Make ordering the Education Yearb...
Why not set up a standing order?

To ensure you receive your copy of the Education Yearbook on publication, why not set up a standing order? Our fast and efficient distribution service will guarantee that you receive your copy as soon as the yearbook is published so you do not have to remember to reorder each year.

Setting up a standing order takes the hassle out of ordering each year and you can be sure you have access to the most up-to-date information on the day of publication.

Simply complete the form below and leave the rest to us!

ORDER FORM

☐   Please set up a standing order for the Education Yearbook
(I understand that copies of the 2009/2010 edition and subsequent editions will be dispatched on the day of publication with an invoice)

Do you need extra copies of the 2008/2009 edition?

☐   Please invoice me £ _____ for ____ extra copies of the Education Yearbook 2008/2009 at £110.00 each; ISBN 978-0-273-71875-8

- | **Fold here, then staple** | -

Your details

Title _____ Initial(s) _____ Surname _____

Job Title _____

Organisation _____

Address _____

_____

_____ Postcode _____

Tel _____ Fax _____

E-mail _____

Signed _____ Date _____

If you have any queries, please contact Customer Services on 0870 607 3777

Education Yearbook
2008/2009

PEARSON
Prentice
Hall

Harlow, England • London • N   ey • Singapore • Hong Kong
Tokyo • Seoul • Taipei • New L   dam • Munich • Paris • Milan

Editorial Team	Shamini Sriskandarajah
	Johan Gregory
Marketing	Gemma Williams

Pearson Education Limited
Edinburgh Gate
Harlow CM20 2JE
Tel: +44 (0) 1279 623623
Fax: +44 (0) 1279 431059

To find out more about our business and professional products, you can visit us at
www.pearson-books.com
To view sample pages from Pearson Education yearbook products, please visit
www.pearson-books.com/yearbook
For other Pearson Education publications, visit www.pearsoned.co.uk

A catalogue record for this book is available from the British Library

ISBN-10: 0 273 71875 4
ISBN-13: 978 0 273 71875 8

10 9 8 7 6 5 4 3 2 1

Typeset by 71
Printed by Ashford Colour Press Ltd., Gosport

The publisher's policy is to use paper manufactured from sustainable forests

Contents

Preface

The *Education Yearbook 2008/2009* has been fully updated to provide a comprehensive guide to the broad spectrum of education provision in the United Kingdom. This includes central government offices and local government education departments; complete details of UK secondary schools; private sector secondary and special school provision; higher, further and vocational education; education related organisations and services; and additional resources for education professionals.

The 2008/2009 edition has been organised to present this wide range of institutions and organisations as clearly as possible. Schools are displayed in an easy to use table layout, presenting information such as pupil numbers, age range, gender and residential provision in a standardised format. Throughout the book, entries are listed by the countries of the United Kingdom and by the nine English Government Office Regions (GORs). A guide to these nine regions is provided on pages vii–ix.

We would like to thank all the institutions, organisations and individuals who have assisted us in producing this new edition. If users know of any relevant organisations that are not currently listed, we would be grateful if they could fill in and return the new entry form on page xix, or e-mail directories@pearson.com. Any other suggestions will be received with interest.

The editorial team

Whilst every effort is made to ensure the accuracy of the entries, advertisements, listings and other material in this edition, neither the proprietors, Pearson Education, nor the printers are to be liable in damages or otherwise for omissions or incorrect insertion, whether as to wording, space or position of any entry or advertisement. The listing of any organisation or establishment in this book does not imply recommendation.

The publishers reserve the right of acceptance or rejection in respect of particulars, advertising copy, and other listings submitted for insertion.

Crown copyright material is reproduced with the permission of the Controller of Her Majesty's Stationery Office and the Queen's Printer for Scotland

The Regions of the UK: Scotland and Northern Ireland

KEY

—— Government Office Region —— Health & Social Services Boards

Government Office Regions only occur in England, but Scotland, Wales and Northern Ireland are regarded as an equivalent for statistical purposes. Health and Social Services Boards are often used to report statistics at a sub-regional level in Northern Ireland.

☐ Council Areas (Scotland)   ☐ District Council Areas (Northern Ireland)

Boundaries effective at 1st April, 1998 except Government Office Regions (4th August, 1998)
© Crown Copyright (ONS.GD272183.2004).

Orkney Islands

Shetland Islands

Eilean Siar

Highland

Moray

Aberdeenshire

A

Scotland

Angus

Perth and Kinross

DC

ED   East Dunbartonshire
ER   East Renfrewshire
G   Glasgow City
In   Inverclyde
NL   North Lanarkshire
Rn   Renfrewshire
WD   West Dunbartonshire

Argyll and Bute

Stirling

Fife

Cl

WD
ED
In
Rn G NL
ER
Falkirk
WL
Ed
Md
EL

A   Aberdeen City
Cl   Clackmannanshire
DC   Dundee City
ED   Edinburgh, City of
EL   East Lothian
Md   Midlothian
WL   West Lothian

North Ayrshire

South Lanarkshire

East Ayrshire

Scottish Borders

South Ayrshire

Dumfries and Galloway

Moyle

Limavady
Coleraine
Ba

Derry
Ballymena
Larne

Strabane   Magherafelt
Nta Cf

Omagh   Cookstown
Antrim
Be   ND
Cr   Ards

Dungannon   Craigavon
Lisburn

Fermanagh
Armagh   Banbridge   Down

Newry and Mourne

Ba   Ballymoney
Be   Belfast
Cf   Carrickfergus
Cr   Castlereagh
ND   North Down
Nta Newtownabbey

vii

The Regions of the UK: England and Wales

KEY

—— Government Office Region

Government Office Regions only occur in England, but Scotland, Wales and Northern Ireland are regarded as an equivalent for statistical purposes. Health and Social Services Boards are often used to report statistics at a sub-regional level in Northern Ireland.

Greater London and London Boroughs

Unitary Authorities (England and Wales)

Metropolitan Counties (England)

Counties (England)

Boundaries effective at 1st April, 1998 except Government Office Regions (4th August, 1998) © Crown Copyright (ONS.GD272183.2004).

D   Darlington
H   Hartlepool
M   Middlesbrough
RC   Redcar and Cleveland
ST   Stockton-on-Tees

De   Derby
KH   Kingston upon Hull, City of
Lr   Leicester
NEL North East Lincolnshire
Nt   Nottingham
Pe   Peterborough
R   Rutland

Bpl Blackpool
BnD Blackburn with Darwen
H   Halton
S   Stoke-on-Trent
TW   Telford and Wrekin
W   Warrington

Bd   Bridgend
BG   Blaenau Gwent
Ca   Cardiff
Cy   Caerphilly
MT   Merthyr Tydfil
Mon Monmouthshire
N   Newport
NPT Neath Port Talbot
RCT Rhondda, Cynon, Taff
T   Torfaen
VG   The Vale of Glamorgan

B   City of Bristol
BS   Bath and North East Somerset
NS   North Somerset
SG   South Gloucestershire

L   Luton
MK   Milton Keynes

Mtn Medway
SS   Southend-on-Sea
Tk   Thurrock

BF   Bracknell Forest
Re   Reading
Sl   Slough
Sw   Swindon
W   Wokingham
WM   Windsor and Maidenhead

BH   Brighton and Hove
Bo   Bournemouth
Pl   Poole
Po   Portsmouth
So   Southampton

Ty   Torbay
Py   Plymouth

The Regions of the UK: Counties of England

The nine Government Office Regions of England, listed by county

County	Region	County	Region
Bedfordshire	*East of England*	Leicestershire	*East Midlands*
Berkshire	*South East*	Lincolnshire*	*East Midlands*
Buckinghamshire	*South East*	Norfolk	*East of England*
Cambridgeshire	*East of England*	Northamptonshire	*East Midlands*
Cheshire	*North West*	Northumberland	*North East*
Cornwall	*South West*	Nottinghamshire	*East Midlands*
Cumbria	*North West*	Oxfordshire	*South East*
Derbyshire	*East Midlands*	Rutland	*East Midlands*
Devon	*South West*	Shropshire	*West Midlands*
Dorset	*South West*	Somerset	*South West*
Durham	*North East*	Staffordshire	*West Midlands*
Essex	*East of England*	Suffolk	*East of England*
Gloucestershire	*South West*	Surrey	*South East*
Hampshire	*South East*	Sussex	*South East*
Herefordshire	*West Midlands*	Warwickshire	*West Midlands*
Hertfordshire	*East of England*	Wiltshire	*South West*
Isle of Wight	*South East*	Worcestershire	*West Midlands*
Isles of Scilly	*South West*	Yorkshire	*Yorkshire and the Humber*
Kent	*South East*		
Lancashire	*North West*		

Counties of England, listed by region

East of England
Bedfordshire
Cambridgeshire
Essex
Hertfordshire
Norfolk
Suffolk

East Midlands
Derbyshire
Leicestershire
Lincolnshire*
Northamptonshire
Nottinghamshire
Rutland

London
London Boroughs

North East
Durham
Northumberland

North West
Cheshire
Cumbria
Lancashire

South East
Berkshire
Buckinghamshire
Hampshire
Isle of Wight
Kent
Oxfordshire
Surrey
Sussex

South West
Cornwall
Devon
Dorset
Gloucestershire
Isles of Scilly
Somerset
Wiltshire

West Midlands
Herefordshire
Shropshire
Staffordshire
Warwickshire
Worcestershire

Yorkshire and the Humber*
Yorkshire

* The Unitary Authorities of North Lincolnshire and North East Lincolnshire fall into the Government Office Region of Yorkshire and the Humber

Web Resources

These websites can provide useful further information for people interested in the education sector. The list is not exhaustive and the inclusion of these URLs does not imply that Pearson Education endorses the contents of the sites.

Parliament and Government Departments and Offices

www.berr.gov.uk	Department for Business, Enterprise and Regulatory Reform (formerly Department of Trade and Industry)
www.cabinetoffice.gov.uk	The Cabinet Office
www.comunities.gov.uk	Department for Communities and Local Government
www.dcsf.gov.uk	Department for Children, Schools and Families (formerly Department for Education and Skills)
www.dh.gov.uk	Department of Health
www.direct.gov.uk	Public service information
www.dius.gov.uk	Department of Innovation, Universities and Skills
www.dwp.gov.uk	Department for Work and Pensions
www.learning.wales.gov.uk	Welsh Assembly Government education and skills site
www.lga.gov.uk	Local Government Association
www.niassembly.gov.uk	Northern Ireland Assembly
www.nio.gov.uk	Northern Ireland Office
www.ofsted.gov.uk	Ofsted – Office for Standards in Education, Children's Services and Skills
www.opsi.gov.uk	Office of Public Sector Information
www.parliament.uk	UK Parliament
www.scotland.gov.uk	Scottish Government
www.scotlandoffice.gov.uk	Scotland Office
www.scottish.parliament.uk	The Scottish Parliament
www.standards.dfes.gov.uk	DfES: The Standards Site
www.tsoshop.co.uk	The Stationery Office online bookshop
www.wales.gov.uk	National Assembly for Wales and Welsh Assembly Government
www.walesoffice.gov.uk	Wales Office

News and Information

www.bbc.co.uk/learning	BBC education and learning pages
education.guardian.co.uk	Education section of the Guardian
www.ft.com/businesseducation	Business education section of the Financial Times
www.independent.co.uk/news/education	Education section of the Independent
www.telegraph.co.uk/education	Education section of the Telegraph
www.tes.co.uk	Times Educational Supplement
www.timeshighereducation.co.uk/	Times Higher Education
www.wrx.zen.co.uk	Links to national and local media

Education

www.edulinks.co.uk	Links to education and government websites
www.learningalive.co.uk	Primary and secondary educational resource
www.qca.org.uk	Qualifications and Curriculum Authority
www.scre.ac.uk	Scottish Council for Research in Education
www.specialistschools.org.uk	Specialist Schools and Academies Trust
www.universities.co.uk	Listings and information about universities in the UK
www.youthsporttrust.org	Youth Sport Trust

Terminology and Abbreviations

ABE	Adult Basic Education
ACS	Average Class Size
Adv	Advanced
AMG	Annual Maintenance Grant
APL	Accreditation of Prior Learning
APR	Age Participation Rate
ASB	Aggregated Schools Budget
ASH	Average Student Hours in class per week
AVA	Audio-Visual Aid
BR	Block Release
BSF	Better Schools Fund
CE	Church of England
CAD	Computer Aided Design
CAL	Computer Assisted Learning
CBT	Competency Based Training
CCPR	Central Council of Physical Recreation
CCT	Compulsory Competitive Tendering
CFE	College of Further Education
CIW	Church in Wales
CPD	Continuing Professional Development
CTC	City Technology College
CY	Community School maintained by the LEA
CYS	Community Special School maintained by the LEA
EFL	English as a Foreign Language
ELT	English Language Teaching
EMIE	Education Management Information Exchange
EPA	Educational Priority Areas
FD	Foundation School maintained by the LEA
FDS	Foundation Special School maintained by the LEA
FE	Further Education
FT	Full-time
FTE	Full-Time Equivalent
GSA	The Girls' Schools Association
GTTR	Graduate Teacher Training Registry
HE	Higher Education
HMC	Headmasters' and Headmistresses' Conference
IGDS	Integrated Graduate Development Scheme
IIP	Investors in People
INSET	In-service Training for Teachers
Inter	Intermediate
JCR	Junior Common Room
JEB	Joint Examining Board
LAPP	Lower Attaining Pupils Programme
LMS	Local Management of Schools
MAST	Monitoring and Support Time
MCI	Management Charter Initiative
NAFE	Non-Advanced Further Education
NEC	National Extension College
NRE	Net Revenue Expenditure
OCN	Open College Network
Ofsted	Office for Standards in Education, Children's Services and Skills
PT	Part-time
PTE	Part-Time Equivalent

PTR	Pupil:Teacher Ratio
RC	Roman Catholic
SLA	School Library Association
SSA	Standard Spending Assessment
SSR	Student:Staff Ratio
TCR	Teacher Class Ratio
VA	Voluntary Aided
VC	Voluntary Controlled
WRFE	Work Related Further Education
YT	Youth Training

Special Needs

ADHD	Attention Deficit Hyperactivity Disorder
AS	Asperger's Syndrome
ASD	Autism Spectrum Disorder
CD	Communication Difficulties
DMP	Delicate Medical Problems
Ep	Epilepsy
HI	Hearing Impairment
HS	Hospital School
MLD	Moderate Learning Difficulties
MSI	Multi-Sensory Impairment
PD	Physical Difficulties
PMLD	Profound and Multiple Learning Difficulties
SCU	Special Care Unit
SEBD	Social, Emotional and Behavioural Difficulties
SEN	Special Educational Needs
SLD	Severe Learning Difficulties
SpLD	Specific Learning Difficulties
VI	Visual Impairment

Guide to Legislation

All of the following are available from The Stationery Office and are subject to Crown Copyright protection.

Disability Discrimination Act 1995

An Act to make it unlawful to discriminate against disabled persons in connection with employment, education, the provision of goods, facilities and services or the disposal or management of premises; to make provision about the employment of disabled persons; and to establish a National Disability Council.

Education Act 1980

Parental rights extended to allow them to choose their child's school (resource permitting) and to be represented on school governing bodies. The Assisted Places Scheme was created and funds were released to LEAs wishing to teach or use the Welsh language in schools.

Education Act 1994

An Act to make provision about teacher training and related matters, to make provision with respect to the conduct of students' unions and for connected purposes. Part One establishes the Teacher Training Agency with the object of raising standards of teaching by improving the quality of all training, and promoting teaching as a career. The Act details arrangements for funding, including grants and loans, and defines eligible, institutions. Part Two defines 'students' unions', the establishment to which the Act applies, and the requirements to be observed, including finance and affiliation to other organisations.

Education Act 1996

This legislation repeals totally the following acts: Education Act 1944, Education Act 1946, Education (Miscellaneous Provisions) Act 1948, Education (Miscellaneous Provisions) Act 1953, Education Act 1959, Rating and Valuation Act 1961, Education Act 1964, Education (Handicapped Children) Act 1970, Education (Work Experience) Act 1970, Education Act 1975, Education (School-leaving Dates) Act 1976, Education Act 1976, Education Act 1979, Education Act 1981, Education (Grants and Awards) 1984, Education Act 1993. In addition the following acts were repealed substantially in parts but not totally: Education Act 1980, Education (No 2) Act 1986, Education Reform Act 1988. Part One outlines the statutory system of education; the educational institutions – primary, secondary and middle schools, nursery schools and special schools; the functions of LEAs; the functions and duties of the

Secretary of State; the Funding Agency for Schools and the Schools Funding Council for Wales. Part Two deals with LEA schools and voluntary schools and defines 'maintained' schools, details funding arrangements for voluntary schools and their assistance by LEAs. A further chapter specifies arrangements for the government for the general responsibility for the conduct of the school and in particular all staffing matters. Part Three deals comprehensively with grant-maintained schools; establishment, government and funding. Part Four defines 'special educational needs' and the provision of services by LEAs. Part Five is devoted to the curriculum and the implementation of the National Curriculum in schools and the function of the School Curriculum and Assessment Authority and the Curriculum and Assessment Authority for Wales. Arrangements for the provision of religious education in all categories of schools are given in detail. Part Six outlines arrangements for school admissions attendance and charges for all schools – county and voluntary, nursery, special and grant-maintained. Part Seven is devoted to independent schools and city colleges. Part Eight covers grants. Part Nine deals with ancillary functions including functions of the Secretary of State, LEAs and governing bodies. Part Ten is devoted to other miscellaneous matters including the management of schools premises, the employment of children and young persons, and arrangements for work experience in the last year of compulsory schooling.

Education Act 1997

An Act to amend the law relating to education in schools and further education in England and Wales; to make provision for the supervision of the awarding of external academic and vocational qualifications in England, Wales and Northern Ireland; and for connected purposes.

Education Act 2002

An Act to make provision about education, training and childcare in England and Wales. The Act is divided into 11 Parts. Part One introduces new legal frameworks, including powers to promote innovation. Part Two makes provision for financial assistance, and repeals a significant number of powers to fund education, replacing them with a single general one. Part Three makes provision for the governance of maintained schools and for exclusion of pupils. Part Four makes provision for intervention in schools causing concern and LEAs. Part Five introduces Academies, making changes to the Education Act 1996 and to the Learning and Skills Act 2000; and makes changes to provisions for the establishment, alteration and discontinuance of schools. Part Six and Part Seven replace for England and Wales respectively the curriculum provisions in Part Five of the Education Act 1996. Part Eight makes provision with respect to teachers, making provision for teachers' pay and conditions and making new provision for teachers' qualifications. Part Nine makes adjustments to provision with respect to nursery education and childcare. Part Ten makes provision with respect to independent schools. Part Eleven makes miscellaneous and general provisions.

Education Act 2005

This Act is divided into five Parts. Part One repeals the School Inspections Act 1996 and re-enacts many of the Act's provisions, with some significant changes. It reforms school inspections in England and it gives the National Assembly for Wales the power to introduce similar reforms in the future. It revises the current categorisation for schools causing concern, introducing a new designation of requiring significant improvement, and removes the duty on schools in England to provide an action plan. It aligns the inspection of early years provision with school inspections, and also includes a number of Wales-only provisions. Part Two extends the circumstances in which a local education authority must invite proposals for a new or replacement secondary school. Part Three broadens the objectives of the Teacher Training Agency so that it may carry out activities in relation to the whole school workforce, not just in relation to teaching. Part Four contains a number of miscellaneous provisions relating to maintained schools, information sharing, and attendance for excluded pupils at alternative educational provision. Part Four also provides for LEAs to set annual targets for pupil performance; for the removal of the requirement on schools to produce an annual governors' report and to hold an annual parents meeting, and the introduction of the school profile in England only; for limited courses of higher education to be provided and funded in maintained schools; for admission arrangements to make special provision for children who are looked after by local authorities; and for safeguards to apply to the disposal of publicly-funded, foundation school land. Part Five contains general incidental and supplemental provisions, including those relating to the functions of the National Assembly for Wales, subordinate legislation, general interpretation, repeals, commencement and extent.

Education (No 2) Act 1986

Places extra responsibilities on school governing bodies, which must now have an instrument of government, and articles of government, made by order of the LEA. The Act specifies the composition of the governing body, and the election or co-operation of members. Other matters covered by the Act include freedom of speech in universities and polytechnics, sex education, the abolition of corporal punishment and teacher appraisal. Circular 8/86, December 1986 gives commencement dates for the various sections of the Act.

Education (Scotland) Act 1980

A consolidating Act, covering the general requirements in relation to pupils, public schools of all categories, placing in such schools and independent schools, grant-aided schools and independent schools and makes provision for the Secretary of State for Scotland prescribing regulations to which authorities must conform in carrying out certain functions.

Education (Scotland) Act 1996

Established the Scottish Qualifications Authority.

Education And Inspections Act 2006 Chapter 40

The Act implements proposals contained in the White Paper Higher Standards, Better Schools for All (Cm 6677) which was published in October 2005. This Act also makes provision in consequence of the Chancellor of the Exchequer's announcement in the March 2005 Budget Statement of a reduction in the number of public service inspectorates from eleven to four, with the aim of enabling better co-ordination and reduced duplication.

Education and Training (Scotland) Act 2000

An Act of the Scottish Parliament to make provision for the payment of grants in respect of the education and training of certain individuals.

Education (Disability Strategies and Pupils' Educational Records) (Scotland) Act 2002

An Act of the Scottish Parliament to require bodies responsible for schools to prepare and implement strategies relating to the accessibility, for pupils with a disability, of school education; and to make provision in respect of the educational records of school pupils.

Education (Fees and Awards) Act 1983

An Act to make provision with respect to the fees charged by universities and other institutions to students not having the requisite connection with the United Kingdom, the Channel Islands or the Isle of Man and the exclusion of such students from eligibility for certain discretionary awards.

Education (Graduate Endowment and Student Support) (Scotland) Act 2001

An Act of the Scottish Parliament to make provision for the payment by certain persons of the graduate endowment; to make provision in relation to the use of income arising from the graduate endowment for the purposes of the financial support of students; to make further provision as respects financial support for students; and to make provision exempting students from liability for council tax.

Education Reform Act 1988

This legislation is divided into four main areas. For schools there is to be a national curriculum with three corporate bodies – a National Curriculum Council, a Curriculum Council for Wales and a School Examinations and Assessment Council. Special reference is made to religious education with a requirement for all pupils at maintained schools to attend an act of collective worship. Every LEA is to constitute a standing advisory council on religious education. LEAs are now required to provide the Secretary of State with a scheme for financing county and voluntary schools with provision for the delegation of the management of a school's budget share to the governing of the school. The Act provides for certain schools to apply for grant-maintained status and opt out of the LEA control. The size and composition of the governing body is detailed, together with the powers and financial arrangements, the procedure for the acquisition of grant-maintained status to include a secret postal ballot of parents, after the publication of the proposals initial governors to be elected. The second area is that of higher education and the removal of the LEAs' duty to provide facilities for higher education. The existing institutions (over 50) will become legal entities in their own right. The National Advisory Body for Public Sector Higher Education will be replaced by a Polytechnic and Colleges Funding Council and the University Grants Committee will be replaced by the Universities Funding Council. In further education, colleges will still be maintained by LEAs but at least half of their governors must represent 'employment interests' and will be able to influence staff appointments and dismissals, delegate budgets and the provision of a service relevant to the area. The finance and government of further and higher education is detailed in the Act. The third area covered in the Act details the reorganisation of education in inner London consequent upon the abolition of the ILEA in April 1990. The final part of the Act lists miscellaneous matters such as the establishment of the Education Assets Board and the University Commissioners; grants, unrecognised degrees and the extension of the functions of the Audit Commission are also discussed. This Act affected by the 1996 Act.

Education Reform (Northern Ireland) Order 1989

Financial control delegated to school governing bodies with opt out option (only where schools would fully integrate Protestant and Roman Catholic pupils) A curriculum and assessment pattern, similar to the reforms in England and Wales, was also established.

Education (Schools) Act 1992

An Act to make provision with respect to the inspection of schools and with respect to information about schools and their pupils.

Education (Schools) Act 1997

An Act to make provision for and in connection with the ending of the assisted places schemes in England and Wales and in Scotland.

Education (School Meals) (Scotland) Act 2003

An Act of the Scottish Parliament to confer powers on the Scottish Ministers to prescribe circumstances in which education authorities are obliged to ensure that provision is made for pupils to receive milk, meals or other refreshments free of charge; and to provide that the first exercise of those powers has retrospective effect.

Education (Student Loans) Act 1990

Established system by which students in England, Wales and Scotland can borrow and repay money, for use towards their maintenance whilst in higher education.

Education (Student Loans) Act 1996

An Act to make provision for, and in consequence of, the payment of subsidy in respect of private sector student loans.

Education (Student Loans) Act 1998

An Act to make further provision with respect to public sector student loans connected purposes.

Equality Act 2006

The Act's main provisions: establish the Commission for Equality and Human Rights (CEHR) and define its purpose and functions; make unlawful discrimination on the grounds of religion or belief in the provision of goods, facilities and services, education, the use and disposal of premises, and the exercise of public functions; enable provision to be made for discrimination on the grounds of sexual orientation in the provision of goods, facilities and services, education, the use and disposal of premises and the exercise of public functions; create a duty on public authorities to promote equality of opportunity between women and men ('the gender duty'), and prohibit sex discrimination and harassment in the exercise of public functions. The CEHR will take on the work of the existing equality Commissions (the Equal Opportunities Commission (EOC), the Commission for Racial Equality (CRE), and the Disability Rights Commission (DRC)) and will additionally assume responsibility for promoting equality and combating unlawful discrimination in three new strands, namely sexual orientation, religion or belief, and age. The CEHR will also have responsibility for the promotion of human rights.

Further Education and Training Act 2007 Chapter 25

An Act to make provision about the Learning and Skills Council for England; to make provision about institutions within the further education sector; to make provision with respect to industrial training levies; to make provision about the formation of, and investment in, companies and charitable incorporated organisations by higher education corporations; to enable the making of Assembly Measures in relation to the field of education and training; and for connected purposes.

Further and Higher Education Act 1992

An Act to make new provision about further and higher education. This act establishes two Further Education Funding Councils, one for England and one for Wales. The act also relates to the transfer of Further Education institutions to Higher Education institutions, the power to award degrees and assume the title of University, with the approval of the Privy Council.

Higher Education Act 2004

Makes provision for research in arts and humanities and complaints by students against institutions providing higher education; makes provision for fees payable by students in higher education; provides for the appointment of a Director of Fair Access to Higher Education; makes provision for grants and loans to students in higher or further education; limits the jurisdiction of visitors of institutions providing higher education; and for connected purposes.

Learning and Skills Act 2000

Sets up the Learning and Skills Council, National Council for Education and Training, and Wales and Adult Learning Inspectorate. Other principal concerns of the act are the extension of the remits of the Chief Inspectors of Schools in England and Wales; the dissolution of the English and Welsh FEFC; Inspections Frameworks; Qualifications and Student Support.

Nursery Education and Grant Maintained Schools Act 1996

An Act to provide for the making of grants in respect of nursery education and to permit borrowing by grant-maintained schools. This short act is principally concerned with the detailed arrangements for making grants, delegation requirements and inspections, with specific arrangements for children with special educational needs. Details of amendments to previous legislation, including the Education Act of 1993 and 1994 to permit grant maintained schools to borrow money, are given in section 7 of the Act.

Racial And Religious Hatred Act 2006 Chapter 1

The Act amends the Public Order Act 1986 ("the 1986 Act") by creating new offences of stirring up hatred against persons on religious grounds and amends section 24A of the Police and Criminal Evidence Act 1984 so that the powers of citizens arrest do not apply to the offences of stirring up religious and racial hatred. The new offences apply to the use of words or behaviour or display of written material (new section 29B), publishing or distributing written material (new section 29C), the public performance of a play (new section 29D), distributing, showing or playing a recording (new section 29E), broadcasting or including a programme in a programme service (new section 29F) and the possession of written materials or recordings with a view to display, publication, distribution or inclusion in a programme service (new section 29G). For each offence the words, behaviour, written material, recordings or programmes must be threatening and intended to stir up religious hatred. Religious hatred is defined as hatred against a group of persons defined by reference to religious belief or lack of religious belief.

School Education (Amendment) (Scotland) Act 2002

This Act has two separate but related purposes, in that they both deal with aspects of school education. Section One amends section 28A of the Education (Scotland) Act 1980 so as to ensure that parents have a statutory right to make placing requests for all children who have either started school, or are eligible to start school at the next intake. Section Two amends the School Boards (Scotland) Act 1988 in connection with the abolition of the post of assistant headteacher. To enable existing assistant headteachers to be regraded as deputy headteachers without following the advertisement and appointment procedures required by that Act, the provisions in that Act requiring posts to be advertised and an appointment committee to be set up are disapplied. The section also removes references to assistant headteachers from that Act. These changes complement the introduction of a new career structure for the teaching profession from April 2002 and the abolition of the post of assistant headteacher.

School Inspections Act 1996

Part One deals with school inspections and outlines the functions and powers of the Inspectorate for England and for Wales. Part One also deals with the procedure for inspection and the preparation and destination of reports of inspections. Religious education is also dealt with here. Part Two outlines the power of the inspectorate over schools requiring special measures including educational associations. Part Three deals with the inspection of computer records, financial provisions and consequential amendments, repeals and transitional provisions.

School Standards and Framework Act 1998

An Act to make new provision with respect to school education and the provision of nursery education otherwise than at school; to enable arrangements to be made for the provision of further education for young persons partly at schools and partly at further education institutions; to make provision with respect to the Education Assets Board; and for connected purposes. Part One outlines measures to raise standards of school education. Part Two outlines new framework for maintained schools. Part Three outlines school admissions. Part Four outlines other provisions about school education. Part Five outlines nursery education. Part Six outlines partnership arrangements in Wales. Part Seven outlines miscellaneous and general code of practice for LEAs and maintained schools.

School Teachers' Pay and Conditions Act 1991

Repealed the Teachers' Pay and Conditions Act 1987 and established a review body appointed by the Prime Minister to examine and report on the pay and conditions of teachers in England and Wales. Findings to be submitted to the Secretary of State and published. After consultation with local education authorities associations, bodies representing voluntary schools governors, school teachers and governors of grant-maintained schools, the Secretary of State may make an Order relating to statutory conditions of employment. Special provisions may apply to grant-maintained schools where an application for exemption has been made to the Secretary of State and been granted. The Act contains interpretation, orders and application of provisions of the 1944 Education Act.

Scottish Qualifications Authority Act 2002

An Act of the Scottish Parliament to make provision in relation to the members of the Scottish Qualifications Authority; to confer power on the Scottish Ministers to regulate the procedure of that Authority; to provide for the establishment of a committee to consider and advise on matters relating to qualifications awarded by, and the functions and procedures of, that Authority; and for Further and Higher Education (Scotland) Act 1992 Allowed for similar reforms to those in Further and Higher Education in England and Wales.

Self Governing Schools etc. (Scotland) Act 1989

Allowed Scottish schools to 'opt out' of LEA control and be funded directly by the Scottish Central Government.

Special Educational Needs and Disability Act 2001

An Act to make further provision against discrimination, on grounds of disability, in schools and other educational establishments; and for connected purposes.

Standards in Scotland's Schools etc. Act 2000

An Act of the Scottish Parliament to make further provision as respects school education, the welfare of pupils attending independent schools and corporal punishment of pupils for whom school education is provided; to make further provision as respects School Boards; to make further provision as respects the functions, constitution and structure of the General Teaching Council for Scotland; to abolish the committee known as the Scottish Joint Negotiating Committee for School Education; to make further provision relating to the inspection of institutions within the higher education sector which educate and train persons to be, or persons who are, teachers in schools; and for connected purposes.

Teaching and Higher Education Act 1998

An Act to make provision for the establishment of General Teaching Councils for England and Wales and with respect to the registration, qualifications and training of teachers and the inspection of such training; to make new provision with respect to grants and loans to students in higher or further education and fees payable by them; to make provision with respect to the funding of higher education institutions and certain further education, and other matters relating to further and higher education institutions; to enable the higher and further education funding councils in Scotland to discharge certain functions jointly; to enable young persons to have time off work for study or training; to make provision with respect to the inspection of training and careers services provided in pursuance of arrangements or directions under the Employment and Training Act 1973; to provide that the Scottish Further Education Funding Council shall be a relevant body for the purposes of section 19(5) of the Disability Discrimination Act 1995; and for connected purposes.

New Entry Suggestion Page

In order to ensure that our coverage is complete for the next edition of the *Education Yearbook*, your help would be much appreciated. The form below is for users to complete if they feel an organisation should be included. Please photocopy this page and return it to:

The Directories Editor (Education Yearbook)
Pearson Education
Edinburgh Gate
Harlow
CM20 2JE

Tel 01279 623623
E-mail directories@pearson.com

The following organisation should be included in the directory

Information to be published:

Name of organisation

Address

Postcode

Tel

Fax

E-mail

Website

Contact name(s) of key personnel and position(s)

Type of organisation

Most suited chapter

This information will not be published but will be used for correspondence only:

Information supplied by

Address

Tel

E-mail

Whilst every effort will be made to include suggestions in the next edition, Pearson Education retains the right to decide on all editorial content of the directory.

Central Government

1

Department for Business, Enterprise and Regulatory Reform

Department for Children, Schools and Families

Department for Communities and Local Government

Department for Culture, Media and Sport

Ministry of Defence

Department for Environment, Food and Rural Affairs

Foreign and Commonwealth Office

Department of Health

The Home Office

Department of Innovation, Universities and Skills

Ministry of Justice

Department for Work and Pensions

Government Departments Scotland

Government Departments Wales

Government Departments Northern Ireland

Government Departments Channel Islands and Isle of Man

Other Government and Public Offices

Central Government

Department for Business, Enterprise and Regulatory Reform

www.berr.gov.uk

Three new departments were set up in June 2007 by the Prime Minister. The Department for Business, Enterprise and Regulatory Reform replaces the Department of Trade and Industry. The following information is subject to change.

1 Victoria St, London SW1H 0ET; URL www.berr.gov.uk; e-mail enquiries@berr.gsi.gov.uk; Tel 020 7215 5000; Fax 020 7215 0105

Secretary of State   The Rt Hon John Hutton MP
Minister of State (Employment Relations and Postal Affairs)   Pat McFadden MP
Minister of State (Energy)   Malcolm Wicks MP
Minister of State (Trade and Investment)   Lord Digby Jones of Birmingham
Parliamentary Under Secretary of State (Business and Competitiveness)   Baroness Shriti Vadera
Parliamentary Under Secretary of State (Trade and Consumer Affairs)   Gareth Thomas MP

This department brings together functions from the former Department of Trade and Industry, including responsibilities for enterprise, business relations, regional development, fair markets and energy policy, with the Better Regulation Executive (BRE), previously part of the Cabinet Office. Trade promotion overseas and encouraging inward investment (UK Trade and Investment) is a joint responsibility of the this department and the Foreign and Commonwealth Office.

Department for Children, Schools and Families

www.dcsf.gov.uk

Two new departments were set up in June 2007 by the Prime Minister to replace the Department for Education and Skills. These are the Department for Children, Schools and Families and the Department for Innovation, Universities and Skills. The following information is subject to change.

Sanctuary Bldgs, Gt Smith St, London SW1P 3BT; URL www.dcsf.gov.uk; e-mail info@dcsf.gsi.gov.uk; Tel (public enquiries) 0870 000 2288; Tel (switchboard) 0870 001 2345; Fax 01928 794248

Secretary of State   The Rt Hon Ed Balls MP; e-mail sec-of-state.ps@dcsf.gsi.gov.uk; Tel 020 7925 7510; Fax 020 7925 6995
Minister of State (Children, Young People and Families)   The Rt Hon Beverley Hughes MP; e-mail hughes.ps@dcsf.gsi.gov.uk; Tel 020 7925 6951; Fax 020 7925 5011
Minister of State (Schools and Learners)   Jim Knight MP; e-mail knight.ps@dcsf.gsi.gov.uk; Tel 020 7925 6255; Fax 020 7925 6996;

Parliamentary Under Secretary of State (Children, Young People and Families)   Kevin Brennan MP; e-mail brennan.ps@dcsf.gsi.gov.uk; Tel 020 7925 5177; Fax 020 7925 5011
Parliamentary Under Secretary of State (School and Learners)   Lord Andrew Adonis; e-mail adonis.ps@dcsf.gsi.gov.uk; Tel 020 7925 6388; Fax 020 7925 6996
Permanent Secretary   David Bell
Principal Private Secretary   Mela Watts
Private Secretary   Felicity Read
Parliamentary Clerk   Mike Watts
Board Members
Executive Members David Bell, Jane Cooper, Tom Jeffrey, Lesley Longstone, Stephen Meek, Ralph Tabberer, Jon Thompson, Caroline Wright
Non-Executive Members Philip Augar, Katherine Kerswell

The Department for Children, Schools and Families works to ensure that children and young people stay healthy and safe; secure an education and the highest possible standards of achievement; enjoy their childhood; make a positive contribution to society and the economy; and have lives free from the effects of poverty

Children and Families Directorate

Director General   Tom Jeffery
Deputy Director (Directorate Support)   Kim Sibley

Early Years, Extended Schools and Special Needs Group

Director   Sheila Scales
Deputy Director (Childcare)   Graham Archer
Deputy Director (Children's Centres and Extended Schools)   Anne Gross
Deputy Director (Quality and Standards Division)   Helen Bennett
Deputy Director (SEN and Disability)   Hardip Begol
Head (Strategic Services)   Lucy Smith

Families Group

Director   Vacancy
Deputy Director (Children in Need)   Sally Burlington
Deputy Director (Families, Policy, Development and Delivery)   Julia Gault
Deputy Director (Families, Strategy and Interdepartmental Issues)   Shan Scott

Safeguarding Group

Director   Jeanette Pugh
Deputy Director (Child Protection)   Peter D. Clark
Deputy Director (Safeguarding Operations)   Richard Blows
Deputy Director (Safeguarding Vulnerable Groups Act Implementation Division)   Peter Swift

Improving Information Sharing and Management (IISaM) Programme

Director   Christine Goodfellow
Deputy Director (Business Change)   Denise Blunn

Supporting Delivery Group

Director Peter Lauener
Deputy Director (Analysis and Research)
  Richard Bartholomew
Deputy Director (Commissioning and Market Development)
  Marion Kerr
Deputy Director (Local Implementation Governnment Office and Intelligence) Jacky Tiotto
Deputy Director (Local Policy and Performance)
  Andrew Sargent
Deputy Director (Workforce Development) Anne Frost

Child Wellbeing Group

Director Anne Jackson
Deputy Director (Cross Government Child Poverty) Vacancy
Deputy Director (Health and Wellbeing) Caroline Kelham
Deputy Director (Health and Wellbeing) Richard Vaughan

Schools Directorate

Director General Ralph Tabberer
Deputy Director (School Analysis and Research)
  Audrey Brown
Deputy Director (Schools Directorate Support and Change)
  Leanne Hedden
Deputy Director (Technology Futures Unit) Doug Brown

School Standards Group

School Performance and Reform
Director Vacancy

Curriculum and Pupil Wellbeing
Director Helen Williams
Deputy Director (Curriculum Unit) Julie Bramman
Deputy Director (Curriculum Unit) Alan Clarke
Deputy Director (Improving Behaviour and Attendance)
  Nick Baxter
Deputy Director (Pupil Wellbeing Health and Safety Unit)
  Stuart Miller

Chief Adviser on School Standards
Director Sue Hackman
Deputy Director (Central Advice and Support) Tom Goldman
Deputy Director (City Challenge/Closing Gaps)
  Susanna Todd
Deputy Director (Improving Pupil Performance)
  Michael Stark
Deputy Director (Progression and Personalisation)
  Dawn Taylor
Deputy Director (Raising Standards) Fred Sharrock
Deputy Director (School Improvement) Peter Clough

School Resources Group

Director Dugald Sandeman
Deputy Director (Modernising Supply Project)
  Dominic Hudson
Deputy Director (Pay and Professionalism) Ian Whitehouse
Deputy Director (School Funding Unit) Stephen Kingdom
Deputy Director (School and LEA Funding: Policy)
  Andrew Wye
Deputy Director (School Leadership) Noreen Graham
Policy Head (New Relationship with Schools Data Sub Programme) Nick Tomlinson
Policy Head (Pensions and Medical Fitness) Paul Bleasdale

School Formation and Investment Group

Academies and Capital
Director Peter Houten
Deputy Director (Academies Group) Neil Flint
Deputy Director (Academies Policy Unit) Mary Pooley
Deputy Director (Capital Strategy) Philip Parker (Acting)
Deputy Director (Fair Access) Julian Butcher (Acting)

Deputy Director (Future Academies Delivery) Jenny Loosley
Deputy Director (Independent Schools and School Organisation) Penny Jones
Deputy Director (School Commissioning and Supply)
  Sinead O'Sullivan
Deputy Director (Schools Capital) Sally Brooks
Deputy Director (Schools Design and Assets) Mukund Patel

Schools Commissioner
Schools Commissioner Bruce Liddington
Deputy Director (Deputy Schools Commissioner)
  Paul Schofield

Young People Directorate

Director General Lesley Longstone
Director (Youth Task Force) Anne Weinstock
Deputy Director (Young People Analysis Division)
  Tony Moody

14–19 Reform Group

Director Jon Coles
Deputy Director (14–19 Diplomas) Fiona Jordan
Deputy Director (14–19 Policy and Local Delivery)
  Dominic Herrington
Deputy Director (14–19 Strategy and Implementation)
  Elaine Hendry
Deputy Director (14–19 Targets and Funding)
  Hannah Woodhouse
Deputy Director (Education and Skills Bill) Anna Paige
Deputy Director (External Relations and Flexible Resource)
  Chris Tweedale
Deputy Director (General Qualifications) Jacquie Spatcher
Deputy Director (Young People's Strategic Delivery)
  David Taylor

Supporting Children and Young People Group

Director Andrew McCully
Deputy Director (Activities and Engagement)
  Antony Hughes
Deputy Director (Choice and Opportunity)
  Mohammed Haroon
Deputy Director (Joint Youth Justice) Diana Luchford
Deputy Director (Targeted Support) Marcus Bell
Deputy Director (Youth Inclusion Unit) Vacancy

Joint International Unit

Director Win Harris
Deputy Director (European Social Fund) Gordon Pursglove
Deputy Director (International Co-ordination and Communications) Judith Grant
Deputy Director (International Education, Skills and Youth)
  Peter Drummond
Deputy Director (International Employment and Social Policy)
  Liz Tillett

Corporate Services Directorate

Director General Jon Thompson
Director (Commercial) Ian Taylor
Director (Corporate Services Transformation Programme)
  Mike Daly
Director (Finance) Michael Hearty
Director (Human Resources) Anne Copeland
Director (Strategy, Performance and Analysis) Stephen Meek
Chief Information Officer Tim Wright

Communication Directorate

Director Caroline Wright
Deputy Director (Communications Strategy and Planning)
  Stuart Dickenson

Deputy Director (Corporate and Internal Communication)
Anna Brocklehurst
Deputy Director (Directorate Transformation and Management) Tina Haslam
Deputy Director (Marketing) Karen Smalley
Deputy Director (Press Office) Lee Bailey

Legal Adviser's Office

Legal Adviser Claire Johnston
Deputy Director (Academies, Commercial and School Food)
Brett Welch
Deputy Director (Behaviour, Curriculum and School Workforce) Nick Beach
Deputy Director (Childcare, Early Years and Data)
Aileen Stanton
Deputy Director (Children's Services) Sandra Walker
Deputy Director (Equality, Establishments and EC)
Daniel Jenkins
Deputy Director (School Resources) Penny Halnan

Non-Departmental Public Bodies

Higher Education Funding Council for England (HEFCE)

Northavon Hse, Coldharbour La, Bristol BS16 1QD;
URL www.hefce.ac.uk; e-mail hefce@hefce.ac.uk;
Tel 0117 931 7317; Fax 0117 931 7203
Chair Tim Melville-Ross
Chief Executive Prof David Eastwood
Board Members
Alastair Balls, Jackie Fisher, Dame Patricia Hodgson, Prof
Peter Rubin, Peter Saraga, Prof Nigel Savage, Ed Smith, Sir
Richard Sykes, Anne Tate, Prof Paul Wellings, Prof Dianne
Willcocks, Prof Tim Wilson
The Higher Education Funding Council for England
distributes public money for teaching and research to
universities and colleges. In doing so, it aims to promote
education and research, within a financially healthy sector.
The council also plays a key role in ensuring accountability
and promoting good practice.

Learning and Skills Council

Cheylesmore Hse, Quinton Rd, Coventry, Warwickshire
CV1 2WT; Tel 0845 019 4170; Fax 024 7649 3600
Chair Chris Banks
Chief Executive Mark Haysom
The role of the Learning and Skills Council is to secure
throughout England sufficient and adequate facilities for
further education to meet the needs of students, including
those with learning difficulties and/or disabilities, from the
communities in which they live; distribute the money given
to them by parliament to further education colleges, and
make sure that there are further education opportunities for
all. It is accountable to parliament for the distribution of
those funds. Its work includes inspecting the standards of
quality and achievement in the further education sector.
There are nine regional offices, one for each area in England.
Each region is represented by a regional committee, with
members appointed by the secretary of state. These
committees play a vital role in highlighting local needs and
demands, and are responsible for advising the council on
further education provision in their area. They work closely
with the local community, training and enterprise councils,
local education authorities and business interests.

Quality Improvement Agency for Lifelong Learning (QIA)

Friars Hse, Manor House Dr, Coventry, West Midlands
CV1 2TE; URL www.qia.org.uk; Tel 0870 162 0632;
Fax 0870 162 0633

Chair Sir Geoffrey Holland
Chief Executive Andrew Thomson
Director (Communications and Partnerships)
Margaret Bennett
Director (Improvement and Strategy) Kate Anderson
Director (Strategic Reform and Development) Jenny Burnette
The role of the QIA is to lead the development of a three year
quality improvement strategy for the sector; build
providers' capacity for self-improvement; secure the
commitment of the learning and skills sector to national
strategic priorities; and speed up the pace of improvement
among providers. QIA is a small, strategic organisation. It
does not deliver services itself; it commissions other
organisations to deliver these on its behalf.

Dysg Department for Education, Lifelong Learning and
Skills (DELLS), Welsh Assembly Government, 11 Ty
Nant Ct, Morganstown, Cardiff CF15 8LW;
URL www.dysg.org.uk
Director Sonia Reynolds; Tel 02920 741841;
Fax 02920 741822
**Learning and Skills Development Agency for Northern
Ireland** See Chapter 6: Vocational and Adult Education
Organisations and Associations: Learning and Skills
Network
Director Trevor Carson

Special Educational Needs and Disability Tribunal (SENDIST)

Upper Ground Fl West, Procession Hse, 55 Ludgate Hill,
London EC4M 7JW; URL www.sendist.gov.uk; e-mail
tribunalqueries@sendist.gsi.gov.uk; Tel 0870 241 2555;
Fax 0870 600 6926
SENDIST is an independent tribunal which (i) hears and
decides parents' appeals against the decisions of LEAs about
SEN, and (ii) hears and decides parents' claims of disability
discrimination in schools

Teacher Training Agency Communication Centre

Enquiries: PO Box 3210, Chelmsford, Essex CM1 3WA;
e-mail teaching@ttainfo.demon.co.uk; Tel 01245 454454;
Fax 01245 261668
Head Office, Portland Hse, London SW1E 5TT;
Tel 020 7925 3700
Chair Sir Brian Follett
Chief Executive Ralph Tabberer
Director (Communications and Marketing) Ceol Webb
Director (Corporate Services and Board Secretary)
Leanne Heddon
Director (Quality and Funding) Michael Day
Director (Teacher Supply and Recruitment) Mary Doherty
Director (Teacher Training Strategy) Jill Staley
Director (Teacher Training Strategy) Angela Walsh
Director (Teacher Training Support) Chris Dee
Head (Special Projects) Nigel Vivian

Executive Agency

Teachers' Pensions Agency

Mowden Hall, Staindrop Rd, Darlington DL3 9BG;
Tel 01325 460155
Chief Executive D. Metcalfe
Director (Finance and Business Planning) D.G. Sanders
Director (Policy and Personnel) P.M. Bleasdale
Director (Systems and Employer Operations) A. Allison
Director (Teacher Operations) K.M. Miles
Teachers' Superannuation Scheme policy, legislation and
administration

Department for Communities and Local Government

www.communities.gov.uk

26 Whitehall, London SW1A 2WH;
  URL www.communities.gov.uk; Tel 020 7944 4400
Secretary of State The Rt Hon Hazel Blears MP
Minister of State (Local Government) John Healey MP
Parliamentary Under Secretary of State
  Baroness Kay Andrews OBE
Parliamentary Under Secretary of State Parmjit Dhanda MP
Parliamentary Under Secretary of State Iain Wright MP

Regional Development Group

Riverwalk Hse, 157–161 Millbank, London SW1P 4RR
Director General Rob Smith
The RDG has four key aims: better co-ordination of area-based initiatives; greater involvement of the Government Offices (GOs) in policy making; making the GOs the key representatives of government in the regions; and establishing the RDG as the unified head office for the Gos.
Government Offices for the Regions
The government offices are key agents of government for the English Regions, aiming to ensure effective delivery of government programmes regionally and locally. The group works with regional partners, including local authorities, Regional Development Agencies and other organisations.

Government Office for the East of England

Eastbrook, Shaftesbury Rd, Cambridge, Cambridgeshire
  CB2 2DF; URL www.go-east.gov.uk; Tel 01223 372500;
  Fax 01223 372501
Regional Director Caroline Bowdler
Areas of responsibility
Bedfordshire; Cambridgeshire; Essex; Hertfordshire; Luton; Norfolk; Peterborough; Southend-on-Sea; Suffolk; Thurrock

Government Office for the East Midlands

The Belgrave Centre, Stanley Pl, Talbot St, Nottingham
  NG1 5GG; URL www.go-em.gov.uk; Tel 0115 971 9971;
  Fax 0115 971 2404
Regional Director Jane Todd
Areas of responsibility
Derby; Derbyshire; Leicester; Leicestershire; Lincolnshire; Northamptonshire; Nottingham; Nottinghamshire; Rutland

Government Office for London

Riverwalk Hse, 157–161 Millbank, London SW1P 4RR;
  URL www.go-london.gov.uk; Tel 020 7217 3328;
  Fax 020 7217 3450
Regional Director Liz Meek
Areas of responsibility
Barking and Dagenham; Barnet; Bexley; Brent; Bromley; Camden; City of London; Croydon; Ealing; Enfield; Greenwich; Hackney; Hammersmith and Fulham; Haringey; Harrow; Havering; Hillingdon; Hounslow; Islington; Kensington and Chelsea; Lambeth; Lewisham; Merton; Newham; Redbridge; Richmond; Southwark; Sutton; Tower Hamlets; Waltham Forest; Wandsworth; Westminster

Government Office for the North East

Welbar Hse, Gallowgate, Newcastle upon Tyne, Tyne and
  Wear NE1 4TD; URL www.go-ne.gov.uk;
  Tel 0191 201 3300; Fax 0191 202 3830
Regional Director Jonathon Blackie
Areas of responsibility
Darlington; Durham; Hartlepool; Middlesbrough; Northumberland; Redcar and Cleveland; Stockton-on-Tees; Tyne and Wear

Government Office for the North West

Sunley Tower, Piccadilly Plaza, Manchester M1 4BE;
  Tel 0161 952 4000; Fax 0161 952 4099
Cunard Bldg, Pier Head, Water St, Liverpool, Merseyside
  L3 1QB; Tel 0151 224 6300; Fax 0151 224 6470
Regional Director Keith Barnes
Areas of responsibility
Blackburn with Darwen; Blackpool; Cheshire; Cumbria; Greater Manchester; Halton; Knowsley; Lancashire; Liverpool; St Helens; Sefton; Warrington; Wirral

Government Office for the South East

Bridge Hse, 1 Walnut Tree Cl, Guildford, Surrey GU1 4GA;
  URL www.go-se.gov.uk; Tel 01483 882255;
  Fax 01483 882259
Regional Director Paul Martin
Areas of responsibility
Berkshire; Bracknell Forest; Brighton and Hove; Buckinghamshire; East Sussex; Hampshire; Isle of Wight; Kent; Medway; Milton Keynes; Oxfordshire; Portsmouth; Reading; Slough; Southampton; Surrey; West Sussex; Windsor and Maidenhead; Wokingham

Government Office for the South West

2 Rivergate, Temple Quay, Bristol BS1 6ED;
  URL www.gosw.gov.uk; Tel 0117 900 1700;
  Fax 0117 900 1900
Mast Hse, Shepherds Wharf, 24 Sutton Rd, Plymouth
  PL4 0HJ; URL www.gosw.gov.uk; Tel 01752 635000;
  Fax 01752 227647
Castle Hse, Pydar St, Truro, Cornwall TR1 2UD;
  Tel 01872 264500; Fax 01872 264503
Regional Director Jane Henderson
Areas of responsibility
Bath and North East Somerset; Bournemouth; Bristol; Cornwall; Devon; Dorset; Gloucestershire; Isles of Scilly; North Somerset; Plymouth; Poole; Somerset; South Gloucestershire; Swindon; Torbay; Wiltshire

Government Office for the West Midlands

77 Paradise Circus, Queensway, Birmingham, West
  Midlands B1 2DT; URL www.go-wm.gov.uk;
  Tel 0121 212 5050; Fax 0121 212 1010
Regional Director Graham Garbutt
Areas of responsibility
Birmingham; Coventry; Dudley; Herefordshire; Sandwell; Shropshire; Solihull; Staffordshire; Stoke-on-Trent; Telford and Wrekin; Walsall; Warwickshire; Wolverhampton; Worcestershire

Government Office for Yorkshire and the Humber

City Hse, New Station St, Leeds, West Yorkshire LS1 4US;
  URL www.goyh.gov.uk; Tel 0113 280 0600;
  Fax 0113 283 6394
25 Queen St, Leeds, West Yorkshire LS1 2TW
Regional Director Felicity Everiss
Areas of responsibility
East Riding of Yorkshire; Kingston upon Hull; North East Lincolnshire; North Lincolnshire; North Yorkshire; South Yorkshire; West Yorkshire; York

Department for Culture, Media and Sport

www.culture.gov.uk

2–4 Cockspur St, London SW1Y 5DH;
  URL www.culture.gov.uk; Tel 020 7211 6263;
  Fax 020 7211 6270

Secretary of State   The Rt Hon Andy Burnham MP
Minister of State (Culture, Creative Industries and Tourism)
   The Rt Hon Margaret Hodge MP MBE
Minister of State (Sport)   Gerry Sutcliffe MP

Education, Training, Arts and Sport

Head of Group   P. Drew
Head (Arts)   Vacancy
Head (Heritage Division)   N. Pittman

Libraries, Galleries and Museums Heritage

Head of Group   A. Stewart
Director (British Library St Pancras Project)   D. Trench
Director (Government Art Collection)   P. Johnson
Head (Cultural Property Unit)   H. Bauer
Head (Libraries and Information Services Division)   J. Evans
Head (Museums and Galleries Division)   H. Corner

Finance and Personnel Group

Head of Group   Nicholas Kroll
Head (National Lottery Division)   J. Zeff

Broadcasting Media and Creative Industries

Head of Group   A. Ramsay
Head (Broadcasting Policy Division)   D. Khan
Head (Media Division)   Mr Seeney

Regions, Tourism, Millennium and International Group

Head of Group   B. Leonard
Head (Sports and Recreation Division)   H. Reeves
Head (Tourism Division)   S. Broadley

Information Management Unit

Head (Information Management Projects)   Vacancy

Ministry of Defence
www.mod.uk

Whitehall, London SW1 2HB; URL www.mod.uk;
   Tel 020 7218 9000
Secretary of State   The Rt Hon Des Browne MP
Minister of State   The Rt Hon Bob Ainsworth MP
Parliamentary Under Secretary of State   Baroness Ann Taylor
Parliamentary Under Secretary of State   Derek Twigg MP

Educational and Training Services (Army)

Trenchard Lines, Upavon, Pewsey, Wiltshire SN9 6BE;
   Tel 01980 618710; Fax 01980 618705
Director (Army Education)   Brigadier M.S.T. Filler

Service Children's Education (SCE)

HQ SCE, Bldg 5, Wegberg Military Complex, BFPO 40;
   Tel +49 2161 908 2295; Fax +49 2161 908 2396
Chief Executive   D.G. Wadsworth; Tel (enquiries)
   +49 2161 908 2372
Assistant Chief Executive (Corporate Affairs)   L. Moore-
   Rosindell; Tel (enquiries) +49 2161 908 2323
Assistant Chief Executive (Operations)   P. Niedzwiedzki;
   Tel (enquiries) +49 2161 908 2319
Assistant Chief Executive (Quality Assurance)   J. Morris;
   Tel (enquiries) +49 2161 908 2378
Senior Assistant Education Officer (Cyprus)   D. Munro;
   Tel (enquiries) +357 596 3978
Senior Assistant Education Officer (UK)   O. Denson;
   Tel (enquiries) 01980 618259
SCE is a defence agency responsible for the provision of an
effective and efficient education service, from foundation
stage through to sixth form, for dependent children residing
with MOD personnel serving outside the UK. SCE

administers 39 primary schools, two middle schools and six
secondary schools in 10 countries around the world.
Additionally, the agency aims to enable those children to
benefit from their residence abroad; and will provide advice
and support to service parents on maintained and
independent school provision available in the UK. The aim
is to provide an education system of the highest quality,
modelled on those of the UK. The agency is within the
defence chain of command, the chief executive being
ultimately responsible and formally accountable to the
Secretary of State for Defence.

Flag Officer Training and Recruiting Commander Education and Resettlement

Victory Bldg, HM Naval Base, Portsmouth PO1 3LS;
   Tel 02392 727641

Air Officer Commanding and Air Officer Commanding Training Group

RAF, Bldg 255, Innsworth, Gloucester, Gloucestershire
   GL3 1EZ; Tel 01452 712612

Civilian Management (Training) Division

Ministry of Defence, Empress State Bldg, London SW6 1TR

Department for Environment, Food and Rural Affairs (DEFRA)
www.defra.gov.uk

Nobel Hse, 17 Smith Sq, London SW1P 3JR;
   URL www.defra.gov.uk; e-mail
   defra.library@defra.gsi.gov.uk; Tel 020 7238 6000;
   Fax 020 7238 6591
Secretary of State   The Rt Hon Hilary Benn MP
Minister of State   The Rt Hon Lord Jeff Rooker
Minister of State   Phil Woolas MP
Parliamentary Under Secretary of State   Joan Ruddock MP
Parliamentary Under Secretary of State   Jonathan Shaw

Foreign and Commonwealth Office
www.fco.gov.uk

King Charles St, London SW1A 2AH;
   URL www.fco.gov.uk; Tel 020 7270 3000
Secretary of State   The Rt Hon David Miliband MP
Minister of State (Europe)   Jim Murphy MP
Minister of State   Dr Kim Howells MP
Minister of State   Lord Digby Jones of Birmingham
Minister of State   The Rt Hon Lord Mark Malloch Brown
Parliamentary Under Secretary of State   Meg Munn

Department of Health
www.dh.gov.uk

Richmond Hse, 79 Whitehall, London SW1A 2NS;
   URL www.dh.gov.uk; e-mail
   <firstname>.<surname>@dh.gsi.gov.uk;
   Tel 020 7210 3000
Secretary of State   The Rt Hon Alan Johnson MP
Minister of State (Health Services)   Ben Bradshaw MP
Minister of State (Public Health)
   The Rt Hon Dawn Primarolo MP
Parliamentary Under Secretary of State   Prof Lord Ara Darzi
Parliamentary Under Secretary of State (Care Services)
   Ivan Lewis MP
Parliamentary Under Secretary of State (Health)   Ann Keen
   MP

Departmental Board

Permanent Secretary   Hugh Taylor CB
Chief Medical Officer   Prof Sir Liam Donaldson KB
Chief Nursing Officer; Director General (Chief Nursing Officer Directorate)   Prof Christine Beasley CBE
Deputy Chief Medical Officer; Director General (Health Improvement)   Dr Fiona Adshead
Director General (Capability Development Team)   Bill McCarthy
Director General (Commissioning and System Management)   Mark Britnell
Director General (Communications)   Sian Jarvis
Director General (Connecting for Health; IT)   Richard Granger
Director General (Finance and Investment)   Richard Douglas CB
Director General (Health Protection, International Health and Scientific Development)   Dr David Harper CBE
Director General (Healthcare Quality)   Prof Martin Marshall
Director General (NHS Finance: Performance and Operations)   David Flory
Director General (Policy and Strategy)   Una O'Brien (Acting)
Director General (Programmes)   Dr Bill Kirkup
Director General (Research and Development)   Prof Sally C. Davies
Director General (Social Care: Local Government and Care Partnerships)   David Behan CBE
National Director (Equality and Human Rights)   Surinder Sharma
Chief Statistician; Head (Department of Health Wide Statistics Team)   Richard Willmer
Head (Medicines, Pharmacy and Industry)   Dr Felicity Harvey
Head (NHS Choices: Information Services)   Beverley Bryant

The Home Office

www.homeoffice.gov.uk

Direct Communications Unit, 2 Marsham St, London SW1P 4DF; URL www.homeoffice.gov.uk; e-mail public.enquiries@homeoffice.gsi.gov.uk; Tel 020 7035 4848; Fax 020 7035 4745
Home Secretary   The Rt Hon Jacqui Smith MP
Minister of State   Liam Byrne MP
Minister of State   Tony McNulty MP
Parliamentary Under Secretary of State   Vernon Coaker MP
Parliamentary Under Secretary of State   Meg Hillier MP
Parliamentary Under Secretary of State   Admiral Sir Alan West
Permanent Secretary   Sir David Normington
Home Office statement of purpose and aims
1. To reduce crime and the fear of crime; tackle youth crime and violent, sexual and drug-related crime, anti-social behaviour and disorder, increasing safety in the home and public spaces.
2. To reduce organised and international crime, including trafficking in drugs, people and weapons, and to combat terrorism and other threats to national security, in co-operation with EU partners and the wider international community.
3. To ensure the effective delivery of justice, avoiding unnecessary delay, through efficient investigation, detection, prosecution and court procedures; to minimise the threat to and intimidation of witnesses and to engage with and support victims.
4. To deliver effective custodial and community sentences to reduce reoffending and protect the public, through the Youth Justice Board.
5. To reduce the availability and abuse of dangerous drugs, building a coherent, co-ordinated drugs strategy, covering education and prevention, supply and misuse; to focus on effective intelligence and detection, preventative measures at local level, community regeneration, and – with other relevant departments and agencies – the provision of

necessary treatment and rehabilitation services; to reduce the incidence of drugs in prisons and provide appropriate follow-up and remedial services.
6. To regulate entry to and settlement in the UK effectively in the interests of sustainable growth and social inclusion; to provide an efficient and effective work permit system to meet economic and skills requirements, and fair, fast and effective programmes for dealing with visitors, citizenship and long-term immigration applications and those seeking refuge and asylum; to facilitate travel by UK citizens.
7. To support strong and active communities in which people of all races and backgrounds are valued and participate on equal terms by developing social policy to build a fair, prosperous and cohesive society in which everyone has a stake; to work with other departments and local government agencies and community groups to regenerate neighbourhoods, to support families; to develop the potential of every individual; to build the confidence and capacity of the whole community to be part of the solution; and to promote good race and community relations, combating prejudice and xenophobia; to promote equal opportunities both within the Home Office and more widely; and to ensure that active citizenship contributes to the enhancement of democracy and the development of civil society.

Education Service

Chief Education Officer   Judith Williams (Acting)
Senior Education Development Officer   A. Harris
Senior Education Development Officer   J. Temple
Office Manager   Paul Gomery
Personal Secretary   P. Clark

Physical Education Branch

Tel 020 8760 1776; Fax 020 8760 1855
Senior Development Officer (Physical Education)   A. Tait

Department for Innovation, Universities and Skills

www.dius.gov.uk

Three new departments were set up in June 2007 by the Prime Minister to replace the Department for Education and Skills and the Department of Trade and Industry. The following information is subject to change.
Head Office: Kingsgate Hse, 66–74 Victoria St, London SW1E 6SW; URL www.dius.gov.uk; Tel 020 7215 5555
Postal Address: Castle View Hse, East La, Runcorn, Cheshire WA7 2GJ
Secretary of State (Innovation, Universities and Skills)   The Rt Hon John Denham MP
Minister of State (Lifelong Learning, Further and Higher Education)   Bill Rammell MP
Minister of State (Science and Innovation)   Ian Pearson MP
Parliamentary Under Secretary of State (Skills)   David Lammy MP
Parliamentary Under Secretary of State (Intellectual Property and Quality)   Baroness Delyth Morgan
The Department for Innovation, Universities and Skills brings together functions from the former Department of Trade and Industry, including responsibilities for science and innovation, with further and higher education and skills, previously part of the Department for Education and Skills. The department will promote effective investment in research, science, innovation and skills. It will work closely with the new Department for Business, Enterprise and Regulatory Reform and the Department for Children, Schools and Families as well as other key departments – including the Department for Communities and Local Government and the Department for Culture, Media and Sport to ensure the wider personal, community and cultural benefits of education and science are supported.

UK Intellectual Property Office (An Executive Agency of the Department for Innovation, Universities and Skills)

Concept Hse, Cardiff Rd, Newport NP10 8QQ;
URL www.ipo.gov.uk; e-mail enquiries@ipo.gov.uk;
Tel 0845 950 0505; Fax 01633 813600
Chief Executive Ron Marchant
The UK Intellectual Property Office is the operating name of the Patent Office. The office stimulates innovation and enhances the international competitiveness of British industry and commerce. It offers customers a system, both nationally and internationally, for granting intellectual property rights, including patents, designs, trademark and copyright.

Ministry of Justice
www.justice.gov.uk

Selborne Hse, 54 Victoria St, London SW1E 6QW;
URL www.justice.gov.uk; e-mail
general.queries@justice.gsi.gov.uk; Tel 020 7210 8500
Secretary of State for Justice The Rt Hon Jack Straw MP
Minister of State The Rt Hon David Hanson MP
Minister of State Michael Wills MP
Parliamentary Under Secretary of State Maria Eagle MP
Parliamentary Under Secretary of State
The Rt Hon Lord Philip Hunt
Parliamentary Under Secretary of State Bridget Prentice MP
Responsible for criminal law and sentencing, reducing re-offending, and prisons and probation

HM Prison Service – Education Services

8th Fl, Amp Hse, Dingwall Rd, Croydon, Surrey CR0 2LX;
e-mail pas.hmp@connect.bt.com; Tel 020 8760 1710;
Fax 020 8760 1855

Department for Work and Pensions
www.dwp.gov.uk

Richmond Hse, 79 Whitehall, London SW1A 2NS;
URL www.dwp.gov.uk; e-mail
ministers@dwp.gsi.gov.uk; Tel 020 7210 3000;
Tel (parliamentary branch) 020 7238 0715;
Fax 020 7238 0727
Secretary of State The Rt Hon James Purnell MP
Minister of State The Rt Hon Stephen Timms MP
Minister of State Mike O'Brien MP
Parliamentary Under Secretary of State Barbara Follett MP
Parliamentary Under Secretary of State Anne McGuire MP
Parliamentary Under Secretary of State
Lord Bill McKenzie of Luton
Parliamentary Under Secretary of State James Plaskitt MP
Chief Executive (Jobcentre Plus) Lesley Strathie

Government Departments Scotland

The Scottish Government

St Andrew's Hse, Regent Rd, Edinburgh EH1 3DG;
URL www.scotland.gsi.gov.uk; e-mail
ceu@scotland.gsi.gov.uk; Tel 0131 556 8400;
Fax 01397 795001
First Minister The Rt Hon Alex Salmond MSP; head of the Scottish Government, with the Deputy First Minister responsible for the development, implementation and presentation of SG policies

Cabinet Secretary (Education and Lifelong Learning)
Fiona Hyslop
Cabinet Secretary (Finance and Sustainable Growth)
John Swinney
Cabinet Secretary (Health and Wellbeing) Nicola Sturgeon MSP
Cabinet Secretary (Justice) Kenny MacAskill
MSP; responsible for criminal justice, youth justice, victim support, criminal justice social work, police, prisons, sentencing policy, courts, law reform, including civil law and fire services
Cabinet Secretary (Rural Affairs and the Environment)
Richard Lochhead
Minister (Children and Early Years) Adam Ingram
MSP; responsible for school education, nurseries and childcare, Gaelic, children's services, social work, HMIE, HMSWI and SQA
Minister (Communities and Sport) Stewart Maxwell
MSP; housing, regeneration, the land use planning system, building standards, voluntary sector, anti-poverty measures, land policy responsibility for older people, charity law, religious and faith organisations, equality issues
Minister (Community Safety) Fergus Ewing
Minister (Enterprise, Energy and Tourism) Jim Mather
Minister (Environment) Michael Russell
MSP; responsible for environment and natural heritage, land reform, water, sustainable development, agriculture, fisheries, rural development including aquaculture and forestry
Minister (Europe, External Affairs and Culture)
Linda Fabiani
Minister (Parliamentary Business) Bruce Crawford
MSP; responsible for parliamentary affairs and the management of government business in the parliament
Minister (Public Health) Shona Robison MSP; responsible for the NHS, community care, health service reform, health improvement, health promotion, allied healthcare services, acute, primary and mental health services, addiction services, pharmaceutical services, performance, quality and improvement framework and food safety
Minister (Schools and Skills) Maureen Watt
Minister (Transport, Infrastructure and Climate Change)
Stewart Stevenson MSP; responsible for transport policy and delivery, public transport, road, rail services, lifeline air and ferry services
Permanent Secretary John Elvidge
Lord Advocate The Rt Hon Elish Angiolini QC
Solicitor General Frank Mulholland QC

General Education Directorate

Victoria Quay, Leith, Edinburgh EH6 6QQ
Director General Philip Rycroft
Head (Information and Analytical Services Division)
Bill Maxwell

Schools Directorate
Head Liz Hunter
Head (Curriculum Division) Alison Coull
Head (Qualifications Assessment and Skills Division)
Christine Carlin
Head (Schools Division) Colin Reeves
Head (Support for Learning Division) Mike Gibson
Head (Teachers Division) Michael Kellet

Enterprise, Energy and Tourism Directorate
Head Graeme Dickson
Head (Business Growth and Innovation) Douglas Greig
Head (Energy and Telecommunications Division)
Jane Morgan
Head (Enterprise and Industry) Jamie Hume
Head (Enterprise and Networks Division) Wilson Malone
Head (European Structural Funds Division) John Rigg
Head (Innovation and Investments Grants Division)
David McFadyen
Head (Tourism and Whisky Legislation Division) John Brown

Environmental Quality Directorate

Head John Mason

Health

Director General; Chief Executive (NHS Scotland Office)
Kevin Woods
Chief Medical Officer Dr Harry Burns

Economy

Director General; Chief Economic Advisor
Dr Andrew Goudie

Crown Office and Procurator Fiscal Service

Chief Executive and Crown Agent Norman McFadyen

Office of the Solicitor to the Scottish Executor

Contact Murray Sinclair

Justice Department

Director General (Justice and Communities) Robert Gordon

Children, Young People and Social Care Directorate

Head Colin MacLean
Head (Care and Justice Division) Olivia McLeod
Head (Organisations and Quality Issues Division)
Shane Rankin
Head (Positive Futures Division) Maureen Verrall
Head (Safer Children, Stronger Families Division)
Clare Monaghan
Head (Workforce and Capacity Issues Division)
Moira Hughes

Corporate Analytical Services Directorate

Head Ian Sanderson
Head (Office of Chief Economic Advisor Division)
Gary Gillespie
Head (Office of Chief Researcher Division) Diana Wilkinson
Head (Office of Chief Statistician Division) Rob Wishart

General Group Directorate

*Head (Education Information and Analytical Services
Division)* Bill Maxwell
*Head (Enterprise, Energy and Lifelong Learning Analytical
Services Division)* John Ireland

Lifelong Learning Directorate

Head Mike Batho
Head (Employability and Skills Division) Rosemary Winter-
Scott
*Head (Enterprise and Employability for Young People
Division)* Michael Cross
Head (Further and Adult Education Division)
Aileen McKechnie
Head (Higher Education and Learner Support Division)
Stephen Kerr

Office of the Chief Scientific Adviser Directorate

Head Prof Anne Glover

Non-Departmental Public Bodies

Scottish Funding Council (SFC)
Donaldson Hse, 97 Haymarket Terr, Edinburgh EH12 5HD;
URL www.sfc.ac.uk; e-mail info@sfc.ac.uk;
Tel 0131 313 6500; Fax 0131 313 6501
Chair John McClelland CBE
Chief Executive Roger McClure
*Secretary to the Council; Director (Corporate Policy/Services to
Deputy Chief Executive)* David Wann
Director (Funding) Riona Bell

Director (Governance and Management Appraisal and Policy)
Martin Fairbairn
Director (Learning Policy and Strategy) Laurence Howells
Director (Research Policy and Strategy) David Gavi
The Scottish Funding Council distributes £1.5 billion a year
in funding for teaching and learning, research and other
activities in Scotland's colleges and universities. Established
in 2005, the council provides a strategic overview of tertiary
education in Scotland to help secure a more coherent system
of learning, teaching and research. Working in partnership
with colleges, universities and other bodies with an interest
in learning and research in Scotland, the council supports
colleges and universities in the delivery of programmes for
learners; the investment in modern facilities for learning and
research; and being flexible and responsive in allowing
access to lifelong learning for all.

Scottish Further Education Unit (SFEU)
Argyll Ct, Castle Business Pk, Stirling FK9 4TY;
URL www.sfeu.ac.uk; e-mail sfeu@sfeu.ac.uk;
Tel 01786 892000; Fax 01786 892001
The Scottish Further Education Unit (SFEU) is the primary
national agency whose purpose is to contribute to the
development of learning provision within further education
colleges through the support of staff and the curriculum.
The unit works in partnership with all further education
colleges in Scotland, as well as other national agencies
involved in vocational education and training, and lifelong
learning.
It undertakes its development role through the provision of
consultancy, training and development. Its focus of activity
is on teaching, learning and assessment, quality,
organisation and professional development, research,
design and development.

The Scottish Office

Dover Hse, Whitehall, London SW1A 2AU
Secretary of State for Scotland The Rt Hon Des Browne MP
Minister of State David Cairns MP

Government Departments Wales

Welsh Assembly Government

New Crown Bldg, Cathays Pk, Cardiff CF10 3NQ;
URL www.wales.gov.uk; e-mail
assembly.info@wales.gov.uk; Tel (switchboard)
02920 825111; Tel (information line) 02920 898200;
Fax 02920 898630
First Minister Rhodri Morgan
Deputy First Minister; Minister (Economy and Transport)
Leuan Wyn Jones
Minister (Assembly Business and Communications)
Carwyn Jones
Minister (Children, Education, Lifelong Learning and Skills)
Jane Hutt
Minister (Finance and Public Service Delivery)
Andrew Davies
Minister (Health and Social Services) Edwina Hart
Minister (Heritage) Rhodri Glyn Thomas
Minister (Rural Affairs) Elin Jones
Minister (Social Justice and Local Government)
Dr Brian Gibbons
Minister (Sustainability and Housing) Jane Davidson

Welsh Assembly Government Department for Children, Education, Lifelong Learning and Services

National Assembly for Wales, Cathays Pk, Cardiff
CF10 3NQ; Tel 02920 823284; Fax 02920 825524

Director   Steve Marshall; Tel 02920 823284

Director (Business Improvement and Resource Investment Group)   Lynne Hamilton (Acting); Tel 02920 823965

Director (Children, Young People and School Effectiveness Group)   Elizabeth Taylor; Tel 02920 825686

Acting Director (Qualifications Curriculum and Learning Improvement Group); Head (Qualifications and Learning Division)   Ann Evans; Tel 02920 375438

Director (Skills, Higher Education and Lifelong Learning Group)   Dennis Gunning; Tel 02920 825437

Area Improvement Director (North Wales)   Vacancy

Area Improvement Director (South East Wales)   Chris Burdett; Tel 02920 823936

Area Improvement Director (South Wales)   Vacancy

Area Improvement Director (South West/ Mid Wales)   Sonia Reynolds; Tel 02920 825881

Head (Business and Skills Division)   Grenville Jackson; Tel 01686 620200

Head (Children and Young People's Strategy Division)   Liz Williams; Tel 02920 826523

Head (Corporate Services Division)   Rob Rogers; Tel 01443 663856

Head (Curriculum and Assessment Division)   Linda Badham; Tel 02920 375400

Head (Funding and Student Finance Division)   Simon Brindle; Tel 02920 826092

Head (Knowledge Management Division)   Chris Owen; Tel 02920 825276

Head (Learning Improvement and Professional Development Division)   Phil Rogers; Tel 02920 801331

Head (Lifelong Learning and Providers Division)   Mike Hopkins; Tel 01443 663857

Head (Schools Management and Effectiveness Division)   Sylvia Lindoe; Tel 02920 826087

Head (Strategy Unit)   David Bacon; Tel 02920 825851

Head (Support for Learners Division)   Alan Lansdown; Tel 02920 823368

The Wales Office

Gwydyr Hse, Whitehall, London SW1A 2ER;
    URL www.walesoffice.gov.uk; e-mail
    wales.office@walesoffice.gsi.gov.uk; Tel 020 7270 0534;
    Fax 020 7270 0561

Secretary of State for Wales   The Rt Hon Peter Hain MP

Parliamentary Under Secretary of State   Huw Irranca-Davies MP

The Secretary of State for Wales is the member of the UK cabinet who takes the lead in matters connected with the Government of Wales Act and the transfer of functions to the assembly. The Secretary of State is responsible for consulting the assembly on the government's legislative programme. Parliament will vote the main estimate for Wales to the Secretary of State, who will pass it on to the assembly as a grant in aid.

Government Departments Northern Ireland

The Northern Ireland Office

Stormont Castle, Stormont Estate, Belfast BT4 3TT;
    URL www.nio.gov.uk; Tel 028 9052 0700;
    Fax 028 9052 8473

Secretary of State for Northern Ireland
    The Rt Hon Shaun Woodward MP

Minister of State   Paul Goggins MP

Department of Education

Rathgael Hse, Balloo Rd, Bangor, County Down BT19 7PR;
    URL www.deni.gov.uk; e-mail mail@deni.gov.uk;
    Tel 028 9127 9279; Fax 028 9127 9100

Permanent Secretary   Will Haire

Deputy Secretary   Robson Davison

Deputy Secretary   Eddie Rooney

Minister   Catriona Ruane

Chief Inspector   M. Matchett

Contact (Corporate Services Division)   M. McCusker

Contact (Development and Infrastructure)   E. Rooney

Contact (Early Years Youth and School Finance)   L. Warde-Hunter

Contact (Education and Training Inspectorate)   S. Goudie

Contact (Finance Division)   C. Daly

Contact (Raising Standards)   K. Godfrey

Contact (Review of Public Administration)   C. Stewart

Contact (Strategic Planning and Education and Skills Authority Implementation Team)   Dr M. Brown

Contact (Strategy Performance and Accountability)   D. Woods

Contact (Supporting and Safeguarding Children)   D. Angus

The inspectorate is the main source of professional advice for the department and the sole group with responsibility for inspection in the education service in Northern Ireland. The inspectorate gives objective and independent professional judgement.

Strategy, Performance and Accountability Division

Tel (enquiries) 028 9127 9427

Head   David Woods

Preparing department for post-RPA arrangements and developing appropriate relationship with ESA including corporate governance structures and appointment of ESA board and chair; statistics and research; teacher negotiating committee; teachers pensions policy; departmental/ESA business planning and performance objectives

RPA Programme Management Office

Tel (enquiries) 028 9127 9456

Head of Unit   Mary Cromey

Co-ordination of the overall programme of projects required to implement, by April 2009, the new education structures agreed as a result of the public sector, RPA Reform Agenda programme

Raising Standards Division

Tel (enquiries) 028 9127 9524

Head   Katrina Godfrey

Policy on core education matters including the school curriculum; pupil assessment; public examinations and qualifications; school improvement; literacy and numeracy (including school libraries). Extended schools; the role of ICT in supporting teaching and learning including the provision of a managed service to all schools by Classroom 2000 (C2K). Policy responsibility in the areas of teacher education; school/industry linkages; education provision (in conjunction with the Department for Employment and Learning) for young people aged 14–19, including careers education, information, advice and guidance (CEIAG). Sponsor division for the Council for Curriculum, Examinations and Assessment (CCEA). Business education and employability activities and issues. E2s programme board secretariat, strategic advisory group secretariat, educational ICT, empowering schools, qualifications. Entitlement framework, vocational enhancement programme, development of vocational qualifications, specialist schools. Teacher education – initial induction and early professional development, continuing professional development, CASS, professional qualification for headship, GTC.

Supporting and Safeguarding Children Division

Tel 028 9127 9325

Contact   Dorothy Angus

Divisional responsibilities

Policy on school enrolments; admissions and transfer procedure arrangements. School transport, meals and clothing allowances; school management and administration; special educational needs; disability; English as an additional language; education of children from ethnic minority groups. School attendance; pupil behaviour; children at risk; child protection, health and wellbeing in schools; traveller education; suspensions and expulsions, school discipline, bullying. Independent schools counselling service, alternative education provision, education of looked after children, school-aged mothers programme, young carers, gifted children. Review of pastoral care, input to suicide prevention strategy, parenting initiatives, alcohol and drugs strategies, and knife awareness campaign. School governance issues, educational maintenance allowances, and secretariat to primary and secondary standing conferences; registration of independent schools.

Early Years, Youth and School Finance Division

Tel (enquiries) 028 9127 9263
Head   Louise Warde-Hunter
Policy on provision of integrated education and Irish medium education and funding of NICIE and Comhairle na Gaelscolaiochta; development of early years policy and co-ordination of the delivery of pre-school education, children and young people's fund; development and implementation of policy in respect of the Northern Ireland youth sector and the promotion of community relations between young people; policy on the general local management of schools (LMS) including the development and implementation of the LMS common funding scheme; the equitable distribution of available funding to schools.

Top Management Support Unit

Tel (enquiries) 028 9127 9693
Contact   John Leonard
Co-ordination of business and development of relations with Northern Ireland Assembly; legislation; British Council; international relations

Education and Training Inspectorate

Tel (enquiries) 028 9127 9359
Chief Inspector   Marion Matchett
Divisional responsibilities
Provides inspection services for the Department of Education, the Department for Employment and Learning, and the Department of Culture, Arts and Leisure. Evaluates and reports publicly on the quality of education and training in schools, colleges, the youth service, other educational institutions and training organisations. Provides professional advice to all three departments and assists in the formulation and evaluation of policies.

Education and Skills Authority Implementation Team (ESAIT)

Tel (enquiries) 028 9069 4961
Contact   Dr Mark Browne
To establish the Education and Skills Authority by April 2009, which operates effectively and is positioned to secure the expected efficiencies and improvements in the delivery of education services

Equality Division

Tel (enquiries) 028 9127 9312
Contact   Dr Eddie Rooney
Ensuring that the department complies fully with its obligations in respect of equality and human rights, and in particular the co-ordination of departmental policy on disability rights in the education sector

Government Departments Channel Islands and Isle of Man

Guernsey

Sir Charles Frossard Hse, PO Box 43, St Peter Port, Guernsey GY1 1FH, Channel Islands; URL www.gov.gg

Schools Music Service

States Works Dept, La Hure Mare, Vale, Guernsey GY3 5UD, Channel Islands; e-mail musicservice@cwgsy.net; Tel 01481 248260; Fax 01481 243061
Head of Service   M.C. Grand BMus, PGCE

States of Guernsey Education Department

Education Dept, The Grange, St Peter Port, Guernsey GY1 3AU, Channel Islands; URL www.education.gg; e-mail office@education.gov.gg; Tel 01481 710821; Fax 01481 714475
Education Minister   M.A. Ozanne
Deputy Minister   W. Morgan
Director (Education)   D.T. Neale BA, MA(Ed)
Deputy Director (Education)   John Lamb CertEd, BEd
Assistant Director (Planning and Projects)   D. Bridel CACA
Assistant Director (Resources)   F. Flynn Cert PA, Dip PA, ACMA
Assistant Director (Staffing Services)   G. Dawson
Head (Lifelong Learning)   A. Williams BA, DipCG, MEd
Head (Youth Services)   D. Le Feuvre BSc(Hons), PGC
Manager (Pupil Services)   K.S. Isbister BA(Hons), MScEdPsych
Principal Educational Psychologist   S.M. Hayward BA, MSc, EdPsych, ACP, ABPsS(Principal)
Schools Library Service   M. Falla BA, DipLib, ALA
Number of Schools
12 Primary; 6 Secondary; 2 Special Day; 2 Infants; 1 Junior
Day of Board Meeting
Alternate Tuesdays
Requisition Periods for Schools Supplies
No specific dates
Other Authorities with whom Joint Purchasing Arrangements are made
States of Guernsey interdepartmental agreement

Education Development Centre

Education Department The Grange, St Peter Port, Guernsey GY1 3AU, Channel Islands; e-mail cbibby@education.gov.gg; Tel 01481 720654; Fax 01481 712907
Manager (Training)   C. Bibby BA(Hons), PGCE

Isle of Man Government

Government Office, Bucks Rd, Douglas, Isle of Man IM1 2SF; URL www.gov.im; e-mail ceo@dlge.gov.im

Education Department

St Georges Ct, Upper Church St, Douglas, Isle of Man IMI 2SG; e-mail admin@doe.gov.im; Tel 01624 685820; Fax 01624 685834
Minister   Hon A.V. Craine
Department Member   Mr R.W. Henderson MHK
Department Member   Mr E.G. Lowey MLC
Director (Education)   J.R. Cain MEd
Director (Estates)   R.A. Collister
Director (Finance)   K.A. Halsall
Deputy Director (Education)   Mrs M. Britton
Manager (Careers Service)   J. Potts; Tel 01624 685128
Manager (Human Resources)   H.J. Christian
Manager (Legal and Administrative Support)   J.P. Gill

Educational Psychologist   J. Fisher
Educational Psychologist   J. Hedges
Educational Psychologist   C. Smith
Finance Officer   D. Goldsmith
Assistant Education Officer (SEN)   J. Kermode MSc, ABPsS, PGCE
Senior Adviser   Mr S. Dobson
Co-ordinating Adviser (Primary Education)   M. Barrow
Co-ordinating Adviser (Secondary Education)   P. Craine BA, MPhil
Adviser (Information and Communications Technology)   G. Kinrade
Adviser (Youth and Community)   C.M. Clague
Inspector (Works)   J. Webb
Mobile Librarian   S.M. Henderson; Dept of Education Library, Noble's Hall, Douglas, Isle of Man; Tel 01624 673123; Fax 01624 671043
Children's Librarian   M. Cousins
School Meals Organiser   J. Buckley MHCIMA
Number of Schools
5 Secondary; 1 College
Day of Department Meeting
Monday; monthly
Requisition Periods for Schools Supplies
February, May (main), November

Board of Education
Members of the Board
R.E. Bank-Jones, E.H. Bradley, B.A. Brereton, R. Chatel, A.C. Collister, E.M. Deans, Mrs E. Godby, E.D.R. Killey, Mrs G. Kirk, C.S. Lewin, G.I. Moore, B.C. Potter, Mrs L. Strickett, B. Wooldridge

In-service Centre
Santon, Isle of Man; Tel 01624 823647

Music Service
Douglas, Isle of Man; Tel 01624 686555

Outdoor Pursuits Centres
Ardwhallin   West Baldwin, Isle of Man; Tel 01624 686057; Fax 01624 686060
Youth Officer   P. Young
Eary Cushlin   Dalby, Peel, Isle of Man; Tel 01624 686057; Fax 01624 686060
Youth Officer   P. Young

Jersey

Population: 87 186
States Greffe, Morier Hse, St Helier, Jersey JE1 1DD, Channel Islands; URL www.gov.je; e-mail m.delahaye@gov.je; Tel 01534 441020; Fax 01534 441098
President of the States   Bailiff Sir Philip Bailhache;   Bailiff's Chambers; Tel 01534 441100; Fax 01534 441137

States of Jersey Department of Education, Sport and Culture

PO Box 142, Jersey JE4 8QJ, Channel Islands; URL www.esc.gov.je; Tel 01534 445504
President   Senator M. Vibert
Vice-President   Deputy B. Fox
Treasurer of the States   Ian Black; Tel 01534 603000
Director   T.W. McKeon BEd, MBA
Assistant Director (Lifelong Learning)   D. Greenwood
Assistant Director (Policy and Planning)   M. Heald
Assistant Director (Resources)   E. Middleton
Assistant Director (Schools and Colleges)   M.G. Lundy
Assistant Director (Sport and Leisure)   Derek De La Haye
Manager (Children's Office)   M. Baudains; Maison Le Pape, The Parade, St Helier, Jersey JE2 3PU, Channel Islands; Tel 01534 623500
Consultant Dental Surgeon; Senior School Dental Officer   Dr John Fleet; Tel 01534 71000
School Dental Officer   Mr M. Cassidy RD, BDS, MSc, FDS, DRD, FFD

Medical Officer (Health)   Vacancy; Public Health Dept, Le Bas Centre, St Saviour's Rd, St Helier, Jersey JE1 4HR, Channel Islands; Tel 01534 879111
Consultant Psychologist   Ian Berry Dip(Tech), MBC(DipPsych); Tel 01534 71000
Chief Librarian   Pat Davis;   Central Library; Tel 01534 759991
Number of Schools
7 Secondary; 1 FE College
Requisition Periods for Schools Supplies
No fixed period

Learning Support Unit
Education Sport and Culture   Fax 01534 499400

Other Government and Public Offices

England

Children's Education Advisory Service (CEAS)

Trenchard Lines, Upavon, Pewsey, Wiltshire SN9 6BE; URL www.ceas.mod.uk; e-mail enquiries@ceas.detsa.co.uk; Tel 01980 618244; Fax 01980 618245
Senior Education Officer   Mrs O.M. Denson
CEAS, a Ministry of Defence organisation, is based in the UK to provide advice and assistance for service families. Information and impartial advice can be provided on any aspect of education that might affect a family as they move from one area to another. Information is available on both state and independent schools and colleges within the UK, SEN and admissions to mainstream school. Information can also be provided on educational systems and international schools overseas.

Connexions

Connexions Service National Unit, Department for Education and Skills, Moorfoot, Sheffield S1 4PQ
Chief Executive   Anne Weinstock
Contact (Government Office East of England)   Roger Allen
Contact (Government Office East Midlands)   Peter Ward
Contact (Government Office London)   Cheryl Rose
Contact (Government Office North East)   Eric Bannister
Contact (Government Office North West)   Tony McGee
Contact (Government Office South West)   Nita Murphy
Contact (Government Office West Midlands)   John Robertson
Contact (Government Office Yorkshire and the Humber)   Derek Ireland
Connexions is a governmental advice and guidance service for 13–19 year olds

Equality and Human Rights Commission

In October 2007 the new single body brought together the work of the Commission for Racial Equality, the Disability Rights Commission and the Equal Opportunities Commission. It addresses discrimination on grounds of religion, sexuality, age, gender, race and disability.
3 More London, Riverside, Tooley St, London SE1 2RG; URL www.equalityhumanrights.com
Chief Executive   Dr Nicola Brewer
Chair   Trevor Phillips

HQ Service Children's Education (SCE)

Headquarters Organisation
An agency of the Ministry of Defence
Tel +49 2161 908 2295
Chief Executive   D.G. Wadsworth

Service Children's Education is responsible for providing schooling for the children of service personnel and civilian support staff working outside the UK

Children's Education Advisory Service (CEAS)

Trenchard Lines, Upavon, Pewsey, Wiltshire SN9 6BE;
    URL www.ceas.mod.uk; e-mail
    enquiries@ceas.detsa.co.uk; Tel 01980 618244;
    Fax 01980 618245
Head of Service   Olivia Denson

Office for National Statistics

1 Drummond Gate, London SW1V 2QQ;
    URL www.statistics.gov.uk; e-mail
    info@statistics.gov.uk; Tel 020 7533 6261;
    Fax 020 7533 5880

Ofsted (Office for Standards in Education, Children Services and Skills)

Alexandra Hse, 33 Kingsway, London WC2B 6SE;
    URL www.ofsted.gov.uk; Tel 0845 640 4040;
    Fax 020 7421 6707
Her Majesty's Chief Inspector of Schools (England)
    Christine Gilbert CBE
Director (Children's Services)   Michael Hart
Director (Corporate Services)   Lorraine Langham
Director (Education)   Miriam Rosen
Director (Finance)   Vanessa Howlison
Director (Learning and Skills)   Melanie Hunt
Deputy Director (Corporate Services)   Peter Duffy
Deputy Director (Early Years)   Jean Humphreys
Deputy Director (Education)   David Hinchliffe
Deputy Director (Learning and Skills)   David Ansell

Ombudsmen

Local Government Ombudsman

10th Fl, Millbank Tower, Millbank, London SW1P 4QP;
    URL www.lgo.org.uk; e-mail enquiries@lgo.org.uk;
    Tel (advice line) 0845 602 1983; Tel 020 7217 4620;
    Fax 020 7217 4621; Telex DX 149243 Victoria 13
Local Government Ombudsman
    Tony Redmond;   responsible for London boroughs
    north of the River Thames (including Richmond but not
    Harrow), Berkshire, Buckinghamshire, Coventry City,
    East and West Sussex, Essex, Hertfordshire, Kent, Suffolk
    and Surrey
Local Government Ombudsman   Anne Seex;   responsible
    for Birmingham City, Cheshire, Derbyshire,
    Nottinghamshire, Lincolnshire, Solihull MBC,
    Warwickshire and the North of England (except the cities
    of Manchester, York and Lancaster); Beverley Hse, 17
    Shipton Rd, York YO30 5FZ; e-mail
    enquiries@lgo.org.uk; Tel 01904 380200;
    Fax 01904 380269
Local Government Ombudsman   Jerry White;   responsible
    for London Borough of Harrow and London boroughs
    south of the River Thames, the cities of Manchester, York
    and Lancaster; Trafford and the rest of England not
    covered by Tony Redmond and Anne Seex; The Oaks, 2
    Westwood Way, Westwood Business Pk, Coventry
    CV4 8JB; e-mail enquiries@lgo.org.uk; Tel 024 7682 0000;
    Fax 024 7682 0001
The ombudsmen, established under the Local Government
Act 1974, investigates complaints from citizens alleging
injustice caused by maladministration by local authorities.
There are three (local government ombudsmen), each of
whom investigates complaints arising in a particular area of
the country. A free booklet about the service is called
'Complaint about the council? How to complain to the Local
Government Ombudsman', available from council offices,
citizens advice bureaux or direct from the ombudsmen's
London office. The local government ombudsmen can

investigate complaints about social services matters, which
form about 8% of the total number of complaints received
and about 13% of reports issued by the ombudsmen.
Reports of investigations of social services complaints are
available from the ombudsmen's office in London.

Qualifications and Curriculum Authority (QCA)

83 Piccadilly, London W1J 8QA; URL www.qca.org.uk;
    e-mail (customer relations) info@qca.org.uk
    Tel 020 7509 5555; Fax 020 7509 6666
Chair   Sir Anthony Greener
Chief Executive   Dr Ken Boston
Head (Media Relations)   Matthew Lumby; QCA Press
    Office; Tel 020 7509 6789
Director (Communications and Marketing)   David Robinson
Director (Curriculum)   Mick Waters
Director (Finance)   Arthur Jordan
Director (National Assessment Agency)   David Gee
Director (Qualifications and Skills)   Mary Curnock Cook
Director (Regulation and Standards)   Isabel Nesbit
QCA promotes quality and standards in the curriculum,
examinations and qualifications. Its work includes
preparing advice to the Secretary of State for Education
about the curriculum, assessment, and qualifications;
publishing information and guidance for early years
practitioners, teachers and parents; and developing criteria
for general and vocational qualifications to ensure their
quality and consistency. Most areas of the work relate to the
education and training system in England, but the QCA is
also responsible for accrediting NVQs in Wales and
Northern Ireland.

Royal Mail Group Ltd, Education Service (including Film and Video Library)

PO Box 145, Sittingbourne, Kent ME10 1NH;
    URL www.teacherspost.co.uk; e-mail info@edist.co.uk;
    Tel 01795 426465; Fax 01795 437988
Contact   Linda Gates
Contact   B. Wiles

Scotland

Equality and Human Rights Commission

In October 2007 the new single body brought together the
work of the Commission for Racial Equality, the Disability
Rights Commission and the Equal Opportunities
Commission. It addresses discrimination on grounds of
religion, sexuality, age, gender, race and disability.
The Optima Bldg, 58 Robertson St, Glasgow G2 8DU;
    URL www.equalityhumanrights.com; e-mail
    scotland@equalityhumanrights.com; Tel 0141 228 5910;
    Fax 0141 248 5912
Chief Executive   Dr Nicola Brewer
Chair   Trevor Phillips

Forestry Commission Scotland

231 Corstorphine Rd, Edinburgh EH12 7AT;
    URL www.forestry.gov.uk; e-mail
    sally.york@forestry.gsi.gov.uk; Tel 0131 314 6458;
    Fax 0131 314 6152
Scotland Adviser (Education)   Sally York

Ombudsmen

Scottish Public Services Ombudsman

4 Melville St, Edinburgh EH3 7NS; URL www.spso.org.uk;
    e-mail ask@spso.org.uk; Tel 0800 377 7330;
    Fax 0800 377 7331
Ombudsman   Prof Alice Brown

Wales

Equality and Human Rights Commission

In October 2007 the new single body brought together the work of the Commission for Racial Equality, the Disability Rights Commission and the Equal Opportunities Commission. It addresses discrimination on grounds of religion, sexuality, age, gender, race and disability.
3rd Fl, 3 Callaghan Sq, Cardiff CF10 5BT;
 URL www.equalityhumanrights.com; e-mail
 wales@equalityhumanrights.com; Tel 02920 447710;
 Fax 02920 447712
Chief Executive   Dr Nicola Brewer
Chair   Trevor Phillips

Ombudsmen

Public Services Ombudsman for Wales

1 Ffordd yr Hen Gae, Pencoed CF35 5LJ;
 URL www.ombudsman-wales.org.uk; e-mail
 ask@ombudsman-wales.org.uk; Tel 01656 641150;
 Fax 01656 641999
Public Services Ombudsman for Wales investigates complaints of injustice caused by maladministration or service failure by public bodies in Wales, including local authorities, the NHS, housing associations, and the National Assembly for Wales. The jurisdiction of the ombudsman also extends to the investigation of allegations that members of local authorities have breached the code of conduct.

Northern Ireland

Department of Agriculture and Rural Development for Northern Ireland

Dundonald Hse, Upper Newtownards Rd, Belfast BT4 3SB;
 URL www.dardni.gov.uk; e-mail
 pauline.rooney@dardni.gov.uk; Tel 028 9052 4413;
 Fax 028 9052 4055

Education and Training Policy

Head (SDG Education and Finance)   Pauline Rooney

Ombudsmen

Office of the Northern Ireland Ombudsman, Progressive Hse, 33 Wellington Pl, Belfast BT1 6HN;
 URL www.ni-ombudsman.org.uk; e-mail
 ombudsman@ni-ombudsman.org.uk; Tel 028 9023 3821;
 Fax 028 9023 4912
Northern Ireland Ombudsman   T. Frawley
The Northern Ireland Ombudsman comprises two statutory offices: the Assembly Ombudsman for Northern Ireland and the Northern Ireland Commissioner for Complaints. The Assembly Ombudsman investigates complaints of alleged maladministration against Northern Ireland government departments and their agencies and the Commissioner for Complaints investigates complaints of alleged maladministration against public bodies in Northern Ireland.

Local Government

2

Local Authority Associations

East of England

East Midlands

London

North East

North West

South East

South West

West Midlands

Yorkshire and the Humber

Scotland

Wales

Northern Ireland

Local Government

LOCAL AUTHORITY ASSOCIATIONS

Representative Bodies

Association of Chief Executives of Area Boards for Education and Libraries

Hon Secretary   John McCullough; Belfast Education and Library Board, 40 Academy St, Belfast, County Armagh BT1 2NQ; e-mail john.mccullough@belb.co.uk; Tel 028 9056 4041; Fax 028 9033 1715

Association of Directors of Education in Scotland

General Secretary   A. Wilson; Dundee City Council, Dundee DD1 3RJ; Tel 01382 434000
President   M. O'Neill; North Lanarkshire Council, Coatbridge, North Ayrshire ML5 3LS
Vice-President; Executive Director (Education and Community Services)   K. Bloomer; Clackmannanshire Council, Lime Tree Hse, Alloa, Clackmannanshire FK10 1EX
Vice-President   M. O'Neill; North Lanarkshire Council, Coatbridge, North Ayrshire ML5 3LS
Treasurer   J. Christie; The Scottish Borders Council, Melrose, Scottish Borders TD6 0SA; Tel 01835 824000

Association of Northern Ireland Education and Library Boards

Belfast Education and Library Board, 40 Academy St, Belfast BT1 2NQ; e-mail geraldinem@belb.co.uk; Tel 028 9056 4041; Fax 028 9033 1715
Chief Executive (Belfast Education and Library Board) D. Cargo
Chief Executive (North Eastern Education and Library Board) G. Topping; North Eastern Education and Library Board, County Hall, 182 Galgorm Rd, Ballymena, County Antrim BT42 1HN; Tel 028 2566 2296; Fax 028 2564 4299
Chief Executive (South Eastern Education and Library Board) Mr S. Sloan; South Eastern Education and Library Board, Grahamsbridge Rd, Dundonald, Belfast BT16 0HS; Tel 028 9056 6283; Fax 028 9048 3297
Chief Executive (Southern Education and Library Board) Mrs H. McClenaghan; Southern Education and Library Board, 3 Charlemont Pl, The Mall, Armagh, County Armagh BT61 9AX; Tel 028 3751 2324; Fax 028 3751 2535
Chief Executive (Western Education and Library Board) B. Mulholland; Western Education and Library Board, 1 Hospital Rd, Omagh, County Tyrone BT79 0AW; Tel 028 8241 1205; Fax 028 8224 3557
Hon Secretary   J. McCullough

Confed

Humanities Bldg, University of Manchester, Oxford Rd, Manchester M13 9PL; e-mail confedoffice@confed.org.uk; Tel 0161 275 8810; Fax 0161 275 8811

President   Andrew Seber;   Hampshire
Immediate Past President   Alan Parker;   Ealing
Executive Director   Chris Waterman
Assistant Director   Sarah Caton
Hon Treasurer   Tony Eccleston;   Bracknell Forest; Education Dept, County Hall, Preston, Lancashire PR1 8RJ
Administrator   Jo Dunston
Administrator   Jane Haythorne
Membership of the council is for four years with officers retiring in rotation. Results of annual elections are confirmed at the AGM in January; from January the Vice-President automatically becomes President and the President automatically becomes Immediate Past President.

Regional Secretaries
East Anglia Regional Society   Martin Fog;   Essex
Midlands Regional Society   Paul McGann;   Derbyshire LEA
North Regional Society   Vacancy
North West Regional Society   Stephen Clark;   Lancashire LEA
South East Regional Society   Vacancy
South West Regional Society   Rick Harmes;   Oxfordshire LEA
Yorkshire and the Humber   Gavin Tonkin;   Kirklees
Confed (Wales)   Edgar Lewis

Convention of Scottish Local Authorities

Rosebery Hse, 9 Haymarket Terr, Edinburgh EH12 5XZ; URL www.cosla.gov.uk; e-mail carol@cosla.gov.uk; Tel 0131 474 9200; Fax 0131 474 9292; Telex DX ED407 Edinburgh
Chief Executive   Rory Mair
President (South Lanarkshire)   Cllr Pat Watters
Vice-President (Dumfries and Galloway Council) Cllr Andrew R. Campbell CBE
Vice-President (Stirling Council)   Cllr Corrie McChord
Director (Policy and Legislation)   Jon Harris
Cultural Affairs Spokesperson (Fife)   Vacancy
Education Spokesperson (Fife)   Cllr Helen Law

Advisers
Chair   Bridget McConnell
Executive Director (Education Resources: South Lanarkshire) Maggi Allan
Director (Education: North Lanarkshire)   Michael O'Neill
Director (Leisure and Arts: Dundee City)   Steve Grimmond
Head (Lifelong Learning and Recreation: Aberdeenshire) Rodney Stone
Manager (Libraries, Information and Archives: Dumfries and Galloway)   Alastair Johnston

Local Education Authority Research Group (LEARG)

Education Department, County Hall, Taunton, Somerset TA1 4DY; URL www.learg.org.uk; e-mail learg@somerset.gov.uk
Treasurer (Isle of Wight)   Andy Seaward
A self-help group that brings together education officers, advisers and others involved in research, planning and statistical work in LEAs. The research group does not conduct or manage research projects, but aims to provide a forum for discussion of current issues in educational

research and its management in LEAs and to exchange factual information and to test ideas. Links are maintained with a variety of organisations, including DFE, EMIE, NCET, NFER, SEO and QCA.

Local Government Association

Local Government Hse, Smith Sq, London SW1P 3HZ;
   URL www.lga.gov.uk; e-mail info@lga.gov.uk;
   Tel 020 7664 3131; Fax 020 7664 3030
President   Lord Best
Chair   Lord Bruce-Lockhart
Vice-Chair   Sir Jeremy Beecham (Lab)
Vice-Chair   Cllr Margaret Eaton OBE (Con)
Deputy Chair   Cllr Richard Kemp (LD)
Head (Children and Young People Board)   Caroline Abrahams

Children and Young People Board

Chair (Birmingham City Council)   Cllr Les Lawrence

London Councils

59$^1/_2$ Southwark St, London SE1 0AL;
   URL www.londoncouncils.gov.uk; e-mail
   info@londoncouncils.gov.uk; Tel 020 7934 9999;
   Fax 020 7934 9991
Chair   Cllr Merrick Cockell (Con)
Deputy Chair   Cllr Dame Sally Powell (Lab)
Vice-Chair   Cllr Steve Hitchins (LD)
Vice-Chair   Cllr Edward Lister (Con)
Vice-Chair   Cllr Hugh Malyan (Lab)

Education Steering Group

Chair   Cllr Louisa Woodley (Lab)
Deputy Chair   Cllr Katy Donnelly (Lab)
Vice-Chair   Cllr Malcolm Grimston (Con)
Vice-Chair   Cllr James Kempton (LD)
Vice-Chair   Cllr Leo Thomson (Lab)

Education Division Staff

Contact   Melanie Griffiths; Tel 020 7934 9826

Northern Ireland Local Government Association

123 York St, Belfast BT15 1AB; URL www.nilga.org; e-mail office@nilga.org; Tel 028 9024 9286; Fax 028 9023 3328
President   Cllr Francis Molloy

SCIA

President for 2003–04   Elaine Ball; e-mail
   elaine.ball@towerhamlets.gov.uk
Past President   Clive Wilkinson; e-mail
   c.wilkinson@worcestershire.gov.uk
Treasurer   Caroline Gruen; e-mail
   caroline.gruen@doncaster.gov.uk
Secretary   Tony Stainer; e-mail tstainer@suttonlea.org
SCIA Administrator   Chris Waterman; Confed, Humanities
   Bldg, University of Manchester, Oxford Rd, Manchester
   M13 9PL; e-mail chriswaterman@onet.co.uk
This national organisation aims to provide a forum for the exchange of views, information and experience relating to all aspects of the management of LEA advisory and inspectorial work, quality assurance, school improvement and pupil achievement. Key objectives are to develop a professional response to issues that may influence the work of members and to promote and provide for members' collective professional development.

Welsh Local Government Association

Local Government Hse, Drake Wlk, Cardiff CF10 4LG;
   URL www.wlga.gov.uk; e-mail wlga@wlga.gov.uk;
   Tel 02920 468600; Fax 02920 468601
Chief Executive   Steve Thomas

EAST OF ENGLAND

Bedfordshire County Council
www.bedfordshire.gov.uk

In April 1997 Luton became a unitary authority and is listed separately in this section. The rest of Bedfordshire retains a two-tier structure. Bedfordshire County Council is a commissioner and provider of social services.
Population: 382 120
Political composition: Con: 26, Lab: 13, LD: 9, Ind: 1
County Hall, Cauldwell St, Bedford, Bedfordshire
   MK42 9AP; URL www.bedfordshire.gov.uk; e-mail
   care@bedscc.gov.uk; Tel 01234 363222; Fax 01234 228619
Chief Executive   A. Hill

Education

Director (Children's Services)   Malcolm Newsam
Deputy Director (Children's Services)   Nicky Pace
Assistant Director (Children in Need)   Sue Warboys
Assistant Director (Commissioning)   Wendi Ogle-Welbourn
Assistant Director (School Standards and Strategy)
   Linda Bird
Head (Early Years and Extended Services)   Bob Thompson
Head (School Standards and Improvement Key Stage 1 and 2)
   Patrick Shevlin
Head (School Standards and Improvement Key Stage 3, 4 and 5)
   Jeffrey Hooper
Head (SEN, Access and Inclusion)   Helen Redding
Head (Strategy, Admissions and Planning)   John Goldsmith
Portfolio Holder (Children and Young People)
   Cllr D. Reedman
Portfolio Holder   Cllr R. Drinkwater
Number of Schools
146 Lower; 39 Middle; 17 Upper; 10 Special; 1 PRU

PUPIL REFERRAL UNIT

Greys Education Centre   Manor Dr, Kempston, Bedford,
   Bedfordshire MK42 7AB; Tel 01234 408477;
   Fax 01234 408478
Head (Pupil Referral Unit)   Sue Raffe
9–13; Number of pupils: 89

ADULT CONTINUING EDUCATION CENTRES

Biddenham Community College   Biddenham Upper School,
   Biddenham Turn, Bedford, Bedfordshire MK40 4AZ;
   Tel 01234 244970
Cedars Community College   Mentmore Rd, Linslade,
   Leighton Buzzard, Bedfordshire LU7 7PA;
   Tel 01525 374276
Hastingsbury Community College   Hastingsbury Upper
   School, Hill Rise, Bedford, Bedfordshire MK42 7EB;
   Tel 01234 244970
John Bunyan and Elstow Craft Centre   Mile Rd, Bedford,
   Bedfordshire MK42 9TR; Tel 01234 244970
Manshead Upper School   Dunstable Rd, Caddington,
   Bedfordshire LU1 4BB; Tel 01582 608641
Mark Rutherford Community College   Mark Rutherford
   Upper School, Wentworth Dr, Bedford, Bedfordshire
   MK41 8PX; Tel 01234 244970
Northfields Upper School   Houghton Rd, Dunstable,
   Bedfordshire LU5 5AB; Tel 01582 608011
Queensbury Upper School   Langdale Rd, Dunstable,
   Bedfordshire LU6 3BU; Tel 01582 601241
Redborne Community College   Redborne Upper School,
   Flitwick Rd, Bedford, Bedfordshire MK45 2NU;
   Tel 01525 404412
Samuel Whitbread Community College   Samuel Whitbread
   Upper School, Shefford Rd, Clifton, Bedfordshire
   SG17 5QS; Tel 01462 629906

Sandy Community College Sandy Upper School, Engayne Ave, Sandy, Bedfordshire SG19 1BL; Tel 01767 680574

Sharnbrook Community College Sharnbrook Upper School, Odell Rd, Bedford, Bedfordshire MK44 1JX; Tel 01234 782581

Stratton Community College Stratton Upper School, Eagle Farm Rd, Biggleswade, Bedfordshire SG18 8JB; Tel 01767 318097

Vandyke Community College Vandyke Upper School, Vandyke Rd, Leighton Buzzard LU7 3DY; Tel 01525 375769

RESIDENTIAL AND OUTDOOR EDUCATION CENTRES

Blue Peris Mountain Centre Dinorwic, Caernarfon, Gwynedd LL55 3EY; Tel 01286 870853
Centre Manager Oliver Knowles

The Outdoor Centre Hillgrounds Rd, Kempston, Bedford, Bedfordshire MK42 8RG; Tel 01234 408402; Fax 01234 408403
Centre Manager Mr B. Stanbridge

SERVICES FOR SENSORY IMPAIRMENT AND COMMUNICATION DIFFICULTIES

The Child Development Centre Hill Rise, Kempston, Bedford, Bedfordshire MK42 7EB; Tel 01234 300710; Fax 01234 300720
Centre Manager L. Truscott

Minority Achievement Support Service (includes Home School Liaison) County Hall, Cauldwell St, Bedford, Bedfordshire MK42 9AP; Tel 01234 408454; Fax 01234 408467
Head of Service Christine Herrick

TRAVELLER EDUCATION SERVICE

Regis Education Centre Parkside Dr, Houghton Regis, Bedfordshire LU5 5PX; Tel 01582 861063
Head of Service Mrs S. Bernarde

YOUTH SERVICES

County Hall, Cauldwell St, Bedford, Bedfordshire MK42 9AP; Tel 01234 228311
Manager (Youth Service) Belinda Evans
Co-ordinator (13–19 Learning) Dave Crawford

Biggleswade and Sandy Area Youth Office Sandy Biggleswade AYO, Sandye Place Middle School, Panc Rd, Sandy, Bedfordshire SG19 1JD; Tel 01767 211549
Project Youth Worker Stephanie Large
Youth Mediation Worker Martin Fairhurst

Houghton Regis Community Resource Centre Angels La, Houghton Regis, Bedfordshire LU7 8HS; Tel 01582 890200; Fax 01582 890201
Project Youth Worker (Barton/Caddington/Toddington) Vannett Wilson

Interface 21–23 Gadsby St, Bedford, Bedfordshire MK40 3HP
Project Youth Worker (Bedford) Winnie Manning; Tel 01234 316063

Mid Bedfordshire Area Youth Office Shefford Youth Centre, Samuel Whitbread Campus, Clifton, Bedfordshire SG17 5QS; Tel 01462 639075
Project Youth Worker (Arlesey/Shelford) Claire Turpin

Rufus Centre Steppingley Rd, Flitwick, Bedfordshire MK45 1AH; Tel 01525 630077
Project Youth Worker (Ampthill/Flintwick) Robert Ward

South Bedford Area Youth Office Kempston Youth Centre, Hillgrounds Rd, Bedford, Bedfordshire MK42 8RG; Tel 01234 408400
Project Youth Worker (Kempston) Roy Bedford

South Bedfordshire Area Youth Office Vernon Place, Dunstable, Bedfordshire LU5 4EZ; Tel 01582 708488
Project Youth Worker (Leighton/Linslade) Ken Foulkes
Youth Counselling Project Worker Marett Troostwyk; The Place, 76a High St, Bedford, Bedfordshire LU6 1NF; Tel 01582 890295

Cambridgeshire County Council
www.cambridgeshire.gov.uk

In April 1998 Peterborough became a unitary authority and is listed separately in this section. The rest of Cambridgeshire retains a two-tier structure.
Population: 565 700 (mid 2004 estimate)
Political composition: Con: 42, LD: 23, Lab: 4
Shire Hall, Castle Hill, Cambridge, Cambridgeshire CB3 0AP; URL www.cambridgeshire.gov.uk; e-mail info@cambridgeshire.gov.uk; Tel (Cambridgeshire Direct) 0845 045 5200; Tel (main switchboard) 01223 717111; Fax 01223 717201
Chief Executive Ian Stewart
Deputy Chief Executive (Corporate Resources) Mike Parsons
Director (Human Resources) Stephen Moir
Director (Property and Asset Management) Andrew Rowson

Children and Young People's Services

URL www.cambridgeshire.gov.uk/social; Tel 0845 045 5203; Fax 01223 717307
Deputy Chief Executive Gordon Jeyes
Area Director (East Cambridgeshire and Fenland) Mike Davey
Area Director (Huntingdonshire) Charlotte Black
Area Director (South Cambridgeshire and City) Niki Clemo
Director (Inclusion) Brian Gale
Director (Learning) Helen Whiter
Director (Planning and Development) Adrian Loades
Number of Schools
29 Secondary; 13 Special
Requisition Periods for Schools Supplies
None

EDUCATION COMMITTEE

Con: 6, Lab: 4, LD: 4
Chair R. Wilkinson (Con)
Members of the Committee
Con: R. Driver, L.W. McGuire, A.K. Melton, A.G. Orgee, A.M. White, R. Wilkinson
LD: A.J. Bowen, S.E. Friend-Smith, A.C. Kent, R.B. Martlew
Lab: I.C. Kidman, S.B. Normington, Dr Pegram, J. Percy

Broad Leas Centre Broad Leas, St Ives, Huntingdon, Cambridgeshire PE17 4QB; Tel 01480 462069
Patch Co-ordinator Chris Thompson

Cambridgeshire Advisory Service Lawrence Ct, Princes St, Huntingdon, Cambridgeshire PE18 6PA; Tel 01480 375870; Fax 01480 375853
Head of Service K. Grimwade

Cambridgeshire Race Equality and Diversity (Traveller and Multicultural Unit) CPDC, Foster Rd, Trumpington, Cambridgeshire CB2 2NL
Team Manager Bethan Rees

East Barnwell Centre Newmarket Rd, Cambridge, Cambridgeshire CB5 8RS; Tel 01223 211945
Centre Supervisor Vacancy

Governor Training and Development Unit Castle Ct, Shire Hall, Castle Hill, Cambridgeshire CB3 0AP; Tel 01223 712265; Fax 01223 712268
Team Manager Susie Hall

Education ICT Service 42 West St, Godmanchester, Cambridgeshire PE18 8HJ; Tel 01480 376655; Fax 01480 376660
Cambridge Rd, Waterbeach, Cambridgeshire CB5 9JN; Tel 01223 566456; Fax 01223 863023
Manager Hazel Coulter

March Community Centre 34 Station Rd, March, Cambridgeshire PE15 8LE; e-mail commed.march@education.camcnty.gov.uk; Tel 01354 653148

Queen Mary Centre for Community Education Queens Rd, Wisbech, Cambridgeshire; e-mail commed.wisbech@education.camcnty.gov.uk; Tel 01945 581444

Patch Co-ordinator Penny Andrews

School Library Service Units 1–3, Springwater Business Pk, Peterborough, Cambridgeshire; Tel 01733 758010; Fax 01733 758015

Head of Service Margaret Smith

Secondary Support and Inclusion Service Ascham Rd, Cambridge, Cambridgeshire CB4 2BD; Tel 01223 712900; Fax 01223 712912

Head B. Sproson

Upware Field Studies Centre Upware, Cambridgeshire CB7 5YQ; Tel 01353 720264

Warden N. Rowntree

Wisbech Castle Professional Development Centre The Castle Museum Sq, Wisbech, Cambridgeshire PE13 1EH; Tel 01945 585096; Fax 01945 474929

Centre Co-ordinator I. Reach

OTHER EDUCATIONAL ESTABLISHMENTS

Burwell House North St, Burwell, Cambridgeshire CB5 0BA; Tel 01638 741256

Warden J. Scarborough

Cambridgeshire Instrumental Music Agency The Old School, Ermine St, Papworth Everand, Cambridge, Cambridgeshire CB3 8RH; Tel 01480 831695; Fax 01480 831696

Manager Vacancy

Cambridge Professional Development Centre Foster Rd, Trumpington, Cambridgeshire CB2 2NL; Tel 01223 844880; Fax 01223 844690

Centre Manager A. O'Neil

Grafham Water Centre West Perry, Huntingdon, Cambridgeshire PE18 0BX; e-mail grafham.water@education.camcnty.gov.uk; Tel 01480 810521; Fax 01480 812739

Centre Manager I. Downing

Huntingdon Professional Development Centre Lawrence Ct, Princes St, Huntingdon, Cambridgeshire PE18 6PA; Tel 01480 425869; Fax 01480 425862

Centre Administrator E. Wilson

Huntingdon Youth Centre Sallowbush Rd, Huntingdon, Cambridge, Cambridgeshire PE18 7AF; Tel 01480 375030; Fax 01480 375034

St Neots Youth Centre Priory Rd, St Neots, Huntingdon, Cambridgeshire PE19 3EG; Tel 01480 474948

Stibbington Centre for Environmental Education Gt North Rd, Stibbington, Peterborough PE8 6LP; e-mail rosie.edwards@cambridgeshire.gov.uk; Tel 01780 782386; Fax 01780 783835

Contact Rosie Edwards

Essex County Council

www.essexcc.gov.uk

In April 1998 both Southend and Thurrock councils became unitary authorities and are listed separately in this section. The rest of Essex retains a two-tier structure.

Population: 1 318 400

Political composition: Con: 50, Lab: 13, LD: 8, Ind: 2, Non aligned: 2

County Hall, Chelmsford, Essex CM1 1LX; URL www.essexcc.gov.uk; e-mail learning@essexcc.gov.uk; Tel 0845 743 0430

Chief Executive Joanna Killian

Chair of the Council Gerard McEwen

Directorate for Schools, Children and Young People

Essex County Council, County Hall, PO Box 47, Chelmsford, Essex CM2 6WN; Tel 0845 603 7627

Director (Schools, Children and Young People) Dr Carey Bennet

Deputy Director (Vulnerable Children and Young People) Clair Pyper

Assistant Director (Localities) Jo Smith

Hertfordshire County Council

www.hertsdirect.org

Population: 1 004 600

Political composition: Con: 46, Lab: 16, LD: 14, Green: 1

County Hall, Pegs La, Hertford, Hertfordshire SG13 8DQ; URL www.hertsdirect.org; e-mail hertsdirect@hertscc.gov.uk

Chief Executive Caroline Tapster

Director (Adult Care Services) Sarah Pickup

Director (Community Information) A. Robertson

Deputy Director (Social Care) Ann Domeney

County Secretary A. Laycock; Tel 01992 555501

County Supplies Officer (Refining) S. Gilbey; County Supplies Dept, Mount Pleasant La, Hatfield, Hertfordshire; Tel 01707 268181

Children, Schools and Families

Tel (customer service) 01438 737500

Director John Harris

Deputy Director (Integrated Children's Services) Alan Dinning

Head (Adoption Service) Brenda Simmonds

Head (Child Protection Unit) Carol Taylor

Head (Children's Trust Arrangements) Andrew Wellington

Head (Finance) Claire Cook

Head (Information Services and Lifelong Learning) Andrew Bignell

Head (Learner and Adolescent) David Ring

Head (Learning, Training and Research) Gillian Cawley

Head (Libraries, Culture and Learning) Glenda Wood

Head (Operations, Planning) Derek Knight

Head (School Governance) Carole Connelly

Head (Secondary School Effectiveness) Andy Cunnigham

Head (SEN, Disability and Pupil Support) Debbie Orton

Head (Standards and School Effectiveness) Gill Jones

Head (Strategic Commissioning) Gary Heathcote

Manager (Student Finance) Chris Hicks

Number of Schools

89 Secondary and Middle; 27 Special (19 Day, 8 Residential)

Day of Committee Meeting

Wednesday

CHILDREN, SCHOOLS AND FAMILIES

Con: 12, Lab: 3, LD: 1

Chair T. Kent (Lab)

Vice-Chair R. Clements (Con)

Spokesperson I. Ambrose (LD)

Spokesperson T. Kent (Lab)

Deputy Spokesperson D. Billing (Lab)

Members of the Committee

Con: R. Clements, T. Dodd, B. Engel, K. Gray, F. Guest, D. Hills, B. Lamb, M. O'Neill, S. Quilty, R. Smith, J. Taunton

Lab: D. Billing, T. Kent, L. Kersher

LD: I. Ambrose

GOVERNOR SUPPORT SERVICE

Development Centre, Butterfield Rd, Wheathampstead, Hertfordshire AL4 8PY

Services offered

All services relating to governor support, information and training; clerk support and training; clerking service; co-ordination of forums and consultations

QUADRANT TEAMS

East County Hall, Pegs La, Hertford, Hertfordshire SG13 8DF
Manager Helen Nys
North The Old Grammar School, Broadway, Letchworth, Hertfordshire SG6 3TD
Manager Mike Benaim
South Langleybury School Site, Hunton Bridge, Langleybury, Kings Langley, Hertfordshire WD4 8RW
Manager David Ring
West 4 Porters Wood, St Albans, Hertfordshire AL3 6ST
Manager Paul Wedgbury

Luton Borough Council
www.luton.gov.uk

In April 1997 Luton became a unitary authority. The rest of Bedfordshire retains a two-tier structure and is listed separately in this section.
Population: 184 900
Political composition: Lab: 26, LD: 17, Con: 5

Children and Learning

Unity Hse, 111 Stuart St, Luton LU1 5NP; e-mail debbie.jones@luton.gov.uk; Tel 01582 548400; Fax 01582 548454
Executive Portfolio Lead Member (Children's Services)
Cllr Tahir Khan
Corporate Director Debbie Jones

CHILDREN AND FAMILIES SERVICE

Head (Children and Family Services) Jenny Coles
Head (Youth Offending Service) Anita Briddon
Deputy Head (Youth Offending Team) Jon O'Byrne
Service Manager (Disabled Children and Partnership)
Jo Fisher
Service Manager (Family Support and Child Protection)
Richard Fountain
Service Manager (Looked After Children) Jonathan Whalley
Service Manager (Standards and Performance) Rachel Jones
Team Manager (Children with Disabilities) Kate Burchell
Team Manager (Family Support and Child Protection)
Sharon Power
Team Manager (Intensive Support) Sharon Keenan
Team Manager (Looked After Children)
Rhona Freeman (Acting)
Team Manager (Looked After Children) Trish Rhynas
Manager (16+ Team) Tom Keating
Manager (Fostering) Annie Craig
Manager (Parys Young People's Resource Centre)
Bukky Oginni

RESOURCES AND PERFORMANCE REVIEW SERVICE

Head William Clapp
Manager (BSF: Strategic Programme) Roger Lucas
Manager (Catering) Ferri Fassihi
Manager (Finance) Bob Freeman
Manager (Human Resources) Hazel Burgess
Manager (Knowledge and Information) Gavin Sandmann
Manager (Performance Review) Carole Brooks
Manager (Planning and Admissions) Debbie Craig
Manager (Student Support) June Power

ACCESS SERVICE

Head Anne Futcher
Head (Avenue Centre) Chris Day

Head (Behaviour Support Service and Tuition Service)
David Snape
Head (Orchard Centre) Roger Brown
Head (Psychology, Assessment and Intervention)
Harriet Martin
Manager (Education Support Services) Christine Goldson
Manager (Education Welfare) Simon Ashley
Manager (Principal Youth Service) Nicholas Chamberlain
Manager (SEN Assessment Team) David Newbury
Co-ordinator (Behaviour Improvement Programme) Vacancy

SCHOOL IMPROVEMENT SERVICE

Director (14–19) Alison Batten
Director (Training and Partnerships for the Shire Foundation SCITT and Primary DRB) Graham McFarlane
Head of Service Geoff Headley
Head (Music Service) Stephen Beaven
Manager (Governor Support Services)
Yvonne Jones (Acting)
Manager (LLRC) Sue O'Flynn
Manager (Sure Start and Extended Schools) David Bruce
Chief Adviser (Primary) Chris Spruce
Chief Adviser (Secondary) David Hood

CHANGE FOR CHILDREN UNIT

Head Jenny Williams
Manager (Partnership Commissioning) Stephanie Cash
Manager (Partnership Commissioning) Karen Malone

LUTON ADULT AND COMMUNITY LEARNING

Head Diane Beaven; Tel 01582 490033; Fax 01582 499629
Challney Community College Stoneygate Rd, Luton LU4 9TJ; Tel 01582 576400; Fax 01582 494308
Assistant Head Tracey Thomas
Contact William Merrick
Lea Manor Community College Lea Manor High School, Northwell Dr, Luton LU3 3TL; URL www.luton-acl.ac.uk; e-mail info@ladeadmin.org.uk; Tel 01582 490033
Manager Diane Beaven
Putteridge Community College Putteridge High School, Putteridge Rd, Luton LU2 8HJ; e-mail admin.eladed@ladedadmin.org.uk; Tel 01582 415591; Fax 01582 419357
Manager Diane Beaven
South Luton Community College Cutenhoe Rd, Luton LU1 3NH; e-mail admin.sladed@ladedadmin.org.uk; Tel 01582 480886; Tel 01582 488302
Manager Diane Beaven
Family and Adult Community Learning/ESOL LLRC, Strangers Way, Luton LU4 9ND; Tel 01582 538223; Fax 01582 538206
Manager Gwen Tai

OTHER EDUCATION AND TRAINING CENTRES

Dell Farm Residential Outdoor Education Centre Whipsnade, Luton LU6 2LG; URL www.dellfarm.ik.org; e-mail dell.farm.admin@luton.gov.uk; Tel 01582 872666; Fax 01582 872484
Head Michael Harwin
elearning@luton (City Learning Centre) 230 Sundon Park Rd, Luton LU3 3AL; URL www.luton.gov.uk/elearning; Tel 01582 499670; Fax 01582 499679
Manager Emma Darcy
Luton Learning Resource Centre Strangers Way, Luton LU4 9ND; URL www.luton.gov.uk/llrc; e-mail llrc@luton.gov.uk; Tel 01582 538200; Fax 01582 538206
Manager Sue O'Flynn

YOUTH SERVICE PROVISION

Ashcroft Youth Club Ashcroft High School, Crawley Grn, Luton LU2 9AG; Tel 01582 654445
Manager Ronald Burke

Bushmead Youth Club Bushmead Community Centre, Hancock Dr, Luton LU2 7SF; Tel 01582 654445
Manager Shabnam Iqbal

Centre for Youth and Community Development 94–96 Leagrave Rd, Luton LU4 8HZ; Tel 01582 519500
Manager Sujel Miah

Community Support School (CSS) Denbigh High School, Alexandra Ave, Luton LU3 1HE; Tel 01582 566614
Manager Mick Forshaw

Farley Youth Club Farley Community Centre, Delphine Cl, Luton LU1 5RE; Tel 01582 654445
Manager Taj Hussain

Halyard Youth Centre Emerald Rd, Luton LU4 0NR; e-mail halyardyc@luton.gov.uk; Tel 01582 607688; Fax 01582 662993
Manager Kerrie Virgo

Hockwell Ring Youth Club Hockwell Ring Community Centre, Mayne Ave, Luton LU4 9LB; Tel 01582 561651
Manager Sonia Blackett

Lea Manor Youth Club Northwell Dr, Luton LU3 3TL; e-mail leamanoryouthclub@luton.gov.uk; Tel 01582 579714; Fax 01582 579714
Manager Linda Farmer

Luton Youth Canoe Club Wardown Swimming and Leisure Centre, Bath Rd, Luton LU3 1ES; Tel 01582 566614
Manager Mick Forshaw

Luton Youth Drama Workshop The Hat Factory, 65–67 Bute St, Luton LU1 2EY; Tel 01582 548147
Manager Melanie Skyers

Pakistan and Kashmir Youth Forum (PKYF) Dallow Learning Centre, 234 Dallow Rd, Luton LU1 1TB; Tel 01582 608175
Manager Susan Rivett

Putteridge Youth Club Putteridge High School, Putteridge Rd, Luton LU2 8HJ; Tel 01582 876569; Fax 01582 548232
Manager Jackie Moore

Saints Girl's Group Saints Community Centre, 83–85 Solway Rd North, Luton LU3 1TU; Tel 01582 566614
Manager Mick Forshaw

Saints Youth Club Saints Community Centre, 83–85 Solway Rd North, Luton LU3 1TU; Tel 01582 566614

Starlight Youth Club 88 Inkerman St, Luton LU1 1JD; e-mail bernie.abbey@luton.gov.uk; Tel 01582 425668; Fax 01582 425668
Manager Bernie Abbey

Sundon Park Youth Club Lealands High School, Sundon Park Rd, Luton LU3 2AL; e-mail jackie.moore@luton.gov.uk; Tel 01582 572279; Fax 01582 848782
Manager Geoff Morris

The Welbeck Centre 20–22 High Town Rd, Luton LU2 0DD; e-mail mila.prasad@luton.gov.uk; Tel 01582 654445
Contact Jacky Walsh

CHILDREN AND FAMILY RESOURCE CENTRES

Manor Family Resource Centre Chase St, Luton LU1 3QZ; Tel 01582 415401
Manager Jane Brown

Marsh Farm Children's Centre Redgrave Gdns, Marsh Farm, Luton LU3 3QN; e-mail surestart@luton.gov.uk; Tel 01582 556661
Manager Denise Poore

Young People's Resource Centre Parys Rd, Birdsfoot La, Luton LU3 2EW; Tel 01582 572145
Manager Bukky Oginni

OTHER SERVICE GROUPS

Beechwood Inclusive Learning Development Beechwood School, Linden Rd, Luton LU4 9RD; e-mail beechwood@luton.gov.uk; Tel 01582 656930

PUPIL REFERRAL UNITS

The Orchard Centre Strangers Way, Luton LU4 9ND; e-mail orchard.pupil.admin@luton.gov.uk; Tel 01582 613000
Head Roger Brown

Avenue Centre for Education (ACE) Tomlinson Ave, Luton LU4 0QP; e-mail avenues.centre.admin@luton.gov.uk
Head Chris Day

Norfolk County Council
www.norfolk.gov.uk

Population: 822 500 (mid 2005)
Political composition: Con: 46, Lab: 22, LD: 14, Green: 2
County Hall, Martineau La, Norwich, Norfolk NR1 2DH; URL www.norfolk.gov.uk; e-mail information@norfolk.gov.uk; Tel 0844 800 8020; Fax 01603 306090

Children's Services

County Hall, Martineau La, Norwich, Norfolk NR1 2DL; e-mail education.enquiries.edu@norfolk.gov.uk; Tel 01603 222146; Fax 01603 222119
Area Director (Central) Lesley Witney
Area Director (North) Graham Wright
Area Director (South) Alison Murphy
Area Director (West) David Lennard Jones
Director Lisa Christensen
Deputy Director (Prevention Early Intervention Specialist Support) Meera Spillett
Deputy Director (School, Communities and Early Years) Fred Corbett
Assistant Director (Commissioning and Performance) Frances Kemp
Assistant Director (Resources and Efficiency) Paul Fisher
Head (Business and Efficiency) Mick Sabec
Head (Community Learning and Development) Martyn Livermore
Head (Early Years, Childcare and Extended Schools Service) Marcelle Curtis
Head (Finance) Doug Slade
Head (ICT) Vacancy
Head (Planning and Buildings) Chris Hey
Head (Primary School Development) David Osborne
Head (Pupil and Student Support) Richard Snowden
Head (School Performance, Organisation and Inclusion) Terry Cook
Head (Secondary School Development) Yvonne Barclay
Service Manager (Corporate Parenting) Malcolm Griffiths
Service Manager (Safeguarding Strategy) Mandy Lyons
Service Manager (Special and Additional Needs) Stuart Marpole
Manager (Human Resources and Organisational Development) Elly Starling
Child Protection Officer (Education) G. Cheese
Senior Education Officer (Pupil Access and Support Services) R. Vahey
Senior Education Officer (School and LEA Effectiveness) R. Potts
Number of Schools
384 Primary; 23 Secondary; 12 Special; 3 Nursery

CHILDREN'S SERVICES REVIEW PANEL

Chair Mrs H. Bolt (Con)
Cabinet Member Mrs R. Monriot (Con)
Spokesperson Mrs H. Panting (Lab)
Spokesperson M.J. Scutter (LD)

GOVERNOR SUPPORT SERVICE, NORFOLK EDUCATION ADVICE SERVICE

Professional Development Centre, Woodside Rd, Norwich, Norfolk NR7 9QL; URL www.norfolkesinet.org.uk; e-mail governorsupport@norfolk.gov.uk; Tel 01603 433276; Fax 01603 700236
Full programme of training courses, in-school training for governing bodies; termly newsletter, training helpline and information; resource loans, books, videos and training packs

TEACHERS' CENTRES

Professional Development Centre Woodside Rd, Norwich, Norfolk NR7 9QL; URL www.norfolkesinet.org.uk; Tel 01603 433276; Fax 01603 700236

West Norfolk Professional Development Centre Kilhams Way, King's Lynn, Norfolk PE30 2HU; e-mail janet.atkins@norfolk.gov.uk; Tel 01553 766872; Fax 01553 692374

PUPIL REFERRAL UNITS

Brooklands Centre Shrublands, Magdalen Way, Gorleston, Great Yarmouth, Norfolk NR31 0JJ; e-mail office@brooklandscentre.easternnps.norfolk.sch.uk; Tel 01493 662923; Fax 01493 651373

Brooklands Cottage Shrublands, Magdalen Way, Gorleston, Great Yarmouth, Norfolk NR31 0JJ; e-mail chris.doherty@norfolk.gov.uk; Tel 01493 660223; Fax 01493 651373

Central Area (PRU) 113 Aylsham Rd, Norwich, Norfolk NR2 2HY; Tel 01603 408036; Fax 01603 412529

Earthsea House Education Centre Berry La, Honingham, Norwich, Norfolk NR9 5AX; e-mail office@elmroadcentre.southwestnps.norfolk.sch.uk; Tel 01603 881045; Fax 01603 881045

Elm Road Centre (PRU) Elm Rd, Thetford, Norfolk IP24 3HL; e-mail toni.rainbow@norfolk.gov.uk; Tel 01842 762289; Fax 01842 820478

Northern Area (PRU) Douglas Bader School, Filby Rd, Coltishall, Norfolk NR10 5JW; e-mail justin.blocksidge@norfolk.gov.uk

Contact Justin Blocksidge

Terrapin Centre The Hewett High School, Cecil Rd, Norwich, Norfolk NR1 2PL; e-mail tom.burt@norfolk.gov.uk; Tel 01603 455531; Fax 01603 501818

Peterborough City Council

www.peterborough.gov.uk

In April 1998 Peterborough City Council became a unitary authority. The rest of Cambridgeshire retains a two-tier structure and is listed separately in this section.

Population: 160 000 (July 2006)

Political composition: Con: 36, Ind: 7, LD: 5, Minority Party: 5, Lab: 4

Town Hall, Bridge St, Peterborough, Cambridgeshire PE1 1HL; URL www.peterborough.gov.uk; e-mail ask@peterborough.gov.uk; Tel 01733 747474

Chief Executive Gillian Beasley

Children's Services

Bayard Pl, Broadway, Peterborough PE1 1FB; URL www.thelearningcity.co.uk; Tel 01733 747474; Fax 01733 748002

Director Mohammed Mehmet

Number of Schools

4 Special; 2 Secondary

CABINET

Cabinet Member (Education and Children's Services) Cllr Ridgway (Con)

EDUCATIONAL PSYCHOLOGY SERVICE

Peterborough City Council (Education), Bayard Pl, Broadway, Peterborough PE1 1FB; Tel 01733 748360

Principal Educational Psychologist Sue Dewar

ADULT EDUCATION

Peterborough College of Adult Education Brook St, Peterborough, Cambridgeshire PE1 1TU; Tel 01733 761361

Principal Graham Winton

COMMUNITY EDUCATION

Arthur Mellows Village College Helpston Rd, Glinton, Peterborough PE6 7JX; Tel 01733 252045; Fax 01733 252206

Patch Co-ordinator Fred Mann

Bushfield Community College Orton Goldhay, Peterborough PE2 5RQ; Tel 01733 394407; Fax 01733 371524

Patch Co-ordinator Chris Bird

Fletton Student Support Centre Old Court House, High St, Old Fletton, Peterborough PE2 8EW; Tel 01733 560504; Fax 01733 898435

Peterborough Careers Centre Cavell Ct, 9–11 Lincoln Ct, Peterborough, Cambridgeshire; Tel 01733 311094

Peterborough Centre for Multicultural Education 165a Cromwell Rd, Peterborough, Cambridgeshire PE1 2EL; Tel 01733 703741; Fax 01733 703242

Manager (Youth Work) Rachel Lee

Southend-on-Sea Borough Council

www.southend.gov.uk

In April 1998 Southend became a unitary authority. The rest of Essex retains a two-tier structure and is listed separately in this chapter.

Civic Centre, Victoria Ave, Southend-on-Sea, Essex SS2 6ER; URL www.southend.gov.uk; Tel 01702 215000

Chief Executive Rob Tinlin

Children and Learning Department

e-mail maureencox@southend.gov.uk; Tel 01702 215048

Corporate Director Paul Greenhalgh

Number of Schools

36 Primary; 12 Secondary; 5 Special; 1 PRU

EDUCATION SCRUTINY COMMITTEE

Con: 9, LD: 5, Lab: 3

Civic Centre, Victoria Ave, Southend-on-Sea, Essex SS2 6ER

Chair Mr A.J. Moring

Portfolio Holder Sally Carr

ADULT EDUCATION CENTRES

South East Essex College Southend-on-Sea, Essex SS1 1ND; e-mail learning@southend.ac.uk; Tel 01702 220400; Fax 01702 432320

Contact Jan Hodges

Southend Adult Community College Ambleside Dr, Southend-on-Sea, Essex SS1 2UP; Tel 01702 445700; Fax 01702 445739

Principal Ali Hadawi

Suffolk County Council

www.suffolkcc.gov.uk

Population: 702 000

Political composition: Con: 45, Lab: 22, LD: 7, Ind: 1

Endeavour Hse, 8 Russell Rd, Ipswich, Suffolk IP1 2BX; URL www.suffolkcc.gov.uk; Tel 01473 583000; Fax 01473 214549

Chief Executive M. More CPFA

Director (Adult and Community Services) G. Gatehouse

Director (Children and Young People) R. Turner

Education Offices

Tel 01473 264000; Fax 01473 216848
Service Director (Education) G. Nethercott
Service Director (Vulnerable Children) J. Gregg
Assistant Director (Strategic Finance) G. Bultitude
Head (Children and Young People's Development)
  D. Maynard
Head (Children's Service Infrastructure Development)
  I. Brown
Head (Commissioning and Partnerships) T. Hines
Head (Corporate Parenting) G. Jones
Head (Inclusive School Improvement) J. Wellings
*Head (Integrated Early Years, Extended Schools, Youth
  Services)* V. Muller
Head (Integrated Services – Children and Additional Needs)
  Vacancy
Head (Planning and Strategic Commissioning) C. Carruthers
Head (Safeguarding) C. James
Head (Vulnerable Children's Service) J. Lowe
Head (Youth Offending Service) H. Collyer
County Manager (Catering) R. Glaisher FHCIMA, MIPD,
  MRSH
County Manager (Grounds) K. Rowton
Manager (County Caretaking and Cleaning) C. Cross
Manager (Passenger Transport Operations) S. Harper
Manager (Passenger Transport Operations) T. Vobe
Senior Education Officer (Development) M. Chapman
Senior Education Officer (Social Inclusion) A. Orr
County Adviser (14–19) K. Ridealgh
County Adviser (Art) T. Wilson
County Adviser (Assessment) M. Wyard
County Adviser (Design and Technology) V. Fehners
County Adviser (English) J. Merrion
County Adviser (Humanities) D. Banham
County Adviser (Information Communication Technology)
  G. Rushbrook
County Adviser (Mathematics) P. Jaynes
County Adviser (Modern Languages) Vacancy
County Adviser (Music) P.J. Shaw LTCL, GNSM
County Adviser (Personal and Social Development) C. Moore
County Adviser (Physical Education and Sport) S. Thornton
County Adviser (Professional Development) F. Denny
County Adviser (PSHE) Vacancy
County Adviser (Religious Education) M. Myatt
County Adviser (Science) S. Turp
County Educational Psychologist W.F. Herbert BSc(Hons),
  MEd
Number of Schools
256 Primary; 40 Middle; 38 Comprehensive; 13 PRU; 9
Special; 1 Nursery
Requisition Periods for Schools Supplies
No specific arrangements
**Other Authorities with whom Joint Purchasing Arrangements
are made**
Department of Education and Science and a number of
county, borough and district councils

CABINET

Con: 8
Chair Jeremy Pembroke
Members of the Committee
E. Alcock, G. McGregor, G. Newman, P. O'Brien, J. Spicer, J.
Storey

CHILD GUIDANCE CLINICS

Cases referred to the Institute of Family Psychiatry

AREA OFFICES

Northern Area Adrian Hse, Alexandra Rd, Lowestoft,
  Suffolk NR32 1PL; Tel 01502 405218
  Area Manager S. Simpkin
  *Area Manager (Direct Services to Children and Young
  People)* K. Drake
  Area Manager (Schools and Communities) S. Boardman

  Area Manager (SEN) J. Taylor
  Senior Educational Psychologist E. Price
  Cluster Development Co-ordinator L. Broadhurst
  Cluster Development Co-ordinator C. Besley
Southern Area St Edmunds Hse, Rope Wlk, Ipswich,
  Suffolk IP4 1LZ; Tel 01473 584800
  Area Director A. Cadzow
  *Area Manager (Direct Services to Children and Young
  People)* T. Bailey
  Area Manager (Schools and Communities) J. Lee
  Area Manager (SEN) G. Green
  Area Senior Educational Psychologist M. Smith
  Cluster Development Co-ordinator J. Norden
  Cluster Development Co-ordinator J. Nind
Western Area Shire Hall, Bury St Edmunds, Suffolk
  IP33 IRX; Tel 01284 352000
  Area Director V. Harvey-Samuel
  *Area Manager (Direct Services to Children and Young
  People)* G. Smith
  Area Manager (Schools and Communities) L. Howe
  Area Manager (Schools and Communities) A. Jones
  Area Manager (Schools and Communities) F. Stockley
  Area Manager (SEN) T. Sale
  Senior Educational Psychologist R. Parker
  Cluster Development Co-ordinator M. Miller
  Cluster Development Co-ordinator S. O'Leary

ADULT AND COMMUNITY LEARNING

Head (Service Development) J. Bloomfield; Endeavour Hse,
  Russell Rd, Ipswich, Suffolk; Tel 01473 264649
Manager (Adult and Community Learning) M. Cole;
  Endeavour Hse, Russell Rd, Ipswich, Suffolk;
  Tel 01473 260115
Manager (Learning Standards and Curriculum Development)
  S. Butcher; Endeavour Hse, Russell Rd, Ipswich;
  Tel 01473 260116

PERFORMING ARTS CENTRES

Northgate Arts Centre Sidegate La, Ipswich, Suffolk
  IP4 3DF; Tel 01473 281866
West Suffolk Performing Arts Centre King Edward VI
  Upper School, Grove Rd, Bury St Edmunds, Suffolk
  IP33 3BH; Tel 01284 723105

INFORMATION, SUPPORT AND COUNSELLING FOR YOUNG PEOPLE

Information, Support and Counselling (North) Opportunity
  Hse, London Rd North, Lowestoft NR32 1BH;
  Tel 01502 525941
Information, Support and Counselling (South) Suffolk
  Young Peoples Health Project, 14 Lower Brook St,
  Ipswich IP4 1AP; Tel 01473 225344
Information, Support and Counselling (West)
  Tel 01284 774580
  Contact M. Straw

OUTDOOR EDUCATION CENTRES

Alton Water Sports Centre, Holbrook SWSA Woodbridge
  Youth Centre, The Avenue, Woodbridge, Suffolk
  IP12 4BA; Tel 01394 382007
  Contact S. Harrington-Rutterford
Deben Water Sports Centre, Woodbridge SWSA
  Woodbridge Youth Centre, The Avenue, Woodbridge,
  Suffolk IP12 4BA; Tel 01394 382007
  Contact S. Harrington-Rutterford
Felixstowe Ferry Residential Centre Ferry Rd, Old
  Felixstowe, Suffolk; Tel 01473 712645
Neptune Water Sports Centre, Woolverstone SWSA
  Woodbridge Youth Centre, The Avenue, Woodbridge,
  Suffolk IP12 4BA; Tel 01394 382007
  Contact S. Harrington-Rutterford
Oulton Broad Water Sports Centre, Lowestoft Colman's
  Dyke, Bridge Rd, Lowestoft, Suffolk NR33 9JR;
  Tel 01502 587163
  Contact R. Thomas

Thorpe Woodlands Camping and Outdoor Activity Site
Endeavour Hse; Tel 01473 833321; Fax 01473 216848
Contact T. Edmonds

Thurrock Council
www.thurrock.gov.uk

In April 1998 Thurrock became a unitary authority. The rest
of Essex retains a two-tier structure and is listed separately
in this section.
Population: 145 235
Political composition: Con: 26, Lab: 20, Ind: 2, Independent
Socialist: 1
Civic Offices, New Rd, Grays, Thurrock RM17 6SL;
    URL www.thurrock.gov.uk; e-mail
    general.enquiries@thurrock.gov.uk; Tel 01375 390000
Managing Director Angie Ridgwell

Children, Education and Families

Civic Offices, New Rd, Grays, Thurrock RM17 5RL;
    Tel 01375 652652
Corporate Director Julien Kramer (Acting)
*Executive Head (Resources, Development and Lifelong
    Learning)* Stuart Freel
Executive Head (Universal and Targeted Services)
    Mark Gurrey
Strategic Leader (Assessment and Safeguarding) Chris Miller
Strategic Leader (Assets, Access and Schools Services)
    Mike Singleton
Strategic Leader (Educare 0–5) Sue Green
Strategic Leader (Enhanced Support) Jean Imray
Strategic Leader (Schools and Learning) Christine Tinkler
Strategic Leader (Targeted Intervention) Christine Dove
Contact (Awards and Benefits) Carol Ford
Contact (Education Welfare) Wendy Springham
Contact (Parent and Pupil Services) Brenda Stannard
Number of Schools
45 Primary; 10 Secondary; 2 Special

CABINET MEMBER WITH PORTFOLIO FOR CHILDREN AND LEARNING

Contact Cllr Mike Revel

CABINET MEMBER WITH PORTFOLIO FOR FAMILIES AND YOUNG PEOPLE

Con: 10
Contact Cllr Wendy Herd

ADULT EDUCATION

Adult Community College Richmond Rd, Grays, Thurrock
    RM17 6DN; Tel 01375 372476
    Principal Sharon Walsh

OTHER ESTABLISHMENTS

Environmental and Outdoor Education Centre
    Grangewaters, Buckles La, South Ockendon, Thurrock
    RM15 6RS; Tel 01708 856422
    Manager A. Hodges
Speech and Language Unit c/o Corringham Primary School,
    Herd La, Corringham, Thurrock SS17 9BH;
    Tel 01375 360756
    Teacher-in-Charge Jean Barnes
Thurrock Pupil Support Service The Culver Centre, Daiglen
    Dr, South Ockendon, Thurrock RM15 5RR;
    Tel 01708 853781
    Head D. Hawkins
    Education other than at school, pupil referral unit/
    individual tuition service
Youth Service PO Box 118, New Rd, Grays, Thurrock
    RM17 6SL; e-mail dxmurphy@thurrock.gov.uk;
    Tel 01375 652542
    Manager D. Murphy

EAST MIDLANDS

Derby City Council
www.derby.gov.uk

2

In April 1997 Derby City Council became a separate unitary
authority. Derbyshire County Council retains a two-tier
structure and is listed separately in this section.
Population: 233 700
Political composition: Lab: 24, LD: 15, Con: 11, Ind: 1
The Council Hse, Corporation St, Derby DE1 2FS;
    URL www.derby.gov.uk; e-mail
    enquiries@derby.gov.uk; Tel 01332 293111;
    Fax 01332 255500
Chief Executive R.H. Cowlishaw IPFA

Corporate and Adult Social Services Department/Children and Young People's Department

Norman Hse, Friar Gate, Derby DE1 1NU;
    URL www.derby.gov.uk; Tel (Derby care line 1700-0900
    daily, weekends and bank holidays) 01332 711250;
    Tel (0900–1700) 01332 717777; Fax (0900–1700)
    01332 711254
Tel (Child Protection Register enquiries) 01332 717818
Corporate Director (Children and Young People)
    Andrew Flack
Assistant Director (Learning) Mick Seller

Education Service

Middleton Hse, 27 St Marys Gate, Derby DE1 3NN;
    URL www.derby.gov.uk; e-mail
    margaret.mcinally@derby.gov.uk; Tel 01332 716924;
    Fax 01332 716920
Director (Children and Young People) Andrew Flack
Assistant Director (Integrating Children's Services Project)
    Rachel Dickinson
*Assistant Director (Lifelong Learning and Community
    Services)* Lesley Whitney
Assistant Director (Resources and Strategic Planning)
    Simon Longley
Assistant Director (School Improvement)
    Mick Seller (Acting)
Assistant Director (School Inclusion) Rita Silvester (Acting)
Head (Adult Learning) Jenny German
Head (Asset Management Planning) Gurmail Nizzer
Head (Finance and Contracts) Keith Howkins
Head (ICT) Peter Simpson
Head (Marketing and Communication) Sian Hoyle
Head (Personnel) Jayne Stone
Head (Youth Services) David Finn
Education Officer (Access/EAL) Rajesh Lall
Education Officer (Pupil Services and SEN) Liz Beswick
Education, Attendance and Welfare Officer
    Danny McLaughlin
Principal Educational Psychologist Mick Pitchford
Number of Schools
13 Secondary; 5 Special

SPECIAL UNITS

Ronnie Mackeith Centre for Child Development Derby City
    General Hospital Trust, Uttoxeter Rd, Derby DE22 3NE;
    Tel 01332 340131 ext 6917
    Teacher-in-Charge L. Harahan

Special Educational Needs Support Service (including Pupil Referral Service) Kingsmead Centre, Bridge St, Derby DE1 3LB; Tel 01332 716000; Fax 01332 716006
Head   Sue Bradley

Derbyshire County Council

www.derbyshire.gov.uk

In April 1997 Derby City Council became a separate unitary authority and is listed separately in this section. Derbyshire County Council retains a two-tier structure.
Population: 754 100
Political composition: Lab: 38, Con: 15, LD: 10, Ind: 1
County Hall, Matlock, Derbyshire DE4 3AG;
   URL www.derbyshire.gov.uk; Tel 01629 580000;
   Fax 01629 585279
Chief Executive   A.R.N. Hodgson
Deputy Chief Executive   G.C. Tommy
Strategic Director (Children and Younger Adults)
   A.B. Buckley
Head (Corporate Finance)   G. Hunt
County Procurement Officer   A.C. Ayling

Children and Younger Adults

County Hall, Matlock, Derbyshire DE4 3AG;
   Tel 01629 580000
Cabinet Member (Children's Services)   Cllr A. Western
Cabinet Member (Schools)   Cllr A.F. Charles
Deputy Director   David Connor
Deputy Director   David Shaw
Assistant Director (Children and Family Support)
   Frances James
Assistant Director (Education Improvement)   Jim Hickman
Assistant Director (Engagement and Skills)   Donald Rae
Assistant Director (Resources)   Ian Thomas
Assistant Director (Safeguarding and Specialist Services)
   Ian Johnson
Number of Schools
355 Primary; 47 Secondary; 10 Special; 8 Support Centres; 8 Nursery
Requisition Periods for Schools Supplies
No fixed period

IMPROVEMENT AND SCRUTINY COMMITTEE – SERVICES FOR CHILDREN

Lab: 12, Co-opted: 6, Con: 4, LD: 3, Ind: 1
Members of the Committee
Lab: Sean Bambrick, Sharon Blank, Walter Burrows, David Chapman, Derek Cotterill, Jim Coyle, Charles Cutting, Joan Dixon, Kath. Lauro, Gail Newman, Peter Riggott, Paul Smith
Con: Ray Caswell, Tracy Critchlow, Judith Twigg, George Wharmby
LD: Beth Atkins, Keith Morgan, Izzy Pryce
Ind: Bill Camm
Non-elected Members of the Committee
Parent Governor (with voting rights) J. Smith (primary)
Trade Union Representatives (without voting rights) D. Allen, T. Rawlinson
Church Representatives Ms A. Brown (CE), E. Hayes (RC)

SUPPORT CENTRES

Breadsall Support Centre (KS3) Brookside Rd, Breadsall, Derbyshire DE21 5LF; Tel 01332 832246;
   Fax 01332 833625
   Head of Centre J. Brandt
Breadsall Support Centre (KS4) Brookside Rd, Breadsall, Derbyshire DE21 5LF; Tel 01332 831316;
   Fax 01332 833108
   Head of Centre P. Bancroft
Buxton Support Centre c/o High Peak and Derbyshire Dales Area Education Office, Kents Bank Rd, Buxton, Derbyshire SK17 9HR; Tel 01298 26121; Fax 01298 72191
   Head of Centre J. Walker

Creswell Support Centre at Ashbrook c/o Ashbrook Day Centre, Cuttholme Rd, Chesterfield S40 4RD;
   Tel 01246 235395
   Head of Centre Andrew Sutton
Deincourt Support Centre (KS2) c/o Deincourt Community School, Chesterfield Rd, North Wingfield, Chesterfield, Derbyshire S42 5LE; Tel 01246 855014; Fax 01246 855014
   Head of Centre J. Stuart
Granville Support Centre (KS2) c/o Granville Community School, Burton Rd, Woodville, Swadlincote, Derbyshire DE11 7JR; Tel 01283 522889; Fax 01283 226428
   Head of Centre I. Malloy
Kirk Hallam Support Centre (KS2 and KS3) Windsor Cres, Kirk Hallam, Ilkeston, Derbyshire DE7 4HD;
   Tel 0115 932 6445; Fax 0115 307980
   Head of Centre A. Raynor
Newhall Support Centre (KS3) Memorial Hall, Newhall, Swadlincote, Derbyshire DE11 0TW; Tel 01283 550667; Fax 01283 215321
   Head of Centre V. Fisher

Leicester City Council

www.leicester.gov.uk

In April 1997 Leicester City Council became a unitary authority. Leicestershire County Council retains a two-tier structure and is listed separately in this section.
Population: 279 923
Political composition: Lab: 38, Con: 8, LD: 6, Green: 2
New Walk Centre, Welford Pl, Leicester LE1 6ZG;
   URL www.leicester.gov.uk; Tel 0116 254 9922
Chief Executive   Rodney Green

Children and Young People's Services

Marlborough Hse, 38 Welford Rd, Leicester LE2 7AA;
   e-mail sheila.lock@leicester.gov.uk; Tel 0116 252 7710;
   Fax 0116 233 9922
Corporate Director   Sheila Lock
Service Director (Access, Inclusion and Participation)
   Paul Livock; Tel 0116 252 7704; Fax 0116 233 9922
Service Director (Family Support and Safeguarding)
   Andrew Bunyan; New Walk Centre; Tel 0116 252 8309;
   Fax 0116 233 9922
Service Director (Learning Services)   Joe Pajak;
   Tel 0116 252 7701; Fax 0116 233 9922
Service Director (Strategic Planning, Commissioning and Performance)   Adrian Paterson; Tel 0116 252 7702;
   Fax 0116 233 9922
Head (Children's Resources)   Andy Smith (Acting); St Martin's, c/o 1 Grey Friars; Tel 0116 256 5213;
   Fax 0116 256 5079
Head of Service (Children's Fieldwork)   Peter McEntee; St Martin's, c/o 1 Grey Friars; Tel 0116 256 8252;
   Fax 0116 256 5079
Service Manager (Child Care – Cluster B)   Dave Starling; 1 Grey Friars; Tel 0116 256 5023; Fax 0116 256 5192
Service Manager (Child Care – Cluster C)   Carol Shaw; 1 Grey Friars; Tel 0116 256 8292; Fax 0116 256 5192
Service Manager (Child Protection)   Caroline Tote; Mansion Hse; Tel 0116 225 4703; Fax 0116 225 4748
Service Manager (Children's Duty and Assessment Service)
   Penny Brown; 1 Grey Friars; Tel 0116 256 5082;
   Fax 0116 256 5067
Service Manager (Commissioning; LAC)   Maggie McGrath;
   Eagle Hse; Tel 0116 299 5879; Fax 0116 299 5887
Service Manager (Disabled Children and Young Carers Issues)
   Sue North; Access, Inclusion and Participation Division, Fosse Neighbourhood Centre, Mantle Rd, Leicester, Leicestershire LE3 5HG; Tel 0116 223 2290;
   Fax 0116 223 2291
Service Manager (Family Support – Modernisation)
   Bernice Bennett; 10 York Rd, Leicester, Leicestershire LE1 6NU; Tel 0116 229 4184; Fax 0116 233 3032

Service Manager (LAC Safeguarding) Julie Jordan; Mansion Hse; Tel 0116 225 4726; Fax 0116 223 2337
Service Manager (Leaving Care and Children's Services) Steve Bond; St Martin's, c/o 1 Grey Friars; Tel 0116 256 8231; Fax 0116 256 5079
Service Manager (Placements including Fostering and Adoption) Mark Tingley; Eagle Hse; Tel 0116 299 5876; Fax 0116 299 5887
Service Manager (Residential Care) Mike Evans; Eagle Hse; Tel 0116 299 5875; Fax 0116 299 5887
Service Manager (Specialist Family Support) Lorraine White; Hillview, 1b Blackmore Dr, Leicester, Leicestershire LE3 1LP; Tel 0116 223 2300; Fax 0116 223 2337
Manager (Child Care – Cluster A) Sonia Grant (Acting); Beaumont Way, Leicester LE4 0PQ; Tel 0116 299 5708; Fax 0116 299 5777
Principal Officer (Inclusion, RALAC Services, LAC PSA: Education, Corporate Parenting) Mark Fitzgerald; Mansion Hse; Tel 0116 229 4185; Fax 0116 233 3032
Co-ordinator (Teenage Pregnancy and Sure Start Plus) Kirsty Reid; Mansion Hse; Tel 0116 252 8195; Fax 0116 233 3032

Education and Lifelong Learning Department

Leicester City Council, Marlborough Hse, 38 Welford Rd, Leicester LE2 7AA; URL www.leicester.gov.uk/ education; e-mail education.policy@leicester.gov.uk; Tel 0116 252 7807; Fax 0116 233 2685
Corporate Director Steven Andrews
Service Director (Achievement and Innovation) Louise Goll
Service Director (Lifelong Learning and Community Development) John Crookes
Service Director (Policy and Resources) Adrian Paterson
Service Director (Pupil and Student Support) Paul Livock
Head (Arts in Education) Peter Baker
Head (Education IS) Jen Johnson
Head (Education Policy and Communication Unit) Jay Hardman
Head (Finance) David Wilkin
Head (Human Resources) Gill Stacey
Head (Planning, Property and Procurement) John Garratt
Head (SEN Teaching) Janis Warren
Head (Standards and Effectiveness) Jim Muncey
Manager (Effectiveness Strategies) Richard Whitehouse
Manager (Multicultural Services) Richard Wale
Manager (Student Grants, Awards and Loans) Senitta Mann
Education Officer (Administration and Governor Services) Trevor Pringle
Education Officer (Admissions and Exclusions) Janet Shaw
Education Officer (SEN) Vicky Wibberley
Principal Education Welfare Officer John Broadhead
Education Policy Officer Vacancy
Education Policy Officer (Equalities) Kamljit Obhi
Adviser (Early Years) Josephine Elks
Co-ordinator (Excellence in Cities) Lis Stock (Acting)
Co-ordinator (Traveller Education Service) Margaret Hutchinson

EDUCATION AND LIFELONG LEARNING SCRUTINY COMMITTEE

LD: 7, Lab: 5, Con: 2
Chair Cllr R. Willmott (Lab)
Spokesperson Cllr J. Fitch (LD)
Spokesperson Mrs B. Maw (LD)
Cabinet Link Member (Building Schools for the Future); Deputy Leader of the Council Cllr M. Johnson
Cabinet Link Member (Education and Lifelong Learning) Cllr H. Suleman
Members of the Committee
Lab: Cllr Bhatti, Cllr Kitterick, Cllr Sood, Cllr Waddington
LD: Cllr Garrity, Cllr Henry, Cllr Hunt, Cllr Panchbhaya, Cllr Renold
Con: Cllr Porter, Cllr Thompson

EDUCATIONAL SERVICES

Adult Basic Education Service Leicester College, Abbey Park Campus, Leicester LE1 3WA; Tel 0116 251 1273; Fax 0116 253 6553
Arts in Education Service Knighton Fields Centre, Herrick Rd, Leicester LE2 6DH; e-mail artsined@leicester.gov.uk; Tel 0116 270 0850; Fax 0116 270 4928
Awards and Grants Services 10 York Rd, Leicester LE1 5TS; Tel 0116 229 4305; Fax 0116 222 0682
Connexions Leicestershire Leicester Careerpoint, Halford Hse, 91 Charles St, Leicester LE1 1HL; e-mail enquiry@connexions; Tel 0116 262 7254; Fax 0116 262 0682
Education Welfare Service Collegiate Hse, College St, Leicester LE2 0JX; Tel 0116 221 1260; Fax 0116 221 1261
Educational Psychology Service Collegiate Hse, College St, Leicester LE2 0JX; Tel 0116 221 1200; Fax 0116 221 1216
Forest Lodge Education Centre Charnor Rd, Leicester LE3 6LH; Tel 0116 222 2600; Fax 0116 231 1804
Leicester Learning Zone The Stable Block, Braunstone Pk, Leicester LE3 1HX; e-mail thezone@leicestereaz.gov.uk; Tel 0116 249 2080; Fax 0116 285 6387
Leicestershire Education Business Company Boshouse, Meridian East, Meridian Business Pk, Leicester LE19 1WZ; Tel 0116 240 7000; Fax 0116 240 7001
Leicestershire Learning and Skills Council Ltd 17a Meridian East, Meridian Business Pk, Leicester LE19 1UU; Tel 0116 228 1881; Fax 0116 228 1801
Minority Ethnic Language and Achievement Service (MELAS) Forest Lodge Education Centre, Charnor Rd, Leicester LE3 6LH; Tel 0116 222 2612; Fax 0116 231 1804
Open College Network South East Midlands Ltd 249 Derby Rd, Loughborough, Leicestershire LE11 5HJ; e-mail ocnsem@ocnsem.com; Tel 01509 211881; Fax 01509 211771
Resource Centre for Multicultural Education Forest Lodge Education Centre, Charnor Rd, Leicester LE3 6LH; Tel 0116 222 2610; Fax 0116 231 1804
Special Needs Teaching Services New Parks Hse, Pindar Rd, Leicester LE3 9RN; Tel 0116 225 4800; Fax 0116 225 4806
Traveller Education Service The Bennet Centre, Beaumanor Pk, Loughborough, Leicestershire LE12 8TX; e-mail mhutchinson@leicester.gov.uk; Tel 0150 989 0543; Fax 0150 989 1414

Leicestershire County Council

www.leics.gov.uk

In April 1997 Leicester City and Rutland became separate unitary authorities and are listed separately in this section. Leicestershire County Council retains a two-tier structure.
Population: 623 900
Political composition: Con: 31, Lab: 13, LD: 11
County Hall, Glenfield, Leicester LE3 8RA; URL www.leics.gov.uk; e-mail information@leics.gov.uk; Tel 0116 232 3232

Children and Young People's Service

County Hall, Glenfield, Leicester LE3 8RF; e-mail childrensservices@leics.gov.uk; Tel 0116 265 6631
Director Gareth I. Williams
Assistant Director (Specialist Services) Flick Schofield
Assistant Director (Strategic Services) Nigel Farrow
Assistant Director (Targeted Services) Frances Craven
Assistant Director (Universal Services) Tony Mulhearn
Head (Outdoor and Residential Learning Service) Alan Jacobs
Senior Service Manager (Extended Services: Operations) Brigid Joyce
Service Manager (Access and Welfare) Andy Darvill
Service Manager (Early Years) Michelle Foulds
Service Manager (Leicestershire Arts in Education) Osyth Dolton
Service Manager (School Food Support Service) Wendy Philp
Service Manager (SENA) Chris Bristow

Project Manager (PE and Sports: Leicester-Shire and Rutland Sport) Steve Conway
Manager (Healthy Schools Strategy) Jane Roberts
Senior Adviser (School Development) David Bradley
Senior Adviser (School Development) Allison Davies
Principal Educational Psychologist (Educational Psychology Service) Trevor Holme
Principal Youth Officer (Youth Service) Neil Hanney
Development Officer (Study Support: Great Learning Centre) Heather Rawling
Number of Schools
54 Secondary; 6 Special

GOVERNOR DEVELOPMENT SERVICES

Children and Young People's Service; e-mail governors@leics.gov.uk; Tel 0116 265 6517; Fax 0116 265 7520
Service Manager Ruth Stretton
Services offered
The purpose of the service is to contribute to school improvement. It identifies governors' needs and provides access to training, advice and information to give them the confidence, skills and knowledge to offer leadership and direction to their schools and colleges. The team supports governing bodies in schools causing concern. GDS also supports recruitment and retention of governors.

LEICESTERSHIRE EDUCATIONAL PSYCHOLOGY SERVICE

OEM Bldg, Whiteacres, Leicester LE8 6ZG; Tel 0116 284 5100; Fax 0116 284 5184
Principal Educational Psychologist Trevor Holme

YOUTH AND COMMUNITY CENTRES

Glenfield Youth Centre Co-op Car Pk, Station Rd, Glenfield, Leicester LE3 8BQ; Tel 0116 231 1527
Centre Co-ordinator Jill Sergent
Greenhill Youth Centre Waterworks Rd, Coalville, Leicestershire LE67 4HZ; Tel 01530 832722
Centre Co-ordinator Trish Hoult
Kegworth Community Centre The Dragwell, Kegworth, Derby, Leicestershire DE7 2EL; Tel 01509 672237
Centre Co-ordinator Isabel Osborne
Market Harborough Young People's Centre Farndon Rd, Market Harborough, Leicestershire LE16 9BX; Tel 01858 464355
Centre Co-ordinator Laura Mullen
Moira Community Centre Moira St, Loughborough, Leicestershire LE11 1AX; Tel 01509 267378
Centre Co-ordinator Madeline Gibbard
Mountfields Lodge Youth Centre Epinal Way, Loughborough, Leicestershire LE11 3GE; Tel 01509 236043
Centre Co-ordinator Amanda Weeks
Thringstone Community Centre The Green, Thringstone, Coalville, Leicestershire LE67 8NR; Tel 01572 787358
Centre Co-ordinator Lorraine Whitehurst
Venture House Youth Centre Asfordby Rd, Melton Mowbray, Leicestershire LE13 0HN; Tel 01664 565460
Centre Co-ordinator Carol Pick
Wigston Young People's Centre Holmden Ave, South Wigston, Leicestershire LE18 2EG

CONFERENCE AND RESIDENTIAL CENTRES

Beaumanor Hall Conference Centre Woodhouse, Loughborough, Leicestershire LE12 8TX; URL www.leics.gov.uk/residential_services; e-mail hall@beaumanor.rmplc.co.uk; Tel 01509 890119
Centre Manager Ian Humphreys
Service Manager (Residential Service) Alan Jacobs

INTERNATIONAL EDUCATION CENTRE

Quorn Hall, Meynell Rd, Quorn, Loughborough, Leicestershire LE12 8BQ; URL www.leics.gov.uk/residential_services; e-mail quornhallinfo@beaumanor.rmplc.co.uk; Tel 01509 412223
Head Mark Lantsbery
Service Manager (Residential Service) Alan Jacobs

Lincolnshire County Council
www.lincolnshire.gov.uk

Population: 678 500
Political composition: Con: 48, Lab: 21, LD: 4, Ind: 3
County Offices, Newland, Lincoln, Lincolnshire LN1 1YL; URL www.lincolnshire.gov.uk; Tel 01522 552222; Fax 01522 552323

Children's Services

County Offices, Newland, Lincoln, Lincolnshire LN1 1YQ; Fax 01522 553257
Director Peter Duxbury
Assistant Director Christine Banim
Assistant Director Helen Longland
Assistant Director Rob Mayall
Head (Additional Needs) Peter Broster
Head (Children in Public Care) Philip Hunt
Head (Children with Disabilities) Hilary Barrett
Head (Children's Trust Arrangements) Simon Payne
Head (Extended Provision) Meredith Teasdale
Head (Human Resources) Simon Nearney
Head (ICT) Bertold Weidmann
Head (Modernisation) Jane Mason
Head (Participation and Inclusion) Linda Ozmen
Head (Performance Management) John O'Connor
Head (Provision Planning) Paul Holmes
Head (Regulated Services) Janice Spencer
Head (Safeguarding Children) Jennie Thornton
Head (School Administration) Dick Pike
Head (School Improvement: CfBT) Andy Breckon
Head (Service Development) Justin Hackney
Head (Strategy) Mark Cozens
Head (Strengthening Families) Stuart Carlton
Manager (Financial Strategy) Tony Warnock
Principal School Improvement Adviser (CPD) Dr Tim Lomas
Principal School Improvement Adviser (Primary) Muriel George
Principal School Improvement Adviser (Secondary) Sue Baxter
Principal School Improvement Adviser (Strategic Project) Paul Snook
Number of Schools
286 Primary; 63 Secondary; 21 Special; 5 Nursery; 5 PRU
Requisition Periods for Schools Supplies
None
Other Authorities with whom Joint Purchasing Arrangements are made
Cambridgeshire County Council, Leicestershire County Council, Norfolk County Council and Warwickshire County Council

CHILDREN'S SERVICES POLICY DEVELOPMENT GROUP

Chair Cllr H.G. Wheat
Executive Councillor (Children's Service) Cllr Mrs P. Bradwell
Executive Councillor (Secondary Education and Healthy Communities) Cllr Mrs C. Talbot

GOVERNOR TRAINING UNIT

Governor Support and Development, The Vicarage, County Offices, Newland, Lincolnshire LN1 1YQ; Tel 01522 553357

Senior Administrative Officer   Hilary Wells

Services offered

Training offered to school governors, chairs and clerks to governing bodies, governor helpline, governor appointments, termly newsletter and 18 resource libraries

EMOTIONAL AND BEHAVIOURAL SUPPORT SERVICES

Tel 01522 553390

Head   Sue Fenton-Smith

LEARNING SUPPORT SERVICE

Tel 01522 553265

Head of Service   Penny Fixter

The Learning Support Service is a delegated service from which primary schools can purchase time to provide professional advice or teaching support in respect of children with specific learning difficulties. Headteachers can contact the head of service.

SENSORY IMPAIRED SERVICE

Tel 01522 553364

Head   T.A. Moodley

ETHNIC MINORITY ACHIEVEMENT SERVICE

e-mail jill.chandar-nair@lincolnshire.gov.uk; Tel 01427 787190

Head   Jill Chandar-Nair

TRAVELLER EDUCATION SERVICE

Tel 01522 553320

Head   P. Ingall

GIFTED AND TALENTED SUPPORT SERVICE

Tel 01427 788056

Teacher; Co-ordinator   M. Stopper

COUNTY SERVICE FOR SENSORY IMPAIRED/AUDIOLOGY

County Offices, Newland, Lincoln, Lincolnshire LN1 1YQ; e-mail asoka.moodley@lincolnshire.gov.uk; Tel 01522 553364; Fax 01522 553236

Head of Service   Asoka Moodley

COUNTY PSYCHOLOGY SERVICE

Council Offices   Sleaford, Lincolnshire NG34 7EB; Tel 01529 414144

County Hall   Boston, Lincolnshire PE21 6LX; Tel 01205 310010

Eastfield House   Eastfield Rd, Louth, Lincolnshire LN11 7AN; Tel 01507 600800

49 Newland   Lincoln, Lincolnshire LN1 1YQ; Tel 01522 552222

Northamptonshire County Council

www.northamptonshire.gov.uk

Population: 629 676 (2001 Census)

Political composition: Lab: 39, Con: 33, LD: 1

County Hall, Northampton, Northamptonshire NN1 1DN; URL www.northamptonshire.gov.uk; e-mail genie@northamptonshire.gov.uk; Tel 01604 236236; Fax 01604 236223

Children and Young People's Service

The department operates on a split site

County Hall, PO Box 93, Northampton, Northamptonshire NN1 1AN; Tel 01604 236252; Fax 01604 237121

County Hall, PO Box 233, Northampton, Northamptonshire NN1 1AZ; e-mail mpratt@northamptonshire.gov.uk; Tel 01604 237863; Tel (out-of-hours team) 01604 626938; Fax 01604 237121

Director (Children and Young People)   Andrew Sortwell; Tel 01604 236252

Head (Buildings and Capital Development)   Peter Burrell

Head (Education: Finance)   Rosemary Pallot

Head (Learning and ICT)   Bob Brind-Surch

Head (School Improvement and Performance)   Jan Martin; John Drydron Hse, 8–10 The Lakes, Northampton, Northamptonshire NN4 7DD; e-mail jnmartin@northamptonshire.gov.uk; Tel 01604 237169

Head (Schools Service)   Harry Darby; John Dryden Hse, 8–10 The Lakes, Northampton, Northamptonshire NN4 7DD; Tel 01604 236218

County Manager (Education Welfare)   Anna-Marie Millan; Tel 01604 236203

Manager (ICT Service)   Bob Brid-Surch

SAEO (Corby and Kettering)   Duncan Mills

SAEO (Northampton)   Peter Goringe

SAEO (South and West)   Vacancy

SAEO (Wellingborough and East Northants)   Vacancy

Senior Inspector (Head of Inspection Division)   M. Lovett BSc, ENG, ACGI

Senior Inspector (Head of Management Services)   C. Green MEd, BEd(Hons)

Senior Inspector (Northamptonshire Inspection and Advisory Service)   A. Kent

Senior Education Officer (Social Inclusion)   J.B. Sleet CQSW; Tel 01604 236203

Senior Education Officer (Special Provision)   J. Craig BSc, MPhil PGCE; Tel 01604 236202

Education Officer (Early Years and Childcare)   Kate Yates

Senior Education Inspector (Primary)   Lesley Link

Education Officer (Promoting Equalities: Multi-cultural Education Service)   Roger Tweed; Tel 01604 236213

General Education Inspector   Peter Nickoll

Principal Adviser (School Improvement)   Phil Mason

County Commissioner (Youth Service)   G. Stewart; Tel 01604 236601; Fax 01604 237441

County Officer (Lifelong Learning)   C.R. Dobbs MEd, DipFE; Tel 01604 236319

Principal Educational Psychologist   Michael Brooks; Tel 01604 237464

Number of Schools

250 Primary; 40 Secondary; 13 Special

DIVISIONAL YOUTH OFFICES

Eastern Division Youth Office   Fairlawns Centre, Spring Gdns, Wellingborough, Northamptonshire NN8 2AA; Tel 01933 445830; Fax 01933 445832

Divisional Youth Officer   Alison Barlow

Divisional Administrator   Sandra Draycott

Northampton Division Youth Office   John Clare Centre, Kettering Rd, Northampton, Northamptonshire NN1 4AZ; Tel 01604 604538; Fax 01604 602790

Divisional Youth Officer   R. Tims MA Grad, DipComEd

Northern Division Youth Office   Divisional Youth Office, The William Knibb Centre, Kettering, Northamptonshire NN16 8AE; Tel 01536 417524; Fax 01536 416750

Divisional Youth Officer   Nick Chamberlain

Divisional Administrator   L. Lemaitre

Southern Division Youth Office   St John's Centre, Tiffield, Northamptonshire NN12 8AA; Tel 01604 859380; Fax 01604 858042

Divisional Youth Officer   Carol Taylor

Divisional Administrator   Margaret Daynes

AREA OFFICES

Brackley Youth Centre Manor Rd, Brackley, Northamptonshire NN13 6EE; Tel 01280 703911

Brixworth Youth Centre Church St, Brixworth, Northampton, Northamptonshire NN6 9BZ; Tel 01604 880766

Woodford Halse Youth Club High St, Woodford Halse, Daventry, Northamptonshire NN11 6RE; Tel 01327 261792

HOSPITAL EDUCATION SERVICE

Cromwell St, Northampton, Northamptonshire; Tel 01604 239730
Headteacher Lynn Mayer

Daventry/South West Area Team St John's Centre, St Johns Rd, Tiffield, Northampton, Northamptonshire NN12 8AM; Tel 01604 857382; Fax 01604 857383
Area SEN Officer Jill Timms

Kettering/Corby Area Team William Knibb Centre, Montague St, Kettering, Northamptonshire NN16 8AE
Area SEN Officer Denise Cowther; Tel 01536 533930; Fax 01536 414809

Northampton Area Team Springfield Cliftonville, Northampton, Northamptonshire NN1 5BE; Tel 01604 630082; Fax 01604 630283
Area SEN Officer Tim Bunn

Wellingborough and North East Area Team Fairlawn Centre, Spring Gdns, Wellingborough, Northamptonshire NN8 2AA; Tel 01933 440289; Fax 01933 226744
Area SEN Officer Andrew Avery

MAINTAINED YOUTH CENTRES

Bective Youth Centre Bective Middle School, Whiston Rd, Northampton, Northamptonshire NN2 7AJ; Tel 01604 712924

Brackley Youth Centre Manor Rd, Brackley, Northamptonshire NN13 6EE; Tel 01280 703911

Brixworth Centre Church St, Brixworth, Northampton, Northamptonshire NN6 9BZ; Tel 01604 880766

Corby Youth Centre Connaughty Centre, Cottingham Rd, Corby, Northamptonshire NN17 1SY; Tel 01536 204258

Desborough Youth Centre Paddock La, Desborough, Northamptonshire NN14 6LZ; Tel 01536 761286

Duston Folk Centre Duston Upper School, Berrywood Rd, Northampton, Northamptonshire NN5 6XA; Tel 01604 751303

The Farm Youth Centre Rickyard Rd, The Arbours, Northampton, Northamptonshire NN3 3QZ; Tel 01604 405253

Kingsthorpe Upper School Youth Club, Boughton Green Rd, Northampton, Northamptonshire NN2 7AF; Tel 01604 711953

Lings Upper School Youth Office, Billing Brook Rd, Northampton, Northamptonshire NN3 4NH; Tel 01604 412743

Mereway Upper School Youth Club, Mereway, Northampton, Northamptonshire NN4 9BU; Tel 01604 706244

Rushden Youth Centre Moor Rd, Rushden, Northamptonshire NN10 9TP; Tel 01933 314077; Fax 01933 413983

Thrapston Youth Club King John School, Market Rd, Kettering, Northamptonshire NN14 4JU

Woodford Halse Youth Centre High St, Woodford Halse, Daventry, Northamptonshire NN11 6RE

ADULT EDUCATION SERVICE

Lifelong Learning Education and Community Learning, PO Box 216, Northampton, Northamptonshire NN4 7DD
Principal Adult Education Officer C.R. Dobbs; Tel 01604 236319
Senior Assistant (Planning and Development) Dr D.R. Wilson BA, PhD

ADULT EDUCATION ESTABLISHMENTS

Adult Residential College and Training Centre Irchester Knuston Hall, Wellingborough, Northamptonshire NN9 7EU; Tel 01933 312104; Fax 01933 357596
Principal (East Northamptonshire Area) S. Pollock

East Northants and Wellingborough Adult Education Service 29 Church St, Rushden, Northamptonshire NN10 9YU; Tel 01933 352910; Fax 01933 352915
Principal (Uplands: North West Area) J. Theairs MA

Kettering and Corby Adult Learning Service William Knibb Centre, Montague St, Kettering, Northamptonshire NN16 8AE; Tel 01536 527960; Fax 01536 527975

Northampton Adult Learning Service Russell Hse, Rickyard Rd, Northampton, Northamptonshire NN3 3QZ; Tel 01604 410236

Northampton College Booth La South, Northampton, Northamptonshire NN3 3RF; Tel 01604 734339; Fax 01604 734336
Principal (Northampton Area) R. Starkey

The Old Chapel Watling St, Towcester, Northamptonshire NN12 7DE; Tel 01327 356000; Fax 01327 356016
Principal (South Northamptonshire Area) W. Nicholson MA

ADULT EDUCATION OUTSIDE NORTHAMPTON

Moulton College West St, Moulton, Northampton, Northamptonshire NN3 7RR; Tel 01604 491131; Fax 01604 491127
Headteacher M. Hawkins

Northampton College Daventry Badby Rd, Daventry, Northamptonshire NN11 4HJ; Tel 01327 300232; Fax 01327 300942
Headteacher C. Harris

Tresham Institute of Further and Higher Education Wellingborough Campus: Church St, Wellingborough, Northamptonshire NN8 4PD; Tel 01933 224165; Fax 01933 441832
Corby Campus: George St, Corby, Northamptonshire NN17 1QA; Tel 01536 402252; Fax 01536 413357
Headteacher D. Wedlake BA, MEd

PROFESSIONAL DEVELOPMENT CENTRES

Corby Professional Development Centre Firdale, Cottingham Rd, Corby, Northamptonshire NN17 1TD; Tel 01536 266833; Fax 01536 203642
Centre Manager J. Sheffer

Kettering Professional Development Centre William Knibb Centre, Montague St, Kettering, Northamptonshire NN16 8AE; Tel 01536 410579; Fax 01536 414530
Centre Manager J. Sheffer

Northampton Professional Development Centre Barry Rd, Northampton, Northamptonshire NN1 5JS; Tel 01604 630815; Fax 01604 622547
Centre Manager M. Davison

Wellingborough Professional Development Centre 86 Stanley Rd, Wellingborough, Northamptonshire NN8 1DY; Tel 01933 225104; Fax 01933 223925
Centre Manager G. Graham

OUTDOOR EDUCATION CENTRE

Longtown Outdoor Education Centre The Court House, Longtown, Hereford, Herefordshire HR2 0LD; Tel 01873 860225; Fax 01873 860333
Head R. Burson

TRAINING RESEARCH AND DEVELOPMENT

Adult Education Service, Cultural Services PO Box 216, Northampton, Northamptonshire NN4 7DD; Tel 01604 236319
Manager (Quality Curriculum and Staff Development) J. Theairs
Contact A. Chesney

2

Duke of Edinburgh Award Scheme Grendon Hall Residential Centre, Main Rd, Grendon, Northamptonshire NN7 1JW; Tel 01933 663853; Fax 01933 663853
Manager Jean Moksa
Everdon Field Studies Centre The Green, Everdon, Daventry, Northamptonshire NN11 3BL; Tel 01327 361384; Fax 01327 361384
Manager Tony Kidd
Fletton House Residential Centre Clapthorne Rd, Oundle, Peterborough; Tel 01832 272179
Manager Debbie Goodfellow
Grendon Hall Residential Centre Main Rd, Grendon, Northamptonshire NN7 1JW; Tel 01933 666830
Manager Melanie Leadman
Longtown Outdoor Education Centre The Court House, Longtown, Hereford, Herefordshire; Tel 01873 860225; Fax 01873 860333
Manager Bob Burson

YOUTH SERVICE

Headquarters, John Dryden Hse, 8–10 The Lakes, Northampton, Northamptonshire NN4 7DD; Tel 01604 236601; Fax 01604 237441
County Manager Gordon Stewart
East Northants Area Youth Office 29 Church St, Rushden, Northamptonshire NN10 9YU; Tel 01933 352910; Fax 01933 352915
Area Manager Alison Barlow
Kettering Area Youth Office William Knibb Centre, Montague St, Kettering, Northamptonshire NN16 8AE; Tel 01604 527960; Fax 01536 527975
Area Manager Nelista Cuffy
Northampton Area Youth Office Russell Hse, Rickyard Rd, The Arbours, Northampton, Northamptonshire NN3 3QZ; Tel 01604 410236; Fax 01604 786191
Area Manager Sue Jane
South Northants Area Youth Office The Old Chapel, 186 Watling St, Towcester, Northamptonshire NN12 6DB; Tel 01327 356000; Fax 01327 356016
Area Manager Martin John (Acting)

Nottingham City Council

www.nottinghamcity.gov.uk

In April 1998 Nottingham City Council became a unitary authority. The rest of Nottinghamshire retains a two-tier structure and is listed separately in this section.
The Guildhall, Nottingham NG1 4BT; URL www.nottinghamcity.gov.uk; Tel 0115 915 5555; Fax 0115 915 4636
Chief Executive Michael Frater

Education Department

Sandfield Centre, Sandfield Rd, Lenton, Nottingham NG7 1QH; URL www.nottinghamschools.co.uk; e-mail education@lea.nottinghamcity.gov.uk
Director Robin Aldridge (Acting)
Assistant Director (Equalities, Regeneration and Partnerships) Ian Curryer
Assistant Director (Inclusion) Di Smith
Assistant Director (Resources) Ray Watson
Assistant Director (Standards and Effectiveness) Robin Aldridge
Assistant Director (Support and Intervention) Russell Andrews
Head (Finance) Graham Feek
Head (Human Resources) Nigel Willey
Head (School Organisation Team) Fiona Lewis
Strategy Manager (Excellence in Cities) Chris Archer
Service Manager (Admissions and Inclusion) Mirth Parker
Service Manager (Asset Management Team) Sharon Smith
Service Manager (Community Education Psychology Service) Paula Crosbie
Service Manager (Curriculum Service) Alistair Couquer
Service Manager (Customer Support Service) Sharon Jackson
Service Manager (Early Years Unit) Paulette Thompson-Omeuka
Service Manager (Education Welfare Service) Tom Elvidge
Service Manager (Information Management Service) Matt Varley
Service Manager (SEN Team) Andy Beckett
Co-ordinator (14–19 Partnership and Strategy) Brett Kerton
Principal Secondary Adviser (School Improvement) Louise Adams
Senior Adviser (Early Years and Ethnic Minority Achievement) Alison Day
Schools
19 Secondary; 6 Special; 3 Hospital

EDUCATION COMMITTEE

Chair Cllr Graham Chapman; Council Hse, Market Sq, Nottingham

GOVERNORS' DEVELOPMENT AND SUPPORT SERVICE TEAM

Nottingham City Council, LEA, Sandfield Centre, Sandfield Rd, Lenton, Nottingham NG7 1QH; e-mail leonie.meikle@le.nottinghamcity.gov.uk; Tel 0115 915 0612
Head of Service Leonie Meikle
Standards and Effectiveness Nottingham City Council, LEA, Sandfield Centre, Sandfield Rd, Lenton, Nottingham NG7 1QH; e-mail robin.aldridge@lea.nottinghamcity.gov.uk; Tel 0115 915 0606

COMMUNITY EDUCATIONAL PSYCHOLOGY SERVICE

Sandfield Centre, Sandfield Rd, Lenton, Nottingham NG7 1QH; e-mail paula.crosbie@lea.nottinghamcity.gov.uk; Tel 0115 915 0730
Head Paula Crosbie

HOSPITAL EDUCATION

Inclusion Division City of Nottingham Education Department, The Sandfield Centre, Sandfield Rd, Lenton, Nottingham NG7 1QH; e-mail di.smith@lea.nottinghamcity.gov.uk; Tel 0115 915 0710; Fax 0115 915 0603
Head (Inclusive Education Service) Lynne Duckett; Tel 0115 915 7810
Nottingham City Hospital Education Base Hucknall Rd, Nottingham NG5 1PB; Tel 0115 962 7600; Fax 0115 962 7931
Contact Angie Mindel
Queens Medical Centre Education Base E Fl, East Block, Nottingham NG7 2UH; Tel 0115 970 9753; Fax 0115 924 4292
Contact Hazel Coalwood
Thorneywood Hospital Education Base Fairmead Cl, The Wells Rd, Nottingham NG3 3AL; Tel 0115 915 3862; Fax 0115 915 3863
Contact Graham Marshall

Nottinghamshire County Council

www.nottinghamshire.gov.uk

In April 1998 Nottingham City Council became a unitary authority and is listed separately in this section.
Nottinghamshire County Council retains a two-tier structure.
Population: 762 700
Political composition: Lab: 38, Con: 25, LD: 4

County Hall, West Bridgford, Nottingham NG2 7QP;
URL www.nottinghamshire.gov.uk; Tel 0115 982 3823;
Fax 0115 981 7945

Children and Young People's Services

URL www.nottinghamshire.gov.uk/learningandwork;
e-mail communications.cyp@nottscc.gov.uk
Strategic Director Anthony May (Acting)
Service Director (Inclusion and Engagement)
R. Skelton (Acting)
Service Director (Learning and Achievement) J. Slater
Service Director (Social Care and Health) H. Ryan
Service Director (Strategic Services) M. Taylor
Number of Schools
216 Primary; 47 Secondary; 45 Infant; 38 Junior; 11 Special; 2
Nursery

CABINET MEMBER FOR CHILDREN AND YOUNG PEOPLE'S SERVICES

Cabinet Member J. Bosnjak (Lab); 7 Stanley Rd, Mansfield,
Nottingham NG18 5AA
Ashfield District Meadow Hse, Littleworth, Mansfield,
Nottinghamshire NG18 2TA; Tel 01623 433433;
Fax 01623 433411
Local Education Officer P. Gawthorne
Bassetlaw District Meadow Hse, Littleworth, Mansfield,
Nottinghamshire NG18 2TA; Tel 01623 433433
Local Education Officer M. Kesterton
Broxtowe District Sir John Robinson Way, Arnold,
Nottinghamshire NG5 6DA; Tel 0115 854 6000
Gedling District Sir John Robinson Way, Arnold,
Nottinghamshire NG5 6DA; Tel 0115 854 6000
Local Education Officer A. Coker
Mansfield District Meadow Hse, Littleworth, Mansfield,
Nottinghamshire NG18 2TA; Tel 01623 433433
Local Education Officer J. Littlewood
Newark District Meadow Hse, Littleworth, Mansfield,
Nottinghamshire NG18 2TA; Tel 01623 433433
Local Education Officer T. Kent
Rushcliffe District Sir John Robinson Way, Arnold,
Nottinghamshire NG5 6DA; Tel 0115 854 6000
Local Education Officer B. Dart

EDUCATIONAL PSYCHOLOGY SERVICE

Ashfield, Bassetlaw, Mansfield and Newark Meadow Hse,
Littleworth, Mansfield, Nottinghamshire NG18 2TA;
Tel 01623 433433; Fax 01623 433319
Senior Educational Psychologist (Ashfield/Mansfield)
C. Brett
Senior Educational Psychologist (Bassetlaw/Newark)
C. Savage
Broxtowe, Gedling and Rushcliffe Sir John Robinson Way,
Arnold, Nottinghamshire NG5 6BN; Tel 0115 854 6000;
Fax 0115 854 6037
Senior Educational Psychologist C. Allward

Rutland County Council

www.rutland.gov.uk

In April 1997 Rutland Council became a unitary authority.
Leicestershire County Council retains a two-tier structure
and is listed separately in this section.
Population: 37 000
Political composition: Con: 18, Ind: 3, LD: 2, Others: 1
Catmose, Oakham, Rutland LE15 6HP;
URL www.rutland.gov.uk; e-mail
enquiries@rutland.gov.uk; Tel 01572 722577;
Fax 01572 758375
Chief Executive Helen Briggs

Children and Young People's Services Department

Fax 01572 758479
Director (Children and Young People's Services)
Carol Chambers; e-mail cchambers@rutland.gov.uk
Head (Inclusion) Steven Attwood
Head (Policy and Performance) Kate McKenna
Number of Schools
17 Primary; 3 Community; 1 Special

CABINET AND SCRUTINY COMMITTEE

Con: 5, Ind: 1, LD: 1
Cabinet Portfolio Holder (Children's Services)
Alan Hodgkinson
Cabinet Portfolio Holder (Children's Services) Robert Reid
Scrutiny Chair Ken Boole
Members of the Scrutiny Panel
Ruth Archer, Jeff Dale, John Duckham, Linda Graves, Marc
Oxley, Hugh Rees, David Richardson, Jan Rodger

LONDON

Barking and Dagenham London Borough Council

www.barking-dagenham.gov.uk

Population: 156 962
Political composition: Lab: 41, Con: 3, LD: 3, Residents
Association: 3; BNP: 1
Civic Centre, Dagenham, Essex RM10 7BN;
URL www.barking-dagenham.gov.uk; e-mail
enquiries@barking-dagenham.gov.uk; Tel 020 8592 4500;
Fax 020 8227 2806
Chief Executive Robert Whiteman
Director (Housing and Health) D.W. Woods DMS, MRSH;
Roycraft Hse, 15 Linton Rd, Barking, Essex IG11 8HE
Director (Leisure and Environmental Services) N. Bolger;
Town Hall, Barking, Essex IG11 7LU; Tel 020 8592 4500
Director (Social Services) Ms J. Ross
Community forums meet six times a year. The assembly
meets every fourth week. The executive meets for three
weeks in every month.

Children's Services Department

Town Hall, Barking, Essex IG11 7LU; e-mail
sthomson@barking-dagenham.gov.uk;
Tel 020 8227 3022; Fax 020 8227 3471
Divisional Director (Safeguarding and Rights)
Tolis Vouyloukas
Director R. Luxton OBE
Head (Children's Policy and Trust Commissioning)
Meena Kishinani
Head (Pupil and Family Support) Anna Harskamp
Head (Quality and School Improvement) Jane Hargreaves
Head (Shared Services and Engagement) Christine Pryor
Number of Schools
9 Secondary; 1 Special

GOVERNOR TRAINING UNIT

London Borough of Barking and Dagenham, CIAS,
Westbury Centre, Ripple Rd, Barking, Essex IG11 7PT;
e-mail jens@bardaglea.org.uk; Tel 020 8270 4834;
Fax 020 8270 4811
Contact (Professional Development) A. Jenner

Services offered

A comprehensive training and support programme for all governors, covering a wide area of topics. The programme covers group sessions, whole team approach, residential school-based and individual support. Link governor system in operation.

EDUCATIONAL PSYCHOLOGY SERVICE

Seabrook House 22 Shipton Cl, Bennetts Castle La, Dagenham, Essex RM8 3DR; e-mail bdavis@barking-dagenham.gov.uk; Tel 020 8593 7577; Fax 020 8592 9002
Group Manager (Community Educational Psychology Service) Brian Davis

INSPECTION AND ADVISORY SERVICE

Westbury Centre, Ripple Rd, Barking, Essex IG11 7PT; e-mail lesley.jennings@lbbd.gov.uk; Tel 020 8270 4800; Fax 020 8270 4811
Principal Inspector (IPM and Primary Development) D. Rosenthal
Principal Inspector (Management and Curriculum Development) G.S. Rowe BSc(Econ)
Principal Inspector (Primary Phase) R. Medhurst
General Inspector (Art, Design and Technology) N. Sagar
General Inspector (Humanities) Mary Pattinson
General Inspector (Information Technology) J.S. Lucock
General Inspector (Mathematics) A. Pepper
General Inspector (Physical Education) Miss F. Bevan
General Inspector (Science) B. Singh
General Inspector (SEN); Head (Educational Inclusion) A. Jones

IPM (MATHEMATICS PROJECT)

Westbury Centre, Ripple Rd, Barking, Essex IG11 7PT; e-mail lesley.jennings@lbbd.gov.uk; Tel 020 8270 4800; Fax 020 8270 4811

YOUTH OFFENDING TEAM

5a Parsloes Avenue Dagenham, Essex; Tel 020 8270 6462; Fax 020 8270 6461

ADULT EDUCATION

The Adult College of Barking and Dagenham Fanshawe Cres, Dagenham, Essex RM9 5QA; Tel 020 8270 4722; Fax 020 8270 4733
Head (Adult College) P. Cooney
Barking and Dagenham Music Centre The Adult College, Fanshawe Cres, Dagenham, Essex RM9 5QA; e-mail office@music-service@bardaglea.org.uk; Tel 020 8270 6690; Fax 020 8270 6689
Head (Community Music Service); Adviser (Music) Vacancy

TRAINING SERVICES

Training Centre St Georges Rd, Dagenham, Essex RM9 5AJ; e-mail office@bdts.bardaglea.org.uk; Tel 020 8270 6515; Fax 020 8270 6516
Head of Service C. Applebee

HEARING IMPAIRED UNIT

Westbury Centre Ripple Rd, Barking, Essex IG11 7PT; e-mail office@eshic.bardaglea.org.uk; Tel 020 8270 4611; Fax 020 8270 4612
Head of Service L. Pescud

YOUTH SUPPORT AND DEVELOPMENT

Morline Hse, 2nd Fl, 160 London Rd, Barking, Essex IG11 8BB; e-mail brian.lindsay@lbbd.gov.uk; Tel 020 8270 5050
Group Manager (Youth Support and Development Services) B. Lindsay

YOUTH CENTRES

Beacon Youth Centre 195–211 Becontree Ave, Dagenham, Essex RM8 2UT; Tel 020 8270 6028
Senior Youth Worker B. Kettle
Senior Youth Worker S. Unsworth
Chadwell Heath Youth Centre Warren Comprehensive School, Whalebone La North, Romford, Essex RM6 6SB; Tel 020 8599 8410
Manager (Youth Service) B. Kettle
Erkenwald Youth Centre Marlborough Rd, Dagenham, Essex RM8 2HU; Tel 020 8593 8917
Manager (Youth Service) D. Telfer
Marley Youth Centre Dagenham Priory Comprehensive School, School Rd, Dagenham, Essex RM10 9QH; Tel 020 8592 4143
Manager (Youth Service) S. Unsworth-Tomlinson
Mayesbrook Lake Outdoor Centre Mayesbrook Lake, Lodge Ave, Dagenham, Essex; Tel 020 8593 3539
Advisory Teacher (Outdoor and Environmental Education) L. Montague
New Cambell Youth Centre Arden Cres, Dagenham, Essex RM9 6TD; Tel 020 8592 7793
Manager (Youth Service) D. Telfer
Oaks Centre Collier Row Rd, Romford, Essex RM5 2DD; e-mail oaksyouthoffice@rmplc.co.uk; Tel 020 8270 6100
Senior Youth and Community Worker S. Gooding
Senior Youth and Community Worker L. Muscat
Outdoor Centre Eastbrook Comprehensive School, Dagenham Rd, Dagenham, Essex RM10 7UR; Tel 020 8595 3922
Youth Worker R. Kemp
Thames View Youth Centre c/o Education Department, Town Hall, Barking, Essex IG11 7LU
Manager (Youth Service) S. Unsworth-Tomlinson
Trewern Centre Cusop, Hay-on-Wye, Herefordshire HR3 5RF; e-mail office@trewern.bardaglea.org.uk; Tel 01497 820512; Fax 01497 820056
Head J. Parker-Smith

COLLEGE OF ADULT EDUCATION

Adult College of Barking and Dagenham, Fanshawe Cres, Dagenham, Essex RM9 5QA; Tel 020 8595 3237; Fax 020 8595 1395
Head of College P. Cooney

IN-SERVICE CENTRE

Westbury Centre Ripple Rd, Barking, Essex IG11 7PU; e-mail lesley.jennings@lbbd.gov.uk; Tel 020 8270 4800; Fax 020 8270 4811
Centre Manager L. Jennings

Barnet London Borough Council

www.barnet.gov.uk

Population: 334 800
Political composition: Con: 37, Lab: 20, LD: 6
Hendon Town Hall, The Burroughs, Hendon, London NW4 4BG; URL www.barnet.gov.uk; e-mail first.contact@barnet.gov.uk; Tel 020 8359 2000; Fax 0870 889 6800
North London Business Pk, Oakleigh Rd South, New Southgate, London N11 1NP
Barnet Hse, 1255 High Rd, Whetstone, London N20 0EJ; Fax 020 8359 2561
Chief Executive Leo Boland; North London Business Pk; Tel 020 8359 7001; Fax 0870 889 7152
Director (Adult Social Services) Irene Findlay; North London Business Pk; Tel 020 8359 4123; Fax 020 8359 4810
Chief Finance Officer Clive Medlicott; North London Business Pk; Tel 020 8359 7110; Fax 0870 889 7153

Children's Service

Cabinet Member   Cllr Fiona Bulmer
Cabinet Member (Investment in Learning)   Cllr John Marshall
Director (Children's Services)   Gillian Palmer
Deputy Director (Safeguarding and Social Care)   Mark Gurry;
Barnet Hse; Tel 020 8359 7152; Fax 020 8359 4819
Deputy Director (Schools and Learning)   Martin Baker; North
London Business Pk; Tel 020 8359 7270
Assistant Director (Inclusion)   Graham Durham; North
London Business Pk; Tel 020 8359 7702
Assistant Director (Partnerships, Performance and Planning)
Val White; North London Business Pk; Tel 020 8359 7036
Number of Schools
87 Primary; 19 Secondary; 4 Special

Bexley Council

www.bexley.gov.uk

Population: 218 756
Political composition: Con: 54, Lab: 9
Bexley Civic Offices, Broadway, Bexleyheath, Kent
DA6 7LB; URL www.bexley.gov.uk; e-mail
customer.services@bexley.gov.uk; Tel 020 8303 7777;
Fax 020 8301 2661
Chief Executive   David Berry (Acting)

Directorate of Children's and Young People's Services

Hill View, Hill View Dr, Welling, Kent DA16 3RY;
Tel 020 8303 7777
Director   Dr Deborah Absalom DPhil, PGCE
*Deputy Director (Children's Services: Integrated Youth and
Access)*   Linda Tottman
*Deputy Director (Children's Services: Social Care and Local
Integrated Teams)*   Sheila Murphy
Deputy Director (Performance, Planning and Resources)
Adrian Smith
*Deputy Director (Quality Assurance, Schools and Cluster
Development)*   Jim Rouncefield
*Deputy Director (Special and Additional Needs and Placement
Service)*   Roger Vandevelde
Head (Admissions)   Keith Porter
Head (Knowledge Management)   Gordon Young
Head (Schools HR)   Lea Dehaney
Head (Placements and Provision)   Mel Newell
Manager (Education Finance)   Keith Francis
Principal Primary School Improvement Partner
Moyra Pickering
Principal Secondary School Improvement Partner
Richard Dix-Pincott BA, MBA
Number of Schools
59 Primary; 16 Secondary; 5 Special

CABINET MEMBERS

Contact (Children's Services)   Cllr Teresa O'Neill (Con)
Contact (Schools, Adult Education and Youth Services)
Cllr Simon Windle (Con)

GOVERNOR TRAINING UNIT, SCHOOL SUPPORT SERVICES

URL www.bexley.gov.uk/governors
Governance Officer   Mrs W. Creasy
Services offered
A full support service for school governors, including
training courses

PUPIL REFERRAL UNITS

Primary   The Beeches Primary Centre (Pupil Referral Unit),
Lensbury Way, Abbey Wood SE2 9TA; Tel 020 8312 2746;
Fax 020 8310 1800
Head   John Moore
5–11
Secondary   Howbury Centre, Slade Green Rd, Erith, Kent
DA8 2HX; Tel 01322 356520
Head   John Moore
11–16

INSTITUTES OF ADULT EDUCATION

Adult Education College, Bexley   Administrative
Headquarters, Sidcup Arts and Adult Education Centre,
Alma Rd, Sidcup, Kent DA14 4ED;
URL www.adultedbexley.org; e-mail
saaec@adulted.bexley.org
Principal   R. Easterbrook; Tel 020 8269 8988;
Fax 020 8269 8992
Bexley Lane Evening Centre   Cleeve Park School, Bexley La,
Sidcup, Kent DA14 4JN; Tel (daytime) 020 8300 1056;
Tel (evenings) 020 8302 6418; Fax 020 8269 8992
Contact   Mrs N. Lofts
Brampton Road Education Centre   5 Brampton Rd, Bexley
Heath, Kent DA7 4EZ; Tel 020 8303 2541;
Fax 020 8298 2814
Contact   Mrs S. Palmer
Crayford Manor House   Mayplace Rd East, Crayford, Kent
DA1 4HB; Tel 01332 521463; Fax 01322 552554
Contact   Ms J. Crowhurst

YOUTH AND COMMUNITY CENTRES

Belvedere Youth Centre   Mitchell Cl, Belvedere, Kent
DA17 6AA; Tel 020 8311 5550
Cray Youth Centre   150 Rectory La, Sidcup, Kent DA14 5BT;
Tel 020 8308 1821 ext 201
Crayford and Barnehurst Youth Centre   Woodside Rd,
Bexleyheath, Kent DA7 6EQ; Tel 01322 527176
Danson Youth and Community Centre   Brampton Rd,
Bexleyheath, Kent DA7 4EZ; e-mail
dansonyouth.centre@virgin.net; Tel 020 8303 6052
Manager   Joy Toghill
Erith Cyber Cafe   Erith Library, Walnut Tree Rd, Erith, Kent
DA8 1RS; Tel 01322 345827
Falconwood Community Centre   31–39 Falconwood Pde, The
Green, Welling, Kent DA16 2PG; Tel 020 8303 9793
Howbury Youth Centre   Slade Green Rd, Slade Green, Erith,
Kent DA8 2HX; Tel 020 8855 4046 ext 201
Hurst Community Centre   Hurst Pl, Hurst Rd, Bexley, Kent
DA5 3LH; Tel 020 8300 2076
St Michael's Community Centre   Wrotham Rd, Welling, Kent
DA16 1LS
North Cray Community Centre   Bedens Rd, Sidcup, Kent
DA14 5JH; Tel 020 8302 8973
Parkside Community Centre   1 Parkside Cross, Bexleyheath,
Kent DA7 6NH; Tel 020 8303 7777
Sidcup Youth Centre   Burnt Oak La, Sidcup, Kent DA15 9BZ;
Tel 020 8300 3882 ext 201
Slade Green Community Centre   Bridge Rd, Slade Green,
Erith, Kent DA8 2HS; Tel 01322 330398
Southlake Centre   Seacourt Rd, Thamesmead SE28 9XB;
Tel 020 8320 6396 ext 201
Welling Youth Centre   Youth Service, Administration
Headquarters, Lovel Ave, Welling, Kent DA16 3JQ;
Tel 020 8855 4046 ext 201
Youth and Family Centre   105 West St, Erith, Kent DA8 1AW;
e-mail info@youthandfamily.org.uk; Tel 01322 449178;
Fax 01322 449088
Contact   Jan Blackburn

Brent London Borough Council

www.brent.gov.uk

Population: 263 466
Political composition: LD: 27, Lab: 21, Con: 15
Brent Town Hall, Forty La, Wembley, Greater London
  HA9 9HD; URL www.brent.gov.uk; e-mail
  chief.executive@brent.gov.uk; e-mail cit@brent.gov.uk;
  Tel 020 8937 1234; Fax 020 8937 1444
Chief Executive   Gareth Daniel

Education, Arts and Libraries

Education Offices, Chesterfield Hse, 9 Park La, Wembley,
  Greater London HA9 7RW; Tel 020 8937 3011;
  Fax 020 8937 3010
Chair (Education, Arts and Libraries Committee)
  Cllr Bob Wharton
Director (Education)   John Christie
Head Education Psychologist   M. Hymans; Tel 020 8937 3202
School Adviser (English and Literacy)   Marilyn Richardson
Senior School Improvement Adviser   C. Ross MA(Hons)
Senior School Improvement Adviser (Modern Languages)
  F. Ellks
School Improvement Adviser (Mathematics)
  Christina Rossiter
School Improvement Adviser (Science)   B. Tomlinson
Number of Schools
14 Secondary; 5 Special
Day of Committee Meeting
Five week cycle

BRENT EDUCATION PSYCHOLOGY AND LEARNING SUPPORT

The Education Dept, Chesterfield Hse, 9 Park La, Wembley,
  Greater London HA9 7RW; Tel 020 8937 3202
Principal Officer   M. Hymans

LANGUAGE UNIT

Mitchell Brook School   Bridge Rd, London NW10 9BX;
  Tel 020 8459 5681
Headteacher   Mrs Mathison

SENSORY IMPAIRMENT UNITS

Kingsbury Green School   Old Kenton La, Kingsbury,
  London NW9 9ND; Tel 020 8204 6423
Headteacher   Mr A. Vaughan
Kingsbury High School (Grant-Maintained)   Princes Ave,
  Kingsbury, London NW9 9JR; Tel 020 8204 9814
Headteacher   Mr C. Chung

PUPIL REFERRAL UNIT

364a Stag La, London NW9 9AG; Tel 020 8937 3193
Head of Service   Paul Roper

ENVIRONMENTAL EDUCATION CENTRES

Gordon Brown Environmental Education Centre   Ridge La,
  Rotherwick, Hampshire RG27 9AT; Tel 01256 762824
Head   Teresha Malcolm (Acting)
Welsh Harp Environmental Education Centre   Birchen Gr,
  London NW9 8RY; Tel 020 8200 0087
Contact   Harry Mackie

Bromley London Borough Council

www.bromley.gov.uk

2

Population: 295 530
Political composition: Con: 49, LD: 7, Lab: 4
Civic Centre, Stockwell Cl, Bromley, Kent BR1 3UH;
  URL www.bromley.gov.uk; Tel 020 8464 3333;
  Fax 020 8313 4620
Chief Executive   Doug Patterson

Children and Young People Department

Fax 020 8313 4049
*Chair (Children and Young People/Policy, Development and
  Scrutiny Committee)*   Cllr Michael Turner
Executive Councillor (Children and Young People)
  Cllr Graham Arthur
Director (Children and Young People)   G.L. Pearson MEd
*Assistant Director (Commissioning and Children's Education
  Services)*   Vacancy
Assistant Director (Learning and Achievement in Schools)
  G.W. Searle BSc(Hons), PhD, MRSC, CCChem, DMS
Head (School Improvement)   Merril Haeusler
Principal Adviser (Secondary)   S. Mordecai
Principal Educational Psychologist   D. Farrelly

GOVERNOR TRAINING UNIT

Learning and Achievement in Schools, Education
  Development Centre, Bromley, Kent BR2 8LD;
  Tel 020 8462 8911; Fax 020 8462 7786
Principal Officer   S. Cornish
Services offered
A full support service for school governors, including
training courses

INFORMATION OFFICES

Staff at these offices will answer, as far as possible, questions
relating to any of the council's services

YOUTH CENTRE

Bromley Youth Service   Central Office, c/o The Phoenix
  Youth Centre, Hawes La, West Wickham, Kent BR4 9AE;
  Tel 020 8777 7350; Fax 020 8777 1914
Head (Youth Service)   Rikki Garcia

TEACHERS' CENTRE

Education Development Centre   Church La, Bromley, Kent
  BR2 8LD; Tel 020 8462 8520; Fax 020 8461 6286
  *Assistant Director (Education: Learning and Achievement in
  Schools)*   George W. Searle

ADULT EDUCATION CENTRES

Bromley Adult Education College   The Widmore Centre,
  Nightingale La, Bromley, Kent BR1 2SQ;
  Tel 020 8460 0020; Fax 020 8466 7299
  Principal   Michael Wheeler
Kentwood Adult Education Centre   Kingsdale Rd, Penge,
  London SE20; Tel 020 8659 7976; Fax 020 8778 8362
Poverest Adult Education Centre   Poverest Rd, Orpington,
  Kent BR5 2DQ; Tel 01689 822886; Fax 01689 827641
Widmore Centre   Nightingale La, Bromley, Kent BR1 2SQ;
  Tel 020 8460 0020

London Borough of Camden

www.camden.gov.uk

Population: 227 453 (2006 mid year estimate)
Political composition: LD: 21, Lab: 17, Con: 14, Green: 2
Town Hall, Judd St, London WC1H 9JE;
    URL www.camden.gov.uk; Tel 020 7974 4444
Chief Executive   Moira Gibb; Tel 020 7974 5686;
    Fax 020 7974 5998

Children, Schools and Families

Crowndale Centre, 218 Eversholt St, London NW1 1BD;
    Tel 020 7974 1525; Fax 020 7974 1536
Executive Member (Schools)   Cllr Andrew Mennear
Director (Children, Schools and Families)   Heather Schroeder
Assistant Director (Access and Inclusion)   Andy Knowles
Assistant Director (Finance and Schools Support)
    Richard Lewin
Assistant Director (Learning and School Effectiveness)
    Gail Tolley
*Assistant Director (Partnerships, Strategy and
    Commissioning)*   Yvette Stanley
Assistant Director (Safeguarding and Social Care)
    Anne Turner
Head (Adult and Community Learning Service)
    Brian Mitchell
Head (Building Schools for the Future)   Ian Patterson (Acting)
Head (Commissioning and External Partnerships)
    Olivia Vincenti
Head (Communications and Marketing)   Ben Schofield
Head (Customer Service and Complaints)   Phil Sowter
Head (Early Years and Sure Start Service)   Barbara Sampson
Head (Education Inclusion and Safeguarding)   Lisa Clarke
Head (Ethnic Minority Achievement)   Karen Thomas
Head (Finance)   Gary Jarvis
Head (Human Resources)   Gordon McFarlane
Head (Information Technology Service)   Hilary Simpson
Head (Policy, Planning and Performance)   Pippa Shukla
Head (Primary Learning Support Service)   Ruth Draper
Head (Property and Contracts Service)   Sarah Bourne
Head (Research and Management Information)
    Marilyn Goodman
Head (School Improvement Service)   Sarah Conway
Head (SEN and Psychology Service)   Joan Riddel
Head (Student Finance and Admission)   Stuart Berwick
Head (Training and Media Services)   Gillian Tilbrook
Head (Youth and Connexions Service)   Ronke Martins
Number of Schools
41 Primary; 9 Secondary; 6 Special

EXECUTIVE MEMBER (CHILDREN)

Contact   Cllr John Bryant

UNDER FIVES CENTRES

Acol Centre   16 Acol Rd, London NW6 3AG;
    Tel 020 7624 2937
    Head   Nick Moran
Caversham   Vadnie Bish Hse, 33–43 Caversham Rd, London
    NW5 2DR; Tel 020 7974 3377
    Head   Debbie Hall
Gospel Oak Centre   Lismore Circus, London NW5 3LE;
    Tel 020 7267 4517
    Head   Sue Rushton
Hampden Centre   80 Polygon Rd, London NW1 1HQ;
    Tel 020 7387 1822
    Head   Lydia McEwan
Harmood   1 Forge Pl, London NW1 8DQ; Tel 020 7974 5207
    Head   Paulette Dallas
Kilburn Grange   1 Palmerston Rd, London NW6 2LJ;
    Tel 020 7974 5154
    Head   Carol Lyness-Barr

Konstam Centre   75 Chester Rd, London N19 5DH;
    Tel 020 7272 3594
    Head   Patricia Franks
Langtry Centre   Langtry Rd, London NW8 0AJ;
    Tel 020 7624 0963
    Head   Aisha Ashanti
Regents Park Centre   Augustus St, London NW1 3TJ;
    Tel 020 7387 2382
    Head   Sue Williamson
Thomas Coram   49 Mecklenburgh Sq, London WC1N 2NY;
    Tel 020 7520 0385
    Head   Bernadette Duffy

HOSPITAL SCHOOLS

Children's Hospital School   Gt Ormond St, London
    WC1N 3JH; Tel 020 7813 8269
    Headteacher   Yvonne Hill
Royal Free Hospital School   6th Fl, Royal Free Hospital, Pond
    St, London NW3 2QG; Tel 020 7472 6298
    Headteacher   Jude Chalk

City of London Corporation

www.cityoflondon.gov.uk

Population: 7100 (residential); 357 000 (daytime)
Political composition: Non-political body
PO Box 270, Guildhall, London EC2P 2EJ;
    URL www.cityoflondon.gov.uk; e-mail
    community.services@cityoflondon.gov.uk;
    Tel 020 7332 1750; Fax 020 7332 1621

Education Department

e-mail education@corpoflondon.gov.uk
Head (Adult Learning)   Barbara Hamilton
Head (Support Services)   Graham Watson
Head (Youth Support Service)   S. Webb (Acting)
Education Officer (City)   Ian Comfort
PA to Chief Education Officer; Head of Secretariat
    Marion Pereira

EDUCATION COMMITTEE

12 members of the Court of Common Council, one
representative of the London Diocesan Board for Schools;
two parent representatives, five co-opted. Members do not
represent political parties.
Chair   Mr J. Mayhew
Vice-Chair   W.H. Dove

COMMUNITY EDUCATION CENTRE

Tel 020 7608 2753; Fax 020 7336 8713
Manager   Annie Smuts

London Borough of Croydon

www.croydon.gov.uk

Population: 342 697
Political composition: Con: 43, Lab: 27
Taberner Hse, Park La, Croydon, Surrey CR9 3JS;
    URL www.croydon.gov.uk; Tel 020 8726 6000
Chief Executive   Jon Rouse

Children's Services

Taberner Hse, Park La, Croydon, Surrey CR9 1TP;
    URL www.croydon.gov.uk; Tel 020 8726 6400;
    Fax 020 8760 5603
Cabinet Member (Children's Services and Adult Learning)
    Cllr Maria Gatland

Director Peter Wylie
Assistant Director (Development and Care) Barbara Peacock
Assistant Director (Partnerships) Alison Critchley
Assistant Director (Planning, Performance and Commissioning) Steve Liddicott
Head of Service (Learning and Schools) Vacancy
Head of Service (Partnership) Julie Briant
Head of Service (Planning, Performance and Commissioning) Vacancy
Head of Service (Resources) David Bradshaw
Head of Service (Social Work and Safeguarding) Vacancy
Head of Service (Special Educational Needs/Learning Disability) Vacancy
Head of Service (Youth and Social Inclusion) Linda Wright

GOVERNOR SERVICES TEAM

Governor Services Team, London Borough of Croydon, Croydon, Surrey CR9 1TP; Tel 020 8760 5612; Fax 020 8760 5783
Manager Richard Hill
Services offered
The Governor Services Team provides a full range of advisory, training, administrative and information services to schools, governors, and clerks to governing bodies. Advice and information is also provided for members, headteachers and officers.

EDUCATIONAL PSYCHOLOGY SERVICE

Victoria Hse, Southbridge Pl, Croydon, Surrey CR0 4HA; Tel 020 8686 0393; Fax 020 8680 0890
Chief Educational Psychologist Anne Moore

PUPIL REFERRAL UNITS

Bridge To School 194 Selhurst Rd, London SE25 6XY; Tel 020 8771 8256; Fax 028 8768 2789
Head Peter Jones
Coningsby Centre Pupil Referral Unit 45 Coombe Rd, Croydon, Surrey CR0 1BQ; Tel 020 8680 0949; Fax 020 8680 5497
Headteacher Barbara Gonella (Acting)
Number of places: 44
Cotelands Centre Pupil Referral Unit 105 Cotelands, Park Hill, Croydon, Surrey CR0 5UF; e-mail cotelands.croydon@lgfl.net; Tel 020 8688 2995; Fax 020 8688 2939
Head Jenny Adamson
Number of places: 32
Moving On Pupil Referral Unit 1 Katharine St, Croydon, Surrey CR0 1NX; e-mail sshearer.movingon.croydon@lgfl.net; Tel 020 8604 1414; Fax 020 8604 1295
Headteacher Sue Welling
Number of places: 60
Victoria House Pupil Referral Unit Southbridge Pl, Croydon, Surrey CR0 4HA; e-mail sharon.gammon@victoriahouse.croydon.sch.uk; Tel 020 8686 0393; Fax 020 8680 0890
Headteacher Helen Logan
Number of places: 48

Ealing London Borough Council

www.ealing.gov.uk

Population: 301 600
Political composition: Lab: 48, Con: 17, LD: 4
Town Hall, New Broadway, Ealing, London W5 2BY; URL www.ealing.gov.uk; e-mail webmaster@ealing.gov.uk; Tel 020 8825 5000
Chief Executive Darra Singh

Education Department

Perceval Hse, 14–16 Uxbridge Rd, Ealing, London W5 2HL; e-mail education@ealing.gov.uk; Tel 020 8825 5000; Fax 020 8825 5858
Director (Education) Linda Prince (Acting)
Director (Education Access and Inclusion) H. McCafferty
Director (Education Resources) G. Redhead (Acting)
Director (School Standards Service) Linda Prince (Acting)
Service Head Tracey McNeil (Acting)
Service Head (Educational and Social Work) T. Galvin
Service Head (Planning/ICT/Bursarial Services) G. Redhead BA(Hons), DipSoc Admin
Service Head (Pupil Support and Contract Services) E. Lustig
Service Head (SEN Service to Schools) R. MacConville
Head (Community Learning) S. Jones
Head (Ealing Music Service) Y. Dattani
Head (Early Years Childcare and Play) Charles Barnard
Head (Library and Information Service) Geoff Allen (Acting)
Head (School Effectiveness) B. Anderson BSc, MSc, CertEd
Head (Training and Development) Vacancy
Head (Youth Service) Elaine Cunningham
General Inspector (Cross-Curricular Elements) Vacancy
General Inspector (Early Years) S. John
General Inspector (Key Stage Three) M. Mudd
General Inspector (Primary) Vacancy
General Inspector (Science and Technology) R. Brown
Deputy Principal Educational Psychologist S. Nath
Group Accountant Dave Jefferis
Number of Schools
65 Primary; 13 Secondary; 7 Special

EALING EDUCATION CENTRE

Mansell Rd, Greenford, Greater London UB6 9EG; Tel 020 8578 6154; Fax 020 8578 6163
Manager S. Davies
Services offered
A full and varied programme of courses for governors, including support for headteachers, school teaching and support staff

TRAINING AND DEVELOPMENT UNIT

Development and Training Services (Education), Perceval Hse, London W5 2HL
Principal Support Officer T. Abrahams

AREA OFFICES

Ealing Area Office Perceval Hse, 14–16 Uxbridge Rd, Ealing, London W5 2HL; Tel 020 8579 2424; Fax 020 8280 1291

EDUCATIONAL PSYCHOLOGISTS AND SOCIAL WORKERS

Perceval Hse, 14–16 Uxbridge Rd, Ealing, London W5 2HL; Tel 020 8825 5000; Fax 020 8825 5353

ADULT EDUCATION AND COMMUNITY SERVICES

Central Office Perceval Hse, 14–16 Uxbridge Rd, London W5 2HL; Tel 020 8825 5577

THE STUDY CENTRE

Boston Site Study Centre (Pupil Support) 42 Lower Boston Rd, Hanwell, London W7 2NR; Tel 020 8840 4484; Fax 020 8579 0934
Head Mrs B. Raymond
Assistant Head V. Griffin
Study Centre (KS3 GRO Provision) 9 Longfield Rd, Ealing, London W5 2DH; Tel 020 8998 6583; Fax 020 8571 2507
Assistant Head Kurtis Lewis

Enfield London Borough Council
www.enfield.gov.uk

Population: 281 800
Political composition: Con: 34, Lab: 27, Save Chase Farm 2
Civic Centre, PO Box 61, Enfield, Greater London EN1 3XY;
  URL www.enfield.gov.uk; e-mail
  <firstname>.<surname>@enfield.gov.uk;
  Tel 020 8379 1000
Chief Executive   Rob Leak

Education, Children's Services and Leisure

PO Box 56, Civic Centre, Silver St, Enfield, Greater London
  EN1 3XQ; Fax 020 8379 3243; Minicom 020 8367 8701;
  Telex DX 90615 ENFIELD
Cabinet Member   P. McCannah (Con); 10 Greenbrook Ave,
  Hadley Woods, Hertfordshire N13 4JN
Cabinet Member   G. Vince (Con); 2 The Glen, Enfield,
  Greater London
Director   Peter Lewis
Assistant Director (Children's Services)   Andrew Fraser;
  Tel 020 8379 4541; Fax 020 8379 4274
Assistant Director (Children's Access and Support)
  K. Fletcher-Wright
Assistant Director (School Effectiveness and Inclusion)
  N. Rousell
Assistant Director (Strategy and Resources)   J. Hill
Head (Admissions)   J. Fear
Head (Asset Management and Development)   C. Graham
Head (Behaviour Support)   J. Lowe
Head (Childcare, Early Years and Community Access)
  E. Stickler
Head (Children in Need Services)   J. Edwards
Head (Commissioning Performance and Development)
  T. Theodoulou
Head (Educational Psychology and CAMHS)   D. Grant
Head (Libraries and Museums)   J. Gibson
Head (Looked After Children)   L. Hill
Head (Policy, Quality and Performance)   M. Janaway
Head (Resources and IT)   M. Shukri
Manager (Enfield Education Business Partnership)   P. O'Brien
Manager (Enfield Training Services)   J. Burke
Manager (Excellence in Cities)   B. Firth
Manager (School Improvement: Inclusion)   J. Tosh
Manager (School Improvement: Primary)   R. Barnes
Strategy Manager (Early Years)   R. Moore
Strategy Manager (ICT)   D. Mitchell
Strategy Manager (Primary)   W. Connolly
Strategy Manager (PSHE/Citizenship)   S. Bourne
Strategy Manager (Secondary)   D. Thompson
Service Manager (Lifelong and Community Learning)
  B. Charles
Service Manager (School Improvement Service)   A. Lloyd
Number of Schools
60 Primary; 17 Secondary; 8 Special
Requisition Periods for Schools Supplies
Any time

GOVERNOR TRAINING UNIT

Professional Development Centre, Kimberley Gdns, Enfield,
  Greater London EN1 3ST; Tel 020 8363 4148;
  Fax 020 8367 8554
Co-ordinator (Governor Training)   S. Lotay
Services offered
The LEA offers a central training programme which
includes courses for new governors, courses on the
curriculum, and those dealing with governors'
responsibilities. The training co-ordinator organises
governing body-based sessions in schools; additionally,
advice is available individually for governors on a broad
range of issues. A feature of the training programme is a
series of 'Open Forums' where governors can directly raise
any issue with officers from the authority.

PROFESSIONAL DEVELOPMENT CENTRE

Craddock Road   Enfield, Greater London; Tel 020 8363 4148

YOUTH CENTRES

Alan Pullinger Youth Centre   1 John Bradshaw Rd, London
  N14 6BN; Tel 020 8886 1693; Fax 020 8882 9982
Albany Youth Centre   Bell La, Enfield, Greater London
  EN3 5PA; Tel 020 8443 3586; Fax 020 8482 2261
Craig Park Youth Centre   Lawrence Rd, Edmonton, London
  N18 2HN; Tel 020 8803 8292; Fax 020 8482 2261
Croyland Youth Centre   Croyland Rd, Edmonton, London
  N9 7BA; Tel 020 8351 8320; Fax 020 8351 8329
Detached and Outreach Team   1 Foxglove Cl, Edmonton,
  London N9 8LX; Tel 020 8379 1192
  Unit 51, Island Centre Way, Enfield EN3 6GS;
  Tel 020 8379 1308
Ponders End Youth Centre   129–139 South St, Ponders End,
  Enfield, Greater London EN3 4PX; Tel 020 8804 5908;
  Fax 020 8804 7426
Two 'E' Information and Advice Centre   324 High St, Ponders
  End, London EN3 4HF; Tel 020 8805 9726;
  Fax 020 8805 9721

London Borough of Greenwich
www.greenwich.gov.uk

Population: 215 238
Political composition: Lab: 36, Con: 13, LD: 2
Town Hall, Wellington St, London SE18 6PW;
  URL www.greenwich.gov.uk; e-mail
  mary.ney@greenwich.gov.uk; Tel 020 8854 8888
Chief Executive   Mary Ney

Children's Services

Riverside Hse, Woolwich High St, Woolwich, London
  SE18 6DF; Tel 020 8921 8038; Fax 020 8921 8228
Director   Christine Whatford (Acting)
Senior Assistant Director (Learning and Achievement)
  Les Cragg (Acting)
Senior Assistant Director (Safeguarding and Social Care)
  Andrew O'Sullivan;
Assistant Director (Children's Integration and Partnerships)
  Sheila Norris
Assistant Director (Economic Wellbeing and Youth Support)
  Mick Price
Assistant Director (Strategic Projects)   Mike Bright
Head (Finance)   Sue Peach
Number of Schools
13 Secondary; 4 Special

CHILDREN AND YOUNG PEOPLE SCRUTINY PANEL

Political composition: Lab: 8, Con: 2, LD: 1
Chair   Danny Thorpe (Lab)
Ex-Officio   Mick Hayes (Lab)
Councillors
Lab: Bill Freeman, Beverley Jones, Allan MacCarthy, Clive
Mardner, Claire Morris, Dick Quibell, Elizabeth Truss
Con: Spencer Drury, Dermot Poston
LD: Brian Woodcraft

GREENWICH PROFESSIONAL DEVELOPMENT CENTRE

5th Fl, Eltham Green Complex, Eltham, London SE9 5HH;
  Tel 020 8859 9100; Fax 020 8859 9101
Centre Manager   Jim Johnson

Hackney London Borough Council
www.hackney.gov.uk

Population: 207 700
Political composition: Lab: 44, Con: 9, LD: 3, Green: 1
Hackney Town Hall, Mare St, London E8 1EA;
   URL www.hackney.gov.uk; Tel 020 8356 5000

Children and Young People Services

205 Morning La, London E9 6JX;
   URL www.hackney.gov.uk; Tel 020 8356 5000;
   Fax 020 8356 4726
Director; Chief Executive (Learning Trust)   Alan Wood
Deputy Director (Children and Young People Services)
   Steve Goodman
Assistant Director (Children Social Care)   Isabelle Trowler

The Learning Trust, Technology and Learning Centre

Technology Centre, 1 Reading La, London E8 1GQ;
   Tel 020 8820 7000; Fax 020 8820 7001
Number of Schools
9 Secondary; 1 Academy

CHILDREN AND YOUNG PEOPLE'S SCRUTINY COMMISSION

Chair   Cllr Saleem Siddiqui
Vice-Chair   Muttalip Unluer
Cabinet Member (Children and Young People)
   Cllr Rita Krishma
Cabinet Adviser (Children and Young People)
   Cllr Carol Williams
Members of the Committee
Dawood Akhoon, Brian Bell, Feryat Demirci, Gulay Icoz,
Chris Kennedy, Faizullah Khan, Chris McShane, Harvey
Odze, Shuja Shaikh, Saleem Siddiqui, Muttalip Unluer
Co-optees Eli Anderson, Ralph Bergmann, Andrew
Bridgwater, Vera Edwards, Mary Ludlow, Lucy Quatre,
Mohammed Zeena

Hammersmith and Fulham London Borough Council
www.lbhf.gov.uk

Population: 171 000
Political composition: Con: 33, Lab: 13
Town Hall, King St, Hammersmith, London W6 9JU;
   URL www.lbhf.gov.uk; Tel 020 8753 2001

Children's Services

e-mail enquiries@hafed.org.uk; Tel 020 8753 3625;
   Fax 020 8753 3614
Director   Andrew Christie
Deputy Director (Resources and Lifelong Learning)   Vacancy
Assistant Director (Children, Youth and Community)
   Gill Sewell
*Assistant Director (Commissioning, Performance and
   Partnership)*   Carole Bell
Assistant Director (School Improvement and Standards)
   Janet Lewis
Head (Access and Inclusion)   Vacancy
Head (Admissions, Allegations and School Information)
   Barbara Beese
Number of Schools
8 Secondary; 6 Special

Haringey London Borough Council
www.haringey.gov.uk

Population: 216 507
Political composition: Lab: 42, LD: 15
Civic Centre, High Rd, London N22 8LE;
   URL www.haringey.gov.uk; e-mail
   customer.services@haringey.gov.uk; Tel 020 8489 0000;
   Fax 020 8862 3864
Chief Executive   Ita O' Donovan

2

The Children and Young People's Service

48 Station Rd, Wood Green, London N22 4TY;
   Tel 020 8489 0000; Fax 020 8489 3864
Lead Member (The Children and Young People's Service)
   Cllr Liz Santry
*Deputy Lead Member (The Children and Young People's
   Service)*   Cllr Emma Jones
Director (The Children and Young People's Service)
   Sharon Shoesmith
Deputy Director (Business Support and Development)
   Ian Bailey
Deputy Director (Delivery and Performance)   Vacancy
Deputy Director (School Standards and Inclusion)
   Janette Karklins
Head (Administration)   Norma Downer-Powell
Head (Adult Learning)   Pat Duffy (Acting)
Head (Finance)   Kevin Bartle
Head (Governor Support and Training)   Pat Elcock
Head (Information and Communication Technology)
   Max Riley
Head (Management Information and Research)   Avi Becker
Manager (Recruitment and Retention)   Elizabeth Baldick
Manager (School Funding and Policy)   Steve Worth
Communications and Marketing Relations Officer
   Monica Kochhar
Equalities Officer   Claire Barnes
Project Officer   Jayesh Amin
Principal Budget Accountant   Lorraine Tisseverasinghe
Number of Schools
10 Secondary; 4 Special
Requisition Periods for Schools Supplies
Within the financial year
**Other Authorities with whom Joint Purchasing Arrangements
are made**
Counties Furniture Group, Cleapse, ILEA Supplies

Children and Families

*Head (Services to Children and Young People with Additional
   Disabilities)*   Phil Di Leo
Service Manager (Asylum)   Motak Ahmed
Service Manager (Care Planning and Permanency)
   Clive Preece
Service Manager (Child Protection and Review)
   Teresa Walsh-Jones
Service Manager (Duty and Assessment)   Marion Wheeler
*Service Manager (Family Support and Children with
   Disabilities)*   Lucianna Frederick
Service Manager (Leaving Care and Asylum)   Julia Wise-
   St.Legar
Service Manager (Looked After Children)   Rachel Oakley
Principal Educational Psychologist   Christa Rippon

School Standards and Inclusion

Head (Primary and Special School Standards)   Rachel Singer
Head (Secondary Alternative Provisions)   Sue Panter
Head (Secondary and Special School Standards)
   John Edwards (Acting)
Head (Secondary Innovations)   David Williamson
Head (Student Attendance, Placements and Welfare)   Su Shaw
Head (Youth Services)   Belinda Evans

Manager (Additional Needs Team)   Kristie Watkins
Contact (Attendance and Welfare Society)   Terry O'Reirdan

Delivery and Performance

Head (Children's Network, North); Lead Officer (Early Intervention/Prevention)   Dwynwen Stepien
Head (Children's Network, South); Lead Officer (Safeguarding)   Jan Doust
Head (Children's Network, West); Lead Officer (Workforce Development)   Alison Botham
Head (Children, Young People, Parental and Community Participation)   Jennifer James
Head (Music and Performing Arts)   Peter Desmond
Performance Manager   Christine Jorge
Manager (Extended School Development)   Carol Mackinnon
Community Participation Officer   Leon Joseph
Partnership Officer   Jan Mottram
Policy and Partnership Officer   Patricia Walker
Policy Officer (Children's Network and Safeguarding)   Tom Fletcher
Children and Young People's Participation Officer   Vacancy
Children's Networks Development Officer   Robert Singh

Business Support and Development

Head (Admission)   Sheila Locke
Head (Operational Commissioning, Contracts and Business Management)   Maria Hajipanayi
Head (Pendarren Outdoor Education Centre)   Martin Skinner
Head (Property and Contracts)   Vacancy
Head (Schools Personnel)   Carmelina Tona
Schools Organisation and Development Officer   Corinne Hilton

Finance

Director (Building Schools for the Future)   Gordon Smith

Services

HARINGEY EDUCATION BUSINESS PARTNERSHIP

Tottenham Green Enterprise Centre   Town Hall Approach Rd, London N15 4RX; e-mail haringey.ebp@hebp.co.uk; Tel 020 8375 3500
Centre Manager   D. Wheeler

HARINGEY ADULT LEARNING SERVICES

Unit 5   2nd Fl, Central Library, High Rd, London N22 6XD; Tel 020 8489 2566
Head of Service   M. Wheeler

SCHOOLS LIBRARY SERVICE

Contact   C. Collingbourn; Tel 020 8889 1292
Central Library Service   Central Library, High Rd, London N22 1HE; Tel 020 8489 2759
Contact   Diana Edmonds

OUTDOOR EDUCATION CENTRE

Pendarren House   Llangenny, Crickhowell, Powys NP8 1HE; Tel 01873 810694
Centre Manager   M. Skinner

Harrow London Borough Council

www.harrow.gov.uk

Population: 214 000
Political composition: Con: 38, Lab: 24, LD: 1
Civic 1, Civic Centre, Station Rd, Harrow, Greater London HA1 2XF; URL www.harrow.gov.uk; e-mail info@harrow.gov.uk; Tel 020 8863 5611
Mayor   Cllr Janet Cowan
Chief Executive   Mike Lockwood

People First Directorate

This directorate brings together health, social and learning services (largely comprising the former education services and social services departments)
Civic 1, Civic Centre, Station Rd, Harrow, Greater London HA1 2UL
Bentley Hse, 17–19 Headstone Dr, Harrow, Greater London HA3 5QX
Executive Director   Lorraine O'Reilly
Director (Adult Community Care Services)   Penny Furness-Smith
Director (Children's Services)   Paul Clark
Director (Lifelong Learning and Cultural Services)   Javed Khan
Director (Strategic Services)   Geoff Wingrove
Head of Joint Commissioning (Supporting People)   Lesley Parker
Group Manager (JAR Co-ordination)   Judy Ravenscroft
Group Manager (People First Finance)   Paula Foulds
Senior Professional (Mental Health Services)   Mark Hall-Pearson;   based at Bentley House; Tel 020 8424 7702
Senior Professional (People First Human Resources)   Paul R. Turner

Children's Services

429–433 Pinner Rd, North Harrow, Harrow, Greater London HA1 4HN; Tel 020 8863 5544; Fax 020 8424 8045
Teachers' Centre, Tudor Rd, Wealdstone, Greater London HA3 5PQ
Alexandra Avenue Health and Social Centre, 275 Alexandra Ave, South Harrow, London HA2 9DX
Director   Paul Clark;   based at Civic 1, Civic Centre
Service Manager (Children in Need and Looked After Service)   Jai Batra
Service Manager (Children with Disabilities Service)   Mary Moss (Acting);   based at Alexandra Ave
Service Manager (Education Welfare Service)   Anna Marie Tenconi
Service Manager (Referral and Assessment Team)   Jennifer Noble (Acting)
Sevice Manager (Family Placement Service)   Arlene Bridgewater (Acting)
Service Manager (Safer Harrow)   Joy Shakespeare;   based at Civic 1, Civic Centre
Service Manager (SEN Assessment and Review)   Carole Wells;   based at Alexandra Ave
Service Manager (Youth Engagement)   Joyce Harvie;   based at Civic 9, Civic Centre
Group Manager (Children and Families)   Paul Wedgbury;   based at Civic 1, Civic Centre
Group Manager (Early Years, Childcare and Parenting)   Wendy Beeton; Leisure Centre Annexe, Christchurch Ave, Wealdstone, Harrow, London HA3 5BD
Group Manager (Safeguarding and Family Support)   Gail Hancock
Group Manager (Fostering, Adoption and Residential Care)   Richard Marks
Group Manager (Schools and Children's Development)   Heather Clements;   based at Teachers' Centre
Group Manager (SEN Services)   Roger Rickman;   based at Alexandra Avenue
Group Manager (Young People's Services)   Richard Segalov;   based at Civic 1, Civic Centre
Senior Professional (Achievement and Inclusion)   Adrian Parker;   based at Teachers' Centre
Senior Professional (Achievement and Inclusion)   Brenda Rayson;   based at Teachers' Centre
Senior Professional (Achievement and Inclusion)   Carole Tobin;   based at Teachers' Centre
Senior Co-ordinator (Child Protection)   Steve Spurr;   based at Civic 1, Civic Centre
Senior Co-ordinator (Children Looked After)   Andreas Kyriacou;   based at Civic 1, Civic Centre
Co-ordinator (Local Safeguarding Children Board)   Betty Lynch;   based at Civic 1, Civic Centre

Principal Educational Psychologist (Educational Psychology Service) Gladys de Groot; based at Alexandra Ave

Lifelong Learning and Cultural Services

Civic 1, Civic Centre, Station Rd, Harrow, Greater London HA1 2UW
Director Javed Kahn
Group Manager (Community and Area Development – Central) Kashmir Takhar
Group Manager (Community and Area Development – East) Anita Luthra-Suri (Acting)
Group Manager (Community and Area Development – West) Samia Malik
Group Manager (Library Services) Bob Mills
Group Manager (Lifelong Learning Services) Anita Luthra-Suri
Group Manager (Sports and Cultural Services) Samantha Webster

LIFELONG LEARNING, CULTURAL SERVICES AND ISSUES FACING OLDER PEOPLE

Portfolio Holder Cllr Christine Bednell

PEOPLE FIRST – CHILDREN'S SERVICES

Portfolio Holder Cllr Jane Mote

CHILDREN AND YOUNG PEOPLE SCRUTINY SUB-COMMITTEE

Cons: 8, Lab: 3
Chair Cllr Mark Versallion

ADULT HEALTH AND SOCIAL CARE SCRUTINY SUB-COMMITTEE

Cons: 4, Lab: 3
Chair Cllr Myra Michael

EDUCATION CONSULTATIVE FORUM

Cons: 4, Lab: 3
Chair Cllr Christine Bednell

HARROW ADMISSIONS FORUM

Cons: 2, Lab: 1
Chair Cllr Bill Stephenson

TEACHERS CENTRE

Tudor Rd, Wealdstone, Greater London HA3 5PQ; URL www.harrowtc.org.uk; e-mail bookings.harrowtc@harrow.gov.uk; Tel 020 8427 1291; Fax 020 8427 2418
The Teachers Centre provides resources and specialist accommodation for in-service training and community activities and is also available for hire for training and development purposes

Havering London Borough Council

www.havering.gov.uk

Population: 224 248 (2001 Census)
Political composition: Con: 34, Residents: 13, Rainham and Wennington Residents Independent Association: 3, Lab: 2, Liberal Democrat Focus Team: 1, BNP: 1
Town Hall, Main Rd, Romford, Essex RM1 3BD; URL www.havering.gov.uk; Tel 01708 434343; Fax 01708 432428; Textphone 01708 433175
Chief Executive Cheryl Coppell

Children's Services Directorate

Scimitar Hse, 23 Eastern Rd, Romford, Essex RM1 3NH; Tel 01708 434343; Fax 01708 433837
Cabinet Lead Member Geoff Starns (Con)

Director Andrew Ireland
Head (Pupil and Student Services) Sue Allen
Head (School Improvement) Shirley Ditchburn
Head (Strategy and Commissioning) David Tomlinson
Number of Schools
65 Primary; 18 Secondary; 3 Special

HAVERING COLLEGE OF ADULT EDUCATION

Main Office The Broxhill Centre, Broxhill Rd, Romford, Essex RM4 1XN; e-mail jeff.hooton@havering.gov.uk; Tel 01708 433874
Manager (Lifelong Learning) J. Hooton

HAVERING INSPECTION AND ADVISORY SERVICE

The Broxhill Centre, Broxhill Rd, Romford, Essex RM4 1XN; Tel 01708 773794
Principal Inspector (Development) Sue Butterworth
Principal Inspector (Performance) Russell Sherman
Inspector (Schools) David Maclean
Educational Computer Centre Town Hall Print Unit, Main Rd, Romford, Essex RM1 3BB; Tel 01708 433987; Fax 01708 433974
Head B. Bailey
Europa Centre The Walk, Hornchurch, Essex RM11 3TL; e-mail europacentre@hotmail.com; Tel 01708 440087; Tel 01708 445694
Head (Modern Languages) C. Whitham
Learning Support Service The Broxhill Centre, Broxhill Rd, Romford, Essex RM4 1XN; Tel 01708 433937
Head (Learning Support Service) Anna Williams

MUSIC CENTRE

Havering Music School The Walk, Hornchurch, Essex RM11 3TL; e-mail liebman@haveringmusicschool.org; Tel 01708 450313; Fax 01708 620199
Head (Havering Music School) Mrs I. Liebman

YOUTH HOUSES

Albemarle Youth House Gooshays Dr, Harold Hill, Romford, Essex RM3 9LB; e-mail jacqueline.mann@havering.gov.uk; Tel 01708 340161
Century Youth House Albert Rd, Romford, Essex RM1 2PS; e-mail doris.baffour@havering.gov.uk; Tel 01708 751656
Robert Beard Youth House 233 High St, Hornchurch, Essex RM11 3XU; e-mail maureen.redgwell@havering.gov.uk; Tel 01708 450609

London Borough of Hillingdon

www.hillingdon.gov.uk

Population: 243 000
Political composition: Con: 45, Lab: 18, LD: 2
Civic Centre, High St, Uxbridge, Greater London UB8 1UW; URL www.hillingdon.gov.uk
Chief Executive Dorian Leatham

Education, Youth and Leisure Services Group

Tel 01895 250111
Corporate Director Chris Spencer
Head (Finance and Resources Services) D. Tully
Head (Lifelong Learning) R. Turner GRSM, MA
Educational Psychology Service C. Sullivan
Inspector (Primary: Humanities/RE) J. Dewhurst MA, LCP, DipEd
Inspector (Post-16: Mathematics/Assessment) Dr E. Blaire BA, PhD
Inspector (SEN) Vacancy
Senior Adviser (Standards) M. Baxter BSc, MBA, PGCE

Number of Schools (including Foundation)
18 Secondary; 6 Special
Requisition Periods for Schools Supplies
Various
Other Authorities with whom Joint Purchasing Arrangements are made
CLEAPSE, CFG

EDUCATION COMMITTEE

Con: 12, Lab: 11, LD: 1
Chair David Yarrow (Con)
Vice-Chair Solveig Stone (Con)

EDUCATIONAL PSYCHOLOGY SERVICE

The Lancaster Centre 26 Bennetts Yd, Lancaster Rd, Uxbridge, Greater London UB8 1BN; Tel 01895 256524
Principal Educational Psychologist Christine Sullivan

INSTITUTES OF ADULT EDUCATION

Adult Education Office 86 Long La, Ickenham, Uxbridge, Greater London UB10 8SX; Tel 01895 676690
Harlington Adult Education Centre Harlington Community School, Pinkwell La, Hayes, Greater London UB3 1PE; Tel 020 8569 1613
North Hillingdon Adult Education Centre 86 Long La, Ickenham, Uxbridge, Greater London UB10 8SX; Tel 01895 634616
Open Learning Centre Harlington AEC, Harlington Community School, Hayes, Greater London UB3 1PE; Tel 020 8569 1614

HILLINGDON MUSIC SERVICE

Compass Theatre Glebe Ave, Ickenham, Uxbridge, Greater London UB10 8PD; Tel 01895 630155

Hounslow London Borough Council

www.hounslow.gov.uk

Population: 212 508
Political composition: Lab: 24, Con: 23, LD: 4, Community Group: 6, Hounslow Federation of Independent Councillors: 3
Civic Centre, Lampton Rd, Hounslow, Greater London TW3 4DN; URL www.hounslow.gov.uk; e-mail information.ced@hounslow.gov.uk; Tel 020 8583 2000
Chief Executive Mark Gilks

Children's Services and Lifelong Learning

Tel 020 8583 2600; Fax 020 8583 2613
Leader of the Council Cllr Peter Thompson
Director Judith Pettersen
Assistant Director (Children and Families) Mr Chris Hogan
Assistant Director (Partnerships and Community) Colin Peak
Assistant Director (Resources and Planning) Rodney D'Costa
Assistant Director (Schools) John Bolt
Head (Finance) Mr Alex Taylor
Head (Inclusion) Merle Abbott
Head (Human Resources) John Reece
Head (Safeguarding) Sally Phillips
Senior Education Officer (School Services) Sheena Poley
Education Officer (School Attendance and Exclusions) Ian Whittaker
Education Officer (Operational Planning and Strategy) Mr Kam Bhari
Principal Adviser (School Catering) Bruce Headford
Chief Adviser (School Improvement and Science) Corinne Stevenson
Senior Adviser (National Strategies KS1, 2, 3: English/Drama) Liz Thomas

Senior Adviser (School Monitoring, Education, Assessment and ASTS) Chris Thomas
General Adviser (Design and Technology and ICT) Mr Chris Salt
General Adviser (Equal Opportunities and Ethnic Minority Achievement) Mr Avtar Sherrie
General Adviser (Primary Education; Gifted and Talented) Rebecca Scott-Saunders
General Adviser (Primary Education and NQTs) Val Blackwell
General Adviser (SEN, Inclusion and Disability) Judy Kirby
Senior Adviser (Secondary EIC Post 16, Health and Citizenship) David Brockie (Acting)
Principal Youth Officer (Youth Service) Liz Hassock
Principal Educational Psychologist Nicola D'Aeth
Principal (Adult Education) Debbie Latimer
Number of Schools
60 Primary; 14 Secondary; 5 Special Day; 1 PRU
Requisition Periods for Schools Supplies
As required
Other Authorities with whom Joint Purchasing Arrangements are made
None

COMMITTEE OF THE COUNCIL

Executive Member (Education and Children) Cllr Kinghorn (Con)
Members of the Executive Committee
Andrews, Bowen, P. Fisher, Hibbs, Kinghorn, Lee, McGregor, Reid

GOVERNOR DEVELOPMENT AND TRAINING

Governor Training Programme, Education Dept, Hounslow, Greater London TW3 4DN; Tel 020 8583 2881; Fax 020 8583 2613
Co-ordinator (Governor Training) Mrs Margaret Bonsey
Comprehensive programme of centrally-organised training courses; helpline – advice given on any issue connected with school governance; central resource loan library; school-based governors' libraries; access to regional and national governor services through local authority membership of AGIT, NAGM etc.; training for individual governing bodies

TEACHING SUPPORT SERVICE

Hounslow Education Centre, Martindale Rd, Hounslow, Greater London TW4 7HE; Tel 020 8570 8547; Fax 020 8572 2145
Head Mrs J. Capstick
The service consists of four specialist teams: Behaviour, Learning, Physical Disability and Sensory Impairment

WOOD LANE CENTRE

24 Wood La, Isleworth, Greater London TW7 5ED; Tel 020 8583 2984; Fax 020 8583 2988
Head of Service Ms Carole Carr

EDUCATION CENTRE

Hounslow Education Centre Martindale Rd, Hounslow, Greater London TW4 7HE; Tel 020 8583 4190
Centre Manager M. Baker

London Borough of Islington

www.islington.gov.uk

Population: 185 500
Political composition: LD: 24, Lab: 23, Green: 1
Town Hall, Upper St, London N1 2UD; URL www.islington.gov.uk; Tel 020 7527 2000
Chief Executive Helen Bailey
Assistant Director (Children and Families) David Worlock
Director (Children's Services) Paul Curran; 159 Upper St, London N1 1RE; Tel 020 7527 5662

Executive Member (Children and Young People)
  Cllr Ursula Woolley

Cambridge Education @ Islington

159 Upper St, London N1 1RE; Tel 020 7527 5624;
  Fax 020 7527 5903
Director (Education Services)   Eleanor Schooling
*Assistant Director (Education Transformation and Investment:
  Innovation Champion)*   Kirit Modi
*Assistant Director (Policy and Performance : Children's
  Champion)*   Sandra Bingham
*Assistant Director (School Improvement: Standards
  Champion)*   Mark Taylor
Number of Schools
44 Primary; 9 Secondary; 4 Special; 3 Nursery; 3 PRU

EDUCATION PROFESSIONAL DEVELOPMENT CENTRE

The Barnsbury Centre, Barnsbury Complex, Offord Rd,
  London N1 1QF; Tel 020 7527 5653; Fax 020 7527 5652

Kensington and Chelsea

www.rbkc.gov.uk

Population: 184 000
Political composition: Con: 45, Lab: 9
The Town Hall, Hornton St, Kensington, London W8 7NX;
  URL www.rbkc.gov.uk; e-mail
  information@rbkc.gov.uk; Tel 020 7361 3000;
  Fax 020 7938 1445
Chief Executive; Town Clerk   Derek Myers BA, LLB

Family and Children's Services

e-mail annemarie.carrie@rbkc.gov.uk; e-mail
  <firstname>.<surname>@rbkc.gov.uk;
  Tel (Educationline) 020 7361 3009; Tel 020 7361 3013;
  Fax 020 7361 3481
Chief Executive (Central London Connexions)   C. Heaume
Executive Director   Anne Marie Carrie; Tel 020 7361 3300
Director (Community Learning)   K. Tyerman
Director (Schools)   R. Matthews (Acting)
Head (Access and Inclusion)   R. Sachse
Head (Adult and Family Learning)   P. Hoffman
Head (Child and Family Services)   L. Blake
Head (Early Years, Childcare and Play)   P. Williamson
Head (Language Development Service)   S. Green
Head (Library Service)   J. Battye
Head (Pupil Support Service)   G. Crosbie
Head (Research and Information)   J. Hay
Head (Resources)   M. Salih
*Head (School Organisation, Admissions and Governors
  Support)*   L. Purcell
Head (SEN and Additional Needs)   D. Dyer
Head (Services to Young People)   B. O'Keefe
Manager (Children's Strategic Planning)   O. Butler
Senior Adviser (School Improvement)   D. Hall
Adviser (School Improvement)   F. Beresford
Principal Education Welfare Officer   H. Shaw
Principal Educational Psychologist   P. Wagner
Number of Schools
26 Primary; 4 Secondary; 4 Nursery; 2 Special

CABINET

Cabinet Member (Education and Libraries)   M. Weale (Con);
  39a Kelso Pl, London W8 5QP; Tel 020 7937 0765
Cabinet Member (Family and Children's Services)
  S. Ritchie (Con); The Town Hall, Hornton St, London
  W8 7NX; Tel 020 7376 8151

OVERVIEW AND SCRUTINY COMMITTEE ON FAMILY AND CHILDREN'S SERVICES

Chair   J. Husband
Vice-Chair   B. Campbell
Members of the Committee
Con: V. Borwick, J. Clamp, Prof Sir A. Coates, J. Cox, N.
Halbritter, B. Levitt, S. Redman
Lab: M. Alapini, R. Atkinson, M. Lasharie

GOVERNOR TRAINING UNIT

Isaac Newton Centre for Professional Development, 108a
  Lancaster Rd, London W11 1QS; Tel 020 7598 4801;
  Fax 020 7598 4832
*Principal (including support for organisationally-led
  programmes)*   S. Cobb
Services offered
Central programme including induction of new governors;
helpline; information sheet produced twice termly;
information centre resource section; borough's
representative for AGIT, NAGAM and other related bodies

TEACHERS' CENTRE

Isaac Newton Centre for Professional Development   108a
  Lancaster Rd, London W11 1QS; Tel 020 7598 4801;
  Fax 020 7598 4832
Principal   S. Cobb

COMMUNITY LEARNING

125 Freston Rd, London W10 6TH; URL www.rbkc.gov.uk;
  e-mail community.education@rbkc.gov.uk;
  Tel 020 7938 8000; Fax 020 7938 8020

YOUTH CENTRES

Chelsea Youth Club   Worlds End Est, Blantyre St, London
  SW10 1EQ; Tel 020 7349 9602
Connexions Centre   125 Freston Rd, London W10 6TH;
  Tel 020 7938 8091
East Chelsea Team   John Keys Centre, Pond Pl, London
  SW3 6QT; Tel 020 7225 1631
Golborne Youth Centre   2a Wornington Rd, London
  W10 5QQ; Tel 020 8960 6238
Lancaster West Detached Project   Estate Office, Grenfell
  Tower, London W11 1TQ; Tel 020 7221 9640
Lancaster Youth Centre   128a Lancaster Rd, London
  W11 1QS; Tel 020 7221 2197; Tel 020 7221 2477
Wornington Green Detached Youth Project   Wornington
  Green Est, c/o Residents Association, 8c Chiltern Hse, 15
  Telford Rd, London W10; Tel 020 8964 4608
YCTV Foundation   77 Barlby Rd, London W10 6AZ;
  Tel 020 8964 4646
Youth Inclusion Programme   Dalgarno Community Centre, 1
  Webb Cl, Dalgarno Way, London W10 5QB

Kingston upon Thames

www.kingston.gov.uk

Population: 147 273
Political composition: LD: 25, Con: 21, Ind: 1, Lab: 1
Guildhall, Kingston upon Thames, Surrey KT1 1EU;
  URL www.kingston.gov.uk; e-mail
  <firstname>.<surname>@rbk.kingston.gov.uk;
  Tel 020 8547 5757
Chief Executive   Bruce McDonald; Tel 020 8547 5150;
  Fax 020 8547 5012
Service Director (Planning and Transportation)
  Roy Thompson; Tel 020 8547 5343

Learning and Children's Services

Guildhall 2, Kingston upon Thames, Surrey KT1 1EU;
  Tel 020 8547 5234; Fax 020 8547 5297

Strategic Director Patrick Leeson
Directorate Head (Children's Services and Safeguarding)
  D. Clark; Tel 020 8547 6056
Directorate Head (Cultural Services and Lifelong Learning)
  S. Herbertson
Directorate Head (Learning and School Effectiveness)
  N. Whitfield
Directorate Head (Resources and Commissioning)
  A. Redparth
Head (Assessment and Support for Learning) J. Ely
Head (Early Years and Childcare Services) C. Halstead
Head (Education Welfare Service) M. Zhang
Head (Educational Psychology Service) J. Hardy
Head (Kingston Adult Education) B. Selwyn
Lead Strategic Manager (Family Support and Child Protection)
  Lee Hopkins; Tel 020 8547 6111
Strategic Manager (Early Years and Childcare) C. Halstead;
  Tel 020 8547 5278
Strategic Manager (School Cluster Services) C. Catlow;
  Tel 020 8547 6676
Number of Schools
10 Secondary (5 Community, 3 VA and 2 Foundation); 3
Special

EXECUTIVE MEMBER FOR YOUNG PEOPLE'S SERVICES

Contact Cllr Patricia Bamford (LD)

SOCIAL CARE TEAMS

Dukes Centre Dukes Ave, Kingston upon Thames, Surrey
  KT2 5QY; Tel 020 8547 6699; Fax 020 8439 7794
Team Manager (Educational Psychology Service) J. Hardy
*Team Manager (Family Advice and Support Service: CAMHS
  Tier 2)* J. Hardy
Eagle Chambers 18 Eden St, Kingston, Surrey KT1 1BB;
  Tel 020 8547 6290; Fax 020 8547 6959
Team Manager (Young Offending Team) K. Walker
Team Manager (Young People's Team) K. Walker
Co-ordinator (Teenage Pregnancy) L. Morris
Guildhall 1 Kingston, Surrey KT1 1EU
Team Manager (Family Placement Team) J. Rigby;
  Tel 020 8547 6088
Team Manager (Looked After and Leaving Care) J. Budden;
  Tel 020 8547 6922
Team Manager (Unaccompanied Asylum Seekers)
  A. Thorne; Tel 020 8547 6900
Team Manager (Youth Service) G. Hall; Tel 020 8547 5715
Surbiton Children's Centre Alpha Rd, Surbiton, Surrey
  KT5 8RS; Tel 020 8547 6242; Fax 020 8390 6805
*Team Manager (Children's Fund and Early Intervention
  Services)* A. Carnie
Team Manager (Supporting Families Service) S. Brown

ADULT EDUCATION

Kingston Adult Education and Training Service North
  Kingston Centre, Richmond Rd, Kingston upon Thames,
  Surrey KT2 5PE; Tel 020 8547 6700; Fax 020 8547 6747

London Borough of Lambeth
www.lambeth.gov.uk

Population: 275 800
Political composition: Lab: 28, LD: 28, Con: 7
Town Hall, Brixton Hill, Lambeth, London SW2 1RW;
  URL www.lambeth.gov.uk; Tel 020 7926 1000

Children and Young People's Service

International Hse, Canterbury Cres, London SW9 7QE
Executive Director Phyllis Dunipace; Tel 020 7926 9771
Divisional Director (Community Learning) John Readman;
Divisional Director (Inclusion and Standards Division)
  Chris Ashton

Divisional Director (Social Care Division) Yashi Shah
Divisional Director (Strategy and Performance)
  Doreen Redwood
Programme Director (Building Schools for the Future: BSF)
  Mike Pocock
Programme Director (Change Management)
  Sandra Morrison
Number of Schools
10 Secondary; 3 Special; 1 Academy

GOVERNOR SERVICES

London Borough of Lambeth, International Hse, London
  SW9 7QE; Tel 020 7926 1000
Governor Training and Development Officer Pat Petch
Services offered
Borough-wide training programme for school governors,
covering relevant curriculum; personnel; finance, premises
and pupil-related issues; provides individual governing
body training; advice and support services to governors on
statutory management and policy issues

PROFESSIONAL DEVELOPMENT CENTRE

International House Canterbury Cres, London SW9 7QE;
  Tel 020 7926 1000

Lewisham London Borough Council
www.lewisham.gov.uk

Population: 240 353
Lewisham Town Hall, Catford Rd, London SE6 4RU;
  URL www.lewisham.gov.uk; Tel 020 8314 6000;
  Fax 020 8314 3000
Chief Executive Barry Quirk; Fax 020 8314 6444

Directorate for Children and Young People

London Borough of Lewisham, 3rd Fl, Laurence Hse, 1
  Catford Rd, London SE6 4RU; Tel 020 8314 8527;
  Fax 020 8314 3151
Executive Director Frankie Sulke
Director (Children's Social Care) Alistair Pettigrew
Head (Access and Support Services for Children)
  Christine Grice
Head (Commissioning, Performance and Strategy)
  Warwick Tomsett
Head (Resources) Alan Docksey
Head (School Effectiveness) Chris Threlfall
Number of Schools
12 Secondary; 7 Special

GOVERNORS' SERVICES

Laurence Hse, 1 Catford Rd, London SE6 4SW;
  Tel 020 8695 6000 ext 6233; Fax 020 8690 4392
Services offered
Range of school-based and central training offered on termly
basis; briefing papers produced on termly basis; occasional
borough-wide conferences/events. Telephone advice.

EDUCATIONAL PSYCHOLOGY AND LEARNING SUPPORT SERVICE

Head of Service Mary Cava
Service provided at Kaleidoscope Children's Centre

EARLY YEARS CENTRES

Amersham Road Early Years Centre Amersham Rd, New
  Cross, London SE14 6QH; e-mail
  amersham.eyc@leys.org.uk; Tel 020 8691 1114
  Head Yvonne Ellis

Clyde Early Childhood Centre Alverton St, London
SE8 5NH; e-mail clyde.eyc@leys.org.uk;
Tel 020 8692 3653
Head (Childcare) Neil Robinson

Honor Oak Early Childhood Centre Brockley Way, London
SE4 2LW; e-mail honoroak.eyc@leys.org.uk;
Tel 020 7639 1802
Head Daphne Hollands

Ladywell Early Childhood Centre 30 Rushey Mead, London
SE4 1JJ; e-mail ladywell.eyc@leys.org.uk;
Tel 020 8690 9845
Head Gerry Richards

Louise House Early Childhood Centre Louise Hse,
Dartmouth Rd, London SE23 3HZ; e-mail
louise.house.eyc@leys.org.uk; Tel 020 8291 5771
Head Sylvia Maguire

Rushey Green Early Years Centre 41 Rushey Grn, Catford,
London SE6 4AS; e-mail rushey.green.eyc@leys.org.uk;
Tel 020 8698 1608
Head Joanne Sharpe

Woodpecker Early Years Centre 20 Woodpecker Rd, Forest
Hill, London SE14 6EU; e-mail
woodpecker.eyc@leys.org.uk; Tel 020 8694 9557
Head Gerry Richards (Acting)

FIELD STUDY CENTRES

Horton-Kirby Environmental Studies Centre Dartford, Kent
DA4 9BN; e-mail hortonkirby.widehorizons@lgfl.net;
Tel 01322 863465
Head T. McGregor

Tyn-y-Benth Mountain Centre Corris Uchaf, Machynlleth,
Powys SY20 9RH; e-mail
tynyberth@widehorizons.org.uk; Tel 01654 761678;
Fax 01654 761668
Head T. Dawson

TEACHERS' CENTRE

Professional Development Centre Kilmorie Rd, London
SE23 2SP; Tel 020 8314 6146

Merton London Borough Council

www.merton.gov.uk

Population: 190 000
Merton Civic Centre, London Rd, Morden, Surrey SM4 5DX;
URL www.merton.gov.uk; e-mail
postroom@merton.gov.uk; Tel 020 8274 4901
Chief Executive Ged Curran

Children, Schools and Families Department

Director Dave Hill
Head (Commissioning, Strategy and Performance)
Paul Ballatt
Head (Education) Janet Martin
Head (Social Care and Youth Inclusion) Helen Lincoln
Manager (Community Support and Social Care)
Melissa Caslake
Manager (Contracts, Procurement and School Organisation)
Tom Procter
Manager (Early Years and Children's Centres) Julie Danzey
Manager (Extended Schools) Ann Macrory
Manager (Finance) Tim Gibson
Manager (ICT, Business Support and Project Management)
Paul Whiteman
Manager (Joint Commissioning and Partnerships)
Leanne Wallder
Manager (Looked After Children Permanency and Placements)
Anne Hignett
Manager (Personnel) Sue Watson

Manager (Policy, Planning and Performance)
Michael Sutherland
Manager (Safeguarding and Partnerships) Andrew Wyatt
Manager (School Standards and Quality) Kate Saksena
Manager (SEN) Kaye Beeson
Manager (Youth Inclusion) Keith Shipman
Number of Schools
43 Primary; 6 Secondary; 3 Special; 1 PRU

CHILD GUIDANCE CLINIC

Worsfold House Chapel Orchard, Church Rd, Mitcham,
Surrey CR4 3BE; Tel 020 8648 4066

EDUCATIONAL PSYCHOLOGY SERVICE

Merton Civic Centre London Rd, Morden, Surrey SM4 5DX;
Tel 020 8545 4820

INSTITUTE OF ADULT EDUCATION

Merton Adult College Whatley Ave, London SW20 9NS;
Tel 020 8543 9292
Head (Community Education) Yvonne Tomlin

OTHER CENTRES

Merton Professional Development Centre Chaucer Centre,
Canterbury Rd, Morden, Surrey SM4 6PX;
Tel 020 8288 5678; Fax 020 8288 5600
Worsfold House Church Rd, Mitcham, Surrey CR4 3BE;
Tel 020 8545 4201

YOUTH SERVICES

Youth Office The Pavillion, Farm Rd, Morden, Surrey
SM4 6RA; Tel 020 8640 7050; Fax 020 8646 8273
Principal Youth Officer Mark Clark

Newham London Borough Council

www.newham.gov.uk

Population: 230 000
Town Hall, Barking Rd, London E6 2RP;
URL www.newham.gov.uk; Tel 020 8430 2000
Chief Executive Dave Burbage
Executive Director (Housing) Chris Wood; Bridge Hse, 320
High St, Stratford, London E15
Executive Director (Resources) Bob Heaton

Children and Young People's Services

Executive Director (Children and Young People)
Liz Graham (Acting)
Divisional Director (Strategy and Performance)
Maggie White
Head (Asset Management and Planning) Phil Preston
Head (Business and Achievement) D. Lister
Head (Children, Young People and Families) Jenny Dibsdall
Head (Community Education and Youth Service) S. Cameron
Head (Continuing Professional Development Service)
P. Hoyle
Head (Pupil and Student Services) A. Saad
Head (School Development Unit) D. Haggerstone
Head (School Management) T. Matthews
Head (SEN) J. Cameron
*Principal Service Manager (Capital Strategy and School
Planning)* Andrew Panton
*Principal Service Manager (Continuing Professional
Development)* Andi Smith
Principal Service Manager (Economic Wellbeing and 14–19)
John Douglas
Principal Service Manager (Extended Services) Janet Hicks
Principal Service Manager (Learning Support Services)
Lynda Haddock
Principal Service Manager (Primary Standards) Richard Ray

Principal Service Manager (School Organisation)
Trevor Matthews
Principal Service Manager (Secondary Standards)
Anne Seeley
Primary Service Manager (Young People and Lifelong Learning) Steve Cameron
Principal Educational Psychologist Ian Millward
Senior Adviser (Inclusive Education) B. Burke
Monitoring and Standards Officer J. Grieve
Number of Schools
15 Secondary; 2 Special
Requisition Periods for Schools Supplies
None
Other Authorities with whom Joint Purchasing Arrangements are made
Greater London Supplies, Essex County Supplies

CABINET MEMBERS FOR EDUCATION

Cabinet Member (Education) G. Lane (Lab)
Deputy Cabinet Member (Education) Q. Peppiatt (Lab)

GOVERNOR TRAINING UNIT

Credon Centre, Kirton Rd, London E13 9DR;
Tel 020 8470 0931; Fax 020 8471 4605
Governor Education Co-ordinator M. Saunders
Services offered
Training courses for individual governors and governing bodies; support for governing bodies

EDUCATION WELFARE SERVICE

Education Welfare Service Broadway Hse, 322 High St, Stratford, London E15 1AJ; Tel 020 8430 2000
Chief Education Welfare Officer S. Newman

COMMUNITY EDUCATION CENTRE

Newham Community Education and Youth Service Beckton Globe, 1 Kingsford Way, Beckton, London E6 5JQ;
Tel 020 8430 2000
Head (Youth and Community Education Service)
S. Cameron

OUTDOOR EDUCATION CENTRES

Fairplay House Wickham Bishops, Maldon, Essex CM8 3JL; Tel 01621 891213; Fax 01621 892759
Head A. Clasper
The Barge Haybay Heybridge Basin, Maldon, Essex CM9 4RS; Tel 01621 852096

RESIDENTIAL CENTRE

Debden House Centre Debden Green, Loughton, Essex IG10 2PA; Tel 020 8508 3008; Fax 020 8508 0284
Head L. Turner

TEACHERS' CENTRE

Newham In-Service Education Centre The Credon Centre, Kirton Rd, London E13 9DR; Tel 020 8548 5001;
Fax 020 8471 4605

YOUTH CENTRES

Forest Gate Youth Centre 1 Woodford Rd, Forest Gate, London E7 0DH; Tel 020 8519 0095
Little Ilford Youth Centre 1a Rectory Rd, Manor Pk, London E12 6JB; Tel 020 8478 3668; Fax 020 8514 0352
Shipman Youth Centre Custom Hse, Prince Regent La, London E16; Tel 020 7476 1189
Youth Information and Advice Service 49–51 The Broadway, Stratford, London E15 4BQ; Tel 020 8221 1350

Redbridge London Borough Council
www.redbridge.gov.uk

Population: 251 500 (2005 estimate)
Town Hall, 128–142 High Rd, Ilford, Essex IG1 1DD;
URL www.redbridge.gov.uk; e-mail
customer.cc@redbridge.gov.uk; e-mail
<firstname>.<surname>@redbridge.gov.uk;
Tel 020 8554 5000
Chief Executive Roger Hampson; Tel 020 8708 2100;
Fax 020 8478 2356

Children's Services

Lynton Hse, 255–259 High Rd, Ilford, Essex IG1 1NN; e-mail pat.reynolds@redbridge.gov.uk; Tel 020 8708 3100;
Fax 020 8708 3894
Director (Children's Services) Patricia Reynolds
Chief Education Officer (Premises and Planning)
Frank O'Neill
Senior Education Officer (Governors) Steve Carter
Senior Education Officer (Statutory Assessments) Linda Blyth
Chief Officer (School Improvement) Vacancy
Principal Education Welfare Officer Stephen Clarke
Principal Adviser Peter Shepherd
Consultant (KS3 Literacy) Jane Waters
Consultant (KS3 Numeracy) Nikki Martin
Consultant (Primary Literacy) Vacancy
Consultant (Primary Numeracy) Peter McCarthy

CABINET MEMBER FOR CHILDREN'S SERVICES

Contact Cllr Michael Stark (Con); c/o Members' Secretariat, Town Hall, Ilford, Essex IG1 1DD; e-mail michael.stark@redbridge.gov.uk; Tel 020 8708 9680

CHILDREN'S SERVICES SCRUTINY COMMITTEE

Con: 6, Co-opted: 5, Lab: 3, LD: 2
Chair A. Kumar; Con; c/o Members' Secretariat, Town Hall, Ilford, Essex IG1 1DD; e-mail ashok.kumar@redbridge.gov.uk; Tel 020 8708 9736
Vice-Chair G. Borrott; Con; c/o Members' Secretariat, Town Hall, Ilford, Essex IG1 1DD
Members of the Committee
Con: C. Elliman, E. Griffin, R. Turbefield, B. Waite
Co-opted: Helen Clark, Miss Vimala Devi Ranggasami, Mike Ewers, Mr K. Mallick, Rowena Rudkin
Lab: J. Hughes, E. Norman, D. Sharma
LD: F. Banks, R. Scott

GOVERNOR TRAINING UNIT

Melbourne Rd, Ilford, Essex IG1 4HT; Tel 020 8708 0817;
Fax 020 8708 3595
Team Leader (Governers Support Section) Karen Mount
Services offered
Range of courses offered as part of central programme that includes induction training for new governors, chairship skills, personnel issues, financial administration, curriculum training and training for clerks to governing bodies; tailored sessions for individual governing bodies and clusters, sessions on team building, the effective governing body etc.; production of termly newsletter, out-of-hours telephone helpline; and reference shelves in libraries and resource bank of training materials

EDUCATIONAL PSYCHOLOGY SERVICE

852 Cranbrook Rd, Barkingside, Ilford, Essex IG6 1HZ;
Tel 020 8478 3020 ext 87071; Fax 020 8708 7037
Principal Educational Psychologist David Townley

2

TEACHERS' CENTRE AND SEN SUPPORT SERVICE

The Teachers' Centre Melbourne Rd, Ilford, Essex IG1 4HT;
Tel 020 8478 3706; Fax 020 8514 2367

DRAMA CENTRE

Churchfields, South Woodford, London E182 2RB;
Tel 020 8504 5451
Head of Service Keith Homer

MUSIC SERVICE

Redbridge Music Service John Savage Centre, Fencepiece
Rd, Ilford, Essex IG6 2LJ; Tel 020 8501 3944
Director E. Forder CertEd

OUTDOOR PURSUITS CENTRES

Fairlop Sailing Centre Forest Rd, Hainault, Ilford, Essex
IG6 3HN; Tel 020 8500 1468
Warden P.J. Corti
Glasbury House Outdoor Education Centre Glasbury Hse,
Glasbury, Hereford, Herefordshire HR3 5NW;
Tel 01497 847231
Head J. Middleton

YOUTH CENTRES

Caterham Youth Centre Caterham High School, Caterham
Ave, Ilford, Essex IG5 0QW; Tel 020 8550 6019
Youth and Community Worker Gail McGuigan
Daton Youth Centre Ethel Davis School, Barley La, Ilford,
Essex IG3 8XS; Tel 020 8478 4306
Youth and Community Worker Jeff Cocks
Hainault Youth Centre Hainault Forest High School, 116
Huntsman Rd, Hainault, Greater London IG6 2SY;
Tel 020 8500 8071
Youth and Community Worker Kath Terrell
Loxford Youth Centre Loxford High School, Loxford La,
Essex IG1 2UT; Tel 020 8478 4306
Youth and Community Worker O. Bowes CertEd
Mildmay House Youth Centre 69 Albert Rd, Ilford, Essex
IG1 1HS; Tel 020 8553 3617
Youth and Community Worker Julie Saggers
Wanstead Youth Centre Elmcroft Ave, Wanstead, London
E11 2DB; Tel 020 8989 1711
Youth and Community Worker Tracey Quinn
Woodford Youth Centre Woodbridge High School, St
Barnabas Rd, Woodford Green, Essex IG8 7DH;
Tel 020 8504 1287
Youth and Community Worker Mickey Peacock

REDBRIDGE INSTITUTE OF ADULT EDUCATION

Gaysham Ave, Gants Hill, Ilford, Essex IG2 6TD; e-mail
enquiries@redbridge-iae.ac.uk; Tel 020 8550 2398
Principal M.A. Briggs BSc(Econ), CertEd, DipAdEd

Richmond upon Thames London Borough Council

www.richmond.gov.uk

Population: 186 000
Political composition: LD: 36, Con: 18
Civic Centre, 44 York St, Twickenham, Greater London
TW1 3BZ; URL www.richmond.gov.uk;
Tel 020 8891 1411

Education and Children's Services

Regal Hse, London Rd, Twickenham, Greater London
TW1 3QB; URL www.richmond.gov.uk/education;
e-mail education@richmond.gov.uk; Tel 020 8891 7500;
Fax 020 8891 7714

Chief Executive G. Norton
Director Nick Whitfield
Assistant Director (Youth and Culture) Philip J. Lomax
Assistant Director (School Standards) Louise Soden
Assistant Director (Specialist Children's Services)
Barbara Murray
Assistant Director (Strategy and Resources)
Paul Bettles (Acting)
Head (Arts) Rachel Tranter
Head (Children with Learning Difficulties and Disabilities)
Geraldine Herage
Head (Libraries and Culture) Aileen Cahil
Manager (Building Development) Beverly Butler
Manager (Policy, Performance and Systems) Karen Neill
Manager (Sport and Recreation) Colin Sinclair
Manager (Youth Service) Ivana Price
*Senior Inspector (SEN); Inspector (Children with Learning
Difficulties and Disabilities)* Keith Tysoe
Number of Schools
41 Primary; 8 Secondary; 2 Special; 1 Nursery

EXECUTIVE MEMBERS

*Deputy Leader; Cabinet Member (Children's Services and
Education)* Cllr Malcolm Eady (LD)
Cabinet Member (Youth, Culture and Young People)
Cllr John Coombs (LD)

GOVERNOR TRAINING UNIT

Governor Support Unit, London Borough of Richmond
upon Thames, Twickenham, Greater London TW1 3QB;
Tel 020 8891 7510; Fax 020 8891 7714
Co-ordinator (Governor Support) Angela Langford
Services offered
Advice, guidance and support for individual governors,
governing bodies, school staff and clerks; organisation and
arranging of training programmes for governors within the
authority; distribution of a termly Director of Education and
Children's Services Report and Governors' Information
Bulletin, as well as any information received from
organisations such as AGIT, NAGM or the DCSF etc.

EDUCATION WELFARE SERVICE

Regal House 1st Fl, Twickenham, Greater London
TW1 3QB; Tel 020 487 5479; Fax 020 8891 7714

SCHOOL PSYCHOLOGICAL SERVICE

York Street 1st Fl, 42 York St, Twickenham, Greater London
TW1 3BW; Tel 020 8487 5464; Fax 020 8487 5465

ADULT EDUCATION CENTRES

Richmond Business School/RAC Parkshot, Richmond,
Greater London TW9 2RE; URL www.racc.ac.uk; e-mail
info@racc.ac.uk; Tel 020 8940 0170
Principal C. Conroy
Richmond Community College Main Centre, Clifden Rd,
Twickenham, Greater London TW1 4LT;
URL www.racc.ac.uk; e-mail info@racc.ac.uk;
Tel 020 8891 5907
Principal C. Conroy
Richmond upon Thames College Egerton Rd, Twickenham,
Greater London TW2 7SJ; URL www.rutc.ac.uk;
Tel 020 8607 8000
Principal K. Watson

London Borough of Southwark

www.southwark.gov.uk

Political composition: Lab: 28, LD: 27, Con: 6, Green: 1, Ind: 1
Southwark Town Hall, London SE5 8UB;
URL www.southwark.gov.uk; Tel 020 7525 5000;
Fax 020 7525 5200
Chief Executive Annie Shepperd; Tel 020 7525 7171

Southwark Children's Services

John Smith Hse, 144–152 Walworth Rd, London SE17 1JL; Tel 020 7525 5001; Tel (information) 020 7525 5050

Strategic Director (Children's Services)   Romi Bowen

Director (Nursing and Children's Commissioning)
Donna Kinnair

Deputy Director (Children's Services: Education)
Terry Parkin

Deputy Director (Children's Services: Management Services)
Michael Daniels

Assistant Director (Access and Inclusion)   Pauline Armour

Assistant Director (Community Services)   Mike Smith

Assistant Director (Schools and Early Years Achievement)
Terry Reynolds

Assistant Director (Specialist Children's Services and Safeguarding)   Rory Patterson

Number of Schools

68 Primary; 15 Secondary; 7 Special; 5 Nursery; 2 Hospital Schools

EXECUTIVE COMMITTEE

Leader of the Council   Cllr Nick Stanton

Deputy Leader of the Council   Cllr Kim Humphreys

Executive Membership

Columba Blango, Denise Capstick, Toby Eckersley, Jeff Hook, Caroline Pidgeon, Lisa Rajan, Richard Thomas, Lorraine Zuleta

GOVERNOR DEVELOPMENT

Southwark Education Services, John Smith Hse, 144–152 Walworth Rd, London SE17 1JL; Tel 020 7525 5001; Fax 020 7525 5200

Manager (Governor Development)   David Lister

Services offered

A range of centrally-run briefings and training sessions open to all governors; whole governing body training once a year; specific groups training, i.e. teachers, chairs of governors, parent governors; a traded clerking service; a core advice and support service, including a free termly governor bulletin

HOSPITAL SCHOOLS

Bethlem and Maudsley Hospital School   Monks Orchard Rd, Beckenham, Kent BR3 3BX; Tel 020 8777 1897; Fax 020 8777 1239

Headteacher   J. Ivens

Evelina Hospital School   Level 3 (Beach), Evelina Children's Hospital, Lambeth Palace Rd, London SE1 7EH; Tel 020 7188 2267

Headteacher   Manuela Beste

TRAINING AND DEVELOPMENT

Education Library Service   Education Resource Centre, Wilson Rd, London SE5 8PD; e-mail elvena.brumant@southwark.gov.uk; Tel 020 7525 2830

Manager   E. Brumant

Southwark Adult Education Centre, Thomas Calton Centre   Alpha St, London SE15 4NX; Tel 020 7639 6818; Fax 020 7732 4842

Head   Sheila Tarbard

Southwark Learning and Business Centre   Cator St, London SE15 6AA; Tel 020 7525 2800

Head   Gerri Savage

Sutton London Borough Council

www.sutton.gov.uk

Population: 180 000

Civic Offices, St Nicholas Way, Sutton, Surrey SM1 1EA; URL www.sutton.gov.uk; Tel 020 8770 5000; Fax 020 8770 5404

Chief Executive   Paul Martin

Children, Young People and Learning Services

The Grove, Carshalton, Surrey SM5 3AL; URL www.suttonlea.org; Tel 020 8770 6080

Strategic Director   Ian Birnbaum MA, PhD; Tel 020 8770 6500

Executive Head (Children and Families)   Lynda Crellin; Tel 020 8770 4502; Fax 020 8770 5214

Executive Head (Early Years and Extended Services); Assistant Director (SMPCT)   Kathy Wocial; Tel 020 8254 8211

Executive Head (Parent, Pupil and Student Services)
Sharman Lawson; Tel 020 8770 6513; Fax 020 8770 6532

Executive Head (School Improvement)   Peter Simpson; Tel 020 8770 6516; Fax 020 8770 6545

Executive Head (Service Management)   Stephen Ingram; Tel 020 8770 6684; Fax 020 8770 6636

Head (Policy and Research)   Corinne Delahunt; Tel 020 8770 5992; Fax 020 8770 6016

Head (Sutton Youth Music Service)   Nigel Hiscock; Sutton Youth Music Service, c/o Wandle Valley School, Welbeck Rd, Carshalton, Surrey SM5 1LW; Tel 020 8640 8781

Head (Youth Service)   Neil Sewell

Assistant Head (School Improvement)   Nigel Laing; Tel 020 8770 6491; Fax 020 8409 7082

Manager (Business Systems)   Gary Shambrook; Tel 020 8770 6667; Fax 020 8770 6628

Manager (Secondary Strategy)   Mike Slaughter MA, BSc(Hons); Tel 020 8770 5249

Lead Inspector (Early Years)   Chris Taylor; Tel 020 8770 6857

Lead Inspector (Inclusion)   Maria Marsh; Tel 020 8770 6520

Lead Inspector (Primary)   David Shannon; Tel 020 8770 6547

Lead Inspector (Secondary)   Hugh Betterton BA(Hons), MA;

Inspector (Maths)   Tony Maslin

Chief Borough School Attendance Officer   Eileen Arnold; Tel 020 8770 6606; Fax 020 8770 6545

Principal Educational Psychologist   Brenda Tubbs; Tel 020 8770 6780; Fax 020 8770 6532

Number of Schools

14 Secondary; 3 Special

CHILDREN AND YOUNG PEOPLE SCRUTINY COMMITTEE

LD: 6, Con: 4

Members of the Committee

LD: M. Court, B. Hudson, K. Jerome, J. Keys, J. Slark, S. Stears

Con: C. Dunlop, P. Geiringer, P. Wallis, M. Williams

TRAINING AND SCHOOL GOVERNMENT

Children, Young People and Learning Services, Stonecourt, Carshalton, Surrey SM5 2HU; Tel 020 8770 6696; Fax 020 8770 6636

Manager (Training and Development)   Anne Gould

Services offered

Broad range of training courses for all governors; individual governor body sessions; advice and helpline; governors library and resource centre; briefings for chairs and link governors; primary, special and high planning forum for governors

TEACHERS' CENTRE

The Glastonbury Centre   Hartland Rd, Morden, Surrey SM4 6LZ; Tel 020 8770 6745

YOUTH CENTRES

e-mail youthservice@suttonlea.org

Adventure Education Duke of Edinburgh Awards c/o The Quad, Green Wrythe La, Carshalton, Surrey SM5 1JW; Tel 020 8687 0239
Contact   Paul Matthews

Centre 21 Youth Centre Alcorn Cl, Sutton Common Rd, Sutton, Surrey SM3 9PT; Tel 020 8644 1428
Youth Development Worker   Vacancy

Century Youth Centre Fellowes Rd, Carshalton, Surrey SM5 2SX; Tel 020 8647 3627
Senior Youth Development Worker   H. James

The Quad Youth Centre Green Wrythe La, Carshalton, Surrey SM5 1JW; Tel 020 8648 8715
Senior Youth Development Worker   H. James

Sutton Youth Centre Robin Hood La, Sutton, Surrey SM1 2SD; Tel 020 8642 0634
Youth Development Worker   L. Martinez

Wallington Methodist Town Centre (NM) Beddington Gdns, Wallington, Surrey SM6 0HU; Tel 020 8669 3840
Youth Worker In Charge   D. Lapham

The Youth Zone, Phoenix Centre Mollison Dr, Roundshaw, Wallington, Surrey SM6 9HY; Tel 020 8647 7132
Development Youth Worker   Vacancy

Tower Hamlets London Borough Council

www.towerhamlets.gov.uk

Population: 196 630
Political composition: Lab: 36, LD: 15
Mulberry Pl, 5 Clove Cres, London E14 2BG; URL www.towerhamlets.gov.uk; Tel 020 7364 5000
Tower Hamlets Information Centre, 18 Lamb St, London E1 6EA; Tel 020 7364 4970; Tel 020 7364 4971; Fax 020 7375 2539
Chief Executive   Christine Gilbert

Children's Services

Fax 020 7364 4976
Chair (Learning Achievement and Leisure Scrutiny)   Cllr Louise Alexander
Lead Member (Education and Youth)   Cllr O. Ahmed
Director   Kevan Collins
Head (Access and Inclusion)   Helen Jenner
Head (Standards and School Development Services)   Terry Parkin
Head (Strategic and Operational Services)   Isobel Cattermole
Head (Youth and Community Learning)   Mary Durkin (Acting)
Principal Educational Psychologist   David Carroll
Number of Schools (including Grant-Maintained)
16 Secondary; 7 Special

GOVERNOR TRAINING UNIT

Head (Education Personnel)   Helen Anderson (Acting)
Head (Governor Services)   Frank Solarz
Head (Pupil and Student Services)   Hania Franek

PROFESSIONAL DEVELOPMENT CENTRE

English St, London E3 4TA; Tel 020 7364 6350
Advisers

ADULT EDUCATION CENTRES

Bethnal Green Centre 229 Bethnal Green Rd, London E2 6AB; Tel 020 7613 1135
Bow Ideas Store Roman Rd, London; Tel 020 8983 1047
Olga Centre Lanfranc, Medway Rd, London E3 5DH; Tel 020 8981 6014

Poplar Community Education Centre St Paul's Way School, Shelmerdine Cl, London E3 4AN; Tel 020 7987 6879
Shadwell Centre The Highway, London E1 9HT; Tel 020 7364 5014
St Matthias Centre Bullivant St, London E14 0ER; Tel 020 7538 9054
Tower Hamlets College Centre 112 Poplar High St, London E14 0AF; Tel 020 7510 7510
Wessex Community Centre Hadleigh St, London E2 0LB; Tel 020 8980 2588
Whitechapel Centre Myrdle St, London E1 1HL; Tel 020 7377 0640

Waltham Forest London Borough Council

www.walthamforest.gov.uk

Population: 225 000
Political composition: Lab: 26, LD: 19, Con: 15
Town Hall, Forest Rd, Walthamstow, London E17 4JF; URL www.walthamforest.gov.uk; e-mail jacquie.dean@walthamforest.gov.uk; Tel 020 8496 3000; Fax 020 8527 8313
Municipal Offices, The Ridgeway, Chingford, London E4 6PS
Chief Executive   Jacquie Dean

Education Department

Cabinet Member (Children's Services)   Cllr Chris Robbins
Executive Director (Children's Services)   Chris Kiernan
Head (Core Support Services)   Mark Ballinger
Head (Education and Communities)   Leora Cruddas
Head (Finance)   Duncan Pike
Head (Pupil and Student/School Support Services)   Jim Waddington
Head (Schools Support Services)   Patrick Morgan
Head (Schools Support Services)   Eleanor Schooling
Number of Schools
17 Secondary; 6 Special
Requisition Periods for Schools Supplies (Main)
May

Wandsworth London Borough Council

www.wandsworth.gov.uk

Population: 273 400 (2001 est.)
Political composition: Con: 50, Lab: 11
Wandsworth Town Hall, Wandsworth High St, London SW18 2PU; URL www.wandsworth.gov.uk; Tel 020 8871 6000
Chief Executive   G.K. Jones

Education Department

e-mail eddirectors@wandsworth.gov.uk; Tel 020 8871 8013
Director   Paul Robinson
Deputy Director   Mary Evans
Assistant Director   Adrian Butler
Assistant Director (Quality and Evaluation)   John Johnson
Head (Contracts and Personnel)   P. Gaskin
Head (Early Years and Childcare Service)   R. Nicholson
Head (Financial Management Services)   A. Stokes
Head (ICT and Office Services)   D. Cooper
Head (Integrated Support Services)   J. McSherry
Head (Lifelong Learning and 14–19 Developments)   S. Fragola
Head (Planning, Development and Governor Support)   B. Glockling

Head *(Professional Centre Services)*   D. Bowey
Head *(Research and Evaluation)*   J. Bren
Head *(Special and Family Services)*   A. Harris
Manager *(Pupil Services)*   G. Carter
Manager *(Student Finance)*   C. Green
Principal Education Welfare Officer   S. Macaulay
Principal Educational Psychologist   P. Prior
Number of Schools
10 Secondary; 9 Special

EDUCATION OVERVIEW AND SCRUTINY COMMITTEE

Con: 10, Lab: 2
Chair (Overview and Scrutiny Committee)
   Cllr T. Strickland (Con)
Deputy Chair   Cllr A. Dunn (Con)
Executive Member (Education)   Cllr M. Grimston (Con)
Members of the Committee
Con: Cousins, Dawe, Hime, McNaught-Davis, Nurse,
Prichard, Roberts, Robson
Lab: Belton, Gibbons

Westminster City Council

www.westminster.gov.uk

Population: 222 000
Political composition: Con: 48, Lab: 12
Westminster City Hall, Victoria St, London SW1E 6QP;
   URL www.westminster.gov.uk; Tel (switchboard)
   020 7641 6000

Children and Community Services Department

URL www.westminster.gov.uk/educationandlearning
Deputy Chief Executive (Children and Community Services)
   Julie Jones; Fax 020 7641 2246
Director   Phyl Crawford
Director (Children and Families Social Services)
   Michael O'Connor; Tel 020 7641 2253; Fax 020 7641 3406
Director (Housing)   Rosemary Westbrook;
   Tel 020 7641 2576; Fax 020 7641 1904
Director (Lifelong Learning)   Mike Potter
Director (Older People, Disability and Health Services)
   Marian Harrington; Tel 020 7641 1940
Director (Schools)   Mary Fowler
Director (Specialist Social Care Services and Development)
   Vivienne Lukey; Tel 020 7641 1964
Assistant Director (Contracting and Best Value)
   Terry Cotton; Tel 020 7641 1939
Assistant Director (Finance and Business Services)
   Caroline Holland; Tel 020 7641 2297
Assistant Director (Schools)   Mary Fowler
Assistant Director (Strategy and Performance)   Sean Rafferty;
   Tel 020 7641 2273
Assistant Director (Trading Wing: Westminster Care Services)
   Philip Bradshaw; e-mail
   pbrardshaw@westminster.gov.uk; Tel 020 7641 2262;
   Fax 020 7641 2246
Assistant Director (Young People and Adult Learning)
   Mike Potter
Head *(Early Childhood Services)*   Jennifer Greenwood
Head *(SEN and Additional Needs)*   June Simson
Number of Schools
40 Primary; 8 Secondary; 4 Nursery; 2 Special

CABINET

Cabinet Member (Leisure and Lifelong Learning)   Greg Clark
Cabinet Member (Schools)   Cllr Brian Connell

ARTS AND LEISURE OVERVIEW AND SCRUTINY COMMITTEE

Chair   Cllr Susie Burbridge

EDUCATION OVERVIEW AND SCRUTINY COMMITTEE

Chair   Cllr Carolyn Keam
Members of the Committee
Allum, Bianco, Barns, Bull, Page, Rees-Mogg, Schmeling,
Stockill, Thorne, Rev Bradley, Gabrielle Barry, Michael
Beckett, Christopher Keif

LEARNING SERVICES OVERVIEW AND SCRUTINY COMMITTEE

Nominated Chair   Cllr Tim Mitchell; PO Box 240, City Hall,
   64 Victoria St, London SW1E 6QP
Nominated Vice-Chair   Cllr Susie Burbridge (Con)
Nominated Vice-Chair   Cllr Simon Stockill (Lab)
Members of the Committee
Con: Edward Agar, Frances Blois, Nick Evans, Gwyneth
Hampson, Phillip Roe, Nick Yarker
Lab: Barbara Grahame, Papya Qureshi
Co-opted voting representatives: Mohammed Amieur (Parent
Governor - Primary), Brenda Morrisson (Church of England
Diocese), Dr Sonny Sharma (Parent Governor - Secondary)
Co-opted non-voting representatives: Elizabeth Phillips
(Headteacher, St. Marylebone CE School)

SUPPORTING CHILDREN OVERVIEW AND SCRUTINY COMMITTEE

Chair   Cllr Carolyn Keen

NORTH EAST

Cleveland County Council

In April 1996 Cleveland County Council, Hartlepool
Borough Council, Langbaurgh-on-Tees Borough Council,
Middlesbrough Borough Council and Stockton-on-Tees
Borough Council were replaced by Hartlepool Borough
Council, Middlesbrough Council, Redcar and Cleveland
Borough Council and Stockton-on-Tees Borough Council –
each responsible for all local government services in its area.
These councils are listed separately in this section.

Darlington Borough Council

www.darlington.gov.uk

Population: 77 869
Political composition: Lab: 34, Con: 14, LD: 3, Ind: 2
Town Hall, Darlington DL1 5QT;
   URL www.darlington.gov.uk; e-mail
   enquiries@darlington.gov.uk; Tel 01325 380651;
   Fax 01325 382032
Chief Executive   Ada Burns

Children's Services

Tel 01325 388060; Fax 01325 388688
Director (Children's Services)   Margaret Asquith
Assistant Director (Policy, Planning and Resources)
   George McQueen; e-mail
   george.mcqueen@darlington.gov.uk; Tel 01325 388813
Assistant Director (School Effectiveness Service)
   David Walker
Head *(Capital Programmes)*   Kevin Duffy
Head *(Curriculum, Learning and Development)*
   Sharon Lissaman
Head *(Early Years Service)*   Christine Archer
Head *(Performance and Development)*   Julian Kenshole
Head *(Pupil Support Services)*   Gill Walker
Head *(Resources)*   Ian Coxon
Head *(SEN)*   Cate Crallan
Cabinet Member (Children's Services)   Chris McEwan

Number of Schools
30 Primary; 7 Secondary; 2 Nursery; 1 Special

RESOURCES SCRUTINY

Chair   I.G. Hazeldine
Members of the Committee
R. Francis, C.G. Hutchinson, C.V. Johnson, T. Richmond, E.
Roberts, F.S. Robson, B.Thistlethwaite, G.B. Walker, E.
Wilson

Durham County Council
www.durham.gov.uk

In April 1997 Darlington became a separate unitary
authority and is listed separately in this section. Durham
County Council retains a two-tier structure.
Population: 492 300
Political composition: Lab: 53, LD: 5, Ind: 3, Con: 2
County Hall, Durham, County Durham DH1 5UL;
   URL www.durham.gov.uk; e-mail
   help@durham.gov.uk; Tel 0191 383 3000;
   Fax 0191 383 4500
Chief Executive   Vacancy

Children and Young People's Services

Corporate Director   David Williams
Head (Access and Inclusion Services)   Maureen Clare
Head (Achievement Services)   Dave Ford
Head (Extended Services)   Amanda Johnson
Head (Finance Services)   Phil Barclay
Head (Safeguarding and Specialist Services)   Gail Hopper
Head (Strategic Commissioning)   Carole Payne
Head (Support Services)   Neil Charlton
Number of Schools
233 Primary; 36 Secondary; 12 Nursery; 10 Special; 1 PRU

Gateshead Council
www.gateshead.gov.uk

Population: 191 500
Political composition: Lab: 41, LD: 23, Liberal: 1
Civic Centre, Regent St, Gateshead, Tyne and Wear
   NE8 1HH; URL www.gateshead.gov.uk; e-mail
   enquiries@gateshead.gov.uk; Tel 0191 433 3000;
   Fax 0191 478 3495
Chief Executive   R.M. Kelly

Learning and Children

Fax 0191 490 1168
Chief Executive   R. Kelly
*Group Director (Learning and Children); Director (Children's
   Services)*   Dr M. Atkinson
Director (Learning and Schools)   David Mitchell BA, LTCL
Head (Access and Inclusion)   Bob Campion
Head (Behavioural Support Services)   Jim Nevitt
Head (Business Strategy and Support)   Andy Crabtree
Head (Ethnic Minority and Traveller Achievement Service)
   Veena Soni
Head (Raising Achievement); Chief Inspector   Paul Carvin
Senior Manager (Primary Strategy); Inspector   C. O'Neill
Service Manager (Education of Looked-After Children)
   Dr Liz Hunter
*Manager (Access and Social Inclusion); Education Welfare
   Officer*   Ken Johnson CQSW
Manager (Business Support and Dryden Centre)   M. Howe

Manager (Financial Support Services)   D.M. Cowper DMS
Manager (Individual Needs Service)   Susan Ratliff
Manager (Performance Management and Planning)
   A. Whitfield (Acting)
Manager (Pupil Services)   Deborah Alder
Manager (School Organisation and Development)
   Sandra Punton
Manager (Secondary Strategy); Inspector (Secondary)
   L. Gleave
Manager (Staffing Support)   P. Purvis
Adviser (Data Analysis and Performance)   D. Adamson
Adviser (ICT)   M. Thompson
Adviser (PE/Health Education/Sport)   A. Davies
Senior Inspector (Secondary)   Chris Cottam
Senior Inspector (Secondary Innovations and Development)
   S. Horne
*Inspector (CPD/Primary Education: Leadership/Management/
   Maths/Primary MFL/Primary G and T/NQT Induction)*
   A. Sergison
Inspector (Primary Education: Early Years)   Sue Waugh
*Inspector (Primary Education: Learning and Teaching
   Assessment)*   T. Nelson
Inspector (Primary Education: Literacy/Numeracy)   C. Snee
*Inspector (Secondary Education: Leadership and Management/
   Education Otherwise/Secondary NQTs/NPQH/Ofsted Co-
   ordination/TIPD/ASTs)*   K. Self
Inspector (Secondary EIC Co-ordinator/Post 16)   M.C. Coburn
   MA, BA
Inspector (SEN and Inclusion)   A. Muxworthy
Principal Educational Psychologist   Liz Elliott
Principal Officer (Community Development)   Vacancy
Number of Schools
70 Primary; 10 Secondary; 6 Special

GOVERNOR TRAINING UNIT

Dryden Centre, Evistones Rd, Gateshead, Tyne and Wear
   NE9 5UR; Tel 0191 433 8500; Fax 0191 491 1394
Manager (Governing Bodies)   Jacqui Ridley
Services offered
Training programme support for individual governing
bodies in development of their own training programme
and use of funding through provision of newsletter, training
materials and equipment

BEHAVIOURAL SUPPORT SERVICES

Bleach Green Centre   Ash St, Blaydon, Gateshead, Tyne and
   Wear NE21 5HS; Tel 0191 414 4233
   Teacher-in-Charge   Ms S. Murphy
Heworth Hall Centre   Smithburn Rd, Felling, Gateshead,
   Tyne and Wear NE8 4JN; Tel 0191 438 0111
   Teacher-in-Charge   Les Burns
Millway Centre   Millway, Sheriff Hill, Gateshead, Tyne and
   Wear NE9 5PQ; Tel 0191 420 0606; Fax 0191 491 5114
   Teacher-in-Charge   Susan Arciero
Shipcote Centre   Edendale Terr, Gateshead, Tyne and Wear
   NE8 4JN; Tel 0191 477 4835; Fax 0191 477 1663
   Teacher-in-Charge   Sheila Atkinson

PUPIL SERVICES

Dryden Centre, Evistones Rd, Gateshead, Tyne and Wear
   NE9 5UR; Tel 0191 433 8500; Fax 0191 491 1394

Hartlepool Borough Council
www.hartlepool.gov.uk

Political composition: Lab: 24, Ind: 12, LD: 7, Con: 4
Civic Centre, Victoria Rd, Hartlepool TS24 8AY;
   URL www.hartlepool.gov.uk; Tel 01429 266522;
   Fax 01429 523599
Chief Executive   Paul Walker

Children's Services Department

Fax 01429 523750
Director (Children's Services)   Adrienne Simcock
Assistant Director (Performance and Achievement)
    John Collings
Assistant Director (Planning and Service Integration)
    Sue Johnson
Assistant Director (Resources and Support Services)
    Paul Briggs
Assistant Director (Safeguarding and Specialist Services)
    Vacancy
Head (Finance)   Steve Haley
Senior Adviser (Enrichment)   Paul Wilkinson
Senior Adviser (Primary)   Janice Sheraton-Wright
Number of Schools
30 Primary; 6 Secondary; 2 Special; 1 Nursery; 1 PRU

Cabinet

Portfolio Holder   Cllr Cath Hill

Middlesbrough Council
www.middlesbrough.gov.uk

Population: 137 900
Political composition: Lab: 26, Ind: 12, Con: 6, LD: 2, Miarton
Independent Group: 2
Town Hall, PO Box 99a, Middlesbrough TS1 2QQ;
    URL www.middlesbrough.gov.uk; Tel 01642 245432
Mayor   Ray Mallon
Chief Executive   Jan Richmond
Executive Director (Regeneration)   Tim White

Children, Families and Learning

PO Box 69, Vancouver Hse, Gurney St, Middlesbrough
    TS1 1EL; e-mail jan_douglas@middlesbrough.gov.uk;
    Tel 01642 728301; Fax 01642 728970
Executive Member (Children's Services)   Cllr Jan Brunton
Executive Member (Education and Skills)
    Cllr Paul Thompson
Executive Director   Jan Douglas
Deputy Director; Head (Family Services)   Vacancy
*Assistant Director (Organisational Development and
    Performance)*   Gill Rollings
Head (Capital and Assets Service)   Terry Sutcliffe
Head (Community Education Services)   Andy White
Head (Policy and Resources Services)   Julie Cordiner
Head (Pupil Support Service)   Dave Johnson
Head (School Improvement Service)   Rosemary Morris
Assistant Head (School Improvement Service)   Kevin Buckle
Principal Adviser (Inclusion and Vulnerable Children)
    June Kearns
Principal Adviser (Primary)   Andrew Mackie
Senior Standards Adviser (Primary)   Jennifer Bell
Senior Standards Adviser (Secondary)   David Snaith
Consultant (Human Resources)   Harry Eagling
Strategic Accountant   Fiona Buck
Number of Schools
42 Primary; 6 Secondary; 9 Special; 3 City Academies

GOVERNOR TRAINING UNIT

Governor Support Services, PO Box 69, Vancouver Hse,
    Gurney St, Middlesbrough TS1 1EL; Tel 01642 728108

PSYCHOLOGICAL SERVICES

Children, Families and Learning, MTLC, Tranmere Ave,
    Middlesbrough TS3 8PB; Tel 01642 201851
Principal Education Psychologist   Janet Philpott

OUTDOOR PURSUITS CENTRES

Lanehead Outdoor Pursuits Centre   Lanehead, Coniston,
    Cumbria LA21 8AA; Tel 01539 441293
    Contact   Janet Prier
Stainsacre Hall Residential Youth Centre   Stainsacre, Whitby,
    North Yorkshire YO22 4NT; Tel 01904 603214
    Contact   Mick Prior

Newcastle upon Tyne City Council
www.newcastle.gov.uk

Population: 293 600
Civic Centre, Barras Bridge, Newcastle upon Tyne, Tyne
    and Wear NE1 8PR; URL www.newcastle.gov.uk;
    Tel 0191 232 8520; Fax 0191 211 4972

Education Offices

Lab: 62, LD: 16
City Education Dept, Civic Centre, Barras Bridge, Newcastle
    upon Tyne, Tyne and Wear NE1 8PU
Chair (Education Select Committee)   Cllr Lillian Kennedy
Leader of the Council   Cllr A.G. Flynn
*Deputy Leader of the Council; Spokesperson (Lifelong Learning
    and Training)*   Keith Taylor (Lab)
Executive Director (Children's Services)   Catherine Fitt
Head (Education)   David Clegg
Head (Standards and Effectiveness Unit)   David Clegg
Head (Strategic Management and Performance)
    Marian Howett
Senior Adviser (Early Years)   Helen Cavanagh
Senior Adviser (Performance and Review)   Ray Steele
Senior Adviser (Primary)   Karen Bower
General Adviser (KS3)   David Mulholland
General Adviser (Music)   Steve Halsey
General Adviser (Numeracy)   Gustav MacLeod
General Adviser (PE)   Dot Anderson-Cryer
*General Adviser (Primary Literacy and Leadership and
    Management)*   Vacancy
General Adviser (SEN and Inclusion)   Linda Water
Principal Educational Psychologist
    Kathleen Richardson (Acting)
Co-ordinator (Excellence Challenge)   Judy Norris
Co-ordinator (G and T)   Gair Hedley
Learning Mentor (EIC)   Chris Davison
Number of Schools
72 First/Primary; 11 Secondary; 5 Nursery; 5 Special; 3
Middle; 2 Early Years Centres
School Population
39 624

GOVERNOR TRAINING UNIT

Governor Information Development and Support,
    Education Department, Newcastle upon Tyne, Tyne and
    Wear NE1 8PU; Tel 0191 232 8520; Fax 0191 211 4983
Agency Manager   N. Sanders
Services offered
Training; clerking service; conferences; newsletters;
governor information points; telephone helpline; governor
forums

EDUCATION DEVELOPMENT CENTRE

Newcastle Springfield Centre   Blakelaw Rd, Newcastle upon
    Tyne, Tyne and Wear NE3 5HU; Tel 0191 277 4401
    Contact   W. Banks

North Tyneside Council

www.northtyneside.gov.uk

Population: 193 600
Political composition: Lab: 39, Con: 13, LD: 8
Town Hall, High St East, Wallsend, Tyne and Wear
NE28 7RR; URL www.northtyneside.gov.uk;
Tel 0191 200 6565; Fax 0191 200 7273
Graham Hse, Benton, Newcastle upon Tyne, Tyne and Wear
NE12 9TQ; Tel 0191 200 7575; Fax 0191 200 7440
Head (Legal) Maria Lucas; Tel 0191 200 5317;
Fax 0191 200 5858
Head (Policy) Rob Worrall; Tel 0191 200 1183;
Fax 0191 200 7273
Head (Schools Services) Gill Alexander; Tel 0191 200 5002;
Fax 0191 200 5060

Education Service

Stephenson Hse, Stephenson St, North Shields, Tyne and
Wear NE30 1QA; Tel 0191 200 5022; Fax 0191 200 6090
Strategic Director (Children, Young People and Learning)
Gill Alexander BA, MA
Head (Access and Inclusion) John Scott MA
Head (Planning, Commissioning and Quality Assurance)
Peter Parish MA
Head (Resources and Operation) Mark Longstaff
Head (Standards and Effectiveness) Kevin Willis
Manager (Statutory Assessment and Review Service)
Janet Young
Senior Inspector Jean Griffith
Senior Inspector (English) B. Jordan BEd(Hons), MA
*Senior Inspector (History/Geography/Modern Languages/RE/
Environmental Education)* A.F. Heinzman BA, MEd
Senior Inspector (SEN) Mick McCabe
Inspector (Home Economics/Health/PSE) D. Greaves
Inspector (ICT) Dean Jackson
Inspector (SEN) M. McCabe
General Inspector (KS3) C. Weaver
General Inspector (Leadership and Management) A. James
Education Inspection (Primary) D. Shearsmith MSc
Number of Schools
11 Secondary; 5 Special; 4 Middle

CHILDREN AND YOUNG PEOPLE SELECT COMMITTEE

Con 1, Lab 8, LD 1
*Lead Member (Children and Young People/Policy and Resources
Committee)* R. Lackenby; Town Hall, Wallsend, Tyne
and Wear NE28 7RR
Chair A. McGlade; 3 Park Villas, The Green, Wallsend,
Tyne and Wear NE28 7NW
Deputy-Chair N.J. Huscroft; 146 St Peter's Rd, Wallsend,
Tyne and Wear NE28 7HH

LEARNING SUPPORT SERVICE

Hadrian Education Centre, Addington Dr, Wallsend, Tyne
and Wear NE28 9RT; Tel 0191 200 6981
Manager John Waldron

BEHAVIOUR AND ATTENDANCE SUPPORT SERVICE

Hadrian Education Centre, Addington Dr, Wallsend, Tyne
and Wear NE28 9RT; Tel 0191 200 8641
Manager (Acting) Hazel Brown

LANGUAGE UNITS

Goathland Primary School Goathland Ave, Longbenton,
Newcastle upon Tyne, Tyne and Wear NE12 8LH;
Tel 0191 200 7427
Headteacher Mrs S.A. Tickell
Waterville Primary School Waterville Rd, North Shields,
Tyne and Wear NE29 6SL; Tel 0191 200 6351
Headteacher Mrs J. Forster

ADULT CONTINUING EDUCATION CENTRES

Burnside Community High School Boyd Rd, Wallsend, Tyne
and Wear NE28 7AF; Tel (enquiries) 0191 200 8329
Churchill Community College Churchill St, Wallsend, Tyne
and Wear NE28 7TN; Tel 0191 262 3497
George Stephenson Community High School Stephenson
Centre, Killingworth, Newcastle upon Tyne, Tyne and
Wear NE12 0YB; Tel (enquiries) 0191 200 8329
John Spence Community High School North Rd, Preston,
North Shields, Tyne and Wear NE29 9PU;
Tel 0191 200 5220
Longbenton Community College Hailsham Ave,
Longbenton, Newcastle upon Tyne, Tyne and Wear
NE12 8ER; Tel 0191 200 7423
Marden High School Hartington Rd, North Shields, Tyne
and Wear NE30 3RZ; Tel (enquiries) 0191 200 8329
Monkseaton Community High School Seatonville Rd,
Monkseaton, Whitley Bay, Tyne and Wear NE25 9EQ;
Tel (enquiries) 0191 200 8329
Seaton Burn Community College Dudley La, Seaton Burn,
Newcastle upon Tyne, Tyne and Wear NE13 6HB;
Tel (enquiries) 0191 200 8329
Whitley Bay High School Deneholm, Whitley Bay, Tyne and
Wear NE25 9AS; Tel (enquiries) 0191 200 8329

Northumberland County Council

www.northumberland.gov.uk

Population: 310 000
Political composition: Lab: 38, Con: 17, LD: 9, Ind: 3
County Hall, Morpeth, Northumberland NE61 2EF;
URL www.northumberland.gov.uk; Tel 01670 533000;
Fax 01670 533253
Chief Executive Alan Clarke
Chair of the County Council Ian Swithenbank
Director (Finance) Clive Burns

Education Directorate

Fax 01670 533605
Director B. Edwards (Acting)
Senior Education Officer D.M. Jenkins
Principal Educational Psychologist B.V. Daly
Senior Educational Psychologist J. Taylor
Principal Adviser A. Rusby
Adviser (English) C. Reeves
Adviser (First Schools) H. Wood
Adviser (First Schools/Assessment) V. Cassell
Adviser (IT) R. Taylor
Adviser (Modern Languages) R. Remacle
Adviser (PE) L. Swainston
Adviser (Primary) N. Hogg
Adviser (SEN) S. Pinner
Adviser (Young Peoples Issues) E. O'Connor
Adviser; Inspector (Science) K. Sample
Number of Schools
45 Middle; 15 Secondary

SPOKESPERSON (CHILDREN'S SERVICES)

Member J. Wright (Lab)
Head (Children's Services) J. Morris (Lab)

GOVERNOR TRAINING UNIT

Advisory and Inspection Division, Education Development
Centre, Morpeth, Northumberland NE61 6NF;
Tel 01670 533000; Fax 01670 533591
Education Officer (PRMS) T.M. Richardson
Services offered
Governor training

EDUCATION WELFARE OFFICES

County Hall, Morpeth, Northumberland NE61 2EF;
Tel 01670 533000; Fax 01670 533750
Principal Education Welfare Officer   M.R. Macdonald
Alnwick Education Welfare Office   54 Bondgate Within,
Alnwick, Northumberland NE66 1JD; Tel 01665 605428;
Fax 01665 606121
Senior Education Welfare Officer   L.M. McAvoy
Blyth Education Welfare Office   107a Waterloo Rd, Blyth,
Northumberland NE24 1BY; Tel 01670 361874;
Fax 01670 369236
Senior Education Welfare Officer   L.M. McAvoy
Hexham Education Welfare Office   The Gatehouse, Wanless
La, Hexham, Northumberland NE46 1BU;
Tel 01434 605973; Fax 01434 600357
Senior Education Welfare Officer   S. Lister
Morpeth Education Welfare Office   Newgate Hse, 94
Newgate St, Morpeth, Northumberland NE61 1BU;
Tel 01670 511474; Fax 01670 517616
Senior Education Welfare Officer   A. Cunningham

PSYCHOLOGICAL SERVICES

Tyne House   Hepscott Pk, Stannington, Morpeth,
Northumberland NE61 6NF; Tel 01670 534300;
Fax 01670 534327
Principal Educational Psychologist   B.V. Daly

SERVICES FOR PUPILS WITH A COMMUNICATION DISORDER

Till House Centre   Hepscott Pk, Morpeth, Northumberland
NE61 6NF; Tel 01670 534344; Fax 01670 534343
Head of Service   S. Grigor

UNITS FOR PUPILS WITH A COMMUNICATION DISORDER

Abbeyfields County First School   Abbots Way, Morpeth,
Northumberland NE61 2LZ; Tel 01670 513582
Headteacher   J. Robinson
Hexham East County First School   Beaufront Ave, Hexham,
Northumberland NE46 1JD; Tel 01434 603467;
Fax 01434 603467
Headteacher   J. Palmer

CENTRES AND UNITS FOR HEARING IMPAIRED CHILDREN

Blyth Horton Grange First School   Blyth, Northumberland
NE24 4RE; Tel 01670 353503; Fax 01670 354276
Headteacher   J. Philipson
Cramlington Community High School   Highburn,
Cramlington, Northumberland NE23 6BN;
Tel 01670 712311; Fax 01670 730598
Headteacher   S. Mobberley
Holy Trinity First School   Bell Tower Pl, Berwick-upon-
Tweed, Northumberland TD15 1NB; Tel 01289 306142
Headteacher   S. Churchill
Southlands County Middle School   Westloch Rd,
Cramlington, Northumberland NE23 6LW;
Tel 01670 714475; Fax 01670 734968
Headteacher   L. Bohill
Till House   Hepscott Pk, Stannington, Morpeth,
Northumberland NE61 6NF; Tel 01670 534313;
Fax 01670 534343
Head of Service   P. Loftus

OUTDOOR EDUCATION CENTRE

Ford Castle Residential Centre   Ford, Berwick-upon-Tweed,
Northumberland TD15 2PX; Tel 01890 820257

TEACHERS' CENTRE

Education Development Centre   Hepscott Pk, Stannington,
Morpeth, Northumberland NE61 6NF; Tel 01670 533000

Redcar and Cleveland Borough Council
www.redcar-cleveland.gov.uk

Population: 139 000
Political composition: Lab: 22, LD: 15, Con: 13, Ind: 9
Town Hall, Fabian Rd, South Bank, Middlesbrough
TS6 9AR; URL www.redcar-cleveland.gov.uk;
Tel 01642 444000; Fax 01642 444584
Chief Executive   Colin Moore

Children's Services Department

PO Box 83, Council Offices, Kirkleatham St, Redcar, Redcar
and Cleveland TS10 1YA; Fax 01642 444122
Director   Jenny Lewis; Fax 01642 771184
Head (Achievement and Inclusion)   Vacancy
Head (Community Learning)   Allan Cassidy
*Head (In School Support Service); Principal Education
Psychologist*   Alastair Robertson
Head (Standards)   Brian Lewis
Head (Strategy)   Kaye Mount
Manager (ICT Centre)   David Major
Principal Youth and Community Officer   Rod Weston-
Bartholomew
Senior Adviser (Curriculum and Assessment)   Barry Holley
Senior Adviser (GEST)   Mike Lewis
SEN Officer   Kate Redfern
Number of Schools
12 Secondary; 2 Special
Day of Meeting
Tuesday

COUNCIL EXECUTIVE

Lead Member (Children's Services)   Val Halton
Cabinet Member (Education)   Steve Kay

PSYCHOLOGICAL SERVICE

Children's Services, Corporation Rd, Redcar, Redcar and
Cleveland TS10 1HA; Tel 01642 286644; Fax 01642 282146
Head   A. Robertson (Acting)

EDUCATION DEVELOPMENT CENTRES

City Learning Centre, Eston   Normanby Rd, South Bank,
Middlesbrough TS6 9AE; e-mail enquiries@clceston.com;
Tel 01642 467138; Fax 01642 770579
Director   Mr S. Nimmo
Education ICT Centre   Redcar EDC, Corporation Rd, Redcar
and Cleveland TS10 1HA; Tel 01642 286688;
Fax 01642 282151
Centre Manager   Mr D. Major
Excellence in Cities   Cooper Centre, Beech Gr, South Bank,
Middlesbrough TS6 6SU; e-mail
excellence_in_cities@redcar-cleveland.gov.uk;
Tel 01642 461321; Fax 01642 468751
Co-ordinator   Mr G. Davey
Guisborough Education Development Centre   Old Northgate
School, Wilton La, Guisborough, Redcar and Cleveland
TS14 6JA; Tel 01287 632572; Fax 01287 610177
Literacy Development Centre   Cooper Centre, Beech Gr,
South Bank, Middlesbrough TS6 6SU; e-mail
literacy_centre@redcar-cleveland.gov.uk;
Tel 01642 466507; Fax 01642 468289

YOUTH AND COMMUNITY CENTRES

Brotton Youth Centre   Freebrough Community College,
Brotton Centre, Linden Rd, Brotton, Saltburn-by-the-Sea,
Redcar and Cleveland TS12 2SJ; Tel 01287 677141;
Fax 01287 677222

California Youth Centre Guisborough St, Eston,
Middlesbrough TS6 9LA; e-mail califoyc@aol.co.uk;
Tel 01642 453330; Fax 01642 453330

Eston Park Youth Centre Eston Pk, Burns Rd, South Bank,
Middlesbrough TS6 9AW; Tel 01642 452196;
Fax 01642 452196

Grangetown Youth and Community Centre Broadway,
Grangetown, Middlesbrough TS6 7HP; Tel 01642 455435;
Fax 01642 455435

Grenfell Youth Club/Learning Difficulties Ridley St, Redcar,
Redcar and Cleveland TS10 1RF; Tel 01642 471747;
Minicom 01642 616110

Guisborough Youth Centre Laurence Jackson School,
Church La, Guisborough, Redcar and Cleveland
TS14 6DD; Tel 01287 634332; Fax 01287 634332

Lingdale Youth Centre High St, Lingdale, Saltburn-by-the-
Sea, Redcar and Cleveland TS12 3EP; Tel 01287 653529;
Fax 01287 653529

Loftus Youth and Community Centre Duncan Pl, Loftus,
Saltburn-by-the-Sea, Redcar and Cleveland TS13 4PR;
Tel 01287 640654; Fax 01287 643971

Marske Youth Centre Bydales School, Marlborough Ave,
Marske, Redcar, Redcar and Cleveland TS11 6AR;
Tel 01642 485602; Fax 01642 685602

Nunthorpe Youth Centre Guisborough Rd, Nunthorpe,
Middlesbrough TS7 0LA; Tel 01642 316818;
Fax 01642 316818

Redcar Youth Centre Burnhamthorpe, Coatham Rd, Redcar,
Redcar and Cleveland TS10 1RP; e-mail
redcaryc@aol.com; Tel 01642 482174; Fax 01642 775201

Redcar Youth and Community Centre Ayton Dr, Redcar,
Redcar and Cleveland TS10 4EW; e-mail
ryccayton@aol.com; Tel 01642 487297; Fax 01642 485871

Saltburn Youth Centre Saltburn School Annexe, Marske Rd,
Saltburn-by-the-Sea, Redcar and Cleveland TS12 1QA;
Tel 01287 623783; Fax 01287 623783

Skelton Youth Centre Freebrough Community College,
Skelton Centre, Skelton, Saltburn, Redcar and Cleveland
TS12 2HA; Tel 01287 651276; Fax 01287 651276

South Bank Youth and Community Centre Upper Jackson St,
South Bank, Middlesbrough TS6 6PN; Tel 01642 466748;
Fax 01642 466748

West Redcar Youth Centre Youth Annexe, West Redcar
School, Redcar, Redcar and Cleveland TS10 4AB;
Tel 01642 483949; Fax 01642 483949

ADVICE RESOURCE AND COUNSELLING SERVICES

Awards and Activities Support Service, Duke of Edinburgh's
Award, Youth Achievement Awards c/o Redcar Youth
Centre, Coatham Rd, Redcar, Redcar and Cleveland
TS10 1RP; e-mail awards@7points.co.uk;
Tel 01642 498103

East Cleveland Advice Resource and Counselling Service c/o
Skelton Youth Centre, Freebrough Community College,
Skelton Centre, Marske La, Skelton, Saltburn-by-the-Sea,
Redcar and Cleveland TS12 2HA; Tel 01287 654821;
Fax 01287 654821

Grangetown and South Bank SRB, Advice Resource and
Counselling Service/Youth Voice Project Grangetown
Youth and Community Centre, Broadway, Grangetown,
Redcar and Cleveland TS6 7AP; Tel 01642 206224

Redcar SRB, Advice Resource and Counselling Service
Redcar Youth Centre, Coatham Rd, Redcar, Redcar and
Cleveland TS10 1RP; Tel 01642 775987

Skelton SRB, Advice Resource and Counselling Service
Skelton Youth Centre, Freebrough Community College,
Skelton Centre, Skelton, Saltburn-by-the-Sea, Redcar and
Cleveland TS12 2HA; Tel 01287 654821

Youthwise SRB Detached Youth Work Project, PO Box 69,
South Bank, Redcar and Cleveland TS6 6GF;
Tel 01642 465739

ADULT EDUCATION CENTRES

Bankfields Local Learning Centre Bankfields Primary
School, Mansfield Rd, Eston, Redcar and Cleveland
TS6 0RZ; Tel 01642 756454; Fax 01642 775899
Manager Denise Bollands

Coatham Local Learning Centre Coatham Primary School,
Coatham Rd, Redcar, Redcar and Cleveland TS10 1QY;
Tel 01642 756454; Fax 01642 775899
Manager Denise Bollands

Dormanstown Local Learning Centre Dormanstown
Primary School, South Ave, Dormanstown, Redcar and
Cleveland TS10 5LY; Tel 01642 756454; Fax 01642 489040
Manager Denise Bollands

Gillbrook Adult Education Centre Gillbrook School,
Normanby Rd, South Bank, Redcar and Cleveland
TS6 9AG; Tel 01642 466201; Fax 01642 463905
Manager Richard Oliver

Guisborough Adult Education Centre Laurence Jackson
School, Guisborough, Redcar and Cleveland TS14 6RD;
Tel 01287 631849; Fax 01287 610309
Manager Les Thomson

Nunthorpe Adult Education Centre Nunthorpe Community
School, Nunthorpe, Redcar and Cleveland TS7 0LA;
Tel 01642 310561; Fax 01642 325672
Manager Mike Wright

Redcar Adult Education Centre Corporation Rd, Redcar,
Redcar and Cleveland TS10 1HA; Tel 01642 490409;
Fax 01642 492388
Principal John Harris

Skelton Local Learning Centre Skelton Junior School, Station
La, Skelton, Redcar and Cleveland TS12 2LR;
Tel 01642 756454; Fax 01287 654496
Manager Jacqui Callaghan; c/o Coatham Local
Learning Centre

EDUCATION OTHER THAN AT SCHOOL SERVICE

Normanby Rd, Normanby, Middlesbrough TS6 9AD;
Tel 01642 440225; Fax 01642 463751
Head of Service Ms K. Smith

South Tyneside Council
www.southtyneside.info

Population: 151 489
Political composition: Lab: 34, Ind: 7, Prog: 6, LD: 4, Con: 3
Town Hall and Civic Offices, Westoe Rd, South Shields,
Tyne and Wear NE33 2RL;
URL www.southtyneside.info; Tel 0191 427 1717;
Fax 0191 455 0208

Lifelong Learning and Leisure Directorate

Fax 0191 427 0584
Executive Director Kim Bromley-Derry
Director (Excellence in Cities) L. Howe
Head (Access and Inclusion) A. Bradley
Head (Cultural and Community Services) T. Duggan
Head (Lifelong Learning) C. Smith
Head (School Improvement) M. Dillon
Head (Strategy and Resources) G. Rollings
Senior Manager (Student Finance) D. Morgan
Manager (Adult and Community Learning) S. Chopra
Manager (Community Development) S. Chilton
Manager (Cultural Development) B. Atkinson
Manager (Cultural Operations) R. Jago
Manager (Education Welfare Service) J.A. Soulsby
Manager (Finance) Julie Allison
Manager (Governors' Administration and Support)
A. Locklan
Manager (Libraries) M. Freeman
Manager (Personnel) M.R. Grady

Manager (Pupil Services) B. Davis
Manager (Pupil Services) S. Makin BSc, MA, PGCE
Manager (Schools Services) L.D. Rodgers
Manager (SEN and Assessment Support Service) M. Walsh
Manager (Youth Support Services) V. High
Project Manager J. Burrow
School Improvement Officer M. Brooks
Senior Adviser (Primary) P. Cutts
Senior Adviser (Projects) M. Donnellan
Co-ordinator (Learning Development) K. Hutchinson
Co-ordinator (Outdoor Education) D. Addison
Education Business Partnership M. Riches
Finance Officer (Schools) S. Hope
Personnel Officer M. Dixon
Personnel Officer B. Morris
School Meals Contractor (In House) E. Luke
Under 13s Officer M. Welch
Youth Work Officer S. Southern
Number of Schools
51 Primary; 10 Secondary; 6 Special; 4 Nursery; 1 Pupil
Referral Unit
Other Authorities with whom Joint Purchasing Arrangements are made
North Eastern Purchasing Organisation (certain items only)

GOVERNORS' ADMINISTRATION

Lifelong Learning and Leisure Directorate, Town Hall Civic
Offices, South Shields, Tyne and Wear NE33 2RL;
Tel 0191 427 1717; Fax 0191 427 0584
Governor Support Manager Alex Locklan
Services offered
Comprehensive training package to school governors; link
governor network; resource base; termly newsletter;
telephone helpline

SCHOOL PSYCHOLOGICAL, CHILD GUIDANCE SERVICE AND SPECIAL NEEDS SUPPORT CENTRE

Chuter Ede Education Centre Galsworthy Rd, South Shields,
Tyne and Wear; Tel 0191 519 1909; Fax 0191 519 0600

ADULT EDUCATION, YOUTH AND COMMUNITY CENTRES

All Saints Community Centre Stanley St, South Shields,
Tyne and Wear NE34 0BX; Tel 0191 456 1185
Boldon Colliery Village Hall ASDA Complex, North Rd,
Boldon Colliery, Tyne and Wear NE35 9AR;
Tel 0191 536 3841
Jarrow Community Centre Cambrian St, Jarrow, Tyne and
Wear NE32 3QK; Tel 0191 489 4100
Boldon Lane Learning Centre Boldon La, South Shields,
Tyne and Wear NE34 0LZ; Tel 0191 427 0011
Low Simonside Community Centre Taunton Ave, Jarrow,
Tyne and Wear NE32 3RT; Tel 0191 489 8224
Brinkburn Community Centre Brinkburn Comprehensive
School, McAnany Ave, South Shields, Tyne and Wear
NE34 0PJ; Tel 0191 455 8491; Fax 0191 454 0300
Lukes Lane Community Centre Marine Dr, Lukes Lane Est,
Hebburn, Tyne and Wear NE31 2AX; Tel 0191 489 2358;
Fax 0191 489 2358
Mid Tyne Activities Centre Grange Rd, Jarrow, Tyne and
Wear NE32 3QN; Tel 0191 489 7594; Fax 0191 489 7595
The Cave Youth Centre Captains Row, South Shields, Tyne
and Wear NE33 5AP; Tel 0191 456 3917
Chuter Ede Community Centre Galsworthy Rd, South
Shields, Tyne and Wear NE34 9UG; Tel 0191 536 0515;
Fax 0191 536 0515
Mortimer Community Centre Mortimer Comprehensive
School, Reading Rd, South Shields, Tyne and Wear
NE33 4UG; Tel 0191 456 6680; Fax 0191 427 1176
Clegwell Community Centre Mountbatten Ave, Campbell
Park Rd, Hebburn, Tyne and Wear NE31 2QU;
Tel 0191 489 7575; Fax 0191 489 7575
Cleadon Park Community Centre Sunderland Rd, South
Shields, Tyne and Wear NE34 0BS; Tel 0191 454 4403;
Fax 0191 454 4409

Hartleyburn Community Centre Crawley Ave, Hebburn,
Tyne and Wear NE31 2LW; Tel 0191 428 0555
Derby Terrace Community Centre Derby Terr, South
Shields, Tyne and Wear NE32 3QN; Tel 0191 455 7506;
Fax 0191 455 7506
Hebburn Community Centre Argyle St, Hebburn, Tyne and
Wear NE31 1BQ; Tel 0191 483 2784; Fax 0191 483 2376
Harton Community Centre Crawley Ave, South Shields,
Tyne and Wear NE34 6DL; Tel 0191 456 4226
Hedworthfield Community Centre Cornhill, Hedworth,
Jarrow, Tyne and Wear NE32 4QD; Tel 0191 420 3336;
Fax 0191 420 3330
Horsley Hill Community Centre Marsden Rd, South Shields,
Tyne and Wear NE34 6RQ; Tel 0191 456 4466
Boldon Community Centre Boldon School, New Rd, Boldon
Colliery, Tyne and Wear NE35 9DZ; Tel 0191 536 8085;
Fax 0191 536 8085
Millennium PHAB Club 113 Grange Rd, Jarrow, Tyne and
Wear NE32 5DZ; Tel 0191 489 4336; Fax 0191 489 3400
Ocean Road Community Centre Ocean Rd, South Shields,
Tyne and Wear NE33 2AA; Tel 0191 423 0787;
Fax 0191 456 0080
Percy Hudson Youth Centre Sheridan Rd, Biddick Hall,
South Shields, Tyne and Wear NE34 9JF;
Tel 0191 536 2578
Perth Green Community Centre Inverness Rd, Jarrow, Tyne
and Wear NE32 4JX; Tel 0191 489 3743; Fax 0191 483 5521
Primrose Village Community Centre Lambton Terr, Jarrow,
Tyne and Wear NE32 5QY; Tel 0191 424 9977;
Fax 0191 424 9966
Simonside Youth Centre St Simon St, South Shields, Tyne
and Wear NE34 9SD; Tel 0191 424 0118
Trinity House Social Centre 134 Laygate La, South Shields,
Tyne and Wear NE33 4JD; Tel 0191 456 4239
Whitburn Community Centre Whitburn Comprenhensive
School, Nicholas Ave, Whitburn, Tyne and Wear
SR6 7EX; Tel 0191 529 4202; Fax 0191 529 4202

FIELD STUDY AND OUTDOOR PURSUITS CENTRES

Akenshawburn Centre Akenshawburn Cottages, Kielder,
Northumberland; Tel 0191 424 7759
Thurston Outdoor Education Centre Coniston, Cumbria
LA21 8AB; Tel 01539 441218; Fax 01539 441169
Water Activities Centre The Groyne, South Shields, Tyne
and Wear; Tel 0191 455 5414

SERVICE EDUCATION CENTRE

Chuter Ede Education Centre Galsworthy Rd, South Shields,
Tyne and Wear NE34 9UG; Tel 0191 519 1909;
Fax 0191 519 0600
Contact J. Kranz
SEN Support/Resource Centre/Child Guidance Centre

Stockton-on-Tees Borough Council

www.stockton.gov.uk

Population: 187 100
Political composition: Lab: 27, Con: 12, Ind: 10, LD: 7
PO Box 11, Municipal Bldgs, Stockton-on-Tees TS18 1LD;
URL www.stockton.gov.uk; e-mail
stocktoncouncil@stockton.gov.uk; Tel 01642 393939;
Fax 01642 393092
Chief Executive George Garlick

Children, Education and Social Care

PO Box 228, Municipal Bldgs, Stockton-on-Tees TS18 1XE;
Tel 01642 527049; Fax 01642 527037
Corporate Director (Children, Education and Social Care)
Ann Baxter
Head (Adult Operational Services) Sean McEneany
Head (Adult Strategy) Ruth Hill
Head (Arts and Cultural Services) Reuben Kench

2

Head (Children and Young People's Operational Service)
    Jane Humphreys
Head (Children and Young People's Strategy)   Peter Seller
Head (Performance)   Simon Willson
Head (School Effectiveness)   Julia Morrison
Head (Support Services)   Tony Beckwith
Manager (Assets and Facilities)   Ken Richardson
Manager (Community Education)   Marc Mason
Manager (Information)   Phil Kicks
Manager (Payroll)   Susan Coulson
Manager (Personnel)   Paul Hiser
Manager (Pupils and Students)   Betty Johns
Manager (School and Governor Support)   Ian Short
Manager (Secondary Strategy)   Paul Welford
*Manager (Specialist Learning Support); Principal Educational
    Psychologist*   Ian Edmunds
Education Finance Officer   David New
Chief Adviser   Lesley Reed
Senior Secondary Adviser   Sally Walton
Link Adviser   Michael Reeves
Link Adviser   Gillian Dorman-Smith
Planning and Policy Development Officer   John Hegarty
Number of Schools
62 Primary (1558 nursery places); 14 Secondary; 4 Special
Day of Cabinet Meeting
Thursday; four weekly cycle

CHILDREN AND YOUNG PEOPLE SELECT COMMITTEE

Lab: 6, Con: 3, LD: 2, Thornaby Independent Association: 1,
Ingleby Barwick Independent Society: 1, Diocesan
Representatives: 2, Parent Governor Representatives: 2
Cabinet Member   Alex Cunningham; 10 Lapwing La,
    Norton, Stockton-on-Tees TS20 1LT

ADULTS LEISURE AND CULTURE SELECT COMMITTEE

Lab: 6, Con: 3, LD: 2, Ingleby Barwick Independent Society:
2, Diocesan Representatives: 2, Parent Governor
Representatives: 2
Cabinet Member   Alex Cunningham; 10 Lapwing La,
    Norton, Stockton-on-Tees TS20 1LT

SCHOOL AND GOVERNOR SUPPORT

Education Centre, Junction Rd, Norton, Stockton-on-Tees
    TS19 1PR; Tel 01642 526419; Fax 01642 528676
Manager (School and Governor Support)   Ian Short
Support Officer (Training)   Lucy Emmerson
Foundation training for new governors, together with
information packs. A training programme of specialist
courses, including staff selection, financial management,
health and safety, and premises issues. A programme of
'whole governing body' training, some aspects to include
senior staff, on such topics as Ofsted inspections, building
partnerships and school development planning. There are
also chair briefing sessions, link governor briefings, resource
centres containing distance learning materials, a termly
newsletter and a governors' helpline. School support issues
include curriculum enrichment activities, notes of guidance,
planning the school year, and school complaints.

EDUCATIONAL PSYCHOLOGICAL SERVICE

Wrensfield Hse, Wrensfield Rd, Stockton-on-Tees
    TS19 0AT; Tel 01642 527110; Fax 01642 527154

SPECIAL UNIT FOR PUPILS WITH PHYSICAL DISABILITIES

Bishopsgarth Secondary School   Harrowgate La, Stockton-
    on-Tees TS19 8TF; Tel 01642 586262; Fax 01642 570038
Headteacher   John Golds

YOUTH AND COMMUNITY CENTRES

Chapel Road Youth and Community Centre   Chapel Rd,
    Billingham, Stockton-on-Tees TS23 1DX;
    Tel 01642 361197

Conyers Youth and Community Centre   Green La, Yarm,
    Stockton-on-Tees TS15 9ET; Tel (school) 01642 527975;
    Tel (centre) 01642 783253
Egglescliffe Youth and Community Centre   Egglescliffe
    Comprehensive School, Urlay Nook Rd, Egglescliffe,
    Stockton-on-Tees TS18 0LA; Tel 01642 527975
Elmwood Youth and Community Centre   53 Darlington La,
    Hartburn, Stockton-on-Tees TS18 5EP; Tel 01642 527786
Grangefield Youth and Community Centre   Oxbridge La,
    Stockton-on-Tees TS18 4NY; Tel 01642 393531;
    Fax 01642 608096
Hardwick Youth Centre   Ketton Rd, Hardwick, Stockton-on-
    Tees TS19 8BU; Tel 01642 356633
Kiora Hall Youth and Community Centre   Ragpath La,
    Roseworth, Stockton-on-Tees TS19 9JS; Tel 01642 528010
Long Newton and Elton Youth and Community Centre   Long
    Newton, Stockton-on-Tees; Tel 01642 583749
Norton Youth and Community Centre   Berkshire Rd,
    Stockton-on-Tees TS20 2RD; Tel 01642 528532
Robert Atkinson Youth and Community Centre   Thorntree
    Rd, Thornaby, Stockton-on-Tees TS17 8JP;
    Tel 01642 605712
Stillington Youth and Community Centre   Lawson St,
    Stillington, Stockton-on-Tees TS21 1JE; Tel 01740 630041
Thornaby Youth and Community Centre   Baysdale Rd,
    Thornaby, Stockton-on-Tees TS17 9DF; Tel 01642 527972
Willows Youth and Community Centre   Tilery Youth Centre,
    Tilery Primary School, Stockton-on-Tees TS18 2HU;
    Tel 01642 613345

SPECIAL REFERRAL UNITS FOR PUPILS

Bishopton Centre (Secondary Pupil Support)   Wrensfield Rd,
    Stockton-on-Tees TS19 0AT; Tel 01642 393565;
    Fax 01642 393577
Headteacher   Peter Ewart (Acting)
Greengates (Primary Pupil Support)   Melton Rd, Stockton-
    on-Tees TS19 0JD; Tel 01642 528617; Fax 01642 528631
Headteacher   Dorothy Elliott

Sunderland City Council

www.sunderland.gov.uk

Population: 280 600
Political composition: Lab: 53, Con: 17, Ind: 4, LD: 1
Civic Centre, Sunderland, Tyne and Wear SR2 7DN;
    URL www.sunderland.gov.uk; e-mail
    <firstname>.<surname>@sunderland.gov.uk;
    Tel 0191 520 5000; Fax 0191 553 1099
Chief Executive   Ged Fitzgerald

Children's Services

e-mail childrens.services.info@sunderland.gov.uk;
    Tel 0191 520 5555; Fax 0191 553 1431
Director (Children's Services)   Dr Helen Paterson;
    Tel 0191 553 1355
Deputy Director (Children's Services)   Keith Moore;
    Tel 0191 553 1397
Head (Health Improvement)   Janette Sherratt;
    Tel 0191 553 1353
Head (Performance Improvement and Policy)   Norma Hardy;
    Tel 0191 553 1438
Head (Positive Contribution and Economic Wellbeing)
    Judith Hay; Tel 0191 553 1972
Head (Resources)   Paul Campbell; Tel 0191 553 1356
Head (Safeguarding)   Mick McCracken; Tel 0191 553 1349
Head (Standards)   Lynda Brown; Tel 0191 553 1410
Manager (Performance and Information)
    Andrew Baker (Acting)
Manager (Performance and Information)
    Ken O'Neill (Acting)
Number of Schools
84 Primary; 18 Secondary; 9 Nursery; 7 Special

Day of Committee Meeting
Thursdays; monthly
Requisition Periods for Schools Supplies
Schools requisition supplies when required

CHILDREN'S SERVICES REVIEW COMMITTEE

Members: 12, Voting Representatives: 13, Non-voting
Representatives: 8
Members of the Sub Committee
Lab: Cllr Bell, Cllr Fletcher, Cllr Gofton, Cllr Heron, Cllr
Miller, Cllr Stewart, Cllr J. Walker, Cllr Williams, Cllr
Wilson

Tyne and Wear Metropolitan Area

The following Metropolitan Councils comprise the Tyne and
Wear Metropolitan Area and are listed separately in this
section: Gateshead, Newcastle upon Tyne, North Tyneside,
South Tyneside, Sunderland

NORTH WEST

Blackburn with Darwen Borough Council

www.blackburn.gov.uk

In April 1998 Blackburn with Darwen became a unitary
authority. The rest of Lancashire retains a two-tier structure
and is listed separately in this section.
Population: 140 500
Political composition: Lab: 32, Con: 17, LD: 13, For Darwen:
3
Town Hall, Blackburn BB1 7DY;
    URL www.blackburn.gov.uk; e-mail
    info@blackburn.gov.uk; Tel 01254 585585;
    Fax 01254 587591
Chief Executive   Graham Burgess

Children's Services Department

The Exchange, Ainsworth St, Blackburn BB1 6AD;
    Tel 01254 666425; Fax 01254 666443
Director   Peter Morgan
Director (Children's Services)   Gladys Rhodes
Director (EAZ)   Lisa Bibby
Assistant Director (Inclusion and Access)   Cath Hitchen
Assistant Director (Lifelong Learning)   Bill Lovatt
Assistant Director (School Improvement)   Ian Kendrick
Assistant Director (Strategy and Performance)
    Harry Devonport
Manager (Access Point)   Jackie Waring
Manager (Behaviour and Community Cohesion)   Zaq Patel
Manager (Client Services and Premises)   Helen Olive
Manager (Curriculum and Learning Enhancement)
    Mebz Bobat
Manager (Early Years and Children's Trust)
    Deborah Gornik (Acting)
Manager (Finance)   Helen Seechurn
Manager (Lifelong Learning)   Chris Sivers
Manager (Research and Planning)   Robert Arrowsmith
Manager (Statutory Assessment Team)   Dave Ramsey
Manager (Strategic Support)   Andrew Hutchinson
Manager (Youth Service)   Kate Clements
Service Administration Manager (Inclusions and Access)
    Julie Molineux
Service Administration Manager (Resources and Support)
    Sharifa Ali
Principal Education Psychologist   Dave Crowder

Principal Education Welfare Officer   Lawrence Warburton
Principal Governor Support Officer   Sean Rogers
*Principal Officer (Pupil Progress and Ethnic Minority
    Support)*   Dave Abell
Principal School Improvement Officer   George Carter
Number of Schools
58 Primary; 9 Secondary; 9 Nursery; 5 Special; 1 PRU

LEAD MEMBERS FOR EDUCATION AND LIFELONG LEARNING

Executive Member   Cllr Dave Hollings (Lab)
Lead Member   Cllr Tahimr Mahmood (Lab)
Lead Member   Cllr Dorothy Walsh (Lab)
Shadow Lead Member   Cllr John Williams (Con)
Shadow Portfolio Holder   Cllr Sheila Williams (Con)
Opposition Spokesperson   Cllr Chris Thayne (LD)

ACCESS 2 PROGRESSION

Special Educational Needs Support Service   Education –
    Lifelong Learning, Sunnyhurst Centre, Salisbury Rd,
    Darwen, Blackburn BB3 1HZ; Tel 01254 778280
    Contact   Viviene Smith

SUPPORT FOR ETHNIC MINORITY ACHIEVEMENT

Jubilee Hse, Jubilee St, Blackburn; Tel 01254 587644
    Contact   Dave Abell

Blackpool Council

www.blackpool.gov.uk

In April 1998 Blackpool became a unitary authority. The rest
of Lancashire retains a two-tier structure and is listed
separately in this section.
Political composition: Con: 26, Lab: 13, LD: 3
Town Hall, Blackpool FY1 1AD;
    URL www.blackpool.gov.uk; Tel 01253 477477;
    Fax 01253 477101
Chief Executive   Steve Weaver DipCRP
Executive Director (Business Services)   Julian Kearsley
*Corporate Director (Housing, Environmental and Social
    Services)*   Steve Pullan; Progress Hse, Clifton Rd,
    Blackpool FU4 4US; Tel 01253 477500; Fax 01253 477577
Director (Tourism)   Jane Seddon
Assistant Director (Enterprise and Business Development)
    Alan Cavill; Tel 01253 477006
Head (Economic Development)   Peter Legg; Technology
    Management Centre, Faraday Way, Blackpool FY2 0JW;
    Tel 01253 477320; Fax 01253 476112
Head (ICT)   Philip Baron
Head (Operational Services)   Graham Sharrock
Head (Personnel)   Catherine Wilson
Head (Planning and Transportation)   Reg Haslam
Head (Revenue Services)   Andrew Pollock
Head (Technical Services)   Vacancy
Chief Financial Officer   Mike Hanson

Children and Young People's Department

Progress Hse, Clifton Rd, Blackpool FY4 4US;
    Fax 01253 476504
Executive Member (Children's Services)   Cllr C. Clapham
Executive Director   David Lund BEd(Hons), MSc
Assistant Director (Community and Inclusion)   Sue Crouch
Assistant Director (Learning and Achievement)   Sue Harrison
Assistant Director (Targeted Services)   Sheila Sutherland
Assistant Director (Transforming School)   Robert Brophy
Head (Business Support)   Margaret Rawding
Principal Educational Psychologist   Mike Twistleton
Principal Officer (Integrated Youth)   Mike Taplin
Principal Officer (SEN)   Linda Dawes
Senior Personnel Officer   Linda Dutton

Principal Adviser Stephen Toon
Adviser (SEN) Lorraine Stephens
Adviser (Literacy) Glenn Mascord
Governor Services Officer Ann Dixon
Number of Schools
8 Secondary; 3 Special

CHILD DEVELOPMENT CENTRE

Child Development and Family Support Centre Blenheim Hse, 145–147 Newton Dr, Blackpool FY3 8LZ; Tel 01253 397006; Fax 01253 379008

SPEECH AND LANGUAGE UNIT

Speech and Language SERF c/o Stanley Infants School, Wordsworth Ave, Blackpool FY3 9UR; Tel 01253 763601

HEARING IMPAIRED CHILDREN (DAY UNIT)

Blackpool SERF for the Hearing Impaired (Primary) c/o Waterloo Primary School, Waterloo Rd, Blackpool FY4 3AG; Tel 01253 315370

Bolton Metropolitan Borough Council
www.bolton.gov.uk

Population: 266 100
Political composition: Lab: 23, Con: 21, LD: 15
Civic Centre, Bolton, Greater Manchester BL1 1RU; URL www.bolton.gov.uk; Tel 01204 333333; Fax 01204 331042
Chief Executive Bernard Knight

Children's Services

PO Box 53, Paderborn Hse, Bolton, Greater Manchester BL1 1JW; URL www.boltonlea.org.uk; Tel 01204 333333; Fax 01204 332228
Executive Member (Education) Cllr C. Swarbrick
Director M. Blenkinsop MSc
Deputy Director B. Shaw
Assistant Director (Access and Inclusion Division) S. Fazal
Assistant Director (Heritage) Stephanie Crossley; Fax 01204 332225
Assistant Director (Policy and Resources Division) C. Swift BA, MEd, CertEd
Head (Adult Services) Steve Garland AMA, MBA; Fax 01204 391352
Head (Adult Services) M. Gracey
Head (Youth Service) Moria Hill
Strategic Manager (School Evaluation) T. Birch BEd(Hons), MEd
Manager (Asset Management Unit) S. Sollazzi
Manager (ICT Unit) G.D. Smith MMS, DMS; Tel 01204 332323; Fax 01204 332300
Manager (Information Management Unit) Vacancy
Manager (Office Services Unit) Gill Bird
Manager (Personnel Unit) Kathryn Ball BA, CIPD, BPS
Manager (Pupil and Student Services) V. Fogg
Manager (Regeneration, External Funding and Partnerships) Christine Ellis
Manager (School Finance Unit) C. Davies
Manager (SEN and Transport Service) C.F. Chisholm
Manager (Strategic Services) T. Sinkinson BSc(Hons), PGCE
Manager (Strategy and Performance) A. Gorton
Principal Educational Psychologist Vacancy
Principal Education Social Worker I. Price MA, MSc
EBD Co-ordinator Vacancy
Number of Schools
16 Secondary; 6 Special

Day of Committee Meeting
Wednesday; six week cycle (two weeks prior to council meeting)
Requisition Periods for Schools Supplies
No set period

CHILDREN'S SERVICES SCRUTINY COMMITTEE

Executive Member (Children's Services) Cllr M. Cox (LD)
Executive Member (Education) Cllr C. Swarbrick (LD)
Members of the Committee
Lab: Adia, Alli, Anderton, Eastwood, Evans, Helsby, Mrs Seddon, Stores
Con: Mrs Brierley, Carr, Mrs Fairclough, A. Walsh
LD: Bradwell, Mrs Rothwell, S. Silvester

LEARNING AND DEVELOPMENT UNIT

Castle Hill Centre, Bolton, Greater Manchester BL2 2JW; Tel 01204 332114; Fax 01204 332058
Manager (Learning and Development) Kathryn Ball BA, CIPD, BPS
Services offered
School-based and centre-based training for governors, senior staff and teaching and non-teaching staff of schools; skills training; management; education and law; finance; personnel issues; curriculum issues etc.

EDUCATION WELFARE OFFICE

Castle Hill Centre, Castleton St, Bolton, Greater Manchester BL2 2JW; Tel 01204 338173

Bury Metropolitan Borough Council
www.bury.gov.uk

Population: 181 900
Political composition: Lab: 27, Con: 19, LD: 5
Town Hall, Knowsley St, Bury, Greater Manchester BL9 0SW; URL www.bury.gov.uk; e-mail k.parker@bury.gov.uk; Tel 0161 253 5000; Tel (press office) 0161 253 5007; Fax 0161 253 5079
Education Department, Athenaeum Hse, Market St, Bury, Greater Manchester BL9 0BN; Tel 0161 253 5000
Chief Executive Mark Sanders MBA, BSc(Hons)

Children's Services Department

Athenaeum Hse, Market St, Bury, Greater Manchester BL9 0BN; Tel 0161 253 5652; Fax 0161 253 5653
Executive Member (Children and Young People) Cllr M. Gibb
Executive Director Eleni Ioannides
Director (Culture and Learning) P. Nye
Director (Inclusion and Health Care) T. Dawson
Director (Social Care) Judith Longhill
Head (Curriculum and Language Access Service) M. Griffin
Head (Financial Services) P. Lowe
Head (Personnel Services) J.A. Simms
Head (Quality and Advisory Service) R. Holt
Head (Strategic Planning and Management Services) P.M. Cooke
Manager (SEN Service); Principal Educational Psychologist L. Walker
Manager (Social Inclusion Service) A. Cogswell
Adviser (Humanities) B. Hardman
Adviser (IT) P. Howard
Adviser (Mathematics) B. Roadnight
Adviser (Modern Languages) A. Finbow
Adviser (Primary English/Early Years) P. Pye
Adviser (Science) W. Jackson
Borough Officer (Arts, Libraries and Lifelong Learning) J. Carter
Number of Schools
15 Secondary; 3 Special; 16 Community Education Centres

Teachers' Centres

Development and Training Centre, Parkinson St, Bury; Tel
0161 253 6934

THE EXECUTIVE

Lab: 8, Con: 1, LD: 1
Executive Member (Children and Young People)
   M. Gibb (Lab)
Spokesperson   A. Garner (LD)
Spokesperson   M. Wiseman (Con)

GOVERNOR TRAINING

Development and Training Centre, Parkinson St, Bury,
   Greater Manchester; Tel 0161 253 6934; Fax 0161 253 6928
Senior Adviser (Governor Training)   P. Howard
Services offered
Full support service for school governors, including central
and on-site training, as well as advice and consultancy

INCLUSION AND HEALTHCARE SERVICE

Seedfield Centre, Parkinson St, Bury, Greater Manchester
BL9 6NY; Tel 0161 253 6406
Curriculum and Language Access   Seedfield Centre,
   Parkinson St, Bury, Greater Manchester BL9 6NY;
   Tel 0161 253 6424
Learning Support Service   Seedfield Centre, Parkinson St,
   Bury, Greater Manchester BL9 6NY; Tel 0161 253 6418
   Hospital tuition; home tuition; SpLD; literacy support;
   travellers service; specialist advisory teaching team
Portage Service   Seedfield Centre, Parkinson St, Bury,
   Greater Manchester BL9 6NY; Tel 0161 253 6131
Pupil Learning Centre   New Summerseat Hse, Summerseat
   La, Bury, Greater Manchester BL0 9UD; Tel 01204 885275
   Head   K. Chantrey
Sensory Support Service   School St, Radcliffe, Greater
   Manchester M26 0AW; Tel 0161 724 8337

CHILDREN'S DISABILITY SERVICE

Seedfield Centre, Parkinson St, Bury, Greater Manchester
BL9 6NY; Tel 0161 253 6881

Cheshire County Council

www.cheshire.gov.uk

In April 1998 both Halton and Warrington became unitary
authorities and are listed separately in this section. The rest
of Cheshire retains a two-tier structure.
Population: 668 000
County Hall, Chester, Cheshire CH1 1SF;
   URL www.cheshire.gov.uk; e-mail
   info@cheshire.gov.uk; Tel 01244 602424;
   Fax 01244 603800
Chief Executive   Jeremy Taylor

Children's Services

County Hall, Chester, Cheshire CH1 1SQ; e-mail
   educationhq@cheshire.gov.uk; Tel 01244 602330;
   Fax 01244 603821
Director   J. Feenan
Principal Manager   F. Bradley
County Manager (Education and Community Policy)   L. Rees
County Manager (ISIS)   L. Brown
County Manager (Schools)   Vacancy
Manager (Communications and Information)   D. Plunkett
Manager (Education Business)   Terry Harrop
Manager (ICT Strategy)   A. Curtis
Manager (Personnel)   R. Lewis
Manager (Planning and LMS)   A. Tunnicliffe
Manager (Political Support)   N. Maffingham
Manager (School Development)   Ray Baker

Manager (Sure Start)   Sue Egersdorf
Operations Manager (Student Finance)   M. Boden
Number of Schools
46 Secondary; 14 Special

EXECUTIVE MEMBER FOR CHILDREN'S SERVICES

Contact   D.K. Rowlands (Con)

GOVERNOR TRAINING

Stanney Local Office, Stanney La, Ellesmere Port, Cheshire
   CH65 6QL; Tel 0151 357 6823
Adviser   Ged Hayes
Services offered
Programme of formal courses; in-house courses; governors
update; conferences for governors

AREA EDUCATION OFFICES

Cheshire Parent Partnership Service   The Professional
   Centre, Woodford Lodge, Winsford, Cheshire CW7 4EH;
   URL www.cheshire.gov.uk/parentpartnership; e-mail
   parentpartnership@cheshire.gov.uk; Tel 01606 814375
Children's Services – County Offices   Chapel La, Wilmslow,
   Cheshire SK9 1PU; Tel 01625 534700; Fax 01625 534852
Children's Services – County Offices   Stanney La, Ellesmere
   Port, Cheshire CH65 6QL; Tel 0151 357 6853;
   Fax 0151 357 6844
Children's Services – County Offices   Watling St, Northwich,
   Cheshire CW9 5ET; Tel 01606 814900; Fax 01606 815783

IN-SERVICE CENTRES

Cheshire Lifelong Learning   Community Services
   Department, Rm 328, County Hall, Chester, Cheshire
   CH1 1SQ; Tel 01244 602469; Fax 01270 650351
   Principal Lifelong Learning Officer   Hazel Manning
Kingsley Centre   Middle La, Kingsley, Frodsham, Cheshire
   WA6 6TZ; Tel 01928 787226; Fax 01928 787808
   Contact   K. Harrison
Langley Centre   Main Rd, Langley, Macclesfield, Cheshire
   SK11 0BU; Tel 01260 252713; Fax 01260 253371
   Contact   L. Hodges
Tarvin Meadow Professional Centre   Meadow Cl, Tarvin,
   Chester, Cheshire CH3 8LY; Tel 01829 741118;
   Fax 01829 741592
   Contact   J. Egerton; Tel 01829 742995
Woodford Lodge Professional Centre   Woodford La West,
   Winsford, Cheshire CW7 4EH; Tel 01606 814300;
   Fax 01606 814301
   Contact   Linda Fogg

OUTDOOR EDUCATION CENTRES

Beeston Outdoor Education Centre   Beeston, Tarporley,
   Cheshire CW6 9TR; Tel 01829 260535
   Contact   Chris Pierce
   Residential
Burwardsley Outdoor Education Centre   Tattenhall, Chester,
   Cheshire CH3 9PA; Tel 01829 770424
   Contact   C. Pierce
   Residential
Delamere Forest Outdoor Education Centre   Foxhowl, Ashton
   Rd, Norley, Warrington WA6 6PA; Tel 01928 740393
   Contact   Chris Pierce
   Residential
Langley Education Centre   Main Rd, Langley, Macclesfield,
   Cheshire SK11 0BU; Tel 01260 252713; Fax 01260 253371
   Contact   L.M.A. Hodges
   Day centre with camping facilities

OTHER CENTRES

Conway Centre   Canolfan, LLanfair PG, Isle of Anglesey
   LL61 6DJ; Tel 01248 714501; Fax 01248 714504
   Contact   A.M. Finnegan
   Residential

Tattenhall Centre Tattenhall, Chester, Cheshire CH3 9PX;
Tel 01829 770223; Fax 01829 771117
Contact Margaret Connor
Residential

Cumbria County Council
www.cumbria.gov.uk

Population: 491 400
Political composition: Lab: 39, Con: 32, LD: 11, Ind: 2
The Courts, Carlisle, Cumbria CA3 8NA;
URL www.cumbria.gov.uk; Tel 01228 606369;
Fax 01228 606372
Chief Executive Mr P. Stybelski; Tel 01228 606301;
Fax 01228 606302
Deputy Chief Executive; Corporate Director (Finance and Central Services) R.F. Mather BSc, IPFA; Tel 01228 606260;
Fax 01228 606264
Head (Culture) Jim Grisenthwaite; Tel 01228 607282;
Fax 01228 606728

Children's Services Department

5 Portland Sq, Carlisle, Cumbria CA1 1PU;
URL www.cumbria.gov.uk/education; e-mail
education@cumbriacc.gov.uk; Tel 01228 606877;
Fax 01228 606896
Corporate Director (Children's Services) Mrs M. Swann
Senior Manager (Access and Inclusion) Mr M.D. Watmough
Senior Manager (Children's Services) Mr D. Alexander
Senior Manager (Learning Support) J. Taylor
Senior Manager (Lifelong Learning) Mr P. Davies
Senior Manager (Policy and Resources) Mr D. Johnston
Senior Manager (Standards and School Improvement)
Mr J. Swainston
Manager (Policy) Mr H. Slater
Principal Education Officer (SEN) Mrs A. Henderson
Senior Education Officer (Access and Inclusion)
Mr S. Goodall
Senior Education Officer (Adult Learning) Mr C. Searle
Senior Education Officer (Attendance and Exclusion)
Mr S. Mason
Senior Education Officer (Early Years) Mrs I. Geraghty
Senior Education Officer (Governor Support) Mr S. Cameron
Senior Education Officer (Specialist Teaching) Mr B. White
Senior Education Officer (Performance Review)
Mr T. Whittaker
Assistant Education Officer (School Places) Ms M. Shiels
Principal School Improvement Officer Mr P. McGaw
Principal Educational Psychologist Mr M. Toomey
Education Spokesperson Mr P. Chappelhow
Number of Schools
42 Secondary; 5 Special
Day of Committee Meeting
Quarterly
Requisition Periods for Schools Supplies
No fixed period

GOVERNOR TRAINING UNIT

Governor Support Services, Children's Services
Department, 5 Portland Sq, Carlisle, Cumbria CA1 1PU;
URL www.cumbria.gov.uk/education; e-mail
education@cumbriacc.gov.uk; Tel 01228 606921;
Fax 01228 606920
Governor Development Officer Mrs S. Glendinning
Governor Development Officer Mrs J. Keetley
Services offered
A termly magazine Cumbrian Governor; helpline: support
unit offering development and training

BARROW AREA CHILDREN'S SERVICES OFFICE

The Nan Tait Centre, Abbey Rd, Barrow-in-Furness,
Cumbria LA14 5TY; URL www.cumbria.gov.uk/
education; e-mail education@cumbriacc.gov.uk;
Tel 01229 894400; Fax 01229 894436
Manager (Area Office) Ms A. Bell

KENDAL AREA CHILDREN'S OFFICE

Busher Wlk, Kendal, Cumbria LA9 4RQ;
URL www.cumbria.gov.uk/education; e-mail
education@cumbriacc.gov.uk; Tel 01539 773456;
Fax 01539 773492
Manager (Area Office) Mrs W. Sedgwick

WHITEHAVEN AREA CHILDREN'S SERVICES OFFICE

Union Hall, Scotch St, Whitehaven, Cumbria CA28 7BG;
URL www.cumbria.gov.uk/education; e-mail
education@cumbriacc.gov.uk; Tel 01946 852700;
Fax 01946 852747
Manager (Area Office) Mrs J. Devlin

ADULT EDUCATION ESTABLISHMENTS

Alston Adult Education Centre Samuel King's School,
Church Rd, Alston, Cumbria CA9 3QU; e-mail
adulted@alstoncdc.org.uk; Tel 01434 381236;
Fax 01434 382095
Contact Mr J. Rossouw
Appleby Adult Education Centre Appleby Grammar School,
Battlebarrow, Appleby-in-Westmorland, Cumbria
CA16 6XU; e-mail info@applebyheritagecentre.org.uk;
Tel 01768 353289; Fax 01768 352412
Contact Mr J. Weir
Barrow-in-Furness Sixth Form College Rating La, Barrow-in-
Furness, Cumbria LA13 9LE; e-mail
principal@barrow6fc.ac.uk; Tel 01229 828377;
Fax 01229 836874
Principal Mr E.J. Elvish
Beacon Hill Adult Education Centre Beacon Hill School,
Marke Sq, Aspatria, Wigton, Cumbria CA7 3EZ; e-mail
fified2004@yahoo.co.uk; Tel 01900 815765;
Fax 01900 815765
Contact Ms B. Goldie
Carlisle College Victoria Pl, Carlisle, Cumbria CA1 1HS;
e-mail mtattersall@carlisle.ac.uk; Tel 01228 822700;
Fax 01228 822710
Principal Mrs M. Tattersall
Cartmel Community Education Centre Cartmel Priory CE
School, Headless Cross, Cartmel, Grange-over-Sands,
Cumbria LA11 7SA; e-mail
adulted@cartmelpriory.cumbria.sch.uk;
Tel 01539 536323; Fax 01539 536287
Contact Ms J. Godden
Cockermouth Adult Education Centre Cockermouth School,
Castlegate Dr, Cockermouth, Cumbria CA13 9HF; e-mail
aded@cockermouth.cumbria.sch.uk; Tel 01900 823389;
Fax 01900 325944
Contact Ms E. Nicholson
Cumbria Campus, Newton Rigg University of Central
Lancashire, Newton Rigg, Penrith, Cumbria CA11 0AH;
e-mail cumbriainfo@uclan.ac.uk; Tel 01768 863791;
Fax 01768 867249
Headteacher Dr G. Baldwin
Cumbria Institute of Arts Brampton Rd, Carlisle, Cumbria
CA3 9AY; e-mail liz.belford@cumbria.ac.uk;
Tel 01228 400300; Fax 01228 400333
Principal Prof D. Vaughan
Dalton Adult Education Centre Dowdales School, Dalton-in-
Furness, Cumbria LA15 8AH; e-mail
daltonadulted@yahoo.co.uk; Tel 01229 462168;
Fax 01229 462168
Contact Mrs L. McElroy

Ehenside Adult Education Centre Ehenside School, Towerson St, Cleator, Cumbria CA23 3EL; e-mail stonesj@ehenside.cumbria.sch.uk; Tel 01946 855000; Fax 01946 855002
Contact Ms H. Moore

Furness College Channelside, Barrow-in-Furness, Cumbria LA14 2PJ; e-mail course.enq@furness.ac.uk; Tel 01229 825017; Fax 01229 870964
Principal Mrs A. Attwood

Kendal College Milnthorpe Rd, Kendal, Cumbria LA9 5AY; e-mail enquiries@kendal.ac.uk; Tel 01539 814700; Fax 01539 814701
Principal Mr G. Wilkinson

Keswick Adult Education Centre Keswick School, Vicarage Hill, Keswick, Cumbria CA12 5QB; e-mail chrisclayson@keswick.cumbria.sch.uk; Tel 01768 773565; Fax 01768 774813
Contact Mr C. Clayson

Kirkby Stephen Adult Education Centre Kirkby Stephen Grammar School, Christian Head, Kirkby Stephen, Cumbria CA17 4HA; e-mail adultedks@kirkbystephengrammar.cumbria.sch.uk; Tel 01768 371693; Fax 01768 372387
Contact Christina Collis

Lakes College West Cumbria Hallwood Rd, Lilyhall, Workington, Cumbria CA14 4JN; e-mail pat.glenday@lcwc.ac.uk; Tel 01946 839300; Fax 01946 839301
Centre Manager Ms P. Glenday

Lochinvar Adult Education Centre Lochinvar School, Longtown, Carlisle, Cumbria CA6 5UG; e-mail aecentre@lochinvar.cumbria.sch.uk; Tel 01228 791488; Fax 01228 791701
Contact Mr S. Wylie

Millom Adult Education Centre Millom School, Salthouse Rd, Millom, Cumbria LA18 5AB; e-mail patnelson@btconnect.com; Tel 01229 770084; Fax 01229 770084
Contact Ms P. Nelson

Netherhall Adult Education Centre Netherhall School, Netherhall Rd, Maryport, Cumbria CA15 6NT; e-mail b.goldie@nhall.cumbria.sch.uk; Tel 01900 815765; Fax 01900 815765
Contact Ms B. Goldie

Sedbergh Adult Education Centre The Cottage, Sedbergh Primary School, Long La, Sedbergh, Cumbria LA10 5AL; e-mail admin@sedberghcdc.org.uk; Tel 01539 621031; Fax 01839 622151
Contact Mr C. Wood

Trinity School Strand Rd, Carlisle, Cumbria CA1 1JB; e-mail bfo@trinity.cumbria.sch.uk; Tel 01228 607597; Fax 01228 607499
Contact Ms B. Foster

Ullswater Adult Education Centre Ullswater Community College, Wetheriggs La, Penrith, Cumbria CA11 8NG; e-mail info@ullswater.cumbria.sch.uk; Tel 01768 864120; Fax 01768 242165
Contact Mr N. Kemp

Ulverston Adult Education Centre Ulverston Victoria High School, Springfield Rd, Ulverston, Cumbria LA12 0EB; e-mail adulted@ulverstonvictoria.cumbria.sch.uk; Tel 01229 483901; Fax 01229 483903
Contact Ms H. Ward

Whitehaven Adult Education Centre Whitehaven School, Cleator Moor Rd, Whitehaven, Cumbria CA28 8TY; e-mail mkennedy@whitehaven.cumbria.sch.uk; Tel 01946 852963; Fax 01946 852963
Contact Mr M. Kennedy

Wigton Adult Education Centre Nelson Thomlinson School, High St, Wigton, Cumbria CA7 9PX; e-mail wigtonadulted@aol.com; Tel 01697 321515
Contact Mrs F. Wasteney

William Howard Adult Education Centre William Howard School, Longtown Rd, Brampton, Cumbria CA8 1AR; e-mail whcentre@williamhoward.cumbria.sch.uk; Tel 01697 741771; Fax 01697 741096
Contact Ms F. Kirton

Workington Adult Education Centre Workington Sixth Form Centre, Needham Dr, Workington, Cumbria CA14 3SE; e-mail nicholanelson@uk2.net; Tel 01900 325367; Fax 01900 325269
Contact Ms N. Nelson

Wyndham Adult Education Centre Wyndham School, Main St, Egremont, Cumbria CA22 2DQ; e-mail adult-education@wyndham-school.fsnet.co.uk; Tel 01946 824259; Fax 01946 824259
Contact Mrs L. Close

ADULT EDUCATION RESIDENTIAL CENTRE

Higham Hall College Bassenthwaite Lake, Cockermouth, Cumbria CA13 9SH; e-mail admin@highamhall.com; Tel 01768 776276; Fax 01768 776013
Warden A. Alexandre

COLLEGE OF EDUCATION

University College of St Martin's Ambleside Campus, Rydal Rd, Ambleside, Cumbria LA22 9BB; URL www.ucsm.ac.uk; Tel 01539 430300; Fax 01539 430305
Principal Mrs K. Teasdale

OUTDOOR EDUCATION CENTRES

Cumbria Outdoors Hawse End Centre, Portinscale, Keswick, Cumbria CA12 5UE; e-mail cumbout@dial.pipex.com; Tel 01768 772816; Fax 01768 775108
Contact Mrs B. Hunter

Fellside Centre Fellside Mansion, Caldbeck, Wigton, Cumbria CA7 8HA; e-mail cumbout@dial.pipex.com; Tel 01768 772816; Fax 01768 775108
Contact Mrs B. Hunter

LITERACY CENTRES

Carlisle Literacy Centre The Richmond Centre, Wigton Rd, Carlisle, Cumbria CA2 6LA; e-mail joyce.rogers@cumbriacc.gov.uk; Tel 01228 606955; Fax 01228 606953
Headteacher Mrs J. Rogers

South Cumbria Literacy Centre Ormsgill Primary School, Millbank, Barrow-in-Furness, Cumbria LA14 4AR; Tel 01229 894454
Head Mrs S. Shuttleworth

West Cumbria Literacy Centre Melbreak Hse, Main St, Hensingham, Whitehaven, Cumbria CA28 8TH; Tel 01946 595860; Fax 01946 895861

PUPIL REFERRAL UNITS

Gillford Centre Upperby Rd, Carlisle, Cumbria CA2 4JE; e-mail alan.kemp@cumbriacc.gov.uk; Tel 01228 606957; Fax 01228 606944
Area Co-ordinator Mr A. Kemp
7–16

Kendal Centre Canal Head North, Kendal, Cumbria LA9 7BY; e-mail pru.south@cumbriacc.gov.uk; Tel 01539 732960; Fax 01539 732960
Area Co-ordinator Ms E. Robinson
7–16

Newbridge House Centre Ewan Cl, Barrow-in-Furness, Cumbria LA13 9HU; e-mail pru.south@cumbriacc.gov.uk; Tel 01229 894470; Fax 01229 894469
Area Co-ordinator Ms E. Robinson
4–16

West Cumbria Learning Centre Toll Bar, Distington, Workington, Cumbria CA14 4PJ; e-mail john.graham@cumbriacc.gov.uk; Tel 01946 834848; Fax 01946 834850
Area Co-ordinator Mr J. Graham

Greater Manchester Metropolitan Area

The following Metropolitan Councils comprise the Greater Manchester Metropolitan Area and are listed separately in this section: Bolton, Bury, Manchester, Oldham, Rochdale, Salford, Stockport, Tameside, Trafford and Wigan

Halton Borough Council
www.halton.gov.uk

In April 1998 Halton became a unitary authority. The rest of Cheshire retains a two-tier structure and is listed separately in this section.
Political composition: Lab: 34, LD: 14, Con: 7
Municipal Bldg, Kingsway, Widnes, Halton WA8 7QF;
    URL www.halton.gov.uk; Tel 0151 907 8300
Leader of the Council   Cllr T. McDermott
Chief Executive   David Parr
Executive Director (Children and Young People)   Vacancy

Children and Young People

Grosvenor Hse, Halton Lea, Runcorn, Halton WA7 2WD;
    e-mail hbeduct@halton.gov.uk; Fax 0151 471 7321
Strategic Director   Vacancy
Operational Director   Lorraine Butcher
Operational Director   Ann McIntyre
Operational Director   Kath O'Dwyer
Principal Adviser   Kevin Massey (Acting)
Senior Educational Psychologist   Carol Sheriff
Number of Schools
52 Primary; 8 Secondary; 4 Special; 4 Nursery; 1 PRU

EXECUTIVE BOARD

Lab: 9, LD: 1
Chair   A. McDermott
Vice-Chair   R. Polhill
Members of the Committee
Lab: D. Cargill, A. Gerrard, P. Harris, J. Massey, T. McInerney, S. Nelson, M. Wharton, M. Wright

SCHOOL PSYCHOLOGICAL SERVICE

c/o Hallwood Park Primary School   Hallwood Park Ave, Runcorn, Halton WA7 2FL

YOUTH SERVICE

Halton Youth Service   Youth Service Office, 107 Albert Rd, Widnes, Cheshire WU8 6LB; e-mail hys@hotmail.co.uk; Tel 0151 422 5503; Fax 0151 422 5501
Head   Dave Williams
Operations Manager   Stefan Cadek
Operations Manager   Tracey Walsh
Operations Manager (Special Projects)   Sally Carr
Co-ordinator (Duke of Edinburgh)   Veronica Anderson

COLLEGES

Riverside College, Halton   Kingsway, Widnes, Cheshire WA8 7QQ; Tel 0151 257 2800; Fax 0151 420 2408
Principal; Chief Executive   Alan Harrison
Widnes Campus   Riverside College, Cronton La, Widnes, Cheshire WA8 9WA; Tel 0151 424 1515; Fax 0151 495 1891

RUNCORN CAMPUS

Riverside College, Campus Dr, Runcorn, Cheshire WA7 4RE; URL www.riverside.ac.uk; e-mail info@riverside.ac.uk; Tel 01928 508600; Fax 01928 589481

Knowsley Metropolitan Borough Council
www.knowsley.gov.uk

2

Population: 149 393
Political composition: Lab: 50, LD: 13
PO Box 21, Municipal Bldgs, Archway Rd, Huyton, Knowsley, Merseyside L36 9YU;
    URL www.knowsley.gov.uk; e-mail knowsley@connect.org.uk; Tel 0151 489 6000
Chief Executive   Sheena Ramsey; Tel 0151 443 3772; Fax 0151 443 3030

Education Department

Huyton Hey Rd, Huyton, Merseyside L36 5YH;
    Tel 0151 489 6000
Director   Damian Allen
Assistant Director   Elaine Ayre
Deputy Assistant Director   John Flaterty (Acting)
Head (Early Years)   Linda Richardson
Principal Manager (SEN)   Lois Ward
Manager (School and Community Arts)   Emma Bush
Education Officer (Admissions and Attendance)   Alison Cain
General Adviser (Assessment and Differentiation)   Vacancy
Co-ordinator (Maths)   Ruth Harrison
Co-ordinator (Science)   Tom Costello
Literacy Consultant   Penny France
Contact (Staff Development)   Jane Lyon
Number of Schools
59 Primary; 11 Secondary; 8 Special

EDUCATION COMMITTEE

Cabinet Member with Portfolio (Education and Lifelong Learning)   L.G. Nolan

GOVERNOR TRAINING UNIT

Knowsley Education Department, Education Office, Huyton Hey Rd, Huyton, Knowsley, Merseyside L36 5YH; Tel 0151 443 3263; Fax 0151 480 4411
Contact   Sharon Fryer
Services offered
Training courses and procedural advice; resource library; newsletter; clerking of governors' meetings; governor recruitment publicity; Knowsley governors' forum

SCHOOLS PSYCHOLOGICAL SERVICE

Central Partnership Team   c/o Central Primary Support Centre; Tel 0151 443 5771
    Principal School Psychologist   Vacancy
Northern Partnership Team   c/o Northern Primary Support Centre, Bramcote Wlk, Merseyside; Tel 0151 443 4366

TEACHERS' CENTRE

Knowsley Training and Conference Centre   219 Knowsley La, Huyton, Knowsley, Merseyside L36 8HW; Tel 0151 443 5610
    Head   Patti Soo

Lancashire County Council
www.lancashire.gov.uk

In April 1998 both Blackburn with Darwen and Blackpool councils became unitary authorities and are listed separately in this section. The rest of Lancashire retains a two-tier structure.
Population: 1 134 976
Political composition: Lab: 44, Con: 31, LD: 6, Green: 1, Ind: 1, Idle Toad: 1

PO Box 78, County Hall, Preston, Lancashire PR1 8XJ;
URL www.lancashire.gov.uk; e-mail
enquiries@css.lancscc.gov.uk; Tel 0845 053 0000;
Fax 01772 533553
Chief Executive Chris Trinick
Deputy Chief Executive; Director (Resources) Jim Edney;
Tel 01772 534701; Fax 01772 534702

Education and Cultural Services Directorate (incorporating Children's Services)

PO Box 61, County Hall, Preston, Lancashire PR1 8RJ;
Tel 01772 254868; Fax 01772 261630
Director Sue Mulvany
Number of Schools
493 Primary; 88 Secondary; 33 Special (29 Day, 4
Residential); 26 Nursery

EDUCATION AND CULTURAL CABINET MEMBERS

Cabinet Member (Cultural Services and Communications)
County Cllr Marcus Johnstone
Cabinet Member (Education and Young People)
Cllr Alan Whittaker
Cabinet Member (Children and Families)
Cllr Clive Grunshaw

TRAINING CENTRES/IN-SERVICE TRAINING AND CONFERENCE CENTRE

The Woodlands Centre, Southport Rd, Chorley, Lancashire
PR7 1QR; Tel 01257 265811; Fax 01257 239710
Centre Manager Marion Hindley

SCHOOLS IT CENTRE

Southport Rd, Chorley, Lancashire PR7 1NX;
Tel 01257 516360; Fax 01257 516365
Manager G. Fielden

BUSINESS SERVICES DIVISION

Manager (Buildings and Development) E. Mather;
Tel 01772 531538
Manager (Building Schools for the Future) J. Newton;
Tel 01772 531259
Manager (Business Services Division) M. Hart;
Tel 01772 531648
Manager (Combined Finance Team) D. Kerfoot;
Tel 01772 531733
Manager (Committee and Office Services Team) F. Gore;
Tel 01772 531316
Manager (Personnel Services) P. Durham; Tel 01772 533899
Manager (School Financial Services) A. Taylor;
Tel 01772 531726
Manager (School Management Support Services) C. Garbutt;
Tel 01772 530687
Manager (School Policy and Operations) S.J. Mercer;
Tel 01772 531925
Co-ordinator (Performance and Management Review)
D. Ledsham; Tel 01772 531683
Team Leader (Governor Services) J. Bellis; Tel 01772 531637

THE SCHOOL STANDARDS GROUP

County Hall, Preston, Lancashire PR1 8RJ
Manager (Enterprise and Partnership) C. Lennox;
Tel 01772 531547
Manager (Inclusive Continuum Action Plan) S. Riley;
Tel 01772 532713
Manager (Learning Excellence) P. Carter
Manager (Policy Development) G. Hiscox; Tel 01772 531760
Manager (School Effectiveness Service) G. Dunn;
Tel 01772 531663
Manager (School Standards Group) P. Jefferson;
Tel 01772 531652; Fax 01772 531900

Manager (Service for Learners Out of School)
N. Scanlon (Acting); Tel 01772 531730

LIFELONG LEARNING AND CULTURAL SERVICES GROUP

County Hall, Preston, Lancashire PR1 8RJ
Manager (County Library and Information Services)
D. Lightfoot; Tel 01772 534010
Manager (County Museums Service) E. Southworth;
Tel 01772 530460
Manager (Early Years Development Childcare) Y. Farrow;
Tel 01772 532872
Manager (ICT Team) D. Carr; Tel 01772 532066
Manager (Lancashire Adult Learning) R. Hooper;
Tel 01772 531608
Manager (Lifelong Learning and Cultural Services Group)
R. Wand; Tel 01772 534004
County Archivist B. Jackson; Tel 01772 533026
County Arts Officer E. Roberts; Tel 01772 533012
County Youth and Community Officer J. Goffee;
Tel 01772 531792

CHILDREN SERVICES GROUP

County Hall, Preston, Lancashire PR1 8RJ
Head (SEN Assessment/Educational Psychology Services)
D. Webster; Tel 01772 531661
Manager (Children and Families Social Care Services)
S. Mitchell; Tel 01772 534257
Manager (Children Services Group) G. Rigg;
Tel 01772 534237; Fax 01772 531900
Manager (County Access Team) T. Clark; Tel 01772 531655
Manager (County Youth Justice Services) C. Witt;
Tel 01772 532017
County Education Welfare Officer A. Hazell;
Tel 01772 531613

PERFORMANCE MANAGEMENT AND REVIEW

Team Leader C. Garbutt; Tel 01772 261683
Senior Performance Management Officer S. Blakey;
Tel 01772 262764
Performance Management Officer K. Taylor;
Tel 01772 262838
Strategy Officer P. Bannister; Tel 01772 262739

PORTAGE SERVICES

Lancaster c/o Ridge CP School, Keswick Rd, Lancaster,
Lancashire LA1 3LE; Tel 01524 847140; Fax 01524 847140
Contact Claire Goss

AREA OFFICES

East
The Globe Centre, St James Sq, Accrington, Lancashire
BB5 0RE; Tel 01254 220500; Fax 01254 220501
*District Team Manager (Burnley Youth and Community
Service)* L. Rushton; Tel 01282 831040
*District Team Manager (Hyndburn Youth and Community
Service)* B. Emmett; Tel 01254 876295
*District Team Manager (Pendle Youth and Community
Service)* S. Butters; Tel 01282 862850
*District Team Manager (Ribble Valley Youth and Community
Service)* W. Taylor; Tel 01200 443466
*District Team Manager (Rossendale Youth and Community
Service)* S. Roman; Tel 01706 225180
*Area Assessment Manager; Assistant Principal Educational
Psychologist* K. Fallon; Tel 01254 220526
Area Team Leader (Committee and Office and Services Group)
D. Greaves; Tel 01254 220520
Area Team Leader (School Financial Services Group)
C. Shepherd; Tel 01254 220555
Area Team Leader (School Personnel Group) W. Hindle;
Tel 01254 220510
Senior Education Welfare Officer (Burnley) L. Hunt;
Tel 01282 831033
*Senior Education Welfare Officer (Hyndburn/Ribble Valley/
Rossendale)* J. Lloyd; Tel 01254 220728

Senior Education Welfare Officer (Pendle)   M. Sunderland;
Tel 01282 831204
Area Officer (Pupil Access Officer)   J.C. Thompson;
Tel 01254 220706
Assistant Youth and Community Officer   Vacancy;
Tel 01254 876295
Senior Adviser (Performance Management)   W. Haykin;
Tel 01254 220530

North

Area Education Office, PO Box 606, White Cross Education
Centre, Quarry Rd, Lancaster, Lancashire LA1 3SQ;
Tel 01524 63243; Fax 01524 581149
District Team Manager (Fylde Youth and Community Service)
M. Stott; Tel 01772 682548
*District Team Manager (Lancaster Youth and Community
Service)*   J. Gordon; Tel 01524 581175
District Team Manager (Wyre Youth and Community Service)
M. Piela; Tel 01253 893102
*Area Assessment Manager; Assistant Principal Educational
Psychologist*   J. Bradshaw; Tel 01524 581144
Area Pupil Access Officer   D. Ormerod; Tel 01524 581213
Area Team Leader (Committee and Office Services Group)
G. Gaunt; Tel 01524 581204
Area Team Leader (School Financial Services Group)
R. Livesey; Tel 01524 581101
Area Team Leader (School Personnel Services Group)
D. Singleton; Tel 01524 581102
*Area Team Leader (School Policy and Operations Group:
Governor Services)*   C. Eaves; Tel 01524 581186
Senior Area Education Welfare Officer (Lancaster Team)
Kate Gaskell; Tel 01524 585855

South

Joint Divisional Office, East Cliff, Preston, Lancashire
PR1 3JT; Tel 01772 532719
*District Team Manager (Chorley Youth and Community
Service)*   G. Murdoch; Tel 01257 538251
*District Team Manager (Preston Youth and Community
Service)*   K. Gillies; Tel 01772 531805
*District Team Manager (South Ribble Youth and Community
Service)*   C. Fenning; Tel 01772 621125
*District Team Manager (West Lancashire: Youth and Community
Service)*   A. Blayney-Greene; Tel 01695 585761
*Area Assessment Manager; Assistant Principal Educational
Psychologist*   B. Probin; Tel 01772 531597
*Area Education Welfare Officer (Chorley Education Support
Centre)*   G. Vickers; Tel 01257 517234
Area Officer (Pupil Access)   L. Philipson; Tel 01772 261797
Area Team Leader (Committee and Office Services Group)
D. Wilde; Tel 01772 532718
Area Team Leader (School Financial Services Group)   N. Smith;
Tel 01772 532054
Area Team Leader (School Personnel Group)   C. Allison;
Tel 01772 532106
*Area Team Leader (School Policy and Operations Group:
Governor Services)*   B. Golding; Tel 01772 532162
*Senior Adviser; Team Leader (Lancashire Schools Effectiveness
Service)*   T. Thornton; Tel 01257 517228

COMPLEX LEARNING DIFFICULTIES SERVICE

Hillside School, Longridge   Ribchester Rd, Longridge,
Preston, Lancashire PR3 3XB; Tel 01772 782205;
Fax 01772 782471
Headteacher   Mr G. Fitzpatrick
2–16; ASD

EARLY YEARS (SEN)

Central   8 Eastcliff, Preston, Lancashire PR1 3JE; e-mail
sue.bould@ed.lancscc.gov.uk; Tel 01772 533781
Head of Service   Sue Bould
East Area   The Globe, St James Sq, Accrington, Lancashire
BB5 0RE; Tel 01254 220781; Fax 01254 220787
Team Leader (Early Years: SEN)   Barbara Chapman

North Area   Ridge Primary School, Keswick Rd, Lancaster,
Lancashire LA1 3LE; Tel 01524 847140; Fax 01524 847140
Team Leader (Early Years: SEN)   Claire Goss
South Area   Education Office, Union St, Chorley, Lancashire
PR7 1EB; Tel 01257 239927; Fax 01257 239920
Team Leader (Early Years: SEN)   Win O'Neil

LANCASHIRE EDUCATION MEDICAL SERVICE (LEMS)

Joint Divisional Offices, East Cliff, Preston, Lancashire
PR1 3JT; Tel 01772 531572; Fax 01772 532193
Head   Pat Probin
East Lancashire Education Medical Service   The Globe, St
James Sq, Accrington, Lancashire BB5 0RE;
Tel 01254 220785; Fax 01254 220787
Contact   K. Waddington
North Lancashire Education Medical Service   PO Box 606,
White Cross Est, Quarry Rd, Lancaster, Lancashire
LA1 3SQ; Tel 01524 585838
Contact   D. Wood
South Lancashire Education Medical Service   Joint Divisional
Offices, 5th Fl, East Cliff, Preston, Lancashire PR1 3JT;
Tel 01772 531572
Contact   P. Probin

LANCASHIRE'S EDUCATION INCLUSION SERVICE

East Area   The Globe, St James Sq, Accrington, Lancashire
BB5 0RE; Tel 01254 220777; Fax 01254 220787
Area Manager   Alice Taylor
North Area   Storey Hse, White Cross, Lancaster, Lancashire
LA1 3SQ; Tel 01524 5858732; Fax 01524 585831
Area Manager   Linda Gormally
Area Manager   Annette Pennie
South Area   5th Fl, East Cliff, Preston, Lancashire PR1 3JT;
e-mail margaret.mee@ed.lancscc.gov.uk;
Tel 01772 532196; Fax 01772 262193
Area Manager   Margaret Mee

PUPIL REFERRAL SERVICE/LANCASHIRE EDUCATION MEDICAL SERVICE INCLUDING CAMHS

East Area: The Globe, St James Sq, Accrington, Lancashire
BB5 0RE; Tel 01254 220794; Fax 01254 220787
South Area: 8 East Cliff, Preston, Lancashire PR1 3JR; e-mail
barry.hornby@ed.lancscc.gov.uk; Tel 01772 261853;
Fax 01772 262214
Head of Service (South Area)   Barry Hornby
Senior Manager (East Area)   Kath Waddington (Acting)
Traveller Education Service   8 East Cliff, Preston, Lancashire
PE1 3JE; Tel 01772 263826; Fax 01772 532737
Head of Service   Jeanne Kenyon

PUPIL REFERRAL SERVICE AREA TEAMS

Primary East   Rishton Pupil Referral Unit, 7 Station Rd,
Blackburn, Lancashire BB1 4HF; Tel 01254 887116
Contact   B. Whittaker (Acting)
Primary North   Ringway Pupil Referral Unit, Ringway,
Thornton-Cleveleys, Lancashire FY5 2NL;
Tel 01253 850714
Contact   S. Bonney
Primary South   Centurion Hse, Leyland, Lancaster,
Lancashire PR5 2GR; Tel 01772 455649
Contact   K. Loten
Secondary East   Rawtenstall Education Office, 1 Grange St,
Rawtenstall, Lancashire BB4 7RT; Tel 01706 211149
Contact   P. Cooper
Secondary North   33 Hornby Rd, Caton, Lancaster,
Lancashire LA2 9QW; Tel 01524 771632/3
Contact   L. McKee
Secondary South   Minster Lodge Pupil Referral Unit, Ruff
La, Ormskirk, Lancashire L39 4QX; Tel 01695 575486
Contact   G. Lucy (Acting)

SHORT STAY SCHOOLS

Brookside School Barton Rd, Scotforth, Lancaster, Lancashire LA1 4ER; Tel 01524 389988; Fax 01524 841360
Headteacher Ms L. Greer

Copper House School 7 Station Rd, Rishton, Blackburn BB1 4HF; Tel 01254 887116; Fax 01254 887116
Headteacher Mrs B. Whittaker

Golden Hill School Earnshaw Dr, Leyland, Preston, Lancashire PR25 1QS; Tel 01772 904780;
Fax 01772 904781
Headteacher Mrs S. Parr

Golden Hill School (Preston Centre) Cromwell Rd, Ribbleton, Preston, Lancashire PR2 6YD;
Tel 01772 796603; Fax 01772 652263
Headteacher Mrs S. Parr

Haven School Ringway, Thornton-Cleveleys, Lancashire FY5 2NL; Tel 01253 821516; Fax 01253 850842
Contact Mrs P. Brockbank
SEBD

Hendon Brook School Hendon Brook, Townhouse Rd, Nelson, Lancashire BB9 8BP; Tel 01282 693432;
Fax 01282 693432
Headteacher Mrs G.B. Laycock

Hill View School Swindon St, Burnley, Lancashire BB11 4PF; Tel 01282 434253; Fax 01282 429543
Headteacher Mrs M. Begols (Acting)

Larches House School Larches La, Ashton-on-Ribble, Preston, Lancashire PR2 1QE; Tel 01772 728567;
Fax 01772 723294
Contact Mr A. Dewhurst (Acting)
9–16

Leabrook School Burnley Rd, Rawtenstall, Lancashire BB4 8HY; Tel 01706 215977; Fax 01706 215500
Headteacher Ms H. McLenahan

Marles Hill School 150 Wheatley Lane Rd, Barrowford, Nelson, Lancashire BB9 6QQ; Tel 01282 615862;
Fax 01282 603372
Headteacher Ms J.W. Hart (Acting)
11–16

McKee School Poulton Rd, Fleetwood, Lancashire FY7 7BS; Tel 01253 770714; Fax 01253 770789
Headteacher Ms L. Nixon

Minster Lodge School Ruff La, Ormskirk, Lancashire L39 4QX; Tel 01695 575486; Fax 01695 575150
Headteacher Ms A. Swan
11–16

The Oswaldtwistle School Union Rd, Oswaldtwistle, Lancashire BB5 3DA; Tel 01254 231553; Fax 01254 879544
Headteacher Ms P. Smith

Shaftesbury House School Stratford Rd, Chorley, Lancashire PR6 0AF; Tel 01257 516067; Fax 01257 516069
Headteacher Mrs A. Clark (Acting)

Stepping Stones School Bowerham Rd, Lancaster, Lancashire LA1 4HT; Tel 01524 67164; Fax 01524 841239
Headteacher Mrs J.A. Ashton

ADULT EDUCATION INSTITUTES

The Adult College, Lancaster White Cross Education Centre, PO Box 603, Quarry Rd, Lancaster, Lancashire LA1 3SE; Tel 01524 60141; Fax 01524 849458
Headteacher Mr P. Garrod

Alston Hall College Alston La, Longridge, Preston, Lancashire PR3 3BP; Tel 01772 784661; Fax 01772 785835
Headteacher G. Wilkinson

Lancashire College Southport Rd, Chorley, Lancashire PR7 1NB; Tel 01257 276719; Fax 01257 241370
Headteacher Mr S. Hailstone

OUTDOOR EDUCATION CENTRES

Borwick Hall Borwick, Carnforth, Lancashire LA6 1JU; Tel 01524 732508; Fax 01524 732590
Manager Mrs K. Betley

Hottersall Lodge Field Centre Hothersall La, Longridge, Preston, Lancashire PR3 2XB; Tel 01254 878422;
Fax 01254 878499
Centre Manager Mr D.A. Richardson

Tower Wood Outdoor Education Centre Windermere, Cumbria, Lancashire LA23 3PL; Tel 01539 531519;
Fax 01539 530071
Head of Service Mr S. Baggs

Whitehough Outdoor Education Centre Barley New Rd, Barley, Burnley, Lancashire BB12 9LF; Tel 01282 615688;
Fax 01282 696206
Centre Manager Ms V. Scott

Liverpool City Council
www.liverpool.gov.uk

Population: 447 500
Political composition: LD: 51, Lab: 35, Liberal: 3, Green: 1
Municipal Bldgs, Dale St, Liverpool, Merseyside L69 2DH;
URL www.liverpool.gov.uk; e-mail
gill.jones@liverpool.gov.uk; Tel 0151 233 3000

Education, Library and Sports Services

4th Fl, 4 Renshaw St, Liverpool, Merseyside L1 4NX;
Tel 0151 233 2822
Director (Education) Colin Hilton
Head of Education Services (Education Support) S. Smith
Head of Education Services (School Effectiveness) M. Gill
Head of Education Services (Strategy and Resources)
A. Melville
Head (Strategic Information and Research); Senior Education Officer (Strategic Information) Mike Baker
Manager (Youth and Community) C. Morrison
Principal Education Officer (Client Support) K. Roberts
Principal Education Officer (Personnel and Management Services) T. McNamara
Principal Education Officer (Strategic Development)
R. Richardson Rampling
Principal Educational Psychologist Judy Poole
Principal Educational Welfare Officer R. Collinson
Senior Education Officer (Action Communications Team)
J. Maskell
Senior Education Officer (Additional Needs) K. Gleave
Senior Education Officer (Early Years) H. Winrow
Senior Education Officer (Ethnic Minority Achievement Service) D. Leung-Clifford
Education Officer (Equal Opportunities) S. Brown
Education Officer (Service Review) M. Croft
Area Liaison Officer (Race Equality) John Cole
Finance Officer K. Williams
Number of Schools
32 Secondary; 19 Special
Day of Committee Meeting
Monthly

EDUCATION COMMITTEE

Chair Cllr Paul Clein; 34 Rawlins St, Liverpool, Merseyside L7 0JF
Deputy Chair Jan Clein; 34 Rawlins St, Liverpool, Merseyside L7 0JF
Opposition Spokesperson Alf Flattery (Liv. Lab)
Opposition Spokesperson Steve Radford (LD)
Opposition Spokesperson Geraldine Wilson (Lab)

GOVERNOR TRAINING UNIT

Governor Training, Education, Library and Sports Services, 4th Fl, 4 Renshaw St, Liverpool, Merseyside L1 4NX;
Tel 0151 233 8134; Fax 0151 233 8134
Adviser (Governor Training and Support); Co-ordinator Stella Owen CertEd, AdvDip Special Ed, MEd

Services offered
Training courses; on-site training courses; personal support; telephone helpline; newsletter

ADULT EDUCATION ESTABLISHMENTS

Adult Guidance Service 4th Fl, 4 Renshaw St, Liverpool, Merseyside L1 4NX; Tel 0151 233 1600
   Contact C. Maguire
Burton Manor Residential College of Adult Education Burton, South Wirral, Cheshire L64 5SJ; Tel 0151 336 5172; Fax 0151 336 6586
   Contact K. Chandler
Newsham Drive Adult Education Centre 83 Newsham Dr, Liverpool, Merseyside L6 7UH; Tel 0151 263 5153
   Contact J. Marquis
Phoenix Adult Centre Wellington Rd, Liverpool, Merseyside L8 4TX; Tel 0151 728 9086
   Area Manager A. Phizakerlea
   Assistant Area Manager B. Blanche

EDUCATIONAL CENTRE

Colomendy Centre for Outdoor Education Loggerheads, Near Mold, Clwyd, Conwy CH7 5LB; Tel 01352 810381; Fax 01352 810670
   Contact J. Bannon

Manchester City Council
www.manchester.gov.uk

Population: 442 000
Political composition: Lab: 61, LD: 34, Green: 1
Town Hall, Albert Sq, Manchester M60 2LA;
   URL www.manchester.gov.uk; Tel 0161 234 5000
Chief Executive Sir Howard Bernstein

Children's Services

PO Box 536, Town Hall Extension, Manchester M60 2AF;
   URL www.manchester.gov.uk/ssd
Overseas Hse, Quay St, Manchester M3 3BB;
   URL www.manchester.gov.uk/education-and-learning;
   Fax 0161 234 7147
Director Pauline Newman
Deputy Director John Edwards
Assistant Director Laureen Donnan
Assistant Director Mike Livingstone
Assistant Director Kieran McDermott
Head (Business Services and Access) Nigel Trim; Tel 0161 234 7050; Tel 0161 234 7733
Head (Development, Personnel and Management Support) Vacancy; Tel 0161 234 3926; Tel 0161 234 3980
Head (Education Services 14–19) Vacancy; Tel 0161 234 7721; Fax 0161 234 7733
Head (SEN Casework Service) Brian Seaborn; Tel 0161 234 7134; Tel 0161 234 7728
Head (Strategy and Performance) Graham Mellors; Tel 0161 234 7050; Fax 0161 234 7733
Assistant Chief Education Officer (School Organisation and Redevelopment) Allan Seaborn; Tel 0161 234 7155; Fax 0161 234 7402
Assistant Chief Education Officer (SEN and Inclusion Strategy) Jenny Andrews; Tel 0161 234 7590; Tel 0161 234 7734
Chief Educational Psychologist Maria Heffernan; Central District Centre, Westwood St, Moss Side, Manchester M14 4SW; Tel 0161 226 5404; Fax 0161 226 2221
Contact (Admissions) Linda Ryan; Tel 0161 234 7188; Tel 0161 234 7255
Contact (Admissions) Helen Walsh; Tel 0161 234 7188; Fax 0161 234 7255

Number of Schools
130 Primary; 23 Secondary; 14 Special; 2 Academy
Requisition Periods for Schools Supplies
April-March
Day of Children and Young People Overview and Scrutiny Committee Meeting
Tuesday of week one in six week cycle

EXECUTIVE

Chair Cllr Richard Leese (Lab); Town Hall, Manchester M60 2LA; Tel 0161 234 3004
Members of the Children and Young People Overview and Scrutiny Committee
Lab: Cllr Andrews, Cllr Carmody, Cllr Cooper, Cllr Cox, Cllr Harrison, Cllr Judge, Cllr Keller
LD: Cllr Ali, Cllr Bhatti, Cllr Chohan, Cllr Dobson, Cllr Fisher, Cllr Parkinson
Advisory Members: D. Arnold, Rev R. Chow, Rev Fr Tim Hopkins

EXCLUSIONS AND PUPIL REFERRAL SERVICE

Tel 0161 234 7240; Fax 0161 234 7107
Head (Exclusions and EOTAS) Chris Read

EDUCATIONAL PSYCHOLOGY SERVICE

Central District Centre Westwood St, Moss Side, Manchester M14 4PH; Tel 0161 226 5404; Fax 0161 226 2221
   District Senior Educational Psychologist Patricia Carter
North District Centre 2 Thornaby Wlk, Harpurhey, Manchester M9 5GE; Tel 0161 205 2857; Fax 0161 205 0893
   District Senior Educational Psychologist Teresa Regan

SCHOOL ATTENDANCE IMPROVEMENT SERVICE

Tel 0161 234 7177; Fax 0161 234 7218
East/West Manchester District Education Welfare Office, The Waldway, 537a Stockport Rd, Manchester M12 4LJ; Tel 0161 225 0293; Fax 0161 225 3476
   District Manager (West) Sue Toke
North Manchester District The Old Rectory, 337 St Marys Rd, Moston, Greater Manchester M40 0BF; Tel 0161 682 9054; Fax 0161 681 2715
   District Manager (North East) Sue Toke
South Manchester District 2nd Fl, Hale Top Hse, Wythenshawe, Manchester M22 5SD; Tel 0161 499 1451; Fax 0161 437 6920
   District Manager Beverley Howard

HOSPITAL SCHOOL AND HOME TUITION SERVICE

Leo Kelly Centre Monton St, Greenheys, Manchester M14 4LT; Tel 0161 226 1367; Fax 0161 232 1969
Manchester Hospital Schools and Home Teaching Service Charlestown Rd, Blackley, Manchester M9 7AA; Tel 0161 918 5118; Fax 0161 918 5600
   Head Sandra Hibbert

DIVERSITY AND INCLUSION

Peacock Centre, Peacock Cl, Gorton, Manchester M18 8AX; Tel 0161 223 1653; Tel 0161 223 3158

BEHAVIOUR SUPPORT NEEDS

Peacock Centre, Peacock Cl, Gorton, Manchester M18 8AX; Tel 0161 223 3158; Fax 0161 223 1653
District Co-ordinator Elaine Hillary

INCLUSION SERVICE FOR VISUAL IMPAIRMENT

Shawgrove, Cavendish Rd, West Didsbury, Manchester M20 1QB; Tel 0161 219 6667; Fax 0161 445 0386
Head of Service Tony Bowyer

MANCHESTER INCLUSION SERVICE FOR CHILDREN AND YOUNG PEOPLE WITH HEARING NEEDS OR DEAFNESS

Newbrook, Newholme Rd, West Didsbury, Manchester
M20 2XZ; Tel 0161 445 5172; Fax 0161 438 0058
Head of Service Susan Parsons

INDEPENDENCE DEVELOPMENT SERVICE FOR DISABLED CHILDREN

Abraham Moss Centre Crescent Rd, Crumpsall, Manchester
M8 5UF; Tel 0161 908 8360; Fax 0161 908 8370
Resource Manager Jan Bresnahan

EXCELLENCE IN CITIES

Turing Hse, Archway 5, Birley Fields, Hulme, Manchester
M15 5RL; Tel 0845 450 9595; Fax 0845 450 9596

MUSIC SERVICE

Zion Arts Centre, Stretford Rd, Manchester M15 5ZA;
Tel 0161 226 4411; Fax 0161 226 1010
Head of Service Sue Berry (Acting)
Manchester Dance Centre Zion Arts Centre, Stretford Rd,
Manchester M15 5ZA; Tel 0161 226 4422;
Fax 0161 226 1010

TRAVELLER AND MOBILE CHILDREN

Peacock Centre, Gorton, Manchester M18 8AX;
Tel 0161 223 3158; Fax 0161 223 1653

MISCELLANEOUS ESTABLISHMENTS

Connexions Lee Hse, 90 Gt Bridgewater St, Manchester
M1 5JW; Tel 0161 228 1101
Ghyll Head Outdoor Centre Windermere, Cumbria
LA23 3LN; Tel 01539 443751; Fax 01539 443751

Merseyside Metropolitan Area

The following Metropolitan Councils comprise the
Merseyside Metropolitan Area and are listed separately in
this section: Knowsley, Liverpool, St Helens, Sefton and
Wirral

Oldham Metropolitan Borough Council

www.oldham.gov.uk

Population: 219 000
Civic Centre, West St, Oldham, Greater Manchester
OL1 1UL; URL www.oldham.gov.uk; Tel 0161 911 3000;
Fax 0161 911 4684
Chief Executive Andrew Kilburn

Directorate of Services for Children, Young People and Families

PO Box 40, Civic Centre, Oldham, Greater Manchester
OL1 1XJ; Tel 0161 911 4260; Fax 0161 911 3222
*Chief Executive (Oldham Education Business and Guidance
Services)* Tim Mitchell
Executive Member (Culture, Leisure and Tourism)
Cllr C. Hilyer
Executive Member (Education) Cllr K. Knox
Executive Director Ruth M. Baldwin
Assistant Director (Resources and Planning) Alan Lee
Assistant Director (School Improvement)
Nick Hudson (Acting)

Head (Early Years Development and Childcare) Jackie Stubbs
Head (Education Out-of-School) Nikki Shaw
Head (Finance and Personnel Services) Pauline Kane
Head (Heritage, Libraries and Art) Sheena McFarlane
Head (Libraries, Information and Archives) Richard Lambert
Head (Lifelong Learning and Culture) Lynda Fairhurst
Head (Youth Service) Pam Griffin
Senior Manager (School Improvement) Nina Ascroft
Manager (Buildings/Development) Ron Gregory
Manager (Galleries, Museums and Arts) Sheena MacFarlane
Manager (Personnel and Operational Support)
Gillian Wooley
Manager (School Improvement) Kit Thorne
Manager (Student Services) Jane Barrett
Contact (Early Years SEN Service) Claire Ward
Number of Schools
15 Secondary; 6 Special

EDUCATION AND CULTURAL SERVICES COMMITTEE

Members of the Committee
Battye, Currie, Davies, Dean, Greenwood, Harrison, Hayes,
Heffernan, Hibbert, Hilyer, Jabbar, Jacobs, Jones, Joynes,
Keap, Knox, McArdle, Ritchie, Wingate

OUTDOOR AND ENVIRONMENTAL EDUCATION SERVICE

Castleshaw Centre Waterworks Rd, Delph, Oldham,
Greater Manchester OL3 5LZ; Tel 01457 874276;
Fax 01457 820551
Manager D. Falconbridge

MUSIC CENTRE

The Lyceum Union St, Oldham, Greater Manchester
OL1 1QG; Tel 0161 627 2332; Fax 0161 620 0259
Director (Music) Dr E. Bentley BEd, MEd, GRSM,
ARMCM(P)

THEATRE WORKSHOP

Royton Assembly Hall, Market Sq, Oldham, Greater
Manchester OL2 5QD; Tel 0161 911 3243
Manager James Atherton

SPECIAL NEEDS SUPPORT SERVICES

Cognition and Communication Limeside Primary School,
Third Ave, Oldham, Greater Manchester OL8 3SB;
Tel 0161 688 9833
Head (SEN); Senior Adviser Susan Howe
Educational Psychology Service Centre for Professional
Development, Rosary Rd, Oldham, Greater Manchester
OL8 2QE; Tel 0161 911 4218; Fax 0161 911 3211
Deputy Head (SEN); Principal Educational Psychologist
Stephen Rooney
Governor Support Service CPD, Rosary Rd, Fitton Hill,
Oldham, Greater Manchester OL8 2QE;
Tel 0161 911 3632; Fax 0161 911 3664
Manager (Governor Support and Training Services)
D. Challen
Services offered: To give advice and support to governing
bodies in accordance with their needs; to ensure that the
training needs of governing bodies/governors are met
Home and Hospital Teaching Service Northgate Hse,
Firbank Rd, Oldham, Greater Manchester OL2 6TU;
Tel 0161 911 3234
Manager (Service Unit) Margaret Cadman
Service for Hearing Impairment Greenbank, Firbank Rd,
Royton, Oldham, Greater Manchester OL2 6TU
Service for Visual Impairment Greenbank, Firbank Rd,
Oldham, Greater Manchester OL2 6TU; Tel 0161 911 3110
Social Services Teaching Team c/o Adolescent and Youth
Project, Marion Walker Hse, Oldham, Greater
Manchester; Tel 0161 626 4947
Deputy Teacher-in-Charge J. Hayes

Rochdale Metropolitan Borough Council

www.rochdale.gov.uk

Population: 205 357
Political composition: LD: 27, Lab: 24, Con: 9
PO Box 67, Municipal Offices, Smith St, Rochdale, Greater
Manchester OL16 1YQ; URL www.rochdale.gov.uk;
e-mail council@rochdale.gov.uk; Tel 01706 647474
Chief Executive Roger Ellis

Education Service

PO Box 70, Municipal Offices, Smith St, Rochdale, Greater
Manchester OL16 1YD; Fax 01706 658560
Executive Director T. Piggott
Head (Learners and Young People) A. Tipton
Head (Pupil Referral Service) K. Connolly
Head (Schools) S. Brown
Head (Support) R. Hunter
Manager (Education Welfare) S. Dearden
Manager (Finance) C. Clarkson
Manager (Health Projects and Partnership Team)
K. Sanderson
Manager (Information, Planning and Communications)
C. Kelly
Manager (Operations Support) Vacancy
Manager (Partnership Education Service) Vacancy
Manager (Rochdale Additional Needs Service) S. McKinlay
Team Leader (Access: Inclusion and SEN) M. Boyle
Principal Administration Officer (Governor Support)
M. Matthews
Principal Educational Psychologist J. Stothard
Principal Officer (Early Years) S. Bowness
Principal Buildings Officer Y. Williams
Senior Education Officer (Staffing) M. Moore
Education Officer (Student Support and Finance)
G. Livingstone
*Senior Consultant (Ethnic Minority Achievement Team:
Primary)* S. Robinson
*Senior Consultant (Ethnic Minority Achievement Team:
Secondary)* M. Coates
Senior School Improvement Officer T. Lasan
*Senior Education Officer (School Support); Development
Officer* J. Bollington
Consultant (Behaviour Management Development Team)
J. Hook
Number of Schools
70 Primary; 14 Secondary; 4 Special; 4 Nursery

GOVERNOR SUPPORT UNIT

Governor Support Unit, 8th Fl, Municipal Offices, Smith St,
Rochdale, Greater Manchester OL16 1YD;
Tel 01706 925177; Fax 01706 658560
Principal Administration Officer M. Matthews
Services offered
Governing body support; clerking school governing bodies;
governor training

CHILDREN, SCHOOLS AND FAMILIES OVERVIEW AND SCRUTINY COMMITTEE

Lab: 5, LD: 5, Con: 2
Chair Cllr Clayton (LD)
Vice-Chair Cllr Maguire (LD)
Members of the Committee
Ashworth, Canon Ballard, Clayton, Cooper, Dr Cosgrove,
Fitzsimons, Hardman, B. Jones, Maguire, Marrion, Rev
Mwailu, Noi, Pedley, Rowbotham, Smith, Ward, Williams

PSYCHOLOGY SERVICE

Sutherland Centre Sutherland Rd, Darnhill, Heywood
OL10 3PY; Tel 01706 926400; Fax 01706 926420
Head of Service J. Stothard

SCHOOL SUPPORT SERVICES

Ethnic Minority Achievement Team Highwood Centre,
Highwood, Norden, Rochdale, Greater Manchester
OL11 5XP; Tel 01706 652940; Fax 01706 652958
Contact (Primary) Susan Robinson
Contact (Secondary) Mary Coates
Rochdale Additional Needs Service Sutherland Centre,
Sutherland Rd, Darnhill, Heywood OL10 3PY;
Tel 01706 926400; Fax 01706 926420
Head of Service S. McKinlay
Rochdale Music Service Music Centre, Fieldhouse School,
Rochdale, Lancashire OL12 0HZ; Tel 01706 750288;
Fax 01706 656043
Contact F. Bowker

St Helens Metropolitan Borough Council

www.sthelens.gov.uk

Population: 176 000
Political composition: Lab: 33, LD: 15, Con: 6
Town Hall, St Helens, Merseyside WA10 1HP;
URL www.sthelens.gov.uk; Tel 01744 456000;
Fax 01744 456889
Chief Executive C.A. Hudson BA, IPFA

Children and Young People's Services

The Rivington Centre, Rivington Rd, St Helens, Merseyside
WA10 4ND; Tel 01744 455328; Fax 01744 455350
Executive Member (CYPS) Cllr T. Shields
Executive Member (Social Inclusion) Cllr Ken Pinder
Director (Children and Young People's Services)
Susan Richardson; e-mail
susanrichardson@sthelens.gov.uk; Tel 01744 455320;
Fax 01744 455319
Senior Assistant Director Judith Godley
Senior Assistant Director (Performance and Strategy)
Judith Godley; e-mail judithgodley@sthelens.gov.uk;
Tel 01744 455322; Fax 01744 455319
Assistant Director (Resources and Support) Steve Gaskell
Head (Family Learning) Pam Meredith
Head (Information and Heritage Services) Jill Roughley
Head (Pupil Referral Service) Vacancy
Head (School Improvement) David Law
Head (Service for Children with Hearing Impairment)
Alan McGuffog
Head (Service for Children with Visual Impairment)
Pat Auckland
Head (Sure Start) Cathy Harner
Manager (Early Years and Childcare) Janet Yates
Primary Adviser; Inspector (Early Years) Linda Smith
Primary Adviser; Inspector (ICT) Paul Tomkow
Primary Adviser; Inspector (Literacy) Jean Kendall
Secondary Adviser; Inspector (Modern Foreign Languages)
Patricia Smith
Secondary Adviser; Inspector (Science) Geoff Rate
Principal Personnel Officer Angela Farell
Attendance and Exclusions Officer Geoff Tither
Education Management Accountant Grey Tyrer
Forward Planning Officer John Skinley
Governor Development Officer Joe Heavey
Policy Review Officer George Greenhaigh
Property Officer Hilary Hutchings
Number of Schools
54 Primary; 10 Secondary; 3 Special

Day of Committee Meeting
Friday; eight week cycle
Requisition Periods for Schools Supplies
As and when required

GOVERNOR TRAINING UNIT

Governor Services Section, CYPS, St Helens, Merseyside
WA10 4ND; Tel 01744 455351; Fax 01744 455350
Governor Development Officer Joe Heavey
Services offered
Support and training in all areas of school governance;
provision of information, agenda items, instruments and
articles of government; membership records; clerking
service

SERVICE FOR CHILDREN WITH VISUAL IMPAIRMENT

Park Road Centre, Park Rd, St Helens, Merseyside;
Tel 01744 677333
Manager P. Auckland

Salford City Council
www.salford.gov.uk

Population: 216 103
Political composition: Lab: 44, Con: 8, LD: 8
Salford Civic Centre, Chorley Rd, Swinton, Salford, Greater
Manchester M27 5DA; URL www.salford.gov.uk;
Tel 0161 794 4711; Fax 0161 794 6595
Chief Executive B. Spicer

Children's Services Directorate

Minerva Hse, Pendlebury Rd, Swinton, Salford, Greater
Manchester M27 4EQ; Tel 0161 778 0123
Tel 0161 778 0382
Lead Member Cllr John Warmisham
Executive Support Member Cllr Ann Marie Humphreys
Strategic Director (Children's Services) Jill Baker
Deputy Director (Children's Services) John Stephens
Assistant Director (Inclusion) Paul Woltman
Assistant Director (Resources) Mike Hall
Assistant Director (Strategy and Commissioning)
Paul Greenway
Assistant Director (Transition) Faith Mann
Principal School Improvement Officer (Primary) Paul Ford
Principal School Improvement Officer (Secondary)
Jan Rowney
Principal Group Accountant Robert McIntyre
Number of Schools
82 Primary; 15 Secondary; 5 Special
Day of Children's Services Servicing Committee
Monthly, third Wednesday after council

OUTDOOR EDUCATION CENTRE

Lledr Hall Pont y Pant, Dolwyddelan, Conwy LL25 0PJ;
e-mail lledhall@aol.com; Tel 01690 750214;
Fax 01690 750558
Centre Manager Alistair Cook

CHILDREN'S CENTRES

Barton Moss Children's Centre Barton Moss School, Trippier
Rd, Peel Grn, Eccles, Greater Manchester M30 7PT;
Tel 0161 707 2421; Fax 0161 921 1841
Belvedere Children's Centre Belvedere Rd, Pendleton,
Salford, Greater Manchester M6 5EJ; Tel 0161 737 3171;
Fax 0161 708 8813
Bradshaw Children's Centre Devonshire St, Salford, Greater
Manchester M7 4RF; Tel 0161 792 3271; Fax 0161 708 8313
Irlam Children's Centre Fiddlers Lane Primary School,
Fiddlers La, Irlam, Greater Manchester M44 6QE;
Tel 0161 775 2490; Fax 0161 921 1705

Lark Hill Sure Start Children's Centre Sedgefield Cl, Salford,
Greater Manchester M5 4JL; Tel 0161 921 2348;
Fax 0161 743 0161
Little Hulton Sure Start Children's Centre Longshaw Dr,
Little Hulton, Greater Manchester M28 0BP; e-mail
lhulton.earlyyears@salford.gov.uk; Tel (main)
0161 604 7660; Tel (nursery) 0161 604 7687;
Fax 0161 604 7698
Manager Mrs D. Jones
North Swinton Children's Centre St Charles Primary School,
Moorside Rd, Swinton M27 9PD; Tel 0800 195 5565
Winton Children's Centre Brindley St, Winton, Greater
Manchester M30 8AB; Tel 0161 788 0192;
Fax 0161 789 5822

Sefton Metropolitan Borough Council
www.sefton.gov.uk

Population: 277 400 (ONS mid 2006 est)
Political composition: LD: 26, Lab: 21, Con: 19
URL www.sefton.gov.uk; Tel (contact centre) 0845 140 0845

Children's Services

9th Fl, Merton Hse, Stanley Rd, Bootle, Merseyside L20 3JA;
Fax 0151 934 3349
Strategic Director (Children's Services) Bryn Marsh
*Project Director (Transformational Change, Business and
Strategic Support)* Graham Taylor
Director (Schools and Young People) Vacancy
Assistant Director Andrew Windsor
Assistant Director (Children's Services) Ken Black (Acting)
Assistant Director (Schools) Alan Potter
Assistant Director (Vulnerable Children) Colin Oxley
Assistant Director (Young People Support)
Margaret Loughlin
Head (Family and Community Learning) Olive Carey
Head (Special Advisory Inclusion Service) Daphne Mortimer
Head (Youth Service) Jackie Kerr
Manager (Excellence in Cities) Gill Mullen
Manager (Finance) Nick Carbonaro
Manager (School Organisation and Capital Programme)
Christine Dalziel
Principal Education Psychologist (STEPS Service)
Carol Sherriff
Chief Adviser Danny Roberts
Lead Adviser (School Standards and Effectiveness) Lesley Lee
Lead Adviser (School Support) Vacancy
Co-ordinator (Personal, Social and Health Education)
Norman Scott
Number of Schools
77 Primary; 21 Secondary; 5 Special; 4 Nursery

TRAINING AND GOVERNOR SERVICES

Children's Services, Merton Hse, Stanley Rd, Bootle,
Merseyside L20 3JA; e-mail
training.unit@csf.sefton.gov.uk; Tel 0151 934 3339;
Fax 0151 934 3338
Head (Governance and Training) Joyce Kavanagh
Services offered
Advice and support to enable governors to discharge their
statutory duties; appointment of local authority governors;
training courses for all school based staff and governors;
regular newsletter; helpline for governors and their clerks;
library of books, videos, cassettes; training for individual
governing bodies

CABINET MEMBER – CHILDREN'S SERVICES

Contact Cllr P. Dowd (Lab); c/o Town Hall, Oriel Rd,
Bootle, Merseyside L20 7AE; Tel 0151 934 3319

SEFTON TEACHING AND EDUCATION PSYCHOLOGY SERVICE (STEPS)

Freshfield Primary School Site Watchyard La, Formby, Merseyside L37 3JY; e-mail steps.freshfield@csf.sefton.gov.uk; Tel 01704 385902; Fax 01704 385901

SEFTON MUSIC SERVICE

Central Music Centre Redgate Advisory Centre, Formby, Merseyside L37 4EW; URL www.sefton.gov.uk/ musicservice; e-mail music.service@cs.sefton.gov.uk; Tel 01704 395995; Fax 01704 395996
Head Chris Lennie

YOUTH CLUBS

Aintree Youth Centre Oriel Dr, Aintree, Liverpool, Merseyside L10 6NJ; e-mail chris.burrows@cs.sefton.gov.uk; Tel 0151 526 1177
Area Youth Worker Chris Burrows

Birkdale Youth Centre Windy Harbour Rd, Birkdale, Southport, Merseyside PR8 3DT; e-mail patrice.hey@cs.sefton.gov.uk; Tel 01704 579836
Area Youth Worker Patrice Hey

Crosby Youth Centre Coronation Rd, Crosby, Liverpool, Merseyside L23 5RQ; e-mail paul.riding@cs.sefton.gov.uk; Tel 0151 924 8048
Area Youth Worker Paul Riding

Edge Lane Youth Centre Edge La, Thornton, Liverpool, Merseyside L23; e-mail simon.warner@cs.sefton.gov.uk; Tel 0151 931 3863
Area Youth Worker Simon Warner

The Escape Youth Club NAC Clovers La, Netherton, Merseyside L30 3TL; e-mail lynsey.moran@cs.sefton.gov.uk; Tel 07973 457841
Area Youth Worker Lynsey Moran (Acting)

Formby Youth Centre Redgate, Formby, Liverpool, Merseyside L37 4EW; e-mail claire.tinsley@cs.sefton.gov.uk; Tel 01704 878770
Area Youth Worker Claire Tinsley

Meols Cop Youth Centre Meols Cop Rd, Southport, Merseyside PR8 6JS; e-mail pat.wilson@cs.sefton.gov.uk; Tel 01704 395301
Area Youth Worker Pat Wilson

SPARC Youth Club Orrell Mount Pavillion, Orrell Rd, Bootle, Merseyside L20 6DX; e-mail karen.williams@cs.sefton.gov.uk; Tel 0151 475 5299
Worker in Charge Karen Williams

Stafford Moreton Youth Club Liverpool Rd North, Maghull, Merseyside L31 2PA; e-mail frances.schofield@cs.sefton.gov.uk; Tel 0151 526 3294
Area Youth Worker Frances Schofield

Stanley Youth Centre Marshside Rd, Southport, Merseyside PR9 9TF; e-mail ray.moore@cs.sefton.gov.uk; Tel 01704 225319
Area Youth Worker Ray Moore

TEACHERS' CENTRE

Sefton Professional Development Centre (PDC) 225 Park Rd, Formby, Liverpool, Merseyside L37 6EW; e-mail pdc@csf.sefton.gov.uk; Tel 01704 395352; Fax 01704 395350
Head of Centre Joyce Kavanagh

ADULT AND COMMUNITY LEARNING

Adult and Community Learning 53 Cambridge Rd, Seaforth, Liverpool, Merseyside L21 1EZ; Tel 0151 285 5104
Manager (Community Learning) Jacqui Ball

DISABILITY SERVICES – CHILDREN

Sterrix Centre, Good Shepherd Site, Sterrix La, Litherland, Liverpool, Merseyside L21 0DA; Tel 0151 934 3860

FAMILY PLACEMENT AND ADOPTION

Ellesmere Hse, Crosby Rd North, Waterloo, Liverpool, Merseyside L22 0LG; Tel 0151 285 5019

FAMILY SUPPORT SERVICES – NORTH

Southport Offices, 27–29 Houghton St, Southport, Merseyside PR9 0NS; Tel 0845 140 0845

FAMILY SUPPORT SERVICES – SOUTH

Litherland Sefton Street Offices, 28–30 Sefton St, Litherland, Liverpool, Merseyside L21 7LB; Tel 0151 934 3925

LOOKED AFTER CHILDREN SERVICES

Ellesmere Hse, Crosby Rd North, Waterloo, Liverpool, Merseyside L22 0LG; Tel 0151 285 5019

Stockport Metropolitan Borough Council
www.stockport.gov.uk

Population: 281 600
Political composition: LD: 36, Lab: 15, Con: 9, Ind: 3, Free Social Democrats: 1
Town Hall, Stockport, Greater Manchester SK1 3XE; URL www.stockport.gov.uk; e-mail mail@stockport.gov.uk
Chief Executive John Schultz MA, DipTP, MRTPI, MIMgt

Children and Young People's Directorate

Tel 0161 474 3813; Fax 0161 953 0012
Corporate Director Andrew Webb
Service Director (Social Care and Health) Michael Jameson
Assistant Director (Inclusive Communities) Mark Rogers
Assistant Director (Learning and Achievement) Richard Bates
Assistant Director (Special Projects) Mary Binnie
Head (Continuing Education and Early Years Service) Gay Turner
Head (ICT) Mike Partridge
Head (Support and Development) Celia Newton
Head (Youth Services) Vacancy
Manager (Client Services) Peter Fearn
Senior Adviser (Primary Phase) Sue Guy
Senior Adviser (Secondary Phase) Ron Lofkin
Education Officer (Finance) Terry Conlon
Education Officer (Information and Statistics) Jane Mclennan
Education Officer (IT) John Northwood
Education Officer (Planning and Development) Brian Wainwright
Education Officer (Policy and Development) Lesley Roper
Education Officer (Pupils) Chris Keeble
Education Officer (School Improvement) Richard Skidmore
Education Officer (School Management) Barry Kirkman
Education Officer (School Management) Pat Morgan
Education Officer (SEN) Ian Donegani
Education Officer (Support) Sue Gamon
Number of Schools
76 Primary; 14 Secondary; 9 Nursery; 8 Infant; 8 Junior; 6 Special; 3 PRU
Lifelong Learning Development Meeting
Six week cycle

EDUCATION COMMITTEE

LD: 32, Lab: 25, Ind: 4, Con: 2
Chair M.J. Hunter (LD)
Vice-Chair D. Brailsford (LD)

GOVERNOR TRAINING

Governing Body Training, Schools Management, Town
Hall, Stockport, Greater Manchester SK1 3XE; e-mail
lynn.bray@stockport.gov.uk; Tel 0161 474 3845;
Fax 0161 474 3896
Education Officer (School Management)   P. Morgan
Services offered
Provides, co-ordinates and delivers a comprehensive
training programme for individual governors and collective
governing bodies; an advice and support helpline to assist
governors in the discharging of their duties and
responsibilities

TEACHERS' CENTRE

Dialstone Centre   Lisburne La, Stockport, Greater
Manchester SK2 7LL; Tel 0161 474 2220

Tameside Metropolitan Borough Council
www.tameside.gov.uk

Population: 250 000 (approx.)
Political Compositon: Lab: 46, Con: 6, Ind: 3, LD: 2
Council Offices, Wellington Rd, Ashton-under-Lyne,
Tameside OL6 6DL; URL www.tameside.gov.uk; e-mail
general@tameside.gov.uk; Tel 0161 342 8355;
Fax 0161 342 3070
Chief Executive   J. Orchard

Services for Children and Young People

Council Offices, Wellington Rd, Ashton-under-Lyne,
Tameside OL6 6DL; Tel 0161 342 3766; Fax 0161 342 3260
Cabinet Deputy (Lifelong Learning)   Cllr G. Cooney
Head (Education Partnership)   J. Saunders
Head (Finance, Buildings and Primary School Catering)
Elaine Todd
Head (Human Resources)   J. White
Head (School Improvement)   S. Noble
Head (School Organisation and Social Inclusion)   L.K. Davies
Head (School Library Service)   L. Craigs
Manager (School Catering)   Barbara Hulme
Service Unit Manager (Client Services)   Norman Crawford
Principal Educational Psychologist   Nick Caws
Principal Education Welfare Officer   Briana Bamforth
Principal Officer (Curriculum, Inset and Inspections)
C. Tapper
Education Officer (Capital)   R. Muller
Education Officer (Human Resources)   T. Brennand
Education Officer (School Organisation)   J. Fludder
Assistant Education Officer (Building Unit)   R. Higson
Senior Adviser (Science, Design and Technology)   G. Ashford
General Adviser (Governor and Management Support)
A. Bailey
General Adviser (Humanities)   M. Smith
General Adviser (Mathematics)   J. Hackney
General Adviser (Secondary Arts and Sport)   Zip Dominion
General Adviser (Secondary English)   Max Turton
General Adviser (Vocational and Careers Education)   Vacancy
General Adviser (SEN)   Vacancy
Senior Consultant (Literacy)   M. Huxley
Senior Consultant (Numeracy)   Lindsey Shaw
Consultant (Literacy: Primary)   Shelagh Walton
Consultant (Literacy: Secondary)   Max Turton
Consultant (Numeracy)   Carol Rhodes
Accountant (Financial Resources)   S. Wilde
Advisory Teacher (Health and Drug Education)   A. Holt
Community Languages Teacher   S. Khan
Number of Schools
18 Secondary; 6 Special; 8 Adult Education Centres/
Evening Institutes; 1 Education Development Centre

Requisition Periods for Schools' Supplies
To end of January
**Other Authorities with whom Joint Purchasing Arrangements
are made**
Greater Manchester Purchasing Consortium

LIFELONG LEARNING SERVICES COMMITTEE

Chair   J. Kitchen

GOVERNOR TRAINING UNIT

Governor and Management Support (Rm 2.37), Education
Department, Ashton-under-Lyne, Tameside OL6 6DL;
Tel 0161 342 3218; Fax 0161 342 3260
General Adviser (Governor Support)   David Eccles

CHILD GUIDANCE CLINIC

Springleigh Clinic   Waterloo Rd, Stalybridge, Greater
Manchester SK15 2AU; Tel 0161 303 4902

TUTORIAL CENTRE

Dale Grove Primary Centre (Bankside)   Grange Rd, Hyde,
Tameside SK14 5NU; e-mail
admin@bankside.tameside.sch.uk; Tel 0161 368 1718
Deputy Head   Siobhan Halligan
Emotional and behavioural difficulties

HEARING IMPAIRED SERVICE

Education Development Centre   Lakes Rd, Dukinfield,
Tameside SK16 4TR; Tel 0161 330 1375
Hyde Technology High and Hearing Impaired Unit   Old
Road, Hyde, Tameside SK14 4SP; Tel 0161 368 1353
Secondary

SPECIFIC LEARNING DIFFICULTIES RESOURCE CENTRE

c/o **Two Trees High**   Two Trees La, Denton, Tameside;
Tel 0161 320 7729

EDUCATION DEVELOPMENT CENTRE

Tameside Education Development Centre   Dukinfield Town
Hall, King St, Dukinfield, Greater Manchester SK16 4LA;
e-mail saroj.karpal@tameside.gov.uk; Tel 0161 342 5041
Manager   Ms S. Karpal

ADULT EDUCATION DEPARTMENT

Warrington House   Church St, Ashton-under-Lyne,
Tameside OL6 7PR; Tel 0161 330 2878
Contact   M. Ward

TAMESIDE INSTRUMENTAL MUSIC TEACHING AGENCY (TIMTA)

Denton Festival Hall, Peel St, Denton, Tameside M34 7JY;
e-mail godfrey.calcutt@tameside.gov.uk;
Tel 0161 320 4246
Contact   G.R. Calcutt
School Library Service   Dukinfield Town Hall, King St,
Dukinfield, Tameside SK16 4LA; Tel 0161 342 5084
Manager   L. Craigs

YOUTH CENTRES

Beyer Peacock Youth Project   Kershaw La, Audenshaw,
Tameside M34 5WS; Tel 0161 336 6615
Centre Manager   Steph Brotherton
Broadoak Youth Centre   Broadoak Rd, Ashton-under-Lyne,
Tameside OL6 8RP; Tel 0161 339 6052
Centre Manager   Mike Ashworth
Hattersley Youth Centre   Hattersley Rd East, Hattersley,
Hyde, Cheshire SK14 3EQ
Haughton Green Young People's Centre   Lancaster Rd,
Bakewell Ave, Denton, Tameside M34 7DR;
Tel 0161 336 7535
Centre Manager   Kim McInerney

2

Hyde Youth Centre Lower Bennett St, Hyde, Cheshire
SK14 4PP; Tel 0161 342 3033
Centre Manager Ruhel Ahmed
Jubo Shongho Youth Centre 19 Chapel St, Hyde, Tameside
SK14 1JB; Tel 0161 342 3033
Centre Manager Sanjay Patel
Longdendale/Hollingworth Youth Centre Cannon St,
Hollingworth Hyde, Tameside SK14 8LR;
Tel 0161 342 3033
Centre Manager Vicky Parry
Mossley Youth Base The Rowan, Mossley, Tameside;
Tel 01457 834828
Centre Manager Maurice Chadwick
Centre Manager Sue Embury
Tameside Young People's Centre Duke St, Denton, Tameside
M34 2AN; Tel 0161 336 6615
Centre Manager S. Nathan
West End Youth Centre John St East, Ashton-under-Lyne,
Tameside OL7 0QY; Tel 0161 339 2728
Centre Manager Gillian Nettleton
Youth Adventure Tameside Vicarage Dr, Dukinfield,
Tameside SK16 5LE; Tel 0161 338 2013
Centre Manager Bev Knowles

Trafford Metropolitan Borough Council

www.trafford.gov.uk

Population: 213 000
Political composition: Con: 39, Lab: 20, LD: 4
Trafford Town Hall, Talbot Rd, Stretford, Manchester
M32 0YT; URL www.trafford.gov.uk; Tel 0161 912 1212;
Fax 0161 912 4184
Chief Executive David McNulty

Children and Young People's Service

PO Box 40, Trafford Town Hall, Talbot Rd, Stretford, Greater
Manchester M32 0EL
*Corporate Director (Trafford Children and Young People's
Service)* C. Pratt
Director (Commissioning, Performance and Strategy)
M. Vasic
Director (Education and Early Years Services)
M. Woodhouse
Director (Services for Children, Young People and Families)
F. Waddington
Head (Business Support Services) A.A. Warrington
Manager (Cleaning Services) M. Greenwood
Service Manager (Admissions) M. Golding
Service Manager (Development) R.G. Sigee
Service Manager (Education Catering) H. Dodd
Service Manager (Education Catering) C. Holden
Service Manager (Financial Management) A. Carr
Service Manager (Financial Management) A.M. Steadman
Service Manager (Governing Bodies) C. Peel
Service Manager (Personnel) K. Wilkinson
Chief Adviser (Primary Education) E. Jackson
Chief Adviser (Secondary Education) G. Herbert
General Adviser (SEN) J. Lomas
Principal Educational Psychologist C. Bate
Number of Schools
72 Primary; 11 Secondary High; 7 Secondary Grammar; 6
Special; 3 PRU
Committee Meeting
Six weekly cycle

EXECUTIVE MEMBER (CHILDREN AND YOUNG PEOPLE'S SERVICE)

Contact (Children and Young People's Service)
Cllr I. Mullins; Trafford MBC, PO Box 19, Stretford,
Manchester M33 1YR
Contact (Children's Social Services) Cllr J. Holden

GOVERNOR SERVICES

Children and Young People's Service, 4th Fl, Waterside Hse,
Waterside, Sale, Greater Manchester M33 7ZF;
Tel 0161 912 3218; Fax 0161 912 3088
Service Manager C. Peel
Services offered
Comprehensive governor training programme; governor
support and advice service; termly newsletter; helpline;
resource centres; distance learning packages

Warrington Borough Council

www.warrington.gov.uk

In April 1998 Warrington became a unitary authority. The
rest of Cheshire retains a two-tier structure and is listed
separately in this section.
Population: 193 000
Town Hall, Sankey St, Warrington WA1 1UH;
URL www.warrington.gov.uk; Tel 01925 444400;
Fax 01925 442138
Leader of the Council Ian Marks
Strategic Chief Executive Diana Terris
Strategic Director (Children's Services) Norma Cadwallader
Strategic Director (Community Services) Helen Sumner
Strategic Director (Corporate Services) Yvonne Bottomley
Strategic Director (Environment and Regeneration)
Andy Farrall
Political composition
LD: 27, Lab: 24, Con: 5, Ind: 1

Children's Services Directorate

New Town Hse, Buttermarket St, Warrington WA1 2NJ;
e-mail everychildmatters@warrington.gov.uk;
Fax 01925 442969
Executive Member Cllr S. Woodyalt
Head (Pupil Referral Unit) Mike Frost
Head (Specialist Services) Aileen Greenway
Head of Service (Business Planning and Resources)
Ann McCormack
Head of Service (Children's Social Care and Youth)
John Dunkerley
Head of Service (Community Support Services) Sue Cockerill
Head of Service (Safeguarding) David Johnston
Head of Service (School Improvement and Inclusion)
Pinaki Ghoshal
Head of Service (Strategic Management, Planning and Access)
Sue Cockerill (Acting)
Principal Officer (Admissions, Transport and Pupil Services)
Vacancy
Principal Officer (Capital and Asset Management Planning)
Julie Hall
Principal Officer (Early Years) Vacancy
Principal Officer (Governor Support) Dot Garner
Principal Officer (Personnel) Paul Cunningham
Principal Officer (Personnel) Samantha Hulson
Principal Officer (School Effectiveness) Tonnie Richmond
Principal Officer (Schools and Awards) Janette Lee
Principal Education Welfare Officer Donna Marie Povey
Principal Educational Psychologist Nick Durbin
Chief Adviser Ian Chambers
Principal Accountant David Leadbetter
SEN Consultant Hanneke Van Schelver
Number of Schools
71 Primary; 12 Secondary; 3 Special (2 Day, 1 Residential); 1
Nursery

GOVERNOR TRAINING

Co-ordinator Dot Garner
Services offered
Training courses on various subjects are offered free of
charge to governors of schools buying back the local
authority's service; helpline and termly newsletter; the unit

arranges for speakers to attend individual governing bodies or cluster groups

Wigan Metropolitan Borough Council
www.wigan.gov.uk

Population: 301 000
Political composition: Lab: 46, Community Action: 11; Con: 10, LD: 6, Ind: 2
Town Hall, Library St, Wigan, Greater Manchester WN1 1YN; URL www.wigan.gov.uk; Tel 01942 244991; Fax 01942 827451
Chief Executive   Joyce Redfearn

Children and Young People's Services

Progress Hse, Westwood Park Dr, Wigan, Greater Manchester WN3 4HH; URL www.wiganmbc.gov.uk; e-mail education@wiganmbc.gov.uk; Tel 01942 486123; Fax 01942 486213
Director   Vacancy
Director (Attendance and Child Protection)   Dave Greenhalgh; Tel 01942 705596
Director (Corporate Services)   Tony Dann; Tel 01942 705360
Director (Services in Education)   Sue Astbury; Tel 01942 705357
Director (Services in the Community)   Ray Potts; Tel 01942 705352
Director (Youth Development)   Dave Hill; Tel 01942 705586
Assistant Director (Learning and Attainment)   Richard Powell
Assistant Director (Management and Development)   Vacancy
Assistant Director (School Inclusion)   Lorna Hulme (Acting)
Head (Services for Young People)   D. Hill
Strategic Manager (Finance and IT)   Julie Taylor
Strategic Manager (Development and Premises)   Vacancy
Strategic Manager (Personnel and Governor Services)   Janet Baker
Strategic Manager (Preventative Services and Children's Fund)   Sue Hughes
Strategic Manager (Finance and IT)   Julie Taylor
Strategic Manager (MCCS)   G.S. Long
Strategic Manager (Personnel and Governor Services)   Janet Baker
Manager (Development)   J. Cunliffe
Team Leader (Visual Arts)   N. Leighton
Principal Officer (Educational Placements)   Chris Parry
Principal Officer (Financial Services)   P. Haggart
Principal Officer (Human Resources)   Tess Leyland
Principal Officer (Provision Planning)   Lynn Mappin
Principal Officer (SEN)   A. Patel
Principal Officer (Statutory Assessment)   E. Baulcombe
Senior Officer (Admissions)   Julie Hough
Senior Officer (Exclusion and Transport)   Mike Inman
Senior Officer (Human Resources: Staffing)   Alison Hibbert
Senior Officer (Payroll and Pensions)   Susan Kerslake
Senior Officer (Student Services)   D. Manchester
Senior Adviser (Primary)   Jill Clarke
Senior Adviser (Secondary)   Janet Doherty
Information and Planning Officer   Frances Topping
Number of Schools
106 Primary; 20 Secondary; 8 Special

GOVERNOR TRAINING UNIT

Progress Hse, Westwood Park Dr, Wigan, Greater Manchester WN3 4HH; Tel 01942 486123; Fax 01942 486213
Governor Training Co-ordinator   Ian Doughty
Services offered
Training courses on various subjects are offered free of charge to governors of schools buying back the LEA's service; helpline and termly newsletter; the unit arranges for speakers to attend individual governing bodies or cluster groups

LIFELONG LEARNING PANEL

Cabinet Member (Lifelong Learning Portfolio)   Cllr B.M. Wilson
Special Interest Member   Cllr R. Winkworth
Members of the Panel
Lab: K. Aldred, B. Bourne, C. Rigby, A. Turnock, M.J. Whiteside
LD: N. Hogg
Con: G.W. Fairhurst
Community Action: R. Brierley, D.E. Grace, W.J. Wilkes

Metropolitan Borough of Wirral
www.wirral.gov.uk

Population: 312 289
Political composition: Lab: 25, Con: 21, LD: 20
Town Hall, Brighton St, Wallasey, Wirral CH44 8ED; URL www.wirral.gov.uk; Tel 0151 638 7070
Chief Executive   Steve Maddox; e-mail stephenmaddox@wirral.gov.uk

Children and Young People's Department

Hamilton Bldg, Conway St, Birkenhead, Merseyside CH41 4FD; Tel 0151 606 2000
Director (Children's Services)   Howard Cooper
Head (Children's Social Care)   Julia Lassall
Head (Education Social Welfare Service)   Jill Bennett; Solar Campus, Leasowe Rd, Leasowe, Wirral, Merseyside; Tel 0151 637 6060
Head (Learning and Achievement)   M. Stacey
Head (Participation and Inclusion)   P. Edmondson
Head (Policy and Resources)   C.J. Batman
Senior Inspector (Finance and Resources)   Dave Armstrong
Senior Inspector (Primary Education)   Marie Lawrence
Senior Inspector (Pupil and Student Services)   J. Bulmer
Senior Inspector (Secondary Education)   C. Stretch
General Inspector (Central Services)   P. Bishop
General Inspector (Design and Information Technology)   M. Ellis
General Inspector (Early Years)   C. Kerr
General Inspector (English)   B. Sharkey
General Inspector (Human/Business Education/Home Economics/RE)   D. Smith
General Inspector (Mathematics)   A. Simpson
General Inspector (Personal/Social Education)   C. Lands
General Inspector (Physical Education)   B. Saunders
General Inspector (Primary Curriculum)   Vacancy
General Inspector (Resources)   A. Roberts
General Inspector (Science)   P. Wakefield
Principal Catering Officer   G. Rossiter
Principal Educational Psychologist (SEN Support Service)   Y. Le Lorrain; Solar Campus, 235 Leasowe Rd, Leasowe, Wirral, Merseyside; Tel 0151 637 6090
Principal Youth Officer   Maureen McDaid
Supplies Officer   K. Brooks;
Number of Schools
23 Secondary; 12 Special

EDUCATION AND CULTURAL SERVICES SELECT COMMITTEE

Cabinet Member   Phil Davies (Lab)
Spokesperson   S. Clarke MBE (Con)
Spokesperson   T. Harney (LD)
Members of the Committee
Lab: G. Leech, T. Smith, W. Smith
Con: D. Hunt
LD: P.M. Southwood

GOVERNOR TRAINING UNIT

Tel 0151 666 4334
Senior Inspector (Secondary)   C. Stretch
Services offered
Governors are offered an extensive range of cross-authority
and school-based training courses looking at all aspects of
their role and responsibilities. Attendance at these averages
2000 governors a year. Other resources include a termly
newsletter, data bank, helpline and LEA consultancy
services. Latter include the governor training and support
service plus the presence at every governor meeting of an
LEA officer/inspector to advise and guide participants.

SPECIAL AND REMEDIAL UNITS

Sanderling Ravenswood Unit   Rock Ferry High School,
   Ravenswood Ave, Birkenhead, Wirral CH42 4NY;
   Tel 0151 644 6670
   Head of Unit   R. Rogers
Wimbrick Hey Teaching Support Service for Social Services
   61 Burnley Rd, Moreton, Wirral CH46 9QE;
   Tel 0151 606 0826
   Head of Service   R. Taylor

LEARNING SUPPORT SERVICE

Solar Campus   235 Leasowe Rd, Wallasey, Wirral
   CH45 8LW; Tel 0151 638 8587
   Head of Service   Y. Le Lorrain

HEARING IMPAIRED SERVICE

Solar Campus   235 Leasowe Rd, Wallasey, Wirral
   CH45 8LW; Tel 0151 630 0387
   Head of Service   C. Peake

VISION SUPPORT SERVICE

Solar Campus   235 Leasowe Rd, Wallasey, Wirral
   CH45 8LW; Tel 0151 630 0385
   Head of Service   K. Davies

WIRRAL EDUCATION CENTRE

Acre La, Bromborough, Wirral; Tel 0151 346 6666

SOUTH EAST

Berkshire County Council

In April 1998 Berkshire County Council was replaced by
Bracknell Forest, Reading, Slough, West Berkshire, Windsor
and Maidenhead, and Wokingham Councils, each
responsible for local government services in its area. These
councils are listed separately in this section.

Bracknell Forest Borough Council

www.bracknell-forest.gov.uk

In April 1998 Berkshire County Council was replaced by
Bracknell Forest, Reading, Slough, West Berkshire, Windsor
and Maidenhead, and Wokingham, each responsible for
local government services in its area. They are listed
separately in this section.
Easthampstead Hse, Town Sq, Bracknell, Bracknell Forest
   RG12 1AQ; URL www.bracknell-forest.gov.uk;
   Tel 01344 424642; Fax 01344 352810
Chief Executive   Timothy Wheadon
Director (Corporate Services and Resources)   Alison Sanders

Education, Children Services and Libraries Department

Seymour Hse, 38 Broadway, Bracknell, Bracknell Forest
   RG12 1AU; e-mail ecsl@bracknell-forest.gov.uk;
   Tel 01344 354000
Director (ECSL)   Tony Eccleston
*Assistant Director (Children and Families: Access and
   Inclusion)*   Martin Gocke
Assistant Director (Children and Families: Social Care)
   Alex Walters
Assistant Director (Learning, Achievement and Libraries)
   Allison Fletcher
Assistant Director (Performance and Resources)   Vacancy
Manager (Admissions and Property)   Chris Taylor
Manager (Children and Families)   Gloria King
Manager (Education ICT)   Cherry Bluett
Manager (SEN)   Keith Stapylton
Principal Adviser   Bob Welch
Senior Adviser   Dan Archer
General Adviser   Rosanna Boarder
Principal Educational Psychologist   Anthony Riches
Group Accountant   Paul Clark
Lifelong Learning Officer   David Jones
Number of Schools
6 Secondary; 1 Special; Adult Education provided under
contract largely by Bracknell and Wokingham College

HOME AND HOSPITAL TEACHING SERVICE

West Rd, Old Wokingham Rd, Wokingham RG40 3BT;
   URL www.bracknell-forest.gov.uk; e-mail
   head@office.collegehall-pru.bracknell-forest.sch.uk;
   Tel 0118 989 3378
Co-ordinator   Marion Bent

EDUCATIONAL PSYCHOLOGY SERVICE

Seymour Hse, 38 Broadway, Bracknell, Bracknell Forest
   RG12 1AU; URL www.bracknell-forest.gov.uk; e-mail
   ecsl@bracknell-forest.gov.uk; Tel 01344 354018
Principal Educational Psychologist   Anthony Riches
Co-ordinator (Language and Literacy)   Susan Duffus
Ranelagh School Special Resource (Secondary)   Ranelagh
   School, Ranelagh Dr, Bracknell, Bracknell Forest
   RG12 9DA; e-mail
   head@office.ranelagh.bracknell-forest.sch.uk;
   Tel 01344 421233
   Headteacher   K.M. Winrow

EDUCATION CENTRE

Bracknell Forest Education Centre   Easthampstead Pk,
   Wokingham RG40 3DF;
   URL www.edcentre.bracknell-forest.org.uk; e-mail
   sheila.yates@bracknell-forest.gov.uk

BRACKNELL TEACHING AND SUPPORT SERVICE (TASS)

Adastron Hse, Crowthorne Rd, Bracknell, Bracknell Forest
   RG12 4DG; Tel 01344 451051
Co-ordinator   L. Wales

MEADOW VALE SPECIAL RESOURCE

Meadow Vale Primary School, Moordale Ave, Bracknell,
   Bracknell Forest RG42 1SY; e-mail
   head@office.meadowvale.bracknell-forest.sch.uk;
   Tel 01344 421046
Headteacher   N. Duncan
   Speech and language

COUNTY MUSIC CENTRE

Berkshire Young Musicians Trust   Stoneham Ct, Cockney
   Hill, Reading RG30 4EX; URL www.bymt.org.uk; e-mail
   davidmarcou@bymt.org.uk; Tel 0118 901 2360

Brighton and Hove City Council

www.brighton-hove.gov.uk

In April 1997 Brighton and Hove became a unitary authority. The rest of East Sussex retains a two-tier structure and is listed separately in this section.
Population: 255 000
Political composition: Lab: 23, Con: 20, Green Party: 6, LD: 3, Ind: 2
Kings Hse, Grand Ave, Hove, East Sussex BN3 2SL;
    URL www.brighton-hove.gov.uk; e-mail
    <firstname>.<surname>@brighton-hove.gov.uk;
    Tel 01273 290000
Chief Executive   A. McCarthy
Leader of the Council   B. Oxley
Director (Children, Families and Schools)   David Hawker
Director (Environment)   Jenny Rowlands
Director (Finance and Property)   Catherine Vaughan
Director (Housing and City Support)   Ian Long
Director (Human Resources)   Mark Lamb
Director (Strategy and Governance)   Alex Bailey
Programme Director (Health and Social Care)   Kate Money

Children and Young People's Trust

Brighton and Hove Council, Kings Hse, Grand Ave, Hove,
    East Sussex BN3 2SU; Fax 01273 293596
Chair   Cllr Vanessa Brown; e-mail
    vanessa.brown@brighton-hove.gov.uk; Tel 01273 291012;
    Fax 01273 291003
Clinical Director   Dr Sian Bennett
Director (Children's Services)   Vacancy
Associate Director (Health Care Management)   Jon Ota
Assistant Director (Central Area and School Support)
    Gil Sweetenham
*Assistant Director (East Area, Early Years and NHS
    Commissioning)*   James Dougan
Assistant Director (Learning and Schools)   Jo Lyons
Assistant Director (Quality and Performance)   Steve Barton
Assistant Director (Social Care)   Liz Rugg
Assistant Director (West Area and Youth Support)
    Gillian Cunliffe
Head (Admissions and Transport)   Steve Healey
Head (Children's Workforce Development)   Annie McCabe
Head (Learning Support)   Jacqueline Coe
Head (Schools Capital Strategy and Development Planning)
    Gillian Churchill
Head (SEN and Pupil Support)   Yvonne Ely
Senior Adviser (Secondary)   Linda Ellis
Number of Schools
32 Primary; 12 Junior; 12 Infant; 9 Secondary; 8 Special; 2
Nursery
Brighton and Hove Learning and Development Centre
    Hodshrove La, Brighton, East Sussex BN2 4SE;
    Tel 01273 293699

Buckinghamshire County Council

www.buckscc.gov.uk

Population: 478 400 (est.)
Political composition: Con: 44, LD: 11, Lab: 2
County Hall, Aylesbury, Buckinghamshire HP20 1UA;
    URL www.buckscc.gov.uk; Tel 01296 395000
Chief Executive   Chris Williams
Strategic Director (Adult Social Care)   Rita Lally
Strategic Director (Community Services)   Dean Taylor
Strategic Director (Planning and Transportation)   Neil Gibson
Strategic Director (Resources)   Ian Trenholm
Director (Children and Young People's Services)
    Sue Imbriano

Children and Young People Portfolio

County Hall, Walton St, Aylesbury, Buckinghamshire
    HP20 1UZ
*Cabinet Member (Achievement and Learning); Lead Member
    (Children and Young People's Services)*   Marion Clayton
Cabinet Member (Children and Families Social Care)
    Lin Hazell
Divisional Director (Achievement and Learning)   Louise Goll
*Divisional Director (Commissioning and Business
    Improvement)*   Chris Munday
Number of Schools
184 Primary; 34 Secondary; 12 Special (7 Day, 5 Residential);
6 PRU

Commissioning and Business Improvement Division

Divisional Director   Chris Munday
Divisional Director (Commissioning)   Stephen Bagnall
Divisional Manager (Business Improvement)   David Shaw
*Manager (Communications Development: CYPS Portfolio/
    Contact with Schools)*   Caroline Corcoran

Safeguarding Division

Divisional Director   Trevor R. Boyd
Divisional Manager (Permanency and Placements)
    Diana Large (Acting)
Divisional Manager (Prevention, Assessment and Protection)
    Heather Clarke

Achievement and Learning Division

Divisional Director   Louise Goll

Access and Inclusion
Divisional Manager   Janet Sparrow
Manager (Admissions)   Debbie Munday
Manager (Social Inclusion)   Sarah Dell
Principal Educational Psychologist   Jenny Pearce
Contact (Safeguarding in Education)   Andrea Smith
Contact (Specialist Teaching Service)   Sally Morgan
Contact (Statutory Assessment and SEN)   Ruth Cutler

School Improvement
Divisional Manager   Steve Edgar
Operations Manager (Curriculum Development)   Ian Lenham
Operations Manager (Inclusion, Partnership and Innovation)
    Nigel Cook
Manager (Inclusion: Targeted Support)   Vacancy
Manager (Inclusion: Universal Provision)   Bill Moore
Manager (Primary: Leadership, Standards and Quality)
    Ian Elkington
Manager (Secondary: Leadership, Standards and Quality)
    Christopher Lloyd-Staples
Adviser (14–19)   Brian Cue
Adviser (Assessment and Analysis)   Pauline Cue
Adviser (Early Years)   Julie Hadden
Adviser (English)   Simon Wrigley
Adviser (Humanities)   Simon Lockwood
Adviser (ICT)   Mike Woods
Adviser (Maths)   Lorna Piper
Adviser (Modern Foreign Languages)   Ruth Wilkes
Adviser (Music)   Helen Blakeman
Adviser (PE/Educational Visits)   Ian Park
Contact (Governor Services)   Nicola Cook

Northern Area Office

County Hall, Aylesbury, Buckinghamshire HP20 1UZ;
    Tel 01296 382667; Fax 01296 383532
Operations Manager   David Cousins
Area Adviser   Dan China
Adviser (Primary School Improvement)   Yvonne Davis
Adviser (Primary School Improvement)   Martyn Kitson
Adviser (Primary School Improvement)   Kate Rumboll
Adviser (Primary School Improvement)   Deb Whittle

Southern Area Office

Buckinghamshire County Council, Easton St, High Wycombe, Buckinghamshire HP11 1NH; e-mail wycebu@buckscc.gov.uk; Tel 01494 475343; Fax 01494 475001

Operations Manager   Bob Gibbard

Area Adviser   David Preston

Adviser (Primary School Improvements)   Linda Baily

Adviser (Primary School Improvement)   Tony Fermor

Adviser (Primary School Improvement)   Ruth McGill

HOSPITAL CLASSES

Stoke Mandeville Hospital Aylesbury, Buckinghamshire HP21 8AL; Tel 01296 315067

Teacher-in-Charge   Joanna Jones

Wycombe General Hospital Children's Ward 7, High Wycombe, Buckinghamshire HP11 2TT; Tel 01494 526161 ext 2369

Teacher-in-Charge   Anne Steiner

PUPIL REFERRAL UNITS

Aylesbury Vale Pupil Referral Unit (Primary) Unit 1, Abbey Centre, Weedon Rd, Aylesbury, Buckinghamshire HP19 9NS; e-mail office@aylesburyvale-pri.bucks.sch.uk; Tel 01296 387300; Fax 01296 381506

Head   Gillian Davies

Aylesbury Vale Pupil Referral Unit (Secondary) Unit 8, Abbey Centre, Weedon Rd, Aylesbury, Buckinghamshire HP19 9NS; URL www.avssc.org; e-mail admin@avssc.org; Tel 01296 387600; Fax 01296 339125

Headteacher   Tom Millea

The Chess Valley Grange Pupil Referral Unit Waterside, Chesham, Buckinghamshire HP5 1QD; e-mail chessvg@wycombegrange-pru.bucks.sch.uk; Tel 01494 778146; Fax 01494 772024

Headteacher   George Lloyd

The Oaks Pupil Referral Unit (Primary) Elangeni School Site, Woodside Ave, Amersham, Buckinghamshire HP6 6EG; e-mail office@theoaks-pru.bucks.sch.uk; Tel 01494 721925

Headteacher   Cathy Kirkham

The Wycombe Grange Pupil Referral Unit (Secondary) 56 Amersham Hill, High Wycombe, Buckinghamshire HP13 6PQ; e-mail office@wycombegrange-pru.bucks.sch.uk; Tel 01494 445815; Fax 01494 465860

Headteacher   George Lloyd

Woodlands Pupil Referral Unit (Primary) Philip Rd, High Wycombe, Buckinghamshire HP13 7JS; e-mail office@woodlands.bucks.sch.uk; Tel 01494 523874; Fax 01494 512661

Headteacher   Chris Cartmell

COUNTY MUSIC SERVICE

Amersham Music Centre Woodside School Site, Mitchell Wlk, Amersham, Buckinghamshire HP6 6NW; e-mail ammusic@buckscc.gov.uk; Tel 01494 431900; Fax 01494 431901

Headteacher   David Crook

Aylesbury Music Centre Walton Rd, Aylesbury, Buckinghamshire HP21 7ST; e-mail amcmail@buckscc.gov.uk; Tel 01296 428941; Fax 01296 423036

Head   Hugh Molloy

High Wycombe Music Centre Millbrook Combined School, Mill End Rd, High Wycombe, Buckinghamshire HP12 4BA; e-mail hwmusic@buckscc.gov.uk; Tel 01494 445947; Fax 01494 442773

Headteacher   Simon Salisbury

YOUTH AND COMMUNITY TRAINING CENTRE

Green Park Centre Stable Bridge Rd, Aston Clinton, Aylesbury, Buckinghamshire HP22 5NE; URL www.buckscc.gov.uk/green_park; e-mail gpark@buckscc.gov.uk; Tel 01296 633800; Fax 01296 633848

General Manager   Gary Shackleton

ADULT LEARNING SERVICE

County Hall, Aylesbury, Buckinghamshire HP20 1UZ; URL www.adultlearningbcc.ac.uk; e-mail adultlearning@buckscc.gov.uk; Tel 01296 383048; Fax 01296 382474

Head (Adult Learning)   Paula Buck (Acting)

ADULT LEARNING INFORMATION CENTRE

Winslow Centre, Park Rd, Winslow, Buckinghamshire MK18 3DL; e-mail studentenquiries@buckscc.gov.uk; Tel 0845 045 4040; Fax 01753 651870

COMPUTER CENTRES

ICT Schools Team Great Hampden Centre, Memorial Rd, Great Hampden, Buckinghamshire HP16 9RS; e-mail bemist@buckscc.gov.uk; Tel 01494 488750; Fax 01494 488745

Team Leader   Jenny McFee

ENVIRONMENTAL EDUCATION CENTRE

Shortenills Environmental Education Centre Nightingales La, Chalfont St Giles, Buckinghamshire HP8 4SG; URL www.buckscc.gov.uk/shortenills; Tel 01494 872288

Centre Manager   Ian Duckworth

EDUCATION/BUSINESS PARTNERSHIP

Buckinghamshire Education Business Partnership County Hall, Aylesbury, Buckinghamshire HP20 1UZ; e-mail bucksebp@buckscc.gov.uk; Fax 01296 382383

Manager (Education Business Partnership) Justine Burgess

MULTICULTURAL RESOURCE CENTRE

Minority Ethnic and Traveller Achievement Service Multicultural Resource Centre, Millbrook Combined School, Mill End Rd, High Wycombe, Buckinghamshire HP12 4BA; e-mail metas_millbrook@buckscc.gov.uk; Tel 01494 473046; Fax 01494 472171

Team Leader   Linda Lewins

MULTICULTURAL EDUCATION CENTRE

c/o Elmhurst Junior School, Dunsham La, Aylesbury, Buckinghamshire HP20 2DB; e-mail metas-elmhurst@buckscc.gov.uk; Tel 01296 421038; Fax 01296 330286

East Sussex County Council

www.eastsussex.gov.uk

In April 1997 Brighton and Hove became a unitary authority and is listed separately in this section. The rest of East Sussex retains a two-tier structure.

Population: 503 800 (excluding Brighton and Hove)

County Hall, St Anne's Cres, Lewes, East Sussex BN7 1SG; URL www.eastsussex.gov.uk; e-mail childrenservices@eastsussex.gov.uk; Tel 01273 481000; Fax 01273 481261

Children's Services

PO Box 4, County Hall, St Anne's Cres, Lewes, East Sussex
BN7 1SG; Tel 01273 481000; Fax 01273 481261
Lead Member (Children's and Adult's Services)
Cllr K. Glazier
Director Matt Dunkley
Assistant Director (Planning and Performance Management)
Louise Carter
Assistant Director (Resources) Hazel Cunningham
Deputy Director (Children and Families) Helen Davies
Deputy Director (Learning and School Effectiveness)
Penny Gaunt
Head (School Improvement Service) Bill Lyttle
Manager (Children's Trust) Alison Jaffery
Number of Schools
156 Primary; 27 Secondary; 10 Special
Council Tax Base
£213 230
Non-Domestic Rateable Value
£69 835

CABINET COMMITTEE

Members of Committee
Bill Bentley, Keith Glazier, Peter Jones, Simon Kirby,
Matthew Lock, Anthony Reid, Rupert Simmons, Meg
Stroude, Bob Tidy

EAST SUSSEX MUSIC SERVICE

Performing Arts Centre, Mountfield Rd, Lewes, East Sussex
BN7 2XH; Tel 01273 402555
Director Dr Tony Biggin

Hampshire County Council
www.hants.gov.uk

Population: 1 250 000
The Castle, Winchester, Hampshire SO23 8UG;
URL www.hants.gov.uk; Tel 01962 841841;
Fax 01962 847189
Chief Executive Peter Robertson LLB

Children's Services Department

e-mail enquiries@education.hants.gov.uk; Fax 01962 842355
Assistant Chief Execuitve (Children and Families Branch)
Robin Thomas
Assistant Chief Executive (Resources and Planning)
R.C. Mead MBA, DMA, ACIS
Assistant Chief Executive (Schools) Ann Begley
Director (Children's Services) John Coughlan
Deputy Director (Children's Services) John Clarke
Head (Adult and Community) Lionel Paris
Head (Corporate Unit/Early Education and Childcare)
Tracey Sanders (Acting)
Head (Education Personnel Services) John Wakeling
Head (EFS) Keith Sheppard
Head (Governor Services) Janet Sheriton
Head (Hampshire Music Services) Richard Howlet
Head (ICT) David Woodward
Head (Planning and Communications) Felicity Roe
Deputy Branch Manager (Children and Families)
Felicity Dickinson
Deputy Branch Manager (Children and Families) Cliff Turner
Manager; Principal Educational Psychologist
Hilary Robbins (Acting)
Manager; Principal Educational Psychologist Phil Stringer
Manager (Resource Allocation) Thomas Whiffen
Manager (Strategic Planning) Bob Eardley
Education Officer (EOTAS) Jack Cawthra
Education Officer (Primary) Chris Holt
Education Officer (SEN) Phil Butler

Education Officer (SEN) Sue Dorney-Smith
Education Officer (SEN) Eric Smith
Education Officer (Special Projects) Alex Munro
Education Officer (Special Projects) Terry Rath
Senior Inspector; Adviser (Secondary) Alan Rawlings
Senior Inspector; Adviser (Strategic Management)
Chris Wilson
Principal Education Welfare Officer Rita Crowne
County Inspector (Outdoor Education) Steve Poynton
County Youth Officer Malcolm Rittman
Group Accountant Sheila Little
Number of Schools
437 Primary; 71 Secondary; 27 Special

PROFESSIONAL DEVELOPMENT CENTRE

Central Division Professional Centre Falcon Hse, Romsey
Rd, Winchester, Hampshire SO22 5PW; Tel 01962 874800
Centre Manager Mrs Moran

Isle of Wight Council
www.iwight.com

Political composition: LD: 19, Con: 12, Ind: 12, Lab: 5
County Hall, Newport, Isle of Wight PO30 1UD;
URL www.iwight.com; e-mail
<firstname>.<surname>@iow.gov.uk; Tel 01983 821000;
Fax 01983 823333
Director (Corporate and Environment Services) Mike Fisher
Director (Finance and Information); County Treasurer
Gareth Hughes
Chief Fire Officer Richard Hards

Education Offices

Director (Children's Services) Vacancy
Head (Education Centre) C. Walker
Senior Education Officer A. Seaward BA, ACIS, LIMA
Senior Education Officer; Principal Educational Psychologist
S. Laycock
Education Officer M. Goswell
Principal Youth and Community Officer G. Weech
School Catering Management Officer J. Ewell
Number of Schools
16 Middle; 5 High; 2 Special

EXECUTIVE COMMITTEE

Spokesperson (Children) Patrick Joyce

ADULT EDUCATION SERVICE

Co-ordinator (Adult Education) B. Gould; in co-operation
with Isle of Wight College

POLICY COMMISSION FOR CHILDREN AND SCHOOL RESULTS

Chair Mrs M. Swann (Con)
Members
Con: W. Arnold, G. Camaron, G. Kennett, Lady S. Pigot
Lab: Ms D. Gardiner

FIELD STUDY CENTRE

Branstone Farm Studies Centre Branstone, Sandown, Isle of
Wight PO36 0LT; e-mail moocowiw@aol.com;
Tel 01983 865540; Fax 01983 865540
Warden T. Gurney

EDUCATION CENTRE

Thompson Hse, Sandy La, Newport, Isle of Wight
PO30 3NA; URL edunet.iow.gov.uk; e-mail
eduwight.iow.gov.uk; Tel 01983 529790;
Fax 01983 533644

TUITION CENTRES

Clatterford Watergate Rd, Newport, Isle of Wight
PO30 1XW; Tel 01983 524680; Fax 01983 524680
Teacher-in-Charge Mrs G. Andrew
Newport Tutorial Outreach Service Thompson Hse, Sandy
La, Newport, Isle of Wight PO30 3NA; Tel 01983 533523
Teacher-in-Charge Mrs C. Low
Sandown Tutorial Centre Lake Middle School, Newport Rd,
Lake, Isle of Wight PO36 9PE; Tel 01983 402261
Teacher-in-Charge S. Gee
Thompson House Tuition Centre Thompson Hse, Sandy La,
Newport, Isle of Wight PO30 3NA; Tel 01983 533523
Teacher-in-Charge S. Greenslade

CHILD GUIDANCE CLINIC

Support Teaching and Educational Psychology Service,
Thompson Hse, Newport, Isle of Wight PO30 3NA;
Tel 01983 533523; Fax 01983 528383
Senior Education Officer; Principal Educational Psychologist
S. Laycock

Kent County Council

www.kent.gov.uk

In April 1998 Medway Town Council became a unitary
authority and is listed separately in this section. The rest of
Kent retains a two-tier structure.
Population: 1 610 300
Political composition: Con: 57, Lab: 21, LD: 6
Sessions Hse, County Hall, Maidstone, Kent ME14 1XQ;
URL www.kent.gov.uk; Tel 0845 824 7247;
Fax 01622 690892
Chief Executive P. Gilroy
Managing Director (Adult Services) Oliver Mills
Managing Director (Communities) Amanda Honey
Managing Director (Environment and Regeneration)
Pete Raine

Children, Families and Education

e-mail ebldirector@kent.gov.uk; Fax 01622 694186;
Minicom 0845 824 7905
Managing Director Graham Badman MA, FRSA
Director (Children and Families Social Care) Bill Anderson
Director (Children's Health) Richard Murrells
Director (Commissioning, Specialist Services)
Joanna Wainwright MA, AIMgt
Director (Finance and Corporate Services) Keith Abbott
Director (Operations) Ian Craig PhD, BA, MBA, FRSA
Director (Resources) Grahame Ward BSc(Hons), IPFA
Director (Standards and Achievement) Carol Parsons BEd,
DPSE
Director (Strategy, Policy and Performance) Marilyn Hodges
BA(Hons), CertEd, FAE, MIMgt
Head (Admissions and Transport) Scott Bagshaw
Head (AEN and Resources) Colin Feltham
Head (Attendance and Behaviour Service) Sally Williamson
Head (Children's Safeguards Service Officer) Kel Arthur
Head (Early Years/Childcare) Alex Gamby
Head (EIS) Doug Smart
Head (Extended Schools) Marisa White
Head (Joint Commissioning) Maggie Stephenson
Head (Planning and Performance) Chris Carter
Head (Psychology Service) Andrew Heather (Acting)
Head (Schools Advisory Service) Don Garman
Head (Service Development: Schools Advisory Service)
Peggy Harris
Head (Specialist Teaching Service); Acting Head (MCAs)
Glynis Eley

Manager (Awards) Nick Jordan
Manager (Capital Strategy) Bruce MacQuarrie
Manager (Client Services) Mark Sleep
Manager (Data Collection and Quality Assurance)
Nic Cracknell
Number of Schools
453 Primary; 94 Secondary; 24 Special; 12 PRU; 7 Academies;
3 Middle; 1 Nursery

CABINET

*Cabinet Member (Children, Families and Educational
Standards)* Chris Wells
Cabinet Member (Education) Mark Dance

LOCAL OFFICES

East Kent Office Clover Hse, John Wilson Business Pk,
Whitstable, Kent CT5 3QZ; Tel 01227 772992;
Fax 01227 772290; Minicom 01227 284508
Mid Kent (Ashford) Kroner Hse, Eurogate Business Pk,
Ashford, Kent TN24 8XU; Tel 01233 639677;
Fax 01233 642973; Minicom 01233 652153

MID KENT (MAIDSTONE)

Bishops Terr, Bishops Way, Maidstone, Kent ME14 1AF;
Tel 01622 671411; Fax 01622 605163
West Kent (Joynes House) New Rd, Gravesend, Kent
DA11 0AT; Tel 01474 564701; Fax 01474 320395;
Minicom 01474 564701

WEST KENT (KINGS HILL)

17 Kings Hill Ave, West Malling, Kent ME19 4UL;
Tel 01732 525000; Fax 01732 525319;
Minicom 0845 824 7905

HOSPITAL SPECIAL SCHOOLS

East Kent Health Needs Education Service City View
Hospital, Canterbury, Kent CT2 8PT; Tel 01227 781548
Headteacher Ms R.D.S. Eastwood
West Kent Health Needs Education Service Woodview
Campus, Main Rd, Longfield, Dartford, Kent DA3 7PW;
Tel 01474 365467; Fax 01474 358145
Headteacher Graham Taylor

Medway Council

www.medway.gov.uk

In April 1998 Medway Council became a unitary authority.
The rest of Kent retains a two-tier structure and is listed
separately in this section.
Population: 252 000
Political composition: Con: 33, Lab: 13, LD: 8, Ind: 1
Civic Centre, Strood, Rochester, Medway ME2 4AU;
URL www.medway.gov.uk; Tel 01634 306000
Mayor Cllr Mrs V. Goulden
Chief Executive Neil Davies
Director (Community Services) Ann Windiate
Director (Regeneration and Development) Robin Cooper

Education Department

Fax 01634 331117
Director Rose Collinson
Assistant Director (Children's Care) Caroline Budden
Assistant Director (Learning and Achievement)
Simon Trotter
Assistant Director (Young People) Colin Rees

Milton Keynes Council
www.mkweb.co.uk

Population: 212 810
Political composition: LD: 23, Lab: 15, Con: 13
Civic Offices, 1 Saxon Gate East, Central Milton Keynes,
Buckinghamshire MK9 3HQ; URL www.mkweb.co.uk;
e-mail <firstname>.<surname>@milton-keynes.gov.uk;
Tel (emergency social worker: out of hours) 01908 265545;
Tel 01908 691691; Fax 01908 253556;
Minicom 01908 252727
Chief Executive   John Best

Learning and Development Directorate

PO Box 106, Saxon Ct, 502 Avebury Bvd, Milton Keynes,
Buckinghamshire MK9 3ZE; Fax 01908 253254
*Chief Executive; Corporate Director (Learning and
Development)*   Vanessa Gwynn
Head (Children's Services)   Paul Sutton
Head (Community and Economic Development)   John Cove
Head (Education: Planning and Standards)   David Gamble
Head (Education: SEN and Inclusion)   John O'Donnell
Head (Finance and Performance)   Vacancy
Number of Schools
10 Secondary; 6 Special

CABINET

Lead Member (Schools and Early Years)   Cllr Sandra Clark
Lead Member (Schools and Early Years)
Cllr Euan Henderson

EDUCATION WELFARE SERVICE

Holne Chase Centre, Buckingham Rd, Bletchley, Milton
Keynes, Buckinghamshire MK3 5HP; Tel 01908 657801
Principal Education Welfare Officer   Jayne Murphy
Administrative Officer   Paula Bianco
Administrative Officer   Janet Ellis

EDUCATIONAL PSYCHOLOGISTS

Local Area   Holne Chase Centre, Buckingham Rd, Bletchley,
Milton Keynes, Buckinghamshire MK3 5HP;
Fax 01908 367333; Fax 01908 643256
Principal Psychologist   Meg Timlin
Senior Psychologist (Early Years)   Jackie Andrew-Barrett
Senior Educational Psychologist (Later Years)
Andrew Facherty

SPECIAL NEEDS PROVISION

Primary Behaviour Support Service   Galley Hill Education
Centre, Galley Hill, Stony Stratford, Milton Keynes,
Buckinghamshire MK11 1PA; Tel 01908 254535
Head (Primary Behaviour Support)   Cathy Baker
Pupil Referral Unit – Main Centre   Manor Road Centre,
Bletchley, Milton Keynes, Buckinghamshire MK2 2HP;
Tel 01908 368268; Fax 01908 370154
Teacher-in-Charge   Moyra Forrester
Pupil Resource Base   Romansfield School, Shenley Rd,
Bletchley, Buckinghamshire MK3 7AW;
Tel 01908 376011; Fax 01908 645320
Headteacher   Wayne Marshall
**Special Educational Needs Disability and Inclusion Service
(SENDIS)**   Queensway Centre, Queensway, Bletchley,
Milton Keynes, Buckinghamshire MK2 2HB;
Tel 01908 375072; Fax 01908 630280
Senior Co-ordinator (SENDIS)   Jackie Wheeler

Tuition Service   Fenny Hse, Queensway, Bletchley, Milton
Keynes, Buckinghamshire MK2 2HB; e-mail
shelagh@fenny.milton-keynes.sch.uk; Tel 01908 646034;
Fax 01908 646034
Headteacher   Shelagh Bainbridge
Young People Out of School (YPOS)   Holne Chase Centre,
Buckingham Rd, Bletchley, Milton Keynes,
Buckinghamshire MK3 5HP; Tel 01908 657823;
Fax 01908 649893
Senior Project Worker   Claire Coltman

ADULT CONTINUING EDUCATION SERVICE (ACE)

Lord Grey/Leon ACE Centre   Lord Grey School, Rickley La,
Bletchley, Milton Keynes, Buckinghamshire MK3 6EW;
Tel 01908 647582
Head   Claire Griffin
Milton Keynes Consortium Office   Chaffron Way,
Leadenhall, Milton Keynes, Buckinghamshire MK6 5HJ;
Tel 01908 690538; Fax 01908 690537
Co-ordinator   A. Robinson
Milton Keynes Special Provision Centre (ACE)   The Old
School Hse, 3a The Almhouses, Great Linford, Milton
Keynes, Buckinghamshire MK14 5DZ; Tel 01908 231879;
Fax 01908 231876
Head   Audrey Robinson
Ouesdale ACE Centre   Ouesdale School, The Grove,
Newport Pagnell, Milton Keynes, Buckinghamshire
MK16 0BJ; Tel 01908 210230; Fax 01908 210230
Head   Audrey Robinson
Queensway Centre (ESOL)   Bletchley, Milton Keynes,
Buckinghamshire MK2 2HB; Tel 01908 644036;
Fax 01908 630280
Head   Audrey Robinson
Radcliffe ACE Centre   The Radcliffe School, Aylesbury St
West, Wolverton, Milton Keynes, Buckinghamshire
MK12 5BT; Tel 01908 316853
Head   Audrey Robinson
Shenley ACE Centre   c/o Denbigh School, Burchard Cres,
Milton Keynes, Buckinghamshire MK5 6EX;
Tel 01908 503311; Fax 01908 503376
Head   Claire Griffin
Stantonbury Campus   Community Office, Milton Keynes,
Buckinghamshire MK14 6BN; Tel 01908 220066;
Fax (Community Office) 01908 224201
Principal   Mark Wasserberg
Woughton ACE Centre   Sixth Form Bldg, Woughton
Campus West, Leadenhall, Milton Keynes,
Buckinghamshire MK6 5HJ; Tel 01908 671664;
Fax 01908 690538
Head   Jill Blackwood

EDUCATION/BUSINESS ACTIVITIES

Milton Keynes Education Business Partnership   Countec
Tempus, 249 Midsummer Bvd, Milton Keynes,
Buckinghamshire MK9 1EU; Tel 01908 660005;
Fax 01908 230130
Education Manager (Business Partnership)   Sue Mason

MUSIC SERVICE

Milton Keynes Music Centre   Stantonbury Campus, Milton
Keynes, Buckinghamshire MK14 6BN; Tel 01908 324448;
Fax 01908 225271
Head   Stephen James

OTHER CENTRES

Galley Mill Education Centre   Galley Mill, Stony Stratford,
Milton Keynes, Buckinghamshire MK11 1PA;
Tel 01908 254526
Early years and childcare; primary behaviour support;
parent partnership
Holne Chase Curriculum Centre   Buckingham Rd, Bletchley,
Milton Keynes, Buckinghamshire MK3 5HP;
Tel 01908 275098

Oxfordshire County Council
www.oxfordshire.gov.uk

Population: 617 200
Political composition: Con: 44, LD: 16, Lab: 8, Green: 5, Ind: 1
County Hall, New Rd, Oxford, Oxfordshire OX1 1ND;
    URL www.oxfordshire.gov.uk; e-mail
    online@oxfordshire.gov.uk; Tel 01865 792422;
    Fax 01865 726155
Chief Executive   Joanna Simons
Assistant Chief Executive   S. Capaldi; Tel 01865 810280;
    Fax 01865 815224
Director (Environmental and Economy Directorate)
    Richard Dudding; Speedwell Hse, Speedwell St, Oxford,
    Oxfordshire OX1 1NE
Head (Finance and Procurement)   Sue Scane;
    Tel 01865 816399
Head (Human Resources)   Steve Munn; Tel 01865 815191

Children, Young People and Families

Macclesfield Hse, New Rd, Oxford, Oxfordshire OX1 1NA;
    Tel 01865 815449; Fax 01865 791637
Director   Janet Tomlinson
Head (Raising Achievement Service)
    Sylvia Richardson (Acting)
Head (Raising Achievement Service)   Paula Tansley
Head (Youth Offending Services)   Tan Lea (Acting)
Head of Service (Young People and Access to Education)
    Jan Paine
Assistant Head (Early Learning and Childcare)   Annie Davy
Assistant Head (SEN, Disability and Access)   Simon Adams
Assistant Head (Social Inclusion)   Peter Wild
Assistant Head (Youth Support Services)   Monica Hanaway
Strategic Manager (Planning, Performance and Operations)
    Jackie Hayes
Strategic Manager (Planning and Performance)   Sian Rodway
*Senior Adviser (Educational Achievement and Service
    Monitoring)*   Roy Leach
*Senior Adviser (Partnership Development and Extended
    Learning)*   Judy Dyson
*Senior Adviser (Professional Development and Change
    Management)*   Anne Carter
Number of Schools
33 Secondary; 13 Special

CHILDREN'S SERVICES SCRUTINY COMMITTEE

Chair   Cllr Mrs Anda Fitzgerald-O'Connor (Con)

GOVERNOR SERVICES TEAM

Manager (Governor Services)   Marya Griffiths;
    Tel 01865 458770
Education Officer (Governor Services)   Claudia Wade;
    Tel 01865 458771
Services offered
The team offers a range of courses countrywide, resources
located in public libraries, information and advice, and in-
house training for individual governing bodies. A termly
newsletter is dispatched to every governor.

YOUTH CENTRES

Allandale Centre   Burford Rd, Carterton, Oxfordshire
    OX18 3AA; e-mail carterton.youth@oxfordshire.gov.uk;
    Tel 01993 842416; Fax 01993 847054
Banbury Youth Centre   Hilton Rd, Banbury, Oxfordshire
    OX16 0EJ; e-mail banbury.youth@oxfordshire.gov.uk;
    Tel 01295 264665
Blackbird Leys Youth Centre   Blackbird Leys Rd, Oxford,
    Oxfordshire OX4 6HW; e-mail
    bbleys.youth@oxfordshire.gov.uk; Tel 01865 772886;
    Fax 01865 772886

Botley Youth Centre   The Matrix, Matthew Arnold School,
    Oxford, Oxfordshire OX2 9JE; e-mail
    botley.youth@oxfordshire.gov.uk; Tel 01865 864717
Campus Youth Centre   Wimblestraw Rd, Berinsfield,
    Wallingford, Oxfordshire OX10 7LZ; e-mail
    berinsfield.youth@oxfordshire.gov.uk; Tel 01865 340301;
    Fax 01865 340301
Chiltern Edge Youth Wing   Reades La, Sonning Common,
    Reading RG4 9LN; e-mail
    chilternedge.youth@oxfordshire.gov.uk;
    Tel 0118 972 4418
Chipping Norton Youth Centre   Chipping Norton School, 60
    Burford Rd, Chipping Norton, Oxfordshire OX7 5DY;
    e-mail chippingnorton.youth@oxfordshire.gov.uk;
    Tel 01608 644745
Courtyard Youth Arts Centre, Bicester   Launton Rd, Bicester,
    Oxfordshire OX26 6DJ; e-mail
    bicester.youth@oxfordshire.gov.uk; Tel 01869 602545;
    Fax 01869 603556
Eynsham Youth Centre   Back La, Eynsham, Witney,
    Oxfordshire OX29 4QW; e-mail
    eynsham.youth@oxfordshire.gov.uk; Tel 01865 880630
The Forum Youth Centre   Oxford Rd, Kidlington,
    Oxfordshire OX5 1AB; e-mail
    kidlington.youth@oxfordshire.gov.uk; Tel 01865 375555
Henley Youth Centre   1 Deanfield Ave, Henley-on-Thames,
    Oxfordshire RG9 11UE; e-mail
    henley.youth@oxfordshire.gov.uk; Tel 01491 410836
The Net   Stratton Way, Abingdon, Oxfordshire OX14 3RG;
    e-mail abingdon.youth@oxfordshire.gov.uk;
    Tel 01235 521469; Fax 01235 534680
Rose Hill Youth Centre   The Oval, Oxford, Oxfordshire
    OX4 4UY; e-mail rosehill.youth@oxfordshire.gov.uk;
    Tel 01865 749971
Saxon Youth Centre   Saxon Way, Northway, Oxford,
    Oxfordshire OX3 9DD; e-mail
    headington.youth@oxfordshire.gov.uk;
    Tel 01865 741173; Fax 01865 741173
The Sweatbox   King Alfred's Community College East Site,
    Springfield Rd, Wantage OX12 8ET; e-mail
    grove&wantage.youth@oxfordshire.gov.uk;
    Tel 01235 770577; Fax 01235 225817
Thame Youth Centre   Lord Williams's Lower School,
    Towersey Rd, Thame, Oxfordshire OX9 3NW; e-mail
    thame.youth@oxfordshire.gov.uk; Tel 01844 212973
Union Street Centre for Young People   Union St, Oxford,
    Oxfordshire OX4 1JP; e-mail
    eastoxford.youth@oxfordshire.gov.uk; Tel 01865 248521;
    Fax 01865 200709
The Vibe Youth Centre   Park Rd, Didcot, Oxfordshire
    OX11 8QX; e-mail didcot.youth@oxfordshire.gov.uk;
    Tel 01235 812332; Fax 01235 815132
Wallingford Youth and Community Centre   Clapcot Way,
    Wallingford, Oxfordshire OX10 8HS; e-mail
    wallingford.youth@oxfordshire.gov.uk;
    Tel 01491 837053; Fax 01491 837053
Wheatley Youth Centre   Littleworth Rd, Wheatley,
    Oxfordshire OX33 1NW; e-mail
    wheatley.youth@oxfordshire.gov.uk; Tel 01865 873916
Witney Youth Centre   Witan Way, Witney, Oxfordshire
    OX2 4YA; e-mail witney.youth@oxfordshire.gov.uk;
    Tel 01993 772731; Fax 01993 778016
Wolvercote Young People's Club   St Peters Rd, Wolvercote,
    Oxfordshire OX2 8AU; e-mail
    wolvercote.youth@oxfordshire.gov.uk; Tel 01865 559374;
    Fax 01865 559374

SOCIAL INCLUSION SERVICES

*Contact (Advisory Service for the Education of Travellers –
    ASET)*   Lucy Beckett; Tel 01865 256620
Contact (Behaviour Support Service)   Bernice Smurthwaite;
    Tel 01865 256630
Contact (Educational Psychology Service)   Mark Corness;
    Tel 01865 815751
Contact (Education Social Work Service)   Barry Armstrong;
    Tel 01865 815956

Contact (*Meadowbrook College – Pupil Referral Unit*)
Andrew Creese; Tel 01865 253198

OXFORDSHIRE HOSPITAL SCHOOLS

Nuffield Orthopaedic Centre Headington, Oxfordshire
OX3 7LD; Tel 01865 737259; Fax 01865 737259
Headteacher Barry Jackson

SENSS (SPECIAL EDUCATIONAL NEEDS SUPPORT SERVICES)

The Wheatley Centre, Littleworth Rd, Wheatley OX33 1PH;
Tel 01865 456702; Fax 01865 456710
Head Mark Geraghty

HEARING IMPAIRMENT SUPPORT SERVICE

Central/North

Advisory Service Queensway County Primary School,
Queensway, Banbury, Oxfordshire OX16 9NF
Primary New Marston Primary School, Copse La,
Headington, Oxford, Oxfordshire OX3 0AY;
Tel 01865 761522; Fax 01865 742944
Secondary The Cherwell School, South Site, Marston Ferry
Rd, Oxford, Oxfordshire OX2 7EE; Tel 01865 515966;
Fax 01865 311684

South/East

Primary Rush Common County Primary School, Hendred
Way, Abingdon, Oxfordshire OX14 2AW;
Tel 01235 531070; Fax 01235 531070
Secondary Larkmead School, Faringdon Rd, Abingdon,
Oxfordshire OX14 1RF; Tel 01235 538471;
Fax 01235 538471

VISUAL IMPAIRMENT SUPPORT SERVICE

Advisory Service The Wheatley Centre, Littleworth Rd,
Wheatley, Oxford, Oxfordshire OX33 1PH;
Tel 01865 456711; Fax 01865 456710

LANGUAGE AND COMMUNICATION SUPPORT SERVICE

Central North

Advisory Service SS Mary and John CE Primary School,
Meadow La, Oxford, Oxfordshire OX4 1TJ;
Tel 01865 251485; Fax 01865 251388
Primary Queensway County Primary School, Queensway,
Banbury, Oxfordshire OX16 9NF; Tel 01295 275927;
Fax 01295 269247
Secondary The Marlborough School, Shipton Rd,
Woodstock, Oxfordshire OX20 1LP; Tel 01993 814741;
Fax 01993 813530
Secondary The Warriner School, Bloxham, Banbury,
Oxfordshire OX15 4LJ; Tel 01295 720777;
Fax 01295 721676

South/East

Primary Caldecott Primary School, Caldecott Rd,
Abingdon, Oxfordshire OX14 5HB; Tel 01235 521720;
Fax 01235 521720
Secondary Fitzharrys School, Northcourt Rd, Abingdon,
Oxfordshire O14 1NP; Tel 01235 535542;
Fax 01235 530376

PHYSICAL DISABILITY SUPPORT SERVICE

Early Years Oramerod Bldg, Waynflete Rd, Headington,
Oxfordshire OX3 8DD; Tel 01865 742379;
Fax 01865 762005
Secondary The Marlborough School, Shipton Rd,
Woodstock, Oxfordshire OX20 1LP; Tel 01993 814741;
Fax 01993 813530

Advisory Service Ormerod Bldg, Waynflete Rd,
Headington, Oxfordshire OX3 8DD; Tel 01865 742379;
Fax 01865 762005

DOWN'S SYNDROME AND COMPLEX NEEDS

Ormerod Bldg, Waynflete Rd, Headington, Oxfordshire
OX3 8DD; Tel 01865 744265; Fax 01865 762005

AUTISM SUPPORT SERVICE

Central/North

Primary St Nicholas First School, Raymund Rd, Old
Marston, Oxford, Oxfordshire OX3 0PJ; Tel 01865 726956;
Fax 01865 726956
Secondary The Cherwell School, South Site, Marston Ferry
Rd, Oxford, Oxfordshire OX2 7EE; Tel 01865 316712;
Fax 01865 316712
Secondary The Cherwell School, North Site, Marston Ferry
Rd, Oxford, Oxfordshire OX2 7EE; Tel 01865 559918;
Fax 01865 559918
Secondary The Marlborough School, Shipton Rd,
Woodstock, Oxfordshire OX20 1LP; Tel 01993 814741;
Fax 01993 813530

South/East

Advisory Service The Wheatley Centre, Littleworth Rd,
Wheatley, Oxford, Oxfordshire OX33 1PH;
Tel 01865 456702; Fax 01865 456710
Primary St Andrew's CE Primary School, Station Rd,
Chinnor, Oxfordshire OL9 4PU; Tel 01844 354827;
Fax 01844 354827
Secondary Lord Williams Lower School, Towersey Rd,
Thame, Oxfordshire OX9 3NW; Tel 01844 218412;
Fax 01844 218412
Secondary Lord Wiliams Upper School, Oxford Rd, Thame,
Oxfordshire OX9 2AW; Tel 01844 218800;
Fax 01844 217927

SEN ICT SERVICE

Advisory Service Ormerod Bldg, Waynflete Rd,
Headington, Oxford, Oxfordshire OX3 8DD;
Tel 01865 762776; Fax 01865 762005

Portsmouth City Council
www.portsmouth.gov.uk

Population: 188 500 (2002)
Political composition: LD: 21, Con: 14, Lab: 7
Civic Offices, Guildhall Sq, Portsmouth PO1 2AL;
URL www.portsmouth.gov.uk; e-mail
general@portsmouthcc.gov.uk; Tel 02392 822251
Chief Executive Marion Headicar

Education Authority

Portsmouth City Council, 4th Fl, Civic Offices, Guildhall Sq,
Portsmouth PO1 2EA; e-mail
education@portsmouthcc.gov.uk; Tel 02392 841209;
Fax 02392 841208
Director (Education and Lifelong Learning) Lynda Fisher
Assistant Director (Pupil Services) Andy Hough
Head (Early Years and Childcare) Catherine Kickham
Head (Education Human Resources) Jacqueline Coonie
Head (Education Services) Mike Fowler
Head (Music Service) Andrew Atkins
Head (Schools Standards and Effectiveness) Paddy Bradley
Head (SEN Service) Ken Bowen
Manager (Connexions) Julie Priestley
Manager (Information Development) Helen Handley
Manager (Special Projects) Hayden Ginns
Manager (Sure Start) Jill Fitzgerald

2

Senior Education Officer (SEN)   Steve Parsloe
Senior Education Officer (SEBS)   Philippa Pringle
Senior Adviser (Lifelong Learning)   Robin Johns
Adviser (English)   James Humphries
Adviser (ICT)   Paul Heinrich
Adviser (KS3 Foundation Subjects)   Michael Johns
Adviser (KS3 ICT)   David Ratcliffe
Adviser (Numeracy)   Tracy Potter
Adviser (PSHE)   David Hart
Adviser (School Improvement)   Alison Storey
Adviser (Science)   Vacancy
Principal Officer (Education Welfare)   Richard Harvey
Team Leader (Ethnic Minority Achievement Services)
   Janet Pitt
Exclusions Officer   Richard Barker
Inclusions Officer   Vacancy
Governor Services Officer   Andy Heaword
Group Accountant   Beverley Pennekett
Education Co-ordinator (Looked-After Children)
   Henry Raison
Project Development (Children in Public Care)
   Anne Hutchinson
Child Employment Officer   Mike Harding
Contact (The Pompey Study Centre)   Claire Martin
Contact (Excellence Cluster)   Alan Bartlett
Number of Schools
54 Primary; 11 Secondary; 6 Special; 2 Nursery

EDUCATION COMMITTEE

Chair   Cllr Alistair Thompson (Lab)
Executive Member (Education, Children and Lifelong
   Learning)   Cllr Eleanor Scott (LD)

PUPIL REFERRAL UNITS

Highlands Centre at The Spinnaker Education Centre
   Penhale Rd, Portsmouth PO1 5EF; Tel 02392 816486;
   Fax 02392 816478
   Headteacher   L. Atkinson
North End Centre at The Spinnaker Education Centre
   Penhale Rd, Portsmouth PO1 5EF; Tel 02392 817766;
   Fax 02392 855061
   Headteacher   Linda Atkinson
Primary Behaviour Support Team and Centre at The Crescent
   Centre   151 Lodisway Rd, Milton, Portsmouth PO4 8LD;
   Tel 02392 818547; Fax 02392 818548
   Administration Officer   Jackie Winkworth
The Sevenoaks Centre   Sundridge Cl, Cosham, Portsmouth
   PO6 3JL; Tel 02392 214492; Fax 02392 214509
   Headteacher   Sally Garret

Reading Borough Council
www.reading.gov.uk

In April 1998 Berkshire County Council was replaced by
Bracknell Forest, Reading, Slough, West Berkshire, Windsor
and Maidenhead, and Wokingham, each responsible for
local government services in its area. They are listed
separately in this section.
Political composition:: Lab: 25, Con: 14, LD: 7
Civic Centre, Reading RG1 7TD; URL www.reading.gov.uk;
   e-mail <firstname>.<surname>@reading.gov.uk;
   Tel 0118 939 0900; Fax 0118 958 9770;
   Minicom 0118 939 0700

Education and Children's Services

Civic Centre, PO Box 2623, Reading RG1 7WA;
   Tel 0118 939 0923
Lead Councillor (Children's Services)   Pete Ruhemann
Lead Councillor (Education)   Jon Hartley
Director   Anna Wright; e-mail
   anna.wright@reading.gov.uk
Head (Equality Services)   Jagiro Goodwin

Head (Extended Services)   Melani Oliver
Head (Planning, Performance and Projects)   Vacancy
Head (School Improvement)   Tim Coulson
Manager (Leadership Development)   Lynda Miller
Senior Adviser (Inclusion: Secondary and Primary)
   Jenny Tuck
Senior Co-ordinating Consultant   Ian Muir
Senior SIP (Primary)   Maggie Donaldson
Adviser (14–19)   Peter Shotts
Number of Schools
7 Secondary; 3 Special

EDUCATION WELFARE SERVICE

Reading Education Welfare Service   York Hse, York Rd,
   Reading RG1 8DH; Tel 0118 901 5870
   Head (Attendance)   Lesley Coles

CHILDREN'S EDUCATION SUPPORT SERVICE (CHESS)

Highways PRU   999 Oxford Rd, Reading RG31 6TL;
   Tel 0118 941 1720; Fax 0118 942 1611
   Head (Primary Behaviour Support Service and CHESS)
   Gill Dunlop
Seagulls   Seagulls Hse, Ross Rd, Reading RG1 8DY;
   Tel 0118 901 5583

EDUCATIONAL PSYCHOLOGY SERVICE

23 Craven Rd, Reading RG1 5LE; Tel 0118 901 5400

SPECIAL CLASSES AND UNITS

EP Collier Speech/Language Resource   EP Collier Primary
   School, Ross Rd, Reading RG1 8DZ
Hugh Faringdon Special Resource   Hugh Farringdon
   Secondary School, Fawley Rd, Reading RG30 3EP;
   Tel 0118 957 4730
   Headteacher   P. Barras
   AS
Maple Centre   Geoffrey Field Junior School, Exbourne Rd,
   Reading RG8 8RH; Tel 0118 901 5596

EDUCATION CENTRES

Reading Education Centre   Cranbury Rd, Reading RG30 2TS;
   Tel 0118 901 5581; Fax 0118 901 5597

COUNTY MUSIC CENTRE

County/Finance   BYMT, Stoneham Ct, 100 Cockney Hill,
   Reading RG30 4EZ; Tel 0118 901 2350
   Principal   D. Marcou

Slough Borough Council
www.slough.gov.uk

In April 1998 Berkshire County Council was replaced by
Bracknell Forest, Reading, Slough, West Berkshire, Windsor
and Maidenhead, and Wokingham, each responsible for
local government services in its area. They are listed
separately in this section.
Political composition: Lab: 19, Other: 8, Con: 7, LD: 4,
Liberal: 3
Population: 119 500
Town Hall, Bath Rd, Slough SL1 3UQ;
   URL www.slough.gov.uk; e-mail
   enquiries@slough.gov.uk; Tel 01753 475111;
   Minicom 01753 875030
Chief Executive   Ruth Bagley

Education and Children's Services

Tel 01753 875700; Fax 01753 875716
Strategic Director (Education and Children's Services)
   Clair Pyper

Assistant Director (Children and Families) Nicky Rayner
Assistant Director (Inclusion) Robin Crofts
Assistant Director (Raising Achievements) Bill Alexander
Assistant Director (Resources, Commissioning and Performance) Annal Nayyar
Number of Schools
28 Primary; 11 Secondary; 5 Nursery; 3 Special

CABINET COMMITTEE

Other: 4, Con: 3, Liberal: 2
Chair Richard Stokes

EDUCATION PSYCHOLOGICAL SERVICE

Tel 01753 787640; Fax 01753 787641
Assistant Director (Inclusion) Robin Crofts

RESOURCE FOR CHILDREN WITH PHYSICAL DIFFICULTIES

Priory School Orchard Ave, Slough SL1 6HE; e-mail info@prioryschool.com; Tel 01628 600300
Headteacher Jacqueline Laver
Number of students: 690
Westgate Cippenham La, Slough SL1 5AH; e-mail secretary@westgate.slough.sch.uk; Tel 01753 521320
Headteacher Roger Thomas
Number of students: 835

HEARING IMPAIRED CHILDREN

Foxborough Primary School Common Rd, Slough SL3 8TX; e-mail post@foxborough.slough.sch.uk; Tel 01753 546376
Headteacher Denby Richards
Number of students: 325
Langleywood School Langley Rd, Slough SL3 7EF; e-mail head@langleywood.slough.sch.uk; Tel 01753 541549
Headteacher Paul McAteer
Number of students: 892
St Ethelbert's Catholic Primary School Wexham Rd, Slough SL2 5QR; e-mail post@stethelberts.slough.sch.uk; Tel 01753 522048
Headteacher Theresa Haggart
Number of students: 398

CHILDREN WITH AUTISM AND GENERAL DEVELOPMENT

Arbour Vale School Farnham Rd, Slough SL2 3AE; e-mail office@arbourvale.slough.sch.uk; Tel 01753 515560
Headteacher Debbie Richards
Number of students: 207
Chalvey Nursery Assessment Resource The Green, Slough SL1 2SP; e-mail office@chalveyeyc.slough.sch.uk; Tel 01753 536293
Headteacher Kate Makinson
Number of students: 68
Ryvers Primary Resource Trelawney Ave, Slough SL1 7TS; e-mail office@ryvers.slough.sch.uk; Tel 01753 544474
Headteacher Alan Dean
Number of students: 417

ADULT EDUCATION INSTITUTES

East Berkshire College Station La, Langley, Slough SL3 8BY; e-mail info@eastberks.ac.uk; Tel 0845 373 2500
Principal Jean Robertson
Slough and Eton School Ragstone Rd, Slough SL1 2PE; e-mail post@sloughton.slough.sch.uk; Tel 01753 520824
Contact Graham Lush
Thames Valley University Wellington St, Slough SL1 1YG; e-mail learning.advice@tvu.ac.uk; Tel 01753 534585

Southampton City Council

www.southampton.gov.uk

Population: 209 901
Political composition: Lab: 22, LD: 16, Con: 7

Civic Centre, Southampton SO14 7LY; URL www.southampton.gov.uk; Tel 02380 223855
Chief Executive B. Roynon
Executive Director (Performance and Management) M. Smith

Children's Services and Learning

5th Fl, Frobisher Hse, Southampton SO15 1BZ; URL www.southampton.gov.uk/education
Cabinet Member Cllr Ann Milton
Executive Director Clive Webster; e-mail clive.webster@southampton.gov.uk
Head of Service Sue Allan; Tel 02380 833021

PUPIL REFERRAL UNITS

The Compass Pupil Referral Unit Warren Ave, Shirley Warren, Southampton SO16 6AH; Tel 02380 772572; Fax 02380 776523
Teacher-in-Charge Mr R. Gilroy
Pupil Referral Unit and Exclusion Support Service 18 Melbourne St, Southampton SO14 5RB; Tel 02380 215320; Fax 02380 215329
Headteacher Mr A. Sumner

Surrey County Council

www.surreycc.gov.uk

Population: 1 078 100
Political composition: Con: 58, LD: 12, Ind: 8, Lab: 2
County Hall, Penrhyn Rd, Kingston upon Thames, Surrey KT1 2DN; URL www.surreycc.gov.uk; e-mail contact.centre@surreycc.gov.uk; Tel (contact centre) 0845 600 9009; Fax 020 8541 9004
Chief Executive Dr Richard Shaw

PUPIL REFERRAL UNITS

Guildford Pupil Referral Unit Pewley Hill Centre, Pewley Hill, Guildford, Surrey GU1 3SQ; Tel 01483 452352; Fax 01483 579275
Contact Mrs J. Lindfield
Hersham Teaching Centre 174 Molesey Rd, Hersham, Walton-on-Thames, Surrey KT12 4QY; Tel 01932 229369; Fax 01932 229369
Contact P. Dobbs
11–16
Fordway Centre Stanwell Rd, Ashford, Surrey TW15 3DU; Tel 01784 243365; Fax 01784 423664
Contact Mrs S. Simpson
5–11
Pyrford Centre Engliff La, Pyrford, Woking, Surrey GU22 8SU; Tel 01932 342451; Fax 01932 336517
Contact Mr M. Tozer
14–16
Sidlow Bridge Centre Ironsbottom La, Sidlow, Reigate, Surrey RH2 8PP; Tel 01737 249079; Fax 01737 226520
Contact Mr S. Taylor
14–16
Phoenix Centre Alpine Rd, Redhill, Surrey RH1 2HY; Tel 01737 767521; Fax 01737 760468
Contact Mrs A. Sale
5–11
South East Surrey Pupil Referral Unit 82 Allingham Rd, Reigate, Surrey RH2 8HU; Tel 01737 243806; Fax 01737 240322
Contact Mrs G. Allen
11–16
Sycamore Centre 14 West Hill, Epsom, Surrey KT19 8HR; Tel (admininistration: Tue and Thu only) 01372 722939; Fax 01372 722939
Contact Mrs M.L. McKay-Jones
11–16

Woking Pupil Referral Unit Kingsway Centre, 45 Kingsway, Woking, Surrey GU21 6NT; Tel 01483 728474; Fax 01483 757410
Contact Mrs A. Goebel

SURREY INTEGRATED SERVICE FOR YOUNG PEOPLE

HOPE Epsom West Park Rd, Horton La, Epsom, Surrey KT19 8PB; Tel 01372 203404
Contact Mr J. Dalglish
HOPE Guildford Worplesdon Rd, Guildford, Surrey GU2 6SR; Tel 01483 517190
Contact Ms J.C. Sherington

Children and Young People Directorate

County Hall, Kingston upon Thames, Surrey KT1 2DJ; URL www.surreycc.gov.uk/education
Strategic Director (Services for Families) Andrew Webster
Head (Children and Young People Strategy Unit) Frank Offer
Head (Surrey Children's Service) Felicity Budgen
Head (Schools and Learning) Nick Wilson
Managing Director (Surrey School Support Services: Four S) Dr Marcus Watson
Local Education Officer (Elmbridge/Epsom and Ewell/ Spelthorne) Helen Nowicki; Fairmount Hse, Bull Hill, Leatherhead, Surrey KT22 7AH; Tel 01372 833412
Local Education Officer (Guildford/Waverley) Ian Skelton; South West Area Office, Grosvenor Hse, Cross Lanes, Guildford, Surrey GU1 1FA; Tel 01483 517835
Local Education Officer (Mole Valley/Reigate and Banstead/ Tandridge) Melanie Harris; East Area Office, Omnibus, Lesbourne Rd, Reigate, Surrey RH2 7JA; Tel 01483 517835
Local Education Officer (Runnymede/Surrey Heath/Woking) John Ambrose; Quadrant Ct, 35 Guildford Rd, Woking, Surrey GU22 7QQ; Tel 01483 518106
Number of Schools
314 Primary; 53 Secondary; 24 Special; 13 PRU

CHILDREN AND FAMILIES SELECT COMMITTEE

Chair Yvonna Lay; Tel 01784 457170

GOVERNANCE CONSULTANCY

Four S, Bay Tree Ave, Kingston Rd, Leatherhead, Surrey KT22 7UE; URL www.fours.co.uk; e-mail governance.consultancy@vtplc.com; Tel 01372 834444; Fax 01372 834000
Manager (Governance Consultancy) Sue Boustead
Services offered
Provides statutory and strategic advice for Surrey governors, clerks and headteachers. Produces and distributes a bi-annual newsletter The Surrey Governor. Arranges regular training opportunities on topical issues. Offers an individual service to schools for identified training needs for governors, staff and parents. Provides a help-line for governors, clerks and headteachers. Provides a bespoke clerking service.

HOSPITAL PROVISION

St Peter's Teaching Centre Ash Ward, St Peter's Hospital, Chertsey, Surrey KT16 0PZ; Tel 01932 874761
Contact Mrs J. Ashworth
Surrey Teaching Centre at The Children's Trust The Children's Trust, Tadworth Ct, Tadworth, Surrey KT20 5RU; Tel 01737 354006
Contact Mrs S. West

West Berkshire Council

www.westberks.gov.uk

In April 1998 Berkshire County Council was replaced by Bracknell Forest, Reading, Slough, West Berkshire, Windsor and Maidenhead, and Wokingham, each responsible for local government services in its area. They are listed separately in this section.
Political composition: Con: 26, LD: 26
Council Offices, Market St, Newbury, West Berkshire RG14 5LD; URL www.westberks.gov.uk; Tel 01635 42400; Fax 01635 519431
Chief Executive Nick Carter
Head (Education Service) Ian Pearson

Education Department

Avonbank Hse, West St, Newbury, West Berkshire RG14 1BZ; URL www.westberks.gov.uk/education; Tel 01635 519729; Fax 01635 519624
Chief Adviser (School Improvement) Andy Tubbs
Service Development Manager (Access) Anna Ditchburn
Service Development Manager (Adult and Community) Moyra Blake
Service Development Manger (SEN, Early Years) Jane Seymour
Service Development Manager (Social Inclusion) Caroline Simmonds
School Improvement Adviser (14–19 Strategy) Jeremy Nicholls
School Improvement Adviser (Early Years, The Arts) Avril Allenby
School Improvement Adviser (IT, PSHE, Health Education) Tim Kuhles
School Improvement Adviser (Literacy, Able Pupils) Elaine Ricks
School Improvement Adviser (Numeracy, RE) Maxine Slade
School Improvement Adviser (Primary Leadership Programme) Fay Parkes
School Improvement Adviser (Primary Leadership Programme) Jon Houghton
School Improvement Adviser (Science, PE, Leadership CPD) Andrew Breavington
School Improvement Adviser (Secondary Strategy) Christine Hadrell

CHILDREN AND YOUNG PEOPLE SELECT COMMITTEE

Con: 10, LD: 4
Chair S. Hannon
Vice-Chair S. Ellison
Portfolio Member (Children and Young People) G. Pask
Members of the Committee
Con: P. Argyle, B. Bedwell, P. Bryant, J. Chapman, S. Ellison, A. Kilgour, T. Linden, G. Lundie, T. Metcalfe, I. Neill
LD: S. Hannon, S. Harding, M. Lock, C. Suggett

EDUCATION WELFARE AND PSYCHOLOGY

Avonbank Hse, West St, Newbury, West Berkshire RG14 1BZ
Principal Education Welfare Officer Karen Pottinger; Tel 01635 519785
Principal Educational Psychologist Hilary Mason; Tel 01635 519014

PUPIL REFERRAL UNITS

Alternative Curriculum 14–19 88 Newtown Rd, Newbury, West Berkshire RG14 7BT; e-mail office.alternative@westberks.org; Tel 01635 528048; Fax 01635 36124
Headteacher J. Davies
Badgers Hill Pupil Referral Unit 22 Highview, Calcot, Reading RG31 4XD; e-mail office.badgers@westberks.org; Tel 0118 941 6636; Fax 0118 941 7269
Leading Teacher Mrs D. McDonnell
Bridgeway Pupil Referral Unit 88 Newtown Rd, Newbury, West Berkshire RG14 7BT; e-mail office.bridgeway@westberks.org; Tel 01635 49397; Fax 01635 49397
Leading Teacher Mr B. Woodhart

The Key Riverside Community Centre, Rosemoor Gdns, Newbury, West Berkshire RG14 2FG; e-mail thequay@westberks.gov.uk; Tel 01635 279709; Fax 01635 279769
Leading Teacher Mrs L. Mann

Kingfisher Pupil Referral Unit Moorside Community Centre, Urquhart Rd, Thatcham, West Berkshire RG19 4RE; e-mail office.kingfisher@westberks.org; Tel 01635 861019; Fax 01635 873645
Leading Teacher Ms S. Klaassens

The Oaks Pupil Referral Unit Foxglove Way, Thatcham, West Berkshire RG18 4DH; e-mail office.oaks@westberks.org; Tel 01635 877114; Fax 01635 877107
Leading Teacher Ms F. Holland

Reintegration Service Moorside Community Centre, Urquhart Rd, Thatcham, West Berkshire RG19 4RE; e-mail office.regeneration@westberks.org; Tel 01635 865573; Fax 01635 873645
Headteacher Ms S. Williams

EDUCATION CENTRES

Curriculum Centre West Berkshire Education Centre, Fir Tree La, Newbury, West Berkshire RG14 2HX; Tel 01635 279217; Fax 01635 279279
Administrator (Consultant Support) Sharon Goddard

Learning Support Team West Berkshire Education Centre, Fir Tree La, Newbury, West Berkshire RG14 2HX; Tel 01635 30572
Co-ordinator F. Merchant

West Berkshire Education Centre Fir Tree La, Newbury, West Berkshire RG14 2HX; Tel 01635 43351; Fax 01635 43351
Manager (Education Centre) Rex Wearn

COUNTY MUSIC CENTRE

Berkshire Young Musician Trust Western Office c/o Trinity School, Church Rd, Newbury, West Berkshire RG14 2DU; URL www.bymt.org.uk; e-mail admin@bymt.org.uk; Tel 0118 901 2370

West Sussex County Council

www.westsussex.gov.uk

Population: 764 400
Political composition: Con: 46, LD: 17, Lab: 7
County Hall, West St, Chichester, West Sussex PO19 1RQ; URL www.westsussex.gov.uk; e-mail webmaster@westsussex.gov.uk; Tel 01243 777100; Fax 01243 777952
Chief Executive Mark Hammond MA

Children and Young People's Services

URL www.wsgfl.westsussex.gov.uk; e-mail cyps@westsussex.gov.uk; Tel 0845 075 1007
Director (Children and Young People's Services) Robert Back
Number of Schools
40 Secondary; 12 Special; 4 Nursery

CHILDREN AND YOUNG PEOPLE'S SERVICES CABINET

Chair (Select Committee) Mr C. O'Neill (Con)
Vice-Chair Mrs M. Ball (Con)
Cabinet Member (Children and Young People's Services) Mark Dunn (Con)

Children's Support

Head (Children's Support) John Leaver
Head (Education Welfare) Julie Collick
Head (Locality Care) Nick Longdon
Head (Looked-After Learners) Maureen Giles

Head (SEN and Child Disability) Jon Philpot
Head (Youth Offending Services) Mike Thomas

Learning

Head (Access and Locality Support) Helen Powell
Head (Adult Education) Ros Parker
Head (Educational Inclusion) Hilary Vaughan
Head (Educational Psychology) Peter Emmerson
Head (Educational Psychology) Chris Lewis
Head (Governor Services) Judith Ogan
Head (Learning) David Sword
Head (Out-of-School Learning) Thelma Bartlett
Head (School and Professional Development Services) Brin Martin
Head (School Improvement Primary) Janis Taylor
Head (School Improvement Secondary) John Morrison

Partnerships

Head (Child Protection) Brian Relph
Head (Development) Martin Virr
Head (Early Childhood Service) Marilyn Barton
Head (Independent Reviewing) Jenny Clifton
Head (Integrated Services Development) Nikki Gibbins
Head (Partnerships) Sue Berelowitz
Head (Strategic Partnerships: Children) Jillian Lovejoy
Head (Youth) Carole Aspden
Manager (Integrated Services) Mark Frankland

Resources

Head (Business Support Services) John Goodman
Head (Capital Planning and Client Services) Peter Proudley
Head (Change Programme) Karen Hayler
Head (CYPP/LAA/Policy Development) Tony Drew
Head (Information Management Strategy) Steve Whiting
Head (Performance Development) Vacancy
Head (Resource Planning) Jeanmarie Long
Head (School Organisation Planning) Phil Whiffing

Special Projects

Head (Complaints and Representations) Susie Skipper
Head (Special Projects) Mike Wilson

ADULT EDUCATION CENTRES

Bognor Adult Education Centre Bognor Regis Community College, Westloats La, Bognor Regis, West Sussex PO21 5LH; URL www.westsussex.gov.uk/adulteducation; e-mail baec@westsussex.gov.uk; Tel 01243 872020; Fax 01243 871041

Burgess Hill Adult Education Centre Marle Pl, Leylands Rd, Burgess Hill, West Sussex RH15 8HZ; URL www.westsussex.gov.uk/adulteducation; e-mail oaecburg@westsussex.gov.uk; Tel 01444 236355; Fax 01444 871269

Crawley – Ifield Adult Education Centre Ifield Community College, Crawley Ave, Ifield, Crawley, West Sussex RH11 0DB; URL www.westsussex.gov.uk/adulteducation; e-mail ifield.aec@westsussex.gov.uk; Tel 01293 420505; Fax 01293 420515

Crawley – Thomas Bennett Adult Education Centre Thomas Bennett Community College, Ashdown Dr, Crawley, West Sussex RH11 5AD; URL thomas.bennett.aec.crawley@westsussex.gov.uk; Tel 01293 523811; Fax 01293 538873

Felpham Adult Education Centre Felpham Community College, Felpham Way, Felpham, Bognor Regis, West Sussex PO22 8EL; URL www.westsussex.gov.uk/adulteducation; e-mail felpham.aec@westsussex.gov.uk; Tel 01243 867845; Fax 01243 867845

Haywards Heath Adult Education Centre Oathall Community College, Appledore Gdns, Haywards Heath, West Sussex RH16 2AQ; URL www.westsussex.gov.uk/adulteducation; e-mail oaechayw@westsussex.gov.uk; Tel 01444 452163; Fax 01444 441927

2

Horsham Adult Education Centre The Forest School, Comptons La, Horsham, West Sussex RH13 5NW; URL www.westsussex.gov.uk/adulteducation; e-mail horsham.aec@westsussex.gov.uk; Tel 01403 261088; Fax 01403 756268

Lancing Adult Education Centre Boundstone Community College, Boundstone La, Lancing, West Sussex BN15 9QZ; URL www.westsussex.gov.uk/adulteducation; e-mail boundstone.aec.lancing@westsussex.gov.uk; Tel 01903 755895; Fax 01903 765005

Littlehampton Adult Education Centre The Littlehampton Community School, Hill Rd, Littlehampton, West Sussex BN17 6DQ; URL www.westsussex.gov.uk/adulteducation; e-mail littlehampton.aec@westsussex.gov.uk; Tel 01903 722155; Fax 01903 713200

Midhurst and Petworth Adult Education Centre Midhurst Grammar School, North St, Midhurst, West Sussex GU29 9TD; URL www.westsussex.gov.uk/adulteducation; e-mail midhurst.aec@westsussex.gov.uk; Tel 01730 816683; Fax 01730 816765

Selsey Adult Education Centre Manhood Community College, School La, Selsey, West Sussex PO20 9EH; URL www.westsussex.gov.uk/adulteducation; e-mail manhood.aec.selsey@westsussex.gov.uk; Tel 01243 605030; Fax 01243 607877

Southbourne Adult Education Centre Bourne Community College, Park Rd, Southbourne, Emsworth, Hampshire PO10 8PJ; URL www.westsussex.gov.uk/adulteducation; e-mail bourne.aec.southbourne@westsussex.gov.uk; Tel 01243 379276; Fax 01243 378508

Steyning Adult Education Centre Steyning Grammar School, Shooting Field, Steyning, West Sussex BN44 3RX; URL www.westsussex.gov.uk/adulteducation; e-mail steyning.aec@westsussex.gov.uk; Tel 01903 814880; Fax 01903 814419

Storrington Adult Education Centre Rydon Community College, Rock Rd, Storrington, West Sussex RH20 3AA; URL www.westsussex.gov.uk/adulteducation; e-mail storrington.aec@westsussex.gov.uk; Tel 01903 744129; Fax 01903 741771

Westergate Adult Education Centre Westergate Community School, Lime Ave, Westergate, West Sussex PO20 6UE; URL www.westsussex.gov.uk/adulteducation; e-mail westergate.acc@westsussex.gov.uk; Tel 01243 546820; Fax 01243 544878

Worthing Adult Education Centre Southfield Hse, 2nd Fl, 11 Liverpool Gdns, Worthing, West Sussex BN11 1RY; URL www.westsussex.gov.uk/adulteducation; e-mail worthing.aec@westsussex.gov.uk; Tel 01903 703566; Fax 01903 703575

SPECIAL SUPPORT CENTRES (NORTH)

Crawley Primary Special Support Centre for Children with Additional Learning Needs Maidenbower Junior School, Harvest Rd, Maidenbower, Crawley, West Sussex RH10 7RA; Tel 01293 883758; Fax 01293 889409
Headteacher C. Murphy
Teacher-in-Charge Mrs C. Hiley
7–11

Crawley Primary Special Support Centre for Children with Social Communication Needs Desmond Anderson Primary School, Canterbury Rd, Tilgate, Crawley, West Sussex RH10 5EZ; Tel 01293 525596
Headteacher T. Quinton
Teacher-in-Charge Ms A. Tighe
Mixed; 4–11; Day

Crawley Secondary Special Support Centre for Children with Additional Learning Needs Oriel High School, Maidenbower La, Maidenbower, Crawley, West Sussex RH10 7XW; Tel 01293 880350

Headteacher Ms G. Smith
Teacher-in-Charge Mrs C. Turner
11–18

Crawley Secondary Special Support Centre for Children with Hearing Impairment Hazelwick School, Hazelwick Mill La, Three Bridges, Crawley, West Sussex RH10 1SX; Tel 01293 403344
Headteacher G.M.W. Parry
Teacher-in-Charge Ms C. Simmons
11–18

Crawley Secondary Special Support Centre for Children with Social Communication Needs Thomas Bennett Community College, Ashdown Dr, Tilgate, Crawley, West Sussex RH10 5AD; Tel 01293 526255; Tel (unit) 01293 539310
Headteacher Ms Y. Maskatiya
Teacher-in-Charge Ms J. Fruin
11–18

Crawley Special Support Centre for Children with Hearing Impairment Northgate Primary School, Green La, Crawley, West Sussex RH10 2DX; Tel 01293 526737; Tel (unit) 01293 614878
Headteacher Mrs A. Wood
Teacher-in-Charge Mrs J. Holden
4–11

Crawley Special Support Centre for Children with Physical Disabilities St Margaret's CE Primary School, The Mardens, Ifield, Crawley, West Sussex RH11 0AQ; Tel 01293 521077
Headteacher Ms H. Fletcher-Reilly
Teacher-in-Charge Mrs A. Leighs
5–11

Crawley Special Support Centre for Children with Speech and Language Needs Three Bridges Junior School, Gales Dr, Three Bridges, Crawley, West Sussex RH10 1PD; Tel 01293 526888; Tel (unit) 01293 615864
Headteacher Mrs C. Wharton
Teacher-in-Charge Vacancy
7–11

Crawley Special Support Centre for Children with Speech and Language Needs Three Bridges Infant School, Gales Pl, Three Bridges, Crawley, West Sussex RH10 1QG; Tel 01293 524076; Tel (unit) 01293 615807
Headteacher M. Westgarth
Teacher-in-Charge Mrs J. Triggs
4–7

Haywards Heath Colwood Education Centre Hurstwood La, Haywards Heath, West Sussex RH17 7SH; Tel 01444 456427; Fax 01444 412327
Teacher-in-Charge Grahame Robson

Mid Sussex Primary Special Support Centre for Children with Additional Learning Needs Blackthorns Community Primary School, Blackthorns Cl, Lindfield, Haywards Heath, West Sussex RH16 2AY; Tel 01444 454866
Headteacher Mrs R. Schofield
Teacher-in-Charge Mrs C. Pritchard
7–11

Mid Sussex Secondary Special Support Centre for Children with Additional Learning Needs Warden Park School, Broad St, Cuckfield, Haywards Heath, West Sussex; Tel 01444 457881
Headteacher S. Johnson
Teacher-in-Charge Mrs V. Beckett
11–16

Mid Sussex Special Support Centre for Children with Language Needs London Meed Community Primary School, Chanctonbury Rd, Burgess Hill, West Sussex RH15 9YQ; Tel 01444 232336
Headteacher Mr A. Brown
Teacher-in-Charge (Infants) Mrs A. Holgate
Teacher-in-Charge (Juniors) Mrs A. D'Arcy
4–11

North Pupil Referral Unit (Burgess Hill) Marle Pl, Leylands Rd, Burgess Hill, West Sussex RH15 8JD; Tel 01444 232771; Fax 01444 870229

North Pupil Referral Unit (Crawley) Worth Annex, Turners Hill Rd, Worth, Crawley, West Sussex RH10 7RN; Tel 01293 883209

SPECIAL SUPPORT CENTRES (SOUTH)

Angmering the Lavinia Norfolk Centre for Physically Disabled and Hearing Impaired Children The Angmering Day School, Station Rd, Angmering, Littlehampton, West Sussex BN16 4HH; Tel 01903 772351; Tel (unit) 01903 773146
Headteacher D. Brixey
Teacher-in-Charge Miss G. Tisdall
11–18

Barnham Special Support Centre for Physically Disabled Children Barnham Primary School, Elm Gr, Barnham, Bognor Regis, West Sussex PO22 0HW; Tel 01243 552197; Fax 01243 554588
Headteacher Ms J. Hodgson
Teacher-in-Charge Ms J. Hodgson
4–11

Boundstone Pre-school Class for Children with Speech and Language Problems Boundstone Nursery School, Upper Boundstone La, Lancing, West Sussex BN15 9QX; Tel 01903 753995
Headteacher Mrs S. Smart
Teacher-in-Charge Ms R. Lewis

Chichester Primary Special Support Centre for Children with Social Communication Needs Parklands Community Primary School, Durnford Cl, Chichester, West Sussex PO19 3AG; Tel 01243 788630
Headteacher Mrs H. Faulkner
Teacher-in-Charge Mrs K. Roman
4–11

Chichester Special Support Centre for Speech and Language Impaired Children Portfield Community Primary School, St James Rd, Chichester, West Sussex PO19 4HR; Tel (unit) 01243 781256; Tel 01243 783939
Headteacher Mr S. Morton
Teacher-in-Charge Mrs S. Sheach
Teacher-in-Charge (Infants) Mrs P.R. Denton
4–11

Littlehampton Connaught Special Support Centre for Hearing Impaired Pupils Connaught Junior School, York Rd, Littlehampton, West Sussex BN17 6EW; Tel 01903 715575; Tel (unit) 01903 721677
Headteacher Mrs J. Grevett
Teacher-in-Charge Mrs T. Hayes
7–11

South Pupil Referral Unit (Chichester) Fletcher Place Bldg, North Mundham, Chichester, West Sussex PO20 6JR; Tel 01243 788044
Teacher-in-Charge R. Stepien

South Pupil Referral Unit (Worthing) 37 Richmond Rd, Worthing, West Sussex BN11 1PW; Tel 01903 211855; Fax 01903 216998
Head (South Pupil Referral Units) K. Purbhoo

Steyning Primary Special Support Centre for Children with Additional Learning Needs St Andrew's CE Primary School, Shooting Field, Steyning, West Sussex BN44 3RX; Tel 01903 813420; Tel (unit) 01903 879200
Headteacher C. Luckin
Teacher-in-Charge Mrs L. Latham
4–11

Steyning Secondary Special Support Centre for Children with Additional Learning Needs Steyning Grammar School, Shooting Field, Steyning, West Sussex BN44 3RX; Tel 01903 814555
Headteacher Dr J. Peat
Teacher-in-Charge Mr T. Bostall
11–18

Western Area Secondary Special Support Centre for Children with Additional Learning Needs Bognor Regis Community College, Westloats La, Bognor Regis, West Sussex PO21 5LH; Tel (lower unit) 01243 841026; Tel (upper unit) 01243 871016
Headteacher J.Q. Morrison

Teacher-in-Charge Ms A. Coleman
11–18

Worthing Special Support Centre for Children with Social Communication Needs Lyndhurst First School, Lyndhurst Rd, Worthing, West Sussex BN11 2DG; Tel 01903 235390
Headteacher Mrs A. Lawrenson
Teacher-in-Charge Mrs J. Blewitt
4–7

Worthing Portage Service School Hse, Littlehampton Rd, Durrington, Worthing, West Sussex BN13 1RB; Tel 01903 242558; Fax 01903 242337
Supervisor M. McClelland
Co-ordinator Mrs B. Miles

Worthing Primary Special Support Centre for Children with Additional Learning Needs West Park CE First and Middle School, Marlborough Rd, Worthing, West Sussex BN12 4HD; Tel 01903 243099; Tel 01903 506278
Headteacher P. Neale (Acting)
Teacher-in-Charge Ms G. Woodward
8–12

Worthing Secondary Special Support Centre for Children with Additional Learning Needs Worthing High School, South Farm Rd, Worthing, West Sussex BN14 7AR; Tel 01903 237864
Headteacher Mrs A. Beer
Teacher-in-Charge Mrs S. Lamba
12–16

Worthing Special Support Centre for Children with Social Communication Needs Durrington Middle School, Salvington Rd, Durrington, Worthing, West Sussex BN13 2JD; Tel 01903 260761
Headteacher Mr R. Pavard
Teacher-in-Charge Ms H. Norton
Mixed; 8–12; Day

Worthing Special Support Centre for Physically Disabled Children (Primary) West Park CE First and Middle School, Marlborough Rd, Worthing, West Sussex BN12 4HD; Tel 01903 243099
Headteacher P. Neale (Acting)
Teacher-in-Charge Ms K. Smith
4–12

Worthing Special Support Centre for Speech and Language Impaired Children Field Place First School, Nelson Rd, Worthing, West Sussex BN12 6EN; Tel (unit) 01903 242611; Tel 01903 700234
Headteacher Mrs F. Dunkin
Teacher-in-Charge Mrs J. Arnold
4–8

Worthing Special Support Centre for Speech and Language Impaired Children The Orchards Middle School, Nelson Rd, Worthing, West Sussex BN12 6EN; Tel 01903 520202; Tel (unit) 01903 526155
Headteacher P. Jones
Teacher-in-Charge Miss E. Bellamy
8–12

OTHER PROVISION

Crawley Portage Service c/o Old Robert May Bldgs, Furnace Dr, Furnace Grn, Crawley, West Sussex RH10 6JB; Tel 01293 615325; Fax 01293 537822
Supervisor Ms N. Blackwell
Portage Co-ordinator J. Parry

Ethnic Minority Achievement Team (EMAT) c/o The Mill Primary School, Ifield Dr, Ifield, Crawley, West Sussex RH11 0EL; Tel 01293 525320; Fax 01293 538334
Team Leader Hazel Squire

Horsham and Mid Sussex Portage Service Rm 27, Manor Field Primary School, Junction Rd, Burgess Hill, West Sussex RH15 0PZ; Tel 01444 243150; Fax 01444 232012
Supervisor Ms P. Robbie
Co-ordinator Mrs S. Maskell

Early Childhood Service (incorporating Children's Information Service) (incorporating Children's Information Service) St James Campus, St James Rd, Chichester, West

Sussex PO19 4HR; Tel 01243 520800; Tel (children's information line) 01243 777807; Fax (both units) 01243 520825

Manager   Marilyn Barton

Chichester Portage Service   Orchard St Annexe, Orchard St, Chichester, West Sussex PO19 1DQ; Tel 01243 536182; Fax 01243 779214

Supervisor   Mrs L. Woodhouse

Portage Co-ordinator   Mrs S. Webb

Royal Borough of Windsor and Maidenhead

www.rbwm.gov.uk

In April 1998 Berkshire County Council was replaced by Bracknell Forest, Reading, Slough, West Berkshire, Windsor and Maidenhead, and Wokingham, each responsible for local government services in its area. They are listed separately in this section.

Population: 133 600

Political composition: Con: 36, LD: 16, Ind: 5

Town Hall, St Ives Rd, Maidenhead, Berkshire SL6 1RF; URL www.rbwm.gov.uk; e-mail info@rbwm.gov.uk; Tel 01628 683800; Fax 01628 685757; Minicom 01628 796474

Chief Executive   Ian Trenholm

Corporate Director (Community Services)   David Oram

Corporate Director (Learning and Care)   Jim Gould

Borough Secretary   Vacancy

Learning and Care Directorate

Cabinet Lead Member (Children's Services)   Cllr Eileen Quick

Director   Jim Gould

Unit Manager (Children and Young People)   Cliff Turner

Unit Manager (Strategy and Resources)   Dave Horler

Education Officer (SEN)   Rhidian Jones

Number of Schools: 24 Primary; 14 First; 7 Secondary; 4 Infant; 4 Middle deemed Secondary; 4 Nursery; 3 Junior; 2 Upper; 1 Special

AURAL AND ORAL RESOURCE UNITS FOR CHILDREN WITH HEARING IMPAIRMENT

Wessex Primary School   St Adrians Cl, Cox Grn, Maidenhead, Berkshire SL6 3AT; Tel 01628 626724

Headteacher   Mrs V. Preece

COUNTY MUSIC CENTRES

Berkshire Maestros   Stoneham Ct, 100 Cockney Hill, Reading RG30 4EZ; e-mail admin@berkshiremaestros.org.uk; Tel 0118 901 2370

Windsor Music Centre   Dedworth Green First School, Smiths La, Windsor, Berkshire SL4 5PE

Manager   Ann Brandon

GOVERNOR TRAINING UNIT

Learning and Care   Royal Borough of Windsor and Maidenhead, Town Hall, Maidenhead, Berkshire SL6 1RF; e-mail governors@rbwm.gov.uk; Tel 01628 796680; Fax 01628 796672

Manager (Strategic School Leadership)   Carol Pearce

RESOURCE UNIT FOR CHILDREN WITH A PHYSICAL DISABILITY

Charters Special Resource   Charters School, Charters Rd, Sunningdale, Ascot, Berkshire SL5 9QY; Tel 01344 624826

Headteacher   Mrs M.A. Twelftree

RESOURCE UNIT FOR CHILDREN WITH SPECIFIC LEARNING DIFFICULTIES

Dedworth Special Resource   Dedworth Middle School, Smiths La, Windsor, Berkshire SL4 5PE; Tel 01753 860561

Headteacher   Mr Stuart Muir

SPEECH AND LANGUAGE RESOURCE UNIT

Altwood Special Resource   Altwood CE Secondary School, Altwood Rd, Maidenhead, Berkshire SL6 4PU; Tel (main school) 01628 622236

Headteacher   Miss K.M. Higgins

Ellington Special Resource   Ellington Primary School, Cookham Rd, Maidenhead, Berkshire SL6 7LA; Tel 01628 674096

Headteacher   Mrs Rehana Juna

OTHER ESTABLISHMENTS

Brocket – Alternative Provision   15 Boyn Hill Ave, Maidenhead, Berkshire SL6 4EY; Tel 01628 631624; Fax 01628 635022

Education Welfare Service   Maidenhead Team: Town Hall, St Ives Rd, Maidenhead, Berkshire SL6 1RF; Tel 01628 796585; Fax 01628 796731 Windsor and Ascot Team: York Hse, Sheet St, Windsor, Berkshire SL4 1DD; Tel 01628 683527

Principal Education Welfare and Partnership Officer   Vacancy

Educational Psychological Service   Town Hall, St Ives Rd, Maidenhead, Berkshire SL6 1RF; Tel 01628 796688; Fax 01628 796936

Principal (Psychology and Inclusion)   Mrs H. Green

For the Maidenhead Team and the Windsor and Ascot Team

St Edmunds House Pupil Referral Unit   Ray Mill Rd West, Maidenhead, Berkshire SL6 8SB; Tel 01628 670816; Fax 01628 776971

Co-ordinator   Jean Cole

Sensory Consortium Service   Education Directorate, The Royal Borough of Windsor and Maidenhead, Town Hall, St Ives Rd, Maidenhead, Berkshire SL6 1RF; Tel 01628 796787

Head of Service   Gillian Coles

Specialist Inclusion Services   St Edmunds Hse, Ray Mill Rd West, Maidenhead, Berkshire SL6 8SB; Tel 01628 670816

Head (Specialist Inclusion Services)   Mrs S. Brown

This service is made up of the following teams: pre-school teacher counsellors, learning support teachers, education otherwise than at school, behaviour support team

Wokingham Borough Council

www.wokingham.gov.uk

In April 1998 Berkshire County Council was replaced by Bracknell Forest, Reading, Slough, West Berkshire, Windsor and Maidenhead, and Wokingham, each responsible for local government services in its area. They are listed separately in this section.

Population: 150 229

Political composition: Con: 41, LD: 13

Civic Offices, Shute End, Wokingham RG40 1WN; URL www.wokingham.gov.uk; e-mail wokinghamcc@wokingham.gov.uk; Tel 0118 974 6000; Fax 0118 978 9078

Chief Executive   Paul Turrell (Acting)

Council Leader   Frank Browne (Con)

Children's Services

Tel 0118 974 6105; Fax 0118 974 6135

Director   Wendy Woodcock

Number of Schools

9 Secondary; 2 Special

CHILDREN'S SERVICES EXECUTIVE MEMBER

Contact   F. Browne
Opposition Spokesperson   Beth Rowland (LD)

SOUTH WEST

Avon County Council

In April 1996 Avon County Council, Bath City Council, Bristol City Council, Kingswood Borough Council, Northavon District Council, Wansdyke District Council and Woodspring District Council were replaced by Bath and North East Somerset District Council, Bristol City Council, North Somerset District Council and South Gloucestershire Council, each responsible for all local government services in its area. These councils are listed separately in this section.

Bath and North East Somerset Council

www.bathnes.gov.uk

Political composition: Con: 31, LD: 26, Lab: 5, Ind: 2, Non-affiliated: 1
Guildhall, High St, Bath, Somerset BA1 5AW;
    URL www.bathnes.gov.uk; Tel 01225 477000
Chief Executive   J. Everitt
Strategic Director (Customer Services)   P. Rowntree
Strategic Director (Support Services)
    R. Szadziewski (Acting)
Director (Major Projects)   J. Betty
Head (Human Resources)   W. Harding
Council Solicitor   V. Hitchman

Children's Services

PO Box 25, Riverside, Temple St, Keynsham, Bristol
    BS31 1DN
Strategic Director (Children's Services)   Ashley Ayre
Assistant Director (Children's Health Service)   Mike Bowden
Assistant Director (Children, Young People and Family Support Services)   Maurice Lindsay
Assistant Director (Learning and Inclusion Services)
    Gail Quinton
Assistant Director (Strategic Support Services)   Tony Parker
Head (School Improvement Division)   Sally Boulter (Acting)
Service Manager (Inclusion Support Services)
    Nigel Harrisson
Manager (Assessment and Family Services)   Trina Shane
Manager (Care and Young People's Service)   Charlie Moat
Manager (Early Years and Extended Services)   Sara Willis
Manager (Finance and Resource Services)   Richard Morgan
Manager (Integrated Youth Support Service)
    Christine Hounsell
Manager (Planning and Performance Service)   Liz Price
Manager (Youth Offending Team)   Sally Churchyard
Team Leader (Human Resources)   Jayne Fitton
Team Leader (Schools' Capital and Organisation)
    Chris Kavanagh
Senior Adviser; Team Leader (Primary)   Wendy Hiscock
Senior Adviser; Team Leader (Secondary)   John Beer
Executive Headteacher (Specialist Behaviour Services)
    Dawn Harris
Integrated Safeguarding Officer   Nicola Bennett
Number of Schools
13 Secondary; 3 Special

EXECUTIVE MEMBER

Contact   Cllr Christopher Watt (Con)

COMMUNITY EDUCATION OFFICES

Community Education Office   The Hollies, Midsomer
    Norton, Somerset BA3 1DN; Tel 01225 396452
    Manager   Jan Walker

Bournemouth Borough Council

www.bournemouth.gov.uk

In April 1997 Bournemouth became a separate unitary authority. The rest of Dorset County Council retains a two-tier structure and is listed separately in this section.
Population: 163 600
Political composition: Con: 41, LD: 7, Ind: 3, Lab: 3
Town Hall, Bourne Ave, Bournemouth BH2 6DY;
    URL www.bournemouth.gov.uk; e-mail
    enquiries@bournemouth.gov.uk; Tel 01202 451451

Children's Services

Dorset Hse, 20–22 Christchurch Rd, Bournemouth
    BH1 3NL; Tel 01202 456219; Fax 01202 456191
Director (Children's Services)   Jane Portman
Head (Childcare and Family Support)   Ann Graham
Head (Inclusion and Achievement Business Unit)   Di Mitchell
Head (Support for Children and Young People)
    Neil Goddard (Acting)
Manager (Adult Learning)   Margaret Davidson
Manager (Children's Support Services)   Stephen Richards
Manager (Customer Services)   Felicity Draper
Manager (Governor Services)   Janette Banks
Manager (Human Resources)   Alison Piper
Manager (Planning and Development)   Chris Williams
Manager (Resources)   Karen Gee (Acting)
Manager (SEN Policy/Development)   Michael Dishington
Manager (Youth Service)   Tim Fewell
Number of Schools
10 Secondary; 2 Special

CABINET PORTFOLIO FOR EDUCATION AND LIFELONG LEARNING

LD: 20, Con: 15, Ind: 4, Lab: 4
Cabinet Member; Portfolio Holder   Malcolm Davies
Chair   Stephen Macloughlin
Vice-Chair   John Beesley
Members of the Scrutiny and Review Panel for Education and Lifelong Learning
Eddie Coope, Elaine Cooper, Rod Cooper, Michael Griffiths, Andrew Morgan, Allister Russell, David Shaw, Claire Smith, Ted Taylor

Bristol City Council

www.bristol.gov.uk

Political composition: LD: 31, Lab: 25, Con: 13, Green: 1
The Council Hse, College Grn, Bristol BS1 5TR;
    URL www.bristol.gov.uk; Tel 0117 922 2000
Chief Executive   Nick Gurney

Children and Young People's Services

PO Box 57, The Council Hse, College Grn, Bristol BS99 7EB;
    URL www.bristol-cyps.org.uk; Tel 0117 903 7960;
    Fax 0117 903 7963
Executive Member (Connexions)   Jo Grant
Director   Heather Tomlinson
Programme Director (Health Partnership)
    Claudia McConnell
Programme Director (Integrated Youth Offer)
    Pauline Marson
Programme Director (Partnerships and Localities)   Paul Taylor

Programme Director (Safeguarding and Specialist Support)
Ian McDowall
Programme Director (Standards and Achievement)
Nick Batchelar
Programme Director (Transforming Learning) Kate Campion
Area Manager (Central and East Bristol) Anne Farmer
Area Manager (North Bristol) Mike Nicholson
Area Manager (South Bristol) Katrina Murphy
Manager (Children in Care) Lucy Young
Manager (Human Resources) Mark Williams
Number of Schools
111 Infant, Junior and Primary; 24 Early Years; 18
Secondary; 11 Special

CHILDREN AND YOUNG PEOPLE'S EXECUTIVE

Executive Member Cllr Derek Pickup; (Lab)

PUPIL REFERRAL UNITS

Bristol Hospital Education Service Fairfield Resource Centre
(Embleton School), Fairlawn Rd, Montpelier, Bristol
BS6 5JW; e-mail hosp.embleton@bristol.gov.uk;
Tel 0117 377 2377; Fax 0117 377 2380
Headteacher Carolyne Searle
The Meriton Meriton St, St Philips, Bristol BS2 0SZ; e-mail
the.meriton@bristol.gov.uk; Tel 0117 971 7428;
Fax 0117 971 9765
Headteacher Carol Bowery
St Matthias Park Pupil Referral Service Stafford Rd, St
Werburghs, Bristol BS2 9UR; e-mail
oosps@bristol.gov.uk; Tel 0117 903 1320;
Fax 0117 903 1321
Headteacher Val Neel
The Whitehouse Centre Fulford Rd, Hartcliffe, Bristol
BS13 9PB; e-mail whitehouse.centre@bristol.gov.uk;
Tel 0117 903 8071; Fax 0117 903 8072
Headteacher Marion McMeechan

Cornwall County Council

www.cornwall.gov.uk

Population: 506 100
Political composition: LD: 48, Ind: 19, Con: 9, Lab: 5, Lib: 1
County Hall, Treyew Rd, Truro, Cornwall TR1 3AY;
URL www.cornwall.gov.uk; e-mail
enquiries@cornwall.gov.uk; Tel 01872 322000;
Fax 01872 270340
Chief Executive Sheila Healy
Head (IT) Nigel Blake
County Treasurer Frank Twyning
Contact (Engineering and Architectural Design)
Mark Stephenson

Children, Young People and Families

e-mail general@educationcornwall.gov.uk;
Fax 01872 323818
*Executive Portfolio Holder (Children, Young People and
Families)* Mrs T. Lello
Director Dean Ashton
Deputy Director S. Smith
Assistant Director (Family, Primary and School Services)
H. Williams
Assistant Director (Individual Needs Policy) S.J. Colwill
Assistant Director (Programme Management) D. Cowley
Assistant Director (Secondary, Post-16 and Youth Services)
D. Wood
Assistant Director (Social Care) R. Parry
Head (Admissions and Transport) J. Turner
Head (Capital Strategy) W. Mason
Head (Commissioning and Interagency Service Development)
G. Chappell
Head (Cornwall Learning) F. Perry (Acting)
Head (Education Accountancy) J. Brinson

Head (Family Services) R. Williams
Head (Partnership Support) A. Mankee-Williams
Head (Professional Development: Children's Services)
N. Atfield
Head (Staff Care and Wellbeing) P. Johnson
Head (Statistics and Data Management) C. Hall
Head (Youth Development) D. Pond
Head (Youth Justice) J. Cousins
Senior Manager (CIC) C. Reed
Senior Manager (Performance Management) N. Jackson
Senior Manager (Practice Development) H. Ferris
Senior Manager (Quality Assurance and Planning) D. Rudge
Senior Manager (Social Care County Services) J. Kerrison
Safeguarding Manager (PT) K. Dale
Safeguarding Manager (PT) J. Hampton
Manager (Assessment and Education Provision) J. Murray
Manager (Community Support) A. Bartram
Manager (Education Business Partnership) D. Smith
Manager (Individual Needs Support Services)
J. Ryder Richardson
Manager (Residential and Out of County) K. Brown
Manager (Social Inclusion) S. Chapman
Secondary Inspector D. Wood
Primary Inspector H. Williams
Inspector (SEN) E. Cole
Inspector (SEN) C. Owen
Contact (Personnel Services: Education) H. Andrew
Contact (Student Services) V. Perry
Number of Schools
31 Secondary; 4 Special
Day of Committee Meeting
Thursday; quarterly

CHILDREN, YOUNG PEOPLE AND FAMILIES POLICY DEVELOPMENT AND SCRUTINY COMMITTEE

LD: 10, External: 8, Ind: 4, Con: 2, Lab: 1
Chair M.J. Moyle (Lab)
Vice-Chair R.J. Cooper (LD)
Members of the Committee
LD: B.J. Comber, R.J. Cooper, R.G. Edwards, B.L. Hunkin,
E.L. Parkin, S.J. Rogerson, J.B. Stocker, Ms T.E. Williams
Ind: Mrs A.J. Carlyon, W.V.C. Curnow, D.C. Dent, W.H.
Roberts
Con: J.H. Currie, N.H. Hatton
Lab: M.J. Moyle
Diocesan Board of EDN: Mrs S. Green
RC Diocesan Schools: B. Maitland
Parent Governors: B.G. Adams, K. Dormer
Free Churches: P. Trenberth

CORNWALL LEARNING

Berlewen Bldg, Trevanson La, Pool, Redruth, Cornwall
TR15 3PL; Tel 01209 721400

Devon County Council

www.devon.gov.uk

In April 1998 Plymouth and Torbay became separate unitary
authorities and are listed separately in this section. The rest
of Devon County Council retains a two-tier structure.
Population: 1 009 950
Political composition: LD: 33, Con: 23, Lab: 4, Ind: 2
County Hall, Exeter, Devon EX2 4QD;
URL www.devon.gov.uk; e-mail info@devon.gov.uk;
Tel 0845 155 1015; Fax 0845 155 1003
County Hall, Topsham Rd, Exeter, Devon EX2 4QD
Chief Executive P. Norrey
Director (Children and Young Persons Services)
Anne Whiteley
Director (County Environment) E. Chorlton CEng, MICE,
FIHT, ACIArb, EurIng, FRSA
Director (Social Services) D. Johnstone
Director (Trading Standards and Consumer Protection)
Paul Thomas

Head (Communications and Information)   Mr P. Doyle
Head (Finance and IT)   John Mills
Head (Library and Information Services)   Mrs L.M. Osborne
Head (Personnel and Performance)   Heather Barnes
General Manager (Devon Direct Services)   I. Wasson
County Solicitor   R. Gash

Children and Young People's Services

County Hall, Topsham Rd, Exeter, Devon EX2 4QG; e-mail
  edmail@devon.gov.uk; Tel 0845 155 1019;
  Fax 01392 382203
Director   Anne Whiteley
Director (Personnel and Performance)   Heather Barnes
Deputy Director; Head (Learning and School Improvement)
  Vacancy
Assistant Director; Head (Policy and Strategy)   Ingrid Fisher
Head (Library and Information Services); Group Manager
  (Culture)   Lynn Osborne
Senior Manager (Finance)   Dave Richards
Group Manager   Deborah Booth
Group Manager (Extended Learning)   Debbie Pritchard;
  Tel 01392 383575; Fax 01392 382203
Group Manager (SEN)   Chris Aston
Group Manager (Strategic Planning Group)   Vic Ebdon;
  Tel 01392 382033; Fax 01392 382025
Principal Educational Psychologist   Bea Blair-Smith
Principal Finance Manager (Education Finance Services)
  Dave Richards
Senior Education Officer (Communications and IT)
  Nick Pearce
Number of Schools
316 Primary; 37 Secondary; 10 Special
Day of Committee Meeting
One monthly cycle

COMMUNITY SERVICES OVERVIEW SCRUTINY COMMITTEE

LD: 8, Con: 5, Lab: 1, NAG: 1
Members of the Committee
LD: Chris Bray, Derek Button, Geoff Date, Anne Fry, Rob
Hannaford, Christopher Haywood, Gordon Hook, Eileen
Wragg
Con: Christine Channon, Roger Croad, Andrew Leadbetter,
Michael Lee, James Pennington
Lab: Saxon Spence
NAG: Mary Turner

EXECUTIVE COMMITTEE

LD: 7
Members of the Committee
Roy Connelly, B.C. Greenslade, Sheila Hobden, John
Rawlingson, Margaret Rogers, John Smith, Humphrey
Temperley

DEVON LEARNING RESOURCES

Great Moor Hse, Bittern Rd, Exeter EX2 7NL;
  URL www.devon.gov.uk/dlr; e-mail
  dlres@devon.gov.uk; Tel 01392 385230
Contact   John Houghton

ADULT AND COMMUNITY LEARNING

Buckland Hse, Park Five, Sowton, Exeter EX2 7ND; e-mail
  acl@devon.gov.uk; Tel 01392 386580
Bideford (N) Holsworthy, Torrington; e-mail
  aclbideford-mailbox@devon.gov.uk; Tel 01237 472462
Bideford (N) Bideford Arts Centre, The Quay, Bideford
  EX39 2EY
  Senior Administrator   Sheila Ballard
Cullompton (N) Crediton; e-mail
  aclcullompton-mailbox@devon.gov.uk; Tel 01884 38326
Exmouth (E) Clyst Vale, Honiton; e-mail
  aclexmouth-mailbox@devon.gov.uk; Tel 01395 223851

Exmouth (E) Exmouth Adult and Community Learning, 10–
  12 Victoria Rd, Exmouth EX8 1DL
  Senior Administrator   Ruth Lewis
Ilfracombe (N) Braunton, South Molton; e-mail
  aclifracombe-mailbox@devon.gov.uk; Tel 01271 864171
Newton Abbot (S) Dawlsih, South Dartmoor, Teignmouth;
  e-mail aclnewtonabbot-mailbox@devon.gov.uk;
  Tel 01626 206410
Newton Abbot (S) Newton Abbot AEC, Market St, Newton
  Abbot TQ12 2RJ
  Senior Administrator   Sally Shircliff
Seaton (E) Axe Valley, Ottery St Mary, Sidmouth; e-mail
  aclaxevalley-mailbox@devon.gov.uk; Tel 01297 21904
Tavistock (S) Okehampton; e-mail
  aclbideford-mailbox@devon.gov.uk; Tel 01822 613701
Tavistock (S) The Alexander Centre, 62 Plymouth Rd,
  Tavistock PL19 8BU
  Senior Administrator   Ali Cooper
Totnes (S) Dartmouth, Ivybridge, Kingsbridge; e-mail
  acltotnes-mailbox@devon.gov.uk; Tel 01803 862020

SATELLITE CENTRES

Crediton ACL Queen Elizabeth's Community College,
  Western Rd, Crediton, Devon EX17 3LU;
  Tel 01363 777918; Fax 01363 777918
  Contact   Cherry Hamlyn;   (Tues, Weds and Fri)
Holsworthy ACL The Skills Centre, Western Rd,
  Holsworthy EX22 6DH; Tel 01409 254505
  Contact   Alison Skinner;   (Mon–Fri 1400–1700)
Honiton ACL Honiton Young People's Centre, School La,
  Honiton EX14 1QW; Tel 01404 42102
  Contact   Pam Nicholas;   (Mon–Wed 0900–16.30)
Ivybridge ACL South Devon Tennis Centre, Ermington Rd,
  Ivybridge PL21 9ES; Tel 01752 896662
  Contact   Kaylie Moore
Kingsbridge ACL Tresillian, 12 Fore St, Kingsbridge
  TQ7 1AW; Tel 01548 853298
  Contact   Sue Rowland
Okehampton ACL Mill La, Okehampton EX20 1PW;
  Tel 01837 659436
  Contact   Mandy Gillespie
South Molton ACL Old Alswear Rd, South Molton, Devon
  EX36 4LA; Tel 01769 572834
  Contact   Cherry Hamlyn

DES (DEVON EDUCATION SERVICES)

URL www.deseducation.org; e-mail
  des.info@devon.gov.uk; Tel 01392 384862;
  Fax 01392 384880
Head   Roger Fetherston
Business Manager   Bryan Smith
Support Manager   Hilary Stookes
School Improvement Officer   David Blower
School Improvement Officer   David Lowes
School Improvement Officer   Alison Miller

Governor Services Team
URL www.devon.gov.uk.governors; e-mail
  governor@devon.gov.uk; Tel 01392 383611;
  Fax 01392 383632
Head (Governor Support)   Debbie Clapshaw
Services offered
Administration of appointment of county council
representatives on school governing bodies; maintenance of
records of governing body membership; provision of
training and advice to members of school governing bodies
and clerks; provision of information at local resource
centres; publication of information on policies, procedures
and good practice

Curriculum Advisers
Manager (Primary National Strategy)   Andrew Riley
Manager (Secondary National Strategy)   Graham Cockill
Lead Adviser (Early Years)   Jenny Liggins
Lead Adviser (Primary Phase)   David Chaplin
Adviser (Art and Design)   Phil Creek

2

Adviser (Design and Technology)   Gilly Browning
Adviser (Digital Media)   Tim Arnold
Adviser (E-learning)   Steve Cayley
Adviser (English: Secondary)   Richard Durant
Adviser (Geography and Environmental Education)
    David Weatherly
Adviser (Healthy Schools)   Annette Lyons
Adviser (History)   Jamie Byrom
Adviser (Information Technology)   Steve Cayley
Adviser (Mathematics)   Sue Madgwick
Adviser (Modern Foreign Languages)   Chris Wakely
Adviser (Music)   Fiona Pendreigh
Adviser (Outdoor Education)   Bryan Smith
Adviser (Physical Education)   Steve Kibble
Adviser (Professional Development)   Geoff Tew
Adviser (Religious Education)   Graham Langtree
Adviser (Science)   Philip Knight
Adviser (Secondary Phase)   Hilary Jones
Adviser (SEN)   Linda Chapman
Adviser (Support Staff)   Mark Freeman
Consultant (Workforce Remodelling)   Philipa Court
Statistician   Roland Oxborough

PUPIL REFERRAL UNITS

The Grenville Centre   Ringswell Ave, Exeter, Devon
    EX1 3EG; e-mail admin@grenville-pru.devon.sch.uk;
    Tel 01392 445446; Fax 01392 444755
    Teacher-in-Charge   M. Thompson
Oak Valley Centre   Mulbery Hse, Preston Down Rd,
    Preston, Paignton, Devon TQ3 1RN; e-mail
    windmill@devon.gov.uk; Tel 01803 663830
    Contact   Helen Thomas (Acting)
The Tutorial Centre   St Johns La, Barnstaple, Devon
    EX32 9DD; e-mail bartutor.devon.gov.uk;
    Tel 01271 376641
    Teacher-in-Charge   P. Bowrey

NATIONAL STRATEGIES OFFICE

URL www.deseducation.org/literacy/index.html;
    Tel 01392 386461; Fax 01392 386462
Lead Literacy Consultant   Rebecca Cosgrave
Lead Numeracy Consultant   Ruth Trundley
Reading Recovery Tutor   Janet Ferris

HOSTEL FOR CHILDREN WITH EMOTIONAL AND BEHAVIOURAL DIFFICULTIES

The Gables, Willand, Cullompton, Devon EX15 2PL; e-mail
    gables@dial.devon.gov.uk; Tel 01884 33241;
    Fax 01884 35288
Manager   Paul Cocking
7–12 (Boys), 5–18 (Girls)

DEVON MUSIC SERVICE

Great Moor Hse, Bittern Rd, Sowton, Exeter, Devon
    EX2 7NL; URL www.devony.gov.uk/musicservice;
    e-mail devonmusicservice@devon.gov.uk;
    Tel 01392 385609; Fax 01392 385610
Head of Service   Ken Parr

RESIDENTIAL AND OUTDOOR EDUCATION CENTRES

The Dartmoor Centres   Dartmoor Training Centre
    (residential), Tavistock Rd, Princetown, Devon
    PL20 6QF; e-mail dartcent@devon.gov.uk;
    Tel 01364 631500; Fax 01634 631500
    Pixies Holt Residential Centre, Dartmeet, Princetown,
    Devon PL20 6SG; e-mail
    dartcent@dartcent.devon.gov.uk; Tel 01364 631500;
    Fax 01364 631500
    Contact   P. Berry
Haven Banks Outdoor Education Centre (non-residential)   61
    Haven Banks, Exeter, Devon EX2 8DP; e-mail
    edhaven@devon.gov.uk; Tel 01392 434668;
    Fax 01392 45197

Start Bay Centre (residential)   Slapton, Kingsbridge, Devon
    TQ7 2RA; e-mail startbay@devon.gov.uk;
    Tel 01548 580321; Fax 01548 580321
    Contact   Ali Northcott
Wembworthy Centre (residential)   Wembworthy,
    Chulmleigh, Devon EX18 7QR; e-mail
    wembworth@devon.gov.uk; Tel 01769 580667;
    Fax 01769 580667
    Contact   F. Sendell

DEVON SCHOOL LIBRARY SERVICE

Great Moor Hse, Bittern Rd, Sowton, Exeter, Devon
    EX2 7NL; URL www.devon.sls.org.uk; Tel 01392 381394;
    Fax 01392 381392
Head of Service   Lynne Medlock

Dorset County Council
www.dorsetcc.gov.uk

In April 1997 Bournemouth and Poole became separate
unitary authorities and are listed separately in this section.
The rest of Dorset County Council retains a two-tier
structure.
County Hall, Colliton Pk, Dorchester, Dorset DT1 1XJ;
    URL www.dorsetcc.gov.uk; e-mail
    help@dorsetcc.gov.uk; Tel 01305 251000;
    Fax 01305 224839
Chief Executive   David Jenkins MA
Director (Corporate Resources)   Elaine Taylor

Children's Services

Fax 01305 224499
Director (Education)   Stephen Prewett
Deputy Director; Head (Children and Families)   Jackie Last
Head (Joint Commissioning)   Anne Salter
Head (Lifelong Learning)   Les Gardner
Head (Pupil and School Improvement)   Harry Turner
Number of Schools
20 Secondary; 14 Middle; 5 Special

EDUCATION OVERVIEW AND POLICY DEVELOPMENT COMMITTEE

Con: 10, LD: 3, Lab: 1
Shallowfield, 3 Church Cl, Beer Hackett, Sherborne, Dorset
    DT9 6RA
90 Newland, Sherborne, Dorset DT9 3DT
Chair   D.A. Mildenhall (Con)
Vice-Chair   T.B. Coombs (Con)
Members of the Committee
Con: S.A. Brown, R.W. Coatsworth, T.B. Coombs, P.D.L.
Gaussen, D.W. Hiett, G.E. Hine, J. Lofts, D.A. Mildenhall,
J.E.S. Pay, J.L. Wilson
LD: B. Fox-Hodges, R.A.S. Legg, G. Streets
Lab: M.P. Byatt

SPEECH AND LANGUAGE SPECIALIST MAINSTREAM BASES

Dorchester Speech and Language Base   Damers First School,
    Damers Rd, Dorchester, Dorset DT1 2LB; e-mail
    office@damers.dorset.sch.uk; Tel 01305 264924
    Headteacher   P. Minns
    Teacher-in-Charge   J. Cook
Gillingham CP School Speech and Language Base   School Rd,
    Gillingham, Dorset SP8 4QR; Tel 01747 823245
    Headteacher   Sian Thornton
    Teacher-in-Charge   Mrs G. Harvey

EMOTIONAL AND BEHAVIOURAL DIFFICULTY MAINSTREAM BASE

Bincombe Valley Emotional and Behavioural Difficulty Base
    Culliford Way, Littlemoor, Weymouth, Dorset DT3 6AF;
    Tel 01305 832329

Headteacher L. Strong
Teacher-in-Charge Mrs F. Guppy

ASPERGER'S SYNDROME BASE

Budmouth Technology College Asperger's Syndrome Base Chickerell Rd, Charlestown, Weymouth, Dorset DT4 9SY; Tel 01305 830500
Headteacher D. Akers
Teacher-in-Charge P. McCarthy

SPECIALIST MAINSTREAM BASES FOR MODERATE LEARNING DIFFICULTIES

Beaminster School Newtown, Beaminster, Dorset DT8 3EP; URL www.beaminster.dorset.sch.uk; e-mail office@beaminster.dorset.sch.uk; Tel 01308 862633
Heateacher M. Best
St Mary's CE Primary School Clay La, Beaminster, Dorset DT8 3BY; URL www.stmarysbeaminster.dorset.sch.uk; e-mail office@stmarysbeaminster.dorset.sch.uk; Tel 01308 862201
Headteacher Stuart Bellworthy (Acting)

DAY SPECIAL UNIT FOR PHYSICALLY DISABLED

Dorchester, The Prince of Wales Special Unit Maiden Castle Rd, Dorchester, Dorset DT1 2HH; e-mail office@princeofwales.dorset.sch.uk; Tel 01305 257120
Headteacher P. Farrington

CHILDREN'S HOSPITAL EDUCATION UNIT

Dorchester, Kingfisher Ward Dorset County Hospital, Williams Ave, Dorchester, Dorset DT1 2JY; Tel 01305 254287; Fax 01305 254287
Headteacher H. Finbow

PUPIL REFERRAL UNITS

The Compass Centre 307a Chickerell Rd, Weymouth, Dorset DT4 0QU; Tel 01305 206530
Contact A. Wood
Dorchester Learning Centre Winterborne Monkton, Dorchester, Dorset DT1 9PS; URL www.dorchester-lc.dorset.sch.uk; e-mail john.h.taylor@dorsetcc.gov.uk; Tel 01305 261213
Contact J. Taylor
Sherborne Pupil Referral Unit Simons Rd, Sherborne, Dorset DT9 4DN; e-mail i.hedley@dorsetcc.gov.uk; Tel 01935 814582
Contact Ian Hedley
Wimborne Learning Centre School La, Wimborne, Dorset BH21 1HQ; URL www.wimborne-lc.dorset.sch.uk; e-mail b.smith@dorsetcc.gov.uk; Tel 01202 886947
Contact Kim Rickford

SPEECH AND LANGUAGE SPECIALIST MAINSTREAM BASES

Dorchester Speech and Language Base Damers C First School, Damers Rd, Dorchester, Dorset DT1 2LB; Tel 01305 264924
Headteacher Mr P. Minns
Twynham Speech and Language Base Twynham School, Sopers La, Christchurch, Dorset BH23 1JF; URL www.twynham.dorset.sch.uk; e-mail office@twynham.dorset.sch.uk; Tel 01202 486237
Headteacher Dr T. Fish

SPECIFIC LEARNING DIFFICULTY MAINSTREAM BASES

All Saint's CE School Base All Saint's CE School, Sunnyside Rd, Weymouth, Dorset DT4 9BY; URL www.allsaints.dorset.sch.uk; e-mail office@allsaints.dorset.sch.uk; Tel 01305 783391
Headteacher T. Balmforth
Teacher-in-Charge P. James

Allenbourn Base Allenbourn Middle School, East Borough, Wimborne, Dorset BH21 1PL; URL www.allenbourn.dorset.sch.uk; e-mail office@allenbourn.dorset.sch.uk; Tel 01202 886738; Fax 01202 841242
Headteacher G.L. MacRae
Teacher-in-Charge M. Halliwell
The Gryphon Base The Gryphon School, Bristol Rd, Sherborne, Dorset DT9 4EQ; URL www.gryphon.dorset.sch.uk; Tel 01935 813122
Headteacher S. Hulier
Teacher-in-Charge C. Johnson

ADULT EDUCATION CENTRES

Christchurch Area Christchurch AEC, Old Magistrates' Court, Bargates, Christchurch, Dorset BH23 1QL; Tel 01202 482789; Fax 01202 478344
Contact I. Knott
North and East Dorset Area Ferndown AEC, Mountbatten Dr, Ferndown, Dorset BH22 9EW; Tel 01202 875359; Fax 01202 861088
Contact D. Challis
Contact C. Hewitt
South and West Dorset Area Dorchester AEC, Government Bldgs, Prince of Wales Rd, Dorchester, Dorset DT1 1PY; Tel 01305 251040; Fax 01305 267796
Contact A. Tait

OUTDOOR EDUCATION CENTRES

Ancient Technology Centre, Cranborne Cranborne Middle School, Cranborne, Dorset BH21 5RP; URL www.dorsetcc.gov.uk/educate/does.htm; e-mail atc@dorsetcc.gov.uk; Tel 01725 517618; Fax 01725 517618
Contact L. Winter
Carey Outdoor Education Centre Carey Rd, Wareham, Dorset BH20 7PB; URL www.dorsetcc.gov.uk/education/does.htm; e-mail careyoec@dorsetcc.gov.uk; Tel 01929 552265
Contact M. Dunn
Leeson House Field Studies Centre Langton Matravers, Swanage, Dorset BH19 3EU; URL www.dorsetcc.gov.uk/educate/does.htm; e-mail leeson@dorsetcc.gov.uk; Tel 01929 422126
Contact B. Cullimore
Weymouth Outdoor Education Centre Knightsdale Rd, Weymouth, Dorset DT4 0HS; URL www.dorsetcc.gov.uk/educate/does.htm; e-mail woec@dorsetcc.gov.uk; Tel 01305 784927
Contact J. Perham

YOUTH AND COMMUNITY CENTRES

Beaminster Area Youth and Community Centre 6 Prout Bridge, Beaminster, Dorset DT8 3AY; e-mail p.buxton@dorestcc.gov.uk; Tel 01308 862384
Contact Paula Buxton
Blandford Area Youth and Community Centre Milldown Rd, Blandford, Dorset DT11 7SQ; e-mail a.price@dorsetcc.gov.uk; Tel 01258 455106
Contact A. Price
Bovington Youth Centre – Vision (Part-time) Elles Rd, Bovington, Wareham, Dorset BH20 6JB; Tel 01929 463503
Contact S. Lacey
Bridport Area Youth and Community Centre Gundry La, Bridport, Dorset DT6 3RL; e-mail a.woodgate@dorsetcc.gov.uk; Tel 01308 422500
Contact A. Woodgate
Burton Area Youth and Community Centre Sandy Plot, Burton, Christchurch, Dorset BH23 7NH; e-mail s.cox.orourke@dorsetcc.gov.uk; Tel 01202 470457
Contact S. Cox O'Rourke
Corfe Mullen Youth and Community Centre Blandford Rd, Corfe Mullen, Wimborne, Dorset BH21 3DZ; Tel 01202 697236
Contact C. Murray; e-mail c.murray@dorsetcc.gov.uk

Crossways Youth and Community Centre (Part-time) Old
Farm Way, Crossways, Dorchester, Dorset DT2 8TU;
Tel 01305 853567
Contact C. Moore
Dorchester Area Youth and Community Centre Kings Rd,
Dorchester, Dorset DT1 1NJ; e-mail
c.r.moore@dorsetcc.gov.uk; Tel 01305 262114
Contact C. Moore
Dorset Youth and Community Service Headquarters
Hammick Hse, Bridport Rd, Poundbury, Dorchester,
Dorset DT1 3SD; e-mail d.m.higton@dorsecc.gov.uk;
Tel 01305 254009
Contact D. Higton
Dorset Youth Association Lubbecke Way, Dorchester,
Dorset DT1 1QL; Tel 01305 262440
County Co-ordinator D. Wardell
Gillingham Youth and Community Centre Cemetery Rd,
Gillingham, Dorset SP8 4AZ; e-mail
t.baverstock@dorsetcc.gov.uk; Tel 01747 822267
Contact T. Baverstock
Contact T. Walker
The Planet Advice and Information Centre 4 Church St,
Wimborne, Dorset BH21 1JH; Tel 01202 840628
Contact N. Christopher; e-mail
n.christopher@dorsetcc.gov.uk
Contact C. Murray; e-mail c.murray@dorsetcc.gov.uk
Portland Area Youth and Community Centre Royal Manor
School, Weston Rd, Portland, Dorset DT5 2DB; e-mail
s.j.rose@dorsetcc.gov.uk; Tel 01305 823663
Contact S. Rose
Riffs (Ferndown Area Youth and Community Centre) Church
Rd, Ferndown, Wimborne, Dorset BH22 9ET; e-mail
a.ball@dorsetcc.gov.uk; Tel 01202 874448
Contact A. Ball
Shaftesbury Youth Club Coppice St, Shaftesbury, Dorset
SP7 8PF; Tel 01747 853195
Contact T. Baverstock
Sherborne Area Youth and Community Centre Tinneys La,
Sherborne, Dorset DT9 3DY; e-mail
r.fraiz-brown@dorsetcc.gov.uk; Tel 01935 814202
Contact R. Fraiz-Brown
STEPS – Club for Young People 110 Chickerell Rd,
Weymouth, Dorset DT4 0BT; e-mail
t.s.lane@dorsetcc.gov.uk; Tel 01305 771861
Contact T. Lane
Sturminster Newton Area Youth and Community Centre Bath
Rd, Sturminster Newton, Dorset DT10 1DT; e-mail
a.baverstock@dorsetcc.gov.uk; Tel 01258 472368
Contact A. Baverstock
Contact T. Walker
Swanage Youth and Community Centre Chapel La,
Swanage, Dorset BH19 2PW; e-mail
j.m.andrews@dorsetcc.gov.uk; Tel 01929 423421
Contact J. Andrews
TIDES Project Centre 2 Newstead Rd, Weymouth, Dorset
DT4 8JE; e-mail p.hammond@dorsetcc.gov.uk;
Tel 01305 780563
Contact P. Hammond
Top Club (Littlemoor Youth and Community Centre)
Louviers Rd, Littlemoor, Weymouth, Dorset DT3 6AY;
Tel 01305 833560
Contact G. Evans
TREADS (Blandford Youth Advice and Information Centre)
30a Salisbury St, Blandford, Dorset DT11 7AR;
Tel 01258 455448
Contact M. Hepple
Verwood Youth and Community Centre Howe La, Verwood,
Dorset BH21 6JF; e-mail p.j.cox@dorsetcc.gov.uk;
Tel 01202 825351
Contact P. Cox
Wareham Youth and Community Centre Worgret Rd,
Wareham, Dorset BH20 4PH; Tel 01929 552934
Contact S. Lacey
Weymouth Youth Resource Centre, Waves 'Waves',
Weymouth Youth Resource Centre, 52 St Marys St,
Weymouth, Dorset DT4 8BJ; Tel 01305 766792
Contact O. Stenlake

HOME TUITION BASES

Christchurch Home Tuition Base The Court House,
Bargates, Christchurch, Dorset BH23 1PY;
Tel 01202 471410
Contact Pam Pyke
Southill Home Tuition Base Southill Youth Centre, Radipole
La, Southill, Weymouth, Dorset DT4 9SF;
Tel 01305 771324

CHILDREN'S EDUCATION UNIT

Allington Ward, West Dorset Hospital, Damers Rd,
Dorchester, Dorset DT1 2JX; Tel 01305 254287
Teacher-in-Charge Harriet Finbow

Gloucestershire County Council
www.gloucestershire.gov.uk

Population: 564 000
Political composition: Con: 34, LD: 13, Lab: 12
Shire Hall, Gloucester, Gloucestershire GL1 2TG;
URL www.gloucestershire.gov.uk; e-mail
shrecep@gloucestershire.gov.uk; Tel 01452 425000
Chief Executive Peter Bungard
Chair of the County Council Cllr Mavis Lady Dunrossil
Group Director (Business Management) Stephen Wood
Group Director (Environment) Duncan Jordan; Bearland
Wing, Shire Hall, Gloucester, Gloucestershire GL1 2TG
Press Officer Sarah Wood

Children and Young People

Shire Hall, Westgate St, Gloucester, Gloucestershire
GL1 2TP; Tel 01452 425300; Fax 01452 425496
Group Director Jo Davidson
Head (Contract Services) K. Hill
Head (Education Finance) D. Bennett
Head (Education Planning) G. Black BA, MBA
Head (Education Planning and Lifelong Learning Service)
Susan Robbins
Head (Information Systems) N. Davis
Head (Personnel) M. Thomson
Head (School Improvement and Inclusion Service)
Alan Stubbersfield
Head (Youth and Community Service) M. Counsell BEd,
AdvDipEd Studies
Number of Schools
42 Secondary; 14 Special
Requisition Periods for Schools Supplies
No fixed periods

TUITION CENTRES

The Hatherley Centre Lismore Hse, 3 Horton Rd,
Gloucester, Gloucestershire GL1 3PX; e-mail
thehatherley@easymail.rmplc.co.uk; Tel 01452 309510
St George's Centre 140b St Georges Rd, Cheltenham,
Gloucestershire GL50 3EL; e-mail
stgeorgescentre@easymail.rmplc.co.uk; Tel 01242 581519;
Fax 01242 578836
Whitminster Centre Roxburgh Hse, Nelson St, Stroud,
Gloucestershire GL5 2HP; e-mail
whitminstercentre@easymail.rmplc.co.uk;
Tel 01453 767293

EDUCATIONAL PSYCHOLOGY SERVICE

East Area – Battledown Centre Harp Hill, Battledown,
Cheltenham, Gloucestershire GL52 6PZ;
Tel 01242 525448
Area Manager (SEN Support) Kate Blinston
Area Manager (SEN Support) Mrs E. Rook
East Area – Beeches Green Health Centre Stroud,
Gloucestershire; Tel 01453 751090; Tel 01453 766331
Area Manager (SEN Support) Kate Blinston

West Area – Maitland House Spa Rd, Gloucester,
Gloucestershire GL1 1UY; Tel 01452 42694
Area Manager (SEN Support) Tonia Robinson
Gloucestershire School Improvement and Inclusion Service
The Hucclecote Centre, Churchdown La, Gloucester,
Gloucestershire GL3 3QN
Head (School Support) Martin Skeet MEd
Senior Adviser (Primary) Peter Dunn MEd, BA, CertEd,
DipEd
Senior Adviser (Secondary) N. Batchelar BA(Hons),
PGCE
Adviser (Secondary) Keith Brown BTech(Hons), MSc,
PGCE
Consultant (Secondary) Martin Smith BA(Hons), PCSE
Lifelong Learning Group
Area Education Officer D. Grocott
Area Education Officer D. Haworth BSc, MEd
Area Education Officer C. Williams BA, CertEd
*Education Officer (Adult Continuing Education and Training
– ACET)* J. Austin
Pupil and Student Services (PSS)
Head (Mainstream Services) Tina Browne
Head (SEN) Stewart King
Education Officer (SEN) Sue Meredith

YOUTH AND COMMUNITY SERVICE

Head (Youth and Community Service) Lynne Speak;
Chequers Bridge Centre, Painswick Rd, Gloucester,
Gloucestershire GL4 9PR; Tel 01452 425420;
Fax 01452 426375
Biblins Adventure Centre Symonds Yat, Herefordshire;
Tel (all enquiries to the Wilderness Centre) 01600 890475
Bracelands Adventure Centre Christchurch, Coleford,
Gloucestershire; Tel (enquiries to the Wilderness Centre)
01594 834885
Buckstone Adventure Centre Staunton, Coleford,
Gloucestershire; Tel (enquiries to the Wilderness Centre)
01594 833807

FIELD STUDY CENTRE

Pwll Du Adventure Centre Blaenaven, Abergavenny,
Monmouthshire; Tel (enquiries to the Wilderness Centre)
01495 790357
The Wilderness Centre Mitcheldean, Gloucestershire
GL17 0HA; e-mail wilderness@blueyonder.co.uk;
Tel 01594 542551; Fax 01594 542551
Contact T. Roach

Council of the Isles of Scilly

www.scilly.gov.uk

Population: 2000 (including off-islands)
Political composition: Non-political: 21
Town Hall, St Mary's, Isles of Scilly TR21 0LW;
URL www.scilly.gov.uk; e-mail phygate@scilly.gov.uk;
Tel 01720 422537; Fax 01720 424045
Chief Executive; Clerk P.S. Hygate BA, FRSA

Education Department

Secretary for Education P.S. Hygate BA, FRSA
Number of Schools
1 Federated School
Day of Committee Meetings
Tuesday; nine week cycle
Requisition Periods for Schools Supplies
Vary

EDUCATION COMMITTEE

Chair J.D. May
Vice-Chair Cllr R. Dorrien-Smith

North Somerset District Council

www.n-somerset.gov.uk

Political composition: Con: 43, Ind: 6, LD: 5, Lab: 3, Green: 1
Town Hall, Weston-super-Mare, North Somerset BS23 1ZY;
URL www.n-somerset.gov.uk; Tel 01934 888888;
Fax 01934 888832

Children and Young People's Services

Town Hall, Weston-super-Mare, North Somerset BS23 1ZZ;
e-mail governorsupportunit@n-somerset.gov.uk;
Tel (governor support helpline) 01934 427448;
Fax 01934 426147
Director (Children and Young People's Services)
Colin Diamond
Assistant Director (Children and Families) Steve Tanner
*Assistant Director (Strategy, Commissioning and
Performance)* Craig Bolt
Head (Inclusion) Kate East
Head (Resources) Roger Eggleton
Manager (Admissions) Sally Varley
Manager (Asset Management) Martin Crandon
Manager (Early Years) Jenie Eastman
Manager (Governor Support) Christine Mayer (Acting)
Manager (Governor Support) Jackie Ramplin (Acting)
Manager (Health and Safety/Contracts) Jo Crickson
*Manager (Inclusion Support Service); Principal Educational
Psychologist* Carol Franzen
Manager (IT) N. Thomas
Manager (Lifelong Learning) Lesley Dale
Manager (Music Service) Mark Trego
Manager (Policy and Research) Dave Martin
Manager (Student Funding) Grahame Hughes
Education Manager (Personnel) Amanda Wright
LEA Manager (Finance) Roger Eggleton
Principal Education Welfare Officer Sara Griffiths
Number of Schools
62 Primary; 10 Secondary; 3 Special

EDUCATION CABINET

North Somerset has abolished the committee system and
replaced it with the Education Cabinet
Executive Member (Learning) P. Kehoe

Plymouth City Council

www.plymouth.gov.uk

In April 1998 Plymouth became a unitary authority. The rest
of Devon, apart from Torbay, retains a two-tier structure
and is listed separately in this section.
Population: 246 100 (ONS 2005 mid year estimate)
Political composition: Con: 31, Lab: 26
Civic Centre, Royal Par, Plymouth PL1 2AA;
URL www.plymouth.gov.uk; e-mail
enquiries@plymouth.gov.uk; Tel 01752 668000;
Fax 01752 304880
Chief Executive Barry Keel
Corporate Director (Children's Services) Bronwen Lacey

Department of Children's Services

e-mail childrens.services@plymouth.gov.uk;
Tel 01752 307400; Fax 01752 307403
Assistant Director (Children's Social Care) Mairead MacNeil
Assistant Director (Learner and Family Support)
Maggie Carter
Assistant Director (Lifelong Learning) Stuart Farmer
Assistant Director (Performance and Policy Division)
Verity Jones

2

Service Manager (LAC)   Tony Marchese
Service Manager (Out of Hours)   Richard Lemon
Service Manager (Young People Leaving Care)   Richard Porter
Manager (Commissioning)   Fiona Fleming
Manager (Customer Relations)   Carole Hartley
Manager (Education Catering)   Brad Pearce
Manager (Family Support Service)   Nicky Scutt
Manager (Group Support)   Barbara Buckley
Manager (Information)   Paul Maber-Gill
Manager (Performance)   Claire Cordory
Manager (Placement Service: Fostering and Adoption)
   Karen Morris
Manager (Policy and Planning)   Richenda Broad
Manager (Safeguarding Business)   Simon White
Manager (Strategic Procurement)   Jane Smale
Manager (Youth Offending Team)   Benji Shoker
Senior Education Officer   Graham Peck
Senior Education Officer (Access)   Mary McIntyre
*Senior Education Officer (Capital and Asset Management
   Planning)*   Gareth Simmons
Senior Education Officer (Early Years)   Gay Hickling
Senior Education Officer (Inclusion: SEN)   Vacancy
Senior Education Officer (School Organisation)
   Andrew Leigh
*Principal Education Adviser (Challenge, Support, Standards and
   Intervention)*   Philip Braide
Senior Education Adviser   John Searson
Education Adviser   Stephanie Thomas
Education Adviser   Peter Crispin
Adviser (Inclusion – SEN)   Arnet Donkin
Principal Educational Psychologist   Kevin Rowland
Governor Support Officer   Karen Powell
Continuous Professional Development Officer   Bill May
Community Education Tutor   Linda Aston

COMMUNITY CENTRES

Efford Youth and Community Centre   Blandford Rd,
   Plymouth PL3 6HU; e-mail
   margaretjohns@efford.org.uk; Tel 01752 776853
   Community Education Tutor   M. Johns
Frederick Street Centre   Frederick St, Stonehouse, Plymouth
   PL1 5SX; e-mail mail@frederickstreetcentre.org;
   Tel 01752 228906
   Community Education Tutor   A. Kemp
Honicknowle Youth and Community Centre   Honicknowle
   Grn, Honicknowle, Plymouth PL5 3PX; e-mail
   kathy.tasker@btconnect.com; Tel 01752 705297
   Community Education Tutor   Kathy Tasker
Morley Youth and Community Centre   Broadland Gdns,
   Plymstock, Plymouth PL9 8TU; e-mail
   kerry.mccormick@plymouth.gov.uk; Tel 01752 404370
   Manager (Youth Work)   Kerry McCormick
Plymouth Youth Enquiry Service   14–16 Union St, Derry's
   Cross, Plymouth PL1 2SR; e-mail
   yes@yesplymouth.co.uk; Tel 01752 206626
   Chief Executive   Ruth Marriott
Rees Youth and Community Centre   Mudge Way, Plymton,
   Plymouth PL7 2PS; e-mail
   kerry.mccormick@plymouth.gov.uk; Tel 01752 337267
   Manager (Youth Work)   Kerry McCormick
Southway Youth and Community Centre   Hendwell Cl,
   Southway, Plymouth PL6 6TB; e-mail
   syc@plymouth.gov.uk; Tel 01752 775969
   Centre Manager   Bill McCoy
Tothill Community Centre   Knighton Rd, St Judes, Plymouth
   PL4 9DA; Tel 01752 665919
   Centre Administrator   K. Muller
Trelawny Youth and Community Centres   Ham Dr,
   Plymouth PL2 2NJ; e-mail tycc@plymouth.gov.uk;
   Tel 01752 362263
   Community Education Tutor   K. Morrish
Whitleigh Youth Centre   Lancaster Gdns, Whitleigh,
   Plymouth PL5 4AA; e-mail
   neil.mccartney@plymouth.gov.uk; Tel 01752 771210
   Centre Manager   Bill McCoy
   Youth Development Worker   Neil McCartney

PUPIL REFERRAL UNITS

Plymouth Tuition Service – Years 3–9   Mannamead Centre,
   15 Eggbuckland Rd, Plymouth PL3 5HF; e-mail
   perren.tracey@plymouth.gov.uk; Tel 01752 306269;
   Fax 01752 306269
   Headteacher   Perren Tracey
Plymouth Tuition Service – Years 10–11   Bretonside Tuition
   Centre, Martins Gate, Bretonside, Plymouth PL4 0AT;
   e-mail bretonside.tuition@plymouth.gov.uk;
   Tel 01752 229351; Fax 01752 671236
   Headteacher   Mrs L. Glenister
Plymouth Tuition Service – Centre for Young Parents
   Lancaster Gdns, Whitleigh, Plymouth PL5 4AA; e-mail
   youngparentscentre@plymouth.gov.uk;
   Tel 01752 237696; Fax 01752 237695
   Headteacher   Liz Salway

COMMUNITY EDUCATION – COMMUNITY COLLEGES

Eggbuckland Community Learning   Hartley Hse, Charfield
   Dr, Eggbuckland, Plymouth PL6 5PS;
   URL www.eggbuckland.com; e-mail
   communitylearning@eggbuckland.com;
   Tel 01752 767788
   Manager (Learning Development)   Pam Davis
Estover Community College   Miller Way, Estover, Plymouth
   PL6 8UN; URL www.estover.ac.uk; e-mail
   philstevens@estover.ac.uk; Tel 01752 207907
   Manager (Learning Development)   Vacancy
John Kitto Community College   Honicknowle La,
   Honicknowle, Plymouth PL5 3NE;
   URL www.jkcc.org.uk; e-mail enquiries@jkcc.org.uk;
   Tel 01752 208380
   Manager (Learning Development)   Michelle Costly
   Manager (Learning Development)   Elaine Fordham
Lipson Community College   Bernice Terr, Lipson, Plymouth
   PL4 7PG; URL www.lipson.plymouth.sch.uk; e-mail
   ifleming@lipson.plymouth.sch.uk; Tel 01752 662997
   Manager (Learning Development)   Hayley Alberts
North West Adult and Community Learning   Sir John Hunt
   Community College, Lancaster Gdns, Whitleigh,
   Plymouth PL5 4AA; e-mail
   john.shanahan@plymouth.gov.uk; Tel 01752 201020
   Manager (Learning Development)   Mr J. Shanahan
Plym Adult Learning Centre   Plymstock School Campus,
   Church Rd, Plymouth PL9 9AZ; e-mail
   plymcl@plymouth.gov.uk; Tel 01752 406847
   Manager (Learning Development)   Cheryl Phelps-Moran
Stoke Damerel Community Learning   Somerset Pl, Stoke,
   Plymouth PL3 4BD; e-mail sdcl@plymouth.gov.uk;
   Tel 01752 609128
   Manager (Learning Development)   Lorraine Steer
Swarthmore Adult Education Centre   78 Mutley Plain,
   Plymouth PL4 6LF; e-mail
   railman@swarthmore.eclipse.co.uk; Tel 01752 665268;
   Fax 01752 267196
   Manager (Learning Development)   Clare Fenwick

COMMUNITY EDUCATION

Adult and Community Learning Office   Martins Gate,
   Bretonside, Plymouth PL4 0AT;
   URL www.plymouthoncourse.com; e-mail
   community.learning@plymouth.gov.uk;
   Tel 01752 660713; Fax 01752 255945
   Senior Education Officer   Graham Peck
Devonport Community Learnng   5 Fore St, Devonport,
   Plymouth PL1 4DW; e-mail jeanettedcl@yahoo.co.uk;
   Tel 01752 560374
   Youth Development Worker   J. Lynch
Plymouth Learning Links   The Routeways Centre, 41–43
   Chapel St, Devonport, Plymouth PL1 4DU; e-mail
   pll@plymouth.gov.uk; Tel 01752 606804
   City Co-ordinator   Marlaine Clarke

Sir Joshua Reynolds Centre Longcause, Plympton St Maurice, Plymouth PL7 1JB; e-mail jo.dawe@plymouth.gov.uk; Tel 01752 340328
Centre Administrator Jo Dawe

RESIDENTIAL AND OUTDOOR EDUCATION CENTRES

The Mount Batten Outdoor Education Centre Mount Batton Sailing and Watersports Centre, 70 Lawrence Rd, Plymstock, Plymouth PL9 9SJ;
URL www.mount-batten-centre.com; e-mail enquiries@mount-batten-centre.com; Tel 01752 404567
Centre Manager Fiona Nicholls

PROFESSIONAL AND TEACHERS' CENTRE

Plymouth Professional Development Centre Department for Children's Services, Windsor Hse, Tavistock Rd, Plymouth PL6 5UF; e-mail ppdc@plymouth.gov.uk

CHILDREN'S SERVICES PORTFOLIO

Portfolio Member Cllr Mrs P. Purnell; 28 Valletort Rd, Stoke, Plymouth PL1 5PH; Tel 01752 562281
Chair Cllr Vivien Pengelly (Con)
Vice-Chair Cllr Ted Fry (Con)
Members of the Cabinet
Con: Cllr Ian Bowyer, Cllr Peter Brookshaw, Cllr Delia Ford, Cllr Ted Fry, Cllr Glenn Jordon, Cllr Michael Leaves, Cllr Grant Monahan, Cllr Vivien Pengelly, Cllr Dr David Salter, Cllr Kevin Wigens

Borough of Poole
www.poole.gov.uk

In April 1997 Poole became a separate unitary authority, as did Bournemouth Borough Council. The rest of Dorset County retains a two-tier structure and is listed separately in this section.
Population: 137 500
Political composition: Con: 24, LD: 18
Civic Centre, Poole BH15 2RU; URL www.poole.gov.uk; e-mail enquiries@boroughofpoole.com; Tel 01202 633633; Fax 01202 633706

Children's Services

Strategic Director (Children's Services) John Nash
Head (Children and Young People's Integrated Services) Vicky Wales
Head (Children and Young People's Strategy, Quality and Improvement) Stuart Twiss
Head (Culture and Community Learning Services) Kevin McErlane
Strategy Manager (13–19) Christine White
Operational Manager Brian Bennett
Locality Co-ordinator (East) Colin Dutfield
Locality Co-ordinator (South) Peter Cooper
Senior Youth Worker Simon Harwood
Number of Schools
14 Primary; 8 Middle; 8 Secondary; 7 Combined; 3 Special

CHILDREN'S SERVICES OVERVIEW GROUP

Chair Cllr Carol Evans
Members of the Committee
Cllr Brooke, Cllr Brown, Cllr Butt, Cllr Mrs Dion, Cllr Mrs Evans, Cllr Mrs Lavender, Cllr Mrs Moore, Cllr White, Cllr Miss Wilson, Cllr Woodcock

COMMUNITY SUPPORT AND EDUCATION SCRUTINY COMMITTEE

Chair Judy Butt
Vice-Chair Cllr Xena Dion

Members of the Committee
Cllr Bulteel, Cllr Chandler, Cllr Mrs Lavender, Cllr Martin, Cllr Montrose, Cllr Mrs Moore, Cllr Plummer, Cllr Wilson

YOUTH AND COMMUNITY CENTRES

The Beacon Centre Mitchell Rd, Canford Heath, Poole BH17 8UE; e-mail thebeacon@btconnect.com; Tel 01202 686965
Bourne Valley Youth Centre Northmere Rd, Parkstone, Poole BH12 4DY; Tel 01202 740113
Leader-in-Charge Sarah Evan-Johnson
Broadstone Youth Club Moor Rd, Broadstone, Dorset BH18 8AZ; Tel 01202 697303
Leader-in-Charge Jane Milton
Creekmoor Youth Centre Northmead Dr, Creekmoor, Poole BH17 7YX; Tel 01202 605340
Leader-in-Charge Neil Poulton
Limelights Learoyd Rd, Oakdale, Poole BH17 7PJ; Tel 01202 672318
Leader-in-Charge Nikki Mussell
Merley Youth Centre Chichester Wlk, Merley, Wimborne, Dorset BH21 1ST; Tel 01202 841233
Leader-in-Charge Glenise Dickinson
Parkstone Sports and Arts Centre Recreation Rd, Parkstone, Poole BH12 2EA; Tel 01202 717326
Poole Detached Youth Project Dolphin Centre, Poole BH15 1SA; Tel 01202 262284
Contact Adrian Wilkins
Turlin Moor Youth Centre Turlin Rd, Poole BH16 5AH; Tel 01202 670085
Worker-in-Charge Ruth Caines
Waterloo Youth Centre Kitchener Cres, Waterloo Est, Poole BH17 7HX; Tel 01202 693288
Leader-in-Charge Teresa Murray

PUPIL REFERRAL UNIT

The Gaff Hamworthy Youth Centre, Blandford Rd, Hamworthy, Poole BH15 4AY; Tel 01202 678450

Somerset County Council
www.somerset.gov.uk

Population: 498 700 (mid 2001 estimate)
Political composition: LD: 30, Con: 24, Lab: 4
County Hall, Taunton, Somerset TA1 4DY;
URL www.somerset.gov.uk; Tel (Community Services Directorate) 0845 345 9133; Fax (Community Services Directorate) 01823 355258
Chief Executive Alan Jones

Children and Young People's Directorate

County Hall, Taunton, Somerset TA1 3JR; e-mail somersetdirect@somerset.gov.uk; Tel (Somerset Direct: Mon–Fri 0800–1800, Sat 0900–1600) 0845 345 9122
Please call Somerset Direct for information regarding social care for children and families, and education services including learning and leisure, early years, further education, student finance, play and childcare, pupil services, school admissions, somerset music, youth services or visit the website

South Gloucestershire Council
www.southglos.gov.uk

Political composition: LD: 34, Con: 27, Lab: 9
Castle St, Thornbury, South Gloucestershire BS35 1HF;
URL www.southglos.gov.uk; e-mail mailbox@southglos.gov.uk; Tel 01454 868686
Chief Executive Amanda Deeks

Department for Children and Young People

South Gloucestershire Offices, Bowling Hill, Chipping Sodbury, South Gloucestershire BS37 6JX; e-mail educ.service@southglos.gov.uk; Fax 01454 863263
Director   Therese Gillespie
Deputy Director and Head (Achievement and Inclusion)   Jane Spouse
Head (Asset Management and Capital Planning)   Clare Medland
Head (Central Teaching and Inclusion Service)   Clare Steele
Head (Education Planning and Student Support)   Pat Vedmore
Head (Learning and School Effectiveness)   Richard Swan
Head (Lifelong Learning)   Dennis Cannon
Head (Resources)   Martin Dear
Head (Schools Personnel)   Ron Bull
Head (SEN)   Trevor Daniels
Principal Education Welfare Officer   Fran Bennett
Principal Educational Psychologist   Peter Wiggs
Number of Schools
15 Secondary; 3 Special

Swindon Borough Council

www.swindon.gov.uk

In April 1997 Swindon became a separate unitary authority. The rest of Wiltshire County Council retains a two-tier structure and is listed separately in this section.
Population: 182 600
Political composition: Con: 41, Lab: 13, LD: 3
Civic Offices, Euclid St, Swindon SN1 2JH;
URL www.swindon.gov.uk; e-mail swindon-council@swindon.gov.uk; Tel 01793 463000; Fax 01793 463930
Chief Executive   Gavin Jones
Director (Finance)   Stuart McKellar
Director (Law and Corporate Governance)   Stephen Taylor
Director (Swindon Services)   Bill Fisher
Group Director (Housing and Adult Services)   Caroline Fowles
Group Director (Resources)   Marie Rosenthal

Children

Sanford Hse, Sanford St, Swindon SN1 1QH; e-mail hpitts@swindon.gov.uk; Tel 01793 463902; Fax 01793 488597
Group Director (Children)   Hilary Pitts
Director (Services to Children and Young People)   Geoff Hogg

Torbay Council

www.torbay.gov.uk

In April 1998 Torbay became a unitary authority. The rest of Devon retains a two-tier structure and is listed separately in this section.
Political composition: Con: 24, Liberal: 8, Independent Group: 2, Ind: 1, Independent Liberal: 1,
Town Hall, Torquay, Torbay TQ1 3DR;
URL www.torbay.gov.uk; e-mail webmaster@torbay.gov.uk; Tel 01803 201201
Elected Mayor   Nick Bye
Chief Executive   Elizabeth Raikes

Children's Services

Oldway Mansion, Torquay Rd, Paignton, Devon TQ3 2TE; e-mail csenquiries@torbay.gov.uk; Tel 01803 208208

Assistant Director (Early Intervention)   Ali Matthews
Assistant Director (Learning and Standards)   Tony Porter
Assistant Director (Specialist Services)   Keith Thompson
Section Head (Admissions and Student Services)   Kay Bailey
Section Head (Directorate Services)   Lynda Davison
Section Head (Governor Service)   Hilary Price
Head (Torbay Pupil Referral Unit)   Moira Devlin
Principal Education Welfare Officer   Andy Jones; Tel 01803 206299
Principal Educational Psychologist   Derek Smith; Tel 01803 208261
Principal Youth Officer   Joe Elston
Education Officer (Business Services)   Paul Hope
Education Officer (SEN)   Vacancy
Advisory Teacher (Hearing Impaired)   Hazel Sutherland; Tel 01803 208248
Advisory Teacher (Hearing Impaired)   Denise Tudor
Advisory Teacher (ICT for SEN)   Anne Davenport; Tel 01803 863106
Advisory Teacher (Visually Impaired)   Nicky Simpson; Tel 01803 863397
Group Accountant   Lisa Finn

CABINET MEMBER FOR CHILDREN

Contact   Anna Tolchard

PUPIL REFERRAL UNITS

Pupil Referral Unit, Clennon Valley   c/o YMCA, Dartmouth Rd, Paignton, Torbay TQ4 6NX; e-mail admin@cvec.org.uk; Tel 01803 698018
Teacher-in-Charge   Mrs J. Sharpe
The Polsham Centre   25 Higher Polsham Rd, Paignton, Devon TQ3 2SZ; e-mail margaret.brookes@polsham.centre.torbay.sch.uk; Tel 01803 665735
Teacher-in-Charge   Mrs M. Brookes
Pupil Referral Unit, Waterside   c/o YMCA, Dartmouth Rd, Paignton, Torbay TQ4 6NX; Tel 01803 664801
Teacher-in-Charge   Rachel May
Pupil Referral Unit, Winnicott Centre, Child and Family Service   Hospital Annexe, 187 Newton Rd, Torquay, Torbay TQ2 7AJ; Tel 01803 655695
Teacher-in-Charge   Mary Ings

COMMUNITY EDUCATION

Community Education Torquay   c/o Torquay Community College, Farifield Rd, Torquay, Torbay TQ2 7NU; e-mail torcomed@eclipse.co.uk; Tel 01803 316930; Fax 01803 313961

RESIDENTIAL OUTDOOR AND TRAINING CENTRE

Grenville House Nautical Venture Centre (Residential)   Berry Head Rd, Brixham, Torbay TQ5 9AF; Tel 01803 852797
Centre Manager   M. Bennett

Wiltshire County Council

www.wiltshire.gov.uk

In April 1997 Swindon became a separate unitary authority and is listed separately in this section. The rest of Wiltshire County Council retains a two-tier structure.
Population: 345 500 (2005)
Political composition: Con: 29, LD: 16, Lab: 3, Ind: 1
County Hall, Bythesea Rd, Trowbridge, Wiltshire BA14 8JN; URL www.wiltshire.gov.uk; e-mail keithrobinson@wiltshire.gov.uk; Tel 01225 713000; Fax 01225 713999
Chief Executive   Dr Keith Robinson
Director (Children and Education)   Carolyn Godfrey
Director (Community Services)   Sue Redmond

Department for Children and Education

County Hall, Bythesea Rd, Trowbridge, Wiltshire BA14 8JB;
e-mail directorcel@wiltshire.gov.uk
Director Carolyn Godfrey
Assistant Director (Schools Branch) Stephanie Denovan
Head (Lifelong Learning) Julie Cathcart
Manager (Key Stage Three Strategy) Martin Cooper
Adviser (Design Technology/Assessment/NGFL)
Vince Marriott

GOVERNOR SUPPORT TEAM

Governor Services Schools Branch, Department for Children
and Education, County Hall, Trowbridge, Wiltshire
BA14 8JB; URL www.wiltshire.gov.uk; e-mail
davidmarriott@wiltshire.gov.uk; Tel 01225 713819;
Fax 01225 713892
Head (Governor Support) D. Marriott
Services offered
An annual programme of seminars for governors,
headteachers and clerks to governing bodies; guidance
documents; termly newsletter; helpline; resources library;
distance learning and DIY training kits

RESIDENTIAL CENTRES

Braeside Education and Conference Centre Bath Rd, Devizes,
Wiltshire SN10 2AX; Tel 01380 722637; Fax 01380 721343
Head Keith Browning
Oxenwood Outdoor Education Centre Oxenwood,
Marlborough, Wiltshire SN8 3NQ; Tel 01264 731274;
Fax 01264 731346
Head Stephen Chandler
Urchfont Manor Residential College Urchfont, Devizes,
Wiltshire SN10 4RG; Tel 01380 840495; Fax 01380 840005
Director Jim Ross

SUPPORT CENTRES

Melksham Professional Development Centre 3 Lancaster Pk,
Bowerhill, Melksham, Wiltshire SN12 6TT;
Tel 01225 793349; Fax 01225 793348
Centre Manager Elaine Harbour
Adviser (e-learning) Ian Baker
Salisbury Support Centre Grosvenor Hse, 26 Churchfields
Rd, Salisbury, Wiltshire SP2 7NH; Tel 01722 411356;
Fax 01722 411319
Adviser (Support) Vacancy

YOUTH DEVELOPMENT CENTRES

Amesbury Sports and Community Centre Antrobus Rd,
Amesbury, Wiltshire SP4 7ND; Tel 01980 622173;
Fax 01980 596980
Bradford-on-Avon Youth Development Centre Frome Rd,
Bradford-on-Avon, Wiltshire BA15 1LE;
Tel 01225 868115
Co-ordinator (Youth Development) Dawn Froggatt
Calne Youth and Community Centre Priestley Gr, Calne,
Wiltshire SN11 8EF; Tel 01249 812509
Co-ordinator (Youth Development) Vacancy
Chippenham, The Bridge Youth Development Centre Bath
Rd, Chippenham, Wiltshire SN15 2AA; Tel 01249 655249
Corsham, The Mansion House Youth Development Centre
Pickwick Rd, Corsham, Wiltshire SN13 9BJ;
Tel 01249 712250
Devizes, Southbroom Youth Development Centre The Green,
Devizes, Wiltshire SN10 5AB; Tel 01380 722598
Co-ordinator (Youth Development) Vacancy
Durrington Youth Development Centre The Ham,
Durrington, Salisbury, Wiltshire SP4 8HW;
Tel 01980 654172
Grosvenor House Youth Development Centre 26
Churchfields Rd, Salisbury, Wiltshire SP2 7NH;
Tel 01722 337850
Co-ordinator (Youth Development) R. Saul

Malmesbury, The Cartmell Youth Development Centre
Tetbury Hill, Malmesbury, Wiltshire SN16 9JR;
Tel 01666 823747; Fax 01666 825091
Marlborough Youth Development Centre 30a St Margaret's
Mead, Marlborough, Wiltshire SN8 4BA;
Tel 01672 512762
Co-ordinator (Youth Development) Jan Edwards
Melksham Youth Development Centre 56 Spa Rd,
Melksham, Wiltshire SN12 7NY; Tel 01225 702355
Co-ordinator (Youth Development) Vacancy
Pewsey Swimming and Sports Centre Wilcot Rd, Pewsey,
Wiltshire SN9 5EW; Tel 01672 562469; Fax 01672 563956
Manager I. Richards
Purton and Cricklade Youth Development Centre Reids
Piece, Purton, Swindon, Wiltshire SN5 4AZ;
Tel (Cricklade) 01793 750100; Tel (Purton) 01793 772267
Co-ordinator (Youth Development) H. Wykes
Salisbury Youth Development Centre 124 Wilton Rd,
Salisbury, Wiltshire SP2 7JX; Tel 01722 410963
Co-ordinator (Youth Development) W. Manning
Tidworth/Ludgershall Youth Development Centre St
Andrew's Hall, Bulford Rd, Tidworth, Wiltshire SP9 7RZ;
Tel (Ludgershall) 01264 792845; Tel (Tidworth)
01980 842748
Tisbury and Mere Youth Development Centre The
Recreation Ground, Queens Rd, Mere, Wiltshire
BA13 6EP; Tel (Mere) 01747 861400; Tel (Tisbury)
01747 871454
Co-ordinator (Youth Development) J. Farrell
Trowbridge Court Mills Youth Development Centre
Polebarn Rd, Trowbridge, Wiltshire BA14 7EG;
Tel 01225 776772; Fax 01225 776890
Co-ordinator (Youth Development) Richard Williams
Warminster Youth Development Centre The Close,
Warminster, Wiltshire BA12 9AL; Tel 01985 218561
Co-ordinator (Youth Development) I. Withers
Westbury Youth Development Centre Eden Vale Rd,
Westbury, Wiltshire BA13 3NY; Tel 01373 822335;
Fax 01373 776890
Co-ordinator (Youth Development) Martin Walker
Wootton Bassett Youth Development Centre Lime Kiln,
Wootton Bassett, Swindon, Wiltshire SN4 7HG;
Tel 01793 853198
Co-ordinator (Youth Development) G. Brown

WEST MIDLANDS

Birmingham City Council
www.birmingham.gov.uk

Population: 977 087
Political composition: Con: 43, Lab: 41, LD: 32, Respect
Party: 2, Ind: 1
The Council Hse, Victoria Sq, Birmingham, West Midlands
B1 1BB; URL www.birmingham.gov.uk; e-mail
assist@birmingham.gov.uk; Tel 0121 303 9944
Lord Mayor Randal Brew
Chief Executive Stephen Hughes

Children, Young People and Families Directorate

Council Hse, Extension, Margaret St, Birmingham, West
Midlands B3 3BU; Tel 0121 303 2590; Fax 0121 303 1318
Chair (Children and Education Scrutiny Committee)
Cllr Jon Hunt
Cabinet Member (Children, Young People and Families)
Cllr Les Lawrence
Strategic Director Tony Howell
Service Director (Business Support) Vacancy

Service Director (Inclusion Services)   Chrissie Garrett
Service Director (Specialist Services)   Vacancy
Service Director (Strategy and Commissioning)
    Cheryl Hopkins
Director (Transforming Education)   Sylvia McNamara
Head (School Effectiveness)   Jackie Hughes
Number of Schools
302 Primary; 76 Secondary; 46 Special

Coventry City Council

www.coventry.gov.uk

Population: 304 400
The Council Hse, Coventry, Warwickshire CV1 5RR;
    URL www.coventry.gov.uk; Tel 024 7683 3333;
    Fax 024 7683 1079
Chief Executive   Stella Manzie; Tel 024 7683 1100

Children, Learning and Young People's Directorate

Civic Centre 1, Earl St, Coventry, West Midlands CV1 5RS;
    Tel 024 7683 1511; Fax 024 7683 1620
Director   Colin Green
Head (Children's Neighbourhood Services)   Brian Parker
Head (Services for Schools)   Ruth Snow
Head (Specialist Services)   Amanda Lamb
Head (Strategic Services)   Andy Walmsley
Departmental Manager (Human Resources)   Neelesh Sutaria
Number of Schools
85 Primary, 19 Secondary; 10 Special

CABINET MEMBER (EDUCATION SERVICES)

Contact   John Blundell (Con)

EDUCATIONAL PSYCHOLOGY SERVICE

9 North Ave, Stoke Pk, Coventry, Warwickshire CV2 4DH;
    Tel 024 7678 8400

SPEECH AND LANGUAGE SERVICE

Primary Unit and Administrative Base, Manor Park Primary
    School, Ulverscroft Rd, Coventry, Warwickshire
    CV3 5EZ; Tel 024 7650 2927
Head   Jacqui Tilson
Head   Hilary Union

SPECIAL UNITS

Autism Support Service   c/o Corley Centre, Church La,
    Corley, Coventry, Warwickshire CV7 8AZ;
    Tel 01676 541249; Fax 01676 549116
    Head of Service   Jan Hutchinson
Pre-School Education Service   Limbrick Wood Centre,
    Thomas Naul Crosft, Tile Hill, Coventry, Warwickshire
    CV4 9QX; Tel 024 7669 4736
    Head of Service   Sue Newman
**Sensory Support Service – Includes Hearing and Visual
    Impairment**   Cannon Park School Annexe, Bransford
    Ave, Coventry, Warwickshire CV4 7PS;
    Tel 024 7641 7415; Fax 024 7641 7415
    Head of Service   Peter McCann

SCHOOL OF MUSIC AND DRAMA

Performing Arts Service   City College Tile Centre, Tile Hill
    La, Coventry, West Midlands CV4 9SY;
    Tel 024 7669 5300; Fax 024 7669 4864
    Head   O. Dutton CertEd

Dudley Metropolitan Borough Council

www.dudley.gov.uk

Population: 305 150
Political composition: Con: 40, Lab: 26, LD: 5, UKIP: 1
Council Hse, Priory Rd, Dudley, West Midlands DY1 1HF;
    URL www.dudley.gov.uk; Tel 01384 812345; Tel (out of
    hours) 01384 818182

Children's Services Offices

Westox Hse, 1 Trinity Rd, Dudley, West Midlands DY1 1JQ;
    Tel 01384 814225; Fax 01384 814216
Lead Member   Cllr Liz Walker
Director (Children's Services)   John Freeman
Assistant Director (Children's Specialist Services)
    Pauline Sharratt
Assistant Director (Early Years, Youth and Education
    Services)   Jane Porter
Assistant Director (Partnership and Children's Trust)
    Cindy Peek
Assistant Director (Policy, Performance, Information)
    Chris Wrigley
Assistant Director (Resources)   Raymond Watson
Manager (Dudley Grid for Learning Contracts)   Geoff Baker
    CIPS
Manager (Early Years and Childcare)   Helen Kew
Manager (Pupil Access)   Jon McCabe
General Manager (Purchasing)   Turina Wharton
Adviser (Education Improvement: ICT)   Shirley Hackett
Adviser (Education Improvement: Primary)   Dave Perrett
Adviser (Education Improvement: Secondary)   Ian McGuff
Adviser (Education Improvement: SEN)   Huw Powell
Principal Education Welfare Officer   Keith Bates
Principal Educational Psychologist   Howard Marsh
    BSc(Psych), DipEdPsych
Project and Asset Development Officer   Fay Hayward
    BSc(Hons), ARICS
Student Awards Officer (Grants)   Martin Baker
Training and Development Officer   Lorraine Tozer Assoc,
    IPD
Number of Schools
79 Primary; 22 Secondary; 7 Special

CHILDREN'S SERVICES COMMITTEE

Lead Member   Liz Walker (Con)
Members of the Committee
K. Ahmed, L. Boleyn, L. Coulter, J. Dunn, Rev G. Johnston,
H. Nottingham, G. Partridge, S. Pearce, D. Rogers, C. Wilson

DUDLEY MUSIC CENTRE

Lawnswood Road   Wordsley, Stourbridge, West Midlands
    DY8 5PQ; Tel 01384 813865
    Head (Music Services)   Mr G.V. Johnson

EDUCATION COUNSELLING SERVICE

Church St, Pensnett, Brierley Hill, West Midlands DY5 4EY;
    Tel 01384 814239
Head   Janette Newton

HOME AND HOSPITAL TUITION SERVICE

Office: Saltwells Education Development Centre, Bowling
    Green Rd, Dudley, West Midlands DY2 9LY;
    Tel 01384 813740
Head   Jane Cooper

LEARNING SUPPORT SERVICE

Saltwells Education Development Centre, Bowling Green Rd, Dudley, West Midlands DY2 9LY; Tel 01384 813731
Head   Denise Foxall

ETHNIC MINORITY ACHIEVEMENT SERVICE

Office: Saltwells Education Development Centre, Bowling Green Rd, Dudley, West Midlands DY2 9LY; Tel 01384 813810
Head   Ester Holmes

SCHOOL CAMP SITE – OUTDOOR EDUCATION SERVICE

Astley Burf Camp   Astley Burf, Stourport-on-Severn, Herefordshire DY13 0SD; Tel 01299 823909

PHYSICAL AND SENSORY SERVICE

Church St, Pensnett, Brierley Hill, West Midlands DY5 4EY; Tel 01384 818001
Head   Kim Fisher

SPORTS CENTRES

Coseley Leisure Centre   Coseley School, Coseley, West Midlands; Tel 01384 812857
Cradley Leisure Centre   Cradley High School, West Midlands; Tel 01384 816470
Hillcrest Leisure Centre   Hillcrest School and Community College, West Midlands; Tel 01384 816503
Contact   S. Morgan
Leasowes Sports Centre   Kent Rd, Halesowen, West Midlands; Tel 01384 816287
Thorns Sports Centre   Stockwell Ave, Quarry Bank, Dudley, West Midlands; Tel 01384 816229

EDUCATIONAL DEVELOPMENT CENTRE

Dudley (Saltwells) Educational Development Centre
Bowling Green Rd, Dudley, West Midlands; Tel 01384 813769
Manager   Brenda Proctor

YOUTH CENTRE ENQUIRIES

Claughton Youth and Community Centre   Claughton Hse, Blowers Green Rd, Dudley, West Midlands; Tel 01384 813900
Coseley Youth Centre   Old Meeting Rd, Coseley, Dudley, West Midlands; Tel 01384 813922
Dudley Wood Community Learning Centre   Dudley Wood Rd, Dudley Wood, Dudley, West Midlands; Tel 01384 815175
Greenhill Youth Centre   221a Long La, Halesowen, West Midlands B62 9JT; Tel 01384 812796
Halesowen Youth Centre   Highfield La, Halesowen, West Midlands; Tel 01384 813914
Kingswinford Youth Centre   High St, Kingswinford, Dudley, West Midlands; Tel 01384 813919
Lower Gornal Youth Centre   Temple St, Lower Gornal, Dudley, West Midlands; Tel 01384 813947
Lye Youth Centre   Chapel St, Lye, Stourbridge, West Midlands DY9 8BX; Tel 01384 813940
Meadow Road Youth Centre   Meadow Rd, Dudley, West Midlands; Tel 01384 818240
Nine Lacks Youth Centre   Hill St, Brierley Hill, Dudley, West Midlands DY5 0UE; Tel 01384 813953
Pensnett Neighbourhood Centre   c/o Pensnett School, Tiled House La, Brierley Hill, West Midlands DY5 4LN; Tel 01384 813908
Russells Hall Youth Centre   Overfield Rd, Russells Hall, Dudley, West Midlands; Tel 01384 812265
The Source   Barnett La, Wordsley, Stourbridge, West Midlands; Tel 01384 813969

In April 1998 Hereford and Worcester County Council split to form one unitary authority (Herefordshire Council) and one two-tier authority (Worcestershire County Council). Both are listed separately in this section.
Population: 177 800
Political composition: Con: 32, Ind: 14, LD: 10, Lab: 2
Brockington, 35 Hafod Rd, Hereford, Herefordshire HR1 1SH; URL www.herefordshire.gov.uk; e-mail info@herefordshire.gov.uk; Tel 01432 260000
Chief Executive   Neil Pringle
Chair   Cllr John Edwards
Leader of the Council   Cllr Roger Phillips

Children's and Young People's Directorate

Tel 01432 260000; Tel (emergency duty team: 1700–0900 Mon–Fri; 1600–0900 Fri–Mon; bank holidays) 01432 358116
Director   Sharon Menghini; Tel 01432 260039
Head (Integrated Services and Inclusion)   Anne Heath; Tel 01432 260804
Head (Safeguarding and Assessment Services)   Shaun McLurg; Tel 01432 261603
Head (Schools and Services: Commissioning and Improvement)   George Salmon; Tel 01432 260802
Manager (Children's Service Directorate)   Marcia Perry; Tel 01432 378910
Manager (Community Youth Service)   Jon Ralph; Tel 01432 383377
Manager (Early Years and Extended Services)   Ros Hatherill; Tel 01432 260859
Manager (Finance)   Malcolm Green
Manager (Secondary School Improvement)   Paul Murray
Manager (SEN and Disability)   Linda Nash; Tel 01432 260817
Manager (Social Inclusion)   Dennis Longmore; Tel 01432 260816
Number of Schools
82 Primary, 14 Secondary, 4 Special, 3 PRU

CABINET MEMBER – CHILDREN AND YOUNG PEOPLE

Contact   Cllr Jenny Hyde

Population: 286 300
Political composition: Lab: 51, Con: 11, LD: 5, BNP: 2, Ind: 2
Sandwell Council Hse, PO Box 2374, Oldbury, West Midlands B69 3DE; URL www.sandwell.gov.uk; Tel 0121 569 2200

Children and Young People's Services

Shaftesbury Hse, PO Box 41, 402 High St, West Bromwich, West Midlands B70 9LT; URL www.lea.sandwell.gov.uk; e-mail childrenand_youngpeoplesservices@sandwell.gov.uk; Tel 0121 569 2200; Fax 0121 553 1528
Executive Director   Roger Crouch; Tel 0121 569 8205
Director (Children's Services)   C. Tucker
Director (Partnership and Commissioning)   J. Brown
Director (Schools)   P. Penn-Howard
Head (Extended and Inclusive Learning Service)   P. Watts

Head (Governance and Access Services)   K. Smith
Head (Planning, Performance and Business Services)   P. Cox
Head (Primary Education Service)   B. Aldridge
Head (Secondary Education Service)   N. Fowler
Senior Manager (Finance)   J. Smith
Service Manager (Adult Education Service)   J. Wells
Service Manager (Commissioned Services)   T. Pearce
Service Manager (Planning and Business Support)   B. Griffiths
Service Manager (SEN and Inclusion Support)   P. Evans
Manager (Business Information Services)   M. Parsons
Manager (Organisational Effectiveness)   P. Pulsford
Manager (Personnel)   M. Adams
Manager (Policy, Equalities and Communications Unit)
   J. Massey
Manager (Support Services)   N. Hamer
Unit Manager (Education Welfare)   D. Turner
Unit Manager (School Organisation and Capital
   Commissioning)   C. Wilkes
Senior Adviser (Primary Strategy)   L. Jones
Senior Adviser (Secondary Strategy)   M. Pettit
ICT Adviser (e-Learning Unit)   S. Courtney-Donovan
Principal Officer (Young People's Services)   D. Wright
Number of Schools
77 Primary; 13 Secondary; 9 Infant; 8 Junior; 4 Residential
Centres; 3 Academies; 3 Special Day; 2 Foundation; 1 Special
Residential

CHILDREN AND YOUNG PEOPLE CABINET MEMBER

Cabinet Member   I. Jones (Lab); 18 Pound Rd, Wednesbury,
   West Midlands WS10 9HJ
Adviser   D. Hinton (Lab)

GOVERNOR SERVICES

c/o Children and Young People's Services;
   Tel 0121 569 8144; Fax 0121 553 8258
Services offered
Comprehensive range of training courses; link governor
meetings; clerk support meetings; termly newsletter;
governor advice and support; helplines

INCLUSION SUPPORT

Connor Rd, West Bromwich, West Midlands B71 3DJ;
   Tel 0121 588 8337; Fax 0121 567 5520

RESIDENTIAL ESTABLISHMENTS

Edgmond Hall   41 High St, Newport, Shropshire TF10 8JY;
   URL www.schools.sandwell.net/edgmondhall.com;
   e-mail richard.oakes@edgmondhall.lea.sandwell.net;
   Tel 01952 810799; Fax 01952 812302
   Head   R. Oakes
Frank Chapman Centre   Park End, Ribbesford, Bewdley,
   Worcestershire DY12 2TY;
   URL www.frankchapmancentre.co.uk; e-mail
   headteacher@frankchapman.lea.sandwell.net;
   Tel 01299 403292; Fax 01299 402724
   Head   A. Broome
Ingestre Hall   Ingestre, Stafford, Staffordshire ST18 0RF;
   e-mail enquiries@ingestrehall.lea.sandwell.net;
   Tel 01889 270225; Fax 01889 270225
   Head   J. Thomson
Plas Gwynant   Nantgwynant, Caernarfon, Gwynedd
   LL55 4NR; URL www.plasgwynant.org.uk; e-mail
   enquiries@plasgwynant.lea.sandwell.net;
   Tel 01766 890212; Fax 01766 890431
   Head   J. Handley

Shropshire County Council

www.shropshire.gov.uk

In April 1998 Telford and Wrekin Council became a unitary
authority and is listed separately in this section. The rest of
Shropshire retains a two-tier structure.

Population: 283 300
Political composition: Con: 25, LD: 11, Lab: 9, Ind: 3
The Shirehall, Abbey Foregate, Shrewsbury, Shropshire
   SY2 6ND; URL www.shropshire.gov.uk;
   Tel 0845 678 9000; Fax 01743 252827
Chief Executive   Carolyn Downs; Tel 01743 252702
Corporate Director (Community Services)   Jack Collier;
   Tel 01743 253701

2

Education Services Directorate

Tel 01743 254307; Fax 01743 254415
Chair   J.B. Gillow
Vice-Chair   Mrs E.M.C. Winckler
Corporate Director (Education Services)   E. Nicholson
Assistant Director (Access)   R. Durham
Assistant Director (Advisory and Children's Services)
   C.C. Tiddy
Assistant Director (Community Services)   P. Taylor
Assistant Director (Strategic Management)   I. Budd BA, MA
Head (Multicultural Development Service)   Angela Lidder;
   Tel 01952 291293
Head (Music Service)   K. Havercroft
Head (SEN/Support Services); Principal Educational
   Psychologist   C. Carson
Head (TMBSS)   J. Skeldon
Manager (Education Personnel)   L. Skimins
Manager (Education Premises)   J. Humphreys
Manager (School Support and Communications); Education
   Officer   R.J. Chowdhuri
Senior Adviser (Primary Education)   C. Lister
Senior Adviser (School Improvement Projects)   C. Warn
Senior Adviser (Secondary and Continuing Education)
   J. Rowley
Senior Adviser (SEN)   G. Henderson
Curriculum Adviser (Art)   S. Smith DipAD
Curriculum Adviser (Creative Arts)   N. Rathwell
Curriculum Adviser (Design and Technology/Business
   Studies)   P. Clewes
Curriculum Adviser (English)   A. Gribbin BEd, MA
Curriculum Adviser (Geography and Environmental
   Education)   S. Rogers
Curriculum Adviser (History/Learning Resources)   A. Morgan
Curriculum Adviser (IT)   A. Berkeley
Curriculum Adviser (Mathematics)   B. Robinson
Curriculum Adviser (Modern Languages)   M. McAleavy
Curriculum Adviser (Music)   K. Havercroft MEd
Curriculum Adviser (PE and Outdoor Education)
   C. Matthews
Curriculum Adviser (PSE/Equal Opportunities and
   Citizenship)   F. Phelps MEd
Curriculum Adviser (Religious Education)   J. Williams
Curriculum Adviser (Science)   J. Seymour
Education Officer (LMS)   J. Jones
Governor (Support and Development Services)   S.E. Round
Principal Education Welfare Officer   D. Simpkins
Principal Youth Officer   R. Bell
Team Leader (Sensory Inclusive Service)   A. Broughton
Team Leader (Visually Impaired Service)   A. Lane
Number of Schools
143 Primary; 22 Secondary; 2 Special (1 with hostel)
Day of Cabinet Meeting
Variable
**Other Authorities with whom Joint Purchasing arrangements
are made**
Herefordshire and Worcestershire

CABINET COMMITTEE

LD: 4, Lab: 3, Con: 2, Ind: 1
Chair   R. Walker; 27 Allen Gdns, Market Drayton,
   Shropshire TF9 1BS; Tel 01630 653652
Vice-Chair   Peter Phillips; Frogs Gutter, The Bog,
   Minsterley, Shropshire SY5 0NL; Tel 01588 650335

Members of the Committee

LD: J. Clarke, P. Corston, B. Morris, J. Stevens
Lab: P. Box, J. Jones, D.W. Woodvine
Con: P. Corston, P. Engleheart
Ind: C. Bodenham

EDUCATIONAL PSYCHOLOGICAL SERVICE

The Glebe Centre Glebe St, Wellington, Telford, Shropshire
TF1 1JP; Tel 01952 522610
Education Welfare Service The Glebe Centre, Glebe St,
Telford, Shropshire TF1 1JP; Tel 01952 522620
Principal Education Welfare Officer D. Simpkins

SHROPSHIRE EDUCATIONAL SERVICE FOR HEARING IMPAIRED CHILDREN

The Glebe Centre, Glebe St, Telford, Shropshire TF1 1JP;
Tel 01952 522660; Fax 01952 522661

SHROPSHIRE EDUCATIONAL SERVICE FOR VISUALLY IMPAIRED CHILDREN

The Glebe Centre, Glebe St, Telford, Shropshire TF1 1JP;
Tel 01952 522654; Fax 01952 522651

SHROPSHIRE MULTICULTURAL DEVELOPMENT SERVICE

Hollinswood Junior School, Dale Acre Way, Telford,
Shropshire; Tel 01952 291293; Fax 01952 291294

SPECIAL SUPPORT SERVICE

The Glebe Centre, Glebe St, Telford, Shropshire TF1 1JP;
Tel 01952 522630

SHROPSHIRE EDUCATION WELFARE SERVICE

The Glebe Centre, Glebe St, Telford, Shropshire TF1 1JP;
Tel 01952 522620; Fax 01952 522622

SHROPSHIRE MUSIC SERVICE

Longmeadow, Bayston Hill, Shrewsbury, Shropshire
SY3 0NU; Tel 01743 874145; Fax 01743 872666

PROFESSIONAL CENTRES

Market Drayton Centre Market Drayton Junior School,
Alexandra Rd, Market Drayton, Shropshire TF9 3HU;
Tel 01630 658347
Shrewsbury Centre Racecourse Cres, Shrewsbury,
Shropshire SY2 5BP; Tel 01743 232761; Fax 01743 356251

CHILDREN WITH DISABILITIES

Richmond Hse, Rutland, Harlescott, Shrewsbury,
Shropshire SY1 3QG; Tel 01743 460560
Contact Mike Felstead

Metropolitan Borough of Solihull

www.solihull.gov.uk

Population: 199 517
Political composition: Con: 26, LD: 15, Lab: 7, BNP: 1, Ind: 1,
No Group: 1
Council Hse, PO Box 18, Solihull, West Midlands B91 3QS;
URL www.solihull.gov.uk; e-mail
chiefexecutive@solihull.gov.uk; Tel 0121 704 6000
Chief Executive Katherine Kerswell

Education and Children's Services Directorate

Council Hse, PO Box 20, Solihull, West Midlands B91 9QU;
Fax 0121 704 8129
Cabinet Member (Education and Children) Cllr K.I. Meeson
Chair (Education and Children Scrutiny Board)
Cllr D. Elsmore
Corporate Director (Education and Children's Services)
Mark Rogers
Service Director (Children and Young People) A. Plummer
Service Director (Quality) P.J. Moss
Manager (Business and Performance) S. Fenton
Manager (Inclusion and Access) J. Essex
Chief Education Welfare Officer S. Martin
Education Officer (Information Strategy) D. Butt
Assistant Education Officer (SEN) S. Dewar
Principal Officer (Youth and Community) A. Michell
Senior Adviser (School Improvement) M. Howell
Senior Adviser (School Improvement) N. Lomasney
Senior Adviser (School Improvement) Hugh Wilcock
Principal Educational Psychologist Vacancy
Number of Schools
12 Secondary; 5 Special
Frequency of Committee Meetings
Every six weeks (approx)

EDUCATION AND CHILDREN SCRUTINY BOARD

Cabinet Member Meeson (Con)
Members of the Scrutiny Board
Con: Allport, Burgess, Elsmore, Hall, Mackiewicz, Martin,
Robinson, Mrs Wild
LD: M. Allen, Hodgson, Harber
Lab: Corser, Craig
Non-affiliated: Hall, Murray, Mr Rhind, Mrs Weaver

GOVERNOR DEVELOPMENT UNIT

Keepers Lodge, Chelmsley Rd, Chelmsley Wood,
Birmingham, West Midlands B37 7RS; Tel 0121 788 3161;
Fax 0121 788 0553
Governor Training Co-ordinator S. Crowe
Services offered
Centralised training; governing body training; resource
centres; consultancy; helpline; newsletters; governing body
audits

EDUCATION PSYCHOLOGY SERVICE

Keeper's Lodge, Chelmsley Rd, Chelmsley Wood,
Birmingham, West Midlands B37 7RS; Tel 0121 770 6030;
Fax 0121 770 7608

EDUCATION WELFARE SERVICE

Keeper's Lodge, Chelmsley Rd, Chelmsley Wood,
Birmingham, West Midlands B37 7RS; Tel 0121 788 1505;
Fax 0121 779 7714
Chief Education Welfare Officer S. Martin
Senior Education Welfare Officer I. Wyatt BA, MPhil
Alderbrook School Blossomfield Rd, Solihull, West
Midlands B91 1SN; Tel 0121 704 2146
Headteacher W. Sedgwick
Secondary unit
Langley School Kineton Green Rd, Solihull, West Midlands
B92 7ER; Tel 0121 706 9771
Headteacher V. Duffy-Cross
Secondary unit
Specialist Inclusion Support Service Keepers Lodge,
Chelmsley Rd, Chelmsley Wood, Birmingham, West
Midlands B37 7RS; Tel 0121 770 6267; Fax 0121 770 6267
Manager Ms R. Daws
Lyndon School Daylesford Rd, Solihull, West Midlands
B92 8EJ; Tel 0121 743 3402
Headteacher S. Westwood
Secondary unit

Reynalds Cross Unit   Kineton Green Rd, Solihull, West
  Midlands B92 7ER; Tel 0121 706 0627
  Headteacher   J. Davenport
Secondary Support Centre   Langley School, Kineton Green
  Rd, Solihull, West Midlands; Tel 0121 706 9771
  Headteacher   V. Duffy-Cross

PRE-SCHOOL AND HOME TUITION SERVICE

Triple Crown Centre   Lode La, Solihull, West Midlands
  B91 2HW; Tel 0121 709 0080
  Head of Service   S. Maden

TEACHERS' CENTRE

Solihull Teachers' Centre   Sans Souci, Tanworth La, Solihull,
  West Midlands B90 4DD; Tel 0121 744 1276;
  Fax 0121 733 6173
  Head   Judy King

Staffordshire County Council

www.staffordshire.gov.uk

In April 1997 Stoke-on-Trent became a separate unitary
authority and is listed separately in this section. The rest of
Staffordshire County Council retains a two-tier structure.
Population: 800 000
Political composition: Lab: 32, Con: 28, LD: 2
Martin St, Stafford, Staffordshire ST16 2LH;
  URL www.staffordshire.gov.uk; Tel 01785 223121;
  Fax 01785 215153
Chief Executive   Nigel T. Pursey; e-mail
  nigel.pursey@staffordshire.gov.uk
Director (Development Services)   R. Hilton
Director (Resources)   Olwen Pritchard-Jones;
  Tel 01785 223121
Director (Social Services)   R. Lake; St Chads Pl, Stafford,
  Staffordshire; Tel 01785 223121

Education Department

Education Office, Tipping St, Stafford, Staffordshire
  ST16 2DH; e-mail education@staffordshire.gov.uk;
  Fax 01785 278639
Cabinet Member   Cllr R. Simpson
Corporate Director (Children and Lifelong Learning)
  Peter Traves
Deputy Director (Education: Quality Assurance/Resources)
  K. Cackett
Deputy Director (Education: Raising Achievement)
  Ms Julia Almond
Head (Careers)   E. Manley
Head (County Grounds)   K. Lockley
Head (CPD Unit)   J. Bird
Head (Direct Services)   M. Swanwick
Head (Education Joint Finance Unit)   I. Wilkie
Head (Joint IT Unit)   Martyn Reed
Head (Lifelong Learning)   Jim Brady
Head (Outdoor Education Centres)   E. Gardner
Head (Personnel Services)   Mrs J. Russell
Head (Pupil Support Unit)   P. Parker
Head (Quality Learning Services); Principal Education Officer
  Ms P. Owen
Head (School Effectiveness Unit)   Bill Dewar
Head (Staffordshire Performing Arts)   N. Taylor
Head (Student Finance Service)   G. Davies
Deputy Head (Outdoor Education Centres)   R.K. Griffiths
*Principal Education Officer (Management and Financial
  Services)*   D. Cheeseman IPFA
Principal Education Officer (Pupil and Student Services)
  Mr P. Worrell
*Principal Education Officer (Research and Development
  Services)*   Dr T.C. Hine PhD, BSc
*Principal Education Officer (Youth and Community Education
  Service)*   Mr J. Brady

Chief Educational Psychologist   C. Cherry
District Education Officer (Lichfield/Moorlands)
  Mrs J. Lancaster
District Education Officer (Newcastle/South Staffs)   Vacancy
District Education Officer (Stafford/Cannock)   R.J. Lord
District Education Officer (Tamworth/East Staffs)   P. Moore
Number of Schools
69 Secondary; 22 Special
Day of Committee Meeting
Variable; eight times a year
**Other Authorities with whom Joint Purchasing Arrangements
are made**
Shropshire, Hereford and Worcester

EDUCATION SCRUTINY COMMITTEE

Lab: 7, Con: 5
Chair   S.G. Norman
Members of the Committee
P. Atkins, P. Benion, M.R. Clarke, W. Day, E. Drinkwater,
T.V. Finn, R.L. Gorton, A. Gribbin, D.A. Leech, Mrs M.
Maddox, R. McDermiol, D. Mole, J. Muir, S.G. Norman, E.C.
Perry

EDUCATION CENTRES

Burton Education Centre   Grange St, Burton upon Trent,
  Staffordshire DE14 2ER; Tel 01283 239060;
  Fax 01283 239062
  Centre Manager   Mrs H. Tebbs
Cannock Centre   119 Walsall Rd, Cannock, Staffordshire
  WS11 3JA; Tel 01543 574647; Fax 01543 571571
Kingston Centre   Fairway, Stafford, Staffordshire
  ST16 3TW; e-mail qls.kingston@staffordshire.gov.uk;
  Tel 01785 277900; Fax 01785 256193

COUNTY PSYCHOLOGICAL SERVICE

Flash Ley Resource Centre, Hawksmoor Rd, Stafford,
  Staffordshire ST17 9DR; Tel 01785 356871;
  Fax 01785 356940
District Senior Educational Psychologist   F. Morgan
Specialist Support Service   Flash Ley Resource Centre,
  Hawksmoor Rd, Stafford, Staffordshire ST17 9DR;
  Tel 01785 356917

SPECIAL UNITS (ASSESSMENT CENTRES)

Burton-on-Trent   Horninglow County Infants Speech and
  Language Unit, Horninglow Rd North, Burton upon
  Trent, Staffordshire DE13 0SW; Tel 01283 239537;
  Fax 01283 239537
  Head of Unit   Mrs P. Evans
CEDARS, Newcastle Base   2 Woodlands Ave, Wolstanton,
  Newcastle-under-Lyme, Staffordshire ST5 8AZ;
  Tel 01782 297510; Fax 01782 297510
  Head of Unit   Mr M. Fenton
CEDARS, Wall Lane Base   Wall La Terr, Cheddleton, Leek,
  Staffordshire ST13 7ED; Tel 01538 360917;
  Fax 01538 360917
  Head of Service   Mr M. Fenton
Chancel Special Needs Nursery   Wolesley Rd, Rugeley,
  Staffordshire WS15 2EW; Tel 01889 256141
  Head   Mrs J. Dale
Lichfield, Stowe Teaching Unit   Stowe St, Lichfield,
  Staffordshire WS13 6AF; Tel 01543 510755;
  Fax 01543 510755
  Head of Unit   K.P. Paylor
Pupil and Student Services – Burton and Tamworth District
  Burton Education Centre, Grange St, Burton upon Trent,
  Staffordshire DE14 2ER; Tel 01785 278940;
  Fax 01785 278925
  District Co-ordinator   Mr R. Booth
Pupil and Student Services – Lichfield and Cannock District
  The Old Library, Bird St, Lichfield, Staffordshire
  WS13 6PN; Tel 01543 512052
  District Co-ordinator   Mrs D. Mitchell

Pupil and Student Services – Newcastle and Moorlands District Sidmouth Ave, Newcastle-under-Lyme, Staffordshire ST5 0AM; Tel 01782 297524; Fax 01782 297523
District Co-ordinator   Mr J. Lay-Flurrie

Pupil and Student Services – Stafford and South Staffordshire District Flash Ley Centre, Hawksmoor Rd, Stafford, Staffordshire ST17 9DR; Tel 01785 356949
District Co-ordinator   F. Morgan

Specialist Support Service Flash Ley Centre, Hawksmoor Rd, Stafford, Staffordshire ST17 9DR; Tel 01785 356830; Fax 01785 356841
Head of Service   D. Fran

Stafford, Flash Ley Speech and Language Unit Hawksmoor Rd, Stafford, Staffordshire ST17 9DR; Tel 01785 356643; Fax 01785 356651
Contact   D.I. Lewis

Tamworth, Stoneydelph Hearing Impaired Unit (Pt.Hg.) Crowden Rd, Stoneydelph, Tamworth, Staffordshire B77 4LS; Tel 01827 896666
Head of Unit   Mrs A.M. Mulligan

Tamworth, Torc High, Hearing Impaired Unit Silverlink Rd, Tamworth, Staffordshire B77 2HB; Tel 01827 286305
Head of Unit   P.E. Slusar

Victoria Primary School Speech and Language Unit Victoria Primary School, Victoria Rd, Burton upon Trent, Staffordshire DE14 2LU; Tel 01283 239146
Headteacher   V.E. Warrington

INSTITUTES OF ADULT EDUCATION

Pendrell Hall College of Residential Adult Education Codsall Wood, Wolverhampton, Staffordshire WV8 1QP; Tel 01902 434112; Fax 01902 434113
Headteacher   David Evans

Wedgwood Memorial College Barlaston, Stoke-on-Trent; Tel 01782 372105; Fax 01782 372393
Headteacher   D. Tatton MA, PhD

TEACHERS' CENTRES

Education Joint IT Unit Church La, Hixon, Staffordshire ST18 0PT; Tel 01889 256290; Fax 01889 256291
Head of Unit   M. Reed

Ethnic Minority Achievement Unit Grange St, Burton upon Trent, Staffordshire DE14 2ER; Tel 01283 239089; Fax 01283 239062
Head of Unit   Mrs R. Chowdhrey

Staffordshire ICT Education Programme Kingston Centre, Stafford, Staffordshire ST16 3TU; e-mail qls.kingston@staffordshire.gov.uk; Tel 01785 277974; Fax 01785 256193
Head of Programme   H.C. Bagshaw

MUSIC CENTRE

Staffordshire Music Service Staffordshire Performing Arts Centre, The Green, Stafford, Staffordshire ST17 4BJ; Tel 01785 278278; Fax 01785 278288
Head of Service   Mr N. Taylor

YOUTH CENTRES

Correspondence address: Youth and Community Education Service, Education Offices, Stafford, Staffordshire ST16 2DH; Tel 01785 223121
Principal Officer (Lifelong Learning)   J. Brady
There are 32 youth centres in the county

OUTDOOR EDUCATION CENTRES

Chasewater Outdoor Education Centre Pool Rd, Chasetown, Walsall, West Midlands WS7 8QW; Tel 01543 686524; Fax 01543 672024
Deputy Head (Outdoor Education)   R.K. Griffiths

Coven Outdoor Education Centre Laches La, Slade Heath, Wolverhampton, West Midlands WV10 7PA; Tel 01902 790388; Fax 01902 790376
Centre Manager   R.K. Griffiths

Shugborough Outdoor Education Centre Shugborough Pk, Great Haywood, Staffordshire ST17 0XA; Tel 01889 881357; Fax 01889 881257
Head (Outdoor Education)   E. Gardner

Standon Bowers Outdoor Education Centre Standon, Stafford, Staffordshire ST21 6RD; Tel 01782 791422; Fax 01782 791546
Centre Co-ordinator   E. Gardner

Stoke-on-Trent City Council

www.stoke.gov.uk

In April 1997 Stoke-on-Trent became a separate unitary authority. The rest of Staffordshire County Council retains a two-tier structure and is listed separately in this section.
Population: 240 000
Political composition: Lab: 29, The City First Alliance Group: 10, City Independent Group: 8, Liberal Democrat and Alliance Group: 5, BNP: 5, People's Party: 2, No Party (non-aligned): 1
Civic Centre, PO Box 636, Glebe St, Stoke-on-Trent ST4 1RN; URL www.stoke.gov.uk; e-mail enquiries@stoke.gov.uk; Tel 01782 234567; Fax 01782 232603
Chief Executive   Steve Robinson

Children's Services

Tel 01782 232014
Director   Nigel Rigby
Assistant Director (Achievement)   Peter Taylor
Assistant Director (Continuing Education)   Anne Revell
Assistant Director (Support Services)   Howard Cartlidge
Head (Admissions and Family Services)   Dr Keith Forrest
Head (Finance Unit)   Paul Gerrard
Head (Personnel)   Mary Moran
Head (Premises and Client Services)   Mike Inman
Education Officer (SEN)   Lynne Crockett

PSYCHOLOGICAL SERVICE

Education Psychological Service The Mount, Mount Ave, Penkhull, Stoke-on-Trent ST4 4SY; Tel 01782 234700
Educational Psychologist   C. Barcham

SPECIAL UNITS

Hearing Impaired Unit The Willows Primary School, Greatbach Ave, Penkhill, Stoke-on-Trent ST4 7JU; Tel 01782 233280
Teacher-in-Charge   Janet Payne

SENSS The Mount, Mount Ave, Penkhull, Stoke-on-Trent; Tel 01782 232538
Contact   P. Croft

Stoke, City General Hospital Child Assessment Unit City General Hospital, Newcastle Rd, Stoke-on-Trent ST4 6QG; Tel 01782 552691

Stoke, Thistley Hough Hearing Impaired Support Team Newcastle La, Penkhull, Stoke-on-Trent ST4 5JJ; Tel 01782 418500
Teacher-in-Charge   Margaret Hawkins

TALEEM

Willfield – Community Education Centre, Lauder Pl, Bentilee, Stoke-on-Trent ST2 0QL; Tel 01782 235085
Head (Community Languages)   Javaid Qureshi

Telford and Wrekin Council

In April 1998 Telford and Wrekin Council became a unitary authority. The rest of Shropshire retains a two-tier structure and is listed separately in this section.

Political composition: Con: 25, Lab: 19, Ind: 4, LD: 3, Other: 3
Chief Executive   Steve Wellings

Children and Young People

Civic Offices, PO Box 440, Telford, Wrekin TF3 4WF; e-mail
education@telford.gov.uk; Fax 01952 385000
Director   Graham Foster; Tel 01952 385007
Head (School and Community Services)   John Gilbert;
   Tel 01952 385100
Head (Learning and School Improvement)   Graeme Harkness
Head (Policy Resources and Social Regeneration)
   Graham Foster; Tel 01952 380900
Head (Safeguarding and Corporate Parenting)   Barbara Evens;
   Tel 01952 385005

Walsall Metropolitan Borough Council

www.walsall.gov.uk

Population: 261 599
Civic Centre, Darwall St, Walsall, West Midlands WS1 1TS;
   URL www.walsall.gov.uk; Tel 01922 650000;
   Fax 01922 720885

Children's Services

Rm 29, Council Hse, Lichfield, Walsall, West Midlands
   WS1 1TW; URL www.educationwalsall.com; e-mail
   brownd@walsall.gov.uk; Tel 01922 652081;
   Fax 01922 614210
Executive Director   David Brown
Education Portfolio Holder   Cllr Zahid Ali;
   Mobile 07957 215930
Number of Schools
19 Secondary; 7 Special

Education Walsall

Education Walsall, part of Serco, works in partnership with
Walsall Council for the provision of education services
Education Development Centre, Pelsall La, Rushall, Walsall,
   West Midlands WS4 1NG;
   URL www.educationwalsall.com; Tel 01922 686200;
   Fax 01922 686286
Managing Director   Helen Denton; Tel 01922 686212

Warwickshire County Council

www.warwickshire.gov.uk

Population: 505 860
Political composition: Con: 27, Lab: 23, LD: 11, Ind: 1
Shire Hall, Warwick, Warwickshire CV34 4RR;
   URL www.warwickshire.gov.uk; Tel 01926 410410
Chief Executive   J. Graham

Education Department

22 Northgate St, Warwick, Warwickshire CV34 4SP; e-mail
   edcomms@warwickshire.gov.uk; Fax 01926 412746
Director (Resources)   Jeff Mann
Head (Schools Effectiveness Service)   Stella Blackmore
Manager (ICT Strategy)   John Parmiter
County Education Officer   Eric Wood MSc
Assistant County Education Officer (Community Division)
   Elizabeth Featherstone
Assistant County Education Officer (SEN)   Geoff King
Assistant County Education Officer (Strategy Division)
   Mark Gore

Area Education Officer (Central Area)   Tim Howram
Area Education Officer (Eastern Area)   Peter Thompson
Area Education Officer (North Warwickshire Area)
   Mr D. Potter
Area Education Officer (Nuneaton and Bedworth)   Nigel Mills
Area Education Officer (Southern Area School Team)
   Lynsey Wright
Assistant Education Officer (Business Services)   John Fletcher
Principal Education Social Worker   Viv Sales
14–19 Policy Development Officer   Lynne Upton
Contact (Children Act Project)   Jim Fitzgibbon
Number of Schools
37 Secondary; 10 Special

EDUCATIONAL DEVELOPMENT SERVICE

Manor Hall   Sandy La, Leamington Spa, Warwickshire
   CV32 6RD; e-mail eds@warwickshire.gov.uk
   Tel (schools' library service advice line) 01926 413461;
   Tel (education development service) 01926 413702;
   Tel (numeracy centre) 01926 413717; Tel (governor
   training) 01926 413723; Tel (assessment team)
   01926 413737; Tel (literacy centre) 01926 413749
Marle Hall Residential Centre   Marle La, Llandudno
   Junction, Gwynedd LL31 9JA; e-mail
   marlehall.oec@learnfree.co.uk; Tel 01492 581218;
   Fax 01492 581218

West Midlands Metropolitan Area

The following metropolitan councils comprise the West
Midlands Metropolitan Area and are listed separately in this
section: Birmingham, Coventry, Dudley, Sandwell, Solihull,
Walsall, and Wolverhampton.

Wolverhampton City Council

www.wolverhampton.gov.uk

Population: 240 500
Political composition: Lab: 36, Con: 19, LD: 3, Ind: 1, LIF: 1
Civic Centre, St Peters Sq, Wolverhampton, West Midlands
   WV1 1RT; URL www.wolverhampton.gov.uk; e-mail
   (Chief Executive's Department)
   richard.carr@wolverhampton.gov.uk; Tel 01902 556556;
   Fax (Chief Executive's Department) 01902 554030
Chief Executive   Richard Carr; Tel 01902 554000;
   Fax 01902 554030

Children and Young People's Services

Area 3, St Peter's Sq, Wolverhampton, West Midlands
   WV1 1RR; e-mail educ.mail@wolverhampton.gov.uk;
   Fax 01902 550326
Cabinet Member (Children and Young People)
   Cllr Paula Brookfield
Cabinet Member (Schools)   Cllr Christine Irvine
Director (Children and Young People)   Roy Lockwood
*Deputy Director (Children and Young People: Strategy and
   Resources)*   D. Rawlinson MA
Manager (School Strategy and Policy)   Paul Dean BSc, PGCE,
   ACP
Chief Officer (Quality and Improvement)   Mark Wyatt; Jennie
   Lee Professional Centre, Lichfield Rd, Wolverhampton,
   West Midlands WV11 3HT; Tel 01902 555283;
   Fax 01902 555281
Senior Education Adviser (Intervention)   David Harris
Senior Adviser (Commissioning and Partnership Development)
   John O'Connor BPhil, CertEd
Principal Inspector (Primary)   David Lawrence
Principal Inspector (Service Improvement)   Keith Martin
*Senior Inspector (Secondary: Curriculum Innovation and Co-
   ordination)*   Rita Chowdhury

Senior Inspector (Secondary/EDP)   Peter Wilson
Headteacher Inspector; Adviser (Primary)   Peter Robertson
Number of schools
18 Secondary; 7 Special

GOVERNOR TRAINING SERVICE

The Jennie Lee Professional Centre, Lichfield Rd,
  Wolverhampton, West Midlands WV11 3HT;
  Tel 01902 555271; Fax 01902 555251
Governor Training Co-ordinator   Pam Waldron
Services offered
A varied annual course programme for governors,
including support for specific categories of governor; an on-
site consultancy service to identify governing body training
needs leading to tailor-made training sessions; an
information service which includes the production of a
termly governor newsletter; and provision of training
materials for local and central resource banks

PROFESSIONAL CENTRE

Jennie Lee Professional Centre   Lichfield Rd, Wednesfield,
  Wolverhampton, West Midlands WV11 3HT;
  Tel 01902 555911; Fax 01902 555966

WEST MIDLANDS CONSORTIUM SERVICE FOR TRAVELLING CHILDREN

The Graiseley Centre, Pool St, Wolverhampton, West
  Midlands WV2 4NE; e-mail
  wmcstc@wolverhampton.gov.uk; Tel 01902 714646;
  Fax 01902 714202
Co-ordinator   Kevin Pace

Worcestershire County Council

www.worcestershire.gov.uk

In April 1998 Hereford and Worcester County Council split
to form one unitary authority (Herefordshire Council) and
one two-tier authority (Worcestershire County Council).
Both are listed separately in this section.
Political composition: Con: 29, Lab: 17, LD: 8, Liberal: 2,
Independent Health Concern: 1
County Hall, Spetchley Rd, Worcester, Worcestershire
  WR5 2NP; URL www.worcestershire.gov.uk;
  Tel 01905 763763; Minicom 01905 766399
Chief Executive   Trish Haines
Director (Adult and Community)   Eddie Clarke
Director (Children's Services)   Richard Hubbard
Director (Corporate Services)   Patrick Birch
Director (Environmental Services)   John Hobbs
Director (Financial Services)   Mike Weaver
Director (Planning, Economy and Performance)   Diane Tilley

Children's Services Offices

Fax 01905 766860
Head (Commissioning and Quality)   Richard Keble
Head (Community Partnership)   Geoff Taylor Smith
Head (Integrated Services)   Anne Binney
Head (Raising Achievement and Access to Learning)
  Colin Weeden
Manager (Service Development: 16+ Targeted Services)
  Simon Rushall
Manager (Service Development: Access and Accommodation)
  Geoff Roberts
Manager (Service Development: Additional Needs)
  Kathy Roberts
*Manager (Service Development: Area Services North East
  Worcestershire)*   Enid Noctor
*Manager (Service Development: Area Services North West
  Worcestershire)*   Siobhan Williams

*Manager (Service Development: Area Services South
  Worcestershire)*   Stuart Watkins
*Manager (Service Development: Children with Disabilities/
  Complex Health Needs)*   Chris Parker
*Manager (Service Development: Commissioning and
  Contracting)*   Asa Johnsson Humphries
Manager (Service Development: Community Capacity)
  Peter Sugg
Manager (Service Development: Early Years and Childcare)
  Alison Hitchins
*Manager (Service Development: Education, Performance and
  Development)*   Ray Westwood
Manager (Service Development: Extended Services)
  Zoe Cookson
Manager (Service Development: Family Support)
  Jean Pickering
Manager (Service Development: Learning Opportunities)
  Anne Scarsbrook
*Manager (Service Development: Looked After and Adopted
  Children)*   Julie Elliot
Manager (Service Development: Quality Performance)
  Lisa Peaty
Manager (Service Development: Resources)   Andy McHale
*Manager (Service Development: Safeguarding Quality
  Assurance)*   Alan Ferguson
Manager (Service Development: School Systems)
  Alison Cartwright
Manager (Service Development: Vulnerable Children)
  Chris Golbourne
*Manager (Service Development: Workforce and Practice
  Development)*   Debbie Key
Manager (Service Development: Youth Offending Service)
  Andy McConnochie
Manager (Service Development: Youth Support)
  Bridget Cooper
Number of Schools
179 Primary; 17 Middle Deemed Secondary; 29 Secondary;
10 Special; 9 PRU; 5 Middle Deemed Primary; 1 Nursery

TEACHERS' CENTRES

Finstall Centre   Stoke Rd, Aston Fields, Bromsgrove,
  Worcestershire B60 3EN; Tel 01527 570566;
  Fax 01527 570763
Centre Administrator   Barbara Hedges
Inspection, Advice and Training Centre   Pitmaston Hse,
  Malvern Rd, Worcester, Worcestershire WR2 4LL;
  Tel 01905 425000; Fax 01905 740121
Contact   Kim Drinkwater
Worcestershire Arts Education Centre   The Elgar Centre,
  Crown East La, Lower Broadheath, Worcestershire
  WR2 6RH; Tel 01905 333505; Fax 01905 333506

COUNTY OUTDOOR EDUCATION CENTRES

Llanrug Outdoor Education Centre   Llanrug, Caernarfon,
  Gwynedd LSS 4AP; e-mail office@llanrugoec.org.uk;
  Tel 01286 672136; Fax 01286 675697
Head   Jon Elliott
Malvern Hills Outdoor Education Centre   Old Hollow, West
  Malvern, Worcestershire WR14 4NR; e-mail
  keithfalconer@malvernhills.soc.co.uk; Tel 01684 574546;
  Fax 01684 893931
Head   Phil Ascough
Upton Warren Outdoor Education Centre   Bromsgrove,
  Worcestershire B61 7ER; e-mail
  uwoecenquiries@worcestershire.gov.uk;
  Tel 01527 861426; Fax 01527 861799
Head   Phil Ascough

RESIDENTIAL HOMES

Children's Medium Stay Home   71–72 Walton Cl, Winyates,
  Redditch B98 0NS; e-mail gesson@worcestershire.gov.uk;
  Tel 01527 501394; Fax 01527 515647
Unit Manager   Garry Esson

Green Hill Lodge Green La, Merrimans Hill, Worcester, Worcestershire WR3 8LE; e-mail yyafai@worcestershire.gov.uk; Tel 01905 24378; Fax 01905 24415
Unit Manager Yaf Yafai
Hill View 126 Barnards Green Rd, Malvern; e-mail jshaw3@worcestershire.gov.uk; Tel 01684 575709; Fax 01684 568330
Unit Manager Jake Shaw
Redditch Immediate Response Unit 45 Downsell Rd, Webheath, Redditch B97 5RJ; e-mail sstreather@worcestershire.gov.uk; Tel 01527 543135; Fax 01527 540243
Manager Simon Streather
Vale Lodge Four Pools La, Evesham WR11 1BN; e-mail amcgonigle@worcestershire.gov.uk; Tel 01386 443170; Fax 01386 47287
Unit Manager Alan McGonigle

YORKSHIRE AND THE HUMBER

Barnsley Metropolitan Borough Council
www.barnsley.gov.uk

Population: 223 500
Political composition: Lab: 33, Ind: 21, Con: 5, LD: 2, Non-aligned: 2
Town Hall, Barnsley, South Yorkshire S70 2TA; URL www.barnsley.gov.uk
Chief Executive Phil Coppard
Deputy Chief Executive; Executive Director (Development) David Kennedy
Cabinet Spokesperson (Education) Cllr Linda Burgess
Cabinet Support Member (Education) Cllr Denise Wilde
Executive Director (Children, Young People and Families) Edna Sutton
Executive Director (Environmental Services) Geoff Birkett
Executive Director (Finance) Steve Pick
Director (Public Health) Paul Redgrave
Borough Secretary Andrew Frosdick

Education Department

Berneslai Cl, Barnsley, South Yorkshire S70 2HS; Tel 01226 773500
Executive Director (Education) Edna Sutton
Assistant Director (Learning and Innovation) Rick Lohan
Assistant Director (Performance, Infrastructure and Development) Steven Mair
Head (Business Innovation and Partnerships) Daniel Hennessy
Head (Children and Young Adults Services) M. Vigurs
Head (Information Management Performance and Finance) Louise Nock
Head (Infrastructure for Learning) Tom Storey
Head (Innovation for Learning) David Donnelly
Head (Learning Services) Graham Lund
Manager (Longcar PDC) S. Horton
Manager (Secondary Strategy) Wil Andrews
Chief Libraries Officer Catherine Green
Number of Schools
82 Primary; 14 Secondary; 1 Special

CABINET MEMBERS

Lab: 13
Members of the Committee
Lab: J. Andrews, D. Bostwick, L. Burgess, K. Dyson, A. Gardiner, A. Hancock, S. Houghton, R. Miller, M. Morgan, B. Newman, A. Schofield, M. Stokes, D.. Wilde

EDUCATION WELFARE OFFICE
Berneslai Close Barnsley, South Yorkshire S70 2HS; Tel 01226 773500

PROFESSIONAL DEVELOPMENT CENTRE
Barnsley Learning Services Longcar Professional Development Centre, Longcar La, Barnsley, South Yorkshire S70 6BB; Tel 01226 281961; Fax 01226 731061

City of Bradford Metropolitan District Council
www.bradford.gov.uk

Population: 480 750
City Hall, Bradford, West Yorkshire BD1 1HY; URL www.bradford.gov.uk; e-mail david.kennedy@bradford.gov.uk; Tel 01274 432111; Fax 01274 432065
Chief Executive David Kennedy

Education Bradford

Future Hse, Bolling Rd, Bradford, West Yorkshire BD4 7EB; e-mail info@eb.serco.com; Tel 01274 385500; Fax 01274 385588
Managing Director John Gaskin
Director (Access and Inclusion) Denise Faulconbridge; Tel 01274 385799
Director (Commercial) Nigel Woodworth; Tel 01274 385716
Director (Operations) Steve Humphreys; Tel 01274 385849
Director (Programme Team) Alan Jarvis; Tel 01274 385705
Director (Standards and Effectiveness) Heather Rushton; Tel 01274 385719
Head (Buckden House Outdoor Education Centre) Tony Seddon; Tel 01756 760254
Head (Contract Services) Neil Stoddart; Laisterdyke Offices, Beswick Cl, Bradford, West Yorkshire BD3 8HW; Fax 01274 656077
Head (Education Information Services) Anthony Mugan; Tel 01274 385515
Head (Ingleborough Hall Outdoor Education Centre) Tom Redfern; Tel 01524 251265
Head (Park Primary PRU) Mrs S. Smith
Head (Pupil Referral Unit) Elaine Collins; Tel 01274 620807
Head (School Funding) Alan Jarvis; Tel 01274 385705
Head (SEC Pupil Referral Unit: Woodend) Angela McCullah; Tel 01274 599784
Head (Secondary PRU: College Provision) John Linney; Tel 01274 436423
Head of Service (Greenfield Support Unit) Janet Taylor; Tel 01274 614092
Strategic Manager (Equality and Ethnic Minority Achievement) Ros Garside; Tel 01274 385796
Strategic Manager (Excellence in Cities) David Pye; Fax 01274 385921
Strategic Manager (Key Stage 3) Martin McArthur; Tel 01274 385931
Strategic Manager (Music/Arts/Sport) Graham Cox; Tel 01274 385546
Strategic Manager (PSHE/NHSS) June Sanderson; Tel 01274 385933
Strategic Manager (SEN) Clive Halliwell; Tel 01274 385970
General Manager (West Yorkshire Transport Service) Geoff Binnington; Tel 01274 385584
Manager (Bradford Education Business Partnership) Bob Jones; Tel 01274 385837
Manager (Commercial and Business Support) Susan Wilkinson; Tel 01274 385829
Manager (Facilities) Janine Munday; Tel 01274 385903
Manager (Human Resources Advisory Services) Stephen Pearce; Fax 01274 385884
Manager (ICT: CSMG) Wendell James; Tel 01274 385808

Manager (Learning Support) Bill Turner; Tel 01274 385833
Manager (Pupil Access) Jennie Sadowskyj;
Tel 01274 385617
Manager (School Governor Service) John Hesketh; e-mail
john.hesketh@educationbradford.com; Tel 01274 385629;
Fax 01274 385624
Operations Manager (Human Resources Service)
Richard Boughey; Tel 07771 816967; Fax 01274 385983
Headteacher (SEC Pupil Referral Unit: Aireview) Trevor Loft;
Tel 01274 593123
Headteacher (SEC Pupil Referral Unit: Jesse Street)
Karen Sullivan; Tel 01274 491986
Principal Education Social Worker Barbara Lawrie;
Tel 01274 385789
Co-ordinator (Education Service for Traveller Children)
Paul Johnson; Tel 01274 385557
Co-ordinator (Secondary Support) Kevin McAleese;
Tel 01274 385721
Continuous Professional Development John Williams;
Tel 01274 385912
Education Library Service Graham Cox; Tel 01274 385577;
Fax 01274 385588
Exclusions Officer; Transport Officer (Pupil Access)
Angela Wood; Tel 01274 385612
Lead School Improvement Officer Brendan Grant;
Tel 01274 385736
PSHE Consultant (Life Education) Maria Burton;
Tel 01274 385949
PSHE Consultant (Life Education) Janet Forshaw;
Tel 01274 385949

Education Bradford is part of a strategic partnership for
education in Bradford. The other partners are Bradford
Council, the Education Policy Partnership and schools.
Education Bradford, which signed a 10 year contract with
the council in July 2001, provides support services to schools
and employs most of the central support staff. Nursery
education, lifelong learning and awards remain the
responsibility of the council.
Number of Schools
159 Primary; 28 Secondary; 11 Special; 7 PRU
Requisition Periods for Schools Supplies
1 April to 31 December

EXECUTIVE

Con: 6
c/o City Hall, Bradford, West Yorkshire BD1 1HY
Leader of the Council M. Eaton (Con)
Deputy Leader K. Hopkins (Con)
Education Portfolio Holder D. Smith (Con)
Members of the Committee
Con: S. Cooke, M. Eaton, A. Hawkesworth, K. Hopkins,
B.M. Smith, D. Smith

PUPIL REFERRAL UNITS

Bradford Primary PRU Avenue Rd, West Bowling,
Bradford, West Yorkshire BD5 8DB; e-mail
catherine.carroll@primarypru.ngfl.ac.uk;
Tel 01274 735298; Fax 01274 733795
Headteacher Mrs S. Smith
Bradford Secondary PRU (Aireview) Strong Close Nursery,
Green Head La, Keighley, West Yorkshire BD20 6ER;
e-mail office@aireview.ngfl.ac.uk; Tel 01274 593123;
Fax 01274 594705
Headteacher Mr T. Loft
Bradford Secondary PRU (Ellar Carr) Ellar Carr Rd,
Thackley, Bradford, West Yorkshire BD10 0TD; e-mail
elaine.collins@ellarcarr.ngfl.ac.uk; Tel 01274 612176;
Fax 01274 619050
Headteacher Ms E. Collins
Head (KS3 Centre) Mrs S. Todd
Bradford Secondary PRU (KS4) Firth Bldgs, Wrose Brow,
Shipley, West Yorkshire BD18 1NT; Tel 01274 599784;
Fax 01274 531507
Head Mrs A. McCullough

Bradford College PRU Rm Q6, Old Bldg, BICC, Gt Horton
Rd, Bradford, West Yorkshire BD7 1AY;
Tel 01274 436423; Fax 01274 738723
Head Mr J. Linney
Jesse Street PRU Jesse St, Bradford, West Yorkshire
BD8 0JQ; e-mail office@prejesse.ngfl.ac.uk;
Tel 01274 491986; Fax 01274 548343
Head Mrs K. Sullivan
Newlands (Pregnant Schoolgirl Unit) McMllan Halls of
Residence, Easby Rd, Bradford, West Yorkshire
BD7 1QZ; Tel 01274 626458; Fax 01274 630635
Head of Unit Mrs S. Ahir
Head of Unit Mrs H. English

Calderdale Metropolitan Borough Council

www.calderdale.gov.uk

Population: 194 300
Political composition: Con: 18, LD: 16, Lab: 11, Ind: 3; BNP:
1; English Democrats Party: 1; Other: 1
The Town Hall, Halifax, West Yorkshire HX1 1UJ;
URL www.calderdale.gov.uk; e-mail
chiefexecutive@calderdale.gov.uk; Tel 0845 245 6000;
Fax 01422 393102
Chief Executive Owen Williams

Children and Young People's Services

Northgate Hse, Northgate, Halifax, West Yorkshire
HX1 1UN; e-mail cyps@calderdale.gov.uk;
Tel 01422 392511; Fax 01422 392515
Group Director Carol White
Head (Adult and Community Learning) Eileen Fawcett
Head (Business and Improvement) Ian Dodgson
Head (Care Services) David Ashworth (Acting)
Head (Family Services) Anne Scarborough
Head (Learning Services) Paul Brennan
Head (Partnerships and Commissioning) Sue Rumbold
Head (School Improvement Service) Stewart Bradley
Chief Finance Officer Pete Smith
Principal Psychologist Min O'Hara
Principal Officer (Access and Capital) Alan Winstanley
Principal Officer (Business Support Manager) Mark Woolley
Principal Officer (Child Protection) John Murray
Principal Officer (Commissioning and Partnership); Manager
(Children's Fund Programme) Karen Squillino
Principal Officer (Family Services) Steve Woodhead
Principal Officer (Inclusion Services) Peter Flower
Principal Officer (Integrated Assessments) Iain Low
Principal Officer (Intensive Family Support) Ashley Parkin
Principal Officer (Looked After Children) Sheila Barton
Principal Officer (Performance Support and ICT) Moira Hall
Principal Officer (Placements: Fostering and Adoption)
Lynn Radley
Principal Officer (Placements: Residential) Vacancy
Principal Officer (Policy and Plannning) Andrew Ramsay
Principal Officer (Safeguarding Manager) Paul Sharkey
Principal Officer (School Link) Mary Jackson
Principal Officer (School Link) Lawrence Killian
Principal Officer (Young People's Services) Carol Stone
Number of Schools
15 Secondary; 3 Special
Day of Committee Meeting
Tuesday; three meetings in six weekly cycles
Requisition Periods for Schools Supplies
No fixed dates

CABINET

Chair Megan Swift (Lab)
Portfolio Holder (Children and Young People's Services)
Cllr Craig Whittaker

Members of the Committee
Con: Geraldine Carter, Richard Marshall
Lab: Danielle Coombs, Megan Swift
LD: Nader Fekri, Conrad Winterburn
English Democrats Paul Rogan

GOVERNOR SUPPORT TEAM

Health Training and Development Centre, Free School La,
 Halifax, West Yorkshire HX1 2PT; Tel 01422 394084;
 Fax 01422 394083
Governor Training Programme Administrator Vacancy
Governor Support Officer Vacancy
Services offered
Comprehensive range of courses addressing issues relative
to school government. These courses are available to
governors generally or to individual governing bodies.
Some current courses, including those on personnel issues
and drawing the line, are marketed nationally.

YOUNG PEOPLE'S SERVICE

Headquarters Children and Young People's Services,
 Northgate Hse, Northgate, Education Department,
 Halifax, West Yorkshire HX1 1UN
 Young People's Service Manager Bryan Brooks; e-mail
 bryan.brookssnr@calderdale.gov.uk; Tel 01422 392559;
 Fax 01422 392506
 *Young People's Service Manager (Curriculum
 Development)* Patrick Ambrose; e-mail
 patrick.ambrose@calderdale.gov.uk; Tel 01422 392579;
 Fax 01422 392506
 Principal Officer (Young People's Services) Carol Stone;
 e-mail carol.stone@calderdale.gov.uk; Tel 01422 392495;
 Fax 01422 392506
 Assistant Principal Officer (Young People's Services)
 Chris Eves; e-mail chris.eves@calderdale.gov.uk;
 Tel 01422 392684; Fax 01422 392506
 Area Youth Co-ordinator (Brighouse and Rastrick)
 Mohammed Rahoof; e-mail
 mohammedrahoof@yahoo.co.uk; Tel 01422 205034
 Area Youth Work Co-ordinator (North Halifax)
 Denise Chafer; e-mail denise.chafer@calderdale.gov.uk;
 Tel 01422 254220; Fax 01422 361646
 *Area Youth Work Co-ordinator (Sowerby Bridge and
 Elland)* Ian Hodges; e-mail
 ian.hodges@calderdale.gov.uk; Tel 01422 839526;
 Fax 01422 833642
 Area Youth Work Co-ordinator (Upper Calder Valley)
 Lorraine Daber; e-mail
 lorraine.daber@calderdale.gov.uk; Tel 01706 548186
 Area Youth Work Co-ordinator (West Central Halifax)
 Shabina Mir; e-mail shabina.mir@calderdale.gov.uk;
 Tel 01422 255003; Fax 01422 365757
Adult Learning Horton Hse, Horton St, Halifax, West
 Yorkshire HX1 1PU; Tel 01422 392820; Fax 01422 392821
 Head (Calderdale Adult Learning) Eileen Fawcett
 Manager (Data and Administrative Support Services)
 Jane Hemingway

SCHOOL IMPROVEMENT

Heath Training and Development Centre Free School La,
 Halifax, West Yorkshire HX1 2PT; Tel 01422 394068;
 Fax 01422 394083
 Head (School Improvement Officer) Stewart Bradley
 Principal School Link Officer (3–11) Lawrence Killian
 Principal School Link Officer (11–19) Mary Jackson
 School Link Officer (SIP, Data Analysis and Standards)
 Mike Hull
 School Link Officer (SIP, 11–19) John Burwell
 School Link Officer (SIP, 11–19) Kate Lounds
 *School Link Officer (SIP, 11–19); Secondary Strategy
 Manager* Diane Lightowler
 School Link Officer (SIP, 11–19, SCC Functional Skills)
 Lindsey Murray
 School Link Officer (SIP, Early Years Foundation Stage)
 Kim Porter

School Link Officer (SIP, Inclusive Learning)
Trish Lowson
School Link Officer (SIP, KS1 Assessment for Learning)
Carol Thomas
*School Link Officer (SIP, Primary MFL, Governor Support,
 EOTAS)* Phil Hawker
*School Link Officer (SIP, Quality Marks, CPD, PNS
 Improving Schools Programme)* Tina Warden
*School Link Officer (SIP, Workforce Remodelling, PNS New
 Frameworks)* Jo Campbell
School Improvement Partner (Primary) Pauline Hilling-
Smith
School Improvement Partner (Primary) Linda Wardle
School Improvement Partner (Primary, Special)
Shirley Stoker
School Improvement Partner (Secondary) Neil Donkin
School Improvement Partner (Secondary) Deanna Drake
School Improvement Partner (Secondary) David Farrant
School Improvement Officer (SIP, 11–19) Craig Shipton

Doncaster Metropolitan Borough Council

www.doncaster.gov.uk

Population: 292 877
Political composition: Lab: 28, LD: 12, Con: 9, Ind: 9,
Community Candidate: 6
2 Priory Pl, Doncaster, South Yorkshire DN1 1BN;
 URL www.doncaster.gov.uk; Tel 01302 734444;
 Fax 01302 734040
Managing Director Susan Law
Strategic Director (Development) Peter Dale
*Strategic Director (Neighbourhoods, Communities and Children's
 Services)* Mark Hodson
Strategic Director (Organisational Development and Culture)
 Paul Hart
Strategic Director (Policy, Partnership and Governance)
 Tal Michael
Specialist Director (Education Standards) Mark Eales

Directorate of Education Standards

PO Box 266, The Council Hse, College Rd, Doncaster, South
 Yorkshire DN1 3AD; Tel 01302 737222; Fax 01302 737223
Director M.S. Eales
Group Director (School Improvement) S.P. Chew
Principal Education Officer (Governance) R.P. McCormick
*Principal Education Officer (Inspection, Performance and
 Data)* Mrs S. Howarth
Senior Area Education Standards Officer M. Duffy
Senior Area Education Standards Officer A. Martin
Senior Area Education Standards Officer K. Wildgoose
Principal Adviser N.P. Stewart
Senior Adviser G. Haney
Senior Adviser I. Peel (Acting)
Number of Schools
17 Secondary; 7 Special
**Other Authorities with whom Joint Purchasing Arrangements
are made**
Yorkshire Purchasing Organisation

CABINET RESPONSIBILITIES

Contact (Schools and Children) Cllr Mrs C. Mills; 4 Park
 Ave, Conisbrough, Doncaster, South Yorkshire
 DN12 2EL

PROFESSIONAL DEVELOPMENT CENTRE

Carr House Centre, Danum Rd, Doncaster, South Yorkshire
 DN4 5HF; Tel 01302 734258; Fax 01302 734713
Contact L. Stevenson

GOVERNORS' SUPPORT SERVICE

Doncaster Metropolitan Council, PO Box 266, Doncaster, South Yorkshire DN1 3AD; Tel 01302 737111; Fax 01302 737223

Principal Education Officer (Governance) R.P. McCormick

Services offered

The Governors' Support Service arranges for induction courses to be provided throughout the year to new governors. A comprehensive directory of courses available is circulated to all governors and schools. Courses can be customised to meet the identified needs of individual governing bodies. Governing bodies are also supported by briefing sessions for clerks, a governors' helpline, and the publication of a termly governors' newsletter.

MUSIC CENTRE

Doncaster Music Service Danum Rd, Doncaster, South Yorkshire DN4 5HF; Tel 01302 323556; Fax 01302 323605
Head of Service Vacancy

East Riding of Yorkshire Council

www.eastriding.gov.uk

Population: 327 400 (mid 2005 estimate)
Political composition: Con: 47, LD: 12, Lab: 3, Ind: 4, SDP: 1
County Hall, Beverley, East Riding of Yorkshire HU17 9BA; URL www.eastriding.gov.uk; e-mail info@eastriding.gov.uk; Tel 01482 887700
Chief Executive N. Pearson
Director (Children, Family and Adult Services) Alison Waller
Director (Corporate Policy and Strategy) B. Adams
Director (Corporate Resources) S. Lockwood
Director (Customer Services) H. Roberts

Directorate of Children, Family and Adult Services

e-mail alison.waller@eastriding.gov.uk; Tel 01482 392000; Fax 01482 392002
Assistant Director (Children and Young People's Services) Philip Holmes
Head (Culture and Information) Richard Primmer (Acting)
Head (Improvement and Learning) Mike Furbank
Head (Inclusion) Denise Shaw
Manager (Inclusion and SEN) Roy Thompson
Manager (Learning and Skills) Margaret Walker
Manager (Libraries, Arts and Heritage) Alan Moir
Manager (Performance Team) Lesley Dearing
Manager (School Governance) Bill Jackson
Accountant (Schools Management) Lisa Forster
Number of Schools
18 Secondary; 3 Special

CHILDREN AND YOUNG PEOPLE

Chair Clark (Lab)
Vice-Chair Pickering (Lab)
Members of the Committee
Con: Gilmour, Hudson, Jackson, Pollard, Rudd
LD: Kay, Lynn, McClure, Walker
Ind: Gray

Humberside County Council

In April 1996 Humberside County Council, Beverley Borough Council, Boothferry Borough Council, Cleethorpes Borough Council, East Yorkshire Borough Council, Glanford Borough Council, Great Grimsby Borough Council, Holderness Borough Council, Hull City Council and Scunthorpe Borough Council were replaced by East Riding of Yorkshire Council, Kingston upon Hull City

Council, North East Lincolnshire Council and North Lincolnshire Council, each responsible for all local government services in its area. These councils are listed separately in this section.

Kingston upon Hull City Council

www.hullcc.gov.uk

Population: 269 144
Political composition: LD: 30, Lab: 20, N.E.W. Hull Independent Group: 6, Conservative and Unionist: 2, Ind: 1
Guildhall, Alfred Gelder St, Kingston upon Hull, East Riding of Yorkshire HU1 2AA; URL www.hullcc.gov.uk; Tel 01482 300300
Chief Executive Kim Ryley

Children and Young People's Services

Brunswick Hse, Strand Cl, Beverley Rd, Kingston upon Hull, East Riding of Yorkshire HU2 9DB; Tel 01482 616159
Director (Children and Young People's Services) Nigel Richardson
Head (Commissioning and Business Support) Mike Pinnock
Head (Health and Wellbeing) Pauline Dumble
Head (Learning, Leisure and Achievement) Judith Harwood
Head (Safeguarding and Development) Jon Plant
Assistant Head (Intensive Support) Dez Allenby
Assistant Head (Primary Phase: Universal) Ken Sainty
Assistant Head (Secondary Phase: Universal) Sue Johnson
Assistant Head (Targeted Support) Lyn Banks
Assistant Head of Service (Education Project Adviser) Ingvar Spencer
Manager (Human Resources) S. Herrick

CABINET COMMITTEE

Holder of Portfolio (Lifelong Learning) Cllr Ross (LD)
Members Information Officer Brian Hill
Members of the Cabinet
LD: Baker, Collinson, Healand, Minns, Neal, Randall, Ross, Sloan, Walker, Woods

Kirklees Metropolitan Council

www.kirkleesmc.gov.uk

Population: 390 900
Political composition: LD: 29, Lab: 25, Con: 15, Green: 3
Civic Centre 3, Market St, Huddersfield, West Yorkshire HD1 1WG; URL www.kirkleesmc.gov.uk; Tel 01484 221000; Fax 01484 221777
Chief Executive T. Elson

Education Service

Oldgate Hse, 2 Oldgate, Huddersfield, West Yorkshire HD1 6QW; e-mail gavin.tonkin@kirklees.gov.uk; Tel 01484 225242; Fax 01484 225237
Director (Lifelong Learning) Gavin Tonkin MA
Assistant Director (Community Education and Regeneration) T. Irwin MSc, PhD
Assistant Director (Education Strategy and School Support) M. Parker
Assistant Director (Pupil Support) Liz Dobie
Assistant Director (School Effectiveness) Judith Waddington
Head (Assessment and Performance) J. Brown BSc, MEd
Head (EBD Service) P. Craig
Head (Education 3–11) A. Davis
Head (Education 11–19) D. Gilleard
Head (Education Access) Joe Wilson BSc(Hons), CQSW, DipFT, CMS

Head (Ethnic Minority Achievement and Equalities)   B. Birring
Head (Inclusion)   Liz Godman BSc, PGCE, MEd
Head (Kirklees Early Years Service)   C. Renshaw (Acting)
Head (Management)   Janice Whelan MA, BEd
Head (Monitoring)   Vacancy
Head (Post-16 and Adult Education)   S. Whittingham
Head (Professional Practice: Psychological Service)   J. Bamford
Head (Resources: Lifelong Learning Resources Group)
   Tony Gerrard
Head (SEN Support Services)   G. Sunderland
Head (Service Planning and Development)
   Andrew Pennington
Head (Strategic IT)   C. Williams BSc, DipCE
Head (Young People's Service)   I. York
Manager (Group Catering and Cleaning Resource)
   J.D. Rayner
Manager (Group Finance)   R.W. Askham BA, IPFA
Manager (Group Personnel)   K. Blackburn
School Improvement Officer (The Arts)   Vacancy
School Improvement Officer (Careers Education Guidance and
   Assessment)   K. Massett
School Improvement Officer (Design and Technology)
   A. Likeman
School Improvement Officer (Early Years)   A. Lockett
School Improvement Officer (English)   J. Walsh
School Improvement Officer (Geography and Environmental
   Education)   D. Palfrey
School Improvement Officer (History)   D. Thompson
School Improvement Officer (Management)   S. Thomas
School Improvement Officer (Mathematics)   E. Greenslade
School Improvement Officer (Middle Schools and Primary
   Science)   M. Shimell BA, CertEd
School Improvement Officer (Modern Foreign Languages)
   P. Cummings
School Improvement Officer (Multi-Ethnic Achievement)
   L. Lewis
School Improvement Officer (Music)   B. Lawson
School Improvement Officer (National Literacy Strategy)
   D. Bowgett
School Improvement Officer (PE)   E. Marchant
School Improvement Officer (Primary Education)   J. Bolton
School Improvement Officer (Primary Education)   A. Wathen
School Improvement Officer (Primary Education)   S. Wild
School Improvement Officer (Primary IT)   E. Torr
School Improvement Officer (Primary/Mathematics)
   T. Caulton
School Improvement Officer (PSHE)   G. Hofman
School Improvement Officer (RE)   C. Markham CertEd, BEd,
   CertHealthEd, AdDipEdMgt
School Improvement Officer (Science and Management
   Development)   K. Gueli
School Improvement Officer (Secondary Vocational Education
   and Business Studies)   S. O'Hara
School Improvement Officer (SEN)   A. Tierney
Education Development Officer (Community Partnerships)
   S. Laher
Education Development Officer (Planning and Capital)
   Barbara Challenger
Education Development Officer (Planning and Capital)
   D. Martin
Co-ordinator (Adult Education Planning and Development)
   P. Crosbie
Number of Schools
32 Secondary; 8 Special (under review)

CABINET

Chair   J.R. Smithson (LD); 24 Finthorpe La, Almondbury,
   Huddersfield, West Yorkshire HD5 8TU;
   Tel 01484 312638

GOVERNOR TRAINING UNIT

Oldgate Hse, Oldgate, Huddersfield, West Yorkshire
HD1 6QW; Tel 01484 225183; Fax 01484 225361
School Improvement Officer (Governor Training)   P. Reynolds
Administration Assistant   J. Ross

Services offered
Training; support; development

OUTDOOR PURSUITS AND FIELD STUDY CENTRE

Cliffe House   140 Lane Head Rd, Shepley, Huddersfield,
   West Yorkshire HD8 8DB; e-mail
   cliffe-house@geo2.poptel.org.uk; Tel 01484 222720;
   Fax 01484 222721
Centre Manager   R.C. Swinden

ADULT EDUCATION

Almondbury Adult Education Centre   Fernside Ave,
   Almondbury, Huddersfield, West Yorkshire HD5 8PQ;
   Tel (evenings) 01484 536333
Birkenshaw Adult Education Centre   Tel (evenings)
   01274 871226
Cleckheaton Adult Education Centre   Tel (evenings)
   01274 874695
Deighton Adult Education Centre   Deighton Rd, Deighton,
   Huddersfield, West Yorkshire HD2 1JP;
   Answerphone 01484 453988
Greenhead College Adult Education Centre   Greenhead Rd,
   Huddersfield, West Yorkshire HD1 4ES; Tel (Mon, Wed
   evenings only) 01484 422032
Heckmondwike Adult Education Centre   Tel (evenings)
   01924 402202
Holmfirth Adult Education Centre   Huddersfield Rd,
   Holmfirth, West Yorkshire HD7 1AR; e-mail
   ilister@huddcoll.ac.uk; Tel 01484 682511;
   Fax 01484 680841
   Area Co-ordinator   I. Lister
Holmfirth High School Centre   Tel 01484 437171
Marsden Mechanics Institute   Tel 01484 842692
Meltham Carlisle Institute   Tel 01484 437171
Mirfield Adult Education Centre   Tel (evenings)
   01924 498161
Newsome Adult Education Centre   Newsome High School,
   Castle Ave, Huddersfield, West Yorkshire HD4 6JN;
   Tel 01484 549259 (Mon evening only)
Rawthorpe Adult Education Centre   West Yorkshire;
   Answerphone 01484 516012
Shelley Adult Education Centre   Shelley High School,
   Huddersfield Rd, Huddersfield, West Yorkshire
   HD8 8NL; Tel (evenings – term-time only) 01484 222943
Slaithwaite Adult Education Centre   Town Hall, Carr La,
   Huddersfield, West Yorkshire HD7 5AG; Tel (evening –
   term-time only) 01484 842692

Leeds City Council

www.leeds.gov.uk

Population: 750 000 (approx.)
Political composition: Lab: 40, LD: 25, Con: 24, Morley
Borough Independents: 4, Green: 3, Ind: 2, BNP: 1
Civic Hall, Leeds, West Yorkshire LS1 1UR;
   URL www.leeds.gov.uk; Tel 0113 234 8080
Chief Executive   Paul Rogerson

Education Leeds

10th Fl East, Merrion Hse, 110 Merrion Centre, Leeds, West
   Yorkshire LS2 8DT; URL www.educationleeds.co.uk;
   e-mail info@educationleeds.co.uk; Tel 0113 247 5590
Blenheim Centre (Inclusion and SEN), Crowther Pl, Leeds,
   West Yorkshire LS6 2ST; Tel 0113 395 1100;
   Fax 0113 230 4073
Chief Executive   Chris Edwards
Deputy Chief Executive   Ruth Chiva
Deputy Chief Executive   Dirk Gilleard
Deputy Chief Executive   Ros Vahey
Number of Schools
225 Primary; 40 Secondary; 6 Special

Day of Committee Meeting
Five a year

EDUCATION WELFARE SERVICE

East East Leeds Learning Centre, Brooklands Ave, Leeds, West Yorkshire LS14 1DO; Tel 0113 224 3146
Contact Brian Yeatman
North West Pk Centre, Spen La, Leeds, West Yorkshire LS16 5BE; Tel 0113 274 6711
Contact R. Atkinson
South Morley, West Yorkshire; Tel 0113 256 0622
Contact Colin Whiteley
West Hough Lane Centre, Bramley, Leeds, West Yorkshire LS13 3RD; Tel 0113 256 0622
Contact Colin Whiteley

EDUCATION PSYCHOLOGY SERVICE

Blenheim Centre, Crowther Pl, Leeds, West Yorkshire LS6 2ST; Tel 0113 242 9111
Team Leader Margery Page (Acting)
Peripatetic Service for Deaf and Hearing Impaired Children
Blenheim Centre, Crowther Pl, Leeds, West Yorkshire LS2 2ST; Tel 0113 242 9111
Service Manager M. Pickersgill
Peripatetic Service for Visually Impaired People Blenheim Centre, Crowther Pl, Leeds, West Yorkshire LS2 2ST; Tel 0113 242 9111
Service Manager E. Westwood

PUPIL REFERRAL SERVICE

Bramley Grange, West Yorkshire LS14 3DW; Tel 0113 214 4283
Service Manager P. Armour
Armley Park Centre Rombalds Ave, Armley, West Yorkshire LS12 2BB; Tel 0113 263 6810
Craven Road Centre Woodhouse Community Complex, Woodhouse St, Leeds, West Yorkshire LS6 2SN; Tel 0113 245 8715

OUTDOOR PURSUITS CENTRES (SHARED)

Buckden House Outdoor Pursuits Centre and Local Studies Base Buckden, Skipton, North Yorkshire BD23 5JA; Tel 01756 760254
Manager R. Hird
Manager A. Oates
Humphrey Head Outdoor Pursuits Centre Allithwaite, Grange-over-Sands, Cumbria LA11 7LY; Tel 01539 532881
Head A. Brown
Ingleborough Hall Outdoor Education Centre Clapham, Lancaster, West Yorkshire LA2 8EF; Tel 01524 251265
Manager T. Redfearn

TEACHERS' CENTRES

Elmete Professional Development Centre Elmete La, Leeds, West Yorkshire LS8 1PQ; Tel 0113 214 4068
Head K. Sims
ICT Development Agency Elmete La, Leeds, West Yorkshire LS8 2LJ; Tel 0113 214 4105
Contact R.D. Masterton
The West Park Centre Spa La, West Pk, Leeds, West Yorkshire LS16 5BE; Tel 0113 230 4074
Head C.P.B. Jones

North East Lincolnshire Council

www.nelincs.gov.uk

Population: 157 983
Political composition: Con: 16, LD: 15, Lab: 7, Ind: 4

Municipal Offices, Town Hall Sq, Grimsby, North East Lincolnshire DN31 1HU; URL www.nelincs.gov.uk; e-mail sue.turner@nelincs.gov.uk; Tel 01472 313131
Chief Executive George Krawiec

Directorate of Learning and Child Care

Eleanor St, Grimsby, North East Lincolnshire DN32 9DU; Tel 01472 325432; Fax 01472 323406
Executive Director Vacancy
Deputy Director (Child Care) Martin Eaden
Deputy Director (Learning) P. Lacey
Deputy Director (Support Services) Sarah Mann
Head (Primary Standards) Peter Kipling
Head (Secondary Standards) Derek Kennard
Head of Service (SEN) Vacancy
Service Manager (Business Support) Sally Jack
Principal Education Officer (Schools Services) Anita Green BPharm, MEd
Principal Education Officer (Sites and Buildings) Tony Brumfield
Number of Schools
12 Secondary; 2 Special

CABINET

Portfolio Holder (Childcare) Cllr M. Cracknell
Portfolio Holder (Education) Cllr S. Hocknell
Members of the Cabinet
K. Brooks, M. Cracknell, A. Defreitas, S. Hocknell, D. Khan, G. Lowis, P. Mills, M. Vickers

PUPIL REFERRAL UNITS

Phoenix House Harold St, Grimsby, North East Lincolnshire DN32 7NQ; e-mail office@phoenix.sch.dccl.net; Tel 01472 351412; Fax 01472 351412
Headteacher Vacancy

North Lincolnshire Council

www.northlincs.gov.uk

Population: 159 000
Political composition: Lab: 22, Con: 18, Ind: 2, LD: 1
Pittwood Hse, Ashby Rd, Scunthorpe, North Lincolnshire DN16 1AB; URL www.northlincs.gov.uk; Tel 01724 297240; Fax 01724 297242

Learning, Schools and Communities

PO Box 35, Hewson Hse, Brigg, North Lincolnshire DN20 8XJ; e-mail suzanne.watson@northlincs.gov.uk
Service Director David Lea
Director (BSF Project) Adrian J. Williamson
Head (Learning Services and School Improvement) Jo Moxon
Senior Adviser (Primary School Improvement) Deborah Holland
Senior Adviser (Secondary School Improvement) Jim Garbutt
Senior Adviser (Secondary School Improvement) Tim Harrington
Senior Education Officer (Schools) John Irving
Principal Educational Psychologist; Head (Behaviour Support) Alan Reynolds
Number of Schools
47 Primary; 13 Secondary; 10 Infant; 9 Junior; 2 Special

CHILDREN'S SERVICES

Cabinet Member Tony Gosling
Lead Member (Children's Issues) Linda Cawsey
Lead Member (Schools) Margaret Simpson

OTHER ESTABLISHMENTS

Adult Education Service   Cherry Gr, Ashby, Scunthorpe, North Lincolnshire DN16 2TH; Tel 01724 280323
Head   Andy Boak

Diversity Service and Traveller Education Team   Crosby Primary School, Frodingham Rd, Scunthorpe, North Lincolnshire DN15 7NL; Tel 01724 280207
Head of Service   Sameena Choudry

Education Business Link Organisation   Prince Hse, Arkwright Way, Queensway Industrial Est, Scunthorpe, North Lincolnshire DN16 1AD; Tel 01724 845805
Manager   Julie Duffin

Education Development Centre   South Leys Campus, Enderby Rd, Scunthorpe, North Lincolnshire DN17 2JL; Tel 01724 297177; Fax 01724 297164
Head of Centre   Donna Sumner

Educational Psychology and Behaviour Support Service   Business Link Enterprise Centre, 45a Newdown Rd, South Pk, Scunthorpe, North Lincolnshire DN17 2TX; Tel 01724 847151
Head (Behaviour Support); Principal Educational Psychologist   Alan Reynolds

John Leggott College   West Common La, Scunthorpe, North Lincolnshire DN17 1DS; Tel 01724 282998; Fax 01724 281631
Principal   Nic Dakin

North Lindsey College   Kingsway, Scunthorpe, North Lincolnshire DN17 1AH; Tel 01724 281111; Fax 01724 294020
Principal   Prof R. Bennett

Pupil Referral Unit   The Darley Centre, School Rd, Ashby, Scunthorpe, North Lincolnshire DN16 2TD; Tel 01724 296263; Fax 01724 281704
Head of Service   Mark Snowden

Specialist SEN Teaching Team   Business Link Enterprise Centre, 45a Newdown Rd, South Park Industrial Est, Scunthorpe, North Lincolnshire DN17 2TX; Tel 01724 847151
Senior Educational Psychologist   Peter Smith

Young People's Education Centre   Young People's Education Centre, Henderson Ave, Scunthorpe, North Lincolnshire DN15 7RW; Tel 01724 278668
Head   Coleen Langton

North Yorkshire County Council
www.northyorks.gov.uk

Population: 576 000
Political composition: Con: 42, LD: 18, Lab: 9, Ind: 3
County Hall, Northallerton, North Yorkshire DL7 8AD; URL www.northyorks.gov.uk; e-mail chief.exec@northyorks.gov.uk; Tel 01609 780780; Fax 01609 780447

Education Department – Children and Young People's Service

County Hall, Northallerton, North Yorkshire DL7 8AE; e-mail education@northyorks.gov.uk; Tel 01609 780780; Fax 01609 778611
Executive Member (Children's Services)   C. Patmore
Executive Member (Education)   J. Watson OBE
Corporate Director (Children and Young People's Service)   C. Welbourn MA, FRSA
Head (Continuing Education Unit)   C.J. McGee
Head (Education Finance Unit)   G.C. Bateman IPFA
Head (Policy and Development Unit)   B. Jones
Head (Pupil and Parent Services Unit)   A.P. Terry
Chief Adviser   R.P.N. Geoghegan MA
Number of Schools
328 Primary; 47 Secondary; 11 Special

CONTINUING EDUCATION UNIT

Deputy Head (Unit)   F.A. Lett
Education Officer (Community Learning: Adult)   R. Cannon
Education Officer (Community Learning Development)   T. Begley
Education Officer (Community Learning: Youth, Hambleton/Richmondshire/Scarborough/Ryedale)   R.J. Peters
Education Officer (Community Learning: Youth, Harrogate/Craven/Selby)   P. Carswell

CURRICULUM AND MANAGEMENT ADVISORY SERVICES UNIT

Manager (Music Service Unit)   V.St.D. Morgan
Manager (NYBEP)   D. Christon
Team Leader; Principal Adviser (IT)   J. Owen
Team Leader; Principal Adviser (MFL)   R.P.N. Geoghegan MA
Team Leader; Principal Adviser (RE and PSHE)   R. Lohan MEd
Principal Adviser (SEN)   G. Foster
Senior Adviser (English)   J. Peacock
Senior Adviser (Geography)   R.J. Pike
Senior Adviser (History)   M.C. Holyoak MA
Senior Adviser (Mathematics)   D. Sutherland
Senior Adviser (Physical Education)   A. McCarthy
Senior Adviser (Primary)   J. Ashmore
Senior Adviser (Primary)   G. Lund
Senior Adviser (Science)   J.H. Crossland
Senior Adviser (Secondary)   J. Brown MEd
Senior Adviser (Technology)   G. Howard
Professional Officer   Vacancy

LIBRARIES, ARTS ARCHIVES AND MUSEUMS UNIT

Principal Librarian (School Library Service)   B. Hooper (Acting) DipLibrarianship
Librarian (Public Services)   M. Gibson
Manager (Support Services)   C. Riley DMA, ACIS, MIPD
County Archivist   Vacancy

OUTPOSTED FROM CORPORATE DIRECTOR

Manager (Client Catering)   N. Postma MHCIMA
Manager (Financial Services to Schools)   R. Jacobs IPFA
Manager (Personnel)   C.S. Parkin BA, MIPD
Client Manager (Information Technology)   D.K. Bason
Principal Officer (Non-Schools Budgets)   J. Aihie (Acting)
Principal Officer (Schools-Related Budgets)   J.C. Walls

POLICY AND DEVELOPMENT UNIT

Manager (Early Years and Childcare)   J. Lowery
Manager (Governor Support and Communications)   J.H. Fairburn
Manager (Service Development and Review)   C.A. Bird BA, ALA
Capital Planning Manager (Client Commissioning)   R.E. Allen

PUPIL AND PARENT SERVICES UNIT

Manager (Access)   P.L. Mellor MA, MEd
Manager (Behaviour Support Service)   N. Ogley BA, MSc
Manager (Principal Educational Psychologist)   M. Cotton
Manager (SEN)   M. Bennett

LOCAL OFFICES

Harrogate Local Office   Local Education Office, Ainsty Rd, Harrogate, North Yorkshire HG1 4XU; URL www.northyorks.gov.uk/pps; e-mail pps.harrogate@northyorks.gov.uk; Tel 01423 700100; Fax 01423 700101

Northallerton Local Office   Local Education Office, County Hall, Northallerton, North Yorkshire DL7 8AE; Tel 01609 780780; Fax 01609 760425

Scarborough/Ryedale Local Office Local Education Office, Valley Bridge Par, Scarborough, North Yorkshire YO11 2PL; URL www.northyorks.gov.uk/pps; e-mail pps.scarborough@northyorks.gov.uk; Tel 01723 361376; Fax 01723 501496

Selby/Tadcaster Local Office Local Education Office, 2nd Fl, Selby, North Yorkshire YO8 0PS; Tel 01757 213366; Fax 01757 210205

Skipton Local Office Local Education Office, Water St, Skipton, North Yorkshire BD23 1PD; Tel 01756 792427; Fax 01756 794893

Rotherham Metropolitan Borough Council
www.rotherham.gov.uk

Population: 252 300
Political composition: Lab: 54, Con: 7, Ind: 2
The Crofts, Moorgate St, Rotherham, South Yorkshire S65 1UF; URL www.rotherham.gov.uk; e-mail chiefexecutive@rotherham.gov.uk; Tel 01709 382121
Chief Executive Mike Cuff

Children and Young People's Services

Norfolk Hse, Walker Pl, Rotherham, South Yorkshire S65 1AS; Tel 01709 382121; Fax 01709 372056
Cabinet Member Cllr Amy Rushforth
Cabinet Member Cllr Shaun Wright
Chief Education Welfare Officer Catherine Ratcliffe
Scrutiny Lead Cllr Ann Russell
Senior Director Joyce Thacker
Strategic Director Dr Sonia Sharp
Director (Children's Social Care) Pam Allen
Director (Inclusion, Voice and Influence) Tom Kelly
Director (Planning, Information and Performance) Julie Westwood
Director (Resources and Access) Graham Sinclair
Head (Behaviour Support Service) Katy Edmundson
Head (School Effectiveness Service) David Light
Commissioning Manager Laura Townson
Manager (Assessment Services, SEN and Transport) Helen Barre (Acting)
Manager (Catering Services) Ron Parry
Manager (Community Learning and Wellbeing) Helen Shaw
Manager (External Funding and Regeneration) Jeanette Lane
Manager (Performance, Information and Quality) Sue Wilson
Manager (Policy, Planning and Partnerships) Clare Bailey
Manager (Safeguarding) Jim Stewart
Manager (Schools Organisation, Planning and Development) David Hill
Manager (Student Support) Alison Leone
Manager (Sports and Leisure Facilities) Mark Humphries
Manager (Workforce Planning, Training and Development) Patrick Appleyard
Manager (Young People's Services) George Simpson (Acting)
Project Manager (South Yorkshire e-learning Programme) Dave Ashmore
Principal Educational Psychologist Steve Mulligan
Principal Officer (Admissions and Appeals) Marina Jordan
Principal Officer (Risk Management) Dean Fenton
Principal Officer (School Organisation) Martin Harrop
Number of Schools
102 Primary; 16 Secondary; 7 Special

GOVERNOR TRAINING UNIT

Governors Section, Children and Young People's Services, Norfolk Hse, Walker Pl, Rotherham, South Yorkshire S65 1AS; Tel 01709 822509
Principal Officer (Governors Development) Paul Carney

ROCKINGHAM PROFESSIONAL DEVELOPMENT CENTRE

Roughwood Rd, Rotherham, South Yorkshire S61 4HY; Tel 01709 740226
Centre Manager Sue Drayson

Sheffield City Council
www.sheffield.gov.uk

Population: 512 200 (2002)
Political composition: Lab: 44, LD: 34, Con: 2, Green: 2, Ind: 1, Vacancy: 1
Town Hall, Sheffield, South Yorkshire S1 2HH; URL www.sheffield.gov.uk; e-mail first.point@sheffield.gov.uk; Tel 0114 272 6444
Chief Executive R. Kerslake BSc, IPFA

Children and Young People's Service

Tel 0114 273 5722; Fax 0114 273 6279
Cabinet Member Cllr Harry Harpham
Executive Director (Children and Young People's Service) Jonathan Crossley-Holland
Deputy Director; Head of Service (Planning, Performance and Partnership) Steve Farnsworth
Head of Service (Local Delivery) Paul Makin
Head of Service (Quality Improvment and Support) Vacancy
Head of Service (Resources and Development) Ken Matthews
Number of Schools
25 Secondary; 14 Special

GOVERNOR TRAINING UNIT

Governor Support Team, Bannerdale Centre, 125 Carterknowle Rd, Sheffield, South Yorkshire S7 2EX; URL www.sheffield.gov.uk; Tel 0114 250 6887; Fax 0114 250 6893
Principal Officer Eric Pye
Senior Administrative Officer Rob Johnson
Services offered
Clerking service to governing bodies; support and training package, including negotiated elements

SCHOOL PSYCHOLOGICAL SERVICE

Bannerdale Centre 125 Carterknowle Rd, Sheffield, South Yorkshire S7 2EX; Tel 0114 250 6800; Fax 0114 250 6811
Manager Mary Collins

SPECIAL UNIT

Specialist Support Services c/o Prince Edward School, City Rd, Sheffield, South Yorkshire S12 2AA; Tel 0114 239 8336; Fax 0114 239 8336
Teacher-in-Charge R. Flowerday
Traveller Education Service c/o Lowedges Primary School, Lowedges Rd, Sheffield, South Yorkshire S8 7JG; Tel 0114 237 8705
Teacher-in-Charge S. Stott

INTEGRATED RESOURCES

Abbeydale Grange School Hastings Rd, Sheffield, South Yorkshire S7 2GU; Tel 0114 255 7301; Fax 0114 250 8540
Headteacher K. Bull
SLD
All Saints Catholic High Granville Rd, Sheffield S2 2RJ; Tel 0114 272 4851; Fax 0114 276 5371
Headteacher R. Sawyer
PD
Angram Bank Primary Kinsey Rd, Sheffield S35 4HN; Tel 0114 284 8553; Fax 0114 284 6894
Headteacher P. Sweet-Escott
HI

2

Arbourthorne Primary School Eastern Ave, Sheffield, South Yorkshire S2 2GQ; Tel 0114 239 8163; Fax 0114 249 5125
Headteacher S. Haigh
LD

Birley Community College Thornbridge Ave, Sheffield S12 3AB; Tel 0114 239 2531; Fax 0114 265 5034
Headteacher A. Vicars
CD

Birley Spa Primary Jermyn Cres, Sheffield S12 4QE; Tel 0114 239 9106; Fax 0114 253 1236
Headteacher G. Mawson
CD

Ecclesfield Secondary Chapeltown Rd, Sheffield S35 9WD; Tel 0114 246 1156; Fax 0114 257 0998
Headteacher M. Nolan

Fox Hill NIJ School Keats Rd, Sheffield, South Yorkshire S6 1AZ; Tel 0114 231 3469; Fax 0114 285 3661
Headteacher Mrs V. Marriott
LD

Greystones IJ School Tullibardine Rd, Sheffield, South Yorkshire S11 7GL; Tel 0114 266 3413; Fax 0114 268 6235
Headteacher A. Anwyl
HI

Hallam Primary Hallam Grange Cres, Sheffield S10 4BD; Tel 0114 230 4430; Fax 0114 230 9565
Headteacher Mrs J. Raban
VI

Hartley Brook NIJ School Hartley Brook Rd, Sheffield, South Yorkshire S5 0JF; Tel 0114 245 6882; Fax 0114 240 2544
Headteacher S. Dormand
LD

High Storrs School Ringinglow Rd, Sheffield, South Yorkshire S11 7LH; Tel 0114 267 0000; Fax 0114 266 3624
Headteacher M. Chapman
HI

King Ecgbert School Furniss Ave, Sheffield, South Yorkshire S17 3QN; Tel 0114 236 9931; Fax 0114 236 2468
Headteacher M.R. Evans
CD

Lower Meadow Primary Batemoor Rd, Sheffield S8 8EE; Tel 0114 237 2700; Fax 0114 237 8572
Headteacher Mrs J. O'Connor
HI

Myers Grove Wood La, Sheffield S6 5HG; Tel 0114 234 8805; Fax 0114 285 4246
Headteacher J. Wilkinson
CD

Nether Green J School Fulwood Rd, Sheffield, South Yorkshire S10 3QA; Tel 0114 230 2461; Fax 0114 263 0189
Headteacher S. Jackson
LD

Nook Lane J School Nook La, Stannington, Sheffield, South Yorkshire S6 6BN; Tel 0114 234 1097; Fax 0114 285 4392
Headteacher G. Hodges
LD

Notre Dame Catholic High Fulwood Rd, Sheffield S10 3BT; Tel 0114 230 2536; Fax 0114 230 8833
Headteacher J. Conway

Pipworth J and NI Schools Pipworth Rd, Sheffield, South Yorkshire S2 1AA; Tel 0114 239 1078; Tel (nursery infant) 0114 239 8432; Fax (junior) 0114 239 1989
Headteacher (Junior) J. Storey
Headteacher (Nursery Infant) V. Langley (Acting)
SEBD

St Thomas of Canterbury Catholic Primary Chancet Wood Dr, Sheffield S8 7TR; Tel 0114 274 5597; Fax 0114 274 6499
Headteacher Mrs A. Brighton

Sharrow J School South View Rd, Sheffield, South Yorkshire S7 1DB; Tel 0114 255 1704; Fax 0114 255 1704
Headteacher L. Ley
LD

Silverdale School Bents Cres, Sheffield, South Yorkshire S11 9RT; Tel 0114 236 9991; Fax 0114 262 0627
Headteacher H. Storey
HI

Stradbroke NIJ School Richmond Rd, Sheffield, South Yorkshire S13 8LT; Tel 0114 239 9320; Fax 0114 239 3430
Headteacher B.M. Clarke
LD

Tapton School Darwin La, Sheffield, South Yorkshire S10 5RG; Tel 0114 267 1414; Fax 0114 294 1155
Headteacher D. Bowes
VI

Wharncliffe Side NIJ School Brightholmlee La, Sheffield, South Yorkshire S35 0DD; Tel 0114 286 2379; Fax 0114 229 9582
Headteacher A. Marshall
Nursery; LD

Key Stage 3 Inclusion Support 24 Clarkhouse Rd, Sheffield, South Yorkshire S10 2LB; Tel 0114 268 5357; Fax 0114 267 8146
Headteacher Sue Walker

TEACHERS' CENTRES

Bannerdale Centre 125 Carterknowle Rd, Sheffield, South Yorkshire S7 2EX; Tel 0114 250 6855; Fax 0114 250 6859

Riverside Centre Earl Marshal Rd, Sheffield, South Yorkshire S4 8FB; Tel 0114 244 6846; Fax 0114 243 5393

South Yorkshire Metropolitan Area

The following metropolitan councils comprise the South Yorkshire Metropolitan Area and are listed separately in this section: Barnsley, Doncaster, Rotherham and Sheffield

Wakefield Metropolitan District Council
www.wakefield.gov.uk

Population: 319 760
8 St John's North, Wakefield, West Yorkshire WF1 3QA; URL www.wakefield.gov.uk; e-mail emchale@wakefield.gov.uk; Tel 01924 307700; Fax 01924 307768
Chief Executive John Foster

Family Services

Corporate Director Elaine McHale; Tel 01924 307725
Service Director (Schools and Lifelong Learning) John Edwards; Tel 01924 305500

Education Department

County Hall, Wakefield, West Yorkshire WF1 2QL; e-mail chreception@wakefield.gov.uk; Tel 01924 306090; Fax 01924 305632
Cabinet Member (Children and Young People) Cllr W. Jenkins
Deputy Portfolio Holder (Children and Young People) Cllr J. Holmes
Corporate Director (Education) J. McLeod MA
Head (Access) J. Price
Head (Cultural Services) C. MacDonald
Head (Early Education and Childcare Service) A. Farrell
Head (Education Personnel) I. Metcalfe
Head (ICT and Data Management) K. Watson ACIS
Head (Lifelong Learning) P. Elliott
Head (Planning and Development) P. Mosby LLB, ACIS
Head (School Governor Services) D. Bowen MA
Head (School Improvement, Primary and Early Years) P. Thorburn
Head (School Improvement, Secondary and Post-16) S. Macleod

Head (SEN Inclusion) S. Coleman
Head (Young People's Service) L. Baynes
Manager (Primary Strategy); Senior Adviser (Transforming Primary Education) J. Parkin
Manager (Professional Support) Tim Kitching
Senior Adviser (Partnerships and Planning) J. Smith
Assistant Chief Education Officer (Inclusion and Lifelong Learning) J. Winter
Assistant Chief Education Officer (Resources and Performance Management) K. Jones BSc, IPFA
Assistant Chief Education Officer (School Improvement and Cultural Services) J. Edwards
Number of schools
18 Secondary; 5 Special

CABINET

Cabinet Member (Children and Young People) W. Jenkins; Step Hse, Darrington Rd, Pontefract, West Yorkshire WF8 3DP
Deputy Portfolio Holder (Children and Young People) J. Holmes; 20 Tyndale Ave, Benton Pk, Horbury, West Yorkshire WF4 5QT
Members of the Cabinet
Lab: P. Box (Chair), P. Dobson, G. Isherwood, Mrs D. Jeffery, W.R. Jenkins, P.A. Loosemore, Mrs O.M. Rowley, G. Stokes

HOSPITAL SPECIAL SCHOOL

Pinderfields Hospital School Wrenthorpe Centre, Imperial Ave, Wrenthorpe, Wakefield, West Yorkshire WF2 0LW; e-mail headteacher@hospitalschools.wakefield.sch.uk; Tel 01924 303695
Headteacher Mrs H.M. Ferguson

PUPIL SUPPORT SERVICES

Equality and Diversity Service Rm 204, 2nd Fl, Chantry Hse, 123 Kirkgate, Wakefield, West Yorkshire WF1 1ZS; e-mail abhatti@wakefield.gov.uk; Tel 01924 303677
Head of Service A. Bhatti
The Priory Centre Pontefract Rd, Crofton, Wakefield, West Yorkshire WF4 1LL; e-mail headteacher@priory.wakefield.sch.uk; Tel 01924 303955
Head L. Boyd
Special Educational Needs Support Service The Heath View Centre, Queen Elizabeth Rd, Eastmoor, Wakefield, West Yorkshire WF1 4RJ; e-mail senss@wakefield.gov.uk; Tel 01924 303660
Head of Service B. Young
Springfield Centre St Georges Rd, Lupset, Wakefield, West Yorkshire WF2 8BB; e-mail headteacher@springfield.wakefield.sch.uk; Tel 01924 303770
Head T. Peckham

OTHER CENTRES

EdIT Centre Woolley Hall, New Rd, Woolley, Wakefield, West Yorkshire WF4 2JR; e-mail edithelp@wakefield.gov.uk; Tel 01226 392344
Centre Manager Richard Main
Woolley Hall Conference Centre Woolley Hall, Woolley, Wakefield, West Yorkshire WF4 2JR; e-mail mawilson@wakefield.gov.uk; Tel 01226 392300
Manager B. Jevons

JOINT SERVICES

Hornsea Outdoor Residential Centre Hull Rd, Hornsea, East Riding of Yorkshire HU18 1RW; URL www.wakefield.gov.uk/education/schools/hornseacentre; e-mail headteacher@hornsea-centre.org.uk; Tel 01964 532106
Centre Manager P. Dixon

West Yorkshire Metropolitan Area

The following Metropolitan Councils comprise the West Yorkshire Metropolitan Area and are listed separately in this section: Bradford, Calderdale, Kirklees, Leeds and Wakefield

City of York Council
www.york.gov.uk

Population: 190 000
Guildhall, York YO1 9QN; URL www.york.gov.uk; Tel 01904 613161
Chief Executive Bill McCarthy

Learning, Culture and Children's Services

Mill Hse, North St, York YO1 6JD; Fax 01904 554206
Director Peter Dwyer
Assistant Director (Children and Families) Eoin Rush
Assistant Director (Partnership and Early Intervention) Paul Murphy
Assistant Director (Resource Management) Kevin Hall
Assistant Director (School Improvement and Staff Development) Jill Hodges
Service Manager (Arts) Gill Cooper
Service Manager (Early Years) Heather Marsland
Service Manager (Finance) Richard Hartle
Service Manager (Governance) Sue Pagliaro
Service Manager (Human Resources) Jo Sheen
Service Manager (ICT) Laura Conkar
Service Manager (Lifelong Learning) Alistair Gourlay
Service Manager (Management Information Service) Yasmin Wahab
Service Manager (Planning and Resources) Maggie Tansley
Service Manager (SEN) Steve Grigg
Service Manager (Sport and Active Leisure) Jo Gilliland
Service Manager (Youth) Paul Herring
Number of Schools
10 Secondary; 2 Special

EXECUTIVE MEMBER FOR EDUCATION

Chair (Scrutiny Board) Cllr Madeleine Kirk
Executive Member (Children's Services) Cllr Carol Runciman
Shadow Executive Member (Education) Cllr Dave Merrett

SCOTLAND

Aberdeen City Council
www.aberdeencity.gov.uk

Population: 210 000
Town Hse, Broad St, Aberdeen AB10 1FY; URL www.aberdeencity.gov.uk; Tel 01224 522500; Fax 01224 644346
Chief Executive D. Paterson

Learning and Leisure Service

Summerhill Centre, Stronsay Dr, Aberdeen AB15 6JA; e-mail furen@aberdeencity.gov.uk; Tel 01224 346060; Fax 01224 346061
Corporate Director J. Stodter BA(Hons), PGCE

Head (Quality of Life, Culture and Learning: Neighbourhood Central)   Graham Wark
Head (Quality of Life, Culture and Learning: Neighbourhood North)   Charles Muir MA(Hons)
Head (Quality of Life, Culture and Learning: Neighbourhood South)   Ann Landels MA(Hons), MEd
Head (School Planning and Improvement)   Alex Hunter
Manager (Support Services)   K. Darbyshire
Principal Officer (Education Information)   F. Uren
Principal Officer (Education Staff Support)   Vacancy
Principal Officer (Education Staffing Strategy)   Jean Bell
Principal Officer (Learning Resources)   R. McLeod
Education Officer   David Lang
Adviser (Careers and Guidance)   T. Ashton
Principal Educational Psychologist   W. O'Hara
Adviser (Staff Development)   Hugh Roche
Co-ordinator (DEM)   S. McPhee
Co-ordinator (Music)   Ken McLeod
Organiser (Janitorial Services)   C. Topp

EDUCATION AND LEISURE COMMITTEE

Convener   Cllr P. MacDonald
Vice-Convener   Cllr M. Duncan

Aberdeenshire Council
www.aberdeenshire.gov.uk

Population: 232 850
Political composition: LD, Ind
Woodhill Hse, Westburn Rd, Aberdeen AB16 5GB; URL www.aberdeenshire.gov.uk; e-mail enquiries@aberdeenshire.gov.uk; Tel 01467 620981; Fax 01224 665444
Chief Executive   Alan G. Campbell CBE

Aberdeenshire Education, Learning and Leisure

Tel 01224 664630; Fax 01224 664615
Director   Bruce Robertson
Head (Schools)   Laura Mason
Head (Inclusion)   Pat Scott
Head (Lifelong Learning)   Rod Stone
Number of Schools
152 Primary; 17 Secondary; 4 Special
Day of Committee Meeting
Thursday; six a year

COMMITTEE

LD: 11, Ind: 6, SNP: 6, Con: 4
Chair   Richard Stroud (LD); The Old Hse, Bellabeg, Strathdon, Aberdeenshire AB36 8UX
Vice-Chair   H. Bisset (LD); The Schoolhouse, Keithhall, Inverurie, Aberdeenshire AB51 0LX
Members of the Committee
Wendy Agnew, Jim Anderson, Peter Argyle, Kenneth Benzie, Alan Cameron, Dennis Duthie, John Gibbins, William Howatson, Albert Howie, Moira Ingleby, Alister Leitch, John Loveday, Jack Mair, Sydney Mair, Norma Makin, Paul Melling, Alisan Norrie, Stuart Pratt, Michael Raeburn, Agnes Strachan, Michael Sullivan, Ian Tait, James Towers, Alexander Wallace, Jill Webster

Buchan Area and Banff and Buchan Area

Banff and Buchan Area Education Office   St Leonard's, Sandyhill Rd, Banff, Aberdeenshire AB45 1BH; Tel 01261 813340; Fax 01261 813396
Buchan Area Education Office   Old Infant Bldg, Prince St, Peterhead, Aberdeenshire AB42 1PL; Tel 01779 473269; Fax 01779 470390

Educational Psychology Service   Old Infant Bldg, Prince St, Peterhead, Aberdeenshire AB42 1PL; e-mail peterhead.psych@aberdeenshire.gov.uk; Tel 01779 473269; Fax 01779 470390

Formartine Area and Garioch Area

Formartine Area Education Office   Towie Hse, Manse Rd, Turriff, Aberdeenshire AB53 4AY; Tel 01888 562427; Fax 01888 568559
Garioch Area Education Office   Gordon Hse, Blackhall Rd, Inverurie, Aberdeenshire AB51 3WA; Tel 01467 620981; Fax 01467 622254
Educational Psychology Service   Craigearn Business Pk, Morrison Way, Kintore, Aberdeenshire AB51 0TH; e-mail inverurie.psych@aberdeenshire.gov.uk; Tel 01467 634759; Fax 01467 634698

Kincardine and Mearns Area and Marr Area

Kincardine and Mearns/Marr Area Education Office   Queens Rd, Stonehaven, Aberdeenshire AB39 2QQ; Tel 01569 766960; Fax 01569 768489
Educational Psychology Services Centre   52 Cameron St, Stonehaven, Aberdeenshire AB39 2HE; e-mail stonehaven.psych@aberdeenshire.gov.uk; Tel 01569 764110; Fax 01569 764133

Angus Council
www.angus.gov.uk

Political composition: Angus Alliance: 15, SNP: 13, Con: 5, Ind: 5, lD: 3, Lab: 2, Ind: 1
Angus Hse, Orchardbank Business Pk, Forfar, Angus DD8 1AX; URL www.angus.gov.uk; e-mail chiefexec@angus.gov.uk; Tel 01307 476200; Fax 01307 476140
Chief Executive   David Sawers

Education Department

Angus Hse, Orchardbank Business Pk, Forfar, Angus DD8 1AE; e-mail education@angus.gov.uk; Tel 01307 476301; Fax 01307 461848
Director (Education)   Jim Anderson MA, MEd, MBA, DipEd
Senior Manager (Education)   C. Clement BA, CPFA
Senior Manager (Education)   N. Logue MA(Hons)
Senior Manager (Education)   J. Nowak DCE
Principal Officer (Community Learning and Development)   Graham Hewitson
Principal Officer (Quality Improvement)   P. Duguid
Principal Officer (School and Family Support)   G. Strachan
Principal Psychologist   R. Flavahan

EDUCATION COMMITTEE

Alliance: 8, SNP: 7
Convener   P. Nield (Alliance: LD)
Vice-Convener   M. Thomas (Alliance: Lab)
Members of the Committee
Alliance: A. Andrews, D. Lumgair, D. May, R. Myles, J. Rymer, M. Salmond
SNP: M. Evans, I. Gaul, D. Morrison, R. Murray, H. Oswald, P. Valentine, S. Welsh

Argyll and Bute Council
www.argyll-bute.gov.uk

Kilmory, Lochgilphead, Argyll and Bute PA31 8RT; URL www.argyll-bute.gov.uk; e-mail enquiries@argyll-bute.gov.uk; Tel 01546 602127; Fax 01546 604138

Education Office

Argyll Hse, Alexandra Par, Dunoon, Argyll and Bute
  PA23 8AJ; e-mail suzanne.kerr@argyll-bute.gov.uk;
  Tel 01369 7048525
Director (Community Services)   Douglas Hendry
Head of Service (Planning and Performance)
  Donald MacVicar
Head of Service (Pre-School and Primary Education)
  Carol Walker
Head of Service (Secondary Education and Pupil Support)
  Ronald Gould
Manager (Community, Learning and Regeneration)
  Jim McCrossan
Manager (Quality Standards)   Christopher Shirley
Principal Educational Psychologist   Ted Jefferies
Principal Officer (Early Years)   Margaret Lauder

EXECUTIVE COMMITTEE

Chair   Dick Walsh
Vice-Chair   Robert Macintyre
Spokesperson (Education and Lifelong Learning)
  Cllr Isobel Strong
Learning Spokesperson (Housing and Communities)
  Cllr George Freeman
Learning Spokesperson (Social Services)
  Cllr Donald McIntosh
Learning Spokesperson (Transportation and Infrastructure)
  Cllr Duncan MacIntyre
Infrastructure Spokesperson (Islands)   Cllr Len Scoullar
Infrastruture Spokesperson (21st Century)   Cllr James Robb

COMMUNITY EDUCATION, NEIGHBOURHOOD AND YOUTH CENTRES

Community Education Wing Colgrain Primary School,
  Redgauntlet Rd, Helensburgh, Argyll and Bute G84 7TZ;
  Tel 01436 670481
Dunoon Community Education Centre Edward St, Dunoon,
  Argyll and Bute PA23 7PH; Tel 01369 704669
Kintyre Community Education Centre Stewart Rd,
  Campbeltown, Argyll and Bute PA28 6AT;
  Tel 01586 552732
Lochgilphead Community Education Centre Manse Brae,
  Lochgilphead, Argyll and Bute PA31 8QZ;
  Tel 01546 602177
Lorn Community Learning Centre McCalls Terr, Soroba Rd,
  Oban, Argyll and Bute PA34 4JF; Tel 01631 562466
The Moat Community Education Centre Stuart St, Rothesay,
  Argyll and Bute PA20 0EP; Tel 01700 503696

Clackmannanshire Council

www.clacksweb.org.uk

Population: 49 000
Political composition: Lab: 8, SNP: 7, Con: 1, Ind: 1, LD: 1
Greenfield, Alloa, Clackmannanshire FK10 2AD;
  URL www.clacksweb.org.uk; Tel 01259 450000;
  Fax 01259 452230
Chief Executive   D. Jones

Services To People (Education)

Lime Tree Hse, Alloa, Clackmannanshire FK10 1EX;
  Fax 01259 452440
Director   D. Jones
Head (Education and Community Services)   J. Goodall
Number of Schools
19 Primary; 4 Nursery; 3 Secondary; 2 Special; 10 Nursery
Classes; 2 Family Centres

LEARNING AND LEISURE COMMITTEE

SNP: 10, Lab: 7, Con: 1
Convener   Alison Lindsay (SNP)

Members of the Committee
SNP: William Alexander, Donald Balsillie, Keith Brown,
Charles Forbes, Craig Holden, Provost Walter McAdam,
Tina Murphy, William Wallace
Lab: William Calder, Robert Elder, Margaret Paterson,
Joanne Ross, Alexander Scobbie, Derek Stewart, Jim Watson
Con: Alastair Campbell

PSYCHOLOGICAL SERVICES

Headquarters 15 Mar St, Alloa, Clackmannanshire
  FK10 1HR; e-mail psychological@clacks.gov.uk

SECONDARY SCHOOLS SUPPORT SERVICE

Bedford Pl, Alloa, Clackmannanshire FK10 1LJ; e-mail
  ssss@edu.clacks.gov.uk

Comhairle nan Eilean Siar (Western Isles)

www.cne-siar.gov.uk

Population: 26 260
Council Offices, Sandwick Rd, Stornoway, Western Isles
  HS1 2BW; URL www.cne-siar.gov.uk; Tel 01851 703773;
  Fax 01851 705349
Chief Executive   Malcolm Burr; Fax 01851 706022

Department of Education

Director (Education)   Murdo Macleod MA
Head (Inclusion and Early Education)   Bernard Chisholm
Head (Quality Improvement)   Iain A. Mackinnon
Head (Resources)   Jennet Gordon
Head (Secondary Education and Human Resources)
  Catriona Dunn
Area Manager (Education)   Catherine MacLennan
Educational Psychologist   Bernard Chisholm
Schools Industry Liaison Officer   I. Stewart
Number of Schools
29 Primary; 9 Primary and Secondary; 2 Secondary
Day of Committee Meeting
Wednesday
Requisition Periods for Schools Supplies
March

VOCATIONAL COLLEGE

Lews Castle College Stornoway, Western Isles;
  Tel 01851 770000

Dumfries and Galloway Council

www.dumgal.gov.uk

Population: 147 780
Political composition: Scottish Labour: 14, Ind: 12, Con: 11,
LD: 5, SNP: 5
Council Offices, English St, Dumfries, Dumfries and
  Galloway DG1 2DD; URL www.dumgal.gov.uk; e-mail
  margaretr@dumgal.gov.uk; Tel 01387 260000;
  Fax 01387 260034

Education and Community Services

Woodbank, 30 Edinburgh Rd, Dumfries, Dumfries and
  Galloway DG1 1NW; e-mail frasers@dumgal.gov.uk;
  Tel 01387 260427
Chair   Willie Scobie
Vice-Chair   Jim Dempster
Vice-Chair   Wilma Paterson
Director   F. Sanderson

Group Manager (Business)   C. Taylor
Group Manager (Schools Services)   Vacancy
Operations Manager (Planning and Development)
   Rae Doherty
Operations Manager (Quality, Improvement and Support)
   Keith Best
Chief Social Work Officer   B. Smith
Catering Officer   Judith Borg
Number of Schools
107 Primary; 14 Secondary; 2 Secondary including Primary
Departments; 2 Special; 25 Learning Centres
Requisition Periods for Schools Supplies
As necessary
**Other Authorities with whom Joint Purchasing Arrangements
are made**
Cumbria Contract Services

Dundee City Council
www.dundeecity.gov.uk

Population: 142 170
City Chambers, City Sq, Dundee DD1 3BY;
   URL www.dundeecity.gov.uk; e-mail
   alex.stephen@dundeecity.gov.uk; Tel 01382 434000;
   Fax 01382 434104
Chief Executive   Alex Stephen FCCA
Deputy Chief Executive (Support Services)   P. McIlquham

Education Department

8th–9th Fls, Tayside Hse, 28 Crichton St, Dundee DD1 3RJ;
   Tel 01382 433111; Fax 01382 433080
Director (Education)   Anne Wilson
Head (Education Resources)   S. Weston
Head (Primary Education)   L. Waghorn
Head (Secondary Education)   J. Collins
Head (Support for Learning)   J. Gibson
Convener   Cllr Kevin Keenan
Principal Educational Psychologist   D. Gavine
Number of Schools
40 Primary; 12 Nursery; 10 Secondary; 1 Special; 19 Nursery
Classes; 16 Resourced Locations

EDUCATION COMMITTEE

SNP: 11, Lab: 10, Con: 5, LD: 2, Independent Labour: 1
Members of the Committee
SNP: J. Barrie, R. Beattie, J. Corrigan, A. Dawson, W.
Dawson, N. Don, B. Duncan, J. FitzPatrick, E. Fordyce JP, C.
Roberts, W.W. Sawyers
Lab: C.D.P. Farquhar, F.M. Grant, C. Hind, K. Keenan, J.R.
Letford, J. Morrow, G. Regan, J. Shimi JP, J.M. Sturrock,
H.W. Wright
Con: B. Mackie, N. Powrie, D.J. Scott, R. Wallace, C. Webster
LD: H. Dick, F. MacPherson
Ind Lab: I. Borthwick JP

East Ayrshire Council
www.east-ayrshire.gov.uk

Population: 120 000
Political composition: Elected members: 32 (Lab: 14, SNP:14;
Con: 3; Ind: 1)
Council Headquarters, London Rd, Kilmarnock, East
   Ayrshire KA3 7BU; URL www.east-ayrshire.gov.uk;
   e-mail the.council@east-ayrshire.gov.uk
Chief Executive   Fiona Lees

Department of Educational and Social Services

e-mail education@east-ayrshire.gov.uk; Tel 01563 576000;
   Fax 01563 576210
Executive Director   Graham Short; Tel 01563 576017
Executive Head (Social Work)   Jackie Donnelly;
   Tel 01563 576920; Fax 01563 553507
Head of Service (Community Support)   Kay Gilmour;
   Tel 01563 576104
Head of Service (Schools)   Andrew Sutherland;
   Tel 01563 576126
Head (Facilities Management)   Robin Gourlay;
   Tel 01563 576089
Head (Resources)   Euan Couperwhite; Tel 01563 576090;
   Fax 01563 576123

COMMUNITY EDUCATION OFFICES

**Auchinleck Community Learning and Development Team
   Base** Forgeahead Office, Auchinleck CEC, Well Rd,
   Auchinleck, East Ayrshire KA15 2LE; Tel 01290 426070;
   Fax 01290 423557
   Contact   Suzanne Brodie
Community Learning and Development Team Base Block A,
   St Joseph's Campus, Kilmarnock, East Ayrshire;
   Tel 01563 572929; Fax 01563 571758
   Contact   Bill Hunter
Cumnock Community Learning and Development Team Base
   Bank Ave, Cumnock, East Ayrshire KA18 1PQ;
   Tel 01290 421066; Fax 01290 425850
   Contact   Suzanne Brodie
**Dalmellington Community Learning and Development Team
   Base** High St, Dalmellington, East Ayrshire KA6 7SJ;
   Tel 01292 552940; Fax 01292 552945
   Contact   Suzanne Brodie
**Kilmarnock North and Northern Area Community Learning
   and Development Team Base** Northwest Area Centre,
   Western Rd, Kilmarnock, East Ayrshire KA3 1NQ;
   Tel 01563 578661; Fax 01563 578653
   Contact   Janice Harrison
**Kilmarnock South, Central and Irvine Valley Community
   Learning and Development Team Base** Gateway Centre,
   Foregate, Kilmarnock, East Ayrshire KA1 1LN;
   Tel 01563 554941; Fax 01563 554949
   Contact   Kevin Wells

CAREERS SCOTLAND CENTRES

Cumnock Careers Scotland Centre, Glaisnock Shopping
   Centre, Cumnock, East Ayrshire KA18 1LE;
   URL www.careers-scotland.org.uk; e-mail
   andrew.linton@careers-scotland.org.uk;
   Tel 01290 423422; Fax 01290 420530
   Team Leader   Andrew Linton
Dalmellington 8 High Main St, Dalmellington, East
   Ayrshire KA6 7QN; URL www.careers-scotland.org.uk;
   Tel (Tue, Wed am and Thurs only, contact Cumnock
   Careers Office Mon, Wed pm and Fri) 01292 551191
Kilmarnock 55 John Fimie St, Kilmarnock, East Ayrshire
   KA1 1BH; URL www.careers-scotland.org.uk; e-mail
   pat.mcphee@careers-scotland.org.uk; Tel 01563 527165;
   Fax 01563 525544
   Team Leader   Pat McPhee

NETWORK SUPPORT TEAMS AND SPECIAL UNITS PROJECTS

Network Support Base (North) Playingfield Rd, Crosshouse,
   East Ayrshire KA2 0JJ; Tel 01563 551624;
   Fax 01563 551624
   Co-ordinator (Network Support)   Anne Basford; e-mail
   anne.basford@east-ayrshire.gov.uk
Network Support Base (South) St John's Primary School,
   John Weir Ave, Cumnock, East Ayrshire KA18 1NJ;
   Tel 01290 426137; Fax 01290 426137
   Co-ordinator (Network Support)   Anne Basford; e-mail
   anne.basford@east-ayrshire.gov.uk

SPECIAL UNITS/PROJECTS

Barshare Supported Learning Centre   Barshare Primary School, Dalgleish Ave, Cumnock, East Ayrshire KA18 1QG; e-mail lorraine.facchini@east-ayrshire.gov.uk; Tel 01290 422212
Headteacher   Lorraine Facchini

Crosshouse Communications Centre   Crosshouse Primary School, Playingfield Rd, Crosshouse, East Ayrshire KA2 0JJ; e-mail linda.walker@east-ayrshire.gov.uk; Tel 01563 521459
Headteacher   Linda Walker

Cumnock Supported Learning Centre   Cumnock Academy, Ayr Rd, Cumnock, East Ayrshire KA18 1EH; e-mail gordon.bell@east-ayrshire.gov.uk; Tel 01290 425940; Fax 01290 425812
Headteacher   Gordon Bell

Early Intervention Project (North Base)   Westpark Base, Playingfield Rd, Crosshouse, East Ayrshire KA2 0JJ; e-mail education@east-ayrshire.gov.uks; Tel 01563 570739; Fax 01563 570739
Contact   Lesley Martin

Early Intervention Project (South Base)   St John's Primary School, John Weir Ave, Cumnock, East Ayrshire KA18 1NJ; e-mail hilary.macgillivray@east-ayrshire.gov.uk; Tel 01290 422867; Fax 01290 426137
Contact   Hilary MacGillivray

Early Intervention Project Co-ordinator   Woodstock Centre, Woodstock St, Kilmarnock, East Ayrshire KA1 2BE; e-mail hilary.macgillivray@east-ayrshire.gov.uk; Tel 01563 555650; Fax 01563 574079
Co-ordinator   Hilary MacGillivray

Gaelic Class and Nursery Class   Onthank Primary School, Meiklewood Rd, Kilmarnock, East Ayrshire KA3 2ES; URL www.east-ayrshire.gov.uk; e-mail steven.banks@east-ayrshire.gov.uk; Tel 01563 525477
Headteacher   Steven Banks

Grange Hearing Impaired Unit   Grange Academy, Beech Ave, Kilmarnock, East Ayrshire KA1 2EW; e-mail education@east-ayrshire.gov.uk; Tel 01563 543050; Fax 01563 542648
Contact   Anne Barnaby

Integrated Services   Educational and Social Services Office, Rennie St, Kilmarnock, East Ayrshire KA1 3AR; Tel 01563 578126; Fax 01563 578119
Principal Officer (Children and Young People)   Alison Paterson

Language and Communication Unit   Westpark Base, Playingfield Rd, Crosshouse, East Ayrshire KA2 0JJ; e-mail anne.basford@east-ayrshire.gov.uk; Tel 01563 551624; Fax 01563 551624
Co-ordinator   Anne Basford

Patna Supported Learning Centre   Patna Primary School, Carnshalloch Ave, Patna, East Ayrshire KA6 7NP; e-mail marion.mclean@east-ayrshire.gov.uk; Tel 01292 531271; Fax 01292 532301
Headteacher   Marion McLean

Youth Strategy Project (Base) – Cumnock   Cumnock Academy Campus, Ayr Rd, Cumnock, East Ayrshire KA18 1EH; e-mail julie.muir@east-ayrshire.gov.uk; Tel 01290 427036
Contact   Julie Muir

Youth Strategy Project (Base) – Kilmarnock   Kilmarnock Academy, Elmbank Dr, Kilmarnock, East Ayrshire KA1 3BS; e-mail julie.muir@east-ayrshire.gov.uk; Tel 01563 570851; Fax 01563 570851
Contact   Julie Muir

Youth Strategy Project (Base) – Altonhill Base   Auchencar Dr, Kilmarnock, East Ayrshire; e-mail maggie.fallon@east-ayrshire.gov.uk; Tel 01563 572715
Manager (Youth Strategy)   Maggie Fallon
Principal Teacher (Youth Strategy)   Maggie Murphy

COMMUNITY EDUCATIONAL CENTRES

Auchinleck Community Education Centre   Well Rd, Auchinleck, East Ayrshire KA18 2LE; Tel 01290 420329

Barrhill Community Education Centre   Bank Ave, Cumnock, East Ayrshire KA18 2BE; Tel 01290 421066; Fax 01290 425850

Barshare Community Wing   St John's Primary School, John Weir Ave, Cumnock, East Ayrshire KA18 1NN; Tel 01290 422906

Bellsbank Community Wing   Craiglea Cres, Dalmellington, East Ayrshire KA6 7UA; Tel 01292 551019

Catrine Community Education Centre   2 Institute Ave, Catrine, East Ayrshire KA5 6RT; Tel 01290 550689

Crookedholm Community Education Centre   Grougar Rd, Crookedholm, Kilmarnock, East Ayrshire KA3 6LD; Tel 07791 170223

Crosshouse Community Education Centre   Playingfield Rd, Crosshouse, Kilmarnock, East Ayrshire KA2 0JJ; Tel 01563 572810

Dalmellington Community Education Centre   Ayr Rd, Dalmellington, East Ayrshire KA6 7SJ; Tel 07825 174780

Dalrymple Community Education Centre   38 Barbieston Rd, Dalrymple, East Ayrshire KA6 6DZ; Tel 07854 933239

Drongan Community Education Centre   Millmannoch Ave, Drongan, East Ayrshire KA6 7BY; Tel 01292 591355

Drongan Youth Wing   Millmannoch Ave, Drongan, East Ayrshire KA6 7BY; Tel 01292 590868; Fax 01292 591715

Galston Community Education Centre   38 Orchard St, Galston, East Ayrshire KA4 8EN; Tel 01563 821329

Grange Community Wing   Beech Ave, Kilmarnock, East Ayrshire KA1 2EW; Tel 01563 525628

Hareshaw Community Education Centre   21 Main St, Waterside, Fenwick, East Ayrshire KA3 6JB; Tel 01560 600941

Hurlford Community Education Centre   Cessnock Rd, Hurlford, East Ayrshire KA1 5DD; Tel 01563 524841

Kilmaurs Community Education Centre   East Park Dr, Kilmaurs, East Ayrshire KA3 2QS; Tel 07854 930535

Mauchline Community Education Centre   Kilmarnock Rd, Mauchline, East Ayrshire KA5 5DF; Tel 07837 107604

Muirkirk Community Wing   Burns Ave, Muirkirk, East Ayrshire KA18 3RH; Tel 01290 661350

Netherthird Community Wing   Craigens Rd, Cumnock, East Ayrshire; Tel 07971 329268

New Cumnock Community Education Centre   The Castle, New Cumnock, East Ayrshire KA18 4AH; Tel 01290 338582

Ochiltree Community Education Centre   45 Main St, Ochiltree, East Ayrshire KA18 2PF; Tel 01290 700627

Onthank Community Education Centre   Kirkton Rd, Onthank, Kilmarnock, East Ayrshire KA3 2DF; Tel 07855 093529

Patna Community Education Centre   Doonside Ave, Patna, East Ayrshire KA6 7LX; Tel 01292 531530

Rankinston Community Education Centre   Littlemill Pl, Rankinston, East Ayrshire KA6 7HB; Tel 01292 590675

St Joseph's Community Wing   Grassyards Rd, Kilmarnock, East Ayrshire KA3 7SL; Tel 01563 535913

Shortlees Community Education Centre   Blacksyke Ave, Kilmarnock, East Ayrshire KA1 4QY; Tel 07920 765094

Stewarton Youth and Community Centre   Standalane, Stewarton, East Ayrshire KA3 5BG; Tel 07890 293497

OTHER EDUCATIONAL ESTABLISHMENTS

Ayrshire Technician Support Service   A Block, St Joseph's Academy, Kilmarnock, East Ayrshire KA3 7SL; Tel 01563 544550; Fax 01563 571278
Contact   Alastair Murphy

DMR Office (Devolved Management of Resources)   c/o St Joseph's Academy, Grassyards Rd, Kilmarnock, East Ayrshire; e-mail chris.johnston@east-ayrshire.gov.uk; Tel 01563 573731; Fax 01563 574436
Departmental Finance Officer   Chris Johnston

Education Headquarters   Council Headquarters, London Rd, Kilmarnock, East Ayrshire KA3 7BU; e-mail education@east-ayrshire.gov.uk; Tel 01563 576017; Fax 01563 576210
Executive Director   Graham Short

Education Resource Service (Community Services
Department) Libraries, Council Offices, Lugar, East
Ayrshire KA18 3JQ; Tel 01563 555451; Fax 01563 555455
Contact Pat Standen

Hearing Impairment Peripatetic Service Audiology Unit,
Playingfield Rd, Crosshouse, East Ayrshire KA2 0JJ;
Tel 01563 551219
Co-ordinator Anne Cowgill

Home Visiting Service (Pre 5/SEN) Woodstock Centre,
Woodstock St, Kilmarnock, East Ayrshire KA1 2BE;
Tel 01563 555640; Fax 01563 574079
Home Visiting Teacher Caroline Shaw

Instrumental Service Woodstock Centre, Woodstock St,
Kilmarnock, East Ayrshire KA1 2BE;
URL paul.woods@east-ayrshire.gov.uk;
Tel 01563 555634; Fax 01563 574079
Manager (Instrumental) Paul Woods

Outdoor Education Service Block A, St Joseph's Campus,
Kilmarnock, East Ayrshire KA3 7SL; e-mail
mike.howes@east-ayrshire.gov.uk; Tel 01563 551457;
Fax 01563 571758
Contact Mike Howes

Psychological Service Woodstock Centre, Woodstock St,
Kilmarnock, East Ayrshire KA1 2BE; e-mail
tom.williams@east-ayrshire.gov.uk; Tel 01563 555640;
Fax 01563 574079
Principal Psychologist Dr Tom Williams

Quality Development Team Woodstock Centre, Woodstock
St, Kilmarnock, East Ayrshire KA1 2BE; e-mail
kenneth.mckinlay@east-ayrshire.gov.uk;
Tel 01563 555650; Fax 01563 574079
Contact Kenneth McKinlay

East Dunbartonshire Council

www.eastdunbarton.gov.uk

Population: 107 310
Council Headquarters, Tom Johnston Hse, Civic Way,
Kirkintilloch, East Dunbartonshire G66 4TJ;
URL www.eastdunbarton.gov.uk; Tel 0141 578 8000;
Fax 0141 777 8576
Chief Executive Sue Bruce

Department of Community (Education Service)

Boclair Hse, 100 Milngavie Rd, Bearsden, Glasgow G61 2TQ;
e-mail john.simmons@eastdunbarton.gov.uk;
Tel 0141 578 8000; Fax 0141 578 8653
Corporate Director (Community) David Anderson
Head (Community Services) Gordon Smith
Head (Education) John Simmons
Head (Resources, Planning and Improvement for Children)
Sandy McGarvey
Convener Cllr E. Gotts
Vice-Convener Cllr M. McNaughton
Number of Schools
9 Secondary; 2 Special

EDUCATION AND CULTURAL SERVICES COMMITTEE

LD: 6, Lab: 3, Con: 2, Ind: 1
Members of the Committee
LD: E. Gotts, G. Macdonald, C. McInnes, M. McNaughton,
J. Southcott, P. Steel
Lab: A. Hannah, E. McGaughrin, T. Smith
Con: W. Hendry, A. Jarvis
Ind: J. Young

EDUCATIONAL PSYCHOLOGY SERVICE

Gartconner Primary School Gartshore Rd, Kirkintilloch, East
Dunbartonshire G66 3TH; e-mail psychserviceoffice@
gartconner.e-dunbarton.sch.uk

East Lothian Council

www.eastlothian.gov.uk

Population: 92 830
Political composition: Lab: 7, SNP: 7, LD: 6, Con: 2, Ind: 1
John Muir Hse, Haddington, East Lothian EH41 3HA;
URL www.eastlothian.gov.uk; Tel 01620 827827;
Fax 01620 827888
Chief Executive Alan J. Blackie; e-mail
jblackie@eastlothian.gov.uk

Department of Education and Children's Services

Tel 01620 827631; Fax 01620 827291
Director Vacancy
Head (Children's Services) Alan Ross
Head (Education) Don Ledingham
Service Manager (Practice) Marion Wood
Service Manager (Resources) Robert Swift
Manager (Inclusion and Equality) Sheila Ainslie
Manager (Planning) Gill McMillan
Manager (Teaching and Learning) Maureen Jobson
Business Manager Richard Parker

COUNCIL COMMITTEE FOR EDUCATION

Lab: 5, Liberal: 3, SNP: 3, Con: 1
Convener Peter MacKenzie (SNP)
Vice-Convener Sheena Richardson (LD)
Members of the Committee
Lab: A. Forrest, J. Gillies, W. Innes, J. McNeil, N. Rankin
LD: J. Bell, R. Currie, S. Richardson
SNP: D. Berry, T. Trotter
Con: N. Rankin

OUTDOOR EDUCATION CENTRES

Innerwick Field Study Centre Innerwick, East Lothian;
Tel 01368 840319
Prestonpans Education Centre Gardiner Terr, Prestonpans,
East Lothian EH32 9ET; Tel 01875 814058

PSYCHOLOGICAL SERVICE

East Lothian Psychological Service e-mail
jwilson@eastlothian.gov.uk
Principal Psychologist Jenny Wilson

PUPIL SUPPORT

Outreach Service John Muir Hse, Haddington, East Lothian
EH41 3HA; e-mail fparkingson@eastlothian.gov.uk

East Renfrewshire Council

www.eastrenfrewshire.gov.uk

Population: 89 000
Council Headquarters, Eastwood Pk, Rouken Glen Rd,
Giffnock, East Renfrewshire G46 6UG;
URL www.eastrenfrewshire.gov.uk; Tel 0141 577 3000;
Fax 0141 577 3890
Chief Executive David Dippie

Education Department

East Renfrewshire Council, Council Offices, 211 Main St,
Barrhead, East Renfrewshire G78 1SY; e-mail
john.wilson@eastrenfrewshire.gov.uk; Tel 0141 577 3404;
Fax 0141 577 3276
Director (Education) John Wilson

Head (Education Services: Children and Young People)
Susan Gow
Head (Education Services: Children, Learning, Teaching and Quality Improvement) Mhairi Shaw
Head (Education Services: School Performance and Provision)
Fiona Morrison
Head (Education Services: Staff and Continuing Education)
Ginny Thorburn

The City of Edinburgh Council
www.edinburgh.gov.uk

Political composition: Lab: 31, Con: 13, Scottish Liberal Democrat: 13, SNP: 1
City Chambers, High St, Edinburgh EH1 1YJ;
URL www.edinburgh.gov.uk; Tel 0131 200 2000;
Fax 0131 469 3010
Chief Executive Tom Aitchison
Director (City Development) Andrew Holmes
Director (Corporate Services) Jim Inch
Director (Environmental and Consumer Services)
Mike Drewry
Director (Finance) Donald McGougan
Director (Housing) Mark Turley
Director (Recreation) Lynne Halfpenny
Director (Social Work) Peter Gabbitas

Children and Families

Wellington Ct, 10 Waterloo Pl, Edinburgh EH1 3EG;
Tel 0131 469 3000; Fax 0131 469 3141
Director (Children and Families) Roy Jobson

EXECUTIVE (WITH EDUCATION FUNCTIONS)
Members of the Executive
Lab: Aitken, Burns, Cairns, Child, Cunningham, Fallon, Gilmore, Lord Provost Lesley Hinds, Houston, Kennedy, Kerr, Marshall, Russell, Thomas, Wilson
Con: Berry, Jackson, Meek, Sleigh, Whyte
LD: Edie, Forrest, Lowrie, McLaren
SNP: Munn

REGIONAL PSYCHOLOGICAL SERVICE
Edinburgh 154 McDonald Rd, Edinburgh EH7 4NN;
Tel 0131 469 2800
Principal Psychologist (East) Anna Boni
Principal Psychologist (East) D. Thomson
Principal Psychologist (West) Greg McMillan
Principal Psychologist (West) John Young

PUPIL SUPPORT CENTRE
Panmure House School Support Centre Lochend Cl, Canongate, Edinburgh EH8 8BP; Tel 0131 556 8833
Head of Service D. Simpson

Community Education Service

NORTH EDINBURGH OFFICES AND CENTRES
Area Office Broughton Community Education Office, Carrington Rd, Edinburgh EH4 1EG; Tel 0131 332 6316; Fax 0131 332 3812
Manager (CE Neighbourhood) P. James
Manager (CE Neighbourhood) J. Heywood
Broughton Youth Wing Carrington Rd, Edinburgh EH4 1EG; Tel 0131 332 6316
Craigmount Youth Wing Craigs Rd, Edinburgh EH12 8NH; Tel 0131 339 1884; Tel 0131 339 8278
Craigroyston 1a Pennywell Rd, Edinburgh EH4 4PH; Tel 0131 332 7360
Contact B. Kennedy

Fort Community Wing Fort Primary School, North Fort St, Edinburgh EH6 4HF; Tel 0131 553 1074
Kirkliston Queensferry Rd, Kirkliston, Edinburgh EH29 9AG; Tel 0131 333 4214
Contact D. Hand
Pirniehall Community Education Field Office Pirniehall Primary School, West Pilton Cres, Edinburgh EH4 4HP; Tel 0131 315 2088
Contact M. Gray
Rannoch Rannoch Terr, Edinburgh EH4 7ER; Tel 0131 339 5351
Contact J. McMillan
Ratho 1 School Wynd, Ratho, Edinburgh EH28 8TT; Tel 0131 333 1055
Contact D. Stewart
Royston/Wardieburn Pilton Dr North, Edinburgh EH5 1NF; Tel 0131 552 5700
Contact A. Hosie
South Queensferry and Roseberry Hall Community Education Association Roseberry Hall, High St, South Queensferry, Edinburgh EH30 9LL; Tel 0131 331 2113
Contact S. Stewart

SOUTH-EAST EDINBURGH OFFICES AND CENTRES
Area Office Castlebrae Community Education Office, Greendykes Rd, Edinburgh EH16 4DP; Tel 0131 661 7463; Fax 0131 652 2658
Contact K. Pringle
Bingham Bingham Ave, Edinburgh EH15 3HD; Tel 0131 669 8778
Contact J. McDougall
Burdiehouse/Southhouse Burdiehouse St, Edinburgh EH17 8EZ; Tel 0131 664 2210
Contact L. Markham
Cameron House Cameron House Ave, Edinburgh EH16 5LF; Tel 0131 667 3762
Contact D. McCann
Contact H. Muchamore
Castleview Club Craigmillar Castle Ave, Edinburgh EH16 4DW; Tel 0131 661 4064
Contact J. McDougall
Craigentinny Loaning Rd, Edinburgh EH7 6JE; Tel 0131 661 8188; Tel 0131 661 8189
Contact C. Gough
Gilmerton 4 Drum St, Edinburgh EH17 8QG; Tel 0131 664 2335
Contact C. Lamond
Gracemount Sub-Area Office Lasswade Rd, Edinburgh EH16 6TZ; Tel 0131 664 5101
Contact J. Herriot
Gracemount Youth Centre 128 Lasswade Rd, Edinburgh EH16 6AU; Tel 0131 664 3275
Contact M. Volino
Inch 255 Gilmerton Rd, Edinburgh EH16 5TT; Tel 0131 664 4710; Fax 0131 664 4710
Contact I. Murdoch
Jack Kane 208 Niddrie Mains Rd, Edinburgh EH16 4ND; Tel 0131 657 1595
Contact K. Maclean
Magdalene Magdalene Dr, Edinburgh EH15 3BE; Tel 0131 669 8760
Moredun Moredun Pk View, Edinburgh EH17 7ND; Tel 0131 664 3612
Contact R. Sutherland
Northfield/Willowbrae Northfield Rd, Edinburgh EH8 7PP; Tel 0131 661 5723
Contact G. Coleman
Riddles Court 322 Lawnmarket, Edinburgh EH1 2PQ; Tel 0131 225 4411; Tel 0131 225 8189
Contact A. Burgess
St Ann's 6 South Grays Cl, Cowgate, Edinburgh EH1 1TQ; Tel 0131 557 0469
South Bridge Centre Infirmary St, Edinburgh EH1 1LT; Tel 0131 556 2944
Contact M. Lynch

Southside 117 Nicolson St, Edinburgh EH8 9ER;
Tel 0131 667 0484
Contact K. Smith
Tollcross Tollcross Primary School, Fountainbridge,
Edinburgh EH3 9QG; Tel 0131 229 8448
Contact P. Fordyce

SOUTH-WEST EDINBURGH OFFICES AND CENTRES

Area Office Firrhill Community Education Office, Oxgangs
Rd North, Edinburgh EH14 1DP; Tel 0131 441 6851;
Fax 0131 441 6851
CE Neighbourhood Manager T. McLean
Adult Learning Project (ALP) Tollcross Community Centre,
Edinburgh EH3 9QG; Tel 0131 337 5442
Contact S. Reeves
Balerno Community Wing 5 Bridge St, Balerno, Edinburgh
EH14 7AQ; Tel 0131 477 7733
Contact D. Hillson
Carrickvale Stenhouse St West, Edinburgh EH11 3EP;
Tel 0131 443 6971
Contact D. Bishop
Clovenstone 54 Clovenstone Pk, Edinburgh EH14 3EY;
Tel 0131 453 4561
Contact R. Byfield
Colinton Mains Firrhill Loan, Edinburgh EH13 9EJ;
Tel 0131 441 6597
Contact S. Parnell; at Pentland
Gorgie War Memorial Hall Gorgie Rd, Edinburgh
EH11 2RQ; Tel 0131 337 9098
Contact A. Vardy
Juniper Green Baberton Ave, Edinburgh EH14 5DU;
Tel 0131 453 4427
Contact B. Drysdale
Longstone Redhall Grn, Edinburgh EH14 5DU;
Tel 0131 444 0706
Contact A. McCulloch
Pentland Oxgangs Brae, Edinburgh EH13 9LS;
Tel 0131 445 2871
Contact J. Spence
St Brides Orwell Terr, Edinburgh EH11 2DY;
Tel 0131 346 1405
Contact G. Williamson
Sighthill Sighthill Wynd, Edinburgh EH11 4BL;
Tel 0131 453 6078
Contact K. Mullarkey
Springwell House Ardmillan Terr, Edinburgh EH11 2JN;
Tel 0131 337 1971
Contact A. Vardy
Stenhouse/Whitson 80 Stevenson Dr, Edinburgh EH11 3BQ;
Tel 0131 443 9125
Contact D. Bishop; at Carrickvale
Wester Hailes Sub-Area Office Hailesland Primary School,
Hailesland Pl, Edinburgh EH14 2SL; Tel 0131 442 2001;
Fax 0131 442 4408
Contact A. McCulloch

ADULT BASIC EDUCATION AREA OFFICES AND SERVICES

Edinburgh South Bridge CE Base, Infirmary St, Edinburgh
EH1 1LT; Tel 0131 556 2944
Assistant Community Education Neighbourhood Manager
M. Lynch
The Number Shop 188–190 The Pleasance, Edinburgh
EH8 9RT; Tel 0131 668 4787
Community Education Worker E. McEachern
Regional Office South Bridge Resource Centre, Infirmary
St, Edinburgh EH1 3QN; Tel 0131 558 3545
Community Education Neighbourhood Manager M. Teale
Community Education Worker B. Jamieson
Service for People who are Deaf or Hard of Hearing South
Bridge Resource Centre, Infirmary St, Edinburgh
EH1 3QN; Tel 0131 558 3545
Community Education Worker M. Gilfillan
Community Education Worker S. Kilby

Service for People with Learning Disabilities South Bridge
Resource Centre, Infirmary St, Edinburgh EH1 3QN;
Tel 0131 558 3545
Community Education Worker M. McQueenie

OUTDOOR CENTRES

Benmore Dunoon, Argyll, Argyll and Bute PA23 8QX;
Tel 01369 6337; Fax 01369 3331
Prinicpal A. Beveridge
Lagganlia Kincraig, Kingussie, Inverness, Highland
PH21 1NG; Tel 01540 651265
Contact R.F.J. Arrowsmith

RESOURCE CENTRES

St Bernard's Centre Dean Park St, Edinburgh EH4 1JS;
Tel 0131 311 5600
School Library Service (Primary) Dean Park St, Edinburgh
EH4 1JS; Tel 0131 311 5621
Principal C. Jones
School Library Service (Secondary) Dean Park St, Edinburgh
EH4 1JS; Tel 0131 311 5616

EDUCATION WELFARE SERVICES

Edinburgh Hunters Trust Primary School, Oxgangs Grn,
Edinburgh EH13 9JE; Tel 0131 445 7560
Contact J. Stewart

Falkirk Council

www.falkirk.gov.uk

Population: 143 370
Municipal Bldgs, Falkirk FK1 5RS;
URL www.falkirk.gov.uk; Tel 01324 506070;
Fax 01324 506288
Chief Executive M. Pitcaithly

Education Services

McLaren Hse, Marchmont Ave, Polmont, Falkirk FK2 0NZ;
e-mail director.educ@falkirk.gov.uk; Tel 01324 506600;
Fax 01324 506601
Director (Education) Julia Swan
Head (Educational Resources) Gary Greenhorn
Head (Educational Support) Nigel Fletcher
Head (School Improvement) Ann Carnachan
Manager (Curriculum Support) K. Currie
Manager (Policy and Performance) T. Harrison
Manager (Property Development) A. Livingstone
Manager (Quality Assurance and Communications)
D. MacGregor
Manager (Quality Improvement) M. Graham
Policy Officer Vacancy
Principal Psychologist Graeme King; Moray Pl,
Grangemouth FK3 9DL

SPECIAL CLASSES

Dundas Unit c/o Moray Primary School, Moray Pl,
Grangemouth, Falkirk FK3 9DL; e-mail
dundasdayunit@falkirk.gov.uk; Tel 01324 501311;
Fax 01324 501311
Headteacher Tom Begen
Education Assessment Unit Weedingshall, Polmont, Falkirk
FK2 0XS; e-mail
educationassessmentunit@falkirk.gov.uk;
Tel 01324 506770; Fax 01324 506771
Headteacher May Kydd
Falkirk Day Unit Camelon Education Centre, Abercrombie
St, Camelon, Falkirk FK1 4HA; e-mail
falkirkdayunit@falkirk.gov.uk; Tel 01324 501650;
Fax 01324 503719
Headteacher Gordon Bell

Fife Council
www.fife.gov.uk

Population: 356 000
Political composition: Lab: 24, SNP: 23, LD: 21, Con: 5, Ind: 3, Other: 2
Fife Hse, North St, Glenrothes, Fife KY7 5LT;
 URL www.fife.gov.uk; Tel 0845 155 0000
Chief Executive Ronnie Hinds
Head (Law and Administration) Harry B. Tait
Head (Social Work) S. Moore
Strategic Manager (Education) Ken Greer
Strategic Manager (Environment and Development Services) S. Nicol
Strategic Manager (Local Community and Housing) Eric Byiers
Chief Officer (Information) Terry Trundley
Provost Cllr Frances Melville

Education Service

Rothesay Hse, Rothesay Pl, Glenrothes, Fife KY7 5PQ;
 e-mail education.services@fife.gov.uk; Tel 0845 155 5555;
 Fax 01592 413693
Executive Director Kenneth Greer
Senior Manager (Dunfermline/Inverkeithing) Garry Crosbie
Senior Manager (East/Levenmouth) Bryan Kirkaldy
Senior Manager (Glenrothes/Cowdenbeath/Lochgelly) Anthony Finn
Senior Manager (Kirkcaldy) Craig Munro
Manager (Music Services) G. Wilson
Support Service Manager (Bilingual Support) D. Watson
Support Service Manager (Visiting Teachers) M. Liddell
Principal Psychologist Hamish MacPhee
Principal Client Officer (Cleaning/Janitorial) G. Paterson (Acting)
Education Liaison Officer M. MacDougall
Co-ordinator (PE and Youth Sports) D. Maiden
Co-ordinator (Pre-School Education) C. Miles
Contact (Catering) L. Clark
Number of Schools
141 Primary; 19 Secondary; 17 Nursery; 7 Special
Other Units
10
Requisition Periods for Schools Supplies
No specific dates

CHILDREN'S SERVICES COMMITTEE

Lab: 11, LD: 7, SNP: 4, Ind: 1, Left Alliance: 1
Members of the Committee
Lab: H. Blyth, J. Brennan, A. Brown, P. Callaghan, J. Connelly, T. Dair (Chair), G. Duff, R. Edwards, K. Morrison, A. Paterson, A.J. Smith
LD: J. Bell, S.R. Black, A. Martin, E. Riches, J. Rosiejak, A. Soper, A.M. Watters
SNP: D. Alexander, D. Cunningham, A. Patey, M. Woods
Ind: G. Wood
Left Alliance: W. Clarke

BEHAVIOUR SUPPORT SERVICE

Rimbleton Hse, Rimbleton Pk, Glenrothes, Fife KY6 2BZ;
 e-mail glenrothesbsenquiries@fife.gov.uk;
 Tel 01592 415602; Fax 01592 416994
Manager D. Bruce
Deputy Manager D. Williamson
Alternative Education Support Centre Sandy Brae Community Centre, Sandy Brae, Kennoway, Fife KY8 5JN; Tel 01333 352718
Head R. Duncan
The Bridges Centre 8a MacGrigor Rd, Rosyth, Fife KY11 2AF; Tel 01383 313518; Fax 01383 313512
Deputy Headteacher Mr G. Simpson

Cupar Primary Education Centre Kirkgate Annex, Lovers La, Cupar, Fife KY15 4PE; Tel 01334 654793; Fax 01334 656923
Co-ordinator C. Anderson
Dunfermline Off-Campus Support Centre c/o Psychological Service, 13 Abbey Park Pl, Dunfermline, Fife KY12 7PT; e-mail dunfermlinebsenquiries@fife.gov.uk; Tel 01383 312824; Fax 01383 312821
Co-ordinator Mrs L. Morton
East Fife Off-Campus Support Centre Kirkgate Annexe, Lover La, Cupar, Fife KY15 5AH; Tel 01334 412386; Fax 01334 412386
Co-ordinator Mrs A. Smith
Glenrothes Education Centre Rimbleton Hse, Rimbleton Pk, Glenrothes, Fife KY6 2BZ; Tel 01592 415605; Fax 01592 416994
Deputy Headteacher C. Watson
Glenrothes Off-Campus Support Centre Rimbleton Hse, Rimbleton Pk, Glenrothes, Fife KY6 2BZ; Tel 01952 415624
Co-ordinator E. MacDonald
Kirkcaldy Off-Campus Support Centre Boreland Rd, Dysart, Fife KY1 2YG; e-mail kocsc@itasdarc.demon.co.uk; Tel 01592 653307; Fax 01592 654991
Co-ordinator Mrs J. Geddes
Levenmouth Off-Campus Support Centre Sandy Brae Community Centre, Sandy Brae, Kennoway, Fife KY8 5JN; Tel 01333 352027
Co-ordinator R. Morton

Glasgow City Council
www.glasgow.gov.uk

Population: 585 090
Political composition: Lab: 46; SNP: 22, LD: 5, Scottish Green Party: 5; Con: 1
City Chambers, George Sq, Glasgow G2 1DU;
 URL www.glasgow.gov.uk; e-mail pr@glasgow.gov.uk; Tel 0141 287 2000; Fax 0141 287 5666

Education Services

Glasgow City Council, Wheatley Hse, 25 Cochrane St, Glasgow G1 1HL; e-mail education@glasgow.gov.uk; Tel 0141 287 4271; Fax 0141 287 4895
Convener Bailie Gordon Matheson
Vice-Convener Cllr Patricia Chalmers
Executive Director (Education and Social Work Services) Margaret Doran
Service Director (Education Services) Maureen McKenna
Service Director (Social Work Services) David Crawford
Head of Service Margaret Orr
Head (ASL); Area Manager (North) Brenda Wallace
Head (Early Years); Area Manager (East) John Butcher
Head (Human Resources and Vocational Education) Christine Scalpello
Head (Performance and Asset Management) Jim Wilson
Head (Primary); Area Manager (South East) Anne Marie McGovern
Head (Quality Assurance); Area Manager (South West) Wendy O'Donnell
Head (Secondary); Area Manager (West) Gerry Lyons
Head (Service Department) Moira Abernethy
Head (Vocational Training) John Kane
Number of Schools
34 Special; 29 Secondary

EXECUTIVE COMMITTEE

Lab: 15, SNP: 5, Religious Reps: 3, Scottish Liberal Democrats: 1
Convener Steven Purcell
Vice-Convener James Coleman

Members of the Committee
Shaukat Butt, Aileen Colleran, Stephen Curran, Stephen
Dornan, Archie Graham, Jahangir Hanif, Allison Hunter,
Hanzala Malik, H. Malik, Dr Christopher Mason, John
Mason, Gordon Matheson, Elaine McDougall, Tom
McKeown, C. McMaster, Ifran Rabbani, George Ryan, Ruth
Simpson, Alan Stewart, Alison Thewliss, Martha Wardrop

PSYCHOLOGICAL SERVICES

North East Area Office 48 Gourlay St, Glasgow G21 1AE;
e-mail alan.mclean@education.glasgow.gov.uk;
Tel 0141 558 5303; Fax 0141 558 3211
North West Area Office c/o St Gregory's Primary School,
Glenfinnon Dr, Glasgow G20 8HF; e-mail
susan.reynolds@education.glasgow.gov.uk;
Tel 0141 946 0655; Fax 0141 946 0934
South East Area Office Templeton Business Centre, Bldg 1,
Ground Fl, 62 Templeton St, Glasgow G40 1DA; e-mail
sally.dolan@education.glasgow.gov.uk;
Tel 0141 227 7660; Fax 0141 554 6170
South West Area Office c/o Battlefield Primary, Carmichael
Pl, Glasgow G42 9SY; e-mail
fergal.doherty@education.glasgow.gov.uk;
Tel 0141 632 0638; Fax 0141 649 6483

SPECIAL UNITS WITHIN MAINSTREAM SCHOOLS

Bannerman Autism Unit c/o Bannerman High School,
Glasgow Rd, Glasgow G69 7NS; e-mail
headteacher@bannermanhigh.glasgow.sch.uk
Principal Teacher Robert Stratham; Tel 0141 771 8770
Barlanark Autism Unit 37 Balcurvie Rd, Glasgow G34 9QL
Unit Co-ordinator E. Ann Houston; Tel 0141 773 0841
Caledonia Speech and Language Unit Calderwood Dr,
Baillieston G69 7DJ;
URL unithead@caledoniaunit-pri.glasgow.sch.uk
Unit Co-ordinator Jean Fergusson; Tel 0141 781 4239;
Fax 0141 773 0790
Crookston Speech and Language Unit c/o St Monica's
Primary School, 30 Kempsthorn Rd, Glasgow G53 5SR;
e-mail unithead@crookstonunit-pri.glasgow.sch.uk
Co-ordinator Caroline Dunleavy; Tel 0141 892 0813;
Fax 0141 892 0327
Darnley Visual Impairment Unit c/o Darnley Primary
School, 169 Glen Morriston Rd, Glasgow G53 7HT; e-mail
unithead@darnleyunit-pri.glasgow.sch.uk
Unit Co-ordinator Helen King; Tel 0141 621 2919
Govan Autism Unit c/o Govan High School, 12 Ardnish St,
Glasgow G51 4NB; e-mail
headteacher@govanhigh.glasgow.sch.uk
Head Lorna Wallace; Tel 0141 582 0561;
Fax 0141 582 0091
Hillpark Autism Unit c/o Hillpark Secondary School, 36
Cairngorm Rd, Glasgow G43 2XA; e-mail
headteacher@hillparkunit-sec.glasgow.sch.uk
Co-ordinator Nadine Barber; Tel 0141 582 0112;
Fax 0141 582 0112
Rosshall Visual Impairment Unit c/o Rosshall Academy,
131 Crookston Rd, Glasgow G52 3QF; e-mail
headteacher@rosshallacademy.glasgow.sch.uk
Principal Teacher Moira Gillies; Tel 0141 582 0200;
Fax 0141 582 0201
Royston Speech and Language Unit c/o Royston Primary
School, 102 Royston Rd, Glasgow G21 2NU; e-mail
unithead@roystonunit-pri.glasgow.sch.uk
Co-ordinator Ms Julie Steel; Tel 0141 552 1673
Ruchill Autism Unit c/o Ruchill Primary School, 29 Brassey
St, Glasgow G20 9HW;
URL unithead@ruchillunit-pri.glasgow.sch.uk
Co-ordinator Kay Littlejohn; Tel 0141 498 0073;
Fax 0141 946 7756
St Charles' Speech and Language Unit c/o St Charles'
Primary School, 13 Kelvinside Gdns, Glasgow G20 6BG;
e-mail unithead@st-charlesunit-pri.glasgow.sch.uk
Co-ordinator Mrs Jane Ross; Tel 0141 945 2121

St Joseph's Hearing Impairment Unit St Joseph's Primary
School, 39 Raglan St, Glasgow G4 9QX; e-mail
unithead@st-josephsunit-pri.glasgow.sch.uk
Unit Co-ordinator Mrs Veronica O'Hagan;
Tel 0141 353 6136; Fax 0141 353 6137
St Roch's Hearing Impairment Unit 40 Royston Rd, Glasgow
G21 2NF; e-mail
headteacher@st-rochs-sec.glasgow.sch.uk
Unit Co-ordinator Elizabeth Orr; Tel 0141 582 0273;
Fax 0141 582 0272
For pupils with hearing impairment: Secondary
St Thomas Aquinas Language Unit c/o St Thomas Aquinas
Sec, 112 Mitre St, Glasgow G14 9GW; e-mail
headteacher@st-thomasaquinas-sec.glasgow.sch.uk
Principal Teacher Vacancy; Tel 0141 582 0280;
Fax 0141 582 0281
St Vincent's Autism Unit c/o St Vincent's (Carnwadric)
Primary School, 40 Crebar St, Glasgow G46 8EQ; e-mail
unithead@st-vincentsunit-pri.glasgow.sch.uk
Unit Co-ordinator Isobel McAllister; Tel 0141 621 1968
Toryglen Autism Unit c/o Toryglen Primary School, 6
Drumreoch Pl, Glasgow G42 0ER; e-mail
unithead@toryglenunit-pri.glasgow.sch.uk
Head Mrs Marion McFarlane; Tel 0141 613 3840;
Fax 0141 647 6974

ASSESSMENT CENTRES FOR UNDER-FIVES

Duntarvie Pre School Assessment and Development Centre
c/o Cadder Primary School, 60 Herma St, Glasgow
G23 5AR; e-mail
headteacher@duntarviepre-school.glasgow.sch.uk;
Tel 0141 946 3835
Parkhead Pre-School Assessment Centre 1346 Gallowgate,
Glasgow G31 4DJ; e-mail parkhead-psac@seemis.net;
Tel 0141 551 9591
Teacher-in-Charge M. Morris

PART-TIME CENTRES FOR SPECIAL EDUCATIONAL NEEDS

Drumchapel Learning Centre 77 Hecla Ave, Glasgow
G15 8LX; e-mail
headteacher@drumchapel.glasgow.sch.uk;
Tel 0141 944 8517; Fax 0141 949 1645
Teacher-in-Charge Evelyn Hill
Rosepark Learning Centre 2nd Fl, Rm 9, Thornwood
Primary School, 11 Thornwood Ave, Glasgow G11 7QZ;
e-mail headteacher@rosepark.glasgow.sch.uk
Co-ordinator Margaret Glasgow; Tel 0141 334 5700;
Fax 0141 334 5910

The Highland Council

www.highland.gov.uk

Population: 211 340
Political composition: Joint Ind/SNP
Headquarters, Glenurquhart Rd, Inverness, Highland
IV3 5NX; URL www.highland.gov.uk; e-mail
webmaster@highland.gov.uk; Tel 01463 702000;
Fax 01463 702111
Chief Executive Alistair Dodds

Education, Culture and Sport Service

URL www.highland.gov.uk/educ/default.htm; e-mail
ecs@highland.gov.uk; Tel 01463 702806;
Fax 01463 711177
Director Hugh Fraser
Head (Children's Services) Bill Alexander
Head (Community, Learning and Leisure) Ian Murray
Head (Education Services) D.R.J. MacDonald
Head (Support Services) Ron MacKenzie
*Area Manager (Education, Culture and Sport: Caithness,
Sutherland and Easter Ross)* Graham Nichols; Caithness:
Rhind Hse, West Banks Ave, Wick, Highland KW1 5LZ;

Tel 01955 602362; Fax 01955 602408; Sutherland: Education Office, Brora, Highland KW9 6PG; Tel 01408 623900; Fax 01408 621126

Area Manager (Education, Culture and Sport: Inverness/Nairn/ Badenoch and Strathspey) Hector Robertson BSc, BA; Inverness: 13 Ardross St, Inverness, Highland IV3 5NT; Tel 01463 663800; Fax 01463 663809; Nairn/Badenoch and Strathspey: King St, Kingussie, Highland PH22 1RH; Tel 01540 661009; Fax 01540 662330

Area Manager (Education, Culture and Sport: Ross, Skye and Lochalsh) John Ritchie; The Education Centre, Castle St, Dingwall, Highland IV15 9HU; Tel 01349 863441; Fax 01349 863994

Manager (Community Development) Graham Watson

Manager (Finance) Brenda Dunthorne

Manager (Lifelong Learning) Christopher Phillips

Quality Development Officer (Early Years) Moira Shearer

Quality Development Officer (Pupil Support) Margaret Crombie

Number of Schools

183 Primary; 29 Secondary; 6 Special; 1 Nursery

Number of students

32 163

EDUCATION, CULTURE AND SPORT COMMITTEE

Chair W. Fernie; (Ind)

Vice-Chair (with responsibility for Sport and Recreation) Mr B. Gormley; (SNP)

Members of the Committee

R. Balfour, D. Bremner, I. Campbell, J. Douglas, M. Finlayson, Dr M.E.M. Foxley, C. Fraser, L. Fraser, Rev A. Glass, D. Hendry, E. Hunter, D. MacKay, K. MacNab, E. McAllister, J. McDonald, Rev D.C. Meredith, A.M. Millar, M. Paterson, Dr A. Sinclair, G. Slider, M. Smith, Lady Thurso, J. Urquhart, H. Wood

QUALITY DEVELOPMENT TEAM/SUPPORT FOR LEARNING TEAM

The Education Centre, Castle St, Dingwall, Highland IV15 9HU; Tel 01349 863441; Fax 01349 865637

Manager (Quality Assurance and Development) Tony McCulloch; e-mail tony.mcculloch@highland.gov.uk

Quality Improvement Officer Susan Belford

Quality Improvement Officer Ian Cowie

Quality Improvement Officer Clifford Cooke

Development Officer (Interrupted Learning) Karen MacMaster

Development Officer (Support for Learning) Jane Baines

Autism Outreach Officer Myna Dowds

Autism Outreach Advisory Teacher Roger Bamfield

Autism Outreach Advisory Teacher Dave Sherratt

PSYCHOLOGICAL SERVICE

11–13 Culcabock Ave, Inverness, Highland IV2 3RG; Tel 01463 233494; Fax 01463 713775

Principal Education Psychologist Bernadette Cairns (Acting)

OUTDOOR EDUCATION CENTRES

Kinlocheil Outdoor Centre Kinlocheil, Fort William, Highland; e-mail ron.christie@highland.gov.uk

Manager (Outdoor Education) Ron Christie; Tel 01463 870797; Fax 01463 871044

Torrin Outdoor Centre Torrin, Broadford, Isle of Skye, Highland; e-mail ron.christie@highland.gov.uk

Manager (Outdoor Education) Ron Christie; Tel 01463 870797; Fax 01463 871044

Inverclyde Council

www.inverclyde.gov.uk

Population: 83 050

Political composition: Lab: 9, SNP: 5, LD: 4, Con: 1, Ind: 1

Municipal Bldgs, Greenock, Inverclyde PA15 1LZ; URL www.inverclyde.gov.uk; Tel 01475 724400; Fax 01475 712010

Chief Executive John Mundell

Corporate Director (Education and Social Care) Ian Fraser

Education Services

Inverclyde Council, Municipal Bldgs, Clyde Sq, Greenock, Inverclyde PA15 1LY; e-mail lisa.swann@inverclyde.gov.uk; Tel 01475 712761; Fax 01475 712731

Head (Lifelong Learning and Educational Support) Colin Laird

Head (School Estate) Tom Reid

Head (Schools) Albert Henderson

Manager (SEN Service) Maureen Irving

Quality Improvement Manager Wilma Bain

Quality Improvement Officer Iain Mills

Quality Improvement Officer (Early Years; Primary) Sheena Beaton

Quality Improvement Officer (English) Fiona Norris

Quality Improvement Officer (ICT and Enterprise) Kieran McDevitt

Quality Improvement Officer (Inclusion) Maureen Ruxton

Quality Improvement Officer (Maths) M. Robertson

Quality Improvement Officer (Primary) Irene Watters

EDUCATION SERVICES COMMITTEE

Lab: 5, SNP: 3, LD: 2, Con: 1

Convener S. McCabe (Lab)

Vice-Convener T. Loughran (Lab)

Members of the Committee

Lab: J. Clocherty, G. Dorrian, T. Loughran, S. McCabe, M. McCormick

SNP: K. Brooks, J. Grieve, C. Osborne

LD: A. Blair, G. White

Con: D. Wilson

PSYCHOLOGICAL SERVICE

Highholm Centre Highholm Ave, Port Glasgow, Inverclyde PA14 5JN; e-mail noreen.phillips@inverclydeschools.org.uk; Tel 01475 715430

Principal N. Phillips

SEN NETWORKS

Glenburn Communication Disorder Unit Glenburn School, Inverkip Rd, Greenock, Inverclyde PA16 0QG; e-mail eim571@inverclydeschools.org.uk

Headteacher Eileen McGeer

Communication and language disorders

Midlothian Council

www.midlothian.gov.uk

Population: 79 710

Political composition: Lab: 14, LD: 3, Ind: 1

Midlothian Hse, Buccleuch St, Dalkeith, Midlothian EH22 1DJ; URL www.midlothian.gov.uk; e-mail enquiries@midlothian.gov.uk; Tel 0131 270 7500; Fax 0131 271 3050

Chief Executive Trevor Muir

Director (Education) Donald MacKay

Director (Social Work) Malcolm McEwan

Education Division

Fairfield Hse, 8 Lothian Rd, Dalkeith, Midlothian
  EH22 3ZG; e-mail education@midlothian.gov.uk;
  Tel 0131 271 3718; Fax 0131 271 3751
Director (Education)   Donald MacKay
Head (School and Community Education)   F. Mitchell
Head (Support Services)   J.M. Clarke
Education Officer (Administration)   S. Banks
Education Officer (Community Education)   G. Clayton
Education Officer (Curriculum Development)   M. Tait
Education Officer (Nursery/Primary/Special)   S. Dawe
Education Officer (Nursery/Primary/Special)   S. Thayne
Education Officer (Staff Development)   H. Wylie
Education Officer (Technical and Curriculum Support)
  T. Lawson
Number of Schools
35 Primary; 6 Secondary; 6 Nursery; 1 Special; 18 Nursery
Classes
Day of Cabinet
Every second Tuesday

EDUCATION CABINET

Members of the Midlothian Council
Lab: J. Aitchison, P. Boyes, S. Campbell, W. Chalmers, J.
Dunsmuir, R. Imrie, B. Jenkins, G. Marr, K. McIntosh, D.
Milligan, D. Molloy, A. Montgomery, J. Muirhead, R. Prior,
M. Russell
LD: D. Fletcher, S. Thacker

PUPIL SUPPORT SERVICES

Greenhall Centre Gowkshill, Gorebridge, Midlothian
  EH23 4PE; Tel 01875 823699; Fax 01875 823603
Principal Psychologist   Alan Haughey

COMMUNITY EDUCATION SERVICE OFFICES AND CENTRES

Adult Basic Education Fairfield Hse, 8 Lothian Rd, Dalkeith,
  Midlothian EH22 3ZG; Tel 0131 271 3708
Head   A. McConachy
Beeslack Centre Beeslack High School, Edinburgh Rd,
  Penicuik, Midlothian EH26 0QF; Tel 01968 673893
Head   R. Cooper
Brown Building Gorebridge Primary School, Hunterfield
  Rd, Gorebridge, Midlothian EH23 4XA; Tel 01875 821808
Head   J. McNeill
Carnethy Centre Greenlaw Mains, Penicuik, Midlothian
  EH26 0QP; Tel 01968 673594
Head   Vacancy
Dalkeith Community Learning Centre 29 Elmfield Ct,
  Dalkeith, Midlothian EH22 1DY; Tel 0131 271 3481
Head   L. Reid
Dalkeith Office Dalkeith Community Learning Centre, 6
  Woodburn Rd, Dalkeith, Midlothian EH22 2AR;
  Tel 0131 654 9817
Head   P. Thewlis
Support and Regeneration Service Greenhall Centre,
  Gowkshill, Gorebridge, Midlothian EH23 4PE;
  Tel 01875 823699
Head   P. Jacobs
Greenhall Community Education Centre Gowkshill,
  Gorebridge, Midlothian EH23 4PE; Tel 01875 825091
Head   K. McGowan
Jackson Street Building Jackson St, Penicuik, Midlothian
  EH26 9BQ; Tel 01968 679234
Head   J. Fairgrieve
Lasswade High School Centre Eskdale Dr, Bonyrigg,
  Edinburgh EH19 2LA; Tel 0131 663 8170
Head   A. Lang
Newbattle Centre 67 Gardiner Pl, Newtongrange,
  Midlothian EH22 4RT; Tel 0131 663 6055
Head   P. Johnson

Penicuik YWCA/YMCA 50a Kirkhill Rd, Penicuik,
  Midlothian EH26 8JB; Tel 01968 674851
Head   L. Taylor
Sherwood Community Wing Cockpen Rd, Bonnyrigg,
  Midlothian EH19 3HR; Tel 0131 663 7181
Manager   A. McDonald

Moray Council
www.moray.org.uk

Population: 87 000
Council Office, High St, Elgin, Moray IV30 1BX;
  URL www.moray.org.uk; e-mail hotline@moray.gov.uk;
  Tel 01343 543451; Fax 01343 540183
Chief Executive   Alastair Keddie
Director (Community Services)   Sandy Riddell
Director (Environmental Services)   Robert A. Stewart
Chief Financial Officer   Mark Palmer
Chief Legal Officer   Roderick D. Burns
Convener   George McIntyre

Educational Services

e-mail morag.cantlay@moray.gov.uk; Tel 01343 563397;
  Fax 01343 563478
Director   Donald M. Duncan
Head (Educational Development Services)   George Sinclair
Head (Educational Resource Services)   Alistair Farquhar
Head (Educational Support Services)   Eric Scarborough

EDUCATIONAL SERVICES COMMITTEE

Ind: 11, SNP: 9, Scottish Conservative and Unionists: 3,
Scottish Labour: 2, Vacancy: 1
Joint Chair   Lee Bell (Ind)
Joint Chair   Jeff Hamilton (Ind)
Members of the Committee
Ind: Lee A. Bell, Stewart Cree, Jeff Hamilton, John C. Hogg,
Joe Mackay, Eric M. McGillivray, George McIntyre, Anne C.
McKay, Fiona J. Murdoch, John G. Russell, Ronald H.
Shepherd
SNP: Gary S. Coull, Graham Leadbitter, Michael J.
McConachie, Anita D. McDonald, Gordon McDonald, Irene
Ogilvie, Pearl B. Paul, Mike Shand, David C. Stewart
Scottish Conservative and Unionist: Douglas G. Ross, Allan G.
Wright, Iain Young
Lab: John A. Divers, Barry Jarvis

HEARING IMPAIRED/VISUAL IMPAIRED SERVICE

Central Support Services, Beechbrae Education Centre,
  Elgin, Moray IV30 4NP; e-mail
  kim.stokes@moray.gov.uk; Tel 01343 557921;
  Fax 01343 557935

LANGUAGE SUPPORT AND EARLY YEARS

Central Support Services, Beechbrae Education Centre,
  Elgin, Moray IV30 4NP; e-mail
  kim.stokes@moray.gov.uk; Tel 01343 557921;
  Fax 01343 557935

ENGLISH AS AN ADDITIONAL LANGUAGE

Central Support Services, Beechbrae Education Centre,
  Elgin, Moray IV30 4NP; e-mail
  kim.stokes@moray.gov.uk; Tel 01343 557921;
  Fax 01343 557935

North Ayrshire Council

www.north-ayrshire.gov.uk

Population: 135 830
Political composition: Lab: 12, SNP: 8, Ind: 5, Con: 3, LD: 2
Cunninghame Hse, Irvine, North Ayrshire KA12 8EE;
URL www.north-ayrshire.gov.uk; e-mail
contactus@north-ayrshire.gov.uk; Tel 0845 603 0590;
Fax 01294 324144
Chief Executive   Ian Snodgrass

Educational Services

e-mail education@north-ayrshire.gov.uk; Tel 01294 324400;
Fax 01294 324444
Corporate Director   Carol Kirk
Head (Educational Resources)   Brian Gardner
Head (Educational Services)   Carol Kirk
Head (Educational Services)   James Leckie
Head (Educational Services)   Jan Ward
Number of Schools
53 Primary; 9 Secondary; 4 Special

EDUCATION EXECUTIVE COMMITTEE

Members of the Committee
Lab: Thomas Barr, John Bell, Margaret McDougall, Fr
Matthew McManus, Peter McNamara, David O'Neill, John
Reid, John Scott
Church Representative: Rev David Karoon

PSYCHOLOGICAL SERVICE

6a Kilwinning Rd, Irvine, North Ayrshire KA12 8RU;
Tel 01294 272427; Fax 01294 276308
Contact   Ian Wallace
Kilwinning Road Centre   6a Kilwinning Rd, Vineburgh Pk,
Irvine, North Ayrshire KA12 8RU; Tel 01294 272427;
Fax 01294 276308
Contact   Ian Wallace

OUTDOOR PURSUITS CENTRE

Arran Outdoor Education Centre   Lamlash, Isle of Arran
KA27 8PL; e-mail arranoutdoor@north-ayrshire.gov.uk;
Tel 01770 600532; Fax 01770 600083
Contact   Nigel Marshall

QUALITY IMPROVEMENT SERVICE

Cunninghame Hse, Irvine, North Ayrshire KA12 8EE;
Tel 01294 324400; Fax 01294 324444

EDUCATION RESOURCE SERVICE

Greenwood Centre, Dreghorn, Irvine, North Ayrshire
KA11 4GZ; e-mail nacers@netcentral.co.uk;
Tel 01294 212716; Fax 01294 222509
Contact   Audrey Sutton

North Lanarkshire Council

www.northlan.gov.uk

PO Box 14, Civic Centre, Motherwell, North Lanarkshire
ML1 1TW; URL www.northlan.gov.uk; Tel 01698 302222;
Fax 01698 275125
Chief Executive   Gavin Whitefield; Tel 01698 302452;
Fax 01698 230265
Director (Social Work)   Jim Dickie; Tel 01698 332011;
Fax 01698 332095

Education Department

Municipal Bldgs, Kildonan St, Coatbridge, North
Lanarkshire ML5 3BT; e-mail
education@northlan.gov.uk; Tel 01236 812222;
Fax 01698 403021
Director (Education)   Michael O'Neill
Deputy Director   Christine Pollock
Head (Educational Provision)   Murdo Maciver
Head (Quality and Support Service)   Jane Liddell
Principal Officer (Support for Learning)   Vacancy
Development Officer (Home Education and Gypsy Travellers)
Linda Henderson
Quality Improvement Officer   Gerry Shields;
Tel 01236 812294

EDUCATION COMMITTEE

Lab: 30, SNP: 6, Religious Reps: 3, Teacher Reps: 2, Ind: 1
Convener   C. Gray (Lab)
Vice-Convener   Kevin McKeown
Vice-Convener   Tommy Morgan
Members of the Committee
T. Barrie, B. Brady, J. Brooks, A. Burns, C. Cefferty, A.
Clarke, T. Curley, H. Curran, P. Donnelly, F. Glavin, S.
Grant, C. Gray, F. Griffin, C. Hebenton, E. Holloway, J.
Jones, J. Logue, S. Love, R. Lyle, V. Mathieson, J. McCabe, N.
McCallum, B. McCulloch, I. McGhee, H. McGuigan, K.
McKeown, J. McKinlay, J. Moran, G. Murray, M. Murray, J.
Pentland, B. Scott, J. Smith, D. Stocks, P. Sullivan, B. Wallace

PSYCHOLOGICAL SERVICES

Main Offices   Municipal Bldgs, Kildonan St, Coatbridge,
North Lanarkshire ML5 3BT; e-mail
steeleb@northlan.gov.uk; Tel 01236 812825;
Fax 01236 812247
Principal Educational Psychologist   Christine Vassie
Monklands Area   St Stephen's Primary School, Sikeside St,
Coatbridge, North Lanarkshire ML5 4QH; e-mail
hodonnell@ea.n-lanark.sch.uk; Tel 01236 757664;
Fax 01236 432948
Motherwell Area   St Brendan's Primary School, 45 Barons
Rd, Motherwell, North Lanarkshire ML1 2NB; e-mail
wallace@ea.n-lanark.sch.uk; Tel 01698 262840;
Fax 01698 267180
Contact   Ian Wallace

NETWORK SUPPORT AREA OFFICES

Airdrie Area   c/o St Aloysius' Primary, Main St, Chapelhall,
North Lanarkshire ML6 8SF; e-mail
moyradarroch@en.n-lanark.sch.uk; Tel 01236 748416;
Fax 01236 748416
Contact   Moyra Darroch
Bellshill Area   c/o St Gerard's Primary, Kelvin Rd, Bellshill,
North Lanarkshire ML4 1LN; e-mail
n.reilly@ea.n-lanark.sch.uk; Tel 01698 841743;
Fax 01698 841743
Contact   Nancy Reilly
Bilingual and Support for Learning Section   c/o Baird
Memorial Primary, Glenacre Rd, North Carbrain,
Cumbernauld, North Lanarkshire G67 2NX; e-mail
abdulazizahmed@ea.n-lanark.sch.uk; Tel 01236 612634;
Fax 01236 612634
Contact   Abdul Aziz Ahmed
Coatbridge Area   c/o St Patrick's High, Muiryhall St,
Coatbridge, North Lanarkshire ML5 3NN; e-mail
roma.french@ea.n-lanark.sch.uk; Tel 01236 437039;
Fax 01236 437039
Contact   Roma French
Cumbernauld Area   c/o St Patrick's Primary, Backbrae St,
Kilsyth, North Lanarkshire G65 0NA; e-mail
kathleenmorrison@ea.n-lanark.sch.uk; Tel 01236 824867;
Fax 01236 824867
Contact   Kathleen Morrison (Acting)

Pre-5 Learning Support c/o Petersburn Primary, Petersburn Rd, Airdrie, North Lanarkshire ML6 8DX; e-mail lizleggat@ea.n-lanark.sch.uk; Tel 01236 756276; Fax 01236 756276
Contact Liz Leggat

SEN and Microtec Centre c/o Psychological Services, Kyle Rd, Cumbernauld, North Lanarkshire G67 2DN; e-mail ojkdunn@ea.n-lanark.sch.uk; Tel 01236 731041; Fax 01236 722558
Contact Owen Dunn

Wishaw/Shotts Area 66 Barons Rd, Motherwell, North Lanarkshire ML2 2NB; e-mail wishawsupport@ea.n-lanark.sch.uk; Tel 01698 252041; Fax 01698 252041
Contact Elizabeth Sutters

SERVICES FOR HEARING IMPAIRED PUPILS

Hearing Impaired Unit c/o Cedar Road Nursery, 196 Cedar Rd, Abronhill, North Lanarkshire G67 3BL; e-mail cedarroad@ea.n-lanark.sch.uk; Tel 01236 733604; Fax 01236 733604
Head Elizabeth Sneddon

Hearing Impairment Primary Unit c/o Glencairn Primary, Glencairn St, Motherwell, North Lanarkshire ML1 1TT; e-mail ht@glencairn.n-lanark.sch.uk; Tel 01698 300281; Fax 01236 300283
Head Lorna Galbraith

Hearing Impairment Secondary Unit c/o Dalziel High School, Crawford St, Motherwell, North Lanarkshire ML1 3AG; e-mail rdavidson@dalziel.n-lanark.sch.uk; Tel 01698 328628; Fax 01698 328631
Head Ruby Davidson

SERVICES FOR CHILDREN AND YOUNG PEOPLE WITH SENSORY IMPAIRMENT

Sensory Support Service (Visual and Hearing Impairment) Knowetop Primary, Knowetop Ave, Motherwell, North Lanarkshire ML1 2AG; Tel 01698 269396; Fax 01698 254260
Contact Anne Ferguson

SERVICES FOR PUPILS WITH EMOTIONAL AND BEHAVIOUR DIFFICULTIES

Inclusion Support Base Pentland Rd, Chrystom, North Lanarkshire G69 9DL; e-mail agnesdonnelly@ea.n-lanark.sch.uk; Tel 0141 779 4891; Fax 0141 779 4183
Contact Agnes Donnelly

Language and Communications Unit c/o Castlehill Primary, Brikshaw Brae, Wishaw, North Lanarkshire ML2 0ND; e-mail annefisher@castlehill.n-lanark.sch.uk; Tel 01698 357497; Fax 01698 352491
Contact Anne Fisher

Language Unit c/o St Margaret of Scotland Primary, Broomlands Rd, Cumbernauld, North Lanarkshire G67 2HQ; e-mail ambready@st-margaret-scotland.n-lanark.sch.uk; Tel 01236 726200; Fax 01236 780742
Contact Anne Marie Bready

Newpark Centre 135 New Edinburgh Rd, Uddingston, North Lanarkshire G71 6ND; e-mail sallydykes@ea.n-lanark.sch.uk; Tel 01698 812666; Fax 01698 811978
Contact Sally Dykes

Primary Communication Disorders Unit c/o St Lucy's Primary, Oak Rd, Cumbernauld, North Lanarkshire G67 3LQ; e-mail r.kicinski@st.lucys.n-lanark.sch.uk; Tel 01236 732695; Fax 01236 457266
Contact Rose Kicinski

Secondary Communication Disorders Unit c/o Cumbernauld High, South Carbrain Ring Rd, Cumbernauld, North Lanarkshire G67 2UF; e-mail rpalmer@cumbernauldhigh.n-lanark.sch.uk; Tel 01236 780085; Fax 01236 737158
Contact Ros Palmer

COMMUNITY EDUCATION, NEIGHBOURHOOD AND YOUTH CENTRES

Abronhill Community Education Centre Larch Rd, Cumbernauld, North Lanarkshire G67 3AZ; Tel 01236 733249

Airdrie Community Education Centre 31 North Biggar Rd, Airdrie, North Lanarkshire ML6 6EJ; Tel 01236 751538

Bellshill Community Education Centre John St, Bellshill, North Lanarkshire ML4 1RJ; Tel 01698 844607

Cardinal Newman Community Education Centre Cardinal Newman High School, Main St, Bellshill, North Lanarkshire ML4 3DW; Tel 01698 844952

Coatbridge Community Education Centre 2 Corsewall St, Coatbridge, North Lanarkshire ML5 1QH; Tel 01236 422511

Garrell Vale Community Education Centre Duncansfield, Kilsyth, North Lanarkshire G65 9JX; Tel 01236 823871

Link Community Education Centre Bron Way, Town Centre, Cumbernauld, North Lanarkshire G67 3AZ; Tel 01236 728200

Muirfield Community Education Centre Brown Rd, Cumbernauld, North Lanarkshire G67 1AA; Tel 01236 723966

Newarthill Community Education Centre High St, Newarthill, North Lanarkshire ML1 5JU; Tel 01698 861170

Pivot Community Education Centre Glenmanor Ave, Moodiesburn, North Lanarkshire G67 0DX; Tel 01236 874941

Shotts Community Education Centre Kirk Rd, Shotts, North Lanarkshire ML7 5ET; Tel 01501 821826

Viewpark Community Education Centre Old Edinburgh Rd, Bellshill, North Lanarkshire G71 6PI; Tel 01698 817500

Orkney Islands Council

www.orkney.gov.uk

Population: 19 245
Council Offices, School Pl, Kirkwall, Orkney Islands KW15 1NY; URL www.orkney.gov.uk; Tel 01856 873535; Fax 01856 874615
Chief Executive Alistair Buchan MA, MCIPD

Education and Recreation Services Department

Fax 01856 870302
Director W.L. Manson MA
Head (Community Education) A.G. Clouston DipYCS
Head (Education Resources) D. Sewell
Head (Pupil Support) P. Diamond
Head (Quality Development) M. Richards (Acting)
Manager (Catering) Vacancy
Principal Educational Psychologist Cathy Lyner; Tel 01856 874779; Fax 01856 876049
County Librarian Vacancy; Laing St, Kirkwall, Orkney Islands; Tel 01856 873166; Fax 01856 875260
Number of Schools
17 Primary; 4 Secondary and Primary; 2 Comprehensive
Day of Committee Meeting
Every sixth Wednesday

EDUCATION COMMITTEE

Chair J. Annal
Vice-Chair A. Drever;
Members of the Committee
C. Annal, M.J.F. Drever, S. Hagan, J.M. Hamilton, A. Hutchison, I. Johnstone, A. Leslie, I. Macdonald, R.R. McLeod, J. Moar, S.T. Scott

OUTDOOR CENTRES

Birsay Outdoor Centre Birsay, Orkney, Orkney Islands KW16 2LY; Tel 01856 873535
Warden L. Jones
Hoy Outdoor Centre/Rackwick Outdoor Centre Hoy, Orkney, Orkney Islands KW16 3NJ; Tel 01856 873535
Warden E. Clark

Perth and Kinross Council
www.pkc.gov.uk

Population: 140 190
Political composition: SNP: 18, Con: 12, Scottish Liberal Democrat: 8, Lab: 3
2 High St, Perth, Perth and Kinross PH1 5PH;
URL www.pkc.gov.uk; e-mail enquiries@pkc.gov.uk;
Tel 01738 475000; Fax 01738 475710
Chief Executive Bernadette Malone

Education and Children's Services

Perth and Kinross Council, Pullar Hse, 35 Kinnoull St, Perth, Perth and Kinross PH1 5GD; e-mail ecsgeneralenquiries@pkc.gov.uk; Tel 01738 476200
Executive Director John Fyffe; e-mail jfyffe@pkc.gov.uk
Number of Schools
76 Primary; 10 Secondary; 2 Special; 6 Special Units; 1 Autistic Unit; 1 Gaelic Unit

Renfrewshire Council
www.renfrewshire.gov.uk

Population: 170 000
Political composition: Lab: 17, SNP: 17, LD: 4, Con: 2
Council Headquarters, Renfrewshire Hse, Cotton St, Paisley, Renfrewshire PA1 1LE;
URL www.renfrewshire.gov.uk; Tel 0141 842 5000; Fax 0141 840 3212
Chief Executive David Martin

Education and Leisure Services

e-mail els@renfrewshire.gov.uk; e-mail
<firstname>.<surname>@renfrewshire.gov.uk;
Tel 0141 842 5663; Fax 0141 842 5655
Director John Rooney
Head (Children's Services) Stephen McKenzie
Head (Planning and Community Services) Liz Jamieson
Head (Resource Services) Robert Naylor
Senior Resources Manager George McLachlan
Resources Manager Ian Thomson
Manager (Arts and Museums) John Harding
Manager (Children and Family Services) Kathleen McDonagh
Manager (Community Capacity Services) Gordon Terris
Manager (Community Learning and Information) Derek Bell
Manager (Customer Support) Elaine MacKay
Manager (Estates Support) Julie Telford
Manager (Finance Services) Dougie Paton
Manager (Health Support) Ronnie Gourley
Manager (Home Link Services) Winnie Walker
Manager (Leisure and Cultural Services) Patricia Cassidy
Manager (Library Services) John Laurenson
Manager (Operations Support) Rose Barr
Manager (Performance) Tony McEwan
Manager (Pupil Services) Martin Doherty
Manager (Specialist Peripatetic Services) Anne Craig
Manager (Youth Services) Elizabeth Ireland
Principal Psychologist Richard Woolfson
Depute Principal Psychologist Michael Harker

Senior Adviser (Children and Families) Alan Locke
Senior Adviser (Performance Management) Peter Hempsey (Acting)
Senior Adviser (Policy and Planning) Marjorie Munro
Senior Adviser (School Improvement) Gordon McKinlay (Acting)

EDUCATION POLICY BOARD

Convener Cllr Lorraine Cameron
Depute Convener Cllr Jim McQuade
Members of the Board
SNP: , Cameron, Doig, B. Lawson, McQuade, Noon, Perrie, Provost, Puthucheary
Lab: Bibby, Fee, Harte, M. McMillan, Mullin
Church Reps: Rev Clark, Monsignor Diamond, Mr Hamilton
LD: McDonald, McGurk
Con: Langlands

Scottish Borders Council
www.scotborders.gov.uk

Population: 110 240
Political composition: Con: 11, LD: 10, SNP: 6, Ind: 5, Borders Party: 2,
Council Headquarters, Newtown St Boswells, Melrose, Scottish Borders TD6 0SA;
URL www.scotborders.gov.uk; e-mail enquiries@scotborders.gov.uk; Tel 01835 824000; Fax 01835 825001
Chief Executive David Hume

Education and Lifelong Learning

Fax 01835 825091
Director Glenn Rodger
Head (Business Services) Lynn Mirley
Head (Community Services) Alan Hasson
Head (Primary and Nursery) Yvonne McCracken
Head (Quality Services) Kate Brown
Head (Secondary and ASN) Jackie Swanston
Manager (Additional Support Needs) Maria Lucia MacConnachie MA; Tel 01835 825094
Quality Improvement Officer (QIO) E.M. MacIntosh BA(Hons), DipEd, CertGuid
Number of Schools
12 Special; 9 Secondary
Day of Committee Meeting
Tuesday
Requisition Periods for Schools Supplies
No fixed period
Other Authorities with whom Joint Purchasing Arrangements are made
Cumbria County Council

EDUCATION EXECUTIVE

Members of the Committee
Administration: O.S. Angus, T.R. Dumble, W. Hardie, R.W. Jack, J. Nairn, J.R. Scott, A.R. Younger
Religious Reps: Rev A.C.D. Cartwright, Rev D.A. Gray, Mrs M. Mullen

ADDITIONAL SUPPORT NEEDS PROVISION FOR PRIMARY

Chirnside Primary School Chirnside, Duns, Scottish Borders TD11 3HX; Tel 01890 817002
Principal Teacher Louise Sanders
Langlee Primary School Langlee Dr, Galasheils, Scottish Borders TD1 2EB; Tel 01896 757892; Fax 01896 759316
Depute Headteacher Joan Mackay
Wilton School Wellfield Rd, Hawick, Scottish Borders TD9 7EN; Tel 01450 372075; Fax 01450 370538
Depute Headteacher Linda Turnbull

ADDITIONAL SUPPORT NEEDS PROVISION FOR SECONDARY

Berwickshire High School   Duns, Scottish Borders
TD11 3QQ; Tel 01361 883710; Fax 01361 883018
Headteacher   R. Kelly

Earlston High School   Earlston, Scottish Borders TD4 6HF;
Tel 01896 849282
Headteacher   M. Strong

Eyemouth High School   Eyemouth, Scottish Borders
TD4 6HF; Tel 01890 750363; Fax 01890 751270
Headteacher   D. Watson

Galashiels Academy   Elm Row, Galashiels, Scottish Borders
TD1 3HU; Tel 01896 754788; Fax 01896 755652
Contact   K. Angus

Hawick High School   Buccleuch St, Hawick, Scottish
Borders TD9 0EG; Tel 01450 372429; Fax 01450 377830
Headteacher   A. Williamson

Jedburgh Grammar School   Jedburgh, Scottish Borders
TD8 6DQ; Tel 01835 863273; Fax 01835 863993
Headteacher   D. Bissett (Acting)

Kelso High School   Bowmont St, Kelso, Scottish Borders
TD5 7EG; Tel 01573 224444; Fax 01573 223862
Headteacher   C. Robertson

Peebles High School   Peebles, Scottish Borders EM45 8HB;
Tel 01721 720291; Fax 01721 722563
Headteacher   J. Brown

Selkirk High School   Hillside Terr, Selkirk, Scottish Borders
TD7 4EW; Tel 01750 720246; Fax 01750 723039
Headteacher   W. Burgon

SPECIALIST RESOURCES – SPEECH AND LANGUAGE RESOURCE

Coldstream Primary School   Coldstream, Scottish Borders;
Tel 01890 885807
Principal Teacher   Heather Waldron

Philiphaugh Community School   Selkirk, Scottish Borders;
Tel 01750 720682
Principal Teacher   Margaret Mason

SPECIALIST RESOURCES – SENSORY AND EAL TEAMS

Additional Needs Base   Balmoral Primary School, Balmoral
Ave, Galashiels, Scottish Borders TD1 1JJ
Principal Teacher   Fiona Dove
Principal Teacher   Vicki Logan

SPECIALIST RESOURCES – SEBN

Burnfoot Community School   Kenilworth Ave, Hawick,
Scottish Borders TD9 7SW; Tel 01450 378478;
Fax 01450 372026
Depute Headteacher   Caroline Taggart

Wilton Centre Primary Resource   36 Princes St, Hawick,
Scottish Borders TD9 7AY; Tel 01450 373277;
Fax 01450 370538
Depute Headteacher   Caroline Taggart

Wilton Centre Secondary   Princes St, Hawick, Scottish
Borders TD9 7AY; Tel 01450 378644; Fax 01450 370538
Headteacher   Moira Buckle

SPECIALIST RESOURCE – SEVERE/COMPLEX DIFFICULTIES (POST-16)

Howdenburn School House   Lothian Rd, Jedburgh, Scottish
Borders TD8 6LA; Tel 01835 864577
Principal Teacher   J. Dryburgh

SPECIALIST RESOURCE – AUTISM SPECTRUM DISORDER

St Ronan's Spectrum School   St Ronan's Primary School,
Innerleithen, Peeblesshire, Scottish Borders EH44 6PB;
Mobile 07803 227622
Contact   Sarah Fitch
ASD

Spectrum Support   c/o St Margaret's Primary School,
Hawick, Scottish Borders TD9 0HH; Tel 01450 870619;
Fax 01450 870254
Assistant Headteacher   Sarah Fitch

HOSPITAL CLASS

Children's Ward, Borders General Hospital, Galashiels,
Scottish Borders; Tel 01896 4333
Contact   E. Moon

2

Shetland Islands Council
www.shetland.gov.uk

Population: 22 025
Political composition: Ind: 10, None: 12
Town Hall, Lerwick, Shetland Islands ZE1 0HB;
URL www.shetland.gov.uk; e-mail
info@shetland.gov.uk; Tel 01595 693535;
Fax 01595 744509
Chief Executive   Morgan H. Goodlad

Education and Social Care, Schools Service

Hayfield Hse, Hayfield La, Lerwick, Shetland Islands
ZE1 0QD; Tel 01595 744000; Fax 01595 744010
Executive Director   Hazel Sutherland
Head (Schools)   Helen Budge
Head of Service (Finance)   G. Johnston
Manager (Library and Information Services)   Silvija Crook
Manager (Resources)   Shona Thompson
Quality Improvement Manager   Audrey Edwards
Quality Improvement Officer   Jerry Edwards
Quality Improvement Officer   Lesley Roberts
Quality Improvement Officer   Jim Reyner
Quality Improvement Officer   Maggie Spence
Principal Psychologist   Anne Bain
Senior Officer (Careers)   A. Carter
Number of Schools
24 Primary; 8 Combined Secondary/Primary; 1 Secondary;
1 FE College
Day of Committee Meeting
Wednesday; every six weeks
Requisition Periods for Schools Supplies
April/May

SERVICES COMMITTEE

Chair   Leslie Angus
Vice-Chair   Betty Fullerton
Members of the Committee
L. Angus, L. Baisley, J. Budge, A.J. Cluness, A. Cooper, A.T.
Doull, A. Duncan, C.B. Eunson, B. Fullerton, F.B. Grains, I.J.
Hawkins, R.S. Henderson, J.H. Henry, A.J. Hughson, W.H.
Manson, C.H.J. Miller, R.C. Nickerson, F.A. Robertson, G.
Robertson, J.G. Simpson, C.L. Smith, A.S. Wishart

South Ayrshire Council
www.south-ayrshire.gov.uk

Political composition: Con: 15, Lab: 14, Ind: 1
County Bldgs, Wellington Sq, Ayr, South Ayrshire
KA7 1DR; URL www.south-ayrshire.gov.uk; e-mail
tom.cairns@south-ayrshire.gov.uk; Tel 01292 612000;
Fax 01292 612143
Chief Executive   Tom Cairns
Head (Resource Development)   Brian McInroy
Co-ordinator   R. MacDonald

Department of Education, Culture and Lifelong Learning

County Bldgs, Wellington Sq, Ayr, South Ayrshire
KA7 1DR; e-mail mike.mccabe@south-ayrshire.gov.uk;
Tel 01292 612201; Fax 01292 612258
Director   Michael McCabe
Head (Educational, Achievement and Quality Development)
Bill Clark; Tel 01292 612203
Head (Educational Resources)   Brian McInroy;
Tel 01292 612202
Head (Lifelong Learning)   Pat Whelan; Tel 01292 612473

EDUCATION COMMITTEE

Lab: 5, Con: 5
Convener   A. Murray (Lab)
Vice-Convener   G. Crawley (Lab)
Members of the Committee
Lab: D. Campbell, R. Campbell, I. Fitzsimmons
Con: T. Lewis, P. Paterson, R. Reid, P. Torrance, C. Young

NETWORK SUPPORT TEAMS

Central Peripatetic Support Services   Barassie Primary
School Base, Burnfoot Rd, Troon, South Ayrshire; e-mail
sandra.murdoch@ayracademy.south-ayrshire.gov.uk;
Tel 01292 318195
Official-in-Charge   Sandra Murdoch
Regional Psychology Service   St John's Bldg, Whitletts Rd,
Ayr, South Ayrshire; Tel 01292 261738; Fax 01292 263571
Official-in-Charge   Douglas Hutchison

YOUTH AND COMMUNITY CENTRES

Alloway IFE Wing   Doonholm Rd, Alloway, South Ayrshire
Ballantrae Community Centre   33 Main St, Ballantrae,
Girvan, South Ayrshire; Tel 01465 831595
Barassie IFE Wing   Burnfoot Rd, Barassie, South Ayrshire
Barr Community Centre   Greig Rd, Barr, Girvan, South
Ayrshire; Tel 01465 861229
Barrhill Community Centre   Main St, Barrhill, Girvan, South
Ayrshire; Tel 01465 821473
Belmont Social and Recreation Wing   Belmont Rd, Ayr,
South Ayrshire
Colmonell Community Centre   37 Main St, Colmonell,
Girvan, South Ayrshire
Coylton Community Centre   Hillhead, Coylton, South
Ayrshire; Tel 01292 570539
Crosshill Community Centre   Kirkmichael Rd, Crosshill,
Maybole, South Ayrshire; Tel 01655 740476
Dailly Community Centre   Main St, Dailly, South Ayrshire;
Tel 01465 811624
Doonfoot IFE Wing   Abbots Way, Doonfoot, Ayr, South
Ayrshire; Tel 01292 591355
Girvan Community Centre   80–82 Dalrymple St, Girvan,
South Ayrshire; Tel 01465 713480
Lochside Community Centre   Lochside Rd, Ayr, South
Ayrshire; Tel 01292 263333
Mossblown and Drumley Community Centre   Annbank Rd,
Mossblown, South Ayrshire; Tel 01292 520758
Old Dailly Youth Centre   Old Dailly, By Girvan, South
Ayrshire
Pinwherry Community Centre   Muck Rd, Pinwherry,
Girvan, South Ayrshire; Tel 01465 821291
Prestwick Community Centre   Caerlaverock Rd, Prestwick,
South Ayrshire; Tel 01292 478235
Prestwick Social and Recreation Wing   Newdykes Rd,
Prestwick, South Ayrshire
Queen Margaret Social and Recreation Wing   Dalmellington
Rd, Ayr, South Ayrshire
Tarbolton Community Centre   Montgomerie St, Tarbolton,
South Ayrshire; Tel 01292 541277
Troon Youth Centre   St Meddans St, Troon, South Ayrshire;
Tel 01292 313331
Whitletts and Dalmilling Community Centre   Westwood
Ave, Ayr, South Ayrshire; Tel 01292 264578

OTHER EDUCATION DEPARTMENT ESTABLISHMENTS

Language Provision   Kincaidston Primary School, Cranes
Bill Ct, Kincaidston, Ayr, South Ayrshire; Tel 01292 26686
Official-in-Charge   Marion Law
Harthall Unit   Harthall, Dalmilling, Ayr, South Ayrshire;
Tel 01292 886517
Official-in-Charge   P. Bechelli

COMMUNITY EDUCATION SERVICE – AREA OFFICES

Carrick   Carrick Academy, Maybole, South Ayrshire;
Tel 01655 882105; Fax 01655 882598
Principal Officer   P. Whelan
Girvan Sub-Office   80–82 Dalrymple St, Girvan, South
Ayrshire; Tel 01465 713480; Fax 01465 714729
Kyle   26 Green St, Ayr, South Ayrshire; Tel 01292 618777;
Fax 01292 618777
Community Education Officer   Ronnie Sinclair

South Lanarkshire Council

www.southlanarkshire.gov.uk

Headquarters, Almada St, Hamilton, South Lanarkshire
ML3 0AA; URL www.southlanarkshire.gov.uk;
Tel 01698 454444; Fax 01698 454275
Chief Executive   Michael Docherty

Education Resources

Council Offices, Almada St, Hamilton, South Lanarkshire
ML3 0AE; e-mail education@southlanarkshire.gov.uk;
Tel 01698 454379; Tel (helpline) 01698 454545;
Fax 01698 454465
Executive Director   Ken Arthur
Head (Achievement and Attainment)   John Mulligan
Head (Inclusion)   Andrea Batchelor
Head (Quality)   Larry Forde
Manager (Advisory Service)   Frances Colgan; Hope St,
Hamilton, South Lanarkshire; Tel 01698 427373
Manager (Early Years)   Morag McDonald
Manager (Education)   Lorraine Bell
Manager (Education)   Mary Turley
Manager (Finance Services)   Grace Colthart
Manager (IT Business)   Rea Wallace
Manager (Libraries)   Diana Barr
Manager (Operations Service)   Des Dickson
Manager (Personnel Services)   Jacqui Humphreys
Manager (Psychological Services)   Elizabeth King; Station
Rd, Blantyre, Glasgow G72 9AA; Tel 01698 710568
Manager (Quality Management)   Ann Marie Knowles
Manager (Quality Management)   Carole Mason
Manager (SEN)   Julie Bruce
Manager (Youth Learning)   Roz Gallacher
Education Officer   Jessie McPherson
Parent Support Officer   Alan Milliken

EDUCATION COMMITTEE

Lab: 29, SNP: 2, Con: 1, LD: 1
Chair   Mary Smith
Deputy-Chair   Alice Marie Mitchell
Deputy-Chair   Patrick Morgan
Members of the Committee
Mushtaq Ahmad, Jackie Burns, Pam Clearie, Russell Clearie,
Cathie Condie, Gerry Convery, Jim Daisley, Alan Dick, Jim
Docherty, Rev Bev Gauld, Tommy Gilligan, Carol Hughes,
Hector Macdonald, Anne Maggs, Jim Malloy, Edward
McAvoy, Michael McCann, John McGuinness, Henry
Mitchell, John Ormiston, Brian Reilly, Bob Rooney, Gretel
Ross, Graham Scott, Chris Thompson, Murray Tremble, Jim
Wardhaugh, David Watson, Pat Watters

Stirling Council
www.stirling.gov.uk

Political composition: Lab: 11, Con: 9, SNP: 2
Viewforth, Stirling; URL www.stirling.gov.uk;
Tel 01786 443322; Fax 01786 443078
Chief Executive   K. Yates

Children's Services

Viewforth, Stirling FK8 2ET; e-mail info@stirling.gov.uk;
Tel 0845 277 7000; Fax 01786 442782
Director   D. Cameron
Head (Early Childhood Play and Out of School Care)   L. Kinney
Head (Planning and Resources: Children's Services)
R. Maxwell
Head (Schools)   J. McAlpine (Acting)
Head (Social Work: Children's Services)   F. Eadie
Number of Schools
7 Secondary; 2 Special

PSYCHOLOGICAL SERVICE

Langgarth Stirling FK8 2HA; e-mail liddlei@stirling.gov.uk;
Tel 01786 442553; Fax 01786 442946
Principal Psychologist   Ian Liddle

PRIMARY PUPIL SUPPORT SERVICE

St Mary's, Kildean, Stirling FK8 1RR; e-mail
ppsupser@stirling.gov.uk; Tel 01786 463248
Headteacher   Cathy Mills

SECONDARY STUDENT SUPPORT SERVICE

Edward Rd, Riverside, Stirling FK8 1UP; e-mail
secsser@stirling.gov.uk; Tel 01786 464641
Co-ordinator   Vacancy

MAINSTREAM PRIMARY SCHOOLS WITH EXTENDED PROVISION

Callander Primary School Bridgend, Callander, Stirling
FK17 8AG; e-mail callaps@stirling.gov.uk;
Tel 01877 331576
Headteacher   Ann Genese
Dunblane Primary School Doune Rd, Dunblane, Stirling
FK15 9AU; e-mail dunbps@stirling.gov.uk;
Tel 01786 855351; Fax 01786 821008
Headteacher   Joy McFarlane
Number of students: 412
Fallin Primary School Lamont Cres, Fallin, Stirling FK7 7EJ;
e-mail fallinps@stirling.gov.uk; Tel 01786 812063;
Fax 01786 812803
Headteacher   Ann Harley
Number of students: 275
Riverside Primary School Forrest Rd, Stirling FK8 1UJ;
e-mail rvrsdeps@stirling.gov.uk; Tel 01786 474128
Headteacher   Eleanor Jess

MAINSTREAM SECONDARY SCHOOLS WITH EXTENDED PROVISION

Bannockburn High School Bannockburn Rd, Broomridge,
Stirling FK7 0HG; e-mail
bannockburnhs@stirling.gov.uk; Tel 01786 813519;
Fax 01786 818040
Headteacher   Jim McAlpine
12–16
Stirling High School Ogilvie Rd, Stirling FK8 2PA; e-mail
stirlinghs@stirling.gov.uk; Tel 01786 472451;
Fax 01786 447127
Headteacher   Greig Ingram
Number of students: 868
Wallace High School Ochil Hse, Dumyat Rd, Stirling
FK9 5HW; e-mail wallacehs@stirling.gov.uk;
Tel 01786 449571; Fax 01786 447134
Headteacher   Linda Horsburgh

West Dunbartonshire Council
www.west-dunbarton.gov.uk

Council Offices, Garshake Rd, Dumbarton, West
Dunbartonshire G82 3PU;
URL www.west-dunbarton.gov.uk; Tel 01389 737000;
Fax 01389 737700
Chief Executive   Tim Huntingford

2

Department of Education and Cultural Services

e-mail lizmcginlay@west-dunbarton.gov.uk;
Tel 01389 737301; Fax 01389 737348
Director   Liz McGinlay (Acting)

CHILDREN'S SERVICES COMMITTEE

Convener   Jim McCallum

PSYCHOLOGICAL SERVICE

c/o Aitkenbar Primary School, Whiteford Ave, Dumbarton,
West Dunbartonshire G82 3JZ; e-mail
margaret.connolly@west-dunbarton.gov.uk;
Tel 01389 763279; Fax 01389 734728
Principal Educational Psychologist   Margaret Connolly

COMMUNITY HQ

Area Office, 1st Fl, Alexandria Library, Gilmour St,
Alexandria, West Dunbartonshire G83 0NU;
Tel 01389 608061; Fax 01389 608073
Contact   Sandra Davidson; e-mail
sandra.davidson@west-dunbarton.gov.uk

COMMUNITY LEARNING AND DEVELOPMENT – ADULT LEARNING TEAM

1st Fl, Alexandria Library, Gilmour St, Alexandria, West
Dunbartonshire G83 0NU; e-mail
susan.gardner@west-dunbarton.gov.uk;
Tel 01389 608459; Fax 01389 608073
Team Leader (Adult Learning)   Susan Gardner

COMMUNITY CENTRES

Alexandria Community Centre Main St, Alexandria, West
Dunbartonshire G83 0DA; Tel 01389 608064;
Fax 01389 608063
Bonhill Community Centre Ladyton, Bonhill, Alexandria,
West Dunbartonshire G83 9BH; Tel 01389 608179;
Fax 01389 608149
Clydebank East Community Centre Fleming Ave,
Whitecrook, Clydebank, West Dunbartonshire G81 1AD;
Tel 0141 952 6515; Fax 0141 952 6515
Community Learning and Development Community
Literacies Team, 6–14 Bridge St, Dumbarton, West
Dunbartonshire G82 1NT; Tel 01389 608464;
Fax 01389 608466
Senior Worker (Community Literacies)   Ross Wood
Community Learning and Development Youth Services Team
Dalmuir Community Education Centre, Duntocher Rd,
Clydebank, West Dunbartonshire G81 4RQ;
Tel 0141 562 2395; Fax 0141 562 2397
Team Leader (Youth Services)   Fiona McInnes
Concord Community Centre Town Centre, Dumbarton,
West Dunbartonshire G82 1LJ; Tel 01389 608428;
Fax 01389 762013
Dalmonach Community Centre Second Ave, Bonhill, West
Dunbartonshire G83 9BH; Tel 01389 608178
Glenhead Community Centre Duntiglennan Rd, Duntocher,
West Dunbartonshire G81 6HF; Tel 01389 874130
Hub Community Centre 405 Kilbowie Rd, Clydebank, West
Dunbartonshire G81 2TY; Tel 0141 952 5455;
Fax 0141 952 5455

Phoenix Community Centre Quarryknowe Rd, Castlehill, Dunbarton, West Dunbartonshire G82 5BH; Tel 01389 608026; Fax 01389 608027

Renton Community Centre Main St, Renton, West Dunbartonshire G82 4LY; Tel 01389 608429; Fax 01389 608430

West Lothian Council

www.westlothian.gov.uk

Population: 165 700
West Lothian Hse, Almondvale Bvd, Livingston, West Lothian EH54 6QG; URL www.westlothian.gov.uk; Tel 01506 777141; Fax 01506 777102
Chief Executive Alex Linkston
Director (West Lothian Community Health and Care Partnership) David Kelly

Education Services

Fax 01506 777029
Director (Education and Cultural Services) Gordon Ford

EDUCATION EXECUTIVE

Lab: 14, SNP: 13, Campaign to Save St John's Hospital: 3, Con: 1, Ind:1
Executive Member Cllr Andrew Miller

EDUCATION – CUSTOMER AND INFORMATION

Manager (Customer Services) Brian Innes
Manager (Strategic Customer and Information) Andrew Sneddon

EDUCATION – DEVELOPMENT

Head (Education Development) Moira Niven
Senior Manager (Education) Douglas Short
Manager (Planning and Information) David McKinney
Manager (Strategic Resource) Donna Adam
Project Manager (PPP 3) Craig Henderson

EDUCATION – QUALITY ASSURANCE

Head (Education: Quality Assurance) Patrick Sweeney
Manager (Senior Education Development) Bryan Paterson
Manager (Senior Education Development) Mary Rankine
Education Officer Isobel Chalmers
Education Officer Kay Ryan
Education Officer John Tease
Education Officer (Secondment) Doreen McPhail
Education Officer (Secondment) Margaret Ross
Child Protection Officer (Secondment) Ann Craig
Principal Support Officer Alison Raeburn
Principal Psychologist Liz Gajjar

PSYCHOLOGICAL SERVICE

Ogilvie Hse, Ogilvie Way, Knightsridge, Livingston, West Lothian EH54 8HL; Tel 01506 777462; Fax 01506 777486
Principal Psychologist Liz Gajjer

PUPIL SUPPORT CENTRE

The Avenue, Whitburn, West Lothian EH47 0BX; Tel 01501 678100; Fax 01501 678108
Headteacher Margaret Gibson

CULTURAL SERVICES

Head (Cultural Services) Gerry Fitzpatrick
Manager (Arts Services) Colin Hutcheon
Manager (Community Facilities/International Partnerships) Gordon Connolly
Manager (Community Learning and Development: Work with Adults) Ian McIntosh

Manager (Community Learning and Development: Work with Young People) Alastair Colquhoun
Manager (Library Services) Jeanette Castle
Manager (Outdoor Education) George Thomson
Manager (Sport and Physical Recreation) Charlie Raeburn

OFFICES AND CENTRES

Area Office Community Education Team Office, 2 Court Sq, Linlithgow, West Lothian; Tel 01506 775419; Fax 01506 775424
Team Manager Derek Catto
Area Centre Strathbrock Partnership Centre, 189a West Main St, Broxburn, West Lothian EH52 5LH; Tel 01506 444543; Fax 01506 435572
Senior Community Education Worker John Lockhart
Addiewell Community Wing Church St, Addiewell, West Lothian EH55 8PG; Tel 01501 762796
Centre Co-ordinator Andy Hunter
Armadale North St, Armadale, West Lothian EH48 3QB; Tel 01501 678511; Fax 01501 678511
Centre Co-ordinator Cath Brown
Bathgate Marjoribanks St, Bathgate, West Lothian EH48 1AH; Tel 01506 775151; Fax 01506 775155
Centre Co-ordinator Joyce Murray
Blackburn Ashgrove, Blackburn, West Lothian EH47 7LJ; Tel 01506 653014
Centre Co-ordinator Isobel Smith
Blackridge Community Wing Blackridge Primary School, Main St, Blackridge, West Lothian EH48 3RJ; Tel 01501 752352
Senior Community Education Worker John McGhee; Tel 01501 730708
Bridgend Court Sq, Auldhill Rd, Bridgend, West Lothian EH49 6NZ; Tel 01506 384526; Fax 01506 775424
Broxburn Community Education Centre
Senior Community Education Worker Margo Mitchell (part-time)
Community Education Worker Anne Baikie
Community Education Worker H. D'Arcy
Carmondean Nether Dechmont Farm, Fells Rigg, Livingston, West Lothian EH54 8AX; Tel 01506 439568
Centre Co-ordinator Isobel Darge
Court Square 2 Court Sq, Linlithgow, West Lothian EH49 6NB; Tel 01506 775419; Fax 01506 775424
Craig Inn Main St, Blackridge, West Lothian EH48 3SP; Tel 01501 753227; Fax 01501 753227
Centre Co-ordinator Linda Maxwell
Crofthead Farm Templar Rise, Livingston, West Lothian EH54 8DG; Tel 01506 775991
Deans Community High Eastwood Pk, Deans, Livingston, West Lothian EH54 8PS; Tel 01506 497090; Fax 01506 497025
Dechmont Memorial Strathbrock Partnership Centre, 71 Main St, Dechmont, West Lothian EH52 6LJ; Tel 01506 811022
Dedridge Community Wing Lanthorn Community Education Centre, Dedridge Primary School, Dedridge East, Livingston, West Lothian EH54 6JQ; Tel 01506 412831
East Calder 133 Main St, East Calder, West Lothian EH53 0EP; Tel 01506 881557
Centre Co-ordinator Marlene Burford
East Whitburn Whitburn Community Education Centre, Hen Nest Rd, East Whitburn, West Lothian EH47 8EX; Tel 01501 740938
Centre Co-ordinator Jeanette Wood
Eliburn c/o West Calder Community Education Centre, Peel PS, Garden Pl, Eliburn, Livingstone, West Lothian EH54 6RA; Tel 01506 415492; Fax 01506 871738
Fauldhouse Lanrigg Rd, Fauldhouse, West Lothian EH47 9JA; Tel 01501 770552; Fax 01501 770910
Centre Co-ordinator James Swift
Forestbank West Calder Community Education Centre, Forestbank, Ladywell, Livingston, West Lothian EH54 6DX; Tel 01506 430035
Centre Co-ordinator Sandra McLaughlin

2

Greenrigg c/o Fauldhouse Community Education Centre, Greenrigg PS, Polkemmet Rd, Greenrigg, West Lothian ML7 5RF; Tel 01501 770552; Fax 01501 770910

Inveralmond Community High Willowbank, Ladywell East, Livingston, West Lothian EH54 6HW; Tel 01506 439631

The James Young High Quentin Rise, Dedridge West, Livingston, West Lothian EH54 6NE; Tel 01506 774471; Fax 01506 497014

Knightsridge Adventure Project Knightsridge East, Knightsridge, Livingston, West Lothian EH54 8RA; Tel 01506 433307

Lanthorn Kenilworth Rise, Dedridge, Livingston, West Lothian EH54 6JL; Tel 01506 777707; Fax 01506 417679
Centre Co-ordinator Jim Allan
Centre Co-ordinator Donna Lee

Letham Youth Wing c/o Lanthorn Community Education Centre, Letham Primary School, Forth Dr, Livingston, West Lothian EH54 5LZ; Tel 01506 432013

Livingston Station c/o Livingston Station Youth Centre, 4 Main St, Deans, Livingston, West Lothian EH54 8BE; Tel 01506 414002

Livingston Station Youth Centre 7 Main St, Deans, Livingston, West Lothian EH54 8BE; Tel 01506 411295
Centre Co-ordinator Peter Christie

Livingston Village Kirkton North Rd, Livingston Village, Livingston, West Lothian EH54 7EQ; Tel 01506 417343
Caretaker Shelia Oxley

Mid Calder Institute Hall, 15 Market St, Mid Calder, West Lothian EH53 0AL; Tel 01506 881246
Centre Co-ordinator Jim Brophy

Mosswood 85 Ferguson Way, Knightsbridge, Livingston, West Lothian EH54 8JF; Tel 01506 437761
Centre Co-ordinator Margaret McClafferty

Newton 26 Duddingston Cres, Newton, West Lothian EH52 6QG; Tel 0131 331 3290
Centre Co-ordinator Angela Grant

Newyearfield Farm c/o Almondbank, Hawkbrae, Ladywell West, Livingston, West Lothian EH54 6TW; Tel 01506 462458; Fax 01506 777507

North Area Office Strathbrock Partnership Centre, 189a West Main St, Broxburn, West Lothian EH52 5LH; Tel 01506 771743; Fax 01506 771731
Centre Co-ordinator Linda Sayers

Philpstoun Court Sq, Main St, Philpstoun, West Lothian EH49 6RA; Tel 01506 834360
Centre Co-ordinator Hazel Baff
Contact via area office

Polbeth Community Centre c/o West Calder, Polbeth Rd, Polbeth, West Lothian EH55 8SR; Tel 01506 871034; Fax 01506 871738

Pumpherston Institute c/o Almondbank, Uphall Station Rd, Pumpherston, West Lothian EH53 0LY; Tel 01506 431546; Fax 01506 777507

Riverside Craigsfarm Community Development Project, Riverside Primary School, The Mall, Livingston, West Lothian EH54 5EJ; Tel 01506 777596; Fax 01506 777596

Seafield c/o Blackburn Community Centre, Main St, Seafield, West Lothian EH47 7AL; Tel 01506 631791
Centre Co-ordinator Caroline Fraser

South Area Office Almondbank Primary School, The Mall, Livingston, West Lothian EH54 5EJ; Tel 01506 777505; Fax 01506 777507

Springfield Springfield Primary School, 141 Springfield Rd, Linlithgow, West Lothian EH49 7SN; Tel 01506 847455; Fax 01506 847455

Stoneyburn 75 Main St, Stoneyburn, West Lothian EH47 8BY; Tel 01501 762323
Centre Co-ordinator Joe Smith

Strathbrock Partnership Centre Community Education, 189a West Main St, Broxburn, West Lothian EH52 5LN; Tel 01506 771733; Fax 01506 771737
Centre Co-ordinator Linda Sayers

Toronto Toronto Primary School, Toronto Ave, Howden East, Livingston, West Lothian EH54 6NB; Tel 01506 431465

Torphichen c/o Bathgate Community Education Centre, Bowyett, Torphichen, West Lothian EH48 4LZ; Tel 01506 652383
Centre Co-ordinator Careen Hamilton

Uphall Strathbrock Pl, Uphall, West Lothian EH52 6BN; Tel 01506 854451
Centre Co-ordinator Denise Doig

West Area Office Murrayfield PS, Rowan St, Blackburn, West Lothian EH47 7DX; Tel 01506 776478; Fax 01506 776480
Centre Co-ordinator Alastair Colquhoun

West Calder Dickson St, West Calder, West Lothian EH55 8EG; Tel 01506 871278; Fax 01506 871738
Centre Co-ordinator Danny Graham

Whitburn Manse Rd, Whitburn, West Lothian EH47 8EZ; Tel 01501 743034; Fax 01501 742220
Centre Co-ordinator Archie Munro

Winchburgh Craigton Pl, Winchburgh, West Lothian EH52 6RW; Tel 01506 890348
Centre Co-ordinator Alfie Carmichael

ADULT LEARNING CENTRE

6–10 Glasgow Rd, Bathgate, West Lothian; Tel 01506 776333; Fax 01506 776323
Community Education Worker Lindsey Blackwood
Community Education Worker Elaine Nisbet

OUTDOOR EDUCATION

Low Port Centre, Blackness Rd, Linlithgow, West Lothian EH49 7HZ; Tel 01506 775390; Fax 01506 775399
Manager George Thomson

SPORTS UNIT

Balbardie Pk, Bathgate, West Lothian EH48 4LA
Manager Charlie Raeburn

WALES

Isle of Anglesey County Council
www.anglesey.gov.uk

Population: 67 863
Political composition: Anglesey Forward: 23, Plaid Cymru: 7, Original Independent: 5, Unaffiliated: 5
Swyddfa'r Sir, Llangefni, Isle of Anglesey LL77 7TW; URL www.anglesey.gov.uk; e-mail gjxce@anglesey.gov.uk; Tel 01248 750057; Fax 01248 750839
Corporate Director (Finance) D.G. Elis-Williams MA, MSc, CStat, IPFA; Tel 01248 752601; Fax 01248 752696
Managing Director Geraint F. Edwards BSc, DipTP, MBA, MRTPI; Tel 01248 752102; Fax 01248 750839
Head of Service (Leisure and Community) G. Aled Roberts; Tel 01248 752912; Fax 01248 752999

Education and Leisure Department

Park Mount, Ffordd Glanhwfa Rd, Llangefni, Isle of Anglesey LL77 7EY; Tel 01248 752900; Fax 01248 752999
Director (Education and Leisure) R. Parry Jones MA
Head of Service (Education) G. Elis
Chief Administration Officer Margaret Williams
County Treasurer D.G. Ellis-Williams MA, MSc, CStat, IPFA
Number of Schools
5 Secondary; 1 Special

EDUCATION AND LEISURE COMMITTEE

Plaid Cymru: 5, 99 Group: 5, Ind: 3, Lab: 2, Independent Alliance: 2, Original Independent: 2, Unaff: 1
Vice-Chair   Derlwyn R. Hughes
Lifelong Learning and Leisure Portfolio Member
   Cllr John Merion Davies
Members of the Committee
Bessie Burns, John Byast, P.M. Fowlie, Fflur Mai Hughes, Trefor Ll. Hughes, R. Lloyd Hughes, Robert J. Jones, R. Llewelyn Jones, Rhian Medi, John Williams

SPECIAL EDUCATIONAL NEEDS JOINT-COMMITTEE

Principal Educational Psychologist   R. Coupe;
   Tel 01248 752951
Senior Educational Psychologist   R.E. Owen;
   Tel 01286 679178
Advisory Teacher (Vision Impairment/Physically Disabled)
   S. Thomas; Tel 01286 679295
Statementing Officer   Gwen Lloyd Williams;
   Tel 01286 679180
Joint arrangement with Gwynedd Council

'CYNNAL' – EDUCATION ADVISORY SERVICES

A company in the joint ownership of the Isle of Anglesey and Gwynedd County Council
Chief Executive   Dr G. Jones
Senior Adviser   W. Williams
Adviser (Design and Technology)   B. Portlock
Adviser (Early Childhood)   R.H. Roberts
Adviser (English)   H. Lewis
Adviser (Humanities)   Vacancy
Adviser (Information Technology)   D.W. Williams
Adviser (Mathematics)   H.E. Williams
Adviser (Modern Language)   G.W. Roberts
Adviser (Physical Education)   Ielian Jones
Adviser (Primary Schools)   G. Williams
Adviser (Science)   M. Robertson
Adviser (Secondary Schools)   S. Edwards
Adviser (SEN)   E.A. Evans
Adviser (Welsh)   G. Davies
Advisory Teacher (Music)   B. Roberts
Advisory Teacher (Welsh)   L. Jones

Blaenau Gwent County Borough Council

www.blaenau-gwent.gov.uk

Political composition: Lab: 31, Others: 8, LD: 3
Municipal Offices, Civic Centre, Ebbw Vale, Blaenau Gwent NP23 6XB; URL www.blaenau-gwent.gov.uk; Tel 01495 350555; Fax 01495 301225
Chief Executive   Robin Morrison

Education Department

Festival Hse, Victoria Business Pk, Ebbw Vale, Blaenau Gwent NP23 8ER; e-mail education.department@blaenau-gwent.gov.uk; Tel 01495 355337
Director (Lifelong Learning)   B. Pugh (Acting)
Divisional Head (School Support)
   Hannah Meyrick (Acting);   includes responsibility for LMS, personnel support to schools
Head (School Services)   J. Howells;   includes responsibility for out-of-school-hours childcare, nursery education development, building development and governor support
Manager (Children and Young People's Services)
   S. Annett;   includes responsibility for school admissions, home/school transport, special needs administration, pupil and student growth and awards

Chief Officer (School Improvement)   Jayne Davies
Senior Officer (School Improvement)   Steve Rowland;   all curriculum-related services and school management support
Principal Educational Psychologist   T. Dyson;   also responsible for the service for pupils with specific learning difficulties
Number of Schools
6 Secondary; 1 Special

EDUCATION COMMITTEE

Lab: 31, Ind: 6, LD: 3, Independent Ratepayers: 1
Chair   B. Sutton (Lab)
Vice-Chair   H. Trollope (Lab)
Members of the Committee
Lab: G. Clarke, B.K. Clements, M. Dally, N.J. Daniels, D. Davies, D.L. Elias, K. Hayden, M. Holland, J.J. Hopkins, P. Hopkins, D. Hughes M.M.S. (Dip), G.J. Hughes, M. Lewis, H. McCarthy, J.C. McIlwee, E.G.L. Moore, A. Morgan, D.I. Morris, D.J. Owens, J. Rogers, B.J. Scully, B.M. Sutton (BA, DipEd), S.C. Thomas, H.L. Trollope, J. Watkins, R. Welch, D.W. White, D. Wilcox, D.H. Wilkshire
Ind: K. Barnes, D. Hancock, D. Hillman, J. Mason, C. Meredith, J. Owens
LD: S. Bard, C. Morris, B. Thomas
Ind Lab: E.M. James
Ind Ratepayers: W.J. Williams

FOUNDATION SCHOOL

Brynmawr (Foundation) School   Intermediate Rd, Brynmawr, Blaenau Gwent NP23 4XT; Tel 01495 310527
   Headteacher   M. Norton
   Number of students: 881

Bridgend County Borough Council

www.bridgend.gov.uk

Population: 128 000
Political composition: Lab: 22, LD: 13, Con: 8, Independent Democrat: 6, Ind: 4, Plaid Cymru: 1
Civic Offices, Angel St, Bridgend CF31 4WB;
   URL www.bridgend.gov.uk; e-mail talktous@bridgend.gov.uk; Tel 01656 643643; Fax 01656 668126
Chief Executive   Jo Farrar; e-mail chief.executive@bridgend..gov.uk; Tel 01656 643227; Fax 01656 767152

Education, Leisure and Community Services

Education Office, Sunnyside, Bridgend CF31 4AR; e-mail education@bridgend.gov.uk; Fax 01656 642646
Director   Hilary Anthony
Assistant Director (Children's and Young People's Learning)
   Richard Landy
Assistant Director (Strategy Planning and Support)
   Trevor Guy
Assistant Director (Leisure and Cultural Services)
   Mark Shephard
Unit Manager (Financial Support Services)   D. Exton
Unit Manager (Personnel)   J. Bryant
Unit Manager (Learners' Support)   M. Beauchamp
Number of Schools
9 Secondary; 2 Special

EDUCATION COMMITTEE

Cabinet Member   E.P. Foley

EDUCATIONAL PSYCHOLOGY SERVICE

Ty Morfa Psychological Centre Hafan Deg, Aberkenfig, Bridgend CF32 9AW; e-mail john.noaks@bridgend.gov.uk; Tel 01656 729319; Fax 01656 725806
Principal Educational Psychologist J. Noaks

LEISURE SERVICES

Education and Leisure Department, Sunnyside, Bridgend CF31 4AR; URL www.bridgend.gov.uk; e-mail mark.shephard@bridgend.gov.uk; Tel 01656 642741
Officer (Arts and Culture) G.E. Jones
Officer (Recreation) M. Payne

PUPIL REFERRAL UNIT

Ty Morfa Pupil Referral Unit Heol Persondy, Aberkenfig, Bridgend CF32 9RF; Tel 01656 720225
Head of Unit John Connolly

SPECIAL EDUCATIONAL NEEDS (SPECIALISED SERVICES)

Ty Morfa Heol Persondy, Aberkenfig, Bridgend CF32 9RF; e-mail nichola.jones@bridgend.gov.uk; Tel 01656 720201; Fax 01656 725806
Head of Service N. Jones

ADULT EDUCATION CENTRES

Adult Education Central Office Sunnyside, Bridgend CF31 4AR; Tel 01656 642361
Adult Education Officer Jan Morgan
Bridgend Adult Education Centre Sunnyside, Bridgend CF31 4AR; Tel 01656 642361
Centre Manager Joanne Boxall
Community Education Sunnyside, Bridgend CF31 4AR; Tel 01656 642631; Fax 01656 657882
Principal Officer (Community Education) Jan Morgan
Cwm Ogwr Adult Education Centre Berwyn Centre, Ogwy St, Nantymoel, Bridgend CF32 7SD; Tel 01656 840439
Centre Manager John Webster
Cynffig Adult Education Centre c/o Cynffig Comprehensive School, East Ave, Kenfig Hill, Bridgend CF33 6NP; Tel 01656 740896
Centre Manager Vacancy
Garw Adult Education Centre The Old Junior School, Blaengarw, Bridgend CF32 8NF; Tel 01656 870231
Centre Manager Colin Rees
Maesteg Adult Education Centre Maesteg Lower Comprehensive School, Llwynderw Ave, Maesteg, Bridgend CF34 0AX; Tel (day) 01656 737128; Tel (evening) 01656 738465
Centre Manager Colin Rees
Pencoed Adult Education Centre Pencoed Comprehensive School, Coychurch Rd, Pencoed, Bridgend CF35 5LY
Centre Manager John Webster
Porthcawl Adult Education Centre c/o Porthcawl Comprehensive School, Park Ave, Porthcawl, Bridgend CF36 3ES; Tel 01656 771441
Centre Manager Paula Williams
Ynysawdre Adult Education Centre Ynysawdre Comprehensive School, Tondu, Bridgend CF32 9EH; Tel 01656 702030
Centre Manager John Webster

LIBRARY

Coed Parc Park St, Bridgend CF31 4AZ; Tel 01656 767451; Fax 01656 645719
County Librarian J. Woods

Caerphilly County Borough Council
www.caerphilly.gov.uk

Population: 171 000
Tredomen, Ystrad Mynach, Hengoed, Caerphilly CF82 7WF; URL www.caerphilly.gov.uk; e-mail info@caerphilly.gov.uk; Tel 01443 815588; Fax 01443 864211
Mayor Cllr Elizabeth Aldworth
Chief Executive Stuart Rosser
Leader of Council Cllr Harry Andrews MBE

Directorate of Education and Leisure

Council Offices, Caerphilly Rd, Hengoed, Caerphilly CF82 7EP; e-mail hopkid@caerphilly.gov.uk; Tel 01443 864956; Fax 01443 864869
Director David Hopkins
Head (Inclusion Services) Jill Lawrence
Head (Lifelong Learning) Peter Gomer
Head (Planning and Strategy) Bleddyn Hopkins
Head (School Effectiveness) Bob Howells
Principal Officer (Community Education) Steve Mason
Principal Officer (Finance and Strategic Services) Nicole Skett
Principal Officer (Learning Support) Jacquelyn Elias
Principal Officer (Leisure Services) Mark Lowther
Principal Officer (Library Services) Mary Palmer
Principal Officer (SIMS Support and IT Development) Stuart Lawton
Number of Schools
15 Secondary; 1 Special

CABINET

Chair (Education and Leisure Scrutiny) Cllr Ray Davies
Vice-Chair (Education and Leisure Scrutiny) Cllr Betty Toomer
Cabinet Member (Education and Lifelong Learning) Cllr David Hardacre

EDUCATION AND LEISURE SCRUTINY COMMITTEE

Members of the Scrutiny Committee
E. Adworth, P.J. Bevan, J. Bevan, R. Cook, W. David, M. Davies, K. Dawson, N.S. Dix, E.E. Forehead, L. Gardiner, D.M. Gray, A.J. Higgs, S. Lewis, R. Passmore, D.W.R. Preece, A.J. Pritchard, J.A. Pritchard, M. Sargent, G.D. Simmonds, D.T. Wiltshire

COMMUNITY EDUCATION AND LEISURE CENTRES

Bedwas Leisure Centre Newport Rd, Bedwas, Caerphilly NP1 8BJ; Tel 02920 852538; Fax 02920 884529
Centre Manager Bryan Reynolds
Blackwood Community Education Centre Cefn Rd, Blackwood, Caerphilly NP2 1ER; Tel 01495 227113
Warden Chris Herriott
Caerphilly Leisure Centre Virginia Pk, Caerphilly CS83 3SW; Tel 02920 851403; Fax 02920 868544
Centre Manager John Poyner
Cefn Fforest Sports Centre Cefn Fforest, Blackwood, Caerphilly; Tel 01443 830567; Fax 01443 832819
Centre Manager Jeff Reynolds
Cwmcarn Leisure Centre Chapel Farm, Cwmcarn, Caerphilly NP1 7NG; Tel 01495 272010
Manager Sean Spooner
Heolddu Leisure Centre Mountain Rd, Bargoed, Caerphilly CF819GF; Tel 01443 875886; Fax 01443 875446
Manager Sian Jones
New Tredegar Leisure Centre Grove Pk, New Tredegar, Newport NP2 6NF; Tel 01443 875586
Manager Jeff Reynolds
Newbridge Leisure Centre Bridge St, Newbridge, Caerphilly NP1 5FE; Tel 01495 248100
Manager Sean Spooner

Oakdale Community Education Centre Oakdale, Blackwood, Caerphilly NP2 0DT; Tel 01495 228289
Warden Chris Herriott

Pontllanfraith Leisure Centre Coed Cae Ddu Rd, Pontllanfraith, Blackwood, Caerphilly NP2 2DA; Tel 01495 224562
Manager Bryan Reynolds

Risca Community Education Centre Oxford Hse, Grove Rd, Risca, Caerphilly NP1 6GN; Tel 01633 612245
Warden Matthew Taylor

Risca Leisure Centre Pontymason La, Risca, Caerphilly NP1 6YY; Tel 01633 600940
Manager John Ollman

Skateboard Park Bedwellty Rd, Aberbargoed, Bargoed, Caerphilly CF81 9DN; Tel 01443 875886; Fax 01443 875446
Manager (Centre) Jeff Reynolds

Sue Noake Leisure Centre Pengam Rd, Ystrad Mynach, Caerphilly CF82 8AA; Tel 01443 813982
Manager Ashley Tucker

Cardiff Council

www.cardiff.gov.uk

Population: 315 100
Political composition: LD: 32, Lab: 27, Con: 10, Plaid Cymru: 4, Ind: 2
County Hall, Atlantic Wharf, Cardiff CF10 4UW; URL www.cardiff.gov.uk; e-mail c2c@cardiff.gov.uk; Tel 02920 872087
Chief Executive B. Davies; Tel 02920 872400
Corporate Manager (Children's Services/Adult Services/Social Care/Health) Chris Davies; Tel 02920 872460
Corporate Manager (Schools and Lifelong Learning, Highways and Transportation) Steven Phillips; Tel 02920 873800

Schools and Lifelong Learning Service

e-mail chjones@cardiff.gov.uk; Tel 02920 872000; Fax 02920 872777
Head (Ethnic Minority Achievement Service) Mohammed Evans
Manager (Catering Services) Sue Eakers
Manager (Direct School Services) G. Willmott
Manager (Inclusion) Debbie Mitchem
Manager (Performance Information) David Evans
Manager (Planning and Premises) G. Dalton
Manager (School Support Services) Chris Jones
Manager (Standards and School Effectiveness) Robert Hopkins
Chief Officer (Schools and Lifelong Learning) Chris Jones
Pupil Services Officer Rob FitzGerald
SEN Officer Jennie Hughes
Number of Schools
20 Secondary; 7 Special

SCHOOLS AND CHILDREN

Cabinet Member Bill Kelloway

Carmarthenshire County Council

www.carmarthenshire.gov.uk

Political composition: Ind: 31, Lab: 25, Plaid Cymru: 16, Con: 1, Other: 1
County Hall, Carmarthen, Carmarthenshire SA31 1JP; URL www.carmarthenshire.gov.uk; e-mail information@carmarthenshire.gov.uk; Tel 01267 234567
Chief Executive Mark James

Education and Children's Services

Pibwrlwyd, Carmarthen, Carmarthenshire SA31 2NH; Tel 01267 224532; Fax 01267 221692
Director Vernon Morgan BA, CertEd
Head (Children's Services) J. Morgan
Head (Resources Management) E. Cullen
Head (School Governance and Service Support) B. Stephens
Head (Schools Modernisation) R.A. Sully
Head (Standards and Quality) T.W. Williams
Manager (Governor Support) K. Davies
Manager (Inclusion) M. Provis
Senior Officer (Education Welfare) A. Jones
Number of Schools
123 Primary; 14 Secondary; 2 Special

EDUCATION AND CHILDREN'S SCRUTINY COMMITTEE

Ind: 4, Lab: 4, Plaid Cymru: 2
Chair Cllr G.H. Woolridge
Members of the Committee
Ind: D.W.H. Richards, Mrs L.M. Stephens, D.A. Williams, G.H. Woolridge
Lab: Mrs S.M. Cooke, K.P. Davies, J.D. Evans, W.E. Skinner
Plaid Cymru: W.I.B. James, J.E. Williams

PROFESSIONAL SERVICES

Griffith Jones Centre St Clears, Carmarthen, Carmarthenshire SA33 4BT; Tel 01994 231866; Fax 01994 231255
Business Manager (Lifelong Learning) N. Thomas
Principal Officer (Libraries and Community Learning) D. Thomas
Principal Educational Psychologist A. Davies
Principal School Improvement Officer A. Walters

RESIDENTIAL CENTRES

Ferryside Residential Education Centre Ferryside, Carmarthenshire SA17 5TE; Tel 01267 267207
Centre Administrative Manager W.T. Mountain

Ceredigion County Council

www.ceredigion.gov.uk

Population: 77 000
Political Composition: Coalition Group: 26; Plaid Cymru: 16
Neuadd Cyngor Ceredigion, Penmorfa, Aberaeron, Ceredigion SA46 0PA; URL www.ceredigion.gov.uk; e-mail info@ceredigion.gov.uk; Fax 01545 572009
Chief Executive Owen Watkin OBE
Director (Corporate and Legal Services) Bronwen Morgan
Director (Education and Community Services) Gareth Jones
Director (Environmental Services and Housing) Bryan Thomas
Director (Finance) Gwyn Jones; Town Hall, Aberystwyth, Ceredigion SY23 2EB
Director (Highways, Property and Works) Huw Morgan
Director (Social Services) Parry Davies; Min Aeron, Rhiwgoch, Aberaeron, Ceredigion SA46 0DY

Education Department

County Offices, Marine Terr, Aberystwyth, Ceredigion SY23 2DE; e-mail lisw@ceredigion.gov.uk; Tel 01970 633655; Fax 01970 633663
Chair Cllr W.I. Griffiths
Vice-Chair Cllr D.H. Evans
Director (Education and Community Services) Gareth Jones
Assistant Director (Cultural Services) G. Lewis
Assistant Director (Management Services) D.G. Hughes
Assistant Director (Professional Services) Dr Jeff Jones
Manager (Administration and Financial Services) G.P. Richards

Manager (Professional Services)   S. Fearns
Senior Education Officer (Finance and Administration)
    C. Macey
Senior Inclusion Officer   S. Bradley
Education Link Officer   A. Evans
Senior Peripatetic Music Teacher   C. Lockley
Adviser; Inspector (Early Years)   O. Davies
Adviser; Inspector (Literacy)   G. Jones
Adviser; Inspector (PE)   S. Lloyd
Adviser; Inspector (Science)   C.M.E. Woodward
Adviser; Inspector (Vocational); INSET Manager   C. Henshaw
Advisory Teacher (IT)   H. Roderick
Advisory Teacher (RE)   M. Parry
Advisory Teacher (SEN)   M. Davies
Advisory Teacher (SEN)   A. John
Principal Education Psychologist   Mrs L. Roberts
Education Psychologist   Rhiannon Davies
Education Psychologist   Mrs B. Roberts
Number of Schools
7 Secondary
Committee Meeting
Eight week cycle

EDUCATION, CULTURAL AND LEISURE SERVICES COMMITTEE
Members of the Committee
Ind: B.L. Davies, J.E. Davies, G. Ellis, D.J. Evans, J.G. Jenkins, L.L. Jones, T.J. Jones, J.D. Thomas, T.A. Thomas
LD: W.R. Edwards, J.D.R. Jones, F. Williams
Plaid Cymru: E.E. ap Gwynn, H.G. Evans, D.M. James, W.P. James, C. Llwyd
Lab: H.T. Jones

PROFESSIONAL EDUCATION CENTRE
Felinfach   Lampeter, Ceredigion; Tel 01570 470526
    Head   Dr J. Jones

Conwy County Borough Council
www.conwy.gov.uk

Population: 111 300 (mid 2006 estimate)
Political composition: Ind: 17, Con: 14, Lab: 12, Plaid Cymru: 11, LD: 5
Bodlondeb, Conwy LL32 8DU; URL www.conwy.gov.uk; e-mail information@conwy.gov.uk; Tel 01492 574000; Fax 01492 592114
Chief Executive   C.D. Barker

Education Services

Government Bldgs, Dinerth Rd, Rhos-on-Sea, Colwyn Bay, Conwy LL28 4UL; Tel 01492 575001; Fax 01492 575017
Head (Resources and Performance)   John L.I. Roberts
Head (School Improvement Service)   Dilwyn Price
Service Manager (Education Social Worker)   Noella Roberts
Principal Officer (Youth and Community)   Jane E. Williams
Senior Officer (SEN)   Andrew Wilson
Principal Educational Psychologist (SEN)   Richard Ellis-Owen
Adviser (Expressive Arts)   Julie Meehan
Number of Schools
63 Primary; 7 Secondary; 1 Special

Denbighshire County Council
www.denbighshire.gov.uk

Political composition: Ind: 18, Con: 8, Lab: 8, Plaid Cymru: 8, Democratic Alliance of Wales: 3, LD: 2

County Hall, Wynnstay Rd, Ruthin, Denbighshire LL15 1AT; URL www.denbighshire.gov.uk; e-mail enquiries@denbighshire.gov.uk; e-mail <firstname>.<surname>@denbighshire.gov.uk; Tel 01824 706000; Fax 01824 707446
Corporate Director (Lifelong Learning)   Sioned Bowen
Corporate Director (Personal Services)   Sally Ellis
Assistant Director (Culture and Leisure)   Ann Gosse; Canol y Dre, Ruthin, Denbighshire LL15 1QA; Tel 01824 708009
Head (Education Services)   Ieuan Lloyd Roberts
Head (Strategy and Resources)   Gay Brooks

Lifelong Learning Directorate

Tel 01824 716016
Corporate Director   Huw W. Griffiths
Head (Education Services)
    Ieuan Lloyd Roberts;   responsible for curricular matters; Denbighshire County Council, Trem Clwyd, Canol y Dre, Ruthin, Denbighshire LL15 1QA
Head (Strategy and Resources)
    Gaynor Brooks;   responsible for resources, school support and access to education
Number of Schools
8 Secondary; 2 Special

Flintshire County Council
www.flintshire.gov.uk

Political composition: Lab: 35, Independent and Non-aligned: 18, LD: 10, Con: 4, Non-aligned Plaid Cymru: 1, Non-aligned: 1, Vacancy: 1
County Hall, Mold, Flintshire CH7 6NB; URL www.flintshire.gov.uk; e-mail info@flintshire.gov.uk; Tel 01352 752121; Fax 01352 758240
Chief Executive   Colin Everett

Directorate of Education, Children's Services and Recreation

County Hall, Mold, Flintshire CH7 6ND; Tel 01352 704010
Director   Alun G. Davies (Acting)
Assistant Director (Development Resources)   H. Loveridge BA(Hons), MSc, DMS
Assistant Director (Libraries/Culture/Heritage)   L. Rawsthorne MLib, ALA, MIMGT
Assistant Director (School Improvement)   Elwyn Davies BEd(Hons), MEd, DipManagement
Number of Schools
74 Infants/Primary; 12 Secondary; 3 Special; 1 Nursery

Gwynedd Council
www.gwynedd.gov.uk

Population: 118 000
County Offices, Stryd y Jêl, Caernarfon, Gwynedd LL55 1SH; URL www.gwynedd.gov.uk; e-mail enquiries@gwynedd.gov.uk; Tel 01286 672255; Fax 01286 679488
Chief Executive   Harry Thomas
Director (Social Services)   E.N. Williams
Head (Highways and Municipal Services)   Gwyn Morris Jones
Head (Human Resources)   A.E. Jones

Development Directorate

e-mail addysg@gwynedd.gov.uk; Fax 01286 677347
Strategic Director (Development) Iwan Trefor Jones
Head (Economy and Regeneration) Sioned E. Williams
Head (Lifelong Learning Service) Rhys W. Parri BSc, MEd
Head (Schools Service) Dewi Jones
Head (Student Grants and Youth Service) Peter L. Williams
Senior Manager (Lifelong Learning Service)
   Marianne Jackson BA(Hons), ILAM(Cert)
Senior Manager (Schools Service) I. Roberts BSc, MEd
Manager (Support Services) A. Jones-Griffith
Education Officer (Arfon Area) Keith Parry
Education Officer (Dwyfor Area) Dewi Bowen
Education Officer (Meirionnydd Area) J. Blake CertEd
Education Officer (Social Inclusion) Orina Pritchard
Principal Accountant H. Owen IPFA
Number of Schools
14 Secondary; 3 Special

DEVELOPMENT SCRUTINY COMMITTEE

Chair Cllr Richard H. Jones
Vice-Chair Cllr Thomas Ellis
Leader (Development Directorate) Cllr Dafydd Iwan
Leader (Schools Service) Cllr W. Penri Jones

GOVERNOR TRAINING UNIT

Governor Training Unit
   Education Officer J. Blake; Tel 01341 423191;
   Fax 01341 423723

AREA EDUCATION OFFICES (SWYDDFEYDD ARDAL)

Swyddfa Ardal Arfon Caernarfon, Gwynedd LL55 1SH;
   URL www.gwynedd.gov.uk; Tel 01286 679552;
   Fax 01286 672635
   Education Officer K. Parry
Swyddfa Ardal Dwyfor Pwllheli, Gwynedd;
   Tel 01758 704044; Fax 01758 701178
   Education Officer Dewi Bowen
Swyddfa Ardal Meirion Dolgellau, Gwynedd;
   Tel 01341 423191; Fax 01341 423723
   Education Officer J. Blake

'CYNNAL' EDUCATION ADVISORY SERVICES

A company in the joint ownership of the Isle of Anglesey
and Gwynedd Council
Chief Executive Gareth Williams
Adviser (Design and Technology) B. Portlock
Adviser (English) E. Davies
Adviser (Humanities) B. James
Adviser (Information Technology) P. Roberts
Adviser (Mathematics) E. Davies
Adviser (Modern Language) S. Gartau
Adviser (Physical Education) I. Jones
Adviser (Primary Schools) J. Gruffudd
Adviser (Science) M. Robertson
Adviser (Secondary Schools) S. Edwards
Advisory Teacher (Early Childhood) A. Owen
Advisory Teacher (Music) Huw Gwyn
Advisory Teacher (Welsh) G. Davies

SPECIAL EDUCATIONAL NEEDS JOINT COMMITTEE

Principal Educational Psychologist Angharad Behnan
Advisor (Additional Learning Needs) Delyth Molyneux
Joint arrangement with Isle of Anglesey County Council

MUSIC TEACHING SERVICE

Head (Music) D. Williams; Tel 01286 679838;
   Fax 01286 672633

Merthyr Tydfil County Borough Council

www.merthyr.gov.uk

Population: 59 300
Political composition: Lab: 14, Ind: 13, Plaid Cymru: 4
Ty Keir Hardie, Riverside Ct, Avenue de Clichy, Merthyr
   Tydfil CF47 8XD; URL www.merthyr.gov.uk; e-mail
   socialservices@merthyr.gov.uk; Tel 01685 724600;
   Fax 01685 721965

Integrated Children's Services Department

e-mail officeservices@merthyr.gov.uk
Director Chris Abbott
Head (Children's Service and Partnerships) Leighton Rees
Head (Community Education) Tanis Cunnick
Head (Governance, Inclusion and Support) Stuart Whippey
Head (School Improvement) Margaret Wagner
Principal Educational Psychologist Virginia Board
Number of Schools
4 Secondary; 1 Special

BOARD

Lab: 15, Ind: 14, Plaid Cymru: 4
Board Member (Education) Cllr Ray Thomas (Lab); Crud Yr
   Awel, Station Terr, Dowlais, Merthyr Tydfil CF48 3PU
Shadow Board Member (Education: People in Politics)
   Cllr Paul Brown (Ind); 11 Salisbury Cl, Heolgerrig,
   Merthyr Tydfil CV48 1SD

SPECIAL EDUCATIONAL NEEDS SERVICE

Ty Keir Hardie, Riverside Ct, Merthyr Tydfil CF47 8XD;
   e-mail officeservices@merthyr.gov.uk; Tel 01685 724642

PUPIL REFERRAL UNIT

Alexandra Ave, Penydarren, Merthyr Tydfil CF47 9AF;
   e-mail pru@mtcbc.fsbusiness.co.uk; Tel 01685 721733

COMMUNITY EDUCATION CENTRES

Afon Taf Yew St, Troedyrhiw, Merthyr Tydfil CF48 4ED;
   Tel 01443 691921
Pen y Dre Gurnos Est, Merthyr Tydfil CF47 9DY;
   Tel 01685 722104

Monmouthshire County Council

www.monmouthshire.gov.uk

Population: 85 000
Political composition: Con: 24, Lab: 9, Ind: 5, LD: 3, Plaid
Cymru: 2
County Hall, Cwmbran, Monmouthshire NP44 2XH;
   URL www.monmouthshire.gov.uk; e-mail
   shs@monmouthshire.gov.uk; Tel 01633 644644;
   Fax 01633 644666
Chair Val Smith
Chief Executive Colin Berg
Director (Corporate and Customer Services) S. Greenslade
Director (Social and Housing Services) M. Wilkinson

Lifelong Learning and Leisure Directorate

e-mail andrewkeep@monmouthshire.gov.uk;
   Tel 01633 644487; Fax 01633 644488

Corporate Director   Andrew Keep
Head (Resources and Performance Management)   Paula Ham
Head (School Improvement Service)   Malcolm Morris
School Improvement Officer   B. Knox-Little
School Improvement Officer   J. Murphy
Number of Schools
4 Secondary; 1 Special

LIFELONG LEARNING AND LEISURE

Cabinet Member (Leisure)   Mrs L. Hacket-Pain
Cabinet Member (Lifelong Learning)   P. Joy

Neath Port Talbot County Borough Council
www.npt.gov.uk

Population: 136 000
Political composition: Lab: 36, Plaid Cymru: 10, Ratepayers: 9, Ind: 4, Social Dem: 3, LD: 2
Civic Centre, Port Talbot, Neath Port Talbot SA13 1PJ;
    URL www.npt.gov.uk; e-mail cex@npt.gov.uk;
    Tel 01639 763333; Fax 01639 899930
Chief Executive   K. Sawyers

Education, Leisure and Lifelong Learning Directorate

Corporate Director   K. Napieralla
Head (Access and Support Services)   S.G. Evans
Head (Education Development and Inclusion Services)
    A. Evans
Head (Lifelong Learning, Culture and Leisure)   R. Ward
Principal Officer (Personnel)   Mrs L. Preece
Principal Development Officer (Education Development and Inclusion Service)   A. Herdman
Co-ordinator (Cultural Services)   J.L. Ellis
Co-ordinator (Lifelong Learning)   Mrs M. Dawson
Co-ordinator (Support for Inclusion)   Mrs H. Reid
Number of Schools
11 Secondary; 3 Special
Day of Education, Leisure and Lifelong Learning Cabinet Committee
Thursday; every sixth week
Requisition Periods for Schools Supplies
As required
Member of the Welsh Purchasing Consortium

CHILDREN, YOUNG PEOPLE AND EDUCATION CABINET BOARD

Cabinet Member (Children and Young People)
    Cllr Mrs O. Jones (Lab)
Cabinet Member (Education/Lifelong Learning)   Cllr J. Rogers

ECONOMIC AND COMMUNITY REGENERATION CABINET BOARD

Cabinet Member (Community and Leisure Services)
    Cllr C.J. Crowley (Lab)

Newport City Council
www.newport.gov.uk

Population: 137 011
Political composition: Lab: 31, Con: 11, LD: 6, Ind: 1, Plaid Cymru: 1
Civic Centre, Newport NP20 4UR;
    URL www.newport.gov.uk; e-mail <firstname>.<surname>@newport.gov.uk;
    Tel 01633 656656
Corporate Director   Donald Graham
Managing Director   Chris Freegard

Education Department

Fax 01633 232808
Head (Education, Improvement and Inclusion)   Terry Mackie
Head (Education, Resources and Planning)   James Harris
Chief Education Officer   Brett Pugh
Number of Schools
8 Secondary; 1 Special

CABINET MEMBER FOR YOUNG PEOPLE'S SERVICES

Education Executive Senior Leader   Cllr Bob Poole (Lab); 39 Maesglas Gr, Newport NP20 3DJ

Pembrokeshire County Council
www.pembrokeshire.gov.uk

Population: 117 490
Political composition: Ind: 39, Lab: 11, Plaid Cymru: 5, LD: 4, Non-affilliated: 1
County Hall, Haverfordwest, Pembrokeshire SA61 1TP;
    URL www.pembrokeshire.gov.uk; Tel 01437 764551
Chief Executive   B. Parry-Jones
Director (Development)   Dr Steven Jones
Director (Finance and Leisure)   M. Lewis
Director (Social Care and Housing)   J. Skone
Director (Transportation and Environment)   I. Westley

Education Department

Tel 01437 775861; Fax 01437 775838
Director (Education and Children's Services)   G.W. Davies
Head (Lifelong Learning and Development)
    Mrs J.A. Wakefield
Head (School Improvement and Inclusion)   Mr G. Longster
Manager (LMS Finance)   Huw Jones
Client Manager (CCT)   M. Hicks
Senior Pupil Support Officer   J. Bearne
Pupil Support Officer (North)   Elin Gilderdale
Pupil Support Officer (South)   Sharon Doona
Senior Educational Psychologist; Manager (SEN)
    John Benbow
Professional Officer (Children in Need)   Michelle Rees
Professional Officer (Governing Bodies and Development)
    Steve Russell-Stretch
Professional Officer (People Support Services)
    Cheryl Loughlin
Computer Liaison Officer   Mike Isted
Research and Information Officer   Helen Banner
Adult Services Officer (Community Education)   Chris Davies
Youth Services Officer (Community Education)   Eirian Evans
Co-ordinator (Children in Need)   Karen John
Accountant   Ian Eynon
Number of Schools
66 Primary; 8 Secondary; 1 Special

EDUCATION CABINET

Cabinet Member (Children, Young People and Welsh Language)   Cllr Islwyn Howells
Cabinet Member (Lifelong Learning/Culture and the Arts)
    Cllr David Simpson

PUPIL REFERRAL UNIT

The Pembroke Centre   Pupil Referral Service, The Old College, Neyland, Pembrokeshire; e-mail judy.jones@pembrokeshire.gov.uk; Tel 01646 602473
    Head   J.A. Jones

PROFESSIONAL EDUCATION CENTRE

Pembrokeshire Professional Education Centre   St Clements Rd, Neyland, Pembroke, Pembrokeshire SA73 1SH; Tel 01646 890069; Fax 01646 602154

Powys County Council
www.powys.gov.uk

Population: 130 700
County Hall, Llandrindod Wells, Powys LD1 5LG;
 URL www.powys.gov.uk; e-mail
 webmaster@powys.gov.uk; Tel 01597 826000;
 Fax 01597 826230
Chief Executive   Mark Kerr

Rhondda Cynon Taf County Borough Council
www.rhondda-cynon-taf.gov.uk

Population: 232 581
Council Offices, The Pavillion, Clydach Vale, Tonypandy,
 Rhondda Cynon Taf CF40 2XX;
 URL www.rhondda-cynon-taf.gov.uk; Tel 01443 424000;
 Fax 01443 424027
Chief Executive (Rhondda Cynon Taf)   Keith Griffiths; e-mail
 keith.griffiths@rhondda-cynon-taf.gov.uk
*Group Director (Community and Children's Services); Director
 (Social Services)*   John Wrangham; e-mail
 john.wranghom@rhondda-cynon-taf.gov.uk
Director (Human Resources)   A.R.J. Wilkins; e-mail
 tony.wilkins@rhondda-cynon-taf.gov.uk
Director (Legal and Democratic Services)   P.J. Lucas; e-mail
 paul.j.lucas@rhondda-cynon-taf.gov.uk

Directorate of Education and Lifelong Learning

Ty Trevithick, Abercynon, Mountain Ash, Rhondda Cynon
 Taf CF45 4UQ; URL www.rctednet.net; Tel 01443 744000;
 Fax 01443 744024
Director (Children's Services)   Barbara Brown (Acting)
Director (Education and Lifelong Learning)   M. Keating
Service Director (Lifelong Learning)   G. Newton
Service Director (School Support and Improvement)
 Steve Lamb
Service Director (Strategic Planning and Resources)   G. Kiss
Head (Access and Inclusion)   Ceirion Williams (Acting)
Head (Finance and ICT)   Catrin Edwards
Head (Library and Museum Services)   G. Evans
Area Manager (Governor Support Services)   G. Thomas
Principal Educational Psychologist   V.E. Board
Number of Schools
19 Secondary; 4 Special

CABINET

Leader   R. Roberts
*Deputy Leader; Member (Environmental and Sustainable
 Development)*   A. Christopher
Member (Better Public Services and Transport)   E. Hanagan
Member (Children and Equality)   A. Davies
Member (Cultural Development, Recreation and Tourism)
 G. Thomas
Member (Economic Development)   R. Bevan
Member (Education and Lifelong Learning)   M. Forey
Member (Health and Adult Services)   J. David
*Member (Open Government, Higher Education and Youth
 Services)*   C. Willis
Member (Safer Communities and Housing)   P. Cannon

PUPIL REFERRAL UNIT

Tai Education Centre   Grovefield Terr, Penygraig,
 Tonypandy, Rhondda Cynon Taf CF40 1HL;
 Tel 01443 422666; Fax 01443 436487
Headteacher   Ann Jones

EDUCATION AND BEHAVIOUR DISORDER UNITS

Talbot Green Special Needs Centre   Heol-y-Gyfraith, Talbot
 Grn, Pontyclun, Rhondda Cynon Taf CF72 8AJ;
 Tel 01443 237839; Fax 01443 237839
Headteacher   John Wagstaff
Ty Gwyn Special Needs Centre   Cefn La, Glyncoch,
 Pontypridd, Rhondda Cynon Taf CF37 3BP;
 Tel 01443 408417; Fax 01443 408417
Headteacher   John Wagstaff

City and County of Swansea
www.swansea.gov.uk

Population: 225 500
County Hall, Oystermouth Rd, Swansea SA1 3SN;
 URL www.swansea.gov.uk; Tel 01792 636000;
 Fax 01792 636700
Lord Mayor; Leader   Cllr Chris Holley
Chief Executive   Paul Smith
Deputy Chief Executive   Bob Carter
Assistant Chief Executive (Performance)   Michelle Morris
Strategic Director (Environment)   Reena Owen
Strategic Director (Regeneration)   Phil Roberts
Strategic Director (Social Services and Housing)   Jack Straw

Education Department

e-mail education.department@swansea.gov.uk;
 Tel 01792 636560; Fax 01792 636642
Cabinet Member (Education)   Cllr Mike Day
Strategic Director   Richard Parry
Head of Service (Education Effectiveness)   Robert Barbour
Head of Service (Education Inclusion)   Robin Brown
Head of Service (Education Planning and Resources)
 Brian Roles
Manager (Access to Learning)   Mrs Sharon Davies
Manager (Children and Young People Strategy Unit)
 Alan Twelvetrees
Manager (Employment Training)   Steve Harris
Manager (Performance and Projects Unit)   Dr Julie Sheppard
Manager (Youth Access); Co-ordinator (14–19)   Marcia Vale
Community Education Manager (Lifelong Learning)
 Mike Hughes
Primary Adviser   Keith Day
Primary Adviser   Roger Davies
Primary Adviser   Mrs Leslie Evans
Teacher Adviser (Basic Skills)   Anne Long
Teacher Adviser (Behaviour)   Lesley Williams
Teacher Adviser (ICT)   John Mills
Teacher Adviser (ICT)   Jan Morgan
Teacher Adviser (ICT)   Huw Morris
Teacher Adviser (Inclusion)   Norma Baker
Teacher Adviser (Inclusion)   Debbie Avington
Teacher Adviser (Inclusion)   Sharon Hope
Teacher Adviser (Mathematics and Numeracy)   Jean Bines
Teacher Adviser (Mathematics and Numeracy)   Rob Davies
Adviser (ICT)   Lindsay Harvey
Co-ordinator (PESS)   Wendy Anderson
Co-ordinator (Sixth Form)   Cyril Gray
Web Content Development Officer   Pippa Harris
Number of Schools
90 Primary, 15 Comprehensive; 2 Special

EDUCATION EFFECTIVENESS SERVICE

Manager (Youth Access); Co-ordinator   Marcia Vale
Senior Adviser (Primary)   Paul de Vall
Senior Adviser (Secondary)   Ian James
Primary Adviser (Early Years)   Miss Irene de Lloyd
Teacher Adviser (Early Years)   Sian Williams
Co-ordinator (The Arts)   Carolyn Davies
Co-ordinator (Basic Skills)   Sharon Jones
Co-ordinator (PE and Sports)   Iwan Ellis-Williams
Teacher Adviser (English and Literacy)   Sue Watson

Teacher Adviser (English and Literacy)   Maralyn Griffiths
Teacher Adviser (PSE)   Mark Campion
Adviser (English and Literacy)   D. Taylor
Adviser (Mathematics and Numeracy)   Lynwen Barnsley
Adviser (School Development)   Paul James
Adviser (Science)   Sarah Ford

Torfaen County Borough Council
www.torfaen.gov.uk

Population: 90 400
Civic Centre, Pontypool, Torfaen NP4 6YB;
    URL www.torfaen.gov.uk; e-mail
    your.call@torfaen.gov.uk; Tel 01495 762200;
    Fax 01495 755513
Chief Executive   Alison Ward
Director (Environment)   Vacancy
Director (Finance)   P. Nash CPFA
Director (Housing)   Vacancy
Director (Operational Services)   B. James MSc, CEng, MICE, MCIOB
Head (Leisure and Cultural Services)   D. Congreve

Education Offices

County Hall, Cwmbran, Torfaen NP44 2WN;
    Tel 01633 648610; Fax 01633 648164
Director (Education)   Catherine Simpson
Assistant Director (Education)   T. Mackie
Assistant Director (Education)   P. Matthews
Executive Member (Education)   Cllr J. Turner
Deputy Executive Member   Cllr M. Barnet
Principal Education Adviser   G.H. Buckland
Number of Schools
8 Comprehensive; 1 Special

LEISURE CENTRES AND COMMUNITY EDUCATION CENTRES

Abersychan Leisure Centre   Manor Rd, Abersychan, Pontypool, Torfaen NP4 7DQ; Tel 01495 773140
    Manager   D. Flynn
Blaenavon Community Education Centre   Park St, Blaenavon, Pontypool, Torfaen NP4 9AA; Tel 01495 792013
    Warden   N. Angell
Croesyceiliog Community Education Centre   Woodland Rd, Croesyceiliog, Cwmbran, Torfaen NP4 2YA; Tel 01633 485052
    Warden   M. Slater
Fairwater Leisure Centre   Ty Gwyn Way, Fairwater, Cwmbran, Torfaen NP4 4YZ; Tel 01633 872811
    Manager   D. Flynn
Llantarnam Leisure Centre   Llantarnam Rd, Cwmbran, Torfaen NP4 3XB; Tel 01633 482832
    Manager   D. Flynn
Pontnewydd Community Education Centre   c/o Ashley Hse Youth Centre, Mount Pleasant Rd, Cwmbran, Torfaen NP4 1AN; Tel 01633 482345
    Warden   M. Slater
Pontypool Community Education Centre   The Settlement, Trosnant St, Pontypool, Torfaen; Tel 01495 762266
    Warden   N. Angell
Trevethin Community Education Centre   Trevethin, Pontypool, Torfaen NP4 9UD; Tel 01495 764558
    Warden   N. Angell

Vale of Glamorgan Council
www.valeofglamorgan.gov.uk

Population: 119 292
Political composition: Con: 20, Lab: 16, Plaid Cymru: 8, Ind: 3

Civic Offices, Holton Rd, Barry, Vale of Glamorgan
    CF63 4RU; URL www.valeofglamorgan.gov.uk; e-mail
    enquiries@valeofglamorgan.gov.uk; Tel 01446 700111;
    Fax 01446 745566
Chief Executive   J. Maitland Evans; Tel 01446 709303;
    Fax 01446 421479
Director (Legal and Regulatory)   P. Evans; Tel 01446 709401

Learning and Development

Fax 01446 701820
Director   B. Jeffreys
Head (School Improvement Service)   S. Aspinall
Head (Strategic Planning and Performance)   M. Donovan
Head (Inclusion and Access)   Sheila Kelly
Number of Schools
8 Secondary; 3 Special

LIFELONG LEARNING SCRUTINY COMMITTEE

Chair   C.P. Franks;   Plaid Cymru
Cabinet Member for Lifelong Learning (Education and Training)   A.D. Hampton (Con)
Members of the Committee
Con: C.V.L. Clay, J. Clifford, M. Kelly-Owen, C. Osborne, S. Sharpe, C. Vaughan, E.T. Williams
Lab: M.E. Alexander, Mrs M. Birch, Ms R. Birch, S.C. Egan, F.T. Johnson, A.G. Powell

SPECIAL EDUCATIONAL NEEDS

Pupil Support Service, Directorate of Learning and Development, Barry, Vale of Glamorgan CF63 4RU; e-mail bgrover@valeofglamorgan.gov.uk; Tel 01446 709184; Fax 01446 701821
Head of Service   R. Grover

Wrexham County Borough Council
www.wrexham.gov.uk

Population: 129 300
Political composition: Lab: 19, Liberal Democrat Alliance: 16, Ind: 5, Con: 4, Non-alligned: 4, West Wrexham Independent: 4
PO Box 1284, Guildhall, Wrexham LL11 1WF;
    URL www.wrexham.gov.uk; e-mail
    webmaster@wrexham.gov.uk; Tel 01978 292000;
    Fax 01978 292106
Chief Executive   Isobel Garner
Strategic Director   T. Garner
Strategic Director   Paul Roberts
Strategic Director   Malcolm Russell

Children and Young People Service

Ty Henblas, Queens Sq, Wrexham LL13 8AZ; e-mail education@wrexham.gov.uk; Tel 01978 297400
Number of Schools
10 Secondary; 3 Special

Learning and Achievement Department

Ty Henblas, Queens Sq, Wrexham LL13 8AZ; e-mail education@wrexham.gov.uk; Tel 01978 297400
Head of Service (0–12)   John Davies
Head of Service (10–19)   John O'Roberts
Chief Officer   Hywyn Williams

2

EXECUTIVE BOARD COMMITTEE

Members of the Board
R.W. Caldecott, R.J. Dutton, T. George, P. Jeffares, R.A.
Jenkins, A.G. Jones, R.D. Prince, M. Pritchard, A.R. Robets,
N. Rogers, J.R. Skelland

Prevention and Inclusion

Chief Officer   Clare Field
Head of Service (Education Inclusion)   Graham Edwards
Head of Service (Children and Family Inclusion)   Susan Evans
Head of Service (Young People Inclusion)   Donna Dickenson
Head of Service (Youth Offending Service)   Peter Gill

Safeguarding and Support

Chief Officer   Bob MacLaren
Head of Service (Corporate Parenting)   John Roberts
Head of Service (Family Support)   Margaret Southall
Head of Service (Safeguarding)   Marie Lebacq

NORTHERN IRELAND

Belfast Education and Library Board

www.belb.org.uk

40 Academy St, Belfast BT1 2NQ; URL www.belb.org.uk;
e-mail info@belb.co.uk; Tel 028 9056 4000;
Fax 028 9033 1714
Chief Executive   David Cargo BA(Hons), MA, PGCE;
Tel 028 9056 4040
Chief Education Welfare Officer   M. Devenney
Chief Finance Officer (Finance Department)
David Megaughin FCMA; Tel 028 9056 4190
Senior Education Officer (Education Department)
George Campbell MA, DipEd; Tel 028 9056 4026
Assistant Senior Education Officer (School Support Service)
S. McElhatton CertEd, BEd(Comm)
*Assistant Senior Education Officer (Schools Development
Services)*   N. Todd BEd, MA, MSc, AdvDipEducMgt
Assistant Senior Education Officer (Special)   J. McCullough
BA, MEd, MSc, PGCE
Assistant Senior Education Officer (Technical and Services)
W. McIntaggart BSc, MRICS, MCIOB
Assistant Senior Education Officer (Youth)   G. McGuinness
MSc, BA
Principal Educational Psychologist   M.J. Clarke MSc, PGCE
Secondary Adviser (Behaviour Support)   R.A. Stewart
BEd(Hons), MSc
Adviser (Information Technology)   D. Shufflebottom BA,
BPhI(Hons), MEd
Adviser (Pre-School and Primary Education)   M. Warren
BEd(Hons), BEd, MSc
Adviser (Primary)   G. Mulholland MEd, DASE, BEd
Adviser (Primary)   B. Yeats CertEd, BEd(Hons), MA
Adviser (Religious Education)   William Latimer
Adviser (Secondary Education and Science)   D. McCullough
BSc, DASE, PGradCertinEdMgt
Adviser (Secondary Environment and Society)   Brigid Murray
BSSc, MSSc
Adviser (SEN)   J. Trotter
Chief Librarian (Library Service)   Linda Houston BLS, ALA,
MBA; Tel 028 9050 9151
Purchasing Officer   C. Burnett
Number of Schools
44 Controlled Primary; 41 Maintained Primary; 18
Maintained Nursery; 16 Controlled Nursery; 14 Voluntary
Grammar; 13 Maintained Secondary; 8 Controlled
Secondary; 2 Controlled Grammar; 2 Grant-Maintained
Integrated Primary; 2 Grant-Maintained Integrated
Secondary; 1 Controlled Integrated Primary; 1 School of
Music
Special Schools
11 Controlled; 2 Maintained; 2 Remedial Centres

Education Committee (Schools)

Chair   Jim Caves
Vice-Chair   Cllr D. Browne
Members of the Committee
D. Alderdice, J. Clarke, P. Convery, M.P. Diamond, Dr M.
Harriott, T. Hartley, B. Henry, P. Leeson, J.L. MacVicar, N.
McCausland, S. McIntaggart, Very Rev H. McKelvey, C.
McKinney, C. Molloy, S. O'Prey, E. Paynter, R. Rainey, J.
Rodgers, H. Sioan, Rev E. Smyth, J.J. Toner

MUSIC SERVICE

School of Music   99 Donegall Pass, Belfast BT7 1DR;
Tel 028 9032 2435
Principal Tutor   Dr J. McKeo

North Eastern Education and Library Board

www.neelb.org.uk

County Hall, 182 Galgorm Rd, Ballymena, County Antrim
BT42 1HN; URL www.neelb.org.uk; e-mail
webmaster@neelb.org.uk; Tel 028 2565 3333;
Fax 028 2564 6071
Chief Executive   G. Topping OBE, BA, MSc, MBA, DipEd,
FRSA
Director (Library and Corporate Services)   A.M. Connolly
MBA, MA, BA
Head (Corporate Services)   P. Martin; Library Headquarters,
Demesne Ave, Ballymena, County Antrim
Northern Ireland, BT43 7BG; Tel 028 2566 4100;
Fax 028 2563 2038
Head (Property Services)   G.C. Wylie TCert, BD(Hons),
ADIE; Property Services, 52–56 Ballymoney St,
Ballymena, County Antrim BT43 6AN; Tel 028 2565 5366;
Fax 028 2565 5277
Senior Education Officer   G. Irwin MEd, DASE
Assistant Senior Education Officer   G. Bell
Assistant Senior Education Officer   Mr R. Gilbert
Assistant Senior Education Officer   G. McGeagh
Chief Education Welfare Officer   M.D. Devenney
Chief Administrative Officer   R. Harper BA, MA, CertEd
Chief Officer (Finance)   H. Taylor BA, CPFA
Principal Educational Psychologist   R.M. Crozier BSc, MSc,
PGCE, C.Psychologist, AFBPsS
Information Officer   J.A.D. Kenny BA, DipClPR
Primary Officer   J. Millar
Purchasing Officer   F. Scullion
Secondary Officer   G. Kelly BA, Postgrad Cert, MA
Transport Officer   S.J. McDowell
Adviser (English)   J.A. Wilson
Adviser (Environmental Studies)   V. Quinn
Adviser (Foundation)   L. Gardiner
Adviser (Information and Communications Technology)
M. McCormac
Adviser (Maths)   J. Cormican
Adviser (Religious Education)   P. Hewitt BSc(Hons), PGCE,
CRK, DASE
Adviser (Science and Technology)   S. Maguire
Contact (Human Resources)   G. Laverty
Contact (Key Stage 1 and 2)   S. McKillop
Contact (Modern Languages)   W.A. Brodie MA
Contact (School Improvement/Management Development)
H. Thompson
Number of Schools
216 Primary (including 40 nursery units and 2 nursery
annexes); 38 Other Secondary; 16 Grammar; 15 Controlled
Nursery; 2 Maintained Nursery
Requisition Periods for Schools Supplies
Free books (main) 1 February–10 April
Special Schools
10 Controlled Special, 1 Maintained Special

EDUCATION BOARD

Chair   J.R. Beggs
Vice-Chair   C. Reid
Members of Board
O. Church, T. Clarke, J. Crilly, M. Crockett, J. Donaghy, U. Duncan, J. Finlay, L. Frazer, A. Gilkinson, Rev S. Graham, E. Green, Rev T. Jamieson, M.J. Johnston, S. Kerr, N. Macartney, L. Marsden, W. McCartney, S.A. McCrea, O. McMullan, N.C. Murray, H. Nicholl, U. O'Kane, S. Polley, Dr A. Preston, L. Raven, Prof N. Reid Burley, D. Ritchie, Rev Canon T. Scott, R. Stirling, R. Thompson, D. Walker

EDUCATION COMMITTEE (SCHOOLS)

Members of the Committee
J.R. Beggs, O.M. Church, J. Crilly, M. Crockett, J. Finlay, L. Frazer, Rev D.S. Graham, E. Green, Rev T. Jamieson, M.J. Johnston, S. Kerr, N.S. Macartney, L. Marsden, W. McCartney, S.A. McCrea, O. McMullan, U. O'Kane, Dr A. Preston, L. Raven, J.C. Reid, Prof N. Reid Burley, D. Ritchie, Rev Canon T. Scott, R. Stirling, R. Thompson, D. Walker

BOARD CENTRES

Antrim Board Centre   17 Lough Rd, Antrim, County Antrim BT41 4DG; Tel 028 9448 2200; Fax 028 9446 0794
CLASS Centre   86 Belfast Rd, Ballyclare, County Antrim BT37 9LS; Tel 028 9332 4168
Newtownabbey Educational Guidance Centre   231 Jordanstown Rd, Monkstown, Newtownabbey, County Antrim BT37 0LX; Tel 028 9086 3199; Fax 028 9086 2786
Head of Centre   B. Carruthers
Property Services   52–56 Ballymoney St, Ballymena, County Antrim BT43 6AN; Tel 028 2565 5366; Fax 020 2565 5277
Rathmore Educational Guidance Centre   10 Loughanmore Rd, Antrim, County Antrim BT41 2HQ; Tel 028 9443 2725; Fax 020 9443 3894
Head of Centre   W. Lambe
Sunlea Educational Guidance Centre   180 Ballycastle Rd, Coleraine, County Londonderry BT52 2NL; Tel 028 7035 2377; Fax 028 7032 1041
Head of Centre   A. White

YOUTH OFFICES

Antrim/Ballymena/Moyle   22 Ballymoney Rd, Ballymena, County Antrim BT43 5BY; Tel 028 2564 3625; Fax 028 2563 1287
Coleraine/Ballymoney/Magherafelt   9a Abbey St, Coleraine, County Londonderry BT52 1DS; Tel 028 7035 2279; Fax 028 7032 1157
Larne/Carrickfergus/Newtownabbey   The Bungalow, 134a Ballyclare Rd, Newtownabbey, County Antrim BT36 5HP; Tel 028 9084 0971; Fax 028 9083 3687

RESIDENTIAL YOUTH AND OUTDOOR PURSUITS CENTRES

Ballyhome   51 Ballyhome Rd, Coleraine, County Londonderry BT52 2LX; Tel 028 7082 3212
Bushmills   7 Priestland Rd, Bushmills, County Antrim BT57 8QP; Tel 028 2073 1599; Fax 028 2073 1591
Derganagh House   33 Rathlin Rd, Ballycastle, County Antrim BT54 6LD; Tel 028 2076 2979
Woodhall   27 Moneygran Rd, Kilrea, Coleraine, County Londonderry BT51 5SJ; Tel 028 2954 0331; Fax 028 2954 1075

YOUTH CENTRES

Ballykeel Youth Club   Ballykeel Youth Centre, 46 Crebilly Rd, Ballymena, County Antrim BT42 4DR; Tel 028 2564 1966
Glengormley Youth Club   Glengormley Youth Centre, Glenvarna Dr, Glengormley, Newtownabbey, County Antrim BT36 8JQ; Tel 028 9084 0942
Millgreen Youth Club   Millgreen Youth Centre, 19a Newton Gdns, Newtonabbey, County Antrim BT36 7BX; Tel 028 9085 4440

New Mossley   Campbell Rd, Newtownabbey, County Antrim BT36 8UW; Tel 028 9084 1988
Portrush Youth Club   Portrush Youth Centre, Dunluce Ave, Portrush, County Antrim BT56 8DW; Tel 028 7032 3030
Rathcoole Youth Club   Rathcoole Youth Centre, The Diamond, Newtownabbey, County Antrim BT37 9AH; Tel 028 9085 1172
Sunlea Youth Club   Sunlea Youth Centre, 180 Ballycastle Rd, Coleraine, County Londonderry BT52 2NL; Tel 028 7035 4823
Sunnylands Youth Club   Sunnylands Youth Centre, Hawthorn Ave, Carrickfergus, County Antrim BT38 8ED; Tel 028 9335 1866
Waveney Youth Club   Waveney Youth Centre, Doury Rd, Ballymena, County Antrim BT43 6JX; Tel 028 2564 5522

South Eastern Education and Library Board

www.seelb.org.uk

Grahamsbridge Rd, Dundonald, Belfast BT16 2HS; URL www.seelb.org.uk; e-mail info@seelb.org.uk; Tel 028 9056 6200; Fax 028 9056 6266
Chief Executive   Ms I. Knox BA, MBA, DipLiB, MIPM
Senior Education Officer   S.G. Sloan BSc, DASE, MA(Ed), MSc, MIBiol, CBiol
Assistant Senior Education Officer   J. Peel CertEd, BA, MEd, JP
Assistant Senior Education Officer (Property Services)   T. Walsh BSc, MEd
Assistant Senior Education Officer (SEN)   Mrs S. Skelton BA, MSc, MCPID
Deputy Head (CASS)   David Gillespie BSc, DipEd
Chief Administrative Officer   Vacancy
Chief Education Welfare Officer   K. Bridge CQSW
Chief Finance Officer   K. Brown BSc(Econ), FCA
Chief Librarian   Mrs B. Porter BA(Hons), DipLibStud, MCILIP
Assistant Chief Librarian   A. Adair BA(Hons), DLS, MPHIL, MCILIP
Principal Educational Psychologist   S.R. Irvine BA, MSc
Senior Educational Psychologist   N. Alexander MSc, PGCE
Principal Architect   S. Connolly RIBA, RIAI
Adviser (Behaviour Support/SEN)   Brenda Montgomery
Adviser (Entitlement Framework)   Val Dongherty
Adviser (Environment and Society/Vocational Careers)   Paula Smith
Adviser (ICT)   Eibhlin Tinneny BSc(Hons), MSc
Adviser (Language Studies and International Studies)   Mrs Ann McQuiston BA, CertEd
Adviser (Primary)   Robert Hunter
Adviser (Primary/Early Years)   Peter McAllister
Adviser (Science and Technology)   Peter McAlister
Adviser (Statistics Research and Development/Technology)   Cyril King BEd, MCCEd
Number of Schools
103 Controlled Primary (includes 27 nursery wings); 56 Maintained Primary (includes 12 nursery wings); 18 Controlled Secondary; 11 Controlled Nursery; 9 Maintained Secondary; 7 Maintained Nursery; 7 Voluntary Grammar (includes 4 preparatory departments); 5 Grant- Maintained Integrated Primary (includes 2 nursery units); 3 Grant-Maintained Integrated Secondary; 3 Controlled Grammar with preparatory departments;
Special Schools
18 Units for Primary SEN; 11 Controlled; 7 Secondary SEN; 3 Language and Communication Units; 3 Units for Hearing Imparied; 1 Diagnostic Unit
Requisition Periods for Schools Supplies
None specified
Joint Purchasing Arrangements
All other boards for some items

BOARD MEMBERS

Chair   Rev G.N. Howe
Vice-Chair   Cllr Mrs R.M. Dunlop
Members of the Committee
I. Arbuthnot, Rev Dr J.P.O. Barry, Rev Canon C.W. Bell, Cllr
J. Bell, D. Cahill, Cllr M.A. Coogan, Alderman Mrs M. Craig,
Cllr A.G. Ewat, M.P. Flannagan, F.A. Gault, Cllr P.J. Givan,
B. Henry, Rev J. Honeyford, Mrs S. McKee, Dr L.
McWhurter, Dr R. Montgomery, Mrs V. Morrison, D.G.
Mullan, Cllr Mrs C. O'Boyle, A. Rice, E.M. Robinson, Rev Dr
R.A. Russell, S. Smith, Cllr J. Spratt, D. Tennis, Cllr C. Tosh,
J.D. Uprichard, Cllr W.M. Ward, Cllr P. Weir, J. Williams,
Cllr T. Williams, Alderman B. Wilson

UNITS FOR HEARING IMPAIRED CHILDREN

Cregagh Primary School   Mount Merrion Ave, Belfast
BT6 0FL; e-mail
rmilligan618@cregaghps.belfast.ni.sch.uk;
Tel 028 9040 1246; Fax 028 9040 1246
Headteacher   R.J. Milligan
Holy Family Primary School   1 Drumnaconagher Rd,
Teconnaught, Downpatrick, County Down BT30 9AN;
Tel 028 4483 0319; Fax 028 4483 1879
Headteacher   Mr C. Curran
St Colmcille's High School   1 Killyleagh Rd, Crossgar,
Downpatrick, County Down BT30 9EY; e-mail
info@stcolmcilles.crossgar.ni.sch.uk; Tel 028 4483 0311;
Fax 028 4483 1383
Headteacher   Mrs M.T. McGreevy

LANGUAGE/COMMUNICATION UNIT

Knockmore Primary School   Hertford Cres, Lisburn, County
Antrim BT28 1SA; e-mail
jcooper429@knockmoreps.lisburn.ni.sch.uk;
Tel 028 9266 2600; Fax 028 9266 4279
Headteacher   J.G. Cooper

PRIMARY SEN UNITS

Bloomfield Primary School   Bloomfield Rd South, Bangor,
County Down BT19 7PN; e-mail
gloyers380@bloomfieldps.bangor.ni.sch.uk;
Tel 028 9127 1186; Fax 028 9127 5031
Headteacher   J. Byers
Castlewellan Primary School   2 Church St, Castlewellan,
County Down BT31 9EG; Tel 028 4377 8541;
Fax 028 4377 1721
Headteacher   Mr N.S. McClean
Clandeboye Primary SEN Unit   Clandeboye Rd, Bangor,
County Down BT20 3JW; e-mail
nmckenna618@clandeboyeps.bangor.ni.sch.uk;
Tel 028 9127 1730; Fax 028 9127 1858
Headteacher   N.P. McKenna
Downpatrick Primary School   10 Mount Cres, Downpatrick,
County Down BT30 6AF; e-mail
agreenwood393@dps.downpatrick.ni.sch.uk;
Tel 028 4461 3934; Fax 028 4461 7764
Headteacher   A.J. Greenwood
Knockbreda Primary School   Wynchurch Rd, Belfast BT6 0JJ;
e-mail mhenderson587@knockbredaps.belfast.ni.sch.uk;
Tel 028 9040 1871
Headteacher   Mrs M.E. Henderson
St Colman's Primary School   109 Queensway, Lambeg,
Lisburn, County Antrim BT27 4QS; e-mail
gmcveigh184@stcolmonsps.lisburn.ni.sch.uk;
Tel 028 9260 1532; Fax 028 9260 5892
Headteacher   G. McVeigh
St Colmcille's Primary School   Glebetown Dr, Downpatrick,
County Down BT30 6PZ; e-mail
jmurphy415@stcolmcillesps.downpatrick.ni.sch.uk;
Tel 028 4461 4177; Fax 028 4483 9016
Headteacher   J. Murphy

St Malachy's Primary School   33 Lower Sq, Castlewellan,
County Down BT31 9DN; e-mail
bking387@stmalachysps.castlewellan.ni.sch.uk;
Tel 028 4377 8537; Fax 028 4377 0634
Headteacher   B.A. King
St Mary's Primary School   3 Church Gr, Kircubbin BT22 2SU;
e-mail
jdorrian516@stmaryskircubbin.newtownards.ni.sch.uk;
Tel 028 4273 8581; Fax 028 4273 8037
Headteacher   J. Dorrian
Seymour Hill Primary School   Hazel Ave, Dunmurry, Belfast
BT17 9QX; e-mail
nmeharry236@seymourhillps.lisburn.ni.sch.uk;
Tel 028 9030 1046; Fax 028 9030 8940
Headteacher   N. Meharry
Towerview Primary School   100 Towerview Cres, Bangor,
County Down BT19 6AZ; e-mail
tcowan478@towerviewps.bangor.ni.sch.uk;
Tel 028 9127 0480; Fax 028 9147 3623
Headteacher   T.H. Cowan
West Winds Primary School   Sunderland Pk, Newtownards,
County Down BT23 4RQ; e-mail
jmccoubrie704@westwindsps.newtownards.ni.sch.uk;
Tel 028 9181 5212; Fax 028 9182 2328
Headteacher   Mrs J.A. McCoubrie

SECONDARY SEN UNITS

De La Salle High School   Struell Rd, Downpatrick, County
Down BT30 6JR; e-mail info@dls.downpatrick.ni.sch.uk;
Tel 028 4461 2520; Fax 028 4461 3314
Headteacher   B. Sharvin
Donaghadee High School   Northfield Rd, Donaghadee,
County Down BT21 0BH; e-mail
info@ddee.donaghadee.ni.sch.uk; Tel 028 9188 2361;
Fax 028 9188 3470
Headteacher   S.J. Creber
Down Academy   12 Old Belfast Rd, Downpatrick, County
Down BT30 6SG; e-mail
info@downacademy.downpatrick.ni.sch.uk;
Tel 028 4461 2115; Fax 028 4461 3116
Headteacher   R. Johnston
Dundonald High School   764 Upper Newtownards Rd,
Dundonald, Belfast BT16 1TH; e-mail
info@dundonald.belfast.ni.sch.uk; Tel 028 9048 4271;
Fax 028 9048 2051
Headteacher   Miss J. Cushanhan
St Malachy's High School   3 Dublin Rd, Castlewellan,
County Down BT31 9AG; e-mail
info@stmalachys.castlewellan.ni.sch.uk;
Tel 028 4377 8255; Fax 028 4377 8164
Headteacher   Mrs N. Cunningham
St Mary's High School   23 Ardglass Rd, Downpatrick,
County Down BT30 6JQ; e-mail
info@stmaryshs.downpatrick.ni.sch.uk;
Tel 028 4461 2515; Fax 028 4461 6807
Headteacher   Mrs P. Smyth
St Patrick's High School   Ballinderry Rd, Lisburn, County
Antrim BT28 1TD; e-mail
squinn802@stpats.lisburn.ni.sch.uk; Tel 028 9266 4877;
Fax 028 9266 8606
Headteacher   Dr S. Quinn

OUTDOOR EDUCATION CENTRES

Ardnabannon Outdoor Education Centre   3 Ardnabannon
Rd, Castlewellan, County Down BT31 9EN;
Tel 028 4377 8555; Fax 028 4377 8792
Centre Warden   T.F. Quinn
Killyleagh Outdoor Education Centre   Shore Rd, Killyleagh,
Downpatrick, County Down BT30 9UE;
Tel 028 4482 8511; Fax 028 4482 8482
Centre Warden   K. Balmer

RESOURCE CENTRES

Downpatrick Resource Centre 5–7 Mount Cres, Downpatrick, County Down BT30 6AF; e-mail dpk_rcentre@btconnect.com; Tel 028 4461 3304; Fax 028 4461 7050
Centre Contact A. Dagens
Rathvarna Resource Centre 22 Pond Park Rd, Lisburn, County Antrim BT28 3LF; Tel 028 9267 0662; Fax 028 9263 4140
Centre Manager Mrs V. McClenaghan
Centre Manager Mrs S. Miller
South Eastern Music Centre Church Rd, Ballynahinch, County Down BT24 8LP; URL www.nireland.com/semusic; e-mail semusiccentre@btconnect.com; Tel 028 9756 2030; Fax 028 9756 5120
Director D. McArdle BA, MTD, LTCL

YOUTH CENTRES

Advance Training and Development The Young Adult Centre, 50 Railway St, Lisburn, County Antrim BT28 1XP; Tel 028 9266 6094; Fax 028 9266 6129
Centre Manager C. Dalzell
Centre Manager C. Edgar
Ardcarnet Youth Centre 25 Kinross Ave, Dundonald, Belfast BT5 7GE; Tel 028 9048 0353; Fax 028 9048 0353
Centre Manager Vacancy
Ards Arena Youth Centre 62 South St, Newtownards, County Down BT23 4JU; Tel 028 9181 3987; Fax 028 9182 3470
Centre Manager Ms J. Lewis
Colin Young Development Centre Good Shepherd Rd, Poleglass, Belfast BT17 0PP; Tel 028 9062 9799; Fax 028 9062 9740
Centre Manager A. Quirke
Stevenson Youth Centre Kingsway, Dunmurry, Belfast BT17 9AA; Tel 028 9030 1057

Southern Education and Library Board

3 Charlemont Pl, The Mall, Armagh, County Armagh BT61 9AX; Tel 028 3751 2200
Chief Executive H.M. McClenaghan BA, MEd
Chair Mrs M.E. Donnell
Vice-Chair The Very Rev L.M. McVeigh
Head (Corporate Services) T.M. Heron
Head (Education Services) W. Burke
Head (Human Resources) P. Keating
Head (Support and Property Services) T. Murphy
Manager (Inter-Board Services) J. Curran
Chief Education Welfare Officer Ms A. Barr
Assistant Senior Education Officer (Inclusion, Planning and Development Services) G.P. Butler
Assistant Senior Education Officer (Learning, Advisory and Support Services) Mrs H. Mullan
Procurement Officer R. McMurray
Transport Officer D. Hanna
Chief Librarian Mrs K. Ryan
Senior Organiser (School Meals) Mrs D. Young
Management Accountant Ms L. Ayling
Internal Auditor K. Orr
Number of Schools
Controlled: 102 Primary; 16 Secondary; 2 Nursery; 3 Grammar. Maintained: 138 Primary; 18 Secondary; 12 Voluntary Grammar; 4 Colleges of Further Education; 6 Special; 3 Nursery
Day of board meeting
Third Thursday of each month
Requisition Periods for Schools Supplies
Main: March/April; subsidiary: October
Other Authorities with whom Joint Purchasing Arrangements are made
Other four Northern Ireland Education and Library Boards

BOARD MEMBERSHIP

P.H. Aiken, P. Brannigan, S.R. Brownlee, Rev J. Byrne, M.P. Campbell, P. Cunningham, Cllr F. Dawson, M.E. Donnell, B. Doran, Rev W.R. Ferguson, P. Gildea, I.E.B. Hanna, J. Hanna, Cllr R.A. Harkness, Dr M. Hollinger, A.B. Lewis, C. Mackin, Mrs M. Magennis, W. Mayne, P. McAleer, Mrs C. McCaul, A. McCreesh, Cllr J. McCrum, P. McGinn, Rev Canon McKegney, Cllr K. McKevitt, S. McRoberts, Rev M. McVeigh, B. Monteith, Cllr R. Mulligan, Prof P. Murphy, A.G. Sleator, J.K. Twyble, Cllr Dr P.A. Weir, Mrs E. Wright

EDUCATION WELFARE SERVICE

3 Charlemont Pl, The Mall, Armagh, County Armagh BT61 9AX; Tel 028 3751 2384; Fax 028 3741 5378
Chief Education Welfare Officer A. Barr
Armagh 25 Railway St, Armagh, County Armagh BT61 7HP; Tel 028 3752 5780; Fax 028 3751 8318
Senior Education Welfare Officer E.J. Quinn
Banbridge Banbridge High School, Primrose Gdns, Banbridge, County Down BT32 3EP; Tel 028 4062 8319; Fax 028 4062 8078
Education Welfare Officer Ms C. Fegan
Dungannon Dungannon Primary School, Circular Rd, Dungannon, County Tyrone BT71 6BG; Tel 028 8772 3311; Fax 028 8772 7843
Senior Education Welfare Officer A. Nugent
Dungannon Holy Trinity College, Chapel St, Cookstown, County Tyrone BT80 8QB; Tel 028 8676 2135; Fax 028 8676 7089
Education Welfare Officer Ms C. Comiskey
Newry Kilkeel High School, Knockchree Ave, Kilkeel, Newry, County Down BT34 4BP; Tel 028 4176 3453; Fax 028 4176 5038
Education Welfare Officer Mrs M. Ward
Newry Newry Teachers' Centre, Downshire Rd, Newry, County Down BT34 1EE; Tel 028 3025 3154; Fax 028 3026 4254
Senior Education Welfare Officer Jennifer McCann
Newry St Joseph's High School, 77 Dundalk Rd, Crossmagles, Newry, County Down BT35 9HP; Tel 028 3086 1879; Fax 028 3086 8607
Education Welfare Officer J. Darragh
Portadown Craigavon High School, 26 Lurgan Rd, Craigavon, County Armagh BT63 5BL; Tel 028 3833 0662; Fax 028 3835 2200
Senior Divisional Education Welfare Officer Mrs C. Maxwell
Portadown Tullgally Primary School, 21 Meadowbrook Rd, Lurgan, Craigavon, County Armagh BT66 5AA; Tel 028 3832 6801; Fax 028 3832 6980
Senior Education Welfare Officer Mrs J. McCool

INTEGRATED COLLEGES

Armagh Integrated College 38f Abbey St, Armagh, County Armagh BT61 7EB; Tel 028 3752 2944
Principal Dr O. Griffiths (Acting)
Dungannon College 21 Gortmerron Link Rd, Dungannon, County Tyrone BT71 6LS; e-mail adolan@intcollege.dungannon.ni.sch.uk; Tel 028 8772 4401; Fax 028 8772 5499
Principal A. Sleeth (Acting)
New Bridge College 25 Donard View Rd, Loughbrickland, Banbridge, County Down BT32 3LN; e-mail newbridgecol.banbridgecampus.bt.com; Tel 028 4062 5010; Fax 028 4062 2503
Headteacher P.J. Agnew MA, BA, PGCE, DASE

DIVISIONAL YOUTH OFFICES

Armagh 38 Scotch St, Armagh, County Armagh BT61 7BY; e-mail susan.pollock@selb.org; Tel 028 3752 8681; Fax 028 3751 0277
Divisional Youth Officer Susan Pollock

Banbridge/Craigavon Bann Hse, Bridge St Portadown, Craigavon, County Armagh BT63 5AE; Tel 028 3833 8556; Fax 028 3839 4065
Divisional Youth Officer Miss R. Weir
Cookstown/Dungannon Unit 6, 79 Market Sq, Dungannon, County Tyrone BT70 1JF; e-mail erika.hill@selb.org; Tel 028 8772 2167; Fax 028 8775 3031
Divisional Youth Worker Erika Hill
Newry/Mourne Multipurpose Centre, Downshire Rd, Newry, County Down BT34 1EE; e-mail marie.savage@selb.org; Tel 028 3026 2357; Fax 028 3083 3690
Divisional Youth Officer Marie Savage

MUSIC CENTRES

Dungannon Music Centre Thomas St, Dungannon, County Tyrone BT70 1HW; Tel 028 8772 1753; Fax 028 8775 2138
Officer-in-charge Mrs M. Busby
Newry Music Centre Downshire Rd, Newry, County Down BT34 1EE; Tel 028 3025 3169; Fax 028 3025 7585
Officer-in-Charge Miss S. Hetherington
Portadown Music Centre and SELB Music Service Bann Hse, Bridge St Portadown, Craigavon, County Armagh BT63 5AE; Tel 028 3833 2371; Fax 028 3839 4525
Officer-in-Charge Mrs D. Watt
Head (Music Service) Mrs E. Benson

READING CENTRES

Armagh Reading Centre Armstrong Primary School, College Hill, Armagh, County Armagh; Tel 028 3752 6828; Fax 028 3752 6828
Senior Tutor Ms A. McCreesh
Banbridge Reading Centre Lurgan Rd, Banbridge, County Down BT32 4AF; Tel 028 4062 3724; Fax 028 4062 8607
Senior Tutor D. Evans
Craigavon Reading Centre c/o Drumgor Primary School, Drumgar Rd, Brownlow, Craigavon, County Armagh BT65 5BP; Tel 028 3834 8690; Fax 028 3834 8690
Senior Tutor Mrs A. McKinless
Dungannon Reading Centre c/o Howard Primary School, 2 Main Rd, Moygashel, Dungannon, County Tyrone BT71 7QR; Tel 028 8772 1971; Fax 028 8772 1977
Senior Tutor Ms A. McCreesh
Newry Reading Centre c/o St Patrick's Primary School, Ballinlare Gdns, Newry, County Down BT35 6EX; Tel 020 3026 8590; Fax 028 3026 2917
Senior Tutor Mrs L. Hunt

RESIDENTIAL/OUTDOOR EDUCATION CENTRES

Binnian Outdoor Education Base Head Rd, Annalong, Newry, County Down; Tel 028 4372 3841
Warden A. Carden
Killowen Outdoor Education Centre Killowen Point, Rostrevor, Newry, County Down BT34 3AN; Tel 028 4173 8297; Fax 028 4173 8167
Warden P. Wells
Shannaghmore Residential Centre The Ballagh Kilkeel Rd, Newcastle, County Down BT33 0LA; Tel 028 4372 3841; Fax 028 4372 6602
Warden A. Carden

TEACHERS' CENTRES

Armagh Teachers' Centre Woodford, 1 Markethill Rd, Armagh, County Armagh BT60 1NP; Tel 028 3752 0728; Fax 028 3752 0717
Officer-in-Charge Mrs P. Monaghan
CASS Centre Silverwood Centre, Lough Rd, Lurgan BT66 6LX; URL www.selbcass.org; e-mail hilary.mclean@selb.org; Tel 028 3831 0920; Fax 028 3834 6604
Officer-in-Charge Mrs J. Price
Clounagh Centre 38 Brownstown Rd, Portadown, Craigavon, County Armagh BT62 3PY; Tel 028 3836 8150; Fax 028 3835 1172
Officer-in-Charge E. Anderson

Craigavon Teachers' Centre Tullygally Rd, Craigavon, County Armagh BT65 5BS; Tel 028 3834 2467; Fax 028 3834 9460
Officer-in-Charge J. Price
Dungannon Teachers' Centre Thomas St, Dungannon, County Tyrone BT70 1HW; Tel 028 8772 4379; Fax 028 8775 2138
Officer-in-Charge Mrs F. Hegarty
Newry Teachers' Centre Downshire Rd, Newry, County Down BT34 1BE; Tel 028 3026 2357; Fax 028 3026 4211
Officer-in-Charge Vacancy

YOUTH CENTRES

Armagh Youth Centre 56 Lisanally La, Armagh, County Armagh BT61 7HN; Tel 028 3752 5403; Fax 028 3751 0838
Youth Worker-in-Charge Vacancy
Aughnacloy Youth Centre Aughnacloy High School, 23 Carnteel Rd, Aughnacloy, County Tyrone BT69 6DU; Tel 028 8555 7289; Fax 028 8555 7717
Youth Tutor W. Williams
Banbridge Youth Centre Hill St, Banbridge, County Down BT32 4DP; Tel 028 4066 2509; Fax 028 4066 2509
Youth Worker-in-Charge Ms D. O'Neill
Brownlow Resource Youth Centre Brownlow Rd, Craigavon, County Armagh BT65 5DL; Tel 028 3834 3259; Fax 028 3834 1813
Youth Worker-in-Charge Mrs B. Ringland
Cookstown Youth Centre Cookstown High School, Coolnafrankie Est, Cookstown, County Tyrone BT80 8PQ; Tel 028 8676 9434; Fax 028 8676 1210
Youth Tutor M. Haycock
Dromore Youth Centre Dromore High School, 31 Banbridge Rd, Dromore, County Down BT25 1ND; Tel 028 9269 3473; Fax 028 9269 9825
Youth Tutor M. Teggarty
Drumgor Youth Centre c/o Brownlow Resource Youth Centre, Brownlow Youth Centre, Brownlow Rd, Craigavon, County Armagh BT65 5DL; Tel 028 3834 3259; Fax 028 3834 1813
Youth Worker-in-Charge Mrs B. Ringland
Fivemiletown Youth Centre Fivemiletown High School, Corcreevy Demesne, Fivemiletown, County Tyrone BT75 0SB; Tel 028 8952 1279; Fax 028 8952 1179
Youth Worker K. Graham
Keady Youth Development Project The Old Mill, 2 Main St, Keady, Armagh, County Armagh BT60 3SU; Tel 028 3753 9258; Fax 028 3753 9258
Youth Development Worker Mrs S. Best
Lurgan Youth Annex Toberhewny La, Mourne Rd, County Armagh BT66 8JA; Tel 028 3832 3119; Fax 028 3823 7823
Youth Tutor W. Keegan
Newry Youth Information Point 81a Hill St, Newry, County Down BT34 1DJ; Tel 028 3026 8132; Fax 028 3025 7524
Senior Youth Worker P. Bradley
Taghnevan Youth and Community Centre Glenholme Pk, Lurgan, Craigavon, County Armagh BT66 8SL; Tel 028 3832 4989; Fax 028 3832 5083
Youth Worker-in-Charge Mrs D. McMahon
The Source Cafe Old Town Hall, Banbridge, County Down; Tel 028 4066 9250; Fax 028 4066 9249
Development Worker Miss S. Quinn
Tullygally Youth Centre c/o Brownlow Resource Youth Centre, Brownlow Rd, Craigavon, County Armagh BT65 5DL; Tel 028 3834 3259; Fax 028 3834 1813
Contact Ms B. Ringland

Western Education and Library Board

www.welbni.org

1 Hospital Rd, Omagh, County Tyrone BT79 0AW; URL www.welbni.org; e-mail info@welbni.org; Tel 028 8241 1411; Fax 028 8241 1400

Chief Executive   B. Mulholland CertEd, DASE, MEd
Chair   Rev R. Herron
Vice-Chair   Vacancy
Head (Human Resources)   H. Duffy
Head (Property Services)   I. Barker
Head (Youth Service)   G. Doran
Chief Officer (Finance)   O. Harkin
Chief Officer (Library and Corporate Services)   H. Osborn
Children and Young People's Department Officer
    Dr C. Mangan
Services Department Officer   R. Watterson
Teaching, Learning, Curriculum and Youth Department
    Officer   P. Mackey
Number of Schools
187 Primary; 31 Secondary; 13 Grammar; 12 Nursery; 9
Special

OUTDOOR EDUCATION CENTRES

Corrick Outdoor Education Centre   c/o 19 Main St, Gortin,
Omagh, County Tyrone; Tel 028 8166 2478
    Centre Manager   Mr I. Pentland
Gortatole Outdoor Education Centre   Florencecourt,
Enniskillen, County Fermanagh BT92 1ED; e-mail
gortatole_oec@welbni.org; Tel 028 6634 8888
    Warden   Mr R. Finlay
Magilligan Field Centre   375 Seacoast Rd, Limavady, County
Londonderry BT49 0LF; e-mail liz.wallace@welbni.org;
Tel 028 7775 0234
    Centre Manager   Miss L. Wallace

TEACHERS' CENTRES

North West Teacher's Centre   24 Temple Rd, Strathfoyle,
Londonderry, County Londonderry BT47 6TJ; e-mail
barbara_moore@welbni.org; Tel 028 7186 1116;
Fax 028 7186 1105
Omagh Teachers' Centre   Omagh Library Complex, 1
Spillars Pl, Omagh, County Tyrone BT78 1HL; e-mail
otc@welbni.org; Tel 028 8224 4821; Fax 028 8225 1566
South West Teachers' Centre   Library Headquarters, Hall's
La, Enniskillen, County Fermanagh BT74 7DR; e-mail
stephanie_ritchie@welbni.org; Tel 028 6632 3240;
Fax 028 6632 8607
Strabane Teachers' Centre   Khiva Hse, 55 Urney Rd,
Strabane, County Tyrone BT82 9DB; e-mail
marie-mccullagh@welbni.org; Tel 028 7138 2632;
Fax 028 7138 3252

YOUTH SERVICE

Aileach Youth Club   St Peter's Secondary School, Foyle Hill,
Londonderry, County Londonderry BT48 9SE;
Tel 028 7136 1981; Fax 028 7127 3929
    Centre Manager   J. Morrison
Brollagh Youth Club   St Mary's Secondary School, Brollagh
Belleek, Enniskillen, County Fermanagh BT93 3AH;
Tel 028 6865 8257; Fax 028 6865 8045
    Centre Manager   Vacancy
Carrickmore Youth Club   Termon Rd, Carrickmore, County
Tyrone BT79 9JR; e-mail carrickmore.yc@welbni.org;
Tel 028 8076 1310; Fax 028 8076 1310
    Centre Manager   Vacancy
Caw Youth Club   68 Seymour Gdns, Londonderry, County
Londonderry BT47 6ND; e-mail caw_yc@welbni.org;
Tel 028 7134 2750; Fax 028 7134 2750
    Centre Manager   Vacancy
Derg Valley Youth Centre   Castlederg High School, 16
Castlegore Rd, Castlederg, County Tyrone BT81 7RU;
Tel 028 8167 1272; Fax 028 8167 9801
    Centre Manager   Mr J. Ireland
Derrychara Youth Club   Devenish College, Derrychara,
Enniskillen, County Fermanagh BT74 6JL;
Tel 028 6632 2923; Fax 028 6632 5858
    Centre Manager   Vacancy

Drumgallon Youth Club   James Memorial School,
Mullylogan, Enniskillen, County Londonderry
BT47 5QF; Tel 028 6632 3420
    Manager   Mrs D. Morrison
Glen Club   Strabane High School, 61 Derry Rd, Strabane,
County Tyrone BT82 8LD; Tel 028 8164 8849
    Centre Manager   Mr S. McConnell
Irvinestown Youth Club   Bawnacre Centre, Irvinestown,
Enniskillen, County Fermanagh BT94 1EE; e-mail
irvinestown-yc@welbni.org; Tel 028 6862 1177;
Fax 028 6862 8082
    Centre Manager   Mr G. Beacom
Kesh Youth Club   Devenish College, Kesh, Enniskillen,
County Fermanagh BT93 1TF; Tel 028 6863 1265;
Tel 028 6863 1537
    Centre Manager   Mr R. Beacom
Lakeland Youth Centre   Lakeland Youth Centre, Wellington
Rd, Enniskillen BT74 7HL; e-mail
lakeland_yc@welbni.org; Tel 028 6632 6932;
Fax 028 6632 9209
    Centre Manager   Vacancy
Limavady High School Youth Club   Limavady High School,
Irish Green St, Limavady, County Londonderry
BT49 9AN; Tel (school) 028 7776 2526; Fax 028 7776 4102
    Centre Manager   Mr D. Hornin
Lisnaskea Youth Centre   Lisnaskea High School, Lisnaskea,
Enniskillen, County Fermanagh BT92 OLT;
Tel 028 6772 1239; Tel 028 6772 1283
    Centre Manager   Mr Dr C. Givan
Long Tower Youth Club   Ann St, Londonderry, County
Londonderry BT48 6BP; e-mail
longtower_yc@welbni.org; Tel 028 7126 4012;
Fax 028 7126 4012
    Centre Manager   Mr B. McMenamin
Newbuildings Youth Club   4 Duncastle Rd, Newbuildings,
Londonderry, County Londonderry BT47 2QS;
Tel 028 7131 2252; Fax 028 7132 9937
    Centre Manager   Vacancy
Newtownstewart Model Youth Club   Newtownstewart
Model Primary School, Newtownstewart, County
Londonderry BT82 9GA; Tel 028 8166 2419
    Centre Manager   Vacancy
Omagh Boys and Girls Club   The Station Centre, James St,
Omagh, County Tyrone BT78 1QX; e-mail
omaghbg-yc@welbni.org; Tel 028 8224 3772
    Centre Manager   Vacancy
Omagh Youth Centre   Old Mountfield Rd, Omagh, County
Tyrone BT79 7EG; e-mail omagh-yc@welbni.org;
Tel 028 8224 9349
    Centre Manager   Mrs M. Rodgers
Pennyburn Youth Club   5 Buncrana Rd, Londonderry,
County Londonderry BT48 7QL; e-mail
pennyburn_yc@welbni.org; Tel 028 7126 7959;
Fax 028 7126 7959
    Centre Manager   Mr B. Wilkinson
Pilot's Row Youth and Community Youth Centre   Rossville St,
Londonderry, County Londonderry BT48 6LP; e-mail
pilotsrow_yc@welbni.org; Tel 028 7126 9418;
Fax 028 7137 3296
    Centre Manager   Mr H. Hastings
Rosemount Youth Centre   Rosemount Ave, Londonderry,
County Londonderry BT48 0HH; e-mail
rosemount_yc@welbni.org; Tel 028 7136 9264;
Fax 028 7136 3787
    Centre Manager   Miss M. McCourt
Roslea Youth Club   St Eugene's College, 1 Monaghan Rd,
Roslea, County Londonderry BT92 7SE; Tel 028 6775 1258
    Centre Manager   Vacancy
St Brecan's Youth Club   Immaculate Conception College,
Trench Rd, Londonderry, County Londonderry
BT47 2DS; e-mail pmolly@stbrecans.derry.ni.sch.uk;
Tel 028 7132 9097; Fax 028 7131 1475
    Centre Manager   Mr H. Hegarty
St Brigid's Youth Club   St Brigid's College, Glengalliagh Rd,
Londonderry, County Londonderry BT48 8DU;
Tel 028 7135 1002; Fax 028 7135 4829
    Centre Manager   Vacancy

St Canice's Youth Club St Patrick's College, 9 Curragh Rd, Dungiven, Londonderry, County Londonderry BT47 4SE; Tel 028 7774 1324; Fax 028 7774 2566
Centre Manager Mr C. McCartney

St Eithne's Youth Club St Eithne's Primary School, 26 Springtown Rd, Londonderry, County Londonderry BT48 0LT; Tel 028 7136 1282
Centre Manager Mr D. Haslett

St Joseph's Youth Centre Lenamore Rd, Gallaigh, Londonderry, County Londonderry BT48 8NA; Tel 028 7135 2309
Centre Manager Mr D. O'Kane

St Mary's High School Youth Club St Mary's High School, 72–90 Irish Green St, Limavady, County Londonderry BT49 9AN; Tel 028 7776 5443
Centre Manager Mr T. Campbell

St Patrick's and St Brigid's Youth Club St Patrick's and St Brigid's High School, 55 Main St, Claudy, County Londonderry BT47 4HR; Tel 028 7133 8317
Centre Manager Mrs S. McLaughlin

Shantallow Youth Centre Racecourse Rd, Londonderry, County Londonderry BT48 8DA; e-mail shantallow_yc@welbni.org; Tel 028 7135 3561
Centre Manager Una McCartney

Strabane Youth Association Youth Club Melvin Hall, Strabane, County Tyrone BT82 9PP; e-mail melvinhall_yc@welbni.org; Tel 028 7138 2175
Youth Worker Vacancy

Strathfoyle Youth Centre Deramore Dr, Strathfoyle, Londonderry, County Londonderry BT47 6XL; e-mail strathfoyle_yc@welbni.org; Tel 028 7186 0334
Centre Manager Vacancy

YMCA Youth Club 51 Glenshane Rd, Drumahoe, Londonderry, County Londonderry BT47 3SF; e-mail lderry@ymca-ireland.org; Tel 028 7130 1662; Fax 028 7130 1662
Centre Manager Miss L. Nicholl

Youth Information Service Youth Club 40 Dungiven Rd, Waterside, Londonderry, County Londonderry BT47 1BW; e-mail yis@welbni.org; Tel 028 7131 3444; Fax 028 7131 3555
Manager Mr S. Quigley

CHANNEL ISLANDS AND ISLE OF MAN

See Chapter 1: Government Departments Channel Islands and Isle of Man

Secondary Schools

3

Key

B	Boys
CI	Controlled Integrated
CY	Community
D	Day places
FD	Foundation
G	Girls
GMI	Grant-Maintained Integrated
Ind	Independent/Non-Maintained

MDP	Middle Deemed Primary
MDS	Middle Deemed Secondary
N	Nursery provision
R	Residential provision
Ref	LA Number-DfES Number or regional equivalent
Sp	Special School
VA	Voluntary Aided
VC	Voluntary Controlled

Religious character

Ba	Baptist
Bu	Buddhist
CE	Church of England
CIW	Church in Wales
Cg	Congregational Church
Ch	Christian
CS	Church of Scotland
Es	Episcopalian
FC	Free Church
FP	Free Presbyterian
Gk	Greek Orthodox
Hi	Hindu
ID	Inter/Non-Denominational
IP	Independent Pentecostal
Je	Jewish
Me	Methodist
MF	Multi-Faith
Mu	Muslim
Qk	Quaker
RC	Roman Catholic
SDA	Seventh Day Adventist
UR	United Reformed Church

Special needs

ADHD	Attention Deficit Hyperactivity Disorder
AS	Asperger's Syndrome
ASD	Autism Spectrum Disorder
CD	Communication Difficulties
DMP	Delicate Medical Problems
Ep	Epilepsy
HI	Hearing Impairment
HS	Hospital School
MLD	Moderate Learning Difficulties
MSI	Multi-Sensory Impairment
PD	Physical Difficulties
PMLD	Profound and Multiple Learning Difficulties
SCU	Special Care Unit
SEBD	Social, Emotional and Behavioural Difficulties
SEN	Special Educational Needs
SLD	Severe Learning Difficulties
SpLD	Specific Learning Difficulties
VI	Visual Impairment

Secondary Schools

East of England

Bedfordshire

School name	Address	Tel	Fax	Headteacher	Ref	Type	Ages	Pupils	Other
Biddenham Upper School and Sports College	Biddenham Turn, Bedford, Bedfordshire MK40 4AZ	01234 342521	01234 325646	Mr Mike Berrill	820-4124	CY	13-18	1023	
The Cedars Upper School and Community College	Mentmore Rd, Linslade, Leighton Buzzard, Bedfordshire LU7 2AE	01525 219300	01525 850864	Mr Andrew Warren	820-4011	CY	13-18	1298	
Harlington Upper School	Goswell End Rd, Harlington, Dunstable, Bedfordshire LU5 6NX	01525 755100	01525 755101	Mr Shawn Fell	820-4083	CY	13-18	1252	
Hastingsbury Upper School and Community College	Hill Rise, Kempston, Bedford, Bedfordshire MK42 7EB	01234 290900	01234 290901	Mr Martin Fletcher	820-4064	CY	13-18	946	
John Bunyan Upper School	Mile Rd, Bedford, Bedfordshire MK42 9TR	01234 301500	01234 301501	Mr Neil Smith	820-4081	CY	13-18	657	
Manshead CE VA Upper School	Dunstable Rd, Caddington, Luton, Bedfordshire LU1 4BB	01582 608641	01582 679411	Mr Jim Parker	820-5401	VA	13-18	1036	CE
Mark Rutherford Upper School and Community College	Wentworth Dr, Bedford, Bedfordshire MK41 8PX	01234 290200	01234 290236	Mr J.M. Summers	820-4085	CY	13-18	1045	
The Northfields Technology College	Houghton Rd, Dunstable, Bedfordshire LU5 5AB	01582 619700	01582 619701	Mr Kevin Brown	820-4008	CY	13-18	808	
Queensbury Upper School	Langdale Rd, Dunstable, Bedfordshire LU6 3BU	01582 601241	01582 476988	Mr Nigel Hill	820-5400	FD	13-18	1183	
Redborne Upper School and Community College	Flitwick Rd, Ampthill, Bedford, Bedfordshire MK45 2NU	01525 404462	01525 841246	Mr Nigel Croft	820-4003	CY	13-18	1384	
St Thomas More RC School	Tyne Cres, Bedford, Bedfordshire MK41 7UL	01234 400222	01234 400223	Mr Alan Lee	820-4605	VA	12-18	883	RC
Samuel Whitbread Community College	Shefford Rd, Clifton, Shefford, Bedfordshire SG17 5QS	01462 629900	01462 629901	Mr Robert Robson	820-4079	CY	13-18	1534	
Sandy Upper School and Community College	Engayne Ave, Sandy, Bedfordshire SG19 1BL	01767 680598	01767 683543	Mr David Stevinson	820-4078	CY	13-18	880	
Sharnbrook Upper School and Community College	Odell Rd, Sharnbrook, Bedford, Bedfordshire MK44 1JL	01234 782211	01234 782431	Mr John Clemence	820-5402	FD	13-18	1773	
Stratton Upper School and Community College	Eagle Farm Rd, Biggleswade, Bedfordshire SG18 8JB	01767 220000	01767 220002	Mr N. Bramwell	820-4005	CY	13-18	1172	
Vandyke Upper School and Community College	Vandyke Rd, Leighton Buzzard, Bedfordshire LU7 3DY	01525 636700	01525 636701	Mr T. Carroll	820-4096	CY	13-18	1026	
Wootton Upper School	Hall End Rd, Wootton, Bedford, Bedfordshire MK43 9HT	01234 767123	01234 765203	Mr A. Withell	820-5406	FD	13-18	1242	

Cambridgeshire

School name	Address	Tel	Fax	Headteacher	Ref	Type	Ages	Pupils	Other
Abbey College, Ramsey	Abbey Rd, Ramsey, Cambridgeshire PE26 1DG	01487 812352		Mr Wayne Birks	873-4603	VC	11-18	1742	
Bassingbourn Village College	South End, Royston, Hertfordshire SG8 5NJ	01763 242344	01763 248122	Scott Hudson	873-5401	FD	11-16	658	
Bottisham Village College	Lode Rd, Bottisham, Cambridge, Cambridgeshire CB5 9DL	01223 811250	01223 813123	Mrs Kate Evans	873-4002	CY	11-16	1036	
Chesterton Community College	Gilbert Rd, Cambridge, Cambridgeshire CB4 3NY	01223 712150	01223 300786	Mr M. Patterson	873-4029	CY	11-16	977	
City of Ely Community College	Downham Rd, Ely, Cambridgeshire CB6 2SH	01353 667763	01353 669548	Mr Ian Gartshore	873-4083	FD	11-18	1155	
Coleridge Community College	Radegund Rd, Cambridge, Cambridgeshire CB1 3RJ	01223 712300	01223 712301	C. Meddle	873-4031	FD	11-16	309	
Comberton Village College	West St, Cambridge, Cambridgeshire CB3 7DU	01223 262503	01223 264116	Stephen Munday	873-5406	FD	11-16	1228	R

School name	Address	Tel	Fax	Headteacher	Ref	Type	Ages	Pupils	Other
Cottenham Village College	High St, Cottenham, Cambridge, Cambridgeshire CB24 8UA	01954 288944	01954 288949	Mr Tony Cooper	873-4038	CY	11–16	981	
Cromwell Community College	Wenny Rd, Chatteris, Cambridgeshire PE16 6UU	01354 692193	01354 695952	Mr Jed Roberts	873-4045	CY	11–16	1025	
Hinchingbrooke School	Brampton Rd, Huntingdon, Cambridgeshire PE29 3BN	01480 375700	01480 375699	Mr Keith Nancekievill	873-4503	VC	11–18	1863	
Impington Village College	New Rd, Impington, Cambridge, Cambridgeshire CB4 9LX	01223 200400	01223 200419	Mrs Sandra Morton	873-4004	CY	11–18	1383	
Linton Village College	Cambridge Rd, Cambridge, Cambridgeshire CB1 6JB	01223 891233	01223 894476	Caroline Derbyshire	873-5416	FD	11–16	805	
Longsands College	Longsands Rd, St Neots, Cambridgeshire PE19 1LQ	01480 353535	01480 375757	Robert Whatmough	873-5411	FD	11–18	1665	
The Manor Community College	Arbury Rd, Cambridge, Cambridgeshire CB4 2JF	01223 508742	01223 508747	Mr David Cressey	873-4057	CY	11–16	342	
Melbourn Village College	The Moor, Melbourn, Royston, Hertfordshire SG8 6EF	01763 223400	01763 223411	Mrs Elaine Stephenson	873-4040	CY	11–16	615	
The Neale-Wade Community College	Wimblington Rd, March, Cambridgeshire PE15 9PX	01354 653430	01354 659429	Mr Tim Hitch	873-4501	CY	11–18	1714	
The Netherhall School	Queen Edith's Way, Cambridge, Cambridgeshire CB1 8NN	01223 242931	01223 410473	Mrs Caroline McKenney	873-4061	CY	11–18	1385	
Parkside Community College	Parkside, Cambridge, Cambridgeshire CB1 1EH	01223 712600	01223 712601	Andrew Hutchinson	873-4027	FD	11–16	605	
The Queen's School	Corporation Rd, Wisbech, Cambridgeshire PE13 2SE	01945 585237		S.J. McKenna	873-5402		11–16		
St Bede's Inter-Church School	Birdwood Rd, Cambridge, Cambridgeshire CB1 3TD	01223 568816	01223 576482	Ms Jan Hunt	873-4602	VA	11–16	721	CE/RC
St Ivo School	High Leys, St Ives, Cambridgeshire PE27 6RR	01480 375400	01480 375444	Mr Howard Gilbert	873-4064	CY	11–18	1789	
St Neots Community College	Barford Rd, Eynesbury, St Neots, Cambridgeshire PE19 2SH	01480 374748	01480 375150	Mr Mark Duke	873-4077	CY	11–18	1107	
St Peter's School	St Peter's Rd, Huntingdon, Cambridgeshire PE29 7DD	01480 459581	01480 457968	Valerie Ford	873-5412	FD	11–18	1343	
Sawston Village College	New Rd, Cambridge, Cambridgeshire CB22 3BP	01223 712277	01223 836680	M.J.A. Cannie	873-5408	FD	11–16	1028	
Sawtry Community College	Fen La, Huntingdon, Cambridgeshire PE28 5TQ	01487 830701	01487 831679	James Stewart	873-5403	FD	11–18	1341	
Sir Harry Smith Community College	Eastrea Rd, Whittlesey, Peterborough, Cambridgeshire PE7 1XB	01733 703991	01733 703992	Mr M. Sandeman	873-4051	CY	11–18	1053	
Soham Village College	Sand St, Ely, Cambridgeshire CB7 5AA	01353 724100	01353 624854	Carin Taylor	873-5415	FD	11–16	1336	
Swavesey Village College	Gibraltar La, Swavesey, Cambridge, Cambridgeshire CB24 4RS	01954 230366	01954 230437	Mr Martin Bacon	873-4007	CY	11–16	1176	
Thomas Clarkson Community College	Corporation Rd, Wisbech, Cambridgeshire PE13 2SE	01945 585237	01945 474226	John Bennett	873-4604	FD	11–16		
Witchford Village College	Manor Rd, Witchford, Ely, Cambridgeshire CB6 2JA	01353 662053	01353 662567	Mr John Shield	873-4055	CY	11–16	873	

Essex

School name	Address	Tel	Fax	Headteacher	Ref	Type	Ages	Pupils	Other
Alderman Blaxill School	Paxman Ave, Colchester, Essex CO2 9DQ	01206 216500	01206 549391	Mrs Faith Spinlove	881-5464	FD	11–16	559	
Alec Hunter Humanities College	Stubbs La, Braintree, Essex CM7 3NR	01376 321813	01376 326839	Mr Andrew Hutchinson	881-4350	CY	11–16	898	
Anglo European School	Willow Grn, Ingatestone, Essex CM4 0DJ	01277 354018	01277 355623	Mr Jilldavid Martinbarrs	881-5442	FD	11–18	1317	
The Appleton School	Croft Rd, Benfleet, Essex SS7 5RN	01268 794215	01268 759981	Mrs Karen Kerridge	881-5418	FD	11–16	1189	
Barstable School	Timberlog Cl, Basildon, Essex SS14 1UX	01268 498800	01268 498801	Mrs J. Jones	881-5456	FD	11–16	722	
Beauchamps High School	Beauchamps Dr, Wickford, Essex SS11 8LY	01268 735466	01268 570981	Mr Philip Bell	881-5406	FD	11–18	1309	
The Billericay School	School Rd, Billericay, Essex CM12 9LH	01277 655191	01277 634436	Mrs Susan Hammond	881-5468	FD	11–18	1654	
Bishops Park College	Jaywick La, Clacton-on-Sea, Essex CO16 8BE	01255 424600	01255 424329	Mr Michael Davies	881-4002	CY	11–16	522	R
The Boswells School	Burnham Rd, Chelmsford, Essex CM1 6LY	01245 264451	01245 350142	Mr David Crowe	881-5416	FD	11–18	1483	
Brentwood County High School	Shenfield Common, Brentwood, Essex CM14 4JF	01277 238900	01277 200853	Mrs Carol Mason	881-5459	FD	11–18	1436	
Brentwood Ursuline Convent High School	Queen's Rd, Brentwood, Essex CM14 4EX	01277 227156	01277 229454	Miss Vicky Squirrell	881-5461	VA	11–18	963	RC G
The Bromfords School	Grange Ave, Wickford, Essex SS12 0LZ	01268 471201	01268 762693	Mr R. Thomas	881-5407	FD	11–18	1074	
Burnt Mill Comprehensive School	First Ave, Harlow, Essex CM20 2NR	01279 300555	01279 307234	Mr Stephen Chamberlain	881-4333	CY	11–16	1109	
Castle View School	Meppel Ave, Canvey Island, Essex SS8 9RZ	01268 696811	01268 511585	Mr Russell Sullivan	881-5419	FD	11–16	899	
Chalvedon School	Wickford Ave, Pitsea, Basildon, Essex SS13 3HL	01268 552536	01268 551209	Mr Alan Roach	881-5400	FD	11–18	1804	
Chelmer Valley High School	Court Rd, Broomfield, Chelmsford, Essex CM1 7ER	01245 440232	01245 441774	Mr D. Franklin	881-5429	FD	11–18	1081	
Chelmsford County High School for Girls	Broomfield Rd, Chelmsford, Essex CM1 1RW	01245 352592	01245 345746	Ms G. Howland	881-5410	FD	11–18	872	G
Clacton County High School	Walton Rd, Clacton-on-Sea, Essex CO15 6DZ	01255 424266	01255 473174	Mr John Clay	881-5444	FD	11–18	1643	
Colbayns High School	Pathfields Rd, Clacton-on-Sea, Essex CO15 3JL	01255 428131	01255 428163	Mr Nick Pavitt	881-5445	FD	11–18	1463	

3

School name	Address	Tel	Fax	Headteacher	Ref	Type	Ages	Pupils	Other
Colchester County High School for Girls	Norman Way, Colchester, Essex CO3 3US	01206 576973	01206 769302	Mrs Elizabeth Ward	881-5454	FD	11–18	755	G
Colchester Royal Grammar School	Lexden Rd, Colchester, Essex CO3 3ND	01206 509100	01206 509101	Mr Ken Jenkinson	881-5443	FD	11–18	782	Ch B R
Colne Community School	Church Rd, Brightlingsea, Colchester, Essex CO7 0QL	01206 303511	01206 302258	Mr Terry Creissen	881-5460	FD	11–18	1434	
The Cornelius Vermuyden School and Arts College	Dinant Ave, Canvey Island, Essex SS8 9QS	01268 685011	01268 510290	Mrs Carol Skewes	881-5420	FD	11–16	881	
Davenant Foundation School	Chester Rd, Loughton, Essex IG10 2LD	020 8508 0404	020 8508 9301	Mr Chris Seward	881-5426	VA	11–18	1111	Ch
De La Salle School	Ghyllgrove, Basildon, Essex SS14 2LA	01268 281234	01268 288710	Mr M. Curnock	881-4680	VA	11–16	731	RC
The Deanes School	Daws Heath Rd, Thundersley, Benfleet, Essex SS7 2TD	01268 773545	01268 770157	Mrs Janet Atkiknson	881-5424	FD	11–16	1061	
Debden Park High School	Willingale Rd, Debden, Loughton, Essex IG10 2BQ	020 8500 2979	020 8500 6843	Mr M. Moore	881-4001	CY	11–16	867	
The FitzWimarc School	Hockley Rd, Rayleigh, Essex SS6 8EB	01268 743884	01268 742877	Mr James Fuller	881-5422	FD	11–16	1340	
Furtherwick Park School	Furtherwick Rd, Canvey Island, Essex SS8 7AZ	01268 682157	01268 511718	Ms W. Missons	881-5417	FD	11–16	658	
The Gilberd School	Brinkley La, Colchester, Essex CO4 9PU	01206 842211	01206 854756	Mrs V. Cresswell	881-5441	FD	11–16	1264	
Great Baddow High School	Duffield Rd, Beehive La, Chelmsford, Essex CM2 9RZ	01245 265821	01245 348614	Mr Roger Hunton	881-4390	FD	11–18	1393	
Greensward College	Greensward La, Hockley, Essex SS5 5HG	01702 202571	01702 200083	Mr David Triggs	881-5435	FD	11–18	1518	
The Harwich School A Language College	Hall La, Dovercourt, Harwich, Essex CO12 3TG	01255 245460	01255 241144	Mr Nigel Mountford	881-5453	FD	11–18	1253	
Hedingham School	Yeldham Rd, Sible Hedingham, Halstead, Essex CO9 3QH	01787 460470	01787 462652	Mr John Panayi	881-4026	CY	11–18	1135	
Helena Romanes School and Sixth Form Centre	Parsonage Downs, Dunmow, Essex CM6 2AU	01371 872560	01371 874632	Mr Simon Knight	881-5457	FD	11–18	1467	
The Honywood Community Science School	Westfield Dr, Coggeshall, Colchester, Essex CO6 1PZ	01376 561231	01376 563067	Mr Simon Mason	881-4400	CY	11–16	967	
Hylands School	Hatfield Gr, Chelmsford, Essex CM1 3DF	01245 266766	01245 252570	Mr Terence Mulholland	881-5455	FD	11–18	1013	
The James Hornsby High School	Leinster Rd, Laindon, Basildon, Essex SS15 5NX	01268 545871		Ms J. White	881-4000	CY	11–16	795	
The John Bramston School	Spinks La, Witham, Essex CM8 1EP	01376 512911	01376 501076	Mr E.N. Rowley	881-5451	FD	11–18	1077	
The King Edmund School	Vaughan Cl, Rochford, Essex SS4 1TL	01702 545771	01702 549662	Mr Graham Abel	881-5421	FD	11–19	1537	
King Edward VI Grammar School, Chelmsford	Broomfield Rd, Chelmsford, Essex CM1 3SX	01245 353510	01245 344741	Dr M.J. Walker	881-5411	FD	11–18	857	B
King Harold School	Broomstick Hall Rd, Waltham Abbey, Essex EN9 1LF	01992 714800	01992 654130	Mr Mike Feehan	881-5415	FD	11–16	689	
The King John School	Shipwrights Dr, Thundersley, Benfleet, Essex SS7 1RQ	01702 558284	01702 555636	Miss Margaret Wilson	881-5403	FD	11–18	1834	
Manningtree High School	Colchester Rd, Lawford, Manningtree, Essex CO11 2BW	01206 392852	01206 391512	Miss Deborah Hollister	881-5470	FD	11–16	846	
Mark Hall School	First Ave, Harlow, Essex CM17 9LR	01279 866280	01279 866286	Mr C. Fluskey	881-4263	CY	11–16	1095	
Mayflower High School	Stock Rd, Billericay, Essex CM12 0RT	01277 623171	01277 632256	Mrs L.E. Bamford	881-4471	FD	11–18	1392	
Moulsham High School	Brian Cl, Chelmsford, Essex CM2 9ES	01245 260101	01245 504555	Dr Chris Nicholls	881-4480	CY	11–18	1596	
The Mountfitchet Mathematics and Computing College	Forest Hall Rd, Mountfitchet, Stansted, Essex CM24 8TZ	01279 813384	01279 647182	Miss Jo Mullis	881-4360	FD	11–16	478	
Newport Free Grammar School	Newport, Saffron Walden, Essex CB11 3TR	01799 540237	01799 542189	Mr S. O'Hagan	881-5436	FD	11–18	1028	
Notley High School	Notley Rd, Braintree, Essex CM7 1WY	01376 556300	01376 550991	Mr Simon Thompson	881-4420	CY	11–16	1276	
Passmores School and Technology College	Tendring Rd, Harlow, Essex CM18 6RW	01279 770800	01279 445515	Mr Vic Goddard	881-4323	CY	11–16	731	
Philip Morant School and College	Rembrandt Way, Colchester, Essex CO3 4QS	01206 545222	01206 244000	Mrs Sue Cowans	881-5404	FD	11–18	1617	
Plume School	Fambridge Rd, Maldon, Essex CM9 6AB	01621 854681	01621 855913	Miss Sarah Dignasse	881-5402	FD	11–18	1785	
The Ramsey College	Colne Rd, Halstead, Essex CO9 2HR	01787 472481	01787 474267	Mr Mike Murray	881-4025	CY	11–16	700	
The Rickstones School	Conrad Rd, Witham, Essex CM8 2SD	01376 515756	01376 502194	Mr T. Canty	881-5412	FD	11–16	779	
Roding Valley High School	Alderton Hill, Loughton, Essex IG10 3JA	020 8508 1173	020 8502 4992	Mr J.C. Wincott	881-4499	CY	11–16	1225	
Saffron Walden County High School	Audley End Rd, Saffron Walden, Essex CB11 4UH	01799 513030	01799 513031	Mr John Hartley	881-5408	FD	11–18	1935	
St Benedict's RC College	Norman Way, Colchester, Essex CO3 3US	01206 549222	01206 579342	Mr A. Whelan	881-5466	VA	11–16	827	RC
St Helena School	Sheepen Rd, Colchester, Essex CO3 3LE	01206 572253	01206 543049	Mr Clive Waddington	881-5448	FD	11–16	1002	
St John Payne RC Comprehensive School, Chelmsford	Patching Hall La, Chelmsford, Essex CM1 4BS	01245 256030	01245 352337	Mr Frank McEvoy	881-4701	VA	11–18	1152	RC
St John's CE VC School	Tower Rd, Epping, Essex CM16 5EN	01992 573028	01992 576928	Mr Keith Sharp	881-4530	VC	11–16	746	CE R

School name	Address	Tel	Fax	Headteacher	Ref	Type	Ages	Pupils	Other
St Mark's West Essex RC School	Tripton Rd, Harlow, Essex CM18 6AA	01279 421267	01279 418220	Mr D.J. Brunwin	881-5458	VA	11–18	952	RC
St Martin's School	Hanging Hill La, Hutton, Brentwood, Essex CM13 2HG	01277 238300	01277 238301	Dr N.B. Darby	881-5433	FD	11–18	1722	
St Peters College	Fox Cres, Chelmsford, Essex CM1 2BL	01245 265511	01245 252393	Mr Simon Carpenter	881-4735	VA	11–18	624	CE
St Peter's High School	Southminster Rd, Burnham-on-Crouch, Essex CM0 8QB	01621 782377	01621 785445	Mr David Stephenson	881-4290	CY	11–18	877	
The Sandon School	Molrams La, Sandon, Chelmsford, Essex CM2 7AQ	01245 473611	01245 478554	Mr Jonathan Wincott	881-5463	FD	11–18	1221	
Sawyers Hall College of Science and Technology	Sawyers Hall La, Brentwood, Essex CM15 9DA	01277 220808	01277 228142	Mr John Keller	881-5425	FD	11–18	1095	
Shenfield High School	Alexander La, Shenfield, Brentwood, Essex CM15 8RY	01277 219131	01277 226422	Mr J. Fairhurst	881-5467	FD	11–18	1483	
Sir Charles Lucas Arts College	Hawthorn Ave, Colchester, Essex CO4 3JL	01206 861217	01206 865940	Ms Jude Hanner	881-5450	FD	11–16	1074	
The Stanway School	Winstree Rd, Stanway, Colchester, Essex CO3 0QA	01206 575488	01206 564164	Mr Jonathan Tippett	881-5462	FD	11–16	999	
Stewards School	Parnall Rd, Harlow, Essex CM18 7NQ	01279 421951	01279 435307	Ms Rhonda Murther	881-4343	CY	11–16	954	
The Sweyne Park School	Sir Walter Raleigh Dr, Rayleigh, Essex SS6 9BZ	01268 784721	01268 780293	Mr Andy Hodgkinson	881-4011	CY	11–16	1288	
Tabor Science College	Panfield La, Braintree, Essex CM7 5XP	01376 323701	01376 345834	Mr Steven Clark	881-4470	CY	11–16	1038	
Tendring Technology College	Rochford Way, Frinton-on-Sea, Essex CO13 0AZ	01255 672116	01255 850210	Ms Caroline Haynes	881-5432	FD	11–16	1767	
The Thomas Lord Audley School and Language College	Monkwick Ave, Monkwick, Colchester, Essex CO2 8NJ	01206 547911	01206 760581	Mr Jonathan Tippett	881-4020	CY	11–16	770	
Thurstable School	Maypole Rd, Tiptree, Colchester, Essex CO5 0EW	01621 816526	01621 815409	Mr M. Bacon	881-5413	FD	11–18	1183	
West Hatch High School	High La, Chigwell, Essex IG7 5BT	020 8504 8216	020 8559 2695	Ms Frances Howarth	881-5405	FD	11–18	1258	
William de Ferrers School	Trinity Sq, South Woodham Ferrers, Chelmsford, Essex CM3 5JU	01245 326326	01245 321996	Mr Dennis Parry	881-5427	FD	11–18	1839	
Woodlands School	Takely End, Kingswood, Basildon, Essex SS16 5BA	01268 282146	01268 531655	Mr Andy White	881-4431	CY	11–16	1507	

Hertfordshire

School name	Address	Tel	Fax	Headteacher	Ref	Type	Ages	Pupils	Other
Adeyfield School	Longlands, Hemel Hempstead, Hertfordshire HP2 4DE	01442 406020	01442 252513	Mr Peter Hepburn	919-4029	CY	11–18	773	
Ashlyns School	Chesham Rd, Berkhamsted, Hertfordshire HP4 3AH	01442 863605	01442 876292	Mr Richard Dalziel	919-5406	FD	13–18	820	
The Astley Cooper School	St Agnells La, Hemel Hempstead, Hertfordshire HP2 7HL	01442 394141	01442 401407	Mrs Anne Smithers	919-4499	CY	11–18	781	
Barclay School	Walkern Rd, Stevenage, Hertfordshire SG1 3RB	01438 232221	01438 232300	Mrs Janet Beacom	919-4047	CY	11–18	1094	
Barnwell School	Barnwell, Stevenage, Hertfordshire SG2 9SW	01438 222500	01438 222501	Mr R. Westergreen-Thorne	919-4066	CY	11–18	1501	
Beaumont School	Oakwood Dr, St Albans, Hertfordshire AL4 0XB	01727 854726	01727 847971	Mrs Elizabeth Hitch	919-4043	CY	11–18	1178	
Birchwood High School	Parsonage La, Bishop's Stortford, Hertfordshire CM23 5BD	01279 655936	01279 757459	Mr Chris Ingate	919-4200	CY	11–18	1018	
Bishop's Hatfield Girls' School	Woods Ave, Hatfield, Hertfordshire AL10 8NL	01707 275331	01707 270244	Ms Theodora Nickson	919-4099	CY	11–18	709	G
The Bishop's Stortford High School	London Rd, Bishop's Stortford, Hertfordshire CM23 3LU	01279 868686	01279 868687	Mr Andrew Goulding	919-5405	FD	11–18	1079	B
The Broxbourne School	High Rd, Broxbourne, Hertfordshire EN10 7DD	01992 411060	01992 411061	Mr M.F. Titchmarsh	919-4101	CY	11–18	1251	
Bushey Hall School	London Rd, Bushey, Hertfordshire WD23 3AA	020 8950 9502	020 8420 4038	Mr Jeremy Law	919-5409	FD	11–18	816	
Bushey Meads School	Coldharbour La, Bushey, Hertfordshire WD23 4PA	020 8950 3000	020 8950 6208	Mrs Liz Weddle	919-5408	FD	11–18	1044	
The Cavendish School	Warners End Rd, Hemel Hempstead, Hertfordshire HP1 3DW	01442 404342	01442 404378	Dr Stephen Pam	919-4100	CY	11–18	1125	
Chancellor's School	Pine Gr, Brookmans Pk, Hatfield, Hertfordshire AL9 7BN	01707 650702	01707 663204	Mr Stuart Phillips	919-5419	FD	11–18	1043	
The Chauncy School	Park Rd, Ware, Hertfordshire SG12 0DP	01920 411200	01920 640456	Mr Dennis O'Sullivan	919-4498	CY	11–18	855	
Cheshunt School	College Rd, Cheshunt, Waltham Cross, Hertfordshire EN8 9LY	01992 624375	01992 643411	Mr Stephen Drake	919-5425	FD	11–18	991	
Dame Alice Owen's School	Dugdale Hill La, Potters Bar, Hertfordshire EN6 2DU	01707 643441	01707 645011	Dr A.J. Davison	919-5407	VA	11–18	1434	
Fearnhill School	Icknield Way West, Letchworth, Hertfordshire SG6 4BA	01462 621200	01462 621201	Mr Jeremy Whelan	919-4010	CY	11–18	1065	
Francis Bacon School	Drakes Dr, St Albans, Hertfordshire AL1 5AR	01727 859382	01727 810199	Ms Jacqueline Verrall	919-5402	FD	11–18	737	
Francis Combe School and Community College	Horseshoe La, Watford, Hertfordshire WD25 7HW	01923 672964	01923 665888	Miss Nicky Williams	919-4075	CY	11–18	971	
Freman College	Bowling Green La, Buntingford, Hertfordshire SG9 9BT	01763 271818	01763 273467	Ms Helen Loughran	919-4141	CY	13–18	760	

3

School name	Address	Tel	Fax	Headteacher	Ref	Type	Ages	Pupils	Other
Goffs School	Goffs La, Cheshunt, Waltham Cross, Hertfordshire EN7 5QW	01992 424200	01992 424201	Mrs Jan Cutler	919-5415	FD	11-18	1293	
The Heathcote School	Shephall Grn, Stevenage, Hertfordshire SG2 9XT	01438 222100	01438 222101	Mr Edward Joseph Gaynor	919-4061	CY	11-18	859	
The Hemel Hempstead School	Heath La, Hemel Hempstead, Hertfordshire HP1 1TX	01442 390100	01442 233706	Miss Sandra Samwell	919-4005	CY	11-18	1170	
The Hertfordshire and Essex High School	Warwick Rd, Bishop's Stortford, Hertfordshire CM23 5NJ	01279 654127	01279 508810	Ms Alison Garner	919-5420	FD	11-18	1007	G
Hertswood School	Cowley Hill, Borehamwood, Hertfordshire WD6 5LG	020 8238 7200	020 8238 7290	Mrs Jane Winterbone	919-4001	CY	11-18	1243	
The Highfield School	Highfield, Letchworth Garden City, Hertfordshire SG6 3QA	01462 620500	01462 620501	Mrs Jane Palmer Sayer	919-4122	CY	11-18	1028	
Hitchin Boys' School	Grammar School Wlk, Hitchin, Hertfordshire SG5 1JB	01462 432181	01462 440172	Mr K.S. Wadsworth	919-4008	CY	11-18	1002	B
Hitchin Girls' School	Highbury Rd, Hitchin, Hertfordshire SG4 9RS	01462 621300	01462 621301	Mrs R. Edwards	919-4009	CY	11-18	1060	G
Hockerill Anglo-European College	Dunmow Rd, Bishop's Stortford, Hertfordshire CM23 5HX	01279 658451	01279 755918	Dr Robert Guthrie	919-5427	FD	11-18	737	R
John F Kennedy RC School	Hollybush La, Hemel Hempstead, Hertfordshire HP1 2PH	01442 266150	01442 250014	Mrs Bernadette Jenkins	919-4619	VA	11-18	1132	RC
The John Henry Newman Roman RC School	Hitchin Rd, Stevenage, Hertfordshire SG1 4AE	01438 314643	01438 747882	Mr Michael Kelly	919-5413	VA	11-18	1334	RC
The John Warner School	Stanstead Rd, Hoddesdon, Hertfordshire EN11 0QF	01992 462889	01992 470679	Mr D.J. Kennedy	919-5426	FD	11-18	1138	
Kings Langley School	Love La, Kings Langley, Hertfordshire WD4 9HN	01923 264504	01923 260564	Mr Gary Lewis	919-4096	CY	11-18	1021	
The Knights Templar School	Park St, Baldock, Hertfordshire SG7 6DZ	01462 620700	01462 219276	Mr Andrew Pickering	919-4016	CY	11-18	1372	
The Leventhorpe School	Cambridge Rd, Sawbridgeworth, Hertfordshire CM21 9BY	01279 836633	01279 600339	Mr P.C. Janke	919-5416	FD	11-18	1080	
Longdean School	Rumballs Rd, Bennetts End, Hemel Hempstead, Hertfordshire HP3 8JB	01442 217277	01442 233098	Mr Rhodri Bryant	919-4080	CY	11-18	1179	
Loreto College	Hatfield Rd, St Albans, Hertfordshire AL1 3RQ	01727 856206	01727 833794	Mrs Maire Lynch	919-4620	VA	11-18	792	RC G
Marlborough School	Watling St, St Albans, Hertfordshire AL1 2QA	01727 856874	01727 855285	Ms Annie Thomson	919-5414	FD	11-18	1165	
Marriotts School	Telford Ave, Stevenage, Hertfordshire SG2 0AN	01438 351801	01438 743548	Mr Patrick Marshall	919-4116	CY	11-18	827	
Meridian School	Garden Wlk, Royston, Hertfordshire SG8 7JH	01763 242236	01763 245749	Dr M. Firth	919-4140	CY	13-18	685	
Monks Walk School	Knightsfield, Welwyn Garden City, Hertfordshire AL8 7NL	01707 322846	01707 375080	Mr Philip Bunn	919-4118	CY	11-18	1217	
Mount Grace School	Church Rd, Potters Bar, Hertfordshire EN6 1EZ	01707 655512	01707 663725	Mr Peter Baker	919-4411	CY	11-18	846	
Nicholas Breakspear Catholic School	Colney Heath La, St Albans, Hertfordshire AL4 0TT	01727 860079	01727 848912	Mr Phil Jakszta	919-5412	VA	11-18	1000	RC
The Nobel School	Mobbsbury Way, Stevenage, Hertfordshire SG2 0HS	01438 222600	01438 222606	Mr Alastair C. Craig	919-4104	CY	11-18	1148	
Onslow St Audrey's School	Old Rectory Dr, Hatfield, Hertfordshire AL10 8AB	01707 264228	01707 262332	Ms C. Allen	919-4154	CY	11-18	566	
Parmiter's School	High Elms La, Garston, Watford, Hertfordshire WD25 0UU	01923 671424	01923 894195	Mr Brian Coulshed	919-5404	VA	11-18	1064	
Presdales School	Hoe La, Ware, Hertfordshire SG12 9NX	01920 462210	01920 461187	Mrs Janine Robinson	919-4013	CY	11-18	881	G
The Priory School	Bedford Rd, Hitchin, Hertfordshire SG5 2UR	01462 622300	01462 622301	Mr P. Loach	919-4000	CY	11-18	1626	
Queens' School	Aldenham Rd, Bushey, Hertfordshire WD23 2TY	01923 224465	01923 223975	Mr Terence James	919-5410	FD	11-18	976	
Richard Hale School	Hale Rd, Hertford, Hertfordshire SG13 8EN	01992 583441	01992 503413	Mr Stephen Neate	919-4006	CY	11-18	1247	B
Rickmansworth School	Scots Hill, Rickmansworth, Hertfordshire WD3 3AQ	01923 773296	01923 897314	Dr Stephen Burton	919-5400	FD	11-18	1179	
Roundwood Park School	Roundwood Pk, Harpenden, Hertfordshire AL5 3AE	01582 765344	01582 461404	Mr Nick Daymond	919-4070	CY	11-18	1144	
St Albans Girls' School	Sandridgebury La, St Albans, Hertfordshire AL3 6DB	01727 853134	01727 831157	Mrs Christine Murrell	919-4083	CY	11-18		G
St Clement Danes School	Chenies Rd, Chorleywood, Rickmansworth, Hertfordshire WD3 6EW	01923 284169	01923 284828	Dr Josephine Valentine	919-5421	CY	11-18	1218	
St George's School	Sun La, Harpenden, Hertfordshire AL5 4TD	01582 765477	01582 469830	Mr Norman Hoare	919-4614	VA	11-18	1171	Ch R
St Joan of Arc Roman RC School	High St, Rickmansworth, Hertfordshire WD3 1HG	01923 773881	01923 897545	Mr Peter Sweeney	919-5418	VA	11-18	1223	RC
St Mary's RC School	Windhill, Bishop's Stortford, Hertfordshire CM23 2NQ	01279 654901	01279 653889	Mr A. Sharpe	919-5422	VA	11-18	911	RC
St Mary's High School	Churchgate, Cheshunt, Waltham Cross, Hertfordshire EN8 9ED	01992 629124	01992 643354	Ms Stephanie Benbow	919-5423	VA	11-18	668	CE
St Michael's RC High School	High Elms La, Watford, Hertfordshire WD25 0SS	01923 673760	01923 680511	Mr John Murphy	919-5417	VA	11-18	1038	RC
Sandringham School	The Ridgeway, St Albans, Hertfordshire AL4 9NX	01727 759240	01727 759241	Mr Alan Gray	919-4197	CY	11-18	1170	
The Sele School	Welwyn Rd, Hertford, Hertfordshire SG14 2DG	01992 581455	01992 500408	Mr Nick Binder	919-4117	CY	11-18	422	
Sheredes School	Cock La, Hoddesdon, Hertfordshire EN11 8JY	01992 410800	01992 410801	Mr Michael Smith	919-4137	CY	11-18	859	
Simon Balle School	Mangrove Rd, Hertford, Hertfordshire SG13 8AJ	01992 410400	01992 410401	Mrs Alison Saunders	919-4067	CY	11-18	1051	
Sir Frederic Osborn School	Herns La, Welwyn Garden City, Hertfordshire AL7 2AF	0844 4772515	0844 4772526	Mrs Susan Lewis	919-4087	CY	11-18	974	
Sir John Lawes School	Manland Way, Harpenden, Hertfordshire AL5 4QP	01582 760043	01582 469793	Ms Claire Robins	919-4028	CY	11-18	1167	

School name	Address	Tel	Fax	Headteacher	Ref	Type	Ages	Pupils	Other
Stanborough School	Lemsford La., Welwyn Garden City, Hertfordshire AL8 6YR	01707 321755	01707 387701	Mr Peter J. Brown	919-4014	CY	11–18	1051	
The Thomas Alleyne School	High St, Stevenage, Hertfordshire SG1 3BE	01438 354145	01438 720411	Mr Jonathan M. Block	919-4201	CY	11–18	836	
Townsend CE School	High Oaks. St Albans, Hertfordshire AL3 6DR	01727 853047	01727 834523	Mr A. Wellbeloved	919-4606	VA	11–18	823	CE
Tring School	Mortimer Hill, Tring, Hertfordshire HP23 5JD	01442 822303	01442 890409	Mrs Julia Wond	919-4504	VC	11–18	1507	CE
Turnford School	Mill La., Cheshunt, Waltham Cross, Hertfordshire EN8 0JU	01992 308333	01992 309444	Mr David Rahman	919-4105	CY	11–18	973	
Verulam School	Brampton Rd, St Albans, Hertfordshire AL1 4PR	01727 766100	01727 766256	Mr David Kellaway	919-4011	CY	11–18	1104	B
Watford Grammar School for Boys	Rickmansworth Rd, Watford, Hertfordshire WD18 7JF	01923 208900	01923 208901	Mr M. Post	919-5401	VA	11–18	1239	CE B
Watford Grammar School for Girls	Lady's Cl, Watford, Hertfordshire WD18 0AE	01923 223403	01923 350721	Mrs H. Hyde	919-5403	VA	11–18	1247	CE G
Westfield Community Technology College	Tolpits La., Watford, Hertfordshire WD18 6NS	01923 231560	01923 210568	Ms Jan Spavin	919-4111	CY	11–18	1121	
Yavneh College	Hillside Ave, Borehamwood, Hertfordshire WD6 1HL	020 8736 5580		Ms Dena Coleman	919-4802	VA	11–18	93	Je

Luton

School name	Address	Tel	Fax	Headteacher	Ref	Type	Ages	Pupils	Other
Ashcroft High School	Crawley Green Rd, Luton, Bedfordshire LU2 9AG	01582 436100	01582 436118	Ms Monica Austin	821-5403	FD	11–16	1027	
Barnfield South Academy Luton	Cutenhoe Rd, Luton LU1 3NH	01582 722333	01582 457344	Patrick Hannaway	821-6906		11–18		
Barnfield West Academy Luton	Emerald Rd, Luton LU4 0NE	01582 601221	01582 607948	Rachel De souza	821-6905		11–18		
Bramingham Park Study Centre	Bramingham Park Church, Freeman Ave, Luton, Bedfordshire LU3 4BL	01582 494696	01582 494696	Mrs Dianne Rickett	821-6005		11–16	19	
Cardinal Newman RC School A Specialist Science College	Warden Hill Rd, Luton, Bedfordshire LU2 7AE	01582 597125	01582 503088	Mrs Jane Crow	821-4606	VA	11–18	1446	RC
Challney High School for Boys and Community College	Stoneygate Rd, Luton, Bedfordshire LU4 9TJ	01582 599921		Mr Victor Galyer	821-4102	CY	11–16	804	B
Challney High School for Girls	Stoneygate Rd, Luton, Bedfordshire LU4 9TJ	01582 571427	01582 578133	Miss Mary Arthur	821-4103	CY	11–16	907	G
Denbigh High School	Alexandra Ave, Luton, Bedfordshire LU3 1HE	01582 736611	01582 483937	Mrs Yasmin Bevan	821-4104	CY	11–16	1113	
Halyard High School	Emerald Rd, Luton, Bedfordshire LU4 0NE	01582 601221	01582 607948	Mrs Helen Bailey	821-4105	CY	11–16	728	
Icknield High School	Riddy La., Luton, Bedfordshire LU3 2AH	01582 576561	01582 561533	Mr Christopher Dean	821-5407	FD	11–16	1431	
Lea Manor High School	Northwell Dr, Luton, Bedfordshire LU3 3TL	01582 652600	01582 652601	Ms Christine Lenihan	821-5405	FD	11–16	1120	
Leelands High School	Sundon Park Rd, Luton, Bedfordshire LU3 3AL	01582 611600	01582 612227	Mr Christopher Ginns	821-4111	CY	11–16	932	
Putteridge High School	Putteridge Rd, Luton, Bedfordshire LU2 8HJ	01582 415791	01582 419357	Mr Anthony Smith	821-4108	CY	11–16	1056	
South Luton High School	Cutenhoe Rd, Luton, Bedfordshire LU1 3NH	01582 722333	01582 457344	Mr Tim Westrip	821-4125	CY	11–16	828	
Stopsley High School	St Thomas's Rd, Luton, Bedfordshire LU2 7UX	01582 870900	01582 870928	Mrs Gill Bryan	821-5409	FD	11–16	983	

Norfolk

School name	Address	Tel	Fax	Headteacher	Ref	Type	Ages	Pupils	Other
Acle High School	South Walsham Rd, Acle, Norwich, Norfolk NR13 3ER	01493 751279	01493 751279	Mr Gerard Batty	926-5405	FD	11–16	758	
Alderman Peel High School	Market La., Wells-next-the-Sea, Norfolk NR23 1RB	01328 710476	01328 710767	Mr Jonathan Platten	926-4056	CY	11–16	301	
Archbishop Sancroft High School	Wilderness La., Harleston, Norfolk IP20 9DD	01379 852561	01379 852561	Mr Stephen Carter	926-4602	VA	11–16	426	CE
Attleborough High School	9 Norwich Rd, Attleborough, Norfolk NR17 2AJ	01953 452335	01953 456817	Mr Stuart Bailey	926-4052	CY	11–18	956	
Aylsham High School	Sir Williams La., Aylsham, Norwich, Norfolk NR11 6AN	01263 733270	01263 732918	Mr Paul G Mitchell	926-4046	CY	11–16	915	
The Blyth-Jex School	St Clement's Hill, Norwich, Norfolk NR3 4BX	01603 411721	01603 487575	Ms Karen Topping	926-4070	CY	11–18	890	
Broadland High School	Tunstead Rd, Hoveton, Norwich, Norfolk NR12 8QN	01603 782715	01603 784354	Mr Don Cameron	926-4037	CY	11–16	700	
Caister High School	Windsor Rd, Caister-on-Sea, Great Yarmouth, Norfolk NR30 5LS	01493 720542	01493 728368	Mr George Denby	926-5412	FD	12–16	648	
Charles Burrell High School	Staniforth Rd, Thetford, Norfolk IP24 3LH	01842 763981	01842 766561	Ms Nancy Robinson	926-4048	CY	11–18	657	
City of Norwich School	Eaton Rd, Norwich, Norfolk NR4 6PP	01603 274000	01603 458196	Mr Gordon Boyd	926-4065	CY	11–18	1414	
Cliff Park High School	Kennedy Ave, Gorleston, Great Yarmouth, Norfolk NR31 6TA	01493 661504	01493 440558	Mr Mark Bailie	926-5409	FD	12–16	888	

School name	Address	Tel	Fax	Headteacher	Ref	Type	Ages	Pupils	Other
Costessey High School	Middleton Cres, Norwich, Norfolk NR5 0PX	01603 742310	01603 741875	Mr Philip May	926-5403	FD	11–18	998	
Cromer High School and Language College	Norwich Rd, Cromer, Norfolk NR27 0EX	01263 511433	01263 515378	Mr Ronald Munson	926-5401	FD	11–16	666	
Diss High School	Walcot Rd, Diss, Norfolk IP22 4DH	01379 642424	01379 642428	Mr Stuart Ballantyne	926-4089	CY	11–18	1199	
Downham Market High School – Technology College	Bexwell Rd, Downham Market, Norfolk PE38 9LL	01366 389100	01366 389111	Mr Ian Bloom	926-5402	FD	11–18	1658	
Earlham High School	Earlham Rd, Norwich, Norfolk NR4 7NU	01603 452628	01603 507215	Mr J. Neale	926-4068	CY	11–18	766	
Fakenham High School and College	Field La, Fakenham, Norfolk NR21 9QT	01328 862545	01328 851767	Mr Richard Moore	926-4091	CY	11–18	1429	
Flegg High School	Somerton Rd, Martham, Great Yarmouth, Norfolk NR29 4QD	01493 740349	01493 740223	Mrs Cherry Crowley	926-5410	FD	11–18	779	
Framingham Earl High School	Norwich Rd, Framingham Earl, Norwich, Norfolk NR14 7QP	01508 492547	01508 493597	Mr Trevor Seadon	926-4044	CY	11–16	779	
Great Yarmouth High School	Salisbury Rd, Great Yarmouth, Norfolk NR30 4LS	01493 842061	01493 332848	Mr Jim Nixon	926-5411	VA	12–16	785	Ch
Hamond's High School	Brandon Rd, Swaffham, Norfolk PE37 7DZ	01760 721480	01760 721269	Mrs Yve Srodzinski	926-4086	CY	11–16	716	
Heartsease High School	Marryat Rd, Norwich, Norfolk NR7 9DF	01603 435178	01603 701639	Ms Lindsay Knight	926-4067	CY	11–18	407	
Hellesdon High School	187 Middletons La, Hellesdon, Norwich, Norfolk NR6 5SB	01603 424711	01603 487602	Mr Bill Gould	926-4005	CY	11–18	1161	
Hethersett High School and Science College	Queen's Rd, Hethersett, Norwich, Norfolk NR9 3DB	01603 810924	01603 812697	Mrs Rosemary Allen	926-4082	CY	12–16	603	
The Hewett School	Cecil Rd, Norwich, Norfolk NR1 2PL	01603 628181	01603 764129	Mr Tom Samain	926-4066	CY	11	1055	
Hobart High School	Kittens La, Loddon, Norwich, Norfolk NR14 6JU	01508 520359	01508 528024	Mr John Robson	926-4006	CY	11–16	775	
King Edward VII School	Gaywood Rd, King's Lynn, Norfolk PE30 2QB	01553 773606	01553 769386	Mr Mike Douglass	926-4504	VC	11–18	1313	
Litcham High School	Church St, Litcham, King's Lynn, Norfolk PE32 2NS	01328 701265	01328 701850	Mr Jeremy Nicholls	926-4053	CY	11–16	571	
Long Stratton High School	Manor Rd, Long Stratton, Norwich, Norfolk NR15 2XR	01508 530418	01508 531708	Mr Paul Adams	926-4040	CY	11–16	651	
Lynn Grove VA High School	Lynn Gr, Gorleston, Great Yarmouth, Norfolk NR31 8AP	01493 661406	01493 441368	Mr David Evans	926-5407	VA	12–16	901	Ch
Marshland High School	School Rd, West Walton, Wisbech, Cambridgeshire PE14 7HA	01945 584146	01945 581275	Mr John Bennett	926-5404	FD	11–16	810	
Methwold High School	Stoke Rd, Methwold, Thetford, Norfolk IP26 4PE	01366 728333	01366 728905	Mrs Denise Walker	926-4047	CY	11–18	723	
Neatherd High School	Norwich Rd, Dereham, Norfolk NR20 3AX	01362 697981	01362 698463	Mr John Horsfield	926-4085	CY	11–18	1357	
North Walsham High School	Spenser Ave, North Walsham, Norfolk NR28 9HZ	01692 402581	01692 500643	Mrs Caroline Brooker	926-4008	CY	11–16	841	
Northgate High School	Cemetery Rd, Dereham, Norfolk NR19 2EU	01362 697033	01362 698484	Mr John Smith	926-4002	CY	11–18	1049	
Notre Dame High School, Norwich	Surrey St, Norwich, Norfolk NR1 3PB	01603 611431	01603 763381	Mr John Pinnington	926-4605	VA	11–18	1293	RC
Old Buckenham High School	Abbey Rd, Old Buckenham, Attleborough, Norfolk NR17 1RL	01953 860233	01953 860944	Mr Graham Hodson	926-4054	CY	11–16	584	
Oriel High School	Oriel Ave, Gorleston, Great Yarmouth, Norfolk NR31 7JJ	01493 662966	01493 440715	Mr Geoffrey Best	926-4077	CY	12–16	603	
The Park High School	Queen Mary Rd, Gaywood, King's Lynn, Norfolk PE30 4QG	01553 774671	01553 770740	Dr Robert Rogers	926-4019	CY	11–18	872	
Reepham High School	Whitwell Rd, Reepham, Norwich, Norfolk NR10 4JT	01603 870328	01603 870988	Mr C. Hassell	926-4042	CY	11–16	794	
Rosemary Musker High School, Thetford	Croxton Rd, Thetford, Norfolk IP24 1LH	01842 754875	01842 765036	Mr John Lucas	926-4093	CY	11–18	768	
St Clement's High School	Churchgate Way, Terrington St Clement, King's Lynn, Norfolk PE34 4LZ	01553 828648	01553 829320	Mrs Ros Goudie	926-5408	FD	11–16	626	
Sheringham High School and Sixth Form Centre	Holt Rd, Sheringham, Norfolk NR26 8ND	01263 822363	01263 821413	Mr Tim Roderick	926-5406	FD	11–18	772	
Smithdon High School	Downs Rd, Hunstanton, Norfolk PE36 5HY	01485 534541	01485 535251	Mr Jonathan Goodchild	926-4021	CY	11–18	1116	
Springwood High School	Queensway, Gaywood, King's Lynn, Norfolk PE30 4AW	01553 773393	01553 771405	Mr Peter Hopkins	926-4081	FD	11–18	1481	
Sprowston High School	Cannerby La, Sprowston, Norwich, Norfolk NR7 8NE	01603 485266	01603 426213	Mr Andrew John	926-4043	CY	11–18	1357	
Stalham High School	Brumstead Rd, Stalham, Norwich, Norfolk NR12 9DG	01692 580281	01692 581480	Mr John Chilvers	926-4010	CY	11–16	432	
Taverham High School	Beech Ave, Taverham, Norwich, Norfolk NR8 6HP	01603 860505	01603 261525	Mr Graham Porter	926-4084	CY	12–16	861	
Thorpe St Andrew School	Laundry La, Thorpe St Andrew, Norwich, Norfolk NR7 0XS	01603 497711	01603 497712	Mr Ian Clayton	926-4083	CY	11–18	1751	
Wayland Community High School	Merton Rd, Watton, Thetford, Norfolk IP25 6BA	01953 881514	01953 885677	Mr Michael Rose	926-4031	CY	11–16	707	
Wymondham College	Golf Links Rd, Morley, Wymondham, Norfolk NR18 9SZ	01953 609000	01953 603313	Mr Dominic Findlay	926-5400	FD	11–18	1042	R
Wymondham High School	Folly Rd, Wymondham, Norfolk NR18 0QT	01953 602078	01953 605518	Mr David Brunton	926-4060	CY	11–18	1388	

Peterborough

School name	Address	Tel	Fax	Headteacher	Ref	Type	Ages	Pupils	Other
Arthur Mellows Village College	Helpston Rd, Glinton, Peterborough, Cambridgeshire PE6 7JX	01733 252235	01733 252206	Mr M. Sandeman	874-5417	FD	11–18	1400	
Bushfield Community College	Orton Centre, Peterborough, Cambridgeshire PE2 5RQ	01733 233014	01733 371524	Mr Eric Winstone	874-4080	CY	11–18	623	
Hampton College	Eagle Way, Hampton Vale, Peterborough, Cambridgeshire PE7 8BF	01733 246820		Mr Peter Hains	874-4082	CY	11–16	291	
Jack Hunt School	Ledbury Rd, Peterborough, Cambridgeshire PE3 9PN	01733 263526	01733 330364	Mr Roy Duncan	874-5405	FD	11–18	1430	
Ken Stimpson Community School	Staniland Way, Werrington, Peterborough, Cambridgeshire PE4 6JT	01733 765950	01733 765951	Mr David McPartlin	874-4081	CY	11–18	906	
The King's School	Park Rd, Peterborough, Cambridgeshire PE1 2UE	01733 751541	01733 751542	Mr Gary L. Longman	874-5404	VA	11–18	966	CE
Orton Longueville School	Oundle Rd, Orton Longueville, Peterborough, Cambridgeshire PE2 7EA	01733 368300	01733 368333	Mr David Owen	874-5414	FD	11–18	1172	
St John Fisher RC School	Park La, Peterborough, Cambridgeshire PE1 5JN	01733 343646	01733 347983	Ms M. Mihovilovic	874-5413	VA	11–18	729	RC
Stanground College	Peterborough Rd, Peterborough, Cambridgeshire PE7 3BY	01733 564071	01733 347626	Mr Malcolm Ellison	874-5410	FD	11–18	1479	
Thomas Deacon Academy	Queen's Gdns, Peterborough PE1 2UW	01733 426050	01733 891601	Mr Alan McMurdo	874-6905	CY	11–19		
The Voyager School	Mountsteven Ave, Walton, Peterborough, Cambridgeshire PE4 6HX	01733 383888		Mr Hugh Howe	874-4083	CY	11–18		

Southend-on-Sea

School name	Address	Tel	Fax	Headteacher	Ref	Type	Ages	Pupils	Other
Belfairs High School	Highlands Bvd, Leigh-on-Sea, Essex SS9 3TG	01702 474496	01702 480573	Mr J.R. Duprey	882-5434	FD	11–18		
Cecil Jones College	Eastern Ave, Southend-on-Sea, Essex SS2 4BU	01702 440000	01702 463724	Mr Doug Nichols	882-5452	FD	11–18		
Chase High School	Prittlewell Chase, Westcliff-on-Sea, Essex SS0 0RT	0844 477 3566	0844 477 8907	Mrs Denise Allen	882-4735	CY	11–18	890	
The Eastwood School	Rayleigh Rd, Leigh-on-Sea, Essex SS9 5UU	01702 524341	01702 512181	Mr D. Penketh	882-5414	FD	11–19		
Futures College	Southchurch Rd, Southend on Sea, Essex SS2 4UY	01702 586123	01702 584611	Mrs Jean Alder	882-4736	FD	11–19		
St Bernard's High School and Arts College	Milton Rd, Westcliff-on-Sea, Essex SS0 7JS	01702 343583	01702 390201	Mrs Patricia Barron	882-5465	VA	11–18	843	RC G
St Thomas More High School for Boys	Kenilworth Gdns, Westcliff-on-Sea, Essex SS0 0BW	01702 344933	01702 436990	Mr Peter Travis	882-5447	VA	11–18	986	RC B
Shoeburyness High School	Caulfield Rd, Shoeburyness, Southend-on-Sea, Essex SS3 9LL	01702 292286	01702 292333	Mrs Susan Murphy	882-4034	CY	11–18	1558	
Southend High School for Boys	Prittlewell Chase, Westcliff-on-Sea, Essex SS0 0RG	01702 343074	01702 300028	Mr M. Frampton	882-5446	FD	11–18		B
Southend High School for Girls	Southchurch Bvd, Southend-on-Sea, Essex SS2 4UZ	01702 588852	01702 587181	Mr David Mansfield	882-5428	FD	11–18		G
Westcliff High School for Boys	Kenilworth Gdns, Westcliff-on-Sea, Essex SS0 0BP	01702 475443	01702 470495	Mr Andrew Baker	882-5401	FD	11–18		B
Westcliff High School for Girls	Kenilworth Gdns, Westcliff-on-Sea, Essex SS0 0BS	01702 476026	01702 471328	Dr Paul Hayman	882-5423	FD	11–18		G

Suffolk

School name	Address	Tel	Fax	Headteacher	Ref	Type	Ages	Pupils	Other
The Benjamin Britten High School	Blyford Rd, Lowestoft, Suffolk NR32 4PZ	01502 582312	01502 566779	Mr Trevor Osborne	935-4101	CY	13–18	865	
Bungay High School	Queen's Rd, Bungay, Suffolk NR35 1RW	01986 892140	01986 895319	Mr Sean O'Neill	935-4075	CY	13–18	962	
Bury St Edmunds County Upper School	Beetons Way, Bury St Edmunds, Suffolk IP32 6RF	01284 754857	01284 767313	Mrs Vicky Neale	935-4000	CY	13–18	949	
Castle Manor Business and Enterprise College	Eastern Ave, Haverhill, Suffolk CB9 9JE	01440 705501	01440 714050	Ms Madeleine Vigar	935-4004	CY	13–18	520	
Chantry High School and Sixth Form Centre	Mallard Way, Ipswich, Suffolk IP2 9LR	01473 687181	01473 602693	Mrs Anne Rickwood	935-4091	CY	11–18	1171	
Claydon High School	Church La, Claydon, Ipswich, Suffolk IP6 0EG	01473 836110	01473 836117	Mrs Elizabeth Soule	935-4096	CY	11–18	844	
Copleston High School	Copleston Rd, Ipswich, Suffolk IP4 5HD	01473 277407	01473 274467	Mr Laurence Robinson	935-4092	CY	11–18	1758	
Deben High School	Garrison La, Felixstowe, Suffolk IP11 7RF	01394 282602	01394 278368	Mr Terence Ring	935-4037	CY	11–18	955	
Debenham CE VC High School	Gracechurch St, Debenham, Stowmarket, Suffolk IP14 6BL	01728 860213	01728 860998	Mr Mj Crawshaw	935-4504	VC	11–16	510	CE
The Denes High School	Yarmouth Rd, Lowestoft, Suffolk NR32 4AH	01502 573944	01502 573957	Mr M. Lincoln	935-4066	CY	13–18	842	
East Bergholt High School	Heath Rd, East Bergholt, Colchester, Essex CO7 6RJ	01206 298200	01206 298162	Mrs M.A. Humphreys	935-4097	CY	11–16	883	
Farlingaye High School	Ransom Rd, Woodbridge, Suffolk IP12 4JX	01394 385720	01394 387226	Ms Sue Hargadon	935-4076	FD	11–18	1748	

School name	Address	Tel	Fax	Headteacher	Ref	Type	Ages	Pupils	Other
Great Cornard Upper School and Technology College	Head La, Gt Cornard, Sudbury, Suffolk CO10 0JU	01787 375232	01787 377386	Mr M. Foley	935-4019	CY	13–18	809	
Hadleigh High School	High Lands Rd, Hadleigh, Ipswich, Suffolk IP7 5HU	01473 823496	01473 824720	Mrs Catherine Tooze	935-4017	CY	11–16	764	
Hartismere High School	Castleton Way, Eye, Suffolk IP23 7BL	01379 870315	01379 870554	Mr J. McAtear	935-4036	CY	11–18	823	
Holbrook High School	Ipswich Rd, Holbrook, Ipswich, Suffolk IP9 2QX	01473 328317	01473 327362	Mr Robert Peter Sherington	935-4098	CY	11–16	472	
Holywells High School	Lindbergh Rd, Ipswich, Suffolk IP3 9PZ	01473 729222	01473 718627	Mrs Ruth Everard	935-4093	CY	11–16	875	
Kesgrave High School	Main Rd, Kesgrave, Ipswich, Suffolk IP5 2PB	01473 624855	01473 612317	Mr Nigel Burgoyne	935-4099	CY	11–18	1669	
King Edward VI CE VC Upper School	Grove Rd, Bury St Edmunds, Suffolk IP33 3BH	01284 761393	01284 767474	Mr Geoff Barton	935-4500	VC	13–18	1316	CE
Kirkley Community High School	Kirkley Run, Lowestoft, Suffolk NR33 0UQ	01502 525300	01502 566003	Mr J. Clinton	935-4067	CY	13–18	1302	
Leiston Community High School	Seaward Ave, Leiston, Suffolk IP16 4BG	01728 830570	01728 832227	Mr Ian Flintoff	935-4059	CY	13–18	660	
Mildenhall College of Technology	Bury Rd, Mildenhall, Bury St Edmunds, Suffolk IP28 7HT	01638 714645	01638 510184	Mr Terence Lewis	935-4033	CY	13–18	943	
The Montessori School	Ipswich Rd, Hadleigh, Ipswich, Suffolk IP7 6BG	01473 828682		Mrs C A Prentice	935-6078		5–14	26	
Newmarket College	Exning Rd, Newmarket, Suffolk CB8 0EB	01638 664412	01638 561160	Mr Stephen Dart	935-4027	CY	13–18	622	
Northgate High School	Sidegate La West, Ipswich, Suffolk IP4 3DL	01473 210123	01473 281084	Mr Neil Watts	935-4090	CY	11–18	1660	
Orwell High School	Maidstone Rd, Felixstowe, Suffolk IP11 9EF	01394 282628	01394 278831	Mr Peter Tomkins	935-4038	CY	11–18	856	
St Alban's RC High School	Digby Rd, Ipswich, Suffolk IP4 3NJ	01473 726178	01473 718628	Mr Dennis McGarry	935-4603	VA	11–18	918	RC
St Benedict's RC School	Beetons Way, Bury St Edmunds, Suffolk IP32 6RH	01284 753512	01284 701927	Mr Paul Rossi	935-4600	VA	11–18	566	RC
Samuel Ward Arts and Technology College	Chalkstone Way, Haverhill, Suffolk CB9 0LD	01440 761511	01440 761899	Mr Howard Lay	935-4102	CY	13–18	797	
Sir John Leman High School	Ringsfield Rd, Beccles, Suffolk NR34 9PG	01502 713223	01502 716646	Mr Shaun Common	935-4056	CY	13–18	1349	
Stoke High School	Maidenhall Approach, Ipswich, Suffolk IP2 8PL	01473 601252	01473 601225	Mr Alan Whittaker	935-4087	CY	11–16	809	
Stowmarket High School	Onehouse Rd, Stowmarket, Suffolk IP14 1QR	01449 613541	01449 770436	Mr Keith Penn	935-4057	CY	13–18	1090	
Stowupland High School	Church Rd, Stowupland, Stowmarket, Suffolk IP14 4BQ	01449 674827	01449 774859	Mrs Karen Diana Grimes	935-4103	CY	13–18	683	
Stradbroke Business and Enterprise College	Wilby Rd, Stradbroke, Eye, Suffolk IP21 5JN	01379 384387	01379 388270	Mr Perry Linsley	935-4051	CY	11–16	369	
Sudbury Upper School and Arts College	Tudor Rd, Sudbury, Suffolk CO10 1NW	01787 375131	01787 379101	Mr David Forrest	935-4018	CY	13–18	1035	
Thomas Mills High School	Saxtead Rd, Framlingham, Woodbridge, Suffolk IP13 9HE	01728 723493	01728 621098	Mr Colin Hirst	935-4040	CY	11–18	1113	
Thurleston High School	Defoe Rd, Ipswich, Suffolk IP1 6SG	01473 464545	01473 748723	Mr M. Everett	935-4094	CY	11–16	813	
Thurston Community College	Thurston, Bury St Edmunds, Suffolk IP31 3PB	01359 230885	01359 230880	Miss Diane Helen Wilson	935-4024	CY	13–18	1403	
Westbourne Sports College	Marlow Rd, Ipswich, Suffolk IP1 5JN	01473 742315	01473 464825	Mr Christopher Edwards	935-4095	CY	11–18	1191	

Thurrock

School name	Address	Tel	Fax	Headteacher	Ref	Type	Ages	Pupils	Other
Belhus Chase Specialist Humanities College	Nethan Dr, Aveley, South Ockendon, Essex RM15 4RU	01708 865180	01708 864498	Ms Tess Walker	883-4392	CY	11–16	647	
Chafford Hundred Business and Enterprise College	Chafford Hundred Campus, Mayflower Rd, Chafford Hundred, Grays, Essex RM16 6SA	01375 484580	01375 484581	Mr Christopher Tomlinson	883-4394	FD	11–16	721	
Gable Hall School	Southend Rd, Corringham, Stanford-le-Hope, Essex SS17 8JT	01375 400800	01375 400801	Mr John King	883-5439	FD	11–16	1211	
The Gateway Academy	St Chad's Rd, Tilbury, Essex RM18 8LH	01375 489000	01375 489002	Mr Gary Pratt	883-6905		11–18	819	
The Grays School Media Arts College	Hathaway Rd, Grays, Essex RM17 5LL	01375 371361	01375 382743	Mr Graham Winter	883-5437	FD	11–16	994	
Hassenbrook School Specialist Technology College	Hassenbrook Rd, Stanford-le-Hope, Essex SS17 0NS	01375 671566	01375 644138	Mr Richard Glasby	883-5449	FD	11–16	792	
The Ockendon School	Erriff Dr, South Ockendon, Essex RM15 5AY	01708 851661	01708 851517	Mrs B. King	883-4299	CY	11–16	828	
St Clere's School	Butts La, Stanford-le-Hope, Essex SS17 0NW	01375 641001	01375 675814	Mr Paul Griffiths	883-5440	FD	11–16	1001	
William Edwards School and Sports College	Stifford Clays Rd, Stifford Clays, Grays, Essex RM16 3NJ	01375 486000	01375 486009	Mr John King	883-5438	FD	11–16	1197	

East Midlands

Derby

School name	Address	Tel	Fax	Headteacher	Ref	Type	Ages	Pupils	Other
Bemrose Community School	Uttoxeter New Rd, Derby, Derbyshire DE22 3HU	01332 366711	01332 296955	Ms Jo Ward	831-4177	CY	11–18	821	
Chellaston School	Swarkestone Rd, Chellaston, Derby, Derbyshire DE73 5UB	01332 702502	01332 703779	Mr R. Ruszczynski	831-5402	FD	11–18	1649	
da Vinci Community College	St Andrews View, Breadsall, Derby DE21 4ET	01332 831515	01332 830106	Mr Rob Martlew	831-4608	CY	11–16	573	
Derby Moor Community Sports College	Moorway La, Littleover, Derby, Derbyshire DE23 2FS	01332 766280	01332 270178	Mrs Wendy Whelan	831-4178	CY	11–18	1316	
Landau Forte College	Fox St, Derby DE1 2LF	01332 204040	01332 371867	Mr S. Whiteley	831-6905		11–19	1036	
Lees Brook Community Sports College	Morley Rd, Chaddesden, Derby, Derbyshire DE21 4QX	01332 671723	01332 280794	Mrs C. Dibbs	831-4181	CY	11–16	1111	
Littleover Community School	Pastures Hill, Littleover, Derby, Derbyshire DE23 4BZ	01332 513219	01332 516580	Mr David Nichols	831-4182	CY	11–18	1530	
Merrill College	Brackens La, Alvaston, Derby, Derbyshire DE24 0AN	01332 576777	01332 576796	Dr Roger Shipton	831-5403	FD	11–19	983	
Murray Park Community School	Murray Rd, Mickleover, Derby, Derbyshire DE3 9LL	01332 515921	01332 519146	Mr Eddie Green	831-5406	FD	11–16	1071	
Noel-Baker Community School and Language College	Bracknell Dr, Alvaston, Derby, Derbyshire DE24 0BR	01332 572026	01332 573654	Dr Paul Davies	831-5407	FD	11–18	1535	
St Benedict RC School and Performing Arts College	Duffield Rd, Darley Abbey, Derby, Derbyshire DE22 1JD	01332 557032	01332 553032	Mr Christopher Reynolds	831-4607	VA	11–18	1489	RC
Sinfin Community School	Farmhouse Rd, Sinfin, Derby, Derbyshire DE24 3AR	01332 270450	01332 270455	Mr Steve Monks	831-4158	CY	11–16	994	
West Park School	West Rd, Spondon, Derby, Derbyshire DE21 7BT	01332 662337	01332 280767	Mr Bw Walker	831-5412	FD	11–16	1412	
Woodlands Community School	Blenheim Dr, Allestree, Derby, Derbyshire DE22 2LW	01332 551921	01332 553869	Mr Alan Brady	831-5414	FD	11–18	1183	

Derbyshire

School name	Address	Tel	Fax	Headteacher	Ref	Type	Ages	Pupils	Other
Aldercar Community Language College	Daltons Cl, Langley Mill, Nottingham, Nottinghamshire NG16 4HL	01773 712477	01773 531969	Mr A.W. Cooper	830-4089	CY	11–16	811	
Anthony Gell School	Wirksworth, Matlock, Derbyshire DE4 4DX	01629 825577	01629 824864	Mr David Baker	830-4505	VC	11–18	686	
Belper School	John o'Gaunt's Way, off Kilburn Rd, Belper, Derbyshire DE56 1RZ	01773 825281	01773 820875	Mr Trevor Harding	830-5404	FD	11–18	1503	
Bennerley School	Bennerley Ave, Ilkeston, Derbyshire DE7 8PF	0115 932 8739	0115 932 8739	Mr David Clark	830-4168	CY	11–16	449	
The Bolsover School	Mooracre La, Bolsover, Chesterfield, Derbyshire S44 6XA	01246 822105	01246 240676	Mr Kevin Dean	830-4197	CY	11–16	879	
Brookfield Community School	Chatsworth Rd, Chesterfield, Derbyshire S40 3NS	01246 568115	01246 566827	Mr Russell Barr	830-4196	CY	11–18	1365	
Buxton Community School	College Rd, Buxton, Derbyshire SK17 9EA	01298 23122	01298 27578	Mr Alan Kelly	830-4510	VC	11–18	1374	
Chapel-en-le-Frith High School	Long La, Chapel-en-le-Frith, High Peak, Derbyshire SK23 0TQ	01298 813118	01298 812055	Mr Stuart Ash	830-4019	CY	11–18	949	
Deincourt Community School	Chesterfield Rd, North Wingfield, Chesterfield, Derbyshire S42 5LE	01246 851206	01246 855893	Mr Alun Pelleschi	830-4060	CY	11–16	484	
Dronfield Henry Fanshawe School	Green La, Dronfield, Derbyshire S18 2FZ	01246 412372	01246 412885	Miss Teresa Roche	830-4509	VC	11–18	1924	
The Ecclesbourne School	Wirksworth Rd, Duffield, Belper, Derbyshire DE56 4GS	01332 840645	01332 841871	Mrs Lesley Underhill	830-5401	FD	11–18	1449	
Eckington School	Dronfield Rd, Eckington, Sheffield, Derbyshire S21 4GN	01246 432849	01246 434401	Mr Edward Middlemass	830-4126	CY	11–18	1863	
Frederick Gent School	Mansfield Rd, South Normanton, Alfreton, Derbyshire DE55 2ER	01773 811737	01773 810223	Mr Mike Ainsley	830-4103	CY	11–16	940	
Friesland School	Nursery Ave, Sandiacre, Sandiacre, Nottinghamshire NG10 5AF	0115 939 7326	0115 949 1730	Mr Mike Ruhrmund	830-5409	FD	11–18	1301	
Glossopdale Community College	Talbot Rd, Glossop, Derbyshire SK13 7DR	01457 862336	01457 852811	Mr John Hart	830-4191	CY	11–18	1701	
Granville Community School	Burton Rd, Woodville, Swadlincote, Derbyshire DE11 7JR	01283 216765	01283 552934	Rev Barrie Scott	830-4097	CY	11–16	702	
Hasland Hall Community School	Broomfield Ave, Hasland, Chesterfield, Derbyshire S41 0LP	01246 273985	01246 551362	Miss Heather Boulton	830-4193	CY	11–16	877	
Heanor Gate Science College	Kirkley Dr, Heanor, Derbyshire DE75 7RA	01773 716396	01773 765814	Mr Robert Howard	830-5408	FD	11–18	1359	
Heritage Community School	Boughton La, Clowne, Chesterfield, Derbyshire S43 4QG	01246 810259	01246 811227	Mr Donovan Spencer	830-4198	CY	11–16	1049	
Highfields School	Upper Lumsdale, Matlock, Derbyshire DE4 5NA	01629 581888	01629 57572	Dr Ramsey Tetlow	830-4174	CY	11–18	1455	
Hope Valley College	Castleton Rd, Hope, Hope Valley, Derbyshire S33 6SD	01433 620555	01433 620054	Mr Bernard Hunter	830-4111	CY	11–16	549	

3

School name	Address	Tel	Fax	Headteacher	Ref	Type	Ages	Pupils	Other
Ilkeston School	King George Ave, Ilkeston, Derbyshire DE7 5HS	0115 930 3724	0115 944 1315	Mr Steve Daniels	830-4167	CY	11–18	1211	
John Flamsteed Community School	Derby Rd, Denby, Ripley, Derbyshire DE5 8NP	01332 880260	01332 880260	Mr Danny Holden	830-4172	CY	11–16	589	
John Port School	Etwall, Derby, Derbyshire DE65 6LU	01283 734111	01283 734035	Mr M. Crane	830-5405	FD	11–18	2031	
Kirk Hallam Community Technology College	Godfrey Dr, Kirk Hallam, Ilkeston, Derbyshire DE7 4HH	0115 930 1522	0115 944 5884	Mr Peter Hamer	830-4169	CY	11–16	1052	
Lady Manners School	Shutts La, Bakewell, Derbyshire DE45 1JA	01629 812671	01629 814984	Mr A.D. Meikle	830-5411	FD	11–18	1488	
The Long Eaton School	Thoresby Rd, Long Eaton, Nottingham NG10 3NP	0115 973 2438	0115 973 7349	Mr Richard Vasey	830-4052	CY	11–18	1300	
The Meadows Community School	High St, Old Whittington, Chesterfield, Derbyshire S41 9LG	01246 450825	01246 456014	Ms Lynn Asquith	830-4192	CY	11–16	835	
Mill Hill School	Peasehill, Ripley, Derbyshire DE5 3JQ	01773 746334	01773 570685	Mrs Sarah Graham	830-5416	FD	11–18	1301	
Mortimer Wilson School	Grange St, Alfreton, Derbyshire DE55 7JA	01773 832331	01773 830876	Mrs Wendy Sharp	830-4001	CY	11–18	715	
Netherthorpe School	Ralph Rd, Staveley, Chesterfield, Derbyshire S43 3PU	01246 472220	01246 476116	Mrs Pamela Hedley	830-5400	FD	11–18	1119	
New Mills School and Sixth Form Centre	Church La, New Mills, High Peak, Derbyshire SK22 4NR	01663 743284	01663 745134	Mr Jesse Elms	830-4057	CY	11–18	867	
Newbold Community School	Highfield La, Newbold, Chesterfield, Derbyshire S41 8BA	01246 230550	01246 557994	Mr Terry Gibson	830-4194	CY	11–18	1131	
Parkside Community School	Boythorpe Ave, Boythorpe, Chesterfield, Derbyshire S40 2NS	01246 273458	01246 551361	Mr K.G. Fletcher	830-4195	CY	11–16	576	
The Pingle School	Coronation St, Swadlincote, Derbyshire DE11 0QA	01283 216837	01283 552931	Mrs Susan Tabberer	830-5410	FD	11–18	1273	
Queen Elizabeth's Grammar School	The Green Rd, Ashbourne, Derbyshire DE6 1EP	01335 343685	01335 300637	Dr Roger Wilkes	830-4500	VC	11–18	1375	Ch
St John Houghton RC School	Abbot Rd, Kirk Hallam, Ilkeston, Derbyshire DE7 4HX	0115 932 2896	0115 944 5168	Mr B. Monaghan	830-4199	CY	11–16	619	RC
St Mary's RC High School	Newbold Rd, Upper Newbold, Chesterfield, Derbyshire S41 8AG	01246 201191	01246 279205	Mr Tom Moore	830-5413	VA	11–18	1275	RC
St Philip Howard RC School	St Mary's Rd, Glossop, Derbyshire SK13 8DR	01457 853611	01457 852830	Miss W. Steciuk	830-4602	VA	11–16	462	RC
St Thomas More RC School	Palace Fields, Buxton, Derbyshire SK17 6AF	01298 23167	01298 25816	Mrs Kate Lamb	830-4601	VA	11–16	393	RC
Shirebrook School	Common La, Shirebrook, Mansfield, Nottinghamshire NG20 8QF	01623 742722	01623 742927	Mrs Christine Parker	830-4199	CY	11–16	781	
Springwell Community School	Middlecroft Rd, Staveley, Chesterfield, Derbyshire S43 3NQ	01246 473873	01246 281899	Mr Steve Goddard	830-4200	CY	11–16	941	
Swanwick Hall School	Derby Rd, Swanwick, Alfreton, Derbyshire DE55 1AE	01773 602106	01773 609284	Mr Johnathan Fawcett	830-4000	CY	11–18	1308	
Tibshelf School	High St, Tibshelf, Alfreton, Derbyshire DE55 5PP	01773 872391	01773 590386	Mr Peter Crowe	830-4173	CY	11–16	755	
Tupton Hall School	Station New Rd, Old Tupton, Chesterfield, Derbyshire S42 6LG	01246 863127	01246 250068	Mr Patrick Cook	830-4034	CY	11–18	1867	
William Allitt School	Sunnyside, Newhall, Swadlincote, Derbyshire DE11 0TL	01283 216404	01283 552932	Mr John Crossley	830-4074	CY	11–16	976	
Wilsthorpe Business and Enterprise College	Derby Rd, Long Eaton, Nottingham, Nottinghamshire NG10 4WT	0115 972 9421	0115 946 1974	Mr D.F. Smith	830-4054	CY	11–18	1016	

Leicester

School name	Address	Tel	Fax	Headteacher	Ref	Type	Ages	Pupils	Other
Babington Community Technology College	Strasbourg Dr, Beaumont Leys, Leicester, Leicestershire LE4 0SZ	0116 222 1616	0116 222 1620	Mrs J. Smith	856-4270	CY	11–16	1004	
Beaumont Leys School	Anstey La, Leicester, Leicestershire LE4 0FL	0116 262 0257	0116 251 5356	Mrs Liz Logie	856-4242	CY	11–16	1039	
The City of Leicester College	Downing Dr, Evington, Leicester, Leicestershire LE5 6LN	0116 241 3984	0116 241 6728	Mr Mike Taylor	856-4273	CY	11–18	1437	
Crown Hills Community College	Gwendolen Rd, Leicester, Leicestershire LE5 5FT	0116 273 6893	0116 273 0413	Mr G.A. Coleby	856-4205	CY	11–16	1213	
Darul Arqam Educational Institute	2 Overton Rd, Leicester, Leicestershire LE5 0JA	0116 274 1626		Mr Ahmed Abdul Dadipatel	856-6014		7–16	75	Mu
English Martyrs RC School	Anstey La, Leicester, Leicestershire LE4 0FJ	0116 242 8880	0116 251 4239	Mrs Catherine Fields	856-4721	VA	11–18	1033	RC
Fullhurst Community College	Imperial Ave, Leicester, Leicestershire LE3 1AH	0116 282 4326	0116 282 5781	Mr Michael McPherson	856-4274	CY	11–16	899	
Hamilton Community College	Keyham La West, Netherhall, Leicester, Leicestershire LE5 1RT	0116 241 3371	0116 243 1654	Mr John Morris	856-4249	CY	11–16	968	
Highfields Boys' Secondary School	320 London Rd, Leicester, Leicestershire LE2 2PJ	0116 270 5343		Dr M.H. Mukadam	856-6012		11–16	139	Mu
Judgemeadow Community College	Marydene Dr, Evington, Leicester, Leicestershire LE5 6HP	0116 241 7580	0116 243 2314	Mr W.D. Powell	856-4251	CY	11–16	1221	
The Lancaster School	Knighton La East, Leicester, Leicestershire LE2 6FU	0116 270 3176	0116 244 8513	Mr Paul Craven	856-4246	CY	11–16	1166	B
Moat Community College	Maidstone Rd, Leicester, Leicestershire LE2 0TU	0116 262 5705	0116 251 0653	Mrs F. Hussain	856-4267	CY	11–16	1052	
New College Leicester	Glenfield Rd, Leicester, Leicestershire LE3 6DN	0116 231 8500	0116 232 2286	Mr J. Collins	856-4005	CY	11–18	852	
Riverside Community College	Lyncote Rd, Leicester, Leicestershire LE3 2EL	0116 289 9444	0116 282 4829	Mr Alan Dunsmore	856-4252	CY	11–16	725	
Rushey Mead School	Melton Rd, Leicester, Leicestershire LE4 7PA	0116 266 3730	0116 261 1883	Mrs Carolyn Robson	856-4244	CY	11–16	1360	
St Paul's RC School	Spencefield La, Leicester, Leicestershire LE5 6HN	0116 241 4057	0116 241 9156	Dr Francis Doherty	856-4723	VA	11–18	1077	RC

School name	Address	Tel	Fax	Headteacher	Ref	Type	Ages	Pupils	Other
The Samworth Enterprise Academy	Trenant Rd, Leicester LE2 6UA	0116 278 0232		P. Dubas	856-6905		5–16		CE
Sir Jonathan North Community College	Knighton La East, Leicester, Leicestershire LE2 6FU	0116 270 8116		Mrs Alison Merrills	856-4232	CY	11–16	1212	G
Soar Valley College	Gleneagles Ave, Leicester, Leicestershire LE4 7GY	0116 266 9625	0116 266 0634	Mr Melvin Berry	856-4250	CY	11–16	1215	

Leicestershire

School name	Address	Tel	Fax	Headteacher	Ref	Type	Ages	Pupils	Other
Ashby School	Nottingham Rd, Ashby-de-la-Zouch, Leicestershire LE65 1DT	01530 413748	01530 560665	Mrs Vivien Keller-Garnett	855-4508	VC	14–18	1612	R
The Beauchamp College	Ridge Way, Oadby, Leicester, Leicestershire LE2 5TP	0116 272 9100	0116 271 5454	Mr Richard Parker	855-4045	CY	14–18	2034	
Bosworth Community College	Leicester La, Desford, Leicester, Leicestershire LE9 9JL	01455 822841	01455 828194	Ms Sue Rothwell	855-4048	CY	14–18	1313	
Brockington College	Mill La, Enderby, Leicester, Leicestershire LE19 4LG	0116 286 3722	0116 284 9365	Mrs V. Hood	855-4506	VA	11–14	792	CE
Brookvale High School	Ratby Rd, Groby, Leicester, Leicestershire LE6 0FP	0116 287 7551	0116 232 1670	Ms Katie Rush	855-4051	CY	11–14	672	
Burleigh Community College	Thorpe Hill, Loughborough, Leicestershire LE11 4SQ	01509 554400	01509 554555	Mr John Smith	855-4002	CY	14–18	1226	R
Castle Rock High School	Meadow La, Coalville, Leicestershire LE67 4BR	01530 834368	01530 830485	Mrs Rosemary Baker	855-4035	CY	11–14	495	
Countesthorpe Community College	Winchester Rd, Countesthorpe, Leicester, Leicestershire LE8 5PR	0116 277 1555	0116 277 7027	Mr Brian Myatt	855-4050	CY	14–18	1079	
De Lisle RC Science College	Thorpe Hill, Loughborough, Leicestershire LE11 4SQ	01509 268739	01509 233643	Mr Chris Davies	855-4601	VA	11–18	1313	RC
The Garendon High School	Thorpe Hill, Loughborough, Leicestershire LE11 4SQ	01509 828595	01509 828597	Mrs Jane Walker	855-4030	CY	11–14	628	R
Groby Community College	Ratby Rd, Groby, Leicester, Leicestershire LE6 0GE	0116 287 9921	0116 287 0189	Ms C. Wilkins	855-4052	CY	14–19	885	
Guthlaxton College	Station Rd, Wigston, Leicestershire LE18 2DS	0116 288 1611	0116 288 1432	Mr M.J. Fields	855-4033	CY	14–18	1428	
Hastings High School	St Catherine's Cl, Burbage, Hinckley, Leicestershire LE10 2QE	01455 239414	01455 631629	Mr Matthew Pike	855-4026	CY	11–14	520	
Heathfield High School	Belle Vue Rd, Earl Shilton, Leicester, Leicestershire LE9 7PA	01455 842149	01455 840535	Mr Graham Jones	855-4011	CY	11–14	572	
Hind Leys Community College	Forest St, Shepshed, Loughborough, Leicestershire LE12 9DB	01509 504511	01509 650764	Mrs Yvonne Lee	855-4056	CY	14–18	700	
Humphrey Perkins High School	Cotes Rd, Barrow-upon-Soar, Loughborough, Leicestershire LE12 8JU	01509 412385	01509 620902	Mr J. Edwards	855-4000	CY	11–14	915	
Ibstock Community College	Central Ave, Ibstock, Leicestershire LE67 6NE	01530 260705	01530 265831	Mr Bill Kelly	855-4012	CY	11–14	670	
Ivanhoe College	North St, Ashby-de-la-Zouch, Leicestershire LE65 1HX	01530 412756	01530 412146	Mr Alan Hutchingson	855-4028	CY	11–14	881	R
John Cleveland College	Butt La, Hinckley, Leicestershire LE10 1LE	01455 632183	01455 234126	Mr Andrew Harris	855-4501	VC	14–18	1678	
John Ferneley High School	Scalford Rd, Melton Mowbray, Leicestershire LE13 1LH	01664 565901	01664 480251	Mr Christopher Robinson	855-4044	CY	11–14	570	
Kibworth High School and Community Centre	Smeeton Rd, Kibworth, Leicester, Leicestershire LE8 0LG	0116 279 2238	0116 279 6400	Ms Angela Edwards	855-4055	CY	11–14	708	
King Edward VII School	Burton Rd, Melton Mowbray, Leicestershire LE13 1DR	01664 851010	01664 851011	Mr Chris Williams	855-4005	CY	11–18	1889	
King Edward VII Science and Sport College	Warren Hills Rd, Coalville, Leicestershire LE67 4UW	01530 834925	01530 832268	Mr Noel Melvin	855-4001	CY	14–18	1008	
Leysland High School	Winchester Rd, Countesthorpe, Leicester, Leicestershire LE8 5PR	0116 277 1841	0116 278 3157	Mr Keith McDermott	855-4054	CY	11–14	673	
Limehurst High School	Bridge St, Loughborough, Leicestershire LE11 1NH	01509 263444	01509 230755	Mr Stephen Coneron	855-4014	CY	11–14	365	
The Long Field High School	Ambleside Way, Off Leicester Rd, Melton Mowbray, Leicestershire LE13 0BN	01664 561234	01664 561234	Mr Robert Garrett	855-5400	FD	11–14	442	
Longslade Community College	Wanlip La, Birstall, Leicester, Leicestershire LE4 4GH	0116 267 7107	0116 267 4510	Dr Mike Griffiths	855-4039	CY	14–18	1103	
Lutterworth Grammar School and Community College	Bitteswell Rd, Lutterworth, Leicestershire LE17 4EW	01455 554101	01455 553725	Mr Eddie de Middelaer	855-4503	VC	14–19	1977	CE
Lutterworth High School	Woodway Rd, Lutterworth, Leicestershire LE17 4QH	01455 552710	01455 559635	Mrs Jenny Middleton	855-4015	CY	11–14	728	
Market Bosworth High School and Community College	Station Rd, Market Bosworth, Nuneaton, Warwickshire CV13 0JT	01455 290251	01455 292662	Mr John Hemmingway	855-4016	CY	11–14	614	
Martin High School	Link Rd, Anstey, Leicester, Leicestershire LE7 7EB	0116 236 3291	0116 235 2121	Mr M. Furniss	855-4032	CY	11–14	624	
Mount Grace High School	Leicester Rd, Hinckley, Leicestershire LE10 1LP	01455 238921	01455 890677	Mr John Thomas	855-4010	CY	11–14	593	
Newbridge High School	Forest Rd, Coalville, Leicestershire LE67 3SJ	01530 831561	01530 276440	Mrs Pat Young	855-4007	CY	11–14	508	
Rawlins Community College	Loughborough Rd, Quorn, Loughborough, Leicestershire LE12 8DY	01509 622800	01509 416668	Mr David Brindley	855-4505	VC	14–18	1469	CE
Redmoor High School	Wykin Rd, Hinckley, Leicestershire LE10 0EP	01455 230731	01455 612419	Mr A.W. Coombs	855-4053	CY	11–14	390	

3

School name	Address	Tel	Fax	Headteacher	Ref	Type	Ages	Pupils	Other
The Robert Smyth School	Burnmill Rd, Market Harborough, Leicestershire LE16 7JG	01858 440770	01858 433096	Mr Colin Dean	855-4003	CY	14-19	1335	
Roundhill Community College	997 Melton Rd, Thurmaston, Leicester, Leicestershire LE4 8GQ	0116 269 3896	0116 260 0659	Ms Pauline Munro	855-4022	CY	11-14	634	
St Martin's RC School, Stoke Golding	Stoke Golding, Nuneaton, Warwickshire CV13 6HT	01455 212386	01455 212046	Mrs B M Carson	855-4602	VA	11-14	325	RC
The Stonehill High School	Stonehill Ave, Birstall, Leicester, Leicestershire LE4 4JG	0116 267 3384	0116 267 4224	Mr A. Baker	855-4029	CY	11-14	722	
Thomas Estley Community College	Station Rd, Broughton Astley, Leicester, Leicestershire LE9 6PT	01455 283263	01455 285758	Mr T. Moralee	855-4057	CY	11-14	731	
Welland Park Community College	Welland Park Rd, Market Harborough, Leicestershire LE16 9DR	01858 464795	01858 433702	Mrs Pascale Powell	855-4017	CY	11-14	679	
William Bradford Community College	Heath La, Earl Shilton, Leicester, Leicestershire LE9 7PD	01455 845061	01455 848665	Mrs Betty Hasler	855-4059	CY	14-18	606	
Winstanley Community College	Kingsway North, Braunstone, Leicester, Leicestershire LE3 3BD	0116 289 8688	0116 289 3736	Mrs Rita Nixon	855-4038	CY	11-14	600	
Woodbrook Vale High School	Grasmere Rd, Loughborough, Leicestershire LE11 2ST	01509 557560	01509 557562	Mr Graham Bett	855-4268	CY	11-14	429	
Wreake Valley Community College	Parkstone Rd, Syston, Leicester, Leicestershire LE7 1LY	0116 264 1080	0116 264 1089	Mrs S.H. McDermott	855-4049	CY	11-18	1528	

Lincolnshire

School name	Address	Tel	Fax	Headteacher	Ref	Type	Ages	Pupils	Other
The Aveland High School	Birthorpe Rd, Billingborough, Sleaford, Lincolnshire NG34 0QT	01529 240341	01529 240736	Mrs C.A. Briggs	925-4015	CY	11-16	422	
The Banovallum School, Horncastle	Boston Rd, Horncastle, Lincolnshire LN9 6DA	01507 522232	01507 522752	Mr Ian Carroll	925-4050	CY	11-16	578	
Birkbeck School and Community Arts College	Keeling St, North Somercotes, Louth, Lincolnshire LN11 7PN	01507 358352	01507 358404	Mrs Lynda Dobson	925-4061	CY	11-16	327	
The Boston Grammar School	South End, Boston, Lincolnshire PE21 6JY	01205 366444	01205 310702	Mr John Neal	925-5424	FD	11-18	626	B
Boston High School	Spilsby Rd, Boston, Lincolnshire PE21 9PF	01205 310505	01205 350235	Mrs H.A. McEvoy	925-4022	FD	11-18	762	G
Bourne Grammar School	South Rd, Bourne, Lincolnshire PE10 9JE	01778 422288	01778 394872	Mr Jonathan Maddox	925-4501	VC	11-18	939	Ch
Branston Community College	Station Rd, Branston, Lincoln, Lincolnshire LN4 1LH	01522 880400	01522 880401	Mr P. Beighton	925-5418	FD	11-18	1077	
Caistor Grammar School	Church St, Caistor, Market Rasen, Lincolnshire LN7 6QJ	01472 851250	01472 852248	Mr Roger Hale	925-5406	FD	11-18	622	
Caistor Yarborough School	Grimsby Rd, Caistor, Market Rasen, Lincolnshire LN7 6QZ	01472 851383	01472 851966	Mr Martin Connor	925-4049	CY	11-16	563	
Carre's Grammar School	Northgate, Sleaford, Lincolnshire NG34 7DD	01529 302181	01529 413488	Mr Mike Reading	925-5403	FD	11-18	731	B
The Castle Hills Community Arts College	The Avenue, Gainsborough, Lincolnshire DN21 1PY	01427 612411	01427 677291	Mr John Sargent	925-5410	FD	11-16	624	
Central Technology and Sports College	Rushcliffe Rd, Grantham, Lincolnshire NG31 8ED	01476 566384	01476 575740	Dr K. Atkinson	925-5426	FD	11-16	654	
The Charles Read High School	Bourne Rd, Corby Glen, Grantham, Lincolnshire NG33 4NT	01476 550333	01476 550776	Mr David Airey	925-4017	CY	11-16	236	
Cherry Willingham Community School	Croft La, Cherry Willingham, Lincoln, Lincolnshire LN3 4JP	01522 824250	01522 824251	Mr David Mills	925-4062	CY	11-16	528	
The City of Lincoln Community College	Skellingthorpe Rd, Lincoln, Lincolnshire LN6 0EP	01522 882800	01522 882801	Mr Ian Jones	925-4036	CY	11-18	960	
Cordeaux School	North Holme Rd, Louth, Lincolnshire LN11 0HG	01507 606555	01507 607399	Mr P. Kubicki	925-4056	CY	11-18	629	
Coteland's School Ruskington	Ruskington, Sleaford, Lincolnshire NG34 9BY	01526 834785	01526 834785	Mr David Veal	925-4006	CY	11-16	376	
The Deepings School	Park Rd, Deeping St James, Peterborough, Cambridgeshire PE6 8NF	01778 342159	01778 380590	Mr C Beckett	925-4010	CY	11-18	1349	
The Gartree Community School	Butts La, Tattershall, Lincoln, Lincolnshire LN4 4PN	01526 342379	01526 344418	Dr Glyn Haines	925-5409	FD	11-16	521	
George Farmer Technology and Language College	Park Rd, Holbeach, Spalding, Lincolnshire PE12 7PU	01406 423042	01406 426144	Mr S. Baragwanath	925-4029	CY	11-19	695	
The Giles School	Church La, Old Leake, Boston, Lincolnshire PE22 9LD	01205 870693	01205 871426	Mr C. Walls	925-5423	FD	11-18	968	
Gleed Boys' School	Halmer Gdns, Spalding, Lincolnshire PE11 2EF	01775 722702	01775 712476	Mr Geoffrey Cowley	925-4025	CY	11-16	647	B
The Gleed Girls' Technology College	Neville Ave, Spalding, Lincolnshire PE11 2EJ	01775 722484	01775 760546	Mrs Elizabeth Shawhulme	925-5416	FD	11-19	790	G
The Grantham Church High School	Queensway, Grantham, Lincolnshire NG31 9RA	01476 402200	01476 570140	Mr Robin Castle	925-5419	VA	11-16	541	CE
Grantham The Walton Girls' High School	Harlaxton Rd, Grantham, Lincolnshire NG31 7JR	01476 563251	01476 593243	Mrs Rosalind Gulson	925-4019	FD	11-16	716	G
Haven High Technology College	Marian Rd, Boston, Lincolnshire PE21 9HB	01205 311979	01205 362850	Mr Adrian Reed	925-4072	CY	11-16	725	
John Spendluffe Foundation Technology College	Hanby La, Alford, Lincolnshire LN13 9BL	01507 462443	01507 462013	Mr Paul Kitson	925-4048	FD	11-18	578	
Joseph Ruston Technology College	Shannon Ave, Lincoln, Lincolnshire LN6 7JG	01522 882900	01522 882929	Mr Richard Gilliland	925-5414	FD	11-18	361	

3

School name	Address	Tel	Fax	Headteacher	Ref	Type	Ages	Pupils	Other
Kesteven and Grantham Girls' School	Sandon Rd, Grantham, Lincolnshire NG31 9AU	01476 563017	01476 541155	Mr G. Burks	925-4004	CY	11–18	1061	G
Kesteven and Sleaford High School	Jermyn St, Sleaford, Lincolnshire NG34 7RS	01529 414044	01529 414928	Mrs Alison Ross	925-4005	CY	11–18	843	G
The King Edward VI Grammar School, Louth	Edward St, Louth, Lincolnshire LN11 9LL	01507 600456	01507 600316	Mrs Claire Hewitt	925-5405	FD	11–18	833	
King Edward VI Humanities College	West End, Spilsby, Lincolnshire PE23 5EW	01790 753260	01790 754495	Mrs Margaret Reeve	925-4071	CY	11–16	462	
The King's School, Grantham	Brook St, Grantham, Lincolnshire NG31 6RP	01476 563180	01476 590953	Mr Stephen Howarth	925-5402	FD	11–18	935	B
The Lafford High School, Billinghay	Fen Rd, Billinghay, Lincoln, Lincolnshire LN4 4HU	01526 860410	01526 860775	Mr Paul Watson	925-4016	CY	11–16	255	
Lincoln Christ's Hospital School	Wragby Rd, Lincoln, Lincolnshire LN2 4PN	01522 881144	01522 881145	Dr A. Wright	925-5408	VA	11–18	1270	Ch
The Mablethorpe Tennyson High School	Seaholme Rd, Mablethorpe, Lincolnshire LN12 2DF	01507 473331	01507 474928	Mr Chris Walls	925-4059	CY	11–16	360	
De Aston School Market Rasen	Willingham Rd, Market Rasen, Lincolnshire LN8 3RF	01673 843415	01673 842131	Mrs Ellenor Beighton	925-4514	VC	11–18	1183	Ch R
Middlecott School	Edinburgh Dr, Kirton, Boston, Lincolnshire PE20 1JS	01205 722336	01205 722603	Mrs B. Merrick	925-4028	CY	11–16	495	
Middlefield School of Technology	Middlefield La, Gainsborough, Lincolnshire DN21 1PU	01427 615199	01427 811180	Mrs W.R. Carrick	925-4069	CY	11–16	570	
Monks' Dyke Technology College	Monks' Dyke Rd, Louth, Lincolnshire LN11 9AW	01507 606349	01507 600856	Dr Chris Rolph	925-5417	FD	11–18	1166	
North Kesteven School	Moor La, North Hykeham, Lincoln, Lincolnshire LN6 9AG	01522 881010	01522 881452	Mr Keith Elms	925-5412	FD	11–18	1417	
The Peele School	84 Little London, Long Sutton, Spalding, Lincolnshire PE12 9LF	01406 362120	01406 364940	Ms Julie Chong	925-4030	CY	11–16	649	
The Priory LSST	Cross Cliff Hill, Lincoln, Lincolnshire LN5 8PW	01522 889977	01522 871300	Mr Richard Gilliland	925-5425	CY	11–18	1687	
Queen Eleanor Technology College	Green La, Stamford, Lincolnshire PE9 1HE	01780 751011	01780 752776	Mr Neil Oxborrow	925-4067	CY	11–16	472	
Queen Elizabeth's Grammar School	Station Rd, Alford, Lincolnshire LN13 9HY	01507 462403	01507 462125	Miss Angela Francis	925-5401	FD	11–18	542	
Queen Elizabeth's Grammar School, Horncastle	West St, Horncastle, Lincolnshire LN9 5AD	01507 522465	01507 527711	Mr Tim Peacock	925-5411	FD	11–18	792	
The Queen Elizabeth's High School, Gainsborough	Morton Terr, Gainsborough, Lincolnshire DN21 2ST	01427 612354	01427 612856	Mr David Smart	925-4065	CY	11–18	1163	
The Robert Manning Technology College	Edinburgh Cres, Bourne, Lincolnshire PE10 9DT	01778 422365	01778 393879	Mr Geoff Greatwood	925-4000	CY	11–18	1154	
Robert Pattinson School	Moor La, North Hykeham, Lincoln, Lincolnshire LN6 9AF	01522 882020	01522 880660	Mr Stuart MacFarlane	925-5413	FD	11–18	1277	
St Bede's RC Science College	Tollfield Rd, Boston, Lincolnshire PE21 9PN	01205 365873	01205 368621	Mr Dave Gates	925-4604	VA	11–16	326	RC
St Clements College	Burgh Rd, Skegness, Lincolnshire PE25 2QH	01754 896300		Mr Chris Mcgrath	925-4609	CY	11–18	1026	
The St George's College of Technology	Westholme, Sleaford, Lincolnshire NG34 7PS	01529 302487	01529 414057	Mr P.F. Watson	925-5404	FD	11–18	1595	
The St Guthlac School	Postland Rd, Crowland, Peterborough, Cambridgeshire PE6 0JA	01733 210413	01733 210349	Miss Sheila Paige	925-4032	CY	11–16	382	
St Hugh's CE Mathematics and Computing College	The Avenue, Dysart Rd, Grantham, Lincolnshire NG31 7PX	01476 405200	01476 405252	Mrs Trudy Brothwell	925-5422	FD	11–16	430	CE
St Peter and St Paul, Lincoln's RC High School, A Science College	Western Ave, Lincoln, Lincolnshire LN6 7SX	01522 871400	01522 871404	Mr Mark Kerridge	925-5421	VA	11–18	662	RC
The Sir William Robertson High School, Welbourn	Main Rd, Welbourn, Lincoln, Lincolnshire LN5 0PA	01400 272422	01400 273780	Mr I. Wright	925-5420	FD	11–16	885	
The Skegness Grammar School	Vernon Rd, Skegness, Lincolnshire PE25 2QS	01754 610000	01754 763947	Mr A. Rigby	925-5400	FD	11–18	796	R
Spalding Grammar School	Priory Rd, Spalding, Lincolnshire PE11 2XH	01775 724646	01775 765801	Mr Nigel Ryan	925-4603	VA	11–18	929	B
Spalding High School	Stonegate, Spalding, Lincolnshire PE11 2PJ	01775 722110	01775 762531	Mr Tim Clark	925-4027	CY	11–18	934	G
The Thomas Cowley High School	School La, Donington, Spalding, Lincolnshire PE11 4TF	01775 820254	01775 821899	Mr Martyn A Taylor	925-4507	VC	11–16	597	
William Farr CE Comprehensive School	Lincoln Rd, Welton, Lincoln, Lincolnshire LN2 3JB	01673 866900	01673 862660	Mr Paul Strong	925-5415	FD	11–18	1462	CE
William Lovell CE School	Main Rd, Stickney, Boston, Lincolnshire PE22 8AA	01205 480352	01205 480398	Mr Robert Dring	925-4516	VC	11–16	423	CE
Yarborough School	Riseholme Rd, Lincoln, Lincolnshire LN1 3SP	01522 529203	01522 504007	Mr R. Boothroyd	925-5407	FD	11–18	903	

Northamptonshire

School name	Address	Tel	Fax	Headteacher	Ref	Type	Ages	Pupils	Other
Bishop Stopford School	Headlands, Kettering, Northamptonshire NN15 6BJ	01536 503503	01536 503217	Mrs Margaret Holman	928-4601	VA	11–18	1442	CE
Brooke Weston CTC	Coomb Rd, Gt Oakley, Corby, Northamptonshire NN18 8LA	01536 396366	01536 396867	Mr P.A. Simpson	928-6900		11–18	1154	
Campion School	Bugbrooke, Northampton, Northamptonshire NN7 3QG	01604 833900	01604 833906	Mr Bob Clayton	928-4051	CY	11–18	1488	

School name	Address	Tel	Fax	Headteacher	Ref	Type	Ages	Pupils	Other
Chenderit School	Archery Rd, Middleton Cheney, Banbury, Oxfordshire OX17 2QR	01295 711567	01295 711856	Mr Paul MacIntyre	928-4089	CY	11–18	1084	
Danetre School	Hawke Rd, Southbrook, Daventry, Northamptonshire NN11 4LJ	01327 313400	01327 313416	Mrs Linda Brooks	928-4053	CY	11–16	1079	
The Duston School	Berrywood Rd, Duston, Northampton, Northamptonshire NN5 6XA	01604 460004	01604 454005	Mrs Jane Sara Herriman	928-4066	CY	11–18	1104	
The Ferrers Specialist Arts College	Queensway, Higham Ferrers, Rushden, Northamptonshire NN10 8LF	01933 313411	01933 410755	Dr Rosemary Litawski	928-4094	FD	11–18	1070	
Guilsborough School	West Haddon Rd, Guilsborough, Northampton, Northamptonshire NN6 8QE	01604 740641	01604 740136	Mrs Christine Staley	928-4042	CY	11–18	1336	
Huxlow Science College	Finedon Rd, Irthlingborough, Wellingborough, Northamptonshire NN9 5TY	01933 650496	01933 653435	Mr Michael Malton	928-4017	CY	11–18	814	
Ise Community College	Deeble Rd, Kettering, Northamptonshire NN15 7AA	01536 532700	01536 532709	Mr Mark Lester	928-4019	CY	11–18	1054	
Kingsbrook School	Stratford Rd, Deanshanger, Milton Keynes, Buckinghamshire MK19 6HN	01908 563468	01908 262905	Mr Andy Howlett	928-4041	CY	11–18	971	
Kingsthorpe Community College	Boughton Green Rd, Kingsthorpe, Northampton, Northamptonshire NN2 7HR	01604 716106	01604 720824	Mrs Judith Long	928-4071	CY	11–18	1392	
The Kingswood School	Gainsborough Rd, Corby, Northamptonshire NN18 9NS	01536 741857	01536 460138	Mr David Tristram	928-5402	FD	11–18	1306	
The Latimer Arts College	Castle Way, Barton Seagrave, Kettering, Northamptonshire NN15 6SW	01536 720300	01536 720303	Mr C. Grimshaw	928-4055	FD	11–18	1155	
Lodge Park Technology College	Shetland Way, Corby, Northamptonshire NN17 2JH	01536 203817	01536 403562	Mr Tom Waterworth	928-5405	FD	11–18	1272	
Magdalen College School	Waynflete Ave, Brackley, Northamptonshire NN13 6FB	01280 846300	01280 704953	Mr Ian Colling	928-4550	VC	11–18	1464	
Manor School and Sports College	Mountbatten Way, Raunds, Wellingborough, Northamptonshire NN9 6PA	01933 623921	01933 460818	Mr P. Wingfield	928-5406	FD	11–19	808	
Mereway Community College	Mereway, Northampton, Northamptonshire NN4 8BU	01604 763616	01604 765036	Mr Mark Griffin	928-4069	CY	11–18	1214	
Montagu School	Weekley Glebe Rd, Kettering, Northamptonshire NN16 9NS	01536 515644	01536 510163	Mrs Margaret Gwynne	928-5407	FD	11–18	1047	
Montsaye Community College	Greening Rd, Rothwell, Kettering, Northamptonshire NN14 6BB	01536 418844	01536 418282	Mrs Susan Fennell	928-4015	CY	11–18	1218	
Moulton School and Science College	Pound La, Moulton, Northampton, Northamptonshire NN3 7SD	01604 641600	01604 641601	Mr John Woodhead	928-4022	CY	11–18	1299	
Northampton Academy	Billing Brook Rd, Lings, Northampton NN3 8NH	01604 402811	01604 773830	Mr Martyn Baker	928-6905		11–18	1302	Ch
Northampton School for Boys	Billing Rd, Northampton, Northamptonshire NN1 5RT	01604 230240	01604 258659	Mr Michael Griffiths	928-5404	FD	11–18	1518	B
Northampton School for Girls	Spinney Hill Rd, Devon Way, Northampton, Northamptonshire NN3 6DG	01604 679540	01604 679552	Mrs Penny Westwood	928-4076	CY	11–18	1677	G
Prince William School	Herne Rd, Oundle, Oundle, Northamptonshire PE8 4BS	01832 272881	01832 274942	Mr Malcolm England	928-4052	CY	13–18	1111	
Roade School Sports College	Stratford Rd, Roade, Northampton, Northamptonshire NN7 2LP	01604 862125	01604 863912	Mr R. Parkinson	928-4033	FD	11–18	1377	
The Rushden Community College Specialising in Mathematics and Computing	Hayway, Rushden, Northamptonshire NN10 6AG	01933 350391	01933 411689	Mr Stephen Dommett	928-4098	CY	11–18	1058	
Sir Christopher Hatton School	The Pyghtle, Wellingborough, Northamptonshire NN8 4RP	01933 226077	01933 271424	Mrs Victoria Bishop	928-5409	FD	11–18	1163	
Southfield School for Girls	Lewis Rd, Kettering, Northamptonshire NN15 6HE	01536 513063	01536 518487	Mrs Susan Dunford	928-5400	FD	11–18	928	G
Sponne School Technology College	Brackley Rd, Towcester, Northamptonshire NN12 6DJ	01327 350284	01327 359061	Mr Jamie Clarke	928-4004	FD	11–18	1196	
Thomas Becket RC School	Becket Way, Kettering Rd North, Northampton, Northamptonshire NN3 6HT	01604 493211	01604 497300	Mr Thomas Percy	928-4703	VA	11–18	1032	RC
Unity College	Trinity Ave, Northampton NN2 6JW	01604 778000	01604 778074	Mrs Sharron Goode	928-4103	VA	11–18	1256	CE
Weavers School	Weavers Rd, Wellingborough, Northamptonshire NN8 3JQ	01933 222830	01933 276347	Mr Alan Large	928-5408	FD	11–18	970	
Weston Favell School	Booth La South, Northampton, Northamptonshire NN3 3EZ	01604 402121	01604 773211	Dr Tracey Jones	928-4067	CY	11–18	1376	
William Parker School A Specialist Humanities College	Ashby Rd, Daventry, Northamptonshire NN11 0QF	01327 705816	01327 300156	Mr Jason Brook	928-4035	CY	11–16	1026	
Wollaston School	Irchester Rd, Wollaston, Wellingborough, Northamptonshire NN29 7PH	01933 663501	01933 665272	Mr M. Browne	928-4038	CY	11–18	1342	
Wrenn School	London Rd, Wellingborough, Northamptonshire NN8 2DQ	01933 222039	01933 225334	Mr William Thallon	928-5410	FD	11–18	1424	

Nottingham

School name	Address	Tel	Fax	Headteacher	Ref	Type	Ages	Pupils	Other
Big Wood School	Bewcastle Rd, Warren Hill, Nottingham, Nottinghamshire NG5 9PJ	0115 953 9323	0115 953 9321	Mrs Bernadette Groves	892-4072	CY	11–16	730	
Djanogly City Academy Nottingham	Gregory Bvd, Nottingham NG7 6NB	0115 942 4422	0115 942 4034	Mr Mike Butler	892-6905		11–19	1594	
Elliott Durham School	Ransom Dr, Mapperley, Nottingham, Nottinghamshire NG3 5LR	0115 952 3838	0115 952 3898	Mrs Caroline Churchill	892-4071	CY	11–16	432	
Ellis Guilford School and Sports College	Bar La, Basford, Nottingham, Nottinghamshire NG6 0HT	0115 913 1338	0115 913 1341	Mr P. Plummer	892-4026	CY	11–16	1252	
Fairham Community College	Farnborough Rd, Clifton, Nottingham, Nottinghamshire NG11 9AE	0115 974 4400	0115 974 4401	Mrs Susan Woodward	892-4060	CY	11–16	347	
Farnborough School Technology College	Farnborough Rd, Clifton, Nottingham, Nottinghamshire NG11 8JW	0115 974 4444	0115 974 4445	Mr A.D. Wells	892-4053	CY	11–16	804	
Fernwood School	Goodwood Rd, Wollaton, Nottingham, Nottinghamshire NG8 2FT	0115 928 6326	0115 985 4250	Mrs Ann Witheford	892-4064	CY	11–16	993	
Greenwood Dale School	Sneinton Bvd, Nottingham, Nottinghamshire NG2 4GL	0115 910 3200	0115 910 3204	Mr Barry S. Day	892-5402	FD	11–18	1258	
Hadden Park High School	Harvey Rd, Bilborough, Nottingham, Nottinghamshire NG8 3GP	0115 913 5211	0115 913 5217	Mr Gareth Owen	892-4461	CY	11–16	809	
Haywood School	Edwards La, Sherwood, Nottingham, Nottinghamshire NG5 3HZ	0115 916 1443	0115 967 6802	Mrs Jill Hislop	892-4070	CY	11–16	449	
Henry Mellish Comprehensive School	Highbury Rd, Bulwell, Nottingham, Nottinghamshire NG6 9DS	0115 915 7700	0115 915 7764	Mrs J.B. Young	892-4436	CY	11–16	539	
Manning Comprehensive School	Robins Wood Rd, Aspley, Nottingham, Nottinghamshire NG8 3LD	0115 929 9401	0115 942 5979	Mrs Lesley Lyon	892-4001	CY	11–16	535	G
The Nottingham Bluecoat School and Technology College	Aspley La, Aspley, Nottingham, Nottinghamshire NG8 5GY	0115 929 7445	0115 942 6257	Mr M. Kay	892-4615	VA	11–18	1576	CE
The Nottingham Emmanuel School	Coronation Ave, Wilford, Nottingham NG11 7AD	0115 914 4111	0115 914 4110	Mr David King	892-4462	VA	11–16	833	CE
The River Leen School	Hucknall La, Bulwell, Nottingham, Nottinghamshire NG6 8AQ	0115 915 9750	0115 979 5910	Miss Elizabeth Churton	892-4460	CY	11–16	637	
Top Valley School	Top Valley Dr, Top Valley, Nottingham, Nottinghamshire NG5 9AZ	0115 953 9060	0115 953 9065	Mr Peter A. Brown	892-4067	CY	11–16	823	
The Trinity RC School	Beechdale Rd, Aspley, Nottingham, Nottinghamshire NG8 3EZ	0115 929 6251	0115 942 6560	Mr Michael McKeever	892-5404	VA	11–18	1088	RC
William Sharp School	Bramhall Rd, Bilborough, Nottingham, Nottinghamshire NG8 4HY	0115 929 1492	0115 942 5730	Mr D. Corrall	892-4050	CY	11–16	675	

Nottinghamshire

School name	Address	Tel	Fax	Headteacher	Ref	Type	Ages	Pupils	Other
Alderman White School and Language College	Chilwell La, Nottingham, Nottinghamshire NG9 3DU	0115 917 0424	0115 917 0494	Mrs Janice Addison	891-4117	CY	11–18	645	
All Saints RC Comprehensive School	Broomhill La, Mansfield, Nottinghamshire NG19 6BW	01623 474700	01623 471118	Mr K. Daly	891-4756	VA	11–18	1129	RC
Arnold Hill School and Technology College	Gedling Rd, Nottingham, Nottinghamshire NG5 6NZ	0115 955 4804	0115 955 4805	Mr Robin Fugill	891-4091	CY	11–18	1647	
Ashfield Comprehensive School	Sutton Rd, Nottingham, Nottinghamshire NG17 8HP	01623 455000	01623 455001	Mr I.M. Fraser	891-4009	CY	11–18	2488	
The Becket School	Ruddington La, Nottingham, Nottinghamshire NG11 7DL	0115 981 7742	0115 981 7717	Mr A. Glover	891-4617	VA	11–18	1023	RC
Bramcote Hills Sport and Community College	Moor La, Nottingham, Nottinghamshire NG9 3GA	0115 916 8900	0115 916 8901	Ms Nada Trikic	891-4118	CY	11–18	914	
The Bramcote Park Business and Enterprise School	Bramcote, Nottingham, Nottinghamshire NG9 3GD	0115 913 0013	0115 913 0012	Mr Chris Teal	891-4119	CY	11–16	630	
The Brunts School	The Park, Mansfield, Nottinghamshire NG18 2AT	01623 623149	01623 622746	Mrs Janice Addison	891-4463	CY	11–18	1558	
Carlton le Willows School	Wood La, Nottingham, Nottinghamshire NG4 4AA	0115 956 5008	0115 956 5009	Mr M.H.A. Naisbitt	891-4107	CY	11–18	1310	
Chilwell School	Queen's Rd West, Chilwell, Beeston, Nottingham, Nottinghamshire NG9 5AL	0115 925 2698	0115 925 8167	Mrs H.M.P. Robson	891-4121	FD	11–18	1038	
Christ The King School	Darlton Dr, Nottingham, Nottinghamshire NG5 7JZ	0115 955 6262	0115 955 6363	Mrs Helen Robson	891-4700	VA	11–18	811	RC
Colonel Frank Seely Comprehensive School	Flatts La, Nottingham, Nottinghamshire NG14 6JZ	0115 965 2495	0115 965 5723	Mr I.J. Gage	891-4409	CY	11–18	1109	
Dayncourt School Specialist Sports College	Cropwell Rd, Nottingham, Nottinghamshire NG12 2FQ	0115 911 0091	0115 911 0092	Mr Timothy Mitchell	891-4449	CY	11–18	850	
The Dukeries College	Whinney La, Newark, Nottinghamshire NG22 9TD	01623 860545	01623 836082	Mr P.L. Walker	891-4444	CY	11–18	1201	
Eastwood Comprehensive School	Mansfield Rd, Nottingham, Nottinghamshire NG16 3EA	01773 786212	01773 786211	Mrs Christine Hasty	891-4201	CY	11–18	918	
The Elizabethan High School	Queen St, Retford, Nottinghamshire DN22 7BH	01777 703293	01777 706796	Ms Lynn French	891-4456	CY	11–18	1190	
Garibaldi College	Forest Town, Mansfield, Nottinghamshire NG19 0JX	01623 464220	01623 464221	Mrs Elaine Huckerby	891-4041	CY	11–18	1199	

3

School name	Address	Tel	Fax	Headteacher	Ref	Type	Ages	Pupils	Other
The Gedling School	Wollaton Ave, Nottingham, Nottinghamshire NG4 4HX	0115 952 1171	0115 940 3462	Mrs Jackie Overton	891-4100	CY	11–18	758	
George Spencer Foundation School and Technology College	Arthur Mee Rd, Stapleford, Nottingham, Nottinghamshire NG9 7EW	0115 917 0100	0115 917 0101	Mrs Susan Jowett	891-5401	FD	11–18	1322	
The Grove School	London Rd, Newark, Nottinghamshire NG24 3AL	01636 680200	01636 680201	Mrs P.M. Head	891-4400	CY	11–18	900	
Harry Carlton Comprehensive School	Lantern La, Loughborough, Leicestershire LE12 6QN	01509 852424	01509 856438	Mr Graham Legg	891-4413	CY	11–18	1170	
The Holgate Comprehensive School	Hillcrest Dr, Nottingham, Nottinghamshire NG15 6PX	0115 963 2104	0115 968 1993	Mr R. Kenney	891-4429	CY	11–18	1341	
Joseph Whitaker School	Warsop La, Rainworth, Mansfield, Nottinghamshire NG21 0AG	01623 792327	01623 792419	Mr J.P. Loughton	891-4408	FD	11–18	1298	
Kimberley Comprehensive School	Newdigate St, Nottingham, Nottinghamshire NG16 2NJ	0115 938 3961	0115 945 9970	Mr J. May	891-4226	CY	11–18	1325	
Kirkby College	Tennyson St, Nottingham, Nottinghamshire NG17 7DH	01623 455925	01623 455923	Miss Lynn Parkes	891-4008	CY	11–18	690	
Magnus CE School	Earp Ave, Newark, Nottinghamshire NG24 4AB	01636 680066	01636 680077	Mr D Glenn Evans	891-4583	FD	11–18	1105	CE
The Manor School	Park Hall Rd, Mansfield, Nottinghamshire NG19 8QA	01623 425100	01623 425101	Mr J.P. Hickman	891-4032	CY	11–18	1383	
The Meden School and Technology College	Burns La, Mansfield, Nottinghamshire NG20 0QN	01623 843517	01623 847354	Mrs Kate Reid	891-4075	CY	11–18	1351	
The National School, a CE Technology College	Annesley Rd, Nottingham, Nottinghamshire NG15 7DB	0115 963 5667	0115 963 8955	Mr D. Shannon	891-4635	VA	11–18	1065	CE
The Newark High School	London Rd, Newark, Nottinghamshire NG24 1TT	01636 680440	01636 680444	Mrs Jenni Page	891-4584	VC	11–18	397	
Portland School	Sparken Hill, Worksop, Nottinghamshire S80 1AW	01909 473656	01909 471301	Mr P. Buck	891-4374	CY	11–18	1630	
Quarrydale School	Stoneyford Rd, Sutton-in-Ashfield, Nottinghamshire NG17 2DU	01623 554178	01623 517814	Mr J.C. Weaver	891-4068	CY	11–18	895	
The Queen Elizabeth's (1561) Endowed School	150 Chesterfield Rd South, Mansfield, Nottinghamshire NG19 7AP	01623 623559	01623 659454	Mrs Katherine Sanderson	891-4464	VA	11–18	1153	CE
Redhill School	Redhill Rd, Arnold, Nottingham, Nottinghamshire NG5 8GX	0115 926 1481	0115 967 6922	Mr Andrew Burns	891-4084	FD	11–18	1277	
Retford Oaks High School	Babworth Rd, Retford, Nottinghamshire DN22 7NJ	01777 861618	01777 861620	Mr David Rich	891-4465	CY	11–18	964	
Rushcliffe Comprehensive School	Boundary Rd, Nottingham, Nottinghamshire NG2 7BW	0115 974 4050	0115 974 4051	Mr R. Gullis	891-4329	CY	11–18	1310	
Selston Arts and Community College	Chapel Rd, Nottingham, Nottinghamshire NG16 6BW	01773 810321	01773 510262	Mrs Dianne Stendall	891-4230	CY	11–18	821	
Sherwood Hall School and Sixth Form College	Sherwood Hall Rd, Mansfield, Nottinghamshire NG18 2DY	01623 450025	01623 450026	Mr John Bowers	891-4462	CY	11–18	922	
South Wolds Community School	Church Dr, Nottingham, Nottinghamshire NG12 5FF	0115 937 3506	0115 937 2905	Mr Simon Dennis	891-4454	CY	11–18	1050	
Sutton Centre Community College	High Pavement, Sutton-in-Ashfield, Nottinghamshire NG17 1EE	01623 405500	01623 443220	Mr R. Tanner	891-4069	CY	11–18	953	
Toot Hill School	The Banks, Nottingham, Nottinghamshire NG13 8BL	01949 875550	01949 875551	Mr John Tomasevic	891-4404	CY	11–18	1464	
Tuxford School	Marnham Rd, Newark, Nottinghamshire NG22 0JH	01777 870001	01777 872155	Mr Christopher B Pickering	891-4452	CY	11–18	1288	
Valley Comprehensive School	Baulk La, Worksop, Nottinghamshire S81 7DG	01909 475121	01909 530359	Mr Brian Rossiter	891-4364	CY	11–18	1566	
The West Bridgford School	Loughborough Rd, West Bridgford, Nottingham, Nottinghamshire NG2 7FA	0115 974 4488	0115 974 4489	Mr Robert McDonough	891-4328	FD	11–18	1426	
Wheldon School and Sports College	Coningswath Rd, Nottingham, Nottinghamshire NG4 3SH	0115 955 0010	0115 955 0020	Mr Callum Orr	891-4106	CY	11–18	904	

Rutland

School name	Address	Tel	Fax	Headteacher	Ref	Type	Ages	Pupils	Other
Casterton Business and Enterprise College	Ryhall Rd, Gt Casterton, Stamford, Lincolnshire PE9 4AT	01780 762168	01780 66628	Ms Victoria Crosher	857-5405	FD	11–16	794	
Uppingham Community College	London Rd, Uppingham, Oakham, Rutland LE15 9TJ	01572 823631	01572 821193	Mr Malcolm England	857-5404	FD	11–16	835	
Vale of Catmose College	Cold Overton Rd, Oakham, Rutland LE15 6NU	01572 722286	01572 724429	Mr Peter Green	857-5406	FD	11–16	741	

London

Barking and Dagenham

School name	Address	Tel	Fax	Headteacher	Ref	Type	Ages	Pupils	Other
All Saints RC School and Technology College	Terling Rd, Wood La, Dagenham, Essex RM8 1JT	020 8270 4242	020 8595 4024	Mr Kevin Wilson	301-4703	VA	11–18	1089	RC
Barking Abbey School, A Specialist Sports and Humanities College	Sandringham Rd, Barking, Essex IG11 9AG	020 8270 4100	020 8270 4090	Mr Mark Lloyd	301-4021	CY	11–18	1816	
Dagenham Park Community School	School Rd, Dagenham, Essex RM10 9QH	020 8270 4400	020 8270 4409	Mr J. Torrie	301-4022	CY	11–18	1056	
Eastbrook Comprehensive School	Dagenham Rd, Dagenham, Essex RM10 7UR	020 8270 4567	020 8270 4545	Mrs Valerie Dennis	301-4023	CY	11–18	1454	
Eastbury Comprehensive School	Hulse Ave, Barking, Essex IG11 9UW			Mr Clive Swinton	301-4024	CY	11–18	1651	
Jo Richardson Community School	Gale St, Castle Grn, Dagenham, Essex RM9 4UN	020 8270 6222	020 8270 6223	Mr Andrew Buck	301-4029	CY	11–19	992	
Robert Clack School	Gosfield Rd, Dagenham, Essex RM8 1JU	020 8270 4200	020 8270 4210	Mr P.J.P. Grant	301-4027	CY	11–18	1650	
The Sydney Russell School	Parsloes Ave, Dagenham, Essex RM9 5QT	020 8270 4333	020 8270 4377	Mr R. Leighton	301-4028	CY	11–18	1546	
The Warren Comprehensive School	Whalebone La North, Chadwell Heath, Romford, Essex RM6 6SB	020 8270 4500	020 8270 4484	Mr Kenneth Jones	301-4016	CY	11–18	1304	

Barnet

School name	Address	Tel	Fax	Headteacher	Ref	Type	Ages	Pupils	Other
Ashmole School	Cecil Rd, Southgate, London N14 5RJ	020 8361 2703	020 8368 0315	Mr Derrick Brown	302-5406	FD	11–18	1339	
Bishop Douglass School Finchley	Hamilton Rd, East Finchley, London N2 0SQ	020 8444 5211	020 8444 0416	Ms Angela B. Murphy	302-5408	VA	11–18	743	RC
Christ's College Finchley	East End Rd, East Finchley, London N2 0SE	020 8349 3581	020 8349 8972	Mr Gary Tucker	302-4211	CY	11–18	968	B
The Compton School	Summers La, London N12 0QG	020 8368 1783	020 8368 2097	Mrs T. Tunnadine	302-4215	CY	11–16	849	
Copthall School	Pursley Rd, Mill Hill, London NW7 2EP	020 8959 1937	020 8959 8736	Ms Jane Beaumont	302-4210	CY	11–18	1114	G
East Barnet School	Chestnut Gr, East Barnet, Barnet, Hertfordshire EN4 8PU	020 8445 0105	020 8449 9862	Mr N. Christou	302-4212	CY	11–18	1241	
Finchley RC High School	Woodside La, Finchley, London N12 8TA	020 8445 0105	020 8446 0691	Mr Kevin J. Hoare	302-5405	VA	11–18	1074	RC B
Friern Barnet School	Hemington Ave, Friern Barnet, London N11 3LS	020 8368 2777	020 8368 3208	Mr Jeremy Turner	302-4003	CY	11–16	761	
Hasmonean High School	Holders Hill Rd, Hendon, London NW4 1NA	020 8203 1411	020 8202 4526	Mr Martin Clarke	302-5409	VA	11–18	1044	Je
Hendon School	Golders Rise, Hendon, London NW4 2HP	020 8202 9004	020 8202 3341	Mr Kevin McKellar	302-5400	FD	11–18	1260	
The Henrietta Barnett School	Central Sq, Hampstead Garden Suburb, London NW11 7BN	020 8458 8999	020 8455 8900	Mr Oliver Blond	302-4752	VA	11–18	700	G
London Academy	Spur Rd, Edgware HA8 8DE	020 8238 1100	020 8238 1101	Mr Phil Hearne	302-6905		11–18	1318	
Mill Hill County High School	Worcester Cres, Mill Hill, London NW7 4LL	084 4477 2424	020 8959 6514	Mr G.A. Thompson	302-5402	FD	11–18	1705	
Queen Elizabeth's Girls' School	High St, Barnet, Hertfordshire EN5 5RR	020 8449 2984	020 8441 2322	Mrs Kate Webster	302-4208	CY	11–18	1109	G
Queen Elizabeth's School, Barnet	Queen's Rd, Barnet, Hertfordshire EN5 4DQ	020 8441 4646	020 8440 7500	Dr John Marincowitz	302-5401	FD	11–18	1154	B
The Ravenscroft School a Technology College	Barnet La, London N20 8AZ	020 8445 9205	020 8343 7466	Mrs M.H. Karaolis	302-4009	CY	11–18	877	
St James' RC High School	Gt Strand, Colindale, London NW9 5PE	020 8358 2800	020 8358 2801	Mrs Anne O'Shea	302-5407	VA	11–18	1114	RC
St Mary's CE High School	Downage, Hendon, London NW4 1AB	020 8203 2827	020 8202 5510	Mrs Kate Roskell	302-5403	VA	11–18	895	CE
St Michael's RC Grammar School	Nether St, North Finchley, London N12 7NJ	020 8446 2256	020 8343 9598	Miss Ursula Morrissey	302-5404	VA	11–18	738	RC G
Whitefield School	Claremont Rd, Cricklewood, London NW2 1TR	020 8455 4114	020 8455 4382	Mr Peter Blenkinsop	302-4012	CY	11–18	812	

Bexley

School name	Address	Headteacher	Tel	Fax	Ref	Type	Ages	Pupils	Other
Beths Grammar School	Hartford Rd, Bexley, Kent DA5 1NE	Mr J. Skinner	01322 556538	01322 526224	303-5403	FD	11–18	1134	B
Bexley Grammar School	Danson La, Welling, Kent DA16 2BL	Mr R.I. MacKinnon	020 8304 8538	020 8304 0248	303-4000	FD	11–18	1541	
Bexleyheath School	Woolwich Rd, Bexleyheath, Kent DA7 4HU	Mr M. Noble	020 8303 5696	020 8303 9151	303-4024	CY	11–18	2114	
Blackfen School for Girls	Blackfen Rd, Sidcup, Kent DA15 9NU	Mr Matthew Brown	020 8303 1887	020 8298 1656	303-4008	CY	11–18	1265	G
The Business Academy Bexley	Yarnton Way, Erith DA18 4DW	Mr Duncan Spalding	020 8320 4800	020 8320 4810	303-6905		3–18	1475	
Chislehurst and Sidcup Grammar School	Hurst Rd, Sidcup, Kent DA15 9AG	Dr Joe Vitagliano	020 8302 6511	020 8309 6596	303-4030	CY	11–18	1367	
Cleeve Park School	Bexley La, Sidcup, Kent DA14 4JN	Mr Vince Hodkinson	020 8302 6418	020 8308 1571	303-4030	CY	11–18	1022	
Erith School	Avenue Rd, Erith, Kent DA8 3BN	Mr Toby Hufford	01322 348231	01322 351528	303-4022	FD	11–18	1965	
Hurstmere Foundation School for Boys	Hurst Rd, Sidcup, Kent DA15 9AW	Mr Andrew Stanley Stringer	020 8300 5665	020 8300 2039	303-5404	FD	11–19	1036	B
Merton Court School	38 Knoll Rd, Sidcup, Kent DA14 4QU	Mr D. Price	020 8300 2112	020 8300 1324	303-6053		2–11	319	CE
St Catherine's RC School for Girls	Watling St, Bexleyheath, Kent DA6 7QJ	Ms Susan Powell	01322 556333	01322 555919	303-5402	VA	11–16	918	RC G
St Columba's RC Boys' School	Halcot Ave, Bexleyheath, Kent DA6 7QB	Mr B. Cannon	01322 553236	01322 522471	303-5401	VA	11–16	829	RC B
Townley Grammar School for Girls	Townley Rd, Bexleyheath, Kent DA6 7AB	Mrs L.C. Hutchinson	020 8304 8311	020 8298 7421	303-4001	CY	11–18	1443	G
Trinity School, Belvedere	Erith Rd, Belvedere, Kent DA17 6HT	Mr Ian Collins	01322 441371	01322 436723	303-4603	VA	11–18	980	CE
Welling School	Elsa Rd, Welling, Kent DA16 1LB	Mrs Christine Jefferys	020 8304 8531	020 8301 6414	303-4021	CY	11–18	1562	
Westwood College	The Green, Welling, Kent DA16 2PE	Mrs Corinne Botten	020 8304 4916	020 8298 7121	303-4007	CY	11–16	655	

Brent

School name	Address	Headteacher	Tel	Fax	Ref	Type	Ages	Pupils	Other
Alperton Community School	Stanley Ave, Wembley, Middlesex HA0 4JE	Mrs Margaret Rafee	020 8902 2038	020 8900 1236	304-5405	FD	11–18	1451	
Capital City Academy	Doyle Gdns, London NW10 3ST	Mr Philip O'Hear	020 8838 8700	020 8838 8701	304-6905		11–18	1045	
Cardinal Hinsley Mathematics and Computing College	Harlesden Rd, London NW10 3RN	Mr Richard Kolka	020 8965 3947	020 8965 3430	304-5407	VA	11–19	465	RC B
Claremont High School	Claremont Ave, Kenton, Harrow, Middlesex HA3 0UH	Mr Terry Molloy	0870 350 0093	020 8204 3548	304-5400	FD	11–18	1461	
Convent of Jesus and Mary Language College	Crownhill Rd, London NW10 4EP	Mrs G. Freear	020 8965 2986	020 8838 0071	304-5404	VA	11–18	1016	RC G
Copland – A Specialist Science Community College	Cecil Ave, Wembley, Middlesex HA9 7DX	Sir A. Davies	020 8902 6362	020 8903 1943	304-5401	FD	11–18	1870	
JFS	The Mall, Kenton, Harrow, Middlesex HA3 9TE	Dame Ruth Robins	020 8206 3100	020 8206 3101	304-4033	VA	11–18	1931	Je
John Kelly Boys' Technology College	Crest Rd, London NW2 7SN	Mr Alexander Young	020 8452 8700	020 8208 2281	304-5408	FD	11–18	731	B
John Kelly Girls' Technology College	Crest Rd, London NW2 7SN	Mrs K. Heaps	020 8452 4842	020 8452 6024	304-5409	FD	11–18	939	G
Kingsbury High School	Princes Ave, Kingsbury, London NW9 9JR	Mr C. Chung	020 8204 9814	020 8206 0715	304-5402	FD	11–18	1957	
Preston Manor High School	Carlton Ave East, Wembley, Middlesex HA9 8NA	Mr Matthew Lantos	020 8385 4040	020 8908 2607	304-5410	FD	11–18	1362	
Queen's Park Community School	Aylestone Ave, London NW6 7BQ	Mr Mike Hulme	020 8438 1700	020 8459 1895	304-5403	FD	11–19	1190	
St Gregory RC High School	Donnington Rd, Kenton, Harrow, Middlesex HA3 0NB	Mr M.F. Earley	020 8907 8828	020 8909 1161	304-5406	VA	11–18	1002	RC
Wembley High Technology College	East La, Wembley, Middlesex HA0 3NT	Ms Gill Bal	020 8385 4800	020 8385 4899	304-4006	FD	11–18	1207	

Bromley

School name	Address	Headteacher	Tel	Fax	Ref	Type	Ages	Pupils	Other
Beaverwood School for Girls	Beaverwood Rd, Perry St, Chislehurst, Kent BR7 6HE	Mrs K. Raven	020 8300 3156	020 8300 3251	305-5408	FD	11–18	1290	G
Bishop Justus CE School	Magpie Hall La, Bromley BR2 8HZ	Mrs Kathy Griffiths	020 8315 8130	020 8315 8131	305-4604	VA	11–18	638	CE
Bullers Wood School	St Nicolas La, Logs Hill, Chislehurst, Kent BR7 5LJ	Ms Kathleen Clarke	020 8467 2280	020 8295 1425	305-5400	FD	11–18	1430	G

School name	Address	Tel	Fax	Headteacher	Ref	Type	Ages	Pupils	Other
Cator Park School	Lennard Rd, Beckenham, Kent BR3 1QR	020 8778 5917	020 8778 2043	Ms Meryl Davies	305-4002	FD	11–18	1193	G
Charles Darwin School	Jail La., Biggin Hill, Westerham, Kent TN16 3AU	01959 574043	01959 540036	Mr R.C. Higgins	305-5409	FD	11–18	1298	
Coopers Technology College	Hawkwood La., Chislehurst, Kent BR7 5PS	020 8467 3263	020 8295 0342	Mr R.A. Dilley	305-5401	FD	11–18	1603	
Darrick Wood School	Lovibonds Ave, Orpington, Kent BR6 8ER	01689 850271	01689 857257	Mrs Barbara Rhymaun	305-5418	FD	11–18	1567	
Hayes School	West Common Rd, Hayes, Bromley, Kent BR2 7DB	020 8462 2767	020 8462 0329	Mr Kieran Osborne	305-5407	FD	11–18	1553	
Kelsey Park Sports College	Manor Way, Beckenham, Kent BR3 3SJ	020 8650 8694	020 8658 5527	Mr Brian Lloyd	305-5404	FD	11–18	988	B
Kemnal Technology College	Sevenoaks Way, Sidcup, Kent DA14 5AA	020 8300 7112	020 8300 5619	Mr J.P. Atkins	305-5406	FD	11–18	1163	B
Langley Park School for Boys	Hawksbrook La., South Eden Park Road, Beckenham, Kent BR3 3BP	020 8650 9253	020 8650 5823	Mr Robert Northcott	305-5402	FD	11–18	1588	B
Langley Park School for Girls	Hawksbrook La., South Eden Park Road, Beckenham, Kent BR3 3BE	020 8663 4199	020 8663 6578	Miss Jan Sage	305-5412	FD	11–18	1632	G
Newstead Wood School for Girls	Avebury Rd, Orpington, Kent BR6 9SA	01689 853626	01689 853315	Mrs Elizabeth Allen	305-5419	FD	11–18	980	G
The Priory School	Tintagel Rd, Orpington, Kent BR5 4LG	01689 819219	01689 600842	Mr N. Ware	305-5405	FD	11–18	1322	
Ravens Wood School	Oakley Rd, Bromley, Kent BR2 8HP	01689 856050	01689 850452	Dr G. Berwick	305-5403	FD	11–19	1402	B
The Ravensbourne School	Hayes La., Bromley, Kent BR2 9EH	020 8460 0083	020 8460 7525	Mr P. Murphy	305-5413	FD	11–18	1436	
St Olave's and St Saviour's Grammar School	Goddington La., Orpington BR6 9SH	01689 820101	01689 897943	Mr A. Javis	305-5410	VA	11–18	934	CE B

Camden

School name	Address	Tel	Fax	Headteacher	Ref	Type	Ages	Pupils	Other
Acland Burghley School	Burghley Rd, London NW5 1UJ	020 7485 8515	020 7284 3462	Mr Michael Shew	202-4285	CY	11–18	1279	
The Camden School for Girls	Sandall Rd, London NW5 2DB	020 7485 3414	020 7284 3361	Ms Anne Canning	202-4611	VA	11–18	998	G
Hampstead School	Westbere Rd, Hampstead, London NW2 3RT	020 7794 8133	020 7435 8260	Mr Jacques Szemalikowski	202-4275	CY	11–18	1292	
Haverstock School	24 Haverstock Hill, Chalk Farm, London NW3 2BQ	020 7267 0975	020 7267 3807	Mr John Dowd	202-4104	CY	11–18	1173	
La Sainte Union RC Secondary School	Highgate Rd, London NW5 1RP	020 7428 4600	020 7267 7647	Sr Teresa Finn	202-5401	VA	11–18	1170	RC G
Maria Fidelis Roman RC Convent School FCJ	34 Phoenix Rd, London NW1 1TA	020 7387 3856	020 7388 9558	Mrs Pauline Williams	202-4652	VA	11–18	870	RC G
Parliament Hill School	Highgate Rd, London NW5 1RL	020 7485 7077	020 7485 9524	Ms Susan Higgins	202-4166	CY	11–18	1188	G
South Camden Community School	Charrington St, London NW1 1RG	020 7387 0126	020 7387 0739	Ms Rosemary Leeke	202-4196	CY	11–18	1077	
William Ellis School	Highgate Rd, London NW5 1RN	020 7267 9346	020 7284 1274	Mr Richard Tanton	202-4688	VA	11–18	916	B

City of London

School name	Address	Tel	Fax	Headteacher	Ref	Type	Ages	Pupils	Other
St Paul's Cathedral School	2 New Change, London EC4M 9AD	020 7248 5156	020 7329 6568	Mr A. Dobbin	201-6006		4–13	224	Ch

Croydon

School name	Address	Tel	Fax	Headteacher	Ref	Type	Ages	Pupils	Other
Addington High School	Fairchildes Ave, New Addington, Croydon, Surrey CR0 0AH	01689 842545	01689 843504	Mr Tim Davies	306-4042	CY	11–16	809	
The Archbishop Lanfranc School	Mitcham Rd, Croydon, Surrey CR9 3AS	020 8689 1255	020 8683 3113	Mr D.C. Clark	306-5408	FD	11–16	1017	
Archbishop Tenison's CE High School	Selborne Rd, Croydon, Surrey CR0 5JQ	020 8688 4014	020 8681 6336	Mr Richard Parrish	306-4600	VA	11–16	753	CE
Ashburton Community School	Shirley Rd, Croydon, Surrey CR9 7AL	020 8656 0222	020 8656 1474	Mr R.V. Warne	306-4034	CY	11–16	1071	
BRIT School for Performing Arts and Technology	60 The Crescent, Croydon, Surrey CR0 2HN	020 8665 5242	020 8665 5197	Mr N. Williams	306-6900		14–19	855	
Coloma Convent Girls' School	Upper Shirley Rd, Croydon, Surrey CR9 5AS	020 8654 6228	020 8656 6485	Mrs M. Martin	306-5405	VA	11–18	1053	RC G
Coulsdon High School	Homefield Rd, Old Coulsdon, Coulsdon, Surrey CR5 1ES	01737 551161	01737 557410	Mr Colin Mackinlay	306-5404	FD	11–16	711	
Edenham High School	Orchard Way, Shirley, Croydon, Surrey CR0 7NJ	020 8776 0220	020 8777 3904	Ms Jacinthe Downes	306-5401	FD	11–16	1148	

3

School name	Address	Tel	Fax	Headteacher	Ref	Type	Ages	Pupils	Other
Haling Manor High School	Kendra Hall Rd, South Croydon, Surrey CR2 6DT	020 8681 1141	020 8681 1144	Mr D.J. Troake	306-4036	FD	11–16	811	
Harris Academy South Norwood	South Norwood Hill, London SE25 6AD	020 8404 5100			306-6905		11–19		
Harris City Academy Crystal Palace	Maberley Rd, Upper Norwood, London SE19 2JH	020 8771 2261	020 8771 7531	Dr Daniel Moynihan	306-6906		11–18		
Harris City Technology College	Maberley Rd, Upper Norwood, London SE19 2JH	020 8771 2261	020 8771 7531	Dr Daniel Moynihan	306-6901		11–18	1043	
Norbury Manor Business and Enterprise College for Girls	Kensington Ave, Thornton Heath, Surrey CR7 8BT	020 8679 0062	020 8679 8007	Miss C. Nicholls	306-5406	FD	11–19	962	G
Riddlesdown High School	Honister Heights, Purley, Surrey CR8 1EX	020 8668 5136	020 8660 9025	Dr D.R. Dibbs	306-5400	VA	11–16	1543	
St Andrew's CE VA High School	Warrington Rd, Croydon, Surrey CR0 4BH	020 8686 8306	020 8681 6320	Mr David Matthews	306-4603	VA	11–16	615	CE
St Joseph's College	Beulah Hill, London SE19 3HL	020 8761 1426	020 8761 7667	Mr Eamon Connolly	306-5402	VA	11–18	1031	RC B
St Marys Catholic High School	Woburn Rd, Croydon, Surrey CR0 2AB	020 8686 3837	020 8781 1264	Mr Ejiro Robert Ughwujabo	306-4702	VA	11–16	734	RC
Selhurst Mathematics and Computing Specialist School	The Crescent, Croydon, Surrey CR0 2HN	020 8665 7989	020 8665 0119	Mrs J. Pickering	306-4008	CY	11–16	488	B
Selsdon High School	Farnborough Ave, South Croydon, Surrey CR2 8HD	020 8657 8935	020 8651 6065	Mrs Janet Packer	306-4033	CY	11–16	902	
Shirley High School Performing Arts College	Shirley Church Rd, Croydon, Surrey CR0 5EF	020 8656 9755	020 8654 8507	Mr Nigel Barrow	306-5407	FD	11–18	937	
Stanley Technical High School for Boys	Davidson Rd, Croydon, CR0 6DD	020 8655 3264	020 8771 7588	Mr Paul Morris	306-4602	VA	11–16	607	B
Thomas More RC School	Russell Hill Rd, Purley, Surrey CR8 2XP	020 8668 6251	020 8660 9003	Mr John Casey	306-5403	VA	11–16	735	RC
Virgo Fidelis Convent Senior School	147 Central Hill, Upper Norwood, London SE19 1RS	020 8670 6917	020 8761 4455	Sr Bernadette	306-5900	VA	11–18	787	RC G
Westwood Language College for Girls	Spurgeon Rd, Upper Norwood, London SE19 3UG	020 8653 1661	020 8771 6573	Ms Margaret Hedley	306-4024	CY	11–16	851	G
Woodcote High School	Meadow Rise, Coulsdon, Surrey CR5 2EH	020 8668 6464	020 8660 9038	Mr M.A. Southworth	306-4031	CY	11–16	1035	

Ealing

School name	Address	Tel	Fax	Headteacher	Ref	Type	Ages	Pupils	Other
Acton High School	Gunnersbury La, Acton, London W3 8EY	020 3110 2400	020 3110 2499	Ms Mandy Golding	307-4035	CY	11–16	1027	
Brentside High School	Greenford Ave, Hanwell, London W7 1JJ	020 8575 9162	020 8833 2100	Mr Arwel Jones	307-5400	FD	11–19	1213	
The Cardinal Wiseman Roman RC School	Greenford Rd, Greenford, Middlesex UB6 9AW	020 8575 8222	020 8575 9963	Mr P. Patrick	307-4603	VA	11–18	1809	RC
Dormers Wells High School	Dormers Wells La, Southall, Middlesex UB1 3HZ	020 8813 8671	020 8813 8861	Mrs Janet Leigh	307-5403	FD	11–16	886	
Drayton Manor High School	Drayton Bridge Rd, London W7 1EU	020 8357 1900	020 8357 1901	Sir P. Singh	307-5403	FD	11–19	1563	
The Ellen Wilkinson School for Girls	Queen's Dr, Acton, London W3 0HW	020 8752 1525	020 8993 6632	Ms Chris Sydenham	307-5402	FD	11–18	1379	G
Elthorne Park High School	Westlea Rd, Hanwell, London W7 2AD	020 8566 1166	020 8566 1177	Mr Mohammed Sabur	307-4036	CY	11–16	901	
Featherstone High School	11 Montague Waye, Southall, Middlesex UB2 5HF	020 8843 0984	020 8574 3405	Ms T. Cox	307-4031	CY	11–16	1172	
Greenford High School	Lady Margaret Rd, Southall, Greenford, Middlesex UB1 2GU	020 8578 9152	020 8747 7891	Mrs K. Griffin	307-5401	FD	11–19	1641	
Northolt High School	Eastcote La, Northolt, Middlesex UB5 4HP	020 8864 8544	020 8426 9207	Mr Chris Modi	307-5404	FD	11–18	1327	
Twyford CE High School	Twyford Cres, Acton, London W3 9PP	020 8752 0141	020 8993 7627	Ms Alice Hudson	307-4602	VA	11–18	1293	CE
Villiers High School	Boyd Ave, Southall, Middlesex UB1 3BT	020 8813 8001	020 8574 3071	Ms J. Strang	307-4020	CY	11–16	1141	

Enfield

School name	Address	Tel	Fax	Headteacher	Ref	Type	Ages	Pupils	Other
Albany School	Bell La, Enfield, Middlesex EN3 5PA	020 8804 1648	020 8805 9949	Ms L. Dawes	308-5402	FD	11–18	1452	
Bishop Stopford's School	Brick La, Enfield, Middlesex EN1 3PU	020 8804 1906	020 8805 9434	Mrs Bridget Evans	308-4702	VA	11–18	1076	CE
Broomfield School	Wilmer Way, London N14 7HY	020 8368 1287	020 8368 1287	Mr Angus Walker	308-5401	FD	11–18	1376	
Chace Community School	Churchbury La, Enfield, Middlesex EN1 3HQ	020 8363 7321	020 8342 1241	Ms S. Warrington	308-4037	CY	11–18	1224	
Edmonton County School	Gt Cambridge Rd, Enfield, Middlesex EN1 1HQ	020 8360 3158	020 8364 2218	Ms Siobhan Leahy	308-4007	CY	11–18	1660	
Enfield County School	Holly Wlk, Enfield, Middlesex EN2 6QG	020 8363 3030	020 8367 6569	Miss Irene Byard	308-4030	CY	11–18	1122	G
Enfield Grammar School	Market Pl, Enfield, Middlesex EN2 6LN	020 8363 1095	020 8342 1805	Mr John Kerr	308-5404	FD	11–18	1122	B

School name	Address	Tel	Fax	Headteacher	Ref	Type	Ages	Pupils	Other
Essential Achievers	83 Ridge Ave, Winchmore Hill, London N21 2RH	020 8364 3192	0208 373 2953		308-6066		11–16	6	
The Gladys Aylward School	Windmill Rd, Edmonton, London N18 1NB	020 8803 1738	020 8807 6285	Mr I. Lucas	308-4027	CY	11–18	1359	
Highlands School	148 Worlds End La, London N21 1QQ	020 8370 1100	020 8370 1110	Mrs M. Cross	308-4043	CY	11–18	1394	
Kingsmead School	Southbury Rd, Enfield, Middlesex EN1 1YQ	020 8363 3037	020 8366 3709	Mr G. Bird	308-4015	CY	11–18	1392	
The Latymer School	Haselbury Rd, London N9 9TN	020 8807 4037	020 8807 4125	Mr Mark Garbett	308-5400	VA	11–18	1397	
Lea Valley High School	Bullsmoor La, Enfield, Middlesex EN3 6TW	01992 763666	01992 760152	Ms Janet Cullen	308-4038	CY	11–18	1143	
Oasis Academy Enfield	Kinetic Cres, Innova Park, Enfield EN3 7XH	01992 655400	01992 655401	John Walton	308-6905		11–18		Ch
St Anne's RC High School for Girls	Oakthorpe Rd, Palmers Green, London N13 5TY	020 8886 2165	020 8886 6552	Mrs C. Byamukama	308-4706	VA	11–18	1098	RC G
St Ignatius College	Turkey St, Enfield, Middlesex EN1 4NP	01992 717835	01992 652070	Mr P. Adams	308-5403	VA	11–18	1148	RC B
Salisbury School	Turin Rd, Edmonton, London N9 8DQ	020 8372 5678	020 8372 0303	Mr Trevor Averre-Beeson	308-4041	CY	11–18	1254	
Southgate School	Sussex Way, Cockfosters, Barnet, Hertfordshire EN4 0BL	020 8449 9583	020 8441 6424	Mr Anthony Wilde	308-4023	CY	11–18	1532	
Winchmore School	Laburnum Gr, Winchmore Hill, London N21 3HS	020 8360 7773	020 8360 8409	Mrs Lesley Mansbridge	308-4026	CY	11–18	1468	

Greenwich

School name	Address	Tel	Fax	Headteacher	Ref	Type	Ages	Pupils	Other
Blackheath Bluecoat CE Secondary School	Old Dover Rd, Blackheath, London SE3 8SY	020 8269 4300	020 8853 5978	Mr Paul Petty	203-4715	VA	11–18	866	CE
Crown Woods School	Riefield Rd, Eltham, London SE9 2QN	020 8850 7678	020 8294 1921	Mr M.J. Murphy	203-4271	CY	11–18	1734	
Eltham Green Specialist Sports College	1 Middle Park Ave, Eltham, London SE9 5EQ	020 8859 0133	020 8294 1890	Mrs Anne Barton	203-4257	CY	11–18	1082	
Eltham Hill Technology College for Girls	Eltham Hill, London SE9 5EE	020 8859 2843	020 8294 2365	Mrs M. Findlay-Stone	203-4077	CY	11–16	944	G
The John Roan School	Maze Hill, Blackheath, London SE3 7UD	020 8516 7555	020 8858 9101	Mr Carl Dent	203-4508	VC	11–18	1138	
Kidbrooke School	Corelli Rd, Shooters Hill Rd, London SE3 8EP	020 8516 7977	020 8516 7980	Ms T. Jaffe	203-4243	CY	11–19	1299	
Plumstead Manor-Negus School	Old Mill Rd, London SE18 1QF	020 3260 3333	020 3260 3121	Ms J. Harding	203-4130	CY	11–19	1773	G
St Pauls Academy	Wickham La, Abbey Wood, London SE2 0XX	020 8311 3868	020 8312 1642	Mr Patrick Winston	203-6905		11–16	700	RC
St Thomas More Roman RC Comprehensive School	Footscray Rd, London SE9 2SU	020 8850 6700	020 8294 1855	Mr Markus Ryan	203-4716	VA	11–16	609	RC
St Ursula's Convent School	Crooms Hill, Greenwich, London SE10 8HN	020 8858 4613	020 8305 0560	Mrs Geraldine Scanlan	203-4682	VA	11–16	625	RC G
Thomas Tallis School	Kidbrooke Park Rd, Kidbrooke, London SE3 9PX	020 8856 0115	020 8319 4715	Mr R. Thomas	203-4294	CY	11–19	1654	
Woolwich Polytechnic School for Boys	Hutchins Rd, Thamesmead, London SE28 8AT	020 8310 7000	020 8310 6464	Mr Byron Parker	203-4250	CY	11–18	1188	B

Hackney

School name	Address	Tel	Fax	Headteacher	Ref	Type	Ages	Pupils	Other
The Bridge Academy Hackney	Laburnum St, Hackney, London E2 8BA	020 7729 4623	020 7567 4058	Sunita Bains	204-6907		11–18		
Cardinal Pole Roman RC School	Kenworthy Rd, Homerton, London E9 5RB	020 8985 5150	020 8533 7325	Mr Mannion	204-4714	VA	11–19	999	RC
Clapton Girls' Technology College	Laura Pl, Lower Clapton Rd, London E5 0RB	020 8985 6641	020 8986 4686	Ms C.T. Day	204-4302	CY	11–19	867	G
Hackney Free and Parochial CE Secondary School Specialist Sports College	Paragon Rd, Hackney, London E9 6NR	020 8985 2430	020 8533 5441	Mrs J. Barnes	204-4697	VA	11–16	715	CE
Haggerston School	Weymouth Terr, London E2 8LS	020 7739 7324	020 7739 8603	Ms Maggie Kalnins	204-4283	CY	11–16	867	G
Mossbourne Community Academy	Downs Park Rd, London E5 8JY	020 8525 5200	020 8525 5222	Sir Michael Wilshaw	204-6905		11–16	613	
Our Lady's Convent Roman RC High School	6–16 Amhurst Pk, Stamford Hill, London N16 5AF	020 8800 2158	020 8809 8898	Mrs J. Gray	204-4641	VA	11–18	738	RC G
The Petchey Academy	Shacklewell La, London E8 2HD	020 7254 8722	020 7254 8870	Mr David Daniels	204-6906		11–18	180	
The Skinners' Company's School for Girls	117 Stamford Hill, London N16 5RS	020 8800 7411	020 8809 1382	Ms J.A. Wilkins	204-4686	VA	11–18	796	G
Stoke Newington School	Clissold Rd, Hackney, London N16 9EY	020 7254 0548	020 7923 2451	Mr Mark Emmerson	204-4310	CY	11–16	1285	
Yesodey Hatorah Senior Girls School	Egerton Rd, Stamford Hill, London N16 6UB	020 8826 5500	020 8826 5505	Mrs Rachel Pinter	204-4318	VA	11–16	235	Je G

3

Hammersmith and Fulham

School name	Address	Tel	Fax	Headteacher	Ref	Type	Ages	Pupils	Other
Burlington Danes Academy	Wood La, London W12 0HR	020 8735 4950	020 8740 5659	Mr Malcolm Wheeler	205-6905		11-18	807	CE
Fulham Cross Girls' School and Language College	Munster Rd, London SW6 6BP	020 7381 0861	020 7386 5979	Ms Carol Jones	205-4315	CY	11-16	599	G
Henry Compton Secondary School	Kingwood Rd, Fulham Palace Rd, London SW6 6SN	020 7381 3606	020 7386 9645	Mr D. Ramjee	205-4106	CY	11-16	609	B
Hurlingham and Chelsea Secondary School	Peterborough Rd, Fulham, London SW6 3ED	020 7731 2581	020 7736 7455	Mr Phil Cross	205-4319	CY	11-16	544	
Lady Margaret School	Parson's Grn, London SW6 4UN	020 7736 7138	020 7384 2553	Mrs Sally Whyte	205-4632	VA	11-18	594	CE G
Phoenix High School	The Curve, London W12 0RQ	020 8749 1141	020 8740 0393	Mr W.S. Atkinson	205-4314	CY	11-16	757	
Sacred Heart High School	212 Hammersmith Rd, (Entrance Bute Gardens), Hammersmith, London W6 7DG	020 8748 7600	020 8748 0392	Dr C.T. Carpenter	205-4620	VA	11-16	789	RC G

Haringey

School name	Address	Tel	Fax	Headteacher	Ref	Type	Ages	Pupils	Other
Alexandra Park School	Bidwell Gdns, London N11 2AZ	020 8826 4880	020 8888 2236	Mrs R. Hudson	309-4036	CY	11-18	1200	
Fortismere School	Southwing, Tetherdown, Muswell Hill, London N10 1NE	020 8365 4400	020 8444 7822	Mr A.M. Nixon	309-4032	FD	11-18	1652	
Gladesmore Community School	Crowland Rd, Tottenham, London N15 6EB	020 8800 0884	020 8809 8500	Mr T. Hartney	309-4033	CY	11-18	1290	
Greig City Academy	High St, Hornsey, London N8 7NU	020 8609 0100	020 8341 3290	Mr Paul Sutton	309-6905		11-18	787	CE
Haringey Sixth Form Centre	White Hart La, London N17 8HR				309-4704	CY	16-18		
Highgate Wood Secondary School	Montenotte Rd, London N8 8RN	020 8342 7970	020 8342 7978	Mr Patrick Cozier	309-4030	CY	11-18	1413	
Hornsey School for Girls	Inderwick Rd, London N8 9JF	020 8348 6191	020 8340 1214	Mr Andy Yarrow	309-4029	CY	11-18	1477	G
The John Loughborough School	Holcombe Rd, Tottenham, London N17 9AD	020 8808 7837	020 8801 6719	Dr June M. Alexis	309-5900	VA	11-16	292	SDA
Northumberland Park Community School	Trulock Rd, Tottenham, London N17 0PG	020 8801 0091		Mr Andrew Kilpatrick	309-4031	CY	11-18	1024	
Park View Academy	Langham Rd, London N15 3RB	020 8888 1722	020 8881 8143	Mr Alex Atherton	309-4037	CY	11-18	1268	
St Thomas More Catholic School	Glendale Ave, Wood Green, London N22 5HN	020 8888 7122	020 8826 9370	Dr C.J. Hickey	309-4703	VA	11-18	1140	RC
Woodside High School, a Business and Enterprise Specialist School	White Hart La, Wood Green, London N22 5QJ	020 8889 6761	020 8365 8164	Joan McVittie	309-4034	CY	11-18	1110	

Harrow

School name	Address	Tel	Fax	Headteacher	Ref	Type	Ages	Pupils	Other
Bentley Wood High School	Bridges Rd, Stanmore, Middlesex HA7 3NA	020 8954 3623	020 8954 0427	Ms Janice Howkins	310-4032	CY	12-16	714	G
Canons High School	Shaldon Rd, Edgware, Middlesex HA8 6AN	020 8951 5780	020 8951 2333	Ms Lyn Rowlands	310-4022	CY	12-16	712	
Harrow High School and Sports College	Gayton Rd, Harrow, Middlesex HA1 2JG	020 8861 7300	020 8861 4024	Ms Vivien Swaida	310-4033	CY	12-16	696	
Hatch End High School	Headstone La, Harrow, Middlesex HA3 6NR	020 8428 4330	020 8420 1932	Mr Allan D. Jones	310-4020	CY	12-16	1204	
Nower Hill High School	George V Ave, Pinner, Middlesex HA5 5RP	020 8863 0877	020 8424 0762	Mr Howard Freed	310-4024	CY	12-16	1211	
Park High School	Thistlecroft Gdns, Stanmore, Middlesex HA7 1PL	020 8952 2803	020 8952 6975	Mr A. Barnes	310-4021	CY	12-16	1127	
Rooks Heath High School	Eastcote La, South Harrow, Harrow, Middlesex HA2 9AG	020 8422 4675	020 8422 4407	Dr J. Reavley	310-4027	CY	12-16	934	
The Sacred Heart Language College	High St, Wealdstone, Harrow, Middlesex HA3 7AY	020 8863 9922	020 8861 5051	Mrs M. Waplington	310-4700	VA	12-16	743	RC G
Salvatorian Roman RC College	High Rd, Harrow Weald, Harrow, Middlesex HA3 5DY	020 8863 2706	020 8863 3435	Mr A.M. Graham	310-5400	VA	11-16	700	RC B
Whitmore High School	Porlock Ave, Harrow, Middlesex HA2 0AD	020 8864 7688	020 8869 4870	Ms S. Hammond	310-4026	CY	12-16	1047	

Havering

School name	Address	Tel	Fax	Headteacher	Ref	Type	Ages	Pupils	Other
Abbs Cross School and Arts College	Abbs Cross La, Hornchurch, Essex RM12 4YB	01708 440304	01708 620360	Mr Glenn Mayoh	311-5401	FD	11–16	843	
The Albany, A Business and Enterprise College	Broadstone Rd, off Albany Rd, Hornchurch, Essex RM12 4AJ	01708 441537	01708 437157	Mrs M. Johnson	311-4038	CY	11–16	923	
Bower Park School	Havering Rd North, Romford, Essex RM1 4YY	01708 730244	01708 741748	Mrs Mary Morrison	311-4042	CY	11–16	747	
Brittons School and Technology College	Ford La, Rainham, Essex RM13 7BB	01708 630002	01708 630325	Mr Robert Sheffield	311-4003	CY	11–16	1128	
The Campion School	Wingletye La, Hornchurch, Essex RM11 3BX	01708 452332	01708 456995	Mr John Johnson	311-4700	VA	11–18	995	RC B
The Chafford School, A Specialist Business and Enterprise College	Lambs La South, Rainham, Essex RM13 9XD	01708 552811	01708 522098	Mrs Cheryl Hassell	311-4011	CY	11–16	934	
The Coopers' Company and Coborn School	St Mary's La, Upminster, Essex RM14 3HS	01708 250500	01708 226109	Mr David Parry	311-5402	VA	11–18	1321	Ch
Emerson Park School	Wych Elm Rd, Hornchurch, Essex RM11 3AD	01708 475285	01708 620963	Mr Adrian May	311-4006	CY	11–16	961	
The Frances Bardsley School for Girls	Brentwood Rd, Romford, Essex RM1 2RR	01708 447368	01708 442729	Mrs Suzanne Philipps	311-5400	FD	11–18	1238	G
Gaynes School Language College	Brackendale Gdns, Upminster, Essex RM14 3UX	01708 502900	01708 502901	Mr Russell G. Ayling	311-4026	CY	11–16	939	
Hall Mead School	Marlborough Gdns, Upminster, Essex RM14 1SF	01708 229655	01708 220232	Mr Sam Berwitz	311-4000	CY	11–16	963	
King's Wood School	Settle Rd, Harold Hill, Romford, Essex RM3 9XR	01708 371331		Mrs Delia Mulholland	311-4039	CY	11–16	604	
Marshalls Park School	Pettits La, Romford, Essex RM1 4EH	01708 724134	01708 746021	Mrs P. Mason	311-4037	CY	11–16	771	
Redden Court School	Cotswold Rd, Harold Wood, Romford, Essex RM3 0TS	01708 342293	01708 386550	Mr Peter Townrow	311-4001	CY	11–16	636	
The Royal Liberty School	Upper Brentwood Rd, Romford, Essex RM2 6HJ	01708 730141	01708 723950	Mrs Julia Deery	311-4025	CY	11–16	566	B
Sacred Heart of Mary Girls' School	70 St Mary's La, Upminster, Essex RM14 2QR	01708 222660	01708 226686	Mrs Bernie Williams	311-5403	VA	11–18	807	RC G
St Edward's CofE Comprehensive School, Language College and Sixth Form Centre	London Rd, Romford, Essex RM7 9NX	01708 730462	01708 731485	Mr Giles Drew	311-4600	VA	11–18	1255	CE
The Sanders Draper School and Specialist Science College	Suttons La, Hornchurch, Essex RM12 6RT	01708 443068	01708 479005	Ms Tess Blight	311-4009	CY	11–16	954	

Hillingdon

School name	Address	Tel	Fax	Headteacher	Ref	Type	Ages	Pupils	Other
Abbotsfield School	Clifton Gdns, Hillingdon, Hillingdon, Middlesex UB10 0EX	01895 237350	01895 271995	Mr David Henderson	312-5409	FD	11–18	586	B
Barnhill Community High School	Yeading La, Hayes, Middlesex UB4 9LE	020 8839 0600	020 8839 0661	Mr Ian Marshall	312-5412	FD	11–18	1332	
Bishop Ramsey CE VA Secondary School	Hume Way, Ruislip, Middlesex HA4 8EE	01895 639227	01895 622429	Mr Andrew Wilcock	312-4600	VA	11–18	1209	CE
Bishopshalt School	Royal La, Hillingdon, Uxbridge, Middlesex UB8 3RF	01895 233909	01895 273102	Mr David Bocock	312-5400	FD	11–18	1255	
The Douay Martyrs RC School	Edinburgh Dr, Ickenham, Uxbridge, Middlesex UB10 8QY	01895 679400	01895 678953	Mrs Geraldine Davies	312-5408	VA	11–18	1349	RC
Guru Nanak Sikh VA Secondary School	Springfield Rd, Hayes, Middlesex UB4 0LT	020 8573 6085	020 8561 6772	Mr Rajinder Singh Sandhu	312-4654	VA	11–18	501	Sikh
The Harefield Academy	Northwood Way, Harefield, Uxbridge UB9 6ET	01895 822108	01895 822414	Lynn Gadd	312-6906		11–18	563	
Harlington Community School	Pinkwell La, Harlington, Hayes, Middlesex UB3 1PB	020 8569 1610	020 8569 1624	Mr N. Sherman	312-5411	FD	11–18	1293	
Haydon School	Wiltshire La, Eastcote, Pinner, Middlesex HA5 2LX	020 8429 0005	020 8429 0088	Mr P. Woods	312-5401	FD	11–18	1997	
Mellow Lane School	Hewens Rd, Hayes, Middlesex UB4 8JP	020 8573 1039	020 8813 7058	Ms Marian Lewis	312-5407	FD	11–18	1240	
Northwood School	Potter St, Northwood, Middlesex HA6 1QG	01923 836363	01923 836010	Mrs Carol Ketley	312-5405	FD	11–18	1023	
Queensmead School	Queen's Wlk, Ruislip, Middlesex HA4 0LS	020 8845 6266	020 8845 8852	Mr N. McLaughlin	312-5403	FD	11–18	1238	
Rosedale College	Wood End Green Rd, Hayes, Middlesex UB3 2SE	020 8573 2097	020 8573 0280	Mr C. Neathey	312-5406	FD	11–18	663	
Ruislip High School	Sidmouth Dr, Ruislip, Middlesex HA4 0BY	01895 464064	01895 675331	Mr John Goulborn	312-4023	CY	11–18	150	
Stockley Academy	Park View Rd, Hillingdon UB8 3GA	01895 430066	01895 430062	Mr Fred Groom	312-6905		11–18	739	B
Swakeleys School	Clifton Gdns, Hillingdon, Uxbridge, Middlesex UB10 0EJ	01895 251962	01895 235027	Mrs Sue Pryor	312-5410	FD	11–18	1055	G
Uxbridge High School	The Greenway, Uxbridge, Middlesex UB8 2PR	01895 234060	01895 256738	Mr Peter Lang	312-5404	FD	11–18	1089	
Vyners School	Warren Rd, Ickenham, Uxbridge, Middlesex UB10 8AB	01895 234342	01895 237955	Mr Brian Houghton	312-5402	FD	11–18	1116	

Hounslow

School name	Address	Tel	Fax	Headteacher	Ref	Type	Ages	Pupils	Other
Brentford School for Girls	5 Boston Manor Rd, Brentford, Middlesex TW8 0PG	020 8847 4281	020 8568 2093	Mrs Julie Tomkins	313-4024	CY	11–18	836	G
Chiswick Community School	Burlington La., Chiswick, London W4 3UN	020 8747 0031	020 8747 6620	Mr Alan Howson	313-4020	CY	11–18	1220	
Cranford Community College	High St, Cranford, Hounslow, Middlesex TW5 9PD	020 8897 2001	020 8759 8073	Mr K. Prunty	313-4029	CY	11–18	1417	
Feltham Community College	Browells La., Feltham, Middlesex TW13 7EF	020 8831 3000	020 8751 4914	Mrs G.B. Smith	313-4023	CY	11–18	1235	
The Green School	Busch Corner, Isleworth, Middlesex TW7 5BB	020 8321 8080	020 8321 8081	Mrs P. Butterfield	313-4600	VA	11–18	795	CE G
Gumley House RC Convent School, FCJ	St John's Rd, Isleworth, Middlesex TW7 6XF	020 8568 8692	020 8758 2674	Sr Brenda Wallace	313-5400	VA	11–18	1183	RC G
Gunnersbury RC School	The Ride, Boston Manor Rd, Brentford, Middlesex TW8 9LB	020 8568 7281	020 8569 7946	Mr J. Heffernan	313-5401	VA	11–18	1143	RC B
The Heathland School	Wellington Rd South, Hounslow, Middlesex TW4 5JD	020 8572 4411	020 8569 5126	Mr H.S. Pattar	313-4028	CY	11–18	1837	
Heston Community School	Heston Rd, Heston, Hounslow, Middlesex TW5 0QR	020 8572 1931	020 8570 2647	Mr Philip Ward	313-4026	CY	11–19	1265	
Hounslow Manor School	Prince Regent Rd, Hounslow, Middlesex TW3 1NE	020 8572 4461	020 8577 1605	Mr Roger Shortt	313-4021	CY	11–18	952	
Isleworth and Syon School for Boys	Ridgeway Rd, Isleworth, Middlesex TW7 5LJ	020 8568 5791	020 8568 1939	Mr Euan Ferguson	313-4500	VC	11–18	992	B
Lampton School	Lampton Ave, Hounslow, Middlesex TW3 4EP	020 8572 1936	020 8572 8500	Mrs Susan John	313-4027	CY	11–18	1382	
Longford Community School	Tachbrook Rd, Feltham, Middlesex TW14 9PE	020 8890 0245	020 8844 2441	Mrs A. Dalglish	313-4022	CY	11–18	1193	
St Mark's RC School	106 Bath Rd, Hounslow, Middlesex TW3 3EJ	020 8577 3600	020 8577 0559	Mr Paul Enright	313-4800	VA	11–18	1232	RC

Islington

School name	Address	Tel	Fax	Headteacher	Ref	Type	Ages	Pupils	Other
Central Foundation Boys' School	Cowper St, City Rd, London EC2A 4SH	020 7253 3741	020 7336 7295	Ms J. Fortune	206-4614	VA	11–18	788	B
Elizabeth Garrett Anderson Language College	Risinghill St, off Penton St, London N1 9QG	020 7837 0739	020 7278 9764	Ms Jo Dibb	206-4324	CY	11–16	1097	G
Highbury Fields School	Highbury Hill, London N5 1AR	020 7288 1888	020 7288 2121	Mr B. McWilliams	206-4307	CY	11–18	782	G
Highbury Grove School	Highbury New Pk, London N5 2EG	020 7288 8900	020 7690 8654	Ms Truda White	206-4108	CY	11–18	1109	
Holloway School	Hilldrop Rd, London N7 0JG	020 7607 5885	020 7700 3697	Mr Bob Hamlyn	206-4112	CY	11–16	859	
Islington Arts and Media School	Turle Rd, London N4 3LS	020 7281 3302	020 7281 5514	Mr Richard Ewen	206-4325	CY	11–16	853	
Islington Green School	Prebend St, London N1 8PQ	020 7226 8611	020 7226 9363	Mr Trevor Averre-Beeson	206-4211	CY	11–16	890	
Mount Carmel RC Technology College for Girls	Holland Wlk, Duncombe Rd, London N19 3EU	020 7281 3536	020 7281 0420	Mr John Paul Kehoe	206-4704	VA	11–16	689	RC G
St Aloysius RC College	Hornsey La., Highgate, London N6 5LY	020 7263 1391	020 7263 5963	Mr Tom Mannion	206-4651	VA	11–16	870	RC B
St Mary Magdalene Academy	Liverpool Rd, Islington N7 8PG				206-6905		4–19		CE

Kensington and Chelsea

School name	Address	Tel	Fax	Headteacher	Ref	Type	Ages	Pupils	Other
The Cardinal Vaughan Memorial RC School	89 Addison Rd, London W14 8BZ	020 7603 8478	020 7602 3124	Mr M. Gormally	207-5402	VA	11–18	903	RC B
Holland Park School	Airlie Gdns, Campden Hill Rd, London W8 7AF	020 7727 5631	020 7243 0176	Mr Colin Hall	207-4320	CY	11–18	1401	
St Thomas More Language College	Cadogan St, London SW3 2QS	020 7589 9734	020 7823 7868	Mr G. Connolly	207-4681	VA	11–16	636	RC
Sion-Manning RC School for Girls	St Charles Sq, London W10 6EL	020 8969 7111	020 8969 5119	Mrs C.M. Leach	207-4801	VA	11–16	570	RC G

Kingston upon Thames

School name	Address	Tel	Fax	Headteacher	Ref	Type	Ages	Pupils	Other
Chessington Community College	Garrison La., Chessington, Surrey KT9 2JS	020 8974 1156	020 8974 2603	Mr David Kemp	314-4006	VA	11–18	730	
Coombe Boys' School	College Gdns, Blakes La., New Malden, Surrey KT3 6NU	020 8949 1537	020 8942 6725	Mrs Carol Campbell	314-5403	FD	11–18	508	B
Coombe Girls' School	Clarence Ave, New Malden, Surrey KT3 3TU	020 8942 1242	020 8942 6385	Mrs Carol Campbell	314-4004	CY	11–18	1499	G

School name	Address	Tel	Fax	Headteacher	Ref	Type	Ages	Pupils	Other
The Hollyfield School and Sixth Form Centre	Surbiton Hill Rd, Surbiton, Surrey KT6 4TU	020 8339 4500		Mr S. Chamberlain	314-5404	FD	11–18	1048	
The Holy Cross School	25 Sandal Rd, New Malden, Surrey KT3 5AR	020 8395 4225	020 8395 4234	Mr T. Gibson	314-5402	VA	11–18	923	RC G
Richard Challoner School	Manor Dr North, New Malden, Surrey KT3 5PE	020 8330 5947	020 8330 3842	Mr T. Cahill	314-5401	VA	11–18	859	RC B
Southborough High School	Hook Rd, Surbiton, Surrey KT6 5AS	020 8391 4324	020 8391 0177	Mr J. Rook	314-4009	CY	11–18	745	B
The Tiffin Girls' School	Richmond Rd, Kingston Upon Thames, Surrey KT2 5PL	020 8546 0773	020 8547 0191	Mrs P. Cox	314-4010	CY	11–18	902	G
Tiffin School	Queen Elizabeth Rd, Kingston Upon Thames, Surrey KT2 6RL	020 8546 4638	020 8546 6365	Mr Sean Heslop	314-5400	VA	11–18	1060	CE B
Tolworth Girls' School and Centre for Continuing Education	Fullers Way North, Surbiton, Surrey KT6 7LQ	020 8397 3854	020 8974 2600	Mrs C. Williams	314-4011	FD	11–18	1387	G

Lambeth

School name	Address	Tel	Fax	Headteacher	Ref	Type	Ages	Pupils	Other
Archbishop Tenison's School	55 Kennington Oval, London SE11 5SR	020 7735 3771	020 7587 5186	Mr B. Jones	208-5403	VA	11–18	528	CE B
Bishop Thomas Grant RC Secondary School	Belltrees Gr, London SW16 2HY	020 8769 3294	020 8769 4917	Mr Louis Desa	208-5401	VA	11–16	904	RC
Charles Edward Brooke School	Brooke Site Langton Rd, London SW9 6UL	020 7793 3901	020 7735 8132	Mrs Wendy Cooper	208-4509	VA	11–18	880	CE G
Dunraven School	94–98 Leigham Court Rd, Streatham, London SW16 2QB	020 8677 2431	020 8664 7242	Mr David Boyle	208-5402	FD	11–18	1213	
Elmgreen School	Elmcourt Rd, London SE27 9BZ	020 8766 5020		Ms Asma Mansuri	208-4731	VC	11–19		
La Retraite Roman RC Girls' School	Atkins Rd, London SW12 0AB	020 8673 5644	020 8675 8577	Ms S. Powell	208-5400	VA	11–18	853	RC G
Lambeth Academy	Elms Rd, Clapham, London SW4 9ET	020 7819 4700	020 7819 4701	Mr Stephen Potter	208-6905		11–18	532	Ch
Lilian Baylis Technology School	323 Kennington La, Kennington, London SE11 5QY	020 7091 9500	020 7820 0159	Mr Gary Phillips	208-4321	CY	11–16	623	
London Nautical School	61 Stamford St, Blackfriars, London SE1 9NA	020 7928 6801	020 7261 9408	Mr Gordon Wilson	208-5405	FD	11–18	649	B
Norwood School	Crown Dale, Lambeth, London SE19 3NY	020 8670 9382	020 8761 5933	Mrs Denise Webster	208-4223	CY	11–16	708	
St Martin-in-the-Fields High School for Girls	155 Tulse Hill, London SW2 3UP	020 8674 5594	020 8674 1379	Ms L. Morrison	208-5404	VA	11–18	851	CE G
Stockwell Park School	Clapham Rd, London SW9 0AL	020 7733 6156	020 7738 6196	Miss J. Tapper	208-4322	FD	11–16	983	
Thomas Francis Academy	297–299 Coldharbour La, Brixton, London SW9 8RP	0207 737 7900		Ms Karlene Thomas	208-6405		5–14	20	

Lewisham

School name	Address	Tel	Fax	Headteacher	Ref	Type	Ages	Pupils	Other
Addey and Stanhope School	472 New Cross Rd, New Cross, London SE14 6TJ	020 8305 6100	020 8305 6101	Ms Ann Potter	209-4600	VA	11–16	577	
Allenby Tutorial Centre	1–5 Rojack Rd, London SE23 2DF	020 8699 0717		Roger John Devenish	209-6364		11–16	42	Ch
Bonus Pastor RC College	Winlaton Rd, Downham, Bromley, Kent BR1 5PZ	020 8695 2100	020 8695 2105	Mrs Patricia M. Slonecki	209-4802	VA	11–16	752	RC
Catford High School	Bellingham Rd, London SE6 2PS	020 8697 8911	020 8697 9920	Ms Susan O'Neill	209-4249	CY	11–16	835	
Crofton School	Manwood Rd, Brockley, London SE4 1SA	020 8690 1114	020 8314 1859	Ms Monica Duncan	209-4323	CY	11–16	881	
Deptford Green School	Amersham Vale, New Cross, London SE14 6LQ	020 8691 3236	020 8694 1789	Mr Peter Campling	209-4047	CY	11–18	1098	
Forest Hill School	Dacres Rd, Forest Hill, London SE23 2XN	020 8699 9343	020 8699 9198	Mr P. Walsh	209-4289	CY	11–18	1337	B
Haberdashers' Aske's Hatcham College	Pepys Rd, London SE14 5SF	020 7652 9500	020 7732 1934	Dr Elizabeth Sidwell	209-6905		11–18	1372	
Haberdashers' Aske's Knights Academy	Launcelot Rd, Bromley BR1 5EB	020 8698 1025	020 8698 1025	Ms Yvonne McAllam	209-6906		11–18	733	
Northbrook CE School	Taunton Rd, Lee Grn, London SE12 8PD	020 8852 3311	020 8463 0201	Mr John Ratcliffe	209-4636	VA	11–16	492	CE
Prendergast School	Hilly Fields, Adelaide Ave, London SE4 1LE	020 8690 3710	020 8690 3155	Miss E. Pienaar	209-4646	VA	11–18	771	G
St Joseph's Academy	Lee Terr, Blackheath, London SE3 9TY	020 8852 7433	020 8318 0103	Ms Ange Tyler	209-4664	VA	11–16	466	RC B
St Matthew Academy	St Joseph's Vale, London SE3 0XX	020 8852 5614		M. Cross	209-6907		3–16		RC
Sedgehill School	Sedgehill Rd, London SE6 3QW	020 8698 8911	020 8461 4004	Ms K. Bastick-Styles	209-4267	CY	11–18	1657	
Sydenham School	Dartmouth Rd, London SE26 4RD	020 8699 6731	020 8699 7532	Ms B. Williams	209-4204	CY	11–18	1523	G

3

Merton

School name	Address	Tel	Fax	Headteacher	Ref	Type	Ages	Pupils	Other
Bishopsford Community School	Lilleshall Rd, Morden, Surrey SM4 6DU	020 8687 1157	020 8687 1158	Mr Andrew Barker	315-4061	CY	11–16	1097	
Harris Academy Merton	Wide Way, Mitcham CR4 1BP	020 8623 1000	020 8623 7655	Mr Andy Halpin	315-6905		11–18	651	
Raynes Park High School	Bushey Rd, London SW20 0JL	020 8946 4112	020 8947 0224	Mr Ian Newman	315-4052	CY	11–16	1102	
Ricards Lodge High School	Lake Rd, Wimbledon, London SW19 7HB	020 8946 2208	020 8879 8801	Mrs Alison Jerrard	315-4050	CY	11–16	1179	G
Rutlish School	Watery La, Merton Pk, London SW20 9AD	020 8542 1212	020 8544 0580	Mr R.A. Doyle	315-4500	VC	11–16	1129	B
St Marks CE Academy	Acacia Rd, Mitcham CR4 1SF	020 8648 6627	020 8640 8305	Ms Louise Fox	315-6906	VC	11–18	717	CE
Ursuline High School Wimbledon	Crescent Rd, Wimbledon, London SW20 8HA	020 8255 2688	020 8255 2687	Ms Julia Waters	315-5400	VA	11–18	1299	RC G
Wimbledon College	Edge Hill, London SW19 4NS	020 8946 2533	020 8947 6513	Rev Adrian Porter	315-4701	VA	11–18	1346	RC B

Newham

School name	Address	Tel	Fax	Headteacher	Ref	Type	Ages	Pupils	Other
Brampton Manor School	Roman Rd, London E6 3SQ	020 7540 0500	020 7473 5886	Mr Neil Berry	316-4031	CY	11–16	1491	
Cumberland School	Oban Cl, London E13 8SJ	020 7474 0231	020 7511 2510	Ms J. Noble	316-4033	CY	11–16	1021	
Eastlea Community School	Exning Rd, Canning Town, London E16 4ND	020 7540 0400	020 7540 0041	Ms Ann Palmer	316-4034	CY	11–16	1027	
Forest Gate Community School	Forest St, London E7 0HR	020 8534 8666	020 8519 8702	Mrs M. Wheeler	316-4008	CY	11–16	1023	
Kingsford Community School	Kingsford Way, Beckton, London E6 5JG	020 7476 4700	020 7473 9696	Ms Joan Deslandes	316-4037	CY	11–16	1424	
Langdon School	Sussex Rd, East Ham, London E6 2PS	020 8471 2411	020 8470 7436	Ms V. Wiseman	316-4030	CY	11–16	1761	
Lister Community School	St Mary's Rd, Plaistow, London E13 9AE	020 8471 3311	020 8472 1027	Mr M. Buck	316-4025	CY	11–16	1326	
Little Ilford School	Browning Rd, London E12 6ET	020 8478 8024	020 8478 5954	Ms Yvonne Powell	316-4015	CY	11–16	1277	
Plashet School	Plashet Gr, East Ham, London E6 1DG	020 8471 2418	020 8471 3029	Mrs Bushra Nasir	316-4032	CY	11–16	1352	G
Rokeby School	Pitchford St, London E15 4RZ	020 8534 8946	020 8519 8239	Ms Charlotte Robinson	316-4036	CY	11–16	774	B
The Royal Docks Community School	Prince Regent La, Custom Hse, London E16 3HS	020 7540 2700	020 7540 2701	Mr Sean McGrath	316-4600	VA	11–16	1099	
St Angela's Ursuline School	St George's Rd, Forest Gate, London E7 8HU	020 8472 6022	020 8475 0245	Mrs D. Smith	316-4600	VA	11–18	1322	RC G
St Bonaventure's RC School	Boleyn Rd, Forest Gate, London E7 9QD	020 8472 3844	020 8471 2749	Mr Stephen Foster	316-4601	VA	11–18	1285	RC B
Sarah Bonnell School	Deanery Rd, London E15 4LP	020 8534 6791	020 8555 3793	Ms C. Tooley	316-4035	CY	11–16	1184	G
Stratford School	Upton La, Forest Gate, London E7 9PR	020 8471 2415	020 8471 4684	Mr Andrew Seager	316-5400	FD	11–16	894	

Redbridge

School name	Address	Tel	Fax	Headteacher	Ref	Type	Ages	Pupils	Other
Beal High School	Woodford Bridge Rd, Ilford, Essex IG4 5LP	020 8551 4954	020 8551 4954	Ms Sue Snowdon	317-4030	CY	11–18	1597	
Canon Palmer RC School	Aldborough Rd South, Seven Kings, Ilford, Essex IG3 8EU	020 8590 3808	020 8597 5119	Mr Frank Maguire	317-4800	VA	11–18	1281	RC
Caterham High School	Caterham Ave, Clayhall, Ilford, Essex IG5 0QW	020 8551 4321	020 8551 1933	Dr A. Atkins	317-4006	CY	11–18	1178	
The Chadwell Heath Foundation School	Christie Gdns, Chadwell Heath, Romford, Essex RM6 4RS	020 8252 5151	020 8252 5152	Mr K. Wilkinson	317-5400	FD	11–18	1222	
Hainault Forest High School	Harbourer Rd, Hainault, Ilford, Essex IG6 3TN	020 8500 4266	020 8500 0036	Ms Kathryn Terrell	317-4036	CY	11–18	866	
Ilford County High School	Fremantle Rd, Barkingside, Ilford, Essex IG6 2JB	020 8551 6496	020 8503 9960	Mr S. Devereux	317-4007	CY	11–18	858	B
Ilford Ursuline High School	Morland Rd, Ilford, Essex IG1 4JU	020 8554 1995	020 8554 9537	Mr Alex Burke	317-4605	VA	11–18	607	RC G
King Solomon High School	Forest Rd, Barkingside, Ilford, Essex IG6 3HB	020 8501 2083	020 8559 9445	Rabbi J. Kennard	317-4604	VA	11–18	909	Je
Loxford School of Science and Technology	Loxford La, Ilford, Essex IG1 2UT	020 8514 4666	020 8514 6257	Ms Hazel Farrow	317-4027	CY	11–18	1479	
Mayfield School	Pedley Rd, Dagenham, Essex RM8 1XE	020 8590 5211	020 8597 5729	Mr Andy Rehling	317-4035	FD	11–18	1449	
Oaks Park High School	45–65 Oaks La, Newbury Park, Ilford, Essex IG2 7PQ	020 8590 2245	020 8590 2246	Mr Stephen Wilks	317-4040	CY	11–18	1359	
Seven Kings High School	Ley St, Ilford, Essex IG2 7BT	020 8554 8935	020 8518 2975	Sir Alan Steer	317-4032	CY	11–18	1402	
Trinity RC High School	Mornington Rd, Woodford Green, Essex IG8 0TP	020 8504 3419	020 8505 7546	Dr Paul Doherty	317-4603	VA	11–18	1687	RC

School name	Address	Tel	Fax	Headteacher	Ref	Type	Ages	Pupils	Other
Valentines High School	Cranbrook Rd, Ilford, Essex IG2 6HX	020 8554 3608	020 8518 2621	Mrs S.V. Jones	317-4033	CY	11–18	1256	
Wanstead High School	Redbridge La West, Wanstead, London E11 2JZ	020 8989 2791	020 8530 8879	Mr Christiaan Van Bussel	317-4021	CY	11–18	1481	
Woodbridge High School	St Barnabas Rd, Woodford Green, Essex IG8 7DQ	020 8504 9618	020 8559 0487	Mr Andrew Beaumont	317-4029	CY	11–18	1496	
Woodford County High School	High Rd, Woodford Green, Essex IG8 9LA	020 8504 0611	020 8506 1880	Miss H. Cleland	317-4025	CY	11–18	857	G

Richmond upon Thames

School name	Address	Tel	Fax	Headteacher	Ref	Type	Ages	Pupils	Other
Christ's CE Comprehensive Secondary School	Queens Rd, Richmond, Surrey TW10 6HW	020 8940 6982	020 8332 6085	Mr Richard Burke	318-4603	VA	11–16	552	CE
Grey Court School	Ham St, Ham, Richmond, Surrey TW10 7HN	020 8948 1173	020 8332 2428	Miss Rachel Jones	318-4006	CY	11–16	872	
Hampton Community College	Hanworth Rd, Hampton, Middlesex TW12 3HB	020 8979 3399	020 8783 0086	Dr Sue Demont	318-4011	CY	11–16	820	
Orleans Park School	Richmond Rd, Twickenham, Middlesex TW1 3BB	020 8891 0187	020 8744 0312	Mr D. Talbot	318-4010	CY	11–16	1017	
Shene School	Park Ave, East Sheen, London SW14 8RG	020 8876 8891	020 8392 9694	Ms Sue Raynor	318-4020	CY	11–16	924	
Teddington School	Broom Rd, Teddington, Middlesex TW11 9PJ	020 8943 0033	020 8943 2999	Mr R. Weeks	318-4013	CY	11–16	1141	
Waldegrave School for Girls	Fifth Cross Rd, Twickenham, Middlesex TW2 5LH	020 8894 3244	020 8893 3670	Mrs Philippa Nunn	318-4021	CY	11–16	1026	G
Whitton School	Percy Rd, Twickenham, Middlesex TW2 6JW	020 8894 4503	020 8894 0690	Mr Jon Gillard	318-4016	CY	11–16	776	

Southwark

School name	Address	Tel	Fax	Headteacher	Ref	Type	Ages	Pupils	Other
The Academy at Peckham	112 Peckham Rd, London SE15 5DZ	020 7703 4417	020 7703 4305	Mr Peter Crook	210-6906		11–18	1176	
Archbishop Michael Ramsey Technology College	Farmers Rd, Camberwell, London SE5 0UB	020 7701 4166	020 7701 8461	Mr M. Morrall	210-4725	VA	11–18	904	CE
Aylwin Girls' School	55 Southwark Park Rd, London SE16 3TZ	020 7237 9316	020 7237 9204	Mrs Catharine Loxton	210-4009		11–16	893	
Bacon's College	Timber Pond Rd, Rotherhithe, London SE16 6AT	020 7237 1928	020 7237 4501	Mr T. Perry	210-6911		11–19		
Bacon's College	Timber Pond Rd, Rotherhithe, London SE16 6AT	020 7237 1928	020 7237 4501	Mr T. Perry	210-6900		10–19	1065	
The Charter School	Red Post Hill, London SE24 9JH	020 7346 6600	020 7738 6746	Mr Chris Bowler	210-4318	FD	11–18	1085	
City of London Academy (Southwark)	240 Lynton Rd, London SE1 5LA	020 7394 5100	020 7394 5101	Mr Martyn Coles	210-6905		11–19	798	
Dulwich High School for Boys	Red Post Hill, London SE24 9JH	020 7737 2336	020 7738 6746		210-4281	CY	11–16		B
Geoffrey Chaucer Technology College	Harper Rd, London SE1 6AG	020 7407 6877	020 7403 8922	Ms S. Yardon-Pinder	210-4313	CY	11–16	708	
Harris Academy Bermondsey	55 Southwark Park Rd, London SE16 3TZ	020 7237 9316	020 7237 9204	Ms Cathy Loxton	210-6907		11–18	879	G
Harris Girls' Academy East Dulwich	Homestall Rd, London SE22 0NR	020 7732 2276	020 7277 7785	Ms Lesley Day	210-6908		11–18	775	G
Kingsdale Secondary School	Alleyn Pk, Dulwich, London SE21 8SQ	020 8670 7575	020 8766 7051	Mr S. Morrison	210-4265	FD	11–16	1138	
Notre Dame Roman RC Girls' School	118 St George's Rd, London SE1 6EX	020 7261 1121	020 7620 2922	Ms Anne Marie Niblock	210-5404	VA	11–16	639	RC G
Sacred Heart Roman RC Secondary School	Camberwell New Rd, London SE5 0RP	020 7274 6844	020 7737 1713	Ms Sally Coates	210-5405	VA	11–16	667	RC
St Michael and All Angels CofE Academy	Wyndham Rd, Camberwell, London SE5 0UB	020 7701 4166	020 7701 8461	Mrs S. Graham	210-6910		11–19		CE
St Michael's RC School	John Felton Rd, Bermondsey, London SE16 4UN	020 7237 6432	020 7252 2411	Mrs Grainne Grabowski	210-5403	VA	11–16	650	RC
St Saviour's and St Olave's CE School	New Kent Rd, London SE1 4AN	020 7407 1843	020 7403 9163	Mrs I. Bishop	210-4680	VA	11–18	757	CE G
The St Thomas the Apostle College	Hollydale Rd, Nunhead, London SE15 2EB	020 7639 0106	020 7277 5471	Mr Damian Gerard Fox	210-5402	VA	11–16	733	RC B
Walworth Academy	Shorncliffe Rd, London SE1 5UJ	020 7450 9570	020 7450 9571	Mr Devon Hanson	210-6909		11–16		
Walworth School	Shorncliffe Rd, London SE1 5UJ	020 7450 9570	020 7703 8785	Miss Elizabeth Hanham	210-4215	CY	11–16	1155	

3

Sutton

School name	Address	Tel	Fax	Headteacher	Ref	Type	Ages	Pupils	Other
Carshalton Boys Sports College	Winchcombe Rd, Carshalton, Surrey SM5 1RW	020 8644 7325	020 8641 8721	Mr Simon Barber	319-4000	CY	11–18	1119	B
Carshalton High School for Girls	West St, Carshalton, Surrey SM5 2QX	020 8647 8294	020 8773 8931	Mrs Vivien Jones	319-4002	CY	11–18	1228	G
Cheam High School	Chatsworth Rd, Cheam, Sutton, Surrey SM3 8PW	020 8644 5790	020 8641 8611	Miss Rebecca Allott	319-5403	FD	11–18	1742	
Glenthorne High School	Sutton Common Rd, Sutton, Surrey SM3 9PS	020 8644 6307	020 8641 8725	Mr Stephen Hume	319-4011	FD	11–18	1199	
Greenshaw High School	Grennell Rd, Sutton, Surrey SM1 3DY	020 8715 1001	020 8641 7335	Mr J.K. Fuller	319-4007	CY	11–18	1467	
The John Fisher School	Peaks Hill, Purley, Surrey CR8 3YP	020 8660 4555	020 8763 1837	Mr M.J. Scully	319-5402	VA	11–18	1026	RC B
Nonsuch High School for Girls	Ewell Rd, Cheam, Sutton, Surrey SM3 8AB	020 8394 1308	020 8393 2307	Mrs G.D. Espejo	319-5401	VA	11–18	1222	G
Overton Grange School	36 Stanley Rd, Sutton, Surrey SM2 6TQ	020 8239 2383	020 8239 2382	Mr Stephen Foxwell	319-4019	CY	11–18	1273	
St Philomena's School	Pound St, Carshalton, Surrey SM5 3PS	020 8642 2025	020 8643 7925	Mrs Jackie Johnson	319-5406	VA	11–18	1196	RC G
Stanley Park High School	Stanley Park Rd, Carshalton, Surrey SM5 3HP	020 8647 5842	020 8254 7800	Mr David Taylor	319-4015	CY	11–18	864	
Sutton Grammar School for Boys	Manor La, Sutton, Surrey SM1 4AS	020 8642 3821	020 8770 9070	Mr G. Ironside	319-5404	FD	11–18	830	B
Wallington County Grammar School	Croydon Rd, Wallington, Surrey SM6 7PH	020 8647 2235	020 8254 7921	Dr J.M. Haworth	319-5407	FD	11–18	892	B
Wallington High School for Girls	Woodcote Rd, Wallington, Surrey SM6 0PH	020 8647 2380	020 8773 9884	Mrs B. Greatorex	319-5405	FD	11–18	1281	G
Wilson's School	Mollison Dr, Wallington, Surrey SM6 9JW	020 8773 2931	020 8773 4972	Mr D.M. Charnock	319-5400	VA	11–18	994	CE B

Tower Hamlets

School name	Address	Tel	Fax	Headteacher	Ref	Type	Ages	Pupils	Other
Bethnal Green Technology College	Gosset St, Bethnal Green, London E2 6NW	020 7920 7900	020 7739 4608 / 79207999	Mr Mark Keary	211-4284	CY	11–16	813	R
Bishop Challoner RC Collegiate Boys School	Hardinge St, Stepney, London E1 0EB	020 7790 3634	020 7702 7398	Mrs Catherine Myers	211-4298	VA	11–16	527	RC B
Bishop Challoner RC Collegiate Girls School	Hardinge St, Stepney, London E1 0EB	020 7790 3634	020 7702 7398	Mrs Catherine Myers	211-4726	VA	11–16	965	RC G
Bow School	Paton Cl, Fairfield Rd, London E3 2QD	020 8980 0118	020 8980 1556	Miss B. Dobson	211-4024	CY	11–16	660	B
Central Foundation Girls' School	Harley Gr, Bow, London E3 2AT	020 8981 1131	020 8983 0188	Ms Ann Hudson	211-4507	VA	11–18	1391	G
George Green's School	100 Manchester Rd, Isle of Dogs, London E14 3DW	020 7987 6032	020 7538 2316	Kenny Frederick	211-4505	VC	11–19	1178	
Langdon Park Community School	Byron St, Poplar, London E14 0RZ	020 7987 4811	020 7537 7282	Mr C. Dunne	211-4105	CY	11–16	883	
Morpeth School	Portman Pl, Bethnal Green, London E2 0PX	020 8981 0921	020 8983 0139	Mr A. MacDonald	211-4150	CY	11–16	1165	R
Mulberry School for Girls	Richard St, Commercial Rd, London E1 2JP	020 7790 6327	020 7265 9882	Ms Vanessa Ogden	211-4242	CY	11–18	1410	G
Oaklands School	Old Bethnal Green Rd, Bethnal Green, London E2 6PR	020 7613 1014	020 7729 3756	Patrice Canavan	211-4296	CY	11–16	585	
Raine's Foundation School	Approach Rd, Bethnal Green, London E2 9LY	020 8981 1231	020 8983 0153	Mr P. Hollingum	211-5400	VA	11–18	867	CE
St Paul's Way Community School	Shelmerdine Cl, Bow, London E3 4AN	020 7987 1883	020 7537 4529	Mr Simon Harris	211-4277	CY	11–16	998	
Sir John Cass Foundation and Redcoat CE Secondary School	Stepney Way, Stepney, London E1 0RH	020 7790 6712	020 7790 0499	Mr Hayden Evans	211-4722	VA	11–18	1234	CE
Stepney Green Maths and Computing College	Ben Jonson Rd, Stepney, London E1 4SD	020 7790 6361	020 7265 9766	Mr Paramjit Bhutta	211-4276	CY	11–16	752	B
Swanlea School	31 Brady St, Bethnal Green, London E1 5DJ	020 7375 3267	020 7375 3567	Ms L. Austin	211-4297	CY	11–16	1042	

Waltham Forest

School name	Address	Tel	Fax	Headteacher	Ref	Type	Ages	Pupils	Other
Aveling Park School	Aveling Park Rd, Walthamstow, London E17 4NR	020 8527 5794	020 8531 5063	Mrs K.A. Terrell	320-4060	CY	11–16	566	
Chingford Foundation School	Nevin Dr, Chingford, London E4 7LT	020 8529 1853	020 8559 4329	Mr C. Moore	320-5401	FD	11–18	1302	
Connaught School for Girls	Connaught Rd, Leytonstone, London E11 4AB	020 8539 3029	020 8558 3827	Mrs A. Betts	320-4061	CY	11–16	597	G
George Mitchell School	Farmer Rd, Leyton, London E10 5DN	020 8539 6198	020 8532 8766	Mrs Helen Jeffery	320-4062	CY	11–16	592	
Heathcote School	Normanton Pk, Chingford, London E4 6ES	020 8498 5110	020 8529 3935	Mr Barry Hersom	320-4063	CY	11–16	879	

3

School name	Address	Tel	Fax	Headteacher	Ref	Type	Ages	Pupils	Other
Highams Park School	Handsworth Ave, Highams Pk, London E4 9PJ	020 8527 4051	020 8503 3349	Mr A. Perrett	320-5400	VA	11–18	1472	
The Holy Family RC College	1 Shernhall St, Walthamstow, London E17 3EA	020 8520 0482	020 8521 0364	Mr E. Breen	320-4603	VA	11–18	1043	RC
Kelmscott School	Markhouse Rd, Walthamstow, London E17 8DN	020 8521 2115	020 8521 2115	Mrs Lynnette Parvez	320-4075	CY	11–16	881	
The Lammas School	150 Seymour Rd, Leyton, London E10 7LX	020 8988 5860	020 8988 5861	Ms Shona Ramsay	320-4076	CY	11–16	834	
Leytonstone Business and Enterprise Specialist School	Colworth Rd, Leytonstone, London E11 1JD	020 8988 7420	020 8496 2801	Mr Luke Burton	320-4069	CY	11–16	884	
Norlington School for Boys	Norlington Rd, Leytonstone, London E10 6JZ	020 8539 3055	020 8556 4657	Mr N. Primrose	320-4064	CY	11–16	557	B
Rush Croft Sports College	Rushcroft Rd, Chingford, London E4 8SG	020 8531 9231	020 8523 4779	Ms P. Cutler	320-4074	CY	11–16	861	
Tom Hood Community Science College	Terling Cl, Leytonstone, London E11 3NT	020 8534 3425	020 8534 3317	Mrs Candice Dwight	320-4059	CY	11–16	801	Ch
Walthamstow Academy	Billet Rd, Walthamstow, London E17 5DP	020 8527 3750	020 8527 3606	Ms Fiona Cordeaux	320-6905		11–18	677	Ch
Walthamstow School for Girls	Church Hill, Walthamstow, London E17 9RZ	020 8509 9446	020 8509 9445	Ms Rachel Macfarlane	320-4072	CY	11–16	894	G
Warwick School for Boys	Barrett Rd, Walthamstow, London E17 3ND	020 8520 4173	020 8509 9949	Ms R.A. Woodward	320-4065	CY	11–16	510	B
Willowfield School	Clifton Ave, Walthamstow, London E17 6HL	020 8527 4065	020 8523 4939	Ms E. Wilson	320-4066	CY	11–16	579	

Wandsworth

School name	Address	Tel	Fax	Headteacher	Ref	Type	Ages	Pupils	Other
ADT College	100 West Hill, Wandsworth, London SW15 2UT	020 8877 0357	020 8877 0617	Mr D. Durban	212-6900		11–18	1060	
Ashcroft Technology Academy	100 West Hill, London SW15 2UT	020 8877 0357	020 8877 0617	Mr M. Barker	212-6905		11–18		
Balham Preparatory School	145 Upper Tooting Rd, London SW17 7TJ	020 8767 6057	020 8682 4272	Mr Yusuf Atcha	212-6396		11–16	319	Mu
Battersea Technology College	401 Battersea Park Rd, London SW11 5AP	020 7622 0026	020 7978 2683	Mr Gale Keller	212-4329	CY	11–19	640	
Burntwood School	Burntwood La, London SW17 0AQ	020 8946 6201	020 8944 6592	Mrs Helen Dorfman	212-5401	FD	11–18	1748	G
Chestnut Grove School	Chestnut Gr, Balham, London SW12 8JU	020 8673 8737	020 8675 1190	Ms M. Peacock	212-4328	FD	11–19	852	
Elliott School	Pullman Gdns, Putney, London SW15 3DG	020 8788 3421	020 8789 8280	Mrs Sharon Ferrell	212-5402	FD	11–18	1225	
Ernest Bevin College	Beechcroft Rd, Tooting, London SW17 7DF	020 8672 8582	020 8767 5502	Mr Michael Chivers	212-4297	CY	11–18	1079	B
Graveney School	Welham Rd, Tooting, London SW17 9BU	020 8682 7000	020 8767 5883	Mr G. Stapleton	212-5400	FD	11–18	1933	
John Paul II School	Princes Way, London SW19 6QE	020 8788 8142	020 8780 1393	Mr J. King	212-5404	VA	11–16	461	RC
St Cecilia's, Wandsworth CE School	Sutherland Gr, London SW18 5JR	020 8780 1244	020 8780 2869	Mr Jeffrey Risbridger	212-4734	VA	11–18	599	CE
Salesian College	Surrey La, London SW11 3PB	020 7228 2857	020 7223 4921	Mr S. McCann	212-5403	VA	11–16	632	RC B
Southfields Community College	333 Merton Rd, Wandsworth, London SW18 5JU	020 8875 2600	020 8874 9949	Ms J. Valin	212-5405	FD	11–18	1261	

Westminster

School name	Address	Tel	Fax	Headteacher	Ref	Type	Ages	Pupils	Other
The Grey Coat Hospital	Greycoat Pl, London SW1P 2DY	020 7969 1998	020 7828 2697	Mrs R. Allard	213-4628	VA	11–18	1036	CE G
King Solomon Academy	Penfold St, London NW1 6RX	020 7395 2074		Ms Venessa Willms	213-6907		3–18		
Paddington Academy	Marylands Rd, London W9 2DR	020 7479 3900	020 7479 3995	Mr Phil Hearne	213-6905		11–18	986	Ch
Pimlico School	Lupus St, London SW1V 3AT	020 7828 0881	020 7931 0549	Mr Philip Barnard	213-4279	CY	11–18	1343	
Quintin Kynaston School	Marlborough Hill, London NW8 0NL	020 7722 8141	020 7586 8473	Ms Jo Shuter	213-4295	CY	11–18	1333	
St Augustine's CE High School	Oxford Rd, London NW6 5SN	020 7328 3434	020 7328 3435	Mr Alex Thomas	213-4723	VA	11–18	712	CE
St George RC School	Lanark Rd, Maida Vale, London W9 1RB	020 7328 0904	020 7624 6083	Mr Martin Tissot	213-4809	VA	11–16	595	RC
The St Marylebone CE School	64 Marylebone High St, London W1U 5BA	020 7935 4704	020 7935 4005	Mrs E. Phillips	213-4673	VA	11–18	890	CE G
Westminster Academy	Harrow Rd, London W2 5EZ	020 7641 7700		Mrs Alison Banks	213-6906		11–18	747	
Westminster City School	55 Palace St, London SW1E 5HJ	020 7641 8760	020 7641 8761	Mr David Maloney	213-4687	VA	11–18	783	Ch B

North East

Darlington

School name	Address	Tel	Fax	Headteacher	Ref	Type	Ages	Pupils	Other
Branksome School	Eggleston View, Darlington, County Durham DL3 9SH	01325 380776	01325 282523	Mr Russ Wallace	841-4286	CY	11-16	738	
Carmel RC College	The Headlands, Darlington, County Durham DL3 8RW	01325 254525	01325 254335	Mr James O'Neill	841-4603	VA	11-18	1093	RC
Eastbourne Church of England Academy	The Fairway, Darlington DL1 1ET	01325 254695	01325 267301		841-6905				CE
Eastbourne Comprehensive School	The Fairway, Darlington, County Durham DL1 1ET	01325 267300		Mrs Karen Pemberton	841-4283	CY	11-16	743	
Haughton Community School	Salters Lane South, Darlington, County Durham DL1 2AN	01325 254111	01325 254371	Dame Dela Smith	841-4285	CY	11-16	900	
Hummersknott School and Language College	Edinburgh Dr, Darlington, County Durham DL3 8AR	01325 241191	01325 241122	Mr Patrick Howarth	841-4288	CY	11-16	1224	
Hurworth School	Croft Rd, Hurworth-on-Tees, Darlington, County Durham DL2 2JG	01325 720424	01325 721788	Mr Dean Judson	841-4221	FD	11-16	658	
Longfield School	Longfield Rd, Darlington, County Durham DL3 0HT	01325 380815	01325 254219	Mr Keith B Cotgrave	841-4287	CY	11-16	909	

Durham

School name	Address	Tel	Fax	Headteacher	Ref	Type	Ages	Pupils	Other
Belmont School Community Arts College	Buckinghamshire Rd, Belmont, Durham, County Durham DH1 2QP	0191 386 5715	0191 384 0583	Miss Judith Wilkinson	840-4185	CY	11-16	813	
Bishop Barrington School A Sports with Mathematics College	Woodhouse La, Bishop Auckland, County Durham DL14 6LA	01388 603307	01388 609990	Mr Bruce Guthrie	840-4162	CY	11-16	678	
Consett Community Sports College	Durham Rd, Blackhill, Consett, County Durham DH8 5TW	01207 503515	01207 504633	Mrs Christine Parker	840-4117	CY	11-16	744	
Dene Community School of Technology	Manor Way, Peterlee, County Durham SR8 5RL	0191 586 2140	0191 586 1295	Mrs Jane Low	840-4214	CY	11-16	738	
Durham Community Business College for Technology and Enterprise	Bracken Ct, Ushaw Moor, Durham, County Durham DH7 7NG	0191 373 0336	0191 373 0710	Mrs Anne Lakey	840-4192	CY	11-16	539	
Durham Gilesgate Sports College and Sixth Form Centre	Bradford Cres, Gilesgate, Durham, County Durham DH1 1HN	0191 384 7505	0191 384 8012	Mr M. Brett	840-4191	CY	11-18	1337	
Durham Johnston Comprehensive School	Crossgate Moor, Durham, County Durham DH1 4SU	0191 384 3887	0191 375 5906	Mrs Carolyn Roberts	840-4200	CY	11-18	1443	
Easington Community Science College	Stockton Rd, Easington Village, Peterlee, County Durham SR8 3AY	0191 527 0757	0191 527 0160	Mrs Toni Spoors	840-4280	CY	11-16	907	
Ferryhill Business Enterprise College	Merrington Rd, Ferryhill, County Durham DL17 8RW	01740 651554	01740 654980	Mr Philip Bowden	840-4150	CY	11-16	725	
Framwellgate School Durham	Newton Dr, Framwellgate Moor, Durham, County Durham DH1 5BQ	0191 386 6628	0191 383 0917	Mrs Joan Sjovoll	840-4190	CY	11-18	1248	
Fyndoune Community College	Findon Hill, Sacriston, Durham DH7 6LU	0191 371 0277	0191 371 2269	Mrs Anne Lakey	840-4052	CY	11-16	420	
Greencroft School	Greencroft Road End, Annfield Plain, Stanley, County Durham DH9 8PR	01207 234466	01207 282917	Mr Christopher Espiner	840-4092	CY	11-16	660	
Greenfield School Community and Arts College	Greenfield Way, Newton Aycliffe, County Durham DL5 7LF	01325 300378	01325 318313	Mr David Priestley	840-4176	CY	11-16	772	
The Hermitage School	Waldridge La, Chester-le-Street, County Durham DH2 3AD	0191 388 7161	0191 387 1137	Mr Ian Robertson	840-4054	FD	11-18	1000	
King James I Community Arts College	South Church Rd, Bishop Auckland, County Durham DL14 7JZ	01388 603388	01388 663536	Mr Alan Stephen Rodchester	840-4178	CY	11-18	701	
Moorside Community Technology College	Dunelm Rd, Moorside, Consett, County Durham DH8 8EG	01207 507001	01207 509748	Mr Jonathan Morris	840-4110	CY	11-16	525	
Park View Community School	Church Chare, Chester-le-Street, County Durham DH3 3QA	0191 388 2248	0191 387 1720	Mr Iain Veith	840-4047	CY	11-18	1436	
Parkside School	Hall Lane Est, Willington, Crook, County Durham DL15 0QF	01388 746396	01388 746782	Mr Roland Sterry	840-4128	CY	11-16	841	
Roseberry Sports and Community College	Pelton, Chester-le-Street, County Durham DH2 1NW	0191 370 0300	0191 370 1490	Mrs Ann Bowen	840-4042	CY	11-18	725	
St Bede's RC Comprehensive School	Westway, Peterlee, County Durham SR8 1DE	0191 586 2291	0191 586 1382	Mr Paul Mckenna	840-4693	VA	11-18	944	RC
St Bede's RC Comprehensive School and Sixth Form College, Lanchester	Consett Rd, Lanchester, Durham, County Durham DH7 0RD	01207 520424	01207 521114	Mrs M Bates	840-4694	VA	11-18	1320	RC

3

School name	Address	Tel	Fax	Headteacher	Ref	Type	Ages	Pupils	Other
St John's RCVA Technology School and Sixth Form Centre	Woodhouse La, Bishop Auckland, County Durham DL14 6JT	01388 603246	01388 609988	Mr Francis O'Neill	840-4681	VA	11–18	1296	RC
St Leonard's Roman RC VA Comprehensive School	North End, Durham, County Durham DH1 4NG	0191 384 8575	0191 386 1134	Mr Simon Campbell	840-4691	VA	11–18	1439	RC
Seaham School of Technology	Burnhall Dr, Seaham, County Durham SR7 0EN	0191 516 1600	0191 513 0068	Mr R. Dingle	840-4019	CY	11–16	1084	
Sedgefield Community College Sports Specialist College	Hawthorn Rd, Sedgefield, County Durham TS21 3DD	01740 625300	01740 625334	Ms Lynne Ackland	840-4231	CY	11–18	868	
Shotton Hall School	Waveney Rd, Peterlee, County Durham SR8 1NX	0191 586 2580	0191 586 1328	Mr Ian Mowbray	840-4215	CY	11–16	1083	
Spennymoor Comprehensive School	Whitworth La, Spennymoor, County Durham DL16 7LN	01388 815634	01388 824840	Mr Paul Gillis	840-4154	CY	11–18	734	
Staindrop School A Business and Enterprise College	Cleatlam La, Staindrop, Darlington, County Durham DL2 3JU	01833 660285	01833 660833	Mr B. Kinnair	840-4171	CY	11–16	615	
Stanley School of Technology	Tyne Rd, Stanley, County Durham DH9 6PZ	01207 232506	01207 230825	Ms Janet Bridges	840-4084	CY	11–16	775	
Sunnydale Community College for Maths and Computing	Middridge La, Shildon, County Durham DL4 2EP	01388 772526		Mrs Susan Byrne	840-4180	CY	11–16	556	
Tanfield School, Specialist College of Science and Engineering	Tanfield Lea Rd, Stanley, County Durham DH9 8AY	01207 232881	01207 282922	Mr Graeme Lloyd	840-4099	CY	11–16	631	
Teesdale School	Prospect Pl, Barnard Castle, County Durham DL12 8HH	01833 638166	01833 695127	Mr P. Harrison	840-4174	CY	11–18	786	
Tudhoe Grange School	St Charles Rd, Spennymoor, County Durham DL16 6JY	01388 815000	01388 810211	Mrs Christine Warren	840-4141	CY	11–16	772	
Wellfield Community School a Specialist Maths and Computing College	North Rd East, Wingate, County Durham TS28 5AX	01429 838413	01429 838127	Mrs J.F. Elliott	840-4218	CY	11–16	1070	
Wolsingham School and Community College	Leazes La, Wolsingham, Bishop Auckland, County Durham DL13 3DN	01388 527302	01388 528173	Ms Andrea Crawshaw	840-4139	CY	11–18	780	
Woodham Community Technology College	Washington Cres, Newton Aycliffe, County Durham DL5 4AX	01325 300328	01325 301950	Mr S. Harness	840-4175	CY	11–18	1145	

Gateshead

School name	Address	Tel	Fax	Headteacher	Ref	Type	Ages	Pupils	Other
Cardinal Hume Catholic School	Old Durham Rd, Beacon Lough, Gateshead, Tyne and Wear NE9 6RZ	0191 487 7638	0191 482 4421	Mr N. Hurn	390-4605	VA	11–18	901	RC
Emmanuel College	Consett Rd, Lobley Hill, Gateshead, Tyne and Wear NE11 0AN	0191 460 2099	0191 460 2098	Mr Nigel McQuoid	390-6900		11–18	1225	
Heworth Grange Comprehensive School	High Lanes, Felling, Gateshead, Tyne and Wear NE10 0PT	0191 421 2244	0191 420 2320	Mr Brian Harrison Huddart	390-4036	CY	11–18	1365	
Hookergate School	School La, High Spen, Rowlands Gill, Tyne and Wear NE39 2BX	01207 542862	01207 545050	Mr P. Crabtree	390-4038	CY	11–16	648	
Joseph Swan School	Saltwell Rd South, Gateshead, Tyne and Wear NE9 6LE	0191 442 2000	0191 442 2001	Mr Allan Fuller	390-4043	CY	11–18	1251	
Kingsmeadow Community Comprehensive School	Market La, Dunston, Gateshead, Tyne and Wear NE11 9NX	0191 460 6004	0191 460 0295	Mr Simon Taylor	390-4041	CY	11–16	778	
Lord Lawson of Beamish Community School	Birtley La, Birtley, Chester-le-Street, County Durham DH3 2LP	0191 433 4026	0191 433 4027	Mr D.J. Grigg	390-4027	CY	11–18	1471	
Ryton Comprehensive School	Main Rd, Ryton, Tyne and Wear NE40 3AH	0191 413 2113	0191 413 4844	Mrs S.E. Howarth	390-4031	CY	11–18	1255	
St Thomas More RC School	Croftdale Rd, Blaydon-on-Tyne, Tyne and Wear NE21 4BQ	0191 499 0111	0191 414 1116	Mr Jonathan Parkinson	390-4606	VA	11–18	1494	RC
Thomas Hepburn Community Comprehensive School	Swards Rd, Felling, Gateshead, Tyne and Wear NE10 9UZ	0191 420 4555	0191 420 4554	Mr M. Dawson	390-4042	CY	11–16	894	
Whickham School	Burnthouse La, Whickham, Newcastle upon Tyne, Tyne and Wear NE16 5AR	0191 496 0026	0191 488 0968	Mr N. Morrison	390-4029	CY	11–18	1634	

Hartlepool

School name	Address	Tel	Fax	Headteacher	Ref	Type	Ages	Pupils	Other
Brierton Community School (A Specialist Sports College)	Catcote Rd, Hartlepool, North Yorkshire TS25 4BY	01429 265711	01429 287500	Dr Judith Greene	805-4130	CY	11–16	917	
Dyke House Comprehensive School	Mapleton Rd, Hartlepool, North Yorkshire TS24 8NQ	01429 266377	01429 866404	Mr Bill Jordon	805-4131	CY	11–16	1006	
The English Martyrs School and Sixth Form College	Catcote Rd, Hartlepool TS25 4HA	01429 273790	01429 273998	Mr J. Hughes	805-4603	VA	11–18	1543	RC
High Tunstall College of Science	Elwick Rd, West Pk, Hartlepool, North Yorkshire TS26 0LQ	01429 261446	01429 222856	Mrs Mirjam Bruhler-Willey	805-4133	CY	11–16	1182	
Manor College of Technology	Owton Manor La, Hartlepool, North Yorkshire TS25 3PS	01429 288338	01429 288638	Mr Alan White	805-4134	FD	11–16	1045	
St Hild's CE VA School	King Oswy Dr, West View, Hartlepool TS24 9PB	01429 273041	01429 232235	Mr Andrew Bayston	805-4000	VA	11–16	878	CE

Middlesbrough

School name	Address	Tel	Fax	Headteacher	Ref	Type	Ages	Pupils	Other
Acklam Grange School A Specialist Technology College For Maths and Computing	Lodore Gr, Middlesbrough, North Yorkshire TS5 8PB	01642 277700	01642 816911	Mr John Bate	806-4136	CY	11–16	1355	
Hall Garth Community Arts College	Hall Dr, Acklam, Middlesbrough, North Yorkshire TS5 7JX	01642 813776	01642 816857	Mr Stephen Taylor	806-4000	CY	11–16	701	
The King's Academy	Stainton Way, Coulby Newham, Middlesbrough TS8 0GA	01642 577577	01642 590204	Mr Christopher Drew	806-6906	VA	11–18	1080	Ch
King's Manor School, Specialist Sports College	Hall Dr, Acklam, Middlesbrough TS5 7JY	01642 818200	01642 850560	Mr Morgan Wallace	806-4110	CY	11–16	956	
Macmillan Academy	PO Box 8, Stockton Rd, Middlesbrough TS5 4YU	01642 800800	01642 353000	Mr K.U. Fraser	806-6907		11–19	1478	
The Newlands RC School FCJ	Saltersgill Ave, Middlesbrough TS4 3JW	01642 825311	01642 812709	Mr Stephen Wing	806-4637	VA	11–16	665	RC
Ormesby School	Stockwith Cl, Netherfields, Middlesbrough, Cleveland TS3 0RG	01642 452191	01642 463018	Mr Colin Algie	806-4122	CY	11–16	835	
St David's Roman RC Technology College	St Davids Way, Acklam, Middlesbrough TS5 7EY	01642 298100	01642 298101	Mr Peter Coady	806-4701	VA	11–16	968	RC
Unity City Academy	Ormesby Rd, Middlesbrough TS3 8RE	01642 326262	01642 300663	Mr Robert Dore	806-6905		11–16	1035	RC

Newcastle upon Tyne

School name	Address	Tel	Fax	Headteacher	Ref	Type	Ages	Pupils	Other
All Saints College	West Denton Way, Newcastle upon Tyne, Tyne and Wear NE5 2SZ	0191 267 7036	0191 229 0038	Mr David Scott	391-4500	VC	11–18	932	CE
Benfield School	Benfield Rd, Newcastle upon Tyne, Tyne and Wear NE6 4NU	0191 265 6091	0191 265 5974	Mr L. Brumby	391-4480	CY	11–18	976	
Gosforth High School	Knightsbridge, Gt North Rd, Gosforth, Newcastle upon Tyne, Tyne and Wear NE3 2JH	0191 285 1000	0191 213 2068	Mr Hugh Robinson	391-4429	CY	13–18	1673	
Heaton Manor School	Jesmond Pk West, Newcastle upon Tyne, Tyne and Wear NE7 7DP	0191 281 8486	0191 281 0381	Mr John Dryden	391-4494	CY	11–18	1916	
Kenton School	Drayton Rd, Newcastle upon Tyne, Tyne and Wear NE3 3RU	0191 214 2200	0191 214 2207	Mr David Pearmain	391-4485	CY	11–18	2042	
Sacred Heart High School	Fenham Hall Dr, Fenham, Newcastle upon Tyne, Tyne and Wear NE4 9YH	0191 274 7373	0191 275 1939	Mrs Pat Wager	391-4716	VA	11–18	1360	RC G
St Cuthbert's High School	Gretna Rd, Newcastle upon Tyne, Tyne and Wear NE15 7PX	0191 274 4510	0191 274 2545	Mr J. Gerard Murphy	391-4715	VA	11–18	1090	RC B
St Mary's RC Comprehensive School	Benton Park Rd, Newcastle upon Tyne, Tyne and Wear NE7 7PE	0191 266 8813	0191 266 8813	Mr John Foster	391-4714	VA	11–18	899	RC
Walbottle Campus Technology College	Hexham Rd, Walbottle, Newcastle upon Tyne, Tyne and Wear NE15 9TP	0191 267 8221	0191 264 6025	Mr M.S. Booth	391-4430	CY	11–18	1783	
Walker Technology College	Middle St, Newcastle upon Tyne, Tyne and Wear NE6 4BY	0191 262 0911	0191 263 6758	Mr Steve Gater	391-4450	CY	11–18	1191	
West Gate Community College	West Rd, Newcastle upon Tyne, Tyne and Wear NE4 9LU	0191 241 0200	0191 241 0210	Mr Jim Farnie	391-4498	CY	11–18	1476	

3

North Tyneside

School name	Address	Tel	Fax	Headteacher	Ref	Type	Ages	Pupils	Other
Burnside Business and Enterprise College	St Peters Rd, Wallsend, Tyne and Wear NE28 7LQ	0191 259 8500	0191 259 8501	Mr D. Loveday	392-4032	CY	11–18	1471	
Churchill Community College	Churchill St, Wallsend, Tyne and Wear NE28 7TN	0191 200 7260	0191 200 7264	Mr David Baldwin	392-4033	CY	11–18	941	
George Stephenson Community High School	Southgate, Killingworth, Newcastle upon Tyne, Tyne and Wear NE12 6SA	0191 200 8347	0191 200 8349	Mrs A.L. Welsh	392-4030	CY	11–18	911	
John Spence Community High School	Preston Rd, North Shields, Tyne and Wear NE29 9PU	0191 200 5220	0191 200 5225	Mr B. Davison	392-4038	CY	11–16	871	
Longbenton Community College	Hailsham Ave, Longbenton, Newcastle upon Tyne, Tyne and Wear NE12 8ER	0191 200 7474	0191 200 7850	Mr J. Cockburn	392-4039	CY	11–18	935	
Marden High School A Designated Specialist Media Arts College	Hartington Rd, Cullercoats, North Shields, Tyne and Wear NE30 3RZ	0191 200 6357	0191 200 6361	Mr David Stainthorpe	392-4006	CY	11–16	915	
Monkseaton Community High School	Seatonville Rd, Whitley Bay, Tyne and Wear NE25 9EQ	0191 297 9700	0191 297 0567	Dr P. Kelley	392-4034	FD	13–18	893	
Norham Community Technology College	Alnwick Ave, North Shields, Tyne and Wear NE29 7BU	0191 200 5062	0191 200 5065	Mrs Linda Halbert	392-4008	CY	11–16	802	
St Thomas More Roman RC High School	Lynn Rd, North Shields, Tyne and Wear NE29 8LF	0191 200 6333	0191 200 6336	Mr J.T. Marshall	392-4605	VA	11–18	1687	RC
Seaton Burn College, A Specialist Business and Enterprise School	Dudley La, Seaton Burn, Newcastle upon Tyne, Tyne and Wear NE13 6EJ	0191 236 1700	0191 200 7917	Mr S.J. Prandle	392-4041	CY	11–18	774	
Whitley Bay High School	Deneholm, Whitley Bay, Tyne and Wear NE25 9AS	0191 200 8800	0191 200 8803	Mr A. Chedburn	392-4029	CY	13–18	1528	

Northumberland

School name	Address	Tel	Fax	Headteacher	Ref	Type	Ages	Pupils	Other
Ashington Community High School	Green La, Ashington, Northumberland NE63 8DH	01670 812166	01670 855377	Mr Ken Tonge	929-4415	FD	13–18	1036	
Astley Community High School	Elsdon Ave, Seaton Delaval, Whitley Bay, Northumberland NE25 0BP	0191 237 1505	0191 237 6891	Mr I.G. Knight	929-5400	CY	13–18	796	
Bedlingtonshire Community High School	Palace Rd, Bedlington, Northumberland NE22 7DS	01670 822625	01670 829378	Mr Kieran McGrane	929-4434	CY	13–18	873	
Berwick Community High School	Adams Dr, Berwick-upon-Tweed, Northumberland TD15 2JF	01289 305083	01289 302681	Mr Stephen Quinlan	929-4437	CY	13–18	746	
Blyth Community College	Chase Farm Dr, Blyth, Northumberland NE24 4JP	01670 798100	01670 352765	Mrs Pat Armstrong	929-4442	CY	13–18	1251	
Coquet High School	Acklington Rd, Amble, Morpeth, Northumberland NE65 0NG	01665 710636	01665 713470	Mr Paul Allen	929-4439	CY	13–18	608	
Cramlington Community High School	Highburn, Cramlington, Northumberland NE23 6BN	01670 712311	01670 730598	Mr D.M. Wise	929-4424	CY	13–18	1662	
The Duchess's Community High School	Howling La, Alnwick, Northumberland NE66 1DH	01665 602166	01665 510602	Mr Maurice Hall	929-4438	CY	13–18	1123	
Haydon Bridge Community High School and Sports College	Haydon Bridge, Hexham, Northumberland NE47 6LR	01434 684422	01434 68226	Mr John Dowler	929-4130	CY	13–18	754	R
Hirst High School	Lichfield Cl, Ashington, Northumberland NE63 9RX	01670 816111	01670 522565	Mrs Lesley Craig	929-4433	CY	13–18	703	
The King Edward VI School	Cottingwood La, Morpeth, Northumberland NE61 1DN	01670 515415	01670 504116	Mr Ian Wilkinson	929-4501	VC	13–18	1414	
Ponteland Community High School	Callerton La, Ponteland, Newcastle upon Tyne, Tyne and Wear NE20 9EY	01661 824711	01661 821831	Mr S.J. Prandle	929-4426	CY	13–18	1144	
Prudhoe Community High School	Moor Rd, Prudhoe, Northumberland NE42 5LJ	01661 832486	01661 832859	Dr Iain Shaw	929-4369	CY	13–18	982	
Queen Elizabeth High School	Whetstone Bridge Rd, Hexham, Northumberland NE46 3JB	01434 610300	01434 610320	Mr Tony Webster	929-4417	CY	13–18	1372	
St Benet Biscop RC VA High School	Ridge Terr, Bedlington, Northumberland NE22 6ED	01670 822795	01670 829427	Mr Nick Bowen	929-4632	VA	13–18	848	RC

Redcar and Cleveland

School name	Address	Tel	Fax	Headteacher	Ref	Type	Ages	Pupils	Other
Bydales School – A Specialist Technology College	Coast Rd, Marske-by-Sea, Redcar, North Yorkshire TS11 6AR	01642 482932	01642 477348	Mr Anthony Hobbs	807-4022	CY	11–16	774	
Eston Park School	Burns Rd, Eston, Middlesbrough, North Yorkshire TS6 9AW	01642 466101	01642 466101	Mr J. Rogers	807-4001	CY	11–16	885	
Freebrough Specialist Engineering College	Linden Rd, Brotton, Saltburn-by-the-Sea, Yorkshire TS12 2SJ	01287 676305	01287 677814	Mrs Diane Edwards	807-4000	CY	11–16	895	
Gillbrook College	Normanby Rd, South Bank, Middlesbrough TS6 9AG	01642 466201	01642 463905	Mr John Anthony	807-4120	CY	11–16	669	

School name	Address	Tel	Fax	Headteacher	Ref	Type	Ages	Pupils	Other
Huntcliff School	Marske Mill La, Saltburn-by-the-Sea, North Yorkshire TS12 1HJ	01287 622178	01287 622299	Mrs Ruth Headdon	807-4007	CY	11–16	508	
Laurence Jackson School	Church La, Guisborough TS14 6RD	01287 636361	01287 610309	Mr Robert Campbell	807-4005	CY	11–16	1568	
Nunthorpe School	Guisborough Rd, Nunthorpe, Middlesbrough TS7 0LA	01642 310561	01642 325672	Ms Debbie Clinton	807-4121	CY	11–16	1330	
Redcar Community College A Specialist Visual and Performing Arts Centre	Kirkleatham La, Redcar, North Yorkshire TS10 4AB	01642 289211	01642 489202	Mr Stuart Rees	807-4141	CY	11–16	812	
Rye Hills School	Redcar La, Redcar, North Yorkshire TS10 2HN	01642 484269	01642 484961	Mr H. Joyce	807-4125	CY	11–16	1178	
Sacred Heart Roman RC VA School – A Specialist Science College	Mersey Rd, Redcar, North Yorkshire TS10 1PJ	01642 473221	01642 473741	Mrs Patricia Hibbert	807-4639	VA	11–16	741	RC
St Peter's RC College of Maths and Computing	Normanby Rd, South Bank, Middlesbrough TS6 6SP	01642 453462	01642 455010	Mr Gavin Salvesen-Sawh	807-4638	VA	11–16	478	RC

South Tyneside

School name	Address	Tel	Fax	Headteacher	Ref	Type	Ages	Pupils	Other
Boldon School	New Rd, Boldon Colliery, Tyne and Wear NE35 9DZ	0191 536 2176	0191 5374073	Mr C. Whitfield	393-4019	CY	11–16		
Harton Technology College	Lisle Rd, South Shields, Tyne and Wear NE34 6DL	0191 456 4226	0191 4271478	Mr Ken Gibson	393-4004	CY	11–16		
Hebburn Comprehensive School	Campbell Park Rd, Hebburn, Tyne and Wear NE31 2QU	0191 483 3199	0191 483 2160	Mr N. Anderson	393-4026	CY	11–16		
Jarrow School	Field Terr, Jarrow, Tyne and Wear NE32 5PR	0191 489 3225	0191 489 0088	Mr Les Jones	393-4033	CY	11–16		
Mortimer Community College	Reading Rd, South Shields, Tyne and Wear NE33 4UG	0191 456 6511	0191 427 1176	Ms Claire Mullane	393-4006	CY	11–16		
St Joseph's RC VA Comprehensive School	Mill La, Hebburn, Tyne and Wear NE31 2ET	0191 421 2828	0191 421 0531	Dr J. Campbell	393-4603	VA	11–18	1534	RC
St Wilfrid's RC College	Harton La, South Shields, Tyne and Wear NE34 0PH	0191 456 9121	0191 454 5070	Ms Christine Wright	393-4604	VA	11–16	908	RC
South Shields Community School	McAnany Ave, South Shields, Tyne and Wear NE34 0PJ	0191 456 8929	0191 455 8543	Dr Frain	393-4606	CY	11–16		
Whitburn CE School	Nicholas Ave, Whitburn SR6 7EX	0191 529 3712	0191 529 5569	Miss P.A. Williams	393-4605	VA	11–16	955	CE

Stockton-on-Tees

School name	Address	Tel	Fax	Headteacher	Ref	Type	Ages	Pupils	Other
All Saints CE School	Blair Ave, Ingleby Barwick, Stockton-on-Tees, North Yorkshire TS17 5BL	01642 754650	01642 751917	Mr Kevin Mann	808-4001	VA	11–16	600	CE
Billingham Campus School	Marsh House Ave, Billingham TS23 3HB	01642 560947	01642 370104	Mr David Reach	808-4139	CY	11–16	854	
Bishopsgarth School	Harrowgate La, Bishopsgarth, Stockton-on-Tees, North Yorkshire TS19 8TF	01642 586262	01642 570038	Mr John Golds	808-4105	CY	11–16	515	
Blakeston School – A Community Sports College	Junction Rd, Norton, Stockton-on-Tees, North Yorkshire TS19 9LT	01642 612381	01642 675842	Ms Georgiana Sale	808-4106	CY	11–16	764	
Conyers School	Green La, Yarm, North Yorkshire TS15 9ET	01642 783253	01642 783834	Mr John P. Morgan	808-4023	CY	11–18	1372	
Egglescliffe School	Urlay Nook Rd, Eaglescliffe, Stockton-on-Tees, North Yorkshire TS16 0LA	01642 352570	01642 352571	Mrs Angela Darnell	808-4008	CY	11–18	1421	
Grangefield School and Technology College	Oxbridge Ave, Stockton-on-Tees, North Yorkshire TS18 4LE	01642 353637	01642 673579	Mr Allan Mansfield	808-4138	CY	11–16	1274	
Ian Ramsey CE Aided Comprehensive School	Greens La, Fairfield, Stockton-on-Tees, North Yorkshire TS18 5AJ	01642 585205	01642 570488	Mr Mike Davison	808-4640	VA	11–16	1182	CE
Northfield School and Sports College	Thames Rd, Billingham, North Yorkshire TS22 5EG	01642 557373	01642 360392	Mr D.J. Youldon	808-4102	CY	11–16	1097	
The Norton School Humanities College	Berkshire Rd, Norton, Stockton-on-Tees, North Yorkshire TS20 2RD	01642 557361	01642 360266	Mr Paul Wray	808-4103	CY	11–16	483	
Our Lady and St Bede RC School	Bishopton Rd West, Stockton-on-Tees, North Yorkshire TS19 0QH	01642 890800	01642 603559	Mr Edwin Sherrington	808-4631	VA	11–16	674	RC
St Michael's Roman RC VA Comprehensive School	Beamish Rd, Billingham, Stockton-on-Tees TS23 3DX	01642 870003	01642 370618	Mr Joe White	808-4630	VA	11–16	912	RC
St Patrick's RC Comprehensive School	Baysdale Rd, Thornaby, Stockton-on-Tees TS17 9DE	01642 613327	01642 618227	Mr Kenneth Dyer	808-4632	VA	11–16	553	RC
Thornaby Community School	Baysdale Rd, Thornaby, Stockton-on-Tees TS17 9DB	01642 763244	01642 761318	Mrs Linda Russell-Bond	808-4000	CY	11–16	714	

3

Sunderland

School name	Address	Tel	Fax	Ref	Type	Ages	Pupils	Other
Biddick School Sports College	Biddick La, Washington, Tyne and Wear NE38 8AL	0191 219 3680	0191 219 3688	394-4067	CY	11–16	1115	
Castle View School A Specialist Business and Enterprise College	Cartwright Rd, Hylton Castle, Sunderland, Tyne and Wear SR5 3DX	0191 553 5533	0191 553 5537	394-4036	CY	11–16	888	
Farringdon Community Sports College	Allendale Rd, Sunderland, Tyne and Wear SR3 3EL	0191 553 6013	0191 553 6017	394-4037	CY	11–16	991	
Hetton School	North Rd, Hetton-le-Hole, Houghton-le-Spring, Tyne and Wear DH5 9JZ	0191 553 6756	0191 553 6760	394-4059	CY	11–16	974	
Houghton Kepier Sports College: A Foundation School	Dairy La, Houghton-le-Spring, Tyne and Wear DH4 5BH	0191 553 6528	0191 553 6533	394-4072	FD	11–16	1340	
Hylton Red House School	Rutherglen Rd, Sunderland, Tyne and Wear SR5 5LN	0191 553 5511	0191 553 5515	394-4014	CY	11–16	723	
Monkwearmouth School	Torver Cres, Seaburn Dene, Sunderland, Tyne and Wear SR6 8LG	0191 553 5555	0191 553 5558	394-4041	CY	11–16	1399	
Oxclose Community School	Dilston Cl, Oxclose Village, Washington, Tyne and Wear NE38 0LN	0191 219 3777	0191 219 3780	394-4063	CY	11–16	889	
Pennywell School	Portsmouth Rd, Sunderland, Tyne and Wear SR4 9BA	0191 553 6832	0191 553 6838	394-4017	CY	11–16	876	
St Aidan's RC School	Willow Bank Rd, Ashbrooke, Sunderland, Tyne and Wear SR2 7HJ	0191 553 6073	0191 553 6077	394-4607	VA	11–18	1156	RC B
St Anthony's RC Girls' School	Thornhill Terr, Sunderland, Tyne and Wear SR2 7JN	0191 553 7700	0191 553 7699	394-4610	VA	11–18	1331	RC G
St Robert of Newminster Roman RC School	Biddick La, Washington, Tyne and Wear NE38 8AF	0191 219 3810	0191 219 3815	394-4609	VA	11–18	1542	RC
Sandhill View School	Grindon La, Thorney Cl, Sunderland, Tyne and Wear SR3 4EN	0191 553 6060	0191 553 6063	394-4071	CY	11–16	1009	
Southmoor Community School, Mathematics and Computing College	Ryhope Rd, Sunderland, Tyne and Wear SR2 7TF	0191 553 7600	0191 553 7603	394-4055	CY	11–16	1198	
Thornhill School	Thornholme Rd, Sunderland, Tyne and Wear SR2 7NA	0191 553 7735	0191 553 7740	394-4042	CY	11–16	1238	
Venerable Bede Church of England [Aided] Secondary School	Tunstall Bank, Sunderland, Tyne and Wear SR2 0SX	0191 523 9745	0191 523 9775	394-4073	VA	11–16	919	CE
Washington School	Spout La, Washington, Tyne and Wear NE37 2AA	0191 219 3845	0191 219 3848	394-4065	CY	11–16	1053	

North West

Blackburn with Darwen

School name	Address	Tel	Fax	Ref	Type	Ages	Pupils	Other
Beardwood High School	Preston New Rd, Blackburn, Lancashire BB2 7AD	01254 614980	01254 614981	889-4001	CY	11–16	1032	
Blakewater College	Shadsworth Rd, Blackburn, Lancashire BB1 2HT	01254 505700		889-4799	CY	11–16	508	
Darwen Moorland High School	Holden Fold, Darwen, Lancashire BB3 3AU	01254 819500		889-4189	CY	11–16	821	
Darwen Vale High School	Blackburn Rd, Darwen, Lancashire BB3 0AL	01254 223000	01254 223001	889-4310	CY	11–16	1199	
Our Lady and St John RC Arts College	North Rd, Blackburn, Lancashire BB1 1PY	01254 59055	01254 697308	889-4629	VA	11–16	903	RC
Pleckgate High School Mathematics and Computing College	Pleckgate Rd, Blackburn, Lancashire BB1 8QA	01254 249134	01254 245329	889-4012	CY	11–16	1190	
St Bede's Roman RC High School, Blackburn	Livesey Branch Rd, Blackburn, Lancashire BB2 5BU	01254 202519	01254 207882	889-4632	VA	11–16	1018	RC
St Wilfrid's CE High School and Technology College	Duckworth St, Blackburn, Lancashire BB2 2JR	01254 604000	01254 604004	889-5406	VA	11–18	1580	CE
Tauheedul Islam Girls High School	31 Bicknell St, Blackburn, Lancashire BB1 7EY	01254 54021		889-4800	VA	11–16	313	Mu G
Witton Park High School	Buncer La, Blackburn, Lancashire BB2 6TD	01254 264551	01254 693699	889-4048	CY	11–16	1062	

Blackpool

School name	Address	Tel	Fax	Headteacher	Ref	Type	Ages	Pupils	Other
Beacon Hill High School Business and Enterprise College	Warbreck Hill Rd, Blackpool, Lancashire FY2 0TS	01253 355493	01253 357981	Mr R.M. Wilmore	890-4059	CY	11–16	691	
Bispham High School – an Arts College	Bispham Rd, Blackpool, Lancashire FY2 0NH	01253 353155	01253 500397	Mr Rob Harrison	890-4056	CY	11–16	985	
Collegiate High School Sports College	Blackpool Old Rd, Blackpool, Lancashire FY3 7LS	01253 300460	01253 395700	Ms Gillian Fennel	890-4060	CY	11–16	1176	
Highfield Humanities College	Highfield Rd, Blackpool, Lancashire FY4 3JZ	01253 310925	01253 310929	Mr Ian Evans	890-4053	CY	11–16	1130	
Montgomery High School - A Language College and Full Service School	All Hallows Rd, Bispham, Blackpool, Lancashire FY2 0AZ	01253 356271	01253 352305	Mr P. Moss	890-4057	CY	11–16	1411	
Palatine Community Sports College	St Anne's Rd, Blackpool, Lancashire FY4 2AR	01253 345522	01253 341803	Mr J. McNaughton	890-4404	CY	11–16	1089	
St George's CE High School	Cherry Tree Rd, Marton, Blackpool, Lancashire FY4 4PH	01253 316725	01253 316727	Mrs Elizabeth Warner	890-4405	VA	11–16	882	CE
St Mary's RC College	St Walburga's Rd, Blackpool, Lancashire FY3 7EQ	01253 396286	01253 305475	Mr Stephen Tierney	890-4601	VA	11–18	1227	RC

Bolton

School name	Address	Tel	Fax	Headteacher	Ref	Type	Ages	Pupils	Other
Bolton Muslim Girls School	Swan La, Bolton, Lancashire BL3 6TQ	01204 361103		Muberuck Ibrahin	350-4806	VA	11–16		Mu G
Canon Slade CE School	Bradshaw Brow, Bolton, Lancashire BL2 3BP	01204 333343	01204 333340	Rev Philip Williamson	350-5401	VA	11–18	1728	CE
George Tomlinson School	Springfield Rd, Kearsley, Bolton, Lancashire BL4 8HY	01204 332555	01204 794091	Ms Rachel Glazebrook	350-5402	FD	11–16	539	
Harper Green School	Harper Green Rd, Farnworth, Bolton, Lancashire BL4 0DH	01204 572941	01204 793031	Mr Peter Jefferies	350-4046	CY	11–16	1479	
Hayward School	Lever Edge La, Bolton, Lancashire BL3 3HH	01204 333222	01204 333220	Mrs Jenny Coleman	350-4047	CY	11–16	1011	
Ladybridge High School	New York, Junction Rd, Deane, Bolton, Lancashire BL3 4NG	01204 333355		Ms J. Gabler	350-4805	CY	11–16	794	
Little Lever School Specialist Language College	Church St, Little Lever, Bolton, Lancashire BL3 1BT	01204 333300	01204 333307	Mrs Ann Behan	350-4044	CY	11–16	1092	
Mount St Joseph: Business and Enterprise College	Greenland Rd, Farnworth, Bolton, Lancashire BL4 0HU	01204 391800	01204 389575	Miss Penelope Walker	350-4611	VA	11–16	919	RC
Rivington and Blackrod High School	Rivington La, Horwich, Bolton, Lancashire BL6 7RU	01204 333266	01204 333264	Mr Anthony Purcell	350-4501	VC	11–18	1901	CE
St James's CE School and Sports College	Lucas Rd, Farnworth, Bolton, Lancashire BL4 9RU	01204 333000	01204 333201	Mr C.R. Atkinson	350-5400	VA	11–16	1070	CE
St Joseph's RC High School and Sports College	Chorley New Rd, Horwich, Bolton, Lancashire BL6 6HW	01204 697456	01204 669018	Mr L. Conley	350-4609	VA	11–16	854	RC
Sharples School	Hill Cot Rd, Sharples, Bolton, Lancashire BL1 8SN	01204 333253	01204 333250	Mrs Lynne Porter	350-4048	CY	11–16	1020	
Smithills School	Smithills Dean Rd, Bolton, Lancashire BL1 6JS	01204 842382	01204 847473	Mr J. Lawson	350-4049	CY	11–16	1458	
Thornleigh Salesian College	Sharples Pk, Astley Bridge, Bolton, Lancashire BL1 6PQ	01204 301351	01204 595351	M. Coyle	350-4612	VA	11–18	1577	RC
Turton High School Media Arts College	Bromley Cross Rd, Bromley Cross, Bolton, Lancashire BL7 9LT	01204 333233	01204 333240	Mr John Porteous	350-4034	CY	11–18	1641	
Westhoughton High School	Bolton Rd, Westhoughton, Bolton, Greater Manchester BL5 3BZ	01942 814122	01942 817792	Mr P. Hart	350-4031	CY	11–18	1245	
Withins School	Newby Rd, Breightmet, Bolton, Lancashire BL2 5JB	01204 332533	01204 332530	Mr P. Mather	350-4042	CY	11–16	891	

Bury

School name	Address	Tel	Fax	Headteacher	Ref	Type	Ages	Pupils	Other
Broad Oak High School	Hazel Ave, Bury, Lancashire BL9 7QT	0161 797 6543	0161 797 1149	Mr N. O'Connor	351-4032	CY	11–16	655	
Bury CE High School	Haslam Brow, Bury, Lancashire BL9 0TS	0161 797 6236	0161 705 1872	Mr Philip Grady	351-4603	VA	11–16	728	CE
Castlebrook High School	Parr La, Bury, Lancashire BL9 8LP	0161 796 9820	0161 796 3380	Mr Anthony Roberts	351-4031	CY	11–16	859	
The Derby High School	Radcliffe Rd, Bury, Lancashire BL9 9NH	0161 764 1819	0161 764 9365	Mrs Alyson Byrne	351-4007	CY	11–16	922	
The Elton High School Specialist Arts College	Walshaw Rd, Bury, Lancashire BL8 1RN	0161 763 1434	0161 761 3849	Mr N. Scruton	351-4004	CY	11–16	942	
Manchester Mesivta School	Beechwood, Charlton Ave, Prestwich, Greater Manchester M25 0PH	0161 773 1789	0161 792 4571	Mr P. Pink	351-4005	VA	11–16	189	Je B
Parrenthorn High School	Heywood Rd, Prestwich, Manchester M25 2GR	0161 773 8634	0161 798 7048	Mr Michael Fitzgerald	351-4022	CY	11–16	730	

School name	Address	Tel	Fax	Headteacher	Ref	Type	Ages	Pupils	Other
Philips High School	Higher La., Whitefield, Manchester, Lancashire M45 7PH	0161 351 2200	0161 351 3445	Mr C.J. Trees	351-4025	CY	11–16	849	
Prestwich Arts College	Heys Rd, Prestwich, Manchester, Lancashire M25 1JZ	0161 773 2052	0161 773 5644	Mr Geoffrey Barlow	351-4028	CY	11–16	848	
Radcliffe Riverside School	Spring La., Radcliffe, Manchester M26 2SZ	0161 723 3110	0161 723 1880	Mrs Diana Morton	351-4801	CY	11–16	804	
St Gabriel's RC High School	Bridge Rd, Bury, Lancashire BL9 0TZ	0161 764 3186	0161 761 3469	Mr E.P. Robinson	351-4607	VA	11–16	1028	RC
St Monica's RC High School Specialist Language College	Bury Old Rd, Prestwich, Manchester, Lancashire M25 1JH	0161 773 6436	0161 773 6650	Mr F. McCarron	351-4606	VA	11–16	1138	RC
Tottington High School	Laurel St, Tottington, Bury, Lancashire BL8 3LY	01204 882327	01204 884849	Mr A. Scott	351-4020	CY	11–16	946	
Woodhey High School	Bolton Rd West, Ramsbottom, Bury, Lancashire BL0 9QZ	01706 825215	01706 825989	Mr Martin Braidley	351-4026	CY	11–16	980	

Cheshire

School name	Address	Tel	Fax	Headteacher	Ref	Type	Ages	Pupils	Other
All Hallows RC High School	Brooklands Ave, Macclesfield, Cheshire SK11 8LB	01625 426138	01625 500315	Mr A.S. Billings	875-4801	VA	11–18	1176	RC
Alsager School	Hassall Rd, Alsager, Stoke-on-Trent, Cheshire ST7 2HR	01270 871100	01270 871139	Mr D. Black	875-4121	CY	11–18	1476	
Bishop Heber High School	Chester Rd, Malpas, Cheshire SY14 8JD	01948 860571	01948 860962	Mr David Curry	875-4158	CY	11–18	1038	
The Bishops' Blue Coat CE High School	Vaughans La., Gt Boughton, Chester, Cheshire CH3 5XF	01244 313806	01244 320992	Mr Robert Haigh	875-4623	VA	11–18	1036	CE
Blacon High School, A Specialist Sports College	Melbourne Rd, Blacon, Chester, Cheshire CH1 5JH	01244 371475	01244 374279	Mrs Ella Brett	875-4006	CY	11–16	562	
Brine Leas High School	Audlem Rd, Nantwich, Cheshire CW5 7DY	01270 625663	01270 610373	Mr Michael Butler	875-4220	FD	11–16	1068	
The RC High School, Chester a Specialist Science College	Old Wrexham Rd, Handbridge, Chester, Cheshire CH4 7HS	01244 683473	01244 681773	Mr John Murray	875-4603	VA	11–18	995	RC
Cheshire Oaks High School	Stanney La., Ellesmere Port, Cheshire CH65 9DB	0151 355 5245	0151 357 1834	Mrs L. Fox	875-4154	CY	11–18	741	
Christleton High School	Village Rd, Christleton, Chester, Cheshire CH3 7AD	01244 335843	01244 332173	Mr Tony Lamberton	875-4149	CY	11–18	1274	
Congleton High School	Box La., Congleton, Cheshire CW12 4NS	01260 273013	01260 274580	Mr David Hermitt	875-4226	CY	11–18	1039	
Coppenhall High School	Coronation St, Crewe, Cheshire CW1 4EB	01270 583431	01270 501679	Dr Pam Scott	875-4131	CY	11–16	665	
The County High School Leftwich	Granville Rd, Northwich, Cheshire CW9 8EZ	01606 333300	01606 331483	Miss Julie Brandreth	875-4134	CY	11–16	891	
Eaton Bank School	Jackson Rd, Congleton, Cheshire CW12 1NT	01260 273000	01260 297352	Mr Paul Roberts	875-4227	CY	11–18	1072	
Ellesmere Port RC High School	Capenhurst La., Whitby, Ellesmere Port, Cheshire CH65 7AQ	0151 355 2373	0151 356 9154	Mr P. Lee	875-4611	VA	11–18	1081	RC
Ellesmere Port Specialist School of Performing Arts	Woodchurch La., Ellesmere Port, Cheshire CH66 3NG	0151 339 4807	0151 339 4126	Mrs Christine Needham	875-4161	CY	11–18	892	
Fallibroome High School	Priory La., Upton, Macclesfield, Cheshire SK10 4AF	01625 827898	01625 820051	Mr P.W. Rubery	875-5401	FD	11–18	1500	
Hartford High School a Specialist Languages and Sports College	Hartford Campus, Chester Rd, Hartford, Northwich, Cheshire CW8 1LH	01606 786000	01606 783941	Mr Michael Holland	875-4222	CY	11–16	1107	
Helsby High School	Chester Rd, Helsby, Frodsham, Cheshire WA6 0HY	01928 723551	01928 723093	Mr R. Evans	875-4221	CY	11–18	1407	
Holmes Chapel Comprehensive School	Selkirk Dr, Holmes Chapel, Crewe, Cheshire CW4 7DX	01477 534513	01477 534489	Mr D. Oliver	875-4165	CY	11–18	1117	
Kings Grove School	Buchan Gr, Crewe, Cheshire CW2 7NQ	01270 661223	01270 560789	Mr William Evans	875-4223	CY	11–16	725	
Knutsford High School	Bexton Rd, Knutsford, Cheshire WA16 0EA	01565 633294	01565 633796	Mr K. Hollins	875-4163	CY	11–18	1539	
Macclesfield High School	Park La., Macclesfield, Cheshire SK11 8JR	01625 383100	01625 668635	Mr G.J. Ward	875-5402	FD	11–18	834	
Malbank School and Sixth Form College	Welsh Row, Nantwich, Cheshire CW5 5HD	01270 611009	01270 610350	Mrs Jeannette Walker	875-4143	FD	11–18	1335	
Middlewich High School	King Edward St, Middlewich, Cheshire CW10 9BU	01606 832013	01606 738260	Mr Martin Forster	875-4127	CY	11–16	682	
Neston High School	Raby Park Rd, Neston, Cheshire CH64 9NH	0151 336 3902	0151 353 0408	Mrs R. Winterson	875-4100	CY	11–18	1574	
Poynton High School	Yew Tree La., Poynton, Stockport, Cheshire SK12 1PU	01625 871811	01625 874541	Mrs Susan Adamson	875-4211	CY	11–18	1626	
Queen's Park High School	Queen's Pk, Chester, Cheshire CH4 7AE	01244 675468	01244 679491	Mr A. Firman	875-4007	CY	11–18	1012	
Rudheath Community High School	Shipbrook Rd, Rudheath, Northwich, Cheshire CW9 7DT	01606 42515	01606 46053	Mr M. Hayhurst	875-4126	CY	11–16	762	
Ruskin Sports and Languages College	Ruskin Rd, Crewe, Cheshire CW2 7JT	01270 560514	01270 650248	Mr Philip Mottershead	875-4139	CY	11–16	690	
St Nicholas RC High School	Greenbank La., Hartford, Northwich, Cheshire CW8 1JW		01606 784586	Mr G. Boyle	875-4610	VA	11–18	1277	RC
St Thomas More RC High School	Dane Bank Ave, Crewe, Cheshire CW2 8AE	01270 568014	01270 650860	Mr Peter Walters	875-4612	VA	11–16	630	RC

3

School name	Address	Tel	Fax	Headteacher	Ref	Type	Ages	Pupils	Other
Sandbach High School and Sixth Form College	Middlewich Rd, Sandbach, Cheshire CW11 3NT	01270 765031	01270 768544	Mr J. Leigh	875-4123	FD	11–18	1291	G
Shavington High School	Rope La, Shavington, Crewe, Cheshire CW2 5DH	01270 662111	01270 661305	Mr Robert Knight	875-4144	CY	11–16	862	
Sir William Stanier Community School	Coronation St, Crewe, Cheshire CW1 4EB	01270 537936	01270 537593	Mark Stayner		CY	11–16		
Tarporley Community High School	Eaton Rd, Tarporley, Cheshire CW6 0BL	01829 732558	01829 733945	Ms Sarah Lee	875-4803	CY	11–18	1022	
Tytherington High School	Manchester Rd, Macclesfield, Cheshire SK10 2EE	01625 610220	01625 610925	Mr A. Robinson	875-4116	CY	11–18	1235	
Upton-by-Chester High School	St James Ave, Upton-by-Chester, Chester, Cheshire CH2 1NN	01244 313061	01244 312115	Mr J. Holland	875-4153	CY	11–18	1662	
The Verdin High School	Grange La, Winsford, Cheshire CW7 2BT	01606 592300	01606 863562	Mr Martin Howlett	875-4130	CY	11–19	1037	
Victoria Community Technology School	Meredith Centre, West St, Crewe, Cheshire CW1 2PZ	01270 537936	01270 537953	Mr Mark Stanyer	875-4142	CY	11–16	599	
Weaverham High School	Lime Ave, Weaverham, Northwich, Cheshire CW8 3HT	01606 852120	01606 854033	Mr David Charlton	875-4132	CY	11–16	1068	
The Whitby High School	Sycamore Dr, Whitby, Ellesmere Port, Merseyside CH66 2NU	0151 355 8445	0151 357 2955	Mrs M. Hughes	875-4167	FD	11–18	1571	
Wilmslow High School	Holly Rd, Wilmslow, Cheshire SK9 1LZ	01625 526191	01625 536858	Mrs G. Bremner	875-4225	CY	11–18	1903	
Woodford Lodge High School	Woodford La West, Winsford, Cheshire CW7 4EH	01606 551118	01606 863162	Mr Stephen Meeks	875-4129	CY	11–18	577	

Cumbria

School name	Address	Tel	Fax	Headteacher	Ref	Type	Ages	Pupils	Other
The Alfred Barrow School	Duke St, Barrow-in-Furness, Cumbria LA14 2LB	01229 894644	01229 894640	Dr Linda Potts	909-4304	CY	11–16	401	
Appleby Grammar School	Battlebarrow, Appleby-in-Westmorland, Cumbria CA16 6XU	01768 351580	01768 352412	Mr Terry Hobson	909-5407	FD	11–18	600	
Beacon Hill Community School	Market Sq, Aspatria, Wigton, Cumbria CA7 3EZ	01697 320509	01697 322510	Mrs Julia Richardson	909-4001	CY	11–16	194	
Caldew School	Dalston, Carlisle, Cumbria CA5 7NN	01228 710044	01228 710390	Mr A.B.D. Abernethy	909-5413	FD	11–18	967	
Cartmel Priory CE School	Headless Cross, Cartmel, Grange-over-Sands, Cumbria LA11 7SA	01539 536202	01539 536287	Dr Paul Williams	909-5410	VA	11–16	401	CE
Cockermouth School	Castlegate Dr, Cockermouth, Cumbria CA13 9HF	01900 325940	01900 325944	Mr Stuart Reeves	909-4103	CY	11–18	1387	
Dallam School	Haverflatts La, Milnthorpe, Cumbria LA7 7DD	01539 565165	01539 563913	Mr Steven Holdup	909-5405	FD	11–18	981	
Dowdales School	Dalton-in-Furness, Cumbria LA15 8AH	01229 897911	01229 897913	Mrs E. Moffatt	909-4150	CY	11–16	1096	
Ehenside Community School	Towerson St, Cleator, Cumbria CA23 3EL	01946 855000	01946 855002	Mr G A Orton	909-4200	CY	11–16	259	
John Ruskin School	Lake Rd, Coniston, Cumbria LA21 8EW	01539 441306	01539 441123	Mr Jonathan Longstaffe	909-4151	CY	11–16	164	
Keswick School	Vicarage Hill, Keswick, Cumbria LA12 5QB	01768 772605	01768 774813	Mr Michael Chapman	909-5414	VA	11–18	1058	R
Kirkbie Kendal School	Lound Rd, Kendal, Cumbria LA9 7EQ	01539 727422	01539 729243	Mr Philip Hyman	909-5400	FD	11–18	988	
Kirkby Stephen Grammar School Sports College	Christian Head, Kirkby Stephen, Cumbria CA17 4HA	01768 371693	01768 372387	Mr David Keetley	909-5406	CY	11–18	393	CE
The Lakes School	Troutbeck Bridge, Windermere, Cumbria LA23 1HW	01539 462470	01539 462473	Dr David Selby	909-4056	CY	11–18	724	
Lochinvar School	Longtown, Carlisle, Cumbria CA6 5UG	01228 791416	01228 791701	Mr Alan Smith	909-4005	CY	11–16	173	
Millom School	Salthouse Rd, Millom, Cumbria LA18 5AB	01229 772300	01229 772883	Mr Ian Smith	909-4204	CY	11–18	748	
The Morton School	Wigton Rd, Carlisle, Cumbria CA2 6LB	01228 607545	01228 607546	Mr Mike Bell	909-4501	CY	11–18	522	
The Nelson Thomlinson School	High St, Wigton, Cumbria CA7 9PX	01697 342160	01697 349160	Mr Peter M Ireland	909-4104	CY	11–18	1301	
Netherhall School	Netherhall Rd, Maryport, Cumbria CA15 6NT	01900 813434	01900 814867	Mr David Sibbit		CY	11–18	929	
Newman RC School	Lismore Pl, Carlisle, Cumbria CA1 1NA	01228 607470	01228 607472	Mr John McAuley	909-4630	VA	11–18	531	RC
North Cumbria Technology College	Edgehill Rd, Carlisle, Cumbria CA1 3SL	01228 607507	01228 607590	Mr Mark Yearsley	909-4408	FD	11–18	439	
Parkview School	West Ave, Barrow-in-Furness, Cumbria LA13 9AY	01229 894661	01229 894663	Mrs E. Fraser	909-5409	FD	11–16	962	
Queen Elizabeth Grammar School	Ulswater Rd, Penrith, Cumbria CA11 7EG	01768 864621	01768 890923	Mr Christopher Kirkup	909-5401	FD	11–18	811	
Queen Elizabeth Grammar School	Kirkby Lonsdale, Carnforth, Lancashire LA6 2HJ	01524 272275	01524 272863	Mr Christopher Clarke	909-5411	FD	11–18	1364	
The Queen Katherine School	Appleby Rd, Kendal, Cumbria LA9 6PJ	01539 773640	01539 741223	Mr Stephen Wilkinson	909-5404	FD	11–18	1430	
St Aidan's County High School Specialist Sports College	Lismore Pl, Carlisle, Cumbria CA1 1LY	01228 607587	01228 607590	Mr M.P. Murphy	909-5403	FD	11–18	1480	
St Benedict's RC High School	Red Lonning, Hensingham, Whitehaven, Cumbria CA28 8UG	01946 852680	01946 852684	Mr Mark Condron	909-4622	VA	11–18	1393	RC
St Bernard's RC High School	Rating La, Barrow-in-Furness, Cumbria LA13 9LE	01229 894620	01229 894622	Mr Tumelty	909-4634	VA	11–16	852	RC

School name	Address	Tel	Fax	Headteacher	Ref	Type	Ages	Pupils	Other
St Joseph's RC High School, Business and Enterprise College	Harrington Rd, Workington, Cumbria CA14 3EE	01900 325240	01900 325241	Mr Thomas Ryan	909-4810	VA	11–16	612	RC
Samuel King's School	Church Rd, Alston, Cumbria CA9 3QU	01434 381236	01434 382082	Mr Maurice Peddelty	909-4011	CY	11–16	211	
Settlebeck High School	Long La, Sedbergh, Cumbria LA10 5AL	01539 620383	01539 621024	Mr Dave Smith	909-4060	CY	11–16	202	
Solway Community Technology College	Liddell St, Silloth, Wigton, Cumbria CA7 4DD	01697 331234	01697 332749	Mrs Susie Shepherd	909-4008	CY	11–16	229	
Southfield Technology College	Moorclose Rd, Workington, Cumbria CA14 5BH	01900 325260	01900 325263	Mrs Lynda Dalkin	909-4311	CY	11–18	746	
Stainburn School and Science College	Stainburn Rd, Workington, Cumbria CA14 4EB	01900 325252	01900 325255	Mr Martin Butcher	909-4312	CY	11–18	975	
Thorncliffe School – A Specialist Sports College	Thorncliffe Rd, Barrow-in-Furness, Cumbria LA14 5QP	01229 894605	01229 894603	Mr Paul Segalini	909-4305	CY	11–18	765	
Trinity School	Strand Rd, Carlisle, Cumbria CA1 1JB	01228 607596	01228 607594	Mr A. Mottershead	909-5402	VA	11–18	1861	CE
Ullswater Community College	Wetheriggs La, Penrith, Cumbria CA11 8NG	01768 242160	01768 242165	Mr Stewart Gimber	909-4310	FD	11–18	1419	
Ulverston Victoria High School	Springfield Rd, Ulverston, Cumbria LA12 0EB	01229 894140	01229 894144	Mrs Karen Hanks	909-4152	CY	11–18	1269	
Walney School	Sandy Gap La, Walney, Barrow-in-Furness, Cumbria LA14 3JL	01229 471528	01229 474900	Mr Alan Dickenson	909-4259	CY	11–16	682	
Whitehaven School	Cleator Moor Rd, Hensingham, Whitehaven, Cumbria CA28 8TY	01946 852644	01946 852650	Mr Malcolm Smith	909-4313	CY	11–18	1461	
William Howard School	Longtown Rd, Brampton, Cumbria CA8 1AR	01697 745700	01697 741096	Mr Clive Bush	909-5412	FD	11–18	1489	
Wyndham School	Main St, Egremont, Cumbria CA22 2DQ	01946 820356	01946 823900	Ms Janet Simpson	909-4203	CY	11–18	856	

Halton

School name	Address	Tel	Fax	Headteacher	Ref	Type	Ages	Pupils	Other
The Bankfield School	Liverpool Rd, Widnes, Cheshire WA8 7HU	0151 424 5038	0151 420 8487	Mrs Carole Owen	876-5400	CY	11–16	867	
Fairfield High School	Peelhouse La, Widnes, Cheshire WA8 6TE	0151 423 3571	0151 424 3316	Mr Jeffrey Hughes	876-4203	CY	11–16	811	
Grange Comprehensive School	Latham Ave, Runcorn, Cheshire WA7 5DX	01928 578115	01928 590075	Mr D. Stanley	876-4104	CY	11–16	1072	
Halton High School	Barnfield Ave, Murdishaw, Runcorn, Cheshire WA7 6EP	01928 711643		Mr John Rowlands	876-4218	CY	11–16	563	
The Heath School	Clifton Rd, Runcorn, Cheshire WA7 4SY	01928 576664	01928 568703	Mrs Heather Mullaney	876-4103	CY	11–16	1048	
St Chad's RC High School	Grangeway, Halton Lodge, Runcorn, Cheshire WA7 5YH	01928 564106	01928 572902	Mr Arthur Graley	876-4614	VA	11–18	906	RC
Saints Peter and Paul RC College	Highfield Rd, Widnes, Cheshire WA7 9DW	0151 424 2139	0151 495 1889	Mr Gus Van Cauwelaert	876-4625	VA	11–16	1610	RC
Wade Deacon High School	Birchfield Rd, Widnes, Cheshire WA8 7TD	0151 423 2721	0151 420 5789	Mrs Pamela Wright	876-4207	CY	11–16	1123	

Knowsley

School name	Address	Tel	Fax	Headteacher	Ref	Type	Ages	Pupils	Other
All Saints RC High School	Bewley Dr, Kirkby, Liverpool, Merseyside L32 9PQ	0151 546 6881	0151 549 2879	Mr B. McLoughlin	340-4609	VA	11–18	1346	RC
Bowring Community Sports College	Western Ave, Huyton, Liverpool, Merseyside L36 4PR	0151 489 1566	0151 489 3061	Mrs Yvonne Sharples	340-4017	CY	11–16	665	
Brookfield High School	Bracknell Ave, Southdene, Kirkby, Liverpool, Merseyside L32 9PP	0151 546 6804	0151 549 2958	Mrs P. Jervis	340-4003	CY	11–16	814	
Halewood College	The Ave, Wood Rd, Halewood, Knowsley, Merseyside L26 1UU	0151 486 2951	0151 428 1408	Mr D. Lang	340-4015	CY	11–18	1403	
Higher Side Community Comprehensive School	Cumber La, Whiston, Prescot, Merseyside L35 2XG	0151 426 5715	0151 430 6644	Mr C. Wilkinson	340-4008	CY	11–16	636	
Knowsley Hey School	Seel Rd, Huyton, Liverpool, Merseyside L36 6DG	0151 489 0276	0151 449 3818	Ms Mary Belchem	340-4005	CY	11–16	1007	
Prescot School	Knowsley Park La, Prescot, Merseyside L34 3NB	0151 426 5571	0151 426 0419	Mrs L.J. Heath	340-4014	CY	11–16	920	
Ruffwood School	Roughwood Dr, Northwood, Kirkby, Liverpool, Merseyside L33 8XF	0151 546 4394	0151 549 1591	Mr Colin Wilson	340-4006	CY	11–16	698	
St Edmund Arrowsmith RC High School, A Specialist Technology College	Scotchbarn La, Prescot, Merseyside L35 7JD	0151 477 8520	0151 430 6432	Mr Philip Grice	340-4604	VA	11–16	800	RC
St Edmund of Canterbury RC High School	Lordens Rd, Liverpool, Merseyside L14 8UD	0151 489 3944	0151 489 3058	Dr F.J. Doherty	340-4607	VA	11–16	818	RC

3

Lancashire

School name	Address	Tel	Fax	Headteacher	Ref	Type	Ages	Pupils	Other
Accrington Moorhead Sports College	Queens Rd West, Accrington, Lancashire BB5 4FF	01254 231579	01254 872415	Mr A.D. Bateman	888-4238	CY	11–16	944	
Accrington St Christopher's CE High School	Queen's Rd West, Accrington, Lancashire BB5 4AY	01254 232992	01254 234775	Mr Alasdair Coates	888-4630	VA	11–16	951	CE
Albany Science College	Bolton Rd, Chorley, Lancashire PR7 3AY	01257 244020	01257 244021	Mr D. Higgs	888-4403	CY	11–16	622	
Alder Grange Community and Technology School	Calder Rd, Rawtenstall, Rossendale, Lancashire BB4 8HW	01706 223171	01706 210448	Mr Iain Hulland	888-4030	CY	11–16	658	
All Hallows RC High School	Crabtree Ave, Penwortham, Preston, Lancashire PR1 0LN	01772 746121	01772 900502	Mr Chris Riding	888-4741	VA	11–16	894	RC
All Saints Roman RC High School, Rossendale	Haslingden Rd, Rawtenstall, Rossendale, Lancashire BB4 6SJ	01706 213693	01706 213693	Mr M.J. Brennan	888-4709	VA	11–16	494	RC
Archbishop Temple CE High School and Technology College, Preston	St Vincent's Rd, Fulwood, Preston, Lancashire PR2 8RA	01772 717782	01772 712833	Mr Darren Edward Hugill	888-5405	VA	11–16	772	CE
Ashton Community Science College	Aldwych Dr, Ashton, Preston, Lancashire PR2 1SL	01772 513002	01772 513006	Mr Chris Lickiss	888-4000	CY	11–16	801	
Bacup and Rawtenstall Grammar School	Glen Rd, Waterfoot, Rossendale, Lancashire BB4 7BJ	01706 234500	01706 234505	Mr Marc Morris	888-5400	VA	11–18	1287	
Baines School	Highcross Rd, Poulton-le-Fylde, Lancashire FY6 8BE	01253 883019	01253 892179	Mr Roderick McCowan	888-5404	FD	11–18	1070	
Balshaw's CE High School	Church Rd, Leyland, Lancashire PR25 3AH	01772 421009		Miss J. Venn	888-4500	VC	11–16	921	CE
Bishop Rawstorne CE Language College	Out La, Croston, Leyland, Lancashire PR26 9HJ	01772 600349	01772 601320	Mr George Lloyd	888-4626	VA	11–16	929	CE
Blessed Trinity RC College	Coal Clough La, Ormerod Rd, Burnley, Lancashire BB11 5BT	01282 436314	01282 832198	Ms Bernadette Bleasdale	888-4804	VA	11–16	1439	RC
Bowland High	Riversmead, Grindleton, Clitheroe, Lancashire BB7 4QS	01200 441374	01200 441633	Mr S. Cox	888-4041	CY	11–16	494	
Broughton Business and Enterprise College	Woodplumpton La, Broughton, Preston, Lancashire PR3 5JJ	01772 863849	01772 864710	Mr R. Davies	888-4232	CY	11–16	885	
Burscough Priory Science College	Trevor Rd, Burscough, Ormskirk, Lancashire L40 7RZ	01704 893259	01704 893307	Mr R.N. Leighton	888-4159	CY	11–16	717	
Cardinal Allen RC High School, Fleetwood	Melbourne Ave, Fleetwood, Lancashire FY7 8AY	01253 872659	01253 772143	Mr Philip Mooney	888-4718	VA	11–16	807	RC
Carnforth High School	Kellet Rd, Carnforth, Lancashire LA5 9LS	01524 732424	01524 720167	Mr John Shannon	888-4167	CY	11–16	540	
Carr Hill High School and Sixth Form Centre	Royal Ave, Kirkham, Preston, Lancashire PR4 2ST	01772 682008	01772 673048	Mr John Davies	888-4155	CY	11–18	1313	
Central Lancaster High School	Crag Rd, Lancaster, Lancashire LA1 3LS	01524 32636	01524 849586	Mr Jonathan Wright	888-4405	CY	11–16	641	
Chorley Southlands High School	Clover Rd, Chorley, Lancashire PR7 2NJ	01257 414455	01257 414460	Mr Mark Fowle	888-4131	CY	11–16	1006	
Christ The King RC Maths and Computing College	Lawrence Ave, Frenchwood, Preston, Lancashire PR1 4LX	01772 252072	01772 885674	Mr Anthony Perry	888-4610	VA	11–16	447	RC
City of Preston High School	Ribbleton Hall Dr, Ribbleton, Preston, Lancashire PR2 6EE	01772 651110	01772 652521	Mr Chris Meldrum	888-4004	CY	11–16	417	
Clitheroe Royal Grammar School	York St, Clitheroe, Lancashire BB7 2DJ	01200 423118	01200 442177	Miss Judith Evans	888-5403	FD	11–18	1249	
Colne Park High School	Venables Ave, Colne, Lancashire BB8 7DP	01282 865200	01282 866089	Dr P. Parkin	888-4018	CY	11–16	916	
Colne Primet High School	Dent St, Colne, Lancashire BB8 8JF	01282 863970	01282 871276	Mrs Janet Walsh	888-4019	CY	11–16	774	
Corpus Christi RC Sports College	St Vincent's Rd, Fulwood, Preston, Lancashire PR2 8QY	01772 716912	01772 718779	Mr Martin Callagher	888-4609	VA	11–16	807	RC
Fearns Community Sports College	Fearns Moss, Bacup, Lancashire OL13 0TG	01706 873896	01706 875029	Mr Mark Smallwood	888-4158	CY	11–16	889	
Fleetwood Sports College	Broadway, Fleetwood, Lancashire FY7 8HE	01253 876757	01253 879387	Mr Stephen Roe	888-4408	CY	11–18	1203	
Fulwood High School and Arts College	Black Bull La, Fulwood, Preston, Lancashire PR2 9YR	01772 719060	01772 713573	Mrs K.M. Moss	888-4146	CY	11–16	952	
Garstang High School : A Community Technology College	Bowgreave, Garstang, Preston, Lancashire PR3 1YE	01995 603226	01995 601655	Mr Philip Birch	888-4160	CY	11–16	760	
Glenburn Sports College	Yewdale, Southway, Skelmersdale, Lancashire WN8 6JB	01695 724381	01695 557379	Mrs Hilary Torpey	888-4200	CY	11–16	827	
Hameldon Community College	Byron St, Burnley, Lancashire BB12 6NU	01282 775111	01282 779350	Mrs Gill Broom	888-4802	CY	11–16	1556	
Haslingden High School	Broadway, Haslingden, Rossendale, Lancashire BB4 4EY	01706 215726	01706 219861	Mrs Eve Challenger	888-4402	CY	11–18	1485	
Heysham High School Sports College	Limes Ave, Morecambe, Lancashire LA3 1HS	01524 416830	01524 832622	Mr Maurice Graham	888-4006	CY	11–16	1176	
Hodgson School	Moorland Ave, Poulton-le-Fylde, Lancashire FY6 7EU	01253 882815	01253 899971	Mr Colin Simkins	888-4010	CY	11–18	1154	
The Hollins Technology College	Hollins La, Accrington, Lancashire BB5 2QY	01254 233500	01254 236970	Mr Mark Jackson	888-4195	CY	11–16	749	
Holy Cross RC High School, A Sports aid Science College	Burgh La, Chorley, Lancashire PR7 3NT	01257 262093	01257 232878	Mrs Wendy Anne White	888-4742	VA	11–16	803	RC
Hornby High School	Melling Rd, Hornby, Lancaster, Lancashire LA2 8LH	01524 221471	01524 222115	Mrs Alison Woolerton	888-4170	CY	11–16	174	
Hutton CE Grammar School	Liverpool Rd, Hutton, Preston, Lancashire PR4 5SN	01772 613112	01772 617645	Mr David Pearson	888-4685	VA	11–18	804	CE B

School name	Address	Tel	Fax	Headteacher	Ref	Type	Ages	Pupils	Other
Lancaster Girls' Grammar School	Regent St, Lancaster, Lancashire LA1 1SF	01524 32010	01524 846220	Mrs Pam Barber	888-5402	FD	11–18	880	G
Lancaster Royal Grammar School	East Rd, Lancaster, Lancashire LA1 3EF	01524 580600	01524 847947	Mr Andrew M Jarman	888-5401	VA	11–18	1008	Ch B R
Lathom High School : A Technology College	Glenburn Rd, Skelmersdale, Lancashire WN8 6JN	01695 725653	01695 725654	Mr D. Bruce	888-4411	CY	11–16	634	
Leyland St Mary's RC Technology College	Royal Ave, Leyland, Lancashire PR25 1BS	01772 421909	01772 424705	Mr Trevor Day	888-5407	VA	11–16	774	RC
Longridge High School A Maths and Computing College	Preston Rd, Longridge, Preston, Lancashire PR3 3AR	01772 782316	01772 786486	Mr P.A. Lewis	888-4168	CY	11–16	745	
Lostock Hall Community High School and Arts College	Todd La North, Lostock Hall, Preston, Lancashire PR5 5UR	01772 336293	01772 337083	Mr D.A. Lowe	888-4193	CY	11–16	809	
Lytham St Annes High Technology College	Worsley Rd, Lytham St Annes, Lancashire FY8 4DG	01253 733192	01253 795109	Mr P.S. Wood	888-4137	CY	11–18	1728	
Marsden Heights Community College	Elland Rd, Brierfield, Nelson, Lancashire BB9 5RX	01282 614640	01282 616330	Mr Mike Tull	888-4800	CY	11–16	1138	
Moor Park Business and Enterprise School	Moor Park Ave, Preston, Lancashire PR1 6DT	01772 795428	01772 653912	Mr Peter Cunningham	888-4410	CY	11–16	509	
Morecambe High School	Dallam Ave, Morecambe, Lancashire LA4 5BG	01524 410207	01524 420156	Mr W P Bancroft	888-4302	CY	11–18	1415	
Mount Carmel Roman RC High School, Hyndburn	Wordsworth Rd, Accrington, Lancashire BB5 0LU	01254 233458	01254 236355	Miss Katrina Ryan	888-4797	VA	11–16	790	RC
Norden High School and Sports College	Stourton St, Rishton, Blackburn, Lancashire BB1 4ED	01254 885378	01254 884372	Mr Bob Flood	888-4015	CY	11–16	702	
Ormskirk School	Wigan Rd, Ormskirk, Lancashire L39 2AT	01695 583040	01695 583050	Mr John Doyle	888-4412	VC	11–18	1443	
Our Lady Queen of Peace RC High School and Engineering College	Glenburn Rd, Skelmersdale, Lancashire WN8 6JW	01695 725635	01695 556046	Mrs A.C. Foster	888-4621	VA	11–16	796	RC
Our Lady's RC College	Morecambe Rd, Lancaster, Lancashire LA1 2RX	01524 66689	01524 849441	Mr M.J. Webster	888-4717	VA	11–18	1014	RC
Our Lady's RC High School	St Anthony's Dr, Fulwood, Preston, Lancashire PR2 3SQ	01772 726441	01772 760212	Mr Nigel Ranson	888-4606	VA	11–16	903	RC
Parklands High School	Southport Rd, Chorley, Lancashire PR7 1LL	01257 264596	01257 261215	Mrs J. McGrath	888-4311	CY	11–16	1117	
Pendle Vale College	Oxford Rd, Nelson, Lancashire BB9 8JG	01282 615065	01282 619590	Mr Geoff Walker	888-4799	CY	11–16	816	
Penwortham Girls' High School	Cop La, Penwortham, Preston, Lancashire PR1 0SR	01772 743399	01772 752475	Mrs Joan Fitz-Gibbon	888-4332	CY	11–16	752	G
Priory Sports and Technology College, Penwortham	Crow Hills Rd, Penwortham, Preston, Lancashire PR1 0JE	01772 744448	01772 742426	Mr James Hourigan	888-4135	CY	11–16	945	
Rhyddings Business and Enterprise School	Haworth St, Oswaldtwistle, Accrington, Lancashire BB5 3EA	01254 231051	01254 393242	Mr Barry Burke	888-4026	CY	11–16	1049	
Ribblesdale High School Technology College	Queen's Rd, Clitheroe, Lancashire BB7 1EJ	01200 422563	01200 442506	Mr Simon Smith	888-4013	CY	11–16	1305	
Ripley St Thomas CE High School	Ashton Rd, Lancaster, Lancashire LA1 4RS	01524 64496	01524 847069	Mrs Liz Nicholls	888-4689	VA	11–18	1548	CE
St Aidan's CE Technology College	Cartgate, Preesall, Poulton-le-Fylde, Lancashire FY6 0NP	01253 810504	01253 810244	Mr Alan Porteous	888-4628	VA	11–16	824	CE
St Augustine's Roman RC High School, Billington	Elker La, Billington, Clitheroe, Lancashire BB7 9JA	01254 823362	01254 822147	Mr A. McNamara	888-4725	VA	11–16	1028	RC
St Bede's RC High School	Talbot Rd, Lytham, Lytham St Annes, Lancashire FY8 4JL	01253 737174	01253 731243	Mr P. Grice	888-4627	VA	11–16	726	RC
St Bede's RC High School	St Anne's Rd, Ormskirk, Lancashire L39 4TA	01695 570335	01695 571686	Mr P. Entwistle Obe	888-4631	VA	11–16	692	RC
St Cecilia's RC Technology College	Chapel Hill, Longridge, Preston, Lancashire PR3 2XA	01772 783074	01772 786200	Mrs M. Diffley	888-4721	CY	11–16	448	RC
St Mary's Roman RC High School, Brownedge	Station Rd, Bamber Bridge, Preston, Lancashire PR5 6PB	01772 339813	01772 629236	Mr Martin Reynolds	888-4623	VA	11–16	741	RC
St Michael's CE High School	Astley Rd, Chorley, Lancashire PR7 1RS	01257 264740	01257 224767	Mr Christopher Bagguley	888-4686	VA	11–16	1120	CE
Shuttleworth College	Kiddow La, Burnley, Lancashire BB12 6LH	01282 777705	01282 775054	Mr Andrew Mackenzie	888-4801	CY	11–16	737	
Sir John Thursby Community College	Eastern Ave, Burnley, Lancashire BB10 2AT	01282 436321	01282 830922	Ms Elaine Dawson	888-4803	CY	11–16	876	
Skerton Community High School	Owen Rd, Lancaster, Lancashire LA1 2BL	01524 65143	01524 846121	Mr Martin Burgess	888-4005	CY	11–16	252	
SS John Fisher and Thomas More Roman RC High School, Colne	Gibfield Rd, Colne, Lancashire BB8 8JT	01282 865299	01282 860419	Mr Brendan Conboy	888-4624	VA	11–16	746	RC
Tarleton High School, A Community Technology College	Hesketh La, Tarleton, Preston, Lancashire PR4 6AQ	01772 812644	01772 817901	Mr A.D. Hardiker	888-4178	CY	11–16	876	
Thornton Cleveleys Millfield High School	Belvedere Rd, Thornton-Cleveleys, Lancashire FY5 5DG	01253 865929	01253 857586	Mr Sean Bullen	888-4011	CY	11–16	721	
Tulketh Community Sports College	Tag La, Ingol, Preston, Lancashire PR2 3TX	01772 729773	01772 720037	Mr W. Hill	888-4049	CY	11–16	295	
Unity College	Townley Holmes, Burnley, Lancashire BB11 3EN	01282 436311	01282 430247	Ms Sally Cryer	888-4806	CY	11–16	869	
Up Holland High School	Sandbrook Rd, Orrell, Wigan, Lancashire WN5 7AL	01695 625191	01695 633379	Mr Peter Doyle	888-4173	CY	11–16	917	

3

School name	Address	Tel	Fax	Headteacher	Ref	Type	Ages	Pupils	Other
Walton le Dale Arts College and High School	Brindle Rd, Bamber Bridge, Preston, Lancashire PR5 6RN	01772 335726	01772 339494	Mr Tony Hill	888-4150	CY	11–16	602	
Wellfield High School	Yewlands Dr, Leyland, Lancashire PR25 2TP	01772 421303	01772 454767	Mr M. Ainsworth	888-4036	CY	11–16	435	
West Craven High Technology College	Kelbrook Rd, Barnoldswick, Lancashire BB18 5TB	01282 812292	01282 850427	Mr Arnold Kuchartschek	888-4040	CY	11–16	748	
Whitworth Community High School	Hall Fold, Whitworth, Rochdale, Lancashire OL12 8TS	01706 343218	01706 343218	Mr John Ferguson	888-4184	CY	11–16	557	
Worden Sports College	Westfield Dr, Leyland, Lancashire PR25 1QX	01772 421021	01772 456757	Mrs Susan Rignall	888-4140	CY	11–16	518	

Liverpool

School name	Address	Tel	Fax	Headteacher	Ref	Type	Ages	Pupils	Other
The Academy of St Francis of Assisi	Gardeners Dr, Liverpool L6 7UR	0151 260 7600	0151 260 9222	Mr Jim Burke	341-6905		11–16	661	CE
The Alsop High School A Technology College	Queen's Dr, Liverpool, Merseyside L4 6SH	0151 525 2600	0151 521 1044	Mr P. Jamieson	341-4421	CY	11–18	1740	
Archbishop Beck RC Sports College	Cedar Rd, Walton, Liverpool, Merseyside L9 9AF	0151 525 6326	0151 524 2465	Mr Paul Dickinson	341-4796	VA	11–18	1282	RC
Archbishop Blanch C of E VA High School, A Technology College and Training School	Mount Vernon Rd, Liverpool, Merseyside L7 3EA	0151 709 1452	0151 709 2940	Mr Stephen Brierley	341-4781	VA	11–18	904	CE G
Bellerive FCJ RC College	Windermere Terr, Sefton Park, Liverpool, Merseyside L8 3SB	0151 727 2064	0151 727 8242	Sr Brigid Halligan	341-4787	VA	11–18	884	RC G
Belvedere Academy	17 Belvidere Rd, Princes Park, Liverpool L8 3TF	0151 727 1284	0151 727 0602	Peter Kennedy	341-6907		11–19		G
The Belvedere School GDST	17 Belvedere Rd, Liverpool, Merseyside L8 3TF	0151 727 1284		Mrs G. Richards	341-6039		3–16	541	
The Blue Coat School	Church Rd, Liverpool, Merseyside L15 9EE	0151 733 1407	0151 734 0982	Mr Michael Tittershill	341-5404	VA	11–18	907	
Broadgreen High School a Technology College	Queens Dr, Liverpool, Merseyside L13 5UQ	0151 228 6800	0151 220 9256	Mr I. Andain	341-4425	CY	11–18	1206	
Broughton Hall High School, A Technology College	Yew Tree La, West Derby, Liverpool, Merseyside L12 9HJ	0151 228 3622	0151 228 1980	Mr Gerard Murphy	341-4792	VA	11–18	1258	RC G
Calderstones School	Harthill Rd, Liverpool, Merseyside L18 3HS	0151 724 2087	0151 729 0093	Mr B. Davies	341-4427	CY	11–18	1493	
Cardinal Heenan RC High School	Honeys Green La, Liverpool, Merseyside L12 9HZ	0151 228 3472	0151 252 1246	Mr Dave Forshaw	341-4793	VA	11–18	1394	RC B
Childwall School – A Specialist Sports College	Queen's Dr, Liverpool, Merseyside L15 6XZ	0151 722 1561	0151 737 1698	Mr D.W. Phillips	341-4426	CY	11–18	1253	
Croxteth Community Comprehensive School	Parkstile La, Croxteth, Liverpool, Merseyside L11 0BD	0151 546 4168	0151 548 4347	Mr R. Baker	341-4423	CY	11–18	521	
De La Salle RC High School	Carr La East, Liverpool, Merseyside L11 4SG	0151 546 3134	0151 548 4146	Mr D.G. Richmond	341-4795	VA	11–18	541	RC B
Fazakerley High School	Sherwoods La, Fazakerley, Liverpool, Merseyside L10 1LB	0151 524 4530	0151 523 0524	Mr N. Fleming	341-4420	CY	11–18	794	
Gateacre Community Comprehensive School	Grange La, Gateacre, Liverpool, Merseyside L25 4SD	0151 428 1569	0151 421 1349	Mr Peter Barnes	341-4429	CY	11–18	1581	
Holly Lodge Girls' College	Queen's Dr, Stoneycroft, Liverpool, Merseyside L13 0AE	0151 228 3772	0151 228 0161	Ms Julia Tinsley	341-4404	CY	11–18	1359	G
King David High School	Childwall Rd, Liverpool, Merseyside L15 6UZ	0151 722 7496	0151 738 0259	Mrs Brigid Smith	341-4690	VA	11–18	625	Je
New Heys Comprehensive School	Heath Rd, Liverpool, Merseyside L19 4TN	0151 427 6482	0151 494 2841	Mrs Ann Stahler	341-4428	CY	11–18	963	
North Liverpool Academy	Priory Rd, Liverpool L4 2SL	0151 260 4044	0151 263 5665	Mrs Kay Askew	341-6906		11–18	1145	
Notre Dame RC College	Everton Valley, Liverpool, Merseyside L4 4EZ	0151 263 3104	0151 263 2689	Miss C. McCann	341-4782	VA	11–18	1051	RC G
Parklands High School	Ganworth Rd, Speke, Liverpool, Merseyside L24 2RZ	0151 486 2612	0151 281 6106	Mr A. Smithies	341-4431	CY	11–18	701	
St Benedict's College	Horrocks Ave, Liverpool, Merseyside L19 5PF	0151 427 5302	0151 494 3244	Mr James Finnigan	341-4788	VA	11–18	750	RC
St Edward's College	North Dr, Sandfield Park, Liverpool, Merseyside L12 1LF	0151 281 1999	0151 281 1909	Mr J.E. Waszek	341-5900	VA	11–18	1195	RC
St Francis Xavier's College	High Lee, Beaconsfield Rd, Liverpool, Merseyside L25 6EG	0151 288 1000	0151 288 1001	Mr Leslie David Rippon	341-5400	FD	11–18	1289	RC B R
St Hilda's CE High School	Croxteth Dr, Sefton Park, Liverpool, Merseyside L17 3AL	0151 733 2709	0151 735 0530	Mr J.C. Yates	341-5403	VA	11–18	860	CE G
St John Bosco Arts College	Stonedale Cres, Liverpool, Merseyside L11 9DQ	0151 546 6360	0151 548 5949	Mrs Anne Pontifex	341-4794	VA	11–18	1093	RC G
St Julie's RC High School	Speke Rd, Woolton, Liverpool, Merseyside L25 7TN	0151 428 6421	0151 421 1399	Sr Ann Marie Gammack	341-4797	VA	11–18	1337	RC G
St Margaret's CE High School	Aigburth Rd, Liverpool, Merseyside L17 6AB	0151 427 1825	0151 427 9430	Dr D.F. Dennison	341-5402	VA	11–18	1002	CE B
Shorefields School	Dingle Vale, Liverpool, Merseyside L8 9SJ	0151 727 1387	0151 728 9805	Mr John Charnock	341-4419	CY	11–18	882	
West Derby School	Quarry Wing, Quarry Rd, Liverpool, Merseyside L13 7DB	0151 228 7915	0151 259 4711	Mrs Margaret Rannard	341-4306	CY	11–18	1164	B

Manchester

School name	Address	Tel	Fax	Headteacher	Ref	Type	Ages	Pupils	Other
Abraham Moss High School	Crescent Rd, Crumpsall, Manchester, Lancashire M8 5UF	0161 740 5141	0161 721 4973	Mr D. Watchorn	352-4271	CY	11–16	1179	
The Barlow RC High School and Specialist Science College	Parrs Wood Rd, East Didsbury, Manchester, Lancashire M20 6BX	0161 445 8053	0161 445 6350	Mr Michael O'Neill	352-4768	VA	11–16	899	RC
Brookway High School and Sports College	Moor Rd, Wythenshawe, Manchester, Lancashire M23 9BP	0161 998 3992	0161 998 5144	Ms J.A. Sale	352-4285	CY	11–16	567	
Burnage High School	Burnage La, Burnage, Manchester, Lancashire M19 1ER	0161 432 1527	0161 442 2366	Mr I.D. Fenn	352-4256	CY	11–16	964	B
Cedar Mount High School	Matthews La, Gorton, Manchester, Lancashire M18 7SP	0161 248 7009	0161 248 7914	Mr G. Hutchence	352-4293	CY	11–16	799	
Chorlton High School	Nell La, Chorlton-cum-Hardy, Manchester, Lancashire M21 7SL	0161 882 1150	0161 861 8753	Mr Andrew Park	352-4281	CY	11–16	1463	
The King David High School	Eaton Rd, Crumpsall, Manchester, Lancashire M8 5DY	0161 740 7248	0161 740 0790	Mr B.N. Levy	352-4810	VA	11–18	860	Je
Levenshulme High School	Crossley Rd, Levenshulme, Manchester, Lancashire M19 1FS	0161 224 4625	0161 256 1170	Mr William Skelding	352-4280	CY	11–16	963	G
Manchester Academy	Moss La East, Moss Side, Manchester M14 4PX	0161 232 1639	0161 232 1640	Mrs Kathy August	352-6905	CY	11–16	814	Ch
Newall Green High School	Greenbrow Rd, Wythenshawe, Manchester M23 2SX	0161 499 3878	0161 436 8914	Mr N.G. Wilson	352-4286	CY	11–16	911	
North Manchester High School for Boys	Charlestown Rd, Blackley, Manchester, Lancashire M9 7FS	0161 681 1592	0161 681 8190	Mr M. Woodcock	352-4272	CY	11–16	917	B
North Manchester High School for Girls	Brookside Rd, Moston, Manchester, Lancashire M40 9QJ	0161 681 4678	0161 684 8946	Ms Marian Catterall	352-4273	CY	11–16	1428	G
Our Lady's RC Sports College	Alworth Rd, Higher Blackley, Manchester, Lancashire M9 0RP	0161 795 0711	0161 220 5929	Mrs Teresa Dervin	352-4761	VA	11–16	744	RC
Parklands High School	Simonsway, Wythenshawe, Manchester M22 9RH	0161 499 2726	0161 499 1147	Mr G.B. McHugh	352-4292	CY	11–16	725	
Parrs Wood High School	Wilmslow Rd, East Didsbury, Manchester, Greater Manchester M20 5PG	0161 445 8786	0161 445 5974	Ms Rachel Jones	352-4248	CY	11–18	2012	
Plant Hill Arts College	Plant Hill Rd, Higher Blackley, Manchester, Lancashire M9 0WQ	0161 740 1831	0161 720 7254	Mr R.J. Pemberton	352-4270	CY	11–16	822	
St Matthew's RC High School	Nuthurst Rd, Moston, Manchester, Lancashire M40 0EW	0161 681 6178	0161 681 8590	Mr Kevin Hogan	352-4762	VA	11–16	1137	RC
St Paul's RC High School	Firbank Rd, Newall Grn, Manchester, Lancashire M23 2YS	0161 437 5841	0161 498 2030	Mr W.A. Daron	352-4766	VA	11–16	746	RC
St Peter's RC High School	Kirkmanshulme La, Gorton, Manchester, Lancashire M12 4WB	0161 248 1550	0161 248 1551	Mr J. McNerney	352-4770	VA	11–16	889	RC
St Thomas Aquinas RC High School	Nell La, Chorlton-cum-Hardy, Manchester, Lancashire M21 7SW	0161 881 9448	0161 882 0164	Mr Edwin Wyllie	352-4753	VA	11–16	518	RC
Trinity CE High School	Cambridge St, Hulme, Manchester, Lancashire M15 6HP	0161 226 2272	0161 227 9691	Mr David Ainsworth	352-4765	VA	11–16	1187	CE
Whalley Range 11-18 High School and Business and Enterprise College	Wilbraham Rd, Whalley Range, Manchester, Lancashire M16 8GW	0161 861 9727	0161 881 0617	Ms Patsy Kane	352-4257	CY	11–18	1653	G
William Hulme's Grammar School	Spring Bridge Rd, Manchester, Lancashire M16 8PR	0161 226 2054	0161 232 5544	Mr S.R. Patriarca	352-6031		3–18	579	
William Hulme's Grammar School	Spring Bridge Rd, Manchester M16 8PR	0161 226 2054	0161 232 5544	Steve Patriarca	352-6907		3–18		
Wright Robinson Sports College	Abbey Hey La, Gorton, Manchester, Lancashire M18 8RL	0161 370 5121	0161 371 8287	Mr N. Beischer	352-4276	CY	11–16	1734	

Oldham

School name	Address	Tel	Fax	Headteacher	Ref	Type	Ages	Pupils	Other
The Blue Coat CE School	Egerton St, Oldham, Lancashire OL1 3SQ	0161 624 1484	0161 628 4997	Mrs J.A. Hollis	353-4600	VA	11–18	1367	CE
Breeze Hill School	Roxbury Ave, Salem, Oldham, Lancashire OL4 5JE	0161 911 3251	0161 911 3255	Mr B.F. Phillips	353-4014	CY	11–16	774	
Counthill School	Counthill Rd, Moorside, Oldham, Lancashire OL4 2PY	0161 624 6366	0161 633 5909	Mrs Margaret Ryan	353-4001	CY	11–16	1060	
Crompton House CE School	Rochdale Rd, Shaw, Oldham, Lancashire OL2 7HS	01706 847451	01706 291454	Mrs Victoria Musgrave	353-4605	VA	11–18	1297	CE
Failsworth School	Brierley Ave, Failsworth, Manchester, Lancashire M35 9HA	0161 681 3763	0161 683 5173	Mr D.O. Johnson	353-4023	CY	11–16	1465	
Grange School	Rochdale Rd, Oldham, Lancashire OL9 6DY	0161 652 2428	0161 652 1324	Mr G. Hollinshead	353-4005	CY	11–16	789	
The Hathershaw College of Technology & Sport	Bellfield Ave, Hathershaw, Oldham, Lancashire OL8 3EP	0161 770 8555	0161 770 8556	Mrs Carol Cawkwell	353-4011	CY	11–16	1001	
Kaskenmoor School	Roman Rd, Hollinwood, Oldham, Lancashire OL8 3PT	0161 681 4116	0161 682 8022	Mr John Alder	353-4015	CY	11–16	703	
North Chadderton School	Chadderton Hall Rd, Chadderton, Oldham, Lancashire OL9 0BN	0161 624 9939	0161 628 5995	Mrs Barbara Howse	353-4027	CY	11–18	1492	
Our Lady's RC High School	Vaughan St, Royton, Oldham, Lancashire OL2 5DL	0161 624 9974	0161 627 1871	Mr Roger Whitaker	353-4607	VA	11–18	1081	RC
The Radclyffe School	Broadway, Chadderton, Oldham, Lancashire OL9 9QZ	0161 624 2594	0161 633 2183	Mr H.S. Hayer	353-4028	CY	11–16	1325	
Royton and Crompton School	Blackshaw La, Royton, Oldham, Lancashire OL2 6NT	01706 846474	01706 842874	Mr Desmond Herlihy	353-4022	CY	11–16	1170	

3

School name	Address	Tel	Fax	Headteacher	Ref	Type	Ages	Pupils	Other
Saddleworth School	High St, Uppermill, Oldham, Lancashire OL3 8BU	01457 872072	01457 870190	Mrs Patricia Cornish	353-4026	CY	11–16	1290	
St Augustine of Canterbury RC High School	Grange Ave, Oldham, Lancashire OL8 4ED	0161 911 3225	0161 911 3228	Mr John Kennedy	353-4606	VA	11–16	778	RC
South Chadderton School	Butterworth La, Chadderton, Oldham, Lancashire OL9 8EA	0161 681 4851	0161 683 5183	Ms Christine Hill	353-4021	CY	11–16	711	

Rochdale

School name	Address	Tel	Fax	Headteacher	Ref	Type	Ages	Pupils	Other
Balderstone Technology College	Queen Victoria St, Rochdale, Lancashire OL11 2HJ	01706 649049	01706 644945	Mr Derek Wiggett	354-4085	CY	11–16	991	
Cardinal Langley Roman Catholic High School	Rochdale Rd, Middleton, Manchester, Greater Manchester M24 2GL	0161 643 4009	0871 9941804	Mr C.A. Mason	354-4611	VA	11–18	1101	RC
Falinge Park High School	Falinge Rd, Shawclough, Rochdale, Lancashire OL12 6LD	01706 631246	01706 646538	Mr Robin Lonsdale	354-4086	CY	11–16	1173	
Heywood Community High School	Sutherland Rd, Heywood, Lancashire OL10 3PL	01708 360466	01706 627280	Mr David Yates	354-4084	CY	11–16	552	
Hollingworth Business and Enterprise College	Cornfield St, Milnrow, Rochdale, Lancashire OL16 3DR	01706 641541	01706 644639	Mr C. Burnett	354-5401	FD	11–16	1133	
Holy Family Roman Catholic and Church of England College	Pot Hall, Wilton Gr, Heywood, Lancashire OL10 2AA	01706 360607	01706 363950	Mrs S. Casey	354-4801	VA	11–16		RC
Matthew Moss High School	Matthew Moss La, Marland, Rochdale, Lancashire OL11 3LU	01706 632910	01706 523857	Mr Andrew Raymer	354-4088	CY	11–16	887	
Middleton Technology School	Kenyon La, Middleton, Manchester, Lancashire M24 2GT	0161 643 5116	0161 654 6024	Miss Allison Crompton	354-4091	CY	11–16	1042	
Oulder Hill Community School and Language College	Hudsons Wlk, Rochdale, Lancashire OL11 5EF	01706 645522	01706 648404	Mrs M Dudley	354-4089	CY	11–18	1320	
The Queen Elizabeth School	Hollin La, Middleton, Manchester, Lancashire M24 6XN	0161 643 2643	0161 653 8746	Mr E. Jackson	354-4090	CY	11–16	735	
St Anne's Academy	Hollin La, Middleton, Manchester M24 6XN	0161 643 2643			354-6905		11–18		Ch
St Cuthbert's Roman RC High School, Rochdale	Shaw Rd, Rochdale, Lancashire OL16 4RX	01706 647761	01706 642378	Mr J.V. Wood	354-4612	VA	11–18	1405	RC
Siddal Moor Sports College	Newhouse Rd, Heywood, Lancashire OL10 2NT	01706 369436	01706 620830	Mrs Helen Freeborn	354-4083	CY	11–16	990	
Springhill High School	Turf Hill Rd, Rochdale, Lancashire OL16 4XA	01706 640931	01706 524770	Ms Annabel Bolt	354-4087	CY	11–16	717	
Wardle High School	Birch Rd, Wardle, Rochdale, Lancashire OL12 9RD	01706 373911	01706 377980	Mr Graham Wright	354-5400	FD	11–18	1225	

Salford

School name	Address	Tel	Fax	Headteacher	Ref	Type	Ages	Pupils	Other
The Albion High School	London St, Salford, Lancashire M6 6QT	0161 921 1230	0161 7363219	Mr Steve Aveyard	355-4051	CY	11–16	878	
All Hallows RC Business and Enterprise College	Weaste La, Salford M5 5JH	0161 736 4117	0161 737 2066	Mr S. Almond	355-4620	VA	11–16	494	RC
Beis Yaakov High School	69 Broom La, Bury New Rd, Salford M7 4FF	0161 708 8220	0161 708 9968	Rabbi Yochonon Goldblatt	355-4018	VA	11–16	196	Je G
Buile Hill High School	Eccles Old Rd, Salford, Lancashire M6 8RD	0161 736 1773	0161 737 6556	Ms Gena Merrett	355-4026	CY	11–16	879	
Harrop Fold School	Hilton La, Worsley, Manchester, Lancashire M28 0SY	0161 790 5022	0161 790 4426	Dr Antony Edkins	355-4052	CY	11–16	963	
Hope High School	Prestwood Rd, Salford M6 8GG	0161 736 2637	0161 737 7374	Mr A. Hewitt	355-4016	CY	11–16	706	
Irlam and Cadishead Community High School	Macdonald Rd, Irlam, Manchester, Lancashire M44 5LH	0161 775 5525	0161 775 0599	Mr A. Lamb	355-4036	CY	11–18	944	
Moorside High School	East Lancashire Rd, Swinton, Manchester, Lancashire M27 0BH	0161 794 1045	0161 794 1296	Mr Charlie Mills	355-4039	CY	11–16	1017	
St Ambrose Barlow RC High School	Shaftesbury Dr, Swinton, Manchester M27 5SZ	0161 794 3521	0161 794 1932	Mrs C.M. Garside	355-5400	VA	11–16	734	RC
St George's RC High School	Parsonage Dr, Worsley, Manchester M28 3SH	0161 790 4420	0161 790 5505	Mr Philip Harte	355-4614	VA	11–16	595	RC
St Patrick's RC High School and Arts College	Guilford Rd, Eccles, Manchester M30 7JF	0161 789 4678	0161 707 1335	Mrs Barbara Rogers	355-4616	VA	11–16	909	RC
Salford City Academy	Northfleet Rd, Peel Grn, Manchester M30 7PQ	0161 789 5359	0161 789 2209	Mrs Elizabeth Haddock	355-6905		11–16	570	Ch
The Swinton High School	Sefton Rd, Swinton, Salford, Lancashire M27 6JU	0161 794 6215	0161 728 3383	Mr J. Biddlestone	355-4050	CY	11–16	979	

School name	Address	Tel	Fax	Headteacher	Ref	Type	Ages	Pupils	Other
Walkden High School	Birch Rd, Walkden, Worsley, Manchester, Lancashire M28 7FJ	0161 799 5525	0161 790 5556	Mrs Elaine Hilton	355-4035	CY	11–16	1199	B
Wentworth High School	Wentworth Rd, Eccles, Manchester M30 9BP	0161 789 4565	0161 787 7362	Mr Nigel Harrop	355-4049	CY	11–16	838	

Sefton

School name	Address	Tel	Fax	Headteacher	Ref	Type	Ages	Pupils	Other
Birkdale High School	Windy Harbour Rd, Birkdale, Southport, Merseyside PR8 3DT	01704 577253	01704 570451	Mr Marcus Barker	343-4108	CY	11–16	908	B
Bootle High School	Browns La, Netherton, Bootle, Merseyside L30 5RN	0151 521 1734	0151 525 3517	Mrs C.A. Sweeney	343-4112	CY	11–16	574	
Chesterfield High School	Chesterfield Rd, Crosby, Liverpool, Merseyside L23 9YB	0151 924 6454	0151 931 5089	Mr Simon Penney	343-4105	CY	11–18	1276	
Christ The King RC High School and Sixth Form Centre	Stamford Rd, Southport, Merseyside PR8 4EX	01704 565121	01704 550447	Mr J.K. Gannon	343-4800	VA	11–18	1174	RC
Deyes High School	Deyes La, Maghull, Liverpool, Merseyside L31 6DE	0151 526 3814	0151 526 3713	Mr Peter Reed	343-4100	CY	11–18	1428	
Formby High School	Freshfield Rd, Formby, Liverpool, Merseyside L37 3HW	01704 873100	01704 831748	Mr B. Rourke	343-4101	CY	11–18	968	
Greenbank High School	Hastings Rd, Southport, Merseyside PR8 2LT	01704 567591	01704 568736	Mrs Pat McQuade	343-4109	CY	11–16	976	G
Hillside High School	Breeze Hill, Bootle, Merseyside L20 9NU	0151 525 2630	0151 524 1279	Mrs L. Shemilt	343-4031	CY	11–16	848	
Holy Family RC High School	Virgins La, Thornton, Liverpool, Merseyside L23 4UL	0151 924 6451	0151 932 1417	Mr N. Hutchins	343-4624	VA	11–18	833	RC
Litherland High School	Sterrix La, Litherland, Liverpool, Merseyside L21 0DB	0151 928 4449	0151 949 0247	Mr J.F. Donnelly	343-4104	CY	11–16	818	
Maghull High School	Ormonde Dr, Maghull, Liverpool, Merseyside L31 7AW	0151 526 2711	0151 526 7619	Mrs Maureen Miller	343-4113	CY	11–18	1265	
Maricourt RC High School	Hall La, Maghull, Liverpool, Merseyside L31 3DZ	0151 330 3366	0151 284 6631	Sr Teresa McCarthy	343-4621	VA	11–18	1477	RC
Meols Cop High School	Meols Cop Rd, Southport, Merseyside PR8 6JS	01704 531180	01704 532072	Miss Alison Heaton	343-4110	CY	11–16	559	
Range High School	Stapleton Rd, Formby, Liverpool, Merseyside L37 2YN	01704 879315	01704 833470	Mrs Mo Miller	343-4106	CY	11–18	1261	
Sacred Heart RC College	Liverpool Rd, Crosby, Liverpool, Merseyside L23 5TF	0151 931 2971	0151 924 8715	Mr J. Summerfield	343-4623	VA	11–18	1402	RC
St Ambrose Barlow RC College	Copy La, Netherton, Bootle, Merseyside L30 7PQ	0151 526 7044	0151 527 2153	Mr Paul Davidson	343-4625	VA	11–16	425	RC
St George of England Specialist Engineering College	Fernhill Rd, Bootle, Merseyside L20 6AQ	0151 922 3798	0151 933 9123	Mr V.J. Schwarz	343-4032	CY	11–16	564	
St Michael's CE High School	St Michaels Rd, Crosby L23 7UL	0151 924 6778	0151 924 2994	M.R. Jim	343-4802	VA	11–18	732	CE
St Wilfrid's RC High School	Orrell Rd, Litherland, Liverpool, Merseyside L21 8NU	0151 928 4543	0151 928 9921	Mr B. Eccles	343-4801	VA	11–18	744	RC
Savio High School	Netherton Way, Bootle, Merseyside L30 2NA	0151 521 3088	0151 525 8435	Father James Francis Mageean	343-4611	VA	11–18	792	RC
Stanley High School Sports College	Fleetwood Rd, Southport, Merseyside PR9 9TF	01704 228940	01704 232701	Mr David Tansey	343-4003	CY	11–16	866	

St Helens

School name	Address	Tel	Fax	Headteacher	Ref	Type	Ages	Pupils	Other
Cowley Language College	Hard La, St Helens, Merseyside WA10 6LB	01744 678030	01744 678031	Mr Cameron Sheeran	342-4101	CY	11–18	1768	
De La Salle School	Mill Brow, Eccleston, St Helens, Merseyside WA10 4QH	01744 20511	01744 20543	Mr Will Daunt	342-4714	VA	11–16	1202	RC
Haydock Sports College	Clipsley La, Haydock, St Helens, Merseyside WA11 0JG	01744 678833	01744 678832	Mr S. Fullerton	342-4051	CY	11–16	755	
Newton-le-Willows Community High School	Ashton Rd, Newton-le-Willows, Merseyside WA12 0AQ	01925 227209	01925 291335	Mrs M.B. Rimmer	342-4052	CY	11–16	680	
Rainford High Technology College	Higher La, Rainford, St Helens, Merseyside WA11 8NY	01744 885914	01744 884842	Mrs Ruth Halsall	342-4050	CY	11–18	1628	
Rainhill High School	Warrington Rd, Rainhill, Prescot, Merseyside L35 6NY	01744 677205	01744 677206	Mr John Pout	342-4104	CY	11–18	1381	
St Aelred's RC Technology College	Birley St, Newton-le-Willows, Merseyside WA12 9UW	01925 225974	01925 290759	Mrs Maria Rimmer	342-4710	VA	11–18	1093	RC
St Augustine of Canterbury RC High School	Boardmans La, Blackbrook, St Helens, Merseyside WA11 9BB	01744 678112	01744 678113	Mrs Linda Mousdale	342-4713	VA	11–16	734	RC
St Cuthbert's RC Community College for Business and Enterprise	Berrys La, Sutton, St Helens, Merseyside WA9 3HE	01744 755186	01744 29847	Mr Dave Cairns	342-4801	VA	11–16	901	RC
Sutton High Sports College	Elton Head Rd, St Helens, Merseyside WA9 5AU	01744 678859	01744 678860	Mr Paul Melia	342-4010	CY	11–18	1338	

3

Stockport

School name	Address	Tel	Fax	Ref	Type	Ages	Pupils	Other
Avondale High School	Heathbank Rd, Cheadle Heath, Stockport, Cheshire SK3 0UP	0161 286 0330	0161 286 0331	356-4030	CY	11–16	617	
Bramhall High School	Seal Rd, Bramhall, Stockport, Cheshire SK7 2JT	0161 439 8045	0161 439 8951	356-4038	CY	11–16	1457	
Cheadle Hulme High School	Woods La, Cheadle Hulme, Cheadle, Cheshire SK8 7JY	0161 485 7201	0161 486 6031	356-4039	CY	11–16	1286	
Harrytown RC High School	Harrytown La, Romiley, Stockport, Cheshire SK6 3BU	0161 430 5277	0161 430 1700	356-4601	VA	11–16	807	RC
Hazel Grove High School	Jacksons La, Hazel Gr, Stockport, Cheshire SK7 5JX	0161 456 4888	0161 456 3961	356-4036	CY	11–16	1297	
The Kingsway School	Foxland Rd, Cheadle, Cheshire SK8 4QX	0161 428 7706	0161 491 4335	356-4040	CY	11–16	1539	
Marple Hall School – A Specialist Language College	Hill Top Dr, Marple, Stockport, Cheshire SK6 6LB	0161 427 7966	0161 426 0931	356-4037	CY	11–16	1529	
Offerton School	The Fairway, Offerton, Stockport, Cheshire SK2 5DS	0161 483 9336	0161 419 9160	356-4031	CY	11–16	948	
Priestnall School	Priestnall Rd, Heaton Mersey, Stockport, Cheshire SK4 3HP	0161 432 7727	0161 442 7605	356-4032	CY	11–16	1336	
Reddish Vale Technology College	Reddish Vale Rd, Reddish, Stockport, Cheshire SK5 7HD	0161 477 3544	0161 429 9683	356-4033	CY	11–16	1384	
St Anne's Roman RC High School, Stockport	Glenfield Rd, Heaton Chapel, Stockport, Cheshire SK4 2QP	0161 432 8162	0161 443 1105	356-4603	VA	11–16	666	RC
St James' RC High School – A Specialist Humanities College	St James' Way, Cheadle Hulme, Cheadle, Cheshire SK8 6PZ	0161 486 9211	0161 486 6607	356-4600	VA	11–16	771	RC
Stockport Academy	Heathbank Rd, Cheadle Heath, Stockport SK3 0UP	0161 286 0330	0161 286 0331	356-6905		11–18		Ch
Stockport School	Mile End La, Stockport, Cheshire SK2 6BW	0161 483 3622	0161 456 9452	356-4034	CY	11–16	1036	
Werneth School	Harrytown, Romiley, Stockport, Cheshire SK6 3BX	0161 494 1222	0161 494 1397	356-4035	CY	11–16	1275	

Tameside

School name	Address	Tel	Fax	Ref	Type	Ages	Pupils	Other
Alder Community High School	Mottram Old Rd, Gee Cross, Hyde SK14 5NJ	0161 368 5132	0161 366 6383	357-4006	CY	11–16	793	
All Saints RC College	Kenyon Ave, Dukinfield, Cheshire SK16 5AR	0161 338 2120	0161 303 8861	357-4604	VA	11–18	1004	RC
Astley Sports College and Community High School	Yew Tree La, Dukinfield, Cheshire SK16 5BL	0161 338 2374	0161 304 9251	357-4026	CY	11–16	819	
Audenshaw School	Hazel St, Audenshaw, Manchester, Lancashire M34 5NB	0161 336 2133	0161 320 3046	357-5400	FD	11–18	1250	B
Copley High School	Huddersfield Rd, Stalybridge, Cheshire SK15 3RR	0161 338 6684	0161 303 8517	357-4011	CY	11–16	890	
Droylsden School Mathematics and Computing College for Girls	Manor Rd, Droylsden, Manchester M43 6QD	0161 370 2777	0161 371 7793	357-4013	CY	11–16	965	G
Egerton Park Arts College	Egerton St, Denton, Manchester, Greater Manchester M34 3PB	0161 336 2039	0161 337 8894	357-4015	CY	11–16	1303	
Fairfield High School for Girls	Fairfield Ave, Droylsden, Manchester, Lancashire M43 6AB	0161 370 1488	0161 371 1620	357-5402	FD	11–18	938	G
Hartshead Sports College	Greenhurst Rd, Ashton-under-Lyne, Lancashire OL6 9DX	0161 330 4965	0161 344 2629	357-4016	CY	11–16	1027	
Hyde Technology School and Hearing Impaired Resource Base	Old Rd, Hyde, Cheshire SK14 4SP	0161 368 1353	0161 368 5099	357-4025	CY	11–16	877	
Littlemoss High School for Boys	Cryer St, Droylsden, Manchester, Lancashire M43 7LF	0161 370 3334	0161 371 8459	357-4014	CY	11–16	518	B
Longdendale Community Language College	Spring St, Hollingworth, Hyde, Cheshire SK14 8LW	01457 764006	01457 766483	357-4023	CY	11–16	885	
Mossley Hollins High School	Huddersfield Rd, Mossley, Ashton-under-Lyne, Lancashire OL5 9DJ	01457 832491	01457 837934	357-4018	CY	11–16	722	
St Damian's RC Science College	Lees Rd, Ashton-under-Lyne, Lancashire OL6 8BH	0161 330 5974	0161 331 4744	357-4602	VA	11–16	794	RC
St Thomas More RC College Specialising in Mathematics and Computing	Town La, Denton, Manchester M34 6AF	0161 336 2743	0161 337 9701	357-4603	VA	11–16	784	RC
Stamford High School	Mossley Rd, Ashton-under-Lyne, Lancashire OL6 9SD	0161 330 7437	0161 343 3467	357-4012	CY	11–16	536	
Two Trees Sports College	Two Trees La, Denton, Manchester, Lancashire M34 7QL	0161 336 2719	0161 337 4344	357-4017	CY	11–16	708	
West Hill School	Thompson Cross, Stamford St, Stalybridge, Cheshire SK15 1LX	0161 338 2193	0161 338 8293	357-5401	FD	11–16	843	B

Trafford

School name	Address	Tel	Fax	Headteacher	Ref	Type	Ages	Pupils	Other
Altrincham College of Arts	Green La., Timperley, Altrincham, Cheshire WA15 8QW	0161 980 7173	0161 980 1783	Mr P. Brooks	358-4024	CY	11–16	767	
Altrincham Grammar School for Boys	Marlborough Rd, Bowdon, Altrincham, Cheshire WA14 2RS	0161 928 0858	0161 924 3888	Mr T.J. Gartside	358-5404	FD	11–18	1095	B
Altrincham Grammar School for Girls	Cavendish Rd, Bowdon, Altrincham, Cheshire WA14 2NL	0161 928 0827	0161 941 7400	Mrs D. Ross-Wawrzynski	358-5407	FD	11–18	1218	G
Ashton-on-Mersey School	Cecil Ave, Sale, Cheshire M33 5BP	0161 973 1179	0161 969 4954	Mr T. Kapur	358-5401	FD	11–16	1263	
Blessed Thomas Holford RC College	Urban Rd, Altrincham, Cheshire WA15 8HT	0161 911 8090	0161 911 8049	Mr L.F. Harris	358-5403	VA	11–16	777	RC
Broadoak School	Warburton La., Partington, Urmston, Manchester, Lancashire M31 4BU	0161 776 1977	0161 775 4559	Mr Andrew Griffin	358-4012	FD	11–16	413	
Flixton Girls' High School	Flixton Rd, Flixton, Urmston, Manchester, Lancashire M41 5DR	0161 912 2949	0161 747 1701	Mrs J. Hart	358-4014	CY	11–16	975	G
Loreto Grammar School	Dunham Rd, Altrincham, Cheshire WA14 4AH	0161 928 3703	0161 928 7659	Sr Patricia Goodstadt	358-5901	VA	11–18	1006	RC G
Lostock College	Selby Rd, Stretford, Manchester, Lancashire M32 9PL	0161 864 5700	0161 864 5705	Mrs Dawn Farrent	358-4015	CY	11–16	426	
St Ambrose College	Wicker La., Halebarns, Altrincham, Cheshire WA15 0HE	0161 980 2711	0161 980 2323	Mr M.D. Thompson	358-5900	VA	11–18	887	RC B
St Antony's RC College	Bradfield Rd, Urmston, Manchester, Lancashire M41 9PD	0161 911 8001	0161 748 4571	Mr Bill Byford	358-4602	VA	11–16	702	RC
Sale Grammar School	Marsland Rd, Sale, Cheshire M33 3NH	0161 973 3217	0161 976 4904	Mr D.A. Wilson	358-4029	CY	11–18	1212	
Sale High School	Norris Rd, Sale, Cheshire M33 3JR	0161 973 2713	0161 962 0020	Mrs Kathleen Leaver	358-5402	FD	11–16	964	
Stretford Grammar School	Granby Rd, Stretford, Manchester, Greater Manchester M32 8JB	0161 865 2293	0161 866 9938	Mr M.E. Garbett	358-4025	CY	11–18	671	
Stretford High School Community Language College	Gt Stone Rd, Stretford, Manchester, Lancashire M32 0XA	0161 912 4894	0161 912 4898	Mr Dereck Davies	358-4028	CY	11–16	652	
Urmston Grammar School	Newton Rd, Urmston, Manchester, Lancashire M41 5UG	0161 748 2875	0161 747 2504	Mr M.G. Spinks	358-5405	FD	11–18	879	
Wellacre Technology and Vocational College	Irlam Rd, Flixton, Urmston, Manchester, Lancashire M41 6AP	0161 748 5011	0161 755 3234	Mr Raymond Howell	358-4016	CY	11–16	928	B
Wellington School	Wellington Rd, Timperley, Altrincham, Cheshire WA15 7RH	0161 928 4157	0161 927 9147	Mrs Julie Armstrong	358-5400	FD	11–18	1304	

Warrington

School name	Address	Tel	Fax	Headteacher	Ref	Type	Ages	Pupils	Other
Birchwood Community High School	Brock Rd, Birchwood, Warrington, Cheshire WA3 7PT	01925 853500	01925 853502	Ms Anne Bright	877-4226	CY	11–16	886	
Bridgewater High School	Broomfields Rd, Appleton, Warrington, Cheshire WA4 3AE	01925 263919	01925 861434	Mr Christopher Marks	877-4229	CY	11–18	1684	
Cardinal Newman RC High School	Bridgewater Ave, Latchford, Warrington, Cheshire WA4 1RX	01925 635556	01925 628600	Mr Vincent Love	877-4624	VA	11–16	707	RC
Culcheth High School	Withington Ave, Culcheth, Warrington, Cheshire WA3 4JQ	01925 762136	01925 766373	Mr Martyn Froggett	877-4200	CY	11–18	1181	
Great Sankey High School	Barrow Hall La, Gt Sankey, Warrington, Cheshire WA5 3AA	01925 724118	01925 727396	Mr Alan Yates	877-4206	CY	11–18	1827	
Lymm High VC School	Oughtrington La, Lymm, Cheshire WA13 0RB	01925 755458	01925 758439	Mr Roger A. Lounds	877-4502	VC	11–18	1955	
Padgate Community High School	Insall Rd, Padgate, Warrington, Cheshire WA2 0LN	01925 822632	01925 851418	Mrs Linda Harrison	877-4218	CY	11–18	807	
Penketh High School	Heath Rd, Penketh, Warrington, Cheshire WA5 2BY	01925 722298	01925 723812	Mr Barry Fishwick	877-4201	CY	11–18	1351	
St Gregory's RC High School	Cromwell Ave, Westbrook, Warrington, Cheshire WA5 1HG	01925 574888	01925 243816	Mr S. Clarke	877-4622	VA	11–16	955	RC
Sir Thomas Boteler CE High School	Grammar School Rd, Latchford, Warrington, Cheshire WA4 1JL	01925 636414	01925 417468	Mr John Sharples	877-4230	VA	11–16	715	CE
William Beamont Community High School	Long La, Orford, Warrington, Cheshire WA2 8PX	01925 579500	01925 579505	Mrs Maggie Williams	877-4228	CY	11–16	1015	
Woolston Community High School	Holes La., Woolston, Warrington, Cheshire WA1 4LS	01925 493349	01925 493389	Mrs Jill Robinson	877-4204	CY	11–18	898	

Wigan

School name	Address	Tel	Fax	Headteacher	Ref	Type	Ages	Pupils	Other
Abraham Guest High School	Orrell Rd, Orrell, Wigan, Lancashire WN5 8HN	01942 511987	01942 700811	Mr Robert Caslake	359-4023	CY	11–16	941	
Bedford High School	Manchester Rd, Leigh, Lancashire WN7 2LU	01942 760032	01942 760034	Mr Stephen Preston	359-4019	CY	11–16	1102	
The Byrchall High School	Warrington Rd, Ashton-in-Makerfield, Wigan, Lancashire WN4 9PQ	01942 728221	01942 769612	Mr A.R. Birchall	359-4501	VC	11–16	1194	
Cansfield High Specialist Language College	Old Rd, Ashton-in-Makerfield, Wigan, Lancashire WN4 9TP	01942 727391	01942 720711	Mr Michael Southworth	359-4015	CY	11–16	917	

3

School name	Address	Tel	Fax	Headteacher	Ref	Type	Ages	Pupils	Other
The Deanery CE High School and Sixth Form College	Frog La., Wigan, Lancashire WN1 1HQ	01942 768801	01942 202293	Mrs J.A. Rowlands	359-4608	VA	11–18	1644	CE
Fred Longworth High School	Printshop La., Tyldesley, Manchester, Lancashire M29 8JN	01942 883796	01942 897413	Mr Anthony Colley	359-4025	CY	11–16	1301	
Golborne High School	Lowton Rd, Golborne, Warrington, Cheshire WA3 3EL	01942 726842	01942 273176	Mr David Lythgoe	359-4022	CY	11–16	807	
Hawkley Hall High School	Carr La., Hawkley Hall, Wigan, Lancashire WN3 5NY	01942 204640	01942 403570	Mr Rw Halford	359-4035	CY	11–16	882	
Hesketh Fletcher CE High School, Atherton	Hamilton St, Atherton, Manchester, Lancashire M46 0AY	01942 882425	01942 887310	Dr E. Walker	359-4612	VA	11–16	900	CE
Hindley Community High School – Arts College	Mornington Rd, Hindley, Wigan, Lancashire WN2 4LG	01942 767704	01942 748054	Mrs Jane Lees	359-4026	CY	11–16	932	
Lowton High School A Specialist Sports College	Newton Rd, Lowton, Warrington, Cheshire WA3 1DU	01942 767040	01942 767053	Mr John Shanahan	359-4028	CY	11–16	1138	
PEMBEC High School	Montrose Ave, Pemberton, Wigan, Lancashire WN5 9XL	01942 515370	01942 515375	Mrs Michele Buras-Stubbs	359-4008	CY	11–16	584	
Rose Bridge High School	Holt St, Ince, Wigan, Lancashire WN1 3HD	01942 510712	01942 510939	Mr Jack Pendlebury	359-4017	CY	11–16	654	
St Edmund Arrowsmith RC High School, Ashton-in-Makerfield	Rookery Ave, Ashton-in-Makerfield, Wigan, Lancashire WN4 9PF	01942 728651	01942 730035	Mr P.W. Phillips	359-4805	VA	11–16	1209	RC
St John Fisher RC High School	Baytree Rd, Springfield, Wigan, Lancashire WN6 7RN	01942 510715	01942 519039	Mr S. Gribbon	359-4609	VA	11–16	939	RC
St Mary's RC High School	Manchester Rd, Astley, Tyldesley, Manchester, Lancashire M29 7EE	01942 884144	01942 884357	Mr David Burnett	359-4615	VA	11–18	1594	RC
St Peter's RC High School Visual Arts College	Howards La., Orrell, Wigan, Lancashire WN5 8NU	01942 747693	01942 747694	Miss Helen Jesrstice	359-4614	VA	11–16	906	RC
Shevington High School	Shevington La., Shevington, Wigan, Lancashire WN6 8AB	01257 400990	01257 400992	Mrs Helen Mackenzie	359-4027	CY	11–16	739	
Standish Community High School	Kenyon Rd, Standish, Wigan, Lancashire WN6 0NX	01257 422265	01257 425858	Mr Hugh Crossan	359-4034	CY	11–16	1253	
Westleigh High School – A College of Technology	Westleigh La., Leigh, Lancashire WN7 5NL	01942 202580	01942 202705	Mr John Banks	359-4020	CY	11–16	787	

Wirral

School name	Address	Tel	Fax	Headteacher	Ref	Type	Ages	Pupils	Other
Bebington High Sports College	Higher Bebington Rd, Bebington, Wirral, Merseyside CH63 2PS	0151 645 4154	0151 643 8065	Mr Brian Jordan	344-4070	CY	11–18	1030	
Calday Grange Grammar School	Grammar School La., West Kirby, Wirral, Merseyside CH48 8GG	0151 625 2727	0151 625 9851	Mr Andrew J. Hall	344-5400	FD	11–18	1414	B
Hilbre High School	Frankby Rd, West Kirby, Wirral, Cheshire CH48 6EQ	0151 625 5996	0151 625 3697	Miss Jan Levenson	344-4060	CY	11–18	1022	
The Mosslands School	Mosslands Dr, Wallasey, Merseyside CH45 8PJ	0151 638 8131	0151 639 1317	Mr Mark Rodaway	344-4066	CY	11–18	1431	B
The Oldershaw School	Valkyrie Rd, Wallasey, Merseyside CH45 4RJ	0151 638 2800	0151 691 1581	Mr S.J. Peach	344-4067	CY	11–18	828	
Park High School	Park Rd South, Prenton, Merseyside CH43 4UY	0151 652 1574	0151 653 6760	Mr Steve McMahon	344-4017	CY	11–16	1017	
Pensby High School for Boys: A Specialist Sports College	Irby Rd, Heswall, Wirral, Merseyside CH61 6XN	0151 648 2111	0151 648 3128	Mr Phil Sheridan	344-4057	CY	11–18	718	B
Pensby High School for Girls	Irby Rd, Heswall, Wirral, Merseyside CH61 6XN	0151 648 1941	0151 648 8103	Mr S. Hyden	344-4058	CY	11–18	855	G
Prenton High School for Girls	Hesketh Ave, Rock Ferry, Birkenhead, Merseyside CH42 6RR	0151 644 8113	0151 644 8113	Mr R. Winterson	344-4010	CY	11–16	639	G
Ridgeway High School	Noctorum Ave, Noctorum, Prenton, Merseyside CH43 9EB	0151 678 3322	0151 678 6571	Ms A. Walsh	344-4018	CY	11–16	786	
Rock Ferry High School	Ravenswood Ave, Rock Ferry, Birkenhead, Merseyside CH42 4NY	0151 645 6917	0151 643 1236	Mr P.T. Bennett	344-4011	CY	11–16	798	
St Anselm's College	Manor Hill, Prenton, Merseyside CH43 1UQ	0151 652 1408	0151 652 1957	Mr R.S. Duggan	344-5900	VA	11–18	857	RC B
St John Plessington RC College	Old Chester Rd, Bebington, Wirral, Merseyside CH63 7LF	0151 645 5049	0151 643 1516	Mr T. Quinn	344-4605	VA	11–18	1253	RC
St Mary's RC College	Wallasey Village, Wallasey, Merseyside CH45 3LN	0151 639 7531	0151 691 1452	Ms Tricia McDonough	344-4611	VA	11–18	1584	RC
South Wirral High School	Plymyard Ave, Eastham, Wirral, Merseyside CH62 8EH	0151 327 3213	0151 327 7798	Mrs C.M. McCormack	344-4071	CY	11–18	1161	
Upton Hall School FCJ	Upton, Wirral, Merseyside CH49 6LJ	0151 677 7696	0151 677 6868	Mrs Patricia Young	344-5901	VA	11–18	903	RC G
Wallasey School	Birket Ave, Moreton, Wirral, Merseyside CH46 1RB	0151 677 7825	0151 605 0238	Mr Phil Duffy	344-4073	CY	11–18	1252	
Weatherhead High School Media Arts College	Breck Rd, Wallasey, Wirral CH44 3HS	0151 631 4400		Mr N.R. Dyment	344-4069	VA	11–18	1504	G
West Kirby Grammar School	Graham Rd, West Kirby, Wirral, Merseyside CH48 5DP	0151 632 3449	0151 632 1224	Mrs Glenice Robinson	344-4056	CY	11–18	1202	G

School name	Address	Tel	Fax	Headteacher	Ref	Type	Ages	Pupils	Other
Wirral Grammar School for Boys	Cross La, Bebington, Wirral, Merseyside CH63 3AQ	0151 644 0908	0151 643 8317	Mr A. Cooper	344-5401	FD	11–18	1016	B
Wirral Grammar School for Girls	Heath Rd, Bebington, Wirral, Merseyside CH63 3AF	0151 644 8282	0151 643 1332	Mrs Elaine Cogan	344-4052	CY	11–18	1048	G
Woodchurch High School Engineering College	Carr Bridge Rd, Woodchurch, Wirral, Merseyside CH49 7NG	0151 677 5257	0151 678 1908	Mrs B. Holt	344-4012	CY	11–16	1320	

South East

3

Bracknell Forest

School name	Address	Tel	Fax	Headteacher	Ref	Type	Ages	Pupils	Other
The Brakenhale School	Rectory La, Bracknell, Berkshire RG12 7BA	01344 423041	01344 300397	Mr Paul Salter	867-4030	CY	11–18	604	
Easthampstead Park School	Ringmead, Bracknell, Berkshire RG12 8FS	01344 304567	01344 867862	Mr Gordon Cunningham	867-4061	CY	11–18	1289	
Edgbarrow School	Grant Rd, Crowthorne, Berkshire RG45 7HZ	01344 772658	01344 776623	Mr R. Elsey	867-4032	CY	11–18	1166	
Garth Hill College	Sandy La, Bracknell, Berkshire RG12 2JH	01344 421122	01344 455223	Mr S. Turner	867-4059	CY	11–18	1211	
Ranelagh CE School	Ranelagh Dr, Bracknell, Berkshire RG12 9DA	01344 421233	01344 301811	Mrs Kathy Winrow	867-4603	VA	11–18	884	CE
Sandhurst School	Owlsmoor Rd, Owlsmoor, Sandhurst, Berkshire GU47 0SD	01344 775678	01344 771575	Mr Andrew Fletcher	867-4058	CY	11–18	1098	

Brighton and Hove

School name	Address	Tel	Fax	Headteacher	Ref	Type	Ages	Pupils	Other
Blatchington Mill School and Sixth Form College	Nevill Ave, Hove, East Sussex BN3 7BW	01273 736244	01273 739615	Mr Neil Hunter	846-4067	CY	11–18	1711	
Cardinal Newman RC School	The Upper Dr, Hove, East Sussex BN3 6ND	01273 558551	01273 508778	Mr P. Evans	846-4605	VA	11–18	2033	RC
Dorothy Stringer High School	Loder Rd, Brighton, East Sussex BN1 6PZ	01273 852222	01273 562225	Mr Trevor Allen	846-4016	CY	11–16	1601	
Falmer High School	Lewes Rd, Brighton, East Sussex BN1 9PW	01273 691191	01273 665455	Mr Stuart McLaughlin	846-4022	CY	11–16	662	
Hove Park School and Sixth Form Centre	Nevill Rd, Hove, East Sussex BN3 7BN	01273 295000	01273 295009	Mr Tim Barclay	846-4068	CY	11–18	1730	
Longhill High School	Falmer Rd, Rottingdean, Brighton, East Sussex BN2 7FR	01273 304086	01273 303547	Mr P. Lonsdale	846-4018	CY	11–16	1214	
Patcham High School	Ladies Mile Rd, Brighton, East Sussex BN1 8PB	01273 503908	01273 562896	Mrs Paula Sargent	846-4072	CY	11–16	980	
Portslade Community College	Chalky Rd, Portslade, Brighton, East Sussex BN41 2WS	01273 416300	01273 422129	Mr M. Tait	846-4049	CY	11–18	1032	
Varndean School	Balfour Rd, Brighton, East Sussex BN1 6NP	01273 561281	01273 564614	Mr Andy Schofield	846-4012	CY	11–16	1203	

Buckinghamshire

School name	Address	Tel	Fax	Headteacher	Ref	Type	Ages	Pupils	Other
The Amersham School	Stanley Hill, Amersham, Buckinghamshire HP7 9HH	01494 726562	01494 434181	Mrs Sharon Jarrett	825-4095	CY	11–18	803	
Aylesbury Grammar School	Walton Rd, Aylesbury, Buckinghamshire HP21 7RP	01296 484545	01296 484545	Mr Steve Harvey	825-4500	VC	11–18	1270	B
Aylesbury High School	Walton Rd, Aylesbury, Buckinghamshire HP21 7SX	01296 388222	01296 388200	Mr Alan Rosen	825-4058	CY	11–18	1261	G
Beaconsfield High School	Wattleton Rd, Beaconsfield, Buckinghamshire HP9 1RR	01494 673043	01494 670715	Ms P. Castagnoli	825-5402	FD	11–18	1095	G
The Beaconsfield School	Wattleton Rd, Beaconsfield, Buckinghamshire HP9 1SJ	01494 673450	01494 676404	Mr Alex Russell	825-4082	CY	11–18	782	
Buckingham School	London Rd, Buckingham, Buckinghamshire MK18 1AT	01280 812206	01280 822525	Mrs Christine Jones	825-4004	CY	11–18	1040	
Burnham Grammar School	Hogfair La, Burnham, Slough, Berkshire SL1 7HG	01628 604812	01628 663559	Mrs Cathie Long	825-4051	CY	11–18	846	
Burnham Upper School	Opendale Rd, Burnham, Slough, Buckinghamshire SL1 7LZ	01628 662107	01628 668057	Mr Max Bilsborough	825-4074	CY	11–18	722	
The Chalfonts Community College	Narcot La, Chalfont St Peter, Gerrards Cross, Buckinghamshire SL9 8TP	01753 882032	01753 890716	Mrs Sue Tanner	825-5403	FD	11–18	1793	

School name	Address	Tel	Fax	Headteacher	Ref	Type	Ages	Pupils	Other
Chesham High School	Whitehill, Chesham, Buckinghamshire HP5 1BA	01494 782854	01494 775414	Mr Phillip Wayne	825-4079	CY	11–18	1233	
Chesham Park Community College	Chartridge La., Chesham, Buckinghamshire HP5 2RG	01494 782066	01494 783185	Mr Kevin Patrick	825-4096	CY	11–18	775	
The Cottesloe School	Aylesbury Rd, Wing, Leighton Buzzard, Bedfordshire LU7 0NY	01296 688264	01296 681729	Mr Nigel Fox	825-5407	FD	11–18	1098	
Cressex Community School	Holmers La., High Wycombe, Buckinghamshire HP12 4QA	01494 437729	01494 461502	Mr Richard Marshall	825-4072	CY	11–18	654	
Dr Challoner's Grammar School	Chesham Rd, Amersham, Buckinghamshire HP6 5HA	01494 787500	01494 721862	Dr Mark Fenton	825-4504	VC	11–18	1278	B
Dr Challoner's High School	Cokes La., Little Chalfont, Amersham, Buckinghamshire HP7 9QB	01494 763296	01494 766023	Miss Peg Hulse	825-4061	VC	11–18	1063	G
The Grange School	Wendover Way, Aylesbury, Buckinghamshire HP21 7NH	01296 390900	01296 390991	Mr Vincent Thomas Murray	825-4034	CY	11–18	1238	
Great Marlow School	Bobmore La., Marlow, Buckinghamshire SL7 1JE	01628 483752	01628 475852	Mrs Geralyn Wilson	825-5409	FD	11–18	1181	
Highcrest Community School	Hatters La., High Wycombe, Buckinghamshire HP13 7NQ	01494 529866	01494 472850	Miss Shena Moynihan	825-4001	CY	11–18	768	
Holmer Green Senior School	Parish Piece, Holmer Grn, High Wycombe, Buckinghamshire HP15 6SP	01494 712219	01494 711103	Mr D. Gilbert	825-4070	CY	11–18	839	
John Colet School	Wharf Rd, Wendover, Aylesbury, Buckinghamshire HP22 6HF	01296 623348	01296 622086	Mrs Christine McIntock	825-4044	CY	11–18	1017	
John Hampden Grammar School	Marlow Hill, High Wycombe, Buckinghamshire HP11 1SZ	01494 529589	01494 447714	Mr Stephen Nokes	825-4009	CY	11–18	932	B
Mandeville Upper School	Ellen Rd, Aylesbury, Buckinghamshire HP21 8ES	01296 424472	01296 334666	Mr P.J.R. Patchett	825-4067	CY	11–18	1075	
The Misbourne School	Misbourne Dr, Great Missenden, Buckinghamshire HP16 0BN	01494 862869	01494 890491	Mr Jonathan Howard-Drake	825-4042	CY	11–18	1294	
Princes Risborough	Merton Rd, Princes Risborough, Buckinghamshire HP27 0DT	01844 345496	01844 346147	Mr P. Rowe	825-4036	CY	11–18	933	
Quarrendon School	Weedon Rd, Aylesbury, Buckinghamshire HP19 9PG	01296 428551	01296 486651	Mr Jonathan Johnson	825-4048	CY	11–18	765	
The Royal Grammar School, High Wycombe	Amersham Rd, High Wycombe, Buckinghamshire HP13 6QT	01494 524955	01494 510604	Mr Roy Page	825-5404	FD	11–18	1354	B R
Royal Latin School	Chandos Rd, Buckingham, Buckinghamshire MK18 1AX	01280 813065	01280 813064	Mr Robert Cooper	825-4501	VC	11–18	1227	Ch
St Bernard's RC School	Daws Hill La., High Wycombe, Buckinghamshire HP11 1PW	01494 535196	01494 446523	Mr Robert Simpson	825-4701	VA	11–18	635	RC
Sir Henry Floyd Grammar School and Performing Arts College	Oxford Rd, Aylesbury, Buckinghamshire HP21 8PE	01296 424781	01296 424783	Mr Stephen Box	825-4065	CY	11–18	1009	
Sir William Borlase's Grammar School	West St, Marlow, Buckinghamshire SL7 2BR	01628 816500	01628 477886	Dr Peter Holding	825-4505	VC	11–18	1019	
Sir William Ramsay School	Rose Ave, Hazlemere, High Wycombe, Buckinghamshire HP15 7UB	01494 815211	01494 816734	Mrs Gaynor Comber	825-4084	CY	11–18	943	
Waddesdon CE School	Baker St, Waddesdon, Aylesbury, Buckinghamshire HP18 0LQ	01296 651382	01296 658453	Mr A. Armstrong	825-5408	VA	11–18	959	CE
Wycombe High School	Marlow Rd, High Wycombe, Buckinghamshire HP11 1TB	01494 523961	01494 510354	Ms Jane Wainwright	825-4503	FD	11–18	1350	G
The Wye Valley School	New Rd, Bourne End, Buckinghamshire SL8 5BW	01628 819022	01628 810689	Mrs L. Melton	825-4094	CY	11–18	820	

East Sussex

School name	Address	Tel	Fax	Headteacher	Ref	Type	Ages	Pupils	Other
Beacon Community College	East Beeches Rd, Crowborough, East Sussex TN6 2AS	01892 603000	01892 603001	Mr Peter Swan	845-4026	CY	11–18	1764	
Bexhill High School	Down Rd, Bexhill-on-Sea, East Sussex TN39 4HT	01424 730722	01424 212613	Mr Mike Conn	845-4044	CY	11–16	1555	
The Bishop Bell CE Mathematics and Computing Specialist School	Priory Rd, Eastbourne, East Sussex BN23 7EJ	01323 465400	01323 765126	Mr Terry Boatwright	845-4610	VA	11–16	998	CE
The Causeway School	Larkspur Dr, Eastbourne, East Sussex BN23 8EJ	01323 465700	01323 740097	Mrs Alison Dearden	845-4074	CY	11–16	861	
The Cavendish School	Eldon Rd, Eastbourne, East Sussex BN21 1UE	01323 731340	01323 739572	Mr Mark Dawkins	845-4064	CY	11–16	1006	
Chailey School	Mill La., South Chailey, Lewes, East Sussex BN8 4PU	01273 890407	01273 890893	Mrs Lesley Young	845-4042	CY	11–16	850	
Claverham Community College	North Trade Rd, Battle, East Sussex TN33 0HT	01424 772155	01424 774106	Mr Richard Pitts	845-4025	CY	11–16	1145	
Eastbourne Technology College	Brodrick Rd, Eastbourne, East Sussex BN22 9RQ	01323 514900	01323 514909	Ms Janet Felkin	845-4062	CY	11–16	800	
Filsham Valley School	Edinburgh Rd, St Leonards-on-Sea, East Sussex TN38 8HH	01424 448740	01424 722354	Mrs Lesley Farmer	845-4073	CY	11–18	912	
The Grove	Darwell Cl, St Leonards-on-Sea, East Sussex TN38 9JP	01424 431691	01424 440060	Mrs Jenny Jones	845-4058	CY	11–18	868	
Hailsham Community College	Battle Rd, Hailsham, East Sussex BN27 1DT	01323 841468	01323 848900	Mrs Lesley Farmer	845-4027	CY	11–18	1282	
Heathfield Community College	Cade St, Old Heathfield, Heathfield, East Sussex TN21 8RJ	01435 866066	01435 867155	Mr A. Powell	845-4028	CY	11–18	1474	
Helenswood School	The Ridge, St Leonards-on-Sea, East Sussex TN37 7PS	01424 753040	01424 752529	Dame Sheila Wallis	845-4055	FD	11–18	1214	G

School name	Address	Tel	Fax	Headteacher	Ref	Type	Ages	Pupils	Other
Hillcrest School	Rye Rd, Hastings, East Sussex TN35 5DN	01424 711950	01424 719842	Mrs Lindsay Hart	845-4057	CY	11–18	798	
Peacehaven Community School	Greenwich Way, Peacehaven, East Sussex BN10 8RB	01273 581100	01273 575859	Mrs Helen Cryer	845-4000	CY	11–16	853	
Priory School	Mountfield Rd, Lewes, East Sussex BN7 2XN	01273 476231	01273 486922	Mr Martyn Ofield	845-4047	CY	11–16	1157	
Ratton School	Park Ave, Eastbourne, East Sussex BN21 2XR	01323 504011	01323 520364	Mr David Linsell	845-4063	CY	11–16	1186	
Ringmer Community College	Lewes Rd, Ringmer, Lewes, East Sussex BN8 5RB	01273 812220	01273 813961	Ms Kathryn Stonier	845-4041	CY	11–16	838	
Robertsbridge Community College	Knelle Rd, Robertsbridge, East Sussex TN32 5EA	01580 880360	01580 882120	Ms Karen Roberts	845-4035	CY	11–16	608	
St Richard's RC College	Ashdown Rd, Bexhill-on-Sea, East Sussex TN40 1SE	01424 731070		Mr Anthony Campbell	845-4606	VA	11–16	988	RC
Seaford Head Community College	Arundel Rd, Seaford, East Sussex BN25 4LX	01323 872700	01323 492576	Mrs Lynton Golds	845-4036	CY	11–18	1128	
Thomas Peacocke Community College	The Gr, Rye, East Sussex TN31 7NQ	01797 222545	01797 224343	Mrs Ann Cockerham	845-4045	CY	11–18	629	
Tideway School	Southdown Rd, Newhaven, East Sussex BN9 9JL	01273 517601	01273 611182	Mr Adrian Money	845-4046	CY	11–16	657	
Uckfield Community Technology College	Downsview Cres, Uckfield, East Sussex TN22 3DJ	01825 764844	01825 762946	Mr Craig Pamphilon	845-4037	CY	11–18	1659	
Uplands Community College	Lower High St, Wadhurst, East Sussex TN5 6AZ	01892 782135	01892 782003	Mrs Jayne Edmonds	845-4038	CY	11–18	1026	
William Parker Sports College	Parkstone Rd, Hastings, East Sussex TN34 2NT	01424 439888	01424 461472	Mr Derek Greenup	845-4500	VC	11–18	1317	B
Willingdon Community School	Broad Rd, Lower Willingdon, Eastbourne, East Sussex BN20 9QX	01323 485254	01323 487779	Mr Ian Junglus	845-4039	CY	11–16	937	

Hampshire

School name	Address	Tel	Fax	Headteacher	Ref	Type	Ages	Pupils	Other
Aldworth Science College	Western Way, Basingstoke, Hampshire RG22 6HA	01256 322691	01256 819756	Mrs Julie Churcher	850-4156	CY	11–16	546	
Amery Hill School	Amery Hill, Alton, Hampshire GU34 2BZ	01420 84545	01420 84137	Rev Stephen Crabtree	850-4100	CY	11–16	972	
Applemore College	Roman Rd, Dibden Purlieu, Southampton, Hampshire SO45 4RQ	023 8084 8804	023 8084 8715	Mr Matthew Longden	850-5412	FD	11–16	659	
The Arnewood School	Gore Rd, New Milton, Hampshire BH25 6RS	01425 625400	01425 612036	Mr Christopher Hummerstone	850-5402	FD	11–18	1182	
Bay House School	Gomer La, Gosport, Hampshire PO12 2QP	023 9258 7931	023 9252 4260	Mr Ian Potter	850-5408	FD	11–18	2074	
Bishop Challoner RC Secondary School	St Michael's Rd, Basingstoke, Hampshire RG22 6SR	01256 462661	01256 810359	Mr Anthony Corish	850-4604	VA	11–16	629	RC
Bohunt School	Longmoor Rd, Liphook, Hampshire GU30 7NY	01428 724324	01428 725120	Mr Alan Taylor-Bennett	850-5407	FD	11–16	1290	
Bridgemary Community Sports College	Wych La, Bridgemary, Gosport, Hampshire PO13 0JN	01329 319966	01329 319977	Mrs Cheryl Heron	850-4314	CY	11–16	928	
Brighton Hill Community College	Brighton Way, Basingstoke, Hampshire RG22 4HS	01256 350606	01256 840116	Mr David Eyre	850-4182	CY	11–16	1277	
Brookfield Community School and Language College	Brook La, Sarisbury Grn, Southampton, Hampshire SO31 7DU	01489 576335	01489 579914	Mrs Maria Allan	850-4136	CY	11–16	1754	
Brune Park Community College	Military Rd, Gosport, Hampshire PO12 3BU	023 9261 6000	023 9261 6006	Dr I. Johnson	850-4315	CY	11–16	1675	
The Burgate School and Sixth Form Centre	Salisbury Rd, Fordingbridge, Hampshire SP6 1EZ	01425 652039	01425 656625	Mrs C. Nicholls	850-5401	FD	11–18	956	
Calthorpe Park School	Hitches La, Fleet, Hampshire GU51 5JA	01252 613483	01252 626091	Mrs Catherine Anwar	850-4171	CY	11–16	988	
Cams Hill School	Shearwater Ave, Fareham, Hampshire PO16 8AH	01329 231641	01329 283996	Mr David Wilmot	850-5416	FD	11–16	1042	
The Clere School	Earlstone Common, Burghclere, Newbury, Berkshire RG20 9HP	01635 278372	01635 278538	Ms Sarah Rogers	850-4162	CY	11–16	710	
The Connaught School	Tongham Rd, Aldershot, Hampshire GU12 4AS	01252 343723	01252 322530	Mr J. Hanna	850-4312	CY	11–16	737	
Costello Technology College	Crossborough Hill, London Rd, Basingstoke, Hampshire RG21 4AL	01256 321263	01256 358629	Mrs Julia Mortimore	850-4002	CY	11–16	992	
Court Moor School	Spring Woods, Fleet, Hampshire GU52 7RY	01252 615065	01252 624490	Mrs Beverley Stevens	850-4117	CY	11–16	1094	
Cove School	St John's Rd, Cove, Farnborough, Hampshire GU14 9RN	01252 542397	01252 524223	Ms Megan Davies Jones	850-4203	CY	11–16	1030	
Cowplain Community School	Hart Plain Ave, Cowplain, Waterlooville, Hampshire PO8 8RY	023 9261 2020	023 9261 2030	Mr D.R. Rowlinson	850-4110	CY	11–16	1087	
Cranbourne Business and Enterprise College	Wessex Cl, Basingstoke, Hampshire RG21 3NP	01256 868600	01256 868601	Mrs Betty Elkins	850-4164	CY	11–16	1043	
Crestwood College for Business and Enterprise	Shakespeare Rd, Boyatt Wood, Eastleigh, Hampshire SO50 4FZ	023 8064 1232	023 8062 9373	Mrs Krista Carter	850-4191	CY	11–16	528	
Crofton School	Marks Rd, Stubbington, Fareham, Hampshire PO14 2AT	01329 664251	01329 668525	Mr Antony Forrest	850-5405	FD	11–16	1051	
Crookhorn College of Technology	Stakes Hill Rd, Waterlooville, Hampshire PO7 5UD	023 9225 1120	023 9223 0310	Mr G. Sammons	850-4159	CY	11–16	818	
Eggar's School	London Rd, Holybourne, Alton, Hampshire GU34 4EQ	01420 541194	01420 593412	Mrs F. Martin	850-4000	CY	11–16	797	

3

School name	Address	Tel	Fax	Headteacher	Ref	Type	Ages	Pupils	Other
Everest Community College	Sherborne Rd, Sherborne St John, Basingstoke, Hampshire RG24 9LP	01256 465547	01256 810448	Ms J. Rose	850-4169	CY	11–16	410	
Fernhill School	Neville Duke Rd, Farnborough, Hampshire GU14 9BY	01276 702540	01276 702541	Mr Clive Gilbert	850-4204	CY	11–16	889	
Fort Hill Community School	Kenilworth Rd, Winklebury, Basingstoke, Hampshire RG23 8JQ	01256 354311	01256 365897	Mrs Lesley Lawson	850-4187	CY	11–16	673	
Frogmore Community College	Potley Hill Rd, Yateley, Hampshire GU46 6AG	01252 408444	01252 408445	Mr Peter Green	850-4183	CY	11–18	636	
Hamble Community Sports College	Satchell La, Hamble-le-Rice, Southampton, Hampshire SO31 4NE	023 8045 2105	023 8045 7439	Miss Judith Chambers	850-4119	CY	11–16	1022	
Hardley School and Sixth Form	Long La, Holbury, Southampton, Hampshire SO45 2PA	023 8089 1192	023 8089 2463	Mr R. Underwood	850-5400	FD	11–18	977	
Harrow Way Community School	Harrow Way, Andover, Hampshire SP10 3RH	01264 364533	01264 336982	Mr Charlie Currie	850-4163	CY	11–16	704	
The Hayling College	Church Rd, Hayling Island, Hampshire PO11 0NU	023 9246 6241	023 9246 1835	Mr M. Bullough	850-4147	CY	11–16	691	
Henry Beaufort School	East Woodhay Rd, Harestock, Winchester, Hampshire SO22 6JJ	01962 880073	01962 883667	Miss Sue Hearle	850-4174	CY	11–16	1000	
The Henry Cort Community College	Hillson Dr, Fareham, Hampshire PO15 6PH	01329 843127	01329 846755	Mr Phil Munday	850-4307	CY	11–16	931	
Horndean Technology College	Barton Cross, Horndean, Waterlooville, Hampshire PO8 9PQ	023 9259 4325	023 9257 1108	Mr Glenn Strong	850-4173	CY	11–16	1357	
Hounsdown School	Jacobs Gutter La, Totton, Southampton, Hampshire SO40 9FT	023 8086 2981	023 8066 3160	Miss D.J. Nightingale	850-4168	CY	11–16	1206	
The Hurst Community College	Brimpton Rd, Baughurst, Tadley, Hampshire RG26 5NL	0118 981 7474	0118 981 7976	Mr Malcolm Christian	850-4144	CY	11–16	1067	
John Hanson Community School	Floral Way, Andover, Hampshire SP10 3PB	01264 352546	01264 339685	Mr Stephen Evatt	850-4001	CY	11–16	967	
Kings' School	Romsey Rd, Winchester, Hampshire SO22 5PN	01962 861161	01962 849224	Mrs Susan Lawrence	850-4310	CY	11–16	1641	R
Mill Chase Community Technology College	Mill Chase Rd, Bordon, Hampshire GU35 0ER	01420 472132	01420 479986	Mr S. Mulcahy	850-4152	CY	11–16	749	
The Mountbatten School A Language and Sports College	Whitenap La, Romsey, Hampshire SO51 5SY	01794 502502	01794 502501	Mrs Lesley Morffew	850-4015	CY	11–16	1419	
The Neville Lovett Community School and Continuing Education Centre	St Anne's Gr, Fareham, Hampshire PO14 1JJ	01329 318003	01329 284007	Mr N. Dewhurst	850-4308	CY	11–16	823	
Noadswood School	North Rd, Dibden Purlieu, Southampton, Hampshire SO45 4ZF	023 8084 0025	023 8084 3532	Mr Alex Bernard	850-4128	CY	11–16	1066	
Oak Farm Community School	Ballantyne Rd, Farnborough, Hampshire GU14 8SS	01252 401070	01252 401071	Mr Gren Earney	850-4207	CY	11–16	324	
Oaklands RC School	Stakes Hill Rd, Waterlooville, Hampshire PO7 7BW	023 9225 9214	023 9223 0317	Mr C. Whitfield	850-5411	VA	11–18	1269	RC
Park Community School	Middle Park Way, Leigh Pk, Havant, Hampshire PO9 4BU	023 9247 5254	023 9248 1012	Mr Sean Dickinson	850-4316	CY	11–16	868	
Perins School A Community Sports College	Pound Hill, Alresford, Hampshire SO24 9BS	01962 734361	01962 735930	Mrs J. Bernard	850-4130	CY	11–16	1010	
The Petersfield School	Cranford Rd, Petersfield, Hampshire GU32 3LU	01730 263119	01730 265869	Mr Nigel Poole	850-5418	FD	11–16	1175	
Portchester Community School	White Hart La, Portchester, Fareham, Hampshire PO16 9BD	023 9236 4399	023 9220 1528	Mrs Carolyn Hughan	850-4133	CY	11–16	785	
Priestlands School	North St, Pennington, Lymington, Hampshire SO41 8FZ	01590 677033	01590 670398	Mr Chris Willsher	850-4129	CY	11–16	1163	
Purbrook Park School	Park Ave, Purbrook, Waterlooville, Hampshire PO7 5DS	023 9237 0351	023 9261 7941	Mr K. Clark	850-5414	FD	11–16	870	
Quilley School of Engineering	Cherbourg Rd, Eastleigh, Hampshire SO50 5EL	023 8061 2330	023 8061 8100	Mr Richard Kelly	850-4132	CY	11–16	570	
Ringwood School	Parsonage Barn La, Ringwood, Hampshire BH24 1SE	01425 475000	01425 473063	Miss Chris Edwards	850-5403	FD	11–18	1587	
Robert May's School	West St, Odiham, Hook, Hampshire RG29 1NA	01256 702700	01256 703012	Mrs Susan Rafter	850-4511	VC	11–16	1216	
The Romsey School	Greatbridge Rd, Romsey, Hampshire SO51 8ZB	01794 512334	01794 511497	Mr P. Warburton	850-4143	CY	11–16	1123	
Staunton Park Community Sports College	Wakefords Way, Havant, Hampshire PO9 5JD	023 9247 3031	023 9247 0384	Mr Mike Madden	850-4317	CY	11–16	570	
Swanmore College of Technology	New Rd, Swanmore, Southampton, Hampshire SO32 2RB	01489 892256	01489 891453	Mrs A. Hillier	850-4149	CY	11–16	1327	
Test Valley School	Roman Rd, Stockbridge, Hampshire SO20 6HA	01264 810555	01264 810173	Miss Wendy Morrish	850-4153	CY	11–16	762	
Testbourne Community School	Micheldever Rd, Whitchurch, Hampshire RG28 7JF	01256 892061	01256 896796	Ms Hilary Jackson	850-5410	FD	11–16	762	
Testwood School	Testwood La, Totton, Southampton, Hampshire SO40 3ZW	023 8086 2146	023 8066 6514	Mrs M.A. Capsomidis	850-5406	FD	11–16	990	
Thornden School	Winchester Rd, Chandler's Ford, Eastleigh, Hampshire SO53 2DW	023 8086 6514	023 8026 8393	Dr R.A. Sykes	850-4175	CY	11–16	1383	
The Toynbee School	Bodycoats Rd, Chandler's Ford, Eastleigh, Hampshire SO53 2PL	023 8026 9722	023 8025 1086	Mr D. Jones	850-4113	CY	11–16	1042	
The Vyne Community School	Vyne Rd, Basingstoke, Hampshire RG21 5PB	01256 473003	01256 816956	Mr Peter Michael Hutchinson	850-4180	CY	11–16	749	
Warblington School	Southleigh Rd, Havant, Hampshire PO9 2RR	023 9247 5480	023 9248 6127	Mr Owen Davies	850-4318	CY	11–16	731	
The Wavell School	Lynchford Rd, Farnborough, Hampshire GU14 6BH	01252 341256	01252 345613	Miss Amanda Rowley	850-4206	CY	11–16	853	
The Westgate School	Cheriton Rd, Winchester, Hampshire SO22 5AZ	01962 854757	01962 840080	Mr P. Jenner	850-4012	CY	11–16	1159	R
Wildern School	Wildern La, Hedge End, Southampton, Hampshire SO30 4EJ	01489 783473	01489 790927	Mr Jeffery Threlfall	850-4127	CY	11–16	1811	

School name	Address	Tel	Fax	Headteacher	Ref	Type	Ages	Pupils	Other
Winton School	London Rd, Andover, Hampshire SP10 2PS	01264 351822	01264 332793	Mr Andrew Lessels Clark	850-4184	CY	11–16	801	
Wyvern Technology College	Botley Rd, Fair Oak, Eastleigh, Hampshire SO50 7AN	023 8069 2679	023 8060 3215	Miss Sheila Campbell	850-4161	CY	11–16	1328	
Yateley School	School La, Yateley, Hampshire GU46 6NW	01252 879222	01252 872517	Mr William Sarell	850-4166	CY	11–18	1502	

Isle of Wight

School name	Address	Tel	Fax	Headteacher	Ref	Type	Ages	Pupils	Other
Allbrook Education Trust	Pritchetts Way, Rookley, Isle of Wight PO38 3LT	01983 721597	01983 721597	Mr J. Cowley	921-6043		11–16	14	Ch
Carisbrooke High School	Mountbatten Dr, Newport, Isle of Wight PO30 5QU	01983 524651	01983 825456	Ms Mary Hoather	921-4024	CY	13–18	1379	
Cowes High School	Crossfield Ave, Cowes, Isle of Wight PO31 8HB	01983 203103	01983 203133	Mr David A. Snashall	921-4003	CY	13–18	1025	
Medina High School	Mountbatten Centre, Fairlee Rd, Newport, Isle of Wight PO30 2DX	01983 526523	01983 528791	Mr Richard Williams	921-4028	CY	13–18	992	
Ryde High School	Pell La, Ryde, Isle of Wight PO33 3LN	01983 567331	01983 812948	Ms Linda McGowan	921-4015	CY	13–18	1092	
Sandown High School	The Fairway, Sandown, Isle of Wight PO36 9JH	01983 402142	01983 404948	Mr J. Bradshaw	921-4025	CY	13–18	1469	

Kent

School name	Address	Tel	Fax	Headteacher	Ref	Type	Ages	Pupils	Other
The Abbey School	London Rd, Faversham, Kent ME13 8RZ	01795 532633	01795 539931	Mrs Catrin Woodend	886-4242	CY	11–18	937	
Angley School – A Sports College	Angley Rd, Cranbrook, Kent TN17 2PJ	01580 712754	01580 715434	Mr Philip Morris	886-5419	FD	11–18	1066	
The Archbishop's School	St Stephen's Hill, Canterbury, Kent CT2 7AP	01227 765805	01227 768535	Mr A.J. Hogarth	886-5426	FD	11–18	919	CE
Barton Court Grammar School	Melbourne Ave, Whitfield, Dover, Kent CT16 2EG	01304 820126	01304 821915	Mrs Elaine Hamilton	886-4114	CY	11–18	1013	
Archers Court Maths and Computing College									
Astor College for the Arts	Astor Ave, Dover, Kent CT17 0AS	01304 200106	01304 225170	Mr Christopher Russell	886-4113	CY	11–18	1276	
The Astor of Hever Community School	Oakwood Rd, Maidstone, Kent ME16 8AE	01622 752490	01622 693789	Mr M.E. Carroll	886-4064	CY	11–18	816	
Axton Chase School	Main Rd, Longfield, Kent DA3 7PH	01474 705951	01474 708309	Mr Kevin Stokes	886-4185	CY	11–18	1038	
Aylesford School – Sports College	Teapot La, Aylesford, Kent ME20 7JU	01622 717341	01622 790580	Mr Douglas Lawson	886-5410	FD	11–18	843	
Barton Court Grammar School	Longport, Canterbury, Kent CT1 1PH	01227 464600	01227 781399	Dr S. Manning	886-5444	FD	11–18	844	
Bennett Memorial Diocesan School	Culverden Down, Tunbridge Wells, Kent TN4 9SH	01892 521595	01892 514424	Mr Ian Bauckham	886-5464	VA	11–18	1371	CE
Borden Grammar School	Avenue of Remembrance, Sittingbourne, Kent ME10 4DB	01795 424192	01795 424026	Mr Harold Vafeas	886-4527	VC	11–18	732	B
The Bradbourne School	Bradbourne Vale Rd, Sevenoaks, Kent TN13 3LE	01732 454608	01732 742262	Mrs Mary Boyle	886-5430	FD	11–18	876	G
Brockhill Park Performing Arts College	Sandling Rd, Saltwood, Saltwood, Kent CT21 4HL	01303 265521	01303 262708	Mr Anthony Lyng	886-5466	FD	11–18	1301	
The Canterbury High School	Knight Ave, Canterbury, Kent CT2 8QA	01227 463971	01227 762801	Mr Philip Karnavas	886-5421	FD	11–18	1117	
Castle Community College	Mill Rd, Deal, Kent CT14 9BD	01304 373363	01304 380769	Mrs Christine Chapman	886-4207	CY	11–18	619	
The Charles Dickens School	Broadstairs Rd, Broadstairs, Kent CT10 2RL	01843 862988	01843 865047	Mr Andrew Olsson	886-5438	FD	11–16	1021	
Chatham House Grammar School for Boys	Chatham St, Ramsgate, Kent CT11 7PS	01843 591075	01843 851907	Mr John Mathews	886-5462	FD	11–18	777	B
Chaucer Technology School	Spring La, Canterbury, Kent CT1 1SU	01227 763636	01227 762352	Mr Simon Murphy	886-5452	FD	11–18	1317	
Christ Church CE High School	Millbank Rd, Kingsnorth, Ashford, Kent TN23 3HG	01233 623465	01233 636861	Mr Mulrenan	886-4632	VA	11–16	1111	CE
Clarendon House Grammar School	Clarendon Gdns, Ramsgate, Kent CT11 9BB	01843 591074	01843 851824	Mrs J. Bennett	886-4118	CY	11–18	780	G
The Community College Whitstable	Bellevue Rd, Whitstable, Kent CT5 1PX	01227 272362	01227 770275	Mrs Helena Sullivan-Tighe	886-4091	CY	11–18	1027	
Cornwallis Academy	Hubbards La, Linton, Maidstone ME17 4HX	01622 743152	01622 741866	S. Schwartz	886-6913		11–19		
The Cornwallis School	Hubbards La, Linton, Maidstone, Kent ME17 4HX	01622 743152	01622 741866	Mr M.J. Wood	886-5402	FD	11–18	1681	
Cranbrook School	Waterloo Rd, Cranbrook, Kent TN17 3JD	01580 711800	01580 715365	Mrs Angela Daly	886-5416	VA	13–18	755	Ch R
Dane Court Grammar School	Broadstairs Rd, Broadstairs, Kent CT10 2RT	01843 864941	01843 602742	Mr Paul Luxmoore	886-5460	FD	11–18	1170	
Dartford Grammar School	West Hill, Dartford, Kent DA1 2HW	01322 223039	01322 291426	Mr Anthony Smith	886-5406	FD	11–18	1219	B
Dartford Grammar School for Girls	Shepherds La, Dartford, Kent DA1 2NT	01322 223123	01322 294786	Mrs Jane Wheatley	886-5411	FD	11–18	1029	G
Dartford Technology College	Heath La, Dartford, Kent DA1 2LY	01322 224309	01322 222445	Mrs Patricia Burleigh	886-4026	CY	11–18	819	G

3

School name	Address	Tel	Fax	Headteacher	Ref	Type	Ages	Pupils	Other
Dover Grammar School for Boys	Astor Ave, Dover, Kent CT17 0DQ	01304 206117	01304 206074	Mrs Sally Lees	886-5459	FD	11–18	701	B
Dover Grammar School for Girls	Frith Rd, Dover, Kent CT16 2PZ	01304 206625	01304 242400	Mrs Judith Carlisle	886-4109	FD	11–18	741	G
Ellington School for Girls	Ellington Pl, Ramsgate, Kent CT11 0QQ	01843 593522	01843 852690	Ms Cathy Smith	886-4122	CY	11–16	409	G
Folkestone Academy	Academy La, Folkestone CT19 5FP	01303 241972	01303 252024	John Patterson	886-6908		11–18		Ch
The Folkestone School for Girls	Coolinge La, Folkestone, Kent CT20 3RB	01303 251125	01303 221422	Mrs Tracy Luke	886-5437	FD	11–18	1059	G
Fulston Manor School	Brenchley Rd, Sittingbourne, Kent ME10 4EG	01795 475228	01795 428144	Mr Alan Brookes	886-5414	FD	11–18	1165	
The Grammar School for Girls Wilmington	Wilmington Grange, Parsons La, Wilmington, Dartford, Kent DA2 7BB	01322 226351	01322 222607	Mrs Maggie Bolton	886-5400	FD	11–18	747	G
Gravesend Grammar School	Church Wlk, Gravesend, Kent DA12 2PR	01474 331893	01474 331894	Mr Geoffrey Wybar	886-5465	FD	11–18	1019	B
Gravesend Grammar School for Girls	Pelham Rd, Gravesend, Kent DA11 0JE	01474 352896	01474 331195	Mrs N. Chapman	886-5467	FD	11–18	971	G
Hartsdown Technology College	George V Ave, Margate, Kent CT9 5RE	01843 227957	01843 299642	Mr Andrew Somers	886-4172	CY	11–18	1120	
The Harvey Grammar School	Cheriton Rd, Folkestone, Kent CT19 5JY	01303 252131	01303 220721	Mr Keith Rivers	886-4101	FD	11–18	936	B
The Hayesbrook School	Brook St, Tonbridge, Kent TN9 2PH	01732 500600	01732 500556	Mr Nigel Blackburn	886-5455	FD	11–18	880	B
The Hereson School	Ramsgate Rd, Broadstairs, Kent CT10 1PJ	01843 862729	01843 852475	Mr Antony Hamson	886-4123	CY	11–16	570	B
Herne Bay High School	Bullockstone Rd, Herne Bay, Kent CT6 7NS	01227 361221	01227 742481	Mr Danny DODonovan	886-5448	FD	11–18	1505	
Hextable School	Egerton Ave, Hextable, Swanley, Kent BR8 7LU	01322 668621	01322 668706	Mr Peter Dalton	886-4219	CY	11–18	779	
Highsted Grammar School	Highsted Rd, Sittingbourne, Kent ME10 4PT	01795 424223	01795 429375	Mrs Jennifer Payne	886-4080	CY	11–18	833	G
Highworth Grammar School for Girls	Quantock Dr, Ashford, Kent TN24 8UD	01233 624910	01233 612028	Mr Paul Danielsen	886-4092	CY	11–18	1131	G
Hillview School for Girls	Brionne Gdns, Tonbridge, Kent TN9 2HE	01732 352793	01732 368718	Mr Stephen Bovey	886-5450	FD	11–18	1166	G
Holmesdale Technology College	Malling Rd, Snodland, Kent ME6 5HS	01634 240416	01634 244041	Mr Ian Hobson	886-4065	CY	11–18	759	
Homewood School and Sixth Form Centre	Ashford Rd, Tenterden, Kent TN30 6LT	01580 764222	01580 766267	Mr William Cotterell	886-5408	FD	11–18	2057	
Hugh Christie Technology College	White Cottage Rd, Tonbridge, Kent TN10 4PU	01732 353544	01732 367833	Mr Jon Barker	886-5431	FD	11–18	1192	
Invicta Grammar School	Huntsman La, Maidstone, Kent ME14 5DR	01622 755856	01622 678584	Mr Michael Liddicoat	886-4058	CY	11–18	1308	G
The Judd School	Brook St, Tonbridge, Kent TN9 2PN	01732 770880	01732 771661	Mr Robert Masters	886-4622	VA	11–18	933	B
King Ethelbert School	Canterbury Rd, Birchington, Kent CT7 9BL	01843 831999	01843 831015	Mrs Carole Bailey	886-4120	CY	11–16	721	
The Leigh City Technology College	Green Street Green Rd, Dartford, Kent DA1 1QE	01322 620400	01322 620401	Mr Frank Green	886-6900		10–18	1366	
Leigh Technology Academy	Green St, Green Rd, Dartford DA1 1QE	01322 620400	01322 620401	Frank Green	886-6910		11–19		
Leydenhatch Study Centre	80a The Brent, Dartford, Kent DA1 1YW	01322 223216		Brian Ernest Sambrook	886-6105		11–16	40	Ch
Maidstone Grammar School	Barton Rd, Maidstone, Kent ME15 7BT	01622 752101	01622 753680	Mr Neil Turrell	886-4522	FD	11–18	1250	B
Maidstone Grammar School for Girls	Buckland Rd, Maidstone, Kent ME16 0SF	01622 752103	01622 681947	Mrs Mary Smith	886-4523	VC	11–18	1129	G
The Malling School	Beech Rd, East Malling, West Malling, Kent ME19 6DH	01732 840995	01732 840486	Mrs M Harriott	886-5425	FD	11–18	475	
The Maplesden Noakes School	Buckland Rd, Maidstone, Kent ME16 0TJ	01622 759036	01622 661707	Mrs Jane Prideaux	886-5401	FD	11–19	970	
The Marlowe Academy	Stirling Way, Ramsgate CT12 6NB	01843 593326	01843 591756	Mr Ian Johnson	886-6906	FD	11–19	677	
Marsh Academy	Station Rd, New Romney TN28 8BB	01797 364593	01797 367315	Tracey Luke	886-6909		11–18		
Mascalls School	Maidstone Rd, Paddock Wood, Tonbridge, Kent TN12 6LT	01892 835366	01892 835648	Mrs Vanessa Everett	886-5439	FD	11–18	1292	
Meopham School	Wrotham Rd, Meopham, Gravesend, Kent DA13 0AH	01474 814646	01474 813083	Miss Sara Kemsley	886-5424	FD	11–18	778	
Minster College	Minster Rd, Minster-on-Sea, Sheerness, Kent ME12 3JQ	01795 873591	01795 870107	Mr Alan Klee	886-5417	FD	13–18	1504	
Montgomery School	Bredlands La, Sturry, Canterbury, Kent CT2 0HD	01227 710392	01227 712370	Mr Ian McGinn	886-5453	FD	11–17	291	
New Line Learning Academy	Boughton La, Maidstone ME15 9QL	01622 743286	01622 741963	Jenny Usher	886-6912		11–16		
The North School	Essella Rd, Ashford, Kent TN24 8AL	01233 614600	01233 612906	Mrs Lesley Ellis	886-4246	CY	11–17	810	
Northfleet School for Girls	Hall Rd, Northfleet, Gravesend, Kent DA11 8AQ	01474 534222	01474 335058	Dr J. Key	886-4040	CY	11–18	1137	G
Northfleet Technology College	Colyer Rd, Northfleet, Gravesend, Kent DA11 8BG	01474 533802	01474 536122	Mr John Hassett	886-5456	FD	11–18	890	B
The Norton Knatchbull School	Hythe Rd, Ashford, Kent TN24 0QJ	01233 620045	01233 633668	Mr J.C. Speller	886-4528	VC	11–18	1020	B
Oakwood Park Grammar School	Oakwood Pk, Maidstone, Kent ME16 8AH	01622 726683	01622 721210	Mr Kevin Moody	886-5422	CY	11–18	938	B
Oldborough Manor Community School	Boughton La, Loose, Maidstone, Kent ME15 9QL	01622 743286	01622 741963	Mrs Jane Rouse	886-5413	FD	11–18	403	
Pent Valley School	Surrenden Rd, Folkestone, Kent CT19 4ED	01303 277161	01303 279342	Mr M. Citro	886-5458	FD	11–18	1382	
Queen Elizabeth's Grammar School	Abbey Pl, Faversham, Kent ME13 7BQ	01795 533132	01795 538474	Mrs Jane Percy	886-5449	FD	11–18	852	

3

School name	Address	Tel	Fax	Headteacher	Ref	Type	Ages	Pupils	Other
St Anselm's RC School	Old Dover Rd, Canterbury, Kent CT1 3EN	01227 826200	01227 826201	Mr Philip Wicker	886-5446	VA	11–18	1034	RC
St Edmund's RC School	Old Charlton Rd, Dover, Kent CT16 2QB	01304 201551	01304 202226	Mr C.J. Atkin	886-5440	VA	11–18	828	RC
St George's CE Foundation School	Westwood Rd, Broadstairs, Kent CT10 2LH	01843 861696	01843 609001	Mr K. Rumblo	886-5447	FD	11–18	1158	CE
St George's CE School	Meadow Rd, Gravesend, Kent DA11 7LS	01474 533082	01474 533844	Mrs Ann Hill	886-5404	VA	11–18	1233	CE
St Gregory's RC Comprehensive School	Reynolds La, Tunbridge Wells, Kent TN4 9XL	01892 527444	01892 546621	Ms R. Olivier	886-5435	VA	11–18	1034	RC
St John's RC Comprehensive	Rochester Rd, Gravesend, Kent DA12 2JW	01474 534718	01474 563763	Mr Mike SHShea	886-5461	VA	11–18	1090	RC
St Simon Stock RC School	Oakwood Pk, Maidstone, Kent ME16 0JP	01622 754551	01622 691439	Mr J. McParland	886-5432	VA	11–18	1013	RC
Sandwich Technology School	Deal Rd, Sandwich, Kent CT13 0FA	01304 610000	01304 611886	Mr Richard Wallis	886-5463	FD	11–18	1299	
Senacre Technology College	Sutton Rd, Maidstone, Kent ME15 9DT	01622 679471	01622 661518	Mr Simon Heaton	886-5415	FD	11–18	599	G
Simon Langton Girls' Grammar School	Old Dover Rd, Canterbury, Kent CT1 3EW	01227 463711	01227 458363	Mr A. Stanton	886-4534	VC	11–18	1025	G
Simon Langton Grammar School for Boys	Langton La, Nackington Rd, Canterbury, Kent CT4 7AS	01227 463567	01227 456486	Mr Matthew Baxter	886-5412	FD	11–18	938	B
Sir Roger Manwood's School	Manwood Rd, Sandwich, Kent CT13 9JX	01304 613286	01304 615336	Mr C.R.L. Morgan	886-5428	FD	11–18	892	R
Sittingbourne Community College	Swanstree Ave, Sittingbourne, Kent ME10 4NL	01795 472449	01795 470332	Mr A. Barham	886-4247	CY	11–18	1105	
The Skinners' School	St John's Rd, Tunbridge Wells, Kent TN4 9PG	01892 520732	01892 549356	Mr Simon Everson	886-5418	VA	11–18	768	B
Southlands Community Comprehensive School	Station Rd, New Romney, Kent TN28 8BB	01797 364593	01797 367315	Mr E. Cahill	886-5405	FD	11–18	1148	
Spires Academy	Bredlands La, Sturry, Canterbury CT2 0HD	01227 710392	01227 712370	Lynn Ibeji	886-6911		11–16		
Swadelands School	Ham La, Lenham, Maidstone, Kent ME17 2QJ	01622 858267	01622 850668	Mr Richard Baddeley	886-4059	CY	11–16	864	
Swan Valley Community School	Southfleet Rd, Swanscombe, Kent DA10 0BZ	01322 623100	01322 623108	Mr Nigel Jones	886-4250	CY	11–16	580	
Swanley Technology College	St Mary's Rd, Swanley, Kent BR8 7TE	01322 665231	01322 661006	Mrs Julie Bramley	886-4031	CY	11–18	541	
Thamesview School	Thong La, Gravesend, Kent DA12 4LF	01474 566552	01474 537405	Miss Rhiannon Hughes	886-5407	FD	11–18	812	
Threshold Learning Centre	Howard De Walden, Bluett St, Maidstone, Kent ME14 2UG	01622 676167	01622 761561	Mr Max Heywood	886-6100		15–16	23	
Threshold Learning Centre	The Gateway, Rushenden Rd, Queenborough, Kent ME11 5HX	01622 685635	01622 761561	Ms A. Costello	886-6098		14–16	14	
Tonbridge Grammar School	Deakin Leas, Tonbridge, Kent TN9 2JR	01732 365125	01732 359417	Mrs Rosemary Joyce	886-5443	FD	11–18	1074	G
The Towers School	Faversham Rd, Kennington, Ashford, Kent TN24 9AL	01233 634171	01233 628326	Mr Malcolm Ramsey	886-4196	CY	11–18	1375	
Tunbridge Wells Girls' Grammar School	Southfield Rd, Tunbridge Wells, Kent TN4 9UJ	01892 520902	01892 536497	Mrs Linda Wybar	886-4043	FD	11–18	943	G
Tunbridge Wells Grammar School for Boys	St John's Rd, Tunbridge Wells, Kent TN4 9XB	01892 529551	01892 536833	Mr John Harrison	886-4045	CY	11–18	1256	B
Tunbridge Wells High School	Blackhurst La, Tunbridge Wells, Kent TN2 4PY	01892 534377	01892 516203	Mr Graham Smith	886-5427	CY	11–18	425	
Ursuline College	225 Canterbury Rd, Westgate-on-Sea, Kent CT8 8LX	01843 834431	01843 835363	Sr Alice Montgomery	886-4633	VA	11–18	772	RC R
Valley Park Community School	Huntsman La, Maidstone, Kent ME14 5DT	01622 679421	01622 661671	Mr Victor Ashdown	886-4249	CY	11–18	993	
Walmer Science College	Salisbury Rd, Walmer, Deal, Kent CT14 7QJ	01304 375212	01304 380766	Mr Simon Heaton	886-4169	CY	11–18	806	
Weald of Kent Grammar School	Tudeley La, Tonbridge, Kent TN9 2JP	01732 352819	01732 770536	Mrs Sue Rowell	886-4046	FD	11–18	1047	G
The Westlands School	Westlands Ave, Sittingbourne, Kent ME10 1PF	01795 477475	01795 431946	Mr Jonathan Whitcombe	886-5434	FD	11–18	1602	
The Wilderness School	Seal Hollow Rd, Sevenoaks, Kent TN13 3SN	01732 454617	01732 453675	Mr John Daly	886-5433	FD	11–19	594	B
Wilmington Enterprise College	Common La, Wilmington, Dartford, Kent DA2 7DR	01322 272111	01322 222500	Mr Grahame Price	886-4204	CY	11–18	797	
Wilmington Grammar School for Boys	Common La, Wilmington, Dartford, Kent DA2 7DA	01322 223090	01322 289920	Mrs Fiona Cottam	886-5403	FD	11–18	813	B
Wrotham School	Borough Green Rd, Wrotham, Sevenoaks, Kent TN15 7RD	01732 884207	01732 882178	Mr David Day	886-5409	FD	11–18	707	

Medway

School name	Address	Tel	Fax	Headteacher	Ref	Type	Ages	Pupils	Other
Chapter School	Carnation Rd, Strood, Rochester, Kent ME2 2SX	01634 717121	01634 726643	Miss S. Dore	887-4076	CY	11–18	1101	G
Chatham Grammar School for Boys	Holcombe, Maidstone Rd, Chatham, Kent ME4 6JB	01634 830083	01634 826230	Mr L. David Marshall	887-4068	CY	11–18	1072	B
Chatham Grammar School for Girls	Rainham Rd, Chatham, Kent ME5 7EH	01634 851262	01634 571928	Mr David Gundry	887-5429	FD	11–18	971	G
Chatham South School	Letchworth Ave, Chatham, Kent ME4 6NT	01634 404277	01634 829010	Mr Vincent MAMara	887-4215	CY	11–17	790	
Fort Pitt Grammar School	Fort Pitt Hill, Chatham, Kent ME4 6TJ	01634 842359	01634 817386	Mrs J M Bell	887-4069	CY	11–18	956	G
Greenacre School	157 Walderslade Rd, Walderslade, Chatham, Kent ME5 0LP	01634 861593	01634 869246	Mr Andrew Reese	887-4174	CY	11–18	906	B

School name	Address	Tel	Fax	Headteacher	Ref	Type	Ages	Pupils	Other
The Howard School	Derwent Way, Rainham, Gillingham, Kent ME8 0BX	01634 388558	01634 388765	Mr David Smith	887-5457	FD	11–18	1394	B
The Hundred of Hoo Comprehensive School	Main Rd, Hoo, Rochester, Kent ME3 9HH	01634 251443	01634 254323	Mr Anthony Williams	887-4075	CY	11–18	1652	
Medway Community College	Magpie Hall Rd, Chatham, Kent ME4 5JB	01634 845196	01634 406475	Mrs A.E. Ferris	887-4248	CY	11–17	712	
New Brompton College	Marlborough Rd, Gillingham, Kent ME7 5HT	01634 852341	01634 853574	Ms Judy Rider	887-5454	FD	11–17	1025	
Rainham Mark Grammar School	Pump La, Rainham, Gillingham, Kent ME8 7AJ	01634 364151	01634 260209	Mr Simon Decker	887-5420	FD	11–18	1211	
Rainham School for Girls	Derwent Way, Rainham, Gillingham, Kent ME8 0BX	01634 362746	01634 388334	Mrs Jacquie Dunn	887-4199	CY	11–18	1496	G
The Robert Napier School	Third Ave, Gillingham, Kent ME7 2LX	01634 851157	01634 280972	Miss Fiona Miller	887-5423	FD	11–18	1250	R
The Rochester Grammar School for Girls	Maidstone Rd, Rochester, Kent ME1 3BY	01634 843049	01634 818340	Ms Denise Shepherd	887-5445	FD	11–18	1028	G
St John Fisher RC Comprehensive School	Ordnance St, Chatham, Kent ME4 6SG	01634 842811	01634 825915	Mrs Jennifer Morris	887-5436	VA	11–18	1091	RC
Sir Joseph Williamson's Mathematical School	Maidstone Rd, Rochester, Kent ME1 3EL	01634 844008	01634 818303	Mr Keith Williams	887-4530	VC	11–18	1105	B
Temple School	Cliffe Rd, Strood, Rochester, Kent ME2 3DL	01634 719983	01634 290917	Mr Neil McAree	887-4077	CY	11–16	556	B
The Thomas Aveling School	Arethusa Rd, Rochester, Kent ME1 2UW	01634 844809	01634 818385	Mr Richard Hart	887-5451	FD	11–18	1081	
Walderslade Girls' School	Bradfields Ave, Walderslade, Chatham, Kent ME5 0LE	01634 861596	01634 666506	Mrs P. Conibeer	887-4167	CY	11–18	881	G

Milton Keynes

School name	Address	Tel	Fax	Headteacher	Ref	Type	Ages	Pupils	Other
Denbigh School	Burchard Cres, Shenley Church End, Milton Keynes, Buckinghamshire MK5 6EX	01908 505030	01908 505279	Mrs S. Parker	826-5410	FD	11–19	1451	
Hazeley School	Emperor Dr, Hazeley, Milton Keynes MK8 0PT	01908 555620	01908 508357	Mr Iain Denning	826-4704	FD	11–19	450	
Leon School and Sports College	Fern Gr, Bletchley, Milton Keynes, Buckinghamshire MK2 3HQ	01908 624720	01908 624777	Mr Simon Viccars	826-4077	CY	11–19	820	
Lord Grey School	Rickley La, Bletchley, Milton Keynes, Buckinghamshire MK3 6EW	01908 626110	01908 366139	Ms J. Coughlan	826-5405	FD	11–19	1478	
Oakgrove School	Venturer Gate, Middleton, Milton Keynes MK10 9JQ	01908 545300		Mr Peter Barnes	826-4703	FD	11–19	452	
Ousedale School	The Gr, Newport Pagnell, Buckinghamshire MK16 0BJ	01908 210203	01908 216574	Mr Ken Leaver	826-4018	FD	11–19	2063	
The Radcliffe School	Aylesbury St West, Wolverton, Milton Keynes, Buckinghamshire MK12 5BT	01908 682222	01908 322718	Mr John O'Donnell	826-5406	FD	11–19	957	
St Paul's RC School	Phoenix Dr, Leadenhall, Milton Keynes MK6 5EN	01908 669735	01908 676206	Mr Michael Manley	826-4702	VA	11–19	1629	RC
Shenley Brook End School	Walbank Gr, Shenley Brook End, Milton Keynes, Buckinghamshire MK5 7ZT	01908 520264	01908 520265	Mr Glen Martin	826-4097	FD	11–19	1327	
Sir Frank Markham Community School	Woughton Campus, Chaffron Way, Milton Keynes, Buckinghamshire MK6 5EH	01908 607416	01908 231759	Mr Mike O'Mahony	826-4085	CY	11–19	1436	
Stantonbury Campus	Purbeck, Stantonbury, Milton Keynes, Buckinghamshire MK14 6BN	01908 324400	01908 324401	Mr Mark Wasserberg	826-5400	FD	11–19	2765	
Walton High	Fyfield Barrow, Walnut Tree, Milton Keynes, Buckinghamshire MK7 7WH	01908 677954	01908 677191	Ms Michelle Currie	826-4000	FD	11–19	1284	

Oxfordshire

School name	Address	Tel	Fax	Headteacher	Ref	Type	Ages	Pupils	Other
Heathfield St Mary's School	24-28 Newbury St, Wantage, Oxfordshire OX12 8BZ	01235 773806	01235 760467	S. Sowden	931-6081	FD	11–16	183	CE
Banbury School	Ruskin Rd, Banbury, Oxfordshire OX16 9HY	01295 251451	01295 277682	Dr Fiona Hammons	931-4021	FD	11–18	1434	
Bartholomew School	Witney Rd, Eynsham, Witney, Oxfordshire OX29 4AP	01865 881430	01865 883973	Mr A.S. Hamilton	931-4054	CY	11–18	992	
Bicester Community College	Queen's Ave, Bicester, Oxfordshire OX26 2NS	01869 243331	01869 246396	Mrs C. Bartlect	931-4030	CY	11–18	1227	
Blessed George Napier RC School and Sports College	Addison Rd, Banbury, Oxfordshire OX16 9DG	01295 264216	01295 277952	Mrs Catherine Weaver	931-4600	VA	11–18	840	RC
Burford School and Community College	Cheltenham Rd, Burford, Oxfordshire OX18 4PL	01993 823303	01993 813101	Mr I.P. Sanders	931-4040	CY	11–18	1206	R
Carterton Community College	Upavon Way, Carterton, Oxfordshire OX18 1BU	01993 841611	01993 843710	Mrs Julie Tridgell	931-4041	CY	11–16	751	
Cheney School	Cheney La, Headington, Oxford, Oxfordshire OX3 7QH	01865 765726	01865 767399	Mr A. Lane	931-4120	CY	11–18	1470	

3

School name	Address	Tel	Fax	Headteacher	Ref	Type	Ages	Pupils	Other
The Cherwell School	Marston Ferry Rd, Oxford, Oxfordshire OX2 7EE	01865 558719	01865 311165	Mrs K. Jill Judson	931-4116	CY	11–18	1773	
Chiltern Edge Community School	Reades La, Sonning Common, Reading, Berkshire RG4 9LN	0118 972 1500	0118 972 4116	Mr Paul Leonard	931-4092	CY	11–16	782	
Chipping Norton School	Burford Rd, Chipping Norton, Oxfordshire OX7 5DY	01608 642007	01608 644530	Mr Simon Duffy	931-4010	CY	11–18	1176	
The Cooper School	Churchill Rd, Bicester, Oxfordshire OX26 4RS	01869 242121	01869 320871	Mr Ben Baxter	931-4032	CY	11–16	929	
Didcot Girls' School	Manor Cres, Didcot, Oxfordshire OX11 7AJ	01235 812092	01235 511245	Mrs Paula Taylor-Moore	931-4139	CY	11–18	1381	G
Drayton School	Drayton Rd, Banbury OX16 0UD	01295 253181	01295 279876	Mr Richard Sutton	931-4005	CY	11–16	623	
Faringdon Community College	Fernham Rd, Faringdon, Oxfordshire SN7 7LB	01367 240375	01367 242356	Mr D. Wilson	931-4141	CY	11–18	930	
Fitzharrys School	Northcourt Rd, Abingdon, Oxfordshire OX14 1NP	01235 520698	01235 534590	Mrs Susan Tranter	931-4127	CY	11–18	885	
Gillotts School	Gillotts La, Henley-on-Thames, Oxfordshire RG9 1PS	01491 574315	01491 410509	Ms Catharine Darnton	931-4055	CY	11–16	892	
Gosford Hill School	Oxford Rd, Kidlington, Oxfordshire OX5 2NT	01865 374971	01865 841029	Dr Stephen Bizley	931-4060	CY	11–18	1158	
The Henry Box School	Church Grn, Witney, Oxfordshire OX28 4AX	01993 703955	01993 706720	Mr D.R. Walker	931-4050	CY	11–18	1383	
Icknield Community College	Love La, Watlington, Oxfordshire OX49 5RB	01491 612691	01491 612951	Mr Richard Hudson	931-4082	CY	11–16	611	
John Mason School	Wootton Rd, Abingdon, Oxfordshire OX14 1JB	01235 524664	01235 520711	Mr Paul Corrie	931-4126	CY	11–18	986	
King Alfred's (A specialist Sports College)	Portway, Wantage, Oxfordshire OX12 9BY	01235 225700	01235 760262	Mr Nicholas Young	931-4142	FD	11–18	1697	
Langtree School	Woodcote, Reading, Berkshire RG8 0RA	01491 680514	01491 682411	Mr Rick Holroyd	931-4094	CY	11–16	519	
Larkmead School	Faringdon Rd, Abingdon, Oxfordshire OX14 1RF	01235 520141	01235 533179	Mr C. Harris	931-4125	CY	11–18	821	
Lord Williams's School	Oxford Rd, Thame, Oxfordshire OX9 2AQ	01844 210510	01844 261382	Mr David Wybron	931-4580	VC	11–18	2104	CE
The Marlborough CE School	Shipton Rd, Woodstock, Oxfordshire OX20 1LP	01993 811431	01993 813530	Mrs Julie Fenn	931-4560	VC	11–18	1032	
Matthew Arnold School	Arnolds Way, Oxford, Oxfordshire OX2 9JE	01865 862232	01865 864855	Mrs Katherine Ryan	931-4128	CY	11–18	1071	
North Oxfordshire Academy	Drayton Road, Banbury OX16 0U	01295 253181			931-6905		11–19		
Oxford Community School	Glanville Rd, Oxford, Oxfordshire OX4 2AU	01865 428200	01865 428201	Mr Steve Lunt	931-4117	CY	11–18	1101	
Peers School	Sandy La West, Littlemore, Oxford, Oxfordshire OX4 6JY	01865 774311	01865 715677	Mrs Lorna Caldicott	931-4074	CY	11–18	836	
St Birinus School	Mereland Rd, Didcot, Oxfordshire OX11 8AZ	01235 814444	01235 512258	Mr Christopher Bryan	931-4129	CY	11–18	1274	B
St Gregory the Great VA RC Secondary School	Cricket Rd, Cowley, Oxford, Oxfordshire OX4 3DR	01865 749933	01865 717314	Ms Kathleen KEKeefe	931-4145	VA	11–18	1002	RC
Wallingford School	St George's Rd, Wallingford, Oxfordshire OX10 8HH	01491 837115	01491 825278	Mr Nigel Willis	931-4140	CY	11–18	1063	
The Warriner School	Banbury Rd, Bloxham, Banbury, Oxfordshire OX15 4LJ	01295 720777	01295 721676	Mr Nicholas Hindmarsh	931-4007	CY	11–16	1115	
Wheatley Park School	Holton, Oxford, Oxfordshire OX33 1QH	01865 872441	01865 874712	Ms Kate Curtis	931-4077	CY	11–18	1193	
Wood Green School	Woodstock Rd, Witney, Oxfordshire OX28 1DX	01993 702355	01993 708662	Miss C. Savage	931-4052	CY	11–18	1175	

Portsmouth

School name	Address	Tel	Fax	Headteacher	Ref	Type	Ages	Pupils	Other
Admiral Lord Nelson School	Dundas La, Portsmouth, Hampshire PO3 5XT	023 9236 4536	023 9236 4537	Mr Steven Labedz	851-4320	CY	11–16	1003	
The City of Portsmouth Boys' School	London Rd, Hilsea, Portsmouth, Hampshire PO2 9RJ	023 9269 3521	023 9266 5720	Mr Michael Smith	851-5404	FD	11–16	594	B
City of Portsmouth Girls' School	St Mary's Rd, Portsmouth, Hampshire PO1 5PF	023 9281 2822	023 9287 2022	Mrs Sharon Watt	851-4289	CY	11–16	968	G
King Richard Secondary School	Allaway Ave, Paulsgrove, Portsmouth, Hampshire PO6 4QP	023 9237 0321	023 9238 4811	Mr B. McClarin	851-4302	CY	11–16	919	
Mayfield School	Mayfield Rd, North End, Portsmouth, Hampshire PO2 0RH	023 9269 3432	023 9266 5298	Mr Derek Trimmer	851-4303	CY	11–16	1231	
Miltoncross School	Milton Rd, Fratton, Portsmouth, Hampshire PO3 6RB	023 9273 8022	023 9234 2133	Mr Neil McLeod	851-4000	CY	11–16	978	
Priory School (Specialist Sports College)	Fawcett Rd, Southsea, Hampshire PO4 0DL	023 9281 9115	023 9287 2143	Mr Brian Shimell	851-4283	CY	11–16	1281	
St Edmund's RC School	Arundel St, Portsmouth, Hampshire PO1 1RX	023 9282 3766	023 9287 1874	Mrs Isabelle O Mora	851-5413	VA	11–16	891	RC
St Luke's CE VA Secondary School	Hyde Park Rd, Southsea, Hampshire PO5 4HL	023 9282 4204	023 9282 9867	Mrs Krysia Butwilowska	851-4615	VA	11–16	641	CE
Springfield School	Central Rd, Drayton, Portsmouth, Hampshire PO6 1QY	023 9237 9119	023 9238 8784	Mrs L. Evans	851-4301	CY	11–16	1141	

Reading

School name	Address	Tel	Fax	Headteacher	Ref	Type	Ages	Pupils	Other
Blessed Hugh Faringdon RC School	Fawley Rd, Southcote, Reading, Berkshire RG30 3EP	0118 957 4730	0118 956 8150	Mr P. Barras	870-5411	VA	11–18	831	RC
Highdown School and Sixth Form Centre	Surley Row, Emmer Green, Reading, Berkshire RG4 8LR	0118 901 5800	0118 901 5801	Mr Tim Royle	870-4020	FD	11–18	1174	
John Madejski Academy	Hartland Rd, Reading, Berkshire RG2 8AF	0118 937 0200		Kate Shaw	870-6905		11–18	508	
Kendrick Girls' Grammar School	London Rd, Reading, Berkshire RG1 5BN	0118 901 5859	0118 901 5858	Mrs M. Elms	870-5413	FD	11–18	677	G
Prospect School	Cockney Hill, Tilehurst, Reading, Berkshire RG30 4EX	0118 959 0466	0118 950 4172	Ms Deborah Ajose	870-5410	FD	11–18	1233	
Reading Girls' School	Northumberland Ave, Reading, Berkshire RG2 7PY	0118 986 1336	0118 986 6938	Mrs Ruth Allen	870-5400	FD	11–18	669	G
Reading School	Erleigh Rd, Reading, Berkshire RG1 5LW	0118 901 5600	0118 935 2755	Mr A.J. Linnell	870-5401	FD	11–18	880	B R

Slough

School name	Address	Tel	Fax	Headteacher	Ref	Type	Ages	Pupils	Other
Baylis Court School	Gloucester Ave, Slough, Berkshire SL1 3AH	01753 531760	01753 553719	Mrs M. Ball	871-4082	FD	11–18	762	G
Beechwood School	Long Readings La, Slough, Berkshire SL2 1QE	01753 579632	01753 552985	Ms Julia Shepard	871-4085	CY	11–18	648	
Herschel Grammar School	Northampton Ave, Slough, Berkshire SL1 3BW	01753 520950	01753 530984	Mr J. King-Harris	871-5407	FD	11–18	860	
Langley Grammar School	Reddington Dr, Langley, Slough, Berkshire SL3 7QS	01753 598300	01753 810858	Miss Hilda Clarke	871-5405	FD	11–18	1034	
Langleywood School	Langley Rd, Langley, Slough, Berkshire SL3 7EF	01753 541549	01753 593145	Mr Paul McAteer	871-4086	CY	11–16	803	
St Bernard's Catholic Grammar School	1 Langley Rd, Slough, Berkshire SL3 7AF	01753 527020	01753 576919	Mr John McAteer	871-4700	VA	11–18	882	RC
St Joseph's RC High School	Shaggy Calf La, Slough, Berkshire SL2 5HW	01753 524713	01753 579128	Mr James Welsh	871-4800	VA	11–16	620	RC
Slough and Eton CE Business and Enterprise College	Ragstone Rd, Slough, Berkshire SL1 2PU	01753 520824	01753 574914	Mr Graham Lush	871-4510	VC	11–18	746	CE
Slough Grammar School	Lascelles Rd, Slough, Berkshire SL3 7PR	01753 522892	01753 538618	Mrs Margaret Lenton	871-5408	FD	11–18	1204	
The Westgate School	Cippenham La, Slough, Berkshire SL1 5AH	01753 521320	01753 521200	Mr R. Thomas	871-5409	FD	11–18	790	
Wexham School	Norway Dr, Slough, Berkshire SL2 5QP	01753 526797	01753 573916	Mr J. Richardson	871-4089	CY	11–18	885	

Southampton

School name	Address	Tel	Fax	Headteacher	Ref	Type	Ages	Pupils	Other
Bellemoor School	Bellemoor Rd, Shirley, Southampton, Hampshire SO15 7QU	023 8032 5333	023 8077 0318	Ms C. Ellins	852-4275	CY	11–16	565	B
Bitterne Park School	Copsewood Rd, Bitterne Pk, Southampton, Hampshire SO18 1BU	023 8032 5200	023 8032 5222	Mrs Susan Trigger	852-4278	CY	11–16	1346	
Cantell Maths and Computing College	Violet Rd, Bassett, Southampton, Hampshire SO16 3GJ	023 8032 3111	023 8032 2433	Mrs R. Johnson	852-4311	CY	11–16	1088	
Chamberlayne Park School	Tickleford Dr, Weston, Southampton, Hampshire SO19 9QP	023 8044 7820	023 8044 6847	Ms Chris Kelly	852-4271	CY	11–16	814	
Grove Park Business and Enterprise College	The Grove, Portsmouth Rd, Southampton, Hampshire SO19 9LX	023 8044 8128	023 8032 8228	Mr E.A. Freeman	852-4273	CY	11–16	491	B
Millbrook Community School	Green La, Maybush, Southampton, Hampshire SO16 9RG	023 8077 1881	023 8051 2195	Mr Tony Cotton	852-4274	CY	11–16	423	
Oaklands Community School	Fairisle Rd, Lordshill, Southampton, Hampshire SO16 8BY	023 8039 3660	023 8036 3312	Mrs Sarah Howells	852-4304	CY	11–16	661	
Redbridge Community School	Cuckmere La, Southampton, Hampshire SO16 9RJ	023 8077 1381	023 8051 0004	Mr Richard Schofield	852-4270	CY	11–16	865	
Regents Park Community College	King Edward Ave, Shirley, Southampton, Hampshire SO16 4GW	023 8032 5444	023 8032 2411	Mrs S.R. Hill	852-4262	CY	11–16	918	G
St Anne's RC School	Carlton Rd, Southampton, Hampshire SO15 2WZ	023 8032 2603	023 8033 1767	Mrs B.A. Murtagh	852-5417	VA	11–18	1096	RC G
St George RC School for Boys	Leaside Way, Swaythling, Southampton, Hampshire SO16 3DQ	023 8032 2603	023 8032 2606	Mrs H.M. Knight	852-5415	VA	11–16	466	RC B
The Sholing Technology College	Middle Rd, Sholing, Southampton, Hampshire SO19 8PH	023 8044 8861	023 8042 2998	Miss K.J. Dagwell	852-4264	CY	11–16	982	G
Woodlands Community College	Minstead Ave, Southampton, Hampshire SO18 5FW	023 8046 3303	023 8046 2342	Mr R. Martin	852-4306	CY	11–16	767	
Woolston School Language College	Porchester Rd, Woolston, Southampton, Hampshire SO19 2JD	023 8042 6900	023 8068 5729	Mrs Bernadette Hanly	852-4266	CY	11–16	708	

Surrey

School name	Address	Tel	Fax	Headteacher	Ref	Type	Ages	Pupils	Other
All Hallows RC School	Weybourne Rd, Farnham, Surrey GU9 9HF	01252 319211	01252 328649	Mrs Elizabeth Lutzeier	936-5415	VA	11–18	1245	RC
Ash Manor School	Manor Rd, Ash, Aldershot, Hampshire GU12 6QH	01252 353900	01252 353904	Mr Robert M Linnell	936-4463	CY	11–16	1032	
The Ashcombe School	Ashcombe Rd, Dorking, Surrey RH4 1LY	01306 886312	01306 742537	Mr David Blow	936-4454	CY	11–18	1582	
The Beacon School	Picquets Way, Banstead, Surrey SM7 1AG	01737 359103	01737 365200	Mr J. Darker	936-5406	FD	11–18	1339	
The Bishop David Brown School	Albert Dr, Woking, Surrey GU21 5RF	01932 359118	01932 349175	Mr Stuart Shephard	936-4457	CY	11–16	518	
The Bishop Wand CE School	Laytons La, Sunbury-on-Thames, Middlesex TW16 6LT	01932 787537	01932 771022	Mr N. Dunkley	936-4763	VA	11–18	936	CE
Blenheim High School	Longmead Rd, Epsom, Surrey KT19 9BH	01372 745333	01372 745345	Ms Teresa Leech	936-5417	FD	11–18	1244	
Broadwater School	Summers Rd, Godalming, Surrey GU7 3BW	01483 414516	01483 425782	Mr Chris Lee	936-4058	CY	11–16	571	
Christ's College, Guildford	Larch Ave, Guildford GU1 1JY	01483 537373	01483 452725	Mr S. Green	936-4028	VA	11–18	520	CE
Collingwood College	Kingston Rd, Camberley, Surrey GU15 4AE	01276 457600	01276 457610	Mr Malcolm Jeremy Oddie	936-5401	FD	11–18	2021	
de Stafford School	Burntwood La, Caterham, Surrey CR3 5YX	01883 347818	01883 343194	Mr Mark Phillips	936-5408	FD	11–18	1053	
Epsom and Ewell High School	Ruxley La, West Ewell, Epsom, Surrey KT19 9JW	020 8974 0400	020 8974 0401	Mr Philip Hutchinson	936-5405	FD	11–18	942	
Esher CE High School	More La, Esher, Surrey KT10 8AP	01372 468068	01372 471058	Mr Simon Morris	936-4508	VC	11–16	924	CE
Farnham Heath End School	Hale Reeds, Farnham, Surrey GU9 9BN	01252 733371	01252 712999	Mr David Hoggins	936-4052	CY	11–16	895	
Fullbrook School	Selsdon Rd, New Haw, Addlestone, Surrey KT15 3HW	01932 349301	01932 351224	Mrs Anne Turner	936-5413	FD	11–18	1676	
George Abbot School	Woodruff Ave, Guildford, Surrey GU1 1XX	01483 888000	01483 888001	Mr Danny Moloney	936-4456	CY	11–18	1931	
Glebelands School	Parsonage Rd, Cranleigh, Surrey GU6 7AN	01483 542400	01483 542401	Ms Nikki Knight	936-4162	CY	11–16	884	
Glyn Technology School	The Kingsway, Ewell, Epsom, Surrey KT17 1NB	020 8716 4949	020 8716 4999	Mr Jon Chaloner	936-5404	FD	11–18	1395	B
Gordon's School	Bagshot Road, West End, Woking, Surrey GU24 9PT	01276 858084	01276 855335	Mr Denis Mulkerrin	936-5403	VA	11–16	540	R
Guildford County School	Farnham Rd, Guildford, Surrey GU2 4LU	01483 504089	01483 300849	Mr P. Costello	936-5400	FD	11–18	912	
Heathside School	Brooklands La, Weybridge, Surrey KT13 8UZ	01932 846162	01932 828142	Dr G. Willoughby	936-5409	FD	11–18	1371	
Hinchley Wood School and Sixth Form Centre	Claygate La, Hinchley Wood, Esher, Surrey KT10 0AQ	020 8398 7161	020 8399 3908	Mr S. Poole	936-5416	FD	11–18	1098	
Howard of Effingham School	Lower Rd, Effingham, Leatherhead, Surrey KT24 5JR	01372 453694	01372 456952	Mrs Rhona Barnfield	936-4036	CY	11–18	1561	
Jubilee High School	School La, Addlestone, Surrey KT15 1TE	01932 884800	01932 884803	Mr Gareth Balch	936-4469	FD	11–16	633	
Kings College for the Arts and Technology	Southway, Guildford, Surrey GU2 8DU	01483 458956	01483 458957	Mr Graeme Hawkett	936-4509	VA	11–18	909	
Kings International College for Business and the Arts	Watchetts Dr, Camberley, Surrey GU15 2PQ	01276 683539	01276 709503	Mr John Edwards	936-4468	FD	11–18	740	
The Magna Carta School	Thorpe Rd, Staines, Middlesex TW18 3HJ	01784 454320	01784 441214	Mr Tim Smith	936-4160	CY	11–16	1209	
The Matthew Arnold School	Kingston Rd, Staines, Middlesex TW18 1PF	01784 457275	01784 450037	Mrs J.M. Pearson	936-4202	CY	11–16	932	
Oakwood School	Balcombe Rd, Horley, Surrey RH6 9AE	01293 785363	01293 786465	Mrs S.V. Child	936-4465	CY	11–16	1390	
Oxted School	Bluehouse La, Oxted, Surrey RH8 0AB	01883 712425	01883 723973	Mrs Margaret Hawley	936-4098	CY	11–18	2108	
Parsons Mead School	1 Ottways La, Ashtead, Surrey KT21 2PE	01372 276401		Mrs Jennifer Moran	936-6062		2–16	270	Ch
The Priory CE VA School	West Bank, Dorking, Surrey RH4 3DG	01306 887337	01306 888715	Mr A. Schatski	936-4765	VA	11–18	787	CE
Reigate School	Pendleton Rd, Reigate, Surrey RH2 7NT	01737 243166	01737 226069	Mr John Cain	936-4157	CY	11–16	1180	
Rodborough Technology College	Rake La, Milford, Godalming, Surrey GU8 5BZ	01483 428182	01483 411100	Mr A. Smith	936-4165	CY	11–16	908	
Rosebery School	White Horse Dr, Epsom, Surrey KT18 7NQ	01372 720439	01372 749219	Ms Heather Saunders	936-5407	FD	11–18	1420	G
Rydens School	Hersham Rd, Walton-on-Thames, Surrey KT12 5PY	01932 242994	01932 252896	Mr Mark Jackman	936-4193	CY	11–18	1228	
St Andrew's RC School	Grange Rd, Grange Rd, Leatherhead, Surrey KT22 7JP	01372 277881	01372 279135	Mrs Kim Burke	936-4611	VA	11–18	759	RC
St Bede's School	Carlton Rd, Redhill, Surrey RH1 2LQ	01737 212108	01737 212118	Mr Christopher Curtis	936-4622	VA	11–18	1708	CE/RC
St John The Baptist RC Comprehensive School, Woking	Elmbridge La, Kingfield, Woking, Surrey GU22 9AL	01483 729343	01483 727578	Mrs A. Magill	936-5402	VA	11–18	1162	RC
St Paul's RC College	The Ridings, Green St, Sunbury-on-Thames, Middlesex TW16 6NX	01932 783811	01932 786485	Mr Simon Uttley	936-5411	VA	11–18	1011	RC
St Peter's RC Comprehensive School	Horseshoe La East, Merrow, Guildford, Surrey GU1 2TN	01483 534654	01483 306571	Mr Robert Guinea	936-4619	VA	11–18	1081	RC

School name	Address	Tel	Fax	Headteacher	Ref	Type	Ages	Pupils	Other
Salesian School, Chertsey	Guildford Rd, Chertsey, Surrey KT16 9LU	01932 582520	01932 582521	Mr James Kibble	936-5412	VA	11–18	1230	RC
Sunbury Manor School	Nursery Rd, Sunbury-on-Thames, Middlesex TW16 6LF	01932 784258	01932 772197	Mrs Louise Duncan	936-4259	CY	11–16	1041	
Surrey College	Abbot Hse, Guildford, Surrey GU1 3RL	01483 565887		Ms Louise Cody	936-6561		15–18	31	
Thamesmead School	Manygate La, Shepperton, Middlesex TW17 9EE	01932 219400	01932 219401	Mr Peter Rodin	936-5410	FD	11–16	985	
Therfield School	Dilston Rd, Leatherhead, Surrey KT22 7NZ	01372 818123	01372 818124	Mrs Susan Willman	936-4073	CY	11–18	1349	
Thomas Knyvett College	Stanwell Rd, Ashford, Middlesex TW15 3DU	01784 243824	01784 240050	Mrs Krys Marshall	936-4464	CY	11–16	709	
Tomlinscote School and Sixth Form College	Tomlinscote Way, Frimley, Camberley, Surrey GU16 8PY	01276 709050	01276 709060	Mr A. Ryles	936-4190	FD	11–18	1510	
Warlingham School	Tithe Pit Shaw La, Warlingham, Surrey CR6 9YB	01883 624067	01883 624026	Miss Alison Woodhouse	936-4153	CY	11–18	1548	
The Warwick School	Noke Dr, Redhill, Surrey RH1 4AD	01737 764356	01737 770007	Mr Ronald Searle	936-4460	CY	11–16	1059	
Weydon School	Weydon La, Farnham, Surrey GU9 8UG	01252 725052	01252 717213	Mr J. Winter	936-4151	CY	11–16	1120	
The Winston Churchill School a Specialist Sports College	Hermitage Rd, Stjohns, Woking, Surrey GU21 8TL	01483 476861	01483 476479	Mr David Smith	936-5414	FD	11–16	1551	
Woking High School	Morton Rd, Horsell, Woking, Surrey GU21 4TJ	01483 888447	01483 888448	Mrs Jane Abbott	936-4462	FD	11–16	1188	
Woolmer Hill Technology College	Woolmer Hill, Haslemere, Surrey GU27 1QB	01428 654055	01428 647061	Mrs Susan Bullen	936-4067	CY	11–16	635	

West Berkshire

School name	Address	Tel	Fax	Headteacher	Ref	Type	Ages	Pupils	Other
Denefield School	Long La, Tilehurst, Reading, Berkshire RG31 6XY	0118 941 3458	0118 945 2847	Mr E.F. Joint	869-5404	FD	11–18	1230	
The Downs School	Manor Cres, Compton, Newbury, Berkshire RG20 6NU	01635 270000	01635 578913	Mrs Valerie Houldey	869-5406	FD	11–18	945	
John O'Gaunt Community Technology College	Priory Rd, Hungerford, Berkshire RG17 0AN	01488 682400	01488 681283	Mrs L. Bartlett	869-4034	CY	11–18	575	
Kennet School	Stoney La, Thatcham, Berkshire RG19 4LL	01635 862121	01635 871814	Mr Paul G Dick	869-4042	CY	11–18	1714	
Little Heath School	Little Heath Rd, Tilehurst, Reading, Berkshire RG31 5TY	0118 942 7337	0118 942 1933	Mr Mike Wheale	869-4052	VA	11–18	1670	
Park House School and Sports College	Andover Rd, Newbury, Berkshire RG14 6NQ	01635 573911	01635 528884	Mr Derek Peaple	869-4038	CY	11–19	1348	
St Bartholomew's School	Andover Rd, Newbury, Berkshire RG14 6JP	01635 521255	01635 576320	Mr Stuart Robinson	869-5402	FD	11–18	1581	
Theale Green Community School	Theale, Reading, Berkshire RG7 5DA	0118 930 2741	0118 930 8500	Mrs S. Marshall	869-4054	CY	11–18	1402	
Trinity School	Love La, Shaw, Newbury, Berkshire RG14 2DU	01635 510500	01635 510510	Ms Deborah Forster	869-4055	CY	11–18	910	
The Willink School	School La, Burghfield Common, Reading, Berkshire RG7 3XJ	0118 983 2030	0118 983 2091	Mrs B. Wynn	869-4031	CY	11–16	911	R

West Sussex

School name	Address	Tel	Fax	Headteacher	Ref	Type	Ages	Pupils	Other
Angmering School, The	Station Rd, Angmering, Littlehampton, West Sussex BN16 4HH	01903 772351	01903 850752	Mr David Brixey	938-4060	CY	11–18	1459	
Bishop Luffa CE School, Chichester	Bishop Luffa Cl, Chichester, West Sussex PO19 3LT	01243 787741	01243 531807	Mr Nick Taunt	938-4604	VA	11–18	1379	CE
Bognor Regis Community College	Westloats La, Bognor Regis, West Sussex PO21 5LH	01243 871010	01243 871011	Mr John Morrison	938-4051	CY	11–16	1546	
Boundstone Community College	Upper Boundstone La, Lancing, West Sussex BN15 9QZ	01903 755894	01903 755848	Mr Richard Evea	938-4042	CY	12–18	1032	
Bourne Community College	Park Rd, Southbourne, Emsworth, Hampshire PO10 8PJ	01243 375691	01243 379286	Mrs Margaret M Eva	938-4028	CY	11–16	632	
Chatsmore RC High School	Goring St, Worthing, West Sussex BN12 5AF	01903 241368	01903 240183	Ms Elizabeth York	938-4603	VA	11–16	619	RC
Chichester High School for Boys	Kingsham Rd, Chichester, West Sussex PO19 8AE	01243 787691	01243 531584	Mr John Robinson	938-4000	CY	11–18	1355	B
Chichester High School for Girls	Kingsham Rd, Chichester, West Sussex PO19 8EB	01243 787014	01243 786543	Ms F. Oliver-Watkins	938-4001	CY	11–18	1439	G
Davison CE High School for Girls, Worthing	Selborne Rd, Worthing, West Sussex BN11 2JX	01903 233835	01903 211417	Mrs Della West	938-4502	VC	12–16	1068	CE G
Downlands Community School	Dale Ave, Hassocks, West Sussex BN6 8LP	01273 845892	01273 846358	Mr Walter Clarke	938-4105	CY	11–16	965	
Durrington High School	The Boulevard, Worthing, West Sussex BN13 1JX	01903 244957	01903 245079	Ms Sue Marooney	938-4065	CY	12–16	1344	
Felpham Community College	Felpham Way, Felpham, Bognor Regis, West Sussex PO22 8EL	01243 826511	01243 841021	Mr Peter Cook	938-4059	CY	11–18	1366	
Forest School, The	Comptons La, Horsham, West Sussex RH13 5NW	01403 261086	01403 217150	Mrs Janine Godly	938-4009	CY	11–16	1027	B
Hazelwick School	Hazelwick Mill La, Three Bridges, Crawley, West Sussex RH10 1SX	01293 403344	01293 403446	Mr G.M.W. Parry	938-4029	CY	11–18	1970	

3

School name	Address	Tel	Fax	Headteacher	Ref	Type	Ages	Pupils	Other
Holy Trinity CE Secondary School, Crawley	Buckswood Dr, Gossops Grn, Crawley, West Sussex RH11 8JE	01293 423690	01293 511968	Mr Peter Wickert	938-4606	VA	11–18	1295	CE
Ifield Community College	Crawley Ave, Ifield, Crawley, West Sussex RH11 0DB	01293 420500	01293 420501	Dr W. Lind	938-4030	CY	11–18	941	
Imberhorne School	Imberhorne La, East Grinstead, West Sussex RH19 1QY	01342 323562	01342 317366	Mr Jon Ford	938-4106	CY	11–18	1691	
King's Manor Community College	Kingston La, Shoreham-by-Sea, West Sussex BN43 6YT	01273 274100	01273 274123	Mrs Heidi Brown	938-4057	CY	12–18	1159	
Littlehampton Community School, The	Hill Rd, Littlehampton, West Sussex BN17 6DQ	01903 711120	01903 714361	Mrs Jayne Wilson	938-4062	CY	11–18	1833	
Manhood Community College	School La, Selsey, Chichester, West Sussex PO20 9EH	01243 602558	01243 604097	Mr Mark Vickers	938-4037	CY	11–16	528	
Midhurst Grammar School	North St, Midhurst, West Sussex GU29 9DT	01730 812451	01730 813524	Mr Jonathan Barrott	938-4500	VC	13–18	791	CE
Millais School	Depot Rd, Horsham, West Sussex RH13 5HR	01403 254932	01403 211729	Mr L. Nettley	938-4010	CY	11–16	1486	G
Oakmeeds Community College	Station Rd, Burgess Hill, West Sussex RH15 9EA	01444 241691	01444 235261	Mr Colin Taylor	938-4100	CY	11–16	1029	
Oathall Community College	Appledore Gdns, Lindfield, Haywards Heath, West Sussex RH16 2AQ	01444 414001	01444 417027	Mrs Jill Wilson	938-4102	CY	11–16	1313	
Oriel High School	Matthews Dr, Maidenbower, Crawley RH10 7XW	01293 880350	01293 880351	Mrs Gill Smith	938-4003	CY	11–18	864	
Sackville School	Lewes Rd, East Grinstead, West Sussex RH19 3TY	01342 410140	01342 315544	Mrs Margaret Robson	938-4107	CY	11–18	1592	
St Andrew's CE High School for Boys	Sackville Rd, Worthing, West Sussex BN14 8BG	01903 820676	01903 231880	Mr Steve Jewell	938-4601	VA	12–16	714	CE B
St Paul's RC College	Jane Murray Way, Burgess Hill, West Sussex RH15 8GA	01444 873898	01444 873899	Mr John Flower	938-4610	VA	11–18	867	RC
St Philip Howard RC High School, The	Elm Grove South, Barnham, Bognor Regis, West Sussex PO22 0EN	01243 552055	01243 552900	Mr David Todd	938-4800	VA	11–18	887	RC
St Wilfrid's RC Comprehensive School, Crawley	Oakwood, Old Horsham Rd, Crawley, West Sussex RH11 8PG	01293 421421	01293 421429	Mr Jonathan Morris	938-4602	VA	11–18	916	RC
Steyning Grammar School	Shooting Field, Steyning, West Sussex BN44 3RX	01903 814555	01903 879146	Dr John Peat	938-4501	VC	11–18	2062	CE R
Tanbridge House School	Farthings Hill, Guildford Rd, Horsham, West Sussex RH12 1SR	01403 263628	01403 211830	Mrs M. Johnson	938-4002	CY	11–16	1331	
Thomas Bennett Community College	Ashdown Dr, Tilgate, Crawley, West Sussex RH10 5AD	01293 526255	01293 527704	Ms Yasmin Maskatiya	938-4044	CY	11–18	1358	
Warden Park Community College	Broad St, Cuckfield, Haywards Heath, West Sussex RH17 5DP	01444 457881	01444 417024	Mr Stephen Johnson	938-4103	CY	11–16	1441	
Weald School, The	Station Rd, Billingshurst, West Sussex RH14 9RY	01403 787200	01403 787276	Mr P. May	938-4025	CY	11–18	1512	
Westergate Community School	Lime Ave, Westergate, Chichester, West Sussex PO20 3UE	01243 546800	01243 546810	Mr Steven Nelmes	938-4033	CY	11–16	724	
Worthing High School	South Farm Rd, Worthing, West Sussex BN14 7AR	01903 237864	01903 231709	Mrs Alison Beer	938-4110	CY	12–16	932	

Windsor and Maidenhead

School name	Address	Tel	Fax	Headteacher	Ref	Type	Ages	Pupils	Other
Altwood CE Secondary School	Altwood Rd, Maidenhead, Berkshire SL6 4PU	01628 622236	01628 675140	Ms K Higgins	868-4506	VC	11–18	704	CE
Charters School	Charters Rd, Sunningdale, Ascot, Berkshire SL5 9QY	01344 624826	01344 875182	Mrs M. Twelftree	868-4029	CY	11–18	1552	
Churchmead CE School	Priory Way, Datchet, Slough, Berkshire SL3 9JQ	01753 542707	01753 580046	Mrs Gaynor Goodman	868-4084	VA	11–18	599	CE
Cox Green School	Highfield La, Maidenhead, Berkshire SL6 3AX	01628 629415	01628 637383	Mr Ian Hylan	868-4056	CY	11–18	858	
Desborough School	Shoppenhangers Rd, Maidenhead, Berkshire SL6 2QB	01628 634505	01628 639263	Mr Andrew Linnell	868-5403	CY	11–18	1032	B
Furze Platt Senior School	Furze Platt Rd, Maidenhead, Berkshire SL6 7NQ	01628 625308	01628 782257	Ms Tanya White	868-4055	CY	11–18	1103	
Newlands Girls' School	Farm Rd, Maidenhead, Berkshire SL6 5JB	01628 625068	01628 675352	Mrs Tracey Briggs	868-4036	CY	11–18	1109	G
The Windsor Boys' School	1 Maidenhead Rd, Windsor, Berkshire SL4 5EH	01753 716060	01753 833186	Mr Jeffrey Dawkins	868-4044	CY	13–18	973	B
Windsor Girls' School	Imperial Rd, Windsor, Berkshire SL4 3RT	01753 795155	01753 795156	Mrs Gill Labrum	868-4046	CY	13–18	725	G

Wokingham

School name	Address	Tel	Fax	Headteacher	Ref	Type	Ages	Pupils	Other
The Bulmershe School	Chequers Way, Woodley, Reading, Berkshire RG5 3EL	0118 935 3353	0118 935 2929	Mr P. Lewis	872-4051	VC	11–18	1300	CE
The Emmbrook School	Emmbrook Rd, Wokingham, Berkshire RG41 1JP	0118 978 4406	0118 989 2059	Mr Nigel Matthias	872-4049	CY	11–18	1138	
Forest School	Robin Hood La, Winnersh, Wokingham, Berkshire RG41 5NE	0118 978 1626	0118 977 6018	Mr Keith Quine	872-4050	VA	11–18	1092	B
The Holt School	Holt La, Wokingham, Berkshire RG41 1EE	0118 978 0165	0118 989 0831	Miss Suzanne Richards	872-4047	CY	11–18	1248	G
Maiden Erlegh School	off Silverdale Rd, Earley, Reading, Berkshire RG6 7HS	0118 926 2467	0118 926 6111	Dr P. Thomas	872-4053	CY	11–18	1663	

School name	Address	Tel	Fax	Headteacher	Ref	Type	Ages	Pupils	Other
The Piggott School	Twyford Rd, Wargrave, Reading, Berkshire RG10 8DS	0118 940 2357	0118 940 4892	Dr K. Atton	872-4505	VC	11–18	1098	CE
Ryeish Green School	Ryeish Grn, Spencers Wood, Reading, Berkshire RG7 1ER	0118 988 3133	0118 988 6148	Mrs Jenny Garner	872-4041	CY	11–18	795	
St Crispin's School	London Rd, Wokingham, Berkshire RG40 1SS	0118 978 1144		Mr A. Biddle	872-4048	CY	11–18	1057	
Waingels College	Denmark Ave, Woodley, Reading, Berkshire RG5 4RF	0118 969 0336	0118 944 2843	Mr R. Green	872-4060	CY	11–18	1447	

South West

Bath and North East Somerset

School name	Address	Tel	Fax	Headteacher	Ref	Type	Ages	Pupils	Other
Beechen Cliff School	Alexandra Pk, Bath BA2 4RE	01225 480466	01225 314025	Mr A. Davies	800-5400	FD	11–18	1068	B
Broadlands School	St Francis Rd, Keynsham, Bristol BS31 2DY	0117 986 4791	0117 916 1102	Mrs Linda Ogden	800-4131	CY	11–16	1061	
Chew Valley School	Chew Magna, Bristol, Somerset BS40 8QB	01275 332272	01275 333625	Mr Mark Mallett	800-4130	CY	11–18	1132	
Culverhay School	Rush Hill, Bath, Somerset BA2 2QL	01225 426268	01225 447036	Mr Duncan Fleet	800-4108	CY	11–18	426	B
Hayesfield School Technology College	Upper Oldfield Pk, Bath BA2 3LA	01225 426151	01225 427005	Ms Erica Draisey	800-4107	FD	11–18	1213	G
Norton Hill School	Charlton Rd, Midsomer Norton, Radstock BA3 4AD	01761 412557	01761 410622	Mr P. Beaven	800-4128	FD	11–18	1330	
Oldfield School	Kelston Rd, Bath, Somerset BA1 9AB	01225 423582	01225 464986	Mrs Kim Sparling	800-5401	FD	11–18	869	G
Ralph Allen School	Claverton Down Rd, Combe Down, Bath BA2 7AD	01225 832936	01225 832338	Ms E. Lee	800-4132	CY	11–18	1070	
St Gregory's RC College	Combe Hay La, Odd Down, Bath BA2 8PA	01225 832873	01225 835848	Mr Raymond Friel	800-4608	VA	11–16	793	RC
St Mark's CE School	Baytree Rd, Bath BA1 6ND	01225 312661	01225 429063	Miss Cherril A. Pope	800-4607	VA	11–16	306	CE
Somervale School	Redfield Rd, Midsomer Norton, Midsomer Norton, Somerset BA3 2JD	01761 414276	01761 410613	Mr Michael Gorman	800-4133	CY	11–18	736	
Wellsway School	Chandag Rd, Keynsham, Bristol BS31 1PH	0117 986 4751	0117 986 1504	Mr P.C. Kent	800-4138	CY	11–18	1340	
Writhlington School	Knobsbury La, Writhlington, Radstock BA3 3NQ	01761 433581	01761 432307	Ms M. Getheridge	800-4134	CY	11–18	1170	

Bournemouth

School name	Address	Tel	Fax	Headteacher	Ref	Type	Ages	Pupils	Other
Avonbourne School	Harewood Ave, Bournemouth, Dorset BH7 6NY	01202 398451	01202 304876	Mrs Debbie Godfrey-Phaure	837-5404	FD	11–16	1057	G
The Bishop of Winchester Comprehensive School	Mallard Rd, Bournemouth, Dorset BH8 9PW	01202 512697	01202 513181	Mr Paul McKeown	837-4603	VA	11–16	494	CE
Bournemouth School	East Way, Bournemouth, Dorset BH8 9PY	01202 512609	01202 516095	Mr John Granger	837-5400	FD	11–18	1056	B
Bournemouth School for Girls	Castle Gate Cl, Castle La West, Bournemouth, Dorset BH8 9UJ	01202 526289	01202 548923	Mr Alistair Brien	837-5405	FD	11–18	1115	G R
Glenmoor School	Beswick Ave, Bournemouth, Dorset BH10 4EX	01202 527818	01202 546931	Mrs Pamela Orchard	837-4172	CY	11–16	776	G
Kings High School	Hadow Rd, Bournemouth, Dorset BH10 5HS	01202 528554		Mr Alyn Fendley	837-4001	CY	11–16	603	
Oakmead College of Technology	Duck La, Bournemouth, Dorset BH11 9JJ	01202 774600	0102 774627	Dr A. Minard	837-4189	CY	11–18	1275	
Portchester School	Harewood Ave, Bournemouth, Dorset BH7 6NZ	01202 309841	01202 399615	Mr Christopher Bradey	837-4168	CY	11–16	925	B
St Peter's RC Comprehensive School	St Catherine's Rd, Bournemouth, Dorset BH6 4AH	01202 421141	01202 418886	Mr A. McCaffrey	837-5408	VA	11–18	1542	RC
Winton Arts and Media College	Winton Way, Bournemouth, Dorset BH10 4HT	01202 529738	01202 546281	Mrs Ingrid Masters	837-4173	CY	11–16	845	B

Bristol

School name	Address	Tel	Fax	Headteacher	Ref	Type	Ages	Pupils	Other
Ashton Park School	Blackmoors La., Bower Ashton, Bristol BS3 2JL	0117 377 2777	0117 377 2778	Mr C.C. Gardner	801-4030	CY	11–18	1166	
Bedminster Down School	Donald Rd, Bedminster Down, Bristol BS13 7DQ	0117 964 3530	0117 978 3328	Mr M. Frank	801-4037	CY	11–16	972	
Brislington Enterprise College	Hungerford Rd, Brislington, Bristol BS4 5EY	0117 377 2055	0117 377 2056	Mr John Matthews	801-4032	CY	11–18	1193	
Bristol Brunel Academy	Speedwell Rd, Speedwell, Bristol BS15 1NU	0117 377 2700		Armando Di-Finizio	801-6907		11–19		
The City Academy Bristol	Russell Town Ave, Bristol BS5 9JH	0117 955 8199	0117 954 0962	Mr Ray Priest	801-6905		11–18	1244	
Cotham School	Cotham Lawn Rd, Cotham, Bristol BS6 6DT	0117 908 2200	0117 908 2209	Mr Malcolm Willis	801-4100	CY	11–18	1280	
Fairfield High School	Allfoxton Rd, Horfield, Bristol BS7 9NL	0117 952 7100	0117 952 7168	Mrs N. McAllister	801-4101	CY	11–16	934	
Hartcliffe Engineering Community College	Teyfant Rd, Hartcliffe, Bristol BS13 0RL	0117 964 5155	0117 964 2316	Mr George Croxford	801-4042	CY	11–16	844	
Henbury School	Marissal Rd, Henbury, Bristol BS10 7NJ	0117 903 0100	0117 903 0167	Mrs Clare Bradford	801-4031	CY	11–18	817	
Hengrove Community Arts College	Petherton Rd, Hengrove, Bristol BS14 9BU	0117 377 2800		Mr Stephen Murtagh	801-4028	CY	11–18	670	
Monks Park School	Filton Rd, Horfield, Bristol BS7 0XZ	0117 377 2000	0117 377 2001	Dr Helen Holman	801-4036	CY	11–18	894	
Portway Community School	Penpole La., Shirehampton, Bristol BS11 0EB	0117 353 2600	0117 353 2601	Mr Steve Davies	801-4017	CY	11–18	667	
Redland Green	Redland Court Rd, Redland, Bristol BS6 7EF	0117 353 3200		Mrs Sarah Baker	801-4627	CY	11–16	189	
St Bede's RC College	Long Cross, Lawrence Weston, Bristol BS11 0SU	0117 377 2200	0117 377 2201	Ms C. Hughes	801-4602	VA	11–16	912	RC
St Bernadette RC Secondary School	Fossedale Ave, Whitchurch, Bristol BS14 9LS	0117 377 2050	01275 830127	Mrs Basia Mclaughlin	801-4801	VA	11–16	781	RC
St Mary Redcliffe and Temple School	Somerset Sq, Bristol BS1 6RT	0117 377 2100	0117 377 2101	Mrs E.A. Gilpin	801-4603	VA	11–18	1503	CE
Speedwell Technology College	Speedwell Rd, Speedwell, Bristol BS15 1NU	0117 377 2700	0117 377 2701	Mr Ian Graves	801-4046	CY	11–18		
Whitefield Fishponds Community School	Snowdon Rd, Fishponds, Bristol BS16 2HD	0117 377 2071	0117 958 6962	Mrs Theresa Thorne	801-4045	CY	11–16	737	
Withywood Community School	Molesworth Dr, Withywood, Bristol BS13 9BL	0117 377 2065		Mr B. Eales	801-4038		11–18		

Cornwall

School name	Address	Tel	Fax	Headteacher	Ref	Type	Ages	Pupils	Other
Bodmin College	Lostwithiel Rd, Bodmin, Cornwall PL31 1DD	01208 72114	01208 78680	Mr Robert Mitchell	908-4154	CY	11–18	1469	
Brannel School	Rectory Rd, St Stephen, St Austell, Cornwall PL26 7RN	01726 822485	01726 824613	Mr R. Bell	908-4155	CY	11–16	700	
Budehaven Community School	Valley Rd, Bude, Cornwall EX23 8DQ	01288 353271	01288 353733	Mr David Barton	908-4150	CY	11–18	1286	
Callington Community College	Launceston Rd, Callington, Cornwall PL17 7DR	01579 383292	01579 383562	Mr Stephen Kenning	908-4151	FD	11–18	1332	
Camborne Science and Community College	Cranberry Rd, Camborne, Cornwall TR14 7PP	01209 712280	01209 718139	Mr I.H. Kenworthy	908-4158	CY	11–18	1350	
Cape Cornwall School	Cape Cornwall Rd, St Just, Penzance, Cornwall TR19 7JX	01736 788501	01736 787100	Mr Robin Kneebone	908-4169	CY	11–16	488	
Falmouth School	Trescobeas Rd, Falmouth, Cornwall TR11 4LH	01326 372386	01326 377102	Mrs Sandra Critchley	908-4152	CY	11–18	1181	
Fowey Community College	Windmill, Fowey, Cornwall PL23 1HE	01726 833484	01726 832824	Mr William Gerry	908-4145	CY	11–16	1013	
Hayle Community School	3 High Lanes, Hayle, Cornwall TR27 4DN	01736 753009	01736 752687	Mrs Christine Jackman	908-4171	CY	11–16	716	
Helston Community College	Church Hill, Helston, Cornwall TR13 8NR	01326 572685	01326 572183	Dr Patrick McGovern	908-4146	CY	11–18	1600	
Humphry Davy School	Coombe Rd, Penzance, Cornwall TR18 2TG	01736 363559	01736 331042	Mr Roderick James	908-4173	CY	11–16	807	
Launceston College	Dunheved Rd, Launceston, Cornwall PL15 9JN	01566 772468	01566 777371	Mr Alan Wroath	908-4009	CY	11–18	1367	R
Liskeard School and Community College	Luxstowe, Liskeard, Cornwall PL14 3EA	01579 342344	01579 343350	Mrs Donna Bryant	908-4167	CY	11–18	1363	
Looe Community School	Sunrising, East Looe, Looe, Cornwall PL13 1NQ	01503 262625	01503 265435	Ms Heather Jenkins	908-4168	CY	11–16	607	
Mounts Bay School and Community Sports College	Boscathnoe La., Heamoor, Penzance, Cornwall TR18 3JT	01736 363240	01736 331633	Mrs Sara Davey	908-4172	CY	11–16	887	
Mullion School	Meaver Rd, Mullion, Helston, Cornwall TR12 7EB	01326 240098	01326 241382	Mr Mike Sandford	908-4164	CY	11–16	519	
Newquay Tretherras School	Trevenson Rd, Newquay, Cornwall TR7 3BH	01637 872080	01637 851066	Mr A. Jeavons	908-4165	CY	11–18	1610	
Penair School A Science College	St Clement, Truro, Cornwall TR1 1TN	01872 274737	01872 242465	Dr Barbara Vann	908-4166	CY	11–16	1189	
Penrice Community College	Charlestown Rd, St Austell, Cornwall PL25 3NR	01726 72163	01726 64901	Mr David Parker	908-4156	CY	11–16	1339	
Penryn College	Poltisko Rd, Penryn, Cornwall TR10 8PZ	01326 372379	01326 373194	Mrs M. Hunter	908-4149	CY	11–16	925	
Poltair School	Trevarthian Rd, St Austell, Cornwall PL25 4BZ	01726 874520	01726 874529	Mrs H. McIlroy	908-4157	CY	11–16	871	

3

School name	Address	Headteacher	Tel	Fax	Ref	Type	Ages	Pupils	Other
Pool Business and Enterprise College	Church Rd, Pool, Redruth, Cornwall TR15 3PZ	Mrs Zelma Hill	01209 712220	01209 612070	908-4163	CY	11–16	777	
Redruth School: a Technology College	Tolgus Vean, Redruth, Cornwall TR15 1TA	Mr Paul Sharratt	01209 215507	01209 313604	908-4159	CY	11–18	1425	
Richard Lander School	Higher Besore Rd, Truro, Cornwall TR3 6LT	Mr Trevor Coldman	01872 273750	01872 264372	908-4160	CY	11–16	1264	
The Roseland Community School	Tregony, Truro, Cornwall TR2 5SE	Mrs Jane Black	01872 530675	01872 530498	908-4162	CY	11–16	597	
St Ives School, a Technology College	Higher Tregenna, St Ives, Cornwall TR26 2BB	Mr D.J. Harris	01736 795608	01736 794526	908-4170	CY	11–16	677	
Saltash.net Community School	Wearde Rd, Saltash, Cornwall PL12 4AY	Mrs Isabell Bryce	01752 843715	01752 842825	908-4143	CY	11–18	1339	
Sir James Smith's Community School	Dark La, Camelford, Cornwall PL32 9UJ	Mr Jon Lawrence	01840 213274	01840 212189	908-4141	CY	11–18	659	
Torpoint Community School	Trevol Rd, Torpoint, Cornwall PL11 2NH	Mr David J. Farmer	01752 812511	01752 815014	908-4144	CY	11–18	992	
Treviglas Community College	Bradley Rd, Newquay, Cornwall TR7 3JA	Mrs Helen Mathieson	01637 872076	01637 876026	908-4135	CY	11–18	1097	
Wadebridge School	Gonvena Hill, Wadebridge, Cornwall PL27 6BU	Dr S. Thornton	01208 812881	01208 814883	908-4153	CY	11–18	1228	

Devon

School name	Address	Headteacher	Tel	Fax	Ref	Type	Ages	Pupils	Other
The Axe Valley Community College	Chard St, Axminster, Devon EX13 5EA	Ms E. Pinfield	01297 32146	01297 35851	878-4000	CY	11–18	861	
Bideford College	Abbotsham Rd, Bideford, Devon EX39 3AR	Miss Veronica Matthews	01237 477611	01237 428114	878-4061	CY	11–18	1661	
Braunton School and Community College	Barton La, Braunton, Devon EX33 2BP	Mr David Sharratt	01271 812221	01271 817145	878-4053	CY	11–16	735	
Clyst Vale Community College	Station Rd, Broadclyst, Exeter, Devon EX5 3AJ	Dr Kevin Bawn	01392 461407	01392 460594	878-4009	CY	11–18	1047	
Colyton Grammar School	Whitwell Rd, Colyford, Colyton, Devon EX24 6HN	Mr Barry Sindall	01297 552327	01297 553853	878-5400	FD	11–18	797	
The Community College Chulmleigh	Beacon Rd, Chulmleigh, Devon EX18 7AA	Mr Michael Johnson	01769 580215	01769 581119	878-4054	CY	11–16	600	
Coombeshead College	Coombeshead Rd, Newton Abbot, Devon TQ12 1PT	Mr R.D. Haigh	01626 201810	01626 201810	878-4112	CY	11–18	1537	
Cullompton Community College	Exeter Rd, Cullompton, Devon EX15 1DX	Mrs C. Dunne	01884 33364	01884 38307	878-4010	CY	11–16	647	
Dartmouth Community College	Milton La, Dartmouth, Devon TQ6 9HW	Mrs Julie Stuchbery-Ullah	01803 834921	01803 833358	878-4100	CY	11–16	397	
Dawlish Community College	Elm Grove Rd, Dawlish, Devon EX7 0BY	Mr Andrew Davis	01626 862318	01626 862318	878-4101	CY	11–16	826	
Exmouth Community College	Gipsy La, Exmouth, Devon EX8 3AF	Mr A. Alexander	01395 264761	01395 225355	878-4012	CY	11–18	2472	
Great Torrington Community School and Sports College	Calvesford Rd, Torrington, Devon EX38 7DJ	Mrs Dianne Nicholson	01805 623531	01805 624332	878-4055	CY	11–16	928	
Holsworthy Community College	Victoria Hill, Holsworthy, Devon EX22 6JD	Mr David Fitzsimmons	01409 253430	01409 253121	878-4056	CY	11–16	702	
Honiton Community College	School La, Honiton, Devon EX14 1QT	Mr Norman Tyson	01404 42283	01404 44491	878-4004	CY	11–18	1068	
Ilfracombe Media Arts College	Worth Rd, Ilfracombe, Devon EX34 9JB	Mr Brian Sarahan	01271 863427	01271 863477	878-4058	CY	11–18	1271	
Isca College of Media Arts	Earl Richards Rd South, Exeter, Devon EX2 6AP	Ms Mandi Street	01392 204082	01392 204095	878-4015	CY	11–16	672	
Ivybridge Community College	Harford Rd, Ivybridge, Devon PL21 0JA	Mr G. Rees	01752 691000	01752 691247	878-4184	CY	11–18	2213	
King Edward VI Community College	Ashburton Rd, Totnes, Devon TQ9 5JX	Mr Stephen Jones	01803 869200	01803 869201	878-4109	CY	11–18	1757	
The King's School	Barrack Rd, Ottery St Mary, Devon EX11 1RA	Miss Faith Jarrett	01404 812982		878-4005	CY	11–18	1040	
Kingsbridge Community College	Balkwill Rd, Kingsbridge, Devon TQ7 1PL	Mr Roger Pope	01548 852641	01548 854277	878-4110	CY	11–18	1295	
Knowles Hill School	Old Exeter Rd, Newton Abbot, Devon TQ12 2NF	Dr C. Pope	01626 367335	01626 331369	878-5404	FD	11–16	1088	
Okehampton College	Mill Rd, Okehampton, Devon EX20 1PW	Mr Daryl Chapman	01837 650910	01837 650918	878-4183	CY	11–18	1410	
The Park Community School	Park La, Barnstaple, Devon EX32 9AX	Mr David Atton	01271 373131	01271 373167	878-4059	CY	11–16	1411	
Pilton Community College	Chaddiford La, Barnstaple, Devon EX31 1RB	Mr Mark Juby	01271 374381	01271 324271	878-4060	CY	11–16	1383	
Queen Elizabeth's Community College	Western Rd, Crediton, Devon EX17 3LU	Mr Richard Newton Chance	01363 773401	01363 777859	878-4003	CY	11–18	1569	R
St James School	Summer La, Exeter, Devon EX4 8NN	Mrs Helen Salmon	01392 209922	01392 462506	878-4016	CY	11–16	645	
St Luke's Science and Sports College	Harts La, Exeter, Devon EX1 3RD	Mr Terry Hammond	01392 204600	01392 204601	878-4501	VC	11–16	921	CE
St Peter's CE Aided School	Quarry La, Heavitree, Exeter, Devon EX2 5AP	Mr M.A. Perry	01392 204764	01392 204763	878-4607	VA	11–16	1233	CE
Sidmouth College	Primley Rd, Sidmouth, Devon EX10 9LG	Mr David Birch	01395 514823	01395 578073	878-4011	CY	11–18	867	
South Dartmoor Community College	Balland La, Ashburton, Newton Abbot, Devon TQ13 7EW	Mr Ray Tarleton	01364 652230	01364 654069	878-4108	FD	11–18	1659	

School name	Address	Tel	Fax	Headteacher	Ref	Type	Ages	Pupils	Other
South Molton Community College	Old Alswear Rd, South Molton, Devon EX36 4LA	01769 572129	01769 573351	Mr James Wade	878-4057	CY	11–16	596	CE
Tavistock College	Crowndale Rd, Tavistock, Devon PL19 8DD	01822 614231	01822 612030	Mr Colin Eves	878-4182	FD	11–18	1786	Ch
Teign School	Chudleigh Rd, Kingsteignton, Newton Abbot, Devon TQ12 3JG	01626 366969	01626 335723	Mr Vyv Game	878-5402	FD	11–18	1370	
Teignmouth Community College	Exeter Rd, Teignmouth, Devon TQ14 9HZ	01626 774091	01626 777920	Mr A.P. Gray	878-4120	CY	11–18	1074	
Tiverton High School	Bolham Rd, Tiverton, Devon EX16 6SQ	01884 256655	01884 243364	Mr Andrew Lovett	878-4192	CY	11–16	1176	
Uffculme School	Chapel Hill, Uffculme, Cullompton, Devon EX15 3AG	01884 840458	01884 841570	Mr J.B. Roberts	878-5405	FD	11–16	927	
West Exe Technology College	Hatherleigh Rd, Exeter, Devon EX2 9JU	01392 660100	01392 275134	Mr Steve Maddern	878-4014	CY	11–16	1315	

Dorset

School name	Address	Tel	Fax	Headteacher	Ref	Type	Ages	Pupils	Other
All Saints' CE School, Weymouth	Sunnyside Rd, Wyke Regis, Weymouth, Dorset DT4 9BJ	01305 783391	01305 785291	Mr T. Balmforth	835-4801	VA	11–16	916	CE
Beaminster School	Newtown, Beaminster, Dorset DT8 3EP	01308 862633	01308 863909	Mr Mike Best	835-4505	VC	11–18	721	Ch
The Blandford School	Milldown Rd, Blandford Forum, Dorset DT11 7SQ	01258 451121	01258 454755	Mrs Sally Wilson	835-4510	VC	11–18	1190	
Budmouth Technology College	Chickerell Rd, Weymouth, Dorset DT4 9SY	01305 830500	01305 830555	Mr David Akers	835-5402	FD	11–18	1547	
Ferndown Upper School	Cherry Gr, Ferndown, Dorset BH22 9EY	01202 871243	01202 893383	Mr Alexander Wills	835-4420	CY	13–19	1090	
Gillingham School	Hardings La, Gillingham, Dorset SP8 4QP	01747 822222	01747 825263	Mr M. Lenarduzzi	835-4503	VC	11–18	1748	
The Grange School	Redvers Rd, Christchurch, Dorset BH23 3AU	01202 486536	01202 487621	Mr Mark Stenton	835-4178	CY	11–19	655	
The Gryphon School	Bristol Rd, Sherborne, Dorset DT9 4EQ	01935 813122	01935 816992	Mr S. Hillier	835-4512	VC	11–18	1402	CE
Highcliffe School	Parkside, Highcliffe, Christchurch, Dorset BH23 4QD	01425 273381	01425 271405	Ms Judith Potts	835-5406	FD	11–19	1364	
Lytchett Minster School	Lytchett Minster, Poole, Dorset BH16 6JD	01202 622413	01202 621230	Mr S.R. Clark	835-4035	FD	11–18	1196	
The Purbeck School	Worgret Rd, Wareham, Dorset BH20 4PF	01929 556301	01929 554025	Mr Richard Holman	835-4024	CY	13–18	1170	
Queen Elizabeth's School	Blandford Rd, Pamphill, Wimborne, Dorset BH21 4DT	01202 885233	01202 840703	Mr Andy Puttock	835-4504	VC	13–18	1452	CE
Royal Manor Arts College	Weston Rd, Portland, Dorset DT5 2RS	01305 820262	01305 860417	Mr Paul Green	835-4188	CY	11–16	730	
Shaftesbury School	Salisbury Rd, Shaftesbury, Dorset SP7 8ER	01747 854498	01747 851208	Mr David Booth	835-4511	VC	11–18	992	CE R
The Sir John Colfox School	Ridgeway, Bridport, Dorset DT6 3DT	01308 422291	01308 420036	Mrs Kay Taylor	835-4002	CY	11–18	966	
Sturminster Newton High School	Bath Rd, Sturminster Newton, Dorset DT10 1DT	01258 472642	01258 471521	Mr S. Carrington	835-4179	CY	11–16	638	
The Thomas Hardye School	Queen's Ave, Dorchester, Dorset DT1 2ET	01305 266064	01305 250510	Dr Iain Melvin	835-4615	VA	13–18	2214	
Twynham School	Sopers La, Christchurch, Dorset BH23 1JF	01202 486237	01202 486230	Dr Terry Fish	835-4177	CY	11–19	1469	
The Wey Valley School	Dorchester Rd, Weymouth, Dorset DT3 5AN	01305 817000	01305 815851	Mr Philip Thomas	835-4187	CY	11–16	1095	
The Woodroffe School	Uplyme Rd, Lyme Regis, Dorset DT7 3LX	01297 442232	01297 444762	Dr Richard Steward	835-5401	FD	11–18	1015	

Gloucestershire

School name	Address	Tel	Fax	Headteacher	Ref	Type	Ages	Pupils	Other
Archway School	Paganhill, Stroud, Gloucestershire GL5 4AX	01453 763242	01453 766093	Mr Colin Belford	916-4032	CY	11–18	1132	
Balcarras School	East End Rd, Charlton Kings, Cheltenham, Gloucestershire GL53 8QF	01242 515881	01242 250620	Mr Chris Healy	916-5408	FD	11–18	1306	
Barnwood Park Arts College	St Lawrence Rd, Gloucester, Gloucestershire GL4 3QU	01452 530389	01452 530380	Miss G. Pyatt	916-4012	FD	11–16	712	G
Beaufort Community School	Holmleigh Pk, Tuffley, Gloucester, Gloucestershire GL4 0RT	01452 301381	01452 380779	Mr Malcolm Bride	916-4015	FD	11–18	1197	
Bishops' College	Estcourt Cl, Gloucester, Gloucestershire GL1 3LR	01452 524879		Mr Martin Spoor	916-4608	VA	11–16	537	CE
Brockworth Enterprise School	Mill La, Brockworth, Gloucester, Gloucestershire GL3 4QF	01452 863372	01452 862638	Mr Paul Elliott	916-4040	CY	11–18	867	
Central Technology College	Cotteswold Rd, Gloucester, Gloucestershire GL4 6RN	01452 428800	01452 384290	Mrs Helen Anthony	916-5413	FD	11–18	386	B
Cheltenham Bournside School and Sixth Form Centre	Warden Hill Rd, Cheltenham, Gloucestershire GL51 3EF	01242 235555	01242 226742	Mr A.G. Stafford	916-5418	FD	11–18	1801	
Cheltenham Kingsmead	Howell Rd, Cheltenham, Gloucestershire GL51 0ED	01242 225700	01242 262495	Mr Stephen Jowett	916-5426	FD	11–18	361	
Chipping Campden School	Cider Mill La, Chipping Campden, Gloucestershire GL55 6HU	01386 840216	01386 840498	Mr Jeffrey Price	916-5414	FD	11–18	1191	

3

School name	Address	Tel	Fax	Headteacher	Ref	Type	Ages	Pupils	Other
Chosen Hill School	Brookfield Rd, Churchdown, Gloucester, Gloucestershire GL3 2PL	01452 713488	01452 714976	Mrs Sue Turner	916-5412	FD	11–18	1354	
Christ College	Arle Road, Cheltenham, Gloucestershire GL51 8LE	01242 702220	01242 250217	Teresa Gilpin	916-4609	VA	11–16		RC
Churchdown School	Winston Rd, Churchdown, Gloucester, Gloucestershire GL3 2RB	01452 713340	01452 857367	Mr Simon Packer	916-5409	FD	11–18	1319	
Cirencester Deer Park School	Stroud Rd, Cirencester, Gloucestershire GL7 1XB	01285 653447	01285 640669	Ms Chiquita Henson	916-5420	FD	11–16	1109	
Cirencester Kingshill School	Kingshill La., Cirencester, Gloucestershire GL7 1HS	01285 651511	01285 885652	Miss Christine Oates	916-5419	FD	11–16	822	
Cleeve School	Two Hedges Rd, Bishops Cleeve, Cheltenham, Gloucestershire GL52 8AE	01242 672546	01242 678604	Mr Allen McConaghie	916-4024	FD	11–18	1524	
The Cotswold School	Bourton-on-the-Water, Cheltenham, Gloucestershire GL54 2BD	01451 820554	01451 810658	Mrs Ann Holland	916-5410	FD	11–18	973	
The Crypt School	Podsmead, Gloucester, Gloucestershire GL2 5AE	01452 530291	01452 530292	Mr J.P. Standen	916-5404	FD	11–18	729	B
Dene Magna School	Abenhall Rd, Mitcheldean, Gloucestershire GL17 0DU	01594 542370	01594 544862	Mr Robert Broadbridge	916-5422	FD	11–16	732	
Farmor's School	The Park, Fairford, Gloucestershire GL7 4JQ	01285 712302	01285 713504	Mrs Anne Stokes	916-4513	VC	11–18	1098	
Heywood Community School	Causeway Rd, Cinderford, Gloucestershire GL14 2AZ	01594 822257	01594 823770	Mr Ken Bush	916-5425	FD	11–16	457	
High School for Girls	Denmark Rd, Gloucester, Gloucestershire GL1 3JN	01452 543335	01452 549862	Mrs Ewa Sawicka	916-4002	CY	11–18	832	G
Katharine Lady Berkeley's School	Kingswood Rd, Wotton-under-Edge, Gloucestershire GL12 8RB	01453 842227	01453 845480	Mr Andrew Harris	916-5406	VA	11–18	1521	
Lakers School	Five Acres, Coleford, Gloucestershire GL16 7QW	01594 832263	01594 832486	Ms Alison Elliott	916-5423	FD	11–16	765	
Maidenhill School	Kings Rd, Stonehouse, Gloucestershire GL10 2HA	01453 822469	01453 825615	Mr Adrian Pearson	916-5424	FD	11–16	718	
Marling School	Cainscross Rd, Stroud, Gloucestershire GL5 4HE	01453 762251	01453 756011	Mr Roger Lock	916-5401	FD	11–18	872	B
Newent Community School	Watery La., Newent, Gloucestershire GL18 1QF	01531 820550	01531 820707	Mrs J. Steele	916-5411	FD	11–18	1328	
Pate's Grammar School	Princess Elizabeth Way, Cheltenham, Gloucestershire GL51 0HG	01242 523169	01242 232775	Mr Sean Fenton	916-5403	VA	11–18	951	
Pittville School	Albert Rd, Cheltenham, Gloucestershire GL52 3JD	01242 524787	01242 228750	Mrs Julie Winterman	916-5421	FD	11–16	666	
Rednock School	Rednock Dr, Dursley, Gloucestershire GL11 4BY	01453 543618	01453 545639	Mr David Alexander	916-5407	FD	11–18	1406	
Ribston Hall High School	Stroud Rd, Gloucester, Gloucestershire GL1 5LE	01452 382249	01452 308833	Mrs Amanda Chong	916-5400	FD	11–18	780	G
St Peter's RC High School and Sixth Form Centre	Stroud Rd, Gloucester, Gloucestershire GL4 0DE	01452 520594	01452 509209	Mr L. Montagu	916-4600	VA	11–18	1572	RC
Severn Vale School	School La., Quedgeley, Gloucester, Gloucestershire GL2 4PR	01452 720458	01452 724900	Mr Peter Rowland	916-4064	CY	11–16	1158	
Sir Thomas Rich's School	Oakleaze, Gloucester, Gloucestershire GL2 0LF	01452 338400	01452 382432	Mr Ian Kellie	916-4001	CY	11–18	817	B
Sir William Romney's School	Lowfield Rd, Tetbury, Gloucestershire GL8 8AE	01666 502378	01666 505864	Mr Eric Dawson	916-5428	FD	11–16	569	
Stroud High School	Beards La, Cainscross Rd, Stroud, Gloucestershire GL5 4HF	01453 764441	01453 756304	Mr Timothy Withers	916-5402	FD	11–18	912	G
Tewkesbury School	Ashchurch Rd, Tewkesbury, Gloucestershire GL20 8DF	01684 292152	01684 850742	Mr John Reilly	916-5405	FD	11–18	1731	
Thomas Keble School	Eastcombe, Stroud, Gloucestershire GL6 7DY	01452 770301	01452 770093	Mr Christopher Steer	916-4068	FD	11–16	689	
Vale of Berkeley College	Wanswell, Berkeley, Gloucestershire GL13 9RS	01453 811396	01453 811330	Mr Aidan Farrell	916-4039	FD	11–18	262	
Whitecross School (Foundation)	Church Rd, Lydney, Gloucestershire GL15 5DZ	01594 843202	01594 842025	Mr David Gaston	916-5427	FD	11–16	1017	
Winchcombe School	Greet Rd, Winchcombe, Cheltenham, Gloucestershire GL54 5LB	01242 602233	01242 604211	Mrs Lindsey Cooke	916-5417	FD	11–16	473	
Wyedean School and 6th Form Centre	Beachley Rd, Sedbury, Chepstow, Monmouthshire NP16 7AA	01291 625346	01291 624251	Mr Clive Pemberton	916-5415	FD	11–18	1189	

North Somerset

School name	Address	Tel	Fax	Headteacher	Ref	Type	Ages	Pupils	Other
Backwell School	Station Rd, Backwell, Bristol BS48 3BX	01275 463371	01275 463077	Mr Julian Baldwin	802-4129	CY	11–18	1625	
Broadoak Mathematics And Computing College	Windwhistle Rd, Weston-super-Mare, Somerset BS23 4NP	01934 422000	01934 413903	Mrs Linda Heaven-Woolley	802-4142	CY	11–16	865	
Churchill Community Foundation School and Sixth Form Centre	Churchill Grn, Churchill, North Somerset BS25 5QN	01934 852771	01934 853202	Dr B.T. Wratten	802-4139	FD	11–18	1623	
Clevedon Community School	Valley Rd, Clevedon, Somerset BS21 6AH	01275 876744	01275 340935	Mr John Wells	802-4136	CY	11–18	1246	
Gordano School	St Mary's Rd, Portishead, Bristol, Somerset BS20 7QR	01275 842606	01275 817420	Mr Graham Silverthorne	802-4135	FD	11–18	1704	
Nailsea School	Mizzymead Rd, Nailsea, Bristol, Somerset BS48 2HN	01275 852251	01275 854512	Mr David New	802-4137	CY	11–18	1364	
Priory Community School	Queensway, St George's, Weston-super-Mare, Somerset BS22 6BP	01934 511411	01934 520199	Mr Neville Coles	802-4143	CY	11–16	1188	

School name	Address	Tel	Fax	Headteacher	Ref	Type	Ages	Pupils	Other
St Katherine's School	Pill Rd, Pill, Bristol, Somerset BS20 0HU	01275 373737	01275 372787	Ms Stephanie Quayle	802-4144	CY	11–18	1016	
Worle Community School	Redwing Dr, Mead Vale, Weston-super-Mare, North Somerset BS22 8XX	01934 510777	01934 520941	Mr Trevor Bailey	802-4140	CY	11–16	1481	B
Wyvern Community School	Marchfields Way, Weston-super-Mare, Somerset BS23 3QP	01934 629307	01934 625320	Mr Andrew Russell	802-4141	CY	11–16	866	

Plymouth

School name	Address	Tel	Fax	Headteacher	Ref	Type	Ages	Pupils	Other
Coombe Dean School	Charnhill Way, Elburton, Plymouth, Devon PL9 8ES	01752 406961	01752 482140	Mr Pattrick Frean	879-4181	CY	11–18	1071	
Devonport High School for Boys	Paradise Rd, Stoke, Plymouth, Devon PL1 5QP	01752 208787	01752 208788	Dr N.M. Pettit	879-5406	FD	11–18	1110	B
Devonport High School for Girls	Lyndhurst Rd, Peverell, Plymouth, Devon PL2 3DL	01752 705024	01752 791873	Ms Diane Hill	879-4152	CY	11–18	838	G
Eggbuckland Community College	Westcott Cl, Eggbuckland, Plymouth, Devon PL6 5YB	01752 779061	01752 766650	Miss Katrina Borowski	879-4185	CY	11–18	1443	
Estover Community College	Miller Way, Estover, Plymouth, Devon PL6 8UN	01752 207907	01752 206056	Mr G. Browne	879-4186	CY	11–18	1200	
Hele's School	Seymour Rd, Plympton, Plymouth, Devon PL7 4LT	01752 337193	01752 331460	Mr Andrew Birkett	879-4179	CY	11–18	1318	
John Kitto Community College	Honicknowle La, Pennycross, Plymouth, Devon PL5 3NE	01752 705131	01752 705191	Mr Peter Grainger	879-4188	CY	11–18	1314	
Lipson Community College	Bernice Terr, Lipson, Plymouth, Devon PL4 7PG	01752 671318	01752 252140	Mr Steve Baker	879-4187	CY	11–18	1368	
Notre Dame RC School	Looseleigh La, Derriford, Plymouth, Devon PL6 5HN	01752 775101	01752 768120	Miss Fiona Hutchings	879-4605	VA	11–18	813	RC G
Parkside Community Technology College	Park Ave, Devonport, Plymouth, Devon PL1 4RL	01752 556764	01752 607235	Miss Valena Jones	879-4193	CY	11–16	194	
Plymouth High School for Girls	St Lawrence Rd, Plymouth, Devon PL4 6HT	01752 208308	01752 208309	Mrs Sue Martin	879-4155	CY	11–18	783	G
Plymstock School	Church Rd, Plymstock, Plymouth, Devon PL9 9AZ	01752 402679	01752 484018	Mr David Farmer	879-4180	CY	11–18	1537	
Ridgeway School	Moorland Rd, Plympton, Plymouth, Devon PL7 2RS	01752 338373	01752 331559	Mr John Didymus	879-4178	CY	11–18	1243	
St Boniface's RC College	Tavistock Rd, Crownhill, Plymouth, Devon PL5 3AG	01752 779051	01752 774692	Mr David Kavanagh	879-5403	VA	11–18	815	RC B
Sir John Hunt Community Sports College	Lancaster Gdns, Whitleigh, Plymouth, Devon PL5 4AA	01752 201020	01752 201102	Mrs Wendy Brett	879-4172	CY	11–16	740	
Stoke Damerel Community College	Somerset Pl, Stoke, Plymouth, Devon PL3 4BD	01752 556065	01752 605714	Mrs Carol Hannaford	879-4190	CY	11–18	1393	
Tamarside Community College	Trevithick Rd, Plymouth, Devon PL5 2AF	01752 213939	01752 213909	Mr Keith Ballance	879-4189	CY	11–18	1238	

Poole

School name	Address	Tel	Fax	Headteacher	Ref	Type	Ages	Pupils	Other
Ashdown Technology College	Adastral Rd, Canford Heath, Poole, Dorset BH17 8RE	01202 604222	01202 659181	Mr Ashley Pellegrini	836-4112	CY	12–18	768	
Carter Community College	Blandford Cl, Hamworthy, Poole, Dorset BH15 4BQ	01202 676789	01202 670822	Ms Judy McBlain	836-4104	CY	12–16	383	
Corfe Hills School	Higher Blandford Rd, Broadstone, Dorset BH18 9BG	01202 656300	01202 656356	Mr A. Hinchliffe	836-5410	FD	13–18	1555	
Parkstone Grammar School	Sopers La, Poole, Dorset BH17 7EP	01202 605605	01202 696268	Ms Anne Shinwell	836-5403	FD	12–18	1049	G
Poole Grammar School	Gravel Hill, Poole, Dorset BH17 9JU	01202 692132	01202 606500	Mr Ian Carter	836-5409	FD	12–18	958	B
Poole High School	Harbin Campus, Wimborne Rd, Poole, Dorset BH15 2BW	01202 666988	01202 660674	Mr J.A. Short	836-5407	FD	12–18	1660	
Rossmore Community College	Herbert Ave, Parkstone, Poole, Dorset BH12 4HS	01202 732500	01202 739009	Mrs Sally Apps	836-4111	CY	12–18	727	
St Edward's Roman Catholic/Church of England School, Poole	Dale Valley Rd, Oakdale, Poole, Dorset BH15 3HY	01202 740950	01202 733702	Mrs Pola Bevan	836-4610	VA	12–18	877	CE/RC

Somerset

School name	Address	Tel	Fax	Headteacher	Ref	Type	Ages	Pupils	Other
Ansford School	Maggs La, Castle Cary, Somerset BA7 7JJ	01963 350895	01963 351357	Mr Robert Benzie	933-4250	FD	11–16	693	
Bishop Fox's Community School	Bishop Fox Dr, Taunton, Somerset TA1 3HQ	01823 289211	01823 334582	Mr Paul Scutt	933-4100	CY	11–16	872	
The Blue School	Kennion Rd, Wells, Somerset BA5 2NR	01749 678799	01749 836215	Mr S. Jackson	933-4504	FD	11–18	1460	CE
Brymore School	Cannington, Bridgwater, Somerset TA5 2NB	01278 652369	01278 653244	Mr Malcolm Lloyd	933-5401	FD	13–17	183	B R

3

School name	Address	Tel	Fax	Headteacher	Ref	Type	Ages	Pupils	Other
Bucklers Mead Community School	St John's Rd, Yeovil, Somerset BA21 4NH	01935 424454	01935 431088	Mr Michael Featherstone	933-4451	CY	11-16	985	
The Castle School	Wellington Rd, Taunton, Somerset TA1 5AU	01823 274073	01823 274080	Mr K. Freedman	933-4358	CY	11-16	1204	
Chilton Trinity Technology College	Chilton St, Bridgwater, Somerset TA6 3JA	01278 455631	01278 444361	Mrs P. Hollinghurst	933-4308	CY	11-16	1023	
Court Fields Community School	Mantle St, Wellington, Somerset TA21 8SW	01823 664201	01823 660812	Mrs Elaine Faull	933-4356	CY	11-16	874	
Crispin School	Church Rd, Street, Somerset BA16 0AD	01458 442714	01458 447955	Mr Paul James	933-4283	CY	11-16	1114	
East Bridgwater Community School	Parkway, Bridgwater, Somerset TA6 4QY	01278 422841	01278 446004	Mr Nigel Shipton	933-4307	CY	11-16	866	
Frome Community College	Bath Rd, Frome, Somerset BA11 2HQ	01373 465353	01373 469078	Mr B. Bates	933-4000	CY	13-18	1413	
Haygrove School	Durleigh Rd, Bridgwater, Somerset TA6 7HW	01278 455531	01278 427972	Mr Robert Ward	933-4309	CY	11-16	1080	
Heathfield Community School	School Rd, Monkton Heathfield, Taunton, Somerset TA2 8PD	01823 412396	01823 413119	Mr E. Furneaux	933-4354	CY	11-18	1181	
Holyrood Community School	Zembard La, Chard, Somerset TA20 1JL	01460 260100	01460 64919	Mr M. Hicks	933-4274	CY	11-18	1297	
Huish Episcopi School	Wincanton Rd, Huish Episcopi, Langport, Somerset TA10 9SS	01458 250501	01458 250262	Mr G. Roff	933-4259	CY	11-16	1202	
The King Alfred School	Burnham Rd, Highbridge, Somerset TA9 3EE	01278 784881	01278 782344	Dr Keith Diffey	933-4304	CY	11-18	1368	
King Arthur's Community School	West Hill, Wincanton, Somerset BA9 9BX	01963 32368	01963 33735	Mr Ian Campbell	933-4273	CY	11-16	676	
The Kings of Wessex School	Station Rd, Cheddar, Somerset BS27 3AQ	01934 742608	01934 742757	Mr C.M. Richardson	933-4583	FD	13-18	1174	CE
Kingsmead Community School	Wiveliscombe, Taunton, Somerset TA4 2NE	01984 623483	01984 624230	Mr Geoff Tinker	933-4355	CY	11-16	792	
Ladymead Community School	Cheddon Rd, Taunton, Somerset TA2 7QP	01823 331243	01823 321450	Mr M. Trusson	933-4359	CY	11-16	793	
Preston School	Monks Dale, Yeovil, Somerset BA21 3JD	01935 471131	01935 431216	Mr R.A. Jones	933-4455	CY	11-16	962	
Robert Blake Science College	Hamp Ave, Bridgwater, Somerset TA6 6AW	01278 456243	01278 444987	Mrs Ann Winter	933-4300	CY	11-16	633	
The St Augustine of Canterbury School	Lyngford Rd, Taunton, Somerset TA2 7EF	01823 337128	01823 324214	Mrs Gail Crees	933-4600	VA	11-16	419	CE/RC
St Dunstan's Community School	Wells Rd, Glastonbury, Somerset BA6 9BY	01458 832943	01458 831220	Mrs Pamela G Iles	933-4258	CY	11-16	658	
Sexey's School	Cole Rd, Bruton, Somerset BA10 0DF	01749 813393	01749 812870	Mr Stephen Burgoyne	933-5400	VA	11-18	510	CE R
Stanchester Community School	East Stoke, Stoke-sub-Hamdon, Somerset TA14 6UG	01935 823200	01935 826635	Mr G. Ottery	933-4450	CY	11-16	916	
Wadham School	Mount Pleasant, Yeovil Rd, Crewkerne, Somerset TA18 7NT	01460 270123	01460 270124	Mr David Derbyshire	933-4508	VC	13-18	650	CE
The West Somerset Community College	Bircham Rd, Alcombe, Minehead, Somerset TA24 6AY	01643 706061	01643 705700	Mr Nick Swann	933-4291	CY	13-18	1290	
Westfield Community School	Stiby Rd, Yeovil, Somerset BA21 3EP	01935 423747	01935 411340	Mrs Marguerite Jackson	933-4201	CY	11-16	971	
Whitstone	Charlton Rd, Shepton Mallet, Somerset BA4 5PF	01749 345555	01749 345243	Mr T. Wilson	933-4282	CY	11-16	755	

South Gloucestershire

School name	Address	Tel	Fax	Headteacher	Ref	Type	Ages	Pupils	Other
Bradley Stoke Community School	Fiddlers Wood La, Bradley Stoke, South Gloucestershire BS32 9BS	01454 868840		Mr Dave Baker	803-4104	CY	11-16	395	
Brimsham Green School	Broad La, Yate, Bristol BS37 7LB	01454 868888	01454 868880	Mr R.E. Warrillow	803-4146	CY	11-18	1129	
The Castle School	Park Rd, Thornbury, Thornbury, Gloucestershire BS35 1HT	01454 862100	01454 862101	Ms Melanie Warnes	803-4120	CY	11-18	1716	
Chipping Sodbury School	Bowling Rd, Chipping Sodbury, Bristol, South Gloucestershire BS37 6EW	01454 862900	01454 323173	Mr Philip Lidstone	803-4502	VC	11-18	996	
Downend Comprehensive School	Westerleigh Rd, Downend, Bristol, Gloucestershire BS16 6XA	01454 862300	01454 862301	Mrs Tamryn Savage	803-4148	CY	11-18	1510	
Filton High School	New Rd, Stoke Gifford, Bristol, Gloucestershire BS34 8QT	01454 862400	01454 862401	Miss Ann Duff	803-4113	CY	11-18	1080	
The Grange School and Sports College	Tower Rd North, Warmley, Bristol, South Gloucestershire BS30 8XQ	01454 862800	01454 862801	Mr Philip Steven Cook	803-4149	CY	11-18	954	
Hanham High School	Memorial Rd, Hanham, Bristol, Gloucestershire BS15 3LA	01454 867600	01454 867601	Mrs Peggy Farrington	803-4145	CY	11-18	998	
John Cabot Academy	Woodside Rd, Kingswood, Bristol BS15 8BD	0117 976 3000	0117 976 0630	Mr Jim Wynn	803-6906		11-19	1017	
John Cabot City Technology College	Woodside Rd, Kingswood, Bristol BS15 8BD	0117 976 3000	0117 976 0630		803-6900		11-19	586	
King Edmund Community School	Sundridge Pk, Yate, Bristol BS37 4DX	01454 862626	01454 862627	Mr Roger Gilbert	803-4122	CY	11-18	1198	
Kingsfield School	Brook Rd, Kingswood, Bristol, Gloucestershire BS15 4JT	01454 866538	01454 866541	Mr D.I. Lewis	803-4112	CY	11-18	954	
Mangotsfield School	Rodway Hill, Mangotsfield, Bristol BS16 9LH	01454 862700	01454 862701	Mr Richard Badley	803-4147	CY	11-18	1216	
Marlwood School	Vattingstone La, Alveston, Bristol, Somerset BS35 3LA	01454 862525	01454 411052	Mr Keith Geary	803-4511	VC	11-18	1301	
Patchway Community College	Hempton La, Almondsbury, Bristol, Somerset BS32 4AJ	01454 862020	01454 862021	Mr Alan Howson	803-4117	CY	11-18	1089	

School name	Address	Tel	Fax	Headteacher	Ref	Type	Ages	Pupils	Other
The Ridings High School	High St, Winterbourne, Bristol, Gloucestershire BS36 1JL	01454 252000	01454 250404	Dr Robert Gibson	803-4121	CY	11–18	1884	
Sir Bernard Lovell School	North St, Oldland Common, Bristol, Gloucestershire BS30 8TS	01454 868020	01454 868021	Mr David Turrell	803-4124	CY	11–18	1296	

Swindon

School name	Address	Tel	Fax	Headteacher	Ref	Type	Ages	Pupils	Other
Churchfields School	Salcombe Gr, Swindon, Wiltshire SN3 1HQ	01793 487286	01793 525466	Mr Steve Flavin	866-4065	CY	11–16	1017	
The Commonweal School	The Mall, Old Town, Swindon, Wiltshire SN1 4JE	01793 612727	01793 513437	Mr K. Defter	866-5410	FD	11–16	1099	
Dorcan Technology College	St Paul's Dr, Covingham, Swindon, Wiltshire SN3 5DA	01793 525231	01793 431461	Dr Scott Sissons	866-4060	CY	11–16	1332	
Greendown Community School	Grange Park Way, Grange Pk, Swindon, Wiltshire SN5 6HN	01793 874224	01793 876274	Mr Clive Zimmerman	866-4086	CY	11–16	1264	
Headlands	Headlands Gr, Swindon SN2 7HS	01793 747800	01793 747801	Mrs Janet Shadick	866-4087	CY	11–16	825	
Highworth Warneford School	Shrivenham Rd, Highworth, Swindon, Wiltshire SN6 7BZ	01793 762426	01793 861865	Mr J.G. Saunders	866-4074	CY	11–16	931	
Isambard Community School	The Learning Campus, Redhouse Way, Swindon, Wiltshire SN25 2ND	01793 705400	01793 707596	Mrs Rachel Mattey	866-4088	CY	11–16		
Kingsdown School	Hyde Rd, Stratton Street Margaret, Swindon, Wiltshire SN2 7SH	01793 822284	01793 828726	Mrs Wendy Taylor	866-5407	FD	11–16	1270	
Nova Hreod	Akers Way, Moredon, Swindon, Wiltshire SN2 2NQ	01793 527999	01793 430394	Mr Andrew Fleet	866-4084	CY	11–16	1288	
The Ridgeway School	Inverary Rd, Wroughton, Swindon, Wiltshire SN4 9DJ	01793 846100	01793 815065	Mr Steven Colledge	866-5417	FD	11–18	1398	
St Joseph's RC College	Ocotal Way, Swindon, Wiltshire SN3 3LR	01793 714200	01793 714270	Mr Peter Wells	866-5409	VA	11–18	1221	RC
Swindon Academy	Headlands Gr, Headlands School, Swindon SN2 7HS	01793 747835	01793 747835	Ms Jan Shaddick	866-6905		3–19		

Torbay

School name	Address	Tel	Fax	Headteacher	Ref	Type	Ages	Pupils	Other
Brixham Community College	Higher Ranscombe Rd, Brixham, Devon TQ5 9HF	01803 858271	01803 882726	Mr C.P. Turner	880-4118	FD	11–16	973	
Churston Ferrers Grammar School	Greenway Rd, Churston Ferrers, Brixham, Devon TQ5 0LN	01803 842289	01803 846007	Mr Stephen Kings	880-4116	FD	11–18	888	
Paignton Community and Sports College	Waterleat Rd, Paignton, Devon TQ3 3WA	01803 403005	01803 403004	Miss Jane English	880-4119	CY	11–18	1861	
St Cuthbert Mayne School	Trumlands Rd, Torquay, Devon TQ1 4RN	01803 328725	01803 322273	Mrs Catherine Gilfillan	880-4601	VA	11–18	1099	RC/CE
Torquay Boys' Grammar School	Shiphay Manor Dr, Torquay, Devon TQ2 7EL	01803 615501	01803 614613	Mr Roy Pike	880-5401	FD	11–18	1041	B
Torquay Community College	Fairfield Rd, Torquay, Devon TQ2 7NU	01803 329351	01803 316297	Miss Gillian M. Battye	880-4115	CY	11–16	998	
Torquay Grammar School for Girls	30 Shiphay La, Torquay, Devon TQ2 7DY	01803 613215	01803 616724	Mrs E.J. Cross	880-4114	FD	11–18	860	G
Westlands School and Technology College	Westlands La, Torquay, Devon TQ1 3PE	01803 400660	01803 323210	Mr Michael Stewart	880-4117	FD	11–18	1308	

Wiltshire

School name	Address	Tel	Fax	Headteacher	Ref	Type	Ages	Pupils	Other
Abbeyfield School	Stanley La, Chippenham, Wiltshire SN15 3XB	01249 464500	01249 464500	Mrs Patricia Shubrook	865-4000	CY	11–19	913	
Avon Valley College	Recreation Rd, Durrington, Salisbury, Wiltshire SP4 8HH	01980 652467	01980 623568	Ms Rowena Brookes	865-4071	CY	11–18	646	
Bishop Wordsworth's Grammar School	11 The Close, Salisbury, Wiltshire SP1 2EB	01722 333851	01722 325899	Dr Stuart Smallwood	865-5413	VA	11–18	857	CE B
Bradon Forest School	The Peak, Purton, Swindon, Wiltshire SN5 4AT	01793 770570	01793 771063	Mr Len Spiers	865-5408	FD	11–16	1184	
Castledown School	Tidworth Rd, Ludgershall, Andover, Hampshire SP11 9RR	01264 405060	01264 791894	Mr John Pender	865-5416	FD	11–16	446	
The Clarendon College	Frome Rd, Trowbridge, Wiltshire BA14 0DJ	01225 762686	01225 751034	Mr C. Kay	865-4069	CY	11–18	1326	
The Corsham School A Visual Arts College	The Tynings, Corsham, Wiltshire SN13 9DF	01249 713284	01249 701102	Mr Martin Williams	865-4066	CY	11–18	1387	
Devizes School	The Green, Devizes, Wiltshire SN10 3AG	01380 724886	01380 720955	Mr Malcolm Irons	865-5411	FD	11–18	1193	G
The George Ward School	Shurnhold, Melksham, Wiltshire SN12 8DQ	01225 702771	01225 700913	Mr Stephen Clark	865-4013	CY	11–18	1129	
Hardenhuish School	Hardenhuish La, Chippenham, Wiltshire SN14 6RJ	01249 650693	01249 767388	Mr Colin Smith	865-5414	FD	11–18	1476	
The John Bentley School	White Horse Way, Calne, Wiltshire SN11 8YH	01249 818100	01249 818136	Mr G. Trafford	865-5406	FD	11–18	1233	

3

School name	Address	Tel	Fax	Headteacher	Ref	Type	Ages	Pupils	Other
The John of Gaunt School	Wingfield Rd, Trowbridge, Wiltshire BA14 9EH	01225 762637	01225 777475	Mr Andrew Packer	865-4075	CY	11–18	1360	
Lavington School	The Spring, Market Lavington, Devizes, Wiltshire SN10 4EB	01380 812352	01380 818492	Mr Martin Watson	865-5402	FD	11–16	685	
Malmesbury School	Corn Gastons, Malmesbury, Wiltshire SN16 0DF	01666 829700	01666 829701	Mr Malcolm Trobe	865-4064	CY	11–18	1215	
Matravers School	Springfield Rd, Westbury, Wiltshire BA13 3QH	01373 822666	01373 824283	Mr Chris Dark	865-5415	FD	11–18	1084	
Pewsey Vale School	Wilcot Rd, Pewsey, Wiltshire SN9 5EW	01672 565000	01672 565009	Mrs Carol Grant	865-5403	FD	11–16	386	
St Augustine's RC College	Wingfield Rd, Trowbridge, Wiltshire BA14 9EN	01225 350001	01225 350002	Mr Brendan Wall	865-5400	VA	11–16	961	RC
St Edmund's CE Girls' School and Sports College	Church Rd, Laverstock, Salisbury, Wiltshire SP1 1RD	01722 328565	01722 421391	Mrs Jacqui Goodall	865-4511	VC	11–16	815	CE G
St John's School and Community College	Stedman Bldg, Orchard Rd, Marlborough, Wiltshire SN8 4AX	01672 516156	01672 516664	Dr Patrick Hazlewood	865-5405	FD	11–18	1492	
St Joseph's RC School	Church Rd, Laverstock, Salisbury, Wiltshire SP1 1QY	01722 335380	01722 410741	Mr Paul Hughes	865-4610	VA	11–16	359	RC
St Laurence School	Ashley Rd, Bradford-on-Avon, Wiltshire BA15 1DZ	01225 309500	01225 867694	Mr James Colquhoun	865-4537	VC	11–18	1170	CE
Salisbury High School	Westwood Rd, Salisbury, Wiltshire SP2 9HS	01722 323431	01722 330010	Mr Brian Eales	865-5418	FD	13–19	849	CE
Sheldon School	Hardenhuish La, Chippenham, Wiltshire SN14 6HJ	01249 766020	01249 445732	Mr Gerard MacMahon	865-5404	FD	11–18	1683	
South Wilts Grammar School for Girls	Stratford Rd, Salisbury, Wiltshire SP1 3JJ	01722 323326	01722 320703	Mrs Frances Stratton	865-5412	FD	11–18	959	G
The Stonehenge School	Antrobus Rd, Amesbury, Salisbury, Wiltshire SP4 7ND	01980 623407	01980 625547	Mr Nigel Roper	865-4070	CY	11–16	770	
The Trafalgar School at Downton	Breamore Rd, Downton, Salisbury, Wiltshire SP5 3HN	01725 510610	01725 512841	Mrs Jenny Lawrie	865-4006	CY	11–16	444	
Warminster Kingdown	Woodcock Rd, Warminster, Salisbury, Wiltshire SN4 7HG	01985 215551	01985 846697	Mrs Sheelagh Brown	865-4072	CY	11–18	1402	
Wootton Bassett School	Lime Kiln, Wootton Bassett, Swindon, Wiltshire SN4 7HG	01793 841900	01793 841969	Mr Christopher Montacute	865-4067	CY	11–18	1539	
Wyvern College	Church Rd, Laverstock, Salisbury, Wiltshire SP1 1RE	01722 500700	01722 500900	Mr Richard Butler	865-4001	VA	11–16	624	CE B

West Midlands

Birmingham

School name	Address	Tel	Fax	Headteacher	Ref	Type	Ages	Pupils	Other
Al-Hijrah Secondary School	Cherrywood Centre, Burbidge Rd, Bordesley Grn, Birmingham, West Midlands B9 4US	0121 773 7979	0121 773 7111	Mr M. Saqib	330-4334	VA	11–16	284	Mu
Archbishop Ilsley RC School	Victoria Rd, Acocks Grn, Birmingham, West Midlands B27 7XY	0121 706 4200	0121 707 6597	Mr S. O'Donnell	330-4804	VA	11–18	1252	RC
The Arthur Terry School	Kittoe Rd, Four Oaks, Sutton Coldfield, West Midlands B74 4RZ	0121 323 2221	0121 308 8033	Mr Christopher Stone	330-4307	CY	11–18	1560	
Aston Manor School	Phillips St, Aston, Birmingham, West Midlands B6 4PZ	0121 359 8108	0121 359 2426	Ms Heather Roberts	330-4220	CY	11–16	726	
Bartley Green School A Specialist Technology and Sports College	Adams Hill, Birmingham, West Midlands B32 3QJ	0121 476 9246	0121 478 1585	Mrs C. Owen	330-4108	CY	11–16	863	
Baverstock Foundation School and Specialist Sports College	501 Bells La, Druids Heath, Birmingham, West Midlands B14 5TL	0121 430 7924	0121 474 5313	Mr David Green	330-5400	FD	11–18	1288	
Bishop Challoner RC School	Institute Rd, Kings Heath, Birmingham, West Midlands B14 7EG	0121 444 4161	0121 441 1552	Mrs M.G. Symons	330-5413	VA	11–18	1084	RC
Bishop Vesey's Grammar School	Lichfield Rd, Sutton Coldfield, West Midlands B74 2NH	0121 250 5400	0121 250 5420	Mr David Iddon	330-4660	VA	11–18	886	B
Bishop Walsh RC School	Wylde Green Rd, Sutton Coldfield, West Midlands B76 1QT	0121 351 3215	0121 313 2142	Mr M.A. Moran	330-4661	VA	11–18	959	RC
Bordesley Green Girls' Specialist Business and Enterprise School	Bordesley Green Rd, Birmingham, West Midlands B9 4TR	0121 464 1881	0121 464 3311	Ms C. Considine	330-4115	CY	11–16	601	G
Bournville School and Sixth Form Centre	Griffins Brook La, Birmingham, West Midlands B30 1QJ	0121 475 3881	0121 483 2349	Mrs R. Harker	330-4238	CY	11–18	1235	
Broadway School	The Broadway, Perry Barr, Birmingham, West Midlands B20 3DP	0121 464 8834	0121 464 1122	Mr Emm	330-4227	CY	11–18	1172	
Cardinal Wiseman RC Technology College	Old Oscott Hill, Kingstanding, Birmingham, West Midlands B44 9SR	0121 360 6383	0121 366 6873	Mr Martin Jones	330-4801	VA	11–16	611	RC
Castle Vale School and Specialist Performing Arts College	Farnborough Rd, Castle Vale, Birmingham, West Midlands B35 7NL	0121 464 6101	0121 464 7069	Mr Clive Owen	330-4214	CY	11–16	869	R

3

School name	Address	Tel	Fax	Headteacher	Ref	Type	Ages	Pupils	Other
Cockshut Hill Technology College	Cockshut Hill, Yardley, Birmingham, West Midlands B26 2HX	0121 464 2122	0121 722 2354	Mr Richard Sloan	330-4233	CY	11–18	1449	
The College High Specialist Arts School	395 College Rd, Erdington, Birmingham, West Midlands B44 0HF	0121 373 1647	0121 382 2707	Mrs K.L. Popratnjak	330-4083	CY	11–16	984	
Colmers School and Sports College	Bristol Rd South, Rednal, Birmingham, West Midlands B45 9NY	0121 453 1778	0121 457 7642	Mr P. Jones	330-5416	FD	11–16	1037	
Dame Elizabeth Cadbury Technology College	Woodbrooke Rd, Bournville, Birmingham, West Midlands B30 1UL	0121 464 4040	0121 464 2856	Mrs Lesley Brooman	330-4129	CY	11–18	628	
Fairfax School	Fairfax Rd, Sutton Coldfield, West Midlands B75 7JT	0121 378 1288	0121 378 3176	Mrs S. Calvert	330-5410	FD	11–18	1356	
Four Dwellings High School	Dwellings La, Quinton, Birmingham, West Midlands B32 1RJ	0121 422 0131	0121 423 1352	Mr B.K. Smith	330-4226	CY	11–16	686	
Frankley Community High School	New St, Frankley, Birmingham, West Midlands B45 0EU	0121 464 9901	0121 464 8706	Mr Jonathan Wilding	330-4333	CY	11–16	435	
George Dixon International School and Sixth Form Centre	City Rd, Edgbaston, Birmingham, West Midlands B17 8LF	0121 434 4488	0121 434 3721	Mr R. Dowling	330-5412	FD	11–18	1102	
Golden Hillock School A Specialist College for Sports and The Arts	Golden Hillock Rd, Sparkhill, Birmingham, West Midlands B11 2QG	0121 773 8156	0121 773 8159	Mr Matthew Scarrott	330-4138	CY	11–16	845	
Great Barr School	Aldridge Rd, Gt Barr, Birmingham, West Midlands B44 8NU	0121 366 6611	0121 366 6007	Mrs Catherine Mary Abbott	330-5403	FD	11–18	2400	
Hall Green School	Southam Rd, Hall Green, Birmingham, West Midlands B28 0AA	0121 628 8787	0121 702 2182	Mr A. Greaney	330-5409	FD	11–16	873	
Hamstead Hall School	Craythorne Ave, Handsworth Wood, Birmingham, West Midlands B20 1HL	0121 386 7510	0121 386 7511	Mr K. Morris	330-4240	CY	11–18	1118	
Handsworth Grammar School	Grove La, Handsworth, Birmingham, West Midlands B21 9ET	0121 554 2794	0121 554 5405	Mr R.J. Shephard	330-5402	VA	11–18	952	B
Handsworth Wood Girls' Visual and Performing Arts Specialist College	Church La, Handsworth, Birmingham, West Midlands B20 2HL	0121 554 8122	0121 551 6805	Dr S. Nepaulsingh	330-4207	CY	11–18	667	G
Harborne Hill School	Harborne Rd, Edgbaston, Birmingham, West Midlands B15 3JL	0121 464 2737	0121 464 4695	Mr A.R. Wright	330-4144	CY	11–16	432	
The Heartlands High School	Gt Francis St, Nechells, Birmingham, West Midlands B7 4QR	0121 464 3931	0121 359 6562	Mrs Glynis Jones	330-4332	CY	11–16	622	
Hillcrest School A Specialist Maths and Computing College and Sixth Form Centre	Stonehouse La, Birmingham, West Midlands B32 3AE	0121 464 3172	0121 428 1075	Miss Lynda Roan	330-4012	CY	11–18	761	G
Hodge Hill Girls' School	Bromford Rd, Birmingham, West Midlands B36 8EY	0121 464 3094	0121 464 6814	Mrs E.M. Brown	330-4015	CY	11–18	690	G
Hodge Hill School	Bromford Rd, Hodge Hill, Birmingham, West Midlands B36 8HB	0121 464 7500	0121 685 7517	Ms Marie McMahon	330-4201	CY	11–16	1061	
Holte School	Wheeler St, Lozells, Birmingham, West Midlands B19 2EP	0121 523 7321	0121 523 0321	Mrs Patricia Walters	330-4223	CY	11–16	921	
Holy Trinity RC Media Arts College	Oakley Rd, Small Heath, Birmingham, West Midlands B10 0AX	0121 772 0184	0121 772 9788	Mr T. Temple	330-4664	VA	11–16	615	RC
Holyhead School	Milestone La, Handsworth, Birmingham, West Midlands B21 0HN	0121 523 1960	0121 523 1969	Mr Martin Bayliss	330-4241	FD	11–16	1020	
The International School and Community College, East Birmingham	Gressel La, Tile Cross, Birmingham, West Midlands B33 9UF	0121 464 9600	0121 464 9601	Mr Colin Bateman	330-4244	CY	11–18	1050	
John Willmott School	Reddicap Heath Rd, Sutton Coldfield, West Midlands B75 7DY	0121 378 1946	0121 311 1437	Mr Ken Nimmo	330-4301	CY	11–18	1134	
King Edward VI Aston School	Frederick Rd, Aston, Birmingham, West Midlands B6 6DJ	0121 327 1130	0121 328 7020	Mr Colin Parker	330-5408	VA	11–18	744	Ch B
King Edward VI Camp Hill School for Boys	Vicarage Rd, Kings Heath, Birmingham, West Midlands B14 7QJ	0121 444 3188	0121 441 2796	Mr J.V. Darby	330-5407	VA	11–18	712	Ch B
King Edward VI Camp Hill School for Girls	Vicarage Rd, Kings Heath, Birmingham, West Midlands B14 7QJ	0121 444 2150	0121 444 5123	Mrs Dru James	330-5406	VA	11–18	879	Ch G
King Edward VI Five Ways School	Scotland La, Bartley Green, Birmingham, West Midlands B32 4BT	0121 475 3535	0121 477 8555	Mr D.J. Wheeldon	330-5405	VA	11–18	1109	Ch
King Edward VI Handsworth School	Rose Hill Rd, Birmingham, West Midlands B21 9AR	0121 554 2342	0121 554 3879	Miss E.V. Insch	330-5404	VA	11–18	916	Ch G
King's Heath Boys Mathematics and Computing College	Hollybank Rd, Birmingham, West Midlands B13 0RJ	0121 464 4454	0121 464 5554	Mr Selwyn Calvin	330-4063	CY	11–16	574	B
King's Norton Boys' School	Northfield Rd, Birmingham, West Midlands B30 1DY	0121 628 0010	0121 628 0080	Mr Roy Baylis	330-5415	FD	11–18	748	B
King's Norton Girls' School and Language College	Selly Oak Rd, Birmingham, West Midlands B30 1HW	0121 458 1305	0121 459 2514	Mrs P. Beanland	330-5414	FD	11–18	952	G
King's Norton High School	Shannon Rd, Kings Norton, Birmingham, West Midlands B38 9DE	0121 459 4451	0121 433 3328	Ms Denise Burns	330-4217	CY	11–16	505	
Kingsbury School and Sports College	Kingsbury Rd, Erdington, Birmingham, West Midlands B24 8RE	0121 373 1080	0121 306 4878	Ms P. Exley	330-4330	CY	11–16	885	
Lordswood Boys' School	Hagley Rd, Birmingham, West Midlands B17 8BJ	0121 464 2807	0121 464 2746	Mr Hayden Abbott	330-4057	CY	11–18	683	B
Lordswood Girls' School and Specialist Centre for Media Arts	Knightlow Rd, Harborne, Birmingham, West Midlands B17 8QB	0121 429 2838	0121 429 4840	Mrs J. Hattatt	330-4060	CY	11–18	859	G
Moseley School A Language College	College Rd, Moseley, Birmingham, West Midlands B13 9LR	0121 678 6400	0121 678 1299	Mr David Peck	330-4245	CY	11–18	1352	
Ninestiles School	Hartfield Cres, Birmingham, West Midlands B27 7QG	0121 628 1311	0121 778 4234	Ms Christine Quinn	330-5411	FD	11–18	1432	

School name	Address	Tel	Fax	Headteacher	Ref	Type	Ages	Pupils	Other
Park View School	Naseby Rd, Alum Rock, Birmingham, West Midlands B8 3HG	0121 464 4209	0121 464 2656	Mrs Lindsey Clark	330-4323	CY	11–16	592	
Perry Beeches School	Beeches Rd, Birmingham, West Midlands B42 2PY	0121 360 4242	0121 366 6014	Mrs Ingrid Gallagher	330-4109	CY	11–16	883	
Plantsbrook School	Upper Holland Rd, Sutton Coldfield, West Midlands B72 1RB	0121 362 7310	0121 321 7311	Ms Tracy Campbell	330-4331	CY	11–16	1304	
Queensbridge School	Queensbridge Rd, Moseley, Birmingham, West Midlands B13 8QB	0121 464 5566	0121 683 5588	Mr Tim Boyes	330-4173	CY	11–16	587	
St Alban's CE Specialist Engineering College	Angelina St, Birmingham, West Midlands B12 0UU	0121 464 7811	0121 464 2849	Mr D. Gould	330-4611	VA	11–16	429	CE
St Edmund Campion RC School	Sutton Rd, Erdington, Birmingham, West Midlands B23 5XA	0121 464 7700	0121 250 7702	Mr K.P. Ash	330-4663	VA	11–18	978	RC
St John Wall Catholic School - A Specialist Humanities College	Oxhill Rd, Handsworth, Birmingham, West Midlands B21 8HH	0121 554 1825	0121 507 0993	Mr John Hussey	330-4625	VA	11–16	624	RC
St Paul's School for Girls	Vernon Rd, Edgbaston, Birmingham, West Midlands B16 9SL	0121 454 0895	0121 456 4803	Miss Angela Whelan	330-4606	VA	11–18	945	RC G
St Thomas Aquinas RC School	Wychall La, Kings Norton, Birmingham, West Midlands B38 8AP	0121 464 4643	0121 464 4043	Mr J. Foley	330-4616	VA	11–18	1247	RC
Saltley School and Specialist Science College	Belchers La, Bordesley Grn, Birmingham, West Midlands B9 5RX	0121 464 1801	0121 766 6389	Mrs A. Cole	330-4008	CY	11–16	918	
Selly Park Technology College for Girls	5 Selly Park Rd, Selly Pk, Birmingham, West Midlands B29 7PH	0121 472 1238	0121 414 1143	Miss Michelle Magrs	330-4177	CY	11–16	735	G
Sheldon Heath Community Arts College	Sheldon Heath Rd, Sheldon, Birmingham, West Midlands B26 2RZ	0121 464 4428	0121 464 2357	Mr John Allen	330-4081	CY	11–18	1142	
Shenley Court Specialist Arts College and Sixth Form Centre	Shenley La, Birmingham, West Midlands B29 4HE	0121 464 5191	0121 464 3711	Ms Carol Gumbley	330-4326	CY	11–18	1105	
Small Heath School	Muntz St, Small Heath, Birmingham, West Midlands B10 9RX	0121 464 7997	0121 766 8120	Mr Peter Charles Slough	330-5401	FD	11–16	1306	
Stockland Green Technology College	Slade Rd, Erdington, Birmingham, West Midlands B23 7JH	0121 373 4807	0121 373 0939	Mr Andrew Arnott	330-4206	CY	11–16	591	R
Sutton Coldfield Grammar School for Girls	Jockey Rd, Sutton Coldfield, West Midlands B73 5PT	0121 354 1479	0121 354 9418	Mrs K. Harrison	330-4300	CY	11–18	1006	G
Swanshurst School	Brook La, Billesley, Birmingham, West Midlands B13 0TW	0121 464 2400	0121 464 2401	Mrs Elaine Kenney	330-4237	CY	11–19	1754	G
Turves Green Boys' Technology College	Turves Grn, Northfield, Birmingham, West Midlands B31 4BS	0121 675 4129	0121 478 3705	Mr K. Nimmo	330-4188	CY	11–16	648	B
Turves Green Girls' School and Technology College	Turves Grn, Northfield, Birmingham, West Midlands B31 4BP	0121 464 8346	0121 478 2318	Mrs S. Brehony	330-4187	CY	11–16	736	G
Washwood Heath Technology College	Burney La, Stechford, Birmingham, West Midlands B8 2AS	0121 784 7272	0121 789 9077	Mrs Beverley Mabey	330-4084	CY	11–18	1392	
Waverley School	Hob Moor Rd, Small Heath, Birmingham, West Midlands B10 9BT	0121 464 1780	0121 464 7479	Mr J.P. Allen	330-4009	CY	11–16	732	
Wheelers Lane Technology College	Wheelers La, Kings Heath, Birmingham, West Midlands B13 0SF	0121 444 2864	0121 444 0540	Ms Deborah James	330-4193	CY	11–16	599	B
Yardleys School	Reddings La, Tyseley, Birmingham, West Midlands B11 3EY	0121 464 6821	0121 693 6824	Mrs Rosemary Hughes	330-4246	CY	11–16	901	

Coventry

School name	Address	Tel	Fax	Headteacher	Ref	Type	Ages	Pupils	Other
Barr's Hill School and Community College	Radford Rd, Coventry, West Midlands CV1 4BU	024 7623 4600	024 7623 4609	Mr R. Brabban	331-4000	CY	11–18	611	
Bishop Ullathorne RC School	Leasowes Ave, Coventry, West Midlands CV3 6BH	024 7641 4515	024 7669 2253	Miss J. Byrne	331-4701	VA	11–18	971	RC
Caludon Castle School	Axholme Rd, Wyken, Coventry, West Midlands CV2 5BD	024 7644 4822	024 7663 6282	Mrs Carol Reid	331-4028	CY	11–18	1437	
Cardinal Newman RC School and Community College	Sandpits La, Keresley, Coventry, West Midlands CV6 2FR	024 7633 2382	024 7633 5626	Mrs Carol Buchanan	331-4707	VA	11–18	1148	RC
Cardinal Wiseman RC School and Language College	Potters Green Rd, Coventry, West Midlands CV2 2AJ	024 7661 7231	024 7660 2572	Mrs Helen Knight	331-4710	VA	11–18	1356	RC
Coundon Court School and Community College	Northbrook Rd, Coventry, West Midlands CV6 2AJ	024 7633 5121	024 7633 6842	Mr John Vickers	331-4026	CY	11–18	1702	
The Coventry Blue Coat CE School	Terry Rd, Coventry, West Midlands CV1 2BA	024 7622 3542	024 7655 0927	Mr S. Timbrell	331-4800	VA	11–18	1337	CE
Ernesford Grange Community School A Specialist Science College	Princethorpe Way, Coventry, West Midlands CV3 2QD	024 7645 3121	024 7663 6136	Mr Julian Leslie Chartres	331-4039	CY	11–18	1024	
Finham Park School	Green La, Coventry, West Midlands CV3 6EA	024 7641 8135	024 7684 0803	Mr P. Logan	331-4037	CY	11–18	1457	
Foxford School and Community Arts College	Grange Rd, Longford, Coventry, West Midlands CV6 6BB	024 7636 9200	024 7636 9201	Ms Ruth Williamson	331-4029	CY	11–18	1047	
Lyng Hall School	Blackberry La, Coventry, West Midlands CV2 3JS	024 7672 4960	024 7672 4969	Mr P. Green	331-4030	CY	11–18	674	

School name	Address	Tel	Fax	Headteacher	Ref	Type	Ages	Pupils	Other
President Kennedy School and Community College	Rookery La., Coventry, West Midlands CV6 4GL	024 7666 1416		Mr G. Payne	331-4034	CY	11–18	1452	
Sidney Stringer School – Specialising in Mathematics and Computing	Cox St, Coventry, West Midlands CV1 5NL	024 7625 1756	024 7655 0940	Mr B. Worrall	331-4038	CY	11–18	1141	
Stoke Park Community Technology College	Dane Rd, Coventry, West Midlands CV2 4JW	024 7645 0215	024 7663 6129	Mr W.T. Wolger	331-4005	CY	11–18	1091	
Tile Hill Wood School and Language College	Nutbrook Ave, Coventry, West Midlands CV4 9PW	024 7642 6200	024 7642 6246	Mrs Joanna Shirlaw	331-4033	CY	11–18	1284	G
The Westwood School – A Technology College	Mitchell Ave, Canley, Coventry, West Midlands CV4 8DY	024 7646 7321	024 7646 7321	Mr Roger Whittle	331-4043	CY	11–18	590	
Whitley Abbey Business & Enterprise College	Abbey Rd, Whitley, Coventry, West Midlands CV3 4BD	024 7630 2580	024 7663 9352	Mrs L. Allen	331-4044	CY	11–18	715	
The Woodlands School	Broad La., Coventry, West Midlands CV5 7FF	024 7646 2634	024 7646 7190	Mr Neil Charlton	331-4027	CY	11–18	1011	B
Woodway Park School and Community College	Wigston Rd, Coventry, West Midlands CV2 2RH	024 7661 6155	024 7660 2398	Mr Steve Allen	331-4035	CY	11–18	743	

Dudley

School name	Address	Tel	Fax	Headteacher	Ref	Type	Ages	Pupils	Other
Bishop Milner RC School	Burton Rd, Dudley, West Midlands DY1 3BY	01384 816600	01384 816601	Mr D.A. Fagan	332-4800	VA	11–18	717	RC
Castle High School and Visual Arts College	St James's Rd, Dudley, West Midlands DY1 3JE	01384 816045	01384 816046	Mr T. Johnson	332-4612	VA	11–16	1055	
The Coseley School	Henne Dr, Coseley, Bilston, West Midlands WV14 9JW	01384 816565	01384 816566	Mrs Amanda Elwiss	332-4027	CY	11–16	949	
Cradley High School	Homer Hill, Halesowen, West Midlands B63 2UP	01384 816465	01384 816466	Ms T. Fowler	332-4114	CY	11–16	606	
The Crestwood School	Bromley La., Kingswinford, West Midlands DY6 8QG	01384 816535	01384 816540	Mr D. Francis	332-4025	CY	11–16	750	
The Dormston School	Mill Bank, Sedgley, Dudley, West Midlands DY3 1SN	01384 816395	01384 816396	Ms S.J. Sherwood	332-4023	CY	11–16	1123	
The Earls High School	Furnace La., Halesowen, West Midlands B63 3SL	01384 816105	01384 816106	Mr Thomas Johnston	332-4106	FD	11–16	1154	
The Ellowes Hall School Specialist Sports College	Stickley La., Lower Gornal, Dudley, West Midlands DY3 2JH	01384 817915	01902 880367	Mr Andrew Griffiths	332-5401	FD	11–18	1030	
The High Arcal School	High Arcal Dr, Sedgley, Dudley, West Midlands DY3 1BP	01902 838038	01902 838039	Mrs Joanna Mary Manson	332-5403	FD	11–16	1197	
The Hillcrest School and Community College	Simms La., Netherton, Dudley, West Midlands DY2 0PB	01384 816500	01384 816501	Dame Maureen Brennan	332-4117	CY	11–16	885	
Holly Hall Maths and Computing College	Scotts Green Cl, Russells Hall Est, Dudley, West Midlands DY1 2DU	01384 253722	01384 456705	Mr Graham Lloyd	332-5405	FD	11–16	678	
The Kingswinford School a Science College	Water St, Kingswinford, West Midlands DY6 7AD	01384 296596	01384 401098	Mr Peter Limb	332-5402	FD	11–16	923	
Leasowes Community College	Kent Rd, Halesowen, West Midlands B62 8PJ	01384 816285	01384 816286	Mr J. Howells	332-4110	FD	11–16	1144	
Old Swinford Hospital	Heath La., Stourbridge, West Midlands DY8 1QX	01384 817300	01384 441686	Mr Melvyn Roffe	332-5400	VA	11–18	605	CE B R
Pedmore Technology College and Community School	Grange La., Pedmore, Stourbridge, West Midlands DY9 7HS	01384 816660	01384 816660	Mr D. Kemp	332-4105	CY	11–16	771	
Pensnett High School	Tiled House La., Brierley Hill, West Midlands DY5 4LN	01384 816435	01384 816436	Dr Susan Bains	332-4118	CY	11–16	537	
Redhill School and Specialist Language College	Junction Rd, Stourbridge, West Midlands DY8 1JX	01384 816355	01384 816356	Mr Brian Heavisides	332-4119	CY	11–16	1160	
Ridgewood High School	Park Rd West, Wollaston, Stourbridge, West Midlands DY8 3NQ	01384 818445	01384 818446	Mr C. Nutting	332-4121	CY	11–16	904	
The Summerhill School	Lodge La., Kingswinford, West Midlands DY6 9XE	01384 816165	01384 816166	Mr Ben Warren	332-4020	CY	11–16	1013	
Thorns Community College	Stockwell Ave, Brierley Hill, West Midlands DY5 2NU	01384 816225	01384 816226	Mr David Mountney	332-4018	CY	11–16	1349	
Windsor High School	Richmond St, Halesowen, West Midlands B63 4BB	0121 550 1452	0121 585 0610	Mr K. Sorrell	332-5404	FD	11–16	1353	
The Wordsley School	Brierley Hill Rd, Wordsley, Stourbridge, West Midlands DY8 5SP	01384 816015	01384 482325	Mr Mike Lambert	332-4030	CY	11–16	696	

Herefordshire

School name	Address	Tel	Fax	Headteacher	Ref	Type	Ages	Pupils	Other
Aylestone High School	Broadlands Hse, Broadlands La., Hereford, Herefordshire HR1 1HY	01432 357371	01432 263925	Mr Steve Byatt	884-4015	CY	11-16	1135	
The Bishop of Hereford's Bluecoat School	Hampton Dene Rd, Tupsley, Hereford, Herefordshire HR1 1UU	01432 347500	01432 278220	Mrs Sara Catlow-Hawkins	884-4600	VA	11-16	1185	CE
Fairfield High School	Peterchurch, Hereford, Herefordshire HR2 0SG	01981 550231	01981 550171	Mr C. Barker	884-4032	CY	11-16	359	
John Kyrle High School and Sixth Form Centre	Ledbury Rd, Ross-on-Wye, Herefordshire HR9 7ET	01989 764358	01989 565766	Mr Nigel Griffiths	884-4428	CY	11-18	1124	
John Masefield High School	Mabels Furlong, Ledbury, Herefordshire HR8 2HF	01531 631012	01531 631433	Mr Andrew Evans	884-4058	CY	11-18	948	
Kingstone High School	Kingstone, Hereford, Herefordshire HR2 9HJ	01981 250224	01981 251132	Mr Robert Ridout	884-4021	CY	11-16	679	
Lady Hawkins High School	Park View, Kington, Herefordshire HR5 3AR	01544 230441	01544 230978	Mr Jonathan Barry	884-4022	CY	11-18	465	
The Minster College	South St, Leominster, Herefordshire HR6 8JJ	01568 613221	01568 613622	Mr Richard North	884-4027	CY	11-18	697	
Queen Elizabeth High School	Ashfields, Bromyard, Herefordshire HR7 4QS	01885 482230	01885 483935	Mr Adrian Long	884-4004	CY	11-16	332	
St Mary's RC High School 'A Specialist Science College'	Lugwardine, Hereford, Herefordshire HR1 4DR	01432 850416	01432 851728	Mr Clive Lambert	884-4601	VA	11-16	697	RC
Weobley High School	Burton Wood, Weobley, Hereford, Herefordshire HR4 8ST	01544 318159	01544 318040	Mrs Susan Woodrow	884-4045	CY	11-16	426	
Whitecross Hereford; High School and Specialist Sports College	Three Elms Rd, Hereford, Herefordshire HR4 0RN	01432 359151	01432 350219	Ms Denise Strutt	884-4014	CY	11-16	897	
Wigmore High School	Ford St, Wigmore, Leominster, Herefordshire HR6 9UW	01568 770323	01568 770917	Mr Andrew Shaw	884-4046	CY	11-16	445	
Wyebridge Sports College	Stanberrow Rd, Redhill, Hereford, Herefordshire HR2 7NG	01432 355213	01432 278216	Mr John Sheppard	884-4011	CY	11-16	740	

Sandwell

School name	Address	Tel	Fax	Headteacher	Ref	Type	Ages	Pupils	Other
Alexandra High School and Sixth Form Centre	Alexandra Rd, Tipton, West Midlands DY4 7NR	0121 557 4146	0121 522 2264	Mr I. Binnie	333-4025	CY	11-18	1379	
Bristnall Hall Technology College	Bristnall Hall La., Oldbury, West Midlands B68 9PA	0121 552 5425	0121 511 1325	Mr Steven Venross	333-4129	CY	11-16	940	
Dartmouth High School	Wilderness La., Gt Barr, Birmingham, West Midlands B43 7SD	0121 358 6186	0121 358 5967	Mrs C.J. Badyal	333-4012	CY	11-18	1036	
George Salter Collegiate Academy	Claypit La. West Bromwich B70 9UW	0121 553 4665	0121 558 8377	Mr M Green	333-6907		11-19		
George Salter High School	Claypit La., West Bromwich, West Midlands B70 9UW	0121 553 4665	0121 525 5082	Mr Phillip Clayton	333-4026	FD	11-16	916	
The Heathfield Foundation Technology College	Wrights La., Cradley Heath, West Midlands B64 6QU	01384 566598	01384 638471	Mr John Parker	333-5401	FD	11-18	1874	
Holly Lodge High School College of Science	Holly La., Smethwick, West Midlands B67 7JG	0121 558 0691	0121 558 6136	Mr J. Souter	333-4138	CY	11-16	1326	
Manor High School (Foundation)	Friar Park Rd, Wednesbury, West Midlands WS10 0JS	0121 556 2858	0121 505 3150	Ms Miriam Mole	333-5400	FD	11-18	690	
Menzies High School	Clarkes La. West Bromwich, West Midlands B71 2BX	0121 588 8384	0121 567 5284	Mr Glen Goddard	333-4010	CY	11-18	1520	
Midland Oak School	Bloomfield Rd, Tipton, West Midlands DY4 9AH	0121 520 3497	0121 520 3499	Mr Daryl Edgar	333-6002		11-16	6	
Oldbury College of Sport	Pound Rd, Oldbury, West Midlands B68 8NE	0121 544 7521	0121 552 1517	Mr J. Martin	333-4111	CY	11-16	1686	
Perryfields High School	Oldacre Rd, Oldbury, West Midlands B68 0RG	0121 421 7979	0121 421 5718	Mr D.J. Meredith	333-4111	CY	11-16	954	
Rathbone Choices	First Floor Rowley Business Pk, Tipton, West Midlands DY4 8AH	0121 522 6990	0121 522 6991	Mr Steve Peters	333-6001		14-16	10	
St Michael's CE High School	Throne Rd, Rowley Regis, West Midlands B65 9LD	0121 559 5224	0121 559 4203	Mr R.V. Worthington	333-4500	VC	11-16	987	CE
Sandwell Academy	Halfords La., West Bromwich, West Midlands B71 4LF	0121 525 1700	0121 553 4300	Mr S. Topper	333-6905		11-18	340	
Shireland Collegiate Academy	Waterloo Rd, Smethwick B66 4ND	0121 558 8086	0121 558 8377	Mr M. Grundy	333-6906		11-19		
Shireland Language College	Waterloo Rd, Smethwick, West Midlands B66 4ND	0121 558 8086	0121 558 8377	Mr M. Grundy	333-4117	FD	11-19	1034	
Stuart Bathurst RC High School College of Performing Arts	Wood Green Rd, Wednesbury, West Midlands WS10 9QS	0121 556 1488	0121 556 3985	Mr A.S. Billings	333-4600	VA	11-18	778	RC
Tividale Community Arts College	Lower City Rd, Tividale, Oldbury, West Midlands B69 2HE	0121 552 5501	0121 511 1326	Mr G. Black	333-4120	CY	11-18	967	
Willingsworth High School	Bilston Rd, Gospel Oak, Tipton, West Midlands DY4 0BZ	0121 556 1351	0121 502 0038	Mr P.S. Spoerer	333-4027	CY	11-16	1072	

School name	Address	Tel	Fax	Headteacher	Ref	Type	Ages	Pupils	Other
Wodensborough Community Technology College	Hydes Rd, Wednesbury, West Midlands WS10 0DR	0121 556 4951	0121 556 0134	Mr Ken Ellis	333-4023	CY	11–18	1073	
Wood Green High School College of Sport, Maths and Computing	Wood Green Rd, Wednesbury, West Midlands WS10 9QU	0121 556 4131	0121 506 4609	Mr Pank Patel	333-4024	CY	11–18	1444	

Shropshire

School name	Address	Tel	Fax	Headteacher	Ref	Type	Ages	Pupils	Other
Belvidere School	Crowmere Rd, Shrewsbury, Shropshire SY2 5LA	01743 235073	01743 234090	Mr M. Bamford	893-4396	CY	11–16	815	
Bridgnorth Endowed School	Northgate, Bridgnorth, Shropshire WV16 4ER	01746 762103	01746 768340	Mrs P.M. Chapman	893-4500	VC	11–18	1027	
Church Stretton School	Shrewsbury Rd, Church Stretton, Shropshire SY6 6EX	01694 722209	01694 722417	Mr John Allin	893-4385	CY	11–16	740	
The Community College, Bishop's Castle	Brampton Rd, Bishops Castle, Shropshire SY9 5AY	01588 638257	01588 630034	Mr T.W. Hunt	893-4376	CY	11–18	583	
The Corbet School	Eyton La, Baschurch, Shrewsbury, Shropshire SY4 2AX	01939 260296	01939 262009	Mr R.J. Thompson	893-5401	FD	11–16	721	
The Grange School	Worcester La, Harlescott Grange, Shrewsbury, Shropshire SY1 3LP	01743 445493	01743 243712	Mrs J.M. Thomas	893-4418	CY	11–16	500	
The Grove School	Newcastle Rd, Market Drayton, Shropshire TF9 1HF	01630 652121	01630 658980	Ms Jane Radbourne	893-4423	CY	11–18	1033	
Idsall School	Coppice Green La, Shifnal, Shropshire TF11 8PD	01952 468400	01952 463052	Mr D. Gibbons	893-4394	CY	11–18	1248	
The Lacon Childe School	Love La, Cleobury Mortimer, Kidderminster, Worcestershire DY14 8PE	01299 270312	01299 271037	Mr Allan Gilhooley	893-4412	CY	11–16	557	
The Lakelands School and Sports College	Oswestry Rd, Ellesmere, Shropshire SY12 0EA	01691 622543	01691 623834	Mr I. Sanders	893-4387	CY	11–16	560	
Ludlow CE School	Bromfield Rd, Burway, Ludlow, Shropshire SY8 1GJ	01584 872691	01584 877708	Mr Philip Poulton	893-4501	VC	11–16	798	CE
The Marches School and Technology College	Morda Rd, Oswestry, Shropshire SY11 2AR	01691 664400	01691 671515	Mr Graham Davies	893-4437	CY	11–16	1299	
The Mary Webb School and Science College	Pontesbury, Shrewsbury, Shropshire SY5 0TG	01743 792100	01743 790890	Mrs J. Brown	893-4410	CY	11–16	602	
Meole Brace School Science College	Longden Rd, Shrewsbury, Shropshire SY3 9DW	01743 235961	01743 364017	Mrs Hilary Burke	893-4403	CY	11–16	1056	
Oldbury Wells School	Oldbury Wells, Bridgnorth, Shropshire WV16 5JD	01746 765454	01746 762746	Mrs S. Godden	893-4427	CY	11–18	907	
The Priory School	Longden Rd, Shrewsbury, Shropshire SY3 9EE	01743 284000	01743 360658 284001	Ms Candy Garbett	893-4368	CY	11–16	805	
Rhyn Park School	St Martins, Oswestry, Shropshire SY10 7BD	01691 776500	01691 776501	Mr Richard Hedge	893-4406	CY	11–16	480	
Sir John Talbot's Technology College	Tilstock Rd, Whitchurch, Shropshire SY13 2BY	01948 660600	01948 660610	Mrs M. Roddy	893-4502	VC	11–18	686	
Sundorne School and Sports College	Corndon Cres, Sundorne, Shrewsbury, Shropshire SY1 4LL	01743 276700	01743 461335	Mr Michael Dunning	893-4395	CY	11–16	462	
The Thomas Adams School, Wem	Lowe Hill, Wem, Shrewsbury, Shropshire SY4 5UB	01939 237000	01939 237020	Mr Neil Hemming	893-4503	VC	11–18	1322	R
The Wakeman School	Abbey Foregate, Shrewsbury, Shropshire SY2 6AA	01743 365771	01743 266838	Mrs Karen Moore	893-4374	CY	11–16	586	
William Brookes School	Farley Rd, Much Wenlock, Shropshire TF13 6NB	01952 727606	01952 728289	Mrs P.A. Cooper	893-4391	CY	11–16	933	

Solihull

School name	Address	Tel	Fax	Headteacher	Ref	Type	Ages	Pupils	Other
Alderbrook School and Arts College	Blossomfield Rd, Solihull, West Midlands B91 1SN	0121 704 2146	0121 711 4123	Mr W. Sedgwick	334-4015	CY	11–16	1277	
The Archbishop Grimshaw RC School	Kew Cl, Chelmsley Wood, Birmingham, West Midlands B37 6NY	0121 770 5331	0121 770 0055	Mr M. Corrigan	334-4660	VA	11–18	1115	RC
Arden School	Station Rd, Knowle, Solihull, West Midlands B93 0PT	01564 773348	01564 771784	Mrs Ann Green	334-4017	CY	11–16	1221	
The City Technology College	PO Box 1017, Cooks La, Kingshurst, Birmingham, West Midlands B37 6NZ	0121 329 8300	0121 770 0879	Miss Ann Jones	334-6900		10–19	1546	
Grace Academy	Chapelhouse La, Chelmsey Wood, Birmingham B37 5JS	0121 329 4600	0121 329 4605	Mr David Wootton	334-6905		11–18	1138	
Heart of England School	Gipsy La, Balsall Common, Coventry, West Midlands CV7 7FW	01676 535222	01676 534282	Mrs Annette Croft	334-4030	CY	11–18	1308	
Langley School	Kineton Green Rd, Olton, Solihull, West Midlands B92 7ER	0121 706 9771	0121 706 8715	Mrs Valerie Duffy-Cross	334-4012	CY	11–16	955	
Light Hall School	Hathaway Rd, Shirley, Solihull, West Midlands B90 2PZ	0121 744 3835	0121 733 6148	Mr V. Scutt	334-4018	CY	11–16	1225	
Lode Heath School and Sports College	Lode La, Solihull, West Midlands B91 2HW	0121 704 1421	0121 711 2663	Mr John Burton	334-4019	CY	11–16	997	

3

School name	Address	Tel	Fax	Headteacher	Ref	Type	Ages	Pupils	Other
Lyndon School Humanities College	Daylesford Rd, Solihull, West Midlands B92 8EJ	0121 743 3402	0121 742 6138	Mrs Selina Westwood	334-4020	CY	11–16	1262	
Park Hall School	Water Orton Rd, Castle Bromwich, Birmingham, West Midlands B36 9HF	0121 748 2121	0121 730 1085	Mr N.B. Craven	334-4031	CY	11–18	1293	
St Peter's RC School and Specialist Science College	Whitefields Rd, Solihull, West Midlands B91 3NZ	0121 705 3988	0121 705 9803	Mrs F.M. McGarry	334-4650	VA	11–18	1241	RC
Smith's Wood Sports College	Windward Way, Kingshurst, Birmingham, West Midlands B36 0UE	0121 770 6811	0121 788 2881	Mr R. Hawkins	334-4034	CY	11–16	1032	
Tudor Grange School	Dingle La., Solihull, West Midlands B91 3PD	0121 705 5100	0121 709 0455	Mrs J.A. Bexon-Smith	334-4014	CY	11–16	1259	

Staffordshire

School name	Address	Tel	Fax	Headteacher	Ref	Type	Ages	Pupils	Other
Abbot Beyne School	Linnell Bldg, Osborne St, Burton-on-Trent, Staffordshire DE15 0JL	01283 239835	01283 239852	Mrs Christine Thompson	860-4500	VC	11–18	1030	
Alleyne's High School	Oulton Rd, Stone, Staffordshire ST15 8DT	01785 354200	01785 354222	Mrs Catherine Ann Spears	860-4112	CY	13–18	996	
Belgrave High School	Birds Bush Rd, Belgrave, Tamworth, Staffordshire B77 2NE	01827 285596	01827 261924	Mr S. Turney	860-4156	CY	11–18	1036	
Biddulph High School	Conway Rd, Knypersley, Biddulph, Staffordshire ST8 7AR	01782 523977	01782 519188	Mr Stephen Collier	860-4143	CY	13–18	857	
Blake Valley Technology College	Marston Rd, Hednesford, Cannock, Staffordshire WS12 4JH	01543 512415	01543 512441	Mr John Williams	860-4071	CY	11–18	742	
Blessed William Howard RC School	Rowley Ave, Stafford, Staffordshire ST17 9AB	01785 244236		Mr Philip Smith	860-4607	VA	11–18	1036	RC
Blythe Bridge High School	Cheadle Rd, Blythe Bridge, Stoke-on-Trent, Staffordshire ST11 9PW	01782 392519	01782 388261	Mrs Shan Schanda	860-4067	CY	11–18	1027	
Cannock Chase High School	Hednesford Rd, Cannock, Staffordshire WS11 1JT	01543 502240	01543 577528	Mr N. Hooper	860-5401	FD	11–18	1658	
Cardinal Griffin RC High School	Stafford Rd, Cannock, Staffordshire WS11 4AW	01543 502215	01543 574929	Mr Michael Burrowes	860-5403	VA	11–18	938	RC
Chase Terrace Technology College	Bridge Cross Rd, Chase Terr., Burntwood, Staffordshire WS7 2DB	01543 682286	01543 673337	Mrs Heather Bowman	860-4178	CY	11–18	1334	
Chasetown Specialist Sports College	Pool Rd, Burntwood, Staffordshire WS7 3QW	01543 685828	01543 677485	Mrs P.E. Slusar	860-5404	FD	11–18	865	
Cheadle High School	Station Rd, Cheadle, Stoke-on-Trent, Staffordshire ST10 1LH	01538 483900	01538 483920	Mr Mike Webber	860-4153	CY	11–18	873	
Cheslyn Hay Sport and Community High School	Saredon Rd, Cheslyn Hay, Walsall, West Midlands WS6 7JQ	01922 416024	01922 414411	Mr John Martin	860-4140	CY	11–18	1391	
Chesterton Community High School	Castle St, Chesterton, Newcastle, Staffordshire ST5 7LP	01782 296500	01782 561978	Mrs Lynn Jackson	860-4093	CY	11–16	478	
Clayton Hall Business and Language College	Clayton La., Clayton, Newcastle under Lyme, Staffordshire ST5 3DN	01782 297570	01782 297569	Mr M. Heuston	860-4094	CY	11–16	948	
Clough Hall Technology School	First Ave, Kidsgrove, Stoke-on-Trent, Staffordshire ST7 1DP	01782 783281	01782 771403	Mr Ian Richardson Tait	860-4082	CY	11–18	883	
Codsall Community High School	Elliotts La, Codsall, Codsall, Staffordshire WV8 1PQ	01902 434200	01902 434242	Mrs Marjorie Tunnicliffe	860-4075	CY	13–18	1187	
De Ferrers Specialist Technology College	St Mary's Dr, Burton-on-Trent, Staffordshire DE13 0LL	01283 239936	01283 239950	Mr Michael York	860-4176	CY	11–18	1941	
Edgecliff High School	Enville Rd, Kinver, Stourbridge, West Midlands DY7 6AA	01384 551000	01384 873784	Dr Stuart Jones	860-4083	CY	11–18	629	
Endon High School	Leek Rd, Endon, Stoke-on-Trent, Staffordshire ST9 9EE	01782 502240	01782 502473	Mrs Lynne Spedding	860-4077	CY	11–16	723	
Fair Oak Business and Enterprise College	Penkridge Bank Rd, Rugeley, Staffordshire WS15 2UE	01889 802440	01889 578761	Mr Mark Sutton	860-4171	CY	11–18	1022	
The Friary School	Eastern Ave, Lichfield, Staffordshire WS13 7EW	01543 510631	01543 510634	Mr John M Brough	860-4126	CY	11–18	1308	
Great Wyrley High School	Hall La., Gt Wyrley, Walsall, West Midlands WS6 6LQ	01922 857030	01922 857066	Mr Chris Leach	860-4079	CY	11–18	1099	
Hagley Park Sports College	Burnthill La., Rugeley, Staffordshire WS15 2HZ	01889 256050	01889 256073	Mr John Hall	860-4172	CY	11–18	889	
John Taylor High School	Dunstall Rd, Barton-under-Needwood, Burton-on-Trent, Staffordshire DE13 8AZ	01283 239300	01283 239333	Mr D.M. Osborne-Town	860-4061	CY	11–18	1437	
King Edward VI High School	Westway, Stafford, Staffordshire ST17 9YJ	01785 258546	01785 224231	Mr Colin Elstone	860-4181	CY	11–18	909	
King Edward VI School	Upper St John St, Lichfield, Staffordshire WS14 9EE	01543 255714	01543 418118	Mr K W Maycock	860-4090	CY	11–18	1388	
Kingsmead Technology College	Kings Ave, Littleworth, Hednesford, Cannock, Staffordshire WS12 1DH	01543 512455	01543 512481	Mr Christopher Hilton	860-4070	CY	11–18	1303	
Leek High Specialist Technology School	Springfield Rd, Leek, Staffordshire ST13 6EU	01538 483036	01538 483052	Ms J. Samuel	860-4085	CY	13–18	473	
Madeley High School	Newcastle Rd, Madeley, Crewe CW3 9JJ	01782 297200	01782 297222	Mr Eddie Wilkes	860-4090	CY	11–16	672	
Maryhill High School	Gloucester Rd, Kidsgrove, Stoke-on-Trent, Staffordshire ST7 4DL	01782 296751	01782 296771	Dr Alan Jones	860-4084	CY	11–18	829	
Moorside High School	Cellarhead Rd, Werrington, Stoke-on-Trent, Staffordshire ST9 0HP	08444 778985	01782 550265	Dr Mazda Jenkin	860-4072	CY	11–18	745	

3

School name	Address	Tel	Fax	Headteacher	Ref	Type	Ages	Pupils	Other
Nether Stowe High School	St Chad's Rd, Lichfield, Staffordshire WS13 7NB	01543 263446	01543 414602	Mr B. Cooper	860-4089	CY	11-18	856	
Newcastle Community High School	Ostend Pl, Newcastle, Staffordshire ST5 2QY	01782 667650	01782 297435	Mr Neil Hutchinson	860-4096	CY	11-16	486	
Norton Canes High School	Burntwood Rd, Norton Canes, Cannock, Staffordshire WS11 9SP	01543 514400	01543 514430	Mr Paul Fell	860-4066	CY	11-18	603	
Ounsdale High School	Ounsdale Rd, Wombourne, Wolverhampton, West Midlands WV5 8BJ	01902 892178	01902 892070	Mr P. Jordan	860-4122	CY	11-18	1203	
Paget High School, Business and Enterprise College	Burton Rd, Branston, Burton-on-Trent, Staffordshire DE14 3DR	01283 239000	01283 239019	Mr D.I. Smith	860-4055	CY	11-18	980	
Painsley RC College	Station Rd, Cheadle, Stoke-on-Trent, Staffordshire ST10 1LH	01538 483944	01538 483962	Mr F.R. Tunney	860-4610	VA	11-18	1116	RC
Paulet High School	Violet Way, Stapenhill, Burton upon Trent, Staffordshire DE15 9RT	01283 239710	01283 239735	Mr Alexander Timms	860-4051	CY	11-18	696	
Queen Elizabeth's Mercian School	Ashby Rd, Tamworth, Staffordshire B79 8AH	01827 62241	01827 66712	Mr Kevin Debney	860-4115	CY	11-18	1099	
Rawlett Community Sports College	Comberford Rd, Tamworth, Staffordshire B79 9AA	01827 57178	01827 68423	Mr John Brodie	860-4158	CY	11-18	1119	
Robert Sutton RC School	Bluestone La, Stapenhill, Burton-on-Trent, Staffordshire DE15 9SD	01283 239181	01283 239196	Mr T. Downey	860-4710	VA	11-18	705	RC
St John Fisher RC High School	Ashfields New Rd, Newcastle, Staffordshire ST5 2SJ	01782 615636	01782 717391	Ms F. Hegarty	860-4713	VA	11-18	979	RC
Sir Graham Balfour High School	North Ave, Stafford, Staffordshire ST16 1NR	01785 223490	01785 250145	Mr David Wright	860-4180	CY	11-18	944	
Sir Thomas Boughey High School	Station Rd, Halmer End, Stoke-on-Trent, Staffordshire ST7 8AP	01782 296600	01782 722761	Mr D. Boston	860-4060	CY	11-16	730	
Stafford Sports College	Wolverhampton Rd, Stafford, Staffordshire ST17 9DJ	01785 258383	01785 225913	Dr Rowena Blencowe	860-5402	FD	11-18	495	
Thomas Alleyne's High School	Dove Bank, Uttoxeter, Staffordshire ST14 8DU	01889 561820	01889 561850	Mr P.K. Mitchell	860-4146	CY	13-18	1401	
Walton High School	The Rise, Walton-on-the-Hill, Stafford, Staffordshire ST17 0LJ	01785 356300	01785 356339	Mrs S.J. Kirkham	860-4111	CY	11-18	1306	
Weston Road High School	Blackheath La, Stafford, Staffordshire ST18 0YG	01785 356700	01785 356727	Dr Greg Taylor	860-4183	CY	11-18	970	
Westwood College	Westwood Pk, Leek, Staffordshire ST13 8NP	01538 370930	01538 370932	Mr Keith Hollins	860-4086	CY	13-18	948	
Wilnecote High School	Tinkers Green Rd, Wilnecote, Tamworth, Staffordshire B77 5LF	01827 475111	01827 475114	Mr S. Tonks	860-4123	CY	11-18	1294	
Wolgarston High School	Cannock Rd, Penkridge, Stafford, Staffordshire ST19 5RX	01785 355500	01785 716121	Mr Philip Tapp	860-4100	CY	13-18	828	
Wolstanton High School	Milehouse La, Newcastle, Staffordshire ST5 9JU	01782 297725	01782 297757	Dr Charles Freeman	860-4098	CY	11-16	1110	
Woodhouse High School	Highfield Ave, Amington, Tamworth, Staffordshire B77 3JB	01827 475620	01827 475636	Mr Neil Hemmings	860-4124	CY	11-18	1153	

Stoke-on-Trent

School name	Address	Tel	Fax	Headteacher	Ref	Type	Ages	Pupils	Other
Berry Hill High School and Sports College	Arbourfield Dr, Bucknall, Stoke-on-Trent, Staffordshire ST2 9LR	01782 235235	01782 234949	Ms Ruth Poppleton	861-4041	CY	11-16	745	
Birches Head High School	Birches Head Rd, Hanley, Stoke-on-Trent, Staffordshire ST2 8DD	01782 233595	01782 236647	Ms Karen Ann Healey	861-4046	CY	11-16	781	
Blurton High School	Beaconsfield Dr, Blurton, Stoke-on-Trent, Staffordshire ST3 3JD	01782 234004	01782 234008	Mr Richard Balukiewicz	861-4037	CY	11-16	847	
Brownhills Maths and Computing College	Brownhills Rd, Tunstall, Stoke-on-Trent, Staffordshire ST6 4LD	01782 837508	01782 834637	Mr Andrew Stanier	861-4028	CY	11-16	732	
Edensor Technology College	Greendock St, Longton, Stoke-on-Trent, Staffordshire ST3 2NA	01782 233933	01782 233926	Mr Richrd Mercer	861-4023	CY	11-16	1034	
Haywood High School and Engineering College	High La, Burslem, Stoke-on-Trent, Staffordshire ST6 7AB	01782 853535	01782 853537	Mr D. Dickinson	861-4173	FD	11-16	1070	
Holden Lane High School Specialist Sports College	Milton Rd, Sneyd Grn, Stoke-on-Trent, Staffordshire ST1 6LG	01782 234449	01782 208351	Mrs J. Lewis	861-4038	CY	11-16	1081	
James Brindley High School	St Michael's Rd, Tunstall, Stoke-on-Trent, Staffordshire ST6 6JT	01782 235785	01782 235788	Mr C.S. Rigby	861-4184	CY	11-16	729	
Longton High School	Box La, Meir, Stoke-on-Trent, Staffordshire ST3 5PR	01782 599232	01782 598041	Mrs Jan Webber	861-4040	CY	11-16	569	
Mitchell High School	Corneville Rd, Bucknall, Stoke-on-Trent, Staffordshire ST2 9EY	01782 233633	01782 233638	Ms Deborah Sanderson	861-4185	CY	11-16	587	
St Joseph's College	London Rd, Trent Vale, Stoke-on-Trent, Staffordshire ST4 5NT	01782 848008	01782 745487	Ms Roisin Maguire	861-5901	VA	11-18	925	RC
St Margaret Ward RC School and Arts College	Little Chell La, Tunstall, Stoke-on-Trent, Staffordshire ST6 6LZ	01782 234477	01782 577157	Mr C. Smith	861-4711	VA	11-18	888	RC
St Peter's CE High School and International Language College	Queen's Rd, Penkhull, Stoke-on-Trent, Staffordshire ST4 7LG	01782 233600	01782 233602	Mr Christopher Wright	861-4603	VA	11-16	796	CE
St Thomas More RC College	Longton Hall Rd, Longton, Stoke-on-Trent, Staffordshire ST3 2NJ	01782 234734	01782 598946	Mr Nick Finnigan	861-5400	VA	11-18	1055	RC
Sandon High School	Sandon Rd, Meir, Stoke-on-Trent, Staffordshire ST3 7DF	01782 312782	01782 598197	Miss Barbara Hall	861-4044	CY	11-16	748	

School name	Address	Headteacher	Tel	Fax	Ref	Type	Ages	Pupils	Other
Thistley Hough High School	Newcastle La, Penkhull, Stoke-on-Trent, Staffordshire ST4 5JJ	Mr Robert Haines	01782 418500	01782 418501	861-4175	CY	11–16	899	
Trentham High School	Allerton Rd, Trentham, Stoke-on-Trent, Staffordshire ST4 8PQ	Mrs S. Chesterton	01782 234534	01782 234537	861-4042	CY	11–16	654	

Telford and Wrekin

School name	Address	Headteacher	Tel	Fax	Ref	Type	Ages	Pupils	Other
Abraham Darby Specialist School for Performing Arts	Hill Top, Madeley, Telford, Shropshire TF7 5HX	Miss C. Brown	01952 386000	01952 433002	894-5403	FD	11–16	889	
Adams' Grammar School	High St, Newport, Shropshire TF10 7BD	Mr Jim Richardson	01952 386300	01952 812696	894-5400	VA	11–18	791	B R
Blessed Robert Johnson RC College	Whitchurch Rd, Wellington, Telford, Shropshire TF1 3DY	Mr Robert Hall	01952 386100	01952 417501	894-5405	VA	11–18	765	RC
The Burton Borough School	Audley Ave, Newport, Shropshire TF10 7DS	Mrs U. Vandenburg	01952 387000	01952 417552	894-4405	CY	11–16	1110	
Charlton School	Severn Dr, Dothill, Wellington, Telford, Shropshire TF1 3LE	Mrs Gwen Kelsey	01952 386800	01952 386805	894-5404	FD	11–16	1169	
Ercall Wood Technology College	Golf Links La, Wellington, Telford, Shropshire TF1 2DT	Mrs Kathryn Owen-Reece	01952 387300	01952 387301	894-5402	FD	11–16	841	
Hadley Learning Community – Secondary Phase	Waterloo Rd, Hadley, Telford, Shropshire TF1 5NU	Mr Paul Topping	01952 387000		894-4439	CY	11–16	1056	
The Lord Silkin School	District Centre, Stirchley, Telford, Shropshire TF3 1FA	Mr John Sullivan	01952 387400	01952 387444	894-4425	CY	11–16	689	
Madeley Court School	Court St, Madeley, Telford, Shropshire TF7 5DZ	Mr Vic Maher	01952 680306	01952 582012	894-4424	CY	11–16	623	
Newport Girls' High School	Wellington Rd, Newport, Shropshire TF10 7HL	Mrs Edwina Gleeson	01952 386400	01952 820054	894-4364	CY	11–18	361	G
The Phoenix School	Manor Rd, Dawley, Telford, Shropshire TF4 3DZ	Mr Neil Stonehouse	01952 386700	01952 595145	894-4408	CY	11–16	918	
The Sutherland School	Gibbons Rd, Trench, Telford, Shropshire TF2 7JR	Mr Stephen Wall	01952 387800	01952 605864	894-4438	CY	11–16	605	R
Thomas Telford School	Old Park, Telford, Shropshire TF3 4NW	Sir Kevin Satchwell	01952 200000	01952 293294	894-6900		11–18	1177	
Wrockwardine Wood Arts College	New Rd, Wrockwardine Wood, Telford, Shropshire TF2 6JZ	Mr Richard Williiams	01952 388300	01952 388301	894-4401	CY	11–16	971	

Walsall

School name	Address	Headteacher	Tel	Fax	Ref	Type	Ages	Pupils	Other
Aldridge School – A Science College	Tynings La, Aldridge, Walsall, West Midlands WS9 0BG	Mr Anthony Harrison	01922 743988	01922 740119	335-5405	FD	11–18	1451	
Alumwell Business and Enterprise College	Primley Ave, Walsall, West Midlands WS2 9UA	Miss S. Bradford	01922 720741	01922 641508	335-4017	CY	11–18	933	
Barr Beacon Language College	Old Hall La, Aldridge, Walsall, West Midlands WS9 0RF	Dame Maureen Brennan	0121 366 6600	0121 366 6876	335-5406	FD	11–18	1378	B
Blue Coat CE Comprehensive School A Performing Arts Specialist College	Birmingham St, Walsall, West Midlands WS1 2ND	Mr Ken Yeates	01922 720558	01922 632326	335-4602	VA	11–18	1019	CE
Brownhills Community Technology College	Deakin Ave, Brownhills, Walsall, West Midlands WS8 7QG	Miss Helen Keenan	01543 452886	01543 370105	335-4057	CY	11–18	928	
Darlaston Community Science College	Herberts Park Rd, Darlaston, Wednesbury, West Midlands WS10 8QJ	Mr Stephen Casey	0121 568 6767	0121 568 6607	335-4100	CY	11–18	1090	
Frank F Harrison Community School	Leamore La, Bloxwich, Walsall, West Midlands WS2 7NR	Mr Martin Cain	01922 710257	01922 473134	335-4016	CY	11–18	847	
Joseph Leckie Community Technology College	Walstead Rd West, Walsall, West Midlands WS5 4PG	Mr Keith Whittlestone	01922 721071	01922 641497	335-4007	CY	11–18	1220	
Pool Hayes Community School	Castle Dr, Willenhall, West Midlands WV12 4QZ	Mr Jim Clarke	01902 368147	01902 609501	335-4106	CY	11–18	1142	
Queen Mary's Grammar School	Sutton Rd, Walsall, West Midlands WS1 2PG	Mr S.G. Holtam	01922 720696	01922 725932	335-5404	VA	11–18	691	B
Queen Mary's High School	Upper Forster St, Walsall, West Midlands WS4 2AE	Mrs Diana Woods	01922 721013	01922 32387	335-5403	VA	11–18	709	G
St Francis of Assisi RC Technology College	Erdington Rd, Aldridge, Walsall, West Midlands WS9 0RN	Mrs Philomena Mullins	01922 743696	01922 454362	335-4606	VA	11–18	1077	RC
St Thomas More RC School, Willenhall	Darlaston La, Bilston, West Midlands WV14 7BL	Mr Sean Flynn	01902 368798	01902 630380	335-5401	VA	11–18	1443	RC
Shelfield Sports and Community College	Broad Way, High Heath, Pelsall, Walsall, West Midlands WS4 1BW	Mr Bernard Dickenson	01922 685777	01922 694267	335-4055	CY	11–18	1389	
Shire Oak School (A Science College)	Lichfield Rd, Walsall Wood, Walsall, West Midlands WS9 9PA	Mr Gary Crowther	01543 452518	01543 373204	335-5402	FD	11–18	1330	
Sneyd Community School	Vernon Way, Sneyd La, Bloxwich, Walsall, West Midlands WS3 2PA	Mrs Gail Gregory	01922 710298	01922 473145	335-4107	CY	11–18	1151	
The Streetly School	Queslett Rd East, Sutton Coldfield, West Midlands B74 2EX	Mr David Binnie	0121 353 2709	0121 353 0212	335-5400	FD	11–18	1359	

School name	Address	Headteacher	Tel	Fax	Ref	Type	Ages	Pupils	Other
Walsall Academy	Lichfield Rd, Bloxwich, Walsall WS3 3LX	Mrs Jean Hickman	01922 493910	01922 492186	335-6905		11–18	843	
Willenhall School Sports College	Furzebank Way, Willenhall, West Midlands WV12 4BD	Mrs Vicki Till	01902 368221	01902 634253	335-4105	CY	11–18	1546	

Warwickshire

School name	Address	Headteacher	Tel	Fax	Ref	Type	Ages	Pupils	Other
Alcester Grammar School	Birmingham Rd, Alcester, Warwickshire B49 5ED	Mr I.G. Blaikie	01789 762494	01789 400626	937-5407	FD	11–18	934	
Alcester High School Technology College	Gerard Rd, Alcester, Warwickshire B49 6QQ	Mrs Annabelle Guyver	01789 762285	01789 400095	937-4240	CY	11–16	823	
Alderman Smith School	Radnor Dr, Nuneaton, Warwickshire CV10 7PD	Mr Trevor Nunn	024 7634 1134	024 7637 5459	937-4150	CY	11–16	1189	
Ash Green School	Ash Green La, Ash Grn, Coventry, West Midlands CV7 9AH	Mr Graham Tyrer	024 7636 6772	024 7636 6383	937-5401	FD	11–16	652	
Ashlawn School	Ashlawn Rd, Rugby, Warwickshire CV22 5ET	Mr Peter Rossborough	01788 573425	01788 536159	937-4241	CY	11–18	1526	
The Avon Valley School and Performing Arts College	Newbold Rd, Newbold-on-Avon, Rugby, Warwickshire CV21 1EH	Mr Don NENeill	01788 542355	01788 572050	937-5400	FD	11–16	1057	
Aylesford School, a specialist Language and Music College	Shelley Ave, Warwick, Warwickshire CV34 6LA	Mr Steven Hall	01926 747100	01926 494194	937-4190	CY	11–18	967	
Bilton School – A Maths and Computing College	Lawford La, Bilton, Rugby, Warwickshire CV22 7JT	Mrs Lynda Brodie	01788 840600	01788 840610	937-4238	CY	11–16	1177	
Bishop Wulstan RC School	Oak St, off Dunchurch Rd, Rugby, Warwickshire CV22 5EA	Mr Brendan Higgins	01788 542928	01788 550758	937-4720	VA	11–16	320	RC
Campion School and Community College	Sydenham Dr, Leamington Spa, Warwickshire CV31 1QH	Mr Andrew Chubb	01926 743200	01926 336123	937-4192	CY	11–18	565	
The Coleshill School – a Maths and Computing College	Coventry Rd, Coleshill, Birmingham, West Midlands B46 3EX	Mrs C.M. Kearney	01675 462435		937-4233	CY	11–18	1004	
Etone Technology Language Vocational College	Leicester Rd, Nuneaton, Warwickshire CV11 6AA	Mr P. Kingham	024 7638 2008	024 7635 2320	937-4004	CY	11–16	766	
George Eliot Community School	Raveloe Dr, Caldwell, Nuneaton, Warwickshire CV11 4QP	Mr Tim Over	024 7674 4000	024 7632 6980	937-4156	CY	11–16	713	
Harris School	Harris Dr, Overslade La, Rugby, Warwickshire CV22 6EA	Mrs S. Simms	01788 812549	01788 816123	937-4802	VA	11–16	685	CE
Hartshill School	Church Rd, Hartshill, Nuneaton, Warwickshire CV10 0NA	Mr R. Turner	024 7639 2237	024 7639 4641	937-5402	FD	11–16	954	
Henley in Arden High School	Stratford Rd, Henley-in-Arden, Solihull, Warwickshire B95 6AF	Mr Paul Wright	01564 792364	01564 792411	937-4108	CY	11–16	609	
Higham Lane School	Shanklin Dr, Nuneaton, Warwickshire CV10 0BJ	Mr Phil Kelly	024 7638 8123	024 7637 0550	937-4153	CY	11–16	1228	
Kenilworth School and Sports College	Leyes La, Kenilworth, Warwickshire CV8 2DA	Dr A.L. Begbie	01926 859421	01926 859426	937-4236	CY	11–19	1725	
Kineton High School	Banbury Rd, Kineton, Warwick, Warwickshire CV35 0JX	Mrs Julia Morris	01926 640465	01926 640872	937-4110	CY	11–18	984	
King Edward VI School	Church St, Stratford-upon-Avon, Warwickshire CV37 6HB	Mr T.P. Moore-Bridger	01789 293351	01789 293564	937-4601	VA	11–18	497	B
Kingsbury School, A Specialist Science College with Mathematics	Tamworth Rd, Kingsbury, Tamworth, Staffordshire B78 2LF	Mrs A. Rogerson	01827 872316	01827 873814	937-4111	CY	11–16	610	
Lawrence Sheriff School	Clifton Rd, Rugby, Warwickshire CV21 3AG	Dr Peter Kent	01788 542074	01788 567962	937-4620	VA	11–18	809	B
Manor Park Community School	Beaumont Rd, Nuneaton, Warwickshire CV11 5HJ	Mr Alan Edwards	024 7637 4099	024 7635 1094	937-4154	CY	11–16	608	
Myton School	Myton Rd, Warwick, Warwickshire CV34 6PJ	Mr Geoff Walker	01926 493805	01926 490380	937-5403	FD	11–18	1622	
Nicholas Chamberlaine Technology College	Bulkington Rd, Bedworth, Warwickshire CV12 9EA	Mrs L.B. King	024 7631 2308	024 7664 3183	937-4103	CY	11–18	1668	
North Leamington Community School and Arts College	Cloister Way, Leamington Spa, Warwickshire CV32 6QF	Mr David Hazeldine	01926 338711	01926 429818	937-4237	CY	11–18	1398	
Northfields School	North Fosse, Leamington Spa, Warwickshire CV31 1XQ	Mr C Boardman	01926 614455	01295 277470	937-6103		11–17	66	Ch
Polesworth International Language College	Dordon Rd, Dordon, Tamworth, Staffordshire B78 1QT	Mr A. Clarke	01827 702205	01827 702206	937-4112	CY	11–18	1334	
Queen Elizabeth School	Witherley Rd, Atherstone, Warwickshire CV9 1LZ	Mr Anthony Wilmot	01827 712477	01827 715253	937-5404	FD	11–18	626	
Rugby High School	Longrood Rd, Rugby, Warwickshire CV22 7RE	Ms Charlotte Marten	01788 810518	01788 811794	937-5406	FD	11–18	738	G
St Benedict's RC High School	Kinwarton Rd, Alcester, Warwickshire B49 6PX	Mr T. Sara	01789 762888	01789 400192	937-4730	VA	11–16	550	RC
St Thomas More RC School and Technology College	Greenmoor Rd, Nuneaton, Warwickshire CV10 7EX	Mr M. Moore	024 7664 2400	024 7632 1919	937-4803	VA	11–16	783	RC
Shipston High School – A Specialist Technology College	Darlingscote Rd, Shipston-on-Stour, Warwickshire CV36 4DY	Mr Jonathan Baker	01608 661833	01608 663459	937-4113	CY	11–16	337	

3

School name	Address	Tel	Fax	Headteacher	Ref	Type	Ages	Pupils	Other
Southam College	Welsh Rd West, Southam, Warwickshire CV47 0JW	01926 812560	01926 815807	Mr M.J. Thompson	937-4114	CY	11-18	1114	
Stratford-upon-Avon High School	Alcester Rd, Stratford-upon-Avon, Warwickshire CV37 9DH	01789 268051	01789 261919	Mr David Williams	937-4124	CY	11-18	1267	
Stratford-upon-Avon Grammar School for Girls A Specialist College for Language and Science	Shottery Manor, Stratford-upon-Avon, Warwickshire CV37 9HA	01789 293759	01789 261450	Ms Kate Barnett	937-4002	CY	11-18	597	G
Studley High School	Crooks La, Studley, Warwickshire B80 7QX	01527 852478	01527 854469	Mrs Elaine Elizabeth Young	937-5408	FD	11-16	748	
Trinity RC School	Guy's Cliffe Ave, Leamington Spa, Warwickshire CV32 6NB	01926 428416	01926 337408	Dr James Ferguson	937-4752	VA	11-18	1026	RC

Wolverhampton

School name	Address	Tel	Fax	Headteacher	Ref	Type	Ages	Pupils	Other
Aldersley High School	Barnhurst La, Codsall, Wolverhampton, West Midlands WV8 1RT	01902 556868	01902 747598	Mr Timothy Edward Perry	336-5402	FD	11-18	844	
Colton Hills Community School	Jeremy Rd, Goldthorn Pk, Wolverhampton, West Midlands WV4 5DG	01902 558420	01902 558421	Mr K. Byatt	336-4133	CY	11-18	917	
Coppice Performing Arts School	Ecclestone Rd, Wednesfield, Wolverhampton, West Midlands WV11 2QE	01902 558500	01902 558501	Mr R. Rossides	336-4128	CY	11-18	870	
Deansfield High School	Deans Rd, Wolverhampton, West Midlands WV1 2BH	01902 556400	01902 556401	Mr Steve Hawke	336-4115	CY	11-19	753	
Heath Park Business and Enterprise College	Prestwood Rd, Wolverhampton, West Midlands WV11 1RD	01902 556360	01902 556361	Mr Douglas Selkirk	336-4134	CY	11-18	1154	
Highfields Science Specialist School	Boundary Way, Penn, Wolverhampton, West Midlands WV4 4NT	01902 556530	01902 556531	Mrs Jill Jordan	336-4113	CY	11-18	1451	
The King's CE School	Regis Rd, Tettenhall, Wolverhampton, West Midlands WV6 8XG	01902 558333	01902 558334	Mr Tim Gallagher	336-4731	VA	11-18	846	CE
Moreton Community School	Old Fallings La, Wolverhampton, West Midlands WV10 8BY	01902 558310	01902 558306	Mr Tony Leach	336-4139	CY	11-18	663	
Moseley Park School	Holland Rd, Bilston, West Midlands WV14 6LU	01902 353901	01902 496103	Mrs Lorraine McCarthy	336-5401	FD	11-18	1217	
The Northicote School	Northwood Park Rd, Bushbury, Wolverhampton, West Midlands WV10 8EP	01902 623800	01902 623801	Mr Mark Capel	336-4106	CY	11-18	876	
Our Lady and St Chad RC Sports College	Old Fallings La, Wolverhampton, West Midlands WV10 8BL	01902 558250	01902 558251	Miss M.C. Keelan	336-4606	VA	11-18	821	RC
Parkfield High School	Wolverhampton Rd East, Wolverhampton, West Midlands WV4 6AP	01902 558660		Mr Arthur Thompson	336-4131	CY	11-18	1007	
Pendeford Business and Enterprise College	Marsh La, Fordhouses, Wolverhampton, West Midlands WV10 6SE	01902 551551	01902 551550	Mr Nigel Combellack	336-4129	CY	11-18	564	
St Edmund's RC School	Compton Pk, Compton Rd West, Wolverhampton, West Midlands WV3 9DU	01902 558888	01902 558889	Ms D. Finucane	336-4605	VA	11-18	800	RC
St Peter's Collegiate CE School	Compton Pk, Compton Rd West, Wolverhampton, West Midlands WV3 9DU	01902 558600	01902 558596	Rev Huw Bishop	336-4601	VA	11-18	1005	CE
Smestow School	Windmill Cres, Castlecroft, Wolverhampton, West Midlands WV3 8HU	01902 558585	01902 558586	Mr Des Ennis	336-4117	CY	11-18	970	
Wednesfield High School	Lichfield Rd, Wednesfield, Wolverhampton, West Midlands WV11 3ES	01902 558222	01902 558200	Mr Peter Coates	336-4130	CY	11-18	1079	
Wolverhampton Girls' High School	Tettenhall Rd, Tettenhall, Wolverhampton, West Midlands WV6 0BY	01902 328783	01902 328770	Mrs Julie Grace Lawton	336-5400	FD	11-18	745	G

Worcestershire

School name	Address	Tel	Fax	Headteacher	Ref	Type	Ages	Pupils	Other
The Alice Ottley School	Upper Tything, Worcester, Worcestershire WR1 1HW	01905 27061	01905 724626	Mrs M. Chapman	885-6001		3-19	446	CE
Arrow Vale Community High School – a Specialist Sports College	Green Sward La, Matchborough West, Redditch, Worcestershire B98 0EN	01527 526800	01527 514255	Mr Peter Woodman	885-4034	CY	13-18	920	
Baxter College	Habberley Rd, Kidderminster, Worcestershire DY11 5PQ	01562 741524	01562 827719	Mr David Seddon	885-4007	CY	11-18		
The Bewdley School and Sixth Form Centre	Stourport Rd, Bewdley, Worcestershire DY12 1BL	01299 403277	01299 405480	Mrs Julie Reilly	885-4001	CY	11-18		
Bishop Perowne CE College	Merriman's Hill Rd, Worcester, Worcestershire WR3 8LE	01905 746800	01905 746846	Ms Julie Farr	885-4754	VA	11-16	1053	CE
Blessed Edward Oldcorne RC College	Timberdine Ave, Worcester, Worcestershire WR5 2XD	01905 352615	01905 763041	Mr Sean Devlin	885-5402	VA	11-16	1047	RC
Christopher Whitehead Language College	Bromwich Rd, Worcester, Worcestershire WR2 4AF	01905 423906	01905 420788	Mr N. Morris	885-4432	CY	11-16	1123	

School name	Address	Tel	Fax	Headteacher	Ref	Type	Ages	Pupils	Other
Droitwich Spa High School	Briar Mill, Droitwich Spa, Worcestershire WR9 0AA	01905 774421	01905 777070	Mr Allan Foulds	885-4005	CY	12–18	1405	
Dyson Perrins CE High School	Yates Hay Rd, Malvern, Worcestershire WR14 1WD	01684 564751	01684 573765	Mr David Griffin	885-4801	VA	11–18	949	CE
Elgar Technology College	Bilford Rd, Worcester, Worcestershire WR3 8HN	01905 454627	01905 756517	Mr Anthony James	885-4431	CY	11–16	966	
Evesham High School	Four Pools Rd, Evesham, Worcestershire WR11 1DQ	01386 442060	01386 41734	Mr David Kelly	885-4006	CY	13–18	955	
Hagley Roman RC High School	Brake La, Hagley, Hagley, Worcestershire DY8 2XL	01562 883193	01562 881820	Mr Terence Hammond	885-4800	VA	11–18	1007	RC
Hanley Castle High School	Church End, Hanley Castle, Worcester, Worcestershire WR8 0BL	01684 593241	01684 593910	Mr Robert Haring	885-4500	VC	11–18	887	
Haybridge High School and Sixth Form	Brake La, Hagley, Stourbridge, West Midlands DY8 2XS	01562 886213	01562 887002	Dr M.J. Kershaw	885-4010	FD	11–18	1146	
King Charles I Secondary School	Hill Grove Hse, Comberton Rd, Kidderminster, Worcestershire DY10 1XA	01562 512880	01562 512881	Mr Tim Gulliver	885-4501	VC	11–18		
Kingsley College	Woodrow Dr, Redditch, Worcestershire B98 7UH	01527 523088	01527 514245	Mrs Lesley McGuigan	885-4438	FD	13–18	1074	
Malvern, The Chase	Geraldine La, Malvern, Worcestershire WR14 3NZ	01684 891961	01684 566643	Mr Kevin Peck	885-4028	CY	11–18	1690	
Martley, The Chantry High School	Martley, Worcester, Worcestershire WR6 6QA	01886 887100	01886 887102	Ms Caroline Browne	885-4435	CY	11–16	699	
North Bromsgrove High School	School Dr, Stratford Rd, Bromsgrove, Worcestershire B60 1BA	01527 872375	01527 839730	Mrs Sue Ballard	885-4002	CY	13–18	1033	
Northwick Education	223 Northwick Rd, Worcester WR3 7EJ	01905 575400			885-6037		10–16	24	Ch
Pershore High School	Station Rd, Pershore, Worcestershire WR10 2BX	01386 552471	01386 555104	Mr Clive Corbett	885-4030	CY	12–18	1216	
Prince Henry's High School	Victoria Ave, Evesham, Worcestershire WR11 4QH	01386 765588	01386 40760	Mr Bernard Roberts	885-5403	FD	13–18	1289	
St Augustine's RC High School: A Specialist Science College	Stonepits La, Hunt End, Redditch, Worcestershire B97 5LX	01527 550400	01527 550230	Mrs Yvonne Brennan	885-5400	VA	13–18	859	RC
St James's School	Croft Bank, West Malvern, Malvern, Worcestershire WR14 4DF	01684 560851	01684 569252	Mrs R. Hayes	885-6013		7–16	147	Ch
South Bromsgrove Community High School	Charford Rd, Bromsgrove, Worcestershire B60 3NL	01527 831783	01527 837162	Mr P.W. Copeland	885-4003	CY	13–18	1294	
The Stourport High School and Sixth Form Centre	Minster Rd, Stourport-on-Severn, Worcestershire DY13 8AX	01299 872950	01299 827972	Ms Liz Quinn	885-4004	CY	11–18		
Tenbury High School	Oldwood Rd, Tenbury Wells, Worcestershire WR15 8XA	01584 810304	01584 819921	Mr Stuart Cooke	885-4041	CY	11–16	429	
Trinity High School and Sixth Form Centre	Easemore Rd, Redditch, Worcestershire B98 8HB	01527 585859	01527 65587	Mrs Marian Barton	885-4437	CY	13–18	924	
Waseley Hills High School and Sixth Form Centre	School Rd, Rubery, Rednal, Birmingham, West Midlands B45 9EL	0121 453 5211	0121 457 8850	Mr D. Thurbon	885-4044	CY	11–18	1007	
Wolverley CofE Secondary School	Blakeshall La, Wolverley, Kidderminster, Worcestershire DY11 5XQ	01562 859800	01562 859807	Mr Kevin O'Regan	885-4503	VC	11–18		
Woodrush Community High School	Shawhurst La, Hollywood, Birmingham, West Midlands B47 5JW	01564 826533	01564 822226	Mr Antony Morrison	885-4017	CY	11–18	990	
Worcester, Nunnery Wood High School	Spetchley Rd, Worcester, Worcestershire WR5 2LT	01905 356288	01905 763482	Mr Alun Williams	885-4434	CY	11–16	1337	

Yorkshire and The Humber

Barnsley

School name	Address	Tel	Fax	Headteacher	Ref	Type	Ages	Pupils	Other
The Barnsley Academy	Ardsley Rd, Worsbrough Dale, Barnsley S70 4RL	01226 284606	01226 731793	Mr Dave Berry	370-6905		11–19	441	Ch
Darton High School	Churchfield La, Darton, Barnsley, South Yorkshire S75 5EW	01226 382568	01226 382350	Mr Simon Hill	370-4025	CY	11–16	1137	
The Dearne High School	Goldthorpe Rd, Goldthorpe, Rotherham, South Yorkshire S63 9EW	01709 892211	01709 891192	Mr P. Shenton	370-4037	CY	11–16	1243	
Edward Sheerien School	Carlton Rd, Barnsley, South Yorkshire S71 2BB	01226 291697	01226 207914	Mrs S. Hamby	370-4001	CY	11–16	743	
The Foulstone School	Nanny Marr Rd, Darfield, Barnsley, South Yorkshire S73 9AB	01226 753223	01226 751953	Mr Phillip King	370-4021	CY	11–16	877	
Holgate School and Sports College	Shaw La, Barnsley, South Yorkshire S70 6EP	01226 203720	01226 201489	Miss J. Rothery	370-4500	VC	11–16	952	
The Kingstone School	Broadway, Barnsley, South Yorkshire S70 6RB	01226 215757	01226 215758	Mr Matthew Milburn	370-4035	CY	11–16	1473	
Kirk Balk School	Kirk Balk, Hoyland, Barnsley, South Yorkshire S74 9HX	01226 742286	01226 741267	Mrs Val Malcolm	370-4029	CY	11–16	1219	
Penistone Grammar School	Huddersfield Rd, Penistone, Sheffield, South Yorkshire S36 7BX	01226 762114	01226 370328	Mrs C.G. Gower	370-4027	CY	11–18	1559	
Priory School and Sports College	Littleworth La, Lundwood, Barnsley, South Yorkshire S71 5RG	01226 203110	01226 731013	Mrs Bernadette O'Brien	370-4005	CY	11–16	929	

3

School name	Address	Tel	Fax	Headteacher	Ref	Type	Ages	Pupils	Other
Royston High – A Specialist Science College	Station Rd, Royston, Barnsley, South Yorkshire S71 4EQ	01226 722515	01226 728664	Ms K. Jenkins	370-4023	CY	11–16	620	
St Michael's RC and CE High School	Carlton Rd, Barnsley, South Yorkshire S71 2BD	01226 282845	01226 242820	Mr Karol Grabowski	370-4038	VA	11–16	672	CE/RC
Willowgarth High School	Brierley Rd, Grimethorpe, Barnsley, South Yorkshire S72 7AJ	01226 711542	01226 711560	Mr Anthony Loveday	370-4026	CY	11–16	840	
Wombwell High – A Humanities College	Roebuck St, Wombwell, Barnsley, South Yorkshire S73 0JU	01226 752551	01226 274802	Mr Chris Wilson	370-4024	CY	11–16	971	

Bradford

School name	Address	Tel	Fax	Headteacher	Ref	Type	Ages	Pupils	Other
Beckfoot School	Wagon La, Bingley, West Yorkshire BD16 1EE	01274 771444	01274 771445	Mr David Horn	380-4064	CY	11–18	1579	
Belle Vue Boys' School	Thorn La, Haworth Rd, Bradford, West Yorkshire BD9 6ND	01274 493533	01274 483671	Mr Rick Whittaker	380-4022	VA	11–18	623	B
Belle Vue Girls' School	Thorn La, Bingley Rd, Bradford, West Yorkshire BD9 6NA	01274 492341	01274 490559	Ms M. Platts	380-4041	CY	11–18	1076	G
Bingley Grammar School	Keighley Rd, Bingley, West Yorkshire BD16 2RS	01274 807700	01274 510136	Mr Chris Taylor	380-5400	VA	11–18	1915	
Bradford Academy	Teasdale St, Bradford BD4 7QJ	01274 256789			380-6906		7–13		Ch
Buttershaw Business and Enterprise College	Reevy Rd West, Buttershaw, Bradford, West Yorkshire BD6 3PX	01274 676285	01274 679228	Mr John Midgley	380-4001	CY	11–18	1479	
Carlton Bolling College	Undercliffe La, Bradford, West Yorkshire BD3 0DU	01274 633111	01274 630635	Dr Nigel Jepson	380-4100	CY	11–18	1397	
The Challenge College	North Ave, Bradford, West Yorkshire BD8 7ND	01274 362050	01274 362051	Ms Sian Harris	380-4111	CY	11–18	930	
Dixons City Academy	Ripley St, Bradford BD5 7RR	01274 776777	01274 391928	Mr Nick Weller	380-6905		11–18	1094	
Feversham College	Cliffe Rd, Undercliffe, Bradford, West Yorkshire BD3 0LT	01274 559500		Mrs Tracy McNally	380-4613	VA	11–18	600	Mu G
Grange Technology College	Haycliffe La, Bradford, West Yorkshire BD5 9ET	01274 775335	01274 775665	Mr Paul Burluraux	380-4101	CY	11–18	1802	
Greenhead High School	Greenhead Rd, Utley, Keighley, West Yorkshire BD20 6EB	01535 210333	01535 210182	Mrs P. Mccarthy	380-4066	CY	11–18	1031	
Hanson School	Sutton Ave, Swain House Rd, Bradford, West Yorkshire BD2 1JP	01274 776200	01274 776686	Mrs Susan Horsley	380-5401	FD	11–18	1850	
The Holy Family RC School	Spring Gardens La, Keighley, West Yorkshire BD20 6LH	01535 210212	01535 210242	Mr C. Davis	380-4610	VA	11–18	981	RC
Ilkley Grammar School	Cowpasture Rd, Ilkley, West Yorkshire LS29 8TR	01943 608424	01943 601285	Mrs Gillian James	380-4502	VC	11–18	1538	
Immanuel CE Community College	Leeds Rd, Idle, Bradford, West Yorkshire BD10 9AQ	01274 425900		Mrs J. Tiller	380-4616	VA	11–18	1063	CE
Laisterdyke Business and Enterprise College	Thornbury Rd, Bradford, West Yorkshire BD3 8HE	01274 401140	01274 403477	Mrs Joan Law	380-5404	FD	11–18	1030	
Nab Wood School	Cottingley New Rd, Bingley, West Yorkshire BD16 1TZ	01274 567281	01274 510688	Mrs E. Shoesmith	380-4077	CY	11–18	967	
Oakbank School	Oakworth Rd, Keighley, West Yorkshire BD22 7DU	01535 210111	01535 210555	Mr Chris Thompson	380-5402	FD	11–18	1828	
Parkside School	Parkside Terr, Cullingworth, Bradford, West Yorkshire BD13 5AD	01535 272752		Dr T. Rickwood	380-4112	CY	11–18	1088	
Queensbury School	Deanstones La, Queensbury, Bradford, West Yorkshire BD13 2AS	01274 882214	01274 884853	Mrs D. Shipton	380-4069	CY	11–18	1328	
Rhodesway School	Oaks La, Allerton, Bradford, West Yorkshire BD15 7RU	01274 770230	01274 770231	Mrs Rachel Kidd	380-4034	CY	11–18	1149	
St Bede's RC Grammar School	Highgate, Heaton, Bradford, West Yorkshire BD9 4BQ	01274 541221	01274 498290	Mr Paul Martin	380-4600	VA	11–18	910	RC B
St Joseph's RC College	Cunliffe Rd, Bradford, West Yorkshire BD8 7AP	01274 401500	01274 541060	Mr P. McDermott	380-4611	VA	11–18	990	RC G
Salt Grammar School	Higher Coach Rd, Baildon, Shipley, West Yorkshire BD17 5RH	01274 415551	01274 415552	Mrs Susan Mansfield	380-4074	CY	11–18	1384	
Thornton Grammar School	Leaventhorpe La, Thornton, Bradford, West Yorkshire BD13 3BH	01274 881082	01274 814871	Mr John Weir	380-5403	FD	11–18	1476	
Tong School	Westgate Hill St, Bradford, West Yorkshire BD4 6NR	01274 681455	01274 689547	Mrs Lyn O'Reilly	380-4036	CY	11–18	1434	
Wyke Manor School	Wilson Rd, Wyke, Bradford, West Yorkshire BD12 9PX	01274 414380	01274 414384	Mr Dwayne Saxton	380-4033	CY	11–18	729	
Yorkshire Martyrs RC College	Westgate Hill St, Bradford, West Yorkshire BD4 6NR	01274 681262	01274 689747	Mr J. Tat	380-4612	VA	11–18	1057	RC

Calderdale

School name	Address	Tel	Fax	Headteacher	Ref	Type	Ages	Pupils	Other
Brighouse High School	Finkil St, Brighouse, West Yorkshire HD6 2NY	01484 710408	01484 400638	Mr Graham Soles	381-5406	FD	11–18	1304	
The Brooksbank School	Victoria Rd, Elland, West Yorkshire HX5 0QG	01422 374791	01422 310945	Mrs Jeanne Watson	381-5405	FD	11–18	1593	
Calder High School, A Specialist Technology College	Brier Hey La, Mytholmroyd, Hebden Bridge, West Yorkshire HX7 5QN	01422 883213	01422 882684	Mr Stephen Ball	381-4022	CY	11–18	1302	
The Crossley Heath School	Savile Pk, Halifax, West Yorkshire HX3 0HG	01422 360272	01422 349099	Miss Helen Gaunt	381-5401	FD	11–18	1015	RC

School name	Address	Tel	Fax	Headteacher	Ref	Type	Ages	Pupils	Other
Halifax High at Wellesley Park	Gibbet St, Halifax, West Yorkshire HX2 0BA	01422 301080	01422 301081	Mr Jeremy Waxman	381-4035	CY	11–16	685	
Hipperholme and Lightcliffe High School and Sports College	Stoney La, Lightcliffe, Halifax, West Yorkshire HX3 8TL	01422 201028	01422 204615	Mrs Karen E Mort	381-5404	FD	11–18	1162	
Holy Trinity CE Senior School	Holdsworth Rd, Holmfield, Halifax, West Yorkshire HX2 9TD	01422 244890	01422 240033	Mr Paul Triner	381-5403	VA	11–18	1014	CE
The North Halifax Grammar School	Moorbottom Rd, Illingworth, Halifax, West Yorkshire HX2 9SU	01422 244625	01422 245237	Mr Graham Maslen	381-5400	FD	11–18	1067	
Park Lane High	Park La, Exley, Halifax, West Yorkshire HX3 9LG	01422 362215	01422 363236	Mr Neil Clark	381-4001	CY	11–16	430	
Rastrick High School	Field Top Rd, Rastrick, Brighouse, West Yorkshire HD6 3XB	01484 710235	01484 720043	Mrs Helen Lennie	381-5402	FD	11–18	1403	
The Ridings School	Nursery La, Ovenden, Halifax, West Yorkshire HX3 5SX	01422 352836	01422 363421	Mrs A.M. White	381-4036	CY	11–18	659	
Ryburn Valley High School	St Peter's Ave, Sowerby, Sowerby Bridge, West Yorkshire HX6 1DF	01422 832070	01422 833386	Mr Ian Adam	381-5408	FD	11–18	1349	
St Catherine's RC High School	Holdsworth Rd, Holmfield, Halifax, West Yorkshire HX2 9TH	01422 245411	01422 240008	Miss Pauline Luniw	381-5407	VA	11–18	831	RC
Sowerby Bridge High School	Albert Rd, Sowerby Bridge, West Yorkshire HX6 2NW	01422 831011	01422 835962	Mrs Kate Wood	381-4024	CY	11–18	967	
Todmorden High School	Ewood La, Todmorden, Lancashire OL14 7DG	01706 813558	01706 814821	Mr Patrick Ottley-O'Connor	381-4026	CY	11–18	809	

Doncaster

School name	Address	Tel	Fax	Headteacher	Ref	Type	Ages	Pupils	Other
The Armthorpe School	Mere La, Armthorpe, Doncaster, South Yorkshire DN3 2DA	01302 831582	01302 831385	Mr Nigel Pattinson	371-4021	CY	11–18	833	
Balby Carr Community Sports College	Weston Rd, Balby, Doncaster, South Yorkshire DN4 8ND	0845 345 1629	01302 310774	Mr M. Craig	371-4056	CY	11–18	1251	
Campsmount Technology College	Ryecroft Rd, Norton, Doncaster, South Yorkshire DN6 9AS	01302 700474	01302 700056	Mr Andrew Sprakes	371-4036	CY	11–18	787	
Danum School Technology College	Armthorpe Rd, Doncaster, South Yorkshire DN2 5QD	01302 300757	01302 300109	Dr K.P.J. Simmonds	371-4014	CY	11–18	1944	
Don Valley School and Performing Arts College	Jossey La, Scawthorpe, Doncaster, South Yorkshire DN5 9DD	01302 781528	01302 786252	Mr Robert Johnson	371-4029	CY	11–18	1448	
Edlington School	Tait Ave, Edlington, Doncaster, South Yorkshire DN12 1HH	01709 864100	01709 770026	Mr Kevin Oliver	371-4031	CY	11–18	1143	
Hall Cross School	Thorne Rd, Doncaster, South Yorkshire DN1 2HY	01302 320626	01302 322190	Mr K. Jones	371-4062	CY	11–18	2109	
Hatfield Visual Arts College	Ash Hill, Hatfield, Doncaster, South Yorkshire DN7 6JH	01302 840961	01302 845906	Mr C.D. Coady	371-4023	CY	11–18	1166	
The Hayfield School	Hurst La, Auckley, Doncaster, South Yorkshire DN9 3HG	01302 770589	01302 770179	Mr G.A. Storey	371-5400	FD	11–18	1079	
Hungerhill School A Specialist Centre for Science, Mathematics and Computing	Hungerhill La, Edenthorpe, Doncaster, South Yorkshire DN3 2JY	01302 885811	01302 880384	Mr G. Wakeling	371-4040	CY	11–16	1150	
The McAuley RC High School	Cantley La, Doncaster DN3 3QF	01302 537396	01302 537891	Mrs Mary Lawrence	371-4606	VA	11–18	1713	RC
Mexborough School	Maple Rd, Mexborough, South Yorkshire S64 9SD	01709 585858	01709 578080	Dr J. Campbell	371-4032	CY	11–18	1196	
North Doncaster Technology College	Windmill Balk La, Woodlands, Doncaster, South Yorkshire DN6 7SF	01302 722237	01302 337345	Mr W.G. Blakemore	371-4020	CY	11–18	1370	
Northcliffe School	Gardens La, Conisbrough, Doncaster, South Yorkshire DN12 3JS	01709 864001	01709 770185	Mr David Martin	371-4022	CY	11–16	752	
Ridgewood School	Barnsley Rd, Scawsby, Doncaster, South Yorkshire DN5 7UB	01302 783939	01302 390448	Mr C. Hoyle	371-4033	CY	11–16	1319	
Rossington All Saints CE School – A Sports College	Bond St, Rossington, Doncaster DN11 0BZ	01302 868414		Mr David Rowsell	371-4607	VA	11–18	897	CE
Trinity Academy	Church Balk, Thorne, Doncaster DN8 5BY	01405 813000	01405 818382	Mr Ian Brew	371-6905		11–18	1193	Ch

East Riding of Yorkshire

School name	Address	Tel	Fax	Headteacher	Ref	Type	Ages	Pupils	Other
Beverley Grammar School	Queensgate, Beverley HU17 8NF	01482 881531	01482 881564	Mr G. Broadbent	811-4625	VA	11–18	788	B
Beverley High School	Norwood, Beverley, East Riding of Yorkshire HU17 9EX	01482 881658	01482 870935	Mrs R. Vincent	811-4050	CY	11–18	837	G
Bridlington School Sports College	Bessingby Rd, Bridlington, East Riding of Yorkshire YO16 4QU	01262 672593	01262 672593	Mr J. Wilson	811-4500	VC	11–18	1020	
Cottingham High School	Harland Way, Cottingham, Lincolnshire HU16 5PX	01482 847498	01482 841053	Mr Tom Darbyshire	811-4058	CY	11–18	1568	
Driffield School	Manorfield Rd, Driffield, East Riding of Yorkshire YO25 5HR	01377 253631	01377 256922	Mr Martin Green	811-4057	CY	11–18	1929	
Headlands School and Community Science College	Sewerby Rd, Bridlington, East Riding of Yorkshire YO16 6UR	01262 676198	01262 607907	Dr Steve Rogers	811-4064	CY	11–18	1460	

3

School name	Address	Tel	Fax	Headteacher	Ref	Type	Ages	Pupils	Other
Hessle High School	Tranby Hse, Heads La, Hessle, East Yorkshire HU13 0JQ	01482 648604	01482 643207	Mr David Rose	811-4053	CY	11–18	1455	
Hornsea School and Language College	Eastgate, Hornsea, East Riding of Yorkshire HU18 1DW	01964 532727	01964 533403	Mr Ron Newey	811-4061	CY	11–18	1299	
Howden School and Technology College	Derwent Rd, Howden, Goole, East Riding of Yorkshire DN14 7AL	01430 430870	01430 432435	Mr Andrew Williams	811-4063	CY	11–18	808	
Longcroft School and Performing Arts College	Burton Rd, Beverley HU17 7EJ	01482 862171	01482 862872	Mrs L. Hughes	811-4051	CY	11–18	1538	
The Market Weighton School	Spring Rd, Market Weighton, East Riding of Yorkshire YO43 3JF	01430 873450	01430 871015	Mrs Mary McCorry	811-4055	CY	11–18	707	
The Snaith School	Pontefract Rd, Snaith, Goole, East Riding of Yorkshire DN14 9LB	01405 860327	01405 862748	Mrs Jean Pickerill	811-4102	CY	11–16	808	
South Holderness Technology College	Station Rd, Preston, Hull, East Riding of Yorkshire HU12 8UZ	01482 899315	01482 890514	Mr Martin Cooper	811-4059	CY	11–18	1822	
South Hunsley School	East Dale Rd, Melton, North Ferriby, East Riding of Yorkshire HU14 3HS	01482 631208	01482 634186	Miss Chris Abbott	811-4056	CY	11–18	1820	
Vermuyden School	Centenary Rd, Goole DN14 6AN	01405 768621	01405 768277	Miss A. McErlane	811-4007	CY	11–18	1134	
Withernsea High School Specialising in Humanities and Technology	Hull Rd, Withernsea, Lincolnshire HU19 2EQ	01964 613133	01964 614560	Dr Fiona Ireland	811-4054	CY	11–18	1004	
Woldgate College	92 Kilnwick Rd, Pocklington, York, North Yorkshire YO42 2LL	01759 302395	01759 306535	Mr J. Bower	811-4060	CY	11–18	1354	
Wolfreton College	South Ella Way, Kirk Ella, Kirk Ella, East Riding of Yorkshire HU10 7LU	01482 659356	01482 658598	Mr Roy Cooke	811-4062	CY	11–18	2020	

Kingston upon Hull

School name	Address	Tel	Fax	Headteacher	Ref	Type	Ages	Pupils	Other
Andrew Marvell Business and Enterprise College	Barham Rd, Hull, East Riding of Yorkshire HU9 4EE	01482 799132	01482 786804	Mr David McCready	810-4455	CY	11–16	1158	
Archbishop Thurstan CE VC School	Hopewell Rd, Bilton Grange Est, Hull, East Riding of Yorkshire HU9 4HD	01482 781912	01482 784959	Mr Dennis Palmer	810-4504	VC	11–16	871	CE
David Lister School	Rustenburg St, Hull, East Riding of Yorkshire HU9 2PR	01482 376304	01482 799882	Mrs Lesley Johnson	810-4130	CY	11–16	1105	
Endeavour High School	Fountain Rd, Beverley Rd, Kingston upon Hull, East Riding of Yorkshire HU3 1UR	01482 313600		Mr Christopher Straker	810-4005	CY	11–16	1019	
Hull Trinity House School	Princes Dock St, Hull, East Riding of Yorkshire HU1 2JX	01482 326421	01482 324697	Mr Andrew Twaits	810-4622	VA	11–16	296	B
Kelvin Hall School	Bricknell Ave, Hull, East Yorkshire HU5 4QH	01482 342229	01482 346817	Mr Martin Doolan	810-4113	CY	11–16	990	
Kingswood College of Arts	Wawne Rd, Bransholme, Hull, East Riding of Yorkshire HU7 4WR	01482 879967		Mr Kevin Beaton	810-4004	CY	11–16	1075	
Malet Lambert School Language College	James Reckitt Ave, Hull HU8 0JD	01482 374211	01482 707642	Mrs S. Ireland	810-4020	CY	11–16	1407	
Newland School for Girls	Cottingham Rd, Hull, East Riding of Yorkshire HU6 7RU	01482 343098	01482 441416	Mrs Angela Martinson	810-4030	CY	11–16	841	G
Pickering High School Sports College	Pickering Rd, Hull, East Riding of Yorkshire HU4 7AE	01482 352939	01482 569982	Mrs Elaine Wadsworth	810-4006	CY	11–16	948	
St Mary's College	Cranbrook Ave, Hull, East Riding of Yorkshire HU6 7TN	01482 851136	01482 804522	Mr Ged Fitzpatrick	810-4626	VA	11–18	1534	RC
Sir Henry Cooper School	Thorpepark Rd, Orchard Park Est, Hull, East Riding of Yorkshire HU6 9ES	01482 854687	01482 809690	Mr David White	810-4250	CY	11–16	685	
Sydney Smith School	First La, Anlaby, Hull, Lincolnshire HU10 6UU	08445 444555	01482 651690	Mr Kevin Beaton	810-4267	CY	11–16	1512	
Winifred Holtby School Technology College	Midmere Ave, Leeds Rd, Bransholme, Hull, East Riding of Yorkshire HU7 4PW	01482 826207	01482 839589	Mr Stephen Liddle	810-4001	CY	11–16	1552	

Kirklees

School name	Address	Tel	Fax	Headteacher	Ref	Type	Ages	Pupils	Other
All Saints RC College Specialist in Humanities	Bradley Bar, Huddersfield, West Yorkshire HD2 2JT	01484 426466	01484 456452	Mr Lm H Haaronnixon	382-4613	VA	11–16	868	RC
Almondbury High School and Language College	Fernside Ave, Almondbury, Huddersfield, West Yorkshire HD5 8PQ	01484 223910	01484 223912	Ms Janet Tolley	382-4019	CY	11–16	794	
Batley Business and Enterprise College	Batley Field Hill, Batley, West Yorkshire WF17 0BJ	01924 326343	01924 326348	Mr James Ryan	382-4044	CY	11–16	543	B
Batley Girls' High School	Windmill La, Batley, West Yorkshire WF17 0LD	01924 326352	01924 326357	Mrs Jackie Eames	382-4048	CY	11–18	1094	G

3

School name	Address	Tel	Fax	Headteacher	Ref	Type	Ages	Pupils	Other
Birkdale High School	Wheelwright Dr, Dewsbury, West Yorkshire WF13 4JB	01924 869180	01924 869188	Mrs Christine Caraher	382-4056	CY	11–16	569	
Castle Hall School	Richard Thorpe Ave, Crowlees Rd, Mirfield, West Yorkshire WF14 9PH	01924 520500	01924 520504	Mr A.D. Pugh	382-5400	FD	11–16	859	
Colne Valley High School	Gillroyd La, Linthwaite, Huddersfield, West Yorkshire HD7 5SP	01924 222564	01484 222568	Mrs Linda Wright	382-4042	CY	11–16	1436	
The Community Science College at Thornhill	Valley Dr, Thornhill, Dewsbury, West Yorkshire WF12 0HE	01924 324890	01924 324892	Mr S.A. Valentine	382-4060	CY	11–16	759	
Earlsheaton Technology College	Old Bank Rd, Dewsbury, West Yorkshire WF12 7DW	01924 325230	01924 325232	Mr Paul Levey	382-4058	CY	11–16	859	
Fartown High School	Woodhouse Hall Rd, Fartown, Huddersfield, West Yorkshire HD2 1DJ	01484 226540	01484 226544	Mr Steve Britton	382-4020	CY	11–16	448	
Heckmondwike Grammar School	High St, Heckmondwike, West Yorkshire WF16 0AH	01924 402202	01924 418318	Mr Mark Tweedle	382-5401	FD	11–18	1178	
Holmfirth High School	Heys Rd, Thongsbridge, Holmfirth, West Yorkshire HD9 7SE	01484 691460	01484 691469	Dr Andy Williams	382-4046	CY	11–16	1265	
Honley High School	Station Rd, Honley, Holmfirth, West Yorkshire HD9 6QJ	01484 222347	01484 222314	Mr A. Connor	382-4038	CY	11–16	1233	
King James's School	St Helen's Gate, Almondbury, Huddersfield, West Yorkshire HD4 6SG	01484 223930	01484 223934	Mr Robert Lamb	382-4000	CY	11–16	806	
The Mirfield Free Grammar and Sixth Form	Kitson Hill Rd, Mirfield, West Yorkshire WF14 9EZ	01924 483660	01924 483661	Mrs L. Barker	382-4040	FD	11–18	1341	
Moor End Technology College	Dryclough Rd, Crosland Moor, Huddersfield, West Yorkshire HD4 5JA	01484 222230	01484 222233	Ms Jane Acklam	382-4021	CY	11–16	873	
Newsome High School and Sports College	Castle Ave, Newsome, Huddersfield, West Yorkshire HD4 6JN	01484 226570	01484 226572	Mr G. Hull	382-4022	CY	11–16	769	
Rawthorpe High School	Nether Hall Ave, Rawthorpe, Huddersfield, West Yorkshire HD5 9PG	01484 221892	01484 221894	Mrs Joan Young	382-4009	CY	11–16	350	
Royds Hall High School	Luck La, Paddock, Huddersfield, West Yorkshire HD3 4HA	01484 463366	01484 222223	Mrs Janine Westmoreland	382-4003	CY	11–16	806	
St John Fisher RC High School	Oxford Rd, Dewsbury, West Yorkshire WF13 4LL	01924 527000	01924 527004	Mr Kevin Higgins	382-4800	VA	11–18	1149	RC
Salendine Nook High School	New Hey Rd, Huddersfield, West Yorkshire HD3 4GN	01484 657541	01484 460579	Mrs Christine Spencer	382-4013	CY	11–16	1319	
Shelley College, A Specialist Centre For Science	Huddersfield Rd, Shelley, Huddersfield, West Yorkshire HD8 8NL	01484 868777	01484 222945	Mr John Fowler	382-4049	CY	13–18	1412	
Spen Valley Sports College	Roberttown La, Liversedge, West Yorkshire WF15 7LX	01924 325676	01924 325679	Mr Toby Eastaugh	382-4061	CY	11–16	884	
Westborough High School	Stockhill St, Dewsbury, West Yorkshire WF13 2JE	01924 325223	01924 325226	Mr David Roche	382-4057	CY	11–16	883	
Whitcliffe Mount Specialist Business and Enterprise College	Turnsteads Ave, Cleckheaton, West Yorkshire BD19 3AQ	01274 335182	01274 335187	Mr John Mcgee	382-4500	VC	13–18	1324	

Leeds

School name	Address	Tel	Fax	Headteacher	Ref	Type	Ages	Pupils	Other
Abbey Grange CE High School	Butcher Hill, Leeds, West Yorkshire LS16 5EA	0113 275 7877	0113 275 4794	Mr Alan Key	383-5400	VA	11–18	1249	CE
Allerton Grange School	Talbot Ave, Leeds LS17 6SF	0113 368 4200	0113 368 4201	Mrs Jean Hertrich	383-4040	CY	11–18	1723	
Allerton High School	King La, Leeds LS17 7AG	0113 268 4216	0113 237 0508	Mrs Elaine Silson	383-4032	CY	11–18	1099	
Benton Park School	Harrogate Rd, Leeds LS19 6LX	0113 250 2330	0113 250 9177	Mrs A.M. Clarke	383-4106	CY	11–18	1392	
Boston Spa School	Clifford Moor Rd, Wetherby LS23 6RW	01937 846636	01937 841069	Dr Alun Rees	383-4114	CY	11–18	1810	
Brigshaw High School and Language College	Brigshaw La, Castleford WF10 2HR	0113 336 8100	0113 286 4105	Mr P.J. Laurence	383-4113	CY	11–18	1394	
Bruntcliffe School	Bruntcliffe La, Leeds LS27 0LZ	0113 252 3225	0113 387 8683	Mrs Lynda Johnson	383-4109	VA	11–18	1479	
Cardinal Heenan RC High School	Tongue La, Meanwood, Leeds, West Yorkshire LS6 4QE	0113 294 1166	0113 294 0320	Miss Elizabeth Cox	383-4751	VA	11–16	917	RC
Carr Manor High School	Carr Manor Rd, Leeds LS17 5DJ	0113 268 8352	0113 288 8265	Mr Simon Flowers	383-4041	CY	11–18	655	
City of Leeds School	Bedford Field, Leeds LS6 2LG	0113 336 8310	0113 230 7721	Ms Margaret Hamlet	383-4031	CY	11–18	627	
Cockburn College of Arts	Parkside, Leeds LS11 5TT	0113 270 7451	0113 276 1853	Mr Colin Richardson	383-4047	CY	11–16	1070	
Corpus Christi RC College	Neville Rd, Leeds, West Yorkshire LS9 0TT	0113 248 2666	0113 235 0758	Mrs Sandra Redding	383-4752	VA	11–16	923	RC
Crawshaw School	Robin La, Pudsey LS28 9HU	0113 257 7617	0113 256 4722	Mr N.J. Turner	383-4107	CY	11–18	1188	
David Young Community Academy	Bishop's Way, Off North Parkway, Seacroft, Leeds LS14 6NU	0845 634 0007	0113 273 4216	Ms Ros McMullen	383-6905		11–18	892	CE
Farnley Park Maths and Computing College	Chapel La, Leeds LS12 5EU	0113 263 0741	0113 231 9582	Dr W.T. Pullen	383-4056	CY	11–18	834	
Garforth Community College	Lidgett La, Garforth, Leeds, West Yorkshire LS25 1LJ	0113 286 9091	0113 287 2727	Mr R.P. Edwards	383-4112	FD	11–18	1947	

School name	Address	Tel	Fax	Headteacher	Ref	Type	Ages	Pupils	Other
Guiseley School	Fieldhead Rd, Leeds LS20 8DT	01943 872315	01943 872287	Mr Paul Morrissey	383-4108	CY	11–18	1337	
Horsforth School	Lee La East, Leeds LS18 5RF	0113 226 5454	0113 226 5401	Mr S. Jex	383-4115	CY	11–18	1384	
Intake High School Arts College	Calverley La, Leeds LS13 1AH	0113 229 5454	0113 229 5522	Mrs Annette Hall	383-4054	CY	11–18	1122	
John Smeaton Community High School	Smeaton Approach, Leeds LS15 8TA	0113 293 0484	0113 293 0486	Mr John Daulby	383-4045	CY	11–18	1018	
Lawnswood School	Ring Rd, Leeds LS16 5AG	0113 284 4020	0113 284 4021	Mr M. Davidovic	383-4006	CY	11–18	1556	
Leeds College of Music	3 Quarry Hill, Leeds, West Yorkshire LS2 7PD	0113 222 3400	0113 243 8798	Mr David Hoult	383-8011				
Leeds Girls' High School	Headingley La, Leeds, West Yorkshire LS6 1BN	0113 274 4000	0113 275 2217	Ms Fishburn	383-6111		3–19	974	
Morley High School	Fountain St, Leeds LS27 0PD	0113 253 2952	0113 253 1483	Mr John Townsley	383-4101	CY	11–18	1484	
Mount St Mary's RC High School	Ellerby Rd, Leeds, West Yorkshire LS9 8LA	0113 245 5248	0113 242 8486	Mrs B. King	383-4753	VA	11–16	1125	RC
Otley Prince Henry's Grammar School Specialist Language College	Farnley La, Otley, West Yorkshire LS21 2BB	01943 463524	01943 850978	Mr John Steel	383-4501	VC	11–18	1402	
Parklands Girls' High School	South Parkway, Leeds LS14 6TY	0113 273 1964	0113 232 3591	Mrs M. Bisson	383-4059	CY	11–18	782	G
Priesthorpe School	Priesthorpe La, Pudsey LS28 5SG	0113 257 2618	0113 236 2167	Mr Kenneth Hall	383-4110	CY	11–18	1207	
Primrose High School	Stoney Rock La, Leeds LS9 7HD	0113 336 8320	0113 248 5265	Ms Tonia Bowden	383-4044	CY	11–18	870	
Pudsey Grangefield School	Richardshaw La, Pudsey LS28 7ND	0113 229 6000	0113 229 6001	Mr K. Cornforth	383-4102	CY	11–18	1184	
Ralph Thoresby High School Community Arts College	Holt Pk, Leeds LS16 7RX	0113 336 8181	0113 261 3132	Mr Mark Edwards	383-4062	CY	11–18	988	
Rodillian School	Longthorpe La, Wakefield WF3 3PS	01924 823135	01924 826718	Mr John Barrett	383-4103	CY	11–18	1337	
Roundhay School Technology College	Gledhow La, Leeds LS8 1ND	0113 393 1200	0113 393 1201	Mr N. Clephan	383-4063	CY	11–18	1539	
Royds School Specialist Language College	Pennington La, Leeds LS26 8EX	0113 205 9559	0113 205 9558	Mrs Bernadette Young	383-4104	CY	11–18	1323	
St Mary's RC Comprehensive School, Menston	Bradford Rd, Menston, Ilkley, West Yorkshire LS29 6AE	01943 883000	01943 870242	Mr Michael Pyle	383-4601	VA	11–18	1168	RC
South Leeds High School	Old Run Rd, Leeds LS10 2JU	0113 336 8448	0113 336 8449	Mr Colin Bell	383-4851	CY	11–18	1338	
Temple Moor High School Science College	Field End Gr, Leeds LS15 0PT	0113 264 5278	0113 260 9394	Mr Richard Sheriff	383-4046	CY	11–18	1310	
Victory Academy	Victory Centre, Garnet Road, Beeston, Leeds, West Yorkshire LS11 5JY	0113 277 5042	0113 277 7990	Rev Rosemary Foster	383-6121		3–18	12	Ch
West Leeds High School	Congress Mount, Leeds LS12 3DT	0113 263 3426	0113 214 3568	Mrs M. Brown	383-4058	CY	11–18	1119	
Wetherby High School	Hallfield La, Wetherby LS22 6JS	01937 522500	01937 522504	Ms A K Barnes	383-4111	CY	11–18	1012	
Woodkirk High Specialist Science School	Rein Rd, Wakefield WF3 1JQ	0113 336 8140	0113 252 6456	Mr Jonathan White	383-4105	CY	11–18	1794	
Wortley High School	Swallow Cres, Leeds LS12 4RB	0113 263 0745	0113 231 1829	Mrs Gillian Knutsson	383-4057	CY	11–18	857	

North East Lincolnshire

School name	Address	Tel	Fax	Headteacher	Ref	Type	Ages	Pupils	Other
Havelock Academy	Holyoake Rd, Grimsby, North East Lincolnshire DN32 8JL	08444 772498			812-6907		11–18		
Havelock School	Holyoake Rd, Grimsby DN32 8JL	01472 693946	01472 693375	Mrs J.S. Dyer	812-4008	CY	11–16	758	
Healing School, A Specialist Science College	Low Rd, Healing, Grimsby, Lincolnshire DN41 7QD	01472 502400	01472 502401	Mrs Ann Addison	812-4084	FD	11–16	790	
Hereford Technology School	Westward Ho, Grimsby, Lincolnshire DN34 5AH	01472 310015	01472 310016	Mr Jim Cunningham	812-4009	CY	11–16	1132	
Humberston Comprehensive School	Humberston Ave, Humberston, Grimsby, Lincolnshire DN36 4TF	01472 319990	01472 319993	Ms Carol Sanderson	812-4092	CY	11–16	707	
The Lindsey School and Community Arts College	Grainsby Ave, Cleethorpes DN35 9NX	01472 500123	01472 500446	Mr D. Walsh	812-4086	CY	11–18	1219	
Matthew Humberstone CE School	Chatsworth Pl, Cleethorpes, Lincolnshire DN35 9NF	01472 328888	01472 328400	Mr Ian Cox	812-4503	VC	11–18	1254	CE
Oasis Academy Immingham	Carver Rd, Immingham, Lincolnshire DN40 1JT	08444 771882	01469 556590	Mr Brian Dickson	812-6905		11–18		
Oasis Academy Wintringham	Weelsby Ave, Grimsby, North East Lincolnshire DN32 0AZ	01472 276336	01472 276336	Miss Jane Bowman	812-6906		11–18		
St Mary's RC School	Wootton Rd, Grimsby, North East Lincolnshire DN33 1HE	01472 871811	01472 878869	Mr Richard Mellos	812-4627	VA	11–16	360	RC
Tollbar Business and Enterprise College	Station Rd, New Waltham, Grimsby, N E Lincolnshire DN36 4RZ	01472 500505	01472 500506	Mr David Hampson	812-4078	FD	11–18	1996	

School name	Address	Tel	Fax	Headteacher	Ref	Type	Ages	Pupils	Other
Whitgift School	Crosland Rd, Grimsby DN37 9EH	01472 887117	01472 887634	Mr Mark Rushby	812-4011	CY	11–16	808	
Wintringham School	Weelsby Ave, Grimsby, North East Lincolnshire DN32 0AZ	01472 871811	01472 276336	Ms Jane Bowman	812-4038	CY	11–16	522	

North Lincolnshire

School name	Address	Tel	Fax	Headteacher	Ref	Type	Ages	Pupils	Other
Baysgarth School	Barrow Rd, Barton-upon-Humber DN18 6AE	01652 632576	01652 635973	Mr C. Saywell	813-4491	CY	11–16	974	
Brumby Engineering College	Cemetery Rd, Scunthorpe, North Lincolnshire DN16 1NT	01724 860237	01724 281176	Dr Thomas Clark	813-4075	CY	11–16	744	
Frederick Gough School – A Specialist Language College	Grange La South, Bottesford, Scunthorpe, Lincolnshire DN16 3NG	01724 860151	01724 271007	Mr Ben Lawrance	813-4087	CY	11–16	1189	
FTC (Foxhills Technology College)	Foxhills Rd, Scunthorpe, Lincolnshire DN15 8LJ	01724 860458	01724 270685	Mr Stephen Gallaher	813-4076	CY	11–16	742	
High Ridge School Specialist Sports College	Doncaster Rd, Scunthorpe, North Lincolnshire DN15 7DF	01724 842447	01724 289660	Mrs Karen Parsonage	813-4088	CY	11–16	547	
Huntcliff School	Redbourne Mere, Gainsborough, Lincolnshire DN21 4NN	01652 648276	01652 640390	Mrs Sue Bond	813-4074	CY	11–16	791	
Mellor Community College for Business, Enterprise and the Arts	Chandos Rd, Scunthorpe, North Lincolnshire DN17 1HA	01724 868666	01724 270378	Mrs Angela Briggs	813-4701	CY	11–16		
North Axholme School	Wharf Rd, Crowle, Scunthorpe, Lincolnshire DN17 4HU	01724 710368	01724 711923	Mr Joe Sellars	813-4082	CY	11–16	536	
St Bede's RC School	Collum Ave, Scunthorpe, Lincolnshire DN16 2TF	01724 861371	01724 280878	Mrs Michelle Travers	813-4700	VA	11–16	683	RC
Sir John Nelthorpe School – A Specialist Technology College for Science, Mathematics and Computing	Grammar School Rd, Brigg, Lincolnshire DN20 8AA	01652 656551	01652 658229	Mrs L. Hewlett-Parker	813-4501	VC	11–18	929	
South Axholme Community School	Burnham Rd, Epworth, Doncaster, South Yorkshire DN9 1BY	01427 872121	01427 875028	Mr M. Toms	813-4083	CY	11–16	955	
South Leys Business and Enterprise College	Enderby Rd, Scunthorpe, North Lincolnshire DN17 2JL	01724 868388	01724 280768	Mr Kevin John Maloney	813-4081	CY	11–16	424	
Thomas Sumpter School	Chandos Rd, Scunthorpe, North Lincolnshire DN17 1HA	01724 868666	01724 270378	Mrs Angela Briggs	813-4077	CY	11–16	726	
Vale of Ancholme Technology & Music College	Westmoor Hse, Grammar School Rd, Brigg, North Lincolnshire DN20 8BA	01652 652908	01652 650245	Mrs G. Young	813-4091	CY	11–18	719	
Winterton Comprehensive School with Specialist Status in Engineering	Newport Dr, Winterton, Scunthorpe, Lincolnshire DN15 9QD	01724 732777	01724 733051	Mr John Fitzgerald	813-4090	CY	11–16	688	

North Yorkshire

School name	Address	Tel	Fax	Headteacher	Ref	Type	Ages	Pupils	Other
Aireville School	Gargrave Rd, Skipton, North Yorkshire BD23 1UQ	01756 792965	01756 701075	Mr Stuart Mason	815-4208	CY	11–16	679	
Allertonshire School	Brompton Rd, Northallerton, North Yorkshire DL6 1ED	01609 772888	01609 780517	Mr David Bradley	815-4074	CY	11–14	708	
Bartly High School	York Rd, Bartly, Selby, North Yorkshire YO8 5JP	01757 706161	01757 213699	Rev Francis Loftus	815-4232	CY	11–16	681	
Bedale High School	Fitzalan Rd, Bedale, North Yorkshire DL8 2EQ	01677 422419	01677 425488	Mr Graham Turner	815-4052	CY	11–16	860	
Boroughbridge High School	Wetherby Rd, Boroughbridge, York, North Yorkshire YO51 9JX	01423 323540	01423 324353	Ms E. Dixon	815-4221	CY	11–18	696	
Brayton College	Doncaster Rd, Selby, North Yorkshire YO8 9QS	01757 707731	01757 213389	Mr John G Kesterton	815-4224	CY	11–16	1092	
Caedmon College	Airy Hill, Whitby, North Yorkshire YO21 1QA	01947 602570	01947 820315	Mr Tony Hewitt	815-4059	CY	11–14	489	
The Collegiate Foundation	Undercroft Administration Centre, Thorpe Underwood Estate, York, North Yorkshire YO26 9SS	0870 742 3300	01423 333912	Mr Brian Martin	815-6037		14–18	28	
Easingwold School	York Rd, Easingwold, York, North Yorkshire YO61 3EF	01347 821451	01347 823301	Mrs Carey Chidwick	815-4005	CY	11–18	1369	
Ermysted's Grammar School	Gargrave Rd, Skipton, North Yorkshire BD23 1PL	01756 792186	01756 793714	Mr Tom Ashworth	815-4608	VA	11–16	694	B
Eskdale School	Stainsacre La, Whitby, North Yorkshire YO22 4HS	01947 602856	01947 605748	Mr Keith Prytherch	815-4041	CY	11–14	301	
Filey School	Muston Rd, Filey, North Yorkshire YO14 0HG	01723 512354	01723 512165	Mrs Lorraine Gill	815-4150	CY	11–16	830	
George Pindar Community Sports College	Moor La, Eastfield, Scarborough, North Yorkshire YO11 3LW	01723 582194	01723 583110	Mr Hugh Bellamy	815-4069	CY	11–16	858	
Graham School Science College	Woodlands Dr, Scarborough, North Yorkshire YO12 6QW	01723 366451	01723 364102	Mr Garry Hancock	815-4070	CY	11–16	1318	
Harrogate Grammar School	Arthur Ave, Harrogate, North Yorkshire HG2 0DZ	01423 531127	01423 521325	Mr Richard Sheriff	815-4200	CY	11–18	1759	
Harrogate High School	Ainsty Rd, Harrogate, North Yorkshire HG1 4AP	01423 548800	01423 501664	Mr V. McNicholas	815-4219	CY	11–18	1074	

3

School name	Address	Tel	Fax	Headteacher	Ref	Type	Ages	Pupils	Other
Holy Family RC High School, Carlton	Longhedge La., Carlton, Goole, East Riding of Yorkshire DN14 9NS	01405 860276	01405 860311	Miss Annette Dews	815-4610	VA	11–16	447	RC
Howsham Hall School	Barton-le-Willows, York, North Yorkshire YO60 7PJ	01653 618374	01653 618295	Mr S. Knock	815-6020		5–14	60	RC
King James's School	King James Rd, Knaresborough, North Yorkshire HG5 8EB	01423 866061	01423 861189	Dr David Hudson	815-4202	CY	11–18	1706	
Lady Lumley's School	Swainsea La., Pickering, North Yorkshire YO18 8NG	01751 472846	01751 477259	Mr John Tomsett	815-4054	CY	11–18	1015	
Malton School	Middlecave Rd, Malton, North Yorkshire YO17 7NH	01653 692828	01653 696871	Mr Rob Williams	815-4077	CY	11–18	687	
Nidderdale High School and Community College	Low Wath Rd, Pateley Bridge, Harrogate, North Yorkshire HG3 5HL	01423 711246	01423 711859	Mr David Read	815-4223	CY	11–16	447	
Northallerton College	Grammar School La., Northallerton, North Yorkshire DL6 1DD	01609 773340	01609 770265	Mr Michael Hill	815-4503	VC	14–18	946	
Norton College	Langton Rd, Norton, Malton, North Yorkshire YO17 9PT	01653 693296	01653 693338	Mr Tony Rawdin	815-4152	CY	11–16	668	
Raincliffe School	Lady Ediths Dr, Scarborough, North Yorkshire YO12 5RL	01723 366527	01723 501580	Mr G. Steele	815-4071	CY	11–16	482	
Richmond School	Darlington Rd, Richmond, North Yorkshire DL10 7BQ	01748 850111	01748 828106	Mr Phillip Beever	815-4076	CY	11–18	1650	
Ripon College	Clotherholme Rd, Ripon, North Yorkshire HG4 2DE	01765 604564	01765 604564	Mr P. Lowery	815-4203	CY	11–18	622	
Ripon Grammar School	Clotherholme Rd, Ripon, North Yorkshire HG4 2DG	01765 602647	01765 606388	Mr Martin Pearman	815-4215	CY	11–18	821	R
Risedale Sports and Community College	Hipswell, Catterick Garrison, North Yorkshire DL9 4BD	01748 833501	01748 836149	Mr Tadeusz Zaranko	815-4004	CY	11–16	527	
Rossett School	Green La., Harrogate, North Yorkshire HG2 9JP	01423 564444	01423 502301	Mrs Patricia Hunter	815-4217	CY	11–18	1305	
Ryedale School	Gale La., Nawton, York, North Yorkshire YO62 7SL	01439 771665	01439 770969	Mr Geoffrey Jenkinson	815-4022	CY	11–16	595	
St Aidan's CE High School	Oatlands Dr, Harrogate, North Yorkshire HG2 8JR	01423 885814	01423 884327	Mr Dennis Richards	815-4611	VA	11–18	1823	CE
St Augustine's Roman RC School, Scarborough	Sandybed La., Stepney Hill, Scarborough, North Yorkshire YO12 5LH	01723 363280	01723 500490	Mr Roger Cannon	815-4604	VA	11–16	478	RC
St Francis Xavier School	Darlington Rd, Richmond, North Yorkshire DL10 7DA	01748 823414	01748 823946	Dr Joseph Mc Auley	815-4605	VA	11–16	400	RC/CE
St John Fisher RC High School	Hookstone Dr, Harrogate, North Yorkshire HG2 8PT	01423 887254	01423 881056	Mr P. Jackson	815-4609	VA	11–18	1347	RC
Scalby School	Fieldstead Cres, Newby, Scarborough, North Yorkshire YO12 6TH	01723 362301	01723 369226	Mr Andy Tebay	815-4073	CY	11–16	1011	
Selby High School Specialist School for the Arts	Leeds Rd, Selby, North Yorkshire YO8 4HT	01757 703327	01757 708212	Mr Paul Eckersley	815-4225	CY	11–16	872	
Settle College	Giggleswick, Settle, North Yorkshire BD24 0AU	01729 822451	01729 823830	Mr W. Bancroft	815-4205	CY	13–18	557	
Sherburn High School	Garden La., Sherburn-in-Elmet, Leeds, West Yorkshire LS25 6AS	01977 682442	01977 682752	Mr Carl Sugden	815-4216	CY	11–18	944	
Skipton Girls' High School	Gargrave Rd, Skipton, North Yorkshire BD23 1QL	01756 707600	01756 701068	Mrs Janet Renou	815-4518	FD	11–18	732	G
South Craven School	Holme La., Cross Hills, Keighley, West Yorkshire BD20 7RL	01535 632861	01535 632859	Dr Andrew Cummings	815-4210	FD	11–18	1746	
Stokesley School	Station Rd, Stokesley, North Yorkshire TS9 5AL	01642 710050	01642 710836	Mrs Catherine Brooke	815-4047	CY	11–18	1382	
Tadcaster Grammar School	Toulston La., Tadcaster, North Yorkshire LS24 9NB	01937 833466	01937 836082	Mr G. Mitchell	815-4211	CY	11–18	1668	
Thirsk School and Sixth Form College	Topcliffe Rd, Sowerby, Thirsk, North Yorkshire YO7 1RZ	01845 522024	01845 526617	Mr J.C. Lewis	815-4035	CY	11–18	1132	
Upper Wharfedale School	Wharfeside Ave, Threshfield, Skipton, North Yorkshire BD23 5BS	01756 752215	01756 752363	Mrs Ros Rees	815-4206	CY	11–16	286	
The Wensleydale School	Richmond Rd, Leyburn, North Yorkshire DL8 5HY	01969 622244	01969 624086	Mr David Eaton	815-4075	CY	11–18	537	
Whitby Community College	Prospect Hill, Whitby, North Yorkshire YO21 1LA	01947 602406	01947 821169	Ms R.M. Totton	815-4039	VA	14–18	887	

Rotherham

School name	Address	Tel	Fax	Headteacher	Ref	Type	Ages	Pupils	Other
Aston Comprehensive School	Aughton Rd, Swallownest, Sheffield, South Yorkshire S26 4SF	0114 287 2171	0114 287 6359	Mrs Eunice Newton	372-4021	CY	11–18	1794	
Brinsworth Comprehensive School	Brinsworth Rd, Brinsworth, Rotherham, South Yorkshire S60 5EJ	01709 828383	01709 835937	Mr Mike Gray	372-4024	CY	11–18	1501	
Clifton: A Community Arts School	Middle La., Rotherham, South Yorkshire S65 2SN	01709 515005	01709 515015	Mr Patrick Daley	372-4000	CY	11–16	1321	
Dinnington Comprehensive Specialising in Science and Engineering	Doe Quarry La., Dinnington, Sheffield, South Yorkshire S25 2NZ	01909 550066	01909 550170	Ms Sue Carhart	372-4022	CY	11–18	1454	
Maltby Comprehensive School	Braithwell Rd, Maltby, Rotherham, South Yorkshire S66 8AB	01709 812864	01709 790955	Mr David Sutton	372-4015	CY	11–18	1318	
Oakwood Technology College	Moorgate Rd, Rotherham, South Yorkshire S60 2UH	01709 512222	01709 512244	Mrs Jan Charters	372-4003	CY	11–16	1083	
Pope Pius X RC High School	Wath Wood Rd, Wath-upon-Dearne, Rotherham, South Yorkshire S63 7PQ	01709 767900	01709 875106	Mrs Anne Winfield	372-4601	VA	11–16	671	RC

School name	Address	Tel	Fax	Headteacher	Ref	Type	Ages	Pupils	Other
Rawmarsh Community School – A Sports College	Monkwood Rd, Rawmarsh, Rotherham, South Yorkshire S62 7GA	01709 710672	01709 710078	Mr John Lambert	372-4016	CY	11–16	1107	
St Bernard's RC High School, Specialist School for the Arts	Herringthorpe Valley Rd, Rotherham, South Yorkshire S65 3BE	01709 828183	01709 372609	Mr David Butler	372-4800	VA	11–16	661	RC
Swinton Community School	East Ave, Swinton, Mexborough, South Yorkshire S64 8JW	01709 570586	01709 571563	Mr Dave Shevill	372-4023	CY	11–18	1101	
Thrybergh Comprehensive School	Arran Hill, Thrybergh, Rotherham, South Yorkshire S65 4BJ	01709 850471	01709 854561	Mr David Pridding	372-4020	CY	11–16	591	
Wales High School	Storth La, Kiveton Pk, Sheffield, South Yorkshire S26 5QQ	01909 771291	01909 772849	Mr Lawrence Morton	372-4025	CY	11–18	1519	
Wath Comprehensive School : a Language College	Sandygate, Wath-on-Dearne, Rotherham, South Yorkshire S63 7NW	01709 760222	01709 761094	Mrs Patricia Ward	372-4017	CY	11–18	1749	
Wickersley School and Sports College	Bawtry Rd, Wickersley, Rotherham, South Yorkshire S66 1JL	01709 542147	01709 703364	Mr David Hudson	372-4018	CY	11–18	1815	
Wingfield School	Wingfield Rd, Rotherham, South Yorkshire S61 4AU	01709 513002	01709 511196	Miss Pippa Dodgshon	372-4011	CY	11–16	855	
Winterhill School	High St, Kimberworth, Rotherham, South Yorkshire S61 2BD	01709 740232	01709 740403	Mr Roger Burman	372-4010	CY	11–16	1608	

Sheffield

School name	Address	Tel	Fax	Headteacher	Ref	Type	Ages	Pupils	Other
Abbeydale Grange School	Hastings Rd, Sheffield, South Yorkshire S7 2GU	0114 255 7301	0114 250 8540	Ms Catherine Bull	373-4254	FD	11–16	635	
All Saints' RC High School	Granville Rd, Sheffield, South Yorkshire S2 2RJ	0114 272 4851	0114 276 5371	Mr R.B. Sawyer	373-5401	VA	11–18	1202	RC
Birley Community College	Thornbridge Ave, Sheffield, South Yorkshire S12 3AB	0114 239 2531	0114 265 5034	Mr A. Vicars	373-4276	CY	11–16	1185	
Bradfield School	Kirk Edge Rd, Worrall, Sheffield, South Yorkshire S35 0AE	0114 286 3861	0114 286 2246	Ms Carol Gormley	373-4272	CY	11–16	916	
Chaucer Business and Enterprise College	Wordsworth Ave, Sheffield, South Yorkshire S5 8NH	0114 232 2338	0114 232 1426	Mr Steve Robinson	373-4233	CY	11–16	961	
The City School	Stradbroke Rd, Sheffield, South Yorkshire S13 8SS	0114 239 2571	0114 264 8752	Ms J.M. Warne	373-4002	CY	11–16	1457	
Ecclesfield School	Chapeltown Rd, Ecclesfield, Sheffield, South Yorkshire S35 9WD	0114 246 1156	0114 257 0998	Mrs A.M. Talboys	373-4270	CY	11–16	1745	
Fir Vale School	Owler La, Sheffield, South Yorkshire S4 8GB	0114 243 9391	0114 261 1640	Mrs Lesley Bowes	373-4280	CY	11–16	751	
Firth Park Community Arts College	Fircroft Ave, Sheffield, South Yorkshire S5 0SD	0114 257 6238	0114 257 6239	Mrs M. Laycock	373-4256	CY	11–16	1328	
Handsworth Grange School	Handsworth Grange Rd, Handsworth, Sheffield, South Yorkshire S13 9HJ	0114 269 4801	0114 269 2832	Mr Stephen Burnage	373-4278	CY	11–16	1029	
High Storrs School	High Storrs Rd, Sheffield, South Yorkshire S11 7LH	0114 267 0000	0114 266 3624	Mr M. Chapman	373-4257	CY	11–18	1570	
King Ecgbert School	Totley Brook Rd, Sheffield, South Yorkshire S17 3QU	0114 236 9931	0114 236 2468	Mr B. Evans	373-4230	CY	11–18	1243	
King Edward VII School	Glossop Rd, Sheffield, South Yorkshire S10 2PW	0114 266 2518	0114 268 7690	Mr M.H.A. Lewis	373-4259	CY	11–18	1670	
Meadowhead School	Dyche La, Sheffield, South Yorkshire S8 8BR	0114 237 2723	0114 283 9855	Ms C. James	373-4279	CY	11–16	1641	
Myers Grove School	Wood La, Sheffield, South Yorkshire S6 5HG	0114 234 8805	0114 285 4246	Mr John Wilkinson	373-4236	CY	11–16	769	
Newfield Secondary School	Lees Hall Rd, Sheffield, South Yorkshire S8 9JP	0114 255 7331	0114 258 3625	Mr K. Yeates	373-4260	CY	11–16	1045	
Notre Dame RC High School	Fulwood Rd, Sheffield, South Yorkshire S10 3BT	0114 230 2536	0114 230 8833	Mr J. Conway	373-5400	VA	11–18	1310	RC
Parkwood High School	Penrith Rd, Sheffield, South Yorkshire S5 8UF	0114 231 0221		Mr Chris Mallaband	373-4281	CY	11–16	727	
Sheffield Park Academy	Beaumont Cl, Sheffield S2 1RY	0114 239 2661	0114 265 4616	Mr Andy Gardiner	373-6905		11–19	1059	Ch
Sheffield Springs Academy	East Bank Rd, Sheffield S2 2AL	0114 239 2631	0114 239 9666	Mr G. Inglish	373-6906		11–19	976	Ch
Silverdale School	Bents Cres, Sheffield, South Yorkshire S11 9QH	0114 236 9991	0114 262 0627	Mrs H. Storey	373-4229	CY	11–18	1204	
Stocksbridge High School	Shayhouse La, Stocksbridge, Sheffield, South Yorkshire S36 1FD	0114 288 3153	0114 288 8475	Mrs J. Featherstone	373-4271	CY	11–16	925	
Tapton School	Darwin La, Sheffield, South Yorkshire S10 5RG	0114 267 1414	0114 230 6590	Mr D. Bowes	373-4234	CY	11–18	1596	
Westfield Sports College	Eckington La, Sothall, Sheffield, South Yorkshire S20 1HQ	0114 248 5221		Mr R.W. Porter	373-4252	CY	11–16	1296	
Wisewood School and Community Sports College	Rural La, Sheffield, South Yorkshire S6 4BH	0114 233 3606	0114 231 3725	Ms Diane McKinlay	373-4219	CY	11–16	777	
Yewlands School Technology College	Creswick La, Grenoside, Sheffield, South Yorkshire S35 8NN	0114 232 9010	0114 240 2522	Mrs Angela Armytage	373-4253	CY	11–16	893	

3

Wakefield

School name	Address	Tel	Fax	Headteacher	Ref	Type	Ages	Pupils	Other
Airedale High School	Crewe Rd, Airedale, Castleford, West Yorkshire WF10 3JU	01977 664555	01977 664556	Mr Paul Frazer	384-4026	CY	11–16	1055	
Carleton Community High School A Specialist Science College	Green La, Carleton, Pontefract, West Yorkshire WF8 3NW	01977 722605	01977 722609	Mr Robert Foreman	384-4027	CY	11–16	956	
Castleford High School Technology College	Ferrybridge Rd, Castleford, West Yorkshire WF10 4JQ	01977 605060	01977 605070	Mr Roy Vaughan	384-4015	CY	11–16	1260	
Cathedral CE (VC) High School, The	Thornes Rd, Wakefield, West Yorkshire WF2 8QF	01924 303740	01924 382674	Mr Paul West	384-4506	VC	11–16	986	CE
Crofton High School – Specialists in Maths and Computing	High St, Crofton, Wakefield, West Yorkshire WF4 1NF	01924 303940	01924 303937	Mr Jeremy Horsley	384-4029	CY	11–16	1075	
Featherstone Technology College	Pontefract Rd, Purston, Featherstone, Pontefract, West Yorkshire WF7 5AJ	01977 722805	01977 722809	Dr Stuart Wilson	384-4042	CY	11–16	724	
The Freeston Business and Enterprise College	Favell Ave, Normanton, West Yorkshire WF6 1HZ	01924 302560	01924 302564	Mrs Gillian Metcalfe	384-4504	VC	11–16	1061	
Hemsworth Arts and Community College	Station Rd, Hemsworth, Pontefract, West Yorkshire WF9 4HW	01977 624220	01977 624221	Mrs Pamela Massett	384-4016	CY	11–18	1676	
Horbury School – A Specialist Language College	Wakefield Rd, Horbury, Wakefield, West Yorkshire WF4 5HE	01924 303065	01924 303067	Mrs Deborah Duncan	384-4028	CY	11–16	1078	
Kettlethorpe High School, A Specialist Maths and Computing College	Kettlethorpe Hall Dr, Standbridge La, Sandal, Wakefield, West Yorkshire WF2 7EL	01924 303510	01924 303514	Mr Tudor Griffiths	384-4006	CY	11–16	1589	
The King's School Specialising in Mathematics and Computing	Mill Hill La, Pontefract, West Yorkshire WF8 4JF	01977 601701	01977 602259	Mrs Julie A Craig	384-4020	CY	11–16	1038	
Knottingley High School and Sports College	Middle La, Knottingley, West Yorkshire WF11 0BZ	01977 622850	01977 622899	Mr Arthur Hutchinson	384-4031	CY	11–16	864	
Minsthorpe Community College, A Specialist Science College	Minsthorpe La, South Elmsall, Pontefract, West Yorkshire WF9 2UJ	01977 723810	01977 723814	Mr Richard Brown	384-4030	CY	11–18	1751	
Ossett School	Storrs Hill Rd, Ossett, West Yorkshire WF5 0DG	01924 232820	01924 302852	Mr Martin Shevill	384-4023	CY	11–18	1665	
Outwood Grange College of Technology	Potovens La, Outwood, Wakefield, West Yorkshire WF1 2PF	01924 303815	01924 303820	Mr Michael Wilkins	384-4024	CY	11–18	2097	
St Thomas a Becket RC College Specialist status in Humanities	Barnsley Rd, Sandal, Wakefield, West Yorkshire WF2 6EQ	01924 303545	01924 303548	Mr B.S.L. Donnellan	384-4800	VA	11–16	763	RC
St Wilfrid's RC High School and Sixth Form College	Cutsyke Rd, Featherstone, Pontefract, West Yorkshire WF7 6BD	01977 691000	01977 723569	Mr John McNally	384-4604	VA	11–18	1640	RC
Wakefield City High School – A Specialist Maths and Computing College	Warmfield View, Wakefield, West Yorkshire WF1 4SF	01924 303755	01924 303758	Mr Alan Yellup	384-4009	CY	11–16	644	

York

School name	Address	Tel	Fax	Headteacher	Ref	Type	Ages	Pupils	Other
All Saints RC School	Mill Mount La, York, North Yorkshire YO24 1BJ	01904 647877	01904 647877	Mr Bill Scriven	816-4702	VA	11–18	1203	RC
Archbishop Holgate's School	Hull Rd, York, North Yorkshire YO10 5ZA	01904 411341	01904 414948	Mr J. Harris	816-4500	VA	11–16	835	CE
Burnholme Community College	Bad Bargain La, York, North Yorkshire YO31 0GW	01904 415906	01904 426302	Mr Anthony Gavin	816-4227	CY	11–16	439	
Canon Lee School	Rawcliffe Dr, Clifton Without, York, North Yorkshire YO30 6ZS	01904 560000	01904 610386	Mr Kevin Deadman	816-4003	CY	11–16	941	
Fulford School	Fulfordgate, Heslington La, Fulford, York, North Yorkshire YO10 4FY	01904 633300	01904 626899	Mr Stephen Smith	816-4153	CY	11–18	1288	
Huntington School	Huntington Rd, Huntington, York YO32 9WT	01904 752100	01904 752101	Mr John Tomsett	816-4063	CY	11–18	1512	
Joseph Rowntree School	Haxby Rd, New Earswick, York, North Yorkshire YO32 4BZ	01904 768107	01904 750458	Mr Hugh Porter	816-4508	VC	11–18	1219	
Manor CE VA School, York	Low Poppleton La, York, North Yorkshire YO26 6BB	01904 798722	01904 782902	Mr Brian Crosby	816-4602	VA	11–16	641	CE
Millthorpe School	Nunthorpe Ave, York, North Yorkshire YO23 1WF	01904 686400	01904 630753	Mr Tony Wootton	816-4229	CY	11–16	1025	
York High School	Dijon Ave, Acomb, York, North Yorkshire YO24 3DD	01904 791674		Mr David Ellis	816-4703	CY	11–16		

Scotland

Aberdeen City

School name	Address	Website	E-mail	Tel	Fax	Pupils
Aberdeen Grammar School	Skene St, Aberdeen AB10 1HT	www.grammar.org.uk	office@grammar.org.uk	01224 642299	01224 627413	1172
Bankhead Academy	Bankhead Ave, Bucksburn, Aberdeen AB21 9ES	www.bankhead.aberdeen.sch.uk	enquiries@bankhead.aberdeen.sch.uk	01224 713861	01224 713246	458
Bridge of Don Academy	Braehead Way, Bridge of Don, Aberdeen AB22 8RR	www.bridgeofdon.aberdeen.sch.uk	accboda@mplc.co.uk	01224 707583	01224 706910	725
Cults Academy	Hillview Dr, Cults, Aberdeen AB15 9SA	www.cults-academy.aberdeen.sch.uk	enquiries@cults-academy.aberdeen.sch.uk	01224 868801	01224 869865	1150
Dyce Academy	Riverview Dr, Dyce, Aberdeen AB21 7NF	www.dyceacademy.aberdeen.sch.uk	admin@dyceacademy.aberdeen.sch.uk	01224 725118	01224 772571	494
Harlaw Academy	18–20 Albyn Pl, Aberdeen AB10 1RG		accharlaw@rmplc.co.uk	01224 589251	01224 212794	950
Hazlehead Academy	Groat's Rd, Aberdeen AB15 8BE	www.hazleheadacy.aberdeen.sch.uk	enquiries@hazleheadacy.aberdeen.sch.uk	01224 310184	01224 208434	1032
Kincorth Academy	Kincorth Circle, Kincorth, Aberdeen AB12 5NL	www.kincorth.aberdeen.sch.uk	enquiries@kincorth.aberdeen.sch.uk	01224 872881	01224 878958	777
Northfield Academy	Granitehill Pl, Aberdeen AB16 7AU	www.northfield.aberdeen.sch.uk	enquiries@accnorth.aberdeen.sch.uk	01224 699715	01224 685239	933
Oldmachar Academy	Jesmond Dr, Bridge of Don, Aberdeen AB22 8UR	www.oldmachar.aberdeen.sch.uk	enquiries@oldmachar.aberdeen.sch.uk	01224 820887	01224 823850	1040
St Machar Academy	St Machar Dr, Aberdeen AB24 3YZ	www.rsc.co.uk	enquiries@stmachar.aberdeen.sch.uk	01224 492855	01224 276112	1144
Torry Academy	Tullos Circle, Aberdeen AB11 8HD	www.torry.aberdeen.sch.uk	enquiries@torry.aberdeen.sch.uk	01224 876733	01224 249597	485

Aberdeenshire

School name	Address	Website	E-mail	Tel	Fax	Pupils
Aboyne Academy	Bridgeview Rd, Aboyne, Aberdeenshire AB34 5JN	www.aboyneacademy.com	aboyne.aca@aberdeenshire.gov.uk	01339 887722	01339 885020	645
Alford Academy	Murray Terr, Alford, Aberdeenshire AB33 8PY	atschool.eduweb.co.uk	alford.aca@aberdeenshire.gov.uk	01975 562251	01975 563269	556
Banchory Academy	Schoolhill, Banchory, Aberdeenshire AB31 5TQ	www.banchoryacademy.co.uk	banchory.aca@aberdeenshire.gov.uk	01330 823357	01330 825409	961
Banff Academy	Bellevue Rd, Banff, Aberdeenshire AB45 1BY	atschool.eduweb.co.uk	banff.aca@aberdeenshire.gov.uk	01261 812591	01261 815491	1083
Ellon Academy	Schoolhill, Ellon, Aberdeenshire AB41 9AX	www.ellonacademy.org.uk	ellonac@tsc.co.uk	01358 720715	01358 723758	1200
Fraserburgh Academy	Dennyduff Rd, Fraserburgh, Aberdeenshire AB43 9NA	atschool.eduweb.co.uk	fraserburgh.ac@rmplc.co.uk	01346 515771	01346 510229	1277
The Gordon Schools	Castle St, Huntly, Aberdeenshire AB54 4SE	www.gordonschools.aberdeenshire.sch.uk	gordonschools.aca@aberdeenshire.gov.uk	01466 792181	01466 794715	859
Inverurie Academy	Jackson St, Inverurie, Aberdeenshire AB51 3PX	www.inverurieacademy.co.uk	inverurie.aca@aberdeenshire.gov.uk	01467 621655	01467 624425	918
Kemnay Academy	Bremner Way, Kemnay, Inverurie, Aberdeenshire AB51 5FW	www.kemnayacademy.aberdeenshire.sch.uk		01467 643535	01467 642306	607
Mackie Academy	Slug Rd, Stonehaven, Aberdeenshire AB39 3DF	www.mackie.aberdeenshire.sch.uk	webmaster@mackieacademy.aberdeenshire.sch.uk	01569 762071	01569 767287	1242
Mearns Academy	Aberdeen Rd, Laurencekirk, Aberdeenshire AB30 1AJ	www.mearns.aberdeenshire.sch.uk	mearns.aca@aberdeenshire.gov.uk	01561 378817	01561 378252	644
Meldrum Academy	Colpy Rd, Oldmeldrum, Inverurie, Aberdeenshire AB51 0NT	www.meldrumacademy.co.uk		01651 871300	01651 871313	965
Mintlaw Academy	Station Rd, Mintlaw, Peterhead, Aberdeenshire AB42 5FN	www.mintlawacademy.aberdeenshire.sch.uk	mintlaw.aca@aberdeenshire.gov.uk	01771 622994	01771 624228	863
Peterhead Academy	Prince St, Peterhead, Aberdeenshire AB42 1SY	www.peterheadacademy.aberdeenshire.sch.uk	gmilne@peterheadacademy.aberdeenshire.sch.uk	01779 472231	01779 472055	1352
Portlethen Academy	Bruntland Rd, Portlethen, Aberdeen, Aberdeenshire AB12 4QL	www.portlethenacademy.aberdeenshire.sch.uk		01224 782174	01224 782076	858
Turriff Academy	Victoria Terr, Turriff, Aberdeenshire AB53 4EE	www.turriff.aberdeenshire.sch.uk	turriff.aca@aberdeenshire.gov.uk	01888 563216	01888 568966	770
Westhill Academy	Hays Way, Westhill, Aberdeenshire AB32 6XZ	www.westhillacademy.aberdeenshire.sch.uk	westhill.aca@aberdeenshire.gov.uk	01224 740111	01224 743163	945

3

Angus

School name	Address	Website	E-mail	Tel	Fax	Pupils
Arbroath Academy	Glenisla Dr, Arbroath, Angus DD11 5JD	www.arbroathacademy.angus.sch.uk	arbroathacademy@arbroathacademy.angus.sch.uk	01241 872978	01241 871140	600
Arbroath High School	Keptie Rd, Arbroath, Angus DD11 3EN	www.arbroathhigh.angus.sch.uk	arbroathhigh@arbroathhigh.angus.sch.uk	01241 872033	01241 878693	1088
Brechin High School	Duke St, Brechin, Angus DD9 6LB	www.brechinhigh.angus.sch.uk	brechinhigh@brechinhigh.angus.sch.uk	01356 622135	01356 626774	621
Carnoustie High School	Shanwell Rd, Carnoustie, Angus DD7 7SS	www.carnoustiehigh.angus.sch.uk	carnoustiehigh@carnoustiehigh.angus.sch.uk	01241 852601	01241 855778	868
Forfar Academy	Taylor St, Forfar, Angus DD8 3LB		forfaracademy@forfaracademy.angus.sch.uk	01307 464545	01307 468567	1115
Monifieth High School	Panmurefield Rd, Monifieth, Angus DD5 4QT	www.monifieth-high.org.uk	monifiethhigh@monifiethhigh.angus.org.uk	01382 534466	01382 532987	1073
Montrose Academy	Academy Sq, Montrose, Angus DD10 8HU	www.montroseacademy.angus.sch.uk	montroseacademy@montroseacademy.angus.sch.uk	01674 672626	01674 678919	975
Webster's High School	Kirriemuir, Angus DD8 5BR	www.webstershigh.angus.sch.uk	webstershigh@webstershigh.angus.sch.uk	01575 572840	01575 573692	791

Argyll and Bute

School name	Address	Website	E-mail	Tel	Fax	Pupils
Campbeltown Grammar School	Hutcheon Rd, Campbeltown, Argyll and Bute PA28 6JS		enquiries@campbeltown.argyll-bute.sch.uk	01586 552907	01586 554691	580
Dunoon Grammar School	Ardenslate Rd, Kirn, Argyll and Bute PA23 8LU		enquiries@dunoongrammar.argyll-bute.sch.uk	01369 705010	01369 702168	1006
Hermitage Academy	Campbell Dr, Colgrain, Helensburgh, Argyll and Bute G84 7TB	www.hermitageacademy.argyll-bute.sch.uk	enquiries@hermitageacademy.argyll-bute.sch.uk	01436 672145	01436 671338	1405
Islay High School	Bowmore, Isle of Islay, Argyll and Bute PA43 7LS	www.islay.argyll-bute.sch.uk	enquiries@islay.argyll-bute.sch.uk	01496 810239	01496 810755	249
Lochgilphead High School	Lochgilphead, Argyll and Bute PA31 8JY		enquiries@lochgilpheadhigh.argyll-bute.sch.uk	01546 602598	01546 603084	516
Oban High School	Soroba Rd, Oban, Argyll and Bute PA34 4JB		enquiries@obanhigh.argyll-bute.sch.uk	01631 564231	01631 565916	1104
Rothesay Academy	Academy Rd, Rothesay, Isle of Bute, Argyll and Bute PA20 0BG		enquiries@rothesayacademy.argyll-bute.sch.uk	01700 503097	01700 505297	461
Tarbert Academy	School Rd, Tarbert, Argyll and Bute PA29 6TE	www.tarbert.argyll-bute.sch.uk	enquiries@tarbert.argyll-bute.sch.uk	01880 820269	01880 820957	162
Tiree High School	Isle of Tiree, Argyll and Bute PA77 6XA	www.tiree.argyll-bute.sch.uk	enquiries@tiree.argyll-bute.sch.uk	01879 220795	01879 220721	54
Tobermory High School	Tobermory, Isle of Mull, Argyll and Bute PA75 6PB	www.tobermory.argyll-bute.sch.uk	enquiries@tobermory.argyll-bute.sch.uk	01688 302062	01688 302093	164

Clackmannanshire

School name	Address	Website	E-mail	Tel	Fax	Pupils
Alloa Academy	Claremont, Alloa, Clackmannanshire FK10 2EQ	www.clacksweb.org.uk	alloa@edu.clacks.gov.uk	01259 214979	01259 211022	828
Alva Academy	Queen St, Alva, Clackmannanshire FK12 5LY	www.alvaacademy.clacks.sch.uk		01259 760342	01259 769169	1130
Lornshill Academy	Tullibody Rd, Alloa, Clackmannanshire FK10 2ES	www.clacksweb.org.uk	lornshill@edu.clacks.gov.uk	01259 214331	01259 720402	1057

Comhairle nan Eilean Siar (Western Isles)

School name	Address	Website	E-mail	Tel	Fax	Pupils
Back School	Back, Lewis, Western Isles HS2 0LB	www.sgoilabhac.org.uk	backschool@fnes.net	01851 820230	01851 820620	61
Bayble School	Point, Isle of Lewis, Western Isles HS2 0PX	www.cne-siar.gov.uk	bayble-school@cne-siar.gov.uk	01851 870216	01851 870913	24
Castlebay School	Castlebay, Barra, Western Isles HS9 5XD	www.cne-siar.gov.uk	castelbay-school@cne-siar.gov.uk	01871 810471	01871 810213	107
Daliburgh School	Daliburgh, South Uist, Western Isles HS8 5SS	www.cne-siar.gov.uk	dailburghschool@eileanansiar.biblio.net	01878 700276	01878 700213	15
Lionel	Lionel, Port of Ness, Isle of Lewis, Western Isles HS2 0XB	www.lionelschool.freeuk.com	lionel-school@cne-siar.gov.uk	01851 810208	01851 810742	42
Paible School	Bayhead, North Uist, Western Isles HS6 5DX	www.cne-siar.gov.uk	paible-school@cne-siar.gov.uk	01876 510275	01876 510203	42
Sgoil Lionacleit	Liniclate, Benbecula, Western Isles HS7 5PJ	www.cne-siar.gov.uk	sgoil-lionacleit@cne-siar.gov.uk	01870 602211	01870 602817	302

3

School name	Address	Website	E-mail	Tel	Fax	Pupils
Sgoil-nan-Loch	Cameron Terr, Lochs, Isle of Lewis, Western Isles HS2 9PE	www.cne-siar.gov.uk	sgoilnanloch@eileanansiar.biblio.net	01851 705187	01851 701103	34
Shawbost School	Shawbost, Lewis, Western Isles HS2 9BQ	www.cne-siar.gov.uk	shawbost-school@cne-siar.gov.uk	01851 710212	01851 710582	34
Sir E Scott School	Tarbet, Isle of Lewis, Western Isles HS3 3BG	www.cne-siar.gov.uk	sirescott-school@cne-siar.gov.uk	01859 502339	01859 502014	112

Dumfries and Galloway

School name	Address	Website	E-mail	Tel	Fax	Pupils
Annan Academy	St John's Rd, Annan, Dumfries and Galloway DG12 6AP	www.annanacademy.org.uk	annanacademy@alb.dumgal.org.uk	01461 202954	01461 205955	1075
Castle Douglas High School	Dunmuir Rd, Castle Douglas, Dumfries and Galloway DG7 1LQ		cdhs@alc.dumgal.org.uk	01556 502821	01556 502821	547
Dalbeattie High School	Haugh Rd, Dalbeattie, Dumfries and Galloway DG5 4AR	www.dalbeattiehighschool.com	administrator@ald.dumgal.org.uk	01556 610445	01556 611763	382
Dalry School	Dalry, Castle Douglas, Dumfries and Galloway DG7 3UX	www.dalryscool.ik.org	administrator@ale.dumgal.org.uk	01644 430259	01644 430527	72
Douglas Ewart High School	Newton Stewart, Dumfries and Galloway DG8 6JQ	www.douglasewart@dumgal.sch.uk	administrator@alf.dumgal.org.uk	01671 403773	01671 402807	708
Dumfries Academy	Academy St, Dumfries and Galloway DG1 1DD	www.dumfriesacademy.org.uk	administrator@alg.dumgal.org.uk	01387 252846	01387 252846	769
Dumfries High School	Marchmount, Dumfries, Dumfries and Galloway DG1 1PX	www.dumfrieshighschool.co.uk	jslater@alh.dumgal.org.uk	01387 263061	01387 268951	980
Kirkcudbright Academy	St Mary's Wynd, Kirkcudbright, Dumfries and Galloway DG6 4JN	www.kirkcudbright.dumgal.sch.uk	ht@alj.dumgal.org.uk	01557 330440	01557 330440	510
Langholm Academy	Langholm, Dumfries and Galloway DG13 0BL		langholmac@alk.dumgal.org.uk	01387 380418	01387 380746	281
Lockerbie Academy	Dryfe Rd, Lockerbie, Dumfries and Galloway DG11 2AL	www.lockerbie-academy.co.uk	ht@all.dumgal.org.uk	01576 202626	01576 203032	789
Maxwelltown High School	Lochside Rd, Dumfries, Dumfries and Galloway DG2 0EL	www.maxwelltown.dumgal.sch.uk	edmaxhigh@alm.dumgal.org.uk	01387 720458	01387 721544	383
Moffat Academy	Academy Rd, Moffat, Dumfries and Galloway DG10 9DA		littles@dumgal.orag.uk	01683 220114	01683 220703	272
St Joseph's College	Craigs Rd, Dumfries, Dumfries and Galloway DG1 4UU	www.st-josephscollege.dumgal.sch.uk	supportmanager@alp.dumgal.org.uk	01387 252893	01387 254456	774
Sanquhar Academy	Broomfield, Sanquhar, Dumfries and Galloway DG4 6JN		neilianh@dumgal.orag.uk	01659 50208	01659 50208	362
Stranraer Academy	McMaster's Rd, Stranraer, Dumfries and Galloway DG9 8BY	www.stranraeracademy.co.uk	secretary@alt.dumgal.org.uk	01776 706484	01776 704748	1108
Wallace Hall Academy	Thornhill, Dumfries and Galloway DG3 5DS	www.wallacehallacademy.dumgal.sch.uk	wallacehall@alv.dumgal.org.uk	01848 330294	01848 330294	517

Dundee City

School name	Address	Website	E-mail	Tel	Fax	Pupils
Baldragon Adademy	Burn St, Dundee DD3 0LB	www.baldragon.ea.dundeecity.sch.uk	baldragon@dundeecity.gov.uk	01382 436550	01382 436552	582
Braeview Academy	Berwick Dr, Dundee DD4 0NL		braeview@dundeecity.gov.uk	01382 438452	01382 438446	745
Craigie High School	Garnet Terr, Dundee DD4 7QD		craigie@dundeecity.gov.uk	01382 431111	01382 431130	845
Grove Academy	Camperdown St, Boughty Ferry, Dundee DD5 3AE		grove@dundeecity.gov.uk	01382 436800	01382 436851	951
Harris Academy	Perth Rd, Dundee DD2 1NL	www.harris-academy.com	harris@dundeecity.gov.uk	01382 435700	01382 435701	1165
Lawside RC Academy	West School Rd, Dundee DD3 8RT	www.lawsideacademy.co.uk	lawside.academy@dundeecity.gov.uk	01382 436100	01382 436125	861
Menzieshill High School	Yarrow Terr, Dundee DD2 4DW	www.millenniumschools.co.uk	menzieshill@dundeecity.gov.uk	01382 435677	01382 435664	759
Morgan Academy	Forfar Rd, Dundee DD4 7AX		morgan@dundeecity.gov.uk	01382 307000	01382 307046	925
St John's RC High School	Lawton Rd, Dundee DD3 6SZ		st-johns@dundeecity.gov.uk	01382 436139	01382 436422	862

School name	Address	Website	E-mail	Tel	Fax	Pupils
St Paul's RC Academy	Gilburn Rd, Dundee DD3 0AB		st-pauls@dundeecity.gov.uk	01382 436100	01382 436125	
St Saviour's RC High School	Drumgeith Rd, Dundee DD4 0JX		st-saviours@dundeecity.gov.uk	01382 438200	01382 438229	425

East Ayrshire

School name	Address	Website	E-mail	Tel	Fax	Pupils
Auchinleck Academy	Sorn Rd, Auchinleck, East Ayrshire KA18 2LY	www.auchinleckacademy.e-ayr.sch.uk	colin.maclean@east-ayrshire.gov.uk	01290 420617	01290 425811	1058
Cumnock Academy	Ayr Rd, Cumnock, East Ayrshire KA18 1EH	www.cumnock.e-ayr.sch.uk	gordon.bell@east-ayrshire.gov.uk	01290 421228	01290 425812	1051
Doon Academy	Ayr Rd, Dalmellington, East Ayrshire KA6 7SJ	www.millenniumschools.co.uk	patrick.o'rourke@east-ayrshire.gov.uk	01292 550521	01292 551073	393
Grange Academy	Beech Ave, Kilmarnock, East Ayrshire KA1 2EW	www.millenniumschools.co.ul	fred.wildridge@east-ayrshire.gov.uk	01563 521969	01563 542648	1207
James Hamilton Academy	Sutherland Dr, Kilmarnock, East Ayrshire KA3 7DF		bill.mcgregor@east-ayrshire.gov.uk	01563 533221	01563 534370	789
Kilmarnock Academy	Elmbank Dr, Kilmarnock, East Ayrshire KA1 3BS	www.kilmarnockacademy.co.uk	carole.ford@east-ayrshire.gov.uk	01563 525509	01563 542683	770
Loudoun Academy	Glasgow Rd, Galston, East Ayrshire KA4 8PD		brian.johnston@east-ayrshire.gov.uk	01563 820061	01563 820878	1091
St Joseph's Academy	Grassyards Rd, Kilmarnock, East Ayrshire KA3 7SL		brigid.rooney@east-ayrshire.gov.uk	01563 527197	01563 542418	768
Stewarton Academy	Cairnduff Pl, Stewarton, Kilmarnock, East Ayrshire KA3 5QF	www.millenniumschools.co.uk	derek.mathieson@east-ayrshire.gov.uk	01560 482342	01560 485339	798

East Dunbartonshire

School name	Address	Website	E-mail	Tel	Fax	Pupils
Bearsden Academy	Morven Rd, Bearsden, Glasgow G61 3SU	www.bearsdenacademy.e-dunbarton.sch.uk	office@bearsdenacademy.e-dunbarton.sch.uk	0141 942 2297	0141 942 4681	1303
Bishopbriggs Academy	South Crosshill Rd, Bishopbriggs, East Dunbartonshire G64 2NN	www.bishopbriggsacademy.e-dunbarton.sch.uk	office@bishopbriggsacademy.e-dunbarton.sch.uk	0141 772 1529	0141 762 3059	1294
Bishopbriggs High School	South Crosshill Rd, Bishopbriggs, East Dunbartonshire G64 2NN	www.bishopbriggs-high.co.uk	office@bishopbriggs.e-dunbarton.sch.uk	0141 772 1529	0141 762 3059	1294
Boclair Academy	Inveroran Dr, Bearsden, East Dunbartonshire G61 2PL	www.boclair.e-dunbarton.sch.uk	office@boclair.e-dunbarton.sch.uk	0141 943 0717	0141 943 0216	987
Douglas Academy	Mains Est, Milngavie, East Dunbartonshire G62 7HL	www.douglas.e-dunbartonshire.sch.uk	office@douglas.e-dunbarton.sch.uk	0141 956 2281	0141 956 1533	1062
Kirkintilloch High School	Briar Rd, Kirkintilloch, East Dunbartonshire G66 3SA	www.kirkintilloch.e-dunbarton.sch.uk	office@kirkintilloch.e-dunbarton.sch.uk	0141 776 5293	0141 777 8115	648
Lenzie Academy	Myrtle Ave, Lenzie, East Dunbartonshire G66 4HR	www.lenzieacademy.e-dunbarton.sch.uk	office@lenzieacademy.e-dunbarton.sch.uk	0141 776 6118	0141 777 8121	1379
St Ninian's High School	Wester Cleddens Rd, Bishopbriggs, East Dunbartonshire G64 1HZ	www.st-ninians.e-dunbarton.sch.uk	office@st-ninians.e-dunbarton.sch.uk	0141 762 1444	0141 762 3062	748
Thomas Muir High School	Wester Cleddens Rd, Bishopbriggs, East Dunbartonshire G64 1HZ		office@thomasmuir.e-dunbarton.sch.uk	0141 762 3110	0141 762 3062	567
Turnbull High School	St Mary's Rd, Bishopbriggs, Glasgow G64 2EF	www.turnbull.e-dunbarton.sch.uk	office@turnbull.e-dunbarton.sch.uk	0141 772 9101	0141 762 3671	741

East Lothian

School name	Address	Website	E-mail	Tel	Fax	Pupils
Dunbar Grammar School	Summerfield Rd, Dunbar, East Lothian EH42 1NJ	www.dgs.dunbar.org.uk	dunbar.gs@eastlothian.gov.uk	01368 863339	01368 864798	712
Knox Academy	Pencaitland Rd, Haddington, East Lothian EH41 4DT	web.knox.e-lothian.sch.uk	knoxacademy@eastlothian.gov.uk	01620 823387	01620 823186	891
Musselburgh Grammar School	86 Inveresk Rd, Musselburgh, East Lothian EH21 7BA	www.mgsonline.org.uk	musselburgh.gs@eastlothian.gov.uk	0131 665 4278	0131 653 2152	1368
North Berwick High School	Grange Rd, North Berwick, East Lothian EH39 4QS	www.millenniumschools.co.uk	northberwick.hs@eastlothian.gov.uk	01620 894661	01620 895495	888
Preston Lodge High School	Park View, Prestonpans, East Lothian EH32 9QJ	www.prestonlodge.e-lothian.sch.uk	prestonlodge.hs@eastlothian.gov.uk	01875 811170	01875 810060	965
Ross High School	Well Wynd, Tranent, East Lothian EH33 2EQ	www.rosshigh.co.uk	ross.hs@eastlothian.gov.uk	01875 610433	01875 615462	985

East Renfrewshire

School name	Address	Website	E-mail	Tel	Fax	Pupils
Barrhead High School	Aurs Rd, Barrhead, East Renfrewshire G78 2SJ	www.barrhead.e-renfrew.sch.uk	headteacher@barrhead.e-renfrew.sch.uk	0141 577 2100	0141 577 2143	708
Eastwood High School	Capelrig Rd, Newton Mearns, East Renfrewshire G77 6NQ	www.ea.e-renfrew.sch.uk	headteacher@eastwood.e-renfrew.sch.uk	0141 577 2200	0141 577 2220	1024
Mearns Castle High School	Waterfoot Rd, Newton Mearns, East Renfrewshire G77 5RU	www.ea.e-renfrew.sch.uk	headteacher@mearnscastle.e-renfrew.sch.uk	0141 577 2300	0141 577 2314	1465
St Luke's High School	Springfield Rd, Barrhead, East Renfrewshire G78 2SG	www.ea.e-renfrew.sch.uk	headteacher@st-lukes.e-renfrew.sch.uk	0141 577 2400	0141 577 2440	603
St Ninian's High School	Eastwood Pk, Rouken Glen Rd, Giffnock, East Renfrewshire G46 6UG	www.ea.e-renfrew.sch.uk	headteacher@st-ninians.e-renfrew.sch.uk	0141 577 2000	0141 577 2037	1705
Williamwood High School	Eaglesham Rd, Clarkston, Glasgow G76 8RF	www.williamwood.e-renfrew.sch.uk	headteacher@williamwood.e-refrew.sch.uk	0141 577 2500	0141 577 2545	1458
Woodfarm High School	Robslee Rd, Thornliebank, Glasgow G46 7HG	www.ea.e-renfrew.sch.uk	headteacher@woodfarm.e-renfrew.sch.uk	0141 577 2600	0141 577 2640	766

Edinburgh City

School name	Address	Website	E-mail	Tel	Fax	Pupils
Balerno Community High School	5 Bridge Rd, Balerno, Edinburgh EH14 7AQ	www.balernochs.edin.sch.uk	admin@balernochs.edin.sch.uk	0131 477 7788	0131 477 7707	775
Boroughmuir High School	Viewforth, Edinburgh EH10 4LR	www.boroughmuir.edin.sch.uk	admin@boroughmuir.edin.sch.uk	0131 229 9703	0131 228 9185	1096
Broughton High School	Carrington Rd, Edinburgh EH4 1EG	www.broughton.edin.sch.uk	admin@broughton.edin.sch.uk	0131 332 7805	0131 343 3296	1021
Castlebrae Community High School	2a Greendykes Rd, Edinburgh EH16 4DP	www.castlebrae.edin.sch.uk	admin@castlebrae.edin.sch.uk	0131 661 1282	0131 661 4049	286
Craigmount High School	Craigs Rd, Edinburgh EH12 8NH	www.craigmount.edin.sch.uk	enquiries@craigmount.edin.sch.uk	0131 339 6823	0131 339 9830	1389
Craigroyston Community High School	Pennywell Rd, Edinburgh EH4 4QP		admin@craigroyston.edin.sch.uk	0131 477 7801	0131 477 7805	432
Currie High School	Dolphin Ave, Currie, Edinburgh EH14 5RD	www.currie.edin.sch.uk	admin@currie.edin.sch.uk	0131 449 2165	0131 451 5854	971
Drummond Community High School	41 Bellevue Pl, Edinburgh EH7 4BS	www.drummond.edin.sch.uk	admin@drummond.edin.sch.uk	0131 556 2651	0131 467 7270	471
The Edinburgh Academy School	42 Henderson Row, Edinburgh EH3 5BL	www.edinburghacademy.org.uk	headmaster@edinburghacademy.org.uk	0131 556 4603	0131 556 9353	414
Firrhill High School	9 Oxgangs Rd North, Firrhill, Edinburgh EH14 1DP	www.firrhill.edin.sch.uk	admin@firrhill.edin.sch.uk	0131 441 4501	0131 441 1036	1154
Forrester High School	Broomhouse Rd, Edinburgh EH12 9AE	www.forrester.edin.sch.uk	admin@forrester.edin.sch.uk	0131 334 9262	0131 467 7134	676
Gracemount High School	136 Lasswade Rd, Edinburgh EH16 6TZ	www.gracemount.edin.sch.uk	admin@gracemount.edin.sch.uk	0131 664 7440	0131 664 3902	544
Holy Rood High School	Duddingston Rd West, Edinburgh EH15 3ST	www.holyrood.edin.sch.uk	admin@holyrood.edin.sch.uk	0131 661 5871	0131 659 5868	1000
James Gillespie's High School	Lauderdale St, Edinburgh EH9 1DD	www.jamesgillespies.edin.sch.uk	admin@jamesgillespies.edin.sch.uk	0131 447 1900	0131 466 7035	1080
Leith Academy	20 Academy Pk, Edinburgh EH6 8JQ	www.leith.edin.sch.uk	admin@leith.edin.sch.uk	0131 554 0606	0131 555 2698	951
Liberton High School	Gilmerton Rd, Edinburgh EH17 7PT	www.liberton.edin.sch.uk	admin@liberton.edin.sch.uk	0131 664 7514	0131 467 7173	757
Portobello High School	Duddingston Rd, Edinburgh EH15 1NF	www.portobello.edin.sch.uk	admin@portobello.edin.sch.uk	0131 669 2324	0131 669 0975	1444
Queensferry High School	Ashburnham Rd, South Queensferry, Edinburgh EH30 9JN		admin@queensferry.edin.sch.uk	0131 319 3200	0131 319 3201	841
The Royal High School	East Barnton Ave, Edinburgh EH4 6JP	www.royalhigh.edin.sch.uk	admin@royalhigh.edin.sch.uk	0131 336 2261	0131 312 8592	1168
St Augustine's High School	Broomhouse Rd, Edinburgh EH12 9AD	www.staugustines.edin.sch.uk	admin@staugustines.edin.sch.uk	0131 334 6801	0131 334 7329	775
Trinity Academy	Craighall Ave, Edinburgh EH6 4RT	www.trinity.edin.sch.uk	admin@trinity.edin.sch.uk	0131 478 5050	0131 478 5055	992
Tynecastle High School	McLeod St, Edinburgh EH11 2NJ	www.tynecastle.edin.sch.uk	admin@tyneside.edin.sch.uk	0131 337 3488	0131 337 3915	700
Wester Hailes Education Centre	5 Murrayburn Dr, Edinburgh EH14 2SU	www.whec.edin.sch.uk	admin@whec.edin.sch.uk	0131 442 2201	0131 458 3348	439

Falkirk

School name	Address	Website	E-mail	Tel	Fax	Pupils
Bo'ness Academy	Gauze Rd, Bo'ness, Falkirk EH51 9AS	www.bonessacademy.falkirk.sch.uk	bonessacademy@falkirk.gov.uk	01506 822028	01506 778801	804
Braes High School	Newlands Rd, Reddingmuirhead, Falkirk FK2 0DA	www.braes.falkirk.sch.uk	braeshighschool@falkirk.gov.uk	01324 719551	01324 503878	1110
Denny High School	Shanks Ave, Denny, Falkirk FK6 5EB	www.dennyhigh.falkirk.sch.uk	dennyhighschool@falkirk.gov.uk	01324 823124	01324 508861	1355
Falkirk High School	Blinkbonny Rd, Falkirk FK1 5BZ	www.falkirk.falkirk.sch.uk	falkirkhighschool@falkirk.gov.uk	01324 629511	01324 501891	1125
Graeme High School	Callendar Rd, Falkirk FK1 1SY	www.graeme.falkirk.sch.uk	graemehighschool@falkirk.gov.uk	01324 622576	01324 508681	1165
Grangemouth High School	Tinto Dr, Grangemouth, Falkirk FK3 0HW	www.grangemouth.falkirk.sch.uk	grangemouthhighschool@falkirk.gov.uk	01324 485031	01324 508771	837
Larbert High School	Carrongrange Ave, Stenhousemuir, Larbert, Falkirk FK5 3BL	www.larbert.falkirk.sch.uk	larberthighschool@falkirk.gov.uk	01324 554233	01324 503551	1751
St Mungo's High School	Merchison Ave, Falkirk FK2 7JT	www.st-mungos.falkirk.sch.uk	stmungoshighschool@falkirk.gov.uk	01324 628416	01324 508686	1060

Fife

School name	Address	Website	E-mail	Tel	Fax	Pupils
Auchmuty High School	Dovecot Rd, Glenrothes, Fife KY7 5JL		auchmutyhs.enquiries@fife.gov.uk	01592 583401	01592 415651	1196
Balwearie High School	Balwearie Gdns, Kirkcaldy, Fife KY2 5LY	www.balweariehighschool.org.uk	balweariehs.enquiries@fife.gov.uk	01592 583402	01592 412260	1674
Beath High School	Foulford Rd, Cowdenbeath, Fife KY4 9BH	www.fife-education.org.uk	beaths.enquiries@fife.gov.uk	01383 602401	01383 313061	1258
Bell Baxter High School	Carslogie Rd, Cupar, Fife KY15 4HY	www.bbhs-online.co.uk	rector@bellbaxter.fife.sch.uk	01334 659459	01334 412333	1823
Buckhaven High School	Methilhaven Rd, Buckhaven, Leven, Fife KY8 1HL	www.fife-education.org.uk	buckhavenhs.enquiries@fife.gov.uk	01592 583403	01592 414464	1209
Dunfermline High School	St Leonard's Pl, Dunfermline, Fife KY11 3BQ		dunfermlinehs.enquiries@fife.gov.uk	01383 602402	01383 312599	1722
Glenrothes High School	Napier Rd, Glenrothes, Fife KY6 1HJ		glenrotheshs.enquiries@fife.gov.uk		01592 415554	830
Glenwood High School	South Parks Rd, Glenrothes, Fife KY6 1JX		glenwoodhs.enquiries@fife.gov.uk	01592 583476	01592 415444	1108
Inverkeithing High School	Hillend Rd, Inverkeithing, Fife KY11 1PL	www.fife-education.org.uk	inverkeithinghs.enquiries@fife.gov.uk	01383 602403	01383 313460	1463
Kirkcaldy High School	Dunnikier Way, Kirkcaldy, Fife KY1 3LR	www.fife-education.org.uk	kirkcaldyhs.enquiries@fife.gov.uk	01592 583405	01592 412709	1214
Kirkland High School and Community College	Methil Brae, Methil, Leven, Fife KY8 3LT	www.fife-education.org.uk	kirklandhs.enquiries@fife.gov.uk	01333 659403	01333 592405	682
Lochgelly High School	Station Rd, Lochgelly, Fife KY5 8LZ	www.fife-education.org.uk	lochgellyhs.enquiries@fife.gov.uk	01592 583406	01592 418099	791
Madras College	South St, St Andrews, Fife KY16 9EJ	www.madras.fife.sch.uk	madrashs.enquiries@fife.gov.uk	01334 659402	01334 412555	1683
Queen Anne High School	Broomhead, Dunfermline, Fife KY12 0PQ	members.aol.com	queenannehs.enquiries@fife.gov.uk	01383 502404	01383 312646	1747
St Andrew's RC High School	Overton Rd, Kirkcaldy, Fife KY1 3JL	www.fife-education.org.uk	standrewsrchs.enquiries@fife.gov.uk	01592 583407	01592 418310	801
St Columba's RC High School	Woodhill Rd, Dunfermline, Fife KY11 4UN		stcolumbasrchs.enquiries@fife.gov.uk	01383 602405	01383 312500	908
Viewforth High School	Loughborough Rd, Kirkcaldy, Fife KY1 3DE	www.fife-education.org.uk	viewforthhs.enquiries@fife.gov.uk	01592 583408	01592 418399	359
Waid Academy	St Andrews Rd, Anstruther, Fife KY10 3HD		waidhs.enquiries@fife.gov.uk	01333 659404	01333 592049	823
Woodmill High School	Shields Rd, Dunfermline, Fife KY11 4ER	www.fife-education.org.uk	woodmillhs.enquiries@fife.gov.uk	01383 602406	01383 312580	802

Glasgow City

School name	Address	Website	E-mail	Tel	Fax	Pupils
All Saints Secondary School	299 Ryehill Rd, Glasgow G21 3EN		headteacher@allsaints-sec.glasgow.sch.uk	0141 582 0010	0141 582 0011	1058
Bannerman High School	Glasgow Rd, Baillieston, Glasgow G69 7NS		headteacher@bannermanhigh.glasgow.sch.uk	0141 582 0020	0141 582 0021	1359
Bellahouston Academy	30 Gower Terr, Glasgow G41 5QF		headteacher@bellahoustonacademy.glasgow.sch.uk	0141 582 0030	0141 582 0031	912
Castlemilk High School	223 Castlemilk Dr, Glasgow G45 9JY		headteacher@castlemilkhigh.glasgow.sch.uk	0141 582 0050	0141 582 0051	467
Cleveden Secondary School	42 Cleveden Rd, Glasgow G12 0JW	www.cleveden-sec.glasgow.sch.uk	headteacher@cleveden-sec.glasgow.sch.uk	0141 582 0060	0141 582 0061	1178
Drumchapel High School	45 Cally Ave, Glasgow G15 7SQ	www.drumchapelhigh.glasgow.sch.uk	headteacher@drumchapelhigh.glasgow.sch.uk	0141 582 0070	0141 582 0071	696
Eastbank Academy	26 Academy St, Glasgow G32 9AA	www.eastbankacademy.org.uk	headteacher@eastbankacademy.glasgow.sch.uk	0141 582 0080	0141 582 0081	1256

3

School name	Address	Website	E-mail	Tel	Fax	Pupils
Govan High School	12 Ardnish St, Glasgow G51 4NB	www.govanhigh.glasgow.sch.uk	headteacher@govanhigh.glasgow.sch.uk	0141 582 0090	0141 582 0091	434
Hillhead High School	Oakfield Ave, Glasgow G12 8LJ	www.hillheadhigh.ik.org	headteacher@hillheadhigh.glasgow.sch.uk	0141 582 0100	0141 582 0101	909
Hillpark Secondary School	36 Cairngorm Rd, Glasgow G43 2XA	www.hillpark-sec.glasgow.sch.uk	headteacher@hillpark-sec.glasgow.sch.uk	0141 582 0110	0141 582 0116	1158
Holyrood Secondary School	100 Dixon Rd, Crosshill, Glasgow G42 8AU	www.holyrood-sec.glasgow.sch.uk	headteacher@holyrood-sec.glasgow.sch.uk	0141 582 0120	0141 582 0121	2011
Hyndland Secondary School	Lauderdale Gdns, Glasgow G12 9RQ		headteacher@hyndland-sec.glasgow.sch.uk	0141 582 0130	0141 582 0131	967
John Paul Academy	2 Arrochar St, Glasgow G23 5LY		headteacher@johnpaulacademy.glasgow.sch.uk	0141 582 0140	0141 582 0141	685
King's Park Secondary School	14 Fetlar Dr, Simshill, Glasgow G44 5BL		headteacher@kingspark-sec.glasgow.sch.uk	0141 582 0150	0141 582 0151	1065
Knightswood Secondary School	60 Knightswood Rd, Knightswood, Glasgow G13 2XD	www.knightswoodsecondary.org.uk	headteacher@knightswood-sec.glasgow.sch.uk	0141 582 0160	0141 582 0161	1364
Lochend Community High School	20 Cairnbrook Rd, Easterhouse, Glasgow G34 0NZ		headteacher@lochendcommunityhigh.glasgow.sch.uk	0141 582 0170	0141 582 0171	706
Lourdes Secondary School	47 Kirriemuir Ave, Glasgow G52 3DF		headteacher@lourdes-sec.glasgow.sch.uk	0141 582 0180	0141 582 0181	1247
Notre Dame High School	160 Observatory Rd, Dowanhill, Glasgow G12 9LN	www.notredamehigh.org	headteacher@notredamehigh.glasgow.sch.uk	0141 582 0190	0141 582 0191	802
Rosshall Academy	131 Crookston Rd, Glasgow G52 3PD		headteacher@rosshallacademy.glasgow.sch.uk	0141 582 0200	0141 582 0201	1215
St Andrew's Secondary School	47 Torphin Cres, Glasgow G32 6QE	www.st-andrews-sec.glasgow.sch.uk	headteacher@st-andrews-sec.glasgow.sch.uk	0141 582 0240	0141 582 0241	1562
St Margaret Mary's Secondary School	9 Birgidale Rd, Glasgow G45 9NJ		headteacher@st-margaretmarys-sec.glasgow.sch.uk	0141 582 0250	0141 582 0251	503
St Mungo's Academy	235 Crown Point Rd, Glasgow G40 2RA		headteacher@st-mungosacademy.glasgow.sch.uk	0141 582 0260	0141 582 0261	782
St Paul's High School	36 Damshot Rd, Glasgow G53 5HW		headteacher@st-paulshigh.glasgow.sch.uk	0141 582 0040	0141 582 0041	727
St Roch's Secondary School	40 Royston Rd, Glasgow G21 2NF	www.st-rochs-sec.glasgow.sch.uk	headteacher@st-rochs-sec.glasgow.sch.uk	0141 582 0270	0141 582 0271	661
St Thomas Aquinas Secondary School	112 Mitre Rd, Glasgow G14 9PP		headteacher@st-thomasaquinas-sec.glasgow.sch.uk	0141 582 0280	0141 582 0281	936
Shawlands Academy	31 Moss-side Rd, Shawlands, Glasgow G41 3TR	www.shawlandsacademy.glasgow.sch.uk	headteacher@shawlandsacademy.glasgow.sch.uk	0141 582 0210	0141 582 0211	1273
Smithycroft Secondary School	282 Smithycroft Rd, Glasgow G33 2QU	www.smithycroft-sec.glasgow.sch.uk	headteacher@smithycroft-sec.glasgow.sch.uk	0141 582 0220	0141 582 0221	694
Springburn Academy	151 Edgefauld Rd, Springburn, Glasgow G21 4JL		headteacher@springburnacademy.glasgow.sch.uk	0141 582 0230	0141 582 0231	1035
Whitehill Secondary School	280 Onslow Dr, Dennistoun, Glasgow G31 2QF	rubble.ultralab.ac.uk	headteacher@whitehill-sec.glasgow.sch.uk	0141 582 0290	0141 582 0291	532

Highland

School name	Address	Website	E-mail	Tel	Fax	Pupils
Alness Academy	Alness, Highland IV17 0UY	www.alness.highland.sch.uk	alness.academy@highland.sch.uk	01349 883341	01349 882614	516
Ardnamurchan High School	Drimnatorran, Strontian, Argyll, Highland PH36 4JA	www.ardnamurchan.highland.sch.uk	ardnamurchan.high@highland.gov.uk	01397 700105	01397 709227	137
Charleston Academy	General Booth Rd, Kinmylies, Inverness, Highland IV3 8ET	www.charleston.highland.sch.uk	charleston.primary@highland.gov.uk	01463 234324	01463 715352	862
Culloden Academy	Keppoch Rd, Culloden, Inverness, Highland IV2 7JZ	www.culloden.highland.sch.uk	culloden.academy@highland.gov.uk	01463 790851	01463 790061	1030
Dingwall Academy	Dingwall, Highland IV15 9LT		dingwall.academy@highland.gov.uk	01349 863071	01349 865005	1009
Dornoch Academy	Evelix Rd, Dornoch, Sutherland, Highland IV25 3HR	www.dornochacademy.highland.sch.uk	dornoch.academy@highland.gov.uk	01862 810246	01862 811128	261
Farr High School	Bettyhill, Thurso, Highland KW14 7SS	www.farrhigh.highland.sch.uk	farr.high@highland.gov.uk	01641 521217	01641 521203	92
Fortrose Academy	Academy St, Fortrose, Ross-shire, Highland IV10 8TW	www.fortrose.highland.sch.uk	fortrose.academy@highland.gov.uk	01381 620310	01381 621699	729
Gairloch High School	Achtercairn, Gairloch, Highland IV21 2BP	www.gairlochhigh.highland.sch.uk	gairloch.high@highland.gov.uk	01445 712275	01445 712318	187
Glen Urquhart High School	Pittkerald Rd, Drumnadrochit, Highland IV63 6UG	www.glenurquharthigh.highland.sch.uk	glenurquhart.high@highland.gov.uk	01456 459134	01456 459229	235
Golspie High School	Golspie, Highland KW10 6RF	www.golspiehigh.highland.sch.uk	golspie.high@highland.gov.uk	01408 633451	01408 633833	350
Grantown Grammar School	Cromdale Rd, Grantown-on-Spey, Highland PH26 3HU	www.grantowngrammar.highland.sch.uk	grantown.grammar@highland.gov.uk	01479 872649	01479 873649	372

School name	Address	Website	E-mail	Tel	Fax	Pupils
Invergordon Academy	Academy Rd, Invergordon, Highland IV18 0LD	www.invergordon.highland.sch.uk	invergordon.academy@highland.gov.uk	01349 852362	01349 853748	443
Inverness High School	Montague Row, Inverness, Highland IV3 5DZ		inverness.high@highland.gov.uk	01463 233586	01463 243113	464
Inverness Royal Academy	Culduthel Rd, Inverness, Highland IV2 6RE	www.invernessroyal.highland.sch.uk	ira@highland.gov.uk	01463 222884	01463 243591	924
Kilchuimen Academy	Station Rd, Fort Augustus, Highland PH32 4DL	www.kilchuimenacademy.highland.sch.uk	kilchuimen.academy@highland.gov.uk	01320 366296	01320 366439	78
Kingussie High School	Ruthven Rd, Kingussie, Highland PH21 1ES	www.kingussiehigh.highland.sch.uk	kingussie.high@highland.gov.uk	01540 661475	01540 661123	404
Kinlochbervie High School	Manse Rd, Kinlochbervie, By Lairg, Sutherland, Highland IV27 4RG	www.kinlochberviehigh.highland.sch.uk	kinlochbervie.high@highland.gov.uk	01971 521767	01971 521419	68
Kinlochleven High School	Fort William Rd, Kinlochleven, Argyll, Highland PH50 4QE	www.kinlochlevenhighschool.org	kinlochleven.high@highland.gov.uk	01855 831273	01855 831603	128
Lochaber High School	Fort William, Highland PH33 7ND	www.lochaber.highland.sch.uk	lochaber.high@highland.gov.uk	01397 702512	01397 703667	866
Mallaig High School	Mallaig, Highland PH41 4RG	www.mallaighigh.highland.sch.uk	mallaig.high@highland.gov.uk	01687 462107	01687 462219	144
Millburn Academy	Diriebught Rd, Inverness, Highland IV2 3QR	www.millburn.highland.sch.uk	millburn.academy@highland.gov.uk	01463 233573	01463 232933	1061
Nairn Academy	Duncan Dr, Nairn, Highland IV12 4RD	www.nairn.highland.sch.uk	nairn.academy@highland.gov.uk	01667 453700	01667 453128	822
Plockton High School	Plockton, Ross-shire, Highland IV52 8TU	www.plocktonhigh.highland.sch.uk	plockton.high@highland.gov.uk	01599 530800	01599 544439	320
Portree High School	Viewfield Rd, Portree, Isle of Skye, Highland IV51 9ET	www.portreehigh.highland.sch.uk	portree.high@highland.gov.uk	01478 612030	01478 612154	679
Tain Royal Academy	Scotsburn Rd, Tain, Ross-shire, Highland IV19 1PS	www.tainroyalacademy.org.uk	tainroyal.academy@highland.gov.uk	01862 892121	01862 893334	615
Thurso High School	Ormlie Rd, Thurso, Caithness, Highland KW14 7DS	www.thurso.highland.sch.uk	thurso.high@highland.gov.uk	01847 893822	01847 895509	998
Ullapool High School	Mill St, Ullapool, Ross-shire, Highland IV26 2UN	www.ullapoolhigh.highland.sch.uk	ullapool.high@highland.gov.uk	01854 612078	01854 612793	257
Wick High School	West Banks Ave, Wick, Caithness, Highland KW1 5LU	www.wick.highland.sch.uk	wick.high@highland.gov.uk	01955 603333	01955 602198	849

Inverclyde

School name	Address	Website	E-mail	Tel	Fax	Pupils
Cedars School of Excellence	Lothian Rd, Greenock, Inverclyde PA16 0PG	www.cedars.inverclyde.sch.uk	ajewell@ecosse.net	01475 631074		19
Gourock High School	Fletcher Ave, Gourock, Inverclyde PA19 1TN		christine.robertson@inverclyde.gov.uk	01475 715000	01475 715001	638
Greenock Academy	Madeira St, Greenock, Inverclyde PA16 7XF		headteacher.greenockacademy@inverclyde.gov.uk	01475 715050	01475 715091	849
Notre Dame High School	Dunlop St, Greenock, Inverclyde PA16 9BJ			01475 715150	01475 715151	940
Port Glasgow High School	Marloch Ave, Port Glasgow, Inverclyde PA14 6PT			01475 715200	01475 715201	558
St Columba's High School	Burnside Rd, Gourock, Inverclyde PA19 1XX	www.st-columbas.org	elizabeth.doherty@inverclyde.gov.uk	01475 715250	01475 715251	731
St Stephen's High School	Duchal Rd, Kilmacolm, Inverclyde PA13 4AU	www.st-columbas.org	secretary@st-columbas.org	01505 872238	01505 873995	350
	Southfield Ave, Bardrainney, Port Glasgow, Inverclyde PA14 6PR			01475 715300	01475 715301	620

Midlothian

School name	Address	Website	E-mail	Tel	Fax	Pupils
Beeslack High School	Edinburgh Rd, Penicuik, Midlothian EH26 0QF	www.beeslack.info	beeslack_hs@midlothian.gov.uk	01968 678060	01968 678659	924
Dalkeith High School	2 Cousland Rd, Dalkeith, Midlothian EH22 2PS	www.dalkeith-hs.info	dalkeith_hs@midlothian.gov.uk	0131 654 4701	0131 663 7311	828
Lasswade High School Centre	Eskdale Dr, Bonnyrigg, Midlothian EH19 2LA	www.lasswade.info	lasswade_hs@midlothian.gov.uk	0131 663 7171	0131 663 6634	1281
Newbattle Community High School	64 Easthouses Rd, Dalkeith, Midlothian EH22 4EW	www.newbattle.org.uk	newbattle_hs@midlothian.gov.uk	0131 663 4191	0131 654 2611	898
Penicuik High School	39a Carlops Rd, Penicuik, Midlothian EH26 9EP	www.penicuik.info	penicuik_hs@midlothian.gov.uk	01968 674165	01968 678604	696
St David's RC High School	1 Cousland Rd, Dalkeith, Midlothian EH22 2PS	www.st-davids.info	stdavids_hs@midlothian.gov.uk	0131 654 4702	0131 663 1826	834

Moray

School name	Address	Website	E-mail	Tel	Fax	Pupils
Buckie Community High School	West Cathcart St, Buckie, Moray AB56 1QB	www.buckiehigh.com	admin.buckiehigh@moray-edunet.gov.uk	01542 832605	01542 835758	928
Elgin Academy	Morriston Rd, Elgin, Moray IV30 4ND		admin.elginacad@moray-edunet.gov.uk	01343 543485	01343 543893	957
Elgin High School	High School Dr, New Elgin, Moray IV30 6UD		admin.elginhigh@moray-edunet.gov.uk	01343 545181	01343 540892	661
Forres Academy	Burdsyard Rd, Forres, Moray IV36 1FG		admin.forresacad@moray-edunet.gov.uk	01309 672271	01309 676745	1071
Keith Grammar School	School Rd, Keith, Moray AB55 5ES	www.keithgrammar.com	admin.keithgrammar@moray-edunet.gov.uk	01542 882461	01542 886032	487
Lossiemouth High School	Coulardbank Rd, Lossiemouth, Moray IV31 6JU		admin.lossiehigh@moray-edunet.gov.uk	01343 812047	01343 814343	677
Milne's High School	West St, Fochabers, Moray IV32 7DJ	www.milneshigh.cwc.net	admin.milneshigh@moray-edunet.gov.uk	01343 820611	01343 820306	602
Speyside High School	Mary Ave, Aberlour, Moray AB38 9PN		admin.speysidehigh@moray-edunet.gov.uk	01340 871522	01340 871098	531

North Ayrshire

School name	Address	Website	E-mail	Tel	Fax	Pupils
Ardrossan Academy	Sorbie Rd, Ardrossan, North Ayrshire KA22 8AR	www.methyl.freeserve.co.uk	contactus@ardrossan.n-ayrshire.sch.uk	01294 461931	01294 468646	1065
Arran High School	Lamlash, Isle of Arran, North Ayrshire KA27 8NG	arranhigh.co.uk	contactus@arran.n-ayrshire.sch.uk	01770 600341	01770 600336	328
Auchenharvie Academy	Saltcoats Rd, Stevenston, North Ayrshire KA20 3JW		contactus@auchenharvie.n-ayrshire.sch.uk	01294 605156	01294 604806	676
Garnock Academy	School Rd, Kilbirnie, North Ayrshire KA25 7AX	www.garnockacademy.org	contactus@garnock.n-ayrshire.ac.uk	01505 682685	01505 684876	1030
Greenwood Academy	Dreghorn, Irvine, North Ayrshire KA11 4HL		contactus@greenwood.n-ayrshire.sch.uk	01294 213124	01294 211950	1549
Irvine Royal Academy	Kilwinning Rd, Irvine, North Ayrshire KA12 8SJ	www.irvineroyal.co.uk	contactus@irvineroyal.n-ayrshire.sch.uk	01294 278756	01294 312636	798
Kilwinning Academy	Dalry Rd, Kilwinning, North Ayrshire KA13 7HD		contactus@kilwinning.n-ayrshire.sch.uk	01294 551316	01294 552980	946
Largs Academy	Flatt Rd, Largs, North Ayrshire KA30 9JX	www.largs.n-ayrshire.sch.uk	contactus@largs.n-ayrshire.sch.uk	01475 675421	01475 687479	1052
St Andrew's Academy	Jack's Rd, Saltcoats, North Ayrshire KA21 5NT		school@st-andrews.n-ayrshire.sch.uk	01294 605221	01294 605306	762
St Michael's Academy	Winton Ave, Kilwinning, North Ayrshire KA13 6LJ	stmichaels.kilwinning.com	contactus@st-michaels.n-ayrshire.sch.uk	01294 551564	01294 552990	852

North Lanarkshire

School name	Address	Website	E-mail	Tel	Fax	Pupils
Abronhill High School	Larch Rd, Cumbernauld, North Lanarkshire G67 3AZ		ht@abronhillhigh.n-lanark.sch.uk	01236 731715	01236 729500	527
Airdrie Academy	South Commonhead Ave, Airdrie, North Lanarkshire ML6 6NX		ht@airdrie.n-lanark.sch.uk	01236 607034	01236 747425	1104
Bellshill Academy	Main St, Bellshill, North Lanarkshire ML4 1AR		ht@bellshillacademy.com	01698 747585	01698 842662	662
Braidhurst High School	Dalriada Cres, Motherwell, North Lanarkshire ML1 3XF		ht@braidhurst.n-lanark.sch.uk	01698 275555	01698 275358	559
Brannock High School	Loanhead Rd, Newarthill, Motherwell, North Lanarkshire ML1 5AY		ht@brannock.n-lanark.sch.uk	01698 733905	01698 734327	677
Calderhead High School	Dyfrig St, Shotts, North Lanarkshire ML7 4DH		ht@calderhead.n-lanark.sch.uk	01501 820050	01501 825403	506
Caldervale High St	Towers Rd, Airdrie, North Lanarkshire ML6 8PG		ht@caldervale.n-lanark.sch.uk	01236 766711	01236 747426	939
Cardinal Newman High School	Main St, Bellshill, North Lanarkshire ML4 3DW		ht@cardinalnewman.n-lanark.sch.uk	01698 747593	01698 841562	1092
Chryston High	Lindsaybeg Rd, Chryston, Glasgow, North Lanarkshire G69 9DL		ht@chrystonhigh.n-lanark.sch.uk	0141 779 4131	0141 779 3950	704
Clyde Valley High School	Castlehill Rd, Wishaw, North Lanarkshire ML2 0LS		ht@clydevalley.n-lanark.sch.uk	01698 375011	01698 358725	666
Coatbridge High School	Albert St, Coatbridge, North Lanarkshire ML5 3ET		ht@coatbridge.n-lanark.sch.uk	01236 427676	01236 440313	848
Coltness High School	Mossland Dr, Coltness, Wishaw, North Lanarkshire ML2 8LY		ht@coltnesshigh.n-lanark.sch.uk	01698 384307	01698 386871	922
Columba High School	Wallace St, Whifflet, Coatbridge, North Lanarkshire ML5 4DE		ht@columba.n-lanark.sch.uk	01236 426185	01236 427462	604
Cumbernauld High School	South Carbrain Ring Rd, Kildrum, Cumbernauld, North Lanarkshire G67 2UF		ht@cumbernauldhigh.n-lanark.sch.uk	01236 725511	01236 725343	615

School name	Address	Website	E-mail	Tel	Fax	Pupils
Dalziel High School	Crawford St, Motherwell, North Lanarkshire ML1 3AG	www.dalzielhigh.org.uk	ht@dalziel.n-lanark.sch.uk	01698 328628	01698 328631	970
Greenfaulds High School	Athelstane Dr, Cumbernauld, North Lanarkshire G67 4AQ		ht@greenfauld.n-lanark.sch.uk	01236 727956	01236 451072	1154
Kilsyth Academy	Balmalloch, Kilsyth, Glasgow, North Lanarkshire G65 9NF		ht@kilsythacademy.n-lanark.sch.uk	01236 822244	01236 824974	830
Our Lady's High School	Dalzell Dr, Motherwell, North Lanarkshire ML1 2DG	www.ourladyshighschool.co.uk	ht@ourladyshigh.n-lanark.sch.uk	01698 265191	01698 275361	671
Rosehall High School	Woodhall Ave, Coatbridge, North Lanarkshire ML5 5DB		ht@rosehall.n-lanark.sch.uk	01236 431166	01236 710659	425
St Aidan's High School	Waverley Dr, Wishaw, North Lanarkshire ML2 7EW		ht@staidanshigh.n-lanark.sch.uk	01698 360333	01698 386874	1203
St Ambrose High School	Blair Rd, Coatbridge, North Lanarkshire ML5 2EW		ht@st-ambrose.n-lanark.sch.uk	01236 427671	01236 425961	1393
St Andrew's High School	Wallace St, Coatbridge, North Lanarkshire ML5 4DE		ht@standrewshigh.n-lanark.sch.uk	01236 426185	01236 427462	1241
St Margaret's High School	Waverley Dr, Airdrie, North Lanarkshire ML6 6EU		ht@st-margarets.n-lanark.sch.uk	01236 766881	01236 747429	1345
St Maurice's High School	Westfield, Cumbernauld, North Lanarkshire G68 9AG		afa@st-maurices.n-lanark.sch.uk	01236 732701	01236 728660	1132
St Patrick's High School	Muiryhall St, Coatbridge, North Lanarkshire ML5 3NN		ht@st-patrickshigh.n-lanark.sch.uk	01236 426191	01236 440317	746
Taylor High School	Carfin St, New Stevenston, Motherwell, North Lanarkshire ML1 4JP		ht@taylor.n-lanark.sch.uk	01698 832219	01698 833086	775

Orkney Islands

School name	Address	Website	E-mail	Tel	Fax	Pupils
Kirkwall Grammar School	Kirkwall, Orkney Islands KW15 1QN	www.kgs.orkney.sch.uk	enquiries.kgs@orkneyschools.org.uk	01856 872102	01856 872911	935
North Walls Community School	Lyness, Stromness, Orkney Island KW16 3NX	www.northwalls.orkney.sch.uk	enquiries.northwalls@orkneyschools.org.uk	01856 791246	01856 791229	5
Pierowall Junior High School	Westray, Orkney Islands KW17 2DH	www.pierowall.orkney.sch.uk	enquiries.pierowall@orkneyschools.org.uk	01857 677353	01857 677246	35
Stromness Academy	Stromness, Orkney, Orkney Islands KW16 3JS	www.stromnessacademy.orkney.sch.uk	enquiries.stromnessacad@orkneyschools.org.uk	01856 850660	01856 850171	427
Stronsay Junior High School	Stronsay, Orkney Islands KW17 2AE	www.stronsay.orkney.sch.uk	enquiries.stronsay@orkneyschools.org.uk	01857 616246	01857 616433	18
Sanday Junior High School	Orkney, Orkney Islands KW17 2AY	www.sanday.orkney.sch.uk	enquiries.sanday@orkneyschools.org.uk	01857 600228	01857 600246	31

Perth and Kinross

School name	Address	Website	E-mail	Tel	Fax	Pupils
Blairgowrie High School	Beeches Rd, Blairgowrie, Perth and Kinross PH10 6PW	www.blairgowrie.pkc.sch.uk	headteacher@blairgowrie.pkc.sch.uk	01250 873445	01250 876826	967
Breadalbane Academy	Crieff Rd, Aberfeldy, Perth and Kinross PH15 2DU	www.breadalbane.pkc.sch.uk	headteacher@breadalbane.pkc.sch.uk	01887 820428	01887 820061	485
Community School of Auchterarder	New School La, Auchterarder, Perth and Kinross PH3 1BL	www.auchterarder.pkc.sch.uk	headteacher@auchterarder.pkc.sch.uk	01764 662182	01764 663762	443
Crieff High School	Crieff, Perth and Kinross PH7 3RS	www.crieffhigh.pkc.sch.uk	headteacher@crieffhigh.pkc.sch.uk	01764 653383	01764 654739	699
Kinross High School	8 High St, Kinross, Perth and Kinross KY13 8AN	www.kinrosshigh.pkc.sch.uk	headteacher@kinrosshigh.pkc.sch.uk	01577 862430	01577 862606	911
Perth Academy	Murray Pl, Perth, Perth and Kinross PH1 1NJ	www.perthacademy.pkc.sch.uk	headteacher@perthacademy.pkc.sch.uk	01738 623491	01738 625275	1045
Perth Grammar School	Gowans Terr, Perth, Perth and Kinross PH1 5AZ	www.perthgrammar.pkc.sch.uk	headteacher@perthgrammar.pkc.sch.uk	01738 620071	01738 620073	1098
Perth High School	Oakbank Rd, Perth, Perth and Kinross PH1 1HB	www.perthhigh.co.uk	headteacher@perthhigh.pkc.sch.uk	01738 628271	01738 630938	1540
Pitlochry High	East Moulin Rd, Pitlochry, Perth and Kinross PH16 5ET		headteacher@pitlochry.pkc.sch.uk	01796 472900	01796 472251	188
St Columba's RC High School	Malvina Pl, Perth, Perth and Kinross PH1 5BD	www.st-columbas.pkc.sch.uk	headteacher@st-columbas.pkc.sch.uk	01738 622994	01738 630935	569

Renfrewshire

School name	Address	Website	E-mail	Tel	Fax	Pupils
Castlehead High School	Camphill, Paisley, Renfrewshire PA1 2HL	www.castleheadhigh.renfrewshire.sch.uk	enquiries@castleheadhigh.renfrewshire.sch.uk	0141 887 4261	0141 848 1107	963
Gleniffer High School	Amochrie Rd, Foxbar, Paisley, Renfrewshire PA2 0AQ	www.gleniferhigh.renfrewshire.sch.uk	david.nicholls@renfrewshire.gov.uk	01505 813116	01505 816458	1341
Gryffe High School	Old Bridge, off Wear Rd, Houston, Renfrewshire PA6 7EB	www.gryffehigh.renfrewshire.sch.uk	gryffehs@aol.com	01505 690633	01505 690888	931
Johnstone High School	Beith Rd, Johnstone, Renfrewshire PA5 0JN	www.johnstonehs.org.uk	mpstraining@aol.com	01505 322173	01505 322145	1209
Johnstone Technical Education Centre	Units C and D, Floors Street Ind Est, Johnstone, Renfrewshire PA5 8PE			01505 331700		
Linwood High School	Stirling Dr, Linwood, Paisley, Renfrewshire PA3 3NB	www.linwoodhigh.renfrewshire.sch.uk	keith.hasson@renfrewshire.gov.uk	01505 351170	01505 351174	468
Paisley Grammar School	Glasgow Rd, Paisley, Renfrewshire PA1 3RP	www.paisley-gs.renfrewshire.sch.uk	mail@paisleygs.renfrewshire.sch.uk	0141 889 3484	0141 887 2059	1186
Park Mains High School	Barrhill Rd, Erskine, Renfrewshire PA8 6EY	www.parkmainshigh.renfrewshire.sch.uk	dpurduepmh@aol.com	0141 812 2801	0141 812 0119	1457
Renfrew High School	Haining Rd, Renfrew, Renfrewshire PA4 0AN	www.renfrewhigh.renfrewshire.sch.uk	john.strang@renfrewshire.gov.uk	0141 886 7511	0141 885 0675	864
St Andrew's Academy	Barrhead Rd, Paisley, Renfrewshire PA2 7LG	www.st-andrews.renfrewshire.sch.uk		0141 887 5201	0141 887 2116	1137
St Benedict's High School	Bridge of Weir Rd, Linwood, Paisley, Renfrewshire PA3 3DS	www.st-benedictshigh.renfrewshire.sch.uk	enquiries@st-benedictshigh.renfrewshire.sch.uk	01505 327500	01505 333720	731
St Brendan's High School	Middleton Rd, Linwood, Paisley, Renfrewshire PA3 3BE	www.st-brendanshigh.renfrewshire.sch.uk	michael.canning@renfrewshire.gov.uk	01505 329311	01505 336146	346
St Cuthbert's High School	Hallhill Rd, Spateston, Johnstone, Renfrewshire PA5 0SD	www.st-cuthbertshigh.renfrewshire.sch.uk	alan.ward@renfrewshire.gov.uk	01505 703421	01505 702801	406
Trinity High School	Glebe St, Renfrew, Renfrewshire PA4 8TP	www.trinityhigh.renfrewshire.sch.uk	jack.nellaney@renfrewshire.gov.uk	0141 886 6121	0141 885 0694	1081

Scottish Borders

School name	Address	Website	E-mail	Tel	Fax	Pupils
Berwickshire High School	Duns, Berwickshire, Scottish Borders TD11 3QQ	www.berwickshire.scotborders.sch.uk	rkelly@scotborders.gov.uk	01361 883710	01361 883018	786
Earlston High School	Earlston, Berwickshire, Scottish Borders TD4 6HF	www.earlstonhigh.scotborders.sch.uk	earlstonhs@scotborders.gov.uk	01896 849282	01896 848918	864
Eyemouth High School	Eyemouth, Berwickshire, Scottish Borders TD14 5BY	www.eyemouthhigh.scotborders.sch.uk	eyhs@scotborders.gov.uk	01890 750363	01890 751270	447
Galashiels Academy	Elm Row, Galashiels, Selkirkshire, Scottish Borders TD1 3HU	www.galashiels.scotborders.sch.uk	bkennan@scotborders.gov.uk	01896 754788	01896 755652	959
Hawick High School	Bucleuch Rd, Hawick, Roxburghshire, Scottish Borders TD9 0EG	www.hawick.scotborders.sch.uk	nhorn@scotborders.gov.uk	01450 372429	01450 377830	1012
Jedburgh Grammar School	High St, Jedburgh, Roxburghshire, Scottish Borders TD8 6DQ	www.jedburgh.scotborders.gov.uk	hwatt@scotborders.gov.uk	01835 863273	01835 863993	426
Kelso High School	Bowmont St, Kelso, Roxburghshire, Scottish Borders TD5 7EG	www.kelso.scotborders.sch.uk	crobertson@scotborders.gov.uk	01573 224444	01573 227340	672
Peebles High School	Springwood Rd, Peebles, Peeblesshire, Scottish Borders EH45 9HB	www.peebleshighschool.co.uk	rkerr@scotborders.gov.uk	01721 720291	01721 722563	1254
Selkirk High School	Hillside Terr, Selkirk, Scottish Borders TD7 4EW	www.selkirk.scotborders.sch.uk	selkirkhs@scotborders.gov.uk	01750 720246	01750 723039	549

Shetland Islands

School name	Address	Website	E-mail	Tel	Fax	Pupils
Aith Junior High School	Aith, Bixter, Shetland Isles ZE2 9NB	www.aithschool.shetland.co.uk	aithoffice@shetland.biblio.net	01595 810206	01595 810297	92
Anderson High School	Lovers Loan, Lerwick, Shetland Isles ZE1 0JH	www.anderson.shetland.sch.uk	andersonoffice@shetland.biblio.net	01595 692306	01595 695688	878

School name	Address	Website	E-mail	Tel	Fax	Pupils
Baltasound Junior High School	Baltasound, Unst, Shetland Isles ZE2 9DY	www.baltasound.shetland.sch.uk	baltasoundoffice@shetland.biblio.net	01957 711316	01957 711676	39
Brae High School	Brae, Shetland Isles ZE2 9QG		braeoffice@shetland.biblio.net	01806 522370	01806 522734	234
Mid Yell Junior High School	Mid Yell, Shetland Isles ZE2 9BN	www.midyell.shetland.sch.uk	midyellhead@shetland.biblio.net	01957 702252	01957 702091	49
Sandwick Junior High School	Sandwick, Shetland Isles ZE2 9HH	www.sandwick.shetland.sch.uk	sandwickoffice@shetland.biblio.net	01950 431454	01950 431404	184
Scalloway Junior High School	Scalloway, Shetland Isles ZE1 0TN	www.scalloway.shetland.sch.uk	scallowayoffice@shetland.biblio.net	01595 880546	01595 880787	122
Skerries School	Skerries, Shetland Isles ZE2 9AR		skerrieshead@shetland.biblio.net	01806 515235	01806 515223	2
Whalsay School	Symbister, Whalsay, Shetland Isles ZE2 9AQ	www.symbisterhouse.shetland.sch.uk	whalsayoffice@shetland.biblio.net	01595 743800	01806 566667	60

South Ayrshire

School name	Address	Website	E-mail	Tel	Fax	Pupils
Ayr Academy	7 Fort St, Ayr, South Ayrshire KA7 1HX		mail@ayracademy.south-ayrshire.gov.uk	01292 262302	01292 261105	711
Belmont Academy	Belmont Rd, Ayr, South Ayrshire KA7 2PG		mail@belmontacademy.south-ayrshire.gov.uk	01292 281733	01292 611113	1448
Carrick Academy	72–74 Kirkoswald Rd, Maybole, South Ayrshire KA19 8BN		mail@carrickacademy.south-ayrshire.gov.uk	01655 882389	01655 885748	553
Girvan Academy	62 The Ave, Girvan, South Ayrshire KA26 9DD		mail@girvanacademy.south-ayrshire.gov.uk	01465 713008	01465 715708	657
Kyle Academy	7 Overmills Rd, Ayr, South Ayrshire KA7 3LR		mail@kyleacademy.south-ayrshire.gov.uk	01292 262234	01292 611123	761
Marr College	Dundonald Rd, Troon, South Ayrshire KA10 7AB		mail@marrcollege.south-ayrshire.gov.uk	01292 311082	01292 312208	1144
Prestwick Academy	15 Newdykes Rd, Prestwick, South Ayrshire KA9 2LB	www.south-ayrshire.gov.uk	mail@prestwickacademy.south-ayrshire.gov.uk	01292 477121	01292 671850	1178
Queen Margaret Academy	33a Dalmellington Rd, Ayr, South Ayrshire KA7 3TL		mail@queenmargaretacademy.south-ayrshire.gov.uk	01292 268379	01292 611143	706

South Lanarkshire

School name	Address	Website	E-mail	Tel	Fax	Pupils
Biggar High School	John's Loan, Biggar, South Lanarkshire ML12 6AG		office@biggar.s-lanark.sch.uk	01899 220144	01899 221265	719
Carluke High School	Carnwath Rd, Caluke, South Lanarkshire ML8 4EA	www.carluke.s-lanark.sch.uk	office@carluke.s-lanark.sch.uk	01555 772302	01555 750024	1226
Cathkin High School	Whitlawburn, Cambuslang, Glasgow G72 8YS		office@cathkin.s-lanark.sch.uk	0141 641 4331	0141 641 9003	926
Duncanrig Secondary School	Alberta Ave, East Kilbride, South Lanarkshire G75 8HY	www.duncanrig.s-lanark.sch.uk	office@duncanrig.s-lanark.sch.uk	01355 234254	01355 231340	1790
Hamilton Grammar School	Auchincampbell Rd, Hamilton, South Lanarkshire ML3 6PF	www.hamilton.s-lanark.sch.uk	office@hamilton.s-lanark.sch.uk	01698 285777	01698 891949	1182
Holy Cross High School	Muir St, Hamilton, South Lanarkshire ML3 6EY	www.holycross.s-lanark.sch.uk	office@holycross.s-lanark.sch.uk	01698 283888	01698 891952	1269
John Ogilvie High School	Farm Rd, Burnbank, Hamilton, South Lanarkshire ML3 9LA	www.johnogilvie.s-lanark.sch.uk	office@johnogilvie.s-lanark.sch.uk	01698 820811	01698 829033	900
Lanark Grammar School	Albany Dr, Lanark, South Lanarkshire ML11 9AQ	www.lanark.s-lanark.sch.uk	office@lanark.s-lanark.sch.uk	01555 662471	01555 662340	1063
Larkhall Academy	Cherryhill, Larkhall, South Lanarkshire ML9 1QN	www.larkhallacademy.co.uk	office@larkhall.s-lanark.sch.uk	01698 881570	01698 887051	1272
Lesmahagow High St	School Rd, Lesmahagow, South Lanarkshire ML11 0DL	www.lesmahagow.s-lanark.sch.uk	office@lesmahagow.s-lanark.sch.uk	01555 893456	01555 893115	586
St Andrew's and St Bride's High School	Crosshouse Rd, Greenhills, East Kilbride, South Lanarkshire G75 9DG			01355 234134	01355 225351	1702
Stonelaw High School	140 Calderwood Rd, Rutherglen, Glasgow G73 3SE	www.stonelaw.s-lanark.sch.uk	office@stonelaw.s-lanark.sch.uk	0141 643 0212	0141 647 0325	1177
Strathaven Academy	Crosshouse Rd, Greenhills, East Kilbride, South Lanarkshire G75 9DG	www.strathaven.s-lanark.sch.uk	office@strathaven.s-lanark.sch.uk	01357 520126	01357 529489	808
Trinity High School	Muir St, Hamilton, ML3 6EY	www.trinity.s-lanark.sch.uk	office@trinity.s-lanark.sch.uk	0141 641 7741	0141 641 9004	1000
Uddingston Grammar School	Station Rd, Uddingston, South Lanarkshire G71 7BS	www.uddingston.s-lanark.sch.uk	dgreenshields@uddingston.s-lanark.sch.uk	01698 327400	01698 327409	1221

Stirling

School name	Address	Website	E-mail	Tel	Fax	Pupils
Balfron High School	Roman Rd, Balfron, Glasgow G63 0PW	www.balfronhigh.stirling.sch.uk	balfronhs@stirling.gov.uk	01360 440469	01360 440260	961
Bannockburn High School	Bannockburn Rd, Bannockburn, Stirling FK7 0HQ	www.bannockburnhigh.stirling.sch.uk	bannockburnhs@stirling.gov.uk	01786 813519	01786 818040	852
Dunblane High School	Highfields, Dunblane, Perthshire FK15 9DR	www.dunblanehigh.stirling.sch.uk	dunblanehs@stirling.gov.uk	01786 823823	01786 824462	163
McLaren High School	Mollands Rd, Callander, Stirling FK17 8JH	www.mclarenhigh.com	mclarenhs@stirling.gov.uk	01877 330156	01877 331601	692
St Modan's High School	Barnsdale Rd, Stirling FK7 0PU	www.stmodans.ik.org	stmodans@stirling.gov.uk	01786 470962	01786 447117	922
Stirling High School	Ogilvie Rd, Stirling FK8 2PA	www.stirling.stirling.sch.uk	stirlinghs@stirling.gov.uk	01786 472451	01786 447127	914
Wallace High School	Dumyat Rd, Stirling FK9 5HW	www.wallace.stirling.sch.uk	wallacehs@stirling.gov.uk	01786 462166	01786 447134	942

West Dunbartonshire

School name	Address	Website	E-mail	Tel	Fax	Pupils
Braidfield High School	Queen Mary Ave, Clydebank, West Dunbartonshire G81 2LR		schooloffice@braidfield.w-dunbarton.sch.uk	0141 952 3265	0141 941 3784	414
Clydebank High School	Shelley Dr, Clydebank, West Dunbartonshire G81 3EJ		schooloffice@clydebank.w-dunbarton.sch.uk	0141 952 0001	0141 941 2160	1499
Dumbarton Academy	Crosslet Rd, Dumbarton, West Dunbartonshire G82 2AJ		mrsfinn@dumbarton.biblio.net	01389 763373	01389 763981	728
Our Lady and St Patrick's High School	Hawthornhill Rd, Dumbarton, West Dunbartonshire G82 5JF	www.olsp.org.uk	schooloffice@olsp.w-dunbarton.sch.uk	01389 762101	01389 731109	1215
St Andrew's High School	North Douglas St, Clydebank, West Dunbartonshire G81 1NQ		schooloffice@st-andrews.w-dunbarton.sch.uk	0141 952 7761	0141 951 4386	915
St Columba's High School	Gilmour St, Clydebank, West Dunbartonshire G81 2BW	www.wdcweb.info	schooloffice@st-columbas.w-dunbarton.sch.uk	0141 952 3163	0141 941 1413	755
Vale of Leven Academy	Place of Bonhill, Alexandria, West Dunbartonshire G83 0TR		schooloffice@leven.w-dunbarton.sch.uk	01389 757231	01389 721805	1047

West Lothian

School name	Address	Website	E-mail	Tel	Fax	Pupils
Armadale Academy	West Main St, Armadale, West Lothian EH48 3LY		armadale.ac@wled.org.uk	01501 730601	01501 735900	749
Bathgate Academy	Edinburgh Rd, Bathgate, West Lothian EH48 1LF	www.westlothian.org.uk	bathgate.ac@wled.org.uk	01506 653725	01506 652262	1000
Broxburn Academy	Cardross Rd, Broxburn, West Lothian EH52 6AG		broxburn.ac@wled.org.uk	01506 852521	01506 856211	907
Deans High School	Eastwood Pk, Deans, Livingston, West Lothian EH54 8PS	www.westlothian.org.uk	margaret.ross1@wled.org.uk	01506 497090	01506 497025	842
The James Young High School	Willowbank, Ladywell, Livingston, West Lothian EH54 6HN	www.jamesyoung.org	thejamesyoung.hs@wled.org.uk	01506 414244	01506 497014	1105
Linlithgow Academy	Braehead Rd, Linlithgow, West Lothian EH49 6EH	www.linlithgowacademy.org	linlithgow.ac@wled.org.uk	01506 843211	01506 848082	1157
St Kentigern's Academy	West Main St, Blackburn, West Lothian EH47 7LX		kathleen.gibbons@wled.org.uk	01506 656404	01506 651736	1065
St Margaret's Academy	Howden South Rd, Howden, Livingston, West Lothian EH54 6AT		patrick.sweeney@wled.org.uk	01506 497104	01506 497103	1014
West Calder High School	Limefield, Polbeth, West Calder, West Lothian EH55 8QN		bill.gourlay@wled.org.uk	01506 871510	01506 871345	1058
Whitburn Academy	Shanks Rd, Whitburn, West Lothian EH47 0HL	www.whitburn.w-lothian.sch.uk	david.williamson@wled.org.uk	01501 740675	01501 74272	998

Wales

Blaenau Gwent

School name	Address	Tel	Ref
Abertillery Comprehensive School	Alma St, Abertillery, Blaenau Gwent, Blaenau Gwent NP13 1YL	01495 217121	677-4074
Brynmawr School	Rhydw, Intermediate Rd, Brynmawr, Blaenau Gwent, Blaenau Gwent NP23 4XT	01495 310527	677-5401
Ebbw Vale Comprehensive School	Waen-Y-Pound Rd, Ebbw Vale, Blaenau Gwent, Blaenau Gwent NP23 6LE	01495 303409	677-4067
Glyncoed Comprehensive School	Badminton Gr, Ebbw Vale, Blaenau Gwent, Blaenau Gwent NP23 5UW	01495 303216	677-4045
Nantyglo Comprehensive School	Pond Rd, Nantyglo, Brynmawr, Blaenau Gwent NP23 4WX	01495 310776	677-4073
Tredegar Comprehensive School	Stable La, Tredegar, Blaenau Gwent, Blaenau Gwent NP22 4BH	01495 723551	677-4061

Bridgend

School name	Address	Tel	Ref
Archbishop Mcgrath RC School	Bryn Rd, Heol Yr Ysgol, Tondu, Bridgend CF32 9EH	01656 720677	672-4601
Brynteg Comprehensive School	Ewenny Rd, Bridgend CF31 3ER	01656 641800	672-4078
Bryntirion Comprehensive School	Merlin Cres, Cefn Glas, Bridgend, Bridgend CF31 4QR	01656 641100	672-4068
Cynffig Comprehensive School	East Ave, Kenfig Hill, Bridgend, Bridgend CF33 6NP	01656 740294	672-4059
Maesteg Comprehensive School	Llangynwyd, Maesteg CF34 9RW	01656 812700	672-4071
Ogmore Comprehensive School	Spout Hill, Abergarw, Brynmenyn, Bridgend CF32 9NA	01656 721515	672-4084
Pencoed Comprehensive School	Coychurch Rd, Pencoed, Bridgend, Bridgend CF35 5LZ	01656 867100	672-4076
Porthcawl Comprehensive School	52 Park Ave, Porthcawl, Bridgend, Bridgend CF36 3ES	01656 774100	672-4080
Ynysawdre Comprehensive School	Heol-yr-Ysgol, Tondu, Bridgend, Bridgend CF32 9EL	01656 720643	672-4074

Caerphilly

School name	Address	Tel	Ref
Bedwas High School	Newport Rd, Bedwas, Caerphilly, Newport CF83 8BJ	02920 859800	676-4093
Blackwood Comprehensive School	Ty Isha Terr, Cen Fforest, Blackwood, Blackwood NP12 1ER	01495 225288	676-4046
Cwmcarn High School	Chapel Farm, Cwmcarn, Crosskeys, Crosskeys NP11 7NG	01495 270982	676-5400
Heolddu Comprehensive School	Mountain Rd, Caerphilly, Bargoed CF81 8XL	01443 875531	676-4073
Lewis Girls' Comprehensive School	Oakfield St, Ystrad Mynach CF82 7WW	01443 813168	676-4077
Lewis School Pengam	Gilfach, Bargoed CF81 8LJ	01443 873873	676-4075
Newbridge Comprehensive School	Bridge St, Newbridge, Newport, Newport NP11 5FR	01495 243243	676-4031
Oakdale Comprehensive School	Penmaen Rd, Oakdale, Blackwood, Caerphilly NP12 0DT	01495 233600	676-4053
Pontllanfraith Comprehensive School	Coed Caeddu Rd, Pontllanfraith, Blackwood, Blackwood NP12 2YB	01495 224929	676-4032
Rhymney Comprehensive School	Mill Field, Abertysswg, Rhymney, Rhymney NP2 5XF	01685 846900	676-4090
Risca Community School	Pontymason La, Rogerstone, Newport, Newport NP11 6YY	01633 612425	676-4068
St Cenydd Comprehensive School	St Cenydd Rd, Trecenydd, Caerphilly, Caerphilly CF83 2RP	02920 852504	676-4065
St Ilan School	Pontygwyndy Rd, Caerphilly CF83 3HD	02920 852533	676-4067
St Martin Comprehensive School	Hillside, Caerphilly CF83 1UW	02920 858050	676-4070
Ysgol Gyfun Cwm Rhymni	Heol Gelli Hat, Fleur De Lys, Blackwood, Caerphilly NP12 3JQ	01443 875227	676-4103

Cardiff

School name	Address	Tel	Ref
The Bishop Of Llandaff CIW High School	Rookwood Cl, Llandaff, Llandaff, Cardiff CF5 2NR	02920 562485	681-4608
Cantonian High School	Fairwater Rd, Fairwater, Cardiff CF5 3JR	02920 415250	681-4049
Cardiff High School	Llandennis Rd, Cyncoed, Cardiff CF23 6WG	02920 680850	681-4039
Cathays High School	Crown Way, New Zealand Road, Cardiff CF14 3XG	02920 544400	681-4054
Corpus Christi RC High School	Ty Draw Rd, Lisvane, Cardiff CF23 6XL	02920 761893	681-4611
Ely Presbyterian Church School	Archer Rd, Cardiff CF5 4FR		681-6023
Fitzalan High School	Lawrenny Ave, Leckwith, Cardiff CF11 8XB	02920 232850	681-4042
Glyn Derw High School	Penally Rd, Ely, Cardiff CF5 5XP	02920 590920	681-4035
Llanedeyrn High School	Roundwood, Llanedeyrn, Cardiff CF23 9US	02920 734718	681-4047
Llanishen High School	Heol Hir, Llanishen, Cardiff CF14 5YL	02920 680800	681-4051
Llanrumney High School	Ball Rd, Llanrumney, Cardiff CF3 4YW	02920 365500	681-4052
Mary Immaculate RC High School	Caerau La, Wenvoe, Cardiff CF5 5QZ	02920 593465	681-4607
Michaelston Community College	Michaelston Rd, Ely, Ely CF5 4SX	02920 672700	681-4073
Radyr Comprehensive School	Heol Isaf, Radyr, Cardiff CF15 8XG	02920 845100	681-4070
Rumney High School	Quarry Hill, Newport Road, Cardiff CF3 3XG	02920 792751	681-4030
St Illtyds RC High School	Newport Rd, Rumney, Cardiff CF3 1XQ	02920 778174	681-4600
St Teilo's CIW High School	Llanedeyrn Rd, Pen-y-lan, Cardiff CF23 9DT	02920 434700	681-4609
Whitchurch High School	Penlline Rd, Whitchurch, Cardiff CF14 2XJ	02920 629700	681-4050
Willows High School	Willows Ave, Tremorfa, Cardiff CF24 2YE	02920 414243	681-4041
Ysgol Gyfun Gymraeg Glantaf	Heol Y Bont, Gogledd Llandaf, Cardiff CF14 2JL	02920 333090	681-4071
Ysgol Gyfun Gymraeg Plasmawr	Pentrebane Rd, Tyllgoed, Cardiff CF5 3PZ	02920 405498	681-4072

Carmarthenshire

School name	Address	Tel	Ref
Amman Valley Comprehensive School	Margaret St, Ammanford, Carmarthenshire, Carmarthenshire SA18 2NW	01269 592441	669-4029
Bryngwyn Comprehensive School	Dafen, Llanelli, Carmarthenshire, Carmarthenshire SA14 8RP	01554 750661	669-4054
Coedcae School	Trostre Rd, Llanelli, Carmarthenshire, Carmarthenshire SA15 1LJ	01554 750574	669-4050
Queen Elizabeth High	Llansteffan Rd, Johnstown Road, Carmarthenshire, Carmarthenshire SA31 3NL	01267 237650	669-4063
St John Lloyd R C School	Havard Rd, Llanelli, Carmarthenshire, Carmarthenshire SA14 8SD	01554 772589	669-4600
Ysgol Glan-Y-Mor School	Heol Elfed, Burry Port, Carmarthenshire, Carmarthenshire SA16 0AL	01554 832507	669-4053
Ysgol Gyfun Dyffryn Taf	North Rd, Whitland, Carmarthenshire, Carmarthenshire SA34 0BD	01994 242100	669-4512
Ysgol Gyfun Emlyn	Newcastle Emlyn, Carmarthenshire, Carmarthenshire SA38 9LN	01239 710447	669-4060
Ysgol Gyfun Gymraeg Bro Myrddin	Croesyceiliog, Carmarthen, Sir Gaerfyrddin, Carmarthenshire SA32 8DN	01267 234829	669-4056
Ysgol Gyfun Maes Yr Yrfa	74 Heol Y Parc, Cefneithin, Llanelli, Carmarthenshire SA14 7DT	01269 833900	669-4061
Ysgol Gyfun Pantycelyn	Cilycwm Rd, Llandovery, Carmarthenshire, Carmarthenshire SA20 0DY	01550 720395	669-4024
Ysgol Gyfun Tregib	Ffairfach, Llandeilo, Carmarthenshire, Carmarthenshire SA19 6TB	01558 823477	669-4028
Ysgol Gyfun Y Strade	Heol Sandy, Llanelli, Carmarthenshire, Carmarthenshire SA15 4DL	01554 745100	669-4052
Ysgol Y Gwendraeth	Drefach, Llanelli, Carmarthenshire, Carmarthenshire SA14 7AB	01269 841322	669-4062

Ceredigion

School name	Address	Tel	Ref
Cardigan County Secondary	Park Pl, Aberteifi, Ceredigion, Ceredigion SA43 1AD	01239 612670	667-4044
Penglais Comprehensive School	Waunfawr, Aberystwyth, Ceredigion, Ceredigion SY23 3AW	01970 624811	667-4047

School name	Address	Tel	Ref
Ysgol Gyfun Aberaeron	Stryd Y Fro, Aberaeron, Ceredigion, Ceredigion SA46 0DT	01545 570217	667-4042
Ysgol Gyfun Dyffryn Teifi	Heol Llyn y Fran, Llandysul, Ceredigion, Ceredigion SA44 4HP	01559 362310	667-4059
Ysgol Gyfun Llanbedr-Pont-Steffan	Peterwell Terr, Llanbedr Pont Steffan, Ceredigion, Ceredigion SA48 7BX	01570 422214	667-4041
Ysgol Gyfun Penweddig	Ffordd Llanbadarn, Llangawsai, Aberystwyth, Aberystwyth SY23 3QN	01970 639499	667-4048
Ysgol Uwchradd Tregaron	Tregaron, Ceredigion SY25 6HG	01974 298231	667-4046

Conwy

School name	Address	Tel	Ref
Eirias High School	Eirias Rd, Colwyn Bay LL29 7SP	01492 532025	662-5402
Ysgol Aberconwy	Morfa Dr, Conwy LL32 8ED	01492 593243	662-4023
Ysgol Bryn Elian	Windsor Dr, Colwyn Bay, Conwy, Conwy LL29 8HU	01492 518215	662-5403
Ysgol Dyffryn Conwy	Nebo Rd, Llanrwst LL26 0AP	01492 640649	662-4035
Ysgol Emrys Ap Iwan	Faenol Ave, Abergele, Conwy, Conwy LL22 7HE	01745 832287	662-5400
Ysgol John Bright	Maesdu Rd, Llandudno LL30 1DF	01492 864200	662-4022
Ysgol Y Creuddyn	Ffordd Dderwen, Bae Penrhyn, Llandudno, Llandudno LL30 3LB	01492 544344	662-4038

Denbighshire

School name	Address	Tel	Ref
Blessed Edward Jones RC School	Cefndy Rd, Rhyl, Denbighshire, Denbighshire LL18 2EU	01745 343433	663-4601
Denbigh High School	Ruthin Rd, Denbigh, Denbighshire, Denbighshire LL16 3EX	01745 812485	663-4026
Prestatyn High School	2 Princes Ave, Prestatyn, Denbighshire, Denbighshire LL19 8RS	01745 852312	663-4014
Rhyl High School	Grange Rd, Rhyl, Denbighshire, Denbighshire LL18 4BY	01745 343533	663-4003
St Brigid's School	Plas Yn Grn, Mold Rd, Denbigh LL16 4BH	01745 815228	663-5900
Ysgol Brynhyfryd	Mold Rd, Ruthin, Denbighshire, Denbighshire LL15 1EG	01824 703933	663-4031
Ysgol Dinas Bran	Dinbren Rd, Llangollen, Denbighshire, Denbighshire LL20 8TG	01978 860669	663-4027
Ysgol Uwchradd Glan Clwyd	Ffordd Dinbych, Llanelwy, Sir Ddinbych, Sir Ddinbych LL17 0RP	01745 582611	663-4020

Flintshire

School name	Address	Tel	Ref
Argoed High School	Bryn Rd, Bryn Y Baal, Nr Mold, Flintshire CH7 6RY	01352 756414	664-4042
Castell Alun High School	Hope, Flintshire LL12 9PY	01978 760238	664-4017
Connah's Quay High School	Golftyn La, Connah's Quay, Flintshire, Flintshire CH5 4BH	01244 813491	664-4022
Elfed High School	Mill La, Buckley, Flintshire, Flintshire CH7 3HQ	01244 550217	664-4011
Flint High School	Maes Hyfryd, Flintshire CH6 5LL	01352 732268	664-4021
Hawarden High School	The Highway, Hawarden, Deeside, Flintshire CH5 3DJ	01244 526400	664-4000
Holywell High School	The Strand, Holywell, Flintshire, Flintshire CH8 7AW	01352 710011	664-4012
John Summers High School	Chester Rd West, Queensferry, Deeside, Flintshire CH5 1SE	01244 831575	664-4019
Mold Alun School	Wrexham Rd, Mold, Flintshire, Flintshire CH7 1EP	01352 750755	664-4006
St David's High School	St David's Terr, Saltney, Chester, Flintshire CH4 0AE	01244 671583	664-4013
St Richard Gwyn Roman RC High School	Ffordd Llewelyn, Flint CH6 5JZ	01352 736900	664-4600
Ysgol Maes Garmon	Stryd Conwy, Yr Wyddgrug, Sir Y Fflint, CH7 1JB	01352 750678	664-4018

3

Gwynedd

School name	Address	Tel	Ref
Ysgol Ardudwy	Ffordd y Traeth, Harlech, Gwynedd, Gwynedd LL46 2UH	01766 780331	661-4034
Ysgol Botwnnog	Botwnnog, Llyn, Gwynedd, Gwynedd LL53 8PY	01758 730220	661-4003
Ysgol Brynrefail	Llanrug, Caernarfon, Gwynedd, Gwynedd LL55 4AD	01286 672381	661-4004
Ysgol Dyffryn Nantlle	Ffordd Y Brenin, Penygroes, Gwynedd, Gwynedd LL54 6RL	01286 880345	661-4007
Ysgol Dyffryn Ogwen	Ffordd Coetmor, Bethesda, Gwynedd, Gwynedd LL57 3NN	01248 600291	661-4002
Ysgol Eifionydd	Porthmadog, Gwynedd LL49 9HS	01766 512114	661-4009
Ysgol Friars	Lon y Bryn, Bangor, Gwynedd, Gwynedd LL57 2LN	01248 364905	661-4036
Ysgol Glan Y Mor	Ffordd Caerdydd, Pwllheli, Gwynedd, Gwynedd LL53 5NU	01758 701244	661-4040
Ysgol Syr Hugh Owen	Bethel Rd, Caernarfon, Gwynedd, Gwynedd LL55 1HW	01286 673076	661-4039
Ysgol Tryfan	Lon Powys, Bangor, Gwynedd, Gwynedd LL57 2TU	01248 352633	661-4037
Ysgol Uwchradd Tywyn	Station Rd, Tywyn, Gwynedd, Gwynedd LL36 9EU	01654 710256	661-4032
Ysgol Y Berwyn	Y Bala, Gwynedd LL23 7BN	01678 520259	661-4033
Ysgol Y Gader	Dolgellau, Gwynedd LL40 1HY	01341 422578	661-4030
Ysgol Y Moelwyn	Heol Wynne, Blaenau Ffestiniog, Gwynedd, Gwynedd LL41 3DW	01766 830435	661-4031

Isle of Anglesey

School name	Address	Tel	Ref
Ysgol David Hughes	Ffordd Pentraeth, Porthaethwy, Ynys Mn, Ynys Môn LL59 5SS	01248 712287	660-4028
Ysgol Gyfun Llangefni	Llangefni, Ynys Mn, Ynys Môn LL77 7NG	01248 723441	660-4027
Ysgol Syr Thomas Jones	Pentrefelin, Amlwch, Ynys Mon, Ynys Môn LL68 9TH	01407 830287	660-4025
Ysgol Uwchradd Bodedern	Bodedern, Bro Alaw, Ynys Mn, Caergybi, Ynys Môn LL65 3SU	01407 741000	660-4029
Ysgol Uwchradd Caergybi	Caergybi, Ynys Mn, Ynys Môn LL65 1NP	01407 762219	660-4026

Merthyr Tydfil

School name	Address	Tel	Ref
Afon Taf High School	Yew St, Troedyrhiw, Merthyr Tydfil, Merthyr Tydfil CF48 4ED	01443 690401	675-4011
Bishop Hedley High School	Gwaunfarren Rd, Penydarren, Merthyr Tydfil, Merthyr Tydfil CF47 9AN	01685 721747	675-4600
Cyfarthfa High School	Cae Mari Dwn, Queen's Rd, Merthyr Tydfil, Merthyr Tydfil CF47 0LS	01685 721725	675-4013
Pen-Y-Dre High School	Gurnos Est, Merthyr Tydfil CF47 9BY	01685 721726	675-4012

Monmouthshire

School name	Address	Tel	Ref
Caldicot Comprehensive School	Mill La, Caldicot, Monmouthshire, Monmouthshire NP26 5XA	01291 426436	679-4066
Chepstow Comprehensive School	Welsh St, Chepstow, Monmouthshire, Monmouthshire NP16 5LR	01291 635777	679-4065
King Henry VIII Comprehensive School	Old Hereford Rd, Abergavenny, Monmouthshire, Monmouthshire NP7 6EP	01873 735373	679-4064
Monmouth Comprehensive School	Old Dixton Rd, Monmouthshire NP25 3YT	01600 775177	679-4060

Neath Port Talbot

School name	Address	Tel	Ref
Cefn Saeson Comprehensive School	Afan Valley Rd, Cimla, Neath, Neath SA11 3TA	01639 791300	671-4064
Cwmtawe Comprehensive School	Ynysderw Rd, Pontardawe, Swansea, Swansea SA8 4EG	01792 863200	671-4065

School name	Address	Tel	Ref
Cwrt Sart Comprehensive School	Old Rd, Briton Ferry, Neath, Neath SA11 2ET	01639 777890	671-4068
Cymer Afan Comprehensive School	School Rd, Cymmer, Port Talbot, Port Talbot SA13 3EL	01639 850237	671-4047
Dwr-y-Felin Comprehensive School	Dwr-y-Felin Rd, Neath SA10 7RE	01639 635161	671-4067
Dyffryn School	Bertha Rd, Margam, Port Talbot, Port Talbot SA13 2AN	01639 760110	671-4059
Glan Afan Comprehensive School	Station Rd, Port Talbot SA13 1LZ	01639 883964	671-4052
Llangatwg Comprehensive School	Main Rd, Cadoxton, Neath, Neath SA10 8DB	01639 634700	671-4066
St Joseph's Catholic School and 6th form Centre	Newton Ave, Port Talbot SA12 6EY	01639 884305	671-4601
Sandfields Comprehensive School	Southdown View, Sandfields, Port Talbot, Port Talbot SA12 7AH	01639 884246	671-4056
Ysgol Gyfun Ystalyfera	Glan Yr Afon, Ystalyfera, Swansea, Neath, Port Talbot SA9 2JJ	01639 842129	671-4060

Newport

School name	Address	Tel	Ref
Bassaleg School	Forge La, Bassaleg, Newport, Newport NP10 8NF	01633 892191	680-4030
Bettws High School	Bettws La, Newport NP9 5XL	01633 820100	680-4025
Caerleon Comprehensive School	Cold Bath Rd, Caerleon, Newport, Newport NP18 1NF	01633 420106	680-4059
Duffryn High School	Lighthouse Rd, Duffryn, Newport, Newport NP10 8YD	01633 654100	680-4020
Hartridge High School	Hartridge Farm Rd, Newport NP18 2YE	01633 412487	680-4021
Lliswerry High School	Nash Rd, Newport NP19 0RP	01633 277867	680-4026
St Joseph's R.C.High School	Pencarn Way, Tredegar Park, Newport, Newport NP10 8XH	01633 670570	680-4602
St Julian's Comprehensive School	Heather Rd, St Julian's, Newport, Newport NP9 7XU	01633 224490	680-4003

Pembrokeshire

School name	Address	Tel	Ref
The Greenhill School	Heywood La, Tenby, Pembrokeshire, Pembrokeshire SA70 8BN	01834 840100	668-4035
Milford Haven School	Steynton Rd, Milford Haven, Pembrokeshire, Pembrokeshire SA73 1AE	01646 690021	668-4063
Pembroke School/ Ysgol Penfro	Bush, Pembroke, Pembrokeshire, Pembrokeshire SA71 4RL	01646 682461	668-4038
Sir Thomas Picton School	Queensway, Haverfordwest, Pembrokeshire, Pembrokeshire SA61 2NX	01437 765394	668-4055
Tasker-Milward VC School	Off Portfield Ave, Haverfordwest, Pembrokeshire, Pembrokeshire SA61 1EQ	01437 764147	668-4511
Ysgol Bro Gwaun	Heol Dyfed, Fishguard, Pembrokeshire, Pembrokeshire SA65 9DT	01348 872268	668-4031
Ysgol Dewi Sant	St David's, Haverfordwest, Pembrokeshire, Pembrokeshire SA62 6QH	01437 725000	668-4034
Ysgol Gyfun Ddwyieithog Y Preseli	Crymych, Preseli, Sir Benfro, Sir Benfro SA41 3QH	01239 831406	668-4064

Powys

School name	Address	Tel	Ref
Brecon High School	Penlan, Brecon, Powys, Powys LD3 9SR	01874 622361	666-4022
Builth Wells High School	College Rd, Builth Wells, Powys, Powys LD2 3BW	01982 553292	666-4020
Caereinion High School	Llanfair Caereinion, Welshpool, Powys, Powys SY21 0HW	01938 810888	666-4000
Crickhowell High School	New Rd, Crickhowell, Powys, Powys NP8 1AW	01873 813500	666-4024
Gwernyfed High School	Three Cocks, Brecon, Powys, Powys LD3 0SG	01497 847445	666-4023
John Beddoes School	Broadaxe La, Powys LD8 2YT	01544 267259	666-4014
Llandrindod High School	Dyffryn Rd, Llandrindod Wells, Powys, Powys LD1 6AW	01597 822992	666-4019
Llanfyllin High School	Llanfyllin, Powys SY22 5BJ	01691 648391	666-4001
Llanidloes High School	Llanidloes, Powys SY18 6EX	01686 412289	666-4002

School name	Address	Tel	Ref
Newtown High School	Dolfor Rd, Newtown, Powys, Powys SY16 1JE	01686 626304	666-4011
Welshpool High School	Erw Wen Salop Rd, Welshpool, Powys, Powys SY21 7RE	01938 552014	666-4013
Ysgol Bro Ddyfi	Machynlleth, Powys SY20 8DR	01654 702012	666-4003
Ysgol Maes-Y-Dderwen	Tudor St, Ystradgynlais, Swansea, Swansea SA9 1AP	01639 842115	666-4021

Rhondda Cynon Taff

School name	Address	Tel	Ref
Aberdare Boys' School	Cwmdare Rd, Aberdare, Rhondda, Cynon, Taff, Rhondda Cynon Taff CF44 8SS	01685 872642	674-4100
Aberdare Girls' Comprehensive School	Cwmbach Rd, Aberdare, Rhondda, Cynon, Taff, Rhondda Cynon Taff CF44 0NF	01685 872460	674-4101
Blaengwawr Comprehensive School	Club St, Aberaman, Aberdare, Aberdare CF44 6TN	01685 874341	674-4056
Bryncelynnog Comprehensive School	Penycoedcae Rd, Beddau, Pontypridd, Pontypridd CF38 2AE	01443 203411	674-4019
Cardinal Newman RC Comprehensive School	Dynea Rd, Rhydyfelin, Pontypridd, Rhondda, Cynon, Taff, Rhondda Cynon Taff CF37 5DP	01443 494110	674-4602
The Coedylan Comprehensive School	Albion Site, Cilfynydd, Pontypridd, Pontypridd CF37 4SF	01443 486133	674-4022
Ferndale Community School	Ferndale, CF43 4AR	01443 755337	674-4083
Hawthorn High School	School La, Hawthorn, Pontypridd, Pontypridd CF37 5AL	01443 841228	674-4027
Mountain Ash Comprehensive School	New Rd, Mountain Ash CF45 4DG	01443 479199	674-4053
Porth County Community School	Cemetery Rd, Porth, Rhondda, Cynon, Taff, Rhondda Cynon Taff CF39 0BS	01443 682137	674-4087
St John Baptist CIW High School	Glan Rd, Aberdare, Rhondda, Cynon, Taff, Rhondda Cynon Taff CF44 8BW	01685 875414	674-4604
Tonypandy Community College	Llewellyn St, Rhondda, Penygraig, Rhondda, Cynon, Taff, Rhondda Cynon Taff CF40 1HQ	01443 436171	674-4095
Tonyrefail Comprehensive School	Gilfach Rd, Tonyrefail CF39 8HG	01443 670647	674-4057
Treorchy Comprehensive School	Pengelli, Treorchy, Rhondda, Rhondda Cynon Taff CF42 6UL	01443 773128	674-4081
Y Pant Comprehensive School	Cowbridge Rd, Talbot Grn, Pontyclun, Rhondda, Cynon, Taff, Rhondda Cynon Taff CF72 8YQ	01443 237701	674-4096
Ysgol Gyfun Cymer Rhondda	Heol Graigwen, Cymmer, Porth, Porth CF39 9HA	01443 680800	674-4097
Ysgol Gyfun Garth Olwg	St Illtyds Rd, Church Village, Pontypridd, Rhondda, Cynon, Taff CF38 1RQ	01443 486818	674-4054
Ysgol Gyfun Llanhari	Llanhari, Pontyclun, Rhondda, Cynon, Taff, Rhondda Cynon Taff CF72 9XE	01443 237824	674-4088
Ysgol Gyfun Rhydywaun	Rhodfa Lawrence, Penywaun, Hirwaun, Rhondda, Cynon, Taff, Rhondda Cynon Taff CF44 9ES	01685 813500	674-4105

Swansea

School name	Address	Tel	Ref
Birchgrove Comprehensive School	Birchgrove Rd, Birchgrove, Swansea, Swansea SA7 9NB	01792 535400	670-4075
Bishop Gore Comprehensive School	De La Beche Rd, Sketty, Swansea, Swansea SA2 9AP	01792 411400	670-4044
Bishop Vaughan RC School	Mynydd Garnlwyd Rd, Morriston, Swansea, Swansea SA6 7QG	01792 772006	670-4600
Bishopston Comprehensive School	The Glebe, Bishopston, Swansea, Swansea SA3 3JP	01792 234121	670-4069
Cefn Hengoed Community School	Caldicot Rd, Winch Wen, Swansea, Swansea SA1 7HX	01792 773464	670-4031
Daniel James Community School	Heol Ddu, Treboeth, Swansea, Swansea SA5 7HP	01792 771935	670-4077
Dylan Thomas Community School	John St, Cockett, Swansea, Swansea SA2 0FR	01792 610300	670-4076
Gowerton School	Cecil Rd, Gowerton, Swansea, Swansea SA4 3DL	01792 873461	670-4063
Morriston Comprehensive School	Heol Maes Eglwys, Morriston, Swansea, Swansea SA6 6NH	01792 797745	670-4033
Olchfa School	Gower Rd, Sketty, Swansea, Swansea SA2 7AB	01792 534300	670-4032
Pentrehafod School	Pentremawr Rd, Hafod, Swansea, Swansea SA1 2NN	01792 410400	670-4043
Penyrheol Comprehensive School	Pontarddulais Rd, Gorseinon, Swansea, Swansea SA4 4FG	01792 533066	670-4062
Pontarddulais Comprehensive School	Caecerrig Rd, Pontarddulais, Swansea, Swansea SA4 1PD	01792 884556	670-4072
Ysgol Gyfun Bryn Tawe	Heol Gwyrosydd, Penlan, Swansea, Swansea SA5 7BU		670-4078
Ysgol Gyfun Gwyr	Talbot St, Tregwyr, Abertawe, Swansea SA4 3DB	01792 872403	670-4074

3

265

Torfaen

School name	Address	Tel	Ref
Abersychan Comprehensive School	Old La, Abersychan, Pontypool, Gwent NP4 7DQ	01495 773068	678-4070
Croesyceiliog School	Woodland Rd, Croesyceiliog, Cwmbran, Torfaen NP44 2YB	01633 645900	678-4051
Fairwater High School	Ty Gwyn Way, Fairwater, Cwmbran, Torfaen NP44 4YZ	01633 776650	678-4062
Llantarnam School	Llantarnam Rd, Cwmbran, Torfaen, Torfaen NP44 3XB	01633 866711	678-4050
St Alban's RC High School	The Park, Pontypool, Torfaen, Torfaen NP4 6XG	01495 765800	678-4603
Trevethin Community School	Penygarn Rd, Penygarn, Pontypool, Torfaen NP4 8BG	01495 763551	678-4071
West Monmouth Comprehensive School	Blaendare Rd, Pontypool, Torfaen, Torfaen NP4 5YG	01495 762080	678-4072
Ysgol Gyfun Gwynllyw	Heol Folly, Trefddyn, Pontypool, Torfaen NP4 8JD	01495 750405	678-4075

Vale of Glamorgan

School name	Address	Tel	Ref
Barry Comprehensive School	Port Rd West, Barry CF62 8ZJ	01446 411411	673-4061
Bryn Hafren Comprehensive School	Merthyr Dyfan Rd, Barry CF62 9YQ	01446 403500	673-4062
Cowbridge Comprehensive School	Aberthin Rd, Cowbridge CF71 7EN	01446 772311	673-4065
Llantwit Major School	Ham La East, Llantwit Major CF61 1TQ	01446 793301	673-4060
St Cyres Comprehensive School	St Cyres Rd, Penarth, The Vale of Glamorgan, Vale of Glamorgan CF64 2XP	02920 708708	673-5401
St Richard Gwyn RC High School	Argae La, Barry CF63 1BL	01446 729250	673-4612
Stanwell School	Archer Rd, Penarth, The Vale of Glamorgan, Vale of Glamorgan CF64 2XL	02920 707633	673-5400
Ysgol Bro Morgannwg	Colcot Rd, Barry, Vale of Glamorgan, Vale of Glamorgan CF62 8YU	01446 450280	673-4066

Wrexham

School name	Address	Tel	Ref
Darland High School	Darland La, Rossett, Wrexham LL12 0EN	01244 570588	665-4034
The Maelor School	Penley, Wrexham LL13 0LU	01948 830291	665-5401
St Joseph's RC High School	Sontley Rd, Wrexham LL13 7EN	01978 265209	665-4602
Ysgol Bryn Alyn	Gwersyllt, Wrexham LL11 4HB	01978 720700	665-4033
Ysgol Clywedog	Ruthin Rd, Wrexham, Wrexham LL13 7UB	01978 346800	665-4049
Ysgol Morgan Llwyd	Ffordd Cefn, Wrexham LL13 9NG	01978 315050	665-4032
Ysgol Rhiwabon	Ruabon, Wrexham LL14 6BT	01978 822392	665-4044
Ysgol Rhosnesni	Rhosnesni La, Wrexham, Wrexham LL13 9ET	01978 340840	665-4048
Ysgol Y Grango	Vinegar Hill, Rhos, Wrexham LL14 1EL	01978 840082	665-4029

Northern Ireland

Belfast

School name	Address	Tel	Ref	Type
Aquinas Diocesan Grammar School	518 Ravenhill Rd, Belfast, Antrim BT6 0BY	028 9064 3939	142-0277	Voluntary
Ashfield Boys' High School	Holywood Rd, Belfast, Antrim BT4 2LY	028 9065 6812	121-0015	Controlled
Ashfield Girls' High School	Holywood Rd, Belfast, Antrim BT4 2LY	028 9047 1744	121-0014	Controlled

3

School name	Address	Tel	Ref	Type
Balmoral High School	Blacks Rd, Belfast, Antrim BT10 0NB	028 9030 1578	121-0288	Controlled
Belfast Boys' Model School	Ballysillan Rd, Belfast, Antrim BT14 6RB	028 9039 1156	121-0022	Controlled
Belfast Model School For Girls	Dunkeld Gdns, Belfast, Antrim BT14 6NT	028 9039 1768	121-0021	Controlled
Belfast Royal Academy	5-17 Cliftonville Rd, Belfast, Antrim BT14 6JL	028 9075 0610	142-0028	Voluntary
Bloomfield Collegiate	Astoria Gdns, Belfast, Antrim BT5 6HW	028 9047 1214	162-0018	Voluntary
Bloomfield Collegiate	Astoria Gdns, Belfast, Antrim BT5 6HW	028 9047 1214	142-0018	Voluntary
Campbell College	Belmont Rd, Belfast, Antrim BT4 2ND	028 9076 3076	142-0020	Voluntary
Castle High School	Fortwilliam Pk, Belfast, Antrim BT15 4AR	028 9077 8602	121-0258	Controlled
Christian Brothers School	Glen Rd, Belfast, Antrim BT11 8BW	028 9080 8050	123-0146	Maintained
Colaiste Feirste	51-87 Beechview Pk, Falls Rd, Belfast, Antrim BT12 7PY	028 9032 0707	124-0291	Maintained
Corpus Christi College	Ard Na Va Rd, Belfast, Antrim BT12 6FF	028 9024 5645	123-0262	Maintained
De La Salle College	Edenmore Dr, Belfast, Antrim BT11 8LT	028 9050 8800	123-0182	Maintained
Dominican College	38 Fortwilliam Pk, Belfast, Antrim BT15 4AQ	028 9037 0298	142-0082	Voluntary
Grosvenor Grammar School	Cameronian Dr, Belfast, Antrim BT5 6AX	028 9070 2777	141-0079	Controlled
Hazelwood College	70 Whitewell Rd, Newtownabbey, Antrim BT36 7ES	028 9077 4202	126-0269	GMI
Hunterhouse College	Upper Lisburn Rd, Belfast, Antrim BT10 0LE	028 9061 2293	142-0265	Voluntary
Little Flower Girls' School	71a Somerton Rd, Belfast, Antrim BT15 4DE	028 9037 0665	123-0089	Maintained
Malone Integrated College	45 Finaghy Rd, Belfast, Antrim BT10 0JB	028 9038 1988	126-0294	GMI
Methodist College	1 Malone Rd, Belfast, Antrim BT9 6BY	028 9020 5205	142-0022	Voluntary
Mount Gilbert Community College	237 Ballygomartin Rd, Belfast, Antrim BT13 3NL	028 9071 2600	121-0273	Controlled
Orangefield High School	Cameronian Dr, Belfast, Antrim BT5 6AW	028 9080 5040	121-0266	Controlled
Our Lady Of Mercy Girls' School	Ballysillan Rd, Belfast, Antrim BT14 7QR	028 9039 1769	123-0104	Maintained
Rathmore Grammar School	Kingsway, Finaghy, Belfast, Antrim BT10 0LF	028 9061 0115	142-0095	Voluntary
The Royal Belfast Academical Institution	College Square East, Belfast, Antrim BT1 6DL	028 9024 0461	142-0027	Voluntary
St Dominic's High School	135-137 Falls Rd, Belfast, Antrim BT12 6AE	028 9032 0081	142-0029	Voluntary
St Gabriel's School	685 Crumlin Rd, Belfast, Antrim BT14 7GD	028 9039 1518	123-0032	Maintained
St Gemma's High School	51 -59 Ardilea St, Belfast, Antrim BT14 7DG	028 9074 0375	123-0173	Maintained
St Genevieve's High School	Trench Hse, 87 Stewartstown Road, Belfast, Antrim BT11 9JP	028 90925670	123-0155	Maintained
St Joseph's College	518-572 Ravenhill Rd, Belfast, Antrim BT6 0BY	028 9049 1280	123-0275	Maintained
St Louise's Comprehensive College	468 Falls Rd, Belfast, Antrim BT12 6EN	028 9032 5631	123-0053	Maintained
St Malachy's College	36 Antrim Rd, Belfast, Antrim BT15 2AE	028 9074 8285	142-0030	Voluntary
St Mary's Christian Brothers' Grammar School	147a Glen Rd, Belfast, Antrim BT11 8NR	028 9029 4000	142-0021	Voluntary
St Patrick's College	619-622 Antrim Rd, Bearnagheeha, Belfast, Antrim BT15 4DZ	028 9077 0011	123-0026	Maintained
St Rose's High School	Beechmount Ave, Belfast, Antrim BT12 7NA	028 9024 0937	123-0130	Maintained
Strathearn School	188 Belmont Rd, Belfast, Antrim BT4 2AU	028 9047 1595	142-0089	Voluntary
Strathearn School	188 Belmont Rd, Belfast, Antrim BT4 2AU	028 9047 1595	162-0089	Voluntary
Victoria College	Cranmore Pk, Belfast, Antrim BT9 6JA	028 9066 1506	142-0264	Voluntary
Wellington College	18 Carolan Rd, Belfast, Antrim BT7 3HE	028 9064 2539	141-0270	Controlled

North Eastern

School name	Address	Tel	Ref	Type
Antrim Grammar School	Steeple Rd, Antrim BT41 1AF	028 9446 4091	341-0209	Controlled
Ballee Community High School	Ballee Road West, Ballymena, Antrim BT42 2HS	028 2564 9327	321-0233	Controlled
Ballycastle High School	33 Rathlin Rd, Ballycastle, Antrim BT54 6LD	028 2076 2254	321-0124	Controlled
Ballyclare High School	31 Rashee Rd, Ballyclare, Antrim BT39 9HJ	028 9332 2244	341-0008	Controlled

School name	Address	Tel	Ref	Type
Ballyclare Secondary School	Doagh Rd, Ballyclare, Antrim BT39 9BG	028 9332 2610	321-0134	Controlled
Ballymena Academy	89 Galgorm Rd, Ballymena, Antrim BT42 1AJ	028 2565 2782	342-0011	Voluntary
Ballymoney High School	17 Garryduff Rd, Ballymoney, Antrim BT53 7AN	028 2766 2361	321-0133	Controlled
Belfast High School	740 Shore Rd, Newtownabbey, Antrim BT37 0PX	028 9086 4431	342-0077	Voluntary
Cambridge House Grammar School	Cambridge Ave, Ballymena, Antrim BT42 2EH	028 2564 3151	341-0297	Controlled
Carrickfergus College	110 North Rd, Carrickfergus, Antrim BT38 7QX	028 9336 2347	321-0091	Controlled
Carrickfergus Grammar School	120 North Rd, Carrickfergus, Antrim BT38 7RA	028 9336 3615	341-0098	Controlled
Coleraine Academical Institution	Castlerock Rd, Coleraine, Londonderry BT51 3LA	028 7034 4331	342-0032	Voluntary
Coleraine College	Carthall Rd, Coleraine, Londonderry BT51 3LR	028 7035 7000	321-0300	Controlled
Coleraine High School	Lodge Rd, Coleraine, Londonderry BT52 1LZ	028 7034 3178	341-0033	Controlled
Cross And Passion College	Moyle Rd, Ballycastle, Antrim BT54 6LA	028 2076 2473	323-0227	Maintained
Crumlin High School	10 Glenav Rd, Crumlin, Antrim BT29 4LA	028 9445 2497	321-0149	Controlled
Crumlin Integrated College	10 Glenavy Rd, Crumlin, Antrim BT29 4LA	028 9445 2497	325-0149	CI
Cullybackey High School	44 Pottinger St, Cullybackey, Ballymena, Antrim BT42 1BP	028 2588 0771	321-0172	Controlled
Dalriada School	St James' Rd, Ballymoney, Antrim BT53 6BL	028 2766 3066	362-0012	Voluntary
Dalriada School	St James Rd, Ballymoney, Antrim BT53 6BL	028 2766 3066	342-0012	Voluntary
Dominican College	2 Strand Rd, Portstewart, Londonderry BT55 7PF	028 7083 2715	342-0068	Maintained
Downshire School	Downshire Rd, Carrickfergus, Antrim BT38 7DA	028 9336 4334	321-0232	Controlled
Dunclug College	Doury Rd, Ballymena, Antrim BT43 6SU	028 2565 3665	321-0208	Controlled
Dunluce School	Dunluce Rd, Bushmills, Antrim BT57 8QQ	028 2073 1448	321-0222	Controlled
Edmund Rice College	96-100 Hightown Rd, Newtownabbey, Antrim BT36 7TZ	028 9084 8433	323-0203	Maintained
Garvagh High School	142 Main St, Garvagh, Coleraine, Londonderry BT51 5AE	028 2955 8216	321-0013	Controlled
Glengormley High School	134 Ballyclare Rd, Newtownabbey, Antrim BT36 5HP	028 9083 7223	321-0202	Controlled
Larne Grammar School	Lower Cairncastle Rd, Larne, Antrim BT40 1PQ	028 2827 2791	342-0046	Voluntary
Larne High School	20 Sallagh Pk, Larne, Antrim BT40 1NT	028 2827 2159	321-0038	Controlled
Loreto College	Castlerock Rd, Coleraine, Londonderry BT51 3JZ	028 7034 3611	342-0034	Voluntary
Maghera High School	30 Tobermore Rd, Maghera, Londonderry BT46 5DR	028 7964 2454	321-0090	Controlled
Magherafelt High School	30 Moneymore Rd, Magherafelt, Londonderry BT45 6AF	028 7963 2385	321-0035	Controlled
Masserene Community College	Birch Hill Rd, Antrim BT41 2QH	028 9446 4034	321-0292	Controlled
Monkstown Community School	Bridge Rd, Monkstown, Newtownabbey, Antrim BT37 0EA	028 9086 7431	321-0200	Controlled
Newtownabbey Community High School	Whitehouse, Rathcoole Dr, Newtownabbey, Antrim BT37 9AD	028 9085 1558	321-0279	Controlled
North Coast Integrated College	21 Cloyfin Rd, Coleraine, Londonderry BT52 2NU	028 7032 9026	326-0290	GMI
Our Lady Of Lourdes High School	Castle St, Ballymoney, Antrim BT53 6JX	028 2766 2050	323-0075	Maintained
Parkhall High College	Steeple Rd, Antrim BT41 1AF	028 9446 2963	321-0207	Controlled
Rainey Endowed School	72 Rainey St, Magherafelt, Londonderry BT45 5AH	028 7963 2478	342-0058	Voluntary
St Aloysius High School	60 Coast Rd, Cushendall, Ballymena, Antrim BT44 0RX	028 2177 1314	323-0019	Maintained
St Benedict's College	5 Craigstown Rd, Randalstown, Randalstown, Antrim BT41 2AF	028 9447 2411	323-0308	Maintained
St Colm's High School	2 Magherafelt Rd, Draperstown, Magherafelt, Londonderry BT45 7AF	028 7962 8377	323-0132	Maintained
St Comgall's High School	Drumalis, Bankhead's La, Larne, Antrim BT40 1DU	028 2827 2300	323-0066	Maintained
St Joseph's College	Beresford Ave, Coleraine, Londonderry BT52 1HJ	028 7034 3009	323-0110	Maintained
St Louis Grammar School	Cullybackey Rd, Kintullagh, Ballymena, Antrim BT43 5DW	028 2564 9534	342-0010	Voluntary
St Macnissi's College	Garron Tower, 25 Tower Rd, Carnlough, Ballymena, Antrim BT44 0JS	028 2888 5202	342-0094	Voluntary
St Malachy's High School	4 Birch Hill Rd North, Antrim BT41 2QH	028 9446 3939	323-0226	Maintained
St Mary's College	230 Moyagall Rd, Portglenone, Ballymena, Antrim BT44 8NN	028 2582 1370	323-0142	Maintained
St Mary's Grammar School	3 Castledawson Rd, Magherafelt, Londonderry BT45 6AX	028 7963 2320	342-0080	Voluntary
St Olcans High School	5 Craigstown Rd, Randalstown, Antrim BT41 2AF	028 9447 2411	323-0074	Maintained

3

School name	Address	Tel	Ref	Type
St Patrick's Co-ed Comprehensive College	25 Coleraine Rd, Maghera, Londonderry BT46 5BN	028 7964 2451	323-0234	Maintained
St Patrick's College	Broughshane Rd, Ballymena, Antrim BT43 7DZ	028 2564 5059	323-0084	Maintained
St Paul's College	11 Bann Rd, Kilrea, Coleraine, Londonderry BT51 5RU	028 2954 0536	323-0151	Maintained
St Pius X College	59 Moneymore Rd, Magherafelt, Londonderry BT45 6HQ	028 7963 2186	323-0168	Maintained
Slemish College	Larne Rd, Ballymena, Antrim BT42 3HA	028 2563 0156	326-0289	GMI
Sperrin Integrated College	39 Pound Rd, Magherafelt, Londonderry BT45 6NR	028 7963 4177	326-0303	GMI
Ulidia Integrated College	112 Victora Rd, Carrickfergus, Antrim BT38 7JL	028 9335 8500	326-0299	GMI

South Eastern

School name	Address	Tel	Ref	Type
Assumption Grammar School	22-24 Belfast Rd, Ballynahinch, Down BT24 8EA	028 9756 2250	442-0086	Voluntary
Bangor Academy And 6th Form College	Castle Campus, Castle St, Bangor, Down BT20 4TB	028 9127 0535	421-0296	Controlled
Bangor Grammar School	College Ave, Bangor, Down BT20 5HJ	028 9147 3734	442-0015	Voluntary
De La Salle Secondary School	Struell Rd, Downpatrick, Down BT30 6JR	028 4461 2520	423-0224	Maintained
Donaghadee High School	Northfield Rd, Donaghadee, Down BT21 0BH	028 9188 2361	421-0031	Controlled
Down Academy	12 Old Belfast Rd, Downpatrick, Down BT30 6SG	028 4461 2115	425-0272	CI
Down High School	Mount Cres Mount Cres, Downpatrick, Down BT30 6EU	028 4461 2103	441-0085	Controlled
Down High School	Mount Cres, Downpatrick, Down BT30 6EU	028 4461 2103	461-0085	Controlled
Dundonald High School	764 Upper Newtownards Rd, Dundonald, Belfast, Antrim BT16 1TH	028 9048 4271	421-0262	Controlled
Dunmurry High School	River Rd, Dunmurry, Belfast, Antrim BT17 9DS	028 9062 2828	421-0194	Controlled
Fort Hill College	Belfast Rd, Lisburn, Antrim BT27 4TL	028 9266 3670	425-0072	CI
Friends' School	6 Magheralave Rd, Lisburn, Antrim BT28 3BH	028 9266 2156	442-0050	Voluntary
Glastry College	14 Victoria Rd, Newtownards, Down BT22 1DQ	028 4277 1226	421-0046	Controlled
Glenlola Collegiate	Castle Park Rd, Bangor, Down BT20 4TH	028 9147 5356	461-0097	Controlled
Glenlola Collegiate	Castle Park Rd, Castle Pk, Bangor, Down BT20 4TH	028 9147 5340	441-0097	Controlled
The High School Ballynahinch	103 Belfast Rd, Ballynahinch, Down BT24 8EH	028 9756 2424	421-0029	Controlled
Knockbreda High School	43 Upper Knockbreda Rd, Belfast, Antrim BT6 0NE	028 9064 9302	421-0086	Controlled
Lagan College	44 Manse Rd, Castlereagh, Belfast, Antrim BT8 6SA	028 9040 1810	426-0255	GMI
Laurelhill Community College	22 Laurelhill Rd, Lisburn, Antrim BT28 2UH	028 9260 7351	421-0201	Controlled
Lisnagarvey High School	Warren Gdns, Lisburn, Antrim BT28 1HN	028 9266 2636	421-0051	Controlled
Lisnasharragh High School	Stirling Ave, Belfast, Antrim BT6 9LP	028 9040 1041	421-0030	Controlled
Movilla High School	Donaghadee Rd, Newtownards, Down BT23 7HA	028 9181 2283	421-0012	Controlled
Nendrum College	Darragh Rd, Comber, Newtownards, Down BT23 5BX	028 9187 2361	421-0045	Controlled
Newtownbreda High School	Newtownbreda Rd, Belfast, Antrim BT8 6PY	028 9064 5374	421-0183	Controlled
Our Lady And St Patrick's College	Kingsway Gdns, Knock, Belfast, Antrim BT5 7DQ	028 9040 1184	442-0259	Voluntary
Priory College	My Lady's Mile, Holywood, Down BT18 9ER	028 9042 3481	425-0024	CI
Regent House School	Circular Rd, Newtownards, Down BT23 4QA	028 9181 3234	461-0063	Controlled
Regent House School	Circular Rd, Newtownards, Down BT23 4QA	028 9181 3234	441-0063	Controlled
St Colman's High School	52 Crossgar Rd, Ballynahinch, Down BT24 8XR	028 9756 2518	423-0161	Maintained
St Colmcille's High School	1 Killyleagh Rd, Crossgar, Down BT30 9EY	028 4483 0311	423-0102	Maintained
St Colm's High School	Summerhill Dr, Twinbrook, Dunmurry, Belfast, Antrim BT17 0BT	028 9030 1118	423-0223	Maintained
St Columbanus' College	Ballymaconnell Rd, Bangor, Down BT20 5PU	028 9127 0927	423-0107	Maintained
St Columba's College	2 Ballyphilip Rd, Portaferry, Newtownards, Down BT22 1RB	028 4272 8323	423-0067	Maintained
St Malachy's High School	3 Dublin Rd, Castlewellan, Down BT31 9AG	028 4377 8255	423-0211	Maintained
St Mary's High School	23 Ardglass Rd, Downpatrick, Down BT30 6JQ	028 4461 2515	423-0023	Maintained

School name	Address	Tel	Ref	Type
St Patrick's Grammar School	Saul St, Downpatrick, Down BT30 6NJ	028 4461 9722	442-0088	Voluntary
St Patrick's High School	Ballinderry Rd, Lisburn, Antrim BT28 1TD	028 9266 4877	423-0165	Maintained
Saintfield High School	21 Comber Rd, Saintfield, Down BT24 7BB	028 9751 0356	421-0063	Controlled
Shimna Integrated College	The Lawnfield, 5a King St, Newcastle, Down BT33 0HD	028 4372 6107	426-0281	GMI
Strangford Integrated College	Abbey Rd, Carrowdore, Down BT22 2GB	028 9186 1199	426-0295	GMI
Sullivan Upper School	Belfast Rd, Holywood, Down BT18 9EP	028 9042 8780	442-0044	Voluntary
Sullivan Upper School	Belfast Rd, Holywood, Down BT18 9EP	028 9042 8780	462-0044	Voluntary
Wallace High School	12a Clonevin Pk, Lisburn, Antrim BT28 3AD	028 9267 2311	462-0051	Voluntary
Wallace High School	Clonevin Pk, Lisburn, Antrim BT28 3AD	028 9267 2311	442-0051	Voluntary

Southern

School name	Address	Tel	Ref	Type
Abbey Christian Brothers Grammar School	Courtney Hill, Newry, Down BT34 2ED	028 3026 3142	542-0059	Voluntary
Armagh Integrated College	63 Keady Rd, Armagh BT60 3AS	028 3752 2944	526-0307	GMI
Aughnacloy High School	23 Carnteel Rd, Aughnacloy, Tyrone BT69 6DX	028 8555 7289	521-0153	Controlled
Banbridge Academy	Lurgan Rd, Banbridge, Down BT32 4AQ	028 4062 3220	541-0013	Controlled
Banbridge High School	Primrose Gdns, Banbridge, Down BT32 3EP	028 4062 2471	521-0047	Controlled
Brownlow Int College	Tullygally Rd, Craigavon, Armagh BT65 5BS	028 3834 2121	525-0216	CI
City Armagh High School	Alexander Rd, Armagh BT61 7JH	028 3752 2278	521-0121	Controlled
Clounagh Junior High School	Brownstown Rd, Portadown, Armagh BT62 3QA	028 3833 2717	521-0043	Controlled
Cookstown High School	Coolnafrankie Demesne, Molesworth Street, Cookstown, Tyrone BT80 8PQ	028 8676 3620	521-0230	Controlled
Craigavon Senior High School	26-34 Lurgan Rd, Portadown, Armagh BT63 5HJ	028 3834 9222	521-0282	Controlled
Dromore High School	31 Banbridge Rd, Dromore, Down BT25 1ND	028 9269 2278	521-0064	Controlled
Drumcree College	4 Moy Rd, Portadown, Armagh BT62 1QL	028 3833 4725	523-0256	Maintained
Drumglass High School	Carland Rd, Dungannon, Tyrone BT71 4AA	028 8772 2421	521-0231	Controlled
Fivemiletown College	Corcreevy Demesne, Fivemiletown, Tyrone BT75 0SB	028 8952 1279	521-0097	Controlled
Holy Trinity College	Chapel St, Cookstown, Tyrone BT80 8OB	028 8676 2420	523-0278	Maintained
Integrated College Dungannon	21 Gortmerron Link Rd, Dungannon, Tyrone BT71 6LS	028 8772 4401	526-0286	GMI
Kilkeel High School	Knockchree Ave, Kilkeel, Newry, Down BT34 4BP	028 4176 2365	521-0016	Controlled
Killicomaine Junior High School	Upper Church La, Portadown, Armagh BT63 5JE	028 3833 2021	521-0054	Controlled
Lismore Comprehensive School	Drumgask, Craigavon, Armagh BT65 5DU	028 3831 4950	523-0213	Maintained
Lurgan College	Preparatory Department, College Wlk, Lurgan, Craigavon, Armagh BT66 6JW	028 3832 2083	561-0057	Controlled
Lurgan College	College Wlk, Lurgan, Craigavon, Armagh BT66 6JW	028 3832 2083	541-0057	Controlled
Lurgan Junior High	Toberhewny Lane Lower, Lurgan, Armagh BT66 8SU	028 3832 3243	521-0271	Controlled
Markethill High School	61 Mowhan Rd, Markethill, Armagh BT60 1RQ	028 3755 1270	521-0083	Controlled
New-bridge Integrated College	25 Donard View Rd, Loughbrickland, Banbridge, Down BT32 3LN	028 4062 5010	526-0285	GMI
Newry High School	23 Ashgrove Rd, Newry, Down BT34 1QN	028 3026 2383	521-0186	Controlled
Newtownhamilton High School	9 Armagh Rd, Newtownhamilton, Newry, Down BT35 0DG	028 3087 8246	521-0025	Controlled
Our Lady's Grammar School	Chequer Hill, Newry, Down BT35 6DY	028 3026 3552	542-0060	Voluntary
Portadown College	Killycomaine Rd, Portadown, Armagh BT63 5BV		561-0067	Controlled
Portadown College	4 Killycomaine Rd, Portadown, Craigavon, Armagh BT63 5BU	028 3833 2439	541-0067	Controlled
Rathfriland High School	76 Newry St, Rathfriland, Newry, Down BT34 5PZ	028 4063 0374	521-0127	Controlled
The Royal School Armagh	College Hill, Armagh BT61 9DH	028 3752 2807	542-0263	Voluntary
The Royal School Dungannon	1 Ranfurley Rd, Dungannon, Tyrone BT71 6AP	028 8772 2710	542-0260	Voluntary
Sacred Heart Grammar School	10 Ashgrove Ave, Newry, Down BT34 1PR	028 3026 4632	542-0076	Voluntary

3

School name	Address	Tel	Ref	Type
St Brigid's High School	Windmill Hill, Armagh BT60 4BR	028 3752 3849	523-0160	Maintained
St Catherine's College	2 Convent Rd, Armagh BT60 4BG	028 3752 2023	523-0218	Maintained
St Ciaran's High School	15 Tullybryan Rd, Ballygawley, Dungannon, Tyrone BT70 2LY	028 8556 8640	523-0152	Maintained
St Colman's College	46 Armagh Rd, Violet Hill, Newry, Down BT35 6PP	028 3026 2451	542-0062	Voluntary
St Columban's College	127 Newcastle Rd, Kilkeel, Newry, Down BT34 4NL	028 4176 2314	523-0059	Maintained
St Joseph's Boys' High School	20 Armagh Rd, Newry, Down BT35 6DH	028 3026 2595	523-0056	Maintained
St Joseph's College	29 School La, Coalisland, Dungannon, Tyrone BT71 4NW	028 8774 0510	523-0192	Maintained
St Joseph's College	77 Dundalk Rd, Crossmaglen, Newry, Down BT35 9HL	028 3086 1240	523-0167	Maintained
St Joseph's Grammar School	58 Castlecaulfield Rd, Donaghmore, Dungannon, Tyrone BT70 3HE	028 8776 1227	542-0073	Voluntary
St Louis Grammar School	151 Newry Rd, Kilkeel, Down BT34 4EU	028 4176 2747	542-0045	Voluntary
St Mark's High School	Upper Dromore Rd, Warrenpoint, Newry, Down BT34 3PN	028 4175 3366	523-0135	Maintained
St Mary's High School	Upper Chapel St, Newry, Down BT34 2DT	028 3026 2851	523-0108	Maintained
St Mary's High School	Waring St, Lurgan, Craigavon, Armagh BT66 6DQ	028 3832 2446	523-0070	Maintained
St Michael's Grammar	12 Cornakinegar Rd, Lurgan, Craigavon, Armagh BT67 9JW	028 3832 3192	542-0056	Voluntary
St Patrick's Academy	37 Killymeal Rd, Dungannon, Tyrone BT71 6DS	028 8772 7400	542-0304	Voluntary
St Patrick's Boys Academy	37 Killymeal Rd, Dungannon, Tyrone BT71 6DS	028 8772 2668	542-0038	Voluntary
St Patrick's College	Donaghmore Rd, Dungannon, Tyrone BT70 1HA	028 8772 2205	523-0293	Maintained
St Patrick's Girls Academy	35 Killymeal Rd, Dungannon, Tyrone BT71 6DF	028 8772 2474	542-0039	Voluntary
St Patrick's Grammar School	Cathedral Rd, Armagh BT61 7QZ	028 3752 2018	542-0268	Voluntary
St Patrick's High School	Scarva Rd, Banbridge, Down BT32 3AS	028 4066 2309	523-0076	Maintained
St Patrick's High School	Middletown Rd, Keady, Keady, Armagh BT60 3TH	028 3753 1393	523-0187	Maintained
St Paul's High School	108 Camlough Rd, Bessbrook, Newry, Down BT35 7EE	028 3083 0309	523-0157	Maintained
St Paul's Junior High School	Francis St, Lurgan, Craigavon, Armagh BT66 6DL	028 3832 2694	523-0088	Maintained
Tandragee Junior High School	Armagh Rd, Tandragee, Armagh BT62 2AY	028 3884 0278	521-0143	Controlled

Western

School name	Address	Tel	Ref	Type
Castlederg High School	16 Castlegore Rd, Castlederg, Tyrone BT81 7RU	028 8167 1272	221-0065	Controlled
Christian Brothers' Grammar School	Kevlin Rd, Omagh, Tyrone BT78 1LD	028 8224 3567	242-0064	Voluntary
Clondermot High School	Irish St, Londonderry BT47 2DD	028 7134 3487	221-0017	Controlled
Convent Grammar School	Curlyhill Rd, Strabane, Tyrone BT82 8LP	028 7188 2339	242-0072	Voluntary
Dean Brian Maguirc College	26 Termon Rd, Carrickmore, Sixmilecross, Omagh, Tyrone BT79 9JR	028 8076 1272	223-0138	Maintained
Devenish College	1 Algeo Dr, Derrychara, Enniskillen, Fermanagh BT74 6JL	028 6632 2923	221-0305	Controlled
Drumragh College	1 Donaghanie Rd, Omagh, Tyrone BT78 1PN	028 8225 2440	226-0283	GMI
Duke Of Westminster High School	Ederney Rd, Kesh, Enniskillen, Fermanagh BT93 1TA	028 6863 1265	221-0204	Controlled
Enniskillen Collegiate	1 Cooper Cres, Enniskillen, Fermanagh BT74 6DQ	028 6632 2165	241-0040	Controlled
Enniskillen High School	1 Algeo Dr, Derrychara, Enniskillen, Fermanagh BT74 6JL	028 6632 2923	221-0050	Controlled
Erne Integrated College	Drumcoo, Enniskillen, Fermanagh BT74 4FY	028 6632 5996	226-0280	GMI
Faughan Valley High School	35 Drumahoe Rd, Cross, Londonderry BT47 3SD	028 7130 1284	221-0078	Controlled
Foyle & Londonderry College	122 Northland Rd, Londonderry BT48 0AW	028 7126 9321	242-0229	Voluntary
Foyle And Londonderry College	Preparatory Department, Springtown, Londonderry BT48 0LY	028 7126 9321	262-0229	Voluntary
Holy Cross College	Springhill, Strabane, Tyrone BT82 8NQ	028 7188 0315	223-0301	Maintained
Immaculate Conception College	Trench Rd, Waterside, Londonderry BT47 2DS	028 7134 5364	223-0254	Maintained
Limavady Grammar School	3 Ballyquin Rd, Limavady, Londonderry BT49 9ET	028 7776 0950	241-0048	Controlled
Limavady High School	Irish Green St, Limavady, Londonderry BT49 9AN	028 7776 2526	221-0302	Controlled

School name	Address	Tel	Ref	Type
Lisnaskea High School	Castlebalfour, Lisnaskea, Enniskillen, Fermanagh BT92 0LT	028 6772 1283	221-0080	Controlled
Lisneal College	70 Crescent Link, Londonderry BT47 5SQ	028 7134 8888	221-0306	Controlled
Loreto Grammar School	James St, Omagh, Tyrone BT78 1DL	028 8224 3633	242-0065	Voluntary
Lumen Christi College	Bishop St, Londonderry BT48 6UL	028 7136 2595	242-0287	Voluntary
Mount Lourdes Grammar School	Belmore St, Enniskillen, Fermanagh BT74 6AB	028 6632 2265	242-0041	Voluntary
Oakgrove Integrated College	Stradreagh, Gransha Pk, Clooney Rd, Londonderry BT47 6TG	028 7186 0443	226-0276	GMI
Omagh Academy	21-23 Dublin Rd, Omagh, Tyrone BT78 1HF	028 8224 2688	241-0066	Controlled
Omagh High School	14 Crevenagh Rd, Omagh, Tyrone BT79 0EQ	028 8224 2656	221-0125	Controlled
Our Lady Of Mercy High School	Springhill, Strabane, Tyrone BT82 8NQ	028 7138 2331	223-0087	Maintained
Portora Royal School	Derrygonnelly Rd, Enniskillen, Fermanagh BT74 7HA	028 6632 2658	242-0042	Voluntary
Sacred Heart College	Kevlin Rd, Omagh, Tyrone BT78 1LG	028 8224 2717	223-0298	Maintained
St Aidan's High School	Derrylin, Enniskillen, Fermanagh BT92 9LA	028 6774 8337	223-0166	Maintained
St Brigid's College	Glengalliagh Rd, Shantallow, Londonderry BT48 8DU	028 7135 1002	223-0225	Maintained
St Cecilia's College	Bligh's La, Londonderry BT48 9PJ	028 7128 1800	223-0188	Maintained
St Colman's High School	35 Melmount Rd, Strabane, Tyrone BT82 9EF		223-0071	Maintained
St Columb's College	Buncrana Rd, Londonderry BT48 8NH	028 7128 5000	242-0054	Voluntary
St Comhghall's College	Derryree, Lisnaskea, Enniskillen, Fermanagh BT92 0LA	028 6772 1417	223-0190	Maintained
St Eugene's College	Roslea, Enniskillen, Fermanagh BT92 7SE	028 6775 1258	223-0180	Maintained
St Eugene's High School	1 Cavan Rd, Castlederg, Tyrone BT81 7TP	028 8167 1543	223-0111	Maintained
St Fanchea's College	Mill St, Enniskillen, Fermanagh BT74 6AN	028 6632 2919	223-0099	Maintained
St John's High School	37 Omagh Rd, Dromore, Omagh, Tyrone BT78 3AL	028 8289 8284	223-0148	Maintained
St Joseph's Boys' School	Westway, Londonderry BT48 9NX	028 7126 2923	223-0131	Maintained
St Joseph's College	Chanterhill Rd, Enniskillen, Fermanagh BT74 6DE	028 6632 2918	223-0100	Maintained
St Joseph's High School	397 Lisnaragh Rd, Plumbridge, Omagh, Tyrone BT79 8AH	028 8164 8349	223-0141	Maintained
St Mary's College	Lisnarick Rd, Irvinestown, Enniskillen, Fermanagh BT94 1EL	028 6862 1318	223-0109	Maintained
St Mary's College	Fanad Dr, Londonderry BT48 9QE	028 7136 2154	223-0081	Maintained
St Mary's High School	Brollagh, Belleek, Enniskillen, Fermanagh BT93 3AH	028 6865 8257	223-0085	Maintained
St Mary's Limavady	Irish Green St, Limavady, Londonderry BT49 9AN	028 7776 2360	223-0077	Maintained
St Michael's College	Chanterhill Rd, Enniskillen, Fermanagh BT74 6DG	028 6632 2935	242-0043	Voluntary
St Patricks & St Brigids High School	55 Main St, Claudy, Londonderry BT47 4HR	028 7133 8317	223-0122	Maintained
St Patrick's College	9 Curragh Rd, Dungiven, Londonderry BT47 4SE	028 7774 1324	223-0144	Maintained
St Peter's High School	Southway, Foyle Hill, Londonderry BT48 9SE	028 7136 1981	223-0181	Maintained
Strabane Grammar School	Milltown Hse, 4 Liskey Rd, Strabane, Tyrone BT82 8NW	028 7138 2319	241-0096	Controlled
Strabane High School	61 Derry Rd, Strabane, Tyrone BT82 8LD	028 7188 2578	221-0164	Controlled
Templemore Secondary School	Northland Rd, Londonderry BT48 0AP	028 7136 3407	221-0049	Controlled
Thornhill College	Culmore Rd, Londonderry BT48 8JF	028 7135 5800	242-0052	Voluntary

Channel Islands and Isle of Man

Guernsey

School name	Address	Tel	Headteacher	Ref
Beechwood School	The Queen's Rd, St Peter Port, Guernsey, Channel Islands GY1 1PU	01481 722123	Mrs S. Battey	706-6004
Convent of Mercy	Cordier Hill, St Peter Port, Guernsey, Channel Islands GY1 1JH	01481 720729	Sister Carmel	706-6002

3

School name	Address	Tel	Headteacher	Ref
Elizabeth College	The Grange, St Peter Port, Guernsey, Channel Islands GY1 2PY	01481 726544	Mr D.E. Toze	706-6006
The Grammar School	Les Varendes, St Andrew's, Guernsey, Channel Islands GY6 8TD		Mr D. Balls	706-4001
Herm School	Herm Island, Guernsey, Channel Islands GY1 3HR	01481 710962	Mrs J. Sandrey	706-2017
La Mare de Carteret Secondary School	Rue de Galaad, Castel, Guernsey, Channel Islands GY5 7FL	01481 256588	Mr Philip White	706-4003
Le Rondin School	Rue des Landes, Forest, Guernsey, Channel Islands GY8 0DP	01481 268300		706-7004
Les Beaucamps Secondary School	Rue des Delisles, Castel, Guernsey, Channel Islands GY5 7DS	01481 256477	Mr Peter Le Cheminant	706-4002
Ormer House Preparatory School	La Vallee, Alderney, Guernsey, Channel Islands GY9 3XA	01481 823287	Mr A.J. Roberts	706-6007
St Anne's School	Braye Rd, St Annes, Guernsey, Channel Islands GY9 3XP	01481 822173	Mrs Yvonne Locker	706-2015
St Peter Port School	Les Ozouets Rd, St Peter Port, Guernsey, Channel Islands GY1 2UB	01481 720236	Mr Ken Wheeler	706-4004
St Sampson's Secondary School	Rue des Monts, St Sampson's, Guernsey, Channel Islands GY2 4AS	01481 244411	Miss Hazel Tetlaw	706-4005

Isle of Man

School name	Address	Tel	Headteacher	Ref
Anagh Coar School	Darragh Way, Anagh Coar, Isle of Man IM2 2BX	01624 622148	Mr Terry Bates	705-2061
Andreas School	Kirk Andreas, Ramsey, Isle of Man IM7 4EZ	01624 880375	Mr M.J. Barrow	705-2000
Ballacottier School	Clybane Rd, Farmhill, Isle of Man IM2 2ST	01624 612558	Mr P.J. Rhodes	705-2203
Ballakermeen High School	St Catherines Dr, Douglas, Isle of Man IM14 4BE	01624 648700	Mrs Adrienne Burnett	705-4001
The Buchan School	Westhill, Arbory Road, Isle of Man IM9 1RD	01624 822526	G R Shaw-Twilley	705-6000
Castle Rushen High School	Arbory Rd, Castletown, Isle of Man IM9 1RE	01624 826500	Mrs M. Tomaszewska	705-4002
Cronk-y-Berry School	Hailwood Ave, Douglas, Isle of Man IM2 7PA	01624 615995	Mr D. Gorham	705-2204
Michael School	Main Rd, Kirk Michael, Isle of Man IM6 1AJ	01624 878246	Mrs M.J. Cubbon	705-2027
Queen Elizabeth II High School	Douglas Rd, Peel, Isle of Man IM5 1RD	01624 841000	Ms S. Moore	705-4003
Ramsey Grammar School	Lezayre Rd, Ramsey, Isle of Man IM8 2RG	01624 811100	Mr D.J. Trace	705-4004
St Mary's RC School	St Mary's Rd, Douglas, Isle of Man IM2 5RB	01624 673807	Mr Brian Blaire	705-3100
St Ninian's High School	St Ninian's, Douglas, Isle of Man IM2 5RA	01624 648800	Mr J.G. Quayle	705-4005
St Thomas's CE School	Finch Rd, Douglas, Isle of Man IM1 2PL	01624 674230	Mr Jonathan Ayres	705-3000
Scoill Phurt le Moirrey	Plantation Rd, Port St Mary, Isle of Man IM9 5RB	01624 835531	Mrs C.A. Best	705-2063
Scoill Vallajeelt	Meadow Cres, Douglas, Isle of Man IM2 1NN	01624 670844	Mr Ian Walmsley	705-2062

Jersey

School name	Address	Tel	Headteacher	Ref
Beaulieu Convent School	Wellington Rd, St Helier, Jersey, Channel Islands JE2 4RJ	01534 731280	Mrs R. Hill	707-6002
D'Auvergne School	La Pouquelaye, St Helier, Jersey, Channel Islands JE2 3GF			707-2026
De La Salle College	Wellington Rd, St Saviour, Jersey, Channel Islands JE2 7TH	01534 726548	Mr J. Sankey	707-4008
First Tower School	La Route de St Aubin, St Helier, Jersey, Channel Islands JE2 3SD	01534 721066	Mr J. Davenport	707-2002
Grainville School	St Saviours Hill, St Saviour, Jersey, Channel Islands JE2 7XB	01534 822900	Mr Keith Shannon	707-4002
Grands Vaux School	Les Grands Vaux, St Saviour, Jersey, Channel Islands JE2 7NZ	01534 735808	Mr R. Howells	707-2003
Grouville School	La Rue de la Haye du Puits, Grouville, Jersey, Channel Islands JE3 9DL	01534 851089	Ms Gill Shaw	707-2004
Haute Vallee School	La Grande Route de Mont a l'Abbe, St Helier, Jersey, Channel Islands JE2 3HA	01534 736524	Mr Robin Fairhurst	707-4001
Hautlieu School	Wellington Rd, St Saviour, Jersey, Channel Islands JE2 7TH	01534 736242	Mrs Lesley Greenwood	707-4005
Helvetia House School	Elizabeth Pl, St Helier, Jersey, Channel Islands JE2 3PN	01534 724928		707-6170
Janvrin School	Mont Cantel, La Pouquelaye, Jersey, Channel Islands JE2 3ZN	01534 731306	Mr J. du Feu	707-2005
Jersey College for Girls	Le Mont Millais, St Saviour, Jersey, Channel Islands JE2 7YB	01534 516200	Ms C. Marten	707-4006

School name	Address	Tel	Headteacher	Ref
Jersey College for Girls Preparatory School	Claremont Rd, St Saviour, Jersey, Channel Islands JE2 7RT	01534 615900	Miss D.R. Hardiman	707-2006
La Moye School	La Route Orange, St Brelade, Jersey, Channel Islands JE3 8GQ	01534 741390	Mr J. Speight	707-2007
Le Rocquier School	La Grande Route de St Clement, St Clement, Jersey, Channel Islands JE2 6QP	01534 855876	Mr Richard Rolfe	707-4004
Les Chenes Residential School	La Grande Route de St Martin, St Saviour, Jersey, Channel Islands JE2 7GS	01534 872940	Mr K. Mansell	707-7001
Les Landes School	La Rue des Cosnets, St Ouen, Jersey, Channel Islands JE3 2BJ	01534 481013	Ms Mary Bannier	707-2009
Les Quennevais School	Les Quennevais Pk, St Brelade, Jersey, Channel Islands JE3 8JW	01534 743171	Mr J. Thorp	707-4003
Mont Nicolle School	La Route des Genets, St Brelade, Jersey, Channel Islands JE3 8DB	01534 744992	Mrs C. Audrain	707-2011
Plat Douet School	Plat Douet Rd, St Saviour, Jersey, Channel Islands JE2 7PN	01534 725759	Mrs S. Conoops	707-2012
Rouge Bouillon School	Brighton Rd, St Helier, Jersey, Channel Islands JE2 3YN	01534 705705	Mrs W. Hurford	707-2013
St Christopher's School	33 Stopford Rd, St Helier, Jersey, Channel Islands JE2 4LB	01534 724758	Mrs A.J. le Brocq	707-6171
St Clement's School	La Rue de la Chapelle, St Clement, Jersey, Channel Islands JE2 6LN	01534 854007	Mrs Susan J. Birtwhistle	707-2014
St George's Prep School	La Hague Manor, Rue de la Hague, Jersey, Channel Islands JE3 7DB	01534 481593	Mr C. Blackwell	707-6003
St James School	Chapel La., St Helier, Jersey, Channel Islands JE2 4QN	01534 733801	Mr C. Rogers	707-7003
St John's School	La Rue de la Mare Ballam, St John, Jersey, Channel Islands JE3 4EJ	01534 861692	Mr Colin C. Masterman	707-2015
St Lawrence's School	La Grande Route de St. Laurent, St Lawrence, Jersey, Channel Islands JE3 1NG	01534 863172	Mr R. Brown	707-2016
St Luke's School	Elizabeth St, St Saviour, Jersey, Channel Islands JE2 7PG	01534 730657	Mrs Ann Curzons	707-2017
St Martin's School	La Rue de la Croix au Maitre, St Martin, Jersey, Channel Islands JE3 6HW	01534 851812	Mrs Diane Hooper	707-2019
St Mary's School	La Verte Rue, St Mary, Jersey, Channel Islands JE3 3DA	01534 481690	Mrs Linda McKenzie	707-2020
St Michael's School	La Rue de la Houguette, St Saviour, Jersey, Channel Islands JE2 7UG	01534 856904	Mr R. de Figueiredo	707-6001
St Peter's School	La Rue du Presbytere, St Peter, Jersey, Channel Islands JE3 7ZH	01534 481536	Mrs C. Downey	707-2021
St Saviour's School	Bagatelle Rd, St Saviour, Jersey, Channel Islands JE2 7TY	01534 725549	Mr M. Jehan	707-2022
Samares School	School Rd, St Clement, Jersey, Channel Islands JE2 6TG	01534 735415	Mrs Isobel Wood	707-2010
Springfield School	St Marks Rd, St Saviour, Jersey, Channel Islands JE2 7LD	01534 759657	Mr Sam Cooper	707-2025
Trinity School	La Route de la Trinite, Trinity, Jersey, Channel Islands JE3 5JP	01534 864085	Mrs C. Stone	707-2023
Victoria College Preparatory School	Pleasant St, St Helier, Jersey, Channel Islands JE2 4RR	01534 723468	Mr P. Stevenson	707-2024

Independent Schools

4

Key

B	Boys
CI	Controlled Integrated
CY	Community
D	Day places
FD	Foundation
G	Girls
GMI	Grant-Maintained Integrated
Ind	Independent/Non-Maintained

MDP	Middle Deemed Primary
MDS	Middle Deemed Secondary
N	Nursery provision
R	Residential provision
Ref	LA Number-DfES Number or regional equivalent
Sp	Special School
VA	Voluntary Aided
VC	Voluntary Controlled

Religious character

Ba	Baptist
Bu	Buddhist
CE	Church of England
CIW	Church in Wales
Cg	Congregational Church
Ch	Christian
CS	Church of Scotland
Es	Episcopalian
FC	Free Church
FP	Free Presbyterian
Gk	Greek Orthodox
Hi	Hindu
ID	Inter/Non-Denominational
IP	Independent Pentecostal
Je	Jewish
Me	Methodist
MF	Multi-Faith
Mu	Muslim
Qk	Quaker
RC	Roman Catholic
SDA	Seventh Day Adventist
UR	United Reformed Church

Special needs

ADHD	Attention Deficit Hyperactivity Disorder
AS	Asperger's Syndrome
ASD	Autism Spectrum Disorder
CD	Communication Difficulties
DMP	Delicate Medical Problems
Ep	Epilepsy
HI	Hearing Impairment
HS	Hospital School
MLD	Moderate Learning Difficulties
MSI	Multi-Sensory Impairment
PD	Physical Difficulties
PMLD	Profound and Multiple Learning Difficulties
SCU	Special Care Unit
SEBD	Social, Emotional and Behavioural Difficulties
SEN	Special Educational Needs
SLD	Severe Learning Difficulties
SpLD	Specific Learning Difficulties
VI	Visual Impairment

Independent Schools

East of England

Bedfordshire

School name	Address	Tel	Fax	Headteacher	Ref	Ages	Pupils	Other
Bedford High School	Bromham Rd, Bedford, Bedfordshire MK40 2BS	01234 360221	01234 353552	Mrs Julie Pendry	820-6009	7-16	835	G R
Bedford Modern School	Manton La., Bedford, Bedfordshire MK41 7NT	01234 332500	01234 332550	Mr S. Smith	820-6011	7-19	1202	R
Bedford School	De Parys Ave, Bedford, Bedfordshire MK40 2TU	01234 362200	01234 362283	Dr I.P. Evans	820-6002	7-16	1102	B R CE
Dame Alice Harpur School	Cardington Rd, Bedford, Bedfordshire MK42 0BX	01234 340871	01234 344125	Mrs Jill Berry	820-6012	7-16	892	G
Rushmoor School	58-60 Shakespeare Rd, Bedford, Bedfordshire MK40 2DL	01234 352031	01234 348395	Mr Keith Knight	820-6004	2-17	304	B
St Andrew's School	78 Kimbolton Rd, Bedford, Bedfordshire MK40 2PA	01234 267272	01234 355105	Mrs J.E. Marsland	820-6006	3-16	303	G
Sceptre School	Ridgeway Ave, Dunstable, Bedfordshire LU5 4QL	01582 665676		Mrs Monica Bartlett	820-6019	11-17	106	Ch

Cambridgeshire

School name	Address	Tel	Fax	Headteacher	Ref	Ages	Pupils	Other
Beechwood School	Shelford Bottom, Shelford Bottom CB22 3BF	01223 400190	01223 400191	Mr M. Drake	873-6034	7-18	33	Ch
Bellerbys College Cambridge	Queens Campus, Bateman St, Cambridge, Cambridgeshire CB2 1LZ	01223 363159	01223 307425	Mr E.J. Squires	873-6023	14-16	308	R
Cambridge Arts and Sciences Sixth Form and Tutorial College	13-14 Round Church St, Cambridge, Cambridgeshire CB5 8AD	01223 314431	01223 467773	Dr G. Hawkins	873-6022	14-16	291	R
Cambridge Centre for Sixth Form Studies	1 Salisbury Villas, Station Rd, Cambridge, Cambridgeshire CB1 2JF	01223 716890	01223 517530	Mr N. Roskilly	873-6021	15-16	185	R
Cambridge international Preparatory School	17-19 Brookside, Cambridge, Cambridgeshire CB2 1JE	01223 305875		Mr H. Sturdy	873-6042	4-16	46	
Kimbolton School	Kimbolton, Huntingdon, Cambridgeshire PE28 0EA	01480 860505	01480 860386	Mr J. Belbin	873-6012	4-18	863	R
King's College School	West Rd, Cambridge, Cambridgeshire CB3 9DN	01223 365814	01223 461388	Mr N. Robinson	873-6000	4-14	338	R
The King's School Ely	Barton Rd, Ely, Cambridgeshire CB7 4DB	01353 660701	01353 667485	Mrs S. Freestone	873-6005	5-16	913	R
The Leys School	Trumpington Rd, Cambridge, Cambridgeshire CB2 2AD	01223 508900	01223 505333	Mr M. Slater	873-6003	11-16	537	R
Mander Portman Woodward	3-4 Brookside, Cambridge, Cambridgeshire CB2 1JE	01223 350158	01223 366429	Dr N. Marriott	873-6017	14-19	110	R
The Perse School	Hills Rd, Cambridge, Cambridgeshire CB2 2QF	01223 403800	01223 568293	Mr N. Richardson	873-6010	3-16	974	B
Perse School for Girls	Union Rd, Cambridge, Cambridgeshire CB2 1HF	01223 454700	01223 467420	Miss P.M. Kelleher	873-6011	7-19	666	G ND
The Red Balloon Learner Centre at Herbert House	57 Warkworth Terr, Parkside, Cambridge, Cambridgeshire CB1 1EE	01223 357714		Ms J. Lechner	873-6024	11-16	14	
St Andrew's	2a Free School La., Cambridge, Cambridgeshire CB2 3QA	01223 360040	01223 467150	Mrs C. Williams	873-6019	15-16	133	R
St Mary's School	Bateman St, Cambridge, Cambridgeshire CB2 1LY	01223 353253	01223 357451	Mrs M. Triffitt	873-6001	11-18	468	G R RC
Sancton Wood School	2 St Paul's Rd, Cambridge, Cambridgeshire CB1 2EZ	01223 359488	01223 471703	Dr Jack McDonald	873-6009	1-16	292	CE
Wisbech Grammar School	47 North Brink, Wisbech, Cambridgeshire PE13 1JX	01945 583631	01945 476746	Mr R. Repper	873-6013	4-16	713	CE

Essex

School name	Address	Tel	Fax	Headteacher	Ref	Ages	Pupils	Other
Braeside School	Buckhurst Hill, Essex IG9 5SD	020 8504 1133	020 8505 6675	Mrs C. Naismith	881-6000	3-16	209	G
Brentwood School	Brentwood, Essex CM15 8AS	01277 243243	01277 243299	Mr D.I. Davies	881-6035	3-16	1479	R

School name	Address	Tel	Fax	Headteacher	Ref	Ages	Pupils	Other
Chigwell School	Chigwell, Essex IG7 6QF	020 8501 5700	020 8500 6232	Mr D.F. Gibbs	881-6006	7-16	715	R Ch
The Christian School (Takeley)	Bishop's Stortford, Hertfordshire CM22 6QH	01279 871182		Mr M.E. Humphries	881-6041	4-16	43	Ch
Colchester High School	Colchester, Essex CO3 3HD	01206 573389	01206 573114	Mr David E. Wood	881-6015	2-16	428	CE
Felsted School	Dunmow, Essex CM6 3LL	01371 822600	01371 822607	Mr S. Roberts	881-6009	13-16	871	CE
Friends School	Saffron Walden, Essex CB11 3EB	01799 525351	01799 523808	Mr A.D. Waters	881-6012	2-18	375	R Qk
Gosfield School	Halstead, Essex CO9 1PF	01787 474040	01787 478228	Mrs Elizabeth Goodchild	881-6010	4-18	186	R
Guru Gobind Singh Khalsa College	Chigwell, Essex IG7 6BQ	020 8559 9160	020 8559 9064	Mr A.S. Toor	881-6042	3-19	252	Sikh
New Hall School	Chelmsford, Essex CM3 3HS	01245 467588	01245 467188	Mrs K. Jeffrey	881-6001	3-18	768	R RC
Peniel Academy	Brentwood, Essex CM15 0DG	01277 374123	01277 373596	Dr M.S.B. Reid	881-6036	2-19	171	Ch
St Mary's School	Colchester, Essex CO3 3RB	01206 572544	01206 576437	Mrs G.M. Mouser	881-6008	4-16	415	G Ch
St Nicholas School	Old Harlow, Essex CM17 0NJ	01279 429910	01279 450224	Mr R. Cusworth	881-6023	4-16	378	G Ch

Hertfordshire

School name	Address	Tel	Fax	Headteacher	Ref	Ages	Pupils	Other
Abbot's Hill School	Bunkers La., Hemel Hempstead, Hertfordshire HP3 8RP	01442 240333	01442 269981	Mrs K. Lewis	919-6000	2-17	467	G CE
Aldenham School	Elstree, Borehamwood, Hertfordshire WD6 3AJ	01923 858122	01923 854410	Mr J.C. Fowler	919-6003	3-16	661	R CE
The Arts Educational School	Tring Pk, Tring, Hertfordshire HP23 5LX	01442 824255	01442 891069	Mr Stefan Anderson	919-6041	8-18	267	R
Berkhamsted Collegiate School	Castle St, Berkhamsted, Hertfordshire HP4 2BB	01442 358002	01442 358003	Dr P. Chadwick	919-6005	3-19	1484	R Ch
Bishop's Stortford College	10 Maze Green Rd, Bishop's Stortford, Hertfordshire CM23 2PJ	01279 838575	01279 836570	Mr J.G. Trotman	919-6007	4-18	995	R Ch
Edge Grove School	High Cross, Watford, Hertfordshire WD25 8NL	01923 855724	01923 859920	Mr M.T. Wilson	919-6002	7-14	377	R Ch
Egerton-Rothesay School	Durrants La., Berkhamsted, Hertfordshire HP4 3UJ	01442 865275	01442 864977	Mrs N. Boddam-Whetham	919-6062	2-16	310	
Haberdashers' Aske's School for Boys	Butterfly La., Borehamwood, Hertfordshire WD6 3AF	020 8266 1700	020 8266 1800	Mr P.B. Hamilton	919-6221	5-18	1318	B
Haberdashers' Aske's School for Girls	Aldenham Rd, Borehamwood, Hertfordshire WD6 3BT	020 8266 2300	020 8266 2303	Mrs E.J. Radice	919-6222	4-16	1145	G Ch
Haileybury and Imperial Service College	Hertford, Hertfordshire SG13 7NU	01992 462507	01992 467603	Mr S.A. Westley	919-6015	11-18	754	R CE
Immanuel College	87-91 Elstree Rd, Bushey, Hertfordshire WD23 4EB	020 8950 0604	020 8950 8687	Mr Philip Skelker	919-6231	11-19	520	Je
International Stanborough School	Stanborough Pk, Watford, Hertfordshire WD25 9JT	01923 673268	01923 893943	Mr Stephen Rivers	919-6209	11-18	25	R
The King's School	Elmfield, Harpenden, Hertfordshire AL5 4DU	01582 767566	01582 765406	Mr C. Case	919-6224	2-16	208	Ch
Lockers Park School	Lockers Park La., Hemel Hempstead, Hertfordshire HP1 1TL	01442 251712	01442 234150	Mr D. Lees-Jones	919-6024	6-14	140	B R
Merchant Taylors' School	Sandy Lodge, Northwood, Middlesex HA6 2HT	01923 820644	01923 835110	Mr S.N. Wright	919-6036	11-16	827	B CE
The Princess Helena College	Preston, Hitchin, Hertfordshire SG4 7RT	01462 432100	01462 443871	Mrs A.M. Hodgkiss	919-6033	11-16	203	G R Ch
Purcell School	Aldenham Rd, Bushey, Hertfordshire WD23 2TS	01923 331100	01923 331166	Mr J. Tolputt	919-6239	8-19	172	R
Queenswood School	Shepherd's Way, Hatfield, Hertfordshire AL9 6NS	01707 602597	01707 602597	Mrs Paul Edgar	919-6020	11-16	415	G R Me
Redemption Academy	Old Chells Play Area, Stevenage, Hertfordshire SG2 0LL	01438 727370	01438 727370	Mrs S.J. Neale	919-6242	3-18	25	Ch
Royal Masonic School for Girls	Rickmansworth Pk, Rickmansworth, Hertfordshire WD3 4HF	01923 773168	01923 896729	Ms D. Rose	919-6165	4-18	786	G R
Rudolf Steiner School	Langley Hill, Kings Langley, Hertfordshire WD4 9HG	01923 262505	01923 270958		919-6109	3-16	396	
St Albans High School for Girls	4 Townsend Ave, St Albans, Hertfordshire AL1 3SJ	01727 853800	01727 792516	Ms J. Pain	919-6038	4-18	944	G Ch
St Albans School	Abbey Gateway, St Albans, Hertfordshire AL3 4HB	01727 855521	01727 843447	Mr A. Grant	919-6220	11-19	767	Ch
St Albans Tutors	69 London Rd, St Albans, Hertfordshire AL1 1LN	01727 842348		Mr Assim Jemal	919-6243	14-16	44	
St Christopher School	Barrington Rd, Letchworth, Hertfordshire SG6 3JZ	01462 650850	01462 481578	Mr Richard Palmer	919-6028	2-19	513	R
St Columba's College	King Harry La., St Albans, Hertfordshire AL3 4AW	01727 855185	01727 892024	Mr Nicholas O'Sullivan	919-6136	4-18	839	B RC
St Edmund's College	Old Hall Grn, Ware, Hertfordshire SG11 1DS	01920 821504	01920 823011	Mr Chris Long	919-6115	3-19	733	R RC
St Francis College	Broadway, Letchworth, Hertfordshire SG6 3PJ	01462 670511	01462 682361	Miss M.H. Hegarty	919-6029	11-18	298	G R Ch
St Margaret's School	Merry Hill Rd, Bushey, Hertfordshire WD23 1DT	020 8901 0870	020 8950 1677	Mrs Lynne Crighton	919-6047	4-18	432	G Ch
Sherrardswood School	Lockleys, Welwyn, Hertfordshire AL6 0BJ	01438 714282	01438 840616	Mrs Lynda Corry		2-19	345	G R CE

4

School name	Address	Tel	Fax	Headteacher	Ref	Ages	Pupils	Other
Stanborough Secondary School	Stanborough Pk, Watford, Hertfordshire WD25 9JT	01923 673268	01923 893943	Mr R. Murphy	919-6154	3-18	255	R SDA
Westbrook Hay School	London Rd, Hemel Hempstead, Hertfordshire HP1 2RF	01442 256143	01442 232076	Mr K.D. Young	919-6021	3-14	236	CE

Luton

School name	Address	Tel	Fax	Headteacher	Ref	Ages	Pupils	Other
Bury Park Educatiuonal Institute (Al-Hikmah Secondary School)	82-86 Dunstable Rd, Luton, Bedfordshire LU1 1EH	01582 728196	01582 485656	Mr Mufti Muhamad Abdul Hannan	821-6007	9-16	66	B Mu
Jamiatul Uloom Al-Islamia	364-366 Leagrave Rd, Luton, Bedfordshire LU3 1RF	01582 595535	01582 595535	Mr Mohammed Sadek Miah	821-6006	11-15	26	B Mu
Rabia Girls' School	Portland Rd, Luton, Bedfordshire LU4 8AX	01582 493239		Mrs F. Shaikh	821-6001	4-16	340	Mu
Rathbone School	1 Telford Way, Luton, Bedfordshire LU1 1HT	01582 420730		Ms N.J. Khan	821-6008	14-16	16	

Norfolk

School name	Address	Tel	Fax	Headteacher	Ref	Ages	Pupils	Other
All Saints School	School Rd, Lessingham, Stalham, Norwich, Norfolk NR12 0DJ	01692 582083	01692 584999	Mrs Judith Gardiner	926-6140	5-16	89	Ch
Beeston Hall School	West Runton, Cromer, Norfolk NR27 9NQ	01263 837324	01263 838177	I.K. Macaskill	926-6058	6-14	167	R CE
Breckland Park School	Turbine Way, Swaffham, Norfolk PE37 7XD	01760 336939		Mrs Jackie Swift	926-6153	11-17	65	Ch
CfBT Education Trust trading as Include	29 Woodcock Rd, First Fl, Bessemer Rd, Norwich, Norfolk NR3 3UA	01603 401515	01603 301435	Mrs Sue Wootton	926-6150	11-16	23	
Glebe House School	2 Cromer Rd, Hunstanton, Norfolk PE36 6HW	01485 532809	01485 533900	Mr J.P. Crofts	926-6004	4-14	177	R
Gresham's School	Cromer Rd, Holt, Norfolk NR25 6EA	01263 713271	01263 712028	Mr Antony Roy Clark	926-6003	2-16	789	R CE
Hethersett Old Hall School	Hethersett, Norwich, Norfolk NR9 3DW	01603 810390	01603 812094	Mrs J.M. Mark	926-6029	3-19	231	R CE
Langley School	Langley Pk, Norwich, Norfolk NR14 6BJ	01508 520210	01508 528058	Mr J.G. Malcolm	926-6005	10-16	460	R
Norwich High School for Girls GDST	95 Newmarket Rd, Norwich, Norfolk NR2 2HU	01603 453265	01603 259891	Mrs V.C. Bidwell	926-6123	4-16	880	G
Norwich School	70 The Close, Norwich, Norfolk NR1 4DD	01603 728430	01603 627036	Mr James Bruce Hawkins	926-6124	7-18	843	
Sacred Heart Convent School	17 Mangate St, Swaffham, Norfolk PE37 7QW	01760 721330	01760 725557	Miss Diana Wynter	926-6051	3-16	206	R RC
Thetford Grammar School	Bridge St, Thetford, Norfolk IP24 3AF	01842 752840	01842 750220	Mr Gareth James Price	926-6128	4-16	318	
Thorpe House School	7 Yarmouth Rd, Norwich, Norfolk NR7 0EA	01603 433055	01603 436323	Mr Alistair Todd	926-6062	3-16	214	G
Wood-Dene School	Aylmerton Hall, Aylmerton, Norwich, Norfolk NR11 8QA	01263 837224	01263 835037	Mrs Diana Taylor	926-6137	2-17	170	

Peterborough

School name	Address	Tel	Fax	Headteacher	Ref	Ages	Pupils	Other
Peterborough High School	Westwood Hse, Thorpe Rd, Peterborough, Cambridgeshire PE3 6JF	01733 343357	01733 555712	Mrs S. Dixon	874-6000	4-16	361	R CE

Southend-on-Sea

School name	Address	Tel	Fax	Headteacher	Ref	Ages	Pupils	Other
St Hilda's School	15 Imperial Ave, Westcliff-on-Sea, Essex SS0 8NE	01702 344542	01702 344547	Mrs S. O'Riordan	882-6004	3-17	152	
Thorpe Hall School	Wakering Rd, Thorpe Bay, Southend-on-Sea, Essex SS1 3RD	01702 582340	01702 587070	Mr Brian Robinson	882-6001	2-17	341	Ch

Suffolk

School name	Address	Tel	Fax	Headteacher	Ref	Ages	Pupils	Other
Amberfield School	Nacton, Ipswich, Suffolk IP10 0HL	01473 659265	01473 659843	Mrs Helen Kay	935-6032	2–17	262	Ch
Culford School	Culford, Bury St Edmunds, Suffolk IP28 6TX	01284 728615	01284 728631	Mr Julian Johnson-Munday	935-6053	3–19	318	R Me
Felixstowe International College	Maybush La, Felixstowe, Suffolk IP11 7NA	01394 282388	01394 276926	Mrs J.S. Lee	935-6076	10–18	15	R CE
Finborough School	The Hall, Gt Finborough, Stowmarket, Suffolk IP14 3EF	01449 773600	01449 773601	Mr J. Sinclair	935-6062	2–19	224	R
Framlingham College	Framlingham, Woodbridge, Suffolk IP13 9EY	01728 723789	01728 724546	Mrs G.M. Randall	935-6046	3–16	697	R CE
Ipswich High School	Woolverstone, Ipswich, Suffolk IP9 1AZ	01473 780201	01473 400058	Mrs Elaine Purves	935-6055	3–19	672	G
Ipswich School	Henley Rd, Ipswich, Suffolk IP1 3SG	01473 408300		Mr I. Galbraith	935-6039	2–16	1084	R
Larchcroft School	32 Larchcroft Rd, Ipswich, Suffolk IP1 6AR	01473 464975		Mr Alan Webber	935-6082	11–16	50	Ch
Orwell Park School	Nacton, Ipswich, Suffolk IP10 0ER	01473 659225	01473 659822	Mr A. Auster	935-6005	2–14	276	R
Royal Hospital School	Holbrook, Ipswich, Suffolk IP9 2RX	01473 326200	01473 326213	Mr H.W. Blackett	935-6056	11–18	616	R
St Felix School	Halesworth Rd, Reydon, Southwold, Suffolk IP18 6SD	01502 722175	01502 722641	Mr D.A.T. Ward	935-6007	11–16	396	R
St Joseph's College	Birkfield, Belstead Rd, Ipswich, Suffolk IP2 9DR	01473 690281	01473 602409	Mrs S. Grant	935-6044	2–18	556	R Ch
Stoke College	Ashen La, Stoke-by-Clare, Sudbury, Suffolk CO10 8JE	01787 278141	01787 277904	Mr J. Gibson	935-6003	3–16	241	R
Summerhill School	Westward Ho, Leiston, Suffolk IP16 4HY	01728 830540	01728 830540	Mrs Z. Readhead	935-6016	5–16	71	R
Woodbridge School	Burkitt Rd, Woodbridge, Suffolk IP12 4JH	01394 615000	01394 380944	Mr S.H. Cole	935-6054	4–16	954	R CE

East Midlands

Derby

School name	Address	Tel	Fax	Headteacher	Ref	Ages	Pupils	Other
Derby Grammar School	Rykneld Rd, Littleover, Derby, Derbyshire DE23 4BX	01332 523027	01332 518670	Mr Roger D. Waller	831-6004	7–18	305	B CE
Derby High School	Hillsway, Littleover, Derby, Derbyshire DE23 3DT	01332 514267	01332 516085	Mr C.T. Callaghan	831-6001	3–18	583	CE
Friar Gate House School	65 Friar Gate, Derby, Derbyshire DE1 1DJ	01332 342765		Mrs Sandra June Williams	831-6003	3–16	61	
Step Forward Educational Trust (Derby)	St James Centre, Malcolm St, Derby, Derbyshire DE23 8LU	01332 604086		Mrs C. Weightman	831-6007	15–16	20	

Derbyshire

School name	Address	Tel	Fax	Headteacher	Ref	Ages	Pupils	Other
Abbotsholme School	Rocester, Uttoxeter, Staffordshire ST14 5BS	01889 590217	01889 591001	Mr Steve Fairclough	830-6005	7–16	303	R
Foremarke Hall Repton Preparatory School	Formarke Hall, Milton, Derby, Derbyshire DE65 6EJ	01283 703269	01283 702957	Mr P.H. Brewster	830-6019	2–14	467	R Ch
Michael House School	The Field, Shipley, Heanor, Derbyshire DE75 7JH	01773 718050	01773 711784	Mrs Carol Aspinall	830-6010	3–17	148	
Mount St Mary's College	Spinkhill, Sheffield, South Yorkshire S21 3YL	01246 433388	01246 435511	Mr P.G. MacDonald	830-6014	11–16	386	R
Ockbrook School	The Settlement, Ockbrook, Derby, Derbyshire DE72 3RJ	01332 673532	01332 665184	Mrs Alison Steele	830-6002	3–16	590	G R Ch
Repton School	Repton, Derby, Derbyshire DE65 6FH	01283 559200	01283 559210	Mr Robert Holroyd	830-6001	12–16	590	R Ch
Trent College	Long Eaton, Nottingham, Nottinghamshire NG10 4AD	01158 494921	01158 494997	Mr J.S. Lee	830-6000	3–19	1095	R

4

Leicester

School name	Address	Tel	Fax	Headteacher	Ref	Ages	Pupils	Other
Darul Uloom Leicester	119 Loughborough Rd, Leicester, Leicestershire LE4 5LN	0116 2 668922		Mr Shafiq Latif	856-6004	11–16	123	B R Mu
Emmanuel Christian School	The Grounds Of Braunstone, Braunstone, Leicester LE3 1QP	0116 299 7741		Miss P. Wells	856-6018	5–14	15	Ch
Jameah Girls Academy	33 Woodhill, Leicester, Leicestershire LE5 3SP	0116 262 7745		Mrs S. Patel	856-6015	6–16	149	G Mu
Leicester Grammar School	8 Peacock La, Leicester, Leicestershire LE1 5PX	0116 222 0400	0116 291 0505	Mr Christopher King	856-6006	9–19	690	
Leicester High School for Girls	454 London Rd, Leicester, Leicestershire LE2 2PP	0116 270 5338	0116 244 8823	Mr J. Burns	856-6009	3–18	435	G CE
Leicester Islamic Academy	320 London Rd, Leicester, Leicestershire LE2 2PJ	0116 270 5343	0116 244 8503	Dr M.H. Mukadam	856-6007	3–16	712	Mu
Leicester Montessori Grammar School	58 Stoneygate, Leicester, Leicestershire LE2 2BN	0116 255 4441	0116 255 4440	Mrs R. Borland	856-6008	2–16	161	
St Crispin's School	6 St Marys Rd, Leicester, Leicestershire LE2 1XA	0116 270 7648	0116 270 7648	Mrs D. Lofthouse	856-6000	5–16	119	

Leicestershire

School name	Address	Tel	Fax	Headteacher	Ref	Ages	Pupils	Other
Brooke House College	Leicester Rd, Market Harborough, Leicestershire LE16 7AU	01858 462452	01858 462487	Mr J. Stanford	855-6005	14–16	163	R
Dixie Grammar School	Station Rd, Market Bosworth, Nuneaton, Warwickshire CV13 0LE	01455 292244	01455 292151	Mr John Robert Wood	855-6004	3–16	512	
Jamia Islamia (Islamic Studies Centre)	Watling St, Nuneaton, Warwickshire CV11 6BE	024 7664 1333	024 7635 3345	Mr Sabir Khan	855-6015	11–16	59	B R Mu
Loughborough Grammar School	Burton Walks, Loughborough, Leicestershire LE11 2DU	01509 233233	01509 218436	Mr P.B. Fisher	855-6012	10–19	1002	B R
Loughborough High School	Burton Walks, Loughborough, Leicestershire LE11 2DU	01509 212348	01509 215720	Miss Biddie O'Connor	855-6009	11–18	587	G ID
Manor House Preparatory School	South St, Ashby-de-la-Zouch, Leicestershire LE65 1BR	01530 412932	01530 417435	I.R. Clews	855-6003	4–16	155	
Our Lady's Convent School	Burton St, Loughborough, Leicestershire LE11 2DT	01509 263901	01509 236193	Sister Shelagh Fynn	855-6008	3–16	433	G RC
Ratcliffe College	Fosse Way, Ratcliffe-on-the-Wreake, Leicester, Leicestershire LE7 4SG	01509 817006	01509 815541	Mr P. Farrar	855-6001	3–16	627	R RC
Twycross House School	Twycross, Atherstone, Warwickshire CV9 3PL	01827 880651	01827 880651	Mrs N.J. Lilley	855-6006	8–18	313	

Lincolnshire

School name	Address	Tel	Fax	Headteacher	Ref	Ages	Pupils	Other
Excell International School	Well Vale Hall, Alford, Lincolnshire LN13 0ET	01507 462764	01507 462764	Mrs Dulcie M. Kay	925-6024	0–16	10	R
Fen School	Side Bar La, Heckington Fen, Sleaford, Lincolnshire NG34 9LY	01529 460966		Mrs J.M. Dunkley	925-6037	2–16	11	CE
High Leas Education Centre	4 High Leas, Nettleham, Lincoln, Lincolnshire LN2 2TA	01522 754050		Mr Bill Haughton	925-6049	11–17	23	Ch
Kirkstone House School	1–6 Main St, Baston, Peterborough, Cambridgeshire PE6 9PA	01778 560350	01778 560547	Miss Margaret Pepper	925-6017	2–17	233	
Lincoln Minster School	Upper Lindum St, Lincoln, Lincolnshire LN2 5RW	01522 551300	01522 551310	Mr C. Rickart	925-6012	2–16	797	R Ch
Locksley Christian School	Bilney Block, Manby Pk, Manby, Louth, Lincolnshire LN11 8UT	01507 327859	01507 328512	Mrs A. Franklin	925-6039	2–19	56	Ch
Stamford High School	St Martin's, Stamford, Lincolnshire PE9 2LL	01780 484200	01780 484201	Mrs Y.L. Powell	925-6028	11–19	611	G R Ch
Stamford School	St Paul's St, Stamford, Lincolnshire PE9 2BQ	01780 750300	01780 750336	Mr S. Burns	925-6027	11–19	661	B R Ch

Northamptonshire

School name	Address	Tel	Fax	Headteacher	Ref	Ages	Pupils	Other
Bosworth Independent College	Nazareth Hse, Leicester Par, Barrack Rd, Northampton, Northamptonshire NN2 6AF	01604 239995	01604 239996	Mr M. McQuin	928-6062	14–16	315	R
Maidwell Hall School	Maidwell, Northampton, Northamptonshire NN6 9JG	01604 686234	01604 686659	Mr R.A. Lankester	928-6005	7–14	96	R Ch
Northampton High School	Newport Pagnell Rd, Hardingstone, Northampton, Northamptonshire NN4 6UU	01604 765765	01604 709418	Mrs L.A. Mayne	928-6057	3–19	789	G CE
Northamptonshire Grammar School	Pitsford Hall, Moulton La, Pitsford, Northampton, Northamptonshire NN6 9AX	01604 880306	01604 882212	Mr Noel Toone	928-6064	3–16	306	Ch

4

School name	Address	Tel	Fax	Headteacher	Ref	Ages	Pupils	Other
Oundle School	Gt Hall, New St, Oundle, Peterborough, Cambridgeshire PE8 4GH	01832 277112	01832 277123	Dr R.D. Townsend	928-6007	10–16	1071	R
Overstone Park School	Overstone Pk, Overstone, Northampton, Northamptonshire NN6 0DT	01604 643787		Mrs M.F. Brown	928-6063	3–16	102	
Quinton House School	Upton Hall, Upton, Northampton, Northamptonshire NN5 4UX	01604 752050	01604 581707	Mr J.R. Chatburn	928-6043	2–19	328	
St Peter's Independent School	Lingswood Pk, Blackthorn, Northampton, Northamptonshire NN3 8TA	01604 411745	01604 411475	Mr G.J. Smith	928-6056	4–16	140	Ch
Spratton Hall School	Smith St, Spratton, Northampton, Northamptonshire NN6 8HP	01604 847292	01604 820844	S.J. Player	928-6032	2–14	407	CE
Wellingborough School	Irthlingborough Rd, Wellingborough, Northamptonshire NN8 2BX	01933 222427	01933 222339	Mr G.R. Bowe	928-6010	3–19	895	

Nottingham

School name	Address	Tel	Fax	Headteacher	Ref	Ages	Pupils	Other
Hollygirt School	Elm Ave, Nottingham, Nottinghamshire NG3 4GF	0115 958 0596	0115 989 7929	Mrs M. Connolly	892-6001	4–16	294	Ch
Jamia Al-Hudaa Residential College	Forest Hse, Berkeley Ave, Mapperley Pk, Nottingham, Nottinghamshire NG3 5TT	0115 969 0800	0115 969 0818	Maha Abu-Taha	892-6012	5–16	231	G R Mu
The King's School	51 Green St, The Meadows, Nottingham, Nottinghamshire NG2 2LA	0115 953 9194	0115 955 1148	Mr R. Southey	892-6011	4–16	131	Ch
Nottingham High School	Waverley Mount, Nottingham, Nottinghamshire NG7 4ED	0115 978 6056	0115 924 9716		892-6004	3–17	840	B
Nottingham High School for Girls GDST	9 Arboretum St, Nottingham, Nottinghamshire NG1 4JB	0115 941 7663	0115 924 0757	Mrs Susan Gorham	892-6009	4–16	1075	G
Nottingham Islamia School	30 Bentinck Rd, Hyson Grn, Nottingham, Nottinghamshire NG7 4AF	0115 970 5858	0115 912 0813	Dr Musharraf Hussain	892-6013	5–16	86	Mu

Nottinghamshire

School name	Address	Tel	Fax	Headteacher	Ref	Ages	Pupils	Other
Al Karam Secondary School	Eaton Hall, Retford, Nottinghamshire DN22 0PR	01777 706441	01777 711538	Mr Ahmed	891-6021	11–17	132	B R Mu
Bramcote Lorne School	Gamston, Retford, Nottinghamshire DN22 0QQ	01777 838636	01777 838633	Mr Richard Raistrick	891-6011	2–14	180	R
Dagfa House School	57 Broadgate, Beeston, Nottingham, Nottinghamshire NG9 2FU	0115 913 8330	0115 913 8331	Mr Andrew Hampton	891-6003	3–16	244	
Lammas School	Lammas Rd, Sutton-in-Ashfield, Nottinghamshire NG17 2AD	01623 516879	01623 516879	Mr C. Peck	891-6016	4–16	149	
Orchard School	South Leverton, Retford, Nottinghamshire DN22 0DJ	01427 880395	01427 884707	Mrs S. Fox	891-6015	2–16	230	
Saville House School	11 Church St, Mansfield Woodhouse, Mansfield, Nottinghamshire NG19 8AH	01623 625068		Mrs J. Nutter	891-6008	3–16	110	
Three Shires School	Lilac Gr, Beeston, Nottingham, Nottinghamshire NG9 1PJ	0115 925 6965	0870 950 2832	Mr D.M. Berry	891-6023	11–17	57	Ch
Wellow House School	Wellow, Newark, Nottinghamshire NG22 0EA	01623 861054	01623 836665	Mr Peter Cook	891-6013	2–14	152	R Ch
Worksop College	Sparken Hill, Worksop, Nottinghamshire S80 3AP	01909 537100	01909 537102	Mr Roy A. Collard	891-6001	13–19	418	R CE

Rutland

School name	Address	Tel	Fax	Headteacher	Ref	Ages	Pupils	Other
Oakham School	Chapel Cl, Oakham, Rutland LE15 6DT	01572 758500	01572 755786	Dr J.A.F. Spence	857-6000	9–16	1079	R
Uppingham School	Uppingham, Oakham, Leicestershire LE15 9QE	01572 822216	01572 822332	Dr Richard Harman	857-6002	13–16	753	R CE

London

Barnet

School name	Address	Tel	Fax	Headteacher	Ref	Ages	Pupils	Other
The Albany College	21–24 Queen's Rd, Hendon, London NW4 2TL	020 8202 9748	020 8202 8460	Mr J. Arthy	302-6083	14–19	171	R
Ayesha Community Education	133 West Hendon, Broadway, London NW9 7DY	07782 151554		Sayed Shakil Ahmed	302-6119	11–16	23	G Mu

School name	Address	Tel	Fax	Headteacher	Ref	Ages	Pupils	Other
Beis Hamedrash Elyon	211 Golders Green Rd, London NW11 9BY	020 8201 8668	020 8201 8769	Mr C. Steinhart	302-6113	11–14	45	B Je
Beth Jacob Grammar School for Girls	Stratford Rd, Hendon, London NW4 2AT	020 8203 4322	020 8202 8480	Mrs D. Steinberg	302-6092	11–17	264	G Je
Brampton College	Lodge Hse, Lodge Rd, Hendon, London NW4 4DQ	020 8203 5025	020 8203 0052	Mr Bernard Canetti	302-6101	15–19	246	
Ellern Mede School	31 Totteridge Common, London N20 8LR	020 8959 7774	020 8959 6311	Ms Anna Tate	302-6118	13–18	13	
King Alfred School	149 North End Rd, London NW11 7HY	020 8457 5200	020 8457 5249	Mrs Dawn Isobel Moore	302-6004	5–16	603	
London Jewish Girls' High School at The Community Centre	18 Raleigh Cl, Hendon, London NW4 2TA	020 8203 8618	020 8203 8618	Mr Joel Rabinowitz	302-6110	11–16	98	G Je
Menorah Grammar School	Abbots Rd, Edgware, Middlesex HA8 0QS	020 8906 9756		Rabbi A.M. Goldblatt	302-6089	11–18	172	B Je
Mill Hill School Foundation	The Ridgeway, Mill Hill, London NW7 1QS	020 8959 1176	020 8201 0663	Mr William Winfield	302-6000	3–16	1276	R
The Mount School	Milespit Hill, London NW7 2RX	020 8959 3403	020 8959 1503	Mrs J. Kirsten-Jackson	302-6010	5–16	338	G MF
Pardes House Grammar School	Hendon La, Finchley, London N3 1SA	020 8349 4222	020 8349 4777	Rabbi D. Dunner	302-6084	10–16	227	B
St Martha's Senior School	Camlet Way, Hadley, Barnet, Hertfordshire EN4 0NJ	020 8449 6889	020 8441 5632	Mr J. Sheridan	302-6014	11–19	292	G RC
Susi Earnshaw Theatre School	68 High St, Barnet, Hertfordshire EN5 5SJ	020 8441 5010	020 8364 9618	Mr David Earnshaw	302-6111	10–16	59	
Wellgrove School	4 Well Gr, Whetstone, London N20 9EQ	020 8446 8855		Mr W. Jones	302-6117	11–17	75	Ch
Wentworth Tutorial College	6–10 Brentmead Pl, London NW11 9LH	020 8458 8524	020 8209 1288	Mr A. Davies	302-6109	15–16	146	
Woodside Park International School	6 Friern Barnet La, London N11 3LX	020 8920 0600	020 8368 3220	Mr David Rose	302-6098	2–18	374	

Brent

School name	Address	Tel	Fax	Headteacher	Ref	Ages	Pupils	Other
Al-Sadiq and Al-Zahra Schools	134 Salusbury Rd, London NW6 6PF	020 7372 7706	020 7372 2752	Dr M. Movahedi	304-6072	4–16	373	Mu
Brondesbury College for Boys	8 Brondesbury Pk, London NW6 7BX	020 8830 4522	020 8830 4523	Dr Nasim Butt	304-6076	11–16	73	B Mu
Islamia Girls' High School	129 Salusbury Rd, London NW6 6PE	020 7372 3472	020 7604 4061	Miss Asmat Ali	304-6060	11–16	101	G Mu
The School of the Islamic Republic of Iran	100 Carlton Vale, London NW6 5HE	020 7372 8051	020 7372 6367	Mr Farzad Farzan	304-6079	6–16	71	Mu
The Swaminarayan School	260 Brentfield Rd, London NW10 8HE	020 8965 8381	020 8961 4042	Mr M. Savjani	304-6074	2–16	448	Hi

Bromley

School name	Address	Tel	Fax	Headteacher	Ref	Ages	Pupils	Other
Babington House School	Grange Dr, Chislehurst, Kent BR7 5ES	020 8467 5537	020 8295 1175	Mrs D.A. Odysseas Bailey	305-6000	3–16	252	
Baston School	Baston Rd, Hayes, Bromley, Kent BR2 7AB	020 8462 1010	020 8462 0438	Miss Katherine Greenwood	305-6001	2–16	148	G CE
Bishop Challoner School	228 Bromley Rd, Shortlands, Bromley, Kent BR2 0BS	020 8460 3546	020 8466 8885	Mr J.A. de Waal	305-6003	2–18	399	RC
Bromley High School	Blackbrook La, Bickley, Bromley, Kent BR1 2TW	020 8468 7981	020 8295 1062	Mrs L.A. Duggleby	305-6073	4–18	899	G
Darul Uloom London	Foxbury Ave, Chislehurst, Kent BR7 6SD	020 8295 0637	020 8467 0655	Mr M.M. Musa	305-6077	11–19	142	B R Mu
Eltham College	Grove Park Rd, Mottingham, London SE9 4QF	020 8857 1455	020 8857 7160	Paul J. Henderson	305-6074	7–19	823	Ch
Farringtons School	Perry St, Chislehurst, Kent BR7 6LR	020 8467 0256	020 8467 5442	Mrs C.E. James	305-6007	3–19	502	R Me

Camden

School name	Address	Tel	Fax	Headteacher	Ref	Ages	Pupils	Other
The Academy School	2 Pilgrims Pl, Rosslyn Hill, Hampstead, London NW3 1NG	020 7435 6621		Mr Evans	202-6396	6–14	71	
Hampstead College of Fine Arts and Humanities	24 Lambolle Pl, Belsize Pk, London NW3 4PG	020 7586 0312	020 7483 0355	Ms C. Cochrane & Mr N Cave	202-6387	13–19	102	
North Bridge House Senior School	1 Gloucester Ave, London NW1 7AB	020 7485 0661	020 7284 2508	Miss J. Battye	202-6269	11–16	171	R Me

School name	Address	Tel	Fax	Headteacher	Ref	Ages	Pupils	Other
Royal School Hampstead	65 Rosslyn Hill, Hampstead, London NW3 5UD	020 7794 7708	020 7431 6741	Mrs Jo Ebner-Landy	202-6386	3–16	236	G R Ch
St Margaret's School	18 Kidderpore Gdns, London NW3 7SR	020 7435 2439	020 7431 1308	Mrs S. Meaden	202-6014	4–16	139	G CE
South Hampstead High School	3 Maresfield Gdns, London NW3 5SS	020 7435 2899	020 7431 8022	Mrs J.E. Stephen	202-6307	4–16	835	G
Southbank International School	16 Netherhall Gdns, London NW3 5TH	020 7431 1200	020 7794 5858	Ms Jane Treftz	202-6395	3–14	192	
University College School	Frognal, Hampstead, London NW3 6XH	020 7435 2215	020 7433 2111	Mr K.J. Durham	202-6018	7–19	962	B

City of London

School name	Address	Tel	Fax	Headteacher	Ref	Ages	Pupils	Other
City of London School	Queen Victoria St, London EC4V 3AL	020 7489 0291	020 7329 6887	Mr D.R. Levin	201-6007	10–18	894	B
City of London School for Girls	St Giles Terr, Barbican, London EC2Y 8BB	020 7847 5500	020 7638 3212	Dr Y.A. Burne	201-6005	7–18	706	G CE

Croydon

School name	Address	Tel	Fax	Headteacher	Ref	Ages	Pupils	Other
Al-Khair School	109–117 Cherry Orchard Rd, Croydon, Surrey CR0 6BE	020 8662 8664	08700 682979	Mr Usman Qureshi	306-6096	5–16	126	Mu
ALTE School at Open Gate Centre	2 Union Rd, Croydon, Surrey CR0 2XU	020 8665 5533	020 8684 7233	Ms Mary McCauley	306-6097	11–16	16	Ch
CACFO Education Centre	40 Northwood Rd, Thornton Heath, Surrey CR7 8HQ	020 8771 6222	020 8771 9700	Mr Philip Gardiner	306-6094	11–16	6	
Cambridge Tutors College	Water Tower Hill, Croydon, Surrey CR0 5SX	020 8688 5284	020 8686 9220	Mr D.A. Lowe	306-6095	15–18	268	R
Croham Hurst School	79 Croham Rd, South Croydon, Surrey CR2 7YN	020 8688 3863	020 8688 1142	Miss S.C. Budgen	306-6002	3–19	515	G
Croydon High School	Old Farleigh Rd, Selsdon, South Croydon, Surrey CR2 8YB	020 8651 5020	020 8657 5413	Mrs Zelma Braganza	306-6081	3–16	735	G
Folly's End Christian School	9 South Park Hill Rd, South Croydon, Surrey CR2 7DY	020 8649 9121		Mr S. Poole	306-6087	3–14	54	Ch
Lodge School	11 Woodcote La, Purley, Surrey CR8 3HB	020 8660 3179	020 8660 1385	Miss P. Maynard	306-6001	3–16	250	
Old Palace School of John Whitgift	Old Palace Rd, Croydon, Surrey CR0 1AX	020 8688 2027	020 8680 5877	Miss Judy Harris	306-6082	4–18	801	G Ch
Royal Russell School	Coombe La, Croydon, Surrey CR9 5BX	020 8657 4433	020 8657 0207	Dr J.R. Jennings	306-6009	3–19	832	R
Trinity School	Shirley Pk, Croydon, Surrey CR9 7AT	020 8656 9541	020 8655 0522	Mr C.J. Tarrant	306-6077	10–18	879	B CE
Whitgift School	Haling Pk, South Croydon, Surrey CR2 6YT	020 8688 9222	020 8760 0682	Dr C.A. Barnett	306-6014	10–16	1189	B CE

Ealing

School name	Address	Tel	Fax	Headteacher	Ref	Ages	Pupils	Other
Acorn Independent College	39–47 High St, Southall, Middlesex UB1 3HF	020 8571 9900	020 8571 9901	Mrs Gladys Watt	307-6081	13–19	139	
Aston House School	1 Aston Rd, London W5 2RL	020 8566 7300	020 8566 7499	Ms J.S. Lawson	307-6076	5–10	99	
Ayesha Siddiqa Girls School	165–169, The Broadway, Southall, Middlesex UB1 1LS	020 8571 6839	020 8571 0241	Mr Abdullah Dawood	306-6338	11–16	48	G Mu
Barbara Speake Stage School	East Acton La, East Acton, London W3 7EG	020 8743 1306	020 8743 1306	Mr David Speake	307-6050	4–16	139	
Ealing College Upper School	83 The Avenue, Ealing, London W13 8JS	020 8248 2312	020 8248 3765	Mr B. Webb	307-6055	11–16	95	
Ealing Independent College	83 New Broadway, Ealing, London W5 5AL	020 8579 6668	020 8567 8688	Dr Ian Moores	307-6082	14–19	92	
Harvington School	20 Castlebar Rd, Ealing, London W5 2DS	020 8997 1583	020 8810 4756	Mrs Anna Evans	307-6002	3–16	198	G
The Japanese School	87 Creffield Rd, Acton, London W3 9PU	020 8993 7145	020 8992 1224	Mrs Kiyoe Tsuruoka	307-6070	6–16	491	
King Fahad Academy	Bromyard Ave, Acton, London W3 7HD	020 8743 0131	020 8749 7085	Dr Sumaya Alyusuf	307-6068	0–18	511	Mu
Notting Hill and Ealing High School	2 Cleveland Rd, London W13 8AX	020 8799 8400	020 8810 6891	Mrs S. Whitfield	307-6065	5–16	827	G
Perivale Study Centre	10 Walmgate Rd, Perivale, Middlesex UB6 7LH	020 8998 6630		S. Turner	307-6083	11–16	53	Ch
St Augustine's Priory	Hillcrest Rd, Ealing, London W5 2JL	020 8997 2022	020 8810 6501	Mrs F.J. Gumley-Mason	307-6005	4–16	492	G RC
St Benedict's School	5 Montpelier Ave, London W5 2XP	020 8862 2254	020 8862 2199	C.J. Cleugh	307-6006	11–16	862	B RC

Enfield

School name	Address	Tel	Fax	Headteacher	Ref	Ages	Pupils	Other
North London Muslim School	131–133 Fore St, Edmonton, London N18 2XF	020 8345 7008		Mr W. Abdulla	308-6067	0–18	21	Mu
Palmers Green High School	104 Hoppers Rd, London N21 3LJ	020 8886 1135	020 8882 9473	Mrs J.C. Edmundson	308-6001	3–17	318	G
Phoenix Academy	85 Bounces Rd, Edmonton, London N9 8LD	020 8887 6888	020 8885 5007	Mr A. Hawkes	308-6068	11–15	19	Ch
St John's Preparatory and Senior School	North Lodge, The Ridgeway, Enfield, Middlesex EN2 8BE	020 8366 0035	020 8363 4439	Mrs C. Tardios	308-6062	4–18	429	Ch

Greenwich

School name	Address	Tel	Fax	Headteacher	Ref	Ages	Pupils	Other
Belcanto London Academy Theatre School	20 Passey Pl, Eltham Palace, Eltham, London SE9 5DQ	020 8850 9888	020 8850 9944	Mrs Susan Pendergast	203-6298	8–16	51	
Bellerbys College	Bounty Hse, Stowage, London SE8 3DE	020 8694 7000	020 8694 7001	Mr P. Langman	203-6376	15–19	327	R
Blackheath High School	27 Vanbrugh Pk, London SE3 7AG	020 8853 2929	020 8853 3663	Mrs Elizabeth Laws	203-6295	3–16	547	G
Colfes School	Horn Park La. Lee, London SE12 8AW	020 8852 2283	020 8852 2283	Mr Richard Russell	203-6293	3–18	1058	
Right Choice Project	132–134 Powis St, Woolwich, London SE18 6NL	020 8854 6229	020 8855 8181	Mr Banjo Aromolaran	203-6300	13–18	35	
Riverston School	63–69 Eltham Rd, Lee Grn, London SE12 8UF	020 8318 4327	020 8297 0514	Mrs S. Salathiel	203-6169	2–19	292	
Schoolhouse Education	Macbean St, London SE18 6LP	020 8836 9899	020 8854 9757	Lynda Smith	203-6377	14–16	26	

Hackney

School name	Address	Tel	Fax	Headteacher	Ref	Ages	Pupils	Other
Beis Chinuch Lebonos Girls School	Woodberry Down Centre, Woodberry Down, London N4 2SH	020 8809 7737	020 8802 7996	Mrs R. Springer	204-6399	2–16	451	G
Beis Malka Girls' School	93 Alkham Rd, London N16 6XD	020 8806 2070	020 8806 1719	Mr A. Grossman	204-6337	5–16	345	G Je
Beis Rochel d'Satmar Girls' School	51–57 Amhurst Pk, London N16 5DL	020 8800 9060	020 8809 7069	Ms Gita Ruth Smus	204-6296	2–17	866	G Je
Bnois Jerusalem School	79–81 Amhurst Pk, London N16 5DL	020 8211 7136		Mrs Sonnenschein	204-6242	3–16	504	G Je
Getters Talmud Torah	86 Amhurst Pk, London N16 5AR	020 8802 2512		Rabbi P. Ginsbury	204-6405	5–14	182	B Je
Lubavitch House School (Senior Girls)	107–115 Stamford Hill, London N16 5RP	020 8800 0022	020 8809 7324	Rabbi S. Lew	204-6411	11–17	107	G
Mustard School	Parish Hall, Nuttall St, London N1 5LR	020 7739 3499	020 7739 3499	Mr A.F. Johnson	204-6402	2–19	47	Ch
Paragon Christian Academy	233–241 Glyn Rd, London E5 0JP	020 8985 1119		Mrs J.A. Lynch	204-6389	5–14	38	Ch
Tawhid Boys School, Tawhid Educational Trust	21 Cazenove Rd, London N16 6PA	020 8806 2999		Mr Usman Mapara	204-6407	9–16	123	B Mu
Tayyibah Girls' School	88 Filey Ave, Stamford Hill, London N16 6JJ	020 8880 0085	020 8880 0085	Mrs N.B. Qureshi	204-6388	4–16	267	G Mu
Yesodey Hatorah School	2–4 Amhurst Pk, London N16 5AE	020 8800 8612	020 8802 2479	Rabbi A. Pinter	204-6072	5–16	569	Je

Hammersmith and Fulham

School name	Address	Tel	Fax	Headteacher	Ref	Ages	Pupils	Other
The Godolphin and Latymer School	Iffley Rd, Hammersmith, London W6 0PG	020 8741 1936	020 8746 3352	Miss M. Rudland	205-6291	11–16	720	G ID
Latymer Upper School	237 King St, Hammersmith, London W6 9LR	020 8741 1851	020 8748 5212	Mr Peter J. Winter	205-6306	7–19	1231	
Ravenscourt Theatre School	8–30 Galena Rd, Hammersmith, London W6 0LT	020 8741 0707	020 8741 1786	Miss Judi Swinney	205-6208	8–16	77	
St James Independent School for Senior Girls	Earsby St, London W14 8SH	020 7348 1777	020 7348 1717	Mrs Laura Hyde	205-6399	10–18	258	G
St Paul's Girls' School	Brook Grn, London W6 7BS	020 7603 2288	020 7602 9932	Ms Clarissa Farr	205-6011	10–19	691	G

4

Haringey

School name	Address	Tel	Fax	Headteacher	Ref	Ages	Pupils	Other
Channing School	Highgate, London N6 5HF	020 8340 2328	020 8341 5698	Mrs E. Radice	309-6000	4–16	566	G Unitarian
Greek Secondary School of London	Avenue Lodge, Bounds Green Rd, London N22 7EU	020 8881 9320	020 8881 9320	Andreas Kaskabas	309-6081	12–18	71	
Highgate School	North Rd, London N6 4AY	020 8340 1524	020 8340 7674	Mr Adam Pettitt	309-6001	3–19	1240	CE
Wisdom Primary and Secondary School	336 Phillip La, Tottenham, London N15 4AB	020 8880 9070	020 8885 4341	Mr Ramazan Guveli	309-6086	7–16	29	

Harrow

School name	Address	Tel	Fax	Headteacher	Ref	Ages	Pupils	Other
Buckingham College School	15–17 Hindes Rd, Harrow, Middlesex HA1 1SH	020 8427 1220	020 8863 0816	Mr D.F.T. Bell	310-6054	11–16	146	B
Dorset House School	17 Dorset Dr, Edgware, Middlesex HA8 7NT	020 8952 4503		Mr Stanley Drizen	310-6077	5–16	8	
Harrow School	5 High St, Harrow, Middlesex HA1 3HP	020 8872 8000	020 8423 3112	Mr B.J. Lenon	310-6000	13–19	801	B R Ch
Heathfield School Pinner	Beaulieu Dr, Pinner, Middlesex HA5 1NB	020 8868 2346	020 8868 4405	Miss C. Juett	310-6001	3–16	572	G
The John Lyon School	Middle Rd, Harrow, Middlesex HA2 0HN	020 8872 8400	020 8872 8455	Mr Kevin Riley	310-6002	11–18	578	B
North London Collegiate School	Canons Dr, Edgware, Middlesex HA8 7RJ	020 8952 0912	020 8951 1391	Mrs B. McCabe	310-6075	4–16	1057	G
Peterborough and St Margaret's School	Common Rd, Stanmore, Middlesex HA7 3JB	020 8950 3600	020 8421 8946	Mrs S.R. Watts	310-6062	4–16	167	G CE
Regent College	Sai House 167 Imperial Dr, Harrow, Middlesex HA2 7JP	020 8966 9900	020 8429 5639	Mr Selva Pankaj	310-6080	11–19	102	
TCS Tutorial College	Fitzgerald House (Main academic campus), Harrow, Middlesex HA3 8ES	020 8909 1432	020 8909 1466	Dr R. Antoine	310-6082	11–19	60	ID

Havering

School name	Address	Tel	Fax	Headteacher	Ref	Ages	Pupils	Other
Immanuel School	Havering Grange Centre, Havering Rd North, Romford, Essex RM1 4HR	01708 764449		Miss Fiona Norcross	311-6060	3–16	127	Ch
Noak Hill School	Church Rd, Noak Hill, Romford, Essex RM4 1LD	01708 378751		Mr Phil Anderson	311-6062	12–17	38	Ch
Raphael Independent School	Park La, Hornchurch, Essex RM11 1XY	01708 744735		Mr N.W. Malicka	311-6057	4–16	130	ND

Hillingdon

School name	Address	Tel	Fax	Headteacher	Ref	Ages	Pupils	Other
ACS Hillingdon International School	108 Vine La, Hillingdon, Uxbridge, Middlesex UB10 0BE	01895 259771	01895 256974	Mrs Ginger G. Apple	312-6060	4–19	582	ND
Northwood College	Maxwell Rd, Northwood, Middlesex HA6 2YE	01923 825446	01923 836526	Ms R. Mercer	312-6001	3–19	799	G
St Helen's School	Eastbury Rd, Northwood, Middlesex HA6 3AS	01923 843210	01923 843211	Mrs M. Morris	312-6004	3–18	1144	G R

Hounslow

School name	Address	Tel	Fax	Headteacher	Ref	Ages	Pupils	Other
The Arts Educational School at Cone Ripman House	14 Bath Rd, Turnham Green Station, Chiswick, London W4 1LY	020 8987 6600	020 8987 6601	Mr Robert Luckham	313-6064	11–16	145	
The Eden SDA School	St Georges Hall, Green Dragon La, Brentford, Middlesex TW8 0LR	020 8568 7756		Mrs L. Osei	313-6070	5–18	60	
International School of London	139 Gunnersbury Ave, London W3 8LG	020 8992 5823	020 8993 7012	Ms E. Whelen	313-6063	4–16	286	
Oak Heights	3 Red Lion Ct, Hounslow, Middlesex TW3 1JS	020 8577 1827	020 8577 1827	Mrs Roswitha Akinola	313-6081	11–18	27	

Islington

School name	Address	Tel	Fax	Headteacher	Ref	Ages	Pupils	Other
Italia Conti Academy of Theatre Arts	23 Goswell Rd, London EC1M 7AJ	020 7608 0047	020 7253 1430	Mr C. Vote	206-6162	10-16	295	ID
St Paul's Steiner School	1 St Pauls Rd, Islington, London N1 2QH	020 7226 4454	020 7226 6062		206-6379	2-14	168	

Kensington and Chelsea

School name	Address	Tel	Fax	Headteacher	Ref	Ages	Pupils	Other
Ashbourne Independent School	17 Old Court Pl, London W8 4PL	020 7937 3858	020 7937 2207	Mr M.J. Hatchard-kirby	207-6348	13-16	160	
Collingham	23 Collingham Gdns, London SW5 0HL	020 7244 7414		Mr G. Hattee	207-6362	13-19	165	
David Game College	69 Notting Hill Gate, Kensington, London W11 3JS	020 7221 6665	020 7243 1730	Mr D. Game	207-6386	13-16	333	
Duff Miller College	59 Queen's Gate, London SW7 5JP	020 7225 0577	020 7589 5155	C.R. Denning	207-6262	13-16	186	
Instituto Espanol Vicente Canada Blanch	317 Portobello Rd, London W10 5SY	020 8969 2664	020 8968 9432	Mr S. Santos	207-6305	5-16	446	
Knightsbridge School	67 Pont St, London SW1X 0BD	020 7581 5044	020 7589 9055	Mr M. Giles	207-6316	2-16	130	Gk
The Lloyd Williamson School	12 Telford Rd, London W10 5SH	020 8962 0345	020 8962 0345	Lucy Williamson	207-6399	0-14	60	
Lycee Francais Charles de Gaulle	35 Cromwell Rd, London SW7 2DG	020 7584 6322		Mrs M. Valette	207-6028	3-16	3392	
Lycee Francais Charles de Gaulle (British Section)	35 Cromwell Rd, London SW7 2DG	020 7584 6322		Mrs Martine Valette	207-6391	3-19	223	
Mander Portman Woodward School	90-92 Queen's Gate, London SW7 5AB	020 7835 1355	020 7370 4769	Mr Steven D. Boyes	207-6363	14-16	434	
More House School	22-24 Pont St, Chelsea, London SW1X 0AA	020 7235 2855	020 7259 6782	Mrs L. Falconer	207-6202	11-16	177	G RC
Queen's Gate School	133 Queen's Gate, Kensington, London SW7 5LE	020 7589 3587	020 7584 7691	Mr A. Holyoak	207-6026	3-16	417	G
Southbank International School	36-38 Kensington Park Rd, London W11 3BU	020 7229 8230	020 7229 3784	Mr Terrence Hedger	207-6383	3-19	464	
Tabernacle School	210 Latimer Rd, London W10 6QY	08702 408207	08702 408207	Mrs P. Wilson	207-6396	3-18	44	Ch
The Walmer Road School	221 Walmer Rd, London W11 4EY	020 7229 2928	020 7313 5258	Ms V. Whiteford	207-6402	14-16	3	

Kingston upon Thames

School name	Address	Tel	Fax	Headteacher	Ref	Ages	Pupils	Other
Canbury School	Kingston Hill, Kingston Upon Thames, Surrey KT2 7LN	020 8549 8622	020 8974 6018	Mr Robin Metters	314-6068	11-16	65	
Kingston Grammar School	London Rd, Kingston Upon Thames, Surrey KT2 6PY	020 8546 5875	020 8974 5177	Mr C.D. Baxter	314-6067	10-19	745	Ch
Marymount International School	George Rd, Kingston Upon Thames, Surrey KT2 7PE	020 8949 0571	020 8336 2485	Sister Kathleen Fagan	314-6058	10-16	233	R RC
Shrewsbury House School	107 Ditton Rd, Surbiton, Surrey KT6 6RL	020 8399 3066	020 8339 9529	Mr C.M. Ross	314-6002	7-14	295	
Surbiton High School	Surbiton Cres, Kingston Upon Thames, Surrey KT1 2JT	020 8546 5245	020 8547 0026	Dr Jennifer Longhurst	314-6003	5-16	1227	Ch

Lambeth

School name	Address	Tel	Fax	Headteacher	Ref	Ages	Pupils	Other
Beechwood School	55 Leigham Court Rd, Streatham, London SW16 2NJ	020 8677 8778	020 7677 5041	Mrs M. Marshall	208-6366	5-14	107	
Streatham and Clapham High School	42 Abbotswood Rd, Streatham, London SW16 1AW	020 8677 8400	020 8677 2001	Mrs S. Mitchell	208-6311	3-19	712	G
Waldorf School of South West London	Woodfields, Abbotswood Rd, Streatham, London SW16 1AP	020 8769 6587	020 8677 5334	Ms Pat Hague	208-6344	3-15	81	

Lewisham

School name	Address	Tel	Fax	Headteacher	Ref	Ages	Pupils	Other
St Dunstan's College	Stanstead Rd, London SE6 4TY	020 8516 7200	020 8516 7300	Mrs J. Davies	209-6032	4-16	918	CE
Schoolhouse Education	10 St Johns Vale, Lewisham, London SE8 4EW	020 8691 7102	020 8691 7961	Mrs Lynda Smith	209-6365	14-16	23	

School name	Address	Tel	Fax	Headteacher	Ref	Ages	Pupils	Other
Sydenham High School GDST	19 Westwood Hill, London SE26 6BL	020 8768 8000	020 8768 8002	Mrs Kathryn E. Pullen	209-6309	5–16	672	G ND

Merton

School name	Address	Tel	Fax	Headteacher	Ref	Ages	Pupils	Other
King's College School	Southside, Wimbledon Common, London SW19 4TT	020 8255 5300	020 8255 5359	Mr A.C.V. Evans	315-6000	7–18	1215	Ch
The Norwegian School in London	28 Arterberry Rd, Wimbledon, London SW20 8AH	020 8947 6617		Mrs Kirsti H. Jacobsen	315-6072	3–16	101	Mu
Wimbledon High School	Mansel Rd, London SW19 4AB	020 8971 0900	020 8944 1989	Mrs Pamela Wilkes	315-6071	4–16	898	Ch

Newham

School name	Address	Tel	Fax	Headteacher	Ref	Ages	Pupils	Other
Azhar Academy	235a Romford Rd, Forest Gate, London E7 9HL	020 8534 5959	020 8534 5960	Mrs R. Rehman	319-6064	11–16	221	G Mu
Imam Zakaria Academy	Romford Rd, Forestgate, London E7 8AB	020 8534 8672		Mr Mian M. Aslam	316-6063	5–14	158	Mu
London Christian Learning Centre	Brickfields Christian Centre, Welfare Raod, London E15 4HT	020 8519 7579		Rev Ricardo D. Bolus JR	316-6067	4–16	12	Ch
Promised Land Academy	St Cedds Hall, Webb Gdns, London E13 8SR	020 8471 3939		Rev Allan Coote	316-6068	4–16	12	Ch

Redbridge

School name	Address	Tel	Fax	Headteacher	Ref	Ages	Pupils	Other
Bancrofts School	611–627 High Rd, Woodford Green, Essex IG8 0RF	020 8505 4821	020 8559 0032	Dr Peter Scott	317-6063	11–16	758	
Cranbrook College	34 Mansfield Rd, Ilford, Essex IG1 3BD	020 8554 1757	020 8518 0317	Mr Andrew Moss	317-6054	4–16	191	B
Park School for Girls	20–22 Park Ave, Ilford, Essex IG1 4RS	020 8554 2466	020 8554 3003	Mrs N. O'Brien	317-6061	6–19	214	G

Richmond upon Thames

School name	Address	Tel	Fax	Headteacher	Ref	Ages	Pupils	Other
The German School	Douglas Hse, Petersham Rd, Petersham, Richmond, Surrey TW10 7AH	020 8940 2510	020 8332 7446	Mrs M. Balkenhd	318-6070	3–19	690	
Hampton School	Hanworth Rd, Hampton, Middlesex TW12 3HD	020 8979 5526	020 8941 7368	Mr B.R. Martin	318-6071	2–19	1270	
The Harrodian School	Lonsdale Rd, London SW13 9QN	020 8748 6117	020 8563 7327	Mr James Hooke	318-6078	4–17	874	
King's House School	68 King's Rd, Richmond, Surrey TW10 6ES	020 8940 1878	020 8939 2501	Stephanie C. Piper	318-6001	4–14	390	B
The Lady Eleanor Holles School	Hanworth Rd, Hampton, Middlesex TW12 3HF	020 8979 1601	020 8941 8291	Mrs G. Low	318-6002	7–18	853	G CE
The Royal Ballet School	White Lodge, Richmond Pk, Richmond, Surrey TW10 5HR	020 8392 8000	020 8392 8037	Mrs Pippa Hogg	318-6074	11–19	203	R
St Catherine's School	Cross Deep, Twickenham, Middlesex TW1 4QJ	020 8891 2898	020 8744 9629	Mrs Zelma Braganza	318-6008	3–17	330	RC
St James Independent School for Boys	19 Cross Deep, Heath Rd, Twickenham, Middlesex TW1 4QG	020 8892 2002	020 8892 4442	Mr David Boddy	318-6080	10–19	287	B R
St Paul's School	Lonsdale Rd, Barnes, London SW13 9JT	020 8748 9162	020 8746 5353	Dr G.M. Stephen	318-6066	7–16	1275	B R CE
The Swedish School	82 Lonsdale Rd, London SW13 9JS	020 8741 1751		Mr J. Drackenberg	318-6076	3–16	209	

Southwark

School name	Address	Tel	Fax	Headteacher	Ref	Ages	Pupils	Other
Alleyn's School	Townley Rd, London SE22 8SU	020 8557 1500	020 8557 1462	Dr Colin Diggory	210-6312	4–16	1141	CE
Dulwich College	Dulwich, London SE21 7LD	020 8693 3601	020 8693 6319	Mr G.G. Able	210-6000	2–16	1680	R
Dulwich College Preparatory School	42 Alleyn Pk, London SE21 7AA	020 8670 3217	020 8766 7586	Mr G. Marsh	210-6001	2–14	826	B R

4

School name	Address	Tel	Fax	Headteacher	Ref	Ages	Pupils	Other
The From Boyhood to Manhood Foundation	1 Newest Cl, London SE15 6EF	020 7703 6415	020 7703 9479	Decima Suamona Francis	210-6394	12–16	16	
James Allen's Girls' School	East Dulwich Gr, London SE22 8TE	020 8693 1181	020 8693 7842	Mrs M. Gibbs	210-6002	5–16	1042	G CE

Sutton

School name	Address	Tel	Fax	Headteacher	Ref	Ages	Pupils	Other
Homefield Preparatory School	Western Rd, Sutton, Surrey SM1 2TE	020 8642 0965	020 8770 1668	Mr P.R. Mowbray	319-6001	2–14	415	B Ch
Stowford College	95 Brighton Rd, Sutton, Surrey SM2 5SJ	020 8661 9444	020 8661 6136	Mr R.J. Shakespeare	319-6070	6–16	99	Ch
Surrey Hills School	Little Woodcote Centre, Telegraph Track, Off Woodmansterne La., Carshalton, Surrey SM5 4AZ	020 8773 9966	020 8647 7101	Mr T.M. Lynes	319-6073	11–17	64	Ch
Sutton High School	55 Cheam Rd, Sutton, Surrey SM1 2AX	020 8642 0594	020 8642 2014	Mr S.J. Callaghan	319-6069	4–16	767	G ND

Tower Hamlets

School name	Address	Tel	Fax	Headteacher	Ref	Ages	Pupils	Other
Darul Hadis Latifiah	1 Cornwall Ave, London E2 0HW	020 8980 2673	020 7709 8540	Maulana M. Hussain	211-6389	11–19	111	B Mu
Jamiatul Ummah School	56 Bigland St, London E1 2ND	020 7790 7878	020 7790 2005	Abdur Rahman Madani	211-6387	11–16	134	B Mu
London East Academy and Muslim Centre	46 Whitechapel Rd, Whitechapel, London E1 1JX	020 7650 3070	020 7650 3071	A.M. Faradhi	211-6394	11–16	96	B Mu
London Islamic School	18–22 Damien St, London E1 2HX	020 7265 9667	020 7790 5536	Mr Abdul Hadi	211-6390	11–16	117	B Mu
Madani Secondary Girls' School	Myrdle St, London E1 1HL	020 7377 1992	020 7377 1992	F. Liyawdeen	211-6383	11–18	221	G Mu
Mazahirul Uloom School	241–243 Mile End Rd, Stepney, London E1 4AA	020 7790 9806	020 7790 9806	Imadur Rahman	211-6391	11–16	112	B Mu

Waltham Forest

School name	Address	Tel	Fax	Headteacher	Ref	Ages	Pupils	Other
Forest School	College Pl, Snaresbrook, London E17 3PY	020 8520 1744	020 8520 3656	Mr A.G. Boggis	320-6000	4–16	1210	R CE
Lantern of Knowledge Secondary School	30–36 Lindley Rd, Leyton, London E10 6QT	020 8539 5183		Mr Irfan Sidyot	320-6501	10–16	38	B Mu
Normanhurst School	68–74 Station Rd, Chingford, London E4 7BA	020 8529 4307	020 8524 7737	Mr P.J. Williams	320-6059	2–16	220	MF

Wandsworth

School name	Address	Tel	Fax	Headteacher	Ref	Ages	Pupils	Other
Emanuel School	Battersea Rise, London SW11 1HS	020 8870 4171	020 8877 1424	Mr Mark Hanley-Browne	212-6292	10–19	664	CE
Hall School Wimbledon	Stroud Cres, Putney Vale, London SW15 3EQ	020 8788 2370	020 8788 2121	Mr T.J. Hobbs	212-6390	4–16	534	
Ibstock Place School	Clarence La., Roehampton, London SW15 5PY	020 8876 9991	020 8878 4897	Mrs A. Sylvester-Johnson	212-6040	3–18	819	
Putney High School	35 Putney Hill, London SW15 6BH	020 8788 4886	020 8789 8068	Dr Denise Lodge	212-6310	4–18	856	G
Putney Park School	Woodborough Rd, London SW15 6PY	020 8788 8316	020 8780 2376	Mrs Ruth Mann	212-6203	4–16	261	
Thames Christian College	The Hornsby Centre, Wye St, London SW11 2HB	020 7228 3933	020 7924 1112	Mr S. Holsgrove	212-6403	11–16	91	Ch

Westminster

School name	Address	Tel	Fax	Headteacher	Ref	Ages	Pupils	Other
The American School in London	1 Waverley Pl, London NW8 0NP	020 7449 1200	020 7449 1352	Mr William C. Mules	213-6215	4–18	1334	
Bales College	2j Kilburn La, London W10 4AA	020 8960 5899	020 8960 8269	Mr W.B. Moore	213-6384	13–16	71	R
Davies Laing and Dick College	100 Marylebone La, London W1U 2QB	020 7935 8411	020 7935 0755	Ms E. Rickards	213-6391	14–19	346	
Francis Holland School	39 Graham Terr, London SW1W 8JF	020 7730 2971	020 7823 4066	Miss S.J. Pattenden	213-6046	4–16	459	G CE
Francis Holland School	Clarence Gate, Ivor Pl, London NW1 6XR	020 7723 0176	020 7706 1522	Mrs Vivienne Durham	213-6037	11–16	428	G CE
International Community School	4 York Terr East, Regents Pk, London NW1 4PT	020 7935 1206	020 7935 7915	Mr P. Hurd	213-6304	3–19	191	
Lansdowne College	40–44 Bark Pl, Bayswater, London W2 4AT	020 7616 4400	020 7616 4401	Mr H. Templeton	213-6389	15–16	199	
Portland Place School	56–58 Portland Pl, London W1B 1NJ	020 7307 8700	020 7436 2676	Mr Richard Tilston Walker	213-6386	11–18	330	
Queen's College London	43–49 Harley St, London W1G 8BT	020 7291 7000	020 7291 7090	Miss M.M. Connell	213-6036	3–18	536	G CE
Sylvia Young Theatre School	Rossmore Rd, Marylebone, London NW1 6NJ	020 7402 0673	020 7723 1040	Ms Frances Chave	213-6319	10–16	154	R
Westminster Abbey Choir School	Dean's Yard, London SW1P 3NY	020 7222 6151	020 7222 1548	Mr J. Milton	213-6044	7–14	30	B R CE
Westminster Cathedral Choir School	Ambrosden Ave, London SW1P 1QH	020 7798 9081	020 7630 7209	Mr John Browne	213-6197	8–14	137	B R RC
Westminster School	Little Dean's Yard, London SW1P 3PF	020 7963 1042	020 7963 1006	Dr M.S. Spurrr	213-6047	12–19	733	R CE
Westminster Under School	27 Vincent Sq, Pimlico, London SW1P 2NN	020 7821 5788	020 7821 0458	Mr J.P. Edwards	213-6182	7–14	264	B CE

North East

Darlington

School name	Address	Tel	Fax	Headteacher	Ref	Ages	Pupils	Other
Hurworth House School	38 The Green, Hurworth-on-Tees, Darlington, County Durham DL2 2AD	01325 720645	01325 720122	Mr C.R.T. Fenwick	841-6001	3–16	178	B
Polam Hall School	Grange Rd, Darlington, County Durham DL1 5PA	01325 463383	01325 383539	Miss M. Green	841-6000	3–19	414	G R

Durham

School name	Address	Tel	Fax	Headteacher	Ref	Ages	Pupils	Other
Barnard Castle School	Newgate, Barnard Castle, County Durham DL12 8UN	01833 690222	01833 638985	Mr D.H. Ewart	840-6003	5–16	736	R Ch
Durham High School for Girls	Farewell Hall, South Rd, Durham, Co Durham DH1 3TB	0191 384 3226	0191 386 7381	Mrs A. Templeman	840-6004	3–16	616	G CE
Durham School	Durham, Co Durham DH1 4SZ	0191 386 4783	0191 383 1025	Mr N.G. Kern	840-6000	3–18	556	R CE
Include – Durham Bridge Year 10/11	Dawden Community Centre, Alexandra St, Dawden, Seaham, Co Durham SR7 7NQ	01388 776911		Mrs Lisa Varadinekova	840-6007	14–16	19	G

Gateshead

School name	Address	Tel	Fax	Headteacher	Ref	Ages	Pupils	Other
Gateshead Jewish Boarding School	10 Rydal St, Gateshead, Tyne and Wear NE8 1HG	0191 477 1431	0191 477 1432	Rabbi M. Kupetz	390-6002	10–16	99	B Je
Gateshead Jewish High School for Girls	6 Gladstone Terr, Gateshead, Tyne and Wear NE8 4DY	0191 477 3471		Rabbi D. Bowden	390-6005	11–16	138	G Je

4

Middlesbrough

School name	Address	Tel	Fax	Headteacher	Ref	Ages	Pupils	Other
Moordale Academy	Sotherbury Hse, Sotherbury Rd, Middlesbrough, Cleveland TS3 8BS	01642 224960		Steven Waugh Myton	806-6001	11–16	26	

Newcastle upon Tyne

School name	Address	Tel	Fax	Headteacher	Ref	Ages	Pupils	Other
Central Newcastle High School	Eskdale Terr, Newcastle upon Tyne, Tyne and Wear NE2 4DS	0191 281 1768	0191 281 3267	Mrs Hilary French	391-6034	3–19	927	G
Dame Allan's Boys' School	Fowberry Cres, Fenham, Newcastle upon Tyne, Tyne and Wear NE4 9YJ	0191 275 0608	0191 274 5428	Dr John Richard Hind	391-6035	8–19	520	B
Dame Allan's Girls' School	Fowberry Cres, Fenham, Newcastle upon Tyne, Tyne and Wear NE4 9YJ	0191 275 0708	0191 275 1502	Dr J.R. Hind	391-6036	8–19	410	G CE
La Sagesse School	North Jesmond, Newcastle upon Tyne, Tyne and Wear NE2 3RJ	0191 281 3474	0191 281 2721	Miss Linda Clark	391-6002	3–16	251	G
Newcastle-upon-Tyne Church High School	Tankerville Terr, Jesmond, Newcastle upon Tyne, Tyne and Wear NE2 3BA	0191 281 4306	0191 281 0806	Mrs L.G. Smith	391-6001	2–16	510	G Ch
Royal Grammar School	Eskdale Terr, Newcastle upon Tyne, Tyne and Wear NE2 4DX	0191 281 5711	0191 212 0392	Mr J.F.X. Miller	391-6037	7–19	1216	B
Westfield School	Oakfield Rd, Gosforth, Newcastle upon Tyne, Tyne and Wear NE3 4HS	0191 285 1948	0191 213 0734	Mrs M. Farndale	391-6012	3–19	334	G Ch

North Tyneside

School name	Address	Tel	Fax	Headteacher	Ref	Ages	Pupils	Other
The King's School	Huntington Pl, Tynemouth, North Shields, Tyne and Wear NE30 4RF	0191 258 5995	0191 296 3826	Mr Philip Cantwell	392-6000	4–16	893	CE

Northumberland

School name	Address	Tel	Fax	Headteacher	Ref	Ages	Pupils	Other
Longridge Towers School	Berwick-upon-Tweed, Northumberland TD15 2XQ	01289 307584	01289 302581	Mr A.E. Clemit	929-6001	4–16	329	R
Rock Hall School	Rock Village, Alnwick, Northumberland NE66 3SB	01665 579224	01665 579467	Mrs L. Bosanquet	929-6044	2–14	46	

Stockton-on-Tees

School name	Address	Tel	Fax	Headteacher	Ref	Ages	Pupils	Other
Red House School	36 The Green, Norton, Stockton-on-Tees TS20 1DX	01642 553370	01642 361031	Mr A. Taylor	808-6000	3–16	430	
Teesside Preparatory and High School	The Avenue, Eaglescliffe, Stockton-on-Tees, Cleveland TS16 9AT	01642 782095	01642 791207	Mr Thomas Packer	808-6001	3–16	380	ND
Yarm School	The Friarage, Yarm, Cleveland TS15 9EJ	01642 786023	01642 789216	Mr D.M. Dunn	808-6002	11–16	623	CE

Sunderland

School name	Address	Tel	Fax	Headteacher	Ref	Ages	Pupils	Other
Argyle House School	19–20 Thornhill Pk, Sunderland, Tyne and Wear SR2 7LA	0191 510 0726	0191 567 2209	Mr C. Johnson	394-6003	2–17	228	
Grindon Hall Christian School	Nookside, Sunderland, Tyne and Wear SR4 8PG	0191 534 4444	0191 534 4111	Mr C.J. Gray	394-6010	3–18	335	Ch
Sunderland High School	Mowbray Rd, Sunderland, Tyne and Wear SR2 8HY	0191 567 4984	0191 565 6510	Dr A.J. Slater	394-6008	2–19	556	Ch

North West

Blackburn with Darwen

School name	Address	Tel	Fax	Headteacher	Ref	Ages	Pupils	Other
Al-Islah Schools	108 Audley Range, Blackburn, Lancashire BB1 1TF	01254 261573	01254 671604	Mr Nizammuddin I. Makda	889-6004	4–16	178	Mu
Islamiyah School	Willow St, Little Harwood, Blackburn, Lancashire BB1 5NQ	01254 661259		Mrs Zarina Seedat	889-6007	11–16	224	G Mu
Jamiatul-Ilm Wal-Huda UK School	15 Moss St, Blackburn, Lancashire BB1 5HW	01254 673105		Mr A. Ahmed	889-6005	11–16	335	B R Mu
Markazul Uloom	Park Lee Rd, Blackburn, Lancashire BB2 3NY	01254 660026	01254 279406	Mrs Asiya Gajaria	889-6009	11–16	288	G R Mu
Queen Elizabeth's Grammar School	West Park Rd, Blackburn, Lancashire BB2 6DF	01254 686300	01254 692314	Dr David S. Hempsall	889-6001	5–16	784	Ch
Rawdhatul Uloom School	19 Dock St, Blackburn, Lancashire BB1 3AT	01254 670017		Mr A.W. Wasway	889-6003	5–14	91	Mu
Westholme School	Wilmar Lodge, Meins Rd, Blackburn, Lancashire BB2 6QU	01254 506070	01254 506080	Mrs L. Croston	889-6000	3–16	1087	G Ch

Blackpool

School name	Address	Tel	Fax	Headteacher	Ref	Ages	Pupils	Other
Arnold School	Lytham Rd, Blackpool, Lancashire FY4 1JG	01253 346391	01253 336250	Mr B.M. Hughes	890-6004	2–19	974	B R Mu

Bolton

School name	Address	Tel	Fax	Headteacher	Ref	Ages	Pupils	Other
Al Jamiah Al Islamiyyah at Mount St Joseph's Convent	Willows La, Deane, Bolton, Lancashire BL3 4HF	01204 361103		Mr S.J. Haneef	350-6017	11–19	145	G Mu
Bolton Muslim Girls' School	Swan La, Bolton, Lancashire BL3 6TQ	01204 840201	01204 849477	Idrish Patel	350-6016	11–16	374	G Mu
Bolton School Boys' Division	Chorley New Rd, Bolton, Lancashire BL1 4PA	01204 840201		Mr M.E.W. Brooker	350-6014	7–16	1075	B
Bolton School Girls' Division	Chorley New Rd, Bolton, Lancashire BL1 4PB	01204 840201	01204 434710	Miss E.J. Panton	350-6015	4–16	1347	G
Lord's Independent School	53 Manchester Rd, Bolton, Lancashire BL2 1ES	01204 523731		Mrs Anne Ainsworth	350-6000	11–16	89	
Madrasatul Imam Muhammad Zakariya	Keswick St, Bolton, Lancashire BL1 8LX	01204 384434		Mrs Amena Sader	350-6018	11–16	114	G Mu

Bury

School name	Address	Tel	Fax	Headteacher	Ref	Ages	Pupils	Other
Bury Grammar School (Boys)	Tenterden St, Bury, Lancashire BL9 0HN	0161 797 2700	0161 763 4655	Rev Steven Harvey	351-6008	7–18	764	B
Bury Grammar School (Girls)	Bridge Rd, Bury, Lancashire BL9 0HH	0161 797 2808	0161 763 4658	Mrs Roberta Georghiou	351-6009	4–16	1031	ND
Darul Uloom Al Arabiya Al Islamiya	Holcombe Hall, Bury, Lancashire BL8 4NG	01706 826106	01706 827907	Mr A.R. Limbada	351-6007	12–16	320	B R Mu

Cheshire

School name	Address	Tel	Fax	Headteacher	Ref	Ages	Pupils	Other
Abbey Gate College	Saighton Grange, Chester, Cheshire CH3 6EN	01244 332077	01244 335510	E.W. Mitchell	875-6018	5–16	436	B
Alderley Edge School for Girls	Wilmslow Rd, Alderley Edge, Cheshire SK9 7QE	01625 583028	01625 590271	K. Mills	875-6012	2–16	598	G RC
Beech Hall School	Beech Hall Dr, Macclesfield, Cheshire SK10 2EG	01625 422192	01625 502424	Mark Atkins	875-6008	1–16	265	Ch
Blacon Young Peoples Project co Blacon Library	Western Ave, Chester, Cheshire CH1 5QY	01244 371716	01244 382095	Louise Jane Davey	875-6030	14–16	6	

School name	Address	Tel	Fax	Headteacher	Ref	Ages	Pupils	Other
Cransley School	Belmont Hall, Northwich, Cheshire CW9 6HN	01606 891747	01606 892122	J.E. Jones	875-6017	5–16	187	
The Grange School	Bradburns La, Northwich, Cheshire CW8 1LU	01606 74007	01606 784581	C.P. Jeffery	875-6005	4–18	1139	
Greater Grace School of Christian Education	Church La, Chester, Cheshire CH2 4BE	01244 851797		Sandrine Goodey	875-6027	5–18	13	Ch
Hammond School	Mannings La, Chester, Cheshire CH2 4ES	01244 305350	01244 305351	M.P. Dangerfield	875-6016	10–16	218	R
The King's School	Cumberland St, Macclesfield, Cheshire SK10 1DA	01625 260000	01625 260009	S. Coyne	875-6007	3–19	1453	CE
The King's School	Wrexham Rd, Chester, Cheshire CH4 7QL	01244 689500	01244 689501	T.J. Turvey	875-6019	7–19	915	CE
Mostyn House School	The Parade, Neston, Cheshire CH64 6SG	0151 336 1010	0151 353 1040	Miss Lloyd	875-6009	3–19	197	
The Queen's School	City Walls Rd, Chester, Cheshire CH1 2NN	01244 312078	01244 321507	C.M. Buckley	875-6020	5–16	571	G Ch
Sandbach School	Crewe Rd, Sandbach, Cheshire CW11 3NS	01270 758870	01270 764787	P.R. Wiles	875-6010	11–19	1169	B

Cumbria

School name	Address	Tel	Fax	Headteacher	Ref	Ages	Pupils	Other
Austin Friars St Monica's	Etterby Scaur, Carlisle, Cumbria CA3 9PB	01228 528042	01228 810327	Mr Christopher Lumb	909-6032	11–19	514	RC
Casterton School	Kirkby Lonsdale, Carnforth, Lancashire LA6 2SG	01524 279200	01524 271146	Dr Peter McLaughlin	909-6005	5–16	339	R CE
Chetwynde School	Rating La, Barrow-in-Furness, Cumbria LA13 0NY	01229 824210	01229 871440	Mrs Isobel E. Nixon	909-6025	3–16	397	Ch
Harecroft Hall School	Gosforth, Seascale, Cumbria CA20 1HS	01946 725220	01946 725885	Mr P. Block	909-6002	3–16	74	R
Lime House School	Holm Hill, Dalston, Carlisle, Cumbria CA5 7BX	01228 710225	01228 710508	Mr N. Rice	909-6001	3–18	257	R ND
St Bees School	St Bees, Cumbria CA27 0DS	01946 828000	01946 823657	Mr P.J. Capes	909-6003	10–16	300	R CE
Sedbergh School	Malim Lodge, Sedbergh, Cumbria LA10 5RY	01539 620535	01539 621301	Mr C.H. Hirst	909-6026	12–16	446	R CE
Windermere St Anne's School	Browhead, Patterdale Rd, Windermere, Cumbria LA23 1NW	01539 446164	01539 446803	Mr Alan M. Graham	909-6008	2–19	413	R

Lancashire

School name	Address	Tel	Fax	Headteacher	Ref	Ages	Pupils	Other
Clifton Tutorial Centre	293 Clifton Dr South, St Annes, Lytham St Annes, Lancashire FY8 1HN	01253 725815		Mr Welsby	888-6028	14–16	15	
Emmanuel Christian School	Fylde Community, Normoss Rd, Blackpool, Lancashire FY3 0BE	01253 882873	01253 892022	Mr M.L. Derry	888-6053	5–16	61	Ch
Ghausia Girls' High School	1–3 Cross St, Nelson, Lancashire BB9 7EN	01282 699214	01282 619011	Mr Jamil Mohammed	888-6033	11–16	51	G Mu
Jamea Al Kauthar	Ashton Rd, Lancaster, Lancashire LA1 5AJ	01524 389898	01524 389333	Miss Ayesha Uddin	888-6034	11–16	417	G R Mu
King Edward VII and Queen Mary School	Clifton Dr South, Lytham St Annes, Lancashire FY8 1DT	01253 784100	01253 784150	Mr R.J. Karling	888-6014	4–16	683	
The Kingsfold Christian School	Moss La, Hesketh Bank, Preston, Lancashire PR4 6AA	01772 813824		Mr S.D. Lamin	888-6019	4–16	48	Ch
Kingswood College	Scarisbrick Hall, Southport Rd, Scarisbrick, Ormskirk, Lancashire L40 9RQ	01704 880200	01704 880032	Mr E.J. Borowski	888-6006	2–16	309	
Kirkham Grammar School	Ribby Rd, Kirkham, Preston, Lancashire PR4 2BH	01772 671079	01772 672747	Mr D.R. Walker	888-6013	3–19	970	R ND
Maharishi School of the Age of Enlightenment	Cobbs Brow La, Lathom, Ormskirk, Lancashire L40 6JJ	01695 729912	01695 729030	Mr Derek Cassells	888-6018	4–16	69	
Moorland School Limited	Ribblesdale Ave, Clitheroe, Lancashire BB7 2JA	01200 423833	01200 429339	Mr Paul Smith	888-6002	2–17	281	R
Oakhill College	Wiswell La, Whalley, Clitheroe, Lancashire BB7 9AF	01254 823546	01254 822662	Mr P.S. Mahon	888-6012	5–16	264	RC
Preston Muslim Girls' High School	36 Deepdale Mill St, Meadow St, Preston, Lancashire PR1 5BY	01772 651906		Mr Y. Seedat	888-6021	11–16	133	G Mu
Rivington Park Independent School	Knowle Hse, Rivington, Lane, Horwich, Lancashire BL6 7RX	01204 669332	01204 696891	Mr Michael Ruaux	888-6031	1–16	87	
Rossall School	Broadway, Fleetwood, Lancashire FY7 8JW	01253 774201	01253 772052	Mr T.J. Wilbur	888-6044	2–16	656	R CE
The St Anne's College Grammar School	293 Clifton Dr South, Lytham St Annes, Lancashire FY8 1HN	01253 725815	01253 782250	Mr S.R. Welsby	888-6001	5–16	133	R
Stonyhurst College	Stonyhurst, Clitheroe, Lancashire BB7 9PZ	01254 826345	01254 826732	Mr A.J.F. Aylward	888-6000	12–19	443	R RC
Whinfield School	317 Golden Hill La, Earnshaw Bridge, Leyland, Lancashire PR25 2YJ	01772 455378	01772 860390	Mr K. Cragg	888-6054	11–17	21	

Liverpool

School name	Address	Tel	Fax	Headteacher	Ref	Ages	Pupils	Other
Auckland College	65–67 Parkfield Rd, Liverpool, Merseyside L17 4LE	0151 727 0083		Ms G. Akaraonye	341-6046	7–18	142	
Christian Fellowship School	Overbury St, Liverpool, Merseyside L7 3HL	0151 709 1642	0151 709 6164	Mr P. Williamson	341-6040	5–16	192	Ch
Clarendon College	Garston Old Rd, Liverpool L19 9AF	0151 427 3911		Mrs P. Thornton	341-6081	3–16	8	N Ch
Liverpool College	Queen's Dr, Liverpool, Merseyside L18 8BG	0151 724 4000	0151 729 0105	Mr Brian Christian	341-6000	3–18	882	CE
Riverside Study Centre	Stretton Way, Liverpool L36 6JF	0151 480 4000		Mr P. Devenish	341-6051	11–17	37	Ch

Manchester

School name	Address	Tel	Fax	Headteacher	Ref	Ages	Pupils	Other
Abbey College	5–7 Cheapside, Manchester M2 4WG	0161 817 2700	0161 817 2705	Mrs J. Thomas	352-6044	14–16	168	Ch
Beis Rochel Girls' School	1–7 Seymour Rd, Manchester, Lancashire M8 5BQ	0161 795 1830	0161 792 3446	Mrs E. Krausz	352-6050	5–16	243	G
Chethams School of Music	Long Millgate, Manchester, Lancashire M3 1SB	0161 834 9644	0161 839 3609	Mrs Claire Hickman	352-6021	8–19	292	R
Crescent Community High School for Girls	23 Dennison Rd, Victoria Pk, Rusholme, Manchester M14 5DX	0161 256 2652	0161 256 2652	Mrs Mary Ann Kabir Usman	352-6058	11–18	103	G Mu
Etz Chaim School at The Belmont	89 Middleton Rd, Crumpsall, Manchester, Lancashire M8 4JY	0161 740 6800	0161 720 9912	Rabbi Eli Cohen	352-6053	11–16	98	B
Kassim Darwish Grammar School for Boys	Hartley Hall, Alexandra Rd South, Chorlton-cum-Hardy, Manchester, Lancashire M16 8NH	0161 860 7676	0161 860 0011	Mrs Mona Mohamed	352-6049	11–16	164	B Mu
King of Kings School	142 Dantzic St, Manchester, Lancashire M4 4DN	0161 834 4214		Mrs B. Lewis	352-6037	3–18	26	Ch
Lighthouse Christian School	193 Ashley La, Moston, Manchester, Lancashire M9 4NQ	0161 205 0957	0161 256 3973	Mr Akintayo Akinyele	352-6046	5–14	19	Ch
The Manchester Grammar School	Old Hall La, Manchester M13 0XT	0161 224 7201	0161 257 2446	Dr C. Ray	352-6029	10–19	1393	B
Manchester High School for Girls	Grangethorpe Rd, Manchester M14 6HS	0161 224 0447	0161 224 6192	Mrs Christine Lee-Jones	352-6030	4–16	931	G
Manchester Islamic High School for Girls	55 High La, Chorlton, Manchester, Lancashire M21 9FA	0161 881 2127	0161 861 0534	Mrs A. Sessay	352-6040	11–16	236	G Mu
St Bede's College	Alexandra Pk, Manchester, Lancashire M16 8HX	0161 226 3323	0161 226 3813	Mr J. Byrne	352-6032	4–16	1144	RC
Withington Girls' School	Wellington Rd, Fallowfield, Manchester, Lancashire M14 6BL	0161 224 1077	0161 248 5377	Mrs J. Pickering	352-6033	7–16	647	G

Oldham

School name	Address	Tel	Fax	Headteacher	Ref	Ages	Pupils	Other
Hulme Grammar School for Boys	Chamber Rd, Oldham, Lancashire OL8 4BX	0161 624 4497	0161 652 4107	Mr K.E. Jones	353-6012	7–16	671	B
Hulme Grammar School for Girls	Chamber Rd, Oldham, Lancashire OL8 4BX	0161 624 2523	0161 620 0234	Miss M. Smolenski	353-6013	7–16	510	G ND

Rochdale

School name	Address	Tel	Fax	Headteacher	Ref	Ages	Pupils	Other
Beech House School	184 Manchester Rd, Rochdale, Lancashire OL11 4JQ	01706 646309	01704 860685	Mr K. Sartain	354-6001	3–16	287	
Emmanuel Christian School	Horse Carrs, Shawclough Rd, Rochdale, Lancashire OL12 6LG	01706 645643	01706 645643	Mr J. Holloway	354-6004	3–16	42	Ch
Rochdale Girls School	36 Taylor St, Rochdale, Lancashire OL12 0HX	01706 646642		Mr A. Razzak	354-6006	11–16	89	G Mu

Salford

School name	Address	Tel	Fax	Headteacher	Ref	Ages	Pupils	Other
Beis Hatalmud School	62 Wellington St West, Broughton, Salford, Lancashire M7 2FD	0161 708 0400	0161 708 0411	Rabbi M. Zahn	355-6054	11–16	20	B Je
Bnos Yisroel Schools	Leicester Rd, Salford, Lancashire M7 4DA	0161 792 3896	0161 792 7784	Rabbi R. Spitzer	355-6011	3–16	496	G Je

4

School name	Address	Tel	Fax	Headteacher	Ref	Ages	Pupils	Other
Bridgewater School	Drywood Hall, Worsley, Manchester, Lancashire M28 2WQ	0161 794 1463	0161 794 3519	Ms Geraldine Ann Shannon-Little	355-6005	3-19	519	B Je
Jewish Senior Boys' School	4 Newhall Rd, Salford, Lancashire M7 4EL	0161 708 9175		Mr M. Schwartz	355-6010	10-16	39	B Je
Mechinoh School	13 Upper Park Rd, Salford, Lancashire M7 4HY	0161 795 9275		Rabbi N. Baddiel	355-6020	11-16	64	B
New Harvest Learning Centre	194 Chapel St, Salford, Lancashire M3 6BY	0161 288 2622	0871 433 7688	Mrs Stephanie Davies	355-6037	4-18	14	Ch
OYY Lubavitch Girls' School	Beis Menachem, Park La, Broughton Pk, Salford, Lancashire M7 4JD	0161 795 0002		Mrs J. Hanson	355-6028	2-16	73	Je
Yeshivah Ohr Torah School	28 Broom La, Salford, Lancashire M7 4FX	0161 792 1230		Rabbi Y. Wind	355-6031	11-16	33	B Je

Sefton

School name	Address	Tel	Fax	Headteacher	Ref	Ages	Pupils	Other
Merchant Taylors' Boys' School	Liverpool Rd, Crosby, Liverpool, Merseyside L23 0QP	0151 949 9405	0151 928 0434	Mr D. Cook	343-6129	7-19	813	B
Merchant Taylors' School for Girls	Crosby, Crosby, Liverpool, Merseyside L23 5SP	0151 924 3140	0151 932 1461	Mrs Louise Anne Robinson	343-6130	4-18	897	G
St Mary's College	Everest Rd, Crosby, Liverpool, Merseyside L23 5TW	0151 924 3926	0151 932 0363	Mrs Jean Marsh	343-6128	1-18	875	RC
Streatham House School	Victoria Rd West, Blundellsands, Liverpool, Merseyside L23 8UQ	0151 924 1514	0151 931 2780	Mrs Clare Baxter	343-6001	2-16	124	

St Helens

School name	Address	Tel	Fax	Headteacher	Ref	Ages	Pupils	Other
Tower College	Mill La, Rainhill, Prescot, Merseyside L35 6NE	0151 426 4333	0151 426 3338	Miss R.J. Oxley	342-6001	2-17	611	Ch

Stockport

School name	Address	Tel	Fax	Headteacher	Ref	Ages	Pupils	Other
Cheadle Hulme School	Claremont Rd, Cheadle Hulme, Cheadle, Cheshire SK8 6EF	0161 488 3330	0161 488 3349	Mr Paul Dixon	356-6019	4-16	1317	
Covenant Christian School	48 Heaton Moor Rd, Heaton Moor, Stockport, Cheshire SK4 4NX	0161 432 3782		Mrs R. Slack	356-6021	5-16	32	Ch
Hillcrest Grammar School	Beech Ave, Stockport, Cheshire SK3 8HB	0161 480 0329	0161 476 2814	Mr D.K. Blackburn	356-6001	2-17	346	
Hulme Hall Grammar School	75 Hulme Hall Rd, Cheadle Hulme, Cheadle, Cheshire SK8 6LA	0161 485 3524	0161 485 5966	Mr P. Marland	356-6009	5-16	392	
Ramillies Hall School	Cheadle Hulme, Cheadle, Cheshire SK8 7AJ	0161 485 3804		Miss D.M. Patterson	356-6008	0-14	191	
Stockport Grammar School	Buxton Rd, Stockport, Cheshire SK2 7AF	0161 456 9000	0161 419 2407	Mr Andrew H. Chicken	356-6018	5-16	1452	

Tameside

School name	Address	Tel	Fax	Headteacher	Ref	Ages	Pupils	Other
Trinity School	Birbeck St, Stalybridge, Cheshire SK15 1SH	0161 303 0674	0161 304 7589	Mr W.R. Evans	357-6000	3-17	109	Ch

Trafford

School name	Address	Tel	Fax	Headteacher	Ref	Ages	Pupils	Other
Afifah High School For Girls	106-108 Stamford St, Old Trafford, Manchester M16 9LR	0161 227 9343		Mr H. Chunara	358-6018	11-16	37	G Mu
Christ The King School	The King's Centre, Raglan Rd, Sale, Cheshire M33 4AQ	0161 969 1906	0161 905 1586	Mr D. Baynes	358-6017	4-16	51	Ch
Culcheth Hall School	Ashley Rd, Altrincham, Cheshire WA14 2LT	0161 928 1862	0161 929 6893	Miss M. Stockwell	358-6000	2-16	186	
Mereside Education Trust	1 Parkside Rd, Sale, Manchester M33 3HT	0161 972 0049		T.J. Simpson	358-6019	11-17	61	Ch
North Cestrian Grammar School	Dunham Rd, Altrincham, Cheshire WA14 4AJ	0161 928 1856	0161 929 8657	Mr D.G. Vanstone	358-6003	11-16	283	ID

Wirral

School name	Address	Tel	Fax	Headteacher	Ref	Ages	Pupils	Other
Birkenhead High School	86 Devonshire Pl, Prenton, Merseyside CH43 1TY	0151 652 5777	0151 670 0639	Mrs C.H. Evans	344-6024	3–19	686	G ND
Birkenhead School	58 Beresford Rd, Oxton, Prenton, Merseyside CH43 2JD	0151 652 4014	0151 651 3091	Mr D.J. Clark	344-6023	3–19	673	B Ch
Highfield School	96 Bidston Rd, Oxton, Prenton, Merseyside CH43 6TW	0151 652 3708	0151 652 3708	Mrs S. Morris	344-6001	2–17	46	
Kingsmead School	Bertram Dr, Hoylake, Wirral, Merseyside CH47 0LL	0151 632 3156	0151 632 0302	Mr E.H. Bradby	344-6014	3–16	234	R Ch

South East

Bracknell Forest

School name	Address	Tel	Fax	Headteacher	Ref	Ages	Pupils	Other
Eagle House School	Crowthorne Rd, Sandhurst, Berkshire GU47 8PH	01344 772134	01344 779039	Mr S.J. Carder	867-6002	2–14	268	R
Heathfield St Mary's School	London Rd, Ascot, Berkshire SL5 8BQ	01344 898306	01344 890958	Mrs Frances King	867-6000	10–19	220	G R CE
The Licensed Victuallers' School	London Rd, Ascot, Berkshire SL5 8DR	01344 882770	01344 890648	Mr I. Mullins	867-6005	4–16	917	R
Wellington College	Crowthorne, Berkshire RG45 7PU	01344 444000	01344 444002	Dr Anthony Seldon	867-6001	13–16	750	B R CE

Brighton and Hove

School name	Address	Tel	Fax	Headteacher	Ref	Ages	Pupils	Other
Bellerbys College	44 Cromwell Rd, Hove, East Sussex BN3 3ER	01273 323374	01273 749322	Mr N. Addison	846-6009	14–16	609	R
Brighton and Hove High School	Montpelier Rd, Brighton, East Sussex BN1 3AT	01273 734112	01273 737120	Mrs Ann Greatorex	846-6014	3–16	660	G
Brighton College	Eastern Rd, Brighton, East Sussex BN2 0AL	01273 704200	01273 704204	Dr R.J. Cairns	846-6008	12–19	693	R CE
Brighton College Prep School	2 Walpole Rd, Brighton, East Sussex BN2 0EU	01273 704210	01273 704286	Mr Brian Melia	846-6015	7–14	297	CE
Brighton Steiner School Limited	Roedean Rd, Brighton, East Sussex BN2 5RA	01273 386300	01273 386313		846-6016	5–16	203	
Drive Preparatory School	5 The Drive, Hove, East Sussex BN3 3JE	01273 738444	01273 738444	Mrs S. Parkinson	846-6020	3–16	98	
K-BIS Theatre School	Clermont Hall, Brighton, East Sussex BN1 6SL	01273 564366	01273 564366	Ms M. King	846-6022	5–18	41	
Roedean School	Roedean Way, Brighton, East Sussex BN2 5RQ	01273 603181	01273 676722	Mrs Carolyn Shaw	846-6006	11–16	385	G R
St Aubyn's School	76 High St, Brighton, East Sussex BN2 7JN	01273 302170	01273 304004	Mr A. Gobat	846-6001	4–14	208	R
St Christopher's School	33 New Church Rd, Hove, East Sussex BN3 4AD	01273 735404	01273 747956	Mrs Heather Beeby	846-6011	3–14	241	
St Mary's Hall	Eastern Rd, Brighton, East Sussex BN2 5JF	01273 606061	01273 620782	Mrs S.M. Meek	846-6003	3–19	311	G R CE
Stonelands School of Ballet and Theatre Arts	170a Church Rd, Hove, East Sussex BN3 2DJ	01273 770445	01273 770444	Mrs D. Carteur	846-6017	5–16	45	

Buckinghamshire

School name	Address	Tel	Fax	Headteacher	Ref	Ages	Pupils	Other
Akeley Wood School	Akeley Wood, Buckingham, Buckinghamshire MK18 5AE	01280 814110		Mr J.C. Lovelock	825-6015	11–17	863	
Beachborough School	Westbury, Brackley, Northamptonshire NN13 5LB	01280 700071	01280 704839	Mr Jonathan Whybrow	825-6002	2–14	259	R Ch
Godstowe School	Shrubbery Rd, High Wycombe, Buckinghamshire HP13 6PR	01494 529273	01494 429001	Mr David Gainer	825-6007	2–14	292	R
Haydon Training Independent School	Slone Hse, 24–30 New St, Manor Pk, Aylesbury, Buckinghamshire HP20 2NL	01296 398469	01296 399501	Mrs T. Meacock	825-6034	15–16	15	
Holy Cross Convent School	Gold Hill East, Chalfont St Peter, Gerrards Cross, Buckinghamshire SL9 9DW	01753 895600		Mrs Margaret Shinkwin	825-6025	3–18	234	G RC

4

School name	Address	Tel	Fax	Headteacher	Ref	Ages	Pupils	Other
Pipers Corner School	Gt Kingshill, High Wycombe, Buckinghamshire HP15 6LP	01494 718255	01494 719806	Mrs V.M. Stattersfield	825-6017	3-19	499	G R CE
St Mary's School	Packhorse Rd, Gerrards Cross, Buckinghamshire SL9 8JQ	01753 883370	01753 890966	Mrs F.A. Balcombe	825-6006	3-18	321	G CE
Sefton Park School	School La, Stoke Poges, Buckinghamshire SL2 4QA	01753 662167	01753 662168	Mr Timothy Thorpe	825-6037	11-16	115	Ch
Stowe School	Stowe, Buckingham, Buckinghamshire MK18 5EH	01280 818000	01280 818181	Dr Anthony Wallersteiner	825-6001	12-19	619	R CE
Teikyo School (UK)	Framewood Rd, Wexham, Slough, Berkshire SL2 4QS	01753 663712	01753 663819	Mr Tokio Matsumoto	825-6013	15-18	50	R
Thornton College	Convent of Jesus and Mary, Thornton, Milton Keynes, Buckinghamshire MK17 0HJ	01280 812610	01280 824042	Miss A.T. Williams	825-6010	2-16	352	G R RC
Thorpe House School	Oval Way, Gerrards Cross, Buckinghamshire SL9 8QA	01753 882474	01753 889755	Mr A.F. Lock	825-6026	7-16	143	B CE
Wycombe Abbey School	Abbey Way, High Wycombe, Buckinghamshire HP11 1PE	01494 520381	01494 473836	Mrs P. Davies	825-6018	11-16	547	G R CE

East Sussex

School name	Address	Tel	Fax	Headteacher	Ref	Ages	Pupils	Other
Ashdown House School	Forest Row, East Sussex RH18 5JY	01342 822574	01342 824380	Mr A.R. Taylor	845-6001	7-14	145	R
Battle Abbey School	Battle Abbey, Battle, East Sussex TN33 0AD	01424 772385	01424 773573	Mr R.C. Clark	845-6018	2-18	330	R
Buckswood School	Broomham Hall, Rye Rd, Guestling, Hastings, East Sussex TN35 4LT	01424 813813	01825 812100	Mr T. Fish	845-6031	11-16	261	R
Claremont School	Baldslow, St Leonards-on-Sea, East Sussex TN37 7PW	01424 751555	01424 754310	Mr Ian Culley	845-6010	2-14	401	
Cumnor House School	Danehill, Haywards Heath, West Sussex RH17 7HT	01825 790347	01825 790910	Mr C. St J. Heinrich	845-6019	4-14	347	R CE
Darvell School	Darvell Bruderhof, Robertsbridge, East Sussex TN32 5DR	01580 883300	01580 883317	Mr Raphael Arnold Meier	845-6003	4-16	109	Ch
Eastbourne College	Old Wish Rd, Headmaster's Hse, Eastbourne, East Sussex BN21 4JX	01323 452300	01323 452327	Mr Simon Davies	845-6014	12-19	613	R Ch
Greenfields School	Priory Rd, Forest Row, East Sussex RH18 5JD	01342 822189	01342 825289	Mrs V. Tupholme	845-6017	2-19	151	R
Lewes Old Grammar School	High St, Lewes, East Sussex BN7 1XS	01273 472634	01273 476948	Mr R. Blewitt	845-6032	3-19	370	
Michael Hall School	Kidbrooke Pk, Forest Row, East Sussex RH18 5JA	01342 822275	01342 826593	E. Van Manen	845-6037	3-16	546	R
Moira House Girls' School	Upper Carlisle Rd, Eastbourne, East Sussex BN20 7TE	01323 644144	01323 649720	Mrs Lesley Watson	845-6015	2-16	388	G R Ch
St Andrew's School	Meads, Eastbourne, East Sussex BN20 7RP	01323 733203	01323 646860	Mr J.R.G. Griffith	845-6016	2-14	404	R CE
St Bede's Preparatory School	Duke's Dr, Eastbourne, East Sussex BN20 7XL	01323 734222		Mr C.P. Pyemont	845-6011	2-15	466	R
St Bede's School	The Dicker, Upper Dicker, Hailsham, East Sussex BN27 3QH	01323 843252	01323 442628	Mr S.W. Cole	845-6006	13-16	835	R
St Leonards-Mayfield School	The Old Palace, Mayfield, East Sussex TN20 6PH	01435 874600	01435 872627	Mrs J. Dalton	845-6035	11-19	435	G R RC
Vinehall School	Vinehall Rd, Mountfield, Robertsbridge, East Sussex TN32 5JL	01580 880413	01580 882119	Mrs Julie Robinson	845-6004	2-14	366	R
Walsh Manor School	Walshes Rd, Crowborough, East Sussex TN6 3RB	01892 610823		Miss Kimberley Bradford	845-6041	10-16	26	

Hampshire

School name	Address	Tel	Fax	Headteacher	Ref	Ages	Pupils	Other
Allbrook School	The Old School, Pitmore Rd, Allbrook, Eastleigh, Hants SO50 4LW	023 8061 6316	023 8061 6313	Mr Robert Ghinn	850-6080	11-16	79	Ch
Alton Convent School	Anstey La, Alton, Hampshire GU34 2NG	01420 82070	01420 541711	Mrs S. Kirkham	850-6073	2-17	476	RC
Ballard School	Fernhill La, New Milton, Hampshire BH25 5SU	01425 611153	01425 622099	Mr Stephen Duckitt	850-6012	2-16	531	CE
Bedales School	Church Rd, Steep, Petersfield, Hampshire GU32 2DP	01730 300100	01730 300500	Mr K. Budge	850-6007	3-19	725	R
Boundary Oak School	Roche Ct, Fareham, Hampshire PO17 5BL	01329 280955	01329 827656	Mr Basil Leslie Brown	850-6047	2-14	138	R ND
Brockwood Park School	Bramdean, Alresford, Hampshire SO24 0LQ	01962 771744	01962 771875	Mr B.W. Taylor	850-6069	14-16	69	R
Churcher's College	Ramshill, Petersfield, Hampshire GU31 4AS	01730 263033	01730 231437	Mr S.H.L. Williams	850-6040	4-16	918	
Ditcham Park School	Ditcham Pk, Petersfield, Hampshire GU31 5RN	01730 825659	01730 825070	Mrs Kathryn Morton	850-6049	5-16	350	
Durlston Court School	Becton La, Barton-on-Sea, New Milton, Hampshire BH25 7AQ	01425 610010	01425 622731	Mr David Wansey	850-6056	2-14	315	CE
Farleigh School	Red Rice, Andover, Hampshire SP11 7PW	01264 710766		Father Simon Everson	850-6015	3-14	411	R RC

School name	Address	Tel	Fax	Headteacher	Ref	Ages	Pupils	Other
Farnborough Hill	Farnborough Rd, Farnborough, Hampshire GU14 8AT	01252 545197	01252 513037	Miss J.M. Thomas	850-6020	11-16	494	G RC
Hampshire Collegiate School Atherley	Grove Pl, Upton La, Nursling, Southampton, Hampshire SO16 0AB	023 8074 1629	023 8074 1631	Mrs Maureen Bradley	850-6083	2-18	387	Ch
Hampshire Collegiate School, Embley Park	Embley Pk, Romsey, Hampshire SO51 6ZE	01794 512206	01794 518737	Mr D.F. Chapman	850-6035	3-16	839	R Ch
Hawley Place School	Fernhill Rd, Blackwater, Camberley, Surrey GU17 9HU	01276 32028	01276 609695	Mr T.G. Pipe	850-6046	2-16	368	Ch
Hordle Walhampton School Trust Limited	Lymington, Hampshire SO41 5ZG	01590 672013	01590 678498	Mr R.H.C. Phillips	850-6028	2-14	340	R CE
The King's School	Basingstoke Community Church, Sarum Hill, Basingstoke, Hampshire RG21 8SR	01256 467092	01256 473605	Mr David Robotham	850-6003	3-16	172	Ch
Kings School Senior	Lakesmere Hse, Allington La, Fair Oak, Eastleigh, Hampshire SO50 7DB	023 8060 0956	023 8060 0956	Mr Paul Johnson	850-6050	5-16	124	Ch
Lord Wandsworth College	Long Sutton, Hook, Hampshire RG29 1TB	01256 862201	01256 862563	Mr I.G. Power	850-6064	11-16	524	R ID
Meoncross School	Burnt House La, Stubbington, Fareham, Hampshire PO14 2EF	01329 662182	01329 664680	Mr C. Ford	850-6026	2-16	411	Ch
Moyles Court School	Moyles Ct, Ringwood, Hampshire BH24 3NF	01425 472856	01425 474715	Mr R. Dean	850-6048	3-16	170	R CE
Norman Court	West Tytherley, Salisbury, Wiltshire SP5 1NH	01980 862345	01980 862082	Mr K.N. Foyle	850-6001	2-14	242	R
Rookwood School	Weyhill Rd, Andover, Hampshire SP10 3AL	01264 352900	01264 325909	Mrs M. Langley	850-6011	3-16	357	R Ch
St Michael's School	Harts La, Burghclere, Newbury, Berkshire RG20 9JW	01635 278137	01635 278601	Father Frank Kurtz	850-6062	4-18	41	R
St Nicholas' School	Redfields Hse, Redfields La, Church Crookham, Fleet, Hampshire GU52 0RF	01252 850121	01252 850718	Mrs A. Whatmough	850-6036	2-16	381	G CE
St Swithun's School	Alresford Rd, Winchester, Hampshire SO21 1HA	01962 835700	01962 835779	Dr H.L. Harvey	850-6038	3-16	666	G R CE
Salesian College	Reading Rd, Farnborough, Hampshire GU14 6PA	01252 893000	01252 893032	Mr Patrick A. Wilson	850-6022	11-16	548	B RC
Sherfield School	Sherfield on Loddon, Hook, Hampshire RG27 0HT	01256 884800	01256 883172	Dr P. Preedy	850-6084	1-16	342	
Winchester College	College St, Winchester, Hampshire SO23 9NA	01962 621100	01962 621106	Dr Ralph Douglas Townsend	850-6037	12-19	687	B R Ch
Wykeham House School	East St, Fareham, Hampshire PO16 0BW	01329 280178	01329 823964	Mrs Lynn Clarke	850-6053	2-17	251	G

Isle of Wight

School name	Address	Tel	Fax	Headteacher	Ref	Ages	Pupils	Other
Priory School	Alverstone Manor, Luccombe Rd, Shanklin, Isle of Wight PO37 6RR	01983 861222		Ms E.K.K. D'Costa	921-6041	3-18	114	CE
Ryde School with Upper Chine	Queen's Rd, Ryde, Isle of Wight PO33 3BE	01983 562229	01983 614973	Dr N.J. England	921-6002	3-19	779	R CE

Kent

School name	Address	Tel	Fax	Headteacher	Ref	Ages	Pupils	Other
Ashford School	East Hill, Ashford, Kent TN24 8PB	01233 625171	01233 647185	Mr Michael Buchanan	886-6000	3-18	702	G R Ch
Bedgebury School	Bedgebury Pk, Goudhurst, Cranbrook, Kent TN17 2SH	01580 878143	01580 879136	Ms H. Moriarty	886-6051	2-19	333	G R CE
Beech Grove School	Beech Grove Bruderhof, Sandwich Rd, Nonington, Dover, Kent CT15 4HH	01304 842980	01304 843734	Chris Meier	886-6073	4-14	55	Ch
Beechwood Sacred Heart School	Pembury Rd, Tunbridge Wells, Kent TN2 3QD	01892 532747	01892 536164	Mr N.R. Beesley	886-6011	3-19	396	R RC
Benenden School	Cranbrook Rd, Benenden, Cranbrook, Kent TN17 4AA	01580 240592	01580 240280	Mrs C.M. Oulton	886-6002	10-19	503	G R
Bethany School	Goudhurst, Cranbrook, Kent TN17 1LB	01580 211273	01580 211151	Mr N. Dorey	886-6036	3-17	404	R
Canterbury Steiner School Ltd	Garlinge Grn, Chartham, Canterbury, Kent CT4 5RU	01227 738285	01227 731158		886-6052	3-17	243	Ch
CATS Canterbury (formerly Stafford House College)	Stafford Hse, 68 New Dover Rd, Canterbury, Kent CT1 3LQ	01227 866550	01227 866550	Ms Marie-Louise Banning	886-6075	15-16	165	R
Cobham Hall	Cobham, Gravesend, Kent DA12 3BL	01474 823371	01474 825902	Mrs Helen Davy	886-6044	11-18	197	G R
Combe Bank School	Sundridge, Sevenoaks, Kent TN14 6AE	01959 563720	01959 561997	Mrs R. Martin	886-6018	3-16	366	G
Co-Operative Independent College	Army Cadet Force Hall, Westwood Rd, Broadstairs, Kent CT10 2NT	07717 772502		Corron Osborn	886-6094	12-16	10	
Dover College	Effingham Cres, Dover, Kent CT17 9RH	01304 205969	01304 242208	Mr Stephen Jones	886-6003	4-18	320	R CE

4

School name	Address	Tel	Fax	Headteacher	Ref	Ages	Pupils	Other
Duke of York's Royal Military School	Guston, Dover, Kent CT15 5EQ	01304 245023	01304 245019	Mr J.A. Cummings	886-6056	11-16	483	R
Gad's Hill School	Higham, Rochester, Kent ME3 7PA	01474 822366	01474 822977	Mr D.G. Craggs	886-6007	3-16	368	
Grace School	Grace Hill, Folkestone, Kent CT20 1HE	01303 221952		Mrs Drion	886-6082	5-16	11	Ch
Holmewood House School	Barrow La, Langton Grn, Tunbridge Wells, Kent TN3 0EB	01892 860000	01892 863970	Mr A.S.R. Corbett	886-6012	3-14	531	R
Junior King's School	Milner Ct, Sturry, Canterbury, Kent CT2 0AY	01227 714000	01227 713171	Mr P.M. Wells	886-6061	3-14	398	R CE
Kent College (Canterbury)	Whitstable Rd, Canterbury, Kent CT2 9DT	01227 763231	01227 764777	Mr Gino Giovanni Carminati	886-6053	11-16	402	R
Kent College International Study Centre	Whitstable Rd, Canterbury, Kent CT2 9DT	01227 763231	01227 764777		886-6097	12-16	55	R Me
Kent College Pembury	Pembury, Tunbridge Wells, Kent TN2 4AX	01892 822006	01892 820221	Mrs Anne Upton	886-6009	11-19	349	G R Me
The King's School Canterbury	25 The Precincts, Canterbury, Kent CT1 2ES	01227 595510	01227 595595	Rev K. Wilkinson	886-6048	13-16	794	R CE
Linton Park School	3 Eccleston Rd, Tovil, Maidstone, Kent ME15 6QN	01622 356611	01622 356622	Mr J. Bruce	886-6104	11-17	101	Ch
The New Beacon School	Brittains La, Sevenoaks, Kent TN13 2PB	01732 452131	01732 459509	Mr R. Constantine	886-6017	4-14	391	B
Oakwood School	Life Church, Bowles Well Gdns, Folkestone, Kent CT19 6PQ	01303 240033	01303 240023	Mrs P. Triffitt	886-6080	3-18	53	Ch
Sackville School	Tonbridge Rd, Hildenborough, Tonbridge, Kent TN11 9HN	01732 838888	01732 838688	Mrs G.M.L. Sinclair	886-6058	11-16	218	
St Edmund's School	St Thomas Hill, Canterbury, Kent CT2 8HU	01227 475600	01227 471083	Mr Jeremy Gladwin	886-6050	2-19	548	R Ch
St Lawrence College	College Rd, Ramsgate, Kent CT11 7AE	01843 572900	01843 851123	Rev C.W.M. Aitken	886-6010	10-16	330	R CE
St Ronan's School	Hawkhurst, Cranbrook, Kent TN18 5DJ	01580 752271	01580 754882	Mr William Trelawney-Vernon	886-6006	2-14	312	
Sevenoaks Preparatory School	Fawke Cottage, Godden Grn, Sevenoaks, Kent TN15 0JU	01732 762336	01732 764279	Mr E. Oatley	886-6015	2-14	366	
Sevenoaks School	Sevenoaks, Kent TN13 1HU	01732 455133	01732 456143	Mrs Catherine Louise Ricks	886-6014	10-18	980	R
Sutton Valence School	Sutton Valence, Maidstone, Kent ME17 3HL	01622 845203	01622 845301	Mr James Selwyn Davies	886-6019	3-19	897	R Ch
Threshold Learning Centre	The Church Hall, Unitarian Church, Adrian St, Dover, Kent CT17 9AT	01304 209217			886-6102	14-16	11	
Threshold Learning Centre	Centre Piece, Bank St, Ashford, Kent TN23 1BA	01233 646637			886-6101	14-16	6	
Tonbridge School	Tonbridge, Kent TN9 1JP	01732 365555	01732 770853	Mr T.H.P. Haynes	886-6020	13-18	751	B R CE
Walthamstow Hall	Hollybush La, Sevenoaks, Kent TN13 3UL	01732 451334	01732 740439	Mrs Jill Milner	886-6054	3-19	497	G
Wellesley House School	114 Ramsgate Rd, Broadstairs, Kent CT10 2DG	01843 862991	01843 602068	Mr R. Steel	886-6001	6-14	116	R CE

Medway

School name	Address	Tel	Fax	Headteacher	Ref	Ages	Pupils	Other
The Cedars School	70 Maidstone Rd, Rochester, Kent ME1 3DE	01634 847163	01634 847163	Mrs B.M.V. Gross	887-6003	2-16	21	Ch
King's School, Rochester	Satis Hse, Rochester, Kent ME1 1TE	01634 888555	01634 888505	Dr I.R. Walker	887-6000	3-16	651	R CE
Rochester Independent College	Star Hill, Rochester, Kent ME1 1XF	01634 828115	01634 405667	Mr B. Pain	887-6004	14-16	137	R

Milton Keynes

School name	Address	Tel	Fax	Headteacher	Ref	Ages	Pupils	Other
Bury Lawn School	Soskin Dr, Stantonbury Fields, Milton Keynes, Buckinghamshire MK14 6DP	01908 220345	01908 220363	Mr F. Roche	826-6001	1-19	385	
Citischool	599 Avebury Bvd, Milton Keynes, Buckinghamshire MK9 3HR	01908 246789	01908 230130	Richard Richard Collier	826-6008	15-16	20	Ch
Extended Training	Milton Keynes Christian Foundation, Foundation Hse, The Square Wolverton, Milton Keynes, Buckinghamshire MK12 5HX	01908 525097	01908 313375	Mr J. Ghaleb	826-6009	14-16	10	Ch
Milton Keynes Wheelright Motor Project	7–8 Hollin La, Stacey Bushes, Milton Keynes, Buckinghamshire MK12 6HT	01908 314111		Mr David Moss-Norbury	826-6006	14-16	8	B
Rathbone – Alternatives	Castle Hse, Dawson Rd, Mount Farm, Milton Keynes, Buckinghamshire MK1 1QT	01908 625460	01908 363625	Mrs Julie Field	826-6007	14-16	24	

4

Oxfordshire

School name	Address	Tel	Fax	Headteacher	Ref	Ages	Pupils	Other
Abingdon School	Park Rd, Abingdon, Oxfordshire OX14 1DE	01235 521563	01235 559851	Mark Turner	931-6095	4–16	1028	B R Ch
Ash-Shifa School	Merton St, Banbury, Oxfordshire OX16 8RU	01295 279954	01295 279954	Ms F. Aslam	931-6121	11–14	29	G Mu
Bloxham School	Bloxham, Banbury, Oxfordshire OX15 4PE	01295 720222	01295 721897	M.E. Allbrook	931-6002	11–16	410	R Ch
Bruern Abbey School	Chesterton Manor, Chesterton, Bicester, Oxfordshire OX26 1UY	01869 242448	01869 243949	Philip Francis Fawkes	931-6106	7–14	67	B R
Cokethorpe School	Witney, Oxfordshire OX29 7PU	01993 703921	01993 773499	D.J. Ettinger	931-6046	5–18	641	
Cothill House School	Cothill, Abingdon, Oxfordshire OX13 6JL	01865 390800	01865 390205	N.R. Brooks	931-6075	8–14	230	B R CE
Cranford House School Trust Limited	Moulsford, Wallingford, Oxfordshire OX10 9HT	01491 651218	01491 652557	Claire Hamilton	931-6083	3–16	323	G CE
d'Overbroeck's College The Swan Building	111 Banbury Rd, Oxford, Oxfordshire OX2 6JX	01865 310000	01865 552296	S.N. Cohen	931-6104	11–16	371	R
Dragon School	Bardwell Rd, Oxford, Oxfordshire OX2 6SS	01865 315400	01865 311664	J.R. Baugh	931-6062	3–14	844	R CE
Headington School	Headington Rd, Oxford, Oxfordshire OX3 7TD	01865 759100	01865 760268	Anne Jane Coutts	931-6064	3–19	972	G R CE
Kingham Hill School	Kingham, Chipping Norton, Oxfordshire OX7 6TH	01608 658999	01608 658658	Martin Morris	931-6004	11–18	219	R CE
The King's School	12 Wesley Wlk, High St, Witney, Oxfordshire OX28 6ZJ	01993 709985	01993 709986	Ann Gibbon	931-6100	4–16	184	Ch
Magdalen College School	Cowley Pl, Oxford, Oxfordshire OX4 1DZ	01865 242191	01865 240379	A.D. Halls	931-6094	7–19	676	B Ch
Moulsford Preparatory School	Moulsford-on-Thames, Moulsford-on-Thames, Wallingford, Oxfordshire OX10 9HR	01491 651438	01491 651868	M. Higham	931-6087	4–14	246	B R CE
The Oratory School	Woodcote, Reading, Berkshire RG8 0PJ	01491 683500	01491 680020	C.I. Dytor	931-6034	11–16	386	B R RC
Our Lady's Abingdon	Radley Rd, Abingdon, Oxfordshire OX14 3PS	01235 524658	01235 535829	Lynne Renwick	931-6076	10–19	395	G RC
Oxford High School GDST	Belbroughton Rd, Oxford, Oxfordshire OX2 6XA	01865 559888	01865 552343	O.F.S. Lusk	931-6093	3–19	926	G
Radley College	Radley, Abingdon, Oxfordshire OX14 2HR	01235 543000	01235 543106	A.W. McPhail	931-6079	13–18	636	B R CE
Rye St Antony School	Pullen's La, Oxford, Oxfordshire OX3 0BY	01865 762802	01865 763611	A.M. Jones	931-6070	3–19	403	G R RC
St Clare's, Oxford	139 Banbury Rd, Oxford, Oxfordshire OX2 7AL	01865 552031	01865 310002	Paula Holloway	931-6120	14–19	238	R
St Edward's School	Woodstock Rd, Oxford, Oxfordshire OX2 7NN	01865 319323	01865 319242	Andrew Trotman	931-6066	12–19	651	R
The School of St Helen and St Katharine	Faringdon Rd, Abingdon, Oxfordshire OX14 1BE	01235 520173	01235 532934	C. Hall	931-6096	9–16	622	G
Shiplake College	Shiplake Ct, Shiplake, Henley-on-Thames, Oxfordshire RG9 4BW	0118 940 2455	0118 940 5204	A.G.S. Davis	931-6050	13–16	304	B R CE
Sibford School	Sibford Ferris, Banbury, Oxfordshire OX15 5QL	01295 781200	01295 781204	Michael Goodwin	931-6005	4–16	395	R Qk
Tudor Hall School	Wykham Pk, Banbury, Oxfordshire OX16 9UR	01295 263434	01295 253264	W. Griffiths	931-6001	11–16	285	G R CE
Wychwood School	74 Banbury Rd, Oxford, Oxfordshire OX2 6JR	01865 557976	01865 556806	S.M.P. Wingfield Digby	931-6068	10–16	142	G R Ch

Portsmouth

School name	Address	Tel	Fax	Headteacher	Ref	Ages	Pupils	Other
Mayville High School	35 St Simon's Rd, Southsea, Hampshire PO5 2PE	023 9273 4847	023 9229 3649	Mrs L. Owens	851-6002	0–16	468	N ND
The Portsmouth Grammar School	High St, Old Portsmouth, Portsmouth, Hampshire PO1 2LN	023 9236 0036	023 9236 4256	Dr T.R. Hands	851-6004	5–16	1577	Ch
Portsmouth High School	25 Kent Rd, Southsea, Hampshire PO5 3EQ	023 9282 6714	023 9281 4814	Miss Peg Hulse	851-6003	3–16	609	G
St John's College	Grove Rd South, Southsea, Hampshire PO5 3QW	023 9281 5118	023 9287 3603	Mr N.W. Thorne	851-6001	2–16	620	R RC

Reading

School name	Address	Tel	Fax	Headteacher	Ref	Ages	Pupils	Other
The Abbey School Reading	Kendrick Rd, Reading, Berkshire RG1 5DZ	0118 987 2256	0118 987 1478	Mrs B. Stanley	870-6008	3–18	1042	Ch
The Elvian School	61 Bath Rd, Reading, Berkshire RG30 2BB	0118 957 2861	0118 957 2220	Mrs S.M. Manser	870-6004	3–18	168	
Hemdean House School	Hemdean Rd, Caversham, Reading, Berkshire RG4 7SD	0118 947 2590	0118 946 4474	Mrs Joanne Harris	870-6003	3–16	176	G
Leighton Park School	Shinfield Rd, Reading, Berkshire RG2 7ED	0118 987 9600	0118 987 9625	Mr J.H. Dunston	870-6001	10–16	462	R Qk
Queen Anne's School	6 Henley Rd, Caversham, Reading, Berkshire RG4 6DX	0118 918 7300	0118 918 7310	Mrs J. Harrington	870-6000	11–16	322	R CE

School name	Address	Tel	Fax	Headteacher	Ref	Ages	Pupils	Other
St Edward's School	64 Tilehurst Rd, Reading, Berkshire RG30 2JH	0118 957 4342	0118 950 3736	Mr P. Keddie	870-6005	5–14	171	
St Joseph's Convent School	Upper Redlands Rd, Reading, Berkshire RG1 5JT	0118 966 1000	0118 926 9932	Mrs M.T. Sheridan	870-6002	3–16	325	

Southampton

School name	Address	Tel	Fax	Headteacher	Ref	Ages	Pupils	Other
The Gregg School	Townhill Park Hse, Cutbush La., Southampton, Hampshire SO18 2GF	023 8047 2133	023 8047 1080	Mr R. Hart	852-6000	11–16	327	
King Edward VI School	Kellett Rd, Southampton, Hampshire SO15 7UQ	023 8070 4561	023 8070 5937	Mr Anthony Julian Thould	852-6006	10–19	969	
St Mary's College	57 Midanbury La., Bitterne Pk, Southampton, Hampshire SO18 4DJ	023 8067 1267	023 8067 1268	Rev Brother Davis	852-6003	5–16	318	RC

Surrey

School name	Address	Tel	Fax	Headteacher	Ref	Ages	Pupils	Other
ACS Cobham International School	Heywood, Cobham, Surrey KT11 1BL	01932 867251	01932 869790	Mr Thomas J. Lehman	936-6529	3–16	1363	R
ACS Egham International School	Woodlee, Egham, Surrey TW20 0HS	01784 430800	01784 430153	Ms Moyra Hadley	936-6577	2–18	559	
Bishopsgate School	Bishopsgate Rd, Egham, Surrey TW20 0YJ	01784 432109	01784 430460	Mr Mark Dunning	936-6024	3–14	316	R Ch
Box Hill School	Mickleham, Dorking, Surrey RH5 6EA	01372 373382	01372 363942	Mr Mark Eagers	936-6259	11–16	399	R
Caterham School	Harestone Valley, Caterham, Surrey CR3 6YA	01883 343028	01883 347795	Mr R.A.E. Davey	936-6538	10–16	749	R Ch
Charterhouse	Godalming, Surrey GU7 2DJ	01483 291600	01483 291607	Rev J.S. Witheridge	936-6041	12–19	733	B R CE
City of London Freemens' School	Ashtead Pk, Ashtead, Surrey KT21 1ET	01372 277933	01372 276165	Mr D.C. Haywood	936-6061	7–18	841	R
Claremont Fan Court School	Claremont Dr, Esher, Surrey KT10 9LY	01372 467841	01372 471109	Mrs P.B. Farrar	936-6032	3–16	640	Ch
The Cornerstone School	22 West Hill, Epsom, Surrey KT19 8JD	01372 742940		Mr G.R. Davies	936-6558	4–16	54	Ch
Cranleigh School	Horseshoe La., Cranleigh, Surrey GU6 8QQ	01483 273666	01483 267398	Mr G. De W. Waller	936-6017	7–19	870	R
Danes Hill Preparatory School	Leatherhead Rd, Leatherhead, Surrey KT22 0JG	01372 842509	01372 844452	Mr R. Parfitt	936-6272	2–14	879	ND
Dunottar Day School for Girls	High Trees Rd, Reigate, Surrey RH2 7EL	01737 761945	01737 779450	Ms J. Hobson	936-6078	3–16	355	G
Epsom College	College Rd, Epsom, Surrey KT17 4JQ	01372 821000	01372 821005	Mr S.R. Borthwick	936-6030	13–18	724	R
Ewell Castle School	Church St, Epsom, Surrey KT17 2AW	020 8393 1413	020 8786 8218	Mr A.J. Tibble	936-6203	3–16	545	
Frensham Heights School	Rowledge, Farnham, Surrey GU10 4EA	01252 792561	01252 794335	Mr Andrew Fisher	936-6038	3–16	519	R
Greenacre School for Girls	Sutton La., Banstead, Surrey SM7 3RA	01737 352114	01737 373485	Mrs P. Wood	936-6001	3–16	404	G
Guildford High School	London Rd, Guildford, Surrey GU1 1SJ	01483 561440	01483 306516	Mrs Fiona Jane Boulton	936-6046	4–16	957	G Ch
Halliford School	Russell Rd, Shepperton, Middlesex TW17 9HX	01932 223593	01932 229781	Mr Philip Cottam	936-6503	11–19	374	B
Haslemere Preparatory School	The Heights, Haslemere, Surrey GU27 2JP	01428 642350	01428 645314	Mr K. Merrick	936-6456	2–14	237	B
The Hawthorns School	Pendell Ct, Redhill, Surrey RH1 4QJ	01883 743048	01883 744256	Mr Timothy Johns	936-6076	2–14	547	
Hurtwood House School	Holmbury St Mary, Dorking, Surrey RH5 6NU	01483 279000	01483 267586	K.R.B. Jackson	936-6564	15–16	308	R
King Edward's School	Witley, Godalming, Surrey GU8 5SG	01428 686700	01428 682850	Mr P. Kerr Fulton-Peebles	936-6103	10–19	476	R
Lingfield Notre Dame	Racecourse Rd, Lingfield, Surrey RH7 6PH	01342 832407	01342 836048	Mrs N. Shepley	936-6255	2–19	750	Ch
Manor House School	Manor House La., Leatherhead, Surrey KT23 4EN	01372 458538	01372 450514	Mrs A.R. Morris	936-6068	2–17	402	G
Moon Hall College/Burys Court	Leigh, Reigate, Surrey RH2 8RE	01306 611372		Mr David Rowlands	936-6251	2–16	75	CE
Notre Dame Senior School	Burwood Hse, Cobham, Surrey KT11 1HA	01932 869990	01932 860992	Mrs Bridget Williams	936-6163	11–18	383	G RC
Oakfield School	Coldharbour Rd, Woking, Surrey GU22 8SJ	01932 342465	01932 342745	Mrs S.M. Goddard	936-6404	2–14	185	ND
Prior's Field School	Priors Field Rd, Godalming, Surrey GU7 2RH	01483 810551	01483 810180	Mrs J.C. Dwyer	936-6010	11–19	333	G R
Reeds School	Sandy La., Cobham, Surrey KT11 2ES	01932 869044	01932 869046	Mr D.W. Jarrett	936-6009	10–19	561	R
Reigate Grammar School	Reigate Rd, Reigate, Surrey RH2 0QS	01737 222231	01737 224201	Mr D.S. Thomas	936-6531	2–16	1102	
Ripley Court School	Rose La., Woking, Surrey GU23 6NE	01483 225217		Mr Andrew Gough	936-6307	2–14	254	R CE

School name	Address	Tel	Fax	Headteacher	Ref	Ages	Pupils	Other
Royal Grammar School	High St, Guildford, Surrey GU1 3BB	01483 880600	01483 306127	Dr J.M. Cox	936-6534	11–16	889	B ID
The Royal School	Farnham La, Haslemere, Surrey GU27 1HQ	01428 605805	01428 603028	Mrs L. Taylor-Gooby	936-6054	3–16	322	G R CE
St Catherine's School	Station Rd, Guildford, Surrey GU5 0DF	01483 893363	01483 894246	Mrs A.M. Phillips	936-6004	4–16	809	G R
St David's School	Church Rd, Ashford, Middlesex TW15 3DZ	01784 252494	01784 248652	Ms P.A. Bristow	936-6504	3–19	330	G R
St Edmund's School	Portsmouth Rd, Hindhead, Surrey GU26 6BH	01428 604808	01428 607898	Mr A.J. Walliker	936-6053	2–14	180	R CE
St George's College Weybridge	Weybridge Rd, Addlestone, Surrey KT15 2QS	01932 839300	01932 839301	Mr J.A. Peake	936-6092	11–19	806	RC
St John's School	Epsom Rd, Leatherhead, Surrey KT22 8SP	01372 373000	01372 386606	Mr N.J.R. Haddock	936-6070	13–16	470	B R Ch
St Teresa's School	Effingham Hill, Dorking, Surrey RH5 6ST	01372 452037	01372 450311	Mrs Prescott	936-6418	10–16	353	G R RC
Sir William Perkins's School	Guildford Rd, Chertsey, Surrey KT16 9BN	01932 574900		Miss S. Ross	936-6535	11–19	545	G
Tasis	Coldharbour La, Egham, Surrey TW20 8TE	01932 565252	01932 560493	Dr James A. Doran	936-6532	3–16	768	R
Three Counties School	70 Frensham Rd, Farnham, Surrey GU10 3QA	01252 794079		Mr C. Blake	936-6585	11–16	49	Ch
Tormead School	27 Cranley Rd, Guildford, Surrey GU1 2JD	01483 575101	01483 450592	Mrs Susan Marks	936-6050	4–16	752	G ND
Wispers School	High La, Haslemere, Surrey GU27 1AD	01428 643646	01428 641120	Mr L.H. Beltran	936-6520	11–18	84	G R CE
Woldingham School	Marden Pk, Caterham, Surrey CR3 7YA	01883 349431	01883 348653	Miss D. Vernon	936-6111	10–16	471	G R RC
Woodcote House School	Snows Ride, Windlesham, Surrey GU20 6PF	01276 472115	01276 472890	Mr N.H.K. Paterson	936-6102	7–14	101	B R
Yehudi Menuhin School	Cobham, Surrey KT11 3QQ	01932 864739	01932 864633	Mr N. Chisholm	936-6539	8–19	66	R

West Berkshire

School name	Address	Tel	Fax	Headteacher	Ref	Ages	Pupils	Other
Bradfield College	Bradfield, Reading, Berkshire RG7 6AU	0118 964 4500	0118 964 4521	Mr P.J.M. Roberts	869-6000	13–19	661	R CE
Downe House School	Cold Ash, Thatcham, Berkshire RG18 9JJ	01635 200286	01635 202026	Mrs E. McKendrick	869-6002	11–16	585	G R CE
Padworth College	Padworth, Reading, Berkshire RG7 4NR	0118 983 2644	0118 983 4515	Mrs Linde Melhuish	869-6009	13–16	99	R
Pangbourne College	Pangbourne, Reading, Berkshire RG8 8LA	0118 984 2101	0118 984 5443	Dr K.M. Greig	869-6005	11–19	364	R CE
St Gabriel's School	Sandleford Priory, Newbury, Berkshire RG20 9BD	01635 555680	01635 37351	Mr A.S. Jones	869-6004	3–18	501	CE

West Sussex

School name	Address	Tel	Fax	Headteacher	Ref	Ages	Pupils	Other
Arabesque School of Performing Arts	Quarry La, Chichester, West Sussex PO19 8NY	01243 531144		Miss Cynthia Ryder	938-6270	11–18	9	
Ardingly College	College Rd, Ardingly, Haywards Heath, West Sussex RH17 6SQ	01444 893000	01444 893001	Mr J. Franklin	938-6200	2–16	759	R CE
Ashton Park School	Brinsbury Campus East, Stane St, North Heath, Pulborough, West Sussex RH20 1DJ	01798 875836		Mr G. Holding	938-6262	11–16	57	Ch
Burgess Hill School for Girls	Keymer Rd, Burgess Hill, West Sussex RH15 0EG	01444 241050	01444 870314	Mrs Ann Aughwane	938-6201	2–19	672	G R
Christ's Hospital	Horsham, West Sussex RH13 0LJ	01403 247432	01403 247468	Dr P.C.D. Southern	938-6011	11–18	819	R CE
Cottesmore School	Buchan Hill, Pease Pottage, Crawley, West Sussex RH11 9AU	01293 520648	01293 614784	Mr I. Tysoe	938-6008	7–14	113	R
Dorset House School	The Manor, Bury, Pulborough, West Sussex RH20 1PB	01798 831456	01798 831141	Mr E. Clarke	938-6015	3–14	132	R CE
Farlington School	Strood Pk, Horsham, West Sussex RH12 3PN	01403 254967	01403 272258	Mrs P. Mawer	938-6144	5–16	487	G R
Handcross Park Preparatory School	Handcross, Haywards Heath, West Sussex RH17 6HF	01444 400526	01444 400527	Mr W.J. Hilton	938-6223	2–14	263	R
Hurstpierpoint College	College La, Hurstpierpoint, Hassocks, West Sussex BN6 9JS	01273 833636	01273 835257	Mr T.J. Manly	938-6206	4–19	720	R CE
Lancing College	Lancing, West Sussex BN15 0RW	01273 452213	01273 464720	Mr P.M. Tinniswood	938-6013	12–16	507	R CE
Lavant House	West Lavant, Chichester, West Sussex PO18 9AB	01243 527211	01243 530490	Mrs M. Scott	938-6139	3–18	162	G R
Our Lady of Sion School	Gratwicke Rd, Worthing, West Sussex BN11 4BL	01903 204063	01903 214434	Mr M. Scullion	938-6030	2–19	495	RC
Prebendal School,The	53 West St, Chichester, West Sussex PO19 1RT	01243 782026	01243 771821	Mr Timothy Richard Cannell	938-6128	2–14	232	R CE
Rikkyo School-in-England	Guildford Rd, Rudgwick, Horsham, West Sussex RH12 3BE	01403 822107	01403 822535	Mr Makio Higashi	938-6188	11–16	130	R CE
Seaford College	Lavington Pk, Petworth, West Sussex GU28 0NB	01798 867392	01798 867606	Mr T.J. Mullins	938-6023	10–16	487	R CE

4

School name	Address	Tel	Fax	Headteacher	Ref	Ages	Pupils	Other
Shoreham College	St Julian's La, Shoreham-by-Sea, West Sussex BN43 6YW	01273 592681	01273 591673	Mr R.K. Iremonger	938-6027	2–17	439	G RC
Slindon College	Slindon, Arundel, West Sussex BN18 0RH	01243 814320	01243 814702	Mr I. Graham	938-6094	10–16	98	B R ID
Towers Convent School,The	The Towers, Upper Beeding, Steyning, West Sussex BN44 3TF	01903 812185	01903 813858	Mrs Carole Ann Baker	938-6138	3–16	278	G R RC
Westbourne House School	Coach Rd, Shopwyke, Chichester, West Sussex PO20 2BH	01243 782739	01243 770759	Mr B.G. Law	938-6007	2–14	375	R
Windlesham House School	London Rd, Washington, Pulborough, West Sussex RH20 4AY	01903 874705	01903 874702	Mr Paul M. Forte	938-6028	3–14	282	R CE
Worth School	Paddockhurst Rd, Turners Hill, Crawley, West Sussex RH10 4SD	01342 710200	01342 710230	Mr Peter Joseph Armstrong	938-6208	11–19	443	B R RC

Windsor and Maidenhead

School name	Address	Tel	Fax	Headteacher	Ref	Ages	Pupils	Other
The Brigidine School	Kings Rd, Windsor, Berkshire SL4 2AX	01753 863779	01753 850278	Mrs J. Dunn	868-6011	2–19	268	G RC
Claires Court Schools	Ray Mill Rd East, Maidenhead, Berkshire SL6 8TE	01628 411470	01628 411466	Mr J.T. Wilding	868-6014	5–16	1033	
Eton College	Windsor, Berkshire SL4 6DW	01753 671000	01753 671159	Mr A.R.M. Little	868-6016	12–19	1300	B R
Hurst Lodge School	Bagshot Rd, Ascot, Berkshire SL5 9JU	01344 622154	01344 627049	Miss V.S. Smit	868-6012	2–19	190	R
Marist Senior School	The Rosary, Sunninghill, Ascot, Berkshire SL5 7PS	01344 624291	01344 874963	Mr K. McCloskey	868-6013	11–16	313	G RC
Papplewick School	Windsor Rd, Ascot, Berkshire SL5 7LH	01344 621488	01344 874639	Mr T.W. Bunbury	868-6000	6–14	200	B R
Redroofs Theatre School	Littlewick Grn, Maidenhead, Berkshire SL6 3QY	01628 674092	01628 822461	Mrs S. Ground	868-6018	7–16	51	
St George's School	Windsor Castle, Windsor, Berkshire SL4 1QF	01753 865553	01753 842093	Mr J.R. Jones	868-6006	3–14	398	R CE
St George's School	Wells La, Ascot, Berkshire SL5 7DZ	01344 629900	01344 629901	Mrs Caroline Jordan	868-6001	11–16	288	G R CE
St Mary's School Ascot	St Mary's Rd, South Ascot, Ascot, Berkshire SL5 9JF	01344 623721	01344 873281	Mrs M. Breen	868-6002	11–16	365	G R RC
Sunningdale School	Dry Arch Rd, Sunningdale, Ascot, Berkshire SL5 9PZ	01344 620159	01344 873304	Mr A.J.N Dawson	868-6007	7–14	83	B R CE

Wokingham

School name	Address	Tel	Fax	Headteacher	Ref	Ages	Pupils	Other
Bearwood College	Bearwood, Wokingham, Berkshire RG41 5BG	0118 974 8300	0118 977 3186	Mr S.G.G. Aiano	872-6001	1–18	423	R CE
Crosfields School	Shinfield, Reading, Berkshire RG2 9BL	0118 987 1810	0118 931 0806	Mr J. Wansey	872-6008	4–13	442	B
Dolphin School	Hinton Rd, Hurst, Reading, Berkshire RG10 0BP	0118 934 1277	0118 934 4110	Mrs H. Brough	872-6010	3–13	277	
Luckley-Oakfield School	Luckley Rd, Wokingham, Berkshire RG40 3EU	0118 978 4175	0118 977 0305	Miss V.A. Davis	872-6000	11–16	305	G R CE
Reading Blue Coat School	Holme Pk, Sonning La, Sonning on Thames, Reading, Berkshire RG4 6SU	0118 944 1005	0118 944 2690	Mr S.J.W. McArthur	872-6006	11–16	668	CE

South West

Bath and North East Somerset

School name	Address	Tel	Fax	Headteacher	Ref	Ages	Pupils	Other
Bath Academy	27 Queens Sq, Bath BA1 2HX	01225 334577	01225 482414	Mrs Laraine Brown	800-6014	13–19	423	R CE
King Edward's School	North Rd, Bath BA2 6HU	01225 464313	01225 481363	Mr Crispin Rowe	800-6010	3–19	933	B
Kingswood School	Lansdown Rd, Bath BA1 5RG	01225 734200	01225 734205	Mr G.M. Best	800-6000	11–16	632	R Me
Monkton Senior School	Monkton Combe, Bath BA2 7HG	01225 721102	01225 721181	Mr Richard P. Backhouse	800-6008	11–18	353	R Ch

School name	Address	Tel	Fax	Headteacher	Ref	Ages	Pupils	Other
Prior Park College	Ralph Allen Dr, Combe Down, Bath BA2 5AH	01225 835353	01225 835753	Dr Giles Mercer	800-6001	10–19	540	R RC
Royal High School	Lansdown Rd, Bath BA1 5SZ	01225 313877	01225 484378	Mr J.M. Graham-Brown	800-6002	3–19	826	G R ND

Bournemouth

School name	Address	Tel	Fax	Headteacher	Ref	Ages	Pupils	Other
Talbot Heath School	Rothesay Rd, Bournemouth, Dorset BH4 9NJ	01202 761881	01202 768155	Ms Christine Dipple	837-6001	3–19	608	R Ch
Wentworth College	College Rd, Bournemouth, Dorset BH5 2DY	01202 423266	01202 418030	Miss S. Coe	837-6002	11–16	181	R

Bristol

School name	Address	Tel	Fax	Headteacher	Ref	Ages	Pupils	Other
Andalusia Academy Bristol	Halston Dr, Bristol BS2 9JE	0117 942 6457	0117 942 6457	Mr Eric Dolling	801-6130	4–16	72	Mu
Badminton School	Westbury Rd, Westbury-on-Trym, Bristol BS9 3BA	0117 905 5200	0117 962 8963	Mrs J.A. Scarrow	801-6003	4–16	406	G R
Bristol Cathedral School	College Sq, Bristol BS1 5TS	0117 929 1872	0117 930 4219	Mrs J.A. Davey	801-6012	8–19	386	CE
Bristol Grammar School	University Rd, Bristol BS8 1SR	0117 973 6006	0117 946 7485	Dr D.J. Mascord	801-6013	7–19	1177	
Bristol Steiner School	Redland Hill Hse, Redland Hill, Bristol BS6 6UX	0117 933 9990	0117 933 9999		801-6011	2–15	195	
Carmel Christian School	817a Bath Rd, Brislington, Bristol BS4 5NL	0117 977 5535	0117 977 5678	Miss S. Watt	801-6021	4–17	39	Ch
Clifton College	32 College Rd, Clifton, Bristol BS8 3JH	0117 315 7000	0117 315 7101	Mr Mark Moore	801-6000	3–19	1290	R Ch
Clifton High School	College Rd, Clifton, Bristol BS8 3JD	0117 973 0201	0117 923 8962	Mrs Colette Culligan	801-6001	3–18	629	R ND
Colstons Girls' School	Cheltenham Rd, Bristol BS6 5RD	0117 942 4328	0117 942 1052	Mrs L.A. Jones	801-6010	10–16	366	G
Colston's School	Bell Hill, Stapleton, Bristol BS16 1BJ	0117 965 5207	0117 958 5652	Mr Peter Fraser	801-6002	11–18	609	R CE
Include Bristol	150–154 East St, Bedminster, Bristol BS3 4EW	0117 966 5427	0117 955 7711	Ms Margaret Macnaughton	801-6023	14–16	29	
Prospect School	Tramway Rd, Brislington, Bristol BS4 3DS	0117 977 2271		Mrs Lucy Sherrin	801-6027	11–17	31	Ch
Queen Elizabeth's Hospital	Berkeley Pl, Clifton, Bristol BS8 1JX	0117 930 3040	0117 929 3106	Mr S.W. Holliday	801-6014	10–18	549	B R
The Red Maids School	Westbury Rd, Westbury-on-Trym, Bristol BS9 3AW	0117 962 2641	0117 962 1687	Mrs Isabel Tobias	801-6015	6–19	500	G
Redland High School For Girls	Redland Ct, Redland Court Rd, Redland, Bristol BS6 7EF	0117 924 5796	0117 924 1127	Mrs Caroline Bateson	801-6016	3–19	279	G
St Ursula's High School	Brecon Rd, Westbury-on-Trym, Bristol BS9 4DT	0117 962 2616	0117 962 2616	Mrs M. MacNaughton	801-6006	3–16	290	RC

Cornwall

School name	Address	Tel	Fax	Headteacher	Ref	Ages	Pupils	Other
The Bolitho School	Polwithen Rd, Penzance, Cornwall TR18 4JR	01736 363271	01736 230960	Mr David Dobson	908-6002	5–19	422	R
Highfields Private School	Cardrew La, Redruth, Cornwall TR15 1SY	01209 210665		Mrs Mary Haddy	908-6093	4–16	64	
Polwhele House School	Polwhele, Truro, Cornwall TR4 9AE	01872 273011	01872 273011	Mr Jeremy Mason	908-6076	2–14	180	R Ch
St Joseph's School	St Stephen's Hill, Launceston, Cornwall PL15 8HN	01566 772580	01566 775902	Dr A.R. Doe	908-6040	3–16	171	Ch
St Michael's RC Small School	St George's Rd, Truro, Cornwall TR1 3JD	01872 242123	01872 242123	Mrs Joyce Sanderson	908-6092	5–16	50	
St Pirans School GB Ltd	Trelissick Rd, Hayle, Cornwall TR27 4HY	01736 752612	01736 752612	Mr Deryck Wilson	908-6089	3–16	97	Ch
Treverbyn Education Trust	Drummers Hill, Scredda, St Austell, Cornwall PL26 8XR	01726 77316		Mr Bruce Davies	908-6094	11–16	15	Ch
Truro High School	Falmouth Rd, Truro, Cornwall TR1 2HU	01872 272830	01872 279393	Mr M.A. Mcdowell	908-6080	3–18	454	G R CE
Truro School	Trennick La, Truro, Cornwall TR1 1TH	01872 272763		Mr P.K. Smith	908-6079	10–16	838	R Me

Devon

School name	Address	Tel	Fax	Headteacher	Ref	Ages	Pupils	Other
Blundell's School	Blundell's Rd, Tiverton, Devon EX16 4DN	01884 252543	01884 242232	Mr Davenport	878-6011	11–16	558	R
Bramdean School	Richmond Lodge, Homefield Rd, Exeter, Devon EX1 2QR	01392 273387	01392 439330	Mr Connett	878-6001	3–16	155	R
Buckeridge International College	Trinity School, Buckeridge Rd, Teignmouth, Devon TQ14 8LY	01626 774138	01626 771541	Mr Ashby	878-6049	10–16	87	R RC
Edgehill College	Northdown Rd, Bideford, Devon EX39 3LY	01237 471701	01237 425981	Mr Nicholson	878-6030	2–16	246	R Me
Emmanuel School Exeter	36–38 Blackboy Rd, Exeter, Devon EX4 6SZ	01392 258150		Mrs Bastone	878-6048	5–16	35	Ch
Exeter School	Victoria Park Rd, Exeter, Devon EX2 4NS	01392 273679	01392 498144	Mr Griffin	878-6033	6–19	837	
Exeter Tutorial College	44–46 Magdalen Rd, Exeter, Devon EX2 4TE	01392 278101	01392 494853	Mr Jack	878-6051	15–16	40	
Grenville College	Belvoir Rd, Bideford, Devon EX39 3JP	01237 472212	01237 477020	Mr Waters	878-6022	2–16	391	R CE
Kelly College	Parkwood Rd, Tavistock, Devon PL19 0HZ	01822 813100	01822 813168	Mr Steed	878-6009	11–16	362	R CE
Magdalen Court School	Mulberry Hse, Victoria Park Rd, Exeter, Devon EX2 4NU	01392 494919	01392 494919	Mr Bushrod	878-6045	1–16	175	
The Maynard School	Denmark Rd, Exeter, Devon EX1 1SJ	01392 273417	01392 355999	D.M. West	878-6034	7–19	483	G Ch
Moor View School	Moor View School, Staplehill Rd, Liverton, Newton Abbot TQ12 6JD	01626 821686		Mr Powell	878-6058	11–17	57	Ch
Rudolf Steiner School	Hood Manor, Dartington, Totnes, Devon TQ9 6AB	01803 762528		Mr Cooper	878-6029	3–17	292	
St John's School	Broadway, Sidmouth, Devon EX10 8RG	01395 513984	01395 514539	Mrs Parry Davies	878-6018	2–14	163	R
St Margaret's School	147 Magdalen Rd, Exeter, Devon EX2 4TS	01392 273197	01392 251402	Miss Edblooke	878-6002	7–19	317	G
St Michael's School	Tawstock Ct, Tawstock, Barnstaple, Devon EX31 3HY	01271 343242	01271 346771	Mr Pratt	878-6013	2–14	203	CE
St Peter's School	Harefield, Lympstone, Exmouth, Devon EX8 5AU	01395 272148	01395 222410	Mr Williams	878-6020	2–14	246	R
St Wilfrid's School	25–29 St David's Hill, Exeter, Devon EX4 4DA	01392 276171	01392 438666	Macdonald-Dent	878-6004	7–16	106	CE
Sands School	48 East St, Ashburton, Newton Abbot, Devon TQ13 7AX	01364 653666		Mr Bellamy	878-6042	11–17	51	
Shebbear College	Shebbear, Beaworthy, Devon EX21 5HJ	01409 281228	01409 281784	Mr Barnes	878-6031	3–19	331	R Ch
The Small School	Fore St, Hartland, Bideford, Devon EX39 6AB	01237 441672	01237 441672	Ms Meiklejohn	878-6036	11–16	22	
Stover School	Stover, Newton Abbot, Devon TQ12 6QG	01626 354505	01626 361475	Mrs Bradley	878-6014	2–16	451	R CE
Trinity School	Buckeridge Rd, Teignmouth, Devon TQ14 8LY	01626 774138	01626 771541	Mr Ashby	878-6010	2–19	516	R RC
West Buckland School	West Buckland, Barnstaple, Devon EX32 0SX	01598 760281	01598 760546	Mr Vick	878-6032	2–18	684	R

Dorset

School name	Address	Tel	Fax	Headteacher	Ref	Ages	Pupils	Other
Bryanston School	Bryanston, Blandford Forum, Dorset DT11 0PX	01258 452411	01258 484657	T.D. Wheare	835-6005	13–16	647	R CE
Clayesmore School	Iwerne Minster, Blandford Forum, Dorset DT11 8LL	01747 813222	01747 813208	Mr Cooke	835-6009	13–19	397	R CE
The Cricket School	The Dorset Cricket Centre, Hurn, Christchurh, Dorset BH23 6DY	01202 470852	01202 470852	J.M. Lucas	835-6035	11–18		B
Dorchester Preparatory School	25–26 Icen Way, Dorchester, Dorset DT1 1EP	01305 264925	01305 264925	J. Miller	835-6027	5–18	55	
International College, Sherborne School	Newell Grange, Sherborne, Dorset DT9 4EZ	01935 814743	01935 816863	Christopher Greenfield	835-6030	11–17	136	R
Milton Abbey School	Blandford Forum, Dorset DT11 0BZ	01258 880484	01258 881194	W.J. Hughes-D'Aeth	835-6015	13–19	225	B R CE
Port Regis Preparatory School	Motcombe Pk, Shaftesbury, Dorset SP7 9QA	01747 852566	01747 854684	P.A.E. Dix	835-6010	2–14	431	R CE
Ringwood Waldorf School	Folly Farm La, Ashley, Ringwood, Hampshire BH24 2NN	01425 472664			835-6022	5–14	202	
St Antony's Leweston School	Sherborne, Dorset DT9 6EN	01963 210691	01963 210786	Adrian Aylward	835-6025	3–16	241	G R RC
Sherborne Preparatory School	Acreman St, Sherborne, Dorset DT9 3NY	01935 812097	01935 813948	P.S. Tait	835-6026	3–14	249	R Ch
Sherborne School	Abbey Rd, Sherborne, Dorset DT9 3AP	01935 812249	01935 816628	Michael Weston	835-6006	12–16	564	B R CE
Sherborne School for Girls	Bradford Rd, Sherborne, Dorset DT9 3QN	01935 812245	01935 818290	Jenny Dwyer	835-6024	11–19	370	G R CE

Gloucestershire

School name	Address	Tel	Fax	Headteacher	Ref	Ages	Pupils	Other
The Acorn School	Church St, Stroud, Gloucestershire GL6 0BP	01453 836508		Mr G. Whiting	916-6068	3-18	122	Ch
Cheltenham College	Bath Rd, Cheltenham, Gloucestershire GL53 7LD	01242 265600	01242 265630	Mr John Richardson	916-6033	3-19	974	R
The Cheltenham Ladies' College	Bayshill Rd, Cheltenham, Gloucestershire GL50 3EP	01242 520691	01242 227882	Mrs A.V. Tuck	916-6036	11-16	864	G R Ch
Dean Close School	Shelburne Rd, Cheltenham, Gloucestershire GL51 6HE	01242 258000	01242 258003	Rev T.M. Hastie-Smith	916-6035	12-18	475	R CE
Eastbrook College	7a Eastbrook Education Trust, Gloucester, Gloucestershire GL4 3DB	01452 417722		Mr J. Griffiths	916-6078	12-17	75	Ch
Gloucestershire Islamic Secondary School for Girls	Sinope St, Gloucester, Gloucestershire GL1 4AW	01452 300465	01452 300465	Mrs C.H. Sandall	916-6073	11-16	67	G Mu
The Kings School	Pitt St, Gloucester, Gloucestershire GL1 2BG	01452 337337	01452 337314	Mr P. Lacey	916-6003	3-16	543	R
Rendcomb College	Cirencester, Gloucestershire GL7 7HA	01285 831213	01285 831121	Mr G.R. Holden	916-6017	3-19	376	R
Rose Hill School	Alderley, Wotton-under-Edge, Gloucestershire GL12 7QT	01453 843196	01453 846126	Mr Paul Cawley-Wakefield	916-6010	2-14	135	R CE
St Edward's School	Cirencester Rd, Cheltenham, Gloucestershire GL53 8EY	01242 538600	01242 538610	Dr A.J. Nash	916-6032	11-18	498	RC
School of the Lion	Beauchamp Hse, Gloucester, Gloucestershire GL2 8AA	01452 525240	01452 525240	Mr Nigel Steele	916-6075	3-16	22	Ch
Westonbirt School	Westonbirt, Tetbury, Gloucestershire GL8 8QG	01666 880333	01666 880364	Mrs M. Henderson	916-6019	4-19	306	R CE
Wycliffe College	Bath Rd, Stonehouse, Gloucestershire GL10 2JQ	01453 822432	01453 827634	Mrs M.E. Burnet Ward	916-6018	2-16	727	R
Wynstones School	Church La, Gloucester, Gloucestershire GL4 0UF	01452 429220	01452 429221	Mrs Gabriel Kaye	916-6031	3-19	290	R

North Somerset

School name	Address	Tel	Fax	Headteacher	Ref	Ages	Pupils	Other
Rathbone Key Stage 4	M and D Bldgs, Winterstoke Rd, Weston-Super-Mare BS23 3YS	01934 410310	01934 410319	Mr J. Biddle	802-6009	14-16	21	
Sidcot School	Oakridge La, Winscombe BS25 1PD	01934 843102	01934 844181	Mr John Walmsley	802-6002	2-16	495	R Qk

Plymouth

School name	Address	Tel	Fax	Headteacher	Ref	Ages	Pupils	Other
Plymouth College	Ford Pk, Plymouth, Devon PL4 6RN	01752 203300	01752 203246	Mr S. Wormleighton	879-6004	2-19	882	R

Poole

School name	Address	Tel	Fax	Headteacher	Ref	Ages	Pupils	Other
Canford School	Canford Magna, Wimborne, Dorset BH21 3AD	01202 841254	01202 881009	Mr J. Lever	836-6000	12-16	603	R
Uplands School	St Osmund's Rd, Parkstone, Poole, Dorset BH14 9JY	01202 742626	01202 731037	Mrs Sheila Millar Mercer	836-6001	3-16	299	

Somerset

School name	Address	Tel	Fax	Headteacher	Ref	Ages	Pupils	Other
3 Dimensions	Chardleigh Hse, Chardleigh Grn, Wadeford, Chard, Somerset TA20 3AJ	01460 68055	01460 261060	Ms Ann Jenkins	933-6207	11-16		B R
Bruton School for Girls	Sunny Hill, Bruton, Somerset BA10 0NT	01749 814400	01749 812537	Mr John Burrough	933-6003	4-18	361	G R
Chilton Cantelo School	Chilton Cantelo, Yeovil, Somerset BA22 8BG	01935 850555	01935 850482	Mr D. von Zeffman	933-6191	7-16	404	R
Downside School	Stratton-on-the-Fosse, Stratton-on-the-Fosse, Radstock, Somerset BA3 4RJ	01761 235100	01761 235105	Father Leo Maidlow Davis	933-6021	9-18	387	B R RC

4

School name	Address	Tel	Fax	Headteacher	Ref	Ages	Pupils	Other
Hazlegrove King's Bruton Preparatory School	Hazlegrove Hse, Sparkford, Yeovil, Somerset BA22 7JA	01963 440314	01963 440569	Mr R.B. Fenwick	933-6182	3–14	334	R CE
King's College	South Rd, Taunton, Somerset TA1 3DX	01823 328200	01823 334236	Mr Chris Ramsey	933-6023	12–19	401	R CE
King's School	Plox, Bruton, Somerset BA10 0ED	01749 814200	01749 813426	Mr N.M. Lashbrook	933-6004	13–18	325	R Ch
Millfield School	Butleigh Rd, Street, Somerset BA16 0YD	01458 442291	01458 447276	Mr P.M. Johnson	933-6022	12–16	1237	R
The Park School	The Park, Yeovil, Somerset BA20 1DH	01935 423514	01935 411257	Mr P. Bate	933-6035	3–16	267	R Ch
Perrott Hill School	North Perrott, Crewkerne, Somerset TA18 7SL	01460 72051	01460 78246	Mr M.J. Davies	933-6016	2–14	189	R CE
Queen's College	Trull Rd, Taunton, Somerset TA1 4QS	01823 272559	01823 338430	Mr C.J. Alcock	933-6024	3–18	784	R Me
Taunton School	Staplegrove Rd, Taunton, Somerset TA2 6AD	01823 349200	01823 349201	Mr M. Anderson	933-6025	2–16	926	R
Wellington School	South St, Wellington, Somerset TA21 8NT	01823 668800	01823 668844	Mr Martin Reader	933-6178	3–16	999	R CE
Wells Cathedral School	The Liberty, Wells, Somerset BA5 2ST	01749 834200	01749 670724	Mrs E.C. Cairncross	933-6029	2–19	696	R CE

South Gloucestershire

School name	Address	Tel	Fax	Headteacher	Ref	Ages	Pupils	Other
Tockington Manor School	Tockington, Bristol BS32 4NY	01454 613229	01454 613676	Mr R.G. Tovey	803-6004	2–14	238	R CE

Swindon

School name	Address	Tel	Fax	Headteacher	Ref	Ages	Pupils	Other
Maranatha Christian School	Queenlaines Farm, Sevenhampton, Highworth, Swindon, Wiltshire SN6 7SQ	01793 762075	01793 762075	Mr P. Medlock	866-6001	2–19	67	Ch

Torbay

School name	Address	Tel	Fax	Headteacher	Ref	Ages	Pupils	Other
Stoodley Knowle School	Ansteys Cove Rd, Torquay, Devon TQ1 2JB	01803 293160	01803 214757	Sister Perpetua	880-6001	2–19	305	R
Tower House School	Fisher St, Paignton, Devon TQ4 5EW	01803 557077	01803 546038	Mr W. Miller	880-6004	2–16	225	

Wiltshire

School name	Address	Tel	Fax	Headteacher	Ref	Ages	Pupils	Other
Chafyn Grove School	Bourne Ave, Salisbury, Wiltshire SP1 1LR	01722 333423		Mr E.J. Newton	865-6014	3–14	292	R Ch
Dauntsey's School	West Lavington, Devizes, Wiltshire SN10 4HE	01380 814500	01380 814501	Mr S.B. Roberts	865-6007	11–16	756	R
Emmaus School	School La, Staverton, Trowbridge, Wiltshire BA14 6NZ	01225 782684		Mrs M. Wiltshire	865-6032	4–15	47	
The Godolphin School	Milford Hill, Salisbury, Wiltshire SP1 2RA	01722 430500		Miss Horsburgh	865-6006	11–18	436	G R CE
Grittleton House School	Grittleton, Chippenham, Wiltshire SN14 6AP	01249 782434	01249 782669	Mrs C. Whitney	865-6018	2–17	289	
La Retraite Swan	19 Campbell Rd, Salisbury, Wiltshire SP1 3BQ	01722 333094	01722 330868	Mr R.N.S. Leake	865-6026	3–16	326	Ch
Marlborough College	Marlborough, Wiltshire SN8 1PA	01672 892400	01672 892407	Mr Nicholas Sampson	865-6013	12–19	870	R CE
Prior Park Preparatory School	Manor Hse, Calcutt St, Cricklade, Swindon, Wiltshire SN6 6BB	01793 750275	01793 750910	Mr G.B. Hobern	865-6028	6–14	179	R RC
St Mary's School	Donhead St Mary's, Shaftesbury, Dorset SP7 9LP	01747 852416		Mr Richard James	865-6003	9–19	323	G R RC
St Mary's School	Curzon St, Calne, Wiltshire SN11 0DF	01249 857200		Mrs Helen Wright	865-6016	3–19	469	R
Stonar School	Cottles Pk, Atworth, Melksham, Wiltshire SN12 8NT	01225 701740	01225 790830	Mrs C.A. Osborne	865-6001	2–18	406	G R
Tisbury School	Weaveland Rd, Tisbury, Wiltshire SP3 6HJ	01747 873077	01747 870912	Dr P. Evans	865-6037	11–16	96	Ch
Warminster School	Church St, Warminster, Wiltshire BA12 8PJ	01985 210100		Mr Martin Priestley	865-6009	3–16	622	R CE

West Midlands

Birmingham

School name	Address	Tel	Fax	Headteacher	Ref	Ages	Pupils	Other
Abbey College	10 St Paul's Sq, Birmingham, West Midlands B3 1QU	0121 236 7474	0121 236 3937	Mr Andrew Jedras	330-6092	14–16	141	
Al Huda Girls School	74–76 Washwood Heath Rd, Saltley, Birmingham, West Midlands B8 1RD	0121 328 8999	0121 328 5918	Mrs Samina Jawaid	330-6088	11–17	134	G Mu
Al-Burhan Grammar School	28a George St, Balsall Heath, Birmingham, West Midlands B12 9RG	0121 440 5454	0121 440 5454	Dr Mohammed Nasrullah	330-6104	11–16	67	G Mu
Al-Furqan Community College	Reddings La, Tyseley, Birmingham, West Midlands B11 3EY	0121 777 8666	0121 777 1811	Mr A. Ahmed	330-6084	11–19	126	G Mu
Al-Hira School	99–103 Clifton Rd, Balsall Heath, Birmingham, West Midlands B12 8SR	0121 442 6775	0121 440 6118	Mrs Amina Sessay	330-6095	10–16	43	B Mu
Birchfield Independent Girls' School	30 Beacon Hill, Birchfield, Aston, Birmingham, West Midlands B6 6JU	0121 327 7707	0121 327 6888	Mr F. Ali	330-6083	11–17	195	G Mu
The Blue Coat School	Somerset Rd, Edgbaston, Birmingham, West Midlands B17 0HR	0121 410 6800	0121 454 7757	Mr A.D.J. Browning	330-6070	3–14	521	CE
Darul Uloom Islamic High School	521–527 Coventry Rd, Small Heath, Birmingham, West Midlands B10 0LL	0121 772 6408	0121 773 4340	Mr Mujahid	330-6078	11–16	70	B Mu
Edgbaston High School for Girls	Westbourne Rd, Edgbaston, Birmingham, West Midlands B15 3TS	0121 454 5831	0121 454 2363	Dr Ruth Weeks	330-6003	2–19	947	G
Elmhurst School for Dance in Association with Birmingham Royal Ballet	247 Bristol Rd, Edgbaston, Birmingham, West Midlands B5 7UH	0121 472 6655		Mr John McNamara	330-6111	11–19	192	R
Highclare School	10 Sutton Rd, Erdington, Birmingham, West Midlands B23 6QL	0121 373 7400	0121 373 7445	Mrs M. Viles	330-6060	2–19	744	
Jamia Islamia Birmingham	Islamic College, Fallows Rd, Sparkbrook, Birmingham, West Midlands B11 1PL	0121 772 6400	0121 772640	Mohammed Govalia	330-6106	11–16	129	Mu
King Edward VI High School for Girls	Edgbaston Park Rd, Birmingham, West Midlands B15 2UB	0121 472 1834	0121 471 3808	Miss S.H. Evans	330-6077	11–18	547	G
King Edward's School	Edgbaston Park Rd, Birmingham, West Midlands B15 2UA	0121 472 1672	0121 414 1897	Mr John Alan Claughton	330-6076	11–16	848	B CE
Mander Portman Woodward Independent College	38 Highfield Rd, Edgbaston, Birmingham, West Midlands B15 3ED	0121 454 9637	0121 454 6433	Ms Dominica Jewell	330-6079	14–16	110	
The Priory School	Sir Harry's Rd, Edgbaston, Birmingham, West Midlands B15 2UR	0121 440 4103	0121 440 3639	Ms E. Brook	330-6002	2–16	302	RC
St George's School Edgbaston	31 Calthorpe Rd, Birmingham, West Midlands B15 1RX	0121 625 0398	0121 625 3340	Miss H. Phillips	330-6100	2–18	363	Ch
Sporting Edge	St George's Church Centre, Bridge St West, Newtown, Birmingham, West Midlands B19 2YX	01213 337325	01213 337325	Mr S.C. McCullough	330-6109	14–16	19	
Woodstock Girls' School	11–15 Woodstock Rd, Moseley, Birmingham, West Midlands B13 9BB	0781 774 1089	0121 449 6690	Mrs T. Anees	330-6094	11–16	119	G Mu

Coventry

School name	Address	Tel	Fax	Headteacher	Ref	Ages	Pupils	Other
Bablake Junior School	Coundon Rd, Coventry, West Midlands CV1 4AU	024 7627 1260	024 7627 1294	Mr J.S. Dover	331-6023	7–14	172	Ch
Bablake School	Coundon Rd, Bablake, Coventry, West Midlands CV1 4AU	024 7627 1200	024 7627 1290	Dr S. Nuttall	331-6017	11–19	899	Ch
Copsewood School	168–170 Roland Ave, Holbrooks, Coventry, West Midlands CV6 4LX	024 7668 0680		Mr A.R.G. Shedden	331-6027	10–16	93	Ch
Coventry Muslim School	643 Foleshill Rd, Coventry, West Midlands CV6 5JQ	024 7626 1803		Mrs Ashique	331-6022	4–16	59	G Mu
Fairmount School inc Coventry Grammar School	Clarendon St, Coventry, West Midlands CV5 6EX	024 7667 3584		Mrs R. Gillam	331-6025	10–18	9	Ch
King Henry VIII School	Warwick Rd, Coventry, West Midlands CV3 6AQ	024 7627 1111	024 7627 1188	Mr George Fisher	331-6016	7–16	1098	
Pattison College	86–90 Binley Rd, Coventry, West Midlands CV3 1FQ	024 7645 5031	024 7644 1590	Mrs Elizabeth McConnell	331-6011	3–19	146	Ch

4

Dudley

School name	Address	Tel	Fax	Headteacher	Ref	Ages	Pupils	Other
Elmfield Rudolf Steiner School Limited	14 Love La., Stourbridge, West Midlands DY8 2EA	01384 394633	01384 393608	Ms A. O'Reilly	332-6000	3-18	259	R
New Hall Project 20/20	The Huntingtree Park Centre, Halesowen, West Midlands B63 4HY	0121 550 0006			332-6004	14-16	9	
St Thomas Community Network	Bluecoat Base, Beechwood Rd, Dudley, West Midlands DY2 7QA	01384 818990	01384 818991	Ms Janet Hilken	332-6002	14-16	14	
Stephenson House School	292 Stourbridge Rd, Holly Hall, Dudley, West Midlands DY1 2EE	01384 485859	01384 480047	Ms I. Hayes	332-6003	14-16	6	

Herefordshire

School name	Address	Tel	Fax	Headteacher	Ref	Ages	Pupils	Other
The Downs School	Brockhill Rd, Colwall, Malvern, Worcestershire WR13 6EY	01684 540277	01684 540094	Mr A. Ramsay	884-6000	2-14	177	R
Hereford Cathedral School	Old Deanery, The Cathedral Cl, Hereford, Herefordshire HR1 2NG	01432 363522	01432 363525	Mr P.A. Smith	884-6004	10-19	523	CE
Hereford Waldorf School	Much Dewchurch, Hereford, Herefordshire HR2 8DL	01981 540515	01981 541237		884-6005	3-16	265	Ch
Lucton School	Lucton, Leominster, Herefordshire HR6 9PN	01568 782000	01568 782001	Mrs Gill Thorne	884-6007	2-17	266	R Ch
St Richard's School	Bredenbury Ct, Bromyard, Herefordshire HR7 4TD	01885 482491	01885 488982	Mr R.E.H. Coghlan	884-6003	2-14	125	R RC

Shropshire

School name	Address	Tel	Fax	Headteacher	Ref	Ages	Pupils	Other
Adcote School for Girls	Little Ness, Shrewsbury, Shropshire SY4 2JY	01939 260202	01939 261300	Ms D.J. Hammond	893-6003	4-16	97	G R CE
Bedstone College	Bucknell, Shropshire SY7 0BG	01547 530303	01547 530740	Mr M.S. Symonds	893-6000	2-16	265	R CE
Concord College	Acton Burnell Hall, Shrewsbury, Shropshire SY5 7PF	01694 731631	01694 731389	Mr Neil Hawkins	893-6020	12-16	369	R
Ellesmere College	Ellesmere, Shropshire SY12 9AB	01691 622321	01691 623286	Mr B.J. Wignall	893-6001	8-16	553	R CE
Moffats School	Kinlet Hall, Bewdley, Worcestershire DY12 3AY	01299 841230	01299 841444	M. Daborn	893-6002	3-14	63	R
Moreton Hall School	Weston Rhyn, Oswestry, Shropshire SY11 3EW	01691 773671	01691 778552	Mr J. Forster	893-6005	9-16	372	G R
Oswestry School	Upper Brook St, Oswestry, Shropshire SY11 2TL	01691 655711	01691 671194	Mr P.D. Stockdale	893-6011	2-16	413	R ND
Shrewsbury High School	32 Town Walls, Shrewsbury, Shropshire SY1 1TN	01743 362872	01743 364942	Mrs Marilyn Cass	893-6018	2-19	767	G
Shrewsbury School	The Schools, Shrewsbury, Shropshire SY3 7BA	01743 280500	01743 243107	Mr J.W.R. Goulding	893-6009	12-16	674	B R

Solihull

School name	Address	Tel	Fax	Headteacher	Ref	Ages	Pupils	Other
Kingswood School	St James Pl, Shirley, Solihull, West Midlands B90 2BA	0121 744 7883	0121 744 1282	Mr Neil Shaw	334-6009	2-16	45	
St Martin's School	Malvern Hall, Brueton Ave, Solihull, West Midlands B91 3EN	0121 705 1265	0121 711 4529	Mrs J. Carwinthen	334-6002	2-19	517	G
Solihull School	Warwick Rd, Solihull, West Midlands B91 3DJ	0121 705 0958	0121 711 4439	Mr P.J. Griffiths	334-6003	7-19	989	

Staffordshire

School name	Address	Tel	Fax	Headteacher	Ref	Ages	Pupils	Other
Abbots Bromley School for Girls	Abbots Bromley, Rugeley, Staffordshire WS15 3BW	01283 840232	01283 840988	Mrs P.J. Woodhouse	860-6013	4-16	299	G R
Chase Academy c/o Lyncroft House	St John's Rd, Cannock, Staffordshire WS11 3UR	01543 501800	01543 501801	Mr D.R. Holland	860-6020	3-19	203	R Ch
Chase Academy International Study Centre	St John's Rd, Cannock, Staffordshire WS11 0UR	01543 501800	01543 501801	Mr Andrew Evans	860-6023	10-16	76	R Ch
Companions	Hunters Moon, Nr Eccleshall, Sturbridge, Staffordshire ST21 6LF	01785 859455	01785 859277	Mr Graham Cooper	860-6028	14-18	1	R
Denstone College	Denstone, Uttoxeter, Staffordshire ST14 5HN	01889 590484	01889 590744	Mr D.M. Derbyshire	860-6005	11-19	522	R CE
Newcastle-under-Lyme School	Mount Pleasant, Newcastle under Lyme, Staffordshire ST5 1DB	01782 631197	01782 632765	Mrs N. Rugg	860-6015	2-19	1116	
St Bede's School	Bishton Hall, Stafford, Staffordshire ST17 0XN	01889 881277	01889 882749	Mr H.S. Northcote	860-6001	2-14	73	R

School name	Address	Tel	Fax	Headteacher	Ref	Ages	Pupils	Other
St Dominic's Priory School	21 Station Rd, Stone, Staffordshire ST15 8EN	01785 814181	01785 819361	Mr A. Egan	860-6011	3–19	232	RC
St Dominic's School	Bargate St, Stafford, Staffordshire ST19 9BA	01902 850248	01902 851154	Mrs S. White	860-6005	2–18	300	G Ch
Stafford Grammar School	Burton Manor, Stafford, Staffordshire ST18 9AT	01785 249752	01785 255005	Mr M.R. Darley	860-6009	11–18	403	
The Yarlet Schools	Yarlet, Stafford, Staffordshire ST18 9SU	01785 286568	01785 286569	Mr R.S. Plant	860-6000	3–14	161	R CE

Telford and Wrekin

School name	Address	Tel	Fax	Headteacher	Ref	Ages	Pupils	Other
Wrekin College	Sutherland Rd, Wellington, Telford, Shropshire TF1 3BH	01952 240131	01952 415068	Mr S.G. Drew	894-6001	11–16	453	R CE

Walsall

School name	Address	Tel	Fax	Headteacher	Ref	Ages	Pupils	Other
Abu Bakr Independent School	154–160 Wednesbury Rd, Palfrey, Walsall, West Midlands WS1 4JJ	01922 620618	01922 646175	M. Luqman	335-6010	11–16	314	Mu
Emmanuel Girls School	Bath Street Centre, Bath St, Walsall, West Midlands WS1 3DB	01922 635810		J. Swain	335-6009	5–16	59	Ch
Hydesville Tower School	25 Broadway North, Walsall, West Midlands WS1 2QG	01922 624374		Leslie Fox	335-6007	2–16	384	Ch
Palfrey Girls School	72 Queen Mary St, Palfrey, Walsall, West Midlands WS1 4AB	01922 625510		H. Varachia	335-6008	11–16	183	G Mu
Second Chances at The Vine Trust Walsall	33 Lower Hall La, Caldmore, Walsall, West Midlands WS1 1RR	01922 621951	01922 621951	R. Clay	335-6012	14–16		Ch

Warwickshire

School name	Address	Tel	Fax	Headteacher	Ref	Ages	Pupils	Other
Bilton Grange School	Dunchurch, Rugby, Warwickshire CV22 6QU	01788 810217	01788 810122	Mr Peter Kirk	937-6002	3–14	329	R Ch
The King's High School for Girls	Smith St, Warwick, Warwickshire CV34 4HJ	01926 494485	01926 403089	Mrs E. Surber	937-6089	10–16	598	G
The Kingsley School	Beauchamp Ave, Leamington Spa, Warwickshire CV32 5RD	01926 425127	01926 831691	Mrs C.A. Mannion Watson	937-6005	2–19	465	G CE
Princethorpe College	Leamington Rd, Rugby, Warwickshire CV23 9PX	01926 634200	01926 633365	Mr J.M. Shinkwin	937-6084	11–19	717	RC
Rugby School	Lawrence Sheriff St, Rugby, Warwickshire CV22 5EH	01788 556216	01788 556219	Mr P.S.J. Derham	937-6010	11–19	803	R CE
Warwick School	Myton Rd, Warwick, Warwickshire CV34 6PP	01926 776400	01926 401259	Mr E. Halse	937-6020	7–19	1087	B R

Wolverhampton

School name	Address	Tel	Fax	Headteacher	Ref	Ages	Pupils	Other
The Royal Wolverhampton School	Penn Rd, Wolverhampton, West Midlands WV3 0EG	01902 341230	01902 344496	Mr T.L. Waters	336-6000	10–16	450	R CE
Tettenhall College Incorporated	Wood Rd, Tettenhall, Wolverhampton, West Midlands WV6 8QX	01902 751119	01902 741940	Dr P.C. Bodkin	336-6013	2–16	484	R
Wolverhampton Grammar School	Compton Rd, Wolverhampton, West Midlands WV3 9RB	01902 421326	01902 421819	Dr Bernard Trafford	336-6023	10–16	672	G CE

Worcestershire

School name	Address	Tel	Fax	Headteacher	Ref	Ages	Pupils	Other
Abberley Hall School	Abberley, Worcester, Worcestershire WR6 6DD	01299 896275	01299 896875	Mr J.G.W. Walker	885-6005	2–14	264	R
Abbey College	Wells Rd, Malvern, Worcestershire WR14 4JF	01684 892300	01684 892757	Mr Philip Moere	885-6026	14–19	69	R
Bowbrook House School	Peopleton, Pershore, Worcestershire WR10 2EE	01905 841242	01905 840716	Mr C.D. Allen	885-6025	3–17	172	
Bredon School	Pull Ct, Bushley, Tewkesbury, Gloucestershire GL20 6AH	01684 293156	01684 298008	Mr David Keyte	885-6023	8–16	220	R CE
Bromsgrove School	Worcester Rd, Bromsgrove, Worcestershire B61 7DU	01527 579679	01527 576177	Mr Christopher Edwards	885-6006	2–16	1361	R CE

4

School name	Address	Tel	Fax	Headteacher	Ref	Ages	Pupils	Other
Dodderhill School	Crutch La, Droitwich, Worcestershire WR9 0BE	01905 778290	01905 790623	Mrs J.M. Mumby	885-6016	3–16	213	ND
Green Hill School	Greenhill, Evesham, Worcestershire WR11 4NG	01386 442364	01386 442364	Mr O. Lister	885-6004	2–16	88	
Heathfield School	Wolverley, Kidderminster, Worcestershire DY10 3QE	01562 850204		Mr G.L. Sinton	885-6014	3–16	299	
Holy Trinity School	Birmingham Rd, Kidderminster, Worcestershire DY10 2BY	01562 822929	01562 865137	Mrs Y.L. Wilkinson	885-6009	1–19	347	Ch
The King's School	5 College Grn, Worcester, Worcestershire WR1 2LH	01905 721700	01905 721710	Mr R.W. Middleton	885-6027	2–19	1359	CE
Madinatul Uloom Al Islamiya School	Summerfield, Kidderminster, Worcestershire DY10 4BH	01562 66894	01562 862334	Mr A. Hans	885-6031	11–16	213	B R Mu
Malvern College	College Rd, Malvern, Worcestershire WR14 3DF	01684 581504		Mr David Dowdles	885-6011	2–19	769	R CE
Malvern St James	15 Avenue Rd, Malvern, Worcestershire WR14 3BA	01684 892288	01684 566204	Mrs Rosalind Hayes	885-6012	10–18	381	G R
New Elizabethan School	The Village, Hartlebury, Kidderminster, Worcestershire DY11 7TE	01299 250258	01299 250379	Miss Coles	885-6021	4–16	14	
The River School	Oakfield Hse, Droitwich Rd, Worcester, Worcestershire WR3 7ST	01905 457047	01905 754492	Mr D. Climie	885-6030	2–16	141	Ch
Royal Grammar School	Upper Tything, Worcester, Worcestershire WR1 1HP	01905 613391	01905 726892	Mr A. Rattue	885-6028	2–19	1098	
St Mary's Convent School	Mount Battenhall, Worcester, Worcestershire WR5 2HP	01905 357786	01905 351718	Mrs Susan Cookson	885-6000	0–18	356	RC
St Michael's College	Oldwood Rd, St Michaels, Tenbury Wells, Worcestershire WR15 8PH	01584 811300	01584 811221	Mr S. Higgins	885-6036	14–16	103	R
Winterfold House School	Winterfold, Chaddesley Corbett, Kidderminster, Worcestershire DY10 4PW	01562 777234	01562 777234	Mr W. Ibbetson-Price	885-6008	2–14	360	

Yorkshire and The Humber

Barnsley

School name	Address	Tel	Fax	Headteacher	Ref	Ages	Pupils	Other
Barnsley Christian School	Hope Hse, 2 Blucher St, Barnsley, South Yorkshire S70 1AP	01226 211011	01226 211011	Mr G.J. Barnes	370-6001	2–16	92	Ch

Bradford

School name	Address	Tel	Fax	Headteacher	Ref	Ages	Pupils	Other
Bradford Christian School	Livingstone Rd, Bradford BD2 1BT	01274 532649	01274 595819	Mr P. Moon	380-6110	4–16	180	Ch
Bradford Girls' Grammar School	Squire La, Bradford BD9 6RB	01274 545395	01274 482595	Mrs L.J. Warrington	380-6102	2–19	675	G CE
Bradford Grammar School	Keighley Rd, Bradford BD9 4JP	01274 542492	01274 548129	Mr S.R. Davidson	380-6103	6–19	1095	
CJ's Training Base	353 Great Horton Rd, Bradford BD7 3BZ	01274 570232	01274 501724	Mr J. Woodyatt	380-6118	12–16	29	Ch
Darul Uloom Dawatul Imaan	Harry St, Bradford BD4 9PH	01274 402233	01274 402233	Mr Mohamed Bilal Lorgat	380-6114	11–14	117	B R Mu
Jaamiatul Imaam Muhammad Zakaria School	Thornton View Rd, Bradford BD14 6JX	01274 882007	01274 883696	Mrs Z. Hajee	380-6109	11–16	430	G R Mu
Olive Secondary	Byron St, Bradford BD3 0AD	01274 725005		Mr Amjad Mohammed	380-6119	11–18	113	Mu
Shaw House School	150 Wilmer Rd, Bradford BD9 4AH	01274 496299		Mr R.C. Williams	380-6106	11–16	90	MF

Calderdale

School name	Address	Tel	Fax	Headteacher	Ref	Ages	Pupils	Other
Glen House Montessori School	Cragg Vale, Hebden Bridge, West Yorkshire HX7 5SQ	01422 884682		Mrs Margret Scaife	381-6008	2–15	27	
Hipperholme Grammar School	Bramley La, Halifax, West Yorkshire HX3 8JE	01422 202256		Mr C.C. Robinson	381-6006	3–18	292	Ch
Rishworth School	Rishworth, Sowerby Bridge, West Yorkshire HX6 4QA	01422 822217		Mr R.A. Baker	381-6001	3–16	572	R

Doncaster

School name	Address	Tel	Fax	Headteacher	Ref	Ages	Pupils	Other
Hill House St Marys' School	65 Bawtry Rd, Doncaster, South Yorkshire DN4 7AD	01302 535926	01302 534675	Mr Jack Cusworth	371-6000	2–16	458	Ch

East Riding of Yorkshire

School name	Address	Tel	Fax	Headteacher	Ref	Ages	Pupils	Other
Hull Collegiate School	Tranby Croft, Anlaby, Hull HU10 7EH	01482 657016	01482 655389	Mr Rob Haworth	811-6000	2–18	789	Ch
North Moor Education Trust	North Moor Hse, Dunswell Rd, Cottingham HU16 4JS	01482 840722	01482 840723	Mr F. Salt	811-6007	9–17	70	Ch
Pocklington School	West Grn, Pocklington, York, North Yorkshire YO42 2NJ	01759 303125	01759 306366	Mr Nicolas Clements	811-6003	7–16	810	R CE

Kingston upon Hull

School name	Address	Tel	Fax	Headteacher	Ref	Ages	Pupils	Other
Hymers College	Hymers Ave, Hull, East Riding of Yorkshire HU3 1LW	01482 343555	01482 472854	Mr J.C. Morris	810-6001	8–19	977	

Kirklees

School name	Address	Tel	Fax	Headteacher	Ref	Ages	Pupils	Other
Batley Grammar School	Carlinghow Hill, Batley, West Yorkshire WF17 0AD	01924 474980	01924 471960	Mr B. Battye	382-6012	3–16	370	
The Branch Christian School	8–10 Thomas St, Heckmondwike, West Yorkshire WF16 0NW	01924 235637	01924 411021	Mr R. Ward	382-6018	3–16	18	Ch
Brian Jackson College of Open Learning at National Children's Centre	2 New North Par, Westgate, Huddersfield, West Yorkshire HD1 5JP	01484 519988	01484 435150	Mr Peter Joseph	382-6026	14–16	14	
Edgerton College	7 Edgerton Rd, Edgerton, Huddersfield, West Yorkshire HD1 5RA	01484 532412	01484 455564	Mrs Julia Pomeroy	382-6025	14–16	12	
Huddersfield Grammar School	Royds Mount, Luck La, Huddersfield, West Yorkshire HD1 4QX	01484 424549	01484 531835	Mrs J.L. Straughan	382-6005	3–16	437	Ch
Institute of Islamic Education	South St, Savile Town, Dewsbury, West Yorkshire WF12 9NG	01924 455762	01924 455762	Dr M.M. Mulk	382-6013	13–19	312	B R Mu
Islamia Girls' High School	Noor Mosque, Thornton Lodge Rd, Huddersfield, West Yorkshire HD1 3JQ	01484 535674		Mrs Samira El-Turabi	382-6016	9–16	23	G Mu
Madni Muslim Girls' High School	40–42 Scarborough St, Savile Town, Dewsbury, West Yorkshire WF12 9AY	01924 520720	01924 468516	Mrs S. Mirza	382-6017	3–19	219	G Mu
Rathbone Choices	10 Highfield Rd, Huddersfield HD1 5LP	01484 346468	01484 346499	Richard Robson	382-6023	14–16	24	
Zakaria Muslim Girls' High School	111 Warwick Rd, Batley, West Yorkshire WF17 6AJ	01924 444217	01924 444217	Mr Y. Jasat	382-6015	11–16	220	G Mu

Leeds

School name	Address	Tel	Fax	Headteacher	Ref	Ages	Pupils	Other
Brownberrie School	173–179 New Road Side, Horsforth, Leeds, West Yorkshire LS18 4DR	0113 305 3350		Mr M.J. Harding	383-6122	11–17	41	Ch
Fulneck School	Fulneck, Pudsey, West Yorkshire LS28 8DS	0113 257 0235	0113 255 7316	Mr T. Kernohan	383-6117	3–19	378	R Moravian
Gateways School	Harewood, Leeds, West Yorkshire LS17 9LE	0113 288 6345	0113 288 6148	Mr D. Davidson	383-6007	3–16	479	G CE
Grammar School at Leeds	Alwoodley Gates, Harrogate Rd, Leeds, West Yorkshire LS17 8GS	0113 229 1552	0113 228 5111	Dr M. Bailey	383-6112	3–19	1326	B CE
Leeds Menorah School	399 Street La, Leeds, West Yorkshire LS17 6HQ	0113 269 7709		Rabbi Refson	383-6099	5–16	40	Je
New Horizon Community School	Newton Hill Hse, Newton Hill Rd, Leeds, West Yorkshire LS7 4JE	0113 262 4001	0113 262 4912	Mrs Dambatta	383-6119	11–16	73	G Mu
Woodhouse Grove School	Apperley Bridge, Bradford, West Yorkshire BD10 0NR	0113 250 2477	0113 250 5290	Mr D.C. Humphreys	383-6113	4–16	1035	R Me

North East Lincolnshire

School name	Address	Tel	Fax	Headteacher	Ref	Ages	Pupils	Other
St James' School	22 Bargate, Grimsby DN34 4SY	01472 503260	01472 503275	Mrs S.M. Isaac	812-6000	2–16	239	R CE

North Lincolnshire

School name	Address	Tel	Fax	Headteacher	Ref	Ages	Pupils	Other
South Park Enterprise College (14-19)	45a Newdown Rd, South Park Ind Est, Scunthorpe DN17 2TX	01724 291516	01724 291516	Mrs L. Bennett	813-6003	14–19	47	

North Yorkshire

School name	Address	Tel	Fax	Headteacher	Ref	Ages	Pupils	Other
Ampleforth College	Ampleforth, York, North Yorkshire YO62 4ER	01439 766000	01439 788330	Father Gabriel Everitt	815-6006	13–18	590	R
Ashville College	Green La, Harrogate, North Yorkshire HG2 9JP	01423 566358	01423 505142	Mr A.A.P. Fleck	815-6028	4–16	805	R Me
Aysgarth School	Newton-le-Willows, Newton-le-Willows, Bedale, North Yorkshire DL8 1TF	01677 450240		Mr C.A.A. Goddard	815-6009	2–14	166	B R CE
Botton Village School	Danby, Whitby, North Yorkshire YO21 2NJ	01287 661206	01287 661207		815-6003	5–14	61	
Bramcote School	Filey Rd, Scarborough, North Yorkshire YO11 2TT	01723 373086	01723 364186	Mr Andrew Lewin	815-6001	4–14	114	R
Fyling Hall School	Robin Hoods Bay, Whitby, North Yorkshire YO22 4QD	01947 880353	01947 881097	Dr Glenn Horridge	815-6004	5–16	199	R Ch
Giggleswick School	Giggleswick, Settle, North Yorkshire BD24 0DE	01729 893000	01729 893150	Mr Geoffrey P. Boult	815-6011	3–18	435	R CE
Harrogate Ladies' College	Clarence Dr, Harrogate, North Yorkshire HG1 2QG	01423 504543	01423 568893	Dr M.J. Hustler	815-6012	2–18	606	R
Queen Ethelburga's College	Thorpe Underwood Hall, Ouseburn, York, North Yorkshire YO26 9SS	0870 742 3300	0870 742 3310	Mr S. Jandrell	815-6014	2–16	509	R CE
Queen Margaret's School	Escrick Pk, York, North Yorkshire YO19 6EU	01904 728261	01904 728150	Dr G. Chapman	815-6035	10–16	360	G R CE
Queen Mary's School	Baldersby Pk, Topcliffe, Thirsk, North Yorkshire YO7 3BZ	01845 575000	01845 575001	Mr Robert McKenzie Johnston	815-6000	3–16	193	G R CE
Read School	Drax, Selby, North Yorkshire YO8 8NL	01757 618248	01757 617432	Mr R.A. Hadfield	815-6019	3–16	354	R
Scarborough College	Filey Rd, Scarborough, North Yorkshire YO11 3BA	01723 360620	01723 377265	Mr T.L. Kirkup	815-6002	11–19	401	R
Terrington Hall School	Terrington, York, North Yorkshire YO60 6PR	01653 648227	01653 648458	Mr M.J. Glen	815-6003	2–14	171	R Ch

Rotherham

School name	Address	Tel	Fax	Headteacher	Ref	Ages	Pupils	Other
Elsworth House School	Rother Way, Hellaby Est, Rotherham S66 8QN	01709 533770		Mr F. McCabe	372-6003	11–16	40	Ch

Sheffield

School name	Address	Tel	Fax	Headteacher	Ref	Ages	Pupils	Other
Al-Mahad-Al-Islam School	1 Industry Rd, Sheffield, South Yorkshire S9 5FP	0114 242 3138		Mrs F. Messoul	373-6028	11–17	76	G Mu
Bethany School	Finlay St, Sheffield, South Yorkshire S3 7PS	0114 272 6994	0114 272 7003	Mr K. Walze	373-6027	4–16	77	
Birkdale School	Oakholme Rd, Sheffield, South Yorkshire S10 3DH	0114 266 8408	0114 267 1947	Mr R. Court	373-6005	5–16	790	B
Brantwood School	1 Kenwood Bank, Sheffield, South Yorkshire S7 1NU	0114 258 1747	0114 258 1847	Mrs V.A. Barnes	373-6010	4–16	165	G
Handsworth Christian School	231 Handsworth Rd, Handsworth, Sheffield, South Yorkshire S13 9BJ	0114 243 0276	0114 243 4016	Mrs P.E. Arnott	373-6026	5–16	134	Ch
Jamia Al Hudaa	Park Hse, Bawtry Rd, Tinsley, Sheffield S9 1WD	0114 243 8000	0114 243 7041	Mr R. Haq	373-6030	11–16	57	R Mu
Sheffield High School	10 Rutland Pk, Sheffield, South Yorkshire S10 2PE	0114 266 0324	0114 267 8520	Mrs Valerie Dunsford	373-6021	4–18	1012	G
Westbourne School	50 Westbourne Rd, Sheffield, South Yorkshire S10 2QQ	0114 266 0374	0114 267 6518	Mr J. Hicks	373-6001	4–16	312	

Wakefield

School name	Address	Tel	Fax	Headteacher	Ref	Ages	Pupils	Other
Ackworth School	Ackworth, Pontefract, West Yorkshire WF7 7LT	01977 611401	01977 616225	Mr Peter J. Simpson	384-6000	4–18	601	R Qk
Queen Elizabeth Grammar Junior School	158 Northgate, Wakefield, West Yorkshire WF1 3QY	01924 373821	01924 231604	Mr M. Bisset	384-6119	7–14	256	B
Queen Elizabeth Grammar School	154 Northgate, Wakefield, West Yorkshire WF1 3QX	01924 373943	01924 231603	Mr Michael Gibbons	384-6115	11–16	733	B ID
Rathbone	2nd Fl Exchange Hse, Queen St, Wakefield WF1 1JR	01924 299097	01924 299098		384-6122	14–16	6	B
Silcoates School	Wrenthorpe, Wakefield, West Yorkshire WF2 0PD	01924 291614	01924 368693	Mr Paul Spillane	384-6027	7–19	751	UR
Wakefield Girls' High School	Wentworth St, Wakefield, West Yorkshire WF1 2QS	01924 372490	01924 231601	Mrs P.A. Langham	384-6114	11–19	734	G
Wakefield Independent School	Nostell Centre, Doncaster Rd, Nostell, Wakefield, West Yorkshire WF4 1QG	01924 865757	01924 865757	Mrs K.E. Caryl	384-6116	2–17	212	CE

York

School name	Address	Tel	Fax	Headteacher	Ref	Ages	Pupils	Other
Bootham School	51 Bootham, York, North Yorkshire YO30 7BU	01904 623261	01904 652106	Mr J.F.J. Taylor	816-6000	10–19	590	R Qk
The Mount School	Dalton Terr, York, North Yorkshire YO24 4DD	01904 667500	01904 667524	Mrs D.J. Gant	816-6003	3–16	441	G R Qk
Rathbone Choices Centre	6 Nursery Dr, Holgate, York, North Yorkshire YO24 4PE	0161 236 5358	0161 238 6356	Mrs Debbie Malham	816-6009	13–16	15	
St Peter's School (inc St Olave's and Clifton Pre-Prep)	Clifton, York, North Yorkshire YO30 6AB	01904 527300	01904 527302	Mr Andy Falconer	816-6002	3–19	1035	R CE
York Steiner School	Danesmead, Fulford Cross, York, North Yorkshire YO10 4PB	01904 654983	01904 654994	Ms Judy Gray	816-6008	3–14	193	

Scotland

Aberdeen City

School name	Address	Website	E-mail	Tel	Fax	Pupils
Aberdeen Waldorf (Steiner) School	Craigton Rd, Cults, Aberdeen AB15 9QD	www.aberdeenwaldorf.co.uk	aws@talk21.com		01224 868366	34
Albyn School for Girls	17–23 Queens Rd, Aberdeen AB15 4PB	www.albynschool.co.uk	information@albynschool.co.uk	01224 322408	01224 209173	207
International School of Aberdeen	296 North Deeside Rd, Milltimber, Aberdeen AB13 0AB	www.isa.aberdeen.sch.uk	admin@isa.abdn.sch.uk	01224 732267	01224 735648	140
Robert Gordon's College	Schoolhill, Aberdeen AB10 1FE	www.rgc.aberdeen.sch.uk	enquiries@rgc.aberdeen.sch.uk	01224 646346	01224 630301	1040
St Margaret's School for Girls	17 Albyn Pl, Aberdeen AB10 1RU	www.st-margaret.aberdeen.sch.uk	info@st-margaret.aberdeen.sch.uk	01224 584466	01224 585600	339
Springvale Educational Trust	c/o Windmill Printing, Denmore Pl, Bridge of Don, Aberdeen AB23 8JS			01224 798500		24
Total School	1–5 Whitehall Pl, Aberdeen AB25 2RH		aberdeen_french_school@btinternet.com	01224 645545	01224 645565	32

Argyll and Bute

School name	Address	Website	E-mail	Tel	Fax	Pupils
Lomond School	10 Stafford St, Helensburgh G84 9JX	www.lomond-school.demon.co.uk	admin@lomond-school.demon.co.uk	01436 672476	01436 678320	370

4

Clackmannanshire

School name	Address	Website	E-mail	Tel	Fax	Pupils
Dollar Academy	Dollar, Clackmannanshire FK14 7DU	www.dollaracademy.org.uk	rector@dollaracademy.org.uk	01259 742511	01259 742867	848

Dumfries and Galloway

School name	Address	Website	E-mail	Tel	Fax	Pupils
River of Life Christian School	Dumfries Station, Lovers Wlk, Dumfries DG1 1LU	www.riveroflife.org.uk		01387 264646	01387 264200	9

Dundee City

School name	Address	Website	E-mail	Tel	Fax	Pupils
High School of Dundee	Euclid Cres, Dundee DD1 1HU	www.highschoolofdundee.co.uk	enquiries@hsd.dundeecity.sch.uk	01382 202921	01382 229822	679

East Lothian

School name	Address	Website	E-mail	Tel	Fax	Pupils
Belhaven Hill	Dunbar, East Lothian EH42 1NN	www.belhavenhill.e-lothian.sch.uk	belhavenhill@lineone.net	01368 862785	01368 865225	30
Loretto School	Musselburgh, Midlothian EH21 7RE	www.loretto.com	admissions@loretto.com	0131 653 4444	0131 663 4445	338

East Renfrewshire

School name	Address	Website	E-mail	Tel	Fax	Pupils
Belmont House School	Sandringham Ave, Newton Mearns, Glasgow G77 5DU	www.belmontschool.co.uk	headmaster@belmontschool.co.uk	0141 639 2922	0141 639 9860	176

Edinburgh City

School name	Address	Website	E-mail	Tel	Fax	Pupils
Cargilfield School	37 Barnton Ave West, Edinburgh EH4 6HU	www.cargilfield.edin.sch.uk	secretary@cargilfield.edin.sch.uk	0131 336 2207	0131 336 3179	32
The Edinburgh Academy School	42 Henderson Row, Edinburgh EH3 5BL	www.edinburghacademy.org.uk	headmaster@edinburghacademy.org.uk	0131 556 4603	0131 556 9353	402
Fettes College	Carrington Rd, Edinburgh EH4 1QX	www.fettes.com	enquiries@fettes.com	0131 332 2281	0131 332 3081	510
George Heriot's School	Lauriston Pl, Edinburgh EH3 9HE	www.george-heriots.com	headmaster@george-heriots.com	0131 229 7263	0131 229 6363	961
George Watson's College	67–71 Colinton Rd, Edinburgh EH10 5EG	www.gwc.org.uk	info@watsons.edin.sch.uk	0131 446 6000	0131 452 8594	1321
Mannafields Christian School	170 Easter Rd, Edinburgh EH7 5QE	www.mannafields.org.uk	headteacher@mannafields.org.uk	0131 659 5602		3
Mary Erskine School	Ravelston, Edinburgh EH4 3NT	www.esms.edin.sch.uk	schoolsecretary@esmgc.com	0131 347 5700	0131 346 8594	720
Merchiston Castle School	294 Colinton Rd, Edinburgh EH13 0PU	www.merchiston.co.uk	headmaster@merchiston.co.uk	0131 312 2200	0131 441 6060	355
Rudolf Steiner School of Edinburgh	60 Spylaw Rd, Edinburgh EH10 5BR	www.steinerweb.org.uk	info@steinerweb.org.uk	0131 337 3410	0131 538 6066	150
St George's School for Girls	Garscube Terr, Edinburgh EH12 6BG	www.st-georges.edin.sch.uk	head@st-georges.edin.sch.uk	0131 311 8000	0131 315 2035	516
St Margaret's School	East Suffolk Rd, Edinburgh EH16 5PJ	www.st-margarets.edin.sch.uk	contact@st-margarets.edin.sch.uk	0131 668 1986	0131 662 0957	248
St Mary's Music School	Coates Hall, 25 Grosvenor Cres, Edinburgh EH12 5EL	www.st-marys-music-school.co.uk	info@st-marys-music-school.co.uk	0131 538 7766	0131 467 7298	45
St Serf's School	5 Wester Coates Gdns, Edinburgh EH12 5LT	www.st-serfs.edin.sch.uk	office@stserfsschool.freeserve.co.uk	0131 337 1015		79

Falkirk

School name	Address	Website	E-mail	Tel	Fax	Pupils
Oakwood Education Trust	Bog Rd, Laurieston, Falkirk FK2 9BP			01324 630733		51

Fife

School name	Address	Website	E-mail	Tel	Fax	Pupils
Osborne House School	Osborne Hse, West Port, Dysart, Fife KY1 2TD		enquiries@osborne-house.com	01592 651461		16
St Leonards Junior, Middle and Senior Schools and Sixth Form College	St Andrew's, Fife KY16 9QJ	www.stleonards-fife.org	info@stleonards-fife.org	01334 472126	01334 476152	241

Glasgow City

School name	Address	Website	E-mail	Tel	Fax	Pupils
Craigholme School for Girls	72 St Andrews Dr, Glasgow G41 4HS	www.craigholme.co.uk	headteacher@craigholme.glasgow.sch.uk	0141 427 0375	0141 427 6396	259
The Glasgow Academy	Colebrooke St, Glasgow G12 8HE	www.theglasgowacademy.org.uk	enquiries@tga.org.uk	0141 334 8558	0141 337 3473	559
Glasgow Steiner School	52 Lumsden St, Yorkhill, Glasgow G3 8RH	www.glasgowsteinerschool.org.uk	headteacher@glasgowsteiner.glasgow.sch.uk	0141 334 8855	0141 334 8855	75
The High School of Glasgow	637 Crow Rd, Glasgow G13 1PL	www.glasgowhigh.com	rector@hsog.co.uk	0141 954 9628	0141 959 0191	600
Hutchesons' Grammar School	21 Beaton Rd, Glasgow G41 4NW	www.hutchesons.org	rector@hutchesons.org	0141 423 2933	0141 424 0251	1131
Kelvinside Academy	33 Kirklee Rd, Glasgow G12 0SW	www.kelvinsideacademy.org.uk	rector@kelvinsideacademy.org.uk	0141 357 3376	0141 357 5401	314
St Aloysius College	45 Hill St, Garnethill, Glasgow G3 6RJ	www.staloysius.org	mail@staloysius.org	0141 332 3190	0141 353 0426	847

Inverclyde

School name	Address	Website	E-mail	Tel	Fax	Pupils
Cedars School of Excellence	31 Ardgowan Sq, Greenock, Inverclyde PA16 0PG	www.cedars.inverclyde.sch.uk	ajewell@ecosse.net	01475 723905		19
St Columba's School	Knockbuckle Rd, Kilmacolm PA13 4AU	www.st-columbas.org	secretary@st-columbas.org	01505 872768	01505 873995	350

Moray

School name	Address	Website	E-mail	Tel	Fax	Pupils
Gordonstoun School	Elgin, Moray IV30 5RF	www.gordonstoun.org.uk	admissions@gordonstoun.org.uk	01343 837837	01343 837808	515

Perth and Kinross

School name	Address	Website	E-mail	Tel	Fax	Pupils
Ardvreck School	Gwydyr Rd, Crieff, Perthshire PH7 4EX	www.ardvreck.org.uk	headteacher@ardvreck.pkc.sch.uk	01764 653112	01764 654920	62
Craiglowan Preparatory School	Edinburgh Rd, Perth PH2 8PS	www.craiglowan-school.co.uk	mbeale@btconnect.com	01738 626310	01738 440349	32
Glenalmond College	Glenalmond, Perth PH1 3RY	www.glenalmondcollege.co.uk	registrar@glenalmondcollege.co.uk	01738 842056	01738 842063	396
Kilgraston School	Bridge of Earn, Perthshire PH2 9BQ	www.kilgraston.pkc.sch.uk	registrar@killgraston.pkc.sch.uk	01738 812257	01738 813410	157
Morrison's Academy	Ferntower Rd, Crieff, Perthshire PH7 3AN	www.morrisons.pkc.sch.uk	principal@morrisons.pkc.sch.uk	01764 653885	01764 655411	320
Strathallan School	Forgandenny, Perthshire PH2 9EG	www.strathallan.co.uk	headmaster@strathallan.co.uk	01738 812546	01738 812549	450

4

Renfrewshire

School name	Address	Website	E-mail	Tel	Fax	Pupils
Johnstone Technical Education Centre	Units C and D, Floors Street Ind Est, Johnstone PA5 8PE		mpstraining@aol.com	01505 331700		
Spark of Genius Learning Centre	35 Moss St, Paisley PA1 1DL	www.sparkofgenius.co.uk		0141 587 2710	0141 587 2711	

Scottish Borders

School name	Address	Website	E-mail	Tel	Fax	Pupils
St Mary's School	Abbey Pk, Melrose TD6 9LN	www.stmarysmelrose.org.uk	enquiries@stmarys.newnet.co.uk	01896 822517	01896 823550	30

South Ayrshire

School name	Address	Website	E-mail	Tel	Fax	Pupils
Wellington School	Carleton Turrets, Craigwell Rd, Ayr KA7 2XH	www.wellingtonschool.org	info@wellingtonschool.org	01292 269321	01292 272161	286

South Lanarkshire

School name	Address	Website	E-mail	Tel	Fax	Pupils
Fernhill School	Fernbrae Ave, Burnside, Glasgow G73 4SG		fernhill@fschool.fsnet.co.uk	0141 634 2674	0141 631 4343	154
Hamilton College	Bothwell Rd, Hamilton ML3 0AY	www.hamiltoncollege.co.uk	principal@hamiltoncollege.co.uk	01698 282700	01698 281589	412

Stirling

School name	Address	Website	E-mail	Tel	Fax	Pupils
Beaconhurst	52 Kenilworth Rd, Bridge of Allan, Stirling FK9 4RR	www.beaconhurst.com	headmaster@beaconhurst.stirling.sch.uk	01786 832146	01786 833415	163
Queen Victoria School	Dunblane, Perthshire FK15 0JY	www.qvs.org.uk	enquiries@qvs.org.uk	01786 822288	0131 310 2926	233

Wales

Bridgend

School name	Address	Tel	Ref
St Clare's Convent School	Porthcawl CF36 5NR	01656 782509	672-6073

Cardiff

School name	Address	Tel	Ref
Howell's School	Cardiff Rd, Cardiff CF5 2YD	02920 562019	681-6024
Kings Monkton School	6 West Gr, Cardiff CF24 3XL	02920 482854	681-6014

Carmarthenshire

School name	Address	Tel	Ref
Llandovery College	Llandovery, Carmarthenshire SA20 0EE	01550 723002	669-6002
St Michael's School	Bryn, Llanelli SA14 9TU	01554 820325	669-6003

Conwy

School name	Address	Tel	Ref
Rydal Penrhos	Pwllycrochan Ave, Colwyn Bay LL29 7BT	01492 530155	662-6019
St David's College	Llandudno, Conwy LL30 1RD	01492 875974	662-6017

Denbighshire

School name	Address	Tel	Ref
Howell's School	Park St, Denbigh, Denbighshire LL16 3EN	01745 813631	663-6021
Ruthin School	Mold Rd, Ruthin, Denbighshire LL15 1EE	01824 702543	663-6027

Gwynedd

School name	Address	Tel	Ref
St Gerards School Trust	Ffriddoedd Rd, Bangor, Gwynedd LL57 2EL	01248 351656	661-6008

Monmouthshire

School name	Address	Tel	Ref
Monmouth School	Almhouse St, Monmouth, Monmouthshire NP5 3XP	01600 713143	679-6008

Newport

School name	Address	Tel	Ref
Rougemont School	Llantarnam Hall, Malpas Rd, Newport NP20 6QB	01633 820800	680-6003

Powys

School name	Address	Tel	Ref
Christ College	Brecon, Powys LD3 8AG	01874 615440	666-6000

Swansea

School name	Address	Tel	Ref
Flynone House School	36 St James's Cres, Swansea SA1 6DR	01792 464967	670-6018

Vale of Glamorgan

School name	Address	Tel	Ref
Westbourne Schools	4 Hickman Rd, Penarth CF64 2AJ	02920 705705	673-6021

4

Northern Ireland

North Eastern

School name	Address	Tel	Ref	Other
Ballymoney Independent Christian School	55 Market St, Ballymoney, County Antrim BT53 6ED	028 2766 3402	IS3-3	
Hydepark Educational Trust Study Centre	7a Hydepark Rd, Newtownards, County Antrim BT36 4PY	028 9084 2879	IS8-9	
Living Rivers Christian School	2-4 Railway St, Ballymena, County Antrim BT42 2AB	028 2563 8700	IS8-0	
Rowan House	71 Nutts Corner Rd, Nutts Corner, Crumlin, County Antrim BT29 4SJ	028 9082 5180	IS9-8	

South Eastern

School name	Address	Tel	Ref	Other
Bangor Independent Christian School	277 Clandeboye Rd, Bangor, County Down BT19 1AA	028 9145 0240	IS3-6	
Bridge Academy	The Adelboden, 38 Donaghadee Rd, Groomsport, Bangor, County Down BT19 6LH	028 9145 6622	IS9-7	
Holywood Rudolf Steiner Independent School	The Highlands, 34 Croft Rd, Holywood, County Down BT18 0PR	028 9042 8029	IS2-8	
Mourne Independent Christian School	3 Carrigenagh Rd, Kilkeel, County Down BT34 4NE	028 4176 3500	IS4-8	
Newbridge Study Centre	25 Newry Rd, Camlough, Newry, County Down BT35 7JP	028 3083 8399	IS8-8	
Rockport Preparatory Independent School	15 Rockport Rd, Craigavad, Holywood, County Down BT18 0DD	028 9042 8372	IS2-4	
Rowallane Integrated College	Belvoir Park Hospital, Hospital Rd, Belfast, Belfast, County Down BT8 8JP	028 9064 7076	IS9-4	

Southern

School name	Address	Tel	Ref	Other
Buddy Bear Trust Conductive Education Independent School	Killyman Rd, Dungannon, County Tyrone BT71 6DE	028 8775 2025	IS5-9	
Clogher Valley Independent Christian School	Kiltermon, 150 Ballagh Rd, Fivemiletown, County Tyrone BT75 0QP	028 8952 1851	IS4-5	
Clogher Valley Integrated Primary School	Edfield Way, Fivemiletown, Fivemiletown, County Tyrone BT75 0QH	028 8952 2004	IS9-5	
Colaiste Speirin	32 Burn Rd, Cookstown, Cookstown, County Tyrone BT80 8DN	028 8676 0010	IS9-6	
Kilskeery Independent Christian School	Old Junction Rd, Kilskeery, Omagh, County Tyrone BT78 3RN	028 8956 1560	IS3-0	
Portadown Independent Christian School	Levaghery Gdns, Gilford Rd, Portadown, County Armagh BT63 5EQ	028 3833 6733	IS4-9	

Western

School name	Address	Tel	Ref	Other
Gaelscoil na Daróige	12 Coshquinn Rd, Ballymagroarty, Londonderry, County Londonderry BT48 0ND	028 7137 1414	IS9-3	

Channel Islands and Isle of Man

4

Guernsey

School name	Address	E-mail	Tel	Fax	Headteacher
Blanchelande Girls' College	Les Vauxbelets, St Andrew, Guernsey, Channel Islands GY6 8XY		01481 237200	01481 232857	Mrs Lesley Le Page
The Ladies' College	Les Gravees, St Peter Port, Guernsey, Channel Islands GY1 1RW		01481 721602	01481 724209	Mrs Jo Riches

Jersey

School name	Address	E-mail	Tel	Fax	Headteacher
Victoria College	Le Mont Millais, Jersey, Channel Islands JE1 4HT		01534 638200		Mr R. Cook

Sixth Form and Further Education

5

Sixth Form Colleges
Further and Higher Education Colleges
Independent Further Education Establishments

Sixth Form and Further Education

Sixth Form Colleges

East of England

Dereham Sixth Form College
Crown Rd, Dereham, Norfolk NR20 4AG;
URL www.derehamsixthform.norfolk.sch.uk; e-mail
office@derehamsixthform.norfolk.sch.uk;
Tel 01362 696884; Fax 01362 694159
Headteacher Mr D.J. Richardson
Number of students
281

East Norfolk Sixth Form College
Church La, Gorleston, Great Yarmouth, Norfolk NR31 7BQ;
URL www.enorf.ac.uk; e-mail enquiries@enorf-ac.uk;
Tel 01493 662234; Fax 01493 441405
Principal Laurie Poulson

Havering Sixth Form College
Wingletye La, Hornchurch, Essex RM11 3TB;
URL www.havering-sfc.ac.uk; e-mail
mainoffice@havering-sfc.ac.uk; Tel 01708 514400;
Fax 01708 514488
Principal Paul Wakeling

Hills Road Sixth Form College
Hills Rd, Cambridge, Cambridgeshire CB2 2PE;
URL www.hillsroad.ac.uk; e-mail
aclarke@hillsroad.ac.uk; Tel 01223 247251;
Fax 01223 416979
Principal Dr R.E. Wilkinson

Long Road Sixth Form College
Long Rd, Cambridge, Cambridgeshire CB2 2PX;
URL www.longroad.ac.uk; e-mail
enquiries@longroad.ac.uk; Tel 01223 507400;
Fax 01223 507444
Principal Sandra Hamilton-Fox

Luton Sixth Form College
Bradgers Hill Rd, Luton LU2 7EW;
URL www.lutonsfc.ac.uk; e-mail college@lutonsfc.ac.uk;
Tel 01582 877500; Fax 01582 877501
Principal S. Kitchener

Mander Portman Woodward
3–4 Brookside, Cambridge, Cambridgeshire CB2 1JE;
Tel 01223 350158; Fax 01223 366429
Headteacher Mr P. Hill

Palmer's College
Chadwell Rd, Little Thurrock, Grays, Essex RM17 5TD;
URL www.palmers.ac.uk; e-mail
enquiries@palmers.ac.uk; Tel 01375 370121;
Fax 01375 385479
Principal M. Vinall

Paston College
Grammar School Rd, North Walsham, Norfolk NR28 9JL;
URL www.paston.ac.uk; e-mail enquiries@paston.ac.uk;
Tel 01692 402334; Fax 01692 500630
Principal Peter Mayne MA, MEd

SEEVIC College
Runnymede Chase, Thundersley, Benfleet, Essex SS7 1TW;
URL www.seevic-college.ac.uk; e-mail
info@seevic-college.ac.uk; Tel 01268 756111;
Fax 01268 565515
Principal G.P. Arnott

The Sixth Form College, Colchester
North Hill, Colchester, Essex CO1 1SN;
URL www.colchsfc.ac.uk; Tel 01206 500700;
Fax 01206 500770
Principal Ian C. MacNaughton

East Midlands

Bilborough College
College Way, Nottingham, Nottinghamshire NG8 4DQ;
URL www.bilborough.ac.uk; e-mail
enquiries@bilborough.ac.uk; Tel 0115 851 5000;
Fax 0115 942 5561
Principal M.J. Slattery

Gateway College – Leicester
The Newarke, Leicester LE2 7BY; URL www.gateway.ac.uk;
e-mail admin@gateway.ac.uk; Tel 0116 258 0700;
Fax 0116 258 0701
Principal Nicholas Goffin BA, MPhil

Regent College
Regent Rd, Leicester LE1 7LW;
URL www.regent-college.ac.uk; Tel 0116 255 4629;
Fax 0116 254 5680
Principal Eddie Playfair

Welbeck – The Defence Sixth Form College
Forest Road, Woodhouse, Loughborough, Leicestershire
LE12 8WD; Tel 01509 891700; Fax 01509 891701
Principal Mr T. Halliwell

Wyggeston and Queen Elizabeth I College
University Rd, Leicester LE1 7RJ; URL www.wqeic.ac.uk;
e-mail admissions@wqeic.ac.uk; Tel 0116 223 1900;
Tel (admissions office) 0116 223 1968; Fax 0116 223 1969
Principal Ian Wilson

London

The Brooke House Sixth Form College
Kenninghall Rd, Clapton, London E5 8BP;
Tel 020 8525 7150; Fax 020 8525 7151

Brampton College
Lodge Hse, Lodge Rd, Hendon, London NW4 4DQ;
  URL www.bramptoncollege.com; e-mail
  admin@bramptoncollege.com; Tel 020 8203 5025;
  Fax 020 8203 0052
Head of Establishment   Bernard Canetti

Christ the King Sixth Form College
Belmont Gr, Lewisham, London SE13 5GE; e-mail
  enquiries@ctksfc.ac.uk; Tel 020 8297 9433;
  Fax 020 8297 1460
Associate Principal   Shireen Razey

City and Islington Sixth Form College
283–309 Goswell Rd, London EC1V 7LA;
  URL www.candi.ac.uk; Tel 020 7700 9333;
  Fax 020 7520 0602
Director   Keren Abse

Lansdowne College
40–44 Bark Pl, Bayswater, London W2 4AT;
  Tel 020 7616 4400; Fax 020 7616 4401
Headteacher   Mr H. Templeton

Leyton Sixth Form College
Essex Rd, Leyton, London E10 6EQ;
  URL www.leyton.ac.uk; e-mail enquiry@leyton.ac.uk;
  Tel 020 8928 9000; Fax 020 8928 9200
Principal; Chief Executive   Sue Lakeman

Newham Sixth Form College
Prince Regent La, London E13 8SG;
  URL www.newvic.ac.uk; e-mail info@newvic.ac.uk;
  Tel 020 7473 4110; Fax 020 7511 9463
Principal   Sid Hughes

St Charles Catholic Sixth Form College
74 St Charles Sq, London W10 6EY;
  URL www.stcharles.ac.uk; e-mail
  enquiries@stcharles.ac.uk; Tel 020 8968 7755;
  Fax 020 8968 1061
Principal   Paul O'Shea

St Dominic's Sixth Form College
Mount Park Ave, Harrow, Greater London HA1 3HX;
  URL www.stdoms.ac.uk; e-mail stdoms@stdoms.ac.uk;
  Tel 020 8422 8084; Fax 020 8422 3759
Principal   Patrick Harty

St Francis Xavier Sixth Form College
Malwood Rd, London SW12 8EN; URL www.sfx.ac.uk;
  e-mail enquiries@sfx.ac.uk; Tel 020 8772 6000;
  Fax 020 8772 6099
Principal   Bernie J. Borland MA

St Luke's Catholic Sixth Form College
Chislehurst Rd, Sidcup, Kent DA14 6BP; Tel 020 8309 4760;
  Fax 020 8309 4767
Principal   Mr J. Flanner (Acting)

Sir George Monoux College
Chingford Rd, London E17 5AA; e-mail
  info@george-monoux.ac.uk; Tel 020 8523 3544;
  Fax 020 8498 2443
Principal   Kim Clifford

Spelthorne College
Church Rd, Ashford, Greater London TW15 2XD;
  URL www.spelthorne.ac.uk; e-mail
  info@spelthorne.ac.uk; Tel 01784 248666;
  Fax 01784 254132
Principal   K.J.B. Jones

Stanmore College
Elm Pk, Stanmore, Greater London HA7 4BQ;
  Tel 020 8420 7700; Fax 020 8420 6502
Principal   Russell V. Woodrow

Woodhouse College
Woodhouse Rd, London N12 9EY;
  URL www.woodhouse.ac.uk; Tel 020 8445 1210;
  Fax 020 8445 5210
Principal   Keith Murdoch BA, MSc

North East

Bede College
Incorporated sixth form college
Hale Rd, Billingham, Stockton-on-Tees TS23 3ER;
  URL www.bede.ac.uk; e-mail enquiries@bede.ac.uk;
  Tel 01642 808285; Fax 01642 808284
Principal   Miriam Stanton

Hartlepool Sixth Form College
Brinkburn, Blakelock Rd, Hartlepool TS25 5PF; e-mail
  hsfc@hpoolsfc.ac.uk; Tel 01429 294444; Fax 01429 294455
Principal; Chief Executive   R. Wells

Prior Pursglove College – Guisborough
Church Wlk, Guisborough, Redcar and Cleveland
  TS14 6BU; URL www.pursglove.ac.uk; e-mail
  ppc.enquiries@prior.pursglove.ac.uk; Tel 01287 280800;
  Fax 01287 280280
Principal   S.G. Whitehead BA, AdvDipEd

Queen Elizabeth Sixth Form College
Vane Terr, Darlington DL3 7AU; Tel 01325 461315;
  Fax 01325 361705
Principal   Tim Fisher

St Mary's College
Saltersgill Ave, Middlesbrough TS4 3JP; e-mail
  enquiries@stmarys-sfc.ac.uk; Tel 01642 814680;
  Fax 01642 819624
Principal   D.N. Lillistone BA, FRSA

Stockton Sixth Form College
Bishopton Rd West, Stockton-on-Tees TS19 0QD;
  URL www.stocktonsfc.ac.uk; e-mail
  admin@stocktonsfc.ac.uk; Tel 01642 612611;
  Fax 01642 618225
Principal   M.T. Clinton BSc(Econ), PGCE, FRSA

Tynemouth College
Hawkeys La, North Shields, Tyne and Wear NE29 9BZ;
  URL www.tynecoll.ac.uk; e-mail
  enquiries@tynecoll.ac.uk; Tel 0191 257 8414;
  Fax 0191 290 0732
Principal   R.C. Bailey

North West

Abbey College
5–7 Cheapside, Manchester, Greater Manchester M2 4WG;
  Tel 0161 817 2700; Fax 0161 236 1086
Headteacher   Mrs J. Thomas

Aquinas College
Nangreave Rd, Stockport, Cheshire SK2 6TH;
  URL www.aquinas.ac.uk; e-mail
  enquiries@aquinas.ac.uk; Tel 0161 483 3237;
  Fax 0161 487 4072
Principal   Dr Ambrose J. Smith

Ashton-under-Lyne Sixth Form College
Darnton Rd, Ashton-under-Lyne, Lancashire OL6 9RL;
  URL www.asfc.ac.uk; e-mail info@asfc.ac.uk;
  Tel 0161 330 2330; Fax 0161 339 1772
Principal   J.M. Nevin

Barrow-in-Furness Sixth Form College
Rating La, Barrow-in-Furness, Cumbria LA13 9LE;
  Tel 01229 828377; Fax 01229 836874
Principal   D.A. Kelly

Birkenhead Sixth Form College
Park Rd West, Claughton, Prenton, Wirral CH43 8SQ;
Tel 0151 652 5575; Fax 0151 653 4419
Principal   Roger Cracknell MA, FRSA

Blackpool Sixth Form College
Blackpool Old Rd, Blackpool FY3 7LR;
URL www.blackpoolsixth.ac.uk; e-mail
enquiries@blackpoolsixth.ac.uk; Tel 01253 394911;
Fax 01253 300459
Principal   Felicity Greeves

Bolton Sixth Form College
Lever Edge La, Bolton, Greater Manchester BL3 3HH; e-mail
enquiries@bolton-sfc.ac.uk; Tel 01204 846215;
Fax 01204 660218
Principal   R. Whittle OBE, MA, MPhil

Cardinal Newman College
Lark Hill, Preston, Lancashire PR1 4HD;
URL www.cardinalnewman.org.uk; e-mail
admissions@cardinalnewman.ac.uk; Tel 01772 460181;
Fax 01772 204671
Principal   S. Pegg

Carmel College
Prescot Rd, St Helens, Merseyside WA10 3AG;
URL www.carmel.ac.uk; e-mail info@carmel.ac.uk;
Tel 01744 452200; Fax 01744 452222
Principal   Rob Peacock

Cheadle and Marple Sixth Form College
Cheadle Campus, Cheadle Rd, Cheadle Hulme, Cheshire
SK8 5HA; URL www.camsfc.ac.uk; e-mail
info@camsfc.ac.uk; Tel 0161 486 4600; Fax 0161 482 8129
Chief Executive   Christina Cassidy

Eccles College
Chatsworth Rd, Eccles, Greater Manchester M30 9FJ;
URL www.ecclescollege.ac.uk; e-mail
admin@ecclescollege.ac.uk; Tel 0161 789 5876;
Fax 0161 789 1123
Principal   Stuart Wattam

Holy Cross College
Manchester Rd, Bury, Greater Manchester BL9 9BB; e-mail
information@holycross.ac.uk; Tel 0161 762 4500;
Fax 0161 762 4501
Principal   M.J. O'Hare

King George V College
Scarisbrick New Rd, Southport, Merseyside PR8 6LR;
URL www.kgv.ac.uk; e-mail admin@kgv.ac.uk;
Tel 01704 530601; Fax 01704 548656
Principal   Mrs H.M. Anslow OBE, BA, MEd

Loreto College
Chichester Rd, Manchester M15 5PB;
URL www.loreto.ac.uk; e-mail principal@loreto.ac.uk;
Tel 0161 226 5156; Fax 0161 227 9174
Principal   Ms A. Clynch

North Area College Stockport
Buckingham Rd, Heaton Moor, Stockport, Greater
Manchester SK4 4RA; URL www.nacstock.ac.uk; e-mail
nac@nacstock.ac.uk; Tel 0161 442 7494; Fax 0161 442 2166
Principal   Fred Alexander

Oldham Sixth Form College
Union St West, Oldham, Greater Manchester OL8 1XU;
URL www.osfc.ac.uk; e-mail admissions@osfc.ac.uk;
Tel 0161 287 8000; Fax 0161 633 7577
Principal   N.M. Brown OBE, BA, MPhil
Main qualifications offered:
More than 50 AS/A-level subjects and a range of vocational
courses

Pendleton College
Dronfield Rd, Salford, Greater Manchester M6 7FR;
URL www.pendcoll.ac.uk; e-mail
admission@pendcoll.ac.uk; Tel 0161 736 5074;
Fax 0161 737 4103
Principal   Peter Crompton

Priestley College
Loushers La, Warrington WA4 6RD; Tel 01925 633591;
Fax 01925 413887
Principal   David Henderson

St John Rigby College
Gathurst Rd, Orrell, Wigan, Greater Manchester WN5 0LJ;
URL www.sjr.ac.uk; e-mail jennifer.okubo@sjr.ac.uk;
Tel 01942 214797; Fax 01942 216514
Principal   J.A. Crowley BA, MA

St Mary's College
Shear Brow, Blackburn BB1 8DX;
URL www.stmarysblackburn.com; e-mail
reception@stmarysblackburn.com; Tel 01254 580464;
Fax 01254 665991
Principal   Kevin McMahon

Sir John Deane's College
Northwich, Cheshire CW9 8AF; URL www.sjd.ac.uk;
Tel 01606 46011; Fax 01606 47170
Principal   Andrew Jones

Riverside College Halton
Kingsway, Widnes, Cheshire WA8 7QQ; e-mail
info@riversidecollege.ac.uk; Tel 0151 257 2020;
Fax 0151 420 2408
Principal   Pat Grunwell

Winstanley College
Winstanley Rd, Billinge, Wigan, Greater Manchester
WN5 7XF; URL www.winstanley.ac.uk;
Tel 01695 633244; Fax 01695 633409
Principal   Steve Wood

Xaverian College
Lower Park Rd, Manchester M14 5RB;
URL www.xaverian.ac.uk; e-mail
college@xaverian.ac.uk; Tel 0161 224 1781;
Fax 0161 248 9039
Principal   Anthony Andrews

South East

Barton Peveril College
Chestnut Ave, Eastleigh, Hampshire SO50 5ZA;
URL www.barton-peveril.ac.uk; e-mail
enquiries@barton.ac.uk; Tel 02380 367200;
Fax 02380 367228
Principal   Godfrey Glyn

Bexhill College
Penland Rd, Bexhill, East Sussex TN40 2JG;
URL www.bexhillcollege.ac.uk; e-mail
enquiries@bexhillcollege.ac.uk; Tel 01424 214545;
Fax 01424 215050
Principal   Karen Hucker

Brighton, Hove and Sussex Sixth Form College
205 Dyke Rd, Hove, East Sussex BN3 6EG;
URL www.bhasvic.ac.uk; e-mail
admissions@bhasvic.ac.uk; Tel 01273 552200;
Fax 01273 563139
Principal   Chris Thomson

Central Sussex College Sixth Form Haywards Heath
Harlands Rd, Haywards Heath, West Sussex RH16 1LT;
URL www.centralsussex.ac.uk; e-mail
info.hh@centralsussex.ac.uk; Tel 01444 456281;
Fax 01444 417047
Principal   Russell Strutt

Coulsdon College

Placehouse La, Old Coulsdon, Surrey CR5 1YA;
URL www.coulsdon.ac.uk; e-mail
gen.enquiries@coulsdon.ac.uk; Tel 01737 551176;
Fax 01737 551282
Principal David Goodlet BEd, MSc
Director (Finance) Tracey Trotter

Esher College

Weston Green Rd, Thames Ditton, Surrey KT7 0JB;
URL www.esher.ac.uk; e-mail eshercollege@esher.ac.uk;
Tel 020 8398 0291; Fax 020 8339 0207
Principal K. Blackwell MA(Ed)

Farnham College

Morley Rd, Farnham, Surrey GU9 8LU;
URL www.farnham.ac.uk; e-mail
enquiries@farnham.ac.uk; Tel 01252 716988;
Fax 01252 723969
Principal Sally Francis BSc, MA

Godalming College

Tuesley La, Godalming, Surrey GU7 1RS;
URL www.godalming.ac.uk; e-mail
college@godalming.ac.uk; Tel 01483 423526;
Fax 01483 417079
Principal D. Adelman

Havant College

New Rd, Havant, Hampshire PO9 1QL;
URL www.havant.ac.uk; e-mail enquiries@havant.ac.uk;
Tel 02392 483856; Fax 02392 470621
Principal John McDougall

The Henley College

Deanfield Ave, Henley-on-Thames, Oxfordshire RG9 1UH;
Tel 01491 579988; Fax 01491 410099
Headteacher David Ansell

Itchen College

Middle Rd, Bitterne, Southampton SO19 7TB;
URL www.itchen.ac.uk; e-mail info@itchen.ac.uk;
Tel 02380 435636; Fax 02380 421911
Chair Nick Short
Principal Barry Hicks

John Ruskin College

Selsdon Park Rd, South Croydon, Surrey CR2 8JJ;
URL www.johnruskin.ac.uk; e-mail
info@johnruskin.ac.uk; Tel 020 8651 1131;
Fax 020 8651 4011
Principal Jennifer Sims

Peter Symonds College

Owens Rd, Winchester, Hampshire SO22 6RX;
URL www.psc.ac.uk; e-mail psc@psc.ac.uk;
Tel 01962 857500; Fax 01962 857501
Principal N.A. Hopkins BSc, MEd

Portsmouth College

Tangier Rd, Portsmouth PO3 6PZ;
URL www.portsmouth-college.ac.uk; e-mail
registry@portsmouth-college.ac.uk; Tel 02392 667521;
Fax 02392 344363
Principal Steve Frampton

Queen Mary's College

Cliddesden Rd, Basingstoke, Hampshire RG21 3HF; e-mail
postmaster@qmc.ac.uk; Tel 01256 417500;
Fax 01256 417501
Principal Stephen Sheedy

Reigate College

Castlefield Rd, Reigate, Surrey RH2 0SD;
URL www.reigate.ac.uk; e-mail enquiries@reigate.ac.uk;
Tel 01737 221118; Fax 01737 222657
Principal Dr P.L. Rispoli BSc, PhD

College of Richard Collyer in Horsham

Hurst Rd, Horsham, West Sussex RH12 2EJ;
Tel 01403 210822; Fax 01403 211915
Principal Dr J. Johnston BA, MA, DPhil

St Vincent College

Mill La, Gosport, Hampshire PO12 4QA;
URL www.stvincent.ac.uk; e-mail info@stvincent.ac.uk;
Tel 02392 588311; Fax 02392 511186
Principal P. Lynn Lee

The Sixth Form College – Farnborough

Prospect Ave, Farnborough, Hampshire GU14 8JX;
URL www.farnboroughsfc.ac.uk; e-mail
admin@farnboroughsfc.ac.uk; Tel 01252 688200;
Fax 01252 688206
Principal John J. Guy OBE, BSc, MA, MEd, PhD, FRSA

Strode's College

High St, Egham, Surrey TW20 9DR;
URL www.strodes.ac.uk; e-mail info@strodes.ac.uk;
Tel 01784 437506; Fax 01784 471794
Principal Frank Botham BA, PhD

Taunton's College

Hill La, Southampton SO15 5RL; URL www.tauntons.ac.uk;
e-mail email@tauntons.ac.uk; Tel 02380 511811;
Fax 02380 511991
Principal Jonathan Prest

Totton College

Calmore Rd, Totton, Southampton SO40 3ZX;
URL www.totton.ac.uk; e-mail info@totton.ac.uk;
Tel 02380 874874; Fax 02380 874879
Principal Mark Bramwell BA(Hons), MA

Varndean College

Surrenden Rd, Brighton, East Sussex BN1 6WQ;
URL www.varndean.ac.uk; e-mail
office@varndean.ac.uk; Tel 01273 508011;
Fax 01273 542950
Principal Dr Philip Harland

Woking College

Rydens Way, Woking, Surrey GU22 9DL;
URL www.woking.ac.uk; e-mail
wokingcoll@woking.ac.uk; Tel 01483 761036;
Fax 01483 728144
Principal Martin Ingram

Worthing College

Bolsover Rd, Worthing, West Sussex BN13 1NS;
URL www.worthing.ac.uk; e-mail info@worthing.ac.uk;
Tel 01903 243389; Fax 01903 243390
Principal Peter Corrigan

South West

The Richard Huish College

South Rd, Taunton, Somerset TA1 3DZ;
URL www.richuish.ac.uk; e-mail petera@richuish.ac.uk;
Tel 01823 320800; Fax 01823 320801
Principal P. Avery

St Brendan's Sixth Form College

Broomhill Rd, Brislington, Bristol BS4 5RQ;
URL www.stbrn.ac.uk; e-mail info@stbrn.ac.uk;
Tel 0117 977 7766; Fax 0117 972 3351
Principal D. Bodey

West Midlands

Abbey College

10 St Pauls Sq, Birmingham, West Midlands B3 1QU;
Tel 0121 236 7474
Headteacher Dr Colum Devine

Cadbury Sixth Form College

Downland Cl, Redditch Rd, Birmingham, West Midlands
B38 8QT; URL www.cadcol.ac.uk; Tel 0121 458 3898;
Fax 0121 459 4434

Principal   D. Igoe

City of Stoke-on-Trent Sixth Form College

Victoria Rd, Fenton, Stoke-on-Trent ST4 2RR;
URL www.stokesfc.ac.uk; Tel 01782 848736;
Fax 01782 747456

Principal   Helen Pegg

Hereford Sixth Form College

Folly La, Hereford, Herefordshire HR1 1LU; e-mail
sixth-form@hereford.ac.uk; Tel 01432 355166;
Fax 01432 346901

Principal   Dr J.T. Godfrey

Joseph Chamberlain Sixth Form College

Balsall Heath Rd, Highgate, Birmingham, West Midlands
B12 9DS; Tel 0121 446 2200; Fax 0121 440 0798

Principal   Lynne Morris

Josiah Mason College

Slade Rd, Erdington, Birmingham, West Midlands B23 7JH;
URL www.jmc.ac.uk; e-mail enquiries@jmc.ac.uk;
Tel 0121 603 4757; Fax 0121 377 6076

Principal   Chris Grayson

King Edward VI College

Stourbridge, West Midlands DY8 1TD; Tel 01384 398100;
Fax 01384 398123

Principal   John Glazier PhD

King Edward VI College – Nuneaton

King Edward Rd, Nuneaton, Warwickshire CV11 4BE;
URL www.kingednun.demon.co.uk; e-mail
enquiries@kinged6nun.ac.uk; Tel 024 7632 8231;
Fax 024 7632 6686

Principal   Martin Ward BA(Hons), ACCA

Ludlow College

Castle Sq, Ludlow, Shropshire SY8 1GD;
URL www.ludlow-college.ac.uk; e-mail
abrown@ludlow-college.ac.uk; Tel 01584 872846;
Fax 01584 876012

Principal   Ann Brown

New College – Telford

King St, Wellington, Telford, Wrekin TF1 1NY;
URL www.newcollegetelford.ac.uk; Tel 01952 641892;
Fax 01952 243564

Principal   Helen Pegg (Acting)

Shrewsbury Sixth Form College

Priory Rd, Shrewsbury, Shropshire SY1 1RX;
Tel 01743 235491; Fax 01743 242735

Principal   William E. Dowell

The Sixth Form College, Solihull

Widney Manor Rd, Solihull, West Midlands B91 3WR;
URL www.solihullsfc.ac.uk; e-mail
enquiries@solihullsfc.ac.uk; Tel 0121 704 2581;
Fax 0121 711 1598

Principal   Colleen Chater

Worcester Sixth Form College

Spetchley Rd, Worcester, Worcestershire WR5 2LU;
Tel 01905 362600; Fax 01905 362633

Principal   John Tredwell

Yorkshire and the Humber

Franklin College

Chelmsford Ave, Grimsby, North East Lincolnshire
DN34 5BY; URL www.franklin.ac.uk; e-mail
college@franklin.ac.uk; Tel 01472 875000;
Fax 01472 875019

Principal   Peter Newcome

Greenhead College

Greenhead Rd, Huddersfield, West Yorkshire HD1 4ES;
URL www.greenhead.ac.uk; e-mail
college@greenhead.ac.uk; Tel 01484 422032;
Fax 01484 518025

Principal   M.K. Rostron

Huddersfield New College

New Hey Rd, Huddersfield, West Yorkshire HD3 4GL;
URL www.huddnewcoll.ac.uk; e-mail
info@huddnewcoll.ac.uk; Tel 01484 652341;
Fax 01484 649923

Vice-Principal   Steve Wetton

John Leggott College

West Common La, Scunthorpe, North Lincolnshire
DN17 1DS; URL www.leggott.ac.uk; e-mail
nicholasdakin@leggott.ac.uk; Tel 01724 282998;
Fax 01724 281631

Principal   N. Dakin

NEW College – Pontefract

Park La, Pontefract, West Yorkshire WF8 4QR;
URL www.newcollpont.ac.uk; e-mail
reception@newcollpont.ac.uk; Tel 01977 702139;
Fax 01977 600708

Principal   Peter Hillman

Notre Dame Catholic Sixth Form College

St Marks Ave, Leeds, West Yorkshire LS2 9BL;
Tel 0113 294 6644; Fax 0113 294 6006

Principal   Dr A. Adlard

Scarborough Sixth Form College

Sandybed La, Scarborough, North Yorkshire YO12 5LF;
URL www.scarb-6-form.ac.uk; e-mail
<initial>.<surname>@scarb-6-form.ac.uk;
Tel 01723 365032; Fax 01723 367049

Principal   Tom Potter

Thomas Rotherham College

Moorgate, Rotherham, South Yorkshire S60 2BE;
URL www.thomroth.ac.uk/links; e-mail
enquiries@thomroth.ac.uk; Tel 01709 300600;
Fax 01709 300601

Principal   Dr Richard Williams

Wilberforce College

Saltshouse Rd, Kingston upon Hull, East Riding of
Yorkshire HU8 9HD; URL www.wilberforce.ac.uk;
Tel 01482 711688; Fax 01482 798991
Number of students
690

Wyke College

Grammar School Rd, Kingston upon Hull, East Riding of
Yorkshire HU5 4NX; URL www.wyke.ac.uk; e-mail
info@wyke.ac.uk; Tel 01482 346347; Fax 01482 473336

Principal   Dr Richard Smith BA(Hons), PhD

Wales

St David's Catholic College

Ty Gwyn Rd, Penylan, Cardiff CF23 5QD;
URL www.st-davids-coll.ac.uk; e-mail
enquiries@st-davids-coll.ac.uk; Tel 02920 498555;
Fax 02920 472594

Principal   Mark Leighfield BA, MSc

Further and Higher Education Colleges

East of England

Barking College
Dagenham Rd, Romford, Essex RM7 0XU;
URL www.barkingcollege.ac.uk; e-mail
admissions@barkingcollege.ac.uk; Tel 01708 770007;
Fax 01708 770000
Principal Ted Parker

Barnfield College
York St, Luton LU2 0EZ; URL www.barnfield.ac.uk; e-mail
elm@barnfield.ac.uk; Tel 01582 569500; Fax 01582 492928
Principal Pete Birkett

Basildon College
Nethermayne, Basildon, Essex SS16 5NN;
URL www.basildon.ac.uk; e-mail basinfo@rmplc.co.uk;
Tel 01268 532015
Principal John Gould (Acting)

Bedford College
Cauldwell St, Bedford, Bedfordshire MK42 9AH;
URL www.bedford.ac.uk; e-mail info@bedford.ac.uk;
Tel (freephone) 0800 074 0234; Tel 01234 291000;
Fax 01234 342674
Principal; Chief Executive Ian Pryce

Braintree College
Church La, Bocking, Braintree, Essex CM7 5SN;
URL www.braintree.ac.uk; e-mail
enquiries@braintree.ac.uk; Tel 01376 321711;
Fax 01376 340799
Principal J.S. Watts

Cambridge Regional College
Kings Hedges Rd, Cambridge, Cambridgeshire CB4 2QT;
URL www.camre.ac.uk; e-mail enquiry@camre.ac.uk;
Tel 01223 418200; Fax 01223 426425
Principal; Chief Executive Rick Dearing

Chelmsford College
Moulsham St, Chelmsford, Essex CM2 0JQ; e-mail
information@chelmsford-college.ac.uk;Tel 01245 265611;
Fax 01245 266908
Principal D. Law BA(Hons), MBA, CertEd

Colchester Institute
Sheepen Rd, Colchester, Essex CO3 3LL;
URL www.colchester.ac.uk; e-mail
info@colchester.ac.uk; Tel 01206 518000; Tel (enquiry
line) 01206 518777; Fax 01206 763041

Dunstable College
Kingsway, Dunstable, Bedfordshire LU5 4HG;
URL www.dunstable.ac.uk; e-mail
enquiries@dunstable.ac.uk; Tel 01582 477776
Chief Executive C. Vesey

Epping Forest College
Borders La, Loughton, Essex IG10 3SA;
URL www.epping-forest.ac.uk; e-mail
informationcentre@epping-forest.ac.uk;
Tel 020 8508 8311
Principal David Butler BA, MSc

Great Yarmouth College
Southtown, Great Yarmouth, Norfolk NR31 0ED;
URL www.gyc.ac.uk; e-mail info@gyc.ac.uk;
Tel 01493 655261; Fax 01493 653423
Principal Robin Parkinson BA, MSc

Harlow College
Velizy Ave, Town Centre, Harlow, Essex CM20 3LH;
URL www.harlow-college.ac.uk; e-mail
learninglink@harlow-college.ac.uk; Tel 01279 868000;
Fax 01279 868260
Principal Colin Hindmarch

Havering College of Further and Higher Education
Ardleigh Green Rd, Hornchurch, Essex RM11 2LL;
URL www.havering-college.ac.uk; Tel 01708 455011;
Tel (prospectus) 01708 462801; Fax 01708 462788
Principal Noel Otley BA(Hons), MA, PGCE

Hertford Regional College
Broxbourne Centre, Turnford, Broxbourne, Hertfordshire
EN10 6AE; URL www.hrc.ac.uk; e-mail info@hrc.ac.uk;
Tel (information centre) 01992 411411; Fax 01992 411650
Principal Paul Harvey

Huntingdonshire Regional College
California Rd, Huntingdon, Cambridgeshire PE29 1BL;
URL www.huntingdon.ac.uk; e-mail
college@huntingdon.ac.uk; Tel 01480 379100;
Tel (Information Officer) 01480 379106; Fax 01480 379127
Principal A. Constantine BA(Hons), MBA

College of West Anglia, Isle Campus
Ramnoth Rd, Wisbech, Cambridgeshire PE13 2JE;
URL www.col-westanglia.ac.uk; Tel 01945 466302;
Fax 01945 582706
Principal David Pomfret

Lowestoft College
St Peters St, Lowestoft, Suffolk NR32 2NB;
URL www.lowestoft.ac.uk; e-mail info@lowestoft.ac.uk;
Tel 01502 583521; Fax 01502 500031

North Hertfordshire College
Stevenage Centre, Monkswood Way, Stevenage,
Hertfordshire SG1 1LA; URL www.nhc.ac.uk; e-mail
enquiries@nhc.ac.uk; Tel 01462 424242; Fax 01462 443054
Principal Fintan Donohue

City College Norwich
Ipswich Rd, Norwich, Norfolk NR2 2LJ;
URL www.ccn.ac.uk; e-mail information@ccn.ac.uk;
Tel 01603 773311; Tel (prospectus) 01603 773773;
Fax 01603 773301
Principal Dick Palmer

Oaklands College
Oaklands Campus, Hatfield Rd, St Albans, Hertfordshire
AL4 0JA; URL www.oaklands.ac.uk; e-mail
helpline@oaklands.ac.uk; Tel 01727 737000;
Fax 01727 737752
Principal Helen Parr

Peterborough Regional College
Park Cres, Peterborough, Cambridgeshire PE1 4DZ;
URL www.peterborough.ac.uk; e-mail
info@peterborough.ac.uk; Tel 0845 872 8722;
Fax 01733 767986
Principal Don Lawson

Redbridge College
Little Heath, Romford, Essex RM6 4XT; e-mail
info@redbridge-college.ac.uk; Tel 020 8548 7400;
Fax 020 8599 8224
Principal Theresa Drowley

South East Essex College
Luker Rd, Southend-on-Sea, Essex SS1 1ND;
URL www.southend.ac.uk; e-mail
marketing@southend.ac.uk; Tel 01702 220400;
Fax 01702 432320; Minicom 01702 220642
Principal; Chief Executive Jan Llodges BA(Hons), MA,
MBA

Suffolk New College

Rope Wlk, Ipswich, Suffolk IP4 1LT;
URL www.suffolk.ac.uk; e-mail info@suffolk.ac.uk;
Tel 01473 255885; Tel (prospectus requests) 01473 296606;
Fax 01473 296558
Principal   Prof Dave Muller BEd, PhD, CPsychol, FBPsP, FCMI, Hon FRCSLT

Thurrock and Basildon College

Woodview Campus, Grays, Essex RM16 2YR;
URL www.tab.ac.uk; e-mail enquire@tab.ac.uk;
Tel 0845 601 5746; Fax 01375 373356;
Minicom 01375 362740

Canvey Learning Centre, 3 Knightswick Centre, 7 Furtherwick, Canvey, Essex SS18 7AD; Tel 01268 697908

Eastgate Learning Centre, Suite 11, Eastgate Business Centre, Souternhay, Basildon, Essex SS14 1EB; Tel 01268 820130

Lakeside Training Centre, Unit 507, Brompton Wlk, Lakeside Shopping Centre, West Thurrock, Essex RM20 2ZL; Tel 01708 680627

Nethermayne Campus, Nethermayne, Basildon, Essex SS16 5NN; Fax 01268 522139
Principal   Denise Fielding

College of West Anglia

Tennyson Ave, King's Lynn, Norfolk PE30 2QW;
URL www.col-westanglia.ac.uk; e-mail enquiries@col-westanglia.ac.uk; Tel 01553 761144;
Fax 01553 815555
Principal; Chief Executive   David Pomfret

West Herts College

Watford Campus, Hempstead Rd, Watford, Hertfordshire WD17 3EZ; URL www.westherts.ac.uk; e-mail admissions@westherts.ac.uk; Tel 01923 812345
Principal   Elizabeth Rushton

West Suffolk College

Out Risbygate, Bury St Edmunds, Suffolk IP33 3RL;
URL www.westsuffolk.ac.uk; e-mail info@wsc.ac.uk;
Tel 01284 701301; Fax 01284 750561
Principal   Dr Ann Williams
Head (Professional Development and Standards)   Barbara Beaton
Adviser (Connexions)   Michelle Bird

East Midlands

Bishop Grosseteste University College, Lincoln

Newport, Lincoln, Lincolnshire LN1 3DY;
URL www.bishopg.ac.uk; e-mail info@bishopg.ac.uk;
Tel 01522 527347; Fax 01522 530243
Principal   Prof Muriel Robinson
Number of students
1500
Main qualifications offered
MA, BA(Hons), BSc(Hons), QTS, PGCE, Dip, SENDip, Cert

Boston College

Skirbeck Rd, Boston, Lincolnshire PE21 6JF;
URL www.boston.ac.uk; e-mail info@boston.ac.uk;
Tel 01205 365701; Fax 01205 313252
Principal   S. Daley

Brooksby Melton College

Asfordby Rd, Melton Mowbray, Leicestershire LE13 0HJ;
URL www.brooksbymelton.ac.uk; e-mail course.enquiries@brooksbymelton.ac.uk;
Tel 01664 850850; Tel (student services) 01664 855444;
Fax 01664 855455
Principal   Jim Horrocks

Buxton College of Further Education (University of Derby, Buxton)

1 Devonshire Rd, Buxton, Derbyshire SK17 6RY;
URL www.derby.ac.uk/udb; e-mail enquiriesudb@derby.ac.uk; Tel 01298 71100;
Fax 01298 27261
Dean of Faculty   Prof David Gray
Manager (Student Support)   Ben Bailey

Castle College Nottingham

Maid Marian Way, Nottingham NG1 6AB;
URL www.castlecollege.ac.uk; e-mail learn@castlecollege.ac.uk; Tel 0845 845 0500;
Fax 0115 912 8600
Principal   Nick Lewis

Chesterfield College

Infirmary Rd, Chesterfield, Derbyshire S41 7NG;
URL www.chesterfield.ac.uk; e-mail advice@chesterfield.ac.uk; Tel 01246 500500;
Fax 01246 500587
Principal   P.I. Murray

Derby College

Prince Charles Ave, Derby DE22 4LR;
URL www.derby-college.ac.uk; e-mail enquiries@derby-college.ac.uk; Tel (prospectus) 0800 028 0289; Tel 01332 520200; Fax 01332 520234
Principal   D. Croll BA(Hons), PGCE, DipEdMan

Grantham College

Stonebridge Rd, Grantham, Lincolnshire NG31 9AP;
URL www.grantham.ac.uk; e-mail enquiry@grantham.ac.uk; Tel 01476 400200;
Fax 01476 400291
Principal   M.D. Saville BSc(Soc), MA(Ed), PGCE

Leicester College

Freemans Park Campus, Aylestone Rd, Leicester LE2 7LW;
URL www.leicestercollege.ac.uk; Tel 0116 224 2000;
Tel (prospectus information) 0116 224 2240;
Fax 0116 224 2190
Principal   Maggie Galliers

Lincoln College

Monks Rd, Lincoln, Lincolnshire LN2 5HQ;
URL www.lincolncollege.ac.uk; e-mail gainsenquiries@lincolncollege.ac.uk; Tel 01522 876000;
Tel (prospectus) 01522 876276; Fax 01522 876200
Principal   John S. Allen BSc, PhD

Loughborough College

Radmoor Rd, Loughborough, Leicestershire LE11 3BT;
URL www.loucoll.ac.uk; e-mail info@loucoll.ac.uk;
Tel 0845 166 2950; Fax 0845 166 2951
Principal; Chief Executive   Jim Mutton

New College Nottingham

The Adams Bldg, Stoney St, The Lace Market, Nottingham NG1 1NG; URL www.ncn.ac.uk; e-mail enquiries@ncn.ac.uk; Tel 0115 910 0100
Chief Executive   Geoff Hall

North Nottinghamshire College

Carlton Rd, Worksop, Nottinghamshire S81 7HP;
URL www.nnc.ac.uk; e-mail contact@nnc.ac.uk;
Tel 01909 504504; Tel (direct line to principal) 01909 504600; Fax 01909 504505
Principal   J. Connolly

Northampton College

Booth La, Northampton, Northamptonshire NN3 3RF;
URL www.northamptoncollege.ac.uk; e-mail enquiries@northamptoncollege.ac.uk; Tel (prospectus) 0845 300 4401; Tel 01604 734567

Badby Rd West, Daventry, Northamptonshire NN11 4HJ;
Tel 01327 300232

Lower Mounts, Northampton, Northamptonshire NN1 3DE; Tel 01604 734567
Principal   Len Closs

Chair of Governors   R. Morris
Director (Finance)   H. Morgan
Director (Information and Learner Services)   C. Leggitt
Director (Planning and Business Development)   R. Starkey
Student facilities
Industrial placement

University College Northampton
Park Campus, Boughton Green Rd, Northampton,
    Northamptonshire NN2 7AL;
    URL www.northampton.ac.uk; Tel 01604 735500;
    Fax 01604 720636
Director   Ann Tate BSc, MSc, FRSA

South East Derbyshire College
Field Rd, Ilkeston, Derbyshire DE7 5RS; e-mail (admissions)
    admissions@sedc.ac.uk; e-mail enquiries@sedc.co.uk;
    Tel 0115 849 2000; Fax 0115 849 2121
M.F. Brown BA(Econ), MA

South Leicestershire College
Station Rd, Wigston, Leicestershire LE18 2DW;
    URL www.slcollege.ac.uk; e-mail lgs@slcollege.ac.uk;
    Tel 0116 288 5051; Fax 0116 288 0823
Principal; Chief Executive   Lowell Williams BA(Hons), MBA

South Nottingham College
Greythorn Dr, West Bridgford, Nottingham NG2 7GA;
    URL www.snc.ac.uk; e-mail enquiries@snc.ac.uk;
    Tel 0115 914 6400; Fax 0115 914 6444
Principal   Malcolm Cowgill

New College Stamford
Drift Rd, Stamford, Lincolnshire PE9 1XA;
    URL www.stamford.ac.uk; e-mail
    enquiries@stamford.ac.uk; Tel 01780 484300;
    Fax 01780 484301
Principal   Miles Dibsdall

Stephenson College
Thornborough Rd, Coalville, Leicestershire LE67 3TN;
    URL www.stephensoncoll.ac.uk; e-mail
    services@stephensoncoll.ac.uk; Tel 01530 836136;
    Fax 01530 814253
Principal; Chief Executive   Nigel Leigh BEd(Hons), MA,
    MBA, MCIPD

Tresham Institute of Further and Higher Education
Windmill Avenue Campus, Kettering, Northamptonshire
    NN15 6ER; URL www.tresham.ac.uk; e-mail
    info@tresham.ac.uk; Tel 0845 658 8990; Fax 01536 522500
Principal   Mark Silverman

West Nottinghamshire College
Derby Rd, Mansfield, Nottinghamshire NG18 5BH; e-mail
    info@westnotts.ac.uk; Tel (prospectus) 0808 100 3626;
    Tel 01623 627191; Fax 01623 623063
Principal   Di McEvoy-Robinson

London

Barnet College
Wood St, Barnet, Greater London EN5 4AZ;
    URL www.barnet.ac.uk; e-mail info@barnet.ac.uk;
    Tel 020 8200 8300; Tel (prospectus) 020 8266 4000;
    Fax 020 8441 5236
Grahame Park Centre, Grahame Park Way, London
    NW9 5RA; Fax 020 8205 7177
Montagu Road Centre, Hendon, London NW4 3ES;
    Fax 020 8205 7177
Bldg 3, North London Business Pk, Oakleigh Rd South,
    London N11 1GN; Fax 020 8441 5236
Stanhope Road Centre, Stanhope Rd, Finchley, London
    N12 9DX
Principal   M. Hawkins

To obtain a prospectus
Telephone or e-mail the college

Bexley College
Tower Rd, Belvedere, Kent DA17 6JA;
    URL www.bexley.ac.uk; e-mail courses@bexley.ac.uk;
    Tel 01322 442331; Fax 01322 448403
Principal   David Gleed (Acting)

Bromley College of Further and Higher Education
Rookery La, Bromley Common, Bromley, Kent BR2 8HE;
    URL www.bromley.ac.uk; e-mail info@bromley.ac.uk;
    Tel 020 8295 7000; Tel (prospectus) 020 8295 7001;
    Fax 020 8295 7099
Principal   Peter Jones

City and Islington College
Centre for Health, Social and Child Care, The Marlborough
    Bldg, 383 Holloway Rd, London N7 0RN;
    URL www.candi.ac.uk; Tel 020 7700 9333;
    Fax 020 7700 9222

City Lit
1–10 Keeley St, Covent Gdn, London WC2B 4BA;
    URL www.citylit.ac.uk; Tel 020 7831 7831;
    Fax 020 7492 2735
Principal   Peter Davies CB, CBE

City of Westminster College
25 Paddington Grn, London W2 1NB; URL www.cwc.ac.uk;
    e-mail customer.services@cwc.ac.uk; Tel 020 7723 8826;
    Fax 020 7258 2747
Principal   Robin Shreeve

College of North East London
Tottenham Centre, High Rd, London N15 4RU;
    URL www.conel.ac.uk; e-mail
    guidance@staff.conel.ac.uk; Tel (prospectus)
    020 8442 3055; Tel 020 8802 3111; Fax 020 8442 3091
Principal   Paul Head

College of North West London
Dudden Hill La, London NW10 2XD;
    URL www.cnwl.ac.uk; e-mail cic@cnwl.ac.uk;
    Tel 020 8208 5000; Tel (course enquiries) 020 8208 5050;
    Fax 020 8208 5151
Principal   Vicki Fagg

Community College, Hackney
Shoreditch Campus, Falkirk St, London N1 6HQ;
    URL www.thecommunitycollege.co.uk; e-mail
    enquiries@comm-coll-hackney.ac.uk; Tel 020 7613 9123;
    Fax 020 7613 9003
Principal   C.P. Farley

Croydon College
College Rd, Croydon, Greater London CR9 1DX;
    URL www.croydoncollege.com; e-mail
    info@croydon.ac.uk; Tel 020 8686 5700
Principal; Chief Executive   Mariane Cavalli

Ealing, Hammersmith and West London College
College Information Centre at HWLC, Gliddon Rd, Barons
    Ct, London W14 9BL; URL www.wlc.ac.uk; e-mail
    cic@wlc.ac.uk; Tel 0800 980 2175; Fax 020 8741 2491
Principal   Amarjit Basi (Acting)

Enfield College
73 Hertford Rd, Enfield, Greater London EN3 5HA;
    URL www.enfield.ac.uk; e-mail
    courseinformation@enfield.ac.uk; Tel (prospectus)
    020 8372 7600; Tel 020 8443 3434; Fax 020 8804 7028
Principal; Chief Executive   Jean Carter

Greenwich Community College
Plumstead Centre, 95 Plumstead Rd, London SE18 7DQ;
    Tel 020 8488 4800; Fax 020 8488 4899
Principal   Geoff Pine BSc(Econ), DipEdAdmin, PGCE

Harrow College

Lowlands Rd, Harrow, Greater London HA1 3AQ;
URL www.harrow.ac.uk; e-mail
enquiries@harrow.ac.uk; Tel 020 8909 6000;
Fax 020 8909 6060
Principal   Dr Barbara Field

Kensington and Chelsea College

Hortensia Rd, London SW10 0QS; URL www.kcc.ac.uk;
e-mail info@kcc.ac.uk; Tel (course information line)
020 7573 5333; Fax 020 7351 0956
Principal   Mike Jutsum

Lambeth College

45 Clapham Common South Side, London SW4 9BL;
URL www.lambethcollege.ac.uk; e-mail
courses@lambethcollege.ac.uk; Tel 020 7501 5000;
Fax 020 7501 5041
Principal   Richard Chambers

Lewisham College

Lewisham Way, London SE4 1UT;
URL www.lewisham.ac.uk; e-mail info@lewisham.ac.uk;
Tel (course information) 0800 834 545; Tel 020 8692 0353;
Fax 020 8694 9163
Principal   Ruth Silver CBE

Marine Society College of the Sea

202 Lambeth Rd, London SE1 7JW; URL www.mscos.ac.uk;
e-mail education@ms-sc.org; Tel 020 7654 7000;
Fax 020 7401 2537
Director (Education)   Brian G. Thomas

The Mary Ward Centre

42 Queen Sq, London WC1N 3AQ;
URL www.marywardcentre.ac.uk; e-mail
info@marywardcentre.ac.uk; Tel 020 7269 6000;
Fax 020 7269 6001
Principal   Ceri Williams

Merton College

Morden Pk, London Rd, Morden, Surrey SM4 5QX;
URL www.merton.ac.uk; e-mail info@merton.ac.uk;
Tel 020 8408 6400; Fax 020 8408 6666

Morley College

61 Westminster Bridge Rd, London SE1 7HT;
URL www.morleycollege.ac.uk; e-mail
enquiries@morleycollege.ac.uk; Tel 020 7450 1889;
Fax 020 7928 4074
Principal   Philip Meadon

Newham College of Further Education

East Ham Campus, High St South, London E6 6ER;
Tel 020 8257 4000; Fax 020 8257 4300
Principal   Martin Tolhurst

The Open University

Walton Hall, Milton Keynes MK7 6AA;
URL www.open.ac.uk; e-mail
general-enquiries@open.ac.uk; Tel 0845 300 6090
Director   Alan Myles (Acting)

Richmond Adult Community College

Parkshot, Richmond TW9 2RE; Tel 020 8891 5907;
Fax 020 8892 6354
Principal; Chief Executive   Christina Conroy

Richmond upon Thames College

Egerton Rd, Twickenham, Greater London TW2 7SJ;
URL www.rutc.ac.uk; e-mail courses@rutc.ac.uk;
Tel 020 8607 8000; Tel (course enquiries) 020 8607 8305;
Fax 020 8744 9738
Principal   Kevin Watson MA

St Mary's College

Waldegrave Rd, Strawberry Hill, Twickenham, Greater
London TW1 4SX; URL www.smuc.ac.uk;
Tel 020 8240 4000

Principal   Dr A. Naylor MA, MEd, PhD, MBA, FRSA
Deputy Registrar   A. Hume
Number of students
3000

South Thames College

Wandsworth High St, London SW18 2PP;
URL www.south-thames.ac.uk; e-mail
studentservices@south-thames.ac.uk; Tel 020 8918 7480;
Tel (student services) 020 8918 7777
Principal   Sue Rimmer

Southgate College

High St, Southgate, London N14 6BS;
URL www.southgate.ac.uk; e-mail
admiss@southgate.ac.uk; Tel 020 8982 5050;
Fax 020 8982 5051
Principal   M. Blagden JP, BSc, MSc, CEng, MIMechE

Southwark College

Bermondsey Centre, Keetons Rd, London SE16 4EE; e-mail
info@southwark.ac.uk; Tel 020 7815 1500;
Fax 020 7815 1525
Principal   Dorothy Jones BA(Hons), MSc, CertEd

Tower Hamlets College

Poplar Centre, Poplar High St, London E14 0AF;
URL www.tower.ac.uk; e-mail advice@tower.ac.uk;
Tel 020 7510 7510; Tel (course advice line) 020 7510 7777;
Fax 020 7538 9153
Principal   Joanna Gaukroger

Uxbridge College

Park Rd, Uxbridge, Greater London UB8 1NQ;
URL www.uxbridgecollege.ac.uk; e-mail
enquiries@uxbridgecollege.ac.uk; Tel 01895 853333;
Fax 01895 853377
Principal   Laraine Smith

Waltham Forest College

Forest Rd, London E17 4JB; URL www.waltham.ac.uk;
e-mail info@waltham.ac.uk; Tel 020 8501 8501;
Fax 020 8501 8001
Principal; Chief Executive   Robin Jones (Acting)

West Thames College

London Rd, Isleworth, Greater London TW7 4HS;
URL www.west-thames.ac.uk; e-mail
info@west-thames.ac.uk; Tel 020 8326 2000;
Fax 020 8326 2001
Principal   Thalia Marriott

Westminster Kingsway College

Vincent Square Centre, Vincent Sq, London SW1P 2PD;
URL www.westking.ac.uk; e-mail
courseinfo@westking.ac.uk; Tel 020 7556 8001;
Fax 020 7556 8003
Battersea Park Centre, Battersea Park Rd, London SW11 4JR;
Tel 020 7556 8000; Fax 020 7556 8082
Castle Lane Centre, Castle La, London SW1E 6DR;
Tel 020 7556 8000; Fax 020 7963 8518
Gray's Inn Centre, Sidmouth St, London WC1H 8JB;
Tel 020 7556 8000; Fax 020 7306 5000
Kentish Town Centre, 87 Holmes Rd, London NW5 3AX;
Tel 020 7556 8000; Fax 020 7428 2910
Regent's Park Centre, Longford St, London NW5 0HS;
Tel 020 7556 8000; Fax 020 7391 6400
Principal   Richard Williams

The Working Men's College

44 Crowndale Rd, London NW1 1TR;
URL www.wmcollege.ac.uk; e-mail
info@wmcollege.ac.uk; Tel 020 7255 4700;
Fax 020 7383 5561
Principal   Mr Satnam Gill OBE

5

North East

Bishop Auckland College
Woodhouse La, Bishop Auckland, County Durham
DL14 6JZ; e-mail enquiries@bacoll.ac.uk;
Tel 01388 443000; Fax 01388 609294
Principal; Chief Executive   Joanna Tait

Darlington College
Central Pk, Haughton Rd, Darlington DL1 1DR;
URL www.darlington.ac.uk; e-mail
enquire@darlington.ac.uk; Tel (student services)
01325 503030; Tel 01325 503050; Fax 01325 503000
Principal; Chief Executive   S.E. Robinson

Derwentside College
Front St, Consett, County Durham DH8 5EE;
URL www.derwentside.ac.uk; e-mail
enquiries@derwentside.ac.uk; Tel 01207 585900;
Fax 01207 585919
Principal   Albert Croney

East Durham and Houghall Community College
Burnhope Way Campus, Burnhope Way, Peterlee, County
Durham SR8 1NU; URL www.edhcc.ac.uk; e-mail
enquiries@edhcc.ac.uk; Tel 0191 518 2000; Tel (student
services) 0191 518 8222; Fax 0191 586 7125
Chair of Governors   I. Williams

Gateshead College
Baltic Campus, Baltic Business Quarter, Quarryfield Rd,
Gateshead, Tyne and Wear NE8 3BE;
URL www.gateshead.ac.uk; e-mail
start@gateshead.ac.uk; Tel 0191 490 0300;
Tel (prospectus) 0191 490 2246; Fax 0191 490 2313
Principal   David Cheetham
Main qualifications offered
A-level, NatCert, Dip, FirstDip, NVQ

Hartlepool College of Further Education
Stockton St, Hartlepool TS24 7NT;
URL www.hartlepoolfe.ac.uk; e-mail
enquiries@hartlepoolfe.ac.uk; Tel (student services)
01429 295000; Tel 01429 295111; Fax 01429 292999
Principal   D. Waddington

Middlesbrough College
Marton Rd, Middlesbrough TS4 3RZ;
URL www.mbro.ac.uk; e-mail courseinfo@mboro.ac.uk;
Tel 01642 296600; Fax 01642 313290
Principal; Chief Executive   John Hogg LLB(Hons)

New College Durham
Framwellgate Moor Campus, Durham, County Durham
DH1 5ES; URL www.newcollegedurham.ac.uk; e-mail
help@newdur.ac.uk; Tel 0191 375 4000; Fax 0191 375 4222
Principal; Chief Executive   John Widdowson

Newcastle College
Rye Hill Campus, Scotswood Rd, Newcastle upon Tyne,
Tyne and Wear NE4 7SA;
URL www.newcastlecollege.co.uk; e-mail
enquiries@ncl-coll.ac.uk; Tel 0191 200 4000;
Fax 0191 200 4517
Principal; Chief Executive   Jackie Fisher

Northumberland College
College Rd, Ashington, Northumberland NE63 9RG;
Tel 01670 841200; Fax 01670 841201
Principal   Rachel Ellis-Jones

Redcar and Cleveland College
Corporation Rd, Redcar, Redcar and Cleveland TS10 1EZ;
URL www.cleveland.ac.uk; e-mail
cinfo@cleveland.ac.uk; Tel 01642 473132;
Fax 01642 490856
Principal   Gary Groom

South Tyneside College
St Georges Ave, South Shields, Tyne and Wear NE34 6ET;
URL www.stc.ac.uk; e-mail info@stc.ac.uk;
Tel 0191 427 3500; Tel (prospectus) 0191 427 3900;
Fax 0191 427 3535
Principal; Chief Executive   Jim Bennett CertEd, BEd(Hons),
MSc

Stockton Riverside College
Harvard Ave, Thornaby, Stockton-on-Tees TS17 6FB;
Tel 01642 865400; Tel (prospectus) 01642 865566;
Fax 01642 865470
Chief Executive   Sujinder Singh Sangha

City of Sunderland College
Bede Centre, Durham Rd, Sunderland, Tyne and Wear
SR3 4AH; URL www.citysun.ac.uk; Tel (freephone
prospectus information) 0191 511 6060; Tel 0191 511 6327;
Fax 0191 511 6380
The Teleport, 4 Grayling Ct, Doxford International Business
Pk, Sunderland, Tyne and Wear SR3 3XD;
Tel 0191 511 6000; Fax 0191 511 6803
Principal   Angela O'Donoghue

Tyne Metropolitan College
Embleton Ave, Wallsend, Tyne and Wear NE28 9NJ;
URL www.tynemet.ac.uk; Tel 0191 229 5000;
Fax 0191 229 5301
Principal   Phil Green
Strategic Director (Studies 19+)   Eileen Baldwin

North West

Accrington and Rossendale College
Broad Oak Campus, Broad Oak Rd, Accrington, Lancashire
BB5 2AW; URL www.accross.ac.uk; Tel (prospectus)
01254 354354; Tel 01254 389933; Fax 01254 354001
Principal   Stephen Carlisle

Blackburn College
Feilden St, Blackburn BB2 1LH; URL www.blackburn.ac.uk;
Tel (prospectus) 01254 292929; Tel 01254 55144;
Fax 01254 682700
Principal   I. Clinton

Blackpool and The Fylde College
Bispham Campus, Ashfield Rd, Blackpool FY2 0HB;
URL www.blackpool.ac.uk; e-mail
visitors@blackpool.ac.uk; Tel 01253 352352;
Fax 01253 356127
Principal   Pauline Watehouse BA(Hons), PGCE,
AdDipEdMan

Bolton Community College
Manchester Rd, Bolton, Greater Manchester BL2 1ER;
URL www.bolton-community-college.ac.uk;
Tel 01204 907000; Fax 01204 907351
Principal   Alison Bowes

Bridge College
Curzon Rd, Offerton, Stockport, Cheshire SK2 5DG;
Tel 0161 487 4293
Principal   Maggie Thompson

Burnley College
Ormerod Rd, Burnley, Lancashire BB11 2RX;
URL www.burnley.ac.uk; e-mail
student.services@burnley.ac.uk; Tel 01282 711200;
Fax 01282 415063
Principal   John T. Smith
Director (Finance and Resources)   Colin Crowther

Bury College
Woodbury Centre, Market St, Bury, Greater Manchester
BL9 0BG; URL www.burycollege.ac.uk; e-mail
information@burycollege.ac.uk; Tel 0161 280 8280;
Tel (prospectus) 0161 280 8546; Fax 0161 280 8228
Principal   L.M. Chatburn

Carlisle College

Victoria Pl, Carlisle, Cumbria CA1 1HS;
URL www.carlisle.ac.uk; e-mail info@carlisle.ac.uk;
Tel 01228 822700; Tel (information unit) 01228 822703;
Fax 01228 822710
Principal Moira Tattersall

City College Manchester

Northenden Campus, Sale Rd, Northenden, Manchester
M23 0DD; URL www.ccm.ac.uk; e-mail
admissions@ccm.ac.uk; Minicom 0800 013 0123
Principal Mr W. Mills

Co-operative College

Holyoake Hse, Hanover St, Manchester M60 0AS;
URL www.co-op.ac.uk; e-mail enquiries@co-op.ac.uk;
Tel 0161 246 2902; Fax 0161 246 2946
Principal; Chief Executive Mervyn Wilson

Furness College

Channelside, Barrow-in-Furness, Cumbria LA14 2PJ;
URL www.furness.ac.uk; e-mail (prospectus)
course.enq@furness.ac.uk; Tel 01229 825017;
Fax 01229 870964
Principal Anne Attwood (Acting)

Hopwood Hall College

Middleton Campus, Rochdale Rd, Middleton, Greater
Manchester M24 6XH; URL www.hopwood.ac.uk; e-mail
enquiries@hopwood.ac.uk; Tel 0161 643 7560; Tel (course
enquiries) 0800 834 297; Fax 0161 643 2114
Principal Derek O'Toole MSc

Hugh Baird College

Balliol Rd, Bootle, Merseyside L20 7EW;
URL www.hughbaird.ac.uk; e-mail
info@hughbaird.ac.uk; Tel 0151 353 4444;
Fax 0151 353 4469
Principal B. Howarth BA, MA, DASE, CertEd

Kendal College

Milnthorpe Rd, Kendal, Cumbria LA9 5AY;
URL www.kendal.ac.uk; e-mail enquiries@kendal.ac.uk;
Tel 01539 814700; Fax 01539 814701
Principal Graham Wilkinson

Knowsley Community College

Cherryfield Dr, Kirkby, Merseyside L32 8SF;
URL www.knowsleycollege.ac.uk; e-mail
info@knowsleycollege.ac.uk; Tel 0845 155 1055
Principal F. Gill

Lakes College West Cumbria

Hallwood Rd, Lillyhall Business Pk, Workington, Cumbria
CA14 4JN; URL www.lcwc.ac.uk; e-mail
info@lcwc.ac.uk; Tel 01946 839300; Fax 01946 839302
Principal Pat Glenday

Lancaster and Morecambe College

Morecambe Rd, Lancaster, Lancashire LA1 2TY;
URL www.lmc.ac.uk; e-mail marketing@lmc.ac.uk;
Tel (prospectus) 0800 306 306; Tel 01524 66215;
Fax 01524 843078
Principal David Wood
Manager (Quality Improvement) Stuart Rimmer

Liverpool Community College

Old Swan, Broad Green Rd, Liverpool, Merseyside L13 5SQ
Principal Wally Brown

Macclesfield College

Park La, Macclesfield, Cheshire SK11 8LF;
URL www.macclesfield.ac.uk; e-mail
info@macclesfield.ac.uk; Tel 01625 410000;
Tel (prospectus) 01625 410002; Fax 01625 410001
Principal Wendy Wright

Manchester College of Arts and Technology (Adult Centres)

St John's Centre, New Quay St, Manchester M3 3BE;
URL www.mancat.ac.uk; e-mail
enquiries@mancat.ac.uk; Tel (course enquiries)
0800 068 8585; Tel 0161 953 5995; Fax 0161 953 2259
Principal P. Tavernor BASocSc(Hons), PGCE

Mid Cheshire College

Hartford Campus, Northwich, Cheshire CW8 1LJ;
Tel 01606 74444; Fax 01606 720700
Principal John Reilly

Nelson and Colne College

Scotland Rd, Nelson, Lancashire BB9 7YT;
URL www.nelson.ac.uk; e-mail reception@nelson.ac.uk;
Tel 01282 440200; Tel (prospectus) 01282 440258;
Fax 01282 440274
Principal John Farrington (Acting)

North Trafford College of Further Education

Talbot Rd, Stretford, Manchester M32 0XH;
URL www.ntc.ac.uk; Tel (course enquiries)
0161 886 7000; Tel 0161 886 7070; Fax 0161 872 7921
Principal David Lawrence

Oldham College

Rochdale Rd, Oldham, Greater Manchester OL9 6AA;
URL www.oldham.ac.uk; e-mail info@oldham.ac.uk;
Tel (prospectus) 0800 269 480; Tel 0161 624 5214;
Fax 0161 785 4234
Principal Kathleen Thomas

Preston College

St Vincents Rd, Fulwood, Preston, Lancashire PR2 8UR;
e-mail reception@prestoncoll.ac.uk; Tel 01772 772200;
Fax 01772 772201
Principal M.A. Clegg BA, FRSA

Reaseheath College

Reaseheath, Nantwich, Cheshire CW5 6DF;
URL www.reaseheath.ac.uk; e-mail
enquiries@reaseheath.ac.uk; Tel (prospectus)
01270 613242; Tel 01270 625131; Fax 01270 625665
Principal Meredydd David

Riverside College Halton

Kingsway, Widnes, Halton WA8 7QQ;
URL www.riversidecollege.ac.uk; Tel 0151 257 2020;
Fax 0151 420 2408
Principal Pat Grunwell

Runshaw College

Langdale Rd, Leyland, Lancashire PR25 3DQ;
Tel 01772 622677; Fax 01772 642009
Chair Lynne Duckworth
Principal; Chief Executive Michael Sheehan

St Helens College

Brook St, St Helens, Merseyside WA10 1PZ;
URL www.sthelens.ac.uk; e-mail
<initial>.<surname>@sthelens.ac.uk; Tel 01744 733766;
Fax 01744 623400
Principal Ms Pat Bacon BA(Hons), MA, MBA

Salford College

Worsley Campus, Walkden Rd, Worsley, Greater
Manchester M28 7QD; URL www.salford-col.ac.uk;
e-mail centad@salford-col.ac.uk; Tel (central admissions)
0161 211 5001; Tel 0161 702 8272; Fax 0161 211 5020
Principal; Chief Executive Tony Craven MA, PGCE,
AdvDip, BFA, CIPFA

Skelmersdale and Ormskirk Colleges

Westbank Campus, Yewdale, Skelmersdale, Lancashire
WN8 6JA; URL www.skelmersdale.ac.uk; e-mail
enquiries@skelmersdale.ac.uk; Tel 01695 728744;
Fax 01695 51890
Principal; Chief Executive Philip Lewis

5

South Cheshire College

Dane Bank Ave, Crewe, Cheshire CW2 8AB;
URL www.s-cheshire.ac.uk; e-mail
info@s-cheshire.ac.uk; Tel 01270 654654;
Fax 01270 651515
Principal; Chief Executive   David Collins CBE, MA(Hons),
PhD

Southport College

Mornington Rd, Southport, Merseyside PR9 0TT;
URL www.southport-college.ac.uk; e-mail
guidance@southport-college.ac.uk; Tel 0845 006 6236
Principal   B. Mitchell

Stockport College of Further and Higher Education

Wellington Rd South, Stockport, Greater Manchester
SK1 3UQ; URL www.stockport.ac.uk; e-mail
admissions@stockport.ac.uk; Tel 0161 958 3448;
Fax 0161 480 6636
Principal   Peter Roberts BA(Hons), MA, MEd

Tameside College

Ashton Centre, Beaufort Rd, Ashton-under-Lyne, Greater
Manchester OL6 6NX; URL www.tameside.ac.uk; e-mail
info@tameside.ac.uk; Tel 0161 908 6600;
Fax 0161 908 6611

Trafford College

Manchester Rd, West Timperley, Altrincham, Cheshire
WA14 5PQ; URL www.stcoll.ac.uk; e-mail
enquiries@stcoll.ac.uk; Tel 0161 952 4600; Tel (student
services) 0161 952 4686; Fax 0161 952 4672
Principal   W. Moorcroft

Warrington Collegiate

Winwick Road Campus, Warrington, Cheshire WA2 8QA;
URL www.warrington.ac.uk; e-mail
learner.services@warrington.ac.uk; Tel 01925 494494;
Fax 01925 418328
Chair of Governors   Colin Daniels
Principal; Chief Executive   Paul Hafien
Director (Management Information Systems)   Julie Hindley
Contact (Learner Services)   Ellen Parry
Number of students
1709 full-time, 11 378 part-time

West Cheshire College

Chester Campus, Handbridge, Eaton Rd, Chester, Cheshire
CH4 7ER; URL www.west-cheshire.ac.uk; e-mail
info@west-cheshire.ac.uk; Tel 01244 670600;
Fax 01244 670676
Principal   Sara Mogel

Wigan and Leigh College

PO Box 53, Parsons Wlk, Wigan, Greater Manchester
WN1 1RS; URL www.wigan-leigh.ac.uk; e-mail
admissions@wigan-leigh.ac.uk; Tel 01942 761600
Principal   Jim Crewdson

Wirral Metropolitan College

Conway Park Campus, Europa Bvd, Birkenhead,
Merseyside CH41 4NT; URL www.wmc.ac.uk;
Tel 0151 551 7777; Fax 0151 551 7001
Principal   Mike Potter CBE

South East

Abingdon and Witney College

Wootton Rd, Abingdon, Oxfordshire OX14 1GG;
URL www.abingdon-witney.ac.uk; e-mail
inquiry@abingdon-witney.ac.uk; Tel 01235 555585;
Fax 01235 553168
Principal   Teresa Kelly

Alton College

Old Odiham Rd, Alton, Hampshire GU34 2LX;
URL www.altoncollege.ac.uk; e-mail
enquiries@altoncollege.ac.uk; Tel 01420 592200;
Fax 01420 592253
Principal   Jane Machell BA(Hon), MA, PGCE

Amersham and Wycombe College

Chesham Campus, Lycrome Rd, Chesham,
Buckinghamshire HP5 3LA; URL www.amersham.ac.uk;
e-mail info@amersham.ac.uk; Tel (customer services)
0800 614 016; Tel 01494 735555; Fax 01494 735588
Principal   John Eaton

Andover College

Charlton Rd, Andover, Hampshire SP10 1EJ;
URL www.andover.ac.uk; e-mail info@andover.ac.uk;
Tel 01264 360000; Tel (prospectus) 01264 360036;
Fax 01264 360010
Principal   Tim Jackson

Aylesbury College

Oxford Rd, Aylesbury, Buckinghamshire HP21 8PD;
URL www.aylesbury.ac.uk; e-mail
studserv@aylesbury.ac.uk; e-mail
customerservices@aylesbury.ac.uk; Tel 01296 588588;
Fax 01296 588589
Principal   Pauline Odulinski

Basingstoke College of Technology

Worting Rd, Basingstoke, Hampshire RG21 8TN;
URL www.bcot.ac.uk; Tel 01256 354141;
Fax 01256 306444
Principal   J. Armstrong MA, FRSA

Bracknell and Wokingham College

Church Rd, Bracknell, Bracknell Forest RG12 1DJ;
URL www.bracknell.ac.uk; e-mail
study@bracknell.ac.uk; Tel 0845 330 3343
Principal; Chief Executive   Howard O'Keeffe BA, MBA,
ACIS, MCMI, PGCE

Brockenhurst College

Lyndhurst Rd, Brockenhurst, Hampshire SO42 7ZE;
URL www.brock.ac.uk; e-mail enquiries@brock.ac.uk;
Tel 01590 625555; Fax 01590 625526
Principal   D. Roberts BA(Hons), CertEd

Brooklands College

Heath Rd, Weybridge, Surrey KT13 8TT;
URL www.brooklands.ac.uk; e-mail
info@brooklands.ac.uk; Tel 01932 797700;
Tel (prospectus) 01932 797797; Fax 01932 797800
Principal   C.B. Staff BSc(Hons), MSc, CPhys, MInstP

Canterbury College

New Dover Rd, Canterbury, Kent CT1 3AJ;
URL www.cant-col.ac.uk; e-mail
courseenquiries@cant-col.ac.uk; Tel 01227 811111;
Tel (student information centre) 01227 811188
Principal; Executive Director   Alison Clarke

Carshalton College

Nightingale Rd, Carshalton, Surrey SM5 2EJ;
URL www.carshalton.ac.uk; e-mail cs@carshalton.ac.uk;
Tel 020 8544 4444
Principal   David Watkins BA(Hons), PhD, CChem, FRSC,
FRSA

Central Sussex College

College Rd, Crawley, West Sussex RHI0 INR;
URL www.centralsussex.ac.uk; e-mail
info@centralsussex.ac.uk; Tel 01293 442200;
Tel (admissions) 01293 442205; Fax 01293 442399
Principal   Dr Russell Strutt

Chichester College

Chichester Campus, Westgate Fields, Chichester, West Sussex PO19 1SB; URL www.chichester.ac.uk; e-mail info@chichester.ac.uk; Tel 01243 786321; Fax 01243 539481

Principal   R.N. Parker BA(Hons), PhD

City College Brighton and Hove

Pelham St, Brighton, East Sussex BN1 4FA; URL www.ccb.ac.uk; e-mail info@ccb.ac.uk; Tel 01273 667788; Fax 01273 667703

Principal   Phil Frier

College of Estate Management

e-mail prospectuses@cem.ac.uk; Tel 0118 921 4696

Chair   Vacancy

Principal   Dr A. Heywood PhD, BSc(Hons), FRICS, FRGS, MiMgt

Director; Secretary (Finance)   Grahame Smith BA, FCCA

Director (Studies)   P.J.S. Batho MA, MRICS

Web-supported distance learning courses, post-qualification education and training, research and publications

University College for the Creative Arts at Canterbury, Epsom, Farnham, Maidstone and Rochester

See Chapter 6: Universities and University Colleges

East Berkshire College

Station Rd, Langley, Slough SL3 8BY; Tel 0845 373 2500; Fax 01753 793316

Principal   Jean Robertson

East Surrey College

Gatton Point, Redhill, Surrey RH1 2JX; URL www.esc.ac.uk; e-mail student-services@esc.ac.uk; Tel 01737 772611; Tel (prospectus) 01737 788444; Fax 01737 768641

Principal   Frances Wadsworth

Eastleigh College

Chestnut Ave, Eastleigh, Hampshire SO50 5FS; URL www.eastleigh.ac.uk; e-mail goplaces@eastleigh.ac.uk; Tel 02380 911000; Fax 02380 322131

Chief Executive   Tony Lau-Walker

Fareham College

Bishopsfield Rd, Fareham, Hampshire PO14 1NH; URL www.fareham.ac.uk; e-mail info@fareham.ac.uk; Tel 01329 815200; Fax 01329 822483

Principal   Carl Groves BSc, MA, MBA, PGCE DMS, FCMI

Farnborough College of Technology

Boundary Rd, Farnborough, Hampshire GU14 6SB; URL www.farn-ct.ac.uk; e-mail info@farn-ct.ac.uk; Tel 01252 405555; Fax 01252 407041

Principal   Christine Davis BA(Hons), MCIM

Guildford College of Further and Higher Education

Stoke Pk, Guildford, Surrey GU1 1EZ; URL www.guildford.ac.uk; e-mail info@guildford.ac.uk; Tel 01483 448500; Fax 01483 448600

Principal   Clive Cooke

Hastings College of Arts and Technology

Archerty Rd, St Leonards-on-Sea, East Sussex TN38 0HX; URL www.hastings.ac.uk; e-mail studentadvisers@hastings.ac.uk; Tel 01424 442222; Fax 01424 721763

Principal   Sue Middlehurst

Hilderstone College – English Studies Centre

St Peters Rd, Broadstairs, Kent CT10 2JW; URL www.hilderstone.ac.uk; e-mail info@hilderstone.ac.uk; Tel 01843 869171; Fax 01843 603877

Principal   Peter Worley

Isle of Wight College

Medina Way, Newport, Isle of Wight PO30 5TA; URL www.iwcollege.ac.uk; e-mail info@iwcollege.ac.uk; Tel 01983 526631; Tel (prospectus) 01983 535210; Fax 01983 521707

Principal; Chief Executive   Debbie Lavin

Kingston College

Kingston Hall Rd, Kingston upon Thames, Surrey KT1 2AQ; URL www.kingston-college.ac.uk; e-mail info@kingston-college.ac.uk; Tel 020 8546 2151; Fax 020 8268 2900

Lewes Tertiary College

Mountfield Rd, Lewes, East Sussex BN7 2XH; URL www.lewescollege.ac.uk; e-mail info@lewescollege.ac.uk; Tel 01273 483188; Fax 01273 478561

Principal   Peter Gibson

Mid-Kent College of Higher and Further Education

Horsted, Maidstone Rd, Chatham, Kent ME5 9UQ; URL www.midkent.ac.uk; e-mail course.enquiries@midkent.ac.uk; Tel (central college helpline for information on all courses) 01634 402020; Tel 01634 830633; Fax 01634 830224

Principal; Chief Executive   S. Grix

Milton Keynes College

Chaffron Way Campus, Woughton Campus West, Milton Keynes, Buckinghamshire MK6 5LP; URL www.mkcollege.ac.uk; e-mail info@mkcollege.ac.uk; Tel 01908 684444; Tel (admissions) 01908 684452; Fax 01908 684399

Principal; Chief Executive   Rob Badcock

NESCOT – North East Surrey College of Technology

Reigate Rd, Ewell, Epsom, Surrey KT17 3DS; URL www.nescot.ac.uk; e-mail info@nescot.ac.uk; Tel 020 8394 3038; Fax 020 8394 3030

Principal   S. Mann

Newbury College

Monks La, Newbury, West Berkshire RG14 7TD; URL www.newbury-college.ac.uk; e-mail info@newbury-college.ac.uk; Tel 01635 845 000; Fax 01635 845312

Principal   Dr Anne Murdoch BSc, PGCE, PhD, MBA, FRSA, MCMI

North West Kent College

Dartford Campus, Oakfield La, Dartford, Kent DA1 2JT; URL www.nwkcollege.ac.uk; e-mail courseenquiries@nwk.ac.uk; Tel (helpline) 0800 074 1447; Tel 01322 629400; Fax 01322 629468

Gravesend Campus, Dering Way, Gravesend, Kent DA12 2JJ; Fax 01322 629682

Principal   R.M. Bell

Northbrook College Sussex

Littlehampton Rd, Goring-by-Sea, Worthing, West Sussex BN12 6NU; URL www.northbrook.ac.uk; e-mail enquiries@nbcol.ac.uk; Tel 0845 155 6060; Fax 01903 606073

Principal   D. Percival

Orpington College

The Walnuts, Orpington, Kent BR6 0TE; URL www.orpington.ac.uk; e-mail guidance@orpington.ac.uk; Tel 01689 899700; Fax 01689 877949

Principal; Chief Executive   Simon Norton

Oxford and Cherwell Valley College

Banbury Campus, Broughton Rd, Banbury, Oxfordshire OX16 9QA; URL www.oxford-cherwell.ac.uk; e-mail enquiries@occ.ac.uk; Tel 01865 551755; Fax 01865 248871

5

Oxford Campus, Oxpens Rd, Oxford, Oxfordshire OX1 1SA;
  URL www.occ.ac.uk; e-mail
  enquiries@oxford.ocvc.ac.uk; Tel (general enquiries)
  01865 550550; Fax 01865 248871

Priest End, Thame, Oxfordshire OX9 2AF
Chair of Governors   Michael Leech
Principal   Sally Dicketts
Vice-Principal (Development)   Lesley Donoghue
Vice-Principal (Operations)   Hilary Stone
Vice-Principal (Strategic Finance and Planning)
  Stephen McCormick

Plater College

Pullens La, Oxford, Oxfordshire OX3 0DT; e-mail
  reception@plater.ac.uk; Tel 01865 740500;
  Fax 01865 740510
Principal   M. Blades MA, MBA

Rose Bruford College

Lamorbey Pk, Sidcup, Kent DA15 9DF;
  URL www.bruford.ac.uk; e-mail
  enquiries@bruford.ac.uk; Tel 020 8308 2600;
  Fax 020 8308 0542; Minicom 020 8302 5734

Ruskin College

Walton St, Oxford, Oxfordshire OX1 2HE;
  URL www.ruskin.ac.uk; e-mail enquiries@ruskin.ac.uk;
  Tel 01865 554331
Principal   Dr Audrey Mullender FRSA, AcSS, PhD, CQSW

South Downs College

College Rd, Waterlooville, Hampshire PO7 8AA;
  URL www.southdowns.ac.uk; e-mail
  college@southdowns.ac.uk; Tel (Freephone)
  0800 056 0511; Tel 02392 797979; Fax 02392 797940
Principal   Michael Oakes

South Kent College

Shorncliffe Rd, Folkestone, Kent CT20 2NA;
  URL www.southkent.ac.uk; e-mail
  admissions@southkent.ac.uk; Tel 01304 244337;
  Fax 01303 858400
Principal   C. Cooke

Southampton City College

St Mary St, Southampton SO14 1AR;
  URL www.southampton-city.ac.uk; e-mail
  information@southampton-city.ac.uk; Tel (course
  information) 02380 484848; Tel (switchboard)
  02380 577400; Fax 02380 577473
Principal   Lindsey Noble BA, MBA

Sussex Downs College

Cross Levels Way, Eastbourne, East Sussex BN21 2UF;
  URL www.sussexdowns.ac.uk; e-mail
  info@sussexdowns.ac.uk; Tel 01323 637637;
  Fax 01323 637472
Principal   John D. Blake BA(Hons), DPhil

Thanet College

Ramsgate Rd, Broadstairs, Kent CT10 1PN;
  URL www.thanet.ac.uk; e-mail
  student_admissions@thanet.ac.uk; Tel (main
  switchboard) 01843 605040; Tel (central admissions)
  01843 605049; Fax 01843 605013
Principal   Sue Buss

West Kent College

Brook St, Tonbridge, Kent TN9 2PW; URL www.wkc.ac.uk;
  e-mail enquiries@wkc.ac.uk; Tel 01732 358101;
  Fax 01732 771415
Chief Executive   Bill Fearon

South West

Anglo-European Chiropractic College

13–15 Parkwood Rd, Boscombe, Bournemouth, Dorset
  BH5 2DF; URL www.aecc.ac.uk; e-mail
  jlewis@aecc.ac.uk; Tel 01202 436200; Fax 01202 436312

Bournemouth and Poole College

Poole Centre (Main Office), North Rd, Poole BH14 0LS;
  URL www.thecollege.co.uk; e-mail
  enquiries@thecollege.co.uk; Tel (course enquiries)
  01202 205205; Tel 01202 747600; Fax 01202 205719
Principal; Chief Executive   Rowland Foote FRSA
Marketing; Public Relations   Julie-Anne Houldey

Bridgwater College

Bath Rd, Bridgwater, Somerset TA6 4PZ; Tel 01278 455464;
  Fax 01278 444363
Principal   Fiona McMillan

Cirencester College

Fosse Way Campus, Stroud Rd, Cirencester, Gloucestershire
  GL7 1XA; URL www.cirencester.ac.uk; e-mail
  principal@cirencester.ac.uk; Tel 01285 640994;
  Fax 01285 644171
Principal   Nigel Robbins MA, MEd, PGCE

City of Bath College

Avon St, Bath, Somerset BA1 1UP;
  URL www.citybathcoll.ac.uk; e-mail
  courses&enquiries@citybathcoll.ac.uk; Tel 01225 312191;
  Fax 01225 444213
Principal   Matt Atkinson

City of Bristol College

College Green Centre, St Georges Rd, Bristol BS1 5UA;
  URL www.cityofbristol.ac.uk; e-mail
  enquiries@cityofbristol.ac.uk; Tel 0117 312 5000;
  Fax 0117 312 5051; Minicom 0117 312 5503
Principal   Keith Elliott
The college of further education offers courses at nine main
centres across the city

Cornwall College

Trevenson Rd, Redruth, Cornwall TR15 3RD;
  URL www.cornwall.ac.uk; e-mail
  enquiries@cornwall.ac.uk; Tel 01209 611611;
  Fax 01209 611612
Principal   Dr A. Stanhope

Cornwall College St Austell

Tregonissey Rd, St Austell, Cornwall PL25 4DJ;
  URL www.st-austell.ac.uk; e-mail info@st-austell.ac.uk;
  Tel 01726 226626; Fax 01726 226627

East Devon College

Bolham Rd, Tiverton, Devon EX16 6SH;
  URL www.edc.ac.uk; Tel 01884 235200; Fax 01884 235262
Principal   M. Edwards

Exeter College

Hele Rd, Exeter, Devon EX4 4JS; URL www.exe-coll.ac.uk;
  e-mail reception@exe-coll.ac.uk; Tel 0845 111 6000;
  Fax 01392 205842
Principal   Richard Atkins

Filton College

Filton Ave, Bristol BS34 7AT; URL www.filton.ac.uk; e-mail
  info@filton.ac.uk; Tel 0117 931 2121; Fax 0117 931 2233
Principal   Kevin Hamblin

Gloucestershire College of Arts and Technology

Cheltenham, Gloucestershire GL51 7SJ;
  URL www.gloscol.ac.uk; e-mail info@gloscol.ac.uk;
  Tel 01242 532000; Fax 01242 532196
Gloucester Campus, Llanthony Rd, Gloucester,
  Gloucestershire GL2 5JQ; URL www.gloscol.ac.uk;
  e-mail info@gloscol.ac.uk; Tel 01452 532000;
  Fax 01452 563441

Principal   Greg Smith BA, MBA, PGCE
Number of students
3300 full-time, 32 000 part-time

New College – Swindon
New College Dr, Swindon SN3 1AH;
  URL www.newcollege.ac.uk; e-mail
  info@newcollege.ac.uk; Tel 01793 611470;
  Fax 01793 436437
Principal   V. MacLeod

North Devon College
Old Sticklepath Hill, Barnstaple, Devon EX31 2BQ;
  URL www.ndevon.ac.uk; e-mail
  marketing@ndevon.ac.uk; Tel 01271 345 291;
  Fax 01271 338 121
Principal   David Dodd MSc, MIEE, MBCS, CEng

Norton Radstock College
South Hill Pk, Radstock, Somerset BA3 3RW;
  URL www.nortcoll.ac.uk; e-mail
  <initial><surname>@nortcoll.ac.uk; Tel 01761 433161;
  Fax 01761 436173
Principal   Shirley Arayan

Penwith College
St Clare St, Penzance, Cornwall TR18 2SA;
  URL www.penwith.ac.uk; e-mail
  courses@penwith.ac.uk; Tel 01736 335000;
  Fax 01736 335100
Principal   R.M. Andruszko

City College Plymouth
Kings Rd, Devonport, Plymouth, Devon PL1 5QG;
  URL www.cityplym.ac.uk; e-mail
  reception@cityplym.ac.uk; Tel 01752 305300;
  Fax 01752 305343
Principal   Viv Gillespie

Royal Forest of Dean College
Five Acres Campus, Coleford, Gloucestershire GL16 7JT;
  URL www.rfdc.ac.uk; e-mail enquiries@rfdc.ac.uk;
  Tel 01594 833416; Fax 01594 837497
Principal   Dawn Ward OBE

The College of St Mark and St John
Derriford Rd, Plymouth, Devon PL6 8BH;
  URL www.marjon.ac.uk; e-mail
  admissions@marjon.ac.uk; Tel 01752 636890
Principal   Dr David Baker
Head (Careers)   Elaine Young

Salisbury College
Southampton Rd, Salisbury, Wiltshire SP1 2LW;
  URL www.salisbury.ac.uk; e-mail
  enquiries@salisbury.ac.uk; Tel 01722 344344;
  Fax 01722 344345
Principal   Gill Thompson

Somerset College of Arts and Technology
Wellington Rd, Taunton, Somerset TA1 5AX;
  URL www.somerset.ac.uk; e-mail
  enquiries@somerset.ac.uk; Tel 01823 366331;
  Fax 01823 366418
Principal; Chief Executive   Alison Scott BA, FRSA

South Devon College
Newton Rd, Torquay, Torbay TQ2 5BY;
  URL www.southdevon.ac.uk; Tel 01803 400700;
  Fax 01803 400701
Principal   Heather Maxwell

Strode College
Church Rd, Street, Somerset BA16 0AB;
  URL www.strode-college.ac.uk; e-mail
  courseinfo@strode-college.ac.uk; Tel 01458 844422;
  Fax 01458 844411
Principal; Chief Executive   Ian Bennett

Stroud College
Stratford Rd, Stroud, Gloucestershire GL5 4AH; e-mail
  enquire@strouda.demon.co.uk; Tel 01453 763424;
  Fax 01453 753543
Principal   H. Pollock

Swindon College
North Star, Swindon SN2 1DY; Tel 01793 491591;
  Fax 01793 430503
Principal   Jonquil Brooks

Truro College
College Rd, Truro, Cornwall TR1 3XX;
  URL www.trurocollege.ac.uk; e-mail
  enquiry@trurocollege.ac.uk; Tel 01872 267000;
  Fax 01872 267100
Principal   Jonathan Burnett

Weston College
Knightstone Rd, Weston-super-Mare, North Somerset
  BS23 2AL; URL www.weston.ac.uk; e-mail
  mktg@weston.ac.uk; Tel 01934 411411; Fax 01934 411410
Principal; Chief Executive   Dr P. Phillips

Weymouth College
Cranford Ave, Weymouth, Dorset DT4 7LQ;
  URL www.weymouth.ac.uk; e-mail
  igs@weymouth.ac.uk; Tel (prospectus) 01305 208808;
  Tel 01305 761100; Fax 01305 208892

Wiltshire College
Cocklebury Rd, Chippenham, Wiltshire SN15 3BD;
  URL www.wiltscoll.ac.uk; e-mail info@wiltcoll.ac.uk;
  Tel (call centre) 0845 330 2232; Tel 01249 464644;
  Fax 01249 465326
Principal   Di Dale

Yeovil College
Mudford Rd, Yeovil, Somerset BA21 4DR;
  URL www.yeovil.ac.uk; e-mail info@yeovil.ac.uk;
  Tel 01935 423921; Fax 01935 429962
Principal; Chief Executive   James Hampton

West Midlands

Birmingham College of Food, Tourism and Creative Studies
Summer Row, Birmingham, West Midlands B3 1JB;
  URL www.bcftcs.ac.uk; e-mail marketing@bcftcs.ac.uk;
  Tel 0121 604 1000; Tel (marketing unit) 0121 693 2282
Principal   E.F. McIntyre CBE, BA(Hons), MSc, CertEd, MHCIMA

Bournville College
Bristol Rd South, Northfield, Birmingham, West Midlands
  B31 2AJ; URL www.bournville.ac.uk; e-mail
  info@bournville.ac.uk; Tel 0121 483 1000;
  Tel (prospectus) 0121 483 1111; Fax 0121 411 2231
Principal   N. Cave BA, MA, CertEd

Burton College
Lichfield St, Burton upon Trent, Staffordshire DE14 3RL;
  URL www.burton-college.ac.uk; Tel 01283 494400;
  Fax 01283 494800
Principal; Chief Executive   Keith Norris MA, MSc, MCIOB, AIMBM

Cannock Chase Technical College
The Green, Cannock, Staffordshire WS11 1UE;
  URL www.cannock.ac.uk; e-mail
  enquiries@cannock.ac.uk; Tel 01543 462200;
  Fax 01543 574223
Principal; Chief Executive   G.R. Morley

City College Birmingham
East Birmingham Campus, Garrets Green La, Birmingham,
West Midlands B33 0TS; URL www.citycol.ac.uk; e-mail
enquiries@citycol.ac.uk; Tel 0121 204 0000;
Fax 0121 204 0150
Handsworth Campus, The Council Hse, Soho Rd,
Birmingham, West Midlands B21 9DP; Fax 0121 523 4447
Chief Executive   Vacancy

City College Coventry
Butts and Maxwell Centre, Butts, Coventry, Warwickshire
CV1 3GD; URL www.covcollege.ac.uk; e-mail
info@covcollege.ac.uk; Tel (prospectus) 0800 616202;
Tel 024 7679 1000
Principal   Paul Taylor

Dudley College of Technology
The Broadway, Dudley, West Midlands DY1 4AS;
URL www.dudleycol.ac.uk; e-mail
student.services@dudleycol.ac.uk; Tel 01384 363363;
Fax 01384 363311
Principal   Lowell Williams

Evesham and Malvern Hills College
Davies Rd, Evesham, Worcestershire WR11 1LP;
URL www.evesham.ac.uk; e-mail
enquiries@evesham.ac.uk; Tel 01386 712600;
Fax 01386 712640
Principal   D. Blades LLB, CertEd

Fircroft College of Adult Education
1018 Bristol Rd, Selly Oak, Birmingham, West Midlands
B29 6LH; URL www.fircroft.ac.uk; e-mail
accesscourses@fircroft.ac.uk; Tel 0121 472 0116;
Fax 0121 471 1503
Principal   Fiona Larden

Halesowen College
Whittingham Rd, Halesowen, West Midlands B63 3NA;
URL www.halesowen.ac.uk; e-mail
info@halesowen.ac.uk; Tel 0121 602 7777;
Tel (admissions) 0121 602 7888; Fax 0121 585 0369
Principal   Keith Bate

Henley College Coventry
Henley Rd, Bell Grn, Coventry, Warwickshire CV2 1ED;
e-mail principal@henley-cov.ac.uk; Tel 024 7662 6300;
Fax 024 7661 1837
Principal   Ray Goy BA(Hons), PGCE

Herefordshire College of Technology
Folly La, Hereford, Herefordshire HR1 1LS;
URL www.hct.ac.uk; e-mail enquiries@hct.ac.uk;
Tel 0800 032 1986; Fax 01432 353449
Principal   Mr I. Peake BSc, FCIPD (Acting)

Hereward College
Bramston Cres, Tile Hill La, Coventry, Warwickshire
CV4 9SW; URL www.hereward.ac.uk; e-mail
enquiries@hereward.ac.uk; Tel (student services)
02476 426101; Tel 02476 426104; Fax 02476 694305
Principal   Janis Firminger BA, MPhil, MEd, CertEd
General further education college specialising in provision
for disabled people. Residential students with disabilities
from across the UK study alongside their non-disabled peers
in a supportive environment

Kidderminster College
Market St, Kidderminster, Worcestershire DY10 1LX;
Tel 01562 820811
Principal; Chief Executive   Andrew Miller

Leek College
Stockwell St, Leek, Staffordshire ST13 6DP;
URL www.leek.ac.uk; e-mail admissions@leek.ac.uk;
Tel 01538 398866; Fax 01538 399506
Principal   Robert Morrey
Vice-Principal   Julia Leonard
Director (Quality and Development)   Penny Meakin CertEd
Director (Support for Studies)   Valerie Smith

Matthew Boulton College of Further and Higher Education
Jennens Rd, Birmingham, West Midlands B4 7PS;
URL www.mbc.ac.uk; e-mail ask.mbc.ac.uk;
Tel 0121 446 4545; Tel (information centre) 0121 503 8500;
Fax 0121 503 8590
Principal; Chief Executive   Christine Braddock

Newcastle-under-Lyme College
Liverpool Rd, Newcastle-under-Lyme, Staffordshire
ST5 2DF; URL www.nulc.ac.uk; e-mail
enquiries@nulc.ac.uk; Tel 01782 715111;
Fax 01782 717396
Principal; Chief Executive   K.G. Dobson

Newman College of Higher Education
Genners La, Bartley Grn, Birmingham, West Midlands
B32 3NT; URL www.newman.ac.uk; e-mail
registry@newman.ac.uk; Tel 0121 476 1181;
Fax 0121 476 1196
Chair of Governors   The Most Rev Vincent Nichols Phil,
MA, MEd, STL;   Archbishop of Birmingham
Principal   Pamela Taylor BA, MA, MPhil, PGCE, DipEd
Vice-Principal   Dr Kathryn Southworth
Registrar   Heather Somerfield BA, MSc
Director (External Affairs)   Anthony Davenport BA, MA,
PhD, CertEd
Director (Finance)   Tony Sharma ACMA, BA
Director (Quality)   Lysandre de la Haye
Director (Research)   Dr Yahya Al-Nakeeb
Head (Library and Learning Resources)   Chris Port BA, MLib,
MCLIP
Head (School of Community and Professional Development)
Dr Stan Tucker
Head (School of Science and Humanities)   Stephen Bulman
BA, PhD
Head (School of Teacher Education, Training and CPD)
Art Lavelle BA, MSc, MPhil, DASE, DPSE

North East Worcestershire College
Chair   Prof Dick Bryant
Principal   Neil Bromley BA, MA, PGCE

North Warwickshire and Hinckley College
Hinckley Rd, Nuneaton, Warwickshire CV11 6BH;
URL www.nwhc.ac.uk; e-mail the.college@nwhc.ac.uk;
Tel 024 7624 3000; Fax 024 7632 9056
Principal   Marion Plant

Sandwell College
Oldbury Business Centre, Pound Rd, Oldbury, Sandwell,
West Midlands B68 8NA; Tel 0121 556 6000

Shrewsbury College of Arts and Technology
London Rd, Shrewsbury, Shropshire SY2 6PR;
URL www.shrewsbury.ac.uk; e-mail
prospects@shrewsbury.ac.uk; Tel 01743 342342;
Fax 01743 342343
Principal   Greg Molan

Solihull College
Blossomfield Rd, Solihull, West Midlands B91 1SB;
Tel 0121 678 7000; Fax 0121 678 7200
Principal   Brenda Sheils
Vice-Principal (Resources)   Lindsey Stewart

South Birmingham College
SBC Hall Grn, Cole Bank Rd, Birmingham, West Midlands
B28 8ES; URL www.sbc.ac.uk; e-mail info@sbc.ac.uk;
Tel 0121 694 5000; Fax 0121 694 5007
Principal   Mike Hopkins

Stafford College
Earl St, Stafford, Staffordshire ST16 2QR;
URL www.staffordcoll.ac.uk; e-mail
enquiries@staffordcoll.ac.uk; Tel 01785 223800;
Fax 01785 259953
Principal   Stephen Willis

Stoke-on-Trent College
Cauldon Campus, Stoke Rd, Stoke-on-Trent ST4 2DG;
   URL www.stokecollege.ac.uk; e-mail
   info@stokecoll.ac.uk; Tel 01782 208208; Fax 01782 603504
Principal   Graham Moore BSc(Econ), MA

Stourbridge College
Hagley Rd, Stourbridge, West Midlands DY8 1QU;
   URL www.stourbridge.ac.uk; Tel 01384 344344;
   Fax 01384 344345
Principal   Lynette Cutting

Stratford-upon-Avon College
The Willows North, Alcester Rd, Stratford-upon-Avon,
   Warwickshire CV37 9QR; URL www.stratford.ac.uk;
   e-mail college@stratford.ac.uk; Tel 01789 266245;
   Fax 01789 267524
Principal   Martin Penny

Sutton Coldfield College
Lichfield Rd, Sutton Coldfield, West Midlands B74 2NW;
   URL www.sutcol.ac.uk; e-mail infoc@sutcol.ac.uk;
   Tel 0121 355 5671; Fax 0121 355 0799
Great Barr Campus, Aldridge Rd, Great Barr, Birmingham,
   West Midlands B44 8NU; URL www.sutcol.ac.uk;
   Tel 0121 360 3545
Principal   Graham Jones

Tamworth and Lichfield College
Croft St, Upper Gungate, Tamworth, Staffordshire B79 8AE;
   URL www.tlc.ac.uk; e-mail enquiries@tamworth.ac.uk;
   Tel 01827 310202; Fax 01827 59437
Principal   Ann Neville

Telford College of Arts and Technology
Haybridge Road Campus, Haybridge Rd, Wellington,
   Telford, Wrekin TF1 2NP; Tel 01952 642237;
   Fax 01952 642293
Principal   D.F. Boynton BSc, MSc, PGCE, CEng, MIMechE,
   FRSA

Tile Hill College of Further Education
Tile Hill La, Coventry, Warwickshire CV4 9SU;
   Tel 024 7679 1000; Fax 024 7646 4903
Principal   Paul Taylor BSc(Hons), ACA

Walford and North Shropshire College
Oswesty Campus, Oswestry, Shropshire SY11 4QB;
   URL www.wnsc.ac.uk; e-mail enquiries@wnsc.ac.uk;
   Tel 01691 688000; Fax 01691 688001
Principal   Andrew Tyley

Walsall College
St Pauls St, Walsall, West Midlands WS1 1XN;
   URL www.walsallcollege.ac.uk; e-mail
   info@walsallcollege.ac.uk; Tel 01922 657000;
   Fax 01992 657083
Principal; Chief Executive   Chris Ball

**Warwickshire College, Royal Leamington Spa, Rugby,
Moreton Morrell**
Leamington Centre, Warwick New Rd, Leamington Spa,
   Warwickshire CV32 5JE; e-mail
   enquiries@warkscol.ac.uk; Tel 01926 318000;
   Fax 01926 318111
Rugby Centre, Lower Hillmorton Rd, Rugby, Warwickshire
   CV21 3QS; Tel 01788 338800; Fax 01788 338575
Trident Technology and Business Centre, Poseidon Way,
   Leamington Spa, Warwickshire CV34 6SW;
   Tel 01926 884900; Fax 01926 470214
Principal   I.H. Morgan

Wolverhampton College
Wulfrun Campus, Paget Rd, Wolverhampton, West
   Midlands WV6 0DU; URL www.wulfrun.ac.uk; e-mail
   mail@wolverhamptoncollege.ac.uk; Tel 01902 317700;
   Fax 01902 423070
Principal   Jane Williams

Worcester College of Technology
Deansway, Worcester, Worcestershire WR1 2JF;
   URL www.wortech.ac.uk; Tel 01905 725555;
   Fax 01905 725600
Principal; Chief Executive   C.D. Morecroft BSc(Hons), MSc,
   CertEd

Yorkshire and the Humber

Barnsley College
PO Box 266, Church St, Barnsley, South Yorkshire S70 2YW;
   URL www.barnsley.ac.uk; e-mail
   programme.enquiries@barnsley.ac.uk; Tel 01226 216216;
   Fax 01226 298514

Bradford College
Gt Horton Rd, Bradford, West Yorkshire BD7 1AY;
   URL www.bradfordcollege.ac.uk; e-mail (admissions
   office) admissions@bradfordcollege.ac.uk;
   Tel (admissions office for course enquiries and
   applications) 01274 433333; Fax (admissions office)
   01274 431060
Principal; Chief Executive   Michele Sutton

Calderdale College
Francis St, Halifax, West Yorkshire HX1 3UZ;
   URL www.calderdale.ac.uk; e-mail
   info@calderdale.ac.uk; Tel 01422 357357;
   Tel (information and guidance centre) 01422 399399;
   Fax 01422 399320
Chief Executive   Chris Jones

Craven College
High St, Skipton, North Yorkshire BD23 1JY;
   URL www.craven-college.ac.uk; e-mail
   enquiries@craven-college.ac.uk; Tel 01756 791411;
   Fax 01756 794872
Principal   Alan Blackwell

Dearne Valley College
Manvers Pk, Wath upon Dearne, Rotherham, South
   Yorkshire S63 7EW; URL www.dearne-coll.ac.uk; e-mail
   learn@dearne-coll.ac.uk; Tel 01709 513355;
   Fax 01709 513110
Principal; Chief Executive   Sue Ransom

Dewsbury College
Halifax Rd, Dewsbury, West Yorkshire WF13 2AS;
   URL www.dewsbury.ac.uk; e-mail
   info@dewsbury.ac.uk; Tel (Information Officer)
   01924 436221; Tel 01924 465916; Fax 01924 457047
Principal; Chief Executive   Wendy Pawson

Doncaster College
The Hub, Chappell Dr, Doncaster, South Yorkshire
   DN1 2RF; URL www.don.ac.uk; e-mail
   infocentre@don.ac.uk; Tel (prospectus) 0800 358 7575;
   Tel 01302 553553; Fax 01302 553559
Principal; Chief Executive   Rowland Foote

East Riding College
Longcroft Hall, Gallows La, Beverley, East Riding of
   Yorkshire HU17 7DT;
   URL www.eastridingcollege.ac.uk; e-mail
   info@eastridingcollege.ac.uk; Tel 0845 120 0037;
   Fax 01482 306675
St Marys Wlk, Bridlington, East Riding of Yorkshire
   YO16 7JW; Tel 01262 458801
Chair of Governors   D. Thacker
Principal; Chief Executive   D. Branton

Grimsby Institute of Further and Higher Education
Nuns Corner, Grimsby, North East Lincolnshire DN34 5BQ;
   URL www.grimsby.ac.uk; e-mail
   infocent@grimsby.ac.uk; Tel 01472 311222;
   Tel (freephone course enquiries) 0800 315002;
   Fax 01472 879924

5

Principal; Chief Executive   Daniel Khan OBE, MA, FCCA, FAIA

Huddersfield Technical College
New North Rd, Huddersfield, West Yorkshire HD1 5NN; URL www.huddcoll.ac.uk; e-mail info@huddcoll.ac.uk; Tel (freephone: prospectus) 0500 162100; Tel 01484 536521; Fax 01484 511885
Principal   C. Sadler

Joseph Priestley College
Beeston Campus, Burton Ave, Beeston, Leeds, West Yorkshire LS11 5ER; URL www.joseph-priestley.ac.uk; e-mail info@joseph-priestley.ac.uk; Tel 0113 307 6111; Fax 0113 271 6495
Principal   Carolyn Wright

Park Lane College Keighley
Cavendish St, Keighley, West Yorkshire BD21 3DF; URL www.keighley.ac.uk; Tel 01535 618555; Fax 01535 618556
Principal   Maxine Room

Leeds College of Building
North St, Leeds, West Yorkshire LS2 7QT; URL www.lcb.ac.uk; e-mail info@lcb.ac.uk; Tel 0113 222 6000; Tel (student services) 0113 222 6002; Fax 0113 222 6001
Principal   I. Billyard

Leeds College of Technology
Cookridge St, Leeds, West Yorkshire LS2 8BL; Tel 0113 297 6300; Fax 0113 297 6301
Principal   Peter Ryder

Leeds Thomas Danby
Roundhay Rd, Leeds, West Yorkshire LS7 3BG; URL www.leedsthomasdanby.ac.uk; e-mail info@thomasdanby.ac.uk; Tel (freephone: prospectus) 0800 096 2319; Tel 0113 249 4912; Fax 0113 240 1967
Principal; Chief Executive   Roy Thorpe

Leeds Trinity and All Saints
Brownberrie La, Horsforth, Leeds, West Yorkshire LS18 5HD; URL www.leedstrinity.ac.uk; e-mail enquiries@leedstrinity.ac.uk; Tel 0113 283 7150; Fax 0113 283 7200

North Lindsey College
Kingsway, Scunthorpe, North Lincolnshire DN17 1AJ; e-mail info@northlindsey.ac.uk; Tel 01724 281111; Fax 01724 294020
Principal   Roger Bennett

Park Lane College Leeds
Park La, Leeds, West Yorkshire LS3 1AA; URL www.parklanecoll.ac.uk; e-mail course.enquiry@parklanecoll.ac.uk; Tel 0845 045 7275; Fax 0113 216 2020
Principal   Maxine Room

Rother Valley College
Doe Quarry La, Dinnington, South Yorkshire S25 2NF; URL www.rothervalley.ac.uk; e-mail studentservices@rothervalley.ac.uk; Tel 0800 328 8008
Principal   T. Ashurst (Acting)

Rotherham College of Arts and Technology
Eastwood La, Rotherham, South Yorkshire S65 1EG; URL www.rotherham.ac.uk; Tel 01709 362111
Principal; Chief Executive   George Trow

Selby College
Abbots Rd, Selby, North Yorkshire YO8 8AT; URL www.selbycollege.co.uk; e-mail info@selby.ac.uk; Tel 01757 211000; Tel (student services) 01757 211040; Fax 01757 213137
Principal   A. Stewart

Sheffield College
Head Office, PO Box 345, Sheffield, South Yorkshire S2 2YY; URL www.sheffcol.ac.uk; e-mail course-enquiry@sheffcol.ac.uk; Tel 0114 260 2600; Tel (prospectus) 0114 260 3603; Fax 0114 260 2601
Chief Executive   John Taylor

Shipley College
Exhibition Rd, Saltaire, Shipley, West Yorkshire BD18 3JW; URL www.shipley.ac.uk; e-mail enquiries@shipley.ac.uk; Tel 01274 327222; Fax 01274 327201
Principal   Jean McAllister

Wakefield College
Margaret St, Wakefield, West Yorkshire WF1 2DH; URL www.wakefield.ac.uk; e-mail courseinfo@wakefield.ac.uk; Tel 01924 789789; Fax 01924 789340
Principal   H. MacDonald BSc(Hons), PGCE

York College
Sim Balk La, York YO23 2BB; URL www.yorkcollege.ac.uk; e-mail customerservice@yorkcollege.ac.uk; Tel 01904 770200; Fax 01904 770499
Principal   Alison Birkinshaw

Yorkshire Coast College
Lady Ediths Dr, Scarborough, North Yorkshire YO12 5RN; URL www.yorkshirecoastcollege.ac.uk; e-mail admissions@ycoastco.ac.uk; Tel (central admissions) 01723 356112; Tel 01723 372105; Fax 01723 501918
Principal   Carole Kitching

Scotland

Aberdeen College of Further Education
Gallowgate Centre, Aberdeen AB25 1BN; URL www.abcol.ac.uk; e-mail enquiry@abcol.ac.uk; Tel 01224 612000; Tel (information and booking centre) 01224 612330; Fax 01224 612001

Adam Smith College
St Brycedale Ave, Kirkcaldy, Fife KY1 1EX; URL www.adamsmith.ac.uk; e-mail enquiries@adamsmith.ac.uk; Tel 01592 223402; Tel (freephone) 0800 413280; Fax 01592 640225
Principal   Dr C. Thomson

Angus College
Keptie Rd, Arbroath, Angus DD11 3EA; URL www.angus.ac.uk; e-mail marketing@angus.ac.uk; Tel 01241 432600; Fax 01241 876169
Principal   John Burt

Anniesland College
Hatfield Dr, Glasgow G12 0YE; URL www.anniesland.ac.uk; e-mail reception@anniesland.ac.uk; Tel 0141 357 3969; Fax 0141 357 6557
Deputy Principal   B. Hughes

Ayr College
Dam Pk, Ayr, South Ayrshire KA8 0EU; URL www.ayrcoll.ac.uk; e-mail enquiries@ayrcoll.ac.uk; Tel (admissions unit) 0800 199 798; Tel 01292 265184; Fax 01292 263889
Principal   Diane Rawlinson

Banff and Buchan College
Henderson Rd, Fraserburgh, Aberdeenshire AB43 9GA; URL www.banff-buchan.ac.uk; e-mail info@banff-buchan.ac.uk; Tel 01346 586100; Fax 01346 515370
Principal   Robert Sinclair

Borders College
Thorniedean Hse, Melrose Rd, Galashiels, Scottish Borders TD1 2AF; URL www.borderscollege.ac.uk; e-mail admissions@borderscollege.ac.uk; Tel 0870 050 5152; Fax 01896 758179
Principal   Dr R.B. Murray BSc(Hons), MBA, PhD, MBIM

Cambuslang College
85 Hamilton Rd, Cambuslang, Glasgow G72 7NY; Tel 0141 641 6600; Fax 0141 641 4296
Principal; Chief Executive   Gordon Robbins BA(Hons), MIMgt

Cardonald College
690 Mosspark Dr, Glasgow G52 3AY; URL www.cardonald.ac.uk; e-mail enquiries@cardonald.ac.uk; Tel 0141 272 3333; Fax 0141 272 3444
Principal   Ros Micklem

Carnegie College
Halbeath, Dunfermline, Fife KY11 8DY; URL www.carnegiecollege.ac.uk; e-mail info@carnegiecollege.ac.uk; Tel 0844 248 0115; Fax 0844 248 0116
Principal   Prof Bill McIntosh BA(Hons), FCHI

Central College of Commerce
300 Cathedral St, Glasgow G1 2TA; URL www.centralcollege.ac.uk; e-mail information@central-glasgow.ac.uk; Tel 0141 552 3941; Fax 0141 553 2368
Principal   Peter Duncan

Clackmannan College of Further Education
Branshill Rd, Alloa, Clackmannanshire FK10 3BT; Tel 01259 215121; Fax 01259 722879
Principal   John M. Taylor MA, DipEd

Clydebank College
Kilbowie Rd, Clydebank, West Dunbartonshire G81 2AA; URL www.clydebank.ac.uk; e-mail info@clydebank.ac.uk; Tel (student information and advice centre) 0141 951 2122; Tel 0141 952 7771; Fax 0141 951 1574
Principal; Chief Executive   Matt Mochar

Coatbridge College
Kildonan St, Coatbridge, North Lanarkshire ML5 3LS; URL www.coatbridge.ac.uk; e-mail admissions@coatbridge.ac.uk; Tel 01236 422316; Tel (admissions hotline) 01236 436000; Fax 01236 440266
Principal   John Doyle

Cumbernauld College
Tryst Rd, Town Centre, Cumbernauld, North Lanarkshire G67 1HU; Tel 01236 731811; Fax 01236 723416
Principal   B.G.H. Lister BSc(Hons), DipEd

Dumfries and Galloway College
Heathhall, Dumfries, Dumfries and Galloway DG1 3QZ; URL www.dumgal.ac.uk; e-mail info@dumgal.ac.uk; Tel 01387 261261; Fax 01387 250006
Principal   T. Jakimciw

Dundee College
Kingsway Campus, Old Glamis Rd, Dundee DD3 8LE; Tel 01382 834834; Fax 01382 858117
Constitution Road Campus, Constitution Rd, Dundee DD3 6TB; Fax 01382 223299
Principal   Dr I.S. Ovens BA, MA, DMS, OBE

Edinburgh College of Art
Lauriston Pl, Edinburgh EH3 9DF; Tel 0131 221 6000
Principal   Prof Ian G. Howard MA, RSA
Head (School of Architecture)   Leslie Forsyth

Edinburgh's Telford College
350 West Granton Rd, Edinburgh EH5 1QE; URL www.ed-coll.ac.uk; e-mail mail@ed-coll.ac.uk; Tel 0131 559 4000; Fax 0131 559 4111
Principal; Chief Executive   Dr Ray Harris

Forth Valley College of Further and Higher Education
Grangemouth Rd, Falkirk FK2 9AD; URL www.forthvalley.ac.uk; e-mail info@forthvalley.ac.uk; Tel 01324 403000; Tel (prospectus) 0845 634 4444; Fax 01324 403222

Glasgow College of Building and Printing
60 North Hanover St, Glasgow G1 2BP; URL www.gcbp.ac.uk; e-mail enquiries@gcbp.ac.uk; Tel 0141 332 9969; Fax 0141 332 5170
Principal   T.B. Wilson BSc, CEng, MBCS

Glasgow College of Nautical Studies
21 Thistle St, Glasgow G5 9XB; URL www.gcns.ac.uk; e-mail enquiries@glasgow-nautical.ac.uk; Tel 0141 565 2500; Fax 0141 565 2599
Principal   J. Okten

Glasgow Metropolitan College
60 North St, Glasgow G1 2BP; URL www.glasgowmet.ac.uk; e-mail enquiries@glasgowmet.ac.uk; Tel 0141 566 6222; Fax 0141 566 6226
Principal   Prof Thomas B. Wilson OBE, BSc, CEng, MBCS, FRSA

Glenrothes College
Stenton Rd, Glenrothes, Fife KY6 2RA; URL www.glenrothes.ac.uk; e-mail ask@glenrothes.ac.uk; Tel 01592 772233; Fax 01592 568317
Principal   Dr Craig Thomson

Inverness College
3 Longman Rd, Longman South, Inverness, Highland IV1 1SA; Tel 01463 236681; Fax 01463 711977
Principal   Janet Price

James Watt College of Further and Higher Education
Finnart Campus, Finnart St, Greenock, Inverclyde PA16 8HF; URL www.jameswatt.ac.uk; e-mail information@jameswatt.ac.uk; Tel 01475 724433; Fax 01475 888079
Principal   W. Wardle MA, PhD

Jewel & Esk College
Edinburgh Campus, 24 Milton Rd East, Edinburgh EH15 2PP; URL www.jevc.ac.uk; e-mail info@jevc.ac.uk; Tel 0131 660 1010; Tel (information) 0845 850 0060; Fax 0131 657 2276
Principal; Chief Executive   Howard McKenzie MBA, CertEd, DipCurricDevel, PgCertIndustPsychol

John Wheatley College
2 Haghill Rd, Glasgow G31 2SR; URL www.jwheatley.ac.uk; e-mail advice@jwheatley.ac.uk; Tel 0141 588 1500; Fax 0141 588 1503
Principal   Ian Graham

Kilmarnock College
Holehouse Rd, Kilmarnock, East Ayrshire KA3 7AT; e-mail enquiries@kilmarnock.ac.uk; Tel (prospectus) 0800 389 6817; Tel 01563 523501; Fax 01563 538182
Principal   Dr Gordon M.F. Jenkins

Langside College
50 Prospecthill Rd, Glasgow G42 9LB; URL www.langside.ac.uk; e-mail enquireuk@langside.ac.uk; Tel 0141 636 6066; Fax 0141 632 5252
Principal   A.G. Hyslop BA(Hons), MSc

5

Lews Castle College

Stornoway, Isle of Lewis HS2 0XR;
URL www.lews.uhi.ac.uk; e-mail
aofficele@lews.uhi.ac.uk; Tel 01851 770000;
Tel (information officer) 01851 770202; Fax 01851 770001
Principal   D.R. Green BA, MA

Moray College

Moray St, Elgin, Moray IV30 1JJ; URL www.moray.ac.uk;
e-mail registry@moray.uhi.ac.uk; Tel 01343 576000;
Fax 01343 576001
Principal   Mike Devenney

Motherwell College

Dalzell Dr, Motherwell, North Lanarkshire ML1 2DD;
URL www.motherwell.ac.uk; e-mail
information@motherwell.ac.uk; Tel 01698 232323;
Tel (customer services) 01698 232425; Fax 01698 232527
Principal; Chief Executive   Hugh Logan

North Glasgow College

Springburn Campus, 110 Flemington St, Glasgow G21 4BX;
URL www.north-gla.ac.uk; Tel 0141 558 9001;
Fax 0141 558 9905
Principal; Chief Executive   Ronnie Knox

North Highland College

Ormlie Rd, Thurso, Highland KW14 7EE;
URL www.nhcscotland.com; e-mail
nhc.admissions@thurso.uhi.ac.uk; Tel 01847 889000;
Fax 01847 889001
Principal   Rosemary Thompson
Head (Management – Professional Studies)   Tara Morrison

Northern College of Education

Dundee Campus, Gardyne Rd, Dundee DD5 1NY;
Tel 01382 464000
Principal   D.A. Adams MA
Head of School   Ian Ball

Orkney College

Kirkwall, Orkney Islands KW15 1LX;
URL www.orkney.uhi.ac.uk; e-mail
orkney.college@orkney.uhi.ac.uk; Tel 01856 569000;
Fax 01856 569001
Principal   Bill Ross

Perth College

Crieff Rd, Perth, Perth and Kinross PH1 2NX;
URL www.perth.ac.uk; e-mail
pc.enquiries@perth.uhi.ac.uk; Tel (prospectus
information) 0845 270 1177; Tel 01738 877000;
Fax 01738 877001
Principal   Mandy Exley

Reid Kerr College

Renfrew Rd, Paisley, Renfrewshire PA3 4DR;
URL www.reidkerr.ac.uk; e-mail
sservices@reidkerr.ac.uk; Tel (student services)
0800 052 7343; Tel 0141 581 2222; Fax 0141 581 2204
Principal   Joe Mooney

St Andrew's College

Duntocher Rd, Bearsden, Glasgow G61 4QA;
Tel 0141 943 3400
Principal   Prof B.J. McGettrick BSc, MEd, FRSA
Vice-Principal   John McCarney
Number of students
1000

Shetland College

Gremista, Lerwick, Shetland Islands ZE1 0PX; e-mail
hazel.anderson@shetland.uhi.ac.uk; Tel 01595 771000;
Fax 01595 771001
Principal   Prof John McClatchey

Stevenson College Edinburgh

Bankhead Ave, Edinburgh EH11 4DE;
URL www.stevenson.ac.uk; e-mail
info@stevenson.ac.uk; Tel 0131 535 4600;
Fax 0131 535 4666
Principal   S. Bird

Stow College

43 Shamrock St, Glasgow G4 9LD; URL www.stow.ac.uk;
e-mail enquiries@stow.ac.uk; Tel 0141 332 1786;
Fax 0141 332 5207
Principal; Chief Executive   Robert McGrory

Stromness Academy Maritime Studies

Stromness, Orkney Islands KW16 3BS; e-mail
fred.breck@orkney.uni.ac.uk; Tel 01856 569401
Principal   David Sillar BSc, MEd

West Lothian College

Almondvale Cres, Livingston, West Lothian EH54 7EP;
URL www.west-lothian.ac.uk; e-mail
enquiries@west-lothian.ac.uk; Tel 01506 418181;
Fax 01506 409980
Principal   Susan Pinder

Wales

Barry College

Colcot Rd, Barry, Vale of Glamorgan CF62 8YJ;
URL www.barry.ac.uk; e-mail enquiries@barry.ac.uk;
Tel 01446 725000; Fax 01446 732667
Principal; Chief Executive   P.V. Halstead BSc, MSc, PGDCS,
PGCE

Bridgend College

Cowbridge Rd, Bridgend CF31 3DF;
URL www.bridgend.ac.uk; e-mail
markjones@bridgend.ac.uk; Tel 01656 302302;
Fax 01656 663912
Principal   Mark Jones MED, FCA, BSc

Carmarthenshire College/Coleg Sir Gâr

Sandy Rd, Llanelli, Carmarthenshire SA15 4DN;
URL www.colegsirgar.ac.uk; e-mail
admissions@colegsirgar.ac.uk; Tel 01554 748000;
Fax 01554 756088
Principal; Chief Executive   Brian Robinson MSc, CertEd,
OBE

Coleg Ceredigion

Aberystwyth Campus, Aberystwyth, Ceredigion SY23 3BP;
URL www.ceredigion.ac.uk; Tel 01970 624511
Cardigan Campus, Park Pl, Cardigan, Ceredigion
SA43 1AB; Tel 01239 612032
Principal   A. Morgan BA, MA, PGCE

Deeside College/Coleg Glannau Dyfrdwy

Kelsterton Rd, Connah's Quay, Deeside, Flintshire
CH5 4BR; URL www.deeside.ac.uk; e-mail
enquiries@deeside.ac.uk; Tel 01244 831531; Tel (student
services) 01244 834511; Fax 01244 814305
Principal   David B. Jones

Coleg Glan Hafren

Trowbridge Rd, Rumney, Cardiff CF3 1XZ;
URL www.glan-hafren.ac.uk; e-mail
info@glan-hafren.ac.uk; Tel 02920 250250; Tel (advice
shop) 02920 250400; Fax 02920 250339
Principal   Malcolm Charnley MPhil, BSc(Hons), MBA(Ed),
CEng

Gorseinon College

Belgrave Rd, Gorseinon, Swansea SA4 6RD;
URL www.gorseinon.ac.uk; e-mail pr@gorseinon.ac.uk;
Tel 01792 890700; Fax 01792 898729
Principal   Nick Bennett BEd(Hons), MEd, CertEd

Coleg Gwent

The Rhadyr, Usk, Monmouthshire NP15 1XJ;
    URL www.coleggwent.ac.uk; e-mail
    info@coleggwent.ac.uk; Tel 01495 333333;
    Fax 01495 333526
Principal; Chief Executive   Howard Burton

Coleg Harlech WEA (NW)

Harlech, Gwynedd LL46 2PU; URL www.harlech.ac.uk;
    e-mail info@harlech.ac.uk; Tel 01766 780363;
    Fax 01766 780169
Principal   Annie Williams
Director (Residential Studies)   Dr D.R. Wiltshire BA, DPhil

Coleg Llandrillo Cymru

Llandudno Rd, Colwyn Bay, Conwy LL28 4HZ;
    URL www.llandrillo.ac.uk; e-mail
    admissions@llandrillo.ac.uk; Tel 01492 546666;
    Fax 01492 543052
Principal   Huw Evans OBE, BSc, MPhil, FBIM;
    Tel 01492 542301; Fax 01492 542891

Coleg Meirion-Dwyfor

Ffordd Ty'n y Coed, Dolgellau, Gwynedd LL40 2SW;
    URL www.meirion-dwyfor.ac.uk; e-mail
    coleg@meirion-dwyfor.ac.uk; Tel 01341 422827;
    Fax 01341 422393
Principal   Dr Ian Rees

Coleg Menai

Ffriddoedd Rd, Bangor, Gwynedd LL57 2TP;
    URL www.menai.ac.uk; e-mail
    student.services@menai.ac.uk; Tel 01248 370125;
    Tel (prospectus) 01248 383333; Fax 01248 370052
Principal   Dr Haydn. E. Edwards BSc, MBA, PhD, CChem,
    FRSC

Merthyr Tydfil College

Ynysfach, Merthyr Tydfil CF48 1AR;
    URL www.merthyr.ac.uk; e-mail college@merthyr.ac.uk;
    Tel 01685 726000; Tel (student services) 01685 726006;
    Fax 01685 726100
Principal   Howard Jenkins

Coleg Morgannwg

Pontypridd Campus, Ynys Terr, Rhydyfelin, Pontypridd,
    Rhondda Cynon Taf CF37 5RN;
    URL www.morgannwg.ac.uk; e-mail
    college@morgannwg.ac.uk; Tel 01443 662800;
    Fax 01443 663028
Aberdare Campus, Cwmdare Rd, Aberdare, Rhondda
    Cynon Taf CF44 8ST; Tel 01685 887500; Fax 01685 876635
Principal   J. Knight MA, CertEd

Neath Port Talbot College/Coleg Castell Nedd

Dwr-y-Felin Rd, Neath, Neath Port Talbot SA10 7RF;
    URL www.nptc.ac.uk; e-mail admissions@nptc.ac.uk;
    Tel 01639 648000; Tel (prospectus) 01639 648032;
    Fax 01639 648009
Principal   Mark Dacey BSc, MSc, DipBS, MCIOB, FIMBM,
    ACLaRb

Pembrokeshire College

Haverfordwest, Pembrokeshire SA61 1SZ;
    URL www.pembrokeshire.ac.uk; e-mail
    admissions@pembrokeshire.ac.uk; Tel (admissions)
    0800 716 236; Tel 01437 753000; Fax 01437 753001
Principal   Glyn Jones

Coleg Powys

Spa Rd, Llandrindod Wells, Powys LD1 5ES;
    URL www.coleg-powys.ac.uk; e-mail
    enquiries@coleg-powys.ac.uk; Tel 01597 822696;
    Fax 01597 825122
Principal   J.L. Stephenson MA, MSc, MInstP

Swansea College

Tycoch Rd, Tycoch, Swansea SA2 9EB;
    URL www.swancoll.ac.uk; e-mail
    admissions@swancoll.ac.uk; e-mail
    enquiries@swancoll.ac.uk; Tel 01792 284000;
    Fax 01792 284074
Principal   Jeff Gunningham

Workers' Educational Association South Wales

7 Coopers Yard, Curran Rd, Cardiff CF10 5NB;
    URL www.swales.wea.org.uk; e-mail
    weasw@swales.wea.org.uk; Tel 02920 235277;
    Fax 02920 233986
General Secretary   Margaret Hilary Dawson MA, DipASS

Yale College

Grove Park Rd, Wrexham LL12 7AB;
    URL www.yale-wrexham.ac.uk; e-mail
    admissions@yale-wrexham.ac.uk; e-mail
    marketing@yale-wrexham.ac.uk; Tel 01978 311794;
    Fax 01978 364254
Principal   Paul Croke

The College Ystrad Mynach

Twyn Rd, Ystrad Mynach, Hengoed, Caerphilly CF82 7XR;
    URL www.ystrad-mynach.ac.uk; e-mail
    enquiries@ystrad-mynach.ac.uk; Tel (prospectus)
    01443 810054; Tel 01443 816888; Fax 01443 816973
Principal   Bryn Davies

Northern Ireland

Belfast Institute of Further and Higher Education

Park Hse, 87–91 Gt Victoria St, Belfast BT2 7AG;
    URL www.belfastinstitute.ac.uk; e-mail
    information_services@belfastinstitute.ac.uk;
    Tel 028 9026 5000
Director   Prof P. Murphy

Castlereagh College

Montgomery Rd, Belfast BT6 9JD; Tel 028 9079 7144;
    Fax 028 9040 1820
Principal   M. Shankey BA, MSc, CertEd, MCGLI

Causeway Institute of Further and Higher Education

Union St, Coleraine, County Londonderry BT52 1QA; e-mail
    admin@causeway.ac.uk; Tel 028 7035 4717;
    Fax 028 7035 6377
Director   I. Williams

East Antrim Institute of Further and Higher Education

Newtownabbey Campus, 400 Shore Rd, Newtownabbey,
    County Antrim BT37 9RS; URL www.eaifhe.ac.uk; e-mail
    info@eaifhe.ac.uk; Tel 028 9085 5000; Fax 028 9086 2076

East Down Institute of Further and Higher Education

Market St, Downpatrick, County Down BT30 6ND;
    URL www.edifhe.ac.uk; e-mail admin@edifhe.ac.uk;
    Tel 028 4461 5815; Fax 028 4461 5817
Director   Mr T.L. Place BA, MSc, DPM, FIPD, FRSA, MIOD

Limavady College of Further and Higher Education

Main St, Limavady, County Londonderry BT49 0EX;
    URL www.limavady.ac.uk; e-mail info@limavady.ac.uk;
    Tel 028 7776 2334; Fax 028 7776 1018
Chief Executive; Director   Dr A. Heaslett

Lisburn Institute of Further and Higher Education

39 Castle St, Lisburn, County Antrim BT27 4SU;
    URL www.liscol.ac.uk; e-mail courses@liscol.ac.uk;
    Tel 028 9267 7225; Fax 028 9267 7291
Principal   A.J. McReynolds BEd, MA, DASE, DLIS, FRSA

North Down and Ards Institute of Further and Higher Education

Castle Park Rd, Bangor, County Down BT20 4TF;
URL www.ndai.ac.uk; e-mail information@ndai.ac.uk;
Tel 028 9127 6600; Fax 028 9127 6601

Chief Executive; Director   Brian Henry

North West Institute of Further and Higher Education

Strand Rd, Londonderry, County Londonderry BT48 7AL;
URL www.nwi.ac.uk; e-mail info@nwi.ac.uk;
Tel 028 7127 6000; Tel (prospectus) 028 7127 6022;
Fax 028 7126 0520

Director   Seamus Murphy BA, MED, DipEd, DASE

Northern Regional College

Ballymena Campus, Trostan Ave, Ballymena, County
Antrim BT43 7BN; URL www.nrc.ac.uk; e-mail
info@nrc.ac.uk; Tel 028 2565 2871; Fax 028 2565 9245

Principal; Chief Executive   Trevor Neilands

South West College

In August 2007 Omagh College merged with East Tyrone
College and Fermanagh College to become South West
College

2 Mountjoy Rd, Omagh, County Tyrone BT79 7AH;
URL www.swc.ac.uk; Tel 028 8224 5433;
Fax 028 8224 1440

Cookstown Campus

Burns Rd, Cookstown, County Tyrone BT80 8DN;
Tel 028 8676 2620; Fax 028 8676 1818

Dungannon Campus

Circular Rd, Dungannon, County Tyrone BT71 6BQ;
Tel 028 8772 2323; Fax 028 8775 2018;
Textphone 028 8772 0625

Enniskillen Campus

Fairview, 1 Dublin Rd, Enniskillen, County Fermanagh
BT74 6AE; Tel 028 6632 2431; Fax 028 6632 6357

Omagh Campus

Tel (enrolment) 0800 032 7890; Tel (admissions)
028 8225 5210

Southern Regional College

Newry Campus, Patrick St, Newry, County Down
BT35 8DN; URL www.src.ac.uk; e-mail info@src.ac.uk;
Tel 028 3026 1071; Fax 028 3025 9679

Chief Executive; Director   Brian Doran

Channel Islands and Isle of Man

Guernsey College of Further Education

Route des Coutanchez, St Peter Port, Guernsey GY1 2TT,
Channel Islands; e-mail college@cfe.edu.org;
Tel 01481 737500; Fax 01481 714153

President (Education)   Deputy M. Ozanne
Principal   Trevor Wakefield

Highlands College

PO Box 1000, St Saviour, Jersey JE4 9QA, Channel Islands;
e-mail reception@highlands.ac.uk; Tel 01534 608608;
Fax 01534 608600

Principal; Chief Executive   Dr Edward Sallis

Isle of Man College

Homefield Rd, Douglas, Isle of Man IM2 6RB;
URL www.iomcollege.ac.im; e-mail
enquiries@iomcollege.ac.im; Tel 01624 648200;
Fax 01624 648201

Principal   Ian Killip PhD, BEng, MEng, MCIOB, MIMgt

Independent Further Education Establishments

Key

*	Includes a course of English for foreign students
†	Recognised by the British Council English Language Schools Programme
‡	Accredited by the Open and Distance Learning Quality Council
§	Accredited by the British Accreditation Council for Independent Further and Higher Education

British Accreditation Council for Independent Further and Higher Education

Registered Charity Number 326652

44 Bedford Row, London WC1R 4LL;
URL www.the-bac.org; e-mail info@the-bac.org;
Tel 020 7447 2584; Fax 020 7447 2585

President   Lord Alan Watson of Richmond-upon-Thames
Chief Executive   Dr Stephen Vickers
Chair   Tim Cox

Profile

Established in 1984 in succession to an earlier scheme run by
the former Department of Education and Science, its
sponsors include the chief bodies responsible for the
maintenance of academic standards in Britain: universities
and colleges, national validating bodies, public and
professional examining boards, and those bodies, such as
the British Council, with a particular concern for overseas
students. The BAC is constituted as a Company Limited by
Guarantee and, at present, 262 institutions are accredited by
the BAC enrolling almost 70 000 students from Britain and
overseas on a range of courses.

Aims and Objectives

The BAC defines, monitors and improves standards in
independent further and higher education institutions in
Britain by inspecting institutions which are recognised as
efficient by BAC, if they meet its criteria for accreditation.

Criteria

Institutions seeking BAC accreditation must satisfy the BAC
under all of the following: Premises and learning resources;
administration and staffing; quality control, including the
effectiveness of the monitoring of experiences of students in
joining and pursuing the programmes provided; welfare
arrangements, including career advice and counselling
where appropriate; teaching, involving assessment of the
professional competence of academic staff.

In addition, the BAC receives legal and financial
information from institutions. The criteria used by the BAC
are consistent with those required by the Home Office for
bona fide institutions enrolling overseas students. The BAC
inspectorate which carries out all inspections contains more
than 80 inspectors and includes former HM inspectors of
education; former local education authority advisers and
inspectors; current and former heads and senior staff
members of universities, colleges and institutions of higher
education and colleges of further education.

Procedures

The process of accreditation involves an initial application;
the determination of eligibility for accreditation, including a
preliminary visit by an inspector; and a full institutional
inspection followed by a decision on accreditation by the
Accreditation and Recognition Committee of the BAC.
Accreditation is conditional upon re-inspection within four
years. The BAC reserves the right, however, to review the
accreditation of an institution at any time if reasonable
grounds exist.

East of England

Abbey College, Cambridge §
17 Station Rd, Cambridge CB1 2JB;
URL www.abbeycolleges.co.uk; e-mail
admincam@abbeycolleges.co.uk; Tel 01223 578280;
Fax 01223 519425
Head of Establishment   Dr Julian Davies

Bellerbys College, Cambridge *§
Queens Campus, Bateman St, Cambridge, Cambridgeshire
CB2 1LZ; URL www.bellerbys.com; e-mail
cambridge@bellerbys.com; Tel 01223 363159
Principal   John Rushton
Number of students
350
Residential, day

Cambridge Arts and Sciences *§
Round Church St, Cambridge, Cambridgeshire CB5 8AD;
URL www.ceg-uk.com; e-mail
enquiries@catscollege.com; Tel 01223 314431;
Fax 01223 467773
Principal   Mr H. MacDonald
Number of students
276

Cambridge Centre for Sixth Form Studies *
1 Salisbury Villas, Station Rd, Cambridge, Cambridgeshire
CB1 2JF; URL www.ccss.co.uk; e-mail office@ccss.co.uk;
Tel 01223 716890; Fax 01223 517530
Principal   Neil Roskilly
Number of students
210
Residential, day

Cambridge Seminars *§
4 Hawthorn Way, Cambridge, Cambridgeshire CB4 1AX;
e-mail admissions@camsem.co.uk; Tel 01223 313464;
Fax 01223 355352
Residential

International Boatbuilding Training College
Sea Lake Rd, Oulton Broad, Lowestoft, Suffolk NR32 3LQ;
URL www.users.globalnet.co.uk/~ibtc; e-mail
ibtc@globalnet.co.uk; Tel 01502 569663; Fax 01502 500661

Mander Portman Woodward, Cambridge §
3–4 Brookside, Cambridge CB2 1JE;
URL www.mpw.co.uk/camb; e-mail
enquiries@cambridge.mpw.co.uk; Tel 01223 350158;
Fax 01223 366429
Head of Establishment   Dr Nick Marriott

Queen's Marlborough College
Bateman St, Cambridge, Cambridgeshire CB2 1LU;
URL www.qmbsc.ac.uk; e-mail info@qmbsc.ac.uk;
Tel 01223 367016; Fax 01223 364054
Executive Principal   C. Bickford

St Andrew's, Cambridge *§
2a Free School La, Cambridge, Cambridgeshire CB2 3QA;
URL www.standrewscambridge.co.uk; e-mail
wayne.marshall@standrewscambridge.co.uk;
Tel 01223 358046
Residential, day

East Midlands

Bosworth Independent College *§
Nazareth Hse, Barrack Rd, Northampton,
Northamptonshire NN2 6AF;
URL www.bosworthcollege.com; e-mail
mkt3@bosworthcollege.com; Tel 01604 239995;
Fax 01604 239996
Principal   M. McQuin MEd

Number of students
320
Residential, day

Brooke House College *§
Market Harborough, Leicestershire LE16 7AU;
URL www.brookehouse.com; e-mail
enquiries@brookehouse.com; Tel 01858 462452;
Fax 01858 462487
Contact   Robert Price
Number of students
170
Residential, day

Irwin College *
164 London Rd, Leicester LE2 1ND; URL www.cife.org.uk/
irwin/index.htm; e-mail
enquiries@irwincollege.tele2.co.uk; Tel 0116 255 2648
Principal   S.J. Wytcherley
Number of students
200
Residential, day

London

Abbey College, London *§
22 Grosvenor Gdns, Belgravia, London SW1W 0DH;
URL www.abbeylondon.co.uk; e-mail
adminlon@abbeylondon.co.uk; Tel 020 7824 7300;
Fax 020 7824 7309
Head of Establishment   Mark Love

Acorn Independent College §
39–47 High St, Southall, London UB1 3HF;
URL www.acorn-college.co.uk; e-mail
enquiries@acorn-college.co.uk; Tel 020 8571 9900;
Fax 020 8571 9901
Head of Establishment   Gladys Watt

Albany College *§
21–24 Queens Rd, London NW4 2TL;
URL www.albany-college.co.uk; e-mail
info@albany-college.co.uk; Tel 020 8202 9748;
Fax 020 8202 8460
Principal   Robert J. Arthy BSc, MPhil, MRSC
Secretary   Mary Rooney
Number of students
200

Ashbourne Independent Sixth Form College §
17 Old Court Pl, London W8 4PL;
URL www.ashbournecollege.co.uk; e-mail
admin@ashbournecollege.co.uk; Tel 020 7937 3858;
Fax 020 7937 2207
Head of Establishment   Mr M.J. Hatchard-Kirby

Bales College §
Kilburn La, London W10 4AA;
URL www.balescollege.co.uk; e-mail
pr1@balescollege.co.uk; Tel 020 8960 5899
Principal   W.B. Moore
Number of students
100
Residential, day

Cavendish College *§
35–37 Alfred Pl, London WC1E 7DP;
URL www.cavendish.ac.uk; e-mail
learn@cavendish.ac.uk; Tel 020 7580 6043;
Fax 020 7255 1591

The City College *§
University Hse, 55 East Rd, London N1 6AH;
URL www.citycollege.ac.uk; e-mail
admissions@citycollege.ac.uk; Tel 020 7253 1133;
Fax 020 7251 6610
Principal   A. Andrews

College of Central London ***
73 Gt Eastern St, London EC2A 3HR;
 URL www.central-college.co.uk; e-mail
 ccl@btinternet.com; Tel 020 7739 5555; Fax 020 7739 9005
Principal Nicolas Kailides
Number of students
500

Collingham Independent Sixth Form College *§
23 Collingham Gdns, London SW5 0HL;
 URL www.collingham.co.uk; e-mail
 london@collingham.co.uk; Tel 020 7244 7414;
 Fax 020 7370 7312
Principal Gerald Hattee MA, DipEd
Number of students
300

Concepts College London
40 Thorne Rd, London SW8 2BZ;
 URL www.conceptscollege.co.uk; e-mail
 info@conceptscollege.co.uk; Tel 020 7978 1885;
 Fax 020 7622 1490
Principal; Director Dr E. Marcel BSc(Hons), MInstD

**David Game College and Kensington Academy
of English *§**
David Game Hse, 69 Notting Hill Gate, London W11 3JS;
 URL www.davidgame-group.com; e-mail
 david_game@easynet.co.uk; Tel 020 7221 6665;
 Fax 020 7243 1730
Contact David Game
Number of students
300
Residential, day

Davies, Laing and Dick (DLD) *§
100 Marylebone La, London W1U 2QB; URL www.dld.org;
 e-mail dld@dld.org; Tel 020 7935 8411; Fax 020 7935 0755
Principal David Lowe
Number of students
350

Dean College of London *§
97–101 Seven Sisters Rd, Holloway, London N7 7QP;
 URL www.deancollege.co.uk; e-mail
 deancollegeuk@aul.edu; Tel 020 7281 4461;
 Fax 020 7281 7849

Duff-Miller Sixth Form College §
59 Queens Gate, London SW7 5JP;
 URL www.duffmiller.com; e-mail enqs@duffmiller.com;
 Tel 020 7225 0577; Fax 020 7589 5155

Ealing Independent College §
83 New Broadway, Ealing, London W5 5AL;
 URL www.ealingindependentcollege.com; e-mail
 ealingcollege@btconnect.com; Tel 020 8579 6668;
 Fax 020 8567 8688
Head of Establishment Dr Ian Moores

FTC Kaplan, London §
Emile Woolf International, 4 Tannery Hse, Tannery La,
 Send, Woking, Surrey GU23 7EF; URL www.atew.com

Hampstead College of Fine Arts and Humanities
24 Lambolle Pl, London NW3 4PG;
 URL www.hampsteadfinearts.safeweb.co.uk; e-mail
 mail@hampsteadfinearts.com; Tel 020 7586 0312;
 Fax 020 7483 0355

Hogarth Tutors ***
17 Queens Gate Pl, London SW7 5NY; Tel 020 8584 7196
Contact N.N. Browne

Holborn College *§
Woolwich Rd, London SE7 8LN;
 URL www.holborncollege.ac.uk; e-mail
 admissions@holborncollege.ac.uk; Tel 020 8317 6000;
 Fax 020 8317 6001

The Institute
11 High Rd, East Finchley, London N2 8LL;
 URL www.hgsi.ac.uk; e-mail office@hgsi.ac.uk;
 Tel 020 8829 4141; Fax 020 8829 4131
Principal Fay Naylor BA, Dip ACE

Kensington College of Business
52a Walham Gr, London SW6 1QR; Tel 020 7381 6360;
 Fax 020 7386 9650
4 Wild Ct, London WC2 4UB
Number of students
1000

Lansdowne Independent Sixth Form College *§
7–9 Palace Gate, London W8 5LS; Tel 020 7616 4400;
 Fax 020 7616 4401
Principal Paul Murphy
Number of students
300
Residential

London City College *§
Waterloo Hse, 51–55 Waterloo Rd, London SE1 8TX;
 URL www.londoncitycollege.com; e-mail
 admissions@londoncitycollege.com; Tel 020 7928 0029;
 Fax 020 7401 2231
Principal N. Kyritsis
Residential, day

London College of Beauty Therapy
Elsley Hse, 24–30 Gt Titchfield St, London W1P 7AD; e-mail
 info@lcbt.co.uk; Tel 020 7580 2929; Fax 020 7580 3553
Contact Eileen Cavalier

London Electronics College ***
20 Penywern Rd, Earls Court, London SW5 9SU;
 Tel 020 7373 8721; Fax 020 7244 8733
Principal M.D. Spalding BSc, MSc, CEng, MIEE, PGCE,
 MCybSoc, MIOD, FRSA

Lucie Clayton Secretarial College
4 Cornwall Gdns, London SW7 4AJ;
 URL www.sjlccollege.co.uk; Tel 020 7581 0024;
 Fax 020 7589 9693

Mander Portman Woodward, London §
90–92 Queen's Gate, London SW7 5AB;
 URL www.mpw.co.uk/lon; e-mail london@mpw.co.uk;
 Tel 020 7835 1355; Fax 020 7259 2705
Head of Establishment Matthew Judd

Montessori Centre International ‡§
18 Balderton St, London W1K 6TG;
 URL www.montessori.ac.uk; e-mail
 mci@montessori.ac.uk; Tel 020 7493 0165;
 Fax 020 7629 7808
Chief Executive Barbara Isaacs

Montessori Society, AMI(UK)
26 Lyndhurst Gdns, London NW3 5NW;
 URL www.montessori-uk.org; e-mail
 montessorisoc.amiuk@tiscali.co.uk; Tel 020 7435 7874
Chair A. Grebot
Member of the Independent Schools Association

Oxford House College *§
28 Market Pl, Oxford Circus, London W1W 8AW;
 URL www.oxfordhousecollege.co.uk; e-mail
 admission@oxfordhouse.co.uk; Tel 020 7580 9785;
 Fax 020 7323 4582
Principal Tim Matthew
Residential

Pitman Training Group plc
Sandown Hse, Sandbeck Way, Wetherby, West Yorkshire
 LS22 7DN; URL www.pitman-training.com; e-mail
 info@pitman-training.com; Tel 0800 220454
Managing Director Claire Lister
Manager (Franchise) Mike Cressey

Queen's Business and Secretarial College *

4 Wetherby Gdns, London SW5 0JN; URL www.qbsc.ac.uk;
  e-mail info@qbsc.ac.uk; Tel 020 7589 8583;
  Fax 020 7370 3303
Principal   C. Bickford

Regent College §

Sai Hse, 167 Imperial Dr, Harrow, London HA2 7HD;
  URL www.rtc.uk.net; e-mail info@rtc.uk.net;
  Tel 020 8966 9900; Fax 020 8429 5639
Head of Establishment   Selva Pankaj

St Dominic's, London §

King's Head Hse, King's Head Yard, London SE1 1NA;
  URL www.stdominicslondon.co.uk; e-mail
  info@stdominicslondon.co.uk; Tel 020 7378 9061;
  Fax 020 7403 1163
Head of Establishment   Prof Geoff Lancaster

Wentworth Tutorial College §

8–10 Brentmead Pl, London NW11 9LH;
  URL www.wentworthcollege.co.uk; e-mail
  karen.nedas@wentworthcollege.co.uk; Tel 020 8458 8524;
  Fax 020 8458 8524
Head of Establishment   Alan Davies

North West

Abbey College, Manchester §

5–7 Cheapside, Manchester, Greater Manchester M2 4WG;
  URL www.abbeymanchester.co.uk; e-mail
  admin@abbeymanchester.co.uk; Tel 0161 817 2700;
  Fax 0161 817 2705
Head of Establishment   Jenny Thomas

Beaumont College of Further Education

Slyne Rd, Lancaster, Lancashire LA2 6AP; e-mail
  beaumontcollege@hotmail.com; Tel 01524 541400;
  Fax 01524 846896
Principal   Graeme Pyle

South East

Abacus College *†§

Threeways Hse, George St, Oxford, Oxfordshire OX1 2BJ;
  URL www.abacuscollege.co.uk; e-mail
  principal@abacuscollege.co.uk; Tel 01865 240111;
  Fax 01865 247259
Principal   Dr R. Carrington
Principal   Mrs J. Wasilewski
Residential, day

Bellerbys College, Hove *

44 Cromwell Rd, Hove, East Sussex BN3 3ER;
  URL www.bellerbys.com; e-mail info@bellerbys.com;
  Tel 01273 323374
Principal   RichardN. Addison
Number of students
550
Residential, day

Cambridge Tutors Sixth Form College *§

Water Tower Hill, Croydon, Surrey CR0 5SX;
  URL www.ctc.ac.uk; e-mail admin@ctc.ac.uk;
  Tel 020 8688 5284
Principal   D.A. Lowe
Number of students
300
Residential, day

Cherwell College *§

Greyfriars, Paradise St, Oxford, Oxfordshire OX1 1LD;
  URL www.cherwell-college.co.uk; e-mail
  chercoll@rmplc.co.uk; Tel 01865 242670
Principal   Andy Thompson

Number of students
150

College of International Education *†§

Bocardo Hse, 24b St Michael's St, Oxford OX1 2EB;
  URL www.cie-oxford.com; e-mail
  principal@cie-oxford.com; Tel 01865 202238;
  Fax 01865 202241
Head of Establishment   John Hudson

College of Petroleum and Energy Studies

52 New Inn Hall St, Oxford, Oxfordshire OX1 2QD;
  URL www.colpet.ac.uk; e-mail registrar@colpet.ac.uk;
  Tel 01865 250521; Fax 01865 791474

d'Overbroeck's College *

The Swan Bldg, 111 Banbury Rd, Oxford, Oxfordshire
  OX2 6JX; URL www.doverbroecks.com; e-mail
  mail@doverbroecks.com; Tel 01865 310000;
  Fax 01865 552296
Principal   Sami Cohen
Number of students
270
Residential, day

Greene's Tutorial College *

45 Pembroke St, Oxford, Oxfordshire OX1 1BP;
  URL www.greenes.org.uk; e-mail
  enquiries@greenes.org.uk; Tel 01865 248308;
  Fax 01865 240700
Residential, day

Hurtwood House School *

Holmbury St Mary, Dorking, Surrey RH5 6NU; e-mail
  info@hurtwood.net; Tel 01483 279000
Principal   K.R.B. Jackson MA
Number of students
300
Residential

International Management Centres Association §

Buckingham, Buckinghamshire MK18 1BP;
  URL www.i-m-c.org; e-mail imc@imc.org.uk;
  Tel 01280 817222; Fax 01280 813297

King's School Oxford *†§

St Joseph's Hall, Temple Rd, Oxford, Oxfordshire OX4 2UJ;
  URL www.kingsoxford.co.uk; e-mail
  info@kingsoxford.co.uk; Tel 01865 711829;
  Fax 01865 747791
Principal   Simon Fenn BA, Dip, RSA
Number of students
150

Modes Study Centre §

73–75 George St, Oxford OX1 2BQ; URL www.cife.org.uk/
  cife_colleges/modes.cfm; e-mail
  enquiries@modesstudycentre.co.uk; Tel 01865 245172;
  Fax 01865 722443
Head of Establishment   Dr Stephen Moore

Oxford Business College §

Kings Mead Hse, Oxpens Rd, Oxford 0X1 1RX;
  URL www.oxfordbusinesscollege.co.uk; e-mail
  enquiries@oxfordbusinesscollege.co.uk;
  Tel 01865 791908; Fax 01865 245059
Head of Establishment   Stanley D. Hunter

Oxford Media and Business School *§

Rose Pl, St Aldates, Oxford, Oxfordshire OX1 1SB;
  URL www.oxfordbusiness.co.uk; e-mail
  courses@oxfordbusiness.co.uk; Tel 01865 240963;
  Fax 01865 242783
Principal   David Wilkins

5

Number of students
100
Residential, day

Padworth College *†§
Padworth, Reading, Berkshire RG7 4NR;
    URL www.padworth.com; e-mail info@padworth.com;
    Tel 0118 983 2644; Fax 0118 983 4515
Principal   Linde Melhuish

Richmond, The American International University in London *
Queens Rd, Richmond, Surrey TW10 6JP; e-mail
    enroll@richmond.ac.uk; Tel (admissions enquiries)
    020 8332 9000
Dean (Admissions)   Julie L. Williams
Number of students
1200
Residential

Rochester Independent College *§
Star Hill, Rochester, Kent ME1 1XF;
    URL www.rochester-college.org; e-mail
    rochester@mcmailcom; Tel 01634 828115;
    Fax 01634 405667
Principal   Pauline Bailey
Principal   Alistair Brownlow
Principal   Brian Pain
Residential, day

St Clare's, Oxford *†§
139 Banbury Rd, Oxford, Oxfordshire OX2 7AL; e-mail
    admissions@stclares.ac.uk; Tel 01865 552031;
    Fax 01865 513359
Principal   Boyd Roberts MA, CertEd, CBiol, MIBiol
Number of students
358
Residential, day

St Giles College *†
13 Silverdale Rd, Eastbourne, East Sussex BN20 7AJ;
    URL www.stgiles-international.com; e-mail
    english@stgiles-eastbourne.co.uk; Tel 01323 729167;
    Fax 01323 721332
Contact   J. Sutherland
Number of students
180

Stafford House College *§
68 New Dover Rd, Canterbury, Kent CT1 3LQ;
    URL www.staffordhouse.com; e-mail
    admissions@staffordhouse.com; Tel 01227 866540;
    Fax 01227 866550
Registrar   Miss Laurakay
Number of students
170
Residential, day

Surrey College *†§
Administration Centre, Abbot Hse, Guildford, Surrey
    GU1 3RL; Tel 01483 565887; Fax 01483 534777
Principal   Louise Cody BA, MA, PGCE
Residential

Tante Marie School of Cookery *§
Woodham Hse, Carlton Rd, Woking, Surrey GU21 4HF;
    URL www.tantemarie.co.uk; e-mail
    info@tantemarie.co.uk; Tel 01483 726957;
    Fax 01483 724173
Principal   M.C. O'Donovan
Career and lifestyle cookery courses

Tobias School of Art and Therapy
Coombe Hill Rd, East Grinstead, Sussex RH19 4LZ;
    URL www.tobiasart.org; e-mail info@tobiasart.org;
    Tel 01342 313655; Fax 01342 328125

West Dean College of Visual and Applied Arts, Conservation and Restoration §
West Dean, Chichester, West Sussex PO18 0QZ;
    URL www.westdean.org.uk; e-mail
    diplomas@westdean.org.uk; Tel 01243 811299;
    Fax 01243 811343
Principal   Bob Pulley
Residential

South West

Bath Academy *§
27 Queen Sq, Bath, Somerset BA1 2HX;
    URL www.bathacademy.co.uk; e-mail
    principal@bathacademy.co.uk; Tel 01225 334577;
    Fax 01225 482414
Principal   Laraine Brown
Residential, day

Bath Tutors *
23 Bloomfield Ave, Bath, Somerset BA2 3AB;
    Tel 01225 310162
Contact   M. O'Hanlon
Tutorial agency; all subjects

Exeter Tutorial College *§
44–46 Magdalen Rd, Exeter, Devon EX2 4TE;
    URL www.tutorialcollege.com; e-mail
    info@tutorialcollege.com; Tel 01392 278101
Principal   Kenneth Jack
Residential, day

Mander Portman Woodward College, Bristol
10 Elmdale Rd, Clifton, Bristol BS8 1SL;
    URL www.mpw.co.uk; e-mail bristol@mpw.co.uk;
    Tel 0117 925 5688; Fax 0117 925 5690
Contact   C. Harrow

National Star College
Ullenwood, Cheltenham, Gloucestershire GL53 9QU;
    URL www.natstar.ac.uk; e-mail principal@natstar.ac.uk;
    Tel 01242 527631; Fax 01242 222234
Residential, day; 16–25; disabilities

West Midlands

Abbey College §
251–3 Wells Rd, Malvern, Worcestershire WR14 4JF;
    URL www.abbeycollege.co.uk; e-mail
    enquiries@abbeycollege.co.uk; Tel 01684 892300;
    Fax 01684 892757
Head of Establishment   Mr P. Moere

Abbey College, Birmingham §
10 St Paul's Sq, Birmingham, West Midlands B3 1QU;
    URL www.abbeycolleges.co.uk; e-mail
    adminbir@abbeycolleges.co.uk; Tel 0121 236 7474;
    Fax 0121 236 3937
Head of Establishment   Andrew Jedras

The Cable and Wireless College §
320 Westwood Heath Rd, Coventry, Warwickshire
    CV4 8GP; Tel 024 7686 8600; Fax 024 7686 8650

Concord College *
Acton Burnell Hall, Shrewsbury, Shropshire SY5 7PF;
    URL www.concordcollegeuk.com; e-mail
    theprincipal@concordcollegeuk.com; Tel 01694 731631;
    Fax 01694 731389
Residential, day

Mander Portman Woodward, Birmingham *§
38 Highfield Rd, Edgbaston, Birmingham, West Midlands
    B15 3ED; URL www.mpw.co.uk; e-mail
    enq@birmingham.mpw.co.uk; Tel 0121 454 9637;
    Fax 0121 454 6433
Principal   D. Jewell BA, MA

Yorkshire and the Humber

Harrogate Tutorial College *†§
2 The Oval, Harrogate, North Yorkshire HG2 9BA;
    URL www.htcuk.org; e-mail study@htcuk.org;
    Tel 01423 501041; Fax 01423 531110
Principal   Keith Pollard BSc, DipMaths, DipEd
Residential, day

North of England College
Cavendish Hse, 92 Albion St, Leeds, West Yorkshire
    LS1 6AG; URL www.noec.co.uk; e-mail info@noec.co.uk;
    Tel 0113 245 3073
Director   Roger Gibbeson

Scotland

Basil Paterson Tutorial College §
66 Queen St, Edinburgh EH2 4NA;
    URL www.basilpaterson.co.uk; e-mail
    info@basilpaterson.co.uk; Tel 0131 225 3802;
    Fax 0131 226 6701
Principal   Colin M. Smith
All examination levels catered for; full-time and part-time
study with accommodation available

Wales

New College *
Bute Terr, Cardiff CF1 2TE; Tel 02920 463355;
    Fax 02920 489616
Principal   W. Hoole BSc, CChem, MRSc, PhC
Residential, day

United World College of the Atlantic *
St Donat's Castle, Llantwit Major, Vale of Glamorgan
    CF61 1WF; URL www.uwc.org; e-mail
    principal@uwcac.uwc.org; Tel 01446 799000
Principal   M.H. McKenzie
Number of students
340
Residential, day

5

Higher and Vocational Education

6

Higher Education Councils and Committees

Universities and University Colleges

Vocational and Adult Education Organisations and Associations

Adult Colleges

English Language Schools

Secretarial Colleges

Correspondence Education

Management Education

Armed Forces Education

Agriculture and Horticulture Colleges

Colleges and Faculties of Art and Design

Music, Dancing and Drama Colleges

Higher and Vocational Education

Higher Education Councils and Committees

British Accreditation Council for Independent Further and Higher Education (BAC)

44 Bedford Row, London WC1R 4LL;
URL www.the-bac.org; e-mail info@the-bac.org;
Tel 020 7477 2584; Fax 020 7447 2585

Chief Executive   Dr Stephen Vickers

Acts as the principal non-EFC accreditation authority for independent further and higher education

General Teaching Council for Scotland

Clerwood Hse, 96 Clermiston Rd, Edinburgh EH12 6UT;
URL www.gtcs.org.uk; e-mail gtcs@gtcs.org.uk;
Tel 0131 314 6000; Fax 0131 314 6001

GuildHE

Woburn Hse, 20 Tavistock Sq, London WC1H 9HB;
URL www.guildhe.ac.uk; e-mail info@guildhe.ac.uk;
Tel 020 7387 7711; Fax 020 7387 7712

Chair   Pamela Taylor; Newman College of Higher Education, Genners La, Bartley Green, Birmingham B32 2NT; Tel 0121 476 1181

Executive Secretary   Patricia Ambrose

Policy Adviser   Elaine Clarke

Policy Adviser   Helen Bowles

GuildHE comprises the principals and directors of colleges and institutes of higher education in the UK and it was established by the colleges themselves. GuildHE's primary function is to provide a forum in which the executive heads of institutions are able to discuss and take action on matters of common concern. Through its corporate voice, GuildHE has had an impact on national planning and debate concerning higher education in the university sector. It also promotes the interests of the colleges to the government, the media, national and international agencies, and to industry, commerce and the professions.

Higher Education Funding Council for England (HEFCE)

Northavon Hse, Coldharbour La, Bristol BS16 1QD;
URL www.hefce.ac.uk; e-mail hefce@hefce.ac.uk;
Tel 0117 931 7317; Fax 0117 931 7203

Chief Executive   Prof David Eastwood

Chair   Tim Melville-Ross

The Higher Education Funding Council for England distributes public money for teaching and research to universities and colleges. In doing so, it aims to promote education and research, within a financially healthy sector. The council also plays a key role in ensuring accountability and promoting good practice.

Higher Education Funding Council for Wales (HEFCW)

Linden Ct, The Orchards, Llanishen, Cardiff CF14 5DZ;
URL www.hefcw.ac.uk; e-mail info@hefcw.ac.uk;
Tel 02920 761861; Fax 02920 763163

Chief Executive   Prof Philip Gummett

Chair   Prof Sir Roger Williams

Director (Finance and Corporate Services)   Richard Hirst

Director (Strategic Development)   Dr David Blaney

The Higher Education Funding Council for Wales is a Welsh Assembly Government sponsored body. Under the Further and Higher Education Act 1992, HEFCW is responsible for the administering funds made available by the Welsh Assembly Government to support education, and research at higher education institutions, and higher education prescribed courses at further education institutions; under the Education Act 1994, the HEFCW is responsible for accrediting providers of initial teaching training for school teachers and commissioning research to improve the standards of teachers and teacher training.

Qualifications and Curriculum Authority (QCA)

83 Piccadilly, London W1J 8QA; URL www.qca.org.uk;
e-mail info@qca.org.uk; Tel 020 7509 5555;
Fax 020 7509 6666

Chief Executive   Dr Ken Boston

Chair   Sir Anthony Greener

Deputy Chair   Sir Dominic Cadbury

Head (Assessment)   Linda O'Sullivan

Head (Qualifications)   Keith Weller

Contact (Strategy and Communications)   Dugald Sandeman

Contact (Curriculum Division)   Chris Jones

Contact (Quality Audit)   Bill Kelly

Contact (Resources and Internal Development)   David Ackland

The Qualifications and Curriculum Authority (QCA) is a public body responsible for promoting quality and coherence in education and training

QCA's remit ranges from early years education to higher level vocational qualifications. It is responsible for ensuring that the curriculum and qualifications available to children, young people and adults are coherent and flexible.
As a body committed to enhancing quality in education, QCA aims to help raise national standards of achievement. This includes promoting greater access to, and participation in, education and training, enhancing lifelong learning opportunities, creating ways of giving credible national recognition for all learners and encouraging greater achievement.

Scottish Further and Higher Education Funding Council (SFC)

Donaldson Hse, 97 Haymarket Terr, Edinburgh EH12 5HD;
URL www.sfc.ac.uk; Tel 0131 313 6500;
Fax 0131 313 6501

Chief Executive   Roger McClure

Chair   John McClelland

SFC is a non-departmental public body responsible to, but operating at arm's length from, the Scottish Government. It distributes more than £1.6 billion of public funds annually on behalf of the Scottish Government. The council provides financial support for learning and teaching, and research and associated activities in Scotland's 19 higher education institutions. As well as providing financial support for learning and teaching in Scotland's 43 further education colleges, the council provides resources to enable colleges to offer bursaries to students on non-advanced courses.

Society for Research into Higher Education (SRHE)

3 Devonshire St, London W1N 2BA; URL www.srhe.ac.uk; e-mail srheoffice@srhe.ac.uk; Tel 020 7637 2766; Fax 020 7637 2781

Standing Conference on University Teaching and Research in the Education of Adults (SCUTREA)

Chair Barbara Merrill; University of Nottingham, School of Continuing Education, Pilgrim College, South Sq, Fydell Hse, Boston, Lincolnshire PE21 6HU; URL www.scutrea.ac.uk; e-mail david.jones@nottingham.ac.uk; Tel 01205 351520; Fax 01205 358363

Hon Secretary A. Jackson; 19 Hillcrest Ave, Hessle, East Riding of Yorkshire HU13 0NP; e-mail a.jackson@freenet.co.uk; Tel 01482 648450

SCUTREA's objective is to further the study of and research into the education of adults. Through its annual conferences, seminars, study groups and published papers, it provides the opportunity for adult educators to share experiences and to discuss research priorities. Membership is open to individuals and institutions who are making a contribution to the study of or research into any aspect of learning, education or training in adulthood.

Student Loans Company Ltd

100 Bothwell St, Glasgow G2 7JD; Tel 0141 306 2000; Fax 0141 306 2005

Chief Executive Ralph Seymour-Jackson

Administration of the government's student loans schemes

Universities UK

Woburn Hse, 20 Tavistock Sq, London WC1H 9HQ; URL www.universitiesuk.ac.uk; e-mail info@universitiesuk.ac.uk; Tel 020 7419 4111; Fax 020 7388 8649

President Prof Rick Trainor

Chief Executive Diana Warwick; e-mail diana.warwick@universitiesuk.ac.uk

Director (External Relations and Communications) Lesley Perry; e-mail lesley.perry@universitiesuk.ac.uk

Director (Policy Development) Rannia Leontaridi; e-mail rannia.leontaridi@universitiesuk.ac.uk

Director (Research) Tony Bruce; e-mail tony.bruce@universitiesuk.ac.uk

Director (Resources Group) Chris Lambert; e-mail chris.lambert@universitiesuk.ac.uk

Universities UK represents the executive heads of UK universities, and exists to promote, encourage and develop the universities in the UK. It aims to improve the funding, regulatory and marketing environment within which UK universities pursue their diverse missions; promote public understanding of the roles, achievements, needs and objectives of UK universities; and to assist in developing good practice in all spheres of university activity by sharing ideas and experience. It represents the universities in dealings with government, parliament, funding councils, and other organisations and individuals worldwide, and provides information and central services, some of which are run by satellite offices and the higher education executive agencies. Universities UK is a company limited by guarantee with charitable status.

Universities and University Colleges

England

Anglia Ruskin University

Victoria Rd South, Chelmsford, Essex CM1 1LL; URL www.anglia.ac.uk; e-mail planning-dept@anglia.ac.uk; Tel 01245 493131; Fax 01245 252646

East Rd Campus, East Rd, Cambridge, Cambridgeshire CB1 1PT; Tel 01223 363271

Bishop Hall La, Chelmsford, Essex CM1 1SQ; Tel 01245 493131

Chair of Governors A. Cherry MBE
Vice-Chancellor M. Malone-Lee CB
Deputy Vice-Chancellor A. Powell
Secretary S.G. Bennett
Number of students
6000 full-time, 15 000 part-time

Aston University

Aston Triangle, Birmingham, West Midlands B4 7ET; URL www.aston.ac.uk; Tel 0121 204 3000

Chancellor Sir Michael Bett CBE, MA, CCIPD, HonDBA, HonDSc
Vice-Chancellor Prof Julia King
Number of students
Undergraduate: 6762 full-time; postgraduates: 939 full-time, 861 part-time

University of Bath

Claverton Down, Bath, Somerset BA2 7AY; URL www.bath.ac.uk; Tel 01225 388388

Chancellor Lord Tugendhat Kt, MA, LLD
Vice-Chancellor Prof G. Breakwell PhD
The university is strongly orientated towards the sciences and technology, undertaking teaching and research which is both challenging and relevant to the outside world
Number of students
8340 undergraduate, 2365 full-time postgraduate
Faculties/schools/departments
Faculties: Science; Engineering and Design; Humanities and Social Sciences. Schools: Health; Management.

Bath Spa University

Newton Pk, Newton St Loe, Bath, Somerset BA2 9BN; URL www.bathspa.ac.uk; e-mail enquiries@bathspa.ac.uk; Tel 01225 875875; Fax 01225 875444

Sion Hill, Lansdown, Bath, Somerset BA1 5SF; Tel 01225 875875; Fax 01225 875666

Vice-Chancellor Prof Frank Morgan BA, MSc, CPFA
Faculties/schools/departments
Art and Design; Education; Historical and Cultural Studies; Music and Performing Arts, English and Creative Studies; Science and the Environment; Social Science

University of Bedfordshire

Park Square Campus, Park Sq, Luton LU1 3JU; URL www.beds.ac.uk; Tel 01234 400400
Faculties/schools/departments
University of Bedfordshire Business School; Health and Social Science; Creative Arts Technologies and Science; School of Education and Sport

Putteridge Bury Campus
Hitchin Rd, Luton LU2 8LE; Tel 01582 489069

University of Birmingham

Edgbaston, Birmingham, West Midlands B15 2TT;
Tel 0121 414 3365; Tel (estate management office)
0121 414 5950
Chancellor   Sir Alex Jarratt CB, BCom, HonLLD, HonDSc,
HonDUniv
Pro Vice-Chancellor   L. Clark
Vice-Chancellor; Principal   Prof M.J.H. Sterling BEng, PhD,
DEng, CEng, FREng, FIEE, FInstMC, FRSA
Registrar; Secretary   J.W. Nicholls
Number of students
13 500 undergraduate, 5000 postgraduate

School of Education

University of Birmingham, Edgbaston, Birmingham, West
Midlands B15 2TT; URL www.education.bham.ac.uk;
e-mail education@bham.ac.uk; Tel 0121 414 4831
Head   Prof Hywel Thomas PhD, BA, MEd, PGCE

Birmingham City University

Perry Barr, Birmingham, West Midlands B42 2SU;
URL www.bcu.ac.uk; e-mail choices@bcu.ac.uk;
Tel 0121 331 5595; Fax 0121 331 7994
Vice-Chancellor   D. Tidmarsh BSc(Hons), PhD, CEng,
FIMechE, FCMI
Registrar; Secretary   M. Penlington
Pro Vice-Chancellor   M. Martin MA, FCA
Pro Vice-Chancellor   P.H. Walking BA, DASE, MEd
Pro Vice-Chancellor   S. Westney BA, CertEd
Number of students
24 375

University of Bolton

Chadwick St, Bolton, Greater Manchester BL2 1JW;
URL www.bolton.ac.uk; e-mail enquiries@bolton.ac.uk;
Tel 01204 900600; Fax 01204 903201
Vice-Chancellor   Mrs M. Temple MA, BA(Hons)
Pro Vice-Chancellor   Dr Peter Marsh
Head (Education)   A.T. Graham BSc(Hons), CertEd, MEd,
MIEE, ILTM
Number of students
500 teacher education
Main qualifications offered
CertEd, PGCE, BA, MEd, specialist PGCE/CertEd for basic
skills, Level 4 CPD Basic Skills

Bournemouth University

Fern Barrow, Poole BH12 5BB;
URL www.bournemouth.ac.uk; e-mail
enquiries@bournemouth.ac.uk; Tel 01202 524111;
Fax 01202 595287
Vice-Chancellor   Prof G. Slater BA, MSc, MA, DPhil, FIMA
Pro Vice-Chancellor (Academic)   Prof Paul Luker BSc(Eng),
MSc, PhD, CEng, FBCS
Pro Vice-Chancellor (Finance and Corporate Development)
David Willey BSc, MBA, MRICS
Director (Human Resources)   M. Riordan BA, BD
Number of students
14 400 full-time and part-time
Faculties/schools/departments
Design, Engineering and Computing; Conservation
Sciences; Business and Law; Institute of Health and
Community Services; Bournemouth Media School Services
Management

University of Bradford

Richmond Rd, Bradford, West Yorkshire BD7 1DP;
URL www.bradford.ac.uk; e-mail
course-enquiries@bradford.ac.uk; Tel 0800 073 1225;
Fax 01274 236260
Chancellor   Imran Khan
Pro-Chancellor; Chair of Council   Paul Jagger
Pro-Chancellor   Diana Chambers
Vice-Chancellor; Principal   Prof Mark Cleary MA, PhD

Deputy Vice-Chancellor   Prof Jeff Lucas BSc, MPhil, PhD,
CBiol, PgD(EdMan)
University Secretary and Legal Adviser   Vacancy
Pro Vice-Chancellor (Learning and Teaching)
Prof Geoff Layer OBE, LLB, FRSA
Pro Vice-Chancellor (Research and Knowledge Transfer)
Prof Phil Coates BSc, MSc, PhD, ARCS, FIMechE, FIM,
CEng, FREng
Pro Vice-Chancellor (e-Strategy)   Prof Rae Earnshaw PhD,
FBCS, MIEEE
Deputy Principal   Vacancy
Treasurer   Roland Clark
Number of students
Undergraduate: 7502 full-time, 1142 part-time;
postgraduate: 1411 full-time, 1233 part-time

University of Brighton

Mithras Hse, Lewes Rd, Brighton, East Sussex BN2 4AT;
URL www.brighton.ac.uk; e-mail
business.services@brighton.ac.uk; Tel 01273 643222
Director   Prof D. Watson MA, PhD
Number of students
9745 full-time undergraduate, 921 full-time postgraduate

School of Education

Falmer, Brighton, East Sussex BN1 9PH; Tel 01273 600900
Head of School   Maggie Carroll

University of Bristol

Senate Hse, Tyndall Ave, Bristol BS8 1TH;
URL www.bristol.ac.uk; Tel 0117 928 9000
Chancellor   Sir Jeremy Morse KCMG, MA, DLitt, DSc, LLD
Vice-Chancellor   Sir John Kingman FRS, MA, ScD, DSc,
LLD
Registrar   D. Pretty
Number of students
9839 undergraduate, 3105 postgraduate

Graduate School of Education

Helen Wodehouse Bldg, 35 Berkeley Sq, Bristol BS8 1JA;
Tel 0117 928 9000; Fax 0117 925 1537
Professor of Education; Head of School   Prof R.M. Hughes BA,
PhD

Brunel University

Uxbridge, Greater London UB8 3PH;
URL www.brunel.ac.uk; e-mail
admissions@brunel.ac.uk; Tel 01895 274000;
Fax 01895 232806
Chancellor   The Rt Hon Lord Wakeham DL, PC, JP, FCA,
DHonUniv, HonPhD
Pro-Chancellor   Sir Robert Balchin MEd, DLitt, DL
Vice-Principal   Prof M. Sarhadi BSc, MSc, PhD, CEng,
MIEE
Vice-Chancellor; Principal   Prof C. Jenks BSc, MSc(Econ),
PhD, PGCE, AcSS

School of Sport and Education

Brunel University, Uxbridge, Greater London UB8 3PH;
URL www.brunel.ac.uk/about/aceol/sse; e-mail
sse-ugcourses@brunel.ac.uk; Tel 01895 266472;
Fax 01895 269769

University of Buckingham

Hunter Street, Buckingham, Buckinghamshire MK18 1EG;
URL www.buckingham.ac.uk; e-mail
info@buckingham.ac.uk; Tel 01280 814080;
Fax 01280 822245
Vice-Chancellor   Dr Terence Kealey
Chair of the Council   Chloe Woodhead
Vice-Chair of Council   Ian Plaistowe
Secretary to Council   Prof John Clarke
Director (Finance)   C. Wilkes
Number of students
814

6

6 Higher and Vocational Education

Buckingham Chilterns University College
See Colleges and Faculties of Art and Design

University of Cambridge
Chancellor   HRH The Prince Philip, Duke of Edinburgh
    HonLLD
Vice-Chancellor   Prof Alison Richard
Registrar   Jonathan Nicholls; University Registry, The Old
    Schools, Cambridge, Cambridgeshire; Tel 01223 332200
Chief Executive (Local Examinations)   Simon Lebus;
    Syndicate Bldgs, Hills Rd, Cambridge, Cambridgeshire;
    Tel 01223 553311
Director (Careers Syndicate)   Gordon Chesterman; Stuart
    Hse, Mill La, Cambridge, Cambridgeshire;
    Tel 01223 338288
Number of students
11 731 undergraduate, 5800 postgraduate

Institute of Continuing Education
Madingley Hall, Madingley, Cambridge, Cambridgeshire
    CB3 8AV; Tel 01954 280280
Director   Prof R.K.S. Taylor

Faculty of Education
184 Hills Rd, Cambridge, Cambridgeshire CB2 2PQ;
    Tel 01223 767600; Fax 01223 767602
Head of Department   Mike Younger MA

Colleges for Men and Women
With date of foundation
Christ's (1505)   St Andrew's St, Cambridge, Cambridgeshire
    CB2 3BU; Tel 01223 334900; Fax 01223 334967
    Master   Prof Frank Kelly
Churchill (1960)   Storey's Way, Cambridge, Cambridgeshire
    CB3 0DS; Tel 01223 336000; Fax 01223 336180
    Master   Sir David Wallace CBE
Clare (1326)   Trinity La, Cambridge, Cambridgeshire
    CB2 1TL; Tel 01223 333200; Fax 01223 333219
    Master   Prof A.J. Badger
Clare Hall (1965)   Herschel Rd, Cambridge, Cambridgeshire
    CB3 9AL; Tel 01223 332360; Fax 01223 332333
    President   Prof Ekhard Salje FRS
    Graduates only
Corpus Christi (1352)   Trumpington St, Cambridge,
    Cambridgeshire CB2 1RH; Tel 01223 338000;
    Fax 01223 338061
    Master   Dr Oliver Rackham
Darwin (1964)   Silver St, Cambridge, Cambridgeshire
    CB3 9EU; Tel 01223 335660; Fax 01223 335667
    Master   Prof William Brown
    Graduates only
Downing (1800)   Regent St, Cambridge, Cambridgeshire
    CB2 1DQ; Tel 01223 334800; Fax 01223 467934
    Master   Prof Barry Everitt
Emmanuel (1584)   St Andrew's St, Cambridge,
    Cambridgeshire CB2 3AP; Tel 01223 334200;
    Fax 01223 334426
    Master   Lord Richard Wilson of Dinton
Fitzwilliam (1966)   Huntingdon Rd, Cambridge,
    Cambridgeshire CB3 0DG; Tel 01223 332000;
    Fax 01223 477976
    Master   Prof Robert David Lethbridge
Girton (1869)   Huntingdon Rd, Cambridge, Cambridgeshire
    CB3 0JG; Tel 01223 338999; Fax 01223 338896
    Mistress   Prof Dame M. Strathern
Gonville and Caius (1348)   Trinity St, Cambridge,
    Cambridgeshire CB2 1TA; Tel 01223 332400;
    Fax 01223 332456
    Master   Sir Christopher Hum
Homerton (1976)   Hills Rd, Cambridge, Cambridgeshire
    CB2 2PH; Tel 01223 507111; Fax 01223 507120
    Principal   K.B. Pretty MA, PhD
Hughes Hall (1885)   Mortimer Rd, Cambridge,
    Cambridgeshire CB1 2EW; Tel 01223 334898;
    Fax 01223 311179
    President   Sarah Squire

Jesus (1497)   Jesus La, Cambridge, Cambridgeshire CB5 8BL;
    Tel 01223 339339; Fax 01223 324910
    Master   Prof Robert Mair
King's (1441)   Kings Par, Cambridge, Cambridgeshire
    CB2 1ST; Tel 01223 331100; Fax 01223 331315
    Provost   Prof Ross Harrison
Magdalene (1428)   Magdalene St, Cambridge,
    Cambridgeshire CB3 0AG; Tel 01223 332100;
    Fax 01223 363637
    Master   Duncan Robinson
Pembroke (1347)   Trumpington St, Cambridge,
    Cambridgeshire CB2 1RF; Tel 01223 338100;
    Fax 01223 338163
    Master   Sir Richard Dearlove
Peterhouse (1284)   Trumpington St, Cambridge,
    Cambridgeshire CB2 1RD; Tel 01223 338200;
    Fax 01223 337578
    Master   Lord David Wilson of Tillyorn
Queen's (1448)   Silver St, Cambridge, Cambridgeshire
    CB3 9ET; Tel 01223 335511; Fax 01223 335522
    President   Prof Lord John Eatwell
Robinson (1979)   Grange Rd, Cambridge, Cambridgeshire
    CB3 9AN; Tel 01223 339100; Fax 01223 351794
    Warden   David Yates
St Catharine's (1473)   Trumpington St, Cambridge,
    Cambridgeshire CB2 1RL; Tel 01223 338300;
    Fax 01223 338340
    Master   Dame Jean Thomas
St Edmund's (1896)   Mount Pleasant, Cambridge,
    Cambridgeshire CB3 0BN; Tel 01223 336250;
    Fax 01223 336111
    Master   Prof Paul Luzio
St John's (1511)   St John's St, Cambridge, Cambridgeshire
    CB2 1TP; Tel 01223 338600; Fax 01223 337720
    Master   Prof Chris Dobson
Selwyn (1882)   Grange Rd, Cambridge, Cambridgeshire
    CB3 9DQ; Tel 01223 335846; Fax 01223 335837
    Master   Prof Richard Bowring
Sidney Sussex (1596)   Sidney St, Cambridge,
    Cambridgeshire CB2 3HU; Tel 01223 338800;
    Fax 01223 338884
    Master   Prof Sandra Dawson
Trinity (1546)   Trinity St, Cambridge, Cambridgeshire
    CB2 1TQ; Tel 01223 338400; Fax 01223 338564
    Master   Lord Martin Rees of Ludlow
Trinity Hall (1350)   Trinity La, Cambridge, Cambridgeshire
    CB2 1TJ; Tel 01223 332500; Fax 01223 332537
    Master   Prof Martin Daunton
Wolfson (1965)   Barton Rd, Cambridge, Cambridgeshire
    CB3 9BB; Tel 01223 335900; Fax 01223 335937
    President   Dr Gordon Johnson MA, PhD
    Graduates only

Colleges for Women
Lucy Cavendish (1965)   Lady Margaret Rd, Cambridge,
    Cambridgeshire CB3 0BU; Tel 01223 332190;
    Fax 01223 332178
    President   Dame Veronica Sutherland
New Hall (1954)   Huntingdon Rd, Cambridge,
    Cambridgeshire CB3 0DF; Tel 01223 762100;
    Fax 01223 352941
    President   Mrs A. Lonsdale MA
Newnham (1871)   Sidgwick Ave, Cambridge,
    Cambridgeshire CB3 9DF; Tel 01223 335700;
    Fax 01223 357898; Fax 01223 359155
    Principal   Dame Patricia Hodgson

Canterbury Christ Church University
Canterbury Christ Church University, North Holmes Rd,
    Canterbury, Kent CT1 1QU;
    URL www.canterbury.ac.uk; e-mail
    admissions@canterbury.ac.uk
Principal; Vice-Chancellor   Prof Michael Wright
Director (Admissions and Recruitment)   John Slater
Number of students
15 000 resident and day

356

Faculty of Education
Dean (Education)   Dr John Moss

University College for the Creative Arts at Canterbury, Epsom, Farnham, Maidstone and Rochester

URL www.ucreative.ac.uk; e-mail info@ucreative.ac.uk
Rector   Elaine Thomas

University College for the Creative Arts at Canterbury
New Dover Rd, Canterbury, Kent CT1 3AN;
Tel 01252 722441

University College for the Creative Arts at Epsom
Ashley Rd, Epsom, Surrey KT18 5BE; Tel 01372 728811

University College for the Creative Arts at Farnham
Falkner Rd, Farnham, Surrey GU9 7DS; Tel 01252 722441

University College for the Creative Arts at Maidstone
Oakwood Pk, Maidstone, Kent ME16 8AG; Tel 01622 620000

University College for the Creative Arts at Rochester
Fort Pitt, Rochester, Kent ME1 1DZ; Tel 01634 888702

University of Central Lancashire

Preston, Lancashire PR1 2HE
Vice-Chancellor   Malcolm McVicar BA, MA, PhD
University Secretary   Vacancy
Number of students
36 000

Department of Education and Social Science
University of Central Lancashire, Preston, Lancashire
PR1 2HE; URL www.uclan.ac.uk; e-mail
cenquiries@uclan.ac.uk
Head of Department   Ken Phillips

Faculty of Science and Technology
Dean   Prof Dave Phoenix PhD, MAEd, MBA, CBiol, FBiol,
CChem, FRSC, MIMA

University of Chester

Chester Campus, Parkgate Rd, Chester, Cheshire CH1 4BJ;
URL www.chester.ac.uk; e-mail enquiries@chester.ac.uk;
Tel 01244 511000; Fax 01244 511300
Warrington Campus, Crab La, Warrington WA2 0DB;
URL www.chester.ac.uk; e-mail enquiries@chester.ac.uk;
Tel 01925 530000; Fax 01925 530001
Vice-Chancellor   Prof Timothy Wheeler BA(Hons), PhD,
FETeachersCert, CPsychol, AFBPsS
Bursar; Clerk to the Governing Body   J.D. Stevens BA, ACIS

University of Chichester

Bishops Otter Campus, College La, Chichester, West Sussex
PO19 6PE; URL www.chiuni.ac.uk; e-mail
enquiries@admissions@chi.ac.uk; Tel 01243 816000;
Fax 01243 816080
Bognor Regis Campus, Upper Bognor Rd, Bognor Regis,
West Sussex PO21 1HR
Vice-Chancellor   Prof Philip E.D. Robinson
Number of students
4851
Main qualifications offered
Awards own taught degrees: research degrees validated by
University of Southampton

City University

Northampton Sq, London EC1V 0HB; URL www.city.ac.uk;
e-mail registry@city.ac.uk; Tel 020 7040 5060
Chancellor   The Rt Hon The Lord Mayor of London
Pro-Chancellor   Sir Paul Newall TD, DL, MA
Vice-Chancellor; Principal   Prof D. Rhind BSc, PhD, FRGS,
FRICS

Academic Registrar   A.H. Seville MA, PhD
Officer (Schools Liaison)   M. Sanders
Number of students
8324 undergraduate, 6321 postgraduate (including 476
research students)

Department of Continuing Education
Head   Andrew Lewis BA, MSc, PhD, DMS, CertEd(Tech)

Coventry University

Priory St, Coventry, West Midlands CV1 5FB;
URL www.coventry.ac.uk; e-mail
info.rao@coventry.ac.uk; Tel 024 7688 7688;
Fax 024 7688 8069
Vice-Chancellor   Prof Madeleine Atkins PhD
Pro Vice-Chancellor   John Latham
Pro Vice-Chancellor   Prof Ian Marshall
Pro Vice-Chancellor   Prof Donald Pennington
Pro Vice-Chancellor   David Soutter
Number of students
15 612 undergraduate (including HND), 2509 postgraduate
Student facilities
Drop-in student centre, Lanchester library
Sports facilities
Sports centre

Cranfield University

Cranfield, Bedfordshire MK43 0AL;
URL www.cranfield.ac.uk; e-mail info@cranfield.ac.uk;
Tel 01234 750111; Fax 01234 750875
Chancellor   Lord Richard Vincent of Coleshill GBE, KCB,
DSO
Pro-Chancellor   Sir Colin Chandler

University of Cumbria

Carlisle Campus, Fusehill St, Carlisle, Cumbria CA1 2HH;
URL www.cumbria.ac.uk
Ambleside Campus, Rydal Rd, Ambleside, Cumbria
LA22 9BB
Brampton Road Campus, Brampton Rd, Carlisle, Cumbria
CA3 9AY
Lancaster Campus, Bowerham Rd, Lancaster, Lancashire
LA1 3JD
London Campus, English St, Bow, London E3 4TA
Newton Rigg Campus, Newton Rigg, Penrith, Cumbria
CA11 0AH
Chair of Board of Directors   The Ven Peter Ballard
Chancellor   Prof Christopher J. Carr
Pro Vice-Chancellor   Helen Marshall
Director (Finance, Resources and Estates)   Peter Armer
Secretary   Neil Harris
Number of students
15 000
Main qualifications offered
Nat Award, NatDip, NatCert, NVQ, BA, BSc, PGCE, PGDip,
MA, MPhil, PhD

De Montfort University

The Gateway, Leicester LE1 9BH; URL www.dmu.ac.uk;
e-mail enquiry@dmu.ac.uk; Tel 0116 255 1551;
Fax 0116 255 0307
Chair (Governors)   Prof Bill Dawson
Vice-Chancellor; Chief Executive   Prof Philip Tasker
Deputy Vice-Chancellor   Prof David Asch
Pro Vice-Chancellor   Prof Stephen Baskerville
Pro Vice-Chancellor   Prof Jeffrey Knight
Pro Vice-Chancellor   Prof Philip Martin
Pro Vice-Chancellor   Prof Judy Simons
Academic Registrar   E. Critchlow
Head (Student Services)   Stephen Robinson
Number of students
Undergraduate: 13 960 full-time, 3163 part-time;
postgraduate: 747 full-time, 2535 part-time

6

Student facilities

Residential; lodgings assistance; industrial placement; counselling; careers guidance; health service

University of Derby

Kedleston Rd, Derby DE22 1GB; URL www.derby.ac.uk; e-mail askadmissions@derby.ac.uk; Tel 01332 590500; Fax 01332 294861
Vice-Chancellor Prof John Coyne
Pro Vice-Chancellor (Academic Development) Prof Musa Mihsein
Pro Vice-Chancellor (Learning, Teaching and Scholarship) Prof Michael Gunn
Pro Vice-Chancellor; Director (Finance) Mr Hari Punchihewa
Dean (Faculty of Arts, Design and Technologies) Prof Huw Davies
Dean (Faculty of Business, Computing and Law) Fiona Church
Dean (Faculty of Education, Health and Sciences) Helen Langton
Dean (University of Derby Buxton) Prof David Gray
Company Secretary Dr Paul Bridges
Number of students
Approx 24 000

University of Durham

University Office, Durham, County Durham DH1 3HP; URL www.dur.ac.uk; e-mail registrar@durham.ac.uk; Tel 0191 334 2000; Fax 0191 334 6250
Chancellor Bill Bryson BA, HonDLitt, HonDSc, HonDCL
Vice-Chancellor; Warden Prof Christopher F. Higgins BSc, PhD, FRSE, FRSA, FMedSci
Pro Vice-Chancellor Prof Ray Hudson BA, PhD, DSc, FBA
Pro Vice-Chancellor Prof W.J. Stirling MA, PhD, CPhys, FInstP, FRS
Registrar; Secretary L. Sanders
Head (Careers Advisory Service) Mrs C.L. Richardson; University Careers Advisory Service, 49 New Elvet, Durham, County Durham DH1 3PF; Tel 0191 334 1430; Fax 0191 334 1436

School of Education

Leazes Rd, Durham, County Durham DH1 1TA; URL www.dur.ac.uk/education; Tel 0191 334 8310; Fax 0191 334 8311
Head of Department Prof L. Newton MA(Ed), PhD

Colleges in Durham

College of St Hild and St Bede Durham, County Durham DH1 1SZ; URL www.dur.ac.uk/hild-bede; Tel 0191 334 8300; Fax 0191 334 8301
Principal Dr J.A. Pearson BSc, PhD
Collingwood College South Rd, Durham, County Durham DH1 3LT; URL www.dur.ac.uk/collingwood; e-mail collingwood.college@dur.ac.uk; Tel 0191 334 5000; Fax 0191 334 5035
Principal Prof E. Corigan MA, PhD, FRS
George Stephenson College University Bvd, Thornaby, Stockton-on-Tees TS17 6BH; URL www.dur.ac.uk/stephenson; e-mail stephenson@dur.ac.uk; Tel 0191 334 0040; Fax 0191 334 0054
Principal Prof A.C. Darnell BA, MA
Grey College South Rd, Durham, County Durham DH1 3LG; URL www.dur.ac.uk/grey.college; e-mail grey.college@dur.ac.uk; Tel 0191 334 5900; Fax 0191 334 5901
Master Prof J.M. Chamberlain MA, DPhil, FInstP
Hatfield College North Bailey, Durham, County Durham DH1 3RQ; URL www.dur.ac.uk/hatfield.college; e-mail hatfield.reception@dur.ac.uk; Tel 0191 334 2633; Fax 0191 334 3101
Master Prof T.P. Burt MA, PhD, DSc, FRGS

John Snow College University Bvd, Thornaby, Stockton-on-Tees TS17 6BH; URL www.dur.ac.uk/johnsnow.college; e-mail snow.college@dur.ac.uk; Tel 0191 334 0034; Fax 0191 334 0010
Principal Prof H.M. Evans BA, PhD
Josephine Butler College South Rd, Durham, County Durham DH1 3TQ; URL www.dur.ac.uk/butler.college; e-mail butler.reception@dur.ac.uk; Tel 0191 334 7260; Fax 0191 334 7259
Principal Mr A. Simpson
St Aidan's College Windmill Hill, Durham, County Durham DH1 3LJ; URL www.dur.ac.uk/st-aidens.college; Tel 0191 334 5769; Fax 0191 334 5770
Principal Prof J.S. Ashworth BA, MA
St Chad's College North Bailey, Durham, County Durham DH1 3RH; URL www.dur.ac.uk/stchads; e-mail st-chads.www@dur.ac.uk; Tel 0191 334 3358; Fax 0191 334 3371
Principal Rev Dr J.P. Cassidy BA, MA, STB, MDiv, PhD, ThD
St Cuthbert's Society 12 South Bailey, Durham, County Durham DH1 3EE; URL www.dur.ac.uk/st-cuthberts; e-mail st-cuthberts.society@dur.ac.uk; Tel 0191 334 3400; Fax 0191 334 3401
Principal Prof R.D. Boyne BSoc.Sc, Phd
St John's College 3 South Bailey, Durham, County Durham DH1 3RJ; URL www.dur.ac.uk/st-johns.college; Tel 0191 334 3500; Fax 0191 334 3501
Principal Rev Dr D.A. Wilkinson BSc, PhD, MA, PhD, FRAS
St Mary's College Elvet Hill Rd, Durham, County Durham DH1 3LR; URL www.dur.ac.uk/st-marys.college; Tel 0191 334 5719; Fax 0191 334 5720
Principal Dr P. Gilmartin BSc, PhD
Trevelyan College Elvet Hill Rd, Durham, County Durham DH1 3LN; URL www.dur.ac.uk/trevelyan.college; Tel 0191 334 7000; Fax 0191 334 5371
Principal Dr N. Martin MA, PhD
University College The Castle, Palace Grn, Durham, County Durham DH1 3RW; URL www.dur.ac.uk/university.college; Tel 0191 334 4099; Fax 0191 334 3801
Master Prof M.E. Tucker BSc, PhD, FGS, CGeol
Ushaw College Durham, County Durham DH7 9RH; URL www.ushaw.ac.uk; Tel 0191 373 8517; Fax 0191 373 8503
Rector Rev T. Drainey
Ustinov College Howlands Farm, Durham, County Durham DH1 3TQ; URL www.dur.ac.uk/ustinov.college; e-mail ustinov.college@durham.ac.uk; Tel 0191 334 5470; Fax 0191 334 7231
Principal Dr P.B. Wilson MA, DPhil, FRSA
Van Mildert College Mill Hill La, Durham, County Durham DH1 3LH; URL www.dur.ac.uk/van-mildert.college; Tel 0191 334 7100; Fax 0191 334 7152
Principal Prof P. O'Meara BA, MA, DPhil

University of East Anglia

University Plain, Norwich, Norfolk NR4 7TJ; URL www.uea.ac.uk; Tel 01603 456161; Fax 01603 458553
Vice-Chancellor Prof David Eastwood MA, DPhil, FRHists
Registrar; Secretary B.J. Summers
Number of students
9852 undergraduate, 3328 postgraduate

University of East London

Docklands Campus, University Way, London E16 2RD; URL www.uel.ac.uk; e-mail publicity@uel.ac.uk; Tel 020 8223 3000; Fax 020 8223 2900
Vice-Chancellor Prof Martin Everett
Number of students
18 000

School of Education

Stratford Campus, Ranford Rd, London E15 4LZ; Tel 020 8223 2150
Head of Department Ann Slater

School of Social Sciences, Media and Cultural Studies
University Way, London E16 2RD; Tel 020 8223 4216
Head   Andrew Blake (Acting)

Edge Hill University
St Helens Rd, Ormskirk, Lancashire L39 4QP;
 URL www.edgehill.ac.uk; e-mail
 enquiries@edgehill.ac.uk; Tel 01695 575171;
 Fax 01695 579997
Vice-Chancellor   Dr J. Cater
Clerk to the Governing Body   J. McNamara
Wide range of undergraduate and postgraduate full-time
and part-time courses including Arts, Humanities and Law,
Health Studies, Management and Social Sciences, Science
and Information Technology, Teacher Education, Sport and
Performing Arts
Number of students
More than 13 000 on degree and diploma courses.
Accommodation available on-campus and in the locality

University of Essex
Wivenhoe Pk, Colchester, Essex CO4 3SQ;
 URL www.essex.ac.uk; Tel 01206 873333;
 Fax 01206 873598
Vice-Chancellor   Prof Sir Ivor Crewe BA, MSc(Econ)
Registrar; Secretary   Dr T. Rich BA(Hons), PhD
Director (Educational Development Services)   Stella Heath
 BA, MA
Number of students
5700 undergraduate, 2210 postgraduate, 850 continuing
education

University of Exeter
Northcote Hse, The Queen's Dr, Exeter, Devon EX4 4QJ;
 URL www.exeter.ac.uk; e-mail s.d.franklin@exeter.ac.uk;
 Tel 01392 661000; Fax 01392 263108
Chancellor   Floella Bentamin
Vice-Chancellor   Prof Steven M. Smith BSc, MSc, PhD
Registrar; Secretary   D.J. Allen MA
Number of students
9179 undergraduates (full-time), 741 undergraduates (part-
time), 2303 postgraduates (full-time), 1140 postgraduates
(part-time)

School of Education and Lifelong Learning
Heavitree Rd, Exeter, Devon EX1 2LU; URL www.ex.ac.uk/
 education; e-mail ed-student@exeter.ac.uk;
 Tel 01392 264892; Fax 01392 264922
Head of School   Prof Debra Myhill

University College Falmouth
Woodlane, Falmouth, Cornwall TR11 4RH;
 URL www.falmouth.ac.uk; e-mail
 admissions@falmouth.ac.uk; Tel 01326 211077;
 Fax 01326 213880

University of Gloucestershire
The Park, Cheltenham, Gloucestershire GL50 2QF;
 URL www.glos.ac.uk; e-mail admissions@glos.ac.uk;
 Tel (schools and colleges liaison officer) 0870 720 1100;
 Tel 0870 721 0210
Principal   Prof Patricia Broadfoot CBE
Executive Director (Marketing)   Paul Drake
Executive Director (Resources)   Mike Jesnick BA(Hons),
 ACMA
Director (Human Resources)   Paul van Rossum BSc, PGCE,
 MA
Number of students
9986 total, 3200 part-time
Faculties/schools/departments
Education, Humanities and Sciences; Media, Art and
Communications; Sport, Health and Social Care; Business
School

Department of Education
Francis Close Hall Campus, Swindon Rd, Cheltenham,
 Gloucestershire GL50 4AZ; URL www.glos.ac.uk;
 Tel 01242 714551
Head   Dr Kevin Richardson

University of Greenwich
Park Row, Greenwich, London SE10 9LS;
 URL www.greenwich.ac.uk; e-mail
 courseinfo@gre.ac.uk; Tel 0800 005 006; Tel 020 8331 8000
Vice-Chancellor   Prof Rick Trainor BA, MA, DPhil, FRHistS
Pro Vice-Chancellor   Prof Mark Cross
Pro Vice-Chancellor   Prof John Humphreys
Head (School of Architecture and Construction)
 Dr R. Hayward
Head (School of Business)   Prof Les Johnson
Head (School of Chemical and Life Sciences)   E. Briggs
 ACTWA
Head (School of Computing and Mathematics)
 Prof Martin Everett
Head (School of Education and Training)   M. Stiasney
Head (School of Health and Social Care)   Prof L. Meerabeau
Head (School of Humanities)   Jane Longmore
Head (School of Natural Resources Institute)   Tony Clayton
Head (School of Social Services and Law)   Prof D. Chambers

Avery Hill Campus
Mansion Site, Bexley Rd, Eltham, London SE9 2PQ;
 Tel 020 8331 8000
Campus Director   Dr R. Allen

Kings Hill Institute
6 Alexander Gr, Kings Hill, West Malling, Kent ME19 4GR;
 URL www.khi.gre.ac.uk

Medway University Campus
Pembroke, Central Ave, Chatham Maritime, Chatham, Kent
 ME4 4AW; Fax 020 8331 8000

Harper Adams University College
Newport, Shropshire TF10 8NB;
 URL www.harper-adams.ac.uk; e-mail
 admissions@harper-adams.ac.uk; Tel 01952 820280;
 Fax 01952 814783
Chair of Governors   Alison Blackburn
Principal   Prof E.W. Jones BSc, PhD, FRAgS
Director (Corporate Affairs)   D.G. Llewellyn BSc, MSc, ACIS
Dean (Academic Affairs)   Prof A.H. Cobb BSc, PhD
Dean (External Liaison)   Prof B.J. Revell BA, MA
Head (Educational Development and Quality Assurance)
 Abigail Hind BSc, PhD
Head (Information Services)   C. Taylor BSc, MSc, FCMI
Head (Liaison and Marketing)   R.J. Jopling BA, MA, PGCE
Head (Research)   Prof A.H. Cobb
Academic Registrar   N. Morrison BA, PhD
Number of students
2000
Students' Union facilities
Cafeteria, bars, common rooms, shop, bookshop, doctor's
surgery, laundry, halls for dramatic and musical
entertainments; offices and boardroom
Student facilities
Residential accommodation for 600 students; lodgings
assistance; farmlands, grounds and gardens
Sports facilities
Floodlit astroturf pitch, sports hall and multigym, heated
outdoor swimming pool, billiards, snooker, tennis and
squash courts, playing fields, floodlit rugby pitch
Annual Gross Expenditure Budget
£21 million
Main qualifications offered
BSc(Hons)
To obtain a prospectus
Contact admissions

6

University of Hertfordshire

College La, Hatfield, Hertfordshire AL10 9AB;
URL www.herts.ac.uk; e-mail
main.reception@herts.ac.uk; Tel 01707 284000;
Fax 01707 286386
De Havilland Campus, Hatfield, Hertfordshire AL10 9AB;
Tel 01707 284000
Vice-Chancellor; Chief Executive   Prof R.J.T. Wilson
*Pro Vice-Chancellor (Academic Quality and Graduate
Development)*   Prof R.M. Pittilo PhD, BSc, FIBMS, FRSH,
FLS
Pro Vice-Chancellor (Academic Staffing and Services)
Prof T.H.P. Hanahoe PhD, CBiol, FIBiol
Registrar; Secretary   P.E. Waters
Number of students
15 190 undergraduates, 3240 postgraduates

Law

St Albans Campus, 7 Hatfield Rd, St Albans, Hertfordshire
AL1 3RS; Tel 01707 284000
Dean   Prof Diana Tribe LLB, MA

University of Huddersfield

Queensgate, Huddersfield, West Yorkshire HD1 3DH;
URL www.hud.ac.uk; Tel 01484 422288;
Fax 01484 516151
Vice-Chancellor   Bob Cryan
Head of Registry   Mrs K.A. Sherlock
University Secretary   A.E. Mears
Number of students
10 899 full-time, 5723 part-time

School of Education and Professional Development

Dean of School   Dr F. Bridge MSc, BA, DipMathEd,
DipCompEd, PGCRM, MinMgt, PhD
Number of students
2688 full-time and part-time

School of Computing and Engineering

School of Computing and Engineering, The University of
Huddersfield, Queensgate, Huddersfield, West
Yorkshire HD1 3DH
HND, HNC, degree MSc and professional courses in
business computing software engineering, multimedia and
information technology; research; consultancy; short
courses

University of Hull

Cottingham Rd, Kingston upon Hull, East Riding of
Yorkshire HU6 7RX; Tel 01482 346311

University of Hull Scarborough Campus

Filey Rd, Scarborough, East Riding of Yorkshire YO11 3AZ;
URL www.hull.ac.uk; Tel 01723 362392

Keele University

Chancellor   Prof Sir David Weatherall Kt, DL, MB, ChB,
MD, DSc, FRCP, FRCPE, FRS
Vice-Chancellor   Prof J.V. Finch CBE, DL, BA, PhD, AcSS
Registrar; Secretary   S.J. Morris
*Head (School of Criminology, Education, Sociology and Social
Work)*   Prof Charlotte Williams
Number of students
Undergraduate: 5962 full-time, 556 part-time; postgraduate:
744 full-time, 603 part-time

University of Kent

Canterbury, Kent CT2 7NZ; URL www.kent.ac.uk;
Tel 01227 764000
Chancellor   Sir Robert Worcester KBE, DL. BSc
Chair of the Council   Valerie Marshall MA, MBA, MSI, LRM
Vice-Chancellor   Prof David Melville CBE, BSc, PhD,
CPhys, FInstP, FRSA

Chair (Finance and Resources Committee)   John Simmonds
AIB
Senior Deputy Vice-Chancellor   David R. Nightingale MA
Deputy Vice-Chancellor   Prof Keith Mander BSc, PhD,
CEng, MBCS, MCMI
Pro Vice-Chancellor   Dr Robin Baker BA, PhD, FRSA
Pro Vice-Chancellor   Prof John Baldock BA, MA
Dean (Faculty of Humanities)   Prof David Turley MA, PhD
Dean (Faculty of Science, Technology and Medical Studies)
Prof Peter Jeffries BSc, PhD
Master (Darwin College)   Dr Anthony Ward MA, PhD
Master (Eliot College)   Dr M.J. Hughes MA, EdD, BEd,
CertEd, DipRSA
Master (Keynes College)   David Reason
Master (Rutherford College)   Dr Rachel Forrester-Jones BSc,
Econ(Hons), PhD
Undergraduate: 10 605 full-time, 2685 part-time;
postgraduate: 1057 full-time, 761 part-time

Kingston University

Student Information and Advice Centre, Cooper Hse,
Kingston upon Thames, Surrey KT1 2HX;
Tel 020 8547 2000; Fax 020 8547 7080
Chair of Governors   Jerry Cope
Vice-Chancellor   Peter Scott HonDLitt, HonLLD
Deputy Vice-Chancellor   Caroline Gipps
University Secretary   Raficq Abdulla MA, Barrister
Number of students
12 213 undergraduates, 3500 postgraduates

Faculty of Education

Kingston Hill Centre, Kingston Hill, Kingston upon Thames,
Surrey KT2 7LB
Head   Prof Mike Gibson BA, MA, PhD, CertEd
Number of students
1274

Lancaster University

Chancellor   Sir Christian Bonington CBE
Pro-Chancellor   Bryan Gray BA, MBE
Director (Department of Continuing Education)   Prof K. Percy
MA, BSc(Soc), MA, PhD
Head (Continuing Education, Training and Development)
Jane O'Brien MA
Head (Department of Educational Research)   M. Hamilton BA,
Phd
Head (Department of Management Learning and Leadership)
V. Hodgson BSc, PhD
Number of students
8149 full-time undergraduate, 1701 full-time postgraduate

Lancaster Colleges

With date of foundation
Bowland (1964)
Principal   Dr L. Banton BA, MPhil, PhD, CPsychol,
MCIM; Tel 01524 65201
Cartmel (1966)
Principal   J. Corless; Tel 01524 65201
The County (1967)
Principal   Prof D. Smith MA, BPhil; Tel 01524 65201
Furness (1968)
Principal   Dr R. Edwards BSc, PhD; Tel 01524 65201
Fylde (1969)
Principal   Mr F. Wareing BA, MA; Tel 01524 65201
The Graduate (1990)
Principal   Prof M.W. Kirby BA, PhD, FRHistS;
Tel 01524 65201
Grizedale (1975)
Principal   H. Pollock BA, STL; Tel 01524 65201
Lonsdale (1964)
Principal   Dr K. Davidson BSc, PhD; Tel 01524 65201
Pendle (1974)
Principal   Peter Scullion; Tel 01524 65201

Office for the Associated Institutions

Contact   J.S.W. Dickinson

University of Leeds

Leeds, West Yorkshire LS2 9JT; URL www.leeds.ac.uk;
  e-mail enquiry@leeds.ac.uk; Tel 0113 243 1757;
  Fax 0113 244 3921
Chancellor   The Rt Hon Lord Bragg MA, DUniv, LLD,
  DLitt, DCL, FRSL, FRTS
Pro-Chancellor   Mrs L. Pollard OBE, JP, FRSA, DL
Vice-Chancellor   Prof M.J.P. Arthur BM, DM, FRCP,
  FMedSci
Deputy Vice-Chancellor   Prof J. Fisher BSc, DEng, PhD,
  FIMechE, CEng
Pro Vice-Chancellor   Prof M.K. Atack BA, PhD
Pro Vice-Chancellor   Prof V.M. Jones MA, DPhil
Pro Vice-Chancellor   Prof S.K. Scott BSc, PhD
Pro Vice-Chancellor   Prof R.A. Williams BSc(Eng), PhD,
  FREng, CEng, CSci, ARSM, DIC, FIMMM
Director (Estates)   D.R. Sladdin FRICS
Director (Finance and Commercial)   B.S. Smith BA, ACMA
Director (Human Resources)   M. Knight MA, FCIPD
Director (Marketing)   M. Holmes
University Secretary   J.R. Gair MA
Number of students
32 500

School of Education

Hillary Pl, University of Leeds, Leeds, West Yorkshire
  LS2 9JT; URL www.education.leeds.ac.uk; e-mail
  enquiries@education.leeds.ac.uk; Tel 0113 343 4545;
  Fax 0113 343 4541
Chair   T. Roper BSc, MSc, CMath, FIMA

Leeds Trinity All Saints

Brownberrie La, Horsforth, Leeds, West Yorkshire
  LS18 5HD; Tel 0113 283 7100; Fax 0113 283 7200
Principal   Dr F.A. Bridge
Assistant Principal (Academic)   Ms A. Christou
Assistant Principal (Finance)   Mrs J. Bancroft
Assistant Principal (Registrar)   Ms J. Share
Assistant Principal (Resources and External Development)
  Mr M. Shields
Number of students
2500

York St John University

See separate entry

Leeds Metropolitan University

Civic Quarter, Leeds, West Yorkshire LS1 3HE;
  URL www.leedsmet.ac.uk; e-mail
  course-enquiries@leedsmet.ac.uk; Tel 0113 283 3113;
  Fax 0113 283 3129
Vice-Chancellor   Prof S. Lee BA, LLM
Deputy Vice-Chancellor   F.J. Griffiths BSc, MSc
Deputy Vice-Chancellor   G.D. Hitchins BSc, MSc, PhD
Number of students
More than 41 000

University of Leicester

Chancellor   Sir M. Atiyah OM, FRS, MA, PhD, DSc
Registrar   David Hall
Number of students
Undergraduate: 6870; postgraduate: 1746 full-time, 780 part-
time; 2728 distance learning

School of Education

Leicester University, 21 University Rd, Leicester LE1 7RF;
  Tel 0116 252 3688; Fax 0116 252 3653
Secretary   J.M. Wilkinson BEd, MSc

Department of Adult Education

128 Regent Rd, Leicester LE1 7PA; Tel 0116 252 5911;
  Fax 0116 252 5909
Head   Dr R. Carter BA, PhD

University of Lincoln

Central Admissions Unit, Brayford Pool, Lincoln,
  Lincolnshire LN6 7TS; URL www.lincoln.ac.uk; e-mail
  admissions@lincoln.ac.uk; Tel 01522 837027

University of Liverpool

Senate Hse, Abercromby Sq, Liverpool, Merseyside
  L69 3BX; Tel 0151 794 2000; Fax 0151 708 6502
Chancellor   Lord David Owen CH, PC, MB, BChir, MA
Vice-Chancellor   Prof P.N. Love CBE, MA, LLB
Registrar   M.D. Carr MA
Academic Secretary   J. Latham
Number of students
10 127 undergraduate, 2052 postgraduate

Centre for Continuing Education

19 Abercromby Sq, Liverpool, Merseyside L69 3BX;
  Tel 0151 794 2528
Director (Continuing Education)   R. Derricott BA, MEd,
  DCP, FRSA

Department of Education

University of Liverpool, Liverpool, Merseyside L69 3BX;
  Tel 0151 794 2517
Sydney Jones Professor of Education   D.F. Hamilton
Head of Department   Dr N.M. Beattie MA, PhD

College Studies Unit

SCILAS, University of Liverpool, Liverpool, Merseyside
  L69 3GD; Tel 0151 794 5932

Liverpool Hope University

Hope Pk, Liverpool, Merseyside L16 9JD;
  URL www.hope.ac.uk; e-mail enquiry@hope.ac.uk;
  Tel 0151 291 3000; Fax 0151 291 3100
Vice-Chancellor; Rector   Prof Gerald J. Pillay
Number of students
7500, resident and day

Liverpool John Moores University

Customer Relationship, Roscoe Ct, 4 Rodney St, Liverpool,
  Merseyside L1 2TZ; URL www.ljmu.ac.uk; e-mail
  recruitment@ljmu.ac.uk; Tel 0151 231 5090;
  Fax 0151 231 3462
Vice-Chancellor; Chief Executive
  Eur Ing Prof Michael Brown
Number of students
15 756 full-time, 7200 part-time, 3666 postgraduate, 2500
sandwich course
External income from research over the last three years is
almost £10 million a year (not including HEFCE)

Faculty of Education, Community and Leisure

Liverpool John Moores University, IM Marsh Campus,
  Barkhill Rd, Liverpool, Merseyside L17 6BD;
  URL www.ljmu.ac.uk; e-mail
  pcl-recruitment@ljmu.ac.uk; Tel 0151 231 5340;
  Fax 0151 231 5379
Admissions and Information Officer   Jenny Craddock

University of London

Senate Hse, Malet St, London WC1E 7HU;
  URL www.london.ac.uk; e-mail enquiries@london.ac.uk;
  Tel 020 7862 8360; Fax 020 7862 8358
Chancellor   HRH The Princess Royal
Pro-Chancellor   Lord Stewart Sutherland of Houndwood
Vice-Chancellor   Sir Graeme Davies
Director (Administration)   Catherine Swarbrick
Head (External and Internal Student Administration)
  J. McConnell BA, MA
Colleges and Institutes of the University (see separate entries)
Birkbeck, University of London Institute in Paris, Central
School of Speech and Drama, Institute of Musical Research,
Institute of Philosophy, Courtauld Institute of Art,
Goldsmiths College, Heythrop College, Imperial College
London, Institute for the Study of the Americas, Institute of

6

Advanced Legal Studies, Institute of Cancer Research, Institute of Classical Studies, Institute of Commonwealth Studies, Institute of Education, Institute of English Studies, Institute of Germanic and Romance Studies, Institute of Historical Research, King's College London, London Business School, London School of Economics and Political Science, London School of Hygiene and Tropical Medicine, Queen Mary, Royal Academy of Music, Royal Holloway, Royal Veterinary College, St George's Hospital Medical School, School of Advanced Study, School of Oriental and African Studies, School of Pharmacy, University College London, Warburg Institute

Birkbeck, University of London

Malet St, London WC1E 7HX; URL www.bbk.ac.uk; e-mail admissions@bbk.ac.uk; Tel 020 7631 6000

The Central School of Speech and Drama, University of London

See Music, Dancing and Drama Colleges

Courtauld Institute of Art, University of London

North Block, Somerset Hse, Strand, London WC2R 0RN; URL www.courtauld.ac.uk; Tel 020 7848 2777

Goldsmiths College, University of London

Lewisham Way, New Cross, London SE14 6NW; URL www.goldsmiths.ac.uk; Tel 020 7919 7171

Heythrop College, University of London

Kensington Sq, London W8 5HQ; URL www.heythrop.ac.uk; Tel 020 7795 6600

Imperial College London, University of London

Faculty Bldg, Exhibition Rd, London SW7 2AZ; URL www.ic.ac.uk; e-mail rector@imperial.ac.uk; Tel 020 7594 5002

Institute of Advanced Legal Studies, University of London

Charles Clore Hse, 17 Russell Sq, London WC1B 5DR; URL www.ials.sas.ac.uk; e-mail ials@sas.ac.uk; Tel 020 7862 5800

Institute of Cancer Research, University of London

123 Old Brompton Rd, London SW7 3RP; URL www.icr.ac.uk; Tel 020 7352 8133; Fax 020 7370 5261

Institute of Classical Studies, University of London

Senate Hse, Malet St, London WC1E 7HU; URL www.sas.ac.uk/icls; Tel 020 7862 8700

Institute of Commonwealth Studies, University of London

28 Russell Sq, London WC1B 5DS; URL www.sas.ac.uk/commonwealthstudies; e-mail ics@sas.ac.uk; Tel 020 7862 8844

Institute of Education, University of London

20 Bedford Way, London WC1H 0AL; URL www.ioe.ac.uk; Tel 020 7612 6000; Fax 020 7612 6089

Institute of English Studies, University of London

Senate Hse, Malet St, London WC1E 7HU; URL www.sas.ac.uk/ies; e-mail ies@sas.ac.uk; Tel 020 7862 8675

Institute of Germanic and Romance Studies, University of London

Senate Hse, Malet St, London WC1E 7HU; URL igrs.sas.ac.uk; e-mail igrs@sas.ac.uk; Tel 020 7862 8677

Institute of Historical Research, University of London

Senate Hse, Malet St, London WC1E 7HU; URL www.history.ac.uk; e-mail ihrdir@sas.ac.uk; Tel 020 7862 8740

Institute of Musical Research

Senate Hse, Malet St, London WC1E 7HU; URL www.music.sas.ac.uk; Tel 020 7664 4865

Institute of Philosophy

Senate Hse, Malet St, London WC1E 7HU; URL www.philosophy.sas.ac.uk; Tel 020 7862 8682

Institute for the Study of the Americas, University of London

31 Tavistock Sq, London WC1H 9HA; URL americas.sas.ac.uk; e-mail americas@sas.ac.uk; Tel 020 7862 8870

King's College London, University of London

Strand, London WC2R 2LS; URL www.kcl.ac.uk; e-mail principal@kcl.ac.uk; Tel 020 7836 5454; Fax 020 7836 3430

London Business School, University of London

Regent's Pk, London NW1 4SU; URL www.london.edu; Tel 020 7000 7000

London School of Economics and Political Science, University of London

Houghton St, London WC2A 2AE; URL www.lse.ac.uk; Tel 020 7405 7686

External Programme (Distance Learning)

The Information Centre, Senate Hse, Malet St, London WC1E 7HU; URL www.londonexternal.ac.uk; e-mail enquiries@lon.ac.uk; Tel 020 7862 8360
University of London degrees and diplomas are available by distance learning. More than 90 undergraduate and postgraduate courses are offered for study.

London School of Hygiene and Tropical Medicine, University of London

Keppel St, London WC1E 7HT; URL www.lshtm.ac.uk; Tel 020 7636 8636

Queen Mary, University of London

Incorporating Barts and The London, School of Medicine and Dentistry
Mile End Rd, London E1 4NS; URL www.qmul.ac.uk; Tel 020 7882 5555

Royal Academy of Music, University of London

See Music, Dancing and Drama Colleges

Royal Holloway, University of London

Egham Hill, Egham, Surrey TW20 0EX; URL www.rhul.ac.uk; Tel 01784 434455

Royal Veterinary College, University of London

Royal College St, London NW1 0TU; URL www.rvc.ac.uk; Tel 01707 666333

St George's, University of London
Cranmer Terr, Tooting, London SW17 0RE;
 URL www.sgul.ac.uk; Tel 020 8672 9944

School of Advanced Study, University of London
Senate Hse, Malet St, London WC1E 7HU;
 URL www.sas.ac.uk; e-mail school@sas.ac.uk;
 Tel 020 7862 8000

School of Oriental and African Studies, University of London
Thornhaugh St, Russell Sq, London WC1H 0XG;
 URL www.soas.ac.uk; Tel 020 7637 2388

School of Pharmacy, University of London
29–39 Brunswick Sq, London WC1N 1AX;
 URL www.pharmacy.ac.uk; Tel 020 7753 5800

University College London, University of London
Gower St, London WC1E 6BT; URL www.ucl.ac.uk;
 Tel 020 7679 2000

University of London Institute in Paris
London address: Senate Hse, Malet St, London WC1E 7HU;
 URL www.ulip.lon.ac.uk; Tel 020 7862 8000
Paris address: 9–11 rue de Constantine, 75340 Paris Cedex
 07, France; Tel +33 1 44 11 73 73

University of the Arts London
Communications and Development, 65 Davies St, London
W1K 5DA; URL www.arts.ac.uk; e-mail info@arts.ac.uk;
Tel 020 7514 6000; Fax 020 7514 6131
University of the Arts London consists of Camberwell
College of Arts, Central Saint Martins College of Art and
Design, Chelsea College of Art and Design, London College
of Communication, London College of Fashion and
Wimbledon College of Art. See Art and Design and
Performing Arts Colleges.

London Metropolitan University
166–220 Holloway Rd, London N7 8DB;
 URL www.londonmet.ac.uk; e-mail
 admissions@londonmet.ac.uk; Tel 020 7133 4202;
 Fax 020 7133 2677
Chair of Governors   Peter Anwyl
Vice-Chancellor; Chief Executive   Brian Roper
Academic Secretary   John McParland
The department of education at London Metropolitan
University has experience in providing initial teacher
education, early years work and continuing professional
development courses for teachers. The department works in
partnership with nursery, primary and secondary schools
and other educational settings.
Number of students
34 000
Number of staff
3300
Student Facilities
Two campuses, 14 main sites; five sport facilities; award-
winning social facilities; five libraries, as well as special
collections, including the Women's Library

Department of Education
London Metropolitan University, 166–220 Holloway Rd,
 London N7 8DB; URL www.londonmet.ac.uk;
 Tel 020 7133 2661; Fax 020 7133 2628
Head of Department   Roddy Gallacher

London South Bank University
103 Borough Rd, London SE1 0AA; URL www.lsbu.ac.uk;
 Tel 020 7815 7815

Chair (Governors)   David Longbottom BSc, ARCS, FCIPD
Vice-Chancellor   Prof D. Hopkin
Number of students
13 250 full-time, 9992 part-time
Arts and Human Sciences; Business, Computing and
Information Management; Engineering, Science and the
Built Environment; Health and Social Care

Faculty of Arts and Human Sciences
Dean   Prof Mike Molan BA(Hons), Barrister, LL.M, FHEA
Head (Division of Education)   Prof Sally Inman BA, MA
Faculty Manager   Nicola Hallas

Loughborough University
Vice-Chancellor   Prof S. Pearce CBE, BA, MPhil, PhD
Director (Careers)   J. Jones BA, PGDip, CGHE
Head (Social Sciences)   Prof Dennis Smith BA, MSc, PhD
Chief Operating Officer   W. Spinks BSc, MCIPD, PGDip
Number of students
10 171 undergraduate, 2060 postgraduate

Teacher Education Unit
Loughborough University, Loughborough, Leicestershire
 LE11 3TU; URL www.lboro.ac.uk/departments/teu;
 e-mail f.mclaughlin@lboro.ac.uk; Tel 01509 222762;
 Fax 01509 223912
Head of Unit   Jo Harris BA, MA, PhD

University of Manchester
3rd Fl, Beyer Bldg, Manchester M13 9PL; Tel 0161 275 2000
Chancellor   Lord Brian Flowers FRS
Vice-Chancellor   Prof M.B. Harris CBE, MA, PhD
Registrar; Secretary   E. Newcomb BA, DipEd, FRSA
Number of students
15 358 undergraduate, 3278 postgraduate

Centre for the Development of Continuing Education
Director   J.M. Hostler MA, PhD, MEd

Hester Adrian Research Centre
Director   Prof C.C. Kiernan BA, PhD
For the study of learning processes in people with learning
difficulties

School of Education
Dean of Faculty; Professor (SEN and Educational Psychology)
 Mel Ainscow MEd, PhD
Dean (Research and Graduate School)/Professor (Education)
 G.K. Verma BA, MA, DipEd, PhD, FBPsS, CPsychol
*Director of the School; Professor (Educational Assessment and
 Evaluation)*   Prof Thomas Christie MA, MEd, PGCE
Professor (Audiological Medicine)   Valerie E. Newton MD,
 MSc, MRCP, FRCPCH
Professor (Audiology and Education of the Deaf)   J.M. Bamford
 BA, PhD
Professor (Child Language and Learning)   Gina M. Conti-
 Ramsden BA, MPhil, MSc, PhD
Professor (Clinical Bioethics)   Sir David Alliance
Professor (Education)   N.C. Boreham MA, MPhil, PhD,
 CPsychol
Professor (Education)   D.J. Reid JP, BSc, PGCE, MA(Ed),
 PhD
Professor (SEN)   P.J. Mittler CBE, MA, MEd, PhD, FBPS,
 CPsychol
Hon Visiting Professor (Education)   D.G. Graham CBE, MA,
 Teachers' Cert
Hon Visiting Professor (Education)   C.D. Shaw CBE, MA

Manchester Metropolitan University
All Saints, Manchester M15 6BH; Tel 0161 247 2000;
 Fax 0161 247 6390
Vice-Chancellor   Prof J.S. Brooks BSc, PhD, DSc, CEng,
 CPhys, FInstP
Deputy Vice-Chancellor   Prof B. Plumb DipEE, MSc, CEng,
 MIEE, FRSA
Pro Vice-Chancellor (Art and Design)   Prof M. Wayman
 DipAD, FRSA

Pro Vice-Chancellor (Business School)   Prof Huw Morris
    MSc, BSc, FCIPD
Pro Vice-Chancellor (Health, Psychology and Social Care)
    Prof V. Ramprogus PhD, MSc, CPN, BA(Hons), RMN,
    RGN
Pro Vice-Chancellor (Humanities, Law and Social Science)
    Prof A. Holmes BA, MPhil, GPDip, FRSA, FHEA
Pro Vice-Chancellor (MMU Cheshire)   Mr D. Dunn MA,
    BA(Hons)
Pro Vice-Chancellor (Science and Engineering)
    Prof Maureen Neal DipSS, PhD, BSc(Hons)
Director (Financial)   L. Grant MBA, FCMA
Director (Human Resources)   Gill Hemus MA, LLB, DPA,
    DPM, FCIPD
Secretary   Kai Hughes
Number of students
23 411 full-time and sandwich, 7083 part-time

Faculty of Health, Psychology and Social Care
799 Wilmslow Rd, Manchester M20 2RR; Tel 0161 247 2020
Pro Vice-Chancellor; Dean of Faculty   Prof Vince Ramprogus

Middlesex University (MU)

North London Business Pk, Oakleigh Rd South, London
    N11 1QS; URL www.mdx.ac.uk; e-mail
    admissions@mdx.ac.uk; Tel 020 8411 5555
Vice-Chancellor   Prof M. Driscoll BA, CCIM, FRSA
Deputy Vice-Chancellor   Terry Butland BA, MA, PhD,
    CPhys, FInstPhys, FRSA
Deputy Vice-Chancellor   Prof Margaret House BSc, PhD
Deputy Vice-Chancellor; Director (Finance)   Melvyn Keen
    MA, FCA
Assistant Vice-Chancellor; Director (Research)
    Prof Q. Ahmad BA, PhD
Academic Registrar   Colin Davis BSc, PGCE, DIC, CEng,
    MBCS
Number of students
17 930 undergraduate, 4482 postgraduate

Archway Health Campus (including Hospitals)
Highgate Hill, London N19 3UA

Cat Hill Campus (Art and Design)
Barnet, Hertfordshire EN4 8HT

Hendon Campus (Business School)
The Burroughs, London NW4 4BT

School of Arts and Education
Trent Pk, Bramley Rd, London N14 4YZ

Newcastle University

Newcastle upon Tyne, Tyne and Wear NE1 7RU;
    URL www.ncl.ac.uk/postgraduate; e-mail
    enquiries@ncl.ac.uk; Tel 0191 222 5594
Number of students
14 163 undergraduate, 4249 postgraduate

**School of Education, Communication and Language
Sciences**
Joseph Cowen Hse, St Thomas' St, Newcastle University,
    Newcastle upon Tyne, Tyne and Wear NE1 7RU;
    URL www.ncl.ac.uk/ecls; Tel 0191 222 8830
Main qualifications offered
PGCE, MPhil, PhD, Integrated PhD, Educational
Psychology (DEdPsy, MSc), MEd, TESOL, Cert, Dip, MA

University of Northampton

Park Campus, Boughton Green Rd, Northampton,
    Northamptonshire NN2 7AL;
    URL www.northampton.ac.uk; e-mail
    marketing@northampton.ac.uk; Tel 0800 358 2232;
    Tel (switchboard) 01604 735500; Fax 01604 722083
Vice-Chancellor   Ann Tate BSc, MSc, FRSA
Number of students
10 000

Faculties/schools/departments
Applied Sciences; Arts, Social Sciences; Business; Education
and Health

Northumbria University

21–22 Ellison Pl, Newcastle upon Tyne, Tyne and Wear
    NE1 8ST; URL www.northumbria.ac.uk;
    Tel 0191 232 6002; Fax 0191 227 4017
Chair (Board of Governors)   G. Black
Vice-Chancellor; Chief Executive   Prof Kel Fidler BSc, PhD,
    FRSA, CEng, FIEE
Deputy Vice-Chancellor (Development)   Prof A.R.D. Dickson
    BSc(Hon), PhD
University Registrar   Paul Kelly
Number of students
Undergraduate: 12 979 full-time, 6578 part-time;
postgraduate: 877 full-time, 2360 part-time

Division of Teacher Education and Development
Coach La Campus, Coach La, Newcastle upon Tyne, Tyne
    and Wear NE7 7XA; Tel 0191 232 6002
Assistant Dean   Ray Stephens
Division Leader   Christine Taylor
SEN; primary; secondary; part day/part residential; part-
time or full-time
Number of students
618 teacher trainees
Correspondence should be addressed to the Assistant Dean

University of Nottingham

University Pk, Nottingham NG7 2RD;
    URL www.nottingham.ac.uk; Tel 0115 951 5151
Chancellor   Prof Fujia Yang BSc, DSc, DHumanities and
    Letters
Vice-Chancellor   Prof Sir Colin M. Campbell DL, LLB,
    FRSA, CIM, LLD
Registrar   Dr Paul Greatrix BA, MA, PhD
Director (Centre for Career Development)   Steven McAuliffe
Head (School of Education)   Dr C.A. Hall BA, PhD
Chief Financial Officer   C. Thompson BA, FCA
Number of students
35 600

School of Continuing Education
Jubilee Campus, Wollaton Rd, Nottingham N68 1BB;
    Tel 0115 846 6466
Deputy Head of School   Prof P. Olleson MA, PhD, CertEd,
    LRSM, LTCL, ARCO, FRSA, ITLM

Nottingham Trent University

Burton St, Nottingham NG1 4BU; URL www.ntu.ac.uk;
    e-mail cor.web@ntu.ac.uk; Tel 0115 941 8418
Vice-Chancellor   Prof Neil Gorman
Number of students
Undergraduate: 15 807 full-time, 1758 part-time

School of Education
Dean of School   Dr Gill Scott
Number of students
Undergraduate: 1325 full-time, 235 part-time

The Open University

Initial enquiries: Walton Hall, Milton Keynes,
    Buckinghamshire MK7 6AA; URL www.open.ac.uk;
    e-mail gen-enquiries@open.ac.uk; Tel 01908 274066;
    Fax 01908 652247
Chancellor   The Rt Hon Betty Boothroyd
Pro-Chancellor   Lord Christopher Haskins
Vice-Chancellor   Prof B. Gourley MBL, HonLLB
Pro Vice-Chancellor (Curriculum and Awards)   Prof A. Tait
    MA
Pro Vice-Chancellor (Learning and Teaching)
    Prof Denise Kirkpatrick BEd, MEd, DPhil
Pro Vice-Chancellor (Research and Enterprise)
    Prof Brigid Heywood BSc, PhD

Pro Vice-Chancellor (Strategy, Planning and External Affairs)
Prof D. Vincent BA, PhD, FR, HisOS, FRSA
Dean (Arts Faculty)   Dr R.F. Allen BA, PhD
Dean (Faculty of Education and Language Studies)
Dr Sharon Ding BA, PhD
Dean (Faculty of Health and Social Care)   Prof S. Reveley BA, MA, PhD
Dean (Faculty of Mathematics, Computing and Technology Faculty)   Prof Chris Earl BA, MSc, PhD
Dean (School of Management)   Prof James Fleck BSc, MSc, MA
Dean (Science Faculty)   Dr Phil Potts BSc, PhD
Dean (Social Science Faculty)   Prof Dorothy Miell
Director (Institute of Educational Technology)
Josie Taylor (Acting)
Director (Students)   Will Swann
Secretary   A.F. Woodburn BSc, DPA
General enquiries should be addressed to Course Information and Advice Centre
To obtain a prospectus
Admissions information is available in the following guides: Studying with the Open University; Undergraduate Courses; Research Degree Prospectus. All these guides can be obtained from the Course Information and Advice Centre.

Regional Directors
Contact (The Open University in the East of England)
Helen Wildman MBA, MSc, BA, PGCE, FCIPD
Contact (The Open University in the East Midlands)
G.A. Lammie MA
Contact (The Open University in London)   Rosemary Mayes
Contact (The Open University in the North)   Dr David Knight
Contact (The Open University in the North West)
Lynda Brady LLB
Contact (The Open University in the South)   Celia Cohen MA, BSc
Contact (The Open University in the South East)   Liz Gray BA, PGCE (Acting)
Contact (The Open University in the South West)
Linda Brightman
Contact (The Open University in the West Midlands)
Mike Rookes
Contact (The Open University in Yorkshire)   Nick Berry
Contact (The Open University in Scotland)   P.W. Syme MA
Contact (The Open University in Wales)   Rob Humphreys
Contact (The Open University in Ireland)   Dr R. Hamilton BSc, PhD, CBE

University of Oxford

University Offices, Wellington Sq, Oxford, Oxfordshire OX1 2JD; URL www.ox.ac.uk; Tel 01865 270000; Fax 01865 270708

Department of Education
15 Norham Gdns, Oxford, Oxfordshire OX2 6PY; URL www.education.ox.ac.uk; e-mail general.enquiries@education.ox.ac.uk; Tel 01865 274024; Fax 01865 274027
Main qualifications offered
PGCE, MSc, DPhil

Colleges of the University
All Souls Oxford OX1 4AL; URL www.all-souls.ox.ac.uk; Tel 01865 279379; Fax 01865 279299
Balliol Oxford OX1 3BJ; URL www.balliol.ox.ac.uk; Tel 01865 277777; Fax 01865 277803
Blackfriars St Giles, Oxford OX1 3LY; URL www.bfriars.ox.ac.uk
Brasenose Oxford OX1 4AJ; URL www.bnc.ox.ac.uk; Tel 01865 277830; Fax 01865 277822
Campion Hall Oxford OXI lQS; URL www.campion.ox.ac.uk; Tel 01865 286100; Fax 01865 286148
Christ Church Oxford OX1 1DP; URL www.chch.ox.ac.uk; Tel 01865 276150; Fax 01865 286588

Corpus Christi Merton Street, Oxford OX1 4JF; URL www.ccc.ox.ac.uk; Tel 01865 276700; Fax 01865 276767
Exeter Turl Street, Oxford OX1 3DP; URL www.exeter.ox.ac.uk; Tel 01865 279600; Fax 01865 279645
Green Templeton Woodstock Road, Oxford OX2 6HG; URL www.gtc.ox.ac.uk; Tel 01865 274770; Fax 01865 274796
Harris Manchester Mansfield Rd, Oxford OX1 3TD; URL www.hmc.ox.ac.uk; e-mail enquiries@hmc.ox.ac.uk; Tel 01865 271006; Fax 01865 271012
Hertford Catte St, Oxford OX1 3BW; URL www.hertford.ox.ac.uk; Tel 01865 279400; Fax 01865 79437
Jesus Turl St, Oxford OX1 3DW; URL www.jesus.ox.ac.uk; e-mail enquiries@jesus.oxford.ac.uk; Tel 01865 279700; Fax 01865 279687
Keble Parks Rd, Oxford OX1 3PG; URL www.keble.ox.ac.uk; e-mail college.office@keble.ox.ac.uk; Tel 01865 272727; Fax 01865 272705
Kellogg 62 Banbury Rd, Oxford, Oxfordshire OX2 6PN; URL www.kellogg.ox.ac.uk; e-mail college.office@kellogg.ox.ac.uk; Tel 01865 612000; Fax 01865 612001
Lady Margaret Hall Norham Gdns, Oxford OX2 6QA ; URL www.lmh.ox.ac.uk; Tel 01865 274300; Fax 01865 274313
Linacre St Cross Rd, Oxford OX1 3JA; URL www.linacre.ox.ac.uk; e-mail college.secretary@linacre.ox.ac.uk; Tel 01865 271650; Fax 01865 271668
Lincoln Turl St, Oxford OX1 3DR; URL www.lincoln.ox.ac.uk; e-mail info@lincoln.ox.ac.uk; Tel 01865 279800; Fax 01865 279802
Magdalen High St, Oxford OX1 4AU; URL www.magd.ox.ac.uk; Tel 01865 276000; Fax 01865 276030
Mansfield Mansfield Rd, Oxford OX1 3TF; URL www.mansfield.ox.ac.uk; e-mail admissions@mansfield.ox.ac.uk; Tel 01865 270999; Fax 01865 270970
Merton Merton St, Oxford OX1 4JD; URL www.merton.ox.ac.uk; Tel 01865 276310; Fax 01865 276361
New College Holywell St, Oxford OX1 3BN; URL www.new.ox.ac.uk; Tel 01865 279555; Fax 01865 279590
Nuffield New Rd, Oxford OX1 1NF; URL www.nuff.ox.ac.uk; Tel 01865 278500; Fax 01865 278621
Oriel Oriel Sq, Oxford OX1 4EW; URL www.oriel.ox.ac.uk; e-mail lodge@oriel.ox.ac.uk; Tel 01865 276555
Pembroke St Aldates, Oxford OX1 1DW; URL www.pmb.ox.ac.uk; Tel 01865 276444; Fax 01865 276418
Queen's High St, Oxford OX1 4AW; URL www.queens.ox.ac.uk; Tel 01865 279120; Fax 01865 790819
Regent's Park Pusey St, Oxford OX1 2LB; URL www.rpc.ox.ac.uk; Tel 01865 288120; Fax 01865 288121
St Anne's Woodstock Rd, Oxford OX2 6HS; URL www.stannes.ox.ac.uk; Tel 01865 274800; Fax 01865 274899
St Antony's Woodstock Rd, Oxford OX2 6JF; URL www.sant.ox.ac.uk; e-mail coll.sec@sant.ox.ac.uk; Tel 01865 284700; Fax 01865 274526
St Benet's Hall St Giles, Oxford OX1 3LN; URL www.st-benets.ox.ac.uk; Tel 01865 280556; Fax 01865 280792
St Catherine's Manor Rd, Oxford OX1 3UJ; URL www.stcatz.ox.ac.uk; e-mail admissions@stcatz.ox.ac.uk; Tel 01865 271700

6

St Cross St Giles, Oxford OX1 3LZ; URL www.stx.ox.ac.uk; e-mail college.secretary@stx.ox.ac.uk; Tel 01865 278458; Fax 01865 278484

St Edmund Hall Queens La, Oxford OX1 4AR; URL www.seh.ox.ac.uk; e-mail college.secretary@seh.ox.ac.uk; Tel 01865 279000

St Hilda's Cowley Pl, Oxford OX4 1DY; URL www.sthildas.ox.ac.uk; e-mail outreach@st-hildas.ox.ac.uk; Tel 01865 276884; Fax 01865 276816

St Hugh's St Margarets Rd, Oxford OX2 6LE; URL www.st-hughs.ox.ac.uk; e-mail admissions@st-hughs.ox.ac.uk; Tel 01865 274900

St John's St Giles, Oxford OX1 3JP; URL www.sjc.ox.ac.uk; e-mail college.office@sjc.ox.ac.uk; Tel 01865 277318; Fax 01865 277435

St Peter's New Inn Hall St, Oxford OX1 2DL; URL www.spc.ox.ac.uk; Tel 01865 278864; Fax 01865 278855

St Stephen's House 16 Marston St, Oxford OX4 1JX; URL www.ssho.ox.ac.uk; e-mail enquiries@ssho.ox.ac.uk; Tel 01865 247874; Fax 01865 794338

Somerville Woodstock Rd, Oxford OX2 6HD; URL www.some.ox.ac.uk; e-mail secretariat@some.ox.ac.uk; Tel 01865 270619

Trinity Broad St, Oxford OX1 3BH; URL www.trinity.ox.ac.uk; Tel 01865 279900; Fax 01865 279902

University College High St, Oxford OX1 4BH; URL www.univ.ox.ac.uk; e-mail college.office@univ.ox.ac.uk; Tel 01865 276601; Fax 01865 276790

Wadham Parks Rd, Oxford OX1 3PN; URL www.wadham.ox.ac.uk; e-mail admissions@wadh.ox.ac.uk; Tel 01865 277900; Fax 01865 277937

Wolfson Linton Rd, Oxford OX2 6UD; URL www.wolfson.ox.ac.uk; e-mail membership.secretary@wolfson.ox.ac.uk; Tel 01865 274100; Fax 01865 274125

Worcester Walton St, Oxford OX1 2HB; URL www.worcester.ox.ac.uk; e-mail admissions@worc.ox.ac.uk; Tel 01865 278300; Fax 01865 278369

Wycliffe Hall Banbury Rd, Oxford OX2 6PW; URL www.wycliffe.ox.ac.uk; e-mail enquiries@wycliffe.ox.ac.uk; Tel 01865 274200; Fax 01865 274215

Oxford Brookes University

Gipsy La, Headington, Oxford, Oxfordshire OX3 0BP; URL www.brookes.ac.uk; e-mail query@brookes.ac.uk; Tel 01865 484848; Fax 01865 483616
Vice-Chancellor Prof Janet Beer BA, MA, PhD
Deputy Vice-Chancellor (Academic Affairs) Dr Petra Wend
Deputy Vice-Chancellor (Business and Resources); Registrar Rex Knight
Pro Vice-Chancellor (External Affairs) Prof John Raffery
Pro Vice-Chancellor (Research) Prof Diana Woodhouse
Librarian Helen Workman BSc, MA, PhD, ALA, MIInfSc
Number of students
18 000

University of Plymouth

Drake Circus, Plymouth PL4 8AA; URL www.plymouth.ac.uk; e-mail prospectus@plymouth.ac.uk; Tel 01752 232232
Vice-Chancellor; Chief Executive Prof Wendy Purcell
Deputy Vice-Chancellor Prof Steve Newstead
Deputy Vice-Chancellor; Director (Finance) Graham Raikes
Deputy Vice Chancellor Prof Mary Watkins

Faculty of Education
Drake Circus, Plymouth PL4 8AA; URL www.plymouth.ac.uk/education; e-mail education.enq@plymouth.ac.uk; Tel 01395 255522; Fax 01395 255303
Dean of Faculty Prof Michael Totterdell BA, MA, MID, PGCE, FInstAM, FRSA

University of Portsmouth

University Hse, Winston Churchill Ave, Portsmouth PO1 2UP; URL www.port.ac.uk; e-mail info.centre@port.ac.uk; Tel 02392 848484; Fax 02392 842733
Chancellor Lord Palumbo
Vice-Chancellor Prof John A.G. Craven
Pro Vice-Chancellor A.H. Glasner BSc, MSc
Pro Vice-Chancellor C. Monk BSc, MBA
Dean (Business School) M. Dunn
Dean (Faculty of the Environment) L. Shurmer-Smith
Dean (Faculty of Humanities and Social Sciences) M. Mitchell BA, MSc
Dean (Faculty of Science) Prof D. Rogers
Dean (Faculty of Technology) D. Arrell MSc, PhD
Number of students
12 800 undergraduate, 1700 postgraduate and research assistants

University of Reading

Whiteknights, PO Box 217, Reading RG6 6AH; URL www.reading.ac.uk; e-mail student.recruitment@reading.ac.uk; Tel 0118 378 6586; Fax 0118 378 8924
Chancellor Dr John Madejski OBE, DL
Vice-Chancellor Prof R.G. Marshall BA, DPhil
Number of students
10 786 undergraduates, 5374 postgraduates
Faculties/schools/departments
Faculty of Arts and Humanities; Faculty of Economic and Social Sciences; Faculty of Life Sciences; Faculty of Science
To obtain a prospectus
Visit the website or telephone the college

Institute of Education
University of Reading, Bulmershe Ct, Earley, Reading RG6 1HY; URL www.education.rdg.ac.uk
Head of Institute Prof D. Malvern

School of Continuing Education
The University, London Rd, Reading RG1 5AQ; e-mail cont-ed@reading.ac.uk; Tel 0118 378 8347
Head of School Dr Brian O'Callaghan

School of Health and Social Care
The University of Reading, Bulmershe Ct, Reading RG6 1HY; URL www.reading.ac.uk/health; e-mail d.r.matthews@reading.ac.uk; Tel 0118 378 8855; Fax 0118 378 6808
Head of School Prof Christina Victor

Roehampton University

Erasmus Hse, Roehampton La, London SW15 5PU; URL www.roehampton.ac.uk; e-mail enquiries@roehampton.ac.uk; Tel 020 8392 3232; Fax 020 8392 3470
Vice-Chancellor Prof Paul O'Prey
Number of students
6473 undergraduates, 1371 postgraduate (including mature and residential places)
Faculties/schools/departments
Arts; Business and Social Science; Education; Human and Life Sciences
Qualifications offered
BA, BSc, BMus, BEd, MA, MRes, MS, MPhil, PhD, PGCE, INSETDip and Cert

Royal Agricultural College

See Agricultural and Horticultural Colleges

Royal College of Art

See Colleges and Faculties of Art and Design

Royal College of Music

See Music, Dancing and Drama Colleges

University of Salford

Salford, Greater Manchester M5 4WT;
    URL www.salford.ac.uk
Chancellor   Sir M. Harris
Vice-Chancellor   Prof Michael Harloe MA, PhD, BA, ACCS
Pro Vice-Chancellor   Prof Peter Barrett BA, MA, PhD
Registrar   Dr Adrian Graves BA(Hons), DPhil
Number of students
14 937 full-time, 4369 part-time

University of Sheffield

Firth Ct, Western Bank, Sheffield, South Yorkshire S10 2TN;
    URL www.sheffield.ac.uk; e-mail
    j.a.smith1@sheffield.ac.uk; Tel 0114 222 5300;
    Fax 0114 273 8496
Pro-Chancellor   P. Firth
Pro-Chancellor   G.H.N. Peel
Pro-Chancellor   K.E. Riddle JP, BA, LLB
Vice-Chancellor   Prof R.F. Boucher PhD, HonDHL, CEng,
    FIMechE, FASME, MIEEE, HonRCM
Registrar; Secretary   D.E. Fletcher BA, PhD

School of Education
Head   Prof W. Carr BA, MA
Deputy Head   Vacancy

Institute for Lifelong Learning
Professor; Director   S.C. Webb BA, PGCE, MA, PhD
Lecturer; Director (Part-time Studies)   R. Toynton BSc, PhD,
    AMA, FGS

Sheffield Hallam University

City Campus, Howard St, Sheffield, South Yorkshire
    S1 1WB; URL www.shu.ac.uk; e-mail
    enquiries@shu.ac.uk; Tel 0114 225 5555;
    Fax 0114 225 2430
Vice-Chancellor   Prof Philip Jones LLb, LLm, MA
University Secretary   Liz Winders
Director (Finance)   Philip Severs
Director (Student and Academic Services)   Clive Macdonald
Number of students
21 152 full-time and sandwich, 7903 postgraduate, 6392
part-time

**Division of Education and Humanities, Faculty of
Development and Society**
Collegiate Crescent Campus, Sheffield Hallam University,
    Sheffield, South Yorkshire S10 2BP
Dean   Prof Sylvia Johnson

University of Southampton

Highfield, Southampton SO17 1BJ;
    URL www.southampton.ac.uk; e-mail
    prospenq@soton.ac.uk; Tel 02380 595000;
    Fax 02380 593131
Chancellor   The Rt Hon John Palmer, Earl of Selborne KBE,
    FRS
Vice-Chancellor   Prof Bill Wakeham PHd, DSC, FPEng,
    FInstP, FIChemE, FIEE
Registrar; Secretary   J.F.D. Lauwerys BEd, MA
Academic Registrar   Vacancy
Number of students
16 730 undergraduates, 6089 postgraduates

Degree subjects offered
Education (PGCE and part-time BA), Health and Social Care
Foundation Degree, Medicine, Midwifery, Nursing,
Occupational Therapy, Physiotherapy, Podiatry, and Sports
Studies
Faculties/schools/departments
Law; Arts and Social Sciences, including Education;
Engineering; Science; Mathematics; Medicine; Health and
Life Sciences

Southampton Solent University

East Park Terr, Southampton, Hampshire SO14 OYN;
    URL www.solent.ac.uk; e-mail enquiries@solent.ac.uk;
    Tel 02380 319000; Fax 02380 334161

Staffordshire University

Stoke Campus, College Rd, Stoke-on-Trent, Staffordshire
    ST4 2DE; URL www.staffs.ac.uk; e-mail
    admissions@staffs.ac.uk; Tel 01782 294000;
    Fax 01782 745422
Vice-Chancellor   Prof C.E. King, DL BA, MA, PhD,
    HonDLitt, CIM, FRSA, FRHistS
University Secretary   K.B.G. Sproston DMA
Academic Registrar; Dean (Students)   F. Francis
Head (Student Recruitment)   Linda Bradbury
Number of students
12 270 full-time and sandwich, 6040 part-time

Stafford Campus
Beaconside, Stafford, Staffordshire ST18 0AD

Business School
Leek Rd, Stoke-on-Trent ST4 2DF; Tel 01782 294060;
    Fax 01782 747006
Dean   Susan Foreman

University of Sunderland

Edinburgh Bldg, Chester Rd, Sunderland, Tyne and Wear
    SR1 3SD; e-mail student-helpline@sunderland.ac.uk;
    Tel 0191 515 2000
Vice-Chancellor; Chief Executive   Prof Peter Fidler MBE,
    MSc, DipTP, DipSoc, MRTPI
University Secretary   J.D. Pacey LLB
Academic Registrar   Beatrice Ollerenshaw MA, PGCE, MBA
Number of students
Undergraduate: 11 517 full-time; postgraduate: 1521 full-
time, 4379 part-time

School of Education
Forster Bldg, Chester Rd, Sunderland, Tyne and Wear
    SR1 3SD; Tel 0191 515 2000
Director of School   Prof Gary Holmes
Number of students
937 full-time, 656 part-time

University of Surrey

Guildford, Surrey GU2 7XH; URL www.surrey.ac.uk;
    Tel 01483 300800; Fax 01483 300803
Chair of Council   Mr M. Taylor
Clerk to the Council   J.W.A. Strawson MA, MSc, CertEd
Chancellor   HRH The Duke of Kent KG, GCMG, GCVO
Vice-Chancellor; Chief Executive
    Prof Christopher M. Snowden FRS, FREng, FIEE, FIEEE,
    FCGI
Pro Vice-Chancellor   Prof B.G. Evans BSc, FIEE, FRSA,
    FREng
Pro-Chancellor   Prof B.L. Weiss BSc, PhD, DSc, DEng,
    CEng, CPhys, FIET, FInstP
Pro-Chancellor Emeritus   Sir Idris Pearce CBE, TD, DL,
    FRICS, FRSA
Deputy Vice-Chancellor   Prof J.A. Turner MA, DPhil,
    FRHistS
Director (Corporate Services)   G.K. Melly MBA, CAIB
Director (External Academic Relationships)   Prof J.E. Harding
    ACGI, BSc, MSc, DICPhD, CEng, FIStructE, FICE

6

Director (Finance)   Mr D.J. Sharkey LLB, ACA
Director (Information Services); University Librarian
    T.J.A. Crawshaw BEng, DipLib
Registrar   Mr P. Henry BSc, GradCertEd, MBA, MCMI, TD
Number of students
7362 undergraduates, 4362 postgraduates (2005/06)

University of Sussex

Sussex Hse, Falmer, Brighton, East Sussex BN1 9RH;
    URL www.sussex.ac.uk; e-mail
    information@sussex.ac.uk; Tel 01273 606755
Chancellor   Lord Richard Attenborough Kt, CBE,
    HonDLitt, HonDCL, HonLLD
Vice-Chancellor   Prof Michael Farthing
Deputy Vice-Chancellor   Prof Paul Layzell
Registrar; Secretary   Dr Philip Harvey
Number of students
7427 undergraduate, 3136 postgraduate

University of Teesside

Middlesbrough TS1 3BA; URL www.tees.ac.uk;
    Tel 01642 342301; Fax 01642 342399
Vice-Chancellor   Prof G. Henderson
Deputy Vice-Chancellor (Academic and Development)
    Prof Katherine Leni Oglesby
Deputy Vice-Chancellor (External and Research)
    Prof Cliff Hardcastle
Dean (Social Sciences and Law)   E. Barnes BEd, MMedSci

Thames Valley University

St Mary's Rd, Ealing, London W5 5RF; URL www.tvu.ac.uk;
    e-mail learning.advice@tvu.ac.uk; Tel 020 8579 5000;
    Fax 020 8231 2056
Vice-Chancellor   Prof Geoff Crispin
TVU is the leading provider of higher education in the West
London and Thames Valley area
Faculties/schools/departments
Faculty of Professional Studies; London College of Music
and Media; Faculty of Health and Human Sciences

Slough Campus
Wellington St, Slough SL1 1YG; Tel 01753 534585;
    Fax 01753 574264

Reading Campus
Crescent Rd, Reading RG1 5RQ; e-mail
    reading.enquiries@tvu.ac.uk; Tel 0800 036 8888;
    Fax 0118 967 5301
Pro Vice-Chancellor (Further Education)   Lee Nicholls
Head (14–19 Academy)   Jo Burford
Head (Faculty of the Arts)   Mark Langley
Head (Faculty of Professional Studies)   Pat Prime
Head (Faculty of Technology)   Ann Osler

Warburg Institute, University of London

Woburn Sq, London WC1H 0AB; URL warburg.sas.ac.uk;
    e-mail warburg@sas.ac.uk; Tel 020 7862 8949

University of Warwick

Coventry, Warwickshire CV4 7AL;
    URL www.warwick.ac.uk
Chancellor
    Sir Nicholas Scheele, (BA, Hon DBA, Hon DUniv, Hon
    DTech Hon LLD, Hon DSc, Hon RCM, Hon FIMechE
Pro-Chancellor   J. Leighfield CBE, MA, HonDUniv,
    HonDTech, FBCS, FIDAm, FINstD
Vice-Chancellor   Prof N. Thrift BA, MA, PhD, DSC, FBA
Assistant Registrar   R.E. Lees MA, PGCE
Academic Registrar   D. Law BA, MPhil, PhD
Director (Department of Physical Education and Sport)
    T. Monnington BA, MA, TCert
Director (Institute of Education)   A. Hams BA, MEd, PhD,
    PGCE
Director (Lifelong Learning)   R. Moseley BSc, MSc, DPhil

Registrar   J.F. Baldwin BA, MBA, HonDLitt, MIMgt, FCIS,
    FRSA
Contact (Lifelong Learning: Open Studies)   K. Rainsley BA,
    MA
Number of students
11 370 undergraduates, 4805 postgraduates (2005/06)

University of the West of England

Frenchay Campus, Coldharbour La, Bristol BS16 1QY;
    URL www.uwe.ac.uk; e-mail admissions@uwe.ac.uk;
    Tel 0117 328 3333; Fax 0117 328 2810
Chancellor   The Rt Hon The Baroness Butler-Sloss GBE
Vice-Chancellor   Prof Steven West (Acting) BSc, DPodM,
    FChS, MPodA, MIPEMS
Academic Registrar   Tessa Harrison BA, PGDip
Head of Careers   John Clarke BA, PGDip, MSc
Number of students
18 959 full-time, 6640 part-time (2006/07)
Faculties/schools
Bristol Business School; Creative Arts; Environment and
Technology; Health and Life Sciences; Social Sciences and
Humanities

University of Westminster

Headquarters Bldg, 309 Regent St, London W1B 2UW;
    URL www.westminster.ac.uk; e-mail
    course-enquiries@westminster.ac.uk; Tel 020 7911 5000;
    Fax 020 7911 5858
Chair (Court of Governors)   Sir Alan Thomas
Vice-Chancellor; Rector   Prof Geoff Petts
*Deputy Vice-Chancellor (External Affairs); Provost (Regent
    Campus)*   Prof Margaret Blunden BA, MA, DPhil
*Deputy Vice-Chancellor (Internal Affairs); Provost (Cavendish
    Campus)*   Dr Maud Tyler BA, PhD
Academic Registrar   Evelyne Rugg
Number of students
12 282 full-time and sandwich, 10 142 part-time; 16 678
undergraduate, 5746 postgraduate

University of Winchester

West Hill , Winchester , Hampshire SO22 4NR ;
    URL www.winchester.ac.uk; e-mail
    course.enquiries@winchester.ac.uk; Tel 01962 841515;
    Fax 01962 842280
Vice-Chancellor   Prof Paul Light
Pro Vice-Chancellor (Academic)   Prof C.M.D. Turner
Pro Vice-Chancellor (Administration)   T.P. Geddes
Faculties/schools/departments
Community and Performing Arts; Cultural Studies;
Education; Social Sciences

Faculty of Education
Sparkford Rd, Winchester, Hampshire SO22 4NR;
    URL www.winchester.ac.uk; e-mail
    course.enquiries@winchester.ac.uk
Dean of Faculty   Prof A. Williams

University of Wolverhampton

City Campus, Wulfruna St, Wolverhampton, West
    Midlands WV1 1SB; URL www.wlv.ac.uk; e-mail
    enquiries@wlv.ac.uk; Tel 01902 321000; Fax 01902 322680
Vice-Chancellor   Prof Caroline Gipps
Number of students
13 480 full-time sandwich, 9226 part-time

School of Education
Gorway Rd, Walsall, West Midlands WS1 3BD;
    URL www.wlv.ac.uk/sed; e-mail enquiries@wlv.ac.uk;
    Tel 01902 321050; Fax 01902 323177
Dean   Sir Geoff Hampton KBE, CertEd, BEd, MEd;
    Tel 01902 323258; Fax 01902 323180
Number of students
3078 full-time, 2362 part-time

University of Worcester

Henwick Gr, Worcester, Worcestershire WR2 6AJ;
URL www.worcester.ac.uk; e-mail study@worc.ac.uk;
Tel 01905 855000; Fax 01905 855132
Vice-Chancellor　Prof David Green MA
Deputy Vice-Chancellor　Prof Judith Elkin BA, PhD, FLA,
FIInfSc, AcSS, FCLIP
Registrar; Secretary　John Ryan BA, MLitt
Number of students
4500 full-time, 3100 part-time

Institute of Education

University of Worcester, Henwick Gr, Worcester,
Worcestershire WR2 6AJ; URL www.worcester.ac.uk;
e-mail c.robertson@worc.ac.uk; Tel 01905 855231;
Fax 01905 855132
Head　Mrs Chris Robertson MA

University of York

Heslington, York YO10 5DD; URL www.york.ac.uk;
Tel 01904 430000; Fax 01904 433433
Chancellor　Dame Janet Baker CH, DBE
Vice-Chancellor　Prof R.U. Cooke BSc, MSc, PhD, DSc
Registrar　D.J. Foster
Head (Department of Educational Studies)　Dr R. Campbell
BSc, MSc, PhD, CertEd, CBiol, MBiol
Number of students
5200 undergraduates, 1900 postgraduates

Centre for Performance Evaluation and Resource Management

Director　Prof David Mayston MA, MSc, PhD, FRSA;
e-mail dm3@york.ac.uk; Tel 0190 443 3761;
Fax 0190 443 3759
Associate Director　Prof David Jesson; e-mail
dj2@york.ac.uk; Tel 0114 222 3015; Fax 0114 275 0878

York St John University

Lord Mayor's Wlk, York YO31 7EX; URL www.yorksj.ac.uk;
e-mail admissions@yorksj.ac.uk; Tel 01904 624624;
Fax 01904 612512
Chancellor　Dr J.T.M. Sentamu Archbishop of York
Vice-Chancellor　Prof Dianne Willcocks
Deputy Vice-Chancellor　Prof M. Brown
Pro Vice-Chancellor　Prof S. Billingham
Director (Finance)　J. Gallacher
Number of students
6000 (including part-time and mature)
Faculties/schools/departments
Humanities; Social, Environmental, Health and Life
Sciences; Teaching; Professional and Management Studies;
Creative and Performing Arts

Scotland

University of Aberdeen

King's College, Aberdeen AB24 3FX; URL www.abdn.ac.uk;
e-mail m.clark@abdn.ac.uk; Tel 01224 272000
Chancellor　Lord David Wilson of Tillyorn
Vice-Chancellor; Principal　Prof C. Duncan Rice
Number of students
10 323 undergraduates, 3265 postgraduates

Centre for Lifelong Learning

University of Aberdeen, Regent Bldg, King's College,
Aberdeen AB24 3FX; URL www.abdn.ac.uk; e-mail
lifelonglearning@abdn.ac.uk; Tel 01224 273528
Director　Julie McAndrews

School of Education

University of Aberdeen, MacRobert Bldg, Kings College,
Aberdeen AB24 SUA; URL www.abdn.ac.uk;
Tel 01224 274776

University of Abertay Dundee

Bell St, Dundee DD1 1HG; URL www.abertay.ac.uk; e-mail
sro@abertay.ac.uk; Tel 01382 308000; Fax 01382 308877
Chair (University Court)　Prof G. Hewitt MA(Hons), DBA
Vice-Chancellor; Principal　Prof B. King CBE, CCIMgt,
FIWSc, CBiol, FIBiol
Vice-Principal　Prof M.T. Swanston MA, PhD
Vice-Principal　Prof N. Terry BSc, MSocSci, MPhil
Number of students
4500

University of Dundee

Nethergate, Dundee DD1 4HN; URL www.dundee.ac.uk;
e-mail secretary@dundee.ac.uk; Tel 01382 383000;
Fax 01382 201604
Chancellor　Lord Naren Patel Kt, FMedSci, FRSE
Vice-Chancellor; Principal　Sir Alan Langlands BSc, FRSE
Number of students
Undergraduate: 9395 full-time, 3111 part-time/distance
learning; postgraduate: 1749 full-time, 3628 part-time/
distance learning

Continuing Education

Tower Bldg, Nethergate, Dundee DD1 4HN;
URL www.dundee.ac.uk/learning/conted; e-mail
s.z.norrie@dundee.ac.uk; Tel 01382 384809;
Fax 01382 386713
Community Learning Officer　Jill McKay

School of Education, Social Work and Community Education

Dundee University, Dundee DD1 4HN;
URL www.dundee.ac.uk/eswce; e-mail
educsocwk@dundee.ac.uk; Tel 01382 381400;
Fax 01382 381511
Dean　Prof Elizabeth Leo

Medical Education

Tay Park Hse, 484 Perth Rd, Dundee DD2 1LR;
URL www.dundee.ac.uk/meded; e-mail
c.m.e.courses@dundee.ac.uk; Tel 01382 381952;
Fax 01382 645748
Head　Prof Margery Davis MBChB, MRCP

University of Edinburgh

Adam Ferguson Bldg, School of Social and Political Studies,
40 George Sq, Edinburgh EH8 9LL;
URL www.sps.ed.ac.uk; e-mail ssps@ed.ac.uk;
Tel 0131 650 1000
Chancellor　HRH The Prince Philip, Duke of Edinburgh
KG, KT, PC, OM, GBE, LLD, FRS
Vice-Chancellor; Principal　Prof Timothy O'Shea BSc, PhD
Head (School of Social and Political Studies)
Prof Anthony Good
Vice-Principal; Head of College　Prof V. Bruce
Vice-Principal; Head of College　Prof G. Bulfield
Vice-Principal; Head of College　Prof J. Savill
Number of students
Undergraduate: 16 930 full-time, 697 part-time;
postgraduate: 3186 full-time, 2247 part-time

University of Glasgow

Glasgow G12 8QQ; URL www.gla.ac.uk; Tel 0141 330 2000
Chancellor　Prof Sir Kenneth Colman
Vice-Chancellor; Principal　Sir Muir Russell KCB, FRSE
Secretary (University Court)　David Newall
Academic Secretary　Jan Hulme MA
Number of students
16 000 undergraduate, 4000 postgraduate

Department of Adult and Continuing Education

St Andrews Bldg, 11 Eldon St, Glasgow G3 6NH;
URL www.gla.ac.uk/departments/adulteducation;
e-mail enquiry@ace.gla.ac.uk; Tel 0141 330 1835 ext 394
Head of Department　Dr Martin Cloonan

6

Faculty of Education

St Andrews Bldg, 11 Eldon St, Glasgow G3 6NH;
URL www.gla.ac.uk/faculties/education;
Tel 0141 330 2000
Dean (Education) Prof James Conroy

Glasgow Caledonian University

Cowcaddens Rd, Glasgow G4 0BA;
URL www.caledonian.ac.uk; e-mail helpline@gcal.ac.uk;
Tel 0800 027 9171; Fax 0141 331 3005
Chair (University Court) Martin Cheyne
Principal; Vice-Chancellor Prof Pamela Gillies BSc, PGCE,
MEd, MMedSci, PhD, FRSA, FFPH
Pro Vice-Chancellor (International) Prof G. Galbraith BSc,
PhD, CEng, MCIBSE, MILT
Pro Vice-Chancellor (Learning and Teaching)
Prof Caroline MacDonald BSc, PhD, CBiol, FIBiol, FHEA
Pro Vice-Chancellor (Research) Prof Mike Smith BA, MA
Dean (Caledonian Business School) Dr Ian Robson
Dean (School of Engineering and Computing)
Prof Mike Mannion BSc, PhD, MBCS, CEng, MBA
Dean (School of Health and Social Care) Dr Brian Durward
MSc, PhD, MCSP
Dean (School of Law and Social Sciences)
Prof William Hughes
Dean (School of Life Sciences) Prof Kevin M.A. Gartland
Dean (School of Nursing, Midwifery and Community Health)
Frank Crossan (Acting)
Dean (School of the Built and Natural Environment)
Peter Kennedy MSc, LLM, MCIOB, MCIM
*Executive Director (Business Development and
Commercialisation)* Robert Crawford
Executive Director (Human Resources) Mike Ellis
Director (Marketing and Communications) Alison Steel MSc,
MCIPR
Head (Academic Administration) E.B. Ferguson BSc, DMS
Head (Academic Practice Unit) Prof J.T. Mayes BSc, PhD,
AFBPsS
University Secretary Alison Rooney BSc, MBA
Principal Administrator (Court Office) Lesley McGinley
Number of students
14 961

Heriot-Watt University

Edinburgh EH14 4AS; URL www.hw.ac.uk;
Tel 0131 449 5111; Fax 0131 449 5153
Chancellor Lord James Mackay of Clashfern PC, QC, MA,
LLB, BA, LLD, DUniv, HonFRCSE, HonFRIC
Vice-Chancellor; Principal Prof J.S. Archer FREng, FCGI,
BSc, PhD, DIC, MSPE, FInstE, FIMM, FI
Vice-Principal Prof J.E.L. Simmons FRSE, FIMechE, FIEE,
BSc, PhD
Secretary of the University P.L. Wilson BSc, MA, FRSA,
FIMgt, FIPD
Number of students
4531 undergraduate, 1144 postgraduate

Scottish Borders Campus

Netherdale, Galashiels, Scottish Borders TD1 3HF;
URL www.hw.ac.uk/sbc; e-mail
enquiries@tex.hw.ac.uk; Tel 01896 892133;
Fax 01896 758965
Head (School of Textiles and Design) Prof D.G. Owen
Number of students
600 full-time

Napier University Edinburgh

Craiglockhart Campus, Edinburgh EH14 1DJ;
URL www.napier.ac.uk; e-mail info@napier.ac.uk;
Tel (information office) 0845 260 6040; Fax 0131 455 6464
Principal Prof J. Stringer CBE
Secretary G. Webber BA, MBA, DPhil
Number of students
9775 full-time, 4227 part-time

Queen Margaret University, Edinburgh

Craighall Campus, Edinburgh EH21 6UU;
URL www.qmu.ac.uk; e-mail admissions@qmu.ac.uk;
Tel 0131 317 3000
Vice-Chancellor; Principal Prof Anthony Cohan
Vice-Principal (International Strategy and Commercialisation)
Prof Richard Kerley
Vice-Principal (Learning and Teaching) Prof David Kirk
Vice-Principal (Research Development) Prof Alan Gilloran
Vice-Principal; University Secretary Rosalyn Marshall
Number of students
5421

The Robert Gordon University

Schoolhill, Aberdeen AB10 1FR; URL www.rgu.ac.uk;
e-mail admissions@rgu.ac.uk; Tel 01224 262000;
Fax 01224 263000
Chair (Governors) Dr Allan Bruce
Principal Prof Mike Pittilo
Number of students
7780 full-time, 5529 part-time

University of St Andrews

St Andrews, Fife KY16 9AJ; URL www.st-andrews.ac.uk;
Tel 01334 476161; Fax 01334 462543
Chancellor Sir Menzies Campbell CBE, QC, MP
Vice-Chancellor; Principal Dr Brian Lang MA, PhD
Registrar; Secretary Mr M. Butler
Number of students
5780 undergraduate (2005/06)

Research and Enterprise Services

Director Dr Ewan D. Chirnside BSc, PhD
Associate Director (Life and Environmental Sciences)
Lorna Sillar
Associate Director (Physical and Mathematical Sciences)
Alistair B. Main BSc, MSc, MBA, CEng, MIEE

University of Stirling

Stirling FK9 4LA; URL www.stir.ac.uk; Tel 01786 473171
Chancellor Dame Diana Rigg
Vice-Chancellor; Principal Prof Christine Hallett
University Secretary Kevin J. Clarke
Number of students
6000 undergraduate, 1200 postgraduate

Institute of Education

University of Stirling, Stirling FK9 4LA;
URL www.stir.ac.uk/education; e-mail
h.cameron@stir.ac.uk
Head Peter Cope

University of Strathclyde

Centre for Lifelong Learning

Graham Hills Bldg, 40 George St, Glasgow G1 1QE;
URL www.cll.strath.ac.uk; e-mail learn@cll.strath.ac.uk
Director L.A. Hart MA, MBE, MSc

Royal Scottish Academy of Music and Drama

See Music, Dancing and Drama Colleges

University of the West of Scotland

Paisley Campus, Paisley PA1 2BE; e-mail info@uws.ac.uk;
Tel 0141 848 3000
Principal; Vice Chancellor Prof Seamus McDaid

Wales

Cardiff University

PO Box 921, Cardiff University, Cardiff CF10 3BB;
URL www.cardiff.ac.uk; e-mail
prospectus@cardiff.ac.uk; Tel 02920 874839

prospectus office: Cardiff University, 46 Park Pl, Cardiff CF10 3AT; Tel 02920 874899
Vice-Chancellor   Dr David Grant CBE, PhD, FREng, FIEE
Director (Careers)   Mr N.R. Thomas BA, DipCG
Number of students
25 997 undergraduate and postgraduate
Main qualifications offered
BSc, BSc Econ, LLB, BEng, MEng, BArch, MPharm, MChem, BA, BMus, BTh, MESci, MPhys, BDS, MB, BCH, BMid, BN, DipHE
To obtain a prospectus
Telephone, e-mail or write to the college

School of Social Sciences
Director   Prof H. Beynon BA, DSc

Cardiff Centre for Lifelong Learning
21 Senghenydd Rd, Cardiff CF24 4AG; e-mail learn@cardiff.ac.uk; Tel 02920 870000
Head   Dr Richard Evans

University of Glamorgan

Vice-Chancellor   Prof David Halton BA(Hons), PGCE, MSc, EdD
Number of students
10 722 full-time, 9875 part-time

North East Wales Institute of Higher Education

Plas Coch, Wrexham LL11 2AW; URL www.newi.ac.uk; e-mail sid@newi.ac.uk; Tel 01978 293439; Fax 01978 290008
Principal; Chief Executive   Prof Michael Scott BA, MA, PhD, PGCE FRSA
Faculties/schools/departments
Art and Design; Business; Computing and Communications Technology; Education and Community; Health, Social Care and Exercise Sciences; Humanities; Science and Technology

Royal Welsh College of Music and Drama

See Music, Dancing and Drama Colleges

Swansea Institute of Higher Education

Mount Pleasant, Swansea SA1 6ED; URL www.sihe.ac.uk; e-mail enquiry@sihe.ac.uk; Tel 01792 481000; Fax 01792 481085
Principal; Chief Executive   Prof David Warner
Higher education corporation
Number of students
3300 full-time, 1700 part-time
Faculties/schools/departments
Applied Design and Engineering; Humanities; Art and Design

Trinity College

Carmarthen, Carmarthenshire SA31 3EP; URL www.trinity-cm.ac.uk; e-mail registry@trinity-cm.ac.uk; Tel 01267 676767; Fax 01267 676766
Principal; Clerk to the Governing Body   Medwin Hughes BA, DPhil, FRSA
Vol; Church in Wales; Bilingual
Number of students
2200 day and resident
Faculties
Creative Arts and Humanities; Computing, Business and Tourism; Sport, Health and Outdoor Education; Theatre and Performance; Initial Teacher Education Training; Early Years Education; Education and Social Inclusion; Theology and Religious Studies

University of Wales

University Registry, Cathays Pk, Cardiff CF10 3NS; URL www.wales.ac.uk; e-mail uniwales@wales.ac.uk; Tel 02920 376999; Fax 02920 376984

Vice-Chancellor   R.M. Clement BSc, PhD, CEng, CPhys, FIET
Number of students
103 500 undergraduate and postgraduate

Aberystwyth University

King St, Aberystwyth, Ceredigion SY23 2AX; URL www.aber.ac.uk; e-mail ug-admissions@aber.ac.uk; Tel 01970 623111; Fax 01970 611446
Vice-Chancellor; Principal   Prof Noel Lloyd BSc, PhD
Registrar; Secretary   Catrin Hughes BA, PhD
Senior Adviser (Careers)   E. Harrison
Number of students
7500 undergraduate and postgraduate

Department of Educational and Life-long Learning
Old College, King St, Aberystwyth, Ceredigion SY23 2AX; URL www.aber.ac.uk/sell; Tel 01970 617616
Contact   Prof P. Neil BA, PhD

Bangor University

College Rd, Bangor, Gwynedd LL57 2DG; URL www.bangor.ac.uk; Tel 01248 351151; Fax 01248 370451
Vice-Chancellor   Prof R.M. Jones BA, MA, PhD, FRHistS
Deputy Vice-Chancellor   Prof C.F. Lowe BA, PhD, CPsychol, FBPsS
Pro Vice-Chancellor   Prof C.R. Baker BA, PhD, FBPsS
Pro Vice-Chancellor   Prof J.F. Farrar MA, DPhil
Pro Vice-Chancellor   Prof S. Hope BSc, MPhil
Pro Vice-Chancellor   Prof M. Huws BSc, MSc
Registrar   D.M. Roberts MA, PhD
Head (Centre for Careers and Opportunities)   J. Preece (Acting)
Head (College of Arts and Humanities)   Prof A.M. Claydon BA, PhD (Acting)
Head (College of Business, Social Sciences and Law)   Prof E.P.M. Gardener MSc, PhD, Hon DEcon, FCIS
Head (College of Education and Lifelong Learning)   Dr K.J. Pritchard BSc, PhD
Head (College of Natural Sciences)   Prof S.J. Hawkins BSc, PhD, CBiol
Head (College of Physical and Applied Sciences)   Prof G.J. Ashwell BSc, PhD, DrHabil, FRSC
Head (Health and Behavioural Sciences)   Prof L. Hardy MA, PhD
Number of students
10 130 undergraduate and postgraduate

University of Wales Institute, Cardiff (UWIC)

PO Box 377, Llandaff Campus, Western Ave, Cardiff CF5 2SG; URL www.uwic.ac.uk; e-mail uwicinfo@uwic.ac.uk; Tel 02920 416044; Fax 02920 416286
Vice-Chancellor; Principal   Prof A.J. Chapman BSc, PhD, FBPsS, CPsychol, FRSA
Number of students
Approx. 9000
Faculties/schools/departments
Art and Design; Education; Health Sciences; Management; Sport

University of Wales, Lampeter

Lampeter, Ceredigion SA48 7ED; URL www.lamp.ac.uk; e-mail admissions@lamp.ac.uk
Vice-Chancellor   Prof R.A. Pearce BCL, MA, FRSA
Number of students
9000 undergraduate and postgraduate

Department of Voluntary Sector Studies
Lampeter, Ceredigion SA48 7ED; URL www.volstudy.ac.uk; e-mail enquiries@volstudy.ac.uk; Tel 01570 424785; Fax 01570 423600
Course Director   C. Matera-Rogers

6

University of Wales, Newport

Caerleon Campus, PO Box 179, Newport NP18 3YG;
  URL www.newport.ac.uk; e-mail uic@newport.ac.uk;
  Tel 01633 430088; Tel 01633 432432
Vice Chancellor Prof James R. Lusty
Academic Registrar P. Folan
8000 students
Faculties/schools/departments
Schools of Art, Media and Design; Business and
Management; Community and Lifelong Learning;
Computing and Engineering; Education; Humanities and
Sciences; Social Studies

Swansea University

Singleton Park, Swansea SA2 8PP; URL www.swan.ac.uk;
  e-mail admissions@swansea.ac.uk; Tel 01792 205678

Northern Ireland

Queen's University of Belfast

University Rd, Belfast BT7 1NN; e-mail g.kelly@qub.ac.uk;
  Tel 028 9033 5426; Fax 028 9066 5465
Chancellor Sir David Orr Kt, LLB, HonLLD, HonLLD,
  HonL
Pro-Chancellor Clare Macmahon OBE, BSc, MIBiol
Pro-Chancellor John B. McGuickian BSc(Econ)
Vice-Chancellor Prof George Bain MA(Hons), DPhil,
  HonDBA, HonLLD(NUI)
Pro Vice-Chancellor Prof Malcolm R. Andrew MA, DPhil,
  DLit
Pro Vice-Chancellor Prof Robert J. Cormack MA
Pro Vice-Chancellor Prof Brian W. Hogg BE, DSc(NUI),
  PhD, CEng, EurIng, FIEE, SMIEE
Dean (College of Legal, Social and Educational Sciences)
  K. Brown BA, MA, PhD, FRHistS
Director (Institute of Continuing Education)
  M.P. Patten (Acting) OBE
Director (Physical Education Centre) Maureen Cusdin MSc
Registrar John Tain
Bursar J.P.J. O'Kane BA(CNAA), CIPFA
Secretary to Academic Council Prof R.J. Cormack (Acting)
Administrative Secretary D.H. Wilson BSc, DipEd, JP
Number of students
10 822 undergraduate, 4621 postgraduate

St Mary's University College – a College of the Queen's University of Belfast

191 Falls Rd, Belfast BT12 6FE; URL www.smucb.ac.uk;
  e-mail admis@smucb.ac.uk; Tel 028 9032 7678;
  Fax 028 9033 3719
Number of students
1090
Main qualifications offered
BEd, BA, postgraduate courses

Stranmillis University College

Stranmillis Rd, Belfast BT9 5DY; URL www.stran.ac.uk;
  e-mail registry@stran.ac.uk; Tel 028 9038 4263
Principal A. Measlett BA, MA, DPhil, MSc, FRSA
Vice-Principal; Registrar Mae Watson MBE, BA, MSc,
  FRSA, MIMgt
University College of Education; a college of Queen's
University Belfast
Number of students
Approx. 1000 full-time undergraduate

University of Ulster

Cromore Rd, Coleraine, Co. Londonderry BT52 1SA;
  Tel 0870 040 0700
Chancellor Sir Richard Nichols DCL, LLD

Pro-Chancellor Dr G. Burns MBE, DUniv BSc, FRSA
Pro-Chancellor Prof R.A.J. Spence OBE, MA, MD, FRCS, JP
Vice-Chancellor Prof R. Barnett BSc, PhD
*Pro Vice-Chancellor (Academic Development and Student
  Services)* Prof N. Black BSc, PhD, FRSM, MIEE, MIEEE
*Pro Vice-Chancellor (Communication and Institutional
  Development); Provost (Magee Campus)* Prof J.M. Allen
  BSc, PhD, CBiol, FIBiol
Pro Vice-Chancellor (Research and Innovation)
  Prof B. Hannigan BA(Mod), PhD, FIBMS
Pro Vice-Chancellor (Teaching and Learning)
  Prof D. McAlister BSc, MSc, DipHealthEcon
Hon Treasurer Mr G.D.B. Harkness MA, FCA
Provost (Coleraine Campus) Prof A. Sharp BA, PhD,
  FRHistS
Provost (Jordanstown and Belfast campus) Prof W. Clarke
  BSc, MSc, MCIM, FCIM
Director (Communication and Development)
  Ms N.E.R. Taggart
Director (Corporate Planning and Governance) Ms I.I. Aston
Director (Finance) Mr P. Hope BA, MBA, FCA
Director (Human Resources) Mr R. Magee BA, PGDipPM,
  MCIPD
Director (Information Services) Mr N. Macartney BA, MA,
  DipLib, CertEd
Director (Physical Resources) Mr P.P.G. Donnelly DipQs,
  MRICS, MBIFM
Number of students
More than 23 000

Vocational and Adult Education Organisations and Associations

Adult Residential Colleges Association (ARCA)

6 Bath Rd, Felixstowe, Suffolk IP11 7JW;
  URL www.arca.uk.net; e-mail arcasec@aol.com;
  Tel 01394 278161; Fax 01394 271083
Hon Secretary Janet Dann
The aim of the association is to promote and disseminate
knowledge of the working of the short-term residential
colleges, its primary objective being to provide short-term,
residential, liberal adult education

Amicus – MSF/WEA

3 Acton Sq, The Crescent, Salford, Greater Manchester
  M5 4NY; Tel 0161 745 7300
Contact Michael Payne
Recognised union for staff who work for the Workers'
Educational Association

Association of Business Schools (ABS)

137 Euston Rd, London NW1 2AA;
  URL www.the-abs.org.uk; e-mail abs@the-abs.org.uk;
  Tel 020 7388 0007; Fax 020 7388 0009
Represents all of the major providers of business and
management education across universities and colleges.
ABS aims to advance the education of the public in business
and management, in particular through the promotion of
business and management education, training and
development, so as to improve the quality and effectiveness
of the practice of management in the UK.

The Basic Skills Agency

Commonwealth Hse, 1–19 New Oxford St, London
  WC1A 1NU; URL www.basic-skills.co.uk; e-mail
  enquiries@basic-skills.co.uk; Tel 020 7405 4017;
  Fax 020 7440 6626
Director A. Wells OBE

ContinYou

Unit C1, Grovelands Ct, Grovelands Est, Longford Rd,
  Coventry, Warwickshire CV7 9NE;
  URL www.continyou.org.uk; e-mail
  info@continyou.org.uk; Tel (switchboard) 024 7658 8440;
  Fax 024 7658 8441
Chief Executive   Laurence Blackhall
Chair (Trustees)   Ian Caulfield
ContinYou is the national centre for community-based
learning. It is a charitable trust, which aims to promote a
fairer distribution of learning opportunities, particularly to
those who have benefited least from education. ContinYou
works in the fields of education, health improvement and
economic and community development; provides training
and consultancy, manages projects and produces and
disseminates publications; and runs various subscription
services through which it provides services to thousands of
schools throughout the country.

Educational Centres Association

21 Ebbisham Dr, Norwich, Norfolk NR4 6HQ;
  URL www.e-c-a.ac.uk; e-mail info@e-c-a.ac.uk;
  Tel 0870 161 0302; Fax 01603 469292
Chair   Bernard Godding

The Essentia Group

Lower Ground, Skypark, 72 Finnieston Sq, Glasgow G3 8ET;
  URL www.essentiagroup.com; Tel 0141 568 4000;
  Fax 0141 568 4001
Provides information services by way of telephone
counselling and data processing and analysis. National
helplines in the public information/health sector.

Financial Times Management

Portland Tower, Portland St, Manchester M1 3LD;
  Tel 0161 245 3300; Fax 0161 245 3367
Managing Director   John Trasler
Manager (Marketing)   Nina Clifton

Learning and Skills Network

Regent Arcade Hse, 19–25 Argyll St, London W1F 7LS;
  URL www.lsneducation.org.uk; Tel 020 7297 9000;
  Fax 020 7297 9001
Chief Executive   John Stone
Director (Business Development)   Stephen Bartle
Director (Operations)   Jill Lanning
Manager (Business Development)   Frank Villeneuve-
  Smith;   media enquiries
The Learning and Skills Network (LSN) is one of two
successor organisations formed out of the Learning and
Skills Development Agency (LSDA); the other is the Quality
and Improvement Agency for Lifelong Learning (QIA). LSN
continues the work of LSDA in delivery of support
programmes, research, training , consultancy and other
support services for the education sector. LSN bids for
contracts to provide services for the sector, for the QIA and
for other agencies, and provides services directly to
organisations involved in education and training.

**Learning and Skills Development Agency for Northern
Ireland**
19–21 Alfred St, Belfast BT2 8ED; URL www.lsda.org.uk/ni
Director   Trevor Carson

NIACE (National Institute of Adult Continuing Education)

For information on the NIACE journals: Adults Learning,
Concept – The Journal of Contemporary Community
Education Practice Theory, Journal of Access Policy and
Practice, Journal of Adult and Continuing Education, and
Studies in the Education of Adults; see Chapter 18:
Education Journals

Registered Charity Number 1002775; Registered Company
Number 2603322
21 De Montfort St, Leicester LE1 7GE;
  URL www.niace.org.uk; e-mail
  information@niace.org.uk; Tel 0116 204 4200;
  Fax 0116 285 4514
President   Christine King
Director   Alan Tuckett
NIACE is a national centre for research and information on
all forms of adult continuing education. Its governing
council has representatives of Local Education Authorities
(appointed by the LGA, and Welsh Joint Education
Committee), the universities, colleges, armed forces, Home
Office, the BBC, and numerous national voluntary bodies.
The Department for Children, Schools and Families
appoints assessors. The membership comprises national
bodies promoting all forms of adult education, and there are
provisions for corporate and individual membership.
NIACE also carries out enquiries, publishes journals,
maintains a library and information centre and organises
conferences. Other regulars include the Year Book of Adult
Learning (January). NIACE promotes public awareness of
study opportunities by organising Adult Learners' Week
each year.

6

Northern Ireland Adult Education Association (NIAEA)

c/o 42 Northland Rd, Londonderry, County Londonderry
  BT48 7ND; Tel 028 7126 5007
Chair   M. Maginn
Vice-Chair   P. Patten
Secretary   M. Baumann
Treasurer   E. Kelly

Scottish Qualifications Authority

Optima, 58 Robertson, Glasgow G2 8DQ;
  URL www.sqa.org.uk; e-mail customer@sqa.org.uk;
  Tel 0845 279 1000
The Scottish Qualifications Authority (SQA) is Scotland's
national body for qualifications. It is responsible for the
development, assessment, quality assurance and
certification of all qualifications except degrees and some
professional qualifications.
National Qualifications which include Standard Grade,
Access, Intermediate 1, Intermediate 2, Higher and
Advanced Higher are taken at school and/or college.
National Courses and Group Awards are made up of groups
of National Units. Higher National Certificates (HNCs) and
Higher National Diplomas (HNDs) have been developed in
partnership with colleges, universities and industry. Made
up of Higher National units, these qualifications are
delivered within colleges. Scottish Vocational Qualifications
(SVQs) are flexible, work-based qualifications. Made up of
SVQ units, they are designed to prove competence at a
particular job.

Workers' Educational Association

Registered Charity Number 1112775; a company limited by
guarantee and registered in England number 2806910
3rd Fl, 70 Clifton St, London EC2A 4HB;
  URL www.wea.org.uk; e-mail national@wea.org.uk;
  Tel 020 7426 3450; Fax 020 7426 3451
President   Colin Barnes
General Secretary   Richard Bolsin
The Workers' Educational Association (WEA) is the largest
voluntary sector provider of adult education in Britain and
provides learning opportunities for more than 95 000 people
each year. It operates in all nine English regions and in
Scotland, and it employs more than 3000 part-time tutors.
The WEA creates and delivers courses in response to local
need, often in partnership with community groups, local
charities and other organisations. The WEA believes that
education is lifelong and should continue beyond school,
college and university, in order to help people develop their
full potential.

REGIONAL SECRETARIES

Eastern
Regional Director　Carolyn Daines; Cintra Hse, 12 Hills Rd, Cambridge, Cambridgeshire CB2 1JP; e-mail eastern@wea.org.uk; Tel 01223 350978; Fax 01223 300911

East Midlands
Regional Director　Mike Attwell; 39 Mapperley Rd, Mapperley Pk, Nottingham, Nottinghamshire NG3 5AQ; e-mail eastmidlands@wea.org.uk; Tel 0115 962 8400; Fax 0115 962 8401

London
Regional Director　Soraya Patrick; 4 Luke St, London EC2A 4XW; e-mail london@wea.org.uk; Tel 020 7426 1950; Fax 020 7383 5668

North East
Regional Director　Nigel Todd; 1st Fl, Unit 6, Metro Riverside Business Pk, Delta Bank Rd, Gateshead, Tyne and Wear NE11 9DJ; e-mail northeast@wea.org.uk; Tel 0191 461 8100; Fax 0191 461 8117

North West
Regional Director　Greg Coyne; The Cotton Exchange Bldg, Suite 405, Old Hall St, Liverpool, Merseyside L3 9JR; e-mail northwest@wea.org.uk; Tel 0151 243 5340; Fax 0151 243 5359

Southern
Regional Director　John Williams; Unit 57, Riverside 2, Sir Thomas Longley Rd, Rochester, Kent ME2 4DP; e-mail southern@wea.org.uk; Tel 01634 298600; Fax 01634 298601

South West
Bradninch Ct, Castle St, Exeter, Devon EX4 3PL; e-mail southwest@wea.org.uk; Tel 01392 490970; Fax 01392 474330
Regional Director　Steve Martin

West Midlands
Regional Director　Peter Caldwell; 4th Fl, Lancaster Hse, 67 Newhall St, Birmingham, West Midlands B3 1NQ; e-mail westmidlands@wea.org.uk; Tel 0121 237 8120; Fax 0121 237 8121

Yorkshire and Humber
Regional Director　Ann Walker; 6 Woodhouse Sq, Leeds, West Yorkshire LS3 1AD; e-mail yorkshumber@wea.org.uk; Tel 0113 245 3304; Fax 0113 245 0883

WEA Scotland
Scottish Secretary　Joyce Connon; Riddle's Ct, 322 Lawnmarket, Edinburgh EH1 2PG; e-mail hq@weascotland.org.uk; Tel 0131 226 3456; Fax 0131 220 0306

World ORT
ORT Hse, 126 Albert St, London NW1 7NE; URL www.ort.org; e-mail wo@ort.org; Tel 020 7446 8500; Fax 020 7446 8650
Director General　Robert Singer
Independent, technological education and training organisation with schools, colleges and teacher training and resource centres worldwide.

Adult Colleges

University of Birmingham, Selly Oak Campus
Elmfield Hse, Birmingham, West Midlands B29 6LQ; Tel 0121 415 2286; Fax 0121 415 2296
Course Director　Ralph Thomas BA(Hons), MA, DipAppSocSt

Diploma in Social Work, for both non-graduates and graduates (2 years), 3rd year leading to BA(Hons) Applied Social Sciences. Development Studies, training courses for experienced field workers and headquarters' staff of voluntary aid agencies and church development organisations from different countries. NVQ 4 in Care for workers in Social Work/Social Care.

Ruskin College
Walton St, Oxford, Oxfordshire OX1 2HE; URL www.ruskin.ac.uk; e-mail enquiries@ruskin.ac.uk; Tel 01865 554331; Fax 01865 554372
Principal　Prof Audrey Mullender
Academic Co-ordinator　Teresa Munty
Number of students
130

Sutton College of Learning for Adults
St Nicholas Way, Sutton, Surrey SM1 1EA; URL www.scola.ac.uk; e-mail reception@scola.ac.uk; Tel 020 8770 6901; Fax 020 8770 6933
Principal　Chris Jones MA, MCIM
Director (Administration)　Cherry Yates
An adult college offering both vocational and non-vocational courses. The college incorporates seven evening and two daytime centres as well as the main centre for both day and evening courses. There are music practice rooms for hire housed in the purpose-built headquarters building.
To obtain a prospectus
Telephone or e-mail the college

English Language Schools

Key
*	Includes a course of English for foreign students
†	Recognised by the British Council English Language Schools Programme
‡	Accredited by the Open and Distance Learning Quality Council
§	Accredited by the British Accreditation Council for Independent Further and Higher Education

British Council – Accreditation UK
British Council, Bridgewater Hse, 58 Whitworth St, Manchester M1 6BB; URL www.britishcouncil.org/accreditation; e-mail accreditation.unit@britishcouncil.org; Tel 0161 957 7692; Fax 0161 957 7074
Profile
Accreditation UK was established in succession to an earlier scheme run by the Department of Education and Science. It is a voluntary quality assurance scheme, administered by the British Council in partnership with English UK and is open to all educational organisations offering courses in English language in the UK. At present more than 420 organisations are accredited.
Aims and Objectives
Accreditation UK monitors and improves standards in English language teaching in the UK, in the interest of overseas students, of the proprietors and staff of accredited schools, and in the national interest.
Organisations undergo a rigorous inspection under the four headings: Management; Resources and Environment; Teaching and Learning; Welfare and Student Services. Details of the criteria are set out in the handbook of the scheme, available on the website. Accreditation UK has been approved to accredit private educational organisations so they can apply to be on the Home Office sponsors' register (necessary for student visas from 2009).
Procedures
Organisations are inspected once every four years by independent British Council inspectors. In addition to the

regular inspections, spot checks may be carried out at any time, without prior warning to the provider, to ensure that standards are maintained. There is also a student complaints procedure – details are on the website.

East of England

Aspect College Cambridge *†
75 Barton Rd, Cambridge, Cambridgeshire CB3 9LJ;
    URL www.aspectworld.com; e-mail
    rebecca.andreo@aspectworld.com; Tel 01223 357702;
    Fax 01223 311939
Principal   Isabel Ribeiro
Director (Studies)   Stu Proudfoot
    Number of students: 150

Bell Cambridge *†
1 Red Cross La, Cambridge, Cambridgeshire CB2 2QX;
    URL www.bell-centres.com; e-mail
    info.cambridge@bell-centres.com; Tel 01223 278800;
    Fax 01223 412410

Bell Central Registration Department *†
Hillscross, Red Cross La, Cambridge, Cambridgeshire
    CB2 2QX; URL www.bell-centres.com; e-mail
    info@bell-centres.com; Tel 01223 212333;
    Fax 01223 410282
Senior Registrar   Vacancy
    Residential

Bell International *†
Bowthorpe Hall, Bowthorpe, Norwich, Norfolk NR5 9AA;
    URL www.bell-centres.com; www.bell-centres.com/
    norwich; e-mail info.norwich@bell-centres.com;
    Tel 01603 745615; Fax 01603 747669
Centre Manager   Philip Goddard
    Number of students: 150

Bell Young Learners *†
Lancaster Hse, South Rd, Saffron Walden, Essex CB11 3DP;
    URL www.bell-centres.com/younglearners; e-mail
    info.yl@bell-centres.com; Tel 01799 527511;
    Fax 01799 527499
Contact   Hannah Moore
    8–17; Residential, day; Number of students: 200

Cambridge Academy of English *†
65 High St, Girton, Cambridge, Cambridgeshire CB3 0QD;
    URL www.cambridgeacademy.co.uk; e-mail
    cae@cambridgeacademy.co.uk; Tel 01223 277230;
    Fax 01223 277606
Principal   John Barnett BA(Hons), Cert TEFL, ADELTM
    Number of students: 70–90 (Winter), 130–160 (Summer)

Cambridge Centre for Languages (CCL) *†
Sawston Hall, Sawston, Cambridge, Cambridgeshire
    CB2 4JR; URL www.camlang.co.uk; e-mail
    ar70@dial.pipex.com; Tel 01223 835099; Fax 01223 837424
Contact   Mrs R. Muir
    Residential; Number of students: 160

Colchester English Study Centre *†
19 Lexden Rd, Colchester, Essex CO3 3PW;
    URL www.cesc.co.uk; e-mail info@cesc.co.uk;
    Tel 01206 544422; Fax 01206 761849
Contact   Sarah Greatorex
    Number of students: 280

EF International School of English *†
221 Hills Rd, Cambridge, Cambridgeshire CB2 2RW;
    URL www.ef.com; e-mail alan.wilson@ef.com;
    Tel 01223 240020; Fax 01223 412474
Principal   Alan Wilson MA, PGCE, DTEFLA

Embassy CES Newnham *†
8 Grange Rd, Cambridge, Cambridgeshire CB3 9DU;
    URL www.studygroupintl.com; e-mail
    cambridge@embassyces.com; Tel 01223 311344;
    Fax 01223 461411
Contact   David Rouson
    Number of students: 140

Eurocentres Cambridge *†
62 Bateman St, Cambridge, Cambridgeshire CB2 1LR;
    URL www.eurocentres.com; e-mail
    cam-info@eurocentres.com; Tel 01223 353607;
    Fax 01223 368531
Centre Manager   Lorraine Smith
    Number of students: 225

International Language Academy *†
12–13 Regent Terr, Cambridge, Cambridgeshire CB2 1AA;
    e-mail admissions@ilacambridge.com; Tel 01223 350519;
    Fax 01223 464730
Contact   J. Bloomfield

Language Studies International *†
41 Tenison Rd, Cambridge, Cambridgeshire CB1 2DG;
    URL www.lsi.edu; e-mail cam@lsi.edu; Tel 01223 361783;
    Fax 01223 467725
Registrar   Alison Bingham

Regent Language Training Ltd *†
119 Mill Rd, Cambridge, Cambridgeshire CB1 2AZ;
    URL www.regent.org.uk; e-mail
    cambridge@regent.org.uk; Tel 01223 312333;
    Fax 01223 323257
Manager (Administration)   Simon Gray

London

Academy International *†
3 Queen's Gdns, London W2 3BA;
    URL www.central-london-english.co.uk; e-mail
    info@central-london-english.co.uk; Tel 020 7262 6982;
    Fax 020 7262 0854
Contact   John Murphy

Anglo European Study Tours Ltd *†
8 Celbridge Mews, London W2 6EU;
    URL www.plus-ed.com; e-mail plus@plus-ed.com;
    Tel 020 7229 4435; Fax 020 7792 8717

Bell Language School *†
34 Fitzroy Sq, London W1T 6BP;
    URL www.bell-centres.com; e-mail
    info.london@bell-centres.com; Tel 020 7637 8338;
    Fax 020 7637 4811
Centre Manager   Victoria Martin
Office Manager   Maggie Linfeld
    Number of students: 130

Cambridge School of English *†
7–11 Stukeley St, London WC2B 5LT; e-mail
    info@cambridgeschool.co.uk; Tel 020 7242 3787;
    Fax 020 7242 3626
Contact   René Durand
    Number of students: 150

The Canning School *
10 Knaresborough Pl, London SW5 0TG;
    URL www.canning.com; Tel 020 7370 1055
Contact (Partner)   R.R. Pooley

Central School of English *†
1 Tottenham Court Rd, London W1T 1BB; e-mail
    enquiry@centralschool.co.uk; Tel 020 7580 2863;
    Fax 020 7255 1806
School Director   G. Mitchell
    Number of students: 200

6

Ebury Executive English *†
132 Ebury St, London SW1W 9QQ; e-mail eburyee@aol.com;
   Tel 020 7730 3991; Fax 020 7730 1794

EF International School of English *†
74 Roupell St, London SE1 8SS; URL www.ef.com;
   Tel 020 7401 8399; Fax 020 7401 3717
School Director   Nick Stratford

ELS Language Centres *†
3–5 Charing Cross Rd, London WC2H 0QX; e-mail
   info@els-london.com; Tel 020 7976 1066;
   Fax 020 7976 1055
Managing Director   Rupert Johnstone

English and Cultural Studies Centres (ESC) †
40 Village Rd, Enfield, Greater London EN1 2EN;
   Tel 020 8360 4118

Eurocentres Lee Green *†
21 Meadowcourt Rd, Lee Green, London SE3 9EU;
   URL www.eurocentres.com; e-mail
   lee-info@eurocentres.com; Tel 020 8318 5633
Contact   D. Barrett
   Residential; Number of students: 360

Eurocentres London Central *†
56 Eccleston Sq, London SW1V 1PH;
   URL www.eurocentres.com; e-mail
   vic-info@eurocentres.com; Tel 020 7834 4155;
   Fax 020 7834 1866
Centre Manager   Simon Rickets
   Number of students: 252

Frances King School of English *†
77 Gloucester Rd, London SW6 6SS;
   URL www.francesking.co.uk; e-mail
   info@francesking.co.uk; Tel 020 7870 6533;
   Fax 020 7341 9771

GEOS English Academy *†§
16–20 New Broadway, London W5 2XA;
   URL www.geos-london.co.uk; e-mail
   info@geos-london.co.uk; Tel 020 8566 2188;
   Fax 020 8566 2011
Principal   Jane Flynn
   Residential, day

Hampstead School of English *†
553 Finchley Rd, London NW3 7BJ; e-mail
   info@hampstead-english.ac.uk; Tel 020 7794 3533;
   Fax 020 7431 2987
Principal   Kevin McNally

International House *†
16 Stukeley St, London WC2B 5LQ;
   URL www.ihlondon.com; e-mail info@ihlondon.co.uk;
   Tel 020 7611 2400; Fax 020 7117 4177
Contact   Steve Brent BA(Hons), MA, RSA Dip, TEFL
   Number of students: 600

International Language Academy London *†
457–463 Caledonian Rd, London N7 9BA;
   URL www.language-academics.com; e-mail
   ilalond@mplc.co.uk; Tel 020 7700 6438; Fax 020 7607 5783
Principal   Neil Harvey
   Number of students: 80

Language Link London Ltd *†
21 Harrington Rd, South Kensington, London SW7 3EU;
   URL www.languagelink.co.uk; e-mail
   info@languagelink.co.uk; Tel 020 7225 1065;
   Fax 020 7584 3518

Language Studies International
19–21 Ridgmount St, London WC1E 7AH;
   URL www.lsi.edu; e-mail lon@lsi.edu; Tel 020 7467 6500;
   Fax 020 7323 1736
Registrar   Jacqueline McGee

Language Studies International, London Hampstead *†
Heath Hse, 13 Lyndhurst Terr, London NW3 5QA;
   URL www.lsi.edu/en/hampstead.html; e-mail
   ham@lsi.edu/en/hampstead.html; Tel 020 7794 8111;
   Fax 020 7431 5681
Principal   Tania Kyriakides
General English, business English and exam preparation
courses are available with flexible course lengths. Call to
arrange a free trial lesson.

Lansdowne International College Ltd *
9 Palace Gate, Kensington, London W8 5LS;
   Tel 020 7581 9485
Principal   Paul W. Templeton BSc(Econ)
   Residential; Number of students: 2000

Leicester Square School of English *†
22 Leicester Sq, London WC2H 7LE; URL www.lsse.ac.uk;
   e-mail info@lsse.ac.uk; Tel 020 7839 7772;
   Fax 020 7839 2377
Manager (Marketing)   Emma Carter

Linguarama Ltd *†
New London Bridge Hse, 25 London Bridge St, London
   SE1 9SG; URL www.linguarama.com; e-mail
   london@linguarama.com; Tel 020 7939 3200
Contact   Amanda Summers

London School of English *†
15 Holland Park Gdns, London W14 8DZ;
   URL www.londonschool.com; e-mail
   office@londonschool.com; Tel 020 7605 4123;
   Fax 020 7605 4190
Managing Director   Timothy Blake
   Number of students: 200

London Study Centre *†
Munster Hse, 676 Fulham Rd, London SW6 5SA; e-mail
   106153.2344@compuserve.com; Tel 020 7731 3549;
   Fax 020 7731 6060
Contact   Colin D. Gordon MA(Hons)
   Number of students: 850

Mayfair School of English *†
61–65 Oxford St, London W1D 2EL;
   URL www.mayfairschool.co.uk; e-mail
   enquiries@mayfairschool.co.uk; Tel 020 7437 9941;
   Fax 020 7494 3611

Oxford House College *
28 Market Pl, London W1W 8AW;
   URL www.oxfordhousecollege.co.uk; e-mail
   english@oxfordhouse.co.uk; Tel 020 7580 9785
Principal   Fiona Balloch
   Number of students: 500

Poly-Contact Education and Training *
Barley Mow Centre, 10 Barley Mow Passage, London
   W4 4PH; e-mail enquiries@polycontact.co.uk;
   Tel 020 8944 6477
Contact   M. Webb
   Disabled clients especially welcome; Residential

Regent London English Language Training *†
12 Buckingham St, London WC2N 6DF;
   URL www.regent.org.uk; e-mail london@regent.org.uk;
   Tel 020 7872 6660; Fax 020 7872 6630
Principal   Clare Hewitt
   Number of students: 120

St Giles College *†
51 Shepherds Hill, Highgate, London N6 5QP;
   URL www.stgiles-international.com; e-mail
   londonhighgate@stgiles.co.uk; Tel 020 8340 0828;
   Fax 020 8348 9389
Principal   K. Harding MA, DPhil, RSA, DipTEFLA

St John's Wood School of English *†
126 Boundary Rd, London NW8 0RH;
    URL www.sjw-school.co.uk; e-mail
    sjw-school@dial.pipex.com; Tel 020 7624 1925;
    Fax 020 7328 6877
Contact   P. Bulmer

St Patrick's International College *†
24 Gt Chapel St, London W1F 8FS; e-mail
    info@st-patricks.ac.uk; Tel 020 7287 6664;
    Fax 020 7287 6282
Registrar   E. Hardy
    Number of students: 500–1000

Select English *†
144 Church Rd, London SE19 2NT;
    URL www.selectenglish.com; e-mail
    londonenquiries@selectenglish.co.uk; Tel 020 8653 7285;
    Fax 020 8653 9667
Contact   S. Mann BA, DELTA
    Residential; Number of students: 120

SELS College, School of English *
64–65 Long Acre, Covent Gdn, London WC2E 9SX;
    URL www.sels.co.uk; e-mail english@sels.co.uk;
    Tel 020 7240 2581; Fax 020 7379 5793
    Number of students: 120

Shane Global London Central *†
59 South Molton St, London W1K 5SN; e-mail
    londoncentral@shaneglobal.com; Tel 020 7499 8533;
    Fax 020 7499 9374

Skola International Community School London *
12 Porchester Pl, London W2 2BS; URL www.skola.co.uk;
    e-mail ics@skola.co.uk; Tel 020 7298 8877;
    Fax 020 7706 8171
Principal   Kasha Borthwick
    Number of students: 125 (average), 150 (maximum)

Stanton School of English *†
Stanton Hse, 167 Queensway, London W2 4SB; e-mail
    study@stanton-school.co.uk; Tel 020 7221 7259;
    Fax 020 7792 9047
Principal   D.A. Garrett MA

Victoria School of English *†
28 Graham Terr, London SW1W 8JH;
    URL www.victoriaschool.co.uk; e-mail
    ft@victoria-school.co.uk; Tel 020 7730 1333;
    Fax 020 7823 4175
Principal   Jon Hooton
Director   Lotte Hooton DipRSA
    16+; Number of students: 40 (all year), 70 (in summer)

The Wimbledon School of English *†
41 Worple Rd, Wimbledon, London SW19 4JZ;
    URL www.wimbledon-school.ac.uk; e-mail
    principal@wimbledon-school.ac.uk; Tel 020 8947 1921;
    Fax 020 8944 0275
Principal   Jane Dancaster
    Number of students: 180

North East

Durham Language Services *†
14–18 Stowell St, Newcastle upon Tyne, Tyne and Wear
    NE1 4XQ; e-mail ihnew@compuserve.com;
    Tel 0191 232 9551; Fax 0191 232 1126
    Residential; Number of students: 120 (maximum)

International House, Newcastle *†
14–18 Stowell St, Newcastle upon Tyne, Tyne and Wear
    NE1 4XQ; URL www.ihnewcastle.com; e-mail
    info@ihnewcastle.com; Tel 0191 232 9551;
    Fax 0191 232 1126
Principal   G. Mitchell
    Residential, day

North West

Eaton Language Centre Ltd *†
32 York Rd, Sale, Manchester M33 6UU;
    URL www.eaton-languages.co.uk; e-mail
    english@eaton-languages.co.uk; Tel 0161 962 3105;
    Fax 0161 905 2476

English in Chester *†
9–11 Stanley Pl, Chester, Cheshire CH1 2LU;
    URL www.english-in-chester.co.uk; e-mail
    study@english-in-chester.co.uk; Tel 01244 318913;
    Fax 01244 320091
Principal   R.J. Day
    Number of students: 180

Inlingua College Courses *
12 Meadowgate, Urmston, Manchester M41 9LB; e-mail
    inlingua.opt@dial.pipex.com; Tel 0161 748 2621
Principal   D.A. Willey
    Residential

Nord Anglia Education Plc
Centrum Point, Third Ave, Centrum 100, Burton upon
    Trent, Staffordshire DE4 2WD; e-mail
    enquiries@nordanglia.com; Tel 0845 225 3030;
    Fax 0845 225 3031
Nurseries, international schools and learning services

South East

Buckswood School *†
Guestling, Hastings, East Sussex TN35 4LT;
    URL www.buckswood.co.uk; e-mail
    achieve@buckswood.co.uk; Tel 01424 813813;
    Fax 01424 812100
    Residential, day

CES Swandean School of English *†
12 Stoke Abbott Rd, Worthing, West Sussex BN11 1HE;
    e-mail worthing@ces-schools.com; Tel 01903 231330;
    Fax 01903 200953
Principal   M. Quinn
    Number of students: 100 (term), 350 (summer),

Chichester School of English *†
45 East St, Chichester, West Sussex PO19 1HX;
    Tel 01243 789893; 01239 781768; Fax 01243 531378
Contact   A.S. Robertson

Churchill House School of English *†
Spencer Sq, Ramsgate, Kent CT11 9EQ;
    URL www.churchillhouse.co.uk; e-mail
    welcome@churchillhouse.co.uk; Tel 01843 586833;
    Fax 01843 584827
Contact   David Leigh

Cicero Languages International *†
42 Upper Grosvenor Rd, Tunbridge Wells, Kent TN1 2ET;
    e-mail info@cicero.co.uk; Tel 01892 547077;
    Fax 01892 522749
Principal   Christopher Hills
    Residential (family accommodation arranged); Number
    of students: Approx. 40

Concorde International Summer Schools *†
Arnett Hse, Hawks La, Canterbury, Kent CT1 2NU;
    URL www.concorde-international.com; e-mail
    info@concorde-int.com; Tel 01227 451035;
    Fax 01227 762760
    Residential

The East Sussex School of English *†
92 Portland Rd, Hove, East Sussex BN3 5DN;
    Tel 01273 736404

6

Eastbourne School of English *†
8 Trinity Trees, Eastbourne, East Sussex BN21 3LD;
  URL www.esoe.co.uk; e-mail english@esoe.co.uk;
  Tel 01323 721759; Fax 01323 639271
Principal   Graham White
  Number of students: 120

EC Brighton *†
24 Portland Pl, East Sussex BN2 1DH;
  URL www.ecenglish.com; e-mail
  brighton@ecenglish.com; Tel 01273 694618;
  Fax 01273 674775
Principal   J. Camilleri

Eckersley Oxford *†
14 Friars Entry, Oxford, Oxfordshire OX1 2BZ;
  URL www.eckersley.co.uk; e-mail
  english@eckersley.co.uk; Tel 01865 721268;
  Fax 01865 791869
Principal   J.M. Eckersley MA
  Residential; Number of students: 50–80

EF International School of English †
74–80 Warrior Sq, St Leonards-on-Sea, Hastings, East Sussex
  TN37 6BP; Tel 01424 423998

EF International School of English *†
1–2 Sussex Sq, Kempton, Brighton, East Sussex BN2 1FJ;
  Tel 01273 571780; Fax 01273 691232
Contact   Dermot A. Tobin BA(Hons), Dip(TEFL)RSA
  Number of students: 900

The Elizabeth Johnson Organisation Ltd *†
Eagle Hse, Lynchborough Rd, Passfield, Hampshire
  GU30 7SB; URL www.ejo.co.uk; e-mail
  programmes@ejo.co.uk; Tel 01428 751933;
  Fax 01428 751944

ELT Banbury †
49 Oxford Rd, Banbury, Oxfordshire; Tel 01295 263480;
  Tel 01295 263502
Contact   Dr T.J. Gerighty

Embassy CES *†
Palace Ct, White Rock, Hastings, East Sussex TN34 1JY;
  URL www.embassyces.com; e-mail
  rveale@studygroup.com; Tel 01424 720100
Principal   Reginald Veale BA, DipTEFL, MA
  Average class size: 15

The English Language Centre *†
33 Palmeira Mansions, Hove, East Sussex BN3 2GB;
  URL www.elc-brighton.co.uk; e-mail
  info@elc-brighton.co.uk; Tel 01273 721771;
  Fax 01273 720898
Contact   C.N. Harrison FCA
  Number of students: 500

Eurocentres Brighton *†
Huntingdon Hse, 20 North St, Brighton, East Sussex
  BN1 1EB; URL www.eurocentres.com; e-mail
  bri-info@eurocentres.com; Tel 01273 324545;
  Fax 01273 746013
Manager (Centre)   Sara Bailey

GEOS – LTC International College *†
Compton Pk, Compton Place Rd, Eastbourne, East Sussex
  BN21 1EH; URL www.geos-ltc.com; e-mail
  info@geos-ltc.com; Tel 01323 727755; Fax 01323 728279
Principal   Paul Clark MA, DipRSA, MA, TESOL
  Residential; Number of students: 275

GEOS English Academy *†
55–61 Portland Rd, East Sussex BN3 5DQ;
  URL www.geos-brighton.com; e-mail
  info@geos-brighton.com; Tel 01273 735975;
  Fax 01273 732884
Principal   Paul Clark
  Number of students: 150

Greylands School of English *†
315 Portswood Rd, Southampton SO17 2LD;
  URL www.greylands.co.uk; e-mail
  info@greylands.co.uk; Tel 02380 315180;
  Fax 02380 586684
  18+; Residential

Harven School of English *†
Coley Ave, Woking, Surrey GU22 7BT;
  URL www.harven.co.uk; e-mail info@harven.co.uk;
  Tel 01483 770969; Fax 01483 740267
Principal   Joanne Clements

Hastings English Language Centre *†
St Helens Park Rd, Hastings, East Sussex TN34 2JW;
  URL www.helc.co.uk; e-mail english@helc.co.uk;
  Tel 01424 437048; Fax 01424 716442

Kaplan Aspect Oxford *†
108 Banbury Rd, Oxford, Oxfordshire OX2 6JU;
  URL www.kaplanaspect.com; Tel 01865 515808;
  Fax 01865 310068
Principal   Anna Stanton
Director (Studies)   David Meek
  16+; Number of students: 150–220

Kent School of English *
10–12 Granville Rd, Broadstairs, Kent CT10 1QD;
  URL www.kentschoolofenglish.com; e-mail
  enquiries@kentschool.co.uk; Tel 01843 874870;
  Fax 01843 860418

King's School of English *†
25 Beckenham Rd, Beckenham, Kent BR3 4PR;
  URL www.kingslon.co.uk; e-mail info@kingslon.co.uk;
  Tel 020 8650 5891; Fax 020 8663 3224
Principal   A. Townsend BA, PGCE, DTEFLA
  Number of students: 160

King's School Oxford *§
St Joseph's Hall, Temple Rd, Oxford, Oxfordshire OX4 2UJ;
  URL www.kingsoxford.co.uk; e-mail
  info@kingsoxford.co.uk; Tel 01865 711829;
  Fax 01865 747791
Principal   Simon Fenn BA, Dip(TEFL) RSA
  Residential, day

The Lake School of English *†
14 Park End St, Oxford, Oxfordshire OX1 1JQ;
  URL www.englishinoxford.com; e-mail
  enquiries@englishinoxford.com; Tel 01865 724312;
  Fax 01865 251360
Administrator   Lilly Sell
  Residential (host family accommodation)

Language Specialists International *†
1–13 Lord Montgomery Way, Portsmouth PO1 2AH;
  URL www.lsi-international.co.uk; e-mail
  contact@lsi-international.co.uk; Tel 02392 291811;
  Fax 02392 750435
  Residential

Language Studies International Ltd *†
13 Ventnor Villas, Hove, East Sussex BN3 3DD;
  URL www.lsi.edu; e-mail bri@lsi.edu; Tel 01273 722060;
  Fax 01273 746341
Principal   John Jefferys
Registrar   Dan Sherrington
  Residential

Languages Plus *
24 Holland Rd, Hove, East Sussex BN3 1JJ; Tel 01273 779231;
  Fax 01273 207388
Principal   Andy Cowley

Lewis School of English *†
33 Palmerston Rd, Southampton SO14 1LL;
  URL www.lewis-school.co.uk; e-mail
  study@lewis-school.co.uk; Tel 02380 228203;
  Fax 02380 231395

London House School of English *†
51 Sea Rd, Westgate-on-Sea, Kent CT8 8QL;
    URL www.london-house.co.uk; e-mail
    enquiries@london-house.co.uk; Tel 01843 831216;
    Fax 01843 832419
    Residential, day

Marine Parade
69 Marine Par, Brighton, East Sussex BN2 1AD

Meads School of English *†
2 Old Orchard Rd, Eastbourne, East Sussex BN21 1DB;
    URL www.meadsenglish.co.uk; e-mail
    english@meads.co.uk; Tel 01323 734335
Director   Chris Savins
    Number of students: 150

Meridian School of English *†
9 Yarborough Rd, Southsea, Portsmouth PO5 3DZ;
    URL www.meridianenglish.com; e-mail
    meridianenglish@btconnect.com; Tel 02392 816023;
    Fax 02392 833438
Principal   S.C. Kemp

Oxford English Centre *†
Wolsey Hall, 66 Banbury Rd, Oxford, Oxfordshire OX2 6PR;
    Tel 01865 516162; Fax 01865 310910
    Residential, day

Oxford House School of English *†
67 High St, Wheatley, Oxford, Oxfordshire OX33 1XT;
    URL www.oxfordhouseschool.co.uk; e-mail
    study@oxfordhouseschool.co.uk; Tel 01865 874786;
    Fax 01865 873351

Oxford Intensive School of English *†
OISE Hse, Binsey La, Oxford, Oxfordshire OX2 0EY; e-mail
info@oise.com; Tel 01865 258300; Fax 01865 244696
Contact   Angela Radford
    Residential (family and campus accommodation);
    Number of students: 48 (maximum) in each centre (19
    centres)

Padworth College *†
Padworth, Reading RG7 4NR; URL www.padworth.com;
    e-mail info@padworth.com; Tel 0118 983 2644;
    Fax 0118 983 4515
Principal   Mrs Linde Melhuish
    Residential, day; Number of students: 110

Pilgrims Ltd *†
4–6 Orange St, Canterbury, Kent CT1 2JA; e-mail
sales@pilgrims.co.uk; Tel 01227 762111; Fax 01227 459027
    Residential; Number of students: Approx. 1500 each year

Regency School of English *†
Royal Cres, Ramsgate, Kent CT11 9PE;
    URL www.regencyschool.co.uk; e-mail
    regency.school@btinternet.com; Tel 01843 591310;
    Fax 01843 590300
Director (Studies)   David Batten
    Residential, day

Regent Brighton *†
18 Cromwell Rd, Hove, East Sussex BN3 3EW;
    URL www.regent.org.uk; e-mail
    brighton@regent.org.uk; Tel 01273 731684;
    Fax 01273 324542
Principal   Paul Johnston
    Number of students: 175

Regent Language Holidays *†
Imperial Hse, 40–42 Queen's Rd, Brighton, East Sussex
    BN1 3XB; URL www.regent.org.uk; e-mail
    holidays@regent.org.uk; Tel 01273 718620;
    Fax 01273 718621
Manager   Jaqueline Pilkington
Courses for young learners 9–17 at four sites
    Residential; Number of students: Approx. 2000

Regent Margate *†
Northdown Hse, Margate, Kent CT9 3TP;
    URL www.regent.org.uk; e-mail margate@regent.org.uk;
    Tel 01843 865547; Fax 01843 869055
Contact   Wade Winton

Regent Oxford Language School *†
90 Banbury Rd, Oxford, Oxfordshire OX2 6JT;
    URL www.regent.org.uk; e-mail oxford@regent.org.uk;
    Tel 01865 515566; Fax 01865 512538
Principal   Doris Suchet

Richard Lewis Communications *†
Riversdown Hse, Warnford, Southampton SO32 3LH;
    URL www.crossculture.com; Tel 01962 771111;
    Fax 01962 771050
    One-to-one tuition; Residential

St Giles College *†
3 Marlborough Pl, Brighton, East Sussex BN1 1UB;
    URL www.stgiles.co.uk; e-mail stgiles@pavilion.co.uk;
    Tel 01273 682747; Fax 01273 689808
Contact   Dermot A. Tobin MA
    Number of students: 300

St Giles College *†
13 Silverdale Rd, Eastbourne, East Sussex BN20 7AJ;
    URL www.stgiles-international.com; e-mail
    english@stgiles-eastbourne.co.uk; Tel 01323 729167

St Peter's School of English *†
4 St Alphege La, Canterbury, Kent CT1 2EB;
    URL www.stpeters.co.uk; e-mail info@stpeters.co.uk;
    Tel 01227 462016; Fax 01227 458628
Principal   Nick Bendall
    16–70; Teacher training (weekend courses)

School of English Studies Folkestone *†
26 Grimston Gdns, Folkestone, Kent CT20 2PX;
    URL www.ses-folkestone.co.uk; e-mail
    info@ses-folkestone.co.uk; Tel 01303 850007;
    Fax 01303 256544
Principal   Una O'Connell

Stafford House College and School of English *†§
19 New Dover Rd, Canterbury, Kent CT1 3AH;
    URL www.ceg-uk.com; e-mail info@staffordhouse.com;
    Tel 01227 453237; Fax 01227 451685
Principal   Marie-Louise Banning
Principal (School of English)   Patrick O'Donoghue
    Residential, day; Number of students: 200

Summer School in England †
Longlythe, Stairs Hill, Liss, Hampshire GU33 6HW

Surrey Language Centre *
Sandford Hse, 39 West St, Farnham, Surrey GU9 7DR;
    URL www.surreylanguage.co.uk; e-mail
    slc@surreylanguage.co.uk; Tel 01252 723494;
    Fax 01252 717692

Sussex English Language School *†
Seadown Hse, Farncombe Rd, Worthing, West Sussex
    BN11 2BE; URL www.selschool.co.uk; e-mail
    info@selschool.co.uk; Tel 01903 209244; Fax 01903 231402
    16+

Swan School of English *†
111 Banbury Rd, Oxford, Oxfordshire OX2 6JX;
    URL www.swanschool.com; e-mail
    english@swanschool.com; Tel 01865 553201;
    Fax 01865 552923
Principal   H.A. Swan
    Number of students: 120

Thames Valley Cultural Centres Ltd *†
13 Park St, Windsor, Berkshire SL4 1LU; e-mail
    english@tvcc.demon.co.uk; Tel 01753 852001

Twin English Centre, Eastbourne *
25 St Anne's Rd, Eastbourne, East Sussex BN21 2DJ;
URL www.twinuk.com; e-mail astead@twinuk.com;
Tel 01323 725887; Fax 01323 730727
Contact   A. Stead BA(Hons), RSA Dip TEFLA
Number of students: 80

Universal Language Services *†
43–45 Cambridge Gdns, Hastings, East Sussex TN34 1EN;
URL www.universallanguageservices.com; e-mail
enquiries@universallanguageservices.com;
Tel 01424 438025; Fax 01424 438050
Director   Colin Spicer BA(Hons), RSA DipTEFL
Number of students: 150

Vacational Studies *†§
Pepys' Oak, Tydehams, Newbury, West Berkshire RG14 6JT;
URL www.vacstuds.com; e-mail
vacstuds@vacstuds.com; Tel 01635 523333;
Fax 01635 523999
Managing Director   I.G. Mucklejohn
11–17; Residential; Number of students: 100

The West Sussex School of English *†
7 High St, Steyning, West Sussex BN44 3GG; e-mail
info@wsse.uk.com; Tel 01903 814512; Fax 01903 812451
Residential, day

Windsor English Language Centre *
147 Slough Rd, Datchet, Berkshire SL3 9AE;
URL www.windsorenglishlanguagecentre.co.uk; e-mail
study@windsorenglishlanguagecentre.co.uk;
Tel 01753 542907; Fax 01753 542907
Principal   M. Osborn
Average class size: Small group courses (4 maximum)

YES Language Schools *†
12 Eversfield Rd, Eastbourne, East Sussex BN21 2AS;
URL www.yeseducation.co.uk; e-mail
english@yeseducation.co.uk; Tel 01323 644830;
Fax 01323 726260

South West

Abon Language Centre †
St Peter's Bldg, Dorset Cl, Bath, Somerset BA2 3RF;
Tel 01225 332211

Anglo-Continental School of English *†
29–35 Wimborne Rd, Bournemouth BH2 6NA;
URL www.anglo-continental.com; e-mail
english@anglo-continental.com; Tel 01202 557414;
Fax 01202 556156
Managing Director   G. Schillig
Number of students: 1000

Anglo-Continental School for Young Learners *†
29–35 Wimborne Rd, Bournemouth BH2 6NA;
URL www.anglo-continental.com; e-mail
english@anglo-continental.com; Tel 01202 557414;
Fax 01202 556156
Managing Director   G. Schillig
Number of students: 320

Aspect ILA Bournemouth *†
Hinton Chambers, Hinton Rd, Bournemouth BH1 2EN;
URL www.aspectworld.com; e-mail
bournemouthcity@aspectworld.com; Tel 01202 557522;
Fax 01202 297046
Principal   D. Brown MA
Number of students: 200

Anglo World Bournemouth †
136 Poole Rd, Westbourne, Bournemouth BH4 9EF;
Tel 01202 752200

Contact   G. Witt MA, RSA, CertTEFL
Number of students: 100

BEET Language Centre *†
Nortoft Rd, Charminster, Bournemouth, Dorset BH8 8PY;
URL www.beet.co.uk; e-mail admin@beet.co.uk;
Tel 01202 397609

Bournemouth International School *†
2 Owls Rd, Boscombe, Bournemouth BH5 1AA;
URL www.bischool.com; e-mail info@bischool.com;
Tel 01202 393112; Fax 01202 309638
Academic Principal   John Tuffin
Number of students: 50

Canning †
Bath, 1 Brock St, Bath, Somerset BA1 2LN;
URL www.canning.com; e-mail
richard.pooley@canning.co.uk; Tel 01225 335323

Cheltenham School of English *†
87 St George's Rd, Cheltenham, Gloucestershire GL50 3DU;
URL www.cheltenhamschool.co.uk; e-mail
enquiries@cheltenhamschool.co.uk; Tel 01242 570000;
Fax 01242 260000
Director (Studies)   Phillippa Gregory
Number of students: 10 (term), 12 (summer school)

The Devon School of English *†
The Old Vicarage, 1 Lower Polsham Rd, Paignton, Torbay
TQ3 2AF; URL www.devonschool.co.uk; e-mail
english@devonschool.co.uk; Tel 01803 559718;
Fax 01803 551407
Principal; Managing Director   Brian Hawthorne

Eagle International School *†
Tiami, 55 Elm's Ave, Lilliput, Poole BH14 8EE; e-mail
eaglesch@aol.com; Tel 01202 745175; Fax 01202 745175

EF International Language Schools
11 Poole Rd, Bournemouth BH2 5QR; URL www.ef.com;
Tel 01202 767555

English Language Centre Bristol *†
44 Pembroke Rd, Bristol BS8 3DT;
URL www.elcbristol.co.uk; e-mail info@elcbristol.co.uk;
Tel 0117 973 7216; Fax 0117 923 9638
Principal   J. Duncan

Eurocentres UK *†
26 Dean Park Rd, Bournemouth BH1 1HZ;
URL www.eurocentres.com; e-mail
bth-info@eurocentres.com; Tel 01202 554426
Contact   Mrs P. Williams MA, RSA, DipTEFL
Number of students: 200

Exeter Academy *†
64 Sylvan Rd, Exeter, Devon EX4 6HA;
URL www.exeteracademy.co.uk; e-mail
english@exeteracademy.co.uk; Tel 01392 430303;
Fax 01392 437309
Small school for adults (average age 29) with a flexible range
of courses available

International House Salisbury *†
36 Fowlers Rd, Salisbury, Wiltshire SP1 2QU;
URL www.english-school.co.uk; e-mail
info@english-school.co.uk; Tel 01722 331011;
Fax 01722 328324
Part of the WELS Group of International House Schools

International House Summer in England, Junior Courses *†
13 Castle Rd, Torquay, Devon TQ1 3BB;
URL www.ihwelsgroup.com; e-mail
info@ihwelsgroup.com; Tel 01803 299691;
Fax 01803 291946
Contact (Marketing)   Anya Jones
Contact (Marketing)   James Samuel

International Language Academy †
Castle Circus, Union St, Torquay, Torbay TQ1 3DE; e-mail
ila_torquay@rmplc.co.uk; Tel 01803 297166;
Fax 01803 298184
Residential

The International School *†
1 Mount Radford Cres, Exeter, Devon EX2 4EW;
URL www.internationalschool.co.uk; e-mail
study@internationalschool.co.uk; Tel 01392 254102
Principal Trevor Williams
Number of students: 150

International Teaching and Training Centre *†
674 Wimborne Rd, Winton, Bournemouth BH9 2EG;
Tel 01202 531355
Residential, day

The Isca School of English *†
4 Mount Radford Cres, Exeter, Devon EX2 4EN;
URL www.iscaschool.com; e-mail
iscaschoolexeter@yahoo.co.uk; Tel 01392 255342;
Fax 01392 437320
Principal R.F. Tomlinson BA(Hons), PGCE,
PostGradDipEFL, RSADipTEFLA
Average class size: 12 (maximum); Number of students:
100 (summer)

ISI English Language Schools *
Clarendon Hse, 51 Dolphin Cres, Paignton, Torbay
TQ3 1AN; e-mail isi@shines.swis.net; Tel 01803 524169;
Fax 01803 557060

King's School of English *†
58 Braidley Rd, Bournemouth BH2 6LD;
URL www.kingsgroup.co.uk; e-mail
info@kingsschool.uk.com; Tel 01202 293535;
Fax 01202 293922
Principal C. Brent
Number of students: 300

LAL Torbay *†
Conway Rd, Paignton, Torbay TQ4 5LH;
URL www.lalgroup.com; e-mail info@lalgroup.com;
Tel 01803 558555

Millfield Enterprises *†
Millfield School, Street, Somerset BA16 0YD; e-mail
mahc@millfieldenterprises.com; Tel 01458 444458;
Fax 01458 840584
Residential

MLS International College *†
MLS Hse, 8–9 Verulam Pl, Bournemouth BH1 1DW; e-mail
admin@mls-college.co.uk; Tel 01202 291556;
Fax 01202 293846

OISE Bristol
1 Lower Park Row, Bristol BS1 5BJ; URL www.oise.com;
e-mail bristol@oise.com; Tel 0117 929 7667;
Fax 0117 925 1990
Intensive English study in small groups to build skills,
confidence and fluency in a personal and supportive
environment

Richard Language College *†
43–45 Wimborne Rd, Bournemouth BH3 7AB;
URL www.rlc.co.uk; e-mail enquiry@rlc.co.uk;
Tel 01202 555932; Fax 01202 555874
Principal D.P. Vann BA(Hons), CertEd
Number of students: 100

St Hilary School of English *†
2 Midvale Rd, Paignton, Torbay TQ4 5BD;
URL www.sainthilary.co.uk; e-mail
enquiries@sainthilary.co.uk; Tel 01803 559223;
Fax 01803 663020

Scanbrit School of English *†
22 Church Rd, Southbourne, Bournemouth BH6 4AT; e-mail
info@scanbrit.co.uk; Tel 01202 428252; Fax 01202 428926
Principal Mr Robin Garforth

Sidmouth International School *†
May Cottage, Sidmouth, Devon EX10 8EN;
URL www.sidmouth-int.co.uk; e-mail
efl@sidmouth-int.co.uk; Tel 01395 516754;
Fax 01395 579270
Managing Director D.P. Dumenil
Sidmouth International School is a year-round English
language school (students can join on any Monday).
Students from all over the world come to learn English on
various courses including: General, Intensive, Business,
Cambridge Exam, Pre-UK boarding school, Pre-UK Further
Education. The school also runs development courses for
overseas teachers for English, and TEFL courses for native
English speakers wishing to train as teachers of EFL.

Southbourne School of English *†
30 Beaufort Rd, Southbourne, Bournemouth BH6 5AL;
URL www.southbourneschool.co.uk; e-mail
details@southbourneschool.co.uk; Tel 01202 422300;
Fax 01202 417108
Managing Director Italo Gallina
Number of students: 300

Suzanne Sparrow Plymouth Language School *†
'Barncroft', 72–74 North Rd East, Plymouth PL4 6AL;
URL www.sparrow.co.uk; e-mail study@sparrow.co.uk;
Tel 01752 222700; Fax 01752 222040

Torquay International School *†
15 St Marychurch Rd, Torquay, Torbay TQ1 3HY;
URL www.tisenglish.com; e-mail
study@tisenglish.co.uk; Tel 01803 295576;
Fax 01803 299062
Contact J.J.K. Hands

Totnes School of English *†
Gatehouse, 2 High St, Totnes, Devon TQ9 5RZ;
URL www.totenglish.co.uk; e-mail
enquiry@totenglish.co.uk; Tel 01803 865722;
Fax 01803 865722
Authorised TOEIC test centre; Number of students: 50

Twin English Centre *†
The Duchess of Albany Bldg, Ox Row, Salisbury, Wiltshire
SP1 1EU; URL www.twinuk.com; e-mail
cspicer@twinuk.com; Tel 01722 412711; Fax 01722 414604
Principal Colin Spicer
Integration; summer school; one-to-one and group
tuition

The Wessex Academy *†
84–86 Bournemouth Rd, Parkstone, Poole BH14 0HA;
URL www.wessexacademy.com; e-mail
office@wessexacademy.co.uk; Tel 01202 740365;
Fax 01202 716266
Contact A. Doran
Number of students: 100

West Midlands

Abbey College *†§
253 Wells Rd, Malvern Wells, Worcestershire WR14 4JF;
URL www.abbeycollege.co.uk; e-mail
enquiries@abbeycollege.co.uk; Tel 01684 892300;
Fax 01684 892757
Bursar M. Noor
Residential, day; Number of students: 120

Linguarama, Language Training for Business *†
1 Elm Ct, Arden St, Stratford-upon-Avon, Warwickshire
CV37 6PA; e-mail stratford@linguarama.com;
Tel 01789 296535; Fax 01789 266462

Lydbury English Centre *†
Lydbury North, Shropshire SY7 8AU;
  URL www.lydbury.co.uk; e-mail
  enquiry@lydbury.co.uk; Tel 01588 681000;
  Fax 01588 681018

Oxford House College, Stratford-upon-Avon *†
8 Tiddington Rd, Stratford-upon-Avon, Warwickshire
  CV37 7AE; URL www.stratfordschool.com; e-mail
  stratford.school@btinternet.com; Tel 01789 269497;
  Fax 01789 262837
Principal   J. Bull MA, DipTEFLA
  Number of students: 80

Severnvale Academy *†
25 Claremont Hill, Shrewsbury, Shropshire SY1 1RD;
  URL www.severnvale.co.uk; e-mail
  james@severnvale.co.uk; Tel 01743 232505;
  Fax 01743 272637

Yorkshire and the Humber

Anglolang (Scarborough) Ltd *†
20 Avenue Rd, Scarborough, North Yorkshire YO12 5JX;
  e-mail communicate@anglolang.co.uk; Tel 01723 367141;
  Fax 01723 378698

Functional English *†
International Christian Language School, 5 Chubb Hill Rd,
  Whitby, North Yorkshire YO21 1JU; Tel 01947 603933
Contact   Neil McKelvie MA, PGCE, Dip(TEFL)RSA
  17+; Residential; Number of students: 85

Harrogate Language Academy *†
8a Royal Par, Harrogate, North Yorkshire HG1 2SZ;
  URL www.hla.co.uk; e-mail enquiry@hla.co.uk;
  Tel 01423 531969; Fax 01423 531064
Principal   J. Godfrey
  Member of English UK

Melton College *†
137 Holgate Rd, York YO24 4DH;
  URL www.melton-college.co.uk; e-mail
  english@melton-college.co.uk; Tel 01904 622250;
  Fax 01904 629233
Principal   A. Hjort

Scarborough International School of English *†§
Cheswold Hall, 37 Stepney Rd, Scarborough, North
  Yorkshire YO12 5BN;
  URL www.english-language.uk.com; e-mail
  info@english-language.uk.com; Tel 01723 362879;
  Fax 01723 366458
Manager   J. Moore
  Day, home stay

Specialist Language Services (International) †
9 Marsden Business Pk, Clifton, York YO3 4XG;
  Tel 01904 691313; Fax 01904 691102
Contact   B. Stainthorp

Scotland

Basil Paterson Edinburgh *†§
Dugdale–McAdam Hse, 22–23 Abercromby Pl, Edinburgh
  EH3 6QE; URL www.basilpaterson.co.uk; e-mail
  study@bp-tut.demon.co.uk; Tel 0131 556 7698;
  Fax 0131 557 8503
Principal   Iris P. Shewan
  Residential, day; Average class size: 8 (maximum)

Edinburgh School of English *†
271 Canongate, The Royal Mile, Edinburgh EH8 8BQ;
  URL www.edinburghschoolofenglish.com; e-mail
  info@edinburghschoolofenglish.com; Tel 0131 557 9200;
  Fax 0131 557 9192

Registrar   Mary Slater
  Junior and adult courses

Highland Language Centre *†
Marine Terr, Rossmarkie, Fortrose, Highland IV10 8UR;
  Tel 01381 620598; Fax 01381 621247
  Residential

Regent Language Training, Edinburgh *†
29 Chester St, Edinburgh EH3 7EN;
  URL www.regent.org.uk; e-mail
  edinburgh@regent.org.uk; Tel 0131 225 9888;
  Fax 0131 225 2133
  Residential

Wales

Park House Training Ltd *†
Park Hse, Hyssington, Montgomery, Powys SY15 6DZ;
  URL www.parkhousetraining.com; e-mail
  enquiries@parkhousetraining.com; Tel 01588 620611;
  Fax 01588 620673

Trebinshun House *†
Trebinshun Hse, Bwlch, Brecon, Powys LD3 7PX;
  Tel 01874 730653

Secretarial Colleges

Key
*   Includes a course of English for foreign students
†   Recognised by the British Council English
           Language Schools Programme
‡   Accredited by the Open and Distance Learning
           Quality Council
§   Accredited by the British Accreditation Council for
           Independent Further and Higher Education

Basil Paterson College *†§
66 Queen St, Edinburgh EH2 4NA;
  URL www.basilpaterson.co.uk; e-mail
  info@basilpaterson.co.uk; Tel 0131 225 3802;
  Fax 0131 226 6701
Principal   Colin Smith
  14+ (FE studies), 17+ (EFL); Also GCSE, A-level and
  Scottish Highers, taught either one- to- one or in small
  groups, as well as private tuition according to student
  requirements; Residential, day

Beckenham Computer and Secretarial College *
78 Beckenham Rd, Beckenham, Kent BR3 4RH;
  URL www.beckenhamcollege.co.uk; e-mail
  admin@beckenhamcollege.co.uk; Tel 020 8650 3321
Principal   E. Wakeling
  Residential, day

Cleve College Ltd
96 Newport Rd, Cardiff CF2 1DG; Tel 02920 497981
Principal   D.C. Meek PCT, FTBE

GSC Corporate Training *†§
17 Chapel St, Guildford, Surrey GU1 3UL;
  URL www.g-s-c.co.uk; e-mail mail@g-s-c.co.uk;
  Tel 01483 564885; Fax 01483 534777
Manager (Training)   Salma Sams
Corporate Sales Consultant   Melanie Williams
  Residential

The North of England College
Cavendish Hse, 92 Albion St, Leeds, West Yorkshire
  LS1 6AG; URL www.noec.co.uk; e-mail info@noec.co.uk;
  Tel 0113 245 3073

Oxford Business College *§

65 George St, Oxford, Oxfordshire OX1 2BE;
URL www.oxfordbusinesscollege.co.uk; e-mail
enquiries@oxfordbusinesscollege.co.uk;
Tel 01865 791908; Fax 01865 245059
Principal   S.D. Hunter
The Oxford Business College offers two MBA programmes,
a business degree, pre-Master's and pre-degree foundation
courses as well as a full range of CIM Marketing diplomas

Pitman Training Centre

303–306 High Holborn, London WC1V 7JZ; e-mail
highholborn@pitman-training.net; Tel 020 7025 4700
Director (Studies)   Elly Hyde
Centre Administrator   Paul Chin

Purley Secretarial and Language College

14 Brighton Rd, Purley, Surrey CR8 3AB; e-mail
purleycollege@compuserve.com; Tel 020 8660 5060;
Fax 020 8668 4022
Principal   P.W. Kent

Queen's Business and Secretarial College

24 Queensberry Pl, London SW7 2DS;
URL www.qbsc.ac.uk; e-mail info@qbsc.ac.uk;
Tel 020 7589 8583; Fax 020 7823 9915
Executive Principal   C. Bickford

Queen's Marlborough College

Bateman St, Cambridge, Cambridgeshire CB2 1LU;
Tel 01223 367016
Executive Principal   C. Bickford

St James's and Lucie Clayton College

4 Wetherby Gdns, London SW5 0JN;
URL www.sjlccollege.co.uk; e-mail
information@sjlccollege.co.uk; Tel 020 7373 3852;
Fax 020 7370 3303

Correspondence Education

Key

*	Includes a course of English for foreign students
†	Recognised by the British Council English Language Schools Programme
‡	Accredited by the Open and Distance Learning Quality Council
§	Accredited by the British Accreditation Council for Independent Further and Higher Education

Association of British Correspondence Colleges

PO Box 17926, London SW19 3WB;
URL www.homestudy.org.uk; e-mail
info@homestudy.org.uk; Tel 020 8544 9559;
Fax 020 8540 7657
Chair   P. Fisher
Treasurer   E. Vanden Akker
Secretary   H. Owen
Aims
To ensure that its members provide a high standard of
tuition and efficient service; to safeguard the interests of all
students taking correspondence courses; to be a centre of
information and advice on matters pertaining to
correspondence education; to co-operate with the Open and
Distance Learning Quality Council, central government,
local education authorities, universities, professional
societies and institutions, and other bodies and people
concerned with further education; to maintain and enhance
the prestige of correspondence education. Membership is
open only to correspondence colleges that provide a
consistently reliable and efficient tutorial service and who
comply with the criteria for membership approved by the
council of the association.

Open and Distance Learning Quality Council

Registered Charity Number 325125

16 Park Cres, London W1B 1AH; URL www.odlqc.org.uk;
e-mail info@odlqc.org.uk; Tel 020 7612 7090;
Fax 020 7612 7092
Chair   John Ainsworth
Secretary   David Morley
Established as an independent body with the co-operation
of the Secretary of State for Education. The council, which is
non-profitmaking, is a company limited by guarantee, and is
the only organisation in the UK which can award
accreditation to colleges offering courses in Open and
Distance Learning. At present, more than 50 colleges are
accreditated by ODLQC and at least 300 000 students are
enrolled for correspondence courses in these colleges.
ODLQC is established for the public benefit to promote
education and in particular to raise standards of tuition,
education or training carried out wholly or in part at a
distance. It does this by awarding, where appropriate,
accreditation to ensure that a particular college conforms to
such standards.
Institutions accredited by the council are indicated by a
double dagger symbol next to their entry.

6

Correspondence Course Providers

Animal Care College

29a Ascot Hse, High St, Ascot, Berkshire SL5 7HG;
URL www.animalcarecollege.co.uk; e-mail
acc@rtc-mail.org.uk; Tel 01344 628269; Fax 01344 622771

Association of British Dispensing Opticians

ABDO College of Education, Godmersham Pk,
Godmersham, Canterbury, Kent CT4 7DT;
URL www.abdo.org.uk; e-mail education@abdo.org.uk;
Tel 01227 738829; Fax 01227 733900
Head (Examinations and Registration)   Mark Chandler

Business Training Ltd ‡

Sevendale Hse, 7 Dale St, Manchester M1 1JB;
URL www.businesstrain.co.uk; e-mail
diana@businesstrain.com; Tel 0161 228 6735/6

Cambridge International College *‡†

College Hse, Leoville, St Ouen, Jersey JE3 2DB;
URL www.cambridgecollege.co.uk; e-mail
learn@cambridgetraining.com; Tel 01534 485052;
Fax 01534 485071
The college offers accredited flexible diploma and higher
programmes in business management, accounts, marketing
and other subjects, accredited and equated to level NVQ 4
and NVQ 5. Accredited by ASET (QCA approved).

Chartered Institute of Bankers in Scotland (CIOBS) ‡

Drumsheugh Hse, 38b Drumsheugh Gdns, Edinburgh
EH3 7SW; Tel 0131 473 7777; Fax 0131 473 7788
Contact   Colin A. Morrison

Chartered Insurance Institute

20 Aldermanbury, London EC2V 7HY; URL www.cii.co.uk;
e-mail customer.serv@cii.co.uk; Tel 020 8989 8464;
Fax 020 8530 3052
Qualifications and training for the insurance and financial
services industry

Cheltenham Tutorial College ‡

292 High St, Cheltenham, Gloucestershire GL50 3HQ;
URL www.cheltenhamlearning.com; e-mail
info@cheltenhamlearning.co.uk; Tel 01242 241279;
Fax 01242 234256
Director   M.S. Rigby
Registrar   Pat Pennington
Development Manager   Dmytro Bojaniwskyj

Civil Service Correspondence School ‡
Baldock St, Ware, Hertfordshire SG12 9DZ;
  Tel 01920 465927; Fax 01920 484909

College of Estate Management
Whiteknights, Reading RG6 6AW; URL www.cem.ac.uk;
  e-mail prospectuses@cem.ac.uk; Tel 0118 986 1101;
  Fax 0118 975 5344

The College of Law
Braboeuf Manor, Portsmouth Rd, St Catherines, Guildford,
  Surrey GU3 1HA; URL www.college-of-law.co.uk/
  perfectforpractice; e-mail admissions@lawcol.co.uk;
  Tel 01483 216500; Tel (freephone) 0800 3280153
UK provider of legal education. Graduate Diploma in Law,
Legal Practice Course, Bar Vocational Course, LLM in
Professional Legal Practice, LLM in International Legal
Practice. Full-time and part-time study. Centres in
Birmingham, Chester, Guildford, London and York.

Discovering Herbal Medicine Course
Oak Glade, 9 Hythe Cl, Polegate, East Sussex BN26 6LQ;
  URL www.newvitalitytuition.org.uk; e-mail
  pamela.bull@btopenworld.com; Tel 01323 484353
Course Registrar   Pam Bull
A distance learning herbal medicine course. Course
accredited by the British Herbal Medicine Association and
accepted as an entry qualification to the University of East
London's BSc distance learning course. Also University of
Middlesex's BSc Herbal Medicine Course.

Foulks Lynch
4 The Griffin Centre, Staines Rd, Feltham, Greater London
  TW14 0HS; URL www.foulkslynch.com; e-mail
  info@foulkslynch.com; Tel 020 8831 9990;
  Fax 020 8831 9991
Manager (Sales and Marketing)   Lynne Guthrie

Horticultural Correspondence College ‡
Fiveways Hse, Westwells Rd, Hawthorn, Corsham,
  Wiltshire SN13 9RG; URL www.hccollege.co.uk; e-mail
  info@hccollege.co.uk; Tel 01255 816700
Senior Tutor   O.N. Menhinick MBE

Ideal Schools
60 St Enoch Sq, Glasgow G1 4AG;
  URL www.idealschools.co.uk; e-mail
  ideal.schools@btconnect.com; Tel 0141 248 5200

ifs School of Finance
IFS Hse, 4–9 Burgate La, Canterbury, Kent CT1 2XJ;
  URL www.ifslearning.com; e-mail
  customerservices@ifslearning.com; Tel 01227 818609;
  Fax 01227 784331
Chief Executive   Gavin Shreeve

Institute of Chartered Shipbrokers – Tutorship ‡
85 Gracechurch St, London EC3V 0AA;
  URL www.ics.org.uk; e-mail tutorship@ics.org.uk;
  Tel 020 7623 1111; Fax 020 7623 8118

International Correspondence Schools Ltd ‡§
8 Elliot Pl, Clydeway Centre, Glasgow G3 8EP;
  Tel 0141 221 2926
Principal   M. Gordon

International Graphology Association ‡
Tutorial Section, Cedar Hill, Lee Priory, Littlebourne, Kent
  CT3 1UR; URL www.graphology.org.uk; e-mail
  ljw@graphology.org.uk; Tel 01227 721230;
  Fax 01227 721230

JEB Distance Learning
The Joint Examining Board, 30a Dyer St, Cirencester,
  Gloucestershire GL7 2PF; URL www.jeb.co.uk; e-mail
  jeb@jeb.co.uk; Tel 01285 641747; Fax 01285 650449

London School of Journalism ‡
22 Upbrook Mews, Bayswater, London W2 3HG; e-mail
  education@lsjournalism.com; Tel 020 7706 3536;
  Fax 020 7706 3780
Director   H. Hopkins

Maritime Studies ‡
The Docklands Sailing Centre, Millwall South Dock, London
  E14 3QS; Tel 020 8545 0750
Principal   P. Redway FRIN, AMNI

Mercers College ‡
Baldock St, Ware, Hertfordshire SG12 9DZ;
  Tel 01920 465927; Fax 01920 484909

Metropolitan School of Machine Knitting ‡
Correspondence Division, The Pinfold, Nantwich, Cheshire
  CW5 6AL;
  URL www.metropolitanmachineknitting.co.uk; e-mail
  metromachineknit@btconnect.com; Tel 01270 628414

Montessori Centre International ‡
External Programmes Department, 18 Balderton St, London
  W1K 6TG; URL www.montessori.ac.uk; e-mail
  info@montessori.ac.uk; Tel 020 7493 0165
Chief Executive   Barbara Isaacs
Courses leading to a Montessori teaching diploma in
Nursery and Primary Education, SEN, or Teaching English
as an Additional Language

National Extension College ‡
Registered Charity Number 311454
Purbeck Rd, Cambridge, Cambridgeshire CB2 8HN;
  URL www.nec.ac.uk; e-mail info@nec.ac.uk;
  Tel 0800 389 2839; Fax 01223 400399
Chief Executive   Alison West
National Extension College is an educational charity that
helps people to fit learning into their lives. Courses,
resources and tailored training programmes cover GCSEs
and A-levels, vocational and professional training, key skills
and skills for life.

National Marine Correspondence School
30 Woodside Business Pk, Shore Rd, Birkenhead,
  Merseyside CH41 1EL; URL www.nmcs.u-net.com;
  e-mail sail@nmcs.org.uk; Tel 0151 647 6777;
  Fax 0151 649 9078
Principal   Robert Stott

National School of Salesmanship Concessionaires ‡
Sevendale Hse, 7 Dale St, Manchester M1 1JB;
  Tel 0161 228 6733/4
Chair   E.H. Metcalfe

Northern Institute of Massage Ltd
14–16 St Marys Pl, Bury, Lancashire BL9 0DZ;
  URL www.nim.co.uk; e-mail information@nim.co.uk;
  Tel 0161 797 1800
Contact   Mrs R. Pennington
Recognised by the British Association for Open Learning

Northumbria School of Navigation ‡
78 Stuart Ct, Kenton, Newcastle upon Tyne, Tyne and Wear
  NE3 2SG; Tel 0191 271 4401

Open College of the Arts
Unit 1b, Redbrook Business Pk, Wilthorpe Rd, Barnsley,
  South Yorkshire S75 1JN; URL www.oca-uk.com; e-mail
  open.arts@ukonline.co.uk; Tel 01226 730495;
  Fax 01226 730838

Pitman Training Centre
George Hse, The Parade, Royal Leamington Spa,
  Warwickshire CV32 4DG; Tel 01926 435735;
  Fax 01926 435739
The centre offers more than 150 courses covering
professional business, secretarial and leisure studies. It has
more than 3500 students from the Commonwealth.

RRC Business Training ‡

27–37 St George's Rd, London SW19 4DS;
URL www.rrc.co.uk; e-mail info@rrc.co.uk;
Tel 020 8944 3100; Fax 020 8944 7099
RRC Business Training is a specialist provider of business qualifications and health and safety training for individuals and companies, offering distance learning, e-learning, face-to-face training and consultancy services. Subject areas include Health and Safety, Quality, Environmental, Sales, Marketing, Credit Management, Purchasing and Supply, Administrative Management and Book-keeping. RRC operates globally and has developed effective partnerships with training institutions both within and outside the UK.

Society of Financial Advisers

20 Aldermanbury, London EC2V 7HY; Tel 020 8989 8464;
Fax 020 7600 0766
Development Director   Sarah Neighbour

Wolsey Hall Oxford Ltd §

66 Banbury Rd, Oxford, Oxfordshire OX2 6PR;
Tel 01865 310310; Fax 01865 310969
Director (Marketing)   Jonathan Chalstrey

The Writers' Bureau ‡

Sevendale Hse, 7 Dale St, Manchester M1 1JB;
URL www.writersbureau.co.uk; e-mail
diana@writersbureau.com; Tel 0161 228 2362

Management Education

Regional Centres of Management Education

Bristol Business School

University of the West of England at Bristol, Frenchay Campus, Bristol BS16 1QY; URL www.uwe.ac.uk/bbs; e-mail business@uwe.ac.uk; Tel 0117 328 3607
Dean (Bristol Business School)   Prof Ian Gow OBE

Corporate and Postgraduate Programmes Department

University of East London, Duncan Hse, High St, London E15 2JB; URL www.uel.ac.uk; e-mail needle@uel.ac.uk/elbs
Head (Corporate and Postgraduate Programmes)   D.J. Needle BA, TLSc, GradIRD
University of East London, East London Business School

Dundee Business School, University of Abertay Dundee

Old College, Bell St, Dundee DD1 1HG;
URL www.abertay.ac.uk; e-mail
m.malcolm@abertay.ac.uk; Tel 01382 308495
Head of School   Prof Mary Malcolm

Glasgow Caledonian University

Cowcaddens Rd, Glasgow G4 0BA;
URL www.caledonian.ac.uk; e-mail j.mckay@gcal.ac.uk;
Tel 0141 331 3634
Director of Programmes (Caledonian Business School)
John F. McKay BA, MEd

Kingston Business School

Kingston Hill, Kingston upon Thames, Surrey KT2 7LB;
URL www.kingston.ac.uk/business; e-mail
m.beard@kingston.ac.uk; Tel 020 8547 2000;
Fax 020 8547 7026
Dean   Prof Jean-Noël Ezingeard
Management and business education

Sheffield Hallam University

Sheffield Hallam University, Faculty of Organisation and Management, Stoddart Bldg, Sheffield, South Yorkshire S1 1WB; URL www.shu.ac.uk; e-mail ominfo@shu.ac.uk; Tel 0114 225 2820

Staffordshire University

Business School, Brindley Bldg, Leek Rd, Stoke-on-Trent ST4 2DF; URL www.staffs.ac.uk/business; e-mail bs4060@staffs.ac.uk; Tel 01782 294060; Fax 01782 264907
Dean   Susan Foreman
Manager (Business)   D. Shepherd

University of Ulster, Faculty of Business and Management

Shore Rd, Newtownabbey, County Antrim BT37 0QB;
URL www.business.ulster.ac.uk; e-mail
r.hutchinson@ulster.ac.uk; Tel 028 9036 6350;
Fax 028 9036 6834
Dean of Faculty   Prof Robert Hutchinson
The University of Ulster has formal links with the Association of Business Schools and the European Foundation for Management Development

Business and Administrative Colleges and Institutions

Ashridge Business School

Ashridge, Berkhamsted, Hertfordshire HP4 1NS;
URL www.ashridge.org.uk; e-mail
info@ashridge.org.uk; Tel 01442 843491;
Fax 01442 841036
Chief Executive   Kai Peters
6000 participants a year (on one to four-week courses) covering areas such as marketing, strategy, leadership, general management, personal skills, and a one and two-year MBA programme, a Diploma in General Management (one/two/three years) and Master's programmes in Organisation Consulting and Coaching

Aston Business School, Aston University

Aston Triangle, Birmingham, West Midlands B4 7ET;
URL www.abs.aston.ac.uk; e-mail abspg@aston.ac.uk;
Tel 0121 204 3100
Head (Academic Programmes)   Prof John Edwards

University of Bath School of Management

Claverton Down, Bath, Somerset BA2 7AY;
URL www.bath.ac.uk/management; e-mail
recep@management.bath.ac.uk; Tel 01225 386742

University of Birmingham

Edgbaston, Birmingham, West Midlands B15 2TT;
URL www.bham.ac.uk; e-mail admissions@bham.ac.uk;
e-mail prospectus@bham.ac.uk; Tel 0121 415 8900

BPP Law School

68–70 Red Lion St, London WC1R 4NY;
URL www.bpp.com; e-mail law@bpp.com;
Tel 020 7430 2304; Fax 020 7404 1389

Bradford University School of Management

Emm La, Bradford, West Yorkshire BD9 4JL;
URL www.brad.ac.uk/acad/management; e-mail
management@bradford.ac.uk
Contact Admissions Officer, Postgraduate Recruitment Office or Admissions Officer, Undergraduate Office

Cardiff Business School, Cardiff University

Aberconway Bldg, Colum Dr, Cardiff CF10 3EU;
URL www.cardiff.ac.uk/carbs; e-mail
mcnabb@cardiff.ac.uk; Tel 02920 875210;
Fax 02920 870041
Associate Dean (Undergraduate Studies)   Claire Morgan

CASS Business School

106 Bunhill Row, London EC1Y 8TZ;
URL www.cass.city.ac.uk; e-mail cass-mba@city.ac.uk;
Tel 020 7040 8600; Fax 020 7040 8880

Cranfield School of Management

Cranfield, Bedfordshire MK43 0AL;
URL www.cranfield.ac.uk/som; Tel 01234 751122;
Fax 01234 752439

Director   Prof M. Osbaldeston

Cranfield School of Management is a major international business school forming part of Cranfield University. There are approximately 500 postgraduate students, approximately 300 study for the Master's of Business Administration.

De Montfort University

The Gateway, Leicester LE1 9BH; URL www.dmu.ac.uk; e-mail enquiry@dmu.ac.uk; Tel 0845 945 4647; Fax 0116 255 0307

Vice-Chancellor   Prof P. Tasker

University of Derby, Buxton

Kedleston Rd, Derby DE22 1GB; URL www.derby.ac.uk; Tel 01332 622222; Fax 01332 622299

Chancellor   Prof L. Wagner CBE, BA, MA

Vice-Chancellor   Prof J. Coyne

Deputy Vice-Chancellor (Services)   J.M. Fry

Pro Vice-Chancellor (Academic Development)
Prof M. Mihsein BSc, PhD, MBA, FIMechE

Pro Vice-Chancellor (Learning, Teaching and Scholarship)
Prof M. Gunn LLB

Pro Vice-Chancellor; Director (Resources and Finance)
Mr H. Punchihewa FCMA, ACIB, MBA, CDir

Clerk to the Council; Company Secretary   Prof P. Bridges BSc, PhD, FGS
Number of students: 10 500 full-time, 9000 part-time

Durham Business School

Mill Hill La, Durham, County Durham DH1 3LB; URL www.dur.ac.uk/dbs; e-mail dbs.marketing@durham.ac.uk; Tel 0191 334 5200

Subject Areas

Business and management; economics; finance

Main qualifications offered

MBA, MA, MSc, DBA

EEF Western

Engineers' Hse, The Promenade, Clifton Down, Bristol BS8 3NB; Tel 0117 906 4819

Head (Management Development)   S.C. Barnes DipEM, CertEd, MIMgt, FCIPD

Enquiries to the administration centre

University of Greenwich

Maritime Greenwich Campus, 30 Park Row, London SE10 9LS; URL www.gre.ac.uk/schools/business/cmarg/index.ltm; e-mail a.c.slater@greenwich.ac.uk; Tel 020 8331 9036; Fax 020 8331 9005

Course Director   Alix Slater

Heriot-Watt University

School of Management and Languages, Scottish Borders Campus, Galashiels, Scottish Borders TD1 3HF; URL www.hw.ac.uk/sbc; e-mail c.fenton@hw.ac.uk; Tel 01896 892224; Fax 01896 892253

Director (Undergraduate Course)   Cath Fenton

Director (Postgraduate Course)   Andrew Grieve

Heriot Watt University, Scottish Borders Campus, offers three undergraduate Business Management degree courses: BBA Bachelor of Business Administration; BA in Business Management with Industrial Experience (includes 22 week, CV enhancing, paid industrial placement); BBA with Information Technology. It also offers a one-year postgraduate course in Business Management.

Henley Management College

Greenlands, Henley-on-Thames, Oxfordshire RG9 3AU; URL www.henleymc.ac.uk; e-mail mba@henleymc.ac.uk; Tel 01491 571454; Fax 01491 571635

Chair of Governors   Paul Walsh

Principal   Prof Christopher Bones MBA

Huron University USA in London

58 Princes Gate, London SW7 2PG; URL www.huron.ac.uk; e-mail admissions@huron.ac.uk; Tel 020 7581 4899; Fax 020 7589 9406

Provost   Ray Hilditch MBA

Lancaster University Management School

Lancaster, Lancashire LA1 4YX; URL www.lums.lancs.ac.uk; e-mail management@lancaster.ac.uk; Tel 01524 510752

Contact   Prof Sue Cox

Contact   Dr Sally Watson

University of Leeds

Leeds, West Yorkshire LS2 9JT; URL www.leeds.ac.uk; e-mail ask@leeds.ac.uk; Tel 0113 343 2336; Fax 0113 343 2334

Manager (Schools Relations)   Simon Bright

London School of Economics and Political Science

Houghton St, London WC2A 2AE; URL www.lse.ac.uk; e-mail stu.rec@lse.ac.uk; Tel 020 7955 6613; Fax 020 7955 7421

Manchester Business School

Booth St West, Manchester M15 6PB; e-mail marketing@mbs.ac.uk; Tel 0161 275 6399; Fax 0161 275 5862

Director (Manchester Business School)   Prof J. Arnold MSc, MA, FCA

Director (Full-time MBA Programme)   Dr J. Kang BSc, MSc, PhD

Director (Marketing Communications, Alumni Service)
Paula Barrow

Manager (Central Marketing)   Margaret Quinn
Number of students: 2450 on-campus, 3500 distance learning

University of Manchester Institute of Science and Technology, Manchester School of Management

PO Box 88, Sackville St, Manchester M60 1QD; Tel 0161 200 3443; Fax 0161 200 3518

Full-time Professor (Work and Organisational Psychology)
Prof I.T. Robertson

Middlesex University Business School

The Burroughs, London NW4 4BT; URL www.mubs.mdx.ac.uk; e-mail d.parker@mdx.ac.uk; Tel 020 8411 5834; Fax 020 8411 6011

Pro Vice-Chancellor; Dean of School   Prof Dennis J. Parker BA, PhD, ILTM, FCMI, FRGS

Manager (Admissions and Recruitment)   Sheila Sharp; Tel (admissions) 020 8411 5898

Missenden Abbey Conference Centre

Great Missenden, Buckinghamshire HP16 0BD; URL www.missendenabbey.co.uk; e-mail sales@missendenabbey.ltd.uk; Tel 01494 866811; Fax 01494 867911

Manager (Business Development)   Nicole Sadd

Open University Business School

Open University, Walton Hall, Milton Keynes, Buckinghamshire MK7 6AA; URL oubs.open.ac.uk; e-mail oubs-ilgen@open.ac.uk; Tel 0870 010 0311; Fax 01908 654320

Provider of management development programmes and qualifications through distance learning; available throughout the UK and Western Europe

Roffey Park

Forest Rd, Horsham, West Sussex RH12 4TB; URL www.roffeypark.com; e-mail info@roffeypark.com; Tel 01293 851644; Fax 01293 851565

Chief Executive   J. Gilkes

University of Salford, Salford Business School
Salford, Greater Manchester M5 4WT;
URL www.business.salford.ac.uk; e-mail
go-sbs@salford.ac.uk; Tel 0161 295 5854;
Fax 0161 295 5556
Administrative Officer   Lynne Marsland

Sheffield University Management School
9 Mappin St, Sheffield, South Yorkshire S1 4DT;
URL www.shef.ac.uk/management; e-mail
sums@sheffield.ac.uk; Tel 0114 222 3346;
Fax 0114 222 3348
Dean   Prof K. Glaister

University of Southampton
Highfield, Southampton SO17 1BJ; URL www.soton.ac.uk;
Tel 02380 595000; Fax 02380 593131
Degree Subjects Offered
Accounting and Finance; Actuarial Studies;
Entrepreneurship; Management; Sport Management and
Leadership

**Strathclyde Graduate School of Business, University
of Strathclyde**
199 Cathedral St, Glasgow G4 0QU;
URL www.strathclydemba.com; e-mail
admissions@gsb.strath.ac.uk; Tel 0141 553 6118

Sussex School of Education
Sussex Institute, University of Sussex, Falmer, Brighton,
East Sussex BN1 9QQ; URL www.sussex.ac.uk/
education; e-mail si-enquiries@sussex.ac.uk;
Tel 01273 877888
As well as Initial Teacher Education, the school offers a
range of postgraduate taught programmes at diploma and/
or MA level in Education Studies and International
Education. It also offers three research degrees: the
Professional Doctorate in Education, an International
Doctorate in Education and a MPhil/DPhil programme
which is thesis-based.

Tanaka Business School, Imperial College London
South Kensington Campus, Exhibition Rd, London
SW7 2AZ; URL www.imperial.ac.uk/tanaka; e-mail
mba@imperial.ac.uk; Tel 020 7594 9206;
Fax 020 7594 9146
Recruitment Officer (Full-time Executive MBA)
Gavin Harrison

**The Tavistock Institute Advanced Organisational
Consultation Programme**
30 Tabernacle St, London EC2A 4UE;
URL www.tavistockinstitute.org/aoc; Tel 020 7417 0407
The Advanced Organisational Consultation Programme is a
comprehensive professional development course for
organisational, business and process consultants.
Participants may choose from two modes: to study for the
Tavistock Institute qualification in Advanced
Organisational Consultation, or to study also for the
Master's degree in Advanced Organisational Consultation
awarded through City University, London. This modular
course is recommended for people whose current positions
require continual improvement in group development,
organisational change and/or technological innovation. The
qualification course takes 18 months, and the MA course
runs for two years.

University of Warwick, Warwick Business School
Coventry, Warwickshire CV4 7AL; URL www.wbs.ac.uk;
e-mail enquiries@wbs.ac.uk
Dean of School   Prof H. Thomas BSc, MSc, MBA, PhD
Main qualifications offered
BA, BSc, MA, MSc, MBA, MPA, PhD, Dip

Queen Margaret University, Edinburgh
School of Business, Enterprise and Management, Edinburgh
EH21 6UU; Tel 0131 474 0000; Fax 0131 474 0001

Armed Forces Education

Ministry of Defence Military Colleges and Academies

The Defence Academy
Defence Academy of the UK, Greenhill Hse, Headquarters,
Shrivenham, Swindon, Wiltshire SN6 8LA;
Tel 01793 785615
The Defence Academy is the Ministry of Defence's Higher
Educational institution. It comprises the Royal College of
Defence Studies, the Joint Services Command and Staff
College, the Defence College of Management and
Technology, the Advanced Research and Assessment
Group, and the Armed Forces Chaplaincy Centre.

Conflict Studies Research Centre
Defence Academy of the UK, Faringdon Rd, Watchfield,
Swindon, Wiltshire SN6 8LS; e-mail csrc@da.mod.uk;
Tel 01793 788856

Britannia Royal Naval College
Dartmouth, Devon TQ6 0HJ; Tel 01803 677165
Royal Naval officer training college

Joint Services Command and Staff College
Faringdon Rd, Shrivenhaam, Swindon, Wiltshire SN6 8TS;
e-mail infodesk.jscsc@defenceacademy.mod.uk;
Tel 01793 788000
Joint Services Command and Staff College provides
command and staff training

RAF Cranwell
Sleaford, Lincolnshire NG34 8HB; Tel 01400 261201
Royal Air Force officer training college

Royal College of Defence Studies
37 Belgrave Sq, London SW1X 8NS; Tel 020 7915 4800
Royal College of Defence Studies is part of the UK National
Defence Academy

Royal Military Academy Sandhurst
The Adjutant, Camberley, Surrey GU15 4PQ;
Tel 01276 63344
Army officer training academy

Careers and Sponsorship

Army
URL www.armyjobs.mod.uk/education; Tel 0845 730 0111
Sixth form
The Army awards 100 sixth form scholarships each year.
Parents or guardians will receive £1500 a year while the
student completes their last two years of school. This
guarantees acceptance into Royal Military Academy
Sandhurst after school or university, at which point the
student must complete three years' commissioned service.
Applicants need to be aged between 16 years to 16 years and
six months to apply.
Further education
The Army Training Regiment in Bassingbourn is a 20-week
course teaching core military and vocational skills, while the
Army Foundation College at Harrogate offers a 42-week
school-leavers course. Students aged between 16 and 25 who
are thinking of going to into further education can apply for
the Army FE Bursary Scheme. While the student is at
college, the Army will provide work experience with an

Army team and financial support. Students will then be required to commit four years with the Army after their course.

Higher education

The Army undergraduate bursary provides financial security during study for a degree. The student will be guaranteed a place at Sandhurst after graduation, which they must commence before their 29th birthday. They must then serve a minimum of three years as an officer in the British Army. The bursary is £6000 for a three-year course, £7000 for a four-year course, or £8000 for a five-year course. As a member of the University Officer Training Corps, the student will also receive paid training whilst at university and can qualify for an annual payment. Undergraduate medical, dental, nursing or veterinary students who are interested in joining the Army Medical Services can apply for the Army Undergraduate Cadetship. The Army pays for tuition fees, as well as an annual salary of around £14 000 for the last three years of training and a book allowance of £150. Applicants must be within three years of graduating from a UK medical or dental school.

Vocational skills

Financial reward packages are available for people who have studied specific vocational subjects to a set level and want to use their skills in the Army. Depending on the person's qualifications, the reward can range from £500 to £8000. There are also rewards available if a person wishes to enter one of the technically demanding trades at the basic level.

RAF (Royal Air Force)

People can also apply to the Defence Sixth Form College at Welbeck (see Chapter 5: Sixth Form and Further Education). The college is heavily subsidised so this would be at little or no cost.

URL www.raf.mod.uk/careers; Tel (careers advice/ sponsorship: 0700–2300, 7 days a week) 0845 605 5555

Sixth form

There are sixth form scholarships of up to £2000 for people in Year 13 who want to join the RAF as a pilot, air traffic controller, fighter controller, engineer officer or medical officer.

Higher education

The RAF sponsors 50 people each year to study for an engineering degree, with a view to joining the RAF as engineer officers. These people could be paid over £15 000 during their studies, or earn over £12 000 for a work experience year. For those who would like to join the RAF as a medical or dental officer, medical students can receive over £50 000; dental students can receive nearly £30 000 for university. For other officer jobs, it may be possible to sponsor people before they join the RAF. Undergraduate sponsorship can be worth up to £4000 a year. The RAF generally awards grants, not loans, but it does expect a commitment in return.

Royal Navy

URL www.careers.royalnavy.mod.uk/ training_and_education; Tel 0845 607 5555

Sixth form

Sixth form scholarships of £1050 a year are available for students in Years 11 or 12.

Higher education

Degree sponsorship is available for Arts students who can apply for £1500 a year, and engineers who can apply for £4000 a year. Aspiring engineer officers can apply to the Defence Technical Undergraduate Scheme (DTUS), which offers £5500 a year to students at specified universities in the UK (Aston, Loughborough, Newcastle, Northumbria, Southampton, Oxford and Cambridge). Engineering graduates may also be eligible for a bonus of £12 000 on joining the Royal Navy. The University Cadetship scheme provides a year's officer training before going to university and Royal Naval Officer pay while studying.

Agriculture and Horticulture Colleges

East of England

Capel Manor College

Bullsmoor La, Enfield, Hertfordshire EN1 4RQ;
    URL www.capel.ac.uk; Tel 020 8366 4442;
    Fax 01992 717544
Chief Executive   Dr S.R. Dowbiggin PhD, FIHort

Easton College

Easton, Norwich, Norfolk NR9 5DX; Tel 01603 731200;
    Fax 01603 741438
Principal   D.C. Lawrence DMS, LCG, CertEd, MIMgt
Main qualifications offered
FirstDip, NatDip, FdA
To obtain a prospectus
Telephone or e-mail the college

Otley College

Charity La, Otley, Ipswich, Suffolk IP6 9EY;
    URL www.otleycollege.ac.uk; e-mail
    info@otleycollege.ac.uk; Tel 01473 785543;
    Fax 01473 785353
Principal   P. Winfield

Plumpton College

Ditchling Rd, Plumpton, Lewes, East Sussex BN7 3AE;
    URL www.plumpton.ac.uk; e-mail
    enquiries@plumpton.ac.uk; Tel 01273 890454;
    Fax 01273 890071
Principal   D.P. Lambert

Writtle College

Writtle, Chelmsford, Essex CM1 3RR;
    URL www.writtle.ac.uk; e-mail info@writtle.ac.uk;
    Tel 01245 424200; Fax 01245 420456
Principal   Prof David Burcher
To obtain a prospectus
Telephone the college or visit website

East Midlands

University of Lincoln, Lincolnshire School of Agriculture

Riseholme Pk, Lincoln, Lincolnshire LN2 2LG;
    URL www.lincoln.ac.uk/lsa; e-mail
    rfrench@lincoln.ac.uk; Tel 01522 895389;
    Fax 01522 545436
*Director (Riseholme Park); Head (Further Educational
    Department)*   Clive Bound MEd, FTC, HNC, CertEd,
    AMIAgE
Main qualifications offered
First NatDip (Edexcel)

Moulton College

West St, Moulton, Northampton, Northamptonshire
    NN3 7RR; URL www.moulton.ac.uk; e-mail
    enquiries@moulton.ac.uk; Tel 01604 491131;
    Fax 01604 491127
Principal   C. Moody BSc(Hons), MEd, PGCE, MBIM
Main qualifications offered
NatDip, HND, BSc, FdA, ICA
To obtain a prospectus
E-mail the college

Nottingham Trent University, School of Animal, Rural and Environmental Sciences

Brackenhurst Campus, Brackenhurst, Southwell, Nottinghamshire NG25 0QF; URL www.ntu.ac.uk; e-mail enquiries.lbs@ntu.ac.uk; Tel 01636 817000; Tel (prospectus) 01636 817099; Fax 01636 815404

To obtain a prospectus

Telephone or e-mail the college

North East

East Durham and Houghall Community College

Burnhope Way Campus, Burnhope Way, Peterlee, County Durham SR8 1NU; URL www.edhcc.ac.uk; e-mail enquiries@edhcc.ac.uk; Tel 0191 518 2000; Tel (student services) 0191 518 8222; Fax 0191 586 7125

Principal   Ian Prescott

Northumberland College at Kirkley Hall

Ponteland, Northumberland NE20 0AQ; URL www.northland.ac.uk; e-mail advice.centre@northland.ac.ukw; Tel (prospectus) 0800 162100; Tel 01670 841200; Fax 01661 860047

Principal   Dr T. Capron

Main qualifications offered

BTEC FirstDip, NatDip, NatCert, HND

To obtain a prospectus

E-mail, telephone or visit the college website

North West

University of Central Lancashire

Cumbria Campus, Newton Rigg, Penrith, Cumbria CA11 0AH; URL www.uclan.ac.uk/cumbria; e-mail cumbriainfo@uclan.ac.uk; Tel 01768 863791; Fax 01772 894990

Main qualifications offered

NatDip, FD, C&G, Honours Degree

To obtain a prospectus

Tel 0800 027 4767

Myerscough College

Associate college of University of Central Lancashire

Bilsborrow, Preston, Lancashire PR3 0RY; URL www.myerscough.ac.uk; e-mail enquiries@myerscough.ac.uk; Tel (course enquiries) 01995 642211; Tel (main reception) 01995 642222; Fax 01995 642333

Principal   Ann Turner MA, ARAgS

South East

Berkshire College of Agriculture

Hall Pl, Burchetts Grn, Maidenhead, Berkshire SL6 6QR; URL www.bca.ac.uk; e-mail enquiries@bca.ac.uk; Tel (prospectus) 0800 0711 666; Tel 01628 824444; Fax 01628 824695

Principal   P. Thorn BSc(Hons), MCIM

Main qualifications offered

FirstDip, NatDip, NatCert, HND, BA(Hons), FdA

To obtain a prospectus

Telephone or e-mail the college

Hadlow College

Hadlow, Tonbridge, Kent TN11 0AL; URL www.hadlow.ac.uk; e-mail enquiries@hadlow.ac.uk; Tel 01732 850551; Fax 01732 853207

Principal   P. Hannan

Merrist Wood Campus, Guildford College

Worplesdon, Guildford, Surrey GU3 3PE; URL www.guildford.ac.uk; e-mail mwinfo@guildford.ac.uk; Tel 01483 884000; Fax 01483 884001

Principal   Clive Cooke

Royal Botanic Gardens Kew School of Horticulture

Richmond, Surrey TW9 3AB; URL www.kew.org/education/diploma/index.html; e-mail kewdip@kew.org; Tel 020 8332 5545; Fax 020 8332 5574

Principal   E. Fox

Sparsholt College Hampshire

Sparsholt, Winchester, Hampshire SO21 2NF; URL www.sparsholt.ac.uk; e-mail enquiries@sparsholt.ac.uk; Tel 01962 776441; Fax 01962 776587

Principal   T.D. Jackson BTech(Hons), PGCE

6

South West

Bicton College

East Budleigh, Budleigh Salterton, Devon EX9 7BY; URL www.bicton.ac.uk; e-mail enquiries@bicton.ac.uk; Tel 01395 562300; Tel (customer services) 01395 562400; Fax 01395 567502

Principal   Peter Sadler

Main qualifications offered

FirstDip, Modern Apprenticeship, FdA, NatDip, NatCert, NatAward, NVQ, AdvNatCert, Veterinary Nursing

To obtain a prospectus

Telephone customer services or e-mail the college

Bridgwater College, Cannington Centre for Land-Based Studies

Cannington, Bridgwater, Somerset TA5 2LS; URL www.cannington.ac.uk; Tel 01278 655000

Principal   R. Hinxman

Hartpury College

Hartpury Hse, Hartpury, Gloucestershire GL19 3BE; URL www.hartpury.ac.uk; e-mail enquire@hartpury.ac.uk; Tel (general enquiries) 01452 700283; Tel (course information) 01452 702132; Fax 01452 700629

Principal; Assistant Vice Chancellor   M. Wharton BEd(Hons), NDA, MRAC

Kingston Maurward College

Dorchester, Dorset DT2 8PY; e-mail administration@kmc.ac.uk; Tel 01305 215000; Fax 01305 215001

Principal   David Henley

To obtain a prospectus

Contact the college

University of Plymouth, Seale-Hayne Campus

Newton Abbot, Devon TQ12 6NQ; URL www.plymouth.ac.uk; e-mail shoffice@plymouth.ac.uk

Number of students

1000 full-time and sandwich

Royal Agricultural College

Stroud Rd, Cirencester, Gloucester, Gloucestershire
GL7 6JS; URL www.rac.ac.uk; e-mail
admissions@rac.ac.uk; Tel 01285 652531;
Fax 01285 650219
Chair of Governors S.F. Pott FRICS, FRAgs, MRAC
Principal Prof Christopher Gaskill BVSs, PhD, DVR,
MRCVS

Wiltshire College Lackham

Lacock, Chippenham, Wiltshire SN15 2NY;
URL www.wiltscoll.ac.uk; e-mail info@wiltscoll.ac.uk;
Tel (prospectus) 0845 330 2231; Tel 01249 466800;
Fax 01249 466842
Principal D. Dale
To obtain a prospectus
Telephone or visit the website

West Midlands

Pershore College

Avonbank, Pershore, Worcestershire WR10 3JP;
URL www.warkscol.ac.uk; e-mail
pershore@pershore.ac.uk; Tel 01386 552443;
Fax 01386 556528
Principal Ioan Morgan
Part of Warwickshire College

Rodbaston College

Rodbaston, Penkridge, Staffordshire ST19 5PH;
URL www.rodbaston.ac.uk; e-mail
rodenquiries@rodbaston.ac.uk; Tel 01785 712209;
Fax 01785 715701
Principal Dr R. Alcock PhD, MSc, DipEd, CertEd
Main qualifications offered
All levels from entry level to degree
To obtain a prospectus
Contact the college

Walford and North Shropshire College

Walford, Baschurch, Shrewsbury, Shropshire SY4 2HL;
URL www.wnsc.ac.uk; e-mail walford@wnsc.ac.uk;
Tel 01939 262100; Fax 01939 261112
Principal Ron Pugh

Yorkshire and the Humber

Askham Bryan College

Askham Bryan, York YO23 3FR;
URL www.askham-bryan.ac.uk; e-mail
sf@askham-bryan.ac.uk; Tel 01904 772277;
Fax 01904 772288
Principal Prof Gareth Rees

Bishop Burton College

Bishop Burton, Beverley, East Riding of Yorkshire
HU17 8QG; URL www.bishopburton.ac.uk; e-mail
enquiries@bishopburton.ac.uk; Tel 01964 553000;
Fax 01964 553101
Principal Jeanette Dawson

Scotland

Barony College

Parkgate, Dumfries and Galloway DG1 3NE;
URL www.barony.ac.uk; Tel 01387 860251;
Fax 01387 860395

Principal Russell Marchant BSc, CertEd, MBA
Head (Agricultural Engineering and Agriculture) A. Easton

Elmwood College

Cupar, Fife KY15 4JB; URL www.elmwood.ac.uk; e-mail
contact@elmwood.ac.uk; Tel 01334 658800;
Fax 01334 658888
Principal Jim Crooks

Oatridge College

Ecclesmachan, Broxburn, West Lothian EH52 6NH;
URL www.oatridge.ac.uk; Tel 01506 864800;
Fax 01506 853373
Principal David B. James

Royal Botanic Garden Edinburgh

20a Inverleith Row, Edinburgh EH3 5LR;
URL www.rbge.org.uk; e-mail education@rbge.org.uk;
Tel 0131 248 2937; Fax 0131 248 2901

SAC (Scottish Agricultural College)

Chair (Board of Directors) Dr Maitland Mackie CBE
Principal; Chief Executive Prof W.A.C. McKelvey
Head (Education) David McKenzie; SAC Aberdeen

Aberdeen Campus
Craibstone Campus, Bucksburn, Aberdeen AB21 9YA;
URL www.sac.ac.uk/learning; e-mail
aberdeen@sac.ac.uk; Tel 01224 711189

Ayr Campus
Auchincruive, Ayr, Ayrshire KA6 5HW;
URL www.sac.ac.uk/education; e-mail ayr@sac.ac.uk;
Tel (freephone) 0800 269453; Tel 01292 525353;
Fax 01292 525349

Edinburgh Campus
Kings Bldgs, West Mains Rd, Edinburgh EH9 3JG;
URL www.sac.ac.uk/learning; e-mail
edinburgh@sac.ac.uk; Tel 0131 535 4391

Wales

Pencoed College

Pencoed, Bridgend CF35 5LG; Tel 01656 302600;
Fax 01656 302601
Principal M. Davies

Institute of Rural Sciences

University of Wales, Aberystwyth, Ceredigion SY23 3AL;
URL www.irs.aber.ac.uk; e-mail
irs-enquiries@aber.ac.uk; Tel 01970 624471;
Fax 01970 611264
General enquiries Fay Hollick

Llysfasi College

Ruthin, Denbighshire LL15 2LB; URL www.llysfasi.ac.uk;
e-mail admin@llysfasi.ac.uk; Tel 01978 790263;
Fax 01978 790468
Principal D.F. Cunningham

Welsh College of Horticulture

Northop, Mold, Flintshire CH7 6AA;
URL www.wcoh.ac.uk; Tel 01352 841000;
Fax 01352 841031
Principal Dr M.B. Simkin BSc(Hons), DipIC, PhD, FIHort
Student facilities
Horticulture production unit, organic farm, garden centre,
equine areas, floristry studio, machinery workshops, animal
unit

Northern Ireland

College of Agriculture, Food and Rural Enterprise

22 Greenmount Rd, Antrim, County Antrim BT41 4PU;
    URL www.cafre.ac.uk; e-mail enquiries@cafre.ac.uk;
    Tel (prospectus) 028 9442 6624; Tel 028 9442 6700;
    Fax 028 9442 6606
Director   J.D. Fay BAgr, DipAgrComm
To obtain a prospectus
Telephone the college

Enniskillen College

Enniskillen, County Fermanagh BT74 4GF;
    URL www.enniskillencollege.ac.uk; e-mail
    brian.thomson@dardni.gov.uk; Tel 028 6634 4853
Principal   Seamus McAlinney

Loughry Campus, College of Agriculture, Food and Rural Enterprise

Cookstown, County Tyrone BT80 9AA;
    URL www.cafre.ac.uk; e-mail enquiries@cafre.ac.uk;
    Tel (freephone) 0800 216139; Tel 028 8676 8101;
    Textphone 028 9052 4420
Principal   Dr J.G. Speers

Colleges and Faculties of Art and Design

East of England

Norwich School of Art and Design

Francis Hse, 3–7 Redwell St, Norwich, Norfolk NR2 4SN;
    URL www.nsad.ac.uk; e-mail info@nsad.ac.uk;
    Tel 01603 610561; Fax 01603 615728
Chair of Governors   Graham Creelman
Course Leader (BA Creative Writing)   George Maclennan
Course Leader (BA Fine Art)   Carl Rowe
Course Leader (BA Graphic Design)   Phil Gray
Course Leader (BA Textiles)   Nicholas Rodgers
Course Leader (BA Visual Studies)   Chris Locke
Course Leader (FdA Film and Video)   Liam Wells
Course Leader (FdA Games, Art and Design)   Marie-Claire Isaaman
Course Leader (FdA Graphic Communication)   Andy Campbell
Number of students
867 full-time

East Midlands

University of Derby, School of Art and Design

Kedleston Rd, Derby DE22 1GB; URL www.derby.ac.uk;
    e-mail admissions@derby.ac.uk; Tel 01332 590500
Vice-Chancellor   Prof R. Waterhouse MA, HonDUniv
Academic Registrar   June Hughes ICSA
Clerk to the Council   Richard Gillis FRSA, Solicitor
Number of students
25 000 full-time and part-time

University of Lincoln, Faculty of Art, Architecture and Design

Brayford Pool, Lincoln, Lincolnshire LN6 7TS;
    URL www.lincoln.ac.uk/faculties; e-mail
    aadmarketing@lincoln.ac.uk; Tel 01522 837171;
    Fax 01522 837135
Marketing Officer   Amanda Chesson
Number of students
2000
Student facilities
Counselling; welfare; accommodation
To obtain a prospectus
E-mail the college

Loughborough University School of Art and Design

Loughborough University, Loughborough, Leicestershire
    LE11 3TU; URL www.lboro.ac.uk; e-mail
    r.turner@lboro.ac.uk; Tel 01509 228922; Fax 01509 228902
Director   Dr Marsha Meskimmon
Co-ordinator (Learning and Teaching)   Phil Sawdon
Admissions   Rebecca Turner
Contact   Raff Dewing; e-mail r.dewing@lboro.ac.uk;
    Tel 01509 228908
Number of students
1000 full-time
Main qualifications offered
Dip in Foundation Studies, BA(Hons) in Art and Design
To obtain a prospectus
Telephone or e-mail Raff Dewing

Nottingham Trent University School of Art and Design

Burton St, Nottingham NG1 4BU; Tel 0115 941 8418
Vice-Chancellor   Prof R. Cowell BA, PhD

London

Byam Shaw School of Art

2 Elthorne Rd, Archway, London N19 4AG;
    URL www.byam-shaw.ac.uk; e-mail
    info@byam-shaw.ac.uk; Tel 020 7281 4111;
    Fax 020 7281 1632
Principal   A. Warman
The Byam Shaw School of Art is one of the few
establishments in Britain to concentrate wholly on teaching
Fine Art. The core teaching staff is supplemented by visiting
tutors (specialist lecturers and established artists) and each
student's development is overseen by a personal tutor.
Number of students
200

Camberwell College of Arts

Peckham Rd, London SE5 8UF;
    URL www.camberwell.arts.ac.uk; e-mail
    enquiries@camberwell.arts.ac.uk; Tel 020 7514 6302;
    Fax 020 7514 6310
Head of College   Dr Will Bridge

Central St Martin's College of Art and Design

A constituent college of the University of the Arts London
Southampton Row, London WC1B 4AP;
    URL www.csm.arts.ac.uk; e-mail info@csm.arts.ac.uk;
    Tel 020 7514 7022; Fax 020 7514 7254
Head   Prof Margaret Buck MA

Chelsea College of Art and Design

A constituent college of the University of the Arts London
Millbank, London SW1P 4RJ; URL www.chelsea.arts.ac.uk;
    e-mail enquiries@chelsea.arts.ac.uk; Tel 020 7514 7751;
    Fax 020 7514 7777

Dean   Dr Linda Drew
Head of College   Prof Roger Wilson

City and Guilds of London Art School

124 Kennington Park Rd, London SE11 4DJ;
  URL www.cityandguildsartschool.ac.uk; e-mail
  info@cityandguildsartschool.ac.uk; Tel 020 7735 2306;
  Tel 020 7735 5210; Fax 020 7582 5361
Principal   Tony Carter

Hampstead School of Art

King's College Campus, 19–21 Kidderpore Ave, London
  NW3 7ST; URL www.hampsteadschoolofart.co.uk;
  e-mail hsanw3@aol.com; Tel 020 7794 1439;
  Fax 020 7431 1292
Director   Diana Constance

Inchbald School of Design

7 Eaton Gate, London SW1W 9BA;
  URL www.inchbald.co.uk; e-mail
  admissions@inchbald.co.uk; Tel 020 7730 5508;
  Fax 020 7730 4937
Garden Design Department, 32 Eccleston Sq, London
  SW1V 1PB; URL www.inchbald.co.uk; e-mail
  info@inchbald.co.uk; Tel 020 7630 9011;
  Fax 020 7976 5979
Principal   Jacqueline Duncan FIIDA
Number of students
100
Main qualifications offered
MA, PGDip (validated by the University of Wales), Dip,
Cert

London College of Communication

Elephant and Castle, London SE1 6SB;
  URL www.lcc.arts.ac.uk; e-mail info@lcc.arts.ac.uk;
  Tel 020 7514 6569; Fax 020 8514 2035
Head of College   Dr W. Bridge
The London College of Communication offers courses
which have a common focus on media and communications
Number of students
Approx. 9000 (4000 full-time)

London College of Fashion

20 John Princes St, London W1G 0BJ;
  URL www.fashion.arts.ac.uk; e-mail
  enquiries@fashion.arts.ac.uk; Tel 020 7514 7344;
  Fax 020 7514 8388
Head of College   Dr Frances Corner

Middlesex University, School of Arts and Education

Cat Hill, Barnet, London EN4 8HT; URL www.mdx.ac.uk/
  schools/arts; e-mail admissions@mdx.ac.uk;
  Tel 020 8411 5555; Fax 020 8440 9541
Archway Campus, Highgate Hill, London N19 3UA
Hendon Campus, The Burroughs, London NW4 4BT
Trent Park Campus, Bramley Rd, London N14 4YZ
Vice-Chancellor   Prof M. Driscoll BA, FIMgt, FRSA
Dean of School   Prof Gabrielle Parker
Number of students
4272
To obtain a prospectus
Visit the website or telephone the college

Royal Academy Schools

Burlington Hse, Piccadilly, London W1J 0BD;
  URL www.royalacademy.org.uk; e-mail
  schools@royalacademy.org.uk; Tel 020 7300 5650
Keeper   Prof M. Cockrill RA
Main qualifications offered
Dip in Fine Art

Royal College of Art

Kensington Gore, London SW7 2EU; URL www.rca.ac.uk;
  Tel 020 7590 4100; Fax 020 7590 4500
Provost   Sir Terence Conran
Pro-Provost   Ian Hay Davison BSc(Econ), FCA
Vice-Provost; Rector   Prof Sir Christopher Frayling MA,
  PhD, FRSA
Pro-Rector   Prof Alan Cummings
Director (Administration)   Garry Philpott BA, IPFA
Registrar   Alan Selby BSc(Econ), DMS
Number of students
855

Wimbledon College of Art

Merton Hall Rd, London SW19 3QA;
  URL www.wimbledon.arts.ac.uk; e-mail
  info@wimbledon.arts.ac.uk; Tel 020 7514 9641;
  Fax 020 7514 9642

North East

Cleveland College of Art and Design, Middlesbrough

Green La, Linthorpe, Middlesbrough TS5 7RJ;
  URL www.ccad.ac.uk; e-mail
  studentrecruitment@ccad.ac.uk; Tel 01642 288000;
  Tel (student recruitment) 01642 288888; Fax 01642 288828
Principal   D. Willshaw MA, HDFH, BA(Hons), ATC

University of Northumbria at Newcastle, School of Arts and Social Sciences

Lipman Bldg, Sandyford Rd, Newcastle upon Tyne, Tyne
  and Wear NE1 8ST; URL www.northumbria.ac.uk;
  Tel 0191 227 3871; Fax 0191 227 3180
Dean of School   Prof Lynn Dobbs
School Registrar   Debra Shannon
Number of students
2500 full-time and sandwich, 700 part-time

University of Sunderland, School of Arts, Design, Media and Culture

Ashburne Hse, Backhouse Pk, Sunderland, Tyne and Wear
  SR2 7EF; Tel 0191 515 2110; Fax 0191 515 2132
Dean of School   Prof F. Swann BA, FRSA
Chief Administrative Officer   J.D. Pacey LLB
Number of students
1400 full-time, 200 part-time

North West

Liverpool John Moores University, Liverpool Art School

68 Hope St, Liverpool, Merseyside L1 9EB;
  Tel 0151 231 5095; Fax 0151 231 5096
Number of students
539 full-time

Manchester Metropolitan University, Faculty of Art and Design

Ormond Bldg, Lower Ormond St, Manchester M15 6BX;
  URL www.artdes.mmu.ac.uk; e-mail
  artdes.fac@mmu.ac.uk; Tel 0161 247 1705;
  Fax 0161 247 6393
Dean of Faculty   Prof Maureen Wayman
Number of students
3400 full-time and sandwich, 100 part-time

South East

University of Brighton, Faculty of Arts and Architecture

Grand Par, Brighton, East Sussex BN2 0JY; e-mail
a.boddington@brighton.ac.uk; Tel 01273 600900
Dean of Faculty   Anne Boddington MA, FRSA
Vice-Chancellor   Prof Julian Crampton
Number of students
1980 FTE

Buckinghamshire Chilterns University College

Queen Alexandra Rd, High Wycombe, Buckinghamshire
HP11 2JZ; URL www.bcuc.ac.uk; e-mail
marketing@bcuc.ac.uk; Tel (prospectus) 0800 0565 660;
Tel 01494 522141; Fax 01494 461196
Chief Executive; Director   Dr Ruth Farwell BSc(Hons), PhD
Chair of Governors   Peter Moss
Dean   Dr Rod Marshall
Number of students
10 000
Faculties/schools/departments
Applied Social Science and Humanities; Business School;
Design; Leisure and Tourism; Health; Technology
Main qualifications offered
BA/BSc(Hons), FdA; all pre and post-qualifying courses in
professional social work
To obtain a prospectus
Telephone, e-mail or visit the website

University College for the Creative Arts at Canterbury, Epsom, Farnham, Maidstone and Rochester

Falkner Rd, Farnham, Surrey GU9 7DS;
URL www.ucreative.ac.uk; Tel 01252 722441;
Fax 01252 892616
UCCA is a specialist creative arts higher education provider
offering degrees in Art, Architecture, Design, Media and
Communications

Kingston University, Faculty of Art, Design and Architecture

Knights Pk, Kingston upon Thames, Surrey KT1 2QJ;
URL www.kingston.ac.uk; e-mail
artdesignarchitecture@kingston.ac.uk; Tel 020 8547 2000
Vice-Chancellor   Peter Scott BA(Hons), LLD, HonDLitt
Academic Registrar   Allison Stokes BA, PG, DipEdMan
Number of students
1950

Ravensbourne College of Design and Communication

Walden Rd, Chislehurst, Kent BR7 5SN;
URL www.ravensbourne.ac.uk; e-mail info@rave.ac.uk;
Tel 020 8289 4900; Fax 020 8325 8320
Director   Prof R. Baker OBE, MAPes, RCA, FCSD

West Dean College of Art, Craft, Music and Conservation (The Edward James Foundation)

West Dean, Chichester, West Sussex PO18 0QZ;
URL www.westdean.org.uk; e-mail
enquiries@westdean.org.uk; Tel 01243 811301;
Fax 01243 811343
Principal   Robert Pulley

Winchester School of Art (University of Southampton)

Park Ave, Winchester, Hampshire SO23 8DL;
URL www.wsa.soton.ac.uk; e-mail askwsa@soton.ac.uk;
Tel 02380 596900; Fax 02380 596901
Head of School   Prof Bashir Makhoul
Student facilities
Students' Union creative studies, Mac centre, library, digital
print centre, hall of residence
Main qualifications offered
BA(Hons)
To obtain a prospectus
E-mail the college

South West

The Arts Institute at Bournemouth

Wallisdown, Poole BH12 5HH; URL www.aib.ac.uk; e-mail
(course office) courseoffice@aib.ac.uk; e-mail
general@aib.ac.uk; Tel (course office) 01202 363228;
Tel 01202 533011; Fax 01202 537729
Principal; Chief Executive   Stuart Bartholomew
Main qualifications offered
BA(Hons), Degree, MA, FdA
To obtain a prospectus
Telephone course office or e-mail the course office

Bristol School of Art, Media and Design, University of the West of England

Kennel Lodge Rd, Bower Ashton, Bristol BS3 2JT;
URL www.uwe.ac.uk/amd; e-mail
amd.enquiries@uwe.ac.uk; Tel 0117 328 4716
Dean   P. Gough
Faculty Administrator   J. Hughes
Marketing   L. Jennings
Number of students
1600 full-time

Dartington College of Arts

See Music, Dancing and Drama Colleges: South West, in this
chapter

University College Falmouth

Woodlane, Falmouth, Cornwall TR11 4RH;
URL www.falmouth.ac.uk; e-mail
admissions@falmouth.ac.uk; Tel 01326 211077;
Fax 01326 213880
Principal   Prof Alan Livingston BA, FCSD, FRSA, CBE

Plymouth College of Art and Design

Tavistock Pl, Plymouth PL4 8AT; URL www.pcad.ac.uk;
e-mail enquiries@pcad.ac.uk; Tel 01752 203434;
Fax 01752 203444
Principal   Lynne Staley-Brookes

West Midlands

UCE Birmingham Institute of Art and Design

University of Central England in Birmingham, Corporation
St, Birmingham, West Midlands B4 7DX;
URL www.biad.uce.ac.uk; e-mail info@ucechoices.com;
Tel 0121 331 5595
Registrar of Faculty   Frank Johnson
Number of students
4000

6

Coventry University, Coventry School of Art and Design

Priory St, Coventry, Warwickshire CV1 5FB; e-mail
afuture.ad@coventry.ac.uk; Tel 024 7683 8248;
Fax 024 7683 8667
Head M.J. Tovey MDes(RCA), MCSD, FRSA
Number of students
1500 full-time

Hereford College of Arts

Folly La, Hereford, Herefordshire HR1 1LT;
URL www.hca.ac.uk; e-mail enquiries@hca.ac.uk;
Tel 01432 273359; Fax 01432 341099
Principal; Chief Executive Richard Heatly
Main qualifications offered
NatDip, FdA, BA(Hons), Foundation Dip

Staffordshire University, School of Art and Design

College Rd, Stoke-on-Trent, Staffordshire ST4 2DE;
Tel 01782 294565; Fax 01782 294873
Dean of School David Weightman MDes(RCA)
Administrator Mark Terry

Yorkshire and the Humber

Leeds College of Art and Design

Blenheim Wlk, Leeds, West Yorkshire LS2 9AQ;
URL www.leeds-art.ac.uk; e-mail info@leeds-art.ac.uk;
Tel 0113 202 8000; Fax 0113 202 8001
Principal Edmund Wigan
Deputy Principal Simone Goodwill
Assistant Principal (Further Education) Dave Russell

Leeds Metropolitan University

Vice-Chancellor Prof Simon Lee
Dean (Faculty of Arts and Society) Mary Heycock
Main qualifications offered
Post-16, undergraduate, postgraduate
To obtain a prospectus
Contact course enquiries

Sheffield Hallam University, Sheffield Institute of Art and Design

Faculty of Arts, Computing, Engineering and Sciences, City
Campus, Howard St, Sheffield, South Yorkshire S1 1WB;
URL www.shu.ac.uk/art; e-mail aces-info@shu.ac.uk;
Tel 0113 225 5555; Fax 0114 225 4449

Scotland

Duncan of Jordanstone College of Art and Design

University of Dundee, Perth Rd, Dundee DD1 4HT;
URL www.dundee.ac.uk/djcad; e-mail
c.a.white@dundee.ac.uk; Tel 01382 345213;
Fax 01382 227304
Faculty Secretary Cherry White MSc, GradIPD
To obtain a prospectus
Contact the faculty office

Edinburgh College of Art

Lauriston Pl, Edinburgh EH3 9DF; URL www.eca.ac.uk;
e-mail registry@eca.ac.uk; Tel 0131 221 6000
Principal Prof I. Howard
Secretary Michael Wood
Academic Registrar Irene Bruce
Number of students
1620 full-time

Glasgow School of Art

167 Renfrew St, Glasgow G3 6RQ; URL www.gsa.ac.uk;
e-mail info@gsa.ac.uk; Tel 0141 353 4500;
Fax 0141 353 4528
Director Seona Reid BA, DA, FRSA
Academic Registrar S. Clark
All of the school's degrees are validated by the University of
Glasgow
Number of students
1600 full-time
Main qualifications offered
Highers
To obtain a prospectus
Telephone, e-mail or visit the school website

Wales

Newport School of Art, Media and Design

Caerleon Campus, Caerleon, Newport NP6 1YG;
Tel 01633 430088; Fax 01633 432610
Principal K.J. Overshott DEng, CEng, FIEE, CPhys
Vice-Principal G.H. Williams BSc(Econ), DipEd, FBIM
Dean Derek Lawther
Number of students
730 full-time

North East Wales Institute, North Wales School of Art and Design

49 Regent St, Wrexham LL11 1PF; URL www.nwsad.com;
Tel 01978 293169; Fax 01978 293274
Contact (School Office) Alyn Evans

Music, Dancing and Drama Colleges

East of England

Arts Educational School

Tring Pk, Tring, Hertfordshire HP23 5LX;
URL www.aes-tring.com; e-mail info@aes-tring.com;
Tel 01442 824255; Fax 01442 891069
Principal Stefan Anderson MA, BMus, ARCM
Combined academic and vocational training (Dance,
Drama, Musical Theatre) to GCSE and A-level. Entry by
audition.

Britten-Pears Young Artist Programme

Snape Maltings Concert Hall, Saxmundham, Suffolk
IP17 1SP; URL www.aldeburgh.co.uk; e-mail
britten-pears@aldeburgh.co.uk; Tel 01728 688671;
Fax 01728 688171
Director (Artist Development) Anita Crowe
Co-ordinator Vacancy
Assistant Emily Parker
Administrator Caroline Newton
The Britten-Pears Young Artist Programme (founded by
Benjamin Britten and Peter Pears) holds master class courses
for young singers and chamber musicians of outstanding
ability and promise. Each course is taught by distinguished
guest teachers, and students from all over the world are
selected by audition. Observers are welcome to attend all
master class courses. The orchestras of Britten-Pears
(modern and baroque) meet seven or eight times a year for
courses with world-class conductors, culminating in
concerts at Snape Maltings Concert Hall and throughout
East Anglia and the South East.
To obtain a prospectus
Telephone or e-mail the programme

East 15 Acting School

Hatfields, Rectory La, Loughton, Essex IG10 3RY;
URL www.east15.ac.uk; e-mail east15@essex.ac.uk;
Tel 020 8508 5983
Executive Director   Prof Leon Rubin
Academic Administrator   Margaret Taylor

London

The Arts Educational Schools London

14 Bath Rd, Chiswick, London W4 1LY;
URL www.artsed.co.uk; e-mail
receptionist@artsed.co.uk; Tel 020 8987 6666
Dean   Iain Reid MA
Academic education to GCSE combined with training in the
performing arts of theatre and dance (8–16); courses in
acting and musical theatre, postgraduate acting course,
foundation course offering A-levels and vocational training
(post-16)

Barbara Speake Stage School

East Acton La, East Acton, London W3 7EG; e-mail
cpuk@aol.com; Tel 020 8743 1306; Fax 020 8743 1306
Principal   B.M. Speake ARAD
Academic stage school to GCSE
Number of students
150 full-time

Central School of Ballet

10 Herbal Hill, Clerkenwell Rd, London EC1R 5EG;
URL www.centralschoolofballet.co.uk; e-mail
info@csbschool.co.uk; Tel 020 7837 6332;
Fax 020 7833 5571
Director   Bruce Sansom
Three-year full-time course leading to a BA(Hons) in
Professional Dance and Performance, validated by the
University of Kent. Affiliate of the Conservatoire for Dance
and Drama.
Main qualifications offered
BA(Hons) Professional Dance and Performance
To obtain a prospectus
Telephone or e-mail the school

The Central School of Speech and Drama, University of London

Embassy Theatre, 64 Eton Ave, London NW3 3HY;
URL www.cssd.ac.uk; e-mail enquiries@cssd.ac.uk;
Tel 020 7722 8183; Tel (prospectus) 0870 950 3183
Principal; Chief Executive   Prof Gary Crossley

Drama Centre London

Central Saint Martins College of Art and Design, 10 Back
Hill, London EC1R 5EN; URL www.csm.arts.ac.uk/
drama; e-mail drama@arts.ac.uk; Tel (prospectus)
020 7514 7022; Tel 020 7514 8778; Fax 020 7514 8777
Director   Dr V. Mirodan

Guildhall School of Music and Drama

Barbican, London EC2Y 8DT; URL www.gsmd.ac.uk;
Tel 020 7628 2571
Principal   Prof Barry Ife CBE

Laban

Creekside, London SE8 3DZ; URL www.laban.org; e-mail
info@laban.co.uk; Tel 020 8691 8600; Fax 020 8691 8400
Director   Anthony Bowne
Laban is part of Trinity Laban Conservatoire of Music and
Dance and is a centre for professional contemporary dance
training. Laban offers undergraduate and postgraduate
degrees in contemporary dance, as well as evening and

Saturday classes for all ages and abilities. Laban's facilities
include the 294-seat Bonnie Bird Theatre, a studio theatre, an
outdoor theatre, 12 dance studios and a dance health suite
with a pilates studio in the UK. Laban also features Dance
Theatre Journal and Transitions Dance Company, which
bridges the gap between professional training and company
work for dance artists.

London Academy of Music and Dramatic Art (LAMDA)

155 Talgarth Rd, London W14 9DA;
URL www.lamda.org.uk; e-mail
enquiries@lamda.org.uk; Tel 020 8834 0500;
Fax 020 8834 0501
Chair   Luke Rittner
Principal   Peter James FRSA
Vice-Principal (Academic)   Sarah Rowe
Main qualifications offered
Training at LAMDA is vocational and not academic;
however, students graduating from selected acting courses
will receive a BA(Hons) in Professional Acting. Graduates
from the two year Stage Management and Technical Theatre
course will receive a DipHE in Stage Management and
Technical Theatre. All graduates will receive a LAMDADip.
To obtain a prospectus
Telephone, e-mail or visit the website

London Contemporary Dance School

The Place, 17 Dukes Rd, London WC1H 9PY;
URL www.theplace.org.uk; e-mail lcds@theplace.org.uk;
Tel 020 7121 1111; Fax 020 7121 1145
Director   V. Lewis MBE

London Studio Centre

42–50 York Way, London N1 9AB;
URL www.london-studio-centre.co.uk; e-mail
info@london-studio-centre.co.uk; Tel 020 7837 7741;
Fax 020 7837 3248
Director   Nicholas Espinosa
Head (Studies)   Robert Penman
Registrar   Stephanie Ahern

Middlesex University Dance Department

Trent Pk, Bramley Rd, London N14 4YZ; Tel 020 8411 6148;
Tel (admissions) 020 8411 6680; Fax 020 8411 6425
Department Administrator   Ruth Nicholls
Main qualifications offered
BA, MA
To obtain a prospectus
Telephone or write to the Admissions Office

Mountview Academy of Theatre Arts

Ralph Richardson Memorial Studios, Kingfisher Pl,
Clarendon Rd, London N22 6XF;
URL www.mountview.ac.uk; e-mail
enquiries@mountview.ac.uk; Tel 020 8881 2201;
Fax 020 8829 0034
Principal   Paul Clements
Full-time professional training in performance, directing
and technical theatre, and part-time courses.

Royal Academy of Dance

Faculty of Education, 36 Battersea Sq, London SW11 3RA;
URL education.rad.org.uk; e-mail faculty@rad.org.uk;
Tel 020 7326 8000; Tel (prospectus) 020 7326 8086;
Fax 020 7924 8040
Director (Education)   Prof Joan White
Registrar (Faculty of Education)   Alison Hume
Main qualifications offered
BA(Hons), PGCE, Royal Academy of Dance Awards
To obtain a prospectus
Telephone or e-mail the academy

6

Royal Academy of Dramatic Art

62–64 Gower St, London WC1E 6ED; URL www.rada.org; e-mail enquiries@rada.ac.uk; Tel 020 7636 7076
Principal   Nicholas Barter MA
Registrar   Patricia Myers

Royal Academy of Music, University of London

Marylebone Rd, London NW1 5HT; URL www.ram.ac.uk; e-mail registry@ram.ac.uk; Tel 020 7873 7373; Fax 020 7873 7374
Principal   Curtis Price KBE, AM, PhD, HonRAM, FKC, FRCM, FRNCM, KRE
To obtain a prospectus
Telephone or e-mail the college or download from website

Royal Ballet School

46 Floral St, Covent Garden, London WC2E 9DA; URL www.royalballetschool.co.uk; e-mail info@royalballetschool.co.uk Tel 020 7836 8899; Fax 020 7845 7080
Principal (Academic and Pastoral)   Martin Fosten
Director   Gailene Stock
Assistant Director   Jay Jolley
Financial Administrator   Nigel Copeland

Lower School – White Lodge
Richmond Pk, Richmond, Surrey TW10 5HR; Tel 020 8392 8000; Fax 020 8392 8037
Principal   Phillipa Hogg

Royal College of Music

Prince Consort Rd, London SW7 2BS; URL www.rcm.ac.uk; Tel 020 7589 3643; Fax 020 7589 7740
Director   Prof Colin Lawson MA, PhD, DMus, ARCM, FRCM

Royal College of Organists

PO Box 56357, London SE16 7XL; URL www.rco.org.uk; e-mail admin@rco.org.uk
General Manager   Kim Gilbert
Promotes the art of organ playing and choir training, and is the examining body for organ playing, choir training and organ teaching

Thames Valley University, Faculty of the Arts (LCM)

Thames Valley University, St Marys Rd, London W5 5RF; URL www.tvu.ac.uk; e-mail clare.beckett@tru.ac.uk; Tel 020 8231 2304; Fax 020 8231 2546
Head (Art and Design)   Alan Schechner
Head (Media)   Dr Eryl Price Davis
Head (Music)   Dr Christopher Batchelor
The faculty aims to train young people to think for themselves with confidence. Arts programmes are vocational.

Trinity College of Music

King Charles Ct, Old Royal Naval College, Greenwich, London SE10 9JF; URL www.tcm.ac.uk; e-mail enquiries@tcm.ac.uk; Tel 020 8305 4444; Fax 020 8305 9444
Principal   Derek Aviss
Trinity College of Music is part of Trinity Laban Conservatoire of Music and Dance and a centre for the training of professional musicians. Trinity offers undergraduate and postgraduate degrees in music, as well as Saturday classes for school children. Trinity's facilities include practice rooms and the Jerwood Library of the Performing Arts.

Webber Douglas Academy of Dramatic Art

30 Clareville St, London SW7 5AP; URL webber-douglas-academy.sageweb.co.uk; e-mail webberdouglas@btconnect.com; Tel 020 7370 4154
Principal   R.B. Jago

North West

Manchester Metropolitan University, School of Theatre

Mabel Tylecote Bldg, Cavendish St, Manchester M15 6BG; Tel 0161 247 1305
Head (School)   Niamh Dowling

Royal Northern College of Music

124 Oxford Rd, Manchester M13 9RD; URL www.rncm.ac.uk; e-mail info@rncm.ac.uk; Tel 0161 907 5200; Fax 0161 273 7611
Principal   Prof Edward Gregson
Main qualifications offered
BMus(Hons), PGDip, MMus, MPhil

South East

Bird College

Birkbeck Centre, Birkbeck Rd, Sidcup, Kent DA14 4DE; URL www.birdcollege.co.uk; e-mail admin@birdcollege.co.uk; Tel 020 8300 3031; Fax 020 8308 1370
Main qualifications offered
NatDip, BA(Hons)

GSA Conservatoire

Millmead Terr, Guildford, Surrey GU2 4YT; URL www.conservatoire.org; e-mail (admissions) admissions@conservatoire.org; e-mail enquiries@conservatoire.org; Tel 01483 560701
Director   Peter Barlow

Rose Bruford College

Lamorbey Pk, Sidcup, Kent DA15 9DF; URL www.bruford.ac.uk; e-mail enquiries@bruford.ac.uk; Tel 020 8308 2600; Tel (prospectus) 020 8308 2605; Fax 020 8308 0542

Royal School of Church Music

19 The Cl, Salisbury, Wiltshire SP1 2EB; URL www.rscm.com; e-mail enquiries@rscm.com; Tel 01722 424848; Fax (administration) 01722 424849

South West

Bristol Old Vic Theatre School

2 Downside Rd, Clifton, Bristol BS8 2XF; Tel 0117 973 3535
Principal   Christopher Denys
The school is an industry-led vocational training establishment preparing students for careers in the theatre. The school is staffed by working professionals and is an integral part of a working professional theatre company – the Bristol Old Vic Company.

Dartington College of Arts

Dartington Hall Est, Totnes, Devon TQ9 6EJ;
URL www.dartington.ac.uk; e-mail
enquiries@dartington.ac.uk; Tel 01803 862224;
Fax 01803 861666
Principal   Prof Andrew Brewerton

West Midlands

Birmingham Conservatoire

Paradise Pl, Birmingham, West Midlands B3 3HG;
URL www.conservatoire.bcu.ac.uk; e-mail
conservatoire@bcu.ac.uk; Tel 0121 331 5901;
Fax 0121 331 5906
Principal   Prof George Caird MA, FRAM, FRCM, FRNCM,
HonFLCM, FRSA
Vice-Principal   Prof Mark Racz MFA, BA
Main qualifications offered
BMus(Hons), BMus(Hons) with PGCE, BSc(Hons),
GraduateDip, PGCert, PGDip, MMus, AdvPGDip, MPhil,
PhD
To obtain a prospectus
Telephone, e-mail or visit the website

Birmingham School of Acting

62 Millenium Point, Curzon St, Birmingham, West Midlands
B4 7XG
Principal   Stephen Simms BA(Hons), Dip(Hons), RADA,
PGCE

Yorkshire and the Humber

Leeds College of Music

3 Quarry Hill, Leeds, West Yorkshire LS2 7PD;
URL www.lcm.ac.uk; e-mail enquiries@lcm.ac.uk;
Tel 0113 222 3400; Tel (prospectus) 0113 222 3416;
Fax 0113 243 8798

Northern School of Contemporary Dance

98 Chapeltown Rd, Leeds, West Yorkshire LS7 4BH;
URL www.nscd.ac.uk; e-mail info@nscd.ac.uk;
Tel 0113 219 3000; Fax 0113 219 3030
Principal; Artist Director   Gurmit Hukam

Scotland

Royal Scottish Academy of Music and Drama

100 Renfrew St, Glasgow G2 3DB; URL www.rsamd.ac.uk;
e-mail registry@rsamd.ac.uk; Tel 0141 332 4101;
Fax 0141 332 8901
Principal   Prof John Wallace
Registrar   E. Hainey BA, DipHWU, MSc, ACIS
Director (Finance)   A. Smith
Student facilities
Lodgings assistance; counselling
Number of students
652 full-time
Main qualifications offered
BMus, BEd, BA, MMus, MPerf
To obtain a prospectus
Telephone or visit the website

Wales

Royal Welsh College of Music and Drama

Castle Grounds, Cathays Pk, Cardiff CF10 3ER;
URL www.rwcmd.ac.uk; e-mail info@rwcmd.ac.uk;
Tel 02920 342854; Fax 02920 391301
Principal   Hilary Boulding
To obtain a prospectus
E-mail the college

Northern Ireland

Clarke School of Dancing

177 Upper Donegall St, Belfast BT1 2FJ; e-mail
dancerone@genie.co.uk; Tel 028 9024 1949;
Fax 028 9060 0440
Director   Alan Clarke

School of Music

99 Donegall Pass, Belfast BT7 1DR; URL www.cbsm.org.uk;
e-mail jmckee.hms@btopenworld.com; Tel 028 9032 2435;
Fax 028 9032 9201
Head (Music Service)   Dr J. McKee

6

Special Education

7

Special Schools
Independent Special Schools
Special Further Education Colleges

Key

B	Boys	MDP	Middle Deemed Primary
CI	Controlled Integrated	MDS	Middle Deemed Secondary
CY	Community	N	Nursery provision
D	Day places	R	Residential provision
FD	Foundation	Ref	LA Number-DfES Number or regional equivalent
G	Girls	Sp	Special School
GMI	Grant-Maintained Integrated	VA	Voluntary Aided
Ind	Independent/Non-Maintained	VC	Voluntary Controlled

Religious character

Ba	Baptist
Bu	Buddhist
CE	Church of England
CIW	Church in Wales
Cg	Congregational Church
Ch	Christian
CS	Church of Scotland
Es	Episcopalian
FC	Free Church
FP	Free Presbyterian
Gk	Greek Orthodox
Hi	Hindu
ID	Inter/Non-Denominational
IP	Independent Pentecostal
Je	Jewish
Me	Methodist
MF	Multi-Faith
Mu	Muslim
Qk	Quaker
RC	Roman Catholic
SDA	Seventh Day Adventist
UR	United Reformed Church

Special needs

ADHD	Attention Deficit Hyperactivity Disorder
AS	Asperger's Syndrome
ASD	Autism Spectrum Disorder
CD	Communication Difficulties
DMP	Delicate Medical Problems
Ep	Epilepsy
HI	Hearing Impairment
HS	Hospital School
MLD	Moderate Learning Difficulties
MSI	Multi-Sensory Impairment
PD	Physical Difficulties
PMLD	Profound and Multiple Learning Difficulties
SCU	Special Care Unit
SEBD	Social, Emotional and Behavioural Difficulties
SEN	Special Educational Needs
SLD	Severe Learning Difficulties
SpLD	Specific Learning Difficulties
VI	Visual Impairment

Special Schools

East of England

Bedfordshire

School name	Address	Tel	Fax	Headteacher	Ref	Ages	Pupils	Other
Glenwood School	Beech Rd, Dunstable, Bedfordshire LU6 3LY	01582 667106	01582 699538	Mrs Shirley Crosbie	820-7017	2–11	62	VI CD ASD SEBD PD SLD
Grange School	Halsey Rd, Kempston, Bedford, Bedfordshire MK42 8AU	01234 407100	01234 407110	Mrs Ellen Zapiec	820-7005	5–16	141	ASD MLD
Hillcrest School	Regis Education Centre, Parkside Dr, Houghton Regis, Bedfordshire LU5 5PX	01582 866972	01582 472455	Mr P. Skingley	820-7010	11–19	86	ASD SLD
Hitchmead School	Hitchmead Rd, Biggleswade, Bedfordshire SG18 0NL	01767 601010		Mr Tim Walker	820-7007	6–16	62	MLD
Oak Bank School	Sandy La, Leighton Buzzard, Bedfordshire LU7 3BE	01525 374559	01525 374559	Mr Peter Cohen	820-7018	11–16	49	SEBD
Ridgeway School	Hill Rise, Kempston, Bedford, Bedfordshire MK42 7EB	01234 402402		Mr Graham Allard	820-7012	2–19	61	PD
St John's School	Austin Canons, Bedford Rd, Kempston, Kempston, Bedfordshire MK42 8AA	01234 345565	01234 327734	Mr R. Babbage	820-5951	2–19		SLD
Sunnyside School	The Baulk, Biggleswade, Bedfordshire SG18 0PT	01767 222662	01767 222663	Miss J. Mudd	820-7009	2–19	70	ASD SLD DMP
Weatherfield School	Brewers Hill Rd, Dunstable, Bedfordshire LU6 1AF	01582 605632		Mr C.F. Peters	820-7006	7–16	122	MLD

Cambridgeshire

School name	Address	Tel	Fax	Headteacher	Ref	Ages	Pupils	Other
Castle School, Cambridge	Courtney Way, Cambridge, Cambridgeshire CB4 2EE	01223 442400	01223 442401	Mrs Carol McCarthy	873-7026	2–19	161	
Granta School	Cambridge Rd, Linton, Cambridge, Cambridgeshire CB21 4NN	01223 896890		Ms Lucie Calow	873-7025	2–19	90	MLD PMLD SLD
The Harbour School	Station Rd, Wilburton, Ely, Cambridgeshire CB6 3RR	01353 740229	01353 740632	Mr John Steward	873-7001	5–16	79	SEBD
Highfield Special School	Downham Rd, Ely, Cambridgeshire CB6 1BD	01353 662085	01353 662096	Mrs Jennie Moran	873-7007	2–19	92	MLD SLD
Meadowgate School	Meadowgate La, Wisbech, Cambridgeshire PE13 2JH	01945 461836	01945 589967	Mr Neil Sears	873-7021	2–19	117	AS ASD CD DMP MLD PD SEBD SLD SpLD VI
Samuel Pepys School	Cromwell Rd, St Neots, Cambridgeshire PE19 2EZ	01480 375012	01480 215582	Mrs Julia Weston	873-7023	2–19	91	AS ASD CD MLD SLD
Spring Common School	American La, Huntingdon, Cambridgeshire PE29 1TQ	01480 377403	01480 377405	Mrs Kim Taylor	873-7018	2–19	153	AS ASD MLD SLD

Essex

School name	Address	Tel	Fax	Headteacher	Ref	Ages	Pupils	Other
Castledon School	Bromfords Dr, Wickford, Essex SS12 0PW	01268 761252	01268 571861	Ms Carole Clift	881-7045	5–16	94	ASD MLD
Cedar Hall School	Hart Rd, Thundersley, Benfleet, Essex SS7 3UQ	01268 774723	01268 776604	Mr Peter Whelan	881-7036	4–16	113	MLD
The Chelmsford New Model Special School, Haywood Campus	Maltese Rd, Chelmsford, Essex CM1 2PA	01245 258667	01245 347126	Mr Malcolm Reeve	881-7034	4–16	133	ASD MLD
The Chelmsford New Model Special School, Woodlands Campus	Patching Hall La, Chelmsford, Essex CM1 4BX	01245 355854	01245 491749	Mr M. Reeve	881-7052	3–19	102	VI CD ASD SEBD PD MLD SLD SpLD DMP
The Edith Borthwick School	Fennes Rd, Church St, Bocking, Braintree, Essex CM7 5LA	01376 529300	01376 326436	Mr Gary Pocock	881-7048	3–19	160	VI CD ASD SEBD PD MLD SLD SpLD DMP
The Endeavour School	Hogarth Ave, Brentwood, Essex CM15 8BE	01277 217330	01277 225157	Mr Michael Southgate	881-5951	4–16		MLD

School name	Address	Tel	Fax	Headteacher	Ref	Ages	Pupils	Other
Glenwood School	Rushbottom La., New Thundersley, Benfleet, Essex SS7 4LW	01268 792575	01268 750907	Mrs Judith Salter	881-7054	3–19	99	SLD
Harlow Fields School	Tendring Rd, Harlow, Essex CM18 6RN	01279 423670	01279 431412	Miss Sue Davies	881-7070	3–19	113	ASD
Homestead School	School Rd, Langham, Colchester, Essex CO4 5PA	01206 272303	01206 272927	Mr Warwick Lampard	881-7028	11–18	45	B R SEBD
Kingswode Hoe School	Sussex Rd, Colchester, Essex CO3 3QJ	01206 576408		Mrs E. Drake	881-7030	5–16	111	MLD
Lexden Springs School	Halstead Rd, Colchester, Essex CO3 9AB	01206 563321	01206 570758	Mrs J. Wood	881-7069	3–19	73	ASD SLD
Market Field School	School Rd, Elmstead Market, Colchester, Essex CO7 7ET	01206 825195	01206 825234	Mr G.R. Smith	881-7065	4–16	146	ASD MLD
Oak View School	Whitehills Rd, Loughton, Essex IG10 1TS	020 8508 4293	020 8502 1864	Mr S. Armstrong	881-7044	3–19	59	
The Pioneer School	Church Rd, Basildon, Essex SS14 2NQ	01268 522077	01268 533214	Mr Steve Horsted	881-7001	3–19	120	SLD PMLD
Ramsden Hall School	Heath Rd, Billericay, Essex CM11 1HN	01277 624580		Mr Stewart Grant	881-7021	11–16	91	B R SEBD
Shorefields School at Ogilvie House	114 Holland Rd, Marine Par, Clacton-on-Sea, Essex CO15 6HF	01255 424412	01255 475938	Mrs J. Hodges	881-7060	3–19	98	SLD
Southview School	Conrad Rd, Witham, Essex CM8 2TA	01376 503505	01376 503460	Mr Gary Pocock	881-7013	3–19	50	PD
Thriftwood School	Slades La., Galleywood, Chelmsford, Essex CM2 8RW	01245 266880	01245 266880	Mrs Sally Davies	881-7063	5–16	121	MLD
Wells Park School	School La., Lambourne Rd, Chigwell, Essex IG7 6NN	020 8502 6442	020 8502 6729	Mr D. Wood	881-7022	5–12	28	B R SEBD

Hertfordshire

School name	Address	Tel	Fax	Headteacher	Ref	Ages	Pupils	Other
Amwell View School	Stanstead Abbotts, Ware, Hertfordshire SG12 8EH	01920 870027	01920 871664	Mrs J.S. Liversage	919-7028	2–19	104	ASD SLD
Batchwood School	Townsend Dr, St Albans, Hertfordshire AL3 5RP	01727 765195	01727 761784	Mr Keith Putman	919-7016	11–16	59	SEBD
Brandles School	Weston Way, Baldock, Hertfordshire SG7 6EY	01462 892189		Mr David Andrew Vickery	919-7045	11–16	37	B SEBD
Breakspeare School	Gallows Hill La, Abbots Langley, Hertfordshire WD5 0BU	01923 263645	01923 260087	Ms Gill Williamson	919-7024	2–19	62	SLD
The Collett School	Lockers Park La, Hemel Hempstead, Hertfordshire HP1 1TQ	01442 398988	01442 394317	Ms Elaine Gardner	919-7013	4–16	115	ASD MLD
Colnbrook School	Hayling Rd, Watford, Hertfordshire WD19 7UY	020 8428 1281	020 8421 5359	Mr Richard Hill	919-7011	4–11	89	ASD MLD
Falconer School	Falconer Rd, Bushey, Hertfordshire WD23 3AT	020 8950 2505	020 8421 8107	Mr Mark Williamson	919-7033	10–16	64	B R SEBD
Garston Manor School	Horseshoe La, Garston, Watford, Hertfordshire WD25 7HR	01923 673757	01923 440344	Mrs Julie Lowman	919-7008	11–16	121	MLD
Greenside School	Shephall Grn, Stevenage, Hertfordshire SG2 9XS	01438 315356	01438 748034	Mr Dave Victor	919-7042	3–19	109	ASD SLD
Hailey Hall School	Hailey La, Hertford, Hertfordshire SG13 7PB	01992 465208	01992 460851	Mr Steven Watt	919-7014	11–16	66	B R SEBD
Haywood Grove School	St Agnells La, Hemel Hempstead, Hertfordshire HP2 7BG	01442 250077	01442 260058	Miss Judith Williamson	919-7047	5–11	31	SEBD
Heathlands School	Heathlands Dr, St Albans, Hertfordshire AL3 5AY	01727 754060	01727 754064	Ms Mabel Davis	919-7032	3–16	85	R
Knightsfield School	Knightsfield, Welwyn Garden City, Hertfordshire AL8 7LW	01707 376874	01707 321738	Mrs Lucille Leith	919-7007	10–18	55	R
Lakeside School	Lemsford La, Welwyn Garden City, Hertfordshire AL8 6YN	01707 327410	01707 393352	Mrs Judith Chamberlain	919-7023	2–19	61	VI CD ASD SEBD PD SLD DMP
Larwood School	Webb Rise, Stevenage, Hertfordshire SG1 5QU	01438 236333	01438 236363	Mr A. Whitaker	919-7034	5–11	56	R SEBD
Lonsdale School	Webb Rise, Stevenage, Hertfordshire SG1 5QU	01438 357631	01438 742583	Ms Maria White	919-7022	3–18	74	R PD
Meadow Wood School	Coldharbour La, Bushey, Hertfordshire WD23 4NN	020 8420 4720	020 8420 5497	Mr James Boylan	919-7043	3–11	18	PD
Middleton School	Walnut Tree Wlk, Ware, Hertfordshire SG12 9PD	01920 485152	01920 486738	Mrs Alison Middleton	919-7019	4–11	76	ASD MLD
Pinewood School	Hoe La, Ware, Hertfordshire SG12 9PB	01920 412211	01920 412211	Mr Adrian Lloyd	919-7004	11–16	152	MLD
St Luke's School	Crouch Hall La, Redbourn, St Albans, Hertfordshire AL3 7ET	01582 626727	01582 626549	Mr Paul Johnson	919-7012	9–16	143	MLD
Southfield School	Travellers La, Hatfield, Hertfordshire AL10 8TJ	01707 258259	01707 258260	Mr M.B. Philp	919-7044	4–11	66	MLD
The Valley School	Valley Way, Stevenage, Hertfordshire SG2 9AB	01438 747274	01438 747966	Mr David Harrison	919-7010	11–16	169	MLD
Watling View School	Watling View, St Albans, Hertfordshire AL1 2NU	01727 850560	01727 864391	Mrs Fiona Ison-Jacques	919-7026	2–19	84	SLD
Woodfield School	Malmes Croft, Leverstock Grn, Hemel Hempstead, Hertfordshire HP3 8RL	01442 253476	01442 232619	Mrs Rosemary Freestone	919-7025	3–19	69	SLD
Woolgrove School	Pryor Way, Letchworth Garden City, Hertfordshire SG6 2PT	01462 622422	01462 622022	Mrs Bridget Walton	919-7041	4–12	107	ASD MLD DMP

7

Luton

School name	Address	Tel	Fax	Headteacher	Ref	Ages	Pupils	Other
Lady Zia Wernher School	Ashcroft Rd, Stopsley, Luton, Bedfordshire LU2 9AY	01582 728705	01582 722384	Mrs Diane May	821-7016	2–11	48	PD MLD SLD
Richmond Hill School	Sunridge Ave, Luton, Bedfordshire LU2 7JL	01582 721019		Mrs Jill Miller	821-7014	5–11	71	SLD
Woodlands Secondary School	Northwell Dr, Marsh Farm, Luton, Bedfordshire LU3 3SP	01582 572880	01582 565506	Mrs Sheila Read	821-7015	11–19	140	MLD SLD

Norfolk

School name	Address	Tel	Fax	Headteacher	Ref	Ages	Pupils	Other
Alderman Jackson School	Marsh La, Gaywood, King's Lynn, Norfolk PE30 3AE	01553 672779	01553 670344	Mrs Debby McCarthy	926-7009	2–19	62	SLD
Chapel Road School	Chapel Rd, Attleborough, Norfolk NR17 2DS	01953 453116	01953 455931	Mrs Kairn Peap	926-7010	4–18	45	SLD
The Clare School	South Park Ave, Norwich, Norfolk NR4 7AU	01603 454199		Mr Nigel Smith	926-7013	3–19	84	VI PD
Eaton Hall School, Norwich	Pettus Rd, Norwich, Norfolk NR4 7BU	01603 457480	01603 456211	Miss Valerie Theresa Moore	926-7015	10–16	38	B R SEBD
The Ethel Tipple School, King's Lynn	Winston Churchill Dr, Fairstead, King's Lynn, Norfolk PE30 4RP	01553 763679	01553 770321	Mr Gordon Wilkinson	926-7003	6–16	84	MLD
Fred Nicholson School	Westfield Rd, Dereham, Norfolk NR19 1JB	01362 693915	01362 693298	Mrs Alison Kahn	926-7004	7–16	98	R MLD
Hall School	St Faiths Rd, Old Catton, Norwich, Norfolk NR6 7AD	01603 466467	01603 466407	Mrs Jan Wiggins	926-7006	3–19	72	VI CD ASD SEBD PD SLD SpLD DMP
Harford Manor School, Norwich	43 Ipswich Rd, Norwich, Norfolk NR2 2LN	01603 451809		Mr Geoff Kitchen	926-7016	3–19	69	ASD SLD
John Grant School, Caister-on-Sea	St George's Dr, Caister-on-Sea, Great Yarmouth, Norfolk NR30 5QW	01493 720158		Mr Gerald Hampson	926-7020	3–19	101	SLD
The Parkside School, Norwich	College Rd, Norwich, Norfolk NR2 3JA	01603 441126	01603 441128	Mr Barry Payne	926-7014	7–16	139	VI CD ASD SEBD MSI PD SLD SpLD DMP
Sheringham Woodfields School	Holt Rd, Sheringham, Norfolk NR26 8ND	01263 820520	01263 850521	Mrs Diane Whitham	926-7007	2–19	70	SLD
Sidestrand Hall School	Cromer Rd, Sidestrand, Cromer, Norfolk NR27 0NH	01263 578144	01263 579287	Mrs Sarah Fee	926-7001	8–16	96	R MLD

Peterborough

School name	Address	Tel	Fax	Headteacher	Ref	Ages	Pupils	Other
Heltwate School	Heltwate, North Bretton, Peterborough, Cambridgeshire PE3 8RL	01733 262878	01733 331192	Mr Douglas Thompson	874-7020	4–16	103	MLD SLD
Marshfields School	Eastern Cl, Dogsthorpe, Peterborough, Cambridgeshire PE1 4PP	01733 568058		Mrs Janet James	874-7013	11–19	162	MLD
The Phoenix School	Clayton Site, Orton Goldhay, Peterborough, Cambridgeshire PE2 5SD	01733 391666		Mr Phil Pike	874-7024	2–19	78	

Southend-on-Sea

School name	Address	Tel	Fax	Headteacher	Ref	Ages	Pupils	Other
Kingsdown School	Snakes La, Southend-on-Sea, Essex SS2 6XT	01702 527486	01702 526762	Miss Margaret Rimmer	882-7001	2–19	63	CD PD PMLD
Lancaster School	Prittlewell Chase, Westcliff-on-Sea, Essex SS0 0RT	01702 342543	01702 352630	Mr Phil Rodbard	882-7005	2–19	91	PD SLD PMLD
Priory School	Burr Hill Chase, Prittlewell, Southend-on-Sea, Essex SS2 6PE	01702 347490	01702 432164	Mrs Jacqui Faux	882-7003	7–16	32	SEBD
The St Christopher School	Mountdale Gdns, Leigh-on-Sea, Essex SS9 4AW	01702 524193	01702 526761	Mr Tom Wilson	882-5950	3–16		ASD MLD
St Nicholas School	Philpott Ave, Southend-on-Sea, Essex SS2 4RL	01702 462322	01702 600487	Mrs G.M. Houghton	882-7004	5–16	85	ASD MLD

Suffolk

School name	Address	Tel	Fax	Headteacher	Ref	Ages	Pupils	Other
The Ashley School	Ashley Downs, Lowestoft, Suffolk NR32 4EU	01502 574847	01502 531920	Mr David Field	935-7003	7-16	124	R PD SLD PMLD DMP
Beacon Hill School	Stone Lodge La West, Ipswich, Suffolk IP2 9HW	01473 601175	01473 688882	Mr David Stewart	935-7007	5-16	160	SEBD SLD PMLD SpLD
Belstead School	Sprites La, Ipswich, Suffolk IP8 3ND	01473 556200	01473 556209	Mrs S. Chesworth	935-7005	11-19	71	VI CD ASD SEBD MSI PD MLD PMLD SpLD
Heathside School	Heath Rd, Ipswich, Suffolk IP4 5SN	01473 725508	01473 724419	Mr Odran Doran	935-7008	2-11	43	VI CD ASD SEBD MSI PD MLD PMLD SpLD
Hillside Special School	Hitchcock Pl, Sudbury, Suffolk CO10 1NN	01787 372808	01787 375249	Mrs Sue Upson	935-7002	3-19	60	VI CD ASD SEBD MSI PD MLD PMLD SpLD DMP
Priory School	Mount Rd, Bury St Edmunds, Suffolk IP32 7BH	01284 761934	01284 725878	Mr Roger Mackenzie	935-7000	7-16	103	R VI CD ASD SEBD MSI PD SLD PMLD SpLD DMP
Riverwalk School	South Cl, Bury St Edmunds, Suffolk IP33 3JZ	01284 764280		Mr Barry Ellis	935-7001	2-19	105	SLD
Thomas Wolsey School	642 Old Norwich Rd, Ipswich, Suffolk IP1 6LU	01473 467600	01473 462525	Mrs Nancy McArdle	935-7006	3-19	61	VI CD ASD SEBD MSI MLD SLD PMLD SpLD DMP
Warren School	Clarkes La, Oulton Broad, Lowestoft, Suffolk NR33 8HT	01502 561893		Mr Chris Moore	935-7004	2-19	93	VI CD ASD SEBD PD SLD

Thurrock

School name	Address	Tel	Fax	Headteacher	Ref	Ages	Pupils	Other
Beacon Hill School	Errif Dr, South Ockendon, Romford, Essex RM15 5AY	01708 852006	01708 851679	Mr Richard Milligan	883-7072	3-19	77	SLD
Treetops School	Dell Rd, Grays, Essex RM17 5LH	01375 372723	01375 390784	Mr Paul Smith	883-7032	5-16	174	ASD MLD

East Midlands

Derby

School name	Address	Tel	Fax	Headteacher	Ref	Ages	Pupils	Other
Ivy House School	249 Osmaston Rd, Derby, Derbyshire DE23 8LG	01332 344694	01332 344658	Mrs P. Sillitoe	831-7026	2-19	59	SLD
Kingsmead School	Bridge St, Derby, Derbyshire DE1 3LB	01332 715970	01332 715975	Sue Bradley	831-7029	11-16		SEBD
St Andrew's School	St Andrew's View, Breadsall Hilltop, Derby, Derbyshire DE21 4EW	01332 832746	01332 830115	Mr M. Dawes	831-7027	11-19	67	ASD SLD
St Clare's School	Rough Heanor Rd, Mickleover, Derby, Derbyshire DE3 9AZ	01332 511757	01332 519968	Mrs Carmel McKenna	831-7025	11-16	92	CD ASD SEBD PD MLD SLD
St Giles' School	Hampshire Rd, Chaddesden, Derby, Derbyshire DE21 6BT	01332 343039	01332 207321	Mr P. Walsh	831-7024	4-11	68	ASD SLD
St Martin's School	Wisgreaves Rd, Alvaston, Derby, Derbyshire DE24 8RQ	01332 571151	01332 758608	Mrs Melsa Buxton	831-7021	11-16	57	ASD SEBD MLD SLD

Derbyshire

School name	Address	Tel	Fax	Headteacher	Ref	Ages	Pupils	Other
Alfreton Park Community Special School	Wingfield Rd, Alfreton, Derbyshire DE55 7AL	01773 832019	01773 833227	Mrs Rosemary Mackenzie	830-7018	2-19	59	SLD
Ashgate Croft School	Ashgate Rd, Chesterfield, Derbyshire S40 4BN	01246 275111		Mr Mike Meaton	830-7006	2-19	143	MLD SLD
Bennerley Fields School	Stratford St, Cotmanhay, Ilkeston, Derbyshire DE7 8QZ	0115 932 6374	0115 932 6374	Mrs Margaret Stirling	830-7014	2-16	60	CD ASD SEBD MLD SLD
Brackenfield Special School	Bracken Rd, Long Eaton, Nottingham, Nottinghamshire NG10 4DA	0115 973 3710	0115 972 1272	Mr Philip Ormerod	830-7005	5-16	64	MLD

7

School name	Address	Tel	Fax	Headteacher	Ref	Ages	Pupils	Other
The Delves School	Hayes La, Swanwick, Alfreton, Derbyshire DE55 1AR	01773 602198		Mrs Hilary Surga	830-7009	5-16	75	CD ASD SEBD PD MLD SLD SpLD
Holbrook Centre for Autism	Portway, Belper, Derbyshire DE56 0TE	01332 880208		Mr David Heald	830-7001	5-16	41	R ASD
Holly House Special School	Church St North, Old Whittington, Chesterfield, Derbyshire S41 9QR	01246 450530	01246 450530	Mr Peter Brandt	830-7000	7-14	40	R SEBD
Peak School	Buxton Rd, Chinley, High Peak, Derbyshire SK23 6ES	01663 750324		Ms L. Scowcroft	830-7017	2-19	35	R SLD
Stanton Vale School	Thoresby Rd, Long Eaton, Nottingham, Nottinghamshire NG10 3NP	0115 972 9769		Mrs J. Wells	830-7019	2-19	71	ASD SEBD SLD
Stubbin Wood School	Burlington Ave, Langwith Junction, Mansfield, Nottinghamshire NG20 9AD	01623 742795	01623 742122	Mr Lee Floyd	830-7012	2-16	94	MLD SLD DMP

Leicester

School name	Address	Tel	Fax	Headteacher	Ref	Ages	Pupils	Other
Ash Field School	Broad Ave, Leicester, Leicestershire LE5 4PY	0116 273 7151	0116 273 9962	Mr D. Bateson	856-7003	4-19	96	R CD PD
The Children's Hospital School	Leicester Royal Infirmary, Infirmary Sq, Leicester, Leicestershire LE1 5WW	0116 258 5330	0116 247 1060	Mr Alex Osborne	856-5951	2-16		HS
Ellesmere College	Ellesmere Rd, Leicester, Leicestershire LE3 1BE	0116 289 4224	0116 289 4121	Ms F. Moir	856-7218	11-19	249	MLD
Keyham Lodge School	Keyham La, Leicester, Leicestershire LE5 1FG	0116 241 6852	0116 241 6199	Mr Chris Bruce	856-7220	11-16	49	B SEBD
Millgate School	18a Scott St, Leicester, Leicestershire LE2 6DW	0116 270 4922	0116 270 8753	Mrs J. Woolstencroft	856-7215	11-16	45	B R CD SEBD PD SpLD
Nether Hall School	Netherhall Rd, Leicester, Leicestershire LE5 1DT	0116 241 7258	0116 241 7259	Mrs Erica Dennies	856-7213	4-19	77	PD SLD
Oaklands School	Whitehall Rd, Evington, Leicester, Leicestershire LE5 6GJ	0116 241 5921	0116 243 3259	Mrs Andy Moran	856-7217	5-11	41	MLD
West Gate School	Glenfield Rd, Leicester, Leicestershire LE3 6DN	0116 285 6181	0116 285 8298	Ms Alison Standley	856-7221	5-19	136	MF MLD SLD AS

Leicestershire

School name	Address	Tel	Fax	Headteacher	Ref	Ages	Pupils	Other
Ashmount School	Beacon Rd, Loughborough, Leicestershire LE11 2BG	01509 268506	01509 231605	Mrs Sue Horn	855-7006	3-19	70	SLD
Birch Wood	Grange Dr, Melton Mowbray, Leciestershire LE13 1HA	01664 483340	01664 483340	Mrs Kate Waplington	855-7215	5-16	102	MLD SLD
Dorothy Goodman School	Stoke Rd, Hinckley, Leicestershire LE10 0EA	01455 634582		Mr Tony Smith	855-7216	3-19	88	MLD SLD
Forest Way School	Waterworks Rd, Coalville, Leicestershire LE67 4HZ	01530 831899	01530 814069	Mrs Lynn Slinger	855-7008	3-19	129	SLD
Maplewell Hall School	Woodhouse Eaves, Loughborough, Leicestershire LE12 8QY	01509 890237		Miss Susan Yarnall	855-7002	11-19	127	R MLD SLD
Wigston Birkett House Community Special School	Launceston Rd, Wigston, Leicestershire LE18 2FZ	0116 288 5802	0116 257 1932	Mr S. Welton	855-7005	5-19	123	SLD

Lincolnshire

School name	Address	Tel	Fax	Headteacher	Ref	Ages	Pupils	Other
The Ash Villa South Rauceby	Willoughby Rd, South Rauceby, Sleaford, Lincolnshire NG34 8QA	01529 488066	01529 488239	Mr Neil Barton	925-7003	7-16		HS
The Eresby School, Spilsby	Eresby Ave, Spilsby, Lincolnshire PE23 5HU	01790 752441		Mrs Jackie Mcpherson	925-7024	2-19	38	SLD
Fortuna School	Kingsdown Rd, Doddington Pk, Lincoln, Lincolnshire LN6 0FB	01522 705561	01522 705563	Mrs Josephine Richardson	925-7031	4-11	40	SEBD
The Garth School	Pinchbeck Rd, Spalding, Lincolnshire PE11 1QF	01775 725566	01775 728829	Mr Daran Bland	925-7011	2-19	25	SLD
Gosberton House School	11 Westhorpe Rd, Gosberton, Spalding, Lincolnshire PE11 4EW	01775 840250	01775 841017	Mrs Louise Stanton	925-7008	2-11	74	AS ASD MLD
The Grantham Ambergate School	Dysart Rd, Grantham, Lincolnshire NG31 7LP	01476 564957	01476 573870	Mr P. Bell	925-7002	5-16	93	AS ASD CD MLD SpLD
The Grantham Sandon School	Sandon Cl, Sandon Rd, Grantham, Lincolnshire NG31 9AX	01476 564994	01476 592195	Mrs J.M. Roddis	925-7005	2-19	43	SLD

School name	Address	Tel	Fax	Headteacher	Ref	Ages	Pupils	Other
The Horncastle St Lawrence School	Bowl Alley La, Horncastle, Lincolnshire LN9 5EJ	01507 522563	01507 522974	Mr Derek Smith	925-7021	5-16	123	R MLD
The John Fielding Community Special School	Ashlawn Dr, Boston, Lincolnshire PE21 9PX	01205 363395	01205 357696	Mrs Sue Morrison	925-7010	2-19	40	SLD
The Lady Jane Franklin School	Partney Rd, Spilsby, Lincolnshire PE23 5EH	01790 753902	01790 755640	Mr David Fuller	925-7030	11-16	59	SEBD
The Lincoln St Christopher's School	Hykeham Rd, Lincoln, Lincolnshire LN6 8AR	01522 528378	01522 521110	Mr D. Metcalf	925-7015	3-16	161	AS ASD MLD
Lincoln The Sincil School	South Pk, Lincoln, Lincolnshire LN5 8EW	01522 534559	01522 536190	Mr Robert Parkin	925-7032	11-16	40	
The Phoenix School	Gt North Rd, Grantham, Lincolnshire NG31 7UF	01476 574112	01476 579307	Mr William Bush	925-7029	11-16	60	SEBD
The Pilgrim School	Sibsey Rd, Fishtoft, Boston, Lincolnshire PE21 9QS	01205 445641	01205 368151	Mrs C.M. Seymour	925-7012	2-16	5	HS
The Priory School	Neville Ave, Spalding, Lincolnshire PE11 2EH	01775 724080	01775 713860	Mr D. Bland	925-7009	11-16	119	AS ASD MLD
Queen's Park School, Lincoln	South Pk, Lincoln, Lincolnshire LN5 8EW	01522 878112	01522 878113	Mr Allan Lacey	925-7017	3-19	92	SLD
St Bernard's School, Louth	Wood La, Louth, Lincolnshire LN11 8RS	01507 603776	01507 603914	Mr Michael Warren	925-7025	2-19	40	R SLD
The St Francis Special School, Lincoln	Wickenby Cres, Ermine Est, Lincoln, Lincolnshire LN1 3TJ	01522 526498	01522 569128	Mrs Ann Hoffmann	925-7016	2-19	93	R PD
The Willoughby School	South Rd, Bourne, Lincolnshire PE10 9JE	01778 425203	01778 425284	Mr Adam Booker	925-7028	2-19	67	SLD

Northamptonshire

School name	Address	Tel	Fax	Headteacher	Ref	Ages	Pupils	Other
Billing Brook Special School	Penistone Rd, Lumbertubs, Northampton, Northamptonshire NN3 8EZ	01604 773910		Mrs Caroline Grant	928-7020	3-16	154	ASD MLD SLD
Fairfields School	Trinity Ave, Northampton, Northamptonshire NN2 6JN	01604 714777	01604 714245	Mrs Corallie Murray	928-7014	3-11	62	
Friars School	Friars Cl, Wellingborough, Northamptonshire NN8 2LA	01933 304950	01933 304951	Mr Graham Baker	928-7029	11-16	130	ASD
Greenfields School	Harborough Rd, Northampton, Northamptonshire NN2 8LR	01604 843657		Mrs Jean Moralee	928-7019	11-19	70	VI ASD SLD
Isebrook School	Eastleigh Rd, Kettering, Northamptonshire NN15 6PT	01536 500030	01536 503298	Mr Peter Henshaw	928-7008	11-16	90	ASD PD MLD SLD
Kings Meadow School	Manning Rd, Moulton Leys, Northampton, Northamptonshire NN3 7AR	01604 673730	01604 673739	Mrs K. Lewis	928-7028	5-11	26	B SEBD
Kingsley School	Churchill Way, Kettering, Northamptonshire NN15 5DP	01536 316880	01536 415755	Mr Tom O Dwyer	928-7026	2-11	84	ASD PD MLD SLD
Maplefields School	School Pl, Corby, Northamptonshire NN18 0QP	01536 409040	01536 409040	Mrs L. Morgan	928-7033	3-16	29	SEBD
Northgate School	Queen's Park Par, Kingsthorpe, Northampton, Northamptonshire NN2 6LR	01604 714098	01604 791675	Miss Sheralee Webb	928-7017	7-16	80	MLD
The Raeburn School	St John's Centre, t John's Rd, Tiffield, Northampton, Northamptonshire NN12 8AA	01604 460017	01604 460024	Mr David R. Lloyd	928-7018	11-18	43	SEBD
Rowan Gate Primary School	Finedon Rd, Wellingborough, Northamptonshire NN8 4NS	01933 304970		Mrs Laura Clarke	928-7031	3-11	86	
Wren Spinney Community Special School	Westover Rd, off Westhill Dr, Kettering, Northamptonshire NN15 7LB	01536 481939	01536 312689	Mrs D. Withers	928-7010	11-19	53	VI ASD SLD

Nottingham

School name	Address	Tel	Fax	Headteacher	Ref	Ages	Pupils	Other
Aspley Wood School	Robins Wood Rd, Aspley, Nottingham, Nottinghamshire NG8 3LD	0115 913 1400	0115 913 1404	Mrs B. Mole	892-7034	2-16	24	PD
Nethergate School	Swansdowne Dr, Clifton, Nottingham, Nottinghamshire NG11 8HX	0115 915 2959		Mrs S. Johnson-Marshall	892-7026	5-16	55	MLD
Rosehill School	St Matthias Rd, Nottingham, Nottinghamshire NG3 2FE	0115 915 5815	0115 915 5815	Mr John Pearson	892-7035	4-19	79	ASD MLD
Shepherd School	Harvey Rd, off Beechdale Rd, Bilborough, Nottingham, Nottinghamshire NG8 3BB	0115 915 3265	0115 942 6770	Mr D. Stewart	892-7030	3-19	106	SLD
Westbury School	Chingford Rd, Bilborough, Nottingham, Nottinghamshire NG8 3BT	0115 915 5858	0115 913 8006	Mr John Dyson	892-7040	7-16	41	SEBD
Woodlands School	Beechdale Rd, Aspley, Nottingham, Nottinghamshire NG8 3EZ	0115 915 5734		Mrs Sarah Fee	892-7033	3-16	51	MLD

7

Nottinghamshire

School name	Address	Tel	Fax	Headteacher	Ref	Ages	Pupils	Other
Ash Lea School	Owthorpe Rd, Cotgrave, Nottingham, Nottinghamshire NG12 3PA	0115 989 2744	0115 989 3878	Mrs L. Skillington	891-7023	3–19	69	SLD
Beech Hill School	Fairholme Dr, Mansfield, Nottinghamshire NG19 6DX	01623 626008	01623 651459	Mr M. Sutton	891-7011	11–16	73	MLD
Bracken Hill School	Chartwell Rd, Kirkby-in-Ashfield, Nottingham, Nottinghamshire NG17 7HZ	01623 477268	01623 477298	Mr Ron McCrossen	891-7032	3–19	82	MLD SLD
Carlton Digby School	61 Digby Ave, Mapperley, Nottingham, Nottinghamshire NG3 6DS	0115 956 8289	0115 956 8290	Mrs G. Clifton	891-7019	3–19	53	SLD
Derrymount School	Churchmoor La, Arnold, Nottingham, Nottinghamshire NG5 8HN	0115 953 4015	0115 953 4025	Mrs Kathy Mcintyre	891-7012	3–16	48	MLD
Fountaindale School	Nottingham Rd, Mansfield, Nottinghamshire NG18 5BA	01623 792671	01623 797849	Mr Mark Dengel	891-7009	3–19	59	R PD
Foxwood Foundation School and Technology College	Derby Rd, Bramcote, Nottingham NG9 3GF	0115 917 7202	0115 917 7201	Mr Chris Humphreys	891-5950	3–19		SpLD
Newark Orchard School	Appletongate, Newark, Nottinghamshire NG24 1JR	01636 682255	01636 682266	Mrs Sharon Jefferies	891-7041	2–19	82	R ASD SEBD MLD SLD
Redgate School	Somersall St, Mansfield, Nottinghamshire NG19 6EL	01623 455944		Mr Kenneth Fallows	891-7014	3–11	25	MLD
St Giles School	North Rd, Retford, Nottinghamshire DN22 7XN	01777 703683	01777 705324	Mrs C. Kirk	891-7021	3–19	112	MLD SLD
Yeoman Park School	Park Hall Rd, Mansfield Woodhouse, Mansfield, Nottinghamshire NG19 8PS	01623 459540	01623 459526	Mr Paul Betts	891-7018	3–19	63	SpLD

Rutland

School name	Address	Tel	Fax	Headteacher	Ref	Ages	Pupils	Other
The Parks School	Barleythorpe Rd, Oakham, Leicestershire LE15 6NR	01572 756747	01572 722369	Mrs P. Kerridge	857-7015	2–5	12	VI CD ASD SEBD PD MLD SLD

London

Barking and Dagenham

School name	Address	Tel	Fax	Headteacher	Ref	Ages	Pupils	Other
Trinity School	Heathway, Dagenham, Essex RM10 7SJ	020 8270 1601	020 8270 4969	Ms Helena Hardie	301-7005	3–19	235	PD MLD SLD

Barnet

School name	Address	Tel	Fax	Headteacher	Ref	Ages	Pupils	Other
Mapledown School	Claremont Rd, Cricklewood, London NW2 1TR	020 8455 4111	020 8455 4895	Mr Steve Carroll	302-7010	11–19	61	SLD
Northway School	The Fairway, Mill Hill, London NW7 3HS	020 8959 4232	020 8959 6436	Mrs Lesley Burgess	302-7005	3–11	68	ASD MLD
Oak Lodge School	Heath View, off East End Rd, East Finchley, London N2 0QY	020 8444 6711	020 8444 6468	Mrs L. Walker	302-7000	11–19	158	ASD MLD
Oakleigh School	Oakleigh Rd North, Whetstone, London N20 0DH	020 8368 5336	020 8361 6922	Mrs J. Gridley	302-7009	2–11	45	ASD SLD DMP

Bexley

School name	Address	Tel	Fax	Headteacher	Ref	Ages	Pupils	Other
Marlborough School	Marlborough Park Ave, Sidcup, Kent DA15 9DP	020 8300 6896	020 8309 5612	Ms A.R. Chamberlain	303-7002	11–19	74	SLD
Oakwood School	Woodside Rd, Bexleyheath, Kent DA7 6LB	01322 553787	01322 526754	Mrs Rachel Lindsey	303-7004	11–16	48	SEBD

School name	Address	Tel	Fax	Headteacher	Ref	Ages	Pupils	Other
Shenstone School	94 Old Rd, Crayford, Kent DA1 4DZ	01322 524145	01322 523551	Mrs Linda Aldcroft	303-7001	2–11	58	SLD
Westbrooke School	South Gypsy Rd, Welling, Kent DA16 1JB	020 8304 1320	020 8304 6525	Mrs C.A. Hance	303-7003	5–11	30	B SEBD
Woodside School	Halt Robin Rd, Belvedere, Kent DA17 6DW	01322 433494	01322 433442	Ms L.J. Crooks	303-7000	5–16	227	MLD

Brent

School name	Address	Tel	Fax	Headteacher	Ref	Ages	Pupils	Other
Grove Park School	Grove Pk, Kingsbury, London NW9 0JY	020 8204 3293	020 8905 0353	Ms Kay Johnson	304-7003	2–19	90	PD
Hay Lane School	Grove Pk, Kingsbury, London NW9 0JY	020 8204 5396	020 8905 0971	Mrs P.M. Theuma	304-7009	5–11	117	SLD
Manor School	Chamberlayne Rd, Kensal Rise, London NW10 3NT	020 8968 3160	020 8968 3075	Mrs Jo Gilbert	304-7006	4–11	120	ASD MLD
Vernon House School	Drury Way, London NW10 0NQ	020 8451 6961		Mr G.S. Davidson	304-7005	4–12	34	B SEBD
Woodfield School	Glenwood Ave, Kingsbury, London NW9 7LY	020 8205 1977	020 8205 5877	Miss Desiree Collins	304-7000	11–19	115	MLD

Bromley

School name	Address	Tel	Fax	Headteacher	Ref	Ages	Pupils	Other
Burwood School	Avalon Rd, Orpington, Kent BR6 9BD	01689 821205	01689 820593	Mr Terence Patrick Leary Quinn	305-7011	7–16	53	B SEBD
Glebe School	Hawes La, West Wickham, Kent BR4 9AE	020 8777 4540	020 8777 5572	Mr K. Seed	305-5950	11–16		MLD
Marjorie McClure School	Hawkwood La, Chislehurst, Kent BR7 5PS	020 8467 0174	020 8467 3275	Dr J.W. Wardle	305-7005	3–18	69	PD
Riverside School	Main Rd, St Pauls Cray, Orpington, Kent BR5 3HS	01689 870519	01689 898818	V. Hinchcliffe	305-7012	3–19		SLD PMLD

Camden

School name	Address	Tel	Fax	Headteacher	Ref	Ages	Pupils	Other
Chalcot School	Harmood St, London NW1 8DP	020 7485 2147	020 7485 9297	Mrs E. Hales	202-7137	11–16	39	B SEBD
Childrens Hospital School at Gt Ormond Street and UCH	Gt Ormond St, GOS Hospital for Children, London WC1N 3JH	020 7813 8269	020 7813 8269	Mrs Y. Hill	202-5950	4–16		HS
Frank Barnes School for Deaf Children	Harley Rd, Swiss Cottage, London NW3 3BN	020 7586 4665	020 7722 4415	Ms Karen Simpson	202-7008	2–11	30	N
Jack Taylor School	Ainsworth Way, London NW8 0SR	020 7328 6731	020 7328 1590	Mr Stephen Smith	202-7185	5–19	60	SLD
Royal Free Hospital Children's School	6th Fl Special School Malcolm Ward, Pond St, London NW3 2QG	020 7472 6298		Ms Manuela Beste	202-7201	5–19	5	HS
Swiss Cottage School	Avenue Rd, London NW8 6HX	020 7681 8080	020 7681 8082	Ms Kay Bedford	202-7205	2–16	138	PD MLD

Croydon

School name	Address	Tel	Fax	Headteacher	Ref	Ages	Pupils	Other
Beckmead School	Monks Orchard Rd, Beckenham, Kent BR3 3BZ	020 8777 9311	020 8777 6550	Mr Kim Johnson	306-7004	7–16	77	B SEBD
Bensham Manor School	Ecclesbourne Rd, Thornton Heath, Surrey CR7 7BN	020 8684 0116	020 8683 1301	Mr Raymond Knight	306-7000	11–16	161	ASD MLD
Priory School	Tennison Rd, South Norwood, London SE25 5RR	020 8653 8222	020 8771 6761	Ms Jillian Thomas	306-7008	11–19	61	ASD SLD
Red Gates School	489 Purley Way, Croydon, Surrey CR0 4RG	020 8688 1761		Mrs Sue Beaman	306-7006	4–12	71	ASD SLD DMP
St Giles School	Pampisford Rd, South Croydon, Surrey CR2 6DF	020 8680 2141	020 8681 6359	Mrs J.P. Thomas	306-7001	5–19	98	PD PMLD
St Nicholas School	Reedham Dr, Old Lodge La, Purley, Surrey CR8 4DN	020 8660 4861	020 8660 8119	Mrs J. Melton	306-7005	4–11	99	ASD MLD

7

Ealing

School name	Address	Tel	Fax	Headteacher	Ref	Ages	Pupils	Other
Belvue School	Rowdell Rd, Northolt, Middlesex UB5 6AG	020 8841 3616	020 8841 4409	Ms Shelagh O'Shea	307-7005	12–18	118	MLD
Castlebar School	Hathaway Gdns, Ealing, London W13 0DH	020 8998 3135	020 8810 7597	Mr Paul Adair	307-7007	3–12	99	MLD
John Chilton School	Compton Cres, Northolt, Middlesex UB5 5LD	020 8842 1329	020 8841 1328	Mr Simon Rosenberg	307-7012	2–17	80	PD
Mandeville School	Eastcote La, Northolt, Middlesex UB5 4HW	020 8864 4921	020 8423 1096	Mrs S. Blee	307-7010	4–12	58	SLD
St Ann's School	Springfield Rd, Hanwell, London W7 3JP	020 8567 6291	020 8840 4664	Ms Gillian Carver	307-7014	12–19	77	CD SLD
Springhallow School	Compton Cl, Cavendish Ave, Ealing, London W13 0JG	020 8998 2700	020 8810 7610	Ms Jayne Jardine	307-7013	5–16	73	CD ASD

Enfield

School name	Address	Tel	Fax	Headteacher	Ref	Ages	Pupils	Other
Aylands School	Keswick Dr, Enfield, Middlesex EN3 6NY	01992 761229	01992 767032	Mr Finlay Douglas	308-7004	7–16	34	SEBD
Durants School	4 Pitfield Way, Enfield, Middlesex EN3 5BY	020 8804 1980	020 8804 0976	Ms Helen Bruce	308-7000	4–18	94	ASD SLD
Oaktree School	Chase Side, Southgate, London N14 4HN	020 8440 3100	020 8440 4891	Mr Harrison	308-7005	4–18	90	SEBD SLD
Russet House School	11 Autumn Cl, Enfield, Middlesex EN1 4JA	020 8350 0650		Mrs J. Foster	308-7008	3–11	65	CD ASD SEBD MLD DMP
Waverley School	105 The Ride, Enfield, Middlesex EN3 7DL	020 8805 1858	020 8805 4397	Ms L. Gibbs	308-7007	3–19	102	SLD
West Lea School	Haselbury Rd, Edmonton, London N9 9TU	020 8807 2656	020 8803 5203	Mrs A. Fox	308-7002	4–18	88	CD PD SLD

Greenwich

School name	Address	Tel	Fax	Headteacher	Ref	Ages	Pupils	Other
Charlton School	Charlton Park Rd, London SE7 8HX	020 8854 6259	020 8855 1022	Mr Mark Dale Emberton	203-7199	11–19	140	R
Moatbridge School	Eltham Palace Rd, Eltham, London SE9 5LX	020 8850 8081	020 8850 0987	Mr M.S. Byron	203-7118	11–16	44	B SEBD
Waterside School	Robert St, London SE18 7NB	020 8317 7659	020 8317 2315	Miss Susan Vernoit	203-7200	5–11	21	
Willow Dene School	Swingate La, London SE18 2JD	020 8854 9841	020 8854 9846	Ms Pip Hardaker	203-7201	2–11	149	

Hackney

School name	Address	Tel	Fax	Headteacher	Ref	Ages	Pupils	Other
Downsview School	Tiger Way, Downs Rd, London E5 8QP	020 8985 6833	020 8985 4020	Mr William R. Bulman	204-7144	4–11	50	
Horizon School	Wordsworth Rd, London N16 8BZ	020 7254 8096	020 7923 3665	Miss Anne Uhart	204-7161	5–16	83	MLD
Ickburgh School	Ickburgh Rd, Clapton, London E5 8AD	020 8806 4638	020 8806 7189	Ms Shirleyanne Sullivan	204-7171	2–19	78	SLD
Stormont House School	Downs Park Rd, London E5 8NP	020 8985 4245	020 8985 6886	Mr Kevin McDonnell	204-7097	11–16	92	

Hammersmith and Fulham

School name	Address	Tel	Fax	Headteacher	Ref	Ages	Pupils	Other
Cambridge School	Cambridge Gr, London W6 0LB	020 8748 7585	020 8741 9375	Ms Barton	205-7204	11–16	90	MLD
Gibbs Green School	Mund St, West Kensington, London W14 9LY	020 7385 3908	020 7610 3563	Mr Rod Davies	205-7205	5–11	6	B SEBD
Jack Tizard School	South Africa Rd, London W12 7PA	020 8735 3590	020 8735 3591	Ms Catherine Welsh	205-7203	2–19	68	SLD
Queensmill School	Clancarty Rd, Fulham, London SW6 3AA	020 7384 2330	020 7384 2750	Mrs Jude Ragan	205-7014	3–11	50	CD ASD
Woodlane High School	Du Cane Rd, Hammersmith, London W12 0TN	020 8743 5668	020 8743 9138	Mr N. Holt	205-7153	11–16	51	VI

Haringey

School name	Address	Tel	Fax	Headteacher	Ref	Ages	Pupils	Other
Blanche Nevile School	Admin and Secondary Department, Burlington Rd, Muswell Hill, London N10 1NJ	020 8442 2750	020 8352 2101	Mr Pete Makey	309-7000	3–18	62	CD ASD SEBD MLD SLD
Moselle School	Adams Rd, Tottenham, London N17 6HW	020 8808 8869	020 8801 7074	Mr Martin Doyle	309-7006	4–19	126	PD
Vale Resource Base c o Northumberland Park Community School	c/o Northumberland Park Community School, Trulock Rd, Tottenham, London N17 0PG	020 8801 6111	020 8801 1140	Mr G. Hill	309-7001	2–19	78	
William C Harvey School	Adams Rd, London N17 6HW	020 8808 7120	020 8885 2719	Ms M. Sumner	309-7005	3–19	60	SLD

Harrow

School name	Address	Tel	Fax	Headteacher	Ref	Ages	Pupils	Other
Alexandra School	Alexandra Ave, South Harrow, Harrow, Middlesex HA2 9DX	020 8864 2739	020 8864 9336	Mr D. Goldthorpe	310-7004	2–12	102	SEBD MLD
Kingsley High School	Whittlesea Rd, Harrow, Middlesex HA3 6ND	020 8421 3676	020 8421 7597	Ms K. Johnson	310-7005	12–19	58	
Shaftesbury High School	Headstone La, Harrow, Middlesex HA3 6LE	020 8428 2482	020 8420 2361	Mr P. Williams	310-7002	11–17	96	SEBD
Woodlands First and Middle School	Bransgrove Rd, Edgware, Middlesex HA8 6JP	020 8421 3637	020 8731 2360	Mr John Feltham	310-7006	3–12	53	

Havering

School name	Address	Tel	Fax	Headteacher	Ref	Ages	Pupils	Other
Corbets Tey School	Harwood Hall La, Upminster, Essex RM14 2YQ	01708 225888	01708 220430	Mr Colin V. Arthey	311-7001	4–16	105	MLD
Dycorts School	Settle Rd, Harold Hill, Romford, Essex RM3 9YA	01708 343649	01708 386361	Mr G. Wroe	311-7002	4–16	65	ASD PD MLD
Ravensbourne School	Neave Cres, Faringdon Ave, Harold Hill, Romford, Essex RM3 8HN	01708 341800		Mrs Margaret Cameron	311-7003	2–19	89	SLD

Hillingdon

School name	Address	Tel	Fax	Headteacher	Ref	Ages	Pupils	Other
Chantry School	Falling La, Yiewsley, West Drayton, Middlesex UB7 8AB	01895 446747	01895 441525	Mrs P. Black	312-5950	11–16		SEBD
Grangewood School	Fore St, Eastcote, Pinner, Middlesex HA5 2JQ	01895 676401	01895 621584	Mr J. Ayres	312-7012	3–11	63	SLD
Hedgewood School	Weymouth Rd, Hayes, Middlesex UB4 8NF	020 8845 6756	020 8845 6756	Mr M.J. Goddard	312-7009	5–11	91	MLD
Meadow High School	Royal La, Hillingdon, Uxbridge, Middlesex UB8 3QU	01895 443310	01895 420925	Mr Ross Macdonald	312-7004	11–18	154	MLD
Moorcroft School	Bramble Cl, Hillingdon, Uxbridge, Middlesex UB8 3BF	01895 437799	01895 438123	Mrs J. Nuthall	312-7010	11–19	64	SLD
The Willows School	Stipularis Dr, off Glencoe Rd, Hayes, Middlesex UB4 9QB	020 8841 7176	020 8842 4443	Mrs F. King	312-7002	3–11	26	SEBD

Hounslow

School name	Address	Tel	Fax	Headteacher	Ref	Ages	Pupils	Other
The Cedars Primary School	High St, Cranford, Hounslow, Middlesex TW5 9RU	020 8230 0015	020 8230 0016	Mrs Lesley Julian	313-7010	5–11	42	B SEBD
Lindon Bennett School	Main St, Hanworth, Feltham, Middlesex TW13 6ST	020 8898 0479	020 8893 4630	Mr S. Line	313-7007	3–11	81	SLD
Marjory Kinnon School	Hatton Rd, Bedfont, Feltham, Middlesex TW14 9QZ	020 8890 2032	020 8893 7450	Mr Alan Robertson	313-7005	4–16	152	VI CD ASD SEBD PD MLD
Oaklands School	Woodlands Rd, Isleworth, Middlesex TW7 6JZ	020 8560 3569	020 8568 8805	Mrs E. Felstead	313-7006	11–19	63	SLD
Syon Park School	Twickenham Rd, Isleworth, Middlesex TW7 6AU	020 8560 4300	020 8569 8104	Mr Krzysztof Nowobilski	313-7009	11–16		SEBD

7

Islington

School name	Address	Tel	Fax	Headteacher	Ref	Ages	Pupils	Other
The Bridge School	251 Hungerford Rd, London N7 9LD	020 7226 8223	020 7619 1000	Mr J. Wolger	206-7031	2–19	124	ASD PMLD DMP
Richard Cloudesley PH School	Golden La, London EC1Y 0TJ	020 7251 1161		Ms Anne Corbett	206-7030	2–17	62	PD
Samuel Rhodes MLD School	Dowrey St, off Richmond Ave, Islington, London N1 0HY	020 7837 9075	020 7837 4030	Ms Jackie Blount	206-7146	5–16	74	MLD

Kensington and Chelsea

School name	Address	Tel	Fax	Headteacher	Ref	Ages	Pupils	Other
Chelsea Children's Hospital School	369 Fulham Rd, London SW10 9NH	020 8746 8672	020 8746 8683	Mrs Janette Steel	207-7165	3–19	7	HS
Parkwood Hall School	Beechenlea La, Swanley, Kent BR8 8DR	01322 664441	01322 619013	Mr Nick White	207-7164	8–19	72	R CD ASD SEBD MLD SLD SpLD

Kingston upon Thames

School name	Address	Tel	Fax	Headteacher	Ref	Ages	Pupils	Other
Bedelsford School	Grange Rd, Kingston Upon Thames, Surrey KT1 2QZ	020 8546 9838	020 8296 9238	Mr J. Murfitt	314-5950	2–16		PD PMLD
Dysart School	190 Ewell Rd, Surbiton, Surrey KT6 6HL	020 8412 2600	020 8412 2700	Ms Steph James	314-7002	2–19	68	ASD SLD
St Philip's School	Harrow Cl, Leatherhead Road, Chessington, Surrey KT9 2HR	020 8397 2672	020 8739 1969	Mrs H.J. Goodall	314-7001	11–19	119	MLD

Lambeth

School name	Address	Tel	Fax	Headteacher	Ref	Ages	Pupils	Other
Elm Court School	Elmcourt Rd, West Norwood, London SE27 9BZ	020 8670 6577	020 8766 0309	Mr W. Hutcheson	208-7115	6–16	78	SEBD MLD
Lansdowne School	Argyll Cl, Dalyell Rd, London SW9 9QL	020 7737 3713	020 7738 6877	Mrs G. Bealing	208-7001	11–16	116	MLD
The Livity School	Mandrell Rd, Brixton, London SW2 5DW	020 7733 0681	020 7738 7154	Ms Geraldine Lee	208-7194	2–11	65	
The Michael Tippett School	Oakden St, Kennington, London SE11 4UG	020 7735 9081	020 7735 9082	Ms Jan Stogdon	208-7195	11–19	62	
Turney Primary and Secondary Special School	Turney Rd, London SE21 8LX	020 8670 7220	020 8766 7588	Mrs Linda Adams	208-5950	5–16	62	MLD

Lewisham

School name	Address	Tel	Fax	Headteacher	Ref	Ages	Pupils	Other
Brent Knoll School	Mayow Rd, London SE23 2XH	020 8699 1047	020 8291 7216	Mr Jonathan Sharpe	209-7038	4–16	131	VI CD ASD SEBD MSI PD SLD PMLD SpLD DMP
Greenvale School	Waters Rd, Catford, London SE6 1UF	020 8465 0740	020 8465 0764	Mrs Alison Youd	209-7180	11–19	82	VI CD ASD SEBD MSI PD MLD PMLD SpLD DMP
Meadowgate School	Revelon Rd, Brockley, London SE4 2PR	020 7635 9022	020 7635 9174	Mr Cassim Bakharia	209-7149	4–11	70	VI CD ASD SEBD MSI PD SLD PMLD SpLD DMP
New Woodlands School	49 Shroffold Rd, Downham, Bromley, Kent BR1 5PD	020 8314 9911	020 8314 3475	Mr D.H. Harper	209-7141	5–14	13	VI CD ASD MSI PD MLD SLD PMLD SpLD DMP
Pendragon School	Pendragon Rd, Downham, Bromley, Kent BR1 5LD	020 8698 9738	020 8698 9500	Mr P. Martinez	209-7105	11–17	122	VI CD ASD SEBD MSI PD SLD PMLD SpLD DMP
Watergate School	Lushington Rd, Bellingham, London SE6 3WG	020 8695 6555	020 8695 8280	Mrs A. Youd	209-7182	3–11	62	VI CD ASD SEBD MSI PD MLD PMLD SpLD DMP

Merton

School name	Address	Tel	Fax	Headteacher	Ref	Ages	Pupils	Other
Cricket Green School	Lower Grn West, Mitcham, Surrey CR4 3AF	020 8640 1177	020 8640 4539	Mrs Celia Dawson	315-7006	5–16	124	CD ASD SEBD PD MLD SLD SpLD DMP
Melrose School	Church Rd, Mitcham, Surrey CR4 3BE	020 8646 2620	020 8646 7125	Mr D. Eglin	315-7003	11–16	31	SEBD
St Ann's School	Bordesley Rd, Morden, Surrey SM4 5LT	020 8648 9737	020 8640 5185	Mrs Tina Harvey	315-7004	2–19	82	VI ASD PD SLD

Newham

School name	Address	Tel	Fax	Headteacher	Ref	Ages	Pupils	Other
Eleanor Smith School	North St, Plaistow, London E13 9HN	020 8471 0018	020 8472 1388	Mr Andrew Hall	316-7007	5–14		SEBD
John F Kennedy Special School	Pitchford St, Stratford, London E15 4RZ	020 8534 8544	020 8555 3530	Mrs G. Goldsmith	316-7004	2–19	70	VI CD ASD SEBD MSI PD MLD PMLD SpLD DMP

Redbridge

School name	Address	Tel	Fax	Headteacher	Ref	Ages	Pupils	Other
Hatton School and Special Needs Centre	Roding La South, Woodford Green, Essex IG8 8EU	020 8551 4131	020 8503 9066	Mrs Sue Blows	317-7007	4–11	123	CD MLD
Little Heath School	Hainault Rd, Little Heath, Romford, Essex RM6 5RX	020 8599 4864	020 8590 8953	Mr P. Johnson	317-5950	11–16		ASD MLD DMP
The New Rush Hall School	Fencepiece Rd, Hainault, Ilford, Essex IG6 2LJ	020 8501 3951	020 8500 9309	Mr J. D'Abbro	317-7004	5–16	51	SEBD
Newbridge School	Barley Lane Campus, 258 Barley La, Goodmays, Ilford, Essex IG3 8XS	020 8599 1768	020 8599 6898	Mr Peter Bouldstride	317-7009	2–19	130	VI HI CD MLD SLD PMLD

Richmond upon Thames

School name	Address	Tel	Fax	Headteacher	Ref	Ages	Pupils	Other
Clarendon School	Hanworth Rd, Hampton, Middlesex TW12 3DH	020 8979 1165	020 8941 3069	Mrs A. Coward	318-7000	7–16	109	MLD
Strathmore School	Meadlands Dr, Petersham, Richmond, Surrey TW10 7ED	020 8948 0047	020 8948 0047	Mr S. Rosenberg	318-7007	3–19	44	SLD

Southwark

School name	Address	Tel	Fax	Headteacher	Ref	Ages	Pupils	Other
Beormund Primary School	Crosby Row, Long La, London SE1 3PS	020 7525 9027	020 7525 9026	Ms Sharon Gray	210-7167	5–11	26	B SEBD
Bethlem and Maudsley Hospital School	Monks Orchard Rd, Beckenham, Kent BR3 3BX	020 8777 1897	020 8777 1239	Dr John Ivens	210-7073	4–19	17	HS
Bredinghurst School	Stuart Rd, Peckham Rye, London SE15 3AZ	020 7639 2541	020 7732 5502	Ms J. Anderson	210-7064	11–16	38	B R SEBD
Cherry Garden School	Macks Rd, London SE16 3XU	020 7237 4050	020 7237 7513	Ms Teresa Neary	210-7186	2–11	45	CD ASD PD SLD
The Evelina Hospital School	Lambeth Palace Rd, St Thomas' Hospital, London SE1 7EH	020 7188 2267	020 7188 2265	Mrs Manuela Beste	210-7066	3–18	12	HS
Haymerle School	Haymerle Rd, London SE15 6SY	020 7639 6080	020 7277 9906	Miss Elizabeth Nolan	210-7126	5–11	59	
Highshore School	Bellenden Rd, Peckham, London SE15 5BB	020 7639 7211	020 7252 9024	Ms C. Wood	210-7007	11–16	131	CD MLD
Spa School	Monnow Rd, London SE1 5RN	020 7237 3714	020 7237 6601	Mr Simon Eccles	210-7048	11–19	91	ASD
Tuke School	4 Woods Rd, Peckham, London SE15 2PX	020 7639 5584	020 7635 8937	Ms Heidi Tully	210-7174	11–19	53	ASD SLD

7

Sutton

School name	Address	Tel	Fax	Headteacher	Ref	Ages	Pupils	Other
Carew Manor School	Church Rd, Wallington, Surrey SM6 7NH	020 8647 8349	020 8647 1739	Mr M. Midgley	319-7000	7–16	140	MLD
Sherwood Park School	Streeters La, Wallington, Surrey SM6 7NP	020 8773 9930		Mrs Mary Clare Fionda	319-7002	2–19	75	PD SLD DMP
Wandle Valley School	Welbeck Rd, Carshalton, Surrey SM5 1LW	020 8648 1365	020 8646 7840	Mr D.L. Bone	319-7005	5–16	73	SEBD

Tower Hamlets

School name	Address	Tel	Fax	Headteacher	Ref	Ages	Pupils	Other
Beatrice Tate School	St Jude's Rd, London E2 9RW	020 7739 6249	020 7613 1507	Mr Alan Black	211-7168	11–19	60	SLD
Bowden House School	Firle Rd, Seaford, East Sussex BN25 2JB	01323 894138	01323 492057	Mr Asif Arif	211-7084	10–16	31	B R SEBD
The Cherry Trees School	68 Campbell Rd, Bow, London E3 4EA	020 8983 4344	020 8983 9616	Mr. Alan Fletcher	211-7170	5–11	1	B SEBD
Ian Mikardo School	60 William Guy Gdns, Talwin St, London E3 3LF	020 8981 2413	020 8981 2418	Ms Claire Lillis	211-7171	11–16	30	B SEBD
Phoenix School	49 Bow Rd, London E3 2AD	020 8980 4740	020 8980 6342	Mr Stewart Harris	211-7095	4–17	96	CD ASD SEBD MLD DMP
Stephen Hawking School	Brunton Pl, London E14 7LL	020 7423 9848	020 7423 9878	Mr Matthew Rayner	211-7169	2–11	70	SLD

Waltham Forest

School name	Address	Tel	Fax	Headteacher	Ref	Ages	Pupils	Other
Belmont Park School	Leyton Green Rd, Leyton, London E10 6DB	020 8556 0006	020 8556 5680	Ms M. Loizou	320-7011	11–16	55	SEBD
Brookfield House School	Alders Ave, Woodford Green, Essex IG8 9PY	020 8527 2464	020 8527 8328	Mr Martin Bryan	320-7005	2–16	81	PD
Joseph Clarke School	Vincent Rd, London E4 9PP	020 8523 4833	020 8523 5003	Mr F. Smith	320-7000	2–18	101	VI PMLD
Whitefield Schools and Centre	Macdonald Rd, Walthamstow, London E17 4AZ	020 8531 3426	020 8527 0907	Mr N. Chapman	320-5950	2–19	295	R VI CD ASD PD MLD SLD SpLD DMP
William Morris School	Folly La, Walthamstow, London E17 5NT	020 8503 2225	020 8503 2227	Mr Ian Johnston	320-7010	11–19	129	CD ASD SEBD PD MLD SLD SpLD

Wandsworth

School name	Address	Tel	Fax	Headteacher	Ref	Ages	Pupils	Other
Bradstow School	34 Dumpton Park Dr, Broadstairs, Kent CT10 1BY	01843 862123	01843 866648	Mr Bert Furze	212-7077	6–19	50	R ASD SEBD SLD
Elsley School	co Nightingale School, Beechcroft Road, London SW17 7DF	020 7738 2968	020 7738 9119	Mrs Margaret Fisher	212-7208	5–11	18	SEBD
Garratt Park School	Waldron Rd, Earlsfield, Wandsworth, London SW18 3TB	020 8946 5769	020 8947 5605	Mrs J. Price	212-7207	11–18	161	VI CD ASD SEBD MLD
Greenmead School	St Margaret's Cres, Putney, London SW15 6HL	020 8789 1466	020 8788 5945	Ms P. Morley	212-7123	3–11	38	PD
Linden Lodge School	61 Princes Way, Wimbledon Pk, London SW19 6JB	020 8788 0107	020 8780 2712	Mr R. Legate	212-7067	4–18	103	R VI
Nightingale School	Beechcroft Rd, Tooting, London SW17 7DF	020 8874 9096	020 8877 3724	Mr Jonathan Clark	212-7209	11–16	63	B R SEBD
Oak Lodge School	101 Nightingale La, London SW12 8NA	020 8673 3453	020 8673 9397	Mr Peter Merrifield	212-7068	11–19	86	R
Paddock School	Priory La, London SW15 5RT	020 8878 1521	020 8392 9735	Miss Linda Charman	212-7183	3–19	90	SLD

Westminster

School name	Address	Tel	Fax	Headteacher	Ref	Ages	Pupils	Other
College Park School	Garway Rd, London W2 4PH	020 7641 4460	020 7221 4786	Ms Frances Crockwell	213-7042	5–16	78	MLD
Queen Elizabeth II Jubilee School	Kennet Rd, London W9 3LG	020 7641 5825	020 7641 5823	Ms Mary Loughnan	213-7184	5–19	68	SLD

North East

Darlington

School name	Address	Tel	Fax	Headteacher	Ref	Ages	Pupils	Other
Beaumont Hill School	Salters La South, Darlington, County Durham DL1 2AN	01325 254000	01325 254222	Dame Dela Smith	841-7031	2–19	205	CD ASD SEBD PD MLD SLD

Durham

School name	Address	Tel	Fax	Headteacher	Ref	Ages	Pupils	Other
Durham Trinity School	Flambard Premises, Aykley Heads, Durham, County Durham DH1 5TS	0191 386 4612		Miss J.A. Connolly	840-7032	2–19	179	MLD SLD
Elemore Hall School	Pittington, Durham, County Durham DH6 1QD	0191 372 0275	0191 372 1529	Mr Richard Royle	840-7006	11–16	85	R SEBD
Evergreen Primary School	Warwick Rd, Bishop Auckland, Durham DL14 6LS	01388 459721		Mrs Margaret Wilson	840-7034	2–11	106	ASD MLD SLD PMLD
Glendene School	Crawlaw Rd, Easington Colliery, Peterlee, County Durham SR8 3LP	0191 527 0304		Mr E. Baker	840-7029	2–19	157	ASD MLD SLD PMLD
Hare Law School	Catchgate, Annfield Plain, Stanley, County Durham DH9 8DT	01207 234547	01207 234922	Mrs Maggie Collins	840-7013	5–16	92	ASD MLD SLD PMLD
The Meadows School	Whitworth La, Spennymoor, County Durham DL16 7QW	01388 811178		Mr G. Harris	840-7000	11–16	72	SEBD
The Oaks Secondary School	Rock Rd, Spennymoor, Durham DL16 7DB	01388 827380	01388 827314	Mrs Andrea English	840-7033	11–19	220	ASD MLD SLD PMLD
Villa Real School	Villa Real Rd, Consett, County Durham DH8 6BH	01207 503651	01207 500755	Mrs Fiona Wood	840-7028	2–19	85	ASD MLD SLD PMLD
Walworth School	Bluebell Way, Newton Aycliffe, County Durham DL5 7LP	01325 300194	01325 312735	Mr P. Wallbanks	840-7014	4–11	47	R SEBD
Windlestone School	Dene Bridge Row, Chilton, Ferryhill, County Durham DL17 0HP	01388 720337	01388 724904	Mr Pete Jonson	840-7030	11–16	89	B R SEBD

Gateshead

School name	Address	Tel	Fax	Headteacher	Ref	Ages	Pupils	Other
The Cedars School	Ivy La, Low Fell, Gateshead, Tyne and Wear NE9 6QD	0191 433 4046	0191 482 0926	Mr E. Bartley	390-7002	3–16	76	CD PD
Dryden School	Shotley Gdns, Low Fell, Gateshead, Tyne and Wear NE9 5UR	0191 420 3811	0191 420 0608	Mrs Becky Harrison	390-7009	11–19	52	SLD
Eslington Primary School	Hazel Rd, Gateshead, Tyne And Wear NE8 2EP	0191 478 5198	0191 478 7621	Mrs P. Lowrie	390-7010	7–11	25	SEBD
Furrowfield School	Whitehill Dr, Felling, Gateshead, Tyne and Wear NE10 9RZ	0191 433 4071	0191 420 0905	Mrs Emma Bell	390-7006	11–16	52	B R SEBD
Gibside School	Burnthouse La, Whickham, Newcastle upon Tyne, Tyne and Wear NE16 5AT	0191 441 0123	0191 441 0124	Ms P. Gilbert	390-7007	4–11	84	ASD
Hill Top School	Wealcroft, Felling, Gateshead, Tyne and Wear NE10 8LT	0191 469 2462	0191 438 4166	Ms E. Colquhoun	390-7008	11–16	96	CD ASD SEBD

Hartlepool

School name	Address	Tel	Fax	Headteacher	Ref	Ages	Pupils	Other
Catcote School	Catcote Rd, Hartlepool, Tees Valley TS25 4EZ	01429 264036	01429 234452	Mr Robin Campbell	805-7026	11–19	71	
Springwell School	Wiltshire Way, Hartlepool, North Yorkshire TS26 0TB	01429 280600	01429 280600	Mr Karl Telfer	805-7027	3–11	52	

7

Middlesbrough

School name	Address	Tel	Fax	Headteacher	Ref	Ages	Pupils	Other
Beverley School	Beverley Rd, Saltersgill, Middlesbrough TS4 3LQ	01642 277444	01642 277453	Mr Nigel Carden	806-7003	4-19	99	ASD
Holmwood School	Saltersgill Ave, Easterside, Middlesbrough, North Yorkshire TS4 3PT	01642 819157	01642 829981	Mr John Appleyard	806-7005	4-11	79	MLD SEBD
Priory Woods School	Tothill Ave, Netherfields, Middlesbrough, North Yorkshire TS3 0RH	01642 321212	01642 326800	Mrs Bernadette Knill	806-7000	4-19	142	SLD
Tollesby School	Saltersgill Ave, Middlesbrough, North Yorkshire TS4 3JS	01642 815765	01642 823628	Mr Richard Stokoe	806-7004	11-16	109	MLD SEBD

Newcastle upon Tyne

School name	Address	Tel	Fax	Headteacher	Ref	Ages	Pupils	Other
Hadrian School	Bertram Cres, Newcastle upon Tyne, Tyne and Wear NE15 6PY	0191 273 4440	0191 226 1150	Mr Christopher Rollings	391-7034	2-11	125	PD SLD
Newcastle Bridges School c/o Royal Victoria Infirmary Ward 10	c/o Royal Victoria Infirmary Ward 10, Queen Victoria Rd, Newcastle Upon Tyne, Tyne and Wear NE1 4LP	0191 233 0764	0191 233 0765	Mrs Margaret Dover	391-7037	2-19	37	HS
Sir Charles Parsons School	Westbourne Ave, Newcastle upon Tyne, Tyne and Wear NE6 4ED	0191 263 0261	0191 229 0144	Mr Nicholas Sharing	391-7035	11-19	117	SLD
Thomas Bewick School	Hillhead Parkway, Newcastle upon Tyne, Tyne and Wear NE5 1DS	0191 267 5435	0191 267 9857	Mrs Audrey Lindley	391-7036	3-19	66	R ASD
Trinity School	Condercum Rd, Newcastle upon Tyne, Tyne and Wear NE4 8XJ	0191 226 1500	0191 226 1266	Mr Dave Edmondson	391-7033	7-16	140	R SEBD SpLD

North Tyneside

School name	Address	Tel	Fax	Headteacher	Ref	Ages	Pupils	Other
Beacon Hill School	Mullen Rd, High Farm, Wallsend, Tyne and Wear NE28 9HA	0191 200 6339	0191 200 5217	Mrs Helen M. Jones	392-7008	3-19	134	SLD PMLD
Glebe School	Woodburn Dr, Whitley Bay, Tyne and Wear NE26 3HW	0191 200 8776	0191 200 8774	Mrs L. Turner	392-7004	4-11	87	ASD SEBD MLD
Silverdale School	Langdale Gdns, Howdon, Wallsend, Tyne and Wear NE28 0HG	0191 200 5982	0191 200 6710	Mr Brian Hedley	392-7007	7-16	33	MLD
Southlands School	Beach Rd, Tynemouth, North Shields, Tyne and Wear NE30 2QR	0191 200 6348	0191 200 5674	Mr D.J. Erskine	392-7002	11-16	92	SEBD MLD
Woodlawn School	Langley Ave, West Monkseaton, Whitley Bay, Tyne and Wear NE25 9DF	0191 200 8729	0191 200 8616	Mr B. Hickman	392-7001	2-16	58	CD PD

Northumberland

School name	Address	Tel	Fax	Headteacher	Ref	Ages	Pupils	Other
Atkinson House School	North Terr, Seghill, Cramlington, Northumberland NE23 7EB	0191 298 0838	0191 298 0448	Mr Richard McGlashan	929-7024	11-16	37	B SEBD
Barndale House School	Howling La, Alnwick, Northumberland NE66 1DQ	01665 602541		Mr Leslie Gair	929-7010	3-19	39	R SLD
Cleaswell Hill School	School Ave, Guide Post, Choppington, Northumberland NE62 5DJ	01670 823182	01670 823182	Mr K. Burdis	929-7003	5-16	87	MLD
Cramlington Hillcrest School	East View Ave, East Farm, Cramlington, Northumberland NE23 1DY	01670 713632	01670 713920	Mr C. Gibson	929-7006	11-16	52	MLD
East Hartford School	East Hartford, Cramlington, Northumberland NE23 3AR	01670 713881	01670 737199	Mr H. Steel	929-7021	4-11	32	MLD
The Grove Special School	Grove Gdns, Tweedmouth, Berwick-upon-Tweed, Northumberland TD15 2EN	01289 306390		Mrs Elizabeth Brown	929-7012	3-19	27	SLD
Hexham Priory School	Dene Pk, Hexham, Northumberland NE46 1HN	01434 605021	01434 609022	Mr Michael Thompson	929-7018	3-19	36	SLD
Morpeth Collingwood School	Stobhillgate, Morpeth, Northumberland NE61 2HA	01670 516374		Ms C. Hetherington	929-7022	4-16	92	MLD

Redcar and Cleveland

School name	Address	Tel	Fax	Headteacher	Ref	Ages	Pupils	Other
Kilton Thorpe School	Marshall Dr, Brotton, Saltburn-by-the-Sea, North Yorkshire TS12 2UW	01287 677265	01287 677265	Mr Kevin Thompson	807-7030	2–19	107	
Kirkleatham Hall School	Kirkleatham, Kirkleatham Village, Redcar TS10 4QR	01642 483009	01642 480054	Mrs Gill Naylor	807-7008	4–19	133	VI HI CD ASD SEBD MSI PD MLD SLD DMP
Pathways Special School	Tennyson Ave, Grangetown, Middlesborough TS6 7NP	01642 779292		Mrs Christine Fairless	807-7031	7–15	49	MLD

South Tyneside

School name	Address	Tel	Fax	Headteacher	Ref	Ages	Pupils	Other
Bamburgh School	Norham Ave, South Shields, Tyne and Wear NE34 7TD	0191 454 0671	0191 427 1931	Mrs J. Fawcett	393-7000	2–17	141	VI CD ASD SEBD MSI PD MLD SLD PMLD SpLD
Epinay Business and Enterprise School	Clervaux Terr, Jarrow, Tyne and Wear NE32 5UP	0191 489 8949		Mrs H. Harrison	393-7004	4–16	105	VI CD ASD SEBD MSI PD SLD PMLD SpLD DMP
The Galsworthy Centre	Galsworthy Rd, South Shields, Tyne and Wear NE34 9UG	0191 426 8180	0191 519 0600	Mr P.J. Leivers	393-7006	11–16	57	SEBD
Greenfields School	Victoria Rd East, Hebburn, Tyne and Wear NE31 1YQ	0191 489 7480	0191 483 7390	Miss M.C. Conway	393-7005	2–19	49	VI CD ASD SEBD MSI PD MLD PMLD SpLD DMP
Margaret Sutton School	Ashley Rd, South Shields, Tyne and Wear NE34 0PF	0191 455 3309	0191 422 0702	Mr Hugh Steele	393-7002	4–19	84	VI CD ASD SEBD MSI PD SLD PMLD SpLD DMP
Oakleigh Gardens School	Oakleigh Gdns, Cleadon, Sunderland, Tyne and Wear SR6 7PT	0191 536 2590	0191 519 0213	Mr Dereck Cogle	393-7003	2–19	55	VI CD ASD SEBD MSI PD MLD PMLD SpLD DMP

Stockton-on-Tees

School name	Address	Tel	Fax	Headteacher	Ref	Ages	Pupils	Other
Abbey Hill School and Technology College	Ketton Rd, Hardwick Est, Stockton-on-Tees TS19 8BU	01642 677113	01642 679198	Ms C. Devine	808-7029	11–19	242	ASD SEBD
Ash Trees School	Bowes Rd, Billingham TS23 2BU	01642 563712	01642 563728	Mr Ian Bowran	808-7028	3–11	120	ASD
King Edwin School	Mill La, Norton, Stockton-on-Tees, North Yorkshire TS20 1LG	01642 360418	01642 360461	Mr A. Riley	808-7018	11–16	57	B R SEBD
Westlands School	Eltham Cres, Thornaby, Stockton-on-Tees, North Yorkshire TS17 9RA	01642 883030	01642 883070	Mr Mike Vening	808-7024	5–19	118	R ASD SEBD MLD

Sunderland

School name	Address	Tel	Fax	Headteacher	Ref	Ages	Pupils	Other
Barbara Priestman School	Meadowside, Sunderland, Tyne and Wear SR2 7QN	0191 553 6000	0191 553 6004	Mrs Noreen Robinson	394-7004	3–19	90	VI PD
Castlegreen Community School	Craigshaw Rd, Hylton Castle, Sunderland, Tyne and Wear SR5 3NF	0191 553 5335	0191 553 5338	Mr Ian Reed	394-7000	11–19	117	SEBD MLD
Columbia Grange School	Oxclose Rd, Washington NE38 7NY	0191 219 3860	0191 219 3865	Mrs Catherine Elliott	394-7001	2–11	65	ASD SLD
Maplewood School	Redcar Rd, Sunderland, Tyne and Wear SR5 5PA	0191 553 5587	0191 553 5585	Mr Gary Mellefont	394-7014	6–13	68	SEBD
Portland School	Weymouth Rd, Chapelgarth, Sunderland, Tyne and Wear SR3 2NQ	0191 553 6050	0191 553 6048	Mrs Jennifer Ann Chart	394-7018	11–19	143	SLD
Springwell Dene School	Swindon Rd, Sunderland, Tyne and Wear SR3 4EE	0191 553 6067	0191 528 2295	Mrs M.D. Mitchell	394-7015	13–16	63	SEBD
Sunningdale School	Shaftoe Rd, Springwell, Sunderland, Tyne and Wear SR3 4HA	0191 553 5880	0191 553 5882	Mr J. McKnight	394-7016	3–13	57	MLD SLD

7

North West

Blackburn with Darwen

School name	Address	Tel	Fax	Headteacher	Ref	Ages	Pupils	Other
Broadlands Virtual School	Shadsworth Rd, Shadsworth Children's Centre, Blackburn, Lancashire BB1 2HR	01254 268980	01254 278760	Mrs Anne Stanley	889-7105	2–7		VI CD ASD SEBD PD MLD SLD
Crosshill Special School	Shadsworth Rd, Blackburn, Lancashire BB1 2HR	01254 667713	01254 664449	Mr Mike Hatch	889-7003	5–16	87	MLD
Fernhurst Secondary SEBD School	Heys La, Blackburn, Lancashire BB2 4NW	01254 261655	01254 267240	Drew Crawshaw	889-7001	11–16	30	SEBD
Newfield School	Oldbank La, Blackburn, Lancashire BB1 2PW	01254 588600	01254 588601	Mrs Jane Barrie	889-7107	2–19	147	PD SLD

Blackpool

School name	Address	Tel	Fax	Headteacher	Ref	Ages	Pupils	Other
Highfurlong School	Blackpool Old Rd, Blackpool, Lancashire FY3 7LR	01253 392188	01253 305600	Mr E.V. Jackson	890-7020	3–19	51	PD
Park School	158 Whitegate Dr, Blackpool, Lancashire FY3 9HF	01253 764130	01253 791108	Mr Keith Berry	890-7019	4–16	162	MLD
Woodlands School	Whitegate Dr, Blackpool, Lancashire FY3 9HF	01253 316722	01253 316723	Mr Sam Forde	890-7025	2–19	84	SLD

Bolton

School name	Address	Tel	Fax	Headteacher	Ref	Ages	Pupils	Other
Firwood School	Crompton Way, Breightmet, Bolton, Lancashire BL2 3AF	01204 333044	01204 333045	Dr Jonathan Steele	350-7004	11–19	92	SLD
Green Fold School	Highfield Rd, Farnworth, Bolton, Lancashire BL4 0RA	01204 333750	01204 444751	Mrs Jane Grecic	350-7008	2–11	57	SLD
Ladywood School	Masefield Rd, Little Lever, Bolton, Lancashire BL3 1NG	01204 333400	01204 333405	Mrs Sally McFarlane	350-7000	4–11	60	MLD
Lever Park School	Stocks Park Dr, Horwich, Bolton, Lancashire BL6 6DE	01204 332666		Mr Colin Roscoe	350-7009	5–16	40	SEBD
Rumworth School	Armadale Rd, Ladybridge, Bolton, Lancashire BL3 4TP	01204 333600	01204 333602	Mr Bill Bradbury	350-7003	11–19	142	MLD
Thomasson Memorial School	Devonshire Rd, Poynton, Bolton, Lancashire BL1 4PJ	01204 333118	01204 495675	Mr Bill Wilson	350-7002	3–11	49	

Bury

School name	Address	Tel	Fax	Headteacher	Ref	Ages	Pupils	Other
Cloughside School	Bury New Rd, Prestwich, Manchester, Lancashire M25 3BL	0161 772 4625	0161 772 3478	Mr Norman Cooke	351-7009	12–18	9	HI SEBD HS
Elms Bank Specialist Arts College	Ripon Ave, Whitefield, Bury, Greater Manchester M45 8PJ	0161 766 1597	0161 766 4303	Ms L. Lines	351-7011	11–19	152	MLD SLD
Millwood Primary Special School	Fletcher Fold Rd, Bury, Lancashire BL9 9RX	0161 764 6957	0161 797 3290	Ms H Chadwick	351-7010	2–11	66	MLD SLD

Cheshire

School name	Address	Tel	Fax	Headteacher	Ref	Ages	Pupils	Other
Adelaide School	Adelaide St, Crewe, Cheshire CW1 3DT	01270 255661	01270 584577	Mr L. Willday	875-7209	11–16	35	SEBD
Capenhurst Grange School	Chester Rd, Gt Sutton, Ellesmere Port, Cheshire CH66 2NA	0151 339 5141	0151 348 0348	Mr Graham Stothard	875-7208	11–16	54	R SEBD
Cloughwood School	Stones Manor La, Hartford, Northwich, Cheshire CW8 1NU	01606 76671	01606 783486	Mr Adrian Larkin	875-7105	8–18	51	B R SEBD
Dee Banks School	Dee Banks, Sandy La, Chester, Cheshire CH3 5UX	01244 324012	01244 346723	Rev Raymond Elliott	875-7000	2–19	72	ASD SLD
Dorin Park School	Wealstone La, Upton, Chester, Cheshire CH2 1HD	01244 381951	01244 390422	Ms Annie Hinchliffe	875-7118	2–16	70	PD
Greenbank Residential School	Greenbank La, Hartford, Northwich, Cheshire CW8 1LD	01606 781072	01606 783736	Mrs Chris Brennan	875-7106	6–18	92	R ASD MLD SLD
Hebden Green Community School	Woodford La West, Winsford, Cheshire CW7 4EJ	01606 594221	01606 861549	Mr Andrew Farren	875-7109	2–19	85	R PD

School name	Address	Tel	Fax	Headteacher	Ref	Ages	Pupils	Other
Hinderton School	Capenhurst La, Whitby, Ellesmere Port, Cheshire CH65 7AQ	0151 355 2177	0151 356 8765	Mr Liam McCallion	875-7115	3–8	31	B CD ASD
Oaklands School	Montgomery Way, Winsford, Cheshire CW7 1NU	01606 551048	01606 861291	Mr Kevin Boyle	875-7108	11–16	122	SEBD MLD
Park Lane School	Park La, Macclesfield, Cheshire SK11 8JR	01625 423407	01625 511191	Mr Dave Calvert	875-7112	2–19	74	SLD
Rosebank School	Townfield La, Barnton, Northwich, Cheshire CW8 4QP	01606 74975	01606 783564	Mrs Helen Johnson	875-7120	3–7	47	ASD
The Russett School	Middlehurst Ave, Weaverham, Northwich, Cheshire CW8 3BW	01606 853005	01606 854669	Mrs H.M. Watts	875-7110	2–19	89	SLD
St John's Wood Community School	Longridge, Knutsford, Cheshire WA16 8PA	01565 634578	01565 750187	Mr Michael Burgess	875-7210	11–16	50	SEBD
Springfield School	Crewe Green Rd, Crewe, Cheshire CW1 5HS	01270 582446	01270 258281	Mr Mark Swaine	875-7111	2–19	107	ASD SLD

Cumbria

School name	Address	Tel	Fax	Headteacher	Ref	Ages	Pupils	Other
George Hastwell School	Moor Tarn La, Walney Island, Barrow-in-Furness, Cumbria LA14 3LW	01229 475253	01229 471418	Mr B. Gummett	909-7017	2–19	85	PD MLD
James Rennie School	California Rd, Kingstown, Carlisle, Cumbria CA3 0BX	01228 607559	01228 607563	Mr S. Bowditch	909-7022	3–19	122	VI CD ASD SEBD PD MLD SLD SpLD DMP
Mayfield School	Moresby Rd, Hensingham, Whitehaven, Cumbria CA28 8TU	01946 852676	01946 852677	Mrs Susan Leathers	909-7002	2–19	88	SLD SpLD
Sandgate School	Sandylands Rd, Kendal, Cumbria LA9 6JG	01539 773636	01539 792101	Mr Tom Robson	909-7006	3–19	49	VI CD ASD PD SLD SpLD
Sandside Lodge School	Sandside Rd, Ulverston, Cumbria LA12 9EF	01229 894180	01229 894180	Mr Martin Alloway	909-7013	2–19	72	PD MLD

Halton

School name	Address	Tel	Fax	Headteacher	Ref	Ages	Pupils	Other
Ashley School	Cawfield Ave, Widnes, Cheshire WA8 7HG	0151 424 4892	0151 424 5980	Mrs L. King	876-7202	8–16	112	SEBD MLD
Brookfields School	Moorfield Rd, Widnes, Cheshire WA8 3JA	0151 424 4329	0151 495 3460	Mr A. Chryssafi	876-7206	2–19	83	ASD SLD
Cavendish School	Lincoln Cl, Runcorn, Cheshire WA7 4YX	01928 561706	01928 566088	Mrs Celia Dickinson	876-7003	2–19	72	SLD
Chesnut Lodge Special School	Green La, Ditton, Widnes, Cheshire WA8 7HF	0151 424 0679	0151 495 2141	Mrs Susan Lancaster	876-7200	2–16	50	PD SLD

Knowsley

School name	Address	Tel	Fax	Headteacher	Ref	Ages	Pupils	Other
Alt Bridge Secondary Support Centre	Wellcroft Rd, Huyton, Liverpool, Merseyside L36 7TA	0151 477 8310	0151 477 8313	Mr B. Kerwin	340-7013	11–16	122	MLD SpLD
The Elms School	Whitethorn Dr, Stockbridge Village, Liverpool, Merseyside L28 1RX	0151 477 8350	0151 477 8351	Mrs L. Lowe	340-7012	2–19	112	AS ASD SLD
Highfield School	Bailey's La, Halewood, Liverpool, Merseyside L26 0TY	0151 288 8930	0151 448 0417	Ms P. Tunna	340-7006	6–16	40	SEBD
Knowsley Central Primary Support Centre	Mossbrow Rd, Huyton, Liverpool, Merseyside L36 7SY	0151 477 8450	0151 489 9154	Mrs T. Thomas	340-7015	2–11	52	MLD SpLD
Knowsley Northern Primary Support Centre	Bramcote Wlk, Northwood, Kirkby, Liverpool, Merseyside L33 9UR	0151 477 8140	0151 477 8141	Mrs B. Twiss	340-7014	3–11	34	CD MLD SpLD
Knowsley Southern Primary Support Centre	Arncliffe Rd, Halewood, Liverpool, Merseyside L25 9QE	0151 288 8950	0151 288 8951	Miss Naomi Richards	340-7016	4–11	26	MLD
Springfield School	Cawthorne Cl, Southdene, Kirkby, Liverpool, Merseyside L32 3XQ	0151 549 1425	0151 546 8995	Mr J. Parkes	340-7005	2–19	76	PD

7

Lancashire

School name	Address	Tel	Fax	Headteacher	Ref	Ages	Pupils	Other
Beacon School	Tanhouse Rd, Tanhouse, Skelmersdale, Lancashire WN8 6BA	01695 721066	01695 732932	Mr Angela Lazarevic	888-7104	5–16	65	SEBD
Bleasdale House Community Special School	27 Emesgate La, Silverdale, Carnforth, Lancashire LA5 0RG	01524 701217	01524 702044	Mrs Kairen Dexter	888-7007	2–19	22	R PD SLD
Broadfield Specialist School	Fielding La, Oswaldtwistle, Accrington, Lancashire BB5 3BE	01254 381782	01254 396805	Mrs J.E. White	888-7060	4–16	114	VI CD ASD SEBD MSI PD SLD PMLD SpLD DMP
Brookfield School	Fouldrey Ave, Poulton-le-Fylde, Lancashire FY6 7HE	01253 886895	01253 882845	Mrs S.M. Sanderson	888-7100	11–16	26	SEBD
Chorley Astley Park School	Harrington Rd, Chorley, Lancashire PR7 1JZ	01257 262227	01257 269074	Mr J. McAndrew	888-7037	4–17	111	MLD
The Coppice School	Ash Gr, Bamber Bridge, Preston, Lancashire PR5 6GY	01772 336342	01772 620826	Mrs A. Jenkins	888-7098	2–19	58	VI CD ASD SEBD MSI PD MLD PMLD SpLD DMP
Great Arley School	Holly Rd, Thornton-Cleveleys, Lancashire FY5 4HH	01253 821072	01253 865073	Mr Paul Mcseveny	888-7040	4–16	86	MLD
Hillside Specialist School for Autism Spectrum Disorder, Communication and Interaction	Ribchester Rd, Longridge, Preston, Lancashire PR3 3XB	01772 782205	01772 782471	Mr Geoff Fitzpatrick	888-7109	2–16	58	ASD
Holly Grove School	Harrogate Cres, Burnley, Lancashire BB10 2NX	01282 424216	01282 831419	Mrs Sue Kitto	888-7114	2–11	70	PD MLD SLD PMLD
Kingsbury Primary Special School	School La, Chapel Hse, Skelmersdale, Lancashire WN8 8EH	01695 722991	01695 51428	Mr John Hajnrych	888-7117	2–11	24	SLD
Kirkham Pear Tree School	29 Station Rd, Kirkham, Preston, Lancashire PR4 2HA	01772 683609	01772 681553	Mrs Lesley Koller	888-7076	2–19	66	MLD
Lostock Hall Moor Hey School	Far Croft, Lostock Hall, Preston, Lancashire PR5 5SS	01772 336976	01772 696670	Mr C.W.T. Wilson	888-7049	4–16	82	MLD
The Loyne School	Sefton Dr, Lancaster, Lancashire LA1 2PZ	01524 64543	01524 845118	Mrs Carol Murphy	888-7097	2–19	74	VI CD ASD MLD SLD DMP
Mayfield School	Gloucester Rd, Chorley, Lancashire PR7 3HN	01257 263063	01257 263072	Ms Gela Griffiths	888-7089	2–19	71	SLD
Moorbrook School	Ainslie Rd, Fulwood, Preston, Lancashire PR2 3DB	01772 774752	01772 713256	Mr Graham Torbett	888-7014	11–16	37	SEBD
Morecambe Road School	Morecambe Rd, Morecambe, Lancashire LA3 3AB	01524 414384	01524 426339	Mr Terence Pickles	888-7034	3–16	146	CD ASD SEBD MLD
The New Burnley Special School	March St, Burnley, Lancashire BB12 0BU	01282 433946	01282 839141	Mrs Fran Entwistle	888-7113	11–19	155	PD MLD SLD PMLD
New Pendle	Town Row, Nelson, Lancashire BB9 8DG	01282 614013	01282 691970	Mr Debbie Morris	888-7112	2–11	55	PD MLD SLD PMLD
North Cliffe School	Blackburn Old Rd, Gt Harwood, Blackburn, Lancashire BB6 7UW	01254 885245		Mr Kevan Thompson	888-7058	5–16	56	MLD
Oswaldtwistle White Ash School	Thwaites Rd, Oswaldtwistle, Accrington, Lancashire BB5 4QG	01254 235772	01254 385652	Mrs Phillipa Conti	888-7099	3–19	44	MLD SpLD DMP
Pendle Community High School	Gibfield Rd, Colne, Lancashire BB8 8JT	01282 865011	01282 859096	Mr Paul Wright	888-7115	11–19	110	PD MLD SLD PMLD
Rawtenstall Cribden House Community Special School	Haslingden Rd, Rawtenstall, Rossendale, Lancashire BB4 6RX	01706 213048		Mrs Jacqueline Lord	888-7044	5–11	37	VI CD ASD MSI PD MLD SLD PMLD SpLD DMP
The Rose School	Swindon St, Burnley, Lancashire BB11 4PF	01282 453072	01282 426842	Ms Nicola Jennings	888-7111	11–16	38	SEBD
Royal Cross Primary School	Elswick Rd, Ashton-on-Ribble, Preston, Lancashire PR2 1NT	01772 729705		Ms Ruth Nottingham	888-7110	4–11	30	
Thornton-Cleveleys Red Marsh School	Holly Rd, Thornton-Cleveleys, Lancashire FY5 4HH	01253 868451	01253 820045	Mrs Anita Tidwell	888-7102	2–19	54	VI CD ASD SEBD MSI PD MLD PMLD SpLD DMP
Tor View School	Clod La, Haslingden, Rossendale, Lancashire BB4 6LR	01706 214640	01706 214640	Mr A.J. Squire	888-7092	4–19	120	ASD PD MLD SLD
Wennington Hall School	Lodge La, Wennington, Lancaster, Lancashire LA2 8NS	01524 221333	01524 222140	Mr Joseph Prendergast	888-7028	11–16	70	B R SEBD
West Lancashire Community High School	School La, Chapel Hse, Skelmersdale, Lancashire WN8 8EH	01695 721487		Ms Sue Reynolds	888-7116	11–19	88	MLD

Liverpool

School name	Address	Tel	Fax	Headteacher	Ref	Ages	Pupils	Other
Abbot's Lea School	Beaconsfield Rd, Woolton, Liverpool, Merseyside L25 6EE	0151 428 1161	0151 428 6180	Mrs Margaret Lucas	341-7025	5–19	109	ASD MLD
Ashfield Secondary Special School	Childwall Abbey Rd, Childwall, Liverpool, Merseyside L16 5EY	0151 722 6199	0151 722 0802	Mr John Ashley	341-7069	11–16	90	VI HI CD ASD SEBD MSI PD MLD SpLD AS ADHD Ep
Bank View High School	Sherwoods La, Liverpool L10 1LW	0151 525 3451	0151 524 1284	Mr Ian Wright	341-7070	11–16	207	CD MLD

School name	Address	Tel	Fax	Headteacher	Ref	Ages	Pupils	Other
Clifford Holroyde Centre of Expertise	Thingwall La, Liverpool, Merseyside L14 7NX	0151 228 9500	0151 228 9318	Mr M. Rees	341-7042	7–16	51	SEBD
Ernest Cookson School	Mill La, West Derby, Liverpool, Merseyside L12 7JA	0151 220 1874	0151 252 1238	Mr Roberts	341-7045	5–16	35	B SEBD
Hope School	Naylorsfield Dr, Netherley, Liverpool, Merseyside L27 0YD	0151 498 4055	0151 498 4868	Mr Rohit Naik	341-7065	5–16	34	B SEBD
Lower Lee School	Beaconsfield Rd, Woolton, Liverpool, Merseyside L25 6EF	0151 428 4071	0151 428 4737	Mr Adrian Larkin	341-7039	8–16	47	B R SEBD
Millstead School	Old Mill La, Liverpool, Merseyside L15 8LW	0151 722 0974	0151 722 5852	Mrs Shirley Jones	341-7054	2–11	64	ASD SLD
Palmerston School	Beaconsfield Rd, Woolton, Liverpool, Merseyside L25 6EE	0151 428 2128	0151 421 0985	Mr J. Wright	341-7051	11–19	83	VI CD ASD SEBD PD SLD
Princes School	Selborne St, Liverpool, Merseyside L8 1YQ	0151 709 2602	0151 709 2602	Mrs Val Healy	341-7063	2–11	76	ASD SLD
Redbridge High School	Sherwoods La, Fazakerley, Liverpool, Merseyside L10 1LW	0151 525 5733	0151 524 0435	Mr Paul Cronin	341-7052	11–19	86	ASD PD SLD
Sandfield Park School	Sandfield Wlk, Liverpool, Merseyside L12 1LH	0151 228 0324	0151 252 1273	Mr J. Hudson	341-7059	11–19	71	PD

Manchester

School name	Address	Tel	Fax	Headteacher	Ref	Ages	Pupils	Other
Ashgate Specialist Support Primary School	Crossacres Rd, Peel Hall, Wythenshawe, Manchester M22 5DR	0161 219 6642		Mr Brian Frew	352-7749	5–11	35	ASD SEBD SLD PMLD
The Birches School	Newholme Rd, West Didsbury, Manchester, Lancashire M20 2XZ	0161 448 8895	0161 445 4970	Mrs M. Morgan	352-7041	2–11	114	SLD
Buglawton Hall School	Buxton Rd, Congleton, Cheshire CW12 3PQ	01260 274492	01260 288313	Mr C. Leah	352-7014	7–16	40	B R SEBD SLD
Camberwell Park Specialist Support School	Bank House Rd, Blackley, Manchester, Lancashire M9 8LT	0161 740 1897	0161 740 3473	Ms Mary Isherwood	352-7023	2–11	86	SLD
Ewing School	Central Rd, Didsbury, Manchester, Lancashire M20 4ZA	0161 445 0745	0161 438 0510	Mrs Pat Derbyshire	352-7025	5–16	77	CD
Grange School	77 Dickenson Rd, Rusholme, Manchester, Lancashire M14 5AZ	0161 248 4841	0161 248 6715	Mrs A. Fitzpatrick	352-7055	4–19	60	ASD
Lancasterian School	Elizabeth Slinger Rd, West Didsbury, Manchester, Lancashire M20 2XA	0161 445 0123	0161 445 6826	Ms C. Cooper	352-7029	2–16	89	PD
Manchester Hospital Schools and Home Teaching Service	Charlestown Rd, Blackley, Manchester, Lancashire M9 7AA	0161 220 5118		Mrs H.E. Jones	352-7007	3–18	10	HS
Meade Hill School	Middleton Rd, Crumpsall, Manchester, Lancashire M8 4NB	0161 795 8445	0161 795 8445	Mr B. Paprosky	352-7042	11–16	47	SEBD
Melland High School	Holmcroft Rd, Gorton, Manchester, Lancashire M18 7NG	0161 223 9915	0161 230 6919	Mrs J. O'Kane	352-7043	11–19	133	SLD
North Ridge High School	Palmerstone St, Ancoats, Manchester M12 6PT	0161 274 4667	0161 274 4566	Mrs Sandra Hibbert	352-7061	11–19	105	ASD SLD PMLD
Piper Hill High School	200 Yew Tree La, Northen Moor, Manchester, Lancashire M23 0FF	0161 998 4068	0161 945 6625	Mr Linda Jones	352-7039	11–19	101	SLD
Rodney House School	388 Slade La, Burnage, Manchester, Lancashire M19 2HT	0161 224 2774	0161 225 5186	Ms M. Isherwood	352-7047	2–6	31	ASD SEBD SLD
Southern Cross School	Barlow Hall Rd, Chorlton-cum-Hardy, Manchester, Lancashire M21 7JJ	0161 881 2695	0161 861 7190	Mr J. Law	352-7056	11–16	53	SEBD

Oldham

School name	Address	Tel	Fax	Headteacher	Ref	Ages	Pupils	Other
The Kingfisher Community Special School	Foxdenton La, Chadderton, Oldham, Lancashire OL9 9QR	0161 284 5335	0161 284 5225	Mrs Anne Redmond	353-7013	2–11	89	
New Bridge School	Roman Rd, Hollinwood, Oldham, Lancashire OL8 3PH	0161 222 6999	0161 688 8223	Mr Graham Quinn	353-7014	11–16	249	PD MLD SLD PMLD
Spring Brook School	Heron St, Fitton Hill, Oldham, Lancashire OL8 4JD	0161 911 5007	0161 911 5008	Mrs Janet Jones	353-7012	5–11	3	

Rochdale

School name	Address	Tel	Fax	Headteacher	Ref	Ages	Pupils	Other
Brownhill School	Heights La, Rochdale, Lancashire OL12 0PZ	01706 648990	01706 648537	Mrs Linda Parker	354-7006	7–16	40	SEBD
Newlands	Waverley Rd, Middleton, Manchester, Lancashire M24 6JG	0161 655 0220	0161 655 0221	Mrs Anne Richardson	354-7014	3–11		MLD SLD PMLD

7

School name	Address	Tel	Fax	Headteacher	Ref	Ages	Pupils	Other
Redwood	Hudson Wlk, Rochdale, Lancashire OL11 5EF	01706 750815	01706 751890	Mr Stuart Pidgeon	354-7015	11–19		MLD SLD PMLD
Springside	Albert Royds St, Rochdale, Manchester OL16 2SU	01706 764451	01706 764454	Mrs Jane Herring	354-7013	3–11		MLD SLD PMLD

Salford

School name	Address	Tel	Fax	Headteacher	Ref	Ages	Pupils	Other
Chatsworth High	Chatsworth Rd, Eccles, Salford, Manchester M30 9DY	0161 921 1405	0161 921 1414	Mrs June Redhead	355-7026	11–19	91	SLD PMLD
New Park High School	Off Green La, Patricroft, Eccles, Manchester M30 0RW	0161 921 2000	0161 921 2030	Mrs Almut Bever-Warren	355-7027	11–16	64	SEBD
Oakwood High School	Chatsworth Rd, Ellesmere Pk, Eccles, Lancashire M30 9DY	0161 921 2140		Mrs J. Triska	355-7025	11–16	179	VI CD ASD SEBD PD MLD SpLD DMP
Royal Manchester Children Hospital School	Hospital Rd, Pendlebury, Salford, Greater Manchester M27 4HA	0161 794 1151		Mrs Vivienne Cowie	355-7020	2–19	22	HS
Springwood Primary School	Barton Rd, Swinton, Manchester, Lancashire M27 5LP	0161 778 0022	0161 728 5767	Mrs Anthea Darlington	355-7029	2–11	154	

Sefton

School name	Address	Tel	Fax	Headteacher	Ref	Ages	Pupils	Other
Crosby High School	De Villiers Ave, Crosby, Liverpool, Merseyside L23 2TH	0151 924 3671	0151 931 5083	Mr S.J. Dempsey	343-7009	11–16	127	SEBD MLD
Merefield School	Westminster Dr, Southport, Merseyside PR8 2QZ	01704 577163	01704 571265	Ms Alison Foster	343-7006	2–19	60	SLD
Newfield School	Edge La, Crosby, Liverpool, Merseyside L23 4TG	0151 934 2991	0151 931 5025	Ms Sylvia Evans	343-7011	5–16	78	SEBD
Presfield School	Preston New Rd, Churchtown, Southport, Merseyside PR9 8PA	01704 227831	01704 232306	Mrs Gaynor Hirst	343-7004	11–19	58	MLD
Rowan Park School	Sterrix La, Litherland, Bootle, Merseyside L21 0DB	0151 222 4894		Mrs J.A. Kelly	343-7013	2–19	107	ASD SLD

St Helens

School name	Address	Tel	Fax	Headteacher	Ref	Ages	Pupils	Other
Lansbury Bridge School	Lansbury Ave, Parr, St Helens, Merseyside WA9 1TB	01744 678579	01744 678589	Mr R. Brownlow	342-7008	3–16	163	
Mill Green School	Mill La, Newton-le-Willows, Merseyside WA12 8BG	01744 678760	01744 678761	Mr Colin Myers	342-7007	2–19	77	SLD
Penkford School	Wharf Rd, Newton-le-Willows, Merseyside WA12 9XZ	01744 678745	01744 678748	Mr David Hartley	342-7005	9–16	47	SEBD MLD

Stockport

School name	Address	Tel	Fax	Headteacher	Ref	Ages	Pupils	Other
Castle Hill High School	Lapwing La, Brinnington, Stockport, Cheshire SK5 8LF	0161 494 6439	0161 406 6592	Mr M. Marra	356-7508	11–16	143	SEBD MLD
Heaton School	St James Rd, Heaton Moor, Stockport, Cheshire SK4 4RE	0161 432 1931	0161 432 1931	Ms E.A. Seers	356-7509	2–19	71	SLD
Lisburne School	Half Moon La, Offerton, Stockport, Cheshire SK2 5LB	0161 483 5045	0161 456 4220	Mrs Deborah Woods	356-7506	4–11	49	MLD
Oak Grove School	Matlock Rd, Heald Grn, Cheadle, Cheshire SK8 3BU	0161 437 4956	0161 283 6665	Mrs Gill Nash	356-7510	4–11	29	SEBD
Valley School	Whitehaven Rd, Bramhall, Stockport, Cheshire SK7 1EN	0161 439 7343	0161 439 0664	Mrs C.M. Goodlet	356-7504	2–11	48	ASD PD SLD
Windlehurst School	Windlehurst Rd, Hawk Grn, Marple, Stockport, Cheshire SK6 7HZ	0161 427 4788	0161 484 5091	Mr Kevin Lloyd	356-7511	11–16	26	SEBD

Tameside

School name	Address	Tel	Fax	Headteacher	Ref	Ages	Pupils	Other
Cromwell High School	Yew Tree La, Dukinfield, Cheshire SK16 5BJ	0161 338 9730	0161 338 9731	Mr Andrew Foord	357-7005	11–16	73	SLD
Dale Grove School	Wilshaw La, Ashton-under-Lyne, Lancashire OL7 9RF	0161 330 7595		Mr Robin Elms	357-7002	5–16	61	SEBD
Hawthorns Community School	Corporation Rd, Audenshaw, Manchester, Lancashire M34 5 LZ	0161 336 3389	0161 337 9747	Mrs M. Thompson	357-7001	4–11	47	MLD
Oakdale School and Acorn Nursery	Cheetham Hill Rd, Dukinfield, Cheshire SK16 5LD	0161 367 9299	0161 367 9685	Mrs I. Howard	357-7009	2–12	84	SLD
Samuel Laycock School	Mereside, Stalybridge, Cheshire SK15 1JF	0161 303 1321	0161 338 4638	Mr Stan Andrew	357-7006	11–17	114	MLD

Trafford

School name	Address	Tel	Fax	Headteacher	Ref	Ages	Pupils	Other
Brentwood School	Brentwood Ave, Timperley, Altrincham, Cheshire WA14 1SR	0161 928 8109	0161 928 4548	Mrs Bernice Kostick	358-7001	11–19	74	ASD SLD
Delamere School	Irlam Rd, Flixton, Manchester, Greater Manchester M41 6AP	0161 747 5893	0161 747 2960	Mrs S. Nichols	358-7005	2–11	59	ASD SLD
Egerton High School	Kingsway Pk, Urmston, Manchester, Lancashire M41 7FZ	0161 749 7094	0161 749 7096	Mrs Eloise Scroggie	358-7009	11–16	22	SEBD
Longford Park School	Longford Pk, Stretford, Manchester, Lancashire M32 8PR	0161 912 1895	0161 860 4121	Mrs Beverley Owens	358-7003	5–11	14	MLD
Manor High School	Manor Ave, Sale, Cheshire M33 5JX	0161 976 1553	0161 976 5415	Mr Neil Eltringham	358-7008	11–18	165	ASD SEBD MLD
Pictor School	Grove La, Timperley, Cheshire WA15 6PH	0161 962 5432	0161 905 2051	Mrs J. Spruce	358-7000	2–11	83	CD ASD PD MLD SpLD

Warrington

School name	Address	Tel	Fax	Headteacher	Ref	Ages	Pupils	Other
Fox Wood Special School	Chatfield Dr, Birchwood, Warrington, Cheshire WA3 6QW	01925 851393	01925 816795	Mrs Lesley Roberts	877-7002	4–19	72	SLD
Grappenhall Hall School	Church La, Grappenhall, Warrington, Cheshire WA4 3EU	01925 263895	01925 860487	Mrs Angela Findlay	877-7103	5–19	102	B R SEBD MLD
Green Lane Community Special School	Green La, Padgate, Warrington, Cheshire WA1 4JL	01925 480128	01925 480127	Mr Paul King	877-7001	4–16	126	

Wigan

School name	Address	Tel	Fax	Headteacher	Ref	Ages	Pupils	Other
Hope School	Kelvin Gr, Marus Bridge, Wigan, Lancashire WN3 6SP	01942 824150	01942 230361	Mr P. Dahlstrom	359-7002	2–19	181	PD SLD
Landgate School, Bryn	Landgate La, Ashton-in-Makerfield, Wigan, Lancashire WN4 0EP	01942 776688	01942 776689	Mr Martin Antony Hanbury	359-7001	4–14	36	CD ASD
Montrose	Montrose Ave, Pemberton, Wigan WN5 9XN	01942 223431	01942 225911	Mr Alan Farmer	359-7021	4–14	57	MLD SLD
New Greenhall	Green Hall Cl, Atherton, Manchester, Lancashire M46 9HP	01942 883928	01942 870069	Mr Ihor Anthony Triska	359-7020	2–14	73	MLD SpLD
Oakfield High School and College	Close La, Hindley, Wigan, Lancashire WN2 3SA	01942 776142	01942 776143	Mr John Young	359-7022	11–19	182	ID MLD SLD
Willow Grove Primary School	Willow Gr, Ashton-in-Makerfield, Wigan, Lancashire WN4 8XF	01942 727717	01942 271627	Mrs Valda Pearson	359-7018	5–11	44	SEBD

Wirral

School name	Address	Tel	Fax	Headteacher	Ref	Ages	Pupils	Other
Clare Mount School	Fender La, Moreton, Wirral, Merseyside CH46 9PA	0151 606 9440	0151 678 5476	Mrs L.C. Clare	344-7001	11–19	201	MLD
Elleray Park School	Elleray Park Rd, Wallasey, Merseyside CH45 0LH	0151 639 3594	0151 638 8823	Ms Margaret Morris	344-7005	2–11	61	
Foxfield School	Douglas Dr, Moreton, Wirral, Merseyside CH46 6BT	0151 677 8555	0151 678 5480	Mr A. Baird	344-7004	11–19	138	
Gilbrook School	Pilgrim St, Birkenhead, Merseyside CH41 5EH	0151 647 8411	0151 666 1581	Mr Robert Richardson	344-7010	4–12	52	B SEBD
Hayfield School	Manor Dr, Upton, Wirral, Merseyside CH49 4LN	0151 677 9303	0151 677 9303	Ms S.A. Lowy	344-7000	4–11	119	CD MLD
Kilgarth School	Cavendish St, Birkenhead, Merseyside CH41 8BA	0151 652 8071	0151 653 3427	Miss J.M. Dawson	344-7003	11–16	51	B SEBD

7

School name	Address	Tel	Fax	Headteacher	Ref	Ages	Pupils	Other
The Lyndale School	Lyndale Ave, Eastham, Wirral, Merseyside CH62 8DE	0151 327 3682	0151 344 8678	Mrs P. Stewart	344-7014	2–11	33	CD
Meadowside School	Pool La, Woodchurch, Wirral, Merseyside CH49 5LA	0151 678 7711	0151 678 9155	Ms L. Kane	344-7007	11–19	64	
The Observatory School	Bidston Village Rd, Bidston, Wirral CH43 7QT	0151 652 7093	0151 670 0641	Ms Christine Royle	344-7215	10–16	40	
Orrets Meadow School	Chapelhill Rd, Moreton, Wirral, Merseyside CH46 9QQ	0151 678 8070		Mrs S.E. Blythe	344-7020	7–11	63	SpLD
Stanley School	Pensby Rd, Thingwall, Wirral, Merseyside CH61 7UG	0151 648 3171	0151 648 6887	Mr A. Newman	344-7017	2–11	85	CD
Wirral Hospitals School and Home Education Service Community Base	157 Park Rd North, Claughton, Wirral, Merseyside CH41 0EZ	0151 637 6310	0151 637 6287	Miss Anne Cunningham	344-7019	2–17	51	HS

South East

Bracknell Forest

School name	Address	Tel	Fax	Headteacher	Ref	Ages	Pupils	Other
Kennel Lane School	Kennel La, Bracknell, Berkshire RG42 2EX	01344 483872	01344 304224	Miss Andrea de Bunsen	867-7032	2–19	169	ASD PD MLD SLD

Brighton and Hove

School name	Address	Tel	Fax	Headteacher	Ref	Ages	Pupils	Other
The Alternative Centre for Education	Queensdown School Rd, Off Lewes Rd, Brighton, East Sussex BN1 7LA	01273 604472	01273 621811	Mr Mark Whitby	846-7004	7–16	27	SEBD
The Cedar Centre	Lynchet Cl, Hollingdean, Brighton, East Sussex BN1 7FP	01273 558622		Mrs Sue Furdas	846-7034	4–16	111	MLD
Downs Park School	Foredown Rd, Portslade, Brighton, East Sussex BN41 2FU	01273 417448		Ms G. Golding	846-7016	4–16	108	MLD
Downs View Special School	Warren Rd, Woodingdean, Brighton, East Sussex BN2 6BB	01273 601680	01273 699420	Mr Adrian Carver	846-7006	3–19	123	MLD
Hillside School	Foredown Rd, Portslade, Brighton, East Sussex BN41 2FU	01273 416979	01273 417512	Mr Bob Wall	846-7018	3–16	61	AS ASD CD PD SEBD SLD VI
Patcham House Special School	7 Old London Rd, Patcham, Brighton, East Sussex BN1 8XR	01273 551028	01273 550465	Mrs Kim Bolton	846-7005	5–16	54	DMP PD

Buckinghamshire

School name	Address	Tel	Fax	Headteacher	Ref	Ages	Pupils	Other
Alfriston School	Penn Rd, Knotty Grn, Beaconsfield, Buckinghamshire HP9 2TS	01494 673740	01494 670177	Mrs Jinna Male	825-7003	11–18	117	G R MLD
Booker Park Community School	Stoke Leys Cl, Aylesbury, Buckinghamshire HP21 9ET	01296 427441	01296 427441	Mr R. Westwood	825-7028	5–11	61	MLD
Chiltern Gate School	Verney Rd, High Wycombe, Buckinghamshire HP12 3NE	01494 532622	01494 532622	Ms Sarah Snape	825-7017	4–13	83	R ASD SEBD MLD DMP
Furze Down School	Verney Rd, Winslow, Buckinghamshire MK18 3BL	01296 713385	01296 714420	Mrs Sue Collins	825-7023	11	117	SEBD MLD SLD
Heritage House School	Cameron Rd, Chesham, Buckinghamshire HP5 3BP	01494 771445	01494 775892	Mr Mike Barrie	825-7018	2–19	63	SLD
Maplewood School	Faulkner Way, Downley, High Wycombe, Buckinghamshire HP13 5HB	01494 525728	01494 465609	Mr John Rumble	825-7000	2–19	56	SLD
Pebble Brook School	Churchill Ave, Aylesbury, Buckinghamshire HP21 8LZ	01296 415761	01296 434442	Mrs Donna Jolly	825-7010	11–16	60	R MLD
Prestwood Lodge School	Nairdwood La, Prestwood, Great Missenden, Buckinghamshire HP16 0QQ	01494 863514	01494 863154	Mr M. MacCourt	825-7012	11–16	67	B R SEBD
Stocklake Park Community School	Stocklake, Aylesbury, Buckinghamshire HP20 1DP	01296 423507	01296 433353	Mr Ron Westwood	825-7016	11	70	SLD
Stony Dean School	Orchard End Ave, Pineapple Rd, Amersham, Buckinghamshire HP7 9JW	01494 762007	01494 765631	Mrs P. Dichler	825-7014	11–18	117	R CD MLD

School name	Address	Tel	Fax	Headteacher	Ref	Ages	Pupils	Other
Wendover House School	Church La, Wendover, Aylesbury, Buckinghamshire HP22 6NL	01296 622157	01296 622628	Mr Nigel Morris	825-7032	11–18	47	B R SEBD
Westfield School	Highfield Rd, Bourne End, Buckinghamshire SL8 5BE	01628 533125	01628 523345	Mr Geoff Allen	825-7035	4–11	24	SEBD

East Sussex

School name	Address	Tel	Fax	Headteacher	Ref	Ages	Pupils	Other
Cuckmere House School	Eastbourne Rd, Seaford, East Sussex BN25 4BA	01323 893319	01323 897719	Mr Frank Stanford	845-7036	9–16	51	B R SEBD
Glyne Gap School	School Pl, Hastings Rd, Bexhill-on-Sea, East Sussex TN40 2PU	01424 217720	01424 734962	Mr John Hassell	845-7017	2–19	100	VI CD ASD PD MLD SLD
Grove Park School	Church Rd, Crowborough, East Sussex TN6 1BN	01892 663018	01892 653170	Mrs Pippa Clarke	845-7021	2–19	52	ASD MLD SLD PMLD
Hazel Court School	Larkspur Dr, Eastbourne, East Sussex BN23 8EJ	01323 465720	01323 740121	Mr Peter Gordon	845-7032	11–19	96	ASD MLD SLD PMLD
The Lindfield School	Lindfield Rd, Hampden Pk, Eastbourne, East Sussex BN22 0BQ	01323 502988	01323 500433	Ms J.D. Oatey	845-7031	11–16	71	CD ASD MLD SLD
New Horizons School	Beauchamp Rd, St Leonards-on-Sea, East Sussex TN38 9JU	01424 855665	01424 855117	Mr Steven Pugh	845-7035	7–16	78	SEBD
St Mary's School	Horam, Heathfield, East Sussex TN21 0BT	01435 812278	01435 813019	Mr Richard Tracey	845-7011	9–16	57	B R MLD
Saxon Mount School	Edinburgh Rd, St Leonards-on-Sea, East Sussex TN38 8HH	01424 426303	01424 444115	Ms Louise Carlyle	845-7025	11–16	113	CD ASD MLD SLD
The South Downs Community Special School	Beechy Ave, Eastbourne, East Sussex BN20 8NU	01323 730302	01323 640544	Mr Remo Palladino	845-7030	4–11	105	CD ASD MLD SLD PMLD
Torfield School	Croft Rd, Hastings, East Sussex TN34 3JT	01424 428228	08700 941559	Mrs Jean Mockford	845-7024	3–11	72	CD ASD MLD SLD

Hampshire

School name	Address	Tel	Fax	Headteacher	Ref	Ages	Pupils	Other
Baycroft School	Gosport Rd, Stubbington, Fareham, Hampshire PO14 2AE	01329 664151	01329 668601	Ms Chris Toner	850-7032	11–16	179	CD ASD SEBD MLD SpLD
Dove House School	Sutton Rd, Basingstoke, Hampshire RG21 5SU	01256 351555	01256 29749	Mr Colin House	850-7043	11–16	119	MLD
Forest Edge School	Lydlynch Rd, Totton, Southampton, Hampshire SO40 3DW	023 8086 4949	023 8087 2294	Miss Rosemary Wiles	850-7017	4–11	62	ASD MLD
Glenwood School	Washington Rd, Emsworth, Hampshire PO10 7NN	01243 373120	01243 373103	Mr Phillip Johnson	850-7072	11–16	96	MLD
Heathfield Special School	Oldbury Way, Fareham, Hampshire PO14 3BN	01329 845150	01329 846548	Mrs Christine Tuff	850-7018	3–11	99	PD MLD
Henry Tyndale School	Ship La, Farnborough, Hampshire GU14 8BX	01252 544577	01252 377411	Mr Rob Thompson	850-7000	2–19	104	ASD
Hollywater School	Mill Chase Rd, Bordon, Hampshire GU35 0HA	01420 474396	01420 488329	Mrs Barbara Livings	850-7079	2–19	124	MLD SLD
Icknield School	River Way, Andover, Hampshire SP11 6LT	01264 365297	01264 334794	Mr Stephen Steer-Smith	850-7020	2–19	66	SLD
Lakeside School	Winchester Rd, Chandler's Ford, Eastleigh, Hampshire SO53 2DW	023 8026 6633	023 8026 7147	Mr Gareth Evans	850-7014	11–16	59	B R SEBD
Limington House School	St Andrew's Rd, Basingstoke, Hampshire RG22 6PS	01256 322148	01256 58778	Mrs Petra Smillie	850-7026	2–19	67	SLD
Lord Wilson School	Coldeast Way, Sarisbury Grn, Southampton, Hampshire SO31 7AT	01489 582684	01489 582115	Mrs Lynda Strodder	850-7078	11–16	50	B SEBD
Maple Ridge School	Maple Cres, Basingstoke, Hampshire RG21 5SX	01256 323639	01256 841059	Mrs D. Gooderham	850-7016	4–11	70	ASD MLD
The Mark Way School	Batchelors Barn Rd, Andover, Hampshire SP10 1HR	01264 351835	01264 366276	Mr Anthony Oakley	850-7075	11–16	71	ASD MLD
Norman Gate School	Vigo Rd, Andover, Hampshire SP10 1JZ	01264 323423	01264 354891	Mrs Christine Gayler	850-7015	2–11	49	ASD MLD DMP
Oak Lodge School	Roman Rd, Dibden Purlieu, Southampton, Hampshire SO45 4RQ	023 8084 7213	023 8084 5112	Mrs B. Hawker	850-7070	11–16	126	ASD MLD
Osborne School	Athelstan Rd, Winchester, Hampshire SO23 7BU	01962 897000	01962 849419	Mr R. Wakelam	850-5950	11–19	156	R MLD
Rachel Madocks School	Eagle Ave, Cowplain, Waterlooville, Hampshire PO8 9XP	023 9224 1818	023 9226 9521	Mrs C.A. Browne	850-7023	2–19	63	SLD
Riverside School	Scratchface La, Purbrook, Waterlooville, Hampshire PO7 5QD	023 9225 0138		Miss E. Beavan	850-7009	3–11	109	ASD MLD
St Francis Special School	Patchway Dr, Oldbury Way, Fareham, Hampshire PO14 3BN	01329 845730	01329 847217	Mrs Sue Chalmers	850-7033	2–19	89	ASD SLD
Salterns School	Commercial Rd, Totton, Southampton, Hampshire SO40 3AF	023 8086 4211	023 8087 2174	Mrs Nicky Dando	850-7024	2–19	45	SLD
Samuel Cody Specialist Sports College	Lynchford Rd, Farnborough, Hampshire GU14 6BJ	01252 314720	01252 341869	Mrs Anna Dawson	850-7073	11–16	102	ASD MLD

7

School name	Address	Tel	Fax	Headteacher	Ref	Ages	Pupils	Other
Saxon Wood School	Barron Pl, Rooksdown, Basingstoke, Hampshire RG24 9NH	01256 356635	01256 323713	Mrs Lynne Cannon	850-7053	2–11	30	PD
Shepherds Down Special School	Shepherds La, Compton, Winchester, Hampshire SO21 2AJ	01962 713445	01962 713453	Mr Tony Gazzard	850-7076	4–11	107	CD ASD MLD
Sundridge School	Silvester Rd, Cowplain, Waterlooville, Hampshire PO8 8TR	023 9226 1234	023 9224 1188	Mrs Marjike Miles	850-7001	11–16	35	B
The Waterloo School	Warfield Ave, Waterlooville, Hampshire PO7 7JU	023 9225 5956	023 9224 1150	Ms Anna Brown	850-7051	5–11	45	B SEBD
Wolverdene Special School	22 Love La, Andover, Hampshire SP10 2AF	01264 362350		Mr R.A. Ford	850-7067	6–11	53	R SEBD

Isle of Wight

School name	Address	Tel	Fax	Headteacher	Ref	Ages	Pupils	Other
Medina House School	School La, Newport, Isle of Wight PO30 2HS	01983 522917	01983 526355	Mr Robin Goodfellow	921-7003	2–11	62	SLD
St George's School	Watergate Rd, Newport, Isle of Wight PO30 1XW	01983 524634	01983 533911	Mrs Susan Holman	921-7001	11–19	114	ASD MLD SLD PMLD

Kent

School name	Address	Tel	Fax	Headteacher	Ref	Ages	Pupils	Other
Bower Grove School	Fant La, Maidstone, Kent ME16 8NL	01622 726773	01622 725025	Mr Trevor Phipps	886-7032	5–16	196	MLD
Broomhill Bank School	Broomhill Rd, Rusthall, Tunbridge Wells, Kent TN3 0TB	01892 510440	01892 502460	Mr P.A. Barnett	886-7002	9–19	59	G R MLD
Five Acre Wood School	Boughton La, Maidstone, Kent ME15 9QL	01622 743925	01622 744828	Ms Gill Kratochvill	886-7056	4–19	102	SLD
The Foreland School	Lanthorne Rd, Broadstairs, Kent CT10 3NX	01843 863891	01843 860710	Mrs Pam Ashworth	886-7040	2–19	118	SLD
Foxwood School	Seabrook Rd, Hythe, Kent CT21 5QJ	01303 261155	01303 262355	Mr Christopher Soulsby	886-7059	2–19	98	R ASD SLD DMP
Furness School	Rowhill Rd, Hextable, Swanley, Kent BR8 7RP	01322 662937	01322 615033	Mr Doug Dawson	886-7034	10–16	59	B R SEBD
Goldwyn Community Special School	Godinton La, Gt Chart, Ashford, Kent TN23 3BT	01233 622958	01233 662177	Mr R.W. Law	886-7041	11–16	55	B SEBD
Grange Park School	Birling Rd, Leybourne, West Malling, Kent ME19 5QA	01732 842144	01732 848004	Mr Mark Robson	886-7052	11–19	59	ASD MLD SLD
Harbour School	Elms Vale Rd, Dover, Kent CT17 9PS	01304 201964	01304 225000	Mr Tony Berresford	886-7045	5–16	80	MLD
Highview School	Moat Farm Rd, Folkestone, Kent CT19 5DJ	01303 258755	01303 251185	Mr N. Birch	886-7043	4–17	104	MLD
The Ifield School	Cedar Ave, Gravesend, Kent DA12 5JT	01474 365485	01474 569744	Mrs Pam Jones	886-7039	4–16	145	MLD
Laleham Gap School	Northgdown Pk, Margate, Kent CT9 2TP	01843 221946	01843 231368	Mr Keith Mileham	886-7073	3–16	176	R CD ASD
Meadowfield School	Swanstree Ave, Sittingbourne, Kent ME10 4NL	01795 477788		Mr Philip Rankin	886-7072	4–19	184	
Milestone School	Ash Rd, New Ash Grn, Longfield, Kent DA3 8JZ	01474 709420	01474 707170	Miss E. Flanagan	886-7066	2–19	177	ASD SLD
Oakley School	Pembury Rd, Tunbridge Wells, Kent TN2 4NE	01892 823096	01892 823836	Mr Martin Absolom	886-7070	3–19	152	
The Orchard School	Cambridge Rd, Canterbury, Kent CT1 3QQ	01227 769220	01227 781589	Mr Brian Shelley	886-7062	11–16	71	MLD
Portal House School	Sea St, St Margaret's-at-Cliffe, Dover, Kent CT15 6SS	01304 853033	01304 853526	Mr Les Sage	886-7067	7–13	38	B R SEBD
Ridge View School	Cage Green Rd, Tonbridge, Kent TN10 4PT	01732 771384	01732 770344	Mrs Jacqui Tovey	886-7051	2–19	76	ASD SLD
Rowhill School	Stock La, Wilmington, Dartford, Kent DA2 7BZ	01322 225490	01322 291433	Mr Steven McGuinness	886-7044	4–16	113	MLD
St Anthony's School	St Anthony's Way, Margate, Kent CT9 3RA	01843 292015	01843 231574	Mr Ray Dell	886-7033	3–16	117	MLD
St Nicholas' School	Holme Oak Cl, Nunnery Fields, Canterbury, Kent CT1 3JJ	01227 464316	01227 766883	Mr Daniel Lewis	886-7063	3–19	132	SLD
Stone Bay School	70 Stone Rd, Broadstairs, Kent CT10 1EB	01843 863421	01843 866652	Mr R. Edey	886-7058	11–19	67	R ASD MLD SLD DMP
Valence School	Westerham Rd, Westerham, Kent TN16 1QN	01959 562156	01959 565046	Mr R. Gooding	886-7021	4–19	89	R PD
The Wyvern School	Gt Chart Bypass, Ashford, Kent TN23 4ER	01233 621468	01233 660621	Mr D. Spencer	886-7069	3–19	118	ASD MLD SLD

Medway

School name	Address	Tel	Fax	Headteacher	Ref	Ages	Pupils	Other
Abbey Court Community Special School	Rede Court Rd, Strood, Rochester, Kent ME2 3SP	01634 338220	01634 338221	Ms Karen Joy	887-7053	4–19	129	SLD
Bradfields School	Churchill Ave, Chatham, Kent ME5 0LB	01634 683990	01634 828284	Mr Kim Johnson	887-7042	11–19	231	ASD SEBD PD MLD
Danecourt Community School	Hotel Rd, Watling St, Gillingham, Kent ME8 6AA	01634 232589	01634 263822	Mr John Somers	887-7031	2–11	113	MLD
Rivermead School	Forge La, Gillingham, Kent ME7 1UG	01634 338348		Mrs Susan Rogers	887-7016	4–16	1	HS

Milton Keynes

School name	Address	Tel	Fax	Headteacher	Ref	Ages	Pupils	Other
The Gatehouse School	Crosslands, Stantonbury, Stantonbury, Milton Keynes, Buckinghamshire MK14 6AX	01908 313903	01908 221195	Mrs Susanne Bell	826-7033	11–16	61	B R SEBD
The Redway School	Farmborough, Netherfield, Milton Keynes, Buckinghamshire MK6 4HG	01908 206400	01908 206420	Mrs Ruth Sylvester	826-7034	2–19	99	SLD
Romans Field School	Shenley Rd, Bletchley, Milton Keynes, Buckinghamshire MK3 7AW	01908 376011		Mr Wayne Marshall	826-7015	4–11	42	R SEBD
Slated Row School	Old Wolverton Rd, Wolverton, Milton Keynes, Buckinghamshire MK12 5NJ	01908 316017	01908 315082	Mrs Elizabeth Bull	826-7026	4–19	163	MLD
The Walnuts School	Admiral Dr, Hazeley, Milton Keynes, Buckinghamshire MK8 0PU	01908 563885	01908 555617	Mr Nick Jackman	826-7021	4–19	84	R CD ASD AS
White Spire School	Rickley La, Bletchley, Milton Keynes, Buckinghamshire MK3 6EW	01908 373266	01908 643057	Mr P. Jones	826-7009	5–19	123	R MLD

Oxfordshire

School name	Address	Tel	Fax	Headteacher	Ref	Ages	Pupils	Other
Bardwell School	Hendon Pl, Sunderland Dr, Bicester, Oxfordshire OX26 4RZ	01869 242182	01869 243111	Mrs Chris Hughes	931-7029	2–16	47	SpLD
Bishopswood School	Grove Rd, Sonning Common, South Oxfordshire RG4 9RJ	0118 972 4311		Mrs Jennifer Ann Wager	931-7030	2–16	31	SLD
Fitzwaryn School	Denchworth Rd, Wantage, Oxfordshire OX12 9ET	01235 764504	01235 768728	Mrs Barbara Harker	931-7027	3–16	58	MLD SLD
Frank Wise School	Hornbeam Cl, Banbury, Oxfordshire OX16 9RL	01295 263520	01295 273141	Mr K. Griffiths	931-7010	2–16	88	SLD
Iffley Mead School	Iffley Turn, Oxford, Oxfordshire OX4 4DU	01865 747606	01865 711134	Mrs Kay Willett	931-7018	5–16	88	MLD
John Watson School	Littleworth Rd, Wheatley, Oxford, Oxfordshire OX33 1NN	01865 452725	01865 452724	Mrs Sally Withey	931-7011	2–16	56	SLD
Kingfisher School	Radley Rd, Abingdon, Oxfordshire OX14 3RR	01235 555512	01235 554051	Mrs Ann Meara	931-7032	2–16	66	SLD
Mabel Prichard School	Cuddesdon Way, Littlemore, Oxford, Oxfordshire OX4 6SB	01865 777878	01865 775218	Miss J.M. Wallington	931-7020	2–16	59	SLD
Northern House School	South Par, Summertown, Oxford, Oxfordshire OX2 7JN	01865 557004	01865 511210	Mrs Gill Carey	931-7016	5–14	66	SEBD
Northfield School	Knights Rd, Blackbird Leys, Oxford, Oxfordshire OX4 6DQ	01865 771703	01865 773873	Mr Mark Blencowe	931-7031	11–16	60	SEBD
Ormerod School	Waynflete Rd, Headington, Oxford, Oxfordshire OX3 8DD	01865 744173	01865 741489	Mr C. Peters	931-7015	2–16		PD
Oxfordshire Hospitals Education Service	Nuffield Orthopaedic Centre, Headington, Oxford, Oxfordshire OX3 7LD	01865 227554	01865 227554	Mr Barry Jackson	931-7017	3–18	3	HS
Springfield School	At The Bronze Barrow, Cedar Dr, Witney, Oxfordshire OX28 1AR	01993 703963	01993 708796	Mrs S. Niner	931-7012	2–16	102	SLD
Woodeaton Manor School	Woodeaton, Oxford, Oxfordshire OX3 9TS	01865 558722	01865 311561	Mrs A. Pearce	931-7002	11–16	40	R SEBD

Portsmouth

School name	Address	Tel	Fax	Headteacher	Ref	Ages	Pupils	Other
Cliffdale Primary School	Battenburg Ave, North End, Portsmouth, Hampshire PO2 0SN	023 9266 2601	023 9266 0506	Mrs Jane Sansome	851-7047	4–11	93	ASD MLD
The Harbour School	151 Locksway Rd, Milton, Portsmouth, Hampshire PO4 8LD	023 9281 8547	023 9281 8548	Ms Jill Roucroft	851-7472	5–19		SEBD

7

School name	Address	Tel	Fax	Headteacher	Ref	Ages	Pupils	Other
Mary Rose School	Gisors Rd, Southsea, Portsmouth, Hampshire PO4 8GT	023 9285 2330	023 9285 2362	Ms Alison Beane	851-7751	2–19	110	SLD
Redwood Park School	Wembley Gr, Cosham, Portsmouth, Hampshire PO6 2RY	023 9237 7500		Mr Tony Cox	851-7046	11–16	132	CD MLD
Willows Centre for Children	Battenburg Ave, North End, Portsmouth, Hampshire PO2 0SN	023 9266 6918	023 9265 2247	Mrs A.M. Swann	851-7750	3–5	5	CD MLD SLD

Reading

School name	Address	Tel	Fax	Headteacher	Ref	Ages	Pupils	Other
The Avenue School	Basingstoke Rd, Reading, Berkshire RG2 0EN	0118 901 5554	0118 986 0179	Mrs Sue Bourne	870-7001	2–19	84	PD MLD
The Holy Brook School	Ashampstead Rd, Reading, Berkshire RG30 3LJ	0118 901 5489	0118 957 6113	Mrs J. Male	870-7036	7–11	18	SEBD
Phoenix College	40 Christchurch Rd, Reading, Berkshire RG2 7AY	0118 901 5524	0118 931 1637	Mrs E. Lansdown-Bridge	870-7031	11–16	50	SEBD

Slough

School name	Address	Tel	Fax	Headteacher	Ref	Ages	Pupils	Other
Arbour Vale School	Farnham Rd, Farnham Royal, Slough, Berkshire SL2 3AE	01753 525113	01753 691415	Mrs Debbie Richards	871-7035	2–19	218	R ASD
Haybrook College	112 Burnham La., Slough, Berkshire SL1 6LZ	01628 696076	01628 696080	Mrs Jan Paine	871-7036	11–16	24	SEBD
Littledown School	Queen's Rd, Slough, Berkshire SL1 3QW	01753 521734		Mrs Jan Paine	871-7030	5–12	15	B SEBD

Southampton

School name	Address	Tel	Fax	Headteacher	Ref	Ages	Pupils	Other
The Cedar School	Redbridge La. Nursling, Southampton, Hampshire SO16 0XN	023 8073 4205	023 8073 8231	Mr Brian Hart	852-7037	3–16	58	VI CD ASD SEBD MSI PD SLD PMLD SpLD DMP
Great Oaks School	Vermont Cl, off Winchester Rd, Southampton, Hampshire SO16 7LT	023 8076 7660		Mr P. Crockett	852-7036	11–18	130	SLD PMLD SpLD DMP
The Polygon School	Handel Terr, Southampton, Hampshire SO15 2FH	023 8063 6776	023 8033 6066	Mrs Anne Mary Hendon-John	852-7039	11–16	51	B VI CD ASD MSI PD MLD SLD PMLD SpLD DMP
Springwell School	Hinkler Rd, Netley Abbey, Southampton, Hampshire SO19 6DH		023 8042 6874	Mrs J. Partridge	852-7035	3–11	50	VI CD ASD SEBD MSI PD SLD PMLD SpLD DMP
Vermont School	Vermont Cl, off Winchester Rd, Southampton, Hampshire SO16 7LT	023 8076 7988	023 8076 6902	Mrs Jacqueline Wills	852-7040	7–11	25	B VI CD ASD MSI PD MLD SLD PMLD SpLD DMP

Surrey

School name	Address	Tel	Fax	Headteacher	Ref	Ages	Pupils	Other
The Abbey School	Menin Way, Farnham, Surrey GU9 8DY	01252 725059	01252 737300	Mr Chris Gardiner	936-7061	11–16	87	ASD MLD
Brooklands School	27 Wray Park Rd, Reigate, Surrey RH2 0DF	01737 249941	01737 224787	Mrs Susan Wakenell	936-7051	2–11	63	SLD
Carwarden House Community School	118 Upper Chobham Rd, Camberley, Surrey GU15 1EJ	01276 709080	01276 709081	Mr J.G. Cope	936-7034	11–19	129	MLD
Clifton Hill School	Chaldon Rd, Caterham, Surrey CR3 5PH	01883 347740	01883 349617	Mrs M. Unsworth	936-7049	10–19	90	SLD
Freemantles School	Pyrcroft Rd, Chertsey, Surrey KT16 9ER	01932 563460	01932 569679	Mrs Sue Stephens	936-7062	4–11	100	ASD
Gosden House School	Horsham Rd, Bramley, Guildford, Surrey GU5 0AH	01483 892008	01483 894057	Mr Jon David	936-7003	4–16	112	R CD MLD
Limpsfield Grange School	89 Bluehouse La. Oxted, Surrey RH8 0RZ	01883 713928	01883 730578	Mrs J. Humphreys	936-7019	11–16	60	G R
Linden Bridge School	Grafton Rd, Worcester Park, Surrey KT4 7JW	020 8330 3009	020 8330 6811	Mrs R. Smith	936-7060	4–17	115	R ASD
Manor Mead School	Laleham Rd, Shepperton, Middlesex TW17 8EL	01932 241834		Mrs Fiona Neal	936-7053	2–12	62	VI CD ASD SEBD PD SLD
The Park School	Onslow Cres, Woking, Surrey GU22 7AT	01483 772057	01483 740976	Ms Karen Eastwood	936-7023	8	106	CD MLD
Philip Southcote School	Addlestone Moor, Addlestone, Surrey KT15 1SN	01932 562326	01932 567092	Mr Geoff Rogers	936-7065	11	96	HI MLD
Pond Meadow School	Pond Meadow, Guildford, Surrey GU2 8YG	01483 532239	01483 537049	Mr David Monk	936-7042	2–19	55	ASD SLD

School name	Address	Tel	Fax	Headteacher	Ref	Ages	Pupils	Other
Portesbery School	Portesbery Rd, Camberley, Surrey GU15 3SZ	01276 63078	01276 683641	Mr Justin Price	936-7056	2-19	58	SLD
The Ridgeway Community School	14 Frensham Rd, Farnham, Surrey GU9 8HB	01252 724562	01252 737247	Mr Darryl Morgan	936-7050	2-19	94	SLD
St Nicholas School	Taynton Dr, Merstham, Redhill, Surrey RH1 3PU	01737 215488	01737 646173	Mr Craig Anderson	936-7012	11-16	40	B R SEBD MLD
Starhurst School	Chart La South, Dorking, Surrey RH5 4DB	01306 883763	01306 889819	Mr J. Watson	936-7027	11-16	34	B R SEBD
Sunnydown School at Portley House	152 Whyteleafe South Station, Caterham, Surrey CR3 5ED	01883 342281	01883 341342	Mr M. Armstrong	936-7014	11-16	68	B R SpLD
Walton Leigh School	Queen's Rd, Hersham, Walton-on-Thames, Surrey KT12 5AB	01932 223243	01932 254320	Mrs Linda Curtis	936-7043	11-19	65	SLD
West Hill School	Kingston Rd, Leatherhead, Surrey KT22 7PW	01372 814714	01372 814710	Ms Judy Nettleton	936-7025	11-16	110	ASD MLD
Wey House School	Horsham Rd, Bramley, Guildford, Surrey GU5 0BJ	01483 898130	01483 894642	Mr Paul Sanderson	936-7035	7-11	33	R SEBD
Wishmore Cross School	Alpha Rd, Chobham, Woking, Surrey GU24 8NE	01276 857555	01276 855420	Ms Derry Close	936-7024	11-16	44	B R SEBD
Woodfield School	Sunstone Gr, Merstham, Redhill, Surrey RH1 3PR	01737 642623	01737 642775	Mrs Sharon Lawrence	936-7066	11-19	115	MLD
Woodlands School	Fortyfoot Rd, Leatherhead, Surrey KT22 8RY	01372 377922	01372 376434	Mrs H.D.J. Taylor	936-7048	2-19	55	SLD

West Berkshire

School name	Address	Tel	Fax	Headteacher	Ref	Ages	Pupils	Other
Brookfields School	Sage Rd, Tilehurst, Reading, Berkshire RG31 6SW	0118 942 1382	0118 945 5176	Mr J. Byrne	869-7028	2-19	172	SpLD
The Castle School	Love La, Donnington, Newbury, Berkshire RG14 2JG	01635 42976	01635 551725	Mrs Kerry Gray	869-7007	2-19	130	ASD

West Sussex

School name	Address	Tel	Fax	Headteacher	Ref	Ages	Pupils	Other
Cornfield School, Littlehampton	Cornfield Cl, Littlehampton, West Sussex BN17 6HY	01903 731277	01903 731288	Mr Andy Parker	938-7022	11-16	44	SEBD
Court Meadow School, Cuckfield	Hanlye La, Cuckfield, Haywards Heath, West Sussex RH17 5HN	01444 454535	01444 412289	Ms Kathy Thomas	938-7016	2-19	82	SLD
Fordwater School, Chichester	Summersdale Rd, Chichester, West Sussex PO19 6PP	01243 782475	01243 539210	Mr Bob Rendall	938-7012	2-19	106	SLD
Herons Dale School	Hawkins Cres, Shoreham-by-Sea, West Sussex BN43 6TN	01273 596904	01273 591126	Mrs Sally Pritchard	938-7021	3-11	55	ASD MLD
Littlegreen School, Compton	Compton, Chichester, West Sussex PO18 9NW	023 9263 1259	023 9263 1740	Mrs Susan Harding Roberts	938-7005	7-15	40	B R SEBD
Manor Green College	Lady Margaret Rd, Ifield, Crawley, West Sussex RH11 0DX	01293 520351	01293 535596	Mr Richard Turney	938-7006	11-19	158	ASD MLD SLD
Manor Green Primary School	Lady Margaret Rd, Ifield, Crawley, West Sussex RH11 0DU	01293 526873	01293 510363	Mr D. Reid	938-7011	2-11	122	ASD MLD SLD
Newick House School	Birchwood Grove Rd, Burgess Hill, West Sussex RH15 0DP	01444 233550	01444 870043	Ms Gillian Perry	938-7015	4-16	146	VI CD ASD SEBD PD MLD SLD SpLD DMP
Oak Grove College	The Boulevard, Worthing, West Sussex BN13 1JX	01903 708870	01903 705439	Mr Graham Elliker	938-7010	11-19	237	SLD
Palatine School	Palatine Rd, Worthing, West Sussex BN12 6JP	01903 242835	01903 700264	Mr J. Clough	938-7008	3-11	102	ASD MLD
Queen Elizabeth II Silver Jubilee School, Horsham	Comptons La, Horsham, West Sussex RH13 5NW	01403 266215	01403 270109	Mrs Lesley Dyer	938-7009	2-19	55	SLD
St Anthony's School	Woodlands La, Chichester, West Sussex PO19 5PA	01243 785965	01243 530206	Mr Robert Griffin	938-7004	4-16	200	CD ASD MLD

Windsor and Maidenhead

School name	Address	Tel	Fax	Headteacher	Ref	Ages	Pupils	Other
Holyport Manor School	Ascot Rd, Holyport, Maidenhead, Berkshire SL6 3LE	01628 623196	01628 623608	Mrs Frances Larner	868-7009	2-19	153	R VI CD ASD

7

Wokingham

School name	Address	Tel	Fax	Headteacher	Ref	Ages	Pupils	Other
Addington School	Woodlands Ave, Woodley, Reading, Berkshire RG5 3EL	0118 954 0444	0118 927 2480	Ms Elizabeth Meek	872-7029	2–19	181	VI CD SEBD PD MLD SLD SpLD
Southfield School	Gipsy La, Wokingham, Berkshire RG40 2HR	0118 977 1293	0118 977 6598	Mr Michael J. Pedley	872-7033	11–16	58	R SEBD

South West

Bath and North East Somerset

School name	Address	Tel	Fax	Headteacher	Ref	Ages	Pupils	Other
Fosse Way School	Longfellow Rd, Radstock, Bath, Somerset BA3 3AL	01761 412198	01761 411751	Mr D. Gregory	800-7035	3–19	80	R ASD MLD
The Link School	Frome Rd, Bath BA2 5RF	01225 832212		Ms Dawn Harris	800-7037	9–16	32	SEBD
Three Ways School	180 Frome Rd, Coombe Pk, Bath, Sommerset BA2 5RF	01225 838070	01225 824223	Mrs Julie Dyer	800-7036	2–19	137	AS ASD CD HI MLD MSI PD PMLD SLD SpLD VI

Bournemouth

School name	Address	Tel	Fax	Headteacher	Ref	Ages	Pupils	Other
The Bicknell School	Petersfield Rd, Bournemouth, Dorset BH7 6QP	01202 424361	01202 430592	Mr Brian Hooper	837-7021	11–16	52	SEBD
Linwood School	Alma Rd, Bournemouth, Dorset BH9 1AJ	01202 525107	01202 525107	Mr Stephen Brown	837-7012	3–19	171	ASD MLD SLD

Bristol

School name	Address	Tel	Fax	Headteacher	Ref	Ages	Pupils	Other
Briarwood School	Briar Way, Fishponds, Bristol BS16 4EA	0117 353 2651	0117 353 2658	Mr D. Hussey	801-7042	2–19	80	SLD
Bristol Gateway School	Long Cross, Lawrence Weston, Bristol BS11 0QA	0117 377 2275	0117 377 2283	Mr M. Lewis	801-7001	14–16	50	
Claremont School	Henleaze Pk, Westbury-on-Trym, Bristol BS9 4LR	0117 924 7527	0117 942 6942	Mrs Alison Ewins	801-7011	2–11	39	PD SLD
Elmfield School for Deaf Children	Greystoke Ave, Westbury-on-Trym, Bristol BS10 6AY	0117 903 0366	0117 903 0370	Ms R. Way	801-7000	3–16	20	PD SpLD
The Florence Brown Community School	Leinster Ave, Knowle, Bristol BS4 1NN	0117 353 2011	0117 966 6537	Mr P. Evans	801-7012	5–16	125	SEBD PD MLD
Kingsdon Manor School	Kingsdon, Somerton, Somerset TA11 7JZ	01935 840323	01935 840591	Mr John Holliday	801-7009	9–16	30	B R SEBD MLD
Kingsweston School	Napier Miles Rd, Kingsweston, Bristol BS11 0UT	0117 903 0400	0779 872915	Mr D. Capel	801-7002	2–19	154	ASD MLD SLD
New Fosseway School	New Fosseway Rd, Hengrove, Bristol BS14 9LN	0117 903 0220	0117 903 0221	Mrs Valerie Davis	801-7014	6–19	75	SLD
Notton House School	28 Notton, Lacock, Chippenham, Wiltshire SN15 2NF	01249 730407	01249 730007	Mr Gerry Gamble	801-7015	9–16	43	B R SEBD
Woodstock School	Rectory Gdns, Henbury, Bristol BS10 7AH	0117 377 2175	0117 967 1474	Mr G. Parsons	801-7025	7–11	42	B SEBD

Cornwall

School name	Address	Tel	Fax	Headteacher	Ref	Ages	Pupils	Other
Curnow School	Drump Rd, Redruth, Cornwall TR15 1LU	01209 215432	01209 314205	Dr Bob Coburn	908-7004	2–19	108	SLD
Doubletrees School	St Blazey Gate, St Blazey, Par, Cornwall PL24 2DS	01726 812757	01726 812896	Ms Kim Robertson	908-7003	2–19	88	SLD
Nancealverne School	Madron Rd, Penzance, Cornwall TR20 8TP	01736 365039	01736 331941	Mrs Fiona Cock	908-7005	2–19	80	SLD
Pencalenick School	St Clement, Truro, Cornwall TR1 1TE	01872 520385	01872 520729	Mr Andy Barnett	908-7002	11–16	118	R MLD

Devon

School name	Address	Tel	Fax	Headteacher	Ref	Ages	Pupils	Other
Barley Lane School	Barley La, St Thomas, Exeter, Devon EX4 1TA	01392 430774	01392 433193	Mr Paul Wright	878-7008	10-16	29	B SEBD
Bidwell Brook School	Shinner's Bridge, Dartington, Totnes, Devon TQ9 6JU	01803 864120	01803 868025	Mrs Audrey Finch	878-7044	3-19	88	SLD PMLD
Ellen Tinkham School	Hollow La, Pinhoe, Exeter, Devon EX1 3RW	01392 467168	01392 464011	Mrs Jacqui Warne	878-7002	3-19	102	SLD PMLD
The Lampard Community School	St John's La, Barnstaple, Devon EX32 9DD	01271 345416	01271 345416	Miss Jackie Edwards	878-7020	5-16	71	ASD MLD
Marland School	Peters Marland, Torrington, Devon EX38 8QQ	01805 601324	01805 601298	Mr Keith Bennett	878-7088	11-16	40	B R SEBD
Mill Water School	Honiton Bottom Rd, Honiton, Devon EX14 2ER	01404 43454	01404 43402	Mrs S. Leathlean	878-7006	3-19	89	
Oaklands Park School	John Nash Dr, Dawlish, Devon EX7 9SF	01626 862363	01626 888566	Mr Robert Pugh	878-7043	3-19	52	R SLD
Pathfield School	Abbey Rd, Pilton, Barnstaple, Devon EX31 1JU	01271 342423	01271 323252	Mr Rod Conway	878-7021	3-19	111	SLD
Ratcliffe School	John Nash Dr, Dawlish, Devon EX7 9RZ	01626 862939		Mrs Cherie White	878-7087	8-17	60	R SEBD
Southbrook College	Bishop Westall Rd, Topsham Rd, Exeter, Devon EX2 6JB	01392 258373	01392 494036	Mrs Hilary Green	878-7005	6-16	100	MLD

Dorset

School name	Address	Tel	Fax	Headteacher	Ref	Ages	Pupils	Other
Beaucroft Foundation School	Wimborne Rd, Colehill, Wimborne, Dorset BH21 2SS	01202 886083	01202 848459	Mr Paul McGill	835-5950	4-16		ASD MLD
Mountjoy School	Flood La, Bridport, Dorset DT6 3QG	01308 422250	01308 458664	Mrs Pam Stewart	835-7007	3-19	37	SLD
Westfield Technology College	Littlemoor Rd, Preston, Weymouth, Dorset DT3 6AA	01305 833518	01305 835414	Mr Phil Silvester	835-5953	3-16		ASD MLD
Wyvern School	Dorchester Rd, Weymouth, Dorset DT3 5AL	01305 783660	01305 770965	Mrs Sue Hoxey	835-7008	2-19	72	SLD
Yewstock School	Honeymead La, Sturminster Newton, Dorset DT10 1EW	01258 472796	01258 473577	Mr J.S. Lineton	835-7019	2-19	123	ASD

Gloucestershire

School name	Address	Tel	Fax	Headteacher	Ref	Ages	Pupils	Other
Alderman Knight School	Ashchurch Rd, Tewkesbury, Gloucestershire GL20 8JJ	01684 295639	01684 295639	Mrs Clare Steel	916-7019	4-16	56	MLD
Amberley Ridge School	Rodborough Common, Stroud, Gloucestershire GL5 5DB	01453 872536	01453 872557	Mrs Beverly Cheal	916-7008	5-11	37	R SEBD
Battledown Children's Centre	Harp Hill, Battledown, Cheltenham, Gloucestershire GL52 6PZ	01242 525472	01242 257557	Ms Jane Cummings	916-7022	2-7	25	VI CD ASD SEBD PD MLD SLD DMP
Belmont School	Warden Hill Rd, Cheltenham, Gloucestershire GL51 3AT	01242 216180	01242 227827	Dr Anne Maddison	916-7023	4-16	46	MLD
Bettridge School	Warden Hill Rd, Cheltenham, Gloucestershire GL51 3AT	01242 514934	01242 584107	Mrs Mary Saunders	916-7015	2-19	95	VI CD ASD SLD
Cam House School	Drake La, Cam, Dursley, Gloucestershire GL11 5HD	01453 542130	01453 547067	Mr Ian Johnstone	916-7011	10-16	58	B R SEBD
Coln House School	Horcott Rd, Fairford, Gloucestershire GL7 4DB	01285 712308	01285 713011	Mr C. Clarke	916-7005	9-16	47	R SEBD
Heart of the Forest Community Special School	Speech Hse, Coleford, Gloucestershire GL16 7EJ	01594 822175		Mr Howard Jones	916-7025	3-19	68	SLD PMLD
The Milestone School	Longford La, Gloucester, Gloucestershire GL2 9EU	01452 500499	01452 500602	Mrs Lyn Dance	916-7024	2-16	274	VI CD ASD SEBD PD MLD SLD SpLD DMP
Paternoster School	Watermoor Rd, Cirencester, Gloucestershire GL7 1JS	01285 652480	01285 642490	Ms Julie Mantell	916-7018	2-17	35	SLD
Sandford School	Seven Springs, Cheltenham, Gloucestershire GL53 9NG	01242 870224	01242 870331	Mrs Helen Bartleman	916-7013	6-16	54	SEBD
The Shruberies School	Oldends La, Stonehouse, Gloucestershire GL10 2DG	01453 822155	01453 822155	Ms Jane Jones	916-7017	2-19	87	SLD

North Somerset

School name	Address	Tel	Fax	Headteacher	Ref	Ages	Pupils	Other
Baytree School	The Campus, Highlands La, Weston-super-Mare, North Somerset BS24 7DX	01934 427555	01934 625567	Mrs C. Penney	802-7039	3–19	59	SLD
Ravenswood School	Pound La, Nailsea, Bristol, North Somerset BS48 2NN	01275 854134		Mrs Philippa Clark	802-7037	3–19	94	ASD SLD
Westhaven School	Ellesmere Rd, Uphill, Weston-super-Mare, Somerset BS23 4UT	01934 632171	01934 645596	Mrs Jenny Moss	802-7036	7–16	73	SLD

Plymouth

School name	Address	Tel	Fax	Headteacher	Ref	Ages	Pupils	Other
Courtlands School	Widey La, Crownhill, Plymouth, Devon PL6 5JS	01752 776848	01752 769102	Mr G.H.J. Dunkerley	879-7065	4–12	72	MLD
Downham Special School	Horn La, Plymstock, Plymouth, Devon PL9 9BR	01752 403214	01752 481539	Mr Michael Loveman	879-7063	3–16	71	R SLD
Hillside School	Bodmin Rd, Whitleigh, Plymouth, Devon PL5 4DZ	01752 773875	01752 775761	Mr Clifford Edwards	879-7066	11–19	85	MLD
Longcause Community Special School	Longcause, Plympton St Maurice, Plympton, Plymouth, Devon PL7 1JB	01752 336881	01752 341151	Mr Mike Jelly	879-7068	5–17	85	MLD
Mill Ford School	Rochford Cres, Ernesettle, Plymouth, Devon PL5 2PY	01752 300270	01752 300109	Mrs P. Greenwood	879-7069	3–19	92	SLD
Mount Tamar School	Row La, Higher St Budeaux, Plymouth, Devon PL5 2EF	01752 365128	01752 351227	Mr B.J. Jones	879-7067	5–16	82	R SEBD
Plymouth Hospital School	12th Fl, Derriford Hospital, Plymouth, Devon PL6 8DH	01752 792476	01752 792476	Mrs Jill Jones	879-7064	3–16	9	HS
Woodlands School	Bodmin Rd, Whitleigh, Plymouth, Devon PL5 4DZ	01752 300101	01752 300102	Mrs Frances Larner	879-7062	2–17	66	R VI CD SEBD PD MLD SLD

Poole

School name	Address	Tel	Fax	Headteacher	Ref	Ages	Pupils	Other
Longspee School	Learoyd Rd, Canford Heath, Poole, Dorset BH17 8PJ	01202 380266	01202 380270	Mr Colin Fisher	836-7015	5–14	34	ASD SEBD
Montacute School	3 Canford Heath Rd, Poole, Dorset BH17 9NG	01202 693239	01202 657363	Mrs Marion Sammons	836-5951	2–18	85	ASD SLD
Winchelsea Special School	Guernsey Rd, Parkstone, Poole, Dorset BH12 4LL	01202 746240	01202 733024	Mr Stephen Cook	836-7005	3–16	90	MLD

Somerset

School name	Address	Tel	Fax	Headteacher	Ref	Ages	Pupils	Other
Avalon School	Brooks Rd, Street, Somerset BA16 0PS	01458 443081	01458 447380	Mr Neil Galloway	933-7018	3–16	42	CD SLD
Critchill School	Nunney Rd, Frome, Somerset BA11 4LB	01373 464148	01373 453481	Mr M. Armstrong	933-7019	4–16	41	VI CD DMP
Elmwood School	Hamp Ave, Bridgwater, Somerset TA6 6AP	01278 422866	01278 445157	Mrs Jaqui Tobin	933-7003	4–16	58	
Fairmead School	Mudford Rd, Yeovil, Somerset BA21 4NZ	01935 421295	01935 410552	Mrs Valerie Brookham	933-7007	4–16	65	CD
Fiveways Special School	Victoria Rd, Yeovil, Somerset BA21 5AZ	01935 476227	01935 411287	Mr M.D. Collis	933-7016	4–19	64	SLD
Penrose School	Albert St, Bridgwater, Somerset TA6 7ET	01278 423660	01278 431075	Mrs Susan Neale	933-7013	2–19	54	SLD
The Priory School	Pickeridge Cl, Taunton, Somerset TA2 7HW	01823 275569	01823 275569	Mr G. Toller	933-7006	11–16	59	B R SEBD
Selworthy Special School	Selworthy Rd, Taunton, Somerset TA2 8HD	01823 284970	01823 336519	Ms Karen Milton	933-7014	2–19	64	VI SEBD MSI MLD PMLD SpLD DMP

South Gloucestershire

School name	Address	Tel	Fax	Headteacher	Ref	Ages	Pupils	Other
Culverhill School	Kelston Cl, Yate, Bristol, Gloucestershire BS37 8SZ	01454 866930	01454 866931	Miss N. Jones	803-7000	7–16	130	
New Siblands School	Easton Hill Rd, Thornbury, Bristol, Gloucestershire BS35 2JU	01454 866754	01454 866759	Mr P. Casson	803-7031	4–16	59	SLD
Warmley Park School	Tower Rd North, Warmley, Bristol, Gloucestershire BS30 8XL	01454 867272	01454 867273	Mr Steve Morris	803-7028	2–19	101	SLD

Swindon

School name	Address	Tel	Fax	Headteacher	Ref	Ages	Pupils	Other
Brimble Hill Special School	Tadpole La, Redhouse, Swindon, Wiltshire SN25 2NB	01793 707577		Mr Robert Walker	866-7013	2–11	52	SLD
The Chalet School	Liden Dr, Liden, Swindon, Wiltshire SN3 6EX	01793 534537		Miss Katharine Bryan	866-7011	3–11	36	SLD
Crowdys Hill School	Jefferies Ave, Swindon, Wiltshire SN2 7HJ	01793 332400	01793 511894	Mr Peter Crockett	866-7006	11–16	138	MLD
Nyland School	Nyland Rd, Nythe, Swindon, Wiltshire SN3 3RD	01793 535023	01793 535023	Mr P. Sunners	866-7000	5–11	34	SEBD
St Luke's School	Cricklade Rd, Swindon, Wiltshire SN2 7AS	01793 705566	01793 705858	Mrs Zoe Lattimer	866-7004	11–16	54	SEBD
Uplands School	The Learning Campus, Tadpole La, Swindon, Wiltshire SN25 2NB	01793 707590	01793 703396	Miss Mary Bishop	866-7012	11–19	77	SLD

Torbay

School name	Address	Tel	Fax	Headteacher	Ref	Ages	Pupils	Other
Combe Pafford School	Steps La, Watcombe, Torquay, Devon TQ2 8NL	01803 327902	01803 327902	Mr Mike Lock	880-7041	6–16	162	MLD
Mayfield School	Moor La, Watcombe, Torquay, Devon TQ2 8NH	01803 328375	01803 552014	Mrs J. Palmer	880-7042	2–19	97	SLD
Torbay School	170b Torquay Rd, Paignton TQ3 2AL	01803 665522	01803 521915	Mr Paul Wright	880-7046	9–16	53	SEBD

Wiltshire

School name	Address	Tel	Fax	Headteacher	Ref	Ages	Pupils	Other
Downland School	Downlands Rd, Devizes, Wiltshire SN10 5EF	01380 724193	01380 728441	Mr W. Spear	865-7007	11–16	66	B R SEBD SpLD
Exeter House Special School	Somerset Rd, Salisbury, Wiltshire SP1 3BL	01722 334168	01722 334168	Mr Andrew Mears	865-7008	2–19	96	VI CD ASD SEBD PD MLD SLD SpLD DMP
Larkrise School	Ashton St, Trowbridge, Wiltshire BA14 7EB	01225 761434	01225 774585	Mrs C. Goodwin	865-7010	4–19	75	MLD SLD
Rowdeford School	Rowde, Devizes, Wiltshire SN10 2QQ	01380 850309		Mrs Ingrid Lancaster-Gaye	865-7002	11–16	122	R MLD
St Nicholas School	Malmesbury Rd, Chippenham, Wiltshire SN15 1QF	01249 650435	01249 447033	Mrs Jill Owen	865-7009	2–19	70	SLD
Springfields School	Curzon St, Calne, Wiltshire SN11 0DS	01249 814125	01249 814125	Mr Trystan Williams	865-7015	10–16	59	SEBD

West Midlands

Birmingham

School name	Address	Tel	Fax	Headteacher	Ref	Ages	Pupils	Other
Baskerville School	Fellows La, Harborne, Birmingham, West Midlands B17 9TS	0121 427 3191	0121 428 2204	Ms Rosemary Adams	330-7016	11–19	68	R ASD
Beaufort School	Stechford Rd, Hodge Hill, Birmingham, West Midlands B34 6BJ	0121 783 3886	0121 783 6994	Mrs Debbie Jenkins	330-7052	2–11	28	SLD
Braidwood School for The Deaf	Bromford Rd, Birmingham, West Midlands B36 8AF	0121 464 5558	0121 382 5844	Mrs Karen Saywood	330-7030	11–19	72	
Brays School	Brays Rd, Sheldon, Birmingham, West Midlands B26 1NS	0121 743 5730	0121 742 1567	Mrs Jane Edgerton	330-7038	2–11	79	PD
The Bridge School	290 Reservoir Rd, Erdington, Birmingham, West Midlands B23 6DE	0121 464 8265	0121 377 7619	Mr S. White	330-7049	2–11	54	R ASD SLD PMLD
Calthorpe School Sports College	Darwin St, Highgate, Birmingham, West Midlands B12 0TJ	0121 773 4637	0121 773 0708	Mr Graham Hardy	330-7013	2–19	267	SLD
Cherry Oak School	60 Frederick Rd, Birmingham, West Midlands B29 6PB	0121 464 2037	0121 464 5219	Mrs L. Fowler	330-7051	3–11	38	SLD
The Dame Ellen Pinsent School	Ardencote Rd, Birmingham, West Midlands B13 0RW	0121 444 2487	0121 464 7295	Mrs Debbie Allen	330-7035	5–11	114	MLD
Fox Hollies School and Performing Arts College	Highbury Community Campus, Queensbridge Rd, Moseley, Birmingham, West Midlands B13 8QB	0121 464 6566	0121 464 4148	Mr Paul Roberts	330-7050	11–19	68	SLD

7

School name	Address	Tel	Fax	Headteacher	Ref	Ages	Pupils	Other
Hallmoor School	Hallmoor Rd, Kitts Grn, Birmingham, West Midlands B33 9QY	0121 783 3972	0121 789 8815	Mrs S. Charvis	330-7027	4–19	238	MLD
Hamilton School	Hamilton Rd, Handsworth, Birmingham, West Midlands B21 8AH	0121 464 1676	0121 554 4808	Mrs R. Green	330-7006	4–11	62	MLD
Hunters Hill Technology College	Spirehouse La, Blackwell, Bromsgrove, Worcestershire B60 1QD	0121 445 1320	0121 445 2496	Mr K. Lewis	330-7026	11–16	93	R SEBD MLD
James Brindley School	Bell Barn Rd, Edgbaston, Birmingham, West Midlands B15 2AF	0121 666 6409	0121 666 6956	Mrs Lynne John	330-7063	2–19	107	HS
Langley School	Lindridge Rd, Sutton Coldfield, West Midlands B75 7HU	0121 329 2929	0121 311 1513	Mrs Fiona Woolford	330-7060	3–11	90	MLD
Lindsworth School	Monyhull Hall Rd, Kings Norton, Birmingham, West Midlands B30 3QA	0121 693 5363	0121 693 5369	Mr Francis Kelley	330-7062	11–16	186	R SEBD
Longwill School for the Deaf	Bell Hill, Northfield, Birmingham, West Midlands B31 1LD	0121 475 3923	0121 476 6362	Ms Babs Day	330-7012	2–12	42	
Mayfield School	Heathfield Rd, Handsworth, Birmingham, West Midlands B19 1HJ	0121 464 3354	0121 4644279	Mr Paul Jenkins	330-7040	3–19	149	ASD SEBD
Oscott Manor School	Old Oscott Hill, Kingstanding, Birmingham, West Midlands B44 9SP	0121 360 8222	0121 366 6394	Ms Joy Hardwick	330-7053	11–19	53	SLD
The Pines Special School	Dreghorn Rd, Birmingham, West Midlands B36 8LL	0121 464 6136	0121 747 6136	Mr S.G. Tuft	330-7045	2–11	89	CD ASD
Priestley Smith School	Perry Beeches Campus, Beeches Rd, Gt Barr, Birmingham, West Midlands B42 2PY	0121 325 3900	0121 382 5471	Mr C. Lewis	330-7034	2–17	47	VI
Queensbury School	Wood End Rd, Erdington, Birmingham, West Midlands B24 8BL	0121 373 5731	0121 382 6147	Mr John Higgins	330-7036	11–19	231	MLD
Selly Oak Special School	Oak Tree La, Selly Oak, Birmingham, West Midlands B29 6HZ	0121 472 0876	0121 415 5379	Mr G. Ridley	330-7033	11–19		MLD
Skitts School	Gorcott Hill, Redditch, Worcestershire B98 9ET	01527 853851	01527 857949	Mr S.C. Herriotts	330-7037	5–12	54	R SEBD
Springfield House Community Special School	Kenilworth Rd, Knowle, Solihull, West Midlands B93 0AJ	01564 775696	01564 771767	Mrs Janet Collins	330-7047	5–12	56	R ASD SEBD MLD SLD
Uffculme School	Queensbridge Rd, Birmingham, West Midlands B13 8QB	0121 464 5250	0121 442 2207	Mr A. MacDonald	330-7014	3–11	113	ASD
Victoria School	Bell Hill, Northfield, Birmingham, West Midlands B31 1LD	0121 476 9478	0121 411 2357	Mr James Kane	330-7009	2–19	164	PD
Wilson Stuart School	Perry Common Rd, Erdington, Birmingham, West Midlands B23 7AT	0121 373 4475	0121 373 9842	Mrs A. Tomkinson	330-7031	2–19	121	PD

Coventry

School name	Address	Tel	Fax	Headteacher	Ref	Ages	Pupils	Other
Alice Stevens School	Ashington Gr, Coventry, West Midlands CV3 4DE	024 7630 3776	024 7630 6173	Mr R.I. McAllister	331-7004	11–19	167	MLD
Baginton Fields School	Sedgemoor Rd, Coventry, West Midlands CV3 4EA	024 7630 3854	024 7630 1904	Mr Simon Grant	331-7019	11–19	99	SLD
Corley Centre	Church La, Corley, Coventry CV7 8AZ	01676 540218	01676 542577	Mrs Helen Bishton	331-7022	11–16	76	R PMLD
Sherbourne Fields School	Rowington Cl, Coventry, West Midlands CV6 1PS	024 7659 1501	024 7659 0517	Mr David Southeard	331-7009	2–19	84	PD
Three Spires School	Kingsbury Rd, Coventry, West Midlands CV6 1PJ	024 7659 4952	024 7659 3798	Mrs J. Brook	331-7006	3–11	71	MLD
Tiverton School	Rowington Cl, Coundon, Coventry, West Midlands CV6 1PS	024 7659 4954	024 7659 1575	Mr A. Chave	331-7017	3–11	37	SLD
Woodfield	Stoneleigh Rd, Coventry CV4 7AB	024 7641 8755	024 7669 0809	Mr Mick Chilvers	331-7021	7–16	127	SEBD

Dudley

School name	Address	Tel	Fax	Headteacher	Ref	Ages	Pupils	Other
The Brier School	Bromley La, Kingswinford, West Midlands DY6 8QN	01384 816000	01384 816001	Mr Russell Hinton	332-7002	4–16	138	CD MLD
Halesbury School	Feldon La, Halesowen, West Midlands B62 9DR	01384 818630	01384 818631	Mrs Margaret Winstone	332-7005	4–16	81	MLD
The Old Park School	Corbyn Rd, Russells Hall Est, Dudley, West Midlands DY1 2JZ	01384 818905	01384 818906	Mrs Gill Cartwright	332-7004	3–19	117	SLD
Pens Meadow School	Ridge Hill, Brierley Hill Rd, Wordsley, Stourbridge, West Midlands DY8 5ST	01384 818945	01384 818946	Mr Grahame Robertson	332-7009	3–19	57	SLD
Rosewood School	Overfield Rd, Russells Hall Est, Dudley, West Midlands DY1 2NX	01384 816800		Mr Nigel Griffiths	332-7008	11–16	40	B SEBD

School name	Address	Tel	Fax	Headteacher	Ref	Ages	Pupils	Other
The Sutton School and Specialist College	Scotts Green Cl, Russells Hall Est, Dudley, West Midlands DY1 2DU	01384 818670	01384 818671	Mr David Bishop-Rowe	332-7001	11–16	117	MLD
The Woodsetton School	Tipton Rd, Woodsetton, Dudley, West Midlands DY3 1BY	01384 818265	01384 818266	Mr Philip Rhind-Tutt	332-7003	4–11	80	CD ASD MLD

Herefordshire

School name	Address	Tel	Fax	Headteacher	Ref	Ages	Pupils	Other
Barrs Court School	Barrs Court Rd, Hereford, Herefordshire HR1 1EQ	01432 265035	01432 353988	Mr Richard Aird	884-7003	11–19	57	SLD
Blackmarston School	Honddu Cl, Hereford, Herefordshire HR2 7NX	01432 272376	01432 272376	Mrs Sian Bailey	884-7004	3–11	47	SLD
Brookfield School	Grandstand Rd, Hereford, Herefordshire HR4 9NG	01432 265153		Mrs Oremi Evans	884-7008	7–16	59	SEBD MLD
Westfield School	Westfield Wlk, Leominster, Herefordshire HR6 8HD	01568 613147	01568 613147	Mrs Susan Harris	884-7007	2–19	30	SLD

Sandwell

School name	Address	Tel	Fax	Headteacher	Ref	Ages	Pupils	Other
The Meadows Sports College	Dudley Rd East, Oldbury, West Midlands B69 3BU	0121 569 7080	0121 569 7081	Mr Gordon Phillips	333-7017	11–19	137	VI CD ASD PD SLD
The Orchard School	Coopers La, Smethwick, West Midlands B67 7DW	0121 558 1069	0121 565 0940	Mrs Atkins	333-7018	2–11	85	DMP
Shenstone Lodge School	Birmingham Rd, Shenstone, Lichfield, Staffordshire WS14 0LB	01543 480369	01543 481104	Mr S. Butt	333-7001	5–12	14	B R SEBD
The Westminster School	Westminster Rd, West Bromwich, West Midlands B71 2JN	0121 588 2421	0121 588 5451	Mrs D. Williams	333-7019	11–19	101	MLD

Shropshire

School name	Address	Tel	Fax	Headteacher	Ref	Ages	Pupils	Other
Severndale	Hearne Way, Monkmoor, Shrewsbury, Shropshire SY2 5SL	01743 281600	01743 281601	Mr C. Davies	893-7016	2–19	238	VI CD ASD SEBD PD SLD SpLD
Woodlands School	The Woodlands Centre, Tilley Grn, Wem, Shrewsbury, Shropshire SY4 5PJ	01939 232372	01939 233002	Mr Robin Wilson	893-7006	11–16	37	SEBD

Solihull

School name	Address	Tel	Fax	Headteacher	Ref	Ages	Pupils	Other
Forest Oak School	Windward Way, Birmingham, West Midlands B36 0UE	0121 717 0088	0121 749 7534	Mrs Alison Murking	334-7005	4–16	100	MLD
Hazel Oak School	Hazel Oak Rd, Shirley, Solihull, West Midlands B90 2AZ	0121 744 4162	0121 733 8861	Mr P.A. Wright	334-7001	3–16	102	MLD
Lanchester School	Lanchester Way, Castle Bromwich, Birmingham, West Midlands B36 9LF	0121 776 7465	0121 748 7889	Mrs Susan Williams	334-7009	11–16	29	SEBD
Merstone School	Windward Way, Kingshurst, Birmingham, West Midlands B36 0UE	0121 717 1040	0121 717 1041	Mrs Amanda Mordey	334-7007	2–18	56	SLD
Reynalds Cross School	Kineton Green Rd, Olton, Solihull, West Midlands B92 7ER	0121 707 3012		Mrs Jane Davenport	334-7002	2–19	93	SLD

Staffordshire

School name	Address	Tel	Fax	Headteacher	Ref	Ages	Pupils	Other
Blackfriars School	Priory Rd, Newcastle under Lyme, Staffordshire ST5 2TF	01782 297780	01782 297784	Mr Clive Lilley	860-7026	2–19	169	PD
Chasetown Community School	Church St, Chasetown, Burntwood, Staffordshire WS7 3QL	01543 686315		Dr Linda James	860-7000	4–11	40	
Cherry Trees School	Giggetty La, Wombourne, Wolverhampton, West Midlands WV5 0AX	01902 894484	01902 894484	Mrs L.J. Allman	860-7034	2–11	35	SLD

7

School name	Address	Tel	Fax	Headteacher	Ref	Ages	Pupils	Other
Cicely Haughton School	Westwood Manor, Mill La, Wetley Rocks, Stoke-on-Trent, Staffordshire ST9 0BX	01782 550202	01782 550202	Mr N. Phillips	860-7006	5–11	38	B R SEBD
Coppice School	Abbots Way, Westlands, Newcastle, Staffordshire ST5 2EY	01782 297490	01782 297496	Mrs Sandra Baker	860-7027	11–19	100	SEBD MLD
The Fountains High School	Bitham La, Stretton, Burton-on-Trent, Staffordshire DE13 0HB	01283 239161	01283 239168	Mr Philip Nickless	860-7015	11–18	141	MLD
The Fountains Primary School	Bitham La, Stretton, Burton-on-Trent, Staffordshire DE13 0HB	01283 239700	01283 239700	Mr Philip Nickless	860-7016	2–11	75	SLD
Greenhall Nursery	Second Ave, Holmcroft, Stafford, Staffordshire ST16 1PS	01785 246159	01785 215490	Mrs K.E. Milligan	860-7750	3–5	29	PD
Hednesford Valley High School	Stanley Rd, Hednesford, Hednesford, Staffordshire WS12 4JS	01543 423714	01543 423714	Mrs A. Rattan	860-7023	11–19	123	CD ASD SEBD MLD SpLD DMP
Horton Lodge Community Special School	Rudyard, Leek, Staffordshire ST13 8RB	01538 306214	01538 306006	Mrs R. Zimmerman	860-7003	2–12	52	R PD
Loxley Hall School	Stafford Rd, Uttoxeter, Staffordshire ST14 8RS	01889 256390	01889 256397	Mr M. Pearce	860-7024	11–16	66	B R SEBD
Marshlands School	Lansdowne Way, Wildwood, Stafford, Staffordshire ST17 4RD	01785 356385		Ms Belinda Whale	860-7037	2–11	47	SLD
Meadows School	High St, Knutton, Newcastle-under-Lyme, Staffordshire ST5 6BX	01782 297920	01782 297920	Mr Christian Williams	860-7028	11–19	76	MLD
Merryfields School	Hoon Ave, Newcastle, Staffordshire ST5 9NY	01782 296076		Mrs Sarah Poyner	860-7038	2–11	51	SLD
Queen's Croft Community School	Birmingham Rd, Lichfield, Staffordshire WS13 6PJ	01543 510669	01543 510673	Mr John Edwards	860-7041	11–19	152	MLD
Rocklands School	Wissage Rd, Lichfield, Staffordshire WS13 6SW	01543 510760		Mr A.J. Dooley	860-7036	2–11	78	ASD SLD
Saxon Hill School	Kings Hill Rd, Lichfield, Staffordshire WS14 9DE	01543 510615	01543 510626	Mr Nigel Carter	860-7039	2–19	87	R PD
Sherbrook Primary School	Brunswick Rd, Cannock, Staffordshire WS11 5SA	01543 510216	01543 510222	Mrs Sarah Ashley	860-7032	2–11	77	SLD
Springfield Community Special School	Springfield Rd, Leek, Staffordshire ST13 6LQ	01538 383558	01538 383558	Mrs Irene Corden	860-7033	2–11	53	SLD
Two Rivers High School	Solway Cl, Leyfields, Tamworth, Staffordshire B79 8EB	01827 475690	01827 475697	Mrs Victoria Vernon	860-7030	11–18	113	MLD
Two Rivers Primary School	Quince, Tamworth, Staffordshire B77 4EN	01827 475740	01827 475746	Mrs V.A. Vernon	860-7042	2–11	106	SLD
Walton Hall School	Stafford Rd, Eccleshall, Stafford, Staffordshire ST21 6JR	01785 850420	01785 850225	Mr R. Goldthorpe	860-7021	11–19	132	R
Wightwick Hall School	Tinacre Hill, Compton, Wolverhampton, West Midlands WV6 8DA	01902 761889	01902 765080	Mr Paul Elliott	860-7043	11–19	73	R ASD MLD

Stoke-on-Trent

School name	Address	Tel	Fax	Headteacher	Ref	Ages	Pupils	Other
Abbey Hill School and Performing Arts College	Greasleys Rd, Bucknall, Stoke-on-Trent, Staffordshire ST2 8LG	01782 234727	01782 234729	Mrs M. Coutouvidis	861-7007	2–18	218	ASD MLD DMP
Aynsley Special School	Aynsleys Dr, Blythe Bridge, Stoke-on-Trent, Staffordshire ST11 9HJ	01782 392071	01782 388911	Mrs Angela Hardstaff	861-7005	3–16	117	SEBD MLD
Heathfield Special School	Chell Heath Rd, Chell Heath, Stoke-on-Trent, Staffordshire ST6 6PD	01782 234494	01782 236514	Mrs Catherine Lewis	861-7010	2–19	55	VI SLD
Kemball Special School	Duke St, Fenton, Stoke-on-Trent, Staffordshire ST4 3NR	01782 234879	01782 234880	Mrs Elizabeth Spooner	861-7011	2–19	60	VI CD ASD SEBD PD MLD SLD SpLD DMP
Middlehurst Special School	Turnhurst Rd, Chell, Stoke-on-Trent, Staffordshire ST6 6NQ	01782 234612		Mr Johnathon May	861-7008	5–16	85	MLD

Telford and Wrekin

School name	Address	Tel	Fax	Headteacher	Ref	Ages	Pupils	Other
The Bridge at HLC	Waterloo Rd, Hadley, Telford, Shropshire TF1 5NU	01952 417020	01952 417022	Mrs Una van-den-Berg	894-7017	2–18	218	SLD
Haughton School	Queen St, Madeley, Telford, Shropshire TF7 4BW	01952 387540	01952 583616	Mrs G. Knox	894-7001	5–11	102	MLD
Mount Gilbert School	Hinkshay Rd, Dawley, Telford, Shropshire TF4 3PP	01952 387670		Ms A. Valentini	894-7018	11–16	44	SEBD
Southall School	off Rowan Ave, Dawley, Telford, Shropshire TF4 3PX	01952 592485	01952 591207	Mr Alistair Bates	894-7012	11–16	149	CD ASD MLD SLD

Walsall

School name	Address	Tel	Fax	Headteacher	Ref	Ages	Pupils	Other
Castle School	Odell Rd, Leamore, Walsall, West Midlands WS3 2ED	01922 710129	01922 710835	Mrs Kathy Yates	335-7002	4-19	94	MLD
Daw End School	Floyds La, Rushall, Walsall, West Midlands WS4 1LF	01922 721081	01922 631687	Mr Alastair Fairfull	335-7006	5-16	44	R SEBD
Jane Lane School	Churchill Rd, Bentley, Walsall, West Midlands WS2 0JH	01922 721161	01922 631695	Mrs Heather Lomas	335-7004	4-18	120	VI CD ASD SEBD PD MLD SpLD DMP
Mary Elliot School	Brewer St, Walsall, West Midlands WS2 8BA	01922 720706	01922 612298	Mrs Elizabeth Jordan	335-7005	13-19	61	SLD
Oakwood School	Druids Wlk, Walsall Wood, Walsall, West Midlands WS9 9JS	01543 452040	01543 453982	Mrs K. Mills	335-7011	2-14	57	SLD
Old Hall School	Bentley La, Walsall, West Midlands WS2 7LU	01902 368045	01902 634144	Mr Nigel Smith	335-7007	3-14	82	SLD

Warwickshire

School name	Address	Tel	Fax	Headteacher	Ref	Ages	Pupils	Other
Brooke School	Overslade La, Rugby, Warwickshire CV22 6DY	01788 812324		Mrs S. Cowen	937-7023	2-19	114	SLD
Exhall Grange School and Science College	Wheelwright La, Ash Grn, Coventry, Warwickshire CV7 9HP	024 7636 4200	024 7664 5055	Mr J.D. Truman	937-7000	2-19	138	VI PD
Oak Wood Primary School	Morris Dr, Nuneaton, Warwickshire CV11 4QH	024 7674 0907	024 4767 0921	Mrs Rosemary Scott	937-7002	2-11	73	VI HI ASD MSI PD MLD SLD PMLD SpLD
Oak Wood Secondary School	Morris Dr, Nuneaton, Warwickshire CV11 4QH	024 7674 0901	024 4767 0915	Mrs Rosemarie Scott	937-7046	11-19	118	VI HI ASD MSI PD MLD SLD PMLD SpLD
The Ridgeway School	Montague Rd, Warwick, Warwickshire CV34 5LW	01926 491987	01926 407317	Mrs P.A. Flynn	937-7028	2-10	77	N MLD SLD
River House School	Stratford Rd, Henley-in-Arden, Henley in Arden, Warwickshire B95 6AD	01564 792514	01564 792179	Mr Michael J. Turner	937-7001	11-16	40	B SEBD
The Round Oak School and Support Service	Brittain La, Lillington, Warwick, Warwickshire CV34 6DX	01926 423311	01926 886163	Miss Puffin Pocock	937-7030	11-19	82	MLD SLD
Welcombe Hills School	Blue Cap Rd, Stratford-upon-Avon, Warwickshire CV37 6TQ	01789 266845	01789 204121	Mrs Judith Humphry	937-7044	2-19	135	
Woodlands	Packington La, Coleshill, Birmingham, West Midlands B46 3JE	01675 463590	01675 463584	Mrs Gillian Simpson	937-7047	2-19	84	VI HI ASD MSI PD MLD SLD PMLD SpLD

Wolverhampton

School name	Address	Tel	Fax	Headteacher	Ref	Ages	Pupils	Other
Broadmeadow Nursery School	Lansdowne Rd, Wolverhampton, West Midlands WV1 4AL	01902 558330		Miss Karen Warrington	336-7011	2-6	41	PD SLD
Green Park School	Green Park Ave, Stowlawn, Bilston, West Midlands WV14 6EH	01902 556429	01902 408076	Mrs Lorraine Dawney	336-7008	5-19	99	ASD PD SLD
New Park School	Valley Park Campus, Cromer Gdns, Wolverhampton, West Midlands WV6 0UB	01902 551642		Mrs S.J. Humphreyson	336-7015	8-14	46	SEBD
Penn Fields School	Birches Barn Rd, Penn Fields, Wolverhampton, West Midlands WV3 7BJ	01902 339786	01902 831911	Mr Brian Brigginshaw	336-7004	4-16	158	MLD
Penn Hall School	Vicarage Rd, Penn, Wolverhampton, West Midlands WV4 5HP	01902 558355	01902 620335	Mr Alun Stoll	336-7012	3-19	79	PD
Tettenhall Wood School	School Rd, Tettenhall Wood, Wolverhampton, West Midlands WV6 8EJ	01902 556519	01902 744835	Mr Mostyn Mahoney	336-7007	5-19	56	SLD
Westcroft School and Sports College	Greenacres Ave, Underhill, Wolverhampton, West Midlands WV10 8NZ	01902 558350	01902 558342	Ms A. Brown	336-7005	4-16	165	MLD

7

Worcestershire

School name	Address	Tel	Fax	Headteacher	Ref	Ages	Pupils	Other
Blakebrook School	Bewdley Rd, Kidderminster, Worcestershire DY11 6RL	01562 753066	01562 824533	Mr Michael Russell	885-7005	3–19	68	CD ASD SLD
Chadsgrove School	Meadow Rd, Catshill, Bromsgrove, Worcestershire B61 0JL	01527 871511	01527 579341	Mr R. Aust	885-7015	2–19	120	PD
Fort Royal	Wyld's La, Worcester, Worcestershire WR5 1DR	01905 355525	01905 358867	Mr David Charles Palmer	885-7025	2–11		PD MLD SLD PMLD ADHD
The Kingfisher School	Clifton Cl, Matchborough, Redditch, Worcestershire B98 0HF	01527 502486	01527 502290	Mrs Tania Craig	885-7023	7–16	43	
Pitcheroak School	Willow Way, Batchley, Redditch, Worcestershire B97 6PQ	01527 65576	01527 67845	Mrs Olwen Bird	885-7009	3–19	124	ASD MLD SLD SpLD
Regency High School	Windermere Rd, Warndon, Worcester WR4 9JL	01905 454828	01905 453695	Mr Francis William Steele	885-7024	11–19		PD MLD SLD PMLD ADHD
Rigby Hall Day Special School	Rigby La, Astonfields, Bromsgrove, Worcestershire B60 2EP	01527 875475		Mrs M. Calvert	885-7001	4–18	99	
Riversides School	Thorneloe Rd, Barbourne, Worcester, Worcestershire WR1 3HZ	01905 21261		Mrs B.L. Scott	885-7022	7–16	62	SEBD
Stourminster Special School	Comberton Rd, Kidderminster, Worcestershire DY10 3DX	01562 823156	01562 824552	Mr Ian Hardicker	885-7010	7–16	120	MLD
Vale of Evesham School	Four Pools La, Evesham, Worcestershire WR11 1BN	01386 443367	01386 765787	Mrs Ann Starr	885-7011	2–19	141	R ASD

Yorkshire and The Humber

Barnsley

School name	Address	Tel	Fax	Headteacher	Ref	Ages	Pupils	Other
Greenacre School	Keresforth Hill Rd, Barnsley, South Yorkshire S70 6RG	01226 287165	01226 295328	Mrs Susan Hayter	370-7009	3–19	152	
Springwell Centre	St Helen's Bvd, Barnsley S71 2AY	01226 206683	01226 779244	Josie Thirkell	370-7010	7–16		SEBD

Bradford

School name	Address	Tel	Fax	Headteacher	Ref	Ages	Pupils	Other
Bolling Special School	Anerley St, Bradford, West Yorkshire BD4 7SY	01274 721962		Mrs Susan Gill	380-7028	11–19	94	PD SLD
Braithwaite Special School	Braithwaite Rd, Keighley, West Yorkshire BD22 6PR	01535 603041	01535 691227	Mrs P. Pearson	380-7020	2–19	94	MLD
Branshaw School	Oakworth Rd, Keighley, West Yorkshire BD21 1QX	01535 662739	01535 663834	Mrs J. Graveson	380-7024	2–19	39	SLD
Chapel Grange School	Rhodesway, Bradford, West Yorkshire BD8 0DQ	01274 773307	01274 774088	Mrs H. Morrison	380-7008	11–19	94	ASD SEBD MLD SLD
Greenfield School	Boothroyd Dr, Idle, Bradford, West Yorkshire BD10 8LU	01274 614092	01274 613840	Mrs J. Taylor	380-7010	2–11	52	MLD
Haycliffe School	Haycliffe La, Little Horton, Bradford, West Yorkshire BD5 9ET	01274 576123	01274 502716	Mr K. Fair	380-7025	11–19	140	VI CD ASD SEBD PD MLD SLD SpLD
Heaton Royds School	Redburn Dr, Shipley, West Yorkshire BD18 3AZ	01274 583759	01274 589397	Mrs M. Fowler	380-7021	2–11	48	SLD
Lister Lane School	Lister La, Bradford, West Yorkshire BD2 4LL	01274 777107	01274 773623	Mrs Louise Shinn	380-7002	2–13	64	PD
Netherlands Avenue School and Community Nursery	Netherlands Ave, Odsal, Bradford, West Yorkshire BD6 1EA	01274 677711	01274 677711	Mr G. Bowden	380-7007	2–11	112	CD SEBD
Thorn Park School for Deaf Children	Thorn La, Bingley Rd, Bradford, West Yorkshire BD9 6RY	01274 773770	01274 770387	Mrs Christine Roche	380-7026	2–19	61	
Wedgwood School and Community Nursery	Landscove Ave, Holmewood, Bradford, West Yorkshire BD4 0NQ	01274 687236	01274 686735	Mrs J. Godward	380-7012	2–11	87	

Calderdale

School name	Address	Tel	Fax	Headteacher	Ref	Ages	Pupils	Other
Highbury School	Lower Edge Rd, Rastrick, Brighouse, West Yorkshire HD6 3LD	01484 716319	01484 721893	Miss Pam Sellers	381-7010	2–11	43	VI CD ASD PD SLD
Ravenscliffe High School	Skircoat Grn, Halifax, West Yorkshire HX3 0RZ	01422 358621		Mr Michael Hirst	381-7009	11–19	120	VI CD ASD SEBD PD MLD SLD SpLD DMP
Wood Bank School	Dene View, Luddendenfoot, Halifax, West Yorkshire HX2 6PB	01422 884170	01422 884671	Mrs Jane Ingham	381-7008	2–11	49	VI CD ASD PD MLD SLD

Doncaster

School name	Address	Tel	Fax	Headteacher	Ref	Ages	Pupils	Other
Anchorage School	Barnsley Rd, Scawsby, Scawsby, Doncaster, South Yorkshire DN5 7UB	01302 391006	01302 390135	Mrs Ann Roberts	371-7008	5–16	94	MLD
Athelstane School	Old Rd, Conisbrough, Doncaster, South Yorkshire DN12 3LR	01709 864978	01709 864996	Mr G. Davies	371-7010	5–16	92	MLD
Cedar Special School	Cedar Rd, Balby, Doncaster, South Yorkshire DN4 9HT	01302 853361		Mrs J. Boyda	371-7005	3–19	61	SLD
Chase School	Ash Hill, Hatfield, Doncaster, South Yorkshire DN7 6JH	01302 844883	01302 841052	Mr Glyn Williams	371-7004	2–19	89	ASD SLD
Fernbank School (Severe Learning Difficulties)	Village St, Adwick-le-Street, Doncaster, South Yorkshire DN6 7AA	01302 723571	01302 724196	Mr M. Wright	371-7009	3–19	51	SLD
Rossington Hall School	Gt North Rd, Rossington, Doncaster, South Yorkshire DN11 0HS	01302 868365		Mr S. Leone	371-7003	5–16	91	R ASD SEBD MLD
Sandall Wood School	Leger Way, Doncaster, South Yorkshire DN2 6HQ	01302 322044	01302 739927	Mrs Carol Ray	371-7011	2–19	41	PD

East Riding of Yorkshire

School name	Address	Tel	Fax	Headteacher	Ref	Ages	Pupils	Other
King's Mill School	Victoria Rd, Driffield, East Riding of Yorkshire YO25 6UG	01377 253375		Ms Sarah Young	811-7016	2–16	73	R ASD PD SLD
Riverside Special School	Ainsty St, Goole, East Riding of Yorkshire DN14 5JS	01405 763925		Ms Lynne Jarred	811-7025	5–16	77	CD ASD MLD
St Anne's Community Special School	St Helen's Dr, Welton, Brough, East Yorkshire HU15 1NR	01482 667379		Mr M. Stubbins	811-7018	3–16	70	R SLD

Kingston upon Hull

School name	Address	Tel	Fax	Headteacher	Ref	Ages	Pupils	Other
Bridgeview	Ferriby Rd, Hessle, East Yorkshire HU13 0HR	01482 640115	01482 646603	Mr E. Sykes	810-7029	8–16	83	R SEBD
Frederick Holmes School	Inglemire La, Hull, East Riding of Yorkshire HU6 8JJ	01482 804766	01482 806967	Mr Dominic Boyes	810-7006	2–19	77	PD
Ganton Special School	Springhead La, Willerby Rd, Hull, Humberside HU5 5YJ	01482 564646		Mrs P. Glover	810-7028	3–19	126	SLD
Northcott School	Dulverton Cl, Bransholme, Hull, East Riding of Yorkshire HU7 4EL	01482 825311		Mr Mel Johnson	810-7000	5–16	109	VI ASD SEBD PD MLD
Oakfield	Inglemire La, Hull, East Riding of Yorkshire HU6 8JH	01482 854588	01482 855496	Ms Sykes Edward	810-7007	4–16	74	SEBD MLD
Tweendykes School	Tweendykes Rd, Hull, East Riding of Yorkshire HU7 4XJ	01482 826508	01482 839597	Mrs Bernadette Dobson	810-7008	3–19	81	SLD

Kirklees

School name	Address	Tel	Fax	Headteacher	Ref	Ages	Pupils	Other
Castle Hill School	Newsome Rd South, Huddersfield, West Yorkshire HD4 6JL	01484 226659		Mrs Gill Robinson	382-7015	3–19	100	ASD SLD PMLD
Fairfield School	White Lee Rd, Batley, West Yorkshire WF17 8AS	01924 325700	01924 325702	Mr Richard Ware	382-7011	3–19	98	SLD
Longley School	Dog Kennel Bank, Huddersfield, West Yorkshire HD5 8JE	01484 223937	01484 511520	Mr P. Gibbins	382-7001	5–16	127	ASD SEBD MLD
Lydgate School	Kirkroyds La, New Mill, Holmfirth, West Yorkshire HD9 1LS	01484 222484	01484 222485	Mr Martin Ord	382-7010	5–16	79	MLD

7

School name	Address	Tel	Fax	Headteacher	Ref	Ages	Pupils	Other
Nortonthorpe Hall School	Busker La, Scissett, Huddersfield, West Yorkshire HD8 9JU	01484 222921	01484 222966	Mr Andrew Hodkinson	382-7013	7–16	70	SEBD
Ravenshall School	Ravensthorpe Rd, Thornhill Lees, Dewsbury, West Yorkshire WF12 9EE	01924 325234		Mr C. Newby	382-7005	5–16	160	MLD

Leeds

School name	Address	Tel	Fax	Headteacher	Ref	Ages	Pupils	Other
Broomfield School	Broom Pl, Leeds, West Yorkshire LS10 3JP	0113 277 1603	0113 277 1622	Mrs Sue Steward	383-7062	2–19	144	VI CD ASD SEBD PD MLD SLD SpLD
Elmete Wood	Elmete La, Leeds, West Yorkshire LS8 2LJ	0113 265 5457	0113 265 5450	Mr W.J. Chatwin	383-7068	11–19	117	MLD
John Jamieson School	Hollin Hill Dr, Leeds, West Yorkshire LS8 2PW	0113 293 0236	0113 293 0237	Miss Diane Reynard	383-7015	2–19	120	PD MLD
North West Specialist Inclusive Learning Centre	Tongue La, Meanwood, Leeds, West Yorkshire LS6 4QE	0113 278 3577	0113 278 3577	Mr Michael K. Purches	383-7073	2–19	194	PD MLD SpLD
West Oaks School North East Specialist Inclusive Learning Centre	Westwood Way, Boston Spa, Wetherby, West Yorkshire LS23 6DX	01937 844772	01937 845122	Ms Sue Towers	383-7072	2–19	132	MLD SLD
West Specialist Inclusive Learning Centre	4 Town St, Stanningley, Pudsey, Leeds LS28 6HL	0113 386 2450	0113 255 9162	Mr Peter J. Miller	383-7074	2–19	145	PD SpLD

North East Lincolnshire

School name	Address	Tel	Fax	Headteacher	Ref	Ages	Pupils	Other
Cambridge Park School	Cambridge Rd, Grimsby, North East Lincolnshire DN34 5EB	01472 230110	01472 230113	Mrs G. Kendall	812-7033	4–16	173	ASD MLD
Humberston Park School	St Thomas Cl, Humberston, Grimsby, Lincolnshire DN36 4HS	01472 590645	01472 590643	Mr Andrew Zielinski	812-7011	3–19	89	SLD

North Lincolnshire

School name	Address	Tel	Fax	Headteacher	Ref	Ages	Pupils	Other
St Hugh's School	Bushfield Rd, Scunthorpe, North Lincolnshire DN16 1NB	01724 842960	01724 842960	Mr Chris Darlington	813-7019	11–19	121	CD ASD PD MLD PMLD
St Luke's Primary School	Grange La North, Scunthorpe, North Lincolnshire DN16 1BN	01724 844560	01724 279090	Dr Rob Ashdown	813-7020	3–11	87	ASD PD MLD SLD PMLD

North Yorkshire

School name	Address	Tel	Fax	Headteacher	Ref	Ages	Pupils	Other
Baliol School	Cautley Rd, Sedbergh, Cumbria LA10 5LQ	01539 620232	01539 621275	Mr Drew Anderson	815-7030	11–16	35	B R SEBD
Brompton Hall School	High St, Brompton-by-Sawdon, Scarborough, North Yorkshire YO13 9DB	01723 859121	01723 850239	Mr Mark Mikkelson	815-7000	8–16	49	B R SEBD
Brooklands School	Burnside Ave, Skipton, North Yorkshire BD23 2DB	01756 794028	01756 794200	Mr Keith Shorrock	815-7027	2–19	33	MLD SLD
The Dales School	Morton-on-Swale, Northallerton, North Yorkshire DL7 9QW	01609 772932	01609 780278	Mrs Hanne Barton	815-7015	2–19	65	SLD
The Forest School	Park La, Knaresborough, North Yorkshire HG5 0DQ	01423 864583	01423 861145	Mrs M. Uden	815-7022	2–16	108	MLD
Mowbray School	Masham Rd, Bedale, North Yorkshire DL8 2SD	01677 422446	01677 426056	Mr Jonathan Tearle	815-7029	2–16	127	CD ASD SEBD PD MLD SLD SpLD
Netherside Hall School	Threshfield, Skipton, North Yorkshire BD23 5PP	01756 752324	01756 753227	Dr Morris Charlton	815-7019	10–16	23	B R SpLD
Springhead School	Barry's La, Scarborough, North Yorkshire YO12 4HA	01723 367829	01723 360021	Mrs Debbie Wilson	815-7017	2–19	44	SLD
Springwater School	High St, Starbeck, Harrogate, North Yorkshire HG2 7LW	01423 883214		Mr G. Cook	815-7024	2–19	38	SLD
Welburn Hall School	Kirkbymoorside, York, North Yorkshire YO62 7HQ	01751 431218	01751 433157	Mr David Coram	815-7004	8–18	36	R CD PD MLD DMP
The Woodlands School	Woodlands Dr, Scarborough, North Yorkshire YO12 6QN	01723 373260	01723 371715	Mr P.G. Edmondson	815-7009	2–16	81	R ASD SEBD MLD

Rotherham

School name	Address	Tel	Fax	Headteacher	Ref	Ages	Pupils	Other
Abbey School	Little Common La, Kimberworth, Rotherham, South Yorkshire S61 2RA	01709 740074	01709 553465	Mrs Fiona Jane Naylor	372-7001	7–16	114	MLD
Hilltop School	Larch Rd, Maltby, Rotherham, South Yorkshire S66 8AZ	01709 813386	01709 798383	Mr Peter Leach	372-7011	2–19	99	SLD
Kelford School	Oakdale Rd, Kimberworth, Rotherham, South Yorkshire S61 2NU	01709 512088	01709 512091	Mr Nick Whittaker	372-7003	2–19	92	SLD
Milton School	Storey St, Swinton, Mexborough, South Yorkshire S64 8QG	01709 570246	01709 570547	Mrs Brenda Hughes	372-7006	7–16	93	ASD MLD
Newman School	East Bawtry Rd, Whiston, Rotherham, South Yorkshire S60 3LX	01709 828262	01709 821162	Mrs Suzette Garland-Grimes	372-7000	2–19	57	PD
The Willows School	Locksley Dr, Thurcroft, Rotherham, South Yorkshire S66 9NT	01709 542539	01709 703198	Mrs Anne Sanderson	372-7009	7–16	78	CD MLD

Sheffield

School name	Address	Tel	Fax	Headteacher	Ref	Ages	Pupils	Other
Bents Green School	Ringinglow Rd, Sheffield, South Yorkshire S11 7TB	0114 236 3545	0114 262 1904	Mrs A. Scott-Jones	373-7010	11–19	136	R MLD
Heritage Park Community School	Norfolk Park Rd, Sheffield, South Yorkshire S2 2RU	0114 279 6850		Mr John Hill	373-7040	7–16	75	SEBD
Holgate Meadows Community Special School	Lindsay Rd, Sheffield, South Yorkshire S5 7WE	0114 245 6305	0114 257 6761	Ms Kathryn Stallard	373-7041	7–16	80	SEBD
Mossbrook School	Bochum Parkway, Sheffield, South Yorkshire S8 8JR	0114 237 2768		Mrs M. Brough	373-7036	4–11	75	AS ASD MLD SLD
Norfolk Park School	Park Grange Rd, Sheffield, South Yorkshire S2 3QF	0114 272 6165	0114 272 5932	Ms G.M. Croston	373-7023	2–11	66	SLD
Oakwood School	Northern General Hospital, Herries Rd, Sheffield, South Yorkshire S5 7AU	0114 226 1691	0114 226 1692	Mrs Wendy Dudley	373-7038	12–18		HS
The Rowan School	4 Durvale Ct, Furniss Ave, Sheffield, South Yorkshire S17 3PT	0114 235 0479	0114 235 0478	Mrs Avril Young	373-7013	4–11	63	AS ASD CD
Shirle Hill Hospital School	6 Cherry Tree Rd, Sheffield, South Yorkshire S11 9AA	0114 271 6877	0114 271 6877	Mr G.D. Lewis	373-7021	5–13		HS
Talbot School	Matthews La, Norton, Sheffield, South Yorkshire S8 8JS	0114 250 7394	0114 250 7857	Mr J. Irwin	373-7024	11–19	134	SEBD
Woolley Wood School	Oaks Fold Rd, Sheffield, South Yorkshire S5 0TG	0114 245 6885	0114 257 0269	Ms M.J. Holly	373-7026	3–11	53	

Wakefield

School name	Address	Tel	Fax	Headteacher	Ref	Ages	Pupils	Other
Highfield School	Gawthorpe La, Ossett, West Yorkshire WF5 9BS	01924 302980	01924 302983	Mr Alan Spalding	384-7002	11–17	140	ASD SEBD PD MLD SLD
Kingsland Primary School	Aberford Rd, Stanley, Wakefield, West Yorkshire WF3 4BA	01924 303100		Mrs Nitsa Wainwright	384-7054	2–11	39	
Oakfield Park School, Ackworth	Barnsley Rd, Ackworth, Pontefract, West Yorkshire WF7 7DT	01977 723145	01977 723148	Ms Wendy E. Fereday	384-7055	11–19	113	SLD PMLD
Pinderfields Hospital School	Wrenthorpe Centre, Imperial Ave, Wrenthorpe, Wakefield, West Yorkshire WF2 0LW	01924 303695	01924 303695	Mrs Helen Ferguson	384-7000	2–19	15	HS
Wakefield District Community School	High Well Hill La, South Hiendley, Barnsley, South Yorkshire S72 9DF	01226 718613	01226 714183	Mrs Carol McDermott	384-7056	11–16		R SEBD
Wakefield Pathways School	Poplar Ave, Townville, Castleford, West Yorkshire WF10 3QJ	01977 723085	01977 723088	Miss Yvonne Limb	384-7053	5–11	59	

York

School name	Address	Tel	Fax	Headteacher	Ref	Ages	Pupils	Other
Applefields School	Bad Bargain La, York, North Yorkshire YO31 0LW	01904 553900	01904 553901	Mr George Gilmore	816-7032	11–19	142	ASD MLD SLD PMLD
Hob Moor Oaks School	Green La, Acomb, York, North Yorkshire YO24 4PS	01904 555000		Mrs Susan Williams	816-7033	3–11	59	ASD MLD SLD PMLD

7

Scotland

Aberdeen City

School name	Address	E-mail	Tel	Fax
Aberdeen School for the Deaf	Regent Wlk, Aberdeen AB24 1SX	enquiries@schoolfordeaf.aberdeen.sch.uk	01224 480303	01224 276675
Beechwood School	Raeden Park Rd, Aberdeen AB15 5PD	enquiries@beechwood.aberdeen.sch.uk	01224 323405	01224 311192
Cordyce School	Riverview Dr, Dyce, Aberdeen AB21 7NF	cordyce@rmplc.co.uk	01224 724215	01224 772738
Hazelwood School	Fernielea Rd, Aberdeen AB15 6GU	enquiries@hazlewood.aberdeen.sch.uk	01224 321363	01224 311162
Hospital and Home Tuition Service	Lowit Unit, Royal Aberdeen Children's Hospital, Cornhill Rd, Aberdeen AB25 2ZG	lowitunit@rmplc.co.uk	01224 550317	01224 550417
Marlpool School	Cloverfield Gdns, Bucksburn, Aberdeen AB21 9QN	enquiries@marlpool.aberdeen.sch.uk	01224 712735	01224 712524
Newhills Visual Impairment Unit	Wagley Par, Bucksburn, Aberdeen AB21 9UB		01224 715648	01224 714957
Pupil Support Service	Craighill School, Hetherwick Rd, Kincorth, Aberdeen AB12 5ST		01224 891430	01224 893316
Pupil Support Service	Unit A2 Cordyce, Riverview Dr, Dyce, Aberdeen AB21 7NF		01224 774046	01224 774046
The Raeden Centre Nursery School	Midstocket Rd, Aberdeen AB15 5PD	raeden@rmplc.co.uk	01224 321381	01224 311109
Woodlands School	Craigton Rd, Cults, Aberdeen AB15 9PR	enquiries@woodlands.aberdeen.sch.uk	01224 524393	01224 483116

Aberdeenshire

School name	Address	E-mail	Tel	Fax
Aberdeenshire EPS School	Woodhill Hse, Westburn Rd, Aberdeenshire AB16 5GB	lesley.shearer@aberdeenshire.gov.uk	01224 664026	01224 664615
Anna Ritchie School	Grange Gdns, Peterhead, Peterhead AB42 2AP	annaritchie.sch@aberdeenshire.gov.uk	01779 473293	01779 491063
Carronhill School	Mill of Forest Rd, Stonehaven, Kincardineshire AB39 2GZ	carronhill.sch@aberdeenshire.gov.uk	01569 763886	01569 762332
St Andrew's School	St Andrew's Gdns, Inverurie, Aberdeenshire AB51 3XT	standrewsinv.sch@aberdeenshire.gov.uk	01467 621215	01467 621954
Westfield School	Argyll Rd, Fraserburgh, Aberdeenshire AB43 9BL	westfield.sch@aberdeenshire.gov.uk	01346 518699	01346 516633

Angus

School name	Address	E-mail	Tel	Fax
COMPASS Project	Kingsmuir Resource Centre, Dunnichen Rd, Kingsmuir DD8 2RQ	edncompass@angus.sol.co.uk	01307 462096	01307 469387
MAP Project	Friockheim Resource Centre, Eastgate, Friockheim DD11 4TG	frctaylorf@angus.gov.uk	01241 829006	01241 828666
SSS Project	70 Addison Pl, Arbroath DD11 2BB	3sproject@angus.gov.uk	01241 879799	

Argyll and Bute

School name	Address	E-mail	Tel	Fax
Drummore School	Soroba Rd, Oban, Argyll PA34 4SB	enquiries@drummore.argyll-bute.sch.uk	01631 564811	01631 570331
Parklands School	27 Charlotte St, Helensburgh G84 7EZ	enquiries@parklands.argyll-bute.sch.uk	01436 673714	01436 677864
White Gates Learning Centre	White Gates Rd, Lochgilphead PA31 8SY	enquiries@whitegates.argyll-bute.sch.uk	01546 602583	01546 606026

Clackmannanshire

School name	Address	Tel	Fax	E-mail
Fairfield School	Pompee Rd, Sauchie FK10 3BX	01259 721660	01259 725832	fairfield@edu.clacks.gov.uk
Lochies School	c/o Deerpark Primary School, Gartmorn Rd, Sauchie FK10 3PB	01259 216928	01259 725833	lochies@edu.clacks.gov.uk
Primary School Support Service	c/o Park Primary School, East Castle St, Alloa FK10 1AN	01259 212151	01259 720935	
South School	Bedford Pl, Alloa FK10 1LJ	01259 724345		

Dumfries and Galloway

School name	Address	Tel	Fax	E-mail
Elmbank Special School	Lovers Wlk, Dumfries DG1 1DD	01387 254438	01387 248259	
Langlands School	Loreburn Pk, Dumfries DG1 1LS	01387 267834		

Dundee City

School name	Address	Tel	Fax	E-mail
Kingspark School	Gillburn Rd, Dundee DD3 0AB	01382 436284	01382 436286	kingspark@dundeecity.gov.uk

East Ayrshire

School name	Address	Tel	Fax	E-mail
Barshare Unit	Barshare Primary School, Dalgleish Ave, Cumnock KA18 1QC	01290 422212	01290 422212	
Crosshouse Communication Unit	Crosshouse Primary School, Gateshead Rd, Crosshouse KA2 0JJ	01563 521459	01563 521459	
Hillside School	Dalgleish Ave, Cumnock KA18 1QQ	01290 423239	01290 425870	jim.mccaffrey@east-ayrshire.gov.uk
Park School	Grassyards Rd, Kilmarnock KA3 7BB	01563 525316	01563 525465	anne.wilson@east-ayrshire.gov.uk
Witchhill School	Witch Rd, Kilmarnock KA3 1JF	01563 533863	01563 574517	nana.lauchlan@east-ayrshire.gov.uk
Woodstock School	30 North Hamilton St, Kilmarnock KA1 2QJ	01563 533550	01563 573808	linda.macphee@east-ayrshire.gov.uk

East Dunbartonshire

School name	Address	Tel	Fax	E-mail
Campsie View School	Boghead Rd, Lenzie G66 4DP	0141 777 6269	0141 775 3551	office@campsieview.e-dunbarton.sch.uk
Communications Disorder Unit	Rosslyn Rd, Bearsden G61 4DL	0141 942 1338	0141 931 5499	
Language and Communication Unit	c/o St Ninian's High School, Bellfield Rd, Kirkintilloch G66 1DT	0141 776 1585	0141 777 8123	
Merkland School	Langmuir Rd, Kirkintilloch G66 2QF	0141 578 0177	0141 777 8139	office@merkland.e-dunbarton.sch.uk
Milngavie SEBD Support Unit	c/o St Joseph's Primary School, North Campbell Dr, Milngavie G62 7AA	0141 578 5029	0141 776 7109	
Twechar Language and Communication Unit	Main St, Twechar G65 9TA	01236 827455	01236 826766	
Woodhead Support Service	Woodhead CE Centre, Woodhead Pk, Kirkintilloch G66 3DD	0141 578 2116	0141 776 7109	

East Renfrewshire

School name	Address	Tel	Fax	E-mail
Isobel Mair School	1a Drumby Cres, Clarkston, Glasgow G76 7HN	0141 577 4546	0141 571 7737	headteacher@isobelmair.e-renfrew.sch.uk

Edinburgh City

School name	Address	E-mail	Tel	Fax
Braidburn Special School	107 Oxgangs Rd North, Edinburgh EH14 1ED	admin@braidburn.edin.sch.uk	0131 312 2320	0131 443 7567
Cairnpark School	17 Redhall House Dr, Edinburgh EH14 1JE	admin@cairnpark.edin.sch.uk	0131 443 0903	0131 557 5709
Canonmills School	Rodney St, Edinburgh EH7 4EL	admin@canonmills.edin.sch.uk	0131 556 6000	0131 557 5709
Howdenhall and St Katharine's Special School	39 Howdenhall Rd, Edinburgh EH16 6PG	admin@howdenhall.edin.sch.uk	0131 664 8488	0131 664 3549
Kaimes School	140 Lasswade Rd, Edinburgh EH16 6RT	admin@kaimes.edin.sch.uk	0131 664 8241	0131 672 2086
Kingsinch School	233 Gilmerton Rd, Edinburgh EH16 5UD	admin@kingsinch.edin.sch.uk	0131 664 1911	0131 672 3035
Oaklands Special School	40 Broomhouse Cres, Edinburgh EH11 3UB	admin@oaklands.edin.sch.uk	0131 467 7867	0131 443 5100
Pilrig Park School	12 Balfour Pl, Edinburgh EH6 5DW	admin@pilrigpark.edin.sch.uk	0131 467 7960	0131 467 7961
Prospect Bank School	81 Restalrig Rd, Edinburgh EH6 8BQ	admin@prospectbank.edin.sch.uk	0131 553 2239	0131 554 5119
Rowanfield Special School	67c Groathill Rd North, Edinburgh EH4 2RY	admin@rowanfield.edin.sch.uk	0131 343 6116	0131 343 1725
St Crispin's School	Watertoun Rd, Edinburgh EH9 3HZ	admin@stcrispins.edin.sch.uk	0131 667 4831	0131 668 1487
St Nicholas' School	349 Gorgie Rd, Edinburgh EH11 2RG	admin@stnicholas.edin.sch.uk	0131 337 6077	0131 337 6077
Wellington School	Peebles Rd, Penicuik, Midlothian EH26 8PT	admin@wellington.edin.sch.uk	01968 672515	01968 675812

Falkirk

School name	Address	E-mail	Tel	Fax
Carrongrange School	Carrongrange Ave, Stenhousemuir FK5 3BH	carrongrangeschool@falkirk.gov.uk	01324 555266	01324 503555
Dundas Unit	c/o Moray Primary School, Moray Pl, Grangemouth FK3 9DL		01324 501311	01324 501311
Education Assessment Unit	Weedingshall, Polmont, Falkirk FK2 0XS		01324 506770	01324 506771
Falkirk Day Unit	c/o Camelon Education Centre, Abercrombie St, Camelon, Falkirk FK1 4HA		01324 501650	01324 503719
Torwood School	Stirling Rd, Torwood, Larbert FK5 4SR	torwoodschool@falkirk.gov.uk	01324 503470	01324 503471
Windsor Park School	Bantaskine Rd, Falkirk FK1 5HT	windsorparkschool@falkirk.gov.uk	01324 508640	01324 508647

Fife

School name	Address	E-mail	Tel	Fax
Alternative Education Support Centre	Sandy Brae Centre, Sandy Brae, Kennoway KY8 5JW		01333 352718	01333 353195
Benarty Primary Education Centre	Benarty Community Centre, Hill Rd, Ballingry KY5 8NN		01592 414392	01592 414340
The Bridges Centre	West Fife Alternative Day Resource, 8a McGrigor Rd, Rosyth KY11 2AE		01383 313518	01383 313512
Cupar Primary Education Centre	Kirkgate Annexe, Lovers La, Cupar KY15 5PE		01334 654793	
Dunfermline Support Centre	13 Abbey Park Pl, Dunfermline KY12 7PT		01383 312824	01383 312821
East Fife Support Centre	Kirkgate Annexe, Lovers La, Cupar KY15 5AH		01334 656923	01334 412386
Glenrothes Education Centre	Rimbleton Pk, Glenrothes KY6 2BZ		01592 415605	01592 415628
Glenrothes Off Campus Support Centre	Wayside Halls, Balbirnie Rd, Glenrothes KY7 5ED		01592 760051	01592 757113
Headwell School	Headwell Ave, Dunfermline KY12 0JU		01383 721589	
Hyndhead School	Barncraig St, Buckhaven, Leven KY8 1JE	hyndhead@fife.gov.uk	01592 414499	01592 414484
John Fergus School	Erskine Pl, Glenrothes KY7 4JB	johnfergus@fife.gov.uk	01592 415335	
Kilmaron School	Balgarvie Rd, Cupar KY15 4PE	kilmaron@fife.gov.uk	01334 653125	01334 653105
Kirkcaldy Support Centre	Boreland Rd, Dysart KY1 2YG	kocsc@itasdarc.demon.co.uk	01592 653307	01592 654991
Levenmouth Support Centre	Sandy Brae Centre, Sandy Brae, Kennoway KY8 5JW		01333 352027	
Lochgelly North School	6 McGregor Ave, Lochgelly KY5 9PE	lochgellyn@fife.org.uk	01592 418110	
Robert Henryson School	Linburn Rd, Dunfermline KY11 4LD	rhenryson@fife.gov.uk	01383 312027	01383 314346
Rosslyn School	Viewforth Terr, Kirkcaldy KY1 3BP	rosslyn@fife-education.org	01592 415930	01592 415909

Glasgow City

School name	Address	E-mail	Tel	Fax
Abercorn School	195 Garscube Rd, Glasgow G4 9QH		0141 332 6212	0141 353 2180
Ashcraig School	100 Ave End Rd, Glasgow G33 3SW	headteacher@ashcraig-sec.glasgow.sch.uk	0141 774 3428	0141 774 5571
Barlanark Communication Disorder Unit	c/o Barlanark Primary School, 343 Barlanark Rd, Glasgow G33 4RY		0141 773 0841	
Broomlea School	168 Broomhill Dr, Glasgow G11 7NH	headteacher@broomlea-pri.glasgow.sch.uk	0141 339 6494	0141 337 1630
Carnbooth School	Carnbooth Hse, Carmunnock, Glasgow G76 9EG	headteacher@carnbooth.aol.com	0141 644 2773	0141 644 3136
Cartvale School	80 Vicarfield St, Govan, Glasgow G51 2DF	headteacher@cartvale-sec.glasgow.sch.uk	0141 445 5272	0141 445 4198
Croftcroighn School	180 Findochty St, Glasgow G33 5EP	headteacher@croftcroighn-pri.glasgow.sch.uk	0141 774 7777	0141 774 8957
Darnley Visual Impairment Unit	c/o Darnley Primary, 169 Glen Moriston Rd, Glasgow G53 7HT		0141 621 2919	
Drumchapel Learning Centre	77 Hecla Ave, Glasgow G15 8LX		0141 944 8517	0141 949 1645
Drummore School	129 Drummore Rd, Glasgow G15 7NH	headteacher@drummore-pri.glasgow.sch.uk	0141 944 1323	0141 944 6612
Duntarvie Pre-School Assessment Centre	c/o Cadder Primary School, 60 Herma St, Glasgow G23 5AR		0141 946 3835	
Eastmuir School	211 Hallhill Rd, Glasgow G33 4QL	headteacher@eastmuir-pri.glasgow.sch.uk	0141 771 3464	0141 781 9609
Gadburn School	70 Rockfield Rd, Glasgow G21 3DZ	headteacher@gadburn-pri.glasgow.sch.uk	0141 558 5373	0141 557 5054
Glasgow Secondary Bi-lingual Support Unit	31 Moss-side Rd, Glasgow G41 3TR		0141 632 5718	
Greenview School	Buckley St, Glasgow G22 6DJ	headteacher@greenview-pri.glasgow.sch.uk	0141 336 8391	0141 347 1148
Hampden School	80 Ardnahoe Ave, Glasgow G42 0DL	headteacher@hampden-pri.glasgow.sch.uk	0141 647 7720	0141 647 7720
Hollybrook School	135 Hollybrook St, Govanhill, Glasgow G42 7HU	headteacher@hollybrook-sec.glasgow.sch.uk	0141 423 5937	0141 422 1394
Howford School	487 Crookston Rd, Glasgow G53 7TX	headteacher@howford-pri.glasgow.sch.uk	0141 882 2605	0141 883 2146
Kelbourne School	109 Hotspur St, Glasgow G20 8LH	headteacher@kelbourne-pri.glasgow.sch.uk	0141 946 1405	0141 945 0044
Kelvin School	69 Nairn St, Glasgow G3 8SE	headteacher@kelvin.glasgow.sch.uk	0141 339 5835	0141 339 5835
Kennyhill School	375 Cumbernauld Rd, Glasgow G31 3LP	headteacher@kennyhill-sec.glasgow.sch.uk	0141 554 2765	0141 554 0846
Kirkriggs School	500 Croftfoot Rd, Glasgow G45 0NJ	headteacher@kirkriggs-pri.glasgow.sch.uk	0141 634 7158	
Ladywell School	12a Victoria Park Dr South, Glasgow G14 9RN	headteacher@ladywell-sec.glasgow.sch.uk	0141 959 6665	0141 954 0178
Langlands School	100 Mallaig Rd, Glasgow G51 4PE	headteacher@langlands-pri.glasgow.sch.uk	0141 445 1132	0141 445 1132
Linburn School	77 Linburn Rd, Glasgow G52 4EX	headteacher@linburn-sec.glasgow.sch.uk	0141 883 2082	0141 810 1071
Middlefield Residential School	26 Partickhill Rd, Glasgow G11 5BP	headteacher@middlefield-res.glasgow.sch.uk	0141 334 0159	0141 339 8832
Milton School	6 Liddesdale Terr, Glasgow G22 7HL	headteacher@milton-sec.glasgow.sch.uk	0141 762 2102	0141 762 5650
Nerston Residential School	Nerston Village, East Kilbride G74 4PD	headteacher@nerston-res-pri.glasgow.sch.uk	01355 279242	01355 279289
Newhills School	42 Newhills Rd, Glasgow G33 4HJ	headteacher@newhills-sec.glasgow.sch.uk	0141 773 1296	0141 773 3977
Richmond Park School	30 Logan St, Glasgow G5 0HP	headteacher@richmondpark-pri.glasgow.sch.uk	0141 429 6095	0141 429 6047
Rosepark Tutorial Centre	2nd Fl, Rm 9 Thornwood Primary, 11 Thornwood Ave, Glasgow G11 7QZ		0141 334 5700	0141 334 5910
Rosevale School	48 Scalpay St, Glasgow G22 7DD	headteacher@rosevale-pri.glasgow.sch.uk	0141 772 1756	0141 762 1116
Ruchill Communication Disorder Unit	c/o Ruchill Primary School, 29 Bassey St, Glasgow G20 9HW		0141 948 0073	0141 946 7756
St Aidan's School	255 Rigby St, Glasgow G32 6DJ	headteacher@st-aidans-sec.glasgow.sch.uk	0141 556 6276	0141 556 3328
St Charles' Language Unit	c/o St Charles Primary, 13 Kelvinside Gdns, Glasgow G20 6BG		0141 945 2121	0141 945 2121
St Joan of Arc School	722 Balmore Rd, Glasgow G22 6QS	headteacher@st-joanofarc-sec.glasgow.sch.uk	0141 336 6885	0141 336 6375
St Joseph's Hearing Impairment Unit	c/o St Joseph's Primary, 39 Raglan St, Glasgow G4 9QX		0141 353 6136	0141 353 6137
St Kevin's School	25 Fountainwell Rd, Glasgow G21 1TN	headteacher@st-kevins-pri.glasgow.sch.uk	0141 557 3722	0141 558 4299
St Oswald's School	83 Brunton St, Glasgow G44 3NF	headteacher@st-oswalds-sec.glasgow.sch.uk	0141 637 3952	0141 633 0669
St Raymond's School	384 Drakemire Dr, Castlemilk, Glasgow G45 9SR	headteacher@st-raymonds-pri.glasgow.sch.uk	0141 634 1551	0141 630 1293
St Vincent's Communication Disorder Unit	c/o St Vincent's Primary, 40 Crebar St, Carnwadric, Glasgow G46 8EQ		0141 621 1968	0141 621 1968
St Vincent's School	30 Fullarton Ave, Tollcross, Glasgow G32 8NJ	headteacher@st-vincents.glasgow.sch.uk	0141 778 2254	0141 764 1482

7

Highland

School name	Address	E-mail	Tel	Fax
Black Isle Education Centre	Raddery, By Fortrose, Highland IV10 8SN	gavin@biec.fsnet.co.uk	01381 621600	
Caithness Early Years Autism Centre	Seaforth Ave, Wick KW1 5ND	margaret.mcghee@hcs.uhi.ac.uk	01955 609424	01955 602649
Drummond School	Drummond Rd, Inverness IV2 4NZ	drummond.school@highland.gov.uk	01463 233091	01463 713106
St Clement's School	Tulloch St, Dingwall IV15 9JZ	stclements.primary@highland.gov.uk	01349 863284	01349 863284
St Duthus School	Academy St, Tain IV19 1ED	stduthus.primary@highland.gov.uk	01862 894407	01862 894407

Inverclyde

School name	Address	E-mail	Tel	Fax
Garvel School	Chester Rd, Larkfield, Greenock PA16 0TT		01475 635477	01475 637230
Glenburn School	Inverkip Rd, Greenock PA16 0QG		01475 715400	01475 715401
Lilybank School	Birkmyre Ave, Port Glasgow PA14 5AN		01475 715703	01475 715705
Mearns Centre	Mearns St, Greenock PA15 4QD		01475 715805	01475 715808

Midlothian

School name	Address	E-mail	Tel	Fax
Cuiken House	150 Cuiken Terr, Penicuik EH26 0AH		01968 675025	
Saltersgate School	3 Cousland Rd, Dalkeith, Midlothian EH22 2PS	saltersgate@midlothian.gov.uk	0131 654 4703	0131 561 9524

North Ayrshire

School name	Address	E-mail	Tel	Fax
Haysholm School	Bank St, Irvine KA12 0NE	contactus@haysholm.n-ayrshire.sch.uk	01294 272481	01294 276673
James McFarlane School	Dalry Rd, Ardrossan KA22 7DQ	contactus@jamesmcfarlane.n-ayrshire.sch.uk	01294 461370	01294 470225
James Reid School	Primrose Pl, Saltcoats KA21 6LH	contactus@jamesreid.n-ayrshire.sch.uk	01294 467105	01294 470702
Stanecastle School	Burns Cres, Irvine KA11 1AQ	contactus@stanecastle.n-ayrshire.sch.uk	01294 211914	01294 211792

North Lanarkshire

School name	Address	E-mail	Tel	Fax
Bothwellpark High School	Annan St, Motherwell ML1 2DL	ht@bothwellpark.n-lanark.sch.uk	01698 230700	01698 261515
Clydeview School	Magna St, Motherwell ML1 3QZ	ht@clydeview.n-lanark.sch.uk	01698 264843	01698 276038
Drumpark School	Bargeddie, Baillieston, Glasgow G69 7TW	ht@drumpark.n-lanark.sch.uk	01236 423955	01236 423879
Fallside School	Sanderson Ave, Bothwell Park Viewpark, Uddingston G71 6JZ	ht@fallside.n-lanark.sch.uk	01698 747721	01698 747166
Firpark School	Firpark St, Motherwell ML1 2PR	ht@firpark.n-lanark.sch.uk	01698 251313	01698 276189
Glencryan School	Greenfaulds, Cumbernauld G67 2XJ	ht@glencryan.n-lanark.sch.uk	01236 724125	01236 732625
Mavisbank School	Mitchell St, Airdrie ML6 0EB	ht@mavisbank.n-lanark.sch.uk	01236 752725	01236 755421
Pentland School	Tay St, Coatbridge ML5 2NA	ht@pentland.n-lanark.sch.uk	01236 420471	01236 434844
Portland High School	31–33 Kildonan St, Coatbridge ML5 3LG	ht@portland.n-lanark.sch.uk	01236 440634	01236 440176
Redburn School	Kildrum Rd, Cumbernauld, Glasgow G67 2EL	ronalogan@redburn.n-lanark.sch.uk	01236 720405	01236 720405
Willowbank School	299 Bank St, Coatbridge ML5 1EG	ht@willowbank.n-lanark.sch.uk	01236 421911	

Perth and Kinross

School name	Address	Tel	E-mail	Fax
Cherrybank School	Viewlands Terr, Perth PH1 1DA	01738 622147	headteacher@cherrybank.pkc.sch.uk	01738 445266
The Glebe School	Abbey Rd, Scone PH2 6LW	01738 551493	headteacher@glebe.pkc.sch.uk	01738 553575

Renfrewshire

School name	Address	Tel	E-mail	Fax
Clippens School	Brediland Rd, Linwood PA3 3RX	01505 325333		01505 336097
Kersland School	Ben Nevis Rd, Paisley PA2 7BU	0141 889 8251		0141 849 6729
The Mary Russell School	Hawkhead Rd, Paisley PA2 7BE	0141 889 7628		0141 889 8682

Scottish Borders

School name	Address	Tel	E-mail	Fax
Howdenburn Schoolhouse	Lothian Rd, Jedburgh TD8 6LA	01835 864577		
The Wilton Centre	36 Princes St, Hawick TD9 7AY	01450 378644	itopping@scotborders.gov.uk	01450 370538

South Ayrshire

School name	Address	Tel	E-mail	Fax
Craigpark School	Belmont Ave, Ayr KA7 2ND	01292 288982	mail@craigparkschool.south-ayrshire.gov.uk	01292 618764
Invergarven School	15 Henrietta St, Girvan KA26 9AL	01465 712035	kathyfaulder-bransom@invergarvenschool.south-ayrshire.gov.uk	01465 712035
South Park School	38 Belmont Ave, Ayr KA7 2ND	01292 282259	mail@southparkschool.south-ayrshire.gov.uk	01292 618310

South Lanarkshire

School name	Address	Tel	E-mail	Fax
Craighead School	Whistleberry Rd, Hamilton ML3 0EG	01698 285678	office@craighead.s-lanark-sch.uk	01698 459137
Greenburn School	Maxwellton Ave, East Kilbride G74 3DU	01355 237278	office@greenburn.s-lanark.sch.uk	01355 265170
Hamilton School for the Deaf	Wellhall Rd, Hamilton ML3 9UE	01698 286618	office@hamiltonschooldeaf.s-lanark.sch.uk	01698 425172
Kittoch School	Livingstone Dr, Murray, East Kilbride G75 0AB	01355 244348	office@kittoch.s-lanark.sch.uk	01355 267372
Ridgepark School	Mousebank Rd, Lanark ML11 7RA	01555 662151	office@ridgepark.s-lanark.sch.uk	01555 662859
Rutherglen High School	Reid St, Rutherglen G73 3DF	0141 647 4230	office@rutherglen-high.s-lanark.sch.uk	0141 647 0680
Sanderson High School	High Common Rd, St Leonards, East Kilbride G74 2LX	01355 249073	office@sanderson.s-lanark.sch.uk	01355 249081
Victoria Park School	Market Rd, Carluke ML8 4BE	01555 750591	office@victoriapark.s-lanark.sch.uk	01555 750591
West Mains School	Logie Pk, East Kilbride G74 4BU	01355 249938	office@westmains.s-lanark.sch.uk	01355 225814

Stirling

School name	Address	Tel	E-mail	Fax
Kildean School	Drip Rd, Kildean, Stirling FK8 1RW	01786 473985	kildeans@stirling.gov.uk	01786 448382
Primary Pupil Support Service	c/o St Mary's Primary School, Kildean Toll Drip Rd, Stirling FK8 1RR	01786 463248		01786 448573
Secondary Student Support Service	Edward Ave, Riverside, Stirling FK8 1XN	01786 464641		01786 464641
Whins of Milton	Fairhill Rd, Whins of Milton, Stirling FK7 0LL	01786 812667	wofmps@stirling.gov.uk	01786 812873

7

445

West Dunbartonshire

School name	Address	E-mail	Tel	Fax
The Choices Project	Faifley Skypoint Community Centre, Lennox Dr, Faifley G81 5JY		01389 876442	01389 877374
Cunard School	Cochno St, Clydebank G81 1RQ	schooloffice@cunard.w-dunbarton.sch.uk	0141 952 6614	0141 952 6463
Kilpatrick School	Mountblow Rd, Dalmuir, Clydebank G81 4SW	schooloffice@kilpatrick.w-dunbarton.sch.uk	01389 872168	01389 875646

West Lothian

School name	Address	E-mail	Tel	Fax
Beatlie School Campus	The Mall, Craigshill, Livingston EH54 5EJ	kathy.white@wled.org.uk	01506 777598	01506 777 594
Burnhouse School	The Avenue, Whitburn, West Lothian EH47 0BX	burnhouse@wled.org.uk	01501 678100	01501 678108
Cedarbank School	Ladywell East, Livingston EH54 6DR	cedarbank@wled.org.uk	01506 442172	01506 775805
Ogilvie School Campus	Ogilvie Way, Livingston EH54 8UL	sharon.johnston@wled.org.uk	01506 777460	
Pinewood School	Elm Gr, Blackburn EH47 7QX	pinewood@wled.org.uk	01506 656374	01506 650716

Wales

Blaenau Gwent

School name	Address	Tel	Fax	Ref
Pen-Y-Cwm Special School	Beaufort Hill, Beaufort, Ebbw Vale, Blaenau Gwent NP3 5QG	01495 304031	01495 304031	677-7011
St Illtyd's	Llanhilleth, Abertillery, Blanau Gwent NP13 3JT			677-2312
Thomas Richards Centre	Sirhowy, Tredegar NP2 4PY	01495 724980		677-1101

Bridgend

School name	Address	Tel	Fax	Ref
Bridgend Pupil Referral Unit	Heol Persondy, Aberkenfig, Bridgend CF32 9RF	01656 720225		672-1102
Frontline Christian School	59–63 High St, Laleston, Bridgend CF32 0AL	01656 768028		672-6090
Heronsbridge School	Ewenny Rd, Bridgend CF31 3HT	01656 653974	01656 766270	672-7003
St John's School	Newton, Porthcawl CF36 5NP	01656 783404		672-6083
Ysgol Bryn Castell	Llangewydd Rd, Cefn Glas, Bridgend CF31 4JP	01656 767517	01656 768437	672-7012

Caerphilly

School name	Address	Tel	Fax	Ref
Emmanuel Christian School	High St, Crosskeys NP1 7BU	01495 270433		676-6013
Glanynany Learning Centre	Hanbury St, Glanynant, Pengam, Blackwood NP12 3XP	01433 875520		676-1104
Rhiw Syr Dafydd Primary	Oakdale, Blackwood, Caerphilly NP12 0NA	01495 222829		676-2392
Trinity Fields Special School	Caerphilly Rd, Ystrad Mynach, Hengoed CF82 7DT	01443 866000		676-7011
Whiterose Primary	Whiterose Way, New Tredegar NP24 6DF			676-2387
Wyclif Independent Christian School	Ebenezer Baptist Chapel, Wyndham St, Machen, Caerphilly NP1 8PU	01633 441582		676-6088
Ysgol Bro Sannan	Ty Fry Rd, Aberbargoed, Bargoed CF81 9FN	01443 828000		676-2388

Cardiff

School name	Address	Tel	Fax	Ref
The Academy	40–41 The Parade, Cardiff CF24 3AB	02920 409630		681-6090
Bryn Y Deryn School and Student Support Unit	The Rise, Canton, Cardiff CF10 9PR	02920 733564		681-1107
Cardiff Muslim School	Merthyr St, Cardiff CF24 4JL	02920 342040		681-6093
Cardiff Steiner Early Years Centre	17–18 Iron Street Adamsdown, Cardiff CF24 0LL	02920 190099		681-6091
The Cathedral School	Cardiff Rd, Cardiff CF5 2YH			681-6012
The Court Special School	96a Station Rd, Llanishen, Cardiff CF14 5UX	02920 752713	02920 763895	681-7005
Green Pastures Christian Academy	158b Fidlas Rd, Cardiff CF14 5AZ	02920 765556		681-6089
Greenhill Special School	Heol Brynglas, Cardiff CF4 6UJ	02920 693786	02920 621991	681-7001
Herbert Thompson Primary	Plymouthwood Rd, Ely, Cardiff CF5 4XD	02920 564342		681-2312
The Hollies Special School	Bryn Heulog, Cardiff CF23 7XG	02920 734411	02920 540239	681-7019
Meadowbank Special School	Colwill Rd, Gabalfa, Cardiff CF14 2QQ	02920 616018	02920 529272	681-7021
Riverbank Special School	Vincent Rd, Cardiff CF5 5AQ	02920 563860	02920 563860	681-7008
St Francis VA Primary	Wilspn Rd, Cardiff CF5 4JL	02920 591989		681-3375
St Johns College	Newport Rd, Old St Mellons, Cardiff CF3 5YX			681-6004
Taibah School	22 Wordsworth Ave, Cardiff CF2 1AR			681-6029
Ty Gwyn Special School	Ty Gwyn Rd, Cardiff CF2 5JG	02920 485570	02920 453922	681-7011
Welsh Centre For Conductive Education	Hammond Way, Cardiff CF3 7DH			681-6028
Woodlands High School	Vincent Rd, Cardiff CF5 5AQ	02920 561279	02920 561279	681-7006

Carmarthenshire

School name	Address	Tel	Fax	Ref
Carmarthen Christian School	11 The Parade, Carmarthen, Carmarthenshire SA31 1LY	01267 221436		669-6010
Cilddewi Uchaf	11–16 Llannon, Llanelli SA14 8JZ			669-6012
Heol Goffa Special School	Heol Goffa, Llanelli, Carmarthenshire SA15 3LS	01554 759465		669-7000
Maes Werdd	Greenfields Cottage, Broadway, Ferryside SA17 5UE			669-6013
Nant Y Cwm School	Llanycefn, Nr Clynderwen, Pembrokeshire SA66 7QJ	01437 563640		669-6008
Penygaer House	1 Brynsirol, Penygaer, Llanelli, Carmarthenshire SA14 8AB			669-6011
ysgol Bro Brynach	Hen dy Gwyn Ar Daf, Caerfyddin, Sir Gaerfyrddin SA34 0EL			669-2389
Ysgol Gymunedol Cwmamman Community School	Cwmamman Rd, Glanamman, Ammanford SA18 1DZ			669-2388
Ysgol Rhydygors	Llansteffan Rd, Johnstown, Carmarthenshire SA31 3NQ	01267 231171		669-7010

Ceredigion

School name	Address	Tel	Fax	Ref
Ceredigion Pupil Referral Centre	Felinfach Campus, Felinfach, Lampeter, Ceredigion SA48 8AF	01570 471262		667-1103

Conwy

School name	Address	Tel	Fax	Ref
Alternative Education Centre	Douglas Road Education Centre, Douglas Rd, Colwyn Bay, Conway LL29 7PE	01492 534720		662-1103
Cedar Court	65 Victoria Pk, Colwyn Bay, Conwy LL29 7AJ	01492 533199		662-1100
Conwy Secondary Pupil Referral Unit	c/o Cadant Education Centre, Rosemary La, Conwy LL32 8HY	01492 581661		662-1104
Gyffin Education Centre	Maes Y Llan, Gyffin, Conway LL32 8NB	01492 592859		662-1102

School name	Address	Tel	Fax	Ref
Lyndon School	Grosvenor Rd, Colwyn Bay, Conwy LL29 7YF	01492 523247		662-6029
Ysgol Y Gogarth / Y Graig	Nant-y-Gamar Rd, Craig y Don, Llandudno LL30 1YF	01492 860077	01492 870109	662-7001

Denbighshire

School name	Address	Tel	Fax	Ref
The Branas School	Branas Isaf, Llandrillo, Corwen, Denbighshire LL21 0TA	01490 440343		663-6040
Fairholme Prep. School	The Mount, Mount Rd, St Asaph, Denbighshire LL17 0DH	01745 583505		663-6013
Rhuallt Education Centre	Rhuallt School, Rhuallt, Nr Saint Asaph, Denbighshire LL17 0TD	01745 583375		663-1100
Ysgol Plas Brondyffryn	Ystrad Rd, Denbigh LL16 4RH	01745 813841		663-7010
Ysgol Tir Morfa	Ffordd Derwen, Rhyl, Denbighshire LL18 2RN	01745 350388	01745 343193	663-7000
Ysgol Trefnant	henllan, Trefnant, Nr. Denbigh, Denbighshire LL16 5UF	01745 730276		663-3316

Flintshire

School name	Address	Tel	Fax	Ref
The Lighthouse School	Pwll Glas, Mold, Flintshire CH7 1RA	01352 700022		664-6001
Llwyn Onn Special Education Centre	Halkyn Rd, Holywell, Flintshire CH8 7TZ	01352 714148		664-1102
St Gregory's Preparatory School	Village Hall, Llanasa, Flintshire CH8 9ND	01745 857371		664-6002
Ysgol Belmont	Windmill Rd, Buckley, Flintshire CH7 3HA	01244 543971	01244 545272	664-7014
Ysgol Delyn	Alexandra Rd, Mold, Flintshire CH7 1HJ	01352 755701	01352 755701	664-7013
Ysgol Y Bryn	King George St, Shotton, Deeside, Flintshire CH5 2EQ	01244 830281	01244 815009	664-7018

Gwynedd

School name	Address	Tel	Fax	Ref
Aran Hall School	Rhydymain, Dolgellau, Gwynedd LL40 2AR	01341 450641		661-6022
Bangor Centre for Developmental Disabilities	University of Wales Bangor, Bangor, Gwynedd LL57 2DG			661-6031
Canolfan Brynffynnon	Ffordd Brynffynnon, Y Felinheli, Caernarfon, Gwynedd LL56 8SW	01248 670924		661-1100
Hillgrove School	Ffriddoedd Rd, Bangor, Gwynedd LL57 2TW	01248 353568		661-6007
Little Islands Arthog	7 Nys Fechan Hall, Gwynedd LL39 1YT			661-6032
Ysgol Coedmenai	Treborth, Bangor, Gwynedd LL57 2RX	01248 353527		661-7000
Ysgol Hafod Lon	Y Ffor, Pwllheli, Gwynedd LL53 6US	01766 810626	01766 810002	661-7010
Ysgol Pendalar	Ffordd Victoria, Caernarfon, Gwynedd LL55 2RN	01286 672141	01286 678186	661-7002

Isle of Anglesey

School name	Address	Tel	Fax	Ref
Treffos School	Llansadwrn, Nr Menai Bridge, Anglesey LL59 5SL	01248 712322		660-6027
Uned Gyfeirio	Stryd y Bont, Llangefni, Ynys Mon LL77 7HL	01248 750012		660-1100
Ysgol Y Bont	Stad Ddiwydiannol, Llangefni, Ynys Mon LL77 7JA	01248 750151	01248 724056	660-7011

Merthyr Tydfil

School name	Address	Tel	Fax	Ref
Edward Ville Primary	Cardiff Rd, Edwardsville, Treharris CF46 5NE	01443 410663		675-2353
Greenfield Special School	Duffryn Rd, Pentrebach, Merthyr Tydfil CF48 4BJ	01443 690468	01443 692010	675-7013
Merthyr Tydfil Pupil Referral Unit	Tram Road La, Alexandra Ave, Penydarren, Merthyr Tydfil CF47 9AF	01685 721733		675-1101

Monmouthshire

School name	Address	Tel	Fax	Ref
Agincourt School	Dixton La, Monmouthshire NP5 3SJ	01600 713970	01600 714097	679-6010
Greenfields Adolescent Development Ltd	PO Box 31, monmouthshire NP15 12W	01291 671480		679-6016
Haberdashers Monmouth School For Girls	24 Hereford Rd, Monmouthshire NP5 3XT	01600 711100		679-6009
Llangattock School	Llangattock, Vibon, Avel, Monmouth, Monmouthshire NP25 5NG	01600 772213	01600 772213	679-6013
Mounton House Special School	Pwllmeyric, Chepstow, Monmouthshire NP6 6LA	01291 630871	01291 635055	679-7006
Pentwyn Farmhouse	Gwehelog, Nr Usk, Monmouthshire NP15 1RE			679-6015
Talocher Farm	Wonastow Rd, Monmouth NP25 4DN	01600 740143		679-6014

Neath Port Talbot

School name	Address	Tel	Fax	Ref
Briton Ferry Special School	Ynysmaerdy Rd, Briton Ferry, Neath SA11 2TL	01639 813100	01639 814707	671-7006
Bryncoch Tuition Centre	Ysgol Hendre Campus, Main Rd, Bryncoch, Neath SA10 7TY			671-1104
Ty Afan Primary Centre	Severn Cres, Sandfields, Port Talbot SA12 6TA			671-1103
Ty Afan Secondary Centre	Pendarvis Terr, Port Talbot SA12 6AX			671-1102
Velindre Community Special School	Reginald St, Velindre, Port Talbot, Neath SA13 1YY			671-7007
Ysgol Hendre Special School	Main Rd, Bryncoch, Neath SA10 7TY		01639 644294	671-7005

Newport

School name	Address	Tel	Fax	Ref
Maes Ebbw School	Maesglas Rd, Maesglas, Newport NP20 3DG	01633 815480	01633 817956	680-7002
Queen's Hill PRU	Queen's Hill, Newport NP9 5XN	01633 262564		680-1100
Trinity House	c/o Trinity Methodist Church, Glasllwch La, Newport NP20 3PU			680-6004

Pembrokeshire

School name	Address	Tel	Fax	Ref
Landsker Education	New Moat, Haverfordwest SA63 4RX	01437 532924		668-6016
Netherwood School	Saundersfoot, Pembrokeshire SA69 9BE	01834 811057		668-6004
Pembrokeshire Pupil Referral Service	Off High St, Neyland, Milford Haven SA73 17F	01646 602473		668-1104
Portfield Special School	Off Portfield, Haverfordwest, Pembrokeshire SA61 1BS	01437 762701	01437 769158	668-7001
Redhill Preparatory School	Pembroke Rd, Haverfordwest, Pembrokeshire SA62 4LA	01437 768472		668-6015
St David's Education Unit	Pembroke Hse, Brawdy Business Pk, Haverfordwest SA62 6NP	01437 721234		668-6014
Ysgol Ger y Llan V.C School	St Davids Rd, Letterson, Haverford West SA62 5SL			668-3058
Ysgol Glannau Gwaun	West St, Abergwaun, Fishguard SA65 9AH	01348 872505		668-2389
Ysgol y Frenni	Crymch SA41 3QH	01239 831427		668-2390

449

Powys

School name	Address	Tel	Fax	Ref
Amberleigh Residential Therapeutic School	Golfa La, Welshpool, Powys SY21 9AF			666-6042
Brynllywarch Hall School	Kerry, Nr Newtown, Powys SY16 4PB	01686 670276	01686 670894	666-7001
The Corn Mill School	Safe and Sound, Brithdir La, Berriew, Nr Welshpool SY21 8AW	01686 640889		666-6045
The Crows Nest	Church Stoke, Montgomery, Powys SY15 6TP			666-6046
Hillcrest Pentwyn School	Clyro, Hereford HR3 5SE	01497 821591		666-6007
Llwyn Gwilym Farmhouse	Rhayder, Powys LD6 5NS			666-6044
Macintyre Care – Womaston School	Walton, Presteigne, Powys LD8 2PT	01544 230308		666-6008
Ridgeway School	Sarn, Newtown, Powys SY16 4EW			666-6043
Ysgol Cedewain	Maesyrhandir, Newtown, Powys SY16 1LH	01686 627454	01686 621867	666-7002
Ysgol Penmaes	Canal Rd, Brecon, Powys LD3 7HL	01874 623508	01874 623508	666-7004

Rhondda Cynon Taff

School name	Address	Tel	Fax	Ref
Maesgwyn Special School	Cwmdare Rd, Cwmdare, Aberdare, Rhondda Cynon Taff CF44 8RE	01685 873933	01685 873933	674-7006
Park Lane Special School	Park La, Trecynon, Aberdare, Rhondda Cynon Taff CF44 8HN	01685 874489	01685 883207	674-7008
Rhondda Special School	Brithweunydd Rd, Trealaw, Tonypandy, Rhondda Cynon Taff CF40 2UH	01443 433046	01443 440034	674-7011
Tai Educational Centre	Grovefield Terr, Penygraig, Rhondda Cynon Taff CF40 1HL	01144 422666		674-1108
Ty Gwyn	Heol-y-Gyfraith, Talbot Grn, Pontyclun CF7 8AJ	01443 237839		674-1106
Ysgol Ty Coch	Lansdale Dr, Tonteg, Pontypridd, Rhondda Cynon Taff CF38 1PG	01443 203471		674-7015
Ysgol yr Eos Primary	Bishop St, Penygraig, Rhondda Cynon Taff CF40 1PQ	01443 433209		674-2377

Swansea

School name	Address	Tel	Fax	Ref
Adolescent Girls Group Bonymaen Family Centre	Cefn Hengoed Community School, Coldicot school, Bonymaen, Swansea SA1 7HX			670-1104
Craig Y Nos School	Clyne Common, Bishopston, Swansea SA3 3JB	01792 234288	01792 233813	670-6008
Gorseinon Home Tuition	Youth Network Centre, Pontardulais Rd, Gorseinon, Swansea SA4 2FE	01792 584435		670-1103
Key Stage 4 Education Centre	Brondeg Hse, St John's Rd, Manselton, Swansea SA5 8PR	01792 581221		670-1102
Keystone Education Trust	Keystone Education Trust, Unit A, Queensway, Fforestfach, Swansea SA5 4DG	01792 298537		670-6023
Oakleigh House School	38 Penlan Cres, Uplands, Swansea SA2 0RL	01792 799064		670-6001
Penybryn Senior Special School	Glasbury Rd, Morriston, Swansea SA6 7PA	01792 884486		670-7000
Pontardulais Support Centre	Oakfield St, Pontardulais, Swansea SA4 1LN	01792 404470		670-1101
Primary Education Centre	Dan y Coed Hse, West Cross Ave, West Cross, Swansea SA3 5TS	01792 582139		670-1100
Trehafod Day Unit	Waunarlwydd Rd, Sketty, Swansea SA2 0GB	01792 652388	01792 457774	670-1105
Ysgol Crug Glas	Croft St, Swansea SA1 1QA			670-7008

Torfaen

School name	Address	Tel	Fax	Ref
Crownbridge Special Day School	Greenhill Rd, Sebastopol, Pontypool, Torfaen NP4 5YW	01495 758739		678-7012

Vale of Glamorgan

School name	Address	Tel	Fax	Ref
Ashgrove School	Sully Rd, Penarth CF64 2TP	02920 704212	02920 701945	673-7018
Key Stage 3 PRU	The Amelia Trust Farm, Whitton Rosser, Five Mile Lane, Barry CF62 3AS	01446 781427		673-1109
Pregnant Schoolgirls Unit	Maes Y Coed Family Centre, Gladstone Rd, Barry CF63 1NH	01446 732755		673-1110
Ysgol Enw'r Delyn	St Cyres Rd, Penarth CF64 2WR	02920 707225	02920 706277	673-7012
Ysgol Maes Dyfan	Gibbonsdown Rise, Barry CF63 1DT	01446 732112	01446 742316	673-7015

Wrexham

School name	Address	Tel	Fax	Ref
Cyfle Young Mothers Unit	Abenbury Community Centre, Bridge Rd, Pentre Maelor LL13 9PT			665-1103
Gwersyllt Support centre	Yr Hen Gegin, Dodds La, Gwersyllt LL11 4NT			665-1102
Laurel Park School	Kiln La, Cross Lanes, Wrexham LL13 0TF			665-6044
Riverside School	Bramble Hse, Bersham Rd, Bersham LL14 4HT			665-6043
St Christopher's School	Holt Rd, Wrexham LL13 8NE	01978 346910	01978 346944	665-7005
St Josephs RC and Anglican Secondary School	Sontley Rd, Wrexham LL13 7EN			665-4603
St Pauls VA Primary	Bowling Bank, Isycoed LL13 9RL	01978 661556		665-3347
Woodlands Children's Development Centre	27 Pentrefelyn Rd, Wrexham LL13 7NB	01978 262777	01978 290893	665-6042
Wrexham Support Centre	1 Park Ave, Wrexham LL12 7AH			665-1101

Northern Ireland

Belfast

School name	Address	Tel	Ref	Other
Belfast Hospital School	Royal Bel.hos. Sick Children, Falls Rd, Belfast, Antrim BT12 6BE	028 9024 0503	131-6560	Controlled
Cedar Lodge Special School	24 Landsdowne Pk North, Belfast, Antrim BT15 4AE	028 9077 7292	131-0003	Controlled
Clarawood Special School	Clarawood Pk, Belfast, Antrim BT5 6FR	028 9047 2736	131-6584	Controlled
Fleming Fulton Special School	35 Upper Malone Rd, Belfast, Antrim BT9 6TY	028 9061 1917	131-0012	Controlled
Glenveagh Special School	Harberton Pk, Belfast, Antrim BT9 6TX	028 9066 9907	131-6569	Controlled
Greenwood House Assessment Centre	Greenwood Ave. Upper Newtownards Rd, Belfast, Antrim BT4 3JJ	028 9047 1000	131-0017	Controlled
Harberton Special School	Harberton Pk, Belfast, Antrim BT9 6TX	028 9038 1525	131-0014	Controlled
Mitchell House Special School	1a Marmont Dr, 405 Holywood Rd, Belfast, Antrim BT4 2GT	028 9076 0292	131-0016	Controlled
Oakwood Special School	Harberton Pk, Belfast, Antrim BT9 6TX	028 9060 5116	131-6582	Controlled
Park Education Resource Centre	145 Ravenhill Rd, Belfast, Antrim BT6 8GH	028 9045 0513	131-6500	Controlled
St Francis De Sales Special School	Beechmount Dr, Belfast, Antrim BT12 7LU	028 9024 5599	133-6012	Maintained
St Gerard's Education Resource Centre	12 Upper Springfield Rd, Belfast, Antrim BT12 7QP	028 9032 5249	133-6548	Maintained

North Eastern

School name	Address	Tel	Ref	Other
Castletower School	91 Fry's Rd, Ballymena, Antrim BT43 7EN		331-6676	Controlled
Hill Croft Special School	Manse Way, Newtownabbey, Antrim BT36 5UW	028 9083 7488	331-6510	Controlled

7

School name	Address	Tel	Ref	Other
Jordanstown Special School	85 Jordanstown Rd, Newtownabbey, Antrim BT37 0QE	028 9086 3541	334-0002	Maintained
Kilronan Special School	46 Kilronan Rd, Magherafelt, Londonderry BT45 6EN	028 7963 2168	331-6570	Controlled
Riverside Special School	Fennel Rd, Antrim BT41 4PB	028 9442 8946	331-6609	Controlled
Roddensvale Special School	The Roddens, Larne, Antrim BT40 1PU	028 2827 2802	331-6514	Controlled
Rosstulla Special School	2–12 Jordanstown Rd, Newtownabbey, Antrim BT37 0QF	028 9086 2743	331-0018	Controlled
Sandelford Special School	4 Rugby Ave, Coleraine, Londonderry BT52 1JL	028 7034 3062	331-6512	Controlled
Thornfield Special School	2–12 Jordanstown Rd, Newtownabbey, Antrim BT37 0QF	028 9086 5968	331-6547	Controlled

South Eastern

School name	Address	Tel	Ref	Other
Ardmore House Special School	95a Saul St, Downpatrick, Down BT30 6NJ	028 4461 4881	431-0019	Controlled
Beechlawn Special School	3 Dromore Rd, Hillsborough, Down BT26 6PA	028 9268 2302	431-0008	Controlled
Brookfield Special School	6 Halfpenny Gate Rd, Moira, Craigavon, Armagh BT67 0HN	028 9261 1498	431-6022	Controlled
Clifton Special School	292a Old Belfast Rd, Bangor, Down	028 9127 0210	431-6518	Controlled
Killard House Special School	North Rd, Newtownards, Down BT23 7AP	028 9181 3613	431-0013	Controlled
Knockevin Special School	33 Racecourse Hill, Downpatrick, Down BT30 6PU	028 4461 2167	431-6516	Controlled
Lakewood Special School	169 Rathgael Rd, Bangor, Down BT19 1TA	028 9127 5900	431-6614	Controlled
Longstone Special School	Millar's La, Dundonald, Belfast, Antrim BT16 2DA	028 9048 0071	431-6273	Controlled
Parkview Special School	2 Brokerstown Rd, Lisburn, Antrim BT28 2EE	028 9260 1197	431-6515	Controlled
Tor Bank Special School	718 Upper Newtownards Rd, Dundonald, Belfast, Antrim BT16 1RG	028 9048 4147	431-6517	Controlled

Southern

School name	Address	Tel	Ref	Other
Ceara Special School	Sloan St, Lurgan, Armagh BT66 8NY	028 3832 3312	531-6521	Controlled
Donard Special School	22a Castlewellan Rd, Banbridge, Down BT32 4XY	028 4066 2357	531-6520	Controlled
Lisanally Special School	85 Lisanally La, Armagh BT61 7HF	028 3752 3563	531-6577	Controlled
Rathore Special School	23 Martin's La, Carnagat, Newry, Down BT35 8PJ	028 3026 1617	531-6519	Controlled
Sperrinview Special School	8 Coalisland Rd, Dungannon, Tyrone BT71 6FA	028 8772 2467	531-6523	Controlled

Western

School name	Address	Tel	Ref	Other
Altnagelvin Hospital School	Altnagelvin Area Hospital, Londonderry BT47 6SB		231-0029	Controlled
Arvalee School And Resource Centre	17 Deverney Rd, Omagh, Tyrone BT79 0ND	028 8224 9182	231-6661	Controlled
Belmont House Special School	17 Racecourse Rd, Londonderry BT48 7RE	028 7135 1266	231-0015	Controlled
Elmbrook Special School	Derrygonnelly Rd, Enniskillen, Fermanagh BT74 7EY	028 6632 9947	231-6601	Controlled
Erne Special School	Derrygonnelly Rd, Enniskillen, Fermanagh BT74 7EY	028 6632 3942	231-6234	Controlled
Foyleview Special School	15 Racecourse Rd, Londonderry BT48 7RB	028 7126 3270	231-6525	Controlled
Glasvey Special School	15 Loughermore Rd, Ballykelly, Limavady, Londonderry BT49 9PB	028 7776 2462	231-6526	Controlled
Knockavoe School And Resource Centre	10a Melmount Gdns, Strabane, Tyrone BT82 9EB	028 7188 3319	231-6528	Controlled
Limegrove School	2 Ballyquin Rd, Limavady, Londonderry BT49 9ET	028 7776 2351	231-0007	Controlled

Channel Islands and Isle of Man

Guernsey

School name	Address	E-mail	Tel	Fax	Pupils	Other
Oakvale School	Collings Rd, St Peter Port, Guernsey, Channel Islands GY1 1FW	office@oakvale.sch.gg	01481 723045	01481 701071	32	

Jersey

School name	Address	E-mail	Tel	Fax	Pupils	Other
D'Hautree House School	St Saviour's Hill, St Saviour, Jersey, Channel Islands JE2 7LF	admin@dhautree.sch.je	01534 618042			
Mont l'Abbe School	La Grande Route de St Jean, St Helier, Jersey, Channel Islands JE2 3FN	admin@montlabbe.sch.je	01534 875801			SEBD

7

Independent Special Schools

East of England

Bedfordshire

School name	Address	Tel	Fax	Headteacher	Ref	Ages	Pupils	Other
Holme Court School	Great North Rd, Biggleswade, Bedfordshire SG18 9ST	01767 312766		Mrs Julia Hewerdine	820-6020	5–13	31	SLD
Trent Lodge	Avenue La, Wilden, Bedfordshire MK44 2PY	01536 725998		Mr Adam Snook	820-6021	11–18		G

Cambridgeshire

School name	Address	Tel	Fax	Headteacher	Ref	Ages	Pupils	Other
The Bridge School	11–14 South Brink, Wisbech, Cambridgeshire PE13 1JJ	01945 429043	01945 475748	Ms Jean Jordan	873-6033	10–16	13	SEBD
Castle Lodge School	The Manor Hse, High St, Rothwell, Kettering, Northamptonshire NN14 6BQ	01354 610439	01354 610398	Miss Lucy O'Brien	873-6039	10–16	1	B R MLD
Chartwell House School	Goodens La, Newton, Wisbech, Cambridgeshire PE13 5HQ	01945 870793	01945 870885	Mr C.E. Wright	873-6018	11–16	5	B R SEBD
Downham Lodge School	1 Second Dr, Little Downham, Ely, Cambridgeshire CB6 2UD	01353 862309	01353 862309	Mrs Sharon Sewell	873-6026	10–16	6	B R SEBD
March House	c/o The Manor Hse, High St, Rothwell, Kettering, Northamptonshire NN14 6BQ	01354 740529	01354 740529	Karen O'Brien	873-6040	11–17	5	B MLD
Meldreth Manor School – A Scope School	Fenny La, Meldreth, Royston, Hertfordshire SG8 6LG	01763 268000	01763 268009	Mr Eric Nash	873-6008	9–21	32	R PD MLD SLD
The Old School House	1 March Rd, Friday Bridge, Wisbech, Cambridgeshire PE14 0HA	01945 861114	01945 861188	Mr Arie Ramp	873-6032	8–13	3	B R
On Track Training Centre	Enterprise Hse, Old Field La, Wisbech, Cambridgeshire PE13 2RJ	01945 580898		Ms Jane Hales	873-6041	11–17	15	SEBD
Shelldene House School	20 Main Rd, Wisbech, Cambridgeshire PE14 0HJ	01945 861122	01945 861115		873-6044	12–17		B SEBD
Station Education Centre	5 Station Approach, March, Cambridgeshire PE15 8SJ	01354 658768	01354 659356	Ms Jane Breckon	873-6037	11–16	3	SEBD
Waypoint House	Ebenezer Farm, Ely, Cambridgeshire CB6 2DA	01353 668206	01223 718436	Mr A. Downie	873-6043	8–16		SEBD

Essex

School name	Address	Tel	Fax	Headteacher	Ref	Ages	Pupils	Other
Donyland Lodge	Fingringhoe Rd, Rowhedge, Colchester, Essex CO5 7JL	01206 728869	01206 729806	Mrs Lesley Wright	881-6044	11–18	10	B R SEBD
Doucecroft School	Abbotts La, Eight Ash Grn, Colchester, Essex CO6 3QL	01206 771234	01206 571964	Ms K. Cranmer	881-6032	2–19	44	R ASD SLD
Essex Fresh Start	WI Bldg, Rectory La, Chelmsford, Essex CM1 1RE	01245 490008	01245 490449	Miss Sharina Klaasens	881-6056	14–16	32	SEBD
Jacques Hall Foundation	Jacques Hall, Harwich Rd, Bradfield, Manningtree, Essex CO11 2XW	01255 870311	01255 870377	Mrs Charu Kashyap	881-6039	11–19	13	R SEBD
The Ryes School	Ryes La, Little Henny, Sudbury, Suffolk CO10 7EA	01787 374998	01787 468725	Torsten Friedag	881-6033	7–16	30	R SEBD
St John's RC School	Turpins La, Woodford Bridge, Essex IG8 8AX	020 8504 1818	020 8559 2409	Mr Brian Sainsbury	881-7050	5–19		CD MLD SLD
St John's School	Billericay, Essex CM12 0AR	01277 623070	01277 651288	Ms Fiona Armour	881-6013	3–16	445	
Woodcroft School	Whitakers Way, Baldwins Hill, Loughton, Essex IG10 1SQ	020 8508 1369	020 8502 4855	Mrs M. Newton	881-6031	5–11	32	CD ASD MLD SLD SpLD AS ADHD
The Yellow House School	1 Alderford St, Sible Hedingham, Halstead, Essex CO9 3HX	01787 462504			881-6048	13–17	4	SEBD

Hertfordshire

School name	Address	Tel	Fax	Headteacher	Ref	Ages	Pupils	Other
The Chrysalis School for Autism	St Giles Parish Centre, Bury La, Codicote, Hitchin, Hertfordshire SG4 8XX	01727 760677	01727 760677	Mrs Astrid Hansen	919-6257	4–13	4	ASD
Education and Youth Services	10 Willows Link, Stevenage, Hertfordshire SG1 4QX	01438 745566	01438 316324		919-6258	14–16		
Radlett Lodge School	Harper La, Radlett, Hertfordshire WD7 9HW	01923 854922	01923 859922	Mrs L. Tucker	919-6215	4–16	49	R ASD SLD
St Elizabeth's School	South End, Much Hadham, Hertfordshire SG10 6EW	01279 844270	01279 843903	Mr Philip Poulton	919-7006	5–19		R CD ASD MLD SLD Ep

Norfolk

School name	Address	Tel	Fax	Headteacher	Ref	Ages	Pupils	Other
Avocet House	The Old Vicarage, School La, Heckingham, Norfolk NR14 6QP	01508 549320	01508 549164	Mr Jonathan Lees	926-6419	8–16	6	B R SEBD SpLD
Eagle House	Mill Rd, Banham, Norwich, Norfolk NR16 2HU	01953 888656	01953 887021	Mr Tom Coulter	926-6152	4–19	17	R ASD
The New Eccles Hall School	Quidenham, Norwich, Norfolk NR16 2NZ	01953 887217	01953 887397	Mr R. Allard	926-6041	3–16	170	ID R SpLD
Red Balloon – Norwich	St Barnabas Church Hall, Russell St, Heigham, Norwich, Norfolk NR2 4QT			Ms Marilyn Oakley	926-6158	11–17		
St Andrew's School	Lower Common, East Runton, Cromer, Norfolk NR27 9PG	01263 511727	01263 511727	Ms G. Baker	926-6145	6–12	4	
Sheridan House School	Southburgh, Thetford, Norfolk IP25 7TJ	01953 850494	01953 851498	Mr Bobby Evans	926-6133	10–16	9	B R SEBD
Stubbs House Education Unit	Stubbs Hse, Stubbs Grn, Loddon, Norfolk NR14 6EA	01508 521190	01508 528017	Mrs Valerie Freear	926-6156	5–13	3	R SEBD SpLD

Peterborough

School name	Address	Tel	Fax	Headteacher	Ref	Ages	Pupils	Other
Park House	Wisbech Rd, Thorney, Peterborough, Cambridgeshire PE6 0SA	01733 271187	01733 271187	Mr Alan Crossland	874-6035	4–13	2	
Windsor House	Gt North Rd, Thornhaugh, Peterborough PE8 6HJ	01780 784190	01780 781458	Lucy O'Brien	874-6002	10–17	4	B R SEBD

Southend-on-Sea

School name	Address	Tel	Fax	Headteacher	Ref	Ages	Pupils	Other
Kites Independent School	820 London Rd, Leigh on Sea SS9 3Nh	01702 482588	01702 482599	Mrs Gillian Howard Smith	882-6053	13–18	4	R
Trinity Lodge	6 Trinity Ave, Westcliff-On-Sea, Essex SS0 7PU	01702 434184	01702 338503	Ms Anne Jackson	882-6009	12–18		MLD

Suffolk

School name	Address	Tel	Fax	Headteacher	Ref	Ages	Pupils	Other
Acorn Cottage	Ipswich Rd, Elmsett, Ipswich, Suffolk IP7 6NY	01473 657030	01473 658779	Ms Clare Rowland	935-6084	11–16	3	G R SEBD
Bramfield House School	Walpole Rd, Bramfield, Halesworth, Suffolk IP19 9AB	01986 784235	01986 784645	Mrs D. Jennings	935-6036	10–16	40	B R SEBD MLD
Broadlands Hall	Nr Haverhill, Suffolk CB9 7UA	01440 713006	01440 713007	Colonel K.A. Boulter	935-6086	11–16		R
Four Elms Residential School	Four Elms, Stowmarket, Suffolk IP14 5LB	01449 711105	01449 711307	Raymond Kenneth Saunders	935-6074	11–16	5	B R SEBD
Gable End	Fen La, Hitcham, Suffolk IP7 7NL	01449 744928	01449 744913	Mr Terry Woolard	935-6085	11–16	2	R
The Old Rectory School	Brettenham, Ipswich, Suffolk IP7 7QR	01449 736404	01449 737881	Ms Cynthia Murdoch-Watson	935-6058	7–14	55	ID R
On Track Training Centre	Unit 2 and 3 Wallis Ct, James Carter Rd, Mildenhall, Suffolk IP28 7DD	01638 715555	01638 715555	Mrs Penny Harris	935-6083	13–17	16	SEBD

7

East Midlands

Derby

School name	Address	Tel	Fax	Headteacher	Ref	Ages	Pupils	Other
Royal School for The Deaf	Ashbourne Rd, Derby, Derbyshire DE22 3BH	01332 362512	01332 299708	Ms C. Ford	831-7023	3–16		R HI

Derbyshire

School name	Address	Tel	Fax	Headteacher	Ref	Ages	Pupils	Other
Alderwasley Hall School	Alderwasley, Belper, Derbyshire DE56 2SR	01629 822586	01629 826661	Ms Veronica Jenkins	830-6016	5–19	110	R CD ASD AS
Arnfield Independent School	Manchester Rd, Tintwistle, Glossop, Derbyshire SK13 1NE	01457 860200	01457 860214	Mr Paul Knowles	830-6034	12–17		R SEBD
Bladon House School	Newton Solney, Burton-on-Trent, Staffordshire DE15 0TA	01283 563787	01283 510980	Mrs Kathleen Britt	830-6009	5–19	74	R CD ASD MLD SLD
Boyd House	Slayley La, Clowne, Chesterfield, Derbyshire S43 4LG	01246 810696	01246 812032		830-6036	11–17		SEBD
Eastwood Grange School	Eastwood Grange, Milken La, Ashover, Chesterfield, Derbyshire S45 0BA	01246 590255	01246 590215	Mr Stephen Magson	830-6013	11–16	25	B R SEBD
Glendale House	255 Tamworth Rd, Long Eaton, Nottingham, Nottinghamshire NG10 1AS	01253 316160	01253 316511	Mr Paul Heaven	830-6032	11–17	3	R SEBD
The Linnet Independent Learning Centre	Mount Pleasant Rd, Castle Gresley, Derbyshire DE11 9JG	01283 213989		Jan Sullivan	830-6033	9		SEBD
The Meadows	Country Care, The Meadows, Beech La, Dove Holes, Derbyshire SK17 8DJ	01298 814000	01298 814777	Ms Rachael Dowle	830-6035	11–16		SEBD
Pegasus School	Main St, Caldwell, Swadlincote, Derbyshire DE12 6RS	01283 761352	01283 761312	Mr H. Rodger	830-6024	8–16	21	R

Leicestershire

School name	Address	Tel	Fax	Headteacher	Ref	Ages	Pupils	Other
The Cedars	33 Ashby Rd, Stapleton, Hinckley, Leicestershire LE9 8JF	01455 844205		Mr Troy Scrimshaw	855-6022	11–16	3	B R SEBD
The Grange Therapeutic School	Knossington, Oakham, Leicestershire LE15 8LY	01664 454264	01664 454234	Mr B. Batten	855-6010	8–16	77	B R SEBD
Lewis Charlton School	North St, Ashby-de-la-Zouch, Leicestershire LE65 1HU	01530 560775	01530 563013	Mrs Georgina Pearson	855-6020	11–16	19	R SEBD
Oakwood School	20 Main St, Chantry La, Groby Rd, Leicester, Leicestershire LE3 8DG	0116 287 6218		Mr Peter Kilty	855-6021	8–16	13	SEBD
Sketchley Horizon	Manor Way, Sketchley Village, Burbage, Leicestershire LE10 3HT	01455 890023		Mr Nick Thornber	855-6026	8–16		SEBD
Trinity College	Moor La, Loughborough, Leicestershire LE11 1BA	01509 218906		Mrs Dorothy Yates	855-6025	11–16	15	SEBD

Lincolnshire

School name	Address	Tel	Fax	Headteacher	Ref	Ages	Pupils	Other
Hambling School	Paga Hse, Hulls Drove, Postland, Crowland, Peterborough, Lincolnshire PE6 0JU	01406 331900	01406 331901	Mr Stewart Yeagers	925-6050	11–18	4	SEBD
Kisimul School	The Old Vicarage, 61 High St, Swinderby, Lincoln, Lincolnshire LN6 9LU	01522 868279	01522 866000	Mrs Jean Gardner	925-6034	8–19	49	R SLD
Midsummer House	Roman Hse, Saracens Head, Spalding, Lincolnshire PE12 8AY	01406 420430	01406 420299	Ms Lynne Yeagers	925-6051	8–19	5	R ASD

Northamptonshire

School name	Address	Tel	Fax	Headteacher	Ref	Ages	Pupils	Other
Alderwood	302 Wellingborough Rd, Rushden, Northamptonshire NN10 6BB	01933 359861	01604 811878	Mrs Jacqueline Wadlow	928-6068	8–19	8	R
Ashmeads School	Buccleuch Farm, Haigham Hill, Burton Latimer, Kettering, Northamptonshire NN15 5PH	01536 725998	01536 420847	Mr Adam Snook	820-6017	11–16	6	SEBD
Farrow House School Northampton	67 Queens Park Par, Kingsthorpe, Northampton, Northamptonshire NN2 6LR	01604 719711	01604 791195	Kimberley Sando-Reynolds	928-6067	11–16	3	SEBD MLD
Potterspury Lodge School	Potterspury Lodge, Towcester, Northamptonshire NN12 7LL	01908 542912	01908 543399	Mrs Christine Haylett	928-6039	8–16	52	B R SEBD
Thornby Hall School	Naseby Rd, Thornby, Northampton, Northamptonshire NN6 8SW	01604 740001	01604 740311	Mrs R.M. Jelly	928-6061	12–18	16	R SEBD

Nottingham

School name	Address	Tel	Fax	Headteacher	Ref	Ages	Pupils	Other
Rutland House School	Elm Bank, Mapperley Rd, Nottingham, Nottinghamshire NG3 5AJ	0115 962 1315	0115 962 2867	Mrs C. Oviatt-ham	892-6008	5–19	21	R PD SLD
Sutherland House School	Sutherland Rd, Carlton, Nottingham, Nottinghamshire NG3 7AP	0115 987 3375	0115 940 0483	Ms Maria Allen	892-7041	3–19		ASD

Nottinghamshire

School name	Address	Tel	Fax	Headteacher	Ref	Ages	Pupils	Other
Blue Mountain School	Willow Farm, Newton La, Cossall, Ilkston, Nottinghamshire NG16 2SD	0115 932 1153	0115 932 1149	Ms Maureen Broad	891-6026	8–16	6	R MLD
Dawn House School	Helmsley Rd, Rainworth, Mansfield, Nottinghamshire NG21 0DQ	01623 795361	01623 491173	Dr Jeff Wardle	891-7022	5–19		R CD
Freyburg School	2 South Par, Bawtry, Doncaster, South Yorkshire DN10 6JH	01302 719914	01302 718210	Ms Andrea Conway	891-6022	11–16	6	B
Hope House School	Barnby Rd, Newark, Nottinghamshire NG24 3NE	01636 700380			891-6032	5–14		
Middlehay	c/o The Manor Hse, High St, Rothwell, Kettering, Northamptonshire NN14 6BQ	0115 965 5812	0115 965 4892	Mrs S. Bray	891-6025	10–18	2	R MLD
Nookin Cottage	c/o The Manor Hse, High St, Rothwell, Kettering, Northamptonshire NN14 6BQ	01777 871076	01777 872793		891-6027	10–18	1	R MLD
The Old Farmhouse	c/o The Manor Hse, High St, Rothwell, Kettering, Northamptonshire NN14 6BQ	01400 283928	01400 282881	Mrs S. Bray	891-6024	10–18	2	R MLD
Villa Real Farmhouse	c/o The Manor Hse, Squires Hill, Rothwell, Northants NN14 6BQ	01623 823259	01623 823259	Mrs S. Bray	891-6029	10–17		R SEBD

Rutland

School name	Address	Tel	Fax	Headteacher	Ref	Ages	Pupils	Other
The Shires at Stretton	Gt North Rd, Stretton, Oakham, Rutland LE15 7QT	01780 411101	01780 411102	Mrs Marina Gough	857-6004	11–19	7	R ASD SLD
Wilds Lodge School	Stamford Rd, Epingham, Oakham, Rutland LE15 8QQ	01780 751279			857-6005	7–16		R SEBD

London

Barking and Dagenham

School name	Address	Tel	Fax	Headteacher	Ref	Ages	Pupils	Other
Hopewell School	1 Strathfield Gdns, Barking, Essex IG11 9UJ	020 8591 6333	020 8594 4803	Carol Barlow	301-6002	11–16	4	R SEBD MLD

Barnet

School name	Address	Tel	Fax	Headteacher	Ref	Ages	Pupils	Other
Kisharon Day School	1011 Finchley Rd, London NW11 7HB	020 8455 7483	020 8731 7005	Mrs Lilian Amdurer	302-6085	5–19	16	Je MLD
Southover Partnership School	322a Ballards La, London N12 0EY			Helen Jackson	302-6121	11–17	8	SEBD

Bromley

School name	Address	Tel	Fax	Headteacher	Ref	Ages	Pupils	Other
Browns School	Cannock Hse, Hawstead La, Chelsfield, Orpington, Kent BR6 7PH	01689 876816	01689 827118	Mr M.F. Brown	305-6078	7–12	36	CE SpLD

Camden

School name	Address	Tel	Fax	Headteacher	Ref	Ages	Pupils	Other
The Tavistock Mulberry Bush Day Unit	33 Daleham Gdns, London NW3 5BU	020 7794 3353		Ms Ellenore Nicholson	202-6401	5–12	13	B SEBD

Croydon

School name	Address	Tel	Fax	Headteacher	Ref	Ages	Pupils	Other
Hillcrest Mulberry School	69 to 71 Outram Rd, Croydon, Surrey CR0 6XJ	020 8655 3338	020 8655 3948		306-6104	11–17	3	R SEBD
Kingsdown Secondary School	112 Orchard Rd, Sanderstead, Croydon CR2 9LQ	020 8657 1200		Ms Carole Nicholson	306-6089	11–16	12	B R SEBD
Little David's School	The Time Bridge Centre, Fieldway, New Addington, Croydon, Surrey CR0 9AZ	01689 800822	01689 800822	Mrs Patricia Bhola	306-6093	3–11	15	ASD MLD
Rutherford School	1a Melville Ave, South Croydon, Surrey CR2 7HZ	020 8688 7560	020 8406 8220	Ms Diane Muir	306-6078	2–12	21	PMLD
Tudor Lodge School	92 Foxley La, Woodcote, Purley, Surrey CR8 3NA	020 8763 8785	020 8763 8785	Ms Patricia Lines	306-6091	12–16	6	ID R SEBD

Ealing

School name	Address	Tel	Fax	Headteacher	Ref	Ages	Pupils	Other
Sybil Elgar School	Havelock Rd, Southall, Middlesex UB2 4NZ	020 8813 9168	020 8571 7332	Ms C. Phillips	307-6064	11–19	100	R ASD SLD

Hackney

School name	Address	Tel	Fax	Headteacher	Ref	Ages	Pupils	Other
Side by Side Kids School	9 Big Hill, London E5 9HH	020 8880 8300	020 8880 8341	Ms R. Atkins	204-6409	2–16	47	CD MLD SLD

Hammersmith and Fulham

School name	Address	Tel	Fax	Headteacher	Ref	Ages	Pupils	Other
The Moat School	Bishops Ave, Fulham, London SW6 6ED	020 7610 9018	020 7610 9098	Mr R. Carlysle	205-6395	11–19	91	SpLD
Parayhouse School	New Kings School Annex, New Kings Rd, Fulham, London SW6 4LY	020 7751 0914	020 7751 0914	Mrs S.L. Jackson	205-7206	7–16		CD MLD

Haringey

School name	Address	Tel	Fax	Headteacher	Ref	Ages	Pupils	Other
Conductive Education	54 Muswell Hill, London N10 3ST	020 8444 7242	020 8444 7241	Ms Charlotte Millward	309-6070	2–6	8	PD
Treehouse School	Woodside Ave, Muswell Hill, London N10 3JA	020 8815 5424	020 8815 5420	Ms Gillian Mary Bierschenk	309-6085	3–16	53	ASD SLD

Hillingdon

School name	Address	Tel	Fax	Headteacher	Ref	Ages	Pupils	Other
Hillingdon Manor School	Moorcroft Complex, Harlington Rd, Hillingdon, Uxbridge, Middlesex UB8 3HD	01895 813679	01895 813679	Mr Sean Pavitt	312-6063	3–19	78	ASD SLD AS
Field Heath House School	Field Heath Rd, Uxbridge, Middlesex UB8 3NW	01895 233092	01895 256497	Sister Julie Rose	312-7006	7–19		RC R MLD SLD
RNIB Sunshine House Northwood	33 Dene Rd, Northwood, Middlesex HA6 2DD	01923 822538	01923 826227	Mrs L. Stewart	312-7005	2–11		R VI

Kensington and Chelsea

School name	Address	Tel	Fax	Headteacher	Ref	Ages	Pupils	Other
Abingdon House School	4–6 Abingdon Rd, Kensington, London W8 6AF	0845 230 0426	020 7361 0751	Mr Nicholas Rees	207-6405	4–11	37	ASD AS

Lambeth

School name	Address	Tel	Fax	Headteacher	Ref	Ages	Pupils	Other
Five Bridges	331 Kennington La, Vauxhall, London SE11 5QY	020 7735 1151	020 7587 5301	Mr Craig Smillie	208-6403	13–16	35	SEBD

Merton

School name	Address	Tel	Fax	Headteacher	Ref	Ages	Pupils	Other
Blossom House School	8a The Drive, Wimbledon, London SW20 8TG	020 8946 7348		Mrs Joanna Burgess	315-6076	3–16	104	CD
Eagle House School	224 London Rd, Mitcham, Surrey CR4 3HD	020 8687 7050	020 8687 7055	Mr Tom Coulter	315-6081	4–19	60	ASD AS

Newham

School name	Address	Tel	Fax	Headteacher	Ref	Ages	Pupils	Other
Laurel Leaf School	362 Romford Rd, Forest Gate, London E7 8BS	020 8586 7884			316-6069	11–16		R SEBD MLD

Southwark

School name	Address	Tel	Fax	Headteacher	Ref	Ages	Pupils	Other
Cavendish School	58 Hawkstone Rd, Southwark Pk, London SE16 2PA	020 7394 0088	020 7734 4101	Mrs Sara Graggs	210-6391	11–16	37	

Sutton

School name	Address	Tel	Fax	Headteacher	Ref	Ages	Pupils	Other
The Anchor School	Sutton Junior Tennis Centre, Rose Hill, Sutton, Surrey SM1 3HD	07734 110054		Mrs Wendy Holmes	319-6071	4–11	6	Ch SpLD
Link Primary School	138 Croydon Rd, Beddington, Croydon, Surrey CR0 4PG	020 8688 5239	020 8667 0828	Mrs Beverley Dixon	319-7006	5–12	40	CD
Link Secondary School	82–86 Croydon Rd, Beddington, Croydon, Surrey CR0 4PD	020 8688 7691	020 8688 5522	Mr Joe Pearson	319-7007	11–16	40	CD

7

Wandsworth

School name	Address	Tel	Fax	Headteacher	Ref	Ages	Pupils	Other
Centre Academy	92 St John's Hill, Battersea, London SW11 1SH	020 7738 2344	020 7738 9862	Dr Duncan Rollo	212-6408	7–19	61	SpLD ADHD
The Dominie	55 Warriner Gdns, Battersea, London SW11 4DX	020 7720 8783	020 7720 8783	Mrs L. Robertson	212-6368	6–13	26	SpLD
L'Ecole des Petits	L'Ecole des Battersea, Trott St, Battersea, London SW11 3DS	020 7924 3186	020 7924 7058	Mrs M. Otten	212-6411	3–11		N
Rainbow School for Autistic Children	520 Garratt La, Summerstown, London SW17 0NY	020 8879 7700	020 8947 5300	Mrs Sally Anne Palmer	212-6405	4–11	14	ASD

Westminster

School name	Address	Tel	Fax	Headteacher	Ref	Ages	Pupils	Other
Fairley House School	30 Causton St, London SW1P 4AU	020 7976 5456	020 7976 5905	Ms J. Murray	213-6327	5–14	121	
The Westside Independent School	3–7 Third Ave, London W10 4RS	07866 455119		Mr Paul Moody	213-6394	14–16	4	SEBD MLD

North East

Darlington

School name	Address	Tel	Fax	Headteacher	Ref	Ages	Pupils	Other
Pear Tree Projects	Toy Top Farm, Houghton Bnak, Heighington, Darlington, County Durham DL2 2UQ	01388 776799	01388 776428	Mr David Bartlett	841-6003	8–18	5	R MLD

Durham

School name	Address	Tel	Fax	Headteacher	Ref	Ages	Pupils	Other
The Daltons	Dalton-le-Dale, Seaham, Durham SR7 8QT	0191 513 1999	0191 581 6021	Mr David Carter	840-6009	12–19	3	R ASD SEBD MLD SLD

Hartlepool

School name	Address	Tel	Fax	Headteacher	Ref	Ages	Pupils	Other
Hartlepool School Educational and Vocational Training Centre	c/o 1st and 2nd Fl, Leeds Hse, 11a Yorkshire St, Rochdale OL16 1BH	01706 644471			805-6002			SEBD

Newcastle upon Tyne

School name	Address	Tel	Fax	Headteacher	Ref	Ages	Pupils	Other
Northern Counties School	Gt North Rd, Newcastle upon Tyne, Tyne and Wear NE2 3BB	0191 281 5821	0191 281 5060	Mrs Judith James	391-7004	3–19		R VI HI ASD MSI SLD PMLD
Talbot House School Newcastle	Hexham Rd, Walbottle, Newcastle Upon Tyne, Tyne and Wear NE15 8HW	0191 229 0111	0191 267 4021	Mr A.P. James	391-7038	11–16		R SEBD

North Tyneside

School name	Address	Tel	Fax	Headteacher	Ref	Ages	Pupils	Other
Parkside House School	Station Rd, Backworth, Tyne and Wear NE27 0AB	0191 216 1051	0191 216 1051	Mrs Belinda Young	392-6011	11–16	10	SEBD MLD
Percy Hedley School	Station Rd, Forest Hall, Newcastle upon Tyne, Tyne and Wear NE12 8YY	0191 266 5491	0191 266 8435	Mrs Lynn Watson	392-7006	3–18		R HI CD PD

Northumberland

School name	Address	Tel	Fax	Headteacher	Ref	Ages	Pupils	Other
Howard House	Netherton Colliery, Bedlington, Northumberland NE22 6BB	01670 820320	01670 820320	Mr Colin Lynch	929-6046	10–18	1	B R SEBD
Nunnykirk Centre for Dyslexia	Netherwitton, Morpeth, Northumberland NE61 4PB	01670 772685	01670 772434	Mr Simon Dalby-Ball	929-7023	7–16		R SpLD

Sunderland

School name	Address	Tel	Fax	Headteacher	Ref	Ages	Pupils	Other
Thornhill Park School	21 Thornhill Pk, Sunderland, Tyne and Wear SR2 7LA	0191 514 0659	0191 510 8242	Mr D. Walke	394-6015	4–16	75	R ASD SLD

North West

Blackburn with Darwen

School name	Address	Tel	Fax	Headteacher	Ref	Ages	Pupils	Other
Cumberland School	4 East Park Rd, Blackburn, Lancashire BB1 8DW	01254 691195		Mr Philip Meadows	889-6008	11–16	2	SEBD
Darwen Education Centre	Sudwell La, Darwen, Lancashire BB3 3HW	01254 777154			889-6011	7–14		SEBD

Blackpool

School name	Address	Tel	Fax	Headteacher	Ref	Ages	Pupils	Other
Pennsylvania House	1 Barclay Ave, Blackpool FY4 4HH	01253 313101	01253 313102	Mr Chris Nock	890-6008	11–17	5	R SEBD
Piers House	334 St Annes Rd, Blackpool, Lancashire FY4 2QN	01253 319651	01253 319652	Mr Keith Parker	890-6005	11–16	6	R SEBD

Bolton

School name	Address	Tel	Fax	Headteacher	Ref	Ages	Pupils	Other
Birtenshaw Hall (Children's Charitable Trust)	Darwen Rd, Bromley Cross, Bolton, Lancashire BL7 9AB	01204 304230	01204 597995	Mr C.D. Jamieson	350-7007	3–19		R PD
Booth Greencorns Independent School	1st and 2nd Fl, Leeds Hse, 11a Yorkshire St, Bolton BL3 1JY	01706 644471	01706 656065		350-6019	10–18		R SEBD

Bury

School name	Address	Tel	Fax	Headteacher	Ref	Ages	Pupils	Other
Primrose Cottage	c/o Northern Care 214 Whitegate Dr, Blackpool, Lancashire FY3 9JL	01253 316160	01253 316511	Annabel Fenning	351-6013	11–16	2	G R SEBD

7

Cheshire

School name	Address	Tel	Fax	Headteacher	Ref	Ages	Pupils	Other
Brook House Farm	The Manor Hse, High St, Kettering, Northamptonshire NN14 6BQ	01606 354648	01606 354649	Mr Geoff Southall	875-6033	10–17	2	R SEBD
Dane House	c/o The Manor Hse, High St, Rothwell, Kettering, Northamptonshire NN14 6BQ	01260 279786	01260 279753	Mr Geoff Southall	875-6034	8–16	1	R MLD
David Lewis School	Mill La, Warford, Alderley Edge, Cheshire SK9 7UD	01565 640066	01565 640166	Mr C.D. Dean	875-7101	7–19		R Ep
Delamere Forest School	Blakemere La, Norley, Frodsham, Cheshire WA6 6NP	01928 788263	01928 788263	Mr Harvey Burman	875-7102	6–17		R VI HI CD SEBD MLD SpLD AS
Inscape House School	Schools Hill, Cheadle, Cheshire SK8 1JE	0161 283 4750	0161 283 4751	Dr Steven Tyler	875-7103	4–16		CD ASD SpLD
Lambs Grange School	Forest Rd, Cuddington, Northwich, Cheshire CW8 2EH	01606 301514	01606 301516	Mr Jonathan Wilkins	875-6028	14–19	20	R ASD
Lambs House School	Buxton Rd, Buglawton, Congleton, Cheshire CW12 2DT	01260 272089		Miss Lisa Foster	875-6024	5–16	22	R AS ASD SLD
Oracle	Unit 2 Dane Valley Mill, Unit 2, Dane Valley Mill, Congleton, Cheshire CW12 2AH	0870 850 2949	01260 297673	Mr Steven Bromley	875-6035	7	2	R SEBD

Cumbria

School name	Address	Tel	Fax	Headteacher	Ref	Ages	Pupils	Other
Appletree School	Natland, Kendal, Cumbria LA9 7QS	01539 560253	01539 561301	Mr Rob Davies	909-6048	7–12	7	R SEBD
Cedar House School	Kendal Rd, Kirkby Lonsdale, Carnforth, Lancashire LA6 2HW	01524 271181	01524 271910	Mrs Gillian Ridgway	909-6037	7–16	60	R SEBD
Eden Grove School	Bolton, Appleby-in-Westmorland, Cumbria CA16 6AJ	01768 361346	01768 361356	Mr Stephen Salt	909-6010	8–16	63	B R SEBD MLD
Fell House School	Grange Fell Rd, Grange-over-Sands, Cumbria LA11 6AS	01539 535926	01539 534847	Mr Rob Davies	909-6051	7–12	4	R SEBD
Fellside School	Queens Rd, Kendal, Cumbria LA9 4PH	01539 737381	01539 737382	Mr F.W. Grist	909-6052	7–19	13	R SEBD
Kirby Moor School	Longtown Rd, Brampton, Nr Carlisle, Cumbria CA8 2AB	01697 742598		Mr Simon Ringrose	909-6056	14–17		B R SEBD
Radical Education	119 Warwick Rd, Carlisle, Cumbria CA1 1JZ	01228 631770	01228 631770	Ms Elspeth Anne Forrest	909-6050	14–16	3	SEBD
Underley Garden School	Kirkby Lonsdale, Carnforth, Lancashire LA6 2HE	01524 271569	01524 72581		909-6044	9–19	43	R ASD SLD
Underley Hall School	Kirkby Lonsdale, Carnforth, Lancashire LA6 2HE	01524 271206	01524 272581	Mr John Parkinson	909-6036	9–16	41	B R SEBD
Whinfell School	110 Windermere Rd, Kendal, Cumbria LA9 5EZ	01539 723322		Mr Richard David Tyson	909-6054	11–19	4	B R ASD
Wings School	Whassett, Milnthorpe, Cumbria LA7 7DN	01539 562006	01539 564811	Mrs Pam Redican	909-6053	11–16	40	R SEBD
Witherslack Hall School	Witherslack, Grange-over-Sands, Cumbria LA11 6SD	01539 552397	01539 552419	Mr Robert Hartlebury	909-6027	11–19	63	B R SEBD

Halton

School name	Address	Tel	Fax	Headteacher	Ref	Ages	Pupils	Other
110 Peel House Lane Green Corns	c/o 11a Yorkshire St, 1st and 2nd Fl, Rochdale OL16 1BH	01706 644471	01706 644599		876-6006			R ASD SEBD MLD
Fairholme	170 Greenway Rd, Runcorn, Cheshire WA7 4NN	01928 589047	01928 589047	Mr Shahram Mesdaghi	876-6002	10–16		R SEBD
Greenway Green Corns	c/o 11a Yorkshire St, 1st and 2nd Fl, Rochdale OL16 1BH	01706 644471	01706 644599		876-6003			R ASD SEBD
Halton School	31–33 Main St, Halton, Runcorn, Cheshire WA7 2AN	01928 589810	01928 592475	Mrs Kelley Fray	876-6000	8–14	12	SEBD
Halton View Green Corns	c/o 11a Yorkshire St, 1st and 2nd Fl, Rochdale OL16 1BH	01706 644471	01706 644599		876-6007			R ASD SEBD MLD
Liverpool Green Corns	c/o 11a Yorkshire St, 1st and 2nd Fl, Rochdale OL16 1BH	01706 644471	01706 644599		876-6005			R ASD SEBD MLD
Middleton Lodge	174 Hale Rd, Ditton, Widnes, Cheshire WA8 8SZ	0151 420 1271	0151 420 2252	Mr Shahram Mesdaghi	876-6001	10–16		R SEBD
Saxon Road Green Corns	c/o 11a Yorkshire St, 1st and 2nd Fl, Rochdale OL16 1BH	01706 644471	01706 644599		876-6004			R ASD SEBD MLD
South Parade Green Corns	c/o 11a Yorkshire St, 1st and 2nd Fl, Rochdale OL16 1BH	01706 644471	01706 644599		876-6008			R ASD SEBD MLD

Lancashire

School name	Address	Tel	Fax	Headteacher	Ref	Ages	Pupils	Other
Applegate School	51–53 Albert Rd, Colne, Lancashire BB8 0BP	01253 316160	01253 316511	Mr Gordon Smith	888-6090	11–17	4	B R SEBD
Beech Tree School – A Scope School	Meadow La, Bamber Bridge, Preston, Lancashire PR5 8LN	01772 323131	01772 322187	Mr Paul Boldy	888-6017	7–19	5	R SLD
Belmont School	Haslingden Rd, Rawtenstall, Rossendale, Lancashire BB4 6RX	01706 221043	01706 221043	Mr G.S. McEwan	888-6029	10–16	86	B SEBD
The Birches	106 Breck Rd, Poulton Le Fylde, Lancashire FY6 7HT	01253 899102	01253 892305	Mr Bill Baker	888-6095	11–17	6	B R SEBD
Broadclough Lodge	Meadows Ave, Rossendale, Lancashire OL13 8DF	01706 873874			888-6099	10–16		B R SEBD
Crookhey Hall School	Crookhey Hall, Garstang Rd, Cockerham, Lancaster, Lancashire LA2 0HA	01524 792618	01524 792684	Mr J. Rider	888-6022	11–16	64	B SEBD AS
The Evaglades	Main St, Low Bentham, Lancashire LA2 7BX	01524 262210	01524 261857		888-6098	11–16		
Langdale Academy for Personalised Learning	265 Tag La, Ingol, Preston, Lancashire PR2 3TY	01772 725976		Mr Steve Ellis	888-6087	8–14	2	
Learn 4 Life	Quarry Bank Community Centre, 364 Ormskirk Rd, Tanhouse, Skelmersdale, Lancashire WN8 9AL	01695 558698		Ms Elaine Booth	888-6089	11–16	4	SEBD
Linkway House School	25 Clifton St, Burnley, Lancashire BB12 0QZ	01282 831649	01282 831649	Mrs Jean Stretton	888-6088	11–18	4	R AS ASD MLD
Mill House School	Mill La, Farington Moss, Leyland, Lancashire PR26 6PS	01772 624953	01772 458558	Mr C. Nook	888-6091	11–17	4	B R SEBD
Moorlands View School	Manchester Rd, Dunnockshaw, Burnley, Lancashire BB11 5PQ	01282 431144	01282 455411	Pat Amick	888-6046	11–17	8	R SEBD
The Nook	The Nook, Knotts La, Colne, Lancashire BB8 8HH	01282 862433		Mrs Pamela Woods	888-6023	8–16	6	B R SEBD
Oakfield House School	Station Rd, Salwick, Preston, Lancashire PR4 0YH	01772 672630		Mr Kevin Peter Lusk	888-6037	5–11	19	SEBD
Oliver House School	Hallgate, Astley Village, Chorley, Lancashire PR7 1XA	01257 220011	01257 220033	Ms Gill Hughes	888-6094	6–19	3	AS ASD Ep SLD SpLD
Park View School	73 Grange St, Clayton-le-Moors, Accrington, Lancashire BB5 5PJ	01254 388382	01254 388383	Mr Chris Nock	888-6092	11–17	4	B R SEBD
Pontville Residential School	Black Moss La, Ormskirk, Lancashire L39 4TW	01695 578734	01695 579224	Mr Iain Sim	888-6050	11–19	64	R MLD
Progress School	Gough La, Bamber Bridge, Preston, Lancashire PR5 6AQ	01772 334832	01772 314933	Ms Lyn Lewis	888-6030	7–19	21	R SLD
Rawdhatul Uloom	North St, Jamia Masjid-E-Farooq-Azam, Burnley, Lancashire BB10 1LU	07817 555034			888-6097	4–11		Mu
Red Rose School	28–30 North Promenade, St Annes on Sea, Lytham St Annes, Lancashire FY8 2NQ	01253 720570	01253 720570	Mr Colin Lannen	888-6032	5–16	49	Ch SpLD
Regent School – Green Corns	1st and 2nd Fl, Rochdale, Lancashire OL16 1BH	01706 644471	01706 644599	Mrs Mandy Reddick	888-6100	10–18		R SEBD
Ridgway Park	Jenny Browns Point, Silverdale, Carnforth, Lancashire LA5 0UA	01524 702072	01524 702073	Mrs Gaynor Llewellyn	888-6049	11–16	19	R SEBD
Roselyn House School	Wigan Rd, Off Moss La, Leyland, Lancashire PR25 5SD	01772 435948			888-6095	11–16		SEBD
Rossendale School	Bamford Rd, Ramsbottom, Bury, Lancashire BL0 0RT	01706 822779	01706 821457	Mr D.G. Duncan	888-6020	8–16	53	R SEBD
Trax Academy	Riverside Pk, Walland Rd, Preston, Lancashire PR2 2HW	01772 731832	01772 731871	Miss Jeanette Wallace	888-6093	14–18	4	SEBD
Waterloo Lodge School	Preston Rd, Chorley, Lancashire PR6 7AX	01257 230894	01257 230894	Mr G. Sinclair	888-6026	11–16	44	SEBD
Westmorland School	Weldbank La, Chorley, Lancashire PR7 3NQ	01257 278899	01257 265505	Mr J. Martin Hayhurst	888-6048	5–11	22	SEBD
White House Park School	Chorley Rd, Withnell, Chorley, Lancashire PR6 8BN	01254 831731	01254 831726	Mrs Gail Neasham	888-6055	11–16	2	R
Whitebeam School – Green Corns	11a Yorkshire St, Rochdale, Lancashire OL16 1BH	01706 644471	01706 644599		888-6101	10–18		R SEBD

Liverpool

School name	Address	Tel	Fax	Headteacher	Ref	Ages	Pupils	Other
Lakeside School	Naylors Rd, Liverpool L27 2YA	0151 487 7211	0151 487 7214	Miss V. Shaw	340-6004	5–11	25	B SLD
Royal School for The Blind	Church Rd North, Wavertree, Liverpool, Merseyside L15 6TQ	0151 733 1012	0151 733 1703	Mr J.P. Byrne	341-7023	2–19		R VI HI
St Vincent's School for Blind and Partially Sighted Children	68 Yew Tree La, West Derby, Liverpool, Merseyside L12 9HN	0151 228 9968	0151 230 5070	Mr Stephen Roberts	341-7018	4–17		R VI
Walton Progressive School	Progressive Lifestyles Education Services, Rice La, Liverpool, Merseyside L9 1NR	0151 525 4004	0151 521 5804	Ms Diane Jones	341-6047	8–19	21	CD
Willowfield School	3–4 Tuffins Corner, Liverpool, Merseyside L27 7BR	0151 487 6280		Mr Christian Whelan	341-6053	12–16	5	SEBD

7

Manchester

School name	Address	Tel	Fax	Headteacher	Ref	Ages	Pupils	Other
Birch House School	Birch La, Longsight, Manchester, Lancashire M14 0WN	0161 224 7500	0161 224 7500	Mr Bilal Mahmood	352-6045	11–16	33	R SEBD
The Meadows School	71 Victoria Ave East, Blackley, Manchester M9 6HE	0161 795 4482	0161 795 4482	Mr Graham Mcewan	352-6047	5–11	18	
T'Mimei Lev School	Manchester Jewish Community Centre, Jubilee School, Bury Old Rd, Manchester M7 4QY	0161 795 2253	0161 792 2068	Mrs M. Gold	352-6062	4–16	2	Je MLD

Oldham

School name	Address	Tel	Fax	Headteacher	Ref	Ages	Pupils	Other
The Croft	9 The Croft, Shaw, Oldham, Lancashire OL2 8LU	07917 894088		Ms Shellie Barcroft	353-6018	10–18	1	R SEBD

Rochdale

School name	Address	Tel	Fax	Headteacher	Ref	Ages	Pupils	Other
Argyle – Green Corns	1st and 2nd Fl, Leeds Hse, Rochdale, Lancashire OL16 1BH	01706 644471		Mrs Mandy Reddick	354-6024	11–18		R SEBD MLD
Bankfield	16 Bankfld La, Norden, Rochdale, Lancashire OL11 5RJ	01706 359042	01706 359042	Ms Shellie Barcroft	354-6012	10–18	1	R SEBD MLD
Cronkeyshaw – Green Corns	1st and 2nd Fl, Leeds Hse, 11a Yorkshire St, Rochdale, Lancashire OL16 1BH	01706 644471		Mrs Mandy Reddick	354-6022	11–18		R SEBD MLD
Elmsfield	153 Elmsfield Ave, Norden, Rochdale, Lancashire OL11 5XA	01706 359512	01706 359512	Shellie Barcroft	354-6014	10–18		R SEBD MLD
Fox – Green Corns	1st and 2nd Fl, Leeds Hse, Rochdale, Lancashire OL16 1BH	01706 644471		Mrs Mandy Reddick	354-6023	11–18	1	R SEBD MLD
Further Heights – Green Corns	1st and 2nd Fl, Leeds Hse, Rochdale, Lancashire OL16 1BH	01706 644471		Mrs Mandy Reddick	354-6026	11–18	1	R SEBD MLD
Gloucester – Green Corns	1st and 2nd Fl, Leeds Hse, Rochdale, Lancashire OL16 1BH	01706 644471		Mrs Mandy Reddick	354-6025	11–18	1	R SEBD MLD
Meadows – Green Corns	1st and 2nd Fl, Leeds Hse, 11a Yorkshire St, Rochdale, Lancashire OL16 1BH	01706 644471		Ms E. Jones	354-6063	11–18	1	B R SEBD
Moorgate	22 Moorgate Ave, Bamford, Rochdale, Lancashire OL11 5JY	01706 868055	01706 630033	Shellie Barcroft	354-6013	10–18	1	R SEBD MLD
Norden Way	64 Norden Way, Norden, Rochdale, Lancashire OL11 5TD	01706 357174	01706 630033	Ms Shellie Barcroft	354-6010	10–18	2	R SEBD MLD
Park Hill – Green Corns	1st and 2nd Fl, Leeds Hse, 11a Yorkshire St, Rochdale, Lancashire OL16 1BH	01706 644471		Mrs Mandy Reddick	354-6016	11–18	1	R SEBD MLD
Pilsworth – Green Corns	1st and 2nd Fl, Leeds Hse, 11a Yorkshire St, Rochdale, Lancashire OL16 1BH	01706 644471		Mrs Mandy Reddick	354-6017	11–18	1	R SEBD MLD
Pleasant Street	9 Pleasant St, Castleton, Rochdale, Lancashire OL11 3BE	01706 643406		Ms Shellie Barcroft	354-6011	10–18	1	R SEBD MLD
Queens Park – Green Corns	1st and 2nd Fl, Leeds Hse, 11a Yorkshire St, Rochdale, Lancashire OL16 1BH	01706 644471		Mrs Mandy Reddick	354-6019	11–18		R SEBD MLD
Rooley Moor – Green Corns	1st and 2nd Fl, Leeds Hse, 11a Yorkshire St, Rochdale, Lancashire OL16 1BH	01706 644471		Mrs Mandy Reddick	354-6020	11–18	1	R SEBD MLD
Roughbank Farm	Ogden, Newhey, Rochdale, Lancashire OL16 3QH	01706 630033		Ms Shellie Barcroft	354-6027	10–18		R SEBD MLD
Shelfield	114 Shelfield La, Norden, Rochdale, Lancashire OL11 5XZ	01706 630022		Mr Frederick Kearsley	354-6008	10–18		SEBD MLD
Shelfield Greencorns	c/o 1st and 2nd Fl, Leeds Hse, 11a Yorkshire St, Rochdale OL16 1BH	01706 644471		Mandy Reddick	354-6028	10–18		R SEBD
Summit Greencorns	c/o 1st and 2nd Fl, Leeds Hse, 11a Yorkshire St, Rochdale OL16 1BH	01706 644471		Mandy Reddick	354-6029	10–18		R SEBD
Thames – Green Corns	1st and 2nd Fl, Leeds Hse, 11a Yorkshire St, Rochdale, Lancashire OL16 1BH	01706 644471		Mrs Mandy Reddick	354-6018	11–18	1	R SEBD MLD
Weston – Green Corns	1st and 2nd Fl, Leeds Hse, 11a Yorkshire St, Rochdale, Lancashire OL16 1BH	01706 644471		Mrs Mandy Reddick	354-6015	11–18	1	R SEBD MLD

Salford

School name	Address	Tel	Fax	Headteacher	Ref	Ages	Pupils	Other
Inscape House School Salford – The Together Trust	Walkden Rd, Worsley, Manchester M28 7FG	0161 975 2340	0161 975 4751	Mr Keith Cox	355-7030	4–16		ASD

Sefton

School name	Address	Tel	Fax	Headteacher	Ref	Ages	Pupils	Other
Chestnut Tree School	85–87 Liverpool Rd, Crosby, Liverpool, Merseyside L23 5TD	0151 931 5444	0151 931 5888	Mr Stephen Christopherson	343-6052	11–16	21	SEBD
Clarence High School	West La, Freshfield, Formby, Liverpool, Merseyside L37 7AZ	01704 872151	01704 831001	Mr McKillop	343-6131	10–18	41	R SEBD
Peterhouse School	Preston New Rd, Churchtown, Southport, Merseyside PR9 8PA	01704 506682	01704 506683	Mr Graham Birtwell	343-7014	5–19		ASD

St Helens

School name	Address	Tel	Fax	Headteacher	Ref	Ages	Pupils	Other
Nugent House School	Carr Mill Rd, Wigan, Lancashire WN5 7TT	01744 892551	01744 895697	Mrs J. Bienias	342-6004	7–19	57	B R SEBD
Wargrave House School	449 Wargrave Rd, Newton-le-Willows, Merseyside WA12 8RS	01925 224899	01925 291368	Mrs W. Mann	342-7009	5–19		R ASD

Stockport

School name	Address	Tel	Fax	Headteacher	Ref	Ages	Pupils	Other
Acorns School	19b Hibbert La, Marple, Stockport, Cheshire SK6 7NN	0161 449 5820	0161 449 5820	Mr Tim Whitwell	356-6027	5–16	19	SEBD
Child and Youth Care Education Service – The Together Trust	Schools Hill, Cheadle, Cheshire SK8 1JE	0161 283 4848	0161 283 4843	Mr Steve Grimley	356-6025	8–16	37	R SEBD
Royal Schools for The Deaf and Communication Disorders	Stanley Rd, Cheadle Hulme, Cheadle, Cheshire SK8 6RQ	0161 610 0100	0161 610 0101	Mrs Hilary Ward	356-7502	4–19		R HI ASD SEBD MSI
St John Vianney School	Rye Bank Rd, Firswood, Stretford, Manchester, Lancashire M16 0EX	0161 881 7843	0161 881 6948	Mrs Eileen McMorrow	356-7503	5–16		MLD

Tameside

School name	Address	Tel	Fax	Headteacher	Ref	Ages	Pupils	Other
Lime Meadows	73 Taunton Rd, Ashton-Under-Lyne, Tameside OL7 9DU	0161 339 9412	0161 343 4368	Mr W. Baker	357-6056	14–19	5	B R SEBD

Warrington

School name	Address	Tel	Fax	Headteacher	Ref	Ages	Pupils	Other
Chaigeley School	Lymm Rd, Thelwall, Warrington, Cheshire WA4 2TE	01925 752357	01925 757983	Mr Drew Crawshaw	877-7100	8–16	57	B R SEBD
Cornerstones	2 Victoria Rd, Grappenhall, Warrington, Cheshire WA4 2EN	01925 211056	01925 211092		877-6001	7–16	7	B R ASD SEBD
Fletcher Street Greencorns	c/o 1st and 2nd Fl, Leeds Hse, 11a Yorkshire St, Rochdale, Lancs OL16 1BH	01706 644471	01706 644599	Mrs Mandy Reddick	877-6004	10–18		R ASD SEBD MLD SLD
High Trees	3 Clay La, Burtonwood, Warrington, Cheshire WA5 4HH	01925 227119	01925 227119	Mr Shahram Mesdaghi	877-6002	10–16		R SEBD
Hunt Close Greencorns	c/o 1st and 2nd Fl, Leeds Hse, 11a Yorkshire St, Rochdale, Lancashire OL16 1BH	01706 644471	01706 644599	Gail Downey	877-6006	10–18		R ASD SEBD MLD SLD
Kingsway Greencorns	c/o 1st and 2nd Fl, Leeds Hse, 11a Yorkshire St, Rochdale, Lancashire OL16 1BH	01706 64471	01706 644599	Gail Downey	877-6005	10–18		R ASD SEBD MLD SLD

School name	Address	Tel	Fax	Headteacher	Ref	Ages	Pupils	Other
Park View	1 Park View, Orford, Warrington, Cheshire WA2 0LF	01925 831495	01925 831495	Mr Shahram Mesdaghi	877-6003	10–16		R SEBD

Wirral

School name	Address	Tel	Fax	Headteacher	Ref	Ages	Pupils	Other
West Kirby Residential School	Meols Dr, West Kirby, Wirral, Merseyside CH48 5DH	0151 632 3201	0151 632 0621	Mr G.W. Williams	344-7015	5–16	100	R SEBD

South East

Bracknell Forest

School name	Address	Tel	Fax	Headteacher	Ref	Ages	Pupils	Other
SWAAY	PO Box 2929, Earley, Reading, Berkshire RG6 7XQ	0118 926 1010	0118 9665454	Ms J. Collighan	870-6580	11–16	12	B SEBD

Brighton and Hove

School name	Address	Tel	Fax	Headteacher	Ref	Ages	Pupils	Other
Hamilton Lodge School for Deaf Children	Walpole Rd, Brighton, East Sussex BN2 0LS	01273 682362	01273 695742	Mr Chris Owen	846-7003	5–18		R HI
Ovingdean Hall School	Greenways, Ovingdean, Brighton, East Sussex BN2 7BJ	01273 301929	01273 305884	Mrs Pauline Hughes	846-7001	10–19		R HI
St John's School	Firle Rd, Seaford, East Sussex BN25 2HU	01323 872940	01323 872940	Mr D. Kent	846-7002	7–19		R MLD SLD
Springboard Education Junior	39 Whippingham Rd, St Wilfred's Upper Hall, Brighton, East Sussex BN2 3PS	01273 885109	01273 885109	Ms Elizabeth Freeman	846-6050	7–13	8	SEBD ADHD

Buckinghamshire

School name	Address	Tel	Fax	Headteacher	Ref	Ages	Pupils	Other
Include – Buckinghamshire	Suite 9, Lloyd Berkeley Pl, Pebble La, Aylesbury, Buckinghamshire HP20 1NA	01296 394668	01296 437549	Mr Nathan Crawley-Lyons	825-6035	14–16	23	SEBD
MacIntyre School	Leighton Rd, Wingrave, Wingrave, Aylesbury, Buckinghamshire HP22 4PD	01296 681274	01296 681091	Mr Stephen Smith	825-6011	10–19	36	R ASD SLD
The PACE Centre	Philip Green Hse, Coventon Rd, Aylesbury, Buckinghamshire HP19 9JL	01296 392739	01296 334836	Mrs H. Last	825-6031	2–12	24	PD MLD
Penn School	Church Rd, Penn, High Wycombe, Buckinghamshire HP10 8LZ	01494 812139	01494 811400	Mrs Mary-Nest Richardson	825-7001	11–18		R HI CD

East Sussex

School name	Address	Tel	Fax	Headteacher	Ref	Ages	Pupils	Other
Chailey Heritage School	Haywards Heath Rd, North Chailey, Lewes, East Sussex BN8 4EF	01825 724444	01825 723773	Ms Sylvia Lamb	845-7012	3–19		R PD
Cornerstones School	87 Payne Ave, Hove, East Sussex BN3 5HD	01273 734164	01273 716171	Mrs J. Dance	845-6043	7–16	8	SEBD
Frewen College	Northiam, Rye, East Sussex TN31 6NL	01797 252494	01797 252567	Mrs Linda Smith	845-6002	5–17	92	ID R SpLD AS
Grove Bridge Education	Bartletts Farm, Bodle Street Grn, BN27 4QU	01435 830818	01435 830818	Mr S. Cleeve	845-6050	11–19	1	B SEBD
Headstart	Crouch La, Ninfield, Battle, East Sussex TN33 9EG	01424 893803	01424 893803	Ms Nicola Dann	845-6051	12–17	9	SEBD

School name	Address	Tel	Fax	Headteacher	Ref	Ages	Pupils	Other
Northease Manor School	Rodmell, Lewes, East Sussex BN7 3EY	01273 472915	01273 472202	Mr Paul Stanley	845-6028	10–17	80	ID R SpLD
Owlswick School	Newhaven Rd, Kingston, Lewes, East Sussex BN7 3NF	01273 473078	01273 473721	Mr A.K. Harper	845-6007	10–17	5	Ch R SEBD MLD
St Mary's Wrestwood Children's Trust	Wrestwood Rd, Bexhill-on-Sea, East Sussex TN40 2LU	01424 730740	01424 733575	Mr David Cassar	845-7000	7–19		Ch R HI CD ASD MSI PD MLD SpLD AS DMP Ep
Step by Step, School for Autistic Children Ltd	Neylands Farm, Grinstead La, Sharpthorne, East Sussex RH19 4HP	01342 811852	01342 811853	Miss Cathryn Jones	845-6054	4–16	9	ASD

Hampshire

School name	Address	Tel	Fax	Headteacher	Ref	Ages	Pupils	Other
Chiltern Tutorial School	Otterbourne Halls, Cranbourne Dr, Otterbourne, Winchester, Hampshire SO21 2ET	01962 860482	01962 860482	Mrs Jane Gaudie	850-6063	7–11	19	SpLD
Coxlease School	High Coxlease Hse, Clayhill, Lyndhurst, Hampshire SO43 7DE	023 8028 3633	023 8028 2515	S.F. Cliffen	850-6017	9–17	49	B R SEBD
Fairways School	New Rd, Manor Farm Cottage, Swanwick, Hampshire SO31 7HE	01489 579011	023 8023 0400	Ian Thorsteinsson	850-6088	11–16		
Grateley House School (part of Cambian Education)	Grateley, Andover, Hampshire SP11 8TA	0800 288 9779	020 7348 5223	Mrs Susan Elizabeth King	850-6058	9–19	43	R CD AS ADHD
Hill House School (part of Cambian Education)	Rope Hill, Boldre, Lymington, Hampshire SO41 8NE	0800 288 9779	020 7348 5223	Ms J. Wright	850-6031	11–25	22	R CD ASD SLD ADHD Ep
Hillcrest – Hayling Island	24 Alexandra Ave, Hayling Island, Hampshire PO11 9AL	023 9246 9691	023 9246 6413	Mr David MacAskill	850-6086	8–16	4	B R SEBD
The Loddon School	Wildmoor, Sherfield-on-Loddon, Hook, Hampshire RG27 0JD	01256 882394	01256 882929	Miss Karen Rookes	850-6005	8–18	27	R SLD
St Edward's School	Melchet Ct, Sherfield English, Romsey, Hampshire SO51 6ZR	01794 884271	01794 884903	Mr L. Bartel	850-6032	11–17	44	B R SEBD
Southlands School (part of Cambian Education)	Vicars Hill, Boldre, Lymington, Hampshire SO41 5QB	0800 288 9779	020 7348 5223	Ms Angela Marion Nightingale	850-6030	7–16	77	B R CD AS ADHD
Stanbridge Earls School	Stanbridge La, Romsey, Hampshire SO51 0ZS	01794 529400	01794 511201	Mr Geoff Link	850-6065	11–18	175	R SpLD
Tadley Horizon	Tadley Common Rd, Tadley, Basingstoke, Hampshire RG26 3TB	0118 981 7720	0118 981 7720	Vanessa Wilkinson	850-6085	4–19	11	R ASD
Treloar School	Upper Froyle, Alton, Hampshire GU34 4LA	01420 526400	01420 526426	Mr Harry Dicks	850-7068	5–19		R PD

Isle of Wight

School name	Address	Tel	Fax	Headteacher	Ref	Ages	Pupils	Other
St Catherine's School	Grove Rd, Ventnor, Isle of Wight PO38 1TT	01983 852722	01983 857219	Mr Grenville Shipley	921-7000	7–19		R CD

Kent

School name	Address	Tel	Fax	Headteacher	Ref	Ages	Pupils	Other
Alexandra House	c/o The Manor Hse, High St, Rothwell, Kettering, Northamptonshire NN14 6BQ	01536 711111	01536 711155	Mrs Karen Burke	886-6111	10–17		R SEBD
The Annex School House	Leyden Hatch La, Pembroke Hse, Hextable, Kent BR8 7PS	01322 618776		Wendy McLoughin	886-6122	8–16		B
Arundel House	The Manor Hse, High St, Rothwell, Kettering, Northamptonshire NN14 6BQ	01536 711111	01536 712994	Karon Hopwood	886-6119	8–17		R
The Ashbrook Centre	8 Almond Cl, Broadstairs, Kent CT10 2NQ	01843 869240	01843 869240	Ms Lesley Gibson	886-6110	5–18	3	SEBD
Brewood Middle School	146 Newington Rd, Ramsgate, Kent CT12 6PT	01304 620971		Mr Donald Wilton	886-6103	5–13	7	SEBD
Brewood Secondary School	86 London Rd, Deal, Kent CT14 9TR	01304 363000	01304 363099	Mr Daniel Jonathan Radlett	886-6070	11–18	11	SEBD MLD
Caldecott Foundation School	Station Rd, Smeeth, Ashford, Kent TN25 6PW	01303 815665		Mrs Valerie Miller (Acting)	886-7003	5–18		R SEBD
The Davenport Centre	Princess Margaret Ave, Ramsgate, Kent CT12 6HX	01843 589018	01843 589018	Mr Franklyn Brown	886-6089	7–12	5	B SEBD

7

School name	Address	Tel	Fax	Headteacher	Ref	Ages	Pupils	Other
Dorton House School	Seal Dr, Seal, Sevenoaks, Kent TN15 0EB	01732 592650	01732 592670	Ms Jude Thompson	886-7035	5–16		R VI
East Court School	Victoria Par, Ramsgate, Kent CT11 8ED	01843 592077	01843 592418	Dr M.E. Thomson	886-6055	7–14	74	R SpLD
Farm Cottage	The Manor Hse, High St, Rothwell, Kettering, Northamptonshire NN14 6BQ	01536 711111	01536 712994	Ms Karon Hopwood	886-6118	8–17	2	R
Great Oaks Small School	Ebbsfleet Farmhouse, Ebbsfleet La, Minster, Ramsgate, Kent CT12 5DJ	01843 822022		Mrs J. Kelly	886-6093	13–16	15	SpLD
Greenfields School	Tenterden Rd, Biddenden, Ashford, Kent TN27 8BS	01580 292523	01580 292354	Mr Darin Nobes	886-6084	5–10	9	SEBD
Haven House	Squire's Hill, c/o Castlecare Manor Hse, Rothwell, Northants NN14 6BQ	01536 711111	01536 712994	Mrs Karon Hopwood	886-6121	8–18	3	R SEBD MLD
Heath Farm School	Heath Farm, Ashford, Kent TN27 0AX	01233 712030	01233 712066	Ms Elizabeth Cornish	886-6060	5–18	38	SEBD
Helen Allison School	Longfield Rd, Gravesend, Kent DA13 0EW	01474 814878	01474 812033	Mrs J. Ashton-Smith	886-6046	5–16	64	R AS ASD SLD
Hill View School	Cleve Farm Hse, Cleve Hill, Graveney, Kent ME13 9EE	01795 537649		Mr P.D. Pritchard	886-6088	11–17		SEBD
Hobbit House	c/o The Manor Hse, Squires Hill, Rothwell, Northants NN14 6BG	01536 711111	01536 711155	Mrs Karon Burke	886-6112	8–17	2	R SEBD
Hythe House Education	Power Station Rd, Sheerness, Kent ME12 3AB	01795 581006		Mr Paul Paul	886-6107	11–16	5	
Integrated Services Programme	Church St, Sittingbourne, Kent ME10 3EG	01795 422044	01795 477088	Ms Sharon McDermott	886-6065	11–16	15	SEBD
ISP Teynham	Conyer Rd, Barrow Grn, Teynham, Sittingbourne, Kent ME9 9EA	01795 523900	01795 520035	S. McDermott	886-6090	7–16	16	SEBD MLD
Learning Opportunities Centre Primary	The Street, Canterbury, Kent CT4 6HE	01227 831236	01227 831236	Ms Diana Ward	886-6068	8–11	9	SEBD
Learning Opportunities Centre Secondary	Ringwould Rd, Deal, Kent CT14 8DW	01304 381906	01304 381906	Ms Diana Ward	886-6063	11–16	17	SEBD
Little Acorns School	London Beach Farm, Ashford Rd, St Michaels, Tenterden, Kent TN30 6SR	01233 850422	01233 850422	Mr David Wilmshurst	886-6085	8–11	6	R SEBD
Meadows School (Barnardo's)	London Rd, Southborough, Tunbridge Wells, Kent TN4 0RN	01892 529144	01892 527787	Mr Mike Price	886-7011	11–16		R SEBD
NCH Westwood School	479 Margate Rd, Westwood, Broadstairs, Kent CT10 2QA	01843 600820	01843 600827	Mr C.L. Walter	886-7071	11–16		R SEBD
The New School at West Heath	Ashgrove Rd, Sevenoaks, Kent TN13 1SR	01732 460553	01732 456734	Mrs Valerie M. May	886-6079	11–18	102	R SEBD
The Old Priory School	Priory Rd, Ramsgate, Kent CT11 9PG	01843 599322	01843 599333	Mr Peter Pritchard	886-6076	11–16	30	SEBD
The Old School	Capel St, Capel-le-Ferne, Folkestone, Kent CT18 7EY	01303 251116	01303 251116	Martyn Jordan	886-6086	9–17	28	B
The Quest School	Church Farm, Church Rd, The Old Stables, Offham, Kent ME19 5NX	01732 522700		Mrs Anne Martin	886-6108	4–14	7	ASD
Ripplevale School	Chapel La, Deal, Kent CT14 8JG	01304 373866	01304 381011	Mr Ted Schofield	886-6047	9–16	28	B R SEBD
Royal School for Deaf Children and Westgate College for Deaf People	Victoria Rd, Margate, Kent CT9 1NB	01843 227561	01843 227637	Mr Christopher Owen	886-7017	4–19		R HI MSI
The Symbol Academy	Woodlands Farm, Paddlesworth Rd, Snodland, Kent ME6 5DL	01634 244000		Mrs Lyne Kingsmill	886-6120	9–16	5	CD
Toadstool Cottage	c/o The Manor Hse, High St, Rothwell, Kettering, Northamptonshire NN14 6BQ	01536 711111	01536 711155	Karon Hopwood	886-6114	8–17		R SEBD
Victoria House	c/o The Manor Hse, High St, Rothwell, Kettering, Northamptonshire NN14 6BQ	01536 711111	01536 711155	Karen Burke	886-6115	9–17	2	R SEBD
Wilford Court	c/o The Manor Hse, High St, Rothwell, Kettering, Northamptonshire NN14 6BQ	01536 711111	01536 711155	Karon Burke	886-6117	8–17	1	R SEBD
The Willows	144–146 Mickleburgh Hall, Eddington, Herne Bay, Kent CT6 6JZ	01227 369125	01227 742223	Mr Paul Heaven	886-6116	5–11	4	R SEBD

Medway

School name	Address	Tel	Fax	Headteacher	Ref	Ages	Pupils	Other
Trinity School	13 New Rd, Rochester, Kent ME1 1BG	01634 812233	01634 812233	Mrs Claire Dunn	887-6006	6–16	43	SpLD

Oxfordshire

School name	Address	Tel	Fax	Headteacher	Ref	Ages	Pupils	Other
Bellerby's College	Boswell Hse, 1–5 Broad St, Oxford, Oxfordshire OX1 3AJ	01256 320250		Jane Collis	931-6126	14–19		R
Bessels Leigh School	Bessels Leigh, Abingdon, Oxfordshire OX13 5QB	01865 390436	01865 390688	Mr John Boulton	931-7026	10–17		B R SEBD SpLD
Chilworth House School	Thames Rd, Wheatley, Oxford, Oxfordshire OX33 1JP	01844 339077	01844 339088	Mr B. Marchbank	931-6125	5–12	6	SEBD SLD
Hillcrest Park School	Southcombe, Chipping Norton, Oxford, Oxfordshire OX7 5QH	01608 644621	01608 644295	Miss Patricia Bradley	931-6115	7–16	11	R SEBD
Mulberry Bush School	Abingdon Rd, Standlake, Witney, Oxfordshire OX29 7RW	01865 300202	01865 300084	Mr Andy Lole	931-7005	5–12		R SEBD
Penhurst School	New St, Chipping Norton, Oxfordshire OX7 5LN	01608 647020	01608 647029	Mr Derek Lyseight-Jones	931-7001	5–19		R PD PMLD
Swalcliffe Park School Trust	Swalcliffe, Banbury, Oxfordshire OX15 5EP	01295 780302	01295 780006	Mr R. Hooper	931-7007	11–19		B R SEBD AS
The Unicorn School	18 Park Cres, Wildmoor, Whitefield, Abingdon, Oxfordshire OX14 1DD	01235 530222	01235 530222	Mrs Jacqueline Vaux	931-6109	7–11	41	

Southampton

School name	Address	Tel	Fax	Headteacher	Ref	Ages	Pupils	Other
Cornerstone School	101 Portsmouth Rd, Woolston, Southampton, Hampshire SO19 9BE	023 8023 0463	023 8023 0234		852-6010	8–16		SpLD
Hope Lodge School	22 Midanbury La., Bitterne Pk., Southampton, Hampshire SO18 4HP	023 8063 4346	023 8023 1789	Mr Mike Robinson	852-6004	5–19	50	R ASD SLD AS
Rosewood School	300 Aldermoor Rd, Bradbury Centre, Southampton SO16 5NA	023 8072 1234	023 8051 3473	Mrs Jenny Boyd	852-7050	2–19		PMLD
The Serendipity Centre	399 Hinkler Rd, Thornhill, Southampton, Hampshire SO19 6DS	023 8042 2255	023 8042 2255	Mrs Sue Tinson	852-6009	11–16	5	G

Surrey

School name	Address	Tel	Fax	Headteacher	Ref	Ages	Pupils	Other
Apple Orchard Education Unit	Apple Orchard, Birtley Grn, Bramley, Guildford, Surrey GU5 0LE	01483 894075	01483 894075	Mr Jim Martin	936-6574	13–16	9	B R SEBD
Cornfield School	53 Hanworth Rd, Redhill, Surrey RH1 5HS	01737 779578	01737 771927	Mrs Jayne Telfer	936-6581	12–18	12	Ch G SEBD
Grafham Grange School	Grafham, Bramley, Guildford, Surrey GU5 0LH	01483 892214	01483 894297	Mr R. Norman	936-6567	10–17		B R SEBD
The Jigsaw School	Building 21, Dunsfold Pk, Stovolds Hill, Cranleigh, Surrey GU6 8TB	01483 273874	01252 516816	Ms Kate Grant	936-6579	4–16	30	ID ASD
Knowl Hill School	School La., Pirbright, Woking, Surrey GU24 0JN	01483 797032	01483 797641	Mr James Dow-Grant	936-6554	7–16	46	Ch SpLD
Meath School	Brox Rd, Otershaw, Chertsey, Surrey KT16 0LF	01932 872302	01932 875180	Mrs Janet Dunn	936-7063	5–12		R CD
Moon Hall School for Dyslexic Children	Feldemore, Holmbury St Mary, Dorking, Surrey RH5 6LQ	01306 731464	01306 731504	Mrs P. Lore	936-6551	7–13	98	CE R SpLD
Moor House School	Mill La., Hurst Grn, Oxted, Surrey RH8 9AQ	01883 712271	01883 716722	Mrs Hilary Dobbie	936-7007	7–16		R CD
More House School	Moons Hill, Frensham, Farnham, Surrey GU10 3AP	01252 792303	01252 797601	Mr Barry Huggett	936-6420	9–19	270	RC B R CD SpLD
National Centre for Young People with Epilepsy, St Piers School	St Piers La, Lingfield, Surrey RH7 6PW	01342 832243	01342 834639	Mr Nicholas Byford	936-7005	5–19		R MLD SLD Ep
Papillon House	Pebble Cl, Tadworth, Surrey KT20 7PA	01737 365810			936-6590	4–11		SEBD
St Dominic's School	Mount Olivet, Hambledon, Godalming, Surrey GU8 4DX	01428 684693	01428 684693	Mrs Susan Russam	936-7010	7–17		R CD SpLD
St Joseph's School	Amlets La, Cranleigh, Surrey GU6 7DH	01483 272449	01483 276003	Mrs Mary Fawcett	936-7011	7–19		R CD ASD MLD SLD
St Margaret's School	Tadworth Ct, Tadworth, Surrey KT20 5RU			Mrs J.E. Cunningham	936-7069	5–19		R PMLD
Stepping Stones School	Tower Rd, Hindhead, Surrey GU26 6SU	01428 609083	01428 609083	Mr Neil Clark	936-6584	7–16	5	PD MLD
Unsted Park School	Munstead Heath Rd, Godalming, Surrey GU7 1UW	01483 892061	01483 892061		936-6592	7–16		R ASD

7

West Berkshire

School name	Address	Tel	Fax	Headteacher	Ref	Ages	Pupils	Other
Mary Hare Grammar School	Arlington Manor, Snelsmore Common, Newbury, Berkshire RG14 3BQ	01635 244200	01635 244200	Dr I. Tucker	869-7005	4–19	240	R HI
Priors Court School	Priors Ct, Hermitage, Thatcham, Berkshire RG18 9NU	01635 247202	01635 247203	Mr Robert Hubbard	869-6014	5–19	53	R ASD

West Sussex

School name	Address	Tel	Fax	Headteacher	Ref	Ages	Pupils	Other
The Amicus School	No 2 Yeoman's Nursery, Warningcamp, Arundel, West Sussex BN18 9QY	01903 885135	01903 885135	Mrs Olga Cumberland	938-6265	7–12	3	R MLD SpLD
Ark House	190 Sompting Rd, Worthing, West Sussex BN14 9EY	01903 537892	01903 537834	Mrs Rosenfeld	938-6269	12–16	3	R SEBD MLD
Brantridge School	Staplefield Pl, Staplefield, Haywards Heath, West Sussex RH17 6EQ	01444 400228	01444 401083	Mrs Tamsin Gent	938-7019	7–12	37	B R SEBD
The Education Centre	56 Rowlands Rd, Worthing, West Sussex BN11 3JT	01903 824166	01903 535350		938-6274	13–17		Ch R CD ASD ADHD
Education Centre, The	17–21 Boltro Rd, Haywards Heath, West Sussex RH16 1BT	01444 450111	01444 450666	Mrs Jacqueline Roffe	938-6249	13–16	40	SEBD
Farney Close School	Bolney Ct, Bolney, Haywards Heath, West Sussex RH17 5RD	01444 881811	01444 881957	Mr B.C. Robinson	938-6217	11–17	61	R SEBD
Gleniffer House Residential School	Five Oaks Rd, Slinfold, Horsham, West Sussex RH13 0RQ	01403 783416	01403 786082	Ms Janet Parsons	938-6258	14–16	3	B R SEBD
Hillcrest Slinfold	Stane St, Slinfold, Horsham, West Sussex RH13 0QX	01403 790939	01403 790954	Miss Nikki Forsyth	938-6255	11–16	16	B R SEBD
Ingfield Manor School	Five Oaks, Billingshurst, West Sussex RH14 9AX	01403 782294	01403 785066	Mr Alistair Bruce	938-6175	3–16	25	R PD
Kestral House	27 Valebridge Rd, Burgess Hill, Burgess Hill RH15 0RA	01444 446920	01444 446929	Ms Annie Murphy	938-6271	11–16	2	R PD
Muntham House School	Barns Grn, Horsham, West Sussex RH13 0NU	01403 730302	01403 730510	Mr Richard Boyle	938-7003	8–18	50	B R SEBD ADHD
Ocean Pearl	North Dr, Angmering, Angmering BN16 4JJ	01903 859502	01903 859502	Ms Annie Murphy	938-6272	11–16	2	G R SEBD
Philpots Manor School	West Hoathly, East Grinstead, West Sussex RH19 4PR	01342 810268	01342 811363	Ms Linda Churnside	938-6219	7–19	49	Ch R SEBD
S and P Educational Services	69 Mill Rd, Worthing, West Sussex BN11 5DX	0870 421 5767		Mrs Susan Evans	938-6263	11–18	5	R SEBD MLD SLD
Shopham Bridge	Shopham Bridge, Petworth, Petworth GU28 0JP	01444 446920	01444 446929		938-6273	11–16		R SEBD
Southways School	The Vale Hse, Findon Rd, Findon, Worthing, West Sussex BN14 0RA	01903 877448	01903 877449	Mrs Brenda Ruth Bailey	938-6253	7–11	3	SEBD
Springboard Education	55 South St, Lancing, West Sussex BN15 8HA	01903 605980	01903 605980		938-6266	8–16	11	SEBD
Strides Learning Support Centre	66 Livesay Cres, Broadwater, Worthing, West Sussex BN14 8AT	01903 216552	01903 216552	Ms Christine Silvester	938-6264	13–16	2	B R

Windsor and Maidenhead

School name	Address	Tel	Fax	Headteacher	Ref	Ages	Pupils	Other
Heathermount, The Learning Centre	Devenish Rd, Ascot, Berkshire SL5 9PG	01344 875101	01344 875102	Ms Stephanie Lord	868-7206	5–19	42	R AS

Wokingham

School name	Address	Tel	Fax	Headteacher	Ref	Ages	Pupils	Other
Annie Lawson School	Ravenswood Village, Nine Mile Ride, Crowthorne, Berkshire RG45 6BQ	01344 755508	01344 762317	Mr M. Hughes	872-6009	11–20	21	R SEBD PD SLD
High Close School (Barnardo's)	Wiltshire Rd, Wokingham, Berkshire RG40 1TT	0118 978 5767	0118 989 4220	Mr Sandy Paterson	872-7006	7–16	59	R SEBD

South West

Bristol

School name	Address	Tel	Fax	Headteacher	Ref	Ages	Pupils	Other
Belgrave School	10 Upper Belgrave Rd, Clifton, Bristol BS8 2XH	0117 974 3133	0117 973 9405	Mrs P.J. Jones	801-6019	7–12	18	SpLD
Greenfields	c/o PO Box 31, USK NP15 1ZW	01291 671480	01291 671473	Judy Raudon-Hill	801-6131	11–18	3	R SEBD
Little Islands Henbury	22 Todmarton Cres, Henbury, Bristol BS10 7LW	0117 950 8176	0117 950 8575	Mr A. Date	801-6129	12–16	6	AS
St Christopher's School	2 Carisbrooke Lodge, Westbury Pk, Bristol BS6 7JE	0117 973 3301	0117 974 3665	Ms O. Matz	801-6008	7–19	48	Ch R SLD PMLD

Cornwall

School name	Address	Tel	Fax	Headteacher	Ref	Ages	Pupils	Other
T Plus Centre (Taliesin Education)	Heathlands Rd, Liskeard, Cornwall PL14 6DH	01579 344999			908-6096	11–16		
Three Bridges	East Hill, Blackwater, Truro, Cornwall TR4 8EG	01872 561010		Mr Tyler Collins	908-6095	11–16	7	R ASD
Whitstone Head School	Whitstone, Holsworthy, Devon EX22 6TJ	01288 341251	01288 341207	Mr David McLean-Thorne	908-7001	10–16		R SEBD

Devon

School name	Address	Tel	Fax	Headteacher	Ref	Ages	Pupils	Other
Bishop Dunstan School	16–18 South Rd, Newton Abbot, Devon TQ12 1HH	01626 356395	01626 366657	Ms Alice Morris	878-6057	11–16	20	B R SEBD
Blackmoor School	Moorlands Farm, Luppitt, Honiton, Devon EX14 4SX	01404 891035	01404 891030	Mr Peter Taylor	878-6059	11–16	6	SEBD
Broomhayes School and Children's Centre	Kingsley Hse, Alverdiscott Rd, Bideford, Devon EX39 4PL	01237 473830	01237 421097	Ms M. Vallely	878-6038	10–19	24	R ASD SLD
Chelfham Mill School	Chelfham, Barnstaple, Devon EX32 7LA	01271 850448	01271 850235	Mrs K. Roberts	878-6024	7–13	38	B R SEBD
Chelfham Senior School	Bere Alston, Yelverton, Devon PL20 7EX	01822 840379	01822 841489	Mr Andrew Arnold	878-6039	11–19	66	B R SEBD
Dame Hannah Rogers School	Woodland Rd, Ivybridge, Devon PL21 9HQ	01752 892461	01752 898101	Ms Angela Murray	878-6082	8–19		R PD
On Track Training Centre	Unit 8, Paragon Bldgs, Ford Rd, Totnes, Devon TQ9 5LQ	01803 866462	01803 866462	Mrs J. Fox	878-6060	11–17	15	SEBD MSI SpLD AS
Royal School for the Deaf Exeter	50 Topsham Rd, Exeter, Devon EX2 4NF	01392 272692	01392 431146	Mr Lee Fullwood	878-7083	5–19		R VI HI
Vranch House School	Pinhoe Rd, Exeter, Devon EX4 8AD	01392 468333	01392 463818	Miss M. Boon	878-6007	2–12	20	PD MLD
West of England School	Countess Wear, Exeter, Devon EX2 6HA	01392 454200	01392 454200	Mr Paul Holland	878-7081	2–19		R VI
Willows	Loyalty Hall, Cullompton, Devon EX15 2BY	01884 266145		Taryn Stanton	878-6061	11–16		G R SEBD
Woodhouse School	Hawkchurch, Axminster, Devon EX13 5UF	01297 678577	01297 678561	Mrs Chris Moore	878-6056	9–18	3	G R SEBD

Dorset

School name	Address	Tel	Fax	Headteacher	Ref	Ages	Pupils	Other
The Forum School (part of Cambian Education)	Shillingstone, Blandford Forum, Dorset DT11 0QS	0800 288 9779	020 7348 5223	Mrs Gay Waters	835-6033	7–19	41	R CD ASD MLD SLD ADHD Ep
Philip Green Memorial School	Boveridge Hse, Cranborne, Wimborne, Dorset BH21 5RU	01725 517218	01725 517968	Mrs L.M. Walter	835-6020	11–19	39	R MLD SLD
Portfield School	Parley La, Christchurch, Dorset BH23 6BP	01202 573808	01202 580532	Mrs Janis Rogers	835-6008	2–19	64	R ASD SLD
Purbeck View School (part of Cambian Education)	Northbrook Rd, Swanage, Dorset BH19 1PR	0800 288 9779	020 7348 5223	Mrs S. Goulding	835-6016	9–19	43	R CD ASD MLD SLD ADHD Ep
Sheiling School	Horton Rd, Ashley, Ringwood, Hampshire BH24 2EB	01425 477488	01425 479536		835-6004	6–19	38	R SLD

7

Gloucestershire

School name	Address	Tel	Fax	Headteacher	Ref	Ages	Pupils	Other
Althea Park Education Unit	51 Stratford Pk, Stroud, Gloucestershire GL5 4AJ	01453 757356	01453 757356	Mrs Cheryl Byford	916-6079	13–18	1	G R
Cotswold Chine Home School	Box, Stroud, Gloucestershire GL6 9AG	01453 837550	01453 837555	Maureen Smith	916-6040	9–18	36	Ch R SEBD
The Marlowe Education Unit	Hartpury Old School, Gloucester Rd, Hartpury, Gloucester, Gloucestershire GL19 3BG	01452 700855	01452 700866	Mrs Diana Mcqueen	916-6072	8–16	10	
St Rose's Special School	Stratford Lawn, Stroud, Gloucestershire GL5 4AP	01453 763793	01453 752617	Sister M. Quentin	916-7006	2–18		R VI CD PD
Three Castles College	The Marina, Oridge St, Corse, Lydney, Gloucestershire GL15 5ET	01594 844114	01452 840528	Mrs Joy Price-Bish	916-6080	11–18	5	B R

Plymouth

School name	Address	Tel	Fax	Headteacher	Ref	Ages	Pupils	Other
Wolsdon Street School	39 Wolsdon St, Plymouth, Devon PL1 5EH	01752 550479	01752 265228	Mr J. Greenfield	879-6007	13–19	8	SEBD

Poole

School name	Address	Tel	Fax	Headteacher	Ref	Ages	Pupils	Other
Langside School	Langside Ave, Parkstone, Poole, Dorset BH12 5BN	01202 518635	01202 531513	Mr John Ashby	836-7016	2–19		PD MLD SLD PMLD SpLD
Victoria Education Centre	12 Lindsay Rd, Branksome Pk, Poole, Dorset BH13 6AS	01202 763697	01202 768078	Mrs Christina Davies	836-7004	3–19		R CD PD

Somerset

School name	Address	Tel	Fax	Headteacher	Ref	Ages	Pupils	Other
Blackford Education Limited T/A Libra	Blackford Hse, Blackford, Minehead, Somerset TA24 8SY	01598 752666	01598 752630	Ms J.E. Wilkes	933-6202	8–18	9	SEBD
Edington and Shapwick School	Shapwick Manor, Bridgwater, Somerset TA7 9NJ	01458 210384	01458 210111	Mr D.C. Walker	933-6173	8–18	157	R SpLD
Farleigh College	Newbury Manor, Frome, Somerset BA11 3RG	01373 814980	01373 814984	Mr A.R. Mulcahy	933-6195	11–16	41	R AS
Marchant Holliday School	North Cheriton, Templecombe, Somerset BA8 0AH	01963 33234	01963 33432	Mr T.J. Kitts	933-6089	7–13	30	B R SEBD
Mark College	Mark, Highbridge, Somerset TA9 4NP	01278 641632	01278 641426	Mrs J. Kay	933-6185	10–18	79	R SpLD
Merryhay School	Merryhay Hse, Ilton Business Pk, Ilton, Ilminster, Somerset TA19 9DU	01460 53232	01460 53232	Mrs Lesley Chudley	933-6208	11–16	2	SEBD MLD
New Horizon Centre School	Bath House Farm, West Hatch, Taunton, Somerset TA3 5RH	01823 481902	01823 481901	Jennie Meadows	933-6203	11–16	17	SEBD
North Hill House	Fromefield, Frome, Somerset BA11 2HB	01373 466222	01373 475175	Mr Andy Cobley	933-6200	7–16	50	B R ASD AS
Periton Mead Independent School	Periton Rd, Minehead, Somerset TA24 8DT	01643 702247	01643 704040	Linda Moss	933-6201	11–18	7	SEBD
Phoenix School	Westport Hse, Langport Rd, Hambridge, Somerset TA10 0BH	01460 281854	01460 281854	Ms Liz Sharpe	933-6211	11–16	10	B HI ASD SEBD
Sarah Biffin School	Lillesdon Hse, Lillesdon La, North Curry, Taunton, Somerset TA3 6BY	01823 492025	01823 492026	Ms Liz Sharpe	933-6213	11–16	15	G HI SEBD
Staddlestones School	Staddons, Cheddon Fitzpaine, Taunton, Somerset TA2 8LD	01823 451789	01823 451789	Ms Liz Sharpe	933-6212	11–16	14	B HI SEBD
Wessex College	Wessex Lodge, Nuney Rd, Frome, Wiltshire BA11 4LA	01985 218486	01985 218347	Ms C. Smith	933-6210	11–16	8	SEBD

South Gloucestershire

School name	Address	Tel	Fax	Headteacher	Ref	Ages	Pupils	Other
Sabis International School UK	Ashwicke Hall, Marshfield, Wiltshire SN14 8AG	01225 891841	01225 891011		803-6006	10–14		R
Sheiling School	Thornbury Pk, Thornbury, Bristol BS35 1HP	01454 412194	01454 411860		803-6000	6–19	16	Ch R MLD SLD AS Ep

Torbay

School name	Address	Tel	Fax	Headteacher	Ref	Ages	Pupils	Other
Wychbury House School	22 Cleveland Rd, Torquay, Devon TQ2 5BE	01803 293460	01803 293460	Mr D. Simpson	880-6005	9–16	10	R SEBD MLD

Wiltshire

School name	Address	Tel	Fax	Headteacher	Ref	Ages	Pupils	Other
Appleford School	Elston La, Shrewton, Salisbury, Wiltshire SP3 4HL	01980 621020	01980 621366	Ms Stella Marie Wilson	865-6008	7–13	78	
Calder House School	Thickwood La, Colerne, Chippenham, Wiltshire SN14 8BN	01225 742329	01225 742329	Mrs Katherine Walling	865-6024	5–12	36	SpLD
Cotswold Community	Ashton Keynes, Swindon, Wiltshire SN6 6QU	01285 861239	01285 860114	Mr Andrew Thomas	865-6030	8–16	17	B R SEBD
Sherant Education	Acorn Hse, 38 Forest Rd, Melksham, Wiltshire SN12 7AB	01225 706361		Mrs Paula Hayden	865-6038	11–16	3	B R SEBD
Tumblewood Community School at The Laurels	The Laurels, 4 Hawkeridge Rd, Westbury, Wiltshire BA13 4LF	01373 824466	01373 824321	Ms Helen Twiggs	865-6034	11–18	11	G R SEBD

West Midlands

Birmingham

School name	Address	Tel	Fax	Headteacher	Ref	Ages	Pupils	Other
Birmingham Rathbone Society	Longmore Hse, Cromer Rd, Moseley, Birmingham, West Midlands B12 9QP	0121 449 1011	0121 449 8977	Mr Ian Hinksman	330-6118	14–16		MLD SLD
The Collegiate Centre for Values Education for Life	51 Hockley Hill, Newtown, Birmingham, West Midlands B18 5AQ	0121 523 0222	0121 523 5111	Mr David Rowse	330-6101	14–17	18	SEBD
National Institute for Conductive Education	Cannon Hill Hse, Russell Rd, Moseley, Birmingham, West Midlands B13 8RD	0121 449 1569	0121 449 1611	Mrs W. Baker	330-6080	3–11	7	
St James College	St James Hse, St James Pl, Birmingham, West Midlands B7 4JE	0121 333 3001	0121 359 5863	Mr G.J. Franks	330-6117	14–16		
St Paul's	Hertford St, Balsall Heath, Birmingham B12 8NJ	0121 464 4376	0121 464 2555	Mr John Colwell	330-6115	9–19	59	
Spring Hill High School	c/o 36 Hunton Rd, Erdington, Birmingham, West Midlands B23 6AH	0121 384 2453	0121 384 3782	Mrs Barbara Scrivens	330-6112	11–19	4	R SEBD
Trade Based Training	Units 10, 1 and 16, Stetchford Trading Est, Lyndon Rd, Stetchford, Birmingham, West Midlands B33 8BU	0121 789 6602	0121 789 6603	Mr Christopher Dawe	330-6114	11–16	39	B SEBD
Ward End Community College	962–968 Alum Rock Rd, Ward End, Birmingham, West Midlands B8 2LS	0121 789 7060	0121 789 7708		330-6116	14–19		G

Coventry

School name	Address	Tel	Fax	Headteacher	Ref	Ages	Pupils	Other
RNIB Rushton School and Children's Home	Wheelwright La, Ash Grn, Coventry CV7 9RA	024 7636 9500	024 7636 9501	Ms Judy Bell	331-7020	4–19		R VI
Rowan House	135 Broad La, Coventry, West Midlands CV5 7AL	024 7671 2401		Ms Frances Cubitt	331-6028	11–16		B R SEBD

Herefordshire

School name	Address	Tel	Fax	Headteacher	Ref	Ages	Pupils	Other
Coddington Court School	Coddington, Ledbury, Herefordshire HR8 1JL	01531 640541	01531 640731	Miss Ruth Burton	884-6014	9–19	25	R
Larches School	Coningsby Rd, Leominster, Herefordshire HR6 8LL	01568 610279	01568 610279	Mr Andrew McDouall	884-6010	11–16	22	R SEBD

7

School name	Address	Tel	Fax	Headteacher	Ref	Ages	Pupils	Other
Melrose School	Hardwicke, Hay on Wye, Hertfordshire HR3 5TA	01497 831661		Ms Liz Sharp	884-6015	11-16		B SEBD
Queenswood School	The Old Rectory, Hope-under-Dinmore, Leominster, Herefordshire HR6 0PW	01568 620403		Mr Spencer Thomas	884-6011	9-16	6	R SEBD
Rowden House School	Rowden Hse, Winslow, Bromyard, Herefordshire HR7 4LS	01885 488096	01885 48336	Mr I. Gateley	884-6006	11-19	40	R SLD

Shropshire

School name	Address	Tel	Fax	Headteacher	Ref	Ages	Pupils	Other
Access School	Holbrook Villa Farm, Harmer Hill, Broughton, Shrewsbury SY4 3EW	01939 220789	01939 220701	Mr Stephen Ellis	893-6096	7-16	9	SEBD
Condover Horizon School	Condover Hall, Condover, Shrewsbury, Shropshire SY5 7AH	01743 875100	01743 873310	Mrs Joan Pearson	893-6101	4-19	5	R ASD
Cruckton Hall School	Cruckton, Shrewsbury, Shropshire SY5 8PR	01743 860206	01743 860206	Mr P.D. Mayhew	893-6017	9-19	79	B R AS
David Banks School	Oteley Island, Oteley Rd, Shrewsbury, Shropshire SY2 6QP	01743 240971	01743 249019	Mrs Glen Hulse	893-6100	11-17	17	R
Farleigh College	Condover Hall, Condover, Shrewsbury, Shropshire SY7 7AH	01743 872320		Mr Alun Maddocks	893-6104	14-19	10	R
Highlea School	Astbury La, Chelmarsh, Bridgnorth, Shropshire WV16 6AX	01746 862423	01746 862635	Ms Tony Milosvorov	893-6023	10-16	11	SEBD
Hillgate School	Hemford, Minsterley, Shrewsbury, Shropshire SY5 0HJ	01743 891862		Mr H. Cullen	893-6099	8-16	2	R SEBD
Hurst Farm	c/o Castlecare Group, The Manor Hse, Squires Hill, Rothwell, Northamptonshire NN14 6BQ	01536 711111	01536 712664	Mr Wallace Robinson	893-6103	10-17	2	R
Learning for Life Education Centre	Station Rd, Ditton Priors, Bridgnorth, Shropshire WV16 6SS	01746 712985	01584 877393	Mr Stephen Piper	893-6024	11-16	10	SEBD
Minor Lodge	The Oaks Business Pk, Shepherds La, Bicton, Shrewsbury, Shropshire SY3 8BT	01743 850840	01743 851060	Julie Dodd	893-6097	4-16	4	SEBD
The Orchard School	Middletown, Welshpool, Powys SY21 8EW	01743 884145	01743 884081	Mrs E. Yeomans	893-6021	12-19	8	R
Rubicon	Smallbrook Lodge, Smallbrook Rd, Whitchurch, Shropshire SY13 1BX	01948 661110	01948 666979	Mr I.J. Phillips	893-6026	11-19	5	R SEBD
The Stubbs	Leigh, Minsterley, Shrewsbury, Shropshire SY5 0DT	01743 891296	01743 891296	Mr J. Hanley	893-6098	8-16		R SEBD
Ty Newydd	Ford Heath, Shrewsbury, Shropshire SY5 9GZ	01743 792273		Alaistair Craib	893-6105	11-16		SEBD
Whitty Tree House	c/o Castlecare Group, The Manor Hse, High St, Rothwell, Kettering, Northamptonshire NN14 6BQ	01536 711111	01536 712994	Mr Geoffrey Southall	893-6102	10-17	2	R MLD
Young Options College	Lamledge La, Shifnal, Shropshire TF11 8SD	01952 468220	01952 468221	Mr A. Large	893-6025	9-18	20	R SEBD

Staffordshire

School name	Address	Tel	Fax	Headteacher	Ref	Ages	Pupils	Other
Corporation Farmhouse	CastleCare Group, The Manor Hse, Squire's Hill, Rothwell, Northants NN14 6BQ	01543 411604		Ms Rose M.K. Montgomery	860-6030	10-19		R MLD
Highfields Farmhouse	Clifton La, Clifton Campuille, Tamworth, Staffordshire B79 0AQ	01827 830066	01827 830066		860-6031	10-16		R SEBD
Hillcrest Kings Bromley	Alrewas Rd, Kings Bromley, Burton on Trent, Staffordshire DE13 7HR	01543 473772	01543 473283	Mr Mark Hollinshead	860-6029	11-16	7	B R SEBD
Horizon School for Children with Autism	Blithbury Rd, Blithbury, Rugeley, Staffordshire WS15 3JQ	01889 504400	01889 504010	Mrs Marisa Kelsall	860-6024	4-19	41	R ASD SLD
The Manor House School	High St, Knutton, Newcastle under Lyme, Staffordshire ST5 6BX	01782 623153	01782 618206	Mr T. Whitwell	860-6026	11-16	14	SEBD
Maple Hayes Hall School	Abnalls La, Lichfield, Staffordshire WS13 8BL	01543 264387	01543 262022	Dr E.N. Brown	860-6022	7-17	91	SpLD
Roaches School	Tunstall Rd, Knypersley, Stoke-on-Trent, Staffordshire ST8 7AB	01782 523479	01782 511875	Mr Matt Wilson	860-6017	7-16	24	R SEBD

Stoke-on-Trent

School name	Address	Tel	Fax	Headteacher	Ref	Ages	Pupils	Other
Aidenswood	214 Whitegate Dr, Blackpool, Lancashire FY3 9JL	01253 316160	01253 316511	Mr Bill Baker	861-6003	13-17	4	B R SEBD MLD

Telford and Wrekin

School name	Address	Tel	Fax	Headteacher	Ref	Ages	Pupils	Other
Acorn School	By Hollinswood, Medical Practice, Dale Acre Way Hollinswood, Telford TF3 2EN	01952 200410	01952 210048	Ms Sarah Morgan	894-6006	11–19	8	SEBD
Castle Homes Upper Forge	The Upper Forge, Dale Rd, Coalbrookdale, Telford, Shropshire TF8 7DT	01952 432660	01952 432873	Mr G. Southall	894-6005	12–17	5	R SEBD
Eastgate House	Castlecare Group, The Manor Hse, Squires Hill, Rothwell, Northants NN14 6BQ	01536 711111	01536 712994	Mr Wallace Robinson	894-6008	8–16	2	R SEBD
Jigsaw School	Hadley, Telford TF1 6AJ	01952 388555		Jacqueline Ann Cooper	894-6007	11–16	17	R SEBD SpLD
Overley Hall School	Wellington, Telford, Shropshire TF6 5HE	01952 740262	01952 740262	Gill Flannery	894-6003	10–16	21	R SLD

Warwickshire

School name	Address	Tel	Fax	Headteacher	Ref	Ages	Pupils	Other
The Old School	Church End, Ansley, Nuneaton, Warwickshire CV10 0QR	024 7639 4801	024 7639 6535	Mr Mike Ross	937-6092	11–16	26	SEBD
Valley House	Nuneaton Rd, Fillongley, Warwickshire CV7 8DL	01676 542875	01676 542597	Mr Chris Liddell	937-6105	12–17		R ASD MLD SLD ADHD
Wathen Grange School	Church Wlk, Royal Leamington Spa, Nr Atherstone, Warwickshire CV9 1PZ	01827 714454	01827 716509	Mr Chris Nock	937-6104	11–16	2	R SEBD

Worcestershire

School name	Address	Tel	Fax	Headteacher	Ref	Ages	Pupils	Other
New College Worcester	Whittington Rd, Worcester, Worcestershire WR5 2JX	01905 763933	01905 763277	Mr N.A. Ratcliffe	885-7019	11–19	83	R VI
Sunfield School	Clent Gr, Clent, Stourbridge, West Midlands DY9 9PB	01562 882253	01562 883856	Mrs L. Ross	885-6024	6–19	71	R SLD

Yorkshire and The Humber

Barnsley

School name	Address	Tel	Fax	Headteacher	Ref	Ages	Pupils	Other
Dove Adolecent Services	194 New Rd, Barnsley S75 6PP	01226 381380	01226 381380	Mrs Margaret Naylor	370-6005	9–16		SEBD
Grasmere School	12–14 Waterfield Pl, Stairfoot, Barnsley S70 3PZ	01226 282656	01226 282656	Ms R. Bhella	370-6003	8–16	11	SEBD
The Robert Ogden School	Clayton La, Thurnscoe, Rotherham, South Yorkshire S63 0BG	01709 874443	01709 870701	Mrs G. Roberts	370-6004	7–19	125	R ASD SLD

Bradford

School name	Address	Tel	Fax	Headteacher	Ref	Ages	Pupils	Other

Calderdale

School name	Address	Tel	Fax	Headteacher	Ref	Ages	Pupils	Other
Broadwood High School	252 Moor End Rd, Halifax, West Yorkshire HX2 0RU	01422 366202		Mr Andy Christie	381-6010	10–16	27	B SEBD
Elland House School	Unit 1, Ripponden Mill, Mill Fold, Ripponden, West Yorkshire HX6 4DH	01422 820510	01422 820642	Mr David Bailey	381-6013	11–16		SEBD

7

School name	Address	Tel	Fax	Headteacher	Ref	Ages	Pupils	Other
Norset House	West View, Boothtown, Halifax, West Yorkshire HX3 6PG	01422 329045	01422 329046	Mr Chris Nock	381-6011	12–16	6	SEBD
William Henry Smith School	Boothroyd, Brighouse, West Yorkshire HD6 3JW	01484 710123	01484 721658	Mr B.J. Heneghan	381-7005	8–16		B R SEBD SpLD

Doncaster

School name	Address	Tel	Fax	Headteacher	Ref	Ages	Pupils	Other
Doncaster School for the Deaf	Leger Way, Doncaster, South Yorkshire DN2 6AY	01302 386733	01302 361808	Mr David Gadd	371-7002	5–16		R HI
Fullerton House School (The Hesley Group)	Tickhill Sq, Denaby, Doncaster, South Yorkshire DN12 4AR	01709 861663	01709 869635	Mr D. Whitehead	371-6011	8–19	39	R ASD SLD
Wilsic Hall School (The Hesley Group)	Wadworth, Doncaster, South Yorkshire DN11 9AG	01302 856382	01302 853608	Mr M.V. Henderson	371-6005	11–19	29	R ASD SLD
York House	c/o Castlecare Group, The Manor Hse, Squires Hill, Rothwell, Northamptonshire NN14 6BQ	01536 711111	01536 712994	Ms Catherine Dalton	371-6013	11–17		R SEBD

East Riding of Yorkshire

School name	Address	Tel	Fax	Headteacher	Ref	Ages	Pupils	Other
New Haven	3 Wilton Rd, Hornsea, East Riding of Yorkshire HU18 1QU	01964 537407	01964 537319	Mr C. Nock	811-6010	11–17	5	B R SEBD
Prospect School	West Lambwath Rd, Withernwick, Hull, East Yorkshire HU11 4TP	01964 529300	01964 529300	Mrs Lynda Casey	811-6008	10–16	3	R
Sycamore House	365 Queens St, Withernsea, East Yorkshire HU19 2NT	01253 316160	01253 316511	Mr W. Baker	811-6011	11–17	3	B R SEBD

Kingston upon Hull

School name	Address	Tel	Fax	Headteacher	Ref	Ages	Pupils	Other
Farrow House	20 Priory Road Ind Est, Beverley, East Riding of Yorkshire HU17 0EW	01482 307830	01482 307832	Miss Sarah Pulford	810-6003	10–16	11	SEBD
Horton House School	Hill Top Farm, Sutton Rd, Warne, Hull, Kingston Upon Hull HU7 5YY	01482 820112	01482 820112	Mr David King	810-6004	8–16	18	R SEBD

Kirklees

School name	Address	Tel	Fax	Headteacher	Ref	Ages	Pupils	Other
Holly Bank School	Roe Head, Far Common Rd, Mirfield, West Yorkshire WF14 0DQ	01924 490833	01924 491464	Ms Pam L. King	382-7000	5–19		R CDPD MLD SLD PMLD
Rosedale c/o Central Office	c/o Central Office, 21–22 Queen's Sq, Leeds Rd, Huddersfield, West Yorkshire HD2 1XN	01484 452761	01484 452761	Mr J. Rudd	382-6024	11–18	2	R ASD SLD

Leeds

School name	Address	Tel	Fax	Headteacher	Ref	Ages	Pupils	Other
Meadowcroft School	Tingley Common, Morley, Leeds LS27 0HT	0113 307 5345	01274 587974	Mrs Susan Smith	383-6123	10–19	2	B R SEBD
St John's RC School for the Deaf	Church St, Boston Spa, Wetherby, West Yorkshire LS23 6DF	01937 842144	01937 541471	Mr T. Wrynne	383-7016	3–19		R HI

North Lincolnshire

School name	Address	Tel	Fax	Headteacher	Ref	Ages	Pupils	Other
Barton School	Barrow Rd, Barton upon Humber, North Lincolnshire DN18 6DA	01745 563258		Mr Mark Eames	813-6004	8–19	4	R
Demeter House	98–100 Oswald Rd, Scunthorpe, North Lincolnshire DN15 7PA	01724 277877		Dr R. Wardlaw	813-6005	7–14		SEBD

North Yorkshire

School name	Address	Tel	Fax	Headteacher	Ref	Ages	Pupils	Other
Breckenbrough School	Sand Hutton, Thirsk, North Yorkshire YO7 4EN	01845 587238	01845 587385	Mr T. Bennett	815-7002	9–17		B R SEBD
Farrow House Educational Centre	19 Alma Sq, Scarborough, North Yorkshire YO11 1JR	01723 350750	01723 350750	Mrs Jacqui Macauley	815-6036	8–17	10	SEBD
Learning to Listen	Hill Top Farm, Ilton, Masham, North Yorkshire HG4 4JY	01765 689368	01765 689368	Sarah Middleton	815-6038	13–19	5	SEBD
Spring Hill School (Barnardo's)	Palace Rd, Ripon, North Yorkshire HG4 3HN	01765 603320	01765 607549	Mrs Linda Nelson	815-7020	9–19		R SEBD MLD SLD

Sheffield

School name	Address	Tel	Fax	Headteacher	Ref	Ages	Pupils	Other
Emmaus School	Grove Rd, Totely Rise Methodist Church, Totely, Sheffield SK17 4DJ	0114 267 1065			373-6031	4–11		Ch
Paces High Green School for Conductive Education	Paces High Green Centre, Pack Horse La, High Grn, Sheffield, South Yorkshire S35 3HY	0114 284 5298	0114 284 4444	Mr Gabor Fellner	373-6029	1–18	20	PD MLD SLD

Wakefield

School name	Address	Tel	Fax	Headteacher	Ref	Ages	Pupils	Other
Denby Grange School	Off Stocksmoor Rd, Midgley, Wakefield, West Yorkshire WF4 4JQ	01924 830096	01924 830824	Miss Jennie Littleboy	384-6120	11–16	21	
Dove Adoloscent Services	170 Southgate, Pontefract, West Yorkshire WF8 1QJ	01226 381380		Mrs Margaret Naylor	384-6124	13–16		SEBD

Scotland

Aberdeen City

School name	Address	E-mail	Tel	Fax
Camphill Rudolf Steiner Schools	Murtle Hse, Bieldside, Aberdeen AB15 9EP	office@crss.org.uk	01224 867935	01224 868420
Linn Moor Residential School	Peterculter, Aberdeen AB14 0PJ	info@linnmoorschool.co.uk	01224 732246	01224 735261
Oakbank School	Midstocket Rd, Aberdeen AB15 5XP	audrey.anderson@oakbank.aberdeen.sch.uk	01224 313347	01224 312017

Angus

School name	Address	E-mail	Tel	Fax
Rossie Secure Accommodation Services	Montrose, Angus DD10 9TW		01674 820204	01674 820249

Clackmannanshire

School name	Address	E-mail	Tel	Fax
Struan House School	27 Claremont, Alloa, Clackmannanshire FK10 2DF	taylor@autism-n-scotland.org.uk	01259 213435	01259 211851

Dumfries and Galloway

School name	Address	E-mail	Tel	Fax
Closeburn Centre	Closeburn, Dumfries DG3 5HP	closeburncentre@btconnect.com	01848 331352	01848 331594
Life Gateway	Kirkgunzeon Mill, Kirkgunzeon, Dumfries DG2 8LA	catha@appliedcare.co.uk	01387 760292	01387 760591

7

School name	Address	Tel	Fax	E-mail
Maben House	Gilmour Banks – Parkfoot, Lochmaben, Dumfries DG11 1RW	01387 871995	01387 331594	mabenhouse@btconnect.com
Mill Hill School	45 High St, Lockerbie DG11 2JL	01576 204777	01576 204422	carol.long@carevisions.co.uk

Dundee City

School name	Address	Tel	Fax	E-mail
Parkview School	309 Blackness Rd, Dundee DD2 1SH	01382 667903	01382 669914	genoffice@parkviewschool.co.uk

East Ayrshire

School name	Address	Tel	Fax	E-mail
Daldorch House School	Sorn Rd, Catrine, East Ayrshire KA5 6NA	01290 551666	01290 553399	daldorch@nas.org.uk

Edinburgh City

School name	Address	Tel	Fax	E-mail
Blackford Brae Project (Barnardo's)	91 South Oswald Rd, Edinburgh EH9 2HH	0131 662 4997	0131 668 3280	blackford.brae@barnardos.org.uk
Donaldson's College	West Coates, Edinburgh EH12 5JJ	0131 337 9911	0131 3371654	admin@donaldsons-coll.edin.sch.uk
Dunedin School	Millar Hall, 5 Gilmerton Rd, Edinburgh EH16 5TY	0131 664 1328		staff@dunedin.edin.sch.uk
Harmeny Education Trust	Mansfield Rd, Balerno, Midlothian EH14 7JY	0131 449 3938	0131 449 7121	school@harmeny.org.uk
Royal Blind School	Craigmillar Pk, Edinburgh EH16 5NA	0131 667 1100	0131 229 4060	office@royalblindschool.org.uk
Westerlea Special Education Unit	11 Ellersley Rd, Edinburgh EH12 6HY	0131 337 1236	0131 346 4412	westerlea.school@capability-scotland.org.uk

Falkirk

School name	Address	Tel	Fax	E-mail
Lecropt School (Barnardo's)	108 Glasgow Rd, Camelon, Falkirk FK1 4HS	01324 621304	01324 629682	hugh.jones@barnardos.org.uk

Fife

School name	Address	Tel	Fax	E-mail
Falkland House School	Falkland Est, Falkland KY15 7AE	01337 857268	01337 857778	fhs@supanet.com
Hillside School	Hillside, Aberdour, Fife KY3 0RH	01383 860731	01383 860929	marr_p@hillsideschool.co.uk
Starley Hall School	Aberdour Rd, Burntisland KY3 0AG	01383 860314	01383 860956	info@starleyhallschool.co.uk
Sycamore School	6 Bellyeoman Rd, Dunfermline, Fife KY1 3HD	01592 591500	01592 591500	

Glasgow City

School name	Address	Tel	Fax	E-mail
East Park School	1092 Maryhill Rd, Glasgow G20 9TD	0141 946 8315	0141 946 2838	enquiries@eastpark.org.uk
St Francis Day Boy Unit	1190 Edinburgh Rd, Shettleston, Glasgow G33 4EH	0141 774 4499	0141 774 4613	headteacher@st-francisday.glasgow.sch.uk
St Mary's Kenmure	St Mary's Rd, Bishopbriggs, Glasgow G64 3EH	0141 586 1200	0141 586 1200	administrator@stmaryskenmure.org.uk
Springboig St John's	1190 Edinburgh Rd, Glasgow G33 4EH	0141 774 9791	0141 774 4613	headteacher@springboig-st-johns.glasgow.sch.uk

North Ayrshire

School name	Address	Tel	Fax	E-mail
Geilsland School	Geilsland Rd, Beith, Ayrshire KA15 1HD	01505 504044	01505 502635	admin@geilsland.bosr.org.uk
Seafield School	86 Eglinton Rd, Ardrossan KA22 8NL	01294 470355	01294 470355	seafieldschool@totalise.co.uk

North Lanarkshire

School name	Address	Tel	Fax	E-mail
The Craighalbert Centre	1 Craighalbert Way, Cumbernauld, North Lanarkshire G68 0LS	01236 456100	01236 736889	
St Francis Unit	Beechwood Hse, Plains, by Airdrie ML6 7SF	01236 750888	01236 755637	
St Philip's School	Beechwood, Plains, by Airdrie ML6 7SF	01236 765407	01236 755637	paddy.hanrahan@cora.org.uk

Perth and Kinross

School name	Address	Tel	Fax	E-mail
Balnacraig School	Fairmount Terr, Perth PH2 7AR	01738 636456	01738 441863	admin@balnacraig.net
The New School Butterstone	Butterstone, Dunkeld, Perthshire PH8 0HJ	01350 724216	01350 724283	info@thenewschool.co.uk
Ochil Tower School	140 High St, Auchterarder, Perthshire PH3 1AD	01764 662416	01786 662416	office@ochiltowerschool.org.uk
Seamab School	Rumbling Bridge, Kinross KY13 0PT	01577 840307	01577 840107	anne@seamab.org.uk

Renfrewshire

School name	Address	Tel	Fax	E-mail
Coresford Residential School	Howwood Rd, Kilbarchan, Renfrewshire PA10 2NT	01505 702141	01505 702445	coresford.school@capability-scotland.org.uk
Good Shepherd Centre	Greenock Rd, Bishopton, Renfrewshire PA7 5PF	01505 862814	01505 864167	goodshepc@aol.com
Kibble Education and Care Centre	Goudie St, Paisley PA3 2LG	0141 889 0044	0141 887 6694	mailbox@kibble.org
Northview House	11 North Rd, Johnstone PA5 8NE	01505 336690		paullennon@northviewhouse.com
St Francis Day Unit	Cora Campus, Bishopton PA7 5PF	01505 862899		

South Lanarkshire

School name	Address	Tel	Fax	E-mail
Stanmore House School	Lanark ML11 7RR	01555 665480	01555 665480	stanmore.school@capability-scotland.org.uk

Stirling

School name	Address	Tel	Fax	E-mail
Ballikinrain Residential School	Fintry Rd, Balfron, Renfrewshire G63 0LL	01360 440244	01360 440946	cmcnaught.cos@uk.uumail.com
Snowdon School	31 Spittal St, Stirling FK8 1DU	01786 473449	01786 470383	snowdonschool@aol.com

West Lothian

School name	Address	Tel	Fax	E-mail
Moore House School	21 Edinburgh Rd, Bathgate, West Lothian EH48 1EX	01506 652312	01506 635306	mail@moorehouseschool.com

7

Wales

Cardiff

School name	Address	Tel	Ref
Craig Y Parc School – A Scope School	Heol y Parc, Cardiff CF4 8NB	02920 890397	681-6087

Gwynedd

School name	Address	Tel	Ref
Bryn Melyn for Young People	Llandderfel, Bala, Gwynedd LL23 7RA	01678 530330	

Powys

School name	Address	Tel	Ref
Tregynon Hall School	Tregynon, Newtown, Powys SY16 3PG	01686 650330	666-6009

Vale of Glamorgan

School name	Address	Tel	Ref
Headlands School	2 St Augustines Rd, Penarth, CF64 1YY	02920 709771	673-6025

Wrexham

School name	Address	Tel	Ref
Prospects Centre For Young People	Bersham Rd, Bersham, Wrexham LL14 4HS		665-6039

Special Further Education Colleges

East of England

Bedfordshire

School name	Address	Tel	Fax	Headteacher	Ref	Ages	Pupils	Other
Hinwick Hall Further Education College	Hinwick, Wellingborough, Northamptonshire NN29 7JD				820-7904	16+		

Peterborough

School name	Address	Tel	Fax	Headteacher	Ref	Ages	Pupils	Other
SENSE East	72 Church St, Market Deeping, Peterborough PE6 8AL	01778 382230	01778 380078	Mr Roger Gale	874-7904	16+		SEBD

East Midlands

Derbyshire

School name	Address	Tel	Fax	Headteacher	Ref	Ages	Pupils	Other
Landmarks	Upper Mill Farm, Creswell, Worksop S80 4HP	01909 724724	01909 724725	Mr Victor Hartwell	830-7904	16+		MLD SEBD

Leicestershire

School name	Address	Tel	Fax	Headteacher	Ref	Ages	Pupils	Other
Homefield College	42 St Mary's Rd, Sileby LE12 7TL	01509 815696	01509 815696	Chris Berry	855-7904	16-25		AS MLD SEBD
RNIB Vocational College Loughborough	Radmoor Rd, Loughborough LE11 3BS	01509 611077	01509 232013	Mr Tony Warren	855-7905	16+		

Nottinghamshire

School name	Address	Tel	Fax	Headteacher	Ref	Ages	Pupils	Other
Portland College	Nottingham Rd, Mansfield, Nottinghamshire NG18 4TJ	01623 499111	01623 499134	Mr Mike Syms	891-7904	16+		MLD
Whitegates College	Dukeries Centre, Worksop S80 1HH	01909 509400	01909 488204	Ms Karen Bulmer	891-7905	16-25		ASD

7

London

Barnet

School name	Address	Tel	Fax	Headteacher	Ref	Ages	Pupils	Other
Kisharon College	54 Parson St, Hendon, London NW4 1TP	020 8457 2525	020 8457 2535	Ms Yitzchak Freeman	302-7904	16+		Je AS MLD

Bromley

School name	Address	Tel	Fax	Headteacher	Ref	Ages	Pupils	Other
Nash College of Further Education Centre	Croydon Rd, Hayes, Bromley BR2 7AG	020 8315 4800	020 8315 0347	Mr Andrew Giles	305-7904	16–25		MLD

Ealing

School name	Address	Tel	Fax	Headteacher	Ref	Ages	Pupils	Other
Leap Service – The National Autistics Society	Woodlands Bldg, Mill Hill Rd, Acton W3 8RR	020 8992 6611	020 8992 6644	Mr Sadat Aslam	307-7904	16+		AS ASD

Hillingdon

School name	Address	Tel	Fax	Headteacher	Ref	Ages	Pupils	Other
West Middlesex College	Colne Lodge, Longbridge Way, Uxbridge UB8 2YG	01895 619700	01895 619711	Ms Alison White	312-7904	18+		AS ASD

Sutton

School name	Address	Tel	Fax	Headteacher	Ref	Ages	Pupils	Other
Orchard Hill College	Old Town Hall, Woodcote Rd, Wallington, Surrey SM6 0NB	020 8254 7820	020 8254 9800	Ms Caroline Allen	319-7904	16+		MLD

North East

Newcastle upon Tyne

School name	Address	Tel	Fax	Headteacher	Ref	Ages	Pupils	Other
Northern Countries College	Gt North Rd, Jesmond, Newcastle NE2 3BB	0191 281 5821		Ms Angela Gilbert	391-7904	16–25		MLD

Northumberland

School name	Address	Tel	Fax	Headteacher	Ref	Ages	Pupils	Other
Dilston College of Further Education	Dilston Hall, Corbridge NE45 5RJ	01434 632692	01434 633721	Mr John Jameson	929-7904	16–25		MLD

Sunderland

School name	Address	Tel	Fax	Headteacher	Ref	Ages	Pupils	Other
European Services for People with Autism (ESPA) Limited	6–7 The Cloisters, Sunderland SR2 7BD	0191 565 9800	0191 565 9271	Mr Stephen Levy	394-7904	16–25		AS ASD
Tyne and Wear Autistic Society Adult Services	14 Thornhill Pk, Sunderland SR2 7LA	0191 510 2038	0191 567 2902	Mr Allan Tutty	394-7905	16+		AS ASD

North West

Cheshire

School name	Address	Tel	Fax	Headteacher	Ref	Ages	Pupils	Other
David Lewis College	Mill La, Warford, Nr Alderley Edge, Cheshire SK9 7UD	01565 640160	01565 640260	Ms Angela Heppenstall	875-7904	16–25		R

Cumbria

School name	Address	Tel	Fax	Headteacher	Ref	Ages	Pupils	Other
Beaumont College – A Scope College	Slyne Rd, Lancaster LA2 6AP	01524 541400	01524 846896	Mr Graham Pyle	909-7904	16–25		
Lindeth Collgege of Further Education	The Oaks, Bowness on Windermere LA23 3NH	01539 446265	01539 488840	Ms Nicky Buckley	909-7905	16–25		MLD

Oldham

School name	Address	Tel	Fax	Headteacher	Ref	Ages	Pupils	Other
Belford College Limited	Grange Ave, Werneth, Oldham OL8 4EL	0161 626 9905	0161 626 9906	Ms Sally Harte	353-7904	16+		MLD SEBD

Salford

School name	Address	Tel	Fax	Headteacher	Ref	Ages	Pupils	Other
Langdon College	9 Leicester Ave, Salford, Manchester M7 4HA	0161 740 5900	0161 741 2500	Mr Arthur O'Brien	355-7904	16+		MLD

Stockport

School name	Address	Tel	Fax	Headteacher	Ref	Ages	Pupils	Other
Bridge College – The Together Trust	Curzon Rd, Offerton, Stockport, Cheshire SK2 5DG	0161 487 4293	0161 487 4294	Ms Maggie Thompson	356-8605	19–23	75	PD

South East

Brighton and Hove

School name	Address	Tel	Fax	Headteacher	Ref	Ages	Pupils	Other
St John's College	Walpole Rd, Brighton BN2 0AF	01273 244000	01273 244038	Ms Coral Romain	846-7904	16–22		MLD

7

East Sussex

School name	Address	Tel	Fax	Headteacher	Ref	Ages	Pupils	Other
Mount Camphill Community	Faircrouch La, Wadhurst TN5 6PT	01892 782025	01892 782917	Ms Gillian Brand	845-7904	16+		AS ASD MLD SEBD

Hampshire

School name	Address	Tel	Fax	Headteacher	Ref	Ages	Pupils	Other
Minstead Training Project	Minstead Lodge, Nr Lyndhurst, Hampshire SO43 7FT	023 8081 2254	023 8081 2297	Mr Martin Lenaerts	850-7904	16+		MLD
Wing Centre (part of Cambian Education)	Vicars Hill, Lymington, Hampshire SO41 5QB	0800 288 9779	020 7348 5223	Ms Angela Nightingale	850-7905	16–19	29	AS

Kent

School name	Address	Tel	Fax	Headteacher	Ref	Ages	Pupils	Other
Dorton College	Seal Dr, Seal, Nr Sevenoaks TN15 0AH	01732 592600	01732 592601	Mr Graham Williams	886-7905	16–25		
Westgate College at Westcliff House	37 Sea Rd, Westbrook, Westgate on Sea CT8 8QP	01843 836300	01843 830001	Mr Chris Owen	886-7904	16+		

Surrey

School name	Address	Tel	Fax	Headteacher	Ref	Ages	Pupils	Other
The National Centre for Young People with Epilepsy, St Piers FE College	St Piers La, Lingfield, Surrey RH7 6PW	01342 832243	01342 834639	Ms Amanda Quincey	936-7005	16–25	99	R, D ADHD AS ASD CD Ep HI MLD PD PMLD SEBD SLD VI
Orpheus Centre	North Park La, Godstone, Surrey RH9 8ND	01883 744664	01883 744994	Ms Megan Johnson	936-7904	18–25		MLD
Queen Elizabeth's Foundation Brain Injury Centre	Banstead Pl, Banstead, Surrey SM7 3EE	01737 356222	01737 359467	Ms Eileen Jackman	936-7905	16–35		
RNIB Redhill College	Philanthropic Rd, Redhill, Surrey RH1 4DG	01737 768935	01737 778776	Ms Tracey De Bernhardt Dunkin	936-7906	16+		

South West

Devon

School name	Address	Tel	Fax	Headteacher	Ref	Ages	Pupils	Other
Education and Care	Oak Park Rd, Dawlish EX7 0DE	01626 864066	01626 866770	Mr Frank Loft	878-7904	16–25		AS MLD SEBD
Oakwood Court College	Oak Park Villas, Dawlish, Devon EX7 0DE	01626 864066	01626 864066	Ms Jeana Butler	878-7905	16–25		MLD SEBD
Royal West of England School for the Deaf	Countess Wear, Exeter, Devon EX2 6HA	01392 454218	01392 430517	Mr Richard Ellis	878-7906	16+		MLD
West of England College	Countess Wear, Exeter, Devon EX2 6HA	01392 454218	01392 430517	Mr Richard Ellis	878-7907	16+		

Dorset

School name	Address	Tel	Fax	Headteacher	Ref	Ages	Pupils	Other
Fortune Centre of Riding Therapy	Bransgore, Avon Tyrrell BH23 8EE	01425 693297	01425 674320	Ms Jennifer Dixon-Clegg	835-7904	16–25		MLD SEBD
Ivers College	Hains La, Marnhull, Sturminster Newton DT10 1JU	01258 820164	01258 820258	Ms Linda Matthews	835-7905	18+		MLD SEBD

Gloucestershire

School name	Address	Tel	Fax	Headteacher	Ref	Ages	Pupils	Other
National Star College	Ullenwood, Cheltenham GL53 9QU	01242 527631	01242 222234	Ms Helen Sexton	916-7904	16+		
William Morris (Camphill) Community	William Morris Hse, Stonehouse GL10 3SH	01453 824025	01453 825807	Ms Suzanne Pickering	916-7905	16+		MLD

Somerset

School name	Address	Tel	Fax	Headteacher	Ref	Ages	Pupils	Other
Fairfield Opportunity Farm	Dilton Marsh, Westbury BA13 4DL	01373 823028	01373 859032	Ms Janet Kenward	933-7904	16–25		MLD
Farleigh Further Education College – Frome	North Par, Frome BA11 2AB	01373 475470	01373 475473	Mr Andrew Chiffers	933-7905	16+		AS MLD
Foxes Academy	The Esplanade, Minehead TA24 5QP	01643 704450	01643 708249	Ms Lorraine Atkins	933-7906	18–25		MLD
Lufton College of Further Education	Lufton, Yeovil BA22 8ST	01935 403120	01935 403126	Ms Tess Baber	933-7907	18+		MLD

Wiltshire

School name	Address	Tel	Fax	Headteacher	Ref	Ages	Pupils	Other
Farleigh Further Education College – Swindon	105 Bath St, Old Town, Swindon SN1 4AX	01793 484031		Mr Jonathan Hammond	865-7904	16–22		AS

West Midlands

Birmingham

School name	Address	Tel	Fax	Headteacher	Ref	Ages	Pupils	Other
Queen Alexandra College	49 Court Oak Rd, Harborne, Birmingham B17 9TG	0121 428 5050	0121 428 5048	Mr Alex Mellon	330-7904	16–63		

Dudley

School name	Address	Tel	Fax	Headteacher	Ref	Ages	Pupils	Other
Glasshouse College	Wollaston Rd, Amblecote, Stourbridge, West Midlands DY8 4HF	01384 399400	01384 399401	Mr Tim Christenson	332-7904	16+		AS MLD SEBD

Herefordshire

School name	Address	Tel	Fax	Headteacher	Ref	Ages	Pupils	Other
Royal National College for the Blind	College Rd, Hereford, Herefordshire HR1 1EB	01432 765725		Ms Roisin Burge	884-7905	16+		
St Elizabeth's College	South End, Much Hadham, Herefordshire SG10 6EW	01279 844423	01279 842981	Mr Frank Boyle	884-7904	16–19		

7

Shropshire

School name	Address	Tel	Fax	Headteacher	Ref	Ages	Pupils	Other
Condover College Limited	Condover Hse, Shropshire SY5 7AH	01743 871076	01743 874815	Ms Pauline Carmichael	893-7904	18-24		
Derwen College	Whittington Rd, Oswestry SY11 3JA	01691 661234	01691 670714		893-7906	16-25		R
Loppington House	Loppington, Shropshire SY4 5NF	01939 233926	01939 235255	Mr Paul Harris	893-7905	18+		AS ASD

Stoke-on-Trent

School name	Address	Tel	Fax	Headteacher	Ref	Ages	Pupils	Other
Regent College	77 Shelton New Rd, Stoke on Trent ST4 7AA	01782 263326	01782 209800	Ms Wendy Williams	861-7904	16-25		SEBD
Strathmore College	107 Trentham Rd, Stoke on Trent ST3 4EG	01782 333366	01782 333366	Ms Kathleen Smith	861-7905	16+		MLD

Yorkshire and The Humber

Doncaster

School name	Address	Tel	Fax	Headteacher	Ref	Ages	Pupils	Other
Doncaster College for the Deaf	Leger Way, Doncaster DN2 6AY		01302 361808	Mr Alan Robinson	371-7904	16-63		
Hesley Village and College (The Hesley Group)	Hesley Hall, Stripe Rd, Tickhill, Doncaster, South Yorkshire DN11 9HH	01302 866906	01302 865473	Mrs S.P. Ekins		16+	67	R AS ASD SLD

North East Lincolnshire

School name	Address	Tel	Fax	Headteacher	Ref	Ages	Pupils	Other
Linkage Colege	The Vine Hse, The Sleight Centre, Grimsby DN32 9RU	01472 372400	01472 242375	Mr Hugh Williams	812-7904	16-25		AS

North Lincolnshire

School name	Address	Tel	Fax	Headteacher	Ref	Ages	Pupils	Other
AALPS College	Winterton Rd, Roxby, Scunthorpe DN15 0BJ	01724 733777	01724 733666	Ms Pat Clendining	813-7904	16-30		AS ASD
Broughton House College (part of Cambian Education)	Brant Broughton, Lincolnshire LN5 0SL	0800 288 9779	020 7348 5223	Mr Keith Salmon	813-7905	16-30	29	AS ASD SEBD

Sheffield

School name	Address	Tel	Fax	Headteacher	Ref	Ages	Pupils	Other
Freeman College, RMET	27 Leadmill Rd, Ruskin Mill Educational Trust, Sheffield, South Yorkshire S1 3JA	0114 213 0290	0114 213 0299		373-7904	16+		AS MLD

Wakefield

School name	Address	Tel	Fax	Headteacher	Ref	Ages	Pupils	Other
Penine Camphill Community	Boyne Hall, Chapelthorpe, Wakefield WF4 3JH	01924 255281	01924 240257	Mr Steve Hopewell	384-7904	16+		MLD

Wales

Carmarthenshire

School name	Address	Tel	Fax	Ref
Coleg Elidyr	Rhandirmwyn, Carmarthenshire SA20 0NL	01550 760400	01550 760331	669-7904

Denbighshire

School name	Address	Tel	Fax	Ref
Pengwern College	Sarn La, Rhuddlan, Denbighshire LL18 5UH	01745 592300		663-7904

Vale of Glamorgan

School name	Address	Tel	Fax	Ref
Beechwood College	Hayes Rd, Sully, Penarth, Vale of Glamorgan CF64 5SE	02920 532210	02920 531774	673-7904

7

Special Needs Organisations

8

Communication Impairment

Visual Impairment

Physical and Learning Disabilities

Special Educational Needs

Special Needs Organisations

Communication Impairment

AFASIC

50–52 Gt Sutton St, London EC1V 0DJ;
URL www.afasic.org.uk; e-mail info@afasic.org.uk;
Tel (helpline) 0845 355 5577; Tel 020 7490 9410;
Fax 020 7251 2834

British Association of Teachers of the Deaf

175 Dashwood Ave, High Wycombe, Buckinghamshire
HP12 3DB; URL www.batod.org.uk; e-mail
secretary@batod.org.uk; Tel 01494 464190;
Fax 01494 464190

National Secretary   Paul Simpson

British Deaf Association (BDA)

1–3 Worship St, London EC2A 2AB; URL www.bda.org.uk;
e-mail helpline@bda.org.uk; Tel 020 7588 3520;
Tel (charged at national rate) 0870 770 3300;
Fax 020 7588 3527; Textphone 0800 652 2965

Chief Executive   Jeff McWhinney

British Stammering Association

15 Old Ford Rd, Bethnal Green, London E2 9PJ;
URL www.stammering.org; e-mail
info@stammering.org; Tel (Scotland helpline)
0845 330 3800; Tel (UK helpline Mon–Thurs 1000–1600)
0845 603 2001; Tel 020 8983 1003; Fax 020 8983 3591

Chief Executive   Norbert Lieckfeldt

CACDP

Durham University Science Pk, Block 4, Stockton Rd,
Durham, County Durham DH1 3UZ;
URL www.cacdp.org.uk; e-mail durham@cacdp.org.uk;
Tel 0191 383 1155; Fax 0191 383 7914;
Answerphone 0191 383 7915

Chief Executive   Jim Edwards

Cued Speech Association UK

9 Jawbone Hill, Dartmouth, Devon TQ6 9RW;
URL www.cuedspeech.co.uk; e-mail
info@cuedspeech.co.uk; Tel 01803 832784;
Fax 01803 835311

Deafblind UK

National Centre for Deafblindness, John and Lucille van
Geest Pl, Cygnet Rd, Hampton, Peterborough
Cambridgeshire, PE7 8FD; e-mail info@deafblind.org.uk;
Tel 01733 358100; Fax 01733 358100

One to one support for deafblind people includes
communicator guides, housing support workers, home care,
interpreters; registered with CSCI. Volunteers, membership
and 24 hour helpline available.

deafPLUS

National Office, 1st Fl, Trinity Centre, Key Cl, Whitechapel,
London E1 4HG; URL www.deafplus.org; e-mail
paul.bartlett@deafplus.org; Tel 020 7790 6147;
Fax 020 7790 6147; Textphone 020 7790 5999

Chief Executive   Paul Bartlett

Hearing Concern

Registered Charity Number 1094497
95 Gray's Inn Rd, London WC1X 8TX;
URL www.hearingconcern.org.uk; e-mail
info@hearingconcern.org.uk; Tel (helpdesk: voice and
text) 0845 074 4600; Fax 020 7440 9872

Chief Executive   Damian Barry

I CAN

8 Wakley St, London EC1V 7QE; URL www.ican.org.uk;
www.talkingpoint.org.uk; e-mail info@ican.org.uk;
Tel 0845 225 4073; Fax 0845 225 4072

I CAN is the children's communication charity. I CAN
works to develop speech, language and communication
skills for all children, with a particular focus on children
who find communication difficult. I CAN provides a
combination of specialist therapy and education for children
with severe and complex disabilities, information for
parents, and training and advice for teachers and other
professionals. It also works to ensure that the needs of these
children are taken into account in all children's policy.

National Association for Tertiary Education for Deaf People (NATED)

The Flash Ley Centre, Hawksmoor Rd, Stafford ST17 9DR;
e-mail nated@btopenworld.com

Secretary   Mandy Tucker

Aims to promote education and training opportunities for
deaf and hard of hearing students and trainees across the
tertiary sector

National Deaf Children's Society

15 Dufferin St, London EC1Y 8UR; URL www.ndcs.org.uk;
e-mail helpline@ndcs.org.uk; Tel (freephone helpline:
voice and textphone Mon–Fri 1000–1700) 0808 800 8880;
Fax 020 7251 5020

Paget Gorman Society (Paget Gorman Signed Speech)

2 Dowlands Bungalows, Dowlands La, Smallfield, Surrey
RH6 9SD; URL www.pgss.org; e-mail
prup@compuserve.com ; Tel 01342 842308

Chief Examiner   Mrs P.R. Philips

Royal Association for Deaf People (RAD)

18 Westside Centre, London Rd, Colchester, Essex
CO3 8PH; URL www.royaldeaf.org.uk; e-mail
info@royaldeaf.org.uk; Tel 0845 668 2525;
Fax 0845 668 2526; Minicom 0845 668 2527

Chief Executive   Tom Fenton

8

RAD promotes the welfare and interests of deaf people, working with the deaf community, deaf clubs, deaf individuals and the parents of deaf children. Most of RAD's work is in London, Essex and the South East. RAD provides the following services: deaf community development, advice and advocacy, learning disability, mental health, sign language interpreting and training.

Sense, The National Deafblind and Rubella Association

11–13 Clifton Terr, Finsbury Pk, London N4 3SR; URL www.sense.org.uk; e-mail info@sense.org.uk; Tel 020 7272 7774; Fax 020 7272 6012
Chief Executive   Dr Tony Best

Young Sound Vision

Educational Service for Sensory Impairment, 17 Greek St, Stockport, Greater Manchester SK3 8AB; e-mail headteacher.essi@stockport.gov.uk; Tel 0161 474 3906; Fax 0161 474 3906
Chair   Angela Fawley

Visual Impairment

British Retinitis Pigmentosa Society (BRPS)

Registered Charity Number 271729
PO Box 350, Buckingham, Buckinghamshire MK18 1GZ; URL www.brps.org.uk; e-mail info@brps.org.uk; Tel (helpline) 0845 123 2354; Tel 01280 821334; Fax 01280 815900
Hon President; Trustee   Lynda Cantor MBE
Membership annual subscription £15, quarterly newsletter available in large print, braille, on tape, or by email. Publications list available.

British Wireless for the Blind Fund

Gabriel Hse, 34 New Rd, Chatham, Kent ME4 4QR; URL www.blind.org.uk; e-mail info@blind.org.uk; Tel 01634 832501; Fax 01634 817485
Chief Executive   Mrs M.R. Grainger

CALIBRE Audio Library

Registered Charity Number 286614
Aylesbury, Buckinghamshire HP22 5XQ; URL www.calibre.org.uk; e-mail enquiries@calibre.org.uk; Tel 01296 432339; Fax 01296 392599
Director   M. Lewington
Calibre provides a free postal library of recorded books for people of all ages who have sight problems or other disabilities. The books are recorded on standard cassettes or MP3 discs which can be played back on a commercially available listening device. All books are unabridged and there are 7000 titles to choose from (1200 for children).

English National Association of Visually Handicapped Bowlers

Registered Charity Number 273134
6 Sherburn Gr, Birkenshaw, West Yorkshire BD11 2JH; URL www.englishblindbowls.co.uk; e-mail newcombe1@btopenworld.com
Chair   John Newcombe MBE

The Guide Dogs for the Blind Association

Registered Charity Number 209617
Hillfields, Burghfield Common, Reading RG7 3YG; URL www.guidedogs.org.uk; e-mail guidedogs@guidedogs.org.uk; Tel 0118 983 5555; Fax 0118 983 5433

International Glaucoma Association (IGA)

Registered Charity Number 274681
Woodcote Hse, 15 Highpoint Business Village, Henwood, Ashford, Kent TN24 8DH; URL www.glaucoma-association.com; e-mail info@iga.org.uk; Tel (Sightline) 01233 648170; Fax 01233 648179
Patient Support Secretary   Valerie Greatorex

National Federation of the Blind of the United Kingdom

Registered Charity Number 236629
Sir John Wilson Hse, 215 Kirkgate, Wakefield, West Yorkshire WF1 1JG; URL www.nfbuk.org; e-mail nfbuk@nfbuk.org; Tel 01924 291313; Fax 01924 200244
President   Peter Westwood

RNIB National Library Service

Far Cromwell Rd, Bredbury, Stockport, Greater Manchester SK6 2SG; URL www.rnib.org.uk/reading; e-mail cservices@rnib.org.uk; Tel 0845 762 6843; Fax 0161 355 2098
Head of Service   Helen Brazier
It provides a library service with more than 45 000 titles in braille, giant print and unabridged audio, and free access to online reference material. It also provides braille sheet music, themed book lists and a quarterly reader magazine.

Partially Sighted Society

PO Box 322, Doncaster, South Yorkshire DN1 2XA; e-mail info@partsight.org.uk; Tel 01302 323132; Fax 01302 368998
General Secretary   Norman Stenson

Royal National Institute of the Blind (RNIB)

Registered Charity Number 226227
105 Judd St, London WC1H 9NE; URL www.rnib.org.uk; e-mail helpline@rnib.org.uk; Tel (RNIB helpline) 0845 766 9999; Fax 020 7388 2034
Chief Executive   Lesley-Anne Alexander
Director (Education and Employment)   E. Fetton
RNIB advises on benefits, mobility, staying independent, housing, employment, education, leisure, accessible information and eye health. It offers a wide range of services to people of all ages cross the UK, including Talking Books, schools, colleges, rehabilitation training, products for the home and information in large print, braille and on tape.

Visual Impairment Centre for Teaching and Research

University of Birmingham, School of Education, Edgbaston, Birmingham, West Midlands B15 2TT; URL www.education.bham.ac.uk/research/victar; e-mail victar-enquiries@bham.ac.uk; Tel 0121 414 6733; Fax 0121 414 4865

Physical and Learning Disabilities

AbilityNet

PO Box 94, Warwick, Warwickshire CV34 5WS; URL www.abilitynet.org.uk; e-mail enquiries@abilitynet.org.uk; Tel (freephone advice line) 0800 269545; Tel 01926 312847; Fax 01926 407425
AbilityNet is a national charity, providing advice on computing and disability. It helps people with a wide range of disabling or limiting conditions to access computer technology. It provides a freephone advice and information line, individual assessments, awareness training and courses for professionals.

Acting Up

Registered Charity Number 281428
Unit 304, Mare St Studios, 203–213 Mare St, London E8 3QE;
    URL www.acting-up.org.uk; e-mail
    info@acting-up.org.uk; Tel 020 8533 3344
Director   John Ladle
A Matchbox Theatre Trust project

Advocacy Resource Exchange

Registered Charity Number 1035082
162 Lee Valley Technopark, Ashley Rd, London N17 9LN;
    URL www.advocacyresource.net; e-mail
    cait@citizenadvocacy.co.uk; Tel 020 8880 4545;
    Fax 020 8880 4113
Director   Sally Carr
Aims to promote the development of independent advocacy
in the UK and provides information and networking on a
national basis

Association of Disabled Professionals

BCM ADP, London WC1N 3XX; URL www.adp.org.uk;
    e-mail adp.admin@ntlworld.com; Tel 01204 431638;
    Fax 01204 431638
Chair   Jane Hunt

Association for Spina Bifida and Hydrocephalus (ASBAH)

ASBAH Hse, 42 Park Rd, Peterborough, Cambridgeshire
    PE1 2UQ; URL www.asbah.org; e-mail info@asbah.org;
    Tel 01733 555988
Executive Director   A. Russell

British Institute of Learning Disabilities

Campion Hse, Green St, Kidderminster, Worcestershire
    DY10 1JL; URL www.bild.org.uk; e-mail
    enquiries@bild.org.uk; Tel 01562 723010;
    Fax 01562 723029
Chief Executive   Mr K. Smith
Finance and Administration Officer   A. Massey
Information Officer   J. Edwards
Information Assistant   Kate Brackley

British Society for Music Therapy

Registered Charity Number 260837
61 Church Hill Rd, East Barnet, Hertfordshire EN4 8SY;
    URL www.bsmt.org ; e-mail info@bsmt.org;
    Tel 020 8441 6226; Fax 020 8441 4118
Chair   Dr Wendy Magee

Capability Scotland

11 Ellersly Rd, Edinburgh EH12 6HY;
    URL www.capability-scotland.org.uk; e-mail
    capability@capability-scotland.org.uk; Tel 0131 337 9876;
    Fax 0131 346 7864
Chief Executive   A.D.J. Dickson

Dovetail Enterprises

Dunsinane Ave, Dundee DD2 3QN;
    URL www.dovetailenterprises.co.uk; e-mail
    sales@dovetailenterprises.co.uk; Tel 01382 833890;
    Fax 01382 814816
Manager (Sales)   Jim Pearce

Employment Opportunities

Registered Charity Number 280112
53 New Broad St, London EC2M 1SL;
    URL www.opportunities.org.uk; e-mail info@eopps.org;
    Tel 020 7448 5420; Fax 020 7374 4913;
    Textphone 020 7374 6684

Employment opportunities is a national charity dedicated to
creating routes into employment for people with all
disabilities and health conditions

Foundation for Assistive Technology (FAST)

12 City Forum, 250 City Rd, London EC1V 8AF;
    URL www.fastuk.org; e-mail info@fastuk.org;
    Tel 020 7253 3303
Director   Keren Down
FAST works with the assistive technology (AT) community
to support innovation in AT product development and good
practice in AT service provision. FAST provides an online
database of UK research projects, organisations, events,
training and jobs. It is the secretariat for the AT Forum, a
coalition of organisations representing AT stakeholders.

IMPACT Foundation

151 Western Rd, Haywards Heath, West Sussex RH16 3LH;
    URL www.impact.org.uk; e-mail impact@impact.org.uk;
    Tel 01444 457080; Fax 01444 457877
Chief Executive   Claire Hicks

Kith and Kids

c/o the Irish Centre, Pretoria Rd, London N17 8DX;
    URL www.kithandkids.org.uk; e-mail
    projects@kithandkids.org.uk; Tel 020 8801 7432;
    Fax 020 8885 3035
Director   Marjolein de Vries
Family Support Co-ordinator   Carol Schaffer
Parent self-help group actively working for empowerment
and inclusion of the whole family, through a range of project
services

Lead Scotland (Linking Education and Disability)

Princes Hse, 5 Shadwick Pl, Edinburgh EH2 4RG;
    URL www.lead.org.uk; e-mail enquiries@lead.org.uk;
    Tel 0131 228 9441; Fax 0131 229 8082
Supports disabled adults and carers into post-16 education

Limbless Association

Queen Mary's Hospital, Roehampton La, London
    SW15 5PN; URL www.limbless-association.org; e-mail
    enquiries@limbless-association.org; Tel 020 8788 1777;
    Fax 020 8788 3444

MacIntyre Care

Registered Charity Number 250840
602 South Seventh St, Milton Keynes, Buckinghamshire
    MK9 2JA; URL www.macintyrecharity.org; e-mail
    mail@macintyre-care.org.uk; Tel 01908 230100;
    Fax 01908 234379
A national charity providing a wide range of flexible
services across the UK for more than 500 adults and children
with learning disabilities; services include residential
accommodation, support living schemes, day services and
education and training opportunities, as well as two
residential schools

MENCAP

4 Swan Courtyard, Coventry Rd, Birmingham B26 1BU;
    URL www.mencap.org.uk; e-mail help@mencap.org.uk;
    e-mail info@mencap.org.uk; Tel 0121 707 7877;
    Tel (helpline) 0808 808 1111; Fax 0121 707 3019
Chief Executive   Jo Williams DBE
Chair   Brian Baldock CBE
President   Lord Rix CBE, DL
Royal MENCAP Society is a registered charity that offers
services to adults and children with learning disabilities. It
offers help and advice on benefits, housing and employment
via the helpline. It can also provide information and support
for leisure, recreational services (Gateway Clubs),
residential services and holidays.

8

Norwood

Broadway Hse, 80–82 The Broadway, Stanmore, Greater
London HA7 4HB; URL www.norwood.org.uk; e-mail
norwood@norwood.org.uk; Tel 020 8954 4555;
Fax 020 8420 6800
Patron HM The Queen
Chief Executive Norma Brier
President Richard Desmond
Chair Michael Teacher
Norwood is Anglo-Jewry's largest children and family
services organisation, supporting children and their
families, and adults, in coping with learning disabilities and
social difficulties
Covering Ravenswood Village; Learning Disability Services;
Special Education Services; Fostering and Adoption Services
and Children and Family Services

Phab

Summit Hse, Wandle Rd, Croydon, Surrey CRO 1DF;
URL www.phabengland.org.uk; e-mail
info@phabengland.org.uk
Manager (Fundraising) Anne Joyce

Queen Elizabeth's Foundation

Registered Charity Number 251051
Leatherhead Ct, Woodlands Rd, Leatherhead, Surrey
KT22 0BN; URL www.qef.org.uk; e-mail
info@qef.org.uk; Tel 01372 841100; Fax 01372 844072
Chief Executive; Secretary Cynthia Robinson

Remploy Ltd

Stonecourt, Siskin Dr, Coventry, Warwickshire CV3 4FJ;
URL www.remploy.co.uk
Leading provider of employment opportunities for disabled
people

Scope

Scope Response, PO Box 833, Milton Keynes,
Buckinghamshire MK12 5NY; URL www.scope.org.uk;
e-mail response@scope.org.uk; Tel (publications line)
01908 321049; Tel (freephone) 0808 800 3333;
Fax 01908 321051
Scope is for people with disabilities achieving equality, and
focuses particularly on cerebral palsy. Scope's work is
focused around early years, education, work and daily
living. In addition to its range of national and local services,
Scope has more than 250 local affiliated groups. For
information and support about cerebral palsy or
information about Scope's services, contact Scope Response.
Open 0900–1700 weekdays, 1000–1900 weekends.

Skill: National Bureau for Students with Disabilities

4th Fl, Chapter Hse, 18–20 Crucifix La, London SE1 3JW;
URL www.skill.org.uk; e-mail info@skill.org.uk;
Tel (information service Tue 1130–1330; Thu 1330–1530)
0800 328 5050; Tel (general: voice/minicom)
020 7450 0620; Fax 020 7450 0650; Minicom (information
service) 0800 068 2422
Chief Executive Barbara Waters
Skill Northern Ireland Unit 2, Jennymount Ct, North Derby
St, Belfast BT15 3HN; URL www.skillni.org.uk; e-mail
admin@skillni.org.uk; Tel (voice and minicom)
028 9028 7000; Fax 028 9028 7002
Director Alison Anderson
Director Maria Murray
Skill Scotland Norton Pk, 57 Albion Rd, Edinburgh
EH7 5QY; e-mail admin@skillscotland.org.uk;
Tel 0131 475 2348 (and Minicom); Fax 0131 475 2397
Director John Ireson
Skill Wales Suite 14, 2nd Fl, The Executive Centre, Temple
Ct, Cathedral Rd, Cardiff CF11 9HA; e-mail
paul@skillwales.org.uk; Tel 02920 786506;
Fax 02920 786666
Development Officer Paul Warren

United Kingdom Sports Association for People with Learning Disability (UKSAPLD)

1st Fl, 12 City Forum, 250 City Rd, London EC1V 2PU;
URL www.uksportsassociation.org; e-mail
office@uksapld.freeserve.co.uk; Tel 020 7490 3057;
Fax 020 7251 8861
National Director Tracey McCillen
Provides increased opportunities for people with learning
disabilities to participate in sport and recreation; co-
ordinates the work of member organisations; acts as a
national forum; increases awareness of the value of physical
activity to professionals involved with people with learning
disabilities

Values into Action

Oxford Hse, Derbyshire St, London E2 6HG;
URL www.viauk.org; e-mail general@viauk.org;
Tel 020 7729 5436; Fax 020 7729 7797
Chief Executive Kiran Dattani Pitt
Research and campaigning organisation working for a
better quality of life for people with learning difficulties
through publications, newsletters and lobbying

Special Educational Needs

British Dyslexia Association

98 London Rd, Reading RG1 5AU;
URL www.bdadyslexia.org.uk; e-mail
helpline@bdadyslexia.org.uk; Tel (helpline)
0118 966 8271; Fax 0118 935 1927
Chief Executive Judi Stewart
Advice; helpline; befriending; publications; encourages
research; accreditation of specialist dyslexia courses

Dyslexia Action (National Training and Resource Centre)

National Training and Resource Centre, Park Hse, Wick Rd,
Egham, Surrey TW20 0HH;
URL www.dyslexiaaction.org.uk; e-mail
info@dyslexiaaction.org.uk; Tel 01784 222300;
Fax 01784 222333
Chief Executive S. Cramer
Advice and counselling; teaching and teacher training
services offered by nationwide centres. Further information
from head office (enclose an SAE).

Dyslexia Scotland

Stirling Business Centre, Stirling FK8 2DZ;
URL www.dyslexiascotland.org.uk; e-mail
helpline@dyslexiascotland.org.uk; Tel 01786 446650;
Tel (helpline) 0844 800 8484; Fax 01786 471235
Provides information and practical help for children and
adults with dyslexia (specific learning difficulties). Resource
centre open Mon–Fri 1000–1600, free to members.

Enquire

Princes Hse, 5 Shandwick Pl, Edinburgh EH2 4RG;
URL www.enquire.org.uk; e-mail info@enquire.org.uk;
Tel 0845 123 2303; Fax 0131 228 9852
Senior Manager Sally Cavers
Senior Manager Anne Lennon
Enquire is the Scottish advice service for additional support
for learning. It is managed by Children in Scotland and
funded by the Scottish Government. Enquire provides
information and advice, free publications, training and
outreach services to parents, professionals and voluntary
organisations working with and for children and young
people who have additional support needs. Its services are
also available to children and young people themselves.

Hyperactive Children's Support Group

71 Whyke La, Chichester, West Sussex PO19 7PD;
   URL www.hacsg.org.uk; e-mail
   hyperactive@hacsg.org.uk; Tel 01243 539966
Founder; Director   Sally Bunday
To help and support children with hyperactivity, ADHD or
allergies, and their parents; to conduct research and
promote investigation into the incidence of hyperactivity in
the UK–its causes and treatments; to disseminate
information concerning this condition. Send an SAE for
details.

nasen

nasen Hse, 4–5 Amber Business Village, Amber Cl,
   Amington, Tamworth, Staffordshire B77 4RP;
   URL www.nasen.org.uk; e-mail welcome@nasen.org.uk;
   Tel 01827 311500

National Autistic Society

393 City Rd, London EC1V 1NG; URL www.autism.org.uk;
   e-mail (autism helpline) autismhelpline@nas.org.uk;
   e-mail nas@nas.org.uk; Tel (autism helpline)
   0845 070 4004; Tel 020 7833 2299; Fax 020 7833 9666
Chief Executive   Vernon Beauchamp
Runs the autism helpline offering impartial and confidential
information, advice and support for people with an autistic
spectrum disorder, their families and professionals. It also
manages a library which is open by appointment.

Rathbone

4th Fl, Churchgate Hse, Oxford St, Manchester M1 6EU;
   e-mail info@rathbonetraining.co.uk; Tel 0161 236 5358;
   Tel (special education advice line) 0800 917 6790;
   Fax 0161 238 6356
Chief Executive   Richard Williams

Scottish Society for Autism (SSAC)

Hilton Hse, Alloa Business Pk, Whins Rd, Alloa,
   Clackmannanshire FK10 3SA;
   URL www.autism-in-scotland.org.uk; e-mail
   autism@autism-in-scotland.org.uk; Tel 01259 720044;
   Fax 01259 720051
Chief Executive   John McDonald

The Scottish Society for Autism runs a residential school for
children; residential and specialist day services for adults; a
respite care centre for autism; nationwide family support
services; training for carers and professionals; supports self-
help groups and local societies; produces information and a
members' magazine; undertakes community care
assessments and gives guidance on diagnosis, assessment
and care management. Advice on all aspects of autism is
available from professional staff.

Southern England Psychological Services

Allington La, Fair Oak, Eastleigh, Hampshire SO50 7DE;
   URL www.drludwigredlowenstein.com;
   www.parental-alienation.info; e-mail
   ludwig.lowenstein@btinternet.com; Tel 02392 692621;
   Fax 02392 692621
Consultant Psychologist   Dr L.F. Lowenstein MA,
   DipPsych, PhD, BPs, Chartered Psychologist
Diagnosis therapy and advice; vocational assessment;
assessment of dyslexic children. From average to below
average ability and children of superior intelligence with
moderate to fairly severe learning and/or behavioural
difficulties and general problems for children.

Volunteer Reading Help (VRH)

Registered Charity Number 296454
Charity Hse, 14–15 Perseverance Works, 38 Kingsland Rd,
   London E2 8DD; URL www.vrh.org.uk; e-mail
   info@vrh.org.uk; Tel 020 7729 4087; Fax 020 7729 7643
Chief Executive   Gill Astarita
Volunteer Reading Help (VRH) is a registered charity which
encourages aged six to 11 children to become confident and
literate through the support of trained volunteers. Also
provides training for adults on how to help children with
reading. It is currently funded by DCSF, LEAs, schools,
charitable trusts, companies and individual supporters, and
has a network of branches across the country.

8

Assessment Bodies, Research and Advisory Bodies

9

Assessment Bodies

Research Councils

Research and Advisory Bodies

Assessment Bodies, Research and Advisory Bodies

Assessment Bodies

Assessment and Qualifications Alliance (AQA)

Devas St, Manchester M15 6EX; URL www.aqa.org.uk;
e-mail mailbox@aqa.org.uk; Tel 0161 953 1180;
Fax 0161 273 7572
Director General Dr M.J. Cresswell
Deputy Director General A.J. Bird
Director (Examination Services) C.R. Adams
Director (Finance) R.J. Cox
Director (ICT) P.G. Dawson
Director (Market Strategy) G. Hurst
Director (People, Environment and Research) J.D. Milner
Director (Qualifications Development and Support)
C.J. Mitchell; Stag Hill Hse, Guildford, Surrey GU2 7XJ;
Tel 01483 506506; Fax 01483 300152
Harrogate Office 31–33 Springfield Ave, Harrogate, North
Yorkshire HG1 2HW; Tel 01423 840015; Fax 01423 523678

Associated Board of the Royal Schools of Music

24 Portland Pl, London W1B 1LU; URL www.abrsm.org;
e-mail abrsm@abrsm.ac.uk; Tel 020 7636 5400;
Fax 020 7637 0234
Chief Executive Richard Morris
Head (Marketing) Giles Morris
The Associated Board offers a graded system of music
exams in 35 instruments, jazz, singing, choral singing,
practical musicianship and theory. A Professional
Development Course is available for instrumental and
singing teachers, leading to the qualification of CT ABRSM.

Cambridge Assessment

See also OCR
1 Hills Rd, Cambridge, Cambridgeshire CB1 2EU;
URL www.cambridgeassessment.org.uk; e-mail
public.affairs@cambridgeassessment.org.uk
Group Chief Executive Mr S.D. Lebus;
URL www.ucles.org.uk; Tel 01223 553311;
Fax 01223 460278
Chief Executive (Cambridge ESOL)
Dr Mike Milanovic; provides English examinations for
speakers of other languages, and qualifications for
language teachers around the world;
URL www.cambridgeesol.org; Tel 01223 553355;
Fax 01223 460278
Chief Executive (Cambridge International Examinations) (CIE)
Ann Puntis; provides assessment services to many
governments and supplies international qualifications
and vocational awards worldwide; URL www.cie.org.uk;
Tel 01223 553554; Fax 01223 553558
*Group Director (Assessment, Research and Development
Department)* Tim Oates; focuses on research,
expanding e-assessment capabilities and operates the
university entrance tests; Tel 01223 553311;
Fax 01223 460278
Cambridge Assessment plays a leading role in developing
and delivering assessment across the globe by offering
qualifications through three exam boards: OCR in the UK,
Cambridge International Examinations (CIE) and
Cambridge English for Speakers of Other Languages
(Cambridge ESOL). Cambridge Assessment is a department
of the University of Cambridge and is a not-for-profit
organisation.

CCEA

29 Clarendon Rd, Belfast BT1 3BG; URL www.ccea.org.uk;
e-mail info@ccea.org.uk; Tel 028 9026 1200; Tel (press
office) 028 9026 1216
The role of CCEA is to review all aspects of the curriculum,
examinations and assessment; advise the Department of
Education in Northern Ireland (DE); publish and
disseminate curriculum, examinations and assessment
materials; conduct and award certificates for examinations;
conduct the moderation of relevant examinations and
assessments; ensure that standards of the relevant
examinations and assessments are recognised and
maintained; develop, conduct and mark the transfer tests;
develop and produce teaching support materials; carry out
other activities as directed by the Department of Education
in Northern Ireland. It also has a regulatory role in relation
to standards in all general and vocational examinations, the
development of educational technology and the production
of multimedia resources. The council takes account of the
effect of its work on teachers to ensure services are helpful
and supportive. Further information may be obtained from
the press office.

City & Guilds

1 Giltspur St, London EC1A 9DD;
URL www.cityandguilds.com; Tel 020 7294 2800;
Fax 020 7294 2405
An organisation offering more than 400 vocational
qualifications, including NVQs, SVQs and Modern
Apprenticeships

College of Teachers

Institute of Education, 20 Bedford Way, London
WC1H 0AL; URL www.collegeofteachers.ac.uk; e-mail
enquiries@cot.ac.uk; Tel 020 7911 5536; Fax 020 7612 6482

Council for Awards in Children's Care and Education (CACHE)

Incorporating CEYA and NNEB
Beaufort Hse, 23 Grosvenor Rd, St Albans, Hertfordshire
 AL1 3AW; URL www.cache.org.uk; e-mail
 info@cache.org.uk; Tel 0845 347 2123; Fax 01727 818618
Chief Executive   Richard C. Dorrance

Edexcel

One90 High Holborn, London WC1V 7BH;
 URL www.edexcel.org.uk; e-mail
 enquiries@edexcel.org.uk; Tel 0844 499 1900;
 Fax 020 7190 5628
Chief Executive   Jerry Jarvis
Chair   Martin Cross
Edexcel, a Pearson company, is a UK awarding body
offering a range of academic and vocational learning across
schools and colleges. It offers GCSEs, A-levels, BTEC and
vocational qualifications. It is accredited by its English
regulator to offer all five lines of learning in the new diploma
in English schools. Other services include occupational and
specific programmes for employers around the world, and a
range of work experience placements for students through
its Trident and Edexcel service.

English Speaking Board (International) Ltd

26a Princes St, Southport, Merseyside PR8 1EQ;
 URL www.esbuk.org; e-mail admin@esbuk.org;
 Tel 01704 501730; Fax 01704 539637

Faculty of the Arts

Thames Valley University, St Marys Rd, London W5 5RF;
 URL www.tvu.ac.uk; Tel 020 8231 2304;
 Fax 020 8231 2546
Pro Vice-Chancellor; Dean   Chris O'Neil
Head (Art and Design)   Alan Schechner
Head (Media)   Dr Jeremy Strong
Head (Music)   Christopher Batchelor
TVU aims to train young people to be confident and self-
assured. The music programmes focus on twentieth century
music, and all Faculty of the Arts programmes are
vocational.
Faculty of the Arts runs undergraduate programmes in
Advertising; Graphic Design and Film; Digital Animation;
Fine Art; Film and TV Studies; Journalism; Media Arts;
Media Studies; Games Development; Digital Media
Production; Music Technology; Photography; Popular
Music Performance (Performance/Composition);
Broadcasting;Video Production. There are also
postgraduate programmes available: PGDip and MMus;
Performance; MMus in Composing Concert Music; MMus in
Composing for Film and Television; MA/PGDip in Film
and The Moving Image, MA Media, MA Computer Arts;
MA Video; MA Creative Screenwriting; MA Photography;
MA Computer Arts; MA Performance and Media Health.

IATEFL

Darwin College, University of Kent, Canterbury, Kent
 CT2 7NY; URL www.iatefl.org; e-mail
 generalenquiries@iatefl.org; Tel 01227 824430;
 Fax 01227 824431

Independent Schools Examinations Board

Jordan Hse, Christchurch Rd, New Milton, Hampshire
 BH25 6QJ; e-mail enquiries@iseb.co.uk; Tel 01425 621111;
 Fax 01425 620044
General Secretary   Mrs J. Williams
The Independent Schools Examinations Board sets
examinations for entry to senior schools at 11 and 13.
Examinations take place in the spring term for both age
groups and in June for 13.

Institute of Leadership and Management

1 Giltspur St, London EC1A 9DD; Tel 020 7294 2470;
 Fax 020 7294 2402
Director (Professional Development)   Dr Sally Messenger

International Baccalaureate Organisation

Peterson Hse, Malthouse Ave, Cardiff Gate, Cardiff
 CF23 8GL; URL www.ibo.org; e-mail ibca@ibo.org;
 Tel 02920 547777; Fax 02920 547778

Joint Council for Qualifications

Veritas Hse, 125 Finsbury Pavement, London EC2A 1NQ;
 URL www.jcq.org.uk; e-mail info@jcq.org.uk
Director   Dr Ellie Johnson Searle
The Joint Council for Qualifications (JCQ) enables member
awarding bodies to act together in: providing, wherever
possible, common administrative arrangements for the
schools, colleges and other providers that offer their
qualifications; dealing with the regulatory authorities, in
responding to proposals and initiatives on assessment and
the curriculum; and dealing with the media on issues
affecting all member bodies. In this respect, the JCQ office
acts as an administrative hub for the joint and collaborative
work of the members.

Joint Examining Board

30a Dyer St, Cirencester, Gloucestershire GL7 2PF;
 URL www.jeb.co.uk; e-mail jeb@jeb.co.uk;
 Tel 01285 641747; Fax 01285 650449
Director   M. Cooch
The Joint Examining Board offers Education Practice
Certificates and Diplomas for Education Principles,
Educational Management, ICT Skills and ICT Advanced.
These courses are run by registered centres and are also
available through distance learning. Educational Use of ICT
has also been introduced for teachers who would like to use
information communication technology skills and integrate
them into their teaching. The course is run by registered
centres and leads to a JEB Certificate in Educational Use of
ICT. Additionally, the board has launched a course leading
to the Certificate in Delivering Learning using a VLE.

London Chamber of Commerce and Industry Examinations Board

Athena Hse, 112 Station Rd, Sidcup, Kent DA15 7BJ;
 URL www.lccieb.org.uk; Tel 020 8302 0261;
 Fax 020 8302 4169
Manager (Marketing)   Liam Wynne

National Examination Board in Occupational Safety and Health (NEBOSH)

Dominus Way, Meridian Business Pk, Leicester LE19 1QW;
 URL www.nebosh.org.uk; e-mail info@nebosh.org.uk;
 Tel 0116 263 4700; Fax 0116 282 4000
Chief Executive   Teresa Budworth BSc(Hons), MBA,
 CFIOSH

OCR (Oxford Cambridge and RSA Examinations)

9 Hills Rd, Cambridge, Cambridgeshire CB2 1BP;
 URL www.ocr.org.uk; Tel 01223 552552;
 Fax 01223 552553
Chief Executive   Greg Watson MA, FRSA
OCR is one of the UK's leading awarding bodies, providing
a wide range of qualifications which recognise the
achievements of learners in all phases of life and work. OCR
qualifications include AS/A-levels, VCEs and GNVQs,
GCSEs, Key Skills, Entry Level qualifications, NVQs and
'own brand' qualifications covering areas such as IT,
business, languages, teaching and training, administration
and secretarial skills.
Registered Office   1 Hills Rd, Cambridge, Cambridgeshire
 CB1 2EU; Tel 01223 552552; Fax 01223 552553

OCR Information Bureau (General Qualifications) 9 Hills Rd, Cambridge, Cambridgeshire CB2 1BP; Tel 01223 553998; Fax 01223 552627

Pitman Qualifications

1 Giltspur St, London EC1A 9DD; Tel 020 7294 2471; Fax 020 7294 2403

Scottish Qualifications Authority

The Optima Bldg, 58 Robertson St, Glasgow G2 8DQ; URL www.sqa.org.uk; e-mail customer@sqa.org.uk; Tel 0845 279 1000; Fax 0845 213 5000

SQA is the national body in Scotland responsible for the development, accreditation, assessment and certification of qualifications other than degrees, and some professional qualifications. The main functions of SQA are to devise, develop and validate qualifications and keep them under review; accredit qualifications; approve education and training establishments as being suitable for delivering SQA qualifications; arrange for, assist in and carry out assessment of candidates; quality assure education and training establishments; issue certificates to SQA candidates. Standards are designed in collaboration with experts in education, employers, industry bodies, Sector Skills Councils, and professional and technical bodies. SQA's qualifications are designed to provide a variety of recognisable routes to careers and to further study through the workplace, college or university.

Welsh Joint Education Committee

245 Western Ave, Cardiff CF5 2YX; URL www.wjec.co.uk; e-mail info@wjec.co.uk; Tel 02920 265000
Chief Executive   Gareth Pierce
Chair   Cllr John W. Turner
Vice-Chair   Cllr Arwel G. Jones
Director (Examinations and Assessment)   Derec Stockley
Assistant Director (Communications)   Len Belton
Assistant Director (Compliance)   Sandra Anstey
Assistant Director (Curriculum)   Arthur Parker

Research Councils

Biotechnology and Biological Sciences Research Council

Polaris Hse, North Star Ave, Swindon SN2 1UH; Tel 01793 413200; Fax 01793 413201
Chair   Dr Peter Ringrose
Deputy Chair; Chief Executive   Prof Julia Goodfellow

Economic and Social Research Council (ESRC)

Polaris Hse, North Star Ave, Swindon SN2 1UJ; URL www.esrcsocietytoday.ac.uk; Tel 01793 413000; Fax 01793 413001
Chief Executive   Prof Ian Diamond
The ESRC is the UK's largest funding agency for research and postgraduate training relating to social and economic issues. It provides independent, relevant research to business, the public sector and Government. At any one time the RSRC supports more than 4000 researchers and postgraduate students in academic institutions and research policy institutes.
ESRC aims to provide research on issues of importance to business, the public sector and government. The issues considered include economic competitiveness, the effectiveness of public services and policy, and quality of life.

Engineering and Physical Sciences Research Council (EPSRC)

Polaris Hse, North Star Ave, Swindon SN2 1ET; URL www.epsrc.ac.uk; e-mail infoline@epsrc.ac.uk; Tel 01793 444000; Tel (helpline) 01793 444100
Chief Executive   Dr Randal Richards (Acting)
Chair   Prof Dame Julia Higgins FRS, FREng

Medical Research Council

20 Park Cres, London W1B 1AL; Tel 020 7636 5422; Fax 020 7436 6179
Chair   Sir John Chisholm
Chief Executive   Prof Colin Blakemore

Natural Environment Research Council

Polaris Hse, North Star Ave, Swindon SN2 1EU; Tel 01793 411500; Fax 01793 411501
Chair   James C. Smith CBE, FEng, FRSE
Chief Executive   Prof John Lawton CBE, FRS

Science and Technology Facilities Council

Polaris Hse, North Star Ave, Swindon SN2 1SZ; URL www.scitech.ac.uk; e-mail pr.pus@stfc.ac.uk; Tel 01793 442000; Fax 01793 442002

Research and Advisory Bodies

British Educational Research Association

Association Hse, South Park Rd, Macclesfield, Cheshire SK11 6SH; URL www.bera.ac.uk; e-mail admin@bera.ac.uk; Tel 01625 504062; Fax 01625 267879
Administrative Secretary   Dan Hollingshurst

Centre for Design and Technology Education

University of Wolverhampton, Castle View, Dudley DY1 3HR; Tel 01902 321000; Fax 01902 323540
Senior Lecturer   J.N. Atkins

Centre for Education and Finance Management Ltd (CEFM)

Red Lion Hse, 9–10 High St, High Wycombe, Buckinghamshire HP11 2AZ; URL www.cefm.co.uk; e-mail info@cefm.co.uk; Tel 01494 459183; Fax 01494 474480
Managing Director   Christine Dickson
Support Services   Jason Foster
Professional Development   Val Forrest
CEFM provides a range of services to support schools and aims to deliver the highest levels of information and advice to schools. CEFM has more than 500 client schools and specialises in a range of support and consultancy programmes that include salary reviews, management audits and financial consultancy. Helplines operate throughout the school day, every day of the year; the centre tracks development and trends in the education sector and provides a practical commentary.

Centre for Institutional Studies (CIS)

University of East London, Docklands Campus, 4–6 University Way, London E16 2RD; e-mail cis@uel.ac.uk; Tel 020 8223 4230; Fax 020 8223 4298
Director   M. Locke
CIS undertakes research studies and consultancy into public policy and public institutions, specialising in education in the UK and overseas countries, urban regeneration and voluntary organisations. It offers vocational postgraduate programmes for public and voluntary sectors and public enterprise.

9

Centre for the Study of Education and Training (CSET)

University of Lancaster, County South, Lancaster, Lancashire LA1 4YD; URL www.lancs.ac.uk/fss/centres/cset; e-mail d.daglish@lancaster.ac.uk; Tel 01524 592679; Fax 01524 592914
Director   Prof M. Saunders

CILT

3rd Fl, 111 Westminster Bridge Rd, London SE1 7HR; URL www.cilt.org.uk; e-mail info@cilt.org.uk; Tel (general enquiries) 020 7379 5101; Fax 020 7379 5082
Director   Isabella Moore
Press Enquiries   Catherine Mansfield
CILT, the National Centre for Languages is the government's recognised centre for expertise on languages. The centre serves education, business and the wider community, supporting and developing plurilingualism in all sectors of society.

Department of Sociology

School of Social Sciences, The University of Birmingham, Edgbaston, Birmingham, West Midlands B15 2TT; Tel 0121 414 6060; Fax 0121 414 6061
Head   J. Holmwood

EMFEC

Robins Wood Hse, Robins Wood Rd, Aspley, Nottinghamshire NG8 3NH; URL www.emfec.co.uk; e-mail enquiries@emfec.co.uk; Tel 0115 854 1616; Fax 0115 854 1617

EMIE at NFER

NFER, The Mere, Upton Pk, Slough SL1 2DQ; URL www.nfer.ac.uk/emie; e-mail emie@nfer.ac.uk; Tel 01753 523156; Fax 01753 531458
Head of Service   Geoff Gee
EMIE provides an information service on policy and practice issues for local authority staff in education and children's services departments in the UK. It enables them to share documentation, good practice and common problems. Funded by local government, it is a collaborative enterprise involving authorities as the major users and contributors of information. EMIE at NFER offers a range of information services, including regular reports, current awareness bulletins and research briefings, all available on its website. Local authority documents can be downloaded from an online database, and there are e-mail discussion forums and an enquiry service.

European Institute of Education and Social Policy

Université de Paris IX-Dauphine, Place du Maréchal de Lattre de Tassigny, 75775 Paris Cedex 16, France; URL www.e-education-europe.org; e-mail leeps@dauphine.fr; Tel +33 1 44 05 40 01; Fax +33 1 44 05 40 02
Director   Jean Gordon

Eurydice Unit for England, Wales and Northern Ireland

The Mere, Upton Pk, Slough SL1 2DQ; URL www.nfer.ac.uk/eurydice; www.eurydice.org; e-mail eurydice@nfer.ac.uk; Tel 01753 637036; Fax 01753 531458
Based at the National Foundation for Educational Research (NFER), Eurydice at NFER is the national Eurydice Unit for England, Wales and Northern Ireland. A separate unit for Scotland is based at the Scottish Government. Eurydice at NFER provides information on education in Europe to support and enhance the policy making process.

Examinations Appeals Board (EAB)

83 Piccadilly, London W1J 8QA; URL www.theeab.org.uk; e-mail bryan.whittaker@theeab.org.uk; Tel 020 7509 5995; Fax 020 7509 6975
Chair   Jeff Thompson
Deputy Chair   Mike Moran
Deputy Chair   Robin Trebilcock
The EAB seeks to ensure that those using the examination system can have confidence that the grades awarded are as fair as possible. In hearing appeals for AS, A, GCSE, VCE, GNVQ and Entry Levels, it considers whether an awarding body's procedures were appropriately and properly applied. It has powers to make recommendations and to require an awarding body to reconsider a case.

Further Education Research Association

Lifelong Learning Office, University of Worcester, Henwick Gr, Worcester, Worcestershire WR2 6AJ; URL www.worc.ac.uk; e-mail g.elliott@worc.ac.uk; Tel 01905 855145; Fax 01905 855132
Chair   Prof Geoffrey Elliott

Further Education Research Network

FERN Centre, De Montfort University, Leicester LE7 9SU; Tel 0116 257 8651
Co-ordinator   David G. Rogers
FERN is an independent, self-financing charity, established and organised by teachers seeking to equip themselves with the knowledge and techniques relevant to contemporary changes in further and higher education. Membership is available to all teachers in further and higher education and the network is administered by an annually elected executive committee.
FERN supports a wide variety of investigations initiated by members, and current research projects include the development of new teaching materials, textbook readability studies and the analysis of classroom interaction. Members receive the FERN Journal, published twice a year, and a FERN Newsletter three times a year. Libraries and other organisations may subscribe to these publications.

The Grubb Institute of Behavioural Studies

Cloudesley St, London N1 0HU; URL www.grubb.org.uk; e-mail info@grubb.org.uk; Tel 020 7278 8061; Fax 020 7278 0728
The Grubb Institute is an applied research foundation working globally to mobilise values, faiths and beliefs as a resource for the transformation of organisations, people and society. Its learning programmes and consultancy programme enable leaders, managers and activists to achieve personal and organisational purpose. The institute is active in schools, LEAs and educational and leadership institutions across the country.

ISCG (Information for School and College Governors)

Avondale Park School, Sirdar Rd, London W11 4EE; URL www.governors.uk.com; e-mail iscg@governors.uk.com; Tel 020 7229 0200
Director   M. Jones
Director   E. al Qadhi
Director   F. Taylor
Company Secretary   S. Shiel

Learning and Teaching Scotland

Headquarters, The Optima, 58 Robertson St, Glasgow G2 8JD; URL www.ltscotland.org.uk; e-mail enquiries@ltscotland.org.uk; Tel 0870 010 0297 Gardyne Rd, Broughty Ferry, Dundee DD5 1NY; Tel 01382 443600; Fax 01382 443645
Chair   John Mulgrew
Chief Executive   Bernard McLeary
Learning and Teaching Scotland is an executive non-departmental public body sponsored by the Scottish Government. Learning and Teaching Scotland is the main

organisation for the development and support of the Scottish curriculum and Scottish education. Its role is to provide advice, support, resources and staff development to enhance the quality of learning and teaching in Scotland, combining expertise in the 3–18 curriculum with advice on the use of ICT in education. Learning and Teaching Scotland works in close partnership with the Scottish Government, HMIE, SQA, ADES, COSLA, education authorities, schools and a range of professional associations.

The Leverhulme Trust

1 Pemberton Row, London EC4A 3BG;
  URL www.leverhulme.ac.uk; e-mail
  gdupin@leverhulme.ac.uk; Tel 020 7822 6938
Director Prof Sir Richard Brook OBE, ScD, FEng
Awards grants to institutions and individuals, mainly for research

Mayfair School of English

61–65 Oxford St, London W1D 2EL;
  URL www.mayfairschool.co.uk; e-mail
  enquiries@mayfairschool.co.uk; Tel 020 7437 9941;
  Fax 020 7494 3611
Principal Naeem Ahmad

National Advisory Council for Education and Training Targets (NACETT)

Dunford Lodge, Storth La, Sheffield, South Yorkshire
S10 3LL; Tel 0114 259 7887
Head of Secretariat V. Nowell
Contact D. Stephen
Contact G. Thompson
Advisory body to the government

National Children's Bureau

8 Wakley St, London EC1V 7QE; Tel 020 7843 6000;
  Fax 020 7278 9512
Chief Executive Paul Ennals
Vice-President Prof Philip Graham
Vice-President Dr Patricia Hamilton
Vice-President Sir William Utting
Chair Dame Gillian Pugh
Vice-Chair Harry Marsh
Treasurer Barry Gifford

National Education Business Partnership Network

188 Main St, New Greenham Pk, Thatcham, Berkshire
RG19 6HW; URL www.nebpn.org; e-mail
office@nebpn.org; Tel 01635 279914; Fax 01635 279919
Operations Manager Hazel Meaney

National Foundation for Educational Research in England and Wales

The Mere, Upton Pk, Slough SL1 2DQ;
  URL www.nfer.ac.uk; e-mail enquiries@nfer.ac.uk;
  Tel 01753 574123; Fax 01753 691632
President Sir Brian Fender CMG
Vice-President J.E.L. Baird OBE, MA, FEIS
Vice-President N. Harrison CBE, FCP
Chair R.D.C. Bunker MA
Vice Chair and Hon Treasurer Mr D.A.L. Whitbread
Director Sue Rossiter

National Primary Trust

Martineau Education Centre, Balden Rd, Birmingham, West
  Midlands B32 2EH; URL www.npt.org.uk; e-mail
  nptrust@tesco.net
Chief Executive Peter Mamer

Northern Ireland Council for the Curriculum, Examinations and Assessment (CCEA)

Clarendon Dock, 29 Clarendon Rd, Belfast BT1 3BG;
  URL www.ccea.org.uk; e-mail info@ccea.org.uk;
  Tel 028 9026 1200; Fax 028 9026 1234
Chief Executive Neil Anderson
Chair David McKee
CCEA is a unique educational body in the UK, bringing together the three areas of curriculum, examiniations and assessment: Advising Government – on what should be taught in Northern Ireland's schools and colleges; Monitoring Standards – ensuring that the qualifications and examinations offered by awarding bodies in Northern Ireland are of an appropriate quality and standard; Awarding Qualifications – offering a diverse range of qualifications, such as GCSEs, including the GCSE Double Award specifications in vocational subjects, GCE A and AS levels, Entry Level Qualifications, and Graded Objectives in Modern Languages.

The Nuffield Foundation

28 Bedford Sq, London WC1B 3JS;
  URL www.nuffieldfoundation.org; Tel 020 7631 0566
Chair of the Trustees Baroness O'Neill CBE, PBA, FMedSci,
  Hon FRS
Director Anthony Tomei

Policy Studies Institute

50 Hanson St, London W1W 6UP; URL www.psi.org.uk
Chair Sir Leonard Peach
Director Malcolm Rigg

Public Management and Policy Association

3 Robert St, London WC2N 6RL; URL www.pmpa.co.uk;
  e-mail info@pmpa@cipfa.org; Tel 020 7543 5600
Director (Development) Janet Grauberg
The Public Management and Policy Association (PMPA) is a national membership organisation which promotes the value of public management and public policy. It serves public sector managers, academics, policy-makers, commentators and those with an interest in public services. It arranges events, lectures, publications and other opportunities for this community to meet, discuss and comment on public policy and management issues. Membership includes subscription to Public Money and Management; the quarterly member newsletter, The PMPA Review; 20% discount off Public Finance; priority places at Public Management and Policy Association lectures and other events; Public Management and Policy Association Reports. The Individual member rate is £80; student rate available.

Qualifications and Curriculum Authority

83 Piccadilly, London W1J 8QA; URL www.qca.org.uk;
  e-mail info@qca.org.uk; Tel 020 7509 5555;
  Fax 020 7509 6976
Chair Sir Anthony Greener
Deputy Chair Richard Greenhalgh
Chief Executive Ken Boston
Managing Director (NAA) David Gee
Director (Curriculum) Mick Waters
Director (Qualifications and Skills) Mary Curnock Cook
Director (Regulations and Standards) Isabel Nisbit
Director (Strategic Resource Management) Andrew Hall
Head (Communications and Marketing Division)
  David Robinson
Principal Manager (Customer Services) Mark Hunter
Principal Manager (Marketing) Adeloa Akande
Principal Manager (Publishing) Roger Davies
Senior Media Officer Alan Cox
QCA is a guardian of standards in education and training. It works with others to maintain and develop the school curriculum and associated assessments, and to accredit and monitor qualifications in schools, colleges and at work.

9

The SCRE Centre, University of Glasgow

11 Eldon St, Glasgow G3 6NH; URL www.scre.ac.uk; e-mail
  scre@scre.ac.uk; Tel 0141 330 3490; Fax 0141 330 3491
Director   Paul Brna
Information Officer   Jon Lewin

Standing Committee for the Education and Training of Teachers (SCETT)

University of Worcester, Worcester, Worcestershire
  WR2 6AJ; URL www.scett.org.uk; e-mail
  scett@worc.ac.uk; Tel 01905 855055; Fax 01905 855132
Chair   D. Hayes
Hon Treasurer   S. Rogers
Academic Secretary   Cliff Jones
Office Secretary   Tracey Allman
Provides a forum for teacher training organisations and
higher educational establishments with responsibility for
teacher training. Members include the representative bodies
for teacher education including all the teacher associations,
universities and colleges, LEA personnel and schools.

The Tavistock Institute

See also Chapter 6: Management Education; Business and
Administrative Colleges and Institutions
30 Tabernacle St, London EC2A 4UE;
  URL www.tavinstitute.org; Tel 020 7417 0407;
  Fax 020 7417 0566
Institute Secretary   Debbie Sorkin
The Tavistock Institute is an independent, non-profitmaking
research, consultancy and professional development
organisation. The institute applies ideas from across the
social sciences to provide practical help to individuals and
organisations needing to deal with issues of change,
innovation and policy delivery.

Universities Council for the Education of Teachers (UCET)

Whittington Hse, 19–30 Alfred Pl, London WC1E 7EA;
  URL www.ucet.ac.uk; e-mail info@ucet.ac.uk;
  Tel 020 7580 8000; Fax 020 7323 0577
Chair   M. Totterdell
Chair (Elected)   Roger Woods
Treasurer   C. Cook
Executive Director   J. Rogers
Academic Secretary   G. Kirk
Universities and university-sector colleges in England,
Wales, Scotland and Northern Ireland involved in teacher
education at any level are members of UCET. UCET acts as
a national forum for discussion of all matters relating to the
education of teachers and the study of education in
universities. It also campaigns and lobbies on behalf of its
member institutions.

World Association for Educational Research

President   Prof Dr Wolfgang Mitter; Deutsches Institut fuer
  Internatinale Paedagogische Forschung, German
  Institute for International Educational Research,
  Frankfurt am Main Schloss-Strasse 29, Germany; e-mail
  mitter@dipf.de; Tel +49 692 4708 107;
  Fax +49 692 4708 444
Secretary General   Prof Dr Anthony Hourdakis; University
  of Crete, Faculty of Educational Sciences, Gallos
  74100; Crete, Greece; e-mail hourd@edc.uch.gr;
  Fax +30 2831 0 77596

Employment and Careers

10

Employment and Careers

Government Offices for the Regions and Learning and Skills Councils

England

Government Office for the East of England

Eastbrook, Shaftsbury Rd, Cambridge, Cambridgeshire CB2 2DF; URL www.go-east.gov.uk; e-mail jstreet.go-east.go-regions.gsi.gov.uk; Tel 01223 372536; Fax 01223 372861
Regional Director Caroline Bowdler

Bedfordshire and Luton Learning and Skills Council

Woburn Ct, 2 Railton Rd, Woburn Road Industrial Est, Kempston, Bedfordshire MK42 7DN; Tel 0845 019 4160; Fax 01234 843211
Chair Jim McGivern
Executive Director Linda Hockey

Cambridgeshire Learning and Skills Council

Stuart Hse, St Johns St, Peterborough, Cambridgeshire PE1 5DD; Tel 0845 019 4165; Fax 01733 895260
Chair Sal Brinton
Executive Director Stephen Catchpole

Essex Learning and Skills Council

Redwing Hse, Hedgerows Business Pk, Colchester Rd, Chelmsford, Essex CM2 5PB; Tel 0845 019 4179; Fax 01245 451430
Chair Mike Malone-Lee
Executive Director Alison Webster

Hertfordshire Learning and Skills Council

45 Grosvenor Rd, St Albans, Hertfordshire AL1 3AW; Tel 0845 019 4167; Fax 01727 813443
Chair Stelio Stefanou
Executive Director Roy Bain

Norfolk Learning and Skills Council

St Andrews Hse, St Andrews St, Norwich, Norfolk NR2 4TP; Tel 0845 019 4173; Fax 01603 218802
Chair Geoff Loades
Executive Director John Brierley

Suffolk Learning and Skills Council

Felaw Maltings, 42 Felaw St, Ipswich, Suffolk IP2 8SJ; Tel 0845 019 4180; Fax 01473 883090
Chair Tony Preston
Executive Director John McLeod

Government Office for the East Midlands

The Belgrave Centre, Stanley Pl, Talbot St, Nottingham NG1 5GG; URL www.go-em.gov.uk; Tel 0115 971 9971; Fax 0115 971 2404
Regional Director Jane Todd

Derbyshire Learning and Skills Council

St Helens Ct, St Helens St, Derby, Derbyshire DE1 3GY; Tel 0845 019 4183; Fax 01332 292188

Chair John Kirkland OBE
Executive Director Peter Brammall

Leicestershire Learning and Skills Council

Meridian East, Meridian Business Pk, Leicester, Leicestershire LE19 1UU; Tel 0845 019 4177; Fax 0116 228 1801
Chair Maureen Milgram Forrest
Executive Director Mary Rogers

Lincolnshire/Rutland Learning and Skills Council

Lindum Business Pk, Station Rd, North Hykeham, Lincoln, Lincolnshire LN6 3FE; Tel 0845 019 4178; Fax 01522 508540
Chair Roger Begy
Executive Director Nick Rashley

Northamptonshire Learning and Skills Council

Royal Pavilion, Summerhouse Rd, Moulton Park Industrial Est, Northampton, Northamptonshire NN3 6BJ; Tel 0845 019 4175; Fax 01604 533046
Chair Christopher Ripper
Executive Director Liz Searle

Nottinghamshire Learning and Skills Council

Castle Marina Rd, Castle Marina Pk, Nottingham, Nottinghamshire NG7 1TN; Tel 0845 019 4187; Fax 0115 948 4589
Chair Keith Stanyard
Executive Director Mick Brown

Government Office for London

Riverwalk Hse, 157–161 Millbank, London SW1P 4RR; URL www.go-london.gov.uk; Tel 020 7217 3328; Fax 020 7217 3450
Regional Director David Warwick (Acting); Tel 020 7217 3151; Fax 020 7217 3036
Director (Skills and Education) Richard Wragg; e-mail rwragg.gol@go-regions.gsi.gov.uk
Contact Ian McNab; e-mail imcnab.gol@go-regions.gsi.gov.uk

London Central Learning and Skills Council

Centre Point, 103 New Oxford St, London WC1A 1DR; Tel 0845 019 4144; Fax 020 7896 8686
Chair Yvonne Thompson
Executive Director Jacqueline Henderson

London East Learning and Skills Council

Boardman Hse, 64 Broadway, Stratford, London E15 1NT; Tel 0845 019 4151; Fax 020 8929 3802
Chair Ken Coello
Executive Director Mary Conneely

London North Learning and Skills Council

Dumayne Hse, 1 Fox La, Palmers Grn, London N13 4AB; Tel 0845 019 4158; Fax 020 8882 5931
Chair Peter Lyne
Executive Director Verity Bullough

London South Learning and Skills Council

Canius Hse, 1 Scarbrook Rd, Croydon, Surrey CR0 1SQ; Tel 0845 019 4172; Fax 020 8929 4706

10

Chair Roy Charles
Executive Director Victor Seddon

London West Learning and Skills Council
West London Centre, 15–21 Staines Rd, Hounslow,
Middlesex TW3 3HA; Tel 0845 019 4164;
Fax 020 8929 8403
Chair Vacancy
Executive Director Peter Pledger

Government Office for the North East
Wellbar Hse, Gallowgate, Newcastle upon Tyne, Tyne and
Wear NE1 4TD; URL www.go-ne.gov.uk;
Tel 0191 201 3300; Fax 0191 202 3830
Head (Central Secretariat) Helen Parks

County Durham Learning and Skills Council
Horndale Ave, Aycliffe Industrial Pk, Newton Aycliffe,
County Durham DL5 6XS; Tel 0845 019 4174;
Fax 01325 372302
Chair Olivia Grant
Executive Director Austin McNamara

Northumberland Learning and Skills Council
Suite 2, Craster Ct, Manor Wlk, Cramlington,
Northumberland NE23 6XX; Tel 0845 019 4185;
Fax 01670 706212
Chair Barry Morgan
Executive Director Susan Bickerton

Tees Valley Learning and Skills Council
3 Queens Sq, Middlesborough, Cleveland TS2 1AA;
Tel 0845 019 4166; Fax 01642 232480
Chair Miles Middleton OBE
Executive Director Pam Eccles

Tyne and Wear Learning and Skills Council
Moongate Hse, 5th Avenue Business Pk, Team Valley,
Gateshead, Tyne and Wear NE11 0HF; Tel 0845 019 4181;
Fax 0191 491 6159
Chair Ashley Winter
Executive Director Chris Roberts

Government Office for the North West
Sunley Tower, Piccadilly Plaza, Manchester M1 4BE;
URL www.go-nw.gov.uk; e-mail
bbendell.gonw@go-regions.gov.uk; Tel 0161 952 4000;
Fax 0161 952 4099
Regional Director Keith Barnes
Manager (Communications) Bruce Bendell

Bolton and Bury Education Business Partnership
EBP Hse, 9 Chorley New Rd, Bolton, Greater Manchester
BL1 4QR; URL www.boltonburyebp.co.uk; e-mail
thopkins@boltonburyebp.co.uk; Tel 01204 375790
Director Tracy Hopkins

Cheshire/Warrington Learning and Skills Council
Dalton Hse, Dalton Way, Middlewich, Cheshire CW10 0HU;
Tel 0845 019 4163; Fax 01606 320082
Chair Brian Fleet
Executive Director Julia Dowd

Cumbria Learning and Skills Council
Venture Hse, Regents Ct, Guard St, Workington, Cumbria
CA14 4EW; Tel 0845 019 4159; Fax 01900 733302
Chair Rober Cairns
Executive Director Mick Farley

Greater Manchester Learning and Skills Council
Arndale Hse, Arndale Centre, Manchester M4 3AQ;
Tel 0845 019 4142; Fax 0161 261 0370
Chair Anthony Goldstone OBE
Executive Director Liz Davis

Greater Merseyside Learning and Skills Council
3rd Fl, Tithebarn Hse, Tithebarn St, Liverpool, Merseyside
L2 2NZ; Tel 0845 019 4150; Fax 0151 672 3533
Executive Director Paul Holme

Lancashire Learning and Skills Council
Caxton Rd, Fulwood, Preston, Lancashire PR2 9ZB;
Tel 0845 019 4157; Fax 01772 443002
Chair John Oliver
Executive Director Steve Palmer

Government Office for the South East
Bridge Hse, 1 Walnut Tree Cl, Guildford, Surrey GU1 4GA;
URL www.go-se.gov.uk; e-mail
reception.gose@go-regions.gsi.gov.uk; Tel 01483 882255;
Fax 01483 882259
Regional Director Rolande Anderson
Contact Carey Johnson

Berkshire Learning and Skills Council
Pacific Hse, Imperial Way, Reading, Berkshire RG2 0TF;
Tel 0845 019 4147; Fax 0118 908 2109
Chair Thomas Melvin
Executive Director Jay Mercer

Hampshire/Isle of Wight Learning and Skills Council
25 Thackeray Mall, Fareham, Hampshire PO16 0PQ;
Tel 0845 019 4182; Fax 01329 237733
Chair Penelope Melville-Brown

Kent/Medway Learning and Skills Council
26 Kings Hill Ave, Kings Hill, West Malling, Kent
ME19 4AE; Tel 0845 019 4152; Fax 01732 841641
Chair Allan Chisholm
Executive Director Simon Norton

Oxford/Buckinghamshire/Milton Keynes Learning and Skills Council
24 The Quadrant, Abingdon Science Pk, Barton La,
Oxfordshire OX14 3YS; Tel 0845 019 4154;
Fax 01235 556201
Chair Dr Patrick Upson
Executive Director Christine Doubleday

Surrey Learning and Skills Council
Technology Hse, 48–54 Goldsworth Rd, Woking, Surrey
GU21 1LE; Tel 01483 803209; Fax 01483 803330
Chair Robert Douglas
Executive Director Nick Wilson

Sussex Learning and Skills Council
Prince's Hse, 53 Queens Rd, Brighton, East Sussex BN1 3XE;
Tel 01273 783555; Fax 01273 783565
Chair Norman Boyland
Executive Director Henry Ball

Government Office for the South West
2 Rivergate, Temple Quay, Bristol BS1 6ED;
URL www.gosw.gov.uk; Tel 0117 900 1700;
Fax 0117 900 1900
Mast Hse, Shepherds Wharf, 24 Sutton Rd, Plymouth
PL4 0HJ; Tel 01752 635000; Fax 01752 227647
Castle Hse, Pydar St, Truro, Cornwall TR1 2UD;
Tel 01872 264500; Fax 01872 264503
Regional Director Bronwyn Hill

Bournemouth, Dorset and Poole Learning and Skills Council
Provincial Hse, 25 Oxford Rd, Bournemouth BH8 8EY;
Tel 0845 019 4148; Fax 01202 652666
Chair Graham Yates
Executive Director Patricia Taylor

Devon and Cornwall Learning and Skills Council
Foliot Hse, Budshead Rd, Crownhill, Plymouth PL6 5XR;
Tel 0845 019 4155; Fax 01752 754040
Chair Prof Sir John Bull
Executive Director Paul Lucken

Gloucestershire Learning and Skills Council
Conway Hse, 33–35 Worcester St, Gloucester,
Gloucestershire GL1 3AJ; Tel 01452 450001;
Fax 01452 450002

Chair Brian Kemp
Executive Director Roger Crouch

Somerset Learning and Skills Council
The Business Centre, East Reach, Taunton, Somerset TA1 3EN; Tel 0845 019 4161; Fax 01823 256174
Chair Jane Barrie
Executive Director Dugald Sandeman

West of England Learning and Skills Council
St Lawrence Hse, 29–31 Broad St, Bristol BS99 7HR; Tel 0845 019 4168; Fax 0117 922 6664
Chair John Savage
Executive Director Paul May

Wiltshire and Swindon Learning and Skills Council
The Bora Bldg, Westlea Campus, Westlea Down, Swindon SN5 7EZ; Tel 0845 019 4176; Fax 01793 608003
Chair Bryan McGinty
Executive Director Penny Hachett

Government Office for the West Midlands
5 St Philip's Pl, Colmore Row, Birmingham, West Midlands B3 2PW; URL www.go-wm.gov.uk; e-mail enquiries@go-wm.gov.uk; Tel 0121 212 5050; Fax 0121 212 5310

Birmingham and Solihull Learning and Skills Council
Chaplin Ct, 80 Hurst St, Birmingham, West Midlands B5 4TG; URL www.lsc.gov.uk/birminghamsolihull; Tel 0845 019 4143; Fax 0121 345 4503
Chair John Towers
Executive Director David Cragg

Black Country Learning and Skills Council
Black Country Hse, Rounds Green Rd, Oldbury B69 2DG; URL www.lsc.gov.uk/blackcountry; e-mail blackcountryinfo@lsc.gov.uk; Tel 0121 345 4811; Fax 0121 345 4777
Executive Director Andrew Brown

Learning and Skills Council Shropshire
Hollinswood Hse, Suite G1, Stafford Ct, Stafford Pk, Telford, Shropshire TF3 3DD; URL www.lsc.gov.uk/shropshire; e-mail shropshireinfo@lsc.gov.uk; Tel 0845 019 4190; Fax 01952 235556
Area Director Sharon Gray

National LSC
Cheylesmore Hse, Quinton Rd, Coventry, Warwickshire CV1 2WT; URL www.lsc.gov.uk/cw; Tel 02476 823946; Fax 02476 825736

Staffordshire Learning and Skills Council
Festival Way, Festival Pk, Stoke-on-Trent, Staffordshire ST1 5TQ; URL www.lsc.org.uk/staffordshire; e-mail staffordshireinfo@lsc.gov.uk; Tel 0845 019 4149; Fax 01782 463104
Executive Director Gill Howland

Government Office for Yorkshire and the Humber
PO Box 213, City Hse, New Station St, Leeds, West Yorkshire LS1 4US; e-mail rporritt.goyh@go-regions.gsi.gov.uk; Tel 0113 283 5252; Fax 0113 283 5405
Contact Roy Porritt

Humberside Learning and Skills Council
The Maltings, Silvester Sq, Silvester St, Kingston upon Hull, East Riding of Yorkshire HU1 3HL; Tel 0845 019 4153; Fax 01482 383595
Chair Robert Smith
Executive Director Sheilah Burden

North Yorkshire Learning and Skills Council
7 Pioneer Business Pk, Amy Johnson Way, York, North Yorkshire YO30 4YN; Tel 0845 019 4146; Fax 01904 385503
Executive Director David Harbourne

South Yorkshire Learning and Skills Council
The Straddle, Victoria Quays, Wharf St, Sheffield, South Yorkshire S2 5SY; Tel 0845 019 4171; Fax 0114 267 5012
Executive Director John Korzeniewski

West Yorkshire Learning and Skills Council
Mercury Hse, 4 Manchester Rd, Bradford, West Yorkshire BD5 0QL; Tel 0845 019 4169; Fax 01274 444009
Chair Clive Leach
Executive Director Margaret Coleman

Scotland – Local Enterprise Companies

Argyll and The Islands Enterprise
The Enterprise Centre, Kilmory, Lochgilphead, Argyll and Bute PA31 8SH; URL www.hie.co.uk/aie; e-mail info@aie.co.uk; Tel 01546 602281; Fax 01546 603964

Scottish Enterprise Ayrshire
17–19 Hill St, Kilmarnock, East Ayrshire KA3 1HA; Tel 01563 526623; Fax 01563 543636
Chief Executive Evelyn McCann
Chair Simon Foster
Company Secretary Craig Nimmo

Scottish Enterprise Borders
Bridge St, Galasheils, Scottish Borders TD1 1SW; Tel 01896 758991; Fax 01896 758625
Chief Executive David Gass
Chair Hugh Tasker
Company Secretary Julian Pace

Scottish Enterprise Edinburgh and Lothian
Apex Hse, 99 Haymarket Terr, Edinburgh EH12 5HD; URL www.scottish-enterprise.com/edinburghandlothian; e-mail lothian@scotent.co.uk; Tel 0131 313 4000; Fax 0131 313 4231
Chief Executive David Crichton
Chair Charles Hammond
Company Secretary John Fanning

Scottish Enterprise Fife
Kingdom Hse, Saltire Centre, Glenrothes, Fife KY6 2AQ; Tel 01592 623000; Fax 01592 623149
Chief Executive Robert McKenzie
Chair Ray Baker

Scottish Enterprise Forth Valley
Laurel Hse, Laurelhill Business Pk, Stirling FK7 9JQ; Tel 01786 451919; Fax 01786 478123
Chief Executive Charlene O'Connor
Chair Tom Shields
Company Secretary Ken Goodwin

Scottish Enterprise Glasgow
Atrium Ct, 50 Waterloo St, Glasgow G2 6HQ; URL www.scottish-enterprise.com/glasgow; Tel 0141 204 1111; Fax 0141 248 1600
Operations Director Stuart Patrick

Grampian Education Business Partnership
27 Albyn Pl, Aberdeen AB10 1DB; Tel 01224 252048; Fax 01224 213417
Manager Isobel Maughan

HIE Innse Gall
James Sq, 9 James St, Stornoway, Isle of Lewis HS1 2QN; URL www.hie.co.uk/innse-gall; e-mail innse-gall@hient.co.uk; Tel 01851 703703; Fax 01851 704130
Regional Director Donnie Macaulay

HIE Inverness and East Highland
The Green Hse, Beechwood Business Pk North, Inverness, Highland IV2 3BL; URL www.hie.co.uk/ieh; Tel 01463 713504; Fax 01463 712002
Chief Executive Stuart Black

10

Chair   Freda Rapson
Head of Executive Office   Billy Macrae

Scottish Enterprise Lanarkshire

New Lanarkshire Hse, Strathclyde Business Pk, Bellshill, North Lanarkshire ML4 3AD;
    URL www.scottish-enterprise-com/lanarkshire; e-mail selenquiry@scotent.co.uk; Tel 01698 745454;
    Fax 01698 842211
Chief Executive   Liz Connolly
Chair   Neil MacDonald
SEL creates and delivers innovative business development, training, skills and environmental programmes throughout Lanarkshire

Lochaber Enterprise

St Mary's Hse, Gordon Sq, Fort William, Highland PH33 6DY; URL www.hie.co.uk/lochaber; e-mail lochaber@hient.co.uk; Tel 01397 704326;
    Fax 01397 705309
Chief Executive   Charlotte Wright (Acting)
Chair   Andrew McFarlane-Slack

Moray, Badenoch and Strathspey Enterprise

The Apex, Forres Enterprise Pk, Forres IV36 2AB;
    URL www.hie.co.uk/mbse; Tel 01309 696000;
    Fax 01309 696001
Chief Executive   Douglas Yule
Chair   Derek Bedford

Scottish Enterprise Renfrewshire

27 Causeyside St, Paisley, Renfrewshire PA1 1UL;
    URL www.scottish-enterprise.com; Tel 0141 848 0101;
    Fax 0141 848 6930

Ross and Cromarty Enterprise

69–71 High St, Invergordon, Highland IV18 0AA;
    URL www.hie.co.uk/race; e-mail info@race.co.uk;
    Tel 01349 853666; Fax 01349 853833
Chief Executive   Gordon Cox
Head (Skills Development)   David Caddick

Shetland Enterprise

Toll Clock Shopping Centre, 26 North Rd, Lerwick, Shetland Islands ZE1 0DE; URL www.hie.co.uk/shetland;
    Tel 01595 693177; Fax 01595 693208
Chief Executive   Dr Ann Black
Chair   Brian Anderson

Skye and Lochalsh Enterprise

Kings Hse, The Green, Portree, Highland IV51 9BS;
    URL www.hie.co.uk/sale; e-mail sale@hient.co.uk;
    Tel 01478 612841; Fax 01478 612164
Chief Executive   Robert D. Muir
Chair   Muriel Jones

Scottish Enterprise Tayside

Enterprise Hse, 45 North Lindsay St, Dundee DD1 1HT;
    e-mail reception@scotent.co.uk; Tel 01382 223100;
    Fax 01382 201319
Chief Executive   Shana Cormack
Chair   Ian McMillan
Company Secretary   Jack Robertson

Highlands and Islands Enterprise

Tollemache Hse, High St, Thurso, Caithness, Highland KW14 8AZ; URL www.hie.co.uk/
    caithness-and-sutherland; e-mail
    caithness-and-sutherland@hient.co.uk; Tel 01847 896115;
    Fax 01847 893383
Area Director   Carroll Buxton

Wales

ELWa

Waterside Business Pk, Clos Llyn Cwm, Swansea Enterprise Pk, Swansea SA6 8AH; URL www.elwa.org.uk; e-mail info@elwa.org.uk; Tel 01792 765800; Fax 01792 765801

ELWa Mid Wales   1st Fl, St David's Hse, Newtown, Powys SY16 1RB; URL www.elwa.org.uk; e-mail info@elwa.org.uk; Tel 01686 622494; Fax 01686 622716
Regional Director   Robin Beckmann
ELWa North Wales   St Asaph Business Pk, St Asaph, Denbighshire LL17 0LJ; URL www.elwa.org.uk; e-mail info@elwa.org.uk; Tel 01745 538500; Fax 01745 538501
Regional Director   Katie Blackburn
ELWa South East Wales   Ty'r Afon, Bedwas Rd, Bedwas, Caerphilly CF83 8WT; URL www.elwa.org.uk; e-mail info@elwa.org.uk; Tel 01443 663663; Fax 01443 663653
Regional Director   David Morgan
ELWa South West Wales   Waterside Business Pk, Clos Llyn Cwm, Swansea Enterprise Pk, Llansamlet, Swansea SA6 8AH; URL www.elwa.org.uk; e-mail info@elwa.org.uk; Tel 01792 765800; Fax 01792 765801
Regional Director   Richard Hart

National Council for Education and Training for Wales

Area covered: Conwy, Denbighshire, Flintshire, Gwynedd, Isle of Anglesey, Wrexham
Unit 6, St Asaph Business Pk, St Asaph, Denbigh, Denbighshire LL17 0LJ; Tel 01745 538500;
    Fax 01745 538501
Regional Director   Katie Blackburn

Northern Ireland

Northern Ireland Employment Service

Headquarters, Belfast BT2 8DJ; Tel 028 9025 7777
Director (Employment Service)   J.D. Noble

Industrial Training

Careers Service

Department for Employment and Learning, 3rd Fl, Lesley Bldgs, 61 Fountain St, Belfast BT1 5EX;
    URL www.careersserviceni.com; e-mail john.mckeown@delni.gov.uk; Tel 028 9044 1840;
    Fax 028 9044 1820
Head (Careers and Guidance Services)   John McKeown

Cogent SSC Ltd

Minerva Hse, Bruntland Rd, Portlethen, Aberdeen AB12 4QL; URL www.cogent-ssc.com; e-mail john.ramsay@cogent-ssc.com; Tel 01224 787800;
    Fax 01224 787830
Contact   J. Ramsay
Sector Skills Council
Development and approval of standards of training and competence for the offshore oil and gas industry, training registrars, accreditors and verifiers

Construction Skills

Bircham Newton, King's Lynn, Norfolk PE31 6RH;
    URL www.constructionskills.net; Tel 01485 577577;
    Fax 01485 577793
Chair   Sir Michael Latham
Deputy Chair   Peter Rogerson
Scope
Construction Skills is the sector skills council for the construction industry. Construction Skills provides assistance in all aspects of recruiting, training and qualifying the construction workforce. It also works with partners in industry and government to improve the competitiveness of the industry as a whole.

Officials of the Board

Chief Executive   Peter Lobban

Regional Offices

Construction Skills Greater London and East 1a Peel St, Luton, Bedfordshire LU1 2QR; Tel 01582 727462; Fax 01582 456318
Area Manager Vacancy

Construction Skills Midlands Belton Road Industrial Est, 20 Prince William Rd, Loughbrough, Leicestershire LE11 0GU; Tel 01509 610266; Fax 01509 210241
Area Manager Sandra Bell

Construction Skills North East 2nd Fl, Tower Hse, Sunderland, Tyne and Wear SR5 3XJ; Tel 0191 516 3900; Fax 0191 516 9978
Area Manager Ben Dures

Construction Skills North West 10–12 Waterside Ct, St Helens Tech Campus, St Helens, Merseyside WA9 1HA; Tel 01744 616004; Fax 01744 617003
Area Manager Steve Howsley

Construction Skills South West 7 Kew Ct, Pynes Hill, Exeter, Devon EX2 5AZ; Tel 01392 444900; Fax 01392 445044
Area Manager Stella Rose Williams

Construction Skills Southern Counties Eastleigh Hse 1st Fl, Upper Market St, Eastleigh SO50 9FD; Tel 02380 620505; Fax 02380 612056
Area Manager John Course

Construction Skills Yorkshire and Humber Milton Hse, Queen St, Leeds, West Yorkshire LS27 9EL; Tel 0113 252 1966; Fax 0113 220 3116
Area Manager Ken Parker

Construction Skills Scotland 4 Edison St, Hillington, Glasgow G52 4XN; Tel 0141 810 3044; Fax 0141 882 1100
Director Graeme Ogilvy

Construction Skills Wales Unit 4 and 5 Bridgend Business Centre, David St, Bridgend Industrial Est, Bridgend CF31 3SH; Tel 01656 655226; Fax 01656 655232
Director Wyn Prichard

EMTA Training Organisation for Engineering Manufacture

EMTA Hse, 14 Upton Rd, Watford, Hertfordshire WD18 0JT; URL www.emta.org.uk; Tel 01923 238441; Fax 01923 256086
Chair Lord David Trefgarne
The training organisation for engineering manufacture, and aspirant SSC for science, engineering, manufacture and technology. EMTA is responsible for the development of standards of competence for occupations at all levels in the industry and for the development of national training frameworks for modern apprenticeships and similar programmes. EMTA wholly owns an awarding body – EMTA Awards Ltd – which is accredited to award NVQs and SVQs at levels 1–5.

Officials of the Board
Chief Executive Dr M.D. Sanderson
Director (Finance); Company Secretary P.W. Whiteman

Improvement and Development Agency (IDeA)

Layden Hse, 76–86 Turnmill St, London EC1M 5LG; URL www.idea.gov.uk; Tel 020 7296 6600; Fax 020 7296 6666
Chair Cllr Ian Swithenbank
Scope
Local authorities in England and Wales. The IDeA exists to help local government meet the current agenda for change, both in response to initiatives generated by central government and those introduced by local government itself. The IDeA aims to help local authorities improve the way they work; help local authorities develop the skills of those working in local government; recognise the future challenges facing local government, and respond to those challenges on behalf of local government; disseminate local government's achievements at a national level.

Officials of the Board
Executive Director Lucy de Groot
Director (IDeA Solutions) John O'Brien
Director (Knowledge and Learning) Martin Horton

Institute for the Management of Information Systems (IMIS)

Registered Charity Number 291495
5 Kingfisher Hse, New Mill Rd, Orpington, Kent BR5 3QG; e-mail central@imis.org.uk; Tel 0700 002 3456; Fax 0700 002 3023
Manager (Business Development) Vanessa Hymas
IMIS is one of the leading professional associations in the IT sector. It fosters greater understanding of the importance of information systems management, works to enhance the status of those engaged in the profession, and promotes higher standards through better education and training, in the UK and overseas.

Lantra Limited

Lantra Hse, Stoneleigh Pk, Coventry, Warwickshire CV8 2LG; URL www.lantra.co.uk; e-mail connect@lantra.co.uk; Tel 024 7669 6996; Fax 024 7669 6732
Chief Executive Peter Martin
Manager (Corporate Communications) Annabel Shackleton
Lantra is the Sector Skills Council for the environmental and land-based sector, representing the training and business development interests of more than 230 000 businesses, including 1 million workers and 400 000 volunteers. The sector covers 17 related industries, including agriculture, animal care, animal technology, aquaculture, environmental conservation, equine, farriery, fencing, fisheries management, floristry, game and wildlife management, land-based engineering, landscape, production horticulture, trees and timber, and veterinary nursing. Lantra aims to raise the level of skills, knowledge and enterprise of individuals working in the sector to increase competitiveness, productivity and to boost sustainable development.

Man-Made Fibres Industry Training Trust

Stowe Hse, Netherstowe, Lichfield, Staffordshire WS13 6TJ; URL www.man-made-fibres.co.uk; e-mail trust@man-made-fibres.co.uk Tel 01543 254223; Fax 01543 257848
Chair N.D. Wallace
General Manager P.A. Grice FISM, MCIPD

NAITeC Ltd

Bradbury Rd, Aycliffe Industrial Pk, Newton Aycliffe, County Durham DL5 6DA; URL www.naitec.co.uk; e-mail naitec@aycliffe.itecne.co.uk; Tel 01325 304351; Fax 01325 304351
Contact Barbara Hay
NAITeC has approximately 35 members who have established themselves as leading national providers of IT related training and qualifications, including the delivery and assessment of NVQs. NAITeC members adhere to a national code of practice, and are undertaking ISO 9000 or equivalent quality standards. Standard or personalised short courses are available in almost all popular computer packages and applications. The centres are also approved by many awarding bodies, including BTEC, RSA, City and Guilds, EnTra and SQA. Further information on the ITeC in your area and how it might help you is available from the above office.

National Education Business Partnership Network

188 Main St, New Greenham Pk, Thatcham, Berkshire RG19 6HW; URL www.nebpn.org; e-mail jenny@nebpn.org; Tel 01635 279918; Fax 01635 279919
Development Manager Jenny Asher

10

National School of Government

Sunningdale Pk, Larch Ave, Ascot, Berkshire SL5 0QE;
URL www.nationalschool.gov.uk; e-mail
customer.services@nationalschool.gsi.gov.uk;
Tel 01344 634000; Fax 01344 634787

Director   Robin Ryde

The National School of Government is the centre of
excellence for learning and development in support of the
strategic business priorities of government

People 1st

2nd Fl, Armstrong, 38 Market Sq, Uxbridge, Greater London
UB8 1LH; URL www.people1st.co.uk; e-mail
info@people1st.co.uk; Tel 0870 060 2550;
Fax 0870 060 2551

Chief Executive   Brian Wisdom

People 1st is the Sector Skills Council for the hospitality,
leisure, travel and tourism industry throughout the UK. It
advocates the value of skills development to employers,
employees, educators and the government, and aims to
make business more productive and individuals more
employable through skills.

People 1st Scotland   28 Castle St, Edinburgh EH2 2HT;
e-mail info@people1st.co.uk

Polymer Training

Halesfield 7, Telford, Shropshire TF7 4NA; e-mail
general@ptlonline.org; Tel 01952 587020;
Fax 01952 582065

Manager (Communications)   Wendi Beamson

Services offered

Technical training, human resource consultancy,
development courses, computer-based training, young
people training, technical publications, Modern
Apprenticeships, Scottish/National Vocational
Qualifications

RTITB Ltd

Access Hse, Halesfield 17, Telford, Shropshire TF7 4PW;
URL www.rtitb.co.uk; e-mail rtitb@rtitb.co.uk;
Tel 01952 520200; Fax 01952 520201

Managing Director   A. Nelson

Scope

RTITB Ltd accredits the training arrangements of
organisations providing training in lift truck instructor
training; lift truck operations (operator training); large
goods vehicle driving assessor training; large goods vehicle
specialist/job trainer instruction; other transport related
training. There are more than 600 organisations accredited
by RTITB to offer transport, distribution, warehousing and
logistics training in the UK.

Officials of the Board

Managing Director   A. Nelson

All enquiries to Marketing Department

Number of firms on the board's register

27 000

Skillfast-UK

80 Richardshaw La, Pudsey, Leeds, West Yorkshire
LS28 6BN; URL www.skillfast-uk.org; e-mail
enquiries@skillfast-uk.org; Tel 0113 227 3333;
Fax 0113 227 3388

CAPITB Trust is the National Training Organisation for the
British Apparel and allied products industry. Its
responsibilities include vocational education and promoting
clothing careers and training programmes.

Officials of the Board

Chief Executive   J.W. Dearden

Connexions Head Offices

East of England

Connexions Bedfordshire and Luton

1–27 Bolton Rd, Luton, Bedfordshire LU1 3HY;
URL www.connx.org.uk; e-mail info@connx.org.uk;
Tel (freephone) 0800 032 1319; Tel 0845 612 3300;
Fax 0845 612 7921

Connexions Cambridgeshire and Peterborough

7 The Meadows, Meadow La, St Ives, Huntingdon,
Cambridgeshire PE27 4LG;
URL www.connexionscp.co.uk; e-mail
stivesccg@cambscg.co.uk; Tel 01480 376000;
Tel (freephone helpline 0900–1700 Mon–Fri; 0930–1300
Sat) 0800 561 3219

Chief Executive   Stephanie Luke (Acting)

Essex, Southend and Thurrock Connexions Ltd

Westergaard Hse, The Matchyns, London Rd, Rivenhall,
Essex CM8 3HA; URL www.estconnexions.co.uk; e-mail
enquiries@estconnexions.co.uk; Tel 01376 533060;
Fax 01376 533061

Connexions Hertfordshire

28 Castle St, Hertford, Hertfordshire SG14 1HH;
URL www.connexions-hertfordshire.co.uk; e-mail
andrew.simmons@hertscc.gov.uk; Tel 01992 531963

Connexions Norfolk

Norwich City FC, Carrow Rd, Norwich, Norfolk NR1 1HU;
URL www.connexions-norfolk.co.uk; e-mail
enquiries@connexions-norfolk.co.uk; Tel 01603 215300

Suffolk Youth and Connexions Service

Suffolk County Council, Endeavour Hse, Gold Block PL3,
Russell Rd, Ipswich, Suffolk IP1 2BX;
URL www.connexionssuffolk.org.uk; e-mail
enquiries@connexionssuffolk.org.uk; Tel (0900–1700
Mon–Fri)) 0800 085 4448; Tel 01473 260169;
Fax 01473 266848

East Midlands

Connexions Derbyshire

2 Godkin Hse, Park Rd, Ripley, Derbyshire DE5 3EF;
URL www.connexions-derbyshire.org; e-mail
angela.calvert@debp.co.uk; Tel (freephone) 0800 269 468;
Tel 01773 570939

Chief Executive   Hugh Hastie

Connexions Leicester Shire

2nd Fl, 6 Millstone La, Leicester, Leicestershire LE1 5JN;
URL www.connexions-leics.org; e-mail
enquiries@connexions-leics.org; Tel 0116 261 5900

Chief Executive   Rosemary Beard

Connexions Lincolnshire

Lincolnshire County Council, County Office, Newland,
Lincoln, Lincolnshire LN1 1YL; Tel 01522 552222

Head (Teenager Services)   Sal Thirlway

Connexions Northamptonshire

Wood Burcote Hse, Burcote Rd, Towcester NN12 6TF;
Tel 01604 356124

Connexions Nottinghamshire

Head Office, Heathcote Bldgs, Heathcote St, Nottingham,
Nottinghamshire NG1 3AA; URL www.cnxnotts.co.uk;
e-mail ask@cnxnotts.co.uk; Tel 0115 912 6611;
Fax 0115 912 6612

Chief Executive   Jean Pardoe

London

Connexions Central London

Partnership Office, 125 Freston Rd, London W10 6TH;
URL www.centrallondonconnexions.org.uk; e-mail
info@centrallondonconnexions.org.uk; Tel (help and
advice) 0808 001 3219; Tel 020 7938 8087;
Fax 020 7938 8020

Central London Connexions provides information, advice
and practical support to all 13–19 year olds (up to the age of
25 if a person has learning difficulties or disabilities); it helps
young people within the seven central London boroughs of
Camden, Islington, Kensington and Chelsea, Lambeth,
Southwark, Wandsworth and Westminster

London East Connexions Partnership

Head Office, 4th Fl, Solar Hse, Stratford, London E15 4LJ;
URL www.yourroutes.co.uk; e-mail
info@londoneastconnexions.co.uk; Tel 020 8534 2830;
Tel (Mon–Fri 0900–1700) 020 8536 3630

Connexions North London

New Gallery, Haringey Pk, Crouch End, London N8 9JA;
URL www.connexions-northlondon.co.uk; e-mail
feedback@connexions-northlondon.co.uk;
Tel 020 8347 2380; Fax 020 8347 2390

Connexions South London

Canius Hse, 1 Scarbrook Rd, Croydon, Surrey CR0 1SQ;
URL www.connexions-southlondon.org.uk;
Tel 020 8929 4802

Connexions London West

Suite 4, 2nd Fl, Alperton Hse, Bridgewater Rd, Wembley,
London HA1 1EH;
URL www.connexions-londonwest.com; e-mail
enquiries@connexions-londonwest.com;
Tel 020 8453 5000; Fax 020 8453 5001

North East

Connexions County Durham

Aykley Heads Hse, Aykley Heads, Durham, County
Durham DH1 5TS; URL www.connexions-durham.org;
e-mail info@connexions-durham.org; Tel 0191 383 1777;
Fax 0191 383 2777

Executive Director   J.M. Bray MBE, BA, DipYESTB

Connexions Northumberland

7 Sextant Hse, Freehold St, Blyth, Northumberland
NE24 2BA;
URL www.connexions-northumberland.org.uk; e-mail
enquiries@connexions-northumberland.org.uk;
Tel 01670 798180; Fax 01670 798181

Connexions Tees Valley

Head Office, Calverts La, Stockton-on-Tees TS18 1SW;
URL www.cxtv.co.uk; e-mail
enquiries@connexionsteesvalley.co.uk; Tel 01642 601600;
Fax 01642 633663

Manager (Marketing)   Martin Barrett

Connexions Tyne and Wear

City Library Bldg, 30–32 Fawcett St, Sunderland, Tyne and
Wear SR1 1RE; URL www.connexions-tw.co.uk; e-mail
helpline@connexions-tw.co.uk; Tel 0191 443 2986;
Fax 0191 443 2858

Local Manager   Ray Reay

Connexions Tyne and Wear (Gateshead)

The Interchange Centre, West St, Gateshead, Tyne and Wear
NE8 1BH; URL www.connexions-tw.co.uk;
Tel (freephone) 0800 073 8700; Tel 0191 490 1717;
Fax 0191 4434 264

North West

Connexions Cheshire and Warrington

No. 2 The Stables, Gadbrook Pk, Northwich, Cheshire
CW9 7RJ; URL www.connexions-cw.co.uk; e-mail
info@connexions-cw.co.uk; Tel 01606 305200;
Fax 01606 49158

Chief Executive   Steve Hoy

Connexions Cumbria

24–26 Portland Sq, Carlisle, Cumbria CA1 1PE;
URL www.connexionscumbria.co.uk; e-mail
info@connexionscumbria.co.uk; Tel 01228 597600;
Fax 01228 598080

Chief Executive   Sian Rees

Connexions Greater Manchester

Turing Hse, Archway 5, Birley Fields, Greater Manchester
M15 5RL; URL www.gmconnexions.com; e-mail
info@connexions-gmcr.org.uk; Tel 0161 227 7000;
Fax 0161 342 0095

Connexions Greater Merseyside

The Tea Factory, 3rd Fl, 82 Wood St, Liverpool, Merseyside
L1 4DQ; URL www.connexions-gmerseyside.co.uk;
e-mail hq@connexions-gmerseyside.co.uk;
Tel 0151 703 7400

Connexions Lancashire

Business and Meeting Centre, Chorley Hse, Centurion Way,
Leyland, Lancashire PR26 6TT; URL www.cxl-uk.com;
e-mail info@cxl-uk.com; Tel 01772 642400;
Fax 01772 642401

Managing Director   Karen O'Donoghue

South East

Connexions Berkshire

Pacific Hse, Imperial Way, Reading RG2 0TF;
URL www.connexions-berkshire.org.uk; e-mail
info@connexions-berkshire.org.uk; Tel 0845 408 5001;
Fax 0845 408 5003

Connexions Buckinghamshire

Walker Hse, George St, Aylesbury, Buckinghamshire
HP20 2HU; Tel 01296 397738

Connexions Kent and Medway

Woodstock Hse, 15 Ashford Rd, Maidstone, Kent
ME14 5DA;
URL www.connexionskentandmedway.co.uk; e-mail
website@connexionskentandmedway.co.uk;
Tel 01622 683155; Fax 01622 683129

Connexions Milton Keynes

662 North Row, Milton Keynes MK9 3AP; Tel 01908 232808

Connexions Oxfordshire

Macclesfield Hse, New Rd, Oxford, Oxfordshire OX1 1NA;
Tel 01865 815166

Connexions South Central

4 Gloster Ct, Whittle Ave, Fareham, Hampshire PO15 5SH;
URL www.connexions-southcentral.org;
Tel 01489 566990; Fax 01489 578340

Connexions Surrey

2nd Fl, Connexions Hse, 83 East St, Epsom, Surrey
KT17 1DN; URL www.connexionssurrey.co.uk; e-mail
info@connexionssurrey.co.uk; Tel 01372 746500;
Fax 01372 720400

Connexions Sussex

53 Queens Rd, Brighton, East Sussex BN1 3XB;
URL www.connexions-sussex.org.uk; e-mail
admin@connexions-sussex.org.uk; Tel 01273 783648;
Fax 01273 730055

10

South West

Connexions across Bournemouth, Dorset and Poole
Ansbury Hse, 2 Pendruffle La, Poundbury, Dorchester
DT1 3WJ; URL www.connexions-bdp.co.uk; e-mail
headoffice@connexions-bdp.co.uk; Tel 0800 358 3888

Connexions Cornwall and Devon Ltd
Partnership Office, Tamar Business Pk, Pennygillam
Industrial Est, Pennygillam Way, Launceston, Cornwall
PL15 7ED; URL www.connexions-cd.org.uk; e-mail
partnership@connexions-cd.org.uk; Tel 01566 777672;
Tel (freephone) 0800 975 5111; Fax 01566 777713
Chief Executive   Jenny Rudge OBE

Connexions Gloucestershire
Southgate Hse, Southgate St, Gloucester, Gloucestershire
GL1 1UW; URL www.connexionsglos.org.uk; e-mail
info@connexionsglos.org.uk; Tel (information)
01452 524800; Tel 01452 833600; Fax 01452 833601

Connexions Somerset
1 Mendip Hse, High St, Taunton, Somerset TA1 3SX;
URL www.connexions-somerset.org.uk; e-mail
info@connexions-somerset.org.uk; Tel 01823 423450;
Fax 01823 423479
Chief Executive   Peter Renshaw

Connexions West of England
2nd Fl, 4 Colston Ave, Bristol BS1 4ST;
URL www.connexionswest.org.uk; e-mail
enquiries@connexionswest.org.uk; Tel (0930–1630 Mon–
Thu; 0930–1600 Fri) 0800 923 0323; Fax 0117 074517

Connexions Wiltshire and Swindon
Wiltshire County Council, Unit 7, Avon Reach, Monkton
Hill, Chippenham, Wiltshire SN15 1EE; Tel 01249 448855

West Midlands

Connexions Birmingham and Solihull
100 Broad St, Birmingham, West Midlands B15 1AE;
URL www.connexions-bs.co.uk; e-mail
info@connexions-bs.co.uk; Tel 0121 248 8001

Connexions Black Country
40 Lower High St, Wednesbury, West Midlands WS10 7AQ;
URL www.blackcountryconnexions.co.uk; e-mail
info@blackcountryconnexions.co.uk; Tel 0121 502 7400;
Fax 0121 502 7401

Connexions Coventry and Warwickshire
1st Fl, Tower Ct, Foleshill Enterprise Pk, Courtaulds Way,
Coventry, Warwickshire CV6 5QT;
URL www.connexions-covandwarks.org.uk; e-mail
mailbox@cswpconnexions.org.uk; Tel (0830–1730 Mon–
Fri) 024 7670 7400; Tel 024 7670 7401

Connexions Herefordshire and Worcestershire
County Bldgs, St Marys St, Worcester, Worcestershire
WR1 1TW; URL www.connexions-hw.org.uk; e-mail
headoffice@connexions-hw.org.uk; Tel 01905 765428;
Fax 01905 765527

Connexions Shropshire, Telford and Wrekin
1st Fl, Victoria Hse, Victoria Quay, Welsh Bridge,
Shrewsbury, Shropshire SY1 1HH; URL www.13–
19.org.uk; e-mail enquiry@connexionsstw.org.uk;
Tel 01743 284428

Connexions Staffordshire
Foregate Hse, 70 Foregate St, Stafford, Staffordshire
ST16 2PX; URL www.cxstaffs.co.uk; e-mail
info@cxstaffs.co.uk; Tel (customer services)
0808 1000 434; Tel 01785 355700; Fax 01785 355747;
Minicom 0800 083 7034

Yorkshire and the Humber

Connexions Humber
24 Priory Tec Pk, Saxon Way, Hessle, West Yorkshire
HU13 9PB; URL www.connexionshumber.co.uk; e-mail
cburgess@connexionshumber.co.uk; Tel (0900–1700
Mon–Thu; 0900–1630 Fri) 0808 180 4636; Tel 01482 350151

Connexions South Yorkshire
1 Arena Link, Broughton La, Don Valley, Sheffield, South
Yorkshire S9 2DD; URL www.connexionssy.org.uk;
e-mail info@connexions-sy.org.uk; Tel 0114 261 9393

Connexions West Yorkshire
Parkview Hse, Woodvale Office Pk, Woodvale Rd,
Bridghouse, West Yorkshire HD6 4AB;
URL www.connexionswestyorkshire.co.uk; e-mail
enquiries@connexionswestyorkshire.co.uk;
Tel 01484 727500

Connexions York and North Yorks
2nd Fl, Marlborough Hse, Westminster Pl, York Business Pk,
York YO26 6RS; URL www.connex.me.uk; e-mail
info@connexionsyny.org.uk; Tel 01904 799931

Other Careers Offices

East of England

Connexions
1a St Nicholas Ct, North Walsham, Norwich, Norfolk
NR28 9BY; e-mail nwcc@connexions-norfolk.co.uk;
Tel 01692 408200; Fax 01692 408229
Manager   Mary Lambert

Hertfordshire Careers Services Ltd
Delta Hse, Ave One, Letchworth, Hertfordshire SG6 2HU;
URL www.hcs.co.uk; e-mail info@hcs.co.uk;
Tel 01462 705000; Fax 01462 705001
Chief Executive   Shaun Reason

London

Careers Management, Capital
Head Office, 27b Dalston La, London E8 3DF;
URL www.vtplc.com/careersmanagement; e-mail
enterprisecareers@vtplc.com; Tel 020 7275 0346;
Fax 020 7254 8602

Lifetime Careers Brent and Harrow Ltd
Careers Service Headquarters, 3rd Fl, Lyon Rd, Harrow,
Greater London HA1 2EN;
URL www.careers-london.com; e-mail
enquiries@london.lifetime-careers.co.uk;
Tel 020 8863 1243; Fax 020 8901 3723
Chief Executive   Liam Duffy

Prospects Services Ltd
Prospects Hse, 19 Elmfield Rd, Bromley, Kent BR1 1LT;
URL www.prospects.co.uk; e-mail hq@prospects.co.uk;
Tel 020 8315 1500; Fax 020 8315 1549
Executive Chairman   Ray Auvray
Managing Director   Vincent McDonnell
Director (Group Finance)   Kevin Beerling

North East

Northumberland Guidance Company
1st Fl, 27–12 Bamburgh Hse, Manor Wlks, Cramlington,
Northumberland NE23 6QE; URL www.ngcl.co.uk;
e-mail enquiries@ngcl.co.uk; Tel 01670 597810;
Fax 01670 597811
Managing Director   John Cooke

North West

Lifetime Careers Stockport and High Peak Ltd

2nd Fl, Royal and Sun Alliance Hse, 1–13 Wellington Rd
  North, Stockport, Cheshire SK4 1AF; e-mail
  enquiries@connexions-stockport.co.uk;
  Tel 0161 475 7700; Fax 0161 476 6760
Director (Operations)   Mike Brown

St Helens Careers Services Ltd

SmithKline-Beecham Bldg, Westfield St, St Helens,
  Merseyside WA10 1QQ; Tel 01744 633500;
  Fax 01744 633501
Chief Executive   John Foster

South East

Berkshire and Oxfordshire Careers Services

CfBT Advice and Guidance, Highbridge Hse, 16–18 Duke St,
  Reading RG1 4RU; URL www.wayahead-careers.co.uk;
  e-mail aandg@cfbt-hq.org.uk; Tel 0118 971 9400;
  Fax 0118 971 9422
Managing Director   Lesley Moore

Careers Management Buckinghamshire and Milton Keynes

Head Office, 662 North Row, Milton Keynes,
  Buckinghamshire MK9 3AP; URL www.vtplc.com/
  careersmanagement; e-mail buckscareers@vtplc.com;
  Tel 01908 232808; Fax 01908 208901
General Manager   Julia Valentine

Kent Adult Careers Guidance (Prospects Group)

Joynes Hse, 1–5 New Rd, Gravesend, Kent DA11 0AT;
  URL www.prospects.co.uk; Tel 01474 544475;
  Fax 01474 544377
Marketing Assistant   Mary Webb; e-mail
  mary.webb@prospects.co.uk

Sussex Careers Ltd

Reed Hse, 47 Church Rd, Hove, East Sussex BN3 2BE;
  URL www.sussexcareers.com; e-mail
  hq@sussexcareers.com; Tel 01273 223040;
  Fax 01273 223041
Chief Executive   Stephen Gauntlett

VT Careers Management Surrey

2nd Fl, Sutton Hse, Weyside Pk, Catteshall La, Godalming,
  Surrey GU7 1XJ; URL www.vtplc.com/
  careersmanagement; e-mail surreycareers@vtplc.com;
  Tel 01483 528852; Fax 01483 528860
General Manager   Mike Reeves

VT Careers Management West Sussex

1–2 The Chambers, Chapel St, Chichester, West Sussex
  PO19 1DL; URL www.vtplc.com/careersmanagement;
  e-mail westsussexcareers@vtplc.com; Tel 01243 537799;
  Fax 01243 533111
General Manager   Stephen Tregidgo

South West

Dorset Careers Headquarters

South Grove Cottage, Dorchester, Dorset DT1 1TU;
  URL www.dorset-careers.co.uk; Tel 01305 755100;
  Fax 01305 264545
Chief Executive   Vacancy

Wiltshire Careers Services

Lifetime Careers Wiltshire Ltd, 7 Ascot Ct, White Horse
  Business Pk, Trowbridge, Wiltshire BA14 0XA;
  Tel 01225 716000; Fax 01225 716019
Chief Executive   Linda Kidd

West Midlands

Central Careers

331–333 Stratford Rd, Shirley, Solihull, West Midlands
  B90 3BL; URL www.centralcareers.co.uk; e-mail
  info@centralcareers.co.uk; Tel 0121 251 1800
Chief Executive   Doreen Taylor

Connexions – Birmingham and Solihull

Charter Hse, 100 Broad St, Birmingham, West Midlands
  B15 1AE; URL www.connexions-bs.co.uk; e-mail
  info@connexions-bs.co.uk
Chief Executive   John Ling

Hereford and Worcester Careers Service Ltd

County Bldgs, St Marys St, Worcester, Worcestershire
  WR1 1TW; e-mail careershq@hwcareers.co.uk;
  Tel 01905 765479; Fax 01905 765527
Chief Executive   Jane D. Crysell (Acting)

Prospects Services Ltd

See also London
Castlemill, Tipton, West Midlands DY4 7UF;
  URL www.prospects.co.uk; e-mail
  prospects@prospects.co.uk; Tel 0121 521 2300;
  Fax 0121 557 1502
Chief Executive   Ray Auvray
Director (Operations)   Sue Mattock

Yorkshire and the Humber

Calderdale and Kirklees Careers Ltd

78 John William St, Huddersfield, West Yorkshire HD1 1EH;
  URL www.workabout.org.uk; e-mail
  careers@ckcareers.org.uk; Tel 01484 226700;
  Fax 01484 226767
Chief Executive   G.V. Costello

Careers Bradford Ltd

Onward Hse, Baptist Pl, Bradford, West Yorkshire BD1 2PS;
  URL www.careersb.co.uk; e-mail
  careersdirect@careersb.co.uk; Tel (corporate services)
  01274 829345; Tel 01274 829400; Fax 01274 829401

Guidance Enterprises Group Ltd

Corporate Services, Guidance Hse, York Rd, Thirsk, West
  Yorkshire YO7 3BT; e-mail
  info@guidance-enterprises.co.uk; Tel 01845 526699;
  Fax 01845 526633

Guidance Services Ltd

Guidance Hse, York Rd, Thirsk, North Yorkshire YO7 3BT;
  URL www.guidance-enterprises.co.uk; e-mail
  geginfo@vtplc.com; Tel 01845 526699; Fax 01845 526633
Executive Manager   Allan Hunton

Leeds Careers

No. 1 Eastgate, Leeds, West Yorkshire LS2 7LY;
  URL www.leedscareers.co.uk; e-mail
  enquiries@leedscareers.co.uk; Tel 0113 225 9000;
  Fax 0113 225 9090
Director   Terry Walsh

Nord Anglia Lifetime Development

Lifetime Careers Ltd, Enterprise Ct, Farfield Pk, Manvers
  Way, Wath upon Dearne, Rotherham, South Yorkshire
  S63 5DB;
  URL www.nordanglialifetimedevelopment.co.uk; e-mail
  info@nald-ne.co.uk; Tel 01709 310600; Fax 01709 310624
Regional Director   Sue Holland

Sheffield Futures

Star Hse, 43 Division St, Sheffield, South Yorkshire S1 4SL;
  URL www.sheffieldfutures.org.uk; e-mail
  enquiries@sheffieldfutures.org.uk; Tel 0114 201 2800;
  Fax 0114 273 5190
Chief Executive   John Evans

10

Scotland

Careers Scotland Headquarters, 150 Broomielaw, Atlantic
Quay, Glasgow G2 8LU;
URL www.careers-scotland.org.uk; e-mail
hq@careers-scotland.org.uk; Tel 0845 850 2502;
Fax 0141 228 2851

Careers Scotland, Highlands and Islands

c/o Highlands and Islands Enterprise, Cowan Hse,
Inverness Retail Pk, Inverness, Highland IV2 7GF;
URL www.careers-scotland.org.uk; e-mail
info@careers-scotland.org.uk; Tel 0845 850 2502

Careers Scotland North East Region Headquarters

31 Albert Sq, Dundee DD1 1DJ; Fax 01592 416031
Regional Manager M. Barron
Fife, Grampian and Tayside

Careers Scotland South East Region Headquarters

17 Logie Mill, Edinburgh EH7 4HG; e-mail
southeast@careers-scotland.org.uk; Tel 0131 556 7384;
Fax 0131 556 0841
Regional Manager P.A. Gierthy
Borders, Edinburgh and Lothians, and Forth Valley

Careers Scotland South West Region Headquarters

Scottish Enterprise, New Lanarkshire Hse, Strathclyde
Business Pk, Bellshill, South Lanarkshire ML4 3AD;
URL www.careers-scotland.org.uk; e-mail
southwest@careers-scotland.org.uk; Tel 01698 745454;
Fax 01698 842211
Regional Manager Marjory Logue
Ayrshire, Dumfries and Galloway, and Lanarkshire

Careers Scotland West Region Headquarters

Scottish Enterprise, Atrium Ct, Waterloo St, Glasgow
G2 6HQ; e-mail west@careers-scotland.org.uk;
Tel 0141 204 1111; Fax 0141 248 1600
Chief Executive Catriona Eagle
Dunbartonshire, Glasgow and Renfrewshire

Wales

Careers Wales Association, Suite 6, Block D, Van Ct,
Caerphilly Business Pk, Van Rd, Caerphilly CF83 3ED;
URL www.careerswales.com; e-mail
enquiries@careerswalesassociation.co.uk;
Tel 02920 854880; Fax 02920 854889

Careers Wales Cardiff and Vale

Careers Wales Cardiff and Vale, Cardiff Careers Centre, 53
Charles St, Cardiff CF10 2GD; e-mail
mark.freeman@cardiffandvale.org.uk; Tel 02920 906700;
Fax 02920 906799
Chief Executive Mark Freeman

Careers Wales Gwent

Head Office, Ty Glyn, Albion Rd, Pontypool, Torfaen
NP4 6GE; URL www.careerswalesgwent.com; e-mail
headoffice@careerswalesgwent.org.uk; Tel 01495 756666;
Fax 01495 768950
Chief Executive Trina Neilson

Careers Wales Mid Glamorgan

11 Centre Ct, Main Ave, Treforest Industrial Est,
Pontypridd, Rhondda Cynon Taf CF37 5YR;
URL www.cwmg.co.uk; e-mail hqadmin@cwmg.co.uk;
Tel 01443 842207; Fax 01443 842208
Chief Executive Wayne Feldon

Careers Wales Mid Glamorgan and Powys

10 Centre Ct, Treforest Industrial Est, Pontyrpidd CF37 5YR;
URL www.careerswales.com; e-mail
hqadmin@cwmgp.co.uk; Tel 01443 842207;
Fax 01443 842208
Chief Executive Wayne Feldon

Careers Wales North East

Careers Wales North East, St Davids Bldg, Earl Rd, Mold,
Flintshire CH7 1DD; URL www.careerswales.com;
e-mail enquiries@cwne.org; Tel 01352 750456;
Fax 01352 756470
Chief Executive Joyce M'Caw

Careers Wales North West

Careers Wales North West, Head Office, 5 Castle St,
Caernarfon, Gwynedd LL55 1SE; e-mail
admin@cwne.org; Tel 01286 679199; Fax 01286 679222
Chief Executive Dr John Llewellyn
Information Officer Sarah Jones-Morris

Careers Wales West

Heol Nantyreos, Cross Hands, Carmarthenshire SA14 6RJ;
URL www.careerswaleswest.co.uk; e-mail
mail@careerswaleswest.co.uk; Tel 01269 846000;
Fax 01269 846001
Chief Executive Ray Collier

Northern Ireland

Department for Education and Learning (DEL),
Headquarters Adelaide Hse, 39–49 Adelaide St, Belfast
BT2 8FD; URL www.delni.gov.uk;
www.teaonline.gov.uk; e-mail info@delni.gov.uk;
Tel 028 9025 7777; Fax 028 9025 7795
The main government department in Northern Ireland
concerned with lifelong learning and employment, DEL has
responsibility for the policy, planning and support of higher
and further education; employment rights; equality of
opportunity. The Training and Employment Agency is
responsible for developing and implementing the training
and employment functions of the department. The agency's
overall aim is to assist economic development and to help
people to find work through training and employment
services delivered on the basis of equality of opportunity.

Andersonstown Job Centre

1st Fl, Kennedy Centre, 564–566 Falls Rd, Belfast BT11 9AE;
e-mail andersonstown.jc@delni.gov.uk;
Tel 028 9087 1880; Fax 028 9087 1888

Antrim Jobs and Benefits Office

20 Castle St, Antrim, County Antrim BT41 4JE; e-mail
antrim.jc@delni.gov.uk; Tel 028 9442 6500;
Fax 028 9442 6515

Armagh Jobs and Benefits Office

Alexander Rd, Armagh, County Armagh BT61 7JL; e-mail
armagh-jc@delni.gov.uk; Tel 028 3752 9777;
Fax 028 3752 9749

Ballymena Job Centre

35–39 Bridge St, Ballymena, County Antrim BT43 5EL;
e-mail ballymena.jc@delni.gov.uk; Tel 028 2566 0777;
Fax 028 2566 0766

Ballymoney Jobs and Benefits Office

Crown Bldgs, 37–45 John St, Ballymoney, County Antrim
BT53 6DT; e-mail ballymoney.jc@delni.gov.uk;
Tel 028 2766 0100; Fax 028 2766 0147

Ballynahinch Job Centre

18 Crossgar Rd, Ballynahinch, County Down BT24 8XP;
e-mail ballynahinch.jc@delni.gov.uk; Tel 028 9756 0500;
Fax 028 9756 0545

Banbridge Jobs and Benefits Office

18 Castlewellan Rd, Banbridge, County Down BT32 4AZ;
e-mail banbridge.jc@delni.gov.uk; Tel 028 4062 0800;
Fax 028 4062 3840

Bangor Job Centre

65 High St, Bangor, County Down BT20 5BE; e-mail
bangor.jc@delni.gov.uk; Tel 028 9127 9999;
Fax 028 9146 5747

Belfast North Job Centre
Gloucester Hse, 57 Chichester St, Belfast BT1 4RA; e-mail
northbelfast.jc@delni.gov.uk; Tel 028 9025 2222;
Fax 028 9025 2341
Falls Road Jobs and Benefits Office   19 Falls Rd, Belfast
BT12 4PH; e-mail fallsroad.jc@delni.gov.uk;
Tel 028 9054 2800; Fax 028 9054 2823
Knockbreda Jobs and Benefits Office   Crown Bldgs, 8 Upper
Knockbreda Rd, Belfast BT8 4SX; e-mail
knockbreda.jc@delni.gov.uk; Tel 028 9054 5600;
Fax 028 9054 5610
Shankill Jobs and Benefits Office   15–25 Snugville St, Belfast
BT13 1PP; e-mail shankillroad.jc@delni.gov.uk;
Tel 028 9054 3456; Fax 028 9054 3474

Carrickfergus Jobs and Benefits Office
Davy St, Carrickfergus, County Antrim BT38 8EJ; e-mail
carrickfergus.jc@delni.gov.uk; Tel 028 9335 1811;
Fax 028 9335 6909

Coleraine Jobs and Benefits Office
Artillery Rd, Coleraine, County Londonderry BT52 2AA;
e-mail coleraine.jc@delni.gov.uk; Tel 028 7034 1000;
Fax 028 7034 1187
Contact   F. O'Hara

Cookstown Job Centre
17 Oldtown St, Cookstown, County Tyrone BT80 8EE;
e-mail cookstown.jc@delni.gov.uk; Tel 028 8676 6950;
Fax 028 8676 1231

Downpatrick Job Centre
Rathkeltair Hse, Market St, Downpatrick, County Down
BT30 6LZ; e-mail downpatrick.jc@delni.gov.uk;
Tel 028 4461 8023; Fax 028 4461 8026

Dungannon Jobs and Benefits Office
5 Thomas St, Dungannon, County Tyrone BT70 1HN; e-mail
dungannon.jc@delni.gov.uk; Tel 028 8775 4870;
Fax 028 8775 4327

Enniskillen Jobs and Benefits Office
Crown Bldgs, Queen Elizabeth Rd, Enniskillen, County
Fermanagh BT74 7JD; e-mail enniskillen.jc@delni.gov.uk;
Tel 028 6634 3333; Fax 028 6634 3261

Foyle Jobs and Benefits Office
Crown Bldgs, Asylum Rd, Londonderry, County
Londonderry BT47 7EA; e-mail foyle.jc@delni.gov.uk;
Tel 028 7131 9500; Fax 028 7132 1820

Kilkeel Jobs and Benefits Office
Newry St, Kilkeel, Newry, County Down BT34 4DN; e-mail
kilkeel.jc@delni.gov.uk; Tel 028 4176 1425;
Fax 028 4176 1433

Larne Jobs and Benefits Office
59 Pound St, Larne, County Antrim BT40 1SB; e-mail
larne.jc@delni.gov.uk; Tel 028 2826 3200;
Fax 028 2826 3297

Limavady Jobs and Benefits Office
9 Connell St, Limavady, County Londonderry BT49 0TZ;
e-mail limavady.jc@delni.gov.uk; Tel 028 7776 0500;
Fax 028 7776 0589

Lisburn Jobs and Benefits Office
71 Bow St, Lisburn, County Antrim BT28 1BB; e-mail
lisburn.jc@delni.gov.uk; Tel 028 9262 3300;
Fax 028 9262 3401

Lurgan Jobs and Benefits Office
Alexandra Cres, Lurgan, Craigavon, County Armagh
BT66 6BB; e-mail lurgan.jc@delni.gov.uk;
Tel 028 3831 5600; Fax 028 3831 3244

Magherafelt Jobs and Benefits Office
31 Station Rd, Magherafelt BT45 5DJ; e-mail
magherafelt.jc@delni.gov.uk; Tel 028 7930 2000;
Fax 028 7930 2052

Newcastle Job Centre
113 Main St, Newcastle, County Down BT33 0AE; e-mail
newcastle.jc@delni.gov.uk; Tel 028 4372 5001;
Fax 028 4372 6302

Newry Jobs and Benefits Office
Phoenix Hse, Bridge St, Newry BT35 8AG; e-mail
newry.jc@delni.gov.uk; Tel 028 3026 5522;
Fax 028 3025 4185

Newtownabbey Jobs and Benefits Office
39–41 Church Rd, Glenmount Rd, Newtownabbey, Belfast
BT36 7LB; e-mail newtownabbey.jc@delni.gov.uk;
Tel 028 9054 8133; Fax 028 9054 8110

Newtownards Job Centre
9 Conway St, Newtownards, County Down BT23 4DA;
e-mail newtownards.jc@delni.gov.uk; Tel 028 9181 8653;
Fax 028 9182 4911

Omagh Jobs and Benefits Office
7 Mountjoy Rd, Omagh BT79 7BB; e-mail
omagh.jc@delni.gov.uk; Tel 028 8225 5500;
Fax 028 8225 5511

Portadown Jobs and Benefits Office
140 Jervis St, Portadown, County Armagh BT62 3HA; e-mail
portadown.jc@delni.gov.uk; Tel 028 3839 7200;
Fax 028 3829 6255

Strabane Job Centre
23 Upper Main St, Strabane, County Tyrone BT82 8AS;
e-mail strabane.jc@delni.gov.uk; Tel 028 7138 2332;
Fax 028 7138 2172

Channel Islands, Isle of Man and Isles of Scilly

Guernsey Careers Services
Education Department, The Grange, St Peter Port, Guernsey
GY1 3AU, Channel Islands; URL www.careers.gg; e-mail
careers@education.gov.gg; Tel 01481 710821;
Fax 01481 713015

Isle of Man Careers Services
Careers Advisory Service, Careers Centre, St Georges Ct,
Hill St, Douglas, Isle of Man IM1 1EE;
URL www.gov.im/careers; e-mail careers@gov.im;
Tel 01624 685128; Fax 01624 687016

Jersey Careers Service
Department for Education, Sport and Culture, St Helier,
Jersey JE4 8QJ, Channel Islands; URL www.gov.je/
careers; e-mail careers@gov.je; Tel 01534 449440;
Fax 01534 449470

Careers Advice and Counselling

Association of Graduate Recruiters
The Innovation Centre, Warwick Technology Pk, Gallows
Hill, Warwick, Warwickshire CV34 6UW;
URL www.agr.org.uk; e-mail info@agr.org.uk;
Tel 01926 623236; Fax 01926 623237
Chief Executive   Carl Gilleard

Cambridge University Careers Service
Stuart Hse, Mill La, Cambridge, Cambridgeshire CB2 1XE;
URL www.careers.cam.ac.uk; e-mail
enquiries@careers.cam.ac.uk; Tel 01223 338288
Head of Department   Gordon Chesterman

Career Analysts Ltd
120 Crawford St, London W1U 6BL;
URL www.careeranalysts.co.uk; e-mail
info@careeranalysts.co.uk; Tel 020 7935 5452
Managing Director   Leo Soloman
For career advice in all aspects of education

Career Counselling Services
46 Ferry Rd, Barnes, London SW13 9PW;
URL www.career-counselling-services.co.uk; e-mail
careercs@dial.pipex.com; Tel 020 8741 0335
Managing Director   Robert Nathan MSc, DipCouns,
CPsychol

Career Guidance
4 Cadogan La, London SW1X 9EB; Tel 020 7631 1209
Director   J.F. Stevenson MA, MSc

Careers Guidance Consultants
Hooton Lawn, Benty Heath La, Hooton, Merseyside
L66 6AG; Tel 0151 327 3894
Contact   Dr D.W. Blything

Careers Research and Advisory Centre (CRAC)
Sheraton Hse, Castle Pk, Cambridge, Cambridgeshire
CB3 0AX; URL www.crac.org.uk; e-mail
enquiries@crac.org.uk; Tel 01223 460277;
Fax 01223 311708
CRAC Chief Executive   Gill Wilson (Acting)

Graduate Prospects
Prospects Hse, 25 Booth St East, Manchester M13 9EP;
URL www.prospects.ac.uk; e-mail
sales@prospects.ac.uk; Tel 0161 277 5200;
Fax 0161 277 5210
Chief Executive   Mike Hill
Head (Sales)   Alan Brown

ECCTIS Ltd
Oriel Hse, Oriel Rd, Cheltenham, Gloucestershire GL50 1XP;
URL www.postgraduk.com; e-mail
enquiries@ecctis.co.uk; Tel 01242 252627;
Fax 01242 258600
UK Course Information Service

Educational Guidance Service for Adults
4th Fl, 40 Linenhall St, Belfast BT2 8BA;
URL www.connect2learn.org.uk; e-mail
info@egsa.org.uk; Tel (helpline) 0845 602 6632;
Tel 028 9024 4274; Fax 028 9027 1507
Director   E. Kelly BA, DCG

Gabbitas Educational Consultants Ltd
Carrington Hse, 126–130 Regent St, London W1B 5EE;
URL www.gabbitas.co.uk; e-mail
market@gabbitas.co.uk; Tel 020 7734 0161;
Fax 020 7437 1764

Inspiring Futures Foundation
St Georges Hse, Knoll Rd, Camberley, Surrey GU15 3SY;
URL www.inspiringfutures.org.uk; e-mail
helpline@inspiringfutures.org.uk; Tel 01276 687500;
Fax 01276 28258
Chief Executive   Andrew Airey

Institute of Career Guidance
3rd Fl, Copthall Hse, New Rd, Stourbridge, West Midlands
DY8 1PH; URL www.icg-uk.org; e-mail hq@icg-uk.org;
Tel 01384 376464; Fax 01384 440830

Institution of Civil Engineers
1 Gt George St, London SW1P 3AA; URL www.ice.org.uk;
e-mail careers@ice.org.uk; Tel 020 7665 2194;
Fax 020 7233 0515

National Institute for Careers Education and Counselling
Sheraton Hse, Castle Pk, Cambridge, Cambridgeshire
CB3 0AX; URL www.crac.org.uk/nicec; e-mail
nicec@crac.org.uk; Tel 01223 460277; Fax 01223 311708
Administrator   Sally Fielder

Springboard UK
3 Denmark St, London WC2H 8LP;
URL www.springborduk.org.uk; e-mail
info.london@springboarduk.org.uk; Tel 020 7497 8654;
Fax 020 7497 2466

**WISE (Women Into Science, Engineering
and Construction)**
2nd Fl, Weston Hse, 246 High Holborn, London WC1V 7EX;
URL www.wisecampaign.org.uk; e-mail
info@wisecampaign.org.uk; Tel 020 3206 0408;
Fax 020 3206 0401
Director   Terry Marsh

The Services

Army

Scholarship Schemes and Undergraduate Sponsorship
Enquiries about Army Scholarship Schemes may be sent to
Recruiting Group, Army Training and Recruiting Agency,
Ministry of Defence, Room 1, Bldg 165, Trenchard Lines,
Upavon, Wiltshire, SN9 6BE; Tel 01980 618181

Headquarters, Director of Army Education
Army Foundation College   Uniacke Barracks, Penny Pot La,
Harrogate, North Yorkshire HG3 2SE; e-mail
ci-afc@itg.mod.uk; Tel 01904 664426
Commandant   Lieut Col Lap Drakeley
Chief Instructor   Major T. Farthing
Army School of Training Support   Trenchard Lines, Upavon,
Pewsey, Wiltshire SN9 6BE; Tel 01494 676121 ext 3289
Duke of York's Royal Military School   Dover, Kent
CT15 5EQ; URL www.doyrms.mod.uk; e-mail
headmaster@doyrms.com; Tel 01304 245024;
Fax 01304 245019
Queen Victoria School   Dunblane, Stirling FK15 0JY;
URL www.qvs.org.uk; e-mail enquiries@qvs.org.uk;
Tel 0131 310 2927; Fax 0131 310 2926
Head   W. Bellars MA(Hons), PGCE, DipEd, MA(Ed
MgMt)

Joint Services Command and Staff College
Faringdon Rd, Shrivenham, Swindon SN6 8TS
Commandant   Major General T.J. Granville-Chapman CBE

Royal Military Academy
Sandhurst, Camberley, Surrey GU15 4PQ; Tel 01276 63344
Commandant   Major General T.P. Toyne Sewell
Director (Studies)   B.T. Jones RD, MA

Royal Military College of Science
Cranfield Institute of Technology, Shrivenham, Swindon,
Wiltshire SN6 8LA; Tel 01793 782551
Commandant   Major General S.A. Cowan CBE
Principal   Prof A.C. Baynham BSc, PhD, RCDS

Royal Military School of Music
Kneller Hall, Twickenham, Greater London TW2 7DU;
Tel 020 8898 5533
Commandant   Brig C.H. Bond OBE
Director (Music)   Lieutenant Colonel F.A. Renton ARCM,
DSM

Merchant Navy

11–16 Boys Secondary School
Hull Trinity House School, Princes Dock St, Kingston upon
Hull, East Riding of Yorkshire HU1 2JX;
URL www.hulltrinity.net; Tel 01482 326421;
Fax 01482 324697
Headmaster   A. Twaits

Courses for Officer Cadets
The following colleges undertake residential courses
leading to ONC/OND in Nautical Studies approved by the
Department of Trade for which remission of qualifying
service is given. Students attending these courses are
sponsored by shipping companies.

Blackpool and The Fylde College Ashfield Rd, Bispham, Blackpool, Lancashire FY2 0HB; e-mail visitors@blackpool.ac.uk; Tel 01253 504343; Fax 01253 356127

City of Liverpool Community College Clarence Street Centre, Clarence St, Liverpool, Merseyside L3 5TP; Tel 0151 252 4703; Fax 0151 252 4721
Principal Wally Brown
Head of Faculty Marie Allen

South Tyneside College St Georges Ave, South Shields, Tyne and Wear NE34 6ET; URL www.stc.ac.uk; e-mail bdu@stc.ac.uk; Tel 0191 427 3910; Fax 0191 427 9830
Principal J. Bennett CertEd, BEd(Hons), MSc

University of Wales Institute, Cardiff (UWIC) PO Box 377, Western Ave, Cardiff CF5 2SG; URL www.uwic.ac.uk; e-mail uwicinfo@uwic.ac.uk; Tel 02920 406044 ext 4316; Fax 02920 416286

Warsash Maritime Academy Newtown Rd, Warsash, Southampton SO31 9ZL; URL www.warsashacademy.co.uk; e-mail wma@solent.ac.uk; Tel 01489 576161; Fax 01489 573988
Manager (Marketing) Nigel Holloway

Courses for Deck, Catering and Engine Room Ratings and Other Merchant Navy Personnel

National Sea Training Centre, Dering Way, Gravesend, Kent DA12 2JJ; URL www.nwkcollege.ac.uk; e-mail iangoodwin@nwkcollege.ac.uk; Tel 01322 629600; Fax 01322 629687

Navigation Systems

DTI Radiocommunications Agency is responsible for examinations for radio officers. Enquiries should be addressed to Maritime Radio Operators Exams, AMERC NAC, PO Box 4, Ambleside, Cumbria LA22 0BF; Tel 015394 32255; Fax 015394 34663.
Contact S. Parkinson; Radiocommunications Agency, Wyndham Hse, 189 Marsh Wall, London E14 9SX; URL www.radio.gov.uk; Tel 020 7211 0210

Kelvin Hughes Ltd New North Rd, Hainault, Ilford, Essex IG6 2UR; URL www.kelvinhughes.com; Tel 020 8500 1020

NATS

Corporate and Technical Centre, 2000 Parkway, Whiteley, Fareham, Hampshire PO15 7FL; URL www.natscareers.co.uk; Tel 01489 616090
Air traffic services in the UK, both air traffic control and telecommunications, are provided and managed by NATS. Training opportunities: Trainee Air Traffic Controller (TATC); graduate engineers. Training schemes and salary packages are offered; for further information please visit NATS website. Aircrew and aircraft engineers are generally employed by airline operators; aircraft manufacturers have their own training schemes.

Courses of instruction

The Flight Directory of British Aviation, which may be seen at most public libraries, includes a complete list of universities, colleges, schools and clubs giving training. Requirements for the issue of licences to those seeking a career in civil aviation are set out in appropriate civil aviation publications, which may be obtained from the Civil Aviation Authority.

Aeroplane Licences

Course duration is approximately nine months for the basic Commercial Pilot's Licence and 12 months for the Commercial Pilot's Licence and Instrument Rating
British Aerospace Flying College Ltd Prestwick Airport, South Ayrshire KA9 2BW
GB Air Academy Ltd Goodwood Airfield, Chichester, West Sussex PO18 0PH
Oxford Air Training School Oxford Airport, Kidlington, Oxfordshire OX5 1RA
Perth Aerodrome Perth Aerodrome, Perth, Perth and Kinross PH2 6NP

Trent Air Services Cranfield Aerodrome, Bedford, Bedfordshire MK3 0AL

Helicopter Licences

Course duration is nine months
Bristow Helicopters Ltd Redhill Aerodrome, Redhill, Surrey RH1 5JZ
Oxford Air Training School Oxford Airport, Kidlington, Oxfordshire OX5 1RA
Trent Air Services Cranfield Aerodrome, Bedford, Bedfordshire MK3 0AL

Professional Bodies

Accountancy

ACCA

2 Central Quay, 89 Hydepark St, Glasgow G3 8BW; URL www.accaglobal.com; e-mail info@accaglobal.com; Tel 0141 582 2000; Fax 020 7396 5858

Association of Accounting Technicians (AAT)

140 Aldersgate St, London EC1A 4HY; URL www.aat.org.uk; e-mail patricia.mcdonagh@aat.org.uk; Tel 020 7397 3065; Fax 020 7397 3009
Head (Education and Training Operations and Development) Patricia McDonagh

Association of International Accountants

Staithes 3, The Watermark, Metro Riverside, Newcastle upon Tyne, Tyne and Wear NE11 9SN; URL www.aiaworldwide.com; e-mail newsdesk@aiaworldwide.com; Tel 0191 493 0277; Fax 0191 493 0278

Chartered Institute of Management Accountants

26 Chapter St, London SW1P 4NP; URL www.cimaglobal.com; Tel 020 7663 5441; Fax 020 7663 5442
Chief Executive Charles Tilley
Director (Education) Robert Jelly

CIPFA (Chartered Institute of Public Finance and Accountancy)

3 Robert St, London WC2N 6RL; URL www.cipfa.org.uk; e-mail marketing@cipfa.org; Tel 020 7543 5600; Fax 020 7543 5700
President Mike Burnes
Chief Executive Steve Freer CPFA

Institute of Chartered Accountants in England and Wales

Level 1, Metropolitan Hse, 321 Avebury Bvd, Milton Keynes, Buckinghamshire MK9 2GA; URL www.icaew.com/careers; e-mail careers@icaew.com; Tel 01908 248040; Fax 01908 248006
The largest professional accountancy body in Europe, with 128 000 members worldwide. It offers the ACA qualification which leads to a diversity of careers in every sector of business.

Institute of Chartered Accountants in Ireland

The Linenhall, 32–38 Linenhall St, Belfast BT2 8BG; URL www.icai.ie; e-mail ca@icai.ie; Tel 028 9023 1541; Fax 028 9031 9320
Director (Education and Training) Ronan O'Loughin; Dublin Office
Administrator Mary Armstrong; Belfast Office

Institute of Chartered Accountants of Scotland

CA Hse, 21 Haymarket Yards, Edinburgh EH12 5BH; URL www.icas.org.uk; e-mail caeducation@icas.org.uk; Tel 0131 347 0161; Fax 0131 347 0108

10

Institute of Company Accountants
40 Tyndalls Park Rd, Bristol BS8 1PL; Tel 0117 973 8261;
  Fax 0117 923 8292
Director General   B.T. Banks

Institute of Cost and Executive Accountants
Tower Hse, 139 Fonthill Rd, London N4 3HF;
  Tel 020 7272 3925; Fax 020 7281 5723
Secretary General   S.K. Das Gupta BCom, ACIS

Institute of Financial Accountants
Burford Hse, 44 London Rd, Sevenoaks, Kent TN13 1AS;
  URL www.ifa.org.uk; e-mail mail@ifa.org.uk;
  Tel 01732 458080; Fax 01732 455848
Chief Executive   David Woodgate

International Association of Book-Keepers
Burford Hse, 44 London Rd, Sevenoaks, Kent TN13 1AS;
  URL www.iab.org.uk; e-mail mail@iab.org.uk;
  Tel 01732 458080; Fax 01732 455848
Chief Executive   Malcolm Trotter

Acoustics

Institute of Acoustics
77a St Peters St, St Albans, Hertfordshire AL1 3BN;
  URL www.ioa.org.uk; e-mail education@ioa.org.uk;
  Tel 01727 848195; Fax 01727 850553
Chief Executive   Kevin Macan-Lind
The Institute of Acoustics is the UK's professional body for
those working in acoustics, noise and vibration

Actuaries

See also Insurance

The Actuarial Profession
Napier Hse, 4 Worcester St, Oxford, Oxfordshire OX1 2AW;
  URL www.actuaries.org.uk; e-mail
  careers@actuaries.org.uk; Tel 01865 268228;
  Fax 01865 268233
Chief Executive   C.M. Instance

Faculty of Actuaries
Maclaurin Hse, 18 Dublin St, Edinburgh EH1 3PP;
  URL www.actuaries.org.uk; e-mail
  faculty@actuaries.org.uk; Tel 0131 240 1300;
  Fax 0131 240 1313
Secretary   Mr R. Maconachie FCCA, MBA

Administration

Institute of Agricultural Secretaries and Administrators Ltd
NAC Stoneleigh, Kenilworth, Warwickshire CV8 2LZ;
  URL www.iagsa.co.uk; e-mail iagsa@iagsa.co.uk;
  Tel 024 7669 6592; Fax 024 7641 7937
Secretary   Charlotte O'Kane

Institute of Chartered Secretaries and Administrators
16 Park Cres, London W1B 1AH; URL www.icsa.org.uk;
  e-mail info@icsa.co.uk; Tel 020 7580 4741;
  Fax 020 7323 1132
Chief Executive; Secretary   M.J. Ainsworth DipEd, FCIS

Institute of Healthcare Management
18–21 Morley St, London SE1 7QZ; URL www.ihm.org.uk;
  e-mail education@ihm.org.uk; Tel 020 7593 0462;
  Fax 020 7620 1040

Institute of Paralegal Training (incorporating the Association of Legal Secretaries)
The Mill, Clymping St, Clymping, Littlehampton, Sussex
  BN17 5RN; e-mail amanda@ibberson.fsbusiness.co.uk;
  Tel 01903 714276
Secretary General   Mrs A.Y. Ibberson

Institute of Qualified Professional Secretaries Ltd
1st Fl, 6 Bridge Ave, Maidenhead, Berkshire SL6 1RR;
  URL www.iqps.org; e-mail office@iqps.org;
  Tel 01628 625007; Fax 01628 624990
Membership Secretary   J. Jerrum FIQPS

Advertising

See Marketing/Advertising/Public Relations

Aeronautics

Royal Aeronautical Society
4 Hamilton Pl, London; URL www.raes.org.uk; e-mail
  raes@raes.org.uk; Tel 020 7499 3515; Fax 020 7499 6230
Director   Keith Mans
Incorporates the Institution of Aeronautical Engineers, the
Helicopter Association of Great Britain and the Society of
Licensed Aircraft Engineers and Technologists

Agriculture

Farming and Countryside Education (FACE)
Royal Agricultural Society of England, Stoneleigh Pk,
  Warwickshire CV8 2LZ; URL www.face-online.org.uk;
  e-mail enquiries@face-online.org.uk; Tel 024 7685 8261;
  Fax 024 7641 4808
FACE helps young people learn more about food and
farming in a sustainable countryside and is a non-
campaigning organisation with members representing the
full spectrum of views across the agricultural sector. Its
website highlights the challenges both locally and globally
that have an impact on people's lives through issues such as
fair trade, food security, biotechnology and environment.

Apothecaries

Society of Apothecaries
Apothecaries' Hall, Black Friars La, London EC4V 6EJ;
  URL www.apothecaries.org; e-mail
  examoffice@apothecaries.org; Tel 020 7236 1180;
  Fax 020 7329 3177

Arbitration

Chartered Institute of Arbitrators
International Arbitration Centre, 12 Bloomsbury Sq, London
  WC1A 2LP; URL www.arbitrators.org; e-mail
  info@arbitrators.org; Tel 020 7421 7444;
  Fax 020 7404 4023

Archaeology

Council for British Archaeology
St Mary's Hse, 66 Botham, York, North Yorkshire YO30 7BZ;
  URL www.britarch.ac.uk; e-mail info@britarch.ac.uk;
  Tel 01904 671417; Fax 01904 671384
Director   Mike Heyworth BA, MA, PhD, FSA, MIFA
Education Officer   D. Henson BA, MPhil, FSA, MIFA

Architecture

Architecture and Surveying Institute
St Mary Hse, 15 St Mary St, Chippenham, Wiltshire
  SN15 3WD; Tel 01249 444505; Fax 01249 443602
Chief Executive   Ian Norris FASI, RIBA, FRSA
Education and Training Executive   Keith Roberts

Association of Building Engineers
Lutyens Hse, Billing Brook Rd, Northampton,
  Northamptonshire NN3 8NW; URL www.abe.org.uk;
  e-mail building.engineers@abe.org.uk; Tel 01604 404121;
  Fax 01604 784220
Membership and Education Officer   Mrs C. Braybrook

Chartered Institute of Architectural Technologists

397 City Rd, London EC1V 1NH; URL www.ciat.org.uk;
e-mail careers@ciat.org.uk; Tel 020 7278 2206;
Fax 020 7837 3194
Chief Executive Francesca Berriman
Director (Education and Research) Tara Pickles

Commonwealth Association of Architects

66 Portland Pl, London; e-mail
caa@gharchitects.demon.co.uk; Tel 020 7490 3024;
Fax 020 7253 2592
Executive Director Tony Godwin

Royal Institute of British Architects

66 Portland Pl, London W1B 1AD; Tel 020 7580 5533;
Fax 020 7255 1541
Director General Richard Hastilow
Director (Education) Leonie Milliner

Archivists

Society of Archivists

Registered Charity Number 1041063
Prioryfield Hse, 20 Canon St, Taunton, Somerset TA1 1SW;
URL www.archives.org.uk; e-mail
societyofarchivists@archives.org.uk; Tel 01823 327030;
Fax 01823 271719

Banking

Chartered Institute of Bankers in Scotland (CIOBS)

Drumsheugh Hse, 38b Drumsheugh Gdns, Edinburgh
EH3 7SW; URL www.ciobs.org.uk; e-mail
info@ciobs.org.uk; Tel 0131 473 7777; Fax 0131 473 7788
Chief Executive Simon Thompson

ifs School of Finance

6th Fl, 100 Cannon St, London EC4N 6EU;
URL www.ifslearning.ac.uk; e-mail
customerservices@ifslearning.ac.uk; Tel 020 7444 7111;
Fax 020 7444 7115
Head (Marketing) Simon Ashmore
IFS House 4–9 Burgate La, Canterbury, Kent CT1 2XJ;
URL www.ifslearning.ac.uk; e-mail
customerservices@ifslearning.ac.uk; Tel 01227 818609;
Fax 01277 786696

Biology

Institute of Biology

9 Red Lion Ct, London EC4A 3EF; URL www.iob.org; e-mail
n.roscoe@iob.org; Tel 020 7936 5930; Fax 020 7936 5931
Head (Education and Training) Neil Roscoe
Administrator (Education and Training) Sarah Blench

Brewing

Institute of Brewing & Distilling

33 Clarges St, London W1J 7EE; URL www.ibd.org.uk;
e-mail enquiries@ibd.org.uk; Tel 020 7499 8144;
Fax 020 7499 1156
Executive Director Simon J. Jackson

Building

Chartered Institute of Building (CIOB)

Englemere, Kings Ride, Ascot, Berkshire SL5 7TB;
URL www.ciob.org.uk; e-mail reception@ciob.org.uk;
Tel 01344 603700
Press Officer Saul Townsend

Careers

Association of Graduate Careers Advisory Services

Millennium Hse, 30 Junction Rd, Sheffield, South Yorkshire
S11 8XB; URL www.agcas.org.uk; e-mail
mike.proctor@agcas.org.uk; Tel 0114 251 5750
Office Manager Mike Proctor

Institute of Career Guidance

27a Lower High St, Stourbridge, West Midlands DY8 1TA;
URL www.icg-uk.org; e-mail hq@icg.uk.org;
Tel 01384 376464

Cartography

British Cartographic Society

c/o Royal Geographical Society (with IBG), 1 Kensington
Gore, London SW7 2AR; URL www.cartography.org.uk;
e-mail admin@cartography.org.uk; Tel 01823 665775;
Fax 01823 665775
President Ms M. Spence MBE

Ordnance Survey

Romsey Rd, Southampton SO16 4GU;
URL www.ordnancesurvey.co.uk; e-mail
roger.jeans@ordnancesurvey.co.uk; Tel 02380 792022;
Fax 02380 792230
Education Sector Manager Roger Jeans

Caseworkers

See Social Work

Chemistry

Chemical Industries Association

Kings Bldgs, Smith Sq, London SW1P 3JJ;
URL www.cia.org.uk; e-mail enquiries@cia.org.uk;
Tel 020 7834 3399; Fax 020 7834 4469

Royal Society of Chemistry

Burlington Hse, Piccadilly, London W1J 0BA;
URL www.rsc.org; www.chemsoc.org; e-mail
education@rsc.org; Tel 020 7437 8656; Fax 020 7287 9825
Chief Executive Dr Richard Pike

Chiropody

Society of Chiropodists and Podiatrists

1 Fellmongers Path, Tower Bridge Rd, London SE1 3LY;
URL www.feetforlife.org; e-mail enq@scpod.org;
Tel 0845 450 3720; Fax 0845 450 3721

Choreology

Benesh Institute

36 Battersea Sq, London SW11 3RA; URL www.benesh.org;
e-mail beneshinstitute@rad.org.uk; Tel 020 7326 8031;
Fax 020 7924 3129
Director Liz Cunliffe
The Benesh Institute is the international centre for Benesh
Movement Notation

Civil Service

Civil Service

Civil Service Careers, Pilgrims Well, 427 London Rd,
Camberley, Surrey GU15 3HZ;
URL www.careers.civil-service.gov.uk; e-mail
civilservicecareers@parity.net; Tel 01276 400333
The civil service consists of more than 100 government
departments and agencies providing customer-focused
services. It delivers the priorities of any elected government.
People join at every level – directly from school or
university, or switching from another career and from every
kind of background. The work is varied and includes
economists, engineers, lawyers, scientists, weather

10

forecasters, courts ushers, driving examiners and forest rangers.

Cleaning

British Institute of Cleaning Science Ltd (BICS)
9 Premier Ct, Boarden Cl, Moulton Pk, Northampton, Northamptonshire NN3 6LF; URL www.bics.org.uk; e-mail info@bics.org.uk; Tel 01604 678710; Fax 01604 645988
Chief Executive   M. Sweeney

Clerks of Works

Institute of Clerks of Works of Great Britain Incorporated
Equinox, 28 Commerce Rd, Peterborough, Cambridgeshire PE2 6LR; URL www.icwgb.org; e-mail info@icwgb.co.uk; Tel 01733 405160; Fax 01733 405161
Chair (Examination Board)   Mr Jerry Shoolbred FICW
Company Secretary   Rachel Morris

Clinical Radiology and Oncology

Royal College of Radiologists
38 Portland Pl, London W1B 1JQ; URL www.rcr.ac.uk; Tel 020 7636 4432

Colour Technology

See Dyers and Colourists

Commodities

Federation of Commodity Associations (FCA)
Gafta Hse, 6 Chapel Pl, London EC2A 3SH; Tel 020 7814 9666; Fax 020 7814 8383
Secretary   Pamela Kirby Johnson

Computer Science

British Computer Society (BCS)
1st Fl, Block D, North Star Hse, North Star Ave, Swindon, Wiltshire SN2 1FA; URL www.bcs.org.uk; e-mail bcshq@hq.bcs.org.uk; Tel 01793 417417; Fax 01793 417444

Concrete

The Concrete Society
Riverside Hse, 4 Meadows Business Pk, Station Approach, Blackwater, Camberley, Surrey GU17 9AB; e-mail enquiries@concrete.org.uk; Tel 01276 607140; Fax 01276 607141

Credit Management

Institute of Credit Management
The Water Mill, Station Rd, South Luffenham, Oakham, Leicestershire LE15 8NB; URL www.icm.org.uk; e-mail education@icm.org.uk; Tel 01780 722909; Fax 01780 721333

Dance

Imperial Society of Teachers of Dancing
Imperial Hse, 22–26 Paul St, London EC2A 4QE; e-mail admin@istd.org; Tel 020 7377 1577; Fax 020 7247 8979
Chief Executive   Michael J. Browne FFA, FFBA, FCES, FIAB, FRSA, FInstD

Dentistry

General Dental Council
37 Wimpole St, London W1G 8DQ; URL www.gdc-uk.org; e-mail information@gdc-uk.org; Tel 020 7887 3800; Fax 020 7224 3294
Chief Executive; Registrar   A. Townsend

Design

Chartered Society of Designers
1 Cedar Ct, Royal Oak Yard, Bermondsey St, London SE1 3GA; URL www.csd.org.uk; e-mail info@csd.org.uk; Tel 020 7357 8088; Fax 020 7407 9878
Chief Executive   Frank Peters

National Association of Advisers and Inspectors in Design and Technology
London; URL www.naaidt.org.uk
Administration Officer   John Culpin

Dietetics

British Dietetic Association
5th Fl, Charles Hse, 148–149 Gt Charles St, Queensway, Birmingham, West Midlands B3 3HT; URL www.bda.uk.com; e-mail info@bda.uk.com; Tel 0121 200 8079
Team Co-ordinator   Saar De Wagter

Dyers and Colourists

Society of Dyers and Colourists
PO Box 244, Perkin Hse, Bradford, West Yorkshire BD1 2JB; Tel 01274 725138; Fax 01274 392888
Qualifications Officer   Clare Moore

Energy

The Energy Institute
61 New Cavendish St, London W1G 7AR; URL www.energyinst.org; e-mail info@energyinst.org; Tel 020 7467 7100; Fax 020 7255 1472

Engineering

Chartered Institution of Building Services Engineers
222 Balham High Rd, London SW12 9BS; URL www.cibse.org; e-mail info@cibse.org; Tel 020 8675 5211; Fax 020 8675 5449
Chief Executive; Secretary   Stephen Matthews CEng, FIMechE

Chartered Institution of Water and Environmental Management
15 John St, London WC1N 2EB; URL www.ciwem.org; e-mail membership@ciwem.org; Tel 020 7831 3110; Fax 020 7405 4967
Executive Director   Nick Reeves
Director (Professional Development)   Rosemary Butler

IChemE
Davis Bldg, Railway Terr, Rugby, Warwickshire CV21 3HQ; URL www.icheme.org; e-mail info@icheme.org; Tel 01788 578214; Fax 01788 560833
1 Portland Pl, London W1B 1PN; e-mail london@icheme.org; Tel 020 7927 8200
Chief Executive   Dr D.J. Brown PhD, CPhys, CSci, FInstP

Institute of Domestic Heating and Environmental Engineers
Unit 35a, New Forest Enterprise Centre, Chapel La, Totton, Southampton SO40 9LA; e-mail info@idhee.org.uk
Chair   W.V. Bucknell

Institute of Marine Engineering, Science and Technology

80 Coleman St, London EC2R 5BJ; URL www.imarest.org/
  careers; e-mail holly.sheridan@imarest.org;
  Tel 020 7382 2600; Fax 020 7382 2670
Co-ordinator (Membership Development)   Holly Sheridan

Institute of Physics and Engineering in Medicine

Fairmount Hse, 230 Tadcaster Rd, York YO24 1ES;
  URL www.ipem.ac.uk; e-mail office@ipem.ac.uk;
  Tel 01904 610821; Fax 01904 612279
President   Dr T.K. Ison
Hon Secretary   Dr D.C. Crawford

Institution of Agricultural Engineers

Barton Rd, Silsoe, Bedford, Bedfordshire MK45 4FH;
  URL www.iagre.org; e-mail secretary@iagre.org;
  Tel 01525 861096; Fax 01525 861660
Chief Executive; Secretary   Christopher Whetnall CEnv,
  IEng, FIAgrE, MemASABE

Institution of Civil Engineers

1 Gt George St, London SW1P 3AA; URL www.ice.org.uk/
  education; e-mail careers@ice.org.uk; Tel 020 7665 2150;
  Fax 020 7222 7500

Institution of Engineering Designers

Courtleigh, Westbury Leigh, Westbury, Wiltshire
  BA13 3TA; URL www.ied.org.uk; e-mail
  staff@ied.org.uk; Tel 01373 822801; Fax 01373 858085
Secretary   E.K. Brodhurst

Institution of Engineering and Technology

Savoy Pl, London WC2R 0BL; URL www.theiet.org; e-mail
  schools@theiet.org; Tel 020 7240 1871
Chief Executive   Robin McGill

Institution of Highways and Transportation

6 Endsleigh St, London WC1H 0DZ; URL www.iht.org;
  e-mail info@iht.org; Tel 020 7387 2525; Fax 020 7387 2808
Chief Executive; Secretary   Mary Lewis

Institution of Mechanical Engineers

1 Birdcage Wlk, London SW1H 9JJ; e-mail
  enquiries@imeche.org.uk; Tel 020 7222 7899;
  Fax 020 7222 4557
Director General   Sir Michael Moore KBE, LVO
Director (Qualifications)   Harvey Spindler

Institution of Nuclear Engineers

Allan Hse, 1 Penerley Rd, London SE6 2LQ;
  URL www.inuce.org.uk; e-mail
  rosburton@nuceng.freeserve.co.uk; Tel 020 8698 1500;
  Fax 020 8695 6409
Secretary   W.J. Hurst

Institution of Structural Engineers

11 Upper Belgrave St, London SW1X 8BH;
  URL www.istructe.org.uk; e-mail mail@istructe.org.uk;
  Tel 020 7235 4535; Fax 020 7235 4294
Chief Executive   Dr K.J. Eaton BSc(Eng), PhD, CEng,
  FIStructE, FCGI

Society of Operations Engineers

22 Greencoat Pl, London SW1P 1PR; URL www.soe.org.uk;
  e-mail soe@soe.org.uk; Tel 020 7630 1111;
  Fax 020 7630 6677
Chief Executive   Nick Jones FCA

The Welding Institute (TWI)

Granta Pk, Great Abington, Cambridge, Cambridgeshire
  CB1 6AL; Tel 01223 891162; Fax 01223 894219
Associate Director (Professional Affairs and Certification)
  T.J. Jessop

Women's Engineering Society

22 Old Queen St, London SW1H 9HW;
  URL www.wes.org.uk; e-mail info@wes.org.uk;
  Tel 020 7233 1974
Secretary   C.J. MacGillivray

Engineering and Technology

Committee of the Engineering Professors' Conference

Chair   Prof Graham Ellison; Department of Mechanical
  Engineering, University of Bristol, Bristol BS8 1TR;
  Tel 0117 930 3243

Engineering and Technology Board (ETB)

2nd Fl, Weston Hse, 246 High Holborn, London WC1V 7EX;
  URL www.scenta.co.uk; www.enginuity.org.uk;
  www.etechb.co.uk; e-mail careers@etechb.co.uk;
  Tel 020 3206 0400; Fax 020 3206 0401

Institute of Science Technology

Kingfisher Hse, 90 Rockingham St, Sheffield S1 4EB;
  URL www.istonline.org.uk; e-mail
  office@istonline.org.uk; Tel 0114 276 3197;
  Fax 0114 272 6354

International Society for Soil Mechanics and Geotechnical Engineering

Geotechnical Engineering Research Centre, City University,
  London EC1V 0HB; URL www.issmge.org; e-mail
  secretariat@issmge.org; Tel 020 7040 8154;
  Fax 020 7040 8832
Secretary General   Prof R.N. Taylor

English Language Teaching

English UK

56 Buckingham Gate, London SW1E 6AG;
  Tel 020 7802 9200; Fax 020 7802 9201
Chief Executive   Tony Millns
English UK is the national association of British Council
accredited English Language teaching centres

Estate Agents

National Federation of Property Professionals (NFOPP)

Arbon Hse, 6 Tournament Crt, Edgehill Dr, Warwick,
  Warwickshire CV34 6LG; URL www.nfopp.co.uk; e-mail
  quals@nfopp.co.uk; Tel 01926 417794; Fax 01926 417789

10

Export

Institute of Export

Registered Charity Number 266395
Export Hse, Minerva Business Pk, Lynchwood,
  Peterborough, Cambridgeshire PE2 6FT;
  URL www.export.org.uk; e-mail institute@export.org.uk;
  Tel 01733 404400
Director General   Maria McCaffery MIEX, MBE

Farriers

Farriery Training Agency

Sefton Hse, Adam Ct, Newark Rd, Peterborough,
  Cambridgeshire PE1 5PP;
  URL www.farrierytraining.co.uk; e-mail
  fta@farrierytraining.co.uk; Tel 01733 319770;
  Fax 01733 319771

Food

Food and Drink Qualifications (FDQ)

PO Box 141, Winterhill Hse, Snowdon Dr, Winterhill, Milton
  Keynes, Buckinghamshire MK6 1YY; e-mail
  info@fdq.org.uk; Tel 01908 231062; Fax 01908 231063
Awards Executive   Nikki Taylor

Institute of Food Science and Technology

5 Cambridge Ct, 210 Shepherds Bush Rd, London W6 7NJ;
  URL www.ifst.org; www.foodtechcareers.org; e-mail
  info@ifst.org; Tel 020 7603 6316
Chief Executive   H.G. Wild

Forestry

Forestry Commission
Silvan Hse, 231 Corstorphine Rd, Edinburgh EH12 7AT;
URL www.forestry.gov.uk; e-mail
enquiries@forestry.gsi.gov.uk; Tel 0131 334 0303;
Fax 0131 334 3047

Institute of Chartered Foresters
59 George St, Edinburgh EH2 2JG;
URL www.charteredforesters.org; e-mail
icf@charteredforesters.org; Tel 0131 240 1425;
Fax 0131 240 1424
Chair (Professional and Educational Standards Committee)
Pat Hunter-Blair FICFor
Executive Director   Shireen Chamers MICFor

Geology

The Geological Society
Burlington Hse, Piccadilly, London W1J 0BG;
URL www.geolsoc.org.uk; e-mail
enquiries@geolsoc.org.uk; Tel 020 7434 9944;
Fax 020 7439 8975
Chair (External Relations Committee)
Prof Edward Derbyshire;   responsibility for training
and education
Contact (Education and Training)   Ms J. Lakin

Hairdressing

National Hairdressers' Federation
1 Abbey Ct, Fraser Rd, Priory Business Pk, Bedford,
Bedfordshire MK44 3NH; URL www.nhf.biz; e-mail
enquiries@nhf.info; Tel 0845 345 6500; Fax 01234 838875
General Secretary   Ray J. Seymour FCIS, MIMgt

Health

Association of Medical Secretaries, Practice Managers, Administrators and Receptionists (AMSPAR)
Tavistock Hse North, Tavistock Sq, London WC1H 9LN;
URL www.amspar.com; e-mail info@amspar.co.uk;
Tel 020 7387 6005; Fax 020 7388 2648
Manager (Qualifications)   M. Kay

Chartered Institute of Environmental Health
Chadwick Ct, 15 Hatfields, London SE1 8DJ;
URL www.cieh.org; Tel 020 7928 6006
Director (Education and Professional Standards)   P. Robinson

Royal Institute of Public Health
28 Portland Pl, London W1B 1DE; URL www.riph.org.uk;
e-mail exams@riph.org.uk; Tel 020 7580 2731;
Fax 020 7580 6157
Director (Standards)   Heather Davison

Royal Society for the Promotion of Health
38a St Georges Dr, London SW1V 4BH; URL www.rsph.org;
e-mail rsph@rsph.org; Tel 020 7630 0121;
Fax 020 7976 6847
Chief Executive   Richard Parish

Health and Safety Inspectors

Health and Safety Executive
2 Southwark Bridge, London SE1 9HS;
URL www.hse.gov.uk; e-mail
richard.broughton@hse.gov.uk; Tel 020 7717 6605;
Fax 020 7717 6190
Contact   R. Broughton

Horticulture

Royal Horticultural Society's Garden
Wisley, Woking, Surrey GU23 6QB; URL www.rhs.org.uk/
education/mn_training.asp; e-mail
careerinfo@rhs.org.uk; Tel 01483 212419;
Fax 01483 212382

Hospitality, Leisure and Tourism

Institute of Hospitality
Trinity Ct, 34 West St, Sutton, Surrey SM1 1SH;
URL www.instituteofhospitality.org; e-mail
awardingbody@instituteofhospitality.org;
Tel 020 8661 4900; Fax 020 8661 4901
Co-ordinator (Qualifications and Accreditation)
Maria Lockwood

Local Authority Caterers Association
Bourne Hse, Horsell Pk, Woking, Surrey GU21 4LY;
URL www.laca.co.uk; e-mail admin@laca.co.uk;
Tel 01483 766777; Fax 01483 751991
LACA Secretariat   Vic Laws

Housing

Chartered Institute of Housing (CIH)
Octavia Hse, Westwood Way, Coventry, Warwickshire
CV4 8JP; URL www.cih.org; Tel 024 7685 1700
Head (Education)   Roger Keller

Hypnotherapy

British Society of Hypnotherapists
37 Orbain Rd, London SW6 7JZ;
URL www.britishhypnotherapists.org.uk; e-mail
enquiries@britishhypnotherapists.org.uk;
Tel 020 7385 1166; Fax 020 7385 1166
General Secretary   S.C. Young MBSH

British Society of Medical and Dental Hypnosis (Metropolitan and South)
73 Ware Rd, Hertford, Hertfordshire SG13 7ED;
Tel 020 8905 4342
Secretary   Dr L. Gevertz

Hypnotherapy Training Institute of Britain
37 Orbain Rd, London SW6 7JZ;
URL www.hypnotherapytraininginstitute.org; e-mail
enquiries@hypnotherapytraininginstitute.org;
Tel 020 7385 1166; Fax 020 7385 1166
Director   Dr John Butler
Provider of training courses in hypnotherapy

Indexers

Society of Indexers
Woodbourn Business Centre, 10 Jessell St, Sheffield, South
Yorkshire S9 3HY; URL www.indexers.org.uk; e-mail
admin@indexers.org.uk; Tel 0114 244 9561;
Fax 0114 244 9563
Administrator   Wendy Burrow

Industrial Art and Design

Chartered Society of Designers
32–38 Saffron Hill, London EC1N 8SG; e-mail
csd@csd.org.uk; Tel 020 7831 9777; Fax 020 7831 6277

Insurance
See also Actuaries

British Insurance Brokers' Association
BIBA Hse, 14 Bevis Marks, London EC3A 7NT;
Tel 020 7623 9043; Fax 020 7626 9676

Chartered Insurance Institute
20 Aldermanbury, London EC2V 7HY; URL www.cii.co.uk;
e-mail customer.serv@cii.co.uk; Tel 020 8989 8464;
Fax 020 8530 3052
Chief Executive   Dr Alexander W.M. Scott

Journalism

National Council for the Training of Journalists
The New Granary, Station Rd, Newport, Essex CB11 3PL;
URL www.nctj.com; e-mail info@nctj.com;
Tel 01799 544014; Fax 01799 544015
Chief Executive   Joanne Butcher

Landscape, Architecture, Sciences and Management

The Landscape Institute (The Chartered Professional Institute for Landscape Architects)
6–8 Barnard Mews, London SW11 1QU;
URL www.l-i.org.uk; e-mail mail@l-i.org.uk;
Tel 020 7350 5200; Fax 020 7350 5201
Director General   Stuart Royston
Education Officer   Cathy Collins

Languages

Chartered Institute of Linguists
Saxon Hse, 48 Southwark St, London SE1 1UN;
URL www.iol.org.uk; e-mail info@iol.org.uk;
Tel 020 7940 3100; Fax 020 7940 3101

Laundry and Drycleaning

TSA (Textile Services Association)
7 Churchill Ct, 58 Station Rd, North Harrow, Harrow,
Greater London HA2 7SA; URL www.tsa-uk.org; e-mail
tsa@tsa-uk.org; Tel 020 8863 7755; Fax 020 8861 2115
Chief Executive   M. Simpson

Law

Faculty of Advocates
Advocates Library, Parliament Hse, Edinburgh EH1 1RF;
URL www.advocates.org.uk; Tel 0131 226 5071
Co-ordinator   Scott Brownridge

Inns of Court School of Law
City University, 4 Grays Inn Pl, London WC1R 5DX;
URL www.city.ac.uk/icsl; e-mail icsl-courses@city.ac.uk;
Tel 020 7404 5787; Fax 020 7831 4188
Director (CPD)   Penny Cooper Barrister
Provider of the Bar Vocational Course (BVC), which is taken
by those intending to qualify for call to the Bar of England
and Wales. It offers a Legal Practice Course (LPC) and a
specialist LLM course in Criminal Litigation and bespoke
CPD courses for legal and non-legal professionals.

Institute of Legal Executives
Kempston Manor, Kempston, Bedford, Bedfordshire
MK42 7AB; URL www.ilex.org.uk; e-mail
info@ilex.org.uk; Tel 01234 841000; Fax 01234 840373

The Law Society
Law Society's Hall, 113 Chancery La, London WC2A 1PL;
URL www.lawsociety.org.uk; Tel 020 7242 1222;
Fax 020 7831 0344
Head (Education and Training)   Julie Swan

The Law Society of Scotland
26 Drumsheugh Gdns, Edinburgh EH3 7YR;
URL www.lawscot.org.uk; e-mail
legaleduc@lawscot.org.uk; Tel 0131 476 8155;
Fax 0131 476 8109
Co-ordinator (New Lawyers')   Collette Paterson

Libraries and Information

Chartered Institute of Library and Information Professionals
7 Ridgmount St, London WC1E 7AE;
URL www.cilip.org.uk; e-mail careers@cilip.org.uk;
Tel 020 7255 0500; Fax 020 7255 0501;
Textphone 020 7255 0505
Chief Executive   Bob McKee PhD, MCLIP, FRSA

Local Government

Chartered Institution of Wastes Management
9 Saxon Ct, St Peters Gdns, Northampton,
Northamptonshire NN1 1SX; URL www.ciwm.co.uk;
e-mail education@ciwm.co.uk; Tel 01604 620426;
Fax 01604 621339
Manager (Education and Training)   Claire Poole

Chartered Institution of Water and Environmental Management
15 John St, London WC1N 2EB; URL www.ciwem.org.uk;
e-mail admin@ciwem.org.uk; Tel 020 7831 3110;
Fax 020 7405 4967
Executive Director   Nick Reeves

Institute of Maintenance and Building Management (IMBM)
Keets Hse, 30 East St, Farnham, Surrey GU9 7SW;
URL www.imbm.org.uk; e-mail info@imbm.org.uk;
Tel 01252 710994; Fax 01252 737741
Chief Executive   Simon P. Sinclair

Institute of Sport and Recreation Management
Sir John Beckwith Centre for Sport, Loughborough
University, Loughborough, Leicestershire LE11 3TU;
URL www.isrm.co.uk; e-mail martinsteer@isrm.co.uk;
Tel 01509 226474; Fax 01509 226475
Manager (Education Development)   Martin Steer

Management

ASLIB
The Association for Information Management, Holywell
Centre, 1 Phipp St, London EC2A 4PS;
URL www.aslib.com; e-mail training@aslib.com;
Tel 020 7613 3031; Fax 020 7613 5080

Association of Business Executives
5th Fl, Cl Tower, High St, New Malden, Surrey KT3 4TE;
URL www.abeuk.com; e-mail info@abeuk.com;
Tel 020 8329 2930; Fax 020 8329 2945

Chartered Institute of Personnel and Development (CIPD)
51 The Broadway, London SW15 1JQ;
URL www.cipd.co.uk; e-mail cipd@cipd.co.uk;
Tel 020 8612 6200; Fax 020 8612 6201
Director General   Geoff Armstrong
Manager (Professional Education)   Peter Herrman

The Chartered Management Institute
Management Hse, Cottingham Rd, Corby,
Northamptonshire NN17 1TT;
URL www.managers.org.uk; e-mail
cmd.customerservice@managers.org.uk;
Tel 01536 207373; Fax 01536 207384
Head (Accreditation)   Liz Wilson
Head (Information Centre)   Bob Norton
Contact (Management Development)   Carlem Sadler

Institute of Administrative Management
Caroline Hse, 55–57 High Holborn, London WC1V 6DX;
URL www.instam.org; e-mail info@instam.org;
Tel 020 7841 1100; Fax 020 7841 1119
Chief Executive   David Woodgate FInstAM
The IAM is the leading provider of qualifications for
professional administrators. The institute's objectives are to
promote and develop, for public benefit, the science of

10

administrative management in all branches; to encourage the attainment of professional academic qualifications; to provide, via conferences, seminars, meetings and publications, information to enable members to keep up to date with the latest techniques and developments in the field of administrative management.

Institute of Association Management
1 Queen Anne's Gate, Westminster, London SW1H 9BT
President   D.J. Pryke

Institute of Leadership and Management
Stowe Hse, Netherstowe, Lichfield, Staffordshire WS13 6TJ;
   URL www.i-l-m.com; e-mail
   ism@ismstowe.demon.co.uk; Tel 01543 251346;
   Fax 01543 266811
1 Giltspur St, London EC1A 9DD; URL www.i-l-m.com;
   e-mail customer@i-l-m.com; Tel 020 7294 3053;
   Fax 020 7294 2402
Chief Executive   Penny De Valk
Information Officer   Bernice Conlin BA(Hons), MInstLM
Now part of the City and Guilds Group, the Institute of Leadership and Management (ILM) is an awarding body for management-related qualifications with more than 75 000 candidates. It also offers informal personal and professional support to practising leaders and managers across all disciplines and at every career stage. ILM gives its 20 000 members strategic, ongoing support to enhance their skills, add to their professional expertise and to develop a wider network of valuable business contacts.

Institute of Management Consultancy
5th Fl, 32–33 Hatton Gdn, London EC1N 8DL;
   URL www.imc.co.uk; e-mail consult@imc.co.uk;
   Tel 020 7242 2140; Fax 020 7831 4597
Head (Membership Services)   Wendy Gerber

Institute of Management Services
Brook Hse, 24 Dam St, Lichfield, Staffordshire WS13 6AA;
   URL www.ims-productivity.com; e-mail
   admin@ims-stowe.fsnet.co.uk
Co-ordinator (IMS Administration)   Lynette Gill

Women in Management Association
5th Fl, 45 Beech St, London EC2Y 8AD; Tel 020 7382 9978;
   Fax 020 7382 9979
Association Secretary   Marion Watson

Market Research

Market Research Society
15 Northburgh St, London EC1V 0JR;
   URL www.mrs.org.uk; e-mail info@mrs.org.uk;
   Tel 020 7490 4911; Fax 020 7490 0608

Marketing/Advertising/Public Relations

Chartered Institute of Marketing (CIM)
Moor Hall, Cookham, Maidenhead, Berkshire SL6 9QH;
   URL www.cim.co.uk; Tel 01628 427500;
   Fax 01628 427399
Head (Awarding Body)   Neil Scurlock BSc(Hons), DipM,
   MBA, MCIM, Chartered Marketer
Contact (Operations)   C. Lenton DipM, FCIM, ACCA, FCIS

Institute of Practitioners in Advertising
44 Belgrave Sq, London SW1X 8QS; Tel 020 7235 7020;
   Fax 020 7245 9904

Institute of Public Relations
The Old Trading Hse, 15 Northburgh St, London EC1V 0PR;
   Tel 020 7253 5151; Fax 020 7490 0588
President   Anne Gregory
Director General   Colin Farrington

Marketing Education Group
Chair   Prof David Carson
Membership Secretary   Sean Ennis; Marketing, University of Strathclyde, Glasgow

Materials

Institute of Materials, Minerals and Mining
1 Carlton House Terr, London SW1Y 5DB;
   URL www.iom3.org; e-mail admin@iom3.org;
   Tel 020 7451 7300; Fax 020 7839 1702
Chief Executive   Dr B.A. Rickinson CEng, FIM

Mathematics

Institute of Mathematics and its Applications
Catherine Richards Hse, 16 Nelson St, Southend-on-Sea,
   Essex SS1 1EF; e-mail post@ima.org.uk; Tel 01702 354020;
   Fax 01702 354111
Executive Director   David Jordan

Measurement

Institute of Measurement and Control
87 Gower St, London WC1E 6AF; URL www.instmc.org.uk;
   e-mail education@instmc.org.uk; Tel 020 7387 4949;
   Fax 020 7388 8431
Secretary   M.J. Yates MA

Medical Laboratory Sciences

Institute of Biomedical Science
12 Coldbath Sq, London EC1R 5HL; URL www.ibms.org;
   e-mail mail@ibms.org; Tel 020 7713 0214;
   Fax 020 7436 4946
Executive Head (Education)   Alan Wainwright

Society of Cardiological Technicians
c/o Cardiac Dept, The Royal London Trust, London E1 1BB;
   Tel 020 7377 7659
Public Relations Officer   Deirdre Harrington

Mining and Metallurgy

Institute of Materials, Minerals and Mining
See Materials

Institute of Quarrying
7 Regent St, Nottingham NG1 5BS; Tel 0115 945 3880;
   Fax 0115 948 4035
General Manager   Dr M.R. Smith

Motor Industry

Institute of the Motor Industry
Fanshaws, Brickendon, Hertford, Hertfordshire SG13 8PQ;
   URL www.motor.org.uk; e-mail imi@motor.org.uk;
   Tel 01992 511521; Fax 01992 511548

Museums

The Museums Association
24 Calvin St, London E1 6NW;
   URL www.museumsassociation.org; e-mail
   info@museumsassociation.org; Tel 020 7426 6910;
   Fax 020 7426 6961

Nature Conservation

Joint Nature Conservation Committee (JNCC)
Monkstone Hse, City Rd, Peterborough, Cambridgeshire
   PE1 1JY; URL www.jncc.gov.uk; e-mail
   communications@jncc.gov.uk; Tel 01733 562626;
   Fax 01733 555948
The Joint Nature Conservation Committee is a forum through which the four country nature conservation agencies (the Countryside Council for Wales, English Nature, the Scottish Natural Heritage, and the Council for Nature Conservation and the Countryside, Northern Ireland) deliver their special statutory responsibilities for the UK as a whole and internationally. These special

responsibilities, known as the special functions, contribute to sustaining and enriching biological diversity, enhancing geological features and sustaining natural systems. The special functions are to devise and maintain common standards and protocols for nature conservation; to promote, through common standards, the free interchange of data between the country agencies and with external partners; to advise on nature conservation issues affecting the UK as a whole; to pursue wider international goals for nature conservation (encouraging sustainable development, biological diversity and earth science conservation), including the provision of relevant advice to the government; to commission new research and collate existing knowledge in support of these activities, and to disseminate the results.

Naval Architects

Royal Institution of Naval Architects
10 Upper Belgrave St, London SW1X 8BQ;
    URL www.rina.org.uk; e-mail hq@rina.org.uk;
    Tel 020 7235 4622; Fax 020 7259 5912
Chief Executive   Trevor Blakeley

Nursing

NHS Careers
PO Box 2311, Bristol BS2 2ZX; URL www.nhs.uk/careers;
    e-mail advice@nhscareers.nhs.uk; Tel 0845 606 0655;
    Fax 0845 850 8866
NHS Careers provides careers information about nursing; midwifery; the allied health professions (formerly known as the professions allied to medicine); therapies (e.g. speech and language therapy, physiotherapy, occupational therapy etc); healthcare scientists; medicines dentistry; health informatics; management and the wider healthcare team

Royal College of Nursing
20 Cavendish Sq, London W1G 0RN; URL www.rcn.org.uk;
    Tel 020 7409 3333; Fax 020 7647 3425
Director (RCN Institute)   Geraldine Cunningham
General Secretary   Dr Beverly Malone

Occupational Therapy

College of Occupational Therapists
106–114 Borough High St, Southwark, London SE1 1LB;
    URL www.cot.org.uk; www.baot.org.uk; e-mail
    anne.lawsonporter@cot.co.uk; Tel 020 7357 6480;
    Fax 020 7450 2299
Group Head (Education)   A. Lawson-Porter

Operational Research

Operational Research Society
Seymour Hse, 12 Edward St, Birmingham, West Midlands
    B1 2RX; URL www.theorsociety.com; e-mail
    email@theorsociety.com; Tel 0121 233 9300;
    Fax 0121 233 0321
Secretary; General Manager   Mr G. Blackett

Optics (Ophthalmic Dispensing)

Association of British Dispensing Opticians
6 Hurlingham Business Pk, Sulivan Rd, London SW6 3DU;
    Tel 020 7736 0088; Fax 020 7731 5531
General Secretary   Sir Anthony Garrett CBE
Registrar   D.G. Baker

College of Optometrists
42 Craven St, London WC2N 5NG;
    URL www.college-optometrists.org; e-mail
    optometry@college-optometrists.org; Tel 020 7839 6000;
    Fax 020 7839 6800
Chief Executive   Bryony Pawinska

General Optical Council
41 Harley St, London W1G 8DJ; URL www.optical.org;
    e-mail goc@optical.org; Tel 020 7580 3898;
    Fax 020 7436 3525
Registrar   Peter C. Coe

Osteopathy

British College of Osteopathic Medicine
Lief Hse, 120–122 Finchley Rd, London NW3 5HR;
    URL www.bcom.ac.uk; e-mail ipd@bcom.ac.uk;
    Tel 020 7435 6464; Fax 020 7431 3630
Principal   Dr I.P. Drysdale

British School of Osteopathy
275 Borough High St, London SE1 1JE; URL www.bso.ac.uk;
    e-mail chunt@bso.ac.uk; Tel 020 7407 0222;
    Fax 020 7089 5300
Principal   Charles Hunt

General Osteopathic Council
Osteopathy Hse, 176 Tower Bridge Rd, London SE1 3LU;
    URL www.osteopathy.org.uk; e-mail
    info@osteopathy.org.uk; Tel 020 7357 6655;
    Fax 020 7357 0011

Packaging

The Institute of Packaging
Willoughby Hse, Broad St, Stamford, Lincolnshire PE9 1PB;
    URL www.iop.co.uk
Contact (Training Department)   Alan Kinnear

Patent Attorneys

Chartered Institute of Patent Attorneys
95 Chancery La, London WC2A 1DT;
    URL www.cipa.org.uk; e-mail mail@cipa.org.uk;
    Tel 020 7405 9450; Fax 020 7430 0471
Registrar; Secretary   Michael Ralph

Petroleum

Energy Institute
61 New Cavendish St, London W1G 7AR;
    URL www.energyinst.org.uk; e-mail
    info@energyinst.org.uk; Tel 020 7467 7100;
    Fax 020 7255 1472
Manager (Education)   Alex Hartley

Pharmacy

Pharmaceutical Society of Northern Ireland
73 University St, Belfast BT7 1HL; URL www.psni.org.uk;
    Tel 028 9032 6927; Fax 028 9043 9919

Royal Pharmaceutical Society of Great Britain
1 Lambeth High St, London SE1 7JN;
    URL www.rpsgb.org.uk; e-mail
    rdewdney@rpsgb.org.uk; Tel 020 7572 2380;
    Fax 020 7572 2506
Head (Education Division)   Dr Robert Dewdney

Photography and Photographic Technicians

British Institute of Professional Photography
2 Amwell End, Ware, Hertfordshire SG12 9HN;
    URL www.bipp.com; e-mail info@bipp.com;
    Tel 01920 464011

Physicians

British Medical Association
BMA Hse, Tavistock Sq, London WC1H 9JP;
    Tel 020 7387 4499; Fax 020 7383 6400
Chief Executive; Secretary   A.R. Bourne

10

Royal College of Physicians of London
11 St Andrews Pl, Regent's Pk, London NW1 4LE;
URL www.rcplondon.ac.uk; e-mail
infocentre@rcplondon.ac.uk; Tel 020 7935 1174;
Fax 020 7487 5218

Royal Society of Medicine
1 Wimpole St, London W1G 0AE; URL www.rsm.ac.uk;
e-mail events@rsm.ac.uk; Tel 020 7290 2991;
Fax 020 7290 2992
Director (Education and Professional Development)
J. Parkinson

Physics

Institute of Physics
76 Portland Pl, London W1B 1NT; URL www.iop.org;
e-mail physics@iop.org; Tel 020 7470 4800;
Fax 020 7470 4848
Chief Executive   Dr Robert Kirby-Harris CPhys, FInstP
Manager (Public Relations)   D. Stilwell

Physiotherapy

Chartered Society of Physiotherapy
14 Bedford Row, London WC1R 4ED;
URL www.csp.org.uk; e-mail csp@csp.org.uk;
Tel 020 7306 6666; Fax 020 7306 6611
Chief Executive   Phil Gray

Printing

British Printing Industries Federation (BPIF)
11 Bedford Row, London WC1R 4DX;
URL www.bpif.org.uk; e-mail info@bpif.org.uk;
Tel 020 7915 8300; Fax 020 7405 7784
Chief Executive   Tom Machin
Director (Education and Training)   Andrew Brown
Manager (Corporate Marketing)   Daphne Carter

Institute of Printing
The Mews, Hill Hse, Clanricarde Rd, Tunbridge Wells, Kent
TN1 1PJ; URL www.instituteofprinting.org; e-mail
admin@instituteofprinting.org; Tel 01892 538118;
Fax 01892 518028
Secretary General   D. Freeland DMS

Psychology

British Psychological Society
St Andrew's Hse, 48 Princess Rd East, Leicester LE1 7DR;
URL www.bps.org.uk; e-mail mail@bps.org.uk;
Tel 0116 254 9568; Fax 0116 247 0787
Hon General Secretary   Prof Ann Colley

Public Relations
See Marketing/Advertising/Public Relations

Publishing

Booktrust
Book Hse, 45 East Hill, London SW18 2QZ;
URL www.booktrusted.com; e-mail
query@booktrust.org.uk; Tel 020 8516 2977;
Fax 020 8516 2978

The Publishers Association
29b Montague St, London WC1B 5BW;
URL www.publishers.org.uk; e-mail
mail@publishers.org.uk; Tel 020 7691 9191;
Fax 020 7691 9199
President   Mike Boswood
Vice-President   Ian Hudson
Chief Executive   Simon Juden

Society of Young Publishers
c/o 12 Dyott St, London WC1A 1DF
Chair   Suzanne Collier

Women in Publishing
c/o 1 Kingsway, London WC2
Information Officer   Marina Vakos

Purchasing

Chartered Institute of Purchasing and Supply
Easton Hse, Easton on the Hill, Stamford, Lincolnshire
PE9 3NZ; URL www.cips.org; e-mail
membership.enquiry@cips.org; Tel 01780 756777;
Fax 01780 751610
Manager (Membership Operations)   C. Bain

Radiographers

College of Radiographers
207 Providence Sq, Mill St, London SE1 2EW;
URL www.sor.org; e-mail info@sor.org;
Tel 020 7740 7200; Fax 020 7740 7233
Director (Professional Policy)   Prof Audrey Paterson

Refrigeration

Institute of Refrigeration
Kelvin Hse, 76 Mill La, Carshalton, Surrey SM5 2JR;
URL www.ior.org.uk; e-mail ior.org.uk;
Tel 020 8647 7033; Fax 020 8773 0165
Secretary   M. Rodway

Retail Trades

National Association of Colleges in Distributive Education and Training
39 The Birches, Winchmore Hill, London N21 1NJ;
Tel 020 8360 4409

Secretaries
See Administration

Shipping

Institute of Chartered Shipbrokers
85 Gracechurch St, London EC3V 0AA;
URL www.ics.org.uk; Tel 020 7623 1111;
Fax 020 7623 8118
Director   A. Phillips FRGS, FCMI

Social Work

British Association of Social Workers
16 Kent St, Birmingham, West Midlands B5 6RD;
URL www.basw.co.uk; Tel 0121 622 3911;
Fax 0121 622 4860
Director   Ian Johnston

Speech and Language Therapy

Royal College of Speech and Language Therapists
2 White Hart Yard, London SE1 1NX; Tel 020 7378 1200;
Fax 020 7403 7254
Professional Director   K. Gadhok MRCSLT

Statistics

Royal Statistical Society
12 Errol St, London EC1Y 8LX; URL www.rss.org.uk; e-mail
rss@rss.org.uk; Tel 020 7638 8998; Fax 020 7614 3905
Director General   I. Goddard

Supervisory Management

The Institute for Supervision and Management (ISM) has merged with NEBS Management to become the Institute of Leadership and Management (ILM); please see entry under Management

Surgeons

Royal College of Surgeons of England
35–43 Lincolns Inn Fields, London WC2A 3PE;
   Tel 020 7405 3474
Executive General Manager   David Munn

Surveyors

Institution of Civil Engineering Surveyors
Dominion Hse, Sibson Rd, Sale, Cheshire M33 7PP;
   URL www.ices.org.uk; e-mail membership@ices.org.uk;
   Tel 0161 972 3100; Fax 0161 972 3118
Chair (Education Training and Membership Committee)
   Jason Smith
Manager (Education, Training and Membership)   Paul Brown

Royal Institution of Chartered Surveyors
12 Gt George St, Parliament Sq, London SW1P 3AD;
   URL www.rics.org; e-mail contactrics@rics.org;
   Tel 020 7222 7000; Fax 020 7334 3811
Chief Executive   J. Armstrong

Town Planning

Royal Town Planning Institute
41 Botolph La, London EC3R 8DL; URL www.rtpi.org.uk;
   e-mail careers@rtpi.org.uk; Tel 020 7929 9494;
   Fax 020 7929 9490
Secretary General   Robert Upton
*Director (Membership, Education and Lifelong Learning
   Department)*   Sue Percy

Transport

Institute of Highway Incorporated Engineers
20 Queensberry Pl, London SW7 2DR;
   URL www.ihie.org.uk; e-mail information@ihie.org.uk;
   Tel 020 7823 9093; Fax 020 7581 8087
Secretary   J.M. Walker

Institute of Logistics and Transport
80 Portland Pl, London W1N 4DP; e-mail
   enquiry@iolt.org.uk; Tel 020 7467 9400;
   Fax 020 7467 9440
Chief Executive   Graham Ewer FCIT
Director (Education)   Dorothea Cavvalho
Manager (Qualifications)   Helen Chambers

Travel and Tourism

Institute of Travel and Tourism
PO Box 217, Ware, Hertfordshire SG12 8WY;
   URL www.itt.co.uk; e-mail admin@itt.co.uk;
   Tel 01727 854395; Fax 01727 847415

International Association of Tour Managers
397 Walworth Rd, London SE17 2AW;
   URL www.iatm.co.uk; e-mail iatm@iatm.co.uk;
   Tel 020 7703 9154; Fax 020 7703 0358
Manager   R. Julian

The Tourism Society
Trinity Ct, 34 West St, Sutton, Surrey SM1 1SH;
   URL www.tourismsociety.org; e-mail
   admin@tourismsociety.org; Tel 020 8661 4636;
   Fax 020 8661 4637
Chair   Alison Cryer
Executive DIrector   Flo Powell

Underwater Technology

Society for Underwater Technology
80 Coleman St, London EC2R 5BJ; URL www.sut.org.uk;
   e-mail cheryl.ince@sut.org; Tel 020 7382 2601;
   Fax 020 7382 2684
Administrative Secretary   Cheryl Ince
SUT provides careers information packs on careers in marine sciences, engineering and technology, and student sponsorship at undergraduate and MSc levels

Veterinary Science

Institute of Animal Technology (IAT)
5 South Par, Summertown, Oxford, Oxfordshire OX2 7JL;
   URL www.iat.org.uk; e-mail website@iat.org.uk
Professional body for Career Animal Technologists;
enquiries to the Hon Secretary

Royal College of Veterinary Surgeons
Belgravia Hse, 62–64 Horseferry Rd, London SW1P 2AF;
   URL www.rcvs.org.uk; e-mail registrar@rcvs.org.uk;
   Tel 020 7222 2001; Fax 020 7222 2004
Registrar; Secretary   J.C. Hern MA

Wood

Institute of Wood Science
3rd Fl D, Carpenters' Hall, 1 Throgmorton Ave, London
   EC2N 2BY; URL www.iwsc.org.uk; e-mail
   info@iwsc.org.uk; Tel 020 7256 2700; Fax 020 7256 2701

Youth and Community Work

The National Youth Agency
Eastgate Hse, 19–23 Humberstone Rd, Leicester LE5 3GJ;
   URL www.nya.org.uk; e-mail nya@nya.org.uk;
   Tel 0116 242 7350; Fax 0116 242 7444
Chief Executive   Fiona Blacke

10

Sponsored Training and Apprenticeships

Acordis Acetate Chemicals Ltd
PO Box 5, Spondon, Derby DE21 7BP; Tel 01332 681603;
   Fax 01332 662410
Adviser (Human Resources)   Kieran Grimshaw
Acetate Products, a sub-business unit of the Acordis group, offers occasional vocational training for engineering and science degree courses; industrial training placements; and vocational training for all employees

Aeroflex International Ltd
Longacres Hse, Six Hills Way, Stevenage, Hertfordshire
   SG1 2AN; URL www.aeroflex.com; e-mail
   caroline.miles@aeroflex.com; Tel 01438 742200;
   Fax 01438 772041
Adviser (Human Resources)   Caroline Miles
Aeroflex employs 500 people at sites in Stevenage, manufacturing electronic test and measurement equipment. Sponsored student training in electronic engineering on either thick or thin (integrated) sandwich courses; technician and technician engineer training, leading to HNC by day release at a local college.

Air Products plc
Hersham Pl, Molesey Rd, Walton-on-Thames, Surrey
   KT12 4RZ; Tel 01932 249200; Fax 01932 249893
Sponsorship available for students wishing to study for chemical engineering, mechanical engineering and electrical engineering

ALSTOM Power, Rugby
Newbold Rd, Rugby, Warwickshire CV21 2NH;
Tel 01788 531871
Training Development Officer David Huntington;
Tel 01788 531871
ALSTOM Power is a world leader in power generation
equipment. Opportunities include craft and technician
apprenticeships in mechanical engineering; student
sponsorships include bursary and salary during industrial
periods; graduate traineeships of up to two years' duration
in engineering design, manufacturing, construction, service,
and project management.

AMEC
URL www.amec.com/careers
Programmes aimed at school and college leavers, covering a
range of career routes, including craft, other vocational and
technician options. Trainees are encouraged to become
qualified in their trade or discipline and, where appropriate,
are given opportunities for day release so that they can
study at universities or colleges of further education.

Arup
URL www.arup.com; e-mail graderec@arup.com;
Tel 01635 584146
Up to 10 sponsorships a year are available to young people
of academic distinction expecting to take degrees in civil,
structural, mechanical, electrical, building services
engineering or general engineering followed by
specialisation in those fields. Sponsored students are
normally expected to gain nine to 10 months' gap year
experience.
Degree applicant requirements
Six good GCSE grades, including English, Mathematics and
Sciences with an expectation of at least three good A-levels
or five good grades at SCE Higher Level

Automotive Products plc
Tachbrook Rd, Leamington Spa, Warwickshire CV31 3ER;
Tel 01926 472351
Manager (Training) W.L. Clarkson
A range of engineering apprenticeships is offered mainly for
local applicants. Commercial apprenticeships for GCSE or
A-level school-leavers are more widely offered for training
in accountancy, purchasing, marketing and computer
applications. These apprenticeships are usually combined
with appropriate sandwich courses in cost and management
accountancy or business studies, for which financial
assistance is given. Day release may be offered as an
alternative part-time study where appropriate.

Avdel Textron Ltd
Mundells, Welwyn Garden City, Hertfordshire AL7 1EZ;
Tel 01707 668668; Fax 01707 338828
President R. Ayotte
Managing Director Andrew Taylor
Director K. Denham
Engineering apprenticeships in technician or engineer for
school-leavers with GCSE Grade C; involving college to
National or Higher National Certificate level. Craft
apprenticeships in toolroom or maintenance leading to C&G
qualifications. Sponsored student training scheme to study
mechanical or manufacturing engineering or closely-related
subject at university. Bursary whilst at university; salary
during industrial placement in company.

Baker Perkins Ltd
Manor Dr, Paston Parkway, Peterborough, Cambridgeshire
PE4 7AP; URL www.bakerperkinsgroup.com; e-mail
bpltd@bakerperkinsgroup.com; Tel 01733 283000;
Fax 01733 283018
Summer vacation placements for local undergraduates
studying general, mechanical, manufacturing, electrical,
electronic engineering or business studies

BBC (British Broadcasting Corporation)
Broadcasting Hse, London W1A 1AA; Tel 020 7927 5442;
Fax 020 7631 5491

Engineering and technical operations recruitment
(engineering and technical enquiries), secretarial and
clerical services (secretarial and clerical enquiries) or
corporate recruitment services (all other enquiries).
Principal training schemes: secretarial, data preparation,
studio management, news, local radio reporters,
production, film, make-up, engineers, camera operation,
recording operation. Write to above address for literature
regarding entry qualification.

Bentley Motors Limited
Crewe, Cheshire CW1 3PL; URL www.bentleymotors.com;
www.bentleycareers.com; Tel 01270 255155;
Fax 01270 586548
GCSE Level
Craft/technical and business/commercial apprenticeships
starting in September each year
A-Level
Sponsored degree apprenticeships allowing successful
applicants to undertake a part-time degree as well as on-the-
job training
Undergraduate Level
10-week summer placements for 12-month industrial
placements for students studying for engineering or
business-related degrees
Graduate level
12 to 24 month graduate development programme for
students interested in engineering or other business
functions

C-Mac Quartz Crystals Limited
Dowsett Hse, Sadler Rd, Lincoln, Lincolnshire LN6 3RS;
Tel 01522 883611
Personnel Officer J.M. Wass
Sponsorships for university undergraduates following
sandwich courses in electronic engineering, production
engineering, manufacturing studies, or engineering with
marketing

CROWN Packaging
Downsview Rd, Wantage, Oxfordshire OX12 9BP;
Tel 01235 772929; Fax 01235 402541
Manager (Graduate Recruitment and Training) P. Axtell
CROWN Packaging manufactures cans, tins, plastic bottles
and containers, aerosols and closures for bottles and glass
jars. Sponsorship is available to students planning to study
engineering at university in the UK.

Haden Young Limited
44 Clarendon Rd, Watford, Hertfordshire WD17 1DR;
URL www.hadenyoung.co.uk; e-mail
recruitment@hadenyoung.co.uk; Tel 01923 232959
Director (Personnel) P. Jackson
The company recruits school-leavers for engineering
student training programmes, commercial student
programmes and craft apprenticeships in the fields of
heating, ventilating, air-conditioning, electrical installation,
plumbing, quantity surveying and fire protection. The
company has branches in Bristol, Edinburgh, Glasgow,
Horley, Leeds, London, Newcastle, Tamworth, Warrington
and Watford.

HBG UK Ltd
Merit Hse, Edgware Rd, London NW9 5AF;
URL www.hbgc.co.uk; e-mail (enquiries only)
careers@hbgc.co.uk; Tel 020 8200 7070; Fax 020 8200 3997
Training Officer Roo Modasia; Tel 020 8338 2818;
Fax 020 8200 0974
Major building contractor offering day release, sandwich
course, postgraduate employment in Construction,
Quantity Surveying, Civil Engineering, Design and
Architecture related fields. It also sponsors undergraduates
at selected universities, and offer summer placements and
unpaid work experience.

Laing Construction Services Ltd
Paramount Hse, Maylands Ave, Hemel Hempstead,
Hertfordshire HP2 4XH; Tel 01442 275500;
Fax 01442 275552

Manager (Human Resources: Administration)   D. Whitehouse
Three-year training agreements for estimators, planners, buyers, site engineers and quantity surveyors; degree sponsorships for building and quantity surveying degree sandwich sources; craft apprenticeships in bricklaying and carpentry/joinery through two-year modern apprenticeship scheme. Day release for technical and professional study given.

London Regional Transport
Engineering Training Centre, 123 Gunnersbury La, London W3 8J; Tel 020 7918 6682
Apprenticeships in mechanical engineering, electrical engineering, electronics, fabrication (welding and sheet metal), vehicle building. Day or block release for college, depending on trade.

Marconi Radar Systems Ltd
Writtle Rd, Chelmsford, Essex CM1 3BN; Tel 01245 267111 ext 2075
Student apprenticeships for A-level school-leavers; training schemes offered are principally in electronics engineering and software production and application. Sponsored students following a recognised sandwich course will be given relevant industrial training.

Ofrex Group Holdings plc
Acco–Rexel Ltd, Bretton Way, Peterborough, Cambridgeshire PE3 8YZ; Tel 01733 264711
Director (Personnel and Training)   C.G. Winchester
Normal apprenticeships in engineering; industrial training in business studies sandwich degree courses; training in finance, marketing, sales, computing and distribution. Day and block release given for part-time and professional courses; financial assistance for examinations and books.

Quarry Products Training Council (QPTC)
Sterling Hse, 20 Station Rd, Gerrards Cross, Buckinghamshire SL9 8HT; Tel 01753 891808; Fax 01753 891132
Senior Adviser (Training)   J.R. George
Adviser (Training)   I.V. Dickinson
Youth training based on Stages 1 and 2 of the Extractives Industries Apprenticeship Scheme. Some 20 sponsorships a year to take BEng (Ordinary) Degree in Quarry and Road Surface Engineering at Doncaster College.

Rolls Royce Plc
Queens Engineering Works, Ford End Rd, Bedford, Bedfordshire MK40 4JB; Tel 01234 272000

Royal Ordnance plc
PO Box 40, Chorley, Lancashire PR7 6AD; Tel 01257 65511 ext 2455
Senior Training and Studies Officer   K. Gaskill
Intake of 100 craft apprenticeships, 12 sponsored students taking a first degree

Shell Ship Management Ltd
Manannan Hse, Market Sq, Castletown, Isle of Man IM9 1RB; URL www.shell.com/shipping; e-mail recruitment@shell.com; Tel 01624 821500
Opportunities for sponsorship as deck or engineer cadets to become future officers in worldwide shipping fleet. Training spent partly in technical/nautical colleges ashore and partly at sea. Nationally recognised qualifications and Department of Transport certificates obtained by cadets during training. Entry qualifications are A-level passes in Maths or Physics.

Shell UK Ltd
Shell–Mex Hse, Strand, London WC2R 0DX; Tel 020 7257 1825
Head (Sponsorship)   R.M. Smeeton (UKPS/3)
Undergraduate sponsorship is available to those applying for a place on courses in engineering and science disciplines at selected universities

Shepherd Construction Ltd
Frederick Hse, Fulford Rd, York YO10 4EA; Tel 01904 660364; Fax 01904 660559
Manager (Learning and Development)   P.A. Blackburn
Building craft apprenticeships, building studentships, undergraduate sponsorship and graduate trainees in management, planning, quantity surveying, and occasionally more specialist careers, with appropriate release to attend further and higher education courses. Located at Birmingham, Darlington, Huntingdon, Leeds, London, Manchester and York.

Vickers Shipbuilding and Engineering Limited
Barrow-in-Furness, Cumbria LA14 1AF; Tel 01229 873736
Head (Personnel, Development and Training)   R.D. Clark
Student and graduate apprenticeships

Vosper Thornycroft (UK) Ltd
Company Training Manager, Victoria Rd, Southampton SO9 5GR; Tel 02380 445144
Student sponsorship; postgraduate training; maximum period of two years. Disciplines include naval architecture, all mechanical/marine engineering, electronic/electrical engineering, computer applications, and business/commercial training. Training will be given within the company's three divisions, as appropriate.

Westinghouse Brakes Limited
PO Box 74, Chippenham, Wiltshire SN15 1HY; Tel 01249 442829
Manager (Human Resources)   J. Walters
Westinghouse Brakes is an engineering company specialising in the supply of brake and door equipment to the railway industry. Sponsored student training in mechanical engineering; financial assistance given during academic periods; schemes of training meet the requirements of the relevant professional institution.

10

Physical Education and Sport

11

Physical Education and Sport

National Sports Councils and Committees

Sport England
3rd Fl, Victoria Hse, Bloomsbury Sq, London WC1B 4SE;
  URL www.sportengland.org; e-mail
  info@sportengland.org; Tel 0845 850 8508
Chief Executive   Jennie Price
Chair   Vacancy
Sport England is the brand name of the English Sports
Council which is the distributor of the lottery funds to sport.
The English Sports Council is a body, constituted from the
Sports Council, and is responsible for providing the strategic
lead for sport in England to deliver government sporting
objectives. It also receives grants in aid from the Department
for Culture, Media and Sport. There is also UK Sport and
Sports Councils for Wales, Scotland and Northern Ireland.

Sport England Regional Offices
East Region   19 The Crescent, off Tavistock St, Bedford,
  Bedfordshire MK40 2QP; Tel 01234 345222
  Regional Director   Chris Perks
East Midland Region   Grove Hse, Bridgford Rd, Nottingham
  NG2 6AP; Tel 0115 982 1887
  Regional Director   T. Garfield
London Region   3rd Fl, Victoria Hse, Bloomsbury Sq,
  London WC1B 4SE; Tel 020 7242 2801
  Regional Director London   Sean Holt
North East Region   Aykley Heads, Durham, County
  Durham DH1 5UU; Tel 0191 384 9595
  Regional Director   J. Rasmussen
North West Region   Astley Hse, Quay St, Manchester
  M3 4AE; Tel 0161 834 0338
  Regional Director   Stewart Kellett
South East Region   51a Church St, Caversham, Reading
  RG4 8AX; Tel 0118 948 3311
  Regional Director   Judith Dean
South West Region   Ashlands Hse, Ashlands, Crewkerne,
  Somerset TA18 7LQ; Fax 01460 73491
  Regional Director   Jim Clarke
West Midlands Region   5th Fl, No 3 Broadway, Five Ways,
  Birmingham, West Midlands B15 1BQ; Tel 0121 616 6700
  Regional Director   Steve Town
Yorkshire Region   4th Fl, Minerva Hse, East Par, Leeds, West
  Yorkshire LS1 5PS; Tel 0113 243 6443
  Regional Director   David Gent

National Sports Centres
Bisham Abbey National Sports Centre   Marlow,
  Buckinghamshire SL7 1RT; Tel 0162 847 6911
  Director   Vacancy
Crystal Palace National Sports Centre   Crystal Palace
  National Sports Centre, Norwood, London SE19 2BB;
  Tel 020 8778 0131
  Director   Vacancy
Holme Pierrepont National Water Sports Centre   Adbolton
  La, Holme Pierrepont, Nottingham NG12 2LU;
  Tel 0115 982 1212
  Director   Vacancy

Lilleshall Hall National Sports Centre   Newport, Shropshire
  TF10 9AT; Tel 01952 603003
  Director   Vacancy
The National Centre for Mountain Activities   Plas y Brenin,
  Capel Curig, Gwynedd LL24 0ET; Tel 01690 14214;
  Tel 01690 14280
  Director   Dave Alcock

Central Council of Physical Recreation
Francis Hse, Francis St, London SW1P 1DE;
  URL www.ccpr.org.uk; e-mail admin@ccpr.org.uk;
  Tel 020 7854 8500
The umbrella organisation for national governing and
representative bodies of sport and recreation in the UK. An
independent voice working to promote, protect and develop
sport and recreation.

Sports Council for Wales
Welsh Institute of Sport, Sophia Gdns, Cardiff CF11 9SW;
  URL www.sports-council-wales.co.uk; e-mail
  scw@scw.co.uk; Tel 02920 300500
Chair   G. Davies MA
Chief Executive   Dr H.G. Jones

Sports Centres
Plas Menai National Watersports Centre   Caernarfon,
  Gwynedd LL55 1UE; e-mail plas.menai@scw.co.uk;
  Tel 01248 670964
Welsh Institute of Sport   Sophia Gdns, Cardiff CF11 9SW;
  e-mail wis@scw.co.uk; Tel 02920 300500

sportscotland
Caledonia Hse, South Gyle, Edinburgh EH12 9DQ;
  URL www.sportscotland.org.uk; e-mail
  library@sportscotland.org.uk; Tel 0131 317 7200;
  Fax 0131 317 7202
Chief Executive   Stewart Harris
sportscotland was set up by Royal Charter with a mission to
encourage people in Scotland to develop their own sporting
experience, helping to increase participation and improve
performances in Scottish sport. sportscotland also
distributes National Lottery funds for sport through the
Lottery Sports Fund.

sportscotland National Centres
sportscotland National Centre – Cumbrae   Isle of Cumbrae,
  Ayrshire KA28 0HQ;
  URL www.nationalcentrecumbrae.org.uk; e-mail
  cumbraecentre@sportscotland.org.uk; Tel 01475 530757;
  Fax 01475 530013
  Principal   John Kent
sportscotland National Centre – Glenmore Lodge   Aviemore,
  Highland PH22 1QU; URL www.glenmorelodge.org.uk;
  e-mail enquiries@glenmorelodge.org.uk;
  Tel 01479 861256; Fax 01479 861212
  Principal   Tim Walker
sportscotland National Centre – Inverclyde   Burnside Rd,
  Largs, Ayrshire KA30 8RW;
  URL www.nationalcentreinverclyde.org.uk; e-mail
  in.enquiries@sportscotland.org.uk; Tel 01475 674666;
  Fax 01475 674720
  Principal   John Kent

11

National Sports Organisations

General Sports Organisations

Association for Physical Education
Bldg L25, London Rd, Reading RG1 5AQ;
  URL www.afpe.org; e-mail enquiries@afpe.org.uk;
  Tel 0118 378 6240
Membership and Company Secretary   John Matthews
Organisation for the physical education profession

British Association of Advisers and Lecturers in Physical Education
Sports Development Centre, Loughborough University,
  Loughborough, Leicestershire LE11 3TU;
  URL www.baalpe.org; e-mail baalpe@lboro.ac.uk;
  Tel 01509 228378; Fax 01509 228378
General Secretary   Peter Whitlam

British Olympic Association
1 Wandsworth Plain, London SW18 1EH;
  URL www.olympics.org.uk; e-mail boa@boa.org.uk;
  Tel 020 8871 2677; Fax 020 8871 9104
To develop and promote the Olympic Movement in Great
Britain in accordance with the Olympic Charter and prepare
and send the Great Britain Olympic Team (Team GB) to the
Olympic and Olympic Winter Games

British Universities Sports Association
20–24 King's Bench St, London SE1 0QX;
  URL www.busa.org.uk; e-mail office@busa.org.uk;
  Tel 020 7633 5080; Fax 020 3268 2120

British Veterans' Athletic Federation (BVAF)
67–71 Goswell Rd, London EC1V 7EN; Tel 020 7250 1881
Hon Administrative Officer   J.F. Fitzgerald
Provides athletic competition at national and international
level for men over 40 and women over 35 years of age

The Commonwealth Games Federation
Walkden Hse, 3–10 Melton St, London NW1 2EB;
  URL www.thecgf.com; e-mail office@thecgf.com;
  Tel 020 7383 5596
President   HRH The Prince Edward, CVO
Cheif Executive Officer   Michael Hooper
Promotes at four-yearly intervals the Commonwealth
Games, establishes rules and regulations for the conduct of
the Games (in conformity with technical rules of
International Federations governing sports concerned) and
encourages amateur sport throughout the Commonwealth
by efficient organisation of the Games' competitions

Institute of Leisure and Amenity Management
Professional Development Department, ILAM Hse, Lower
  Basildon, Reading RG8 9NE; URL www.ilam.co.uk;
  e-mail profdev@ilam.co.uk; Tel 01491 874831;
  Fax 01491 874800

The Institute of Sport and Recreation Management
Giffard Hse, 36–38 Sherrard St, Melton Mowbray,
  Leicestershire LE13 1XJ; URL www.isrm.co.uk; e-mail
  education+training@isrm.co.uk; Tel 01664 565531;
  Fax 01664 501155

The Institute of Sport and Recreation Management (Scottish Branch)
Kirktown Depot, Broomhill Rd, Stonehaven, Aberdeenshire
  AB3 2NH; Tel 01569 767202
Training and Education Officer   T. Parker

The Institute of Sports Medicine (ISM)
The Royal Free and University College Medical School,
  Charles Bell Hse, 67–73 Riding Hse St, London W1W 7EJ;
  e-mail m.hobsley@ucl.ac.uk; Tel 020 7813 2832;
  Fax 020 7813 2832
Hon Secretary   Dr W.T. Orton MB, BCh, DPH, MFPHM
Postgraduate medical education in sports medicine

National Council for School Sport
19 Davy's Cl, St Albans, Hertfordshire AL4 8TL;
  URL www.yst.org.uk/ncss; e-mail
  gilliangilyead@aol.com; Tel 01509 226680;
  Fax 01509 210851
Chair   John Arnold; 17 Cyprus Mount, St John's,
  Wakefield, West Yorkshire WF1 2RJ; Tel 01924 372597;
  Fax 01924 372597
Hon Treasurer   Jean Gates; 11 Hazells La, Shrivenham,
  Swindon SN6 8DS; Tel 01793 783066
The NCSS is an umbrella body for national associations
dealing with school sport, with more than 30 sports in
membership. The NCSS is the development of a national
competition framework with a range of sports as part of the
government's Physical Education, School Sport and Club
Links programme; working in partnership with the
Department for Culture, Media and Sport, the Department
for Children, Schools and Families, Sport England and the
Youth Sport Trust. Helping to enhance the structure of
competitive school sport from local to national level is a
prime aim. In addition, The NCSS encourages school sports
associations and national governing bodies of sport to work
together. This will provide an opportunity for more young
people to participate in competition and to develop their
talent. The NCSS is affiliated to the International School
Sport Federation.

National Sports Medicine Institute
National Sports Medicine Institute, 32 Devonshire St,
  London W1G 6PX; e-mail isabel.lancoma@nsmi.org.uk;
  Tel 020 7908 3643; Fax 020 7908 3635
Manager (Education)   Isabel Lancoma
The NSMI gives information on aspects of postgraduate
sport and exercise medicine training to individuals and
organisations

Northern Ireland Commonwealth Games Council
22 Mountcoole Pk, Cave Hill, Belfast BT14 8JR;
  Tel 028 9071 6558; Fax 028 9071 6558
General Secretary   R.J. McColgan MBE

Royal Air Force Sports Board
RAF Halton, Aylesbury, Buckinghamshire HP22 5PG;
  e-mail sportsboard-dsb1@halton.raf.mod.uk;
  Tel 01296 657133; Fax 01296 657138

Scottish Local Authority Network of Physical Education
Auchterderran Centre, Woodend Rd, Cardenden, Fife
  KY5 0NE; e-mail david.maiden@fife.gov.uk;
  Tel 0845 155 5555 ext 442015; Fax 01592 583175
Chair   C. Watson; Education Service, Sir John Maxwell
  Primary School, 3 Christian St, Glasgow G43 1RH;
  Tel 0141 632 1370; Fax 0141 632 1370

Scottish Universities Sport
3rd Fl, 48 Pleasance, Edinburgh EH8 9TJ
Manager (Sports Programme)   Stew Fowlie
Executive Officer   Jacqui Stone

Sports Coach UK
114 Cardigan Rd, Headingley, Leeds, West Yorkshire
  LS6 3BJ; URL www.sportscoachuk.org; e-mail
  coaching@sportscoachuk.org; Tel 0113 274 4802
Chief Executive   Steve Parkin
sports coach UK (scUK) is the focus for all issues relating to
sports coaching. Its overall aim is to work with key partners
to develop better coaches for better sport. Supported by the
Sports Councils in England, Scotland, Wales and Northern
Ireland (and the UK Sports Council), scUK works closely
with the national governing bodies of sport, local authorities
and higher and further education, to provide a
comprehensive range of services for sports coaches of all
levels of experience and from all sports. scUK's work
programmes are delivered locally throughout the UK via a
network of coaching development officers and scUK
products and resources are sold through its trading
subsidiary, Coachwise Ltd.

SPRIG
URL www.sprig.org.uk
Secretary Peter Drake; Local Studies and History, Central
  Library, Chamberlain Sq, Birmingham, West Midlands
  B3 3HQ; Tel 0121 303 4220; Fax 0161 835 3678
Chair Martin Scarrott; Information Centre, St Mary's
  College, Waldegrave Rd, Twickenham, Greater London
  TW1 4SX; Tel 020 8240 2304
Acts as a special interest group for those involved in
disseminating and managing information in leisure, tourism
and sport. Disseminates information to users with an
interest in leisure, tourism and sport. Lobbies information
providers (such as government organisations, publishers
and specialist libraries) in leisure, tourism and sport for
better co-ordination in provision and to identify gaps in that
provision. Aims to improve awareness of leisure, tourism
and sport information sources, particularly to those outside
the library and information profession.

Welsh Council for School Sport
28 Deysbrook La, Liverpool, Merseyside L12 8RF;
  Tel 0151 220 9961
Hon Secretary Courteney Owen

Angling

Anglers' Conservation Association (ACA)
Shalford Dairy, Shalford Hill, Aldermaston, Reading
  RG7 4NB; e-mail admin@a-c-a.org; Tel 0118 971 4770;
  Fax 0118 971 4799
Director Jane James
Common Law actions to prevent pollution of waterways

Confederation of English Fly Fishers (CEFF)
31 Meadow Rd, Hartshill, Nuneaton, Warwickshire
  CV10 0NL
Hon Secretary John Hedges
Organises international fly fishing events

National Federation of Anglers
National Water Sports Centre, Adbolton La, Holme
  Pierrepont, Nottingham NG12 2LU;
  URL www.nfadirect.com; e-mail office@nfadirect.com;
  Tel 0115 981 3535; Fax 0115 981 9039
Governing body for freshwater angling

National Federation of Sea Anglers
Level 5, Hamlyn Hse, Mardle Way, Buckfastleigh, Devon
  TQ11 0NS; URL www.nfsa.org.uk; e-mail
  ho@nfsa.org.uk; Tel 01364 644643; Fax 01364 644486
Development Officer David Rowe
The NFSA is the governing body of the sport within
England, and looks after the interests of individual anglers,
sea angling clubs, their members, and the development of
the sport. Enquiries to development officer.

Archery

The British Crossbow Society
2 Vicarage Rd, Chellaston, Derbyshire DE73 1SD;
  URL www.british-crossbow.co.uk; e-mail
  keith@bullseye.force9.co.uk; Tel 01332 700180
President A. Gunn
Represents crossbowmen in all matters appertaining to their
sport and promotes competitive amateur competition
throughout the UK

Grand National Archery Society
Lilleshall National Sports Centre, Newport, Shropshire
  TF10 9AT; URL www.gnas.org; e-mail
  enquiries@gnas.org; Tel 01952 677888; Fax 01952 606019

National Field Archery Society
Sweetbrier Cottage, Bedford Rd, Northill, Bedfordshire
  SG18 9AW; Tel 01767 626197
Hon Secretary Chris Cox
Organisation of archery competitions in wooded terrain in
which hunting skills are simulated

Northern Ireland Archery Society
Hon Secretary Stephen Ward; 8 Ballynahinch Rd,
  Hillsborough, County Down BT26 6AR; Tel (home)
  028 9268 2432

Athletics

Amateur Athletic Association of England
Edgbaston Hse, 3 Duchess Pl, Hagley Rd, Birmingham,
  West Midlands B16 8NM;
  URL www.englandathletics.org

Athletics UK
Apex 6, 10 Harborne Rd, Edgbaston, Birmingham, West
  Midlands B15 3AA; e-mail
  information@ukathletics.org.uk; Tel 0121 456 5098;
  Fax 0121 456 8752

British Triathlon Association (BTA)
PO Box 25, Loughborough, Leicestershire LE11 3WX;
  URL www.britishtriathlon.org; e-mail
  info@britishtriathlon.org; Tel 01509 226161;
  Fax 01509 226165
Chief Executive Norman Brook
Controls and promotes the Olympic sport of triathlon
(swimming, cycling and running) and duathlon (any two of
previous three)

**Cymdeithas Athletau Ysgolion Cymru (Welsh Schools'
Athletic Association)**
Hon Secretary G. Coldwell; 21 John St, Neyland, Milford
  Haven, Pembrokeshire; Tel 01646 602187;
  Tel 01437 764147 (school)
Hon Treasurer C.E. Hughes MBE; Coleyne, Roe Pk, St
  Asaph, Denbighshire; Tel (home) 01745 582409

English Cross-Country Association (ECCA)
22 Denham Dr, Basingstoke, Hampshire RG2 6LR;
  Tel 01256 328401
Hon Secretary I. Byett
Encourages and promotes cross–country running and lays
down guidelines for affiliated clubs and associations

English Schools' Athletic Association
26 Newborough Grn, New Malden, Surrey KT3 5HS;
  URL www.esaa.net; Tel 020 8949 1506; Fax 020 8942 0943
Hon Secretary D.R. Littlewood

International Association of Athletics Federations
17 Rue Princesse Florestine, BP 359, MC-98007, Monaco;
  URL www.iaaf.org; e-mail info@iaaf.org;
  Tel +377 93 10 88 88; Fax +377 93 15 95 15
President Lamine Diack
General Secretary Pierre Weiss
World governing body for track and field athletics

Kangaroo Club
'Oakdene', The Old Rectory, Lowe Hill Rd, Wem, Shropshire
  SY4 5UA; Tel 01939 233220; Fax 01939 233220
Long and Triple Jump

Northern Ireland Athletic Federation
Athletics Hse, Old Coach Rd, Belfast BT9 5PR;
  URL www.niathletics.org; e-mail info@niathletics.org;
  Tel 028 9060 2707; Fax 028 9030 9939

Modern Pentathlon Association of Great Britain
Norwood Hse, University of Bath, Claverton Down, Bath
  BA2 7AY; URL www.mpagb.org.uk; Tel 01225 386808;
  Fax 01225 386995

Road Runners' Club
2 Hodgson Hse, Eton, Hertfordshire SL4 6DE
Secretary R.M. Fisher

Scottish Athletics
9a South Gyle Cres, South Gyle, Edinburgh EH12 9EB;
  URL www.scottishathletics.org.uk; e-mail
  admin@scottishathletics.org.uk; Tel 0870 145 1500;
  Fax 0870 145 1501

11

Scottish Schools' Athletic Association

11 Muirfield St, Kirkcaldy, Fife KY2 6SY; Tel (home)
01592 260168; Fax 01592 772013
Contact A. Jack

Badminton

Badminton England

National Badminton Centre, Bradwell Rd, Loughton Lodge,
Milton Keynes, Buckinghamshire MK8 9LA;
URL www.badmintonengland.co.uk; e-mail
enquiries@badmintonengland.co.uk; Tel 01908 268400;
Fax 01908 268412

Badminton Scotland

Cockburn Centre, 40 Bogmoor Pl, Glasgow G51 4TQ;
URL www.badmintonscotland.org.uk; e-mail
enquiries@badmintonscotland.org.uk; Tel 0141 445 1218;
Fax 0141 425 1218

International Badminton Federation (IBF)

Manor Park Pl, Rutherford Way, Cheltenham,
Gloucestershire GL51 9TU; URL www.intbadfed.org;
www.worldbadminton.net; e-mail info@intbadfed.org;
Tel 01242 234904
Chief Executive Neil M. Cameron
Promotion and development of badminton worldwide

Schools and Youth Board, Badminton Association of England Ltd

Chair E.W. Brown; 25 Bounds Green Ct, London N11 2EX;
Tel 020 8888 0554
Vice-Chair M.J. Smith; 66 Slayleigh La, Fulwood, Sheffield,
South Yorkshire S10 3RH; Tel 0114 230 5618
Events Co-ordinator (Schools and Youth Board)
Nikki Tarrant; Badminton England, National Badminton
Centre, Bradwell Rd, Loughton Lodge, Milton Keynes,
Buckinghamshire MK8 9LA;
URL www.badmintonengland.co.uk; e-mail
nikkitarrant@badmintonengland.co.uk;
Tel 01908 268400; Fax 01908 268412

Ulster Badminton

National Badminton Centre, 36 Belfast Rd, Lisburn
BT27 4AS; e-mail ulsterbadminton@btconnect.com;
Tel 028 9266 8392; Fax 028 9262 9674

Welsh Badminton Union

4th Fl, 3 Westgate St, Cardiff CF1 1JF;
URL www.welshbadminton.net; e-mail
welsh@welshbadminton.force9.co.uk; Tel 02920 222082;
Fax 02920 394282
Contact L. Williams

Baseball and Softball

Guernsey Softball Association (GSA)

c/o The Secretary, Millefleur, La Retot, Castel, Guernsey
GY5 7EG, Channel Islands; e-mail moby@guernsey.net;
Tel 01481 721666
Contact Melissa Green
To foster and promote softball to all age groups. Men's and
women's open tournaments held every season.

Welsh Baseball Union

63 Shakespeare Cres, Newport NP20 3JA; Tel 01633 64311
Contact L.C. Mort

Basketball

Basketball Wales

30 Eileen Pl, Treherbert, Rhondda Cynon Taff CF42 5BU;
URL www.basketballwales.com; e-mail
wj.incentevents@virgin.net; Tel 07768 044443

basketballscotland

Caledonia Hse, South Gyle, Edinburgh EH12 9DQ;
URL www.basketball-scotland.com; e-mail
enquiries@basketball-scotland.com; Tel 0131 317 7260;
Fax 0131 317 7489
Chief Executive Rodger Thompson
Youth Development basketballscotland, Caledonia Hse,
South Gyle, Edinburgh EH12 9DQ;
URL www.basketball-scotland.com; e-mail
david.sarnowski@basketball-scotland.com;
Tel 0131 317 7260; Fax 0131 317 7489

England Basketball

48 Bradford Rd, Stanningley, Leeds, West Yorkshire
LS28 6DF; URL www.basketballengland.org.uk; e-mail
ebba@basketballengland.net; Tel 0113 236 1166;
Fax 0113 236 1022
Chief Executive Simon Kirkland

Mini-Basketball England

4 Fairmead Rise, Northampton, Northamptonshire
NN2 8PP; URL www.mini-basketball.org.uk; e-mail
martin.spencer12@ntlworld.com; Tel 01604 517732;
Fax 01604 517732
Education Officer Martin Spencer
Promotes the development of mini-basketball in schools and
youth organisations

Billiards and Snooker

International Billiards and Snooker Federation (IBSF)

92 Kirkstall Rd, Leeds, West Yorkshire LS3 1LT;
Tel 01532 440586; Fax 01532 468418
Secretary David Ford
World governing body

Bowling

British Crown Green Bowling Association

94 Fishers La, Pensby, Wirral CH61 8SB;
URL www.bowls.org; e-mail jac21up@aol.com;
Tel 0151 648 5740; Fax 0151 648 0733
Chief Executive J.A. Crowther
Promotes the game of crown green bowls and develops it
throughout the UK

English Bowling Association

Lyndhurst Rd, Worthing, West Sussex BN11 2AZ;
URL www.bowlsengland.com; e-mail
eba@bowlsengland.com; Tel 01903 820222;
Fax 01903 820444

English Bowling Federation (EBF)

84 School Rd, Beighton, Sheffield, South Yorkshire S20 1EH;
URL www.fedbowls.co.uk; Tel 0114 2477 763
Secretary John Heppel
Promotes, fosters and safeguards the flatgreen game of
bowls and formulates rules and laws

English Women's Bowling Association (EWBA)

EWBA Office, Victoria Pk, Archery Rd, Leamington Spa,
Warwickshire CV31 3PT;
URL www.englishwomensbowling.net; e-mail
office@englishwomensbowling.net; Tel 01926 430686
Chief Executive Pauline Biddlecombe
Brings together all women's county associations and mixed
bowls associations in England and encourages the sport
generally

Guernsey Bowling Association

Meadow View, Mount Row, St Peter Port, Guernsey
GY1 1NS, Channel Islands; Tel 01481 25556
Hon Secretary Simon D. Masterton

Guernsey Indoor Bowling Association
Hougue du Pommier, Vale, Guernsey GY6 8BD, Channel
　　Islands; URL www.giba.org.gg; e-mail giba@giba.org.gg;
　　Tel 01481 257100; Fax 01481 251251
Secretary　　P.R. Harris

Scottish Bowling Association
National Centre for Bowling, Hunters Ave, Ayr, Ayrshire
　　RA8 9AL; Tel 01292 294683
Secretary　　Ian Pickavance

Scottish Women's Bowling Association
Kingston Hse, 3 Jamaica St, Greenock, Inverclyde PA15 1XX;
　　e-mail eleanor@swba.co.uk; Tel 01475 724676

Boxing

The Amateur Boxing Association of England Ltd
Crystal Palace, National Sports Centre, London SE19 2BB;
　　e-mail hq@abae.org.uk; Tel 020 8778 0251;
　　Fax 020 8778 9324
Company Secretary　　C. Brown

Welsh Amateur Boxing Association
8 Erw Wen, Rhiwbina, Cardiff CF4 6JW

Camping

Camping and Caravanning Club
Greenfields Hse, Westwood Way, Coventry, Warwickshire
　　CV4 8JH;
　　URL www.campingandcaravanningclub.co.uk; e-mail
　　paul.jones@thefriendlyclub.co.uk; Tel 024 7647 5230;
　　Fax 024 7647 5416

Camping and Caravanning Club (Scottish Region)
20 The Oval, Clarkston, Glasgow G76 8LY
Secretary　　P. McIlraith

Canoeing

**British Canoe Union (Paddlesport Participation
Programme)**
18 Market Pl, Bingham, Nottinghamshire NG13 8AP;
　　URL www.bcu.org.uk; e-mail youth@bcu.org.uk;
　　Tel 0845 370 9500; Fax 0845 370 9501
Chief Executive　　P. Owen
The young people's wing of the British Canoe Union,
incorporating the British Schools' Canoeing Association

Canoe Camping Club
25 Waverley Rd, South Norwood, London SE25 4HT

Scottish Canoe Association
Caledonia Hse, South Gyle, Edinburgh EH12 9DQ;
　　URL www.canoescotland.com; e-mail
　　general.office@canoescotland.com; Tel 0131 317 7314;
　　Fax 0131 317 7319

Caving

British Cave Research Association (BCRA)
The Old Methodist Chapel, Great Hucklow, Buxton,
　　Derbyshire SK17 8RG; URL www.bcra.org.uk; e-mail
　　secretary@bcra.org.uk; Tel 01298 873800;
　　Fax 01298 873801
Administrator (Membership)　　Glenn Jones
Promotion of speleological research and related activities
and the provision of support services. Publications:
Speleology, Cave and Karst Science; for full details see
website.

British Caving Association
The Old Methodist Chapel, Buxton, Derbyshire SK17 8RG;
　　URL www.british-caving.org.uk; e-mail
　　secretary@british-caving.org.uk

Cricket

Cricket Scotland
National Cricket Academy, MES Sports Centre, Ravelston,
　　Edinburgh EH4 3NT; URL www.cricketscotland.com;
　　e-mail admin@cricketscotland.com; Tel 0131 313 7420;
　　Fax 0131 313 7430

England and Wales Cricket Board
Lord's Cricket Ground, London NW8 8QZ;
　　URL www.ecb.co.uk; e-mail peter.ackerley@ecb.co.uk;
　　Tel 020 7432 1200; Fax 020 7286 5583
Head (Development)　　Pete Ackerley

English Schools' Cricket Association
Patron　　G.H.G. Doggart OBE; 19 Westgate, Chichester,
　　West Sussex
President　　J.R.T. Barclay; Spindlewood, High St, Amberley,
　　Nr Arundel, West Sussex; Tel 01798 831561
General Secretary　　K.S. Lake; 38 Mill Hse, Woods La,
　　Kingston upon Hull, East Riding of Yorkshire
　　HU16 4HQ; Tel 01482 844446
Assistant Secretary　　G.A. Hemingway; 1 Ash Gr, Rainford,
　　St Helens, Merseyside WA11 8DU; e-mail
　　tony.hemingway@blueyounder.co.uk; Tel 01744 88204;
　　Fax 01744 632349
Treasurer　　B.L. Johns; 52 Hatherley Rd, Reading RG1 5QE
Assistant Treasurer　　H. Cherry; 19 Raddington Dr, Solihull,
　　West Midlands B92 7DU; Tel 0121 707 4285

Marylebone Cricket Club (MCC)
Lord's Cricket Ground, London NW8 8QN;
　　URL www.lords.org; e-mail tours@mcc.org.uk;
　　Tel 020 7616 8595; Fax 020 7616 8504
Contact　　Peter Stray
Guided tours of Lord's Cricket Ground and MCC Museum
available to schools throughout the year, including some
match days. Indoor school available for net practice.

Northern Cricket Union of Ireland
House of Sport, Upper Malone Rd, Belfast BT9 5LA;
　　URL www.ncucricket.org; e-mail
　　cricket.ncu@nireland.com; Tel 028 9038 1222

Welsh Schools' Cricket Association
President　　A.R. Lewis MA
Chair　　P. Hourahane; 4 Wool Row, Brecon Rd, Builth Wells,
　　Powys LD2 3ED
General Secretary　　J. Prickett; 'Laurieknowe', Pencoed Rd,
　　Llanelli, Carmarthenshire SA16 0PW; Tel 01554 832539
Treasurer　　B.R. Williams; 105 High Cross Rd, Rogerstone,
　　Newport NP1 9AN; Tel 01633 664159

Croquet

The Croquet Association
Cheltenham Croquet Club, Old Bath Rd, Cheltenham,
　　Gloucestershire GL53 7DF; URL www.croquet.org.uk;
　　e-mail caoffice@croquet.org.uk; Tel 01242 242318
Secretary　　Klim Seabright

Curling

Royal Caledonian Curling Club
Cairnie Hse, Ingliston Showground, Newbridge,
　　Midlothian EH28 8NB;
　　URL www.royalcaledoniancurlingclub.org; e-mail
　　office@royalcaledoniancurlingclub.org;
　　Tel 0131 333 3003; Fax 0131 333 3323

Cycling

British Cycling
National Cycling Centre, Stuart St, Manchester M11 4DQ;
　　URL www.britishcycling.org.uk; e-mail
　　coaching@britishcycling.org.uk; Tel 0161 274 2060;
　　Tel 0870 871 2000

11

CTC – The National Cyclists' Organisation

Parklands, Guildford, Surrey GU2 9JX;
   URL www.ctc.org.uk; e-mail cycling@ctc.org.uk;
   Tel 0870 873 3060; Fax 0870 873 0064
CTC, the national cyclists' organisation, is the UK's largest
and oldest cycling body providing information on all
aspects of cycling, travel and route expertise, free third party
cover and legal aid to members and representing all 22
million UK cyclists in the corridors of power. CTC
campaigns for better cycle training, provision for cyclists
both on and off road and for improved bike carriage on
public transport.

Cycling Time Trials

77 Arlington Dr, Pennington, Leigh, Greater Manchester
   WN7 3QP; URL www.ctt.org.uk; e-mail
   phil.heaton@cyclingtimetrials.org.uk; Tel 01942 603976;
   Fax 01942 262326
National Secretary   P.A. Heaton

English Schools' Cycling Association

Patron   R.F. Butlin
President   R. Thorn
Chair   G. Banham
General Secretary   P.A.W. Dixon; 6 Malmers Well Rd, High
   Wycombe, Buckinghamshire HP13 6LX;
   Tel 01494 446857
Membership Secretary; Treasurer   D. Shrubbs; 18 St Blaise
   Rd, Four Oaks, Sutton Coldfield, West Midlands;
   Tel 0121 308 0455

Northern Ireland Cycling Federation

Contact   M.K. Wright; 8 Wyncairn Rd, Larne, County
   Antrim BT40 2DX

Scottish Cycling

The Velodrome, Meadowbank Stadium, London Rd,
   Edinburgh EH7 6AD; URL www.scottishcycling.com;
   e-mail info@scottishcycling.com; Tel 0131 652 0187;
   Fax 0131 661 0474
Director (Operations)   Jackie Davidson
Governing body for cycle sport. Promotes the sport of
cycling for all ages, encourages the leisure aspect of cycling
and runs mountain bike leader courses.

Dancing, Movement and Keep Fit

The Clarke School of Dancing

177 Upper Donegall St, Belfast BT1 2FJ; e-mail
   dancerone@onetel.net.uk; Tel 028 9024 1949;
   Tel 028 9038 1076

The College of Chinese Physical Culture

26 Roundhay Rd, Leeds, West Yorkshire LS7 1AB;
   URL www.ccpc.ac.uk; e-mail office@ccpc.ac.uk;
   Tel 0113 293 0630; Fax 0113 293 0631
CPC is fun to learn and perform and leads to nationally
recognised qualifications in Performing, Coaching and Basic
Skills. Teachers are qualified to relevant NVQ levels through
the governing body and deliver community based classes
for adults and the unemployed, classes in schools for young
people at risk of exclusion and work-based learning for
people with no up-to-date qualifications.

The Dalcroze Society UK (Incorporated)

7 Canada Rise, Market Lavington, Devizes, Wiltshire
   SN10 4AD; URL www.dalcroze.org.uk; e-mail
   admin@dalcroze.org.uk; Tel 01380 813198
Administrator   Greta Price
Develops the basic principles of eurythmics, understanding
music through movement, in the light of modern
educational needs through training courses and recreational
classes. Summer course annually.

Dance Council for Wales/Cyngor Dawns Cymru

Thurgarton Hse, Longdown Bank, St Dogmaels, Ceredigion
   SA43 3DU; Tel 01239 612138

The English Folk Dance and Song Society

Cecil Sharp Hse, 2 Regent's Park Rd, London NW1 7AY;
   URL www.efdss.org; e-mail info@efdss.org;
   Tel 020 7485 2206
Manager (National Education)   Diana Campbell Jewitt

The Fitness League

Registered Charity Number 226127
52 London St, Chertsey, Surrey KT16 8AJ; e-mail
   tfl@thefitnessleague.com; Tel 01932 564567;
   Fax 01932 567566
Exercise system for women and children, with emphasis on
correct body alignment, mobility, strength, stretch and tone.
More than 300 classes nationwide. Supported by Sport
England.

Imperial Society of Teachers of Dancing

Imperial Hse, 22–26 Paul St, London EC2A 4QE;
   URL www.istd.org; e-mail marketing@istd.org;
   Tel 020 7377 1577; Fax 020 7247 8979
Chief Executive   J.R. Singleton

International Association of MMM (Margaret Morris Movement)

Brook Cottage, Buildwas, Shropshire TF8 7DA;
   URL www.margaretmorrismovement.com; e-mail
   jacqueline.harper@margaretmorrismovement.com;
   Tel 07043 345666
Administrator   Jacqueline D. Harper
MMM is a unique form of recreative movement and dance.
Classes are held for all ages. Teacher training programmes
available plus INSET courses for Key Stages 1 and 2 of the
national curriculum.

International Dance Teachers' Association

International Hse, 76 Bennett Rd, Brighton, East Sussex
   BN2 5JL; URL www.info@idta.co.uk; e-mail
   info@idta.co.uk; Tel 01273 685652; Fax 01273 674388

Keep Fit Exercise Association, Northern Ireland

8 Barnett's Cres, Belfast BT5 7BQ; Tel 028 9048 9141
Contact   Rosaleen Henry

National Association of Teachers of Dancing

44–47 The Broadway, Thatcham, Berkshire RG19 3HP;
   URL www.natd.org.uk; e-mail info@natd.org.uk;
   Tel 01635 868888; Fax 01635 872301

Royal Scottish Country Dance Society

12 Coates Cres, Edinburgh EH3 7AF; URL www.rscds.org;
   e-mail info@rscds.org; Tel 0131 225 3854;
   Fax 0131 225 7783

Scottish Official Board of Highland Dancing

32 Grange Loan, Edinburgh EH9 2NR;
   URL www.sobhd.net; e-mail admin@sobhd.net;
   Tel 0131 668 3965; Fax 0131 662 0404

Welsh Folk Dance Society/Cymdeithas Ddawns Werin Cymru

Ffynnonlwyd, Trelech, Carmarthen, Carmarthenshire
   SA33 6QZ; URL www.welshfolkdance.org.uk; e-mail
   dafydd.evans@ic24.net; Tel 01994 484496
Contact   Dafydd M. Evans

Diving

British Sub-Aqua Club

Telford's Quay, South Pier Rd, Ellesmere Port, Cheshire
   CH65 4FL; URL www.bsac.com; Tel 0151 350 6200;
   Fax 0151 350 6253
c/o Hempel Paints (Bahrain), WLL, Manama, Bahrain;
   e-mail nigelp@batelco.co.bh
c/o Galadari Automobiles, PO Box 4069, Abu Dhabi, United
   Arab Emirates
Regional Coach for Eastern (Bedfordshire/Cambridgeshire/Essex/
   Hertfordshire/Norfolk/Suffolk)   Mark Cooper; 4 Burnett
   Wlk, Wittering, Peterborough, Cambridgeshire PE8 6ED;
   e-mail eastern.coach@bsac.com; Tel 01780 783799

Regional Coach for East Midlands (Derbyshire/Leicestershire/Lincolnshire/Northamptonshire/Nottinghamshire)
Arthur Johnson; Willow Farm, Fen La, Marsham-le-Fen, Boston PE22 7SD; e-mail east.midlands.coach@bsac.com; Tel 01507 568546

Regional Coach for Greater London Roy Sherwin; 7 Bear Rd, Hanworth, Middlesex TW13 6RJ; e-mail london.coach@bsac.com; Tel 020 8230 6531

Regional Coach for the North East (Cleveland/Durham/Northumberland/Tyne and Wear) Sandra Cooper; 7 Dene Cres, Plawsworth Rd, Sacriston, Durham, County Durham DH7 6PJ; e-mail northeast.coach@bsac.com; Tel 0191 371 0454

Regional Coach for the North West (Cheshire/Cumbria/Greater Manchester/Isle of Man/Lancashire/Merseyside) James Donbavand; 1 Cornfield, Stalybridge, Cheshire SK15 2UA; e-mail northwest.coach@bsac.com; Tel 01457 764607

Regional Coach for the South (Berkshire/Buckinghamshire/Channel Islands/Hampshire/Isle of Wight/Oxfordshire/Wiltshire) Richard Trevithick; Elderslie, Oaksey Rd, Upper Minety, Malmesbury SN16 9PY; e-mail southern.coach@bsac.com; Tel 07709 542886

Regional Coach for South East (East and West Sussex/Kent/Surrey) Dave Tressider; 4 Avenue Rd, New Malden, Surrey KT3 3QF; e-mail southeast.coach@bsac.com; Tel 07841 431689

Regional Coach for the South West (Bristol/Cornwall/Devon/Dorset/Somerset) Sophie Rennie; 49 Maritime Ct, Haven Rd, Exeter, Devon EX2 8GP; e-mail southwest.coach@bsac.com; Tel 01392 215333

Regional Coach for West Midlands (Gloucestershire/Herefordshire/Shropshire/Staffordshire/Warwickshire/West Midlands/Worcestershire) Eugene Farrell; 62 Stafford Rd, Bloxwich, Walsall WS3 3NS; e-mail west.midlands.coach@bsac.com; Tel 01922 405306

Regional Coach for Yorkshire (East, North, South and West Yorkshire/North East Lincolnshire) Hilary Child; 3 Calder Way, Daleswater Mews, Waterside Silsden, West Yorkshire BD20 0QU; e-mail yorkshire.coach@bsac.com; Tel 01535 655380

Regional Coach for North Scotland (Grampian/Highlands/Islands/Tayside) Dave Sydenham; 44 Braehead Cres, Stonehaven AB39 2PS; e-mail scotland.north.coach@bsac.com; Tel 01569 760553

Regional Coach for South Scotland (Borders/Central/Dumfries and Galloway/Fife/Lothian/Strathclyde) Sandra Castro; 16c Melbourne Rd, North Berwick, East Lothian EH39 4JX; e-mail scotland.south.coach@bsac.com; Tel 01620 890346

Regional Coach for Wales Hywel Dyer; 5 Tylchawen Cres, Mid Glamorgan CF39 8AL; e-mail wales.coach@bsac.com

Regional Coach for Northern Ireland Sam Moffett; 5 Elm Corner, Seymour Hill, Dunmurry BT17 9PZ; e-mail northern.ireland.coach@bsac.com; Tel 028 9094 7435

National Snorkellers' Club

13 Langham Gdns, Wembley, Greater London HA0 3RG; Tel 020 8959 6013

Director L.F. Blandford

More than 450 branches throughout the UK, training children aged 9–16 years in safe and efficient snorkel diving

Sub-Aqua Association

26 Breckfield Rd North, Liverpool, Merseyside; Tel 0151 287 1001; Fax 0151 287 1026

Represents independent sub-aqua diving clubs and promotes safe diving within a club environment

Scottish Sub-Aqua Club

The Cockburn Centre, 40 Bogmoor Pl, Glasgow G51 4TQ; URL www.scotsac.com; e-mail ab@hqssac.demon.co.uk; Tel 0141 425 1021; Fax 0141 425 1021

Fencing

British Fencing Association

1 Barons Gate, 33–35 Rothschild Rd, London W4 5HT; URL www.britishfencing.com

Fishing

The Scottish Federation of Sea Anglers

Unit 6, Evans Business Centre, Mitchelston Dr, Mitchelston Industrial Est, Kirkcaldy, Fife KY1 3NB; Tel 01592 657520

Fives

Eton Fives Association (EFA)

3 Bourchier Cl, Sevenoaks, Kent TN13 1PD; URL www.etonfives.co.uk; e-mail efa@etonfives.co.uk; Tel 01732 458775

Hon Secretary M.R. Fenn

The promotion and extension of the game of Eton Fives, laws and rules, membership, competitions, sponsorship and facilities

Flying

Aircraft Owners' and Pilots' Association (AOPA)

50a Cambridge St, London SW1V 4QQ; URL www.aopa.co.uk; e-mail info@aopa.co.uk; Tel 020 7834 5632; Fax 020 7834 8623

Chair George Done

Promotes and protects the safety, aims and interests of the general aviation sector. Headquarters of the European General Aviation Safety Foundation (EGASF).

British Microlight Aircraft Association (BMAA)

Bullring, Deddington, Banbury, Oxfordshire OX15 0TT; URL www.bmaa.org; e-mail general@bmaa.org; Tel 01869 338888

Chief Executive Chris Finnigan

The governing body for microlight aviation in the UK

Football

11

Amateur Football Alliance

55 Islington Park St, London N1 1QB; URL www.amateur-fa.com; e-mail info@amateur-fa.com; Tel 020 7359 3493; Fax 020 7359 5027

Chief Executive M.L. Brown

Administration and development of amateur football for member clubs and referees of the Amateur Football Alliance

English Schools' Football Association

4 Parker Ct, Staffordshire Technology Pk, Stafford, Staffordshire ST18 0WP; URL www.esfc.co.uk; e-mail john.read@schoolsfa.com; Tel 01785 785970; Fax 01785 256246

Chief Executive J.A. Read

The Football Association

25 Soho Sq, London W1D 4FA; URL www.thefa.com; e-mail info@thefa.com; Tel 020 7745 4545

The Football Association is the governing body of the sport in England and protects and promotes the game at all levels

Football Association of Wales

11 and 12 Neptone Ct, Vanguard Way, Cardiff CF24 5PJ; URL www.faw.org.uk; e-mail info@faw.co.uk; Tel 02920 435830

Irish Football Association

20 Windsor Ave, Belfast BT9 6EG; URL www.irishfa.com; e-mail enquiries@irishfa.com; Tel 028 9066 9458; Fax 028 9066 7620

The Schools' Association Football International Board (SAFIB)

Chair W. Leslie Donaldson MBE

Hon Secretary; Treasurer Allen McKinstry; 33 Huntingdale Lodge, Dough Rd, Ballyclare; e-mail allen.mckinstry@btinternet.com; Tel 028 9332 4090; Fax 028 9332 4090

Victory Shield competition for under 16s in the UK, Centenary Shield competition for under 18s in the UK; control of national schoolboy football. Organises international matches at schoolboy level within the UK and in Europe. 21 member associations.
The board also covers Scotland and Northern Ireland.

Scottish Amateur Football Association

'Beechwood', Gateside Rd, Barrhead, Glasgow G78 1EP

Contact I. McTweed

Scottish Football Association Ltd

Hampden Pk, Glasgow G42 9AY; URL www.scottishfa.co.uk; e-mail info@scottishfa.co.uk; Tel 0141 616 6000; Fax 0141 616 6001

Chief Executive; Company Secretary G. Smith

Scottish Youth Football Association

Hampden Pk, Glasgow G42 9AY; Tel 0141 620 4590

Welsh Schools' Football Association

Chair P. Hughes-Griffiths

Hon Secretary D. Painter; 49 Lanpark Rd, Pontypridd, Rhondda Cynon Taf; Tel 01443 404442

Hon Assistant Secretary P. Fowler; 77 Somerset St, Abertillery, Newport BP3 1DH; Tel 01495 213047

Hon Treasurer C.M. Evans; Watcombe, 170 Cardiff Rd, Newport NP20 3AE

Hon Under 15 Secretary E. Blackmore; 48 Trevallen Ave, Neath, Neath and Port Talbot; Tel 01639 639378

Hon Under 18 Secretary D.E. Flye; 66 Aberfan Rd, Aberfan, Merthyr Tydfil CF48 4QJ; Tel 01443 690401

Gliding

British Gliding Association

Kimberley Hse, Vaughan Way, Leicester LE1 4SE; URL www.gliding.co.uk; e-mail office@gliding.co.uk; Tel 0116 253 1051

British Hang Gliding and Paragliding Association (BHPA)

The Old Schoolroom, Loughborough Rd, Leicester LE4 5PJ; URL www.bhpa.co.uk; e-mail office@bhpa.co.uk; Tel 0116 261 1322; Fax 0116 261 1323

Public Relations Officer David Wootton

Administrator Jennie Burdett

Promotion, development and co-ordination of paragliding and hang gliding in the UK. Responsible to the CAA for the sport.

Scottish Gliding Centre

Portmoak Airfield, Scotlandwell, Perth and Kinross KY13 9JJ; URL www.scottishglidingcentre.co.uk; e-mail office@scottishglidingcentre.co.uk; Tel 01592 840543

Course Secretary Irene Donald

Gliding instruction holidays, trial flights of 20 minutes, new members welcome

Golf

Council of National Golf Unions

19 Birch Grn, Formby, Liverpool, Merseyside L37 1NG; Tel 01704 831800; Fax 01704 831800

Hon Secretary A. Thirlwell

Co-ordinates golf administration between the four National Golf Unions (England, Wales, Scotland and Ireland)

English Golf Union

The National Golf Centre, Woodhall Spa, Lincolnshire LN10 6PU; URL www.englishgolfunion.org; e-mail info@englishgolfunion.org; Tel 01526 354500; Fax 01526 354020

English Ladies' Golf Association

Edgbaston Golf Club, Church Rd, Birmingham, West Midlands B15 3TB; URL www.englishladiesgolf.org; e-mail office@englishladiesgolf.org; Tel 0121 456 2088; Fax 0121 454 5542

Chief Executive; Secretary Pauline A. Perla

Administers ladies' amateur golf in England and organises the English ladies' and girls' championships

Golf Foundation

The Spinning Wheel, High St, Hoddesdon, Hertfordshire EN11 8BP; URL www.golf-foundation.org; e-mail info@golf-foundation.org; Tel 01992 449830; Fax 01992 449840

Ladies' European Tour

The Tytherington Club, The Old Hall, Macclesfield, Cheshire SK10 2LQ; URL www.ladieseuropeantour.com; e-mail mail@ladieseuropeantour.com; Tel 01625 611444; Fax 01625 610406

Chief Operating Officer Ian Randell

Promotes and administers women's professional golf tournaments throughout Europe

Ladies' Golf Union

The Scores, St Andrews, Fife KY16 9AT; URL www.lgu.org; e-mail info@lgu.org; Tel 01334 475811

National Golf Clubs' Advisory Association

Suite 2, Angel Hse, Bakewell, Derbyshire DE45 1HB; Tel 01629 813844

Secretary Jean Brock

Safeguards the interests of member clubs and provides them with legal advice under opinion of counsel where necessary

The Professional Golfers' Association

Centenary Hse, The Belfry, Sutton Coldfield, West Midlands B76 9PW; Tel 01675 470333

Chief Executive Sandy Jones

Protects and advances the interests of golf professionals, identifies and fulfils the needs and interests of the membership, acting as custodians for the traditions of the game, while promoting golf for the benefit of all.
The PGA Training Academy provides education and training for PGA professionals and potential PGA professionals. This is a three-year distance learning programme that encompasses all aspects of the role of a golf club professional. Entry requirements are four GCSEs (Grade C or above) or equivalent and a golf handicap of four for men and six for women.

PGA National Training Academy Ping Hse, The Belfry, Sutton Coldfield, West Midlands B76 9PW; Tel 01675 470333

Director (Training and Education) Gerry Paton

Provides a three-year training programme for golf professionals leading to membership of the association. Training and education programmes are also provided for qualified professionals.

Royal and Ancient Golf Club of St Andrews

St Andrews, Fife KY16 9JD; URL www.randagc.org; www.opengolf.com; e-mail thesecretary@randagc.org; Tel 01334 460000; Fax 01334 460001

Scottish Golf Union Ltd (SGU)

Drumoig, St Andrews, Fife KY16 0DW; URL www.scottishgolfunion.org; e-mail sgu@scottishgolfunion.org; Tel 01382 549500; Fax 01382 549510

Chief Executive Hamish Grey

Governing body of men's amateur golf in Scotland

Scottish Ladies' Golfing Association

The Den, 2 Dundee Rd, Perth, Perth and Kinross PH2 7DW;
URL www.slga.co.uk; e-mail secretary@slga.co.uk;
Tel 01738 442357; Fax 01738 442380

Co-ordinates all aspects of women's and girls' amateur golf
in Scotland, including organising the national
championships and other competitions

Welsh Golfing Union

Catsash, Newport NP18 1JQ; URL www.welshgolf.org;
e-mail wgu@welshgolf.org; Tel 01633 430830;
Fax 01633 430843

Gymnastics

British Gymnastics

Ford Hall, Lilleshall National Sports Centre, Newport,
Shropshire TF10 9NB; URL www.british-gymnastics.org;
e-mail info@british-gymnastics.org; Tel 0845 129 7129;
Fax 0845 124 9089

Chief Executive   Brian Stocks

President   Paul Carber

Director (Performance and Technical)   M. Greenwood

Head (Media and Publicity)   Vera Atkinson

Head (Publications)   Mark Young

British Gymnastics and Trampolining Efficiency Awards

British Schools' Gymnastic Association

Chair   V.J. Jackman; Goldrood, South Rd, Burnham-on-
Sea, Somerset TA8 2SE; e-mail
joan@goldrood.demon.co.uk; Tel 01278 751702;
Fax 01278 751702

Vice-Chair   R. Jeavons; 1 Rainbow Mead, Hatfield Peverel,
Chelmsford, Essex CM3 2EB; Tel 01245 381741

General Secretary   Clive Hamilton; Orchard Hse, 15 North
Common Rd, Uxbridge, Greater London UB8 1PD; e-mail
cvhamilton@lineone.net; Tel 01895 233377;
Fax 01895 814031

Competition Secretary; Judges Convener   K. McLoughlin; 16
Sheerstock, Haddenham, Buckinghamshire HP17 8EU;
e-mail mcloughlinkaren@aol.com; Tel 01844 290540

Treasurer; Board of Control Representative   H. Todd; 184
Dalston Rd, Carlisle, Cumbria CA2 6DY; e-mail
howard.todd@cumbriacc.gov.uk; Tel 01228 539745

Board of Control Representative   R. Currier; 137 Hazelhurst
Rd, Birmingham, West Midlands B14 6AG;
Tel 0121 444 1278

Hockey

British Octopush Association (BOA)

25 Brunswick St, Waltham Forest, London E17 9NB;
URL www.gbuwh.co.uk; e-mail
contactus@gbuwh.co.uk; Tel 020 8520 8823

Past President   Cliff Underwood

The BOA is the controlling and ruling body for all
underwater hockey (octopush) in the UK and is part of the
world body for the sport (CMAS)

England Hockey

The Stadium, Silbury Bvd, Milton Keynes, Buckinghamshire
MK9 1HA; URL www.englandhockey.co.uk; e-mail
info@englandhockey.org; Tel 01908 544644;
Fax 01908 241106

English Mixed Hockey Association

4 The Sycamore, Horbury, Wakefield, West Yorkshire
WF4 5QG; Tel 01924 274620

Hon Secretary   J. White

Promotes the game of mixed hockey throughout England
and the UK at all levels

English Schoolboys' Hockey Association

6 St John's, Worcester, Worcestershire WR2 5AH;
Tel 01905 426009

Chair   D.A. Billson; 28 Thorburn Rd, Weston Favell,
Northampton, Northamptonshire NN3 3DA;
Tel 01604 411685

Hon Secretary   J.E. Law; 16 Clover Dr, Hardwicke,
Gloucester, Gloucestershire GL2 6TG; Tel 01452 721247

Hon Match Secretary   K. Billson; 28 Thorburn Rd, Weston
Favell, Northampton, Northamptonshire NN3 3DA;
Tel 01604 411685

Hon Treasurer   A.J. Barton; The Pines, 30 Roundwood Ave,
Brentwood, Essex CM13 2LZ; Tel 01277 211999

Assistant Secretary (Mini Hockey)   R.S. Price; 70 Pownall St,
Macclesfield, Cheshire SK10 1DG; Tel 01625 614105

Great Britain Olympic Hockey Board (GBOHB)

The Stadium, Silbury Bvd, Milton Keynes, Buckinghamshire
MK9 1HA; Tel 01908 544626; Fax 01908 544640

Administrator   Debbie Smith

Administers the needs of the board and its sub-committees,
prepares and manages men's and women's squads for each
Olympic Games. Liaises with the British Olympic
Association and other agencies.

National Roller Hockey Association (UK) Ltd

82 Greenfield Rd, Farnham, Surrey GU9 8TQ;
URL www.playrollerhockey.net; e-mail
gail-whattingham@tinyonline.co.uk; Tel 01252 723635;
Fax 01252 723635

*President (South East Counties Roller Hockey Association); Hon
Vice President (National Roller Hockey Association)*
Gail Whattingham

Schools and Youth Committee of Hockey Association

16 Clover Dr, Hardwicke, Gloucestershire GL2 6TG;
Tel 01452 721247

Secretary   J.E. Law

Scottish Hockey Union (SHU)

589 Lanark Rd, Edinburgh EH14 5DA;
URL www.scottish-hockey.org.uk; e-mail
youth@scottish-hockey.org.uk; Tel 0131 453 9070;
Fax 0131 453 9079

Officer (Youth Development)   Ally Blair

Controls, promotes, develops and encourages the playing of
hockey in Scotland

Welsh Hockey Union

Welsh Hockey Union, Severn Hse, Station Terr, Ely, Cardiff
CF5 4AA; URL www.welsh-hockey.co.uk; e-mail
info@welsh-hockey.co.uk; Tel 02920 573940;
Fax 02920 573941

Horse Driving

British Driving Society (BDS)

27 Dugard Pl, Barford, Warwickshire CV35 8DX;
URL www.britishdrivingsociety.co.uk; e-mail
email@britishdrivingsociety.co.uk; Tel 01926 624420;
Fax 01926 624633

Executive Secretary   J.M. Dillon

Encourages and assists those interested in the driving of
horses and ponies. Examining body for carriage driving,
including teaching and carriage grooms.

Guernsey Horse Driving Society

19 Clos de Carteret, Guernsey GY5 7UU, Channel Islands;
Tel 01481 57868

Promotes horse driving and encourages preservation of
horse drawn vehicles, harnesses and their use

Lacrosse

English Lacrosse Union (ELU)

Ryecroft Mills, Smith St, Ashton-under-Lyne, Tameside
OL7 0DB; Tel 0161 339 7508

Chief Executive   David Shuttleworth

Promotion and development of lacrosse in England

11

Welsh Lacrosse Association

Welsh Lacrosse Association, 6 Chantry Rise, Penarth , Vale of Glamorgan CF64 5RS; URL www.welshlacrosse.com; e-mail chrisshumack@yahoo.com; Tel 02920 708966; Fax 02920 708588

Lifesaving

Lifesavers – The Royal Life Saving Society UK

River Hse, High St, Broom, Warwickshire B50 4HN; URL www.lifesavers.org.uk; e-mail lifesavers@rlss.org.uk; Tel 01789 773994; Fax 01789 773995
Chief Executive   Di Standley

Martial Arts

British Aikido Association (BAA)

2 Heather Rise, Burley-in-Wharfedale, Ilkley, West Yorkshire LS29 7RA; URL www.aikido-baa.org.uk; e-mail jonesbinw@btinternet.com; Tel 01943 863857
Chair; Senior Coach   R. Jones
The promotion and development of the sport aikido within Great Britain

British Schools Judo Association (BSJA)

21 Finborough Rd, Tooting, London SW17 9HY; Tel 020 8640 6083
Hon General Secretary   Simon R.W. Hicks
Promotion of schools' and colleges' judo, national and international competitions, star award scheme and publication of judo-related curricula and policies

Judo Scotland

Caledonia Hse, 40 Bogmoor Pl, South Gyle, Edinburgh EH12 9DQ; Tel 0131 317 7270; Fax 0131 317 7050
Office Manager   Kirsteen Hogg

Scottish Karate Board

48 Ryde Rd, Wishaw, North Lanarkshire ML2 7DX; Tel 01698 357739; Fax 01698 357739
Chair   T. Morris
Secretary   A. Murdoch

Motor Sport

Amateur Motor Cycle Association (AMCA)

28 Navigation Way, Hill Pk, Cannock, Staffordshire WS11 2XT; URL www.amca.uk.com; e-mail amca.office@btinternet.com; Tel 01543 466282; Fax 01543 466283
Chair   D.T. Green
An organisation with 150 clubs who run off-road motor cycle sporting events – motocross, scrambling trials, enduros – at amateur level

Auto-Cycle Union Ltd (ACU)

ACU Hse, Wood St, Rugby, Warwickshire CV21 2YX; URL www.acu.org.uk; e-mail admin@acu.org.uk; Tel 01788 566400; Fax 01788 573585
General Secretary   Gary Thompson MBE, BEM
Governing body of motorcycle sport, controlling and promoting all forms of the sport for all age groups

British Automobile Racing Club (BARC)

Thruxton Circuit, Andover, Hampshire SP11 8PN; URL www.barc.net; e-mail info@barc.net; Tel 01264 882200; Fax 01264 882233
Chief Executive   Dennis Carter
Organises motor race, sprint and hillclimb meetings and social events in the UK and training of motorsport marshals

British Cycle Speedway Council (BCSC)

Central Office, 57 Rectory La, Norwich, Norfolk NR14 7SW; Tel 0150 86 3880

General Secretary   Rod Witham
Unification of cycle speedway organisations, gaining national recognition, obtaining grant aid assistance, co-ordination of leagues and competitions

British Motorcyclists' Federation (BMF)

Jack Wiley Hse, 129 Seaforth Ave, New Malden, Surrey KT3 6JU; Tel 020 8942 7914
Office Administrator   Aisha Latif
Pursues, protects and promotes the interests of motorcyclists

Mountaineering

British Mountaineering Council

177–179 Burton Rd, Manchester M20 2BB; URL www.thebmc.co.uk; e-mail office@thebmc.co.uk; Tel 0870 010 4878; Fax 0161 445 4500
Chief Executive   Dave Turnbull
Representative body for climbers, hillwalkers and mountaineers in England and Wales, providing membership, insurance, information and advice on all aspects of the sport

Mountaineering Council of Scotland (MCofS)

The Old Granary, West Mill St, Perth, Perth and Kinross PH1 5QP; URL www.mountaineering-scotland.org.uk; e-mail info@mountaineering-scotland.org.uk; Tel 01738 638227; Fax 01738 442095
MCofS is the national representative organisation for hill walkers, climbers and mountaineers. It is recognised by sportscotland as the national governing body for the sport of climbing. Specialist staff offer advice on mountain safety; access rights and legislation; conservation of upland areas; skills development; climbing ethics and personal development at all levels of the sport/recreation. MCofS also offers benefits to both club and individual members.

Netball

England Netball

Netball Hse, 9 Paynes Pk, Hitchin, Hertfordshire SG5 1EH; URL www.englandnetball.co.uk; e-mail info@englandnetball.co.uk; Tel 01462 442344; Fax 01462 442343
National Development Director   Vanessa Brown
Head (Netball Development)   Sue Sanford
Manager (Events)   Esther Nicholls
Manager (Marketing and Media)   Mark Pritchard

Northern Ireland Netball Association

26 Cresslough Pk, Belfast BT11 9HH
Hon Secretary   A. Hamill

Welsh Netball Association

33–35 Cathedral Rd, Cardiff CF11 9HB; URL www.welshnetball.co.uk; e-mail welshnetball@welshnetball.com; Tel 02920 237048; Fax 02920 226430

Orienteering

British Orienteering

8a Stancliffe Hse, Whitworth Rd, Darley Dale, Matlock, Derbyshire DE4 2HJ; URL www.britishorienteering.org.uk; e-mail info@britishorienteering.org.uk; Tel 01629 734042; Fax 01629 733769
Chief Executive   Mike Hamilton
Director (Coaching)   Derek Allison

Scottish Orienteering Association

6 Newark Cres, Doonfoot, Ayr KA7 4HP; URL www.scottish-orienteering.org

Parachuting

British Parachute Association

5 Wharf Way, Glen Parva, Leicester LE2 9TF;
URL www.bpa.org.uk; e-mail skydive@bpa.org.uk;
Tel 0116 278 5271; Fax 0116 247 7662

Governing body for the sport in the UK. Examines all sport parachute instructors.

Scottish Sport Parachute Association

1b Rosebery Cres, Edinburgh EH12 5JP
Secretary Kevin McPhillips

Polo

The Hurlingham Polo Association

Manor Farm, Little Coxwell, Faringdon, Oxfordshire
SN7 7LW; URL www.hpa-polo.co.uk; e-mail
enquiries@hpa-polo.co.uk; Tel 01367 242828;
Fax 01367 242829

Chief Executive David Woodd

Every April publishes a yearbook at £10 (including postage) which gives detailed information on clubs, rules, fixtures, results etc.

Racing

National Greyhound Racing Club Ltd (NGRC)

Twyman Hse, 16 Bonny St, London NW1 9QD;
URL www.ngrc.org.uk; e-mail mail@ngrc.org.uk;
Tel 020 7267 9256

Chief Executive A. McLean

Regulatory and disciplinary body for greyhound racing in England, Scotland and Wales

The Racecourse Association Ltd

Winkfield Rd, Ascot, Berkshire SL5 7HX;
URL www.britishracecourses.org; e-mail
info@racecourseassociation.co.uk; Tel 01344 625912;
Fax 01344 627233

Chief Executive Stephen Atkin
Chair David Thorpe

Considers all questions affecting the welfare of racecourse owners and initiates the improvement in regulations affecting racecourses

Racketball

The English Racketball Association

50 Tredegar Rd, Wilmington, Dartford, Kent DA2 7AZ;
e-mail idw@kentsra.co.uk; Tel 01322 272200;
Fax 01322 289295

Secretary Ian Wright

Promotes the playing of racketball in England and enforces standard rules via SRA

Rambling

Ramblers' Association

2nd Fl, Camelford Hse, 87–90 Albert Embankment, London
SE1 7TW; URL www.ramblers.org.uk; e-mail
ramblers@ramblers.org.uk; Tel 020 7339 8500;
Fax 020 7339 8501

Scottish Rights of Way and Access Society

24 Annandale St, Edinburgh EH7 4AN;
URL www.scotways.com; e-mail info@scotways.com;
Tel 0131 558 1222; Fax 0131 558 1222

Secretary Judith Lewis

Riding

Association of British Riding Schools

Queen's Chambers, 38–40 Queen St, Penzance, Cornwall
TR18 4BH; e-mail office@abrs-info.org; Tel (exams
department) 01736 365777; Tel 01736 369440;
Fax 01736 351390

British Horse Society

Stoneleigh Deer Pk, Kenilworth, Warwickshire CV8 2XZ;
URL www.bhs.org.uk; e-mail enquiry@bhs.org.uk;
Tel 0870 120 2244; Fax 01926 707800

Scottish Equestrian Association

Sunnylea, Ormiston, Hawick, Roxburghshire TD9 9SJ;
URL www.w.s-e-a.org.uk; Tel 01450 373861;
Fax 01450 373861

Chair Janey Roncoroni

Rowing

Amateur Rowing Association

The Priory, 6 Lower Mall, London W6 9DJ;
URL www.ara-rowing.org; e-mail info@ara-rowing.org;
Tel 020 8237 6700

National Manager Rosemary E. Napp
Manager (Youth and Community) Simon Dickie

Rugby

British Amateur Rugby League Association (BARLA)

West Yorkshire Hse, 4 New North Par, Huddersfield, West
Yorkshire HD1 5JP; URL www.barla.org.uk; e-mail
info@barla.org.uk; Tel 01484 544131

Governs and promotes ARLF throughout Great Britain and represents the sport on the International Federation

Irish Rugby Football Union (Ulster Branch)

85 Ravenhill Pk, Belfast BT6 0DG;
URL www.ulsterrugby.com; e-mail
reception@ulsterrugby.com; Tel 028 90493111;
Fax 028 90491522

Rugby Football League

Red Hall, Red Hall La, Leeds, West Yorkshire LS17 8NB;
URL www.rfl.uk.com; e-mail rfl@rfl.uk.com;
Tel 0113 232 9111; Fax 0113 232 3666

Rugby Football Schools' Union

Rugby Football Union, Rugby Hse, Rugby Rd, Twickenham
TW1 1DZ; URL www.rfu.com; e-mail
marksaltmarsh@rfu.com

President E.J. Blackman; 4 Merchants Rd, Clifton, Bristol
BS8 4EP; e-mail ericblackman@therfu.com;
Tel 0117 973 3510; Fax 0117 973 1208
Vice-President R. Whittle
Hon Treasurer F.U. Batchelor
Executive Officer M. Saltmarsh

Rugby Football Union

Twickenham, Greater London TW1 1DZ; Tel 020 8892 8161;
Fax 020 8892 9816

Scottish Rugby Union plc

Murrayfield, Edinburgh EH12 5PJ; Tel 0131 346 5000;
Fax 0131 346 5001

Chief Executive W.S. Watson

Welsh Rugby Union

Golate Hse, 101 St Mary St, Cardiff CF10 1GE;
URL www.wru.co.uk; e-mail martynrees@wru.co.uk;
Tel 02920 781700; Fax 02920 781722

Welsh Schools' Rugby Union

Chair Adrian Davies; 6 Rhyddings Pk Rd, Brynmill,
Swansea SA2 0AQ; Tel 01792 466261; Fax 01792 466261
Hon Secretary (Junior Group) Mike Farley; 9 Augusta Rd,
Penarth, Vale of Glamorgan CF64 5RH; Tel 02920 701712

11

Sailing

British Federation of Sand and Land Yacht Clubs (BFSLYC)
23 Piper Dr, Long Whatton, Loughborough, Leicestershire
LE12 5DJ; e-mail mike.hampton4@virgin.net;
Tel 01509 842292
General Secretary M. Hampton
Governs and promotes the sport, assisting new participants
and clubs, providing training and other support

National School Sailing Association
c/o 49 West St, Hertford, Hertfordshire SG13 8EZ;
URL www.nssa.org.uk; e-mail
ak.blannin@ntlworld.com; Tel 01992 423665
Secretary Anna Blannin
The NSSA is an organisation that brings together schools,
clubs and individuals interested in helping the development
of young people via activity afloat

Royal Yachting Association
RYA Hse, Romsey Rd, Eastleigh, Hampshire SO50 9YA;
URL www.rya.org.uk; e-mail jon.challis@rya.org.uk;
Tel 02380 627400; Fax 02380 627417

Royal Yachting Association Scotland
Caledonia Hse, South Gyle, Edinburgh EH12 9DQ;
URL www.ryascotland.org.uk; e-mail
admin@ryascotland.org.uk; Tel 0131 317 7388;
Fax 0131 317 8566

School Sailing Association of Wales
President A.K. Corey
Chair A.F. Bond; 22 Bryn Estyn Rd, Wrexham,
Denbighshire LL13 9NB; Tel 01978 352747
Hon Secretary H. Jones; Glan Llyn, Llanuwchllyn, Bala,
Gwynedd
There is a committee of five elected members and
representatives from each County Sailing Association in
Wales

Tall Ships Youth Trust
2a The Hard, Portsmouth PO1 3PT; Tel 02392 832055;
Fax 02392 815769
Chief Executive Chris Law

Services

Army Sport Control Board
Clayton Barracks, Aldershot, Hampshire GU11 2BG;
URL www.army.mod.uk/sportandadventure; e-mail
secretary@ascb.uk.com

HMS Temeraire, Directorate of Naval Physical Training and Sport and Royal Navy School of Physical Training
Burnaby Rd, Portsmouth PO1 4QS

Royal Air Force
GCPEd, HQPTC, Innsworth, Gloucester, Gloucestershire
GL3 1EZ; e-mail gcped.tgda@ptc.raf.mod.uk;
Tel 01452 712612 ext 5446

Royal Air Force School of Physical Training
RAF Cosford, Wolverhampton, Staffordshire WV7 3EX;
Tel 01902 372393 ext 7271

Royal Air Force Sports Board
RAF Innsworth, Gloucester, Gloucestershire GL3 1EZ;
e-mail dsbla.cos@ptc.raf.mod.uk;
Tel 01452 712612 ext 5443

Royal Navy and Royal Marines Sports Control Board
Ministry of Defence, HMS Temeraire, Portsmouth PO1 2HB;
Tel 02392 723994; Fax 02392 724923

Royal Navy – Scotland and Northern Ireland Area
Base Instructor Officer, HMS Cochrane, Rosyth KY11 2XT;
Tel 01383 412121 ext 62998

Shinty

Camanachd Association
Queen Anne Hse, 111 High St, Fort William PH33 6DG;
URL www.shinty.com; e-mail enquiries@shinty.com;
Tel 01397 703903; Fax 01397 703903

Shooting

The British Association for Shooting and Conservation (BASC)
Marford Mill, Rossett, Wrexham LL12 0HL;
URL www.basc.org.uk; Tel 01244 573018
Director (Shooting Standards) Richard Thorne
The national representative body for sporting shooting
seeks to promote the highest standards of safety,
sportsmanship and courtesy among the shooting public and
fosters a practical interest in the countryside, wildlife
management and conservation

Clay Pigeon Shooting Association
Earlstrees Ct, Earlstrees Rd, Corby, Northamptonshire
NN17 4AX; Tel 01536 443566; Fax 01536 443438

Great Britain Target Shooting Federation
1 The Cedars, Great Wakering, Southend-on-Sea, Essex
SS3 0AQ; e-mail gbtsf@aol.com; Tel 01702 219395;
Fax 01702 219250
Hon Secretary K. Murray
Co-ordination of action and policy on matters affecting the
interests of target shooting associations

National Rifle Association
Bisley Camp, Brookwood, Woking, Surrey GU24 0PB;
URL www.nra.org.uk; e-mail info@nra.org.uk;
Tel 01483 797777; Fax 01483 797285
Secretary General R.C. Fishwick

National Small-Bore Rifle Association
Bisley Camp, Woking, Surrey GU24 0NP;
URL www.nsra.co.uk; e-mail info@nsra.co.uk;
Tel 01483 485500

Skating

National Ice Skating Association of UK Ltd
1st Fl, 114–116 Curtain Rd, London EC2A 3AH;
URL www.iceskating.org.uk; e-mail
nisa@iceskating.org.uk; Tel 020 7613 1188;
Fax 020 7739 2445

The Scottish Ice Skating Association
c/o The Ice Sports Centre, Riversdale Cres, Edinburgh
EH12 5XN; e-mail office@sisa.org.uk; Tel 0131 337 3976;
Fax 0131 337 9239
Chair Barry Messetter
Administrator Vacancy

Scottish Speed Skating Union
Hartley Hse, Racecourse View, Ayr, South Ayrshire
KA7 2TX; Tel 01292 261183

Skiing and Snowboarding

British Association of Snowsport Instructors
Glenmore, Aviemore, Highland PH22 1QU;
URL www.basi.org.uk; e-mail basi@basi.org.uk;
Tel 01479 861717; Fax 01479 861718

Scottish National Ski Council
Caledonia Hse, South Gyle, Edinburgh EH12 9DQ;
URL www.snsc.demon.co.uk; e-mail
admin@snsc.demon.uk; Tel 0131 317 7280;
Fax 0131 339 8602

Ski Club of Great Britain

The White Hse, 57–63 Church Rd, Wimbledon, London SW19 5SB; URL www.skiclub.co.uk; e-mail skiers@skiclub.co.uk; Tel 0845 458 0780; Fax 0845 458 0781

Manager (Marketing)   Fiona Sweetman
PR   Vanessa Haines

The club responds to the requirements of today's winter sports enthusiasts, encouraging and providing enjoyable and safe skiing and snowboarding. It offers members specialist ski and snowboarding holidays and courses including organised holidays for the under 20s, representatives in resorts, social events, school races at UK dry ski slopes, ski and snowboarding insurance, equipment advice, resort information, snow conditions, Ski and Board magazine, clubhouse with room hire, discounts offering savings. Individual, with under 24s at a special rate of only £12, family or commercial memberships available including school affiliations.

Snowsport England

Area Library Bldg, Queensway Mall, Halesowen, West Midlands B63 4AJ; URL www.snowsportengland.org.uk; e-mail info@snowsportengland.org.uk; Tel 0121 501 2314; Fax 0121 585 6448

Chief Executive   Trish Ball
Company Secretary   Andrew Jolly

Snowsport GB

Hillend, Biggar Rd, Midlothian EH10 7EF; URL www.snowsportgb.com; e-mail info@snowsportgb.com; Tel 0131 445 7676; Fax 0131 445 4949

Squash

International Squash Rackets Federation (ISRF)

93 Cathedral Rd, Cardiff CF1 9PG; Tel 02920 374771; Fax 02920 374409

Executive Director   Roger Eady

Promoting, administering and legislating the game worldwide. The ISRF is now the recognised world governing body of the sport incorporating the leading squash playing nations.

Scottish Squash Limited

Caledonia Hse, South Gyle, Edinburgh EH12 9NQ; URL www.scottishsquash.org; e-mail info@scottishsquash.org; Tel 0131 317 7343; Fax 0131 317 7734

Surfing

British Surfing Association (BSA)

Fistral Beach, Newquay, Cornwall TR7 1HY; URL www.britsurf.co.uk; Tel 01637 876474; Fax 01637 878608

National Director   Karen Walton

Promotion and development of the sport of surfing in the UK. Coaching and competition organisation. Representation of members' interests.

Swimming

Amateur Swimming Association

Harold Fern Hse, Derby Sq, Loughborough, Leicestershire LE11 5AL; URL www.britishswimming.org; e-mail customerservices@swimming.org; Tel 01509 618700

English Schools' Swimming Association

'Mulina', Pyrford Woods, Woking, Surrey GU22 8QT
President   D. Teale; 8 Ashbrook, Buckingham St, Kingston upon Hull, East Riding of Yorkshire HU8 8TT
Hon Awards Secretary   J. Stiven; Tel 01932 346832
Hon General Secretary   N. Bramwell; 'Brackenridge', Guilsborough Hill, Hollowell, Northamptonshire NN6 8RN; Tel 01604 740919; Fax 01604 740919

Hon Treasurer   John Beddoe; 319 Berry Hill La, Mansfield, Nottinghamshire NG18 4JB; Tel 01623 656757 (home); Tel 01623 882494 (school)
Hon Press and Publicity Secretary   Frank Stockley; 48 Papermill La, Bramford, Ipswich, Suffolk IP8 4BS; e-mail f.stockley@essa-schoolswimming.com; Tel 01473 463487
Hon Championships Co-ordinator   M. Fox; Rylstone, Wolverhampton Rd, Middle Hill, nr Shareshill, Staffordshire WV10 7LT; Tel 01922 416959
Hon Assistant Championships Secretary   E. Hartley; 49 The Millbank, Ifield, Crawley, West Sussex RH11 0JQ; Tel 01293 515519
ESSA Representatives
British Sports Association for Disabled and National Water Safety Committee   N. Bramwell
National Council for School Sport; Central Council of Physical Recreation   E. Hartley
WISE Committee   J. Beddoe
WISE Committee   C. Turner
Annual Championships
ESSA national championships, school team and diving championships, schools' water polo championships, synchronised team championships
Dolphin Trophy Learn to Swim Award Scheme
Organiser   C. Matthews; 93 Kennedy Rd, Hanwell, London W7 1JW; Tel 020 8578 8785
The Dolphin Trophy Learn to Swim Scheme is open to all schools in England and Wales, the Channel Isles and the Service Children's Education Authority, with primary-aged pupils on their roll, where swimming is part of the curriculum. Special schools may ignore the upper age limit. The aim of the scheme is to make every child a safe swimmer before the age of 12.

Institute of Swimming Teachers and Coaches Ltd (ISTC)

41 Granby St, Loughborough, Leicestershire LE11 3DU; e-mail istc@swimming.org.uk; Tel 01509 264357; Fax 01509 231811

Chief Executive   D.L. Freeman-Wright MBA

The education and in–service training of swimming teachers and coaches

Scottish Amateur Swimming Association (SASA)

National Swimming Academy, University of Stirling, Stirling FK9 4LA; URL www.scottishswimming.com; e-mail info@scottishswimming.com; Tel 01786 466520; Fax 01786 466521

Chief Executive   Ashley Howard

Promotes and encourages the knowledge of swimming, diving, water-polo, synchronised swimming, long-distance swimming and masters swimming

Swim Ulster Ltd

House of Sport, Upper Malone Rd, Belfast BT9 5LA; URL www.swim-ulster.com; e-mail ruth@swim-ulster.com; Tel 028 9038 3807; Fax 028 9068 2757

Secretary   Frank Stevens

Swimming Teachers' Association

Anchor Hse, Birch St, Walsall, West Midlands WS2 8HZ; URL www.sta.co.uk; e-mail sta@sta.co.uk; Tel 01922 645097; Fax 01922 720628

Table Tennis

English Schools' Table Tennis Association

White Lodge, 24 Springfield Rd, Hinckley, Leicestershire LE10 1AN; URL www.estta.org.uk; e-mail eileen.shaler@ntlworld.com; Tel 01455 635138
President   J. Arnold; 17 Cyprus Mount, St John's, Wakefield, West Yorkshire WF1 2RJ; Tel 01924 372597; Fax 01924 372597
Chair   John Blackband; 5 Fairfield Mount, Highgate, Walsall, West Midlands WS1 3HZ; Tel 0121 556 4131 (school); Tel 01922 627081 (home)
Vice-Chair   P. Birch; 23 Kestrel Rd, Bedford, Bedfordshire MK41 7HR; Tel 01234 341988

11

General Secretary   Eileen Shaler
Hon Treasurer   Peter Embling; 77a Coxtie Green Rd, Brentwood, Essex CM14 5PS; Tel (home) 01277 372420
Hon Assistant General Secretary   Hugh Cherry; 19 Raddington Dr, Olton, Solihull B92 7DU, West Midlands; Tel (home) 0121 707 4285
Hon Individual Competition Secretary   Dennis Worrell; 36 Richmond Dr, Richmond Lakes, North Hykeham, Lincolnshire LN6 8QY; Tel (home) 01522 683027
Hon Team Competition Secretary   R. Hudson; 14 Rufford Cres, Yeadon, Leeds, West Yorkshire LS19 7QX; Tel 0113 250 2110
Hon Handbook Editor   John Wilde; 60 Hollinwell Ave, Wollaton, Nottingham NG8 1JZ
Hon Press and PR Officer   Vacancy
ESTTA promotes and encourages the playing of table tennis in schools, encourages the formation of county and local schools' table tennis associations, organises courses for teachers and players, arranges schools' competitions at any level and assists in the development of schools' table tennis

English Table Tennis Association
Queensbury Hse, 3rd Fl, Havelock Rd, Hastings, East Sussex TN34 1HF; URL www.etta.co.uk; e-mail admin@etta.co.uk; Tel 01424 722525; Fax 01424 422103

The International Table Tennis Federation
Chemin de la Roche 11, 1020 Renens, Lausanne 1020, Switzerland; URL www.ittf.com; e-mail ittf@ittf.com; Tel +41 21 3407090; Fax +41 21 3407099
President   Adham Sharara
Executive Director   Jordi Serra
Control of the sport of table tennis worldwide and the organisation of the world championships and other world title table tennis events

Table Tennis Association of Wales
31 Maes-y-Celyn, Griffithstown, Pontypool, Torfaen NP4 5DG; URL www.btinternet.com/wttaw; e-mail steve-gibbs@btinternet.com; Tel 01495 756112; Fax 01495 763025
Contact   S. Gibbs

Tennis

British Schools Tennis Association
c/o The Tennis Foundation, National Tennis Centre, 100 Priory La, Roehampton, London SW15 5JQ
Chair   Cathie Sabin
Manager (Schools)   Alison Connell
The British Schools Tennis Association is administered by the Tennis Foundation. Initiatives including in-service training for teachers, coaching programmes and a competitive structure for all ages are available. County Schools Tennis Associations have been established in most areas; any school requiring advice or help should write to the BSTA Manager.

Real Tennis and Rackets Association
c/o The Queen's Club, Palliser Rd, London W14 9EQ; URL www.tennisandrackets.com; e-mail james.wyatt@tennis-rackets.net; Tel 020 7386 3447; Fax 020 7385 7424
Chief Executive; Secretary   J.D. Wyatt
Administers and controls the games of Real Tennis and Rackets and preserves and strengthens their future in Great Britain

Tennis Scotland
177 Colinton Rd, Edinburgh EH14 1BZ; URL www.tennisscotland.org; e-mail info@tennisscotland.org; Tel 0131 444 1984; Fax 0131 444 1973

Ulster Council of the Irish Lawn Tennis Association
c/o 17 Tennyson Ave, Bangor, County Down BT20 3SS

Tenpin Bowling

British Tenpin Bowling Association
114 Balfour Rd, Ilford, Essex IG1 4JD; Tel 020 8478 1745; Fax 020 8514 3665
Chair   Pat White

Volleyball

English Volleyball Association
Suite B, Loughborough Technology Centre, Epinal Way, Loughborough, Leicestershire LE11 3GE; URL www.volleyballengland.org; e-mail info@volleyballengland.org; Tel 01509 631699; Fax 01509 631689
Chief Executive   Lisa Wainwright
National Development Manager   Craig Handford
Partnerships Officer   Laura Brown

Scottish Volleyball Association
48 The Pleasance, Edinburgh EH8 9TJ; URL www.scottishvolleyball.org; e-mail admin@scottishvolleyball.org; Tel 0131 556 4633; Fax 0131 557 4314

Water Skiing

British Water Ski
The Tower, Thorpe Rd, Chertsey, Surrey KT16 8PH; URL www.britishwaterski.org.uk; e-mail info@bwsf.co.uk; Tel 01932 570885; Fax 01932 566719

Scottish Board Sailing Association
Beinn Bhan, Kilmory Rd, Lochgilphead, Argyll and Bute; Tel 01546 2024
Contact   Forbes Johnston

Waterskiscotland
Scottish National Water Ski Centre, Townhill Country Pk, Dunfermline, Fife KY12 0HT; URL www.waterskiscotland.co.uk; e-mail info@waterskiscotland.co.uk; Tel 01383 620123

Weight Lifting

British Amateur Weight-Lifters' Association
131 Hurst St, Oxford, Oxfordshire OX4 1HE; URL www.bawla.com; e-mail jane@bawla.com; Tel 01865 200339; Fax 01865 790096
Chief Executive   Steve Cannon

Wrestling

British Wrestling Association Ltd
The Wrestling Academy, 41 Gt Clowes St, Manchester M7 1RQ; URL www.britishwrestling.org; Tel 01246 236443; Fax 01246 236443

Scottish Wrestling Association
60 Braehead Ave, Milngavie, Glasgow G62 6EL; Tel 0141 956 2307

Yoga

The British Wheel of Yoga
25 Jermyn St, Sleaford, Lincolnshire NG34 7RU; URL www.bwy.org.uk; e-mail office@bwy.org.uk; Tel 01529 306851

Youth Hostels

Scottish Youth Hostels Association
7 Glebe Cres, Stirling FK8 2JA; URL www.syha.org.uk; e-mail info@syha.org.uk; Tel 01786 891400; Fax 01786 891333
Chief Executive   Keith Legge

Youth Hostels Association (England and Wales) Ltd
PO Box 6028, Dimple Rd, Matlock, Derbyshire DE4 3XB;
 URL www.yha.org.uk; e-mail
 grouppreservations@yha.org.uk; Tel 0870 770 6117;
 Fax 0870 770 6127

Youth Hostel Association of Northern Ireland
22 Donegall Rd, Belfast BT12 5JN; URL www.hini.org.uk;
 e-mail info@hini.org.uk; Tel 028 9032 4733;
 Fax 028 9043 9699

Playing Fields

The London Playing Fields Society
Fraser Hse, 29 Albemarle St, London W1S 4JB;
 Tel 020 7493 3211; Fax 020 7409 3405
The Post Office Sports and Social Association Sports
 Ground, Forest Rd, Hainault, Essex IG6 3HJ
Chief Executive   Dr C. Goodson-Wickes DL
The aim of the London Playing Fields Society is to help
protect, provide and promote playing fields for the adults
and youths of Greater London. Seven are currently
operated:
Boston Manor Playing Field   Boston Gdns, Brentford,
 Greater London TW8 9LR
Douglas Eyre Sports Centre   Coppermill La, Walthamstow,
 London E17 7HE
Fairlop Oak Playing Field   Forest Rd, Hainault, Ilford, Essex
**London Post Office Sports and Social Association Sports
 Ground**   Forest Rd, Hainault, Ilford, Essex IG6 3HJ
Morden Park Sports Centre   Hillcross Ave, Morden, Surrey
 SM4 4AF
The Peter May Sports Centre   Wadham Rd, Walthamstow,
 London E17 4HR

National Playing Fields Association
Stanley Hse, St Chad's Pl, London WC1X 9HH; e-mail
 info@npfa.org; Tel 020 7833 5360; Fax 020 7833 5365
Patron   HM The Queen
President   HRH The Duke of Edinburgh KG, KT
Director   Alison Moore-Gwyn
The NPFA is the only independent organisation specialising
in play and sports environments. It offers advice on safety
and design matters, arranges seminars on grounds
maintenance and site management and provides an
independent playground and sport safety inspection
service.

STRI (The Sports Turf Research Institute)
Bingley, West Yorkshire D16 1AU; URL www.stri.co.uk;
 e-mail info@stri.co.uk; Tel 01274 565131;
 Fax 01274 561891
Patron   HRH The Duke of Edinburgh KG, KT
President   The Rt Hon Lord Hugh Griffiths MC
Chief Executive   Dr G.I. McKillop BSc, PhD, CBiol, MBNA
Director (Finance); Company Secretary   Mark Godfrey
STRI is officially recognised as the national centre for sports
and amenity turf. It is a non-profitmaking distributing
company limited by guarantee and registered as a scientific
research association with the Department for Business,
Enterprise and Regulatory Reform. The STRI is managed by
a small executive committee drawn from its members' body
comprising of the major sports controlling bodies. Activities
include research, consultancy and advisory services, books
and publications and training.
Advisory and Consultancy Services
STRI advises throughout the British Isles and beyond on the
management and maintenance of sports grounds (soccer,
rugby, hockey, cricket etc.) and golf courses. The service
functions through annual advisory visits supplemented by
postal advice, information, regular publications and the
testing of samples via its laboratory services. STRI also
specialises in golf course architecture, ecology and land
management, irrigation and the construction and drainage
of sports grounds. Sport England, represented on the
members' body, has expressed the wish that education

authorities should generally make full use of STRI as a
source of information and technical advice.
Objectives
To raise the standard of turf used for all sports, recreational
and amenity purposes through scientific research and
innovation, practical trials, advisory and consultancy
services, education and publications.
Research
The research programme includes contract work
commissioned by government departments, sports
controlling bodies and commercial companies. Additionally
STRI finances its own programme within the limits of
available funds.

Sport for People with Disabilities

See also Chapter 8

British Blind Sport
4–6 Victoria Terr, Leamington Spa, Warwickshire
 CV31 3AB; URL www.britishblindsport.org.uk; e-mail
 blindsport@btinternet.com; Tel 01926 424247;
 Fax 01926 427775
Chief Executive   Maurice J. Bright

British Deaf Sports Council
7 Bridge St, Otley, West Yorkshire LS21 1BQ; Tel (voice)
 01943 850214; Fax 01943 850828; Minicom 01943 850081
Promotes and controls amateur sports and games for deaf
people of Great Britain on a national and international plane

British Disabled Water Ski Association (BDWSA)
The Tony Edge National Centre, Heron Lake, Hythe End,
 Wraysbury, Greater London TW19 6HW;
 URL www.bdwsa.org.uk; e-mail info@bdwsa.org.uk;
 Tel 01784 483664; Fax 01784 482747
Teaches people with a disability to water ski

British Wheelchair Sports Foundation
Registered Charity Number 265498
Guttmann Rd, Stoke Mandeville, Buckinghamshire
 HP21 9PP; URL www.bwsf.org.uk; e-mail
 info@bwsf.org.uk; Tel 01296 395995; Fax 01296 424171
Office opening hours: Mon–Fri 0900–1730
BWSF aims to develop disabled sport for children and
adults and encourage both recreational and competitive
participation; to organise and host a range of sports events
for children and adults at the Stoke Mandeville Stadium and
throughout the UK; to work with the 17 wheelchair sports
associations to deliver a programme of opportunities for all
ability levels. Its activities include sports camps for
beginner, intermediate and experienced participants; sports
events including, junior, national and international games;
support for British wheelchair teams at home and abroad;
education and training of athletes, officials and volunteers;
disability awareness training; provides information services
on wheelchair sport through a range of publications and a
website.

The Calvert Trust
Little Crosthwaite, Underkiddaw, Keswick, Cumbria
 CA12 4QD; URL www.calvert-trust.org.uk; e-mail
 enquiries.calvert.keswick@dial.pipex.com;
 Tel 01768 772255; Fax 01768 771920
Centre Director   John Crosbie
Outdoor activities centre for people with disabilities,
activity courses, courses for education (PE, PSE or field
studies), for personal development designed to meet the
needs of individual clients. Activities include rock climbing,
abseiling, hill walking, sailing, canoeing, kayaking, horse
riding, trap driving, swimming, fishing, bird watching,
indoor archery and hockey; standard or specially adapted
equipment available. Staff hold national governing body
awards where appropriate, and are empathetic to the needs
of clients. Comfortable fully serviced accommodation in a
converted farmhouse with wheelchair access throughout,
heated indoor swimming pool, large games room, sports

11

hall with climbing wall, TV and video lounge, library and quiet room accessible throughout. Special diets catered for.

English National Association of Visually Handicapped Bowlers

Registered Charity Number 273134
18 Hervey St, Lowestoft, Suffolk NR32 2JG;
  Tel 01502 514700
Hon Secretary Gail Hepworth
Patron Tony Alcock MBE
Charity for blind bowlers in England with 53 member clubs and 600 members. Promotes national and international tournaments. Affiliated to IBBA and BBS.

Great Britain Wheelchair Basketball Association

The Woodlands, Brook End, Keysoe, Bedfordshire
  MK44 2HR; URL www.gbwba.org.uk; e-mail
  perrygbwba@aol.com; Tel 01234 708741
National Development Manager Gordon Perry
Promotes and governs the game of wheelchair basketball in Great Britain

Kids, National Development Division

Registered Charity Number 275936
6 Aztec Row, Berners Rd, London N1 0PW;
  URL www.kids.org.uk; e-mail pip@kids.org.uk;
  Tel 020 7359 3073; Fax 020 7359 3520
Established in 1970, Kids is a national charity providing a wide range of services for disabled children, young people and their families. Operating in five English regions, it provides early years support and childcare as well as specialist and inclusive play provision.
Kids National Development Division promotes the inclusion of disabled children in play and childcare nationally through the Playwork Inclusion Project. This is carried out through a programme of training, consultancy, publications and advice to professionals in the play, children and young people's sector. Kids sits on the Central Council of the SkillsActive Playwork Unit, the Executive Committee of the Children's Play Council and is a member of the Council for Disabled Children.

Mencap/Gateway

MENCAP, 4 Swan Courtyard, Coventry Rd, Birmingham,
  West Midlands B26 1BU; Tel 0121 707 7877
Chair Brian Baldock
National organisation developing opportunities together with individuals and groups to enhance the personal development of people with learning disabilities

National Association of Swimming Clubs for the Handicapped

The Willows, Mayles La, Wickham, Hampshire PO17 5ND;
  URL www.nasch.org.uk; e-mail
  naschswim-willows@yahoo.co.uk; Tel 01329 833689
Administrator Rosemary O'Leary
Recognises the value of swimming for the rehabilitation of disabled people and encourages, promotes and develops swimming among disabled people; produces a register of swimming clubs and organised swimming sessions for disabled people

Riding for the Disabled Association

Norfolk Hse, 1a Tournament Ct, Edgehill Dr, Warwick,
  Warwickshire CV34 6LG; URL www.rda.org.uk; e-mail
  info@rda.org.uk; Tel 0845 658 1082; Fax 0845 658 1083
Provides the opportunity of riding to disabled people to benefit their general health and wellbeing

Scottish Disability Sport

Head Office, Caledonia Hse, South Gyle, Edinburgh
  EH12 9DQ; URL www.scottishdisabilitysport.com;
  e-mail admin@scottishdisabilitysport.com;
  Tel 0131 317 1130; Fax 0131 317 1075
Chair Gordon McCormack
Chief Executive Gavin MacLeod
National Development Officer Claire Mands
Performance Development Officer Ruari Davidson
Administrator Caroline Ellis
National governing body for sport for all people with a disability in Scotland with a nationwide structure of branches

Sports Club for the Blind (London)

64 Antrim Mansions, Antrim Rd, London NW3 4XL
Chair Keith De Jersey
For a very small membership fee, many sports and activities are made available

United Kingdom Sports Association for People with Learning Disability

1st Fl, 12 City Forum, 250 City Rd, London EC1V 2PU;
  URL www.uksportsassociation.org; e-mail
  office@uksapld.freeserve.co.uk; Tel 020 7490 3057;
  Fax 020 7251 8861
Chief Executive Geoff Smedley
National co-ordinating body for sport and recreational activities for people with learning disabilities. UK Sports is the umbrella organisation for all agencies involved in the provision of sport for people with learning disability and is the member organisation representing the UK to the International Federation of Sport for Persons with Intellectual Disability (INAS-FID).

Welsh Paraplegic and Tetraplegic Sports Association

1 Greenway Ave, Rumney, Cardiff CF3 8HQ;
  Tel 02920 778026; Fax 02920 360483
Secretary J. Bridgeman
Welfare and sports for paraplegic and tetraplegic people

YOU and ME Yoga

Dacrelands Clinic, Owen Rd, Skerton, Lancaster, Lancashire
  LA1 2DU; URL www.youandmeyoga.com;
  Tel 01524 782103
Project Co-ordinator Maria Gunstone
Trains teachers, therapists, carers and parents, together with students who have learning difficulties, in a simple systematic yoga approach combined with teaching materials, designed to meet the needs of people with learning difficulties and the development of their potential. Competence-based programmes are available for both students and trainers. You and Me Yoga training package comprising teaching video and handbook also available.

Religious Education Organisations

Religious Education Organisations

Agency for Jewish Education

Bet Meir, 44a Albert Rd, London NW4 2SJ;
Tel 020 8457 9700; Fax 020 8457 9707
Chair   D. Rose
Chief Executive   Simon Goulden
Director (Education)   J. Leader

Teaching and Learning Centre

44b Albert Rd, London NW4 2SG; URL www.theus.org.uk/
aje; e-mail resources@aje.org.uk; Tel 020 8457 9717;
Fax 020 8457 9707
The Agency for Jewish Education provides training and
resources in support of more effective and forward-looking
Jewish education. A programme of lectures, workshops and
other events are organised for Jewish educators and
resources are provided for the wider community. Agency
personnel regularly visit schools. Teachers meet and learn
from each other at conferences, seminars and symposia both
in the UK and abroad. The Teaching and Learning Centre
has the latest educational publications and technology and
is used by teachers to research and produce their own
material. The resource centre sells publications produced by
the Agency for Jewish Education and teaching aids.

Association of Religious Education

53 Cromwell Rd, London SW7 2EH; Tel 020 7584 6617

Baptist Union of Great Britain

Head (Mission Department)   Rev Derek Allan
Mission Department   Baptist Hse, PO Box 44, Didcot,
Oxfordshire OX11 8RT; e-mail mission@baptist.org.uk;
Tel 01235 517700; Fax 01235 517715

British Humanist Association

1 Gower St, London WC1E 6HD;
URL www.humanism.org.uk; e-mail
info@humanism.org.uk; Tel 020 7079 3580;
Fax 020 7079 3588

Catholic Education Service for England and Wales

39 Eccleston Sq, London SW1V 1BX; Tel 020 7901 4880;
Fax 020 7901 4893
Chief Executive   Oona Stannard
Chair   The Rt Rev Vincent Nichols
Trustee   Rev Vincent Malone

Diocesan Schools' Commissioners

Chair   The Rt Rev Vincent Nichols
Arundel and Brighton   Diocesan Schools Commission,
Christian Education Centre, 4 Southgate Dr, Arundel,
West Sussex RH10 6RP
Commissioner   Mary Reynolds MA
Birmingham   Diocesan Schools Commission, Don Bosco
Hse, 61 Coventry Rd, Coleshill, Birmingham, West
Midlands B46 3EA
Commissioner   Rev Canon Stock
Director (RE)   Fr Jonathan Veasey

Brentwood   Cathedral Hse, 28 Ingrave Rd, Brentwood,
Essex CM15 8AT
Commissioner; Director (RE)   Monsignor George Stokes
Cardiff/Menevia   Diocesan Schools Commission,
Archbishop's Hse, 41–43 Cathedral Rd, Cardiff CF1 9HD
Commissioner   Anne Robertson
Director (RE)   Sr A. Murray OSU; Curia Office, 27
Convent St, Swansea SA1 2BY
Clifton   Diocesan Schools Commission, Alexander Hse, 160
Pennywell Rd, Bristol BS5 0TX
Commissioner   Peter Bradshaw
Director (RE)   David Byrne; Clifton Religious Education
Centre, 160 Pennywell Rd, Bristol BS5 0TX
East Anglia   Diocesan Schools Commission, The White Hse,
21 Upgate Poringland, Norwich, Norfolk NR14 7SH
Commissioner   Mrs J. O'Connor
Hallam   Diocesan Schools' Commission, Hallam Pastoral
Centre, Sheffield, South Yorkshire S9 3WU
Director (Schools)   Marian Bolton
Director (Schools)   Jim Conway
Hexham and Newcastle   St Vincents Offices, St Cuthbert's
Hse, West Rd, Newcastle upon Tyne, Tyne and Wear
NE15 7PY
Commissioner; Director (RE)   Dr Harry O'Neill
Lancaster   Cathedral Bldg, Balmoral Rd, Lancaster,
Lancashire LA1 3BT
Director (Education)   Fr Luiz Ruscillo
Leeds   Diocesan Schools' Commission, Hinsley Hall, 62
Headingley La, Leeds, West Yorkshire LS6 2BX
Commissioner   Trina Hagerty
Director (RE)   Fr John Wilson
Liverpool   Diocesan Education Department, LACE,
Croxteth Dr, Sefton Pk, Liverpool, Merseyside L17 1AA
Commissioner   F. Cogley
Director (RE)   Rev Desmond Seddon
Middlesbrough   Curial Office, 50a The Avenue,
Middlesbrough T55 6QT
Commissioner   Vacancy
Director (RE)   Kathleen Stead
Northampton   Our Lady of Lourdes, Lloyds Coffee Hall,
Milton Keynes, Buckinghamshire MK6 5EB
Commissioner   Frances Image
Director (RE)   Fr Kevin McGinnell
Nottingham   The Diocesan Centre, Mornington Cres,
Mackworth, Derby, Derbyshire DE22 4BD
Commissioner   Edward Hayes
Director (RE)   Sr Margaret Horan; The Education and
Formation Commision, The Diocesan Centre,
Mornington Cres, Mackworth, Derby DE22 4BD
Plymouth   Newman Hse, Wonford Rd, Exeter EX2 4PF
Commissioner   John Mannix
Co-Director (RE)   David Wells; Department for
Formation, Newman Hse, Wonford Rd, Exeter, Devon
EX2 4PF
Portsmouth   Park Place Pastoral Centre, Winchester Rd,
Wickham, Fareham, Hampshire PO17 5HA
Commissioner   Chris Richardson
Director (RE)   Nicky Stevens
Salford   Diocesan Schools' Commission, 5 Gerald Rd,
Salford, Greater Manchester M6 6DL
Commissioner   Martin Lochery

12

Director (RE) Bernard Stuart; Salford Diocese Religious Education Centre, Plymouth Gr, Longsight, Manchester M13 0AS
Shrewsbury Diocesan Schools' Commission, 2 Park Rd South, Birkenhead, Merseyside L43 4UX
Commissioner; Director (RE) Michael Clarke
Director (RE) Fr David Roberts
Southwark Southwark Diocesan Schools' Commission, St Edward's Hse, Orpington, Kent BR5 2SR
Commissioner D. Wadman
Director (RE) Rev J. O'Toole; Christian Education Centre, 21 Tooting Bec Rd, London SW17 8BS
Westminster
Commissioner; Director (RE) Paul Barber
Wrexham Bishop's Hse, Sontley Rd, Wrexham LL13 7EW
Contact Rita Price

Catholic Teachers Federation (of England and Wales)

General Secretary M.H. Emm BA, MEd; 24 Knowlands Rd, Monkspath, Solihull, West Midlands B90 4UG; Tel 0121 745 4265

The Children's Society

Chief Executive Bob Reitemeier; Edward Rudolf Hse, Margery St, London WC1X 0JL; URL www.childrenssociety.org.uk; Tel 020 7841 4500

Christian Education

1020 Bristol Rd, Selly Oak, Birmingham, West Midlands B29 6LB; URL www.christianeducation.org.uk; www.retoday.org.uk; e-mail enquiries@christianeducation.org.uk; Tel 0121 472 4242; Fax 0121 472 7575
Christian Education Publications, International Bible Reading Association and RE Today Services

Church of England Board of Education

Chair The Rt Rev Kenneth Stevenson; Bishop of Portsmouth
Head (School Development) Rev David Whittington
National Children's Adviser (Higher Education and Chaplaincy) Rev Hugh Shilson-Thomas
National Children's Adviser Rev Mary Hawes
Deputy Secretary; Head (School Improvement) Mr N. McKemey
Chief Education Officer Rev Jan Ainsworth; Church Hse, Gt Smith St, London SW1P 3NZ; Tel 020 7898 1500
Further Education Officer Alan Murray
School Support Officer Liz Carter
Youth Adviser Peter Ball
Youth Adviser Yvonne Criddle
Adviser (Lay Discipleship and Shared Ministry) Joanna Cox

Welsh Provincial Consultant for Education
Director Edwin Counsell; The Court, Coychurch, Bridgend CF35 5HF

Diocesan Directors of Education (Church of England and Wales)
Bangor Diocesan Centre, Cathedral Cl, Bangor, Gwynedd LL57 1RL
Contact Rev Tegid Roberts
Bath and Wells The Old Deanery, Wells, Somerset
Contact Maureen Bollard
Birmingham Church Hse, Harborne Park Rd, Birmingham, West Midlands B17 0BH
Contact Mary Edwards
Blackburn Diocesan Office, Cathedral Cl, Blackburn BB1 5AA
Contact Rev Canon P. Ballard
Bradford, Ripon and Leeds
Contact Mr C. Sedgewick
Bristol All Saints' Centre, 1 All Saints' Ct, Bristol BS1 1JN

Contact Jackie Waters-Dewhurst
Canterbury Diocesan Hse, Lady Wootton's Grn, Canterbury, Kent CT1 1TL
Contact R. Bristow
Carlisle Diocesan Church Centre, West Walls, Carlisle, Cumbria CA3 8UE
Contact Rev Canon D. Jenkins
Chelmsford Diocesan Education Centre, 53 New St, Chelmsford, Essex CM1 1NG
Contact Rev Canon Peter Hartley
Chester Church Hse, Lower La, Aldford, Chester, Cheshire CH3 6HP
Contact Jeffrey Turnbull
Chichester Diocesan Church Hse, 211 New Church Rd, Hove, East Sussex
Contact Jeremy Taylor
Coventry 1 Hilltop, Coventry, Warwickshire CV1 5AR
Contact Linda Wainscot
Derby Church Hse, Full St, Derby DE1 3DY
Contact P. Moncur
Durham Carter Hse, Pelaw Leazes La, Durham, County Durham CH1 1TB
Contact Sheila Bamber
Ely Diocesan Office, Bishop Woodford Hse, Barton Rd, Ely, Cambridgeshire CB7 4DX
Contact Rev Canon T. Elbourne
Exeter Diocesan Board of Education, The Old Deanery, The Cloisters, Cathedral Cl, Exeter, Devon EX1 1HS
Gloucester Diocesan Education Office, 4 College Gr, Gloucester, Gloucestershire GL1 2LR
Contact Phil Metcalf
Guildford Education Centre, The Cathedral, Guildford, Surrey GU2 5UP
Contact Derek Holbird
Hereford Diocesan Office, The Palace, Hereford, Herefordshire HR4 9BL
Contact Rev Ian Terry
Leicester 3–5 St Martin's East, Leicester LE1 5FX
Contact Rev Canon Peter Taylor
Lichfield St Mary's Hse, The Close, Lichfield, Staffordshire WS13 7LD; e-mail colin.hopkins@lichfield.anglican.org; Tel 01543 306040; Fax 01543 306039
Contact C. Hopkins
Lincoln Diocesan Education Centre, The Old Palace, Lincoln, Lincolnshire LN2 1PU
Contact Peter Staves
Liverpool St James Hse, 20 St James Rd, Liverpool, Merseyside L1 7BY
Contact Jon Richardson
Llandaff The Court, Coychurch, Llandaff, Cardiff CF35 5HF
Contact Rev Edwin Counsell
London 36 Causton St, London SW1P 4AU
Contact Tom Peryer
Manchester Diocesan Church Hse, 90 Deansgate, Manchester M3 2GJ
Contact Maurice Smith
Monmouth 64 Caerau Rd, Newport NP9 4HU
Contact Rev Canon Dr Keith Denison
Newcastle upon Tyne Diocesan Office, Church Hse, St John's Terr, North Shields, Tyne and Wear NE29 6HS; e-mail m.nicholson@newcastle.anglican.org; Tel 0191 270 4100; Fax 0191 270 4101
Director of Education Margaret Nicholson
Norwich Diocesan Hse, 109 Dereham Rd, Easton, Norfolk NR9 5ES
Contact Andy Mash
Oxford Diocesan Church Hse, North Hinksey, Oxford, Oxfordshire OX2 0NB
Contact Leslie Stephen
Peterborough Education Department, Bouverie Ct, The Lakes, Northampton, Northamptonshire NN4 7YD
Contact Dr S. Partridge
Portsmouth 1st Fl, Peninsular Hse, Wharf Rd, Portsmouth PO2 8HB
Contact T. Blackshaw

Ripon, Leeds and Bradford Windsor Hse, Cornwall Rd, Harrogate, North Yorkshire GE1 2PW
Contact Rev Clive Sedgewick
Rochester Diocesan Office, St Nicholas Church, Boley Hill, Rochester ME1 1SL
Contact Rev Canon J. Smith
St Albans Diocesan Office, Holywell Lodge, 41 Holywell Hill, St Albans, Hertfordshire AL1 1HE
Contact J. Reynolds
St Asaph Diocesan Office, High St, St Asaph, Denbighshire LL17 0RD
St David's Brynheulog, Heol Penlanffos, Carmarthen SA31 2HL
Contact Rev Mary Thorley
St Edmundsbury and Ipswich Churchgate Hse, Cutler St, Ipswich, Suffolk IP1 1VQ
Contact The Ven John Cox
Salisbury Diocesan Education Centre, Devizes Rd, Salisbury, Wiltshire SP2 9LY
Contact C. Shepperd
Sheffield Diocesan Church Hse, 95–99 Eftingham St, Rotherham, South Yorkshire S65 1BL
Contact Heather Morris
Southwark 48 Union St, London SE1 1TD; Tel 020 7407 7911
Contact Barbara Lane
Southwell Dunham Hse, 8 Westgate, Southwell, Nottinghamshire NG25 0JL
Contact Rev Howard Worsley
Swansea and Brecon The Rectory, Maes Glas, Llangammarch Wells LD4 4EE
Contact Rev Catherine Haynes
Truro Kenwyn, Truro, Cornwall TR1 1JQ
Contact Susan Green
Wakefield Church Hse, 1 South Par, Wakefield, West Yorkshire WF1 1LP
Contact Rev Ian Wildey
Winchester 1st Fl, Peninsular Hse, Wharf Rd, Portsmouth PO2 8HB
Contact Tony Blackshaw
Worcester The Old Palace, Deansway, Worcestershire WR1 1JE
Contact Rev D. Morphy
York Diocesan Hse, Aviator Ct, Clifton Moor, York YO30 4SW; e-mail alees@yorkdiocese.org.uk; Tel 01904 699 512; Fax 01904 699 510
Contact Dr Ann Lees

Church Schools Foundation Ltd/Church Schools Company

Chief Executive Ewan Harper MA; Church Schools Hse, Titchmarsh, Kettering, Northamptonshire NN14 3DA; Tel 01832 735105; Fax 01832 734760

Churches' Joint Education Policy Committee

Chair The Rt Rev Dr Kenneth Stevenson; Bishop of Portsmouth
Secretary Sarah Lane; Free Church Education Unit, Churches Together in England, 27 Tavistock Sq, London WC1H 9HH
Committee Members
Anglican Members Peter Bruinvels, Rev Dr John Gay, Rev Canon Peter Hartley, Rev Canon John Hall, Peter Williams
Free Churches' Council Members Graham Hanscomb, Sarah Lane, Rheinallt Thomas, Phyllis Thompson, Mary Whalley, Gillian Wood
Roman Catholic Members Very Rt Rev Vincent Nichols, Sister Margaret, Canon Peter Humphrey, Dr Arthur Naylor, Mary Reynolds, Oona Stannard
Other Churches' Members Sup Apos James, Janet Scott, Rev Father Antonious Thabit Shenouda, Mike Simmonds
Observers Rev John Kennedy, Rev Bill Snelson, Rev Gethin Abraham-Williams

Community Issues Division

Director Marlena Schmool

Education Officer Samantha Blendis; Commonwealth Hse, 1–19 New Oxford St, London WC1A 1NU; Tel 020 7543 5400; Fax 020 7543 0010

Council of Christians and Jews

Camelford Hse, 89 Albert Embankment, London SE1 7TP; URL www.ccj.org.uk; e-mail cjrelations@ccj.org.uk; e-mail jane@ccj.org.uk Tel 020 7820 0090; Fax 020 7820 0504
Executive Director Sr Margaret Shepherd
Education Officer Jane Clements
Education Officer Rabbi Rachel Montagu
Education Adviser Jonathan Gorsky

First Church of Christ, Scientist

Christian Science Committees on Publication for the UK and the Republic of Ireland
District Manager Tony Lobl; Claridge Hse, 29 Barnes High St, London SW13 9LW; e-mail londoncs@csps.com; Tel 020 8282 1645; Fax 020 8487 1566

Free Church of England (otherwise called Reformed Episcopal Church)

Contact The Rt Rev Paul Hunt; 329 Wolverhampton Rd West, County Bridge, Willenhall, West Midlands WV13 2RL; e-mail church@revpaulhunt.wanadoo.co.uk; Tel 01902 607335; Fax 01902 607335

Free Churches Group

27 Tavistock Sq, London WC1H 9HH; URL www.churches-together.org.uk; e-mail education@cte.org.uk; Tel 020 7529 8145; Fax 020 7529 8134
Chair Mary Whalley
Education Officer (Free Churches and Churches Together in England) Sarah Lane
Methodist Education Officer Kathleen Wood; 66 Balfour Rd, West Ealing, London W13 9TW

Education Committee

Chair Mary Whalley; Churches Together in England, 27 Tavistock Sq, London WC1H 9HH
HE Chaplaincy Co-ordinator Rev Robert Jones; Southlands College, 80 Roehampton La, London SW15 5SL
Contact Sarah Lane; Churches Together in England, 27 Tavistock Sq, London WC1H 9HH
Also members of the Churches' Joint Education Policy Committee which brings together members of the Church of England Board of Education, the Catholic Education Service and the Free Churches' Group together with representatives of the Religious Society of Friends, the Orthodox Churches, the black majority churches and the Evangelical Alliance.

Friends' Schools' Joint Council

Friends Hse, Euston Rd, London NW1 2BJ; URL www.quakerschools.co.uk; e-mail debbiet@quaker.org.uk; Tel 020 7663 1038
There are seven Quaker boarding schools, each managed separately by a representative committee of the society

Independent Methodist Churches

Contact William C. Gabb; 66 Kirkstone Dr, Loughborough, Leicestershire LE11 3RW; URL www.imcgb.org.uk; Tel 01509 268566; Fax 01509 227014

Islamic Academy

Registered Charity Number 287003
205 Gilbert Rd, Cambridge, Cambridgeshire CB4 3PA; e-mail info@islamicacademy.ac.uk; Tel 01223 350976; Fax 01223 350976
Director General Dr S.A. Mabud

12

A religious-educational charity and research-oriented body, aimed at making religious values the basis of education. Publishes educational books and the journal Muslim Education Quarterly.

Islamic Academy of Manchester

19 Chorlton Terr, Upper Brook St, Brunswick, Manchester M13 9TD; Tel 0161 273 1145
Director Dr Khalid Mahmud MA, PhD

Jewish Education Bureau

8 Westcombe Ave, Leeds, West Yorkshire LS8 2BS; URL www.jewisheducationbureau.co.uk; e-mail jeb@jewisheducationbureau.co.uk; Tel 0844 873 1044; Fax 0844 873 1046
Director Rabbi D.S. Charing

The King David Foundation

Administering the King David High School, King David Primary School and King David Kindergarten
120 Childwall Rd, Liverpool, Merseyside L15 6WU; e-mail admin@kdf.org.uk; Tel 0151 737 1214; Fax 0151 722 9375
President (King David Foundation) B. Michaelson (Acting)
Chair of Governors (High School) M. Steinberg OBE
Chair of Governors (Primary School) Mrs L. Lesin-Davis

Leo Baeck College

Sternberg Centre for Judaism, 80 East End Rd, London N3 2SY; URL www.lbc.ac.uk; e-mail info@lbc.ac.uk; Tel 020 8349 5600; Fax 020 8349 5619
Director (Finance and Administration) Stephen Ross
Head (Administration) Rhona Lesner
Sandra Vigon Resource Centre c/o Manchester Reform Synagogue, Jackson's Row, Manchester M2 5NH; Tel 0161 831 7092

Methodist Church

Education Secretary G. Russell MA

Moravian Church

Provincial Board Jackie Morten; Moravian Church Hse, 5 Muswell Hill, London N10 3TJ; Tel 020 8883 3409
Two boarding and day schools

Multifaith Education Centre

Sacred Trinity Church, Chapel St, Salford, Greater Manchester M3 7AJ; Tel 0161 832 3709
Co-ordinator Trish Hardy

Muslim Educational Trust

130 Stroud Green Rd, London N4 3RZ; URL www.muslim-ed-trust.org.uk; e-mail info@muslim-ed-trust.org.uk; Tel 020 7272 8502; Fax 020 7281 3457
Director Ghulam Sarwar

Muslim Teachers' Association (MTA)

Islamic Cultural Centre, 146 Park Rd, London NW8 7RG; Tel 020 8393 7335
President S.N. Bokhari
Vice-President N. Mustafa
Secretary Mrs B. Nasir

National Society (CE) for Promoting Religious Education

Church Hse, Gt Smith St, London SW1P 3NZ; e-mail info@natsoc.c-of-e.org.uk; Tel 020 7898 1518; Fax 020 7898 1520
General Secretary; Chief Education Officer Rev Jan Ainsworth; e-mail jan.ainsworth@c-of-e.org.uk
Deputy Secretary; Head (School Improvement) Mr N. McKemey
Head (School Development) Rev David Whittington

Presbyterian Church of Wales

General Secretary Rev Ifan R. Roberts; 81 Merthyr Rd, Whitchurch, Cardiff CF14 1DD; URL www.ebcpcw.org.uk; e-mail swyddfa.office@ebcpcw.org.uk; Tel 02920 627465; Fax 02920 616188

Church and Society Department

Chair Mervyn Phillips
Secretary Parch G.T. Jones; 18 Richs Rd, Birchgrove, Cardiff CF14 4AA; e-mail glyntudwal@lycos.co.uk; Tel 02920 621268

Religious Education Council of England and Wales

c/o RE Today, 1020 Bristol Rd, Selly Oak, Birmingham, West Midlands B29 6LB; URL www.religiouseducationcouncil.org
Chair Prof Brian Gates
Treasurer Dr John Gay
Registrar; Secretary Mrs Sue Hart; Teaching Matters, PO Box 148, Goole, South Yorkshire DN14 0YD
Member Organisations
Alkhoei Foundation; Association of University Departments of Theology and Religious Studies; The Association of Christian Teachers; Association of Jewish Teachers; The Maha Bohdi Society (UK); The Baptist Union of Great Britain; The Board of Deputies of British Jews; The British Humanist Association; The British Sikh Education Council; The Buddhist Society; The Catholic Association of Teachers in Schools and Colleges; The Catholic Bishops' Conference and Education Services; The Catholic Education Service; The Church in Wales; Christian Education (Wales); Christian Education; Christian Education Movement (Wales); The Church of England Board of Education; Conference of University Lecturers in RE; Council of African and Afro Caribbean Churches UK; Council of Christians and Jews; Culham College Institute; The Farmington Institute for Christian Studies; Federation of National and Regional RE Centres; Free Churches Education Unit; Independent Schools Religious Studies Association; The Interfaith Network UK; The IQRA Trust; ISKCON Education Services; Islamic Academy; The Islamic Cultural Centre; The Muslim Educational Trust; NATFHE (Religious Studies Section); The Association of RE Inspectors, Advisers and Consultants; National Association of Standing Advisory Councils for RE; National Council of Hindu Temples; The National Society (CE) for Promoting Religious Education; The National Spiritual Assembly of the Baha'is of the UK; The Norham Foundation; The Professional Council for Religious Education; The Religious Society of Friends; Roman Catholic National Board of Religious Inspectors and Advisers; Russian Orthodox Diocese of Sourozh; The SHAP Working Party on World Religions in Education; The Stapleford Centre; The Union of Muslim Organisations NMEC; Wales Association of Standing Advisory Councils; The World Congress of Faiths; Observers NFER; Ofsted; DCSF, ACCAC, ESTYN, EFTRE, QCA

Scottish Joint Committee on Religious and Moral Education

Joint Secretary L. Bradley; 6 Clairmont Gdns, Glasgow G3 7LW; Tel 0141 353 3595; Fax 0141 332 2778

Scripture Union Schools Ministry

207–209 Queensway, Bletchley, Milton Keynes, Buckinghamshire MK2 2EB; URL www.scriptureunion.org.uk; e-mail schools@scriptureunion.org.uk; Tel 01908 856168; Fax 01908 856012
Schools Consultant Gill Marchant

Society for Promoting Christian Knowledge (SPCK)

36 Causton St, London SW1P 4ST; URL www.spck.org.uk; Tel 020 7592 3900; Fax 020 7592 3939
Chair The Rt Rev Michael Perham
Chief Executive Simon Kingston

Union of Muslim Organisations of UK and Ireland

109 Campden Hill Rd, London W8 7TL; Tel 020 7221 6608; Fax 020 7792 2130

Houses the National Muslim Education Council of UK and UMO Youth Council of UK and Eire

Union of Welsh Independents Incorporated

General Secretary Rev Dr Geraint Tudur BA, BD; The Welsh Congregational Union, Ty John Penry, 5 Axis Ct, Riverside Business Pk, Swansea Vale, Swansea SA7 0AJ; Tel 01792 795888; Fax 01792 795376

United Reformed Church

General Secretary Rev Dr D.G. Cornick; United Reformed Church, 86 Tavistock Pl, London WC1H 9RT; Tel 020 7916 2020; Fax 020 7916 2021

Urban Theology Unit

210 Abbeyfield Rd, Sheffield, South Yorkshire S4 7AZ; URL www.utusheffield.org.uk; e-mail office@utusheffield.org.uk; Tel 0114 243 5342

Director Rev Christine Jones

Manager (Support Services) Kate Thompson

12

Voluntary Services and Groups for Children and Young People

National Voluntary Youth Organisations
Local Councils for Voluntary Youth Services

Voluntary Services and Groups for Children and Young People

National Voluntary Youth Organisations

Army Cadet Force Association

Holderness Hse, 51–61 Clifton St, London EC2A 4DW;
URL www.armycadets.com; e-mail
acfa@armycadets.com; Tel 020 7426 8377
General Secretary   Brig Mike Wharmby
The army's voluntary youth organisation with a strength of approximately 41 000 boys and girls between the ages of 13 and 18 years

Boys' Brigade

Felden Lodge, Felden, Hemel Hempstead, Hertfordshire
HP3 0BL; URL www.boys-brigade.org.uk; e-mail
enquiries@boys-brigade.org.uk; Tel 01442 231681;
Fax 01442 235391
Brigade Secretary   Steve Dickinson

Brathay Hall Trust

Brathay Hall, Ambleside, Cumbria LA22 0HP;
URL www.brathay.org.uk; e-mail
brathay@brathay.org.uk; Tel 01539 439760;
Fax 01539 439701
Brathay is an educational trust that works with children and young people, and professionals who work with children and young people. Brathay offers professional development courses.

British Red Cross

44 Moorfields, London EC2Y 9AL;
URL www.redcross.org.uk; e-mail
information@redcross.org.uk; Tel 020 7877 7000;
Fax 020 7562 2000
National Officer (Youth and Schools)   Mairi Allan

British Youth Council

2 Downstream Bldg, 1 London Bridge, London SE1 9BG;
URL www.byc.org.uk; e-mail mail@byc.org.uk;
Tel 0845 458 1489; Fax 0845 458 1847
Chair   Dan Wood
Chief Executive   Kathleen Cronin
BYC represents and involves young people from more than 140 youth organisations and a network of 700 local groups; promotes the active citizenship of young people and organises a range of events and training that develop young people's skills and abilities to participate fully within organisations, their communities and wider society

BTCV

See also BTCV entry in Chapter 14: Working Holidays
Sedum Hse, Mallard Way, Doncaster, South Yorkshire
DN4 8DB; URL www.btcv.org; e-mail
information@btcv.org.uk; Tel 01302 388883
BTCV builds healthy, sustainable communities and increases people's life skills. It aims to create an environment where people from all cultures feel valued, included and involved. BTCV supports 140 000 volunteers a year to improve their urban and rural environments, and a community network supports local groups. Local, community-based programmes for young people to engage with e.g. Young Volunteer Challenge, GetREAL, Millennium Volunteers.

Campaigner Ministries

6 Eaton Ct, Colmworth Business Pk, Eaton Socon, St Neots,
Cambridgeshire PE19 8YH;
URL www.campaigners.org.uk; e-mail
information@campaigners.org.uk; Tel 01480 215622
Executive Director   John D. Radcliffe

Catholic Youth Services (CYS)

39 Eccleston Sq, London SW1V 1BX; e-mail
cys@cbcew.org.uk; Tel 020 7901 4870
Development Officer   Adam Berry

Church Lads' and Church Girls' Brigade

St Martin's Hse, 2 Barnsley Rd, Wath upon Dearne,
Rotherham, South Yorkshire S63 6PY;
URL www.clcgb.org.uk; e-mail
brigadesecretary@clcgb.org.uk; Tel 01709 876535;
Fax 01709 878089
Brigade Secretary   Col (Retd) Alan J. Millward
A uniformed organisation within the Church of England which offers adventure, challenge and responsibility for children and young people through fun, faith and fellowship

Clubs for Young People

371 Kennington La, London SE11 5QY;
URL www.clubsforyoungpeople.org.uk; e-mail
office@clubsforyoungpeople.org.uk; Tel 020 7793 0787;
Fax 020 7820 9815
Director (Programmes)   David Springett

Combined Cadet Force Association

Holderness Hse, 51–61 Clifton St, London EC2A 4DW;
e-mail ccfa@armycadets.com; Tel 020 7426 8377;
Fax 020 7426 8378
Secretary   Brigadier Mike Wharmby

13

Council for Environmental Education

c/o Field Studies Council, Preston Montford, Shrewsbury, Shropshire SY4 1HW; URL www.cee.org.uk; e-mail marion@field-studies-council.org; Tel 01743 852121; Fax 01743 852101

Council for Wales of Voluntary Youth Services (CWVYS)

Baltic Hse, Mount Stuart Sq, Cardiff CF10 5FH; URL www.cwvys.org.uk; e-mail swyddfa@cwvys.org.uk; Tel 02920 473498; Fax 02920 451245

Endeavour Training

Sheepbridge Centre, Sheepbridge La, Chesterfield, Derbyshire S41 9RX; e-mail info@endeavour.org.uk; Tel 0870 770 3250; Fax 0870 770 3254
Patron HRH The Duke of Kent KG, GCMG, GCVO, ADC
President
Lord Phillips of Worth Matravens, Lord Chief Justice
Founder R.S. Allcock OBE
Chair Richard de Lacy QC
Chief Executive Les Roberts
Endeavour provides long-term programmes for the personal development of young people aged 14–25. Clients are recruited through schools and are offered a wide curriculum. After two years they may take part in the national programme of outdoor residential courses for a nominal charge. There are groups of volunteers who meet regularly and are supported to run activities and expeditions for themselves and for others both at home and overseas.

Fairbridge

Registered Charity Number 206807
207 Waterloo Rd, London SE1 8XD;
URL www.fairbridge.org.uk; e-mail info@fairbridge.org.uk; Tel 020 7928 1704; Fax 020 7928 6016
Fairbridge is a leading youth charity supporting 13–25 year olds, who are outside education, training and employment, or are at risk of becoming so, in 15 of the most disadvantaged areas in the country. The aim of the programme is to develop motivation, confidence and personal, social and life skills using a wide range of challenging activities from abseiling to business projects.

Field Studies Council

SY4 1HW; URL www.field-studies-council.org; e-mail fsc.enquiries@field-studies-council.org; Tel 0845 345 4071
President Prof Ian D. Mercer
Chair Prof Tim Burt MA, PhD, DSc, FRGS
Hon Treasurer G. Brown
Director (Communications) S.M. Tilling
Director A.D. Thomas BA, CertEd, AcDipEd
Director (Operations) R. Lucas
Secretary; Treasurer C.J. Bayliss FCA; Head Office, Preston Montford, Montford Bridge, Shrewsbury, Shropshire SY4 1HW; Tel 01743 852100

RESIDENTIAL AND DAY CENTRES ADMINISTERED BY THE COUNCIL

Amersham Field Centre Mop End, Amersham, Buckinghamshire HP7 0QR; URL www.field-studies-council.org; e-mail fsc@amershamfc.freeserve.co.uk; Tel 01494 721054
Blencathra Field Centre Threlkeld, Keswick, Cumbria CA12 4SG; URL www.field-studies-council.org; e-mail enquiries.bl@field-studies-council.org; Tel 017687 79601
Brockhole Visitor Centre Lake District National Park Authority, Windermere, Cumbria LA23 1LJ; URL www.field-studies-council.org; e-mail education@lake-district.gov.uk; Tel 01539 440800

Castle Head Field Centre Grange-over-Sands, Cumbria LA11 6QT; URL www.field-studies-council.org; e-mail enquiries.ch@field-studies.council.org; Tel 0845 330 7364
Dale Fort Field Centre Haverfordwest, Pembrokeshire SA62 3RD; URL www.field-studies-council.org; e-mail enquiries.df@field-studies-council.org; Tel 0845 330 7365
Derrygonnelly Field Centre Derrygonnelly, Fermanagh, County Fermanagh BT93 6HW; URL www.field-studies-council.org; e-mail enquiries.dg@field-studies-council.org; Tel 028 6864 1673
Epping Forest Field Centre High Beach, Loughton, Essex IG10 4AF; URL www.field-studies-council.org; e-mail enquiries.ef@field-studies-council.org; Tel 020 8502 8500 Caters mainly for primary and secondary schools in the areas of London, Essex and Hertfordshire although it is used by higher education and adult groups as well
Flatford Mill Field Centre East Bergholt, Colchester, Essex CO7 6UL; URL www.field-studies-council.org; e-mail enquiries.fm@field-studies-council.org; Tel 0845 330 7368
Juniper Hall Field Centre Dorking, Surrey RH5 6DA; URL www.field-studies-council.org; e-mail enquiries.jh@field-studies-council.org; Tel 0845 458 3507
Kindrogan Field Centre Enochdhu, Blairgowrie, Perthshire PH10 7PG; URL www.field-studies-council.org; e-mail enquiries.kd@field-studies-council.org; Tel 01250 870150
Malham Tarn Field Centre Settle, North Yorkshire BD24 9PU; URL www.field-studies-council.org; e-mail enquiries.mt@field-studies-council.org; Tel 01729 830331
Margam Park Education Service Neath Port Talbot SA13 2TJ; URL www.field-studies-council.org; e-mail margam_sustainable_centre@hotmail.com; Tel 01639 895636
Nettlecombe Court The Leonard Wills Field Centre, Williton, Taunton, Somerset TA4 4HT; URL www.field-studies-council.org; e-mail enquiries.nc@field-studies-council.org; Tel 01984 640320
Orielton Field Centre Pembroke, Pembrokeshire SA71 5EZ; URL www.field-studies-council.org; e-mail enquiries.or@field-studies-council.org; Tel 0845 330 7372
Preston Montford Field Centre Montford Bridge, Shrewsbury, Shropshire SY4 1DX; URL www.field-studies-council.org; e-mail enquiries.pm@field-studies-council.org; Tel 0845 330 7378
Rhyd-y-Creuau The Drapers' Field Centre, Betws-y-Coed, Conwy LL24 0HB; URL www.field-studies-council.org; e-mail enquiries.rc@field-studies-council.org; Tel 01690 710494
Slapton Ley Field Centre Slapton, Kingsbridge, Devon TQ7 2QP; URL www.field-studies-council.org; e-mail enquiries.sl@field-studies-council.org; Tel 01548 580466

Frontier Youth Trust

Unit 208b, The Big Peg, 120 Vyse St, Birmingham, West Midlands B18 6NF; URL www.fyt.org.uk; e-mail frontier@fyt.org.uk; Tel 0121 687 3505
Chief Executive; Team Leader Dave Wiles
FYT is a christian-based organisation working with young people at risk from all types of exclusion

Girlguiding UK

17–19 Buckingham Palace Rd, London SW1W 0PT; URL www.girlguiding.org.uk; e-mail chq@girlguiding.org.uk; Tel 020 7834 6242; Fax 020 7828 8317
Chief Executive Denise King

Girls' Brigade England and Wales

PO Box 196, 129 Broadway, Didcot, Oxfordshire OX11 8XN; URL www.girlsbrigadeew.org.uk; e-mail gbco@girlsbrigadeew.org.uk; Tel 01235 510425; Fax 01235 510429
National Director Ruth Gilson
Uniformed Christian youth organisation for girls

Girls Venture Corps Air Cadets

Phoenix Hse, 3 Handley Sq, Finningley Airport, Doncaster, South Yorkshire DN9 3GH; e-mail gvcachqi@btopenworld.com; Tel 01302 775019; Fax 01302 775020

Corps Director   Mrs B. Layne MBE

Uniformed organisation for girls aged 11–20. Opportunities for flying, skiing, outdoor pursuits. Aims to develop members into responsible citizens.

Hope UK

25f Copperfield St, London SE1 0EN; URL www.hopeuk.org; e-mail enquiries@hopeuk.org; Tel 020 7928 0848; Fax 020 7401 3477

Representative   George Ruston

Alcohol and drug awareness sessions provided by educators trained using an Open College Network (OCN) accredited course. OCN-accredited training for children, youth and family workers.

Inter-Action Special Enterprise Trust

HMS President (1918), nr Blackfriars Bridge, Victoria Embankment, London EC4Y 0HJ; Tel 020 7583 2652

Representative   Ed Berman

Jewish Lads' and Girls' Brigade (JLGB)

Registered Charity Number 286950

Camperdown, 3 Beechcroft Rd, South Woodford, London E18 1LA; URL www.jlgb.org; e-mail office@jlgb.org; Tel 020 8989 5743; Fax 020 8530 3332

Chair of Council   Charles Skay MBE

Learning South West

Bishops Hull Hse, Bishop's Hull, Taunton, Somerset TA1 5EP; URL www.learning-southwest.org.uk; e-mail tim_boyes_watson@learning-southwest.org.uk; Tel 01823 335491; Fax 01823 323388

Chief Executive   Tim Boyes-Watson

The Marine Society and Sea Cadets

202 Lambeth Rd, London SE1 7JW; URL www.ms-sc.org; e-mail info@ms-sc.org; Tel 020 7654 7000; Fax 020 7928 8914

Captain of the Sea Cadet Corps   Captain J.M.S. Fry Royal Navy

Chief Executive   Michael Cornish

The Marine Society and Sea Cadets was formed in November 2004 following the merger of The Marine Society (the UK's oldest nautical charity) and Sea Cadet Association (the UK's oldest nautical youth organisation). It has two operational arms dedicated to providing personal development opportunities and support in a maritime context. It provides education, library services and financial support to those who go to sea, promotes careers at sea and enhances the wellbeing of professional seafarers; it is responsible for the activities of the Sea Cadet Corps, providing young people aged 12–18 with nautical, life and citizenship skills.

MAYC – Supporting Youth Work in the Methodist Church

Methodist Church Hse, 25 Marylebone Rd, London NW1 5JR; URL www.mayc.info; e-mail info@mayc.info; Tel 020 7486 5502

National Secretary   Mike Seaton

National Council for Voluntary Youth Services (NCVYS)

2nd Fl, Solecast Hse, 13–27 Brunswick Pl, London N1 6DX; URL www.ncvys.org.uk; e-mail mail@ncvys.org.uk; Tel 020 7253 1010; Fax 020 7253 1012

Chief Executive   S. Rauprich

NCVYS is the independent voice of the voluntary sector in England. A diverse network of more than 160 national voluntary and community youth organisations and regional and local youth networks, NCVYS has been working since 1936 to raise the profile of youth work, share good practice and influence policy that has an impact on young people and the organisations that support them.

National Federation of 18 Plus Groups

Church St Chambers, 8–10 Church St, Newent, Gloucestershire GL18 1PP; e-mail office@18plus.org.uk; Tel 01531 821210

National Chair   Wayne Fenton

Administration Officer   Christine George

National Federation of Young Farmers' Clubs (NFYFC)

YFC Centre, Stoneleigh Pk, Kenilworth, Warwickshire CV8 2LG; e-mail post@nfyfc.org.uk; Tel 024 7685 7200; Fax 024 7685 7229

Operations Manager   James Eckley

The National Youth Agency

Eastgate Hse, 19–23 Humberstone Rd, Leicester LE5 3GJ; URL www.nya.org.uk; e-mail nya@nya.org.uk; Tel 0116 242 7350; Fax 0116 242 7393

Chief Executive   Fiona Blacke

The National Youth Agency aims to advance youth work to promote young people's personal and social development, and their voice, influence and place in society. Funded primarily by the Local Government Association and government departments it works to improve and extend youth services and youth work; enhance and demonstrate youth participation in society and to promote effective youth policy and provision. The NYA provides resources to improve work with young people and its management; creates and demonstrates innovation in service and methods; supports the leadership of organisations to deliver 'best value' and manage change; influences public perception and policy; and secures standards of education and training for youth work.

National Youth Theatre

443–445 Holloway Rd, London N7 6LW; e-mail info@nyt.org.uk; Tel 020 7281 3863

Contact   Sid Higgins

Outward Bound Trust

Hackthorpe Hall, Hackthorpe, Penrith, Cumbria CA10 2HX; Tel 0870 513 4227; Fax 01931 74000

Director (Sales and Marketing)   Lynn Petersen

CENTRES

Outward Bound Professional   Eskdale Grn, Holmrook, Cumbria CA19 1TE; Tel 019467 23281; Fax 019467 23393
General Manager   Alan Brenton

Outward Bound Ullswater   Watermillock, Penrith, Cumbria CA11 0JL; Tel 017684 85000; Fax 017684 86405
General Manager   Simon Waring

Outward Bound Scotland   Loch Eil Centre, Fort William, Highland PH33 7NN; Tel 013977 72866; Fax 013977 73905
General Manager   Tony Shepherd

Outward Bound Wales   Aberdovey Centre, Aberdovey, Gwynedd LL35 0RA; Tel 01654 767464; Fax 01654 767835
General Manager   Andy Jeffrey

The Prince's Trust

18 Park Sq East, London NW1 4LH; URL www.princes-trust.org.uk; e-mail info@princes-trust.org.uk; Tel (freephone) 0800 842842; Fax 020 7543 1200

President   HRH The Prince of Wales KG, KT, GC

Chief Executive   Martina Milburn

13

The Prince's Trust is a youth charity that helps young people to overcome barriers and get their lives working. Through practical support, including training, mentoring and financial assistance, the trust helps 14–30 year olds realise their potential and transform their lives; it focuses its efforts on those who have struggled at school, been in care, been in trouble with the law or are long-term unemployed.

Reform Synagogue Youth Netzer

The Sternberg Centre for Judaism, 80 East End Rd, London N3 2SY; URL www.rsy-netzer.org.uk; e-mail admin@rsy-netzer.org.uk; Tel 020 8349 5680; Fax 020 8349 5696

Religious Society of Friends (Quakers)

Children and Young People's Committee, Friends Hse, Euston Rd, London NW1 2BJ; URL www.quaker.org.uk; e-mail bevelies@quaker.org.uk; Tel 020 7663 1013
Representative   Howard Nurden

RSPB Wildlife Explorers

The Lodge, Sandy, Bedfordshire SG19 2DL; URL www.rspb.org/youth; e-mail rspb.org.uk; Tel 01767 680551; Fax 01767 292365
Youth Manager   Mark Boyd
Junion membership of Royal Society for Protection of Birds. The national club for young people interested in birds and wildlife conservation. Members receive magazines and take part in competitions, projects, local groups, holidays and award schemes. Schools affiliation available.

Salvation Army

101 Newington Causeway, London SE1 6BN; URL www.salvationarmy.org.uk; Tel 020 7367 4501; Fax 020 7364 4702

The Scout Association

Gilwell Pk, Chingford, London E4 7QW; URL www.scouts.org.uk; e-mail info.centre@scout.org.uk; Tel 020 8433 7100; Fax 020 8433 7103
Secretary   David J.C. Shelmerdine
Scouting promotes the development of young people in achieving their full physical, intellectual, social and spiritual potentials, as individuals, as responsible citizens and as members of their local, national and international communities

Scripture Union

207–209 Queensway, Bletchley, Milton Keynes, Buckinghamshire MK2 2EB; URL www.scriptureunion.org.uk; e-mail info@scriptureunion.org.uk; Tel 01908 856 1000; Fax 01908 856 1111
Chief Executive   K. Civval

Sea Ranger Association

10 Ellesmere Orchard, Westbourne, Emsworth, Hampshire PO10 8TR; e-mail d.s.cox@btinternet.com
Hon Secretary   Dorothy Cox

Trident

The Trident Trust, The Smokehouse, Smokehouse Yard, 44–46 St John St, London EC1M 4DF; URL www.thetridenttrust.org.uk; www.trident-transnational.org; e-mail trident@trid.demon.co.uk; Tel 020 7014 1400; Fax 020 7336 8561
Chief Executive   Paul Poulter
Trident, through its Skills for Life programme, provides a progression of personal challenge, community involvement and work experience. Key skills learning is recorded and certificated. Nationally, Trident supports more than 50 offices involving more than 160 000 students, in partnership with education, business and voluntary agencies.

UK Youth

Kirby Hse, 20–24 Kirby St, London EC1N 8TS; URL www.ukyouth.org; e-mail info@ukyouth.org; Tel 020 7242 4045; Fax 020 7242 4125
Chief Executive   John Bateman OBE
Supports and develops youth work and informal educational opportunities for all young people, thereby helping them to achieve their full potential and develop life skills to help them make a successful transition to adulthood.

United Reformed Church, Youth and Childrens Work Committee

Youth Office, United Reformed Church Hse, 86 Tavistock Pl, London WC1H 9RT; URL www.urc.org.uk; e-mail youth@urc.org.uk; Tel 020 7916 8682

Urban Saints

Kestin Hse, 45 Crescent Rd, Luton, Bedfordshire LU2 0AH; URL www.urbansaints.org; e-mail email@urbansaints.org; Tel 01582 589850; Fax 01582 721702
Executive Director   Matt Summerfield
Urban Saints works with children and young people who have no church connection, helping them to realise their potential

Woodcraft Folk

13 Ritherdon Rd, London SW17 8QE; URL www.woodcraft.org.uk; e-mail info@woodcraft.org.uk; Tel 020 8672 6031
General Secretary   Kirsty Palmer

YMCA England

640 Forest Rd, London E17 3DZ; URL www.ymca.org.uk; Tel 020 8520 5599; Fax 020 8509 3190
National Secretary   Angela Sarkis

Young Christian Workers

St Joseph's, off St Joseph's Gr, Hendon, London NW4 4TY; URL www.ycwimpact.com; e-mail info@ycwimpact.com; Tel 020 8203 6290; Fax 020 8203 6291
Representative   J.M. O'Brien

Young Explorers' Trust

Stretton Cottage, Wellow Rd, Ollerton, Newark, Nottinghamshire NG22 9AX; URL www.theyet.org; e-mail info@theyet.org; Tel 01623 861027
Hon General Secretary   N.E. Grey

Youth Hostels Association (YHA)

Trevelyan Hse, Dimple Rd, Matlock, Derbyshire DE4 3YH; URL www.yha.org.uk; www.learn4real.co.uk; e-mail groupreservations@yha.org.uk; Tel 0870 770 8868; Fax 0870 770 6127

YWCA England and Wales

Clarendon Hse, 52 Cornmarket St, Oxford, Oxfordshire OX1 3EJ; URL www.ywca.org.uk; e-mail info@ywca.org.uk; Tel 01865 304200
Chief Executive   Deborah Annetts
YWCA is the leading charity working with disadvantaged young women in England and Wales

Youthlink Scotland

Rosebery Hse, 9 Haymarket Terr, Edinburgh EH12 5EZ;
URL www.youthlink.co.uk; e-mail
info@youthlink.co.uk; Tel 0131 313 2488;
Fax 0131 313 6800
Chief Executive   Jim Sweeney MSc, DipYCS
YouthLink Scotland, the national youth work agency in
Scotland, supports the developmant of accessible youth
work services, which promote the wellbeing and
development of young people. This is achieved by being the
voice of the youth work sector; influencing policy affecting
the youth work sector and lives of young people; enabling
the sector to make best use of resources; being a source of
expert advice and information for youth work practitioners
and policy makers; facilitating innovative youth work
through research and development; and supporting
partnerships working across the youth work sector.

ORGANISATIONS IN MEMBERSHIP

Aberlour Child Care Trust   36 Park Terr, Stirling FK8 2JR;
e-mail kelly.bayes@aberlour.org.uk; Tel 01786 895024;
Fax 01786 473238
Head (Policy and Communication)   Kelly Bayes
Association of Chief Police Officers in Scotland (ACPOS)
Central Scotland Police, Police Office, Perth Rd,
Dunblane, Stirling FK15 0EY; e-mail
fiona.barker@centralscotland.police.uk; Tel 01786 826005
Inspector   Chief Inspector Fiona Barker
Barnardo's Scotland   235 Corstorphine Rd, Edinburgh
EH12 7AR; e-mail tam.baillie@barnardos.org.uk;
Tel 0131 334 9893; Fax 0131 316 4008
Assistant Director (Policy)   Mr Tam Baillie
Boys' and Girls' Clubs of Scotland   88 Giles St, Edinburgh
EH6 6BZ; e-mail bgcofscotland@line1.net;
Tel 0131 555 1729; Fax 0131 555 5921
Chief Adviser   Tom Leishman
The Boys' Brigade   Carronvale Hse, Carronvale Rd, Larbert,
Falkirk FK5 3LH; e-mail tom.boyle@boys-brigade.org.uk;
Tel 01324 562008; Fax 01324 552323
Director (Scotland)   Tom Boyle
British Red Cross Scotland   Bradbury Hse, Grangemouth
Rd, Falkirk FK2 9AA; e-mail mallan@redcross.org.uk;
Tel 01324 679065; Fax 01324 679076
Manager (Youth Development)   Mairi Allan
BTCV Scotland   Balallan Hse, 24 Allan Pk, Stirling FK8 2QG;
e-mail d.jamieson@btcv.org.uk; Tel 01786 479697;
Fax 01786 465359
Director (Scotland)   David Jamieson
Campaigners Scotland   36 Auld Kirk Rd, Tullibody,
Clackmannanshire FK10 2TG; e-mail
marketing@campaigners.org.uk; Tel 01259 212866;
Fax 01480 405550
Executive Development Officer   Mark Smith
Careers Scotland   150 Broomielaw, Atlantic Quay, Glasgow
G2 8LU; e-mail
julie-anne.jamieson@careers-scotland.org.uk;
Tel 0141 228 2362; Fax 0141 228 2851
Head (Inclusion and Employability)   Julie-Ann Jamieson
Catholic Youth Council (Glasgow)   196 Clyde St, Glasgow
G1 4JY; Tel 0141 226 5898; Fax 0141 225 2600
Youth Officer   Chris Docherty
Catholic Youth Council Scotland   Diocesan Youth Service,
Gillis College, 113 Whitehouse Loan, Edinburgh
EH9 1BB; Tel 0131 452 8247; Fax 0131 452 9153
Community Education Worker   Rhona Kennedy
Children 1st   83 Whitehouse Loan, Edinburgh EH9 1AT;
e-mail neil.mathers@children1st.org.uk;
Tel 0131 446 2300; Fax 0131 446 2339
Services Manager   Neil Mathers
Chinese Community Development Project   Napiershall St
Centre, 39 Napiershall St, Glasgow G20 6EZ; e-mail
cydt@gisp.net; Tel 0141 341 0026; Fax 0141 341 0020
Contact   Gar-Ming Hui

Church of Scotland   Board of Parish Education, 121 George
St, Edinburgh EH2 4YN; e-mail
smallon@cofscotland.org.uk; Tel 0131 225 5722
Adviser (National Youth and Young People)   Steve Mallon
Clubs for Young People (Scotland)   88 Giles St, Edinburgh
EH6 6BZ; e-mail secretary@cypscotland.co.uk;
Tel 0131 555 1729; Fax 0131 555 5921
Chief Officer   Tom Leishman
Commonwealth Youth Exchange Council   30 Wyvis Cres,
Conon Bridge, Dingwall, Highland IV7 8BX; e-mail
cyecscotland@btinternet.com; Tel 01349 861110;
Fax 01349 861110
Development Officer (Scotland)   Jim Morrison
CSV Scotland   Wellgate Hse, 200 Cowgate, Edinburgh
EH1 1NQ; e-mail cstevens@csv.org.uk; Tel 0131 622 7766;
Fax 0131 622 7755
Director   Claire Stevens
Duke of Edinburgh's Award   69 Dublin St, Edinburgh
EH3 6NS; e-mail janet.shepherd@theaward.org;
Tel 0131 556 9097
Secretary for Scotland   Janet Shepherd
Fairbridge In Scotland   Norton Pk, 57 Albion Rd, Edinburgh
EH7 5QY; e-mail twatson@fairbridgescot.org.uk;
Tel 0131 475 2303; Fax 0131 475 2312
Director   Tom Watson
Fast Forward   4 Bernard St, Leith, Edinburgh EH6 6PP;
e-mail alastair@fastforward.org.uk; Tel 0131 554 4300;
Fax 0131 554 4330
Director   Alastair MacKinnon
Forces and Cadets Association   Lowland Reserve, 60
Avenuepark St, Glasgow G20 8LW; e-mail
lo-cedep@lo.rfca.mod.uk; Tel 0141 945 4951;
Fax 0141 945 4869
Deputy Secretary   Major John Menzies
Girlguiding Scotland   16 Coates Cres, Edinburgh EH3 7AH;
e-mail sally@girlguiding-scot.org.uk; Tel 0131 226 4511;
Fax 0131 220 4828
Executive Director   Sally Pitches
Glasgow Anti Racist Alliance (GARA)   30 Bell St, Glasgow
G1 1LG; e-mail jatin@gara.org.uk; Tel 0141 572 1140;
Fax 0141 572 1141
Manager (Partnership)   Mr Jatin Haria
Iona Community   Rm MG10, The Scottish Parliament,
Edinburgh EH99 1SP; e-mail
peter.mccoll@scottish.parliament.uk; Tel 0131 348 6419
Contact   Peter McColl
LGBT Youth Scotland   John Cotton Centre, 10 Sunnyside,
Edinburgh EH7 5RA; e-mail jamie@lgbtyouth.org.uk;
Tel 0131 622 2266; Fax 0131 622 2266
Chief Executive   Mr Jamie Rennie
MAYC   Scottish Churches' Hse, Kirk St, Dunblane, Stirling
FK15 0AJ; e-mail closcotland@methodist.plus.com;
Tel 01786 820295; Fax 01786 820295
Connexional Liaison Officer (Scotland)   Dr William Reid
NHS Scotland   Woodburn Hse, Canaan La, Edinburgh
EH10 4SG; e-mail gary.wilson@health.scot.nhs.uk;
Tel 0131 536 5500; Fax 0131 536 5501
Manager (Programme: Young People)   Gary Wilson
Ocean Youth Trust Scotland   191 West George St, Glasgow
G2 2LJ; e-mail nick@oytscotland.org.uk;
Tel 0141 221 1200; Fax 0141 221 2002
General Manager   Nick Flemming
Penumbra   Norton Pk, 57 Albion Rd, Edinburgh EH7 5QY;
e-mail patrick.little@penumbra.org.uk;
Tel 0131 475 2380; Fax 0131 475 2391
Manager (Scottish Development)   Patrick Little
PHAB Scotland   5a Warriston Rd, Edinburgh EH3 5LQ;
URL www.phab.org.uk; e-mail info@phab.org.uk;
Tel 0131 558 9912; Fax 0131 558 9913
Chief Executive   Fiona Hird
Prince's Trust Scotland   1st Fl, The Guildhall, 57 Queen St,
Glasgow G1 3EN; e-mail
geraldine.gammell@princes-trust.org.uk;
Tel 0141 204 4409; Fax 0141 221 8221
Director   Geraldine Gammell

13

ProjectScotland 49 Melville St, Edinburgh EH3 7HL; e-mail kate.mavor@projectsotland.co.uk; Tel 0131 226 0700; Fax 0131 226 0770
Chief Executive Kate Mavor

RNID Scotland Dunedin Hse, 2nd Fl, 24 Ravelston Terr, Edinburgh EH4 3TP; e-mail michelle.donoghue@rnid.org.uk; Tel 0131 311 8522
Manager (Youth Programme) Michelle Donoghue

RSPB Scotland Dunedin Hse, Scottish Headquarters, 25 Ravelston Terr, Edinburgh EH4 3TP; e-mail jean.burns@rspb.org.uk; Tel 0131 311 6500; Fax 0131 331 6569
Manager (Public Affairs) Jean Burns

Save the Children Prospect Hse, 2nd Fl, 5 Thistle St, Edinburgh EH2 1DF; e-mail s.fisher@scfuk.org.uk; Tel 0131 527 8200; Fax 0131 527 8201
Assistant Director (Programme) Sue Fisher

Scotland Girls' Brigade 11a Woodside Cres, Glasgow G3 7UL; e-mail national.director@girls-brigade-scotland.org.uk; Tel 0141 332 1765; Fax 0141 331 2681
National Director Caroline Goodfellow

Scottish Association of Young Farmers' Clubs Young Farmers' Centre, Ingliston, Edinburgh EH28 8NE; e-mail natsec@saytc.org; Tel 0131 333 2445; Fax 0131 333 2488
National Secretary Fiona Bain

Scottish Centres Loaningdale Hse, Carwood Rd, Biggar, South Lanarkshire ML12 6LX; Tel 01899 221115; Fax 01899 220644
Chief Executive David Spence

Scottish Community Fire Safety Forum SFR Headquarters, Bothwell St, Hamilton, South Lanarkshire ML3 0EA; e-mail macintosha@strathclydefire.org; Tel 01698 300999; Fax 01698 338257
Strategic Youth Development Officer Alistair MacIntosh

Scottish Crusaders Challenge Hse, 29 Canal St, Glasgow G4 0AD; e-mail rrawson@scottishcrusaders.org.uk; Tel 0141 331 2400; Fax 0141 331 2400
Director Rob Rawson

Scottish Wildlife Trust Cramond Hse, Kirk Craymond, Cramond Glebe Rd, Edinburgh EH4 6NS; e-mail ecochrane@swt.org.uk; Tel 0131 312 4770; Fax 0131 312 8705
Members Centre and Watch Officer Emma Cochrane

Scottish Youth Football Association (SYFA) Hampden Pk, Glasgow G42 9BF; e-mail nationalsecretary@scottish-football.com; Tel 0141 620 4590; Fax 0141 620 4591
National Secretary David Little

Scottish Youth Parliament Rosebery Hse, 9 Haymarket Terr, Edinburgh EH12 5EZ; e-mail kelly.c@scottishyouthparliament.org.uk; Tel 0131 313 2488; Fax 0131 313 6800
General Manager Kelly Chambers

Scout Association Fordell Firs, Hillend, Dunfermline, Fife KY11 7HQ; e-mail jimduffy@scouts-scotland.org.uk; Tel 01383 419073; Fax 01383 414892
Chief Executive Jim Duffy

Scripture Union Scotland 70 Milton St, Glasgow G4 0HR; e-mail andy@suscotland.org.uk; Tel 0141 352 7607; Fax 0141 352 7600
Chief Executive Andy Bathgate

Sea Cadets HMS Caledonia, Rosyth, Fife KY11 2XH; e-mail sreeve@ms-sc.org; Tel 01383 425109; Fax 01383 425106
Director (Business and Management: North) Syd Reeve

SSC 88 Giles St, Edinburgh EH6 6BZ; e-mail breive@thessc.com; Tel 0131 555 6123; Fax 0131 555 6345
Youth Development Worker Steven Hughes

Support Training Action Group c/o Enable Scotland, 6th Fl, 7 Buchanan St, Glasgow G1 3HL; e-mail elaine.darling@enable.org.uk; Tel 0141 225 1615; Fax 0141 204 4398
Chair Elaine Darling

University of Strathclyde Community Education Division, 76 Southbrae Dr, Glasgow G13 1PP; e-mail annette.coburn@strath.ac.uk; Tel 0141 950 3374; Tel 0141 950 3602

Lecturer (Department of Educational and Professional Studies) Annette Coburn

Venture Scotland Norton Pk, 57 Albion Rd, Edinburgh EH7 5QY; e-mail sarah@venturescotland.org.uk; Tel 0131 475 2395; Fax 0131 475 2396
Director Jane Bruce

Volunteer Development Scotland Stirling Enterprise Pk, Stirling FK7 7RP; e-mail morven.brooks@vds.org.uk; Tel 01786 479593; Fax 01786 449285
Information and Internal Communications Officer Ms Morven Brooks

Who Cares? Scotland Oswald Chambers, 5 Oswald St, Glasgow G1 4QR; e-mail d.watson@whocaresscotland.org; Tel 0141 226 4441; Fax 0141 226 4445
Director Deirdre Watson

Woodcraft Folk 87 Bath St, Glasgow G2 2EE; Tel 0141 304 5552; Fax 0141 304 5554
Scottish Officer Fleur Gayet

Young Scot Rosebery Hse, 9 Haymarket Terr, Edinburgh EH12 5EZ; e-mail sarahjt@youngscot.org; Tel 0131 313 2488; Fax 0131 313 6800
Office Manager Sarah-Jane Turnbull

Youth Link Ayrshire 12 Craignaw Pl, Irvine, North Ayrshire KA11 1EZ; e-mail youth.link@ic24.net; Tel 01294 214178
Contact Tom Bark

Youth Scotland Balfour Hse, 19 Bonnington Gr, Edinburgh EH6 4BL; e-mail carol@youthscotland.org.uk; Tel 0131 554 2561; Fax 0131 555 5223
Chief Executive Carol Downie

YWCA Scotland 7b Randolph Cres, Edinburgh EH3 7TH; e-mail elaine@ymcascotland.org; Tel 0131 225 7592; Fax 0131 225 7592
11 Rutland St, Edinburgh EH1 2AE; e-mail peter@ymcascotland.org; Tel 0131 228 1464; Fax 0131 228 5462
Chief Executive Elaine Samson
National General Secretary Peter Crory

YouthNet

The Voluntary Youth Network for Northern Ireland
5th Fl, Premier Business Centre, Belfast BT2 8GD; URL www.youthnetni.org.uk; e-mail info@youthnet.co.uk; Tel 028 9033 1880; Fax 028 9033 1977
Communications Officer Linda Gordon
The Voluntary Youth Network for Northern Ireland has in membership the major voluntary youth work agencies in the province. Its role is that of an umbrella pressure group, working to provide a platform for the voluntary sector, representing the interests of its member organisations and acting on their behalf on issues of common concern.

MEMBERS

Action Mental Health – VOTE Project Mourne Hse, Knockbracken Healthcare Pk, Saintfield Rd, Belfast BT8 8BH; URL www.actionmentalhealth.org.uk; Tel 028 9040 3726

Army Cadet Force Association 35 Manse Rd, Carryduff, Belfast, County Down BT8 8DA; URL www.armycadets.com

Baptist Youth 117 Lisburn Rd, Belfast BT9 7AF; URL www.baptistyouth.org

Belfast Community Circus School 23–25 Gordon St, Belfast BT1 2LG; URL www.belfastcircus.org; Tel 028 9023 6007; Fax 028 9043 4971

Boys' Brigade Rathmore Hse, 126 Glenarm Rd, Larne, County Antrim BT40 1DZ; URL www.boys-brigade.org.uk

British Red Cross – Youth and Schools 87 University St, Belfast BT7 1HP; URL www.redcross.org.uk; Tel 028 9024 6400; Fax 028 9032 6102
First aid and humanitarian education training for young people.

Brook, Belfast 29a North St, Belfast BT1 1NA; URL www.brook.org.uk; e-mail belfast.brook@talk21.com; Tel 028 9032 8866; Fax 028 9023 5735

The Bytes Project Unit 5, The Filor Bldg, Twin Spires Complex, 155 Northumberland St, Belfast BT13 2JF; URL www.bytesproject.org; e-mail admin@bytes.org; Tel 028 9028 8810

CATHOG 68 Berry St, Belfast BT1 1FJ

Catholic Guides of Ireland 285 Antrim Rd, Belfast BT15 2GZ; URL www.girlguidesireland.ie; e-mail admin.nr@catholicguides.org.uk; Tel 028 9074 0835; Fax 028 9074 1311

Centre for Global Education 9 University St, Belfast BT7 1FY; URL www.centreforglobaleducation.com; e-mail info@centreforglobaleducation.com; Tel 028 9024 1879; Fax 028 9024 4120

Challenge for Youth 2nd Fl, Donegall Hse, 98–102 Donegall St, Belfast BT1 2LP; URL www.challengeforyouth.org; Tel 028 9023 6893

Children's Law Centre 3rd Fl, Phillip Hse, 123–137 York St, Belfast BT15 1AB; URL www.childrenslawcentre.org; e-mail info@childrenslawcentre.org; Tel 028 9024 5704; Fax 028 9024 5679

Chinese Welfare Association 133–135 University St, Belfast BT7 1HQ; URL www.cwa-ni.org; e-mail contact@cwa-ni.org; Tel 028 9028 8277; Fax 028 9028 8278

Church of Ireland Youth Council 7 Elmwood Ave, Belfast BT9 6AZ; URL www.ciyd.org; e-mail admin@ciyd.org; Tel 028 9066 0052; Fax 028 9066 0053

Cinemagic 49 Botanic Ave, Belfast BT7 1JL; URL www.cinemagic.org.uk; e-mail info@cinemagic.org.uk; Tel 028 9031 1900; Fax 028 9031 9709

Clubs for Young People NI Ground Fl, 22 Stockman's Way, Musgrave Pk Industrial Est, Belfast BT9 7JU; URL www.cypni.net; e-mail post@cypni.net; Tel 028 9066 3321; Fax 028 9066 3306

Contact Youth Counselling Service 2a Ribble St, Belfast BT4 1HW

Co-operation Ireland 2nd Fl, Glendinning Hse, 6 Murray St, Belfast BT1 6DN; URL www.cooperationireland.org; e-mail info@cooperationireland.org; Tel 028 9032 1462; Fax 028 9089 1000

Corrymeela Community 8 Upper Cres, Belfast BT7 1NT; URL www.corrymeela.org; e-mail belfast@corrymeela.org; Tel 028 9050 8080

Department of Youth and Childrens Work – Methodist Church Aldersgate Hse, University Rd, Belfast BT7 1NA; URL www.irishmethodist.org/dycw; e-mail online@irishmethodist.org; Tel 028 9032 7191; Fax 028 9024 1322

Disability Action Portside Business Pk, 189 Airport Rd West, Belfast BT3 9ED; URL www.disabilityaction.org; e-mail hq@disabilityaction.org; Tel 028 9029 7880; Fax 028 9029 7881

Down's Syndrome Association Knockbracken Healthcare Pk, Saintfield Rd, Belfast BT8 8BH; URL www.downs-syndrome.org.uk; Tel 028 9070 4606; Fax 028 9070 4075

Duke of Edinburgh Award Scheme 28 Wellington Pk, Belfast BT9 6DL; URL www.theaward.org/northernireland; e-mail nirleand@theaward.org; Tel 028 9050 9550; Fax 028 9050 9555

The Extern Organisation Hydepark Hse, 54 Mallusk Rd, Newtownabbey BT36 4WU; URL www.extern.org; e-mail info@extern.org; Tel 028 9084 0555; Fax 028 9084 7333

Girls' Brigade 16 May St, Belfast BT1 4NL; URL www.gbni.co.uk; e-mail info@gbni.co.uk; Tel 028 9023 1157; Fax 028 9032 3633

Girls' Friendly Society 36 Upper Leeson St, Dublin 4, Republic of Ireland; URL www.gfs.ie; e-mail office@girlsfriendlysociety.ie; Tel +353 1 660 3754; Fax +353 1 660 3754

GLYNI 64 Donegall St, Belfast BT1 1SH; URL www.glyni.org.uk; e-mail mail@glyni.org.uk; Tel 020 9027 8636

The Guide Association (Province of Ulster) Lorne Hse, Station Rd, Holywood, Craigavad, County Down BT18 0BP; URL www.girlguidingulster.org.uk; e-mail info@girlguidingulster.org.uk; Tel 028 9042 5212; Fax 028 9042 6025

Harmony Community Trust Glebe Hse, Downpatrick, County Down BT30 7NZ

Hope UK (NI) Ebrington Manse, 19 Clearwater Caw, Londonderry, County Londonderry BT47 1BE; URL www.hopeuk.org

Hostelling International NI 22–32 Donegall Rd, Belfast BT12 5JN; URL www.hini.org.uk; e-mail info@hini.org.uk; Tel 028 9032 4733; Fax 028 9031 5889
General Secretary K. Canavan

International Voluntary Service 34 Shaftesbury Sq, Belfast BT2 7DB; URL www.ivsni.org.uk; e-mail info@ivsni.org; Tel 028 9023 8147; Fax 028 9024 4356

Mencap Segal Hse, 4 Annadale Ave, Belfast BT7 3JH; URL www.mencap.org; e-mail mencaph@mencap.org.uk; Tel 028 9069 1351; Fax 028 9064 0121

Multicultural Resource Centre 9 Lower Cres, Belfast BT7 1NR; URL www.mcrc-ni.org; Tel 028 9024 4639; Fax 028 9032 9581

National Council of YMCAs Memorial Hse, Waring St, Belfast BT1 2EU; URL www.ymca-ireland.org

NICHS 547 Antrim Rd, Belfast BT15 3BU; URL www.nichs.org; e-mail info@nichs.org; Tel 028 9037 0373; Fax 028 9078 1161

Northern Ireland Children's Holiday Scheme 547 Antrim Rd, Belfast BT15 3B4

Northern Ireland Council for Ethnic Minorities 3rd Fl, Ascot Hse, 24–31 Shaftesbury Sq, Belfast BT2 7DB; URL www.nicem.org.uk; e-mail info@nicem.org.uk; Tel 028 9023 8645; Fax 028 9031 9485

Northern Ireland Deaf Youth Association Wilton Hse, 5 College Sq North, Belfast BT1 6AR; URL www.nidya.org.uk; Tel 028 9043 8566; Fax 028 9043 8566

Northern Ireland Forces Youth Service Education and Training Services Branch, HQ Northern Ireland

Northern Ireland Scout Council 109 Old Mill Town Rd, Belfast BT8 4SP; URL www.scoutsni.com; e-mail info@scoutsni.com; Tel 028 9049 2829; Fax 028 9049 2830

Northern Ireland Women's Aid Federation – Young Person's Development Project 129 University St, Belfast BT7 1HP; URL www.womensaidni.org; e-mail info@womensaidni.org; Tel 028 9024 9041; Fax 028 9023 9296

Order of Malta Ambulance Corps St John's Hse, Sloan St, Dungannon, County Tyrone

Peace People 224 Lisburn Rd, Belfast BT9 66E

PHAB (NI) PO Box 780, Belfast BT15 3YG; URL www.inclusionmatters.org; Tel 028 9074 6555; Fax 028 9074 6444

Playboard 59–65 York St, Belfast BT15 1AA; URL www.playboard.org; e-mail info@playboard.org; Tel 028 9080 3380; Fax 028 9080 3381

Presbyterian Board of Youth and Children's Ministry Church Hse, Fisherwick Pl, Belfast BT1 6DW; URL www.pciyouth.org; Tel 028 9032 2284

Prince's Youth Business Trust Block 5, Jennymount Ct, North Derby St, Belfast BT15 3HN; URL www.princes-trust.org.uk; e-mail webinfoni@princes-trust.org.uk; Tel 028 9074 5454; Fax 028 9074 8416

The Rainbow Project 2–8 Commercial Ct, Belfast BT1 2NB; URL www.rainbow-project.org; e-mail manager@rainbow-project.org; Tel 028 9031 9030; Fax 028 9031 9031

St John Ambulance Brigade ERNE, Purdysburn Hospital, Belfast BT8 8RA; URL www.sja.org.uk; e-mail districthq@ni.sja.org.uk

13

Scout Foundation Northern Ireland Unit 12a Lisburn Enterprise Centre, Lisburn, County Antrim; URL www.scouts.ie; Tel 028 9266 7696; Fax 028 9266 7696

Share Centre Smith's Strand, Lisnaskea, County Fermanagh BT92 0EQ; URL www.sharevillage.org; e-mail info@sharevillage.org; Tel 028 6772 2122; Fax 028 6772 1893

The Spirit of Enniskillen Trust 97 Malone Ave, Belfast BT9 6EQ; URL www.soetrust.co.uk; e-mail info@soetrust.co.uk; Tel 028 9038 1500; Fax 028 9038 1500

St Columb's Park House 4 Limavady Rd, Londonderry, County Londonderry BT47 6JY; URL www.stcolumbsparkhouse.org; e-mail brian@stcolumbsparkhouse.org; Tel 028 7134 3080; Fax 028 7134 3443

Voice of Young People in Care 9–11 Botanic Ave, Belfast BT7 1JG; Tel 028 9024 4888

VS B – Young Citizens in Action The Centre for Citizenship, 34 Shaftesbury Sq, Belfast BT2 7DB; URL www.vsb.org.uk; e-mail info@vsb.org.uk; Tel 028 9020 0850; Fax 028 9020 0860

Young Farmers' Club of Ulster 475 Antrim Rd, Belfast BT15 3BD; URL www.yfcu.org; e-mail info@yfcu.org; Tel 028 9037 0713; Fax 028 9077 7946

Youth Action Northern Ireland Hampton, Glenmachan Pk, Belfast BT4 2PJ; URL www.youthaction.org; e-mail info@youthaction.org; Tel 028 9076 0067; Fax 028 9076 8799

Youth Com 68 Berry St, Belfast BT1 1FJ; URL www.youthcom.org; e-mail info@youthcom.org; Tel 028 9023 2432; Fax 028 9023 9598

Youth Initiatives 128b Lisburn Rd, Belfast BT9 6AH; URL www.youthinitiatives.com

Youth Link 143a University St, Belfast BT7 1HP; URL www.youthlink.org.uk; e-mail info@youthlink.org.uk; Tel 028 9032 3217; Fax 028 9032 3247

AFFILIATE MEMBERS

Belfast Education and Library Board; North Eastern Education and Library Board; South Eastern Education and Library Board; Southern Education and Library Board; Western Education and Library Board; Probation Board for Northern Ireland; PSNI Community Affairs; NUS/USI; NSPCC

Local Councils for Voluntary Youth Services

0-25 Network
14 Castle St, Liverpool, Merseyside L2 0NJ; e-mail ellen.hawkins@liverpoolcss.org; Tel 0151 236 7728
Facilitator Ellen Hawkins

Avon Council Scouts
Avon County Scout Council, Woodhouse Pk, Fernhill, Almondsbury, South Gloucestershire BS32 4LX; URL www.avonscouts.org.uk; e-mail office@avonscouts.org.uk; Tel 01454 613006
County Secretary P. Hanna

Bailiwick of Guernsey Youth Association
c/o Youth Office, Brock Rd, St Peter Port, Guernsey GY1 1RU, Channel Islands; e-mail davel@gcfe.net; Tel 01481 715363; Fax 01481 715379
Secretary David Le Feuvre

Berkshire Council for Voluntary Youth Services
452 Basingstoke Rd, Reading RG2 0QE; e-mail admin@bacyp.co.uk; Tel 0118 923 1267; Fax 0118 923 1226
Secretary Ray Tapken

Cambridgeshire and Peterborough Council for Voluntary Youth Services
20 St Benedicts Ct, Huntingdon, Cambridgeshire PE29 3PN; URL www.ccvys.org.uk; e-mail admin@ccvys.org.uk; Tel 01480 375638
Administrator Heather Laing

Coventry Council for Voluntary Youth Services
67 Momus Bvd, Coventry, Warwickshire CV1 5NA; Tel 024 7645 5749
Representative Kamla Granger

Croydon Voluntary Youth Sector (CVYS)
Bensham Manor School, Ecclesbourne Rd, Thornton Heath, Surrey CR7 7BN; e-mail patriciacreighton@tiscali.co.uk; Tel 020 8684 7060; Fax 020 8684 7060
Chair Patricia Creighton

Derbyshire Council for Voluntary Youth Services
65 Matthew St, Alvaston, Derby DE24 0ES

Devon Voluntary Youth Services
YFC Centre, Retail Park Cl, Marsh Barton Rd, Exeter, Devon EX2 8LG; URL www.vysdevon.org.uk; e-mail admin@vysdevon.org.uk; Tel 01392 250976; Fax 01392 250976
Manager Mark Goodman

Dorset Youth Partnership
Diocesan Education Office, Audley Hse, Salisbury, Wiltshire SP1 2PU; Tel 01722 411977
Chair Tony Nye

Essex Council for Voluntary Youth Services
46 High St, Great Dunmow, Essex CM6 1AN; URL www.ecvys.org.uk; e-mail brenda@ecvys.org.uk; Tel 01371 874273
Executive Officer B. Towle

Gateshead Borough Youth Organisation Council
12 Gladstone Terr, Gateshead, Tyne and Wear NE8 4DY; URL www.gbyoc.org.uk; e-mail info@gbyoc.org.uk; Tel 0191 490 1900
Co-ordinator Terry Eccles

Gloucestershire Council for Voluntary Youth Services (GCVYS)
Gloucestershire Youth and Community Service, Chequers Bridge Centre, Painswick Rd, Gloucester, Gloucestershire GL4 6PR; Tel 01452 425416
c/o Gloucestershire Youth and Community Service, Chequers Bridge Centre, Gloucester, Gloucestershire GL4 6PR
Chair Mike Counsell; 74 Sandy La, Charlton Kings, Cheltenham, Gloucestershire GL53 9DH
Administration Officer K. Tilling

Hereford and Worcester Council of Voluntary Youth Services
49 Brookside Cl, Shifnal, Shropshire TF11 8HN; Tel 01952 460364
Representative Martin Lambourne

Hull Council for Voluntary Youth Services
15 Park Ave, Kingston upon Hull, East Riding of Yorkshire HU5 3EN; Tel 01482 446095
Representative Eleanor Griffiths

Kent Council for Voluntary Youth Services
The Youth Hse, Upbury Manor, Marlborough Rd, Gillingham, Kent ME7 5HR; e-mail kcvys@hotmail.com; Tel 01634 579833; Fax 01634 338750
Executive Officer B. Clout

Knowsley Council for Voluntary Service
Nutgrove Villa, 1 Griffiths Rd, Huyton, Liverpool, Merseyside L36 6NA; URL www.knowsleycvs.org.uk; e-mail f.villanova@knowsleycvs.org; Tel 0151 489 1222; Fax 0151 443 0251
Representative Fiona Villanova

Leicestershire Council for Voluntary Youth Services

The Fosse Centre, Mantle Rd, Leicester LE3 5HG; e-mail info@leicestershirecvys.org.uk; Tel 0116 222 1896; Fax 0116 222 1897

Lincolnshire Council for Voluntary Youth Services

3 Christopher Cl, Heckington, Sleaford, Lincolnshire NG34 9SA; Tel 01529 60670

Hon Secretary   Capt N. Thomson

Norfolk Council for Voluntary Youth Services (Norfolk CVYS)

Youth Work Development Unit, School La, Sprowston, Norwich, Norfolk NR7 8TR; URL norfolkcvys.org.uk; e-mail info@norfolkcvys.org.uk; Tel 01603 423995; Fax 01603 416079

Chair   Richard Draper

Administrator   Julie Eldred

Northumberland Federation of Young Farmers Clubs

YFC Office, Kirkley Hall College, Ponteland, Northumberland NE20 0AQ; e-mail countyoffice@northumberlandfc.co.uk; Tel 01661 872562; Fax 01661 872562

Representative   Sally A. Milner

Oxfordshire Children and Voluntary Youth Services

Macclesfield Hse, New Rd, Oxford, Oxfordshire OX1 1NA; URL www.ocvys.org; e-mail ocvys@oxfordshire.gov.uk; Tel 01865 810650; Fax 01865 810656

Manager   Colette Selwood

The Prince's Trust, Milton Keynes, Oxfordshire and Buckinghamshire

c/o Glaxo Smith Kline, 11 Stoke Poges La, Slough, Berkshire SL1 3NW; e-mail offseslo@princes-trust.org.uk; Tel 01753 502234; Fax 01753 502109

Area Manager   Calvin Silvester

Staffordshire Council of Voluntary Youth Services

c/o YFC Centre, County Showground, Weston Rd, Stafford, Staffordshire ST18 0BD; e-mail barry.halls@staffordshire.gov.uk; Tel 01785 240378

Sussex Youth Ltd

Tim Jones Hse, Rochester Gdns, Hove, East Sussex BN3 3AW; e-mail sussex.youthclubs.uk@ukonline.co.uk; Tel 01273 821789; Fax 01273 734621

Chief Executive   R. Graham Gordon

Wiltshire Council for Voluntary Youth Services

Wiltshire Youth Service Council, 34 Luxfield Rd, Warminster, Wiltshire BA12 8HN; Tel 01985 217992

Representative   C. Rowberry

Wirral Council for Voluntary Youth Services

c/o Shaftesbury Youth Club, Mendip Rd, Birkenhead, Merseyside LA2 8NU; URL www.shaftsburyyouthclub.org.uk; e-mail pnugent@onetel.com; Tel 0151 608 7165

Representative   P. Nugent

YMCA Cornwall

International Hse, Alverton Rd, Penzance, Cornwall TR18 4TE; URL www.cornwall.ymca.org.uk; e-mail admin@cornwall.ymca.org.uk; Tel 01736 365016

Chief Executive   Emma Lesaux

Young Suffolk (The Independent Voice of the Voluntary Children and Young People's Sector)

Rm 9, Castle Hill Community Centre, Highfield Rd, Ipswich, Suffolk IP1 6DG; URL www.youngsuffolk.com; e-mail youngsuffolk@suffolkonline.net; Tel 01473 744187

Chief Executive   Dr Bud Simpkin

Youth Focus (Buckinghamshire Council for Voluntary Youth Services)

Green Pk, Aylesbury, Buckinghamshire HP22 5NE; URL www.youthfocus.org.uk; e-mail office@youthfocus.org.uk; Tel 01296 631911

13

Educational Visits, Travel and Services

14

Administrative and Co-ordinating Bodies

National Travel Organisations

Exchange Visits and School Travel

Recreational and Residential Courses

Voluntary Service and Working Holidays (Home and Abroad)

Educational Visits, Travel and Services

Association of Independent Museums

President Sir Neil Cossons OBE; English Heritage, 23 Savile Row, London W1S 2ET

Chair Bill Ferris; The Old Surgery, Chatham Historic Dockyard, Chatham, Kent ME4 4TZ

Hon Secretary Matthew Tanner; SS Great Britain, Gt Western Dock Yard, Bristol BS1 6TY; e-mail matthewt@ss-great-britain.com; Tel 0117 926 0680; Fax 0117 925 5788

Editor Diana Zeuner; Lindford Cottage, Church La, Cocking, Midhurst, West Sussex GU29 0HW; e-mail heavyhorse@mistral.co.uk; Tel 01730 812419; Fax 01730 812419

Membership Secretary Michael Cope; Vintage Carriages Trust, 30 Gledhow Dr, Oxenhope, Keighley, West Yorkshire BD22 9SA; e-mail michael@mwdjcope.demon.co.uk; Tel 01535 646472

Cadw

Plas Carew, Unit 5–7 Cefn Coed, Parc Nantgarw, Cardiff CF15 7QQ; URL www.cadw.wales.gov.uk; e-mail cadw@wales.gsi.gov.uk; Tel 01443 336006; Fax 01443 336001

Carries out the statutory responsibilities of the Welsh Assembly Government for protecting and conserving monuments and historic buildings in Wales. These range from prehistoric tombs to Victorian blast furnaces and include most of the castles and abbeys in Wales. In order that teachers and lecturers may make full use of these monuments to inform and educate their pupils, parties of school children and students in full-time education receive free entry to those properties where an admission charge is levied. To take advantage of these arrangements, an application form, obtainable from the above address and website, should be completed and returned. Details of Cadw's education packs and videos are contained in the catalogue of publications obtainable from the same address.

Council for National Parks

6–7 Barnard Mews, London SW11 1QU; URL www.cnp.org.uk; e-mail info@cnp.org.uk; Tel 020 7924 4077; Fax 020 7924 5761

President Ben Fogle

Chair Kate Ashbrook

Chief Executive Kathy Moore

The council aims to uphold and promote the twin purposes (conservation and recreation) of national park designation, by representing these interests nationally and through educational and visitor information. Public membership scheme and speaker service.

English Heritage

Education, 1 Waterhouse Sq, 138–142 Holburn, London EC1N 2ST; e-mail education@english-heritage.org.uk; Tel 020 7973 3384; Fax 020 7973 3443

The official body in England responsible for conserving the historic features of the built environment, English Heritage produces a wide range of educational material, including publications and videos, and offers a professional service for teachers and those working in the heritage education field

Historic Houses Association

2 Chester St, London SW1X 7BB; URL www.hha.org.uk; e-mail info@hha.org.uk; Tel 020 7259 5688; Fax 020 7259 5590

President James Hervey-Bathurst

Director General Nick Way

Association of privately-owned historic houses. Many of those open to the public offer educational facilities. In 2006 the association launched a learning advisory service to develop new educational initiatives.

Historic Royal Palaces

Hampton Court Palace, Surrey KT8 9AU; URL www.hrp.org.uk; e-mail education.info@hrp.org.uk; Tel 0870 751 5190

Education Manager Susie Batchelor

The education manager is responsible for educational provision at Hampton Court Palace, the Tower of London, Kensington Palace, Kew Palace and the Banqueting House, Whitehall.

A range of curriculum related teachers' materials is available, and teachers' courses, study days and on-site tuition (storytelling, artefact handling and costumed interpretation) are run at Hampton Court and, in partnership with the Royal Armouries, at the Tower of London.

Special schools rate charge applies September to the end of May for pre-booked education groups (September to April at the tower).

National Trust

Registered Charity Number 205846

Rowan, Kembrey Pk, Swindon SN2 8YL; URL www.nationaltrust.org.uk/learning; e-mail learning@nationaltrust.org.uk; Tel 01793 462789; Fax 01793 469813

Director General Fiona Reynolds

An independent charity established by Act of Parliament to preserve land and buildings of beauty and historic interest for the benefit of the nation. Properties include more than 200 houses and castles, 160 gardens, countryside and coastline. The trust is committed to the educational use of its properties by people of all ages and has extensive programmes and facilities to support this. There is a special

14

573

membership scheme for education groups; details from the above address.

Cragside House, Gardens and Estate

Cragside, Rothbury, Northumberland NE65 7PX; e-mail pam.dryden@nationaltrust.org.uk;
Tel 01669 620333 ext 7; Fax 01669 620066
Education Officer   Pam Dryden

National Trust Regional Office Devon and Cornwall

Landhydrock, Bodmin, Cornwall PL30 4DE;
URL www.nationaltrust.org.uk; e-mail
hannah.jones@nationaltrust.org.uk; Tel 01208 265251
Education Development Officer   G. O'Callaghan

National Trust Regional Office East of England

Westley Bottom, Bury St Edmunds, Suffolk IP33 3WD;
URL www.nationaltrust.org.uk; e-mail
karen.chancellor@nationaltrust.org.uk; Tel 01284 747568
Regional Learning and Interpretation Officer
Karen Chancellor

National Trust Regional Office East Midlands

Clumber Park Stableyard, Worksop, Nottinghamshire
S80 3BE; e-mail shelley.fielder@nationaltrust.org.uk;
Tel 01909 486411; Fax 01909 486377
Regional Officer (Learning and Interpretation)   Shelley Fielder
Curriculum-linked visits for schools. Subjects covered
include History, Science and Geography.

National Trust Regional Office Kent and East Sussex

Scotney Castle, Lamberhurst, Tunbridge Wells, Kent
TN3 8JN; Tel 01892 890651; Fax 01892 890110
Contact (Education)   Anne Whitley

National Trust Regional Office North West

The Hollens, Grasmere, Cumbria LA22 9QZ;
URL www.nationaltrust.org.uk; e-mail
clare.perry@nationaltrust.org.uk; Tel 015394 35599;
Fax 015394 35353
Regional Learning and Interpretation Officer   Clare Perry

National Trust Regional Office South East

Polesden Lacey, Dorking, Surrey RH5 6BD;
URL www.nationaltrust.org.uk/regions/southeast;
e-mail anita.goodwin@nationaltrust.org.uk;
Tel 01372 455011; Fax 01372 452023
Regional Learning and Interpretation Officer   Anita Goodwin

National Trust Regional Office Thames and Solent

Hughenden Manor, High Wycombe, Buckinghamshire
HP14 4LA; URL www.nationaltrust.org.uk/regions/
thamessolent; e-mail sally.stafford@nationaltrust.org.uk;
Tel 01494 528051; Fax 01494 463310

National Trust Regional Office Wessex

Eastleigh Ct, Bishopstrow, Warminster, Wiltshire
BA12 9HW; URL www.nationaltrust.org.uk/education;
e-mail barbara.webber@nationaltrust.org.uk;
Tel 01985 843622; Fax 01985 843624
Regional Community Learning and Volunteering Officer
Barbara Webber

National Trust Regional Office West Midlands

Attingham Pk, Shrewsbury, Shropshire SY4 4TP; e-mail
keith.robinson@nationaltrust.org.uk; Tel 01743 708100;
Fax 01743 708150
Education Contact   Keith Robinson

National Trust Regional Office Yorkshire

Goddards, 27 Tadcaster Rd, York YO24 1GG;
URL www.nationaltrust.org.uk/learning;
Tel 01904 771956; Fax 01904 771970
*Learning and Interpretation Officer (Yorkshire and the North
East)*   Katie Croft
*Learning and Interpretation Officer (Yorkshire and the North
East)*   Jo Foster

Contact for details of educational opportunities at National
Trust properties throughout Yorkshire and the North East

National Trust Office for Wales

Trinity Sq, Llandudno, Conwy LL30 2DE;
URL www.nationaltrust.org.uk/education; e-mail
heledd.jones@nationaltrust.org.uk; Tel 01492 860123;
Fax 01492 860233
Communications Officer   Heledd Jones

National Trust Regional Office Northern Ireland

Rowallane Hse, Saintfield, Ballynahinch, County Down
BT24 7LH; URL www.nationaltrust.org.uk;
Tel 028 9751 0721

For further details about the National Trust Education
Programme, which is supported by the BT Community
Partnership Programme and the Department of Education,
please contact the regional learning manager at the above
address

National Trust for Scotland

Wemyss Hse, 28 Charlotte Sq, Edinburgh EH2 4ET;
URL www.nts@education.org.uk; e-mail
education@nts.org.uk; Tel 0131 243 9300;
Fax 0131 249 9301
Head (Education and Interpretation)   Colin MacConnachie
Education in the Trust

Trust properties offer opportunities to all sectors of
education; primary, secondary, tertiary and community
groups are all welcome and specific programmes of study
may be arranged to match the requirements of visiting
students and groups. Regional education officers are able to
advise and help prepare for visits to trust properties; school
parties are welcome and the trust encourages teachers and
leaders to make use of extensive facilities. The trust can
provide in-service courses at the property or an education
centre venue, and can host an open day to facilitate the
planning of visits. The countryside properties offer
environmental education outdoors and have their own
ranger service, while many of the trust's smaller properties
offer the opportunity to study the built environment. The
facilities include costumes, history-based drama activities,
and spaces for project work.

Standard Grade, Higher and SVQ students, and Tourism,
Ecology, and Environmental Studies students may find the
trust's properties a useful resource; videos and slides may be
borrowed from the library; a range of educational
publications is available, including property-based study
packs, special children's guides and leaflets. Educational
membership is available which allows a teacher or lecturer a
free preliminary tour before each visit, and then allows the
school, college or group free visits to all properties
throughout the year. Copies of the schools programme are
available from the above address.

Annual membership rates: nursery up to 50: £20; special
needs: £20; school roll up to 50: £20; school roll 51–100: £40;
school roll 101–200: £50; school roll 201–500: £70; school roll
over 500: £80; tertiary education: £120.

Highland Region

Balnain Hse, 40 Huntly St, Inverness, Highland IV3 5HR;
Tel 01463 232034

North East Region

The Stables, Castle Fraser, Sauchen, Inverurie,
Aberdeenshire AB51 7LD; Tel 01330 833225

South Region

Northgate Hse, 32 Northgate, Peebles, Scottish Borders
EH45 8RS; Tel 01721 722502; Fax 01721 724700

West Region

Greenbank Hse, Flewders Rd, Clarkston, Glasgow G76 8RB;
Tel 0141 616 2266; Fax 0141 616 2266

National Travel Organisations

The British Council, Youth Department

10 Spring Gdns, London SW1A 2BN;
  URL www.connectyouthinternational.com; e-mail
  connectyouth.enquiries@britishcouncil.org;
  Tel 020 7389 4030; Fax 020 7389 4033

Youth Department at the British Council promotes
international youth exchanges, voluntary work and other
activities between the UK and other countries. It administers
grants to youth groups aged 13–30, runs projects and
provides information, advice and training services to British
youth services on international exchanges. The British
Council is the national agency for the European Youth in
Action programme which is sponsored by the European
Commission of the EU.

The English-Speaking Union of the Commonwealth

Registered Charity Number 273136

Dartmouth Hse, 37 Charles St, London W1X 8AB; e-mail
esu@esu.org; Tel 020 7493 3328

English Speaking Union Scotland

23 Atholl Cres, Edinburgh EH3 8HQ;
  URL www.esuscotland.org.uk; e-mail
  director@esuscotland.org.uk; Tel 0131 229 1528;
  Fax 0131 229 1533

ESU Scotland works to promote global understanding
through the English language. It runs programmes of
debating and public speaking for school and university
students; organises a creative writing competition with the
National Galleries of Scotland and Scottish Poetry Library
and runs a creative workshop group; offers a number of
travel scholarships each year for professional development;
provides English language tuition to non-native speakers;
offers training in presentation and public speaking skills;
organises regular public debates on issues of topical
concern; and works actively with other ESU branches
around the world. It has produced resources on debating in
schools for LT Scotland.

ISTC (International Student Travel Confederation)

Keizersgracht 174–176, 1016 DW Amsterdam, The
  Netherlands; e-mail istc@istc.org; Tel +31 20 421 28 00;
  Fax +31 20 421 28 10

The International Student Travel Confederation was
established by unversity student unions to make travel
affordable for students

LECT (League for the Exchange of Commonwealth Teachers)

Commonwealth Hse, 7 Lion Yard, Tremadoc Rd, London
  SW4 7NQ; URL www.lect.org.uk; e-mail
  info@lect.org.uk; Tel 0870 770 2636; Fax 0870 770 2637

LECT connects teachers and educators throughout the
Commonwealth

VisitBritain

Thames Tower, Blacks Rd, London W6 9EL;
  URL www.visitbritain.com; e-mail
  visitbritain@visitbritain.org; Tel 020 8846 9000;
  Fax 020 8563 0302

Chief Executive   Tom Wright

As the national tourism agency VisitBritain is responsible
for marketing Britain worldwide and for developing
England's visitor economy. Please check the website for
details of local tourist boards.

Exchange Visits and School Travel

This does not claim to be a complete list of firms and
organisations offering educational travel facilities. Inclusion
of an editorial entry does not imply approval; equally,
exclusion does not imply disapproval.

Accueil Familial des Jeunes Étrangers

23 rue du Cherche-Midi, 75006 Paris, France;
  URL www.afje-paris.org; e-mail accueil@afje-paris.org;
  Tel +33 1 42 22 50 34; Fax +33 1 45 44 60 48

Arranges au pair places for students (18–27) for the whole
school year (beginning of September to the end of June) or
for a minimum of six months, in Paris, suburbs and major
provincial cities; and summer stays (June to September)
seaside, mountains and countryside. Paying guest service
(aged 18 and over) in Paris and suburbs, minimum stay 15
days.

AFS Intercultural Programmes UK

Registered Charity Number 284174

Leeming Hse, Vicar La, Leeds, West Yorkshire LS2 7JF;
  URL www.afsuk.org; e-mail unitedkingdom@afs.org
  info-unitedkingdom@afs.org; Tel 0113 242 6136;
  Fax 0113 243 0631

Voluntary work opportunities in Latin America, Asia and Africa

People aged over 18 can spend six months abroad living
with a volunteer host family. Work alongside local people
on development projects, in areas such as protection of
human rights, public health, environment and conservation,
community development, business development,
education, or serving disabled people. Departures in
January/February or July/August.

Study opportunities abroad

For those aged 15–18, AFS offers the opportunity to spend a
year abroad. Participants live with a volunteer host family
and attend a local school. There is a choice of 55 countries,
including Brazil, Italy, Germany, Argentina, Spain and the
USA. AFS provides full support prior, during and after the
exchange programme. AFS is an international, voluntary,
non-profitmaking and non-governmental organisation.

Atherfield Bay Holidays

Chale, Ventnor, Isle of Wight PO38 2JD;
  URL www.atherfieldbay.co.uk; e-mail
  info@atherfieldbay.co.uk; Tel 01983 740307

Accommodation and entertainment for school parties from
March to October

Avalon Student Travel

11 Marlborough Pl, Brighton, East Sussex BN1 1UB;
  URL www.avalontravel.co.uk ; e-mail
  aart@avalontravel.co.uk; Tel 01273 243395;
  Fax 01273 243396

Arranges group travel to Western and Eastern European
countries. Arranges study tours, family accommodation,
sight-seeing and English language training for foreign
students for individuals and groups.

BREAK

Davison Hse, 1 Montague Rd, Sheringham, Norfolk
  NR26 8WN; URL www.break-charity.org; e-mail
  office@break-charity.org; Tel 01263 822161;
  Fax 01263 822181

BREAK provides supported holidays and respite care for
children and young adults with learning disabilities from all
areas of the country at our centre on the Norfolk coast.
Individuals and groups welcome, with or without
accompanying staff. Full 24 hour care, special diets catered
for, varied holiday programme including outings, indoor
heated swimming pools, transport with wheelchair lift.
Centre staff are available to assist with activities and provide
relief cover if required, e.g. extra help on outings, cover
while staff have time off, waking night duties. BREAK can
arrange recreational and educational outings with transport
provided free of charge.

14

British Deaf Association (BDA)

Registered Charity Number 1031687

1–3 Worship St, London EC2A 2AB; URL www.bda.org.uk; e-mail helpline@bda.org; Tel (Videophone for BSL callers) 020 7496 9539; Tel (helpline: national rate) 0870 770 3300; Fax 020 7588 3527; Textphone (helpline) 0800 652 2965

The BDA is a democratic, membership-led national charity campaigning on behalf of nearly 70 000 deaf sign language users in the UK. It exists to advance and protect the interests of deaf people, to increase deaf people's access to facilities and lifestyles, and to ensure greater awareness of their rights and responsibilities. The association has teams covering education and youth, information, health promotions, and community services, offering advice and help. There is a national helpline that provides information and advice on subjects such as welfare rights, the Disability Discrimination Act (DDA) and education. The BDA also publishes Sign Matters. The BDA is based in London and has regional offices in Belfast, Cardiff, Edinburgh and Warrington. It represents Britain within the European Union of the Deaf, and in the World Federation of the Deaf (affiliated to the United Nations).

BUNAC

16 Bowling Green La, London EC1R 0QH; Tel 020 7251 3472

Work and travel programmes arranged in the USA and Canada during summer months. The Summer Camp USA programme offers jobs to individuals working with children and teaching sports, arts and crafts etc. There are private sports camps, church camps, inner-city and disabled children's camps. Return flight, visa and insurance arranged by BUNAC. Board, lodging and salary ($935–1075) provided by camp. Up to six weeks to travel after camp.

Camp America

Dept EYB, 37a Queens Gate, London SW7 5HR; URL www.campamerica.co.uk; e-mail brochure@campamerica.co.uk; Tel 020 7581 7333; Fax 020 7581 7377

This programme arranges for young people (18 and over) to work on American summer camps for nine weeks, either as a counsellor (looking after children), or as a worker (kitchen, laundry, office etc.). There are also places for special needs counsellors. Camp America offers free return flight, board and lodging, pocket money and up to two months for independent travel. Applicants must be available from June to September.

Centre de Rencontres Internationales et de Sejour de Dijon

1 Bvd Champollion, 21000 Dijon, France; URL auberge_cri_dijon.com; e-mail reservation@auberge_cri_dijon.com; Tel +33 380 72 9520; Fax +33 380 70 0061

Accommodation in Burgundy (France) for groups (up to 220) and individuals. Study tours, linguistic programmes and cultural programmes can only be arranged for groups.

CESA Languages Abroad

CESA Hse, Pennance Rd, Lanner, Cornwall TR16 5TQ; URL www.cesalanguages.com; e-mail info@cesalanguages.com; Tel 01209 211800; Fax 01209 211830

Information and enrolment service on a wide range of centres in Europe and South America, courses for juniors (France, Germany and Spain), holiday programmes for adults, short-term intensive courses for business executives, courses for students working for language exams and private tuition. Year out long-term courses for all ability levels. Free colour brochure available on request. Full range of languages covered includes: Arabic, Chinese, French, German, Greek, Italian, Japanese, Portuguese, Russian and Spanish; French and German can be offered with skiing in the afternoons.

Club du Vieux Manoir

Ancienne Abbaye du Moncel, 60700 Pont-Point, France; URL www.clubduvieuxmanoir.asso.fr; e-mail clubduvieuxmanoir@free.fr; Tel +33 3 44 72 33 98; Fax +33 3 44 70 13 14

Club Europe Holidays

Fairway Hse, 53 Dartmouth Rd, London SE23 3HN; URL www.club-europe.co.uk; e-mail travel@club-europe.co.uk; Tel 0800 496 4996; Fax 020 8699 7770

Specialists in ski, concert and educational school tours. Ski tours to Austria, France and Italy; concert tours throughout Europe; educational tours (Art, Geography, History, Technology) and cultural tours across Europe. Member of ABTA and ATOL protected.

Commonwealth Youth Exchange Council

7 Lion Yard, Tremadoc Rd, London SW4 7NQ; URL www.cyec.org.uk; e-mail mail@cyec.org.uk; Tel 020 7498 6151

Promotes contact between groups of young people aged 15–25 from all Commonwealth countries by means of two-way youth exchanges and projects promoting skills for global citizenship. Publishes a starter pack: safety welfare guidelines for youth exchange organisers, 'Crossing Frontiers' (with Christian Aid) – an intercultural learning pack for youth groups planning international travel, Journeys Outward, Journeys Inward – a personal record of achievement tool kit, and a newsletter. Guidelines for funding leaflet and publications list available on request (send an SAE).

Curriculum Travel Ltd

78 Beckenham Rd, Beckenham, Kent BR3 4RH; URL www.ukschooltravel.com; e-mail info@ukschooltravel.com; Tel 020 8658 9219; Fax 020 8658 5269

Educational and recreational travel for school groups; tours and centres on UK mainland, Isle of Wight and Europe

Dick Phillips

Whitehall Hse, Nenthead, Alston, Cumbria CA9 3PS; e-mail icelandick@nent.enta.net; Tel 01434 381440

Iceland only. Operators of long-distance walking and motor-assisted tours in uninhabited areas. Full expeditionary service.

Don Quijote UK, In-Country Language Courses Ltd

2–4 Stoneleigh Park Rd, Epsom, Surrey KT19 0QT; URL www.donquijote.org; e-mail uk@donquijote.org; Tel 020 8786 8081; Fax 020 8786 8086

Don Quijote is Europe's largest organisation for Spanish language courses in Spain, operating centres in Barcelona, Granada, Madrid, Malaga, Salamanca, Seville, Tenerife, Valencia. Courses for all levels start regularly throughout the year. Also in Guanajuato (Mexico), Cuzco (Peru) and Alicante (Marbella).

Dove Nest Group

Millness Mill, Crooklands, Milnthorpe, Cumbria LA7 7NS; URL www.dovenest.co.uk; e-mail admin@dovenest.co.uk; Tel 015395 67878; Fax 015395 68838

Provides residential courses and a range of outdoor pursuits courses, including a variety of activities such as canoeing, abseiling, gorge walking, sailing, archery, orienteering, overnight camps, assault course etc., for colleges and industrial groups

En Famille Overseas

La Maison Jaune, Avenue Du Stade, 34210 Siran, France; URL www.enfamilleoverseas.co.uk; e-mail clare.cox@wanadoo.fr; Tel +33 468 329447

Arranges individual paying-guest stays with host families in France, Germany, Spain and Italy at any time of year. Language courses including Easter and summer holidays in Barcelona and Madrid, Florence, Loire Valley, Paris, Frankfurt, Regensburg, Ravenna and Bagno di Romagna, and Tours. Intensive tuition in Paris, Montpellier and the west coast of France. School groups at reduced rates to France and Spain. All combined with home stays.

Euro-Academy

67–71 Lewisham High St, Lewisham, London SE13 5JX; URL www.euroacademy.co.uk; e-mail enquiries@euroacademy.co.uk; Tel 020 8297 0505; Fax 020 8297 0984

School group and individual language travel; tailor-made programmes throughout Europe as well as Central and South America are suitable for all ages, all levels and group sizes. It has a vast range of courses from beginner to advanced levels, including exam revision, one-to-one, immersion home stays, and junior summer schools.

Experiment in International Living

287 Worcester Rd, Malvern, Worcestershire WR14 1AB; URL www.eiluk.org; e-mail info@eiluk.org; Tel 01684 562577; Fax 01684 562212

Home stay and education programmes arranged in about 30 countries, promoting learning through direct personal experience. Special home stays arranged for language students, individuals and groups. Scholarship opportunities available. European Voluntary Service programme.

Families in Britain

Martins Cottage, Martins La, Birdham, Chichester, Sussex PO20 7AU; URL www.families-in-britain.com; e-mail gillift@martinscottages.plus.com; Tel 01243 512222; Fax 01243 512222

Paying-guest visits; all ages. It also recommends small residential language courses and English boarding schools.

FIAP Jean Monnet

30 rue Cabanis, 75014 Paris, France; URL www.fiap-paris.org; e-mail fiap@fiap-paris.org; Tel +33 1 43 13 17 00; Fax +33 1 45 81 63 91

200 rooms, two restaurants. Hosts groups and individuals.

Frango Travel

Pentlands, 13 Kingswood Firs, Grayshott, Surrey GU26 6EU; URL www.frango-travel.com; e-mail frangott@aol.com; Tel 01428 606169; Fax 01428 606169

Overseas travel for pupils aged 8–18. From brief 'Taste of France' tours to cultural visits to Czech Republic, Hungary and Russia, and historical tours to Turkey. Programme includes flexible four and five-day tours of Normandy and Paris, with historical, cultural and linguistic content; 10-day French course with activities in the Swiss Alps; small group tours to Albania.

French Government Tourist Office

Lincoln Hse, 300 High Holborn, London WC1V 7JH; URL www.franceguide.com; e-mail info@uk@franceguide.com; Tel 0906 824 4123 (calls charged at 60p per minute) Cultural Department, French Embassy: 23 Cromwell Rd, London SW7; Tel 020 7838 2055; Fax 020 7838 2088 French Institute: e-mail library@ambafrance.org.uk; Tel 020 7073 1350; Fax 020 7073 1355

Provides heads and teachers with a list of British tour operators and travel agents specialising in school and group travel and offering a wide range of tours, day visits, educational tours, holidays, ski-holidays all over France. For information on exchanges, sporting holidays and stays with French families or French courses in France, contact Cultural Department, French Embassy or the French Institute.

HF Holidays Ltd

Imperial Hse, Edgware Rd, London NW9 5AL; e-mail info@hfholidays.co.uk; Tel 020 8905 9557; Fax 020 8205 0506

School party accommodation in the UK, in term-time and holiday periods; low-cost travel; free preview visits; one free place for every 10

Interchange

Interchange Hse, 27 Stafford Rd, Croydon, Surrey CR0 4NG; e-mail interchange@interchange.uk.com; Tel 020 8681 3612; Fax 020 8760 0031

Educational visits to most East European countries for school pupils, young people at work and adult education students. Specialist visits to the former Soviet Union, China, Cuba and Venezuela for teachers, youth leaders and student teachers. Travel concessions available.

International Study Programmes (ISP)

The Manor, Hazleton, Cheltenham, Gloucestershire GL54 4EB; URL www.international-study-programmes.org.uk; e-mail discover@international-study-programmes.org.uk; Tel 01451 860379; Fax 01451 860482

Home stays and study programmes in various locations in England, Scotland and Wales for school/youth groups; courses in Britain for overseas teachers of English; work experience for young visitors to Britain

Interski/Interschool Travel Ltd

Acorn Pk, Commercial Gate, Mansfield, Nottinghamshire NG18 1EX; URL www.interski.co.uk; e-mail email@interski.co.uk; Tel 01623 456333; Fax 01623 456353 *Sales and Marketing*   Trisha Scott; e-mail trisha@interski.co.uk

INTERVAC International Home Exchange Service

24 The Causeway, Chippenham, Wiltshire SN15 3DB; URL www.intervac.com; www.intervac.co.uk; e-mail holiday@intervac.co.uk; Tel 01249 461101; Fax 01249 461101

A home exchange organisation that helps professional people to arrange holiday home exchanges. 12 500 listings from around 50 countries are represented throughout the season, on the international website at www.intervac.com. Directory listings are available as part of the membership. Current information and online registration details are available on the national website.

IPFS (International Pen Friend Service)

10015 Ivrea, Italy; URL www.ipfs.org; e-mail info@ipfs.org; Tel +39 01 25 23 44 33

Arranges penfriend links between students in the UK and most foreign countries; services are free of charge for the UK; age range 8–20. Member of FIOCES.

La Magnanarie

Villedieu, 84110 Vaison-la-Romaine, France; URL www.magnanarie.com; e-mail infos@magnanarie.com; Tel +33 4 90 28 92 58

Board and lodging with garden and swimming pool, for groups (up to 60 places) on touring or study holidays

Le Fosso in Brittany

Registered Charity Number 1037092 Le Fosso, 22230 Gomené, France; e-mail lefosso@club-internet.fr; Tel +33 2 96 28 47 97 *Director*   M. Townsend *Bookings Secretary*   H. Townsend

Holidays and residential field trips in Brittany, France. Full accreditation for families, youth and school groups. Two houses provide up to 29 places in spacious bedrooms, all accessible to people with disabilities. Options include self-catering and full board; a smaller apartment is available for couples or small families, fully accessible; gardens and grounds, including a mini-farm. A programme of visits and organised activities (cultural, educational, sports etc.) can be arranged if required, as part of an all-inclusive package. Le Fosso UK can assist groups with special needs wishing to visit Le Fosso from the UK, including providing a qualified driver or giving bursaries to individuals or groups.

MIJE

6 Rue de Fourcy, 75004 Paris, France; URL www.mije.com; e-mail info@mije.com; Tel +33 1 42 74 23 45; Fax +33 1 42 74 08 93

14

Advises on and organises journeys to and stays in Paris, all French provinces and all European countries. MIJE has three hotels in Paris and can provide transportation, meals, visits and guides. Programmes may be suggested or organised in advance by group leaders, or can be drawn up by the educational services of MIJE.

MS Language
41 Rue H.Bergé, 1030 Brussels, Belgium;
URL www.macbaron.net; e-mail macbaron@chello.be;
Tel +32 2 242 27 66; Fax +32 2 242 25 36
Manager X.M. Mouffe
The work experience abroad programme enables students to practise French (in Brussels) or German (in Lubeck) while gaining work experience and sharing the daily life of a French or German-speaking family

National Association of Youth Orchestras
Central Hall, West Tollcross, Edinburgh EH3 9BP;
URL www.nayo.org.uk; e-mail admin@nayo.org.uk;
Tel 0131 221 1927; Fax 0131 229 2921
Courses include European Youth Music Week in conjunction with Internationaler Arbeitskreis für Musik; Festival of British Youth Orchestras, Edinburgh and Glasgow in August/September

NST Educational Visits
Chiltern Hse, Bristol Ave, Blackpool FY2 0FA;
URL www.nstgroup.co.uk; e-mail info@nstgroup.co.uk;
Tel 01253 352525; Fax 01253 356955
Educational visit programmes to the UK, Europe and worldwide covering History, Modern Languages, English and Drama, Geography, and Art and Design. Additional programmes include Concert Tours for Music Groups, Sports Coaching and Tournament courses, Ardeche Adventure and a Key Stage 2 ICT and Activity course at NST's own centre. NST's externally verified safety management system meets latest DCSF guidelines.

OIK – Organisation für Internationale Kontakte
Postfach 201051, 53140 Bonn, Germany; URL www.oik.org;
e-mail oik@tronet.de; Tel +49 228 82 09 70;
Fax +49 228 36 43 68
A non-profitmaking organisation for groups only, arranges stays in youth centres and hotels throughout Germany and Europe. Study tours, field trips, and home stays with German families; language courses; sports programmes, music programmes and cultural visits. Own international youth music festival every July.

Progress Travel
4 Garden St, Hebden Bridge, West Yorkshire HX7 8AQ;
URL www.progress-travel.net; e-mail
sales@progress-travel.net; Tel 01422 844028
Contact E. Simpson
Student travel office, Australian specialist, group travel, round-the-world tickets, small group adventure tours

Rayburn Tours
Rayburn Hse, Parcel Terr, Derby DE1 1LY;
URL www.rayburntours.com; e-mail
enquiries@rayburntours.com; Tel 01332 347828;
Fax 01332 371298
Specialist group tour operator, arranging worldwide performance tours for school music groups and educational tours based on the national curriculum, throughout Europe. Rayburn Tours is a member of ABTA, ATOL protected, and is a founding member of the School Travel Forum.

St Denis International School
19 avenue du Général de Gaulle, BP146-37601 Loches,
France; e-mail elit@saint-denis.net; Tel +33 2 47 59 17 33;
Fax +33 2 47 94 04 50
French language courses for individuals or groups of children or adults. Summer courses and boarding school offering the French national curriculum in French and English. Registered centre for IGCSE. Accommodation with a host family or in the school residence. Activities and excursions in July and August.

The School Travel Forum
Katepwa Hse, Ashfield Park Ave, Ross-on-Wye,
Herefordshire HR9 5AX;
URL www.schooltravelforum.com; e-mail
info@schooltravelforum.com; Tel 01989 764242;
Fax 01989 567676
National association of school tour operators that promotes good practice and safety in school travel. All full members adhere to a code of practice and safety management standards.

Séjours Internationaux Linguistiques et Culturels (SILC)
32 Rempart de l'Est, 16022 Angouleme Cedex, France;
URL www.silc-international.com; e-mail
info@silc-international.com; Tel +33 5 45 97 41 00;
Fax +33 5 45 97 41 42
SILC organises educational, cultural and language travel programmes for juniors, students and professionals in France and around the world.
SILC offers a wide range of short and long-term programmes, for groups and individuals throughout France, Spain and the UK: immersion programmes with or without tuition, international language schools and university courses, work experience, cultural and educational tours, academic programmes, holiday camps, international summer courses, tailor-made programmes for groups.

Sing for Pleasure
Bolton Music Centre, New York, Bolton BL3 4NG;
URL www.singforpleasure.org.uk; e-mail
admin@singforpleasure.org.uk; Tel 01484 860404;
Fax 01484 860404
National and regional choral events throughout the year and short courses for singers, teachers and conductors held in the UK each summer. Singing days, weekends and residential summer courses for children. Residential and one-day teachers' courses. Choral music published for choirs, singing groups and for use in schools. Choir exchanges and visits to festivals in Europe in co-operation with 'A Cur Joie'.

SkiBound/TravelBound
Olivier Hse, 18 Marine Par, Brighton, East Sussex BN2 1TL;
URL www.travelbound.co.uk; e-mail
enquiries@travelbound.co.uk; Tel 0870 900 3200;
Fax 0870 333 2329
Director Bryn Robinson; e-mail
bryn.robinson@firstchoice.co.uk
Manager Natalie Evans; e-mail
natalie.evans@firstchoice.co.uk
Offers school tours to a large number of destinations in Europe and worldwide. Disneyland Paris school tour operator; also offers subject-specific project tours and study courses. TravelBound's active and sports programme offers coaching, tournaments and individual fixture tours and sailsport and activity adventures.

Society for Co-operation in Russian and Soviet Studies
Registered Charity Number 1104012
320 Brixton Rd, London SW9 6AB; URL www.scrss.org.uk;
e-mail ruslibrary@scrss.co.uk; Tel 020 7274 2282;
Fax 020 7274 3230
An educational charity which organises Russian language courses in London with teachers from Russia; help and advice for school parties on pre-departure study, contacts in FSU, but no travel arrangements

Studentours Group Travel
Gaveston Hall, Nuthurst, Horsham, West Sussex RH13 6RF;
URL www.gavestonhll.com; e-mail
info@gavestonhall.com; Tel 01403 891431;
Fax 01403 891439
Budget accommodation for group visits to London and educational visits arranged throughout the UK. School journeys and educational visits at the residential centre.

UK Connection

A division of Kuoni Travel Ltd

Deepdene Lodge, Deepdene Ave, Dorking, Surrey
RH5 4AZ; e-mail ukconnection@kuoni.co.uk;
Tel 01306 744666; Fax 01306 744667

Specialists in school and college group travel worldwide.
From a one-night stay to a complete educational
programme, for groups of all ages. Contracted hotels are
located close to places of entertainment and interest. Also
sports tours, theatre visits, weekend packages, special event
stopovers etc.

Venture Abroad

Rayburn Hse, Parcel Terr, Derby DE1 1LY;
URL www.ventureabroad.co.uk; e-mail
tours@ventureabroad.co.uk; Tel 01332 342050;
Fax 01332 224960

Inclusive holidays for cubs, Scouts, Brownies and Guide
groups both small and large in size. Chalets in the Bernese
Oberland region of Switzerland; holidays in Iceland,
Croatia, Spain, Belgium, France and Disneyland Paris.

VENUEMASTERS

The Workstation, Paternoster Row, Sheffield, South
Yorkshire S1 2BX; URL www.venuemasters.co.uk; e-mail
info@venuemasters.co.uk; Tel 0114 249 3090;
Fax 0114 249 3091

Manager (Marketing) Jo Mitchell

Promoting the meeting and accommodation facilities
available at more than 90 universities and colleges
throughout the UK

Worldwide Christian Travel and Worldwide Group Travel

36 Coldharbour Rd, Bristol BS6 7NA;
URL www.hadlertours.ltd.uk; e-mail
info@hadlertours.ltd.uk; Tel 0845 458 8308;
Fax 0845 458 8307

Managing Director Mrs J. Pimm

Group travel and air tickets

Youth Hostels Association (YHA)

See Chapter 13

Youth Travel Bureau, Israel Youth Hostels Association

International Convention Center, PO Box 6001, Jerusalem
ZC 91060, Israel; URL www.iyha.org.il; e-mail
iyhtb@iyha.org.il; Tel +972 2 6558400; Fax +972 2 6558432

Arranges educational tours for school and student groups
throughout the year. Special programmes for school groups
12–20 year olds. Archaeological excavations 18–35 year olds.
Professional study tours for student groups.

Recreational and Residential Courses

This does not claim to be a complete list of firms and
organisations offering recreational and residential courses.
Inclusion of an editorial entry does not imply approval;
equally exclusion does not imply disapproval. Details of
such courses may also be obtained from many of the
national sports and youth organisations listed in Chapters
11 and 13, and the educational organisations in Chapter 21.

Academia Hispanica de Cordoba

Rodriguez Sanchez 15, 14003 Cordoba, Spain;
URL www.academiahispanica.com; e-mail
info@academiahispanica.com; Tel +34 9 57 488 002;
Fax +34 9 57 488 199

Year round Spanish courses; intensive, one-to-one, DELE
preparation; Spanish and flamenco, cookery.
Accommodation and activities

Académie Internationale d'Eté de Nice

Cloître du Monastère du Cimiez, Nice F06000, France;
URL www.hexagone.net/nice; e-mail
academies@hexagone.net; Tel +33 4 93 81 01 23;
Fax +33 4 93 53 33 91

Higher and professional education, instrumental and
singing master classes (from July to August)

The Active Training and Education Trust (ATE)

8 St Ann's Rd, Malvern, Worcestershire WR14 4RG;
URL www.ate.org.uk; e-mail info@ate.org.uk; Tel (local
rate) 0845 456 1205; Fax 01684 562716

Director Barry Walmsley BEd, MSc

ATE runs residential superweeks for children in school
holidays and trains students and sixth formers for
residential work with children. ATE also offers supertrips
(residential weeks for schools), superweekends for teachers
with pupils (subject based), ideas weekends for teachers,
and INSET in schools.

ATE is a successor body to Colony Holidays for
Schoolchildren.

Activity Island Ltd

35 Lowdham, Wilnecote, Tamworth, Staffordshire B77 4LX;
URL www.activityisland.com; e-mail
sales@activityisland.com; Tel 01827 331100;
Fax 01827 331188

Specialises in educational visits to the Isle of Wight for
primary and junior schools

Aigas Field Centre

Aigas, Beauly, Inverness IV4 7AD; URL www.aigas.co.uk;
e-mail info@aigas.co.uk; Tel 01463 782443;
Fax 01463 782097

Aigas Field Centre runs day visits and residential field
studies programmes for children of all ages. Aigas is
situated in the Highlands and runs Natural History,
Geography, Geology, Biology and Archaeology based
programmes which are tailor-made for each group's needs.

Allnatt Centres

Allnatt Group Ltd, 35 Ulwell Rd, Swanage, Dorset
BH19 1LG; URL www.allnatt.co.uk; e-mail
sales@allnatt.co.uk; Tel 01929 421075; Fax 01929 421075

Educational visit centres in the Isle of Wight and Dorset, able
to accommodate whole year groups or small groups.
Adventure, environmental and field study courses; AALA
license.

Auberge de la Jeunesse

rue Trencavel, La Cite, 11000 Carcassonne, France;
URL www.fuaj.srg; e-mail carcassonne@fuaj.srg;
Tel +33 4 68 25 23 16; Fax +33 4 68 71 14 84

Excursions; youth hostel accommodation, 120 beds; groups;
meals if required, individual cooking facilities

BACH to Bacchus Weekends, Germany

Willowdown, Megg La, Chipperfield, Hertfordshire
WD4 9JN; URL www.musicholiday.com; e-mail
bhmc@musicholiday.com; Tel 01923 263715;
Fax 01923 268412

Wine and music – May and October 2008; instrumentalists
and singers

Berwang Holiday Music Course Austria

Willowdown, Megg La, Chipperfield, Hertfordshire
WD4 9JN; URL www.musicholiday.com; e-mail
bhmc@musicholiday.com; Tel 01923 263715;
Fax 01923 268412

Holiday and music courses in Tyrolean alpine village.
Classes, concerts, wind, strings, singers, walks, swimming,
excursions from August to September.

Berwang Winter Music Holiday, Austria

Willowdown, Megg La, Chipperfield, Hertfordshire
WD4 9JN; URL www.musicholiday.com; e-mail
bhmc@musicholiday.com; Tel 01923 263715;
Fax 01923 268412

14

Winter sports, walks and music; singers and instrumentalists. One week in January each year.

Bowles Outdoor Centre

Sandhill La, Eridge Grn, Tunbridge Wells, Kent TN3 9LW; URL www.bowles.ac; e-mail admin@bowles.ac; Tel 01892 665665

Multi-activity courses including rock climbing, abseiling, canoeing, dry-skiing, ropes course, problem-solving. 96 residential places, year six upwards. ISO9001 approved.

Bradwell Outdoors

Waterside, Bradwell-on-Sea, Southminster, Essex CM0 7QY; URL www.bradwelloutdoors.com; e-mail info.bradwelloutdoors@essexcc.gov.uk; Tel 01621 776256; Fax 01621 776378

Sailing, canoeing, multi-activity courses and offshore cruising courses from April to October; self-programming courses from October to March. Fully residential or daily from £23 a day.

Brathay Hall Trust

See Chapter 13: Voluntary Services and Groups

BSES Expeditions (British Schools Exploring Society)

The Royal Geographical Society, 1 Kensington Gore, London SW7 2AR; URL www.bses.org.uk; e-mail info@bses.org.uk; Tel 020 7591 3141

Executive Director   Will Taunton-Burnett

Manager (Marketing)   Charlie Masding

BSES Expeditions is a youth development charity which organises scientific research expeditions to remote arctic, jungle and mountainous environments for 16–23 year olds. Those over 19 and with previous expedition experience can gain more leadership qualifications through BSES's Leadership Development Course, which provides mountain leader, GNVQ3, first aid and expedition leader training.

In 2008/09, BSES is planning expeditions to Svalbard, the Peruvian Amazon, the Indian Himalaya, Arctic Norway and South Georgia.

The Camping and Caravanning Club

Greenfield Hse, Westwood Way, Coventry, Warwickshire CV4 8JH; URL www.campingandcaravanningclub.co.uk; Tel 024 7669 4995; Fax 024 7669 4886

Advice on camping and caravanning in Britain, Europe and the rest of the world. 320 000 UK members.

Canford Summer School of Music

PO Box 629, Godstone, Surrey RH9 8WQ; URL www.canfordsummerschool.co.uk; e-mail canfordsummersch@aol.com; Tel 020 8660 4766; Fax 020 8668 5273

Varied courses, tuition, musical and social activities

Cape Adventure International Ltd

Ardmore, Rhiconich, Lairg, Sutherland IV27 4RB; URL www.capeadventure.co.uk; e-mail info@capeadventure.co.uk; Tel 01971 521006; Fax 01971 521006

Outdoor activity courses and holidays set in the Highlands. Sea kayaking, land yachting, surfing, walking, climbing, abseiling, orienteering and survival.

Centre Audio-visuel de Royan pour l'Etude des Langues

C.A.R.E.L., BP 219C, 17205 Royan, France; URL www.carel.org; e-mail info@carel.org; Tel +33 546 39 50 00; Fax +33 546 05 27 68

Full-time French courses throughout the year; minimum age 18. Intensive courses in July and August for juniors (12–17) and residential facilities for supervised groups of teenagers. Residential facilities for adult and junior students. Teacher-training courses in July and August.

Centre International d'Etudes Françaises

Université Catholique de l'Ouest, 3 Pl André Leroy, 49008 Angers Cedex 01, France; URL cidef.uco.fr; e-mail cidef@uco.fr; Tel +33 2 41 88 30 15; Fax +33 2 41 87 71 67

Director   Marc Melin

Three holiday courses in July, August and September; all levels of French; from age 16; language and culture credit courses; grades sent to admissions offices at the end of each session. Board and lodging provided.

Offers two semesters: September–December (or October–January) and February–June.

Centro Velico Caprera

Corso Italia 10, Milan 20122, Italy; URL www.centrovelicocaprera.it; e-mail info.cvc@cvcaprera.it; Tel +39 2 86 45 21 91; Fax +39 2 89 01 08 26

Sailing school on the island of Caprera, north-east of Sardinia and in Lerici in Liguria, offering one or two-week courses from May to October, and spring–winter weekend courses in Lerici. Three levels of instruction from elementary sailing to offshore cruising. For 16 year olds (without limits) and special courses for 14–16 year olds.

Council for British Archaeology

St Mary's Hse, 66 Bootham, York YO30 7BZ; URL www.britarch.ac.uk; e-mail education@britarch.ac.uk; Tel 01904 671417; Fax 01904 671384

Head (Education and Outreach)   D. Henson

Head (Information and Communication)   D. Hall

The Council for British Archaeology (CBA) works to promote the study and safeguarding of Britain's historic environment, to provide a forum for archaeological opinion, and to improve public knowledge of Britain's past, and provides educational advice and resources through its web site

The CBA produces a magazine, British Archaeology (six issues a year; subscription £25), which includes news on current developments in British archaeology and lists excavations and other projects, conferences and courses. The magazine is available as part of CBA individual membership (£32 a year, £19 for those in full-time education). The CBA also runs the Young Archaeologists' Club (YAC) for members aged 9–16. Its members receive a quarterly magazine, Young Archaeologist, and other benefits. Annual membership £12, with family membership of CBA and YAC at £40.

Cranedale Field Study Centre

Kirby Grindalythe, Malton, North Yorkshire YO17 8DB; URL www.cranedale.com; e-mail admin@cranedale.com; Tel 01944 738687

Field study courses (A2/AS level, GCSE and junior) in Biology, Geography, Geology and Environmental Studies. Courses tailored to specific requirements. Courses offer a combination of outdoor activities and environmental studies. Facilities available for self-tutored groups.

CSSM

5 Bushey Cl, Old Barn La, Kenley, Surrey CR8 5AU; URL www.cssmamateurmusiccourses.co.uk; e-mail cssm.music@aol.com; Tel 020 8660 4766; Fax 020 8668 5273

Varied courses, tuition, musical and social activities including concerts

CTC

69 Meadrow, Godalming, Surrey GU7 3HS; URL www.ctc.org.uk; e-mail cycling@ctc.org.uk; Tel 0870 873 0060; Fax 0870 873 0064

Provides information and advice on cycle training and a wide range of membership services (insurance, magazine and events)

Dartmoor Expedition Centre

Rowden, Widecombe in the Moor, Newton Abbot, Devon TQ13 7TX; URL www.dartmoorbase.co.uk; e-mail earle@clara.co.uk; Tel 01364 621249

Barn bunkhouse accommodation (maximum 35) and two leader's rooms; self-catering or meals provided. Year-round multi-activity and specialist residential courses for schools, youth groups; details from John Earle at above address.

Det Danske Kulturinstitut
Vartov, Farvergade 27L,2, DK-1463 Copenhagen K, Denmark; URL www.dankultur.dk; e-mail dankultur@dankultur.dk; Tel +45 33 13 54 48; Fax +45 33 15 10 91
Institute for information about Denmark and cultural co-operation with other countries. Offers seminars on different aspects and problems of Danish education from pre-school and childcare to education for adults and care for older people, on Danish social policy, library problems, architecture, arts and crafts and design.

Early Music Days Sopron
Budapest Filharmonia Kht, H-1075 Budapest, Kazinczy u 24–26, Hungary; URL www.filharmoniabp.hu; e-mail liszkay.maria@hu.inter.net; Tel +36 1 266 14859; Fax +36 1 302 4962
Manager   M. Liszkay
Workshops, public concerts and master classes in harpsichord, violin, chamber music, recorder, voice and dance

The English Folk Dance and Song Society
Cecil Sharp Hse, 2 Regents Park Rd, London NW1 7AY; URL www.efdss.org; e-mail info@efdss.org; Tel 020 7485 2206; Fax (library) 020 7284 0523; Fax 020 7284 0534
Resources for schools and information on festivals, events, courses, workshops and clubs; specialist library

Estudio Internacional Sampere
Lagasca 16, E-28001 Madrid, Spain; URL www.sampere.es; e-mail sampere@sampere.es; Tel +34 9 14 31 43 66; Fax +34 9 15 75 95 09
Different Spanish courses throughout the year
EIS El Puerto   Pagador 18, 11500 El Puerto Santa Maria, Cádiz, Spain; e-mail puerto@sampere.es; Tel +34 9 56 87 20 21; Fax +34 9 56 87 41 09
Intensive Spanish courses, open February to November
EIS Salamanca   Vazquez Coronado 9, E-37002 Salamanca, Spain; e-mail salamanca@sampere.es; Tel +34 9 23 26 22 18; Fax +34 9 23 26 84 88

Europa Cantat – European Federation of Young Choirs
Weberstrasse 59a, D-53113 Bonn, Germany; URL www.europacantat.org; e-mail info@europacantat.org; Tel +49 228 9125663; Fax +49 288 9125658
Europa Cantat organises a European choir festival and holds international singing weeks all over Europe. It also maintains the European Academy for Young Choral Conductors and leads study tours for choral conductor in partner countries. It runs the World Youth Choir in co-operation with IFCM and Jeunesses Musicales. There is a newspaper for members, EC magazine.

Fédération Unie des Auberges de Jeunesse
27 Rue Pajol, 75018 Paris, France; URL www.fuaj.org; e-mail fuaj@fuaj.org; Tel +33 1 44 89 87 27
Runs more than 160 youth hostels throughout France, open to members only. Winter and summer activities for individuals and groups. Accommodation for groups and special programmes.

FLT
Binderton, Chichester, West Sussex PO18 0JT; e-mail bob@flt-education.com; Tel 01243 528421; Fax 01243 528421
Specialists in organising visits to England for foreign schools, including contact with English school pupils. School holiday courses for individual foreign students; English language lessons, sports, activities and accommodation included. One term to one year in an

English school or college, and English language courses for adults of all levels.

Folk Camps Society Ltd
43 Mill St, Tonyrefail, Porth CF39 8AB; URL www.folkcamps.co.uk; e-mail info@folkcamps.co.uk; Tel 020 8123 2136
Camping holidays, January, February, May, June, July, August in England and France. Minimum age 18 unless accompanied by an adult. From £190 a week, including all food and folk entertainment.

Geography Outdoors
Royal Geographical Society (IBG), 1 Kensington Gore, London SW7 2AR; URL www.rgs.org/go; e-mail go@rgs.org; Tel 020 7591 3030; Fax 020 7591 3031
Geography Outdoors supports field research, exploration and outdoor learning. It is funded by the Royal Geographical Society to provide information and training to those planning scientific or adventurous expeditions overseas from schools, universities or in private groups.

Glencoe Outdoor Centre
Glencoe, Highland PH49 4HS; URL www.glencoeoutdoorcentre.org.uk; e-mail gocbook@aol.com; Tel 01855 811350; Fax 01855 811644
Located in the Highlands, offering multi-activity courses for schools. Activities include archery, kayaking, canoeing, hill-walking, skiing, orienteering, sailing and wind-surfing, climbing and abseiling. Accommodation; facilities include drying room, lounge and games room; maximum 35 guests. Qualified instruction.

Harrow House International College
Harrow Dr, Swanage, Dorset BH19 1PE; URL www.harrowhouse.com; e-mail harrowhouse@mailhost.lds.co.uk; Tel 01929 424421; Fax 01929 427175
Residential centre open to groups of all ages and interests. Facilities include tennis and squash courts, swimming pool, gym, sports dome, bar, video, TV, computer rooms

Humboldt-Institut
Schloss Ratzenried, Argenbuehl D-88260, Germany; URL www.humboldt-institut.org; e-mail info@humboldt-institut.org; Tel +49 7522 9880; Fax +49 7522 988 988
Director   Norbert Guethling
The Humboldt-Institute has 19 language centres in Germany where international students are taught by native speakers. The course centre at Freudental Castle runs one-to-one and mini-group courses for executives; summer centres in Ratzenried, Berlin and Cologne cater for university students; and the school in Lindenberg is designed for 10–17 year olds. Special courses offered include 'German language plus skiing' and TestDaF preparation courses. Leisure programme included in course fees.

Institut Catholique de Paris
Institut de Langue et de Culture Françaises, ILCF, 21 rue d'Assas, 75270 Paris Cedex 06, France; URL www.icp.fr/ilcf; e-mail ilcf@icp.fr; Tel +33 1 44 39 52 68; Fax +33 1 44 39 52 09
Termly courses (all levels, three to 24 hours a week); French language, written French, oral French, phonetics, business French, arts and culture; teacher training (annual course and a monthly course in July); evening classes; short-term intensive French programmes for one to three months for all levels.

International Association of Music
49565 Bramsche–Malgarten, Germany; URL www.iam-ev.de; e-mail iamev@t-online.de; Tel +49 5461 9963 0; Fax +49 5461 9963 10
Courses for young and adult musicians in Germany and other European countries during Easter, summer and Christmas holidays. Singing, orchestral and chamber music, dancing, improvisation etc, for ages 15–60.

14

International Bartók Seminar and Festival

Organised by Filharmonia Concert Agency
1066 Budapest, Hungary; URL www.filharmoniabp.hu;
    e-mail kadar.csilla@hu.inter.net; Tel +36 1 266 1459;
    Fax +36 1 302 4962

Workshops, public concerts, special events, folklore
programmes and master classes in piano, singing,
composition and conducting, viola, trumpet and
improvisation with professors. Located in Szombathely,
West Hungary.

International Centre for the Study of Mosaic (CISIM)

c/o Consorzio Provinciale di Formazione Professionale di
    Ravenna, via M. Monti, 32-48100 Ravenna, Italy;
    Tel +39 544 450345; Fax +39 544 451788

International courses on mosaics at Lido Adriano-Ravenna

International Junior Camp

PO Box 329, CH-3780 Gstaad, Switzerland;
    URL www.itc-ijc.com; e-mail mail@itc-ijc.com;
    Tel +41 56 222 6778; Fax +41 56 222 6775

Summer courses in English, French, German and Spanish
from July to August, for ages 7–14; sports, excursions,
hiking, summer skiing

International Teen Camp

PO Box 400, CH-1000, Lausanne 12, Switzerland;
    URL www.itc-ijc.com; e-mail mail@itc-ijc.com;
    Tel +41 21 654 6550; Fax +41 56 222 6775

Summer courses in English, French, German and Spanish
from July to August, for ages 14–19; sports, excursions,
hiking, summer skiing.

Internationales Musikinstitut Darmstadt (IMD)

D-64285 Darmstadt, Nieder-Ramstädter Strasse 190,
    Germany; URL www.imd.darmstadt.de; e-mail
    imd@darmstadt.de; Tel +49 6151 132416;
    Fax +49 6151 132405

Information and documentation centre. International
vacation courses for the composition and interpretation of
contemporary music (biennial, even-numbered years). Also
music information centre.

IST Plus Ltd

Rosedale Hse, Rosedale Rd, Richmond, Surrey TW9 2SZ;
    URL www.istplus.com; Tel 020 8939 9057;
    Fax 020 8332 7858

Work abroad and study abroad opportunities for students
and recent graduates: Internship USA – up to 12 months of
course and future career related work; Internship Canada –
up to 12 months of course related work; Australia Work and
Travel – casual work for up to 12 months; Work and Travel
USA – summer work anywhere in the USA; Teach in China
or Thailand – 5/10 month renewable contracts teaching
English (TEFL not required).

Jeunesses Musicales de Suisse

Rue Merle d'Aubigné, Genève 1207, Switzerland;
    URL www.jmsuisse.ch; e-mail info@jmsuisse.ch;
    Tel +41 22 786 32 73; Fax +41 22 786 32 73

Courses, competitions and music camps

John Hall Pre-University Course in Venice

12 Gainsborough Rd, Ipswich, Suffolk IP4 2UR;
    URL www.johnhallvenice.co.uk; e-mail
    info@johnhallvenice.co.uk; Tel 01473 251223;
    Fax 01473 288009

One week in London, six in Venice (February/March);
extension weeks in Florence and Rome. Lectures, visits,
excursions and independent student groupwork on
Architecture, Art History, Cinema, History, Literature,
Music; classes in Italian, life-drawing and photography.

Jugendreise-Sekretariat Tyrol

A-6020 Innsbruck, Meinhardstrasse 9/IV, Austria;
    URL www.jugendreisen-tyrol.at; e-mail
    jrt@jugendreisen-tyrol.at; Tel +43 512 582 744;
    Fax +43 512 573 274

Recreational holidays for youth groups, family and adult
groups, May to September; winter ski courses for school
groups begin December. Centres in Salzburg, Tyrol and
Vorarlberg.

Kunstfactor (LCA)

Plompetorengracht 3, 3512 CA Utrecht, The Netherlands;
    URL www.kunstfactor.nl; e-mail info@kunstfactor.nl;
    Tel +31 30 2334255; Fax +31 30 2332721

Kunstfactor is the institute for amateur art in the
Netherlands. It organises festivals and exchange
programmes in amateur art, courses and lectures

Les Glénans

Quai Louis Blériot, Paris Cedex 16 75781, France;
    URL www.glenans.asso.fr; e-mail
    stagiaires@glenans.asso.fr; Tel +33 1 53 92 86 00

European sailing school with 1000 instructors and 450 boats;
courses in English or French; all types of boats from
catamarans to large units; beginners to experts and
instructors; two-day to 49-day long courses; hundreds of
one-week long sailing courses; individuals or groups; girls
and boys 13–17; adults 18 and over (no maximum); five
centres in Brittany and in the Mediterranean; partnerships in
Italy (Venice and Genova) and Ireland.

Loch Morlich Watersports

Glenmore Forest Pk, Aviemore, Highland PH22 1QU;
    URL www.lochmorlich.com; e-mail
    office@lochmorlich.com; Tel 01479 861221;
    Fax 01479 861221

Canoeing and kayaking, mountain biking, orienteering,
sailing, walking, windsurfing. Mixed activity and
educational packages available May to September.

Longtown Outdoor Education Centre

The Courthouse, Longtown, Herefordshire HR2 0LD;
    URL www.longtownoec.co.uk; e-mail
    longtown@northamptonshire.gov.uk; Tel 01873 860225;
    Fax 01873 860482

Outdoor education for young people aged 7 and over.
School groups during term time; youth groups and adult
courses during weekends and school holidays; individuals
during summer holiday period. Courses can include
outdoor and adventurous activities, history, geography and
biology, as well as National Governing Body Award
courses. Sponsored by Northamptonshire County Council.

Luftsportjugend des DAeC

Hermann-Blenk St 28, D-38108, Braunschweig, Germany;
    URL www.luftsportjugend.com; e-mail
    p.weber@daec.de; Tel +49 531 2354072;
    Fax +49 531 2354011

International airport youth meetings in gliding in Germany
from April to September. Courses in: aeromodelling,
gliding, hot air ballooning, parachuting.

Medina Valley Centre

Dodnor La, Newport, Isle of Wight PO30 5TE;
    URL www.medinavalleycentre.org.uk; e-mail
    info@medinavalleycentre.org.uk; Tel 01983 522195;
    Fax 01983 825962

80-bedded residential outdoor education centre. Some en
suite facilities for visiting staff; three fully equipped
classrooms/laboratories; separate lounge, dining and
games rooms. Fully tutored, self-tutored, or tutor-assisted
courses Key Stage 2 to A-level: GCSE and A-level Biology
and Geography; Environmental Studies activity weeks;
evening programmes organised for Key Stage 2 or Key Stage
3; RYA dinghy sailing; BOF orienteering; BCU open
canoeing.

Mountain Water Experience

Courtlands, Kingsbridge, Devon TQ7 4BN;
    URL www.mountainwaterexperience.com; e-mail
    mwe@mountainwaterexp.demon.co.uk;
    Tel 01548 550675; Fax 01548 550675

Managing Director   Mark Agnew
Business Administrator   Mrs Stevie Wrigley

Activity, field study and adventure courses for groups. Facilities for self-run courses. Close to Dartmoor and south Devon coast. Wide range of options from eight years old, all year round.

The National Trust
Heelis, Kemble Dr, Swindon, Wiltshire SN2 2NA; URL www.nationaltrust.org.uk; Tel 01793 817575; Fax 01793 817401
Head (Learning and Interpretation) Laura Hetherington
The National Trust offers an educational resource with coast and countryside, historic buildings and gardens, archeological sites and historical monuments. More than 600 000 pupil visits a year; offer professional staff support, on-site study bases, residential opportunities, theatre projects, special projects and programmes across the curriculum.
Education Group membership provides free group entry to trust properties for one year.

Neige et Merveilles
Hameau de la Minière de Vallauria, 06430 St Dalmas-de-Tende, France; URL www.neige-merveilles.com; e-mail doc@neige-merveilles.com; Tel +33 4 93 04 62 40
Two-week to two-month holiday courses in Mercantour national park and the Vallée des Merveilles in the south of France, Alpes Maritimes. For ages 18 and over.

Orford Arts Centre
3165 Chemin du Parc, Orford, Québec J1X 7A2, Canada; URL www.arts-orford.org; e-mail centre@arts-orford.org; Tel +1 819 843 3981; Fax +1 819 843 7274
Courses and master class on bassoon, cello, chamber music, clarinet, flute, double bass, French horn, oboe, piano, viola, violin, voice

Outward Bound Scotland
Fort William, Highland PH33 7NN; URL www.outwardbound.org.uk; e-mail enquiries@outwardbound.org.uk; Tel 01397 772866
Courses in the Highlands, using a wide range of outdoor activities. Also courses using one particular activity, from specialised ice-climbing to outward bound land journeys and sea voyages. Courses open to individuals and groups; from age 14.

PGL Travel Ltd
Alton Ct, Penyard La, Ross-on-Wye, Herefordshire HR9 5GL; URL www.pgl.co.uk; e-mail enquiries@pgl.co.uk; Tel 0870 055 1551; Fax 0870 055 1561
One of Britain's leading school travel operators, with a range of 20 UK outdoor activity centres in the Wye Valley, Brecon Beacons, Devon, Dorset, Isle of Wight, Shropshire, Lincolnshire, Surrey and Scotland. Full board and accommodation in dormitories, chalets or tents. AALA licensed for activities in scope; BAHA, BCU and RYA inspected centres. Also canoeing, rafting, windsurfing and sailing in southern France and Spain at BCU and RYA approved centres; tours to three PGL centres in northern France and to hotels in Belgium, France, Germany, Holland, London and Eastern Europe; ski trips to Austria, France, Italy and Switzerland.

The Pony Club
NAC, Stoneleigh Pk, Kenilworth, Warwickshire CV8 2RW; URL www.pcuk.org; e-mail enquiries@pcuk.org; Tel 024 7669 8300; Fax 024 7669 6836
Youth organisation for those interested in riding and ponies. 360 branches throughout the British Isles; both sexes, up to the age of 25.

Ramblers Holidays Ltd
Box 43, Welwyn Garden City, Hertfordshire AL8 6PQ; URL www.ramblersholidays.co.uk; e-mail info@ramblersholidays.co.uk; Tel 01707 331133; Fax 01707 333276
General Manager Kathy Cook

Walking, trekking, cross-country skiing, alpine mountaineering worldwide; botany, bird-watching, city sightseeing and exploring tours

Scouts de Wiltz
Château de Wiltz, 9516 Wiltz, Grand Duchy of Luxembourg; URL www.scoutswiltz.lu; e-mail scoutswi@pt.lu; Tel +352 958 199
International European Scouting centre, providing camping facilities for schools, guides and scouts at 10 homes and 10 campsites, as well as site leaders and families

Scripture Union
207–209 Queensway, Bletchley, Milton Keynes MK2 2EB; URL www.scriptureunion.org.uk; e-mail media@scriptureunion.org.uk; Tel 01908 856000; Fax 01908 856111
Christian holidays and training courses for children and young people aged 8–18

Sealyham Activity Centre
Sealyham Mansion, Wolfscastle, Haverfordwest, Pembrokeshire SA62 5NF; URL www.sealyham.com; e-mail enquiries@sealyham.com; Tel 01348 840763; Fax 01348 841919
Outdoor pursuits courses for schools, including canoeing, climbing, abseiling, sailing, surfing, mountain biking. For ages 8–18; full-board and dormitory accommodation for more than 100 staff; field study groups also catered for. Licence ref R0044.

SOEC
Loaningdale Hse, Carwood Rd, Biggar, South Lanarkshire ML12 6LX; URL www.soec.org.uk; e-mail info@soec.org.uk; Tel 01899 221115; Fax 01899 220644
Four residential outdoor education centres situated in Aberfoyle, Biggar, Meigle and West Linton. Accommodation for groups of 10–250 people. Outdoor and environmental activities.

Sterts Theatre and Environmental Centre
Upton Cross, Liskeard, Cornwall PL14 5AZ; URL www.sterts.co.uk; e-mail sterts@btinternet; Tel 01579 362382
450-seat covered amphitheatre, studio, art gallery, conference and training centre, craft workshops, bistro/bar. Drama, music and ballet classes; performances in theatre May–September; October–April in the studio.

Tall Ships Youth Trust
2a The Hard, Portsmouth PO1 3PT; Tel 02392 832055; Fax 02392 815769
Chief Executive Christine Law

Union Belge de Spéléologie (UBS)
93 Rue Belvaux, B4030 Liege, Belgium; URL www.speleo.be/ubs; e-mail ubs@speleo.be; Tel +32 04 342 61 42; Fax +32 04 342 11 56
Caving school. Mountaineering and caving tuition (beginners to advanced); equipment available for hire; permanent organisation of technical and cultural activities. Initiation stage, for ages 15 and over.

14

Universidad Internacional de Malaga
Facultad de Filosofia y Letras, Campus de Teatinos s/n, Màlaga, Spain; URL www.filosofia.uma.es; e-mail mhm@uma.es; Tel +34 95 21 31682
Spanish language courses, summer and winter. Literature, History, Art, Music, Geography and Spanish culture; Diploma in Hispanic studies or Certificate of Proficiency in Spanish.

Universite d'été de Menton
c/o Office du Tourisme, Palais de l'Europe, 8 Avenue Boyer, BP 239, 06506 Menton, Cedex, France; URL www.univ-menton.com; e-mail ot@villedementon.com; Tel +33 4 92 41 76 90; Fax +33 4 92 41 76 58

Three-week summer school course in French for foreigners in July and August, minimum age 16. Classes for beginners, intermediate and advanced students and teacher training.

University of Dublin, Trinity College

Accommodation Office, Trinity College, Dublin 2, Republic of Ireland; URL www.tcd.ie/conferences; e-mail reservations@tcd.ie; Tel +353 1 896 1177; Fax +353 1 671 1267

Summer schools, language courses, group and individual accommodation

University of London Institute in Paris

An Institute of Advanced Study of the University of London

9–11 rue de Constantine, 75340, Paris Cedex 07, France; URL www.ulip.lon.ac.uk; e-mail d.shepheard@ulip.lon.ac.uk; Tel +33 1 44 11 73 73; Fax +33 1 45 50 31 55

BA, MA and diploma courses in French, translation and language teaching

The Venture Centre

Lewaigue Farm, Maughold, Isle of Man IM7 1AW; URL www.adventure-centre.co.uk; e-mail enquiries@adventure-centre.co.uk; Tel 01624 814240; Fax 01624 815615

Multi-activity adventure courses for groups and individuals. Activities include canoeing, climbing, abseiling, archery, assault course etc. Bunkhouse accommodation, maximum 130 people, March to October, two to seven nights, residential and non-residential courses. BAHA, BCU and RYA approved.

YHA (England and Wales) Ltd

Registered Charity Number 301657

PO Box 6028, Dimple Rd, Matlock, Derbyshire DE4 3YH; URL www.yha.org.uk; e-mail groupreservations@yha.org.uk; Tel 0870 770 8868; Fax 0870 770 6127

YHA provides low-cost accommodation for school groups, with a network of more than 220 youth hostels throughout England and Wales. Maximum support, with free leader places, a group reservations office and a range of more than 100 packages to meet the needs of each group.

Scottish Youth Hostels Association 7 Glebe Cres, Stirling FK8 2JA; URL www.syha.org.uk; e-mail info@syha.org.uk; Tel 01786 891400; Fax 01786 891333

Hostelling International Northern Ireland 22–32 Donegall Rd, Belfast BT12 5JN; URL www.hini.org.uk; e-mail info@hini.org.uk; Tel 028 9032 4733; Fax 028 9043 9699

YMCA – Fairthorne Manor

Fairthorne Manor, Curdridge, Southampton SO30 2GH; URL www.ymca-fg.org; e-mail info@ymca-fg.org; Tel 01489 785228; Fax 01489 798936

An outdoor education and training centre for schools, colleges, youth service and industry, located on the River Hamble. Open daily throughout the year, it welcomes groups with a wide range of special needs. Fully programmed or project-based programmes available; activities include sailing, canoeing, climbing, archery, assault courses, aerial runway and environmental activities. Registered with the AALA, BCU and RYA.

YMCA – Isle of Wight

Winchester Hse, Sandown Rd, Shanklin, Isle of Wight PO37 6HU; URL www.ymca-fg.org; e-mail winchesterhouse@ymca-fg.org; Tel 01489 785228; Tel 01983 862441; Fax 01983 863513

Winchester House has accommodation for 10–135 people. Lounges, teaching rooms and function rooms are available. Full board including packed lunches for days out. For smaller groups the lodge can accommodate 10–24 people.

Voluntary Service and Working Holidays (Home and Abroad)

Co-ordinating Committee for International Voluntary Service

Unesco, 1 rue Miollis, 75732 Paris - Cedex 15, France; URL www.unesco.org/ccivs; e-mail ccivs.@unesco.org; Tel +33 1 45 68 49 36; Fax +33 1 42 73 05 21

Administration Regis Colin
Director S. Costanzo

CCIVS is a co-ordinating body for short, medium or long-term voluntary services organisations worldwide. It can provide lists of contacts in many countries, but applicants should apply in the first instance to organisations in their own country. Publications include National Service – what are the choices?, Running a Workshop, How to Present a Project, The Volunteer's Handbook, Volunteering in Conflict Areas, The Leader Trainer Handbook, Fundraising Strategies for Non-Governmental Organisations, Report of South-South: North-South Exchanges Seminar, International Cookbook for Workcamps, Games and Exercises, Games North/South. Enquirers should check the information online.

CSV (Community Service Volunteers)

Registered Charity Number 291222

237 Pentonville Rd, London N1 9NJ; URL www.csvcommunitypartners.org.uk; e-mail education@csv.org.uk; Tel 020 7643 1435; Fax 020 7833 0149

Director (CSV Education for Citizenship) Peter Hayes

CSV (Community Service Volunteers) is a UK charity that provides support for schools to help develop citizenship as an active part of their curriculum. Practical tools, training materials and learning workshops provide teachers, parents and pupils with a practical approach to citizenship. Projects include peer learning; role play situations highlighting bullying, racism and sexism; surveying social attitudes amongst pupils and local residents; intergenerational projects and initiatives to develop communities through the arts, sciences and sport.

International Voluntary Service

South: Old Hall, East Bergholt, Colchester, Essex CO7 6TQ; URL www.ivs-gb.org.uk; e-mail ivssouth@ivs-gb.org.uk; Tel 01206 298215

North: Oxford Place Centre, Oxford Pl, Leeds LS1 3AX; e-mail ivsnorth@ivs-gb.org.uk; Tel 0113 246 9900; Fax 0113 246 9910

Hon Treasurer Amy Fox
Secretary S. Davies

International Voluntary Service is the UK Branch of Service Civil International – an international peace movement. It exists to promote true international understanding by bringing together people of different nationalities, backgrounds, ages and beliefs in effective community service. It organises about 60 international workcamps a year in Britain, and sends British volunteers to workcamps in more than 30 countries (minimum age 18).

Voluntary Service Overseas

Registered Charity Number 313757

317 Putney Bridge Rd, London SW15 2PN; URL www.vso.org.uk; e-mail enquiry@vso.org.uk; Tel 020 8780 7500

Director M. Goldring

VSO is an international development charity that works through volunteers. VSO enables people aged 18–75 to share their skills and experience with communities and organisations across the developing world. Placements are in education, health, natural resources, technical trades, engineering, business, communications and social development; more than 1500 volunteers work in 40 countries in Africa, Asia, and the Pacific. Standard VSO placements are usually for one to two years; VSO youth programmes offer shorter placements. Volunteers must be willing to work for a modest living allowance.

Other Organisations Concerned with Voluntary Service Abroad

Church Mission Society

157 Waterloo Rd, London SE1 8UU; URL www.cms-uk.org; e-mail info@cms-uk.org; Tel 020 7928 8681; Fax 020 7401 3215

Experience Exchange Programme

USPG: Anglicans in World Mission, 200 Great Dover St, London SE1 4YB; URL www.uspg.org.uk; e-mail eep@uspg.org.uk; Tel 020 7378 5677

Contact   Habib Nader

This programme provides the opportunity for people aged 18 and over to experience life in another part of the world for six months to a year. Participants work as volunteers alongside local people in church-based projects such as schools, community development programmes and hostels. No special skills are necessary, although those with particular expertise can be placed accordingly. Placements are in Africa, Asia, the Caribbean, Europe and Latin America. The programme is run jointly by USPG, an Anglican mission agency, and the Methodist Church.

Girlguiding UK

17–19 Buckingham Palace Rd, London SW1W 0PT; URL www.girlguiding.org.uk; e-mail chq@girlguiding.org.uk; Tel 020 7834 6242; Fax 020 7828 8317

Chief Executive   Denise King

International Service

Hunter Hse, 57 Goodramgate, York YO1 7FX; URL www.internationalservice.org.uk; e-mail is@internationalservice.org.uk; Tel 01904 647799; Fax 01904 652353

UNAIS, Suite 3a, York YO1 7FX

Administrator (Recruitment)   Stella Hobbs

International Service works to promote self-reliance and long-term, sustainable development in West Africa, Latin America, and the West Bank and Gaza. It provides skilled and experienced personnel to collaborate with locally organised initiatives. Contact the recruitment administrator for further details.

Liverpool Hope University

Liverpool Hope University, Hope Pk, Liverpool, Merseyside L16 9JD; URL www.hope.ac.uk; e-mail enquiry@hope.ac.uk; Tel 0151 291 3000; Fax 0151 291 3100

Hope One World is Liverpool Hope University's overseas education charity which runs summer projects to aid the development of communities in Africa, the Indian sub-continent and Brazil.

Returned Volunteer Action

76 Wentworth St, London E1 7SA; e-mail retvolact@lineone.net; Tel 020 7247 6406

RVA is an independent membership organisation of and for serving overseas volunteers and development workers, and those interested or active in development work. RVA does not send people overseas. RVA's main aims are to press for improvements in overseas programmes, especially in training, support and project evaluation; to help returned workers evaluate their overseas experience and feed it into action in this country; to encourage those seeking placements overseas to examine their personal and political motivations and expectations. The membership database enables returned workers to be in touch on a cross-agency

basis, and enables prospective volunteers to learn from their knowledge.

RVA is a small organisation and much of its work is done through its regular newsletter and its publications, Thinking about Volunteering and Volunteering Overseas, and Development: A Guide to Opportunities. Available as a joint pack for £3.50 and 58p SAE; cheques payable to RVA. Full resources list or membership form available on request.

The Salvation Army Schools and Colleges Unit

Territorial Headquarters, 101 Newington Causeway, London SE1 6BN; URL www.salvationarmy.org.uk/schools; e-mail schools@salvationarmy.org.uk; Tel 020 7367 4706; Fax 020 7367 4728

Save the Children UK

1 St John's La, London EC1M 4AR; URL www.savethechildren.org.uk; e-mail supporter.care@savethechildren.org.uk; Tel 020 7012 6400; Fax 020 7012 6963

Development Education Unit provides a range of teaching packs and resources. Details available from above address.

The Scout Association

Gilwell Pk, Bury Rd, Chingford, London E4 7QW; URL www.scouts.org.uk; e-mail info.centre@scout.org.uk; Tel 0845 300 1818; Fax 020 8433 7103

Toc H

The Stable Block, The Firs, High St, Whitchurch, Aylesbury, Buckinghamshire HP22 4JU; URL www.toch.org.uk; e-mail info@toch.org.uk; Tel 01296 642020; Fax 01296 640022

Working Holidays

This does not claim to be a complete list of firms and organisations offering voluntary work and working holidays. The inclusion of an editorial entry does not imply approval; equally exclusion does not imply disapproval.

ATD-Fourth World

48 Addington Sq, London SE5 7LB; URL www.atd-uk.org; e-mail atd@atd-uk.org; Tel 020 7703 3231; Fax 020 7252 4276

ATD Fourth World is an international human rights organisation whose aim is to combat extreme poverty and social exclusion by working in partnership with poor people themselves. It runs a respite home in Surrey, creative workshops for young families in Southwark, and has a family support team helping families to build and strengthen their own support networks.

BTCV

See also BTCV entry in Chapter 13: Voluntary Services and Groups

Sedum Hse, Mallard Way, Doncaster, South Yorkshire DN4 8DB; URL www.btcv.org; e-mail information@btcv.org.uk; Tel 01302 388883

Work includes tailored educational activities to engage children in practical environmental tasks, advice to schools, youth-focused activities, active community groups network, training courses, publications. It runs more than 400 conservation working holidays a year throughout the UK, ranging from a weekend to a fortnight; tree planting, habitat management, waterways and wetlands, hills, heaths and coasts. For ages 16–70; from £40, including accommodation and food; international working holidays in countries such as America, Ecuador, Hungary, Iceland, Japan and New Zealand for people over 18. Book holidays via online shop www.btcv.org/shop which also sells insurance, trees, wildflowers, tools and clothing.

BTCV Scotland

Balallan Hse, 24 Allan Pk, Stirling FK8 2QG; URL www.btcv.org.uk; e-mail scotland@btcv.org.uk; Tel 01786 479697; Fax 01786 465359

14

Concordia

Registered Charity Number 305991
19 North St, Portslade, East Sussex BN41 1DH;
URL www.concordia-iye.org.uk; e-mail
info@concordia-iye.org.uk; Tel 01273 422218;
Fax 01273 421182

International Volunteer Projects

Concordia is a charity committed to international
volunteering as a means to promoting intercultural
understanding. Its International Volunteer Programme
offers volunteers aged 18 and over the opportunity to join
international teams of volunteers working on short-term
projects in more than 60 countries in Europe, North
America, the Middle East, Latin America, Africa and Asia. A
selection of projects is available for teenagers aged 16 and 17.
Projects include conservation, restoration, archaeology,
construction, arts, children's play schemes and teaching.
Projects last for two–four weeks with the main season from
June to September. Volunteers pay a registration fee of £150
and fund their own travel and insurance. Board and
accommodation is free of charge

Corrymeela Community

Ballycastle, County Antrim BT54 6QU;
URL www.corrymeela.org; e-mail
ballycastle@corrymeela.org; Tel 028 2076 2626
8 Upper Cres, Belfast BT7 1NT; Tel 028 9050 8080
An ecumenical Christian community working for
reconciliation with a wide range of youth, school, family and
community groups from all backgrounds, who stay for three
to four days at the 120-bedded complex. During July and
August, volunteers are invited to apply to help for one to
three weeks with families, youth projects and as resource
people in arts and crafts, recreation, kitchen etc.

Friday Bridge International Farm Camp

March Rd, Wisbech, Cambridgeshire PE14 0LR;
URL www.fridaybridge.com; e-mail
info@fridaybridge.com; Tel 01945 860255;
Fax 01945 861088
Fruit picking for individuals and groups, for ages 17 and
over; hostel accommodation, meals and entertainment
provided

Frontiers Foundation/Operation Beaver

419 Coxwell Ave, Toronto, Ontario M4L 3B9, Canada;
URL www.frontiersfoundation.ca; e-mail
frontiersfoundation@on.aibn.com; Tel +1 416 690 3930;
Fax +1 416 690 3934
Voluntary service for people aged 18 and over. Work with
native and/or low income Canadians on housing
construction and/or renovation; three months minimum.

GAP Activity Projects (GAP) Ltd

44 Queen's Rd, Reading RG1 4BB; e-mail
volunteer@gap.org.uk; Tel 0118 959 4914;
Fax 0118 957 6634
Offers voluntary work opportunities overseas in 24
countries for 17–25 year olds. Placements include teaching
English, medical care and caring, environmental work and
outdoor education. They last three to 12 months, leaving
time to travel independently. Those interested should apply
as early as possible; for details or a brochure please contact
GAP at the above number.

Jeunesse et Reconstruction

10 rue de Trevise, 75009 Paris, France;
URL www.volontariat.org; e-mail info@volontariat.org;
Tel +33 1 4770 15 88
International workcamps in Africa, the Far East, North
America, Western and Eastern Europe. Grape-picking in
France; long-term voluntary work in France; social and
educational long-term stays in Costa Rica, Europe, Japan,
Kenya and the USA.

Kibbutz Representatives

16 Accommodation Rd, London NW11 8EP; e-mail
enquiries@kibbutz.org.uk; Tel 020 8458 9235;
Fax 020 8455 7930

The kibbutz volunteer programme is for young people aged
18–40 from all over the world, who wish to spend time living
on a kibbutz in Israel, while helping its community.
Minimum stay eight weeks; maximum eight months, the
price includes return flight and airport taxes, full-board and
lodging, and insurance in return for working eight hours a
day, six days a week. Medical certificate and two character
references required; informal interview and full orientation
given.

Project Trust

Hebridean Centre, Isle of Coll, Argyll and Bute PA78 6TE;
URL www.projecttrust.org.uk; e-mail
info@projecttrust.org.uk; Tel 01879 230444;
Fax 01879 230357
Gap year organisation. Projects in Africa, Southern and
Central America, Middle and Far East for young people
aged between 17 and 19 who are about to leave school. Work
as teacher-aides, in social service, in development projects
etc. for 12 months. Applications must be made at least eight
months before departure in August/September.

The Royal Society for the Protection of Birds

Residential Volunteering Scheme, Volunteering
Development Dept, RSPB, The Lodge, Sandy,
Bedfordshire SG19 2DL; URL www.rspb.org.uk/
volunteering/residential; e-mail
volunteers@rspb.org.uk; Tel 01767 680551;
Fax 01767 692365
Residential volunteering on 39 nature reserves throughout
the UK

Scripture Union

207–209 Queensway, Bletchley, Milton Keynes,
Buckinghamshire MK2 2EB; e-mail
info@scriptureunion.org.uk; Tel 01908 856000;
Fax 01908 856111
Working with children, young people and families for one–
two weeks on Christian holidays and missions (mainly July
to August); longer overseas placements. Minimum age 18.

Service archeologique de Douai

227 Rue Jean Perrin, 59500 Douai, France; e-mail
pdemolon@douaisis-agglo.com; Tel +33 3 27 08 88 50;
Fax +33 3 27 08 88 88
Work on archaeological digs during school summer
holidays. Minimum stay two weeks.

Tunstead International Farm Camp

c/o Place UK Ltd, Church Farm, Tunstead, Norwich,
Norfolk NR12 8RQ; URL www.ifctunstead.co.uk; e-mail
info@ifctunstead.co.uk; Tel 01692 536337;
Fax 01692 535493
International farm camp, January to December. Fruit
picking and market gardening; for ages 18 and over.

Union REMPART

1 rue des Guillemites, 75004 Paris, France;
URL www.rempart.com; e-mail contact@rempart.com;
Tel +33 1 42 71 96 55; Fax +33 1 42 71 73 00
Work-camps in all parts of France at weekends and in Easter
and summer holidays; normally for ages 13 and over.
Restoration and conservation work on historic monuments
and archaeology.

VentureCo

The Ironyard, 64–66 The Market Pl, Warwick, Warwickshire
CV34 4SD; URL www.ventureco-worldwide.com; e-mail
mail@ventureco-worldwide.com; Tel 01926 411122;
Fax 01926 411133

Zentralstelle fur Arbeitsvermittlung der Bundesanstalt fur Arbeit (ZAV)

53107 Bonn, Germany; URL www.arbeitsamt.de;
Tel +49 228 1713 1400; Fax +49 228 1713 1400
ZAV is the federal government office which deals with
applications for temporary and permanent employment
from people from abroad

Overseas Education

15

International Education Organisations

Embassies – Educational and Cultural Attachés

Overseas Education

British Council

Headquarters, 10 Spring Gdns, London SW1A 2BN;
Tel 020 7930 8466
Chair   The Rt Hon Lord Neil Kinnock
Director General   Sir David Green
Secretary to the British Council   Julia Race; Tel 020 7389 4675
Director (Education UK Marketing)   Christine Bateman;
Tel 0161 389 7072
Director (Education, Science and Society)   Gordon Slaven;
Tel 020 7389 4487
Director (Higher Education)   Pat Killingley;
Tel 0161 957 7135
Director (Northern Ireland)   Colm McGivern;
Tel 028 9024 8220 ext 224
Director (Schools and Teachers)   Olga Stanojlovic;
Tel 020 7389 4693
Director (Scotland)   Roy Cross; Tel 0131 524 5700
Director (Vocational Partnerships)   Katie Epstein
Director (Wales)   Kevin Higgins; Tel 02920 397357
Head (Vocational Partnerships)   Kate Epstein;
Tel 020 7389 4382
Manager (Scottish Education and Training)   Julia Amour;
Tel 0131 524 5753
*Manager (Seminars and Visits, Contracts Projects and Scholar
Management)*   Sheila Lumsden; Tel 0161 957 7554

Commonwealth Institute

New Zealand Hse, 80 Haymarket, London SW1Y 4TQ;
URL www.commonwealth.org.uk; e-mail
information@commonwealth-institute.org;
Tel 020 7024 9822; Fax 020 7024 9833

Council of British International Schools (COBIS)

Oxford Brookes University, Harcourt Hill Campus, Oxford,
Oxfordshire OX2 4AT; URL www.cobis.org.uk; e-mail
general.secretary@cobis.org.uk; Tel 01865 488564;
Fax 01865 488666
Chair   Roger Fry CBE
Treasurer   Mike Roberts OBE

Belgium

British International School of Brussels
163 Ave Emile Max, 1030 Brussels, Belgium;
URL www.bisb.org; e-mail schooloffice@bisb.org;
Tel +32 2 736 8981; Fax +32 2 736 8981
Headteacher   Stephen Prescott BEng, MA, PGCE

The British Junior Academy of Brussels
83 Bvd St Michel, 1040 Brussels, Belgium;
URL www.bjab.org; e-mail bjabrussels@yahoo.com;
Tel +32 2 732 5376; Fax +32 2 732 5376
Headteacher   Diane Perry

The British School of Brussels
Leuvensesteenweg 19, 3080, Tervuren, Belgium;
URL www.britishschool.be; e-mail
principal@britishschool.be; Tel +32 2 766 0430;
Fax +32 2 767 8070
Principal   Roland S. Chant MA

St Paul's British Primary School
Stationsstraat 3, 3080 Tervuren, Belgium;
URL www.stpaulsbsb.com; e-mail info@stpaulsbsb.com;
Tel +32 2 767 3098; Fax +32 2 767 0351
Headteacher   Katie Tyrie

Czech Republic

The English College in Prague
Sokolovska 320, 190 00 Praha 9, Vysocany, Czech Republic;
URL www.englishcollege.cz; e-mail
headmaster@englishcollege.cz; Tel +420 283 893 113
Headteacher   Peter de Voil

Prague British School
Charlese de Gaulla 19/91, 160 00 Prague 6, Czech Republic;
URL www.pbschool.cz; e-mail info@pbschool.cz;
Tel +420 226 096 200; Fax +420 226 096 201
Educational Director   Jeremy Long

Riverside School, Prague
Roztocka 9, Sedlec, 160 00 Prague 6, Czech Republic;
URL www.riversideschool.cz; e-mail
director@riversideschool.cz; Tel +420 224 315 336;
Fax +420 224 325 765
Director   Peter Daish

Denmark

Rygaards School
Bernstorffsvej 54, 2900 Hellerup, Denmark;
URL www.rygaards.com; e-mail admin@rygaards.com;
Tel +45 39 621053; Fax +45 39 621081
Headteacher   Charles Dalton

France

British School of Paris
38 Quai de l'Ecluse, 78290 Croissy-sur-Seine, France;
URL www.britishschool.fr; e-mail
registrar@britishschool.fr; Tel +33 1 34 80 45 90;
Fax +33 1 39 76 12 69
Headteacher   Richard Woodhall

15

Mougins School

615 Ave Dr Maurice Donat, Font de l'Arme, BP 401, 06251
  Mougins Cedex, France;
  URL www.mougins-school.com; e-mail
  information@mougins-school.com; Tel +33 4 93 90 15 47;
  Fax +33 4 93 75 31 40
Headteacher   Brian Hickmore

Germany

Berlin British School

Dickensweg 17–19, 14055 Berlin, Germany;
  URL www.berlinbritishschool.de; e-mail
  bbs.enq@t-online.de; Tel +49 30 351 09190;
  Fax +49 30 351 09199
Headteacher   Suzanne Owen-Hughes

Independent Bonn International School

Tulpenbaumweg 42, 53177 Bonn, Germany;
  URL www.ibis-school.com; e-mail ibis@ibis-school.com;
  Tel +49 228 32 31 66; Fax +49 228 32 39 58
Headteacher   Irene Bolik MA, CertEd

Greece

Campion School, Athens

PO Box 67484, Pallini 153 02, Greece;
  URL www.campion.edu.gr; e-mail sather@hol.gr;
  Tel +30 210 607 1700; Fax +30 210 607 1750
Headteacher   Stephen Atherton

Italy

Andersen School

International Institute of Child Studies srl, Via Don Carlo
  San Martino 8, 20133 Milano, Italy;
  URL www.andersen-school.it; e-mail
  info@andersen-school.it; Tel +39 02 70 006580;
  Fax +39 02 71 094459
Consultant Head   Sheila Stokes

The New School Rome

Via della Camilluccia 669, 00135 Rome, Italy;
  URL www.newschoolrome.com; e-mail
  info@newschoolrome.com; Tel +39 06 329 4269;
  Fax +39 06 329 7546
Headteacher   Domini MacRory

St George's British International School

Via Cassia Km 16, La Storta, 00123 Rome, Italy;
  URL www.stgeorge.school.it; e-mail
  principal@stgeorge.school.it; Tel +39 06 308 6001;
  Fax +39 06 308 92490
Principal   Nicholas Johnson

Sir James Henderson British School, Milan

Via Pisani Dossi 16, 20134 Milano, Italy;
  URL www.sjhschool.com; e-mail
  trevor.church@sjhschool.com; Tel +39 02 210 941;
  Fax +39 02 210 94225
Principal   Trevor Church

St Louis School

Via Caviglia 1, 20139 Milano, Italy;
  URL www.stlouisschool.it; e-mail
  info@stlouisschool.com; Tel +39 02 55 231235;
  Fax +39 02 56 610885
Head   Natasha Croad

Luxembourg

St George's International School, Luxembourg

Rue des Marguerites, L-2127 Weimershof, Luxembourg;
  URL www.st-georges.lu; e-mail info@st-georges.lu;
  Tel +352 42 32 24; Fax +352 42 32 34
Headteacher   Heather Duxbury

The Netherlands

British School of Amsterdam

Anthonie van Dijckstraat 1, 1077 ME Amsterdam, The
  Netherlands; URL www.britams.nl; e-mail
  info@britams.nl; Tel +31 20 679 7840; Fax +31 20 675 8396
Principal   Mr M.W.G. Roberts OBE, MA, MBA

The British School in The Netherlands

Rosenburgherlaan 2, 2252 BA Voorschoten, The
  Netherlands; URL www.britishschool.nl; e-mail
  info@britishschool.nl; Tel +31 70 315 4064;
  Fax +31 71 560 2290
Principal   Trevor Rowell MA

Norway

British International School of Stavanger

Gauselbakken 107, 4032, Stavanger, Norway;
  URL www.stavanger-british-school.no; e-mail
  principal@biss.no; Tel +47 51 95 0250; Fax +47 51 95 5025
Principal   Anne Howells

Oslo International School

PO Box 53, 1318 Bekkestua, Norway;
  URL www.oslointernationalschool.no; e-mail
  ois.main@aktivepost.no; Tel +47 67 81 8290;
  Fax +47 67 81 8291
Principal   Barbara Carlsen

Portugal

St Julian's School, Portugal

Quinta Nova 2776–601, Carcavelos, Lisbon, Portugal;
  URL www.stjulians.com; e-mail mail@stjulians.com;
  Tel +351 21 458 5300; Fax +351 21 458 5312
Headteacher   David Smith

Romania

Fundatia International British School of Bucharest

Str Agricultori Nr 21, Sector 2, Bucharest, Romania;
  URL www.ibsb.ro; e-mail office@ibsb.ro;
  Tel +40 21 252 3704; Fax +40 21 253 1697
Principal   Julian Hingley

Serbia and Montenegro

Chartwell School

Teodora Drajzera 38, 11 000 Belgrade, Serbia and
  Montenegro; URL www.chartwellinternational.org;
  e-mail reception@chartwellinternational.org;
  Tel +381 11 367 5299; Fax +381 11 367 5340
Principal   Michael O'Grady

Spain

The British School of Alicante

c/del Reino Unido 5, Alicante 03008, Spain;
  URL www.bsalicante.com; e-mail bsa@kingsgroup.org;
  Tel +34 96 510 6351; Fax +34 96 510 8096
Headteacher   Elaine Blaus

The British School of Gran Canaria

Crta Tafira a Marzagan, El Sabinal, 35017 Las Palmas, Gran
  Canaria, Spain; URL www.bs-gc.net; e-mail
  hardes@bs-gc.net; Tel +34 928 351167;
  Fax +34 928 351065
Director   Steven Hardes

The English International College

Urb Ricmar, Carretera de Cádiz Km. 189.5, 29600 Marbella,
  Málaga, Spain; URL www.eic.edu; e-mail
  director@eic.edu; Tel +34 95 283 1058;
  Fax +34 95 283 8992
Headteacher   Yvonne Stevenson (Acting)

King's College

Paseo de los Andes, 35, 28761 Soto de Viñuelas, Madrid,
Spain; URL www.kingscollege.es; e-mail
info@kingscollege.es; Tel +34 91 803 4800;
Fax +34 91 803 6557
Headteacher   David Johnson MSc

Sierra Bernia School

Apartado 121, La Caneta s/n, San Rafael 03580, Alfaz Del Pi,
Alicante, Spain; e-mail duncan@ctv.es;
Tel +34 96 687 5149; Fax +34 96 687 3633
Headteacher   Duncan M. Allan

Sweden

British International Primary School of Stockholm

Östra Valhallavägen 17, 182~68 Djursholm, Sweden;
URL www.britishinternationalprimaryschool.se; e-mail
borgen@britishinternationalprimaryschool.se;
Tel +46 8 755 23 75; Fax +46 8 755 26 35
Principal   Jane Crowley

Switzerland

Aiglon College

1885 Chesières-Villars, Switzerland; URL www.aiglon.ch;
e-mail info@aiglon.ch; Tel +41 24 496 6161;
Fax +41 24 496 6162
Headteacher   Peter Armstrong

Turkey

British Embassy Study Group, Ankara

Sehit Ersan Caddesi 46/a, Çankaya 06680, Ankara, Turkey;
URL www.besg.org; e-mail admin@besg.org;
Tel +90 312 468 6239; Tel +90 312 468 6563
Headteacher   David J. Draper BEd, MA, FCollP

British International School of Istanbul

Dihayat Spok No 18, Etiler, 34337 Istanbul, Turkey;
URL www.bis.k12.tr; Tel +90 21 22 027027

Council of Europe

F-67075 Strasbourg CEDEX, France; URL www.coe.int;
Tel +33 3 88 41 20 00

European Cultural Convention

Tel +33 3 88 41 21 12

Council of Europe, Directorate of School, Out-of-School and
Higher Education, F-67075 Strasbourg CEDEX, France

The European Cultural Convention is the legal framework
for the Council of Europe's activities in education and
culture. Co-operation with 46 member states and
Mediterranean countries.

Education programmes

European dimension of education; education for democratic
citizenship and human rights; management of diversity and
intercultural and interreligious dialogue; targeted assistance
for education systems in priority countries; history teaching;
teacher training; language education policies; education of
Roma children in Europe; higher education and research –
recognition of qualifications, public responsibility for higher
education and research, higher education governance, and
establishment of a European Higher Education Area by
2010.

Partnerships

European Union, Unesco, OECD, OSCE, Nordic Council of
Ministers, World Bank, Euro-Arab/Euro-Mediterranean co-
operation, relations with non-European countries

European Commission

8 Storey's Gate, London SW1P 3AT; URL ec.europa.eu/
unitedkingdom
Head of Representation   Reijo Kemppinen
The European Commission's Representation is directly
responsible to the commission's headquarters in Brussels. Its
representative offices are independent of the governments
of the countries in which they are based. The commission's
principal functions are to propose legislation, to manage
established community policies, and to be the guardian of
the treaties setting up the union. The representation in the
UK, through its four offices, reports directly to the
commission on political, economic and social developments
throughout the UK; in partnership with others, it explains
the likely impact of policies, programmes, and proposals for
future action, and stimulates debate on the future of the
European Union. The European Commission supports a
network of information providers throughout the country,
thereby enabling the public to have access to EU information
at a local level.

European Resource Centre Scotland

Rosebery Hse, 9 Haymarket Terr, Edinburgh EH12 5EZ;
URL www.eurodesk.org.uk; Tel 0131 313 2488;
Fax 0131 313 6800
Information Officer   Catherine Thwaites
The European Resource Centre deals with enquiries relating
to Europe from pupils, students and their teachers from
schools and colleges. The information held by the ERC
includes information on EU institutions and both free and
priced publications relating to Europe and European
countries.

European Commission Office in Wales

2 Caspian Point, Caspian Way, Cardiff CF10 4QQ;
URL www.cec.org.uk/wales/index.htm; e-mail
christine.mcgrath@ec.europa.eu; Tel 02920 895020;
Fax 02920 895035

European Commission Office in Northern Ireland

Windsor Hse, 9–15 Bedford St, Belfast BT2 7EG;
URL ec.europa.eu/northernireland; e-mail
eddie.mcveigh@ec.europa.eu; Tel 028 9024 0708;
Fax 028 9024 8241
Head of Office   Eddie McVeigh

Eurodesk UK (Scotland)

Rosebery Hse, 9 Haymarket Terr, Edinburgh EH12 5EZ;
URL www.eurodesk.org.uk; Tel 0131 3132 2488;
Fax 0131 313 6800
Information Officer   Catherine Thwaites
Eurodesk deals with enquiries from young people and those
who work with them relating to European opportunities
and European funding

EC Members – Education Ministries

Belgium

Flemish Ministry of Education

Rijksadministrarief Centrum, Arcadengebouw Blk F, 1010
Brussels, Belgium; Tel +32 2 210 5511

Ministry of National Education (French Speaking)

1 Rue Ad Lavalee, 1080 Brussels, Belgium;
URL www.cfwb.be/infosup; e-mail
chantal.kaufman@cfwb.be; Tel +32 2 690 87 02;
Fax +32 2 690 87 60

Denmark

Undervisningsministeriet

Frederiksholms Kanal 21, DK-1220 Copenhagen K,
Denmark; Tel +45 33 92 50 00; Fax +45 33 92 55 47
Minister (Education)   Margrethe Vestager

15

France

Ministry of National Education

110 rue de Grenelle, 75357 Paris 07SP, France;
URL www.education.gouv.fr; Tel +33 1 55 55 10 10

Federal Republic of Germany

Federal Ministry for Economic Co-operation and Development

53113 Bonn, Friedrich-Ebert-Allee 40, Bonn, Germany;
Tel +49 228 5350

Federal Minister   Carl-Dieter Spranger

Federal Ministry of Education and Research

Heinemannstrasse 2, D-53175 Bonn, Germany; e-mail
bmbf@bmbf.bund.de; Tel +49 1888 57 0;
Fax +49 1888 57 83601

Minister (Education and Research)   Edelgard Bulmahn

Staendige Konferenz der Kultusminister der Laender in der Bundesrepublik Deutschland (Standing Conference of the Ministers of Education and Cultural Affairs of the Lander in the Federal Republic of Germany)

Lenné Str 6, 53113 Bonn, Germany; URL www.kmk.org;
e-mail presse@kmk.org; Tel +49 228 5010;
Fax +49 228 501 777

Ireland

Department of Education

Marlborough St, Dublin 1, Republic of Ireland;
Tel +353 1 734 700

Minister (Education)   Micheal Martin TD

Examinations Section

Cornamaddy, Athlone, County Westmeath, Republic of
Ireland; Tel 01902 74621

Post-Primary Branch   Hawkins Hse, Dublin 2, Republic of
Ireland; Tel +353 1 734700

Primary Branch   Cornamadd, Athlone, County Westmeath,
Republic of Ireland

Italy

Ministero dell'Istruzione, dell' Università e della Ricera

Viale Trastevere 76A, 00153 Roma, Italy;
URL www.istruzione.it; e-mail
communicazione.uff4@istruzione.it; Tel 390 658 491

Luxembourg

Ministère de l'Education Nationale, et de la Formation Professionnelle et des Sports

Ministere de l'Education Nationale, de la Formation
Professionelle, 29 rue Aldringen, L-2926 Luxembourg;
URL www.men.lu; Tel +352 478 5185

Minister (Education)   Mady Delvaux-Stehres

General Co-ordinator of the Ministry
M. Siggy Koenig;   Conseiller de Gouvernement 1ère
Classe

The Netherlands

The Ministry of Education, Culture and Science

PO Box 25000, NL-2700 LZ Zoetermeer, The Netherlands;
URL www.minocw.nl; e-mail webmaster@minocw.nl;
Tel +31 79 3232323; Fax +31 79 3232320;
Telex 32636 MINO NL

Minister (Education and Science)   Drs L.M.L.H.A. Hermans

European Council of International Schools (ECIS)

21b Lavant St, Petersfield, Hampshire GU32 3EL;
URL www.ecis.org; e-mail ecis@ecis.org;
Tel 01730 268244; Fax 01730 267914

Executive Director   Dixie McKay

ECIS is an independent, non-profitmaking membership
organisation representing the interests of more than 400
international schools in Europe and throughout the world,
which provide education for the children of the local
expatriate community. Professional development services
include conferences, online learning, the international
teacher certification program, fellowship grants and
awards. Resources available from ECIS include the
International Schools Directory, International Schools
Journal, Effective International Schools publications and the
annual statistical survey. ECIS currently has 31 subject and
administrative committees which are a resource covering
every discipline.

Institut Français d'Ecosse/French Institute (IFE)

13 Randolph Cres, Edinburgh EH3 7TT; e-mail
contact@ifecosse.org.uk; Tel 0131 225 5366;
Fax 0131 220 0648

Director   Anne Laval

Deputy Director; Education Attaché   Aziza Ouardani

The French Institute of Scotland (IFE) develops cultural,
educational and linguistic co-operation between France and
Scotland, on behalf of the French Foreign Office; it is placed
under the authority of the cultural service of the French
Embassy in the UK. It is supported by a consultive
committee, the Society of Friends of the Institut français
d'Ecosse.

IFE is a place for cultural dialogue between Scotland and
France, which sets up cultural events around Scotland; a
linguistic centre which offers French language courses; an
education service to develop co-operation between France
and Scottish educational institutions, and promote the
teaching of French in schools and universities in Scotland;
and an information centre about contemporary France, with
a multimedia library.

The educational co-operation office, headed by a linguistic
attaché, gives support to teachers, academics of various
disciplines and education administrators who are actively
involved in the promotion of the French language in
Scotland.

Royal Commonwealth Society

25 Northumberland Ave, London WC2N 5AP;
URL www.rcsint.org; e-mail info@rcsint.org;
Tel 020 7930 6733; Fax 020 7930 9705

Director General   Stuart Mole

Schola Europaea – European Schools

European Commission, rue Joseph II, 30, 2nd Fl, B-1049
Brussels, Belgium; URL www.eursc.org;
Tel +32 2 95 37 46; Tel +32 2 95 62 70

The European schools are official educational
establishments controlled jointly by the governments of the
member states of the European Union. In all of these
countries they are legally regarded as public institutions.
The mission of the European schools is to provide a
multilingual, multicultural and multidenominational
education for nursery, primary and secondary level pupils.

Alicante European School

Avenida Locutor Vicente Hipólito s/n, 03540 Playa de San Juan, Alicante, Spain; e-mail beatriz.font@eursc.org; Tel +34 965 15 56 10; Fax +34 965 26 97 77

Bergen European School

Molenweidtje 5, Postbus 99, NL-1860 AB Bergen (NH), The Netherlands; URL www.eursc.org; e-mail info.esbergen@eursc.org; Tel +31 72 5890109; Fax +31 72 5896862

Headteacher   S. Gardeli

Kindergarten; primary and secondary education in five language sections

Brussels I European School

Ave du Vert Chasseur 46, 1180 Brussels, Belgium; e-mail kari.kivinen@eursc.org; Tel +32 2 373 86 11; Fax +32 2 375 47 16

Headteacher   Kari Kivinen

Brussels II European School

Ave Oscar Jespers 75, B-1200 Brussels, Belgium; Tel +32 774 22 11; Fax +32 774 22 43

Brussels III European School

Bvd du Triomphe, 135, 1050 Brussels, Belgium; URL www.eeb3.eu; Tel +32 629 47 00; Fax +32 629 47 92

Culham European School

Culham, Abingdon, Oxfordshire OX14 3DZ; URL www.eursc.org; e-mail esculham@eursc.org; Tel 01235 522621; Fax 01235 554609

Headteacher   Mr U. Pedersen

Frankfurt European School

Praunheimer Weg 126, D-60439 Frankfurt am Main, Germany; e-mail peter.friss@eursc.org; Tel +49 69 92 88 74 0; Fax +49 69 92 88 74 74

Karlsruhe European School

Albert-Schweitzer-Strasse 1, D-76139 Karlsruhe, Germany; URL www.eursc.org; www.eskar.org; e-mail info@eskar.org; Tel +49 721 680090; Fax +49 721 6800950

Headteacher   Tom Høyem

Luxembourg European School

Bvd Konrad Adenauer, 23, L-1115 Luxembourg/Kirchberg, Luxembourg; Tel +352 43 20 821; Fax +352 43 20 823 44

Luxembourg II European School (Mamer)

Rue Richard Coudenhove-Kalergi, L-1115 Luxembourg, Luxembourg; Tel +352 26 685 900; Fax +352 26 685 909

Mol European School

Europawijk 100, 2400 Mol, Belgium; URL www.esmol.net; Tel +32 14 56 31 04; Tel +32 14 56 31 11

Headteacher   R. Galvin

Munchen European School

Elise-Aulinger-Str 21, D-81739 München, Germany; URL www.esmunich.de; Tel +49 89 628 16 0; Fax +49 89 628 16 444

Varese European School

Via Montello 118, I-21100, Varese, Italy; URL www.scuolaeuropeadivarese.it; Tel +39 332 80 61 11; Fax +39 332 80 62 02

Other Organisations

Centre for Educational Research and Innovation (CERI)

Directorate for Education, OECD, 2 Rue André Pascal, 75775 Paris, Cedex 16, France; URL www.oecd.org/edu/ceri; e-mail ceri.contact@oecd.org; Tel +33 1 45 24 92 53

Communications   Delphine Grandrieux

Centre for International Mobility (CIMO)

PO Box 343, FI-00531, Helsinki, Finland; URL www.cimo.fi; www.iaeste.org.uk; e-mail cimoinfo@cimo.fi; Tel +358 9 7747 7033; Fax +358 0 7747 7064

Runs IAESTE trainee exchange in Finland. Offers placements in the field of engineering and natural sciences; see IAESTE website. Offers scholarships for international postgraduates and young researchers in Finland. Study periods 3–12 months. Provides information on study opportunities in Finnish higher education.

CESA Languages Abroad

CESA Hse, Pennance Rd, Lanner, Cornwall TR16 5TQ; URL www.cesalanguages.com; e-mail info@cesalanguages.com; Tel 01209 211800; Fax 01209 211830

Language courses abroad. Information and enrolment service on a wide range of centres in Europe and South America, courses for juniors (France, Germany and Spain), holiday programmes for adults, short-term intensive courses for business executives, courses for students working for language exams and private tuition. Year out long-term courses for all ability levels. Free colour brochure available on request. Full range of languages covered includes: Chinese, Dutch, French, German, Greek, Italian, Japanese, Portuguese, Russian and Spanish. French and German can be offered with skiing in the afternoons.

EIL Cultural and Educational Travel

287 Worcester Rd, Malvern, Worcestershire WR14 1AB; URL www.eiluk.org; e-mail eil@eiluk.org; Tel 01684 562577; Fax 01684 562212

Manager (European Voluntary Service: EVS)
Lorraine Lockyer
Chief Executive   David Shaddick

English Speaking Board (International) Ltd

26a Princes St, Southport, Merseyside PR8 1EQ; URL www.esbuk.org; e-mail admin@esbuk.org; Tel 01704 501730; Fax 01704 539637

English-Speaking Union of the Commonwealth

Dartmouth Hse, 37 Charles St, London W1J 5ED; URL www.esu.org; e-mail esu@esu.org; Tel 020 7759 1550; Fax 020 7495 6108

Chair   Lord David Hunt of Wirral MBE, PC
Director (Education)   Elizabeth Stokes

European Association of Teachers

Hon Secretary (UK Section)   Brian Sandford; e-mail eat_uk@tiscali.co.uk; Tel 01702 586622

Resource material for teaching European Studies. Approved assessment tests in European Knowledge at three levels.

European Centre for the Development of Vocational Training – CEDEFOP

PO Box 22427, GR-55 102 Thessaloniki, Greece; URL www.cedefop.europa.eu; e-mail info@cedefop.europa.eu; Tel +30 231 0490 111; Fax +30 231 0490 102

Director   A. Bulgarelli
Deputy Director   C. Lettmayr

European Trade Union Committee for Education (ETUCE)

5 Bvd du Roi Albert II, 9th Fl, 1210 Brussels, Belgium; URL www.csee-etuce.org; e-mail secretariat@csee-etuce.org

Policy Co-ordinator   Anne Marie Falktoft

15

Eurydice Network

Avenue Louise 240, B-1050 Brussels, Belgium; URL www.eurydice.org; e-mail info@eurydice.org; Tel +32 2 600 53 53; Fax +32 2 600 53 63

Eurydice is the information network on education in Europe. It provides information on education systems in Europe and is specifically targeted at education policy makers in government departments, government agencies and local authorities. The network gathers, monitors, processes and circulates reliable and readily comparable information on education systems and policies throughout Europe. The Eurydice Unit for England, Wales and Northern Ireland is based at the National Foundation for Educational Research (NFER). A separate unit for Scotland is based at the Scottish Government.

International Bureau of Education

UNESCO, PO Box 199, 1211 Geneva 20, Switzerland; URL www.ibe.unesco.org; e-mail doc.centre@ibe.unesco.org; Tel +41 22 917 7800; Fax +41 22 917 7801
Director   Clementina Acedo

IST Plus

Rosedale Hse, Rosedale Rd, Richmond, Surrey TW9 2SZ; URL www.istplus.com; e-mail info@istplus.com; Tel 020 8939 9057; Fax 020 8332 7858
Work and study abroad opportunities for students and graduates. Internship USA – students can obtain course-related work experience anywhere in the USA for up to 12 months. Internship Canada – up to 12 months of course-related work experience. PCT-USA – young professionals and graduates can obtain professional career training anywhere in the USA for up to 18 months. Work and Travel Australia or New Zealand – up to 12 months of casual work. Work and Travel USA – work in almost any job, anywhere in the USA from May to October. Teach in China or Thailand – five or 10 month renewable contracts teaching English in either China or Thailand (no TEFL required).

North Atlantic Treaty Organisation (NATO)

1110 Brussels, Belgium; URL www.nato.int; e-mail natodoc@hq.nato.int; Tel +32 2 707 4111; Fax +32 2 707 4579

UK Socrates-Erasmus Council

Rothford, Giles La, Canterbury, Kent CT2 7LR; URL www.erasmus.ac.uk; e-mail info@erasmus.ac.uk; Tel 01227 762712; Fax 01227 762711
Director   John E. Reilly
The UK national agency for the European Commission's Socrates-Erasmus and Erasmus Mundus programme

University Association for Contemporary European Studies

UACES Secretariat, King's College London, London WC2R 2LS; URL www.uaces.org; e-mail admin@uaces.org; Tel 020 7240 0206; Fax 020 7836 2350
Chair   Prof J. Shaw
This active membership association welcomes involvement of all those interested in exchanging ideas on Europe

Western European Union

15 rue de l'Association, 1000 Bruxelles, Belgium; URL www.weu.int; e-mail secretariatgeneral@weu.int; Tel +32 2 500 4412; Fax +32 2 500 4470

Embassies – Educational and Cultural Attachés

Embassy of the Islamic State of Afghanistan

31 Princes Gate, London SW7 1QQ; Tel 020 7589 8891; Fax 020 7581 3452

Albania

British Embassy, Rruga Skenderbeg 12, Tirana, Albania; URL www.uk.al; e-mail enquiries.tirana@fco.gov.uk; Tel +355 42 34974; Fax +355 42 47697

Algerian Embassy

Cultural Section, 6 Hyde Park Gate, London SW7; Tel 020 7589 6885

Argentine Embassy

65 Brook St, London W1K 4AH; URL www.argentine-embassy-uk.org; e-mail info@argentine-embassy-uk.org; Tel 020 7318 1300; Fax 020 7318 1301

Austrian Cultural Forum

28 Rutland Gate, London SW7 1PQ; URL www.austria.org.uk/culture; e-mail culture@austria.org.uk; Tel 020 7225 7300; Fax 020 7225 0470
Director   Dr Johannes Wimmer

Austrian Embassy

18 Belgrave Mews West, London SW1X 8HU; URL www.bmaa.gv.at/london; e-mail embassy@london-obobmaa.gv.at; Tel 020 7344 3250; Fax 020 7344 0292

Embassy of the State of Bahrain

98 Gloucester Rd, London SW7 4AU; Tel 020 7370 5978
Cultural Attaché   Mrs Safia Al-Awadhi

Belgian Embassy

17 Grosvenor Cres, London SW1X 7EE; URL www.diplomatie.be/london; e-mail london@diplobel.be; Tel 020 7470 3700; Fax 020 7470 3795
Officer (Press and Education Affairs)   K. Dockx

Bolivian Embassy

106 Eaton Sq, London SW1W 9AD; URL bolivia.embassyhomepage.com; e-mail embolivia-londres@rree.gov.bo; Tel 020 7235 4248; Tel (consulate) 020 7235 4255

Brazilian Embassy

32 Green St, London W1K 7AT; e-mail ffortuna@brazil.org.uk; Tel 020 7399 9000; Fax 020 7399 9100
Head (Cultural Section)   Felipe Fortuna

Embassy of the Republic of Bulgaria

186–188 Queen's Gate, London SW7 5HL; URL www.bulgarianembassy-london.org; e-mail press@bulgarianembassy.org.uk; Tel 020 7584 9400; Fax 020 7584 4948
Press and Culture   Irena Dimitrova

High Commission for the Republic of Cameroon

84 Holland Pk, London W11 3SB; Tel 020 7792 4825
Cultural Counsellor   K.W. Mbeboh

Chilean Embassy

12 Devonshire St, London W16 7DS; e-mail embachile@embachile.co.uk; Tel 020 7580 6392; Fax 020 7436 5204
Third Secretary   Andrea Concha

Embassy of the People's Republic of China

49–51 Portland Pl, London W1; Tel 020 7636 5197
Ambassador   Ma Zhengang

Colombian Embassy

3 Hans Cres, London SW1X 0LN; URL www.colombianembassy.co.uk; e-mail mail@colombianembassy.co.uk; Tel 020 7589 9177; Fax 020 7581 1829

Côte d'Ivoire Embassy

2 Upper Belgrave St, London SW1X 8BJ; Tel 020 7201 9601; Tel (Cultural and Education Section) 020 7201 9608; Fax 020 7259 5320
Consular Affairs   Mr Yeboue

Embassy of Cuba

167 High Holborn, London WC1; e-mail oficult@cubaldn.com; Tel 020 7240 2488; Fax 020 7837 8739

Counsellor (Scientific and Cultural Affairs)
Mrs T. Domingue
Assistant Cultural Counsellor   Mrs Y. Hernandez

Danish Cultural Institute
3 Doune Terr, Edinburgh EH3 6DY;
URL www.dancult.co.uk; e-mail dci@dancult.co.uk;
Tel 0131 225 7189; Fax 0131 220 6162
Director (Great Britain)   Dorthe Foged

Embassy of Denmark
Press, Culture and Information Section, 55 Sloane St,
London SW1X 9SR; URL www.ambloudou.um.dk;
e-mail lonamb@um.dk; Tel 020 7333 0200;
Fax 020 7333 0270
Head of Section   Lone Britt Molloy

**Office of the High Commissioner for the Commonwealth
of Dominica**
1 Collingham Gdns, London SW5 0HW;
URL www.dominica.co.uk; e-mail
dominicahighcom@btconnect.com; Tel 020 7370 5194;
Fax 020 7373 8743

Ecuadorian Embassy
Flat 3b, 3 Hans Cres, London SW1X 0LS; e-mail
eecugranbretania@mmrree.gov.ec; Tel 020 7584 1367;
Fax 020 7823 9701
Ambassador   Teodoro Maldonado
Minister   Deborah Salgado
Second Secretary (Consul)   Gonzalo Vega
Second Secretary (Multilateral Affairs)   Paul Moreno

Embassy of the Arab Republic of Egypt
Egyptian Educational and Cultural Bureau, 4 Chesterfield
Gdns, London W1Y 8BR;
URL www.egypt-culture.org.uk; e-mail
egypt.culture@ukonline.co.uk; Tel 020 7491 7720
Cultural Attaché   Dr Amr I.A. Elatraby

Embassy of El Salvador
Mayfair Hse, 34 Gt Portland St, London W1W 7JZ;
Tel 020 7436 8282; Fax 020 7436 8181
Chargé d'Affaires   Margareto Aragon-Pineda

Ethiopian Embassy
Education Dept, 17 Princes Gate, London SW7 1PZ;
URL www.ethioembassy.org.uk; e-mail
info@ethioembassy.org.uk; Tel 020 7589 7212

Embassy of Finland
38 Chesham Pl, London SW1X 8HW;
URL www.finemb.org.uk; e-mail sanomat.lon@formin.fi;
Tel 020 7838 6200

Gabonese Embassy
27 Elvaston Pl, London SW7 5NL; Tel 020 7823 9986

Embassy of the Federal Republic of Germany
23 Belgrave Sq, London SW1X 8PZ;
URL www.london.diplo.de; e-mail
kultur@german-embassy.org.uk; Tel 020 7824 1300;
Fax 020 7824 1525
Education Attaché   Darius Rahimi

Goethe-Institut London (German Cultural Centre)
50 Princes Gate, Exhibition Rd, London SW7 2PH;
Tel 020 7596 4000
Director   A. Wassener

Greek Embassy
1a Holland Pk, London W11 3TP; Tel 020 7229 3850

Hungarian Cultural Centre
10 Maiden La, London WC2E 7NA;
URL www.hungary.org.uk; e-mail
culture@hungary.org.uk; Tel 020 7240 8448;
Fax 020 7240 4847

Embassy of Iceland
2a Hans St, London SW1X 0JE; URL www.iceland.org/uk;
e-mail icemb.london@utn.stjr.is; Tel 020 7259 3999;
Fax 020 7245 9649

Indonesian Embassy
38 Grosvenor Sq, London W1K 2HW;
URL www.indonesianembassy.org.uk; e-mail
atdikbud-london@indonesian-embassy.org.uk;
Tel 020 7499 7661; Fax 020 7491 4993
Education and Cultural Attaché   Bambang Wasito
Minister Counsellor (Information)   Ahmad Rusdi

**Scientific Representative and Director of Iranian Students
in the UK and Ireland**
Education Department, 50 Kensington Ct, London W8 5DB;
URL www.iran-student.net; e-mail
academic-coordinator@iran-student.net;
Tel 020 7598 0023

Embassy of the Republic of Iraq
Cultural Department, 20 Queen's Gate, London SW7 5JG;
Tel 020 7584 7141
Cultural Counsellor   M.A. Al-Hasson (Acting)

Embassy of Ireland
Embassy of Ireland, 17 Grosvenor Pl, London SW1X 7HR;
Tel 020 7235 2171

Embassy of Israel
2 Palace Grn, London W8; Tel 020 7957 9500

Italian Cultural Institute
39 Belgrave Sq, London SW1X 8NX;
URL www.icilondon.esteri.it; e-mail icilondon@esteri.it;
Tel 020 7235 1461; Fax 020 7235 4618
Director   Prof Pierluigi Barrotta

Italian Embassy
14 Three Kings Yard, London W1K 4EH;
URL www.embitaly.org.uk; e-mail
emblondon@embitaly.org.uk; Tel 020 7312 2200;
Tel (education officer) 020 7312 2224
Italian Institute of Culture, 39 Belgrave Sq, London
SW1X 8NX; Tel 020 7235 1461

Embassy of Japan
101–104 Piccadilly, London W1V 9FN;
URL www.embjapan.org.uk; e-mail
education@jicc.demon.co.uk; Tel 020 7465 6500;
Fax 020 7491 9347

Embassy of the Hashemite Kingdom of Jordan
6 Upper Phillimore Gdns, London W8 7HB;
URL www.jordanembassyuk.gov.jo; www.jislondon.org;
e-mail lonemb@dircon.co.uk; Tel 020 7937 3685
Cultural Attaché   Nader Tarawneh

Embassy of the Republic of Korea
60 Buckingham Gate, London SW1E 6AJ; e-mail
education-uk@mofat.go.kr
Director (Education)   Lee Hwasung; Tel 020 7227 5547;
Fax 020 7227 5503

Lebanese Embassy
21 Kensington Palace Gdns, London W8 4QM;
Tel 020 7229 7265

Embassy of the Republic of Liberia
23 Fitzroy Sq, London W1T 6EW
Chargé d'Affaires   Ismael Ar Es Ish Mael Grant

Luxembourg Embassy
27 Wilton Cres, London SW1X 8SD; e-mail
londres.amb@mae.etat.lu; Tel 020 7235 6961;
Fax 020 7235 9734

15

Mexican Embassy
42 Hertford St, London W1Y 7TF;
URL www.embamex.co.uk; Tel 020 7499 8586
Ambassador Alma-Rosa Moreno

Embassy of Mongolia
7 Kensington Ct, London W8 5DL;
URL www.embassyofmongolia.co.uk; Tel 020 7937 0150;
Fax 020 7937 1117

Embassy of the Kingdom of Morocco
49 Queen's Gate Gdns, London SW7 5NE; Tel 020 7581 5001;
Tel (consulate) 020 7724 0719; Fax 020 7225 3862

Embassy of the Union of Myanmar
19a Charles St, London W1J 5DX; URL myanmar.com;
e-mail memblondon@aol.com; Tel 020 7493 7397
Cultural Attaché (Counsellor) Wai Lwinthan

Embassy of Nepal
12a Kensington Palace Gdns, London W8;
URL www.nepembassy.org.uk; e-mail
info@nepembassy.org.uk; Tel 020 7229 1594;
Tel 020 7229 6231
Minister; Counsellor Dipendra P. Bista
Military Attaché Colonel Himalaya Thapa
Third Secretary Mohan Basnet
Attaché Lawa Subedi

Royal Netherlands Embassy
38 Hyde Park Gate, London SW7 5DP;
URL www.netherlands-embassy.org.uk; e-mail
cultural@netherlands-embassy.org.uk; Tel 020 7590 3270

Nicaraguan Consulate
Vicarage Hse, 58–60 Kensington Church St, London
W8 4DB; e-mail embanic1@yahoo.co.uk;
Tel 020 7938 2373; Fax 020 7937 0952

Royal Norwegian Embassy
25 Belgrave Sq, London SW1X 8QD;
URL www.norway.org.uk; e-mail
presse.london@mfa.no; Tel 020 7591 5500;
Fax 020 7245 6993

Embassy of the Sultanate of Oman
Cultural Attachés Office, 64 Ennismore Gdns, London
SW7 1NH; URL www.omanculturalattache.org.uk;
e-mail cao@omanembassy.org.uk; Tel 020 7589 0220;
Fax 020 7584 6435

High Commission for Pakistan
Counsellor for Welfare, Education and Culture, 36 Lowndes
Sq, London SW1X 9JN; Tel 020 7664 9208

Embassy of Panama
40 Hertford St, London W1J 7SH; e-mail
panama1@btconnect.com; Tel 020 7493 4646;
Fax 020 7493 4333

Paraguayan Embassy
3rd Fl, 344 Kensington High St, London W14 8NS;
URL www.paraguayembassy.co.uk; e-mail
embapar@btconnect.com; Tel 020 7610 4180;
Fax 020 7371 4297
Counsellor Cristina Acosta
First Secretary Raúl Montiel

Embassy of Peru
52 Sloane St, London SW1X 9SP;
URL www.peruembassy-uk.com; e-mail
postmaster@peruembassy-uk.com; Tel 020 7235 1917;
Fax 020 7235 4463

Embassy of the Philippines
9a Palace Grn, London W8 4QE; URL www.philemb.org.uk;
e-mail londonpe@dfa.gov.ph; Tel 020 7937 1600;
Fax 020 7937 2925

Ambassador Edgardo B. Espiritu
Deputy Chief of Mission Reynaldo Catapang

Polish Embassy
47 Portland Pl, London W1B 1JH;
URL www.polishembassy.org.uk; Tel 020 7580 5430;
Fax 020 7637 2190
Counsellor (Science and Education) Krystyna Milewska

Portuguese Embassy
11 Belgrave Sq, London SW1X 8PP; e-mail
culture@portembassy.co.uk; Tel 020 7235 5331;
Fax 020 7235 0739
Press Counsellor Maria Monteiro

Embassy of Romania
Embassy of Romania, 4 Palace Grn, Kensington, London
W8 4QD; URL www.roemb.co.uk; e-mail
roemb@roemb.co.uk; Tel 020 7937 8125;
Fax 020 7937 8069
Cultural Counsellor Sinziana Dragos

Saudi Arabian Cultural Bureau
29 Belgrave Sq, London SW1X 8QB; e-mail sacb@sacb.co.uk;
Tel 020 7245 9944; Fax 020 7245 9895
Cultural Attaché A. Al-Naser

Embassy of the Slovak Republic
25 Kensington Palace Gdns, London W8 4QY;
URL www.slovakembassy.co.uk; Tel 020 7243 0803;
Fax 020 7313 6481
Secretary for Culture and Education Vacancy

South African High Commission
Trafalgar Sq, London WC2N 5DP; Tel 020 7451 7299
Third Secretary (Cultural Affairs) J. Denyer

Spanish Embassy
Cultural Office, 39 Chesham Pl, London SW1X 8BZ;
Tel 020 7201 5522; Tel 020 7201 5524
Education Office, 20 Peel St, London W8 7PD;
URL www.sgci.mec.es/uk; e-mail
conserjeria.uk@correo.mec.es; Tel 020 7727 2462;
Fax 020 7229 4965
Cultural Counsellor Juan Hazarredo
Education Counsellor J.A. Del Tejo

Embassy of Sweden
11 Montagu Pl, London W1H 2AL;
URL www.swedenabroad.com/london;
Tel 020 7917 6400
Cultural Counsellor Johanna Garpe

Swiss Embassy
16–18 Montagu Pl, London W1H 2BQ;
URL www.swissembassy.org.uk; e-mail
swissembassy@lon.rep.admin.ch; Tel 020 7616 6000;
Fax 020 7724 7001

Royal Thai Embassy
29–30 Queen's Gate, London SW7 5JB; e-mail
thaiduto@btinternet.com; Tel 020 7584 4530; Tel (Thai
Government Students' Office) 020 7589 2944

Tunisian Embassy
29 Princes Gate, London SW7 1QG; e-mail
amilcan@globalnet.co.uk; Tel 020 7584 8117
Cultural Counsellor Mrs Lamia Siala

Turkish Embassy
Educational Counsellor's Office, Tigris Hse, 256 Edgware
Rd, London W2 1DS; URL www.meblem.org.uk; e-mail
meblem06@gmail.com; Tel 020 7724 1511;
Fax 020 7724 9989

United States Embassy

Grosvenor Sq, London W1A 2LH; Tel 020 7499 9000;
  Fax 020 7491 2485

Venezuelan Embassy

Miranda Hse and Bolívar Hall, Cultural Section, London
  W1P 5LB; e-mail embvenuk_ccm@pipex.dial.com;
  Tel 020 7388 5788; Fax 020 7383 3253
Cultural Attaché   G. Carnevali

**Embassy of the Socialist Republic
of Vietnam**

12–14 Victoria Rd, London W8; Tel 020 7937 1912

Embassy of the Republic of Yemen

57 Cromwell Rd, London SW7 2ED;
  URL www.yemenembassy.org.uk; Tel 020 7584 6607;
  Fax 020 7589 3350

15

Education Consultants

16

The Society of Education Consultants

Aspect

Other Consultants

Education Consultants

The Society of Education Consultants

25 Dickenson Rd, London N8 9ER; URL www.sec.org.uk;
  e-mail sec@sec.org.uk; Tel 0845 345 7932
Chair   Nick Zienau
Secretary   Patrick Allan
Treasurer   Richard Beeden
The Society of Education Consultants is a membership
organisation for consultants who work in the field of
education and children's services. The aim of the society is to
advance the profession and support its members.

Bernard Abrams (Education Management Associates)

28 Windyridge Gdns, Cheltenham, Gloucestershire
  GL51 0AF; e-mail abrams@rmplc.co.uk;
  Tel 01242 700461; Fax 0870 136 8721
School improvement, self-valuation, class management,
specialist schools programme, leadership development

Rizwan Ahmad (UK Direct)

101 Colchester Rd, Leyton, London E10 6HD; e-mail
  info@ukdirect.org.uk; Tel 020 8989 1564

James Aleander (Principal Learning Limited)

7 Rushley Manor, Nottingham Rd, Mansfield NG18 5BG;
  URL jaleander@ja12.freeserve.co.uk;
  Mobile 07966 388663

Patrick Allan (TimePlan Consulting)

Patrick Allan (TimePlan Consulting), 25 Dickenson Rd,
  London N8 9ER; URL www.timeplan.com; e-mail
  patrick.allan@timeplan.net; Tel 020 8340 6729
Human resources consultancy specialising in management
support to the education sector

Christopher John Archer

Hollybank, 107 Main St, Calverton, Nottingham NG14 6FG;
  e-mail chris.archer107@btinternet.com; Tel 01159 653916;
  Mobile 07871 844245

Anthony Ashwino (A.A. Consulting UK Ltd)

8a Stannington Path, Borehamwood, Hertfordshire
  WD6 5EP; e-mail anthonyashwino@yahoo.com;
  Tel 020 8236 0027; Mobile 07960 076438

Michael Aston

8 Causeway Cl, Potters Bar, Hertfordshire EN6 5HW; e-mail
  mike@kcited.demon.co.uk; Tel 01707 658644;
  Fax 01707 856565
Independent advice and consultancy on the use of ICT in
education

John Atkins

1 Littleton Cl, Kenilworth, Warwickshire CV8 2WA; e-mail
  john@atconsult.co.uk; Tel 01926 864409;
  Fax 01926 864840
All phases and sectors of education, at home and overseas;
resource generation and allocation; organisational issues

Gordon Bailey

The Coop, Inksmoor Ct, Tedstone Wafre, Herefordshire
  HR7 4PP; e-mail gordonatazahar@aol.com;
  Tel 01885 483130

Jill Barton (Seneca Partnerships)

78 Hillway, Highgate, London N6 6DP; e-mail
  jillcb78@aol.com; Tel 020 8340 2252; Fax 020 8340 2252
Specialisms include the single conversation, school self-
evaluation, and school improvement partnerships

Richard Beeden (Beeden Educational Consultancy)

Beeden Educational Consultancy, 1 Finch La, Bushey,
  Hertfordshire WD23 3AH; e-mail rbeeden@aol.com;
  Tel 020 8420 4411; Fax 020 8420 4411;
  Mobile 07711 655078
LEA, change and resource management, strategic planning,
disability and SEN planning and funding

Paul Bench

1 Whitehall Terr, Shrewsbury, Shropshire SY2 5AA; e-mail
  pfbench@aol.com; Tel 01743 233164;
  Mobile 07711 392 777

Mark Biddiss (ProEducation Limited and Dr Mark)

23 St John's St, Keswick, Cumbria CA12 5AE; e-mail
  mark.biddiss@btinternet.com; Tel 01768 772869

Tim Blanchard (Gordon House Education Consultancy Ltd)

Gordon Hse, 126 Mercers Rd, London N19 4PU; e-mail
  timblanchard@tiscali.co.uk; Tel 020 7263 3171;
  Mobile 07739 874499

Jim Bolton

8 Fairfield Cl, Nafferton, Driffield, East Riding of Yorkshire
  YO25 0JH; e-mail jhbolton@jhbolton.com;
  Tel 01377 254404; Fax 01377 254404
Human resources consultancy, child protection issues,
governors' training

Owen Booker (People and Places)

People and Places Training and Consultancy, The Chapel
  Hse, Newton on the Hill, Harmer Hill, Shrewsbury,
  Shropshire SY4 3EH; URL pptc.fsnet.co.uk; e-mail
  ob@pptc.co.uk; Tel 01939 290830
Safe practice concerning behaviour and SEBDs, including
policy and classroom management

Peter Boshier (Adult Learning Education and Research Consultancy)

Yeomans, Aythorpe Roding, Gt Dunmow, Essex CM6 1PD;
  e-mail peterboshier@hotmail.com; Tel 01245 231003;
  Fax 01245 231003
A former college principal with more than 30 years'
experience in the education of adults as tutor, manager,
tutor-trainer, consultant and researcher

Karen Boynton (Highcliffe St Mark Primary School)

Greenways, Highcliffe, Dorset BH23 5AZ; e-mail
  kboynton@highcliffeprimary.dorset.sch.uk;
  Tel 01424 273029

Larry Braim (BPT3 Educational Site Consultants)

PO Box 492, Wakefield WF1 9AQ; e-mail
  enquiry@bpt3.co.uk; Tel 07843 784599

David Michael Braybrook

Rigg Hse West, Hawes, North Yorkshire DL8 3LR; e-mail
  braybrook5@aol.com; Tel 01969 666015; Fax 01969 667177

16

SEN, strategic review and QA work, trainer, PFI work, SEN tribunal, care standards tribunal

Professor Steve Bristow (Open Direction)
Open Direction Ltd, 2 Shelton Oak Priory, Shelton, Shrewsbury, Shropshire SY3 8BH;
URL www.open-direction.com; e-mail slbristow@open-direction.com; Tel 01743 341565; Fax 01743 341565; Mobile 07799 533222
Governance, strategy, evaluation, organisational development, leadership, quality assurance, higher education

Daniel Britton (Live2Learn)
e-mail d.j.britton@hotmail.co.uk; Tel 01202 717587

Robin Brooke-Smith (Creative Consulting Group)
73 Woodfield Rd, Shrewsbury, Shropshire SY3 8HU; e-mail ccg@creativeconsulting.fsnet.co.uk; Tel 01743 232145

Bill Brown (The Education Partnership)
9 Harnleigh Grn, Hanham Rd, Salisbury, Wiltshire SP2 8JN; e-mail bill.brown@sec.org.uk; Tel 01722 336815

Dr John Browne
Strategic Advantage Ltd, 26 Ringley Park Ave, Reigate, Surrey RH2 7ET; URL www.strategic-advantage.co.uk; e-mail john_browne@strategic-advantage.co.uk; Fax 01737 771099; Mobile 07775 810656
Communications, marketing, stakeholder engagement, reputation risk management

John Bryson (educare)
10 Derwent Ave, North Ferriby, East Riding of Yorkshire HU14 3DZ; e-mail johnbryson1@aol.com; Tel 07947 825358; Fax 01482 632938
Training and consultancy support, including performance improvement programmes in primary and secondary schools in the UK and overseas

Steve Butterworth Ltd
York Cottage, York Rd, Barlby, Selby, North Yorkshire YO8 5JH; e-mail butterworth@tinyonline.co.uk; Tel 01757 705657; Fax 01757 705657; Mobile 07740 434688
Countrywide advice, support and training for school leadership and management, staff and governors. Professional development and performance management.

Penny Bysshe
School Guidance Consultancy, Orchard Hse, High Rd, Cookham, Berkshire SL6 9JT;
URL www.school-guidance.co.uk; e-mail consult@school-guidance.co.uk; Tel 01628 810696; Fax 01628 810696
Professional, independent advice and assistance to parents on the choice of school for their child. Schools researched throughout the UK including state, independent, international and SEN schools. Professional help with the preparation and presentation of admission, transfer and selection appeals and complaints to the ombudsman. Expert witness in cases involving disputes about education.

Italo Cafolla
19 Thorn Dr, George Grn, Wexham, Buckinghamshire SL3 6SA; e-mail italo@castleview.slough.sch.uk; Tel 07887 726660

Evelyn Carpenter
4 Clare Gdns, Barking, Essex IG11 9JG; e-mail e.carpenter@btinternet.com; Tel 020 8594 4993; Fax 020 8594 4993
Community education consultant helps schools and colleges develop links with arts organisations and museums

Peter Clarke
76 Fitzalan St, London SE11 6QU; e-mail peterjmclarke@yahoo.co.uk; Tel 020 7820 8385; Fax 0015 303 488 235
Primary mathematics education, including in-service training and writing

Steve Clarke
41 Velvet Lawn Rd, New Milton, Hampshire BH25 5GE;
URL www.personalsafety.org.uk; e-mail clarkepsa@aol.com; Tel 01425 629992; Fax 01425 622292
Safe practice issues in the public sector, including dealing with challenging and difficult behaviour

Dr Julia Coop
The Poplars, Greenhill Rd, Griffithstown, Torfaen NP4 5BE; e-mail julia@coopand.co.uk; Tel 01495 758220; Fax 01495 760856
Primary, SEN, early years; support and advice on: inspection, SEN school improvement, self-evaluation, leadership and management

Helen Cooper CertEd, FCIPD (HC Associates Limited)
26 New Wlk, Beverley, East Riding of Yorkshire HU17 7DJ; e-mail helen.cooper@hcassociates.co.uk; Tel 01482 866534; Fax 0870 052 2708; Mobile 07808 739404

Philippa Cordingley, CUREE
4 Copthall Hse, Station Sq, Coventry, Warwickshire CV1 2FL; URL www.curee.co.uk; e-mail info@curee.co.uk; e-mail info@curee.org.uk; Tel 024 7652 4036; Fax 024 7663 1646
CUREE specialises in the use of research for continuing professional development, mentoring and coaching

Michael Gerard Coward (MCG Consulting Ltd)
49 Haywards Rd, Haywards Heath, West Sussex RH16 4HX; e-mail mgcoward@btinternet.com; Tel 01444 412632

John Crossman
117 Lenthay Rd, Sherborne, Dorset DT9 6AQ; e-mail john.crossman@ukonline.co.uk; Tel 01935 813962; Mobile 07721 616003

Louise Davies
60 Meadowview Rd, Ewell, Surrey KT19 9UB; e-mail louise@brightideas.plus.com; Tel 020 8786 8821; Fax 020 8786 8821
Experience as Design and Technology curriculum leader, lecturer in teacher training, teaching

Jeffrey Deakin
Old Rectory, Farmhouse School La, Warmington, Warwickshire OX17 1DE; e-mail jeff.deakin@ukgateway.net; Tel 01295 690663; Fax 01295 690663; Mobile 07776 157343
Acting senior manager and consultant in children's services for local authorities, LSCs and the DCSF

Philip Done
Granscott, East Down, Barnstaple, Devon EX31 4LX; e-mail p.j.done@btinternet.com; Tel 01271 850432; Fax 01271 850432
Post-16 curriculum, quality review, target setting, governor and senior management support, risk management

Ian M. Dutton (Murray Martin – Consultants)
Murray Martin Consultants, 2 The Meadow, Stichill, Kelso, Scottish Borders TD5 7TG; e-mail imd@scottishborders.co.uk; Tel 01573 470605; Fax 01573 470605
Education and management advice

Margaret Edgington
27 Holyoake St, Enderby, Leicester LE19 4NS; e-mail edgington@madasafish.com; Tel 0116 286 4987; Fax 0116 286 4987
Advice and in-service training on all aspects of foundation stage practice

Martin Edwards (MJE Services)
71 North Rd, West Bridgford, Nottingham NG2 7NG; e-mail mjeservices@aol.com; Tel 0115 981 4025; Fax 0115 981 4025
Project management, best value and FE governance

Janet Elliott
40 Temple Fortune La, London NW11 7UE; e-mail
janetelliottuk@aol.com; Tel 020 8455 2191

Sandra Ernstoff
39 Kinloch Dr, Kingsbury, London NW9 7JY; e-mail
sandra@ernstoff.net; Tel 020 8205 4213;
Mobile 07941 189430
Finance and resourcing, SEN, Building Schools for the
Future, parents, investigations and reviews

Karen Jane Evans (Twenty Twenty Learning)
12 The Leys, Springfield, Chelmsford, Essex CM2 6AU;
e-mail info@20-20learning.com; Tel 01245 352020

Roger Evans
11 Avondale Ave, Esher, Surrey KT10 0DB; e-mail
rogevans@aol.com; Tel 020 8224 1985
Advice to school governing bodies on governance,
personnel management, resolution of complaints and
grievances

Dennis Farrington
16 New Whinchelsea Rd, Rye, East Sussex TN31 7TA; e-mail
dennisfarrington@yahoo.co.uk; Tel 01797 226196

Kate Foale (Initiative Consulting)
120 Cotgrave La, Tollerton, Nottinghamshire NG12 4FY;
e-mail kate@thefoales.net; Tel 0115 937 6531

Peter Foale (Initiative Consulting)
120 Cotgrave La, Tollerton, Nottinghamshire NG12 4FY;
e-mail peter@initiative-consulting.com; Tel 01159 376531;
Mobile 07977 929205

Tim Foot Ltd
1 Lyster Ave, Great Baddow, Chelmsford, Essex CM2 7DF;
e-mail timjfoot@aol.com; Tel 01245 477891;
Fax 01245 477891
Study skills seminars

Pauline Fraser (PRF Solutions)
PO Box 220, Morpeth, Northumberland NE61 9AW; e-mail
pauline@prfsolutions.com; Tel 01670 505530

Leon Freedman (Terry Freedman Ltd)
45 Douglas Rd, Goodmayes, Essex IG3 8UZ; e-mail
terry@terry-freedman.org.uk; Mobile 07816 279103

John Reginald Fuller
14 Woodberry Way, London N12 0HG; e-mail
johnrfuller@hotmail.co.uk; Tel 01992 785547

Nigel Gann
Hamdon Education Ltd, The Old Hay Barn, East St,
Chiselborough, Stoke-sub-Hamdon, Somerset
TA14 6TW; URL www.hamdoneducation.co.uk; e-mail
nigel.gann@hamdoneducation.co.uk; Tel 01935 881100;
Fax 01935 881729
Management of consultancy company; national and
international work with local authorities, schools and
governing bodies on leadership in schools; consultancy on
governor development, extended schools and
supplementary schools

Joan Greenfield
Yew Tree Cottage, Stanbrook, Thaxted, Essex CM6 2NL;
e-mail joangreenfieldec@tiscali.co.uk; Tel 01371 830416
Ofsted lead inspector and accredited trainer; organisational
reviews, management of change, school improvement.

David Griffiths (Monitor Educational Services)
1 Fulshaw Ave, Wilmslow, Cheshire SK9 5JA;
URL www.monitortimetabling.com; e-mail
admin@monitortimetabling.com; Tel 01625 524474;
Fax 01625 524474
Consultancy and training in timetabling the secondary
school

Andrew Harris (Andrew Harris Consulting Ltd)
48 Stoughton Rd, Oadby, Leicester LE2 4FL; e-mail
aha3312838@aol.com; Tel 0116 271 2359

Glenn Harrison (Education Consultancy)
Gerdavatn, Baltasound, Unst, Shetland ZE2 9DY; e-mail
harrisonunst@btinternet.com; Tel 01957 711578 ext 583

Kirby Haye
1 Muirfield, Whitley Bay, Tyne and Wear NE25 9HY; e-mail
kirbyhaye1@tiscali.co.uk; Tel 0191 291 3480
All aspects of further education, monitoring the quality of
teaching and quality assurance

Paul Herbert (Edge Media)
60 Silver St, Dursley, Gloucestershire GL11 4ND; e-mail
paul@edge-media.co.uk; Tel 01453 544900;
Mobile 07957 864875

David Hill
Pendelton Hse, Hospital La, Mickleover, Derby DE3 0DR;
e-mail dave.hill@btinternet.com; Tel 01332 510951

Bridget Holland (Human Resourceful Limited)
London; e-mail humanresourcefulbh@tiscali.co.uk;
Mobile 07913 224017

Peter Hook (Gillmans Limited)
12 Calderbrook Rd, Littlebrorough, Lancashire OL15 9HL;
e-mail peterhook@phtc.demon.co.uk; Tel 01706 376817
All phases of education, including primary, secondary,
further and special

Paul Howard
109 Willingdon Rd, Eastbourne, East Sussex BN21 1TX;
e-mail paulhoward109@btinternet.com; Tel 07880 745891
Training and consultancy in behaviour management,
restorative approaches to conflict, preferred learning styles,
extended schools, multi-agency practice

Pete Hrekow (Education and Management Consultant)
The Old Chapel, High St, Figheldean, Salisbury, Wiltshire
SP4 8JT; e-mail hrekow@globalnet.co.uk;
Mobile 07976 715010
Experience in managing educational provision for children
with emotional and behavioural difficulties

John Hucker (Simple Solutions for Education)
1 Bracken Ave, Loggerheads, Market Drayton TF9 4RD;
e-mail john.hucker@ssfe.org.uk; e-mail
johnhucker@rocketmail.com; Tel 01630 672017;
Mobile 07703 182458

Graham Jones (School Select)
Merlin St, Johnston, Wrexham LL14 1NL; e-mail
grahamjones@schoolselect.co.uk; Tel 01978 842797;
Mobile 07747 634975

Gill Keene
68 Oaken Gr, Maidenhead SL6 6HH; e-mail
gillkeene@btinternet.com; Tel 01628 639004;
Mobile 07831 822643

Regina Kibel
7 Barham Hse, 39–40 Molyneux St, London W1H 5JA;
Tel 020 7262 9153
Training needs analysis and the design of programmes,
distance learning organisation, committee administration
training

Sa'ad Khaldi
2 Vicar's Cl, Hackney, London E9 7HT; e-mail
saadkhaldi@btinternet.com; Tel 020 8985 1538

Dr Jawad Khan
The Education Centre London, 63 Broadway London,
London E15 4BQ; URL www.edu-centre.co.uk; e-mail
admin@edu-centre.co.uk; Tel 020 8519 7362;
Fax 020 8221 1174
Student recruitment, consultancy for people who want to
study abroad

16

Sue King

18 Battlefield Rd, St Albans, Hertfordshire AL1 4DD; URL suebruce.king@ntlworld.com; Tel 01727 760677

Jenny Knowles

Mile House Farm, Boston Rd, Heckington, Sleaford, Lincolnshire NG34 9JQ; e-mail jkedcon@aol.com; Tel 01529 460282; Mobile 07753 686726

Jorj Kowszun (Cogency Research and Consultancy Ltd)

94 Upper Ratton Dr, Eastbourne, East Sussex BN20 9DJ; e-mail jorj@cogency.info; Tel 01323 503296

Max Krafchik (Inspira Consulting Ltd)

69 Cavendish Rd, Highams Pk, London E4 9NQ; URL www.inspiraconsulting.co.uk; e-mail maxkrafchik@inspiraconsulting.co.uk; Tel 020 8531 0728; Mobile 07967 552103

Strategic planning, lifelong learning, regeneration and neighbourhood renewal, project evaluation

Ismo Kuhanen (FinnTrack)

4 Stod Fold, Ogden, Halifax, West Yorkshire HX2 8XL; e-mail info@finntrack.com; Tel 01422 240267; Mobile 07858 774834

Martyn Kenneth Lane

19 The Bailiwick, East Harling, Norfolk NR16 2NF; e-mail martynklane@yahoo.co.uk; Tel 01953 717583

Judy Larsen

82 Leverton St, Kentish Town, London NW5 2NY; e-mail j.larsen@blueyonder.co.uk; Tel 020 7419 0342

Tony Leach (Tony Leach [Consultants] Ltd)

3 Oshawa Dell, Canal La, Pocklington, York YO42 1NN; URL www.tonyleach.com; e-mail tony@tonyleach.com; Tel 01759 305576; Fax 0870 056 0484

Leadership development and best practice research

Grahame Leon-Smith

Tele-School, The Niven Suite, The Mansion, Ottershaw Pk, Ottershaw, Chertsey, Surrey KT16 0QG; URL www.tele-school.org; e-mail grahame.leon-smith@tele-school.org; Tel 01932 874067; Fax 01932 874068

Principal consultant of Tele-School, designed to promote the internet as an educational resource

Gari Lewis

165 Frampton Rd, Gorseinon, Swansea SA4 4YG; e-mail gari.lewis@btinternet.com; Tel 01792 891699

Alternative curriculum, social inclusion, Welsh language, youth provision

Charles Richard Thomas Lindsay

18 Russell Ave, Bedford MK40 3TD; e-mail charles.lindsay7@ntlworld.com; Tel 01234 405256

Cornelius (Kees) Maxey

48 St Thomas Rd, Brentwood, Essex CM14 4DF; e-mail kees.maxey@geo2.poptel.org.uk; Tel 01277 212357; Fax 01277 212357

Twenty years as an industrial chemist and 10 years as director of the Africa Educational Trust. Consultancies include evaluation of Swedish funding of UNESCO's International Institute of Educational Planning, Paris; evaluation of Save the Children Fund's secondary school child support programme in Swaziland and Lesotho, and analysis of international student mobility in the Commonwealth.

John McDermott

26 Clarence Rd, Four Oaks, Sutton Coldfield, Birmingham, West Midlands B74 4AE

Peter McKenzie

East Grange, High Rd, Carlton in Lindrick, Worksop, Nottinghamshire S81 9DT; URL www.educationleadership.co.uk; e-mail peter.mckenzie@educationleadership.co.uk; Tel 01909 733094; Fax 01909 733094

Governors' support and training, MFL, preparation for inspection, asset management planning, teaching and learning (including monitoring), self-evaluation

Jennifer Mellor

e-mail jennifer_mellor@hotmail.com

Sylvina Mellor

22 Vincent Rd, Dorking, Surrey RH4 3JB; e-mail sylvinamellor@freenet.co.uk; Tel 01306 880906

Philip Mervyn

Philip Mervyn Associates Limited, 42 Grange Rd, Heswall, Wirral CH60 7RZ; e-mail philmervyn@waitrose.com; Tel 0151 342 3315; Mobile 07720 716065

Evaluation and identification of good practice within 14–19 education, inclusion projects, information, advice and guidance etc

Graham Morris

Chi Alegre, Plaidy Park Rd, Plaidy, Looe, Cornwall PL13 1LG; e-mail grahammorris@springwater.fsnet.co.uk; Tel 01503 264324

Experience of working with LLSCs, government offices, local authorities, employers and community organisations on learning strategies, regeneration and economic development

Janet Morrison (Transforming Education Ltd)

The Tile Hse, Bagshot Rd, Woking, Surrey GU22 0QY; e-mail janet.morrison@transformingeducation.co.uk; Tel 020 8244 4200; Mobile 07768 741049

Anita Moss (Bright Tutors: EduNation Ltd)

6 Wilton Cl, Bishop's Stortford, Hertfordshire CM23 5JN; e-mail anita@brighttutors.co.uk; Mobile 07903 881184

Gordon Mott

28 Greenhalgh Wlk, London N2 0DJ; e-mail gordonmott@bulldoghome.com; Tel 020 8458 8059

Experience of working with schools and LEAs on performance and management issues, including primary, secondary, post-16 and SEN

John Murfitt

Haven Cottage, Gorran Churchtown, St Austell, Cornwall PL26 6HF; e-mail johnmurfitt@hotmail.com; Mobile 07941 106371

Roseanne Musgrave

e-mail fortisgreen@clara.net

Mel Myers (Reflective Practice)

203 Rugby Rd, Milverton, Leamington Spa, Warwickshire CV32 6DY; URL www.reflectiveprocess.co.uk; e-mail mm@reflectiveprocess.co.uk; Tel 01926 885033; Fax 01926 885033; Mobile 07977 463193

Over the phone coaching and consultancy on people problems such as difficult people and difficult situations

Annie Nelson

Rose Cottage, Sawyers Hill, Minety, Wiltshire SN16 9QL; e-mail annie.nelson@btopenworld.com; Tel 01666 860354; Mobile 07990 970753

Secondary education with a focus on 14–19 developments; recruitment, teaching, learning and multiple intelligence, mentoring, coaching, training, evaluation and monitoring, and reviews

Susan O'Reilly

129 Ramsden Rd, London SW12 8RF; e-mail oreillysusan@hotmail.com; Tel 020 8675 3874; Mobile 07711 502334

Shan Oakes (Rigby)
3 Norwood, Beverley, East Yorkshire HU17 9ET; e-mail stan@voice-international.net; Tel 01482 862085; Mobile 07769 607710

Lorna Margaret Ogilvie
29 Maywater Cl, Sanderstead, Surrey CR2 0RS; e-mail lornao@tiscali.co.uk; Tel 020 8657 9585

Ray Page (Ray Page Associates)
21 Rodway Rd, Bromley, Kent BR1 3JJ; Tel 020 8460 1960; Fax 020 8313 0152
Governor training sessions for schools, behaviour management, help with senior management appointments

James M.H. Parke
Kennington Educational Services, 2 The Paddock, Kennington, Oxford, Oxfordshire OX1 5SB; e-mail jmh.parke@btinternet.com; Tel 01865 730664; Mobile 07801 820070
School organisation, planning and implementation of capital programmes, project management of building projects

Sue Parker
Learning etc, Ramsey Rd, Ramsey Forty Foot, Huntingdon, Cambridgeshire PE26 2XN; URL www.learning-etc.co.uk; e-mail sue@learning-etc.co.uk; Tel 01487 710856; Fax 01487 710866; Mobile 07793 014218
Learning etc offers consultancy, interim management and training in the learning and skills sector

Helen Rebecca Parry (Twenty Twenty Learning)
12 The Leys, Springfield, Chelmsford, Essex CM2 6AU; e-mail info@20-20learning.com; Tel 01245 352020

Stuart Parry
4 The Banks, Bingham, Nottinghamshire NG13 8BL; e-mail stuartparryeducational@yahoo.com; Tel 01949 839280; Fax 01949 838944
Building Schools for the Future, Private Finance Initiative and Public Private Partnerships, section 106 advice

Adam Parsons (Verwood CE First School)
Verwood CE First School, Howe La, Verwood BH31 6JF; e-mail office@verwoodfirst.dorset.sch.uk; Tel 01202 822652

Ian William Pollard
27 Lyndhurst Rd, Forset Hall, Newcastle-upon-Tyne NE12 9NT; e-mail ian@ianpollard.com; Tel 0191 259 9034

Gareth Allen Powell (Imagine the Possibilities)
6 Bank Cl, Little Neston, Cheshire CH64 4DJ; e-mail gareth.powell64@btinternet.com; Tel 0151 336 2283

Toby Quibell (The Learning Challenge)
Ouseburn Bldg, Albion Row, East Quayside, Newcastle upon Tyne NE6 1LL; e-mail toby.quibell@learningchallenge.org.uk; Tel 0191 275 5023; Mobile 07799 060323

Elizabeth Quinn (Child Behaviour Specialist)
Kelvin Square E 1/3, 25 Mingarry St, Glasgow G20 8NS; URL www.equinn.com; e-mail liz@equinn.com; Tel 0141 576 4252; Fax 0141 576 4252
25 years' experience teaching children with challenging behaviour in inner-city schools

Allan Randall (Focused Learning and Interpretation)
Glebe Hse, Ashby Rd, Ticknall, Derbyshire DE73 7JJ; URL www.focusedlearning.co.uk; e-mail allanrandall@btinternet.com; Tel 01332 862975; Fax 01332 862993
Consultancy services to heritage, museum, tourism and environmental sites; educational strategy and development plans; educational resources development; HLF learning and ADP plans

Dr C.J. Rattew (Dorchester Preparatory and Independent School)
25–26 Icen Way, Dorchester, Dorset DT1 1EP; URL www.dorchesterprepschool.co.uk; e-mail info@dorchesterprepschool.co.uk; Tel 01305 264925

Peter Richardson (Peter Richardson Associates Ltd)
Gelli Aur, Penrherber, Newcastle Emlyn, Carmarthenshire SA38 9RP; e-mail peter.richardson@mac.com; Mobile 07733 231794
Performance and project management, policy and partnership development, charge management, independent reviews

Stephen Richardson (Richardson Training Consultancy Ltd)
Barnsdale, The Street, Shalford, Braintree, Essex CM7 5HL; e-mail info@richardsontraining.co.uk; Tel 01371 850225; Mobile 07846 185432

Colin Rickard
24 Daintree, Needingworth, St Ives, Huntingdon PE27 4SP; e-mail colinrickard@aol.com; Tel 01480 468132

Bill Rigby
3 Norwood, Beverley, Yorkshire HU17 9ET; URL www.voice-international.net; e-mail bill@voice-international.net; Tel 01482 862085
Expertise includes 14–19 diplomas, re-engagement programmes and school-college links. Bid-writing, research and evaluation of programmes undertaken.

Barbara Lynne Roberts (Aidan Consulting)
Aidan Hse, St George's Terr, Roker, Sunderland, Tyne and Wear SR6 9LX; Tel 0191 510 1318

Michael Rocks (MJR Consultancy)
10–16 Tiller Rd, Docklands, London E14 8PX; e-mail mikerocks@mjrconsultancy.co.uk; Tel 020 7345 5033
Provision of human resources and governors support and training services to schools and LEAs

Allan Russell (Battle Education Consultancy)
27 Bowmans Dr, Battle, East Sussex TN33 0LT; e-mail battleeducation@aol.com; Tel 01424 775270

Yvonne Ryszkowska
78 Queen Elizabeth's Wlk, London N16 5UQ; e-mail yvonner@blueyonder.co.uk; Tel 020 8809 7280; Fax 020 8800 2684; Mobile 07803 051029
Expertise in 14–19 diplomas, re-engagement programmes and school-college links. Bid-writing, research and evaluation of programmes undertaken.

Christopher Mark Sanderson (Amadeus Consulting and Training)
8 Grandsmere Pl, Manor Dr, Halifax HX3 0DP; e-mail cmsanderson@hotmail.com; Tel 01422 356249

James Stanford (Milton-on-Stour CE VA Primary School)
Trehurst, Melbury Abbas, Shaftesbury, Dorset SP7 0DA; e-mail jstanford@milton.dorset.sch.uk; Tel 01747 854938

Keith Richard Stevens
Amwell Consultancy and Training Ltd, White Cottage, Whinburgh Rd, Westfield, Nr Dereham, Norfolk NR19 1QJ; URL www.act-for-success.com; e-mail keith@act-for-success.com; Tel 01362 822402
Change management, performance management, recruitment, planning, feasibilities, personnel, training and funding regimes, interim management

John Stibbs (School Management Services)
93 Ashurst Rd, Barnet, Hertfordshire EN4 9LH; e-mail john.l.stibbs@talk21.com; Tel 020 8449 5342
Mentoring senior managers; timetable design and preparation

16

Blaine Stothard

42 Dalyell Rd, London SW9 9QR;
URL www.healthed.org.uk; e-mail
blaine@healthed.demon.co.uk; Tel 020 7733 7194;
Fax 020 7733 7194

Consultancy and support in implementing and evaluating
PSHE and public health issues in school and other settings

David Streatfield (Information Management Associates)

28 Albion Rd, Twickenham, Greater London TW2 6QZ;
e-mail streatfield@blueyonder.co.uk; Tel 020 8755 0471;
Fax 020 8755 0471

Information management in education and public services

Bart Taylor-Harris

19 Coley Rise, Lyddington, Rutland LE15 9LL; e-mail
bart@theoldparsonage.net; Tel 01572 822210;
Mobile 07753 840585

Interim management and consultancy work on school
access, admissions, best value, data analysis, PFI, service
planning and target setting

David Terry

24 Alexander Ave, Droitwich, Worcestershire WR9 8NH;
e-mail terrydroit@aol.com; Tel 01905 774907;
Fax 01905 797478

Governor and board support, head and principal support,
performance management, personnel; assessment

John Tierney

e f g Education for Foundations and Growth, 59 Birdham
Rd, Chichester, West Sussex PO19 8TB; e-mail
john.tierney@virgin.net; Tel 01243 776042

Education for foundation academic learning and emotional
development

Jeanette Townsend (Townsend Consultancy)

48 Tower Rd West, St Leonards on Sea, East Sussex
TN38 0RG; e-mail jt48@btinternet.com; Tel 01424 437720

Dinah Tuck (DMT Associates Ltd)

16 Lodge Dr, Hatfield, Hertfordshire AL9 5HN; e-mail
dinah.tuck@ntlworld.com; Tel 01707 887687;
Fax 01707 887687

Strategic planning and best value analysis

William Tyler

16 Saxon Dr, Witham, Essex CM8 2HL; e-mail
williamtyleruk@yahoo.co.uk; Tel 01376 518867

Former principal of the City Literary Institute and LEA
adviser; adult continuing education

Rob Valentine

16 Hine Ave, Beaconfield, Newark, Nottinghamshire
NG24 2LH; e-mail rob.valentine21@virgin.net;
Tel 01636 706617; Mobile 07730 680789

Hugh Waller

QUORUM Consultancy, 41 Branksome Hill Rd, Talbot
Woods, Bournemouth, Dorset BH4 9LF;
URL www.quorum-consultancy.co.uk; e-mail
hughmwaller@hotmail.com; Mobile 07986 774188

Training, consultancy and research in school governance
and improvement. Organisation, management and clerking
of admission appeals. Supporting parents in presenting
their case at admission appeals (but not CE schools within
the Winchester and Portsmouth Dioceses).

David Watson (Oxford Educational Consulting)

353 Woodstock Rd, Oxford, Oxfordshire OX2 8AA; e-mail
education@oxconsulting.u-net.com; Tel 01865 557182;
Fax 01865 516540

School search for relocating families (all levels of education,
all of UK). All aspects of school/college development,
including student recruitment at home and abroad.

Clio Whittaker (Ampersand Learning Ltd)

39 Ospringe Rd, London NW5; e-mail
clio@ampersand-learning.com; Tel 020 7485 4906;
Mobile 07748 476 136

Christopher Wightwick

19 Nottingham Rd, London SW17 7EA; e-mail
ccbwightwick@aol.com; Tel 020 8767 6161;
Fax 020 8767 6161

School organisation, management and curriculum; Modern
Languages, including INSET and inspection.

Judith Wilson (Judith Wilson Consulting)

4 Rockhill, Sydenham Hill, London SE26 6SW; e-mail
judithwilsonconsulting@compuserve.com;
Tel 020 8670 0500; Fax 020 8670 0500

Project management, SEN, school improvement

Gaynor Wingham (Gaynor Wingham Associates)

17 Greenholm Rd, Eltham Pk, London SE9 1UQ; e-mail
gwingham@aol.com; Tel 020 8859 4678

Training and consultancy on child protection, including
allegations against staff; school attendance; training for
boarding school staff; interagency working; complaints
investigations and management development

Aspect (The Association of Professionals in Education and Children's Trusts)

Woolley Hall, Woolley, Wakefield, West Yorkshire
WF4 2JR; URL www.aspect.org.uk; e-mail
info@aspect.org.uk; Tel 01226 383428; Fax 01226 383427

General Secretary John Chowcat LIB

Aspect is the professional association and trade union for
professionals in education and children's trusts. The
association now represents more than 4000 professionals in
the field, including directors of children's services, local
authority advisers, SEN advisers, educational inspectors,
advisory teachers and independent consultants working in
education and children's services, parent partnership staff,
and co-ordinators of governor services.

J.A. I'Anson

139 Amyand Park Rd, Twickenham, Greater London
TW1 3HN; e-mail j.lanson45@btinternet.com;
Tel 020 8892 0139; Fax 020 8744 3980

Secondary, primary; PE and school sport

David Frank Ayres

6 Purbeck Cl, Aylesbury, Buckinghamshire HP21 9UU;
e-mail davidfayres@btopenworld.com; Tel 01296 422412

Diana Barbara Batt

Espirit Educational Consultants Ltd, Farndale, Marshalls
Heath La, Wheathampstead, Hertfordshire AL4 8HS;
e-mail dianabattednc@aol.com; Tel 01582 833885;
Fax 01582 833885

Foundation and primary, educational advice and Ofsted
inspector

Martin W. Baxter

Sage Interim Management Solutions Ltd, Southside, Kings
Ash, The Lee, Great Missenden, Buckinghamshire
HP16 9NP; e-mail mail@sageinterim.co.uk;
Tel 07947 819765

School improvement and children's services
implementation programmes

Dr David Biltcliffe

Smithy Ridge, Huddersfield Rd, Haigh, Barnsley, South
Yorkshire S75 4BX; e-mail
davidbiltcliffe@smithyridge.freeserve.co.uk;
Tel 01924 830541; Fax 01924 830541

Education consultant, expert witness, free discussions; chief
and registered inspector

Dr Thomas Peter Borrows

Troye Cottage, 32 Whielden St, Old Amersham,
Buckinghamshire HP7 0HU; e-mail
peter@borrows.demon.co.uk; Tel 01494 728422

All key stages; practical science, including health and safety,
and laboratory design

Philip Frank Braide

Tuckers Lodge, 3 Tuckers Cl, Yealmpton, Devon PL8 2LS; e-mail philip.braide@plymouth.gov.uk; Tel 01752 881583; Fax 01752 881583

Secondary, post-16; senior LEA adviser, NPQH tutor, school improvement partner

Anthony Edward Bridge

1 St Mary's Cl, Stockbridge Pk, Elloughton, Brough, East Yorkshire HU15 1JF; e-mail glc@anthonybridge.karoo.co.uk; Tel 01482 662250; Fax 01482 662250

Primary, nursery

Joy Bristow

Deblin, 19 Swan Cl, Stafford, Staffordshire ST16 1AU; e-mail joybristow@btinternet.com; Tel 01785 255824

Primary education; consultant and trainer, SIP

Jane Burnett

The Quarter Hse, Wittersham, Kent TN30 7NP; e-mail janeb.b@virgin.net; Tel 01797 270378; Fax 01797 270935

Primary, post-16, 14–19, Key Stages 2–5, secondary, sixth form, X-phase; evaluation and management development

CADOC Associates

20 Centurion Gate, Caerleon NP18 3NS; e-mail rob.isaac@monmouth.co.uk; Tel 01633 430566; Fax 07971 863246

Managing Director   Robert Alun Isaac MSc, MBCS, CEd, FRSA

Primary, secondary, Key Stages 1–2; curriculum design, pre and post-inspection support, Ofsted and Estyn registered inspector

Gwen Cavill

Highview Hse, Broomfield, Bridgwater, Somerset TA5 2EJ; e-mail gwencavill@aol.com; Tel 01823 451897; Fax 01823 451456

Primary, secondary; consultancy and training in leadership and management, performance management, LPSH and NPQH, work with local authorities in coach development

Patricia Ann Chick

36 Victoria Quay, Ashton-on-Ribble, Preston PR2 2YW; e-mail chick_pat@hotmail.com; Tel 01772 720572; Fax 01772 720572

Chiltern Education Ltd

Box Tree Cottage, The Row, Lane End, High Wycombe, Buckinghamshire HP14 3JU; e-mail phillmann@chilterneducation.co.uk; Tel 01494 883644; Fax 01494 883644

Primary education; Ofsted registered inspector

Partick Kevin Commons

11 Rosedale Rd, Wigston, Leicester LE18 3XT; e-mail kevin.commons@ntlworld.com; Tel 0116 292 8655; Fax 0116 292 8655

Consultancy and training in management, quality assurance and interpersonal skills

Roger Hugh Crowther

14 Dene View, Gosforth, Newcastle upon Tyne NE3 1PU; e-mail rogercrowther@talktalk.net; Tel 0191 284 6615

Secondary, post-16, sixth form, adult, vocational and further education; consultancy, research and training

Esther Elizabeth Digby

Beehive Cottage, Northleigh, Colyton, Devon EX24 6DA; e-mail estherdigby@btinternet.com; Tel 01404 871283

Primary, Key Stages 1–2, early years, nursery; SEN and management

Terence Dillon

The Farthings, Broad Campden, Chipping Campden, Gloucestershire GL55 6UU; e-mail terrydillon@msn.com; Tel 01386 840643; Fax 01386 840643

Ofsted inspections (primary and secondary); training for inspectors; advice and consultancy on curriculum, management and amalagmation of schools; improving failing schools

Neil Donkin

5 Bilberry Cl, Clayton, Bradford, West Yorkshire BD14 6ND; e-mail donkin.education@btinternet.com; Tel 01274 814908

Secondary; performance management, recruitment, self-evaluation training, school improvement work, Ofsted departmental reviews and lesson observations

Colin R. DuQueno

21 Cleveland Rd, Huddersfield, West Yorkshire HD1 4PP; e-mail colin.duqueno@ntlworld.com; Tel 01484 530917; Fax 01484 340842

Primary, secondary, post-16; independent advisor, inspector consultant and trainer

Geoffrey Edwards

15 Sussex Rd, Ickenham, Uxbridge, Greater London UB10 8PN; e-mail geoffrey.edwards@btinternet.com; Tel 01895 638796; Fax 01895 638796; Mobile 07912 209515

Primary leadership and management, school improvement

Excellence Through Education

5 Dennis David Cl, Lutterworth, Leicestershire LE17 4GB; URL www.the-e-group.co.uk; e-mail janstokes1950@hotmail.co.uk; Tel 01455 554722

Michael J. Fitzgerald

47 Mount Park Ave, South Croydon, Surrey CR2 6DW; e-mail m_fitzgerald@freenet.co.uk; Tel 020 8660 5065; Fax 020 8660 5065

Primary and secondary consultant; Ofsted additional inspector; Education London school programme manager

Michael David Gibson

31 Manor La, Sunbury-on-Thames, Greater London TW16 5EB; e-mail mike.gibson94@btinternet.com; Tel 01932 780252

Primary and secondary consultant, Science

Kathleen Gilbert

9 Burnsall Cl, Farnborough, Hampshire GU14 8NN; e-mail kathygilbe@aol.com; Tel 07812 604032; Fax 01252 662757

RE adviser, Section 48 inspector, consultant and threshold assessor, Ofsted inspector, primary external adviser

Vera May Grigg

2 Windy Hill, Hutton, Brentwood, Essex CM13 2HF; e-mail petergrigg1@aol.com; Tel 01277 215596

Under fives, primary, secondary and sixth form education; Ofsted team inspector

Malcolm Groves (Nexus Consulting)

26 Priestgate, Peterborough, Cambridgeshire PE1 1WG; URL www.nexusconsulting.org; e-mail malcolm@nexusconsulting.org; Tel 01733 865010; Fax 01733 865013

Secondary, specialist schools; enterprise, citizenship, QA, development planning, 14–19, community adult learning and youth work, evaluation

P.A. Hanage

50 Grey Towers Dr, Nunthorpe, Middlesbrough TS7 0LT; e-mail pat@hanage.com; Tel 01642 317309

Secondary, post-16, sixth form and FE; management consultancy and training, external adviser, threshold assessor

Daphne Margaret Harris

Combe Down, Sandheath Rd, Hindhead, Surrey GU26 6RU; e-mail daphne.john@btinternet.com; Tel 01428 604926

Experience as a headteacher, inspector, adviser and SIP

Isabel Danice M. Iles

41 Clarendon Sq, Leamington Spa, Warwickshire CV32 5QZ; URL www.clarendon.uk.com; e-mail clarendon@clarendon.uk.com; Tel 01926 316793; Fax 01926 883278

16

Primary, secondary; Ofsted team inspector, ISI reporting inspector, director of Clarendon International Education, former head

Dr Trevor M. James

36 Heritage Ct, Lichfield, Staffordshire WS14 9ST;
   Tel 01543 301097

Director of Young Historian Project

Angela Jensen

10 Portwell, Cricklade, Wiltshire SN6 6SA; e-mail
   angela@jensen92.freeserve.co.uk; e-mail
   ajensen@swindon.gov.uk; Tel 01793 752698

Primary and early years; LEA adviser, Ofsted inspector

Dr Vivien Johnston

23 Mountfield Gdns, Tunbridge Wells, Kent TN1 1SJ; e-mail
   vivien@e-qualitas.co.uk; Tel 01892 513881;
   Fax 01892 513881

Consultancy in school self-evaluation and school
improvement

Maria Landy

The Meeting Hse, School Rd, Barnack, Stamford,
   Lincolnshire PE9 3DZ; URL www.marialandy.co.uk;
   e-mail maria@marialandy.co.uk; Tel 01780 740024;
   Mobile 07803 602434

SEN adviser for special and mainstream schools, PRUs and
local authorities; adviser, inspector and trainer for all
phases; managing director of More Time for Learning Ltd.
Pre-inspection advice, special schools improvement partner,
INSET and Keynotes.

Dorothy Latham

2a Hind Cl, Shipfield, Dymchurch, Romney Marsh, Kent
   TN29 0LG; e-mail dorothy.latham@virgin.net;
   Tel 01303 872665

Consultant for English: reading, writing, speaking and
listening; advises schools, English co-ordinators and
advisers

Dr Tim Lomas

36 Hewson Rd, Lincoln, Lincolnshire LN1 1RX; e-mail
   tlomas@cfbt.com; Tel 01522 546591; Fax 01522 546591

Primary, secondary education; consultancy, INSET, Ofsted
inspector, consultant on workforce development and
primary and secondary History

Margaret Elizabeth Lynch

Ashbank, 50 Prospect Rd, Ash Vale, Surrey GU12 5EL;
   e-mail margaret.lynch@talktalk.net; Tel 01252 326409

Education consultant, inspector and tutor; English and
Drama specialist; primary

Ian Massey

46 Morgan Rd, Reading, Berkshire RG1 5HG; e-mail
   ian.massey@ntlworld.com; Tel 0118 954 1478

Primary, secondary, X-phase; inspector

David Meaden

31 First Cross Rd, Twickenham, Surrey TW2 5QA; e-mail
   david.meaden@hounslow.gov.uk; Tel 020 8583 2875;
   Fax 020 8583 2888

Senior adviser: national strategies

Dr Faysal Mikdadi

1 Cedar Rd, Charlton Down, Dorchester, Dorset DT2 9UL;
   e-mail fhm481812@aol.com; Tel 01305 213702;
   Fax 01305 213702

Additional inspector, novelist and essayist; management,
inclusion, EAL, English, Modern Languages, Law, Arabic

Elizabeth Mildner

Sundown, Drifton Hill, West Kington, Chippenham,
   Wiltshire SN14 7JH; e-mail liz.mildner@virgin.net

Consultant, external adviser

C. Parsons

67 Camrose Way, Basingstoke, Hampshire RG21 3AN;
   e-mail colin@donaldparsons.freeserve.co.uk;
   Tel 01256 472014; Fax 01256 472014

Primary, secondary; LEA adviser, Ofsted registered
inspector

John George F. Parsons

6 Hitcham Hse, Hitcham La, Burnham, Buckinghamshire
   SL1 7DP; e-mail parsons@hitchamh.demon.co.uk;
   Tel 01628 603526

Primary; accredited school improvement partner; Ofsted;
additional inspector

John Pearce (JP Consultancy)

Mathom Hse, 152 Carter La East, Alfreton, Derbyshire
   DE55 2DZ; e-mail johnpearce@ntlworld.com;
   Tel 01773 778013; Fax 01773 778013; Mobile 07970 892807

Consultant, NCSL head facilitator, Ofsted qualified

Dr Richard Perkin

3 Weetwood Ave, Leeds, West Yorkshire LS16 5NG; e-mail
   richard.perkin@ntlworld.com; Tel 0113 225 2807;
   Fax 0113 225 2807

Pre and post-inspection support; interpersonal skills
training, drama in education; Ofsted registered

Avril Marsha Phillips

4 Garth Mews, Ealing, London W5 1HF; e-mail
   avril.phillips@btconnect.com; Tel 020 8810 7620

Alan William Perks

Balneath, 35 Whitefield Cl, Westwood Heath, Coventry,
   West Midlands CV4 8GY; e-mail info@awpec.co.uk;
   Tel 024 7646 9226; Fax 024 7646 9226

Consultant for primary; retired Ofsted registered inspector
and trainer

Nigel Albert Pett

Troy Hse, 29 Priams Way, Stapleford, Cambridgeshire
   CB2 5DT; e-mail npa.cantab@ntlworld.com;
   Tel 01223 562241; Fax 01223 562241

Primary, secondary, post-16; education consultants and
school inspectors (Nigel Pett Associates), Ofsted additional
inspector, National Society Section 48 inspector

Andy Piggott

71 Field Way, Chalfont St Peter, Gerrards Cross,
   Buckinghamshire SL9 9SQ;
   URL www.andy-piggott.co.uk; e-mail
   andy.piggott@btinternet.com; Tel 01753 885222;
   Fax 01753 887634

Secondary Science: laboratory design, health and safety
audits, departmental support, INSET

Patrick Nigel Playfair

Lambourn Cottage, Childs Ercall, Market Drayton,
   Shropshire TF9 2DG; e-mail pnplayfair@aol.com;
   Tel 01952 840469; Fax 01952 840469

Independent education consultant and assessor

Colin H. Press

43 Hydepark Rd, Newtownabbey, County Antrim
   BT36 4PY; e-mail press.colin@btinternet.com;
   Tel 028 9084 9389; Fax 028 9084 9389

Science, project development

Sue Rogers

16 Coniston Ct, 5 Carlton Dr, Putney, London SW15 2BZ;
   e-mail sue@suerogers.net

Jon Rosser

Ty Newdydd Isa, Bontuchel, Ruthin, Denbighshire
   LL15 2DE; e-mail jonrosser@dsl.pipex.com; e-mail
   jon.rosser@flintshire.gov.uk; Tel 01824 704416;
   Fax 0871 661 0627

Key Stages 1–4, post-16; English, Drama, Media

Dr Claude John Scott

17 Lime Tree Rd, Norwich, Norfolk NR2 2NQ; e-mail
cjscott@talktalk.net; Tel 01603 455686; Fax 01603 455686
Educational consultancy, leadership, management training,
primary, secondary, NPQH, head for the future programme

Douglas Sharp

76 Lugtrout La, Solihull, West Midlands B91 2SN; e-mail
dsharp@solihull.gov.uk; Tel 0121 705 3002
Key Stages 1–4; Geography, History, Humanities,
leadership and management

Philip J. Shaw

East View, Ashfield Rd, Elmswell, Bury St Edmunds,
Suffolk IP30 9HG; e-mail philip.shaw@fsmail.net;
Tel 01359 241192; Fax 01359 241192
Local authority county adviser for Music, head of county
music service, artists in residence consultancy and projects;
music performance, management, secondary curriculum
Music

Keith Spencer

GK Partnership, 17 Laburnum St, Wollaston, Stourbridge,
West Midlands DY8 4NX;
URL www.gkpartnership.co.uk; e-mail
gkpartners@blueyonder.co.uk; Tel 01384 835690;
Fax 01384 356847
Development, research and training organisation in
physical education, the arts and sport, national PESS CPD
programme, school sport co-ordinator programme,
Artsmark, Leading Aspect Award, child protection etc.

Deena Tatham

9 Cross Grn, Rothley, Leicester, Leicestershire LE7 7PF;
e-mail deena@peteandeena.co.uk; Tel 0116 230 3014;
Fax 0116 230 1496
Consultant head for schools in difficulty, management
issues

Judith Thomas

20 Oxford St, Liverpool, Merseyside L15 8HX; e-mail
jdmthomas@aol.com; Tel 0151 234 9273;
Fax 0151 234 9273

Elizabeth Thomson

8 Welby Gdns, Grantham, Lincolnshire NG31 8BN; e-mail
lizthomson@aol.com; Tel 01476 562362; Fax 01476 561058
Primary, middle, higher education, X-Phase; evaluation and
management development, international development

Kristine Tutton

Bridleway Cottage, Woodperry, Oxford, Oxfordshire
OX33 1AH; e-mail kris.tutton@oxfordshire.gov.uk;
Tel 01865 358463; Fax 01865 358463
Training and development consultancy for LEA, voluntary
and private sector organisations; foundation stage outdoor
areas for Learning, Design and Technology.

Sandra Tweddell

145 New Dover Rd, Canterbury, Kent CT1 3EG; e-mail
s.tweddell@bbinternet.com; Tel 01227 457855
Literacy, X-Phase; CPD and curriculum planning

Mervyn Wakefield

11 Teasdale Rd, Carlisle, Cumbria CA3 0HF;
URL www.mervynwakefield.co.uk; e-mail
mervyn@cumbria.f9.co.uk; Tel 01228 594040;
Fax 01228 590808
Secondary; curriculum organisation, timetabling training,
timetable construction, costing the curriculum

Dr David Eric Ward

46 Broad Rd, Sale, Cheshire M33 2BN; e-mail
davidwardsalford@aol.com; Tel 0161 962 5490;
Fax 0161 295 2655
Primary, secondary, lifelong learning support; Science –
industry, technology

Graham Warner

3 Bramstead Ave, Compton, Wolverhampton, West
Midlands WV6 8AH; e-mail grew@r3514.fsnet.co.uk;
Tel 01902 762798
Primary, secondary, early years, SEN

Megan (Margaret Anne) Warner

Trading as MAW Education – Education Trainer and
International Consultant
50 Five Mile Dr, Oxford, Oxfordshire OX2 8HW;
URL www.maweducation.co.uk; e-mail
maweducation@easynet.co.uk; Tel 01865 310578;
Fax 01865 310576
Assessor for higher level teaching assistants, performance
management consultant, international and UK education
consultant and teacher trainer, experience as registered
inspector, NFER researcher, primary headteacher and head
of department for secondary and special schools

Dr Anne Watkinson

1 Woodcutters, Littlefield, Wivenhoe, Colchester, Essex
CO1 9LW; URL www.teaching-assistants.net; e-mail
anne@watsnees.co.uk; Tel 01206 823199;
Fax 01206 823199
Training, role, deployment and management of teaching
assistants and higher level teaching assistants in schools

Brian G. Williamson

10 Warren Dr, Wallasey, Wirral CH45 0JR; e-mail
brian.mathsforall@tiscali.co.uk; Tel 0151 639 8744
Mathematics, X-phase, learning support

Dr Ian Francis Wilson

Senior Advisor, London Borough of Bromley, Education
Development Centre, Church Lane, Princes Plain, Kent
BR2 8LD; e-mail ian.wilson@bromley.gov.uk;
Tel 020 8462 8911; Fax 020 8461 6286
Primary, secondary; leadership and management,
assessment; Ofsted registered inspector, NCSL consultant

Ros Wilson

1 Sandringham Ct, Bradley, Huddersfield HD2 1PY;
URL www.andrelleducation.com; e-mail
ros.wilson@andrelleducation.com; Tel 07866 581623
Raising standards in writing

Lynda Jane Woods

Silver Birches, Bramlands La, Woodmancote, Henfield,
West Sussex BN5 9TG; e-mail lynda.woods@virgin.net;
Tel 01273 492373; Fax 01273 492373
Nursery, primary; independent registered inspector and
consultant

Other Consultants

The Adams Consultancy Ltd

Chilterns, Bellingdon, Chesham, Buckinghamshire
HP5 2XL; URL www.theadamsconsultancy.co.uk; e-mail
mail@theadamsconsultancy.co.uk; Tel 01494 791045;
Fax 01494 778045
Director   Margaret Adams
Helps colleges to do more business with businesses.
Training, consultancy, master classes and coaching options
available.

Jane Bower

9 Marks Way, Girton, Cambridge, Cambridgeshire
CB3 0PW; e-mail jane-bower@ntlworld.com;
Tel 01223 502628
Key Stages 1–2; Art, Drama, Dance, Literacy, INSET,
classroom, murals; consultant and advisor

Bill Boyle

Foxbank Cottage, Forest Rd, Cotebrook, Tarporley, Cheshire
CW6 9DZ; e-mail bill.boyle@man.ac.uk; Tel 01829 760126
Assessment consultancy services

16

Dr James Martin Brown

122 Bryansburn Rd, Bangor, County Down BT20 3RG;
e-mail martin@oldcross.u-net.com; Tel 028 9146 0459;
Fax 028 9147 1249

Thinking and learning development, departmental
management, project management; Science

Ronald Bulman

Loftwood, Casterton, Carnforth LA6 2SF; e-mail
r.bulman@talk21.com; Tel 015242 71075;
Fax 015242 71075

Key Stages 3–4, sixth form; languages

H.G. Lyn Clement

22 Old Rd, Llanelli, Carmarthenshire SA15 3HP; e-mail
lyn@clemav.fsnet.co.uk; Tel 01554 772847;
Fax 01554 772847

Secondary; leadership and management

George Crowther

Little Hill, Colley Manor Drive, Reigate, Surrey RH2 9JS;
URL www.georgecrowther.co.uk; e-mail
geocrowther@hotmail.com; Tel 01737 243286;
Fax 01737 243286; Mobile 07710 214349

Judith Annette Dawson

Wellington Hse, 123 Chediston St, Halesworth, Suffolk
IP19 8BJ; e-mail judy@wellhouse123.freeserve.co.uk;
Tel 01986 872975; Fax 01986 872975

Primary; external adviser, Ofsted additional inspector

Tom Dodd

Cedarwood, Grove La, Chalfont St Peter, Buckinghamshire
SL9 9LN; e-mail tomdodd9@aol.com; Tel 01753 885188

Education and training, school inspection, management of
Design and Technology

The Education Officer, Free Church Education Unit

27 Tavistock Sq, London WC1H 9HH;
URL www.churches-together.org.uk; e-mail
education@cte.org.uk; Tel 020 7529 8145;
Fax 020 7529 8134

Set up by the Methodist Church and the Free Church
Federal Council to co-ordinate the 21 member
denominations' work in public education

Educational Management Services Ltd

Bedford Heights, Brickhill Dr, Bedford, Bedfordshire
MK41 7PH; e-mail info@edplus.co.uk; Tel 01234 760300;
Fax 01234 760301

Chief Executive David Ford

Non-curricular management support services for schools

John F.K. Evans

5 Maple Leaf, Coldwaltham, Pulborough, West Sussex
RH20 1LN; e-mail jfkyachts@jfkevans.fsnet.co.uk;
Tel 01798 874034

Leadership development; creativity, change and innovation
management; performance management and personal
development; vocational curriculum development and
international development

James George Forrest

7 Foley Rd, Claygate, Esher, Surrey KT10 0LU; e-mail
jim@jimfo.freeserve.co.uk; Tel 01372 470392;
Fax 01372 470392

Secondary, special, further education; work related
learning, key skills, academic target setting, Ofsted science,
widening HE participation

Terry Freedman Ltd

PO Box 1472, Ilford, Essex IG3 8QX;
URL www.terryfreedman.com; e-mail
terry@terryfreedman.com; Tel 020 8599 4661;
Fax 020 8599 4661

Tom Hinds

Hinds Education and Review, 40 Grove Rd, Windsor,
Berkshire SL4 1JQ; Tel 01753 858123

Local management, governing bodies, performance
indicators, group relations

JM Consulting Ltd

Glenthorne Hse, 20 Henbury Rd, Westbury on Trym, Bristol
BS9 3HJ; Tel 0117 959 3687; Fax 0117 959 3686

Director M. Burdett
Director J. Port

Strategic and business planning, organisational and
management development, financial management

Eric V. Needham

4a Leicester Rd, Broughton Astley, Leicestershire LE9 6QE;
Tel 01455 286486

Experience of inspections (management, history and PE),
school advice; Ofsted team member; management trained

Northern Education Consultancy

Northern Education Consultancy, 61 Moyle Rd, Ballycastle,
County Antrim BT54 6LG; URL www.noredco.com;
e-mail chrisferguson5@btopenworld.com;
Tel 028 2076 2949; Fax 028 2076 8099

Contact Chris Ferguson

Specialises in marketing, public relations and teacher
recruitment

Marjorie Ouvry

78 Hervey Rd, Blackheath, London SE3 8BU; e-mail
ouvry@hervey.demon.co.uk; Tel 020 8856 6050;
Fax 020 8856 6050

In-service courses for practitioners about the foundation
stage curriculum e.g. outdoor play, play, music

Dr Kate Seager

Littlestone Hse, Wall Hill, Ashurst Wood, East Grinstead,
West Sussex RH19 3TQ; e-mail seagerkate@aol.com;
Tel 01342 823588; Fax 01342 823885

Inspector of state and independent schools; consultancies in
the UK and abroad; management of schools and
departments, curriculum and assessment, Modern
Languages, SEN, teacher training

Graham F. Todd

Education Consultancy Services, 12 Christmas La, High
Halstow, Rochester, Kent ME3 8SN; e-mail
grajilltodd@aol.com; Tel 01634 255366; Fax 01634 254076

Advice and training, Ofsted SEN inspector

Teachers' and Other Sectoral Organisations

17

Joint Negotiating Councils and Committees

Trades Unions and Teachers' Associations

Subject Teaching Associations

Professional Educational Associations

Parent–Teacher Associations

Social Work, Disability and Counselling

Teachers' and Other Sectoral Organisations

Joint Negotiating Councils and Committees

Local Government Employers

Local Government Employers, Local Government Hse, Smith Sq, London SW1P 3HZ; e-mail info@lge.gov.uk; Tel 020 7187 7373; Fax 020 7664 3030

Chief Executive Paul Coen

Works with local authorities, regional employers and other bodies to create solutions in relation to pay, pensions and the employment contract, to ensure the provision of efficient and affordable local services

Joint Negotiating Committee for Teachers in Residential Establishments

Layden Hse, 76–86 Turnmill St, London EC1M 5QU

Secretary (Employers' Side) Charles Nolda

Secretary (Staff Side) Barry Fawcett

Joint Negotiating Committee for Youth and Community Workers

Secretary (Employers' Panel) Charles Nolda; Layden Hse, 76–86 Turnmill St, London EC1M 5QU; Tel 020 7296 6600

Secretary (Staff Side) Barry Fawcett; National Union of Teachers, Hamilton Hse, Mabledon Pl, London WC1H 9AJ

Reports

Employers Organisation, Layden Hse, 26–86 Turnmill St, London EC1M 5LG

The reports embodying the scales for teachers in social service establishments and youth workers and community centre wardens and for inspectors, organisers and advisory officers employed by local education authorities are published by the Employers Organisation

Soulbury Committee (Inspectors, Organisers and Advisory Officers of Local Education Authorities)

Secretary (Employers' Side) Charles Nolda; Layden Hse, 76–86 Turnmill St, London EC1M 5QU

Leader (Officers' Side) Steve Sinnott; Hamilton Hse, Mabledon Pl, London WC1H 9BD

Trades Unions and Teachers' Associations

Association of School and College Leaders (ASCL)

130 Regent Rd, Leicester LE1 7PG; URL www.ascl.org.uk; e-mail info@ascl.org.uk; Tel 0116 299 1122; Fax 0116 299 1123

ASCL is the professional association for secondary school and college leaders. ASCL has more than 13 000 members of school and college leadership teams. It is the only association to speak exclusively for the leaders of Britain's secondary schools and colleges, and is influential on government and other education policy makers throughout the UK. It offers a wide range of services to its members, including valued guidance and publications on educational issues.

Association of Secondary Teachers, Ireland

Asti Hse, Winetavern St, Dublin 8, Republic of Ireland; URL www.asti.ie; e-mail info@asti.ie; Tel +353 1 671 9144; Fax +353 1 671 9280

General Secretary John White

Association of Teachers and Lecturers

7 Northumberland St, London WC2N 5RD; URL www.atl.org.uk; e-mail info@atl.org.uk; Tel 020 7930 6441; Fax 020 7930 1359

President Julia Neal
Senior Vice-President Andy Ballard
Junior Vice-President Lesley Ward
Hon Secretary Shelagh Hirst
Hon Secretary Chris Wilson
Hon Treasurer Angie Rutter
Hon Treasurer Martin Lawes
General Secretary Mary Bousted BA(Hons), MA, PhD
Assistant General Secretary Martin Johnson
Deputy General Secretary Gerald Imison
Deputy General Secretary Paul Day
Director (Finance) Paul Jennings
Head (Communications) Victoria Irvine
Head (Education, Research and Policy) Martin Johnson
Head (IT) Ann Raimondo
Head (Legal and Member Services) Martin Pilkington
Head (Membership) Catherine Parry
Head (Pay, Conditions and Pensions) Martin Freedman
Head (Recruitment and Organisation) Mark Holden
Deputy Head (Education, Research and Policy) Nansi Ellis
Deputy Head (Legal and Member Services) Andy Peart
Manager (Human Resources) Nicki Landau
National Official (Pay and Conditions) Steven Crane
Senior Solicitor Philip Lott
National Official (IAMs) Andy Peart

17

National Official (Independent Schools)   John Richardson
National Official (Pensions)   Marion Bird
Organiser (Conference and Events)   Chris Broughton
Training Officer   Abbie Jenkinson

Association of Teachers and Lecturers Office in Northern Ireland

10 Cromac Quay, Ormeau Rd, Belfast BT7 2JD; e-mail
ni@atl.org.uk; Tel 028 9032 7990; Fax 028 9032 7992
Director (Northern Ireland)   Mark Langhammer
Officer (Research and Information)   Theresa Devenney

Association of Teachers and Lecturers Office in Wales

1st Fl, Empire Hse, Mount Stuart Sq, Cardiff CF10 5FN;
e-mail cymru@atl.org.uk; Tel 02920 465000;
Fax 02920 462000
Director (Wales)   Philip Dixon
Organiser   Helen Cole

Centre for Studies in Enterprise, Career Development and Work

Jordanhill Campus, University of Strathclyde, Southbrae Dr,
Glasgow G13 1PP; URL www.strath.ac.uk/
enterprisingcareers; e-mail
enterprising.careers@strath.ac.uk; Tel 0141 950 3141;
Fax 0141 950 3919
Deputy Director   Linda Brownlow

Educational Institute of Scotland

46 Moray Pl, Edinburgh EH3 6BH; URL www.eis.org.uk;
e-mail enquiries@eis.org.uk; Tel 0131 225 6244;
Fax 0131 220 3151
General Secretary   Ronald A. Smith

Irish National Teachers' Organisation (INTO)

35 Parnell Sq, Dublin 1, Republic of Ireland;
URL www.into.ie; e-mail info@into.ie;
Tel +353 1 804 7700; Fax +353 1 872 2462
President   Sheila Nunan
General Secretary   John Carr
General Treasurer   Sheila Nunan
Aims to unite and organise the teachers of Ireland and to
provide a means for the expression of their collective
opinion on educational matters; to safeguard and improve
the conditions of employment of its members; to afford
advice and assistance to individual members on
professional matters; to promote the interests of education;
and to cultivate a spirit of fraternal co-operation with
kindred organisations in this and other countries.

Regional Office

23 College Gdns, Belfast BT9 6BS; URL www.into.ie; e-mail
info@ni.into.ie; Tel 028 9038 1455; Fax 028 9066 2803
Northern Secretary   Frank Bunting

National Association of Head Teachers (NAHT)

1 Heath Sq, Boltro Rd, Haywards Heath, West Sussex
RH16 1BL; URL www.naht.org.uk; e-mail
info@naht.org.uk; Tel 01444 472472; Fax 01444 472473
General Secretary   Mike Brookes BA, MEd
Deputy General Secretary   Carole Whitty

National Association of Schoolmasters Union of Women Teachers (NASUWT)

Hillscourt Education Centre, Rose Hill, Rednal,
Birmingham, West Midlands B45 8RS;
URL www.teachersunion.org.uk; e-mail
nasuwt@mail.nasuwt.org.uk; Tel 0121 453 6150;
Fax 0121 457 6208
President   Amanda Haechner
Senior Vice-President   Julian Chapman
Junior Vice-President   Chris Lines
Ex-President   John Moyes

Hon Treasurer   Sue Rogers
General Secretary   Chris Keates
Deputy General Secretary   Jerry Bartlett
Assistant General Secretary (Administration and Resources)
Roger Darke
Assistant General Secretary (Policy and Communications)
Patrick Roach
*Assistant General Secretary (Regional Development and
Support)*   Mary Howard
National Official (Education)   Darren Northcott
National Official (Equality and Training)   Jennifer Moses
National Official (Finance)   Jane Smith
National Official (Legal and Casework)   Jim Quigley
National Official (Personnel and Development)   Nick Parker
National Official (Recruitment)   Tracey Twist
National Official (Resources)   Paul MacLachlan
National Official (Salaries, Pensions and Conditions of Service)
Bob Johnson

NASUWT (Scotland)

34 West George St, Glasgow G2 1DA; Tel 0141 332 2688;
Fax 0141 332 0608
President   J. Kelly; 9 Woodside Ave, Rutherglen, Glasgow
G73 3HX; Tel 0141 647 2966; Tel (St Ninians High)
0141 776 1585
Scottish Regional Official   Carol Fox BSc, CQSW,
MSc;   NASUWT (Scotland) Office, 34 West George St,
Glasgow G2 1DA; Tel 0141 332 2688
National Executive Member for Scotland   T. Ferri;   St
Margarets High School, Airdrie; Tel 01236 766881; 8
Clydeford Dr, Uddingston, Glasgow G71 7DH;
Tel 01698 813405

National Primary Teacher Education Council (NaPTEC)

University of Greenwich, School of Education and Training,
Eltham, London SE9 2PQ; e-mail r.m.young@gre.ac.uk;
Tel 020 8331 9432
Chair   Robert Young; Tel 020 8331 9491
Treasurer   Alan Haigh; 11 Parkhead Cres, Sheffield, South
Yorkshire S11 9RD; Tel 0114 236 3317

National Society for Education in Art and Design (NSEAD)

The Gatehouse, Corsham Ct, Corsham, Wiltshire SN13 0BZ;
URL www.nsead.org; e-mail johnsteers@nsead.org;
Tel 01249 714825; Fax 01249 716138
General Secretary   J. Steers NDD, ATC, DAE, PhD
President   G. Coutts
Hon Treasurer   A. Laing; 108e North Woodside Rd,
Glasgow G20 7DN

National Union of Teachers (NUT)

Hamilton Hse, Mabledon Pl, London WC1H 9BD;
URL www.teachers.org.uk; Tel 020 7388 6191;
Fax 020 7387 8458
President   Judy Moorhouse
Ex-President   Hilary Bills
Senior Vice-President   Baljeet Ghale
Junior Vice-President   Bill Greenshields
Hon Treasurer   Ian Murch
General Secretary   Steve Sinnott
Deputy General Secretary   Christine Blower
Senior Solicitor   G. Clayton
Assistant Secretary (Accountant)   A.G. Wills
Assistant Secretary (Education and Equal Opportunities)
J. Bangs
Assistant Secretary (Legal and Professional Services)
Amanda Brown
Assistant Secretary (Membership and Communications)
A. Jarman
Assistant Secretary (Organisation and Administration)
D. Macfarlane
*Assistant Secretary (Salaries, Conditions of Service and
Superannuation)*   G.B. Fawcett

Eastern Regional Office

Regional Secretary Hilary Bucky; Elm Hse, Hennett Pk, Malten Rd, Kentford, Suffolk CB8 8GF; Tel 01638 555300; Fax 01638 555330

London East Regional Office

Regional Secretary T. Harrison; NUT Regional Office, 103 Cranbrook Rd, Ilford, Essex IG1 4PU; Tel 020 8477 1234; Fax 020 8477 1230

London West Regional Office

Regional Secretary S. Cankett; London West Regional Office, Ravenscourt Hse, 322a King St, London W6 0RR; Tel 020 8846 0600; Fax 020 8563 8877

Midlands Regional Office

Regional Secretary B. Carter; NUT Regional Office, Jarvis Hse, 96 Stone St, Stafford, Staffordshire ST16 2RS; Tel 01785 244129; Fax 01785 233138

Northern Regional Office

Regional Secretary Elaine Kay; NUT Regional Office, Auckland Hse, High Chare, Chester-le-Street, County Durham DH3 3PX; Tel 0191 389 0999; Fax 0191 389 2074

North West Regional Office

Regional Secretary R. Palframan; NUT Regional Office, 25 Chorley New Rd, Bolton, Greater Manchester BL1 4QR; Tel 01204 521434; Fax 01204 362650

South East Regional Office

Regional Secretary Marian Darke; NUT Regional Office, 14–16 Sussex Rd, Haywards Heath, West Sussex RH16 4EA; Tel 01444 452073; Fax 01444 415095

South West Regional Office

Regional Secretary Andy Woolley; NUT Regional Office, 1 Lower Ave, Heavitree, Exeter, Devon EX1 2PR; Tel 01392 258028; Fax 01392 412801

Yorkshire/Midlands Regional Office

Regional Secretary M. Anderson; NUT Regional Office, 7/9 Chequer Rd, Doncaster, South Yorkshire DN1 2AA; Tel 01302 342448; Fax 01302 341021

Wales (NUT Cymru)

Regional Secretary Gethin Lewis; NUT Regional Office, 122 Bute St, Cardiff CF10 5AE; Tel 2920 491818; Fax 02920 492491

Principals Professional Council

1 Heath Sq, Boltro Rd, Haywards Heath, West Sussex RH16 1BL; e-mail apc@naht.org.uk; Tel 01444 472499; Fax 01444 472493
Chair Joanna Tait
General Secretary Dr Michael Thrower

School Teachers' Review Body (STRB)

Office of Manpower Economics, 6th Fl, Kingsgate Hse, 66–74 Victoria St, London SW1E 6SW; URL www.ome.uk.com; e-mail john.perrett@berr.gsi.gov.uk; Tel 020 7215 8314
Chair Bill Cockburn CBE
Secretary John Perrett
Examines and reports on such matters relating to the statutory conditions of employment of school teachers in England and Wales as may from time to time be referred to the Review Body by the Secretary of State; takes formal evidence from bodies representative of LEAs, governors of schools and school teachers. Nine members.

Scottish Secondary Teachers' Association

14 West End Pl, Edinburgh EH11 2ED; URL www.ssta.org.uk; e-mail info@ssta.org.uk; Tel 0131 313 7300; Fax 0131 346 8057
President Ann Ballinger; Bishopbriggs Academy

Vice-President Peter Wright; Broxburn Academy
General Secretary David Eaglesham
Deputy General Secretary James Docherty
General Treasurer Norman Geekie; Milne's High School, Fochabers

Transport and General Workers Union (TGWU)

Transport Hse, 128 Theobalds Rd, Holborn, London WC1X 8TN; URL www.tgwu.org.uk; e-mail tgwu@tgwu.org.uk; Tel 020 7611 2500; Fax 020 7611 2555

Ulster Teachers' Union (UTU)

94 Malone Rd, Belfast BT9 5HP; URL www.utn.edu; e-mail office@utn.edu; Tel 028 9066 2216; Fax 028 9068 3296
General Secretary A.E. Hall-Callaghan
Senior Field Officer Mike Graves
Field Officer Jude Ford
The UTU is an organisation of teachers in Northern Ireland. Recognised teachers of all types, irrespective of status, belong to this union and have access to its protection, benefits and services.

Undeb Cenedlaethol Athrawon Cymru (Welsh Teachers' Union)

Swyddfa UCAC, Pen Roc, Aberystwyth, Ceredigion SY23 2AZ; URL www.athrawon.com; e-mail ucac@athrawon.com; Tel 01970 639950; Fax 01970 626765
President Robert Howells
General Secretary Gruff Hughes
Deputy General Secretary Dilwyn Roberts-Young
Field Officer (North Wales) Eryl Owain
Field Officer (South Wales) Dilwyn Roberts-Young
Policy Officer Elaine Edwards
Treasurer J.D.E. Jones

Representatives
Isle of Anglesey
  Contact Mari Sexton
Blaenau Gwent and Caerphilly Ysgol y Castell, Caerphilly; Tel 02920 864790
  Contact Gwenllian Jenkins
  Contact Gail Jones; Ysgol Gymraeg Brynmawr, Blaenau Gwent; Tel 01495 310735
Cardiff Ysgol Maes Llyn, Llanelli; Tel 01554 773843
  Contact Bethan E. Williams
Ceredigion Ysgol Gyfun Dyffryn Teifi, Llandysul, Ceredigion; Tel 01559 362310
  Contact Julia James
Conwy Ysgol Gynradd, Llanddoged; Tel 01492 640363
  Contact Gwynn Griffith
Denbigh Ysgol Uwchradd Dinas Brân, Llangollen, Denbighshire; Tel 01978 860669
  Contact Emrys Wynne
Flint Ysgol Uwchradd, Maes Garmon, Yr Wyddgrug; Tel 01352 750678
  Contact Gwilym Evans
Vale of Glamorgan
  Contact Fflur Bedwyr; Ysgol Bro Morgannwg, Y Barri, Vale of Glamorgan; Tel 01446 450280
Gwynedd Ysgol Glan y Môr, Pwllheli, Gwynedd; Tel 01758 701244
  Contact Dilwyn Ellis Hughes
Neath Port Talbot and Swansea Ysgol Gyfun Ystalyfera, Swansea; Tel 01639 842129
  Contact Gareth Morgan
Monmouth, Torfaen and Newport Ysgol Gyfun Gwynllyw, Pontypool, Torfaen; Tel 01495 750405
  Contact Nia Goode
Pembroke
  Contact Phil Higginson
Powys Ysgol Uwchradd, Llanfair, Caereinion, Powys; Tel 01938 810888
  Contact Huw Richards

17

615

Wrexham
Contact Ioan Rhys Jones; Ysgol Morgan Llwyd,
Wrexham; Tel 01978 315050
Rhondda Cynon Taff and Merthyr Ysgol Gynradd,
Gymraeg, Bronllwyn; Tel 01443 435294
Contact Sian Cadifor

UNISON

1 Mabledon Pl, London WC1H 9AJ;
URL www.unison.org.uk; e-mail
localgovernment@unison.co.uk; Tel 020 7551 1121;
Fax 020 7551 1195
General Secretary Dave Prentis
National Officer (Social Services) Helga Pile

University and College Union (UCU)

NATFHE merged with the Association of University
Teachers in 2006 to form the University and College Union
27 Britannia St, London WC1X 9JP; URL www.ucu.org.uk;
e-mail hq@ucu.org.uk; Tel 020 7837 3636
President Linda Newman
President Elect Sasha Callaghan
Vice-President Alastair Hunter

Further Education Regional Offices

Anglia, Buckinghamshire and Parts of Outer London 27
Britannia St, London WC1X 9JP; Tel 020 7520 1038;
Fax 020 7837 4399
Head Liz Martins
East Midlands, Oxford, Parts of Yorkshire 2nd Fl, Alpha
Tower, Suffolk St, Queensway, Birmingham, West
Midlands B1 1TT; Tel 0121 634 7380; Fax 0121 634 7387
Head Russ Escritt
Head Adrian Jones
Inner and Parts of Outer London 27 Britannia St, London
WC1X 9JP; Tel 020 7833 3886; Fax 020 7278 2440
Head Christiane Ohsan
North Western, Merseyside and Cheshire Lancastrian Office
Centre, Talbot Rd, Old Trafford, Manchester M32 0FP;
Tel 0161 772 7010; Fax 0161 772 7013
Head Colin Gledhill
Northern, Yorkshire and the Humber J31 The Avenues,
Eleventh Ave, Team Valley Trading Est, Gateshead, Tyne
and Wear NE11 0NJ; Tel 0191 487 7220; Fax 0191 487 7255
Head Iain Owens
South West 26b Clifton Hall, Exeter, Devon EX1 2DJ;
Tel 01392 412525; Fax 01392 412418
Head Jim McCracken
Southern Counties, South West and South East 27 Britannia
St, London WC1X 9JP; Tel 020 7278 0256;
Fax 020 7278 2440
Head Mary Cooper
West Midlands, Western 2nd Fl, Alpha Tower, Suffolk St,
Queensway, Birmingham, West Midlands B1 1TT;
Tel 0121 634 7382; Fax 0121 634 6648
Head Chris Powell

Higher Education Regional Offices

London, South East and East Anglia 27 Britannia St, London
WC1X 9JP; Tel 020 7833 5527; Fax 020 7837 9214
Head Jenny Golden
Midlands, Southern and South West 2nd Fl, Alpha Tower,
Suffolk St, Queensway, Birmingham, West Midlands
B1 1TT; Tel 0121 634 7384; Fax 0121 634 6648
Head Sue Davis
Northern, North West, Yorkshire and the Humber
Lancastrian Office Centre, Talbot Rd, Old Trafford,
Manchester M32 0FP; Tel 0161 772 7012;
Fax 0161 772 7015
Head Adrian Jones

Further and Higher Education Regional Offices

Northern Ireland 475 Lisburn Rd, Belfast BT9 7EZ;
Tel 028 9066 5501; Fax 028 9066 9225
Head Jim McKeown

Wales Unit 33, The Enterprise Centre, Tondu, Bridgend
CF32 9BS; Tel 01656 721951; Fax 01656 723834
Head Margaret Phelan

Voice

Union for education professionals
2 St James' Ct, Friar Gate, Derby DE1 1BT;
URL www.voicetheunion.org.uk; e-mail
hq@voicetheunion.org.uk; Tel 01332 372337;
Fax 01332 290310
Founder President R. Bryant MSc
National Chair Geraldine Everett
Vice-Chair Andrew Broadhurst
Hon Secretary David Whitewright
General Secretary Philip Parkin BA, MEd, DipEd, DipSE
Director (Wales); Professional Officer (Wales: South/West)
Nick Griffin DipEd, FRSA; e-mail
nickgriffin@voicetheunion.org.uk; Tel 01332 378029
Senior Professional Officer (Fieldwork); Regional Co-ordinator
Mark Essex BA, MSc
Senior Professional Officer (PANN/PAtT Sections)
Tricia Pritchard
Senior Professional Officer (Scotland) Maureen Laing; e-mail
scotland@voicetheunion.org.uk; Tel 0131 220 8241
Principal Professional Officer (Education) Alison Johnston
Principal Professional Officer (Pay and Conditions and Wales)
Deborah Simpson BA, MA
Professional Officer (Communications) Richard Fraser BA,
MCIPR
Professional Officer (Independent Section) Sharon Sherratt
Professional Officer (Legal Services) Sheila Barnes
Professional Officer (Publications; Marketing; Conference)
Lynch Wraith ACIM, MIAM
Professional Officer (Wales: North/Mid) John Till MA, DPA,
DipEd; e-mail johntill@voicetheunion.org.uk;
Tel 01332 378031
Regional Officer (Southern Scotland) Ken Newberry; e-mail
kennewberry@voicetheunion.org.uk
Accountant Sue Cornish BA(Law), FCCA
Solicitor David J. Brierley MA

Professional Association of Teachers in Scotland (PAT, PANN, PAET)

1–3 St Colme St, Edinburgh EH3 6AA;
URL www.pat.org.uk; e-mail scotland@pat.org.uk;
Tel 0131 220 8241; Fax 0131 220 8350
Administrative Officer Isabelle Cameron
Senior Professional Officer Maureen Laing
Regional Officer Ken Newberry

Council Members

Representing geographic areas
East Anglia Region
Contact Mr I. Pringle
(Cambridgeshire, Essex, Norfolk, Peterborough,
Southend, Suffolk, Thurrock)
East Midlands Region
Contact Mrs R. Stokes
(City of Nottingham, Derby City, Derbyshire, Leicester
City, Leicestershire, Lincolnshire, North East
Lincolnshire, North Lincolnshire, Nottinghamshire,
Rutland)
Greater London Region
Contact Mrs N. Foster
Contact Miss C. Wigmore
(Barking and Dagenham, Barnet, Bexley, Brent, Bromley,
Camden, City of London, Croydon, Ealing, Enfield,
Greenwich, Hackney, Hammersmith and Fulham,
Haringey, Harrow, Havering, Hillingdon, Hounslow,
Islington, Kensington and Chelsea, Kingston upon
Thames, Lambeth, Lewisham, Merton, Newham,
Redbridge, Richmond upon Thames, Southwark, Sutton,
Tower Hamlets, Waltham Forest, Wandsworth,
Westminster)

North East Region
Contact Mr W. Barton
Contact Mrs L.M. Cross
(Barnsley, Bradford, Calderdale, Darlington, Doncaster, Durham, East Riding of Yorkshire, Gateshead, Hartlepool, Kingston upon Hull, Kirklees, Leeds, Middlesbrough, Newcastle upon Tyne, North Tyneside, North Yorkshire, Northumberland, Redcar and Cleveland, Rotherham, Sheffield, South Tyneside, Stockton-on-Tees, Sunderland, Wakefield, York)

North West Region
Contact Mrs V. Parkinson
(Blackburn, Blackpool, Bolton, Bury, Cheshire, Cumbria, Halton, Knowsley, Lancashire, Liverpool, Manchester, Oldham, Rochdale, St Helens, Salford, Sefton, Stockport, Tameside, Trafford, Warrington, Wigan, Wirral)

South East Region
Contact Mrs K.M. Barraclough
Contact Mr M. Barton
(Brighton and Hove, East Sussex, Kent, Medway, Surrey, West Sussex)

South Midlands Region
Contact Mr G. Clement
Contact Mrs V. Park
(Bedfordshire, Bracknell Forest, Buckinghamshire, Hertfordshire, Luton, Milton Keynes, Northamptonshire, Oxfordshire, Reading, Slough, West Berkshire, Windsor and Maidenhead, Wokingham)

South West Region
Contact Mrs R. Taylor
(Bath and North East Somerset, Bournemouth, Bristol, Cornwall, Devon, Dorset, Hampshire, Isle of Wight, Isles of Scilly, North West Somerset, Plymouth, Poole, Portsmouth, Somerset, South Gloucestershire, Southampton, Swindon, Torbay, Wiltshire)

West Midlands Region
Contact Mrs Lynn Edwards
Contact Mrs M. Volpé
(Birmingham, Coventry, Dudley, Gloucestershire, Herefordshire, Sandwell, Shropshire, Solihull, Staffordshire, Stoke-on-Trent, Telford and Wrekin, Walsall, Warwickshire, Wolverhampton, Worcestershire)

Edinburgh Region
(City of Edinburgh, Clackmannanshire, East Lothian, Falkirk, Fife Council, Mid Lothian, Scottish Borders, Stirling, West Lothian)

Scotland North Region
Contact Mrs W. Dyble
(Aberdeen, Aberdeenshire, Angus, Dundee, Highland Council, Moray, Orkney, Perthshire and Kinross, Shetland, Western Isles)

Scotland South Region
Contact Mrs E. Lamb
(Argyll and Bute, City of Glasgow, Dumfries and Galloway, East Ayrshire, East Dunbartonshire, East Renfrewshire, Inverclyde, North Ayrshire, North Lanarkshire, Renfrewshire, South Ayrshire, South Lanarkshire, West Dunbartonshire)

Wales Region
Contact Mr P.A. Wilkinson
(Blaenau Gwent, Bridgend, Caerphilly, Cardiff, Carmarthenshire, Ceredigion, Conwy, Denbighshire, Flintshire, Gwynedd, Isle of Anglesey, Merthyr Tydfil, Monmouthshire, Neath and Port Talbot, Newport, Pembrokeshire, Powys, Rhondda Cynon Taff, Swansea, Torfaen, Vale of Glamorgan, Wrexham)

Outside Great Britain
(Northern Ireland, Guernsey, Isle of Man, Jersey, Overseas, SCEA)

Regional Officers
Headquarters Region (East/North Midlands) e-mail hq@voicetheunion.org.uk; Tel 01332 372337
(Derbyshire, Derby, Leicestershire, Leicester, Nottinghamshire, Nottingham, Lincolnshire, North East Lincolnshire, Rutland, Sheffield, Stoke-on-Trent, Staffordshire)

East Anglia
Contact Bob Gale BA; e-mail bobgale@voicetheunion.org.uk
(Northamptonshire, Cambridgeshire, Peterborough, Essex, Thurrock, Southend, Norfolk, Suffolk)

London
Contact Michael Sadler; e-mail michaelsadler@voicetheunion.org.uk
Contact Margaret Taylor; e-mail margarettaylor@voicetheunion.org.uk
(Local education authority in Greater London)

North East England
Contact Stephen Payne BD, DipED; e-mail stephenpayne@voicetheunion.org.uk
(Northumberland, Durham local authorities in Tyne and Wear and Cleveland, North Yorkshire, York, East Riding of Yorkshire, Kingston upon Hull, North Lincolnshire and local authorities in West and South Yorkshire, except Sheffield which is in the Headquarters region)

North West England
Contact Ron Crabtree; e-mail roncrabtree@voicetheunion.org.uk
(Cumbria, Lancashire, Blackpool, Blackburn and Darwen, Cheshire, Isle of Man and local authorities in Merseyside and Greater Manchester)

South East
Contact Janet Martin; e-mail janetmartin@voicetheunion.org.uk
(Kent, Medway, East Sussex, West Sussex, Brighton and Hove, Surrey)

South West England
Contact Ros Griffiths BA; e-mail rosgriffiths@voicetheunion.org.uk
(Cornwall, Plymouth, Isles of Scilly, Devon, Torbay, Dorset, Poole, Bournemouth, Hampshire, Southampton, Portsmouth, Isle of Wight, Somerset, Wiltshire, Guernsey and Jersey)

West/South Midlands
Contact Dick Colligan BEd, MA, FRSA; e-mail dickcolligan@voicetheunion.org.uk
(Shropshire, Telford and Wrekin, Worcestershire, Herefordshire, Gloucestershire, Warwickshire, Oxfordshire, Buckinghamshire, Milton Keynes, Bedfordshire, Luton, Hertfordshire, local authorities in West Midlands, Swindon, Avon and Berkshire)

Subject Teaching Associations

ASET
3 Westbrook Ct, Sharrow Vale Rd, Sheffield, South Yorkshire S11 8YZ; URL www.asetonline.org; e-mail aset@aset.demon.co.uk; Tel 0114 221 2902

Association of Agricultural Education Staffs
Chair (NATFE Agricultural and Allied Education Sector) Chris Gwilt
Sector Official (NATFE Agricultural and Allied Education Sector) Bernice Waugh

Association for Astronomy Education
c/o The Royal Astronomical Society, Burlington Hse, Piccadilly, London W1J 0BQ
Secretary Anne Urquhart-Potts

Association for Language Learning
School of Modern Languages, University of Leicester, University Rd, Leicester LE1 7RH; URL www.all-languages.org.uk; e-mail info@all-languages.org.uk; Tel 0116 229 7453
President Helen Myers
The Association for Language Learning (ALL) is the subject teaching association for all involved in the teaching of modern foreign languages. Its membership comprises university lecturers, teacher trainers, advisers, teachers in primary, preparatory and secondary schools and colleges, as well as trainers in adult education and industry. Members

17

are supported with a quarterly newsletter, six journals a year, advice, information and in-service training courses. The major annual event is the ALL conference and exhibition Language World. The association is consulted by official bodies and plays an active part in national and international organisations, which aim to improve and promote language learning.

Association for Latin Teaching
c/o Stonycroft, Bighton, Alresford, Hampshire SO24 9RE; URL www.arlt.co.uk
Hon Secretary   Liz Scott

Association of Law Teachers
UK Centre for Legal Education, University of Warwick, Coventry CV4 7AL; Tel 024 7652 2394; Fax 024 7652 3290
Secretary   Amanda Fancourt

Association of Motor Vehicle Teachers
Diactec Hse, 19 Peel St, Marsden, West Yorkshire HD7 6BW; Tel 01484 845039; Fax 01484 844828
National Chair   J. Warner

Association for Schools' Science Engineering and Technology (ASSET)
1 Giltspur St, London EC1A 9DD; e-mail asset@scsst.uk.com; Tel 020 7294 2431; Fax 020 7294 2442
President   HRH The Duke of Edinburgh KG, KT, FRS
Chair   J.S. Fraser
Chief Executive   A. Parkin
ASSET aims to excite young people about science and technology through innovatory approaches in teaching and joint activities between schools and industry. This is done via the activities of the CREST Award Scheme, Young Engineers clubs, and the 50 Science and Technology Regional Organisations (SATROs) throughout the UK (list available). Other activities include accredited science updating INSET courses for teachers.

Association for Science Education
College La, Hatfield, Hertfordshire AL10 9AA; URL www.ase.org.uk; e-mail derekbell@ase.org.uk; Tel 01707 283000; Fax 01707 266532
Chief Executive   Dr Derek Bell

Association of Teachers of German
See Association for Language Learning

Association of Teachers of Italian
See Association for Language Learning

Association of Teachers of Mathematics
Unit 7, Prime Industrial Pk, Shaftesbury St, Derby DE23 8YB; Tel 01332 346599; Fax 01332 204357
Administrative Officer   Su Strange
Hon Secretary   Margaret Jones
Hon Treasurer   Alison Parish

Association of Teachers of Russian
See Association for Language Learning

Association of Teachers of Spanish and Portuguese
See Association for Language Learning

Association for the Teaching of Psychology
c/o British Psychology Society, St Andrew's Hse, Leicester LE1 7DR; URL www.theatp.org; Tel 0116 245 9568

British Association for American Studies (BAAS)
Department of Humanities, Fylde 425, University of Central Lancashire, Preston, Lancashire PR1 2HE; URL www.baas.ac.uk; e-mail heidi.macpherson@baas.ac.uk; Tel 01772 893039
Secretary   Dr Heidi Macpherson

The British Association for Chinese Studies
22 Chepstow Cres, London W11 3EB; e-mail s.feuchtwang@lse.ac.uk; Tel 020 7727 0820
President   Stephan Feuchtwang

British Association of Dramatherapists
Waverley, Battledown Approach, Cheltenham, Gloucestershire GL52 6RE; URL www.badth.org.uk; e-mail enquiries@badth.org.uk; Tel 01242 235515
Administrator   Heidi Jockelson

British Association for Language Teaching
See Association for Language Learning

British Association of State English Language Teaching (BASELT)
c/o Baselt Secretariat, University of Gloucestershire, Cornerways, The Park Campus, The Park, Cheltenham, Gloucestershire GL50 2QF; URL www.baselt.org.uk; e-mail baselt@glos.ac.uk; Tel 01242 227099; Fax 01242 227055
Chief Executive   Richard Truscott

Centre for Information on Language Teaching and Research
See CILT under Chapter 9: Research and Advisory Bodies

Christian Education Movement
Royal Bldgs, Victoria St, Derby DE1 1GW; URL www.cem.org.uk; e-mail cem@cem.org.uk; Tel 01332 296655; Fax 01332 343253
Director   Peter Fishpool

Classical Association
36 Station Rd, Blackrod, Bolton, Greater Manchester BL6 5BW; e-mail barbara@finney41.fsnet.co.uk; Tel 01204 698010
Branches Secretary   Barbara Finney

Council for Hospitality Management Education
Department of Hotel and Catering Studies, Westminster College, London W1 2PD
Chair   Prof D.A. Mogendorff; Glasgow Caledonian University, Park Dr, Glasgow G3 6LP; Tel 0141 337 4313; Fax 0141 337 4141

Council of Specialist Teaching Associations
The Niven Suite, The Mansion, Ottershaw Pk, Chertsey, Surrey KT16 0QG
General Secretary   Grahame Leon-Smith MA, FBEA, DipRSA
COSTA was established with the following aims: to provide an effective means of involving specialist teaching associations in decision and policy making at national and regional levels; to provide a means of communication between associations on their activities, methods of organisation and economic planning; to provide a forum for discussion of matters of common interest; to take common action, where appropriate, on behalf of member associations, without thereby committing member associations as a whole, and protecting the right of any constituent association to act individually or to record a dissenting view.
Membership of COSTA is open to all subject and specialist teaching associations.

The Design and Technology Association (DATA)
16 Wellesbourne Hse, Walton Rd, Wellesbourne, Warwickshire CV35 9JB; URL www.data.org.uk; e-mail data@data.org.uk; Tel 01789 470007; Fax 01789 841955
Chief Executive   Richard Green

Earth Science Teachers' Association
c/o The Geological Society, Burlington Hse, London W1V 0JU; URL www.esta-uk.org; e-mail dawn.windley@thomroth.ac.uk; Tel 020 7434 9944; Fax 020 7439 8975
Secretary   Dawn Windley

The Economics and Business Education Association
The Forum, 277 London Rd, Burgess Hill, West Sussex RH15 9QU; URL www.ebea.org.uk; e-mail office@ebea.org.uk; Tel 01444 240150; Fax 01444 240101
Chief Executive   Duncan Cullimore
Administrator   Claire Johnson

The English Association

University of Leicester, University Rd, Leicester LE1 7RH;
Tel 0116 252 3982; Fax 0116 252 2301
President   P.J. Kitson
Chair   M. Moran
Secretary   H. Lucas
Treasurer   R.J. Claxton
To further knowledge, understanding, and enjoyment of the
English Language and its literature, by means of conferences
(five annually), lectures and publications (journals and
annual publications)

European Association of Teachers (UK Section)

(Representing teachers of European Studies on Council of
Subject Teaching Associations)
Chair   Andrew P. Clarke; Modern Language Dept:
Wisbech Grammar School, Wisbech, Cambridgeshire
PE13 1UX
Promotes education about Europe

General Studies Association

6 New Row, Wass, North Yorkshire YO61 4BG;
Tel 01347 868388
Chair   F.I. Magee

Geographical Association

160 Solly St, Sheffield, South Yorkshire S1 4BF;
URL www.geography.org.uk; e-mail
info@geography.org.uk; Tel 0114 296 0088;
Fax 0114 296 7176

Historical Association

59a Kennington Park Rd, London SE11 4JH; e-mail
enquiry@history.org.uk; Tel 020 7735 3901;
Fax 020 7582 4989

Incorporated Society of Musicians

10 Stratford Pl, London W1C 1AA; URL www.ism.org;
e-mail membership@ism.org; Tel 020 7629 4413;
Fax 020 7408 1538
Chief Executive   Neil Hoyle

Joint Association of Classical Teachers

Senate Hse, Malet St, London WC1E 7HU;
URL www.jact.org; e-mail office@jact.org;
Tel 020 7862 8719; Fax 020 7255 2297
Administrator   Anna Bayraktar

London Mathematical Society

De Morgan Hse, 57–58 Russell Sq, London WC1B 4HS;
URL www.lms.ac.uk; e-mail lms@lms.ac.uk;
Tel 020 7637 3686; Fax 020 7323 3655
Executive Secretary   Mr P.R. Cooper
General Secretary   Prof C.M. Goldie
Administrator   Miss S.M. Oakes

Mathematical Association

259 London Rd, Leicester LE2 3BE; URL www.m-a.org.uk;
e-mail office@m.a.org.uk; Tel 0116 221 0013;
Fax 0116 212 2835
Senior Administrator   Marcia Murray

Music Masters' and Mistresses' Association

Membership Secretary   Carol Hawkins; c/o St Edmunds
School, St Thomas' Hill, Canterbury, Kent CT2 8HU;
Tel 01227 475600

National Association for Design Education

General Secretary   F. Zankor MA(Ed), NDD, DLC, FRSA; 26
Dorchester Cl, Mansfield, Nottinghamshire NG18 4QW;
Tel 01623 631551

National Association for Teaching English and Other Community Languages to Adults (NATECLA)

NATECLA, Rm HB110, South Birmingham College, Hall
Green Campus, Cole Bank Rd, Birmingham, West
Midlands B28 8ES; URL www.natecla.org.uk; e-mail
co-ordinator@natecla.fsnet.co.uk; Tel 0121 688 8121;
Fax 0121 694 5062

National Co-ordinator   Cathy Burns
Assistant Co-ordinator   Jane Arstall

National Association for the Teaching of Drama

30 Heathdene Rd, Streatham, London SW16 3PD;
Tel 020 8679 3361
Hon Secretary   Maggie McNeill

National Association for the Teaching of English

NATE Office, 50 Broadfield Rd, Sheffield, South Yorkshire
S8 0XJ; URL www.nate.org.uk; e-mail info@nate.org.uk;
Tel 0114 255 5419; Fax 0114 255 5296
Chair   Elaine Millard
Director (Development and Communications)   Ian McNeilly
Company Secretary   Lyn Fairfax
Secretary   Moyra Beverton
Publications Manager   Anne Fairhall

National Association of Advisers and Inspectors in Design and Technology (NAAIDT)

Secretary   S.J. Kendall; 44 Davenport Rd, London SE6 2AZ;
Tel (office) 020 8655 1299; Tel (home) 020 8698 5676

Association for Careers Education and Guidance

9 Lawrence Leys, Bloxham, Banbury, Oxfordshire
OX15 4NU; URL www.aceg.org.uk; e-mail
alan@aceg.org.uk; Tel 01295 720809; Fax 01295 720809
President   J. Jenson
General Secretary   A. Vincent

National Association of Language Advisers

Hon Secretary   R.S. Heald; Education Services Adviser,
Education Dept, Birmingham, West Midlands B3 3BU;
Tel 0121 235 2706

National Association of Mathematics Advisers

Chair   Graham Smart; Kingston Centre, Fairway, Stafford,
Staffordshire ST16 3TW; Tel 01785 278258

National Association of Music Educators

Administrator   Helen Fraser; Gordon Lodge, Snitterton Rd,
Matlock, Derbyshire DE4 3LZ; URL www.name.org.uk;
e-mail musiceducation@name.org.uk; Tel 01629 760791;
Fax 01629 760791

National Drama

Co-Chair   Pam Bowell; 56 Empress Ave, Wanstead,
London E12 5EU
Co-Chair   Jan MacDonald; St Andrew's Campus,
University of Glasgow, Bearsden, Glasgow G61 4QA
Secretary   Marie Jeanne McNaughton; 21a Dundonald,
Glasgow G12 9LL
Treasurer   Stephanie Partridge; 124 Allestree Cl, Alvaston,
Derby DE24 8SX

Professional Council for Religious Education

1020 Bristol Rd, Selly Oak, Birmingham, West Midlands
B29 6LB; URL www.pcfre.org.uk; e-mail
rachel@retoday.org.uk; Tel 0121 472 4242;
Fax 0121 472 7575
PCfRE is the professional subject association for all who
teach Religious Education. It has members in around 2500
primary and secondary schools.

Schools Music Association of Great Britain

71 Margaret Rd, New Barnet, Hertfordshire EN4 9NT;
URL www.schoolsmusic.org; e-mail
maxwellpryce@educamus.free-online.co.uk;
Tel 020 8440 6919; Fax 020 8440 6919
Chief Executive; Honorary Secretary   Maxwell Pryce MBE
Supports music in schools

The Society for Italic Handwriting

Chair   G. Last; 23 Granby Rd, Old Town, Stevenage,
Hertfordshire SG1 1ER
Secretary; Editor of the quarterly magazine   N. Caulkin; 205
Dyas Ave, Great Barr, Birmingham, West Midlands
B42 1HN; Tel 0121 358 0032

17

Society for the Promotion of Hellenic Studies
Executive Secretary R.W. Shone; Senate Hse, Malet, London WC1E 7HU; e-mail hellenic@sas.ac.uk; Tel 020 7862 8730; Fax 020 7862 8731

Society of Teachers in Business Education
88 Springfield Rd, Millhouses, Sheffield, South Yorkshire S7 2GF; e-mail stbesec@aol.com; Tel 0114 236 3659; Fax 0114 235 2671
General Secretary; Membership Secretary Margaret Maxfield BA(Hons), FSBT

Society of Teachers of Speech and Drama
73 Berry Hill Rd, Mansfield, Nottinghamshire NG18 4RU; URL www.stsd.org.uk; e-mail ann.k.jones@btinternet.com; Tel 01623 627636
Hon General Secretary Ann Jones LRAM, LGSM
Publications:
Journal and newsletters; journal available to non-members; annual conferences in London and Liverpool

Swimming Teachers' Association
Anchor Hse, Birch St, Walsall, West Midlands WS2 8HZ; URL www.sta.co.uk; e-mail sta@sta.co.uk; Tel 01922 645097; Fax 01922 720628
Chief Executive Roger Millward
Encouragement of high professional swimming standards, provision of educational teaching syllabus and certification of teachers of swimming

Voice Care Network UK
Registered Charity Number 1087751
25 The Square, Kenilworth, Warwickshire CV8 1EF; URL www.voicecare.org.uk; e-mail info@voicecare.org.uk; Tel 01926 864000; Fax 01926 864000
Educational charity; disseminates information on vocal health – provides practical voice and speaking skills workshops in schools and ITT

Professional Educational Associations

Examination Officers

Examination Officers' Association (EOA)
Regus Hse (GIZ), 400 Thames Valley Park Dr, Reading RG6 1PT; URL www.examofficers.org; e-mail info@examofficers.org; Tel 0118 963 7904; Fax 0118 963 7600
Chief Executive Andrew Harland

Heads, Governing Bodies and Administrators (Schools)

ACRA
ACRA National Office, Kingston College, PO Box 1136, 55 Richmond Rd, Kingston upon Thames, Surrey KT2 5XD; Tel 020 8541 4940; Fax 020 8546 0718
National Officer Mrs J. Gould

AGBIS
Renshaw Barns, Upper Woodford, Salisbury, Wiltshire SP4 6FA; URL www.agbis.org.uk; e-mail gensec@agbis.org.uk; Tel 01722 782900; Fax 05601 264801
General Secretary Shane Rutter-Jerome
Secretary (Training and Membership) Nigel Noble
Personal Assistant; Office Manager Caroline Higton

Aspect
Woolley Hall, Woolley, Wakefield, West Yorkshire WF4 2JR; URL www.aspect.org.uk; e-mail info@aspect.org.uk; Tel 01226 383428; Fax 01226 383427
President Carolyn Poulter
General Secretary John Chowcat
Head (Professional Development) Judith Hibbert

Association of Headteachers and Deputes in Scotland
PO Box 18532, Inverurie AB51 0WS; URL www.ahds.org.uk; e-mail info@ahds.org.uk; Tel 0845 260 7560

Association of Heads of Outdoor Education Centres
The Priestly Centre, Hoathwaite Farm, Torver, Coniston, Cumbria LA21 8AX; URL www.ahoec.org; e-mail n.e.beech@tham.ac.uk; Tel 01539 441364; Fax 01539 488567
Secretary Norman Beech

Association of University Administrators (AUA)
Executive Director Alison Robinson; AUA National Office, University of Manchester, Oxford Rd, Manchester M13 9PL; URL www.aua.ac.uk; e-mail aua@manchester.ac.uk; Tel 0161 275 2063; Fax 0161 275 2036
The AUA is the professional body for all those with managerial and administrative responsibilities in higher education in the UK and the Republic of Ireland. It seeks to promote the highest standards of professionalism through training and development initiatives, publications and its national conference and implementation of a continuing professional development scheme. The AUA publishes a quarterly journal, Perspectives, focusing on policy and practice in higher education, a quarterly news magazine, Newslink, and a weekly electronic bulletin. AUA's Postgraduate Certificate in Professional Practice (higher education and management) is validated by the Open University. The AUA has established links with administrators and managers in higher education overseas and supports international study visits. Further details can be found on AUA's website. Travel awards are available for AUA members. Awards for excellence are announced annually.

Girls' Day School Trust
100 Rochester Row, London SW1P 1JP; URL www.gdst.net; e-mail reception@wes.gdst.net; Tel 020 7393 6666; Fax 020 7393 6789
Chief Executive Barbara Harrison

Girls' Schools Association
130 Regent Rd, Leicester LE1 7PG; URL www.gsa.uk.com; e-mail office@gsa.uk.com; Tel 0116 254 1619; Fax 0116 255 3792
Executive Director Sheila Cooper MA, MLS, MBA

The Headmasters' and Headmistresses' Conference (HMC)
12 The Point, Rockingham Rd, Market Harborough, Leicestershire LE16 7QU; URL www.hmc.org.uk; e-mail hmc@hmc.org.uk; Tel 01858 469059; Fax 01858 469532
Chair Dr B.St. J. Trafford; Wolverhampton Grammar School, Compton Rd, Wolverhampton WV3 9RB
Vice-Chair Dr N.P.V. Richardson; The Perse School, School Hills Rd, Cambridge CB2 8QF
Hon Treasurer Mr B.R. Martin; Hampton School, Hanworth Rd, Hampton, Greater London TW12 3HD
Secretary G.H. Lucas
Membership Secretary R.V. Peel

Headteachers' Association of Scotland
University of Strathclyde, Jordanhill Campus, Glasgow G13 1PP; e-mail head.teachers@strath.ac.uk; Tel 0141 950 3038; Tel 0141 950 3298; Fax 0141 950 3434
General Secretary Bill McGregor MA, MEd

Independent Schools Association
ISA Boys' British School, East St, Saffron Walden, Essex CB10 1LS; URL isaschools.org.uk; e-mail isa@isaschools.org.uk; Tel 01799 523619; Fax 01799 524892
General Secretary T.M. Ham MA, DipEd

Independent Schools' Bursars Association
General Secretary J.R.B. Cook; Unit 11–12 Manor Farm,
Cliddesden, Basingstoke, Hampshire RG25 2JB;
URL www.theisba.org.uk; e-mail office@theisba.org.uk;
Tel 01256 330369; Fax 01256 330376

Independent Schools Council (ISC)
St Vincent Hse, 30 Orange St, London WC2H 7HH;
URL www.isc.co.uk; e-mail office@isc.co.uk;
Tel 020 7766 7070; Fax 020 7766 7071
Chairman Dame Judith Mayhew Jonas
Director (Communications) Andy Cook
The Independent Schools Council (ISC) represents 1280
independent schools educating more than 500 000 children.
Its schools are accredited by the Independent Schools
Inspectorate (ISI) and the head of each ISC school is a
member of one of its five heads' associations. ISC staff
represent the independent schools sector to government and
to the media. It carries out authoritative research and
statistical analysis, much of which is published in the ISC
Bulletins. ISC also run conferences and events, including an
annual SEN conference in November.
The Independent Schools Council information and advice
service (ISCias) is the information and advice centre for all
enquiries relating to independent schools. ISCias utilises
local contacts, allowing schools access to information and
advice. It gives parents advice on choosing and applying to
ISC schools, and is a resource of printed and electronic
material covering related areas such as SEN provision and
assistance with fees. ISCias also provides information and
advice to parents living overseas who are interested in
finding suitable schools in the UK for their children.
Member Associations
Girls' Schools Association (GSA), Association of Governing
Bodies of Independent Schools (AGBIS), Headmasters' and
Headmistresses' Conference (HMC), Incorporated
Association of Preparatory Schools (IAPS), Independent
Schools Association (ISA), Independent Schools' Bursars
Association (ISBA) and Society of Headmasters and
Headmistresses of Independent Schools (SHMIS)

National Governors Association
2nd Fl, SBQI, 29 Smallbrook, Queensway, Birmingham,
West Midlands B5 4HG; URL www.nga.org.uk; e-mail
governorhq@nga.org.uk; Tel 0121 643 5787;
Fax 0121 633 7141
Chair Judith Bennett
Vice-Chair Stephen Adamson
Vice-Chair Clare Collins
Secretary Terry Douris
Treasurer Carol Woodhouse
Contact Colleen Arnold

Society of Headmasters and Headmistresses of Independent Schools
5 Tolethorpe Cl, Oakham, Rutland LE15 6GF; e-mail
gensec@shmis.org.uk; Tel 01572 755726

Standing Conference of Tertiary and Sixth Form College Principals
Victoria Rd, Fenton, Stoke-on-Trent ST4 2RR;
Tel 01782 848736; Fax 01782 747456

Universities UK
Woburn Hse, 20 Tavistock Sq, London WCH 9HQ;
URL www.universitiesuk.ac.uk; e-mail
info@universitiesuk.ac.uk; Tel 020 7419 4111;
Fax 020 7388 8649

Universities Scotland
53 Hanover St, Edinburgh EH2 2PJ;
URL www.universities-scotland.ac.uk; e-mail
jill@universities-scotland.ac.uk; Tel 0131 226 1111;
Fax 0131 226 1100
Director David Caldwell

Welsh Secondary Schools Association
17 Page St, Swansea SA1 4EZ; URL www.wssa.org.uk;
e-mail wssa@supanet.co.uk; Tel 01792 455933;
Fax 01792 455944
General Secretary R.J. Ashley

Higher and Further Education – Staff and Administration

Association of Colleges (AoC)
2–5 Stedham Pl, London WC1A 1HU; e-mail
communications@aoc.co.uk; Tel 020 7034 9900;
Fax 020 7034 9950
AoC is the national representative body for colleges of
further education, including sixth form colleges, in England,
Wales and Northern Ireland. AoC provides a national
framework for the pay and conditions of all staff, excluding
senior postholders, and provides a wide range of advisory
services to its members. AoC maintains a programme of
lobbying relevant agencies and providing information on all
relevant post-16 and lifelong learning policies and practice.

Association of Principals of Colleges (Northern Ireland Branch)
Deputy Director S. Murphy BA(Hons), DipEd, DASE,
MEd; Belfast Institute of Further and Higher Education,
Park Hse, 87–91 Gt Victoria St, Belfast BT2 7AG;
Tel 028 9026 5457; Fax 028 9026 5451

In-Service and Professional Development Association
University of Worcester, Henwick Gr, Worcester,
Worcestershire WR2 6AJ; URL www.ipda.org.uk; e-mail
t.batesworc@btinternet.com; Tel 01905 855055;
Fax 01905 855132
Individual membership; HE, FE, LEAs, Schools

National Association for Staff Development in the Post-16 Sector (NASD)
Chair Wynne Handley; Basingstoke College
Hon Association Co-ordinator J. Faccenda; 36 Kimbolton
Ave, Bedford, Bedfordshire MK40 3AA; Tel 01234 309678

Librarians

Librarians of Institutes and Schools of Education
Secretary Sue Chubb; Education Library, University of
Bristol, 35 Berkeley Sq, Bristol BS8 1JA; Tel 0117 928 7062

Society of County Children's and Education Librarians
Hon Secretary; Assistant Head (Library Service)
Catherine Blanshard ALA; Hertfordshire Libraries Arts
and Information, New Barnfield, Hatfield, Hertfordshire
AL10 8XG

Management

Cambridge Education Associates (CEA) Ltd
Demeter Hse, Station Rd, Cambridge, Cambridgeshire
CB1 2RS; URL www.cea.co.uk; e-mail cea@cea.co.uk;
Tel 01223 578500; Fax 01223 578501
Consultancy and advice to LEAs, schools, and inspection
contracts for Ofsted. Located in Cambridge, Manchester,
Birmingham, Bristol, North East and London, CEA is
committed to the creation of a lasting improvement in the
quality of leadership and the management of learning.

Chelstoke Educational Consultants Ltd
2 Heathcoat Bldg, Nottingham Science and Technology Pk,
University Bvd, Nottingham, Nottinghamshire NG7 2QS;
URL www.chelstoke.com; e-mail info@chelstoke.co.uk;
Tel 0115 922 9214; Fax 0115 922 9330
Managing Director Neill Ransom
Chelstoke offers support through six divisions: Educational
Management Consultants – management support and
training, curriculum and timetabling, review and
development of schools and departments using
Achievementbuilder and Changebuilder process
consultancy; Educational Building Consultants –
specialising in accommodation needs analysis and
masterplans with advice on refurbishments, extensions and
new building; Educational Financial Consultants – financial
and strategic planning support to headteachers, bursars and
governors; Educational Courses – management and
curriculum courses particularly school-based INSET for
teachers and administrators; Educational Computing
Consultants – advice and training on administrative and
curriculum ICT with School ICT Development Plans;

17

Educational Recruitment – appointment of headteachers and deputies. Chelstoke is the only educational consultancy accredited by the Achievement Network Worldwide.

Department of Management Learning Management School

University of Lancaster, Lancaster, Lancashire LA1 4YX; e-mail m.easterley-smith@lancaster.ac.uk; Tel 01524 65201 ext 4019
Contact   Prof J.G. Burgoyne

Education Management – North West

Padgate Campus, Fearnhead, Warrington, Cheshire WA2 0DB; Tel 01925 816882; Fax 01925 838675
Director   David Ward
Directorate   R. Heron
Directorate   S. Rogers
Educational management consultancy service and INSET training for staff and governors in Primary and Secondary Schools

Educational Courses

Waterside Centre, Abbey Meadows, Abbey Park Rd, Leicester LE4 5AE; Tel 0116 251 6953; Fax 0116 251 0624
Specialists in management courses for teachers and administrators

Regional Training Unit

Blacks Rd, Belfast BT10 0NB; URL www.rtuni.org; e-mail admin@rtuni.org; Tel 028 9061 8121; Fax 028 9061 8123

Scottish Centre for Studies in School Administration

Moray House School of Education, The University of Edinburgh, Holyrood Rd, Edinburgh EH8 8AQ; URL www.scssa.ed.ac.uk; e-mail graham.thomson@ed.ac.uk; Tel 0131 651 6114; Fax 0131 651 6264
Director   Graham Thomson
Administrator   Pam Flockhart

Teachers

Association of Christian Teachers

94a London Rd, St Albans, Hertfordshire AL1 1NX; URL www.christians-in-education.org.uk; e-mail act@christians-in-education.org.uk; Tel 01727 840298; Fax 01727 848966

CfBT Education Trust

60 Queens Rd, Reading RG1 4BS; URL www.cfbt.com; e-mail enquiries@cfbt.com; Tel 0118 902 1000; Fax 0118 902 1434
Chief Executive   Neil McIntosh
Chair   John Harwood
CfBT Education Trust is a charity providing education services for people worldwide. It provides support for school improvement, it teaches in schools and special projects and it provides advice and trains education professionals. Every year CfBT finances a programme of public benefit research and development.

Education International (EI)

5 Bvd du Ro: Albert II (8), 1210 Brussels, Belgium; URL www.ei-ie.org; e-mail educint@ei-ie.org; Tel +33 2 224 0611; Fax +32 2 224 0606
President   M. Hatwood Futrell
General Secretary   F. Van Leeuwen
Founded from the merger of the World Confederation of Organisation of the Teaching Profession (WCOPT/CMOPE) and the International Federation of Free Teachers' Unions (IFFTU/SPIE). Aims to further the cause of organisations of teachers and education employees, promote status, interests and welfare of members and defend their trade union and professional rights; to promote peace, democracy, social justice, equality and application of the Universal Declaration on Human Rights through development of education and collective strength of teachers and education employees; to seek and maintain recognition of the trade union rights of workers in general and of teachers and education employees in particular.

General Teaching Council for England

344–354 Gray's Inn Rd, London WC1X 8BP; URL www.gtce.org.uk; e-mail info@gtce.org.uk; Tel 0870 001 0308; Fax 020 7841 2909
Chief Executive   Carol Adams
Director (Communications)   Fiona Simpson
Director (Policy)   Sarah Stephens
Head (Finance and Administration)   Dennis Jones
Registrar   Alan Meyrick
Elected Members (Teachers)
Andy Barker, David Belfield, Sarah Bowie, Peter Britcliffe, Rosemary Clarke, Andrew Connell, Anthony Cuthbert, David Dewhirst, Mary Gibbon, Jo Gough, Anthony Handley, Marilyn Harrop, Derek Johns, Ralph Manning, Helen Meaney, Gail Mortimer, Sheila Mountain, Tony Neal, Vicki Paterson, Norma Redfearn, Carole Regan, Alice Robinson, Margaret Rudland, Martin Scotchmer, Anthea Tulloch Bisgrove
Nominated Members
Eileen Baker, Andrew Baxter, John Beattie, Peter Bishop, Michael Carney, Chris Cook, Valerie Cox, Mabel Davis, Christine Gale, Sonja Hall, John Hall, Conchita Henry, Anne Madden, Judy Moorhouse, Margaret Morgan, Ann Mullins, Ronnie Norman, Elizabeth Paver, Roy Pinney, Gillian Stainthorpe, Oona Stannard, Philippa Stobbs, Dame Janet Trotter, Ralph Ullmann, Philip Whithers
Secretary of State Appointees
Karen Brown, Ian Chambers, Valerie Dennis, Elizabeth Diggory, Clare Easterbrook, Alison Fisher, Lynn Lee, Bushra Nasir, Shashikala Sivaloganathan, Eugene Sullivan, Naila Zaffar
The GTC serves as the regulatory body for teachers in England and has a statutory duty to provide advice on key educational issues.

Teacher Support Network

Hamilton Hse, Mabledon Pl, London WC1H 9BE; URL www.teachersupport.info; e-mail enquiries@teachersupport.info; Tel (teacher support) 0800 0562 561; Tel 020 7554 5200; Fax 020 7554 5239

Ulster Teachers' Union

94 Malone Rd, Belfast BT9 5HP; URL www.utu.edu/home.html; e-mail office@utu.edu; Tel 028 9066 2216; Fax 028 9068 3296
General Secretary   Avril Hall-Callaghan
Senior Field Officer   Mike Graves

University and College Union (UCU)

27 Britannia St, London WC1X 9JP; URL www.ucu.org.uk; e-mail hq@ucu.org.uk; Tel (NATFHE) 020 7837 3636
25–31 Tavistock Pl, London WC1H 9UT; Tel (AUT) 020 7670 9700
General Secretary   Sally Hunt
General Secretary   Paul Mackney

World Confederation of Teachers

33 Rue de Trèves, 1040 Brussels, Belgium; URL www.wctcsme.org; e-mail wct@cmt_wcl.org.; Tel +32 2 285 4729; Fax +32 2 230 8722
Secretary General   Gaston De la Haye

Tutors

Association of Tutors

Hon Secretary   Dr D.J. Cornelius; Sunnycroft, 63 King Edward Rd, Northampton, Northamptonshire NN1 5LY; Tel 01604 624171; Fax 01604 624718

Parent–Teacher Associations

Campaign for State Education (CASE)

98 Erlanger Rd, London SE14 5TH; URL www.campaignforstateeducation.org.uk; e-mail contact@campaignforstateeducation.org.uk
Contact   Judy Harrington

A pressure group, campaigning for the right of all to experience the highest quality state education regardless of race, gender, home circumstances, ability or disability. It supports a fully comprehensive and locally accountable education system and campaigns for the development of partnership between home, school and the community and a recognition of the achievements of state education. CASE is politically non-aligned.

Membership £15 a year, £5 unwaged.

National Confederation of Parent Teacher Associations (NCPTA)

39 Shipbourne Rd, Tonbridge, Kent TN10 3DS; URL www.ncpta.org.uk; e-mail info@ncpta.org.uk; Tel 01732 375460; Fax 01732 375461

National Education Association

Secretary M. Smith; 1 Hinchley Way, Hinchley Wood, Esher, Surrey KT10 0BD; Tel 020 8398 1253

Voluntary non-political body representing parents throughout the country. It has more than 20 branches and is financed entirely by members' subscriptions and donations.

Social Work, Disability and Counselling

Association for Education Welfare Management

Hon General Secretary Jennifer A. Price; 'The Whiskers', 1 The Boundary, Bradford, West Yorkshire BD8 0BQ; Tel 01274 542295; Fax 01274 505646

Association of Educational Psychologists

26 The Avenue, Durham, County Durham DH1 4ED; Tel 0191 384 9512; Fax 0191 386 5287

Association for University and College Counselling

Division of BAC, BACP Hse, 35–37 Albert St, Rugby, Warwickshire CV21 2SG; URL www.aucc.uk.com; e-mail bacp@bacp.co.uk; Tel 0870 443 5252; Fax 0870 443 5160

British Association of Art Therapists

24–27 White Lion St, London N1 9PD; URL www.baat.org; e-mail info@baat.org; Tel 020 7686 4216

Chair Neil Springham

Office Manager Charles Williams

British Association for Counselling and Psychotherapy

15 St John's Business Pk, Lutterworth, Leicestershire LE17 4HB; URL www.bacp.co.uk; e-mail bacp@bacp.co.uk; Tel 01455 883300; Fax 01455 550243

British Association of Teachers of the Deaf

Secretary Paul Simpson; 21 The Haystacks, High Wycombe, Buckinghamshire HP13 6PY; URL www.batod.org.uk; Tel 01494 464190; Fax 01494 464190

The British Association of Teachers of the Deaf represents the interests of teachers of the deaf in this country. Regional and national meetings are organised to promote issues connected with the education of hearing impaired children. BATOD publishes a refereed journal in February, June and October and an association magazine in February, April, June, October and December. Articles may be submitted to the association secretary or directly to the editor.

British Hypnotherapy Association (BHA)

67 Upper Berkeley St, London W1H 7QX; URL www.hypnotherapy-association.org; e-mail hypnotherapy@the-wordsmith.co.uk; Tel 020 7723 4443

Chair R.K. Brian

Secretary E. Wookey

Maintains a register of qualified, trained practitioners who comply with high standards of competence and ethics. Supplies training, publications, talks and reports. Aims to care for the interests of patients and members, to collate and disseminate information on hypnotherapy and to raise standards in therapy. A voluntary organisation, funded by donations, legacies and subscriptions.

Centre for Educational Sociology (CES)

University of Edinburgh, St John's Land, Holyrood Rd, Edinburgh EH8 8AQ; URL www.ces.ed.ac.uk; e-mail ces@ed.ac.uk; Tel 0131 651 6238; Fax 0131 651 6239

Administrator Marcia Wright

Community and Youth Workers' Union

Unit 302, The Argent Centre, 60 Frederick St, Hockley, Birmingham, West Midlands B1 3HS; URL www.cywu.org.uk; e-mail kerry@cywu.org.uk; Tel 0121 244 3344; Fax 0121 244 3345

Dyslexia Action

Park Hse, Wick Rd, Egham, Surrey TW20 0HH; URL www.dyslexiaaction.org.uk; e-mail info@dyslexiaaction.org.uk; Tel 01784 222300; Fax 01784 222333

Chief Executive Shirley Cramer

Dyslexia Scotland

Stirling Business Centre, Stirling FK8 2DZ; URL www.dyslexiascotland.org.uk; e-mail info@dyslexiascotland.org.uk; Tel 01786 446650; Fax 01786 471235

nasen (The National Association for Special Educational Needs)

nasen Hse, 4–5 Amber Business Village, Amber Cl, Amington, Tamworth, Staffordshire B77 4RP; URL www.nasen.org.uk; e-mail welcome@nasen.org.uk; Tel 01827 311500; Fax 01827 313005

National Association of Advisory Officers for Special Educational Needs

Hon Secretary L. Samson; 22 St Peter St, Sandwich, Kent CT13 9BW; Tel 01304 620179

National Association for Pastoral Care in Education

c/o Institute of Education, The University of Warwick, Coventry, Warwickshire CV4 7AL; URL www.napce.org.uk; e-mail base@napce.org.uk; Tel 024 7652 3810; Fax 024 7657 4110

Chair Ms Jae Bray

President Prof R. Best

Secretary Jill Robson

Treasurer Ethel Southern

Journal Editor Colleen McLaughlin

National Association of Professionals Concerned with Language Impairment in Children (NAPLIC)

Churchill Gardens School, Ranelagh Rd, London SW1 3EU

Chair C. Withey

President David Crystal

Membership Secretary A. Phillips

Treasurer D. Goodger

NAPLIC aims to promote professional awareness of the needs of the language-impaired child and encourage teaching skills

National Association of Social Workers in Education (NASWE)

Hon General Secretary Sue Howe; Rosebank, Beech Hill Rd, Headley, Hampshire GU35 8DB; Tel 020 8541 9559

Social, Emotional and Behavioural Difficulties Association

Rm 211, The Triangle, Exchange Sq, Manchester M4 3TR; URL www.sebda.org; e-mail admin@sebda.org; Tel 0161 240 2418

Director Dr Ted Cole

17

Educational Publishing

18

Educational Publishing

Education Correspondents

National Daily and Sunday Newspapers

Daily Express and Sunday Express
10 Lower Thames St, London EC3R 6EN; Tel 0871 520 7985
Education Correspondent   Tom Wainwright

Daily Mail and Mail on Sunday
Northcliffe Hse, 2 Derry St, London W8 5TT;
Tel 020 7938 6000; Fax 020 7937 5287
Education Correspondent   Tony Halpin
Contact (Mail on Sunday)   Alison Brace

Daily Mirror
1 Canada Sq, Canary Wharf, London E14 5AP;
Tel 020 7293 3000
Education Correspondent   Richard Garner

Daily Star
Ludgate Hse, 245 Blackfriars Rd, London SE1 9UX;
Tel 020 7928 8000
Education Correspondent   David Mertens

The Evening Standard
Northcliffe Hse, 2 Derry St, London W8 5EE;
Tel 020 7938 6000

Financial Times (UK) Ltd
Number One, Southwark Bridge, London SE1 9HL;
URL www.ft.com; e-mail news.desk@ft.com;
Tel 020 7873 3000
Education Correspondent   Jon Boone

The Guardian and Observer
119 Farringdon Rd, London EC1R 3ER;
URL education.guardian.co.uk; e-mail
education@guardian.co.uk
Editor (Education Guardian)   Will Woodward
Deputy Editor (Education Guardian)   Alice Woolley
Education Editor   Rebecca Smithers

The Independent and Independent on Sunday
1 Canada Sq, Canary Wharf, London E14 5DL;
Tel 020 7293 2000
Education Editor   Richard Garner

News of the World
1 Virginia St, London E1; Tel 020 7481 4100

The People
1 Canada Sq, Canary Wharf, London E14 5AP; e-mail
peoplenews@mgn.co.uk; Tel 020 7293 3201

The Scotsman
108 Holyrood Rd, Edinburgh EH8 8AS;
URL www.scotsman.com; Tel 0131 620 8579

The Sun
c/o Press Gallery, House of Commons, London SW1A 0AA;
URL www.thesun.co.uk; e-mail
david.wooding@the-sun.co.uk; Tel 020 7219 0140;
Fax 020 7222 2355
Education Editor   David Wooding

The Times and Sunday Times
1 Pennington St, London E1 9XN; Tel 020 7782 5673
Education Correspondent (Sunday Times)   Geraldine Hackett

Provincial Daily Newspapers

Birmingham Evening Mail
PO Box 78, Weaman St, Birmingham, West Midlands
B4 6AY; URL www.icbirmingham.co.uk; e-mail
eveningmail@mrn.co.uk; Tel 0121 236 3366
Contact   Tony Collins

Birmingham Post
PO Box 78, 78 Weaman St, Birmingham, West Midlands
B4 6AY; Tel 0121 236 3366
Contact   Shahid Naqui

Cambridge Evening News
Winship Rd, Milton, Cambridge, Cambridgeshire CB4 6PP;
URL www.cambridge-news.co.uk; e-mail
catherinebruce@cambridge-news.co.uk;
Tel 01223 434434; Fax 01223 434415
Education Reporter   Stephen Exley

Coventry Evening Telegraph
Corporation St, Coventry, Warwickshire CV1 1FP;
URL www.go2coventry.co.uk; e-mail
news@coventry-telegraph.co.uk; Tel 024 7663 3633
Contact   Julie Chamberlain

Dorset Evening Echo
Fleet Hse, Hampshire Rd, Weymouth, Dorset DT4 9X;
URL www.thisisdorset.net; e-mail echo@wdi.co.uk;
Tel 01305 830930; Fax 01305 830856
Editor   David Murdock

Evening Post
8 Tessa Rd, Reading; e-mail editorial@reading-epost.co.uk;
Tel 0118 918 3000; Fax 0118 959 9363
Editor's Secretary   Sue Norman

Express and Star (Evening)
Queen St, Wolverhampton, West Midlands WV1 3BU;
Tel 01902 313131; Fax 01902 319721
News Editor   Steve Cornell

Herald
200 Renfield St, Glasgow G2 3QB;
URL www.theherald.co.uk; e-mail
rights@glasgow.newsquest.co.uk; Tel 0141 302 7000;
Fax 0141 302 7383
Contact   Elizabeth Buie

Huddersfield Daily Examiner

Queen St South, Huddersfield, West Yorkshire HD1 2TD;
URL www.ichuddersfield.co.uk; e-mail
editorial@examiner.co.uk; Tel 01484 430000;
Fax 01484 437789
Contact   Neil Atkinson

Irish Independent

90 Middle Abbey St, Dublin 1, Republic of Ireland;
Tel +353 1 705 5333; Fax +353 1 872 7997;
Fax +353 1 873 1787
Contact   Fergus Black

Irish News

113–117 Donegall St, Belfast BT1 2GE;
URL www.irishnews.com; e-mail
a.bonner@irishnews.com; Tel 028 9032 2226;
Fax 028 9033 7505
Education Correspondent   Aeneas Bonner

Irish Press, Evening Press and Sunday Press

Irish Press Newspapers Ltd, Burgh Quay, Dublin 2,
Republic of Ireland; Tel +353 1 671 3333
Contact   Patrick Holmes

Irish Times

10–16 D'Olier St, Dublin 2, Republic of Ireland;
Tel +353 1 675 8484; Tel (London) 020 7353 8970;
Fax +353 1 679 2789
Contact   Sean Flynn

Jersey Evening Post

PO Box 582, St Saviour, Jersey JE4 8XQ, Channel Islands;
URL www.thisisjersey.com; e-mail
editorial@jerseyeveningpost.com; Tel 01534 611611;
Fax 01534 611622
Editor   C. Bright

The Journal

Groat Market, Newcastle upon Tyne, Tyne and Wear
NE1 1ED; URL www.thejournal.co.uk; e-mail
jnl.newsdesk@ncjmedia.co.uk; Tel 0191 232 7500;
Fax 0191 221 0172
Editor   Brian Aitken

Lancashire Evening Post

Olivers Pl, Eastway, Preston, Lancashire PR2 9ZA;
Tel 01772 254841; Fax 01772 880173
Editor   Gerrie Burns

Lancashire Evening Telegraph

Newspaper Hse, High St, Blackburn BB1 1HT;
Tel 01254 678678; Fax 01254 680429
Editor   Peter Butterfield

Leicester Mercury

Leicester Mercury Group Ltd, St George St, Leicester
LE1 9FQ; URL www.leicestermercury.co.uk;
www.thisisleicestershire.co.uk; Tel 0116 251 2512;
Fax 0116 253 0645

Northern Echo

Priestgate, Darlington DL1 1NF;
URL www.thisisthenortheast.co.uk; e-mail
echo@nne.co.uk; Tel 01325 381313; Fax 01325 380539
Televisual Data Ltd, Sanbank Business Pk, Dunoon, Argyll
and Bute PA23 8PB; Tel 01369 703448; Fax 01369 703159
Information Officer   Peter Chapman
CD-ROM available from Televisual Data Ltd

North West Evening Mail

Furness Newspapers Ltd, Abbey Rd, Barrow-in-Furness,
Cumbria LA14 5QS; URL www.nwemail.co.uk; e-mail
reporters@nwemail.co.uk; Tel 01229 821835

Oxford Mail (Evening)

Osney Mead, Oxford, Oxfordshire OX2 0EJ; e-mail
news@nqo.com; Tel 01865 425262; Fax 01865 425554
Education Correspondent   Monica Sloan

Paisley Daily Express

14 New St, Paisley, Renfrewshire PA1 1YA;
Tel 0141 887 7911; Fax 0141 887 6254

Press and Journal Aberdeen

Aberdeen Journals, PO Box 43, Lang Stracht, Mastrick,
Aberdeen AB15 6DF;
URL www.thisisnorthscotland.co.uk; e-mail
pj.newskesk@ajl.co.uk; Tel 01224 690222;
Fax 01224 663575
News Editor   Fiona McWhirr

The Press, York

PO Box 29, 76–86 Walmgate, York YO1 9YN;
URL www.yorkpress.co.uk; e-mail newsdesk@ycp.co.uk;
Tel 01904 653051; Fax 01904 612853
Education Reporter   Haydn Lewis

Scottish Daily Express

Also Scottish Sunday Express, Scottish and Universal
Newspapers (Lanarkshire, Ayrshire and West Lothian titles)
24 Borden Rd, Glasgow G13 1QX; Tel 0141 959 1454;
Fax 0141 954 1880

Shields Gazette (Evening)

Chapter Row, South Shields, Tyne and Wear NE33 1BL;
URL www.southtynesidetoday.co.uk; e-mail
gazette.news@northeast-press.co.uk; Tel 0191 427 4800;
Fax 0191 456 8270

Shropshire Star (Evening)

Ketley, Telford TF1 5HU; URL www.shropshirestar.com;
e-mail ypritchard@shropshirestar.co.uk;
Tel 01952 242424; Fax 01952 254605

The Star – Sheffield (Evening)

York St, Sheffield, South Yorkshire S1 1PU;
Tel 0114 276 7676; Fax 0114 272 5978
Education Reporter   Michael Russell

Telegraph and Argus (Evening)

Hall Ings, Bradford, West Yorkshire BD1 1JR;
Tel 01274 729511; Fax 01274 723634
Editor   Kathie Griffiths

Western Daily Press

Temple Way, Bristol BS99 7HD;
URL www.westerndailypress.co.uk; e-mail
wdnews@bepp.co.uk; Tel 0117 934 3000;
Fax 0117 934 3574
Education Correspondent   Ruth Wood

The Western Mail

Thomson Hse, Cardiff CF1 1WR; Tel 02920 583583;
Fax 02920 583652
Contact   Ruth Davies

Wigan Observer

Lancashire Publications Ltd, Martland Mill, Wigan, Greater
Manchester WN5 0LX; Tel 01942 228000
Contact   Allan Rimmer

Yorkshire Evening Post

Wellington St, Leeds, West Yorkshire LS1 1RF;
URL www.thisisleeds.co.uk; e-mail
ian.rosser@ypn.co.uk; Tel 0113 238 8917;
Fax 0113 238 8536
News Editor   Gillian Haworth

Weekly Journals

Nature

4 Crinan St, London N1 9XW; URL www.nature.com;
Tel 020 7833 4000
Manager (Nature Marketing)   Katy Dunningham

New Scientist

Lacon Hse, 84 Theobald's Rd, London WC1X 8NS;
URL www.newscientist.com; e-mail
maggie.mcdonald@rbi.co.uk; Tel 020 8652 3500

New Statesman
3rd Fl, 52 Grosvenor Gardens, London SW1W 0AU; e-mail
info@newstatesman.co.uk; Tel 020 7730 3444;
Fax 020 7828 1881
Editor   John Kampfner
Editor (Books)   Rachel Aspden

Education Journals

ACE Bulletin
Advisory Centre for Education, 1c Aberdeen Studios, 22
Highbury Gr, London N5 2DQ;
URL www.ace-ed.org.uk; e-mail
enquiries@ace-ed.org.uk; Tel 020 7704 3370;
Fax 020 7354 9069

Adults Learning
The National Institute of Adult Continuing Education, 21
Montfort St, Leicester LE1 7GE; URL www.niace.org.uk;
e-mail adultslearning@niace.org.uk; Tel 0116 204 4200;
Fax 0116 204 4262
Editor   Paul Stanistreet
Frequency: Monthly (10 issues)
Annual subscription: £37, £61 (institutions), £20 (adult
learners and part-time tutors)

Amateur Stage
Platform Publications Ltd, Hampden Hse, 2 Weymouth St,
London W1W 5BT; URL amstage.cvtheatre.co.uk; e-mail
magazine@charlesvance.co.uk; Tel 020 7636 4343;
Fax 020 7636 2323
Publisher   Charles Vance
Editor   Mark Thorburn
All aspects of stagecraft, new book and play reviews,
amateur stage diary, news and opinion covering the whole
spectrum of amateur and community theatre and training
Frequency: Monthly
Annual subscription: £24

Antiquaries Journal
Society of Antiquaries of London, Burlington Hse, London
W1J 0BE; URL www.sal.org.uk; e-mail
kowen@sal.org.uk; Tel 020 7479 7089; Fax 020 7287 6967
Manager (Publications)   Kate Owen
Reports of excavations in Britain and abroad; descriptions of
finds, the history of antiquarian studies and studies in
ancient and medieval art crafts, heraldry, and social and
economic life
Frequency: Annual
Annual subscription: £85

Antiquity
King's Manor, York YO1 7EP; URL www.antiquity.ac.uk;
e-mail editor@antiquity.ac.uk; Tel 01904 433994;
Fax 01904 433994
Editor   Martin Carver
Managing Editor   Jo Tozer
Reviews Editor   Madeleine Hummler
Journal of world archaeology, aimed at scholars, students
and interested amateurs. The journal and its back archive of
more than 80 years of archaeological research are available
online.
Formats: Online
Frequency: Quarterly
Annual subscription: Premium subscription (including
access to the back archive) £75 for individuals and £256
for institutions. Online only version £37.

Applied Linguistics
Oxford Journals, Oxford University Press, Great Clarendon
Street, Oxford, Oxfordshire OX2 6DP;
URL www.oxfordjournals.org; Tel 01865 556767;
Fax 01865 267485
Published by: Oxford Journals
Frequency: Four a year
Price of single issue: £51 (institutions), £19 (individuals)

Annual subscription: £173 (institutions), £61 (individuals),
£48.80 (members), £34 (students)

AV Magazine
Haymarket Business Subscriptions, 12–13 Cranleigh
Gardens Industrial Est, Southall, Surrey UB1 2DB;
URL www.avinteractive.co.uk; e-mail
subscriptions@haynet.com; Tel 020 8606 7500;
Fax 020 8606 7301
Editor-in-Chief   Peter Lloyd
Frequency: Monthly
Annual subscription: £72

Books for Keeps
1 Effingham Rd, Lee, London SE12 8NZ;
URL www.booksforkeeps.co.uk; e-mail
enquiries@booksforkeeps.co.uk; Tel 020 8852 4953;
Fax 020 8318 7580
Editor   Rosemary Stones
Reviews of children's books, articles, author profiles,
features and news
Published by: Books for Keeps
Frequency: Bi-monthly
Price of single issue: £4.25
Annual subscription: £25.50
Circulation: 8500

La Brita Esperantisto (The British Esperantist)
Esperanto Hse, Station Rd, Barlaston, Stoke-on-Trent
ST12 9DE; URL www.esperanto-gb.org; e-mail
eab@esperanto-gb.org; Tel 0845 230 1887;
Tel 01782 372141
Editor   P. Gubbins
News and articles on Esperanto in Esperanto
Frequency: Bi-annually
Price of single issue: £1.80
Annual subscription: £3.60 including postage

British Education Index
The Brotherton Library, The University of Leeds, Leeds,
West Yorkshire LS2 9JT; URL www.bei.ac.uk; e-mail
bei@leeds.ac.uk; Tel 0113 343 5525; Fax 0113 343 5525
Editor   Philip W. Sheffield
Subject and author index to more than 300 journals
published in the UK and Europe (more than 5000 article
references a year). Coverage of report and conference
literature.

British Journal of Aesthetics
Oxford Journals, Oxford University Press, Oxford,
Oxfordshire OX2 6DP; Tel 01865 556767;
Fax 01865 267485
Editor   Prof Peter Lamarque
Discussions of general and philosophical aesthetics and
articles on the principles of appraisal which apply in the
various arts, working towards a better understanding of
them all and the analogies and differences between them
Published by: Oxford Journals
Price of single issue: £37
Annual subscription: £132 (institutions), £29 (members)

British Journal of Criminology
Oxford Journals, Oxford University Press, Clarendon St,
Oxford, Oxfordshire OX2 6DP; Tel 01865 556767;
Fax 01865 267485
Editor   Geoff Pearson
Criminology, including social deviance. Has a British and an
international focus.
Published by: Oxford Journals
Frequency: Quarterly
Price of single issue: £58 (institutions), £13 (individuals)
Annual subscription: £292 (institutions), £62 (individuals),
£25 (members)

British Journal of Educational Psychology
The British Psychological Society, St Andrews Hse, 48
Princess Road East, Leicester LE1 7DR; e-mail
enquiry@bps.org.uk; Tel 0116 254 9568;
Fax 0116 227 1314

18

Organisation: British Psychological Society
Annual subscription: £130 (institutions), £42 (individuals),
£20 (members)

British Journal of Educational Studies
Wiley Blackwell, 9600 Garsington Rd, Oxford, Oxfordshire
OX4 2DQ; URL www.blackwellpublishing.com/bjes;
Tel 01865 776868
Editor   James Arthur
Editor   Paul Croll
Published by: Wiley-Blackwell on behalf of the Society for
Educational Studies (SES)
Frequency: Quarterly

British Journal of Educational Technology
Wiley-Blackwell, 9600 Garsington Rd, Oxford, Oxfordshire
OX4 2DQ; URL www.thebjet.com; Tel 01865 776868
Editor   Nick Rushby
Organisation: Published on behalf of the British Educational
Communications and Technology Agency (Becta)
Frequency: Bimonthly

British Journal of Guidance and Counselling
Taylor and Francis Journals, 4 Park Sq, Milton Pk,
Abingdon, Oxfordshire OX14 4RN;
URL www.informaworld.com/bjgc; e-mail
info.education@tandf.co.uk; Tel 020 7017 6000;
Fax 020 7017 6336
Editor   Jennifer M. Kidd
Editor   Paul Wilkins
The major British academic and professional journal in the
guidance and counselling field. It explores the interface
between the various areas of guidance and counselling and
their relationship to such cognate fields as education,
psychotherapy and social work.
Published by: Routledge
Frequency: Quarterly
Annual subscription: £338 (institutions – print and online),
£321 (institutions – online only), £140 (individuals)

British Journal of Music Education
Cambridge University Press, The Edinburgh Bldg,
Shaftesbury Rd, Cambridge, Cambridgeshire CB2 2RU;
URL www.journals.cambridge.org/jid-bme; e-mail
bme@cambridge.org; Tel 01223 312393; Fax 01223 315052
Editor   Gordon Cox;   University of Reading
Editor   Stephen Pitts;   University of Sheffield
BJME provides accounts of current issues in music
education worldwide, together with a section containing
extended book reviews. It strives to strengthen professional
development and improve practice within the field of music
education. Articles cover classroom music teaching,
individual instrumental teaching and vocal teaching, music
in higher education and international comparative music
education.
Published by: Cambridge Journals
Annual subscription: £102 (institutions – online and print),
£92 (institutions – online only), £37 (individuals – print
only)

British Journal for the Philosophy of Science
Oxford Journals, Oxford University Press, Gt Clarendon St,
Oxford, Oxfordshire OX2 6DP; Tel 01865 556767;
Fax 01865 267485
Addresses the study of the logic, method, and philosophy of
science, including the social sciences
Published by: Oxford Journals
Frequency: Quarterly
Annual subscription: £100 (institutions), £88 (individuals),
£30 (members)

British Journal of Special Education
Registered Office: Nasen Hse, 4–5 Amber Business Village,
Amber Cl, Amington, Tamworth, Staffordshire B77 4RP
Editorial Office: The University of Cambridge, School of
Education, Shaftesbury Rd, Cambridge, Cambridgeshire
CB2 2BX; URL rb218@cam.ac.uk
Editor   Richard Byers

Organisation: Journal of The National Association for
Special Educational Needs
Frequency: March, June, September and December
Annual subscription: Individuals £66, institutions £85–125

Bulletin of Hispanic Studies
18 Oxford St, Liverpool, Merseyside L69 7ZN; e-mail
d.s.severin@liv.ac.uk; Tel 0151 794 2773;
Tel 0151 794 2774
General Editor   Dorothy Sherman Severin
Frequency: Six issues a year
Annual subscription: £220, individuals £60

Cambridge Journal of Education
Carfax Publishing Company, 4 Park Sq, Milton Pk,
Abingdon, Oxfordshire OX14 4RN
Managing Editor   Anne Chippindale; University of
Cambridge Faculty of Education, 184 Hills Rd,
Cambridge, Cambridgeshire CB2 8PQ; Tel 01223 767600
Published by: Carfax Publishing, Taylor and Francis Ltd
Organisation: Journal of the University of Cambridge School
of Education
Frequency: Four times a year
Annual subscription: Institutional (print and online) £495

The Cambridge Quarterly
Administration: 73 Selwyn Rd, Cambridge, Cambridgeshire
CB39 9EA; Tel 01223 461009
Editorial: Clare College, Cambridge, Cambridgeshire
CB2 1TL; Tel 01223 461009
Subscriptions: Oxford University Press, Oxford Journals, Gt
Clarendon St, Oxford, Oxfordshire OX2 6DP;
Tel 01865 556767; Fax 01865 267485
Editor   D.C. Gervais
Principally literary criticism, but also articles on painting,
sculpture, music and cinema. Each issue contains reviews of
new books as well as major articles on classic and
contemporary work.
Published by: Oxford Journals
Frequency: Quarterly
Price of single issue: £41 (institutions), £13 (individuals)
Annual subscription: £139 (institutions), £40 (individuals),
£33 (members)

Career Guidance Today
Editor   Rebecca Goodman; 3rd Fl, Copthall Hse, New Rd,
Stourbridge, West Midlands DY8 1PH
Organisation: Journal of the Institute of Careers Guidance
Frequency: Four times a year

Careers Education and Guidance
The Journal of the Association for Careers Education and
Guidance
9 Lawrence Leys, Bloxham, Banbury, Oxfordshire
OX15 4NU; URL www.aceg.org.uk; e-mail
alan@aceg.org.uk; Tel 01295 720809; Fax 01295 720809
Editor   Sylvia Thomson
Organisation: Journal of the Association for Careers
Education and Guidance
Annual subscription: £50

CASE notes
98 Erlanger Rd, London SE14 5TH;
URL www.campaignforstateeducation.org.uk; e-mail
contact@campaignforstateeducation.org.uk;
Tel 07932 149942
Contact   Judy Harrington
News and campaigning information on current issues in
education
Organisation: Campaign for State Education (CASE)
Frequency: Five times a year
Annual subscription: Schools, governing bodies and PTAs,
LEAs, libraries £20; free to members of CASE

Child Education Plus
Scholastic Magazines, Westfield Rd, Southam,
Warwickshire CV47 ORA; URL www.scholastic.co.uk;
e-mail childedplus@scholastic.co.uk; Tel 0845 850 4411
Published by: Scholastic Magazines

Frequency: Monthly
Price of single issue: £4.25
Annual subscription: £42.50; direct debit £39.99
Circulation: 25 000

Child: Care, Health and Development

Blackwell Publishing Ltd, 25 John St, London WC1N 2BS;
Tel 020 7404 4101
Editor   Dr Stuart Logan
Bimonthly; Europe £363
Frequency: Six a year
Annual subscription: £605 (institutions – print and online),
£82 (members)

Childhood, British Association for Early Childhood Education (Early Education)

136 Cavell St, London E1 2JA;
URL www.early-education.org.uk; e-mail
office@early-education.org.uk; Tel 020 7539 5400;
Fax 020 7539 5409
Chief Executive   Anne Nelson
Frequency: Three times a year, also a newsletter three times
a year
Price of single issue: Free to members

Civil Engineering Surveyor

Editor   Darrell Smart; Dominion Hse, Sibson Rd, Sale,
Cheshire M33 7PP; e-mail editor@ices.org.uk;
Tel 0161 972 3110; Fax 0161 972 3119
Organisation: Journal of the Institution of Civil Engineering
Surveyors
Frequency: 10 times a year as well as four supplements
Annual subscription: UK £38, Europe £43, worldwide £48

Classical Quarterly

Oxford Journals, Oxford University Press, Gt Clarendon St,
Oxford, Oxfordshire OX2 6DP; Tel 01865 556767;
Fax 01865 267485
Editor   Miriam Griffin
Editor   Judith Mossman
Graeco-Roman antiquity in the English-speaking world.
Includes research papers and short notes in the fields of
language, literature, history and philosophy, normally in
English but sometimes in other languages.
Published by: Cambridge Journals
Annual subscription: £90 (institutions – online and print),
£83 (institutions – online only)

Classical Review

Oxford Journals, Oxford University Press, Oxford,
Oxfordshire OX2 6DP; Tel 01865 882283;
Fax 01865 882890
Editor   Roy Gibson
Editor   Neil Hopkinson
Critical reviews by experts of new publications in the fields
of Graeco-Roman antiquity from all countries
Published by: Cambridge Journals
Annual subscription: £97 (institutions – online and print),
£91 (institutions – online only)

Collaborative Action Research Network (CARN) Publications

Manchester Metropolitan University, Institute of Education,
799 Wilmslow Rd, Manchester M20 2RR;
URL www.mmu.ac.uk/carn; e-mail carn@mmu.ac.uk;
Tel 0161 247 2318; Fax 0161 247 6353
Member (Co-ordination Team)   Prof Bridget Somekh
Directory of members' activities
Frequency: Biennial
Annual subscription: £40, includes directory and
subscription to Educational Action Research Journal

Concept – The Journal of Contemporary Community Education Practice Theory

National Institute of Adult Continuing Education, 21 De
Montfort St, Leicester, Leicestershire LE1 7GE;
URL www.niace.org.uk; e-mail
subscriptions@niace.org.uk; Tel 0116 204 4200

Editor   Mae Shaw
Concept features articles on a wide range of topics of interest
for those involved in educational activities with
communities. It promotes debate on issues of current
significance and represents a wide variety of perspectives.
Frequency: Tri-annually
Annual subscription: £27 (institutions), £22 (individuals),
£12 (part-time tutors and learners)

Conference and Common Room

John Catt Educational Ltd, Grt Glennham, Saxmundham,
Suffolk IP17 2DH; URL www.johncatt.com; e-mail
enquiries@johncatt.co.uk; Tel 01728 663666;
Fax 01728 663415
Editor   Dr Andrew Cunningham
Frequency: February, May, October
Price of single issue: £4.16 post paid
Annual subscription: £12.50 post paid

Contemporary Physics

Taylor and Francis Journals, 4 Park Sq, Milton Pk,
Abingdon, Oxfordshire OX14 4RN; Tel 020 7017 6000;
Fax 020 7017 6336
Review articles from leading scientists worldwide for
teachers of physics and research workers in educational
institutions and industry
Published by: Taylor & Francis
Frequency: Six a year
Annual subscription: £605 (institutions – print and online),
£574 (institutions – online only), £193 (individuals – print
only)

Critical Survey

Berghahn Books, 3 Newtec Pl, Magdalen Rd, Oxford,
Oxfordshire OX4 1RE; URL www.berghahnbooks.com;
e-mail journals@berghahnbooks.com; Tel 01865 250011;
Fax 01865 250056
Editor (University of Hertfordshire)   Graham Holderness
Literary and cultural studies. The journal publishes detailed
readings on individual texts, wide-ranging debates on the
nature of critical practice, discussion of current educational
issues, original short stories and poetry, book reviews and
arts coverage, with a particular emphasis on theatre, TV and
the cinema.
Frequency: Three a year

Deutsch Lehren und Lernen

German Journal of the Association for Language Learning,
School of Modern Languages, University of Leicester,
University Rd, Leicester LE1 7RH;
URL www.all-languages.org.uk; e-mail
info@all-languages.org.uk; Tel 0116 229 7453
Editor   Uta Smail
Articles, reviews and information of special interest to
learners and teachers of German
Frequency: Twice a year (March and September)
Annual subscription: £70 (UK), £85 (EU), £95 (overseas),
membership £50 (reduced for students and part-time and
retired teachers)

Dutch Crossing

c/o Germanic Studies, University of Sheffield, Sheffield,
South Yorkshire S10 2TN;
URL www.alcs.group.shef.ac.uk; e-mail
alcs@sheffield.ac.uk; Tel 0114 222 4396;
Fax 0114 222 2160

Dyslexia Institute

Park Hse, Wick Rd, Egham, Surrey TW20 0HH;
URL www.dyslexia_inst.org.uk; e-mail
info@dyslexia-inst.org.uk; Tel 01784 222300;
Fax 01784 222333
Chief Executive   Shirley Crammer
Information about the Dyslexia Institute: teaching,
assessment, courses, publications and services
Organisation: Dyslexia Institute

18

Early Music

Oxford Journals, Oxford University Press, Gt Clarendon St, Oxford, Oxfordshire OX2 6DP
Editor   Tess Knighton
Extensively illustrated journal in the field of medieval, renaissance, baroque and classical music
Published by: Oxford Journals
Frequency: Quarterly
Price of single issue: £43 (institutions), £16 (individuals)
Annual subscription: £143 (institutions), £53 (individuals), £43 (members), £33 (students)

Education

The Education Publishing Company Ltd., Devonia Hse, 4, Union Terr, Crediton, Devon EX17 3DY; URL www.educationpublishing.com; e-mail education@educationpublishing.com; Tel 01363 774455
Published by: Education Publishing Company Ltd
Formats: Online, CD-ROM, print
Frequency: Weekly
Annual subscription: Free (online), £240 (CD-ROM), £88 (print)

Education & Health

Schools Health Education Unit, Renslade Hse, Bonhay Rd, Exeter, Devon EX4 3AY; URL www.sheu.org.uk; e-mail sheu@sheu.org.uk; Tel 01392 667272; Fax 01392 667269
Editor   David McGeorge
To pass on the results of recent research into health-related behaviour, and to provide a forum for debate among teachers, health education specialists, and others concerned with the healthy development of young people
Published by: SHEU
Frequency: Four times a year
Annual subscription: £20

Education and Training

Emerald, 62 Toller La, Bradford, West Yorkshire BD8 9BY; URL www.emeraldinsight.com/insight; Tel 01274 777700
Editor   Dr Richard Holden
Frequency: Annual; Nine issues a volume

Education in Chemistry

The Royal Society of Chemistry, Burlington Hse, Piccadilly, London W1J 0BA; URL www.rsc.org/education/eic/index.asp; e-mail eic@rsc.org; Tel 020 7437 8656
Editor   Kathryn Roberts
UK journal devoted to chemistry teaching at all levels, from secondary school to university
Published by: Royal Society fo Chemistry
Formats: Print and online
Frequency: Bimonthly
Annual subscription: £227 (non-members), £56 (members), US$452 (overseas). Online version £204, US$406
Circulation: ca 6000

Education in Science

The Association for Science Education, College La, Hatfield, Hertfordshire AL10 9AA; URL www.ase.org.uk; e-mail eiseditor@ase.org.uk; Tel 01707 266532
Editor   D. Bell
Articles relating to current issues in science education
Frequency: February, April, June, September and November

Education Journal

Education Publishing Company Ltd, Devonia Hse, 4 Union Terr, Crediton, Devon EX17 3DY; URL www.educationpublishing.com; e-mail ej@educationpublishing.com; Tel 01363 774455
Covers general management, research, and policy and administration issues. Includes document research and statistical digests.
Published by: Education Publishing Company Ltd
Frequency: 11 a year
Annual subscription: £38 (print), £240 (CD-ROM)

Education Libraries Journal

Leicester University, Education Library, 21 University Rd, Leicester LE1 7RF; e-mail rwk3@leicester.ac.uk; Tel 0115 848 3421
Editor   John Makin
All aspects of bibliography, librarianship and information science applied to education or to related areas of social science
Published by: Librarians of Institutes and Schools of Education
Frequency: Three times a year
Annual subscription: £30, single issues £11

Education Parliamentary Monitor

Education Publishing Company Ltd, Devonia Hse, 4 Union Terr, Crediton, Devon EX17 3DY; URL www.educationpublishing.com; e-mail epm@educationpublishing.com; Tel 01363 774455
Covers everything about education at Westminster and the devolved institutions in Scotland, Wales and Northern Ireland.
Published by: Education Publishing Company Ltd
Formats: Electronic and in print
Annual subscription: £264.38, £229.12 (electronic only), £57.58 (Scottish/Welsh/schools editions)

Education Review

The Education Publishing Company Ltd, Devonia Hse, 4 Union Terr, Crediton, Devon EX17 3DY; URL www.educationpublishing.com; e-mail er@educationpublishing.com; Tel 01363 774455
Published by: Education Publishing Company Ltd
Organisation: Journal of the NUT
Frequency: Twice a year (June and December)

Education Today

Datateam Publishing Ltd, 15a London Rd, Maidstone, Kent ME16 8LY; URL www.education-today.co.uk; e-mail education@datateam.co.uk
Editor   Stephanie Norbury
Frequency: 11 a year
Annual subscription: £32.50; free to qualifying readers

Education Worldwide

Education Publishing Company Ltd, 73 Marine Ave, Hove, East Sussex BN3 4LG; URL www.educationpublishing.com
Reports on education policy and research findings from around the world
Published by: Education Publishing Company Ltd
Formats: Electronic, print
Frequency: Monthly
Annual subscription: free (electronic), £42 (print)

Educational Psychology in Practice

Taylor and Francis Journals, 4 Park Sq, Milton Pk, Abingdon, Oxfordshire OX14 4RN; Tel 020 7017 6000; Fax 020 7017 6336
Editor   Dr Jeremy Monsen
Published by: Taylor and Francis Journals
Organisation: Journal of the Association of Educational Psychologists
Frequency: Quarterly
Annual subscription: £216 (institutions – print and online), £205 (institutions – online only), £72 (individuals – print only)

Educational Review

School of Education, University of Birmingham, Edgbaston, Birmingham, West Midlands B15 2TT; URL www.tandf.co.uk/journals; e-mail d.m.martin@bham.ac.uk
Orders: Carfax Publishing Company, PO Box 25, Abingdon, Oxfordshire OX14 3UE
Executive Editor   D. Martin
Annual index and title page bound in the November issue

Educational Review is a journal for generic educational research and scholarship, and publishes peer-reviewed papers from international contributors
Frequency: February, May, August and November

Electronic British Library Journal
Scholarly research journal of the British Library
Early Printed Collections, The British Library, 96 Euston Rd, London NW1 2DB; URL www.bl.uk/collections/eblj/eblj.html; Tel 020 7412 7576; Fax 020 7412 7577
Editor   Dr Barry Taylor
Frequency: Biannual
Price of single issue: £17.50, available free online
Annual subscription: £35

Electronics Education
The Institution of Electrical Engineers, Michael Faraday Hse, Six Hills Way, Stevenage, Hertfordshire SG1 2AY; e-mail cfaulkner@iee.org.uk
Managing Editor   J. Stapleton
Journal for secondary school teachers of Design and Technology, and Electronics
Frequency: Three times a year
Annual subscription: Direct mailing by subscription; mailed free to all secondary schools in the UK

ELT Journal
English as a Foreign or Second Language, Oxford University Press, Gt Clarendon St, Oxford, Oxfordshire OX2 6DP; Tel 01865 556767; Fax 01865 267485
Editor   Keith Morrow
Published by: Oxford Journals
Price of single issue: £33 (institutions), £14 (individuals)
Annual subscription: £110 (institutions), £44 (individuals), £38 (members), £24 (students)

English Drama Media
National Association for the Teaching of English, 50 Broadfield Rd, Sheffield, South Yorkshire S8 0XJ; URL www.nate.org.uk; e-mail info@nate.org.uk; Tel 0114 255 5419; Fax 0114 255 5296
Annual subscription also includes magazine NATE Classroom and NATE News
Organisation: NATE's professional journal
Frequency: Three times a year

English Historical Review
Journals Department, Oxford University Press, Gt Clarendon St, Oxford, Oxfordshire OX2 6DP; URL www.oxfordjournals.org; e-mail ehr@oup.com; Tel 01865 353000
Editor (Articles)   Prof G.W. Bernard
Editor (Reviews)   Dr Martin Conway
Frequency: Five times a year
Annual subscription: £136, individual subscribers £65, from Journals Subscription Department

English in Education
National Association for the Teaching of English, 50 Broadfield Rd, Sheffield, South Yorkshire S8 0XJ; URL www.nate.org.uk; e-mail info@nate.org.uk; Tel 0114 255 5419; Fax 0114 255 5296
Vice-Chair   Elaine Millard
Director (Development and Communications)   Ian McNeilly
Manager (Publications)   Anne Fairhall
NATE is the UK subject association for all aspects of English, pre-school to university.
Annual subscription also includes magazine NATE Classroom, and NATE News.
Published by: Wiley-Blackwell
Organisation: Research journal of the National Association for the Teaching of English (NATE)
Frequency: Three times a year
Number of members: Approximately 4000 members

Equals
The Mathematical Association, 259 London Rd, Leicester LE2 3BE; URL www.m-a.org.uk; e-mail equals@m-a.org.uk; Tel 0116 221 0013; Fax 0116 212 2835
Editor   Ray Gibbons
A journal on mathematics and SEN
Frequency: Three times a year

European Journal of Physics
Institute of Physics Publishing Ltd, Dirac Hse, Temple Back, Bristol BS1 6BE; e-mail ejp@ioppublishing.co.uk; Tel 0117 929 7481; Fax 0117 929 4318
Publisher   Therese Quinton
Education and scholarly studies in physics and closely related sciences at university level
Annual subscription: £499 (EU/rest of world)

Evaluation and Research in Education
Editor   Keith Morrison; Frankfurt Lodge, Clevedon Hall, Victoria Rd, Clevedon, North Somerset BS21 7HH; Tel 01275 876519; Fax 01275 871673
Education, review articles; reviews.
Frequency: Three times a year
Annual subscription: Libraries £149; individuals £49 (including postage)

Folk Music Journal
English Folk Dance and Song Society, Cecil Sharp Hse, 2 Regents Park Rd, London NW1 7AY; URL fmj.efdss.org; e-mail fmj@efdss.org; Tel 020 7485 2206; Fax 020 7284 0534
Editor   David Atkinson
Articles on folk music, song and dance
Frequency: Annual
Price of single issue: Free to members of the English Folk Dance and Song Society; back issues £9 and postage and packing

Forum for Modern Language Studies
Oxford Journals, Oxford University Press, Oxford, Oxfordshire OX2 6DP; Tel 01865 556767; Fax 01865 267485
Aspects of literary and linguistic studies from the middle ages to the present day
Published by: Oxford Journals
Price of single issue: £43 (institutions), £15 (individuals)
Annual subscription: £146 (institutions), £47 (individuals), £39 (members)

Francophonie
French Journal of the Association for Language Learning, School of Modern Languages, University of Leicester, University Rd, Leicester LE1 7RH; URL www.all-languages.org.uk; e-mail info@all-languages.org.uk; Tel 0116 229 7453
Editor   Shirley Lawes; Institute of Education, University of London
Articles, reviews and information of special interest to learners and teachers of French
Frequency: Biannual; March and September
Annual subscription: £70 (UK), £85 (EU), £95 (overseas)

French History
Oxford Journals, Oxford University Press, Oxford, Oxfordshire OX2 6DP; Tel 01865 556767; Fax 01865 267485
Editor   Prof Malcolm Crook
Principally French history from Francia to the Fifth Republic, but also includes historically-orientated articles from other disciplines (e.g. art, music, literature, language and social sciences)
Published by: Oxford Journals
Price of single issue: £45
Annual subscription: £152 (institutions), £45 (members)

18

Geography

The Geographical Association, 160 Solly St, Sheffield, South
  Yorkshire S1 4BF; URL www.geography.org.uk; e-mail
  info@geography.org.uk; Tel 0114 296 0088;
  Fax 0114 296 7176
Editorial   Peter Jackson
Editorial   Stuart Lane
Editorial   John Morgan
Editorial   Eleanor Rawling
Frequency: Termly
Annual subscription: Rates available

Geology Today

Blackwell Publishing, 9600 Garsington Rd, Oxford,
  Oxfordshire OX4 2DQ; Tel 01865 776868
Editor   Peter Doyle
A magazine for both amateur and professional earth
scientists. Articles by specialists on pure and applied topics;
also opinions, news items, book reviews, earthquake and
volcano reports etc.
Published by: Blackwell Publishing
Organisation: Published on behalf of The Geologists'
  Association and The Geological Society of London
Formats: Print, online
Frequency: Six a year
Annual subscription: £437 (institutions), £337 (institutions –
  online only), £47 (individuals), £37 (members), £29
  (students)

German History

Hodder Arnold, 338 Euston Rd, London NW1 3BH;
  URL www.germanhistoryjournal.com; e-mail
  hodderarnoldjournals@hodder.co.uk; Tel 020 7873 6337;
  Fax 020 7873 6376
Editor (University of Aberdeen)   Karin Friedrich
Editor (University of Sussex, Brighton)   Prof Paul Betts
Principally the history of Germany and other German-
speaking areas, but also other aspects of German life and
culture which have a clear historical relevance
Frequency: Four a year
Annual subscription: Details available

Gifted Education International

AB Academic Publishers, PO Box 42, Bicester, Oxfordshire
  OX26 6NW; e-mail jrnls@abapubl.demon.co.uk;
  Tel 01869 320949; Fax 01869 320949
Editor   Belle Wallace
Includes evaluation, curriculum development, psychology,
practice, resources, reviews, news
Frequency: Three issues a volume
Annual subscription: £99 a volume (post paid)

Greece and Rome

Cambridge Journals, The Edinburgh Bldg, Shaftesbury Rd,
  Cambridge, Cambridgeshire CB2 2RU; Tel 01223 312393
Published by: Cambridge Journals
Annual subscription: £75 (institutions – print and online),
  £70 (institutions – online only)

GSSE

11 Malford Gr, Gilwern, Abergavenny, Monmouthshire
  NP7 0RN; URL www.gsse.org.uk/educational; e-mail
  gsse@zoo.co.uk; Tel 01873 830872
Educational Publisher   Dr David P Bosworth
Application of educational technology

Health Development Today

National Institute for Health and Clinical Excellence,
  MidCity Pl, 71 High Holborn, London WC1V 6NA;
  URL www.nice.org.u; Tel 020 7067 5800;
  Fax 020 7067 5801
The magazine is aimed at everyone whose remit includes
health improvement.
Formats: Online
Frequency: Six issues a year

Higher Education Quarterly

Wiley-Blackwell, 9600 Garsington Rd, Oxford, Oxfordshire
  OX4 2DQ; URL www.blackwellpublishing.com/hequ;
  Tel 01865 776868
Main Editor   Lee Harvey
Associate Editor   Celia Whitchurch
Published by: Published in association with the Society for
  Research into Higher Education (SRHE)
Frequency: Quarterly

History

Historical Association, 59a Kennington Pk Rd, London
  SE11 4JH; e-mail enquiry@history.org.uk;
  Tel 020 7735 3901
Editor (Exeter University)   Dr Joe Smith
Available as additional journals to annual subscriptions or
from Blackwell Publishing
Frequency: October, February, June

History and Computing

Edinburgh University Press, 22 George Sq, Edinburgh
  EH8 9LF; URL www.eup.ed.ac.uk; e-mail
  journals@eup.ed.ac.uk; Tel 0131 650 4223;
  Fax 0131 662 0053
Editor   Vacancy
Aimed at historians using computers for research. Covers all
aspects of computer applications, from quantitive methods
to free text analysis and image processing.
Annual subscription: Individual £30 (UK/EC); institution
  £65 (UK/EC)

History Today

History Today Ltd, 20 Old Compton St, London W1D 4TW;
  URL www.historytoday.com; e-mail
  admin@historytoday.com; Tel 020 7534 8000
Editor   Peter Furtado
English language history magazine. Reviews, articles,
feature series, news and views from professional historians
and writers on all aspects of British, European and
international history.
Frequency: Monthly
Price of single issue: £4.20
Annual subscription: £42 (UK)

History Workshop Journal

Oxford Journals, Oxford University Press, Oxford,
  Oxfordshire OX2 6DP; Tel 01865 556767;
  Fax 01865 267485
Administrative Editor   Bertie Mandelblatt
Exploration of the everyday in a historical context,
providing new perspectives on the past and present
Published by: Oxford Journals
Frequency: Twice a year
Price of single issue: £54 (institutions), £25 (individuals)
Annual subscription: £90 (institutions), £40 (individuals),
  £32 (members), £17 (students)

Hospitality

Trinity Ct, 34 West St, Sutton, Surrey SM1 1SH;
  URL www.hcima.org.uk; e-mail
  marketing@hcima.co.uk; Tel 020 8661 4900;
  Fax 020 8661 4901
Publisher   Petra Clayton
Hospitality is produced four times a year. It contains
management articles relating to the hotel and catering
industry and associated disciplines.
Published by: Magazine of the Hotel and Catering
  International Management Association
Annual subscription: £38 UK, £48 overseas

Iberian Studies

Centre for Iberian Studies, Department of Earth Sciences
  and Geography, University of Keele, Newcastle,
  Staffordshire ST5 5BG; e-mail w-naylon@s-chesire.ac.uk;
  Tel 01782 627243
Managing Editor   John Naylon
Historical and social science studies of modern Spain and
Portugal

Frequency: Twice a year, spring and autumn
Annual subscription: £12 UK, £20 other countries

Industrial and Commercial Training

Emerald, 62 Toller La, Bradford, West Yorkshire BD9 9BY;
    URL www.emeraldinsight.com/insight;
    Tel 01274 777700
Editor   Bryan Smith
Frequency: Seven issues a volume
Annual subscription: Available

Industrial and Corporate Change

Oxford Journals, Oxford University Press, Oxford,
    Oxfordshire OX2 6DP; Tel 01865 556767;
    Fax 01865 267485
Managing Editor   J. Chytry
Presentation and interpretation of evidence on corporate
and industrial change, drawn from an interdisciplinary set
of approaches and theories
Published by: Oxford Journals
Price of single issue: £68 (institutions), £13 (individuals)
Annual subscription: £342 (institutions), £61 (individuals),
    £49 (members)

Industrial Law Journal

Oxford Journals, Oxford University Press, Oxford,
    Oxfordshire OX2 6DP; Tel 01865 556767;
    Fax 01865 267485
Editor   Prof Paul L. Davies
Comment, in-depth analysis and information for academics,
practising lawyers and lay industrial relations experts on all
aspects of UK labour law
Published by: Oxford Journals
Frequency: Quarterly
Price of single issue: £27 (institutions), £25 (individuals)
Annual subscription: £89 (institutions), £79 (individuals),
    £65 (members)

Horizons Magazine

Institute for Outdoor Learning, The Barn, Plumpton Old
    Hall, Plumpton, Penrith, Cumbria CA11 9NP;
    URL www.outdoor-learning.org; e-mail
    iol@outdoor-learning.org; Tel 01768 885800;
    Fax 01768 885801
Institute for Outdoor Learning also publishes the Outdoor
Source Book, the directory of providers, training, services
and equipment. Mail order bookshop. Call for free copy of
booklist.
Published by: Institute for Outdoor Learning
Frequency: Quarterly
Annual subscription: £30

International Journal of Electrical Engineering Education

Published by Manchester University Press, Oxford Rd,
    Manchester M13 9NR;
    URL www.manchesteruniversitypress.co.uk; e-mail
    mup@manchester.ac.uk; Tel 0161 275 2310
Editor   J. Johnson; School of Electrical and Electronic
    Engineering, University of Manchester, Sackville St,
    Manchester M60 1QD; e-mail ijeee@manchester.ac.uk;
    Tel 0161 306 4799
Frequency: Quarterly
Annual subscription: £197 institution (includes online
    access), £61 individual

International Journal of Law, Policy and the Family

Pembroke College, Oxford, Oxfordshire OX1 1DW;
    Tel 01865 276429; Fax 01865 276418
Editor (University of Nottingham)   Robert Dingwall
Editor ((University of Oxford)   John Eekelaar
Theoretical analysis of family law; sociological literature
concerning the family, of special interest to law and legal
policy; literature in related disciplines (such as medicine,
psychology demography) of special relevance to law and the
family
Frequency: Three a year
Annual subscription: UK and Europe £117

International Journal of Lexicography

Oxford Journals, Oxford University Press, Oxford,
    Oxfordshire OX2 6DP; Tel 01865 556767;
    Fax 01865 267773
Editor   Dr Paul Bogaards
Theoretical, practical, diachronic and synchronic aspects of
lexicography. Dictionaries and reference works of all types,
phrase books, usage guides, encyclopaedia etc. Related
disciplines such as lexicology, terminology, semantics,
pragmatics, are also included.
Published by: Oxford Journals
Frequency: Quarterly
Price of single issue: £47 (institutions), £46 (individuals)
Annual subscription: £158 (institutions), £148 (individuals),
    £70 (members)

International Journal of Lifelong Education

Taylor and Francis Journals, 4 Park Sq, Milton Pk,
    Abingdon, Oxfordshire OX14 4RN; Tel 020 7017 6000;
    Fax 020 7017 6336
Editor   Prof P. Jarvis; Department of Educational Studies,
    University of Surrey, Guildford, Surrey GU2 5XH;
    Tel 01483 71281
Editor   Prof Stella Parker; Department of Adult Education,
    University of Nottingham, Education Bldg, University
    Pk, Nottingham NG7 2RD; Tel 0115 948 4848
Adult, lifelong and continuing education
Published by: Taylor & Francis
Frequency: Six a year
Annual subscription: £532 (institutions – print and online),
    £505 (institutions – online only), £101 (individuals)

International Journal of Mathematical Education in Science and Technology

Taylor and Francis Ltd, 4 Park Sq, Milton Pk, Abingdon,
    Oxfordshire OX14 4RN; Tel 01235 828600;
    Fax 01235 829000
New teaching aids and techniques are a feature
Published by: Taylor & Francis
Frequency: Eight a year
Annual subscription: £879 (institutions – print and online),
    £835 (institutions – online only), £419 (individuals – print
    only)

International Journal of Refugee Law

Oxford Journals, Oxford University Press, Oxford,
    Oxfordshire OX2 6DP; Tel 01865 556767;
    Fax 01865 556646
Editor   Prof Geoff Gilbert
Published by: Oxford Journals
Frequency: Quarterly
Price of single issue: £58 (institutions), £18 (individuals)
Annual subscription: £401 (institutions), £126 (individuals),
    £45 (members)

International Journal of School Disaffection

Trentham Books Ltd, Westview Hse, 734 London Rd,
    Oakhill, Stoke-on-Trent, Staffordshire ST4 5NP;
    URL www.trentham-books.co.uk; e-mail
    tb@trentham-books.co.uk; Tel 01782 745567;
    Fax 01782 745553
Editor   Reva Klein
Journal about the issues and theories surrounding
disaffection
Frequency: Twice a year
Price of single issue: £20
Annual subscription: £53 UK, £63 overseas; online £148

International Journal of Science Education

Routledge, 4 Park Sq, Milton Pk, Abingdon, Oxfordshire
    OX14 4RN; Tel 020 7017 6000
Editor   John Gilbert
International perspectives on science and technology
education; research in science education
Published by: Routledge
Frequency: Monthly
Annual subscription: £1211 (institutions – print and online),
    £1150 (institutions – online only), £423 (individuals)

18

International Schools Journal
European Council of International Schools (ECIS), Council of International Schools (CIS), 21 Lavant St, Petersfield, Hampshire GU32 3EL; e-mail publications@ecis.org; Tel 01730 268244; Fax 01730 267914
Editor Dr Caroline Ellwood
Articles and reviews for educators interested in international education
Frequency: Biannual
Annual subscription: Available as part of individual membership of ECIS/CIS

International Studies in Educational Administration
Education Publishing Company Ltd., Devonia Hse, 4 Union Terr, Crediton, Devon EX17 3DY; URL www.educationpublishing.com; e-mail isea@educationpublishing.com; Tel 01363 774455
Editor Kam-Cheung Wong
Organisation: Journal of Commonwealth Council for Educational Administration and Management
Frequency: Three issues a year
Annual subscription: Individuals £35, institutions £140

Journal of Access Policy and Practice
21 De Montfort St, Leicester LE1 7GE; URL www.niace.org.uk; e-mail subscriptions@niace.org.uk; Tel 0116 204 4200
Editor Prof Mary Stuart
Encourages debate between practitioners and academics interested in participation and accessibility issues in education and training. Reflects critically on education policy and practices as it affects access to learning.
Frequency: Biannual
Annual subscription: £33 (individuals), £88 (institutions); rest of Europe, North America, Australasia, Japan: £44 (individuals), £104 (institutions); rest of world: £22 (individuals), £33 (institutions)

Journal of Adult and Continuing Education
National Institute of Adult Continuing Education, 21 De Montfort St, Leicester, Leicestershire LE1 7GE; URL www.niace.org.uk; e-mail subscriptions@niace.org.uk; Tel 0116 204 4200
Editor Prof Mike Osborne
Provides theoretical and practical work in the field of lifelong learning and adult, community and continuing education. The journal focuses on international and national issues and is aimed at researchers, professionals and practitioners in all sectors.
Formats: Online
Frequency: Biannually
Annual subscription: £33 (individuals), £88 (institutions); rest of Europe, North America, Australasia, Japan: £44 (individuals), £104 (institutions); rest of world: £22 (individual), £33 (institutions). Online access available to subscribers.

Journal of African Economies
Oxford Journals, Oxford University Press, Oxford, Oxfordshire OX2 6DP; URL www.oup.co.uk/jafecol; Tel 01865 556767; Fax 01865 267485
Editor Marcel Fafchamps
Published by: Oxford Journals
Frequency: Five a year
Price of single issue: £70 (institutions), £15 (individuals)
Annual subscription: £296 (institutions), £61 (individuals)

Journal of Biological Education
Institute of Biology, 9 Red Lion Ct, London EC4 3EF; URL www.iob.org; e-mail jbe@iob.org; Tel 020 7936 5900; Fax 020 7936 5901
Editor David Slingsby
Production Editor Jacqui Lagrue
Features Editor Simon Napper
Frequency: Quarterly
Annual subscription: £34 (institute members); £57 (personal UK); £100 (institutional UK); £72 (personal overseas); £130 (institutional overseas)

The Journal of Classics Teaching
Registered Charity Number 313165
Journal of the Joint Association of Classical Teachers (JACT), Senate Hse, Malet St, London WC1E 7HU; URL www.jact.org; e-mail office@jact.org; Tel 020 7862 8719; Fax 020 7255 2297
Contact Anna Bayraktar
Professional association for classics teachers and lecturers at all levels. Journal for classics teachers and lecturers, termly bulletin of events, reports, surveys, proceedings, reviews, summer schools, competitions.
Organisation: Joint Association of Classical Teachers (JACT)
Frequency: Three issues a year
Annual subscription: Available through membership of JACT: standard £40, student £16 (free for one year to classics PGCE and graduate students), retired rates also available
Circulation: 1500

Journal of Computer Assisted Learning
Blackwell Publishing, 9600 Garsington Rd, Oxford, Oxfordshire OX4 2DQ; Tel 01865 776868; Fax 01865 714591
Editor Charles Crook
Published by: Blackwell Publishing
Formats: Print, online
Frequency: Six a year
Annual subscription: £608 (institutions), £525 (institutions – online only), £98 (individuals), £84 (members)

Journal of Curriculum Studies
Taylor and Francis Ltd, 4 Park Sq, Milton Pk, Abingdon, Oxfordshire OX14 4RN; Tel 01235 828600; Fax 01235 829000
All aspects of curriculum studies
Published by: Taylor & Francis
Formats: Online or in print
Frequency: Six a year
Annual subscription: £684 (institutions – print and online), £649 (institutions – online only), £129 (individuals – print only)
Circulation: Approximately 1250

Journal of Design and Technology Education
Trentham Books Ltd, Westview Hse, 734 London Rd, Oakhill, Stoke-on-Trent ST4 5NP; URL www.trentham-books.co.uk; e-mail tb@trentham-books.co.uks; Tel 01782 745567; Fax 01782 745553
Editor R. Kimbell
Presents new approaches to design and technology teaching in schools, colleges and teacher training
Frequency: Three times a year
Price of single issue: £21
Annual subscription: UK £59; overseas £64

Journal of Education and Christian Belief
The Stapleford Centre, Frederick Rd, Stapleford, Nottingham NG9 8FN; URL www.jecb.org; e-mail subs@jecb.org; Tel 0115 939 6270; Fax 0115 939 2076
A journal concerned with current educational thinking from a Christian standpoint sponsored by the Association of Christian Teachers and the Stapleford Centre
Frequency: Twice a year
Annual subscription: £24.10

Journal of Environmental Law
Oxford Journals, Oxford University Press, Oxford, Oxfordshire OX2 6DP; Tel 01865 556767; Fax 01865 267485
Editor Prof Richard Macrory
This journal provides a source of informed analysis in the field. The range of subjects encompassed within environmental law is broad, extending from the more traditional fields of pollution control, waste management, and habitat protection to challenging newer areas such as biotechnology, regulation of hazardous substances, and international regimes for common natural resources.

Published by: Oxford Journals
Frequency: Three a year
Price of single issue: £65 (institutions), £26 (individuals)
Annual subscription: £163 (institutions), £62 (individuals), £45 (members), £24 (students)

Journal of European Industrial Training

Emerald, 60–62 Toller La, Bradford, West Yorkshire BD8 9BY; URL www.emeraldinsight.com/insight; Tel 01274 777700
Editor   Dr Thomas Garavan
Frequency: Nine issues a volume
Annual subscription: Available

Journal of Further and Higher Education

Taylor and Francis Journals, 4 Park Sq, Milton Pk, Abingdon, Oxfordshire OX14 4RN
Editor   Jennifer Rowley
Published by: Routledge
Frequency: Quarterly
Annual subscription: £295 (institutions – print and online), £280 (institutions – online only), £96 (individuals – print only)

Journal of the History of Collections

Oxford Journals, Oxford University Press, Oxford, Oxfordshire OX2 6DP; Tel 01865 556767; Fax 01865 267485
Editor   Dr Kate Heard
Editor   Dr Arthur MacGregor
This journal is dedicated to the study of collections, ranging from the contents of palaces and accumulations in more modest households, to the most systematic collections of academic institutions. The journal covers the content of these collections, the processes that initiated and controlled their formation, and the circumstances of the collections themselves.
Published by: Oxford Journals
Frequency: Two a year
Price of single issue: £84 (institutions), £29 (individuals)
Annual subscription: £141 (institutions), £46 (individuals), £39 (members), £30 (students)

Journal of Islamic Studies

Oxford Centre for Islamic Studies, George St, Oxford, Oxfordshire OX1 2AR; URL www.jis.oupjournals.org; e-mail publications@oxcis.ac.uk; Tel 01865 278730; Fax 01865 248942
Editor   Dr Farhan Ahmad Nizami
Dedicated to the multidisciplinary study of all aspects of Islam and the Islamic world
Frequency: Three a year
Annual subscription: UK and Europe £145; online only: annual price UK and Europe £127

Journal of Logic and Computation

Oxford Journals, Oxford University Press, Oxford, Oxfordshire OX2 6DP; Tel 01865 556767; Fax 01865 267485
Editor-in-Chief   D.M. Gabbay
Logic has found applications in virtually all aspects of IT, from software engineering and hardware to programming and artificial intelligence. This journal covers an interdisciplinary area of logic and computation.
Published by: Oxford Journals
Frequency: Six a year
Price of single issue: £103 (institutions), £49 (individuals)
Annual subscription: £519 (institutions), £233 (individuals), £166 (members)

Journal of Refugee Studies

Refugee Studies Centre, Queen Elizabeth Hse, Mansfield Rd, Oxford, Oxfordshire OX1 3TB; URL www.jrs.oxfordjournals.org; e-mail jrs@qeh.ox.ac.uk; Tel 01865 270267; Fax 01865 270721
Editor   Dr Richard Black
Editor   Dr Joanne van Selm
Academic and policy exploration of the complex problems of forced migration and national and international

responses. Includes anthropology, economics, health and education, international relations, law, politics, psychology and sociology.
Published by: Oxford University Press
Frequency: Quarterly
Annual subscription: UK and Europe £193, individuals and developing world institutions £52/$99

Journal of Research in Reading

Wiley-Blackwell, 9600 Garsington Rd, Oxford, Oxfordshire OX4 2DQ; URL www.jrir.org; Tel 01865 776868
Editor   Rhona Stainthorp
Published by: Published on behalf of The United Kingdom Literacy Association (UKLA)
Frequency: Quarterly

Journal of the Royal Musical Association

Department of Music, Royal Holloway University of London, Egham, Surrey TW20 0EX; URL www.jrma.oupjournals.org; Tel 01784 443532; Fax 01784 439441
Editor   K. Ellis
New research into all branches of musical scholarship – historical musicology and ethnomusicology, theory and analysis, textual criticism, archival research, organology and performing practice
Frequency: Twice a year
Annual subscription: UK and Europe £57

Journal of Semantics

Oxford University Press, Journal Subscription Department, Oxford, Oxfordshire OX2 6DP; Tel 01865 556767; Fax 01865 267485
Editor   Bart Geurts
This journal publishes articles, notes, discussions, and book reviews in the area of natural language semantics. It is explicitly interdisciplinary in that it aims for an integration of philosophical, psychological, and linguistic semantics, as well as semantic work carried out in artificial intelligence and anthropology.
Published by: Oxford Journals
Frequency: Four a year
Price of single issue: £50 (institutions), £19 (individuals)
Annual subscription: £167 (institutions), £62 (individuals), £49 (members)

Journal of Semitic Studies

Middle Eastern Studies, School of Languages, Linguistics and Cultures, Oxford Rd, Manchester M13 9PL; Tel 0161 275 3551; Fax 0161 275 3551
Editor (University of Manchester)   P.S. Alexander
Modern and ancient Near East, with special emphasis on research into the languages and literature of the area
Frequency: Twice a year
Annual subscription: £142 (institutional); £49 (personal); special rates for developing countries

Journal of Theological Studies

Journals Department, Oxford University Press, Oxford, Oxfordshire OX2 6DP; Tel 01865 556767; Fax 01865 556646
Editor   Prof M. Hooker
Editor   Rev Prof M. Wiles
Published by: Oxford Journals
Frequency: Two a year
Price of single issue: £119 (institutions), £26 (individuals)
Annual subscription: £201 (institutions), £41 (individuals)

Junior Education Plus

Scholastic Magazines, Westfield Rd, Southam, Warwickshire CV47 0RA; URL www.scholastic.co.uk; e-mail junioredplus@scholastic.co.uk; Tel 0845 850 4411
Magazine with KS2 resources, including posters and curriculum-linked ideas for the classroom. Linked community website for KS2.
Published by: Scholastic Magazines
Frequency: Monthly
Price of single issue: £4.25

18

Annual subscription: £42.50; direct debit £39.99
Circulation: 17 000

Language Learning Journal

Association for Language Learning, 150 Railway Terr,
Rugby, Warwickshire CV21 3HN;
URL www.all-languages.org.uk; e-mail
info@all-languages.org.uk; Tel 01788 546443;
Fax 01788 544149
Editor   Dr Douglas Allford
Editor   Dr Norbert Pachler
Articles on teaching and learning of languages, applied
linguistics, language policy, current issues, and ideas for
practical classroom teaching. Also reviews and information.
Membership subscription £50, reduced for students and
part-time, retired teachers. See also entries for Deutsch
Lehren and Lernen, Dutch Crossing, Francophonie,
Tuttialia, Vida Hispanica.
Frequency: Twice a year
Annual subscription: £78 UK, £107 overseas

Language Teaching

Cambridge University Press, The Edinburgh Bldg,
Shaftesbury Rd, Cambridge, Cambridgeshire CB2 2RU;
URL www.journals.cambridge.org/jid-lta; e-mail
lta@cambridge.org; Tel 01223 312393; Fax 01223 315052
Editor   Sue Wharton;   Aston University
Experts select articles from about 400 relevant journals for
publication in language teaching. In this way, teachers are
kept up to date with the latest developments in linguistics
and applied linguistics. The journal also shares ideas for use
in the classroom and by discussing methods of effective
language learning.
Published by: Cambridge Journals
Annual subscription: £128 (institutions – online and print),
£108 (institutions – online only)

Leader

The Association of School and College Leaders (Formerly
SHA), 130 Regent Rd, Leicester LE1 7PG;
Tel 0116 299 1122
Editor   Sara Gadzik
Frequency: Three times a term
Price of single issue: £6
Annual subscription: £32

Lebende Sprachen

Langenscheidt K6, Mies-van-der-Rohe-Strasse 1, D-80807
München, Germany; URL www.langenscheidt.de; e-mail
wb@langenscheidt.de; Tel +49 89 3 6096 0;
Fax +49 89 3 6096 222
Editor   Prof Dr Peter A. Schmitt
Editor   Prof Dr Reinhold Werner
Frequency: Four issues a year

The Lecturer

NATFHE, 27 Britannia St, London WC1X 9JP;
URL www.natfhe.org.uk; e-mail
thelecturer@natfhe.org.uk; Tel 020 7837 3636
Editor   Brenda Kirsch
Frequency: Five a year
Annual subscription: £12

Library and Information Update

Subscriptions:: World Wide Subscription Service Ltd, Unit 4,
Gibbs Reed Farm, Ticehurst, East Sussex TN5 7HE;
URL www.cilip.org.uk/update; e-mail
admin@worldwidesubscriptions.com; Tel 01580 200657;
Fax 01580 200616
Editor   Elspeth Hyams
Professional concerns in librarianship, education, recreation
and information
Frequency: 10 issues a year
Annual subscription: £85

The Library

Oxford Journals, Oxford University Press, Oxford,
Oxfordshire OX2 5DP; Tel 01865 556767;
Fax 01865 267485
Editor   Dr Oliver Pickering
The history of books, both manuscript and printed, and the
role of books in history
Published by: Oxford Journals
Organisation: Journal of the Bibliographical Society
Frequency: Quarterly
Price of single issue: £40 (institutions), £16 (individuals)
Annual subscription: £136 (institutions), £50 (individuals),
£99 (members)

Literacy

Wiley-Blackwell, 9600 Garsington Rd, Oxford, Oxfordshire
OX4 2DQ; URL www.blackwellpublishing.com/literacy;
Tel 01865 776868
Editor   Kathy Hall
Published by: Published on behalf of The United Kingdom
Literacy Association (UKLA)
Frequency: Three times a year

Literacy Time Plus

Scholastic Magazines, Westfield Rd, Southam,
Warwickshire CV47 0RA; URL www.scholastic.co.uk;
e-mail littimefeedback@scholastic.co.uk;
Tel 0845 850 4411
There are three versions of this literacy resource (ages 5–7,
ages 7–9 and ages 9–11) which offers a bimonthly printed
magazine and linked online resources
Published by: Scholastic Magazines
Frequency: Bimonthly
Price of single issue: Subscription only
Annual subscription: £54.00
Circulation: Average 2500

Literacy Today

Education Publishing Company Ltd, 73 Marine Ave, Hove,
East Sussex BN3 4LG;
URL www.educationpublishing.com; e-mail
lt@educationpublishing.com; Tel 01273 882338;
Fax 01273 423641
Published by: Education Publishing Company Ltd
Organisation: Magazine of the National Literacy Trust
Frequency: Four issues a year
Annual subscription: £205 (print), £18 (electronic), £18 (CD-
ROM)

Literary and Linguistic Computing

Oxford Journals, Oxford University Press, Oxford,
Oxfordshire OX2 6DP; Tel 01865 556767;
Fax 01865 267773
Editor   Dr Marilyn Deegan
Papers selected for publishing in the Literary and Linguistic
Computing journal cover a wide variety of subjects. These
have included: authorship attribution, bibliographies,
databases, dialect analysis, computer dictionaries,
computerised minimisation, concordances, corpus
linguistics, expert systems, Greek syntax, language
processing, literary statistics, machine translation,
morphological analysis, neural networks, parsers,
phonetics, pronouns, standards, word order etc. Special
sections in the journal provide a regular and timely update
on current issues. The journal also publishes special
sections, such as: full text retrieval systems; machine
translation; computers and language; literary criticism and
computing; computers and teaching in the humanities;
computers and medieval studies; corpora; and information
technology as an aid to literary research.
Published by: Oxford Journals
Frequency: Quarterly
Price of single issue: £55 (institutions), £18 (members)
Annual subscription: £186 (institutions), £58 (members)

Literature and Theology

Oxford Journals, Oxford University Press, Oxford, Oxfordshire OX2 6DP; Tel 01865 882283; Fax 01865 882890

Editor   Dr Andrew Hass

Interdisciplinary study of serious interest to theologians and students of literature

Published by: Oxford Journals

Frequency: Quarterly

Price of single issue: £44 (institutions), £13 (individuals)

Annual subscription: £148 (institutions), £42 (individuals), £38 (members)

Management in Education

The Education Publishing Company Ltd, Devonia Hse, 4 Union Terr, Crediton, Devon EX17 3DY; URL www.educationpublishing.com; e-mail mie@educationpublishing.com; Tel 01363 774455

Published by: Education Publishing Company Ltd

Organisation: Magazine of the British Educational Management and Administration Society

Frequency: Five issues a year

Annual subscription: £85 (print), £49 (electronic), £35 (CD-ROM)

Managing Education Matters

The Education Publishing Company Ltd, Devonia Hse, 4 Union Terr, Crediton, Devon EX17 3DY; URL www.educationpublishing.com; e-mail mem@educationpublishing.com; Tel 01363 774455

International view of educational management and administration from the CCEAM

Published by: Education Publishing Company Ltd

Formats: Electronic and print

Frequency: Two a year

Annual subscription: £105 (print), £12 (electronic)

Mathematical Gazette

The Mathematical Association, 259 London Rd, Leicester LE2 3BE; URL www.m-a.org.uk; Tel 0116 221 0013; Fax 0116 212 2835

Editor   Gerry Leversha

Problems Editor   Nick Lord

Production Editor   Bill Richardson

Reviews Editor   Hugh Williams

Organisation: Publication of the Mathematical Association

Frequency: March, July, November

Annual subscription: Postal subscription £55

Mathematical Pie

Mathematical Pie Ltd, 259 London Rd, Leicester LE2 3BE; URL www.m-a.org.uk

Editor   Wil Ransom

Discounts on bulk orders, details on request

Frequency: Termly

Mathematics in School

The Mathematical Association, 259 London Rd, Leicester LE2 3BE; URL www.m-a.org.uk; Tel 0116 221 0013

Editor   John Berry

Editor   Lesley Jones

Editor   Chris Pritchard

Journal reflecting current thinking and practice in mathematics.

Frequency: Five times a year

Mind

Oxford Journals, Oxford University Press, Gt Clarendon St, Oxford, Oxfordshire OX2 6DP

Editor   Prof Thomas Baldwin

Journal in philosophy. Presents new thinking from epistemology, metaphysics, philosophy of language, philosophy of logic, and philosophy of mind.

Published by: Oxford Journals

Frequency: Quarterly

Price of single issue: £30(institutions), £10 (individuals)

Annual subscription: £100 (institutions), £30 (individuals), £32 (members)

Minerva – A Review of Science, Learning and Policy

Springer SBM, PO Box 17, 3300 AA Dordrecht, The Netherlands

Quarterly; annual subscription, $180 individual, $355 institution

Organisation: Quarterly

/ Annual subscription:

Modern Language Review

Subscription: Suite 1c, Joseph's Well, Hanover Wlk, Leeds LS3 1AB; URL www.mhra.org.uk; e-mail mlr@mhra.org.uk

General Editor   B. Richardson

Organisation: A journal of the Modern Humanities Research Association

Frequency: Quarterly; January, April, July, October

Music and Letters

Oxford Journals, Oxford University Press, Oxford, Oxfordshire OX2 6DP; Tel 01865 556767; Fax 01865 556646

All fields of musical enquiry, from earliest times to present day. Includes wide range of reviews, books, and scholarly editions of music of the past.

Published by: Oxford Journals

Frequency: Quarterly

Price of single issue: £39 (institutions), £16 (individuals)

Annual subscription: £133 (institutions), £50 (individuals)

Music Teacher

Rhinegold Publishing, 241 Shaftesbury Ave, London WC2H 8TF; URL www.rhinegold.co.uk; e-mail music.teacher@rhinegold.co.uk; Tel 020 7333 1747; Fax 020 7333 1769

Editor   Clare Stevens

Deputy Editor   Jonathan Wikeley

Assistant Editor   Ruth Garner

Frequency: Monthly

Price of single issue: £3.75

Annual subscription: £40 UK, £43 worldwide surface mail, £46 Europe airmail, £53 outside Europe airmail

Muslim Education Quarterly

The Islamic Academy, 205 Gilbert Rd, Cambridge, Cambridgeshire CB4 3PA; e-mail info@islamicacademy.ac.uk; Tel 01223 350976; Fax 01223 350976

Editor   Dr Shaikh Abdul Mabud

A review of Muslim education in the modern world, in both Muslim majority and Muslim minority countries, intended as a means of communication for scholars dedicated to the task of making education Islamic in character; also to act as an open forum for exchange of ideas between such scholars and others, including non-Muslims who hold contrary views

Annual subscription: £22.50 (individual), £35 (institutional); airmail: £35 (individual), £45 (institutional)

NASUWT 'Teaching Today'

NASUWT, Hills Court Centre, Rednal, Birmingham, West Midlands B45 8RS; e-mail lena.davies@mail.nasuwt.org.uk; Tel 0121 453 6150

Editor   Lena Davies

A 32 page full-colour journal

Frequency: Six times a year

New Era in Education

54 Fox Lane, London N13 4AL; e-mail subscriptions@neweraineducation.co.uk; Tel 01707 285677; Fax 01707 285616

Editor   Dr Dave Hinton

Education in an international context

Organisation: Journal of World Education Fellowship

Frequency: Three times a year

Annual subscription: £18 (individuals), £30 (institutions)

18

New Humanist

One Gower St, London WC1E 6HD;
URL www.newhumanist.org.uk; e-mail
info@newhumanist.org.uk; Tel 020 7436 1151;
Fax 020 7079 3588
Editor Caspar Melville
Frequency: Six a year
Annual subscription: £18

Newscheck

Trotman Publishing, 2 The Green, Richmond, Surrey
TW9 1PL; URL www.newscheck.co.uk; e-mail
helen.stokes@trotman.co.uk; Tel 020 8486 1217;
Fax 020 8486 1161
Editor Helen Stokes
Brings together careers and occupation-related information
and comment
Frequency: 10 issues a year
Annual subscription: Available

Notes and Queries

Oxford Journals, Oxford University Press, Oxford,
Oxfordshire OX2 6DP; Tel 01865 556767;
Fax 01865 267485
English language and literature, lexicography, history and
scholarly antiquarianism. Notes, readers' queries and
replies, book reviews. Each issue gives emphasis to the work
of a particular period.
Published by: Oxford Journals
Frequency: Quarterly
Price of single issue: £43 (institutions), £15 (individuals)
Annual subscription: £145 (institutions), £47 (individuals),
£41 (members), £30 (students)

Nursery Education Plus

Scholastic Magazines, Westfield Rd, Southam,
Warwickshire CV47 0RA; URL www.scholastic.co.uk;
e-mail nurseryedplus@scholastic.co.uk; Tel 0845 850 4411
Magazine with early years resources, including posters and
curriculum linked ideas. Linked community website for
early years.
Published by: Scholastic Magazines
Frequency: Monthly
Price of a single issue: £4.25
Annual subscription: £42.50; direct debit £39.99
Circulation: 22 000

Omnibus

Magazine of the Joint Association of Classical Teachers
(JACT), London WC1E 7HU; URL www.jact.org; e-mail
office@jact.org; Tel 020 7862 8719; Fax 020 7255 2297
Magazine of general classical interest, colour and fully
illustrated
Frequency: Two issues, Spring (January) and Autumn
(September)
Price of single issue: £3.30 plus postage
Annual subscription: £8.20 (UK), £10.60 (overseas)

Oxford Art Journal

Oxford Journals, Oxford University Press, Oxford,
Oxfordshire OX2 6DP; Tel 01865 556767;
Fax 01865 267485
Published by: Oxford Journals
Frequency: Three a year
Price of single issue: £52 (institutions), £17 (individuals)
Annual subscription: £142 (institutions), £40 (individuals),
£33 (members), £31 (students)

Oxford Journal of Legal Studies

Oxford Journals, Oxford University Press, Oxford,
Oxfordshire OX2 6DP; Tel 01865 556767;
Fax 01865 267485
Editor Ewan McKendrick
Emphasis on matters of theory and on broad issues arising
from the relationship of law to other disciplines, in
particular, legal philosophy and socio-legal matters. Articles
cover comparative and international law, EEC law, legal
history and philosophy and interdisciplinary material from
fields such as economics and sociology.

Published by: Oxford Journals
Frequency: Quarterly
Price of single issue: £58 (institutions), £22 (individuals)
Annual subscription: £196 (institutions), £71 (individuals),
£57 (members)

Paragraph

Edinburgh University Press, 22 George Sq, Edinburgh
EH8 9LF; URL www.eup.ed.ac.uk; e-mail
journals@eup.ed.ac.uk; Tel 0131 650 1000;
Fax 0131 662 0053
Editor Keith Reader
Journal in modern critical theory
Frequency: Three a year
Annual subscription: (Institutions) £68 UK; (individuals)
£30 UK/EU

Parliamentary History

Edinburgh University Press, 22 George St, Edinburgh
EH8 9 LF; URL www.eup.ed.ac.uk; e-mail
journals@eup.ed.ac.uk
Editor Clyve Jones
Research articles and papers of a general appeal on all
aspects of parliamentary history (including the Scottish and
Irish parliaments) from the middle ages to the twentieth
century, and legislatures in Britain's colonies before
independence, covering parliamentary management,
political structure, elections and the electorate, architecture
and representative art of the various parliaments
Frequency: Three a year
Annual subscription: (Individual) £40 UK/EC; (institution)
£85 UK/EC

Past and Present

Oxford Journals, Oxford University Press, Oxford,
Oxfordshire OX2 6DP; Tel 01865 556767;
Fax 01865 514010
Editor Lyndal Roper
Editor Chris Wickham
Primarily concerned with social, economic and cultural
changes, their causes and consequences, this highly readable
journal publishes a wide variety of scholarly and original
historical articles
Published by: Oxford Journals
Frequency: Quarterly
Price of single issue: £38 (institutions), £12 (individuals)
Annual subscription: £129 (institutions), £39 (individuals),
£38 (members), £22 (students)

Physics Education

Insititute of Physics Publishing Ltd, Dirac Hse, Temple Back,
Bristol BS1 6BE; Tel 0117 929 7481
Publisher Therese Quinton
Physics teaching for the 14–19 age level
Annual subscription: Institutions £268 (EU/rest of world),
special rates available for UK schools

Practical Pre-School

URL www.practicalpreschool.com; e-mail
enquiries@practicalpreschool.com; Tel 020 7738 5454;
Fax 020 7733 2325
Editor Sonali Hindmarch
Practical guidance for the foundation stage. Eight pages of
news, 32 pages of information and a colour frieze.
Frequency: 12 times a year
Practical Funding For Schools St Jude's Church, Dulwich Rd,
London SE24 0PB; URL www.practicalfunding.com;
e-mail enquiries@practicalfunding.com;
Tel 020 7738 5454; Fax 020 7733 2325
Editorial Director Rebecca Linssen
Monthly journal giving practical guidance on fundraising
for schools

Prep School

John Catt Educational Ltd, Gt Glemham, Saxmundham,
Suffolk IP17 2DH; URL www.johncatt.com; e-mail
enquiries@johncatt.co.uk; Tel 01728 663666;
Fax 01728 663415

Editor David Tytler; Abbey Cottage, Blythburgh, Suffolk IP19 9LH; Tel 01502 478521; Fax 01502 478776
Frequency: February, May and October
Price of single issue: £3
Annual subscription: £9

Primary Mathematics

The Mathematical Association, 259 London Rd, Leicester LE2 3BE; URL www.m-a.org.uk; e-mail equals@m-a.org.uk; Tel 0116 221 0013
Editor Lynne McClure
Frequency: Spring, summer, autumn

Primary Science Review

College La, Hatfield, Hertfordshire AL10 9AA; URL www.ase.org.uk; e-mail psreditor@ase.org.uk; Tel 01707 283000; Fax 01707 266532
Editor A. Peacock
Organisation: Association for Science Education
Frequency: September, November, January, March, May

Quarterly Journal of Mechanics and Applied Mathematics

Oxford Journals, Oxford University Press, Oxford, Oxfordshire OX2 6DP; Tel 01865 556767; Fax 01865 267485
Published by: Oxford Journals
Frequency: Quarterly
Price of single issue: £106 (institutions), £101 (individuals)
Annual subscription: £358 (institutions), £322 (individuals), £214 (members)

Race Equality Teaching

Trentham Books Ltd, Westview Hse, 734 London Rd, Oakhill, Stoke-on-Trent ST4 5NP; URL www.trentham-books.co.uk; e-mail tb@trentham-books.co.uk; Tel 01782 745567; Fax 01782 745553
Editor Gillian Klein
Focuses on teaching and learning in multi-ethnic schools and communities
Formats: Online
Frequency: Three times a year
Price of single issue: £16
Annual subscription: UK £39 (including postage), overseas £49 (including surface postage); online £176

RE Today

RE Today, 1020 Bristol Rd, Selly Oak, Birmingham, West Midlands B29 6LB; URL www.retoday.org.uk; e-mail lat@retoday.org.uk; Tel 0121 472 4242; Fax 0121 472 7575
Editor Lat Blaylock
Magazine for religious education teachers
Frequency: Three times a year
Annual subscription: £28
Circulation: Approx. 5000

Renaissance Studies

Blackwell Publishing, 9600 Garsington Rd, Oxford, Oxfordshire OX4 2DQ; Tel 01865 776868; Fax 01865 714591
Editor Andrew Hadfield
All aspects of Renaissance history and culture. The journal prints multidisciplinary papers on the history, art, architecture, religion, literature and language of any European country or any country influenced by Europe during the Renaissance period.
Published by: Blackwell Publishing
Formats: Print, online
Annual subscription: £212 (institutions), £183 (institutions – online only), £24 (members)

Report

Editorial, 7 Northumberland St, London WC2N 5RD; URL www.atl.org.uk; e-mail info@atl.org.uk; Tel 020 7782 1591; Fax 020 7925 0529
Organisation: Magazine of the Association of Teachers and Lecturers (ATL)
Frequency: 10 times a year
Annual subscription: £16 UK

Research in Education

Manchester University Press, Oxford Rd, Manchester M13 9PL; URL www.manchesteruniversitypress.co.uk; Tel 0161 273 5539
Executive Editor Prof Ivan Reid
International, interdisciplinary research in education.
Published by: Manchester University Press
Frequency: Twice a year

Review of English Studies

Oxford Journals, Oxford University Press, Oxford, Oxfordshire OX2 6DP; Tel 01865 556767; Fax 01865 267485
English literature and the English language from the earliest period up to the present day. Articles, notes, reviews of recent books, and a summary of periodical literature.
Published by: Oxford Journals
Frequency: Five a year
Price of single issue: £46 (institutions), £13 (individuals)
Annual subscription: £192 (institutions), £51 (individuals), £43 (members), £33 (students)

Safety Education

RoSPA, Royal Society for the Prevention of Accidents, Birmingham, West Midlands B5 7ST; URL www.rospa.com; e-mail jcave@rospa.com; Tel 0121 248 2000; Fax 0121 248 2001
Managing Editor Janice Cave
Head (Safety Education) Peter Cornall
Frequency: Termly
Annual subscription: £12.50 members, £15 non-members

Sage Publications

1 Olivers Yard, 55 City Rd, London EC1Y 1SP; URL www.sagepub.co.uk; e-mail order@sagepub.co.uk; Tel 020 7324 8500; Fax 020 7324 8600
Price of single issue: Single print back issues: £32 (individual), £66 (institutions)
Annual subscription: £98 (individual), £249 (institutions)

School Leadership and Management

Taylor and Francis Journals, 4 Park Sq, Milton Pk, Abingdon, Oxfordshire OX14 4RN; URL www.tandf.co.uk/journals; e-mail enquiries@tandf.co.uk; e-mail journal.orders@tandf.co.uk
A journal concerned with the relationship between leadership and organisational change.
ISSN: 1363-2434 available online (applied for). Online ISSN 1364-2626
Published by: Routledge
Formats: Online
Frequency: Five issues a year
Annual subscription: £641 (institutions – print and online), £608 (institutions – online only), £132 (individuals – print only)

The School Librarian

School Library Association, Unit 2, Lotmead Business Village, Wanborough, Swindon SN4 0UY; URL www.sla.org.uk; e-mail info@sla.org; Tel 01793 791787; Fax 01793 791786
Editor Steve Hird
Reviews Editor Chris Brown
ICT Website Reviews Editor Elspeth Scott
Articles and extensive review sections on books, websites and CD-ROMs for school use
Frequency: Four times a year
Annual subscription: Current rates available from the chief executive

School Science Review

The Association for Science Education, College La, Hatfield, Hertfordshire AL10 9AA; URL www.ase.org.uk; e-mail ssreditor@ase.org.uk; Tel 01707 283000; Fax 01707 266532
Editor Geoff Auty
Frequency: March, June, September and December

18

Schools ETC

ContinYou,, 17 Old Ford Rd, London E2 9PJ;
    URL www.continyou.org.uk; e-mail
    schoolsetc@continyou.org.uk; Tel 020 8709 9900;
    Fax 020 8709 9933
Editor   Paddy O'Dea

Science Teacher Education

College La, Hatfield, Hertfordshire AL10 9AA;
    URL www.ase.org.uk; e-mail steeditor@ase.org.uk;
    Tel 01707 283000; Fax 01707 266532
Editor   Neil Burton
Organisation: Association for Science Education
Frequency: Three times a year

Scottish Educational Journal

46 Moray Pl, Edinburgh EH3 6BH; URL www.eis.org.uk;
    e-mail kblackwell@eis.org.uk; Tel 0131 225 6244;
    Fax 0131 220 3151

Scottish Journal of Political Economy

Department of Economics, University of Stirling, Stirling
    FK9 4LA; URL www.blackwellpublishing.com; e-mail
    sjpe@stir.ac.uk; Tel 01786 466412; Fax 01786 466414
Subscriptions: Blackwell Publishing Ltd, PO Box 1269, 9600
    Garsington Rd, Oxford, Oxfordshire OX4 2ZE
Editor   Prof Robert Hart
Frequency: Five times a year
Annual subscription: Personal £44; institutional £209

Screen (incorporating Screen Education)

Subscriptions/Enquiries: Oxford Journals, Oxford
    University Press, Oxford, Oxfordshire OX2 6DP;
    Tel 01865 556767; Fax 01865 267485
Editorial: Screen, John Logie Baird Centre, Glasgow
    University, Glasgow G12 8QQ; Tel 0141 330 5035;
    Fax 0141 330 8010
Journal of film and television studies. Contributions by
leading critics, academics, and film makers.
Published by: Oxford Journals
Frequency: Quarterly
Price of single issue: £35 (institutions), £15 (individuals)
Annual subscription: £119 (institutions), £47 (individuals),
    £38 (members), £28 (students)

Social History of Medicine

Oxford Journals, Oxford University Press, Oxford,
    Oxfordshire OX2 6DP; Tel 01865 556767;
    Fax 01865 267485
Editor   Dr Brian Dolan
Editor   Prof Bill Luckin
Concerned with all aspects of health, illness and medical
treatment in the past, and committed to publishing work on
the social history of medicine from a variety of disciplines
Published by: Oxford Journals
Frequency: Three a year
Price of single issue: £50 (institutions)
Annual subscription: £126 (institutions), £37 (members)

Speaking English – ideas and developments in oral education

Journal of the English Speaking Board (International), 26a
    Princes St, Southport, Merseyside PR8 1EQ;
    URL www.esbuk.org; e-mail admin@esbuk.org;
    Tel 01704 501730
Editor   Rosemary Ham
Frequency: Twice a year (March and September)
Annual subscription: £35 individual, £50 corporate, UK and
    overseas

Statute Law Review

Oxford Journals, Oxford University Press, Gt Clarendon St,
    Oxford, Oxfordshire OX2 6DP
Editor   Prof T. St John N. Bates;   Strathclyde University
The legislative process, use of legislation as an instrument of
public policy, and the drafting and interpretation of
legislation
Published by: Oxford Journals
Frequency: Three a year

Annual subscription: £169 (institutions), £76 (individuals),
    £61 (members)
Circulation: £67 (institutions), £32 (individuals)

Studies in the Education of Adults

The National Institute of Adult Continuing Education, 21 De
    Montfort St, Leicester LE1 7GE; URL www.niace.org.uk;
    e-mail subscriptions@niace.org.uk; Tel 0116 204 4200
Editor   Prof Miriam Zukas
An international refereed journal, it is aimed at academic
specialists, postgraduate students, practitioners and
educational managers who wish to keep abreast of theory-
building and empirical research in continuing education
Formats: Online access available to subscribers
Frequency: Biannual
Annual subscription: UK: £33 (individuals), £88
    (institutions); rest of Europe, North America, Australasia,
    Japan: £44 (individuals), £104 (institutions); rest of world:
    £22 (individuals), £33 (institutions)

Support for Learning (The British Journal of Learning Support)

University of Northampton School of Education, Boughton
    Green Rd, Northampton, Northamptonshire NN2 7AL;
    e-mail philip.garner@northampton.ac.uk;
    Tel 01604 892418; Fax 01604 716375
Subcriptions: Basil Blackwell, 108 Cowley Rd, Oxford,
    Oxfordshire OX4 1JF; Tel 01865 791100
Editor   Philip Garner
Organisation: A journal of NASEN
Frequency: Quarterly
Annual subscription: Institutions £103

Supporting Teaching and Learning About the Environment and Birds

RSPB, Youth and Education Dept, The Lodge, Sandy,
    Bedfordshire SG19 2DL; URL www.rspb.org.uk/youth;
    Tel 01767 680551
The RSPB is the charity which takes action for wild birds.
The RSPB Youth and Education Department provides a
range of classroom resources and projects for primary
teachers and students, based on birds and the environment
and linked to the national curriculum.
Organisation: RSPB
Frequency: Three times a year

Symmetry Plus

The Mathematical Association, 259 London Rd, Leicester
    LE2 3BE; URL www.m-a.org.uk; Tel 0116 221 0013
Editor   Martin Perkins
Aimed at pupils and students of all ages, but particularly
10–18. Each issue includes articles, puzzles, problems and
competitions for those who enjoy mathematics.

The Teacher

The National Union of Teachers, Hamilton Hse, Mabledon
    Pl, London WC1H 9BD; e-mail teacher@nut.org.uk;
    Tel 020 7380 4708; Fax 020 7383 7230
Editor   Ellie Campbell-Barr
Journalist   Janey Hulme
Administration   Maryam Hulme
Circulation Department Records and Subscription Services
Department
Frequency: Eight issues a year
Annual subscription: Free to NUT members

Teaching Geography

The Geographical Association, 160 Solly St, Sheffield, South
    Yorkshire S1 4BF; URL www.geography.org.uk; e-mail
    info@geography.org.uk; Tel 0114 296 0088;
    Fax 0114 296 7176
Hon Editor   Margaret Roberts
Frequency: Termly
Annual subscription: Rates available

Teaching History

The Historical Association, 59a Kennington Park Rd,
    London SE11 4JH; e-mail enquiry@history.org.uk;
    Tel 020 7735 3901; Fax 020 7582 4939

Editor Christine Counsell; The Historical Association, 59a Kensington Pk Rd, London SE11 4JH
Frequency: January, April, June, October
Annual subscription: £45 (including membership)

Theatre Research International

Cambridge Journals, The Edinburgh Bldg, Shaftesbury Rd, Cambridge, Cambridgeshire CB2 2RU
Editor Freddie Rokem
History of criticism of drama conceived as the art of the theatre, providing both a medium of communication for scholars and a service to students of art, architecture, design, music and dramatic literature
Published by: Cambridge Journals
Annual subscription: £118 (institutions – print and online), £106 (institutions – online only), £31 (individuals)

The Times Educational Supplement

26 Red Lion Sq, Holborn, London WC1R 4HQ; URL www.tes.co.uk; e-mail (letters to editor) letters@tes.co.uk; e-mail (magazine features)features@tes.co.uk; Tel 020 3194 3289; Fax (advertising) 020 7782 3333; Fax 020 3194 3200
Editor Karen Dempsey
Frequency: Weekly; Friday
Price of single issue: £1.40
Annual subscription: £9.00 for 13 weeks by direct debit. After 13 weeks £45 a year by direct debit.

The Times Higher Education

26 Red Lion Sq, Holborn, London WC1R 4HQ; URL www.thes.co.uk; e-mail editor@thes.co.uk; Tel 020 3194 3000; Fax 020 3194 3300
Editor Gerard Kelly
Formats: Online
Frequency: Weekly; Friday
Price of single issue: £1.40
Annual subscription: £55; direct debit £45

TJ Online

10 Bartholomews Wlk, The Cambridgeshire Business Pk, Ely, Cambridgeshire CB7 4EH; URL www.trainingjournal.com; e-mail contact@trainingjournal.com; Tel 01353 654877; Fax 01353 663644
Editor Debbie Carter
Publication for learning and development.
Frequency: 12 times a year
Annual subscription: £137 UK

T Mag

11 King's Par, Cambridge, Cambridgeshire CB2 1SJ; URL www.tmag.co.uk; e-mail mail@tmag.co.uk; Tel 01223 358700; Fax 01223 358766
Editor Ester Reid
Frequency: 10 issues a year
Annual subscription: £99.95

Tuttitalia

Italian Journal of Association for Language Learning, School of Modern Languages, University of Leicester, University Rd, Leicester LE1 7RH; URL www.all-languages.org.uk; e-mail info@all-languages-org.uk; Tel 0116 229 7453
Editor Dr Sonia Cunico
Articles, reviews and information of special interest to learners and teachers of Italian
Frequency: Twice a year (March and September)
Annual subscription: £70 (UK), £85 (EU), £95 (overseas). Available to members of the Association for Language Learning as part of their membership package. Membership subscription £50, reduced for students and part-time and retired teachers.

UC

University and College Union, 27 Britannia St, London WC1X 9JP; URL www.ucu.org.uk; e-mail britannia@ucu.org.uk; Tel 020 7837 3636; Fax 020 7837 4403

Articles of general interest on higher education and trade union matters; incorporates 'Equalise' Section (Equal Opportunities Section)
Frequency: Termly; October, January and April
Price of single issue: Free to members

Under 5

Pre-school Learning Alliance, The Fitzpatrick Bldg, 185 York Way, London N7 9AD; URL www.pre-school.org.uk; e-mail editor.u5@pre-school.org.uk; Tel 020 7697 2500; Fax 020 7697 8607
Editor Anna Roberts
Play and learning for under-fives, at home and in pre-school
Frequency: Monthly except August and December
Annual subscription: Included in annual subscription for members. Magazine only: £30 non-members, £12.50 staff/parent in member groups.

The Use of English

The English Association University of Leicester, University Rd, Leicester LE1 7RH; URL www.le.ac.uk/engassoc; e-mail engassoc@le.ac.uk; Tel 0116 252 3982; Fax 0116 252 2301
Editor Ian BointonBrinton
Frequency: Three times a year; autumn, spring, summer
Annual subscription: £27 individuals, £54 institutions

UTU News

Ulster Teacher's Union, 94 Malone Rd, Belfast BT9 5HP; URL www.utu.edu; e-mail office.utu.edu; Tel 028 9066 2216; Fax 028 9068 3296
Editor Vacancy
Frequency: Termly
Annual subscription: Free to members

Vida Hispanica

Spanish and Portuguese journal
School of Modern Languages, University of Leicester, University Rd, Leicester LE1 7RH; URL www.all-languages.org.uk; e-mail info@all-languages.org.uk; Tel 0116 229 7453
Editor Prof Richard Littlejohns
Organisation: A journal of the Association for Language Learning
Annual subscription: £70 (UK), £85 (EU), £95 (overseas)

Viewpoint

123 Golden La, London EC1Y 0RT; e-mail viewpoint@mencap.org.uk; Tel 020 7696 5599
Organisation: Newspaper of MENCAP and Gateway

The Voice Journal

Journal of the Voice: the union for education professionals, Friar Gate, Derby DE1 1BT; URL www.voicetheunion.org.uk; e-mail pressoffice@voicetheunion.org.uk; Tel 01332 372337; Fax 01332 290310; Fax 01332 292431
Editorial Richard Fraser
Advertising R. Fraser
Frequency: Four times a year
Annual subscription: Free to members; £9.20 a year for non-members

Welsh Journal of Education

Cardiff School of Social Sciences, Glamorgan Bldg, King Edward VII Ave, Cardiff CF10 3WT; e-mail orders@press.wales.ac.uk; Tel 02920 875093; Fax 02920 230908
Editor Prof John Fitz
Reviews Editor Dr Sian Rhiannon Williams
The journal contains articles on issues of general educational interest
Frequency: Annual
Annual subscription: £30

18

Women: A Cultural Review

Taylor and Francis Journals, 4 Park Sq, Milton Pk, Abingdon, Oxfordshire OX14 4RN; Fax 020 7017 6000

Explores the role and representation of gender in culture and the arts

Published by: Routledge

Frequency: Three a year

Annual subscription: £216 (institutions – print and online), £205 (institutions – online only), £52 (individuals – print only)

The World Today

Chatham Hse, 10 St James Sq, London SW1Y 4LE; URL www.theworldtoday.org; e-mail wt@chathamhouse.org.uk; Tel 020 7957 5712; Fax 020 7957 5710

Editor Graham Walker

Assistant Editor Francesca Broadbent

Offers authoritative analysis and background on international political, economic and environmental issues for business people, academics, students, journalists, politicians and diplomats

Frequency: Monthly

Price of single issue: £2.50

Annual subscription: UK: students £28, individuals £35, institutions £80

Young People Now

Haymarket Publications, 174 Hammersmith Rd, London W6 7JP; Tel 020 8267 4707

Contact Steve Barrett

The weekly magazine for everyone working with young people

Frequency: Monthly

Annual subscription: Available

Educational Publishers

A & C Black (Publishers) Ltd

38 Soho Sq, London W1D 3HB; e-mail educationalsales@acblack.com; Tel 020 7758 0200; Fax 020 7758 0222

Managing Director Jill Coleman

Educational and children's books (including music) for primary, middle and secondary schools

Abacus Educational Services

20 Malvern Cl, Worthing, West Sussex BN11 2HE; e-mail peter.sussex@ntlworld.com; Tel 01903 521086

Proprietor Peter Cole

Abacus publishes booklets and organises conferences and insets for teachers and students of Religious Studies and Philosophy

Accelerated Learning Centre

Crown Bldgs, Bancyfelin, Carmarthenshire SA33 5ND; URL www.accelerated-learning.co.uk; e-mail learn@accelerated-learning.co.uk; Tel 01267 211880; Fax 01267 211882

Managing Director David Bowman

Articles of Faith Ltd

Resource Hse, Kay St, Bury, Lancashire BL9 6BU; URL www.articlesoffaith.co.uk; e-mail faith@resourcehouse.co.uk; Tel 0161 763 6232; Fax 0161 763 5366

Religious and historical artefacts and resource publishers

Barefoot Books

124 Walcot St, Bath, Somerset BA1 5BG; URL www.barefootbooks.com; e-mail info@barefootbooks.co.uk; Tel 01225 322400; Fax 01225 322499

Publishes a wide range of multicultural and cross-curricular books on many topics

Beam Education

Maze Workshops, 72a Southgate Rd, London N1 3JT; URL www.beam.co.uk; e-mail info@beam.co.uk; Tel 020 7684 3323; Fax 020 7684 3334

Managing Director Sheila Ebbutt

Primary maths publisher with range of games, books and materials. Runs courses for teachers and headteachers. Offers consultancy service to schools, LEAs and government departments.

Better Books and Software

3 Paganel Dr, Dudley, West Midlands DY1 4AZ; URL www.betterbooks.com; e-mail sales@betterbooks.com; Tel 01384 253276; Fax 01384 253285

Books on dyslexia, dyspraxia, autism, ADHD and other specific learning difficulties

Brilliant Publications

Unit 10, Sparrow Hall Farm, Edlesborough, Dunstable, Bedfordshire LU6 2ES; URL www.brilliantpublications.co.uk; e-mail info@brilliantpublications.co.uk; Tel 01525 222292; Fax 01525 222720

Publisher Priscilla Hannaford

BSB Publishers and Education Consultants

Bhatia Hse, 174 Peartree St, Derby DE23 8PL; URL www.alternative-energy-source.co.uk; e-mail brijindersingh.bhatia@ntlworld.com; Tel 01332 608279; Fax 01332 608279; Mobile 07888 840114

Contact M.K. Bhatia BSc(Hons), MA

Publishers and distributors of education, power station maintenance, electricity generation by alternative methods books and education consultants

Butterworth-Heinemann

Linacre Hse, Jordan Hill, Oxford, Oxfordshire OX2 8DP; Tel 01865 474110; Fax 01865 474111

Engineering and technology, business, media, scientific and technical

Cambridge University Press

The Edinburgh Bldg, Shaftesbury Rd, Cambridge, Cambridgeshire CB2 2RU; URL www.cambridge.org; e-mail <initial><surname>@cambridge.org; Tel 01223 312393; Fax 01223 315052

Archaeology, art and architecture, educational (primary, secondary, tertiary, FE, micro software, information books), history, language and literature, law, linguistics, medicine, music, oriental studies, philosophy, economics, psychology, politics, sociology, anthropology, science (physical and biological), mathematics and computer science, social sciences, theology and religion, Bibles, reference books and prayer books, English language teaching, learned and scientific journals, examination papers.

Chambers Harrap Publishers Ltd

7 Hopetoun Cres, Edinburgh EH7 4AY; URL www.chambersharrap.co.uk; e-mail admin@chambersharrap.co.uk; Tel 0131 556 5929

Managing Director Patrick White

Monolingual and bilingual dictionaries, reference books and EFL titles

Child's Play (International) Ltd

Ashworth Rd, Bridgemead, Swindon SN5 7YD; URL www.childs-play.com; e-mail office@childs-play.com; Tel 01793 616286; Fax 01793 512795

Co-ordinator (Educational Sales and Liaison) Beth Cox

Collins Education, HarperCollins

77–85 Fulham Palace Rd, Hammersmith, London W6 8JB; URL www.collinseducation.com; e-mail education@harpercollins.co.uk; Tel 020 8741 7070; Fax 020 8307 4440

Primary, secondary and further education publishing in all major subject areas: Literacy, Numeracy, English and

Drama, Mathematics, Modern Foreign Languages, ICT, Religious Education, PSHE and Citizenship, Special Needs, Business, Economics, Sociology, Psychology, Leisure and Tourism, Health and Social Care. Collins Education is an imprint of HarperCollins Publishers who also publish English and bilingual dictionaries for all levels, children's books and study and revision guides for Key Stages 2–3, GCSE and AS level.

Continuum International Publishing Group
The Tower Bldg, 11 York Rd, London SE1 7NX;
URL www.continuumbooks.com; e-mail
mgreen@continuumbooks.com; e-mail
<initial><surname>@continuumbooks.com;
Tel 020 7922 0880; Fax 020 7928 7894
Commissioning Editor (Education and Childcare)   Jo Allcock
Continuum International publishes professional books for teachers, students and academics

Dorling Kindersley
Penguin Group, 80 Strand, London WC2R 0RL;
URL www.dk.com; Tel 020 7010 3000; Fax 020 7010 6694
Marketing Director   Catherine Bell

Drake Educational Associates
St Fagans Rd, Fairwater, Cardiff CF5 3AE;
URL www.drakeed.com; e-mail info@drakeed.com;
Tel 02920 560333; Fax 02920 560313
Language Master System and extensive range of audio card programmes and Learning to Listen, Action Phonics, Word Power, alphabet, modern languages. Support cards for Oxford Reading Tree, Ginn 360, Fuzzbuzz, Wellington Square and Jolly Phonics. Phonics study mats, wallcharts, audio-cassettes, Wonder Mats and Wonder Blocks. Teacher reference books.

Easylearn
Trent Hse, Fiskerton, Southwell, Nottinghamshire
NG25 0UH; URL www.easylearn.co.uk; e-mail
enquiry@easylearn.co.uk; Tel 01636 830240;
Fax 01636 830162
Wide variety of English and maths materials for pupils with SEN. Includes a large number of photocopiable books all with clear, easy-to-use worksheets, games, software and posters. All materials designed with the small steps approach in mind.

Education Publishing Company Ltd
Devonia Hse, 4 Union Terr, Crediton, Devon EX17 3DY;
URL www.educationpublishing.com; e-mail
info@educationpublishing.com; Tel 01363 774455
Managing Director   D. Coryton

Edu-Fax
PO Box 94, Hadleigh, Suffolk IP7 5AA;
URL www.edu-fax.com; e-mail info@edu-fax.com;
Tel 01473 652822; Fax 01473 652822
Contact   Julie Girling
Contact   Simon Girling
Reference and planning documents for teachers, governors and inspectors in the nursery, primary, secondary and FE areas, including the Edu-Fax range of curricula, associated orders, and frameworks. Everything published is loose-leaf within a personal organiser binder.

Emerald Group Publishing Ltd
60–62 Toller La, Bradford, West Yorkshire BD8 9BY;
URL www.emeraldinsight.com/insight;
Tel 01274 777700; Fax 01274 785200

The English Association
University of Leicester, University Rd, Leicester LE1 7RH;
URL www.le.ac.uk/engassoc; e-mail engassoc@le.ac.uk;
Tel 0116 252 3982; Fax 0116 252 2301
President   Peter J. Kitson
Chief Executive   Helen Lucas
Chair   Maureen Moran
Treasurer   Roger J. Claxton

To further knowledge, understanding and enjoyment of the English language and its literature, by means of conferences (five annually), lectures, journals and annual publications

English Heritage
Waterhouse Sq, 138–142 Holborn, London EC1N 2NH;
URL www.english-heritage.org.uk; e-mail
education@english-heritage.org.uk; Tel 020 7973 3000
English Heritage Education offers interactive workshops and guided tours for school groups; extensive learning resources and teacher training opportunities

European Schoolbooks Ltd
Ashville Trading Est, The Runnings, Cheltenham,
Gloucestershire GL51 9PQ; URL www.eurobooks.co.uk;
e-mail direct@esb.co.uk; Tel 01242 245252;
Fax 01242 224137
Books, video and other audio-visual and multimedia materials for foreign language teaching at all levels; paperback literature and background books in French, German, Spanish and Italian; subscription service for foreign newspapers and magazines; topic maps for geography and current affairs

Evans Brothers Ltd
2a Portman Mansion, Chiltern St, London W1U 6NR;
URL www.evanbooks.co.uk; e-mail
sales@evansbrothers.co.uk; Tel 020 7487 0920;
Fax 020 7487 0921
Managing Director   Stephen Pawley

Folens Ltd
Albert Hse, Apex Business Centre, Boscombe Rd, Dunstable,
Bedfordshire LU5 4RL; URL www.folens.com; e-mail
folens@folens.com; Tel 0870 609 1237
Managing Director   Adrian Cockell
Director (Publishing)   Peter Burton
All subjects for primary and secondary education, including Personal and Social Education, Mathematics, English, Science, Geography, History, Religious Education

Highflyers Publishing Ltd
25 St Leonards Ave, Stafford, Staffordshire ST17 4LT;
URL www.highflyerspublishing.co.uk; e-mail
info@highflyerspublishing.co.uk; Tel 01785 257744;
Fax 01785 228765

Hilda King Educational
Ashwells Manor Dr, Penn, High Wycombe,
Buckinghamshire HP10 8EU;
URL www.hildaking.co.uk; e-mail hkinged@aol.com;
Tel 01494 813947; Fax 01494 813947
Director   Hilda King
Publishes educational books for both mainstream and SEN (English Language, Mathematics, History, Geography, French and nursery)

James Clarke & Co
PO Box 60, Cambridge, Cambridgeshire CB1 2NT;
URL www.jamesclarke.co.uk; e-mail
publicity@jamesclarke.co.uk; Tel 01223 350865;
Fax 01223 366951
The academic imprint of Lutterworth Press
Academic and scholarly books, reference, the biennial Libraries Directory.

John Catt Educational Ltd
Gt Glemham, Saxmundham, Suffolk IP17 2DH;
URL www.schoolsearch.co.uk; e-mail
enquiries@johncatt.co.uk; Tel 01728 663666;
Fax 01728 663415
Managing Director   Jonathan Evans

Kube Publishing Ltd
Ratby La, Markfield, Leicestershire LE67 9SY;
URL www.islamic-foundation.com;
www.kubepublishing.com; e-mail
info@kubepublishing.com; Tel 01530 249230;
Fax 01530 249656

18

Publisher of academic and scholarly books on Islam with more than 900 titles

Ladybird Books

Penguin UK, 80 Strand, London WC2R 0RL;
URL www.ladybird.co.uk; Tel 020 7010 3000;
Fax 020 7010 6707

Director (Marketing)   Gill Thomas
Director (Publishing)   Stephanie Barton
Publishers of colour-illustrated children's books

Learning Materials Ltd

Dixon St, Wolverhampton, West Midlands WV2 2BX;
URL www.learningmaterials.co.uk; e-mail
learning.materials@btinternet.com; Tel 01902 454026;
Fax 01902 457596

Managing Director   A.S. Wood
Educational suppliers for SEN

Letts Educational

The Chiswick Centre, 414 Chiswick High Rd, London
W4 5TF; URL www.letts-education.com; e-mail
schools@lettsed.co.uk; Tel 020 8996 3333;
Fax 020 8742 8390

Manager (Schools Marketing)   Charis Evans
Letts Educational is part of the Granada Learning Group
Providers of primary, secondary and further education
classroom and revision resources, both print and electronic.

Lifetime Publishing

Mill Hse, 58 Stallard St, Trowbridge, Wiltshire BA14 8HH;
URL www.lifetime-publishing.co.uk; e-mail
sales@lifetime-publishing.co.uk; Tel 01225 716023;
Fax 01225 716025

Publishers of careers information books and software;
careers education, citizenship and PSHE resources

Lion Hudson Plc

Mayfield Hse, 256 Banbury Rd, Oxford, Oxfordshire
OX2 7DH; URL www.lionhudson.com; e-mail
enquiries@lionhudson.com; Tel 01865 302750;
Fax 01865 302757

Director (Sales)   John O'Nions
Manager (Marketing: Children's)   Georgina Elms
Religious Education books (primary and secondary) for
class and library use

The Lutterworth Press

PO Box 60, Cambridge, Cambridgeshire CB1 2NT;
URL www.lutterworth.com; e-mail
publicity@lutterworth.com; Tel 01223 350865;
Fax 01223 366951

Main range: religious education for primary, secondary and
sixth form levels, extensive school library list

McGraw-Hill Education

Shoppenhangers Rd, Maidenhead SL6 2QL;
URL www.mcgraw-hill.co.uk; Tel 01628 502500;
Fax 01628 777342

Managing Director   Paul Maraviglia
Textbooks for computer science, engineering, economics
and business studies at colleges and universities, business
computing and engineering at professional levels. Reference
books, dictionaries and encyclopedias.

Music Sales Ltd

Newmarket Rd, Bury St Edmunds, Suffolk IP33 3YB;
URL www.musicroom.com; e-mail
music@musicsales.co.uk; Tel 01284 702600;
Fax 01284 768301

Marketing   Ruth McKegney
Music publisher incorporating Chester Music, Golden
Apple, Novello, Schirmer, UME, Bosworth, Shawnee Press
and Hal Leonard. Pre-school to further education.

Nelson Thornes Ltd

Delta Pl, 27 Bath Rd, Cheltenham, Gloucestershire
GL53 7TH; URL www.nelsonthornes.com; e-mail
cservice@nelsonthornes.com; Tel 01242 267100;
Fax (general) 01242 221914; Fax (orders) 01242 253695

Managing Director   Fred Grainger

Network Continuum Education

The Tower Bldg, 11 York Rd, London SE1 7NX;
URL www.networkcontinuum.co.uk; e-mail
enquiries@networkcontinuum.co.uk; Tel 020 7922 0880;
Fax 020 7922 0881

Old Vicarage Publications

Reades La, Dane in Shaw, Congleton, Cheshire CW12 3LL;
e-mail williamball@supanet.com; Tel 01260 279276;
Fax 01260 298913

Primary Classics and Art and Craft, secondary Classics and
Rural and Environmental Studies; tertiary Classics, History
and Rural and Environmental Studies

Ordnance Survey

Romsey Rd, Southampton SO16 4GU;
URL www.ordnancesurvey.co.uk; e-mail
enquiries@ordsvy.gov.uk; Tel 0845 605 0505

The official mapping agency for Britain which publishes a
full range of maps and guides of the country in both
conventional and digital format

Oxford University Press

Educational Division, Gt Clarendon St, Oxford, Oxfordshire
OX2 6DP; Tel 01865 267684; Fax 01865 267989

Wide range of textbooks and reference books for infant,
primary and secondary schools, and colleges; children's
picture books, poetry, encyclopedias and information books
and fiction for children and young adults.

Palgrave Macmillan Ltd

Brunel Rd, Houndmills, Basingstoke, Hampshire RG21 6XS;
URL www.palgrave.com; e-mail
d.knight@palgrave.com; Tel 01256 329242;
Fax 01256 479476

Managing Director   Dominic Knight
Director (Sales)   Lorraine Keelan
Journals, textbooks and monographs for universities and
colleges

Pearson Assessment

80 Strand, London WC2R 0RL; URL www.pearson-uk.com;
e-mail info@pearson-uk.com; Tel 01865 888188

Primary, middle, secondary and educational psychology
tests and assessment systems

Pearson Education

Edinburgh Gate, Harlow, Essex CM20 2JE;
Tel 01279 623623; Fax 01279 431059

Pearson Education is the world's largest educational
publisher and the largest English-language teaching
publisher. It produces materials for pupils, students and
professionals from nursery school to postgraduate level
throughout the world.

Penguin Books Ltd

80 Strand, London WC2R 0RL; URL www.penguin.co.uk;
Tel 020 7010 2000

Product Development Office

Abbeygate Hse, East Rd, Cambridge, Cambridgeshire
CB1 1DB; URL www.ldalearning.com; Tel 0845 120 4776;
Fax 01223 460557

Manager (Product Development)   Cathy Griffin
Marketing   Steven Robinson
Publishers of educational books and materials for children
with SEN, from nursery to secondary education. Also
suitable for mainstream education.

Random House Children's Books

61–63 Uxbridge Rd, London W5 5SA;
URL www.kidsatrandomhouse.co.uk; e-mail
childrenspublicity@randomhouse.co.uk;
Tel 020 231 6439; Fax 020 8231 6767

Publish under the following imprints: Doubleday (hardback
fiction for all ages), ISBN prefix 0385; Corgi (Picture Corgi,
Corgi Pups, Young Corgi, Corgi – paperback fiction), ISBN
prefix 0552; Corgi Yearling (paperback fiction for 8–12),
ISBN prefix 0440; Random Imprints, ISBN prefix 0099 Red
Fox; 00917 Hutchinson Children's Books; 0224 Jonathan
Cape; 0370 The Bodley Head; 086264 Anderson Press; 18565
Tellastory

Routledge Education

4 Park Sq, Milton Pk, Abingdon, Oxfordshire OX14 4RN;
URL www.routledge.com/education; e-mail
info.education@tandf.co.uk; Tel 020 7017 6248

Early years, primary, secondary, tertiary, university

Sangam Books Ltd

57 London Fruit Exchange, Brushfield St, London E1 6EP;
e-mail sangambks@aol.com; Tel 020 7377 6399;
Fax 020 7375 1230

General list for all levels

Scripture Union

207–209 Queensway, Bletchley, Milton Keynes MK2 2EB;
URL www.scriptureunion.org.uk; e-mail
media@scriptureunion.org.uk; Tel 01908 856000;
Fax 01908 856111

Sound Ideas

117 Athelstan Rd, Bitterne, Southampton SO19 4DG;
Tel 02380 333405; Fax 02380 235128

Contact   Peter Webb

Produces educational materials for children, teenagers and
adults

Storysack Ltd

Resource Hse, Kay St, Bury, Lancashire BL9 6BU;
URL www.storysack.com; e-mail
hello@resourcehouse.co.uk; Tel 0161 763 6232;
Fax 0161 763 5366

Suppliers and publishers of storysacks for literacy,
numeracy, and other cross-curricular studies

Thomas Nelson and Sons Ltd

See Nelson Thornes Limited

THRASS (UK) Ltd

Units 1–3 Tarvin Sands, Barrow La, Tarvin, Chester,
Cheshire CH3 8JF; URL www.thrass.co.uk; e-mail
enquiries@thrass.co.uk; Tel 01829 741413;
Fax 01829 741419

Director   Alan Davies

Education Consultant   Hilary Davies

Office Manager   Rachel Woodward

Trains teachers in Europe, the Middle East, Africa, South
America, Central America and the USA to use the THRASS
(Teaching Handwriting Reading And Spelling Skills)
printed, audio and software materials, published by
THRASS (UK) Ltd

Trentham Books Ltd

Westview Hse, 734 London Rd, Oakhill, Stoke-on-Trent
ST4 5NP; URL www.trentham-books.co.uk; e-mail
tb@trentham-books.co.uk; Tel 01782 745567

Business Manager   Barbara Wiggins

Member of Education Publishers' Council

Trotman and Company Ltd

2 The Green, Richmond, Surrey TW9 1PL;
URL www.trotman.co.uk; e-mail
mina.patria@trotman.co.uk; Tel 020 8486 1150;
Fax 020 8486 1161

Editorial Director   Mina Patria

Careers and higher education material

Ward Lock Educational Co Ltd

Bic Ling Kee Hse, 1 Christopher Rd, East Grinstead, West
Sussex RH19 3BT; URL www.lingkee.com/wardlock;
e-mail orders@wleducat.freeserve.co.uk;
Tel 01342 318980; Fax 01342 410980

Company Secretary   E. Parsons

Books for teachers and students. Infant, junior and
secondary books. Kent Mathematics Project, Reading
Workshop, Target Science and Geography, Take Part series.

Wiley-Blackwell

9600 Garsington Rd, Oxford, Oxfordshire OX4 2DQ;
URL www.blackwelleducation.com; Tel 01865 776868;
Fax 01865 714591

National Library and Publishing Organisations

Advisory Councils

Community Service Volunteers – Education for Citizenship (CSV)

Registered Charity Number 291222

237 Pentonville Rd, London N1 9NJ;
URL ww.csvcommunitypartners.org.uk; e-mail
education@csv.org.uk; Tel 020 7643 1435;
Fax 020 7833 0149

Director   Peter Hayes

CSV – Education for Citizenship is a UK charity that
provides support for schools to help develop citizenship as
an active part of their curriculum. Practical tools, training
materials and learning workshops provide teachers, parents
and pupils with a no-nonsense approach to citizenship.
Projects include peer learning; role play situations
highlighting bullying, racism and sexism; surveying social
attitudes among pupils and local residents; and
intergenerational projects and initiatives to develop
communities through the arts, sciences and sport.

National Libraries

British Library

96 Euston Rd, London NW1 2DB; URL www.bl.uk; e-mail
visitor-services@bl.uk; Tel 020 7412 7332

Document Supply Services/Bibliographic Standards and
Systems: Boston Spa, Wetherby, West Yorkshire
LS23 7BQ; URL www.bl.uk/docsupply; e-mail (BLDS)
dsc-customer-services@bl.uk; e-mail (BSS)
bss-info@bl.uk; Tel (BLDS) 01937 546060; Tel (BSS)
01937 546548; Fax (BSS) 01937 546586; Fax (BLDS)
01937 546333

Director (British Library Document Supply Services)
Natalie Ceeney

British Library Document Supply Services (BLDS)

The BLDS offers remote supply of loans and copies,
delivered by mail, fax or secure PDF, in every field of study
and research, either direct to registered customers or
through a national network of local and academic libraries.
Registration is free. Many of the library's catalogues are
available on the internet through the British Library's public
catalogue (URL www.bl.uk/catalogue). This site offers a
document ordering link for registered and non-registered
customers. It is the largest organisation of this kind in the
world.

Bibliographic Standards and Systems (BSS)

The bibliographic services are widely used by libraries to
support current awareness, referencing and cataloguing.
The British National Bibliography (BNB) records UK and
Irish publications received on legal deposit: available as
MARC Exchange datafile, a CD-ROM and as a printed
publication. British Library Net, a free ISP, provides access
to cultural and educational websites.

18

British Library Sound Archive 96 Euston Rd, London
NW1 2DB; URL www.bl.uk/soundarchive; e-mail
sound-archive@bl.uk; Tel 020 7412 7676;
Fax 020 7412 7441
Co-ordinator (Service Development) S. Maskell

Listening Books
12 Lant St, London SE1 1QH;
URL www.listening-books.org.uk; e-mail
info@listening-books.org.uk; Tel 020 7407 9417;
Fax 020 7403 1377
Deputy Director Sam Fletcher

National Library for the Blind (NLB)
Far Cromwell Rd, Bredbury, Stockport, Greater Manchester
SK6 2SG; URL www.nlb-online.org; e-mail
enquiries@nlbuk.org; Tel 0161 355 2000;
Fax 0161 355 2098; Minicom 0161 355 2043
Chief Executive Helen Brazier
NLB lends a wide range of reading material from its
extensive collection of braille and Moon books and braille
music. NLB also provides access to electronic books and
reference material via its website.

National Library of Scotland
George IV Bridge, Edinburgh EH1 1EW; URL www.nls.uk;
e-mail enquiries@nls.uk; Tel 0131 623 3700;
Fax 0131 623 3701
Librarian Martyn Wade BA, MLib, ALA

National Library of Wales
National Library of Wales, Aberystwyth, Ceredigion
SY23 3BU; URL www.llgc.org.uk; e-mail
holi@llgc.org.uk; Tel 01970 632800; Fax 01970 632882
Librarian Andrew M.W. Green

**REACH – National Advice Centre for Children with
Reading Difficulties**
California Country Pk, Nine Mile Ride, Finchampstead,
Berkshire RG40 4HT; e-mail
reach@reach-reading.demon.co.uk; Tel (information
helpline) 0845 604 0414; Tel (voice and text)
0118 973 7575; Fax 0118 973 7105

Library and Publishers Associations

**ASCEL (Association of Senior Children's and Education
Librarians)**
Warwickshire Schools Library Service, Unit 11G, Montague
Rd, Warwick, Warwickshire CV34 5LT; e-mail
celiamerriman@warwickshire.gov.uk; Tel 01926 413462
Hon Secretary Celia Merriman
ASCEL's members are those librarians who have senior
managerial responsibility for providing library services to
children and young people in England and Wales. The
association covers both public library services and school
library services (those provided by education departments
and those provided by public libraries).

ASLIB
Staple Hall, Stone House Ct, London EC3A 7PB;
URL www.aslib.com; e-mail aslib@aslib.com;
Tel 020 7903 0000; Fax 020 7903 0011
Chief Executive Roger N. Bowes
Chair of Council Prof C. Turner
Manager (Training) Catherine Clarke

**Association of Learned and Professional Society
Publishers**
8 Rickford Rd, Nailsea, Bristol BS48 4PU;
URL www.alpsp.org; e-mail ian.russell@alpsp.org
Chief Executive Ian Russell
Manager (Finance and Admin) Ian Hunter
Manager (Member Services) Nick Evans
Co-ordinator (Membership and Advertising)
Sazy Fotheringham
Co-ordinator (Seminars and Website) Lesley Ogg

Co-ordinator (Training) Amanda Whiting
Administrative Assistant Diane French

Books for Keeps
1 Effingham Rd, London SE12 8NZ;
URL www.booksforkeeps.co.uk; e-mail
enquiries@booksforkeeps.co.uk; Tel 020 8852 4953;
Fax 020 8318 7580
Managing Director Richard Hill

Booksellers Association of the UK and Ireland Ltd
Minster Hse, 272 Vauxhall Bridge Rd, London SW1V 1BA;
URL www.booksellers.org.uk; e-mail
mail@booksellers.org.uk; Tel 020 7802 0802;
Fax 020 7802 0803
Chief Executive T.E. Godfray

Booktrust
Book Hse, 45 East Hill, London SW18 2QZ;
URL www.booktrust.org.uk; e-mail
query@booktrust.org.uk; Tel 020 8516 2977;
Tel 020 8516 2987
Chair Prof Kimberley Reynolds
Executive Director Viv Bird
Executive Director Allison Morrison
Hon Treasurer Nigel Williams

Federation of Children's Book Groups
2 Bridge Wood View, Horsforth, Leeds, West Yorkshire
LS18 5PE; URL www.fcbg.org.uk; e-mail
info@fcbg.org.uk; Tel 0113 258 8910

**Chartered Institute of Library and Information
Professionals**
7 Ridgmount St, London WC1E 7AE; e-mail
info@cilip.org.uk; Tel 020 7255 0620; Fax 020 7255 0501;
Textphone 020 7255 0505
Chief Executive Bob McKee PhD, MIInfSc, FRSA, ALA

The Publishers Association
29b Montague St, London WC1B 5BW;
URL www.publishers.org.uk; e-mail
mail@publishers.org.uk; Tel 020 7691 9191;
Fax 020 7691 9199
President Mike Boswood
Vice-President Ian Hudson
Chief Executive Simon Juden
Academic and Professional Division 29b Montague St,
London WC1B 5BW; URL www.publishers.org.uk;
e-mail mail@publishers.org.uk; Tel 020 7691 9191;
Fax 020 7691 9199
Chair Jon Walmsley
Vice-Chair Richard Greener
Director Graham Taylor
The Academic and Professional Division is a division of
the Publishers' Association, whose function is to control
policy and activities concerning academic and
professional publishing in the UK
Educational Publishers' Council
Chair Kate Harris
Vice-Chair Robert Ince
Director Graham Taylor

School Library Association
Registered Charity Number 313660
Unit 2 Lotmead Business Village, Lotmead Farm,
Wanborough, Swindon, Wiltshire SN4 0UY;
URL www.sla.org.uk; e-mail info@sla.org.uk;
Tel 0870 777 0979; Fax 0870 777 0987
President Gervase Phinn
Chief Executive Kathy Lemaire BA, DipLib, MCLIP, FRSA
Production Editor Usha Cooper
The School Library Association is a charity which supports
and promotes the aims and development of school libraries
and school library services through advocacy, training,
advice and publications

Welsh Books Council
Castell Brychan, Aberystwyth, Ceredigion SY23 2JB;
URL www.wbc.org.uk; e-mail
castellbrychan@wbc.org.uk; Tel 01970 624151;
Fax 01970 625385
Director   Gwerfyl Pierce Jones

Welsh Books Council   Distribution Centre, Glanyrafon
Enterprise Pk, Aberystwyth, Ceredigion SY23 3AQ;
URL www.gwales.com; e-mail
distribution.centre@wbc.org.uk; Tel 01970 624455;
Fax 01970 625506

Broadcasting, Audio-Visual Education, Computers in Education

19

Educational Broadcasting

Audio-Visual Education

Computers in Education

Broadcasting, Audio-Visual Education, Computers in Education

Educational Broadcasting

BBC (British Broadcasting Corporation)

BBC Media Centre, 201 Wood La, London W12 7TS;
  URL www.bbc.co.uk/learningoverview
Head (BBC Northern Ireland); Editor (Learning)   Jane Cassidy
Head (BBC Scotland); Executive Editor (Learning)
  Nick Simons
Head (BBC Wales: Education and Learning)
  Dr Eleri Wyn Williams; e-mail eleriwyn.lewis@bbc.co.uk
Head (Learning)   Liz Cleaver
Head (Learning: Policy and Public Affairs)   Wendy Jones
The BBC provides educational output, both formal and
informal, across a range of public service media in the UK. It
offers extensive learning content for both children and
adults online, and supports a range of life skills. The BBC
uses digital technology to build on the strengths and
popularity of factual TV and radio programmes and make
them the starting point for online learning through which
people are encouraged to foster general interests in subjects
such as science or history, or to develop specific skills for
work, life and leisure. The BBC works with a range of
educational partners, including government agencies,
libraries, colleges and schools, and it has a longstanding
relationship with the Open University, based on a mutual
commitment to lifelong learning.

BBC Regional Offices

BBC Birmingham   BBC Broadcasting Centre, Pebble Mill Rd,
  Birmingham, West Midlands B5 7QQ;
  URL www.bbc.co.uk; Tel 0121 432 8888;
  Fax 0121 432 9949
BBC North   New Broadcasting Hse, PO Box 27, Manchester
  M60 1SJ; Tel 0161 200 2020
BBC Scotland   Broadcasting Hse, Queen Margaret Dr,
  Glasgow G12 8DG; URL www.bbc.co.uk/education/
  scotland; e-mail aileenmccoll@bbc.co.uk;
  Tel 0141 338 1527
  *Administrator (Educational Broadcasting Council for
  Scotland)*   Aileen McColl
BBC Wales   Broadcasting Hse, Llantrisant Rd, Llandaff,
  Cardiff CF5 2YQ; URL www.bbc.co.uk/wales/
  education; Tel 02920 322834
BBC Northern Ireland   BBC Northern Ireland, Broadcasting
  Hse, Ormeau Ave, Belfast BT2 8HQ; e-mail
  education.ni@bbc.co.uk; Tel 028 9033 8000
  Editor (Learning)   Jane Cassidy

Broadcasting Support Services
Director   Keith Smith
This service is independent of the BBC and offers support
for a wide range of broadcasts in the areas of social concern
and education

Independent Television Companies

Anglia Television Ltd
Anglia Hse, Norwich, Norfolk NR1 3JG;
  URL www.angliatv.com; Tel 01603 615151
Managing Director   Graham Creelman
Controller (Regional Programmes)   Neil Thompson
Head (Regional Affairs)   Jim Woodrow
Anglia Television broadcasts to the East of England
covering Norfolk, Suffolk, Cambridgeshire, Essex,
Bedfordshire, Northamptonshire and parts of Hertfordshire
and Buckinghamshire

Carlton Television
101 St Martins La, London WC2N 4AZ;
  URL www.carlton.com; Tel 020 7240 4000

Channel Four Television Corporation
124 Horseferry Rd, London SW1P 2TX;
  URL www.channel4.com; Tel 01926 436444;
  Fax 01926 436446

Channel Television
Television Centre, St Helier, Jersey JE1 3ZD, Channel
  Islands; URL www.channeltv.co.uk; e-mail
  broadcast@channeltv.co.uk; Tel 01534 816816;
  Fax 01534 816817
Managing Director   Karen Rankine

Discovery Network Europe
160 Gt Portland St, London W1W 5QA; Tel 020 7462 3600;
  Fax 020 7462 3700
Managing Director (Home and Leisure)   Joyce Taylor
Director (Corporate Communications)   Virginia Lee

ITV Central
Gas St, Birmingham, West Midlands B1 2JT;
  URL www.itvlocal.com/central; e-mail
  caroline.newman-belshaw@itv.com; Tel 0844 881 4000
Regional Affairs Assistant   Caroline Newman-Belshaw

ITV Wales
Television Centre, Culverhouse Cross, Cardiff CF5 6XJ;
  URL www.itvwales.com; e-mail
  public.relations@itvwales.com; Tel 0844 881 0100

ITV West Country
Western Wood Way, Language Science Pk, Plymouth
PL7 5BQ; URL www.itv.com/westcountry; e-mail
news@westcountry.co.uk; Tel 01752 333333

ITV Yorkshire
The Television Centre, Kirkstall Rd, Leeds, West Yorkshire
LS3 1JS; URL www.itvlocal.com/yorkshire;
Tel 0113 243 8283; Fax 0113 243 3655
Editor (Calendar, Daily News Magazine Programme)
Will Venters

Independent Local Radio

Bath's GWR (103 FM Stereo)
PO Box 2000, 1 Passage St, Bristol BS99 7SN;
URL www.gwrfmbath.co.uk; Tel (studio) 01225 448888;
Tel (sales) 01793 663019

BRMB Radio Group
Nine Brindley Pl, 4 Oozells Sq, Birmingham, West Midlands
B1 2DJ; URL www.brmb.co.uk; Tel 0121 250 0964
Managing Director Jane Turnbull
Editor (News) Kevin Pashby

Radio Broadland (102.4 FM)
St George Plain, Colegate, Norwich, Norfolk NR3 1DB;
URL www.radiobroadland.co.uk; e-mail
sara.hardman@gcapmedia.com; Tel 01603 671148
Programme Controller Steve Martin
Manager (Sales) Ros Walker
Editor (News) Harry Mitchell

95.8 Capital FM (95.8FM, 1548AM)
30 Leicester Sq, London WC2H 7LA;
URL www.capitalfm.com; Tel 020 7766 6000;
Fax 020 7766 6195
Programme Director Scott Muller

Chiltern Radio
South: Hertfordshire, Bedfordshire and Buckinghamshire –
VHF 97.6 and 828AM; North: Bedford and South West
Cambridgeshire – VHF 96.9 and 792AM
Broadcast Centre, Chiltern Rd, Dunstable, Bedfordshire
LU6 1HQ; Tel 01582 666001
Managing Director C.R. Mason

Classic Gold Digital WABC (330m/990KHz MW)
267 Tettenhall Rd, Wolverhampton, West Midlands
WV6 0DE; Tel 01902 461297; Fax 01902 461266
A Beacon sister-station

Clyde 1 (102.5FM)
PO Box 1025, Clydebank, Glasgow G81 2HQ;
URL www.clyde1.com; e-mail clyde1@srh.co.uk;
Tel 0141 565 2200; Fax 0141 565 2265

Clyde 2 (1152KHz)
PO Box 1152, Clydebank, Glasgow G81 2RX;
URL www.clyde2.com; e-mail clyde2@srh.co.uk;
Tel 0141 565 2200; Fax 0141 565 2265

2 CR-FM (102.3FM) Classic Gold 828 (828AM)
5–7 Southcote Rd, Bournemouth BH1 3LR;
URL www.2crfm.co.uk; e-mail
newsbournemouth@gcapmedia.com; Tel 01202 234900;
Fax 01202 234909
Programme Controller Lucinda Holman

Downtown Radio (96.4, 96.6, 97.1, 102.3, 102.4, 103.1, 103.4 FM; 1026 AM)
Newtownards, County Down BT23 4ES;
URL www.downtown.co.uk; e-mail
programmes@downtown.co.uk; Tel 028 9181 5555;
Fax 028 9181 5252
Managing Director Mark Mahaffy

102.7 Hereward FM Gold (1332 AM)
Queensgate Centre, PO Box 225, Peterborough,
Cambridgeshire PE1 1XJ; URL www.hereward.co.uk;
e-mail <firstname>.<surname>@gcapmedia.com;
Tel 01733 460460; Fax 01733 281379
Programme Controller Tom Haynes
Editor (News) Sarah Spence
Manager (Admininistration) Carole Smith

Magic AM; South Yorkshire (990, 1305, 1548 MW)
Radio Hse, 900 Herries Rd, Sheffield, South Yorkshire
S6 1RH; URL www.magicam.co.uk; Tel 0114 209 1000;
Fax 0114 285 3159
Programme Director Anthony Gay
Deputy Programme Director Darrell Woodman

Marcher Sound/Sain-Y-Gororau (VHF 103.4 and 238m)
The Studios, Gwersyllt, Wrexham LL11 4AF;
Tel 01978 722266
Managing Director Clive Douthwaite
Programme Controller Lisa Marrey
Head (News) Alina Cavanagh

Mercury FM (102.7 and 97.5FM)
The Stanley Centre, Kelvin Way, Crawley, West Sussex
RH10 9SE; e-mail
<firstname>.<surname>@gcapmedia.com;
Tel 01293 519161; Fax 01293 560927
Programme Controller Andrew Danley
Manager (Sales Centre) Jo Lee
Team Leader (Sales) Sarah Barnfield

Northants 96
19–21 St Edmunds Rd, Northampton, Northamptonshire
NN1 5DY; URL www.musicradio.com; e-mail
reception@northants96.musicradio.com;
Tel 01604 795600; Fax 01604 795601
Programme Controller Colin Paterson
Programme Controller Richard Neale
Office Manager Julie Boyall

Northsound Radio (1035AM and 96.9FM)
Abbotswell Rd, Aberdeen AB12 3RS; Tel 01224 337000;
Fax 01224 400003
Managing Director Adam Findlay
Editor (News) Russ Cadlan
Head (Northsound One and Two) Luke McCullough

Radio Aire/Magic 828
51 Burley Rd, Leeds, West Yorkshire LS3 1LR;
URL www.radioaire.co.uk; Tel 0113 283 5500;
Fax 0113 283 5501
Chair R.M. Walker
Managing Director Steve King
Director (Programmes) Stuart Baldwin
Technical Manager Bob Fox
Editor (News) Tim White
Contact (Sales) Roz Whitney

Radio City 96.7 and Magic 1548
St John's Beacon, 1 Houghton St, Liverpool, Merseyside
L1 1RL; URL www.radiocity.co.uk; Tel 0151 472 6800;
Fax 0151 472 6821
Managing Director Iain McKenna
Programme Director Richard Maddock

Radio Forth Ltd
Forth One (97.3 MHz, 97.6 MHz and 102.2 MHz); Forth Two
(1548 KHz)
Forth Hse, Forth St, Edinburgh EH1 3LE;
URL www.forthone.com; www.forth2.com; e-mail
info@forthone.com; e-mail info@forth2.com;
Tel 0131 556 9255; Fax 0131 558 3277
Managing Director Adam Findlay

Red Dragon FM
The Red Dragon Centre, Cardiff CF10 4DJ;
URL www.reddragonfm.co.uk; e-mail
mail@reddragonfm.co.uk; Tel 02920 942954

Red Rose Radio Ltd (VHF 97.3 and 301m) Red Rose Gold (AM 999) Red Rose Rock (FM 97.4)

PO Box 301, St Paul Sq, Preston, Lancashire PR1 1YE;
Tel 01772 556301
Managing Director   A.J. Dewhurst
Joint Programme Director (AM and FM)   Jeff Graham
Editor (News)   Marian Kenny

SGRfm – Ipswich (97.1FM) and Bury St Edmunds (96.4FM)

Alpha Business Pk, 6–12 Whitehouse Rd, Ipswich, Suffolk
IP1 5LT; URL sgrfm.co.uk; e-mail
enquiries@musicradio.com; Tel 01473 461000;
Fax 01473 741200
Managing Director   Gavin Marshall
Programme Controller   Dan Thorpe
Head (News)   Sonia Clark
Manager (Sales)   Nick Maley

Signal Radio (102.6 and 96.9FM) and BIG (1170AM)

Stoke Rd, Shelton, Stoke-on-Trent, Staffordshire ST4 2SR;
URL www.signal1.co.uk; www.big1170.co.uk; e-mail
info@signalradio.com; e-mail
<initial>.<surname>@signalradio.com; Tel 01782 441300;
Fax 01782 441341
Director (Station)   Chris Hurst
Director (Sales)   Lisa Hughes
Programme Manager (BIG AM)   Mark Chivers
Programme Manager (Signal 1)   Mark Franklin
Editor (News)   Paul Sheldon
Engineer   Simon Davies

Southern FM (102.4FM, 103.5FM)

PO Box 2000, Brighton, East Sussex BN41 2SS;
URL www.southernfm.com; e-mail
info@southernradio.co.uk; Tel 01273 430111;
Fax 01273 430098
Managing Director   R. Hoad
Programme Controller   Tony Aldridge
Director (Sales)   Deirdre Lythe

TFM Radio (96.6FM) and Magic (1170MW)

Yale Cres, Teesdale, Thornaby, Stockton-on-Tees TS17 6AA;
URL www.tfmradio.co.uk; Tel 01642 888222;
Fax 0870 429 9104
Chair   Jack Charlton OBE
Managing Director   Sally Aitchison
Programme Director   Chris Rick
Director (Sales)   Matthew Bromham
Head (News and Sport)   Hayley Brewer
Manager (Marketing)   Ben Murphy
Station Engineer   Richard Craig

TRENT FM (Nottingham 96.2FM and Mansfield 96.5FM)

Chapel Quarter, Maid Marian Way, Nottingham NG1 6JR;
URL www.trentfm.co.uk; e-mail
reception.nottingham@gcapmedia.com;
Tel 0115 873 1500; Fax 0115 873 1569
Managing Director   Howard Bradley

Viking FM (96.9FM) and Magic 1161

Commercial Rd, Kingston upon Hull, East Riding of
Yorkshire HU1 2SG; URL www.vikingfm.co.uk;
www.magic1161.co.uk; e-mail
reception@vikingfm.co.uk; Tel 01482 325141
Programme Director   Darrell Woodman
Director (Sales)   Matthew Bromham
Viking Radio is part of EMAP Group

96.4FM The Wave and Swansea Sound (1170MW)

Victoria Rd, Gowerton, Swansea SA4 3AB;
URL www.thewave.co.uk; e-mail info@thewave.co.uk;
Tel 01792 511170 (Swansea Sound);
Tel 01792 511964 (The Wave);
Fax 01792 511965 (The Wave);
Fax 01792 511171 (Swansea Sound)
Chair   John Josephs

West Sound (1035AM; 96.7, 97.5, 103, 97, 96.5FM Stereo)

Radio Hse, 54a Holmston Rd, Ayr, South Ayrshire KA7 3BE;
URL www.westsound.co.uk; e-mail
west-sound@srh.co.uk; Tel 01292 283662;
Fax 01292 262607
Chair   Richard Findlay
Managing Director   Sheena Borthwick
Programme Director   Alan Toomey

Wiltshire's GWR FM (97.2 and 102.2 FM Stereo)

1st Fl, Chiseldon Hse Swindon Wiltshire, Stonehill Grn,
Westlea, Swindon, Wiltshire SN5 7HB;
URL www.gwrfm.co.uk; Tel 01793 663010;
Fax 01793 663009

19

Audio-Visual Education

National Bodies

British Film Institute

21 Stephen St, London W1T 1LN; URL www.bfi.org.uk/
education; e-mail education@bfi.org.uk;
Tel 020 7255 1444
Chair of Board of Governors   Greg Dyke
Director   Amanda Nevill
Head (Education)   Mark Reid
BFI Education develops education about film, television and
video at all levels of the education system through events,
publishing, research and lobbying. It holds conferences,
INSET, events for schools and for the general public. More
information about resources, events and research reports is
available on the website.

British Universities Film and Video Council

77 Wells St, London WIT 3QJ; URL www.bufvc.ac.uk;
e-mail ask@bufvc.ac.uk; Tel 020 7393 1500;
Fax 020 7393 1555
Director   Murray Weston

Children's Film and Television Foundation Ltd

Elstree Studios, Borehamwood, Hertfordshire WD6 1JG;
e-mail annahome@cftf.onyxnet.co.uk; Tel 020 8953 0844;
Fax 020 8207 0860
Chief Executive; Director   Grainne Marmon;   Development
Executive
The foundation is a non-profitmaking organisation which
helps to finance the development of scripts for children and
family feature films through its subsidiary company CFF
Enterprises. This company administers a £300 000 fund,
jointly financed by the foundation, the BBC and the Film
Council. The foundation also has a back catalogue of more
than 200 hours of film, available from Granada
International.

National Film and Television School

Beaconsfield Studios, Station Rd, Beaconsfield,
Buckinghamshire HP9 1LG; URL www.nftsfilm-tv.ac.uk;
e-mail admin@nftsfilm-tv.ac.uk; Tel 01494 671234;
Tel (short course unit) 01494 677903; Fax 01494 674042
President   Lord Richard Attenborough CBE
Director   Nik Powell
Chair (Board of Governors)   Michael Kuhn
Deputy Chair (Board of Governors)   Peter Bazalgette
The UK's leading film school, the NFTS offers a variety of
programmes. A two-year MA allows students to specialise
in one of 10 professional disciplines: Screenwriting,
Producing, Directing (Animation, Documentary or Fiction),
Production Design, Cinematography and Post-production
(Editing, Composing and Sound). Diploma courses varying
in length from 12 to 15 months are available in Digital Post-
production; Sound Recording; Producing for Television –
Entertainment; and Visual and Special Effects Producing;
and a two-year part-time Diploma in Script Development is
run in partnership with The Script Factory.

Annual intake is in January for MA courses and most diploma courses; the Diploma in Visual and Special Effects Producing starts at Easter while the Sound Recording Diploma starts in September. Application deadlines are between March and October, depending on specialism. Applicants usually have a first degree and/or relevant experience, and must be able to demonstrate talent, commitment to team working and some experience in their chosen specialisation. For a prospectus, call the registry The NFTS Short Course Unit is the leading provider of cost-effective short courses for people already working in the industry. A wide range of courses of varying length allows people to upgrade their skills, learn to handle new technologies and develop their careers. Further information from the Short Course Unit.

Other Film, Visual and Aural Education Organisations

Abacus Teaching Systems
Bryn Hir, Blaenau Ffestiniog, Gwynedd LL41 4LG;
   Tel 01766 762576; Fax 01766 762579
Managing Director   G. Price
Pneumatic teaching equipment, including electropneumatic and PLC

Active Visual Supplies Ltd
5 High St, Wellington, Telford, Shropshire TF1 1JW;
   URL www.activeuk.com; e-mail sales@activeuk.com;
   Tel 01952 250166; Fax 01952 249766
Director   M. Doughty
Manufacture, supply and installations of a full range of audio-visual teaching, presentation, and display equipment for schools, colleges, and private training organisations. Products include TV, video, LCD projectors, plasma screens, interactive whiteboards, overhead projection, rear projection equipment, general presentation equipment (including whiteboards, flipcharts etc.) and furniture.

ASLIB Multimedia Group
Staple Hall, Stone Hse Ct, London EC3A 7PB;
   URL www.aslib.com; e-mail aslib@aslib.com;
   Tel 020 7903 0000; Fax 020 7903 0011
Secretary   Sergio Angelini; British Film Institute, 21 Stephen St, London W1P 2LN; URL www.bfi.org.uk; e-mail sergio.angelini@bfi.org.uk; Tel 020 7255 2268; Fax 020 7436 2338

Audio-Visual Association
Herkomer Hse , 156 High St, Bushey, Hertfordshire WD23 3HF; Tel 020 8950 5959
Secretary   M.A. Simpson FBIPP

AVP
School Hill Centre, Chepstow, Monmouthshire NP16 5PH;
   URL www.avp.co.uk; e-mail info@avp.co.uk;
   Tel 01291 625439; Fax 01291 629671
Managing Director   Mark Thomas
AVP is a publisher and one stop shop for educational software and resources. Supplies online resources, CD-ROMS, DVDs, cameras, books and finger puppets.

British Federation of Film Societies
21 Stephen St, London W1P 1PL; URL www.filmsoc.org/bffs-scotland; Tel 020 7255 1444; Fax 020 7255 2315
General Secretary   Tom Brownlie

British Federation of Film Societies Scotland
28 Thornyfiat Rd, Ayr, South Ayrshire KA8 0LX;
   URL www.filmsoc.org/bffs-scotland; e-mail scotland@bffs.org.uk; Tel 01292 283136; Fax 01292 283435
Secretary   R. Currie

British Library Sound Archive
96 Euston Rd, London NW1 2DB; URL www.bl.uk/soundarchive; e-mail sound-archive@bl.uk;
   Tel 020 7412 7676; Fax 020 7412 7441
Service Development Officer   Richard Fairman

BSS
Registered Charity Number 282264
International Hse, 7 High St, London W5 5DB;
   URL www.bss.org; e-mail marketing@bss.org
Chief Executive   Peter Calderbank
A non-profitmaking charity, BSS provides impartial information services to the public on behalf of broadcasters, voluntary and public sector organisations, in order to promote social inclusion and diversity, educational, health and social issues

Camerawork
121 Roman Rd, London E2 0QN; e-mail cam@camwork.demon.co.uk; Tel 020 8980 6256; Fax 020 8983 4714
Gallery and photographic darkroom; exhibitions, short courses, workshops, talks

Community Service Volunteers (CSV)
237 Pentonville Rd, London N1 9NJ; URL www.csv.org.uk;
   Tel 020 7278 6601; Fax 020 7833 0149
CSV creates opportunities for people to participate actively in their community through volunteering training, education and the media.
Each year CSV works with more than 150 000 volunteers, provides more than 123 000 weeks of training, and works in partnerships with more than 1600 schools and colleges, and 100 radio and TV stations nationwide.

Concord Media
22 Hines Rd, Ipswich, Suffolk IP3 9BG;
   URL www.concordmedia.org.uk; e-mail sales@concordmedia.org.uk; Tel 01473 726012; Fax 01473 274531
An educational audio-visual library specialising in social documentary material, the arts and medical subjects

CTVC
Hillside Studios, Merry Hill Rd, Bushey, Watford, Hertfordshire WD23 1DR; e-mail barrie.allcott@ctvc.co.uk; Tel 020 8950 4426; Fax 020 8950 1437
Director   Barrie Allcott

Education Services at the Puppet Centre Trust
The Puppet Centre, Battersea Arts Centre, Lavender Hill, London SW11 5TN; URL www.puppetcentre.com;
   Tel 020 7228 5335
Workshops, courses, school visits, co-ordination of schools, residencies, publication

English Teaching Theatre
c/o 26 Petley Rd, London W6 9ST; e-mail ett@arcinter.net;
   Tel 020 7254 9199; Fax 020 275 8235
Director   Doug Case
Director   Hazel Imbert
Director   Ken Wilson
A professional theatre group producing shows for teenage and adult learners of EFL. Tours worldwide, with occasional performances in the UK.

Flite Electronics International Ltd
Church Hse Farm, Clewers Hill, Waltham Chase, Hampshire SO32 2LN; URL www.flite.co.uk; e-mail sales@flite.co.uk; Tel 01489 892422; Fax 01489 897929
Managing Director   Max D. Soffe
UK Sales   Suzanne Kittow
Educational micro electronics systems and instrumentation

Focal Point Audio Visual Ltd
1 Kew Pl, Cheltenham, Gloucestershire GL53 7NQ;
   URL www.focalpoint.f9.co.uk; e-mail cservice@focalpoint.force9.co.uk; Tel 01242 699051; Fax 01242 693118
General Manager   David Vincent
Suppliers of audio-visual resources for all levels of education: audio and video cassettes and CD-ROMs. Agents for BBC educational videos. Free lists available on request.

Gateway Television Productions

Gemini Hse, 10 Bradgate, Cuffley, Hertfordshire EN6 4RL;
URL www.gatewaytelevision.co.uk; Tel 01707 872054
Managing Director   G.L. Smart
Producers of video, film and tape/slide programmes for
training and education

ICA Films

Institute of Contemporary Arts, The Mall, London
SW1Y 5AH; Tel 020 7930 0493; Fax 020 7873 0051
Production and distribution of educational videos featuring
contemporary writers and artists

Institute of Amateur Cinematographers

24c West St, Epsom, Surrey KT18 7RJ; Tel 01372 739672;
Fax 01372 739672

Iris Audio Visual

Unit M, Forest Industrial Pk, Forest Rd, Hainault, Essex
IG6 3HL; URL www.iris-av.com; e-mail irisav@dasu.net;
Tel 020 8500 2846; Fax 020 8559 8780
Proprietor   Raymond Klarnett
Suppliers of audio-visual and photographic materials to
technical, scientific and educational users

JVC Professional Europe Ltd

JVC Hse, JVC Business Pk, 12 Priestley Way, London
NW2 7BA; URL www.jvcpro.co.uk
Director (Sales)   I. Scott
JVC Professional, through its Educational Partnership
initiative and network of specialist dealers, markets a full
range of standard and high definition video production,
storage, security, presentation and display products that
provide a comprehensive end-to-end solution for tutorial
staff and students

Learning and Teaching Scotland

The Optima, 58 Robertson St, Glasgow G2 8JD;
URL www.ltscotland.org.uk; e-mail
enquiries@ltscotland.org.uk; Tel 0141 282 5000;
Fax 0141 282 5050
Gardyne Rd, Dundee DD5 1NY; e-mail
t.wallace@itscotland.org.uk; Tel 01382 443600;
Fax 01382 443645
Chief Executive   Bernard McLeary
Chair   John Mulgrew

Listening Books

12 Lant St, London SE1 1QH;
URL www.listening-books.org.uk; e-mail
info@listening-books.org.uk; Tel 020 7407 7476;
Fax 020 7403 1377
Director   Bill Dee
Education and Children's Officer   Becky Perkes
Listening Books provides a postal audio library service to
anyone who has difficulty reading in the usual way, as a
result of illness, disability or learning difficulty. Its 'Sound
Learning' initiative aims to provide a wide range of
education audio texts for use by both schools and
individuals.
The audio books support the national curriculum from Key
Stage 2 to A-level. Listening Books offers set texts for English
and English Literature as well as books to support other
curriculum subjects such as History, Citizenship, Science,
Geography and Religious Studies.

London Film School Ltd

24 Shelton St, London WC2H 9UB; e-mail
film.school@lfs.org.uk; Tel 020 7836 9642
Director   Ben Gibson
Director (Student Services)   Flo Austin

Magiboards Ltd

Stafford Pk II, Telford, Shropshire TF3 3AY;
URL www.magiboards.com; e-mail
sales@magiboards.com; Tel 01952 292111
Contact   Julie Weston
Manufacturers and suppliers of visual aids for teaching and
training

BKSTS (The Moving Image Society)

5 Walpole Ct, Ealing Studios, Ealing Green, London
W5 5ED; URL www.bksts.com; e-mail
movimage@bksts.demon.co.uk; Tel 020 8584 5220;
Fax 020 8584 5230
Administration Officer   Katharine Osinska
Training Officer   Dominic O'Brien

Museums Association

42 Clerkenwell Cl, London EC1R 0PA; e-mail
info@museumsassociation.org; Tel 020 7608 2933;
Fax 020 7250 1929
Director   M. Taylor

The Other Cinema Film and Video Library

65 Hopton St, Bankside, London SE1 9LR; e-mail
sarah.claxton@principalmedia.com; Tel 020 7928 9287

Peakdean Interactive Limited

9 The South West Centre, Troutbeck Rd, Sheffield, South
Yorkshire S7 2QA; URL www.peakdean.co.uk; e-mail
peter.ross@peakdean.co.uk; Tel 0114 262 9230;
Fax 0114 255 2431
Director   Peter Ross
Peakdean Interactive is a specialist in open learning,
including interactive multimedia and web-based training. It
offers training for practitioners in the design of e-learning
and develops commissioned courseware for specific clients.

Pictorial Charts Educational Trust Ltd

27 Kirchen Rd, West Ealing, London W13 0UD;
URL www.pcet.co.uk; e-mail info@pcet.co.uk;
Tel 020 8567 9206; Fax 020 8566 5120
Manager (Production)   C. McNicholas
Publishers of wallcharts on a wide range of subjects to
support the national curriculum

Puppet Centre Trust

The Administrator, BAC, Lavender Hill, London
SW11 5TN; e-mail pct@puppetcentre.demon.co.uk;
Tel 020 7228 5335; Fax 020 7228 8863

The Royal Photographic Society

The Octagon, Milsom St, Bath, Somerset BA1 1DN;
URL www.rps.org; e-mail rps@rps.org; Tel 01225 462841
Manager (Education and Commercial)   Liz Williams

Royal Television Society

Registered Charity Number 313728
Kildare Hse, 3 Dorset Rise, London EC4Y 8EN;
URL www.rts.org.uk; e-mail info@rts.org.uk;
Tel 020 7822 2820; Fax 020 7822 2811
An educational charity with around 2000 members. The
society organises regional events where the arts, science and
politics of television can be discussed.

RSPB Education, The Royal Society for the Protection of Birds

Registered Charity Number 207076
The Lodge, Sandy, Bedfordshire SG19 2DL;
URL www.rspb.org.uk; e-mail education@rspb.org.uk;
Tel 01767 680551
The Royal Society for the Protection of Birds is a charity that
takes action for wild birds and the environment
RSPB Education provides resources for teachers using
electronic media and printed visual display materials. The
range of classroom resources is for primary teachers, linked
to the curriculum, and has been tested in classrooms by
teachers. Materials are free of charge. They focus on all the
main UK curricular subjects, and will help teachers cater for
new citizenship and education for sustainable development
requirements.
It also runs curriculum-linked teaching programmes for 5–
16 year olds on its reserves, and has a regional network of
education advisors. It produces bilingual resources for
teachers in Wales, and materials for teachers in Scotland. It
has an annual 'Big Schools Birdwatch' in January. For
downloadable resources, ideas and activities for children,
both in and out of the classroom, see the website.

RSPB Film Hire Library
Education Distribution Services, Education Hse, Drywall
Est, Castle Rd, Sittingbourne, Kent ME10 3RL; e-mail
info@edist.co.ukk; Tel 01795 427614
Manager Linda Gates

S&B UK Limited
Labtec St, Swinton, Manchester M27 8SE; Tel 0161 793 9333
Chair; Managing Director J. Goemans
Director (Sales and Marketing) M. Serridge
Company Secretary J.M. Almond
Manufacturers, distributors and installers of complete
science laboratories and design technology furniture

Scripture Union
207–209 Queensway, Bletchley, Buckinghamshire MK2 2EB;
URL www.scriptureunion.org.uk; e-mail
michaelw@scriptureunion.org.uk; Tel 01908 856000;
Fax 01908 856111
Publishers and suppliers of videos and cassettes on the Bible
and Christian life for all ages

The Society for Screen-Based Learning (Learning on Screen)
URL www.learningonscreen.org.uk
Administrator J. Key; Tel 01937 530520
Membership of Learning on Screen provides access to and
support from the society's growing number of specialists in
the UK and from overseas, including individual video
producers, broadcasters, multimedia developers, education
and online learning specialists. Learning on Screen members
share their expertise and knowledge about the field of
screen-based learning. Production awards (including
student category). Apply to the administrator for
membership and information.

Sound Ideas
117 Athelstan Rd, Bitterne, Southampton SO19 4DG;
URL www.sound-ideas.co.uk; e-mail
peterwebb@sound-ideas.co.uk; Tel 02380 333405;
Fax 02380 235128
Contact Peter Webb
Produces educational materials for children, teenagers and
adults

Tecmedia Ltd
Bruce Hse, 258 Bromham Rd, Biddenham, Bedfordshire
MK40 4AA; Tel 01234 325223; Fax 01234 353524
Managing Director J.D. Baxter
Company Secretary K. Paxton
Specialist in the design, development and production of
information and training packages, newsletters and other
publications

Tribal Tree
66c Chalk Farm Rd, London NW1 8AN;
URL www.musictree.net; www.tribaltreemusic.co.uk;
e-mail enquiries@tribaltreemusic.co.uk;
Tel 020 7482 6945; Fax 020 7485 9244
Aims to promote new talent and encourage new
opportunities for young producers from inner cities. Works
with charities and youth groups; runs music courses.

Uniview Worldwide Ltd
PO Box 20 Hoylake, Wirral CH48 7HY;
URL www.uniview.co.uk; e-mail sales@uniview.co.uk;
Tel 0151 625 3453; Fax 0151 625 3707
Provides online multimedia DVDs, CD-ROMs, videos and
games for education and health professionals covering
Psychology, Biology, Sociology, Sports Science, Philosophy,
Health and Social Care, Child Studies, PSHE and
Citizenship. See website for free resources and secure
ordering.

Wilson and Garden
17–21 Newtown St, Kilsyth, Glasgow G65 0JX;
URL www.wilsonandgarden.com; e-mail
info@wilsonandgarden.com; Tel 01236 823291;
Fax 01236 825683

Sales Manager (Scotland) Derek Hale
Part of The Ultralon Group.
Manufacturers of rollerboards, chalkboards, whiteboards,
display boards, notice boards, information boards,
flipcharts, projection screens and nursery furniture.

Computers in Education

National Bodies

Becta
Milburn Hill Rd, Science Pk, Coventry, West Midlands
CV4 7JJ; URL www.becta.org.uk; e-mail
becta@becta.org.uk; Tel 024 7641 6994; Fax 024 7641 1418
Chief Executive Stephen Crowne
Becta promotes the use of technology through learning

Other National Organisations

AVP
School Hill Centre, Chepstow, Monmouthshire NP16 5PH;
URL www.avp.co.uk; e-mail info@avp.co.uk;
Tel 01291 625439; Fax 01291 629671

British Computer Society
1st Fl, Block D, North Star Hse, North Star Ave, Swindon,
Wiltshire SN2 1FA; URL www.bcs.org; e-mail
customerservice@hq.bcs.org.uk; Tel 01793 417417

Ceefax
Rm 7013, BBC Television Centre, Wood La , London
W12 7RJ; Tel 020 8576 1801
Manager (Systems) Aidan Stowe
Editor Peter Clifton
Subtitling Ruth Griffiths
Ceefax, the BBC's teletext service, offers more than 2500
pages of current news and information

Joint Information Systems Committee
Northavon Hse, Coldharbour La, Bristol BS16 1QD;
URL www.jisc.ac.uk; e-mail m.read@jisc.ac.uk;
Tel 0117 931 7403; Fax 0117 931 7255
JISC Secretary Dr M. Read

University of London Computer Centre
20 Guildford St, London WC1N 1DZ; URL www.ulcc.ac.uk;
e-mail enquiries@ulcc.ac.uk; Tel 020 7692 1000;
Fax 020 7692 1234
Director Dr D. Rippon
Head (Application Services) J.M. Kahn
Head (Information Systems) D. Geary
Head (Infrastructure Services) S. Knibbs
Head (Support Services) D. Bramman

Micros and Primary Education
Chair Heather Govier; c/o Newman College, Bartley Grn,
Birmingham, West Midlands B32 3NT;
URL www.mape.org; Tel 0121 476 1181 ext 2270
Secretary Val Siviter

NCC Education
The Towers, Towers Business Pk, Wilmslow Rd, Didsbury,
Manchester M20 2EZ; URL www.nccedu.com; e-mail
marketing@nccedu.com; Tel 0161 438 6200;
Fax 0161 438 6240
Manager (Marketing) Emma Lowther
Global provider of IT training and education course
materials, education programmes and competence testing
software (ATS). Operates in more than 40 countries.

Scottish Regional Computer Education Centres
Head of Department Norman M. Smart
Department of Business Technology and Administration
Clyde Bank College, Kilbowie Rd, Clydebank, West
Dunbartonshire G81 2AA; Tel 0141 952 7771
Senior Lecturer in Computing R. Elliott

Edinburgh Centre for Computer Education, Moray Hse, College of Edinburgh, Holyrood Rd, Edinburgh EH8 8AQ; Tel 0131 556 8455
Contact P. Barker

Falkirk Computer Studies and Operations, Falkirk College of Technology, Grangemouth Rd, Falkirk F2 9AD; Tel 01324 24981
Head of Department Dr J.M. Sharp

Glasgow Department of Computer Education, Jordanhill, College of Education, Southbrae Dr, Glasgow G13 1PP; Tel 0141 950 3233
Contact J. Hawthorn

Schools' Computer Centre Dundas Vale Teachers' Centre, 6 New City Rd, Glasgow G4 9JR; Tel 0141 332 6762
Teacher-in-Charge K.W. Stapely

Universities and Colleges Information Systems Association (UCISA)
University of Oxford, 13 Banbury Rd, Oxford, Oxfordshire OX2 6NN; URL www.ucisa.ac.uk; e-mail admin@ucisa.ac.uk; Tel 01865 283425; Fax 01865 283426
Business Manager Sue Fells

Training

Advisory Unit – Computers in Education
The Innovation Centre, Hatfield, Hertfordshire AL10 9AB; URL www.advisory-unit.org.uk; e-mail sales@advisory-unit.org.uk; Tel 01707 281102; Fax 01707 281103
Director Diana Freeman
Provides school-based and in-service ICT training, both in schools and at the centre in Hatfield. Bespoke courses in all aspects of computer education are available on request.

City & Guilds
1 Giltspur St, London EC1A 9DD; URL www.cityandguilds.com; e-mail enquiry@cityandguilds.com; Tel 020 7294 2800; Fax 020 7294 2805
The UK's leading assessment and awarding body. An internationally recognised organisation offering more than 400 vocational qualifications, including NVQs, SVQs and modern apprenticeships. Qualifications are available in most job sectors.

City & Guilds Scotland
144 West George St, Glasgow G2 2HG; URL www.cityandguilds.com; e-mail scotland@cityandguilds.com; Tel 0141 341 5700; Fax 0141 341 5725
City & Guilds Scotland is part of the UK's largest vocational assessment and awarding body. A leading provider of SVQs and NVQs, offering a portfolio of more than 500 qualifications and a wide range of services to meet the needs of Scotland's business and education communities.

Computer Education Group
Staffordshire University, School of Computing, Beaconside, Stafford, Staffordshire ST18 0AD; Tel 01785 53511
The association for people involved with IT in education. Publishers of a journal written by teachers for teachers.

Department of Computer Science, University of York
Heslington, York YO10 5DD; URL www.cs.york.ac.uk; e-mail hod@cs.york.ac.uk; Tel 01904 432782; Fax 01904 432708
Education, research and consultancy in computing

Department of Computing, Imperial College London, Technology and Medicine
180 Queens Gate, London SW7 2BZ; URL www.doc.ic.ac.uk/go/admissions; e-mail ugadmissions@doc.ic.ac.uk; Tel 020 7594 8267
Contact Dr J.T. Bradley
Provides training in use of computers, undergraduate and postgraduate full-time courses in Computing Science, Software Engineering and MSc in Advanced Computing

Flite Electronics International Ltd
Church Hse Farm, Clewers Hill, Waltham Chase, Hampshire SO32 2LN; URL www.flite.co.uk; e-mail sales@flite.co.uk; Tel 01489 892422; Fax 01489 897929
Managing Director Max D. Soffe
Manager (IT) Josh Soffe
Office Manager Suzanne Kittow
Educational microelectronic systems and instrumentation

University of Huddersfield
School of Computing and Engineering, The University of Huddersfield, Queensgate, Huddersfield, West Yorkshire HD1 3DH; e-mail scom@hud.ac.uk; Tel 01484 472450; Fax 01484 421106
Admissions Co-ordinator Mrs J.M. Eastwood
HND, HNC, degree, MSc and professional courses in business computing software engineering, multimedia and IT. Research, consultancy, short courses.

University of Kent, MSc Computer Science
Computing Laboratory, The University of Kent, Canterbury, Kent CT2 7NF; URL www.cs.kent.ac.uk; e-mail computer-science@kent.ac.uk; Tel 01227 764000 ext 7694; Fax 01227 762811
Director (Computing Lab) Prof Simon Thompson
Course Convener Dr P. Kenny
Course Convener (MSc Distributed Systems and Networks) Gerald Tripp
Admissions Officer Dr Eerke Boiten
Admissions Officer (MSc Information Security and Biometrics) Dr Gareth Howells
Contact (MSc IT Consultancy) Dr Andrew Runnalls

LJ Group Ltd
Francis Way, Bowthorpe Industrial Est, Norwich, Norfolk NR5 9JA; URL www.ljgroup.com; e-mail sales@ljgroup.com; Tel 01603 748001
Managing Director L.J. Rowe
Director (Marketing) D.T. Breeze
Director (Sales) S.G. Jones
Director (Works) T.D. Whiting
Integrated learning systems for science and technology education, including computer-based classroom management, multimedia coursework and computer-linked hardware

Marjon Television Productions
College of St Mark and St John, Plymouth PL6 8BH; Tel 01752 777188; Fax 01752 761120
General Director Dr Paul Rolph
Projects Officer Richard Wallis
Produces a wide variety of video-based learning material and broadcasts television programmes

NEMEC National Electronics and Microtechnology Education Centre
University of Southampton, Southampton SO17 1BJ; Tel 02380 908800; Fax 02380 908888
Director P. Barnes
Develops and disseminates in-service training and publications in electronics and microtechnology to trainers and teaching staff from schools and further education

Origin Training
Origin UK Ltd, Walsall Rd, Cannock, Staffordshire WS11 3HZ; Tel 01543 463456
Manager (Training) R. Thorley
Specialists in development and delivery of tailored IT end user training solutions for all aspects of IT within the business

RM plc
New Mill Hse, 183 Milton Pk, Abingdon, Oxfordshire OX14 4SE; URL www.rm.com; Tel 0845 070 0300
RM is a leading supplier of ICT software, infrastructure and services to UK education. RM's work can include furnishing a single ICT suite, or providing complete, managed ICT services for whole regions.

School of Informatics

Appleton Tower, Crichton St, Edinburgh EH8 9LE;
    URL www.inf.ed.ac.uk; Tel 0131 650 2690

Undergraduate and postgraduate degrees in Computer
Science and Software Engineering. Joint degrees with
Electronic Engineering, Physics, Management Science and
Mathematics. MSc in Informatics, MSc by Research, PhD by
Research.

School of Computing Science, University of Newcastle upon Tyne

Newcastle upon Tyne, Tyne and Wear NE1 7RU;
    URL www.cs.ncl.ac.uk; e-mail
    chris.phillips@newcastle.ac.uk; Tel 0191 222 7975;
    Fax 0191 222 8232

Head of School   Prof P.A. Lee

Postgraduate and undergraduate degrees in computing
science

SITEC Training Ltd

Montford St, Salford, Greater Manchester M5 2SE;
    Tel 0161 745 8442; Fax 0161 745 9436

General Manager   George Robinson

Part-time IT training, PC installation, networking, business
computing for adults.

Full-time IT training for 16–18 year olds in PC installation
and networking; work placement and in-house training.
Full-time adult networking training and work placement.

Staff Development Management Systems Ltd (SDMS)

9 Pearson Rd, Central Pk, Telford, Shropshire TF2 9TX;
    URL www.sdmsltd.com; e-mail sales@sdmsltd.com;
    Tel 01952 200911; Fax 01952 201563

Managing Director   David Stevens

SDMS specialises in the design of computer systems for
human resource management and quality development. It
provides training management software for education and
social services in the UK, and has a growing customer base
in industry and other areas of public services. The current
software range includes Personnel, Staff Development and
Training Management, Training Needs Analysis, Training
Evaluation, Staff Review and Appraisal. Other specialist
areas include NVQ Learning and Skills Management,
Payroll and web-based INSET Management (Welsh
language version available). All products are fully
supported and are available across all the usual computer
platforms.

Wessex Institute of Technology (WIT)

Ashurst Lodge, Ashurst, Southampton SO40 7AA;
    URL www.wessex.ac.uk; e-mail carlos@wessex.ac.uk;
    Tel 02380 293223; Fax 02380 292853

Director   Prof C.A. Brebbia

WIT's activities include: an international conference
programme; graduate programmes at Master's and PhD
level; advanced research; publications, including books,
conference proceedings and journals; e-publishing
comprising the transactions of Wessex Institute; software
services

Educational Suppliers

Suppliers Associations and Purchasing Organisations

Equipment and Suppliers

Educational Suppliers

20

SUPPLIERS ASSOCIATIONS AND PURCHASING ORGANISATIONS

British Educational Suppliers Association (BESA)

See Equipment and Suppliers, for details of member organisations
20 Beaufort Ct, Admirals Way, London E14 9XL;
    URL www.besa.org.uk; e-mail besa@besa.org.uk;
    Tel 020 7537 4997; Fax 020 7537 4846
Director General   D.J.S. Savage
Director   Ray Barker
BESA is the trade association for the British educational supply industry. Members include manufacturers and distributors of equipment, materials, consumables, furniture, technology, ICT hardware and software related services. BESA members supply to the UK and international markets worldwide, across the curriculum and at all levels from early years to vocational training. All members agree to abide by the BESA Code of Practice.
Free access and advice from 300 members available in print (BESAbook 2007), online and in person.

CLAW, Consortium Local Authorities, Wales

Council Offices, Llangefni, Anglesey LL77 LTW;
    Fax 01248 752300
Chair of the Board of Officers   Michael Barton
The consortium is a unique association of Welsh local authorities. It assists its members with their technical requirements and problems associated with their varied building programmes. It provides to all participating members a wide range of sponsored building components and services obtained through competitive tendering for their building, maintenance and refurbishment programmes. Membership offers quality products approved by the consortium and preferential prices and services.
Specialised activities concentrate upon matters of energy efficiency, anti-vandal and property security measures, and a programme of computer aided design work.
Linking all together is a series of regular forums in which all member authorities are able to participate in wide-ranging exchanges of technical topics of mutual interest, currently highlighting 'best value' and 'fair funding'.
Members
County Councils: Anglesey, Blaenau Gwent, Bridgend, Caerphilly, Carmarthenshire, Ceredigion, Conwy, Denbighshire, Flintshire, Gwynedd, Merthyr Tydfil, Monmouthshire, Neath Port Talbot, Newport, Pembrokeshire, Powys, Rhondda Cynon Taf, Swansea, Torfaen, Vale of Glamorgan, Wrexham
Associate Member
North Wales Policy Authority

The Consortium

Hammond Way, Trowbridge, Wiltshire BA14 8RR;
    URL www.theconsortium.co.uk; e-mail
    enquiries@theconsortium.co.uk; Tel 0845 330 7733;
    Tel (customer enquiries) 0845 330 7780; Fax 0845 330 7785

Chief Executive   J.R. Gould FCIPS
Manager (Customer Support)   Vicky Elliott
Offers a wide choice of products, ranging from educational resources to catering services

Counties Furniture Group

Design Office, The Shirehall, Shrewsbury, Shropshire
    SY2 6ND; URL www.cfg.gov.uk; e-mail info@cfg.gov.uk;
    Tel 01743 253371; Fax 01743 253374
Design Officer   M. Davies;   Shropshire County Council
A non-profitmaking local authority company that provides furniture for education and office environments. Counties Furniture Group has 79 local authority members. It caters for nursery through to further education.

Engineering Training Equipment Manufacturers Association (ETEMA)

ETEMA/BESA, 20 Beaufort Ct, Admirals Way, London
    E14 9XL; URL www.etema.org.uk; e-mail
    besa@besa.org.uk; Tel 020 7537 4997; Fax 020 7537 4846
Chair   Vacancy
Co-ordinator (Member Services)   Mark Rosser
An association of UK manufacturers of teaching and training equipment for all forms and levels of engineering and technology for higher education and vocational training

Scape System Build Ltd

Chartwell Hse, 67–69 Hounds Gate, Nottingham NG1 6BB;
    URL www.scapebuild.co.uk; e-mail
    general@scapebuild.co.uk; Tel 0115 958 3200;
    Fax 0115 958 3232
An organisation dedicated to adding value into building projects. As a local authority controlled company its procedures and practices are right for the public sector.

Yorkshire Purchasing Organisation

41 Industrial Pk, Wakefield, West Yorkshire WF2 0XE;
    URL www.ypo.co.uk; Tel 01924 824477
Chair (Management Committee)   Cllr A. Senior
Director   Steve P. Atherton
A consortium of local authorities in the North of England which, on local government reorganisation in 1974, took over the functions of the former West Riding County Council Supplies Department. Its agency facilities are available to other local authorities and public bodies outside the consortium.
Operating on a commercial budget, the organisation is currently meeting the requirements of member and user authorities, either via its central stores complex or through the media of contractual arrangements.
Member Authorities
Barnsley, Bolton, Bradford, Bury, Calderdale, Doncaster, Kirklees, Knowsley, North Yorkshire, Rotherham, St Helens, Wakefield, Wigan, City of York
User Authorities
Most of the authorities throughout the North of England and beyond

EQUIPMENT AND SUPPLIERS

BESA-Accredited Suppliers

See Suppliers Associations and Purchasing Organisations
for BESA information

@Schools
Jupiter Hse, Calleva Pk, Aldermaston, Berkshire RG7 8NN;
URL www.schools.plc.uk; e-mail info@ukplc.net;
Tel 0870 486 6003; Fax 0870 486 6001

2Simple Software Ltd
Enterprise Hse, 2 The Crest, Hendon, London NW4 2HN;
URL www.2simple.com; e-mail info@2simple.com;
Tel 020 8203 1781; Fax 020 8202 6370

A to Z Supplies Ltd
PO Box 777, Chelmsford, Essex CM2 5AZ;
URL www.atozsupplies.co.uk; e-mail
enquiries@atozsupplies.co.uk; Tel 01245 398000;
Fax 01245 592325
Manager (Customer Services)   Karen Payne;
Tel 01245 398155

The Accelerated Learning Centre
Crown Bldgs, Bancyfelin, Carmarthen SA33 5ND;
URL www.accelerated-learning.co.uk; e-mail
learn@accelerated-learning.co.uk; Tel 01267 211880;
Fax 01267 211882

Aclass Technology (UK) Ltd
Technology Hse, 46b Bradford Rd, Brighouse HD6 1RY;
URL www.aclasstechnology.com; e-mail
info@aclasstechnology.com; Tel 01484 717070;
Fax 01484 404795

Activa Solutions
Activia Hse, Commerce Way, Edenbridge, Kent TN8 6ED;
URL www.activa.co.uk; e-mail info@activa.co.uk;
Tel 0870 754 4514; Fax 0870 754 4516

Adam Equipment Co Ltd
Bond Ave, Denbigh East Industrial Est, Bletchley, Milton
Keynes; URL www.adamequipment.com; e-mail
sales@adamequipment.co.uk; Tel 01908 274545;
Fax 01908 641339

Adobe Systems Europe Ltd
3 Roundabout Ave, Stockley Pk, Uxbridge UB11 1AY;
URL www.adobe.co.uk/education; e-mail
english-custserv@adobe.com; Tel 020 8606 1100;
Fax 020 8606 4004

Advisory Unit – Computers in Education
See also entry in Chapter 19: Computers in Education;
Training
126 Gt North Rd, Hatfield, Hertfordshire AL9 5JZ;
URL www.advisory-unit.org.uk; e-mail
sales@advisory-unit.org.uk; Tel 01707 266714;
Fax 01707 273684
Customer Services   Faye Geal

AJS Furniture
Huntington, York YO32 9PT; URL www.ajsfurniture.com;
e-mail help@ajsfurniture.com; Tel 01904 611808;
Fax 01904 681721
Customer Services   Mike Culpin; Tel 01904 681580

Akhter Computers plc
Akhter Hse, Perry Rd, Harlow, Essex CM18 7PN;
URL www.akhter.co.uk; e-mail
anita.upton@akhter.co.uk; Tel 01279 821200;
Fax 01279 821300
Customer Services   Anita Upton

Alite Ltd
Bourne Pk, Cores End Rd, Bourne End, Buckinghamshire
SL8 5AS; URL www.alite.co.uk; e-mail office@alite.co.uk;
Tel 01628 810700; Fax 01628 810310
Customer Services   Irene Warnock

Alligan Ltd
5 Primrose Gdns, London NW3 4UJ;
URL www.alligan.co.uk; e-mail info@alligan.co.uk;
Tel 020 7722 3254; Fax 020 7813 2435

AlphaSmart Europe
Northway Hse, 1379 High Rd, London N20 9LP;
URL www.alphasmart.co.uk; e-mail
uk-info@alphasmart.com; Tel 020 8492 3690;
Fax 020 8446 7953

Apple
2 Furzeground Way, Stockley Pk, Uxbridge, Greater London
UB11 1BB; URL www.apple.com/uk/education; e-mail
ukschoolsales@euro.apple.com; Tel 020 8218 1500;
Fax 020 8218 1580

Articles of Faith Ltd
Resource Hse, Kay St, Bury, Lancashire BL9 6BU;
URL www.articlesoffaith.co.uk; e-mail
hello@articlesoffaith.co.uk; Tel 0161 763 6232;
Fax 0161 763 5366

ASCO Educational Supplies Ltd
19 Lockwood Way, Leeds, West Yorkshire LS11 5TH;
URL www.ascoeducational.co.uk; e-mail
sales@ascoeducational.co.uk; Tel 0113 270 7070;
Fax 0113 277 5585

ASCOL – Academic Sciences Company
Unit 5, Eldon Rd, Attenborough, Beeston, Nottingham
NG9 6DZ; URL www.ascol.co.uk; e-mail
sales@ascol.co.uk; Tel (sales) 0115 925 6049;
Fax 0115 925 4511

ASG Stage Products Ltd
Redgate Rd, South Lancs Industrial Estate, Ashton-in-
Makerfield, Lancashire WN4 8DT;
URL www.asgstage.co.uk; e-mail post@asgstage.co.uk;
Tel 01942 718347; Fax 01942 718219
Customer Services   Paul McFerran

Audio Visual Material Ltd
AVM Hse, Hawley La, Farnborough, Hampshire
GU14 9EH; URL www.avmltd.co.uk; e-mail
mnisbet@avmltd.co.uk; Tel 01252 510363;
Fax 01252 519874

Autodesk Ltd
1 Meadow Gate Ave, Farnborough Business Pk,
Farnborough, Hampshire GU14 6FG;
URL www.autodesk.co.uk/education; e-mail
gb-info@autodesk.com; Tel 01252 456600;
Fax 01252 456601
Customer Services   Alistair Brook; Tel 01252 456789

Avantis Ltd
See Other Suppliers: Maintenance and Consultancy Services

AVP
School Hill Centre, Chepstow, Monmouthshire NP16 5PH;
URL www.avp.co.uk; e-mail info@avp.co.uk;
Tel (customer services) 01291 625439; Fax 01291 629671

AVS – Multimedia
Item Hse, Beacon Rd, Crowborough, East Sussex TN6 1AS;
URL www.avsmultimedia.com; e-mail
avs@avsmultimedia.com; Tel 01892 668288;
Fax 01892 668266

20

Axminster Power Tool Centre Ltd

Unit 10, Weycroft Ave, Millway Rise Industrial Estate, Axminster EX13 5PH; URL www.axminster.co.uk; e-mail educationsales@axminster.co.uk; Tel 0845 070 7870; Fax 0845 604 0034

Contact   Andrew Cross

Azzurri Communications

Goulton St, Hull HU3 4DD; URL www.azzurrieducation.com; e-mail gerard.toplass@azzu.co.uk; Tel 01482 601100; Fax 01482 587703

Ballicom International

Unit 110, The Saturn Centre, 101 Lockhurst La, Coventry, West Midlands CV6 5SF; URL www.ballicom.co.uk; e-mail education@ballroom.co.uk; Tel 0870 751 5050; Fax 0870 751 5052

The Big Bus

7 Dukes Ct, Chichester, West Sussex PO19 8FX; URL www.thebigbus.com; e-mail learnmore@thebigbus.com; Tel 01243 815845; Fax 01243 815805

Contact   Clare Mogridge

Birchfield Interactive Plc

The Media Centre, Culverhouse Cross, Cardiff CF5 6XJ; URL www.birchfield.co.uk; e-mail enquiries@birchfield.co.uk; Tel 02920 597000; Fax 02920 599456

Bluesky International Ltd (Wildgoose)

The Old Toy Factory, 10 The Business Pk, Jackson St, Coalville, Leicestershire LE67 3NR; URL www.wildgoose.ac; e-mail sales@wildgoose.ac; Tel (Education Department) 01530 518568; Tel 01530 835685; Fax 01530 811900

Boardworks Ltd

The Gallery, 54 Marston St, Oxford, Oxfordshire OX4 1LF; URL www:boardworks.co.uk; e-mail enquiries@boardworks.co.uk; Tel 0870 350 5560; Fax 0870 350 5565

Boxford Ltd

Wheatley, Halifax, West Yorkshire HX3 5AF; URL www.boxford.co.uk; e-mail sales@boxford.co.uk; Tel 01422 358311; Fax 01422 355924

Brainwaves

Unit 2, Bodmin Business Pk, Bodmin, Cornwall PL31 2RT; URL www.brainwaves.net; e-mail sales@brainwaves.net; Tel 0800 032 5454; Fax 0800 032 5464

British Nuclear Group

Community Affairs, H440, Risley, Warrington WA3 6AS; URL www.britishnucleargroup.com; e-mail pauline.j.deans@britishnucleargroup.com; Tel 01925 832826; Fax 01925 835619

British Thornton ESF Ltd

Prospect Works, South St, Keighley, West Yorkshire BD21 5AA; URL www.british-thornton.co.uk; e-mail admin@british-thornton.co.uk; Tel 01535 683250; Fax 01535 680226

Broadway Leasing Ltd

Churchfield Hse, 5 The Crescent, Cheadle, Cheshire SK8 1PS; URL www.broadwayleasing.com; e-mail lpeppi@broadwayleasing.com; Tel 0161 491 5230; Fax 0161 491 5231

BT Plc

BT Plc, BT Centre, 81 Newgate St, London EC1A 7AJ; URL www.bt.com/education; e-mail btlearningcentre@bt.com; Tel 0800 032 9330; Fax 01634 290175

Bytronic Ltd

The Courtyard, Reddicap Trading Est, Sutton Coldfield, West Midlands B75 7BU; URL www.bytronic.net; Tel 0121 378 0613; Fax 0121 311 1774

Sales and Customer Service   Deborah Tweed; e-mail debbie@bytronic.co.uk

Cambridge University Press

The University Printing Hse, Shaftesbury Rd, Cambridge, Cambridgeshire CB2 2BS; URL www.cambridge.org/education; e-mail educustserv@cambridge .org; Tel 01223 358331; Fax 01223 325573

Cambridge-Hitachi

University Printing Hse, Shaftesbury Rd, Cambridge, Cambridgeshire CB2 2BS; URL www.cambridge-hitachi.com; e-mail marketing@cambridge-hitachi.com; Tel 01223 325896; Fax 01223 325167

Canford Audio plc

Crowther Rd, Washington, Tyne and Wear NE38 0BW; URL www.canford.co.uk/education; e-mail info@canford.co.uk; Tel 0191 418 1199; Fax 0191 418 1001

Capita Education Services

Franklin Ct, Priory Business Pk, Cardington, Bedfordshire MK44 3JZ; URL www.sims.co.uk; e-mail sales@capitaes.co.uk; Tel 01234 838080; Fax 01234 838091

Caspian Learning

St Peters Gate, Sunderland Science Pk, Charles St, Sunderland SR6 0AN; URL www.caspianlearning.co.uk; e-mail info@caspianlearning.co.uk; Tel 0191 556 1043; Fax 0191 556 1044

Customer Services   Melanie Trotter

CEM Centre

Mountjoy Research Centre 4, University of Durham, Stockton Rd, Durham DH1 3UZ; URL www.cemcentre.org; e-mail cem@cem.dur.ac.uk; Tel 0191 334 4189; Fax 0191 334 4180

CENTRA Education and Training

Duxbury Pk, Duxbury Hall Rd, Chorley PR7 4AT; URL www.centra.org.uk; e-mail seanh@centra.org.uk; Tel 01257 241428; Fax 01257 260357

Certwood Ltd

Laporte Way, Luton LU4 8EF; URL www.certwood.com; e-mail sales@certwood.com; Tel 01582 456955; Fax 01582 485855

Channel 4 Learning

Channel 4 Television Corporation, 124 Horseferry Rd, London SW1P 2TX; URL www.channel4.com/learning; e-mail 4learning@channel4.co.uk; Tel 0870 124 6444; Fax 0870 124 6446

CIE-Group Ltd

Widdowson Cl, Blenheim Industrial Estate, Bulwell, Nottingham NG6 8WB; URL education@cie-group.com; e-mail education@cie-group.com; Tel 0115 977 0075; Fax 0115 977 0081

Customer Services   Chris Edwards

CIS Office Furniture Ltd

Office Furniture Hse, Potters La, Wednesbury, West Midlands WS10 7LP; URL www.cisoffice.co.uk; e-mail sales@cisoffice.co.uk; Tel 0121 556 0880; Fax 0121 556 9588

Cisco Systems

See Other Suppliers: Maintenance and Consultancy Services

Claire Publications

Unit 8, Tey Brook Craft Centre, Great Tey, Colchester, Essex CO6 1JE; URL www.clairepublications.com; e-mail mail@clairepublications.com; Tel (sales) 01206 211020; Fax 01206 212755

Claranet Ltd

21 Southampton Row, Holborn, London WC1B 5HA; URL www.clara.net; e-mail publicsector@uk.clara.net; Tel 0845 111 8844; Tel (customer services) 020 7685 8000; Fax 020 7685 8084

Cochranes of Oxford Ltd

Leafield, Witney, Oxfordshire OX29 9NY; URL www.cochranes.co.uk; e-mail cochranes@mailbox.co.uk; Tel 01993 878 641; Fax 01993 878 416

Collins Education

77–85 Fulham Palace Rd, London W6 8JB; URL www.collinseducation.com; Tel 020 8741 7070

Commotion Group

Commotion Hse, Morley Rd, Tonbridge, Kent TN9 1RA; URL www.commotiongroup.co.uk; e-mail enquiries@commotiongroup.co.uk; Tel 01732 773399; Fax 01732 773390

Community Playthings

Brightling Rd, Robertsbridge, East Sussex TN32 5DR; URL www.communityplaythings.co.uk; e-mail sales@communityproducts.co.uk; Tel 01304 843701; Fax 01304 843731

Connetix Ltd

24 Lime St, London EC3M 7HS; URL www.connetix.co.uk; e-mail enquiries@connetix.co.uk; Tel 020 7621 3500; Fax 020 7621 3502

The Consortium

Hammond Way, Trowbridge, Wiltshire BA14 8RR; URL www.theconsortium.co.uk; e-mail enquiries@theconsortium.co.uk; Tel 0845 330 7733; Fax 0845 330 7785

Continental Sports Ltd

Hilltop Rd, Paddock, Huddersfield, West Yorkshire HD1 4SD; URL www.continentalsports.co.uk; e-mail sales@contisports.co.uk; Tel 01484 542051; Fax 01484 539148

Senior Sales Administrator Joyce Allen

Coomber Electronic Equipment Ltd

Croft Wlk, Worcester, Worcestershire WR1 3NZ; URL www.coomber.co.uk; e-mail sales@coomber.co.uk; Tel 01905 25168; Fax 01905 612701

Customer Service Heather Hancocks

Costcutters

41 Avery Par, Sutton Coldfield B73 6QB; URL www.costcuttersuk.com; e-mail enquiries@costcuttersuk.com; Tel 0121 244 7070; Fax 0121 244 6868

CR Clarke and Co (UK) Ltd

Betws Industrial Pk, Ammanford, Carmarthenshire SA18 2LS; URL www.crclarke.co.uk; e-mail info@crclarke.co.uk; Tel (sales) 01269 590530; Fax 01269 590540

CRB Solutions

32 Dryden Rd, Bilston Glen Industrial Est, Loanhead, Midlothian EH20 9LZ; URL www.crbsolutions.co.uk; e-mail enquiries@crbsolutions.co.uk; Tel 0131 440 6100; Fax 0131 440 6101

Creativity International Ltd

16 Narrowboat Way, Hurst Business Pk, Netherton, Dudley DY5 1UF; URL www.cilimited.co.uk; e-mail enquiries@cilimited.co.uk; Tel 01384 485550; Fax 01384 485551

Crick Software Ltd

Crick Hse, Boarden Cl, Moulton Pk, Northampton, Northamptonshire NN3 6LF; URL www.cricksoft.com; e-mail info@cricksoft.com; Tel 0845 121 1691; Fax 0845 121 1692

Crocodile Clips

43 Queensferry Street La, Edinburgh EH2 4PF; URL www.crocodile-clips.com; e-mail sales@crocodile-clips.com; Tel 0131 226 1511; Fax 0131 226 1522

Crossbrook Furniture Ltd

Unit 8, Marshgate Trading Est, Marshgate Dr, Hertford, Hertfordshire SG13 7AJ; URL www.crossbrook.co.uk; e-mail sales@crossbrook.co.uk; Tel 01992 557000; Fax 01992 501666

Sales M. Dobson

Cupboard Love for Schools

Unit1, Thornhill Rd, Solihull, West Midlands B91 2HB; URL www.cupboardloveforschools.com; e-mail sales@cupboardloveforschools.com; Tel (schools/commercial) 0121 711 8383; Fax 0121 711 3777

Dalen Ltd (Top-Tec)

See Other Suppliers: IT and Audio-Visual

DAMS International

Head Office and Export Office, Gores Rd, Knowsley Industrial Pk North, Knowsley, Merseyside L33 7XS; URL www.dams.com; e-mail education@dams.com; Tel 0151 548 7111; Fax 0115 548 6369

Manager (Educational Division) Sean Doherty

Data Harvest Group Ltd

1 Eden Ct, Leighton Buzzard, Bedfordshire LU7 4FY; URL www.data-harvest.co.uk; e-mail sales@data-harvest.co.uk; Tel 01525 373666; Fax 01525 851638

Davies Sports

Findel Hse, Excelsior Rd, Ashby Pk, Ashby de la Zouch, Leicestershire LE65 1NG; URL www.daviessports.co.uk; e-mail customerservice@daviessports.co.uk; Tel 0845 120 4515; Fax 01530 418182

Daydream Education

Unit 8, Denvale Trade Pk, Ocean Way, Cardiff CF24 5PF; URL www.daydreameducation.co.uk; e-mail enquiries@daydreameducation.co.uk; Tel 02920 440029; Fax 02920 454595

Deanestor plc

Warren Way, Crown Farm Business Pk, Mansfield, Nottinghamshire NG19 0FL; URL www.deanestor.co.uk; e-mail sales@deanestor.co.uk; Tel 01623 420041; Fax 01623 420061

Denford Ltd

Birds Royd, Brighouse, West Yorkshire HD6 1NB; URL www.denford.co.uk; e-mail info@denford.co.uk; Tel 01484 728000; Fax 01484 728100

Manager (Commercial Dept) John Swallow; Tel 01484 712264

Direct Educational Services

Unit 3, Bowers Par, Harpenden, Hertfordshire AL5 2SH; e-mail enquiries@des-uk.com; Tel 0870 162 0042; Fax 0870 162 0043

D-Link (Europe) Ltd

4th Fl, Merit Hse, Edgware Rd, Colindale, London NW9 5AB; URL www.dlink.co.uk; e-mail sales@dlink.co.uk; Tel 020 8731 5555; Fax 020 8731 5551

Dolphin Computer Access Ltd

See Other Suppliers: IT and Audio-Visual

20

Don Johnston
18–19 Clarendon Ct, Calver Rd, Winwick Quay, Warrington WA2 8QP; URL www.donjohnston.co.uk; e-mail info@djsn.co.uk; Tel 01925 256500; Fax 01925 241745
Customer Service   Denise Whyman

DRS Data Services Ltd
1 Danbury Ct, Linford Wood, Milton Keynes, Buckinghamshire MK14 6LR; URL www.drs.co.uk; e-mail schools@drs.co.uk; Tel 01908 666088; Fax 01908 607668
Customer Service   Peter Adshead

Duncan Roberts Projects
Arkwright Rd, Bicester, Oxfordshire OX26 4UU; URL www.duncanroberts.co.uk; e-mail sales@duncanroberts.co.uk; Tel 01869 366166; Fax 01869 366167

E & L Instruments Ltd
Aerial Rd, Llay, Wrexham LL12 0TU; URL www.eandl-group.com; e-mail info@eandl-group.com; Tel 01978 853920; Fax 01978 854564

Eagle Scientific Ltd
Regent Hse, Lenton St, Sandiacre, Nottingham NG10 5DJ; URL www.eagle-scientific.co.uk; e-mail equip@eagle-scientific.co.uk; Tel 0115 949 1111; Fax 0115 939 1144

EasyTrace Ltd
Cowdown Farm, Micheldever, Winchester, Hampshire SO21 3DN; URL www.easytrace.co.uk; e-mail sales@easytrace.co.uk; Tel 01962 795014; Fax 01962 795015

Eclipse Books Ltd
62–65 Chandos Pl, Covent Garden, London WC2N 4LP; URL www.eclipsebooks.com; e-mail emma@eclipsebooks.com; Tel 0870 242 2269; Fax 020 7407 4659
Customer Services   A. Cousin-Bedford

Economatics Education Ltd
Darnall Rd, Attercliffe, Sheffield, South Yorkshire S9 5AA; URL www.economatics-education.co.uk; e-mail education@economatics.co.uk; Tel (customer service) 0114 281 3311; Tel 0114 281 3344; Fax 0114 243 9306

EDCO
Hyde Park Hse, 54 Mallusk Rd, Newtownabbey, County Antrim BT36 4WU; URL www.edco.co.uk; e-mail info@edco.co.uk; Tel 028 9084 4023; Fax 028 9084 6466

edtech
Locomotion Way, Camperdown Industrial Est, Newcastle upon Tyne, Tyne and Wear NE12 5US; URL www.edtech.co.uk; e-mail sales@edtech.co.uk; Tel 01912 682222; Fax 01912 681137

Education Business
Public Sector Publishing, 226 High Rd, Loughton, Essex IG10 1ET; URL www.educationbusinessuk.com; e-mail sarah@psp-media.co.uk; Tel 020 8532 0055; Fax 020 8532 0066
Customer Services   Laura Micallef

Education Executive
223 The Business Design Centre, 52 Upper St, London N1 0QH; URL richard.johnson@intelligentmedia.co.uk; e-mail www.edexec.co.uk; Tel 020 7288 6833; Fax 020 7288 6834
Customer Services   Richard Johnson

The Education Publishing Company Ltd
Devonia Hse, 4 Union Terr, Crediton, Devon EX17 3DY; URL www.educationpublishing.com; e-mail info@educationpublishing.com; Tel 01363 774455

Education Today
Datateam Publishing Ltd, 15a London Rd, Maidstone, Kent ME16 8LY; URL www.education-today.co.uk; e-mail education@datateam.co.uk; Tel 01622 687031; Fax 01622 757646

Educational and Scientific Products Ltd
A2 Dominion Way, Rustington, West Sussex BN16 3HQ; URL www.espmodels.co.uk; e-mail sales@espmodels.co.uk; Tel 01903 773340; Fax 01903 771108

Educational ICT Services (EdICTs)
7 Dovedale Rd, Hoylake, Wirral CH47 3AN; URL www.edicts.com; e-mail yearbook@edicts.com; Tel 0870 243 0013; Fax 0870 243 0014

Educational Printing Services Ltd
Albion Mill, Water St, Great Harwood BB6 7QR; URL www.eprint.co.uk; e-mail susanbroadley@eprint.co.uk; Tel 01254 882080; Fax 01254 882010
Customer Services   Susan Broadley

EducationCity.com
Pera Innovation Pk, Nottingham Rd, Melton Mowbray, Leicestershire LE13 0PB; URL www.educationcity.com; e-mail sales@educationcity.com; Tel 0870 350 1860; Fax 0870 350 1861

EDUK8 Worldwide Ltd
Wilson Lodge, Great Whittington, Newcastle upon Tyne, Tyne and Wear NE19 2HP; e-mail enquiries@eduk8worldwide.co.uk; Tel 01434 672336; Fax 0870 162 0043

Edu-play
Morris Rd, Leicester, Leicestershire LE2 6BR; URL www.edu-play.co.uk; e-mail info@taskmasteronline.co.uk; Tel 0116 270 4286; Fax 0116 270 6992

EFM – Chesterfield
Pottery La West, Whittington Moor, Chesterfield, Derbyshire S41 9BN; URL www.efmchesterfield.co.uk; e-mail sales@efmchesterfield.co.uk; Tel (sales) 01246 455191; Fax 01246 456506

eInstruction UK Ltd
Family Hall Est, The Square, Farnley, Otley, North Yorkshire LS21 2QF; URL www.optivote.com; e-mail enquiries@optivote.com; Tel 01943 850119; Fax 01943 850714
Customer Services   Sandra Brooke

ELE International Ltd
Chartmoor Rd, Charwell Business Pk, Leighton Buzzard, Bedfordshire LU7 4WG; URL www.ele.com; e-mail sales@eleint.co.uk; Tel 01525 249200; Fax 01525 249249

EME Furniture
See Other Suppliers: Furniture; Classroom and Office

Emmerich (Berlon) Ltd
See Other Suppliers: Furniture; Classroom and Office

Enabling Computer
Castlefields, Newport Rd, Stafford, Staffordshire ST16 1BU; URL www.enablingcomputers.com; e-mail sales@enablingcomputers.com; Tel 01785 243111; Fax 01785 243222

Encyclopaedia Britannica (UK) Ltd
2nd Fl, Unity Wharf, 13 Mill St, London SE1 2BH; URL www.britannica.co.uk; e-mail enquiries@britannica.co.uk; Tel 020 7500 7800; Fax 020 7500 7878

Equanet

Dixons Hse, Maylands Ave, Hemel Hempstead NP2 7TG;
URL www.pcwb.com/education; e-mail
education@pcwb.com; Tel 0870 166 4670;
Fax 0870 166 4603

Equiinet Ltd

Edison Hse, Edison Rd, Dorcan, Swindon, Wiltshire
SN3 5JX; URL www.equiinet.com; e-mail
sales@equiinet.com; e-mail (customer services)
support@equiinet.com; Tel 01793 603700;
Fax 01793 603701

ESA McIntosh Ltd

Mitchelston Dr, Kirkcaldy KY1 3LX;
URL www.esamcintosh.co.uk; e-mail
sales@esamcintosh.co.uk; Tel 01592 656200;
Fax 01592 656299

Esmond Hellerman Ltd

Hellerman Hse, Harris Way, Windmill Rd, Sunbury on
Thames, Surrey TW16 7EW; URL www.hellermans.com;
e-mail sales@hellermans.com; Tel 01932 781888;
Fax 01932 789573

Espresso Education Ltd

Riverside Studios, Crisp Rd, London W6 9RL;
URL www.espresso.co.uk; e-mail info@espresso.co.uk;
Tel 020 8237 1200; Fax 020 8237 1201
Customer Service   Jane Nash; Tel 0800 034 5200

Etech Group Europe Ltd

63 Baring Rd, Hengistbury Head, Bournemouth, Dorset
BH6 4DT; URL www.studywiz.com; e-mail
mike@etechgroup.com; Tel 0845 434 8087;
Fax 01202 422732
Manager (European Client Services)   Helen Baker

Eurotek Office Furniture Ltd

Southern Cross Trading Est, Bognor Regis, West Sussex
PO22 9SB; URL www.eof.co.uk; e-mail
marketing@eof.co.uk; Tel 01243 828921;
Fax 01243 871240

Exclusive Contract Furniture Ltd

Butts Pond Industrial Estate, Sturminster Newton, Dorset
DT10 1AZ; URL www.exclusive-furniture.co.uk; e-mail
sales@exclusive-furniture.co.uk; Tel 01258 472001;
Fax 01258 473884

EYE (Early Years Educator)

MA Education Ltd, St Jude's Church, Dulwich Rd, London
SE24 0PB; URL www.earlyyearseducator.co.uk;
Tel 020 7501 6735; Fax 020 7326 4835

Featherstone Education Ltd

PO Box 6350, Lutterworth LE17 6LP;
URL www.featherstone.uk.com; e-mail
mail@featherstone.uk.com; Tel 01858 881212;
Fax 01858 880362

Feedback Instruments Ltd

Park Rd, Crowborough, East Sussex TN6 2QR;
URL www.fbk.com; e-mail feedback@fdbk.co.uk;
Tel 01892 653322; Fax 01892 663719

Firefly Entertainment Ltd

1st Fl, 110 Harley St, London W1G 7JG;
URL www.earlylearningskills.com; e-mail
info@fireflyentertainment.co.uk; Tel 020 7034 3410;
Fax 020 7034 3419
Customer Services   Sarah Ellis

First Choice Solutions Ltd

1L Merrow Business Centre, Merrow La, Guildford, Surrey
GU4 7WA; URL www.firstchoicesolutionsltd.co.uk;
e-mail bob@fcs.me.uk; Tel 01483 302333;
Fax 01483 306789

Fisher-Marriott Software

58 Victoria Rd, Woodbridge, Suffolk IP12 1EL;
URL www.fishermarriott.com; e-mail
enquiries@fishermarriott.com; e-mail
sales@fishermarriott.com; Tel 01394 387050;
Fax 01394 380064
Customer Service   Cass Davies

Fiskars Brands UK Ltd

Newlands Ave, Bridgend, Mid Glamorgan CF31 2XA;
URL www.fiskars.com; e-mail
info@fiskars.demon.co.uk; Tel 01656 655595;
Fax 01656 649425

Flamefast (UK) Ltd

See Other Suppliers: Maintenance and Consultancy Services

Flite Electronics International Ltd

Church House Farm, Clewers Hill, Waltham Chase,
Hampshire SO32 2LN; URL www.flite.co.uk; e-mail
sales@flite.co.uk; Tel 01489 892422; Fax 01489 897929
Customer Service   Suzanne Kittow

Formech International Ltd

Unit 4, Thrales End Farm, Thrales End La, Harpenden,
Hertfordshire AL5 3NS; URL www.formech.com/
educational; e-mail sales@formech.com; Tel (sales)
01582 469797; Fax 01582 469646

Frank Berry Otter

North Wingfield Rd, Grassmoor, Chesterfield, Derbyshire
S42 5EB; URL www.frankberry.co.uk; e-mail
sales@frankberry.co.uk; Tel 01246 852244;
Fax 01246 855317

FrogTrade Ltd

G423, Dean Clough, Halifax, West Yorkshire HX3 5AX;
URL www.frogteacher.com; e-mail info@frogtrade.com;
Tel 01422 250800; Fax 01422 354232
Operations Manager   Kate Heal

Furniture@Work Ltd

333 Bath St, Glasgow G2 4ER;
URL www.furnitureatwork.co.uk; e-mail
info@furnitureatwork.co.uk; Tel 0870 241 5938;
Fax 0870 238 8259

Galt Educational

Johnsonbrook Rd, Hyde, Cheshire SK14 4QT;
URL www.galt-educational.co.uk; e-mail
enquiries@galt-educational.co.uk; Tel 0845 120 3005;
Fax 0800 056 0314

Genesis Capital

Capital Hse, Unit B Kingsway Business Pk, Oldfield Rd,
Hampton TW12 2HD; URL www.genesiscapital.co.uk;
e-mail education@genesiscapital.co.uk;
Tel 020 8255 5505; Fax 020 8255 5510
Customer Services   Tim Hughes

Geopacks

1st Fl, Omega Bldg, Smugglers Way, London SW18 1AZ;
URL www.geopacks.com; e-mail
service@geopacks.co.uk; Tel 0870 513 3168;
Fax 0870 120 0006
Customer Service   Christine Hinckley

GLS Educational Supplies Ltd

1 Mollison Ave, Enfield, Greater London EN3 7XQ;
URL www.glsed.co.uk; e-mail sales@glsed.co.uk;
Tel 020 8805 8333; Fax 0800 917 2246

GOAL

The Old School, Holly Wlk, Leamington Spa, Warwickshire
CV32 4GL; URL www.goalonline.co.uk; e-mail
customerservice@ediplc.com; Tel 01926 458686;
Fax 01926 887676

Gopak Ltd

See Other Suppliers: Furniture; Classroom and Office

Granada Learning
Chiswick Centre, 414 Chiswick High Rd, London W4 5TF;
URL www.granada-learning.com; e-mail
info@granada-learning.com; Tel 020 8996 3333;
Fax 020 8742 8390

Gratnells Ltd
See Other Suppliers: Furniture; Classroom and Office

Gresswell
Freepost ANG 0802, Hoddesdon, Hertfordshire EN11 0BR;
URL www.gresswell.co.uk; e-mail
orders@gresswell.co.uk; Tel 01992 454511;
Fax 0800 616634

Grid Learning Ltd
53 Chandos Pl, London WC2N 4HS;
URL www.gridlearning.com; e-mail
info@gridlearning.com; Tel 020 7812 6600;
Fax 020 7812 6601

Griffin Education
Bishop Meadow Rd, Loughborough, Leicestershire
LE11 5RG; URL www.griffineducation.co.uk; e-mail
griffinmbx@thermofisher.com; Tel 01509 233344;
Fax 01509 555200

Hand Made Places Ltd
Unit 14, Bordon Trading Estate, Old Station Way, Bordon,
Hampshire GU35 9HH;
URL www.handmadeplaces.co.uk; e-mail
info@handmadeplaces.co.uk; Tel 01420 474111;
Fax 01420 474222

Harcourt
Halley Court, Jordan Hill, Oxford, Oxfordshire OX2 8EJ;
URL www.harcourt.co.uk; e-mail
enquiries@harcourt.co.uk; Tel 01865 888000;
Fax 01865 314091

Heckmondwike FB
PO Box 7, Wellington Mills, Liversedge, West Yorkshire
WF15 7XA; URL www.heckmondwike-fb.co.uk; e-mail
marketing@heckmondwike-fb.co.uk; Tel 01924 410544;
Fax 01924 413620

Henkel Loctite Ltd
Apollo Ct, Bishops Sq, Hatfield, Hertfordshire AL10 9EY;
URL www.prittworld.com; Tel 01707 289041;
Fax 01707 289099
Customer Service   Rod Chesworth

Hindleys Ltd
See Other Suppliers: Educational Resource Suppliers

Hitachi Software Engineering (UK) Ltd
26 Old Bailey, London EC4M 7HW;
URL www.hitachisoft-eu.com; e-mail
marketing@hitachi-software.co.uk; Tel 020 7246 6868;
Fax 020 7246 6860
Customer Services   Peter Kerrison

HME Technology
Priory Hse, Saxon Pk, Hanbury Rd, Stoke Prior,
Worcestershire B60 4AD; URL www.hme-tech.com;
e-mail contactus@hme-tech.com; Tel 01527 839000;
Fax 01527 839001

Hope Education
Hyde Bldgs, Ashton Rd, Hyde, Cheshire SK14 4SH;
URL www.hope-education.co.uk; e-mail
enquiries@hope-education.co.uk; Tel 0845 120 2055;
Fax 0800 929139

Hopscotch Educational Publishing Ltd
Unit 2, The Old Brushworks, 56 Pickwick Rd, Corsham,
Wiltshire SN13 9BX; URL www.hopscotchbooks.com;
e-mail sales@hopscotchbooks.com; Tel 01249 701701;
Fax 01249 701987

Horizon Wimba Limited
Sentry Hse, 110b Northgate St, Bury St Edmunds, Suffolk
IP33 1HP; URL www.horizonwimba.com; e-mail
info@horizonwimba.com; Tel 01284 747780;
Fax 01284 753995

iANSYST Ltd
Fen Hse, Fen Rd, Cambridge, Cambridgeshire CB4 1UN;
URL www.dyslexic.com; e-mail sales@dyslexic.com;
Tel 01223 420101; Fax 01223 426644
Sales   Jenny Cormack; e-mail sales@dyslexic.com;
Tel 0800 018 0045

i-desk Solutions Ltd
Unit 11, Ivanhoe Rd, Finchampstead, Berkshire RG40 4QQ;
URL www.i-desk.co.uk; Tel 0118 973 9720;
Fax 0870 777 1481

Inclusive Technology Ltd
Riverside Crt, Huddersfield Rd, Delph, Oldham OL3 5FZ;
URL www.inclusive.co.uk; e-mail
inclusive@inclusive.co.uk; Tel 01457 819790;
Fax 01457 819799

Innovative Technologies in Education Ltd
212 Piccadilly, London W1J 9HG; URL www.iteltd.com;
e-mail kamal@iteltd.com; Tel 020 7830 9664;
Fax 020 7830 9665

Interactive Education Ltd
PO Box 3256, Willenhall, Wolverhampton, West Midlands
WV13 2HA; URL www.interactive-education.co.uk;
e-mail enquiries@interactive-education.co.uk;
Tel (customer service) 0870 043 4024; Fax 0870 043 4025
Customer Service   Mandy Kaur

Interform Contract Furniture
8 West Hampstead Mews, London NW6 3BB;
URL www.interform-furniture.co.uk; e-mail
sales@interform-furniture.co.uk; Tel 020 7328 2340;
Fax 020 7624 1777
Sales Director   John Rodgers

InterLinx Ltd
8a Windmill Bank, Wombourne, South Staffordshire
WV5 9JD; URL www.interlinx.co.uk; e-mail
nigel@interlinx.co.uk; Tel 0870 743 0999;
Fax 0870 746 0999

Intuitive Media Ltd
Sterndale Hse, Litton, Derbyshire SK17 8QU;
URL www.intuitivemedia.com; e-mail
tricia.pulfrey@intuitivemedia.com; Tel 01298 872651;
Fax 01298 871685
Customer Services   Tricia Pulfrey

Invicta Plastics Ltd
Harborough Rd, Oadby, Leicester LE2 4LB;
URL www.invictagroup.co.uk; e-mail
sales-edu@invictagroup.co.uk; Tel 0116 272 0555;
Fax 0116 272 8393
Customer Service   Kerry McNamara; Tel 0116 272 8337

ISC Research Ltd
35 Southampton St, Faringdon, Oxfordshire SN7 7AZ;
URL www.iscresearch.com; e-mail
info@iscresearch.com; Tel 01367 241222;
Fax 01367 244976

Isis Concepts Ltd
57 High St, Tetsworth, Oxfordshire OX9 7BS;
URL www.isisconcepts.co.uk; e-mail
info@isisconcepts.co.uk; Tel 01844 280123;
Fax 01844 281373
Customer Services   James Clarke

IT Learning Exchange
Department of Education, Shoreditch Bldg, 35 Kingsland
Rd, London E2 8AA; URL www.title.londonmet.ac.uk;
Tel 020 7749 3777; Fax 020 7749 3778

20

ITS-FEDA Ltd
Coombe Lodge, Blagdon, Bristol BS40 7RG;
　　URL www.itservices.org.uk; e-mail
　　sales@itservices.org.uk; Tel 0870 145 1600

JDS Group Ltd
Park Rd, Faringdon, Oxfordshire SN7 7BP;
　　URL www.jdsgroup.co.uk; e-mail
　　education@jdsgroup.co.uk; Tel 01367 245820;
　　Fax 01367 241705
Customer Services 　　Dave Blackmore-Heal

JEM Education Marketing Services Ltd
Orbital Pk, Ashford, Kent TN24 0GA; URL www.jem.co.uk;
　　e-mail info@jem.co.uk; Tel 01233 214022;
　　Fax 01233 214020
Customer Services 　　Joanna Willmore

Johnson Test Papers
Unit 50, Chapel St, Tipton, West Midlands DY4 8JB;
　　URL www.kaagat.com; e-mail info@kaagat.com;
　　Tel 0121 557 3883; Fax 0121 557 8235
Customer Services 　　Julia Scott

Joskos Solutions and Recruitment
Spitfire Studios, 63–71 Collier St, London N1 9BE;
　　URL www.joskos.com; e-mail solutions@joskos.com;
　　Tel 0845 370 0038; Fax 020 7689 5002
Customer Services 　　James Ray

Just Projectors
Gibbs Hse, Kennel Ride, Ascot, Berkshire SL5 7NT;
　　URL www.projectors.co.uk; e-mail
　　sales@projectors.co.uk; Tel 0870 906 3134;
　　Fax 0870 906 3136

KCP Publications Ltd
Woburn Hse, Wenworth Gdns, Toddington, Dunstable
　　LU5 6DN; URL www.kcppublications.com; e-mail
　　sales@kcppublications.com; Tel 0845 230 2101;
　　Fax 0845 230 2102

Kudlian Soft
8a Nunhold Business Centre, Dark La, Hatton,
　　Warwickshire CV35 8XB; URL www.kudlian.net; e-mail
　　info@kudlian.net; Tel 01926 842544; Fax 01926 843537

LDA
Abbeygate Hse, East Rd, Cambridge, Cambridgeshire
　　CB1 1DB; URL www.ldalearning.com; Tel 01223 357788;
　　Fax 01223 460557

Learning Resources Ltd
5 Merchants Cl, Oldmedow Rd, King's Lynn, Norfolk
　　PE30 4JX; URL www.learningresources.co.uk; e-mail
　　sales@learning-resources.co.uk; Tel 01553 762276;
　　Fax 01553 769943

LEGO Educational, DACTA Ltd
Bryn Business Centre, Bryn La, Wrexham LL13 9UT;
　　URL www.lego.com/education; e-mail
　　enquiries@dacta.eu.com; Tel 01978 664966;
　　Fax 01978 729900

LFC
Freepost ANG 9675, PO Box 188, Hoddesdon, Hertfordshire
　　EN11 0BR; URL www.lfccatalogue.co.uk; e-mail
　　orders@lfccatalogue.co.uk; Tel 0845 850 6507;
　　Fax 0800 616629

LJ Group
69–75 Thorpe Rd, Bowthorpe Industrial Est, Norwich,
　　Norfolk NR5 9JA; URL www.ljgroup.com; e-mail
　　sales@ljgroup.com; Tel 01603 748001; Fax 01603 746340

Logotron Ltd
124 Cambridge Science Pk, Milton Rd, Cambridge,
　　Cambridgeshire CB4 0ZS; URL www.logo.com; e-mail
　　sales@logo.com; Tel 01223 425558; Fax 01223 425349

London Emblem plc
Unit 9, Apex Centre, Speedfields Pk, Fareham, Hampshire
　　PO14 1TP; URL www.londonemblem.com; e-mail
　　badgemakers@londonemblem.com; Tel 01329 822900;
　　Fax 01329 829000
Customer Service 　　Deborah Daw; Tel 0870 366 1254

Marshall Cavendish Ltd
119 Wardour St, London W1F 0UW; URL www.mcelt.com;
　　e-mail mcelt@marshallcavendish.co.uk;
　　Tel 020 7565 6000; Tel (marketing) 020 7565 6119;
　　Fax 020 7565 6133

Masterfoods Education Centre
1 Bedford Ave, London WC1B 3AU;
　　URL www.pet-educationresources.co.uk; e-mail
　　mec@uk.graying.com; Tel 020 7255 1100;
　　Fax 020 7255 5454

Matrix Display Systems
Egham Business Village, Crabtree Rd, Egham, Surrey
　　TW20 8RB; URL www.matrixdisplay.com; e-mail
　　info@matrixdisplay.com; Tel 01784 439000;
　　Fax 01784 439090
Customer Service 　　Jason Turner

Metalliform Holdings Ltd
Chambers Rd, Hoyland, Barnsley, South Yorkshire S74 0EZ;
　　URL www.metalliform.com; e-mail
　　sales@metalliform.co.uk; Tel 01226 350555;
　　Fax 01226 350112
Customer Service 　　Gordon Yates

MICE Health and Education
Enfield Cabinet Works, Smethurst St, Pemberton, Wigan,
　　Greater Manchester WN5 8ER;
　　URL www.micekaymar.com; e-mail
　　education@micegroup.com; Tel (sales) 01942 219191;
　　Fax 01942 219190

Microsoft Ltd
Microsoft Campus, Thames Valley Pk, Reading RG6 1WG;
　　URL www.microsoft.com/uk/education; e-mail
　　askedu@microsoft-contact.co.uk; Tel 0870 601 0800

Mike Ayres Design Ltd
Unit 8, Shepherds Gr, Stanton, Bury St Edmunds, Suffolk
　　IP31 2AR; URL www.mikeayresdesign.co.uk; e-mail
　　enquiries@mikeayresdesign.co.uk; Tel 01359 251551;
　　Fax 01359 251707

Mill Publishing
PO Box 120, Bangor, County Down BT19 7PJ;
　　URL www.millpublishing.com; e-mail
　　info@millpublishing.co.uk; Tel 028 9146 2226;
　　Fax 028 9146 6474

Morley's of Bicester Ltd
Arkwright Rd, Bicester, Oxfordshire OX26 4UU;
　　URL www.morleys.co.uk; e-mail
　　hayleywatson@morleys.co.uk; Tel 01869 366389;
　　Fax 01869 366387

Morphun Education
7 Chesterfield Rd, London W4 3HG;
　　URL www.morphun.com; Tel 020 8987 9768;
　　Fax 020 8747 1700
Customer Services 　　Colin D Simonds

Nelson Thornes Ltd
Delta Pl, 27 Bath Rd, Cheltenham, Gloucestershire
　　GL53 7TH; URL www.nelsonthornes.com; e-mail
　　cservices@nelsonthornes.com; Tel 01242 267100;
　　Fax 01242 221914

NES Arnold Ltd
Findel Hse, Excelsior Rd, Ashby Pk, Ashby de la Zouch,
　　Leicestershire LE65 1NG; URL www.nesarnold.co.uk;
　　e-mail enquiries@nesarnold.co.uk; Tel 0845 120 4525;
　　Fax 0800 328 0001

Netmedia Education

1st Fl, Christ Church, Birmingham St, Oldbury, West
    Midlands B69 4DY; URL www.netmediaeducation.com;
    e-mail enquiries@netmedia-ed.co.uk; Tel 0121 544 4115;
    Fax 0121 544 2111

Nortek Educational Furniture and Equipment Ltd

Vale Business Centre, Priesty Fields, Congleton, Cheshire
    CW12 4AQ; URL www.nortekgroup.co.uk; e-mail
    sales@nortekgroup.co.uk; Tel 01260 298321;
    Fax 01260 298169

Numicon Ltd

12 Pine Cl, Avis Way, Newhaven, East Sussex BN9 0DH;
    URL www.nimicon.com; e-mail info@numicon.com;
    Tel 01273 515591; Fax 01273 515592

Contact   Mark Sawtell

Ocarina Workshop

PO Box 56, Kettering, Northamptonshire NN15 5LX;
    URL www.ocarina.co.uk; e-mail info@ocarina.co.uk;
    Tel 01536 485963; Fax 01536 485051

Office Depot UK Ltd

Andover Hse, Greenwich Way, Andover SP10 4JZ;
    URL www.officedepot.co.uk; e-mail
    schools@officedepot.com; Tel 0870 142 9800;
    Tel (customer services) 0870 403 2005; Fax 0870 142 9801

On-Line Computers (A division of SBL)

7–11 Chapel St, Lancaster LA1 1NZ; URL www.olc.co.uk;
    e-mail sales@olc.co.uk; Tel 01524 386600;
    Fax 01524 386601

Ordnance Survey

Romsey Rd, Southampton, Hampshire SO16 4GU;
    URL www.ordnancesurvey.co.uk/education;
    www.ordnancesurvey.co.uk/mapzone; e-mail
    customerservices@ordnancesurvey.co.uk;
    Tel 0845 605 0505; Fax 02380 792615

Oxford University Press

Great Clarendon St, Oxford, Oxfordshire OX2 6DP;
    URL www.oup.com; Tel 01865 556767; Fax 01865 556646

P & B Weir Electrical

Unit 10, Leafield Way, Leafield Industrial Est, Corsham,
    Wiltshire SN13 9SW; URL www.pbweir.com; e-mail
    sales@pbweir.com; Tel 01225 811449; Fax 01225 810909

PA Hilton Ltd

Horsebridge Mill, King's Somborne, Hampshire SO20 6PX;
    URL www.p-a-hilton.co.uk; e-mail
    sales@p-a-hilton.co.uk; Tel 01794 388382;
    Fax 01794 388129

Pearson Education, Schools Division

Edinburgh Gate, Harlow, Essex CM20 2JE;
    URL www.longman.co.uk; e-mail
    schools@longman.co.uk; Tel 01279 623623;
    Fax 01279 623388

Pearson Phoenix

Cross Keys Hse, Queen St, Salisbury SP1 1EY;
    URL www.pearsonphoenix.com; e-mail
    phoenix.info@pearson.com; Tel 01722 344800;
    Fax 01722 326243

Pebble Learning

e-Innovation Centre, University of Wolverhampton,
    Telford, Shropshire TF2 9NT;
    URL www.pebblepad.co.uk; e-mail
    info@pebblepad.co.uk; Tel 01952 288300;
    Fax 01952 288205

Customer Services   Colin Dalziel

Pentel (Stationery) Ltd

Hunts Rise, South Marston Pk, Swindon, Wiltshire
    SN3 4TW; URL www.pentel.co.uk; e-mail
    salesoffice@pentel.co.uk; Tel 01793 823333;
    Fax 01793 823366

Business Manager   Mark Knibbs

Percussion Plus

A division of Findel Education Ltd
The Mill, Gt Bowden Rd, Market Harborough,
    Leicestershire LE16 7DE;
    URL www.percussionplus.co.uk; e-mail
    jdean@percussionplus.co.uk; Tel 01858 433124;
    Fax 01858 462218

Philip and Tacey Ltd

North Way, Andover, Hampshire SP10 5BA;
    URL www.philipandtacey.co.uk; e-mail
    sales@philipandtacey.co.uk; Tel 01264 332171;
    Fax 01264 384808

Philip Harris Education

Findel Hse, Excelsior Rd, Ashby Pk, Ashby de la Zouch,
    Leicestershire LE65 1NG; URL www.philipharris.co.uk;
    e-mail orders@philipharris.co.uk; Tel (customer service)
    0845 120 4520; Fax 01530 419492

Planet PC

The Old School, 690 Bradford Rd, Birkenshaw, West
    Yorkshire BD11 2DR; URL www.planetdveducation.net;
    e-mail sales@planetdv.net; Tel 01274 713400;
    Fax 01274 713422

Play and Learn

66 Sydney Rd, Watford, Hertfordshire WD18 7QX;
    URL www.playandlearn.co.uk; e-mail
    info@playandlearn.co.uk; Tel 01923 210310;
    Fax 01923 233880

Playforce Ltd

The Old Tannery, The Midlands, Holt, Trowbridge,
    Wiltshire BA14 6RW; URL www.playforce.co.uk; e-mail
    sales@playforce.co.uk; Tel 01225 782881;
    Fax 01225 783699

Contact   Julia Budniak

Playline Design Ltd

72a Gestridge Rd, Kingsteignton, Newton Abbot, Devon
    TQ12 3HH; URL www.playlinedesign.co.uk; e-mail
    enquiries@playlinedesign.co.uk; Tel 01626 363262;
    Fax 01626 200302

Customer Services   Stuart Hunt

Portable Technology Solutions Ltd

West Midlands Hse, Gipsy La, Willenhall WV13 2HA;
    URL www.portabletechnology.co.uk; e-mail
    info@portabletechnology.co.uk; Tel 01902 482540;
    Fax 01902 482541

Prim-Ed Publishing

PO Box 2840, Coventry, Warwickshire CV6 5ZY;
    URL www.prim-ed.com; e-mail sales@prim-ed.com;
    Tel 0870 876 0151; Fax 0870 876 0152

Principal Furniture

Arkwright Rd, Bicester, Oxfordshire OX26 4UU;
    URL www.principalfurniture.co.uk; e-mail
    sales@principalfurniture.co.uk; Tel 01869 324488;
    Fax 01869 324012

Customer Services   Alastair Richie

Profile

A division of Lawtons Ltd
60 Vauxhall Rd, Liverpool, Merseyside L69 3AU;
    URL www.profile-education.co.uk; e-mail
    profile@lawtons.co.uk; Tel 0151 479 3030;
    Fax 0151 479 3032

Customer Service   Karin Downey

20

Promethean Technologies Group Ltd
See Other Suppliers: IT and Audio-Visual

Proquest Information and Learning
The Quorum, Barnwell Rd, Cambridge, Cambridgeshire
CB5 8SW; URL www.proquestlearning.co.uk; e-mail
learning@proquest.co.uk; Tel 01223 215512;
Fax 01223 215514
Sales   Nathan Turner; Tel 01223 271420

Questions Publishing Company Ltd
Leonard Hse, 321 Bradford St, Birmingham, West Midlands
B5 6ET; URL www.education-quest.com; e-mail
sales@questpub.co.uk; Tel 0121 666 7878;
Fax 0121 666 7879

Quizdom UK Ltd
8 Carrowreagh Business Pk, Carrowreagh Rd, Belfast
BT16 1QQ; URL www.qwizdom.co.uk; e-mail
info@qwizdom.co.uk; Tel 028 9048 5015;
Fax 0870 751 5063
Customer Services   Samantha Clarke

Rahmqvist UK Ltd
Crabtree Rd, Thorpe Industrial Est, Egham, Surrey
TW20 8RN; URL www.rahmqvist.com; e-mail
office@rahmqvist.com; Tel 01784 439888;
Fax 01784 471419

Ramesys
See Other Suppliers: Maintenance and Consultancy Services

Ransom Publishing Ltd
Rose Cottage, Howe Hill, Watlington, Oxfordshire
OX49 5HB; URL www.ransom.co.uk; e-mail
ransom@ransom.co.uk; Tel 01491 613711;
Fax 01491 613733
Customer Service   Jenny Ertle; e-mail
jenny@ransompublishing.co.uk

Rapid
Severalls La, Colchester, Essex CO4 5JS;
URL www.rapideducation.co.uk; e-mail
sales@rapidelec.co.uk; Tel 01206 751166;
Fax 01206 751188

The Rapport Group
1st Fl, Buckingham Hse, 6–7 Buckingham St, London
WC2N 6BU; URL www.rapportgroup.com; e-mail
sales@rapportgroup.com; Tel (customer services)
0845 230 1060; Tel 020 7839 6087; Fax 020 7925 8099

Renaissance Learning UK Ltd
32 Harbour Exchange Sq, London E14 9GE;
URL www.renlearn.co.uk; e-mail info@renlearn.co.uk;
Tel (customer service) 020 7184 4000; Fax 020 7538 2625

Resource Education
51 High St, Kegworth, Derbyshire DE74 2DA;
URL www.resourcekt.co.uk; e-mail
office@resourcekt.co.uk; Tel (enquiries) 0870 777 0247;
Fax 01509 672267

Richer Sounds plc
Unit 2 Gallery Ct, 1–7 Pilgrimage St, London SE1 4LL;
URL www.richersounds.com; e-mail
corporatesales@richersounds.com; Tel 020 7407 9090;
Fax 020 7378 6373
Customer Services   Ricky Faust

Richmond Systems
West Hse, West St, Hasemere, Surrey GU27 2AB;
URL www.richmondsys.co.uk; e-mail
info@netopuk.com; Tel 01428 647347; Fax 01428 641717

Rickitt Educational Media Ltd
Gt Western Hse, Langport, Somerset TA10 9YU;
URL www.r-e-m.co.uk; e-mail sales@r-e-m.co.uk;
Tel 01458 254700; Fax 01458 254701

Riverdeep UK Ltd
Richmond Hse, Heath Rd, Hale, Cheshire WA14 2XP;
URL www.riverdeep-learning.co.uk; e-mail
pwatts@riverdeep-learning.co.uk; Tel 0161 925 5630;
Fax 0161 925 5640
Customer Services   Janice Corden

RJH Morrisflex Ltd
Artillery St, Heckmondwike, West Yorkshire WF16 0NR;
URL www.rjheng.co.uk; e-mail sales@rjheng.co.uk;
Tel 01924 402490; Fax 01924 404635
Sales   Sara Whitworth
Grinders, polishers, bandfacers, and vacuum form trimming
and finishing machines for design and technology
workshops

RM plc
New Mill Hse, 183 Milton Pk, Abingdon, Oxfordshire
OX14 4SE; URL www.rm.com; e-mail
salesdesk@rm.com; Tel 0870 920 0200; Fax 01235 826999

ROMPA Ltd
Goyt Side Rd, Chesterfield, Derbyshire S40 2PH;
URL www.rompa.com; e-mail sales@rompa.com;
Tel 01246 211777; Fax 01246 221802
Products, services and concepts for people with sensory
impairments or learning disabilities

Rotatrim Ltd
8 Caxton Pk, Elms Trading Est, Bedford, Bedfordshire
MK41 0TY; URL www.rotatrim.co.uk; e-mail
sales@rotatrim.co.uk; Tel 01234 224545; Fax 01234 224550

SAM Learning Ltd
The Forum, 74–80 Camden St, London NW1 0EG;
URL www.samlearning.com; e-mail
helpdesk@samlearning.com; Tel 0845 130 4160;
Fax 0845 130 4170

Sanford UK (Parker Pen Company)
Estate Rd, Newhaven BN9 0AL; URL www.berol.co.uk;
Tel 01273 513233; Fax 01273 514773

Saville Audio Visual
Unit 5, Millfield La, Nether Poppleton, York YO2 6PQ;
URL www.av-education.com; e-mail
productsales@saville.com; Tel 0845 600 9988;
Fax 01904 781535

SAVTEC Computer Technology Ltd
Rumbridge St, Totton, Southampton SO40 9DR;
URL www.savtec.com; e-mail trowley@savtec.com;
Tel 02380 304314; Fax 02380 667763

Scholastic Ltd
Villiers Hse, Clarendon Ave, Leamington Spa CV32 5PR;
URL www.scholastic.co.uk; e-mail
cratcliffe@scholastic.co.uk; Tel 01926 887799;
Fax 01926 883331
Customer Services   Chris Ratcliffe

The School Planner Company Ltd
80 Carolgate, Retford, Nottinghamshire DN22 6EF;
URL www.school-planners.co.uk; e-mail
enquiries@school-planners.co.uk; Tel 01777 861980;
Fax 01777 711782

ScienceScope
Abington Hse, 146 London Rd West, Bath, Somerset
BA1 7DD; URL www.sciencescope.co.uk; e-mail
sales@auc.co.uk; Tel 0870 225 6175; Fax 01225 350029
Customer Service   Sandra Hares; e-mail sandra@auc.co.uk

Scientific and Chemical Supplies Ltd
Carlton Hse, Livingstone Rd, Bilston, West Midlands
WV14 0QZ; URL www.scichem.co.uk; e-mail
scs@scichem.co.uk; Tel 01902 402402; Fax 01902 402343

20

Sebel Furniture Ltd
7 Canon Harnett Ct, Warren Farm Office Village, Wolverton Mill, Milton Keynes, Buckinghamshire MK12 5NF; URL www.sebelfurniture.com; Tel 01908 317766; Fax 01908 317788
Customer Service   Carol Woodroof; e-mail cwoodroof@sebelfurniture.com

Securus Software Ltd
Claremont Hse, Molesey Rd, Hersham, Surrey KT12 4RQ; URL www.securus-software.com; e-mail info@securus-software.com; Tel 01932 255480; Fax 01932 255481
Manager (Marketing)   Linda Stone

Serco Learning Solutions
Winchester Hse, Stephensons Way, Wyvern Business Pk, Derby DE21 6BF; URL www.serco.com; e-mail enquiries@sercolearning.com; Tel (customer services) 0870 046 8861; Tel 0870 046 8865; Fax 01332 660111

SG World Ltd
Duchy Ltd, Crewe, Cheshire CW1 6ND; URL www.sgworld.com; e-mail enquiries@sgworld.com; Tel 01270 500921; Tel (customer services) 01270 588211; Fax 01270 500220

Sherston Software Ltd
Angel Hse, Sherston, Malmesbury, Wiltshire SN16 0LH; URL www.sherston.com; e-mail info@sherston.co.uk; Tel 01666 843200; Fax 01666 843216
Customer Services   Gill Sparrow; e-mail gsparrow@sherston.co.uk

Sibelius Software Ltd
20–22 City North, Fonthill Rd, London N4 3HF; URL www.sibelius.com; e-mail info@sibelius.com; Tel 020 7561 7999; Fax 020 7561 7888

Sico Europe Ltd
See Other Suppliers: Furniture; Classroom and Office

The Skills Factory
Granada TV, Quay St, Manchester, Greater Manchester M60 2EA; URL www.skillsfactory.com; e-mail admin@akillsfactory.com

Smart Kids (UK) Ltd
5 Station Rd, Hungerford, Berkshire RG17 0DY; URL www.smarktkids.co.uk; e-mail sales@smartkids.co.uk; Tel 01488 644644; Fax 01488 644645

Smart Learning Ltd
PO Box 321, Cambridge, Cambridgeshire CB1 3XU; URL www.smart-learning.co.uk; e-mail admin@smart-learning.co.uk; Tel 01223 477550; Fax 01223 477551
Supervisor (Customer Services)   Carla Mason

Soft Teach Educational
Sturgess Farmhouse, Longbridge Deverill, Warminster, Wiltshire BA12 7EA; URL www.soft-teach.co.uk; e-mail info@soft-teach.co.uk; Tel 01985 840329; Fax 01985 840331

Softease
Market Pl, Ashbourne, Derbyshire DE6 1ES; URL www.softease.com; e-mail sales@softease.com; Tel 01335 343421; Fax 01335 343422
Customer Care   Samantha Fletcher

Spacekraft Limited
Titus Hse, 29 Saltaire Rd, Shipley, West Yorkshire BD18 3HH; URL www.spacekraft.co.uk; e-mail enquiries@spacekraft.co.uk; Tel 01274 581007; Fax 01274 531966
Customer Service   Chris Morton

Sparrowhawk and Heald Ltd
3 Cabot Hse, Compass Point Business Pk, Stocks Bridge Way, St Ives, Cambridgeshire PE27 5JL; URL www.sparrowhawkandheald.co.uk; e-mail projects@sparrowhawkandheald.co.uk; Tel 01480 354340; Fax 01480 354345

Special Agent Ltd
233–235 High St, Epping, Essex CM16 4BP; URL www.specialagent.co.uk; e-mail info@specialagent.co.uk; Tel 0870 161 2007; Fax 0870 161 2008

Specialist Crafts
PO Box 247, Leicester LE1 9QS; URL www.specialistcrafts.co.uk; e-mail info@specialistcrafts.co.uk; Tel 0116 269 7711; Fax 0116 269 7722

Specialist Schools Review
Highbury Business Plc, Media Hse, Azalea Dr, Swanley, Kent BR8 8HU; Tel 01322 611419; Fax 01322 616376

Speechmark Publishing Ltd
Telford Rd, Bicester, Oxfordshire OX26 4LQ; URL www.speechmark.net; e-mail info@speechmark.net; Tel 01869 244644; Fax 01869 320040

Staedtler (UK) Ltd
Cowbridge Rd, Pontyclun, Rhondda Cynon Taf CF72 8YJ; URL www.staedtler.co.uk; e-mail enquiries@uk.staedtler.com; Tel 01443 237421; Fax 01443 237440

Stage Systems
Stage Hse, Prince William Rd, Loughborough, Leicestershire LE11 5GU; URL www.stagesystems.co.uk; e-mail info@stagesystems.co.uk; Tel 01509 611021; Fax 01509 233146
Customer Care   Nikki Brown

Steljes Ltd
Bagshot Manor, Green La, Bagshot GU19 5NL; URL www.steljes.co.uk; e-mail info@steljes.co.uk; Tel 0845 075 8758; Fax 0845 026 1500

Step by Step Ltd
Lee Fold, Hyde, Cheshire SK14 4LL; URL www.sbs-educational.co.uk; e-mail enquiries@sbs-educational.co.uk; Tel 0845 125 2550; Fax 0800 056 1438

The Sticker Factory
The Granary, Walnut Tree La, Sudbury, Suffolk, Surrey CO10 1BD; URL www.thestickerfactory.co.uk; e-mail sales@thestickerfactory.co.uk; Tel 01787 370950; Fax 01787 371890
Customer Services   Fiona Garman

Storysack Ltd
Resource Hse, Kay St, Bury, Lancashire BL9 6LU; URL www.storysack.com; e-mail hello@resourcehouse.co.uk; Tel 0161 763 6232; Fax 0161 763 5366

Sunflower Learning Ltd
35 Weston Rd, Thames Ditton, Surrey KT7 0HN; URL www.sunflowerlearning.com; e-mail mail@sunflowerlearning.com; Tel 0845 130 0680; Fax 0845 130 0681

Super Stickers
PO Box 55, 4 Balloo Ave, Bangor, County Down BT19 7PJ; URL www.superstickers.com; e-mail info@motivationinlearning.com; Tel 028 9145 4344; Fax 028 9146 6474
Stickers, charts, certificates, bookmarks, badges, notepads, books, games, posters, classroom decorations, and customised stickers and stampers

Supplies Team Limited

66–70 Vicar La, Little Germany, Bradford BD1 5AG;
URL www.supplies-team.co.uk; e-mail
info@supplies-team.co.uk; Tel 01274 741111;
Fax 01274 892056

Suregrave (UK) Ltd

4 Faraday Cl, Pattinson Industrial Est, Washington, Tyne
and Wear NE38 8QJ; URL www.cadineeducation.com;
e-mail mail@cadineeducation.com; Tel (sales)
0191 417 4505; Fax 0191 415 3410

Sweet Counter/Playground Pictures

PO Box 472, Kingston, Surrey KT2 7ZW;
URL www.sweetcounter.co.uk; e-mail
sweetcounter@dsl.pipex.com; Tel 07973 152064;
Fax 020 8549 2132

Synergic Limited T/A Synergic Workspace Solutions

Unit 5P, Beverley Business Pk, Oldbeck Rd, Beverley, East
Riding of Yorkshire HU17 0JW;
URL www.synergic-uk.com; e-mail
info@synergic-uk.com; Tel 01482 888010;
Fax 01482 888013
Customer Service   David Eva

Syscap Education

Wimbledon Bridge Hse, 1 Hartfield Rd, Wimbledon,
London SW19 3RU; URL www.syscap.com/education;
e-mail education@syscap.com; Tel 020 8254 1870;
Fax 020 8254 1901

TAG Learning Ltd

25 Pelham Rd, Gravesend, Kent DA11 0HU;
URL www.taglearning.com; e-mail
sales@taglearning.com; Tel 01474 357350;
Fax 01474 537887

Tait Components

20 Couper St, Glasgow G4 0DL;
URL www.tait-components.com; e-mail
sales@tait-components.com; Tel 0141 564 1234;
Fax 0141 564 4644

TallyGenicom

Rutherford Rd, Basingtstoke, Hampshire RG24 8PD;
URL www.tallygenicom.co.uk/education; e-mail
info@tallygenicom.co.uk; Tel 0870 872 2888;
Fax 0870 872 2889

Taskmaster Ltd

Morris Rd, Leicester LE2 6BR;
URL www.taskmasteronline.co.uk; e-mail
info@taskmasteronline.co.uk; Tel 0116 270 4286;
Fax 0116 270 6992
Customer Service   Frank Gillard

TEEM

3 Cabot Hse, Stocks Bridge Way, St Ives, Cambridgeshire
PE27 5JL; URL www.teem.org.uk; e-mail
info@teem.org.uk; Tel 01480 354340; Fax 01480 354345
Contact   Ysanne Heald

Texthelp Systems Ltd

Enkalon Business Centre, 25 Randalstown Rd, Antrim
BT41 4LJ; URL www.texthelp.com; e-mail
louise@texthelp.com; Tel 028 9442 8105;
Fax 028 9442 8574

Thorpe Kilworth Ltd

St George's Hse, Moat St, Wigston, Leicestershire
LE18 2NH; URL www.thorpekilworth.co.uk; e-mail
neillogue@thorpekilworth.co.uk; Tel 0116 288 5588;
Fax 0116 281 3777
Director (Business Development)   Mr Neil Logue

Ticktock Media

Unit 2, Orchard Business Centre, North Farm Rd, Tunbridge
Wells TN2 3XF; URL www.ticktock.co.uk; e-mail
info@ticktock.co.uk; Tel 01892 509400; Fax 01892 509401
Customer Services   George Scudder

The Times Educational Supplement

Admiral Hse, 66–68 East Smithfield, London E1W 9BX;
URL www.tes.co.uk; e-mail sales@tes.co.uk;
Tel 020 7782 3000; Fax 020 7782 3042
Customer Service   Patrick Roberts; e-mail
patrick.roberts@newsint.co.uk; Tel 020 7782 3040

TLO Ltd

Henleaze Hse, Harbury Rd, Bristol BS9 4PN;
URL www.tloltd.co.uk; e-mail office@tloltd.co.uk;
Tel 0117 989 8204; Fax 0117 907 7897
Contact   Olivia Wilson

TM Enterprises

9 Primrose Cres, Hyde, Cheshire SK14 5BX; e-mail
timmorgan@btinternet.com; Tel 0161 367 9343

Toshiba Information Systems (UK) Ltd

Toshiba Ct, Weybridge Business Pk, Addlestone,
Weybridge, Surrey KT15 2UL; URL www.toshiba.co.uk/
education; e-mail educationpcs@toshiba-tiu.co.uk;
Tel 01932 841600; Fax 01932 835864

TQ Education and Training Ltd

Bonsall St, Long Eaton, Nottingham NG10 2AN;
URL www.tq.com; e-mail info@tq.com;
Tel 0115 972 2611; Fax 0115 973 1520

Tracline (UK) Ltd

Grosvenor Hse, 1 High St, Edgware, Greater London
HA8 7TA; URL www.tracline.co.uk; e-mail
education@tracline.co.uk; Tel 020 8952 7770;
Fax 020 8951 5149

TS Harrison & Sons

PO Box 20, Union St, Heckmondwike, West Yorkshire
WF16 0HN; URL www.harrison.co.uk; e-mail
mail@harrison.co.uk; Tel 01924 415010; Fax 01924 415011
Sales   David Smith

TSL Education Ltd

Admiral Hse, 66–68 East Smithfield, London E1W 1BX;
URL www.tsleducation.com; Tel 020 7782 3000;
Fax 020 7782 3333

TTS Ltd

Nunn Brook Rd, Huthwaite, Nottinghamshire NG17 2HU;
URL www.tts-group.co.uk; e-mail sales@tts-group.co.uk;
Tel (customer service) 01623 447800; Fax 01623 447999

Unimatic eduCAM

Unimatic Hse, Granville Rd, London NW2 2LN;
URL www.edu-cam.com; e-mail educam@unimatic.com;
Tel 020 8922 1000; Fax 020 8922 1066

UniServity

9th Fl, Thames Tower, Reading RG1 1LX;
URL www.uniservity.com; e-mail info@uniservity.com;
Tel 0870 855 5751; Fax 0870 199 1109

Valiant Technology Ltd

Valiant Hse, 3 Grange Mills, Weir Rd, London SW12 0NE;
URL www.valiant-technology.com; e-mail
info@valiant-technology.com; Tel 020 8673 2233;
Fax 020 8673 6333

Vari-Tech

Sett End Rd North, Shadsworth, Blackburn, Lancashire
BB1 2PT; URL www.vari-tech.co.uk; e-mail
sales@vari-tech.co.uk; Tel 01254 678777;
Fax 01254 678782

VdotCom Ltd

Mitre Hse, Kirkgate, Birstall, West Yorkshire WF17 9HE; URL www.vdotcom.co.uk; Tel 01924 448800; Fax 01924 448844

Viewtech Educational Media

7–8 Falcons Gate, Northavon Business Centre, Dean Rd, Yate, Bristol BS37 5NH; URL www.viewtech.co.uk; e-mail mail@viewtech.co.uk; Tel 01454 858055; Fax 01454 858056

Viglen Limited

Viglen Hse, Alperton La, Alperton, Greater London HA0 1DX; URL www.viglen.co.uk; e-mail sales@viglen.co.uk; Tel 020 8758 7027; Fax 020 8758 7417

Virtual Image Publishing Ltd

184 Reddish Rd, South Reddish, Stockport SK5 7HS; URL www.virtualimmage.co.uk; e-mail nick@virtualimage.co.uk; Tel 0161 480 1915; Fax 0161 612 2965

Welconstruct in Education

Woodgate Business Pk, Kettles Wood Dr, Birmingham, West Midlands B32 3GH; URL www.welconstructeducation.co.uk; e-mail sales@welconstruct.co.uk; Tel 0870 420 9000; Fax 0870 420 9888

Wesco

Unit 20, Manvers Business Pk, High Hazles Rd, Cotgrave, Nottinghamshire NG12 3GZ; URL www.wesco-group.com; e-mail sales@wescouk.co.uk; Tel 0115 989 9765; Fax 0115 989 2401

White Space (Wordshark)

41 Mall Rd, London W6 9DG; URL www.wordshark.co.uk; e-mail sales@wordshark.co.uk; Tel 020 8747 5927; Fax 020 8748 2120

Authors and distributors of Wordshark and Numbershark

Widgit Software

124 Cambridge Science Pk, Milton Rd, Cambridge, Cambridgeshire CB4 0ZS; URL www.widgit.com; e-mail info@widgit.com; Tel 01223 425558; Fax 01223 425349

Wilson and Garden

Newtown St, Kilsyth, Glasgow G65 0JX; URL www.wgltd.com; e-mail sales@wgltd.com; Tel 01236 823291; Fax 01236 825356

Internal Sales   Alanna Park

Wilson and Garden provide presentation solutions to educational establishments throughout the UK. It offers a product range with economy, standard and premier options, including the roller board.

Winslow

Goyt Side Rd, Chesterfield, Derbyshire S40 2PH; URL www.winslow-cat.com; e-mail sales@winslow-cat.com; Tel 0845 230 2777; Fax 01246 551195

Books, games, software, posters etc covering education, special needs, health and rehabilitation. Includes the Xtra product range.

Witley Jones Furniture Limited

Beech Hse, Barracks Rd, Sandy La Industrial Est, Stourport-on-Severn, Worcestershire DY13 9QA; URL www.witleyjones.com; e-mail sales@witleyjones.com; Tel 01299 828888; Fax 01299 828989

Woodham Ltd

1 Coopers Dr, Springwood Industrial Est, Braintree, Essex CM7 2RF; URL www.woodhamsupplies.com; e-mail sales@woodhamltd.co.uk; Tel 01376 553294; Fax 01376 552649

Woodpecker Products (Steel Division)

Little Heath Industrial Est, Unit B18, Old Church Rd, Coventry, Warwickshire CV6 7NB; URL www.woodpeckercomputersecurity.co.uk; e-mail woodpeckerproducts@yahoo.co.uk; Tel 024 7663 8246; Fax 024 7663 8508

Customer Services   Len Orrick

Worlddidac

Bollwerk 21, PO Box 8866, CH-3001 Berne, Switzerland; URL www.worlddidac.org; e-mail info@worlddidac.org; Tel +41 31 311 76 82; Fax +41 31 312 17 44

Zentek Solutions

Zentek Hse, St Marks St, Bolton, Lancashire BL3 6NR; URL www.zentek.co.uk; e-mail sales@zentek.co.uk; Tel 01204 397878; Fax 01204 397880

Other Suppliers

Building Contractors

Accomodex Ltd

Leofric Hse, Oxford Rd, Ryton-on-Dunmore, Coventry, Warwickshire CV8 3ED; URL www.accomodex.co.uk; e-mail davidbailiff@accomodex.co.uk; Tel 024 7630 1301; Fax 024 7630 1148

Boyd Sport & Play Limited

See also sportsequip.co.uk under Furniture; Playground and Outdoor

The Manor, Tur Langton, Market Harborough, Leicestershire LE8 0PJ; URL www.sportsequip.co.uk; e-mail sales@sportsequip.co.uk; Tel 01858 545854; Fax 01858 545954

Brymac London Ltd

Unit 38a Leyton Industrial Village, Argall Way, Leyton, London E10 7QP; URL www.brymac.co.uk; e-mail tarmac@brymaclondon.freeserve.co.uk; Tel 020 8556 8805; Fax 020 8556 8933

Charles Lawrence Surfaces plc

Brunel Hse, Jessop Way, Newark, Nottinghamshire NG24 2ER; URL www.clgplc.co.uk; e-mail surfaces@clgplc.co.uk; Tel 01636 610777; Fax 01636 610222

Courtmarkers

Indigo Suite C, Rainbow Industrial Est, Trout Rd, West Drayton, London UB7 7XT; URL www.courtmarkers.com; Tel 01895 448588; Fax 01895 448608

Deva Resin Services

Chester Rd, Sandycroft, Flintshire CH5 2QW; URL www.devaresinservices.co.uk; e-mail larry@devaresinservices.co.uk; Tel 01244 533666; Fax 01244 538987

Fingershield Safety UK

The Old School Hse, Lind St, Manchester, Lancashire M40 7ES; URL www.fingershield.co.uk; e-mail info@fingershield.co.uk; Tel 0800 980 9444; Fax 0161 272 7000

Foremans Relocatable Building Systems Limited

Catfoss La, Brandesburton, Driffield, East Riding of Yorkshire YO25 8EJ; URL www.foremansbuildings.co.uk; e-mail sales@foremansbuildings.co.uk; Tel 01964 544344; Fax 01964 542141

20

Framework CDM Ltd
PO Box 393, Chesterfield, Derbyshire S42 6WY;
    URL www.frameworkcdm.com; e-mail
    info@frameworkcdm.com; Tel 0870 071 8728;
    Fax 01246 268789

Machzone
Eagle Terr, Cleveland St, Kingston upon Hull, East Riding of
    Yorkshire HU8 7BJ;
    URL www.machzoneconv.free-online.co.uk; e-mail
    machzone@freewire.co.uk; Tel 01482 212208;
    Fax 01482 588578

Matta Products (UK) Limited
Unit 1d, The Summit, Hanworth Rd, Sunbury, Surrey
    TW16 5DB; URL www.matta-products.com; e-mail
    sales@matta-products.com; Tel 01932 788699;
    Fax 01932 788330

Playgrounds (UK) Ltd
80 High St, Winchester, Hampshire SO23 9AT;
    URL www.playgrounds.uk.com; e-mail
    sales@playgrounds.uk.com; Tel 0845 170 1234;
    Fax 0845 170 1236

SMR Trading
40 Juniper Sq, Havant, Hampshire PO9 1JA;
    URL www.ukrubbermats.co.uk; e-mail
    info@ukrubbermats.co.uk; Tel 02392 473927;
    Fax 02392 473927

Whittle Painting Group Ltd
Daybrook Hse, Merchant St, Bulwell, Nottingham,
    Nottinghamshire NG6 8GT;
    URL www.whittlepaintinggroup.co.uk; e-mail
    sales@whittlepaintinggroup.co.uk; Tel 0115 977 0311;
    Fax 0115 977 1472

Building Equipment and Services

Avanta UK Ltd
Unit B1 Astra Pk, Parkside La, Leeds, West Yorkshire
    LS11 5TD; URL www.avantauk.com; e-mail
    sales@avantauk.com; Tel 0113 384 8777;
    Fax 0113 384 8778

Haes Systems Ltd
Columbia Hse, Packet Boat La, Cowley Uxbridge, London
    UB8 2JP; URL www.haes-systems.co.uk; e-mail
    enquiries@haes-systems.co.uk; Tel 01895 422066;
    Fax 01895 402603

Helmsman
Northern Way, Bury St Edmunds, Suffolk IP32 6NH;
    URL www.helmsman.co.uk; e-mail
    sales@helmsman.co.uk; Tel 01284 757600; Tel (sales)
    01284 757666; Fax 01284 757601

S & D Contracting Services Limited
4–8 Vyner St, London E2 9DG; URL www.s-and-d.com;
    e-mail dermot.connell@s-and-d.com; Tel 020 8983 6168;
    Fax 020 8983 6169

SG Consulting
86 St Peter's Ave, Sowerby, Halifax, West Yorkshire
    HX6 1DB; URL www.sgconsulting.org.uk; e-mail
    sgconsulting00@aol.com; Tel 01422 831765;
    Fax 01748 818798

SICL
SICL Hse, 131 Upper Wortley Rd, Leeds, West Yorkshire
    LS12 4JG; URL www.sicl.co.uk; e-mail info@sicl.co.uk;
    Tel 0113 238 9900; Fax 0113 238 9910

Wintun
Wintun Works, Millerston, Paisley, Renfrewshire PA1 2XR;
    URL www.wintun.co.uk; e-mail mail@wintun.co.uk;
    Tel 0141 889 5969; Fax 0141 887 8907

Classroom and Office Supplies

3M UK Plc
Market Pl, Bracknell, Berkshire RG12 1JU;
    URL www.3m.com/uk; e-mail kwheeldon@mmm.com;
    Tel 0870 536 0036; Fax 01344 858175
Contact   Keith Wheeldon

A to Z Supplies Ltd
PO Box 777, Chelmsford, Essex CM1 6PR;
    URL www.atozsupplies.co.uk; e-mail
    kpayne@atozsupplies.co.uk; Tel 01245 398000;
    Fax 01245 398261
Contact   Karen Payne

ACS Ltd
Oldmedow Rd, Hardwick Industrial Est, King's Lynn,
    Norfolk PE30 4LD; URL www.acssupplies.com; e-mail
    sales@acssupplies.com; Tel 0845 050 0863;
    Fax 0845 050 0864
Contact   Toni Bullock

ACS Office Solutions
ACS Hse, Oxwich Cl, Brackmills, Northampton,
    Northamptonshire NN4 7BH;
    URL www.acsofficesolutions.com; e-mail
    info@acsofficesolutions.com; Tel 01604 704000;
    Fax 01604 704001
Contact   Richard Walker

Ash Computer & Office Supplies
81 Leigh St, Sheffield, South Yorkshire S9 2PR;
    URL www.ashcos.co.uk; e-mail ian@ashcos.co.uk;
    Tel 0114 243 3181; Fax 0114 243 9258
Contact   Ian Smith

ATP Instrumentation Ltd
Tournament Way, Ivanhoe Industrial Est, Ashby de la
    Zouch, Leicestershire LE65 2UU;
    URL www.atp-instrumentation.co.uk; e-mail
    sales@atp-instruments.co.uk; Tel 01530 566800;
    Fax 01530 560373
Manager (Sales Department)   Elaine Tombs
ATP Instrumentation supplies test and measurement
equipment for use in the science department, from timers to
multimeters, thermometers and scales

Baker Ross Ltd
2–3 Forest Works, Forest Rd, London E17 6JF;
    URL www.bakerross.co.uk; e-mail
    sales@bakerross.co.uk; Tel 0870 458 5400;
    Fax 0870 458 5445
Director (Marketing)   Paul Baker

Black Cat Acoustics
Festival Hse, Chapman Way, Tunbridge Wells, Kent
    TN2 3EF; URL www.blackcatacoustics.co.uk; e-mail
    info@blackcatacoustics.co.uk; Tel 01892 619819;
    Fax 01892 619123
Acoustics Engineer   Jeff Craske
Supply, manufacture and installation acoustic products

Black Cat Music
Festival Hse, Chapman Way, Tunbridge Wells, Kent
    TN2 3EF; URL www.blackcatmusic.co.uk; e-mail
    blackcatacoustics@yahoo.co.uk; Tel 01892 619719;
    Fax 01892 619123
Senior Sales Executive   Sharon Simpson

Class Ideas
Freepost (SO6206), Romsey, Hampshire SO51 0ZZ;
    URL www.classideas.co.uk; e-mail
    sales@classideas.co.uk; Tel 0800 028 0785
Class Ideas supplies motivational and display items to UK
primary and early years schools. Class Ideas is a trading
name of the parent company Whitehill Publishing Ltd.

20

Educational Aids
25 Bradfield Cl, Finedon Rd Industrial Est, Wellingborough,
Northamptonshire NN8 4RQ; URL www.edaids.com;
e-mail edaids@aol.com; Tel 01933 274434;
Fax 01933 274313
Customer Service   Stephanie Freer

Express Cleaning Supplies
Unit 14, 190 Malvern Common, Poolbrook Rd, Malvern,
Worcestershire WR14 3JZ;
URL www.expresscleaningsupplies.co.uk; e-mail
sales@expresscleaningsupplies.co.uk; Tel 01684 565552;
Fax 01684 577707
Contact   Chris Ralph

Great Art (Artists' Materials)
Normandy Hse, 1 Nether St, Alton, Hampshire GU34 1EA;
URL www.greatart.co.uk; e-mail
welcome@greatart.co.uk; Tel 01420 593332;
Fax 01420 593333
Contact   James Stock

IBS Office Solutions
URL www.ibs-uk.net; e-mail enquiries@ibs-uk.net;
Tel 01491 411996

Just Lamps
Turnfields Ct, Thatcham, Berkshire RG19 4PT;
URL www.justlamps.net; e-mail peter@justlamps.net;
Tel 01635 876950; Fax 01635 273131
Sales Executive   Peter Healy

Magiboards Ltd
Stafford Pk 12, Telford, Shropshire TF3 3BJ;
URL www.magiboards.com; e-mail
sales@magiboards.com; Tel 01952 292111;
Fax 01952 292280

Micro Librarian Systems (MLS)
Arden Hse, Shepley La, Hawk Grn, Marple, Stockport,
Cheshire SK6 7JW; URL www.microlib.co.uk; e-mail
info@microlib.co.uk; Tel 0161 449 9357;
Fax 0161 449 0055
Contact   Andrew O'Brian

Positive Identity
PO Box 17709, London SE6 4ZQ;
URL www.positive-identity.com; e-mail
info@positive-identity.com; Tel 020 8314 0442;
Fax 0871 661 7920
Manager   Alison Collins

Professional Test Systems
Summer Ct, Manafon, Welshpool, Powys SY21 8BJ; e-mail
sales@proftest.com; Tel 01686 650160; Fax 01686 650170
General Manager   M. Doughty

Ricoh Image Communication
Ricoh Hse, 1 Plane Tree Cres, Feltham, London TW13 7HG;
URL www.ricoh.co.uk; Tel 020 8261 4000;
Fax 020 8261 4004

Standard Forms Ltd
Unit 10, Romsey Industrial Estate, Romsey, Hampshire
SO51 0HR; Tel 01794 830302
Director (Marketing)   I. Stephen
To provide motivational items, personalised stationery and
administration items by mail order to schools

Clothing and Uniforms

A–Z Schoolwear
School Shop (mail order) Ltd, FREEPOST, Harrietsham,
Maidstone, Kent ME17 1BR;
URL www.schoolshop.co.uk; e-mail
info@schoolshop.co.uk; Tel 01622 851447;
Fax 01622 851449
Contact   Mariya May

Anglia Sports & Schoolwear Ltd
8 Paxton Rd, Gorse Lane Industrial Est, Clacton-on-Sea,
Essex CO15 4LR;
URL www.angliasportsandschoolwear.co.uk; e-mail
sales@angliasportsandschoolwear.co.uk;
Tel 01255 474550; Fax 01255 474570
Contact   Lynn Madle

APC Clothing Ltd
Unit 6a Guardian Pk, Station Road Industrial Est, Tadcaster,
North Yorkshire LS24 9SG;
URL www.apc-clothing.co.uk; e-mail
nhall@apcclothing.co.uk; Tel 01937 833449;
Fax 01937 832649
Contact   Nick Hall

Art2go UK Ltd
82 Sweyn Rd, Cliftonville, Margate, Kent CT9 2DD;
URL www.art2go-uk.com; Tel 01843 292333;
Fax 01843 290333
Contact   Ian Biggs

Direct Clothing Company
White Hart Hse, Silwood Rd, Ascot, Berkshire SL5 0PY;
URL www.thedirectclothing.co.uk; e-mail
sales@thedirectclothing.co.uk; Tel 01344 872299;
Fax 01344 872312
Contact   Simon Smith

Directschoolwear & Co
Unit 9, Carey Way, Wembley, London HA9 0LQ; e-mail
michael@magicgroup.co.uk; Tel 020 8733 8100;
Fax 020 8733 8148
Contact   Michael Mirpuri

discountschoolwear.com
1st Fl, 114–116 Queen St, Morley, Leeds, West Yorkshire
LS27 9EB; URL www.discountschoolwear.com; e-mail
sales@discountschoolwear.com; Tel 0113 252 1463
Contact   Mr Aziz

Duvatex Clothing Schoolwear Manufacturers
8 Sunderland St, Halifax, West Yorkshire HX1 5AF;
URL www.duvatex.com; e-mail duvatex@hotmail.com;
Tel 01422 363534; Fax 01422 320335

Kitman.co.uk Ltd
128b Station Rd, Sidcup, Kent DA15 7AF;
URL www.kitman.co.uk; e-mail sales@kitman.co.uk;
Tel 020 8302 5828; Fax 020 8302 5828
Contact   Paul Brisenden

Marcus Shoes
Boleyn Lodge, Marryat Rd, Wimbledon, London SW19 5BD;
URL www.marcusshoes.com; e-mail
post@marcusshoes.com; Tel 07973 371240
Contact   Sam Marcus

National Schoolwear Centres Ltd
Kettering Hall, Church Rd, Wymondham, Norwich, Norfolk
NR18 9RS; URL www.nationalschoolwearcentres.co.uk
Contact   Susan Lee

Noyna Aprons and Playwear
Freepost, Urmston, Manchester, Greater Manchester
M41 7ZZ; URL www.noyna.co.uk; e-mail
info@noyna.co.uk; Tel 0161 748 2724; Fax 0161 747 8775

Schoolyard
Limlow Hse, Royston Rd, Litlington, Royston,
Hertfordshire SG8 0RS; URL www.schoolyard.co.uk;
e-mail sales@schoolyard.co.uk; Tel 0800 132988;
Fax 0800 174137
Contact   Lesley Harvey

Sportec Trading Ltd
Unit 5, Abbey Road Industrial Est, Neath, Vale of
Glamorgan SA10 7DN; URL www.sportec.co.uk; e-mail
sales@sportec.co.uk; Tel 01639 632250; Fax 01639 645222

Embroidered and printed sportswear, workwear, leisurewear, corporate wear, schoolwear, sports equipment and sports accessories

Top Form Clothing Limited
90–91 The Stow, Harlow, Essex CM20 3AP;
  URL www.top-form.com; e-mail sales@top-form.com;
  Tel 01279 434813; Fax 01279 635345
Contact   Claire Harrison

Wren Schoolwear Ltd
20 Telford Way, Severalls Pk, Colchester, Essex CO4 4QP;
  URL www.wrenschoolwear.co.uk; e-mail
  info@wrenschoolwear.co.uk; Tel 01206 841222;
  Fax 01206 841118
Contact   Keith Farrer

Educational Resource Suppliers

Credit Action
Howard Hse, The Point, Weaver Rd, Lincoln, Lincolnshire
  LN6 3QN; URL www.creditaction.org.uk; e-mail
  office@creditaction.org.uk; Tel 01522 699777;
  Fax 01522 697703
National Director   Keith Tondeur
Credit Action provides a range of publications giving information concerning a variety of issues surrounding money

Digitalbrain Ltd
Aspect Hse, 84–87 Queens Rd, Brighton, East Sussex
  BN1 5XE; URL www.digitalbrain.com; e-mail
  info@digitalbrain.com; Tel (customer services)
  0870 077 7655; Tel 01273 201700; Fax 01273 729382

Heinemann, Ginn and Rigby
Halley Ct, Jordan Hill, Oxford, Oxfordshire OX2 8EJ;
  URL www.harcourt.co.uk; e-mail
  enquiries@harcourt.co.uk; Tel 01865 888000;
  Fax 01865 314091

Hindleys Ltd
Hillcrest Works, 230 Woodbourn Rd, Sheffield, South
  Yorkshire S9 3LQ; URL www.hindleys.com; e-mail
  sales@hindleys.com; Tel 0114 278 7828; Fax 0114 278 8558
Customer Service   Richard Henry

Listening Books
12 Lant St, London SE1 1QH;
  URL www.listening-books.org.uk; e-mail
  info@listening-books.org.uk; Tel 020 7407 9417;
  Fax 020 7403 1377

National Advice and Information Centre (Outdoor Education)
DMIHE, High Melton Site, Doncaster, South Yorkshire

National Centre for Language and Literacy
University of Reading, Bulmershe Ct, Woodlands Ave,
  Reading RG6 1HY; URL www.ncll.org.uk; e-mail
  ncll@reading.ac.uk; Tel 0118 378 8820; Fax 0118 378 6801

Newspapers in Education (NIE)
121 Sapley Rd, Hartford, Huntingdon, Cambridgeshire
  PE29 1YU; e-mail cmcint@btconnect.com;
  Tel 01480 435428; Fax 01480 435439
Director   George Kelly

PLATO Learning
Statesman Hse, Stafferton Way, Maidenhead, Berkshire
  SL6 1AD; URL www.platolearning.co.uk; e-mail
  ukinfo@plato.com; Tel 01628 588300

Rosetta Stone
St Stephen's Hse, Arthur Rd, Windsor, Berkshire SL4 1RY;
  URL www.rosettastone.com; Tel 01753 834520;
  Fax 01753 830973

Rosetta Stone publishes language training software for more than 28 languages. Programs are available online, CD-ROM or for network and ancillary materials for students and teachers are available including a student management system and flexibility in tailoring courses to individual students.

Finance and Support

Accutecc UK Limited
West Rd, Templefields, Harlow, Essex CM20 2AL; e-mail
  accutecc@kores.co.uk; Tel 01279 401320;
  Fax 01279 437638
Contact   Marnie Welsh

Alder Broker Group Limited
140 Long La, Bexleyheath, Kent DA7 5AH;
  URL www.abgonline.co.uk; e-mail
  commercial@abgonline.co.uk; Tel 0800 318 228;
  Fax 020 8304 9788
Contact   Denis Waller

Association of School and College Leaders
130 Regent Rd, Leicester, Leicestershire LE1 7PG;
  URL www.ascl.org.uk; e-mail info@ascl.org.uk;
  Tel 0116 299 1122; Fax 0116 299 1123

Cleaford Video Services
46 Hazell Rd, Farnham, Surrey GU9 7BP;
  URL www.videocopy.org.uk; e-mail
  sales@cleaford.co.uk; Tel 0845 124 9402;
  Fax 01252 717137
Contact   Angus Cleaver

Dr Hadwen Trust
84a Tilehouse St, Hitchin, Hertfordshire SG5 2DY;
  URL www.drhadwentrust.org; e-mail
  info@drhadwentrust.org; Tel 01462 436819;
  Fax 01462 436844
Science Officer   Carol Newman

ESL Equipment Finance Limited
Stack Hse, 58 Arcadian Ave, Bexley, Kent DA5 1JW; e-mail
  mark@eslltd.co.uk; Tel 0870 350 1406; Fax 0870 350 1407
Contact   Mark Bailey

Faber Systems
2nd Fl, Unit 2, Century Pl, Lamberts Rd, Tunbridge Wells,
  Kent TN1 3EH; URL www.fabsys.com; e-mail
  info@fabsys.com; Tel 01892 517388
Contact   Chris Smith

Hardy's Publishing
6 Cavendish Bldgs, Hill St, Lydney, Gloucestershire
  GL15 5HD; URL www.hardysyearbooks.co.uk; e-mail
  jonhardy@hardysyearbooks.co.uk; Tel 01594 840400;
  Fax 01594 840401
Contact   Jon Hardy

Leasemaster Business Finance Ltd
106 Carver St, Birmingham, West Midlands B1 3AP;
  URL www.lbf.uk.com; e-mail traceyg@lbf.uk.com;
  Tel 0845 060 1111; Fax 0845 060 1112
Contact   Graeme Ferguson

Money To Schools
Unit D1, Longmead Business Pk, Epsom, Surrey KT19 9UP;
  URL www.moneytoschools.com; e-mail
  info@moneytoschools.com; Tel 01372 723723;
  Fax 01372 743743

Permark Name Tapes
Permark Hse, 4 Lavender Gdns, Harrow, London HA3 6DD;
  URL www.nametapesdirect.com; e-mail
  nametapesdirect@aol.com; Tel 020 8954 6333;
  Fax 020 8954 6677
Contact   Cyril Pulver

Schoolsafe Insurance Services Ltd

65 Baildon Mills, Northgate, Baildon, Shipley, West Yorkshire BD17 6JX; URL www.school-safe.com; e-mail kirstyb@school-safe.com; Tel 01274 411112; Fax 01274 410020

Contact Kirsty Breaks

Systems Capital Plc (Syscap)

Wimbledon Bridge Hse, 1 Hartfield Rd, Wimbledon, London SW19 3RU; URL www.syscap-education.com; e-mail education@syscap.com; Tel 020 8254 1870; Fax 020 8254 1901

Contact Richard Shipley

Voice Connect

8–12 Fir Tree La, Groby, Leicester, Leicestershire LE6 0FH; URL www.voiceconnect.co.uk; e-mail informer@voiceconnect.co.uk; Tel 0116 232 2622; Fax 0116 232 2433

Contact Annie Taylor

Wyse Leasing Plc

Prospect Hse, 25 High St, Chesham, Buckinghamshire HP5 1BG; URL www.wyseleasing.com; e-mail johanna.farndon@wyseleasing.com; Tel 01494 791555; Fax 01494 790699

Contact Johanna Farndon

Furniture

Classroom and Office

Anglepoise

6 Stratfield Pk, Elettra Ave, Waterlooville, Hampshire PO7 7XN; URL www.anglepoise.com; Tel 02392 250934; Fax 02392 250696

Audience Systems Ltd

Washington Rd, West Wilts Trading Est, Westbury, Wiltshire BA13 4JP; URL www.audiencesystems.com; e-mail sales@audiencesystems.com; Tel 01373 865050; Fax 01373 827545

Bridge County Ltd

25 Francis St, Hull HU12 8DT; URL www.bridgecounty.co.uk; Tel 01482 588288; Fax 01482 588388

Bridgtown Furniture & Design Limited

Unit 1 Birch Business Pk, Progress Dr, Bridgtown, Cannock, Staffordshire WS11 0BF; URL www.bridgtownfurnituredesign.co.uk; e-mail enquiries@bridgtownfurnituredesign.co.uk; Tel 01543 500666; Fax 01543 579666

Claire Clifford Office Products

98 Laidlaw St, Glasgow G5 8LA; URL www.claire-clifford.co.uk; Tel 0141 420 6789; Fax 0141 420 3420

Curtis Office Furniture Ltd

Eastmount Rd, Darlington, County Durham DL1 1LA; URL www.curtisoffice.co.uk; e-mail enquiries@curtisoffice.co.uk; Tel 01325 380024; Fax 01325 461003

DAXS (Display and Exhibition Solutions)

36 Brian Ave, Sanderstead, Surrey CR2 9NE; URL www.daxs.co.uk; e-mail sales@daxs.co.uk; Tel 020 8651 3618

Display boards, lecterns and plinths, lightboxes, banner stands and pop-ups, brochure stands and counter units

EME Furniture

Blackaddie Rd, Sanquhar, Dumfries and Galloway DG4 6DE; URL www.emescotland.co.uk; e-mail info@emescotland.co.uk; Tel 01659 50404; Fax 0800 132713

Manager (Sales) Peter Raworth

Emmerich (Berlon) Ltd

Wotton Rd, Ashford, Kent TN23 6JY; URL www.emir.co.uk; e-mail edyrbook@emir.co.uk; Tel 01233 622684; Fax 01233 645801

Everything Office

Vernon Hse, The Marina, Lowestoft, Suffolk NR32 1HH; URL www.owa.co.uk/education.htm; e-mail sales@everythingoffice.co.uk; Tel 01502 508080; Fax 01502 508700

Gopak Ltd

Range Rd, Hythe, Kent CT21 6HG; URL www.gopak.co.uk; e-mail info@gopak.co.uk; Tel 01303 265751; Fax 01303 268282

Gratnells Ltd

8 Howard Way, Harlow, Essex CM20 2SU; URL www.gratnells.com; e-mail trays@gratnells.co.uk; Tel 01279 401550; Fax 01279 419127

GT Cheshire and Son

Coventry St, Kidderminster, Worcestershire DY10 2BW; URL www.cheshires.co.uk; Tel 01562 820491

i-desk Solutions Ltd

Unit B6, Falcon Business Pk, Ivanhoe Rd, Hogwood La, Finchampstead, Berkshire RG40 4QQ; URL www.i-desk.co.uk; e-mail paul.nixon@i-desk.co.uk; Tel 0870 770 6890; Fax 0870 777 1481

K-A Display Systems

Whitehall Workshops, Whitehall La, Grindleton, Lancashire BB7 4RL; URL www.ka-display.co.uk; e-mail contactus@kilnerandaspion.co.uk; Tel 01200 441422; Fax 01200 440866

Laytrad Ltd

30 Harmsworth Way, London N20 8JU; URL www.laytrad.co.uk; Tel 020 8445 1688; Fax 020 8446 5944

Maltbury Staging Ltd

22 Pine Rd, London NW2 6RY; URL www.maltbury.com; Tel 0845 130 8881; Fax 020 8208 1318

Nationwide Office Furniture

40 Warren St, London W1T 6AF; URL www.nationwideofficefurniture.com; e-mail sales@corporateofficeinteriors.com; Tel 0800 594 7654; Fax 0845 451 3695

Norseman Direct

Unit 2, Livingstone Mills, Howard St, Batley, West Yorkshire WF17 6JH; URL www.norsemandirect.com; e-mail sales@norsemandirect.com; Tel 01924 439800; Fax 01924 439801

Officestar Group Ltd

Acorn Bldg, Mushet Pk, Gloucestershire GL16 8RE; URL www.officestar-group.co.uk; e-mail 4schools@officestar-group.com; Tel 01594 810081; Fax 01594 810111

Delivering office supplies, office furniture and a full range of educational needs throughout mainland UK and parts of Europe

Osborne Associates VC Ltd

Arch Villa, 23 High St, Bozeat, Northamptonshire NN29 7NF; URL www.osborne-associates.co.uk; Tel 01933 665983; Fax 01933 665984

Point Eight Limited

Narrowboat Way, Blackbrook Valley Industrial Est, Dudley, West Midlands DY2 0E2; URL www.point8.co.uk; e-mail info@point8.co.uk; Tel 01384 238282; Fax 01384 455746

Contact Gary Flavell

Promethean

Promethean Hse, Lower Philips Rd, Blackburn, Lancashire BB1 5TH; URL www.prometheanworld.com; e-mail info@prometheanworld.com; Tel 01254 298598; Fax 01254 581574

R & A Office Environments Ltd

The Football Ground, Moss La, Altrincham, Cheshire WA15 8AP; URL www.randaoffice.co.uk; Tel 0161 929 4747; Fax 0161 929 3929

Schmidt Industries UK Ltd

19 Stoneley Rd, Crewe, Cheshire CW1 4NQ; URL www.matshop.co.uk; e-mail matshoponline@btconnect.com; Tel 01270 253063; Fax 01270 583162

Contact Ann Brookes

SD-Displays

Lancaster Rd, Cressex Business Pk, High Wycombe, Buckinghamshire HP12 3PY; URL www.sd-displays.co.uk; e-mail sales@sd-displays.co.uk; Tel 01494 465212; Fax 01494 465145

Sico Europe Ltd

Henwood Industrial Est, Ashford, Kent TN24 8DH; Tel 01233 643311; Fax 01233 645143

The Specialist Lighting Company Ltd

49 The Broadway, Cheam, Sutton, Surrey SM3 8BL; e-mail sales@specialistlightingonline.com; Tel 020 8643 3110; Fax 020 8770 1911

A specialist lamp stockist providing lamps to schools throughout the UK, the lamps are used mainly within ICT and drama departments, particularly for overhead projectors, LCD data projectors and theatre lighting equipment

Studikraft Limited

Unit 1, Joshua Business Pk, Cromford Rd, Langley Mill, Nottinghamshire NG16 4EW; URL www.studikraft.co.uk; Tel 01773 713715; Fax 01773 714911

Supplyzone and Devon Procurement Services

2 Trusham Rd, Marsh Barton Industrial Est, Exeter, Devon EX2 8RB; URL www.supplyzone.org.uk; e-mail supplyzone@devon.gov.uk; Tel 01392 384651; Fax 01392 384636

Top Office plc

7 Heron Industrial Est, Cooks Rd, Stratford, London E15 2PW; URL www.topoffice.co.uk; e-mail sales@topoffice.co.uk; Tel 0800 592996; Fax 020 8519 5142

Warwick Fraser & Co Ltd

Unit 9, Alford Business Centre, Loxwood Rd, Alford, Cranleigh, Surrey GU6 8HP; URL www.warwickfraser.co.uk; e-mail sales@warwickfraser.co.uk; Tel 01403 753069; Fax 01403 752469

Withy Grove (Leeds) Ltd

Unit 17, Pontefract Rd, Stourton, Leeds, West Yorkshire LS10 1SP; URL www.withygrovesafes.net; e-mail security.wgoi@ic24.net; Tel 0113 272 1441; Fax 0113 272 1881

Playground and Outdoor

Active Learning

28 Hartley Business Centre, Hucknall Rd, Nottingham, Nottinghamshire NG5 1FD; URL www.activelearning-uk.com; Tel 0115 960 6111; Fax 0115 960 6111

Arts Desire

290 Lynton Rd, London SE1 5DE; URL www.artsdesire.co.uk; Tel 020 7231 4441; Fax 020 7231 4441

Bins-n-Benches

Smithy La, Holmeswood, Ormskirk, Lancashire L40 1UH; URL www.bins-n-benches.co.uk; Tel 01704 821136; Fax 01704 821136

Broxap Cloakroom Furniture

Glen St Works, Glen St, Hebburn, Tyne and Wear NE13 1NE; URL www.broxap.com; e-mail cloakrooms@broxap.com; Tel 0191 496 2699; Fax 0191 483 5552

Easthigh Ltd

13 Kilbourn St, St Anns, Nottingham, Nottinghamshire NG3 1BQ; URL www.easthigh.co.uk; Tel 0115 958 2957; Fax 0115 958 7870

Mercury Sports Equipment

Victoria Rd, Fenton, Stoke-on-Trent, Staffordshire ST4 2HS; URL www.mercurysportsequipment.co.uk; Tel 01782 845577; Fax 01782 744998

Playquest Adventure Play Ltd

Bethania Chapel, Main Rd, Ffynnongroew, Flintshire CH8 9SW; URL www.playquest.co.uk; Tel 01745 561117

sportsequip.co.uk

See also Boyd Sport & Play Limited under Building Contractors

The Manor, Tur Langton, Market Harborough, Leicestershire LE8 0PJ; URL www.sportsequip.co.uk; e-mail sales@sportsequip.co.uk; Tel 01858 545789; Fax 01858 545954

Timberline Ltd

Highlands Pl, Foxwood Industrial Pk, Foxwood Rd, Sheepbridge, Chesterfield, Derbyshire S41 9RN; URL www.timberline.co.uk; e-mail info@timberline.co.uk; Tel 01246 454484; Fax 01246 456000

IT and Audio-Visual

See also Chapter 19: Computers in Education

247av.com

2 Winey Cl, Chessington, Surrey KT9 2SP; URL www.247av.com; e-mail info@247av.com; Tel 0870 745 9692; Fax 0870 745 9693

Contact Kunal Khanna

ADA Computer Systems

The Coach Hse, Rownhams Hse, Rownhams, Southampton, Hampshire SO16 8LS

Contact Costa Adamou

Adboards

Units 3–7 Boundary Industrial Est, Millfield Rd, Bolton, Greater Manchester BL2 6QZ; URL www.adboards.co.uk; e-mail info@adboards.co.uk; Tel 01204 395730; Fax 01204 388018

Contact Paul Howe

Asyst International

Dean Bradley Hse, 52 Horseferry Rd, London SW1P 2AF;
    URL www.asyst.co.uk/schools; e-mail
    pd@asyst-international.com; Tel 020 7976 7545;
    Fax 020 7976 7546
Contact   Phil Duffy

Bellville Associates Ltd

4 Provident Pl, Empson Rd, Peterborough, Cambridgeshire
    PE1 5UU; URL www.bellville-associates.co.uk; e-mail
    trevor@bellville-associates.co.uk; Tel 01733 891414;
    Fax 01733 891415
Contact   Trevor Jackson

Bluepoint Corporation Ltd

Davy Ave, Knowhill, Milton Keynes, Buckinghamshire
    MK5 8PB; URL www.bluepoint.net; e-mail
    edu@bluepoint.net
Contact   Jennie Pinder

Brian Madigan

12 Bladud Bldgs, Bath, Somerset BA1 5LS; Tel 01225 463088
Contact   B. Madigan

BTL Publishing

Salts Wharf, Ashley La, Shipley, West Yorkshire BD17 7DB;
    URL www.btlpublishing.com; e-mail
    lisat@btlpublishing.com; Tel 01274 203250;
    Fax 01274 203251
Contact   Lisa Tilsley

Bullet Point Presentations

Park Hse, Wilmington St, Leeds, West Yorkshire LS7 2BP;
    URL www.innovativetechnology.co.uk; e-mail
    enquiries@bullet-point.co.uk; Tel (enquiries)
    0845 606 7600; Fax 0845 606 7601

Cannon Computing / Cumana

Whitegate, Dunmow Rd, Hatfield Heath, Hertfordshire
    CM22 7ED; URL www.cumana.co.uk; e-mail
    ntaylor@cumana.co.uk; Tel 01279 730800;
    Fax 01279 730809
Contact   Nigel A. Taylor

CBC (Northern) Ltd

10–11 Avenue Cres, Seaton Delaval, Tyne and Wear
    NE25 0DN; URL www.cbcnorthern.com; e-mail
    jen@cbcnorthern.com; Tel 0191 237 4000;
    Fax 0191 237 7788
Contact   Jen Appleby

Cygma Distribution Company Ltd

Kelmercourt Hse, 102 Sale La, Tyldesley, Lancashire
    M29 8PZ; URL www.inkjet-carts.co.uk; e-mail
    keith@europacific.co.uk; Tel 0161 799 6366;
    Fax 0161 799 6313
Contact   Keith Moss

Dalen Ltd (Top-Tec)

Valepits Rd, Garretts Green Industrial Est, Birmingham,
    West Midlands B33 0TD; URL www.top-tec.co.uk; e-mail
    sales@top-tec.co.uk; Tel 0121 783 3838; Fax 0121 784 6348
Contact   Simon Ferguson
Dalen Top-Tec supplies physical security devices for ICT
and audio-visual technology, and a range of secure desk
solutions for classroom or open-learning environments.
Many products are LPCB approved.

Dolphin Computer Access Ltd

Technology Hse, Blackpole Trading Est West, Worcester,
    Worcestershire WR3 8TJ; URL www.yourdolphin.com;
    e-mail info@dolphinuk.co.uk; Tel 01905 754577;
    Fax 01905 754559
Contact   Hazel Shaw
Software solutions for people with visual and print
impairments

DVD

Forward Hse, Oakfield Industrial Est, Eynsham,
    Oxfordshire OX29 4TT; URL www.eved.co.uk; e-mail
    polly.inness@everythingeducation.org; Tel 01865 734466;
    Fax 01865 883371
Contact   Polly Inness

E & L Instruments

Aerial Rd, Llay, Wrexham LL12 0TU;
    URL www.eandl-nida.com; e-mail
    info@eandl-group.com; Tel 01978 853920;
    Fax 01978 854564

Elonex Plc

County Oak Cottage, 9 Amberley Ct, County Oak Way,
    Crawley, West Sussex RH11 7XL;
    URL www.elonex.co.uk; e-mail education@elonex.co.uk;
    Tel 0800 037 4459; Fax 01293 524425

European Electronique

Forward Hse, Oakfield Industrial Est, Eynsham,
    Oxfordshire OX8 1TT; URL www.euroele.com; e-mail
    sales@euroele.com; Tel 01865 883300; Fax 01865 883371
Contact   Sue Livesey

Firstcall Photographic Ltd

Cherry Grove Rise, West Monkton, Taunton, Somerset
    TA2 8LW; URL www.firstcall-photographic.co.uk;
    e-mail sales@firstcall-photographic.co.uk;
    Tel 01823 413007; Fax 01823 413103
Manager   Rodney Bates

Imcomputers

23 Beckside, Settrington, Malton, North Yorkshire
    YO17 8NR; URL www.imcomputers.co.uk; e-mail
    sales@imcomputers.co.uk; Tel 01944 768406;
    Fax 0870 063 3312
Contact   Ian Middleton

Info Tech (PSP Ltd)

U10 Honeyborough Industrial Est, Neyland, Milford
    Haven, Pembrokeshire SA73 1SE;
    URL www.infotech-psp.co.uk; e-mail
    paul@infotech-psp.co.uk; Tel 01646 600808;
    Fax 01646 602288
Contact   Paul Murray

The IT Support Centre Limited

Technology Hse, Chasewater Heaths Business Pk, Cobbett
    Rd, Chase Terr, Burntwood, Staffordshire WS7 3GL;
    URL www.theitsupportcentre.com; e-mail
    rachael.shalloe@theitsupportcentre.com;
    Tel 01543 458714; Fax 01543 458542
Contact   Rachael Shalloe

Kelway

42–48 High Rd, London E18 2TN; URL www.kelway.co.uk;
    e-mail r.saunders@kelway.co.uk; Tel 020 8530 9307
Contact   Roland Saunders

Lanway

Network 65 Business Pk, Burnley, Lancashire BB11 5TE;
    URL www.lanway.co.uk; e-mail sales@lanway.co.uk;
    Tel 01282 418888; Fax 01282 418861

Lightwave Ltd

Units 17–18, Wirral Business Centre, Dock Rd, Birkenhead,
    Merseyside CH41 1JW; URL www.computer-cables.com;
    e-mail sales@computer-cables.com; Tel 0151 630 5003;
    Fax 020 630 6237
Contact   Steve Atkinson

MeasureUp Certification Software

Regal Hse, Mengham Rd, Hayling Island, Hampshire
    PO11 9BS; URL www.measureup.uk.com; e-mail
    sales@measureup.uk.com; Tel 02392 460002
Contact   Bruce Bennett

Mercatum Ltd

1 Southview Business Pk, Guiseley, Leeds, West Yorkshire LS20 9LT; URL www.mercatum.co.uk; e-mail sales@mercatum.co.uk; Tel 01943 883500; Fax 01943 884890

Contact Helen Walker

Micro & Peripheral Computer Services

Thirlmere Hse, 55 Thirlmere Gdns, Wembley, Greater London HA9 8RH; URL www.mpcservices.com; e-mail sales@mpcservices.com; Tel 020 8908 6710; Fax 020 8908 6815

Contact Luke Liberos

Micro 2000 London Ltd

Greenstede Hse, Wood St, East Grinstead, West Sussex RH19 1UZ; URL www.micro2000.co.uk; e-mail info@micro2000.co.uk; Tel 01342 301001; Fax 01342 301101

Promethean Technologies Group

Promethean Hse, Lower Philips Rd, Blackburn, Lancashire BB1 5TH; URL www.prometheanworld.com; e-mail info@prometheanworld.com; Tel 0870 241 3194; Fax 0870 241 2176

Customer Service Sharon Pinard; Tel 01254 298526

PSA Parts Ltd

Faraday Hse, 39 Thornton Rd, Wimbledon, London SW19 4NQ; URL www.psaparts.co.uk; e-mail sales@psaparts.co.uk; Tel 020 8944 1538; Fax 020 8944 6694

Contact Ian Gregory

RPS Data Products

Unit 2, The Old Bakery, South Rd, Reigate, Surrey RH2 7LB; URL www.rpsdataproducts.co.uk; e-mail allan@rpsdataproducts.co.uk; Tel 01737 221228; Fax 01737 223206

Contact Allan Curtis

Sentinel Electronic Registration

1 Marco Polo Hse, Cook Way, Bindon Rd, Taunton, Somerset TA2 6BG; URL www.sentinel-2000.com; e-mail info@sentinel-2000.com; Tel 01823 358911; Fax 01823 352797

Sentinel Electronic Registration, the effective real-time system for attendance, pupil location and security. Using swipe cards to register both students and staff, Sentinel automatically records and analyses attendance data, producing a wide variety of standard and customised reports.

Smart Computers Limited

Unit 2, St George's Business Pk, Alstone La, Cheltenham, Gloucestershire GL51 8HF; URL www.smart-computers.co.uk; e-mail sales@smart-computers.co.uk; Tel 01242 580654; Fax 01242 580652

Contact Michelle Welch

Smart Human Logistics

Node Ct, Codicote, Hertfordshire SG4 8TR; URL www.smarthumanlogistics.com; e-mail marketing@smarthumanlogistics.com; Tel 01438 822222; Fax 01438 822240

Manager (Marketing) Victoria Colbert

Software Manufacturing Corporation Ltd

H14 KG Business Centre, Kingsfield Cl, Gladstone Ind, Northampton, Northamptonshire NN5 7QS; URL smc-limited.co.uk; e-mail info@smc-limited.co.uk; Tel 01604 758888; Fax 01604 589722

Contact Russell Bassett

Systemnet Ltd

250 Thornton Rd, Bradford, West Yorkshire BD1 2LB; URL www.systemnet.co.uk; e-mail clare.tighe@systemnet.co.uk; Tel 0845 245 0056; Fax 0845 245 0201

Contact Clare Tighe

TallyGenicom Ltd

Rutherford Rd, Basingstoke, Hampshire RG24 8PD; URL www.tallygenicom.co.uk; e-mail sales@tallygenicom.co.uk; Tel 0870 872 2888; Fax 0870 872 2889

Contact Nicky Young

Time Education

Time Technology Pk, Burnley, Lancashire BB12 7TG; URL www.timeeducation.com; e-mail sales@timeeducation.com; Tel 01282 777799; Fax 01282 778214

Maintenance and Consultancy Services

AC Computers

20–24 Wigan La, Wigan, Greater Manchester WN1 1XR; URL www.accomputers.co.uk; e-mail info@accomputers.co.uk; Tel 01942 495555; Fax 01942 493033

Contact David Blundell

Ambra Solutions

Ambra Hse, 17 Campion Dr, Romsey, Hampshire SO51 7RD; URL www.ambra-solutions.co.uk; e-mail sales@ambra-solutions.co.uk; Tel 01794 502273; Fax 01794 302352

Contact Greg Goodrum

Applied Data Technologies

92 Bedminster Par, Bedminster, Bristol, Somerset BS3 4HL; URL www.adtsystems.co.uk; e-mail stuart@adtsystems.co.uk; Tel 0117 987 2170; Fax 0117 904 1129

Contact Stuart Lusted

Associated Network Solutions Plc

Ducie Hse, 37 Ducie St, Manchester M1 2JW; URL www.ansplc.com; e-mail neil.turvin@ansplc.com; Tel 0161 279 8800; Fax 0161 279 8833

Contact Neil Turvin

Avantis Ltd

Innovation Centre, Navigation Park, Abercynon CF45 4SN; URL www.avantisworld.com; e-mail sales@avantisworld.com; Tel 0870 873 4800; Tel (Avantis Support Centre) 0870 873 4802; Fax 0870 873 4801

Managing Director Dr Richard Theo
Director (Marketing) Lorna Mitchell
Director (Operations) Rob Davies
Director (Research and Development) Mark Pearce

Avantis provides multimedia CD and DVD servers for schools and colleges in the UK

BVRP UK

2 Durley Rd, Bournemouth, Dorset BH2 5JJ; URL www.bvrp.co.uk; e-mail sales@bvrp.co.uk; Tel 01202 293233; Fax 01202 310241

Contact Lee Ward

Cisco Systems

9–11 New Sq, Bedfont Lakes, Feltham, Greater London TW14 8HA; URL www.cisco.com/global/uk; e-mail uk-education@cisco.com; Tel (education team) 020 8824 3018; Fax 020 8824 1001

CJ Computing (Systems) Ltd
57 Westbury Hill, Westbury on Trym, Bristol,
Gloucestershire BS9 3AD; URL www.cjcomputing.com;
e-mail sales@cjcomputing.com; Tel 0117 962 4553;
Fax 0117 949 0901
Contact   Chris Skipp

Compusys Plc
58 Edison Rd, Rabans La, Aylesbury, Buckinghamshire
HP19 8UT; URL www.compusys.co.uk; e-mail
education@compusys.co.uk; Tel 01296 505100;
Fax 01296 424165
Contact   Terry Fisher

Connect-Up Limited
The Old Tannery, Barras St, Leeds, West Yorkshire LS12 4JS;
URL www.connect-up.co.uk; e-mail
sales@connect-up.co.uk; Tel 0113 263 1904;
Fax 0113 231 9139
Contact   Mark Driver

Cristie Data Products Limited
New Mill, Chestnut La, Stroud, Gloucestershire GL5 3EH;
URL www.cristie.com; e-mail sales@cristie.com;
Tel 01453 847000; Fax 01453 847001

Delta Microsystems Limited
Delta Hse, 62 St Georges Rd, Bolton, Lancashire BL1 2DD;
URL www.deltamicro.co.uk; e-mail
airedale@delta-house.co.uk; Tel 01204 368700;
Fax 01204 382552
Contact   Andrew Iredale

The Education Exchange
Pinnacle Hse, 17–25 Hartfield Rd, Wimbledon, London
SW19 3SE; URL www.edex.net; e-mail info@edex.net;
Tel 020 8239 5000; Fax 020 8239 5001

eved
Forward Hse, Oakfield Industrial Est, Eynsham,
Oxfordshire OX29 4TT; URL www.eved.co.uk; e-mail
louise.murray@everythingeducation.org;
Tel 01865 734466; Fax 01865 883371
Contact   Louise Murray

evesham.com
Gloucester Ct, Gloucester Terr, Leeds, West Yorkshire
LS12 2ER; URL www.evesham.com; e-mail
skerr@evesham.com; Tel 0113 203 2004;
Fax 0113 203 2001
Contact   Simon Kerr

Flamefast (UK) Ltd
Unit 2, Labtec St, Manchester, Greater Manchester M27 8SE;
URL www.flamefast.co.uk; e-mail sales@flamefast.co.uk;
Tel 0161 793 9998; Fax 0161 793 0098
Managing Director   Steve Swinden
Sales Manager   Paul Morris

ICON Business Systems Limited
Unit 27, Murrell Green Business Pk, Hook, Hampshire
RG27 9GR; URL www.iconworld.co.uk; e-mail
sales@iconworld.co.uk; Tel 01256 768080;
Fax 01256 768090
Contact   Andrew Stott

KBR IT and Networking Solutions Ltd
Station Hse, Station La, Birtley, County Durham DH3 1DJ;
URL www.kbr.co.uk; e-mail pricer@kbr.co.uk;
Tel 0191 492 1492; Fax 0191 492 8008
Contact   Robin Price

LETSS
The Lodge, Crown Woods School, Riefield Rd, Eltham,
London SE9 2QL; URL www.letss.com; e-mail
letss@compuserve.com; Tel 020 8850 0100;
Fax 020 8850 0400
Contact   Ron More

Link Systems (Brentwood) Ltd
Fernwood Hse, Roman Rd, Mountnessing, Essex
CM15 0UG; URL www.link-systems.co.uk; e-mail
mike.hickson@link-systems.co.uk; Tel 01277 350777;
Fax 01277 350778
Contact   Mike Hickson

London Web Communications
401–405 Nether St, London N3 1LW; e-mail
everythingeducation@londonweb.net; Tel 020 8349 4500;
Fax 020 8349 4488
Contact   Nicky Wolfe

Matcom UK
PO Box 9133, Birmingham, West Midlands B8 2UA;
URL www.matcomuk.co.uk; e-mail
allan.miah@matcomuk.co.uk; Tel 0121 326 7600;
Fax 0121 326 7605
Contact   Allan Miah

Megabyte Limited
Lakeside Hse, Waltham Business Pk, Brickyard Rd,
Swanmore, Hampshire SO32 2SA;
URL www.megabyte.co.uk; e-mail
mark.stafford@megabyte.co.uk; Tel 01489 896266;
Fax 01489 892045
Contact   Mark Stafford

Millgate Computer Systems Ltd
Claire Ct, Rawmarsh Rd, Rotherham, South Yorkshire
S60 1RU; URL www.millgate.co.uk; e-mail
pauls@millgate.co.uk; Tel 01709 511170;
Fax 01709 511172
Contact   Paul Sheerin

MiS (Millennium Integrated Services Ltd)
27 Crown St, Kettering, Northamptonshire NN16 8QA;
URL www.mis-limited.co.uk; e-mail
johnr@mis-limited.co.uk; Tel 07000 647583;
Fax 01536 763043
Contact   John Radford

Optech Fibres Ltd
4 Andrews Way, Barrow-in-Furness, Cumbria LA14 2UD;
URL www.optechfibres.co.uk; e-mail
pat@optechfibres.co.uk; Tel 01229 469700;
Fax 01229 469701
Contact   Pat Donohue

P3 Computer Services Ltd
2 Healey Wood Rd, Burnley, Lancashire BB11 2HJ;
URL www.p3computers.com; e-mail
paul@p3computers.com; Tel 01282 424041;
Fax 01282 424027
Contact   Paul Cumpstey

PSM Micro Computers Ltd
Corporate Hse, Priorslee, Telford, Shropshire TF2 9PJ;
URL www.psmmicros.com; e-mail
dwilliams@psmmicros.com; Tel 01952 291670;
Fax 01952 291845
Contact   David Williams

Ramesys
Glaisdale Dr, Nottingham, Nottinghamshire NG8 4GU;
URL www.ramesys.com; e-mail
nicola.newman@ramesys.com; Tel 0115 971 2093;
Fax 0115 913 0314
Contact   Nicola Newman

Readycrest Ltd
8 Chestnut Ave, Walderslade, Kent ME5 9AJ;
URL www.readycrest.co.uk; e-mail
sales@readycrest.co.uk; Tel 0845 130 4060;
Fax 0845 130 4070
Contact   Paul Bonathan

RODAIR Systems Ltd
Cussins Hse, Wood St, Doncaster, South Yorkshire
DN1 3LW; URL www.rodairsystems.co.uk; e-mail
education@rodairsystems.co.uk; Tel 01302 340505;
Fax 01506 497800
Contact Chris Headon

Sentinel Products Ltd
Netley Hse, Shere Rd, Gomshall, Surrey GU5 9QA;
URL www.rangersuite.com; e-mail
elliep@rangersuite.com; Tel 01483 205001;
Fax 01483 205125
Contact Ellie Puddle

Special Agent Ltd
98 Curtain Rd, London EC2A 3AF;
URL www.simsjobs.com; e-mail
william@specialagent.co.uk; Tel 020 7613 2030;
Fax 020 7613 3502
Contact William Townsend

Special Telephone System Limited
Bruce Way, Cambridge Rd, Whetstone, Leicester,
Leicestershire LE8 6HP;
URL www.sts-communications.com; e-mail
info@sts-communications.com; Tel 0116 250 4000;
Fax 0116 250 4001
Contact Andrew Dayman

System Software Solutions Ltd
26 The Avenue, Rubery, Birmingham, West Midlands
B45 9AL; URL www.system-software.co.uk; e-mail
solutions@system-software.co.uk; Tel 0121 453 0033;
Fax 0121 457 6611
Contact Greg Evans

Total Catering Solutions
50 Park Dr, Dagenham, Essex RM10 7AB; e-mail
richard@tcsinfo.co.uk; Tel 020 8984 4555;
Fax 020 8984 4555
Contact Richard Ware

Watford Electronics Ltd
Jessa Hse, Finway, Luton, Bedfordshire LU1 1WE;
URL www.watford.co.uk; e-mail
educ.sales@watford.co.uk; Tel 0870 729 5566;
Fax 0870 729 5523

Recreational and Sports Equipment

Sportec Trading Ltd
See Clothing and Uniforms

Staff and Pupil Support

Ascon Education
2 Albert Mews, Albert Rd, London N4 3RD;
URL www.asconeducation.com; e-mail
schools@asconeducation.com; Tel 020 7272 4838;
Fax 020 7272 1564
Contact Clare Norburn

Assist-Ed
59 Tower View, Shirley, Croydon, Surrey CR0 7PY;
URL www.assist-education.com; e-mail
information@assist-education.com; Tel 020 8654 0928
Contact Marian Vincent

Big-Buttons
Big Little Ideas Ltd, PO Box 276, Chorley, Lancashire
PR7 3GX; URL www.big-buttons.co.uk; e-mail
talk@big-buttons.co.uk; Tel 07833 922179
Contact Lindsey Hollis

CASCAiD Ltd
Holywell Bldg, Holywell Way, Loughborough,
Leicestershire LE11 3UZ; URL www.cascaid.co.uk;
e-mail enquiry@cascaid.co.uk; Tel 01509 226868;
Fax 01509 226869

The Effective Teaching and Learning Network
37 Wycke La, Tollesbury, London CM9 8ST;
URL www.etln.org.uk; e-mail email@etln.org.uk;
Tel 01621 860674; Fax 01621 860674
Contact Alison Everitt

Left 'n' Write
5 Charles St, Worcester, Worcestershire WR1 2AQ;
URL www.lefthand-education.co.uk; e-mail
mail@lefthand-education.co.uk; Tel 01905 25798;
Fax 01905 25798
Contact Mark Stewart

Mark Education Ltd
Suite 6, Tannery Ct, Tanners La, Warrington WA2 7NA;
URL www.markeducation.co.uk; e-mail
info@markeducation.co.uk; Tel 01925 241115;
Fax 01925 242029
Managing Director Eddie Austin

Oxford Conferences
66 Sunderland Ave, Oxford, Oxfordshire OX2 8DU;
URL www.oxford-conferences.com; e-mail
chris.sivewright@which.net; Tel 01865 512428;
Fax 01280 706583
Contact Chris Sivewright

SPSS (UK) Ltd
1st Fl, St Andrew's Hse, West St, Woking, Surrey GU21 1EB;
URL www.spss.com; e-mail sales@spss.co.uk;
Tel 01483 719200; Fax 01483 719290
Contact Gary Van Heerden

Teacher Support Network
Hamilton Hse, Mabledon Pl, London WC1H 9BE;
URL www.teachersupport.info; e-mail
enquiries@teachersupport.info; Tel 020 7554 5200;
Fax 020 7554 5239

Teachers Inc
Arlington Hse, Arlington Way, Thetford, Norfolk IP24 2DZ;
URL www.teachersinc.com; e-mail
supply@teachersinc.com; Tel 0871 711 5198;
Fax 0871 277 3908

thelea.com Ltd
Brendan Hse, Victoria Sq, Widnes, Cheshire WA8 6AD;
URL www.thelea.com; e-mail owens@thelea.co.uk;
Tel 0151 257 8666; Fax 0151 257 8668
Contact Eileen Owens

Training

3Com UK Ltd
3Com Centre, Boundary Way, Hemel Hempstead,
Hertfordshire HP2 7YU; URL www.3com.co.uk/
education; e-mail ian_lambden@3com.com;
Tel 07990 595905; Fax 01442 432100
Contact Ian Lambden

Aston Swann
Suite 1, 26–28 Aubrey St, Hereford, Herefordshire HR4 0BU;
URL www.astonswann.co.uk; e-mail
education@astonswann.co.uk; Tel 0845 430 4051;
Fax 0845 430 4052
Contact Debbie Skyrme

Kent First Aid Training
41 Goodwood Cres, Gravesend, Kent DA12 5EZ;
URL www.kentfirstaidtraining.co.uk; e-mail
kent.fa.training@talk21.com; Tel 01474 365731
Contact Peter Scutts

mPowerNet
Anglia Ruskin University, 3rd Fl, Sawyers Bldg, Bishops
 Hall La, Chelmsford, Essex CM1 15Q;
 URL www.mpowernet.apu.ac.uk; e-mail
 raynor.sumner@mpowe4rnet.apu.ac.uk;
 Tel 01245 607565; Fax 01245 607566
Contact   Raynor Sumner

Pitman Training Centre
17 Pittville St, Cheltenham, Gloucestershire GL52 2LN;
 URL www.pitman-training.com/cheltenham; e-mail
 cheltenham@pitman-training.net; Tel 01242 226243;
 Fax 01242 222886
Contact   Tina Hayball
Contact   Brenda Thomas

Power Education
Islington Hse, Brown La West, Leeds, West Yorkshire
 LS12 6BD; URL www.powered.co.uk; e-mail
 davidbr@sphinxcst.co.uk; Tel 0113 261 5009;
 Fax 0113 243 9443
Contact   David Brindle

TQ Education and Training
Bonsall St, Long Eaton, Nottingham, Nottinghamshire
 NG20 2AN; URL www.tq.com; e-mail info@tq.com;
 Tel 0115 972 2611; Fax 0115 973 1520
Head (Sales)   Mark Smith

Transport and Travel

See also Chapter 14

Field Business Solutions
6 Hill Ct, Swingbridge Rd, Grantham, Nottinghamshire
 NG31 7XY; URL www.field-bs.com; e-mail
 tony.banks@field-bs.com; Tel 01476 568339;
 Fax 01476 568339
Contact   Tony Banks

Red Kite Minibuses
3 Haddons Dr, Three Legged Cross, Winborne, Dorset
 BH21 6QU; URL www.redkite-minibuses.com; e-mail
 sales@redkite-minibuses.com; Tel 01202 827678;
 Fax 01202 827029

Education Related Organisations and Resources

21

Arts

Business and Industry

Charities

Children, Young People and Families

Education

Environment

Healthcare/Hospitals/Nursing

Heritage

International and Overseas

Languages

Recruitment

Research

Sciences

Societies and Associations

Students

Training

Voluntary Service

Education Related Organisations and Resources

Arts

Art and Design

National Association of Advisers and Inspectors in Design and Technology
44 Davenport Rd, London SE6 2AZ; Tel 020 8698 5676
Secretary   S.J. Kendall

Arts and Design Councils

Arts Council England
14 Gt Peter St, London SW1P 3NQ;
   URL www.artscouncil.org.uk; e-mail
   enquiries@artscouncil.org.uk; Tel 0845 300 6200;
   Fax 020 7973 6590
Chief Executive   Peter Hewitt
Chair   Sir Christopher Frayling
Arts Council England, East   Eden Hse, 48–49 Bateman St,
   Cambridge, Cambridgeshire CB2 1LR; e-mail
   east@artscouncil.org.uk; Tel 0845 300 6200;
   Fax 0870 242 1271; Textphone 01223 306893
Arts Council England, East Midlands   St Nicholas Ct, 25–27
   Castle Gate, Nottingham, Nottinghamshire NG1 7AR;
   e-mail eastmidlands@artscouncil.org.uk;
   Tel 0845 300 6200; Fax 0115 950 2467
Arts Council England, London   2 Pear Tree Ct, London
   EC1R 0DS; e-mail london@artscouncil.org.uk;
   Tel 0845 300 6200; Fax 020 7608 4100;
   Textphone 020 7608 4101
Arts Council England, North East   Central Sq, Forth St,
   Newcastle upon Tyne, Tyne and Wear NE1 3PJ; e-mail
   northeast@artscouncil.org.uk; Tel 0845 300 6200;
   Fax 0191 230 1020; Textphone 0191 255 8500
Arts Council England, North West   Manchester Hse, 22
   Bridge St, Manchester M3 3AB; e-mail
   northwest@artscouncil.org.uk; Tel 0161 834 6644;
   Fax 0161 834 6969; Textphone 0161 834 9131
   Regional Executive Director   Michael Eakin
Arts Council England, South East   Sovereign Hse, Church St,
   Brighton, East Sussex BN1 1RA; e-mail
   southeast@artscouncil.org.uk; Tel 0845 300 6200;
   Fax 0870 242 1257
Arts Council England, South West   Bradninch Pl, Gandy St,
   Exeter, Devon EX4 3LS; e-mail
   southwest@artscouncil.org.uk; Tel 0845 300 6200;
   Fax 01392 229229; Textphone 01392 433503
Arts Council England, West Midlands   82 Granville St,
   Birmingham, West Midlands B1 2LH; e-mail
   westmidlands@artscouncil.org.uk; Tel 0845 300 6200;
   Fax 0121 643 7239; Textphone 0121 643 2815

Arts Council England, Yorkshire   21 Bond St, Dewsbury,
   West Yorkshire WF13 1AX; e-mail
   yorkshire.executive@artscouncil.org.uk;
   Tel 0845 300 6200; Fax 01924 466522;
   Textphone 01924 438585

Arts Council of Wales
9 Museum Pl, Cardiff CF10 3NX;
   URL www.artswales.org.uk; e-mail
   info@artswales.org.uk; Tel 02920 376500;
   Fax 02920 221447
The Arts Council of Wales (Mid and West Wales Office)   Mid
   and West Wales Office, 6 Gardd Llydaw, Jacksons La,
   Carmarthen, Carmarthenshire SA31 1QD;
   URL www.artswales.org.uk; e-mail
   midandwest@artswales.org.uk; Tel 01267 234248;
   Fax 01267 233084
   Director (Mid and West Wales Office)   Simon Lovell-Jones

Arts Council of Northern Ireland
77 Malone Rd, Belfast BT9 6AQ;
   URL www.artscouncil-ni.org; e-mail
   info@artscouncil-ni.org; Tel 028 9038 5200
Youth Arts Officer   Gavin O'Connor

Crafts Council
44a Pentonville Rd, London N1 9BY;
   URL www.craftscouncil.org.uk; e-mail
   education@craftscouncil.org.uk; Tel 020 7278 7700;
   Fax 020 7837 6891

Mid Pennine Arts
Yorke St, Burnley, Lancashire BB11 1HD;
   URL www.midpenninearts.org.uk; e-mail
   info@midpenninearts.org.uk; Tel 01282 421986;
   Fax 01282 429513
Education Officer   David Smith

Scottish Arts Council
12 Manor Pl, Edinburgh EH3 7DD;
   URL www.scottisharts.org.uk; e-mail
   help.desk@scottisharts.org.uk; Tel 0131 226 6051;
   Fax 0131 225 9833
Chief Executive   Jim Tough (Acting)

Sterts Theatre and Environmental Centre
Sterts, Upton Cross, Liskeard, Cornwall PL14 5AZ;
   URL www.sterts.co.uk; e-mail sterts@btinternet.com;
   Tel 01579 362382

Music and Performing Arts

Association for Dance Movement Therapy UK
32 Meadfood La, Torquay TQ1 2BW;
   URL www.admt.org.uk; e-mail admin@admt.org.uk
ADMT UK embraces a national network of subcommittees
and working teams. The day-to-day running of the
association is carried out by an executive council as
nominated by the general membership. The council also

administers a student loan fund, a bursary fund and a service for peer support and professional development. A major part of ADMT UK and its development depends on the work of its committees, including newsletter, workshops and seminars, membership registration, education and training, publications and research, PR and publicity, DMT in education, ethnics, and funding and professional negotiations.

British and International Federation of Festivals for Music, Dance and Speech

Festivals Hse, 198 Park La, Macclesfield, Cheshire SK11 6UD; URL www.festivals.demon.co.uk; e-mail info@federationoffestivals.org.uk; Tel 0870 7744 290; Fax 0870 7744 292
Chief Executive   E. Whitehead

British Library Sound Archive

96 Euston Rd, London NW1 2DB; URL www.bl.uk/soundarchive; e-mail sound-archive@bl.uk; Tel 020 7412 7676; Fax 020 7412 7441
Service Development Officer   Richard Fairman

Choir Schools' Association and Choir Schools' Association Bursary Trust

Wolvesey, College St, Winchester, Hampshire SO23 9ND; URL www.choirschools.org.uk; e-mail admin@choirschools.org.uk; Tel 01962 890530; Fax 01962 869978

Conference of Drama Schools

PO Box 34252, London NW5 1XJ; URL www.drama.ac.uk
Executive Secretary   Saul Hyman

Dance for Everyone

30 Sevington Rd, London NW4 3RX; e-mail orders@dfe.org.uk; Tel 020 8202 7863; Fax 020 8202 7863
Artistic Director   N. Benari MA
Dance company workshops; performance and teaching videos

Music Education Council

54 Elm Rd, Hale, Altrincham, Greater Manchester WA15 9QP; URL www.mec.org.uk; e-mail ahassan@easynet.co.uk; Tel 0161 928 3085; Fax 0161 929 9648
Chair   Leonora Davies
Vice-Chair   Colin Brackley Jones

National Association of Youth Orchestras

Central Hall, West Tollcross, Edinburgh EH3 9BP; URL www.nayo.org.uk; e-mail admin@nayo.org.uk; Tel 0131 221 1927; Fax 0131 229 2921
General Manager   S. White

National Campaign for the Arts (NCA)

1 Kingly St, London W1B 5PA; URL www.artscampaign.org.uk; e-mail nca@artscampaign.org.uk; Tel 020 7287 3777; Fax 020 7287 4777
Director   Louise De Winter
The NCA is a UK independent campaigning organisation representing all the arts. It seeks to safeguard, promote and develop the arts. For more information on its work with the arts and education and details of how to become a member please see the website or contact directly.

National Operatic and Dramatic Association

58–60 Lincoln Rd, Peterborough, Cambridgeshire PE1 2RZ; URL www.noda.org.uk; e-mail info@noda.org.uk; Tel 0870 770 2480
Chief Executive   Mr A. Gibbs

National Youth Choir of Great Britain

PO Box 67, Holmfirth, West Yorkshire HD9 3YT; URL www.nycgb.net; e-mail office@nycgb.net; Tel 01484 687203; Fax 01484 647023
Company Secretary   Carl Browning

National Youth Orchestra of Great Britain

32 Old School Hse, Britannia Rd, Bristol BS15 8DB; URL www.nyo.org.uk; e-mail info@nyo.org.uk; Tel 0117 960 0477; Fax 0117 960 0376
Education Officer   Jo Beavan

National Youth Theatre of Great Britain

443–445 Holloway Rd, London N7 6LW; URL www.nyt.org.uk; Tel 020 7281 3863; Fax 020 7281 8246

Performing Right Society Ltd

29–33 Berners St, London W1T 3AB; Tel 020 7580 5544; Fax 020 7306 4455
Collects and distributes royalites for the public performance and broadcasting of copyright musical works, on behalf of its composer and publisher members

Radius (The Religious Drama Society of Great Britain)

PO Box 34493, London W6 9WR; URL www.radius.org.uk; e-mail office@radius.org.uk; Tel 020 8748 3569
Co-ordinator   David Dean

The Rehearsal Orchestra

60–62 Clapham Rd, London SW9 0JJ; URL www.rehearsal-orchestra.org; e-mail admin@rehearsal-orchestra.org; Tel 020 7820 9994
The Rehearsal Orchestra provides talented musicians of all ages with the opportunity to study large-scale symphonic repertoire in intensive rehearsal with professional conductors, during weekend rehearsal courses and an annual residential week during the Edinburgh Festival

Scottish Community Drama Association

5 York Pl, Edinburgh EH1 3EB; URL www.scda.org.uk; e-mail headquarters@scda.org.uk; Tel 0131 557 5552; Fax 0131 557 5552

Sesame Institute

27 Blackfriars Rd, London SE1 8NY; Tel 020 7633 9690
Researches and promotes the use of movement and drama as therapy and trains therapists in this method

Society for Theatre Research

c/o Theatre Museum, 1e Tavistock St, London WC2E 7PR; URL www.str.org.uk; e-mail e.cottis@btinternet.com

Sing UK

PO Box 8678, Loughborough, Leicestershire LE11 9EA; URL www.singuk.org; e-mail admin@singuk.org; Tel 01509 260345
Manager (Operations)   Eleri Bristow
Arranges singing days; manages singing schemes involving groups of schools or colleges and other projects; organises training for singing leaders

Business and Industry

ASET

Department of Innovation, Universities and Skills (DIUS), W11, Moorfoot, Sheffield, South Yorkshire S1 4PQ; URL www.asetonline.org; e-mail aset@aset.demon.co.uk; Tel 0114 221 2902; Fax 0114 221 2903
Administrator   K. Fildes

Construction Industry Joint Council

55 Tufton St, London SW1P 3QL

HTI (Heads, Teachers and Industry)

Registered Charity Number 1003627
Herald Ct, University of Warwick Science Pk, Coventry, Warwickshire CV4 7EZ; URL www.hti.org.uk; e-mail a.evans@hti.org.uk; Tel 024 7641 0104; Fax 024 7641 5984
HTI is an independent national charity working in partnership with education, business and government to enhance leadership and management in schools.

Professional development is provided through the HTI Leadership Centre by means of teacher secondments into business of six weeks to one year; leadership skills training for senior teachers; national leadership qualifications.

The HTI Trust is involved in supporting research and development of issues such as employability, inclusivity, risk awareness, the environment and creativity; challenging the thinking of stakeholders; and providing opportunities for dialogue and exchange.

Sellafield Ltd
Hinton Hse, Risley, Warrington WA3 6AS;
URL www.succeedingwithscience.com; Tel 01925 832826

Charities

Albany Trust Counselling
239a Balham High Rd, London SW17 7BE;
URL www.albanytrust.org.uk; e-mail albanytrust@hotmail.co.uk; Tel 020 8767 1827
Counselling Co-ordinator   David Burkle

All Saints Educational Trust
St Katharine Cree Church, 86 Leadenhall St, London EC3A 3DH; URL www.aset.org.uk; e-mail aset@aset.org.uk; Tel 020 7283 4485; Fax 020 7621 9758
Clerk   S.P. Harrow FKC

Anglo-Jewish Association
Suite 4, 107 Gloucester Pl, London W1U 6BY;
URL www.anglojewish.co.uk; e-mail info@anglojewish.co.uk; Tel 020 7486 5055
Chair (Education Committee)   Julia Samuel

ATL Trust Fund
7 Northumberland St, London WC2N 5RD;
URL www.atl.org.uk; e-mail trustfund@atl.org.uk;
Tel 020 7930 6441
Administrator   Ann Rowswell

BC.UK
ACE Centre, 92 Windmill Rd, Headington, Oxfordshire OX3 7DR; Tel 01608 676455
Contact   Gillian Hazell
Disseminates information through workshops, lectures and publications; provides training for instructors

British and Foreign School Society
Maybrook Hse, Godstone Rd, Caterham, Surrey CR3 6RE;
URL www.bfss.org.uk; Tel 01883 331177
Director   C.M.C. Crawford

Calouste Gulbenkian Foundation (Lisbon), United Kingdom Branch
98 Portland Pl, London W1B 1ET;
URL www.gulbenkian.org.uk; e-mail info@gulbenkian.org.uk; Tel 020 7636 5313
Assistant Director (Education)   Simon Richey

Caspari Foundation for Educational Therapy and Therapeutic Teaching (FAETT)
Caspari Hse, 1 Noel Rd, London N1 8HQ;
URL www.caspari.org.uk; e-mail casparihouse@btconnect.com; Tel 020 7704 1977;
Fax 020 7704 1783

Charity Commission Direct
PO Box 1227, Liverpool L69 3UG;
URL www.charitycommission.gov.uk; e-mail enquiries@charitycommission.gov.uk; Tel 0845 300 0218;
Minicom 0845 300 0219
Manager (Public Relations)   Sush Amar

Child Growth Foundation
2 Mayfield Ave, Chiswick, London W4 1PW;
URL www.childgrowthfoundation.org; e-mail cgflondon@aol.com; Tel 020 8994 7625; Fax 020 8995 9075
Hon Chair   Tam Fry

Douglas Bomford Trust
44 Drove Rd, Biggleswade, Bedfordshire SG18 8HD;
URL www.iagre.org; e-mail redmanpl@iagre.org;
Tel 01767 315429

Franco–British Society
Rm 227, Linen Hall, London W1R 5TB; Tel 020 7734 0815;
Fax 020 7734 0815

Leonard Cheshire
30 Millbank, London SW1P 4QD;
URL www.leonard-cheshire.org; e-mail info@lc-uk.org;
Tel 020 7802 8200; Fax 020 7802 8250
Project Manager (Workability)   Andrew Anderson

Leverhulme Trust
1 Pemberton Row, London EC4A 3BG;
URL www.leverhulme.ac.uk; e-mail gdupin@leverhulme.ac.uk; Tel 020 7822 5220
Director   Prof Sir Richard Brook OBE, ScD, FREng
Awards grants to institutions and individuals, mainly for research

Lord Kitchener National Memorial Fund
Salters Green Farm, Mayfield, East Sussex TN20 6NP;
Tel 01892 852472
Each year the fund offers up to 25 UK university scholarships for the children of people who served in the armed forces

MENCAP
MENCAP, 123 Golden La, London EC1Y 0RT;
URL www.mencap.org.uk; e-mail help@mencap.org.uk;
Tel 020 7454 0454; Tel (learning disability helpline: Northern Ireland) 0845 763 6227; Tel (learning disability helpline: Wales) 0808 800 0300; Tel (learning disability helpline: England) 0808 808 1111
Chief Executive   Dame Jo Williams DBE
Chair   Brian Baldock CBE

Mitchell City of London Educational Foundation
Fairway, Round Oak View, Tillington, Hereford, Herefordshire HR4 8EQ; Tel 01432 760409;
Fax 01432 760409
Clerk to the Trustees   Margaret E. Keyte

NIACE (National Institute of Adult Continuing Education)
21 De Montfort St, Leicester LE1 7GE;
URL www.niace.org.uk; e-mail enquiries@niace.org.uk;
Tel 0116 204 4200; Fax 0116 285 4514
Director   Alan Tuckett
Librarian   Helen Kruse

PDSA (People's Dispensary for Sick Animals)
Whitechapel Way, Priorslee, Telford, Shropshire TF2 9PQ;
URL www.pdsa.org.uk; e-mail pr@pdsa.org.uk;
Tel 01952 290999

Royal Society for the Prevention of Cruelty to Animals
Wilberforce Way, Southwater, Horsham, West Sussex RH13 9RS; URL www.rspca.org.uk/education; e-mail education@rspca.org.uk; Tel 0300 123 0100

Schoolmistresses and Governesses Benevolent Institution
SGBI Office, Queen Mary Hse, Manor Park Rd, Chislehurst, Kent BR7 5PY; e-mail sgbi@fsmail.net; Tel 020 8468 7997
Director; Secretary   L.I. Baggott FCA

Sidney Perry Foundation (incorporating the Covenantors Educational Trust)
PO Box 2924, Faringdon SN7 7YJ
Secretary   L.A. Owens

21

Children, Young People and Families

Organisations for Children

4Children
City Reach, 5 Greenwich View Pl, London E14 9NN;
URL www.4children.org.uk; e-mail
info@4children.org.uk; Tel 020 7512 2100;
Fax 020 7512 2010
Chief Executive   A. Longfield
Provide information, publications and training for those
interested in using or developing childcare and community
services for children and families

The Boarding Schools Association
Grosvenor Gardens Hse, 35–37 Grosvenor Gdns, London
SW1W 0BS; e-mail bsa@boarding.org.uk;
Tel 020 7798 1580; Fax 020 7798 1581
National Director   Hilary Moriarty BA(Hons), MA, PGCFE

The Brandon Centre
26 Prince of Wales Rd, London NW5 3LG;
URL www.brandon-centre.org.uk; e-mail
reception@brandon-centre.org.uk; Tel 020 7267 4792
Director   G. Baruch PhD
Counselling and psychotherapy for young people (12–21)
with emotional problems, medical counselling for
contraception, pregnancy and related problems.
Bereavement counsellor for 12–18 year olds.

Childhood First
Station Hse, Waterloo Rd, London SE1 8SB;
URL www.childhoodfirst.org.uk; e-mail
mail@childhoodfirst.org.uk; Tel 020 7928 7388;
Fax 020 7261 1307
Chief Executive   Stephen Blunden
Childhood First is a charity providing therapeutic
residential care, treatment and education for children and
young people from 5–18 years old affected by the
consequences of neglect, abuse and trauma. The charity runs
four therapeutic communities, two schools, as well as
offering family and placement support services, a training
programme in partnership with Middlesex University, and
a research programme based at Salford University.

Community and Youth Workers' Union
National Office, 302 The Argent Centre, Birmingham, West
Midlands B1 3HS; URL www.cywu.org.uk; e-mail
kerry@cywu.org.uk; Tel 0121 244 3344; Fax 0121 244 3345

Joint Educational Trust
6–8 Fenchurch Bldg, London EC3M 5HT;
URL www.jetcharity.org; e-mail admin@jetcharity.org;
Tel 020 3217 1100; Fax 020 3217 1110
Director; Fundraiser   Julie Burns MA
Supports 7–13 year olds

KIDS
6 Aztec Row, Berners Rd, London N1 0PW;
URL www.kids.org.uk; e-mail enquiries@kids.org.uk;
Tel 020 7359 3635; Fax 020 7359 8238
Working in partnership with parents, KIDS provides a range
of services for disabled children in regional centres across
England. Services include home-based learning, shared care
(respite), inclusive nurseries, holiday playschemes, and an
independent educational advisory service.

London Union of Youth Clubs
64 Camberwell Rd, London SE5 0EN; Tel 020 7701 6366;
Fax 020 7701 6320
Chief Executive   S. Abbott MA

The Montessori Society, AMI (UK)
26 Lyndhurst Gdns, London NW3 5NW;
URL www.montessori-uk.org; e-mail
montessorisociety@fsmail.net; Tel 020 7435 7874
Chair   A. Grebot

National Association for Primary Education (NAPE)
Registered Charity Number 289645
Moulton College, Moulton, Northampton,
Northamptonshire NN3 7RR; URL www.nape.org.uk;
e-mail nationaloffice@nape.org.uk; Tel 01604 647646;
Fax 01604 647660
Chair   Philip Marples
General Secretary   Diana Batt
Office Manager   Sally Swallow

National Association of Toy and Leisure Libraries/Play Matters
68 Churchway, London NW1 1LT; URL www.natll.org.uk;
e-mail admin@playmatters.co.uk; Tel 020 7255 4600;
Fax 020 7255 4602
Chief Executive   Pauline Henniker
National body for toy libraries in the UK. Toy libraries loan
toys appropriate to each stage of development; operates as a
preventive service, filling gaps in the existing provision for
all families with babies and young children, including those
with special needs. Leisure libraries loan equipment to
young people and adults with learning difficulties. Various
publications about play – send an SAE for list and details of
nearest toy or leisure library; publishes Good Toy Guide
annually; several training courses available. Please note it
cannot answer enquiries from students.

NCH
85 Highbury Pk, London N5 1UD; URL www.nch.org.uk;
Tel 020 7704 7000; Fax 020 7704 7172
Chief Executive   Clare Tickell

Pre-School Learning Alliance
The Fitzpatrick Bldg, 188 York Way, London N7 9AD;
URL www.pre-school.org.uk; e-mail
info@pre-school.org.uk; Tel 020 7697 2500;
Fax 020 7700 0319
Director (Training and Quality Assurance)   Michael Freeston
The alliance provides practical support to more than 15 000
early years settings and makes a positive contribution to the
care and education of more than 500 000 young children and
their families

Scottish Pre-School Play Association
21 Granville St, Glasgow G3 7EE; URL www.sppa.org.uk;
e-mail info@sppa.org.uk; Tel 0141 221 4148

Trust for the Study of Adolescence
23 New Rd, Brighton, East Sussex BN1 1WZ;
URL www.tsa.uk.com; e-mail publications@tsa.uk.com;
Tel 01273 693311; Fax 01273 647322
The trust has a mail order catalogue of resources for parents,
teenagers and those working with young people. As well as
being involved in research on different aspects of
adolescence, the trust also runs training workshops on
suicide and self-harm, resilience and parenting.

United Nations Association of the UK
3 Whitehall Ct, London SW1A 2EL; URL www.una.org.uk;
e-mail rusling@una.org.uk; Tel 020 7766 3459;
Fax 020 7930 5893

UNICEF UK Committee (United Nations Children's Fund)
Africa Hse, 64–78 Kingsway, London WC2B 6NB;
URL www.unicef.org.uk; Tel 020 7405 5592
Head (Education)   Edward Waller
UNICEF UK works with families, communities and
governments to build a world fit for children. The education
team advises on children's rights and global citizenship
through the Rights Respecting Schools programme.

Organisations for Young People

BSES Expeditions
Royal Geographical Society, 1 Kensington Gore, London
SW7 2AR; URL www.bses.org.uk; e-mail
info@bses.org.uk; Tel 020 7591 3141; Fax 020 7591 3140
Executive Director   Will Taunton-Burnet
Manager (Marketing)   Charlie Masding

Christian Aid

35 Lower Marsh, Waterloo, London SE1 7RL;
URL www.christian-aid.org.uk; Tel 020 7620 4444;
Fax 020 7620 0719
Team Leader (Youth Team: London) Matthew Edwards;
Christian Aid Youth Team, PO Box 100, London SE1 7RT;
Tel 020 7620 4444; Fax 020 7620 0719
Youth Co-ordinator (Aberdeen) Paul Clelland; covers
north Scotland
Youth Co-ordinator (Belfast) Vacancy
Youth Co-ordinator (Birmingham) Vacancy
Youth Co-ordinator (Glasgow) Vacancy
Youth Co-ordinator (Leeds) Vacancy; covers west and
north Yorkshire
Youth Co-ordinator (Wales) Branwen Niclas; covers
Wales
Christian Aid has a growing number of Youth Co-ordinators
who participate in local events and run youth group
sessions

Council for Education in World Citizenship – Cymru

Temple of Peace, Cathays Pk, Cardiff CF10 3AP;
URL www.cewc-cymru.org.uk; e-mail
cewc@wcia.org.uk; Tel 02920 228549; Fax 02920 640333
Secretary Stephen Thomas
Education Officer Martin Pollard
CEWC-Cymru exists to help young citizens develop the
skills, knowledge and self-belief that will enable them to
contribute to society

Peak District National Park Centre for Environmental Learning

Education Visits Team, Losehill Hall, Castleton, Derbyshire
S33 8WB; Tel 01433 620373

The Movement for Reform Judaism

Youth Department and Jeneration, Sternberg Centre, 80 East
End Rd, London N3 2SY;
URL www.reformjudaism.org.uk; www.jeneration.org;
e-mail admin@rsy-netzer.org.uk; Tel 020 8349 5666
Director Judith Williams

Royal Society of St George

127 Sandgate Rd, Folkestone, Kent CT20 2BH;
URL www.royalsocietyofstgeorge.com; e-mail
info@rssg.u-net.com; Tel 01303 241795; Fax 01303 211710

RSPB Phoenix

RSPB Youth and Education Department, The Lodge, Sandy,
Bedfordshire SG19 2DL; e-mail phoenix@rspb.org.uk;
Tel 01767 680551; Fax 01767 692395
Youth Team Leader Mark Boyd
National club for young people interested in birds and
wildlife conservation; produces magazines, competitions,
projects, local activities and holidays

Family Welfare

Association for Education Welfare Management

1 The Boundary, Bradford, West Yorkshire BD8 0BQ;
Tel 01924 305519
National Secretary Jennifer A. Price

British Safety Council

70 Chancellors Rd, London W6 9RS;
URL www.britishsafetycouncil.co.uk; Tel 020 8741 1231
Chief Executive Brian Nimick

Family Education Trust

Jubilee Hse, 19–21 High St, Whitton, Twickenham TW2 7LB;
URL www.famyouth.org.uk; e-mail
fyc@ukfamily.org.uk; Tel 020 8894 2525;
Fax 020 8894 3535

fpa

50 Featherstone St, London EC1Y 8QU;
URL www.fpa.org.uk; e-mail helens@fpa.org.uk;
Tel (general line) 020 7608 5240; Tel (training)
020 7608 5276

Manager (Training: England, Scotland and Wales)
Claire Fanstone
Administrator (Training) Helen Shipley
fpa offers sexual health training for professionals in the UK
working in sexual health. Its training is available on request,
tailor-made, as consultancy or open courses. It also provides
university accreditation for many of its courses.

FSU

Registered Charity Number 212114
14 Clerkenwell Cl, London EC1R 0AN;
URL www.fsu.org.uk; Tel 020 7780 7000;
Fax 020 7490 7460
Chief Executive Philippa Gitlin

Royal Society for the Prevention of Accidents (RoSPA)

Edgbaston Pk, 353 Bristol Rd, Birmingham, West Midlands
B5 7ST; URL www.rospa.com; e-mail help@rospa.com;
Tel 0121 248 2000; Fax 0121 248 2001
Director (Public Affairs) Janice Cave
Head (Safety Education) Peter Cornall
Senior Press Officer Roger Vincent

21

Education

Further Education

Arvon Foundation

Senior Administrator (Totleigh) J. Wheadon; Totleigh
Barton, Sheepwash, Beaworthy, Devon EX21 5NS;
Tel 01409 231338
Administrator (Lumb) Ilona Jones; Lumb Bank, Hebden
Bridge, West Yorkshire HX7 6DF; Tel 01422 843714

EMFEC

Robins Wood Hse, Robins Wood Rd, Aspley, Nottingham
NG8 3NH; URL www.emfec.co.uk; e-mail
enquiries@emfec.co.uk; Tel 0115 854 1616;
Fax 0115 854 1617
Specialists in vocational education and training

National Association for Staff Development in the Post-16 Sector

Chair Wynne Handley; Basingstoke College, Worting Rd,
Basingstoke, Hampshire RG21 8TN
Hon Association Co-ordinator J. Faccenda; 36 Kimbolton
Ave, Bedford, Bedfordshire MK40 3AA; Tel 01234 309678

Tertiary Colleges Association

Chair I.K. Wymer BA(Hons), DipEd; Principal, Bilston
Community College, Wolverhampton, West Midlands
WV14 6ER; Tel 01902 353877

Unilever Home Economics, Technical Management, Nutrition

Brooke Hse, Manor Royal, Crawley, West Sussex
RH10 9RQ; URL www.unilever.com; e-mail
sue.batty@unilever.com; Tel 01293 648000
Manager (Home Economics) Sue Batty

Higher Education

CASE Europe

5–11 Worship St, London EC2A 2BH; URL www.case.org;
e-mail info@eurocase.org.uk; Tel 020 7448 9940;
Fax 020 7628 3570
Vice-President for International Operations Joanna Motion
European office of worldwide membership organisation,
providing information and training to alumni relations,
public relations marketing and development professionals
at educational institutions

London Mathematical Society

London Mathematical Society, De Morgan Hse, 57–58 Russell Sq, London WC1B 4HS; URL www.lms.ac.uk; e-mail lms@lms.ac.uk; Tel 020 7637 3686; Fax 020 7323 3655

Executive Secretary Mr P.R. Cooper; e-mail peter.cooper@lms.ac.uk

Chair (Education Committee) Prof C.J. Budd; e-mail isabelle.robinson@lms.ac.uk; Tel 020 7637 3686

Administration Officer Isabelle Robinson

Sir Richard Stapley Educational Trust

Registered Charity Number 313812

North St Farmhouse, Sheldwich, Faversham, Kent ME13 0LN; URL www.stapleytrust.org; e-mail admin@stapleytrust.org

Society for the Promotion of Hellenic Studies

Senate Hse, Malet St, London WC1E 7HU; e-mail hellenic@sas.ac.uk; Tel 020 7862 8730; Fax 020 7862 8731

Secretary R.W. Shone

Specialist Schools and Academics Trust

16th Fl, Millbank Tower, 21–24 Millbank, London SW1P 4QP; URL www.specialistschoolstrust.org.uk; e-mail info@specialistschoolstrust.org.uk; Tel 020 7802 2371; Fax 020 7802 2345

Chief Executive Elizabeth Reid

Chair Sir Cyril Taylor

The Specialist Schools Trust is the registered educational charity, which acts as the central co-ordinating body for the specialist schools programme. It has the following aims: to extend the range of opportunities available to children that best meet their needs and interests; to raise standards of teaching and learning in the school's specialisms while continuing to offer the full national curriculum; to develop a new identity for the school, which is reflected in ambitious but achievable targets in performance; to demonstrate how the school would benefit other schools in its area by building on existing links and developing new ones; to strengthen links between the school and private or charitable sectors, often allowing sponsors a role in the development of the school.

Universities Association for Lifelong Learning

Secretary Prof K.L. Oglesby; University of Teesside, Middlesbrough TS1 3BA; Tel 01642 342012

University of London External Programme

Senate Hse, Malet St, London WC1E 7HU; URL www.londonexternal.ac.uk; e-mail enquiries@lon.ac.uk; Tel 020 7862 8360; Fax 020 7862 8358

Distance learning

Virgil Society

c/o 8 Purley Oaks Rd, Sanderstead, Surrey CR2 0NP

Hon Treasurer J. Kilsby

Wyvernian Foundation

6 Magnolia Cl, Leicester LEG 8PS; e-mail andrew.york@ukonline.co.uk; Tel 0116 283 5345

Secretary A.R. York FCA

Independent Education

Girls' Day School Trust

100 Rochester Row, London SW1P 1JP; URL www.gdst.net; e-mail info@wes.gdst.net; Tel 020 7393 6666; Fax 020 7393 6788

Chief Executive Barbara Harrison

Girls' Schools Association

130 Regent Rd, Leicester LE1 7PG; URL www.gsa.uk.com; e-mail office~gsa.uk.com; Tel 0116 254 1619; Fax 0116 255 3792

General Secretary S. Cooper BA, MLS, MBA

Independent Schools Association

General Secretary T.M. Ham MA, DipEd; ISA Boys' British School, East St, Saffron Walden, Essex CB10 1LS; Tel 01799 523619; Fax 01799 524892

Independent Schools Council (ISC)

St Vincent Hse, 30 Orange St, London WC2H 7HH; URL www.isc.co.uk; e-mail office@isc.co.uk; Tel 020 7766 7070; Fax 020 7766 7071

The Independent Schools Council (ISC) represents 1280 independent schools educating more than 500 000 children. Its schools are accredited by the Independent Schools Inspectorate (ISI) and the head of each ISC school is a member of one of its five heads' associations.

Members

Girls' Schools Association (GSA), Association of Governing Bodies of Independent Schools (AGBIS), Headmasters' and Headmistresses' Conference (HMC), Incorporated Association of Preparatory Schools (IAPS), Independent Schools Association (ISA), Independent Schools Bursars' Association (ISBA) and Society of Headmasters and Headmistresses of Independent Schools (SHMIS)

Other Educational Organisations

ACE Advisory Centre for Education

1c Aberdeen Studios, 22 Highbury Gr, London N5 2DQ; URL www.ace-ed.org.uk; e-mail enquiries@ace-ed.org.uk; Tel (administration) 020 7354 8318; Tel (exclusion answerphone) 020 7704 9822; Tel (advice: Mon–Fri 1000–1700) 0808 800 5793; Fax 020 7354 9069

An independent non-profitmaking body offering confidential advice on the maintained schools system to parents and others through its free advice lines

Centre for Studies on Inclusive Education (CSIE)

New Redland, Frenchay Campus, Coldharbour La, Bristol BS16 1QU; URL www.csie.org.uk; Tel 0117 328 4007; Fax 0117 328 4005

Promotes inclusive education for all pupils with a wide range of materials

Development Education Association

1st Fl, River Hse, 143–145 Farringdon Rd, London EC1R 3AB; URL www.dea.org.uk; e-mail dea@dea.org.uk; Tel 020 7812 1282; Fax 020 7812 1272

The Development Education Association (DEA) is a national umbrella body of more than 240 member and partner organisations. Development education aims to raise awareness and understanding of global and development issues in the UK for all ages and within all sectors – early years, schools, youth groups, colleges, community education, higher education. The DEA works with national and local organisations, including a network of more than 45 local development education centres, to support educators and learners in bringing a global dimension to education. The development education network publishes guidelines for development education and educational materials, advises members and others interested in development and development education, and offers training, workshops and forums.

Geographical Association

160 Solly St, Sheffield, South Yorkshire S1 4BP; URL www.geography.org.uk; e-mail info@geography.org.uk; Tel 0114 296 0088; Fax 0114 296 7176

Manager (Membership Services) Frances Soar

Heatherbank Museum of Social Work

Glasgow Caledonian University, Cowcaddens Rd, Glasgow G4 0BA; URL www.lib.gcal.ac.uk/heatherbank; e-mail j.powles@gcal.ac.uk; Tel 0141 273 1189; Fax 0141 331 3005

Curator Alastair Ramage

Home Education Advisory Service (HEAS)
PO Box 98, Welwyn Garden City, Hertfordshire AL8 6AN;
URL www.heas.org.uk; e-mail enquiries@heas.org.uk;
Tel (advice line available to subscribers) 01707 371854;
Fax 01707 338467

Learning and Teaching Scotland
The Optima, 58 Robertson St, Glasgow G2 8DU;
URL www.ltscotland.org.uk; e-mail
enquiries@ltscotland.org.uk; Tel 0141 282 5000;
Fax 0141 282 5050
Gardyne Rd, Dundee DD5 1NY; Tel 01382 443600;
Fax 01382 443645
Chief Executive Bernard McLeary
Chair Prof Tom Wilson
Learning and Teaching Scotland is an executive non-departmental public body sponsored by the Scottish Government. Learning and Teaching Scotland is the main organisation for the development and support of the Scottish curriculum and Scottish education. Its role is to provide advice, support, resources and staff development to enhance the quality of learning and teaching in Scotland, combining expertise in the 3–18 curriculum with advice on the use of ICT in education. Learning and Teaching Scotland works in close partnership with the Scottish Government, HMIE, SQA, ADES, COSLA, education authorities, schools and a range of professional associations.

National Literacy Trust
68 South Lambeth Rd, London SW8 1RL;
URL www.literacytrust.org.uk; www.rif.org.uk;
www.readon.org.uk; e-mail contact@literacytrust.org.uk;
Tel 020 7587 1842; Fax 020 7587 1411
Director J. Douglas

Oxfam Education and Youth Programme
John Smith Dr, Oxford, Oxfordshire OX4 2JY;
URL www.oxfam.org.uk/education; oxfam.org.uk/generationwhy; e-mail education@oxfam.org.uk;
Tel 0870 333 2700
Head of Programme Gillian Temple
Head (Publishing) Lucy Melville
International Co-ordinator Pete Davis
Marketing Executive (Resources) Susanna Griffiths
Oxfam Education and Youth Programme works in the UK to ensure young people are taught about global issues. Also provides and publishes resources for teachers and young people.

Environment

Arkleton Trust
The Old Golf Hse, Rectory Rd, Streatley, Berkshire
RG8 1QA; URL www.enstoneuk.demon.co.uk/arkleton;
e-mail arkleton@enstoneuk.demon.co.uk
Charitable trust which studies new approaches to rural development. Aims to encourage discussion about the problems of Europe and the developing world between politicians, administrators and practitioners at all levels.

Centre for Alternative Technology
Machynlleth, Powys SY20 9AZ; URL www.cat.org.uk;
e-mail education@cat.org.uk; Tel 01654 705983;
Fax 01654 702782

Civic Trust
17 Carlton House Terr, London SW1Y 5AW;
URL www.civictrust.org.uk; Tel 020 7930 0914;
Fax 020 7321 0180
Chief Executive M. Bacon

Council for Environmental Education
94 London St, Reading RG1 4SJ; e-mail
enquiries@cee.org.uk; Tel 0118 950 2550;
Fax 0118 959 1955
Director Lisbeth Grundy

Umbrella body for environmental and sustainable development education in England

Countryside Agency
John Dower Hse, Crescent Pl, Cheltenham, Gloucestershire
GL50 3RA; URL www.countryside.gov.uk; e-mail
info@countryside.gov.uk; Tel 01242 521381;
Fax 01242 584270
Chief Executive Richard Wakeford

Countryside Education Trust
Out of Town Centre, Palace La, Beaulieu, Hampshire
SO42 7YG; URL www.cet.org.uk; e-mail
mail@cet.org.uk; Tel 01590 612401; Fax 01590 612405
Director D. Bridges
Environmental and countryside studies from pre-school to A-level at a residential farm centre or a day visit woodland study centre

The Environment Council
212 High Holborn, London WC1V 7BF;
URL www.envcouncil.org.uk; e-mail
info@envcouncil.org.uk; Tel 020 7836 2626;
Fax 020 7242 1180
The Environment Council's Learning and Development open course programme of training courses provides the skills to design, manage and evaluate stakeholder engagement and public dialogue processes. Designed and run by experienced practitioners and engagement experts. It offers training needs analysis, training tailored to needs, and coaching and mentoring. Core activities also include advocacy of engagement, engagement and consultation project delivery, a corporate partners programme, and evaluation of engagement.

National Association for Environmental Education
Wolverhampton University, Walsall Campus, Gorway Rd,
Walsall, West Midlands WS1 3BD;
URL www.naee.org.uk; e-mail info@naee.org.uk;
Tel 01922 631200
Hon Secretary Sue Fenoughty

NEA
St Andrew's Hse, 90–92 Pilgrim St, Newcastle upon Tyne,
Tyne and Wear NE1 6SG; URL www.nea.org.uk; e-mail
info@nea.org.uk; Tel 0191 261 5677; Fax 0191 261 6496
Library Manager Susan Clark
NEA develops and promotes energy efficiency services to tackle the heating and insultation problems of low income households. Working with a variety of partners, NEA aims to alleviate fuel poverty and campaigns for greater investment in energy efficiency to help those who are poor or vulnerable.

North of England Civic Trust
Blackfriars, Monk St, Newcastle upon Tyne, Tyne and Wear
NE1 4XN; e-mail nect@lineone.net; Tel 0191 232 9279;
Fax 0191 230 1474
Director G. Bell

Professional Test Systems
Summer Ct, Manafon, Welshpool, Powys SY21 8BJ;
Tel 01686 650160; Fax 01686 650170
General Manager M. Doughty
Manufacture of scientific equipment, for use in school and college laboratories. Products include experiment, test and demonstration equipment for laboratory use, and portable environmental test equipment for field studies of water and environmental pollution. Also swimming pool water testing equipment for use in educational establishments.

Royal Geographical Society with the Institute of British Geographers
1 Kensington Gore, London SW7 2AR; Tel 020 7591 3000;
Fax 020 7591 3001
Director; Secretary Dr Rita Gardner CBE
Librarian E. Rae

Royal Scottish Geographical Society

40 George St, Glasgow G1 1QE; URL www.rsgs.org; e-mail rsgs@strath.ac.uk; Tel 0141 552 3330; Fax 0141 552 3331

Director; Secretary   Dr David M. Munro

Scottish Civic Trust

The Tobacco Merchants Hse, 42 Miller St, Glasgow G1 1DT; Tel 0141 221 1466; Fax 0141 248 6952

Director   T. Levinthal

Town and Country Planning Association

Registered Charity Number 214348

17 Carlton House Terr, London SW1Y 5AS; URL www.tcpa.org.uk; Tel 020 7930 8903; Fax 020 7930 3280

Director   Gideon Amos MA, RIBA

Healthcare/Hospitals/Nursing

Centre for Medical Education, The University of Dundee

Tay Park Hse, 484 Perth Rd, Dundee DD2 1LR; URL www.dundee.ac.uk/meded; e-mail c.m.e.courses@dundee.ac.uk; Tel 01382 381952

Centre Director   Prof M.H. Davis

Epilepsy Action

New Anstey Hse, Gate Way Dr, Yeadon, Leeds, West Yorkshire LS19 7XY; URL www.epilepsy.org.uk; e-mail epilepsy@epilepsy.org.uk; Tel (head office) 0113 210 8800; Tel (freephone helpline) 0808 800 5050; Fax 0113 391 0300

Health Promotion Agency for Northern Ireland

18 Ormeau Ave, Belfast BT2 8HS; URL www.healthpromotionagency.org.uk; e-mail info@hpani.org.uk; Tel 028 9031 1611; Fax 028 9031 1711

Chief Executive   Dr Brian Gaffney

The Health Promotion Agency is responsible for providing regional leadership and direction for health promotion in Northern Ireland

Institute of Health Promotion and Education

Department of Oral Health and Development, University Dental Hospital, Manchester M15 6FH; URL www.ihpe.org.uk; Tel 0161 275 6610; Fax 0161 275 6299

Secretary   Prof A.S. Blinkhorn

Meningitis Trust

Fern Hse, Bath Rd, Stroud, Gloucestershire GL5 3TJ; URL www.meningitis-trust.org; e-mail info@meningitis-trust.org.uk; Tel 0800 028 1828; Tel 01453 768000; Fax 01453 768001

Mental Health Media

356 Holloway Rd, London N7 6PA; URL www.mhmedia.com; e-mail info@mhmedia.com; Tel 020 7700 8171; Fax 020 7686 0959

TACADE (The Advisory Council on Alcohol and Drug Education)

Old Exchange Bldgs, St Ann's Passage, Manchester M2 6AD; Tel 0161 836 6850; Fax 0161 836 6859

Chief Executive   Martin Buczkiewicz

Manager (Communications)   Mandy Broadbent

TACADE is the leading non-governmental organisation working in the field of preventive education. Its work encompasses the fields of health and personal and social education. TACADE works in three key areas: resource materials, project management, and training and consultancy.

Heritage

British Numismatic Society

c/o Warburg Institute, Woburn Sq, London WC1H 0AB; URL www.britnumsoc.org; e-mail secretary@britnumsoc.org

Coors Visitor Centre

PO Box 220, Horninglow St, Burton upon Trent, Staffordshire DE14 1YQ; URL www.coorsvisitorcentre.com; e-mail enquiries@coorsvisitorcentre.com

Education Co-ordinator   Paula White

The museum tells the story of Burton upon Trent, its brewers and breweries, and links to the national curriculum at all levels. Subjects include business, history, leisure and tourism, and literacy and numeracy.

Council for British Archaeology

St Mary's Hse, 66 Bootham, York, North Yorkshire YO30 7BZ; URL www.britarch.ac.uk; e-mail info@britarch.ac.uk; Tel 01904 671417; Fax 01904 671384

Director   Mike Heyworth BA, MA, PhD, FSA, MIFA

Education Officer   Don Henson BA, MPhil, MIFA

Group for Education in Museums (GEM)

Primrose Hse, 193 Gillingham Rd, Gillingham, Kent ME7 4EP; URL www.gem.org.uk; e-mail gemso@blueyonder.co.uk; Tel 01634 312409; Fax 01634 312409

Ironbridge Gorge Museum Trust

Coach Rd, Coalbrookdale, Telford, Shropshire TF8 7DQ; URL www.ironbridge.org.uk; e-mail education@ironbridge.org.uk; Tel 01952 433970; Fax 01952 432204

Administrator (Education)   Rose Lloyd

From early years to adult, ten museum sites have activities, displays and workshops. Telephone for a free introductory teachers' handbook and ticket.

Ironbridge Institute

Ironbridge Gorge Museum Trust, Coalbrookdale, Telford, Shropshire TF8 7DX; URL www.ironbridge.bham.ac.uk; e-mail ironbridge@bham.ac.uk; Tel 01952 432751; Fax 01952 435937

Programme Director   David de Haan

Royal Archaeological Institute

c/o Society of Antiquaries, Burlington Hse, Piccadilly, London W1J 0BE; URL www.royalarchaeolinst.org; e-mail admin@royalarchaeolinst.org; Tel 0116 243 3839; Fax 0116 243 3839

Administrator   C. Raison

Royal Numismatic Society

Department of Coins and Medals, British Museum, London WC1B 3DG; Tel 020 7323 8577

Secretary   A. Meadows

Society for the Promotion of Roman Studies

Senate Hse, Malet St, London WC1E 7HU; URL www.romansociety.org; e-mail office@romansociety.org; Tel 020 7862 8727

Secretary   Dr F.K. Haarer

International and Overseas

Education Action International

3 Dufferin St, London EC1Y 8NA; URL www.education-action.org; e-mail info@education-action.org; Tel 020 7426 5800; Fax 020 7256 7273

Education International (EI)

5 Bvd Roi Albert II, 1210 Brussels, Belgium;
URL www.ei-ie.org; e-mail headoffice@ei-ie.org;
Tel +32 2 224 06 11; Fax +32 2 224 06 06
President Thulas Nxesi
General Secretary F. van Leeuwen
Education International is a worldwide trade union
organisation of education personnel, whose 29 million
members represent all sectors of education, from pre-school
to university, through its 348 national trade unions and
associations in 166 countries and territories

English-Speaking Union of the Commonwealth

Dartmouth Hse, 37 Charles St, London W1J 5ED;
URL www.esu.org; e-mail education@eas.org;
Tel 020 7529 1550
Director of Education Mary Dawson

Experiment in International Living

287 Worcester Rd, Malvern, Worcestershire WR14 1AB;
URL www.eiluk.org; e-mail info@eiluk.org;
Tel 01684 562577; Fax 01684 562212

International Baccalaureate Organisation

Head Office, 15 Route des Morillons, CH-1218 Grand-
Saconnex, Geneva, Switzerland; URL www.ibo.org;
e-mail ibhq@ibo.org; Tel +41 22 791 7740;
Fax +41 22 791 0277
Director General Jeffrey Beard

International Bureau of Education (UNESCO)

PO Box 199, 1121 Geneva 20, Switzerland;
URL www.ibe.unesco.org; e-mail
doc.centre@ibe.unesco.org; Tel +41 22 917 7800;
Fax +41 22 917 7801
Director Pierre Luisoni (Acting)

International Union of Crystallography

2 Abbey Sq, Chester, Cheshire CH1 2HU;
URL www.iucr.org; e-mail execsec@iucr.org;
Tel 01244 345431; Fax 01244 344843
Executive Secretary Mr M.H. Dacombe

Interserve (International Service Fellowship)

5–6 Walker Ave, Wolverton Mill, Milton Keynes
MK12 5TW; URL www.interserveonline.org; e-mail
enquiries@isewi.org; Tel 01908 552700; Fax 01908 552779
Director (Human Resources) Ruth Millson

Society for Anglo-Chinese Understanding

16 Portland St, Cheltenham, Gloucestershire GL52 2PB;
URL www.sacu.org; e-mail info@sacu.org;
Tel 01229 472010
Book collection housed in Sheffield. Information sheets
available for teachers.

TEAM (The European Atlantic Movement)

1a Blakehill Ave, Bradford, West Yorkshire BD2 3JT;
Tel 01274 780756
Chair J. Schofield
Hon Secretary A.J. Thornton

UK Council for International Student Affairs (UKCISA)

9–17 St Albans Pl, London N1 0NX;
URL www.ukcisa.org.uk; Tel 020 7288 4330;
Fax 020 7288 4360
Chief Executive Dominic Scott

US–UK Fulbright Commission (Fulbright Commission)

62 Doughty St, London WC1N 2JZ;
URL www.fulbright.co.uk; e-mail
education@fulbright.co.uk; Tel 020 7404 6880
Executive Director Carol Madison Graham

Welsh Centre for International Affairs

Temple of Peace, Cathays Pk, Cardiff CF10 3AP;
URL www.wcia.org.uk; e-mail centre@wcia.org.uk;
Tel 02920 228549; Fax 02920 640333
Director Stephen Thomas

The WCIA fosters among the people of Wales an
understanding of global issues and encourages a national
sense of belonging to the international community

Languages

Association for Latin Teaching

Cedarwood, West St, Childrey, Oxfordshire OX12 9UL;
URL www.arlt.co.uk
Hon Secretary Linda Soames

The English Association

University of Leicester, University Rd, Leicester LE1 7RH;
URL www.le.ac.uk/engassoc; e-mail engassoc@le.ac.uk;
Tel 0116 252 3982; Fax 0116 252 2301
President P.J. Kitson
Chief Executive H. Lucas
Chair M. Moran
Treasurer R.J. Claxton
To further knowledge, understanding and enjoyment of the
English language and its literature by means of lectures,
publications (journals and annual publications), and five
annual conferences

English UK

56 Buckingham Gate, London SW1E 6AG;
URL www.englishuk.com; e-mail info@englishuk.com;
Tel 020 7802 9200; Fax 020 7802 9201
Chief Executive Tony Millns

Welsh Baccalaureate Qualification CBAC/WJEC

245 Western Ave, Cardiff CF5 2YX; URL www.wbq.org.uk;
e-mail info@wbq.org.uk; Tel 02920 265010;
Fax 02920 575995

Recruitment

Balfor Education

8th Fl, Warwick Chambers, Corporation St, Birmingham,
West Midlands B2 4RN; URL www.balforeducation.com;
e-mail info@balforeducation.com; Tel 0870 727 2244;
Fax 0870 727 2627

Beacon Education Ltd

Beacon Hse, 2–6 Bull La, Rayleigh, Essex SS6 8JG;
URL www.beaconeducation.co.uk; e-mail
info@beaconeducation.co.uk; Tel 01268 779966;
Fax 01268 777735

Capita Education Resourcing

URL www.capitaers.co.uk; e-mail infoers@capita.co.uk;
Tel 0800 731 6871; Fax 020 8293 6356
15 offices nationwide; for details please see the website

Eteach

Academy Hse, 403 London Rd, Camberley, Surrey
GU15 3HL; URL www.eteach.com; e-mail
enquiries@eteach.com; Tel 0845 226 1906;
Fax 0845 226 1907

Long Term Teachers

26 Mortimer St, London W1W 7RB;
URL www.longtermteachers.com; e-mail
info@longtermteachers.com; Tel 0845 130 6149;
Fax 0871 250 6193

Premier Education

Suite 2, Bank Chambers, Church St, Wilmslow, Cheshire
SK9 1AU; URL www.premier-education.co.uk; e-mail
enquiries@premier-education.co.uk; Tel 01625 538568;
Fax 01625 538569

21

Protocol Education
40–43 Chancery La, London WC2A 1JA;
URL www.protocol-education.com; Tel 020 7440 8440;
Fax 020 7406 1873
Chief Executive   Stephen Lawrence
Director (Operations)   Penny Swain

Sanza Teaching Agency
Suite 145a, Business Design Centre, 52 Upper St, Islington,
London N1 0QH; URL www.teachuk.com; e-mail
sanza@teachuk.co.uk; Tel 020 7288 6644;
Fax 020 7288 6643

Teachers and Academic Personnel Ltd (TAP Ltd)
12 Brookfield, Duncan Cl, Moulton Pk, Northampton,
Northamptonshire NN3 6WL; URL www.tap.ltd.com;
e-mail enquiries@tap.ltd.com; Tel 01604 646333;
Fax 01604 499768

Research

British Curriculum Foundation
Chair   M. Davies; Stranraer Academy, Stranraer, Dumfries
and Galloway DG9 8BY; Tel 01776 706484;
Fax 01776 704748
Secretary   G. Edwards; Goldsmith College, New Cross,
London SE14 6NW; Tel 020 8692 7171

British Educational Research Association
Association Hse, South Park Rd, Macclesfield, Cheshire
SK11 6SH; URL www.bera.ac.uk; e-mail
admin@bera.ac.uk; Tel 01625 504062; Fax 01625 267879
Administrative Secretary   Dan Hollingshurst

Centre for Educational Sociology (CES)
University of Edinburgh, St Johns Land, Holyrood Rd,
Edinburgh EH8 8AQ; URL www.ces.ed.ac.uk; e-mail
ces@ed.ac.uk; Tel 0131 651 6238; Fax 0131 651 6239
Administrator   Marcia Wright

Institute for Employment Studies
Mantell Bldg, University of Sussex Campus, Falmer,
Brighton, East Sussex BN1 9RF;
URL www.employment-studies.co.uk; e-mail
askies@employment-studies.co.uk; Tel 01273 686751;
Fax 01273 690430
Director   Nigel Meager

Modern Humanities Research Association
Department of European Studies and Modern Languages,
University of Bath, Bath, Somerset BA2 7AY;
URL www.mhra.org.uk; e-mail d.c.gillespie@bath.ac.uk
Hon Secretary   Prof D.C. Gillespie

Occupational Research Centre (ORC)
Highlands, Gravel Path, Berkhamsted, Hertfordshire
HP4 2PQ; URL www.kaicentre.com; indstate.edu/soe/
blumberg/kai.html (USA); e-mail
m.j.kirton@kaicentre.com; Tel 01442 871200;
Fax 01442 871200
Director   Dr M.J. Kirton

Sciences

Association for Science Education
Registered Charity Number 313123
College La, Hatfield, Hertfordshire AL10 9AA;
URL www.ase.org.uk; e-mail derekbell@ase.org.uk;
Tel 01707 283014; Fax 01707 266532
The Association for Science Education is the professional
association for teachers of science laboratory technicians,
advisers, lecturers in universities, industrialist and others
contributing to science education, with a membership of

more than 18 000. ASE is financed by members'
subscriptions and receives no direct government funding.

Botanical Society of British Isles
c/o Department of Botany, The Natural History Museum,
Cromwell Rd, London SW7 5BD; URL www.bsbi.org.uk;
Tel 020 7942 5002
Hon General Secretary   Mr D. Pearman
Voluntary interest society whose aim is to gain a better
understanding of British and Irish plants with regard to
their form, distribution and conservation. Please enclose an
SAE with all enquiries.

British Association for the Advancement of Science
Wellcome Wolfson Bldg, 165 Queen's Gate, London
SW7 5HD; URL www.the-ba.net; e-mail
rupa.kundu@the-ba.net; Tel 0870 770 7101;
Fax 0870 770 7102
Chief Executive   Sir Roland Jackson
Director (Young People's Programme)   Annette Smith

British Interplanetary Society
27–29 South Lambeth Rd, London SW8 1SZ; e-mail
mail@bis.spaceflight.com; Tel 020 7735 3160;
Fax 020 7820 1504
Executive Secretary   S. Parry

Geologists' Association South Wales Group
Registered Charity Number 1054303
Department of Geography, Swansea University, Singleton
Pk, Swansea SA2 8PP; URL www.swga.org.uk; e-mail
g.owen@swansea.ac.uk; Tel 01792 295141;
Fax 01792 295955
Secretary   G. Owen

Institute of Mathematics and its Applications
Catherine Richards Hse, 16 Nelson St, Southend-on-Sea,
Essex SS1 1EF; URL www.ima.org.uk; e-mail
post@ima.org.uk; Tel 01702 354020; Fax 01702 354111
President   Prof David Abrahams
Executive Director   Mr D. Youdan

Royal Institution of Great Britain
21 Albemarle St, London W1S 4BS; URL www.rigb.org/
insideout; e-mail schools@ri.ac.uk; Tel 020 7409 2992;
Fax 020 7670 2920
Director   Baroness Susan Greenfield

Royal Meteorological Society
104 Oxford Rd, Reading RG1 7LL; Tel 0118 956 8500;
Fax 0118 956 8571
Manager (Education Resources)   J.M. Walker

Royal Microscopical Society
37–38 St Clements, Oxford, Oxfordshire OX4 1AJ;
URL www.rms.org.uk; e-mail education@rms.org.uk;
Tel 01865 254760; Fax 01865 791237
Education Officer   Elaine Rawle
The Royal Microscopical Society provides funding, support
and resources to encourage the use of microscopes in
schools, and organises courses and meetings for scientists on
all aspects of microscopy

School Mathematics Project
The University of Southampton, Southampton SO17 1BJ;
URL www.smpmaths.org.uk; e-mail
office@smpmaths.org.uk; Tel 02380 593686;
Fax 02380 594300

'Understanding Energy' Educational Service for Schools
The Electricity Association, 30 Millbank, London
SW1P 4RD; URL www.natenergy.org.uk; e-mail
ue@electricity.org.uk; Tel 020 7963 5839

United Nations Educational, Scientific and Cultural Organisation (UNESCO)
7 Place de Fontenoy, 75352 Paris 07 SP, France;
URL www.unesco.org/education; e-mail
tve.section@unesco.org; Tel +33 01 456 80960;
Fax +33 01 456 85545

Societies and Associations

Association of Directors of Education in Scotland
City of Edinburgh Council, 10 Waterloo Pl, Edinburgh
EH1 3EG
General Secretary   Vacancy

Association of MBAs
25 Hosier La, London EC1A 9LQ;
URL www.mbaworld.com; e-mail info@mbaworld.com;
Tel 020 7246 2680; Fax 020 7246 2687
Company Secretary   Jeanette Purcell

Centre for Research and Development in Catholic Education (CRDCE)
University of London, Institute of Education, Bedford Way,
London WC1H 0AL; URL http:/ioewebserver.ioe.ac.uk/
ioe; e-mail crdce@ioe.ac.uk; Tel 020 7612 6003;
Fax 020 7612 6157
Director   Prof Gerald Grace
Deputy Director   Dr Patrick Walsh
Research Associate   Dr Christopher Storr
Research Associate   Dr Clare Watkins

Conservative Future
25 Victoria St, London SW1H 0DL;
URL www.conservativefuture.com; e-mail
ssouthern@conservatives.com; Tel 020 7984 8321;
Fax 020 7222 1135
National Organiser   Sarah Southern

The Galton Institute
19 Northfields Prospect, London SW18 1PE;
URL www.galtoninstitute.org.uk; e-mail
betty.nixon@talk21.com; Tel 020 8874 7257
General Secretary   B. Nixon

Honourable Society of Cymmrodorion
30 Eastcastle St, London W1W 8DJ;
URL www.cymmrodorion1751.org.uk; e-mail
aelodau1751we@yahoo.co.uk; Tel 020 7631 0502
Hon Secretary   John Samuel BA, CPFA, DipSocSt

Institute for Outdoor Learning
The Barn, Plumpton Old Hall, Plumpton, Penrith, Cumbria
CA11 9NP; URL www.outdoor-learning.org; e-mail
institute@outdoor-learning.org; Tel 01768 885800;
Fax 01768 885801
Membership and Sales   Melanie Bardgett
Supporting, developing and promoting learning through
outdoor experiences; online bookshop, professional
insurance, magazines etc.

London Natural History Society
c/o The Linnean Society of London, Burlington Hse,
Piccadilly, London W1J 0BF; URL www.lnhs.org.uk
President   Mr M. Burgess
Secretary   Dr J. Edgington
Treasurer   M. West

Nacro
Park Pl, 10–12 Lawn La, London SW8 1UD
Director (Operations)   Claire Bassett; e-mail
claire.bassett@nacro.org.uk; Tel 020 7582 6500;
Fax 020 7735 4666
Services Manager (Publications and Information)
Selina Corkery; 169 Clapham Rd, London SW9 0PU;
e-mail selina.corkery@nacro.org.uk; Tel 020 7582 6500

PLAYLINK
72 Albert Palace Mansions, Lurline Gdns, London
SW11 4DQ; URL www.playlink.org.uk;
Tel 020 7720 2452
Principal   B. Spiegal

Radio Society of Great Britain
Lambda Hse, Cranborne Rd, Potters Bar, Hertfordshire
EN6 3JE; URL www.rsgb.org; e-mail
gmdept@rsgb.org.uk; Tel 0870 904 7373;
Fax 0870 904 7374
General Manager   P. Kirby

Royal Anthropological Institute of Great Britain and Ireland
50 Fitzroy St, London W1T 5BT; URL www.therai.org.uk;
e-mail admin@therai.org.uk; Tel 020 7387 0455;
Fax 020 7388 8817
Director   H. Callan

The Royal Society
6–9 Carlton House Terr, London SW1Y 5AG;
URL www.royalsociety.org; Tel 020 7451 2500;
Fax 020 7451 2693
President   Lord Martin Rees of Ludlow
Treasurer   Sir Peter Williams CBE, FRS
Secretary (Biological)   Sir David Read FRS
Secretary (Executive)   S.J. Cox CVO
Secretary (Foreign)   Prof Lorna Casselton FRS
Secretary (Physical)   Prof Martin Taylor FRS
Manager (Education)   Ginny Page
UK academy of science

Royal Society of Literature
Somerset Hse, The Strand, London WC2R 1LA; e-mail
info@rslit.org; Tel 020 7845 4676; Fax 020 7845 4679
Secretary   Maggie Fergusson

School Journey Association
48 Cavendish Rd, Clapham, London SW12 0DG;
URL www.sjatours.org; e-mail thesja@btconnect.com;
Tel 0845 658 1063; Fax 0845 658 1064
Hon Treasurer   J.U. Lambert

Society of Authors Educational Writers Group
84 Drayton Gdns, London SW10 9SB; Tel 020 7373 6642
Secretary   Elizabeth Haylett

Students

National Union of Students
2nd Fl, Centro 3, 19 Mandela St, London NW1 0DU;
URL www.nusonline.co.uk; e-mail nusuk@nus.org.uk;
Tel 0871 221 8221; Fax 0871 221 8222
National President   Gemma Tumelty

Open University Students' Association
PO Box 397, Walton Hall, Milton Keynes, Buckinghamshire
MK7 6BE; URL www.ousa.org.uk; e-mail
ousa@student.open.ac.uk; Tel 01908 652026;
Fax 01908 654326
General Manager   Trudi de Haney

Training

Academy of Learning Ltd
Parklands Business Centre, Stortford Rd, Leaden Roding,
Essex CM6 1GF; URL www.academyoflearning.co.uk;
e-mail linda@academyoflearning.co.uk;
Tel 01279 877902; Fax 01279 877903

British Hypnotherapy Association (BHA)
67 Upper Berkeley St, London W1H 7QX;
URL www.british-hypnotherapy-association.org; e-mail
hypnotherapy@the-wordsmith.co.uk; Tel 020 7723 4443
Chair   R.K. Brian
Secretary   E. Wookey
Maintains a register of qualified trained practitioners who
comply with high standards of competence and ethics and
supplies training, publications, talks and reports. Aims to

care for the interests of patients and members, to collate and disseminate information on hypnotherapy and to raise standards in therapy. A voluntary organisation, funded by donations, legacies, subscriptions.

Building Crafts College

Kennard Rd, Stratford, London E15 1AH;
    URL www.thecarpenterscompany.co.uk; e-mail info@thebcc.ac.uk; Tel 020 8522 1705
Manager (Training)   John Appleton

Centre for the Study of Education and Training (CSET)

County South, University of Lancaster, Lancaster,
    Lancashire LA1 4YD; Tel 01524 592679; Fax 01524 592914
Director   Prof M. Saunders

ContinYou

Unit Cl Grovelands Ct, Longford Rd, Coventry,
    Warwickshire CV7 9NE; URL www.continyou.org.uk; e-mail info.coventry@continyou.org.uk;
    Tel 024 7658 8440; Fax 024 7658 8441

Directory of Social Change

24 Stephenson Way, London NW1 2DP;
    URL www.dsc.org.uk; e-mail info@dsc.org.uk;
    Tel 0845 077 7707
Director   D. Allcock Tyler
Publishers of Schools Funding Guide and many other directories of grant-making trusts. Also publishes The Educational Grants Directory and the report School Fundraising in England. Runs training courses.

Eastwood Park

Eastwood Park Training and Conference Centre Ltd,
    Falfield, Wotton-under-Edge, Gloucestershire
    GL12 8DA; URL www.eastwoodpark.co.uk; e-mail events@eastwoodpark.co.uk; Tel 01454 262770;
    Fax 01454 260622

Educational Training and Management Centre

Pearse Hse, Parsonage La, Bishop's Stortford, Hertfordshire
    CM23 5BQ; URL www.pearsehouse.co.uk; e-mail pearsehouse@btconnect.com; Tel 01279 757400
INSET courses for teachers; school visits, activity programmes and specialist creative writing courses in centres based throughout England, but particularly in the South East. Qualified assistance and pastoral help provided.

Lighthouse Professional Development

Unit 12 and 13, Waterside Hse, Basin Rd North, Portslade,
    East Sussex BN41 1UY; URL www.lighthouse.tv; e-mail info@lighthouse.tv; Tel 0800 587 8880; Fax 0845 609 8880
Lighthouse Professional Development provides CPD training courses for teachers of most major subject areas as well as pastoral care and managerial areas of responsibility across the UK

Richmond Language Training

32 Hill St, Richmond, Surrey TW9 1TW;
    URL www.rlt.co.uk; e-mail frank@rlt.co.uk;
    Tel 020 8332 7732; Fax 020 8948 3333
Director   Frank W. Hallam
Richmond Language Training Centre has more than 20 years' experience in corporate language training. RLT's system is based on tailor-made courses designed to meet specific requirements, which are mutually agreed upon prior to commencement during an initial needs analysis assessment. Training is targeted and progress is monitored systematically.

Social Care Association (Education)

Thornton Hse, Hook Rd, Surbiton, Surrey KT6 5AN;
    URL www.socialcareassociation.co.uk; e-mail sca@socialcaring.co.uk; Tel 020 8397 1411;
    Fax 020 8397 1436

Therapy Training College

PO Box 10500, Birmingham , West Midlands B14 4WB;
    URL www.lesserian.co.uk; e-mail courses@lesserian.co.uk; Tel 0121 430 3336
Contact   Helen Lesser

Travel and Tourism Programme

Part of Springboard Charitable Trust
Springboard UK, Rm C201, UWIC, Colchester Ave, Cardiff
    CF23 9XR; URL www.springboarduk.org.uk/ttp; e-mail ttp@springboarduk.org.uk; Tel 02920 416325;
    Fax 02920 416405
Provides up-to-date curriculum resource materials, in-service teacher training events, student events, case studies, teacher placements and online support for travel, tourism, leisure and hospitality-based courses in schools and colleges

World ORT

126 Albert St, London NW1 7NE; URL www.ort.org; e-mail wo@ort.org; Tel 020 7446 8500; Fax 020 7446 8650
Director General   Robert Singer
Independent, technological education and training organisation with schools, colleges and teacher training, and resource centres worldwide. In Britain it supports, sponsors and operates training schemes and co-operates closely with government and local education authorities and industry.

Voluntary Service

Education Otherwise

PO Box 325, Kings Lynn, Norfolk PE34 3XW;
    URL www.education-otherwise.org; e-mail enquiries@education-otherwise.org; Tel 0845 478 6345

London Voluntary Service Council

356 Holloway Rd, London N7 6PA; URL www.lvsc.org.uk;
    www.actionlink.org.uk; e-mail library@lvsc.org.uk;
    Tel 020 7700 8107; Fax 020 7700 8108
Director   Elizabeth Balgobin

NASO (National Adult School Organisation)

Registered Charity Number 227844
NASO, Riverton, 370 Humberstone Rd, Leicester LE5 0SA;
    URL www.naso.org.uk; e-mail gensec@naso.org.uk;
    Tel 0116 253 8333
General Secretary   Patricia C. Dean
Publishes an annual handbook, containing discussion material and studies

Network 81

1–7 Woodfield Terr, Stansted, Essex CM24 8AJ;
    URL www.network81.org; e-mail network81@btconnect.com; Tel 0870 770 3306;
    Fax 0870 770 3263
A national network of parents of children with SEN; publishes Parent Guides – A step-by-step guide to statementing and the journal Network News. Individual annual membership £20, annual group membership £25.

Scottish Council for Voluntary Organisations

Mansfield Traquair Centre, 15 Mansfield Pl, Edinburgh
    EH3 6BB; URL www.scvo.org.uk; Tel 0131 556 3882
Manager (Workforce Policy)   Celia Carson

Index

A & C Black 644
@Schools 664
1116 Boys Secondary School 518
247av.com 680
2Simple Software 664
3Com UK 684
3M UK 676
4Children 692

A

Abacus
    College 347
    Educational Services 644
    Teaching Systems 656
Abbey College 324, 326, 348, 381
    Birmingham 348
    Cambridge 345
    London 345
    Manchester 347
Aberdeen
    City Council 120
    College of Further Education 340
    University 369
Aberdeenshire Council 121
Abertay Dundee University 369
    Dundee Business School 385
Aberystwyth University 371
AbilityNet 492
Abingdon and Witney College 334
Abon Language Centre 380
AC Computers 682
Academy
    International 375
    of Learning 699
ACCA 519
Accelerated Learning Centre 644, 664
Accidents, Royal Society for the Prevention of 693
Accomodex 675
Accountancy, Chartered Institute of Public Finance and 519
Accountants
    Association of International 519
    Chartered Institute of Management 519
    Institute
        of Chartered 519
        of Company 520
        of Cost and Executive 520
        of Financial 520
    in Ireland, Institute of Chartered 519
    of Scotland, Institute of Chartered 519
Accounting Technicians, Association of 519
Accreditation UK, British Council 374
Accrington and Rossendale College 332
Accutecc UK 678
ACE
    Advisory Centre for Education 694
    Bulletin 629
Aclass Technology 664
Acordis Acetate Chemicals 529
Acorn Independent College 345
Acoustics, Institute of 520
ACRA 620

ACS 676
    Office Solutions 676
Acting Up 493
Activa Solutions 664
Active
    Learning 680
    Visual Supplies 656
Actuarial Profession 520
Actuaries, Faculty of 520
ADA Computer Systems 680
Adam
    Equipment 664
    Smith College 340
Adboards 680
Administration
    International Studies in Educational 636
    Scottish Centre for Studies in School 622
Administrative
    Colleges and Institutions, Business and 385
    Management, Institute of 525
Administrators
    Association of University 620
    Institute
        of Agricultural Secretaries and 520
        of Chartered Secretaries and 520
Adobe Systems Europe 664
Adolescence, Trust for the Study of 692
Adult
    Colleges 374
    and Continuing Education, Journal of 636
    Continuing Education, National Institute of 373
    Education 372
        Association, Northern Ireland 373
        Organisations and Associations 372
        Residential Colleges Association 372
Adults Learning 629
Advanced
    Legal Studies, Institute of 362
    Study, School of 363
Advertising, Institute of Practitioners in 526
Advice and Counselling, Careers 517
Advisory
    Centre for Education, ACE 694
    Council on Alcohol and Drug Education 696
    Councils 647
    Unit, Computers in Education 659, 664
Advocacy Resource Exchange 493
Advocates, Faculty of 525
Aeroflex International 529
Aeronautical Society, Royal 520
Aesthetics, British Journal of 629
AFASIC 491
African
    Economies, Journal of 636
    Studies, School of Oriental and 363
AGBIS 620
Agency for Jewish Education 553
Agricultural
    College, Royal 390
    Education Staffs, Association of 617
    Engineers, Institution of 523
    and Horticultural Colleges 388
    Secretaries and Administrators, Institute of 520

People 491
 National Association for Tertiary Education for 491
 Royal Association for 491
 Sports Council, British 549
Deafblind
 and Rubella Association, National 492
 UK 491
deafPLUS 491
Dean College
 of London 346
 Royal Forest of 337
Deanestor 666
Dearne Valley College 339
Deeside College 342
Defence
 Academy 387
 Military Colleges and Academies, Ministry of 387
 Ministry of 7
 Sixth Form College, Welbeck 323
 Studies, Royal College of 387
DEFRA 7
Delta Microsystems 683
Denbighshire County Council 143
Denford 666
Dental Council, General 522
Department
 of Agriculture and Rural Development for Northern
  Ireland 15
 for Business, Enterprise and Regulatory Reform 3
 for Children, Schools and Families 3
 for Communities and Local Government 6
 of Computer Science, University of York 659
 of Computing, Imperial College of Science, Technology
  and Medicine 659
 for Culture, Media and Sport 6
 of Education 11
 for Education and Skills (now Department for Children,
  Schools and Families) 3
 for Environment, Food and Rural Affairs 7
 of Health 7
 for Innovation, Universities and Skills 8
 of Management Learning Management School 622
 of Sociology 502
 of Trade and Industry (now Department for Business,
  Enterprise and Regulatory Reform) 3
 for Work and Pensions 9
Derby
 City Council 27
 College 329
 University 358, 386
  Buxton 329
  School of Art and Design 391
Derbyshire
 College, South East 330
 County Council 28
Dereham Sixth Form College 323
Derwentside College 332
Design
 Colleges and Faculties of Art and 391
 Education, National Association for 619
 National Society for Education in Art and 614
 and Technology
  Association 618
  Education
   Centre for 501
   Journal of 636
  National Association of Advisers and Inspectors in
   522, 619, 689
Designers, Chartered Society of 522, 524
Deutsch Lehren und Lernen 631
Deva Resin Services 675

Development
 Agency, Improvement and 511
 Education Association 694
Devon
 College
  North 337
  South 337
 County Council 93
 Purchasing (now Supplyzone and Devon Procurement
  Services) 680
 School of English 380
Dewsbury College 339
Dietetic Association, British 522
Digitalbrain 678
Direct
 Clothing Company 677
 Educational Services 666
Directors of Education in Scotland, Association of 699
Directory of Social Change 700
Directschoolwear & Co 677
Disabilities
 British Institute of Learning 493
 Physical and Learning 492
 Sport for People with 549
Disability 623
 Rights Commission (now Equality and Human Rights
  Commission) 13, 14, 15
 Sport, Scottish 550
 United Kingdom Sports Association for People with
  Learning 550
Disabled
 Association, Riding for 550
 Professionals, Association of 493
 Water Ski Association, British 549
discountsschoolwear.com 677
Discovering Herbal Medicine Course 384
Discovery Network Europe 653
Display and Exhibition Solutions 679
Distance Learning Quality Council, Open and .0 383
D-Link 666
Dolphin Computer Access 666, 681
Don Johnston 667
Doncaster
 College 339
 Metropolitan Borough Council 113
Dorling Kindersley 645
Dorset County Council 95
Douglas Bomford Trust 691
Dovetail Enterprises 493
Down
 and Ards Institute of Further and Higher Education,
  North 344
 Institute of Further and Higher Education, East 343
Downs College
 South 336
 Sussex 336
Dr Hadwen Trust 678
Drake Educational Associates 645
Drama
 Association, Scottish Community 690
 Central School of Speech and 395
 Centre London 395
 Colleges 394
 National 619
  Association for the Teaching of 619
 Schools, Conference of 690
 Society
  of Great Britain, Religious 690
  of Teachers of Speech and 620
Dramatherapists, British Association of 618
Dramatic Association, National Operatic and 690
Driving Society, British 543

F

G

I

N

Q

R

V

W